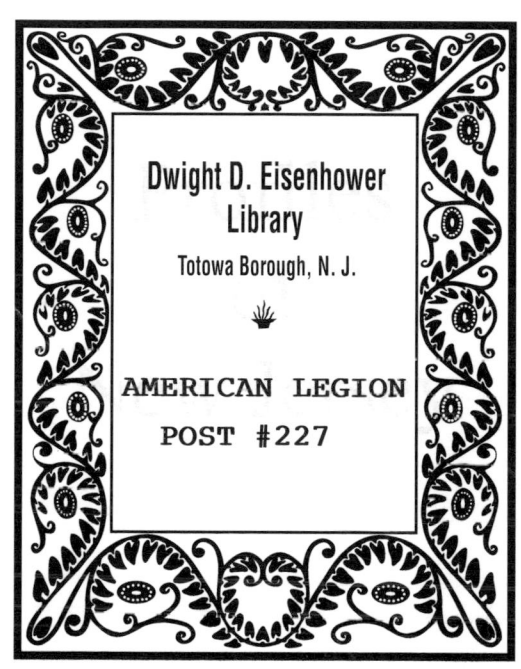

2006

Profiles
of
New Jersey

A Universal Reference Book

Grey House
Publishing

PUBLISHER:	Leslie Mackenzie
EDITOR:	David Garoogian
EDITORIAL DIRECTOR:	Laura Mars-Proietti
RESEARCH ASSISTANTS:	Karynn Ketiinq
MARKETING DIRECTOR:	Jessica Moody

Grey House Publishing, Inc.
185 Millerton Road
Millerton, NY 12546
518.789.8700
FAX 518.789.0545
www.greyhouse.com
e-mail: books @greyhouse.com

While every effort has been made to ensure the reliability of the information presented in this publication, Grey House Publishing neither guarantees the accuracy of the data contained herein nor assumes any responsibility for errors, omissions or discrepancies. Grey House accepts no payment for listing; inclusion in the publication of any organization, agency, institution, publication, service or individual does not imply endorsement of the editors or publisher.

Errors brought to the attention of the publisher and verified to the satisfaction of the publisher will be corrected in future editions.

First edition published 2006
Printed in the USA

ISBN 10: 1-59237-209-0
ISBN 13: 978-1-59237-175-4

Table of Contents

Introduction

This is the first edition of *Profiles of New Jersey – Facts, Figures & Statistics for all 799 Populated Places in New Jersey*. As for the other titles in our *State Profiles* series, we built this work using content from Grey House Publishing's award-winning *Profiles of America* – a 4-volume compilation of data on more than 42,000 places in the United States. We have updated and included the New Jersey chapter from *Profiles of America,* and added entire fresh chapters of demographic information and ranking sections, so that *Profiles of New Jersey* is the most comprehensive portrait of the state of New Jersey ever published.

This first edition provides data on all populated communities and counties in the state of New Jersey, from bustling urban centers to the hard-to-find outposts. It includes seven major sections that cover everything from **Education** to **Ethnic Backgrounds** to **Climate**. All sections include **Comparative Statistics** or **Rankings**, and full-color **Maps** at the back of the book provide valuable information in a quickly processed, visual format. Here's an overview of each section:

1. Profiles
This section, organized by county, gives detailed profiles of 799 places plus 21 counties, and is based on the 2000 Census. This core Census data has been so extensively updated, however, that nearly 80% of this section has 2005 numbers. In addition, we have added current government statistics and original research, so that these profiles pull together statistical and descriptive information on every Census-recognized place in the state. Major fields of information include:

Geography	*Housing*	*Education*	*Religion*
Ancestry	*Transportation*	*Population*	*Climate*
Economy	*Industry*	*Health*	

In addition to place profiles, this section includes an **Alphabetical Place Index** and **Comparative Statistics** that compare New Jersey's 100 largest communities by dozens of data points.

2. Education
This section begins with an *Educational State Profile*, summarizing number of schools, students, diplomas granted and educational dollars spent. Following the state profile are **School District Rankings** on 16 topics ranging from *Teacher/Student Ratios* to *High School Drop-Out Rates*. Following these rankings are *2005 National Assessment of Educational Progress (NAEP), New Jersey Assessment of Skills and Knowledge (NJASK), Grade Eight Proficiency Assessment (GEPA),* and *High School Proficiency Assessment (HSPA)* results.

3. Ancestry
This section provides a detailed look at the ancestral and racial makeup of New Jersey. 217 ethnic categories are ranked three ways: 1) by number, based on all places regardless of population; 2) by percent, based on all places regardless of population; 3) by percent, based on places with populations of 10,000 or more. You will discover, for example, that Jersey City in Hudson County has the greatest number of Egyptians in the state at 4,820, and that Koreans make up 36.4% of the population of Palisades Park in Bergen County.

4. Hispanic Population
This section defines New Jersey's Hispanic population by 23 Hispanic backgrounds from *Argentinian* to *Venezuelan*. It ranks each of 15 categories, from Median Age to Median Home Value, by each Hispanic background. For example, you'll see that Elmwood Park in Bergen County has the highest percentage of

Peruvians who speak Spanish at home, and that Paterson in Passaic County has the greatest number of *Dominicans* who own their own home.

5. Asian Population

Similar in format to the section on Hispanic Population, this section defines New Jersey's Asian population by 21 Asian backgrounds from *Bangladeshi* to *Vietnamese*. It ranks each of 14 categories, from *Median Age* to *Median Home Value*, by each Asian background. You will learn that Camden in Camden County is the place with the greatest number of *Vietnamese* in the state, and that Randolph in Morris County has the highest percent of *Asian Indians* who are college graduates.

6. Weather

This important topic is explored in detail in this section, which includes a *State Summary*, a *map* of the state's weather stations, and profiles of both *National* and *Cooperative Weather Stations*. In addition, you'll find *Weather Station Rankings*, where you'll see that, over the 30-year recorded period, Newark International Airport and Toms River reported the highest annual extreme maximum temperature at 105 degrees Fahrenheit.

This section also includes current *Storm* data, with the most destructive storms ranked by both fatalities and property damage, from 1981-2006. Here you will learn that a flash flood in September 1999 caused $358 million in property damage in Somerset County and that rip currents/heavy surf were responsible for 4 fatalities in eastern Monmouth County in August 1995.

7. Maps

For a more visual point of view, there are 16 full-color maps of New Jersey at the back of the book. They provide information on topics such as Core-Based Statistical Areas and Counties, Population Demographics, Household Size, Median Age, Income, Median Home Values, Educational Attainment, Congressional Districts, and another look at who voted for George Bush in 2004.

Note: The extensive **User's Guide** that follows this Introduction is segmented into six sections and examines, in some detail, each data field in the individual profiles and comparative sections for all chapters. It provides sources for all data points and statistical definitions as necessary.

User's Guide: Profiles

PLACES COVERED

All 21 counties.

942 municipalities. Municipalities are incorporated as either cities (52), towns (15), villages (3), boroughs (254) or townships (241). Townships in New Jersey differ from townships elsewhere in the United States. In most states, townships are an intermediate form of government, between county government and municipalities that are subordinate parts of the township, with different government responsibilities allocated at each level. In New Jersey, there are no subordinate municipalities located within a township, as a New Jersey township is a form of municipal government within a county, equal in status to a village, town, borough, or city, all of which may coexist within a county.

145 census designated places (CDP). The U.S. Bureau of the Census defines a CDP as "a statistical entity, defined for each decennial census according to Census Bureau guidelines, comprising a densely settled concentration of population that is not within an incorporated place, but is locally identified by a name. CDPs are delineated cooperatively by state and local officials and the Census Bureau, following Census Bureau guidelines. Beginning with Census 2000 there are no size limits."

89 unincorporated communities. The communities included have both their own zip code and statistics for their ZIP Code Tabulation Area (ZCTA) available from the Census Bureau. They are referred to as "postal areas." A ZCTA is a statistical entity developed by the Census Bureau to approximate the delivery area for a US Postal Service 5-digit or 3-digit ZIP Code in the US and Puerto Rico. A ZCTA is an aggregation of census blocks that have the same predominant ZIP Code associated with the mailing addresses in the Census Bureau's Master Address File. Thus, the Postal Service's delivery areas have been adjusted to encompass whole census blocks so that the Census Bureau can tabulate census data for the ZCTAs. ZCTAs do not include all ZIP Codes used for mail delivery and therefore do not precisely depict the area within which mail deliveries associated with that ZIP Code occur. Additionally, some areas that are known by a unique name, although they are part of a larger incorporated place, are also included as "postal areas."

Important Notes

- *Profiles of New Jersey* uses the term "community" to refer to all places except counties. The term "county" is used to refer to counties and county-equivalents. All places are defined as of the 2000 Census.

- Several states, including New Jersey, have incorporated municipalities and minor civil divisions in the same county with the same name. Those communities are given separate entries (e.g. Berlin, New Jersey, in Camden County will be listed under both the borough and township of Berlin).

- In each community profile, only school districts that have schools that are physically located within the community are shown. In addition, statistics for each school district cover the entire district, regardless of the physical location of the schools within the district.

- Special care should be taken when interpreting certain statistics for communities containing large colleges or universities. College students were counted as residents of the area in which they were living while attending college (as they have been since the 1950 census). One effect this may have is skewing the figures for population, income, housing, and educational attainment.

- Some information (e.g. unemployment rates) is available for both counties and individual communities. Other information is available for just counties (e.g. election results), or just individual communities (e.g. local newspapers).

- Some statistical information is available only for larger communities. In addition, the larger places are more apt to have services such as newspapers, airports, school districts, etc.

- For the most complete information on any community, you should also check the entry for the county in which the community is located. In addition, more information and services will be listed under the larger places in the county.

- For a more in-depth discussion of geographic areas, please refer to the Census Bureau's Geographic Areas Reference Manual at http://www.census.gov/geo/www/garm.html.

DATA SOURCES

CENSUS 2000

The parts of the data which are from the 2000 Decennial Census are from the following sources: *U.S. Bureau of the Census, Census of Population and Housing, 2000: Summary Files 1 and 3.* Summary File 3 (SF 3) consists of 813 detailed tables of Census 2000 social, economic and housing characteristics compiled from a sample of approximately 19 million housing units (about 1 in 6 households) that received the Census 2000 long-form questionnaire. Summary File 1 (SF 1) contains 286 tables focusing on age, sex, households, families, and housing units. This file presents 100-percent population and housing figures for the total population, for 63 race categories, and for many other race and Hispanic or Latino categories.

Comparing SF 3 Estimates with Corresponding Values in SF 1

As in earlier censuses, the responses from the sample of households reporting on long forms must be weighted to reflect the entire population. Specifically, each responding household represents, on average, six or seven other households who reported using short forms.

One consequence of the weighting procedures is that each estimate based on the long form responses has an associated confidence interval. These confidence intervals are wider (as a percentage of the estimate) for geographic areas with smaller populations and for characteristics that occur less frequently in the area being examined (such as the proportion of people in poverty in a middle-income neighborhood).

In order to release as much useful information as possible, statisticians must balance a number of factors. In particular, for Census 2000, the Bureau of the Census created weighting areas—geographic areas from which about two hundred or more long forms were completed—which are large enough to produce good quality estimates. If smaller weighting areas had been used, the confidence intervals around the estimates would have been significantly wider, rendering many estimates less useful due to their lower reliability.

The disadvantage of using weighting areas this large is that, for smaller geographic areas within them, the estimates of characteristics that are also reported on the short form will not match the counts reported in SF 1. Examples of these characteristics are the total number of people, the number of people reporting specific racial categories, and the number of housing units. The official values for items reported on the short form come from SF 1 and SF 2.

The differences between the long form estimates in SF 3 and values in SF 1 are particularly noticeable for the smallest places, tracts, and block groups. The long form estimates of total population and total housing units in SF 3 will, however, match the SF 1 counts for larger geographic areas such as counties and states, and will be essentially the same for medium and large cities.

SF 1 gives exact numbers even for very small groups and areas, whereas SF 3 gives estimates for small groups and areas such as tracts and small places that are less exact. The goal of SF 3 is to identify large differences among areas or large changes over time. Estimates for small areas and small population groups often do exhibit large changes from one census to the next, so having the capability to measure them is worthwhile.

2005 Estimates and 2010 Projections

Some 2000 Census data has been updated with data provided by Claritas. Founded in 1971, Claritas is the industry leader in applied demography and the preeminent provider of small-area demographic estimates.

INFORMATION FOR COMMUNITIES

PHYSICAL CHARACTERISTICS

Place Type: Lists the type of place (city, town, village, borough, special city, CDP, township, plantation, gore, district, grant, location, reservation, or postal area). *Source: U.S. Bureau of the Census, Census of Population and Housing, 2000: Summary File 1 and U.S. Postal Service, City State File.*

Land and Water Area: Land and water area in square miles. *Source: U.S. Bureau of the Census, Census of Population and Housing, 2000: Summary File 1.*

Latitude and Longitude: Latitude and longitude in degrees. *Source: U.S. Bureau of the Census, Census of Population and Housing, 2000: Summary File 1.*

Elevation: Elevation in feet. *Source: U.S. Geological Survey, Geographic Names Information System (GNIS).*

HISTORY

History: Historical information. *Source: Columbia University Press, The Columbia Gazetteer of North America; Original research.*

POPULATION

Population: 1990 and 2000 figures are a 100% count of population. 2005 estimates and 2010 projections were provided by Claritas. *Source: Claritas; U.S. Bureau of the Census, Census of Population and Housing, 2000: Summary File 1.*

Population by Race: 2005 estimates includes the U.S. Bureau of the Census categories of White alone; Black alone; Asian alone; and Hispanic of any race. Alone refers to the fact that these figures are not in combination with any other race.

The concept of race, as used by the Census Bureau, reflects self-identification by people according to the race or races with which they most closely identify. These categories are socio-political constructs and should not be interpreted as being scientific or anthropological in nature. Furthermore, the race categories include both racial and national-origin groups.

- **White.** A person having origins in any of the original peoples of Europe, the Middle East, or North Africa. It includes people who indicate their race as "White" or report entries such as Irish, German, Italian, Lebanese, Near Easterner, Arab, or Polish.
- **Black or African American.** A person having origins in any of the Black racial groups of Africa. It includes people who indicate their race as "Black, African American, or Negro," or provide written entries such as African American, Afro-American, Kenyan, Nigerian, or Haitian.
- **Asian.** A person having origins in any of the original peoples of the Far East, Southeast Asia, or the Indian subcontinent including, for example, Cambodia, China, India, Japan, Korea, Malaysia, Pakistan, the Philippine Islands, Thailand, and Vietnam. It includes "Asian Indian," "Chinese," "Filipino," "Korean," "Japanese," "Vietnamese," and "Other Asian."
- **Hispanic.** The data on the Hispanic or Latino population, which was asked of all people, were derived from answers to long-form questionnaire Item 5, and short-form questionnaire Item 7. The terms "Spanish," "Hispanic origin," and "Latino" are used interchangeably. Some respondents identify with all three terms, while others may identify with only one of these three specific terms. Hispanics or Latinos who identify with the terms "Spanish," "Hispanic," or "Latino" are those who classify themselves in one of the specific Hispanic or Latino categories listed on the questionnaire — "Mexican," "Puerto Rican," or "Cuban" — as well as those who indicate that they are "other Spanish, Hispanic, or Latino." People who do not identify with one of the specific origins listed on the questionnaire but indicate that they are "other Spanish, Hispanic, or Latino" are those whose origins are from Spain, the Spanish-speaking countries of Central or South America, the Dominican Republic, or people identifying themselves generally as Spanish, Spanish-American, Hispanic, Hispano, Latino, and so on. All write-in responses to the "other Spanish/Hispanic/Latino" category were coded. Origin can be viewed as the heritage, nationality group, lineage, or country of birth of the person or the person's parents or ancestors before their arrival in the United States. People who identify their origin as Spanish, Hispanic, or Latino may be of any race.

Population Density: 2005 population divided by the land area in square miles. *Source: Claritas; U.S. Bureau of the Census, Census of Population and Housing, 2000: Summary File 1.*

Average Household Size: Average household size was calculated by dividing the total population by the total number of households. Figures are 2005 estimates. *Source: Claritas.*

Median Age: Figures are 2005 estimates. *Source: Claritas.*

Male/Female Ratio: Number of males per 100 females. Figures are 2005 estimates. *Source: Claritas.*

Marital Status: Percentage of population never married, now married, widowed, or divorced. *Source: U.S. Bureau of the Census, Census of Population and Housing, 2000: Summary File 3.*

The marital status classification refers to the status at the time of enumeration. Data on marital status are tabulated only for the population 15 years old and over. Each person was asked whether they were "Now married," "Widowed," "Divorced," or "Never married." Couples who live together (for example, people in common-law marriages) were able to report the marital status they considered to be the most appropriate.

- **Never married.** Never married includes all people who have never been married, including people whose only marriage(s) was annulled.
- **Now married.** All people whose current marriage has not ended by widowhood or divorce. This category includes people defined as "separated."
- **Widowed.** This category includes widows and widowers who have not remarried.
- **Divorced.** This category includes people who are legally divorced and who have not remarried.

Foreign Born: Percentage of population who were not U.S. citizens at birth. Foreign-born people are those who indicated they were either a U.S. citizen by naturalization or they were not a citizen of the United States. *Source: U.S. Bureau of the Census, Census of Population and Housing, 2000: Summary File 3.*

Ancestry: Largest ancestry groups reported (up to five). Includes multiple ancestries. *Source: U.S. Bureau of the Census, Census of Population and Housing, 2000: Summary File 3.*

The data represent self-classification by people according to the ancestry group or groups with which they most closely identify. Ancestry refers to a person's ethnic origin or descent, "roots," heritage, or the place of birth of the person, the person's parents, or their ancestors before their arrival in the United States. Some ethnic identities, such as Egyptian or Polish, can be traced to geographic areas outside the United States, while other ethnicities such as Pennsylvania German or Cajun evolved in the United States.

The ancestry question was intended to provide data for groups that were not included in the Hispanic origin and race questions. Therefore, although data on all groups are collected, the ancestry data shown in these tabulations are for non-Hispanic and non-race groups. Hispanic and race groups are included in the "Other groups" category for the ancestry tables in these tabulations.

The ancestry question allowed respondents to report one or more ancestry groups, although only the first two were coded. If a response was in terms of a dual ancestry, for example, "Irish English," the person was assigned two codes, in this case one for Irish and another for English. However, in certain cases, multiple responses such as "French Canadian," "Greek Cypriote," and "Scotch Irish" were assigned a single code reflecting their status as unique groups. If a person reported one of these unique groups in addition to another group, for example, "Scotch Irish English," resulting in three terms, that person received one code for the unique group (Scotch-Irish) and another one for the remaining group (English). If a person reported "English Irish French," only English and Irish were coded. Certain combinations of ancestries where the ancestry group is a part of another, such as "German-Bavarian," were coded as a single ancestry using the more specific group (Bavarian). Also, responses such as "Polish-American" or "Italian-American" were coded and tabulated as a single entry (Polish or Italian).

The Census Bureau accepted "American" as a unique ethnicity if it was given alone, with an ambiguous response, or with state names. If the respondent listed any other ethnic identity such as "Italian-American," generally the "American" portion of the response was not coded. However, distinct groups such as "American Indian," "Mexican American," and "African American" were coded and identified separately because they represented groups who considered themselves different from those who reported as "Indian," "Mexican," or "African," respectively.

The data is based on the total number of ancestries reported and coded. Thus, the sum of the counts in this type of presentation is not the total population but the total of all responses.

ECONOMY

Unemployment Rate: 2005 annual average. Includes all civilians age 16 or over who were unemployed and looking for work. *Source: U.S. Department of Labor, Bureau of Labor Statistics, Local Area Unemployment Statistics (http://www.bls.gov/lau/home.htm).*

Total Civilian Labor Force: 2005 annual average. Includes all civilians age 16 or over who were either employed, or unemployed and looking for work. *Source: U.S. Department of Labor, Bureau of Labor Statistics, Local Area Unemployment Statistics (http://www.bls.gov/lau/home.htm).*

Single-Family Building Permits Issued: Building permits issued for new single-family housing units in 2005. *Source: U.S. Census Bureau, Manufacturing and Construction Division (http://www.census.gov/const/www/permitsindex.html).*

Multi-Family Building Permits Issued: Building permits issued for new multi-family housing units in 2005. *Source: U.S. Census Bureau, Manufacturing and Construction Division (http://www.census.gov/const/www/permitsindex.html).*

Statistics on housing units authorized by building permits include housing units issued in local permit-issuing jurisdictions by a building or zoning permit. Not all areas of the country require a building or zoning permit. The statistics only represent those areas that do require a permit. Current surveys indicate that construction is undertaken for all but a very small percentage of housing units authorized by building permits. A major portion typically get under way during the month of permit issuance and most of the remainder begin within the three following months. Because of this lag, the housing unit authorization statistics do not represent the number of units actually put into construction for the period shown, and should therefore not be directly interpreted as "housing starts."

Statistics are based upon reports submitted by local building permit officials in response to a mail survey. They are obtained using Form C-404 const/www/c404.pdf, "Report of New Privately-Owned Residential Building or Zoning Permits Issued." When a report is not received, missing data are either (1) obtained from the Survey of Use of Permits (SUP) which is used to collect information on housing starts, or (2) imputed based on the assumption that the ratio of current month authorizations to those of a year ago should be the same for reporting and non-reporting places.

Employment by Occupation: Percentage of the employed civilian population 16 years and over in management, professional, service, sales, farming, construction, and production occupations. *Source: U.S. Bureau of the Census, Census of Population and Housing, 2000: Summary File 3.*

- **Management** includes management, business, and financial operations occupations:
  Management occupations, except farmers and farm managers
  Farmers and farm managers
  Business and financial operations occupations:
      Business operations specialists
      Financial specialists

- **Professional** includes professional and related occupations:
  Computer and mathematical occupations
  Architecture and engineering occupations:
      Architects, surveyors, cartographers, and engineers
      Drafters, engineering, and mapping technicians
  Life, physical, and social science occupations
  Community and social services occupations
  Legal occupations
  Education, training, and library occupations
  Arts, design, entertainment, sports, and media occupations
  Healthcare practitioners and technical occupations:
      Health diagnosing and treating practitioners and technical occupations
      Health technologists and technicians

- **Service** occupations include:
  Healthcare support occupations
  Protective service occupations:
      Fire fighting, prevention, and law enforcement workers, including supervisors

Other protective service workers, including supervisors
Food preparation and serving related occupations
Building and grounds cleaning and maintenance occupations
Personal care and service occupations

- **Sales** and office occupations include:
Sales and related occupations
Office and administrative support occupations

- **Farming,** fishing, and forestry occupations

- **Construction,** extraction, and maintenance occupations include:
Construction and extraction occupations:
Supervisors, construction, and extraction workers
Construction trades workers
Extraction workers
Installation, maintenance, and repair occupations

- **Production,** transportation, and material moving occupations include:
Production occupations
Transportation and material moving occupations:
Supervisors, transportation, and material moving workers
Aircraft and traffic control occupations
Motor vehicle operators
Rail, water, and other transportation occupations
Material moving workers

INCOME

Per Capita Income: Per capita income is the mean income computed for every man, woman, and child in a particular group. It is derived by dividing the total income of a particular group by the total population in that group. Per capita income is rounded to the nearest whole dollar. Figures shown are 2005 estimates. *Source: Claritas.*

Median Household Income: Includes the income of the householder and all other individuals 15 years old and over in the household, whether they are related to the householder or not. The median divides the income distribution into two equal parts: one-half of the cases falling below the median income and one-half above the median. For households, the median income is based on the distribution of the total number of households including those with no income. Median income for households is computed on the basis of a standard distribution and is rounded to the nearest whole dollar. Figures shown are 2005 estimates. *Source: Claritas.*

Average Household Income: Average household income is obtained by dividing total household income by the total number of households. Figures shown are 2005 estimates. *Source: Claritas.*

Percent of Households with Income of $100,000 or more: Figures shown are 2005 estimates. *Source: Claritas.*

Poverty Rate: Percentage of population with income in 1999 below the poverty level. Based on individuals for whom poverty status is determined. Poverty status was determined for all people except institutionalized people, people in military group quarters, people in college dormitories, and unrelated individuals under 15 years old. *Source: U.S. Bureau of the Census, Census of Population and Housing, 2000: Summary File 3.*

The poverty status of families and unrelated individuals in 1999 was determined using 48 thresholds (income cutoffs) arranged in a two-dimensional matrix. The matrix consists of family size (from 1 person to 9 or more people) cross-classified by presence and number of family members under 18 years old (from no children present to 8 or more children present). Unrelated individuals and 2-person families were further differentiated by the age of the reference person (RP) (under 65 years old and 65 years old and over).

To determine a person's poverty status, one compares the person's total family income with the poverty threshold appropriate for that person's family size and composition. If the total income of that person's family is less than the threshold appropriate for that family, then the person is considered poor, together with every member of his or her family. If a person is not living with anyone related by birth, marriage, or adoption, then the person's own income is compared with his or her poverty threshold.

TAXES

Total City Taxes Per Capita: Total city taxes collected divided by the population of the city. *Source: U.S. Bureau of the Census, State and Local Government Finances, 2002 (http://www.census.gov/govs/www/estimate.html).*

Taxes include:
- Property Taxes
- Sales and Gross Receipts Taxes
- Federal Customs Duties
- General Sales and Gross Receipts Taxes
- Selective Sales Taxes (alcoholic beverages; amusements; insurance premiums; motor fuels; pari-mutuels; public utilities; tobacco products; other)
- License Taxes (alcoholic beverages; amusements; corporations in general; hunting and fishing; motor vehicles motor vehicle operators; public utilities; occupation and business, NEC; other)
- Income Taxes (individual income; corporation net income; other)
- Death and Gift
- Documentary & Stock Transfer
- Severance
- Taxes, NEC

Total City Property Taxes Per Capita: Total city property taxes collected divided by the population of the city. *Source: U.S. Bureau of the Census, State and Local Government Finances, 2002 (http://www.census.gov/govs/www/estimate.html).*

Property Taxes include general property taxes, relating to property as a whole, taxed at a single rate or at classified rates according to the class of property. Property refers to real property (e.g. land and structures) as well as personal property; personal property can be either tangible (e.g. automobiles and boats) or intangible (e.g. bank accounts and stocks and bonds). Special property taxes, levied on selected types of property (e.g. oil and gas properties, house trailers, motor vehicles, and intangibles) and subject to rates not directly related to general property tax rates. Taxes based on income produced by property as a measure of its value on the assessment date.

EDUCATION

Educational Attainment: Figures shown are 2005 estimates and show the percent of population age 25 and over with a:

- **High school diploma (including GED) or higher:** includes people whose highest degree was a high school diploma or its equivalent, people who attended college but did not receive a degree, and people who received a college, university, or professional degree. People who reported completing the 12th grade but not receiving a diploma are not high school graduates.
- **Bachelor's degree or higher**
- **Master's degree or higher:** Master's degrees include the traditional MA and MS degrees and field-specific degrees, such as MSW, MEd, MBA, MLS, and Meng. *Source: Claritas.*

School Districts: Lists the name of each school district, the grade range (PK=pre-kindergarten; KG=kindergarten), the student enrollment, and the district headquarters' phone number. In each community profile, only school districts that have schools that are physically located within the community are shown. In addition, statistics for each school district cover the entire district, regardless of the physical location of the schools within the district. *Source: U.S. Department of Education, National Center for Educational Statistics, Directory of Public Elementary and Secondary Education Agencies, 2003-04.*

Four-year Colleges: Lists the name of each four-year college, the type of institution (private or public; for-profit or non-profit; religious affiliation; historically black college), the student enrollment, the phone number, and the annual tuition (including fees) for full-time, first-time undergraduate students (in-state and out-of-state). *Source: U.S. Department of Education, National Center for Educational Statistics, Directory of Postsecondary Institutions, 2004-05.*

Two-year Colleges: Lists the name of each two-year college, the type of institution (private or public; for-profit or non-profit; religious affiliation; historically black college), the student enrollment, the phone number, and the annual tuition (including fees) for full-time, first-time undergraduate students (in-state and out-of-state). *Source: U.S. Department of Education, National Center for Educational Statistics, Directory of Postsecondary Institutions, 2004-05.*

HOUSING

Homeownership Rate: Percentage of housing units that are owner-occupied. Figures shown are 2005 estimates. *Source: Claritas.*

Median Home Value: Median value of all owner-occupied housing units as reported by the owner. Figures shown are 2005 estimates. *Source: Claritas.*

Median Rent: Median monthly contract rent on specified renter-occupied and specified vacant-for-rent units. Specified renter-occupied and specified vacant-for-rent units exclude 1-family houses on 10 acres or more. Contract rent is the monthly rent agreed to or contracted for, regardless of any furnishings, utilities, fees, meals, or services that may be included. For vacant units, it is the monthly rent asked for the rental unit at the time of enumeration. *Source: U.S. Bureau of the Census, Census of Population and Housing, 2000: Summary File 3.*

Median Age of Housing: Median age of housing was calculated by subtracting median year structure built from 2000 (e.g. if the median year structure built is 1967, the median age of housing in that area is 33 years—2000 minus 1967). Year structure built refers to when the building was first constructed, not when it was remodeled, added to, or converted. For housing units under construction that met the housing unit definition—that is, all exterior windows, doors, and final usable floors were in place—the category "1999 or 2000" was used for tabulations. For mobile homes, houseboats, RVs, etc, the manufacturer's model year was assumed to be the year built. The data relate to the number of units built during the specified periods that were still in existence at the time of enumeration. *Source: U.S. Bureau of the Census, Census of Population and Housing, 2000: Summary File 3.*

HOSPITALS

Lists the hospital name and the number of licensed beds. *Source: Grey House Publishing, Directory of Hospital Personnel, 2005.*

SAFETY

Violent Crime Rate: Number of violent crimes reported per 10,000 population. Violent crimes include murder, forcible rape, robbery, and aggravated assault. *Source: Federal Bureau of Investigation, Uniform Crime Reports 2004 (http://www.fbi.gov/ucr/ucr.htm).*

Property Crime Rate: Number of property crimes reported per 10,000 population. Property crimes include burglary, larceny-theft, and motor vehicle theft. *Source: Federal Bureau of Investigation, Uniform Crime Reports 2004 (http://www.fbi.gov/ucr/ucr.htm).*

NEWSPAPERS

Lists the names of daily and weekly newspapers. Also includes the newspaper type and circulation, if available. *Source: BurrellesLuce MediaContacts 2005 (http://www.burrellesluce.com/MediaConnect).*

TRANSPORTATION

Commute to Work: Percentage of workers 16 years old and over that use the following means of transportation to commute to work: car; public transportation; walk; work from home. *Source: U.S. Bureau of the Census, Census of Population and Housing, 2000: Summary File 3.*

The means of transportation data for some areas may show workers using modes of public transportation that are not available in those areas (e.g. subway or elevated riders in a metropolitan area where there actually is no subway or elevated service). This result is largely due to people who worked during the reference week at a location that was different from their usual place of work (such as people away from home on business in an area where subway service was available) and people who used more than one means of transportation each day but whose principal means was unavailable where they lived (e.g. residents of non-metropolitan areas who drove to the fringe of a metropolitan area and took the commuter railroad most of the distance to work).

Travel Time to Work: Travel time to work for workers 16 years old and over. Reported for the following intervals: less than 15 minutes; 15 to 30 minutes; 30 to 45 minutes; 45 to 60 minutes; 60 minutes or more. *Source: U.S. Bureau of the Census, Census of Population and Housing, 2000: Summary File 3.*

Travel time to work refers to the total number of minutes that it usually took the person to get from home to work each day during the reference week. The elapsed time includes time spent waiting for public transportation, picking up passengers in carpools, and time spent in other activities related to getting to work.

Amtrak: Indicates if Amtrak service is available. Please note that the cities being served continually change. *Source: National Railroad Passenger Corporation, Amtrak National Timetable, 2005 (www.amtrak.com).*

AIRPORTS

Lists the local airport(s) along with type of service and hub size. *Source: U.S. Department of Transportation, Bureau of Transportation Statistics (http://www.bts.gov).*

ADDITIONAL INFORMATION CONTACTS

The following phone numbers are provided as sources of additional information: Chambers of Commerce; Economic Development Agencies; Boards of Realtors; Convention & Visitors Bureaus. Efforts have been made to provide the most recent area codes. However, area code changes may have occurred in listed numbers. *Source: Original research.*

INFORMATION FOR COUNTIES

PHYSICAL CHARACTERISTICS

Physical Location: Describes the physical location of the county. *Source: Columbia University Press, The Columbia Gazetteer of North America and original research.*

Land and Water Area: Land and water area in square miles. *Source: U.S. Bureau of the Census, Census of Population and Housing, 2000: Summary File 1.*

Time Zone: Lists the time zone. *Source: Original research.*

Year Organized: Year the county government was organized. *Source: National Association of Counties (www.naco.org).*

County Seat: Lists the county seat. If a county has more than one seat, then both are listed. *Source: National Association of Counties (www.naco.org).*

Metropolitan Area: Indicates the metropolitan area the county is located in. Also lists all the component counties of that metropolitan area. The Office of Management and Budget (OMB) defines metropolitan and micropolitan statistical areas. The current definitions are as of November 2004. *Source: U.S. Bureau of the Census (http://www.census.gov/population/www/estimates/metrodef.html).*

Climate: Includes all weather stations located within the county. Indicates the station name and elevation as well as the monthly average high and low temperatures, average precipitation, and average snowfall. The period of record is generally 1970-1999, however, certain weather stations contain averages going back as far as 1900. *Source: Grey House Publishing, Weather America: A Thirty-Year Summary of Statistical Weather Data and Rankings, 2001.*

POPULATION

Population: 1990 and 2000 figures are a 100% count of population. 2005 estimates and 2010 projections were provided by Claritas. *Source: Claritas; U.S. Bureau of the Census, Census of Population and Housing, 2000: Summary File 1.*

Population by Race: 2005 estimates includes the U.S. Bureau of the Census categories of White alone; Black alone; Asian alone; and Hispanic of any race. Alone refers to the fact that these figures are not in combination with any other race.

The concept of race, as used by the Census Bureau, reflects self-identification by people according to the race or races with which they most closely identify. These categories are socio-political constructs and should not be interpreted as being scientific or anthropological in nature. Furthermore, the race categories include both racial and national-origin groups.

- **White.** A person having origins in any of the original peoples of Europe, the Middle East, or North Africa. It includes people who indicate their race as "White" or report entries such as Irish, German, Italian, Lebanese, Near Easterner, Arab, or Polish.
- **Black or African American.** A person having origins in any of the Black racial groups of Africa. It includes people who indicate their race as "Black, African American, or Negro," or provide written entries such as African American, Afro-American, Kenyan, Nigerian, or Haitian.
- **Asian.** A person having origins in any of the original peoples of the Far East, Southeast Asia, or the Indian subcontinent including, for example, Cambodia, China, India, Japan, Korea, Malaysia, Pakistan, the Philippine Islands, Thailand, and Vietnam. It includes "Asian Indian," "Chinese," "Filipino," "Korean," "Japanese," "Vietnamese," and "Other Asian."
- **Hispanic.** The data on the Hispanic or Latino population, which was asked of all people, were derived from answers to long-form questionnaire Item 5, and short-form questionnaire Item 7. The terms "Spanish," "Hispanic origin," and "Latino" are used interchangeably. Some respondents identify with all three terms, while others may identify with only one of these three specific terms. Hispanics or Latinos who identify with the terms "Spanish," "Hispanic," or "Latino" are those who classify themselves in one of the specific Hispanic or Latino categories listed on the questionnaire — "Mexican," "Puerto Rican," or "Cuban" — as well as those who indicate that they are "other Spanish, Hispanic, or Latino." People who do not identify with one of the specific origins listed on the questionnaire but indicate that they are "other

Spanish, Hispanic, or Latino" are those whose origins are from Spain, the Spanish-speaking countries of Central or South America, the Dominican Republic, or people identifying themselves generally as Spanish, Spanish-American, Hispanic, Hispano, Latino, and so on. All write-in responses to the "other Spanish/Hispanic/Latino" category were coded. Origin can be viewed as the heritage, nationality group, lineage, or country of birth of the person or the person's parents or ancestors before their arrival in the United States. People who identify their origin as Spanish, Hispanic, or Latino may be of any race.

Population Density: 2005 population divided by the land area in square miles. *Source: Claritas; U.S. Bureau of the Census, Census of Population and Housing, 2000: Summary File 1.*

Average Household Size: Average household size was calculated by dividing the total population by the total number of households. Figures are 2005 estimates. *Source: Claritas.*

Median Age: Figures are 2005 estimates. *Source: Claritas.*

Male/Female Ratio: Number of males per 100 females. Figures are 2005 estimates. *Source: Claritas.*

RELIGION

Religion: Lists the largest religious groups (up to five) based on the number of adherents divided by the population of the county. Adherents are defined as "all members, including full members, their children and the estimated number of other regular participants who are not considered as communicant, confirmed or full members." The data is based on a study of 149 religious bodies sponsored by the Association of Statisticians of American Religious Bodies. The 149 bodies reported 268,254 congregations and 141,371,963 adherents. *Source: Glenmary Research Center, Religious Congregations & Membership in the United States 2000.*

ECONOMY

Unemployment Rate: 2005 annual average. Includes all civilians age 16 or over who were unemployed and looking for work. *Source: U.S. Department of Labor, Bureau of Labor Statistics, Local Area Unemployment Statistics (http://www.bls.gov/lau/home.htm).*

Total Civilian Labor Force: 2005 annual average. Includes all civilians age 16 or over who were either employed, or unemployed and looking for work. *Source: U.S. Department of Labor, Bureau of Labor Statistics, Local Area Unemployment Statistics (http://www.bls.gov/lau/home.htm).*

Leading Industries: Lists the three largest industries (excluding government) based on the number of employees. *Source: U.S. Bureau of the Census, County Business Patterns 2004 (http://www.census.gov/epcd/cbp/view/cbpview.html).*

Farms: The total number of farms and the total acreage they occupy. *Source: U.S. Department of Agriculture, National Agricultural Statistics Service, 2002 Census of Agriculture (http://www.nass.usda.gov/census).*

Companies that Employ 500 or more persons: The numbers of companies that employ 500 or more persons. Includes private employers only. *Source: U.S. Bureau of the Census, County Business Patterns 2004 (http://www.census.gov/epcd/cbp/view/cbpview.html).*

Companies that Employ 100 - 499 persons: The numbers of companies that employ 100 - 499 persons. Includes private employers only. *Source: U.S. Bureau of the Census, County Business Patterns 2004 (http://www.census.gov/epcd/cbp/view/cbpview.html).*

Companies that Employ 1 - 99 persons: The numbers of companies that employ 1 - 99 persons. Includes private employers only. *Source: U.S. Bureau of the Census, County Business Patterns 2004 (http://www.census.gov/epcd/cbp/view/cbpview.html)*

Black-Owned Businesses: Number of businesses that are majority-owned by a Black or African-American person(s). Majority ownership is defined as having 51 percent or more of the stock or equity in the business. Black or African American is defined as a person having origins in any of the black racial groups of Africa, including those who consider themselves to be "Haitian." *Source: U.S. Bureau of the Census, 2002 Economic Census, Survey of Business Owners: Black-Owned Firms, 2002 (http://www.census.gov/csd/sbo/index.html).*

Hispanic-Owned Businesses: Number of businesses that are majority-owned by a person(s) of Hispanic or Latino origin. Majority ownership is defined as having 51 percent or more of the stock or equity in the business. Hispanic or

Latino origin is defined as a person of Cuban, Mexican, Puerto Rican, South or Central American, or other Spanish culture or origin, regardless of race. *Source: U.S. Bureau of the Census, 2002 Economic Census, Survey of Business Owners: Hispanic-Owned Firms, 2002 (http://www.census.gov/csd/sbo/index.html).*

Women-Owned Businesses: Number of businesses that are majority-owned by a woman. Majority ownership is defined as having 51 percent or more of the stock or equity in the business. *Source: U.S. Bureau of the Census, 2002 Economic Census, Survey of Business Owners: Women-Owned Firms, 2002 (http://www.census.gov/csd/sbo/index.html).*

The Survey of Business Owners (SBO), formerly known as the Surveys of Minority- and Women-Owned Business Enterprises (SMOBE/SWOBE), provides statistics that describe the composition of U.S. businesses by gender, Hispanic or Latino origin, and race. Additional statistics include owner's age, education level, veteran status, and primary function in the business; family- and home-based businesses; types of customers and workers; and sources of financing for expansion, capital improvements, or start-up. Economic policymakers in federal, state and local governments use the SBO data to understand conditions of business success and failure by comparing census-to-census changes in business performances and by comparing minority-/nonminority- and women-/men-owned businesses.

Retail Sales per Capita: Total dollar amount of estimated retail sales divided by the estimated population of the county in 2006. *Source: Editor & Publisher Market Guide 2006*

Single-Family Building Permits Issued: Building permits issued for new, single-family housing units in 2005. *Source: U.S. Census Bureau, Manufacturing and Construction Division (http://www.census.gov/const/www/permitsindex.html).*

Multi-Family Building Permits Issued: Building permits issued for new, multi-family housing units in 2005. *Source: U.S. Census Bureau, Manufacturing and Construction Division (http://www.census.gov/const/www/permitsindex.html).*

Statistics on housing units authorized by building permits include housing units issued in local permit-issuing jurisdictions by a building or zoning permit. Not all areas of the country require a building or zoning permit. The statistics only represent those areas that do require a permit. Current surveys indicate that construction is undertaken for all but a very small percentage of housing units authorized by building permits. A major portion typically get under way during the month of permit issuance and most of the remainder begin within the three following months. Because of this lag, the housing unit authorization statistics do not represent the number of units actually put into construction for the period shown, and should therefore not be directly interpreted as "housing starts."

Statistics are based upon reports submitted by local building permit officials in response to a mail survey. They are obtained using Form C-404 const/www/c404.pdf, "Report of New Privately-Owned Residential Building or Zoning Permits Issued." When a report is not received, missing data are either (1) obtained from the Survey of Use of Permits (SUP) which is used to collect information on housing starts, or (2) imputed based on the assumption that the ratio of current month authorizations to those of a year ago should be the same for reporting and non-reporting places.

INCOME

Per Capita Income: Per capita income is the mean income computed for every man, woman, and child in a particular group. It is derived by dividing the total income of a particular group by the total population in that group. Per capita income is rounded to the nearest whole dollar. Figures shown are 2005 estimates. *Source: Claritas.*

Median Household Income: Includes the income of the householder and all other individuals 15 years old and over in the household, whether they are related to the householder or not. The median divides the income distribution into two equal parts: one-half of the cases falling below the median income and one-half above the median. For households, the median income is based on the distribution of the total number of households including those with no income. Median income for households is computed on the basis of a standard distribution and is rounded to the nearest whole dollar. Figures shown are 2005 estimates. *Source: Claritas.*

Average Household Income: Average household income is obtained by dividing total household income by the total number of households. Figures shown are 2005 estimates. *Source: Claritas.*

Percent of Households with Income of $100,000 or more: Figures shown are 2005 estimates. *Source: Claritas.*

Poverty Rate: Estimated percentage of population with income in 2003 below the poverty level. *Source: U.S. Bureau of the Census, Small Area Income & Poverty Estimates.*

Bankruptcy Rate: The personal bankruptcy filing rate is the number of bankruptcies per thousand residents in 2005. Personal bankruptcy filings include both Chapter 7 (liquidations) and Chapter 13 (reorganizations) based on the county of residence of the filer. *Source: Federal Deposit Insurance Corporation, Regional Economic Conditions (http://www2.fdic.gov/recon/index.html).*

TAXES

Total County Taxes Per Capita: Total county taxes collected divided by the population of the county. *Source: U.S. Bureau of the Census, State and Local Government Finances, 2002 (http://www.census.gov/govs/www/estimate.html).*

Taxes include:
- Property Taxes
- Sales and Gross Receipts Taxes
- Federal Customs Duties
- General Sales and Gross Receipts Taxes
- Selective Sales Taxes (alcoholic beverages; amusements; insurance premiums; motor fuels; pari-mutuels; public utilities; tobacco products; other)
- License Taxes (alcoholic beverages; amusements; corporations in general; hunting and fishing; motor vehicles motor vehicle operators; public utilities; occupation and business, NEC; other)
- Income Taxes (individual income; corporation net income; other)
- Death and Gift
- Documentary & Stock Transfer
- Severance
- Taxes, NEC

Total County Property Taxes Per Capita: Total county property taxes collected divided by the population of the county. *Source: U.S. Bureau of the Census, State and Local Government Finances, 2002 (http://www.census.gov/govs/www/estimate.html).*

Property Taxes include general property taxes, relating to property as a whole, taxed at a single rate or at classified rates according to the class of property. Property refers to real property (e.g. land and structures) as well as personal property; personal property can be either tangible (e.g. automobiles and boats) or intangible (e.g. bank accounts and stocks and bonds). Special property taxes, levied on selected types of property (e.g. oil and gas properties, house trailers, motor vehicles, and intangibles) and subject to rates not directly related to general property tax rates. Taxes based on income produced by property as a measure of its value on the assessment date.

EDUCATION

Educational Attainment: Figures shown are 2005 estimates and show the percent of population age 25 and over with a:

- **High school diploma (including GED) or higher:** includes people whose highest degree was a high school diploma or its equivalent, people who attended college but did not receive a degree, and people who received a college, university, or professional degree. People who reported completing the 12th grade but not receiving a diploma are not high school graduates.
- **Bachelor's degree or higher**
- **Master's degree or higher:** Master's degrees include the traditional MA and MS degrees and field-specific degrees, such as MSW, MEd, MBA, MLS, and Meng. *Source: Claritas.*

HOUSING

Homeownership Rate: Percentage of housing units that are owner-occupied. Figures shown are 2005 estimates. *Source: Claritas.*

Median Home Value: Median value of all owner-occupied housing units as reported by the owner. Figures shown are 2005 estimates. *Source: Claritas.*

Median Rent: Median monthly contract rent on specified renter-occupied and specified vacant-for-rent units. Specified renter-occupied and specified vacant-for-rent units exclude 1-family houses on 10 acres or more. Contract rent is the monthly rent agreed to or contracted for, regardless of any furnishings, utilities, fees, meals, or services that may be included. For vacant units, it is the monthly rent asked for the rental unit at the time of enumeration. *Source: U.S. Bureau of the Census, Census of Population and Housing, 2000: Summary File 3.*

Median Age of Housing: Median age of housing was calculated by subtracting median year structure built from 2000 (e.g. if the median year structure built is 1967, the median age of housing in that area is 33 years — 2000 minus 1967). Year structure built refers to when the building was first constructed, not when it was remodeled, added to, or converted. For housing units under construction that met the housing unit definition—that is, all exterior windows, doors, and final usable floors were in place—the category "1999 or 2000" was used for tabulations. For mobile homes, houseboats, RVs, etc, the manufacturer's model year was assumed to be the year built. The data relate to the number of units built during the specified periods that were still in existence at the time of enumeration. *Source: U.S. Bureau of the Census, Census of Population and Housing, 2000: Summary File 3.*

HEALTH AND VITAL STATISTICS

Birth Rate: Estimated number of births per 10,000 population in 2004. *Source: U.S. Census Bureau, Population Estimates, July 1, 2003 - July 1, 2004 (http://www.census.gov/popest/births.html).*

Death Rate: Estimated number of deaths per 10,000 population in 2004. *Source: U.S. Census Bureau, Population Estimates, July 1, 2003 - July 1, 2004 (http://www.census.gov/popest/births.html).*

Age-adjusted Cancer Mortality Rate: Number of age-adjusted deaths from cancer per 100,000 population in 2002. Cancer is defined as International Classification of Disease (ICD) codes C00 - D48.9 Neoplasms. *Source: Centers for Disease Control, CDC Wonder (http://wonder.cdc.gov).*

Age-adjusted death rates are weighted averages of the age-specific death rates, where the weights represent a fixed population by age. They are used because the rates of almost all causes of death vary by age. Age adjustment is a technique for "removing" the effects of age from crude rates, so as to allow meaningful comparisons across populations with different underlying age structures. For example, comparing the crude rate of heart disease in New York to that of California is misleading, because the relatively older population in New York will lead to a higher crude death rate, even if the age-specific rates of heart disease in New York and California are the same. For such a comparison, age-adjusted rates would be preferable. Age-adjusted rates should be viewed as relative indexes rather than as direct or actual measures of mortality risk.

Death rates based on counts of twenty or less (<=20) are flagged as "Unreliable". Death rates based on fewer than three years of data for counties with populations of less than 100,000 in the 1990 Census counts, are also flagged as "Unreliable" if the number of deaths is five or less (<=5).

Air Quality Index: The percentage of days in 2005 the AQI fell into the Good (0-50), Moderate (51-100), Unhealthy for Sensitive Groups (101-150), and Unhealthy (151+) ranges. *Source: Air Quality Index Report, 2005, U.S. Environmental Protection Agency, Office of Air and Radiation (http://www.epa.gov/oar).*

The AQI is an index for reporting daily air quality. It tells you how clean or polluted your air is, and what associated health concerns you should be aware of. The AQI focuses on health effects that can happen within a few hours or days after breathing polluted air. EPA uses the AQI for five major air pollutants regulated by the Clean Air Act: ground-level ozone, particulate matter, carbon monoxide, sulfur dioxide, and nitrogen dioxide. For each of these pollutants, EPA has established national air quality standards to protect against harmful health effects.

The AQI runs from 0 to 500. The higher the AQI value, the greater the level of air pollution and the greater the health danger. For example, an AQI value of 50 represents good air quality and little potential to affect public health, while an AQI value over 300 represents hazardous air quality. An AQI value of 100 generally corresponds to the national air quality standard for the pollutant, which is the level EPA has set to protect public health. So, AQI values below 100 are generally thought of as satisfactory. When AQI values are above 100, air quality is considered to be unhealthy—at first for certain sensitive groups of people, then for everyone as AQI values get higher. Each category corresponds to a different level of health concern. For example, when the AQI for a pollutant is between 51 and 100, the health concern is "Moderate." Here are the six levels of health concern and what they mean:

- "Good" The AQI value for your community is between 0 and 50. Air quality is considered satisfactory and air pollution poses little or no risk.
- "Moderate" The AQI for your community is between 51 and 100. Air quality is acceptable; however, for some pollutants there may be a moderate health concern for a very small number of individuals. For example, people who are unusually sensitive to ozone may experience respiratory symptoms.
- "Unhealthy for Sensitive Groups" Certain groups of people are particularly sensitive to the harmful effects of certain air pollutants. This means they are likely to be affected at lower levels than the general public. For example, children and adults who are active outdoors and people with respiratory disease are at greater risk from exposure to ozone, while people with heart disease are at greater risk from carbon monoxide. Some people may be sensitive to more than one pollutant. When AQI values are between 101 and 150, members of sensitive groups may experience health effects. The general public is not likely to be affected when the AQI is in this range.
- "Unhealthy" AQI values are between 151 and 200. Everyone may begin to experience health effects. Members of sensitive groups may experience more serious health effects.
- "Very Unhealthy" AQI values between 201 and 300 trigger a health alert, meaning everyone may experience more serious health effects.
- "Hazardous" AQI values over 300 trigger health warnings of emergency conditions. The entire population is more likely to be affected.

Number of Physicians: The number of active, non-federal physicians per 10,000 population in 2004. *Source: Area Resource File (ARF). February 2005. U.S. Department of Health and Human Services, Health Resources and Services Administration, Bureau of Health Professions, Rockville, MD.*

Number of Hospital Beds: The number of hospital beds per 10,000 population in 2003. *Source: Area Resource File (ARF). February 2005. U.S. Department of Health and Human Services, Health Resources and Services Administration, Bureau of Health Professions, Rockville, MD.*

Number of Hospital Admissions: The number of hospital admissions per 10,000 population in 2003. *Source: Area Resource File (ARF). February 2005. U.S. Department of Health and Human Services, Health Resources and Services Administration, Bureau of Health Professions, Rockville, MD.*

ELECTIONS

Elections: 2004 Presidential election results. *Source: Dave Leip's Atlas of U.S. Presidential Elections (http://www.uselectionatlas.org).*

NATIONAL AND STATE PARKS

Lists National and State parks located in the area. *Source: U.S. Geological Survey, Geographic Names Information System.*

ADDITIONAL INFORMATION CONTACTS

The following phone numbers are provided as sources of additional information: Chambers of Commerce; Economic Development Agencies; Boards of Realtors; Convention & Visitors Bureaus. Efforts have been made to provide the most recent area codes. However, area code changes may have occurred in listed numbers. *Source: Original research.*

User's Guide: Education

School District Rankings

Number of Schools: Total number of schools in the district. *Source: U.S. Department of Education, National Center for Education Statistics, Common Core of Data, Public Elementary/Secondary School Universe Survey: School Year 2003-2004.*

Number of Teachers: Teachers are defined as individuals who provide instruction to pre-kindergarten, kindergarten, grades 1 through 12, or ungraded classes, or individuals who teach in an environment other than a classroom setting, and who maintain daily student attendance records. Numbers reported are full-time equivalents (FTE). *Source: U.S. Department of Education, National Center for Education Statistics, Common Core of Data, Local Education Agency (School District) Universe Survey: School Year 2003-2004.*

Number of Students: A student is an individual for whom instruction is provided in an elementary or secondary education program that is not an adult education program and is under the jurisdiction of a school, school system, or other education institution. *Sources: U.S. Department of Education, National Center for Education Statistics, Common Core of Data, Local Education Agency (School District) Universe Survey: School Year 2003-2004 and Public Elementary/Secondary School Universe Survey: School Year 2003-2004*

Individual Education Program (IEP) Students: A written instructional plan for students with disabilities designated as special education students under IDEA-Part B. The written instructional plan includes a statement of present levels of educational performance of a child; statement of annual goals, including short-term instructional objectives; statement of specific educational services to be provided and the extent to which the child will be able to participate in regular educational programs; the projected date for initiation and anticipated duration of services; the appropriate objectives, criteria and evaluation procedures; and the schedules for determining, on at least an annual basis, whether instructional objectives are being achieved. *Source: U.S. Department of Education, National Center for Education Statistics, Common Core of Data, Local Education Agency (School District) Universe Survey: School Year 2003-2004*

English Language Learner (ELL) Students: Formerly referred to as Limited English Proficient (LEP). Students being served in appropriate programs of language assistance (e.g., English as a Second Language, High Intensity Language Training, bilingual education). Does not include pupils enrolled in a class to learn a language other than English. Also Limited-English-Proficient students are individuals who were not born in the United States or whose native language is a language other than English; or individuals who come from environments where a language other than English is dominant; or individuals who are American Indians and Alaskan Natives and who come from environments where a language other than English has had a significant impact on their level of English language proficiency; and who, by reason thereof, have sufficient difficulty speaking, reading, writing, or understanding the English language, to deny such individuals the opportunity to learn successfully in classrooms where the language of instruction is English or to participate fully in our society. *Source: U.S. Department of Education, National Center for Education Statistics, Common Core of Data, Local Education Agency (School District) Universe Survey: School Year 2003-2004*

Migrant Students: A migrant student as defined under federal regulation 34 CFR 200.40: 1) (a) Is younger than 22 (and has not graduated from high school or does not hold a high school equivalency certificate), but (b), if the child is too young to attend school-sponsored educational programs, is old enough to benefit from an organized instructional program; and 2) A migrant agricultural worker or a migrant fisher or has a parent, spouse, or guardian who is a migrant agricultural worker or a migrant fisher; and 3) Performs, or has a parent, spouse, or guardian who performs qualifying agricultural or fishing employment as a principal means of livelihood; and 4) Has moved within the preceding 36 months to obtain or to accompany or join a parent, spouse, or guardian to obtain, temporary or seasonal employment in agricultural or fishing work; and 5) Has moved from one school district to another; or in a state that is comprised of a single school district, has moved from one administrative area to another within such district; or resides in a school district of more than 15,000 square miles, and migrates a distance of 20 miles or more to a temporary residence to engage in a fishing activity. Provision 5 currently applies only to Alaska. *Source: U.S. Department of Education, National Center for Education Statistics, Common Core of Data, Public Elementary/Secondary School Universe Survey: School Year 2003-2004*

Students Eligible for Free Lunch Program: The free lunch program is defined as a program under the National School Lunch Act that provides cash subsidies for free lunches to students based on family size and income criteria. *Source: U.S. Department of Education, National Center for Education Statistics, Common Core of Data, Public Elementary/Secondary School Universe Survey: School Year 2003-2004*

Students Eligible for Reduced-Price Lunch Program: A student who is eligible to participate in the Reduced-Price Lunch Program under the National School Lunch Act. *Source: U.S. Department of Education, National Center for Education Statistics, Common Core of Data, Public Elementary/Secondary School Universe Survey: School Year 2003-2004*

Student/Teacher Ratio: The number of students divided by the number of teachers (FTE). See Number of Students and Number of Teachers above for for information.

Student/Librarian Ratio: The number of students divided by the number of library and media support staff. Library and media support staff are defined as staff members who render other professional library and media services; also includes library aides and those involved in library/media support. Their duties include selecting, preparing, caring for, and making available to instructional staff, equipment, films, filmstrips, transparencies, tapes, TV programs, and similar materials maintained separately or as part of an instructional materials center. Also included are activities in the audio-visual center, TV studio, related-work-study areas, and services provided by audio-visual personnel. Numbers are based on full-time equivalents. *Source: U.S. Department of Education, National Center for Education Statistics, Common Core of Data, Local Education Agency (School District) Universe Survey: School Year 2003-2004.*

Student/Counselor Ratio: The number of students divided by the number of guidance counselors. Guidance counselors are professional staff assigned specific duties and school time for any of the following activities in an elementary or secondary setting: counseling with students and parents; consulting with other staff members on learning problems; evaluating student abilities; assisting students in making educational and career choices; assisting students in personal and social development; providing referral assistance; and/or working with other staff members in planning and conducting guidance programs for students. The state applies its own standards in apportioning the aggregate of guidance counselors/directors into the elementary and secondary level components. Numbers reported are full-time equivalents. *Source: U.S. Department of Education, National Center for Education Statistics, Common Core of Data, Local Education Agency (School District) Universe Survey: School Year 2003-2004.*

Current Spending per Student: Expenditure for Instruction, Support Services, and Other Elementary/Secondary Programs. Includes salaries, employee benefits, purchased services, and supplies, as well as payments made by states on behalf of school districts. Also includes transfers made by school districts into their own retirement system. Excludes expenditure for Non-Elementary/Secondary Programs, debt service, capital outlay, and transfers to other governments or school districts. This item is formally called "Current Expenditures for Public Elementary/Secondary Education."

Instruction: Includes payments from all funds for salaries, employee benefits, supplies, materials, and contractual services for elementary/secondary instruction. It excludes capital outlay, debt service, and interfund transfers for elementary/secondary instruction. Instruction covers regular, special, and vocational programs offered in both the regular school year and summer school. It excludes instructional support activities as well as adult education and community services. Instruction salaries includes salaries for teachers and teacher aides and assistants.

Support Services: Relates to support services functions (series 2000) defined in Financial Accounting for Local and State School Systems (National Center for Education Statistics 2000). Includes payments from all funds for salaries, employee benefits, supplies, materials, and contractual services. It excludes capital outlay, debt service, and interfund transfers. It includes expenditure for the following functions:

- Business/Central/Other Support Services
- General Administration
- Instructional Staff Support
- Operation and Maintenance
- Pupil Support Services
- Pupil Transportation Services
- School Administration
- Nonspecified Support Services

Values shown are dollars per pupil per year. They were calculated by dividing the total dollar amounts by the fall membership. Fall membership is comprised of the total student enrollment on October 1 (or the closest school day to October 1) for all grade levels (including prekindergarten and kindergarten) and ungraded pupils. Membership includes students both present and absent on the measurement day. *Source: U.S. Department of Education, National Center for Education Statistics, Common Core of Data, School District Finance Survey (F-33), Fiscal Year 2001.*

Number of Diploma Recipients: A student who has received a diploma during the previous school year or subsequent summer school. This category includes regular diploma recipients and other diploma recipients. A High School Diploma is a formal document certifying the successful completion of a secondary school program prescribed by the state education agency or other appropriate body. *Source: U.S. Department of Education, National Center for Education Statistics, Common Core of Data, Local Education Agency (School District) Universe Survey: School Year 2003-2004.*

High School Drop-out Rate: A dropout is a student who was enrolled in school at some time during the previous school year; was not enrolled at the beginning of the current school year; has not graduated from high school or completed a state or district approved educational program; and does not meet any of the following exclusionary conditions: has transferred to another public school district, private school, or state- or district-approved educational program; is temporarily absent due to suspension or school-approved illness; or has died. The values shown cover grades 9 through 12. *Source: U.S. Department of Education, National Center for Education Statistics, Common Core of Data, Local Education Agency Universe Dropout File: School Year 2000-2001*

Note: n/a indicates data not available.

New Jersey Educational Profile

Please refer to the District Rankings section in the front of this User's Guide for an explanation of data for all items except for the following:

Average Salary: The average teacher salary in 2003-2004. *Source: American Federation of Teachers, Survey & Analysis of Teacher Salary Trends 2004*

College Entrance Exam Scores:

Scholastic Aptitude Test (SAT). *Note: The College Board strongly discourages the comparison or ranking of states on the basis of SAT scores alone. Source: The College Board, Mean SAT Reasoning Test™ Verbal and Math Scores by State, with Changes for Selected Years, 2005*

American College Testing Program (ACT). *ACT, 2005 ACT National and State Scores*

National Assessment of Educational Progress (NAEP)

The National Assessment of Educational Progress (NAEP), also known as "the Nation's Report Card," is the only nationally representative and continuing assessment of what America's students know and can do in various subject areas. As a result of the "No Child Left Behind" legislation, all states are required to participate in NAEP. For more information please visit the U.S. Department of Education, National Center for Education Statistics at http://nces.ed.gov/nationsreportcard.

No Child Left Behind (NCLB)

The federal No Child left Behind Act of 2001 (NCLB) requires public accountability reports at the school, district, and state levels that include the status of adequate yearly progress (AYP), attendance and dropout/graduation rates, student assessment data disaggregated into subgroups, and information on "highly qualified" teachers.

To meet these requirements, the New Jersey Department of Education (NJDOE) produces the NCLB Report, which provides statewide information incorporating all NCLB conditions (see below), as required by NCLB. The NCLB Report, which identifies data by school is available on the NJDOE Web site at http://education.state.nj.us/rc/NCLB05/NCLB.html. Data are presented at the school level and organized by district. The NJDOE also produces an annual New Jersey School Report Card, required under a 1995 state law.

Guide to the Data Fields in the 2005 NCLB Report

Adequate Yearly Progress (AYP) Status

Adequate yearly progress (AYP) is calculated primarily on the state assessment results for language arts literacy (LAL) and mathematics. These results are applied for performance for the total school population and disaggregated subgroups. Assessment participation is also applied for the total student population and the disaggregated subgroups . A secondary indicator is used for the final AYP calculation. Attendance is the secondary indicator for elementary and middle schools; dropout/graduation rate for high schools. More detail on how AYP is calculated is provided in the document Understanding Accountability in New Jersey for 2005 State Assessments, available on the NJDOE Web site at www.nj.gov/njded/grants/NCLB/guidance/understanding.pdf.

Data Components

The NCLB Report includes a school summary showing proficiency percentages for the school, district, and state. The percentages are shown for the current and previous years for comparison. Results are presented by content area and the state standard is given. The proficiency percentages reflect state assessment data by grade spans: Elementary – NJ Assessment of Skills and Knowledge 3 and 4 (NJASK 3 & 4); Middle - Grade Eight Proficiency Assessment (GEPA); and High School - High School Proficiency Assessment (HSPA). Alternate Proficiency Assessment (APA) data are included in these results. The percent of students not tested is also shown.

A link is given for the results, which are disaggregated by the subgroups required under NCLB. The same information provided on the proficiency summary (proficiency percentages, the state standard, and the percentage of students not tested for the school, district, and state) is listed by content area and grade span for each student subgroup, disaggregated by race/ethnicity, students with disabilities, limited English proficient, and economically disadvantaged. Additionally, data are broken down by gender and migrant students; however, data for these subgroups are not used in the AYP calculation.

Proficiency benchmarks are set by the state for each grade span. Schools must achieve these benchmarks to achieve AYP. Schools must achieve proficiency in the total population and in each student subgroup (except gender and migrant students). If a school does not achieve proficiency or participation in any indicator, it does not make AYP. If the school does not make AYP for two or more consecutive years in the same content area, it is designated a school in need of improvement (SINI).

If all grades within a school are not subject to testing, assessment information for that school is not given.

User's Guide: Ancestry

Places Covered

The ranking tables are based on 701 places in New Jersey. Places covered fall into one of the following categories: 52 cities; 3 villages; 15 towns; 254 boroughs; 205 townships; and 172 Census Designated Places (CDP). The U.S. Bureau of the Census defines a CDP as "a statistical entity, defined for each decennial census according to Census Bureau guidelines, comprising a densely settled concentration of population that is not within an incorporated place, but is locally identified by a name. CDPs are delineated cooperatively by state and local officials and the Census Bureau, following Census Bureau guidelines. Beginning with Census 2000 there are no size limits."

Source of Data

The ancestries shown in this chapter were compiled from three different sections of the 2000 Census: Race; Hispanic Origin; and Ancestry. While the ancestries are sorted alphabetically for ease-of-use, it's important to note the origin of each piece of data. Data for Race and Hispanic Origin was taken from Summary File 1 (SF1) while Ancestry data was taken from Summary File 3 (SF3). The distinction is important because SF1 contains the 100-percent data, which is the information compiled from the questions asked of all people and about every housing unit. SF3 was compiled from a sample of approximately 19 million housing units (about 1 in 6 households) that received the Census 2000 long-form questionnaire.

Ancestries Based on Race

The data on race were derived from answers to the question on race that was asked of all people. The concept of race, as used by the Census Bureau, reflects self-identification by people according to the race or races with which they most closely identify. These categories are sociopolitical constructs and should not be interpreted as being scientific or anthropological in nature. Furthermore, the race categories include both racial and national-origin groups.

If an individual did not provide a race response, the race or races of the householder or other household members were assigned using specific rules of precedence of household relationship. For example, if race was missing for a natural-born child in the household, then either the race or races of the householder, another natural-born child, or the spouse of the householder were assigned. If race was not reported for anyone in the household, the race or races of a householder in a previously processed household were assigned.

African-American/Black:
  Not Hispanic
  Hispanic
Alaska Native tribes, specified:
  Alaska Athabascan
  Aleut
  Eskimo
  Tlingit-Haida
  All other tribes
Alaska Native tribes, not specified
American Indian or Alaska Native
  tribes, not specified
American Indian tribes, specified:
  Apache
  Blackfeet
  Cherokee
  Cheyenne
  Chickasaw
  Chippewa
  Choctaw
  Colville
  Comanche
  Cree

Creek
Crow
Delaware
Houma
Iroquois
Kiowa
Latin American Indians
Lumbee
Menominee
Navajo
Osage
Ottawa
Paiute
Pima
Potawatomi
Pueblo
Puget Sound Salish
Seminole
Shoshone
Sioux
Tohono O'Odham
Ute
Yakama

Yaqui
Yuman
All other tribes
American Indian tribes,
  not specified
Asian:
  Bangladeshi
  Cambodian
  Chinese, except Taiwanese
  Filipino
  Hmong
  Indian
  Indonesian
  Japanese
  Korean
  Laotian
  Malaysian
  Pakistani
  Sri Lankan
  Taiwanese
  Thai
  Vietnamese
  Other Asian, specified

  Other Asian, not specified
Hawaii Native/Pacific Islander:
  Melanesian:
    Fijian
    Other Melanesian
  Micronesian:
    Guamanian/Chamorro
    Other Micronesian
  Polynesian:
    Native Hawaiian
    Samoan
    Tongan
    Other Polynesian
  Other Pacific Islander,
    specified
  Other Pacific Islander,
    not specified
White:
  Not Hispanic
  Hispanic

African American or Black: A person having origins in any of the Black racial groups of Africa. It includes people who indicate their race as "Black, African Am., or Negro," or provide written entries such as African American, Afro American, Kenyan, Nigerian, or Haitian.

American Indian or Alaska Native: A person having origins in any of the original peoples of North and South America (including Central America) and who maintain tribal affiliation or community attachment. It includes people who classified themselves as described below.

American Indian - Includes people who indicated their race as "American Indian," entered the name of an Indian tribe, or reported such entries as Canadian Indian, French American Indian, or Spanish-American Indian.

Respondents who identified themselves as American Indian were asked to report their enrolled or principal tribe. Therefore, tribal data in tabulations reflect the written entries reported on the questionnaires. Some of the entries (for example, Iroquois, Sioux, Colorado River, and Flathead) represent nations or reservations. The information on tribe is based on self identification and therefore does not reflect any designation of federally or state-recognized tribe. Information on American Indian tribes is presented in summary files. The information for Census 2000 is derived from the American Indian Tribal Classification List for the 1990 census that was updated based on a December 1997 Federal Register Notice, entitled "Indian Entities Recognized and Eligible to Receive Service From the United States Bureau of Indian Affairs," Department of the Interior, Bureau of Indian Affairs, issued by the Office of Management and Budget.

Alaska Native - Includes written responses of Eskimos, Aleuts, and Alaska Indians, as well as entries such as Arctic Slope, Inupiat, Yupik, Alutiiq, Egegik, and Pribilovian. The Alaska tribes are the Alaskan Athabascan, Tlingit, and Haida. The information for Census 2000 is based on the American Indian Tribal Classification List for the 1990 census, which was expanded to list the individual Alaska Native Villages when provided as a written response for race.

Asian: A person having origins in any of the original peoples of the Far East, Southeast Asia, or the Indian subcontinent including, for example, Cambodia, China, India, Japan, Korea, Malaysia, Pakistan, the Philippine Islands, Thailand, and Vietnam. It includes "Asian Indian," "Chinese," "Filipino," "Korean," "Japanese," "Vietnamese," and "Other Asian."

Asian Indian - Includes people who indicated their race as "Asian Indian" or identified themselves as Bengalese, Bharat, Dravidian, East Indian, or Goanese.

Chinese - Includes people who indicate their race as "Chinese" or who identify themselves as Cantonese, or Chinese American.

Filipino - Includes people who indicate their race as "Filipino" or who report entries such as Philipino, Philipine, or Filipino American.

Japanese - Includes people who indicate their race as "Japanese" or who report entries such as Nipponese or Japanese American.

Korean - Includes people who indicate their race as "Korean" or who provide a response of Korean American.

Vietnamese - Includes people who indicate their race as "Vietnamese" or who provide a response of Vietnamese American.

Cambodian - Includes people who provide a response such as Cambodian or Cambodia.

Hmong - Includes people who provide a response such as Hmong, Laohmong, or Mong.

Laotian - Includes people who provide a response such as Laotian, Laos, or Lao.

Thai - Includes people who provide a response such as Thai, Thailand, or Siamese.

Other Asian - Includes people who provide a response of Bangladeshi; Bhutanese; Burmese; Indochinese; Indonesian; Iwo Jiman; Madagascar; Malaysian; Maldivian; Nepalese; Okinawan; Pakistani; Singaporean; Sri Lankan; or Other Asian, specified and Other Asian, not specified.

Native Hawaiian or Other Pacific Islander: A person having origins in any of the original peoples of Hawaii, Guam, Samoa, or other Pacific Islands. It includes people who indicate their race as "Native Hawaiian," "Guamanian or Chamorro," "Samoan," and "Other Pacific Islander."

Native Hawaiian - Includes people who indicate their race as "Native Hawaiian" or who identify themselves as "Part Hawaiian" or "Hawaiian."

Guamanian or Chamorro - Includes people who indicate their race as such, including written entries of Chamorro or Guam.

Samoan - Includes people who indicate their race as "Samoan" or who identify themselves as American Samoan or Western Samoan.

Other Pacific Islander - Includes people who provide a write-in response of a Pacific Islander group, such as Carolinian, Chuukese (Trukese), Fijian, Kosraean, Melanesian, Micronesian, Northern Mariana Islander, Palauan, Papua New Guinean, Pohnpeian, Polynesian, Solomon Islander, Tahitian, Tokelauan, Tongan, Yapese, or Pacific Islander, not specified.

White: A person having origins in any of the original peoples of Europe, the Middle East, or North Africa. It includes people who indicate their race as "White" or report entries such as Irish, German, Italian, Lebanese, Near Easterner, Arab, or Polish.

Ancestries Based on Hispanic Origin

Hispanic or Latino:	Salvadoran	Argentinean	Uruguayan
Central American:	Other Central American	Bolivian	Venezuelan
Costa Rican	Cuban	Chilean	Other South American
Guatemalan	Dominican Republic	Colombian	Other Hispanic/Latino
Honduran	Mexican	Ecuadorian	
Nicaraguan	Puerto Rican	Paraguayan	
Panamanian	South American:	Peruvian	

The data on the Hispanic or Latino population were derived from answers to a question that was asked of all people. The terms "Spanish," "Hispanic origin," and "Latino" are used interchangeably. Some respondents identify with all three terms while others may identify with only one of these three specific terms. Hispanics or Latinos who identify with the terms "Spanish," "Hispanic," or "Latino" are those who classify themselves in one of the specific Spanish, Hispanic, or Latino categories listed on the questionnaire ("Mexican," "Puerto Rican," or "Cuban") as well as those who indicate that they are "other Spanish/Hispanic/Latino." People who do not identify with one of the specific origins listed on the questionnaire but indicate that they are "other Spanish, Hispanic, or Latino" are those whose origins are from Spain, the Spanish-speaking countries of Central or South America, the Dominican Republic, or people identifying themselves generally as Spanish, Spanish-American, Hispanic, Hispano, Latino, and so on. All write-in responses to the "other Spanish/Hispanic/Latino" category were coded.

Origin can be viewed as the heritage, nationality group, lineage, or country of birth of the person or the person's parents or ancestors before their arrival in the United States. People who identify their origin as Spanish, Hispanic, or Latino may be of any race.

In all cases where the origin of households, families, or occupied housing units is classified as Spanish, Hispanic, or Latino, the origin of the householder is used. If an individual could not provide a Hispanic origin response, their origin was assigned using specific rules of precedence of household relationship. For example, if origin was missing for a natural-born daughter in the household, then either the origin of the householder, another natural-born child, or spouse of the householder was assigned. If Hispanic origin was not reported for anyone in the household, the Hispanic origin of a householder in a previously processed household with the same race was assigned.

Other Ancestries

Acadian/Cajun	Moroccan	French, except Basque	Scottish
Afghan	Palestinian	French Canadian	Serbian
African, Subsaharan:	Syrian	German	Slavic
African	Other Arab	German Russian	Slovak
Cape Verdean	Armenian	Greek	Slovene
Ethiopian	Assyrian/Chaldean/Syriac	Guyanese	Soviet Union
Ghanian	Australian	Hungarian	Swedish
Kenyan	Austrian	Icelander	Swiss
Liberian	Basque	Iranian	Turkish
Nigerian	Belgian	Irish	Ukrainian
Senegalese	Brazilian	Israeli	United States or American
Sierra Leonean	British	Italian	Welsh
Somalian	Bulgarian	Latvian	West Indian, excluding Hispanic:
South African	Canadian	Lithuanian	Bahamian
Sudanese	Carpatho Rusyn	Luxemburger	Barbadian
Ugandan	Celtic	Macedonian	Belizean
Zairian	Croatian	Maltese	Bermudan
Zimbabwean	Cypriot	New Zealander	British West Indian
Other Subsaharan African	Czech	Northern European	Dutch West Indian
Albanian	Czechoslovakian	Norwegian	Haitian
Alsatian	Danish	Pennsylvania German	Jamaican
Arab:	Dutch	Polish	Trinidadian and
Arab/Arabic	Eastern European	Portuguese	Tobagonian
Egyptian	English	Romanian	U.S. Virgin Islander
Iraqi	Estonian	Russian	West Indian
Jordanian	European	Scandinavian	Other West Indian
Lebanese	Finnish	Scotch-Irish	Yugoslavian

The data on ancestry were derived from answers to long-form questionnaire Item 10, which was asked of a sample of the population. The data represent self-classification by people according to the ancestry group or groups with which they most closely identify. Ancestry refers to a person's ethnic origin or descent, "roots," heritage, or the place of birth of the person, the person's parents, or their ancestors before their arrival in the United States. Some ethnic identities, such as Egyptian or Polish, can be traced to geographic areas outside the United States, while other ethnicities, such as Pennsylvania German or Cajun, evolved in the United States.

The intent of the ancestry question was not to measure the degree of attachment the respondent had to a particular ethnicity. For example, a response of "Irish" might reflect total involvement in an Irish community or only a memory of ancestors several generations removed from the individual. Also, the question was intended to provide data for groups that were not included in the Hispanic origin and race questions. Official Hispanic origin data come from long-form questionnaire Item 5, and official race data come from long-form questionnaire Item 6. Therefore, although data on all groups are collected, the ancestry data shown in these tabulations are for non-Hispanic and non-race groups.

The ancestry question allowed respondents to report one or more ancestry groups, although only the first two were coded. If a response was in terms of a dual ancestry, for example, "Irish English," the person was assigned two codes, in this case one for Irish and another for English. However, in certain cases, multiple responses such as "French Canadian," "Greek Cypriote," and "Scotch Irish" were assigned a single code reflecting their status as unique groups. If a person reported one of these unique groups in addition to another group, for example, "Scotch Irish English," resulting in three terms, that person received one code for the unique group (Scotch-Irish) and another one for the remaining group (English). If a person reported "English Irish French," only English and Irish were coded. Certain combinations of ancestries where the ancestry group is a part of another, such as "German-Bavarian," were coded as a single ancestry using the more specific group (Bavarian). Also, responses such as "Polish-American" or "Italian-American" were coded and tabulated as a single entry (Polish or Italian).

The Census Bureau accepted "American" as a unique ethnicity if it was given alone, with an ambiguous response, or with state names. If the respondent listed any other ethnic identity such as "Italian-American," generally the "American" portion of the response was not coded. However, distinct groups such as "American Indian," "Mexican American," and "African American" were coded and identified separately because they represented groups who considered themselves different from those who reported as "Indian," "Mexican," or "African," respectively.

Census 2000 tabulations on ancestry are presented using two types of data presentations — one using total people as the base, and the other using total responses as the base. This chapter uses total responses as the base and includes the total number of ancestries reported and coded. If a person reported a multiple ancestry such as "French Danish," that response was counted twice in the tabulations — once in the French category and again in the Danish category. Thus, the sum of the counts in this type of presentation is not the total population but the total of all responses.

An automated coding system was used for coding ancestry in Census 2000. This greatly reduced the potential for error associated with a clerical review. Specialists with knowledge of the subject matter reviewed, edited, coded, and resolved inconsistent or incomplete responses. The code list used in Census 2000, containing over 1,000 categories, reflects the results of the Census Bureau's experience with the 1990 ancestry question, research, and consultation with many ethnic experts. Many decisions were made to determine the classification of responses. These decisions affected the grouping of the tabulated data. For example, the Italian category includes the responses of Sicilian and Tuscan, as well as a number of other responses.

Although some people consider religious affiliation a component of ethnic identity, the ancestry question was not designed to collect any information concerning religion. Thus, if a religion was given as an answer to the ancestry question, it was listed in the "Other groups" category which is not shown in this chapter.

Ancestry should not be confused with a person's place of birth, although a person's place of birth and ancestry may be the same.

Ranking Section

In the ranking section of this chapter, each ancestry has three tables. The first table shows the top 10 places sorted by number (based on all places, regardless of population), the second table shows the top 10 places sorted by percent (based on all places, regardless of population), the third table shows the top 10 places sorted by percent (based on places with populations of 10,000 or more).

Within each table, column one displays the place name, the state, and the county (if a place spans more than one county, the county that holds the majority of the population is shown). Column two displays the number of people reporting each ancestry, and column three is the percent of the total population reporting each ancestry. For tables representing ancestries based on race or Hispanic origin, the 100-percent population figure from SF1 is used to calculate the value in the "%" column. For all other ancestries the sample population figure from SF3 is used to calculate the value in the "%" column.

Alphabetical Ancestry Cross-Reference Guide

Acadian/Cajun
Afghan
African *See African, sub-Saharan: African*
African American/Black
African American/Black: Hispanic
African American/Black: Not Hispanic
African, sub-Saharan
African, sub-Saharan: African
African, sub-Saharan: Cape Verdean
African, sub-Saharan: Ethiopian
African, sub-Saharan: Ghanian
African, sub-Saharan: Kenyan
African, sub-Saharan: Liberian
African, sub-Saharan: Nigerian
African, sub-Saharan: Other
African, sub-Saharan: Senegalese
African, sub-Saharan: Sierra Leonean
African, sub-Saharan: Somalian
African, sub-Saharan: South African
African, sub-Saharan: Sudanese
African, sub-Saharan: Ugandan
African, sub-Saharan: Zairian
African, sub-Saharan: Zimbabwean
Alaska Athabascan *See Alaska Native: Alaska Athabascan*
Alaska Native tribes, not specified
Alaska Native tribes, specified
Alaska Native: Alaska Athabascan
Alaska Native: Aleut
Alaska Native: All other tribes
Alaska Native: Eskimo
Alaska Native: Tlingit-Haida
Albanian
Aleut *See Alaska Native: Aleut*
Alsatian
American *See United States or American*
American Indian or Alaska Native tribes, not specified
American Indian tribes, not specified
American Indian tribes, specified
American Indian: All other tribes
American Indian: Apache
American Indian: Blackfeet
American Indian: Cherokee
American Indian: Cheyenne
American Indian: Chickasaw
American Indian: Chippewa
American Indian: Choctaw
American Indian: Colville
American Indian: Comanche
American Indian: Cree
American Indian: Creek
American Indian: Crow
American Indian: Delaware
American Indian: Houma
American Indian: Iroquois
American Indian: Kiowa
American Indian: Latin American Indians
American Indian: Lumbee
American Indian: Menominee
American Indian: Navajo
American Indian: Osage
American Indian: Ottawa
American Indian: Paiute
American Indian: Pima
American Indian: Potawatomi
American Indian: Pueblo
American Indian: Puget Sound Salish
American Indian: Seminole
American Indian: Shoshone

American Indian: Sioux
American Indian: Tohono O'Odham
American Indian: Ute
American Indian: Yakama
American Indian: Yaqui
American Indian: Yuman
Apache *See American Indian: Apache*
Arab
Arab/Arabic *See Arab: Arab/Arabic*
Arab: Arab/Arabic
Arab: Egyptian
Arab: Iraqi
Arab: Jordanian
Arab: Lebanese
Arab: Moroccan
Arab: Other
Arab: Palestinian
Arab: Syrian
Argentinean *See Hispanic: Argentinean*
Armenian
Asian
Asian: Bangladeshi
Asian: Cambodian
Asian: Chinese, except Taiwanese
Asian: Filipino
Asian: Hmong
Asian: Indian
Asian: Indonesian
Asian: Japanese
Asian: Korean
Asian: Laotian
Asian: Malaysian
Asian: Other Asian, not specified
Asian: Other Asian, specified
Asian: Pakistani
Asian: Sri Lankan
Asian: Taiwanese
Asian: Thai
Asian: Vietnamese
Assyrian/Chaldean/Syriac
Australian
Austrian
Bahamian *See West Indian: Bahamian, excluding Hispanic*
Bangladeshi *See Asian: Bangladeshi*
Barbadian *See West Indian: Barbadian, excluding Hispanic*
Basque
Belgian
Belizean *See West Indian: Belizean, excluding Hispanic*
Bermudan *See West Indian: Bermudan, excluding Hispanic*
Blackfeet *See American Indian: Blackfeet*
Bolivian *See Hispanic: Bolivian*
Brazilian
British
British West Indian *See West Indian: British West Indian, excluding Hispanic*
Bulgarian
Cambodian *See Asian: Cambodian*
Canadian
Cape Verdean *See African, sub-Saharan: Cape Verdean*
Carpatho Rusyn
Celtic
Central American: *See Hispanic: Central American*
Cherokee *See American Indian: Cherokee*

Cheyenne *See American Indian: Cheyenne*
Chickasaw *See American Indian: Chickasaw*
Chilean *See Hispanic: Chilean*
Chinese, except Taiwanese *See Asian: Chinese, except Taiwanese*
Chippewa *See American Indian: Chippewa*
Choctaw *See American Indian: Choctaw*
Colombian *See Hispanic: Colombian*
Colville *See American Indian: Colville*
Comanche *See American Indian: Comanche*
Costa Rican *See Hispanic: Costa Rican*
Cree *See American Indian: Cree*
Creek *See American Indian: Creek*
Croatian
Crow *See American Indian: Crow*
Cuban *See Hispanic: Cuban*
Cypriot
Czech
Czechoslovakian
Danish
Delaware *See American Indian: Delaware*
Dominican Republic *See Hispanic: Dominican Republic*
Dutch
Dutch West Indian *See West Indian: Dutch West Indian, excluding Hispanic*
Eastern European
Ecuadorian *See Hispanic: Ecuadorian*
Egyptian *See Arab: Egyptian*
English
Eskimo *See Alaska Native: Eskimo*
Estonian
Ethiopian *See African, sub-Saharan: Ethiopian*
European
Fijian *See Hawaii Native/Pacific Islander: Fijian*
Filipino *See Asian: Filipino*
Finnish
French Canadian
French, except Basque
German
German Russian
Ghanian *See African, sub-Saharan: Ghanian*
Greek
Guamanian or Chamorro *See Hawaii Native/Pacific Islander: Guamanian or Chamorro*
Guatemalan *See Hispanic: Guatemalan*
Guyanese
Haitian *See West Indian: Haitian, excluding Hispanic*
Hawaii Native/Pacific Islander
Hawaii Native/Pacific Islander: Fijian
Hawaii Native/Pacific Islander: Guamanian or Chamorro
Hawaii Native/Pacific Islander: Melanesian
Hawaii Native/Pacific Islander: Micronesian
Hawaii Native/Pacific Islander: Native Hawaiian
Hawaii Native/Pacific Islander: Other Melanesian
Hawaii Native/Pacific Islander: Other Micronesian

Hawaii Native/Pacific Islander: Other Pacific Islander, not specified
Hawaii Native/Pacific Islander: Other Pacific Islander, specified
Hawaii Native/Pacific Islander: Other Polynesian
Hawaii Native/Pacific Islander: Polynesian
Hawaii Native/Pacific Islander: Samoan
Hawaii Native/Pacific Islander: Tongan
Hispanic or Latino
Hispanic: Argentinean
Hispanic: Bolivian
Hispanic: Central American
Hispanic: Chilean
Hispanic: Colombian
Hispanic: Costa Rican
Hispanic: Cuban
Hispanic: Dominican Republic
Hispanic: Ecuadorian
Hispanic: Guatemalan
Hispanic: Honduran
Hispanic: Mexican
Hispanic: Nicaraguan
Hispanic: Other
Hispanic: Other Central American
Hispanic: Other South American
Hispanic: Panamanian
Hispanic: Paraguayan
Hispanic: Peruvian
Hispanic: Puerto Rican
Hispanic: Salvadoran
Hispanic: South American
Hispanic: Uruguayan
Hispanic: Venezuelan
Hmong *See Asian: Hmong*
Honduran *See Hispanic: Honduran*
Houma *See American Indian: Houma*
Hungarian
Icelander
Indian, American *See American Indian*
Indian, Asian *See Asian: Indian*
Indonesian *See Asian: Indonesian*
Iranian
Iraqi *See Arab: Iraqi*
Irish
Iroquois *See American Indian: Iroquois*
Israeli
Italian
Jamaican *See West Indian: Jamaican, excluding Hispanic*
Japanese *See Asian: Japanese*
Jordanian *See Arab: Jordanian*
Kenyan *See African, sub-Saharan: Kenyan*
Kiowa *See American Indian: Kiowa*
Korean *See Asian: Korean*
Laotian *See Asian: Laotian*
Latin American Indians *See American Indian: Latin American Indians*
Latino *See Hispanic or Latino*
Latvian
Lebanese *See Arab: Lebanese*
Liberian *See African, sub-Saharan: Liberian*
Lithuanian
Lumbee *See American Indian: Lumbee*
Luxemburger
Macedonian
Malaysian *See Asian: Malaysian*
Maltese
Melanesian: *See Hawaii Native/Pacific Islander: Melanesian*

Menominee *See American Indian: Menominee*
Mexican *See Hispanic: Mexican*
Micronesian: *See Hawaii Native/Pacific Islander: Micronesian*
Moroccan *See Arab: Moroccan*
Native Hawaiian *See Hawaii Native/Pacific Islander: Native Hawaiian*
Navajo *See American Indian: Navajo*
New Zealander
Nicaraguan *See Hispanic: Nicaraguan*
Nigerian *See African, sub-Saharan: Nigerian*
Northern European
Norwegian
Osage *See American Indian: Osage*
Ottawa *See American Indian: Ottawa*
Paiute *See American Indian: Paiute*
Pakistani *See Asian: Pakistani*
Palestinian *See Arab: Palestinian*
Panamanian *See Hispanic: Panamanian*
Paraguayan *See Hispanic: Paraguayan*
Pennsylvania German
Peruvian *See Hispanic: Peruvian*
Pima *See American Indian: Pima*
Polish
Polynesian: *See Hawaii Native/Pacific Islander: Polynesian*
Portuguese
Potawatomi *See American Indian: Potawatomi*
Pueblo *See American Indian: Pueblo*
Puerto Rican *See Hispanic: Puerto Rican*
Puget Sound Salish *See American Indian: Puget Sound Salish*
Romanian
Russian
Salvadoran *See Hispanic: Salvadoran*
Samoan *See Hawaii Native/Pacific Islander: Samoan*
Scandinavian
Scotch-Irish
Scottish
Seminole *See American Indian: Seminole*
Senegalese *See African, sub-Saharan: Senegalese*
Serbian
Shoshone *See American Indian: Shoshone*
Sierra Leonean *See African, sub-Saharan: Sierra Leonean*
Sioux *See American Indian: Sioux*
Slavic
Slovak
Slovene
Somalian *See African, sub-Saharan: Somalian*
South African *See African, sub-Saharan: South African*
South American: *See Hispanic: South American*
Soviet Union
Sri Lankan *See Asian: Sri Lankan*
sub-Saharan African *See African, sub-Saharan*
Sudanese *See African, sub-Saharan: Sudanese*
Swedish
Swiss
Syrian *See Arab: Syrian*
Taiwanese *See Asian: Taiwanese*
Thai *See Asian: Thai*

Tlingit-Haida *See Alaska Native: Tlingit-Haida*
Tohono O'Odham *See American Indian: Tohono O'Odham*
Tongan *See Hawaii Native/Pacific Islander: Tongan*
Trinidadian and Tobagonian *See West Indian: Trinidadian and Tobagonian, excluding Hispanic*
Turkish
U.S. Virgin Islander *See West Indian: U.S. Virgin Islander, excluding Hispanic*
Ugandan *See African, sub-Saharan: Ugandan*
Ukrainian
United States or American
Uruguayan *See Hispanic: Uruguayan*
Ute *See American Indian: Ute*
Venezuelan *See Hispanic: Venezuelan*
Vietnamese *See Asian: Vietnamese*
Welsh
West Indian, excluding Hispanic
West Indian: Bahamian, excluding Hispanic
West Indian: Barbadian, excluding Hispanic
West Indian: Belizean, excluding Hispanic
West Indian: Bermudan, excluding Hispanic
West Indian: British West Indian, excluding Hispanic
West Indian: Dutch West Indian, excluding Hispanic
West Indian: Haitian, excluding Hispanic
West Indian: Jamaican, excluding Hispanic
West Indian: Other, excluding Hispanic
West Indian: Trinidadian and Tobagonian, excluding Hispanic
West Indian: U.S. Virgin Islander, excluding Hispanic
West Indian: West Indian, excluding Hispanic
White
White: Hispanic
White: Not Hispanic
Yakama *See American Indian: Yakama*
Yaqui *See American Indian: Yaqui*
Yugoslavian
Yuman *See American Indian: Yuman*
Zairian *See African, sub-Saharan: Zairian*
Zimbabwean *See African, sub-Saharan: Zimbabwean*

User's Guide: Hispanic Population

Places Covered

Ranking tables cover all counties and all places in New Jersey with populations of 10,000 or more.

Source of Data

CENSUS 2000

Data for this chapter was derived from following source: *U.S. Bureau of the Census, Census of Population and Housing, 2000: Summary File 4.* Summary File 4 (SF 4) contains sample data, which is the information compiled from the questions asked of a sample (generally 1-in-6) of all people and housing units. Summary File 4 is repeated or iterated for the total population and 335 additional population groups. This chapter focuses on the following 24 population groups:

Hispanic or Latino (of any race)
    Central American
        Costa Rican
        Guatemalan
        Honduran
        Nicaraguan
        Panamanian
        Salvadoran
    Cuban
    Dominican (Dominican Republic)
    Mexican
    Puerto Rican
    South American
        Argentinian
        Bolivian
        Chilean
        Colombian
        Ecuadorian
        Paraguayan
        Peruvian
        Uruguayan
        Venezuelan
    Spaniard
    Other Hispanic or Latino

Please note that the above list only includes Spanish-speaking population groups. Groups such as Brazilian are not classified as Hispanic by the Bureau of the Census because they primarily speak Portugese.

In order for any of the tables for a specific group to be shown in Summary File 4, the data must meet a minimum population threshold. For Summary File 4, all tables are repeated for each race group, American Indian and Alaska Native tribe, and Hispanic or Latino group if the 100-percent count of people of that specific group in a particular geographic area is 100 or more. There also must be 50 or more unweighted people of that specific group in a particular geographic area. For example, if there are 100 or more 100-percent people tabulated as Chilean in County A, and there are 50 or more unweighted people, then all matrices for Chilean are shown in SF 4 for County A.

To maintain confidentiality, the Census Bureau applies statistical procedures that introduce some uncertainty into data for small geographic areas with small population groups. Therefore, tables may contain both sampling and nonsampling error.

In an iterated file such as SF 4, the universes *households, families,* and *occupied housing units* are classified by the race or ethnic group of the householder. In any population table where there is no note, the universe classification is always based on the race or ethnicity of the person. In all housing tables, the universe classification is based on the race or ethnicity of the householder.

Comparing SF 4 Estimates with Corresponding Values in SF 1 and SF 2

As in earlier censuses, the responses from the sample of households reporting on long forms must be weighted to reflect the entire population. Specifically, each responding household represents, on average, six or seven other households who reported using short forms. One consequence of the weighting procedures is that each estimate based on the long form responses has an associated confidence interval. These confidence intervals are wider (as a percentage of the estimate) for geographic areas with smaller populations and for characteristics that occur less frequently in the area being examined (such as the proportion of people in poverty in a middle-income neighborhood). In order to release as much useful information as possible, statisticians must balance a number of factors. In particular, for Census 2000, the Bureau of the Census created weighting areas—geographic areas from which about two hundred or more long forms were completed—which are large enough to produce good quality estimates. If smaller weighting areas had been used, the confidence intervals around the estimates would have been significantly wider, rendering many estimates less useful due to their lower reliability. The disadvantage of using weighting areas this large is that, for smaller geographic areas within them, the estimates of characteristics that are also reported on the short form will not match the counts reported in SF 1 or SF 2. Examples of these characteristics are the total number of people, the number of people reporting specific racial categories, and the number of housing units. The official values for items reported on the short form come from SF 1 and SF 2. The differences between the long form estimates in SF 4 and values in SF 1 or SF 2 are particularly noticeable for the smallest places, tracts, and block groups. The long form estimates of total population and total housing units in SF 4 will, however, match the SF 1 and SF 2 counts for larger geographic areas such as counties and states, and will be essentially the same for medium and large cities. This phenomenon also occurred for the 1990 Census, although in that case, the weighting areas included relatively small places. As a result, the long form estimates matched the short form counts for those places, but the confidence intervals around the estimates of characteristics collected only on the long form were often significantly wider (as a percentage of the estimate). SF 1 gives exact numbers even for very small groups and areas; whereas, SF 4 gives estimates for small groups and areas such as tracts and small places that are less exact. The goal of SF 4 is to identify large differences among areas or large changes over time. Estimates for small areas and small population groups often do exhibit large changes from one census to the next, so having the capability to measure them is worthwhile.

Topics

POPULATION

Total Population: Sample count of total population.

Hispanic Population: The data on the Hispanic or Latino population, which was asked of all people, were derived from answers to long-form questionnaire Item 5, and short-form questionnaire Item 7. The terms "Spanish," "Hispanic origin," and "Latino" are used interchangeably. Some respondents identify with all three terms, while others may identify with only one of these three specific terms. Hispanics or Latinos who identify with the terms "Spanish," "Hispanic," or "Latino" are those who classify themselves in one of the specific Hispanic or Latino categories listed on the questionnaire — "Mexican," "Puerto Rican," or "Cuban" — as well as those who indicate that they are "other Spanish, Hispanic, or Latino." People who do not identify with one of the specific origins listed on the questionnaire but indicate that they are "other Spanish, Hispanic, or Latino" are those whose origins are from Spain, the Spanish-speaking countries of Central or South America, the Dominican Republic, or people identifying themselves generally as Spanish, Spanish-American, Hispanic, Hispano, Latino, and so on. All write-in responses to the "other Spanish/Hispanic/Latino" category were coded. Origin can be viewed as the heritage, nationality group, lineage, or country of birth of the person or the person's parents or ancestors before their arrival in the United States. People who identify their origin as Spanish, Hispanic, or Latino may be of any race.

Population groups whose primary language is not Spanish are not classified as Hispanic by the Bureau of the Census and are not included in this chapter (eg. Brazilian).

AGE

Median Age: Divides the age distribution into two equal parts: one-half of the cases falling below the median age and one-half above the median. Median age is computed on the basis of a single year of age standard distribution.

The data on age, which was asked of all people, were derived from answers to the long-form questionnaire Item 4 and short-form questionnaire Item 6. The age classification is based on the age of the person in complete years as of April 1, 2000. The age of the person usually was derived from their date of birth information. Their reported age was used only when date of birth information was unavailable.

HOUSEHOLD SIZE

Average Household Size: A measure obtained by dividing the number of people in households by the total number of households (or householders). In cases where household members are tabulated by race or Hispanic origin, household members are classified by the race or Hispanic origin of the householder rather than the race or Hispanic origin of each individual. Average household size is rounded to the nearest hundredth.

LANGUAGE SPOKEN AT HOME

English Only: Number and percentage of population 5 years and over who report speaking English-only at home.

Spanish: Number and percentage of population 5 years and over who report speaking Spanish at home.

Language spoken at home data were derived from answers to long-form questionnaire Items 11a and 11b, which were asked of a sample of the population. Data were edited to include in tabulations only the population 5 years old and over. Questions 11a and 11b referred to languages spoken at home in an effort to measure the current use of languages other than English. People who knew languages other than English but did not use them at home or who only used them elsewhere were excluded. Most people who reported speaking a language other than English at home also speak English. The questions did not permit determination of the primary or dominant language of people who spoke both English and another language.

FOREIGN-BORN

Foreign Born: Number and percentage of population who were not U.S. citizens at birth. Foreign-born people are those who indicated they were either a U.S. citizen by naturalization or they were not a citizen of the United States.

Foreign-Born Naturalized Citizens: Number and percentage of population who were not U.S. citizens at birth but became U.S. citizens by naturalization.

The data on place of birth were derived from answers to long-form questionnaire Item 12 which was asked of a sample of the population. Respondents were asked to report the U.S. state, Puerto Rico, U.S. Island Area, or foreign country where they were born. People not reporting a place of birth were assigned the state or country of birth of another family member or their residence 5 years earlier, or were imputed the response of another person with similar characteristics. People born outside the United States were asked to report their place of birth according to current international boundaries. Since numerous changes in boundaries of foreign countries have occurred in the last century, some people may have reported their place of birth in terms of boundaries that existed at the time of their birth or emigration, or in accordance with their own national preference.

EDUCATIONAL ATTAINMENT

High School Graduates: Number and percentage of the population age 25 and over who have a high school diploma or higher. This category includes people whose highest degree was a high school diploma or its equivalent, people who attended college but did not receive a degree, and people who received a college, university, or professional degree. People who reported completing the 12th grade but not receiving a diploma are not high school graduates.

4-Years College Graduates: Number and percentage of the population age 25 and over who have a 4-year college, university, or professional degree.

Data on educational attainment were derived from answers to long-form questionnaire Item 9, which was asked of a sample of the population. Data on attainment are tabulated for the population 25 years old and over.

The order in which degrees were listed on the questionnaire suggested that doctorate degrees were "higher" than professional school degrees, which were "higher" than master's degrees. The question included instructions for people currently enrolled in school to report the level of the previous grade attended or the highest degree received. Respondents who did not report educational attainment or enrollment level were assigned the attainment of a person of the same age, race, Hispanic or Latino origin, occupation and sex, where possible, who resided in the same or a nearby area. Respondents who filled more than one box were edited to the highest level or degree reported.

The question included a response category that allowed respondents to report completing the 12th grade without receiving a high school diploma. It allowed people who received either a high school diploma or the equivalent (Test of General Educational Development—G.E.D.) and did not attend college, to be reported as "high school graduate(s)." The category "Associate degree" included people whose highest degree is an associate degree, which generally requires 2 years of college level work and is either in an occupational program that prepares them for a specific occupation, or an academic program primarily in the arts and sciences. The course work may or may not be transferable to a bachelor's degree. Master's degrees include the traditional MA and MS degrees and field-specific degrees, such as MSW, MEd, MBA, MLS, and MEng. Some examples of professional degrees include medicine, dentistry, chiropractic, optometry, osteopathic medicine, pharmacy, podiatry, veterinary medicine, law, and theology. Vocational and technical training such as barber school training; business, trade, technical, and vocational schools; or other training for a specific trade, are specifically excluded.

INCOME AND POVERTY

Median Household Income (in dollars): Includes the income of the householder and all other individuals 15 years old and over in the household, whether they are related to the householder or not. The median divides the income distribution into two equal parts: one-half of the cases falling below the median income and one-half above the median. For households, the median income is based on the distribution of the total number of households including those with no income. Median income for households is computed on the basis of a standard distribution and is rounded to the nearest whole dollar.

Per Capita Income (in dollars): Per capita income is the mean income computed for every man, woman, and child in a particular group. It is derived by dividing the total income of a particular group by the total population in that group. Per capita income is rounded to the nearest whole dollar.

The data on income in 1999 were derived from answers to long-form questionnaire Items 31 and 32, which were asked of a sample of the population 15 years old and over. "Total income" is the sum of the amounts reported separately for wage or salary income; net self-employment income; interest, dividends, or net rental or royalty income or income from estates and trusts; social security or railroad retirement income; Supplemental Security Income (SSI); public assistance or welfare payments; retirement, survivor, or disability pensions; and all other income.

Receipts from the following sources are not included as income: capital gains, money received from the sale of property (unless the recipient was engaged in the business of selling such property); the value of income "in kind" from food stamps, public housing subsidies, medical care, employer contributions for individuals, etc.; withdrawal of bank deposits; money borrowed; tax refunds; exchange of money between relatives living in the same household; and gifts and lump-sum inheritances, insurance payments, and other types of lump-sum receipts.

The eight types of income reported in the census are defined as follows:

Wage or salary income. Wage or salary income includes total money earnings received for work performed as an employee during the calendar year 1999. It includes wages, salary, armed forces pay, commissions, tips, piece-rate payments, and cash bonuses earned before deductions were made for taxes, bonds, pensions, union dues, etc.

Self-employment income. Self-employment income includes both farm and nonfarm self-employment income. Nonfarm self-employment income includes net money income (gross receipts minus expenses) from one's own business, professional enterprise, or partnership. Gross receipts include the value of all goods sold and services rendered. Expenses include costs of goods purchased, rent, heat, light, power, depreciation charges, wages and salaries paid, business taxes (not personal income taxes), etc. Farm self-employment income includes net money income (gross receipts minus operating expenses) from the operation of a farm by a person on his or her own account, as an owner, renter, or sharecropper. Gross receipts include the value of all products sold, government farm programs, money received from the rental of farm equipment to others, and incidental receipts from the sale of wood, sand, gravel, etc. Operating expenses include cost of feed, fertilizer, seed, and other farming supplies, cash wages paid to farmhands, depreciation charges, cash rent, interest on farm mortgages, farm building repairs, farm taxes (not state and federal personal income taxes), etc. The value of fuel, food, or other farm products used for family living is not included as part of net income.

Interest, dividends, or net rental income. Interest, dividends, or net rental income includes interest on savings or bonds, dividends from stockholdings or membership in associations, net income from rental of property to others and receipts from boarders or lodgers, net royalties, and periodic payments from an estate or trust fund.

Social Security income. Social security income includes social security pensions and survivors benefits, permanent disability insurance payments made by the Social Security Administration prior to deductions for medical insurance, and railroad retirement insurance checks from the U.S. government. Medicare reimbursements are not included.

Supplemental Security Income (SSI). Supplemental Security Income (SSI) is a nationwide U.S. assistance program administered by the Social Security Administration that guarantees a minimum level of income for needy aged, blind, or disabled individuals. The census questionnaire for Puerto Rico asked about the receipt of SSI; however, SSI is not a federally administered program in Puerto Rico. Therefore, it is probably not being interpreted by most respondents as the same as SSI in the United States. The only way a resident of Puerto Rico could have appropriately reported SSI would have been if they lived in the United States at any time during calendar year 1999 and received SSI.

Public assistance income. Public assistance income includes general assistance and Temporary Assistance to Needy Families (TANF). Separate payments received for hospital or other medical care (vendor payments) are excluded. This does not include Supplemental Security Income (SSI).

Retirement income. Retirement income includes: (1) retirement pensions and survivor benefits from a former employer; labor union; or federal, state, or local government; and the U.S. military; (2) income from workers' compensation; disability income from companies or unions; federal, state, or local government; and the U.S. military; (3) periodic receipts from annuities and insurance; and (4) regular income from IRA and KEOGH plans. This does not include social security income.

All other income. All other income includes unemployment compensation, Veterans' Administration (VA) payments, alimony and child support, contributions received periodically from people not living in the household, military family allotments, and other kinds of periodic income other than earnings.

Poverty Status: Number and percentage of population with income in 1999 below the poverty level. Based on individuals for whom poverty status is determined. Poverty status was determined for all people except institutionalized people, people in military group quarters, people in college dormitories, and unrelated individuals under 15 years old.

The poverty status of families and unrelated individuals in 1999 was determined using 48 thresholds (income cutoffs) arranged in a two dimensional matrix. The matrix consists of family size (from 1 person to 9 or more people) cross-classified by presence and number of family members under 18 years old (from no children present to 8 or more children present). Unrelated individuals and 2-person families were further differentiated by the age of the reference person (RP) (under 65 years old and 65 years old and over).

To determine a person's poverty status, one compares the person's total family income with the poverty threshold appropriate for that person's family size and composition. If the total income of that person's family is less than the threshold appropriate for that family, then the person is considered poor, together with every member of his or her family. If a person is not living with anyone related by birth, marriage, or adoption, then the person's own income is compared with his or her poverty threshold.

HOUSING

Homeownership: Number and percentage of housing units that are owner-occupied.

The data on tenure, which was asked at all occupied housing units, were obtained from answers to long-form questionnaire Item 33, and short-form questionnaire Item 2. All occupied housing units are classified as either owner occupied or renter occupied.

A housing unit is owner occupied if the owner or co-owner lives in the unit even if it is mortgaged or not fully paid for. The owner or co-owner must live in the unit and usually is Person 1 on the questionnaire. The unit is "Owned by you or someone in this household with a mortgage or loan" if it is being purchased with a mortgage or some other debt arrangement, such as a deed of trust, trust deed, contract to purchase, land contract, or purchase agreement. The unit is also considered owned with a mortgage if it is built on leased land and there is a mortgage on the unit. Mobile homes occupied by owners with installment loans balances are also included in this category.

Median Gross Rent (in dollars): Median monthly gross rent on specified renter-occupied and specified vacant-for-rent units. Specified renter-occupied and specified vacant-for-rent units exclude 1-family houses on 10 acres or more.

The data on gross rent were obtained from answers to long-form questionnaire Items 45a-d, which were asked on a sample basis. Gross rent is the contract rent plus the estimated average monthly cost of utilities (electricity, gas, water and sewer) and fuels (oil, coal, kerosene, wood, etc.) if these are paid by the renter (or paid for the renter by someone else). Gross rent is intended to eliminate differentials that result from varying practices with respect to the inclusion of utilities and fuels as part of the rental payment. The estimated costs of utilities and fuels are reported on an annual basis but are converted to monthly figures for the tabulations. Renter units occupied without payment of cash rent are shown separately as "No cash rent" in the tabulations.

Housing units that are renter occupied without payment of cash rent are shown separately as "No cash rent" in census data products. The unit may be owned by friends or relatives who live elsewhere and who allow occupancy without charge. Rent-free houses or apartments may be provided to compensate caretakers, ministers, tenant farmers, sharecroppers, or others.

Contract rent is the monthly rent agreed to or contracted for, regardless of any furnishings, utilities, fees, meals, or services that may be included. For vacant units, it is the monthly rent asked for the rental unit at the time of enumeration.

If the contract rent includes rent for a business unit or for living quarters occupied by another household, only that part of the rent estimated to be for the respondent's unit was included. Excluded was any rent paid for additional units or for business premises.

If a renter pays rent to the owner of a condominium or cooperative, and the condominium fee or cooperative carrying charge also is paid by the renter to the owner, the condominium fee or carrying charge was included as rent.

If a renter receives payments from lodgers or roomers who are listed as members of the household, the rent without deduction for any payments received from the lodgers or roomers was to be reported. The respondent was to report the rent agreed to or contracted for even if paid by someone else such as friends or relatives living elsewhere, a church or welfare agency, or the government through subsidies or vouchers.

The median divides the rent distribution into two equal parts: one-half of the cases falling below the median contract rent and one-half above the median. Median contract rents are computed on the basis of a standard distribution and are rounded to the nearest whole dollar. Units reported as "No cash rent" are excluded.

Median Home Value (in dollars): Reported by the owner of specified owner-occupied or specified vacant-for-sale housing units. Specified owner-occupied and specified vacant-for-sale housing units include only 1-family houses on less than 10 acres without a business or medical office on the property. The data for "specified units" exclude mobile homes, houses with a business or medical office, houses on 10 or more acres, and housing units in multi-unit buildings.

The data on value (also referred to as "price asked" for vacant units) were obtained from answers to long-form questionnaire Item 51, which was asked on a sample basis at owner-occupied housing units and units that were being bought, or vacant for sale at the time of enumeration. Value is the respondent's estimate of how much the property (house and lot, mobile home and lot, or condominium unit) would sell for if it were for sale. If the house or mobile home was owned or being bought, but the land on which it sits was not, the respondent was asked to estimate the combined value of the house or mobile home and the land. For vacant units, value was the price asked for the property. Value was tabulated separately for all owner-occupied and vacant-for-sale housing units, owner-occupied and vacant-for-sale mobile homes, and specified owner-occupied and specified vacant-for-sale housing units.

The median divides the value distribution into two equal parts: one-half of the cases falling below the median value of the property (house and lot, mobile home and lot, or condominium unit) and one-half above the median. Median values are computed on the basis of a standard distribution and are rounded to the nearest hundred dollars.

User's Guide: Asian Population

Places Covered

Ranking tables cover all counties and places in New Jersey with Asian and/or Native Hawaiian and other Pacific Islander residents.

Source of Data

CENSUS 2000

Data for this chapter was derived from following source: *U.S. Bureau of the Census, Census of Population and Housing, 2000: Summary File 4.* Summary File 4 (SF 4) contains sample data, which is the information compiled from the questions asked of a sample (generally 1-in-6) of all people and housing units. Summary File 4 is repeated or iterated for the total population and 335 additional population groups. This chapter focuses on the following 23 population groups:

Asian
    Asian Indian
    Bangladeshi
    Cambodian
    Chinese (except Taiwanese)
    Filipino
    Hmong
    Indonesian
    Japanese
    Korean
    Laotian
    Malaysian
    Pakistani
    Sri Lankan
    Taiwanese
    Thai
    Vietnamese
Native Hawaiian and Other Pacific Islander
    Fijian
    Guamanian or Chamorro
    Hawaiian, Native
    Samoan
    Tongan

Please note that this chapter only includes people who responded to the question on race by indicating only one race. These people are classified by the Census Bureau as the race *alone* population. For example, respondents reporting a single detailed Asian group, such as Korean or Filipino, would be included in the Asian *alone* population. Respondents reporting more than one detailed Asian group, such as Chinese and Japanese or Asian Indian and Chinese and Vietnamese would also be included in the Asian *alone* population. This is because all of the detailed groups in these example combinations are part of the larger Asian race category. The same criteria apply to the Native Hawaiian and Other Pacific Islander groups.

In order for any of the tables for a specific group to be shown in Summary File 4, the data must meet a minimum population threshold. For Summary File 4, all tables are repeated for each race group, American Indian and Alaska Native tribe, and Hispanic or Latino group if the 100-percent count of people of that specific group in a particular geographic area is 100 or more. There also must be 50 or more unweighted people of that specific group in a particular geographic area. For example, if there are 100 or more 100-percent people tabulated as Korean in County A, and there are 50 or more unweighted people, then all matrices for Korean are shown in SF 4 for County A.

To maintain confidentiality, the Census Bureau applies statistical procedures that introduce some uncertainty into data for small geographic areas with small population groups. Therefore, tables may contain both sampling and nonsampling error.

In an iterated file such as SF 4, the universes *households, families,* and *occupied housing units* are classified by the race or ethnic group of the householder. In any population table where there is no note, the universe classification is always based on the race or ethnicity of the person. In all housing tables, the universe classification is based on the race or ethnicity of the householder.

Comparing SF 4 Estimates with Corresponding Values in SF 1 and SF 2

As in earlier censuses, the responses from the sample of households reporting on long forms must be weighted to reflect the entire population. Specifically, each responding household represents, on average, six or seven other households who reported using short forms. One consequence of the weighting procedures is that each estimate based on the long form responses has an associated confidence interval. These confidence intervals are wider (as a percentage of the estimate) for geographic areas with smaller populations and for characteristics that occur less frequently in the area being examined (such as the proportion of people in poverty in a middle-income neighborhood). In order to release as much useful information as possible, statisticians must balance a number of factors. In particular, for Census 2000, the Bureau of the Census created weighting areas—geographic areas from which about two hundred or more long forms were completed—which are large enough to produce good quality estimates. If smaller weighting areas had been used, the confidence intervals around the estimates would have been significantly wider, rendering many estimates less useful due to their lower reliability. The disadvantage of using weighting areas this large is that, for smaller geographic areas within them, the estimates of characteristics that are also reported on the short form will not match the counts reported in SF 1 or SF 2. Examples of these characteristics are the total number of people, the number of people reporting specific racial categories, and the number of housing units. The official values for items reported on the short form come from SF 1 and SF 2. The differences between the long form estimates in SF 4 and values in SF 1 or SF 2 are particularly noticeable for the smallest places, tracts, and block groups. The long form estimates of total population and total housing units in SF 4 will, however, match the SF 1 and SF 2 counts for larger geographic areas such as counties and states, and will be essentially the same for medium and large cities. This phenomenon also occurred for the 1990 Census, although in that case, the weighting areas included relatively small places. As a result, the long form estimates matched the short form counts for those places, but the confidence intervals around the estimates of characteristics collected only on the long form were often significantly wider (as a percentage of the estimate). SF 1 gives exact numbers even for very small groups and areas; whereas, SF 4 gives estimates for small groups and areas such as tracts and small places that are less exact. The goal of SF 4 is to identify large differences among areas or large changes over time. Estimates for small areas and small population groups often do exhibit large changes from one census to the next, so having the capability to measure them is worthwhile.

Topics

POPULATION

Total Population: Sample count of total population of all races.

Asian Population: A person having origins in any of the original peoples of the Far East, Southeast Asia, or the Indian subcontinent including, for example, Cambodia, China, India, Japan, Korea, Malaysia, Pakistan, the Philippine Islands, Thailand, and Vietnam. It includes Asian Indian, Bangladeshi, Cambodian, Chinese (except Taiwanese), Filipino, Hmong, Indonesian, Japanese, Korean, Laotian, Malaysian, Pakistani, Sri Lankan, Taiwanese, Thai, and Vietnamese.

Native Hawaiian or Other Pacific Islander (NHPI) Population: A person having origins in any of the original peoples of Hawaii, Guam, Samoa, or other Pacific Islands. It includes people who indicate their race as Fijian, Guamanian or Chamorro, Native Hawaiian, Samoan, and Tongan.

The data on race, which was asked of all people, were derived from answers to long-form questionnaire Item 6 and short-form questionnaire Item 8. The concept of race, as used by the Census Bureau, reflects self-identification by people according to the race or races with which they most closely identify. These categories are socio-political constructs and should not be interpreted as being scientific or anthropological in nature. Furthermore, the race categories include both racial and national-origin groups.

If an individual did not provide a race response, the race or races of the householder or other household members were assigned using specific rules of precedence of household relationship. For example, if race was missing for a natural-born child in the household, then either the race or races of the householder, another natural-born child, or the spouse of the householder were assigned. If race was not reported for anyone in the household, the race or races of a householder in a previously processed household were assigned.

AGE

Median Age: Divides the age distribution into two equal parts: one-half of the cases falling below the median age and one-half above the median. Median age is computed on the basis of a single year of age standard distribution.

The data on age, which was asked of all people, were derived from answers to the long-form questionnaire Item 4 and short-form questionnaire Item 6. The age classification is based on the age of the person in complete years as of April 1, 2000. The age of the person usually was derived from their date of birth information. Their reported age was used only when date of birth information was unavailable.

HOUSEHOLD SIZE

Average Household Size: A measure obtained by dividing the number of people in households by the total number of households (or householders). In cases where household members are tabulated by race or Hispanic origin, household members are classified by the race or Hispanic origin of the householder rather than the race or Hispanic origin of each individual. Average household size is rounded to the nearest hundredth.

LANGUAGE SPOKEN AT HOME

English Only: Number and percentage of population 5 years and over who report speaking English-only at home.

Language spoken at home data were derived from answers to long-form questionnaire Items 11a and 11b, which were asked of a sample of the population. Data were edited to include in tabulations only the population 5 years old and over. Questions 11a and 11b referred to languages spoken at home in an effort to measure the current use of languages other than English. People who knew languages other than English but did not use them at home or who only used them elsewhere were excluded. Most people who reported speaking a language other than English at home also speak English. The questions did not permit determination of the primary or dominant language of people who spoke both English and another language.

FOREIGN-BORN

Foreign Born: Number and percentage of population who were not U.S. citizens at birth. Foreign-born people are those who indicated they were either a U.S. citizen by naturalization or they were not a citizen of the United States.

Foreign-Born Naturalized Citizens: Number and percentage of population who were not U.S. citizens at birth but became U.S. citizens by naturalization.

The data on place of birth were derived from answers to long-form questionnaire Item 12 which was asked of a sample of the population. Respondents were asked to report the U.S. state, Puerto Rico, U.S. Island Area, or foreign country where they were born. People not reporting a place of birth were assigned the state or country of birth of another family member or their residence 5 years earlier, or were imputed the response of another person with similar characteristics. People born outside the United States were asked to report their place of birth according to current international boundaries. Since numerous changes in boundaries of foreign countries have occurred in the last century, some people may have reported their place of birth in terms of boundaries that existed at the time of their birth or emigration, or in accordance with their own national preference.

EDUCATIONAL ATTAINMENT

High School Graduates: Number and percentage of the population age 25 and over who have a high school diploma or higher. This category includes people whose highest degree was a high school diploma or its equivalent, people who attended college but did not receive a degree, and people who received a college, university, or professional degree. People who reported completing the 12th grade but not receiving a diploma are not high school graduates.

Four-Year College Graduates: Number and percentage of the population age 25 and over who have a 4-year college, university, or professional degree.

Data on educational attainment were derived from answers to long-form questionnaire Item 9, which was asked of a sample of the population. Data on attainment are tabulated for the population 25 years old and over.

The order in which degrees were listed on the questionnaire suggested that doctorate degrees were "higher" than professional school degrees, which were "higher" than master's degrees. The question included instructions for people currently enrolled in school to report the level of the previous grade attended or the highest degree received. Respondents who did not report educational attainment or enrollment level were assigned the attainment of a person of the same age, race, Hispanic or Latino origin, occupation and sex, where possible, who resided in the same or a nearby area. Respondents who filled more than one box were edited to the highest level or degree reported.

The question included a response category that allowed respondents to report completing the 12th grade without receiving a high school diploma. It allowed people who received either a high school diploma or the equivalent (Test of General Educational Development—G.E.D.) and did not attend college, to be reported as "high school graduate(s)." The category "Associate degree" included people whose highest degree is an associate degree, which generally requires 2 years of college level work and is either in an occupational program that prepares them for a specific occupation, or an academic program primarily in the arts and sciences. The course work may or may not be transferable to a bachelor's degree. Master's degrees include the traditional MA and MS degrees and field-specific degrees, such as MSW, MEd, MBA, MLS, and MEng. Some examples of professional degrees include medicine, dentistry, chiropractic, optometry, osteopathic medicine, pharmacy, podiatry, veterinary medicine, law, and theology. Vocational and technical training such as barber school training; business, trade, technical, and vocational schools; or other training for a specific trade, are specifically excluded.

INCOME AND POVERTY

Median Household Income (in dollars): Includes the income of the householder and all other individuals 15 years old and over in the household, whether they are related to the householder or not. The median divides the income distribution into two equal parts: one-half of the cases falling below the median income and one-half above the median. For households, the median income is based on the distribution of the total number of households including those with no income. Median income for households is computed on the basis of a standard distribution and is rounded to the nearest whole dollar.

Per Capita Income (in dollars): Per capita income is the mean income computed for every man, woman, and child in a particular group. It is derived by dividing the total income of a particular group by the total population in that group. Per capita income is rounded to the nearest whole dollar.

The data on income in 1999 were derived from answers to long-form questionnaire Items 31 and 32, which were asked of a sample of the population 15 years old and over. "Total income" is the sum of the amounts reported separately for wage or salary income; net self-employment income; interest, dividends, or net rental or royalty income or income from estates and trusts; social security or railroad retirement income; Supplemental Security Income (SSI); public assistance or welfare payments; retirement, survivor, or disability pensions; and all other income.

Receipts from the following sources are not included as income: capital gains, money received from the sale of property (unless the recipient was engaged in the business of selling such property); the value of income "in kind" from food stamps, public housing subsidies, medical care, employer contributions for individuals, etc.; withdrawal of bank deposits; money borrowed; tax refunds; exchange of money between relatives living in the same household; and gifts and lump-sum inheritances, insurance payments, and other types of lump-sum receipts.

The eight types of income reported in the census are defined as follows:

Wage or salary income. Wage or salary income includes total money earnings received for work performed as an employee during the calendar year 1999. It includes wages, salary, armed forces pay, commissions, tips, piece-rate payments, and cash bonuses earned before deductions were made for taxes, bonds, pensions, union dues, etc.

Self-employment income. Self-employment income includes both farm and nonfarm self-employment income. Nonfarm self-employment income includes net money income (gross receipts minus expenses) from one's own business, professional enterprise, or partnership. Gross receipts include the value of all goods sold and services rendered. Expenses include costs of goods purchased, rent, heat, light, power, depreciation charges, wages and salaries paid, business taxes (not personal income taxes), etc. Farm self-employment income includes net money income (gross receipts minus operating expenses) from the operation of a farm by a person on his or her own account, as an owner, renter, or sharecropper. Gross receipts include the value of all products sold, government farm programs, money received from the rental of farm equipment to others, and incidental receipts from the sale of wood, sand, gravel, etc. Operating expenses include cost of feed, fertilizer, seed, and other farming supplies, cash wages paid to farmhands, depreciation charges, cash rent, interest on farm mortgages, farm building repairs, farm taxes (not state and federal personal income taxes), etc. The value of fuel, food, or other farm products used for family living is not included as part of net income.

Interest, dividends, or net rental income. Interest, dividends, or net rental income includes interest on savings or bonds, dividends from stockholdings or membership in associations, net income from rental of property to others and receipts from boarders or lodgers, net royalties, and periodic payments from an estate or trust fund.

Social Security income. Social security income includes social security pensions and survivors benefits, permanent disability insurance payments made by the Social Security Administration prior to deductions for medical insurance, and railroad retirement insurance checks from the U.S. government. Medicare reimbursements are not included.

Supplemental Security Income (SSI). Supplemental Security Income (SSI) is a nationwide U.S. assistance program administered by the Social Security Administration that guarantees a minimum level of income for needy aged, blind, or disabled individuals. The census questionnaire for Puerto Rico asked about the receipt of SSI; however, SSI is not a federally administered program in Puerto Rico. Therefore, it is probably not being interpreted by most respondents as the same as SSI in the United States. The only way a resident of Puerto Rico could have appropriately reported SSI would have been if they lived in the United States at any time during calendar year 1999 and received SSI.

Public assistance income. Public assistance income includes general assistance and Temporary Assistance to Needy Families (TANF). Separate payments received for hospital or other medical care (vendor payments) are excluded. This does not include Supplemental Security Income (SSI).

Retirement income. Retirement income includes: (1) retirement pensions and survivor benefits from a former employer; labor union; or federal, state, or local government; and the U.S. military; (2) income from workers' compensation; disability income from companies or unions; federal, state, or local government; and the U.S. military; (3) periodic receipts from annuities and insurance; and (4) regular income from IRA and KEOGH plans. This does not include social security income.

All other income. All other income includes unemployment compensation, Veterans' Administration (VA) payments, alimony and child support, contributions received periodically from people not living in the household, military family allotments, and other kinds of periodic income other than earnings.

Poverty Status: Number and percentage of population with income in 1999 below the poverty level. Based on individuals for whom poverty status is determined. Poverty status was determined for all people except institutionalized people, people in military group quarters, people in college dormitories, and unrelated individuals under 15 years old.

The poverty status of families and unrelated individuals in 1999 was determined using 48 thresholds (income cutoffs) arranged in a two dimensional matrix. The matrix consists of family size (from 1 person to 9 or more people) cross-classified by presence and number of family members under 18 years old (from no children present to 8 or more children present). Unrelated individuals and 2-person families were further differentiated by the age of the reference person (RP) (under 65 years old and 65 years old and over).

To determine a person's poverty status, one compares the person's total family income with the poverty threshold appropriate for that person's family size and composition. If the total income of that person's family is less than the threshold appropriate for that family, then the person is considered poor, together with every member of his or her family. If a person is not living with anyone related by birth, marriage, or adoption, then the person's own income is compared with his or her poverty threshold.

HOUSING

Homeownership: Number and percentage of housing units that are owner-occupied.

The data on tenure, which was asked at all occupied housing units, were obtained from answers to long-form questionnaire Item 33, and short-form questionnaire Item 2. All occupied housing units are classified as either owner occupied or renter occupied.

A housing unit is owner occupied if the owner or co-owner lives in the unit even if it is mortgaged or not fully paid for. The owner or co-owner must live in the unit and usually is Person 1 on the questionnaire. The unit is "Owned by you or someone in this household with a mortgage or loan" if it is being purchased with a mortgage or some other debt arrangement, such as a deed of trust, trust deed, contract to purchase, land contract, or purchase agreement. The unit is also considered owned with a mortgage if it is built on leased land and there is a mortgage on the unit. Mobile homes occupied by owners with installment loans balances are also included in this category.

Median Gross Rent (in dollars): Median monthly gross rent on specified renter-occupied and specified vacant-for-rent units. Specified renter-occupied and specified vacant-for-rent units exclude 1-family houses on 10 acres or more.

The data on gross rent were obtained from answers to long-form questionnaire Items 45a-d, which were asked on a sample basis. Gross rent is the contract rent plus the estimated average monthly cost of utilities (electricity, gas, water and sewer) and fuels (oil, coal, kerosene, wood, etc.) if these are paid by the renter (or paid for the renter by someone else). Gross rent is intended to eliminate differentials that result from varying practices with respect to the inclusion of utilities and fuels as part of the rental payment. The estimated costs of utilities and fuels are reported on an annual basis but are converted to monthly figures for the tabulations. Renter units occupied without payment of cash rent are shown separately as "No cash rent" in the tabulations.

Housing units that are renter occupied without payment of cash rent are shown separately as "No cash rent" in census data products. The unit may be owned by friends or relatives who live elsewhere and who allow occupancy without charge. Rent-free houses or apartments may be provided to compensate caretakers, ministers, tenant farmers, sharecroppers, or others.

Contract rent is the monthly rent agreed to or contracted for, regardless of any furnishings, utilities, fees, meals, or services that may be included. For vacant units, it is the monthly rent asked for the rental unit at the time of enumeration.

If the contract rent includes rent for a business unit or for living quarters occupied by another household, only that part of the rent estimated to be for the respondent's unit was included. Excluded was any rent paid for additional units or for business premises.

If a renter pays rent to the owner of a condominium or cooperative, and the condominium fee or cooperative carrying charge also is paid by the renter to the owner, the condominium fee or carrying charge was included as rent.

If a renter receives payments from lodgers or roomers who are listed as members of the household, the rent without deduction for any payments received from the lodgers or roomers was to be reported. The respondent was to report the rent agreed to or contracted for even if paid by someone else such as friends or relatives living elsewhere, a church or welfare agency, or the government through subsidies or vouchers.

The median divides the rent distribution into two equal parts: one-half of the cases falling below the median contract rent and one-half above the median. Median contract rents are computed on the basis of a standard distribution and are rounded to the nearest whole dollar. Units reported as "No cash rent" are excluded.

Median Home Value (in dollars): Reported by the owner of specified owner-occupied or specified vacant-for-sale housing units. Specified owner-occupied and specified vacant-for-sale housing units include only 1-family houses on less than 10 acres without a business or medical office on the property. The data for "specified units" exclude mobile homes, houses with a business or medical office, houses on 10 or more acres, and housing units in multi-unit buildings.

The data on value (also referred to as "price asked" for vacant units) were obtained from answers to long-form questionnaire Item 51, which was asked on a sample basis at owner-occupied housing units and units that were being bought, or vacant for sale at the time of enumeration. Value is the respondent's estimate of how much the property (house and lot, mobile home and lot, or condominium unit) would sell for if it were for sale. If the house or mobile home was owned or being bought, but the land on which it sits was not, the respondent was asked to estimate the combined value of the house or mobile home and the land. For vacant units, value was the price asked for the property. Value was tabulated separately for all owner-occupied and vacant-for-sale housing units, owner-occupied and vacant-for-sale mobile homes, and specified owner-occupied and specified vacant-for-sale housing units.

The median divides the value distribution into two equal parts: one-half of the cases falling below the median value of the property (house and lot, mobile home and lot, or condominium unit) and one-half above the median. Median values are computed on the basis of a standard distribution and are rounded to the nearest hundred dollars.

User's Guide: Weather

Inclusion Criteria — How the Data and Stations Were Selected

There were two central goals in the preparation of the weather chapter. The first was to select those data elements which would have the broadest possible use by the greatest range of potential users. For most of the National Weather Service stations there is a substantial quantity and variety of climatological data that is collected, however for the majority of stations the data is more limited. After evaluating the available data set, the editors chose nine temperature measures, five precipitation measures, and heating and cooling degree days — sixteen key data elements that are widely requested and are believed to be of the greatest general interest.

The second goal was to provide data for as many weather stations as possible. Although there are over 10,000 stations in the United States, not every station collects data for both precipitation and temperature, and even among those that do, the data is not always complete for the last thirty years. As the editors used a different methodology than that of NCDC to compute data, a formal data sufficiency criteria was devised and applied to the source tapes in order to select stations for inclusion.

Sources of the Data

The data in the weather chapter is compiled from several sources. The majority comes from the original National Climactic Data Center computer tapes (TD-3220 Summary of Month Co-Operative). This data was used to create the entire table for each Cooperative station and part of each National Weather Service station. The remainder of the data for each NWS station comes from the International Station Meteorological Climate Summary, Version 4.0, September 1996, which is also available from the NCDC.

NCDC has two main classes or types of weather stations; first order stations which are staffed by professional meteorologists and cooperative stations which are staffed by volunteers. In the weather chapter all first order stations operated by the National Weather Service are included, as well as every cooperative station that met our selection criteria.

Potential Cautions

First, as with any statistical reference work of this type, users need to be aware of the source of the data. The information here comes from NOAA, and it is the most comprehensive and reliable core data available. Although it is the best, it is not perfect. Most weather stations are staffed by volunteers, times of observation sometimes vary, stations occasionally are moved (especially over a thirty year period), equipment is changed or upgraded, and all of these factors affect the uniformity of the data. the weather chapter does not attempt to correct for these factors, and is not intended for either climatologists or atmospheric scientists. Users with concerns about data collection and reporting protocols are both referred to NCDC technical documentation, and also, they are perhaps better served by using the original computer tapes themselves as well.

Second, users need to be aware of the methodology used, which is described later in this User's Guide. Although this methodology has produced fully satisfactory results, it is not directly compatible with other methodologies, hence variances in the results published here and those which appear in other publications will doubtlessly arise.

Third, is the trap of that informal logical fallacy known as "hasty generalization," and its corollaries. This may involve presuming the future will be like the past (specifically, next year will be an average year), or it may involve misunderstanding the limitations of an arithmetic average, but more interestingly, it may involve those mistakes made most innocently by generalizing informally on too broad a basis. As weather is highly localized, the data should be taken in that context. A weather station collects data about climatic conditions at that spot, and that spot may or may not be an effective paradigm for an entire town or area. For example, the weather station in Burlington, Vermont is located at the airport about 3 miles east of the center of town. Most of Burlington is a lot closer to Lake Champlain, and that should mean to a careful user that there could be a significant difference between the temperature readings gathered at the weather station and readings that might be gathered at City Hall downtown. How much would this difference be? How could it be estimated? There are no answers here for these sorts of questions, but it is important for users of this book to raise them for themselves. (It is interesting to note that similar situations abound across the country. For example, compare different readings for the multiple stations in San Francisco, CA or for those around New York City.)

Our source of data has been consistent, so has our methodology. The data has been computed and reported consistently as well. As a result, the the weather chapter should prove valuable to the careful and informed reader.

Weather Station Tables

The weather station tables are grouped by type (National Weather Service and Cooperative) and then arranged alphabetically. The station name is almost always a place name, and is shown here just as it appears in NCDC data. The station name is followed by the county in which the station is located, the elevation of the station (at the time beginning of the thirty year period) and the latitude and longitude.

The National Weather Service Station tables contain 30 data elements which were compiled from two different sources, the International Station Meteorological Climate Summary (ISMCS) and NCDC TD-3220 data tapes. The following 14 elements are from the ISMCS: maximum precipitation, minimum precipitation, maximum 24-hour precipitation, maximum snowfall, maximum 24-hour snowfall, thunderstorm days, foggy days, predominant sky cover, relative humidity (morning and afternoon), dewpoint, wind speed and direction, and maximum wind gust. The remaining 16 elements come from the TD-3220 data tapes. The period of record (POR) for data from the TD-3220 data tapes is 1970-1999. The POR for ISMCS data varies from station to station.

Weather Elements (National Weather Service and Cooperative Stations)

The following elements were compiled by the editor from the NCDC TD-3220 data tapes using a period of record of 1970-1999.

The average temperatures (maximum, minimum, and mean) are the average (see Methodology below) of those temperatures for all available values for a given month. For example, for a given station the average maximum temperature for July is the arithmetic average of all available maximum July temperatures for that station. (Maximum means the highest recorded temperature, minimum means the lowest recorded temperature, and mean means an arithmetic average temperature.)

The extreme maximum temperature is the highest temperature recorded in each month over the period 1970-1999. The extreme minimum temperature is the lowest temperature recorded in each month over the same time period.

The days for maximum temperature and minimum temperature are the average number of days those criteria were met for all available instances. The symbol >= means greater than or equal to, the symbol <= means less than or equal to. For example, for a given station, the number of days the maximum temperature was greater than or equal to 90°F in July, is just an arithmetic average of the number of days in all the available Julys for that station.

Heating and cooling degree days are based on the median temperature for a given day and its variance from 65°F. For example, for a given station if the day's high temperature was 50°F and the day's low temperature was 30°F, the median (midpoint) temperature was 40°F. 40°F is 25 degrees below 65°F, hence on this day there would be 25 heating degree days. The also applies for cooling degree days. For example, for a given station if the day's high temperature was 80°F and the day's low temperature was 70°F, the median (midpoint) temperature was 75°F. 75°F is 10 degrees above 65°F, hence on this day there would be 10 cooling degree days. All heating and/or cooling degree days in a month are summed for the month giving respective totals for each element for that month. These sums for a given month for a given station over the past thirty years are again summed and then arithmetically averaged. It should be noted that the heating and cooling degree days do not cancel each other out. It is possible to have both for a given station in the same month.

Precipitation data is computed the same as heating and cooling degree days. Mean precipitation and mean snowfall are arithmetic averages of cumulative totals for the month. All available values for the thirty year period for a given month for a given station are summed and then divided by the number of values. The same is true for days of greater than or equal to 0.1" and 1.0" of precipitation, and days of greater than or equal to 1.0" of snow depth on the ground. The word trace appears for precipitation and snowfall amounts that are too small to measure.

Finally, remember that all values presented in the tables and the rankings are averages of available data (see Methodology below) for that specific data element for the last thirty years (1970-1999).

Weather Elements (National Weather Service Stations Only)

The following elements were taken directly from the International Station Meteorological Climate Summary. The periods of records vary per station.

Maximum precipitation, minimum precipitation, maximum 24-hour precipitation, maximum snowfall, maximum 24-hour snowfall, thunderstorm days, foggy days, relative humidity (morning and afternoon), dewpoint, prevailing wind speed and direction, and maximum wind gust are all self-explanatory.

The word trace appears for precipitation and snowfall amounts that are too small to measure.

Predominant sky cover contains four possible entries: CLR (clear); SCT (scattered); BRK (broken); and OVR (overcast).

How Cooperative Stations Were Selected

The basic criteria is that a station must have data for temperature, precipitation, heating and cooling degree days of sufficient quantity in order to create a meaningful average. More specifically, the definition of sufficiency here has two parts. First, there must be 22 values for a given data element (with the exception of cooling degree days which required only 14 values in order to be considered sufficient- more about this later), and second, eight of the sixteen elements included in the table must pass this sufficiency test. For example, in regard to average maximum temperature (the first element on every data table), a given station needs to have a value for every month of at least 22 of the last thirty years in order to meet the criteria, and, in addition, every station included must have at least eight of the sixteen elements at least this minimal level of completeness in order to fulfill the criteria. By using this procedure, 3,933 stations met these requirements and are included here.

Methodology

The following discussion applies only to data compiled from the NCDC TD-3220 data tapes.

The weather chapter is based on an arithmetic average of all available data for a specific data element at a given station. For example, the average maximum daily high temperature during July for Newark, New Jersey was abstracted from NCDC source tapes for the thirty Julys, starting in July, 1970 and ending in July, 1999. These thirty figures were then summed and divided by thirty to produce an arithmetic average. As might be expected, there were not thirty values for every data element on every table. For a variety of reasons, NCDC data is sometimes incomplete. Thus the following standards were established.

For those data elements where there were 26-30 values, the data was taken to be essentially complete and an average was computed. For data elements where there were 22-25 values, the data was taken as being partly complete but still valid enough to use to compute an average. Such averages are shown in **bold italic** type to indicate that there was less than 26 values. For the few data elements where there were not even 22 values, no average was computed and 'na' appears in the space. If any of the twelve months for a given data element reported a value of 'na', no annual average was computed and the annual average was reported as 'na' as well.

This procedure was followed for 15 of the 16 data elements. The one exception is cooling degree days. The collection of this data began in 1980 so the following standards were adopted: for those data elements where there were 17-20 values, the data was taken to be essentially complete and an average was computed. For data elements where there were 14-16 values, the data was taken as being partly complete but still valid enough to use to compute an average. Such averages are shown in **bold italic** type to indicate that there was 14-16 values. For the few data elements where there were not even 14 values, no average was computed and 'na' appears in the space. If any of the twelve months for a given data element reported a value of 'na', no annual average was computed and the annual average was reported as 'na' as well.

Thus the basic computational methodology of the weather chapter is to provide an arithmetic average. Because of this, such a pure arithmetic average is somewhat different from the special type of average (called a "normal") which NCDC procedures produces and appears in federal publications.

Perhaps the best outline of the contrasting normalization methodology is found in the following paragraph (which appears as part of an NCDC technical document titled, CLIM81 1961-1990 NORMALS TD-9641 prepared by Lewis France of NCDC in May, 1992):

Normals have been defined as the arithmetic mean of a climatological element computed over a long time period. International agreements eventually led to the decision that the appropriate time period would be three consecutive decades (Guttman, 1989). The data record should be consistent (have no changes in location, instruments, observation practices, etc.; these are identified here as "exposure changes") and have no missing values so a normal will reflect the actual average climatic conditions. If any significant exposure changes have occurred, the data record is said to be "inhomogeneous," and the normal may not reflect a true climatic average. Such data need to be adjusted to remove the nonclimatic inhomogeneities. The resulting (adjusted) record is then said to be "homogeneous." If no exposure changes have occurred at a station, the normal is calculated simply by averaging the appropriate 30 values from the 1961-1990 record.

In the main, there are two "inhomogeneities" that NCDC is correcting for with normalization: adjusting for variances in time of day of observation (at the so-called First Order stations data is based on midnight to midnight observation times and this practice is not necessarily followed at cooperative stations which are staffed by volunteers), and second, estimating data that is either missing or incongruent.

A long discussion of the normalization process is not required here but a short note concerning comparative results of the two methodologies is appropriate.

When the editors first started compiling the weather chapter a concern arose because the normalization process would not be replicated: would our methodology produce strikingly different results than NCDC's? To allay concerns, results of the two processes were compared for the time period normalized results are available (1961-1990). In short, what was found was that the answer to this question is no. Never-the-less, users should be aware that because of both the time period covered (1970-1999) and the methodology used, data in the weather chapter is not compatible with data from other sources.

Atlantic County

Located in southeastern New Jersey, on the Atlantic coast. Covers a land area of 561.07 square miles, a water area of 110.37 square miles, and is located in the Eastern Time Zone. The county government was organized in 1837. County seat is Mays Landing.

Atlantic County is part of the Atlantic City, NJ Metropolitan Statistical Area. The entire metro area includes: Atlantic County, NJ

Weather Station: Atlantic City Int'l Airport   Elevation: 59 feet

	Jan	Feb	Mar	Apr	May	Jun	Jul	Aug	Sep	Oct	Nov	Dec
High	42	44	52	61	71	80	85	83	77	66	56	47
Low	23	25	32	40	50	59	65	64	56	44	36	27
Precip	3.5	3.0	4.0	3.6	3.4	2.8	3.7	4.2	3.0	3.0	3.2	3.1
Snow	4.8	5.1	1.1	0.4	tr	tr	tr	0.0	0.0	tr	0.3	1.6

High and Low temperatures in degrees Fahrenheit; Precipitation and Snow in inches

Weather Station: Atlantic City State Marina   Elevation: 9 feet

	Jan	Feb	Mar	Apr	May	Jun	Jul	Aug	Sep	Oct	Nov	Dec
High	41	43	49	58	66	75	81	80	74	64	55	47
Low	28	30	36	45	54	63	69	68	62	51	42	34
Precip	3.4	3.0	3.8	3.2	3.0	2.4	3.2	3.8	2.8	2.8	3.0	3.4
Snow	na	na	na	na	na	na	na	na	na	na	na	na

High and Low temperatures in degrees Fahrenheit; Precipitation and Snow in inches

Population: 224,327 (1990); 252,552 (2000); 269,202 (2005); 286,615 (2010 projected); Race: 67.5% White, 16.9% Black, 5.7% Asian, 13.7% Hispanic of any race (2005); Density: 479.8 persons per square mile (2005); Average household size: 2.66 (2005); Median age: 37.7 (2005); Males per 100 females: 94.3 (2005).
Religion: Five largest groups: 24.9% Catholic Church, 5.8% Jewish Estimate, 2.0% The United Methodist Church, 1.5% Muslim Estimate, 1.3% Evangelical Lutheran Church in America (2000).
Economy: Unemployment rate: 5.2% (2005); Total civilian labor force: 137,697 (2005); Leading industries: 39.9% accommodation & food services; 13.3% retail trade; 11.7% health care and social assistance (2004); Farms: 456 totaling 30,337 acres (2002); Companies that employ 500 or more persons: 20 (2004); Companies that employ 100 to 499 persons: 285 (2004); Companies that employ less than 100 persons: 13,085 (2004), Black-owned businesses: 1,272 (2002); Hispanic-owned businesses: 594 (2002); Asian-owned businesses: 1,361 (2002); Women-owned businesses: 4,476 (2002); Retail sales per capita: $17,455 (2006). Single-family building permits issued: 1,839 (2005); Multi-family building permits issued: 163 (2005).
Income: Per capita income: $23,296 (2005); Median household income: $47,878 (2005); Average household income: $60,735 (2005); Percent of households with income of $100,000 or more: 14.2% (2005); Poverty rate: 10.8% (2003); Bankruptcy rate: 8.39% (2005).
Taxes: Total county taxes per capita: $446 (2004); County property taxes per capita: $446 (2004).
Education: Percent of population age 25 and over with: High school diploma (including GED) or higher: 78.4% (2005); Bachelor's degree or higher: 18.8% (2005); Master's degree or higher: 5.9% (2005).
Housing: Homeownership rate: 67.1% (2005); Median home value: $193,218 (2005); Median rent: $601 per month (2000); Median age of housing: 31 years (2000).
Health: Birth rate: 140.4 per 10,000 population (2004); Death rate: 110.1 per 10,000 population (2004); Age-adjusted cancer mortality rate: 243.3 deaths per 100,000 population (2002); Air Quality Index: 87.5% good, 11.6% moderate, 0.8% unhealthy for sensitive individuals, 0.0% unhealthy (percent of days in 2005); Number of physicians: 26.3 per 10,000 population (2004); Hospital beds: 30.6 per 10,000 population (2003); Hospital admissions: 1,494.1 per 10,000 population (2003).
Elections: 2004 Presidential election results: 46.6% Bush, 52.5% Kerry, 0.5% Nader, 0.1% Badnarik
National and State Parks: Absecon State Wildlife Management Area; Absecon State Wildlife Management Areas; Brigantine National Wildlife Refuge; Edwin B Forsythe National Wildlife Refuge
Additional Information Contacts
Atlantic County Government . . . . (609) 343-2201
   http://www.aclink.org
Atlantic City Chamber of Commerce . . . . (609) 345-5600
   http://www.atlanticcitychamber.com
Atlantic City Convention and Visitors Authority . . . . (888) 228-4748
   http://www.atlanticcitynj.com

Atlantic County Chamber of Commerce . . . . (609) 646-2214
   http://www.atlanticcountychamber.com
Brigantine Beach Chamber of Commerce . . . . (609) 266-3437
   http://www.brigantinechamber.com
Buena Vista Township . . . . (856) 697-2100
   http://www.buenavistatownship.org
City of Atlantic City . . . . (704) 347-5510
   http://www.cityofatlanticcity.org
City of Brigantine . . . . (609) 266-7600
   http://www.brigantinebeachnj.com
City of Margate City . . . . (609) 822-2605
   http://www.margate-nj.com
City of Ventnor City . . . . (609) 823-7906
   http://www.ventnorcity.org
Greater Mercer County Chamber of Commerce . . . . (609) 393-4143
   http://mercerchamber.org
Hammonton Chamber of Commerce . . . . (609) 561-9080
   http://www.hammontonnj.us

Atlantic County Communities

ABSECON (city). Covers a land area of 5.717 square miles and a water area of 1.209 square miles. Located at 39.43° N. Lat.; 74.50° W. Long. Elevation is 25 feet.
History: Settled c. 1780, incorporated 1902.
Population: 7,298 (1990); 7,638 (2000); 7,976 (2005); 8,355 (2010 projected); Race: 81.2% White, 6.5% Black, 8.6% Asian, 4.4% Hispanic of any race (2005); Density: 1,395.1 persons per square mile (2005); Average household size: 2.74 (2005); Median age: 41.1 (2005); Males per 100 females: 92.6 (2005); Marriage status: 25.2% never married, 55.8% now married, 6.8% widowed, 12.1% divorced (2000); Foreign born: 10.4% (2000); Ancestry (includes multiple ancestries): 28.0% Irish, 21.4% Italian, 16.7% German, 16.5% Other groups, 12.8% English (2000).
Economy: Manufactures concrete blocks, consumer goods. Primary crops are nursery products and poultry. Single-family building permits issued: 79 (2005); Multi-family building permits issued: 0 (2005); Employment by occupation: 8.8% management, 19.0% professional, 29.3% services, 29.0% sales, 0.1% farming, 7.5% construction, 6.4% production (2000).
Income: Per capita income: $27,860 (2005); Median household income: $60,652 (2005); Average household income: $75,627 (2005); Percent of households with income of $100,000 or more: 20.7% (2005); Poverty rate: 4.8% (2000).
Education: Percent of population age 25 and over with: High school diploma (including GED) or higher: 85.8% (2005); Bachelor's degree or higher: 22.3% (2005); Master's degree or higher: 7.3% (2005).
School District(s)
Absecon City (PK-08)
   2003-04 Enrollment: 971 . . . . (609) 641-5375
Housing: Homeownership rate: 85.3% (2005); Median home value: $197,522 (2005); Median rent: $718 per month (2000); Median age of housing: 35 years (2000).
Safety: Violent crime rate: 46.9 per 10,000 population; Property crime rate: 310.5 per 10,000 population (2004).
Transportation: Commute to work: 88.3% car, 6.2% public transportation, 1.5% walk, 3.3% work from home (2000); Travel time to work: 33.2% less than 15 minutes, 47.4% 15 to 30 minutes, 9.5% 30 to 45 minutes, 3.5% 45 to 60 minutes, 6.4% 60 minutes or more (2000); Amtrak: Service available.

ATLANTIC CITY (city). Covers a land area of 11.350 square miles and a water area of 6.003 square miles. Located at 39.36° N. Lat.; 74.43° W. Long. Elevation is 8 feet.
History: The history of Atlantic City is a success story of a city that knew what it wanted to be from its very infancy. Before 1852, Atlantic City was an island waste five miles off the mainland. It was known as Absecon Island or Absecon Beach. Once the climate and beach of the Island were appraised, it was not long before a railroad from Camden was under construction. The city was incorporated in 1854 and the first train arrived from Camden that same year. Many dined at a still incomplete hotel. Other hotels were being built, and a second railroad arrived in 1877. The boardwalk was the joint conception in 1870 of a local hotel man, Jacob Keim, and a conductor on the Camden and Atlantic, Alexander Boardman. The next milestone in the history of the resort was the invention of the rolling chair in 1884 by M.D. Shill. In 1895, the picture postcard was brought to Atlantic City, the idea being adopted from Germany. Salt water taffy and an amusement pier followed.

Population: 37,986 (1990); 40,517 (2000); 40,543 (2005); 41,058 (2010 projected); Race: 25.6% White, 41.3% Black, 12.0% Asian, 28.8% Hispanic of any race (2005); Density: 3,572.1 persons per square mile (2005); Average household size: 2.58 (2005); Median age: 35.3 (2005); Males per 100 females: 97.4 (2005); Marriage status: 38.8% never married, 40.5% now married, 9.6% widowed, 11.2% divorced (2000); Foreign born: 24.7% (2000); Ancestry (includes multiple ancestries): 65.1% Other groups, 4.9% Italian, 4.1% Irish, 2.4% United States or American, 2.0% German (2000).
Economy: Unemployment rate: 8.0% (2005); Total civilian labor force: 17,676 (2005); Single-family building permits issued: 70 (2005); Multi-family building permits issued: 31 (2005); Employment by occupation: 5.4% management, 8.3% professional, 48.5% services, 22.3% sales, 0.2% farming, 4.9% construction, 10.4% production (2000).
Income: Per capita income: $16,826 (2005); Median household income: $29,580 (2005); Average household income: $42,429 (2005); Percent of households with income of $100,000 or more: 7.3% (2005); Poverty rate: 23.6% (2000).
Taxes: Total city taxes per capita: $3,341 (2004); City property taxes per capita: $3,261 (2004).
Education: Percent of population age 25 and over with: High school diploma (including GED) or higher: 61.7% (2005); Bachelor's degree or higher: 10.4% (2005); Master's degree or higher: 3.2% (2005).

School District(s)

Agency - Learning Center CS (04-08)
  2003-04 Enrollment: n/a . . . . (609) 340-8823
Agency - Oceanside CS (PK-08)
  2003-04 Enrollment: 316 . . . . (609) 348-3485
Atlantic City (PK-12)
  2003-04 Enrollment: 7,290 . . . . (609) 343-7200
Housing: Homeownership rate: 29.2% (2005); Median home value: $146,634 (2005); Median rent: $502 per month (2000); Median age of housing: 39 years (2000).
Hospitals: Atlantic City Medical Center: City Division (442 beds)
Safety: Violent crime rate: 170.2 per 10,000 population; Property crime rate: 1,143.2 per 10,000 population (2004).
Newspapers: Atlantic City Weekly (General - Circulation 45,000)
Transportation: Commute to work: 46.7% car, 27.9% public transportation, 21.0% walk, 1.2% work from home (2000); Travel time to work: 38.1% less than 15 minutes, 42.4% 15 to 30 minutes, 12.0% 30 to 45 minutes, 3.2% 45 to 60 minutes, 4.3% 60 minutes or more (2000); Amtrak: Service available.
Additional Information Contacts
Atlantic City Chamber of Commerce . . . . (609) 345-5600
  http://www.atlanticcitychamber.com
Atlantic City Convention and Visitors Authority . . . . (888) 228-4748
  http://www.atlanticcitynj.com
City of Atlantic City . . . . (704) 347-5510
  http://www.cityofatlanticcity.org

BRIGANTINE (city). Covers a land area of 6.429 square miles and a water area of 3.357 square miles. Located at 39.40° N. Lat.; 74.37° W. Long. Elevation is 6 feet.
Population: 11,354 (1990); 12,594 (2000); 12,688 (2005); 12,893 (2010 projected); Race: 80.6% White, 4.1% Black, 6.6% Asian, 11.2% Hispanic of any race (2005); Density: 1,973.6 persons per square mile (2005); Average household size: 2.29 (2005); Median age: 42.0 (2005); Males per 100 females: 95.7 (2005); Marriage status: 26.0% never married, 55.0% now married, 7.5% widowed, 11.5% divorced (2000); Foreign born: 12.3% (2000); Ancestry (includes multiple ancestries): 24.5% Irish, 22.2% Italian, 20.6% Other groups, 16.3% German, 10.0% English (2000).
Economy: Resort city. Single-family building permits issued: 158 (2005); Multi-family building permits issued: 6 (2005); Employment by occupation: 11.9% management, 16.9% professional, 33.7% services, 25.8% sales, 0.5% farming, 5.8% construction, 5.5% production (2000).
Income: Per capita income: $25,956 (2005); Median household income: $47,026 (2005); Average household income: $59,462 (2005); Percent of households with income of $100,000 or more: 13.3% (2005); Poverty rate: 9.4% (2000).
Education: Percent of population age 25 and over with: High school diploma (including GED) or higher: 84.7% (2005); Bachelor's degree or higher: 24.1% (2005); Master's degree or higher: 8.5% (2005).

School District(s)

Brigantine City (PK-08)
  2003-04 Enrollment: 1,248 . . . . (609) 266-7671

Housing: Homeownership rate: 63.7% (2005); Median home value: $241,107 (2005); Median rent: $685 per month (2000); Median age of housing: 26 years (2000).
Safety: Violent crime rate: 7.9 per 10,000 population; Property crime rate: 177.7 per 10,000 population (2004).
Newspapers: The Beachcomber News - Brigantine Edition (General - Circulation 5,000)
Transportation: Commute to work: 86.0% car, 8.0% public transportation, 2.1% walk, 2.4% work from home (2000); Travel time to work: 32.5% less than 15 minutes, 42.0% 15 to 30 minutes, 12.6% 30 to 45 minutes, 2.8% 45 to 60 minutes, 10.2% 60 minutes or more (2000)
Additional Information Contacts
Brigantine Beach Chamber of Commerce . . . . (609) 266-3437
  http://www.brigantinechamber.com
City of Brigantine . . . . (609) 266-7600
  http://www.brigantinebeachnj.com

BUENA (borough). Covers a land area of 7.607 square miles and a water area of 0 square miles. Located at 39.52° N. Lat.; 74.94° W. Long. Elevation is 108 feet.
History: Incorporated after 1940.
Population: 4,441 (1990); 3,873 (2000); 3,822 (2005); 3,805 (2010 projected); Race: 78.0% White, 8.3% Black, 0.4% Asian, 23.9% Hispanic of any race (2005); Density: 502.4 persons per square mile (2005); Average household size: 2.64 (2005); Median age: 36.9 (2005); Males per 100 females: 96.2 (2005); Marriage status: 30.7% never married, 49.9% now married, 9.8% widowed, 9.6% divorced (2000); Foreign born: 6.4% (2000); Ancestry (includes multiple ancestries): 34.6% Italian, 27.5% Other groups, 12.9% German, 8.9% Irish, 4.8% Polish (2000).
Economy: Single-family building permits issued: 6 (2005); Multi-family building permits issued: 0 (2005); Employment by occupation: 9.9% management, 11.8% professional, 18.1% services, 24.6% sales, 6.3% farming, 11.6% construction, 17.7% production (2000).
Income: Per capita income: $17,803 (2005); Median household income: $36,542 (2005); Average household income: $46,543 (2005); Percent of households with income of $100,000 or more: 8.0% (2005); Poverty rate: 18.7% (2000).
Education: Percent of population age 25 and over with: High school diploma (including GED) or higher: 62.2% (2005); Bachelor's degree or higher: 8.8% (2005); Master's degree or higher: 2.5% (2005).

School District(s)

Buena Regional (PK-12)
  2003-04 Enrollment: 2,627 . . . . (856) 697-0800
Housing: Homeownership rate: 62.8% (2005); Median home value: $166,846 (2005); Median rent: $557 per month (2000); Median age of housing: 40 years (2000).
Safety: Violent crime rate: 57.0 per 10,000 population; Property crime rate: 251.4 per 10,000 population (2004).
Transportation: Commute to work: 90.3% car, 0.8% public transportation, 2.8% walk, 3.8% work from home (2000); Travel time to work: 37.3% less than 15 minutes, 26.3% 15 to 30 minutes, 19.0% 30 to 45 minutes, 9.1% 45 to 60 minutes, 8.3% 60 minutes or more (2000)

BUENA VISTA (township). Covers a land area of 41.364 square miles and a water area of 0.163 square miles. Located at 39.53° N. Lat.; 74.89° W. Long.
History: Incorporated 1867.
Population: 7,655 (1990); 7,436 (2000); 7,626 (2005); 7,878 (2010 projected); Race: 79.0% White, 14.2% Black, 0.2% Asian, 9.1% Hispanic of any race (2005); Density: 184.4 persons per square mile (2005); Average household size: 2.76 (2005); Median age: 39.6 (2005); Males per 100 females: 95.3 (2005); Marriage status: 26.2% never married, 54.9% now married, 10.0% widowed, 9.0% divorced (2000); Foreign born: 3.5% (2000); Ancestry (includes multiple ancestries): 27.6% Italian, 22.5% Other groups, 17.4% German, 15.4% Irish, 8.2% English (2000).
Economy: Single-family building permits issued: 24 (2005); Multi-family building permits issued: 0 (2005); Employment by occupation: 6.8% management, 12.9% professional, 17.3% services, 27.0% sales, 1.2% farming, 15.9% construction, 19.0% production (2000).
Income: Per capita income: $21,583 (2005); Median household income: $50,164 (2005); Average household income: $59,038 (2005); Percent of households with income of $100,000 or more: 11.4% (2005); Poverty rate: 12.1% (2000).

Education: Percent of population age 25 and over with: High school diploma (including GED) or higher: 71.0% (2005); Bachelor's degree or higher: 12.6% (2005); Master's degree or higher: 4.0% (2005).

Housing: Homeownership rate: 87.5% (2005); Median home value: $149,360 (2005); Median rent: $598 per month (2000); Median age of housing: 32 years (2000).

Transportation: Commute to work: 91.2% car, 4.1% public transportation, 1.6% walk, 2.0% work from home (2000); Travel time to work: 26.0% less than 15 minutes, 31.0% 15 to 30 minutes, 18.1% 30 to 45 minutes, 14.0% 45 to 60 minutes, 10.9% 60 minutes or more (2000)

Additional Information Contacts

Buena Vista Township . . . . (856) 697-2100
    http://www.buenavistatownship.org

COLLINGS LAKES (CDP). Covers a land area of 0.670 square miles and a water area of 0.036 square miles. Located at 39.59° N. Lat.; 74.88° W. Long. Elevation is 81 feet.

Population: 2,046 (1990); 1,726 (2000); 1,761 (2005); 1,790 (2010 projected); Race: 87.6% White, 4.4% Black, 0.2% Asian, 8.7% Hispanic of any race (2005); Density: 2,626.7 persons per square mile (2005); Average household size: 3.03 (2005); Median age: 34.4 (2005); Males per 100 females: 101.0 (2005); Marriage status: 30.3% never married, 47.0% now married, 9.6% widowed, 13.0% divorced (2000); Foreign born: 3.0% (2000); Ancestry (includes multiple ancestries): 32.5% Irish, 25.9% German, 17.9% Italian, 9.9% English, 8.9% Other groups (2000).

Economy: Employment by occupation: 7.6% management, 8.8% professional, 19.8% services, 27.0% sales, 0.0% farming, 15.3% construction, 21.4% production (2000).

Income: Per capita income: $21,279 (2005); Median household income: $63,297 (2005); Average household income: $64,497 (2005); Percent of households with income of $100,000 or more: 13.6% (2005); Poverty rate: 8.6% (2000).

Education: Percent of population age 25 and over with: High school diploma (including GED) or higher: 80.2% (2005); Bachelor's degree or higher: 9.7% (2005); Master's degree or higher: 1.2% (2005).

Housing: Homeownership rate: 90.2% (2005); Median home value: $147,441 (2005); Median rent: $717 per month (2000); Median age of housing: 35 years (2000).

Transportation: Commute to work: 95.3% car, 0.0% public transportation, 0.0% walk, 3.7% work from home (2000); Travel time to work: 16.9% less than 15 minutes, 20.1% 15 to 30 minutes, 28.0% 30 to 45 minutes, 24.7% 45 to 60 minutes, 10.4% 60 minutes or more (2000)

CORBIN CITY (city). Covers a land area of 7.887 square miles and a water area of 1.098 square miles. Located at 39.30° N. Lat.; 74.75° W. Long. Elevation is 13 feet.

Population: 412 (1990); 468 (2000); 419 (2005); 413 (2010 projected); Race: 93.1% White, 2.9% Black, 1.7% Asian, 4.5% Hispanic of any race (2005); Density: 53.1 persons per square mile (2005); Average household size: 2.65 (2005); Median age: 36.6 (2005); Males per 100 females: 99.5 (2005); Marriage status: 21.2% never married, 61.2% now married, 3.9% widowed, 13.7% divorced (2000); Foreign born: 3.2% (2000); Ancestry (includes multiple ancestries): 30.8% German, 27.6% Irish, 18.2% English, 13.0% Italian, 12.0% Other groups (2000).

Economy: Eighteen miles West Southwest of Atlantic City, in cranberry region. Single-family building permits issued: 3 (2005); Multi-family building permits issued: 0 (2005); Employment by occupation: 14.8% management, 19.3% professional, 26.9% services, 13.9% sales, 0.0% farming, 12.6% construction, 12.6% production (2000).

Income: Per capita income: $23,341 (2005); Median household income: $50,735 (2005); Average household income: $61,899 (2005); Percent of households with income of $100,000 or more: 18.4% (2005); Poverty rate: 4.9% (2000).

Education: Percent of population age 25 and over with: High school diploma (including GED) or higher: 85.3% (2005); Bachelor's degree or higher: 20.8% (2005); Master's degree or higher: 5.0% (2005).

School District(s)

Atlantic County Special Services (UG-UG)
    2003-04 Enrollment: 1,036 . . . . (609) 625-5796

Housing: Homeownership rate: 82.3% (2005); Median home value: $229,412 (2005); Median rent: $592 per month (2000); Median age of housing: 32 years (2000).

Transportation: Commute to work: 97.7% car, 0.0% public transportation, 0.0% walk, 0.9% work from home (2000); Travel time to work: 22.0% less

than 15 minutes, 37.9% 15 to 30 minutes, 24.8% 30 to 45 minutes, 11.2% 45 to 60 minutes, 4.2% 60 minutes or more (2000)

DOROTHY (unincorporated postal area, zip code 08317). Covers a land area of 8.137 square miles and a water area of 0 square miles. Located at 39.40° N. Lat.; 74.82° W. Long. Elevation is 72 feet.

Population: 1,180 (2000); Race: 92.7% White, 4.2% Black, 0.0% Asian, 1.6% Hispanic of any race (2000); Density: 145.0 persons per square mile (2000); Age: 31.2% under 18, 8.9% over 64 (2000); Marriage status: 29.5% never married, 56.1% now married, 4.3% widowed, 10.1% divorced (2000); Foreign born: 1.7% (2000); Ancestry (includes multiple ancestries): 25.8% German, 23.3% Irish, 19.9% Italian, 10.1% English, 9.7% Other groups (2000).

Economy: Employment by occupation: 8.7% management, 14.7% professional, 22.3% services, 28.8% sales, 0.0% farming, 15.2% construction, 10.4% production (2000).

Income: Per capita income: $18,610 (2000); Median household income: $60,455 (2000); Poverty rate: 5.5% (2000).

Education: Percent of population age 25 and over with: High school diploma (including GED) or higher: 79.7% (2000); Bachelor's degree or higher: 15.3% (2000).

School District(s)

Weymouth Township (PK-08)
    2003-04 Enrollment: 261 . . . . (609) 476-2412

Housing: Homeownership rate: 90.2% (2000); Median home value: $127,100 (2000); Median rent: $625 per month (2000); Median age of housing: 24 years (2000).

Transportation: Commute to work: 95.7% car, 1.8% public transportation, 1.1% walk, 1.4% work from home (2000); Travel time to work: 10.3% less than 15 minutes, 40.4% 15 to 30 minutes, 28.1% 30 to 45 minutes, 12.1% 45 to 60 minutes, 9.2% 60 minutes or more (2000)

EGG HARBOR (township). Covers a land area of 67.349 square miles and a water area of 7.007 square miles. Located at 39.39° N. Lat.; 74.59° W. Long.

History: Great Egg Harbor Bay lies South, near Ocean City, and Little Egg Harbor Northeast, near Tuckerton. Settled 1854 by Germans, incorporated 1856.

Population: 24,970 (1990); 30,726 (2000); 37,251 (2005); 43,441 (2010 projected); Race: 78.4% White, 10.1% Black, 5.5% Asian, 8.1% Hispanic of any race (2005); Density: 553.1 persons per square mile (2005); Average household size: 2.74 (2005); Median age: 36.9 (2005); Males per 100 females: 95.1 (2005); Marriage status: 24.2% never married, 59.4% now married, 6.4% widowed, 10.0% divorced (2000); Foreign born: 8.4% (2000); Ancestry (includes multiple ancestries): 23.1% Irish, 23.0% Other groups, 18.2% German, 17.4% Italian, 10.4% English (2000).

Economy: Wine-making center, yacht construction; fruit, poultry, vegetables. Annual agricultural fair. Unemployment rate: 4.2% (2005); Total civilian labor force: 20,689 (2005); Single-family building permits issued: 519 (2005); Multi-family building permits issued: 0 (2005); Employment by occupation: 9.6% management, 17.1% professional, 27.3% services, 25.9% sales, 0.1% farming, 10.9% construction, 9.2% production (2000).

Income: Per capita income: $25,128 (2005); Median household income: $57,882 (2005); Average household income: $68,662 (2005); Percent of households with income of $100,000 or more: 19.0% (2005); Poverty rate: 5.4% (2000).

Education: Percent of population age 25 and over with: High school diploma (including GED) or higher: 82.8% (2005); Bachelor's degree or higher: 19.1% (2005); Master's degree or higher: 5.6% (2005).

School District(s)

Egg Harbor Township (PK-12)
    2003-04 Enrollment: 6,805 . . . . (609) 646-7911
Washington Township (PK-08)
    2003-04 Enrollment: 112 . . . . (609) 965-3520

Two-year College(s)

Star Technical Institute-Egg Harbor
    Fall 2004 Enrollment: 135 . . . . (609) 407-2999

Housing: Homeownership rate: 85.2% (2005); Median home value: $195,580 (2005); Median rent: $608 per month (2000); Median age of housing: 21 years (2000).

Safety: Violent crime rate: 27.2 per 10,000 population; Property crime rate: 272.5 per 10,000 population (2004).

Transportation: Commute to work: 93.8% car, 1.4% public transportation, 1.1% walk, 2.2% work from home (2000); Travel time to work: 27.7% less

than 15 minutes, 48.4% 15 to 30 minutes, 14.5% 30 to 45 minutes, 2.8% 45 to 60 minutes, 6.6% 60 minutes or more (2000)

EGG HARBOR CITY (city). Aka Egg Harbor. Covers a land area of 11.107 square miles and a water area of 0.431 square miles. Located at 39.55° N. Lat.; 74.61° W. Long. Elevation is 58 feet.

Population: 4,583 (1990); 4,545 (2000); 4,468 (2005); 4,429 (2010 projected); Race: 64.9% White, 14.8% Black, 1.3% Asian, 25.0% Hispanic of any race (2005); Density: 402.3 persons per square mile (2005); Average household size: 2.74 (2005); Median age: 35.3 (2005); Males per 100 females: 94.1 (2005); Marriage status: 29.4% never married, 53.8% now married, 7.4% widowed, 9.3% divorced (2000); Foreign born: 5.7% (2000); Ancestry (includes multiple ancestries): 36.2% Other groups, 20.1% German, 15.5% Italian, 15.0% Irish, 8.3% English (2000).

Economy: Single-family building permits issued: 11 (2005); Multi-family building permits issued: 0 (2005); Employment by occupation: 5.2% management, 9.9% professional, 23.2% services, 29.5% sales, 0.0% farming, 12.3% construction, 19.7% production (2000).

Income: Per capita income: $15,060 (2005); Median household income: $32,803 (2005); Average household income: $40,063 (2005); Percent of households with income of $100,000 or more: 5.0% (2005); Poverty rate: 13.1% (2000).

Taxes: Total city taxes per capita: $920 (2004); City property taxes per capita: $920 (2004).

Education: Percent of population age 25 and over with: High school diploma (including GED) or higher: 70.1% (2005); Bachelor's degree or higher: 10.3% (2005); Master's degree or higher: 2.5% (2005).

School District(s)

Egg Harbor City (PK-08)
    2003-04 Enrollment: 562 . . . . (609) 965-1034
Mullica Township (PK-08)
    2003-04 Enrollment: 844 . . . . (609) 561-3868

Housing: Homeownership rate: 63.0% (2005); Median home value: $136,675 (2005); Median rent: $532 per month (2000); Median age of housing: 50 years (2000).

Safety: Violent crime rate: 35.4 per 10,000 population; Property crime rate: 203.7 per 10,000 population (2004).

Transportation: Commute to work: 86.4% car, 5.0% public transportation, 5.5% walk, 0.7% work from home (2000); Travel time to work: 18.0% less than 15 minutes, 43.3% 15 to 30 minutes, 27.5% 30 to 45 minutes, 5.0% 45 to 60 minutes, 6.3% 60 minutes or more (2000); Amtrak: Service available.

Additional Information Contacts
Atlantic County Chamber of Commerce . . . . (609) 646-2214
    http://www.atlanticcountychamber.com

EGG HARBOR TOWNSHIP (unincorporated postal area, zip code 08234). Covers a land area of 60.280 square miles and a water area of 0.432 square miles. Located at 39.37° N. Lat.; 74.61° W. Long.

Population: 30,058 (2000); Race: 79.5% White, 10.1% Black, 5.2% Asian, 6.7% Hispanic of any race (2000); Density: 498.6 persons per square mile (2000); Age: 28.4% under 18, 9.0% over 64 (2000); Marriage status: 24.3% never married, 59.3% now married, 6.4% widowed, 10.0% divorced (2000); Foreign born: 8.0% (2000); Ancestry (includes multiple ancestries): 23.2% Irish, 22.9% Other groups, 18.4% German, 17.3% Italian, 10.6% English (2000).

Economy: Employment by occupation: 9.5% management, 17.2% professional, 27.0% services, 25.9% sales, 0.1% farming, 10.9% construction, 9.2% production (2000).

Income: Per capita income: $22,332 (2000); Median household income: $52,618 (2000); Poverty rate: 5.2% (2000).

Education: Percent of population age 25 and over with: High school diploma (including GED) or higher: 83.0% (2000); Bachelor's degree or higher: 19.0% (2000).

School District(s)

Egg Harbor Township (PK-12)
    2003-04 Enrollment: 6,805 . . . . (609) 646-7911

Housing: Homeownership rate: 85.0% (2000); Median home value: $131,400 (2000); Median rent: $602 per month (2000); Median age of housing: 21 years (2000).

Hospitals: Atlanticare/Atlantic City Medical Center (563 beds)

Newspapers: Current Of Egg Harbor Township (General - Circulation 12,200); Current of Linwood, Northfield, and Somers Point (General - Circulation 9,500); The Current of Downbeach (General - Circulation 13,200)

Transportation: Commute to work: 93.8% car, 1.4% public transportation, 1.1% walk, 2.2% work from home (2000); Travel time to work: 27.5% less than 15 minutes, 48.4% 15 to 30 minutes, 14.7% 30 to 45 minutes, 2.8% 45 to 60 minutes, 6.6% 60 minutes or more (2000)

Additional Information Contacts
Atlantic County Chamber of Commerce . . . . (609) 646-2214
    http://www.atlanticcountychamber.com

ELWOOD-MAGNOLIA (CDP). Covers a land area of 3.225 square miles and a water area of 0 square miles. Located at 39.57° N. Lat.; 74.71° W. Long.

Population: 1,474 (1990); 1,392 (2000); 1,541 (2005); 1,673 (2010 projected); Race: 58.1% White, 9.5% Black, 0.6% Asian, 37.5% Hispanic of any race (2005); Density: 477.9 persons per square mile (2005); Average household size: 3.19 (2005); Median age: 35.3 (2005); Males per 100 females: 100.9 (2005); Marriage status: 28.3% never married, 59.8% now married, 6.7% widowed, 5.2% divorced (2000); Foreign born: 0.0% (2000); Ancestry (includes multiple ancestries): 51.5% Other groups, 17.1% Irish, 14.8% Italian, 13.9% German, 5.2% United States or American (2000).

Economy: Employment by occupation: 8.6% management, 9.5% professional, 32.8% services, 21.1% sales, 0.0% farming, 11.7% construction, 16.3% production (2000).

Income: Per capita income: $15,732 (2005); Median household income: $46,565 (2005); Average household income: $47,971 (2005); Percent of households with income of $100,000 or more: 5.4% (2005); Poverty rate: 24.5% (2000).

Education: Percent of population age 25 and over with: High school diploma (including GED) or higher: 68.1% (2005); Bachelor's degree or higher: 3.6% (2005); Master's degree or higher: 2.0% (2005).

School District(s)

Mullica Township (PK-08)
    2003-04 Enrollment: 844 . . . . (609) 561-3868

Housing: Homeownership rate: 84.9% (2005); Median home value: $131,933 (2005); Median rent: $736 per month (2000); Median age of housing: 38 years (2000).

Transportation: Commute to work: 92.4% car, 3.4% public transportation, 0.0% walk, 3.2% work from home (2000); Travel time to work: 21.8% less than 15 minutes, 31.6% 15 to 30 minutes, 26.2% 30 to 45 minutes, 17.6% 45 to 60 minutes, 2.8% 60 minutes or more (2000)

ESTELL MANOR (city). Aka Risley. Covers a land area of 53.568 square miles and a water area of 1.343 square miles. Located at 39.37° N. Lat.; 74.77° W. Long. Elevation is 25 feet.

Population: 1,404 (1990); 1,585 (2000); 1,766 (2005); 1,910 (2010 projected); Race: 93.9% White, 3.6% Black, 0.4% Asian, 0.9% Hispanic of any race (2005); Density: 33.0 persons per square mile (2005); Average household size: 2.95 (2005); Median age: 37.5 (2005); Males per 100 females: 98.9 (2005); Marriage status: 21.8% never married, 66.5% now married, 4.2% widowed, 7.5% divorced (2000); Foreign born: 4.4% (2000); Ancestry (includes multiple ancestries): 25.2% Irish, 22.9% German, 19.7% Italian, 13.2% English, 8.5% Polish (2000).

Economy: Includes Estelville (or Estellville) village and a game preserve. Single-family building permits issued: 8 (2005); Multi-family building permits issued: 0 (2005); Employment by occupation: 14.4% management, 20.2% professional, 16.2% services, 22.6% sales, 0.3% farming, 15.3% construction, 11.1% production (2000).

Income: Per capita income: $21,353 (2005); Median household income: $56,408 (2005); Average household income: $62,008 (2005); Percent of households with income of $100,000 or more: 14.9% (2005); Poverty rate: 4.9% (2000).

Education: Percent of population age 25 and over with: High school diploma (including GED) or higher: 84.6% (2005); Bachelor's degree or higher: 16.8% (2005); Master's degree or higher: 4.7% (2005).

School District(s)

Estell Manor City (PK-08)
    2003-04 Enrollment: 215 . . . . (609) 476-2267

Housing: Homeownership rate: 95.3% (2005); Median home value: $220,776 (2005); Median rent: $675 per month (2000); Median age of housing: 22 years (2000).

Transportation: Commute to work: 94.4% car, 0.3% public transportation, 1.3% walk, 2.8% work from home (2000); Travel time to work: 12.1% less than 15 minutes, 26.6% 15 to 30 minutes, 39.1% 30 to 45 minutes, 14.1% 45 to 60 minutes, 8.1% 60 minutes or more (2000)

FOLSOM (borough). Covers a land area of 8.270 square miles and a water area of 0.185 square miles. Located at 39.59° N. Lat.; 74.84° W. Long. Elevation is 90 feet.
Population: 2,181 (1990); 1,972 (2000); 1,982 (2005); 2,012 (2010 projected); Race: 91.9% White, 4.2% Black, 0.7% Asian, 3.9% Hispanic of any race (2005); Density: 239.7 persons per square mile (2005); Average household size: 2.89 (2005); Median age: 38.4 (2005); Males per 100 females: 96.0 (2005); Marriage status: 25.4% never married, 59.5% now married, 4.4% widowed, 10.7% divorced (2000); Foreign born: 2.7% (2000); Ancestry (includes multiple ancestries): 33.3% Italian, 24.1% German, 24.0% Irish, 8.1% Other groups, 7.6% English (2000).
Economy: Single-family building permits issued: 2 (2005); Multi-family building permits issued: 0 (2005); Employment by occupation: 8.6% management, 15.4% professional, 14.6% services, 31.2% sales, 0.2% farming, 14.0% construction, 16.0% production (2000).
Income: Per capita income: $23,629 (2005); Median household income: $62,361 (2005); Average household income: $68,087 (2005); Percent of households with income of $100,000 or more: 16.2% (2005); Poverty rate: 5.7% (2000).
Education: Percent of population age 25 and over with: High school diploma (including GED) or higher: 82.7% (2005); Bachelor's degree or higher: 16.4% (2005); Master's degree or higher: 4.6% (2005).
School District(s)
Folsom Borough (PK-08)
    2003-04 Enrollment: 342 . . . . (609) 561-8666
Housing: Homeownership rate: 92.9% (2005); Median home value: $184,072 (2005); Median rent: $754 per month (2000); Median age of housing: 29 years (2000).
Transportation: Commute to work: 91.4% car, 4.4% public transportation, 2.3% walk, 0.9% work from home (2000); Travel time to work: 23.9% less than 15 minutes, 31.7% 15 to 30 minutes, 21.4% 30 to 45 minutes, 13.0% 45 to 60 minutes, 10.0% 60 minutes or more (2000)

GALLOWAY (township). Covers a land area of 90.487 square miles and a water area of 24.314 square miles. Located at 39.49° N. Lat.; 74.55° W. Long.
History: Incorporated 1798.
Population: 23,360 (1990); 31,209 (2000); 35,254 (2005); 39,238 (2010 projected); Race: 74.5% White, 10.5% Black, 9.4% Asian, 7.1% Hispanic of any race (2005); Density: 389.6 persons per square mile (2005); Average household size: 2.89 (2005); Median age: 34.9 (2005); Males per 100 females: 92.3 (2005); Marriage status: 27.8% never married, 57.3% now married, 5.3% widowed, 9.6% divorced (2000); Foreign born: 11.2% (2000); Ancestry (includes multiple ancestries): 23.8% Other groups, 20.7% Irish, 19.5% Italian, 19.1% German, 8.2% English (2000).
Economy: Rural resort area, with population growth in recent decades. Unemployment rate: 4.5% (2005); Total civilian labor force: 18,850 (2005); Single-family building permits issued: 348 (2005); Multi-family building permits issued: 0 (2005); Employment by occupation: 11.2% management, 17.6% professional, 28.5% services, 27.6% sales, 0.0% farming, 8.2% construction, 7.0% production (2000).
Income: Per capita income: $24,897 (2005); Median household income: $60,527 (2005); Average household income: $70,899 (2005); Percent of households with income of $100,000 or more: 20.3% (2005); Poverty rate: 6.6% (2000).
Taxes: Total city taxes per capita: $329 (2004); City property taxes per capita: $300 (2004).
Education: Percent of population age 25 and over with: High school diploma (including GED) or higher: 87.5% (2005); Bachelor's degree or higher: 22.9% (2005); Master's degree or higher: 7.4% (2005).
School District(s)
Galloway Township (PK-08)
    2003-04 Enrollment: 4,138 . . . . (609) 748-1250
Housing: Homeownership rate: 73.8% (2005); Median home value: $203,238 (2005); Median rent: $673 per month (2000); Median age of housing: 16 years (2000).
Safety: Violent crime rate: 22.9 per 10,000 population; Property crime rate: 190.9 per 10,000 population (2004).
Transportation: Commute to work: 93.2% car, 2.6% public transportation, 2.1% walk, 1.5% work from home (2000); Travel time to work: 24.4% less than 15 minutes, 52.3% 15 to 30 minutes, 15.1% 30 to 45 minutes, 2.3% 45 to 60 minutes, 5.9% 60 minutes or more (2000)

HAMILTON (township). Covers a land area of 111.283 square miles and a water area of 1.707 square miles. Located at 39.48° N. Lat.; 74.75° W. Long.
Population: 16,012 (1990); 20,499 (2000); 23,825 (2005); 26,947 (2010 projected); Race: 69.8% White, 20.1% Black, 3.5% Asian, 9.0% Hispanic of any race (2005); Density: 214.1 persons per square mile (2005); Average household size: 2.85 (2005); Median age: 35.5 (2005); Males per 100 females: 99.7 (2005); Marriage status: 25.0% never married, 56.8% now married, 7.2% widowed, 11.0% divorced (2000); Foreign born: 6.6% (2000); Ancestry (includes multiple ancestries): 26.4% Other groups, 19.7% German, 18.4% Irish, 17.2% Italian, 8.8% English (2000).
Economy: Single-family building permits issued: 236 (2005); Multi-family building permits issued: 95 (2005); Employment by occupation: 10.3% management, 19.7% professional, 26.2% services, 25.7% sales, 0.3% farming, 9.3% construction, 8.5% production (2000).
Income: Per capita income: $24,187 (2005); Median household income: $55,738 (2005); Average household income: $66,382 (2005); Percent of households with income of $100,000 or more: 15.0% (2005); Poverty rate: 6.6% (2000).
Education: Percent of population age 25 and over with: High school diploma (including GED) or higher: 80.2% (2005); Bachelor's degree or higher: 19.3% (2005); Master's degree or higher: 5.0% (2005).
Housing: Homeownership rate: 73.1% (2005); Median home value: $167,519 (2005); Median rent: $682 per month (2000); Median age of housing: 20 years (2000).
Safety: Violent crime rate: 35.4 per 10,000 population; Property crime rate: 462.3 per 10,000 population (2004).
Transportation: Commute to work: 93.6% car, 3.1% public transportation, 0.8% walk, 1.9% work from home (2000); Travel time to work: 20.9% less than 15 minutes, 40.0% 15 to 30 minutes, 26.7% 30 to 45 minutes, 6.6% 45 to 60 minutes, 5.9% 60 minutes or more (2000)

HAMMONTON (town). Covers a land area of 41.260 square miles and a water area of 0.213 square miles. Located at 39.64° N. Lat.; 74.78° W. Long. Elevation is 100 feet.
History: Incorporated 1866.
Population: 12,208 (1990); 12,604 (2000); 13,204 (2005); 13,858 (2010 projected); Race: 86.3% White, 1.8% Black, 1.1% Asian, 16.6% Hispanic of any race (2005); Density: 320.0 persons per square mile (2005); Average household size: 2.72 (2005); Median age: 39.4 (2005); Males per 100 females: 95.2 (2005); Marriage status: 25.4% never married, 58.0% now married, 8.4% widowed, 8.2% divorced (2000); Foreign born: 8.1% (2000); Ancestry (includes multiple ancestries): 54.3% Italian, 16.6% Other groups, 14.7% Irish, 12.1% German, 5.8% English (2000).
Economy: Shipping and processing center for fruit and manufacturing of wood products, clothing, medical supplies and pharmaceuticals. Site of a winery. Single-family building permits issued: 79 (2005); Multi-family building permits issued: 0 (2005); Employment by occupation: 10.0% management, 15.6% professional, 18.8% services, 29.7% sales, 1.7% farming, 10.1% construction, 14.1% production (2000).
Income: Per capita income: $20,840 (2005); Median household income: $46,062 (2005); Average household income: $55,633 (2005); Percent of households with income of $100,000 or more: 11.7% (2005); Poverty rate: 9.1% (2000).
Education: Percent of population age 25 and over with: High school diploma (including GED) or higher: 72.3% (2005); Bachelor's degree or higher: 16.1% (2005); Master's degree or higher: 4.6% (2005).
School District(s)
Hammonton Town (PK-12)
    2003-04 Enrollment: 3,372 . . . . (609) 567-7004
Mullica Township (PK-08)
    2003-04 Enrollment: 844 . . . . (609) 561-3868
Housing: Homeownership rate: 70.8% (2005); Median home value: $205,769 (2005); Median rent: $602 per month (2000); Median age of housing: 43 years (2000).
Hospitals: William B Kessler Memorial Hospital (130 beds)
Safety: Violent crime rate: 20.6 per 10,000 population; Property crime rate: 162.0 per 10,000 population (2004).
Newspapers: Atlantic County Record (General - Circulation 1,124); Hammonton Gazette (General - Circulation 6,500); Hammonton News (General - Circulation 6,500); Mainland Journal (General - Circulation 1,874); The Egg Harbor News (General - Circulation 724); The Record Journal (General - Circulation 10,000)

Transportation: Commute to work: 91.0% car, 2.9% public transportation, 2.6% walk, 2.0% work from home (2000); Travel time to work: 44.4% less than 15 minutes, 19.4% 15 to 30 minutes, 19.7% 30 to 45 minutes, 8.6% 45 to 60 minutes, 7.9% 60 minutes or more (2000); Amtrak: Service available.

Additional Information Contacts
Hammonton Chamber of Commerce . . . . (609) 561-9080
  http://www.hammontonnj.us

LANDISVILLE (unincorporated postal area, zip code 08326). Part of the Borough of Buena. Covers a land area of 0.909 square miles and a water area of 0 square miles. Located at 39.52° N. Lat.; 74.93° W. Long. Elevation is 113 feet.

Population: 1,280 (2000); Race: 71.2% White, 5.6% Black, 0.0% Asian, 38.8% Hispanic of any race (2000); Density: 1,408.2 persons per square mile (2000); Age: 27.2% under 18, 18.6% over 64 (2000); Marriage status: 32.9% never married, 44.8% now married, 12.8% widowed, 9.6% divorced (2000); Foreign born: 10.9% (2000); Ancestry (includes multiple ancestries): 38.6% Other groups, 33.4% Italian, 10.0% Irish, 9.3% German, 4.5% Polish (2000).

Economy: Clothing; poultry; vegetables. Employment by occupation: 6.8% management, 11.2% professional, 17.8% services, 23.7% sales, 13.4% farming, 11.2% construction, 15.9% production (2000).

Income: Per capita income: $15,004 (2000); Median household income: $30,625 (2000); Poverty rate: 24.6% (2000).

Education: Percent of population age 25 and over with: High school diploma (including GED) or higher: 50.4% (2000); Bachelor's degree or higher: 4.2% (2000).

School District(s)
Buena Regional (PK-12)
  2003-04 Enrollment: 2,627 . . . . (856) 697-0800
Housing: Homeownership rate: 66.2% (2000); Median home value: $88,300 (2000); Median rent: $576 per month (2000); Median age of housing: 46 years (2000).

Transportation: Commute to work: 92.4% car, 0.0% public transportation, 1.8% walk, 1.2% work from home (2000); Travel time to work: 42.1% less than 15 minutes, 29.9% 15 to 30 minutes, 20.3% 30 to 45 minutes, 5.1% 45 to 60 minutes, 2.6% 60 minutes or more (2000)

LINWOOD (city). Covers a land area of 3.828 square miles and a water area of 0.314 square miles. Located at 39.34° N. Lat.; 74.57° W. Long. Elevation is 28 feet.

History: Incorporated as borough 1889, as city 1931.

Population: 6,874 (1990); 7,172 (2000); 7,477 (2005); 7,813 (2010 projected); Race: 95.1% White, 1.1% Black, 2.3% Asian, 2.0% Hispanic of any race (2005); Density: 1,953.1 persons per square mile (2005); Average household size: 2.66 (2005); Median age: 44.3 (2005); Males per 100 females: 87.6 (2005); Marriage status: 18.9% never married, 65.4% now married, 9.8% widowed, 5.8% divorced (2000); Foreign born: 4.4% (2000); Ancestry (includes multiple ancestries): 23.5% Irish, 22.3% Italian, 17.6% German, 14.6% English, 7.7% Other groups (2000).

Economy: Manufacturing: lightweight boats, lumber products. Single-family building permits issued: 24 (2005); Multi-family building permits issued: 2 (2005); Employment by occupation: 18.1% management, 26.7% professional, 16.9% services, 25.4% sales, 0.0% farming, 8.6% construction, 4.2% production (2000).

Income: Per capita income: $34,456 (2005); Median household income: $62,728 (2005); Average household income: $90,825 (2005); Percent of households with income of $100,000 or more: 26.8% (2005); Poverty rate: 3.9% (2000).

Education: Percent of population age 25 and over with: High school diploma (including GED) or higher: 90.3% (2005); Bachelor's degree or higher: 37.8% (2005); Master's degree or higher: 15.1% (2005).

School District(s)
Agency - Charter Tech High School (09-12)
  2003-04 Enrollment: 248 . . . . (609) 653-9398
Linwood City (PK-08)
  2003-04 Enrollment: 1,042 . . . . (609) 926-6703
Mainland Regional (09-12)
  2003-04 Enrollment: 1,669 . . . . (609) 927-2461
Housing: Homeownership rate: 89.4% (2005); Median home value: $270,598 (2005); Median rent: $708 per month (2000); Median age of housing: 33 years (2000).

Safety: Violent crime rate: 8.1 per 10,000 population; Property crime rate: 129.3 per 10,000 population (2004).

Transportation: Commute to work: 93.5% car, 1.5% public transportation, 1.6% walk, 2.8% work from home (2000); Travel time to work: 35.4% less than 15 minutes, 39.7% 15 to 30 minutes, 14.3% 30 to 45 minutes, 3.9% 45 to 60 minutes, 6.7% 60 minutes or more (2000)

LONGPORT (borough). Covers a land area of 0.381 square miles and a water area of 1.245 square miles. Located at 39.31° N. Lat.; 74.52° W. Long. Elevation is 6 feet.

Population: 1,224 (1990); 1,054 (2000); 1,059 (2005); 1,077 (2010 projected); Race: 98.5% White, 0.1% Black, 1.2% Asian, 0.6% Hispanic of any race (2005); Density: 2,778.3 persons per square mile (2005); Average household size: 1.91 (2005); Median age: 57.8 (2005); Males per 100 females: 87.4 (2005); Marriage status: 17.1% never married, 61.9% now married, 11.2% widowed, 9.8% divorced (2000); Foreign born: 3.0% (2000); Ancestry (includes multiple ancestries): 33.1% Italian, 30.1% Irish, 15.8% German, 9.3% English, 6.2% Russian (2000).

Economy: Single-family building permits issued: 23 (2005); Multi-family building permits issued: 0 (2005); Employment by occupation: 20.0% management, 30.9% professional, 17.9% services, 23.3% sales, 0.0% farming, 3.7% construction, 4.1% production (2000).

Income: Per capita income: $61,192 (2005); Median household income: $63,393 (2005); Average household income: $116,761 (2005); Percent of households with income of $100,000 or more: 33.0% (2005); Poverty rate: 3.7% (2000).

Education: Percent of population age 25 and over with: High school diploma (including GED) or higher: 87.0% (2005); Bachelor's degree or higher: 39.0% (2005); Master's degree or higher: 15.8% (2005).

Housing: Homeownership rate: 84.5% (2005); Median home value: $442,949 (2005); Median rent: $746 per month (2000); Median age of housing: 37 years (2000).

Safety: Violent crime rate: 0.0 per 10,000 population; Property crime rate: 113.1 per 10,000 population (2004).

Transportation: Commute to work: 87.8% car, 3.2% public transportation, 2.1% walk, 6.5% work from home (2000); Travel time to work: 27.2% less than 15 minutes, 37.8% 15 to 30 minutes, 19.8% 30 to 45 minutes, 2.9% 45 to 60 minutes, 12.4% 60 minutes or more (2000)

MARGATE CITY (city). Aka Margate. Covers a land area of 1.406 square miles and a water area of 0.176 square miles. Located at 39.32° N. Lat.; 74.50° W. Long. Elevation is 8 feet.

History: Incorporated 1897.

Population: 8,431 (1990); 8,193 (2000); 8,416 (2005); 8,689 (2010 projected); Race: 95.3% White, 1.0% Black, 1.7% Asian, 3.1% Hispanic of any race (2005); Density: 5,983.9 persons per square mile (2005); Average household size: 2.01 (2005); Median age: 51.1 (2005); Males per 100 females: 89.9 (2005); Marriage status: 21.7% never married, 59.4% now married, 11.5% widowed, 7.3% divorced (2000); Foreign born: 7.4% (2000); Ancestry (includes multiple ancestries): 21.2% Italian, 20.9% Irish, 13.7% Other groups, 10.0% Russian, 9.7% German (2000).

Economy: Resort. Known for its pleasant beaches and for its large, old homes, intermixed with expensive, renovated modern residences. Single-family building permits issued: 31 (2005); Multi-family building permits issued: 29 (2005); Employment by occupation: 18.6% management, 19.0% professional, 20.8% services, 31.9% sales, 0.0% farming, 5.9% construction, 3.8% production (2000).

Income: Per capita income: $34,666 (2005); Median household income: $45,129 (2005); Average household income: $69,468 (2005); Percent of households with income of $100,000 or more: 17.4% (2005); Poverty rate: 7.3% (2000).

Education: Percent of population age 25 and over with: High school diploma (including GED) or higher: 88.1% (2005); Bachelor's degree or higher: 36.2% (2005); Master's degree or higher: 13.4% (2005).

School District(s)
Margate City (PK-08)
  2003-04 Enrollment: 600 . . . . (609) 822-1686
Housing: Homeownership rate: 73.0% (2005); Median home value: $299,043 (2005); Median rent: $649 per month (2000); Median age of housing: 40 years (2000).

Safety: Violent crime rate: 9.5 per 10,000 population; Property crime rate: 152.6 per 10,000 population (2004).

Transportation: Commute to work: 89.1% car, 3.6% public transportation, 2.8% walk, 4.2% work from home (2000); Travel time to work: 29.5% less than 15 minutes, 45.0% 15 to 30 minutes, 10.8% 30 to 45 minutes, 5.5% 45 to 60 minutes, 9.1% 60 minutes or more (2000)

Additional Information Contacts

City of Margate City . . . . (609) 822-2605
http://www.margate-nj.com

MAYS LANDING (CDP). Covers a land area of 1.703 square miles and a water area of 0.212 square miles. Located at 39.45° N. Lat.; 74.72° W. Long. Elevation is 20 feet.

History: Settled c.1710.

Population: 2,041 (1990); 2,321 (2000); 2,574 (2005); 2,831 (2010 projected); Race: 89.7% White, 6.3% Black, 0.9% Asian, 4.8% Hispanic of any race (2005); Density: 1,511.3 persons per square mile (2005); Average household size: 2.56 (2005); Median age: 38.4 (2005); Males per 100 females: 95.0 (2005); Marriage status: 25.8% never married, 55.2% now married, 6.2% widowed, 12.8% divorced (2000); Foreign born: 2.9% (2000); Ancestry (includes multiple ancestries): 29.5% Italian, 24.4% German, 23.8% Irish, 10.2% English, 8.1% Other groups (2000).

Economy: Poultry; vegetables. Employment by occupation: 11.3% management, 19.1% professional, 29.3% services, 21.4% sales, 0.0% farming, 12.0% construction, 6.8% production (2000).

Income: Per capita income: $25,227 (2005); Median household income: $57,592 (2005); Average household income: $63,381 (2005); Percent of households with income of $100,000 or more: 15.3% (2005); Poverty rate: 6.8% (2000).

Education: Percent of population age 25 and over with: High school diploma (including GED) or higher: 83.9% (2005); Bachelor's degree or higher: 22.1% (2005); Master's degree or higher: 4.5% (2005).

School District(s)

Atlantic County Special Services (UG-UG)
2003-04 Enrollment: 1,036 . . . . (609) 625-5796
Atlantic County Vocational (09-12)
2003-04 Enrollment: 273 . . . . (609) 625-2249
Greater Egg Harbor Regional (09-12)
2003-04 Enrollment: 3,844 . . . . (609) 625-1456
Hamilton Township (PK-08)
2003-04 Enrollment: 3,065 . . . . (609) 625-6595

Two-year College(s)

Atlantic Cape Community College (Public)
Fall 2004 Enrollment: 6,515 . . . . (609) 625-1111
2005-06 Tuition: In-state $4,809; Out-of-state $8,100
Atlantic County Vocational Technical School (Public)
Fall 2004 Enrollment: 113 . . . . (609) 625-2249

Housing: Homeownership rate: 72.8% (2005); Median home value: $176,654 (2005); Median rent: $611 per month (2000); Median age of housing: 45 years (2000).

Transportation: Commute to work: 96.1% car, 1.8% public transportation, 1.1% walk, 0.5% work from home (2000); Travel time to work: 29.2% less than 15 minutes, 39.7% 15 to 30 minutes, 21.1% 30 to 45 minutes, 2.1% 45 to 60 minutes, 7.9% 60 minutes or more (2000)

MILMAY (unincorporated postal area, zip code 08340). Covers a land area of 12.429 square miles and a water area of 0.003 square miles. Located at 39.43° N. Lat.; 74.87° W. Long. Elevation is 100 feet.

Population: 872 (2000); Race: 93.8% White, 1.0% Black, 0.0% Asian, 0.7% Hispanic of any race (2000); Density: 70.2 persons per square mile (2000); Age: 34.3% under 18, 9.4% over 64 (2000); Marriage status: 25.6% never married, 56.3% now married, 10.5% widowed, 7.6% divorced (2000); Foreign born: 3.1% (2000); Ancestry (includes multiple ancestries): 43.2% Italian, 22.9% German, 21.5% Irish, 13.4% English, 8.5% Other groups (2000).

Economy: Employment by occupation: 11.5% management, 20.3% professional, 13.3% services, 21.1% sales, 0.0% farming, 18.7% construction, 15.2% production (2000).

Income: Per capita income: $20,094 (2000); Median household income: $43,352 (2000); Poverty rate: 6.7% (2000).

Education: Percent of population age 25 and over with: High school diploma (including GED) or higher: 83.6% (2000); Bachelor's degree or higher: 21.1% (2000).

Housing: Homeownership rate: 77.5% (2000); Median home value: $134,400 (2000); Median rent: $492 per month (2000); Median age of housing: 24 years (2000).

Transportation: Commute to work: 100.0% car, 0.0% public transportation, 0.0% walk, 0.0% work from home (2000); Travel time to work: 13.2% less than 15 minutes, 46.2% 15 to 30 minutes, 15.0% 30 to 45 minutes, 20.8% 45 to 60 minutes, 4.7% 60 minutes or more (2000)

MINOTOLA (unincorporated postal area, zip code 08341). Part of the Borough of Buena. Covers a land area of 2.442 square miles and a water area of 0 square miles. Located at 39.51° N. Lat.; 74.95° W. Long. Elevation is 120 feet.

Population: 2,042 (2000); Race: 78.2% White, 9.1% Black, 1.1% Asian, 17.4% Hispanic of any race (2000); Density: 836.2 persons per square mile (2000); Age: 25.5% under 18, 15.5% over 64 (2000); Marriage status: 30.6% never married, 47.9% now married, 10.2% widowed, 11.3% divorced (2000); Foreign born: 3.7% (2000); Ancestry (includes multiple ancestries): 34.5% Italian, 24.1% Other groups, 15.7% German, 9.1% Irish, 4.6% Polish (2000).

Economy: Employment by occupation: 10.0% management, 11.7% professional, 24.7% services, 23.7% sales, 0.9% farming, 11.1% construction, 17.9% production (2000).

Income: Per capita income: $16,185 (2000); Median household income: $32,204 (2000); Poverty rate: 15.9% (2000).

Education: Percent of population age 25 and over with: High school diploma (including GED) or higher: 65.5% (2000); Bachelor's degree or higher: 9.9% (2000).

School District(s)

Buena Regional (PK-12)
2003-04 Enrollment: 2,627 . . . . (856) 697-0800

Housing: Homeownership rate: 56.6% (2000); Median home value: $104,200 (2000); Median rent: $504 per month (2000); Median age of housing: 36 years (2000).

Transportation: Commute to work: 93.6% car, 0.7% public transportation, 0.7% walk, 3.0% work from home (2000); Travel time to work: 29.0% less than 15 minutes, 27.9% 15 to 30 minutes, 21.8% 30 to 45 minutes, 10.0% 45 to 60 minutes, 11.3% 60 minutes or more (2000)

MULLICA (township). Covers a land area of 56.584 square miles and a water area of 0.357 square miles. Located at 39.58° N. Lat.; 74.68° W. Long.

History: Incorporated 1838.

Population: 5,896 (1990); 5,912 (2000); 6,117 (2005); 6,365 (2010 projected); Race: 80.8% White, 4.8% Black, 0.8% Asian, 17.1% Hispanic of any race (2005); Density: 108.1 persons per square mile (2005); Average household size: 2.84 (2005); Median age: 38.0 (2005); Males per 100 females: 101.2 (2005); Marriage status: 24.7% never married, 61.5% now married, 6.2% widowed, 7.6% divorced (2000); Foreign born: 3.7% (2000); Ancestry (includes multiple ancestries): 26.6% Irish, 25.4% Other groups, 23.5% German, 19.8% Italian, 12.0% English (2000).

Economy: Single-family building permits issued: 24 (2005); Multi-family building permits issued: 0 (2005); Employment by occupation: 9.1% management, 12.7% professional, 24.5% services, 24.5% sales, 1.8% farming, 17.3% construction, 10.2% production (2000).

Income: Per capita income: $23,713 (2005); Median household income: $57,712 (2005); Average household income: $66,712 (2005); Percent of households with income of $100,000 or more: 16.1% (2005); Poverty rate: 7.8% (2000).

Education: Percent of population age 25 and over with: High school diploma (including GED) or higher: 78.5% (2005); Bachelor's degree or higher: 13.8% (2005); Master's degree or higher: 3.8% (2005).

Housing: Homeownership rate: 86.6% (2005); Median home value: $181,491 (2005); Median rent: $602 per month (2000); Median age of housing: 29 years (2000).

Safety: Violent crime rate: 16.4 per 10,000 population; Property crime rate: 174.3 per 10,000 population (2004).

Transportation: Commute to work: 92.4% car, 2.3% public transportation, 1.8% walk, 2.8% work from home (2000); Travel time to work: 17.4% less than 15 minutes, 27.6% 15 to 30 minutes, 29.2% 30 to 45 minutes, 15.7% 45 to 60 minutes, 10.1% 60 minutes or more (2000)

NEWTONVILLE (unincorporated postal area, zip code 08346). Covers a land area of 2.702 square miles and a water area of 0 square miles. Located at 39.56° N. Lat.; 74.85° W. Long. Elevation is 103 feet.

Population: 680 (2000); Race: 18.8% White, 53.4% Black, 0.0% Asian, 18.9% Hispanic of any race (2000); Density: 251.7 persons per square mile (2000); Age: 37.1% under 18, 6.0% over 64 (2000); Marriage status: 36.1% never married, 51.3% now married, 4.4% widowed, 8.2% divorced (2000); Foreign born: 0.0% (2000); Ancestry (includes multiple ancestries): 61.2% Other groups, 11.1% African, 7.2% German, 4.1% United States or American, 2.7% English (2000).

Economy: Employment by occupation: 8.8% management, 7.9% professional, 39.4% services, 19.8% sales, 0.0% farming, 11.6% construction, 12.5% production (2000).
Income: Per capita income: $12,079 (2000); Median household income: $50,357 (2000); Poverty rate: 12.9% (2000).
Education: Percent of population age 25 and over with: High school diploma (including GED) or higher: 55.9% (2000); Bachelor's degree or higher: 3.8% (2000).
Housing: Homeownership rate: 90.5% (2000); Median home value: $88,600 (2000); Median rent: $664 per month (2000); Median age of housing: 36 years (2000).
Transportation: Commute to work: 94.9% car, 5.1% public transportation, 0.0% walk, 0.0% work from home (2000); Travel time to work: 9.6% less than 15 minutes, 40.5% 15 to 30 minutes, 24.1% 30 to 45 minutes, 14.7% 45 to 60 minutes, 11.0% 60 minutes or more (2000)

NORTHFIELD (city). Covers a land area of 3.426 square miles and a water area of 0.025 square miles. Located at 39.37° N. Lat.; 74.55° W. Long. Elevation is 33 feet.
History: Incorporated 1905.
Population: 6,899 (1990); 7,725 (2000); 8,082 (2005); 8,476 (2010 projected); Race: 91.0% White, 2.7% Black, 2.4% Asian, 5.4% Hispanic of any race (2005); Density: 2,359.1 persons per square mile (2005); Average household size: 2.73 (2005); Median age: 41.4 (2005); Males per 100 females: 91.5 (2005); Marriage status: 22.3% never married, 59.9% now married, 9.7% widowed, 8.2% divorced (2000); Foreign born: 5.7% (2000); Ancestry (includes multiple ancestries): 26.0% Irish, 20.1% German, 19.6% Italian, 15.6% English, 11.7% Other groups (2000).
Economy: Single-family building permits issued: 40 (2005); Multi-family building permits issued: 0 (2005); Employment by occupation: 11.9% management, 18.7% professional, 28.9% services, 25.1% sales, 0.0% farming, 8.0% construction, 7.3% production (2000).
Income: Per capita income: $26,980 (2005); Median household income: $61,211 (2005); Average household income: $72,931 (2005); Percent of households with income of $100,000 or more: 19.8% (2005); Poverty rate: 5.6% (2000).
Education: Percent of population age 25 and over with: High school diploma (including GED) or higher: 87.3% (2005); Bachelor's degree or higher: 22.3% (2005); Master's degree or higher: 4.9% (2005).
School District(s)
Northfield City (PK-08)
   2003-04 Enrollment: 1,158 . . . . (609) 407-4000
Housing: Homeownership rate: 92.3% (2005); Median home value: $212,298 (2005); Median rent: $683 per month (2000); Median age of housing: 39 years (2000).
Safety: Violent crime rate: 13.7 per 10,000 population; Property crime rate: 149.8 per 10,000 population (2004).
Transportation: Commute to work: 93.1% car, 1.9% public transportation, 1.6% walk, 2.7% work from home (2000); Travel time to work: 31.3% less than 15 minutes, 51.1% 15 to 30 minutes, 10.9% 30 to 45 minutes, 2.3% 45 to 60 minutes, 4.4% 60 minutes or more (2000)

PLEASANTVILLE (city). Covers a land area of 5.776 square miles and a water area of 1.547 square miles. Located at 39.39° N. Lat.; 74.52° W. Long. Elevation is 22 feet.
History: Settled 1702, incorporated 1888.
Population: 15,999 (1990); 19,012 (2000); 19,145 (2005); 19,442 (2010 projected); Race: 23.7% White, 56.9% Black, 1.9% Asian, 26.6% Hispanic of any race (2005); Density: 3,314.4 persons per square mile (2005); Average household size: 3.03 (2005); Median age: 33.3 (2005); Males per 100 females: 89.6 (2005); Marriage status: 37.9% never married, 43.0% now married, 7.5% widowed, 11.6% divorced (2000); Foreign born: 12.9% (2000); Ancestry (includes multiple ancestries): 63.6% Other groups, 4.9% Irish, 4.8% German, 3.3% Italian, 3.0% Haitian (2000).
Economy: Residential and resort city. It is the trade center of an area known as "the Mainland." Tourism, shellfishing, deep-sea fishing, and boatbuilding. Single-family building permits issued: 92 (2005); Multi-family building permits issued: 0 (2005); Employment by occupation: 6.2% management, 11.5% professional, 39.0% services, 25.9% sales, 0.4% farming, 6.1% construction, 10.9% production (2000).
Income: Per capita income: $17,786 (2005); Median household income: $38,596 (2005); Average household income: $45,573 (2005); Percent of households with income of $100,000 or more: 6.2% (2005); Poverty rate: 15.8% (2000).

Taxes: Total city taxes per capita: $626 (2004); City property taxes per capita: $597 (2004).
Education: Percent of population age 25 and over with: High school diploma (including GED) or higher: 70.0% (2005); Bachelor's degree or higher: 10.1% (2005); Master's degree or higher: 3.1% (2005).
School District(s)
Agency - Pleasantech Academy CS (KG-08)
   2003-04 Enrollment: 259 . . . . (609) 383-1717
Agency - Pleasantville CS for Academy Excellence (KG-08)
   2003-04 Enrollment: 338 . . . . (609) 407-9253
Pleasantville City (PK-12)
   2003-04 Enrollment: 4,067 . . . . (609) 383-6800
Two-year College(s)
Shore Beauty School (Private, For-profit)
   Fall 2004 Enrollment: 37 . . . . (609) 645-3635
Housing: Homeownership rate: 56.4% (2005); Median home value: $133,486 (2005); Median rent: $606 per month (2000); Median age of housing: 38 years (2000).
Safety: Violent crime rate: 100.3 per 10,000 population; Property crime rate: 383.8 per 10,000 population (2004).
Newspapers: Jewish Times of the South Jersey Seashore (Jewish, Religious - Circulation 6,500); The Press of Atlantic City (Circulation 73,489)
Transportation: Commute to work: 82.0% car, 14.2% public transportation, 2.4% walk, 0.4% work from home (2000); Travel time to work: 28.5% less than 15 minutes, 49.7% 15 to 30 minutes, 12.4% 30 to 45 minutes, 3.8% 45 to 60 minutes, 5.6% 60 minutes or more (2000)

POMONA (CDP). Covers a land area of 2.796 square miles and a water area of 0 square miles. Located at 39.46° N. Lat.; 74.54° W. Long. Elevation is 60 feet.
History: Site of Richard Stockton College of New Jersey.
Population: 2,624 (1990); 4,019 (2000); 4,785 (2005); 5,515 (2010 projected); Race: 70.6% White, 8.6% Black, 14.0% Asian, 9.3% Hispanic of any race (2005); Density: 1,711.4 persons per square mile (2005); Average household size: 3.10 (2005); Median age: 35.1 (2005); Males per 100 females: 95.6 (2005); Marriage status: 22.7% never married, 62.4% now married, 5.0% widowed, 9.9% divorced (2000); Foreign born: 17.4% (2000); Ancestry (includes multiple ancestries): 28.3% Other groups, 22.7% Italian, 22.1% Irish, 18.6% German, 9.1% English (2000).
Economy: Employment by occupation: 6.7% management, 12.2% professional, 31.2% services, 29.3% sales, 0.0% farming, 11.2% construction, 9.4% production (2000).
Income: Per capita income: $21,521 (2005); Median household income: $61,973 (2005); Average household income: $65,906 (2005); Percent of households with income of $100,000 or more: 18.1% (2005); Poverty rate: 4.6% (2000).
Education: Percent of population age 25 and over with: High school diploma (including GED) or higher: 84.3% (2005); Bachelor's degree or higher: 15.7% (2005); Master's degree or higher: 3.8% (2005).
School District(s)
Galloway Township (PK-08)
   2003-04 Enrollment: 4,138 . . . . (609) 748-1250
Four-year College(s)
The Richard Stockton College of New Jersey (Public)
   Fall 2004 Enrollment: 7,002 . . . . (609) 652-1776
   2005-06 Tuition: In-state $8,394; Out-of-state $11,792
Housing: Homeownership rate: 85.1% (2005); Median home value: $195,385 (2005); Median rent: $421 per month (2000); Median age of housing: 20 years (2000).
Hospitals: Bacharach Institute for Rehabilitation (80 beds)
Transportation: Commute to work: 96.7% car, 2.6% public transportation, 0.0% walk, 0.3% work from home (2000); Travel time to work: 21.3% less than 15 minutes, 55.3% 15 to 30 minutes, 15.9% 30 to 45 minutes, 3.1% 45 to 60 minutes, 4.4% 60 minutes or more (2000)

PORT REPUBLIC (city). Covers a land area of 7.624 square miles and a water area of 1.052 square miles. Located at 39.52° N. Lat.; 74.49° W. Long. Elevation is 17 feet.
Population: 962 (1990); 1,037 (2000); 1,244 (2005); 1,428 (2010 projected); Race: 94.7% White, 1.8% Black, 0.6% Asian, 1.5% Hispanic of any race (2005); Density: 163.2 persons per square mile (2005); Average household size: 2.81 (2005); Median age: 42.1 (2005); Males per 100 females: 96.8 (2005); Marriage status: 23.1% never married, 59.0% now married, 5.8% widowed, 12.1% divorced (2000); Foreign born: 4.6%

PROFILES OF NEW JERSEY / Atlantic County

(2000); Ancestry (includes multiple ancestries): 29.6% German, 23.8% English, 23.6% Irish, 15.4% Italian, 5.0% Polish (2000).
Economy: Single-family building permits issued: 23 (2005); Multi-family building permits issued: 0 (2005); Employment by occupation: 8.1% management, 20.9% professional, 16.1% services, 27.6% sales, 1.3% farming, 14.3% construction, 11.7% production (2000).
Income: Per capita income: $31,507 (2005); Median household income: $77,964 (2005); Average household income: $87,054 (2005); Percent of households with income of $100,000 or more: 30.7% (2005); Poverty rate: 3.5% (2000).
Education: Percent of population age 25 and over with: High school diploma (including GED) or higher: 90.6% (2005); Bachelor's degree or higher: 28.2% (2005); Master's degree or higher: 7.6% (2005).

School District(s)
Port Republic City (PK-08)
   2003-04 Enrollment: 132 . . . . (609) 652-7377
Housing: Homeownership rate: 90.5% (2005); Median home value: $243,711 (2005); Median rent: $664 per month (2000); Median age of housing: 32 years (2000).
Transportation: Commute to work: 92.9% car, 0.4% public transportation, 1.8% walk, 4.9% work from home (2000); Travel time to work: 27.5% less than 15 minutes, 43.3% 15 to 30 minutes, 19.3% 30 to 45 minutes, 3.4% 45 to 60 minutes, 6.5% 60 minutes or more (2000)

RICHLAND (unincorporated postal area, zip code 08350). Covers a land area of 2.443 square miles and a water area of 0 square miles. Located at 39.49° N. Lat.; 74.87° W. Long. Elevation is 105 feet.
Population: 743 (2000); Race: 75.5% White, 20.7% Black, 2.9% Asian, 3.2% Hispanic of any race (2000); Density: 304.1 persons per square mile (2000); Age: 22.5% under 18, 6.3% over 64 (2000); Marriage status: 35.4% never married, 46.7% now married, 9.3% widowed, 8.5% divorced (2000); Foreign born: 1.4% (2000); Ancestry (includes multiple ancestries): 43.7% Italian, 29.9% Other groups, 21.7% German, 14.7% Irish, 5.3% Swiss (2000).
Economy: In agricultural area; poultry. Employment by occupation: 5.6% management, 16.9% professional, 17.3% services, 26.8% sales, 0.0% farming, 18.3% construction, 15.3% production (2000).
Income: Per capita income: $19,438 (2000); Median household income: $60,833 (2000); Poverty rate: 7.9% (2000).
Education: Percent of population age 25 and over with: High school diploma (including GED) or higher: 72.3% (2000); Bachelor's degree or higher: 18.9% (2000).
Housing: Homeownership rate: 86.0% (2000); Median home value: $99,100 (2000); Median rent: $675 per month (2000); Median age of housing: 37 years (2000).
Transportation: Commute to work: 88.9% car, 6.8% public transportation, 4.3% walk, 0.0% work from home (2000); Travel time to work: 36.1% less than 15 minutes, 36.1% 15 to 30 minutes, 13.9% 30 to 45 minutes, 1.4% 45 to 60 minutes, 12.5% 60 minutes or more (2000)

SOMERS POINT (city). Covers a land area of 4.028 square miles and a water area of 1.137 square miles. Located at 39.31° N. Lat.; 74.60° W. Long. Elevation is 27 feet.
History: Settled c.1695, incorporated 1886.
Population: 11,216 (1990); 11,614 (2000); 11,690 (2005); 11,847 (2010 projected); Race: 84.2% White, 7.8% Black, 3.3% Asian, 7.1% Hispanic of any race (2005); Density: 2,902.0 persons per square mile (2005); Average household size: 2.35 (2005); Median age: 39.2 (2005); Males per 100 females: 90.1 (2005); Marriage status: 30.7% never married, 48.9% now married, 9.2% widowed, 11.2% divorced (2000); Foreign born: 8.2% (2000); Ancestry (includes multiple ancestries): 29.0% Irish, 20.3% Italian, 17.0% German, 15.3% Other groups, 11.6% English (2000).
Economy: Boat-repair facility. Single-family building permits issued: 22 (2005); Multi-family building permits issued: 0 (2005); Employment by occupation: 10.0% management, 17.2% professional, 29.4% services, 25.2% sales, 0.7% farming, 10.0% construction, 7.5% production (2000).
Income: Per capita income: $23,231 (2005); Median household income: $43,901 (2005); Average household income: $54,064 (2005); Percent of households with income of $100,000 or more: 8.6% (2005); Poverty rate: 7.0% (2000).
Education: Percent of population age 25 and over with: High school diploma (including GED) or higher: 84.1% (2005); Bachelor's degree or higher: 19.9% (2005); Master's degree or higher: 5.1% (2005).

School District(s)
Somers Point City (PK-08)
   2003-04 Enrollment: 1,155 . . . . (609) 927-7161
Housing: Homeownership rate: 57.2% (2005); Median home value: $197,088 (2005); Median rent: $604 per month (2000); Median age of housing: 34 years (2000).
Hospitals: Shore Memorial Hospital (344 beds)
Safety: Violent crime rate: 37.6 per 10,000 population; Property crime rate: 295.8 per 10,000 population (2004).
Transportation: Commute to work: 91.0% car, 3.3% public transportation, 2.9% walk, 1.6% work from home (2000); Travel time to work: 35.8% less than 15 minutes, 39.3% 15 to 30 minutes, 14.6% 30 to 45 minutes, 3.8% 45 to 60 minutes, 6.6% 60 minutes or more (2000)

VENTNOR CITY (city). Aka Ventor. Covers a land area of 2.143 square miles and a water area of 1.403 square miles. Located at 39.34° N. Lat.; 74.48° W. Long. Elevation is 12 feet.
Population: 11,005 (1990); 12,910 (2000); 12,740 (2005); 12,671 (2010 projected); Race: 71.6% White, 3.4% Black, 9.1% Asian, 21.7% Hispanic of any race (2005); Density: 5,943.9 persons per square mile (2005); Average household size: 2.38 (2005); Median age: 41.4 (2005); Males per 100 females: 92.3 (2005); Marriage status: 26.6% never married, 51.3% now married, 11.0% widowed, 11.1% divorced (2000); Foreign born: 23.0% (2000); Ancestry (includes multiple ancestries): 29.1% Other groups, 22.8% Italian, 15.5% Irish, 8.7% German, 6.2% English (2000).
Economy: Single-family building permits issued: 15 (2005); Multi-family building permits issued: 0 (2005); Employment by occupation: 12.1% management, 14.9% professional, 38.0% services, 23.7% sales, 0.4% farming, 5.2% construction, 5.7% production (2000).
Income: Per capita income: $23,572 (2005); Median household income: $43,331 (2005); Average household income: $55,676 (2005); Percent of households with income of $100,000 or more: 11.9% (2005); Poverty rate: 7.0% (2000).
Taxes: Total city taxes per capita: $2,128 (2004); City property taxes per capita: $2,095 (2004).
Education: Percent of population age 25 and over with: High school diploma (including GED) or higher: 79.7% (2005); Bachelor's degree or higher: 21.4% (2005); Master's degree or higher: 7.8% (2005).

School District(s)
Ventnor City (PK-08)
   2003-04 Enrollment: 1,143 . . . . (609) 487-7918
Housing: Homeownership rate: 59.8% (2005); Median home value: $207,856 (2005); Median rent: $673 per month (2000); Median age of housing: 40 years (2000).
Safety: Violent crime rate: 15.5 per 10,000 population; Property crime rate: 239.4 per 10,000 population (2004).
Transportation: Commute to work: 78.5% car, 16.0% public transportation, 1.8% walk, 2.0% work from home (2000); Travel time to work: 30.6% less than 15 minutes, 47.7% 15 to 30 minutes, 12.6% 30 to 45 minutes, 2.5% 45 to 60 minutes, 6.7% 60 minutes or more (2000)
Additional Information Contacts
City of Ventnor City . . . . (609) 823-7906
   http://www.ventnorcity.org

WEYMOUTH (township). Covers a land area of 12.200 square miles and a water area of 0.367 square miles. Located at 39.42° N. Lat.; 74.78° W. Long. Elevation is 30 feet.
Population: 1,957 (1990); 2,257 (2000); 2,408 (2005); 2,570 (2010 projected); Race: 92.4% White, 4.3% Black, 0.6% Asian, 4.3% Hispanic of any race (2005); Density: 197.4 persons per square mile (2005); Average household size: 2.61 (2005); Median age: 40.1 (2005); Males per 100 females: 92.9 (2005); Marriage status: 24.8% never married, 57.7% now married, 7.9% widowed, 9.6% divorced (2000); Foreign born: 2.6% (2000); Ancestry (includes multiple ancestries): 24.5% Irish, 23.5% German, 23.4% Italian, 11.3% English, 11.2% Other groups (2000).
Economy: Single-family building permits issued: 2 (2005); Multi-family building permits issued: 0 (2005); Employment by occupation: 9.5% management, 14.7% professional, 21.6% services, 29.4% sales, 0.0% farming, 13.2% construction, 11.7% production (2000).
Income: Per capita income: $20,437 (2005); Median household income: $46,604 (2005); Average household income: $53,144 (2005); Percent of households with income of $100,000 or more: 10.6% (2005); Poverty rate: 5.1% (2000).

Education: Percent of population age 25 and over with: High school diploma (including GED) or higher: 79.4% (2005); Bachelor's degree or higher: 14.1% (2005); Master's degree or higher: 4.3% (2005).
Housing: Homeownership rate: 87.1% (2005); Median home value: $183,549 (2005); Median rent: $569 per month (2000); Median age of housing: 18 years (2000).
Transportation: Commute to work: 95.8% car, 1.4% public transportation, 1.0% walk, 1.9% work from home (2000); Travel time to work: 14.3% less than 15 minutes, 37.4% 15 to 30 minutes, 32.3% 30 to 45 minutes, 8.9% 45 to 60 minutes, 7.0% 60 minutes or more (2000)

Bergen County

Located in extreme northeastern New Jersey; bounded on the east by the Palisades of the Hudson River, and on the north by New York. Covers a land area of 234.17 square miles, a water area of 12.63 square miles, and is located in the Eastern Time Zone. The county government was organized in 1683. County seat is Hackensack.

Bergen County is part of the New York-Northern New Jersey-Long Island, NY-NJ-PA Metropolitan Statistical Area. The entire metro area includes: Edison, NJ Metropolitan Division (Middlesex County, NJ; Monmouth County, NJ; Ocean County, NJ; Somerset County, NJ); Nassau-Suffolk, NY Metropolitan Division (Nassau County, NY; Suffolk County, NY); New York-White Plains-Wayne, NY-NJ Metropolitan Division (Bergen County, NJ; Hudson County, NJ; Passaic County, NJ; Bronx County, NY; Kings County, NY; New York County, NY; Putnam County, NY; Queens County, NY; Richmond County, NY; Rockland County, NY; Westchester County, NY); Newark-Union, NJ-PA Metropolitan Division (Essex County, NJ; Hunterdon County, NJ; Morris County, NJ; Sussex County, NJ; Union County, NJ; Pike County, PA)

Population: 825,261 (1990); 884,118 (2000); 903,206 (2005); 922,933 (2010 projected); Race: 75.2% White, 5.4% Black, 12.6% Asian, 12.8% Hispanic of any race (2005); Density: 3,857.0 persons per square mile (2005); Average household size: 2.67 (2005); Median age: 40.4 (2005); Males per 100 females: 93.5 (2005).
Religion: Five largest groups: 54.1% Catholic Church, 9.5% Jewish Estimate, 1.2% Episcopal Church, 1.1% The United Methodist Church, 1.0% Presbyterian Church (U.S.A.) (2000).
Economy: Unemployment rate: 3.7% (2005); Total civilian labor force: 468,897 (2005); Leading industries: 13.5% health care and social assistance; 12.1% retail trade; 10.3% wholesale trade (2004); Farms: 91 totaling 1,283 acres (2002); Companies that employ 500 or more persons: 173 (2004); Companies that employ 100 to 499 persons: 1,383 (2004); Companies that employ less than 100 persons: 65,386 (2004); Black-owned businesses: 2,712 (2002); Hispanic-owned businesses: 5,806 (2002); Asian-owned businesses: 10,961 (2002); Women-owned businesses: 25,668 (2002); Retail sales per capita: $19,325 (2006). Single-family building permits issued: 1,220 (2005); Multi-family building permits issued: 1,752 (2005).
Income: Per capita income: $38,429 (2005); Median household income: $74,097 (2005); Average household income: $101,921 (2005); Percent of households with income of $100,000 or more: 35.3% (2005); Poverty rate: 6.1% (2003); Bankruptcy rate: 4.37% (2005).
Taxes: Total county taxes per capita: $261 (2004); County property taxes per capita: $253 (2004).
Education: Percent of population age 25 and over with: High school diploma (including GED) or higher: 86.5% (2005); Bachelor's degree or higher: 38.1% (2005); Master's degree or higher: 14.1% (2005).
Housing: Homeownership rate: 67.0% (2005); Median home value: $385,744 (2005); Median rent: $805 per month (2000); Median age of housing: 45 years (2000).
Health: Birth rate: 115.8 per 10,000 population (2004); Death rate: 86.4 per 10,000 population (2004); Age-adjusted cancer mortality rate: 187.7 deaths per 100,000 population (2002); Air Quality Index: 57.3% good, 37.8% moderate, 4.9% unhealthy for sensitive individuals, 0.0% unhealthy (percent of days in 2005); Number of physicians: 51.8 per 10,000 population (2004); Hospital beds: 39.4 per 10,000 population (2003); Hospital admissions: 1,717.4 per 10,000 population (2003).
Elections: 2004 Presidential election results: 47.4% Bush, 51.9% Kerry, 0.5% Nader, 0.1% Badnarik
National and State Parks: Palisades State Park
Additional Information Contacts
Bergen County Government . . . . (201) 336-7300
　http://www.co.bergen.nj.us

Bergen County Chamber of Commerce. . . . . (201) 498-9180
　http://www.co.bergen.nj.us
Bergen County Economic Development Corp. . . . . (201) 336-7500
　http://www.bergen4business.com
Bergen County Economic Development . . . . (201) 646-3072
　http://www.bergen4business.com
Bergenfield Chamber of Commerce . . . . (201) 387-4055
　http://www.bergenfieldboro.com
Borough of Allendale . . . . (201) 818-4400
　http://www.allendale.org
Borough of Closter . . . . (201) 784-0600
　http://www.closterboro.com
Borough of Fair Lawn . . . . (201) 796-1700
　http://www.fairlawn.org
Borough of Fort Lee . . . . (201) 592-3546
　http://www.fortleenj.org
Borough of Glen Rock . . . . (201) 670-3956
　http://www.glenrocknj.net
Borough of Hasbrouck Heights . . . . (201) 288-0195
　http://www.hasbrouck-heights.nj.us
Borough of Hillsdale . . . . (201) 666-4880
　http://www.hillsdalenj.org
Borough of Montvale . . . . (201) 391-5700
　http://www.montvale.org
Borough of Oakland . . . . (201) 337-8111
　http://www.oakland-nj.org
Borough of Old Tappan . . . . (201) 664-1849
　http://oldtappan.net
Borough of Ramsey . . . . (201) 825-3400
　http://www.ramseynj.com
Borough of Rutherford . . . . (201) 460-3000
　http://www.rutherford-nj.com/default.asp
Borough of Tenafly . . . . (201) 568-6100
　http://www.tenaflynj.org
Borough of Waldwick . . . . (201) 652-5300
　http://www.waldwickpd.org
Borough of Wood-Ridge . . . . (201) 939-0202
　http://www.wood-ridgenj.org
Borough of Woodcliff Lake . . . . (201) 391-4977
　http://www.wclnj.com
City of Englewood . . . . (201) 871-6612
　http://www.cityofenglewood.org
City of Hackensack . . . . (201) 646-3980
　http://www.hackensack.org
Elmwood Park Chamber of Commerce . . . . (201) 797-5008
　http://www.teaneckchamber.org
Englewood Chamber of Commerce . . . . (201) 567-2381
　http://www.englewood-chamber.com
Englewood Cliffs Chamber of Commerce . . . . (201) 567-9344
　http://www.englewood-chamber.com
Fairlawn Chamber of Commerce . . . . (201) 796-7050
　http://www.fairlawnchamber.org
Fairview Chamber of Commerce . . . . (201) 945-3707
　http://www.co.bergen.nj.us
Fort Lee Chamber of Commerce . . . . (201) 944-7575
　http://www.fortleechamber.us
Franklin Lakes Chamber of Commerce . . . . (201) 847-2482
　http://www.flcoc.org
Garfield Chamber of Commerce . . . . (973) 773-7500
　http://www.tccweb.org/garfield.htm
Glen Rock Chamber of Commerce . . . . (201) 612-2425
　http://www.glenrocknj.net
Hackensack Chamber of Commerce . . . . (201) 489-3700
　http://www.hackensackchamber.org
Lodi Chamber of Commerce . . . . (973) 777-9687
　http://www.lodichamberofcommerce.org
Mahwah Chamber of Commerce . . . . (201) 529-5566
　http://www.mahwah.com
Maywood New Jersey Chamber of Commerce . . . . (201) 843-3111
　http://www.maywoodnj.org
Meadowlands Chamber of Commerce . . . . (201) 939-0707
　http://www.meadowlands.org
Meadowlands Regional Chamber of Commerce . . . . (201) 939-0707
　http://www.meadowlands.org
Oakland Chamber of Commerce . . . . (201) 337-7117
　http://www.oakland-nj.org

Paramus Chamber of Commerce .... (201) 261-3344
    http://www.paramuschamber.com
Ridgefield Park Chamber of Commerce .... (201) 641-3800
    http://www.ridgefieldpark.org
Ridgewood Chamber of Commerce................... (201) 445-2600
    http://www.ridgewoodchamber.com
Teaneck Township............................... (201) 837-4811
    http://www.teanecknjgov.org
Tenafly Chamber of Commerce..................... (201) 871-3504
    http://www.tenaflynj.org
Tri-County Chamber of Commerce .... (973) 423-5815
    http://www.tricounty.org
Village of Ridgefield Park......................... (201) 641-4950
    http://ridgefieldpark.org
Village of Ridgewood .... (201) 670-5500
    http://www.ridgewoodnj.net
Wyckoff Chamber of Commerce .... (201) 891-3616
    http://www.wyckoffchamber.com
Wyckoff Township .... (201) 891-1907
    http://www.wyckoff-nj.com

Bergen County Communities

ALLENDALE (borough). Covers a land area of 3.125 square miles
and a water area of 0.025 square miles. Located at 41.03° N. Lat.; 74.13°
W. Long. Elevation is 375 feet.
History: Settled 1740, incorporated 1894.
Population: 5,898 (1990); 6,699 (2000); 6,783 (2005); 6,892 (2010
projected); Race: 91.3% White, 0.4% Black, 7.2% Asian, 3.1% Hispanic of
any race (2005); Density: 2,170.8 persons per square mile (2005); Average
household size: 3.16 (2005); Median age: 40.2 (2005); Males per 100
females: 93.7 (2005); Marriage status: 18.0% never married, 68.3% now
married, 9.3% widowed, 4.5% divorced (2000); Foreign born: 11.4%
(2000); Ancestry (includes multiple ancestries): 23.9% Irish, 23.5% Italian,
17.8% German, 11.2% English, 10.8% Other groups (2000).
Economy: Single-family building permits issued: 1 (2005); Multi-family
building permits issued: 0 (2005); Employment by occupation: 26.1%
management, 26.7% professional, 7.2% services, 30.5% sales, 0.0%
farming, 4.0% construction, 4.8% production (2000).
Income: Per capita income: $54,155 (2005); Median household income:
$117,898 (2005); Average household income: $167,588 (2005); Percent of
households with income of $100,000 or more: 57.3% (2005); Poverty rate:
1.8% (2000).
Education: Percent of population age 25 and over with: High school
diploma (including GED) or higher: 94.7% (2005); Bachelor's degree or
higher: 62.3% (2005); Master's degree or higher: 22.5% (2005).
School District(s)
Allendale Borough (PK-08)
    2003-04 Enrollment: 1,216 .... (201) 825-6546
Northern Highlands Regional (09-12)
    2003-04 Enrollment: 1,230 .... (201) 327-8700
Housing: Homeownership rate: 90.5% (2005); Median home value:
$661,955 (2005); Median rent: $1,600 per month (2000); Median age of
housing: 38 years (2000).
Safety: Violent crime rate: 0.0 per 10,000 population; Property crime rate:
64.5 per 10,000 population (2004).
Transportation: Commute to work: 80.0% car, 13.2% public
transportation, 1.9% walk, 4.6% work from home (2000); Travel time to
work: 29.6% less than 15 minutes, 24.2% 15 to 30 minutes, 17.9% 30 to 45
minutes, 9.0% 45 to 60 minutes, 19.4% 60 minutes or more (2000)
Additional Information Contacts
Borough of Allendale .... (201) 818-4400
    http://www.allendale.org

ALPINE (borough). Covers a land area of 6.356 square miles and a
water area of 2.817 square miles. Located at 40.95° N. Lat.; 73.93° W.
Long. Elevation is 450 feet.
Population: 1,675 (1990); 2,183 (2000); 2,358 (2005); 2,524 (2010
projected); Race: 73.3% White, 1.8% Black, 22.6% Asian, 2.7% Hispanic of
any race (2005); Density: 371.0 persons per square mile (2005); Average
household size: 3.03 (2005); Median age: 46.1 (2005); Males per 100
females: 101.7 (2005); Marriage status: 21.2% never married, 70.2% now
married, 4.5% widowed, 4.1% divorced (2000); Foreign born: 27.2%
(2000); Ancestry (includes multiple ancestries): 29.2% Other groups,
12.4% Italian, 7.8% Russian, 6.2% German, 6.0% Irish (2000).

Economy: Residential area. Single-family building permits issued: 18
(2005); Multi-family building permits issued: 8 (2005); Employment by
occupation: 28.2% management, 30.3% professional, 6.1% services,
27.5% sales, 0.0% farming, 4.0% construction, 3.9% production (2000).
Income: Per capita income: $68,556 (2005); Median household income:
$140,854 (2005); Average household income: $205,812 (2005); Percent of
households with income of $100,000 or more: 62.9% (2005); Poverty rate:
6.2% (2000).
Education: Percent of population age 25 and over with: High school
diploma (including GED) or higher: 93.6% (2005); Bachelor's degree or
higher: 62.7% (2005); Master's degree or higher: 27.8% (2005).
School District(s)
Alpine Borough (PK-08)
    2003-04 Enrollment: 142 .... (201) 768-6804
Housing: Homeownership rate: 89.3% (2005); Median home value: $1
million+ (2005); Median rent: $1,597 per month (2000); Median age of
housing: 26 years (2000).
Safety: Violent crime rate: 0.0 per 10,000 population; Property crime rate:
56.1 per 10,000 population (2004).
Transportation: Commute to work: 88.0% car, 4.5% public transportation,
0.4% walk, 7.1% work from home (2000); Travel time to work: 14.0% less
than 15 minutes, 18.9% 15 to 30 minutes, 29.0% 30 to 45 minutes, 14.3%
45 to 60 minutes, 23.9% 60 minutes or more (2000)

BERGENFIELD (borough). Covers a land area of 2.895 square miles
and a water area of 0.004 square miles. Located at 40.92° N. Lat.; 73.99°
W. Long. Elevation is 93 feet.
History: Named for the town of Bergen-op-zoom in the Netherlands. Its
Old South Church was built in 1799. Incorporated 1894.
Population: 24,458 (1990); 26,247 (2000); 26,165 (2005); 26,081 (2010
projected); Race: 54.5% White, 8.2% Black, 25.3% Asian, 21.7% Hispanic
of any race (2005); Density: 9,037.1 persons per square mile (2005);
Average household size: 2.97 (2005); Median age: 38.8 (2005); Males per
100 females: 92.3 (2005); Marriage status: 26.4% never married, 59.5%
now married, 7.9% widowed, 6.2% divorced (2000); Foreign born: 32.1%
(2000); Ancestry (includes multiple ancestries): 42.1% Other groups,
16.8% Italian, 16.2% Irish, 10.7% German, 3.6% English (2000).
Economy: It is mainly residential with some light industry. Unemployment
rate: 3.5% (2005); Total civilian labor force: 13,921 (2005); Single-family
building permits issued: 16 (2005); Multi-family building permits issued: 103
(2005); Employment by occupation: 14.2% management, 23.8%
professional, 14.3% services, 29.3% sales, 0.0% farming, 7.0%
construction, 11.3% production (2000).
Income: Per capita income: $28,880 (2005); Median household income:
$71,057 (2005); Average household income: $85,200 (2005); Percent of
households with income of $100,000 or more: 31.0% (2005); Poverty rate:
3.5% (2000).
Education: Percent of population age 25 and over with: High school
diploma (including GED) or higher: 86.4% (2005); Bachelor's degree or
higher: 32.1% (2005); Master's degree or higher: 9.7% (2005).
School District(s)
Bergenfield Borough (PK-12)
    2003-04 Enrollment: 3,900 .... (201) 385-8202
Housing: Homeownership rate: 68.9% (2005); Median home value:
$290,829 (2005); Median rent: $794 per month (2000); Median age of
housing: 49 years (2000).
Safety: Violent crime rate: 9.5 per 10,000 population; Property crime rate:
99.0 per 10,000 population (2004).
Transportation: Commute to work: 83.1% car, 11.6% public
transportation, 2.7% walk, 1.8% work from home (2000); Travel time to
work: 22.6% less than 15 minutes, 33.1% 15 to 30 minutes, 21.4% 30 to 45
minutes, 9.4% 45 to 60 minutes, 13.6% 60 minutes or more (2000)
Additional Information Contacts
Bergenfield Chamber of Commerce .... (201) 387-4055
    http://www.bergenfieldboro.com

BOGOTA (borough). Covers a land area of 0.761 square miles and a
water area of 0.058 square miles. Located at 40.87° N. Lat.; 74.02° W.
Long. Elevation is 100 feet.
History: Incorporated 1894.
Population: 7,824 (1990); 8,249 (2000); 8,151 (2005); 8,079 (2010
projected); Race: 70.8% White, 7.1% Black, 9.1% Asian, 27.5% Hispanic of
any race (2005); Density: 10,712.5 persons per square mile (2005);
Average household size: 2.90 (2005); Median age: 38.0 (2005); Males per
100 females: 91.4 (2005); Marriage status: 30.7% never married, 54.6%

now married, 7.5% widowed, 7.1% divorced (2000); Foreign born: 22.0% (2000); Ancestry (includes multiple ancestries): 34.9% Other groups, 22.6% Italian, 21.0% Irish, 14.7% German, 4.6% English (2000).
Economy: Manufacturing: machinery. Single-family building permits issued: 5 (2005); Multi-family building permits issued: 0 (2005); Employment by occupation: 12.0% management, 22.3% professional, 14.9% services, 32.2% sales, 0.0% farming, 8.7% construction, 9.9% production (2000).
Income: Per capita income: $28,754 (2005); Median household income: $69,613 (2005); Average household income: $82,247 (2005); Percent of households with income of $100,000 or more: 30.2% (2005); Poverty rate: 4.0% (2000).
Education: Percent of population age 25 and over with: High school diploma (including GED) or higher: 84.6% (2005); Bachelor's degree or higher: 28.5% (2005); Master's degree or higher: 9.3% (2005).
School District(s)
Bogota Borough (PK-12)
    2003-04 Enrollment: 1,060 . . . . (201) 441-4800
Housing: Homeownership rate: 66.4% (2005); Median home value: $268,642 (2005); Median rent: $745 per month (2000); Median age of housing: 60+ years (2000).
Safety: Violent crime rate: 19.4 per 10,000 population; Property crime rate: 133.5 per 10,000 population (2004).
Transportation: Commute to work: 77.4% car, 15.9% public transportation, 2.8% walk, 2.7% work from home (2000); Travel time to work: 20.9% less than 15 minutes, 38.2% 15 to 30 minutes, 19.2% 30 to 45 minutes, 5.9% 45 to 60 minutes, 15.8% 60 minutes or more (2000)

CARLSTADT (borough). Covers a land area of 3.954 square miles and a water area of 0.277 square miles. Located at 40.83° N. Lat.; 74.08° W. Long. Elevation is 187 feet.
History: Incorporated 1894.
Population: 5,510 (1990); 5,917 (2000); 6,033 (2005); 6,167 (2010 projected); Race: 86.8% White, 1.5% Black, 7.5% Asian, 10.2% Hispanic of any race (2005); Density: 1,525.7 persons per square mile (2005); Average household size: 2.46 (2005); Median age: 40.5 (2005); Males per 100 females: 95.2 (2005); Marriage status: 26.7% never married, 54.1% now married, 9.2% widowed, 10.0% divorced (2000); Foreign born: 20.5% (2000); Ancestry (includes multiple ancestries): 39.6% Italian, 19.0% German, 16.6% Irish, 15.4% Other groups, 9.6% Polish (2000).
Economy: Manufacturing: chemicals, clothing, plastics, shoes, textiles, brushes, paints, food products and aluminum products. Single-family building permits issued: 7 (2005); Multi-family building permits issued: 20 (2005); Employment by occupation: 17.9% management, 18.6% professional, 12.4% services, 32.1% sales, 0.0% farming, 8.0% construction, 11.0% production (2000).
Income: Per capita income: $34,380 (2005); Median household income: $66,611 (2005); Average household income: $84,453 (2005); Percent of households with income of $100,000 or more: 26.8% (2005); Poverty rate: 6.1% (2000).
Education: Percent of population age 25 and over with: High school diploma (including GED) or higher: 80.0% (2005); Bachelor's degree or higher: 21.2% (2005); Master's degree or higher: 5.7% (2005).
School District(s)
Carlstadt Borough (PK-08)
    2003-04 Enrollment: 532 . . . . (201) 939-6502
Housing: Homeownership rate: 57.3% (2005); Median home value: $347,686 (2005); Median rent: $776 per month (2000); Median age of housing: 55 years (2000).
Safety: Violent crime rate: 19.9 per 10,000 population; Property crime rate: 429.1 per 10,000 population (2004).
Transportation: Commute to work: 82.1% car, 10.3% public transportation, 4.7% walk, 3.0% work from home (2000); Travel time to work: 34.6% less than 15 minutes, 28.8% 15 to 30 minutes, 19.6% 30 to 45 minutes, 8.4% 45 to 60 minutes, 8.6% 60 minutes or more (2000)

CLIFFSIDE PARK (borough). Covers a land area of 0.965 square miles and a water area of 0 square miles. Located at 40.82° N. Lat.; 73.98° W. Long. Elevation is 250 feet.
History: Named for its location on the cliffs lining the western side of the Hudson River. Incorporated 1895.
Population: 20,393 (1990); 23,007 (2000); 22,839 (2005); 22,682 (2010 projected); Race: 73.9% White, 2.0% Black, 13.9% Asian, 22.9% Hispanic of any race (2005); Density: 23,673.5 persons per square mile (2005); Average household size: 2.30 (2005); Median age: 41.7 (2005); Males per

100 females: 94.4 (2005); Marriage status: 29.2% never married, 52.6% now married, 9.4% widowed, 8.8% divorced (2000); Foreign born: 43.3% (2000); Ancestry (includes multiple ancestries): 32.4% Other groups, 21.9% Italian, 7.0% Irish, 5.2% German, 3.8% Armenian (2000).
Economy: A residential suburb, it has some light industry. Single-family building permits issued: 30 (2005); Multi-family building permits issued: 13 (2005); Employment by occupation: 16.4% management, 18.7% professional, 14.4% services, 29.8% sales, 0.0% farming, 8.5% construction, 12.1% production (2000).
Income: Per capita income: $30,275 (2005); Median household income: $49,054 (2005); Average household income: $69,038 (2005); Percent of households with income of $100,000 or more: 19.0% (2005); Poverty rate: 10.7% (2000).
Taxes: Total city taxes per capita: $782 (2004); City property taxes per capita: $764 (2004).
Education: Percent of population age 25 and over with: High school diploma (including GED) or higher: 78.4% (2005); Bachelor's degree or higher: 32.3% (2005); Master's degree or higher: 12.8% (2005).
School District(s)
Cliffside Park Borough (PK-12)
    2003-04 Enrollment: 2,727 . . . . (201) 313-2310
Housing: Homeownership rate: 45.9% (2005); Median home value: $369,097 (2005); Median rent: $794 per month (2000); Median age of housing: 37 years (2000).
Safety: Violent crime rate: 10.8 per 10,000 population; Property crime rate: 90.7 per 10,000 population (2004).
Transportation: Commute to work: 72.2% car, 19.2% public transportation, 4.4% walk, 3.5% work from home (2000); Travel time to work: 19.0% less than 15 minutes, 30.3% 15 to 30 minutes, 22.0% 30 to 45 minutes, 11.7% 45 to 60 minutes, 17.0% 60 minutes or more (2000)

CLOSTER (borough). Covers a land area of 3.170 square miles and a water area of 0.123 square miles. Located at 40.97° N. Lat.; 73.96° W. Long. Elevation is 62 feet.
History: Incorporated 1903.
Population: 8,079 (1990); 8,383 (2000); 8,628 (2005); 8,883 (2010 projected); Race: 73.1% White, 0.9% Black, 23.5% Asian, 5.0% Hispanic of any race (2005); Density: 2,721.6 persons per square mile (2005); Average household size: 2.99 (2005); Median age: 40.3 (2005); Males per 100 females: 97.5 (2005); Marriage status: 18.9% never married, 69.7% now married, 6.4% widowed, 5.0% divorced (2000); Foreign born: 25.3% (2000); Ancestry (includes multiple ancestries): 27.7% Other groups, 17.2% Italian, 14.6% Irish, 13.0% German, 5.6% Russian (2000).
Economy: Manufacturing: curtains, concrete products. Single-family building permits issued: 43 (2005); Multi-family building permits issued: 0 (2005); Employment by occupation: 25.1% management, 26.2% professional, 7.1% services, 31.6% sales, 0.0% farming, 5.1% construction, 4.8% production (2000).
Income: Per capita income: $44,551 (2005); Median household income: $94,305 (2005); Average household income: $131,479 (2005); Percent of households with income of $100,000 or more: 46.6% (2005); Poverty rate: 2.7% (2000).
Education: Percent of population age 25 and over with: High school diploma (including GED) or higher: 93.2% (2005); Bachelor's degree or higher: 49.9% (2005); Master's degree or higher: 19.6% (2005).
School District(s)
Closter Borough (PK-08)
    2003-04 Enrollment: 1,225 . . . . (201) 768-3001
Housing: Homeownership rate: 86.7% (2005); Median home value: $560,361 (2005); Median rent: $1,070 per month (2000); Median age of housing: 43 years (2000).
Safety: Violent crime rate: 4.7 per 10,000 population; Property crime rate: 73.2 per 10,000 population (2004).
Transportation: Commute to work: 86.1% car, 7.6% public transportation, 1.6% walk, 3.3% work from home (2000); Travel time to work: 23.8% less than 15 minutes, 22.5% 15 to 30 minutes, 22.1% 30 to 45 minutes, 10.1% 45 to 60 minutes, 21.6% 60 minutes or more (2000)
Additional Information Contacts
Borough of Closter . . . . (201) 784-0600
    http://www.closterboro.com

CRESSKILL (borough). Covers a land area of 2.136 square miles and a water area of 0 square miles. Located at 40.94° N. Lat.; 73.96° W. Long. Elevation is 86 feet.
History: Incorporated 1894.

Population: 7,615 (1990); 7,746 (2000); 7,960 (2005); 8,187 (2010 projected); Race: 75.1% White, 1.0% Black, 21.1% Asian, 4.8% Hispanic of any race (2005); Density: 3,726.0 persons per square mile (2005); Average household size: 2.93 (2005); Median age: 41.9 (2005); Males per 100 females: 93.3 (2005); Marriage status: 20.1% never married, 66.8% now married, 8.6% widowed, 4.5% divorced (2000); Foreign born: 24.5% (2000); Ancestry (includes multiple ancestries): 26.2% Other groups, 19.5% Irish, 19.1% Italian, 11.2% German, 6.1% English (2000).
Economy: Single-family building permits issued: 17 (2005); Multi-family building permits issued: 0 (2005); Employment by occupation: 24.6% management, 29.1% professional, 7.8% services, 26.9% sales, 0.0% farming, 8.0% construction, 3.6% production (2000).
Income: Per capita income: $46,442 (2005); Median household income: $98,904 (2005); Average household income: $135,837 (2005); Percent of households with income of $100,000 or more: 49.3% (2005); Poverty rate: 3.0% (2000).
Education: Percent of population age 25 and over with: High school diploma (including GED) or higher: 92.2% (2005); Bachelor's degree or higher: 49.9% (2005); Master's degree or higher: 17.4% (2005).

School District(s)

Cresskill Borough (PK-12)
   2003-04 Enrollment: 1,509 . . . . (201) 567-5919
Housing: Homeownership rate: 89.0% (2005); Median home value: $452,402 (2005); Median rent: $1,521 per month (2000); Median age of housing: 44 years (2000).
Safety: Violent crime rate: 5.0 per 10,000 population; Property crime rate: 124.5 per 10,000 population (2004).
Newspapers: Northern Valley Suburbanite (General - Circulation 26,110); Teaneck Suburbanite (General - Circulation 13,175)
Transportation: Commute to work: 85.1% car, 10.1% public transportation, 1.1% walk, 2.9% work from home (2000); Travel time to work: 21.6% less than 15 minutes, 23.8% 15 to 30 minutes, 23.9% 30 to 45 minutes, 9.8% 45 to 60 minutes, 20.9% 60 minutes or more (2000)

DEMAREST (borough). Covers a land area of 2.067 square miles and a water area of 0.005 square miles. Located at 40.95° N. Lat.; 73.96° W. Long. Elevation is 50 feet.
History: Incorporated 1903.
Population: 4,800 (1990); 4,845 (2000); 4,938 (2005); 5,045 (2010 projected); Race: 75.7% White, 0.4% Black, 21.6% Asian, 3.9% Hispanic of any race (2005); Density: 2,388.7 persons per square mile (2005); Average household size: 3.02 (2005); Median age: 41.4 (2005); Males per 100 females: 96.1 (2005); Marriage status: 18.0% never married, 73.4% now married, 5.2% widowed, 3.4% divorced (2000); Foreign born: 24.4% (2000); Ancestry (includes multiple ancestries): 29.5% Other groups, 18.4% Italian, 14.6% Irish, 10.7% German, 5.9% English (2000).
Economy: Single-family building permits issued: 47 (2005); Multi-family building permits issued: 0 (2005); Employment by occupation: 28.3% management, 33.4% professional, 8.5% services, 23.0% sales, 0.0% farming, 3.4% construction, 3.3% production (2000).
Income: Per capita income: $53,651 (2005); Median household income: $119,608 (2005); Average household income: $161,290 (2005); Percent of households with income of $100,000 or more: 58.6% (2005); Poverty rate: 1.6% (2000).
Education: Percent of population age 25 and over with: High school diploma (including GED) or higher: 94.3% (2005); Bachelor's degree or higher: 59.3% (2005); Master's degree or higher: 24.4% (2005).

School District(s)

Demarest Borough (PK-08)
   2003-04 Enrollment: 718 . . . . (201) 768-6060
Northern Valley Regional (09-12)
   2003-04 Enrollment: 2,327 . . . . (201) 768-2200
Housing: Homeownership rate: 91.8% (2005); Median home value: $587,059 (2005); Median rent: $2,000+ per month (2000); Median age of housing: 43 years (2000).
Safety: Violent crime rate: 6.1 per 10,000 population; Property crime rate: 70.8 per 10,000 population (2004).
Transportation: Commute to work: 82.7% car, 9.9% public transportation, 0.9% walk, 5.3% work from home (2000); Travel time to work: 18.9% less than 15 minutes, 24.1% 15 to 30 minutes, 16.6% 30 to 45 minutes, 12.3% 45 to 60 minutes, 28.0% 60 minutes or more (2000)

DUMONT (borough). Covers a land area of 1.986 square miles and a water area of 0 square miles. Located at 40.94° N. Lat.; 73.99° W. Long. Elevation is 104 feet.

History: Named for Dumont Clarke (1846-1909), banker and mayor of the town. Settled 1677 by the Dutch. Incorporated 1894.
Population: 17,187 (1990); 17,503 (2000); 17,539 (2005); 17,648 (2010 projected); Race: 80.8% White, 1.7% Black, 12.9% Asian, 10.3% Hispanic of any race (2005); Density: 8,830.7 persons per square mile (2005); Average household size: 2.74 (2005); Median age: 39.9 (2005); Males per 100 females: 93.7 (2005); Marriage status: 25.6% never married, 60.6% now married, 7.7% widowed, 6.0% divorced (2000); Foreign born: 18.6% (2000); Ancestry (includes multiple ancestries): 26.8% Irish, 26.2% Italian, 23.2% Other groups, 16.1% German, 4.9% English (2000).
Economy: Residential suburb of Hackensack. Single-family building permits issued: 8 (2005); Multi-family building permits issued: 0 (2005); Employment by occupation: 15.7% management, 22.0% professional, 13.1% services, 31.5% sales, 0.1% farming, 8.7% construction, 8.9% production (2000).
Income: Per capita income: $29,837 (2005); Median household income: $71,807 (2005); Average household income: $81,540 (2005); Percent of households with income of $100,000 or more: 29.8% (2005); Poverty rate: 2.6% (2000).
Taxes: Total city taxes per capita: $536 (2004); City property taxes per capita: $520 (2004).
Education: Percent of population age 25 and over with: High school diploma (including GED) or higher: 88.5% (2005); Bachelor's degree or higher: 27.3% (2005); Master's degree or higher: 8.2% (2005).

School District(s)

Dumont Borough (PK-12)
   2003-04 Enrollment: 2,717 . . . . (201) 387-3082
Housing: Homeownership rate: 74.0% (2005); Median home value: $322,966 (2005); Median rent: $824 per month (2000); Median age of housing: 50 years (2000).
Safety: Violent crime rate: 8.5 per 10,000 population; Property crime rate: 96.9 per 10,000 population (2004).
Transportation: Commute to work: 86.0% car, 9.9% public transportation, 1.6% walk, 1.8% work from home (2000); Travel time to work: 23.5% less than 15 minutes, 32.4% 15 to 30 minutes, 19.1% 30 to 45 minutes, 9.9% 45 to 60 minutes, 15.1% 60 minutes or more (2000)

EAST RUTHERFORD (borough). Covers a land area of 3.808 square miles and a water area of 0.338 square miles. Located at 40.83° N. Lat.; 74.09° W. Long. Elevation is 60 feet.
Population: 7,902 (1990); 8,716 (2000); 8,690 (2005); 8,712 (2010 projected); Race: 75.1% White, 4.2% Black, 13.3% Asian, 13.5% Hispanic of any race (2005); Density: 2,282.2 persons per square mile (2005); Average household size: 2.39 (2005); Median age: 39.7 (2005); Males per 100 females: 95.6 (2005); Marriage status: 31.4% never married, 51.6% now married, 8.4% widowed, 8.6% divorced (2000); Foreign born: 28.8% (2000); Ancestry (includes multiple ancestries): 29.7% Italian, 25.9% Other groups, 20.5% Polish, 10.6% Irish, 10.1% German (2000).
Economy: Single-family building permits issued: 3 (2005); Multi-family building permits issued: 12 (2005); Employment by occupation: 13.7% management, 20.5% professional, 14.2% services, 30.8% sales, 0.3% farming, 6.3% construction, 14.1% production (2000).
Income: Per capita income: $33,981 (2005); Median household income: $62,515 (2005); Average household income: $80,161 (2005); Percent of households with income of $100,000 or more: 24.9% (2005); Poverty rate: 9.6% (2000).
Education: Percent of population age 25 and over with: High school diploma (including GED) or higher: 78.4% (2005); Bachelor's degree or higher: 24.9% (2005); Master's degree or higher: 9.7% (2005).

School District(s)

Carlstadt-East Rutherford (09-12)
   2003-04 Enrollment: 528 . . . . (201) 935-4155
East Rutherford Borough (PK-08)
   2003-04 Enrollment: 845 . . . . (201) 804-3103
Housing: Homeownership rate: 43.2% (2005); Median home value: $320,492 (2005); Median rent: $754 per month (2000); Median age of housing: 42 years (2000).
Safety: Violent crime rate: 9.1 per 10,000 population; Property crime rate: 314.0 per 10,000 population (2004).
Transportation: Commute to work: 75.2% car, 16.0% public transportation, 6.1% walk, 1.2% work from home (2000); Travel time to work: 29.1% less than 15 minutes, 25.7% 15 to 30 minutes, 23.5% 30 to 45 minutes, 10.4% 45 to 60 minutes, 11.3% 60 minutes or more (2000)

EDGEWATER (borough). Covers a land area of 0.847 square miles and a water area of 1.570 square miles. Located at 40.83° N. Lat.; 73.97° W. Long. Elevation is 55 feet.
History: Incorporated 1899.
Population: 5,001 (1990); 7,677 (2000); 9,575 (2005); 11,297 (2010 projected); Race: 59.4% White, 3.8% Black, 29.9% Asian, 10.9% Hispanic of any race (2005); Density: 11,300.6 persons per square mile (2005); Average household size: 1.96 (2005); Median age: 38.5 (2005); Males per 100 females: 95.2 (2005); Marriage status: 34.5% never married, 52.4% now married, 4.3% widowed, 8.8% divorced (2000); Foreign born: 35.5% (2000); Ancestry (includes multiple ancestries): 37.9% Other groups, 13.4% Irish, 12.3% Italian, 11.0% German, 4.1% Polish (2000).
Economy: Manufacturing: chemicals, food products, boats, automobile parts, metal products, linseed oil. Single-family building permits issued: 0 (2005); Multi-family building permits issued: 24 (2005); Employment by occupation: 27.5% management, 26.5% professional, 7.4% services, 26.0% sales, 0.0% farming, 4.4% construction, 8.3% production (2000).
Income: Per capita income: $52,376 (2005); Median household income: $73,939 (2005); Average household income: $102,842 (2005); Percent of households with income of $100,000 or more: 35.5% (2005); Poverty rate: 8.6% (2000).
Education: Percent of population age 25 and over with: High school diploma (including GED) or higher: 90.7% (2005); Bachelor's degree or higher: 51.0% (2005); Master's degree or higher: 18.6% (2005).
School District(s)
Edgewater Borough (PK-06)
    2003-04 Enrollment: 413 . . . . (201) 945-4106
Housing: Homeownership rate: 44.4% (2005); Median home value: $344,170 (2005); Median rent: $1,158 per month (2000); Median age of housing: 20 years (2000).
Safety: Violent crime rate: 15.0 per 10,000 population; Property crime rate: 168.1 per 10,000 population (2004).
Transportation: Commute to work: 69.3% car, 22.4% public transportation, 3.7% walk, 3.6% work from home (2000); Travel time to work: 13.2% less than 15 minutes, 24.1% 15 to 30 minutes, 27.6% 30 to 45 minutes, 16.2% 45 to 60 minutes, 18.8% 60 minutes or more (2000)

ELMWOOD PARK (borough). Aka East Paterson. Covers a land area of 2.654 square miles and a water area of 0.110 square miles. Located at 40.90° N. Lat.; 74.12° W. Long. Elevation is 59 feet.
History: Named, originally, East Paterson for its location southeast of Paterson. Incorporated 1916.
Population: 17,623 (1990); 18,925 (2000); 18,994 (2005); 19,093 (2010 projected); Race: 78.5% White, 2.7% Black, 9.6% Asian, 16.2% Hispanic of any race (2005); Density: 7,155.8 persons per square mile (2005); Average household size: 2.70 (2005); Median age: 40.0 (2005); Males per 100 females: 92.3 (2005); Marriage status: 26.1% never married, 57.4% now married, 8.7% widowed, 7.7% divorced (2000); Foreign born: 30.2% (2000); Ancestry (includes multiple ancestries): 25.9% Other groups, 25.2% Italian, 12.6% Polish, 9.1% Irish, 8.8% German (2000).
Economy: Single-family building permits issued: 0 (2005); Multi-family building permits issued: 6 (2005); Employment by occupation: 11.7% management, 16.6% professional, 12.1% services, 35.4% sales, 0.0% farming, 9.2% construction, 15.0% production (2000).
Income: Per capita income: $24,736 (2005); Median household income: $57,188 (2005); Average household income: $66,574 (2005); Percent of households with income of $100,000 or more: 19.5% (2005); Poverty rate: 6.4% (2000).
Taxes: Total city taxes per capita: $341 (2004); City property taxes per capita: $341 (2004).
Education: Percent of population age 25 and over with: High school diploma (including GED) or higher: 79.9% (2005); Bachelor's degree or higher: 20.6% (2005); Master's degree or higher: 6.0% (2005).
School District(s)
Elmwood Park (PK-12)
    2003-04 Enrollment: 2,114 . . . . (201) 794-2979
Housing: Homeownership rate: 60.2% (2005); Median home value: $302,917 (2005); Median rent: $831 per month (2000); Median age of housing: 47 years (2000).
Safety: Violent crime rate: 16.2 per 10,000 population; Property crime rate: 257.6 per 10,000 population (2004).
Transportation: Commute to work: 90.8% car, 5.0% public transportation, 2.5% walk, 0.9% work from home (2000); Travel time to work: 26.6% less

than 15 minutes, 41.7% 15 to 30 minutes, 18.5% 30 to 45 minutes, 5.0% 45 to 60 minutes, 8.2% 60 minutes or more (2000)
Additional Information Contacts
Elmwood Park Chamber of Commerce . . . . (201) 797-5008
    http://www.teaneckchamber.org

EMERSON (borough). Covers a land area of 2.238 square miles and a water area of 0.184 square miles. Located at 40.97° N. Lat.; 74.02° W. Long. Elevation is 50 feet.
History: Settled 1875, incorporated 1909.
Population: 6,954 (1990); 7,197 (2000); 7,329 (2005); 7,469 (2010 projected); Race: 88.6% White, 0.8% Black, 8.7% Asian, 5.8% Hispanic of any race (2005); Density: 3,275.3 persons per square mile (2005); Average household size: 2.99 (2005); Median age: 42.3 (2005); Males per 100 females: 91.7 (2005); Marriage status: 19.6% never married, 66.6% now married, 9.6% widowed, 4.2% divorced (2000); Foreign born: 15.6% (2000); Ancestry (includes multiple ancestries): 29.1% Italian, 22.7% Irish, 16.5% German, 16.2% Other groups, 6.0% English (2000).
Economy: Largely residential. Single-family building permits issued: 12 (2005); Multi-family building permits issued: 0 (2005); Employment by occupation: 24.3% management, 23.4% professional, 11.8% services, 30.8% sales, 0.0% farming, 5.2% construction, 4.5% production (2000).
Income: Per capita income: $36,109 (2005); Median household income: $87,382 (2005); Average household income: $106,329 (2005); Percent of households with income of $100,000 or more: 41.3% (2005); Poverty rate: 2.4% (2000).
Education: Percent of population age 25 and over with: High school diploma (including GED) or higher: 88.8% (2005); Bachelor's degree or higher: 40.1% (2005); Master's degree or higher: 12.4% (2005).
School District(s)
Emerson Borough (PK-12)
    2003-04 Enrollment: 1,154 . . . . (201) 262-2828
Housing: Homeownership rate: 92.3% (2005); Median home value: $417,409 (2005); Median rent: $944 per month (2000); Median age of housing: 44 years (2000).
Safety: Violent crime rate: 5.5 per 10,000 population; Property crime rate: 60.0 per 10,000 population (2004).
Transportation: Commute to work: 85.2% car, 9.0% public transportation, 2.4% walk, 3.4% work from home (2000); Travel time to work: 23.7% less than 15 minutes, 35.7% 15 to 30 minutes, 17.3% 30 to 45 minutes, 6.0% 45 to 60 minutes, 17.3% 60 minutes or more (2000)

ENGLEWOOD (city). Covers a land area of 4.924 square miles and a water area of 0.014 square miles. Located at 40.89° N. Lat.; 73.97° W. Long. Elevation is 44 feet.
History: Named for the contraction of "English wood". The area was founded in the 17th century. Incorporated as a city 1899.
Population: 24,850 (1990); 26,203 (2000); 26,073 (2005); 25,995 (2010 projected); Race: 40.7% White, 38.8% Black, 5.5% Asian, 25.7% Hispanic of any race (2005); Density: 5,295.6 persons per square mile (2005); Average household size: 2.85 (2005); Median age: 38.8 (2005); Males per 100 females: 89.8 (2005); Marriage status: 29.6% never married, 53.4% now married, 7.7% widowed, 9.4% divorced (2000); Foreign born: 30.8% (2000); Ancestry (includes multiple ancestries): 55.5% Other groups, 5.0% Jamaican, 4.5% Italian, 3.6% United States or American, 3.6% Irish (2000).
Economy: Residential area with light industry in a variety of metals and chemical products. Unemployment rate: 4.6% (2005); Total civilian labor force: 13,380 (2005); Single-family building permits issued: 22 (2005); Multi-family building permits issued: 663 (2005); Employment by occupation: 16.0% management, 22.7% professional, 16.0% services, 27.2% sales, 0.1% farming, 5.6% construction, 12.4% production (2000).
Income: Per capita income: $35,897 (2005); Median household income: $66,853 (2005); Average household income: $101,592 (2005); Percent of households with income of $100,000 or more: 32.5% (2005); Poverty rate: 8.9% (2000).
Taxes: Total city taxes per capita: $2,718 (2004); City property taxes per capita: $2,697 (2004).
Education: Percent of population age 25 and over with: High school diploma (including GED) or higher: 81.9% (2005); Bachelor's degree or higher: 35.2% (2005); Master's degree or higher: 15.6% (2005).
School District(s)
Agency - Englewood on the Palisades CS (KG-07)
    2003-04 Enrollment: 189 . . . . (201) 569-9765
Englewood City (PK-12)
    2003-04 Enrollment: 2,803 . . . . (201) 833-6060

Two-year College(s)
Academy of Massage Therapy (Private, For-profit)
Fall 2004 Enrollment: 121 . . . . (201) 568-3220
2005-06 Tuition: In-state $13,075; Out-of-state $13,075
Housing: Homeownership rate: 58.5% (2005); Median home value: $310,793 (2005); Median rent: $768 per month (2000); Median age of housing: 51 years (2000).
Hospitals: Englewood Hospital and Medical Center (547 beds)
Safety: Violent crime rate: 21.3 per 10,000 population; Property crime rate: 199.3 per 10,000 population (2004).
Transportation: Commute to work: 73.4% car, 16.6% public transportation, 4.6% walk, 3.6% work from home (2000); Travel time to work: 22.9% less than 15 minutes, 29.9% 15 to 30 minutes, 20.6% 30 to 45 minutes, 8.8% 45 to 60 minutes, 17.9% 60 minutes or more (2000)
Additional Information Contacts
City of Englewood . . . . (201) 871-6612
http://www.cityofenglewood.org
Englewood Chamber of Commerce. . . . . (201) 567-2381
http://www.englewood-chamber.com

ENGLEWOOD CLIFFS (borough). Covers a land area of 2.092 square miles and a water area of 1.288 square miles. Located at 40.88° N. Lat.; 73.95° W. Long. Elevation is 350 feet.
Population: 5,634 (1990); 5,322 (2000); 5,682 (2005); 6,024 (2010 projected); Race: 63.1% White, 1.6% Black, 33.0% Asian, 5.1% Hispanic of any race (2005); Density: 2,716.4 persons per square mile (2005); Average household size: 2.87 (2005); Median age: 45.5 (2005); Males per 100 females: 89.5 (2005); Marrlage status: 19.2% never married, 70.3% now married, 7.2% widowed, 3.4% divorced (2000); Foreign born: 38.7% (2000); Ancestry (includes multiple ancestries): 35.4% Other groups, 19.7% Italian, 7.3% Greek, 5.5% Irish, 5.4% Russian (2000).
Economy: Manufacturing of tea and pharmaceuticals. Single-family building permits issued: 34 (2005); Multi-family building permits issued: 0 (2005); Employment by occupation: 27.6% management, 29.5% professional, 5.4% services, 30.5% sales, 0.0% farming, 3.2% construction, 3.8% production (2000).
Income: Per capita income: $61,312 (2005); Median household income: $122,709 (2005); Average household income: $175,660 (2005); Percent of households with income of $100,000 or more: 58.8% (2005); Poverty rate: 2.6% (2000).
Education: Percent of population age 25 and over with: High school diploma (including GED) or higher: 92.3% (2005); Bachelor's degree or higher: 52.5% (2005); Master's degree or higher: 23.7% (2005).
School District(s)
Englewood Cliffs Borough (PK-08)
2003-04 Enrollment: 434 . . . . (201) 567-7292
Housing: Homeownership rate: 91.6% (2005); Median home value: $797,447 (2005); Median rent: $1,941 per month (2000); Median age of housing: 35 years (2000).
Safety: Violent crime rate: 7.1 per 10,000 population; Property crime rate: 187.4 per 10,000 population (2004).
Transportation: Commute to work: 81.1% car, 11.3% public transportation, 1.7% walk, 4.8% work from home (2000); Travel time to work: 18.3% less than 15 minutes, 21.6% 15 to 30 minutes, 31.3% 30 to 45 minutes, 13.0% 45 to 60 minutes, 15.8% 60 minutes or more (2000)
Additional Information Contacts
Englewood Cliffs Chamber of Commerce . . . . (201) 567-9344
http://www.englewood-chamber.com

FAIR LAWN (borough). Covers a land area of 5.169 square miles and a water area of 0.051 square miles. Located at 40.93° N. Lat.; 74.11° W. Long. Elevation is 100 feet.
History: Named to promote the town as a good place to live. Constructed in the 1920s. Incorporated 1924.
Population: 30,548 (1990); 31,637 (2000); 31,564 (2005); 31,559 (2010 projected); Race: 89.8% White, 0.8% Black, 5.9% Asian, 6.9% Hispanic of any race (2005); Density: 6,106.9 persons per square mile (2005); Average household size: 2.69 (2005); Median age: 43.1 (2005); Males per 100 females: 91.4 (2005); Marriage status: 21.9% never married, 63.1% now married, 9.0% widowed, 5.9% divorced (2000); Foreign born: 26.8% (2000); Ancestry (includes multiple ancestries): 19.7% Other groups, 19.7% Italian, 11.7% Russian, 10.0% German, 9.9% Irish (2000).
Economy: Residential with light industries. Includes the Radburn "new town," a suburban housing development that separates pedestrian and vehicle traffic. Unemployment rate: 3.6% (2005); Total civilian labor force:

16,566 (2005); Single-family building permits issued: 13 (2005); Multi-family building permits issued: 14 (2005); Employment by occupation: 17.4% management, 30.7% professional, 9.1% services, 29.3% sales, 0.0% farming, 5.8% construction, 7.8% production (2000).
Income: Per capita income: $37,576 (2005); Median household income: $83,679 (2005); Average household income: $100,775 (2005); Percent of households with income of $100,000 or more: 39.7% (2005); Poverty rate: 3.7% (2000).
Taxes: Total city taxes per capita: $691 (2004); City property taxes per capita: $657 (2004).
Education: Percent of population age 25 and over with: High school diploma (including GED) or higher: 89.9% (2005); Bachelor's degree or higher: 44.7% (2005); Master's degree or higher: 17.5% (2005).
School District(s)
Fair Lawn Borough (PK-12)
2003-04 Enrollment: 4,865 . . . . (201) 794-5510
Housing: Homeownership rate: 78.8% (2005); Median home value: $345,538 (2005); Median rent: $863 per month (2000); Median age of housing: 49 years (2000).
Safety: Violent crime rate: 17.6 per 10,000 population; Property crime rate: 155.0 per 10,000 population (2004).
Newspapers: The Shopper News (General - Circulation 71,816)
Transportation: Commute to work: 82.7% car, 11.4% public transportation, 2.0% walk, 3.7% work from home (2000); Travel time to work: 24.3% less than 15 minutes, 33.5% 15 to 30 minutes, 16.7% 30 to 45 minutes, 8.8% 45 to 60 minutes, 16.6% 60 minutes or more (2000)
Additional Information Contacts
Borough of Fair Lawn. . . . . (201) 796-1700
http://www.fairlawn.org
Fairlawn Chamber of Commerce . . . . (201) 796-7050
http://www.fairlawnchamber.org

FAIRVIEW (borough). Covers a land area of 0.850 square miles and a water area of 0 square miles. Located at 40.81° N. Lat.; 74.00° W. Long. Elevation is 238 feet.
History: Named for its view across the Hackensack River valley. Settled 1860. Incorporated 1894.
Population: 10,733 (1990); 13,255 (2000); 13,434 (2005); 13,632 (2010 projected); Race: 66.8% White, 1.9% Black, 5.6% Asian, 48.0% Hispanic of any race (2005); Density: 15,796.0 persons per square mile (2005); Average household size: 2.78 (2005); Median age: 36.2 (2005); Males per 100 females: 107.3 (2005); Marriage status: 31.8% never married, 53.2% now married, 8.2% widowed, 6.8% divorced (2000); Foreign born: 48.4% (2000); Ancestry (includes multiple ancestries): 40.1% Other groups, 21.8% Italian, 5.8% Irish, 4.8% German, 4.6% Croatian (2000).
Economy: Apparel and embroideries. Single-family building permits issued: 9 (2005); Multi-family building permits issued: 52 (2005); Employment by occupation: 11.1% management, 12.8% professional, 15.9% services, 31.4% sales, 0.0% farming, 11.7% construction, 17.1% production (2000).
Income: Per capita income: $20,507 (2005); Median household income: $44,836 (2005); Average household income: $56,622 (2005); Percent of households with income of $100,000 or more: 13.7% (2005); Poverty rate: 11.8% (2000).
Education: Percent of population age 25 and over with: High school diploma (including GED) or higher: 65.4% (2005); Bachelor's degree or higher: 16.4% (2005); Master's degree or higher: 4.1% (2005).
School District(s)
Fairview Borough (PK-08)
2003-04 Enrollment: 1,073 . . . . (201) 943-1699
Housing: Homeownership rate: 34.3% (2005); Median home value: $310,351 (2005); Median rent: $785 per month (2000); Median age of housing: 43 years (2000).
Safety: Violent crime rate: 43.0 per 10,000 population; Property crime rate: 150.7 per 10,000 population (2004).
Transportation: Commute to work: 73.6% car, 20.1% public transportation, 4.5% walk, 1.2% work from home (2000); Travel time to work: 20.0% less than 15 minutes, 35.7% 15 to 30 minutes, 20.9% 30 to 45 minutes, 8.4% 45 to 60 minutes, 15.0% 60 minutes or more (2000)
Additional Information Contacts
Fairview Chamber of Commerce . . . . (201) 945-3707
http://www.co.bergen.nj.us

FORT LEE (borough). Covers a land area of 2.533 square miles and a water area of 0.348 square miles. Located at 40.85° N. Lat.; 73.97° W. Long. Elevation is 313 feet.

History: Named for Major General Charles Lee, Revolutionary War officer. The fort built here by the Americans as Fort Constitution to command the Hudson during the Revolution was abandoned on Nov. 20, 1776, by Gen. Greene after Fort Washington, on the opposite shore (in New York City), fell to the British. It was renamed Fort Lee and is now an historical park and Museum. Fort Lee was an early center of the motion-picture industry. Settled c.1700. Incorporated 1904.

Population: 31,997 (1990); 35,461 (2000); 37,654 (2005); 39,738 (2010 projected); Race: 57.0% White, 2.0% Black, 36.4% Asian, 9.5% Hispanic of any race (2005); Density: 14,867.6 persons per square mile (2005); Average household size: 2.16 (2005); Median age: 43.3 (2005); Males per 100 females: 88.8 (2005); Marriage status: 23.2% never married, 59.1% now married, 9.1% widowed, 8.6% divorced (2000); Foreign born: 44.7% (2000); Ancestry (includes multiple ancestries): 44.7% Other groups, 11.7% Italian, 8.1% Russian, 4.9% Irish, 4.1% German (2000).

Economy: Unemployment rate: 2.8% (2005); Total civilian labor force: 18,926 (2005); Single-family building permits issued: 29 (2005); Multi-family building permits issued: 8 (2005); Employment by occupation: 25.4% management, 26.2% professional, 8.3% services, 30.9% sales, 0.0% farming, 3.3% construction, 5.9% production (2000).

Income: Per capita income: $39,673 (2005); Median household income: $62,972 (2005); Average household income: $85,780 (2005); Percent of households with income of $100,000 or more: 28.5% (2005); Poverty rate: 7.9% (2000).

Education: Percent of population age 25 and over with: High school diploma (including GED) or higher: 89.4% (2005); Bachelor's degree or higher: 48.6% (2005); Master's degree or higher: 18.6% (2005).

School District(s)
Fort Lee Borough (PK-12)
    2003-04 Enrollment: 3,461 . . . . (201) 585-4610

Housing: Homeownership rate: 55.8% (2005); Median home value: $301,891 (2005); Median rent: $1,042 per month (2000); Median age of housing: 33 years (2000).

Safety: Violent crime rate: 7.2 per 10,000 population; Property crime rate: 124.3 per 10,000 population (2004).

Transportation: Commute to work: 73.5% car, 17.6% public transportation, 4.0% walk, 4.2% work from home (2000); Travel time to work: 20.2% less than 15 minutes, 25.2% 15 to 30 minutes, 21.7% 30 to 45 minutes, 14.0% 45 to 60 minutes, 18.9% 60 minutes or more (2000)

Additional Information Contacts
Borough of Fort Lee . . . . (201) 592-3546
    http://www.fortleenj.org
Fort Lee Chamber of Commerce . . . . (201) 944-7575
    http://www.fortleechamber.us

FRANKLIN LAKES (borough). Aka Campgan. Covers a land area of 9.453 square miles and a water area of 0.376 square miles. Located at 41.01° N. Lat.; 74.20° W. Long. Elevation is 390 feet.

History: Named for Wiliam Franklin (1731-1816), son of Benjamin Franklin. Incorporated 1922.

Population: 9,873 (1990); 10,422 (2000); 11,446 (2005); 12,406 (2010 projected); Race: 90.6% White, 1.1% Black, 6.7% Asian, 3.5% Hispanic of any race (2005); Density: 1,210.9 persons per square mile (2005); Average household size: 3.10 (2005); Median age: 41.4 (2005); Males per 100 females: 97.0 (2005); Marriage status: 20.5% never married, 70.8% now married, 4.3% widowed, 4.4% divorced (2000); Foreign born: 11.8% (2000); Ancestry (includes multiple ancestries): 29.8% Italian, 19.8% Irish, 15.2% German, 11.7% Other groups, 8.4% Polish (2000).

Economy: Manufacturing village: Venetian blinds. Campgaw Mt. ski area nearby. Single-family building permits issued: 36 (2005); Multi-family building permits issued: 0 (2005); Employment by occupation: 29.0% management, 25.4% professional, 6.0% services, 30.1% sales, 0.0% farming, 4.6% construction, 4.9% production (2000).

Income: Per capita income: $64,364 (2005); Median household income: $147,406 (2005); Average household income: $199,223 (2005); Percent of households with income of $100,000 or more: 67.1% (2005); Poverty rate: 3.2% (2000).

Education: Percent of population age 25 and over with: High school diploma (including GED) or higher: 94.7% (2005); Bachelor's degree or higher: 52.9% (2005); Master's degree or higher: 21.5% (2005).

School District(s)
Franklin Lakes Borough (PK-08)
    2003-04 Enrollment: 1,671 . . . . (201) 891-1856
Ramapo-Indian Hill Regional (09-12)
    2003-04 Enrollment: 2,134 . . . . (201) 891-1505

Housing: Homeownership rate: 95.2% (2005); Median home value: $951,354 (2005); Median rent: $1,313 per month (2000); Median age of housing: 30 years (2000).

Safety: Violent crime rate: 1.8 per 10,000 population; Property crime rate: 101.6 per 10,000 population (2004).

Transportation: Commute to work: 85.7% car, 5.8% public transportation, 0.4% walk, 7.3% work from home (2000); Travel time to work: 19.7% less than 15 minutes, 34.6% 15 to 30 minutes, 20.9% 30 to 45 minutes, 8.7% 45 to 60 minutes, 16.1% 60 minutes or more (2000)

Additional Information Contacts
Franklin Lakes Chamber of Commerce . . . . (201) 847-2482
    http://www.flcoc.org

GARFIELD (city). Covers a land area of 2.131 square miles and a water area of 0.063 square miles. Located at 40.88° N. Lat.; 74.10° W. Long. Elevation is 36 feet.

History: Named for James Abram Garfield, 20th President of the U.S. Settled 1679 by the Dutch. Incorporated 1898.

Population: 26,727 (1990); 29,786 (2000); 29,662 (2005); 29,605 (2010 projected); Race: 77.7% White, 3.4% Black, 3.2% Asian, 26.0% Hispanic of any race (2005); Density: 13,917.8 persons per square mile (2005); Average household size: 2.70 (2005); Median age: 37.3 (2005); Males per 100 females: 95.9 (2005); Marriage status: 30.8% never married, 52.7% now married, 8.6% widowed, 7.9% divorced (2000); Foreign born: 39.1% (2000); Ancestry (includes multiple ancestries): 24.9% Polish, 24.4% Other groups, 19.5% Italian, 6.7% Irish, 5.5% German (2000).

Economy: Manufacturing includes paper products, rubber, and printing machinery. Unemployment rate: 6.4% (2005); Total civilian labor force: 15,665 (2005); Single-family building permits issued: 0 (2005); Multi-family building permits issued: 38 (2005); Employment by occupation: 8.2% management, 12.3% professional, 15.5% services, 28.2% sales, 0.5% farming, 14.6% construction, 20.7% production (2000).

Income: Per capita income: $21,832 (2005); Median household income: $48,326 (2005); Average household income: $58,706 (2005); Percent of households with income of $100,000 or more: 14.5% (2005); Poverty rate: 7.8% (2000).

Taxes: Total city taxes per capita: $494 (2004); City property taxes per capita: $456 (2004).

Education: Percent of population age 25 and over with: High school diploma (including GED) or higher: 70.2% (2005); Bachelor's degree or higher: 14.0% (2005); Master's degree or higher: 3.8% (2005).

School District(s)
Garfield City (PK-12)
    2003-04 Enrollment: 4,587 . . . . (973) 340-5000

Housing: Homeownership rate: 40.2% (2005); Median home value: $281,302 (2005); Median rent: $694 per month (2000); Median age of housing: 51 years (2000).

Safety: Violent crime rate: 24.4 per 10,000 population; Property crime rate: 179.2 per 10,000 population (2004).

Newspapers: Messenger (General - Circulation 1,500)

Transportation: Commute to work: 89.5% car, 4.6% public transportation, 3.6% walk, 1.4% work from home (2000); Travel time to work: 26.4% less than 15 minutes, 40.8% 15 to 30 minutes, 20.5% 30 to 45 minutes, 4.9% 45 to 60 minutes, 7.4% 60 minutes or more (2000)

Additional Information Contacts
Garfield Chamber of Commerce . . . . (973) 773-7500
    http://www.tccweb.org/garfield.htm

GLEN ROCK (borough). Covers a land area of 2.719 square miles and a water area of 0.013 square miles. Located at 40.96° N. Lat.; 74.12° W. Long. Elevation is 90 feet.

History: Named for a local rock that was an Indian landmark. George Washington's army used the area for camping grounds during the Revolutionary War. Settled c.1710. Incorporated 1896.

Population: 10,884 (1990); 11,546 (2000); 11,486 (2005); 11,474 (2010 projected); Race: 89.5% White, 1.7% Black, 6.8% Asian, 3.3% Hispanic of any race (2005); Density: 4,224.1 persons per square mile (2005); Average household size: 2.94 (2005); Median age: 40.0 (2005); Males per 100 females: 95.6 (2005); Marriage status: 16.7% never married, 72.5% now married, 6.1% widowed, 4.7% divorced (2000); Foreign born: 11.1%

(2000); Ancestry (includes multiple ancestries): 24.8% Irish, 24.1% Italian, 17.1% German, 13.9% Other groups, 9.3% English (2000).

Economy: Single-family building permits issued: 4 (2005); Multi-family building permits issued: 0 (2005); Employment by occupation: 29.6% management, 33.1% professional, 5.2% services, 25.5% sales, 0.0% farming, 2.8% construction, 3.7% production (2000).

Income: Per capita income: $55,399 (2005); Median household income: $125,428 (2005); Average household income: $162,472 (2005); Percent of households with income of $100,000 or more: 62.2% (2005); Poverty rate: 2.4% (2000).

Education: Percent of population age 25 and over with: High school diploma (including GED) or higher: 96.1% (2005); Bachelor's degree or higher: 61.2% (2005); Master's degree or higher: 24.3% (2005).

School District(s)

Glen Rock Borough (PK-12)
   2003-04 Enrollment: 2,399 . . . . (201) 445-7700

Housing: Homeownership rate: 92.3% (2005); Median home value: $508,276 (2005); Median rent: $991 per month (2000); Median age of housing: 51 years (2000).

Safety: Violent crime rate: 1.7 per 10,000 population; Property crime rate: 84.6 per 10,000 population (2004).

Transportation: Commute to work: 78.2% car, 13.9% public transportation, 2.6% walk, 5.4% work from home (2000); Travel time to work: 23.8% less than 15 minutes, 31.1% 15 to 30 minutes, 15.0% 30 to 45 minutes, 9.4% 45 to 60 minutes, 20.7% 60 minutes or more (2000)

Additional Information Contacts

Borough of Glen Rock . . . . (201) 670-3956
   http://www.glenrocknj.net
Glen Rock Chamber of Commerce . . . . (201) 612-2425
   http://www.glenrocknj.net

HACKENSACK (city). Covers a land area of 4.120 square miles and a water area of 0.187 square miles. Located at 40.88° N. Lat.; 74.04° W. Long. Elevation is 22 feet.

History: Named for the Indian translation of "hook mouth" or "low ground". The name Hackensack may be of Native American origin. Hackensack dates back to 1647 when the Dutch from Manhattan established a trading post on the lands of Chief Oratam. Governed by the Council of New Netherland, the region was later known as New Barbadoes after the island whence came the original grantees. Until 1921, when the town received a city charter, its official name was still New Barbadoes.

Population: 37,049 (1990); 42,677 (2000); 43,636 (2005); 44,742 (2010 projected); Race: 48.4% White, 24.5% Black, 9.0% Asian, 31.5% Hispanic of any race (2005); Density: 10,591.0 persons per square mile (2005); Average household size: 2.38 (2005); Median age: 38.2 (2005); Males per 100 females: 99.3 (2005); Marriage status: 35.3% never married, 46.5% now married, 6.9% widowed, 11.3% divorced (2000); Foreign born: 33.8% (2000); Ancestry (includes multiple ancestries): 48.7% Other groups, 13.7% Italian, 7.4% Irish, 5.7% German, 3.3% Polish (2000).

Economy: Unemployment rate: 5.0% (2005); Total civilian labor force: 24,027 (2005); Single-family building permits issued: 3 (2005); Multi-family building permits issued: 101 (2005); Employment by occupation: 14.5% management, 21.1% professional, 14.9% services, 29.8% sales, 0.0% farming, 6.1% construction, 13.6% production (2000).

Income: Per capita income: $30,382 (2005); Median household income: $56,136 (2005); Average household income: $71,254 (2005); Percent of households with income of $100,000 or more: 19.9% (2005); Poverty rate: 9.3% (2000).

Taxes: Total city taxes per capita: $1,105 (2004); City property taxes per capita: $1,080 (2004).

Education: Percent of population age 25 and over with: High school diploma (including GED) or higher: 79.9% (2005); Bachelor's degree or higher: 29.4% (2005); Master's degree or higher: 10.7% (2005).

School District(s)

Bergen County Vocational (09-12)
   2003-04 Enrollment: 2,331 . . . . (201) 967-2472
Hackensack City (PK-12)
   2003-04 Enrollment: 5,149 . . . . (201) 646-7830

Two-year College(s)

Adult & Continuing Education-BCTS (Public)
   Fall 2004 Enrollment: 62 . . . . (201) 343-6000
Hohokus-Hackensack School of Business and Medical Sciences (Private, For-profit)
   Fall 2004 Enrollment: 327 . . . . (201) 488-9400
   2005-06 Tuition: In-state $7,793; Out-of-state $7,793

Parisian Beauty School (Private, For-profit)
   Fall 2004 Enrollment: 187 . . . . (201) 487-2203

Housing: Homeownership rate: 32.0% (2005); Median home value: $257,745 (2005); Median rent: $790 per month (2000); Median age of housing: 37 years (2000).

Hospitals: Hackensack University Medical Center (614 beds)

Safety: Violent crime rate: 31.7 per 10,000 population; Property crime rate: 266.4 per 10,000 population (2004).

Newspapers: The Record (Circulation 191,034)

Transportation: Commute to work: 74.2% car, 15.6% public transportation, 6.9% walk, 1.6% work from home (2000); Travel time to work: 28.7% less than 15 minutes, 34.9% 15 to 30 minutes, 16.8% 30 to 45 minutes, 7.1% 45 to 60 minutes, 12.5% 60 minutes or more (2000)

Additional Information Contacts

Bergen County Economic Development Corp. . . . . (201) 336-7500
   http://www.bergen4business.com
City of Hackensack . . . . (201) 646-3980
   http://www.hackensack.org
Hackensack Chamber of Commerce . . . . (201) 489-3700
   http://www.hackensackchamber.org

HARRINGTON PARK (borough). Covers a land area of 1.855 square miles and a water area of 0.213 square miles. Located at 40.98° N. Lat.; 73.98° W. Long. Elevation is 62 feet.

History: Incorporated 1904.

Population: 4,623 (1990); 4,740 (2000); 4,904 (2005); 5,074 (2010 projected); Race: 82.6% White, 0.7% Black, 15.3% Asian, 2.9% Hispanic of any race (2005); Density: 2,643.4 persons per square mile (2005); Average household size: 2.99 (2005); Median age: 40.7 (2005); Males per 100 females: 94.8 (2005); Marriage status: 21.7% never married, 69.9% now married, 5.5% widowed, 2.9% divorced (2000); Foreign born: 16.5% (2000); Ancestry (includes multiple ancestries): 26.3% Irish, 24.1% Italian, 20.7% German, 19.2% Other groups, 5.5% English (2000).

Economy: Single-family building permits issued: 15 (2005); Multi-family building permits issued: 0 (2005); Employment by occupation: 27.8% management, 26.7% professional, 5.0% services, 30.3% sales, 0.0% farming, 4.5% construction, 5.7% production (2000).

Income: Per capita income: $44,179 (2005); Median household income: $109,867 (2005); Average household income: $130,420 (2005); Percent of households with income of $100,000 or more: 55.4% (2005); Poverty rate: 2.9% (2000).

Education: Percent of population age 25 and over with: High school diploma (including GED) or higher: 96.0% (2005); Bachelor's degree or higher: 58.5% (2005); Master's degree or higher: 21.9% (2005).

School District(s)

Harrington Park Borough (PK-08)
   2003-04 Enrollment: 681 . . . . (201) 768-5700

Housing: Homeownership rate: 94.2% (2005); Median home value: $562,500 (2005); Median rent: $1,031 per month (2000); Median age of housing: 41 years (2000).

Safety: Violent crime rate: 0.0 per 10,000 population; Property crime rate: 43.2 per 10,000 population (2004).

Transportation: Commute to work: 87.6% car, 7.4% public transportation, 1.0% walk, 3.4% work from home (2000); Travel time to work: 25.0% less than 15 minutes, 22.5% 15 to 30 minutes, 21.0% 30 to 45 minutes, 8.7% 45 to 60 minutes, 22.8% 60 minutes or more (2000)

HASBROUCK HEIGHTS (borough). Covers a land area of 1.508 square miles and a water area of 0 square miles. Located at 40.86° N. Lat.; 74.07° W. Long. Elevation is 130 feet.

History: Named for a Dutch colonist, who settled in the area in 1685. Settled c.1685. Incorporated 1894.

Population: 11,488 (1990); 11,662 (2000); 11,629 (2005); 11,634 (2010 projected); Race: 85.2% White, 2.1% Black, 8.1% Asian, 10.7% Hispanic of any race (2005); Density: 7,713.1 persons per square mile (2005); Average household size: 2.55 (2005); Median age: 41.4 (2005); Males per 100 females: 93.2 (2005); Marriage status: 24.5% never married, 60.3% now married, 9.0% widowed, 6.2% divorced (2000); Foreign born: 17.0% (2000); Ancestry (includes multiple ancestries): 38.5% Italian, 17.2% Other groups, 17.1% Irish, 15.3% German, 10.1% Polish (2000).

Economy: Single-family building permits issued: 26 (2005); Multi-family building permits issued: 0 (2005); Employment by occupation: 17.3% management, 25.9% professional, 10.5% services, 31.7% sales, 0.1% farming, 6.2% construction, 8.3% production (2000).

Income: Per capita income: $36,344 (2005); Median household income: $76,355 (2005); Average household income: $92,202 (2005); Percent of households with income of $100,000 or more: 34.7% (2005); Poverty rate: 4.2% (2000).

Taxes: Total city taxes per capita: $871 (2004); City property taxes per capita: $848 (2004).

Education: Percent of population age 25 and over with: High school diploma (including GED) or higher: 86.9% (2005); Bachelor's degree or higher: 29.8% (2005); Master's degree or higher: 8.0% (2005).

School District(s)

Hasbrouck Heights Borough (PK-12)
   2003-04 Enrollment: 1,558 . . . . (201) 393-8145

Housing: Homeownership rate: 69.2% (2005); Median home value: $346,013 (2005); Median rent: $813 per month (2000); Median age of housing: 50 years (2000).

Safety: Violent crime rate: 3.4 per 10,000 population; Property crime rate: 130.6 per 10,000 population (2004).

Newspapers: Observer (General - Circulation 2,500)

Transportation: Commute to work: 84.9% car, 10.8% public transportation, 2.1% walk, 1.8% work from home (2000); Travel time to work: 25.2% less than 15 minutes, 36.2% 15 to 30 minutes, 19.0% 30 to 45 minutes, 7.4% 45 to 60 minutes, 12.2% 60 minutes or more (2000)

Additional Information Contacts

Borough of Hasbrouck Heights . . . . (201) 288-0195
   http://www.hasbrouck-heights.nj.us

HAWORTH (borough).
Covers a land area of 1.957 square miles and a water area of 0.403 square miles. Located at 40.96° N. Lat.; 73.98° W. Long. Elevation is 90 feet.

History: Incorporated 1894.

Population: 3,384 (1990); 3,390 (2000); 3,416 (2005); 3,457 (2010 projected); Race: 87.9% White, 1.1% Black, 9.2% Asian, 3.0% Hispanic of any race (2005); Density: 1,745.6 persons per square mile (2005); Average household size: 2.98 (2005); Median age: 41.8 (2005); Males per 100 females: 96.4 (2005); Marriage status: 20.6% never married, 69.0% now married, 7.5% widowed, 2.9% divorced (2000); Foreign born: 15.7% (2000); Ancestry (includes multiple ancestries): 19.3% Irish, 18.3% Italian, 18.1% Other groups, 15.1% German, 7.6% Polish (2000).

Economy: Single-family building permits issued: 15 (2005); Multi-family building permits issued: 0 (2005); Employment by occupation: 22.1% management, 37.0% professional, 5.4% services, 28.2% sales, 0.0% farming, 4.3% construction, 3.0% production (2000).

Income: Per capita income: $53,204 (2005); Median household income: $121,238 (2005); Average household income: $158,326 (2005); Percent of households with income of $100,000 or more: 57.6% (2005); Poverty rate: 2.0% (2000).

Education: Percent of population age 25 and over with: High school diploma (including GED) or higher: 94.0% (2005); Bachelor's degree or higher: 57.2% (2005); Master's degree or higher: 23.9% (2005).

School District(s)

Haworth Borough (PK-08)
   2003-04 Enrollment: 530 . . . . (201) 501-7077

Housing: Homeownership rate: 94.5% (2005); Median home value: $605,729 (2005); Median rent: $1,250 per month (2000); Median age of housing: 46 years (2000).

Safety: Violent crime rate: 0.0 per 10,000 population; Property crime rate: 14.6 per 10,000 population (2004).

Transportation: Commute to work: 82.7% car, 6.2% public transportation, 0.9% walk, 8.3% work from home (2000); Travel time to work: 19.7% less than 15 minutes, 34.8% 15 to 30 minutes, 17.6% 30 to 45 minutes, 6.9% 45 to 60 minutes, 21.1% 60 minutes or more (2000)

HILLSDALE (borough).
Covers a land area of 2.982 square miles and a water area of 0.004 square miles. Located at 41.00° N. Lat.; 74.04° W. Long. Elevation is 83 feet.

History: Named for the town's hilly terrain. Incorporated 1923.

Population: 9,750 (1990); 10,087 (2000); 10,092 (2005); 10,140 (2010 projected); Race: 91.6% White, 1.0% Black, 5.5% Asian, 5.3% Hispanic of any race (2005); Density: 3,384.9 persons per square mile (2005); Average household size: 2.85 (2005); Median age: 40.6 (2005); Males per 100 females: 95.5 (2005); Marriage status: 21.3% never married, 67.5% now married, 5.8% widowed, 5.5% divorced (2000); Foreign born: 13.3% (2000); Ancestry (includes multiple ancestries): 24.7% Italian, 24.5% Irish, 18.2% German, 12.2% Other groups, 5.9% English (2000).

Economy: Single-family building permits issued: 13 (2005); Multi-family building permits issued: 0 (2005); Employment by occupation: 19.4% management, 26.5% professional, 10.9% services, 31.9% sales, 0.0% farming, 7.6% construction, 3.7% production (2000).

Income: Per capita income: $41,524 (2005); Median household income: $96,727 (2005); Average household income: $117,723 (2005); Percent of households with income of $100,000 or more: 47.9% (2005); Poverty rate: 3.3% (2000).

Education: Percent of population age 25 and over with: High school diploma (including GED) or higher: 92.3% (2005); Bachelor's degree or higher: 45.8% (2005); Master's degree or higher: 16.9% (2005).

School District(s)

Hillsdale Borough (PK-08)
   2003-04 Enrollment: 1,352 . . . . (201) 664-0282
Pascack Valley Regional (09-12)
   2003-04 Enrollment: 1,614 . . . . (201) 358-7005

Housing: Homeownership rate: 89.1% (2005); Median home value: $465,974 (2005); Median rent: $850 per month (2000); Median age of housing: 44 years (2000).

Safety: Violent crime rate: 8.9 per 10,000 population; Property crime rate: 57.1 per 10,000 population (2004).

Transportation: Commute to work: 86.2% car, 6.9% public transportation, 1.5% walk, 4.2% work from home (2000); Travel time to work: 27.6% less than 15 minutes, 31.8% 15 to 30 minutes, 15.7% 30 to 45 minutes, 8.9% 45 to 60 minutes, 16.1% 60 minutes or more (2000)

Additional Information Contacts

Bergen County Economic Development . . . . (201) 646-3072
   http://www.bergen4business.com
Borough of Hillsdale. . . . . (201) 666-4880
   http://www.hillsdalenj.org

HO-HO-KUS (borough).
Aka Hohokus. Covers a land area of 1.742 square miles and a water area of 0.008 square miles. Located at 41.00° N. Lat.; 74.10° W. Long. Elevation is 113 feet.

History: Has 2 notable 18th-century houses. Incorporated 1908.

Population: 3,915 (1990); 4,060 (2000); 4,078 (2005); 4,115 (2010 projected); Race: 92.6% White, 0.7% Black, 5.1% Asian, 2.3% Hispanic of any race (2005); Density: 2,341.4 persons per square mile (2005); Average household size: 2.82 (2005); Median age: 41.7 (2005); Males per 100 females: 92.4 (2005); Marriage status: 18.1% never married, 72.2% now married, 5.3% widowed, 4.4% divorced (2000); Foreign born: 8.9% (2000); Ancestry (includes multiple ancestries): 28.7% Irish, 24.8% Italian, 18.6% German, 14.5% English, 8.4% Other groups (2000).

Economy: Single-family building permits issued: 13 (2005); Multi-family building permits issued: 0 (2005); Employment by occupation: 33.1% management, 28.5% professional, 4.2% services, 27.4% sales, 0.0% farming, 3.2% construction, 3.5% production (2000).

Income: Per capita income: $68,935 (2005); Median household income: $146,191 (2005); Average household income: $193,960 (2005); Percent of households with income of $100,000 or more: 66.3% (2005); Poverty rate: 2.1% (2000).

Education: Percent of population age 25 and over with: High school diploma (including GED) or higher: 97.7% (2005); Bachelor's degree or higher: 68.5% (2005); Master's degree or higher: 22.6% (2005).

School District(s)

Ho Ho Kus Borough (PK-08)
   2003-04 Enrollment: 620 . . . . (201) 652-4555

Housing: Homeownership rate: 91.6% (2005); Median home value: $735,106 (2005); Median rent: $1,458 per month (2000); Median age of housing: 47 years (2000).

Safety: Violent crime rate: 0.0 per 10,000 population; Property crime rate: 48.7 per 10,000 population (2004).

Transportation: Commute to work: 76.8% car, 16.0% public transportation, 1.7% walk, 5.5% work from home (2000); Travel time to work: 25.8% less than 15 minutes, 26.0% 15 to 30 minutes, 17.2% 30 to 45 minutes, 8.7% 45 to 60 minutes, 22.4% 60 minutes or more (2000)

LEONIA (borough).
Covers a land area of 1.505 square miles and a water area of 0.118 square miles. Located at 40.86° N. Lat.; 73.98° W. Long. Elevation is 100 feet.

History: Incorporated 1894.

Population: 8,365 (1990); 8,914 (2000); 8,889 (2005); 8,873 (2010 projected); Race: 59.3% White, 2.1% Black, 31.5% Asian, 15.7% Hispanic of any race (2005); Density: 5,904.7 persons per square mile (2005); Average household size: 2.76 (2005); Median age: 41.1 (2005); Males per

100 females: 93.2 (2005); Marriage status: 23.8% never married, 61.2% now married, 7.1% widowed, 7.8% divorced (2000); Foreign born: 35.8% (2000); Ancestry (includes multiple ancestries): 43.4% Other groups, 14.5% Italian, 11.7% Irish, 9.7% German, 4.2% Russian (2000).

Economy: Single-family building permits issued: 0 (2005); Multi-family building permits issued: 0 (2005); Employment by occupation: 20.1% management, 31.0% professional, 10.9% services, 26.4% sales, 0.4% farming, 4.6% construction, 6.5% production (2000).

Income: Per capita income: $40,555 (2005); Median household income: $82,732 (2005); Average household income: $111,526 (2005); Percent of households with income of $100,000 or more: 39.6% (2005); Poverty rate: 6.5% (2000).

Education: Percent of population age 25 and over with: High school diploma (including GED) or higher: 92.8% (2005); Bachelor's degree or higher: 49.6% (2005); Master's degree or higher: 20.1% (2005).

School District(s)

Leonia Borough (PK-12)

    2003-04 Enrollment: 1,809 . . . . (201) 947-5655

Housing: Homeownership rate: 64.9% (2005); Median home value: $438,808 (2005); Median rent: $840 per month (2000); Median age of housing: 54 years (2000).

Safety: Violent crime rate: 13.4 per 10,000 population; Property crime rate: 102.8 per 10,000 population (2004).

Transportation: Commute to work: 74.8% car, 18.0% public transportation, 2.8% walk, 4.1% work from home (2000); Travel time to work: 19.6% less than 15 minutes, 26.1% 15 to 30 minutes, 22.2% 30 to 45 minutes, 13.9% 45 to 60 minutes, 18.2% 60 minutes or more (2000)

LITTLE FERRY (borough). Covers a land area of 1.526 square miles and a water area of 0.160 square miles. Located at 40.84° N. Lat.; 74.04° W. Long. Elevation is 9 feet.

History: Settled 1636, incorporated 1894.

Population: 9,989 (1990); 10,800 (2000); 10,803 (2005); 10,828 (2010 projected); Race: 61.7% White, 5.1% Black, 21.8% Asian, 10.9% Hispanic of any race (2005); Density: 7,077.1 persons per square mile (2005); Average household size: 2.47 (2005); Median age: 38.9 (2005); Males per 100 females: 95.4 (2005); Marriage status: 29.3% never married, 55.1% now married, 7.4% widowed, 8.2% divorced (2000); Foreign born: 31.1% (2000); Ancestry (includes multiple ancestries): 33.9% Other groups, 26.3% Italian, 14.1% Irish, 12.4% German, 5.4% Polish (2000).

Economy: Manufacturing: machinery, building materials, metal products. Single-family building permits issued: 1 (2005); Multi-family building permits issued: 0 (2005); Employment by occupation: 16.1% management, 18.3% professional, 11.8% services, 33.4% sales, 0.0% farming, 7.2% construction, 13.2% production (2000).

Income: Per capita income: $27,252 (2005); Median household income: $55,584 (2005); Average household income: $67,246 (2005); Percent of households with income of $100,000 or more: 20.0% (2005); Poverty rate: 6.3% (2000).

Education: Percent of population age 25 and over with: High school diploma (including GED) or higher: 81.6% (2005); Bachelor's degree or higher: 24.1% (2005); Master's degree or higher: 8.0% (2005).

School District(s)

Little Ferry Borough (PK-08)

    2003-04 Enrollment: 974 . . . . (201) 641-6192

Housing: Homeownership rate: 46.4% (2005); Median home value: $309,923 (2005); Median rent: $768 per month (2000); Median age of housing: 39 years (2000).

Safety: Violent crime rate: 9.2 per 10,000 population; Property crime rate: 98.4 per 10,000 population (2004).

Transportation: Commute to work: 87.2% car, 8.5% public transportation, 2.9% walk, 1.0% work from home (2000); Travel time to work: 28.9% less than 15 minutes, 33.8% 15 to 30 minutes, 21.0% 30 to 45 minutes, 6.6% 45 to 60 minutes, 9.7% 60 minutes or more (2000)

LODI (borough). Covers a land area of 2.263 square miles and a water area of 0.005 square miles. Located at 40.87° N. Lat.; 74.08° W. Long. Elevation is 43 feet.

History: Named for the Bridge of Lodi in northern Italy, site of Napoleon's victory in 1796. Incorporated 1894.

Population: 22,355 (1990); 23,971 (2000); 24,294 (2005); 24,692 (2010 projected); Race: 73.9% White, 3.9% Black, 10.6% Asian, 22.9% Hispanic of any race (2005); Density: 10,733.3 persons per square mile (2005); Average household size: 2.53 (2005); Median age: 38.2 (2005); Males per 100 females: 91.4 (2005); Marriage status: 31.0% never married, 51.9%

now married, 8.5% widowed, 8.5% divorced (2000); Foreign born: 29.7% (2000); Ancestry (includes multiple ancestries): 33.3% Italian, 29.7% Other groups, 10.3% Irish, 8.5% German, 7.9% Polish (2000).

Economy: Chemical, plastic, and ink manufacturing. Single-family building permits issued: 3 (2005); Multi-family building permits issued: 70 (2005); Employment by occupation: 10.9% management, 16.6% professional, 12.7% services, 34.2% sales, 0.0% farming, 9.1% construction, 16.5% production (2000).

Income: Per capita income: $24,514 (2005); Median household income: $49,429 (2005); Average household income: $61,640 (2005); Percent of households with income of $100,000 or more: 17.1% (2005); Poverty rate: 8.0% (2000).

Taxes: Total city taxes per capita: $583 (2004); City property taxes per capita: $564 (2004).

Education: Percent of population age 25 and over with: High school diploma (including GED) or higher: 76.0% (2005); Bachelor's degree or higher: 18.9% (2005); Master's degree or higher: 5.1% (2005).

School District(s)

Lodi Borough (PK-12)

    2003-04 Enrollment: 3,176 . . . . (973) 778-4620

Four-year College(s)

Felician College (Private, Not-for-profit, Roman Catholic)

    Fall 2004 Enrollment: 1,699 . . . . (201) 559-6000

    2005-06 Tuition: In-state $17,300; Out-of-state $17,300

Housing: Homeownership rate: 41.7% (2005); Median home value: $294,732 (2005); Median rent: $750 per month (2000); Median age of housing: 44 years (2000).

Safety: Violent crime rate: 17.2 per 10,000 population; Property crime rate: 191.4 per 10,000 population (2004).

Transportation: Commute to work: 88.1% car, 7.7% public transportation, 2.4% walk, 1.1% work from home (2000); Travel time to work: 28.0% less than 15 minutes, 40.1% 15 to 30 minutes, 18.2% 30 to 45 minutes, 7.1% 45 to 60 minutes, 6.5% 60 minutes or more (2000)

Additional Information Contacts

Lodi Chamber of Commerce . . . . (973) 777-9687

    http://www.lodichamberofcommerce.org

LYNDHURST (township). Aka Lyndhurst CDP. Covers a land area of 4.649 square miles and a water area of 0.257 square miles. Located at 40.80° N. Lat.; 74.12° W. Long. Elevation is 101 feet.

History: Named for John Singleton Copley, Lord Lyndhurst, lord chancellor of England. Incorporated 1852.

Population: 18,262 (1990); 19,383 (2000); 19,525 (2005); 19,711 (2010 projected); Race: 87.7% White, 0.7% Black, 6.6% Asian, 11.6% Hispanic of any race (2005); Density: 4,200.2 persons per square mile (2005); Average household size: 2.42 (2005); Median age: 41.2 (2005); Males per 100 females: 91.9 (2005); Marriage status: 28.0% never married, 54.5% now married, 9.9% widowed, 7.5% divorced (2000); Foreign born: 17.9% (2000); Ancestry (includes multiple ancestries): 40.8% Italian, 18.3% Irish, 17.0% Other groups, 12.4% Polish, 9.4% German (2000).

Economy: Manufacturing: machinery, metal products, clothing, paints, asphalt. Single-family building permits issued: 7 (2005); Multi-family building permits issued: 178 (2005); Employment by occupation: 14.7% management, 15.6% professional, 13.0% services, 33.8% sales, 0.0% farming, 9.0% construction, 13.8% production (2000).

Income: Per capita income: $29,920 (2005); Median household income: $60,426 (2005); Average household income: $71,933 (2005); Percent of households with income of $100,000 or more: 22.3% (2005); Poverty rate: 4.6% (2000).

Taxes: Total city taxes per capita: $807 (2004); City property taxes per capita: $807 (2004).

Education: Percent of population age 25 and over with: High school diploma (including GED) or higher: 81.4% (2005); Bachelor's degree or higher: 21.9% (2005); Master's degree or higher: 6.3% (2005).

School District(s)

Lyndhurst Township (PK-12)

    2003-04 Enrollment: 2,192 . . . . (201) 438-5683

Housing: Homeownership rate: 59.8% (2005); Median home value: $307,864 (2005); Median rent: $727 per month (2000); Median age of housing: 53 years (2000).

Safety: Violent crime rate: 10.7 per 10,000 population; Property crime rate: 172.5 per 10,000 population (2004).

Newspapers: News Leader Of Rutherford (General - Circulation 3,200); North Arlington Leader (General - Circulation 3,400); The Commercial

Leader (General - Circulation 3,800); The Leader Free Press (General - Circulation 1,600)
Transportation: Commute to work: 85.1% car, 9.9% public transportation, 3.2% walk, 1.3% work from home (2000); Travel time to work: 28.3% less than 15 minutes, 30.1% 15 to 30 minutes, 23.3% 30 to 45 minutes, 9.4% 45 to 60 minutes, 8.8% 60 minutes or more (2000)

MAHWAH (township). Covers a land area of 25.931 square miles and a water area of 0.267 square miles. Located at 41.07° N. Lat.; 74.16° W. Long. Elevation is 300 feet.
History: Seat of Ramapo College of N.J. Center for the 3,000 Ramapough Mountain people, who also live in nearby Ringwood (N.J.) and Hillbury (N.Y.); subjects of an ongoing dispute regarding their status as a Native American tribe or as descendants of late-16th-century French and Dutch farmers.
Population: 17,895 (1990); 24,062 (2000); 24,646 (2005); 25,277 (2010 projected); Race: 87.0% White, 1.7% Black, 7.4% Asian, 5.1% Hispanic of any race (2005); Density: 950.5 persons per square mile (2005); Average household size: 2.56 (2005); Median age: 38.7 (2005); Males per 100 females: 91.1 (2005); Marriage status: 26.1% never married, 59.9% now married, 5.7% widowed, 8.3% divorced (2000); Foreign born: 13.3% (2000); Ancestry (includes multiple ancestries): 25.5% Italian, 19.7% Irish, 15.8% German, 14.7% Other groups, 8.1% Polish (2000).
Economy: Manufacturing includes transportation equipment and electronics. Former auto plant. Largely residential. Single-family building permits issued: 25 (2005); Multi-family building permits issued: 0 (2005); Employment by occupation: 23.9% management, 25.8% professional, 9.3% services, 30.9% sales, 0.1% farming, 4.2% construction, 5.9% production (2000).
Income: Per capita income: $52,102 (2005); Median household income: $93,543 (2005); Average household income: $132,631 (2005); Percent of households with income of $100,000 or more: 46.3% (2005); Poverty rate: 2.0% (2000).
Taxes: Total city taxes per capita: $569 (2004); City property taxes per capita: $531 (2004).
Education: Percent of population age 25 and over with: High school diploma (including GED) or higher: 93.6% (2005); Bachelor's degree or higher: 49.6% (2005); Master's degree or higher: 17.1% (2005).
School District(s)
Mahwah Township (PK-12)
    2003-04 Enrollment: 3,355 . . . . (201) 529-6803
Four-year College(s)
Ramapo College of New Jersey (Public)
    Fall 2004 Enrollment: 5,617. (201) 684-7500
    2005-06 Tuition: In-state $8,792; Out-of-state $13,709
Two-year College(s)
Lincoln Technical Institute (Private, For-profit)
    Fall 2004 Enrollment: 1,183. (201) 529-1414
    2005-06 Tuition: In-state $20,588; Out-of-state $20,588
Housing: Homeownership rate: 84.2% (2005); Median home value: $425,895 (2005); Median rent: $1,045 per month (2000); Median age of housing: 16 years (2000).
Safety: Violent crime rate: 5.3 per 10,000 population; Property crime rate: 93.8 per 10,000 population (2004).
Transportation: Commute to work: 86.7% car, 6.7% public transportation, 2.3% walk, 4.2% work from home (2000); Travel time to work: 29.0% less than 15 minutes, 28.9% 15 to 30 minutes, 17.7% 30 to 45 minutes, 8.6% 45 to 60 minutes, 15.7% 60 minutes or more (2000)
Additional Information Contacts
Mahwah Chamber of Commerce. . . . . (201) 529-5566
    http://www.mahwah.com

MAYWOOD (borough). Covers a land area of 1.300 square miles and a water area of 0 square miles. Located at 40.90° N. Lat.; 74.06° W. Long. Elevation is 94 feet.
History: Incorporated 1894
Population: 9,536 (1990); 9,523 (2000); 9,483 (2005); 9,458 (2010 projected); Race: 81.3% White, 3.3% Black, 8.5% Asian, 15.1% Hispanic of any race (2005); Density: 7,295.4 persons per square mile (2005); Average household size: 2.57 (2005); Median age: 41.5 (2005); Males per 100 females: 88.1 (2005); Marriage status: 21.0% never married, 59.2% now married, 10.8% widowed, 9.0% divorced (2000); Foreign born: 18.8% (2000); Ancestry (includes multiple ancestries): 28.7% Italian, 23.2% Other groups, 21.4% Irish, 17.1% German, 5.8% English (2000).

Economy: Chemicals. Single-family building permits issued: 1 (2005); Multi-family building permits issued: 0 (2005); Employment by occupation: 14.3% management, 23.3% professional, 8.5% services, 37.7% sales, 0.1% farming, 7.6% construction, 8.4% production (2000).
Income: Per capita income: $32,346 (2005); Median household income: $70,730 (2005); Average household income: $82,365 (2005); Percent of households with income of $100,000 or more: 29.6% (2005); Poverty rate: 3.3% (2000).
Taxes: Total city taxes per capita: $811 (2004); City property taxes per capita: $791 (2004).
Education: Percent of population age 25 and over with: High school diploma (including GED) or higher: 87.6% (2005); Bachelor's degree or higher: 31.2% (2005); Master's degree or higher: 10.1% (2005).
School District(s)
Maywood Borough (PK-08)
    2003-04 Enrollment: 824 . . . . (201) 845-9114
South Bergen Jointure Com (UG-UG)
    2003-04 Enrollment: 508 . . . . (201) 845-8818
Housing: Homeownership rate: 68.2% (2005); Median home value: $324,465 (2005); Median rent: $820 per month (2000); Median age of housing: 50 years (2000).
Safety: Violent crime rate: 2.1 per 10,000 population; Property crime rate: 119.2 per 10,000 population (2004).
Newspapers: Our Town (General - Circulation 3,650)
Transportation: Commute to work: 86.2% car, 7.9% public transportation, 2.3% walk, 2.5% work from home (2000); Travel time to work: 33.1% less than 15 minutes, 34.3% 15 to 30 minutes, 15.0% 30 to 45 minutes, 8.0% 45 to 60 minutes, 9.6% 60 minutes or more (2000)
Additional Information Contacts
Maywood New Jersey Chamber of Commerce . . . . (201) 843-3111
    http://www.maywoodnj.org

MIDLAND PARK (borough). Covers a land area of 1.565 square miles and a water area of 0.004 square miles. Located at 40.99° N. Lat.; 74.14° W. Long. Elevation is 350 feet.
History: Incorporated 1894.
Population: 6,902 (1990); 6,947 (2000); 6,925 (2005); 6,935 (2010 projected); Race: 95.3% White, 0.4% Black, 2.4% Asian, 4.7% Hispanic of any race (2005); Density: 4,425.4 persons per square mile (2005); Average household size: 2.61 (2005); Median age: 40.0 (2005); Males per 100 females: 96.2 (2005); Marriage status: 23.1% never married, 63.1% now married, 7.6% widowed, 6.1% divorced (2000); Foreign born: 8.1% (2000); Ancestry (includes multiple ancestries): 22.6% Italian, 21.8% Irish, 18.9% German, 17.0% Dutch, 8.9% English (2000).
Economy: Manufacturing: textiles, towels. Single-family building permits issued: 2 (2005); Multi-family building permits issued: 0 (2005); Employment by occupation: 20.0% management, 23.4% professional, 11.7% services, 28.9% sales, 0.0% farming, 9.2% construction, 6.8% production (2000).
Income: Per capita income: $41,879 (2005); Median household income: $91,320 (2005); Average household income: $108,179 (2005); Percent of households with income of $100,000 or more: 44.6% (2005); Poverty rate: 2.0% (2000).
Education: Percent of population age 25 and over with: High school diploma (including GED) or higher: 93.1% (2005); Bachelor's degree or higher: 38.4% (2005); Master's degree or higher: 10.5% (2005).
School District(s)
Midland Park Borough (PK-12)
    2003-04 Enrollment: 1,117 . . . . (201) 444-1400
Housing: Homeownership rate: 75.4% (2005); Median home value: $413,176 (2005); Median rent: $967 per month (2000); Median age of housing: 49 years (2000).
Safety: Violent crime rate: 2.9 per 10,000 population; Property crime rate: 87.4 per 10,000 population (2004).
Newspapers: The Ridgewood Times - Zone 2 (General - Circulation 14,100); The Villadom Times - Zone 3 (General - Circulation 11,750); The Villadom Times Midland Park - Zone 1 (General - Circulation 38,500)
Transportation: Commute to work: 87.2% car, 7.3% public transportation, 1.6% walk, 3.4% work from home (2000); Travel time to work: 34.6% less than 15 minutes, 31.3% 15 to 30 minutes, 16.4% 30 to 45 minutes, 5.4% 45 to 60 minutes, 12.2% 60 minutes or more (2000)
Additional Information Contacts
Tri-County Chamber of Commerce . . . . (973) 423-5815
    http://www.tricounty.org

MONTVALE (borough). Covers a land area of 3.974 square miles and a water area of 0.005 square miles. Located at 41.04° N. Lat.; 74.04° W. Long. Elevation is 310 feet.
History: Incorporated 1894.
Population: 6,940 (1990); 7,034 (2000); 7,371 (2005); 7,705 (2010 projected); Race: 92.0% White, 0.3% Black, 6.1% Asian, 3.8% Hispanic of any race (2005); Density: 1,854.6 persons per square mile (2005); Average household size: 2.75 (2005); Median age: 40.9 (2005); Males per 100 females: 97.1 (2005); Marriage status: 18.8% never married, 70.7% now married, 6.0% widowed, 4.5% divorced (2000); Foreign born: 13.1% (2000); Ancestry (includes multiple ancestries): 27.0% Italian, 26.0% Irish, 18.3% German, 11.0% Other groups, 8.9% English (2000).
Economy: Makes clothing and paperboard. Single-family building permits issued: 19 (2005); Multi-family building permits issued: 0 (2005); Employment by occupation: 31.0% management, 24.4% professional, 8.3% services, 28.4% sales, 0.0% farming, 3.5% construction, 4.4% production (2000).
Income: Per capita income: $49,015 (2005); Median household income: $107,508 (2005); Average household income: $133,981 (2005); Percent of households with income of $100,000 or more: 53.7% (2005); Poverty rate: 0.9% (2000).
Taxes: Total city taxes per capita: $1,209 (2004); City property taxes per capita: $1,152 (2004).
Education: Percent of population age 25 and over with: High school diploma (including GED) or higher: 95.0% (2005); Bachelor's degree or higher: 55.6% (2005); Master's degree or higher: 20.1% (2005).

School District(s)
Montvale Borough (PK-08)
    2003-04 Enrollment: 1,018 . . . . (201) 391-1662
Pascack Valley Regional (09-12)
    2003-04 Enrollment: 1,614 . . . . (201) 358-7005
Housing: Homeownership rate: 85.2% (2005); Median home value: $543,951 (2005); Median rent: $973 per month (2000); Median age of housing: 36 years (2000).
Safety: Violent crime rate: 9.5 per 10,000 population; Property crime rate: 69.5 per 10,000 population (2004).
Transportation: Commute to work: 88.2% car, 5.1% public transportation, 1.0% walk, 4.9% work from home (2000); Travel time to work: 28.8% less than 15 minutes, 31.5% 15 to 30 minutes, 17.5% 30 to 45 minutes, 10.9% 45 to 60 minutes, 11.3% 60 minutes or more (2000)
Additional Information Contacts
Borough of Montvale . . . . (201) 391-5700
    http://www.montvale.org

MOONACHIE (borough). Covers a land area of 1.725 square miles and a water area of <.001 square miles. Located at 40.84° N. Lat.; 74.05° W. Long. Elevation is 5 feet.
History: Incorporated 1910.
Population: 2,817 (1990); 2,754 (2000); 2,877 (2005); 3,000 (2010 projected); Race: 81.9% White, 1.1% Black, 8.5% Asian, 16.8% Hispanic of any race (2005); Density: 1,667.8 persons per square mile (2005); Average household size: 2.67 (2005); Median age: 42.1 (2005); Males per 100 females: 96.5 (2005); Marriage status: 24.4% never married, 58.4% now married, 10.4% widowed, 6.8% divorced (2000); Foreign born: 21.9% (2000); Ancestry (includes multiple ancestries): 34.1% Italian, 22.2% Other groups, 15.7% German, 14.1% Irish, 6.1% Polish (2000).
Economy: Headquarters for milk distribution; soy; plastics. Single-family building permits issued: 8 (2005); Multi-family building permits issued: 0 (2005); Employment by occupation: 10.8% management, 11.7% professional, 12.7% services, 36.9% sales, 0.0% farming, 9.6% construction, 18.3% production (2000).
Income: Per capita income: $27,282 (2005); Median household income: $57,489 (2005); Average household income: $72,946 (2005); Percent of households with income of $100,000 or more: 21.7% (2005); Poverty rate: 3.8% (2000).
Education: Percent of population age 25 and over with: High school diploma (including GED) or higher: 72.7% (2005); Bachelor's degree or higher: 13.0% (2005); Master's degree or higher: 3.2% (2005).

School District(s)
Moonachie Borough (PK-08)
    2003-04 Enrollment: 287 . . . . (201) 641-5833
South Bergen Jointure Com (UG-UG)
    2003-04 Enrollment: 508 . . . . (201) 845-8818

Housing: Homeownership rate: 77.7% (2005); Median home value: $240,343 (2005); Median rent: $763 per month (2000); Median age of housing: 35 years (2000).
Safety: Violent crime rate: 10.5 per 10,000 population; Property crime rate: 308.2 per 10,000 population (2004).
Transportation: Commute to work: 89.3% car, 6.4% public transportation, 2.3% walk, 1.1% work from home (2000); Travel time to work: 35.4% less than 15 minutes, 39.9% 15 to 30 minutes, 13.5% 30 to 45 minutes, 4.5% 45 to 60 minutes, 6.7% 60 minutes or more (2000)

NEW MILFORD (borough). Covers a land area of 2.310 square miles and a water area of 0 square miles. Located at 40.93° N. Lat.; 74.01° W. Long. Elevation is 33 feet.
History: Named for a mill located on the Hackensack River. Settled in 1695 by French Huguenots. One of the original homes still stands, and there is a Huguenot cemetery in the city. In 1776, George Washington's forces crossed the Hackensack River here during their retreat from Fort Lee to Trenton. Washington used the New Bridge Inn (still standing). Incorporated 1922.
Population: 15,990 (1990); 16,400 (2000); 16,360 (2005); 16,326 (2010 projected); Race: 73.4% White, 3.2% Black, 18.4% Asian, 10.1% Hispanic of any race (2005); Density: 7,081.7 persons per square mile (2005); Average household size: 2.56 (2005); Median age: 41.2 (2005); Males per 100 females: 93.9 (2005); Marriage status: 24.8% never married, 59.3% now married, 8.9% widowed, 7.0% divorced (2000); Foreign born: 24.8% (2000); Ancestry (includes multiple ancestries): 27.7% Other groups, 23.5% Italian, 19.6% Irish, 14.2% German, 4.7% Polish (2000).
Economy: Primarily residential. Single-family building permits issued: 17 (2005); Multi-family building permits issued: 0 (2005); Employment by occupation: 15.0% management, 26.6% professional, 9.9% services, 33.4% sales, 0.0% farming, 7.0% construction, 8.1% production (2000).
Income: Per capita income: $35,572 (2005); Median household income: $70,684 (2005); Average household income: $90,438 (2005); Percent of households with income of $100,000 or more: 32.9% (2005); Poverty rate: 3.4% (2000).
Taxes: Total city taxes per capita: $674 (2004); City property taxes per capita: $655 (2004).
Education: Percent of population age 25 and over with: High school diploma (including GED) or higher: 87.4% (2005); Bachelor's degree or higher: 32.0% (2005); Master's degree or higher: 11.1% (2005).

School District(s)
New Milford Borough (PK-12)
    2003-04 Enrollment: 1,943 . . . . (201) 261-2952
Housing: Homeownership rate: 59.9% (2005); Median home value: $357,217 (2005); Median rent: $729 per month (2000); Median age of housing: 47 years (2000).
Safety: Violent crime rate: 4.2 per 10,000 population; Property crime rate: 83.7 per 10,000 population (2004).
Newspapers: The Palisadian (General - Circulation 32,000)
Transportation: Commute to work: 86.3% car, 8.9% public transportation, 1.5% walk, 3.1% work from home (2000); Travel time to work: 20.9% less than 15 minutes, 34.6% 15 to 30 minutes, 20.2% 30 to 45 minutes, 9.3% 45 to 60 minutes, 15.1% 60 minutes or more (2000)

NORTH ARLINGTON (borough). Covers a land area of 2.581 square miles and a water area of 0.036 square miles. Located at 40.79° N. Lat.; 74.13° W. Long. Elevation is 122 feet.
History: Named for the home of G. W. P. Custis, named for the 1st Earl of Arlington. Settled 1700s. Incorporated 1896.
Population: 13,790 (1990); 15,181 (2000); 15,221 (2005); 15,300 (2010 projected); Race: 87.4% White, 0.6% Black, 6.6% Asian, 13.4% Hispanic of any race (2005); Density: 5,896.2 persons per square mile (2005); Average household size: 2.35 (2005); Median age: 42.3 (2005); Males per 100 females: 89.6 (2005); Marriage status: 29.7% never married, 53.3% now married, 10.0% widowed, 7.1% divorced (2000); Foreign born: 21.7% (2000); Ancestry (includes multiple ancestries): 27.4% Italian, 23.7% Irish, 18.2% Other groups, 11.5% Polish, 8.4% German (2000).
Economy: A residential and industrial suburb of Newark. Single-family building permits issued: 5 (2005); Multi-family building permits issued: 0 (2005); Employment by occupation: 11.4% management, 18.6% professional, 13.9% services, 35.2% sales, 0.0% farming, 8.4% construction, 12.5% production (2000).
Income: Per capita income: $27,369 (2005); Median household income: $55,801 (2005); Average household income: $64,122 (2005); Percent of

households with income of $100,000 or more: 18.2% (2005); Poverty rate: 5.1% (2000).

Taxes: Total city taxes per capita: $689 (2004); City property taxes per capita: $676 (2004).

Education: Percent of population age 25 and over with: High school diploma (including GED) or higher: 82.1% (2005); Bachelor's degree or higher: 19.4% (2005); Master's degree or higher: 5.3% (2005).

School District(s)
North Arlington Borough (PK-12)
   2003-04 Enrollment: 1,624 . . . . (201) 955-5200

Housing: Homeownership rate: 54.8% (2005); Median home value: $309,788 (2005); Median rent: $707 per month (2000); Median age of housing: 51 years (2000).

Safety: Violent crime rate: 8.5 per 10,000 population; Property crime rate: 90.1 per 10,000 population (2004).

Transportation: Commute to work: 86.0% car, 8.6% public transportation, 3.3% walk, 1.5% work from home (2000); Travel time to work: 20.5% less than 15 minutes, 38.1% 15 to 30 minutes, 22.5% 30 to 45 minutes, 8.1% 45 to 60 minutes, 10.8% 60 minutes or more (2000)

NORTHVALE (borough). Covers a land area of 1.319 square miles and a water area of 0.004 square miles. Located at 41.01° N. Lat.; 73.95° W. Long. Elevation is 50 feet.

History: Incorporated 1916.

Population: 4,563 (1990); 4,460 (2000); 4,561 (2005); 4,673 (2010 projected); Race: 80.7% White, 1.0% Black, 15.7% Asian, 4.9% Hispanic of any race (2005); Density: 3,457.8 persons per square mile (2005); Average household size: 2.78 (2005); Median age: 41.6 (2005); Males per 100 females: 99.4 (2005); Marriage status: 22.6% never married, 64.9% now married, 7.4% widowed, 5.1% divorced (2000); Foreign born: 19.5% (2000); Ancestry (includes multiple ancestries): 30.5% Italian, 20.5% Irish, 19.3% Other groups, 17.1% German, 6.3% English (2000).

Economy: Single-family building permits issued: 11 (2005); Multi-family building permits issued: 0 (2005); Employment by occupation: 18.8% management, 22.3% professional, 14.3% services, 28.1% sales, 0.0% farming, 10.8% construction, 5.7% production (2000).

Income: Per capita income: $32,663 (2005); Median household income: $77,613 (2005); Average household income: $90,570 (2005); Percent of households with income of $100,000 or more: 33.0% (2005); Poverty rate: 3.9% (2000).

Education: Percent of population age 25 and over with: High school diploma (including GED) or higher: 87.2% (2005); Bachelor's degree or higher: 29.4% (2005); Master's degree or higher: 10.7% (2005).

School District(s)
Northvale Borough (PK-08)
   2003-04 Enrollment: 578 . . . . (201) 768-8484

Housing: Homeownership rate: 81.0% (2005); Median home value: $391,416 (2005); Median rent: $782 per month (2000); Median age of housing: 41 years (2000).

Safety: Violent crime rate: 0.0 per 10,000 population; Property crime rate: 74.4 per 10,000 population (2004).

Transportation: Commute to work: 90.2% car, 5.0% public transportation, 2.3% walk, 1.8% work from home (2000); Travel time to work: 31.3% less than 15 minutes, 29.1% 15 to 30 minutes, 22.8% 30 to 45 minutes, 7.9% 45 to 60 minutes, 8.9% 60 minutes or more (2000)

NORWOOD (borough). Covers a land area of 2.750 square miles and a water area of 0.005 square miles. Located at 40.99° N. Lat.; 73.95° W. Long. Elevation is 50 feet.

History: Incorporated 1905.

Population: 4,857 (1990); 5,751 (2000); 6,233 (2005); 6,683 (2010 projected); Race: 75.5% White, 0.8% Black, 21.0% Asian, 3.5% Hispanic of any race (2005); Density: 2,266.7 persons per square mile (2005); Average household size: 3.03 (2005); Median age: 42.2 (2005); Males per 100 females: 89.3 (2005); Marriage status: 19.7% never married, 69.3% now married, 7.6% widowed, 3.4% divorced (2000); Foreign born: 22.4% (2000); Ancestry (includes multiple ancestries): 26.2% Italian, 24.7% Other groups, 17.6% Irish, 16.2% German, 6.1% English (2000).

Economy: Single-family building permits issued: 20 (2005); Multi-family building permits issued: 0 (2005); Employment by occupation: 28.9% management, 21.7% professional, 11.4% services, 27.0% sales, 0.0% farming, 6.3% construction, 4.6% production (2000).

Income: Per capita income: $47,524 (2005); Median household income: $104,657 (2005); Average household income: $142,805 (2005); Percent of

households with income of $100,000 or more: 52.3% (2005); Poverty rate: 4.9% (2000).

Education: Percent of population age 25 and over with: High school diploma (including GED) or higher: 91.0% (2005); Bachelor's degree or higher: 42.6% (2005); Master's degree or higher: 14.0% (2005).

School District(s)
Norwood Borough (PK-08)
   2003-04 Enrollment: 664 . . . . (201) 768-4321

Housing: Homeownership rate: 85.0% (2005); Median home value: $548,002 (2005); Median rent: $966 per month (2000); Median age of housing: 32 years (2000).

Safety: Violent crime rate: 9.7 per 10,000 population; Property crime rate: 69.4 per 10,000 population (2004).

Transportation: Commute to work: 90.2% car, 3.6% public transportation, 0.6% walk, 4.8% work from home (2000); Travel time to work: 26.7% less than 15 minutes, 19.0% 15 to 30 minutes, 26.0% 30 to 45 minutes, 13.1% 45 to 60 minutes, 15.2% 60 minutes or more (2000)

OAKLAND (borough). Covers a land area of 8.604 square miles and a water area of 0.147 square miles. Located at 41.02° N. Lat.; 74.23° W. Long. Elevation is 220 feet.

Population: 11,997 (1990); 12,466 (2000); 14,142 (2005); 15,668 (2010 projected); Race: 94.1% White, 0.7% Black, 3.0% Asian, 4.9% Hispanic of any race (2005); Density: 1,643.7 persons per square mile (2005); Average household size: 2.87 (2005); Median age: 40.2 (2005); Males per 100 females: 95.8 (2005); Marriage status: 18.1% never married, 69.7% now married, 6.0% widowed, 6.2% divorced (2000); Foreign born: 9.2% (2000); Ancestry (includes multiple ancestries): 26.7% Italian, 21.2% Irish, 18.1% German, 9.3% Polish, 9.3% Other groups (2000).

Economy: Single-family building permits issued: 2 (2005); Multi-family building permits issued: 0 (2005); Employment by occupation: 21.9% management, 25.5% professional, 8.0% services, 29.9% sales, 0.0% farming, 8.7% construction, 6.0% production (2000).

Income: Per capita income: $42,469 (2005); Median household income: $98,629 (2005); Average household income: $120,514 (2005); Percent of households with income of $100,000 or more: 49.0% (2005); Poverty rate: 1.7% (2000).

Education: Percent of population age 25 and over with: High school diploma (including GED) or higher: 92.5% (2005); Bachelor's degree or higher: 41.6% (2005); Master's degree or higher: 15.0% (2005).

School District(s)
Oakland Borough (PK-08)
   2003-04 Enrollment: 1,692 . . . . (201) 337-6156
Ramapo-Indian Hill Regional (09-12)
   2003-04 Enrollment: 2,134 . . . . (201) 891-1505

Housing: Homeownership rate: 93.1% (2005); Median home value: $387,787 (2005); Median rent: $1,030 per month (2000); Median age of housing: 42 years (2000).

Safety: Violent crime rate: 5.8 per 10,000 population; Property crime rate: 80.2 per 10,000 population (2004).

Transportation: Commute to work: 89.9% car, 4.3% public transportation, 0.7% walk, 4.7% work from home (2000); Travel time to work: 18.3% less than 15 minutes, 36.4% 15 to 30 minutes, 26.1% 30 to 45 minutes, 7.4% 45 to 60 minutes, 11.7% 60 minutes or more (2000)

Additional Information Contacts
Borough of Oakland . . . . (201) 337-8111
   http://www.oakland-nj.org
Oakland Chamber of Commerce . . . . (201) 337-7117
   http://www.oakland-nj.org

OLD TAPPAN (borough). Covers a land area of 3.230 square miles and a water area of 0.846 square miles. Located at 41.01° N. Lat.; 73.98° W. Long. Elevation is 80 feet.

Population: 4,254 (1990); 5,482 (2000); 5,955 (2005); 6,399 (2010 projected); Race: 79.3% White, 0.5% Black, 19.0% Asian, 3.3% Hispanic of any race (2005); Density: 1,843.9 persons per square mile (2005); Average household size: 3.02 (2005); Median age: 42.1 (2005); Males per 100 females: 92.4 (2005); Marriage status: 18.9% never married, 69.8% now married, 6.4% widowed, 4.9% divorced (2000); Foreign born: 16.8% (2000); Ancestry (includes multiple ancestries): 29.1% Italian, 21.0% Irish, 20.6% Other groups, 16.8% German, 6.7% English (2000).

Economy: Single-family building permits issued: 50 (2005); Multi-family building permits issued: 0 (2005); Employment by occupation: 28.2% management, 26.7% professional, 7.4% services, 30.6% sales, 0.0% farming, 3.4% construction, 3.6% production (2000).

Income: Per capita income: $54,889 (2005); Median household income: $125,895 (2005); Average household income: $164,481 (2005); Percent of households with income of $100,000 or more: 62.5% (2005); Poverty rate: 1.8% (2000).

Education: Percent of population age 25 and over with: High school diploma (including GED) or higher: 93.4% (2005); Bachelor's degree or higher: 49.1% (2005); Master's degree or higher: 18.2% (2005).

School District(s)

Northern Valley Regional (09-12)

    2003-04 Enrollment: 2,327 . . . . (201) 768-2200

Old Tappan Borough (PK-08)

    2003-04 Enrollment: 812 . . . . (201) 664-7231

Housing: Homeownership rate: 93.4% (2005); Median home value: $690,621 (2005); Median rent: $940 per month (2000); Median age of housing: 31 years (2000).

Safety: Violent crime rate: 3.4 per 10,000 population; Property crime rate: 51.4 per 10,000 population (2004).

Transportation: Commute to work: 91.2% car, 3.9% public transportation, 0.6% walk, 4.3% work from home (2000); Travel time to work: 23.0% less than 15 minutes, 25.7% 15 to 30 minutes, 21.4% 30 to 45 minutes, 11.9% 45 to 60 minutes, 18.0% 60 minutes or more (2000)

Additional Information Contacts

Borough of Old Tappan . . . . (201) 664-1849

    http://oldtappan.net

ORADELL (borough). Covers a land area of 2.425 square miles and a water area of 0.126 square miles. Located at 40.95° N. Lat.; 74.03° W. Long. Elevation is 91 feet.

History: Settled by Dutch before the Revolution, incorporated 1894.

Population: 8,000 (1990); 8,047 (2000); 8,014 (2005); 8,013 (2010 projected); Race: 89.1% White, 0.6% Black, 8.8% Asian, 4.0% Hispanic of any race (2005); Density: 3,305.4 persons per square mile (2005); Average household size: 2.86 (2005); Median age: 42.5 (2005); Males per 100 females: 92.2 (2005); Marriage status: 19.0% never married, 70.2% now married, 5.9% widowed, 4.9% divorced (2000); Foreign born: 13.3% (2000); Ancestry (includes multiple ancestries): 23.7% Irish, 23.7% Italian, 14.0% German, 13.8% Other groups, 6.4% English (2000).

Economy: Single-family building permits issued: 5 (2005); Multi-family building permits issued: 0 (2005); Employment by occupation: 23.8% management, 32.8% professional, 6.1% services, 29.1% sales, 0.0% farming, 3.2% construction, 5.0% production (2000).

Income: Per capita income: $43,954 (2005); Median household income: $99,790 (2005); Average household income: $124,619 (2005); Percent of households with income of $100,000 or more: 49.9% (2005); Poverty rate: 2.4% (2000).

Education: Percent of population age 25 and over with: High school diploma (including GED) or higher: 94.8% (2005); Bachelor's degree or higher: 51.8% (2005); Master's degree or higher: 21.3% (2005).

School District(s)

Oradell Borough (PK-06)

    2003-04 Enrollment: 760 . . . . (201) 261-1153

River Dell Regional (07-12)

    2003-04 Enrollment: 1,381 . . . . (201) 599-7206

Housing: Homeownership rate: 89.6% (2005); Median home value: $531,608 (2005); Median rent: $916 per month (2000); Median age of housing: 46 years (2000).

Safety: Violent crime rate: 3.7 per 10,000 population; Property crime rate: 82.9 per 10,000 population (2004).

Transportation: Commute to work: 81.1% car, 14.0% public transportation, 1.5% walk, 2.9% work from home (2000); Travel time to work: 22.6% less than 15 minutes, 30.7% 15 to 30 minutes, 16.3% 30 to 45 minutes, 7.7% 45 to 60 minutes, 22.7% 60 minutes or more (2000)

PALISADES PARK (borough). Covers a land area of 1.210 square miles and a water area of 0.064 square miles. Located at 40.84° N. Lat.; 73.99° W. Long. Elevation is 100 feet.

History: Named for its location on the Palisade Cliffs, which line the west bank of the Hudson River. Incorporated 1899.

Population: 14,536 (1990); 17,073 (2000); 18,392 (2005); 19,649 (2010 projected); Race: 38.9% White, 1.4% Black, 49.0% Asian, 19.2% Hispanic of any race (2005); Density: 15,202.7 persons per square mile (2005); Average household size: 2.79 (2005); Median age: 37.4 (2005); Males per 100 females: 99.5 (2005); Marriage status: 29.8% never married, 57.4% now married, 7.0% widowed, 5.8% divorced (2000); Foreign born: 57.0%

(2000); Ancestry (includes multiple ancestries): 57.7% Other groups, 14.8% Italian, 3.9% Irish, 3.7% German, 3.6% Greek (2000).

Economy: Single-family building permits issued: 43 (2005); Multi-family building permits issued: 178 (2005); Employment by occupation: 16.4% management, 16.6% professional, 16.5% services, 29.4% sales, 0.0% farming, 7.9% construction, 13.0% production (2000).

Income: Per capita income: $26,114 (2005); Median household income: $54,812 (2005); Average household income: $72,680 (2005); Percent of households with income of $100,000 or more: 22.4% (2005); Poverty rate: 9.7% (2000).

Education: Percent of population age 25 and over with: High school diploma (including GED) or higher: 79.4% (2005); Bachelor's degree or higher: 30.7% (2005); Master's degree or higher: 7.5% (2005).

School District(s)

Palisades Park (PK-12)

    2003-04 Enrollment: 1,514 . . . . (201) 947-3560

Housing: Homeownership rate: 37.1% (2005); Median home value: $399,301 (2005); Median rent: $851 per month (2000); Median age of housing: 41 years (2000).

Safety: Violent crime rate: 8.3 per 10,000 population; Property crime rate: 96.5 per 10,000 population (2004).

Newspapers: Bergen News (East Edition) (General - Circulation 13,296); Bergen News (South Edition) (General - Circulation 13,700); Bergen News (West Edition) (General - Circulation 17,887); Korean Bergen News (Asian, General - Circulation 5,000); Press Journal (General - Circulation 10,142); Sun Bulletin (General - Circulation 18,454)

Transportation: Commute to work: 77.3% car, 18.1% public transportation, 2.8% walk, 1.4% work from home (2000); Travel time to work: 21.7% less than 15 minutes, 31.8% 15 to 30 minutes, 23.5% 30 to 45 minutes, 8.6% 45 to 60 minutes, 14.4% 60 minutes or more (2000)

PARAMUS (borough). Covers a land area of 10.472 square miles and a water area of 0 square miles. Located at 40.94° N. Lat.; 74.07° W. Long. Elevation is 56 feet.

History: Named for the Algonquian translation of "Saddle River," which also means "turkey river". Early Dutch church here. Settled 1668. Incorporated 1922.

Population: 25,004 (1990); 25,737 (2000); 26,904 (2005); 27,950 (2010 projected); Race: 75.3% White, 1.3% Black, 20.5% Asian, 5.9% Hispanic of any race (2005); Density: 2,569.1 persons per square mile (2005); Average household size: 3.15 (2005); Median age: 44.5 (2005); Males per 100 females: 94.8 (2005); Marriage status: 22.2% never married, 63.5% now married, 9.4% widowed, 4.8% divorced (2000); Foreign born: 25.1% (2000); Ancestry (includes multiple ancestries): 24.1% Other groups, 23.8% Italian, 14.4% Irish, 12.6% German, 6.8% Polish (2000).

Economy: Large retail-trade center known for its expansive shopping malls, especially the Garden State Plaza, one of the largest shopping centers in the U.S. Unemployment rate: 3.4% (2005); Total civilian labor force: 12,824 (2005); Single-family building permits issued: 46 (2005); Multi-family building permits issued: 15 (2005); Employment by occupation: 17.8% management, 26.3% professional, 9.1% services, 33.3% sales, 0.0% farming, 6.2% construction, 7.2% production (2000).

Income: Per capita income: $34,705 (2005); Median household income: $85,847 (2005); Average household income: $106,144 (2005); Percent of households with income of $100,000 or more: 40.8% (2005); Poverty rate: 3.3% (2000).

Taxes: Total city taxes per capita: $1,036 (2004); City property taxes per capita: $979 (2004).

Education: Percent of population age 25 and over with: High school diploma (including GED) or higher: 86.1% (2005); Bachelor's degree or higher: 38.6% (2005); Master's degree or higher: 14.2% (2005).

School District(s)

Bergen County Special Services (UG-UG)

    2003-04 Enrollment: 1,982 . . . . (201) 343-6000

Bergen County Vocational (09-12)

    2003-04 Enrollment: 2,331 . . . . (201) 967-2472

Paramus Borough (PK-12)

    2003-04 Enrollment: 4,576 . . . . (201) 261-7800

Two-year College(s)

Bergen Community College (Public)

    Fall 2004 Enrollment: 14,325 . . . . (201) 447-7200

    2005-06 Tuition: In-state $4,768; Out-of-state $5,008

Capri Institute of Hair Design (Private, For-profit)

    Fall 2004 Enrollment: 203 . . . . (800) 232-2774

Cittone Institute (Private, For-profit)
    Fall 2004 Enrollment: 582 . . . . (201) 845-6868
Dover Business College (Private, For-profit)
    Fall 2004 Enrollment: 384 . . . . (201) 843-8500
    2005-06 Tuition: In-state $11,575; Out-of-state $11,575
Housing: Homeownership rate: 89.9% (2005); Median home value: $464,742 (2005); Median rent: $1,308 per month (2000); Median age of housing: 42 years (2000).
Hospitals: Bergen Regional Medical Center (1185 beds)
Safety: Violent crime rate: 31.5 per 10,000 population; Property crime rate: 790.2 per 10,000 population (2004).
Newspapers: The Armenian Reporter International (Ethnic - Circulation 5,200)
Transportation: Commute to work: 87.8% car, 6.6% public transportation, 1.8% walk, 3.5% work from home (2000); Travel time to work: 27.0% less than 15 minutes, 35.8% 15 to 30 minutes, 18.7% 30 to 45 minutes, 6.1% 45 to 60 minutes, 12.4% 60 minutes or more (2000)
Additional Information Contacts
Paramus Chamber of Commerce . . . . (201) 261-3344
    http://www.paramuschamber.com

PARK RIDGE (borough). Covers a land area of 2.597 square miles and a water area of 0.042 square miles. Located at 41.03° N. Lat.; 74.04° W. Long. Elevation is 250 feet.
History: Settled c.1770, incorporated 1894.
Population: 8,102 (1990); 8,708 (2000); 8,990 (2005); 9,279 (2010 projected); Race: 93.0% White, 1.0% Black, 3.9% Asian, 7.0% Hispanic of any race (2005); Density: 3,461.9 persons per square mile (2005); Average household size: 2.71 (2005); Median age: 42.1 (2005); Males per 100 females: 92.7 (2005); Marriage status: 21.0% never married, 66.5% now married, 6.8% widowed, 5.6% divorced (2000); Foreign born: 13.8% (2000); Ancestry (includes multiple ancestries): 28.9% Italian, 25.4% Irish, 17.3% German, 12.7% Other groups, 8.1% English (2000).
Economy: Manufacturing: office supplies, clothing. Single-family building permits issued: 16 (2005); Multi-family building permits issued: 2 (2005); Employment by occupation: 22.0% management, 25.2% professional, 11.2% services, 30.9% sales, 0.0% farming, 6.2% construction, 4.5% production (2000).
Income: Per capita income: $45,737 (2005); Median household income: $97,383 (2005); Average household income: $122,456 (2005); Percent of households with income of $100,000 or more: 48.6% (2005); Poverty rate: 3.1% (2000).
Taxes: Total city taxes per capita: $814 (2004); City property taxes per capita: $787 (2004).
Education: Percent of population age 25 and over with: High school diploma (including GED) or higher: 91.3% (2005); Bachelor's degree or higher: 45.0% (2005); Master's degree or higher: 17.5% (2005).
School District(s)
Park Ridge Borough (PK-12)
    2003-04 Enrollment: 1,337 . . . . (201) 573-6000
Housing: Homeownership rate: 81.4% (2005); Median home value: $482,720 (2005); Median rent: $908 per month (2000); Median age of housing: 41 years (2000).
Safety: Violent crime rate: 0.0 per 10,000 population; Property crime rate: 50.3 per 10,000 population (2004).
Transportation: Commute to work: 86.1% car, 8.2% public transportation, 2.2% walk, 3.4% work from home (2000); Travel time to work: 31.5% less than 15 minutes, 28.7% 15 to 30 minutes, 15.4% 30 to 45 minutes, 7.7% 45 to 60 minutes, 16.6% 60 minutes or more (2000)

RAMSEY (borough). Covers a land area of 5.555 square miles and a water area of 0.049 square miles. Located at 41.05° N. Lat.; 74.14° W. Long. Elevation is 330 feet.
History: Named either for Peter Ramsey, local landowner, or for a Ramsey who owned a local tavern in the 1700s. Settled 1846, incorporated 1908.
Population: 13,238 (1990); 14,351 (2000); 14,540 (2005); 14,777 (2010 projected); Race: 90.7% White, 0.8% Black, 6.6% Asian, 3.5% Hispanic of any race (2005); Density: 2,617.2 persons per square mile (2005); Average household size: 2.65 (2005); Median age: 39.8 (2005); Males per 100 females: 94.2 (2005); Marriage status: 20.5% never married, 66.1% now married, 6.2% widowed, 7.2% divorced (2000); Foreign born: 11.9% (2000); Ancestry (includes multiple ancestries): 27.9% Italian, 24.0% Irish, 16.7% German, 10.2% Other groups, 10.1% English (2000).
Economy: Single-family building permits issued: 121 (2005); Multi-family building permits issued: 0 (2005); Employment by occupation: 25.5%

management, 28.2% professional, 6.9% services, 29.3% sales, 0.1% farming, 5.6% construction, 4.3% production (2000).
Income: Per capita income: $50,172 (2005); Median household income: $102,423 (2005); Average household income: $132,634 (2005); Percent of households with income of $100,000 or more: 51.1% (2005); Poverty rate: 1.9% (2000).
Taxes: Total city taxes per capita: $878 (2004); City property taxes per capita: $840 (2004).
Education: Percent of population age 25 and over with: High school diploma (including GED) or higher: 95.4% (2005); Bachelor's degree or higher: 54.3% (2005); Master's degree or higher: 19.8% (2005).
School District(s)
Ramsey Borough (PK-12)
    2003-04 Enrollment: 3,038 . . . . (201) 785-2300
Two-year College(s)
Hohokus School of Business and Medical Sciences (Private, For-profit)
    Fall 2004 Enrollment: 469 . . . . (201) 327-8877
    2005-06 Tuition: In-state $7,800; Out-of-state $7,800
Housing: Homeownership rate: 83.6% (2005); Median home value: $491,609 (2005); Median rent: $1,054 per month (2000); Median age of housing: 35 years (2000).
Safety: Violent crime rate: 10.3 per 10,000 population; Property crime rate: 128.2 per 10,000 population (2004).
Newspapers: Home And Store News (General - Circulation 32,000); Our Town (General - Circulation 24,000)
Transportation: Commute to work: 87.5% car, 5.9% public transportation, 1.9% walk, 3.7% work from home (2000); Travel time to work: 32.7% less than 15 minutes, 27.0% 15 to 30 minutes, 18.8% 30 to 45 minutes, 6.8% 45 to 60 minutes, 14.6% 60 minutes or more (2000)
Additional Information Contacts
Borough of Ramsey . . . . (201) 825-3400
    http://www.ramseynj.com

RIDGEFIELD (borough). Covers a land area of 2.610 square miles and a water area of 0.256 square miles. Located at 40.83° N. Lat.; 74.00° W. Long. Elevation is 70 feet.
History: Named for its geological ridges. Incorporated 1892.
Population: 9,996 (1990); 10,830 (2000); 10,943 (2005); 11,099 (2010 projected); Race: 69.3% White, 0.8% Black, 22.4% Asian, 17.8% Hispanic of any race (2005); Density: 4,193.1 persons per square mile (2005); Average household size: 2.75 (2005); Median age: 41.2 (2005); Males per 100 females: 94.2 (2005); Marriage status: 25.3% never married, 59.9% now married, 9.2% widowed, 5.6% divorced (2000); Foreign born: 33.7% (2000); Ancestry (includes multiple ancestries): 31.9% Other groups, 24.2% Italian, 12.9% Irish, 10.0% German, 3.4% Croatian (2000).
Economy: Several corporate headquarters are located here. Single-family building permits issued: 16 (2005); Multi-family building permits issued: 8 (2005); Employment by occupation: 18.4% management, 17.5% professional, 15.5% services, 27.2% sales, 0.0% farming, 9.6% construction, 11.8% production (2000).
Income: Per capita income: $29,264 (2005); Median household income: $61,177 (2005); Average household income: $80,208 (2005); Percent of households with income of $100,000 or more: 26.8% (2005); Poverty rate: 6.6% (2000).
Education: Percent of population age 25 and over with: High school diploma (including GED) or higher: 79.0% (2005); Bachelor's degree or higher: 26.1% (2005); Master's degree or higher: 6.8% (2005).
School District(s)
Ridgefield Borough (PK-12)
    2003-04 Enrollment: 2,336 . . . . (201) 945-9236
Housing: Homeownership rate: 57.0% (2005); Median home value: $392,837 (2005); Median rent: $837 per month (2000); Median age of housing: 46 years (2000).
Safety: Violent crime rate: 8.2 per 10,000 population; Property crime rate: 85.5 per 10,000 population (2004).
Transportation: Commute to work: 80.1% car, 14.3% public transportation, 3.2% walk, 1.8% work from home (2000); Travel time to work: 25.6% less than 15 minutes, 26.5% 15 to 30 minutes, 23.2% 30 to 45 minutes, 9.4% 45 to 60 minutes, 15.2% 60 minutes or more (2000)

RIDGEFIELD PARK (village). Covers a land area of 1.731 square miles and a water area of 0.192 square miles. Located at 40.85° N. Lat.; 74.02° W. Long. Elevation is 100 feet.
History: Named for its geological ridges. Incorporated 1892.

Population: 12,454 (1990); 12,873 (2000); 12,743 (2005); 12,639 (2010 projected); Race: 73.3% White, 5.0% Black, 9.4% Asian, 29.1% Hispanic of any race (2005); Density: 7,360.6 persons per square mile (2005); Average household size: 2.60 (2005); Median age: 39.1 (2005); Males per 100 females: 92.4 (2005); Marriage status: 29.4% never married, 54.3% now married, 7.2% widowed, 9.1% divorced (2000); Foreign born: 23.9% (2000); Ancestry (includes multiple ancestries): 33.6% Other groups, 21.7% Italian, 21.1% Irish, 13.6% German, 5.4% English (2000).
Economy: Paper goods. Single-family building permits issued: 1 (2005); Multi-family building permits issued: 0 (2005); Employment by occupation: 14.3% management, 17.9% professional, 12.9% services, 34.9% sales, 0.0% farming, 7.9% construction, 12.2% production (2000).
Income: Per capita income: $27,814 (2005); Median household income: $59,248 (2005); Average household income: $72,047 (2005); Percent of households with income of $100,000 or more: 23.5% (2005); Poverty rate: 6.7% (2000).
Education: Percent of population age 25 and over with: High school diploma (including GED) or higher: 85.1% (2005); Bachelor's degree or higher: 26.0% (2005); Master's degree or higher: 8.1% (2005).
School District(s)
Ridgefield Park Township (PK-12)
　　2003-04 Enrollment: 1,959 . . . . (201) 807-2638
Housing: Homeownership rate: 53.1% (2005); Median home value: $278,179 (2005); Median rent: $779 per month (2000); Median age of housing: 57 years (2000).
Safety: Violent crime rate: 9.3 per 10,000 population; Property crime rate: 120.4 per 10,000 population (2004).
Transportation: Commute to work: 81.4% car, 13.5% public transportation, 3.0% walk, 1.4% work from home (2000); Travel time to work: 26.1% less than 15 minutes, 34.8% 15 to 30 minutes, 17.7% 30 to 45 minutes, 10.3% 45 to 60 minutes, 11.1% 60 minutes or more (2000)
Additional Information Contacts
Ridgefield Park Chamber of Commerce . . . . (201) 641-3800
　　http://www.ridgefieldpark.org
Village of Ridgefield Park. . . . . (201) 641-4950
　　http://ridgefieldpark.org

RIDGEWOOD (village).
Covers a land area of 5.787 square miles and a water area of 0.046 square miles. Located at 40.98° N. Lat.; 74.11° W. Long. Elevation is 144 feet.
History: Named for its wooded, hilly terrain. Site of many American and British camps in the Revolutionary War. Incorporated 1876.
Population: 24,245 (1990); 24,936 (2000); 24,795 (2005); 24,691 (2010 projected); Race: 86.8% White, 1.6% Black, 9.5% Asian, 4.6% Hispanic of any race (2005); Density: 4,284.6 persons per square mile (2005); Average household size: 2.89 (2005); Median age: 39.2 (2005); Males per 100 females: 93.7 (2005); Marriage status: 21.6% never married, 68.7% now married, 5.6% widowed, 4.1% divorced (2000); Foreign born: 16.1% (2000); Ancestry (includes multiple ancestries): 22.5% Irish, 18.0% Italian, 16.4% Other groups, 14.5% German, 10.7% English (2000).
Economy: Unemployment rate: 2.4% (2005); Total civilian labor force: 11,885 (2005); Single-family building permits issued: 13 (2005); Multi-family building permits issued: 0 (2005); Employment by occupation: 28.3% management, 33.3% professional, 6.6% services, 26.0% sales, 0.0% farming, 3.3% construction, 2.5% production (2000).
Income: Per capita income: $56,873 (2005); Median household income: $118,546 (2005); Average household income: $163,363 (2005); Percent of households with income of $100,000 or more: 57.4% (2005); Poverty rate: 3.0% (2000).
Taxes: Total city taxes per capita: $939 (2004); City property taxes per capita: $911 (2004).
Education: Percent of population age 25 and over with: High school diploma (including GED) or higher: 95.8% (2005); Bachelor's degree or higher: 66.5% (2005); Master's degree or higher: 28.8% (2005).
School District(s)
Bergen County Special Services (UG-UG)
　　2003-04 Enrollment: 1,982 . . . . (201) 343-6000
Ridgewood Village (PK-12)
　　2003-04 Enrollment: 5,560 . . . . (201) 670-2700
Housing: Homeownership rate: 79.2% (2005); Median home value: $620,281 (2005); Median rent: $1,109 per month (2000); Median age of housing: 55 years (2000).
Hospitals: Valley Hospital (421 beds)
Safety: Violent crime rate: 2.4 per 10,000 population; Property crime rate: 82.4 per 10,000 population (2004).

Newspapers: Glen Rock Gazette (General - Circulation 4,380); Ridgewood News (General - Circulation 7,564); The Town Journal (General - Circulation 9,000); The Village Gazette Of Ridgewood (Ethnic, General - Circulation 9,570); Town News (General - Circulation 31,225); Wyckoff Suburban News (General - Circulation 5,740)
Transportation: Commute to work: 75.5% car, 15.8% public transportation, 2.5% walk, 5.8% work from home (2000); Travel time to work: 25.2% less than 15 minutes, 26.7% 15 to 30 minutes, 13.8% 30 to 45 minutes, 9.6% 45 to 60 minutes, 24.7% 60 minutes or more (2000)
Additional Information Contacts
Ridgewood Chamber of Commerce. . . . . (201) 445-2600
　　http://www.ridgewoodchamber.com
Village of Ridgewood . . . . (201) 670-5500
　　http://www.ridgewoodnj.net

RIVER EDGE (borough).
Aka Riverside. Covers a land area of 1.886 square miles and a water area of 0.019 square miles. Located at 40.92° N. Lat.; 74.03° W. Long. Elevation is 90 feet.
History: Named for its location on the Hackensack River. Incorporated 1894.
Population: 10,603 (1990); 10,946 (2000); 10,986 (2005); 11,041 (2010 projected); Race: 81.5% White, 1.3% Black, 14.6% Asian, 6.6% Hispanic of any race (2005); Density: 5,825.7 persons per square mile (2005); Average household size: 2.64 (2005); Median age: 41.1 (2005); Males per 100 females: 91.9 (2005); Marriage status: 21.0% never married, 65.4% now married, 8.1% widowed, 5.6% divorced (2000); Foreign born: 21.4% (2000); Ancestry (includes multiple ancestries): 25.6% Irish, 21.5% Other groups, 20.6% Italian, 15.1% German, 6.4% Russian (2000).
Economy: Single-family building permits issued: 8 (2005); Multi-family building permits issued: 5 (2005); Employment by occupation: 21.7% management, 29.2% professional, 8.7% services, 30.0% sales, 0.0% farming, 5.1% construction, 5.3% production (2000).
Income: Per capita income: $39,099 (2005); Median household income: $80,910 (2005); Average household income: $102,992 (2005); Percent of households with income of $100,000 or more: 38.2% (2005); Poverty rate: 3.1% (2000).
Education: Percent of population age 25 and over with: High school diploma (including GED) or higher: 93.5% (2005); Bachelor's degree or higher: 45.3% (2005); Master's degree or higher: 16.2% (2005).
School District(s)
River Edge Borough (PK-06)
　　2003-04 Enrollment: 1,055 . . . . (201) 261-3404
Housing: Homeownership rate: 73.6% (2005); Median home value: $400,818 (2005); Median rent: $918 per month (2000); Median age of housing: 51 years (2000).
Safety: Violent crime rate: 6.3 per 10,000 population; Property crime rate: 105.8 per 10,000 population (2004).
Transportation: Commute to work: 83.1% car, 12.1% public transportation, 2.4% walk, 2.3% work from home (2000); Travel time to work: 23.3% less than 15 minutes, 33.0% 15 to 30 minutes, 17.9% 30 to 45 minutes, 6.3% 45 to 60 minutes, 19.6% 60 minutes or more (2000)

RIVER VALE (township).
Aka River Vale CDP. Covers a land area of 4.077 square miles and a water area of 0.235 square miles. Located at 41.01° N. Lat.; 74.01° W. Long. Elevation is 56 feet.
History: Incorporated 1906.
Population: 9,410 (1990); 9,449 (2000); 9,790 (2005); 10,137 (2010 projected); Race: 92.2% White, 0.6% Black, 6.0% Asian, 4.0% Hispanic of any race (2005); Density: 2,401.3 persons per square mile (2005); Average household size: 2.83 (2005); Median age: 41.3 (2005); Males per 100 females: 93.6 (2005); Marriage status: 18.2% never married, 70.7% now married, 6.2% widowed, 4.9% divorced (2000); Foreign born: 11.5% (2000); Ancestry (includes multiple ancestries): 27.6% Italian, 18.7% Irish, 17.3% German, 14.8% Other groups, 6.1% Polish (2000).
Economy: Single-family building permits issued: 17 (2005); Multi-family building permits issued: 0 (2005); Employment by occupation: 24.9% management, 27.6% professional, 7.0% services, 29.4% sales, 0.0% farming, 4.4% construction, 6.7% production (2000).
Income: Per capita income: $50,916 (2005); Median household income: $107,797 (2005); Average household income: $143,758 (2005); Percent of households with income of $100,000 or more: 53.6% (2005); Poverty rate: 2.8% (2000).
Education: Percent of population age 25 and over with: High school diploma (including GED) or higher: 94.2% (2005); Bachelor's degree or higher: 48.5% (2005); Master's degree or higher: 18.4% (2005).

Housing: Homeownership rate: 90.8% (2005); Median home value: $551,016 (2005); Median rent: $1,092 per month (2000); Median age of housing: 36 years (2000).
Safety: Violent crime rate: 12.2 per 10,000 population; Property crime rate: 27.6 per 10,000 population (2004).
Transportation: Commute to work: 87.6% car, 6.3% public transportation, 1.0% walk, 4.9% work from home (2000); Travel time to work: 21.3% less than 15 minutes, 28.9% 15 to 30 minutes, 22.7% 30 to 45 minutes, 9.6% 45 to 60 minutes, 17.5% 60 minutes or more (2000)

ROCHELLE PARK (township). Aka Rochelle Park CDP. Covers a land area of 1.045 square miles and a water area of 0 square miles. Located at 40.90° N. Lat.; 74.07° W. Long. Elevation is 63 feet.
Population: 5,587 (1990); 5,528 (2000); 5,519 (2005); 5,536 (2010 projected); Race: 88.5% White, 0.5% Black, 6.7% Asian, 11.6% Hispanic of any race (2005); Density: 5,279.1 persons per square mile (2005); Average household size: 2.67 (2005); Median age: 44.5 (2005); Males per 100 females: 85.6 (2005); Marriage status: 24.4% never married, 54.8% now married, 15.2% widowed, 5.7% divorced (2000); Foreign born: 16.1% (2000); Ancestry (includes multiple ancestries): 31.8% Italian, 18.6% Other groups, 18.5% German, 17.8% Irish, 8.0% Polish (2000).
Economy: Manufacturing: fabricated metal products, chemicals. Single-family building permits issued: 5 (2005); Multi-family building permits issued: 81 (2005); Employment by occupation: 15.2% management, 22.4% professional, 13.4% services, 31.9% sales, 0.0% farming, 5.7% construction, 11.5% production (2000).
Income: Per capita income: $30,144 (2005); Median household income: $70,486 (2005); Average household income: $79,296 (2005); Percent of households with income of $100,000 or more: 28.9% (2005); Poverty rate: 2.9% (2000).
Education: Percent of population age 25 and over with: High school diploma (including GED) or higher: 85.6% (2005); Bachelor's degree or higher: 23.2% (2005); Master's degree or higher: 7.4% (2005).
Housing: Homeownership rate: 75.5% (2005); Median home value: $311,765 (2005); Median rent: $781 per month (2000); Median age of housing: 48 years (2000).
Safety: Violent crime rate: 5.4 per 10,000 population; Property crime rate: 179.9 per 10,000 population (2004).
Transportation: Commute to work: 89.7% car, 5.2% public transportation, 1.5% walk, 3.3% work from home (2000); Travel time to work: 32.7% less than 15 minutes, 35.7% 15 to 30 minutes, 14.1% 30 to 45 minutes, 4.7% 45 to 60 minutes, 12.8% 60 minutes or more (2000)
Additional Information Contacts

ROCKLEIGH (borough). Covers a land area of 0.972 square miles and a water area of 0 square miles. Located at 41.00° N. Lat.; 73.93° W. Long. Elevation is 50 feet.
Population: 270 (1990); 391 (2000); 407 (2005); 416 (2010 projected); Race: 88.0% White, 3.9% Black, 4.4% Asian, 6.9% Hispanic of any race (2005); Density: 418.6 persons per square mile (2005); Average household size: 5.22 (2005); Median age: 53.3 (2005); Males per 100 females: 95.7 (2005); Marriage status: 21.5% never married, 52.6% now married, 19.1% widowed, 6.8% divorced (2000); Foreign born: 20.1% (2000); Ancestry (includes multiple ancestries): 22.6% Other groups, 20.6% Irish, 16.5% Italian, 13.3% German, 4.3% Polish (2000).
Economy: Single-family building permits issued: 0 (2005); Multi-family building permits issued: 0 (2005); Employment by occupation: 30.7% management, 28.9% professional, 7.9% services, 26.3% sales, 1.8% farming, 2.6% construction, 1.8% production (2000).
Income: Per capita income: $52,290 (2005); Median household income: $160,000 (2005); Average household income: $200,929 (2005); Percent of households with income of $100,000 or more: 64.1% (2005); Poverty rate: 23.1% (2000).
Education: Percent of population age 25 and over with: High school diploma (including GED) or higher: 78.5% (2005); Bachelor's degree or higher: 28.7% (2005); Master's degree or higher: 12.5% (2005).

Housing: Homeownership rate: 85.9% (2005); Median home value: $1 million+ (2005); Median rent: $2,000+ per month (2000); Median age of housing: 60+ years (2000).
Safety: Violent crime rate: 150.4 per 10,000 population; Property crime rate: 100.3 per 10,000 population (2004).
Transportation: Commute to work: 81.7% car, 3.7% public transportation, 7.3% walk, 1.8% work from home (2000); Travel time to work: 31.8% less than 15 minutes, 20.6% 15 to 30 minutes, 27.1% 30 to 45 minutes, 7.5% 45 to 60 minutes, 13.1% 60 minutes or more (2000)

RUTHERFORD (borough). Covers a land area of 2.807 square miles and a water area of 0.116 square miles. Located at 40.82° N. Lat.; 74.11° W. Long. Elevation is 100 feet.
Population: 17,790 (1990); 18,110 (2000); 17,998 (2005); 17,946 (2010 projected); Race: 79.4% White, 2.6% Black, 13.4% Asian, 10.6% Hispanic of any race (2005); Density: 6,411.8 persons per square mile (2005); Average household size: 2.54 (2005); Median age: 40.5 (2005); Males per 100 females: 93.1 (2005); Marriage status: 29.7% never married, 55.3% now married, 8.2% widowed, 6.8% divorced (2000); Foreign born: 20.1% (2000); Ancestry (includes multiple ancestries): 25.9% Italian, 24.0% Other groups, 23.3% Irish, 11.9% German, 8.4% Polish (2000).
Economy: Clothing, chemicals, metal products. Includes Carlton Hill, manufacturing village. Site of the Meadowlands Sports Complex, operated by the N.J. Sports and Exposition Authority. Created 1971, the complex includes the Meadowlands Racetrack, Giants Stadium, and Continental Airlines Meadowlands Arena, on a 750-acre tract. Single-family building permits issued: 13 (2005); Multi-family building permits issued: 4 (2005); Employment by occupation: 17.6% management, 27.2% professional, 10.5% services, 30.3% sales, 0.0% farming, 6.4% construction, 8.0% production (2000).
Income: Per capita income: $36,995 (2005); Median household income: $74,871 (2005); Average household income: $93,629 (2005); Percent of households with income of $100,000 or more: 34.6% (2005); Poverty rate: 3.7% (2000).
Taxes: Total city taxes per capita: $812 (2004); City property taxes per capita: $773 (2004).
Education: Percent of population age 25 and over with: High school diploma (including GED) or higher: 88.4% (2005); Bachelor's degree or higher: 40.4% (2005); Master's degree or higher: 14.0% (2005).
Housing: Homeownership rate: 65.3% (2005); Median home value: $349,003 (2005); Median rent: $780 per month (2000); Median age of housing: 58 years (2000).
Safety: Violent crime rate: 6.1 per 10,000 population; Property crime rate: 181.3 per 10,000 population (2004).
Newspapers: The South Bergenite (General - Circulation 35,537)
Transportation: Commute to work: 75.6% car, 16.9% public transportation, 4.2% walk, 3.0% work from home (2000); Travel time to work: 25.4% less than 15 minutes, 28.7% 15 to 30 minutes, 19.3% 30 to 45 minutes, 10.7% 45 to 60 minutes, 15.8% 60 minutes or more (2000)
Additional Information Contacts

SADDLE BROOK (township). Aka Saddle Brook CDP. Covers a land area of 2.723 square miles and a water area of 0.008 square miles. Located at 40.90° N. Lat.; 74.09° W. Long. Elevation is 50 feet.
History: Named for a local brook. Incorporated 1798.
Population: 13,296 (1990); 13,155 (2000); 13,144 (2005); 13,193 (2010 projected); Race: 88.8% White, 1.6% Black, 5.7% Asian, 8.0% Hispanic of any race (2005); Density: 4,826.7 persons per square mile (2005); Average household size: 2.55 (2005); Median age: 41.8 (2005); Males per 100 females: 90.2 (2005); Marriage status: 25.8% never married, 59.1% now married, 8.2% widowed, 6.9% divorced (2000); Foreign born: 16.1% (2000); Ancestry (includes multiple ancestries): 35.7% Italian, 15.7% Irish, 13.3% Other groups, 13.1% Polish, 11.0% German (2000).
Economy: Single-family building permits issued: 105 (2005); Multi-family building permits issued: 44 (2005); Employment by occupation: 15.2%

management, 20.3% professional, 10.8% services, 33.2% sales, 0.0% farming, 9.2% construction, 11.4% production (2000).

Income: Per capita income: $33,028 (2005); Median household income: $73,201 (2005); Average household income: $83,749 (2005); Percent of households with income of $100,000 or more: 30.1% (2005); Poverty rate: 3.3% (2000).

Education: Percent of population age 25 and over with: High school diploma (including GED) or higher: 85.1% (2005); Bachelor's degree or higher: 25.5% (2005); Master's degree or higher: 6.3% (2005).

School District(s)
Saddle Brook Township (PK-12)
   2003-04 Enrollment: 1,763 . . . . (201) 843-2133

Two-year College(s)
Helma Institute of Massage Therapy
   Fall 2004 Enrollment: 32 . . . . (201) 226-0056

Housing: Homeownership rate: 74.1% (2005); Median home value: $328,770 (2005); Median rent: $838 per month (2000); Median age of housing: 46 years (2000).

Safety: Violent crime rate: 12.8 per 10,000 population; Property crime rate: 357.4 per 10,000 population (2004).

Transportation: Commute to work: 93.5% car, 4.0% public transportation, 1.8% walk, 0.6% work from home (2000); Travel time to work: 32.3% less than 15 minutes, 41.1% 15 to 30 minutes, 15.2% 30 to 45 minutes, 4.0% 45 to 60 minutes, 7.4% 60 minutes or more (2000)

SADDLE RIVER
SADDLE RIVER (borough). Covers a land area of 4.982 square miles and a water area of 0 square miles. Located at 41.02° N. Lat.; 74.09° W. Long. Elevation is 143 feet.

Population: 2,952 (1990); 3,201 (2000); 3,846 (2005); 4,414 (2010 projected); Race: 88.0% White, 0.9% Black, 8.4% Asian, 3.0% Hispanic of any race (2005); Density: 772.0 persons per square mile (2005); Average household size: 2.81 (2005); Median age: 48.7 (2005); Males per 100 females: 93.4 (2005); Marriage status: 18.3% never married, 69.7% now married, 8.6% widowed, 3.4% divorced (2000); Foreign born: 17.6% (2000); Ancestry (includes multiple ancestries): 23.8% Italian, 17.8% Irish, 13.7% Other groups, 12.7% German, 6.8% English (2000).

Economy: Paper products. Single-family building permits issued: 17 (2005); Multi-family building permits issued: 0 (2005); Employment by occupation: 30.9% management, 33.9% professional, 5.3% services, 23.4% sales, 0.0% farming, 2.5% construction, 4.1% production (2000).

Income: Per capita income: $72,045 (2005); Median household income: $141,364 (2005); Average household income: $199,695 (2005); Percent of households with income of $100,000 or more: 63.3% (2005); Poverty rate: 3.6% (2000).

Education: Percent of population age 25 and over with: High school diploma (including GED) or higher: 93.7% (2005); Bachelor's degree or higher: 60.6% (2005); Master's degree or higher: 31.8% (2005).

School District(s)
Saddle River Borough (PK-08)
   2003-04 Enrollment: 196 . . . . (201) 327-0727

Housing: Homeownership rate: 91.4% (2005); Median home value: $1 million+ (2005); Median rent: $1,145 per month (2000); Median age of housing: 31 years (2000).

Safety: Violent crime rate: 5.4 per 10,000 population; Property crime rate: 75.4 per 10,000 population (2004).

Transportation: Commute to work: 83.4% car, 5.5% public transportation, 0.0% walk, 10.6% work from home (2000); Travel time to work: 24.2% less than 15 minutes, 29.9% 15 to 30 minutes, 19.0% 30 to 45 minutes, 7.2% 45 to 60 minutes, 19.8% 60 minutes or more (2000)

SOUTH HACKENSACK
SOUTH HACKENSACK (township). Covers a land area of 0.711 square miles and a water area of 0.020 square miles. Located at 40.86° N. Lat.; 74.04° W. Long. Elevation is 11 feet.

Population: 2,106 (1990); 2,249 (2000); 2,348 (2005); 2,446 (2010 projected); Race: 79.0% White, 2.3% Black, 6.9% Asian, 18.8% Hispanic of any race (2005); Density: 3,300.3 persons per square mile (2005); Average household size: 2.75 (2005); Median age: 39.2 (2005); Males per 100 females: 93.9 (2005); Marriage status: 22.1% never married, 61.6% now married, 9.6% widowed, 6.7% divorced (2000); Foreign born: 27.2% (2000); Ancestry (includes multiple ancestries): 40.2% Italian, 29.4% Other groups, 10.9% German, 9.9% Irish, 2.9% United States or American (2000).

Economy: Single-family building permits issued: 0 (2005); Multi-family building permits issued: 2 (2005); Employment by occupation: 15.6%

management, 11.6% professional, 9.1% services, 37.6% sales, 0.0% farming, 12.8% construction, 13.3% production (2000).

Income: Per capita income: $33,860 (2005); Median household income: $72,668 (2005); Average household income: $92,985 (2005); Percent of households with income of $100,000 or more: 31.7% (2005); Poverty rate: 7.1% (2000).

Education: Percent of population age 25 and over with: High school diploma (including GED) or higher: 75.9% (2005); Bachelor's degree or higher: 13.8% (2005); Master's degree or higher: 4.4% (2005).

School District(s)
South Hackensack Township (PK-08)
   2003-04 Enrollment: 247 . . . . (201) 440-2783

Housing: Homeownership rate: 55.8% (2005); Median home value: $347,596 (2005); Median rent: $882 per month (2000); Median age of housing: 40 years (2000).

Safety: Violent crime rate: 60.4 per 10,000 population; Property crime rate: 280.5 per 10,000 population (2004).

Transportation: Commute to work: 89.3% car, 1.5% public transportation, 6.2% walk, 1.6% work from home (2000); Travel time to work: 45.8% less than 15 minutes, 33.0% 15 to 30 minutes, 9.5% 30 to 45 minutes, 6.8% 45 to 60 minutes, 5.0% 60 minutes or more (2000)

TEANECK
TEANECK (township). Aka Teaneck CDP. Covers a land area of 6.053 square miles and a water area of 0.198 square miles. Located at 40.89° N. Lat.; 74.01° W. Long. Elevation is 92 feet.

History: Named for Teneyck, or Ten Eyck, a local Dutch family name. Developed after the construction of the George Washington Bridge (1931), which connects New Jersey with New York city. Fairleigh Dickinson University has a campus here. The city has several 18th-century homes. Settled in the early 1600s. Incorporated 1895.

Population: 37,825 (1990); 39,260 (2000); 40,406 (2005); 41,593 (2010 projected); Race: 52.4% White, 30.1% Black, 7.9% Asian, 12.9% Hispanic of any race (2005); Density: 6,675.5 persons per square mile (2005); Average household size: 2.94 (2005); Median age: 38.9 (2005); Males per 100 females: 90.6 (2005); Marriage status: 26.1% never married, 59.5% now married, 7.6% widowed, 6.8% divorced (2000); Foreign born: 24.0% (2000); Ancestry (includes multiple ancestries): 43.0% Other groups, 6.2% Italian, 6.0% German, 5.3% Russian, 5.1% Irish (2000).

Economy: Manufacturing includes jewelry, electrical equipment, food seasonings. Unemployment rate: 3.5% (2005); Total civilian labor force: 20,460 (2005); Single-family building permits issued: 9 (2005); Multi-family building permits issued: 85 (2005); Employment by occupation: 20.0% management, 33.2% professional, 9.4% services, 26.8% sales, 0.0% farming, 4.2% construction, 6.4% production (2000).

Income: Per capita income: $37,230 (2005); Median household income: $82,927 (2005); Average household income: $108,402 (2005); Percent of households with income of $100,000 or more: 38.9% (2005); Poverty rate: 4.2% (2000).

Taxes: Total city taxes per capita: $932 (2004); City property taxes per capita: $896 (2004).

Education: Percent of population age 25 and over with: High school diploma (including GED) or higher: 89.5% (2005); Bachelor's degree or higher: 47.2% (2005); Master's degree or higher: 22.6% (2005).

School District(s)
Agency - Teaneck Community CS (KG-08)
   2003-04 Enrollment: 211 . . . . (201) 833-9600
Teaneck Township (PK-12)
   2003-04 Enrollment: 4,512 . . . . (201) 833-5510

Four-year College(s)
Fairleigh Dickinson University-Metropolitan Campus (Private, Not-for-profit)
   Fall 2004 Enrollment: 7,634 . . . . (201) 692-2000
   2005-06 Tuition: In-state $22,604; Out-of-state $22,604

Two-year College(s)
Holy Name Hospital School of Nursing (Private, Not-for-profit, Roman Catholic)
   Fall 2004 Enrollment: 152 . . . . (201) 833-3005
   2005-06 Tuition: In-state $12,340; Out-of-state $12,340

Housing: Homeownership rate: 76.8% (2005); Median home value: $336,536 (2005); Median rent: $818 per month (2000); Median age of housing: 54 years (2000).

Hospitals: Holy Name Hospital (361 beds)

Safety: Violent crime rate: 18.7 per 10,000 population; Property crime rate: 186.1 per 10,000 population (2004).

Newspapers: Jewish Community News (Jewish - Circulation 15,000); Jewish Standard (General, Jewish, Religious - Circulation 25,000); The Connection Newspaper (Black, General - Circulation 41,000)
Transportation: Commute to work: 77.7% car, 15.6% public transportation, 2.4% walk, 3.7% work from home (2000); Travel time to work: 22.6% less than 15 minutes, 27.0% 15 to 30 minutes, 20.7% 30 to 45 minutes, 12.2% 45 to 60 minutes, 17.4% 60 minutes or more (2000)
Additional Information Contacts
Teaneck Township.............................. (201) 837-4811
    http://www.teanecknjgov.org

TENAFLY (borough). Covers a land area of 4.612 square miles and a water area of 0.583 square miles. Located at 40.92° N. Lat.; 73.96° W. Long. Elevation is 52 feet.
History: Named for the Dutch translation of "garden valley". Incorporated 1894.
Population: 13,326 (1990); 13,806 (2000); 14,287 (2005); 14,776 (2010 projected); Race: 73.5% White, 1.0% Black, 21.6% Asian, 5.5% Hispanic of any race (2005); Density: 3,097.7 persons per square mile (2005); Average household size: 2.93 (2005); Median age: 41.4 (2005); Males per 100 females: 93.3 (2005); Marriage status: 22.3% never married, 65.0% now married, 6.8% widowed, 5.9% divorced (2000); Foreign born: 28.6% (2000); Ancestry (includes multiple ancestries): 29.5% Other groups, 11.1% Irish, 8.7% Russian, 8.6% Italian, 7.9% United States or American (2000).
Economy: Single-family building permits issued: 35 (2005); Multi-family building permits issued: 14 (2005); Employment by occupation: 22.5% management, 35.9% professional, 7.7% services, 26.1% sales, 0.1% farming, 2.7% construction, 5.0% production (2000).
Income: Per capita income: $56,818 (2005); Median household income: $106,852 (2005); Average household income: $165,530 (2005); Percent of households with income of $100,000 or more: 52.4% (2005); Poverty rate: 5.2% (2000).
Education: Percent of population age 25 and over with: High school diploma (including GED) or higher: 93.0% (2005); Bachelor's degree or higher: 61.6% (2005); Master's degree or higher: 33.0% (2005).
School District(s)
Tenafly Borough (PK-12)
    2003-04 Enrollment: 3,128 .... (201) 816-4501
Housing: Homeownership rate: 80.3% (2005); Median home value: $634,814 (2005); Median rent: $1,064 per month (2000); Median age of housing: 50 years (2000).
Safety: Violent crime rate: 5.6 per 10,000 population; Property crime rate: 84.5 per 10,000 population (2004).
Transportation: Commute to work: 80.1% car, 10.5% public transportation, 2.7% walk, 6.3% work from home (2000); Travel time to work: 22.1% less than 15 minutes, 24.2% 15 to 30 minutes, 19.1% 30 to 45 minutes, 12.3% 45 to 60 minutes, 22.4% 60 minutes or more (2000)
Additional Information Contacts
Borough of Tenafly................................ (201) 568-6100
    http://www.tenaflynj.org
Tenafly Chamber of Commerce...................... (201) 871-3504
    http://www.tenaflynj.org

TETERBORO (borough). Covers a land area of 1.112 square miles and a water area of 0 square miles. Located at 40.85° N. Lat.; 74.06° W. Long. Elevation is 5 feet.
History: Named Bendix 1937, renamed Teterboro 1943.
Population: 22 (1990); 18 (2000); 18 (2005); 18 (2010 projected); Race: 77.8% White, 0.0% Black, 0.0% Asian, 0.0% Hispanic of any race (2005); Density: 16.2 persons per square mile (2005); Average household size: 2.57 (2005); Median age: 31.7 (2005); Males per 100 females: 100.0 (2005); Marriage status: 37.5% never married, 12.5% now married, 0.0% widowed, 50.0% divorced (2000); Foreign born: 0.0% (2000); Ancestry (includes multiple ancestries): 68.8% Italian, 43.8% Irish, 18.8% German, 12.5% Russian (2000).
Economy: Makes aircraft parts and general aviation equipment; large freight airport here is administered by Port of New York Authority. Single-family building permits issued: 0 (2005); Multi-family building permits issued: 0 (2005); Employment by occupation: 23.1% management, 0.0% professional, 0.0% services, 46.2% sales, 0.0% farming, 30.8% construction, 0.0% production (2000).
Income: Per capita income: $74,306 (2005); Median household income: $70,833 (2005); Average household income: $191,071 (2005); Percent of

households with income of $100,000 or more: 42.9% (2005); Poverty rate: 0.0% (2000).
Education: Percent of population age 25 and over with: High school diploma (including GED) or higher: 100.0% (2005); Bachelor's degree or higher: 54.5% (2005); Master's degree or higher: 0.0% (2005).
School District(s)
Bergen County Vocational (09-12)
    2003-04 Enrollment: 2,331 .... (201) 967-2472
Two-year College(s)
Teterboro School of Aeronautics (Private, For-profit)
    Fall 2004 Enrollment: 122 .... (201) 288-6300
Housing: Homeownership rate: 0.0% (2005); Median home value: $n/a (2005); Median rent: $675 per month (2000); Median age of housing: 40 years (2000).
Safety: Violent crime rate: 1,111.1 per 10,000 population; Property crime rate: 11,111.1 per 10,000 population (2004).
Transportation: Commute to work: 100.0% car, 0.0% public transportation, 0.0% walk, 0.0% work from home (2000); Travel time to work: 23.1% less than 15 minutes, 30.8% 15 to 30 minutes, 0.0% 30 to 45 minutes, 0.0% 45 to 60 minutes, 46.2% 60 minutes or more (2000)

UPPER SADDLE RIVER (borough). Covers a land area of 5.292 square miles and a water area of 0.004 square miles. Located at 41.06° N. Lat.; 74.10° W. Long. Elevation is 220 feet.
Population: 7,204 (1990); 7,741 (2000); 8,508 (2005); 9,227 (2010 projected); Race: 90.1% White, 1.0% Black, 7.2% Asian, 2.4% Hispanic of any race (2005); Density: 1,607.6 persons per square mile (2005); Average household size: 3.11 (2005); Median age: 40.7 (2005); Males per 100 females: 96.7 (2005); Marriage status: 16.2% never married, 74.9% now married, 4.8% widowed, 4.1% divorced (2000); Foreign born: 12.1% (2000); Ancestry (includes multiple ancestries): 23.0% Italian, 17.8% Irish, 12.2% German, 12.0% Other groups, 10.1% English (2000).
Economy: Single-family building permits issued: 26 (2005); Multi-family building permits issued: 0 (2005); Employment by occupation: 32.0% management, 28.9% professional, 3.6% services, 29.2% sales, 0.0% farming, 3.8% construction, 2.5% production (2000).
Income: Per capita income: $66,505 (2005); Median household income: $142,171 (2005); Average household income: $205,969 (2005); Percent of households with income of $100,000 or more: 67.3% (2005); Poverty rate: 0.7% (2000).
Education: Percent of population age 25 and over with: High school diploma (including GED) or higher: 96.6% (2005); Bachelor's degree or higher: 59.8% (2005); Master's degree or higher: 25.6% (2005).
School District(s)
Upper Saddle River Borough (PK-08)
    2003-04 Enrollment: 1,379 .... (201) 934-2950
Housing: Homeownership rate: 96.8% (2005); Median home value: $930,019 (2005); Median rent: $1,717 per month (2000); Median age of housing: 35 years (2000).
Safety: Violent crime rate: 2.4 per 10,000 population; Property crime rate: 54.2 per 10,000 population (2004).
Transportation: Commute to work: 82.4% car, 9.2% public transportation, 1.0% walk, 7.0% work from home (2000); Travel time to work: 20.4% less than 15 minutes, 28.6% 15 to 30 minutes, 18.5% 30 to 45 minutes, 9.4% 45 to 60 minutes, 23.1% 60 minutes or more (2000)

WALDWICK (borough). Covers a land area of 2.084 square miles and a water area of 0.008 square miles. Located at 41.01° N. Lat.; 74.12° W. Long. Elevation is 228 feet.
History: Incorporated 1919.
Population: 9,720 (1990); 9,622 (2000); 9,650 (2005); 9,698 (2010 projected); Race: 92.1% White, 0.6% Black, 4.6% Asian, 6.5% Hispanic of any race (2005); Density: 4,629.7 persons per square mile (2005); Average household size: 2.76 (2005); Median age: 39.5 (2005); Males per 100 females: 95.1 (2005); Marriage status: 21.3% never married, 65.1% now married, 7.5% widowed, 6.2% divorced (2000); Foreign born: 12.3% (2000); Ancestry (includes multiple ancestries): 31.9% Italian, 26.4% Irish, 17.4% German, 11.7% Other groups, 6.7% Polish (2000).
Economy: Single-family building permits issued: 15 (2005); Multi-family building permits issued: 0 (2005); Employment by occupation: 19.9% management, 23.3% professional, 12.5% services, 30.5% sales, 0.0% farming, 7.7% construction, 6.1% production (2000).
Income: Per capita income: $37,579 (2005); Median household income: $88,149 (2005); Average household income: $103,424 (2005); Percent of

households with income of $100,000 or more: 41.7% (2005); Poverty rate: 2.1% (2000).

Education: Percent of population age 25 and over with: High school diploma (including GED) or higher: 92.2% (2005); Bachelor's degree or higher: 36.6% (2005); Master's degree or higher: 9.8% (2005).

School District(s)

Waldwick Borough (PK-12)
   2003-04 Enrollment: 1,512 . . . . (201) 445-3131

Housing: Homeownership rate: 89.3% (2005); Median home value: $370,274 (2005); Median rent: $970 per month (2000); Median age of housing: 44 years (2000).

Safety: Violent crime rate: 5.2 per 10,000 population; Property crime rate: 76.3 per 10,000 population (2004).

Transportation: Commute to work: 89.3% car, 6.0% public transportation, 1.8% walk, 2.9% work from home (2000); Travel time to work: 30.7% less than 15 minutes, 31.3% 15 to 30 minutes, 19.4% 30 to 45 minutes, 7.9% 45 to 60 minutes, 10.7% 60 minutes or more (2000)

Additional Information Contacts

Borough of Waldwick . . . . (201) 652-5300
   http://www.waldwickpd.org

WALLINGTON (borough).
Covers a land area of 0.996 square miles and a water area of 0.042 square miles. Located at 40.85° N. Lat.; 74.10° W. Long. Elevation is 30 feet.

History: Named for George Walling, an early settler and landowner. Incorporated 1895.

Population: 10,828 (1990); 11,583 (2000); 11,497 (2005); 11,419 (2010 projected); Race: 85.0% White, 2.8% Black, 6.3% Asian, 8.3% Hispanic of any race (2005); Density: 11,546.1 persons per square mile (2005); Average household size: 2.46 (2005); Median age: 39.9 (2005); Males per 100 females: 93.8 (2005); Marriage status: 29.2% never married, 55.3% now married, 8.0% widowed, 7.5% divorced (2000); Foreign born: 40.9% (2000); Ancestry (includes multiple ancestries): 51.5% Polish, 15.0% Italian, 13.5% Other groups, 7.1% Irish, 5.0% German (2000).

Economy: Manufacturing includes paint, pens, medical equipment, dairy products and plastics. Single-family building permits issued: 2 (2005); Multi-family building permits issued: 2 (2005); Employment by occupation: 9.6% management, 16.6% professional, 13.3% services, 29.0% sales, 0.0% farming, 12.5% construction, 19.0% production (2000).

Income: Per capita income: $27,648 (2005); Median household income: $53,791 (2005); Average household income: $67,870 (2005); Percent of households with income of $100,000 or more: 18.9% (2005); Poverty rate: 6.3% (2000).

Education: Percent of population age 25 and over with: High school diploma (including GED) or higher: 72.5% (2005); Bachelor's degree or higher: 17.4% (2005); Master's degree or higher: 6.4% (2005).

School District(s)

Wallington Borough (PK-12)
   2003-04 Enrollment: 1,172 . . . . (973) 777-4421

Housing: Homeownership rate: 40.7% (2005); Median home value: $327,458 (2005); Median rent: $691 per month (2000); Median age of housing: 47 years (2000).

Safety: Violent crime rate: 12.9 per 10,000 population; Property crime rate: 173.2 per 10,000 population (2004).

Transportation: Commute to work: 89.2% car, 5.3% public transportation, 2.9% walk, 1.2% work from home (2000); Travel time to work: 26.2% less than 15 minutes, 37.2% 15 to 30 minutes, 21.9% 30 to 45 minutes, 6.9% 45 to 60 minutes, 7.7% 60 minutes or more (2000)

WASHINGTON (township).
Aka Washington Township CDP. Covers a land area of 2.910 square miles and a water area of 0.046 square miles. Located at 40.99° N. Lat.; 74.06° W. Long.

Population: 9,353 (1990); 8,938 (2000); 9,770 (2005); 10,552 (2010 projected); Race: 91.8% White, 1.1% Black, 5.6% Asian, 3.9% Hispanic of any race (2005); Density: 3,357.0 persons per square mile (2005); Average household size: 2.73 (2005); Median age: 43.1 (2005); Males per 100 females: 92.9 (2005); Marriage status: 18.2% never married, 70.4% now married, 7.2% widowed, 4.2% divorced (2000); Foreign born: 14.2% (2000); Ancestry (includes multiple ancestries): 29.2% Italian, 22.0% Irish, 19.2% German, 12.1% Other groups, 4.6% English (2000).

Economy: Single-family building permits issued: 25 (2005); Multi-family building permits issued: 0 (2005); Employment by occupation: 24.6% management, 26.4% professional, 8.5% services, 31.5% sales, 0.0% farming, 5.7% construction, 3.3% production (2000).

Income: Per capita income: $45,849 (2005); Median household income: $97,079 (2005); Average household income: $124,862 (2005); Percent of households with income of $100,000 or more: 48.2% (2005); Poverty rate: 2.4% (2000).

Education: Percent of population age 25 and over with: High school diploma (including GED) or higher: 94.0% (2005); Bachelor's degree or higher: 44.8% (2005); Master's degree or higher: 16.7% (2005).

Housing: Homeownership rate: 96.0% (2005); Median home value: $468,661 (2005); Median rent: $1,715 per month (2000); Median age of housing: 39 years (2000).

Safety: Violent crime rate: 1.0 per 10,000 population; Property crime rate: 41.8 per 10,000 population (2004).

Transportation: Commute to work: 88.7% car, 5.5% public transportation, 0.8% walk, 4.5% work from home (2000); Travel time to work: 23.3% less than 15 minutes, 35.5% 15 to 30 minutes, 20.0% 30 to 45 minutes, 8.5% 45 to 60 minutes, 12.6% 60 minutes or more (2000)

WESTWOOD (borough).
Covers a land area of 2.318 square miles and a water area of 0.004 square miles. Located at 40.98° N. Lat.; 74.03° W. Long. Elevation is 75 feet.

History: Named to promote the town as a pleasant place to live. Incorporated 1894.

Population: 10,446 (1990); 10,999 (2000); 11,015 (2005); 11,048 (2010 projected); Race: 85.5% White, 5.4% Black, 5.0% Asian, 7.8% Hispanic of any race (2005); Density: 4,751.9 persons per square mile (2005); Average household size: 2.41 (2005); Median age: 40.2 (2005); Males per 100 females: 91.5 (2005); Marriage status: 22.2% never married, 59.1% now married, 9.7% widowed, 9.0% divorced (2000); Foreign born: 15.3% (2000); Ancestry (includes multiple ancestries): 24.6% Italian, 20.6% Irish, 17.6% German, 16.7% Other groups, 7.1% English (2000).

Economy: Some light manufacturing. Single-family building permits issued: 7 (2005); Multi-family building permits issued: 0 (2005); Employment by occupation: 19.9% management, 22.6% professional, 14.6% services, 29.2% sales, 0.0% farming, 6.5% construction, 7.3% production (2000).

Income: Per capita income: $37,689 (2005); Median household income: $70,005 (2005); Average household income: $90,027 (2005); Percent of households with income of $100,000 or more: 32.1% (2005); Poverty rate: 4.4% (2000).

Education: Percent of population age 25 and over with: High school diploma (including GED) or higher: 88.0% (2005); Bachelor's degree or higher: 37.4% (2005); Master's degree or higher: 11.7% (2005).

School District(s)

Westwood Regional (PK-12)
   2003-04 Enrollment: 2,663 . . . . (201) 664-2765

Housing: Homeownership rate: 61.5% (2005); Median home value: $378,565 (2005); Median rent: $921 per month (2000); Median age of housing: 45 years (2000).

Hospitals: Pascack Valley Hospital (291 beds)

Safety: Violent crime rate: 9.0 per 10,000 population; Property crime rate: 108.2 per 10,000 population (2004).

Newspapers: America Oggi (Circulation 65,000); Pascack Valley Community Life (General - Circulation 25,000)

Transportation: Commute to work: 82.5% car, 8.8% public transportation, 4.6% walk, 2.9% work from home (2000); Travel time to work: 28.9% less than 15 minutes, 34.2% 15 to 30 minutes, 15.6% 30 to 45 minutes, 7.8% 45 to 60 minutes, 13.5% 60 minutes or more (2000)

Additional Information Contacts

Bergen County Chamber of Commerce. . . . . (201) 498-9180
   http://www.co.bergen.nj.us

WOOD-RIDGE (borough).
Covers a land area of 1.099 square miles and a water area of 0 square miles. Located at 40.84° N. Lat.; 74.08° W. Long. Elevation is 170 feet.

History: Settled before the Revolution, incorporated 1894.

Population: 7,506 (1990); 7,644 (2000); 7,594 (2005); 7,580 (2010 projected); Race: 89.2% White, 0.9% Black, 6.1% Asian, 9.3% Hispanic of any race (2005); Density: 6,913.0 persons per square mile (2005); Average household size: 2.50 (2005); Median age: 41.9 (2005); Males per 100 females: 91.5 (2005); Marriage status: 22.9% never married, 62.7% now married, 8.2% widowed, 6.1% divorced (2000); Foreign born: 15.2% (2000); Ancestry (includes multiple ancestries): 40.3% Italian, 24.6% Irish, 16.5% German, 15.5% Other groups, 9.4% Polish (2000).

Economy: Manufacturing of ceramics, electric lamps; printing. Single-family building permits issued: 5 (2005); Multi-family building permits

issued: 2 (2005); Employment by occupation: 17.5% management, 22.0% professional, 9.5% services, 31.0% sales, 0.0% farming, 8.5% construction, 11.4% production (2000).
Income: Per capita income: $34,621 (2005); Median household income: $72,034 (2005); Average household income: $85,046 (2005); Percent of households with income of $100,000 or more: 31.5% (2005); Poverty rate: 1.6% (2000).
Education: Percent of population age 25 and over with: High school diploma (including GED) or higher: 84.4% (2005); Bachelor's degree or higher: 27.7% (2005); Master's degree or higher: 6.4% (2005).

School District(s)
Wood-Ridge Borough (PK-12)
   2003-04 Enrollment: 1,056 . . . . (201) 933-6778
Housing: Homeownership rate: 76.6% (2005); Median home value: $315,553 (2005); Median rent: $875 per month (2000); Median age of housing: 51 years (2000).
Safety: Violent crime rate: 6.5 per 10,000 population; Property crime rate: 70.4 per 10,000 population (2004).
Newspapers: Wood Ridge Independent (General - Circulation 1,425)
Transportation: Commute to work: 92.2% car, 5.8% public transportation, 1.1% walk, 0.7% work from home (2000); Travel time to work: 26.9% less than 15 minutes, 38.1% 15 to 30 minutes, 20.9% 30 to 45 minutes, 6.8% 45 to 60 minutes, 7.3% 60 minutes or more (2000)
Additional Information Contacts
Borough of Wood-Ridge . . . . (201) 939-0202
   http://www.wood-ridgenj.org

WOODCLIFF LAKE (borough). Covers a land area of 3.330 square miles and a water area of 0.208 square miles. Located at 41.02° N. Lat.; 74.05° W. Long. Elevation is 249 feet.
History: Incorporated 1910.
Population: 5,303 (1990); 5,745 (2000); 5,879 (2005); 6,034 (2010 projected); Race: 93.8% White, 0.9% Black, 4.4% Asian, 3.0% Hispanic of any race (2005); Density: 1,765.5 persons per square mile (2005); Average household size: 3.11 (2005); Median age: 41.1 (2005); Males per 100 females: 92.5 (2005); Marriage status: 16.9% never married, 74.7% now married, 4.9% widowed, 3.5% divorced (2000); Foreign born: 10.1% (2000); Ancestry (includes multiple ancestries): 23.0% Italian, 12.9% Irish, 12.9% Other groups, 11.8% German, 9.2% United States or American (2000).
Economy: Single-family building permits issued: 35 (2005); Multi-family building permits issued: 0 (2005); Employment by occupation: 27.0% management, 30.6% professional, 5.2% services, 30.5% sales, 0.0% farming, 3.6% construction, 3.1% production (2000).
Income: Per capita income: $62,294 (2005); Median household income: $143,306 (2005); Average household income: $193,106 (2005); Percent of households with income of $100,000 or more: 64.2% (2005); Poverty rate: 1.5% (2000).
Education: Percent of population age 25 and over with: High school diploma (including GED) or higher: 96.1% (2005); Bachelor's degree or higher: 58.6% (2005); Master's degree or higher: 27.0% (2005).

School District(s)
Woodcliff Lake Borough (PK-08)
   2003-04 Enrollment: 893 . . . . (201) 391-6570
Housing: Homeownership rate: 95.2% (2005); Median home value: $735,659 (2005); Median rent: $1,134 per month (2000); Median age of housing: 36 years (2000).
Safety: Violent crime rate: 5.1 per 10,000 population; Property crime rate: 74.7 per 10,000 population (2004).
Transportation: Commute to work: 83.6% car, 7.4% public transportation, 1.8% walk, 7.3% work from home (2000); Travel time to work: 19.5% less than 15 minutes, 34.5% 15 to 30 minutes, 17.9% 30 to 45 minutes, 11.6% 45 to 60 minutes, 16.6% 60 minutes or more (2000)
Additional Information Contacts
Borough of Woodcliff Lake. . . . . (201) 391-4977
   http://www.wclnj.com

WYCKOFF (township). Aka Wyckoff CDP. Covers a land area of 6.547 square miles and a water area of 0.024 square miles. Located at 40.99° N. Lat.; 74.16° W. Long. Elevation is 355 feet.
History: Named for Wicaugh, in England. Incorporated 1798.
Population: 15,253 (1990); 16,508 (2000); 17,200 (2005); 17,880 (2010 projected); Race: 93.8% White, 0.5% Black, 4.1% Asian, 2.8% Hispanic of any race (2005); Density: 2,627.3 persons per square mile (2005); Average household size: 2.97 (2005); Median age: 41.4 (2005); Males per 100

females: 91.8 (2005); Marriage status: 17.9% never married, 70.6% now married, 8.0% widowed, 3.5% divorced (2000); Foreign born: 9.3% (2000); Ancestry (includes multiple ancestries): 24.1% Irish, 22.9% Italian, 13.8% German, 10.4% English, 10.0% Other groups (2000).
Economy: Manufacturing of baked goods. Single-family building permits issued: 25 (2005); Multi-family building permits issued: 0 (2005); Employment by occupation: 29.3% management, 27.0% professional, 6.2% services, 28.7% sales, 0.1% farming, 3.9% construction, 4.9% production (2000).
Income: Per capita income: $56,042 (2005); Median household income: $119,675 (2005); Average household income: $165,105 (2005); Percent of households with income of $100,000 or more: 57.2% (2005); Poverty rate: 1.8% (2000).
Education: Percent of population age 25 and over with: High school diploma (including GED) or higher: 93.8% (2005); Bachelor's degree or higher: 56.5% (2005); Master's degree or higher: 23.0% (2005).

School District(s)
Wyckoff Township (PK-08)
   2003-04 Enrollment: 2,446 . . . . (201) 848-5701
Housing: Homeownership rate: 92.8% (2005); Median home value: $655,592 (2005); Median rent: $975 per month (2000); Median age of housing: 40 years (2000).
Hospitals: Christian Health Care Center (52 beds)
Safety: Violent crime rate: 4.1 per 10,000 population; Property crime rate: 71.9 per 10,000 population (2004).
Transportation: Commute to work: 84.7% car, 9.3% public transportation, 1.0% walk, 4.8% work from home (2000); Travel time to work: 30.8% less than 15 minutes, 27.1% 15 to 30 minutes, 14.9% 30 to 45 minutes, 9.4% 45 to 60 minutes, 17.8% 60 minutes or more (2000)
Additional Information Contacts
Wyckoff Chamber of Commerce . . . . (201) 891-3616
   http://www.wyckoffchamber.com
Wyckoff Township . . . . (201) 891-1907
   http://www.wyckoff-nj.com

Burlington County

Located in west and central New Jersey; bounded on the northwest by the Delaware River and the Pennsylvania border. Covers a land area of 804.57 square miles, a water area of 14.86 square miles, and is located in the Eastern Time Zone. The county government was organized in 1694. County seat is Mount Holly.

Burlington County is part of the Philadelphia-Camden-Wilmington, PA-NJ-DE-MD Metropolitan Statistical Area. The entire metro area includes: Camden, NJ Metropolitan Division (Burlington County, NJ; Camden County, NJ; Gloucester County, NJ); Philadelphia, PA Metropolitan Division (Bucks County, PA; Chester County, PA; Delaware County, PA; Montgomery County, PA; Philadelphia County, PA); Wilmington, DE-MD-NJ Metropolitan Division (New Castle County, DE; Cecil County, MD; Salem County, NJ)

Weather Station: Indian Mills 2 W   Elevation: 98 feet

	Jan	Feb	Mar	Apr	May	Jun	Jul	Aug	Sep	Oct	Nov	Dec
High	41	45	53	65	75	83	88	86	79	68	57	46
Low	22	24	31	39	49	58	63	61	54	43	35	27
Precip	4.0	3.1	4.4	4.0	4.0	3.6	4.3	4.9	3.5	3.4	3.7	4.0
Snow	6.7	5.2	2.3	0.6	0.0	0.0	0.0	0.0	0.0	tr	0.3	2.1

High and Low temperatures in degrees Fahrenheit; Precipitation and Snow in inches

Weather Station: Pemberton   Elevation: 59 feet

	Jan	Feb	Mar	Apr	May	Jun	Jul	Aug	Sep	Oct	Nov	Dec
High	42	45	53	64	75	82	87	85	79	68	57	47
Low	22	24	31	39	49	57	63	62	55	43	35	28
Precip	3.9	2.9	4.2	3.8	4.3	4.1	4.5	5.1	3.7	3.5	3.5	3.8
Snow	5.9	5.7	2.5	0.5	0.0	0.0	0.0	0.0	0.0	tr	0.3	2.0

High and Low temperatures in degrees Fahrenheit; Precipitation and Snow in inches

Population: 395,066 (1990); 423,394 (2000); 454,259 (2005); 486,556 (2010 projected); Race: 76.0% White, 16.4% Black, 3.3% Asian, 4.9% Hispanic of any race (2005); Density: 564.6 persons per square mile (2005); Average household size: 2.69 (2005); Median age: 38.1 (2005); Males per 100 females: 97.6 (2005).
Religion: Five largest groups: 31.0% Catholic Church, 3.1% Jewish Estimate, 2.4% The United Methodist Church, 2.0% Muslim Estimate, 1.7% Assemblies of God (2000).

Economy: Unemployment rate: 3.7% (2005); Total civilian labor force: 240,547 (2005); Leading industries: 15.2% retail trade; 11.6% health care and social assistance; 10.4% finance & insurance (2004); Farms: 906 totaling 111,237 acres (2002); Companies that employ 500 or more persons: 59 (2004); Companies that employ 100 to 499 persons: 568 (2004); Companies that employ less than 100 persons: 20,830 (2004); Black-owned businesses: 1,884 (2002); Hispanic-owned businesses: 785 (2002); Asian-owned businesses: 1,056 (2002); Women-owned businesses: 9,243 (2002); Retail sales per capita: $16,237 (2006). Single-family building permits issued: 1,290 (2005); Multi-family building permits issued: 185 (2005).

Income: Per capita income: $31,058 (2005); Median household income: $67,054 (2005); Average household income: $82,720 (2005); Percent of households with income of $100,000 or more: 27.3% (2005); Poverty rate: 5.8% (2003); Bankruptcy rate: 6.08% (2005).

Taxes: Total county taxes per capita: $344 (2004); County property taxes per capita: $315 (2004).

Education: Percent of population age 25 and over with: High school diploma (including GED) or higher: 87.2% (2005); Bachelor's degree or higher: 28.4% (2005); Master's degree or higher: 9.3% (2005).

Housing: Homeownership rate: 77.6% (2005); Median home value: $207,445 (2005); Median rent: $672 per month (2000); Median age of housing: 29 years (2000).

Health: Birth rate: 122.0 per 10,000 population (2004); Death rate: 82.9 per 10,000 population (2004); Age-adjusted cancer mortality rate: 216.9 deaths per 100,000 population (2002); Air Quality Index: 100.0% good, 0.0% moderate, 0.0% unhealthy for sensitive individuals, 0.0% unhealthy (percent of days in 2005); Number of physicians: 33.2 per 10,000 population (2004); Hospital beds: 19.9 per 10,000 population (2003); Hospital admissions: 983.4 per 10,000 population (2003).

Elections: 2004 Presidential election results: 46.1% Bush, 53.1% Kerry, 0.5% Nader, 0.2% Badnarik

National and State Parks: Bass River State Forest; Green Bank State Forest; Mount Laurel State Park; Penn State Forest; Rancocas State Park

Additional Information Contacts

Burlington County Government . . . . (609) 265-5020
    http://www.co.burlington.nj.us
Borough of Medford Lakes . . . . (609) 654-7589
    http://www.medfordlakes.com
Burlington County Chamber of Commerce . . . . (609) 298-7774
    http://www.bccoc.com
Burlington County Chamber of Commerce . . . . (609) 387-0963
    http://www.bccoc.com
Burlington County Chamber of Commerce . . . . (856) 439-2520
    http://www.bccoc.com
Burlington Township . . . . (609) 386-4444
    http://www.twp.burlington.nj.us
Cinnaminson Township . . . . (856) 829-6000
    http://cinnaminsonnj.org
City of Burlington . . . . (609) 386-0200
    http://www.burlingtonnj.us
Eastampton Township . . . . (609) 267-5723
    http://www.eastampton.com
Evesham Township . . . . (856) 983-2900
    http://www.twp.evesham.nj.us
Florence Township . . . . (609) 499-2525
    http://www.florence-nj.com
Lumberton Township . . . . (609) 267-3217
    http://www.lumbertontwp.com/gov
Maple Shade Township . . . . (856) 779-9610
    http://www.mapleshade.com
Medford Township . . . . (609) 654-2608
    http://www.medfordtownship.com
Moorestown Township . . . . (856) 235-0912
    http://www.moorestown.com
Mount Laurel Township . . . . (856) 234-0001
    http://www.mountlaurel.com
Pemberton Township . . . . (609) 894-8201
    http://www.pemberton-twp.com
Shamong Township . . . . (608) 268-2377
    http://www.nothinbut.net/~shamong
Southampton Township . . . . (609) 859-3235
    http://www.southamptonnj.org
Springfield Township . . . . (973) 912-2200
    http://springfield-nj.com

Tabernacle Township . . . . (609) 268-1220
    http://www.townshipoftabernacle-nj.gov
Westampton Township . . . . (609) 267-1891
    http://www.westampton.com
Willingboro Township . . . . (609) 877-2200
    http://www.willingboro.org/twpindex.htm

Burlington County Communities

BASS RIVER (township). Covers a land area of 75.882 square miles and a water area of 2.370 square miles. Located at 39.65° N. Lat.; 74.44° W. Long. Elevation is 5 feet.

Population: 1,580 (1990); 1,510 (2000); 1,589 (2005); 1,678 (2010 projected); Race: 98.7% White, 0.0% Black, 0.1% Asian, 3.1% Hispanic of any race (2005); Density: 20.9 persons per square mile (2005); Average household size: 2.69 (2005); Median age: 38.5 (2005); Males per 100 females: 102.2 (2005); Marriage status: 25.6% never married, 60.4% now married, 6.9% widowed, 7.1% divorced (2000); Foreign born: 3.1% (2000); Ancestry (includes multiple ancestries): 27.6% German, 23.1% Irish, 16.6% English, 16.5% Italian, 8.2% Polish (2000).

Economy: Single-family building permits issued: 9 (2005); Multi-family building permits issued: 0 (2005); Employment by occupation: 8.7% management, 14.4% professional, 15.8% services, 27.8% sales, 0.6% farming, 22.1% construction, 10.6% production (2000).

Income: Per capita income: $25,088 (2005); Median household income: $59,063 (2005); Average household income: $67,568 (2005); Percent of households with income of $100,000 or more: 18.8% (2005); Poverty rate: 5.2% (2000).

Education: Percent of population age 25 and over with: High school diploma (including GED) or higher: 80.4% (2005); Bachelor's degree or higher: 17.9% (2005); Master's degree or higher: 4.9% (2005).

Housing: Homeownership rate: 85.9% (2005); Median home value: $145,856 (2005); Median rent: $508 per month (2000); Median age of housing: 34 years (2000).

Transportation: Commute to work: 92.8% car, 0.5% public transportation, 2.4% walk, 3.1% work from home (2000); Travel time to work: 21.1% less than 15 minutes, 29.1% 15 to 30 minutes, 30.6% 30 to 45 minutes, 7.7% 45 to 60 minutes, 11.4% 60 minutes or more (2000)

BEVERLY (city). Covers a land area of 0.577 square miles and a water area of 0.195 square miles. Located at 40.06° N. Lat.; 74.92° W. Long. Elevation is 28 feet.

History: Site of Civil War camp and hospital, and of a national cemetery. Incorporated 1857.

Population: 2,973 (1990); 2,661 (2000); 2,685 (2005); 2,738 (2010 projected); Race: 59.6% White, 33.1% Black, 0.9% Asian, 5.1% Hispanic of any race (2005); Density: 4,649.8 persons per square mile (2005); Average household size: 2.70 (2005); Median age: 35.9 (2005); Males per 100 females: 88.6 (2005); Marriage status: 32.9% never married, 49.6% now married, 7.2% widowed, 10.3% divorced (2000); Foreign born: 2.4% (2000); Ancestry (includes multiple ancestries): 31.4% Other groups, 21.2% Irish, 20.0% German, 11.2% English, 11.0% Italian (2000).

Economy: Manufacturing: jet engine parts, adhesive labels; vegetables, fruit. Single-family building permits issued: 3 (2005); Multi-family building permits issued: 0 (2005); Employment by occupation: 7.4% management, 14.6% professional, 23.0% services, 24.8% sales, 0.0% farming, 10.1% construction, 20.1% production (2000).

Income: Per capita income: $20,845 (2005); Median household income: $49,831 (2005); Average household income: $56,308 (2005); Percent of households with income of $100,000 or more: 11.1% (2005); Poverty rate: 11.5% (2000).

Education: Percent of population age 25 and over with: High school diploma (including GED) or higher: 77.0% (2005); Bachelor's degree or higher: 11.4% (2005); Master's degree or higher: 4.6% (2005).

School District(s)

Beverly City (PK-08)
    2003-04 Enrollment: 292 . . . . (609) 387-2200

Housing: Homeownership rate: 69.2% (2005); Median home value: $139,335 (2005); Median rent: $534 per month (2000); Median age of housing: 56 years (2000).

Safety: Violent crime rate: 48.2 per 10,000 population; Property crime rate: 274.2 per 10,000 population (2004).

Transportation: Commute to work: 92.4% car, 0.8% public transportation, 4.6% walk, 1.1% work from home (2000); Travel time to work: 30.2% less

than 15 minutes, 38.3% 15 to 30 minutes, 15.7% 30 to 45 minutes, 9.4% 45 to 60 minutes, 6.3% 60 minutes or more (2000)

BORDENTOWN (city). Covers a land area of 0.922 square miles and a water area of 0.050 square miles. Located at 40.14° N. Lat.; 74.71° W. Long. Elevation is 40 feet.

History: Bordentown was settled in 1682 by Thomas Farnsworth, an English Quaker. The village was first known as Farnsworth's Landing. It became a busy shipping center. Thomas Paine, the firebrand of the Revolution, made his home in Bordentown. It was incorporated as a borough in 1825 and rechartered as a city in 1867.

Population: 4,341 (1990); 3,969 (2000); 4,035 (2005); 4,144 (2010 projected); Race: 78.7% White, 13.9% Black, 2.7% Asian, 3.5% Hispanic of any race (2005); Density: 4,375.2 persons per square mile (2005); Average household size: 2.20 (2005); Median age: 39.5 (2005); Males per 100 females: 90.9 (2005); Marriage status: 30.5% never married, 49.1% now married, 10.3% widowed, 10.2% divorced (2000); Foreign born: 1.8% (2000); Ancestry (includes multiple ancestries): 25.8% Irish, 22.3% Other groups, 20.3% German, 17.1% Italian, 10.3% Polish (2000).

Economy: Single-family building permits issued: 0 (2005); Multi-family building permits issued: 0 (2005); Employment by occupation: 13.8% management, 19.9% professional, 18.2% services, 29.9% sales, 0.0% farming, 8.5% construction, 9.7% production (2000).

Income: Per capita income: $30,598 (2005); Median household income: $52,418 (2005); Average household income: $66,508 (2005); Percent of households with income of $100,000 or more: 17.2% (2005); Poverty rate: 6.8% (2000).

Education: Percent of population age 25 and over with: High school diploma (including GED) or higher: 85.8% (2005); Bachelor's degree or higher: 26.3% (2005); Master's degree or higher: 7.8% (2005).

School District(s)
Bordentown Regional (PK-12)
    2003-04 Enrollment: 2,062 . . . . (609) 298-0025
Two-year College(s)
Empire Beauty School-Bordentown (Private, For-profit)
    Fall 2004 Enrollment: 110 . . . . (800) 223-3271

Housing: Homeownership rate: 56.0% (2005); Median home value: $179,065 (2005); Median rent: $641 per month (2000); Median age of housing: 60+ years (2000).

Safety: Violent crime rate: 17.3 per 10,000 population; Property crime rate: 146.0 per 10,000 population (2004).

Newspapers: People Papers (General - Circulation 30,000)

Transportation: Commute to work: 88.5% car, 2.4% public transportation, 5.8% walk, 2.1% work from home (2000); Travel time to work: 27.4% less than 15 minutes, 37.2% 15 to 30 minutes, 19.0% 30 to 45 minutes, 8.3% 45 to 60 minutes, 8.1% 60 minutes or more (2000)

Additional Information Contacts
Burlington County Chamber of Commerce . . . . (609) 298-7774
    http://www.bccoc.com

BORDENTOWN (township). Covers a land area of 8.508 square miles and a water area of 0.773 square miles. Located at 40.14° N. Lat.; 74.69° W. Long. Elevation is 40 feet.

History: Damaged by British in American Revolution. Clara Barton's school (built 1739; now a Red Cross memorial) here. Joseph Bonaparte lived here 1816—1839. Settled 1682; incorporated as borough 1825, as city 1867.

Population: 7,683 (1990); 8,380 (2000); 10,012 (2005); 11,573 (2010 projected); Race: 87.8% White, 5.3% Black, 4.3% Asian, 3.4% Hispanic of any race (2005); Density: 1,176.7 persons per square mile (2005); Average household size: 2.51 (2005); Median age: 39.0 (2005); Males per 100 females: 94.8 (2005); Marriage status: 22.8% never married, 61.8% now married, 6.5% widowed, 8.9% divorced (2000); Foreign born: 7.3% (2000); Ancestry (includes multiple ancestries): 25.7% Italian, 23.8% Irish, 20.0% German, 11.8% English, 11.1% Other groups (2000).

Economy: Manufacturing: animal feed, pre-cast concrete, beverages, electrical equipment, printing; grain, dairy products. Youth correctional facilities here. Single-family building permits issued: 102 (2005); Multi-family building permits issued: 0 (2005); Employment by occupation: 14.0% management, 20.7% professional, 13.9% services, 33.6% sales, 0.2% farming, 8.7% construction, 8.9% production (2000).

Income: Per capita income: $32,201 (2005); Median household income: $69,374 (2005); Average household income: $80,728 (2005); Percent of households with income of $100,000 or more: 27.7% (2005); Poverty rate: 2.8% (2000).

Education: Percent of population age 25 and over with: High school diploma (including GED) or higher: 86.9% (2005); Bachelor's degree or higher: 24.0% (2005); Master's degree or higher: 7.5% (2005).

School District(s)
Bordentown Regional (PK-12)
    2003-04 Enrollment: 2,062 . . . . (609) 298-0025
Two-year College(s)
Empire Beauty School-Bordentown (Private, For-profit)
    Fall 2004 Enrollment: 110 . . . . (800) 223-3271

Housing: Homeownership rate: 77.9% (2005); Median home value: $206,235 (2005); Median rent: $672 per month (2000); Median age of housing: 35 years (2000).

Safety: Violent crime rate: 13.4 per 10,000 population; Property crime rate: 242.4 per 10,000 population (2004).

Newspapers: People Papers (General - Circulation 30,000)

Transportation: Commute to work: 94.6% car, 2.1% public transportation, 0.7% walk, 2.3% work from home (2000); Travel time to work: 22.0% less than 15 minutes, 40.9% 15 to 30 minutes, 21.5% 30 to 45 minutes, 7.8% 45 to 60 minutes, 7.8% 60 minutes or more (2000)

Additional Information Contacts
Burlington County Chamber of Commerce . . . . (609) 298-7774
    http://www.bccoc.com

BROWNS MILLS (CDP). Covers a land area of 5.436 square miles and a water area of 0.214 square miles. Located at 39.97° N. Lat.; 74.57° W. Long. Elevation is 61 feet.

Population: 11,278 (1990); 11,257 (2000); 11,768 (2005); 12,333 (2010 projected); Race: 60.5% White, 26.0% Black, 3.3% Asian, 10.7% Hispanic of any race (2005); Density: 2,164.8 persons per square mile (2005); Average household size: 2.78 (2005); Median age: 34.7 (2005); Males per 100 females: 91.0 (2005); Marriage status: 31.8% never married, 52.2% now married, 5.9% widowed, 10.1% divorced (2000); Foreign born: 7.0% (2000); Ancestry (includes multiple ancestries): 36.6% Other groups, 16.1% German, 15.9% Irish, 9.7% Italian, 6.5% United States or American (2000).

Economy: Employment by occupation: 6.4% management, 11.6% professional, 22.7% services, 30.8% sales, 0.2% farming, 10.1% construction, 18.1% production (2000).

Income: Per capita income: $19,874 (2005); Median household income: $48,527 (2005); Average household income: $54,693 (2005); Percent of households with income of $100,000 or more: 9.2% (2005); Poverty rate: 11.0% (2000).

Education: Percent of population age 25 and over with: High school diploma (including GED) or higher: 79.1% (2005); Bachelor's degree or higher: 7.4% (2005); Master's degree or higher: 2.3% (2005).

School District(s)
Pemberton Township (PK-12)
    2003-04 Enrollment: 6,210 . . . . (609) 893-8141

Housing: Homeownership rate: 79.0% (2005); Median home value: $136,252 (2005); Median rent: $552 per month (2000); Median age of housing: 28 years (2000).

Hospitals: Deborah Heart and Lung Center (161 beds)

Newspapers: Community News (General - Circulation 4,500)

Transportation: Commute to work: 94.4% car, 1.0% public transportation, 1.9% walk, 1.1% work from home (2000); Travel time to work: 24.3% less than 15 minutes, 22.8% 15 to 30 minutes, 24.6% 30 to 45 minutes, 16.8% 45 to 60 minutes, 11.5% 60 minutes or more (2000)

BURLINGTON (city). Covers a land area of 3.000 square miles and a water area of 0.723 square miles. Located at 40.07° N. Lat.; 74.85° W. Long. Elevation is 10 feet.

History: Burlington owes its existence to the Quakers. Two companies of Friends, one from London and one from Yorkshire, began the settlement in 1677. It was first called New Beverly, then Bridlington, and finally Burlington. In 1681, after West New Jersey had become a separate province, the Colonial Assembly designated Burlington as the capital and port of entry. By 1744, Burlington ranked with New York, Philadelphia, and Boston as one of the busiest ports in the country.

Population: 9,835 (1990); 9,736 (2000); 9,845 (2005); 10,034 (2010 projected); Race: 62.9% White, 30.5% Black, 1.8% Asian, 4.4% Hispanic of any race (2005); Density: 3,281.4 persons per square mile (2005); Average household size: 2.46 (2005); Median age: 38.6 (2005); Males per 100 females: 91.2 (2005); Marriage status: 30.4% never married, 49.3% now married, 10.5% widowed, 9.7% divorced (2000); Foreign born: 6.2%

(2000); Ancestry (includes multiple ancestries): 27.9% Other groups, 17.3% Italian, 16.6% Irish, 14.0% German, 9.8% Polish (2000).
Economy: Single-family building permits issued: 7 (2005); Multi-family building permits issued: 0 (2005); Employment by occupation: 8.2% management, 16.3% professional, 16.8% services, 29.9% sales, 0.1% farming, 9.7% construction, 18.8% production (2000).
Income: Per capita income: $24,649 (2005); Median household income: $49,698 (2005); Average household income: $59,859 (2005); Percent of households with income of $100,000 or more: 14.7% (2005); Poverty rate: 8.0% (2000).
Education: Percent of population age 25 and over with: High school diploma (including GED) or higher: 77.7% (2005); Bachelor's degree or higher: 12.3% (2005); Master's degree or higher: 3.7% (2005).
School District(s)
Burlington City (PK-12)
    2003-04 Enrollment: 1,919 . . . . (609) 387-5874
Burlington Township (PK-12)
    2003-04 Enrollment: 4,098 . . . . (609) 387-3955
Housing: Homeownership rate: 65.6% (2005); Median home value: $148,739 (2005); Median rent: $525 per month (2000); Median age of housing: 52 years (2000).
Safety: Violent crime rate: 62.8 per 10,000 population; Property crime rate: 166.0 per 10,000 population (2004).
Transportation: Commute to work: 88.5% car, 5.4% public transportation, 4.2% walk, 1.4% work from home (2000); Travel time to work: 33.0% less than 15 minutes, 36.6% 15 to 30 minutes, 18.0% 30 to 45 minutes, 6.3% 45 to 60 minutes, 6.2% 60 minutes or more (2000)
Additional Information Contacts
Burlington County Chamber of Commerce . . . . (856) 439-2520
    http://www.bccoc.com
City of Burlington . . . . (609) 386-0200
    http://www.burlingtonnj.us

BURLINGTON (township). Covers a land area of 13.474 square miles and a water area of 0.500 square miles. Located at 40.06° N. Lat.; 74.84° W. Long. Elevation is 10 feet.
History: Grew mainly as a port; was also on a Philadelphia—New York coach line, and railroad tracks were laid down Broad St. in 1834. The first colonial money was printed here by Benjamin Franklin in 1726. The first newspaper in N.J. appeared in 1777. St. Mary's Church (built 1703) and The Friends' school (1792) still stand. The birthplaces of James Fenimore Cooper and of James Lawrence are preserved. Settled 1677 by Friends, Incorporated 1733.
Population: 12,452 (1990); 20,294 (2000); 22,380 (2005); 24,494 (2010 projected); Race: 63.6% White, 27.2% Black, 4.6% Asian, 4.6% Hispanic of any race (2005); Density: 1,661.0 persons per square mile (2005); Average household size: 2.84 (2005); Median age: 36.7 (2005); Males per 100 females: 90.7 (2005); Marriage status: 22.4% never married, 61.2% now married, 8.3% widowed, 8.0% divorced (2000); Foreign born: 7.9% (2000); Ancestry (includes multiple ancestries): 29.3% Other groups, 17.5% German, 17.1% Irish, 14.8% Italian, 8.7% English (2000).
Economy: In a rich farm area. A shipping point for farm and dairy products. Manufacturing includes metals, textiles, and clothing. Single-family building permits issued: 17 (2005); Multi-family building permits issued: 0 (2005); Employment by occupation: 16.4% management, 21.1% professional, 14.1% services, 28.2% sales, 0.4% farming, 6.7% construction, 13.2% production (2000).
Income: Per capita income: $29,732 (2005); Median household income: $72,853 (2005); Average household income: $82,699 (2005); Percent of households with income of $100,000 or more: 31.2% (2005); Poverty rate: 5.0% (2000).
Taxes: Total city taxes per capita: $356 (2004); City property taxes per capita: $323 (2004).
Education: Percent of population age 25 and over with: High school diploma (including GED) or higher: 85.1% (2005); Bachelor's degree or higher: 26.3% (2005); Master's degree or higher: 7.4% (2005).
School District(s)
Burlington City (PK-12)
    2003-04 Enrollment: 1,919 . . . . (609) 387-5874
Burlington Township (PK-12)
    2003-04 Enrollment: 4,098 . . . . (609) 387-3955
Housing: Homeownership rate: 77.5% (2005); Median home value: $237,599 (2005); Median rent: $550 per month (2000); Median age of housing: 22 years (2000).

Safety: Violent crime rate: 13.2 per 10,000 population; Property crime rate: 224.7 per 10,000 population (2004).
Transportation: Commute to work: 92.7% car, 3.5% public transportation, 1.3% walk, 1.8% work from home (2000); Travel time to work: 24.4% less than 15 minutes, 33.4% 15 to 30 minutes, 23.7% 30 to 45 minutes, 8.4% 45 to 60 minutes, 10.1% 60 minutes or more (2000)
Additional Information Contacts
Burlington County Chamber of Commerce . . . . (856) 439-2520
    http://www.bccoc.com
Burlington Township . . . . (609) 386-4444
    http://www.twp.burlington.nj.us

CHATSWORTH (unincorporated postal area, zip code 08019). Covers a land area of 63.337 square miles and a water area of 0.614 square miles. Located at 39.77° N. Lat.; 74.53° W. Long. Elevation is 99 feet.
Population: 883 (2000); Race: 86.2% White, 0.5% Black, 2.0% Asian, 13.8% Hispanic of any race (2000); Density: 13.9 persons per square mile (2000); Age: 32.0% under 18, 10.1% over 64 (2000); Marriage status: 23.4% never married, 59.5% now married, 5.5% widowed, 11.6% divorced (2000); Foreign born: 1.0% (2000); Ancestry (includes multiple ancestries): 24.5% Irish, 21.5% German, 18.7% Other groups, 15.8% English, 8.7% United States or American (2000).
Economy: Employment by occupation: 11.9% management, 16.3% professional, 15.5% services, 15.2% sales, 7.9% farming, 16.3% construction, 16.8% production (2000).
Income: Per capita income: $19,854 (2000); Median household income: $55,288 (2000); Poverty rate: 10.4% (2000).
Education: Percent of population age 25 and over with: High school diploma (including GED) or higher: 72.3% (2000); Bachelor's degree or higher: 16.0% (2000).
School District(s)
Woodland Township (PK-08)
    2003-04 Enrollment: 164 . . . . (609) 726-1230
Housing: Homeownership rate: 79.1% (2000); Median home value: $120,200 (2000); Median rent: $517 per month (2000); Median age of housing: 40 years (2000).
Transportation: Commute to work: 91.7% car, 0.0% public transportation, 4.7% walk, 2.5% work from home (2000); Travel time to work: 21.4% less than 15 minutes, 16.4% 15 to 30 minutes, 34.1% 30 to 45 minutes, 17.1% 45 to 60 minutes, 11.1% 60 minutes or more (2000)

CHESTERFIELD (township). Covers a land area of 21.415 square miles and a water area of 0.093 square miles. Located at 40.12° N. Lat.; 74.63° W. Long. Elevation is 90 feet.
History: Incorporated 1798.
Population: 4,932 (1990); 5,955 (2000); 6,339 (2005); 6,639 (2010 projected); Race: 48.3% White, 36.6% Black, 0.9% Asian, 14.0% Hispanic of any race (2005); Density: 296.0 persons per square mile (2005); Average household size: 6.25 (2005); Median age: 24.4 (2005); Males per 100 females: 326.0 (2005); Marriage status: 36.1% never married, 59.6% now married, 2.2% widowed, 2.1% divorced (2000); Foreign born: 3.4% (2000); Ancestry (includes multiple ancestries): 22.4% Other groups, 11.6% German, 11.1% Italian, 10.4% Irish, 7.0% English (2000).
Economy: Single-family building permits issued: 87 (2005); Multi-family building permits issued: 18 (2005); Employment by occupation: 20.4% management, 28.8% professional, 11.4% services, 22.0% sales, 1.3% farming, 8.2% construction, 7.9% production (2000).
Income: Per capita income: $21,605 (2005); Median household income: $101,312 (2005); Average household income: $115,833 (2005); Percent of households with income of $100,000 or more: 50.8% (2005); Poverty rate: 1.8% (2000).
Education: Percent of population age 25 and over with: High school diploma (including GED) or higher: 80.5% (2005); Bachelor's degree or higher: 28.8% (2005); Master's degree or higher: 8.2% (2005).
Housing: Homeownership rate: 92.2% (2005); Median home value: $318,750 (2005); Median rent: $620 per month (2000); Median age of housing: 33 years (2000).
Safety: Violent crime rate: 0.0 per 10,000 population; Property crime rate: 16.4 per 10,000 population (2004).
Transportation: Commute to work: 91.5% car, 2.0% public transportation, 0.7% walk, 5.3% work from home (2000); Travel time to work: 19.4% less than 15 minutes, 33.8% 15 to 30 minutes, 26.4% 30 to 45 minutes, 10.1% 45 to 60 minutes, 10.3% 60 minutes or more (2000)

CINNAMINSON (township). Covers a land area of 7.600 square miles and a water area of 0.456 square miles. Located at 39.99° N. Lat.; 74.99° W. Long. Elevation is 70 feet.

History: Named for the Algonquian translation of "stone-tree" for the sugar maple. Incorporated 1860.

Population: 14,583 (1990); 14,595 (2000); 15,221 (2005); 15,948 (2010 projected); Race: 90.5% White, 5.3% Black, 2.1% Asian, 1.8% Hispanic of any race (2005); Density: 2,002.8 persons per square mile (2005); Average household size: 2.82 (2005); Median age: 43.3 (2005); Males per 100 females: 94.8 (2005); Marriage status: 21.8% never married, 65.9% now married, 7.4% widowed, 4.9% divorced (2000); Foreign born: 4.5% (2000); Ancestry (includes multiple ancestries): 30.9% Irish, 25.5% German, 21.1% Italian, 11.7% English, 9.3% Other groups (2000).

Economy: Light industry, residential and commercial. Single-family building permits issued: 127 (2005); Multi-family building permits issued: 30 (2005); Employment by occupation: 16.3% management, 22.8% professional, 9.1% services, 34.0% sales, 0.1% farming, 7.3% construction, 10.3% production (2000).

Income: Per capita income: $33,831 (2005); Median household income: $79,111 (2005); Average household income: $94,951 (2005); Percent of households with income of $100,000 or more: 35.0% (2005); Poverty rate: 2.4% (2000).

Education: Percent of population age 25 and over with: High school diploma (including GED) or higher: 89.6% (2005); Bachelor's degree or higher: 28.7% (2005); Master's degree or higher: 9.2% (2005).

School District(s)

Cinnaminson Township (PK-12)

    2003-04 Enrollment: 2,642 . . . . (856) 829-7600

Housing: Homeownership rate: 96.1% (2005); Median home value: $245,068 (2005); Median rent: $760 per month (2000); Median age of housing: 36 years (2000).

Safety: Violent crime rate: 17.9 per 10,000 population; Property crime rate: 244.8 per 10,000 population (2004).

Transportation: Commute to work: 90.5% car, 3.5% public transportation, 1.0% walk, 4.3% work from home (2000); Travel time to work: 33.2% less than 15 minutes, 33.1% 15 to 30 minutes, 17.2% 30 to 45 minutes, 8.3% 45 to 60 minutes, 8.2% 60 minutes or more (2000)

Additional Information Contacts

Cinnaminson Township . . . . (856) 829-6000

    http://cinnaminsonnj.org

COLUMBUS (unincorporated postal area, zip code 08022). Covers a land area of 26.251 square miles and a water area of 0.035 square miles. Located at 40.08° N. Lat.; 74.70° W. Long. Elevation is 82 feet.

Population: 5,735 (2000); Race: 93.6% White, 2.7% Black, 3.3% Asian, 2.4% Hispanic of any race (2000); Density: 218.5 persons per square mile (2000); Age: 20.8% under 18, 30.4% over 64 (2000); Marriage status: 14.1% never married, 71.3% now married, 11.6% widowed, 3.0% divorced (2000); Foreign born: 6.2% (2000); Ancestry (includes multiple ancestries): 19.8% German, 19.3% Irish, 19.1% Italian, 16.5% English, 11.4% Other groups (2000).

Economy: Farm and flea market center. Employment by occupation: 15.8% management, 22.3% professional, 12.9% services, 30.2% sales, 0.7% farming, 10.0% construction, 8.1% production (2000).

Income: Per capita income: $29,225 (2000); Median household income: $55,309 (2000); Poverty rate: 3.8% (2000).

Education: Percent of population age 25 and over with: High school diploma (including GED) or higher: 86.3% (2000); Bachelor's degree or higher: 29.0% (2000).

School District(s)

Mansfield Township (PK-06)

    2003-04 Enrollment: 716 . . . . (609) 298-0308

Northern Burlington Regional (07-12)

    2003-04 Enrollment: 1,927 . . . . (609) 298-3900

Housing: Homeownership rate: 96.0% (2000); Median home value: $162,300 (2000); Median rent: $623 per month (2000); Median age of housing: 15 years (2000).

Transportation: Commute to work: 90.4% car, 0.5% public transportation, 4.7% walk, 3.8% work from home (2000); Travel time to work: 23.0% less than 15 minutes, 32.2% 15 to 30 minutes, 29.1% 30 to 45 minutes, 5.7% 45 to 60 minutes, 10.0% 60 minutes or more (2000)

COOKSTOWN (unincorporated postal area, zip code 08511). Covers a land area of 2.366 square miles and a water area of 0.011 square miles. Located at 40.05° N. Lat.; 74.55° W. Long. Elevation is 90 feet.

Population: 1,133 (2000); Race: 91.3% White, 6.4% Black, 0.0% Asian, 8.0% Hispanic of any race (2000); Density: 478.9 persons per square mile (2000); Age: 28.9% under 18, 9.8% over 64 (2000); Marriage status: 25.6% never married, 62.6% now married, 6.5% widowed, 5.3% divorced (2000); Foreign born: 3.5% (2000); Ancestry (includes multiple ancestries): 20.1% Irish, 17.9% Other groups, 14.0% English, 11.7% German, 10.2% Italian (2000).

Economy: Employment by occupation: 19.1% management, 15.5% professional, 20.4% services, 13.0% sales, 0.0% farming, 13.6% construction, 18.4% production (2000).

Income: Per capita income: $20,433 (2000); Median household income: $39,050 (2000); Poverty rate: 2.2% (2000).

Education: Percent of population age 25 and over with: High school diploma (including GED) or higher: 74.5% (2000); Bachelor's degree or higher: 7.6% (2000).

Housing: Homeownership rate: 68.8% (2000); Median home value: $140,700 (2000); Median rent: $553 per month (2000); Median age of housing: 22 years (2000).

Transportation: Commute to work: 94.5% car, 1.8% public transportation, 0.9% walk, 2.8% work from home (2000); Travel time to work: 20.3% less than 15 minutes, 38.2% 15 to 30 minutes, 14.3% 30 to 45 minutes, 14.8% 45 to 60 minutes, 12.4% 60 minutes or more (2000)

COUNTRY LAKE ESTATES (CDP). Covers a land area of 1.111 square miles and a water area of 0.259 square miles. Located at 39.94° N. Lat.; 74.54° W. Long. Elevation is 80 feet.

Population: 4,385 (1990); 4,012 (2000); 4,125 (2005); 4,218 (2010 projected); Race: 65.9% White, 24.3% Black, 2.8% Asian, 10.1% Hispanic of any race (2005); Density: 3,711.9 persons per square mile (2005); Average household size: 2.90 (2005); Median age: 35.8 (2005); Males per 100 females: 98.7 (2005); Marriage status: 24.6% never married, 63.8% now married, 5.2% widowed, 6.4% divorced (2000); Foreign born: 5.6% (2000); Ancestry (includes multiple ancestries): 31.5% Other groups, 19.8% Irish, 19.0% German, 11.4% Italian, 8.3% English (2000).

Economy: Employment by occupation: 9.5% management, 17.3% professional, 21.8% services, 30.2% sales, 0.2% farming, 7.3% construction, 13.6% production (2000).

Income: Per capita income: $24,409 (2005); Median household income: $65,521 (2005); Average household income: $70,857 (2005); Percent of households with income of $100,000 or more: 21.5% (2005); Poverty rate: 5.5% (2000).

Education: Percent of population age 25 and over with: High school diploma (including GED) or higher: 83.3% (2005); Bachelor's degree or higher: 12.1% (2005); Master's degree or higher: 2.2% (2005).

Housing: Homeownership rate: 92.1% (2005); Median home value: $148,804 (2005); Median rent: $648 per month (2000); Median age of housing: 25 years (2000).

Transportation: Commute to work: 95.5% car, 1.0% public transportation, 1.3% walk, 1.8% work from home (2000); Travel time to work: 13.1% less than 15 minutes, 36.0% 15 to 30 minutes, 23.5% 30 to 45 minutes, 11.6% 45 to 60 minutes, 15.7% 60 minutes or more (2000)

CROSSWICKS (unincorporated postal area, zip code 08515). Covers a land area of 0.668 square miles and a water area of 0 square miles. Located at 40.14° N. Lat.; 74.65° W. Long. Elevation is 76 feet.

History: Has 18th-century Quaker meetinghouse. Settled before 1700. Hessians quartered here during the American Revolution.

Population: 290 (2000); Race: 100.0% White, 0.0% Black, 0.0% Asian, 2.6% Hispanic of any race (2000); Density: 434.3 persons per square mile (2000); Age: 27.9% under 18, 13.8% over 64 (2000); Marriage status: 18.1% never married, 68.6% now married, 5.3% widowed, 8.0% divorced (2000); Foreign born: 4.3% (2000); Ancestry (includes multiple ancestries): 22.3% English, 22.0% Irish, 15.4% German, 13.4% Polish, 10.8% Italian (2000).

Economy: Seven miles Southeast of Trenton. Area becoming suburban. Employment by occupation: 13.2% management, 29.9% professional, 12.0% services, 24.0% sales, 0.0% farming, 9.6% construction, 11.4% production (2000).

Income: Per capita income: $28,534 (2000); Median household income: $75,304 (2000); Poverty rate: 2.0% (2000).

Education: Percent of population age 25 and over with: High school diploma (including GED) or higher: 100.0% (2000); Bachelor's degree or higher: 42.4% (2000).

Housing: Homeownership rate: 88.0% (2000); Median home value: $172,000 (2000); Median rent: $441 per month (2000); Median age of housing: 60+ years (2000).

Transportation: Commute to work: 82.6% car, 6.0% public transportation, 0.0% walk, 11.4% work from home (2000); Travel time to work: 16.2% less than 15 minutes, 38.5% 15 to 30 minutes, 25.0% 30 to 45 minutes, 11.5% 45 to 60 minutes, 8.8% 60 minutes or more (2000)

DELANCO (township).
Covers a land area of 2.488 square miles and a water area of 0.898 square miles. Located at 40.05° N. Lat.; 74.95° W. Long. Elevation is 20 feet.

Population: 3,316 (1990); 3,237 (2000); 3,619 (2005); 4,001 (2010 projected); Race: 94.6% White, 2.7% Black, 0.4% Asian, 2.5% Hispanic of any race (2005); Density: 1,454.7 persons per square mile (2005); Average household size: 2.57 (2005); Median age: 38.4 (2005); Males per 100 females: 94.0 (2005); Marriage status: 25.6% never married, 59.9% now married, 5.9% widowed, 8.6% divorced (2000); Foreign born: 5.0% (2000); Ancestry (includes multiple ancestries): 29.7% Irish, 26.7% German, 18.5% Italian, 15.5% English, 11.1% Polish (2000).

Economy: Largely residential. Single-family building permits issued: 117 (2005); Multi-family building permits issued: 4 (2005); Employment by occupation: 10.4% management, 15.7% professional, 13.7% services, 32.5% sales, 0.2% farming, 10.9% construction, 16.5% production (2000).

Income: Per capita income: $24,596 (2005); Median household income: $54,004 (2005); Average household income: $63,264 (2005); Percent of households with income of $100,000 or more: 15.1% (2005); Poverty rate: 9.5% (2000).

Education: Percent of population age 25 and over with: High school diploma (including GED) or higher: 85.2% (2005); Bachelor's degree or higher: 14.7% (2005); Master's degree or higher: 4.8% (2005).

School District(s)
Delanco Township (PK-08)
    2003-04 Enrollment: 374 . . . . (856) 461-0859

Housing: Homeownership rate: 81.4% (2005); Median home value: $173,368 (2005); Median rent: $535 per month (2000); Median age of housing: 55 years (2000).

Safety: Violent crime rate: 17.2 per 10,000 population; Property crime rate: 143.4 per 10,000 population (2004).

Transportation: Commute to work: 93.4% car, 1.8% public transportation, 1.3% walk, 1.6% work from home (2000); Travel time to work: 28.7% less than 15 minutes, 39.6% 15 to 30 minutes, 17.7% 30 to 45 minutes, 7.2% 45 to 60 minutes, 6.9% 60 minutes or more (2000)

DELRAN (township).
Covers a land area of 6.640 square miles and a water area of 0.614 square miles. Located at 40.01° N. Lat.; 74.95° W. Long.

History: Incorporated 1880.

Population: 13,178 (1990); 15,536 (2000); 17,157 (2005); 18,786 (2010 projected); Race: 79.3% White, 11.1% Black, 3.3% Asian, 4.4% Hispanic of any race (2005); Density: 2,583.8 persons per square mile (2005); Average household size: 2.60 (2005); Median age: 37.7 (2005); Males per 100 females: 97.0 (2005); Marriage status: 25.5% never married, 61.5% now married, 5.2% widowed, 7.9% divorced (2000); Foreign born: 10.3% (2000); Ancestry (includes multiple ancestries): 27.3% Irish, 22.3% German, 20.0% Italian, 15.4% Other groups, 10.5% English (2000).

Economy: Residential, light industry, and commercial areas. Single-family building permits issued: 6 (2005); Multi-family building permits issued: 0 (2005); Employment by occupation: 15.9% management, 22.2% professional, 10.2% services, 29.1% sales, 0.1% farming, 8.8% construction, 13.7% production (2000).

Income: Per capita income: $30,769 (2005); Median household income: $67,599 (2005); Average household income: $79,798 (2005); Percent of households with income of $100,000 or more: 25.8% (2005); Poverty rate: 4.1% (2000).

Taxes: Total city taxes per capita: $482 (2004); City property taxes per capita: $473 (2004).

Education: Percent of population age 25 and over with: High school diploma (including GED) or higher: 88.5% (2005); Bachelor's degree or higher: 27.7% (2005); Master's degree or higher: 8.4% (2005).

School District(s)
Delran Township (PK-12)
    2003-04 Enrollment: 2,780 . . . . (856) 461-6800

Two-year College(s)
Harrison Career Institute-Delran (Private, For-profit)
    Fall 2004 Enrollment: 125 . . . . (856) 764-8933

Housing: Homeownership rate: 72.5% (2005); Median home value: $235,187 (2005); Median rent: $626 per month (2000); Median age of housing: 29 years (2000).

Safety: Violent crime rate: 12.6 per 10,000 population; Property crime rate: 158.8 per 10,000 population (2004).

Transportation: Commute to work: 94.1% car, 2.3% public transportation, 0.8% walk, 1.9% work from home (2000); Travel time to work: 27.0% less than 15 minutes, 37.2% 15 to 30 minutes, 17.7% 30 to 45 minutes, 9.4% 45 to 60 minutes, 8.7% 60 minutes or more (2000)

EASTAMPTON (township).
Covers a land area of 5.754 square miles and a water area of 0.079 square miles. Located at 39.99° N. Lat.; 74.75° W. Long.

Population: 5,023 (1990); 6,202 (2000); 6,785 (2005); 7,380 (2010 projected); Race: 73.4% White, 14.3% Black, 6.8% Asian, 5.5% Hispanic of any race (2005); Density: 1,179.3 persons per square mile (2005); Average household size: 2.83 (2005); Median age: 36.2 (2005); Males per 100 females: 98.3 (2005); Marriage status: 23.9% never married, 63.4% now married, 4.0% widowed, 8.7% divorced (2000); Foreign born: 8.0% (2000); Ancestry (includes multiple ancestries): 23.2% German, 23.0% Other groups, 21.3% Irish, 17.0% Italian, 10.0% English (2000).

Economy: Single-family building permits issued: 4 (2005); Multi-family building permits issued: 2 (2005); Employment by occupation: 15.2% management, 20.4% professional, 13.1% services, 30.3% sales, 0.2% farming, 7.5% construction, 13.2% production (2000).

Income: Per capita income: $28,242 (2005); Median household income: $74,253 (2005); Average household income: $79,808 (2005); Percent of households with income of $100,000 or more: 28.2% (2005); Poverty rate: 2.9% (2000).

Education: Percent of population age 25 and over with: High school diploma (including GED) or higher: 89.9% (2005); Bachelor's degree or higher: 29.6% (2005); Master's degree or higher: 8.7% (2005).

School District(s)
Eastampton Township (PK-08)
    2003-04 Enrollment: 842 . . . . (609) 267-9172

Housing: Homeownership rate: 69.1% (2005); Median home value: $215,938 (2005); Median rent: $630 per month (2000); Median age of housing: 23 years (2000).

Safety: Violent crime rate: 16.4 per 10,000 population; Property crime rate: 143.2 per 10,000 population (2004).

Transportation: Commute to work: 95.7% car, 1.1% public transportation, 0.5% walk, 2.3% work from home (2000); Travel time to work: 24.5% less than 15 minutes, 36.4% 15 to 30 minutes, 18.7% 30 to 45 minutes, 8.1% 45 to 60 minutes, 12.4% 60 minutes or more (2000)

Additional Information Contacts
Eastampton Township . . . . (609) 267-5723
    http://www.eastampton.com

EDGEWATER PARK (township).
Covers a land area of 2.911 square miles and a water area of 0.126 square miles. Located at 40.05° N. Lat.; 74.90° W. Long. Elevation is 28 feet.

History: Incorporated 1924.

Population: 8,388 (1990); 7,864 (2000); 8,167 (2005); 8,534 (2010 projected); Race: 61.2% White, 24.9% Black, 4.3% Asian, 8.9% Hispanic of any race (2005); Density: 2,805.9 persons per square mile (2005); Average household size: 2.42 (2005); Median age: 39.0 (2005); Males per 100 females: 92.8 (2005); Marriage status: 25.9% never married, 56.6% now married, 8.0% widowed, 9.5% divorced (2000); Foreign born: 8.6% (2000); Ancestry (includes multiple ancestries): 33.4% Other groups, 17.6% Irish, 17.0% German, 14.0% Italian, 8.2% English (2000).

Economy: Single-family building permits issued: 3 (2005); Multi-family building permits issued: 5 (2005); Employment by occupation: 13.7% management, 20.0% professional, 14.0% services, 26.9% sales, 0.0% farming, 9.5% construction, 16.0% production (2000).

Income: Per capita income: $24,815 (2005); Median household income: $51,387 (2005); Average household income: $60,137 (2005); Percent of households with income of $100,000 or more: 14.0% (2005); Poverty rate: 8.6% (2000).

Taxes: Total city taxes per capita: $360 (2004); City property taxes per capita: $333 (2004).

Education: Percent of population age 25 and over with: High school diploma (including GED) or higher: 85.8% (2005); Bachelor's degree or higher: 19.7% (2005); Master's degree or higher: 4.2% (2005).

School District(s)

Edgewater Park Township (PK-08)

2003-04 Enrollment: 972 . . . . (609) 877-2124

Housing: Homeownership rate: 64.0% (2005); Median home value: $174,134 (2005); Median rent: $600 per month (2000); Median age of housing: 34 years (2000).

Safety: Violent crime rate: 35.8 per 10,000 population; Property crime rate: 291.5 per 10,000 population (2004).

Transportation: Commute to work: 92.9% car, 2.4% public transportation, 1.4% walk, 2.2% work from home (2000); Travel time to work: 28.2% less than 15 minutes, 35.9% 15 to 30 minutes, 21.6% 30 to 45 minutes, 7.0% 45 to 60 minutes, 7.2% 60 minutes or more (2000)

EVESHAM (township). Covers a land area of 29.540 square miles and a water area of 0.166 square miles. Located at 39.87° N. Lat.; 74.90° W. Long.

History: Incorporated 1798.

Population: 35,309 (1990); 42,275 (2000); 48,039 (2005); 53,719 (2010 projected); Race: 89.7% White, 3.5% Black, 4.9% Asian, 2.5% Hispanic of any race (2005); Density: 1,626.2 persons per square mile (2005); Average household size: 2.65 (2005); Median age: 37.0 (2005); Males per 100 females: 94.0 (2005); Marriage status: 23.3% never married, 63.6% now married, 5.3% widowed, 7.8% divorced (2000); Foreign born: 6.5% (2000); Ancestry (includes multiple ancestries): 27.8% Irish, 26.6% Italian, 20.4% German, 11.3% Other groups, 9.9% English (2000).

Economy: Rapidly expanding residential area. Unemployment rate: 2.7% (2005); Total civilian labor force: 27,407 (2005); Single-family building permits issued: 46 (2005); Multi-family building permits issued: 0 (2005); Employment by occupation: 21.2% management, 26.8% professional, 9.7% services, 31.1% sales, 0.0% farming, 5.1% construction, 6.1% production (2000).

Income: Per capita income: $34,686 (2005); Median household income: $77,094 (2005); Average household income: $91,329 (2005); Percent of households with income of $100,000 or more: 33.6% (2005); Poverty rate: 2.8% (2000).

Taxes: Total city taxes per capita: $351 (2004); City property taxes per capita: $315 (2004).

Education: Percent of population age 25 and over with: High school diploma (including GED) or higher: 93.2% (2005); Bachelor's degree or higher: 39.7% (2005); Master's degree or higher: 12.3% (2005).

Housing: Homeownership rate: 77.5% (2005); Median home value: $237,683 (2005); Median rent: $765 per month (2000); Median age of housing: 17 years (2000).

Safety: Violent crime rate: 10.6 per 10,000 population; Property crime rate: 152.3 per 10,000 population (2004).

Transportation: Commute to work: 90.6% car, 4.6% public transportation, 1.2% walk, 3.1% work from home (2000); Travel time to work: 21.9% less than 15 minutes, 35.2% 15 to 30 minutes, 20.4% 30 to 45 minutes, 10.6% 45 to 60 minutes, 11.9% 60 minutes or more (2000)

Additional Information Contacts

Evesham Township . . . . (856) 983-2900

http://www.twp.evesham.nj.us

FIELDSBORO (borough). Covers a land area of 0.272 square miles and a water area of 0 square miles. Located at 40.13° N. Lat.; 74.72° W. Long. Elevation is 67 feet.

Population: 579 (1990); 522 (2000); 588 (2005); 653 (2010 projected); Race: 83.2% White, 13.9% Black, 0.0% Asian, 3.1% Hispanic of any race (2005); Density: 2,163.9 persons per square mile (2005); Average household size: 2.68 (2005); Median age: 36.8 (2005); Males per 100 females: 89.1 (2005); Marriage status: 31.3% never married, 52.0% now married, 6.5% widowed, 10.2% divorced (2000); Foreign born: 3.8% (2000); Ancestry (includes multiple ancestries): 20.3% German, 19.7% Other groups, 19.1% Irish, 17.0% English, 10.2% Hungarian (2000).

Economy: Light manufacturing. Mainly residential. Single-family building permits issued: 1 (2005); Multi-family building permits issued: 0 (2005); Employment by occupation: 13.1% management, 15.8% professional, 13.4% services, 34.0% sales, 0.0% farming, 6.2% construction, 17.5% production (2000).

Income: Per capita income: $29,141 (2005); Median household income: $68,849 (2005); Average household income: $78,242 (2005); Percent of

households with income of $100,000 or more: 25.1% (2005); Poverty rate: 1.9% (2000).

Education: Percent of population age 25 and over with: High school diploma (including GED) or higher: 88.6% (2005); Bachelor's degree or higher: 27.6% (2005); Master's degree or higher: 5.5% (2005).

Housing: Homeownership rate: 75.8% (2005); Median home value: $169,841 (2005); Median rent: $1,014 per month (2000); Median age of housing: 54 years (2000).

Transportation: Commute to work: 91.0% car, 0.7% public transportation, 2.2% walk, 4.3% work from home (2000); Travel time to work: 32.3% less than 15 minutes, 38.0% 15 to 30 minutes, 21.1% 30 to 45 minutes, 3.4% 45 to 60 minutes, 5.3% 60 minutes or more (2000)

FLORENCE (township). Covers a land area of 9.712 square miles and a water area of 0.423 square miles. Located at 40.11° N. Lat.; 74.79° W. Long. Elevation is 20 feet.

Population: 10,266 (1990); 10,746 (2000); 11,416 (2005); 12,143 (2010 projected); Race: 81.5% White, 12.1% Black, 3.3% Asian, 3.0% Hispanic of any race (2005); Density: 1,175.4 persons per square mile (2005); Average household size: 2.53 (2005); Median age: 38.2 (2005); Males per 100 females: 92.2 (2005); Marriage status: 26.1% never married, 57.1% now married, 7.6% widowed, 9.2% divorced (2000); Foreign born: 6.4% (2000); Ancestry (includes multiple ancestries): 24.2% Irish, 20.7% German, 18.6% Italian, 16.4% Other groups, 12.1% English (2000).

Economy: Pipe foundry; manufacturing of dairy products. Single-family building permits issued: 127 (2005); Multi-family building permits issued: 0 (2005); Employment by occupation: 14.5% management, 18.4% professional, 12.7% services, 28.7% sales, 0.1% farming, 9.0% construction, 16.6% production (2000).

Income: Per capita income: $28,598 (2005); Median household income: $64,977 (2005); Average household income: $72,284 (2005); Percent of households with income of $100,000 or more: 23.1% (2005); Poverty rate: 6.1% (2000).

Taxes: Total city taxes per capita: $403 (2004); City property taxes per capita: $377 (2004).

Education: Percent of population age 25 and over with: High school diploma (including GED) or higher: 85.7% (2005); Bachelor's degree or higher: 20.5% (2005); Master's degree or higher: 7.0% (2005).

School District(s)

Florence Township (PK-12)

2003-04 Enrollment: 1,641 . . . . (609) 499-4600

Housing: Homeownership rate: 77.1% (2005); Median home value: $176,558 (2005); Median rent: $593 per month (2000); Median age of housing: 41 years (2000).

Safety: Violent crime rate: 22.1 per 10,000 population; Property crime rate: 124.6 per 10,000 population (2004).

Transportation: Commute to work: 93.3% car, 2.1% public transportation, 2.4% walk, 1.6% work from home (2000); Travel time to work: 20.5% less than 15 minutes, 38.6% 15 to 30 minutes, 25.6% 30 to 45 minutes, 8.8% 45 to 60 minutes, 6.6% 60 minutes or more (2000)

Additional Information Contacts

Florence Township. . . . . (609) 499-2525

http://www.florence-nj.com

FLORENCE-ROEBLING (CDP). Covers a land area of 2.212 square miles and a water area of 0.423 square miles. Located at 40.11° N. Lat.; 74.79° W. Long.

Population: 8,563 (1990); 8,200 (2000); 8,408 (2005); 8,686 (2010 projected); Race: 81.1% White, 12.9% Black, 3.1% Asian, 2.4% Hispanic of any race (2005); Density: 3,801.0 persons per square mile (2005); Average household size: 2.49 (2005); Median age: 37.7 (2005); Males per 100 females: 90.4 (2005); Marriage status: 26.4% never married, 55.3% now married, 8.7% widowed, 9.6% divorced (2000); Foreign born: 6.5% (2000); Ancestry (includes multiple ancestries): 23.0% Irish, 20.0% German, 17.0% Italian, 16.9% Other groups, 11.7% English (2000).

Economy: Employment by occupation: 12.6% management, 16.7% professional, 13.5% services, 27.6% sales, 0.2% farming, 10.2% construction, 19.2% production (2000).

Income: Per capita income: $25,983 (2005); Median household income: $56,100 (2005); Average household income: $64,408 (2005); Percent of households with income of $100,000 or more: 17.3% (2005); Poverty rate: 7.3% (2000).

Education: Percent of population age 25 and over with: High school diploma (including GED) or higher: 83.9% (2005); Bachelor's degree or higher: 16.0% (2005); Master's degree or higher: 5.3% (2005).

Housing: Homeownership rate: 71.8% (2005); Median home value: $155,203 (2005); Median rent: $592 per month (2000); Median age of housing: 48 years (2000).
Transportation: Commute to work: 92.0% car, 2.5% public transportation, 2.8% walk, 2.0% work from home (2000); Travel time to work: 21.9% less than 15 minutes, 38.9% 15 to 30 minutes, 24.2% 30 to 45 minutes, 9.2% 45 to 60 minutes, 5.9% 60 minutes or more (2000)

FORT DIX (CDP).

Covers a land area of 11.243 square miles and a water area of 0.060 square miles. Located at 40.01° N. Lat.; 74.62° W. Long. Elevation is 130 feet.
Population: 10,224 (1990); 7,464 (2000); 7,028 (2005); 6,770 (2010 projected); Race: 57.5% White, 37.4% Black, 1.1% Asian, 29.3% Hispanic of any race (2005); Density: 625.1 persons per square mile (2005); Average household size: 9.45 (2005); Median age: 34.0 (2005); Males per 100 females: 538.9 (2005); Marriage status: 18.3% never married, 77.1% now married, 0.7% widowed, 3.9% divorced (2000); Foreign born: 3.4% (2000); Ancestry (includes multiple ancestries): 18.6% Other groups, 5.6% German, 5.3% Irish, 3.3% Italian, 2.2% Polish (2000)..
Economy: Employment by occupation: 7.8% management, 16.6% professional, 24.1% services, 40.5% sales, 1.2% farming, 4.5% construction, 5.3% production (2000).
Income: Per capita income: $11,195 (2005); Median household income: $46,908 (2005); Average household income: $51,159 (2005); Percent of households with income of $100,000 or more: 4.4% (2005); Poverty rate: 3.2% (2000).
Education: Percent of population age 25 and over with: High school diploma (including GED) or higher: 71.6% (2005); Bachelor's degree or higher: 9.5% (2005); Master's degree or higher: 1.4% (2005).
School District(s)
Pemberton Township (PK-12)
    2003-04 Enrollment: 6,210 . . . . (609) 893-8141
Housing: Homeownership rate: 5.2% (2005); Median home value: $138,333 (2005); Median rent: $831 per month (2000); Median age of housing: 40 years (2000).
Newspapers: The Fort Dix Post (General - Circulation 10,000)
Transportation: Commute to work: 93.7% car, 0.0% public transportation, 4.0% walk, 1.7% work from home (2000); Travel time to work: 51.0% less than 15 minutes, 23.8% 15 to 30 minutes, 8.0% 30 to 45 minutes, 11.2% 45 to 60 minutes, 6.0% 60 minutes or more (2000)

HAINESPORT (township).

Covers a land area of 6.521 square miles and a water area of 0.197 square miles. Located at 39.98° N. Lat.; 74.83° W. Long. Elevation is 41 feet.
Population: 3,249 (1990); 4,126 (2000); 6,401 (2005); 8,488 (2010 projected); Race: 92.2% White, 3.5% Black, 2.4% Asian, 3.0% Hispanic of any race (2005); Density: 981.6 persons per square mile (2005); Average household size: 2.77 (2005); Median age: 39.3 (2005); Males per 100 females: 95.5 (2005); Marriage status: 22.1% never married, 65.9% now married, 5.0% widowed, 7.1% divorced (2000); Foreign born: 2.9% (2000); Ancestry (includes multiple ancestries): 26.8% Irish, 22.8% German, 17.5% Italian, 13.4% English, 9.6% Other groups (2000).
Economy: Single-family building permits issued: 38 (2005); Multi-family building permits issued: 0 (2005); Employment by occupation: 21.1% management, 16.5% professional, 12.4% services, 29.5% sales, 0.2% farming, 8.5% construction, 11.9% production (2000).
Income: Per capita income: $36,555 (2005); Median household income: $86,810 (2005); Average household income: $100,992 (2005); Percent of households with income of $100,000 or more: 39.7% (2005); Poverty rate: 3.0% (2000).
Education: Percent of population age 25 and over with: High school diploma (including GED) or higher: 89.0% (2005); Bachelor's degree or higher: 25.5% (2005); Master's degree or higher: 7.9% (2005).
School District(s)
Hainesport Township (PK-08)
    2003-04 Enrollment: 606 . . . . (609) 265-8050
Housing: Homeownership rate: 89.5% (2005); Median home value: $248,582 (2005); Median rent: $552 per month (2000); Median age of housing: 39 years (2000).
Transportation: Commute to work: 93.2% car, 2.7% public transportation, 0.7% walk, 2.5% work from home (2000); Travel time to work: 29.5% less than 15 minutes, 39.5% 15 to 30 minutes, 13.5% 30 to 45 minutes, 7.7% 45 to 60 minutes, 9.9% 60 minutes or more (2000)

JOBSTOWN (unincorporated postal area, zip code 08041).

Covers a land area of 11.652 square miles and a water area of 0 square miles. Located at 40.03° N. Lat.; 74.68° W. Long. Elevation is 70 feet.
Population: 877 (2000); Race: 96.6% White, 0.6% Black, 0.0% Asian, 4.5% Hispanic of any race (2000); Density: 75.3 persons per square mile (2000); Age: 25.7% under 18, 11.3% over 64 (2000); Marriage status: 28.8% never married, 59.1% now married, 6.0% widowed, 6.1% divorced (2000); Foreign born: 5.3% (2000); Ancestry (includes multiple ancestries): 27.3% German, 20.6% Irish, 17.4% Italian, 12.7% English, 9.8% French (except Basque) (2000).
Economy: Employment by occupation: 15.2% management, 17.3% professional, 9.3% services, 36.8% sales, 2.5% farming, 8.0% construction, 10.9% production (2000).
Income: Per capita income: $28,880 (2000); Median household income: $70,948 (2000); Poverty rate: 2.4% (2000).
Education: Percent of population age 25 and over with: High school diploma (including GED) or higher: 88.8% (2000); Bachelor's degree or higher: 23.1% (2000).
School District(s)
Springfield Township (PK-06)
    2003-04 Enrollment: 341 . . . . (609) 723-2479
Housing: Homeownership rate: 82.7% (2000); Median home value: $193,000 (2000); Median rent: $532 per month (2000); Median age of housing: 29 years (2000).
Transportation: Commute to work: 88.6% car, 0.0% public transportation, 3.5% walk, 7.9% work from home (2000); Travel time to work: 29.7% less than 15 minutes, 34.5% 15 to 30 minutes, 19.4% 30 to 45 minutes, 9.8% 45 to 60 minutes, 6.5% 60 minutes or more (2000)

LEISURETOWNE (CDP).

Covers a land area of 1.786 square miles and a water area of 0.087 square miles. Located at 39.90° N. Lat.; 74.70° W. Long. Elevation is 60 feet.
Population: 2,552 (1990); 2,535 (2000); 2,700 (2005); 2,894 (2010 projected); Race: 97.9% White, 1.6% Black, 0.1% Asian, 0.8% Hispanic of any race (2005); Density: 1,511.9 persons per square mile (2005); Average household size: 1.52 (2005); Median age: 74.6 (2005); Males per 100 females: 68.5 (2005); Marriage status: 4.3% never married, 63.1% now married, 28.5% widowed, 4.1% divorced (2000); Foreign born: 7.1% (2000); Ancestry (includes multiple ancestries): 28.5% German, 23.7% Irish, 18.5% English, 10.6% Italian, 7.3% Polish (2000).
Economy: Employment by occupation: 9.4% management, 9.7% professional, 21.7% services, 37.3% sales, 0.0% farming, 4.3% construction, 17.7% production (2000).
Income: Per capita income: $29,147 (2005); Median household income: $34,613 (2005); Average household income: $44,362 (2005); Percent of households with income of $100,000 or more: 6.0% (2005); Poverty rate: 2.5% (2000).
Education: Percent of population age 25 and over with: High school diploma (including GED) or higher: 76.5% (2005); Bachelor's degree or higher: 12.4% (2005); Master's degree or higher: 4.4% (2005).
Housing: Homeownership rate: 94.8% (2005); Median home value: $128,163 (2005); Median rent: $338 per month (2000); Median age of housing: 24 years (2000).
Transportation: Commute to work: 100.0% car, 0.0% public transportation, 0.0% walk, 0.0% work from home (2000); Travel time to work: 17.5% less than 15 minutes, 43.4% 15 to 30 minutes, 19.0% 30 to 45 minutes, 11.1% 45 to 60 minutes, 9.0% 60 minutes or more (2000)

LUMBERTON (township).

Covers a land area of 12.867 square miles and a water area of 0.168 square miles. Located at 39.96° N. Lat.; 74.80° W. Long. Elevation is 20 feet.
History: Incorporated 1860.
Population: 6,680 (1990); 10,461 (2000); 12,729 (2005); 14,847 (2010 projected); Race: 73.9% White, 16.5% Black, 4.1% Asian, 6.1% Hispanic of any race (2005); Density: 989.3 persons per square mile (2005); Average household size: 2.69 (2005); Median age: 36.8 (2005); Males per 100 females: 92.2 (2005); Marriage status: 19.4% never married, 63.7% now married, 5.7% widowed, 11.2% divorced (2000); Foreign born: 6.5% (2000); Ancestry (includes multiple ancestries): 23.8% Other groups, 21.8% Irish, 21.1% German, 14.7% Italian, 12.0% English (2000).
Economy: Boat manufacturing, printing. Single-family building permits issued: 2 (2005); Multi-family building permits issued: 0 (2005); Employment by occupation: 18.1% management, 26.4% professional,

10.6% services, 26.4% sales, 0.0% farming, 6.7% construction, 11.8% production (2000).

Income: Per capita income: $30,128 (2005); Median household income: $68,060 (2005); Average household income: $80,600 (2005); Percent of households with income of $100,000 or more: 26.8% (2005); Poverty rate: 3.8% (2000).

Education: Percent of population age 25 and over with: High school diploma (including GED) or higher: 85.5% (2005); Bachelor's degree or higher: 30.9% (2005); Master's degree or higher: 9.9% (2005).

School District(s)

Burlington County Spec Serv (UG-UG)

    2003-04 Enrollment: 2,472 . . . . (609) 261-5600

Lumberton Township (PK-08)

    2003-04 Enrollment: 1,844 . . . . (609) 265-7709

Housing: Homeownership rate: 68.3% (2005); Median home value: $248,826 (2005); Median rent: $619 per month (2000); Median age of housing: 16 years (2000).

Safety: Violent crime rate: 27.2 per 10,000 population; Property crime rate: 315.1 per 10,000 population (2004).

Transportation: Commute to work: 94.4% car, 2.2% public transportation, 1.0% walk, 1.8% work from home (2000); Travel time to work: 23.1% less than 15 minutes, 38.8% 15 to 30 minutes, 17.9% 30 to 45 minutes, 9.6% 45 to 60 minutes, 10.6% 60 minutes or more (2000)

Additional Information Contacts

Lumberton Township . . . . (609) 267-3217

    http://www.lumbertontwp.com/gov

MANSFIELD (township). Covers a land area of 21.723 square miles and a water area of 0.141 square miles. Located at 40.08° N. Lat.; 74.71° W. Long. Elevation is 90 feet.

Population: 3,874 (1990); 5,090 (2000); 8,336 (2005); 11,309 (2010 projected); Race: 93.5% White, 2.7% Black, 2.1% Asian, 2.5% Hispanic of any race (2005); Density: 383.7 persons per square mile (2005); Average household size: 2.58 (2005); Median age: 47.2 (2005); Males per 100 females: 94.5 (2005); Marriage status: 13.9% never married, 69.4% now married, 13.6% widowed, 3.1% divorced (2000); Foreign born: 5.2% (2000); Ancestry (includes multiple ancestries): 21.8% German, 18.4% Italian, 18.2% Irish, 16.2% English, 9.4% Other groups (2000).

Economy: Single-family building permits issued: 81 (2005); Multi-family building permits issued: 0 (2005); Employment by occupation: 14.9% management, 18.6% professional, 14.0% services, 28.0% sales, 0.7% farming, 12.8% construction, 11.0% production (2000).

Income: Per capita income: $31,074 (2005); Median household income: $63,484 (2005); Average household income: $80,096 (2005); Percent of households with income of $100,000 or more: 28.5% (2005); Poverty rate: 4.5% (2000).

Education: Percent of population age 25 and over with: High school diploma (including GED) or higher: 86.4% (2005); Bachelor's degree or higher: 25.6% (2005); Master's degree or higher: 12.0% (2005).

Housing: Homeownership rate: 94.4% (2005); Median home value: $260,302 (2005); Median rent: $634 per month (2000); Median age of housing: 16 years (2000).

Safety: Violent crime rate: 2.7 per 10,000 population; Property crime rate: 229.2 per 10,000 population (2004).

Transportation: Commute to work: 91.9% car, 0.4% public transportation, 4.6% walk, 2.5% work from home (2000); Travel time to work: 22.7% less than 15 minutes, 36.5% 15 to 30 minutes, 27.1% 30 to 45 minutes, 5.6% 45 to 60 minutes, 8.2% 60 minutes or more (2000)

MAPLE SHADE (township). Covers a land area of 3.847 square miles and a water area of 0 square miles. Located at 39.95° N. Lat.; 74.99° W. Long. Elevation is 50 feet.

Population: 19,211 (1990); 19,079 (2000); 19,399 (2005); 19,876 (2010 projected); Race: 78.4% White, 8.7% Black, 8.4% Asian, 5.9% Hispanic of any race (2005); Density: 5,042.6 persons per square mile (2005); Average household size: 2.23 (2005); Median age: 37.6 (2005); Males per 100 females: 96.3 (2005); Marriage status: 31.0% never married, 50.1% now married, 7.9% widowed, 11.0% divorced (2000); Foreign born: 9.1% (2000); Ancestry (includes multiple ancestries): 24.9% Irish, 20.4% German, 20.1% Italian, 17.3% Other groups, 9.9% English (2000).

Economy: Manufacturing: clothing, paper products. Single-family building permits issued: 4 (2005); Multi-family building permits issued: 97 (2005); Employment by occupation: 11.3% management, 21.6% professional, 14.1% services, 28.7% sales, 0.0% farming, 8.8% construction, 15.5% production (2000).

Income: Per capita income: $27,714 (2005); Median household income: $51,003 (2005); Average household income: $61,012 (2005); Percent of households with income of $100,000 or more: 13.8% (2005); Poverty rate: 5.4% (2000).

Taxes: Total city taxes per capita: $280 (2004); City property taxes per capita: $264 (2004).

Education: Percent of population age 25 and over with: High school diploma (including GED) or higher: 82.6% (2005); Bachelor's degree or higher: 22.2% (2005); Master's degree or higher: 7.4% (2005).

School District(s)

Maple Shade Township (PK-12)

    2003-04 Enrollment: 2,404 . . . . (856) 779-1750

Housing: Homeownership rate: 49.1% (2005); Median home value: $162,947 (2005); Median rent: $703 per month (2000); Median age of housing: 33 years (2000).

Safety: Violent crime rate: 35.6 per 10,000 population; Property crime rate: 223.7 per 10,000 population (2004).

Newspapers: Maple Shade Progress (General - Circulation 5,000)

Transportation: Commute to work: 91.0% car, 4.3% public transportation, 2.5% walk, 1.7% work from home (2000); Travel time to work: 33.2% less than 15 minutes, 36.5% 15 to 30 minutes, 15.8% 30 to 45 minutes, 6.1% 45 to 60 minutes, 8.4% 60 minutes or more (2000)

Additional Information Contacts

Maple Shade Township . . . . (856) 779-9610

    http://www.mapleshade.com

MARLTON (CDP). Aka Woodstraw. Covers a land area of 3.236 square miles and a water area of 0 square miles. Located at 39.89° N. Lat.; 74.92° W. Long. Elevation is 88 feet.

History: Has Baptist church (1805).

Population: 10,228 (1990); 10,260 (2000); 10,619 (2005); 11,060 (2010 projected); Race: 89.0% White, 3.7% Black, 5.2% Asian, 3.1% Hispanic of any race (2005); Density: 3,281.9 persons per square mile (2005); Average household size: 2.44 (2005); Median age: 38.1 (2005); Males per 100 females: 94.2 (2005); Marriage status: 25.4% never married, 57.3% now married, 7.5% widowed, 9.7% divorced (2000); Foreign born: 6.6% (2000); Ancestry (includes multiple ancestries): 28.8% Irish, 26.1% Italian, 21.7% German, 11.0% Other groups, 8.7% Polish (2000).

Economy: Employment by occupation: 14.5% management, 27.0% professional, 12.0% services, 32.1% sales, 0.1% farming, 5.7% construction, 8.6% production (2000).

Income: Per capita income: $29,365 (2005); Median household income: $61,301 (2005); Average household income: $71,387 (2005); Percent of households with income of $100,000 or more: 20.3% (2005); Poverty rate: 3.5% (2000).

Education: Percent of population age 25 and over with: High school diploma (including GED) or higher: 89.8% (2005); Bachelor's degree or higher: 31.1% (2005); Master's degree or higher: 8.1% (2005).

School District(s)

Evesham Township (PK-08)

    2003-04 Enrollment: 5,708 . . . . (856) 983-1800

Lenape Regional (09-12)

    2003-04 Enrollment: 7,067 . . . . (609) 268-2000

Two-year College(s)

Rizzieri Aveda School for Beauty and Wellness (Private, For-profit)

    Fall 2004 Enrollment: 153 . . . . (856) 988-8600

Housing: Homeownership rate: 68.2% (2005); Median home value: $205,451 (2005); Median rent: $703 per month (2000); Median age of housing: 31 years (2000).

Hospitals: Virtua Health (180 beds)

Transportation: Commute to work: 91.3% car, 3.8% public transportation, 1.9% walk, 2.3% work from home (2000); Travel time to work: 31.9% less than 15 minutes, 33.3% 15 to 30 minutes, 17.5% 30 to 45 minutes, 8.0% 45 to 60 minutes, 9.3% 60 minutes or more (2000)

Additional Information Contacts

Burlington County Chamber of Commerce . . . . (609) 387-0963

    http://www.bccoc.com

MCGUIRE AFB (CDP). Covers a land area of 2.069 square miles and a water area of 0 square miles. Located at 40.04° N. Lat.; 74.58° W. Long.

Population: 7,580 (1990); 6,478 (2000); 6,372 (2005); 6,329 (2010 projected); Race: 68.7% White, 17.9% Black, 3.2% Asian, 10.5% Hispanic of any race (2005); Density: 3,079.7 persons per square mile (2005); Average household size: 4.29 (2005); Median age: 23.4 (2005); Males per 100 females: 129.6 (2005); Marriage status: 31.9% never married, 65.3%

now married, 0.1% widowed, 2.8% divorced (2000); Foreign born: 6.1% (2000); Ancestry (includes multiple ancestries): 34.5% Other groups, 18.9% German, 15.9% Irish, 8.4% English, 7.1% Italian (2000).

Economy: Employment by occupation: 10.7% management, 16.9% professional, 22.3% services, 36.9% sales, 0.5% farming, 4.0% construction, 8.7% production (2000).

Income: Per capita income: $13,458 (2005); Median household income: $39,666 (2005); Average household income: $46,141 (2005); Percent of households with income of $100,000 or more: 5.1% (2005); Poverty rate: 6.0% (2000).

Education: Percent of population age 25 and over with: High school diploma (including GED) or higher: 96.4% (2005); Bachelor's degree or higher: 18.8% (2005); Master's degree or higher: 5.6% (2005).

School District(s)
North Hanover Township (PK-06)
   2003-04 Enrollment: 1,372 . . . . (609) 723-3050

Housing: Homeownership rate: 1.2% (2005); Median home value: $126,471 (2005); Median rent: $829 per month (2000); Median age of housing: 40 years (2000).

Transportation: Commute to work: 92.4% car, 0.2% public transportation, 5.2% walk, 0.6% work from home (2000); Travel time to work: 72.5% less than 15 minutes, 14.9% 15 to 30 minutes, 5.7% 30 to 45 minutes, 3.1% 45 to 60 minutes, 3.8% 60 minutes or more (2000)

MEDFORD (township). Aka Medford Center. Covers a land area of 39.318 square miles and a water area of 0.492 square miles. Located at 39.86° N. Lat.; 74.82° W. Long. Elevation is 40 feet.

History: Friends' meetinghouse here built 1814.

Population: 20,516 (1990); 22,253 (2000); 23,820 (2005); 25,479 (2010 projected); Race: 95.9% White, 1.0% Black, 1.8% Asian, 1.3% Hispanic of any race (2005); Density: 605.8 persons per square mile (2005); Average household size: 2.74 (2005); Median age: 40.7 (2005); Males per 100 females: 93.6 (2005); Marriage status: 19.5% never married, 69.9% now married, 4.8% widowed, 5.8% divorced (2000); Foreign born: 3.9% (2000); Ancestry (includes multiple ancestries): 26.2% Irish, 23.3% German, 21.1% Italian, 12.9% English, 8.3% Polish (2000).

Economy: Single-family building permits issued: 27 (2005); Multi-family building permits issued: 0 (2005); Employment by occupation: 23.7% management, 31.3% professional, 8.9% services, 26.3% sales, 0.1% farming, 4.9% construction, 4.8% production (2000).

Income: Per capita income: $45,319 (2005); Median household income: $95,376 (2005); Average household income: $123,228 (2005); Percent of households with income of $100,000 or more: 47.3% (2005); Poverty rate: 1.9% (2000).

Taxes: Total city taxes per capita: $411 (2004); City property taxes per capita: $391 (2004).

Education: Percent of population age 25 and over with: High school diploma (including GED) or higher: 94.8% (2005); Bachelor's degree or higher: 49.7% (2005); Master's degree or higher: 18.3% (2005).

School District(s)
Burlington County Vocational (09-12)
   2003-04 Enrollment: 1,803 . . . . (609) 267-4226
Lenape Regional (09-12)
   2003-04 Enrollment: 7,067 . . . . (609) 268-2000
Medford Township (PK-08)
   2003-04 Enrollment: 3,028 . . . . (609) 654-6416

Housing: Homeownership rate: 85.1% (2005); Median home value: $319,823 (2005); Median rent: $828 per month (2000); Median age of housing: 23 years (2000).

Safety: Violent crime rate: 4.3 per 10,000 population; Property crime rate: 121.6 per 10,000 population (2004).

Newspapers: The Central Record (General - Circulation 15,000)

Transportation: Commute to work: 91.0% car, 2.6% public transportation, 0.8% walk, 5.1% work from home (2000); Travel time to work: 21.4% less than 15 minutes, 33.5% 15 to 30 minutes, 21.8% 30 to 45 minutes, 9.7% 45 to 60 minutes, 13.6% 60 minutes or more (2000)

Additional Information Contacts
Burlington County Chamber of Commerce . . . . (609) 387-0963
   http://www.bccoc.com
Medford Township . . . . (609) 654-2608
   http://www.medfordtownship.com

MEDFORD LAKES (borough). Covers a land area of 1.205 square miles and a water area of 0.102 square miles. Located at 39.85° N. Lat.; 74.80° W. Long. Elevation is 80 feet.

Population: 4,472 (1990); 4,173 (2000); 4,221 (2005); 4,315 (2010 projected); Race: 97.8% White, 0.7% Black, 0.5% Asian, 1.2% Hispanic of any race (2005); Density: 3,502.9 persons per square mile (2005); Average household size: 2.66 (2005); Median age: 41.3 (2005); Males per 100 females: 94.9 (2005); Marriage status: 17.1% never married, 70.2% now married, 6.4% widowed, 6.3% divorced (2000); Foreign born: 1.7% (2000); Ancestry (includes multiple ancestries): 29.4% Irish, 25.2% German, 21.9% English, 21.0% Italian, 5.3% United States or American (2000).

Economy: Single-family building permits issued: 5 (2005); Multi-family building permits issued: 0 (2005); Employment by occupation: 20.6% management, 28.1% professional, 9.4% services, 31.8% sales, 0.0% farming, 4.2% construction, 5.9% production (2000).

Income: Per capita income: $39,796 (2005); Median household income: $90,109 (2005); Average household income: $106,046 (2005); Percent of households with income of $100,000 or more: 42.0% (2005); Poverty rate: 2.1% (2000).

Education: Percent of population age 25 and over with: High school diploma (including GED) or higher: 95.2% (2005); Bachelor's degree or higher: 50.1% (2005); Master's degree or higher: 13.8% (2005).

School District(s)
Medford Lakes Borough (PK-08)
   2003-04 Enrollment: 563 . . . . (609) 654-0991

Housing: Homeownership rate: 94.2% (2005); Median home value: $255,427 (2005); Median rent: $820 per month (2000); Median age of housing: 40 years (2000).

Safety: Violent crime rate: 9.4 per 10,000 population; Property crime rate: 52.0 per 10,000 population (2004).

Transportation: Commute to work: 90.6% car, 2.7% public transportation, 0.9% walk, 5.8% work from home (2000); Travel time to work: 24.7% less than 15 minutes, 31.2% 15 to 30 minutes, 19.1% 30 to 45 minutes, 11.6% 45 to 60 minutes, 13.3% 60 minutes or more (2000)

Additional Information Contacts
Borough of Medford Lakes. . . . . (609) 654-7589
   http://www.medfordlakes.com

MOORESTOWN (township). Covers a land area of 14.772 square miles and a water area of 0.155 square miles. Located at 39.96° N. Lat.; 74.94° W. Long. Elevation is 76 feet.

History: Of interest are several 18th-century houses. Settled 1682 by Quakers, incorporated 1922.

Population: 16,116 (1990); 19,017 (2000); 20,310 (2005); 21,676 (2010 projected); Race: 87.5% White, 6.4% Black, 3.9% Asian, 2.3% Hispanic of any race (2005); Density: 1,374.9 persons per square mile (2005); Average household size: 2.71 (2005); Median age: 41.3 (2005); Males per 100 females: 89.8 (2005); Marriage status: 18.9% never married, 65.5% now married, 8.4% widowed, 7.3% divorced (2000); Foreign born: 5.8% (2000); Ancestry (includes multiple ancestries): 25.2% Irish, 19.7% German, 15.7% Italian, 14.8% English, 12.4% Other groups (2000).

Economy: Electronic equipment, metal products and chemicals are the principal manufacturing. Single-family building permits issued: 63 (2005); Multi-family building permits issued: 0 (2005); Employment by occupation: 22.6% management, 33.5% professional, 6.9% services, 26.2% sales, 0.1% farming, 4.0% construction, 6.8% production (2000).

Income: Per capita income: $47,347 (2005); Median household income: $86,132 (2005); Average household income: $127,640 (2005); Percent of households with income of $100,000 or more: 42.6% (2005); Poverty rate: 3.4% (2000).

Taxes: Total city taxes per capita: $566 (2004); City property taxes per capita: $555 (2004).

Education: Percent of population age 25 and over with: High school diploma (including GED) or higher: 92.5% (2005); Bachelor's degree or higher: 52.9% (2005); Master's degree or higher: 23.4% (2005).

School District(s)
Moorestown Township (PK-12)
   2003-04 Enrollment: 4,316 . . . . (856) 778-6600

Housing: Homeownership rate: 81.8% (2005); Median home value: $393,457 (2005); Median rent: $701 per month (2000); Median age of housing: 38 years (2000).

Safety: Violent crime rate: 12.5 per 10,000 population; Property crime rate: 217.2 per 10,000 population (2004).

Newspapers: News Weekly (General - Circulation 6,000)

Transportation: Commute to work: 89.5% car, 3.5% public transportation, 1.7% walk, 4.7% work from home (2000); Travel time to work: 31.2% less than 15 minutes, 36.4% 15 to 30 minutes, 15.0% 30 to 45 minutes, 7.5% 45 to 60 minutes, 9.8% 60 minutes or more (2000)

Additional Information Contacts

Burlington County Chamber of Commerce . . . . (609) 387-0963
  http://www.bccoc.com
Moorestown Township . . . . (856) 235-0912
  http://www.moorestown.com

MOORESTOWN-LENOLA (CDP). Covers a land area of 7.044 square miles and a water area of 0.054 square miles. Located at 39.96° N. Lat.; 74.95° W. Long.

Population: 13,242 (1990); 13,860 (2000); 14,098 (2005); 14,451 (2010 projected); Race: 86.7% White, 7.8% Black, 2.6% Asian, 2.7% Hispanic of any race (2005); Density: 2,001.4 persons per square mile (2005); Average household size: 2.62 (2005); Median age: 41.7 (2005); Males per 100 females: 88.0 (2005); Marriage status: 20.2% never married, 62.1% now married, 9.3% widowed, 8.4% divorced (2000); Foreign born: 4.7% (2000); Ancestry (includes multiple ancestries): 24.8% Irish, 19.4% German, 14.9% English, 14.0% Italian, 12.4% Other groups (2000).
Economy: Employment by occupation: 20.7% management, 31.1% professional, 8.3% services, 26.8% sales, 0.2% farming, 4.5% construction, 8.4% production (2000).
Income: Per capita income: $37,142 (2005); Median household income: $71,368 (2005); Average household income: $97,135 (2005); Percent of households with income of $100,000 or more: 32.6% (2005); Poverty rate: 4.3% (2000).
Education: Percent of population age 25 and over with: High school diploma (including GED) or higher: 91.4% (2005); Bachelor's degree or higher: 47.9% (2005); Master's degree or higher: 20.5% (2005).
Housing: Homeownership rate: 78.7% (2005); Median home value: $297,443 (2005); Median rent: $673 per month (2000); Median age of housing: 45 years (2000).
Transportation: Commute to work: 89.4% car, 3.1% public transportation, 2.0% walk, 4.9% work from home (2000); Travel time to work: 34.7% less than 15 minutes, 35.6% 15 to 30 minutes, 13.2% 30 to 45 minutes, 7.0% 45 to 60 minutes, 9.4% 60 minutes or more (2000)

MOUNT HOLLY (township). Covers a land area of 2.860 square miles and a water area of 0.021 square miles. Located at 39.99° N. Lat.; 74.78° W. Long. Elevation is 52 feet.

History: Named for the abundance of local holly plants. In 1676, Thomas Rudyard and John Ridges purchased a share of land from Edward Byllynge and the trustees of West Jersey at the place which was to become Mount Holly. An act of legislature transferred the county seat to Mount Holly in 1786.
Population: 10,603 (1990); 10,728 (2000); 10,808 (2005); 10,969 (2010 projected); Race: 64.3% White, 24.1% Black, 1.6% Asian, 10.6% Hispanic of any race (2005); Density: 3,778.7 persons per square mile (2005); Average household size: 2.68 (2005); Median age: 35.6 (2005); Males per 100 females: 100.7 (2005); Marriage status: 34.1% never married, 48.4% now married, 6.3% widowed, 11.2% divorced (2000); Foreign born: 5.8% (2000); Ancestry (includes multiple ancestries): 27.7% Other groups, 16.8% German, 14.9% Irish, 12.1% English, 11.8% Italian (2000).
Economy: Single-family building permits issued: 14 (2005); Multi-family building permits issued: 0 (2005); Employment by occupation: 7.5% management, 19.8% professional, 17.4% services, 27.9% sales, 0.4% farming, 9.4% construction, 17.7% production (2000).
Income: Per capita income: $23,281 (2005); Median household income: $48,516 (2005); Average household income: $61,470 (2005); Percent of households with income of $100,000 or more: 15.4% (2005); Poverty rate: 9.9% (2000).
Taxes: Total city taxes per capita: $334 (2004); City property taxes per capita: $311 (2004).
Education: Percent of population age 25 and over with: High school diploma (including GED) or higher: 78.0% (2005); Bachelor's degree or higher: 18.9% (2005); Master's degree or higher: 4.2% (2005).

School District(s)

Burlington County Spec Serv (UG-UG)
  2003-04 Enrollment: 2,472 . . . . (609) 261-5600
Eastampton Township (PK-08)
  2003-04 Enrollment: 842 . . . . (609) 267-9172
Mount Holly Township (PK-08)
  2003-04 Enrollment: 1,207 . . . . (609) 267-7108
Rancocas Valley Regional (09-12)
  2003-04 Enrollment: 2,269 . . . . (609) 267-0830

Housing: Homeownership rate: 63.2% (2005); Median home value: $146,122 (2005); Median rent: $635 per month (2000); Median age of housing: 49 years (2000).
Safety: Violent crime rate: 47.0 per 10,000 population; Property crime rate: 374.3 per 10,000 population (2004).
Transportation: Commute to work: 88.5% car, 2.7% public transportation, 6.5% walk, 0.9% work from home (2000); Travel time to work: 31.9% less than 15 minutes, 38.2% 15 to 30 minutes, 16.9% 30 to 45 minutes, 6.1% 45 to 60 minutes, 6.9% 60 minutes or more (2000)

MOUNT LAUREL (township). Covers a land area of 21.808 square miles and a water area of 0.123 square miles. Located at 39.94° N. Lat.; 74.90° W. Long. Elevation is 80 feet.

History: Site of housing dispute resolved by New Jersey Supreme Court in 1975 and clarified in Mount Laurel II (1985), which validated low-and moderate-income housing.
Population: 30,270 (1990); 40,221 (2000); 40,630 (2005); 41,385 (2010 projected); Race: 84.6% White, 8.1% Black, 4.7% Asian, 2.7% Hispanic of any race (2005); Density: 1,863.1 persons per square mile (2005); Average household size: 2.39 (2005); Median age: 40.0 (2005); Males per 100 females: 89.8 (2005); Marriage status: 23.0% never married, 61.9% now married, 7.2% widowed, 7.9% divorced (2000); Foreign born: 6.9% (2000); Ancestry (includes multiple ancestries): 21.1% Irish, 19.7% Italian, 19.0% German, 15.9% Other groups, 12.0% English (2000).
Economy: Unemployment rate: 3.1% (2005); Total civilian labor force: 23,193 (2005); Single-family building permits issued: 1 (2005); Multi-family building permits issued: 0 (2005); Employment by occupation: 21.1% management, 28.4% professional, 9.2% services, 30.2% sales, 0.1% farming, 4.8% construction, 6.2% production (2000).
Income: Per capita income: $37,449 (2005); Median household income: $72,050 (2005); Average household income: $89,049 (2005); Percent of households with income of $100,000 or more: 32.1% (2005); Poverty rate: 3.1% (2000).
Taxes: Total city taxes per capita: $532 (2004); City property taxes per capita: $504 (2004).
Education: Percent of population age 25 and over with: High school diploma (including GED) or higher: 92.2% (2005); Bachelor's degree or higher: 42.1% (2005); Master's degree or higher: 14.1% (2005).

School District(s)

Mount Laurel Township (PK-08)
  2003-04 Enrollment: 4,726 . . . . (856) 235-3387

Two-year College(s)

Cittone Institute (Private, For-profit)
  Fall 2004 Enrollment: 491 . . . . (856) 722-9333
  2005-06 Tuition: In-state $12,512; Out-of-state $12,512
Housing: Homeownership rate: 83.1% (2005); Median home value: $225,130 (2005); Median rent: $816 per month (2000); Median age of housing: 15 years (2000).
Safety: Violent crime rate: 10.8 per 10,000 population; Property crime rate: 191.9 per 10,000 population (2004).
Transportation: Commute to work: 92.1% car, 3.1% public transportation, 0.3% walk, 4.0% work from home (2000); Travel time to work: 24.2% less than 15 minutes, 36.4% 15 to 30 minutes, 19.8% 30 to 45 minutes, 8.4% 45 to 60 minutes, 11.2% 60 minutes or more (2000)

Additional Information Contacts

Burlington County Chamber of Commerce . . . . (856) 439-2520
  http://www.bccoc.com
Mount Laurel Township . . . . (856) 234-0001
  http://www.mountlaurel.com

NEW HANOVER (township). Covers a land area of 22.283 square miles and a water area of 0.104 square miles. Located at 40.03° N. Lat.; 74.58° W. Long.

Population: 9,546 (1990); 9,744 (2000); 9,612 (2005); 9,672 (2010 projected); Race: 63.1% White, 29.5% Black, 1.6% Asian, 24.7% Hispanic of any race (2005); Density: 431.4 persons per square mile (2005); Average household size: 8.43 (2005); Median age: 32.0 (2005); Males per 100 females: 390.7 (2005); Marriage status: 29.4% never married, 66.1% now married, 0.7% widowed, 3.8% divorced (2000); Foreign born: 3.4% (2000); Ancestry (includes multiple ancestries): 21.5% Other groups, 8.3% Irish, 8.1% German, 5.0% English, 4.9% Italian (2000).
Economy: Single-family building permits issued: 0 (2005); Multi-family building permits issued: 0 (2005); Employment by occupation: 16.7% management, 22.1% professional, 21.5% services, 23.5% sales, 0.0% farming, 7.6% construction, 8.6% production (2000).

Income: Per capita income: $13,552 (2005); Median household income: $57,253 (2005); Average household income: $63,518 (2005); Percent of households with income of $100,000 or more: 15.2% (2005); Poverty rate: 3.9% (2000).
Education: Percent of population age 25 and over with: High school diploma (including GED) or higher: 74.9% (2005); Bachelor's degree or higher: 14.9% (2005); Master's degree or higher: 3.3% (2005).
Housing: Homeownership rate: 19.6% (2005); Median home value: $207,732 (2005); Median rent: $905 per month (2000); Median age of housing: 39 years (2000).
Safety: Violent crime rate: 0.0 per 10,000 population; Property crime rate: 18.8 per 10,000 population (2004).
Transportation: Commute to work: 90.3% car, 0.0% public transportation, 7.6% walk, 0.4% work from home (2000); Travel time to work: 68.4% less than 15 minutes, 16.2% 15 to 30 minutes, 4.7% 30 to 45 minutes, 5.0% 45 to 60 minutes, 5.7% 60 minutes or more (2000)

NORTH HANOVER (township). Covers a land area of 17.340 square miles and a water area of 0.042 square miles. Located at 40.05° N. Lat.; 74.57° W. Long.
History: Incorporated 1905.
Population: 10,214 (1990); 7,347 (2000); 7,653 (2005); 7,984 (2010 projected); Race: 80.0% White, 10.6% Black, 2.3% Asian, 6.7% Hispanic of any race (2005); Density: 441.3 persons per square mile (2005); Average household size: 2.86 (2005); Median age: 30.7 (2005); Males per 100 females: 100.3 (2005); Marriage status: 18.8% never married, 69.9% now married, 4.9% widowed, 6.4% divorced (2000); Foreign born: 4.9% (2000); Ancestry (includes multiple ancestries): 23.9% Other groups, 18.8% German, 18.1% Irish, 11.9% Italian, 10.5% English (2000).
Economy: Manufacturing: transmitters, automotive parts, switches, wire, adhesive tape; printing. Single-family building permits issued: 15 (2005); Multi-family building permits issued: 0 (2005); Employment by occupation: 11.0% management, 15.8% professional, 13.6% services, 29.0% sales, 0.9% farming, 13.3% construction, 16.4% production (2000).
Income: Per capita income: $21,288 (2005); Median household income: $45,056 (2005); Average household income: $60,950 (2005); Percent of households with income of $100,000 or more: 15.6% (2005); Poverty rate: 5.3% (2000).
Education: Percent of population age 25 and over with: High school diploma (including GED) or higher: 86.5% (2005); Bachelor's degree or higher: 13.5% (2005); Master's degree or higher: 3.4% (2005).
Housing: Homeownership rate: 52.9% (2005); Median home value: $239,452 (2005); Median rent: $553 per month (2000); Median age of housing: 31 years (2000).
Safety: Violent crime rate: 5.3 per 10,000 population; Property crime rate: 85.4 per 10,000 population (2004).
Transportation: Commute to work: 94.0% car, 0.8% public transportation, 1.5% walk, 3.1% work from home (2000); Travel time to work: 38.7% less than 15 minutes, 27.5% 15 to 30 minutes, 19.6% 30 to 45 minutes, 8.4% 45 to 60 minutes, 5.8% 60 minutes or more (2000)

PALMYRA (borough). Covers a land area of 1.977 square miles and a water area of 0.440 square miles. Located at 40.00° N. Lat.; 75.02° W. Long. Elevation is 18 feet.
History: Incorporated 1923.
Population: 7,056 (1990); 7,091 (2000); 7,822 (2005); 8,564 (2010 projected); Race: 78.0% White, 16.0% Black, 2.0% Asian, 4.0% Hispanic of any race (2005); Density: 3,956.7 persons per square mile (2005); Average household size: 2.29 (2005); Median age: 39.3 (2005); Males per 100 females: 93.5 (2005); Marriage status: 27.2% never married, 52.5% now married, 7.9% widowed, 12.4% divorced (2000); Foreign born: 4.1% (2000); Ancestry (includes multiple ancestries): 27.5% Irish, 25.9% German, 18.0% Other groups, 13.3% Italian, 13.1% English (2000).
Economy: Manufacturing: machinery, metal products, electric signs. Single-family building permits issued: 10 (2005); Multi-family building permits issued: 0 (2005); Employment by occupation: 13.4% management, 19.2% professional, 12.6% services, 32.3% sales, 0.1% farming, 10.2% construction, 12.2% production (2000).
Income: Per capita income: $28,153 (2005); Median household income: $56,801 (2005); Average household income: $64,360 (2005); Percent of households with income of $100,000 or more: 16.2% (2005); Poverty rate: 4.2% (2000).
Education: Percent of population age 25 and over with: High school diploma (including GED) or higher: 85.1% (2005); Bachelor's degree or higher: 21.9% (2005); Master's degree or higher: 6.1% (2005).

Palmyra Borough (PK-12)
    2003-04 Enrollment: 1,184 . . . . (856) 786-2963
Housing: Homeownership rate: 69.7% (2005); Median home value: $169,721 (2005); Median rent: $685 per month (2000); Median age of housing: 50 years (2000).
Safety: Violent crime rate: 14.3 per 10,000 population; Property crime rate: 208.9 per 10,000 population (2004).
Transportation: Commute to work: 92.9% car, 2.9% public transportation, 1.7% walk, 1.9% work from home (2000); Travel time to work: 27.1% less than 15 minutes, 36.9% 15 to 30 minutes, 18.1% 30 to 45 minutes, 9.1% 45 to 60 minutes, 8.8% 60 minutes or more (2000)

PEMBERTON (borough). Covers a land area of 0.595 square miles and a water area of 0.015 square miles. Located at 39.97° N. Lat.; 74.68° W. Long. Elevation is 60 feet.
History: The Pemberton district was settled by Quakers before 1690. Pemberton was first called Hampton Hanover because it lay in both Northampton and Hanover Townships. Later the name was changed to New Mills, and in 1826 the present name was adopted in honor of James Pemberton, a Philadelphia shipping merchant.
Population: 1,367 (1990); 1,210 (2000); 1,270 (2005); 1,339 (2010 projected); Race: 75.8% White, 15.1% Black, 2.8% Asian, 9.7% Hispanic of any race (2005); Density: 2,135.4 persons per square mile (2005); Average household size: 2.50 (2005); Median age: 35.2 (2005); Males per 100 females: 101.9 (2005); Marriage status: 29.9% never married, 53.7% now married, 6.7% widowed, 9.7% divorced (2000); Foreign born: 6.6% (2000); Ancestry (includes multiple ancestries): 24.6% Other groups, 17.6% German, 15.7% Irish, 14.1% English, 10.7% Italian (2000).
Economy: Single-family building permits issued: 31 (2005); Multi-family building permits issued: 0 (2005); Employment by occupation: 8.5% management, 15.0% professional, 22.1% services, 26.3% sales, 0.0% farming, 12.3% construction, 15.8% production (2000).
Income: Per capita income: $21,017 (2005); Median household income: $46,382 (2005); Average household income: $52,530 (2005); Percent of households with income of $100,000 or more: 8.3% (2005); Poverty rate: 7.8% (2000).
Education: Percent of population age 25 and over with: High school diploma (including GED) or higher: 83.8% (2005); Bachelor's degree or higher: 15.6% (2005); Master's degree or higher: 4.4% (2005).

Pemberton Borough (PK-08)
    2003-04 Enrollment: 93 . . . . (609) 894-2261
Pemberton Township (PK-12)
    2003-04 Enrollment: 6,210 . . . . (609) 893-8141
Rancocas Valley Regional (09-12)
    2003-04 Enrollment: 2,269 . . . . (609) 267-0830
Burlington County College (Public)
    Fall 2004 Enrollment: 7,514. . . . . (609) 894-9311
    2005-06 Tuition: In-state $2,925; Out-of-state $4,875
Housing: Homeownership rate: 49.3% (2005); Median home value: $179,825 (2005); Median rent: $580 per month (2000); Median age of housing: 60+ years (2000).
Safety: Violent crime rate: 31.8 per 10,000 population; Property crime rate: 294.4 per 10,000 population (2004).
Transportation: Commute to work: 92.2% car, 1.6% public transportation, 4.0% walk, 1.6% work from home (2000); Travel time to work: 31.6% less than 15 minutes, 37.8% 15 to 30 minutes, 19.9% 30 to 45 minutes, 7.2% 45 to 60 minutes, 3.5% 60 minutes or more (2000)

PEMBERTON (township). Covers a land area of 61.676 square miles and a water area of 0.818 square miles. Located at 39.96° N. Lat.; 74.58° W. Long. Elevation is 60 feet.
History: Settled by Quakers before 1690. Site of Burlington County College.
Population: 31,335 (1990); 28,691 (2000); 29,269 (2005); 30,089 (2010 projected); Race: 63.1% White, 25.3% Black, 3.1% Asian, 9.8% Hispanic of any race (2005); Density: 474.6 persons per square mile (2005); Average household size: 2.78 (2005); Median age: 35.5 (2005); Males per 100 females: 96.6 (2005); Marriage status: 28.3% never married, 56.6% now married, 6.4% widowed, 8.7% divorced (2000); Foreign born: 7.1% (2000); Ancestry (includes multiple ancestries): 34.2% Other groups, 16.1% German, 15.5% Irish, 8.8% Italian, 7.4% English (2000).

Economy: Textiles; poultry; wheat, dairy products. Unemployment rate: 5.5% (2005); Total civilian labor force: 14,780 (2005); Single-family building permits issued: 68 (2005); Multi-family building permits issued: 0 (2005); Employment by occupation: 8.5% management, 12.9% professional, 23.0% services, 28.8% sales, 0.4% farming, 10.1% construction, 16.3% production (2000).
Income: Per capita income: $22,305 (2005); Median household income: $52,803 (2005); Average household income: $61,414 (2005); Percent of households with income of $100,000 or more: 13.6% (2005); Poverty rate: 9.3% (2000).
Taxes: Total city taxes per capita: $385 (2004); City property taxes per capita: $378 (2004).
Education: Percent of population age 25 and over with: High school diploma (including GED) or higher: 79.8% (2005); Bachelor's degree or higher: 9.3% (2005); Master's degree or higher: 2.6% (2005).

School District(s)

Pemberton Borough (PK-08)
    2003-04 Enrollment: 93 . . . . (609) 894-2261
Pemberton Township (PK-12)
    2003-04 Enrollment: 6,210 . . . . (609) 893-8141
Rancocas Valley Regional (09-12)
    2003-04 Enrollment: 2,269 . . . . (609) 267-0830

Two-year College(s)

Burlington County College (Public)
    Fall 2004 Enrollment: 7,514 . . . . (609) 894-9311
    2005-06 Tuition: In-state $2,925; Out-of-state $4,875
Housing: Homeownership rate: 74.1% (2005); Median home value: $143,545 (2005); Median rent: $558 per month (2000); Median age of housing: 29 years (2000).
Safety: Violent crime rate: 21.3 per 10,000 population; Property crime rate: 187.0 per 10,000 population (2004).
Transportation: Commute to work: 95.2% car, 1.0% public transportation, 1.4% walk, 1.5% work from home (2000); Travel time to work: 20.6% less than 15 minutes, 29.2% 15 to 30 minutes, 24.5% 30 to 45 minutes, 13.5% 45 to 60 minutes, 12.2% 60 minutes or more (2000)

Additional Information Contacts
Pemberton Township. . . . . (609) 894-8201
   http://www.pemberton-twp.com

PEMBERTON HEIGHTS (CDP). Covers a land area of 0.930 square miles and a water area of 0 square miles. Located at 39.95° N. Lat.; 74.68° W. Long. Elevation is 70 feet.

Population: 2,941 (1990); 2,512 (2000); 2,482 (2005); 2,456 (2010 projected); Race: 42.2% White, 45.9% Black, 4.3% Asian, 11.4% Hispanic of any race (2005); Density: 2,667.5 persons per square mile (2005); Average household size: 2.28 (2005); Median age: 40.8 (2005); Males per 100 females: 100.2 (2005); Marriage status: 33.7% never married, 47.4% now married, 8.0% widowed, 10.8% divorced (2000); Foreign born: 15.0% (2000); Ancestry (includes multiple ancestries): 49.2% Other groups, 16.1% German, 7.2% Irish, 5.7% English, 2.5% African (2000).
Economy: Employment by occupation: 9.5% management, 8.9% professional, 32.4% services, 27.4% sales, 0.0% farming, 5.9% construction, 15.8% production (2000).
Income: Per capita income: $28,830 (2005); Median household income: $49,063 (2005); Average household income: $65,828 (2005); Percent of households with income of $100,000 or more: 15.8% (2005); Poverty rate: 6.6% (2000).
Education: Percent of population age 25 and over with: High school diploma (including GED) or higher: 86.3% (2005); Bachelor's degree or higher: 11.8% (2005); Master's degree or higher: 3.0% (2005).
Housing: Homeownership rate: 54.9% (2005); Median home value: $168,277 (2005); Median rent: $456 per month (2000); Median age of housing: 30 years (2000).
Transportation: Commute to work: 95.7% car, 2.6% public transportation, 0.0% walk, 1.7% work from home (2000); Travel time to work: 15.0% less than 15 minutes, 43.3% 15 to 30 minutes, 20.0% 30 to 45 minutes, 11.1% 45 to 60 minutes, 10.6% 60 minutes or more (2000)

PRESIDENTIAL LAKES ESTATES (CDP). Aka Presidential Lakes. Covers a land area of 1.043 square miles and a water area of 0.016 square miles. Located at 39.91° N. Lat.; 74.56° W. Long.

Population: 2,493 (1990); 2,332 (2000); 2,270 (2005); 2,250 (2010 projected); Race: 75.1% White, 14.2% Black, 2.4% Asian, 8.1% Hispanic of any race (2005); Density: 2,176.4 persons per square mile (2005); Average household size: 3.07 (2005); Median age: 35.9 (2005); Males per 100

females: 104.0 (2005); Marriage status: 29.5% never married, 59.9% now married, 3.8% widowed, 6.8% divorced (2000); Foreign born: 6.4% (2000); Ancestry (includes multiple ancestries): 22.9% Other groups, 22.9% Irish, 18.4% German, 14.6% English, 10.2% United States or American (2000).
Economy: Employment by occupation: 10.6% management, 16.7% professional, 17.1% services, 27.9% sales, 1.2% farming, 9.7% construction, 16.9% production (2000).
Income: Per capita income: $28,141 (2005); Median household income: $76,389 (2005); Average household income: $86,441 (2005); Percent of households with income of $100,000 or more: 28.1% (2005); Poverty rate: 2.5% (2000).
Education: Percent of population age 25 and over with: High school diploma (including GED) or higher: 84.4% (2005); Bachelor's degree or higher: 8.8% (2005); Master's degree or higher: 1.9% (2005).
Housing: Homeownership rate: 95.8% (2005); Median home value: $157,143 (2005); Median rent: $822 per month (2000); Median age of housing: 27 years (2000).
Transportation: Commute to work: 98.4% car, 0.0% public transportation, 0.4% walk, 0.0% work from home (2000); Travel time to work: 8.2% less than 15 minutes, 21.6% 15 to 30 minutes, 38.3% 30 to 45 minutes, 13.0% 45 to 60 minutes, 18.9% 60 minutes or more (2000)

RAMBLEWOOD (CDP). Covers a land area of 3.388 square miles and a water area of 0 square miles. Located at 39.93° N. Lat.; 74.95° W. Long. Elevation is 40 feet.

Population: 6,181 (1990); 6,003 (2000); 5,804 (2005); 5,664 (2010 projected); Race: 87.1% White, 6.0% Black, 4.6% Asian, 2.5% Hispanic of any race (2005); Density: 1,713.1 persons per square mile (2005); Average household size: 2.54 (2005); Median age: 41.5 (2005); Males per 100 females: 92.8 (2005); Marriage status: 22.7% never married, 63.5% now married, 5.7% widowed, 8.2% divorced (2000); Foreign born: 6.6% (2000); Ancestry (includes multiple ancestries): 25.4% Irish, 21.9% Italian, 16.6% German, 13.2% Other groups, 12.5% English (2000).
Economy: Employment by occupation: 24.2% management, 28.1% professional, 7.6% services, 30.8% sales, 0.0% farming, 5.6% construction, 3.7% production (2000).
Income: Per capita income: $36,811 (2005); Median household income: $81,359 (2005); Average household income: $93,158 (2005); Percent of households with income of $100,000 or more: 35.0% (2005); Poverty rate: 1.7% (2000).
Education: Percent of population age 25 and over with: High school diploma (including GED) or higher: 91.7% (2005); Bachelor's degree or higher: 43.1% (2005); Master's degree or higher: 14.6% (2005).
Housing: Homeownership rate: 72.0% (2005); Median home value: $242,345 (2005); Median rent: $834 per month (2000); Median age of housing: 31 years (2000).
Transportation: Commute to work: 89.9% car, 4.9% public transportation, 0.6% walk, 4.0% work from home (2000); Travel time to work: 30.1% less than 15 minutes, 33.8% 15 to 30 minutes, 16.4% 30 to 45 minutes, 8.8% 45 to 60 minutes, 10.9% 60 minutes or more (2000)

RIVERSIDE (township). Covers a land area of 1.522 square miles and a water area of 0.103 square miles. Located at 40.03° N. Lat.; 74.95° W. Long. Elevation is 20 feet.

Population: 7,974 (1990); 7,911 (2000); 8,048 (2005); 8,264 (2010 projected); Race: 87.0% White, 6.0% Black, 0.5% Asian, 5.3% Hispanic of any race (2005); Density: 5,287.2 persons per square mile (2005); Average household size: 2.64 (2005); Median age: 36.8 (2005); Males per 100 females: 99.8 (2005); Marriage status: 29.4% never married, 52.5% now married, 8.9% widowed, 9.2% divorced (2000); Foreign born: 10.2% (2000); Ancestry (includes multiple ancestries): 24.2% Irish, 22.7% German, 18.6% Italian, 12.9% Other groups, 12.4% Polish (2000).
Economy: Manufacturing: watch cases, clothing, metal products, textiles, cement, boats; printing. Single-family building permits issued: 15 (2005); Multi-family building permits issued: 0 (2005); Employment by occupation: 8.7% management, 11.2% professional, 14.1% services, 30.7% sales, 0.3% farming, 16.1% construction, 18.7% production (2000).
Income: Per capita income: $21,712 (2005); Median household income: $48,500 (2005); Average household income: $56,844 (2005); Percent of households with income of $100,000 or more: 11.6% (2005); Poverty rate: 8.2% (2000).
Education: Percent of population age 25 and over with: High school diploma (including GED) or higher: 75.6% (2005); Bachelor's degree or higher: 11.4% (2005); Master's degree or higher: 3.0% (2005).

School District(s)

Riverside Township (PK-12)

    2003-04 Enrollment: 1,629 . . . . (856) 461-1255

Housing: Homeownership rate: 67.5% (2005); Median home value: $153,723 (2005); Median rent: $580 per month (2000); Median age of housing: 57 years (2000).

Safety: Violent crime rate: 41.0 per 10,000 population; Property crime rate: 159.0 per 10,000 population (2004).

Transportation: Commute to work: 90.9% car, 1.5% public transportation, 3.4% walk, 0.9% work from home (2000); Travel time to work: 29.5% less than 15 minutes, 39.7% 15 to 30 minutes, 16.3% 30 to 45 minutes, 5.2% 45 to 60 minutes, 9.3% 60 minutes or more (2000)

RIVERTON (borough). Covers a land area of 0.656 square miles and a water area of 0.285 square miles. Located at 40.01° N. Lat.; 75.01° W. Long. Elevation is 17 feet.

History: Incorporated 1893.

Population: 2,775 (1990); 2,759 (2000); 2,756 (2005); 2,782 (2010 projected); Race: 94.9% White, 2.1% Black, 1.1% Asian, 1.6% Hispanic of any race (2005); Density: 4,200.5 persons per square mile (2005); Average household size: 2.54 (2005); Median age: 42.7 (2005); Males per 100 females: 90.7 (2005); Marriage status: 21.4% never married, 61.6% now married, 9.4% widowed, 7.6% divorced (2000); Foreign born: 2.6% (2000); Ancestry (includes multiple ancestries): 28.6% Irish, 24.7% German, 18.4% English, 12.4% Italian, 9.5% Polish (2000).

Economy: Ironworking. Single-family building permits issued: 1 (2005); Multi-family building permits issued: 0 (2005); Employment by occupation: 15.8% management, 31.7% professional, 6.2% services, 28.2% sales, 0.0% farming, 8.1% construction, 10.0% production (2000).

Income: Per capita income: $32,238 (2005); Median household income: $65,682 (2005); Average household income: $79,931 (2005); Percent of households with income of $100,000 or more: 26.0% (2005); Poverty rate: 3.1% (2000).

Education: Percent of population age 25 and over with: High school diploma (including GED) or higher: 89.9% (2005); Bachelor's degree or higher: 36.2% (2005); Master's degree or higher: 12.6% (2005).

School District(s)

Riverton (PK-08)

    2003-04 Enrollment: 249 . . . . (856) 829-0087

Housing: Homeownership rate: 76.3% (2005); Median home value: $247,051 (2005); Median rent: $639 per month (2000); Median age of housing: 60+ years (2000).

Safety: Violent crime rate: 18.0 per 10,000 population; Property crime rate: 191.0 per 10,000 population (2004).

Transportation: Commute to work: 88.2% car, 5.4% public transportation, 2.6% walk, 2.9% work from home (2000); Travel time to work: 29.0% less than 15 minutes, 29.0% 15 to 30 minutes, 20.6% 30 to 45 minutes, 13.8% 45 to 60 minutes, 7.6% 60 minutes or more (2000)

ROEBLING (unincorporated postal area, zip code 08554). Covers a land area of 1.097 square miles and a water area of 0 square miles. Located at 40.07° N. Lat.; 74.71° W. Long. Elevation is 40 feet.

Population: 3,656 (2000); Race: 90.5% White, 6.1% Black, 1.4% Asian, 1.4% Hispanic of any race (2000); Density: 3,332.7 persons per square mile (2000); Age: 24.3% under 18, 12.3% over 64 (2000); Marriage status: 26.5% never married, 55.5% now married, 8.1% widowed, 9.8% divorced (2000); Foreign born: 5.6% (2000); Ancestry (includes multiple ancestries): 22.9% Irish, 20.2% German, 15.0% Italian, 12.7% Hungarian, 11.3% Polish (2000).

Economy: Employment by occupation: 10.7% management, 16.3% professional, 12.5% services, 32.1% sales, 0.3% farming, 11.1% construction, 16.9% production (2000).

Income: Per capita income: $22,519 (2000); Median household income: $54,848 (2000); Poverty rate: 6.1% (2000).

Education: Percent of population age 25 and over with: High school diploma (including GED) or higher: 83.4% (2000); Bachelor's degree or higher: 15.7% (2000).

School District(s)

Florence Township (PK-12)

    2003-04 Enrollment: 1,641 . . . . (609) 499-4600

Housing: Homeownership rate: 78.7% (2000); Median home value: $92,000 (2000); Median rent: $668 per month (2000); Median age of housing: 60+ years (2000).

Transportation: Commute to work: 91.7% car, 1.8% public transportation, 3.5% walk, 2.7% work from home (2000); Travel time to work: 25.2% less

---

than 15 minutes, 37.8% 15 to 30 minutes, 22.9% 30 to 45 minutes, 7.8% 45 to 60 minutes, 6.2% 60 minutes or more (2000)

SHAMONG (township). Covers a land area of 44.812 square miles and a water area of 0.249 square miles. Located at 39.77° N. Lat.; 74.73° W. Long.

History: Incorporated 1852.

Population: 5,765 (1990); 6,462 (2000); 6,898 (2005); 7,365 (2010 projected); Race: 96.9% White, 0.7% Black, 0.9% Asian, 1.2% Hispanic of any race (2005); Density: 153.9 persons per square mile (2005); Average household size: 2.96 (2005); Median age: 38.0 (2005); Males per 100 females: 99.2 (2005); Marriage status: 21.5% never married, 68.2% now married, 4.7% widowed, 5.6% divorced (2000); Foreign born: 2.0% (2000); Ancestry (includes multiple ancestries): 29.6% Irish, 25.1% German, 21.7% Italian, 15.1% English, 9.6% Polish (2000).

Economy: Single-family building permits issued: 21 (2005); Multi-family building permits issued: 0 (2005); Employment by occupation: 17.4% management, 24.8% professional, 12.8% services, 29.1% sales, 0.1% farming, 8.5% construction, 7.3% production (2000).

Income: Per capita income: $38,381 (2005); Median household income: $92,442 (2005); Average household income: $113,292 (2005); Percent of households with income of $100,000 or more: 44.4% (2005); Poverty rate: 2.6% (2000).

Education: Percent of population age 25 and over with: High school diploma (including GED) or higher: 92.3% (2005); Bachelor's degree or higher: 37.3% (2005); Master's degree or higher: 11.1% (2005).

School District(s)

Shamong Township (PK-08)

    2003-04 Enrollment: 928 . . . . (609) 268-0120

Housing: Homeownership rate: 95.3% (2005); Median home value: $281,550 (2005); Median rent: $631 per month (2000); Median age of housing: 22 years (2000).

Transportation: Commute to work: 90.5% car, 2.1% public transportation, 0.4% walk, 6.1% work from home (2000); Travel time to work: 16.2% less than 15 minutes, 25.2% 15 to 30 minutes, 22.1% 30 to 45 minutes, 18.3% 45 to 60 minutes, 18.2% 60 minutes or more (2000)

Additional Information Contacts

Shamong Township . . . . (608) 268-2377

    http://www.nothinbut.net/~shamong

SOUTHAMPTON (township). Covers a land area of 44.033 square miles and a water area of 0.245 square miles. Located at 39.91° N. Lat.; 74.71° W. Long.

History: Incorporated 1845.

Population: 10,209 (1990); 10,388 (2000); 11,172 (2005); 11,997 (2010 projected); Race: 96.4% White, 1.7% Black, 0.6% Asian, 1.7% Hispanic of any race (2005); Density: 253.7 persons per square mile (2005); Average household size: 2.22 (2005); Median age: 51.2 (2005); Males per 100 females: 88.4 (2005); Marriage status: 16.4% never married, 64.4% now married, 13.1% widowed, 6.1% divorced (2000); Foreign born: 3.4% (2000); Ancestry (includes multiple ancestries): 26.3% German, 23.1% Irish, 16.4% English, 12.0% Italian, 8.1% Polish (2000).

Economy: Manufacturing of machine tools. Single-family building permits issued: 88 (2005); Multi-family building permits issued: 0 (2005); Employment by occupation: 13.4% management, 18.6% professional, 14.3% services, 27.5% sales, 0.3% farming, 11.4% construction, 14.5% production (2000).

Income: Per capita income: $30,479 (2005); Median household income: $51,046 (2005); Average household income: $67,679 (2005); Percent of households with income of $100,000 or more: 20.4% (2005); Poverty rate: 3.9% (2000).

Education: Percent of population age 25 and over with: High school diploma (including GED) or higher: 83.4% (2005); Bachelor's degree or higher: 17.8% (2005); Master's degree or higher: 6.0% (2005).

School District(s)

Southampton Township (PK-08)

    2003-04 Enrollment: 904 . . . . (609) 859-2256

Housing: Homeownership rate: 93.1% (2005); Median home value: $167,928 (2005); Median rent: $624 per month (2000); Median age of housing: 25 years (2000).

Transportation: Commute to work: 91.6% car, 1.9% public transportation, 0.5% walk, 4.5% work from home (2000); Travel time to work: 22.9% less than 15 minutes, 32.6% 15 to 30 minutes, 26.7% 30 to 45 minutes, 9.3% 45 to 60 minutes, 8.5% 60 minutes or more (2000)

Additional Information Contacts

Southampton Township. . . . . (609) 859-3235
http://www.southamptonnj.org

SPRINGFIELD (township). Covers a land area of 30.035 square miles and a water area of 0.011 square miles. Located at 40.03° N. Lat.; 74.70° W. Long. Elevation is 110 feet.

Population: 3,030 (1990); 3,227 (2000); 3,624 (2005); 4,017 (2010 projected); Race: 89.9% White, 4.0% Black, 3.5% Asian, 2.2% Hispanic of any race (2005); Density: 120.7 persons per square mile (2005); Average household size: 2.91 (2005); Median age: 40.3 (2005); Males per 100 females: 99.6 (2005); Marriage status: 23.7% never married, 65.0% now married, 5.6% widowed, 5.7% divorced (2000); Foreign born: 6.6% (2000); Ancestry (includes multiple ancestries): 25.8% German, 20.1% Irish, 16.1% English, 15.1% Italian, 10.9% Polish (2000).

Economy: Single-family building permits issued: 15 (2005); Multi-family building permits issued: 0 (2005); Employment by occupation: 14.1% management, 22.4% professional, 10.9% services, 32.2% sales, 0.9% farming, 9.3% construction, 10.2% production (2000).

Income: Per capita income: $34,550 (2005); Median household income: $83,186 (2005); Average household income: $99,639 (2005); Percent of households with income of $100,000 or more: 36.2% (2005); Poverty rate: 3.6% (2000).

Education: Percent of population age 25 and over with: High school diploma (including GED) or higher: 87.1% (2005); Bachelor's degree or higher: 26.1% (2005); Master's degree or higher: 8.3% (2005).

Housing: Homeownership rate: 91.0% (2005); Median home value: $291,466 (2005); Median rent: $529 per month (2000); Median age of housing: 28 years (2000).

Safety: Violent crime rate: 11.3 per 10,000 population; Property crime rate: 130.3 per 10,000 population (2004).

Transportation: Commute to work: 90.0% car, 0.3% public transportation, 3.7% walk, 6.1% work from home (2000); Travel time to work: 25.1% less than 15 minutes, 34.6% 15 to 30 minutes, 21.7% 30 to 45 minutes, 9.5% 45 to 60 minutes, 9.2% 60 minutes or more (2000)

Additional Information Contacts
Springfield Township . . . . (973) 912-2200
http://springfield-nj.com

TABERNACLE (township). Covers a land area of 49.456 square miles and a water area of 0.062 square miles. Located at 39.83° N. Lat.; 74.68° W. Long. Elevation is 98 feet.

History: Incorporated 1901.

Population: 7,360 (1990); 7,170 (2000); 7,379 (2005); 7,646 (2010 projected); Race: 95.5% White, 2.7% Black, 0.7% Asian, 2.0% Hispanic of any race (2005); Density: 149.2 persons per square mile (2005); Average household size: 2.98 (2005); Median age: 39.0 (2005); Males per 100 females: 101.7 (2005); Marriage status: 21.6% never married, 70.6% now married, 3.0% widowed, 4.8% divorced (2000); Foreign born: 2.2% (2000); Ancestry (includes multiple ancestries): 27.8% Irish, 25.7% German, 18.0% English, 15.8% Italian, 7.2% Polish (2000).

Economy: Single-family building permits issued: 15 (2005); Multi-family building permits issued: 0 (2005); Employment by occupation: 14.5% management, 27.1% professional, 9.1% services, 29.3% sales, 0.3% farming, 10.2% construction, 9.4% production (2000).

Income: Per capita income: $31,953 (2005); Median household income: $85,964 (2005); Average household income: $94,662 (2005); Percent of households with income of $100,000 or more: 40.8% (2005); Poverty rate: 2.0% (2000).

Education: Percent of population age 25 and over with: High school diploma (including GED) or higher: 92.6% (2005); Bachelor's degree or higher: 30.6% (2005); Master's degree or higher: 9.9% (2005).

School District(s)
Lenape Regional (09-12)
    2003-04 Enrollment: 7,067 . . . . (609) 268-2000
Tabernacle Township (PK-08)
    2003-04 Enrollment: 985 . . . . (609) 268-0153

Housing: Homeownership rate: 95.2% (2005); Median home value: $261,252 (2005); Median rent: $589 per month (2000); Median age of housing: 24 years (2000).

Transportation: Commute to work: 93.9% car, 1.3% public transportation, 0.2% walk, 4.4% work from home (2000); Travel time to work: 18.4% less than 15 minutes, 29.5% 15 to 30 minutes, 28.2% 30 to 45 minutes, 8.4% 45 to 60 minutes, 15.4% 60 minutes or more (2000)

Additional Information Contacts

Tabernacle Township. . . . . (609) 268-1220
http://www.townshipoftabernacle-nj.gov

VINCENTOWN (unincorporated postal area, zip code 08088). Covers a land area of 129.237 square miles and a water area of 0.465 square miles. Located at 39.87° N. Lat.; 74.70° W. Long. Elevation is 40 feet.

Population: 24,372 (2000); Race: 97.4% White, 0.8% Black, 0.8% Asian, 1.5% Hispanic of any race (2000); Density: 188.6 persons per square mile (2000); Age: 24.0% under 18, 17.7% over 64 (2000); Marriage status: 19.3% never married, 67.1% now married, 8.1% widowed, 5.6% divorced (2000); Foreign born: 2.7% (2000); Ancestry (includes multiple ancestries): 26.2% Irish, 26.0% German, 16.6% English, 16.1% Italian, 8.2% Polish (2000).

Economy: Employment by occupation: 14.9% management, 23.3% professional, 12.0% services, 28.4% sales, 0.3% farming, 10.3% construction, 10.8% production (2000).

Income: Per capita income: $28,419 (2000); Median household income: $60,773 (2000); Poverty rate: 3.0% (2000).

Education: Percent of population age 25 and over with: High school diploma (including GED) or higher: 88.3% (2000); Bachelor's degree or higher: 26.3% (2000).

Housing: Homeownership rate: 94.2% (2000); Median home value: $154,100 (2000); Median rent: $611 per month (2000); Median age of housing: 24 years (2000).

Transportation: Commute to work: 92.1% car, 1.7% public transportation, 0.3% walk, 4.9% work from home (2000); Travel time to work: 19.4% less than 15 minutes, 29.4% 15 to 30 minutes, 25.8% 30 to 45 minutes, 11.8% 45 to 60 minutes, 13.6% 60 minutes or more (2000)

WASHINGTON (township). Covers a land area of 100.141 square miles and a water area of 2.718 square miles. Located at 39.69° N. Lat.; 74.56° W. Long. Elevation is 55 feet.

Population: 805 (1990); 621 (2000); 646 (2005); 710 (2010 projected); Race: 77.9% White, 4.2% Black, 0.2% Asian, 21.5% Hispanic of any race (2005); Density: 6.5 persons per square mile (2005); Average household size: 3.57 (2005); Median age: 42.2 (2005); Males per 100 females: 97.6 (2005); Marriage status: 12.4% never married, 61.6% now married, 14.9% widowed, 11.1% divorced (2000); Foreign born: 1.2% (2000); Ancestry (includes multiple ancestries): 25.9% Other groups, 24.4% Irish, 14.3% English, 11.7% German, 7.1% Italian (2000).

Economy: Single-family building permits issued: 4 (2005); Multi-family building permits issued: 0 (2005); Employment by occupation: 11.8% management, 8.3% professional, 15.4% services, 16.0% sales, 17.8% farming, 5.3% construction, 25.4% production (2000).

Income: Per capita income: $13,562 (2005); Median household income: $38,629 (2005); Average household income: $44,199 (2005); Percent of households with income of $100,000 or more: 3.3% (2005); Poverty rate: 16.0% (2000).

Education: Percent of population age 25 and over with: High school diploma (including GED) or higher: 55.7% (2005); Bachelor's degree or higher: 12.1% (2005); Master's degree or higher: 2.8% (2005).

Housing: Homeownership rate: 76.2% (2005); Median home value: $163,043 (2005); Median rent: $400 per month (2000); Median age of housing: 47 years (2000).

Transportation: Commute to work: 91.5% car, 0.0% public transportation, 8.5% walk, 0.0% work from home (2000); Travel time to work: 43.6% less than 15 minutes, 3.0% 15 to 30 minutes, 38.8% 30 to 45 minutes, 14.5% 45 to 60 minutes, 0.0% 60 minutes or more (2000)

WESTAMPTON (township). Covers a land area of 11.041 square miles and a water area of 0.118 square miles. Located at 40.01° N. Lat.; 74.82° W. Long.

History: Incorporated 1850.

Population: 6,004 (1990); 7,217 (2000); 8,462 (2005); 9,662 (2010 projected); Race: 64.4% White, 26.2% Black, 3.5% Asian, 7.1% Hispanic of any race (2005); Density: 766.4 persons per square mile (2005); Average household size: 2.83 (2005); Median age: 37.0 (2005); Males per 100 females: 89.9 (2005); Marriage status: 22.8% never married, 65.1% now married, 3.9% widowed, 8.3% divorced (2000); Foreign born: 6.5% (2000); Ancestry (includes multiple ancestries): 30.1% Other groups, 20.7% German, 16.8% Irish, 13.1% Italian, 11.3% English (2000).

Economy: Single-family building permits issued: 66 (2005); Multi-family building permits issued: 0 (2005); Employment by occupation: 13.4% management, 22.7% professional, 14.5% services, 33.5% sales, 0.0% farming, 4.7% construction, 11.2% production (2000).

Income: Per capita income: $29,313 (2005); Median household income: $69,623 (2005); Average household income: $82,299 (2005); Percent of households with income of $100,000 or more: 25.2% (2005); Poverty rate: 2.5% (2000).

Education: Percent of population age 25 and over with: High school diploma (including GED) or higher: 91.0% (2005); Bachelor's degree or higher: 26.2% (2005); Master's degree or higher: 6.9% (2005).

School District(s)

Burlington County Vocational (09-12)
    2003-04 Enrollment: 1,803 . . . . (609) 267-4226
Westampton (PK-08)
    2003-04 Enrollment: 1,080 . . . . (609) 267-2053

Housing: Homeownership rate: 92.9% (2005); Median home value: $187,994 (2005); Median rent: $1,004 per month (2000); Median age of housing: 19 years (2000).

Safety: Violent crime rate: 26.2 per 10,000 population; Property crime rate: 246.6 per 10,000 population (2004).

Transportation: Commute to work: 94.6% car, 1.0% public transportation, 0.7% walk, 3.7% work from home (2000); Travel time to work: 26.1% less than 15 minutes, 34.1% 15 to 30 minutes, 22.5% 30 to 45 minutes, 6.8% 45 to 60 minutes, 10.6% 60 minutes or more (2000)

Additional Information Contacts
Westampton Township . . . . (609) 267-1891
    http://www.westampton.com

WILLINGBORO (township). Covers a land area of 7.689 square miles and a water area of 0.334 square miles. Located at 40.02° N. Lat.; 74.88° W. Long. Elevation is 60 feet.

History: Named for Thomas Olive of Wellingborough, England. The original name of Willingboro was temporarily changed to Levittown after World War II.

Population: 36,291 (1990); 33,008 (2000); 33,118 (2005); 33,563 (2010 projected); Race: 17.9% White, 72.8% Black, 1.8% Asian, 6.6% Hispanic of any race (2005); Density: 4,307.1 persons per square mile (2005); Average household size: 3.01 (2005); Median age: 38.3 (2005); Males per 100 females: 89.7 (2005); Marriage status: 28.8% never married, 56.0% now married, 6.8% widowed, 8.4% divorced (2000); Foreign born: 8.2% (2000); Ancestry (includes multiple ancestries): 64.2% Other groups, 6.9% German, 6.0% Irish, 3.9% English, 3.5% Italian (2000).

Economy: Residential and commercial town. Unemployment rate: 5.6% (2005); Total civilian labor force: 16,798 (2005); Single-family building permits issued: 42 (2005); Multi-family building permits issued: 29 (2005); Employment by occupation: 12.1% management, 20.5% professional, 15.7% services, 30.6% sales, 0.2% farming, 6.2% construction, 14.8% production (2000).

Income: Per capita income: $25,833 (2005); Median household income: $68,351 (2005); Average household income: $77,304 (2005); Percent of households with income of $100,000 or more: 23.2% (2005); Poverty rate: 5.9% (2000).

Taxes: Total city taxes per capita: $538 (2004); City property taxes per capita: $534 (2004).

Education: Percent of population age 25 and over with: High school diploma (including GED) or higher: 87.2% (2005); Bachelor's degree or higher: 18.9% (2005); Master's degree or higher: 6.0% (2005).

School District(s)

Willingboro Township (PK-12)
    2003-04 Enrollment: 5,875 . . . . (609) 835-8600

Housing: Homeownership rate: 92.5% (2005); Median home value: $144,055 (2005); Median rent: $896 per month (2000); Median age of housing: 35 years (2000).

Hospitals: Rancocas Hospital (350 beds)

Safety: Violent crime rate: 35.1 per 10,000 population; Property crime rate: 216.4 per 10,000 population (2004).

Newspapers: Burlington County Times (Circulation 41,327); McGuire Airtides (General - Circulation 9,872)

Transportation: Commute to work: 91.6% car, 5.7% public transportation, 1.1% walk, 1.1% work from home (2000); Travel time to work: 19.6% less than 15 minutes, 31.4% 15 to 30 minutes, 24.2% 30 to 45 minutes, 10.2% 45 to 60 minutes, 14.6% 60 minutes or more (2000)

Additional Information Contacts
Burlington County Chamber of Commerce . . . . (856) 439-2520
    http://www.bccoc.com
Willingboro Township . . . . (609) 877-2200
    http://www.willingboro.org/twpindex.htm

WOODLAND (township). Covers a land area of 95.940 square miles and a water area of 0.446 square miles. Located at 39.84° N. Lat.; 74.51° W. Long.

Population: 2,063 (1990); 1,170 (2000); 1,249 (2005); 1,335 (2010 projected); Race: 97.8% White, 0.5% Black, 0.3% Asian, 1.6% Hispanic of any race (2005); Density: 13.0 persons per square mile (2005); Average household size: 2.69 (2005); Median age: 39.0 (2005); Males per 100 females: 97.3 (2005); Marriage status: 28.5% never married, 56.5% now married, 5.1% widowed, 9.9% divorced (2000); Foreign born: 3.0% (2000); Ancestry (includes multiple ancestries): 28.8% German, 28.7% Irish, 17.8% English, 13.5% Italian, 8.0% Other groups (2000).

Economy: Single-family building permits issued: 7 (2005); Multi-family building permits issued: 0 (2005); Employment by occupation: 8.6% management, 19.7% professional, 14.3% services, 23.0% sales, 1.3% farming, 18.5% construction, 14.6% production (2000).

Income: Per capita income: $32,804 (2005); Median household income: $73,452 (2005); Average household income: $88,113 (2005); Percent of households with income of $100,000 or more: 33.1% (2005); Poverty rate: 2.9% (2000).

Education: Percent of population age 25 and over with: High school diploma (including GED) or higher: 82.6% (2005); Bachelor's degree or higher: 18.2% (2005); Master's degree or higher: 5.9% (2005).

Housing: Homeownership rate: 84.5% (2005); Median home value: $217,537 (2005); Median rent: $475 per month (2000); Median age of housing: 28 years (2000).

Transportation: Commute to work: 93.4% car, 0.3% public transportation, 1.4% walk, 2.4% work from home (2000); Travel time to work: 14.4% less than 15 minutes, 27.1% 15 to 30 minutes, 30.0% 30 to 45 minutes, 16.5% 45 to 60 minutes, 11.9% 60 minutes or more (2000)

WRIGHTSTOWN (borough). Covers a land area of 1.759 square miles and a water area of 0 square miles. Located at 40.03° N. Lat.; 74.62° W. Long. Elevation is 185 feet.

History: Fort, formerly Camp Dix, was built in World War I, renamed and made a permanent garrison in 1939. It was the US Army's largest training center in World War II; it closed in 1992. Residential and commercial services here served the base.

Population: 3,843 (1990); 748 (2000); 750 (2005); 759 (2010 projected); Race: 46.1% White, 30.0% Black, 8.5% Asian, 12.1% Hispanic of any race (2005); Density: 426.3 persons per square mile (2005); Average household size: 2.34 (2005); Median age: 32.8 (2005); Males per 100 females: 94.3 (2005); Marriage status: 41.7% never married, 40.6% now married, 6.3% widowed, 11.3% divorced (2000); Foreign born: 15.4% (2000); Ancestry (includes multiple ancestries): 39.6% Other groups, 13.5% Irish, 11.8% German, 8.0% Italian, 6.4% Polish (2000).

Economy: Fort Dix Military Reservation and McGuire Air Force Base here. Single-family building permits issued: 1 (2005); Multi-family building permits issued: 0 (2005); Employment by occupation: 6.5% management, 7.1% professional, 34.5% services, 27.7% sales, 0.0% farming, 6.2% construction, 18.0% production (2000).

Income: Per capita income: $17,295 (2005); Median household income: $30,536 (2005); Average household income: $39,781 (2005); Percent of households with income of $100,000 or more: 5.3% (2005); Poverty rate: 24.0% (2000).

Education: Percent of population age 25 and over with: High school diploma (including GED) or higher: 79.7% (2005); Bachelor's degree or higher: 7.7% (2005); Master's degree or higher: 1.5% (2005).

School District(s)

New Hanover Township (PK-08)
    2003-04 Enrollment: 166 . . . . (609) 723-2139
North Hanover Township (PK-06)
    2003-04 Enrollment: 1,372 . . . . (609) 723-3050

Housing: Homeownership rate: 25.0% (2005); Median home value: $154,545 (2005); Median rent: $582 per month (2000); Median age of housing: 44 years (2000).

Transportation: Commute to work: 89.7% car, 1.4% public transportation, 8.9% walk, 0.0% work from home (2000); Travel time to work: 36.1% less than 15 minutes, 27.2% 15 to 30 minutes, 16.9% 30 to 45 minutes, 8.6% 45 to 60 minutes, 11.2% 60 minutes or more (2000)

Camden County

Located in southwestern New Jersey; bounded on the northwest by the Delaware River and the Pennsylvania border; drained by the Great Egg

Harbor and Mullica Rivers. Covers a land area of 222.30 square miles, a water area of 5.28 square miles, and is located in the Eastern Time Zone. The county government was organized in 1844. County seat is Camden.

Camden County is part of the Philadelphia-Camden-Wilmington, PA-NJ-DE-MD Metropolitan Statistical Area. The entire metro area includes: Camden, NJ Metropolitan Division (Burlington County, NJ; Camden County, NJ; Gloucester County, NJ); Philadelphia, PA Metropolitan Division (Bucks County, PA; Chester County, PA; Delaware County, PA; Montgomery County, PA; Philadelphia County, PA); Wilmington, DE-MD-NJ Metropolitan Division (New Castle County, DE; Cecil County, MD; Salem County, NJ)

Population: 502,824 (1990); 508,932 (2000); 517,151 (2005); 525,594 (2010 projected); Race: 68.2% White, 19.5% Black, 3.9% Asian, 11.0% Hispanic of any race (2005); Density: 2,326.4 persons per square mile (2005); Average household size: 2.72 (2005); Median age: 36.8 (2005); Males per 100 females: 93.7 (2005).
Religion: Five largest groups: 35.5% Catholic Church, 7.1% Jewish Estimate, 2.6% The United Methodist Church, 1.9% American Baptist Churches in the USA, 1.6% Evangelical Lutheran Church in America (2000).
Economy: Unemployment rate: 4.7% (2005); Total civilian labor force: 265,373 (2005); Leading industries: 17.9% health care and social assistance; 13.8% retail trade; 8.7% manufacturing (2004); Farms: 216 totaling 10,259 acres (2002); Companies that employ 500 or more persons: 63 (2004); Companies that employ 100 to 499 persons: 575 (2004); Companies that employ less than 100 persons: 24,547 (2004); Black-owned businesses: 2,990 (2002); Hispanic-owned businesses: 1,418 (2002); Asian-owned businesses: 2,458 (2002); Women-owned businesses: 10,050 (2002); Retail sales per capita: $14,948 (2006). Single-family building permits issued: 1,160 (2005); Multi-family building permits issued: 546 (2005).
Income: Per capita income: $26,008 (2005); Median household income: $54,446 (2005); Average household income: $69,911 (2005); Percent of households with income of $100,000 or more: 20.1% (2005); Poverty rate: 10.9% (2003); Bankruptcy rate: 9.13% (2005).
Taxes: Total county taxes per capita: $412 (2004); County property taxes per capita: $411 (2004).
Education: Percent of population age 25 and over with: High school diploma (including GED) or higher: 80.1% (2005); Bachelor's degree or higher: 23.8% (2005); Master's degree or higher: 8.3% (2005).
Housing: Homeownership rate: 69.5% (2005); Median home value: $170,670 (2005); Median rent: $554 per month (2000); Median age of housing: 38 years (2000).
Health: Birth rate: 137.0 per 10,000 population (2004); Death rate: 92.3 per 10,000 population (2004); Age-adjusted cancer mortality rate: 225.6 deaths per 100,000 population (2002); Air Quality Index: 63.6% good, 31.5% moderate, 4.9% unhealthy for sensitive individuals, 0.0% unhealthy (percent of days in 2005); Number of physicians: 43.6 per 10,000 population (2004); Hospital beds: 52.5 per 10,000 population (2003); Hospital admissions: 1,732.4 per 10,000 population (2003).
Elections: 2004 Presidential election results: 36.9% Bush, 62.4% Kerry, 0.4% Nader, 0.1% Badnarik
National and State Parks: Garden State Park; Wharton State Forest
Additional Information Contacts
Camden County Government . . . . (856) 225-5000
   http://www.co.camden.nj.us
Borough of Bellmawr . . . . (856) 933-1313
   http://www.bellmawr.com
Borough of Collingswood . . . . (856) 854-0720
   http://www.collingswood.com
Borough of Gibbsboro . . . . (856) 783-6655
   http://www.gibbsboro.com
Borough of Haddon Heights. . . . . (856) 547-7132
   http://www.haddonheights.lib.nj.us
Borough of Magnolia . . . . (856) 783-1520
   http://www.magnolia-nj.org
Borough of Merchantville . . . . (856) 662-2474
   http://www.merchantville.com
Borough of Pine Hill . . . . (856) 783-7400
   http://www.pinehillboronj.com
Borough of Stratford. . . . . (856) 783-0600
   http://www.stratfordnj.org
Chamber of Commerce Southern New Jersey . . . . (856) 424-7776
   http://www.chambersnj.com

Cherry Hill Regional Chamber of Commerce. . . . . (856) 667-1600
   http://www.cherryhillregional.com
Cherry Hill Township . . . . (856) 488-7878
   http://www.cherryhill-nj.com
City of Camden . . . . (856) 757-7150
   http://www.burlingtonnj.us
Gloucester Township . . . . (856) 228-4000
   http://www.glotwp.com
Pennsauken Township . . . . (865) 665-1000
   http://www.twp.pennsauken.nj.us
Southern New Jersey Chamber of Commerce . . . . (856) 424-7776
   http://www.chambersnj.com
Voorhees Township . . . . (856) 429-7757
   http://voorheesnj.com/Default.aspx
Waterford Township. . . . . (856) 768-2300
   http://www.waterfordtwp.org
Winslow Township . . . . (609) 567-0700
   http://www.winslowtownship.com

Camden County Communities

ASHLAND (CDP). Covers a land area of 2.920 square miles and a water area of 0 square miles. Located at 39.87° N. Lat.; 75.01° W. Long. Elevation is 80 feet.
Population: 8,333 (1990); 8,375 (2000); 8,568 (2005); 8,778 (2010 projected); Race: 86.6% White, 4.9% Black, 6.6% Asian, 3.1% Hispanic of any race (2005); Density: 2,934.6 persons per square mile (2005); Average household size: 2.65 (2005); Median age: 42.1 (2005); Males per 100 females: 92.1 (2005); Marriage status: 22.6% never married, 63.4% now married, 8.0% widowed, 6.1% divorced (2000); Foreign born: 10.6% (2000); Ancestry (includes multiple ancestries): 18.9% Irish, 16.2% Other groups, 15.9% Italian, 15.4% German, 8.7% English (2000).
Economy: Employment by occupation: 17.7% management, 34.5% professional, 10.9% services, 26.5% sales, 0.0% farming, 3.1% construction, 7.2% production (2000).
Income: Per capita income: $34,580 (2005); Median household income: $76,225 (2005); Average household income: $90,703 (2005); Percent of households with income of $100,000 or more: 32.6% (2005); Poverty rate: 4.6% (2000).
Education: Percent of population age 25 and over with: High school diploma (including GED) or higher: 91.1% (2005); Bachelor's degree or higher: 43.6% (2005); Master's degree or higher: 16.2% (2005).
Housing: Homeownership rate: 93.1% (2005); Median home value: $206,145 (2005); Median rent: $902 per month (2000); Median age of housing: 36 years (2000).
Transportation: Commute to work: 86.1% car, 9.0% public transportation, 0.5% walk, 3.7% work from home (2000); Travel time to work: 22.4% less than 15 minutes, 39.1% 15 to 30 minutes, 18.8% 30 to 45 minutes, 10.9% 45 to 60 minutes, 8.9% 60 minutes or more (2000)

ATCO (unincorporated postal area, zip code 08004). Covers a land area of 30.050 square miles and a water area of 0.121 square miles. Located at 39.76° N. Lat.; 74.87° W. Long. Elevation is 146 feet.
Population: 14,299 (2000); Race: 87.1% White, 8.5% Black, 1.6% Asian, 2.3% Hispanic of any race (2000); Density: 475.8 persons per square mile (2000); Age: 25.8% under 18, 10.1% over 64 (2000); Marriage status: 23.7% never married, 63.2% now married, 6.6% widowed, 6.4% divorced (2000); Foreign born: 3.8% (2000); Ancestry (includes multiple ancestries): 26.1% Irish, 24.1% German, 20.6% Italian, 11.4% Other groups, 9.6% English (2000).
Economy: Suburbanizing area. Employment by occupation: 13.7% management, 17.3% professional, 13.5% services, 29.7% sales, 0.1% farming, 13.5% construction, 12.3% production (2000).
Income: Per capita income: $23,579 (2000); Median household income: $57,261 (2000); Poverty rate: 5.9% (2000).
Education: Percent of population age 25 and over with: High school diploma (including GED) or higher: 84.1% (2000); Bachelor's degree or higher: 16.9% (2000).
School District(s)
Waterford Township (PK-06)
   2003-04 Enrollment: 955 . . . . (856) 767-0331
Winslow Township (PK-12)
   2003-04 Enrollment: 6,742 . . . . (856) 767-2850

Housing: Homeownership rate: 87.3% (2000); Median home value: $120,000 (2000); Median rent: $699 per month (2000); Median age of housing: 22 years (2000).
Transportation: Commute to work: 90.5% car, 4.9% public transportation, 1.2% walk, 2.9% work from home (2000); Travel time to work: 21.9% less than 15 minutes, 30.0% 15 to 30 minutes, 21.9% 30 to 45 minutes, 12.0% 45 to 60 minutes, 14.2% 60 minutes or more (2000); Amtrak: Service available.

AUDUBON (borough).
Covers a land area of 1.490 square miles and a water area of 0.015 square miles. Located at 39.89° N. Lat.; 75.07° W. Long. Elevation is 60 feet.
History: Named after John James Audubon, the ornithologist, who studied the birds of the area in 1829. Incorporated 1905.
Population: 9,205 (1990); 9,182 (2000); 9,093 (2005); 9,032 (2010 projected); Race: 96.8% White, 0.7% Black, 0.9% Asian, 1.8% Hispanic of any race (2005); Density: 6,102.6 persons per square mile (2005); Average household size: 2.49 (2005); Median age: 39.2 (2005); Males per 100 females: 92.5 (2005); Marriage status: 26.3% never married, 55.4% now married, 9.6% widowed, 8.7% divorced (2000); Foreign born: 2.7% (2000); Ancestry (includes multiple ancestries): 35.0% Irish, 25.2% Italian, 25.1% German, 13.8% English, 9.6% Polish (2000).
Economy: A suburb of Camden. Mostly residential. Single-family building permits issued: 3 (2005); Multi-family building permits issued: 3 (2005); Employment by occupation: 12.1% management, 23.0% professional, 14.4% services, 29.2% sales, 0.1% farming, 10.6% construction, 10.6% production (2000).
Income: Per capita income: $27,578 (2005); Median household income: $58,525 (2005); Average household income: $68,411 (2005); Percent of households with income of $100,000 or more: 17.5% (2005); Poverty rate: 5.5% (2000).
Education: Percent of population age 25 and over with: High school diploma (including GED) or higher: 87.4% (2005); Bachelor's degree or higher: 25.3% (2005); Master's degree or higher: 6.5% (2005).
School District(s)
Audubon Borough (PK-12)
    2003-04 Enrollment: 1,755 . . . . (856) 547-1325
Housing: Homeownership rate: 73.4% (2005); Median home value: $168,858 (2005); Median rent: $555 per month (2000); Median age of housing: 60+ years (2000).
Safety: Violent crime rate: 18.5 per 10,000 population; Property crime rate: 227.6 per 10,000 population (2004).
Transportation: Commute to work: 86.8% car, 6.7% public transportation, 4.3% walk, 2.0% work from home (2000); Travel time to work: 31.9% less than 15 minutes, 39.1% 15 to 30 minutes, 14.8% 30 to 45 minutes, 7.7% 45 to 60 minutes, 6.6% 60 minutes or more (2000)

AUDUBON PARK (borough).
Covers a land area of 0.146 square miles and a water area of 0.016 square miles. Located at 39.89° N. Lat.; 75.09° W. Long. Elevation is 20 feet.
History: Incorporated after 1940.
Population: 1,150 (1990); 1,102 (2000); 1,097 (2005); 1,097 (2010 projected); Race: 98.5% White, 0.5% Black, 0.5% Asian, 0.9% Hispanic of any race (2005); Density: 7,527.5 persons per square mile (2005); Average household size: 2.19 (2005); Median age: 43.6 (2005); Males per 100 females: 81.3 (2005); Marriage status: 22.8% never married, 50.8% now married, 12.8% widowed, 13.5% divorced (2000); Foreign born: 0.9% (2000); Ancestry (includes multiple ancestries): 34.2% Irish, 26.8% German, 22.9% Italian, 12.2% English, 10.3% Polish (2000).
Economy: Chiefly residential. Single-family building permits issued: 0 (2005); Multi-family building permits issued: 0 (2005); Employment by occupation: 6.8% management, 9.0% professional, 17.6% services, 35.7% sales, 0.0% farming, 8.6% construction, 22.2% production (2000).
Income: Per capita income: $19,325 (2005); Median household income: $37,120 (2005); Average household income: $42,231 (2005); Percent of households with income of $100,000 or more: 4.0% (2005); Poverty rate: 8.8% (2000).
Education: Percent of population age 25 and over with: High school diploma (including GED) or higher: 71.7% (2005); Bachelor's degree or higher: 3.3% (2005); Master's degree or higher: 0.4% (2005).
Housing: Homeownership rate: 23.9% (2005); Median home value: $71,852 (2005); Median rent: $471 per month (2000); Median age of housing: 56 years (2000).
Safety: Violent crime rate: 18.1 per 10,000 population; Property crime rate: 217.0 per 10,000 population (2004).

Transportation: Commute to work: 94.1% car, 1.8% public transportation, 1.2% walk, 1.2% work from home (2000); Travel time to work: 35.4% less than 15 minutes, 41.8% 15 to 30 minutes, 12.2% 30 to 45 minutes, 4.6% 45 to 60 minutes, 6.0% 60 minutes or more (2000)

BARCLAY-KINGSTON (CDP).
Covers a land area of 2.850 square miles and a water area of 0 square miles. Located at 39.91° N. Lat.; 74.99° W. Long.
Population: 10,835 (1990); 10,728 (2000); 10,705 (2005); 10,704 (2010 projected); Race: 86.0% White, 4.4% Black, 6.9% Asian, 2.7% Hispanic of any race (2005); Density: 3,756.8 persons per square mile (2005); Average household size: 2.56 (2005); Median age: 43.0 (2005); Males per 100 females: 94.8 (2005); Marriage status: 22.7% never married, 63.1% now married, 8.4% widowed, 5.8% divorced (2000); Foreign born: 9.1% (2000); Ancestry (includes multiple ancestries): 22.5% Irish, 19.3% German, 17.6% Italian, 17.0% Other groups, 11.8% English (2000).
Economy: Employment by occupation: 18.3% management, 31.6% professional, 9.4% services, 32.3% sales, 0.0% farming, 2.8% construction, 5.6% production (2000).
Income: Per capita income: $38,110 (2005); Median household income: $79,657 (2005); Average household income: $97,019 (2005); Percent of households with income of $100,000 or more: 35.1% (2005); Poverty rate: 2.6% (2000).
Education: Percent of population age 25 and over with: High school diploma (including GED) or higher: 94.4% (2005); Bachelor's degree or higher: 43.7% (2005); Master's degree or higher: 15.7% (2005).
Housing: Homeownership rate: 80.7% (2005); Median home value: $235,269 (2005); Median rent: $792 per month (2000); Median age of housing: 36 years (2000).
Transportation: Commute to work: 87.1% car, 7.1% public transportation, 1.3% walk, 4.5% work from home (2000); Travel time to work: 31.5% less than 15 minutes, 38.9% 15 to 30 minutes, 14.7% 30 to 45 minutes, 6.5% 45 to 60 minutes, 8.3% 60 minutes or more (2000)

BARRINGTON (borough).
Covers a land area of 1.606 square miles and a water area of 0 square miles. Located at 39.87° N. Lat.; 75.05° W. Long. Elevation is 81 feet.
History: Laid out c.1890, incorporated 1917.
Population: 6,774 (1990); 7,084 (2000); 7,072 (2005); 7,086 (2010 projected); Race: 89.4% White, 5.3% Black, 1.5% Asian, 3.6% Hispanic of any race (2005); Density: 4,403.9 persons per square mile (2005); Average household size: 2.30 (2005); Median age: 39.5 (2005); Males per 100 females: 91.7 (2005); Marriage status: 27.5% never married, 54.6% now married, 9.5% widowed, 8.3% divorced (2000); Foreign born: 3.2% (2000); Ancestry (includes multiple ancestries): 30.1% Irish, 25.6% Italian, 25.0% German, 14.1% English, 9.0% Other groups (2000).
Economy: Single-family building permits issued: 9 (2005); Multi-family building permits issued: 0 (2005); Employment by occupation: 15.5% management, 24.0% professional, 12.4% services, 32.8% sales, 0.2% farming, 8.0% construction, 7.1% production (2000).
Income: Per capita income: $28,944 (2005); Median household income: $52,652 (2005); Average household income: $66,623 (2005); Percent of households with income of $100,000 or more: 18.0% (2005); Poverty rate: 1.9% (2000).
Taxes: Total city taxes per capita: $370 (2004); City property taxes per capita: $365 (2004).
Education: Percent of population age 25 and over with: High school diploma (including GED) or higher: 86.2% (2005); Bachelor's degree or higher: 25.7% (2005); Master's degree or higher: 5.8% (2005).
School District(s)
Barrington Borough (PK-08)
    2003-04 Enrollment: 639 . . . . (856) 547-8467
Housing: Homeownership rate: 61.6% (2005); Median home value: $173,654 (2005); Median rent: $565 per month (2000); Median age of housing: 44 years (2000).
Safety: Violent crime rate: 11.2 per 10,000 population; Property crime rate: 110.9 per 10,000 population (2004).
Transportation: Commute to work: 89.9% car, 4.6% public transportation, 1.5% walk, 3.5% work from home (2000); Travel time to work: 22.3% less than 15 minutes, 47.6% 15 to 30 minutes, 13.6% 30 to 45 minutes, 8.4% 45 to 60 minutes, 8.2% 60 minutes or more (2000)

BELLMAWR (borough).
Covers a land area of 3.031 square miles and a water area of 0.104 square miles. Located at 39.86° N. Lat.; 75.09° W. Long. Elevation is 70 feet.

History: Named for the Bell Farm, on which the town was founded by Quakers. Incorporated 1926.
Population: 12,603 (1990); 11,262 (2000); 11,270 (2005); 11,323 (2010 projected); Race: 90.9% White, 1.4% Black, 3.6% Asian, 4.5% Hispanic of any race (2005); Density: 3,718.2 persons per square mile (2005); Average household size: 2.49 (2005); Median age: 41.3 (2005); Males per 100 females: 96.8 (2005); Marriage status: 27.7% never married, 55.7% now married, 10.0% widowed, 6.6% divorced (2000); Foreign born: 7.5% (2000); Ancestry (includes multiple ancestries): 31.2% Irish, 31.1% Italian, 21.5% German, 12.0% Polish, 9.4% Other groups (2000).
Economy: Site of industrial park with manufacturing: machinery, aircraft parts. Single-family building permits issued: 7 (2005); Multi-family building permits issued: 51 (2005); Employment by occupation: 9.1% management, 14.3% professional, 13.5% services, 33.0% sales, 0.1% farming, 11.9% construction, 18.2% production (2000).
Income: Per capita income: $22,915 (2005); Median household income: $48,512 (2005); Average household income: $56,924 (2005); Percent of households with income of $100,000 or more: 11.5% (2005); Poverty rate: 4.0% (2000).
Education: Percent of population age 25 and over with: High school diploma (including GED) or higher: 74.7% (2005); Bachelor's degree or higher: 10.3% (2005); Master's degree or higher: 2.8% (2005).

School District(s)
Bellmawr Borough (PK-08)
    2003-04 Enrollment: 1,138 . . . . (856) 931-3620
Housing: Homeownership rate: 73.7% (2005); Median home value: $144,033 (2005); Median rent: $472 per month (2000); Median age of housing: 44 years (2000).
Safety: Violent crime rate: 15.0 per 10,000 population; Property crime rate: 216.9 per 10,000 population (2004).
Transportation: Commute to work: 91.0% car, 4.2% public transportation, 3.2% walk, 0.6% work from home (2000); Travel time to work: 29.4% less than 15 minutes, 44.5% 15 to 30 minutes, 14.4% 30 to 45 minutes, 6.0% 45 to 60 minutes, 5.7% 60 minutes or more (2000)
Additional Information Contacts
Borough of Bellmawr . . . . (856) 933-1313
    http://www.bellmawr.com

BERLIN (borough). Covers a land area of 3.578 square miles and a water area of 0 square miles. Located at 39.79° N. Lat.; 74.93° W. Long. Elevation is 155 feet.
Population: 5,672 (1990); 6,149 (2000); 7,030 (2005); 7,838 (2010 projected); Race: 92.8% White, 2.8% Black, 1.8% Asian, 2.5% Hispanic of any race (2005); Density: 1,964.8 persons per square mile (2005); Average household size: 2.74 (2005); Median age: 39.4 (2005); Males per 100 females: 98.1 (2005); Marriage status: 27.6% never married, 56.5% now married, 9.4% widowed, 6.5% divorced (2000); Foreign born: 4.1% (2000); Ancestry (includes multiple ancestries): 30.6% Irish, 30.2% Italian, 24.8% German, 12.9% English, 7.4% Other groups (2000).
Economy: Single-family building permits issued: 52 (2005); Multi-family building permits issued: 0 (2005); Employment by occupation: 13.3% management, 23.4% professional, 14.1% services, 29.3% sales, 0.0% farming, 9.6% construction, 10.4% production (2000).
Income: Per capita income: $28,870 (2005); Median household income: $70,374 (2005); Average household income: $78,829 (2005); Percent of households with income of $100,000 or more: 27.0% (2005); Poverty rate: 3.5% (2000).
Taxes: Total city taxes per capita: $456 (2004); City property taxes per capita: $419 (2004).
Education: Percent of population age 25 and over with: High school diploma (including GED) or higher: 84.6% (2005); Bachelor's degree or higher: 24.3% (2005); Master's degree or higher: 6.3% (2005).

School District(s)
Berlin Borough (PK-08)
    2003-04 Enrollment: 892 . . . . (856) 767-6785
Housing: Homeownership rate: 83.1% (2005); Median home value: $216,818 (2005); Median rent: $563 per month (2000); Median age of housing: 34 years (2000).
Hospitals: West Jersey Hospital - Berlin Division (92 beds)
Safety: Violent crime rate: 10.2 per 10,000 population; Property crime rate: 256.3 per 10,000 population (2004).
Transportation: Commute to work: 89.7% car, 5.2% public transportation, 2.5% walk, 2.6% work from home (2000); Travel time to work: 26.9% less than 15 minutes, 31.2% 15 to 30 minutes, 24.6% 30 to 45 minutes, 9.3% 45 to 60 minutes, 8.0% 60 minutes or more (2000)

BERLIN (township). Covers a land area of 3.248 square miles and a water area of 0 square miles. Located at 39.80° N. Lat.; 74.93° W. Long. Elevation is 155 feet.
History: Incorporated 1927.
Population: 5,466 (1990); 5,290 (2000); 5,404 (2005); 5,532 (2010 projected); Race: 81.4% White, 11.8% Black, 2.8% Asian, 6.2% Hispanic of any race (2005); Density: 1,664.0 persons per square mile (2005); Average household size: 2.74 (2005); Median age: 37.3 (2005); Males per 100 females: 99.7 (2005); Marriage status: 25.6% never married, 57.7% now married, 7.8% widowed, 8.9% divorced (2000); Foreign born: 5.2% (2000); Ancestry (includes multiple ancestries): 28.2% Irish, 26.2% German, 19.9% Other groups, 19.1% Italian, 13.4% English (2000).
Economy: Manufacturing: plastics, machine parts, glass products; metal fabrication; vegetable farming. Single-family building permits issued: 21 (2005); Multi-family building permits issued: 0 (2005); Employment by occupation: 10.9% management, 16.3% professional, 19.4% services, 26.0% sales, 0.0% farming, 15.8% construction, 11.6% production (2000).
Income: Per capita income: $27,340 (2005); Median household income: $63,297 (2005); Average household income: $74,191 (2005); Percent of households with income of $100,000 or more: 23.4% (2005); Poverty rate: 5.9% (2000).
Education: Percent of population age 25 and over with: High school diploma (including GED) or higher: 76.3% (2005); Bachelor's degree or higher: 14.9% (2005); Master's degree or higher: 4.3% (2005).

School District(s)
Berlin Borough (PK-08)
    2003-04 Enrollment: 892 . . . . (856) 767-6785
Housing: Homeownership rate: 77.7% (2005); Median home value: $168,583 (2005); Median rent: $527 per month (2000); Median age of housing: 32 years (2000).
Hospitals: West Jersey Hospital - Berlin Division (92 beds)
Safety: Violent crime rate: 38.9 per 10,000 population; Property crime rate: 476.1 per 10,000 population (2004).
Transportation: Commute to work: 92.1% car, 1.9% public transportation, 2.6% walk, 2.7% work from home (2000); Travel time to work: 30.3% less than 15 minutes, 30.5% 15 to 30 minutes, 22.7% 30 to 45 minutes, 5.6% 45 to 60 minutes, 10.9% 60 minutes or more (2000)

BLACKWOOD (CDP). Covers a land area of 1.241 square miles and a water area of 0.012 square miles. Located at 39.79° N. Lat.; 75.06° W. Long. Elevation is 73 feet.
History: Settled 1701.
Population: 5,091 (1990); 4,692 (2000); 4,906 (2005); 5,101 (2010 projected); Race: 89.3% White, 4.7% Black, 2.5% Asian, 3.9% Hispanic of any race (2005); Density: 3,954.6 persons per square mile (2005); Average household size: 2.69 (2005); Median age: 39.2 (2005); Males per 100 females: 99.0 (2005); Marriage status: 25.2% never married, 62.7% now married, 6.4% widowed, 5.7% divorced (2000); Foreign born: 4.3% (2000); Ancestry (includes multiple ancestries): 31.7% Italian, 26.7% Irish, 21.7% German, 13.6% Other groups, 7.9% English (2000).
Economy: Clothing manufacturing. In rapidly suburbanizing area. Employment by occupation: 13.4% management, 13.3% professional, 10.8% services, 33.5% sales, 0.0% farming, 12.4% construction, 16.6% production (2000).
Income: Per capita income: $24,403 (2005); Median household income: $55,530 (2005); Average household income: $64,597 (2005); Percent of households with income of $100,000 or more: 16.7% (2005); Poverty rate: 4.0% (2000).
Education: Percent of population age 25 and over with: High school diploma (including GED) or higher: 83.1% (2005); Bachelor's degree or higher: 14.0% (2005); Master's degree or higher: 4.1% (2005).

School District(s)
Black Horse Pike Regional (09-12)
    2003-04 Enrollment: 4,438 . . . . (856) 227-4106
Gloucester Township (PK-08)
    2003-04 Enrollment: 8,090 . . . . (856) 227-1400
Two-year College(s)
Camden County College (Public)
    Fall 2004 Enrollment: 15,116. . . . . (856) 227-7200
    2005-06 Tuition: In-state $2,700; Out-of-state $2,700
Pennco Tech (Private, For-profit)
    Fall 2004 Enrollment: 376 . . . . (856) 232-0310

Housing: Homeownership rate: 78.5% (2005); Median home value: $163,078 (2005); Median rent: $535 per month (2000); Median age of housing: 43 years (2000).
Hospitals: Camden County Health Services Center (449 beds)
Newspapers: News Report (General - Circulation 15,500); Record Breeze (General - Circulation 10,000); The Plain Dealer (General - Circulation 5,000)
Transportation: Commute to work: 93.0% car, 3.1% public transportation, 1.6% walk, 2.0% work from home (2000); Travel time to work: 18.5% less than 15 minutes, 35.8% 15 to 30 minutes, 26.7% 30 to 45 minutes, 10.1% 45 to 60 minutes, 8.9% 60 minutes or more (2000)

BROOKLAWN (borough).
Covers a land area of 0.470 square miles and a water area of 0.050 square miles. Located at 39.88° N. Lat.; 75.12° W. Long. Elevation is 24 feet.
History: Built in World War I to house shipyard workers. Incorporated 1924.
Population: 1,805 (1990); 2,354 (2000); 2,330 (2005); 2,312 (2010 projected); Race: 86.1% White, 6.2% Black, 1.4% Asian, 6.8% Hispanic of any race (2005); Density: 4,952.4 persons per square mile (2005); Average household size: 2.42 (2005); Median age: 35.9 (2005); Males per 100 females: 90.4 (2005); Marriage status: 31.8% never married, 46.1% now married, 8.4% widowed, 13.8% divorced (2000); Foreign born: 3.0% (2000); Ancestry (includes multiple ancestries): 37.6% Irish, 21.8% German, 20.8% Italian, 10.0% Other groups, 9.4% English (2000).
Economy: Single-family building permits issued: 1 (2005); Multi-family building permits issued: 0 (2005); Employment by occupation: 8.3% management, 11.2% professional, 21.2% services, 28.8% sales, 0.4% farming, 12.7% construction, 17.3% production (2000).
Income: Per capita income: $21,390 (2005); Median household income: $44,605 (2005); Average household income: $51,306 (2005); Percent of households with income of $100,000 or more: 7.5% (2005); Poverty rate: 7.3% (2000).
Education: Percent of population age 25 and over with: High school diploma (including GED) or higher: 80.1% (2005); Bachelor's degree or higher: 8.1% (2005); Master's degree or higher: 3.7% (2005).

School District(s)
Brooklawn Borough (PK-08)
   2003-04 Enrollment: 310 . . . . (856) 456-4039
Housing: Homeownership rate: 61.7% (2005); Median home value: $117,179 (2005); Median rent: $540 per month (2000); Median age of housing: 57 years (2000).
Safety: Violent crime rate: 97.8 per 10,000 population; Property crime rate: 714.3 per 10,000 population (2004).
Transportation: Commute to work: 86.3% car, 5.4% public transportation, 5.8% walk, 1.1% work from home (2000); Travel time to work: 33.6% less than 15 minutes, 43.4% 15 to 30 minutes, 13.1% 30 to 45 minutes, 4.3% 45 to 60 minutes, 5.5% 60 minutes or more (2000)

CAMDEN (city).
Covers a land area of 8.822 square miles and a water area of 1.557 square miles. Located at 39.93° N. Lat.; 75.10° W. Long. Elevation is 33 feet.
History: Named for Sir Charles Pratt, 1st Earl of Camden (1714-1794), English statesman and jurist. Camden's history is tied with that of Philadelphia, on the other side of the Delaware River. Both were permanently colonized by the Quakers, fleeing from religious persecution in England. The first Camden settler was probably William Cooper, who built a home in 1681. After Cooper took over a ferry to Philadelphia, the settlement became known as Cooper's Ferries. Others settled also, but the settlement grew slowly as Philadelphia was more attractive to newcomers. A real estate boom began in 1773 when Jacob Cooper, Philadelphia merchant and descendant of William Cooper, laid out 40 acres as a townsite. He named the place Camden for the first earl of Camden. Camden was incorporated as a city in 1828 and in 1844 was made the seat of Camden County. The city's real growth began in 1834, when it became the terminus of the Camden and Amboy Railroad. Following the Civil War, Camden was caught up in the tremendous industrial expansion that was the sequel to railroad building.
Population: 87,492 (1990); 79,904 (2000); 80,605 (2005); 81,402 (2010 projected); Race: 16.5% White, 51.8% Black, 2.7% Asian, 42.3% Hispanic of any race (2005); Density: 9,136.5 persons per square mile (2005); Average household size: 3.29 (2005); Median age: 27.9 (2005); Males per 100 females: 95.1 (2005); Marriage status: 47.8% never married, 36.6% now married, 6.4% widowed, 9.2% divorced (2000); Foreign born: 8.9%

(2000); Ancestry (includes multiple ancestries): 70.8% Other groups, 2.0% Irish, 1.6% German, 1.5% Italian, 1.3% African (2000).
Economy: Unemployment rate: 10.1% (2005); Total civilian labor force: 27,051 (2005); Single-family building permits issued: 1 (2005); Multi-family building permits issued: 16 (2005); Employment by occupation: 4.9% management, 11.8% professional, 25.5% services, 25.1% sales, 0.3% farming, 6.7% construction, 25.7% production (2000).
Income: Per capita income: $10,697 (2005); Median household income: $26,170 (2005); Average household income: $33,681 (2005); Percent of households with income of $100,000 or more: 3.1% (2005); Poverty rate: 35.5% (2000).
Taxes: Total city taxes per capita: $408 (2004); City property taxes per capita: $383 (2004).
Education: Percent of population age 25 and over with: High school diploma (including GED) or higher: 51.2% (2005); Bachelor's degree or higher: 5.3% (2005); Master's degree or higher: 1.8% (2005).

School District(s)
Agency - Camden Academy Charter HS (09-11)
   2003-04 Enrollment: 305 . . . . (856) 365-1000
Agency - Camden's Promise CS (06-08)
   2003-04 Enrollment: 301 . . . . (609) 365-1000
Agency - Leap Academy University CS (KG-11)
   2003-04 Enrollment: 682 . . . . (856) 614-5600
Camden City (PK-12)
   2003-04 Enrollment: 18,997 . . . . (856) 966-2040
Four-year College(s)
Cooper Health System Center for Allied Health Education (Private, Not-for-profit)
   Fall 2004 Enrollment: 47 . . . . (856) 342-2000
Rutgers University-Camden (Public)
   Fall 2004 Enrollment: 5,563 . . . . (856) 225-6095
   2005-06 Tuition: In-state $9,028; Out-of-state $16,626
Two-year College(s)
Divers Academy International (Private, For-profit)
   Fall 2004 Enrollment: 189 . . . . (856) 966-1871
Housing: Homeownership rate: 45.9% (2005); Median home value: $62,798 (2005); Median rent: $440 per month (2000); Median age of housing: 52 years (2000).
Hospitals: Cooper Hospital - University Medical Center; Our Lady of Lourdes Medical Center (410 beds); West Jersey Health System, Camden Division (224 beds)
Safety: Violent crime rate: 226.2 per 10,000 population; Property crime rate: 656.1 per 10,000 population (2004).
Newspapers: Catholic Star Herald (Catholic, Religious - Circulation 38,000)
Transportation: Commute to work: 67.7% car, 20.8% public transportation, 8.5% walk, 0.9% work from home (2000); Travel time to work: 24.7% less than 15 minutes, 40.1% 15 to 30 minutes, 19.1% 30 to 45 minutes, 7.2% 45 to 60 minutes, 8.9% 60 minutes or more (2000)
Additional Information Contacts
City of Camden . . . . (856) 757-7150
   http://www.burlingtonnj.us

CHERRY HILL (township).
Covers a land area of 24.252 square miles and a water area of 0.114 square miles. Located at 39.90° N. Lat.; 75.00° W. Long. Elevation is 40 feet.
History: Named for a local hilltop farm, approached by a path lined with cherry trees. Has been marked by great development and housing growth, especially since the 1970s. Site of early 19th-century Barclay Farmstead. Formerly called Delaware township (until 1961).
Population: 69,348 (1990); 69,965 (2000); 71,986 (2005); 74,000 (2010 projected); Race: 83.1% White, 5.3% Black, 9.2% Asian, 2.9% Hispanic of any race (2005); Density: 2,968.2 persons per square mile (2005); Average household size: 2.63 (2005); Median age: 43.1 (2005); Males per 100 females: 91.7 (2005); Marriage status: 22.4% never married, 62.3% now married, 8.7% widowed, 6.5% divorced (2000); Foreign born: 12.5% (2000); Ancestry (includes multiple ancestries): 21.0% Other groups, 17.0% Irish, 16.8% Italian, 13.7% German, 8.0% Russian (2000).
Economy: Largely residential. Local industries include corrugating machinery, engineering, electronics, and service and retailing. Site of major racetrack. Unemployment rate: 2.9% (2005); Total civilian labor force: 38,277 (2005); Single-family building permits issued: 31 (2005); Multi-family building permits issued: 124 (2005); Employment by occupation: 19.8% management, 33.1% professional, 9.5% services, 28.4% sales, 0.1% farming, 3.7% construction, 5.5% production (2000).

Income: Per capita income: $37,728 (2005); Median household income: $75,708 (2005); Average household income: $97,965 (2005); Percent of households with income of $100,000 or more: 34.7% (2005); Poverty rate: 4.0% (2000).

Taxes: Total city taxes per capita: $291 (2004); City property taxes per capita: $249 (2004).

Education: Percent of population age 25 and over with: High school diploma (including GED) or higher: 90.9% (2005); Bachelor's degree or higher: 46.1% (2005); Master's degree or higher: 19.0% (2005).

School District(s)

Cherry Hill Township (PK-12)
    2003-04 Enrollment: 11,911 . . . . (856) 429-5600

Two-year College(s)

Empire Beauty School-Cherry Hill (Private, For-profit)
    Fall 2004 Enrollment: 123 . . . . (800) 223-3271
Harris School of Business (Private, For-profit)
    Fall 2004 Enrollment: 167 . . . . (856) 662-5300
Prism Career Institute (Private, For-profit)
    Fall 2004 Enrollment: 30 . . . . (856) 317-0100
The Chubb Institute-Cherry Hill (Private, For-profit)
    Fall 2004 Enrollment: 377 . . . . (856) 755-4800

Housing: Homeownership rate: 82.7% (2005); Median home value: $241,286 (2005); Median rent: $747 per month (2000); Median age of housing: 32 years (2000).

Hospitals: Kennedy Memorial Hospitals: UMC Cherry Hill (225 beds)

Safety: Violent crime rate: 14.1 per 10,000 population; Property crime rate: 309.9 per 10,000 population (2004).

Newspapers: Courier-Post (Circulation 80,635); Jewish Community Voice of Southern New Jersey (Jewish - Circulation 12,000)

Transportation: Commute to work: 87.6% car, 6.9% public transportation, 1.3% walk, 3.9% work from home (2000); Travel time to work: 26.8% less than 15 minutes, 35.3% 15 to 30 minutes, 19.1% 30 to 45 minutes, 8.8% 45 to 60 minutes, 10.1% 60 minutes or more (2000); Amtrak: Service available.

Additional Information Contacts

Cherry Hill Regional Chamber of Commerce. . . . . (856) 667-1600
    http://www.cherryhillregional.com
Cherry Hill Township . . . . (856) 488-7878
    http://www.cherryhill-nj.com

CHERRY HILL MALL (CDP). Covers a land area of 3.696 square miles and a water area of 0 square miles. Located at 39.94° N. Lat.; 75.01° W. Long.

Population: 13,586 (1990); 13,238 (2000); 13,541 (2005); 13,834 (2010 projected); Race: 81.0% White, 5.9% Black, 9.8% Asian, 3.4% Hispanic of any race (2005); Density: 3,663.8 persons per square mile (2005); Average household size: 2.58 (2005); Median age: 43.7 (2005); Males per 100 females: 89.4 (2005); Marriage status: 22.9% never married, 59.6% now married, 10.6% widowed, 6.8% divorced (2000); Foreign born: 14.6% (2000); Ancestry (includes multiple ancestries): 21.5% Other groups, 18.9% Italian, 17.7% Irish, 14.1% German, 6.9% Russian (2000).

Economy: Employment by occupation: 20.2% management, 29.1% professional, 10.7% services, 28.9% sales, 0.3% farming, 4.7% construction, 6.0% production (2000).

Income: Per capita income: $34,059 (2005); Median household income: $68,022 (2005); Average household income: $86,240 (2005); Percent of households with income of $100,000 or more: 28.0% (2005); Poverty rate: 4.8% (2000).

Education: Percent of population age 25 and over with: High school diploma (including GED) or higher: 87.4% (2005); Bachelor's degree or higher: 39.1% (2005); Master's degree or higher: 15.1% (2005).

Housing: Homeownership rate: 79.6% (2005); Median home value: $221,464 (2005); Median rent: $847 per month (2000); Median age of housing: 35 years (2000).

Transportation: Commute to work: 88.9% car, 5.9% public transportation, 1.6% walk, 3.2% work from home (2000); Travel time to work: 28.0% less than 15 minutes, 33.1% 15 to 30 minutes, 20.0% 30 to 45 minutes, 8.2% 45 to 60 minutes, 10.7% 60 minutes or more (2000)

CHESILHURST (borough). Covers a land area of 1.716 square miles and a water area of 0 square miles. Located at 39.73° N. Lat.; 74.87° W. Long. Elevation is 178 feet.

Population: 1,526 (1990); 1,520 (2000); 1,901 (2005); 2,220 (2010 projected); Race: 37.0% White, 54.6% Black, 0.4% Asian, 5.2% Hispanic of any race (2005); Density: 1,107.9 persons per square mile (2005); Average household size: 3.02 (2005); Median age: 43.2 (2005); Males per 100 females: 98.8 (2005); Marriage status: 29.5% never married, 51.6% now married, 12.6% widowed, 6.4% divorced (2000); Foreign born: 2.2% (2000); Ancestry (includes multiple ancestries): 58.8% Other groups, 12.2% German, 7.6% Irish, 6.3% Italian, 3.6% Polish (2000).

Economy: Vegetable-farming center. Single-family building permits issued: 7 (2005); Multi-family building permits issued: 5 (2005); Employment by occupation: 7.4% management, 17.8% professional, 19.3% services, 25.5% sales, 0.7% farming, 12.3% construction, 17.0% production (2000).

Income: Per capita income: $17,265 (2005); Median household income: $43,378 (2005); Average household income: $49,563 (2005); Percent of households with income of $100,000 or more: 8.9% (2005); Poverty rate: 15.1% (2000).

Education: Percent of population age 25 and over with: High school diploma (including GED) or higher: 65.6% (2005); Bachelor's degree or higher: 9.4% (2005); Master's degree or higher: 4.0% (2005).

School District(s)

Chesilhurst (PK-06)
    2003-04 Enrollment: 149 . . . . (856) 767-5451

Housing: Homeownership rate: 88.4% (2005); Median home value: $132,172 (2005); Median rent: $580 per month (2000); Median age of housing: 29 years (2000).

Safety: Violent crime rate: 45.2 per 10,000 population; Property crime rate: 175.3 per 10,000 population (2004).

Transportation: Commute to work: 87.5% car, 8.2% public transportation, 1.4% walk, 2.1% work from home (2000); Travel time to work: 22.6% less than 15 minutes, 24.4% 15 to 30 minutes, 26.3% 30 to 45 minutes, 13.9% 45 to 60 minutes, 12.8% 60 minutes or more (2000)

CLEMENTON (borough). Covers a land area of 1.891 square miles and a water area of 0.055 square miles. Located at 39.80° N. Lat.; 74.98° W. Long. Elevation is 96 feet.

History: Incorporated 1925.

Population: 5,601 (1990); 4,986 (2000); 4,974 (2005); 4,984 (2010 projected); Race: 78.3% White, 13.9% Black, 0.8% Asian, 5.2% Hispanic of any race (2005); Density: 2,629.9 persons per square mile (2005); Average household size: 2.55 (2005); Median age: 36.6 (2005); Males per 100 females: 94.2 (2005); Marriage status: 31.7% never married, 46.3% now married, 9.3% widowed, 12.7% divorced (2000); Foreign born: 3.4% (2000); Ancestry (includes multiple ancestries): 28.2% Irish, 23.3% German, 22.4% Italian, 16.4% Other groups, 11.6% English (2000).

Economy: Makes concrete, plastic products. Single-family building permits issued: 11 (2005); Multi-family building permits issued: 0 (2005); Employment by occupation: 9.3% management, 16.7% professional, 17.6% services, 29.8% sales, 0.0% farming, 12.1% construction, 14.6% production (2000).

Income: Per capita income: $20,566 (2005); Median household income: $48,878 (2005); Average household income: $51,997 (2005); Percent of households with income of $100,000 or more: 7.2% (2005); Poverty rate: 11.4% (2000).

Education: Percent of population age 25 and over with: High school diploma (including GED) or higher: 77.3% (2005); Bachelor's degree or higher: 10.9% (2005); Master's degree or higher: 2.7% (2005).

School District(s)

Clementon Borough (PK-08)
    2003-04 Enrollment: 606 . . . . (856) 783-2300

Housing: Homeownership rate: 66.3% (2005); Median home value: $128,372 (2005); Median rent: $536 per month (2000); Median age of housing: 44 years (2000).

Safety: Violent crime rate: 69.9 per 10,000 population; Property crime rate: 443.1 per 10,000 population (2004).

Transportation: Commute to work: 84.1% car, 12.1% public transportation, 1.9% walk, 1.6% work from home (2000); Travel time to work: 22.0% less than 15 minutes, 32.5% 15 to 30 minutes, 22.2% 30 to 45 minutes, 10.4% 45 to 60 minutes, 12.8% 60 minutes or more (2000)

COLLINGSWOOD (borough). Covers a land area of 1.828 square miles and a water area of 0.094 square miles. Located at 39.91° N. Lat.; 75.07° W. Long. Elevation is 20 feet.

History: Named for the mother of Edward Collings Knight. Settled 1682 by Quakers. Incorporated 1888.

Population: 15,289 (1990); 14,326 (2000); 14,170 (2005); 14,035 (2010 projected); Race: 82.6% White, 8.8% Black, 3.0% Asian, 7.4% Hispanic of any race (2005); Density: 7,749.9 persons per square mile (2005); Average household size: 2.25 (2005); Median age: 38.5 (2005); Males per 100

females: 89.6 (2005); Marriage status: 33.7% never married, 45.9% now married, 9.2% widowed, 11.2% divorced (2000); Foreign born: 5.8% (2000); Ancestry (includes multiple ancestries): 25.5% Irish, 20.3% German, 18.7% Italian, 15.5% Other groups, 13.4% English (2000).
Economy: Largely residential, the borough has some light industry. Single-family building permits issued: 0 (2005); Multi-family building permits issued: 0 (2005); Employment by occupation: 12.1% management, 30.3% professional, 10.6% services, 31.5% sales, 0.0% farming, 8.0% construction, 7.4% production (2000).
Income: Per capita income: $28,060 (2005); Median household income: $49,450 (2005); Average household income: $62,787 (2005); Percent of households with income of $100,000 or more: 16.0% (2005); Poverty rate: 6.1% (2000).
Taxes: Total city taxes per capita: $409 (2004); City property taxes per capita: $394 (2004).
Education: Percent of population age 25 and over with: High school diploma (including GED) or higher: 87.5% (2005); Bachelor's degree or higher: 30.3% (2005); Master's degree or higher: 10.2% (2005).

School District(s)

Collingswood Borough (PK-12)
    2003-04 Enrollment: 2,075 . . . . (856) 962-5732
Housing: Homeownership rate: 54.4% (2005); Median home value: $162,042 (2005); Median rent: $637 per month (2000); Median age of housing: 57 years (2000).
Safety: Violent crime rate: 32.1 per 10,000 population; Property crime rate: 261.9 per 10,000 population (2004).
Newspapers: Haddon Township Monthly Monitor (General - Circulation 9,000); The Retrospect (General - Circulation 4,300);
Transportation: Commute to work: 81.4% car, 11.7% public transportation, 3.7% walk, 1.8% work from home (2000); Travel time to work: 27.6% less than 15 minutes, 36.8% 15 to 30 minutes, 21.8% 30 to 45 minutes, 5.4% 45 to 60 minutes, 8.4% 60 minutes or more (2000)
Additional Information Contacts
Borough of Collingswood . . . . (856) 854-0720
    http://www.collingswood.com

ECHELON (CDP). Covers a land area of 2.836 square miles and a water area of 0.013 square miles. Located at 39.84° N. Lat.; 74.99° W. Long.
Population: 9,423 (1990); 10,440 (2000); 11,484 (2005); 12,344 (2010 projected); Race: 68.7% White, 12.7% Black, 14.7% Asian, 3.7% Hispanic of any race (2005); Density: 4,049.8 persons per square mile (2005); Average household size: 2.09 (2005); Median age: 37.1 (2005); Males per 100 females: 91.7 (2005); Marriage status: 34.4% never married, 46.7% now married, 8.0% widowed, 10.9% divorced (2000); Foreign born: 14.4% (2000); Ancestry (includes multiple ancestries): 27.8% Other groups, 18.8% Italian, 17.3% Irish, 14.2% German, 9.1% English (2000).
Economy: Employment by occupation: 16.9% management, 32.1% professional, 11.6% services, 27.8% sales, 0.4% farming, 4.5% construction, 6.7% production (2000).
Income: Per capita income: $31,332 (2005); Median household income: $53,863 (2005); Average household income: $64,841 (2005); Percent of households with income of $100,000 or more: 17.5% (2005); Poverty rate: 8.3% (2000).
Education: Percent of population age 25 and over with: High school diploma (including GED) or higher: 89.2% (2005); Bachelor's degree or higher: 40.9% (2005); Master's degree or higher: 15.7% (2005).
Housing: Homeownership rate: 40.9% (2005); Median home value: $168,285 (2005); Median rent: $744 per month (2000); Median age of housing: 20 years (2000).
Transportation: Commute to work: 77.7% car, 16.3% public transportation, 2.2% walk, 1.6% work from home (2000); Travel time to work: 19.7% less than 15 minutes, 32.0% 15 to 30 minutes, 25.6% 30 to 45 minutes, 12.8% 45 to 60 minutes, 9.9% 60 minutes or more (2000)

ERLTON-ELLISBURG (CDP). Covers a land area of 1.859 square miles and a water area of 0.025 square miles. Located at 39.91° N. Lat.; 75.01° W. Long.
Population: 8,464 (1990); 8,168 (2000); 8,425 (2005); 8,686 (2010 projected); Race: 85.4% White, 4.6% Black, 7.1% Asian, 4.8% Hispanic of any race (2005); Density: 4,531.0 persons per square mile (2005); Average household size: 2.31 (2005); Median age: 43.2 (2005); Males per 100 females: 85.5 (2005); Marriage status: 23.4% never married, 54.6% now married, 12.8% widowed, 9.2% divorced (2000); Foreign born: 12.5%

(2000); Ancestry (includes multiple ancestries): 22.1% Italian, 20.3% Irish, 18.0% Other groups, 15.1% German, 9.0% English (2000).
Economy: Employment by occupation: 14.6% management, 27.9% professional, 14.7% services, 29.4% sales, 0.2% farming, 5.5% construction, 7.7% production (2000).
Income: Per capita income: $29,116 (2005); Median household income: $54,391 (2005); Average household income: $66,530 (2005); Percent of households with income of $100,000 or more: 19.6% (2005); Poverty rate: 5.4% (2000).
Education: Percent of population age 25 and over with: High school diploma (including GED) or higher: 87.6% (2005); Bachelor's degree or higher: 32.9% (2005); Master's degree or higher: 11.2% (2005).
Housing: Homeownership rate: 63.9% (2005); Median home value: $201,288 (2005); Median rent: $638 per month (2000); Median age of housing: 39 years (2000).
Transportation: Commute to work: 87.7% car, 7.0% public transportation, 2.0% walk, 2.4% work from home (2000); Travel time to work: 28.6% less than 15 minutes, 37.4% 15 to 30 minutes, 18.6% 30 to 45 minutes, 8.2% 45 to 60 minutes, 7.3% 60 minutes or more (2000)

GIBBSBORO (borough). Covers a land area of 2.195 square miles and a water area of 0.038 square miles. Located at 39.83° N. Lat.; 74.96° W. Long. Elevation is 122 feet.
Population: 2,383 (1990); 2,435 (2000); 2,504 (2005); 2,576 (2010 projected); Race: 93.2% White, 3.4% Black, 1.0% Asian, 2.8% Hispanic of any race (2005); Density: 1,140.8 persons per square mile (2005); Average household size: 2.88 (2005); Median age: 39.9 (2005); Males per 100 females: 98.1 (2005); Marriage status: 23.1% never married, 64.4% now married, 6.8% widowed, 5.7% divorced (2000); Foreign born: 4.1% (2000); Ancestry (includes multiple ancestries): 28.5% Irish, 22.1% German, 19.5% Italian, 15.9% English, 8.1% Other groups (2000).
Economy: Single-family building permits issued: 2 (2005); Multi-family building permits issued: 0 (2005); Employment by occupation: 16.4% management, 24.2% professional, 7.7% services, 30.6% sales, 0.0% farming, 11.4% construction, 9.6% production (2000).
Income: Per capita income: $30,026 (2005); Median household income: $67,203 (2005); Average household income: $85,521 (2005); Percent of households with income of $100,000 or more: 25.0% (2005); Poverty rate: 4.2% (2000).
Education: Percent of population age 25 and over with: High school diploma (including GED) or higher: 84.7% (2005); Bachelor's degree or higher: 23.1% (2005); Master's degree or higher: 6.4% (2005).

School District(s)

Gibbsboro Borough (PK-08)
    2003-04 Enrollment: 325 . . . . (856) 783-1140
Housing: Homeownership rate: 91.4% (2005); Median home value: $184,069 (2005); Median rent: $705 per month (2000); Median age of housing: 42 years (2000).
Safety: Violent crime rate: 16.0 per 10,000 population; Property crime rate: 260.2 per 10,000 population (2004).
Transportation: Commute to work: 90.8% car, 3.7% public transportation, 1.8% walk, 3.0% work from home (2000); Travel time to work: 28.1% less than 15 minutes, 29.7% 15 to 30 minutes, 23.3% 30 to 45 minutes, 7.7% 45 to 60 minutes, 11.1% 60 minutes or more (2000)
Additional Information Contacts
Borough of Gibbsboro . . . . (856) 783-6655
    http://www.gibbsboro.com

GLENDORA (CDP). Covers a land area of 1.068 square miles and a water area of 0.006 square miles. Located at 39.84° N. Lat.; 75.06° W. Long. Elevation is 72 feet.
Population: 5,201 (1990); 4,907 (2000); 5,051 (2005); 5,206 (2010 projected); Race: 97.1% White, 0.6% Black, 0.4% Asian, 1.9% Hispanic of any race (2005); Density: 4,731.1 persons per square mile (2005); Average household size: 2.47 (2005); Median age: 41.8 (2005); Males per 100 females: 89.1 (2005); Marriage status: 22.5% never married, 56.9% now married, 13.2% widowed, 7.3% divorced (2000); Foreign born: 4.2% (2000); Ancestry (includes multiple ancestries): 37.4% Italian, 29.0% Irish, 25.0% German, 10.4% English, 7.9% Polish (2000).
Economy: Employment by occupation: 9.0% management, 15.4% professional, 11.8% services, 31.8% sales, 0.0% farming, 17.3% construction, 14.6% production (2000).
Income: Per capita income: $24,522 (2005); Median household income: $48,840 (2005); Average household income: $60,450 (2005); Percent of

households with income of $100,000 or more: 15.4% (2005); Poverty rate: 6.4% (2000).

Education: Percent of population age 25 and over with: High school diploma (including GED) or higher: 70.0% (2005); Bachelor's degree or higher: 9.4% (2005); Master's degree or higher: 2.1% (2005).

School District(s)

Gloucester Township (PK-08)

    2003-04 Enrollment: 8,090 . . . . (856) 227-1400

Housing: Homeownership rate: 76.7% (2005); Median home value: $158,475 (2005); Median rent: $329 per month (2000); Median age of housing: 41 years (2000).

Transportation: Commute to work: 93.0% car, 4.6% public transportation, 0.3% walk, 1.5% work from home (2000); Travel time to work: 23.9% less than 15 minutes, 44.5% 15 to 30 minutes, 19.2% 30 to 45 minutes, 5.0% 45 to 60 minutes, 7.5% 60 minutes or more (2000)

GLOUCESTER (township). Covers a land area of 23.221 square miles and a water area of 0.104 square miles. Located at 39.80° N. Lat.; 75.04° W. Long.

History: Incorporated 1798.

Population: 53,797 (1990); 64,350 (2000); 66,628 (2005); 68,741 (2010 projected); Race: 79.3% White, 14.5% Black, 2.7% Asian, 3.9% Hispanic of any race (2005); Density: 2,869.3 persons per square mile (2005); Average household size: 2.74 (2005); Median age: 35.9 (2005); Males per 100 females: 95.1 (2005); Marriage status: 28.4% never married, 58.4% now married, 5.3% widowed, 7.9% divorced (2000); Foreign born: 4.9% (2000); Ancestry (includes multiple ancestries): 29.3% Italian, 25.8% Irish, 19.1% German, 17.1% Other groups, 8.2% English (2000).

Economy: Residential and commercial. Unemployment rate: 2.4% (2005); Total civilian labor force: 36,895 (2005); Single-family building permits issued: 181 (2005); Multi-family building permits issued: 93 (2005); Employment by occupation: 13.6% management, 20.3% professional, 13.3% services, 31.3% sales, 0.0% farming, 10.1% construction, 11.4% production (2000).

Income: Per capita income: $26,845 (2005); Median household income: $62,190 (2005); Average household income: $73,091 (2005); Percent of households with income of $100,000 or more: 22.0% (2005); Poverty rate: 6.2% (2000).

Taxes: Total city taxes per capita: $320 (2004); City property taxes per capita: $301 (2004).

Education: Percent of population age 25 and over with: High school diploma (including GED) or higher: 85.6% (2005); Bachelor's degree or higher: 21.8% (2005); Master's degree or higher: 6.1% (2005).

Two-year College(s)

P B Cosmetology Education Center (Private, For-profit)

    Fall 2004 Enrollment: 153 . . . . (856) 456-4050

Housing: Homeownership rate: 72.0% (2005); Median home value: $177,891 (2005); Median rent: $631 per month (2000); Median age of housing: 24 years (2000).

Safety: Violent crime rate: 31.3 per 10,000 population; Property crime rate: 244.3 per 10,000 population (2004).

Transportation: Commute to work: 90.3% car, 6.4% public transportation, 0.7% walk, 1.8% work from home (2000); Travel time to work: 18.9% less than 15 minutes, 33.7% 15 to 30 minutes, 24.9% 30 to 45 minutes, 10.3% 45 to 60 minutes, 12.2% 60 minutes or more (2000)

Additional Information Contacts

Gloucester Township . . . . (856) 228-4000

    http://www.glotwp.com

GLOUCESTER CITY (city). Aka Gloucester. Covers a land area of 2.203 square miles and a water area of 0.631 square miles. Located at 39.89° N. Lat.; 75.11° W. Long. Elevation is 19 feet.

History: Named for Henry, Duke of Gloucester, third son of Charles I of England. Site of Fort Nassau, built 1623 by the Dutch; settled c.1682 by Irish Quakers. Incorporated 1868.

Population: 12,649 (1990); 11,484 (2000); 11,419 (2005); 11,386 (2010 projected); Race: 96.3% White, 0.9% Black, 0.8% Asian, 2.4% Hispanic of any race (2005); Density: 5,184.2 persons per square mile (2005); Average household size: 2.71 (2005); Median age: 36.9 (2005); Males per 100 females: 95.5 (2005); Marriage status: 32.2% never married, 48.9% now married, 10.2% widowed, 8.7% divorced (2000); Foreign born: 0.9% (2000); Ancestry (includes multiple ancestries): 42.3% Irish, 22.2% German, 18.9% Italian, 10.0% English, 7.0% Polish (2000).

Economy: Oil refining, light industry, and glass manufacturing. Single-family building permits issued: 6 (2005); Multi-family building permits

---

issued: 0 (2005); Employment by occupation: 9.1% management, 11.0% professional, 15.3% services, 29.9% sales, 0.0% farming, 11.0% construction, 23.7% production (2000).

Income: Per capita income: $18,971 (2005); Median household income: $41,668 (2005); Average household income: $51,266 (2005); Percent of households with income of $100,000 or more: 10.6% (2005); Poverty rate: 10.1% (2000).

Education: Percent of population age 25 and over with: High school diploma (including GED) or higher: 72.6% (2005); Bachelor's degree or higher: 8.2% (2005); Master's degree or higher: 1.7% (2005).

School District(s)

Gloucester City (PK-12)

    2003-04 Enrollment: 2,273 . . . . (856) 456-9394

Housing: Homeownership rate: 73.3% (2005); Median home value: $119,343 (2005); Median rent: $523 per month (2000); Median age of housing: 60+ years (2000).

Safety: Violent crime rate: 26.9 per 10,000 population; Property crime rate: 239.7 per 10,000 population (2004).

Newspapers: Gloucester City News (General - Circulation 5,000)

Transportation: Commute to work: 88.5% car, 4.6% public transportation, 4.7% walk, 1.1% work from home (2000); Travel time to work: 31.5% less than 15 minutes, 43.5% 15 to 30 minutes, 15.8% 30 to 45 minutes, 4.7% 45 to 60 minutes, 4.5% 60 minutes or more (2000)

GOLDEN TRIANGLE (CDP). Covers a land area of 2.864 square miles and a water area of 0.085 square miles. Located at 39.92° N. Lat.; 75.04° W. Long.

Population: 3,512 (1990); 3,511 (2000); 3,779 (2005); 4,041 (2010 projected); Race: 79.3% White, 10.7% Black, 5.3% Asian, 5.9% Hispanic of any race (2005); Density: 1,319.4 persons per square mile (2005); Average household size: 2.55 (2005); Median age: 42.6 (2005); Males per 100 females: 97.1 (2005); Marriage status: 32.3% never married, 47.4% now married, 9.6% widowed, 10.7% divorced (2000); Foreign born: 5.6% (2000); Ancestry (includes multiple ancestries): 22.8% Other groups, 22.6% Italian, 18.1% German, 13.2% Irish, 9.0% Polish (2000).

Economy: Employment by occupation: 16.9% management, 21.5% professional, 14.3% services, 23.7% sales, 0.0% farming, 8.9% construction, 14.6% production (2000).

Income: Per capita income: $23,914 (2005); Median household income: $52,387 (2005); Average household income: $59,181 (2005); Percent of households with income of $100,000 or more: 16.3% (2005); Poverty rate: 7.7% (2000).

Education: Percent of population age 25 and over with: High school diploma (including GED) or higher: 82.2% (2005); Bachelor's degree or higher: 21.5% (2005); Master's degree or higher: 6.0% (2005).

Housing: Homeownership rate: 80.1% (2005); Median home value: $176,102 (2005); Median rent: $718 per month (2000); Median age of housing: 35 years (2000).

Transportation: Commute to work: 90.0% car, 4.7% public transportation, 0.9% walk, 4.2% work from home (2000); Travel time to work: 32.6% less than 15 minutes, 36.1% 15 to 30 minutes, 15.7% 30 to 45 minutes, 8.5% 45 to 60 minutes, 7.1% 60 minutes or more (2000)

GREENTREE (CDP). Covers a land area of 4.672 square miles and a water area of 0.004 square miles. Located at 39.89° N. Lat.; 74.95° W. Long.

Population: 10,366 (1990); 11,536 (2000); 11,865 (2005); 12,194 (2010 projected); Race: 74.5% White, 7.7% Black, 15.6% Asian, 2.3% Hispanic of any race (2005); Density: 2,539.5 persons per square mile (2005); Average household size: 2.91 (2005); Median age: 40.3 (2005); Males per 100 females: 94.2 (2005); Marriage status: 21.3% never married, 69.3% now married, 4.6% widowed, 4.9% divorced (2000); Foreign born: 17.8% (2000); Ancestry (includes multiple ancestries): 27.3% Other groups, 14.7% Irish, 14.3% Italian, 11.3% German, 10.0% Russian (2000).

Economy: Employment by occupation: 21.7% management, 35.5% professional, 7.2% services, 28.7% sales, 0.0% farming, 3.3% construction, 3.5% production (2000).

Income: Per capita income: $38,352 (2005); Median household income: $91,137 (2005); Average household income: $110,407 (2005); Percent of households with income of $100,000 or more: 44.6% (2005); Poverty rate: 2.2% (2000).

Education: Percent of population age 25 and over with: High school diploma (including GED) or higher: 93.8% (2005); Bachelor's degree or higher: 56.4% (2005); Master's degree or higher: 25.6% (2005).

Housing: Homeownership rate: 91.4% (2005); Median home value: $269,098 (2005); Median rent: $991 per month (2000); Median age of housing: 24 years (2000).
Transportation: Commute to work: 88.3% car, 6.3% public transportation, 1.6% walk, 3.3% work from home (2000); Travel time to work: 27.2% less than 15 minutes, 31.2% 15 to 30 minutes, 21.2% 30 to 45 minutes, 9.2% 45 to 60 minutes, 11.2% 60 minutes or more (2000)

HADDON (township).
Covers a land area of 2.691 square miles and a water area of 0.109 square miles. Located at 39.90° N. Lat.; 75.06° W. Long. Elevation is 20 feet.
History: Incorporated 1865.
Population: 14,837 (1990); 14,651 (2000); 14,713 (2005); 14,774 (2010 projected); Race: 94.4% White, 1.5% Black, 2.2% Asian, 2.0% Hispanic of any race (2005); Density: 5,466.5 persons per square mile (2005); Average household size: 2.35 (2005); Median age: 41.9 (2005); Males per 100 females: 89.0 (2005); Marriage status: 25.5% never married, 56.4% now married, 10.6% widowed, 7.5% divorced (2000); Foreign born: 3.9% (2000); Ancestry (includes multiple ancestries): 30.0% Irish, 25.2% German, 24.9% Italian, 15.1% English, 8.2% Polish (2000).
Economy: Suburban residential community. Single-family building permits issued: 4 (2005); Multi-family building permits issued: 20 (2005); Employment by occupation: 13.8% management, 27.8% professional, 12.2% services, 29.3% sales, 0.0% farming, 8.8% construction, 8.1% production (2000).
Income: Per capita income: $30,613 (2005); Median household income: $59,476 (2005); Average household income: $71,913 (2005); Percent of households with income of $100,000 or more: 21.7% (2005); Poverty rate: 4.1% (2000).
Education: Percent of population age 25 and over with: High school diploma (including GED) or higher: 89.4% (2005); Bachelor's degree or higher: 30.3% (2005); Master's degree or higher: 9.6% (2005).
Housing: Homeownership rate: 69.3% (2005); Median home value: $188,493 (2005); Median rent: $634 per month (2000); Median age of housing: 50 years (2000).
Safety: Violent crime rate: 17.6 per 10,000 population; Property crime rate: 239.9 per 10,000 population (2004).
Transportation: Commute to work: 82.1% car, 12.3% public transportation, 2.6% walk, 2.0% work from home (2000); Travel time to work: 30.2% less than 15 minutes, 42.6% 15 to 30 minutes, 15.5% 30 to 45 minutes, 5.6% 45 to 60 minutes, 6.2% 60 minutes or more (2000)

HADDON HEIGHTS (borough).
Covers a land area of 1.554 square miles and a water area of 0.004 square miles. Located at 39.87° N. Lat.; 75.06° W. Long. Elevation is 60 feet.
History: Laid out c.1891, incorporated 1904.
Population: 7,860 (1990); 7,547 (2000); 7,477 (2005); 7,415 (2010 projected); Race: 97.6% White, 0.4% Black, 0.7% Asian, 1.2% Hispanic of any race (2005); Density: 4,810.4 persons per square mile (2005); Average household size: 2.45 (2005); Median age: 41.5 (2005); Males per 100 females: 89.6 (2005); Marriage status: 22.7% never married, 60.9% now married, 9.5% widowed, 6.9% divorced (2000); Foreign born: 2.9% (2000); Ancestry (includes multiple ancestries): 33.7% Irish, 23.8% Italian, 23.6% German, 17.5% English, 8.3% Polish (2000).
Economy: Single-family building permits issued: 1 (2005); Multi-family building permits issued: 0 (2005); Employment by occupation: 18.1% management, 30.9% professional, 11.6% services, 27.3% sales, 0.0% farming, 6.5% construction, 5.6% production (2000).
Income: Per capita income: $33,782 (2005); Median household income: $67,500 (2005); Average household income: $82,121 (2005); Percent of households with income of $100,000 or more: 28.4% (2005); Poverty rate: 2.8% (2000).
Education: Percent of population age 25 and over with: High school diploma (including GED) or higher: 90.6% (2005); Bachelor's degree or higher: 38.5% (2005); Master's degree or higher: 14.0% (2005).
School District(s)
Haddon Heights Borough (PK-12)
    2003-04 Enrollment: 1,320 . . . . (856) 547-1412
Housing: Homeownership rate: 77.9% (2005); Median home value: $230,216 (2005); Median rent: $524 per month (2000); Median age of housing: 56 years (2000).
Safety: Violent crime rate: 10.6 per 10,000 population; Property crime rate: 205.4 per 10,000 population (2004).
Transportation: Commute to work: 88.4% car, 5.0% public transportation, 1.7% walk, 4.4% work from home (2000); Travel time to work: 24.7% less

than 15 minutes, 40.8% 15 to 30 minutes, 17.5% 30 to 45 minutes, 8.5% 45 to 60 minutes, 8.4% 60 minutes or more (2000)
Additional Information Contacts
Borough of Haddon Heights. . . . . (856) 547-7132
    http://www.haddonheights.lib.nj.us

HADDONFIELD (borough).
Covers a land area of 2.827 square miles and a water area of 0.031 square miles. Located at 39.89° N. Lat.; 75.03° W. Long. Elevation is 81 feet.
History: Named for Elizabeth Haddon, a Quaker who founded the town in 1770. Of interest are Indian King Tavern (1750), where the first state legislature met in 1777, and the Haddonfield historical society; downtown area is historic preservation district with many 19th- and some 18th-century structures. Site of first complete dinosaur fossil ever found, Haddonfield Hadrosaur, made national historical landmark 1993. Settled c.1713. Incorporated 1875.
Population: 11,628 (1990); 11,659 (2000); 11,609 (2005); 11,597 (2010 projected); Race: 96.2% White, 1.3% Black, 1.1% Asian, 1.8% Hispanic of any race (2005); Density: 4,107.1 persons per square mile (2005); Average household size: 2.61 (2005); Median age: 42.1 (2005); Males per 100 females: 90.6 (2005); Marriage status: 22.2% never married, 64.9% now married, 7.3% widowed, 5.6% divorced (2000); Foreign born: 3.2% (2000); Ancestry (includes multiple ancestries): 30.2% Irish, 20.9% German, 19.3% English, 19.0% Italian, 7.7% Polish (2000).
Economy: Single-family building permits issued: 16 (2005); Multi-family building permits issued: 0 (2005); Employment by occupation: 24.6% management, 43.0% professional, 6.2% services, 20.5% sales, 0.1% farming, 1.3% construction, 4.3% production (2000).
Income: Per capita income: $50,705 (2005); Median household income: $101,002 (2005); Average household income: $131,835 (2005); Percent of households with income of $100,000 or more: 50.5% (2005); Poverty rate: 2.2% (2000).
Taxes: Total city taxes per capita: $574 (2004); City property taxes per capita: $554 (2004).
Education: Percent of population age 25 and over with: High school diploma (including GED) or higher: 95.1% (2005); Bachelor's degree or higher: 64.8% (2005); Master's degree or higher: 28.8% (2005).
School District(s)
Barrington Borough (PK-08)
    2003-04 Enrollment: 639 . . . . (856) 547-8467
Haddon Township (PK-12)
    2003-04 Enrollment: 2,357 . . . . (856) 869-7700
Haddonfield Borough (PK-12)
    2003-04 Enrollment: 2,317 . . . . (856) 429-4130
Housing: Homeownership rate: 84.5% (2005); Median home value: $362,657 (2005); Median rent: $649 per month (2000); Median age of housing: 60+ years (2000).
Safety: Violent crime rate: 7.7 per 10,000 population; Property crime rate: 130.8 per 10,000 population (2004).
Newspapers: The Haddon Herald (General - Circulation 3,000)
Transportation: Commute to work: 78.2% car, 13.2% public transportation, 2.9% walk, 5.2% work from home (2000); Travel time to work: 24.7% less than 15 minutes, 35.1% 15 to 30 minutes, 21.6% 30 to 45 minutes, 9.6% 45 to 60 minutes, 9.1% 60 minutes or more (2000)
Additional Information Contacts
Southern New Jersey Chamber of Commerce . . . . (856) 424-7776
    http://www.chambersnj.com

HI-NELLA (borough).
Aka Hi Nella. Covers a land area of 0.227 square miles and a water area of 0 square miles. Located at 39.83° N. Lat.; 75.02° W. Long. Elevation is 80 feet.
Population: 1,060 (1990); 1,029 (2000); 1,023 (2005); 1,021 (2010 projected); Race: 64.1% White, 23.1% Black, 3.6% Asian, 9.1% Hispanic of any race (2005); Density: 4,510.4 persons per square mile (2005); Average household size: 2.16 (2005); Median age: 33.4 (2005); Males per 100 females: 88.4 (2005); Marriage status: 33.1% never married, 48.2% now married, 6.4% widowed, 12.3% divorced (2000); Foreign born: 6.6% (2000); Ancestry (includes multiple ancestries): 32.0% Other groups, 23.5% Irish, 22.8% German, 16.8% Italian, 8.7% English (2000).
Economy: Single-family building permits issued: 0 (2005); Multi-family building permits issued: 0 (2005); Employment by occupation: 7.7% management, 16.0% professional, 14.7% services, 38.4% sales, 0.0% farming, 8.1% construction, 15.2% production (2000).
Income: Per capita income: $20,308 (2005); Median household income: $39,205 (2005); Average household income: $43,829 (2005); Percent of

households with income of $100,000 or more: 3.8% (2005); Poverty rate: 12.2% (2000).

Education: Percent of population age 25 and over with: High school diploma (including GED) or higher: 79.2% (2005); Bachelor's degree or higher: 13.9% (2005); Master's degree or higher: 4.0% (2005).

Housing: Homeownership rate: 24.1% (2005); Median home value: $136,301 (2005); Median rent: $610 per month (2000); Median age of housing: 37 years (2000).

Safety: Violent crime rate: 58.1 per 10,000 population; Property crime rate: 387.6 per 10,000 population (2004).

Transportation: Commute to work: 86.2% car, 9.0% public transportation, 1.9% walk, 1.0% work from home (2000); Travel time to work: 19.6% less than 15 minutes, 39.2% 15 to 30 minutes, 20.5% 30 to 45 minutes, 11.0% 45 to 60 minutes, 9.7% 60 minutes or more (2000)

LAUREL SPRINGS (borough). Covers a land area of 0.468 square miles and a water area of 0 square miles. Located at 39.82° N. Lat.; 75.00° W. Long. Elevation is 82 feet.

History: Incorporated 1913.

Population: 2,341 (1990); 1,970 (2000); 1,952 (2005); 1,940 (2010 projected); Race: 93.6% White, 2.9% Black, 1.1% Asian, 1.9% Hispanic of any race (2005); Density: 4,175.0 persons per square mile (2005); Average household size: 2.54 (2005); Median age: 38.6 (2005); Males per 100 females: 100.0 (2005); Marriage status: 27.0% never married, 56.1% now married, 6.8% widowed, 10.0% divorced (2000); Foreign born: 2.1% (2000); Ancestry (includes multiple ancestries): 31.9% Irish, 27.4% German, 20.5% Italian, 15.9% English, 6.9% Polish (2000).

Economy: Single-family building permits issued: 1 (2005); Multi-family building permits issued: 0 (2005); Employment by occupation: 9.7% management, 25.6% professional, 14.7% services, 28.3% sales, 0.0% farming, 9.3% construction, 12.3% production (2000).

Income: Per capita income: $28,924 (2005); Median household income: $61,439 (2005); Average household income: $73,420 (2005); Percent of households with income of $100,000 or more: 22.5% (2005); Poverty rate: 3.7% (2000).

Education: Percent of population age 25 and over with: High school diploma (including GED) or higher: 87.2% (2005); Bachelor's degree or higher: 22.6% (2005); Master's degree or higher: 6.8% (2005).

School District(s)
Laurel Springs Borough (PK-06)
   2003-04 Enrollment: 183 . . . . (856) 783-1086
Two-year College(s)
Empire Beauty School-Laurel Springs (Private, For-profit)
   Fall 2004 Enrollment: 103 . . . . (800) 223-3271

Housing: Homeownership rate: 76.7% (2005); Median home value: $177,128 (2005); Median rent: $547 per month (2000); Median age of housing: 55 years (2000).

Safety: Violent crime rate: 40.6 per 10,000 population; Property crime rate: 258.8 per 10,000 population (2004).

Transportation: Commute to work: 88.7% car, 6.0% public transportation, 2.6% walk, 1.8% work from home (2000); Travel time to work: 31.0% less than 15 minutes, 31.9% 15 to 30 minutes, 20.3% 30 to 45 minutes, 7.7% 45 to 60 minutes, 9.1% 60 minutes or more (2000)

LAWNSIDE (borough). Covers a land area of 1.402 square miles and a water area of 0 square miles. Located at 39.86° N. Lat.; 75.03° W. Long. Elevation is 110 feet.

History: Site bought by abolitionists for free blacks (1840), and first called Free Haven. Population is overwhelmingly African-American. Incorporated 1926.

Population: 2,841 (1990); 2,692 (2000); 2,752 (2005); 2,819 (2010 projected); Race: 1.7% White, 92.8% Black, 0.6% Asian, 2.8% Hispanic of any race (2005); Density: 1,962.5 persons per square mile (2005); Average household size: 2.58 (2005); Median age: 43.2 (2005); Males per 100 females: 84.1 (2005); Marriage status: 35.8% never married, 41.3% now married, 13.7% widowed, 9.2% divorced (2000); Foreign born: 6.0% (2000); Ancestry (includes multiple ancestries): 77.1% Other groups, 2.5% Irish, 1.4% German, 1.2% United States or American, 0.7% Jamaican (2000).

Economy: Single-family building permits issued: 20 (2005); Multi-family building permits issued: 0 (2005); Employment by occupation: 10.6% management, 20.6% professional, 17.9% services, 32.2% sales, 0.0% farming, 3.3% construction, 15.5% production (2000).

Income: Per capita income: $23,223 (2005); Median household income: $50,311 (2005); Average household income: $59,897 (2005); Percent of

households with income of $100,000 or more: 18.4% (2005); Poverty rate: 10.7% (2000).

Education: Percent of population age 25 and over with: High school diploma (including GED) or higher: 79.1% (2005); Bachelor's degree or higher: 18.8% (2005); Master's degree or higher: 7.0% (2005).

School District(s)
Lawnside Borough (PK-08)
   2003-04 Enrollment: 309 . . . . (856) 546-4850

Housing: Homeownership rate: 72.6% (2005); Median home value: $155,786 (2005); Median rent: $455 per month (2000); Median age of housing: 35 years (2000).

Safety: Violent crime rate: 87.4 per 10,000 population; Property crime rate: 407.9 per 10,000 population (2004).

Transportation: Commute to work: 87.2% car, 8.8% public transportation, 3.0% walk, 0.6% work from home (2000); Travel time to work: 27.3% less than 15 minutes, 43.7% 15 to 30 minutes, 15.5% 30 to 45 minutes, 7.0% 45 to 60 minutes, 6.5% 60 minutes or more (2000)

LINDENWOLD (borough). Covers a land area of 3.944 square miles and a water area of 0.028 square miles. Located at 39.81° N. Lat.; 74.99° W. Long. Elevation is 90 feet.

History: Named for Linden, Germany, and for the linden trees brought by early settlers to this area. Settled 1742. Incorporated 1929.

Population: 18,734 (1990); 17,414 (2000); 17,365 (2005); 17,359 (2010 projected); Race: 52.2% White, 35.0% Black, 3.8% Asian, 9.9% Hispanic of any race (2005); Density: 4,403.1 persons per square mile (2005); Average household size: 2.32 (2005); Median age: 34.8 (2005); Males per 100 females: 92.0 (2005); Marriage status: 36.0% never married, 45.3% now married, 6.0% widowed, 12.7% divorced (2000); Foreign born: 7.2% (2000); Ancestry (includes multiple ancestries): 38.1% Other groups, 18.6% Irish, 15.7% Italian, 15.0% German, 6.7% English (2000).

Economy: Manufacturing includes plastics, nails, machinery, food. Terminus for a light railroad line from Philadelphia. Single-family building permits issued: 10 (2005); Multi-family building permits issued: 0 (2005); Employment by occupation: 8.9% management, 14.7% professional, 19.9% services, 32.4% sales, 0.1% farming, 10.3% construction, 13.7% production (2000).

Income: Per capita income: $20,656 (2005); Median household income: $39,390 (2005); Average household income: $47,471 (2005); Percent of households with income of $100,000 or more: 7.6% (2005); Poverty rate: 11.8% (2000).

Education: Percent of population age 25 and over with: High school diploma (including GED) or higher: 77.4% (2005); Bachelor's degree or higher: 13.1% (2005); Master's degree or higher: 3.6% (2005).

School District(s)
Lindenwold Borough (PK-12)
   2003-04 Enrollment: 2,808 . . . . (856) 784-4071

Housing: Homeownership rate: 43.2% (2005); Median home value: $121,074 (2005); Median rent: $548 per month (2000); Median age of housing: 30 years (2000).

Safety: Violent crime rate: 65.1 per 10,000 population; Property crime rate: 317.2 per 10,000 population (2004).

Transportation: Commute to work: 83.0% car, 12.5% public transportation, 2.3% walk, 1.3% work from home (2000); Travel time to work: 22.2% less than 15 minutes, 33.6% 15 to 30 minutes, 20.9% 30 to 45 minutes, 10.2% 45 to 60 minutes, 13.1% 60 minutes or more (2000)

MAGNOLIA (borough). Covers a land area of 0.970 square miles and a water area of 0 square miles. Located at 39.85° N. Lat.; 75.03° W. Long. Elevation is 79 feet.

History: Incorporated 1915.

Population: 4,861 (1990); 4,409 (2000); 4,408 (2005); 4,429 (2010 projected); Race: 75.3% White, 18.6% Black, 0.9% Asian, 5.0% Hispanic of any race (2005); Density: 4,542.3 persons per square mile (2005); Average household size: 2.53 (2005); Median age: 37.5 (2005); Males per 100 females: 94.1 (2005); Marriage status: 29.4% never married, 52.3% now married, 9.1% widowed, 9.3% divorced (2000); Foreign born: 3.2% (2000); Ancestry (includes multiple ancestries): 25.9% Irish, 22.3% Other groups, 21.8% German, 19.8% Italian, 9.9% English (2000).

Economy: Single-family building permits issued: 10 (2005); Multi-family building permits issued: 3 (2005); Employment by occupation: 9.3% management, 18.1% professional, 16.0% services, 29.6% sales, 0.0% farming, 13.2% construction, 13.8% production (2000).

Income: Per capita income: $22,156 (2005); Median household income: $48,070 (2005); Average household income: $55,297 (2005); Percent of

households with income of $100,000 or more: 10.6% (2005); Poverty rate: 7.9% (2000).

Education: Percent of population age 25 and over with: High school diploma (including GED) or higher: 80.6% (2005); Bachelor's degree or higher: 12.2% (2005); Master's degree or higher: 2.7% (2005).

School District(s)

Camden County Ed Serv Comm (UG-UG)
   2003-04 Enrollment: n/a . . . . (856) 784-2100
Magnolia Borough (PK-08)
   2003-04 Enrollment: 451 . . . . (856) 783-6343

Housing: Homeownership rate: 73.2% (2005); Median home value: $136,860 (2005); Median rent: $540 per month (2000); Median age of housing: 42 years (2000).

Safety: Violent crime rate: 56.3 per 10,000 population; Property crime rate: 281.5 per 10,000 population (2004).

Transportation: Commute to work: 88.0% car, 7.7% public transportation, 2.3% walk, 1.6% work from home (2000); Travel time to work: 18.8% less than 15 minutes, 38.7% 15 to 30 minutes, 24.5% 30 to 45 minutes, 6.8% 45 to 60 minutes, 11.2% 60 minutes or more (2000)

Additional Information Contacts
Borough of Magnolia . . . . (856) 783-1520
   http://www.magnolia-nj.org

MERCHANTVILLE (borough). Covers a land area of 0.602 square miles and a water area of 0 square miles. Located at 39.95° N. Lat.; 75.05° W. Long. Elevation is 80 feet.

History: Settled 1852, incorporated 1874.

Population: 4,069 (1990); 3,801 (2000); 3,824 (2005); 3,862 (2010 projected); Race: 81.2% White, 10.1% Black, 2.3% Asian, 7.3% Hispanic of any race (2005); Density: 6,355.4 persons per square mile (2005); Average household size: 2.46 (2005); Median age: 38.0 (2005); Males per 100 females: 90.1 (2005); Marriage status: 30.4% never married, 51.8% now married, 8.0% widowed, 9.7% divorced (2000); Foreign born: 3.9% (2000); Ancestry (includes multiple ancestries): 28.9% Irish, 21.5% German, 14.2% Other groups, 13.6% Italian, 10.3% English (2000).

Economy: Single-family building permits issued: 9 (2005); Multi-family building permits issued: 0 (2005); Employment by occupation: 18.9% management, 17.0% professional, 11.9% services, 32.9% sales, 0.0% farming, 9.5% construction, 9.8% production (2000).

Income: Per capita income: $30,807 (2005); Median household income: $57,578 (2005); Average household income: $75,446 (2005); Percent of households with income of $100,000 or more: 22.8% (2005); Poverty rate: 6.8% (2000).

Education: Percent of population age 25 and over with: High school diploma (including GED) or higher: 81.7% (2005); Bachelor's degree or higher: 27.8% (2005); Master's degree or higher: 8.3% (2005).

School District(s)

Merchantville Borough (PK-08)
   2003-04 Enrollment: 368 . . . . (856) 663-1091

Housing: Homeownership rate: 60.1% (2005); Median home value: $190,614 (2005); Median rent: $605 per month (2000); Median age of housing: 60+ years (2000).

Safety: Violent crime rate: 26.0 per 10,000 population; Property crime rate: 208.2 per 10,000 population (2004).

Transportation: Commute to work: 78.0% car, 7.2% public transportation, 2.6% walk, 8.0% work from home (2000); Travel time to work: 25.3% less than 15 minutes, 45.6% 15 to 30 minutes, 12.6% 30 to 45 minutes, 8.7% 45 to 60 minutes, 7.9% 60 minutes or more (2000)

Additional Information Contacts
Borough of Merchantville . . . . (856) 662-2474
   http://www.merchantville.com

MOUNT EPHRAIM (borough). Covers a land area of 0.881 square miles and a water area of 0.015 square miles. Located at 39.88° N. Lat.; 75.09° W. Long. Elevation is 30 feet.

History: Settled before 1800, incorporated 1926.

Population: 4,517 (1990); 4,495 (2000); 4,502 (2005); 4,516 (2010 projected); Race: 96.7% White, 0.5% Black, 0.8% Asian, 2.5% Hispanic of any race (2005); Density: 5,108.1 persons per square mile (2005); Average household size: 2.47 (2005); Median age: 40.7 (2005); Males per 100 females: 94.1 (2005); Marriage status: 25.2% never married, 54.0% now married, 10.8% widowed, 9.9% divorced (2000); Foreign born: 2.2% (2000); Ancestry (includes multiple ancestries): 34.1% Italian, 27.9% Irish, 25.7% German, 13.8% English, 8.6% Polish (2000).

Economy: Single-family building permits issued: 4 (2005); Multi-family building permits issued: 0 (2005); Employment by occupation: 13.8% management, 17.3% professional, 10.1% services, 31.0% sales, 0.0% farming, 12.0% construction, 15.8% production (2000).

Income: Per capita income: $24,956 (2005); Median household income: $51,947 (2005); Average household income: $61,583 (2005); Percent of households with income of $100,000 or more: 16.6% (2005); Poverty rate: 4.9% (2000).

Education: Percent of population age 25 and over with: High school diploma (including GED) or higher: 78.7% (2005); Bachelor's degree or higher: 13.4% (2005); Master's degree or higher: 3.2% (2005).

School District(s)

Mount Ephraim Borough (PK-08)
   2003-04 Enrollment: 511 . . . . (856) 931-1634

Housing: Homeownership rate: 80.1% (2005); Median home value: $139,946 (2005); Median rent: $482 per month (2000); Median age of housing: 50 years (2000).

Safety: Violent crime rate: 44.2 per 10,000 population; Property crime rate: 439.5 per 10,000 population (2004).

Transportation: Commute to work: 88.8% car, 6.7% public transportation, 2.4% walk, 1.2% work from home (2000); Travel time to work: 28.0% less than 15 minutes, 41.8% 15 to 30 minutes, 16.0% 30 to 45 minutes, 5.7% 45 to 60 minutes, 8.4% 60 minutes or more (2000)

OAKLYN (borough). Covers a land area of 0.614 square miles and a water area of 0.083 square miles. Located at 39.90° N. Lat.; 75.08° W. Long. Elevation is 20 feet.

History: Settled 1682 by Friends, laid out c.1890, incorporated 1905.

Population: 4,430 (1990); 4,188 (2000); 4,146 (2005); 4,115 (2010 projected); Race: 94.7% White, 1.5% Black, 1.1% Asian, 2.9% Hispanic of any race (2005); Density: 6,755.8 persons per square mile (2005); Average household size: 2.32 (2005); Median age: 39.0 (2005); Males per 100 females: 95.1 (2005); Marriage status: 28.0% never married, 49.5% now married, 12.0% widowed, 10.6% divorced (2000); Foreign born: 1.5% (2000); Ancestry (includes multiple ancestries): 34.0% Irish, 20.1% German, 19.6% Italian, 13.2% English, 8.2% Polish (2000).

Economy: Single-family building permits issued: 0 (2005); Multi-family building permits issued: 0 (2005); Employment by occupation: 11.9% management, 20.6% professional, 11.7% services, 33.9% sales, 0.0% farming, 12.7% construction, 9.1% production (2000).

Income: Per capita income: $27,957 (2005); Median household income: $53,154 (2005); Average household income: $64,625 (2005); Percent of households with income of $100,000 or more: 16.3% (2005); Poverty rate: 6.5% (2000).

Education: Percent of population age 25 and over with: High school diploma (including GED) or higher: 82.6% (2005); Bachelor's degree or higher: 19.4% (2005); Master's degree or higher: 5.4% (2005).

School District(s)

Collingswood Borough (PK-12)
   2003-04 Enrollment: 2,075 . . . . (856) 962-5732

Housing: Homeownership rate: 68.0% (2005); Median home value: $145,614 (2005); Median rent: $501 per month (2000); Median age of housing: 59 years (2000).

Safety: Violent crime rate: 35.8 per 10,000 population; Property crime rate: 344.1 per 10,000 population (2004).

Transportation: Commute to work: 88.6% car, 7.2% public transportation, 2.4% walk, 0.8% work from home (2000); Travel time to work: 26.8% less than 15 minutes, 42.8% 15 to 30 minutes, 17.9% 30 to 45 minutes, 4.6% 45 to 60 minutes, 7.9% 60 minutes or more (2000)

PENNSAUKEN (township). Aka Pennsauken CDP. Covers a land area of 10.534 square miles and a water area of 1.655 square miles. Located at 39.95° N. Lat.; 75.05° W. Long. Elevation is 65 feet.

History: Named for the Delaware Indian translation of "tobacco pouch". Settled 1840. Incorporated 1892.

Population: 34,764 (1990); 35,737 (2000); 35,923 (2005); 36,169 (2010 projected); Race: 52.1% White, 28.2% Black, 5.1% Asian, 18.7% Hispanic of any race (2005); Density: 3,410.0 persons per square mile (2005); Average household size: 2.90 (2005); Median age: 37.1 (2005); Males per 100 females: 92.5 (2005); Marriage status: 30.2% never married, 54.6% now married, 7.5% widowed, 7.6% divorced (2000); Foreign born: 7.9% (2000); Ancestry (includes multiple ancestries): 36.8% Other groups, 18.4% Irish, 14.3% Italian, 14.3% German, 6.8% English (2000).

Economy: Manufacturing: beer, plastics, wire products, machinery, packaging supplies, food and beverage processing, automotive engines, construction materials. Unemployment rate: 5.3% (2005); Total civilian labor force: 17,769 (2005); Single-family building permits issued: 15 (2005); Multi-family building permits issued: 79 (2005); Employment by occupation: 11.0% management, 16.8% professional, 16.0% services, 31.1% sales, 0.0% farming, 8.1% construction, 16.9% production (2000).

Income: Per capita income: $21,805 (2005); Median household income: $53,381 (2005); Average household income: $62,753 (2005); Percent of households with income of $100,000 or more: 15.7% (2005); Poverty rate: 8.0% (2000).

Taxes: Total city taxes per capita: $397 (2004); City property taxes per capita: $380 (2004).

Education: Percent of population age 25 and over with: High school diploma (including GED) or higher: 77.0% (2005); Bachelor's degree or higher: 15.3% (2005); Master's degree or higher: 4.8% (2005).

School District(s)
Camden County Vocational (09-12)
    2003-04 Enrollment: 2,620 . . . . (856) 767-7000
Pennsauken Township (PK-12)
    2003-04 Enrollment: 6,646 . . . . (856) 662-8505

Two-year College(s)
Omega Institute (Private, For-profit)
    Fall 2004 Enrollment: 124 . . . . (856) 663-4299

Housing: Homeownership rate: 80.5% (2005); Median home value: $141,329 (2005); Median rent: $531 per month (2000); Median age of housing: 44 years (2000).

Safety: Violent crime rate: 44.0 per 10,000 population; Property crime rate: 366.2 per 10,000 population (2004).

Transportation: Commute to work: 88.1% car, 6.3% public transportation, 2.0% walk, 2.2% work from home (2000); Travel time to work: 30.1% less than 15 minutes, 40.0% 15 to 30 minutes, 16.2% 30 to 45 minutes, 6.8% 45 to 60 minutes, 6.8% 60 minutes or more (2000)

Additional Information Contacts
Pennsauken Township. . . . . (865) 665-1000
    http://www.twp.pennsauken.nj.us

PINE HILL (borough). Aka Clementon Heights. Covers a land area of 3.930 square miles and a water area of 0.030 square miles. Located at 39.78° N. Lat.; 74.98° W. Long. Elevation is 170 feet.

History: Named for its native pine forests. Incorporated 1929.

Population: 9,854 (1990); 10,880 (2000); 11,263 (2005); 11,607 (2010 projected); Race: 70.8% White, 23.4% Black, 1.4% Asian, 4.5% Hispanic of any race (2005); Density: 2,865.8 persons per square mile (2005); Average household size: 2.55 (2005); Median age: 34.4 (2005); Males per 100 females: 90.2 (2005); Marriage status: 30.1% never married, 53.6% now married, 6.1% widowed, 10.3% divorced (2000); Foreign born: 3.6% (2000); Ancestry (includes multiple ancestries): 26.3% Irish, 24.8% Other groups, 22.1% Italian, 19.8% German, 8.8% English (2000).

Economy: Residential and light industry. Single-family building permits issued: 28 (2005); Multi-family building permits issued: 0 (2005); Employment by occupation: 10.7% management, 15.2% professional, 17.6% services, 31.5% sales, 0.1% farming, 13.1% construction, 11.9% production (2000).

Income: Per capita income: $21,212 (2005); Median household income: $47,323 (2005); Average household income: $53,841 (2005); Percent of households with income of $100,000 or more: 10.5% (2005); Poverty rate: 7.1% (2000).

Education: Percent of population age 25 and over with: High school diploma (including GED) or higher: 80.3% (2005); Bachelor's degree or higher: 13.7% (2005); Master's degree or higher: 3.7% (2005).

School District(s)
Pine Hill Borough (PK-12)
    2003-04 Enrollment: 2,431 . . . . (856) 783-6900

Housing: Homeownership rate: 60.5% (2005); Median home value: $136,251 (2005); Median rent: $570 per month (2000); Median age of housing: 29 years (2000).

Safety: Violent crime rate: 37.6 per 10,000 population; Property crime rate: 235.5 per 10,000 population (2004).

Transportation: Commute to work: 91.1% car, 5.2% public transportation, 1.4% walk, 1.4% work from home (2000); Travel time to work: 16.9% less than 15 minutes, 31.7% 15 to 30 minutes, 26.7% 30 to 45 minutes, 12.4% 45 to 60 minutes, 12.3% 60 minutes or more (2000)

Additional Information Contacts
Borough of Pine Hill. . . . . (856) 783-7400
    http://www.pinehillboronj.com

PINE VALLEY (borough). Covers a land area of 0.952 square miles and a water area of 0.009 square miles. Located at 39.78° N. Lat.; 74.97° W. Long. Elevation is 164 feet.

Population: 19 (1990); 20 (2000); 21 (2005); 22 (2010 projected); Race: 100.0% White, 0.0% Black, 0.0% Asian, 0.0% Hispanic of any race (2005); Density: 22.1 persons per square mile (2005); Average household size: 2.63 (2005); Median age: 47.5 (2005); Males per 100 females: 162.5 (2005); Marriage status: 0.0% never married, 100.0% now married, 0.0% widowed, 0.0% divorced (2000); Foreign born: 0.0% (2000); Economy: Single-family building permits issued: 1 (2005); Multi-family building permits issued: 0 (2005); Employment by occupation: 0.0% management, 40.0% professional, 0.0% services, 40.0% sales, 0.0% farming, 0.0% construction, 20.0% production (2000).

Income: Per capita income: $16,905 (2005); Median household income: $30,000 (2005); Average household income: $44,375 (2005); Percent of households with income of $100,000 or more: 0.0% (2005); Poverty rate: 0.0% (2000).

Education: Percent of population age 25 and over with: High school diploma (including GED) or higher: 81.3% (2005); Bachelor's degree or higher: 0.0% (2005); Master's degree or higher: 0.0% (2005).

Housing: Homeownership rate: 87.5% (2005); Median home value: $425,000 (2005); Median rent: $n/a per month (2000); Median age of housing: 17 years (2000).

Safety: Violent crime rate: 0.0 per 10,000 population; Property crime rate: 909.1 per 10,000 population (2004).

Transportation: Commute to work: 60.0% car, 40.0% public transportation, 0.0% walk, 0.0% work from home (2000); Travel time to work: 0.0% less than 15 minutes, 0.0% 15 to 30 minutes, 60.0% 30 to 45 minutes, 0.0% 45 to 60 minutes, 40.0% 60 minutes or more (2000)

RUNNEMEDE (borough). Covers a land area of 2.089 square miles and a water area of 0.031 square miles. Located at 39.85° N. Lat.; 75.07° W. Long. Elevation is 132 feet.

History: Settled 1683 by Friends (Quakers), originally called New Hope. Incorporated 1926.

Population: 9,042 (1990); 8,533 (2000); 8,554 (2005); 8,599 (2010 projected); Race: 90.0% White, 4.4% Black, 1.7% Asian, 4.7% Hispanic of any race (2005); Density: 4,094.2 persons per square mile (2005); Average household size: 2.48 (2005); Median age: 39.0 (2005); Males per 100 females: 92.8 (2005); Marriage status: 27.2% never married, 51.5% now married, 10.0% widowed, 11.4% divorced (2000); Foreign born: 4.1% (2000); Ancestry (includes multiple ancestries): 34.5% Irish, 30.8% Italian, 21.0% German, 10.3% Polish, 8.1% English (2000).

Economy: Single-family building permits issued: 8 (2005); Multi-family building permits issued: 0 (2005); Employment by occupation: 10.4% management, 15.3% professional, 15.9% services, 33.1% sales, 0.0% farming, 9.8% construction, 15.6% production (2000).

Income: Per capita income: $22,890 (2005); Median household income: $46,890 (2005); Average household income: $56,510 (2005); Percent of households with income of $100,000 or more: 12.9% (2005); Poverty rate: 5.6% (2000).

Education: Percent of population age 25 and over with: High school diploma (including GED) or higher: 78.5% (2005); Bachelor's degree or higher: 12.6% (2005); Master's degree or higher: 3.4% (2005).

School District(s)
Black Horse Pike Regional (09-12)
    2003-04 Enrollment: 4,438 . . . . (856) 227-4106
Runnemede Borough (PK-08)
    2003-04 Enrollment: 886 . . . . (856) 931-5365

Housing: Homeownership rate: 69.5% (2005); Median home value: $147,779 (2005); Median rent: $542 per month (2000); Median age of housing: 43 years (2000).

Safety: Violent crime rate: 34.9 per 10,000 population; Property crime rate: 383.7 per 10,000 population (2004).

Transportation: Commute to work: 87.1% car, 5.8% public transportation, 4.4% walk, 1.7% work from home (2000); Travel time to work: 24.2% less than 15 minutes, 40.6% 15 to 30 minutes, 19.4% 30 to 45 minutes, 6.0% 45 to 60 minutes, 9.7% 60 minutes or more (2000)

SICKLERVILLE (unincorporated postal area, zip code 08081). Aka Sicklertown. Covers a land area of 22.346 square miles and a water area of 0.050 square miles. Located at 39.74° N. Lat.; 74.99° W. Long. Elevation is 142 feet.

Population: 42,891 (2000); Race: 68.3% White, 25.9% Black, 2.1% Asian, 3.3% Hispanic of any race (2000); Density: 1,919.4 persons per square mile (2000); Age: 32.9% under 18, 5.6% over 64 (2000); Marriage status: 24.9% never married, 63.5% now married, 4.1% widowed, 7.4% divorced (2000); Foreign born: 4.2% (2000); Ancestry (includes multiple ancestries): 29.2% Other groups, 22.3% Irish, 21.6% Italian, 18.0% German, 7.2% English (2000).
Economy: Employment by occupation: 13.3% management, 21.8% professional, 14.2% services, 28.5% sales, 0.1% farming, 10.2% construction, 11.9% production (2000).
Income: Per capita income: $21,903 (2000); Median household income: $61,366 (2000); Poverty rate: 5.7% (2000).
Education: Percent of population age 25 and over with: High school diploma (including GED) or higher: 86.3% (2000); Bachelor's degree or higher: 22.9% (2000).

School District(s)
Black Horse Pike Regional (09-12)
    2003-04 Enrollment: 4,438 . . . . (856) 227-4106
Housing: Homeownership rate: 87.3% (2000); Median home value: $119,700 (2000); Median rent: $635 per month (2000); Median age of housing: 15 years (2000).
Transportation: Commute to work: 89.9% car, 7.0% public transportation, 0.8% walk, 1.8% work from home (2000); Travel time to work: 14.5% less than 15 minutes, 28.9% 15 to 30 minutes, 27.4% 30 to 45 minutes, 14.3% 45 to 60 minutes, 14.8% 60 minutes or more (2000)

SOMERDALE (borough).
Covers a land area of 1.374 square miles and a water area of 0 square miles. Located at 39.84° N. Lat.; 75.02° W. Long. Elevation is 83 feet.
History: Incorporated 1929.
Population: 5,425 (1990); 5,192 (2000); 5,184 (2005); 5,191 (2010 projected); Race: 72.0% White, 19.9% Black, 3.5% Asian, 4.5% Hispanic of any race (2005); Density: 3,773.1 persons per square mile (2005); Average household size: 2.47 (2005); Median age: 40.5 (2005); Males per 100 females: 95.9 (2005); Marriage status: 25.8% never married, 52.2% now married, 8.7% widowed, 13.3% divorced (2000); Foreign born: 6.7% (2000); Ancestry (includes multiple ancestries): 25.7% Other groups, 23.5% Italian, 22.5% Irish, 14.7% German, 9.2% English (2000).
Economy: Single-family building permits issued: 6 (2005); Multi-family building permits issued: 0 (2005); Employment by occupation: 10.3% management, 20.4% professional, 14.0% services, 29.3% sales, 0.0% farming, 10.0% construction, 16.0% production (2000).
Income: Per capita income: $25,644 (2005); Median household income: $54,299 (2005); Average household income: $63,229 (2005); Percent of households with income of $100,000 or more: 15.8% (2005); Poverty rate: 5.5% (2000).
Education: Percent of population age 25 and over with: High school diploma (including GED) or higher: 84.5% (2005); Bachelor's degree or higher: 16.7% (2005); Master's degree or higher: 6.9% (2005).

School District(s)
Somerdale Borough (PK-08)
    2003-04 Enrollment: 550 . . . . (856) 783-2933
Sterling High School Dist (09-12)
    2003-04 Enrollment: 1,121 . . . . (856) 784-1287
Housing: Homeownership rate: 73.8% (2005); Median home value: $146,024 (2005); Median rent: $499 per month (2000); Median age of housing: 39 years (2000).
Safety: Violent crime rate: 28.7 per 10,000 population; Property crime rate: 226.0 per 10,000 population (2004).
Transportation: Commute to work: 85.5% car, 8.1% public transportation, 3.5% walk, 0.9% work from home (2000); Travel time to work: 24.0% less than 15 minutes, 33.2% 15 to 30 minutes, 24.8% 30 to 45 minutes, 11.8% 45 to 60 minutes, 6.2% 60 minutes or more (2000); Amtrak: Service available.

SPRINGDALE (CDP).
Covers a land area of 5.391 square miles and a water area of 0 square miles. Located at 39.87° N. Lat.; 74.97° W. Long. Elevation is 96 feet.
Population: 14,252 (1990); 14,409 (2000); 15,103 (2005); 15,763 (2010 projected); Race: 87.3% White, 2.8% Black, 8.8% Asian, 1.3% Hispanic of any race (2005); Density: 2,801.3 persons per square mile (2005); Average household size: 2.72 (2005); Median age: 45.4 (2005); Males per 100 females: 91.7 (2005); Marriage status: 19.5% never married, 66.7% now married, 8.2% widowed, 5.7% divorced (2000); Foreign born: 11.4%

(2000); Ancestry (includes multiple ancestries): 22.4% Other groups, 14.0% Russian, 12.6% Italian, 12.2% Irish, 8.5% German (2000).
Economy: Employment by occupation: 23.5% management, 40.4% professional, 5.7% services, 26.4% sales, 0.0% farming, 1.9% construction, 2.1% production (2000).
Income: Per capita income: $50,305 (2005); Median household income: $99,075 (2005); Average household income: $135,897 (2005); Percent of households with income of $100,000 or more: 49.4% (2005); Poverty rate: 3.6% (2000).
Education: Percent of population age 25 and over with: High school diploma (including GED) or higher: 93.5% (2005); Bachelor's degree or higher: 62.3% (2005); Master's degree or higher: 29.6% (2005).
Housing: Homeownership rate: 87.7% (2005); Median home value: $322,244 (2005); Median rent: $369 per month (2000); Median age of housing: 23 years (2000).
Transportation: Commute to work: 86.4% car, 7.2% public transportation, 0.8% walk, 5.3% work from home (2000); Travel time to work: 22.1% less than 15 minutes, 34.1% 15 to 30 minutes, 21.2% 30 to 45 minutes, 9.7% 45 to 60 minutes, 12.8% 60 minutes or more (2000)

STRATFORD (borough).
Covers a land area of 1.579 square miles and a water area of 0 square miles. Located at 39.82° N. Lat.; 75.01° W. Long. Elevation is 70 feet.
History: Founded 1890, incorporated 1925.
Population: 7,614 (1990); 7,271 (2000); 7,238 (2005); 7,207 (2010 projected); Race: 86.1% White, 8.0% Black, 2.7% Asian, 4.8% Hispanic of any race (2005); Density: 4,582.9 persons per square mile (2005); Average household size: 2.61 (2005); Median age: 38.7 (2005); Males per 100 females: 95.0 (2005); Marriage status: 27.1% never married, 58.5% now married, 6.6% widowed, 7.8% divorced (2000); Foreign born: 5.3% (2000); Ancestry (includes multiple ancestries): 26.9% Irish, 23.3% Italian, 22.3% German, 13.2% English, 11.0% Other groups (2000).
Economy: Single-family building permits issued: 1 (2005); Multi-family building permits issued: 0 (2005); Employment by occupation: 15.0% management, 21.5% professional, 13.7% services, 33.5% sales, 0.4% farming, 7.7% construction, 8.2% production (2000).
Income: Per capita income: $25,476 (2005); Median household income: $57,250 (2005); Average household income: $65,967 (2005); Percent of households with income of $100,000 or more: 16.6% (2005); Poverty rate: 4.6% (2000).
Education: Percent of population age 25 and over with: High school diploma (including GED) or higher: 86.1% (2005); Bachelor's degree or higher: 19.4% (2005); Master's degree or higher: 4.3% (2005).

School District(s)
Stratford Borough (PK-08)
    2003-04 Enrollment: 922 . . . . (856) 783-2555
Two-year College(s)
Star Technical Institute (Private, For-profit)
    Fall 2004 Enrollment: 106 . . . . (609) 435-7827
Housing: Homeownership rate: 71.6% (2005); Median home value: $174,266 (2005); Median rent: $542 per month (2000); Median age of housing: 38 years (2000).
Hospitals: Kennedy Memorial Hospitals: UMC Stratford (236 beds)
Safety: Violent crime rate: 24.7 per 10,000 population; Property crime rate: 213.8 per 10,000 population (2004).
Transportation: Commute to work: 84.6% car, 10.5% public transportation, 2.4% walk, 1.4% work from home (2000); Travel time to work: 27.3% less than 15 minutes, 29.8% 15 to 30 minutes, 24.5% 30 to 45 minutes, 9.4% 45 to 60 minutes, 8.9% 60 minutes or more (2000)
Additional Information Contacts
Borough of Stratford. . . . . (856) 783-0600
    http://www.stratfordnj.org

TAVISTOCK (borough).
Covers a land area of 0.254 square miles and a water area of 0 square miles. Located at 39.87° N. Lat.; 75.02° W. Long. Elevation is 40 feet.
History: Started as golf course.
Population: 35 (1990); 24 (2000); 24 (2005); 23 (2010 projected); Race: 91.7% White, 8.3% Black, 0.0% Asian, 0.0% Hispanic of any race (2005); Density: 94.3 persons per square mile (2005); Average household size: 4.00 (2005); Median age: 30.3 (2005); Males per 100 females: 60.0 (2005); Marriage status: 38.5% never married, 46.2% now married, 0.0% widowed, 15.4% divorced (2000); Foreign born: 4.3% (2000); Ancestry (includes multiple ancestries): 56.5% Irish, 17.4% Italian, 8.7% Other groups, 8.7% English, 8.7% German (2000).

Economy: Employment by occupation: 22.2% management, 22.2% professional, 22.2% services, 0.0% sales, 0.0% farming, 11.1% construction, 22.2% production (2000).

Income: Per capita income: $26,458 (2005); Median household income: $87,500 (2005); Average household income: $105,833 (2005); Percent of households with income of $100,000 or more: 33.3% (2005); Poverty rate: 21.7% (2000).

Education: Percent of population age 25 and over with: High school diploma (including GED) or higher: 91.7% (2005); Bachelor's degree or higher: 41.7% (2005); Master's degree or higher: 25.0% (2005).

Housing: Homeownership rate: 83.3% (2005); Median home value: $541,667 (2005); Median rent: $675 per month (2000); Median age of housing: 29 years (2000).

Safety: Violent crime rate: 0.0 per 10,000 population; Property crime rate: 370.4 per 10,000 population (2004).

Transportation: Commute to work: 100.0% car, 0.0% public transportation, 0.0% walk, 0.0% work from home (2000); Travel time to work: 25.0% less than 15 minutes, 37.5% 15 to 30 minutes, 0.0% 30 to 45 minutes, 0.0% 45 to 60 minutes, 37.5% 60 minutes or more (2000)

VOORHEES (township). Covers a land area of 11.603 square miles and a water area of 0.031 square miles. Located at 39.85° N. Lat.; 74.96° W. Long.

Population: 24,559 (1990); 28,126 (2000); 28,741 (2005); 29,316 (2010 projected); Race: 75.6% White, 9.4% Black, 12.1% Asian, 2.8% Hispanic of any race (2005); Density: 2,477.0 persons per square mile (2005); Average household size: 2.65 (2005); Median age: 38.0 (2005); Males per 100 females: 92.6 (2005); Marriage status: 25.6% never married, 61.4% now married, 5.8% widowed, 7.3% divorced (2000); Foreign born: 13.4% (2000); Ancestry (includes multiple ancestries): 25.1% Other groups, 19.5% Italian, 18.1% Irish, 14.3% German, 8.3% English (2000).

Economy: Extensive shopping center. Unemployment rate: 2.8% (2005); Total civilian labor force: 16,079 (2005); Single-family building permits issued: 125 (2005); Multi-family building permits issued: 152 (2005); Employment by occupation: 20.8% management, 33.3% professional, 10.2% services, 27.0% sales, 0.2% farming, 3.4% construction, 5.2% production (2000).

Income: Per capita income: $39,330 (2005); Median household income: $76,287 (2005); Average household income: $103,095 (2005); Percent of households with income of $100,000 or more: 36.2% (2005); Poverty rate: 5.7% (2000).

Taxes: Total city taxes per capita: $498 (2004); City property taxes per capita: $460 (2004).

Education: Percent of population age 25 and over with: High school diploma (including GED) or higher: 91.0% (2005); Bachelor's degree or higher: 45.9% (2005); Master's degree or higher: 19.7% (2005).

School District(s)

Eastern Camden County Regional (09-12)
    2003-04 Enrollment: 2,205 . . . . (856) 346-6740
Voorhees Township (PK-08)
    2003-04 Enrollment: 3,519 . . . . (856) 751-8446

Housing: Homeownership rate: 64.6% (2005); Median home value: $265,019 (2005); Median rent: $773 per month (2000); Median age of housing: 17 years (2000).

Hospitals: Virtua Health Hospital Voorhees

Safety: Violent crime rate: 24.3 per 10,000 population; Property crime rate: 284.2 per 10,000 population (2004).

Newspapers: The Journal (General - Circulation 15,000); Trend of Evesham (General - Circulation 15,300); Trend of Medford (General - Circulation 10,000); Trend of Moorestown (General - Circulation 7,000); Trend of Mount Laurel (General - Circulation 14,500); Trend of Voorhees (General - Circulation 11,600)

Transportation: Commute to work: 82.8% car, 10.8% public transportation, 1.4% walk, 3.9% work from home (2000); Travel time to work: 21.4% less than 15 minutes, 29.2% 15 to 30 minutes, 24.9% 30 to 45 minutes, 12.8% 45 to 60 minutes, 11.7% 60 minutes or more (2000)

Additional Information Contacts

Chamber of Commerce Southern New Jersey . . . . (856) 424-7776
    http://www.chambersnj.com
Voorhees Township . . . . (856) 429-7757
    http://voorheesnj.com/Default.aspx

WATERFORD (township). Covers a land area of 36.192 square miles and a water area of 0.066 square miles. Located at 39.75° N. Lat.; 74.84° W. Long.

History: Incorporated 1798.

Population: 10,940 (1990); 10,494 (2000); 10,714 (2005); 10,958 (2010 projected); Race: 92.3% White, 4.3% Black, 0.8% Asian, 2.4% Hispanic of any race (2005); Density: 296.0 persons per square mile (2005); Average household size: 2.91 (2005); Median age: 37.6 (2005); Males per 100 females: 100.3 (2005); Marriage status: 26.4% never married, 61.4% now married, 5.7% widowed, 6.5% divorced (2000); Foreign born: 3.1% (2000); Ancestry (includes multiple ancestries): 28.5% Irish, 25.4% German, 24.8% Italian, 10.7% English, 9.0% Other groups (2000).

Economy: Single-family building permits issued: 31 (2005); Multi-family building permits issued: 0 (2005); Employment by occupation: 11.1% management, 17.3% professional, 14.7% services, 27.9% sales, 0.1% farming, 16.0% construction, 13.0% production (2000).

Income: Per capita income: $25,900 (2005); Median household income: $66,598 (2005); Average household income: $74,521 (2005); Percent of households with income of $100,000 or more: 24.1% (2005); Poverty rate: 5.6% (2000).

Education: Percent of population age 25 and over with: High school diploma (including GED) or higher: 82.7% (2005); Bachelor's degree or higher: 12.9% (2005); Master's degree or higher: 3.5% (2005).

School District(s)

Waterford Township (PK-06)
    2003-04 Enrollment: 955 . . . . (856) 767-0331

Housing: Homeownership rate: 88.6% (2005); Median home value: $181,316 (2005); Median rent: $604 per month (2000); Median age of housing: 24 years (2000).

Safety: Violent crime rate: 17.7 per 10,000 population; Property crime rate: 194.0 per 10,000 population (2004).

Transportation: Commute to work: 91.4% car, 3.5% public transportation, 0.8% walk, 3.5% work from home (2000); Travel time to work: 22.4% less than 15 minutes, 31.7% 15 to 30 minutes, 22.0% 30 to 45 minutes, 10.3% 45 to 60 minutes, 13.6% 60 minutes or more (2000)

Additional Information Contacts

Waterford Township . . . . (856) 768-2300
    http://www.waterfordtwp.org

WATERFORD WORKS (unincorporated postal area, zip code 08089). Aka Waterford. Covers a land area of 17.582 square miles and a water area of 0.039 square miles. Located at 39.72° N. Lat.; 74.85° W. Long. Elevation is 123 feet.

Population: 3,979 (2000); Race: 71.8% White, 23.1% Black, 0.3% Asian, 5.9% Hispanic of any race (2000); Density: 226.3 persons per square mile (2000); Age: 25.0% under 18, 11.0% over 64 (2000); Marriage status: 27.8% never married, 58.3% now married, 8.7% widowed, 5.2% divorced (2000); Foreign born: 2.1% (2000); Ancestry (includes multiple ancestries): 27.7% Other groups, 24.8% Italian, 20.2% Irish, 16.7% German, 8.1% English (2000).

Economy: Employment by occupation: 7.4% management, 20.6% professional, 17.3% services, 26.9% sales, 0.2% farming, 16.1% construction, 11.6% production (2000).

Income: Per capita income: $19,869 (2000); Median household income: $52,310 (2000); Poverty rate: 7.9% (2000).

Education: Percent of population age 25 and over with: High school diploma (including GED) or higher: 75.5% (2000); Bachelor's degree or higher: 11.9% (2000).

Housing: Homeownership rate: 92.0% (2000); Median home value: $114,100 (2000); Median rent: $466 per month (2000); Median age of housing: 26 years (2000).

Hospitals: Ancora Psychiatric Hospital (626 beds)

Transportation: Commute to work: 94.6% car, 2.9% public transportation, 1.3% walk, 1.0% work from home (2000); Travel time to work: 18.5% less than 15 minutes, 29.5% 15 to 30 minutes, 28.5% 30 to 45 minutes, 12.9% 45 to 60 minutes, 10.6% 60 minutes or more (2000)

WEST BERLIN (unincorporated postal area, zip code 08091). Covers a land area of 3.151 square miles and a water area of 0 square miles. Located at 39.80° N. Lat.; 74.93° W. Long. Elevation is 185 feet.

Population: 5,237 (2000); Race: 82.6% White, 11.7% Black, 2.5% Asian, 4.8% Hispanic of any race (2000); Density: 1,661.8 persons per square mile (2000); Age: 26.0% under 18, 12.4% over 64 (2000); Marriage status: 25.7% never married, 58.0% now married, 7.4% widowed, 8.9% divorced (2000); Foreign born: 5.2% (2000); Ancestry (includes multiple ancestries): 28.3% Irish, 26.3% German, 20.0% Other groups, 19.0% Italian, 13.5% English (2000).

Economy: Employment by occupation: 10.9% management, 16.3% professional, 19.4% services, 26.0% sales, 0.0% farming, 15.8% construction, 11.6% production (2000).
Income: Per capita income: $22,184 (2000); Median household income: $54,708 (2000); Poverty rate: 5.9% (2000).
Education: Percent of population age 25 and over with: High school diploma (including GED) or higher: 76.8% (2000); Bachelor's degree or higher: 15.1% (2000).

School District(s)

Berlin Township (PK-08)
   2003-04 Enrollment: 773 . . . . (856) 767-9480
Housing: Homeownership rate: 77.9% (2000); Median home value: $109,800 (2000); Median rent: $527 per month (2000); Median age of housing: 32 years (2000).
Transportation: Commute to work: 92.1% car, 1.9% public transportation, 2.6% walk, 2.7% work from home (2000); Travel time to work: 30.3% less than 15 minutes, 30.5% 15 to 30 minutes, 22.7% 30 to 45 minutes, 5.6% 45 to 60 minutes, 10.9% 60 minutes or more (2000)

WINSLOW (township). Covers a land area of 57.696 square miles and a water area of 0.395 square miles. Located at 39.71° N. Lat.; 74.91° W. Long. Elevation is 114 feet.
History: Incorporated 1845.
Population: 30,087 (1990); 34,611 (2000); 35,465 (2005); 36,338 (2010 projected); Race: 61.9% White, 32.2% Black, 1.3% Asian, 5.0% Hispanic of any race (2005); Density: 614.7 persons per square mile (2005); Average household size: 2.95 (2005); Median age: 35.4 (2005); Males per 100 females: 97.1 (2005); Marriage status: 25.1% never married, 61.9% now married, 5.2% widowed, 7.7% divorced (2000); Foreign born: 3.8% (2000); Ancestry (includes multiple ancestries): 31.0% Other groups, 20.1% Italian, 19.6% Irish, 17.3% German, 6.7% English (2000).
Economy: Unemployment rate: 5.9% (2005); Total civilian labor force: 19,418 (2005); Single-family building permits issued: 538 (2005); Multi-family building permits issued: 0 (2005); Employment by occupation: 11.4% management, 19.9% professional, 15.0% services, 28.3% sales, 0.5% farming, 12.1% construction, 12.9% production (2000).
Income: Per capita income: $25,288 (2005); Median household income: $64,408 (2005); Average household income: $73,837 (2005); Percent of households with income of $100,000 or more: 22.7% (2005); Poverty rate: 6.0% (2000).
Taxes: Total city taxes per capita: $287 (2004); City property taxes per capita: $262 (2004).
Education: Percent of population age 25 and over with: High school diploma (including GED) or higher: 81.9% (2005); Bachelor's degree or higher: 18.5% (2005); Master's degree or higher: 4.3% (2005).
Housing: Homeownership rate: 82.6% (2005); Median home value: $173,022 (2005); Median rent: $614 per month (2000); Median age of housing: 19 years (2000).
Safety: Violent crime rate: 43.2 per 10,000 population; Property crime rate: 193.2 per 10,000 population (2004).
Transportation: Commute to work: 89.6% car, 6.5% public transportation, 1.0% walk, 1.9% work from home (2000); Travel time to work: 17.2% less than 15 minutes, 28.1% 15 to 30 minutes, 25.5% 30 to 45 minutes, 15.0% 45 to 60 minutes, 14.2% 60 minutes or more (2000)
Additional Information Contacts
Winslow Township . . . . (609) 567-0700
   http://www.winslowtownship.com

WOODLYNNE (borough). Covers a land area of 0.216 square miles and a water area of 0.017 square miles. Located at 39.91° N. Lat.; 75.09° W. Long.
History: Laid out 1892, incorporated 1901.
Population: 2,547 (1990); 2,796 (2000); 2,770 (2005); 2,753 (2010 projected); Race: 36.0% White, 29.1% Black, 13.6% Asian, 26.0% Hispanic of any race (2005); Density: 12,819.1 persons per square mile (2005); Average household size: 3.13 (2005); Median age: 31.3 (2005); Males per 100 females: 95.5 (2005); Marriage status: 38.9% never married, 45.4% now married, 6.5% widowed, 9.1% divorced (2000); Foreign born: 14.1% (2000); Ancestry (includes multiple ancestries): 43.4% Other groups, 12.5% Irish, 10.0% Italian, 7.3% English, 7.3% German (2000).
Economy: Single-family building permits issued: 0 (2005); Multi-family building permits issued: 0 (2005); Employment by occupation: 5.4% management, 16.1% professional, 18.1% services, 28.2% sales, 0.0% farming, 5.7% construction, 26.6% production (2000).

Income: Per capita income: $16,939 (2005); Median household income: $45,463 (2005); Average household income: $53,077 (2005); Percent of households with income of $100,000 or more: 9.4% (2005); Poverty rate: 13.9% (2000).
Education: Percent of population age 25 and over with: High school diploma (including GED) or higher: 69.3% (2005); Bachelor's degree or higher: 8.0% (2005); Master's degree or higher: 1.7% (2005).

School District(s)

Woodlynne Borough (PK-08)
   2003-04 Enrollment: 521 . . . . (856) 962-8822
Housing: Homeownership rate: 74.1% (2005); Median home value: $84,635 (2005); Median rent: $523 per month (2000); Median age of housing: 56 years (2000).
Safety: Violent crime rate: 68.0 per 10,000 population; Property crime rate: 297.0 per 10,000 population (2004).
Transportation: Commute to work: 76.6% car, 18.7% public transportation, 3.3% walk, 0.5% work from home (2000); Travel time to work: 26.0% less than 15 minutes, 43.8% 15 to 30 minutes, 14.4% 30 to 45 minutes, 7.4% 45 to 60 minutes, 8.4% 60 minutes or more (2000)

Cape May County

Located in southern New Jersey, on the Cape May Peninsula between the Atlantic Ocean and Delaware Bay; drained in the north by the Tuckahoe River. Covers a land area of 255.19 square miles, a water area of 365.09 square miles, and is located in the Eastern Time Zone. The county government was organized in 1692. County seat is Cape May.

Cape May County is part of the Ocean City, NJ Metropolitan Statistical Area. The entire metro area includes: Cape May County, NJ

Weather Station: Belleplain State Forest   Elevation: 29 feet

	Jan	Feb	Mar	Apr	May	Jun	Jul	Aug	Sep	Oct	Nov	Dec
High	44	47	55	66	75	82	87	85	79	69	59	49
Low	23	25	31	39	49	58	64	63	56	44	36	28
Precip	3.8	3.0	4.1	3.7	3.7	2.9	3.6	5.2	3.7	3.8	3.3	3.5
Snow	3.2	4.3	1.0	tr	0.0	0.0	0.0	0.0	0.0	tr	0.2	0.8

High and Low temperatures in degrees Fahrenheit; Precipitation and Snow in inches

Weather Station: Cape May 2 NW   Elevation: 19 feet

	Jan	Feb	Mar	Apr	May	Jun	Jul	Aug	Sep	Oct	Nov	Dec
High	41	43	50	60	69	78	84	83	77	66	56	47
Low	27	28	35	43	53	62	67	66	61	50	41	32
Precip	3.6	3.1	4.1	3.5	3.6	3.0	3.2	3.6	3.2	3.6	3.2	3.6
Snow	4.0	6.2	1.7	tr	0.0	0.0	0.0	0.0	0.0	tr	0.3	1.3

High and Low temperatures in degrees Fahrenheit; Precipitation and Snow in inches

Population: 95,089 (1990); 102,326 (2000); 101,848 (2005); 101,320 (2010 projected); Race: 92.1% White, 4.7% Black, 0.6% Asian, 3.7% Hispanic of any race (2005); Density: 399.1 persons per square mile (2005); Average household size: 2.40 (2005); Median age: 43.3 (2005); Males per 100 females: 92.8 (2005).
Religion: Five largest groups: 31.6% Catholic Church, 5.0% The United Methodist Church, 2.1% Evangelical Lutheran Church in America, 1.6% Episcopal Church, 1.5% Jewish Estimate (2000).
Economy: Unemployment rate: 6.4% (2005); Total civilian labor force: 58,378 (2005); Leading industries: 21.8% retail trade; 16.2% health care and social assistance; 15.9% accommodation & food services (2004); Farms: 197 totaling 10,037 acres (2002); Companies that employ 500 or more persons: 1 (2004); Companies that employ 100 to 499 persons: 62 (2004); Companies that employ less than 100 persons: 8,320 (2004); Black-owned businesses: n/a (2002); Hispanic-owned businesses: n/a (2002); Asian-owned businesses: n/a (2002); Women-owned businesses: 2,234 (2002); Retail sales per capita: $17,395 (2006). Single-family building permits issued: 1,125 (2005); Multi-family building permits issued: 1,308 (2005).
Income: Per capita income: $28,363 (2005); Median household income: $48,213 (2005); Average household income: $67,268 (2005); Percent of households with income of $100,000 or more: 18.1% (2005); Poverty rate: 9.6% (2003); Bankruptcy rate: 5.06% (2005).
Taxes: Total county taxes per capita: $745 (2004); County property taxes per capita: $739 (2004).
Education: Percent of population age 25 and over with: High school diploma (including GED) or higher: 81.9% (2005); Bachelor's degree or higher: 22.1% (2005); Master's degree or higher: 6.6% (2005).

Housing: Homeownership rate: 74.2% (2005); Median home value: $235,206 (2005); Median rent: $565 per month (2000); Median age of housing: 30 years (2000).
Health: Birth rate: 98.0 per 10,000 population (2004); Death rate: 122.5 per 10,000 population (2004); Age-adjusted cancer mortality rate: 220.8 deaths per 100,000 population (2002); Number of physicians: 17.4 per 10,000 population (2004); Hospital beds: 20.4 per 10,000 population (2003); Hospital admissions: 1,004.2 per 10,000 population (2003).
Elections: 2004 Presidential election results: 56.8% Bush, 42.3% Kerry, 0.5% Nader, 0.2% Badnarik.
National and State Parks: Belleplain State Forest
Additional Information Contacts
Cape May County Government . . . . (609) 465-1065
   http://www.co.cape-may.nj.us
Avalon Chamber of Commerce . . . . (609) 967-3936
   http://www.avalonbeach.com
Borough of Avalon . . . . (609) 967-4457
   http://www.avalonboro.org
Borough of Stone Harbor . . . . (609) 368-5102
   http://www.stone-harbor.nj.us
Cape May Chamber of Commerce . . . . (609) 884-5508
   http://www.capemaychamber.com
Cape May County Chamber of Commerce . . . . (609) 465-7181
   http://www.capemaycountychamber.com
Cape May County Department of Tourism . . . . (800) 227-2297
   http://www.thejerseycape.net
City of Cape May . . . . (609) 884-9525
   http://www.capemaycity.com
City of Sea Isle City . . . . (609) 263-4461
   http://www.sea-isle-city.nj.us
Dennis Township . . . . (609) 861-9700
   http://www.dennistwp.org
Dennis Township Chamber of Commerce . . . . (609) 624-2276
   http://www.dennistwpchamber.org
Greater Wildwood Chamber of Commerce . . . . (609) 729-4000
   http://www.gwcoc.com
Middle Township . . . . (609) 465-8726
   http://www.middletownship.com
Ocean City Chamber of Commerce . . . . (609) 399-1412
   http://www.oceancityvacation.com
Stone Harbor Chamber of Commerce . . . . (609) 368-6101
   http://stoneharborbeach.com
Upper Township Chamber of Commerce . . . . (609) 628-4343
   http://www.capemaycountychamber.com

Cape May County Communities

AVALON (borough). Covers a land area of 4.215 square miles and a water area of 0.675 square miles. Located at 39.09° N. Lat.; 74.72° W. Long. Elevation is 6 feet.
Population: 1,797 (1990); 2,143 (2000); 2,184 (2005); 2,211 (2010 projected); Race: 98.6% White, 0.1% Black, 0.6% Asian, 0.6% Hispanic of any race (2005); Density: 518.2 persons per square mile (2005); Average household size: 2.02 (2005); Median age: 57.2 (2005); Males per 100 females: 94.7 (2005); Marriage status: 14.0% never married, 70.5% now married, 9.5% widowed, 6.0% divorced (2000); Foreign born: 1.7% (2000); Ancestry (includes multiple ancestries): 31.5% Irish, 21.7% German, 17.9% English, 14.8% Italian, 5.8% Polish (2000).
Economy: Resort borough noted for its high sand dunes. Single-family building permits issued: 107 (2005); Multi-family building permits issued: 89 (2005); Employment by occupation: 26.2% management, 15.3% professional, 12.7% services, 30.1% sales, 0.6% farming, 8.5% construction, 6.5% production (2000).
Income: Per capita income: $63,903 (2005); Median household income: $74,302 (2005); Average household income: $128,796 (2005); Percent of households with income of $100,000 or more: 36.0% (2005); Poverty rate: 4.3% (2000).
Taxes: Total city taxes per capita: $4,672 (2004); City property taxes per capita: $4,174 (2004).
Education: Percent of population age 25 and over with: High school diploma (including GED) or higher: 93.0% (2005); Bachelor's degree or higher: 38.0% (2005); Master's degree or higher: 11.0% (2005).
School District(s)
Avalon Borough (PK-08)
   2003-04 Enrollment: 90 . . . . (609) 967-7544

Housing: Homeownership rate: 87.0% (2005); Median home value: $724,457 (2005); Median rent: $545 per month (2000); Median age of housing: 22 years (2000).
Safety: Violent crime rate: 32.3 per 10,000 population; Property crime rate: 857.1 per 10,000 population (2004).
Transportation: Commute to work: 86.0% car, 1.3% public transportation, 4.9% walk, 6.8% work from home (2000); Travel time to work: 40.1% less than 15 minutes, 24.8% 15 to 30 minutes, 13.3% 30 to 45 minutes, 5.9% 45 to 60 minutes, 15.9% 60 minutes or more (2000)
Additional Information Contacts
Avalon Chamber of Commerce . . . . (609) 967-3936
   http://www.avalonbeach.com
Borough of Avalon . . . . (609) 967-4457
   http://www.avalonboro.org

CAPE MAY (city). Covers a land area of 2.485 square miles and a water area of 0.319 square miles. Located at 38.93° N. Lat.; 74.91° W. Long. Elevation is 10 feet.
History: One of the nation's oldest beach resorts, it became popular in the mid—19th century, when it was known as the President's Playground; Lincoln, Grant, Arthur, Buchanan, Hayes, and Benjamin Harrison vacationed here. There are various mansions and Victorian hotels that display 19th-century architecture. Settled in the 1600s, Incorporated 1857.
Population: 4,668 (1990); 4,034 (2000); 3,891 (2005); 3,739 (2010 projected); Race: 93.1% White, 3.9% Black, 0.3% Asian, 4.3% Hispanic of any race (2005); Density: 1,566.1 persons per square mile (2005); Average household size: 2.19 (2005); Median age: 46.7 (2005); Males per 100 females: 98.4 (2005); Marriage status: 23.6% never married, 54.8% now married, 13.7% widowed, 7.9% divorced (2000); Foreign born: 6.1% (2000); Ancestry (includes multiple ancestries): 26.9% Irish, 21.9% German, 16.2% English, 14.2% Italian, 9.8% Other groups (2000).
Economy: Beach resort. The city is connected by ferry to Delaware, and a coast guard base is nearby. Single-family building permits issued: 13 (2005); Multi-family building permits issued: 4 (2005); Employment by occupation: 15.7% management, 18.0% professional, 21.0% services, 33.3% sales, 0.9% farming, 5.9% construction, 5.2% production (2000).
Income: Per capita income: $32,610 (2005); Median household income: $44,248 (2005); Average household income: $68,421 (2005); Percent of households with income of $100,000 or more: 18.4% (2005); Poverty rate: 9.1% (2000).
Education: Percent of population age 25 and over with: High school diploma (including GED) or higher: 87.6% (2005); Bachelor's degree or higher: 30.5% (2005); Master's degree or higher: 11.6% (2005).
School District(s)
Cape May City (PK-06)
   2003-04 Enrollment: 234 . . . . (609) 884-8485
Lower Cape May Regional (07-12)
   2003-04 Enrollment: 1,845 . . . . (609) 884-3475
Lower Township (PK-06)
   2003-04 Enrollment: 2,000 . . . . (609) 884-9400
Housing: Homeownership rate: 56.4% (2005); Median home value: $393,182 (2005); Median rent: $548 per month (2000); Median age of housing: 34 years (2000).
Safety: Violent crime rate: 22.8 per 10,000 population; Property crime rate: 529.1 per 10,000 population (2004).
Newspapers: Cape May County Gazette (General - Circulation 3,100); Cape May Star & Wave (General - Circulation 5,800)
Transportation: Commute to work: 69.5% car, 0.5% public transportation, 20.9% walk, 3.7% work from home (2000); Travel time to work: 59.1% less than 15 minutes, 23.9% 15 to 30 minutes, 3.7% 30 to 45 minutes, 5.9% 45 to 60 minutes, 7.4% 60 minutes or more (2000)
Additional Information Contacts
Cape May Chamber of Commerce . . . . (609) 884-5508
   http://www.capemaychamber.com
Cape May County Department of Tourism . . . . (800) 227-2297
   http://www.thejerseycape.net
City of Cape May . . . . (609) 884-9525
   http://www.capemaycity.com

CAPE MAY COURT HOUSE (CDP). Covers a land area of 8.975 square miles and a water area of 0.138 square miles. Located at 39.08° N. Lat.; 74.82° W. Long. Elevation is 19 feet.
History: Historical museum here. Laid out 1703.
Population: 4,426 (1990); 4,704 (2000); 4,839 (2005); 4,966 (2010 projected); Race: 85.8% White, 9.8% Black, 2.7% Asian, 1.7% Hispanic of

any race (2005); Density: 539.2 persons per square mile (2005); Average household size: 2.68 (2005); Median age: 42.2 (2005); Males per 100 females: 86.9 (2005); Marriage status: 23.6% never married, 55.6% now married, 11.3% widowed, 9.5% divorced (2000); Foreign born: 4.5% (2000); Ancestry (includes multiple ancestries): 25.7% Irish, 20.7% German, 15.9% Other groups, 15.0% Italian, 13.7% English (2000).
Economy: Agriculture: dairy, sweet potatoes, poultry, vegetables. Food processing. Employment by occupation: 11.1% management, 22.7% professional, 19.4% services, 24.8% sales, 1.2% farming, 14.0% construction, 6.9% production (2000).
Income: Per capita income: $23,662 (2005); Median household income: $50,971 (2005); Average household income: $61,627 (2005); Percent of households with income of $100,000 or more: 14.8% (2005); Poverty rate: 7.0% (2000).
Education: Percent of population age 25 and over with: High school diploma (including GED) or higher: 84.4% (2005); Bachelor's degree or higher: 22.1% (2005); Master's degree or higher: 6.5% (2005).
School District(s)
Cape May County Special Services (UG-UG)
    2003-04 Enrollment: 592 . . . . (609) 465-2720
Cape May County Vocational (09-12)
    2003-04 Enrollment: 460 . . . . (609) 465-2161
Middle Township (PK-12)
    2003-04 Enrollment: 2,949 . . . . (609) 465-1800
Housing: Homeownership rate: 80.7% (2005); Median home value: $200,106 (2005); Median rent: $559 per month (2000); Median age of housing: 29 years (2000).
Hospitals: Burdette Tomlin Memorial Hospital (272 beds)
Transportation: Commute to work: 93.5% car, 0.7% public transportation, 2.2% walk, 2.6% work from home (2000); Travel time to work: 48.3% less than 15 minutes, 29.4% 15 to 30 minutes, 9.9% 30 to 45 minutes, 5.8% 45 to 60 minutes, 6.6% 60 minutes or more (2000)
Additional Information Contacts
Cape May County Chamber of Commerce . . . . (609) 465-7181
    http://www.capemaycountychamber.com

CAPE MAY POINT (borough). Covers a land area of 0.294 square miles and a water area of 0.018 square miles. Located at 38.93° N. Lat.; 74.96° W. Long.
Population: 249 (1990); 241 (2000); 222 (2005); 219 (2010 projected); Race: 95.0% White, 2.7% Black, 0.5% Asian, 2.3% Hispanic of any race (2005); Density: 754.8 persons per square mile (2005); Average household size: 1.82 (2005); Median age: 64.7 (2005); Males per 100 females: 100.0 (2005); Marriage status: 9.3% never married, 65.3% now married, 19.1% widowed, 6.2% divorced (2000); Foreign born: 5.0% (2000); Ancestry (includes multiple ancestries): 26.9% Irish, 26.5% English, 12.2% German, 7.1% Other groups, 5.9% Polish (2000).
Economy: Resort borough. Nearby is a lighthouse. Cape May Point State Park, a popular bird-watching area, is nearby. Single-family building permits issued: 7 (2005); Multi-family building permits issued: 0 (2005); Employment by occupation: 13.5% management, 30.8% professional, 7.7% services, 48.1% sales, 0.0% farming, 0.0% construction, 0.0% production (2000).
Income: Per capita income: $62,095 (2005); Median household income: $69,565 (2005); Average household income: $112,992 (2005); Percent of households with income of $100,000 or more: 32.8% (2005); Poverty rate: 1.7% (2000).
Education: Percent of population age 25 and over with: High school diploma (including GED) or higher: 91.7% (2005); Bachelor's degree or higher: 54.4% (2005); Master's degree or higher: 17.2% (2005).
Housing: Homeownership rate: 96.7% (2005); Median home value: $530,488 (2005); Median rent: $645 per month (2000); Median age of housing: 41 years (2000).
Safety: Violent crime rate: 0.0 per 10,000 population; Property crime rate: 245.9 per 10,000 population (2004).
Transportation: Commute to work: 92.3% car, 0.0% public transportation, 3.8% walk, 0.0% work from home (2000); Travel time to work: 36.5% less than 15 minutes, 25.0% 15 to 30 minutes, 21.2% 30 to 45 minutes, 9.6% 45 to 60 minutes, 7.7% 60 minutes or more (2000)

DENNIS (township). Covers a land area of 61.351 square miles and a water area of 2.935 square miles. Located at 39.21° N. Lat.; 74.81° W. Long.
History: Incorporated 1827.

Population: 5,574 (1990); 6,492 (2000); 6,270 (2005); 6,070 (2010 projected); Race: 97.4% White, 1.1% Black, 0.3% Asian, 1.7% Hispanic of any race (2005); Density: 102.2 persons per square mile (2005); Average household size: 2.96 (2005); Median age: 37.9 (2005); Males per 100 females: 96.1 (2005); Marriage status: 18.7% never married, 65.5% now married, 8.5% widowed, 7.3% divorced (2000); Foreign born: 2.3% (2000); Ancestry (includes multiple ancestries): 26.0% Irish, 24.5% German, 19.5% Italian, 13.2% English, 9.0% United States or American (2000).
Economy: Single-family building permits issued: 18 (2005); Multi-family building permits issued: 0 (2005); Employment by occupation: 10.6% management, 19.6% professional, 17.4% services, 24.0% sales, 0.2% farming, 17.9% construction, 10.2% production (2000).
Income: Per capita income: $25,965 (2005); Median household income: $65,962 (2005); Average household income: $75,857 (2005); Percent of households with income of $100,000 or more: 22.7% (2005); Poverty rate: 5.5% (2000).
Education: Percent of population age 25 and over with: High school diploma (including GED) or higher: 83.3% (2005); Bachelor's degree or higher: 20.6% (2005); Master's degree or higher: 5.2% (2005).
Housing: Homeownership rate: 91.0% (2005); Median home value: $232,214 (2005); Median rent: $724 per month (2000); Median age of housing: 21 years (2000).
Newspapers: The Gazette of Middle & Dennis Townships (General - Circulation 8,100)
Transportation: Commute to work: 93.2% car, 0.0% public transportation, 1.3% walk, 4.6% work from home (2000); Travel time to work: 32.0% less than 15 minutes, 35.9% 15 to 30 minutes, 20.9% 30 to 45 minutes, 6.6% 45 to 60 minutes, 4.7% 60 minutes or more (2000)
Additional Information Contacts
Dennis Township . . . . (609) 861-9700
    http://www.dennistwp.org
Dennis Township Chamber of Commerce . . . . (609) 624-2276
    http://www.dennistwpchamber.org

DIAMOND BEACH (CDP). Covers a land area of 0.155 square miles and a water area of 0 square miles. Located at 38.96° N. Lat.; 74.85° W. Long.
Population: 91 (1990); 218 (2000); 208 (2005); 202 (2010 projected); Race: 96.6% White, 1.9% Black, 1.0% Asian, 1.4% Hispanic of any race (2005); Density: 1,340.3 persons per square mile (2005); Average household size: 2.10 (2005); Median age: 54.3 (2005); Males per 100 females: 103.9 (2005); Marriage status: 0.0% never married, 77.4% now married, 7.8% widowed, 14.8% divorced (2000); Foreign born: 0.0% (2000); Ancestry (includes multiple ancestries): 25.2% Hungarian, 24.4% Italian, 23.7% Lithuanian, 11.9% Polish, 11.9% German (2000).
Economy: Employment by occupation: 63.6% management, 0.0% professional, 0.0% services, 36.4% sales, 0.0% farming, 0.0% construction, 0.0% production (2000).
Income: Per capita income: $66,707 (2005); Median household income: $102,419 (2005); Average household income: $140,152 (2005); Percent of households with income of $100,000 or more: 51.5% (2005); Poverty rate: 0.0% (2000).
Education: Percent of population age 25 and over with: High school diploma (including GED) or higher: 88.2% (2005); Bachelor's degree or higher: 18.2% (2005); Master's degree or higher: 18.2% (2005).
Housing: Homeownership rate: 82.8% (2005); Median home value: $325,714 (2005); Median rent: $n/a per month (2000); Median age of housing: 6 years (2000).
Transportation: Commute to work: 100.0% car, 0.0% public transportation, 0.0% walk, 0.0% work from home (2000); Travel time to work: 0.0% less than 15 minutes, 100.0% 15 to 30 minutes, 0.0% 30 to 45 minutes, 0.0% 45 to 60 minutes, 0.0% 60 minutes or more (2000)

ERMA (CDP). Covers a land area of 3.350 square miles and a water area of 0.019 square miles. Located at 39.00° N. Lat.; 74.88° W. Long. Elevation is 10 feet.
Population: 2,045 (1990); 2,088 (2000); 1,972 (2005); 1,905 (2010 projected); Race: 97.6% White, 0.2% Black, 1.0% Asian, 1.7% Hispanic of any race (2005); Density: 588.7 persons per square mile (2005); Average household size: 2.75 (2005); Median age: 37.5 (2005); Males per 100 females: 95.4 (2005); Marriage status: 24.6% never married, 60.0% now married, 6.0% widowed, 9.4% divorced (2000); Foreign born: 2.6% (2000); Ancestry (includes multiple ancestries): 30.8% Irish, 27.3% German, 19.2% Italian, 12.3% English, 5.3% United States or American (2000).

Economy: Employment by occupation: 14.1% management, 4.9% professional, 27.4% services, 28.0% sales, 2.4% farming, 16.7% construction, 6.5% production (2000).
Income: Per capita income: $27,403 (2005); Median household income: $75,303 (2005); Average household income: $75,139 (2005); Percent of households with income of $100,000 or more: 27.3% (2005); Poverty rate: 3.9% (2000).
Education: Percent of population age 25 and over with: High school diploma (including GED) or higher: 77.5% (2005); Bachelor's degree or higher: 8.6% (2005); Master's degree or higher: 0.7% (2005).
Housing: Homeownership rate: 85.2% (2005); Median home value: $182,452 (2005); Median rent: $675 per month (2000); Median age of housing: 29 years (2000).
Transportation: Commute to work: 94.1% car, 0.0% public transportation, 3.0% walk, 1.1% work from home (2000); Travel time to work: 44.0% less than 15 minutes, 36.1% 15 to 30 minutes, 9.4% 30 to 45 minutes, 3.9% 45 to 60 minutes, 6.6% 60 minutes or more (2000)

LOWER (township). Covers a land area of 28.222 square miles and a water area of 2.850 square miles. Located at 38.99° N. Lat.; 74.92° W. Long.
History: Incorporated 1798.
Population: 20,819 (1990); 22,945 (2000); 22,376 (2005); 21,796 (2010 projected); Race: 96.3% White, 1.5% Black, 0.5% Asian, 2.0% Hispanic of any race (2005); Density: 792.9 persons per square mile (2005); Average household size: 2.46 (2005); Median age: 42.5 (2005); Males per 100 females: 90.5 (2005); Marriage status: 21.0% never married, 58.8% now married, 10.2% widowed, 10.0% divorced (2000); Foreign born: 2.9% (2000); Ancestry (includes multiple ancestries): 32.0% Irish, 24.8% German, 16.6% Italian, 13.1% English, 5.8% Polish (2000).
Economy: Single-family building permits issued: 73 (2005); Multi-family building permits issued: 12 (2005); Employment by occupation: 9.7% management, 14.2% professional, 24.1% services, 27.7% sales, 1.4% farming, 13.7% construction, 9.2% production (2000).
Income: Per capita income: $23,851 (2005); Median household income: $46,236 (2005); Average household income: $58,446 (2005); Percent of households with income of $100,000 or more: 13.2% (2005); Poverty rate: 7.7% (2000).
Education: Percent of population age 25 and over with: High school diploma (including GED) or higher: 77.1% (2005); Bachelor's degree or higher: 13.2% (2005); Master's degree or higher: 3.5% (2005).
Housing: Homeownership rate: 81.1% (2005); Median home value: $162,803 (2005); Median rent: $591 per month (2000); Median age of housing: 31 years (2000).
Safety: Violent crime rate: 20.7 per 10,000 population; Property crime rate: 281.4 per 10,000 population (2004).
Newspapers: Lower Township Gazette (General - Circulation 6,400)
Transportation: Commute to work: 92.8% car, 2.5% public transportation, 1.8% walk, 1.4% work from home (2000); Travel time to work: 36.8% less than 15 minutes, 40.4% 15 to 30 minutes, 7.9% 30 to 45 minutes, 5.2% 45 to 60 minutes, 9.7% 60 minutes or more (2000)

MARMORA (unincorporated postal area, zip code 08223). Covers a land area of 13.462 square miles and a water area of 0.030 square miles. Located at 39.26° N. Lat.; 74.65° W. Long. Elevation is 30 feet.
Population: 4,384 (2000); Race: 95.8% White, 1.8% Black, 0.4% Asian, 1.9% Hispanic of any race (2000); Density: 325.7 persons per square mile (2000); Age: 27.5% under 18, 14.2% over 64 (2000); Marriage status: 21.5% never married, 66.1% now married, 5.9% widowed, 6.5% divorced (2000); Foreign born: 3.5% (2000); Ancestry (includes multiple ancestries): 31.8% Irish, 25.5% German, 22.2% Italian, 16.5% English, 5.5% Other groups (2000).
Economy: Employment by occupation: 17.6% management, 22.7% professional, 19.8% services, 23.2% sales, 1.7% farming, 10.5% construction, 4.6% production (2000).
Income: Per capita income: $26,540 (2000); Median household income: $51,272 (2000); Poverty rate: 3.7% (2000).
Education: Percent of population age 25 and over with: High school diploma (including GED) or higher: 93.5% (2000); Bachelor's degree or higher: 33.1% (2000).

School District(s)
Upper Township (PK-08)
   2003-04 Enrollment: 1,767 . . . . (609) 628-3513

Housing: Homeownership rate: 89.1% (2000); Median home value: $167,300 (2000); Median rent: $684 per month (2000); Median age of housing: 18 years (2000).
Transportation: Commute to work: 92.8% car, 1.5% public transportation, 0.6% walk, 4.5% work from home (2000); Travel time to work: 30.9% less than 15 minutes, 39.7% 15 to 30 minutes, 18.6% 30 to 45 minutes, 4.0% 45 to 60 minutes, 6.8% 60 minutes or more (2000)
Additional Information Contacts
Upper Township Chamber of Commerce . . . . (609) 628-4343
   http://www.capemaycountychamber.com

MIDDLE (township). Covers a land area of 71.274 square miles and a water area of 11.833 square miles. Located at 39.05° N. Lat.; 74.85° W. Long.
History: Incorporated 1798.
Population: 14,771 (1990); 16,405 (2000); 17,173 (2005); 17,876 (2010 projected); Race: 87.0% White, 9.5% Black, 1.4% Asian, 2.2% Hispanic of any race (2005); Density: 240.9 persons per square mile (2005); Average household size: 2.71 (2005); Median age: 40.5 (2005); Males per 100 females: 93.1 (2005); Marriage status: 24.6% never married, 56.1% now married, 10.2% widowed, 9.1% divorced (2000); Foreign born: 3.0% (2000); Ancestry (includes multiple ancestries): 22.3% Irish, 18.6% German, 16.1% Other groups, 13.7% Italian, 12.6% English (2000).
Economy: Single-family building permits issued: 186 (2005); Multi-family building permits issued: 6 (2005); Employment by occupation: 9.7% management, 17.4% professional, 23.6% services, 25.6% sales, 1.0% farming, 13.8% construction, 8.9% production (2000).
Income: Per capita income: $22,504 (2005); Median household income: $47,548 (2005); Average household income: $59,273 (2005); Percent of households with income of $100,000 or more: 13.9% (2005); Poverty rate: 10.2% (2000).
Taxes: Total city taxes per capita: $441 (2004); City property taxes per capita: $408 (2004).
Education: Percent of population age 25 and over with: High school diploma (including GED) or higher: 78.0% (2005); Bachelor's degree or higher: 16.4% (2005); Master's degree or higher: 4.5% (2005).
Housing: Homeownership rate: 82.4% (2005); Median home value: $179,661 (2005); Median rent: $557 per month (2000); Median age of housing: 27 years (2000).
Safety: Violent crime rate: 48.2 per 10,000 population; Property crime rate: 397.2 per 10,000 population (2004).
Newspapers: The Gazette of Middle & Dennis Townships (General - Circulation 8,100)
Transportation: Commute to work: 92.2% car, 1.7% public transportation, 3.2% walk, 2.3% work from home (2000); Travel time to work: 43.1% less than 15 minutes, 35.8% 15 to 30 minutes, 9.3% 30 to 45 minutes, 4.9% 45 to 60 minutes, 6.9% 60 minutes or more (2000)
Additional Information Contacts
Middle Township . . . . (609) 465-8726
   http://www.middletownship.com

NORTH CAPE MAY (CDP). Covers a land area of 1.400 square miles and a water area of 0.070 square miles. Located at 38.98° N. Lat.; 74.95° W. Long. Elevation is 20 feet.
Population: 3,574 (1990); 3,618 (2000); 3,453 (2005); 3,338 (2010 projected); Race: 94.4% White, 2.9% Black, 0.5% Asian, 2.2% Hispanic of any race (2005); Density: 2,465.6 persons per square mile (2005); Average household size: 2.32 (2005); Median age: 42.4 (2005); Males per 100 females: 86.2 (2005); Marriage status: 22.8% never married, 57.9% now married, 8.9% widowed, 10.3% divorced (2000); Foreign born: 3.9% (2000); Ancestry (includes multiple ancestries): 34.3% Irish, 31.2% German, 15.0% Italian, 12.0% English, 6.4% Polish (2000).
Economy: Employment by occupation: 5.3% management, 18.3% professional, 24.3% services, 30.5% sales, 2.5% farming, 10.7% construction, 8.3% production (2000).
Income: Per capita income: $23,486 (2005); Median household income: $46,680 (2005); Average household income: $53,991 (2005); Percent of households with income of $100,000 or more: 8.6% (2005); Poverty rate: 4.1% (2000).
Education: Percent of population age 25 and over with: High school diploma (including GED) or higher: 73.7% (2005); Bachelor's degree or higher: 12.0% (2005); Master's degree or higher: 2.6% (2005).
Housing: Homeownership rate: 76.9% (2005); Median home value: $158,101 (2005); Median rent: $598 per month (2000); Median age of housing: 37 years (2000).

Transportation: Commute to work: 92.2% car, 3.7% public transportation, 2.2% walk, 0.6% work from home (2000); Travel time to work: 43.2% less than 15 minutes, 36.4% 15 to 30 minutes, 5.8% 30 to 45 minutes, 5.4% 45 to 60 minutes, 9.2% 60 minutes or more (2000)

NORTH WILDWOOD (city).
Covers a land area of 1.766 square miles and a water area of 0.357 square miles. Located at 39.00° N. Lat.; 74.79° W. Long. Elevation is 6 feet.

Population: 5,017 (1990); 4,935 (2000); 4,817 (2005); 4,695 (2010 projected); Race: 96.6% White, 0.9% Black, 0.6% Asian, 2.2% Hispanic of any race (2005); Density: 2,727.8 persons per square mile (2005); Average household size: 2.10 (2005); Median age: 48.1 (2005); Males per 100 females: 92.4 (2005); Marriage status: 18.8% never married, 57.3% now married, 11.5% widowed, 12.4% divorced (2000); Foreign born: 4.6% (2000); Ancestry (includes multiple ancestries): 36.3% Irish, 22.4% Italian, 19.7% German, 10.7% English, 7.2% Polish (2000).

Economy: Single-family building permits issued: 53 (2005); Multi-family building permits issued: 298 (2005); Employment by occupation: 13.6% management, 14.8% professional, 23.6% services, 31.6% sales, 0.6% farming, 10.1% construction, 5.6% production (2000).

Income: Per capita income: $21,940 (2005); Median household income: $35,943 (2005); Average household income: $46,058 (2005); Percent of households with income of $100,000 or more: 7.2% (2005); Poverty rate: 11.7% (2000).

Education: Percent of population age 25 and over with: High school diploma (including GED) or higher: 82.3% (2005); Bachelor's degree or higher: 13.4% (2005); Master's degree or higher: 3.8% (2005).

School District(s)
North Wildwood City (PK-08)

   2003-04 Enrollment: 380 . . . . (609) 522-6885

Housing: Homeownership rate: 66.4% (2005); Median home value: $222,578 (2005); Median rent: $531 per month (2000); Median age of housing: 41 years (2000).

Safety: Violent crime rate: 49.1 per 10,000 population; Property crime rate: 591.2 per 10,000 population (2004).

Transportation: Commute to work: 91.9% car, 1.4% public transportation, 4.1% walk, 2.2% work from home (2000); Travel time to work: 47.1% less than 15 minutes, 35.8% 15 to 30 minutes, 5.0% 30 to 45 minutes, 4.1% 45 to 60 minutes, 8.0% 60 minutes or more (2000)

OCEAN CITY (city).
Covers a land area of 6.918 square miles and a water area of 4.156 square miles. Located at 39.26° N. Lat.; 74.59° W. Long. Elevation is 6 feet.

History: Ocean City began catering to families in 1879, many of whom returned year after year to spend their vacation time here.

Population: 15,512 (1990); 15,378 (2000); 15,664 (2005); 15,948 (2010 projected); Race: 94.2% White, 3.8% Black, 0.5% Asian, 2.2% Hispanic of any race (2005); Density: 2,264.1 persons per square mile (2005); Average household size: 2.03 (2005); Median age: 49.3 (2005); Males per 100 females: 86.7 (2005); Marriage status: 22.4% never married, 54.3% now married, 11.2% widowed, 12.1% divorced (2000); Foreign born: 3.6% (2000); Ancestry (includes multiple ancestries): 27.7% Irish, 22.5% German, 19.3% Italian, 14.9% English, 8.3% Other groups (2000).

Economy: Single-family building permits issued: 154 (2005); Multi-family building permits issued: 380 (2005); Employment by occupation: 14.7% management, 23.5% professional, 19.0% services, 29.5% sales, 0.5% farming, 6.6% construction, 6.1% production (2000).

Income: Per capita income: $38,937 (2005); Median household income: $50,618 (2005); Average household income: $77,932 (2005); Percent of households with income of $100,000 or more: 23.5% (2005); Poverty rate: 6.8% (2000).

Taxes: Total city taxes per capita: $2,294 (2004); City property taxes per capita: $2,147 (2004).

Education: Percent of population age 25 and over with: High school diploma (including GED) or higher: 89.4% (2005); Bachelor's degree or higher: 33.4% (2005); Master's degree or higher: 10.3% (2005).

School District(s)
Ocean City (PK-12)

   2003-04 Enrollment: 2,224 . . . . (609) 399-5150

Housing: Homeownership rate: 62.0% (2005); Median home value: $363,819 (2005); Median rent: $632 per month (2000); Median age of housing: 28 years (2000).

Safety: Violent crime rate: 25.5 per 10,000 population; Property crime rate: 629.3 per 10,000 population (2004).

Newspapers: Ocean City Gazette (General - Circulation 9,500); Ocean City Sentinel (General - Circulation 10,500)

Transportation: Commute to work: 87.7% car, 2.1% public transportation, 4.8% walk, 3.5% work from home (2000); Travel time to work: 35.6% less than 15 minutes, 28.7% 15 to 30 minutes, 19.3% 30 to 45 minutes, 5.2% 45 to 60 minutes, 11.2% 60 minutes or more (2000)

Additional Information Contacts

Ocean City Chamber of Commerce . . . . (609) 399-1412
   http://www.oceancityvacation.com

OCEAN VIEW (unincorporated postal area, zip code 08230).
Covers a land area of 20.496 square miles and a water area of 0.071 square miles. Located at 39.20° N. Lat.; 74.70° W. Long. Elevation is 20 feet.

Population: 5,589 (2000); Race: 99.0% White, 0.1% Black, 0.3% Asian, 0.0% Hispanic of any race (2000); Density: 272.7 persons per square mile (2000); Age: 28.9% under 18, 14.3% over 64 (2000); Marriage status: 19.1% never married, 63.6% now married, 12.6% widowed, 4.7% divorced (2000); Foreign born: 2.2% (2000); Ancestry (includes multiple ancestries): 34.0% Irish, 24.4% German, 20.8% Italian, 13.0% English, 5.7% Polish (2000).

Economy: Employment by occupation: 12.2% management, 28.2% professional, 15.4% services, 25.1% sales, 0.3% farming, 11.7% construction, 7.1% production (2000).

Income: Per capita income: $27,717 (2000); Median household income: $65,857 (2000); Poverty rate: 5.3% (2000).

Education: Percent of population age 25 and over with: High school diploma (including GED) or higher: 89.6% (2000); Bachelor's degree or higher: 29.9% (2000).

Housing: Homeownership rate: 92.2% (2000); Median home value: $159,700 (2000); Median rent: $682 per month (2000); Median age of housing: 19 years (2000).

Transportation: Commute to work: 92.2% car, 0.5% public transportation, 1.5% walk, 5.6% work from home (2000); Travel time to work: 22.1% less than 15 minutes, 46.4% 15 to 30 minutes, 22.3% 30 to 45 minutes, 4.0% 45 to 60 minutes, 5.1% 60 minutes or more (2000)

Additional Information Contacts

Dennis Township Chamber of Commerce . . . . (609) 624-2276
   http://www.dennistwpchamber.org

RIO GRANDE (CDP).
Covers a land area of 2.357 square miles and a water area of 0.022 square miles. Located at 39.01° N. Lat.; 74.87° W. Long. Elevation is 22 feet.

Population: 2,505 (1990); 2,444 (2000); 2,289 (2005); 2,240 (2010 projected); Race: 91.9% White, 3.8% Black, 0.8% Asian, 3.1% Hispanic of any race (2005); Density: 971.0 persons per square mile (2005); Average household size: 2.34 (2005); Median age: 42.6 (2005); Males per 100 females: 91.5 (2005); Marriage status: 28.7% never married, 49.3% now married, 8.6% widowed, 13.3% divorced (2000); Foreign born: 1.2% (2000); Ancestry (includes multiple ancestries): 24.5% United States or American, 22.5% Irish, 14.9% German, 12.8% Italian, 12.2% English (2000).

Economy: Employment by occupation: 7.7% management, 9.3% professional, 18.9% services, 34.5% sales, 0.0% farming, 19.7% construction, 9.8% production (2000).

Income: Per capita income: $19,565 (2005); Median household income: $32,532 (2005); Average household income: $45,371 (2005); Percent of households with income of $100,000 or more: 7.4% (2005); Poverty rate: 21.4% (2000).

Education: Percent of population age 25 and over with: High school diploma (including GED) or higher: 69.6% (2005); Bachelor's degree or higher: 10.4% (2005); Master's degree or higher: 1.4% (2005).

Housing: Homeownership rate: 76.5% (2005); Median home value: $133,022 (2005); Median rent: $552 per month (2000); Median age of housing: 27 years (2000).

Newspapers: Cape May County Herald Times (General - Circulation 38,000); Cape May Herald Dispatch (General - Circulation 5,000); Shout News (General - Circulation 22,000)

Transportation: Commute to work: 87.4% car, 2.6% public transportation, 6.5% walk, 3.0% work from home (2000); Travel time to work: 48.9% less than 15 minutes, 31.7% 15 to 30 minutes, 10.9% 30 to 45 minutes, 4.3% 45 to 60 minutes, 4.3% 60 minutes or more (2000)

SEA ISLE CITY (city).
Covers a land area of 2.202 square miles and a water area of 0.348 square miles. Located at 39.14° N. Lat.; 74.69° W. Long. Elevation is 6 feet.

Population: 2,692 (1990); 2,835 (2000); 3,004 (2005); 3,160 (2010 projected); Race: 98.1% White, 0.2% Black, 0.4% Asian, 1.1% Hispanic of any race (2005); Density: 1,364.0 persons per square mile (2005); Average household size: 2.03 (2005); Median age: 52.1 (2005); Males per 100 females: 91.6 (2005); Marriage status: 23.1% never married, 56.8% now married, 11.8% widowed, 8.4% divorced (2000); Foreign born: 3.3% (2000); Ancestry (includes multiple ancestries): 38.9% Irish, 24.1% German, 22.4% Italian, 12.7% English, 6.3% Polish (2000).
Economy: Printing and publishing. Single-family building permits issued: 237 (2005); Multi-family building permits issued: 0 (2005); Employment by occupation: 11.1% management, 23.6% professional, 19.3% services, 29.1% sales, 0.0% farming, 11.0% construction, 6.0% production (2000).
Income: Per capita income: $37,014 (2005); Median household income: $56,529 (2005); Average household income: $75,223 (2005); Percent of households with income of $100,000 or more: 26.7% (2005); Poverty rate: 7.6% (2000).
Education: Percent of population age 25 and over with: High school diploma (including GED) or higher: 85.3% (2005); Bachelor's degree or higher: 28.4% (2005); Master's degree or higher: 9.8% (2005).

School District(s)
Sea Isle City (PK-08)
   2003-04 Enrollment: 132 . . . . (609) 263-8461
Housing: Homeownership rate: 76.9% (2005); Median home value: $442,949 (2005); Median rent: $593 per month (2000); Median age of housing: 19 years (2000).
Safety: Violent crime rate: 70.5 per 10,000 population; Property crime rate: 805.9 per 10,000 population (2004).
Transportation: Commute to work: 90.0% car, 0.0% public transportation, 6.8% walk, 2.1% work from home (2000); Travel time to work: 47.7% less than 15 minutes, 18.9% 15 to 30 minutes, 19.7% 30 to 45 minutes, 3.8% 45 to 60 minutes, 9.8% 60 minutes or more (2000)
Additional Information Contacts
City of Sea Isle City . . . . (609) 263-4461
   http://www.sea-isle-city.nj.us

STONE HARBOR (borough). Covers a land area of 1.417 square miles and a water area of 0.568 square miles. Located at 39.05° N. Lat.; 74.76° W. Long. Elevation is 10 feet.
Population: 1,037 (1990); 1,128 (2000); 1,086 (2005); 1,067 (2010 projected); Race: 98.8% White, 0.8% Black, 0.0% Asian, 0.3% Hispanic of any race (2005); Density: 766.5 persons per square mile (2005); Average household size: 1.86 (2005); Median age: 58.9 (2005); Males per 100 females: 86.0 (2005); Marriage status: 18.2% never married, 57.7% now married, 14.1% widowed, 9.9% divorced (2000); Foreign born: 2.1% (2000); Ancestry (includes multiple ancestries): 26.9% Irish, 26.2% German, 18.1% English, 15.6% Italian, 7.4% United States or American (2000).
Economy: Yachting center; seafood. Bird Sanctuary and the Wetlands Institute, a research and education center on tidal ecology, are here. Single-family building permits issued: 57 (2005); Multi-family building permits issued: 0 (2005); Employment by occupation: 19.0% management, 24.9% professional, 13.2% services, 31.6% sales, 0.6% farming, 5.8% construction, 4.8% production (2000).
Income: Per capita income: $55,771 (2005); Median household income: $63,101 (2005); Average household income: $103,864 (2005); Percent of households with income of $100,000 or more: 30.0% (2005); Poverty rate: 3.5% (2000).
Education: Percent of population age 25 and over with: High school diploma (including GED) or higher: 94.0% (2005); Bachelor's degree or higher: 43.9% (2005); Master's degree or higher: 18.8% (2005).

School District(s)
Stone Harbor Borough (PK-08)
   2003-04 Enrollment: 89 . . . . (609) 368-4413
Housing: Homeownership rate: 83.7% (2005); Median home value: $703,782 (2005); Median rent: $603 per month (2000); Median age of housing: 35 years (2000).
Safety: Violent crime rate: 26.8 per 10,000 population; Property crime rate: 732.8 per 10,000 population (2004).
Transportation: Commute to work: 85.6% car, 3.3% public transportation, 6.2% walk, 4.4% work from home (2000); Travel time to work: 47.2% less than 15 minutes, 25.3% 15 to 30 minutes, 8.6% 30 to 45 minutes, 7.2% 45 to 60 minutes, 11.6% 60 minutes or more (2000)
Additional Information Contacts
Borough of Stone Harbor . . . . (609) 368-5102
   http://www.stone-harbor.nj.us

Stone Harbor Chamber of Commerce . . . . (609) 368-6101
   http://stoneharborbeach.com

STRATHMERE (CDP). Covers a land area of 0.649 square miles and a water area of 0.151 square miles. Located at 39.19° N. Lat.; 74.65° W. Long. Elevation is 7 feet.
Population: 163 (1990); 175 (2000); 174 (2005); 174 (2010 projected); Race: 97.1% White, 0.0% Black, 1.1% Asian, 1.7% Hispanic of any race (2005); Density: 268.0 persons per square mile (2005); Average household size: 1.87 (2005); Median age: 59.9 (2005); Males per 100 females: 97.7 (2005); Marriage status: 12.2% never married, 66.0% now married, 12.8% widowed, 9.0% divorced (2000); Foreign born: 0.0% (2000); Ancestry (includes multiple ancestries): 35.3% Irish, 30.8% German, 23.7% English, 11.5% Polish, 8.3% Dutch (2000).
Economy: Employment by occupation: 55.2% management, 28.4% professional, 0.0% services, 16.4% sales, 0.0% farming, 0.0% construction, 0.0% production (2000).
Income: Per capita income: $49,095 (2005); Median household income: $85,833 (2005); Average household income: $91,855 (2005); Percent of households with income of $100,000 or more: 40.9% (2005); Poverty rate: 0.0% (2000).
Education: Percent of population age 25 and over with: High school diploma (including GED) or higher: 92.9% (2005); Bachelor's degree or higher: 42.3% (2005); Master's degree or higher: 27.6% (2005).
Housing: Homeownership rate: 87.1% (2005); Median home value: $398,077 (2005); Median rent: $n/a per month (2000); Median age of housing: 38 years (2000).
Transportation: Commute to work: 100.0% car, 0.0% public transportation, 0.0% walk, 0.0% work from home (2000); Travel time to work: 0.0% less than 15 minutes, 0.0% 15 to 30 minutes, 49.3% 30 to 45 minutes, 14.9% 45 to 60 minutes, 35.8% 60 minutes or more (2000)

UPPER (township). Covers a land area of 63.153 square miles and a water area of 5.322 square miles. Located at 39.25° N. Lat.; 74.70° W. Long.
Population: 10,681 (1990); 12,115 (2000); 11,897 (2005); 11,680 (2010 projected); Race: 97.9% White, 0.7% Black, 0.5% Asian, 1.3% Hispanic of any race (2005); Density: 188.4 persons per square mile (2005); Average household size: 2.82 (2005); Median age: 38.9 (2005); Males per 100 females: 93.1 (2005); Marriage status: 20.5% never married, 66.4% now married, 7.4% widowed, 5.7% divorced (2000); Foreign born: 2.6% (2000); Ancestry (includes multiple ancestries): 32.5% Irish, 25.7% German, 19.5% Italian, 16.6% English, 4.6% Polish (2000).
Economy: Single-family building permits issued: 48 (2005); Multi-family building permits issued: 0 (2005); Employment by occupation: 14.9% management, 26.9% professional, 17.3% services, 23.6% sales, 0.7% farming, 10.5% construction, 6.1% production (2000).
Income: Per capita income: $32,014 (2005); Median household income: $71,936 (2005); Average household income: $90,101 (2005); Percent of households with income of $100,000 or more: 30.8% (2005); Poverty rate: 3.5% (2000).
Education: Percent of population age 25 and over with: High school diploma (including GED) or higher: 91.2% (2005); Bachelor's degree or higher: 32.2% (2005); Master's degree or higher: 8.9% (2005).
Housing: Homeownership rate: 90.7% (2005); Median home value: $263,090 (2005); Median rent: $671 per month (2000); Median age of housing: 19 years (2000).
Newspapers: The Gazette of Upper Township (General - Circulation 6,300)
Transportation: Commute to work: 94.3% car, 0.7% public transportation, 0.8% walk, 3.8% work from home (2000); Travel time to work: 24.3% less than 15 minutes, 42.6% 15 to 30 minutes, 23.1% 30 to 45 minutes, 3.6% 45 to 60 minutes, 6.4% 60 minutes or more (2000)

VILLAS (CDP). Covers a land area of 3.973 square miles and a water area of 0 square miles. Located at 39.01° N. Lat.; 74.93° W. Long. Elevation is 10 feet.
Population: 8,136 (1990); 9,064 (2000); 8,866 (2005); 8,670 (2010 projected); Race: 96.0% White, 1.5% Black, 0.3% Asian, 2.9% Hispanic of any race (2005); Density: 2,231.6 persons per square mile (2005); Average household size: 2.47 (2005); Median age: 39.4 (2005); Males per 100 females: 92.2 (2005); Marriage status: 22.3% never married, 55.8% now married, 9.5% widowed, 12.4% divorced (2000); Foreign born: 2.1% (2000); Ancestry (includes multiple ancestries): 32.3% Irish, 23.6% German, 17.7% Italian, 12.6% English, 7.0% Polish (2000).

Economy: Employment by occupation: 5.3% management, 13.8% professional, 25.0% services, 27.1% sales, 0.7% farming, 15.2% construction, 12.8% production (2000).

Income: Per capita income: $19,490 (2005); Median household income: $39,290 (2005); Average household income: $47,980 (2005); Percent of households with income of $100,000 or more: 7.6% (2005); Poverty rate: 10.4% (2000).

Education: Percent of population age 25 and over with: High school diploma (including GED) or higher: 72.4% (2005); Bachelor's degree or higher: 9.4% (2005); Master's degree or higher: 2.7% (2005).

School District(s)
Lower Township (PK-06)
   2003-04 Enrollment: 2,000 . . . . (609) 884-9400

Housing: Homeownership rate: 80.0% (2005); Median home value: $133,781 (2005); Median rent: $563 per month (2000); Median age of housing: 39 years (2000).

Transportation: Commute to work: 91.5% car, 4.2% public transportation, 1.8% walk, 0.9% work from home (2000); Travel time to work: 28.9% less than 15 minutes, 44.5% 15 to 30 minutes, 9.9% 30 to 45 minutes, 4.7% 45 to 60 minutes, 12.0% 60 minutes or more (2000)

WEST CAPE MAY (borough).
Covers a land area of 1.186 square miles and a water area of 0 square miles. Located at 38.93° N. Lat.; 74.93° W. Long. Elevation is 6 feet.

Population: 1,026 (1990); 1,095 (2000); 1,081 (2005); 1,065 (2010 projected); Race: 89.1% White, 9.7% Black, 0.0% Asian, 1.9% Hispanic of any race (2005); Density: 911.7 persons per square mile (2005); Average household size: 2.17 (2005); Median age: 48.6 (2005); Males per 100 females: 92.0 (2005); Marriage status: 22.5% never married, 52.7% now married, 12.2% widowed, 12.5% divorced (2000); Foreign born: 4.7% (2000); Ancestry (includes multiple ancestries): 19.5% English, 19.5% Irish, 18.7% German, 17.8% Other groups, 9.0% Italian (2000).

Economy: Single-family building permits issued: 7 (2005); Multi-family building permits issued: 0 (2005); Employment by occupation: 14.5% management, 25.8% professional, 16.6% services, 26.0% sales, 1.6% farming, 11.5% construction, 3.9% production (2000).

Income: Per capita income: $29,646 (2005); Median household income: $46,929 (2005); Average household income: $63,392 (2005); Percent of households with income of $100,000 or more: 17.6% (2005); Poverty rate: 7.4% (2000).

Education: Percent of population age 25 and over with: High school diploma (including GED) or higher: 82.9% (2005); Bachelor's degree or higher: 31.6% (2005); Master's degree or higher: 9.5% (2005).

School District(s)
West Cape May Borough (PK-06)
   2003-04 Enrollment: 79 . . . . (609) 884-4614

Housing: Homeownership rate: 77.2% (2005); Median home value: $287,054 (2005); Median rent: $604 per month (2000); Median age of housing: 41 years (2000).

Safety: Violent crime rate: 18.1 per 10,000 population; Property crime rate: 389.8 per 10,000 population (2004).

Transportation: Commute to work: 79.9% car, 1.7% public transportation, 7.0% walk, 4.4% work from home (2000); Travel time to work: 52.1% less than 15 minutes, 27.3% 15 to 30 minutes, 4.9% 30 to 45 minutes, 6.9% 45 to 60 minutes, 8.9% 60 minutes or more (2000)

WEST WILDWOOD (borough).
Covers a land area of 0.264 square miles and a water area of 0.086 square miles. Located at 39.00° N. Lat.; 74.82° W. Long. Elevation is 10 feet.

Population: 453 (1990); 448 (2000); 385 (2005); 363 (2010 projected); Race: 95.3% White, 0.0% Black, 0.0% Asian, 4.7% Hispanic of any race (2005); Density: 1,459.2 persons per square mile (2005); Average household size: 2.21 (2005); Median age: 46.9 (2005); Males per 100 females: 93.5 (2005); Marriage status: 16.1% never married, 57.1% now married, 12.2% widowed, 14.6% divorced (2000); Foreign born: 0.0% (2000); Ancestry (includes multiple ancestries): 47.0% Irish, 27.4% German, 10.7% Italian, 9.1% Polish, 8.5% English (2000).

Economy: In resort area. Single-family building permits issued: 16 (2005); Multi-family building permits issued: 4 (2005); Employment by occupation: 2.4% management, 14.1% professional, 22.8% services, 35.4% sales, 0.0% farming, 15.0% construction, 10.2% production (2000).

Income: Per capita income: $19,565 (2005); Median household income: $35,625 (2005); Average household income: $43,290 (2005); Percent of households with income of $100,000 or more: 4.0% (2005); Poverty rate: 6.5% (2000).

Education: Percent of population age 25 and over with: High school diploma (including GED) or higher: 68.9% (2005); Bachelor's degree or higher: 5.2% (2005); Master's degree or higher: 1.4% (2005).

Housing: Homeownership rate: 79.3% (2005); Median home value: $153,846 (2005); Median rent: $608 per month (2000); Median age of housing: 41 years (2000).

Safety: Violent crime rate: 69.3 per 10,000 population; Property crime rate: 461.9 per 10,000 population (2004).

Transportation: Commute to work: 93.4% car, 2.5% public transportation, 2.0% walk, 0.0% work from home (2000); Travel time to work: 30.5% less than 15 minutes, 40.1% 15 to 30 minutes, 15.7% 30 to 45 minutes, 3.0% 45 to 60 minutes, 10.7% 60 minutes or more (2000)

WHITESBORO-BURLEIGH (CDP).
Covers a land area of 4.115 square miles and a water area of 0.008 square miles. Located at 39.03° N. Lat.; 74.86° W. Long.

Population: 1,997 (1990); 1,836 (2000); 1,977 (2005); 2,067 (2010 projected); Race: 68.3% White, 27.2% Black, 1.1% Asian, 3.5% Hispanic of any race (2005); Density: 480.4 persons per square mile (2005); Average household size: 2.39 (2005); Median age: 43.0 (2005); Males per 100 females: 91.6 (2005); Marriage status: 27.1% never married, 52.3% now married, 16.1% widowed, 4.4% divorced (2000); Foreign born: 1.7% (2000); Ancestry (includes multiple ancestries): 34.2% Other groups, 16.0% Irish, 15.8% United States or American, 11.5% German, 7.5% Italian (2000).

Economy: Employment by occupation: 11.6% management, 13.6% professional, 39.7% services, 21.8% sales, 0.0% farming, 5.3% construction, 8.0% production (2000).

Income: Per capita income: $21,897 (2005); Median household income: $39,151 (2005); Average household income: $52,409 (2005); Percent of households with income of $100,000 or more: 12.8% (2005); Poverty rate: 9.2% (2000).

Education: Percent of population age 25 and over with: High school diploma (including GED) or higher: 67.7% (2005); Bachelor's degree or higher: 11.3% (2005); Master's degree or higher: 2.7% (2005).

Housing: Homeownership rate: 84.3% (2005); Median home value: $100,578 (2005); Median rent: $521 per month (2000); Median age of housing: 23 years (2000).

Transportation: Commute to work: 87.4% car, 3.3% public transportation, 6.0% walk, 3.3% work from home (2000); Travel time to work: 34.4% less than 15 minutes, 42.4% 15 to 30 minutes, 13.4% 30 to 45 minutes, 6.0% 45 to 60 minutes, 3.8% 60 minutes or more (2000)

WILDWOOD (city).
Covers a land area of 1.290 square miles and a water area of 0.094 square miles. Located at 38.98° N. Lat.; 74.82° W. Long. Elevation is 8 feet.

History: Incorporated 1917.

Population: 4,484 (1990); 5,436 (2000); 5,266 (2005); 5,056 (2010 projected); Race: 69.9% White, 15.4% Black, 0.5% Asian, 21.3% Hispanic of any race (2005); Density: 4,080.9 persons per square mile (2005); Average household size: 2.32 (2005); Median age: 35.1 (2005); Males per 100 females: 96.7 (2005); Marriage status: 31.2% never married, 47.1% now married, 11.3% widowed, 10.4% divorced (2000); Foreign born: 4.5% (2000); Ancestry (includes multiple ancestries): 30.8% Other groups, 21.6% Irish, 15.0% Italian, 11.5% German, 5.6% English (2000).

Economy: Resort city. Single-family building permits issued: 46 (2005); Multi-family building permits issued: 254 (2005); Employment by occupation: 10.9% management, 7.6% professional, 25.6% services, 28.8% sales, 1.6% farming, 10.1% construction, 15.5% production (2000).

Income: Per capita income: $14,952 (2005); Median household income: $26,693 (2005); Average household income: $34,485 (2005); Percent of households with income of $100,000 or more: 4.3% (2005); Poverty rate: 26.4% (2000).

Taxes: Total city taxes per capita: $2,321 (2004); City property taxes per capita: $1,842 (2004).

Education: Percent of population age 25 and over with: High school diploma (including GED) or higher: 66.5% (2005); Bachelor's degree or higher: 7.0% (2005); Master's degree or higher: 2.0% (2005).

School District(s)
Wildwood City (PK-12)
   2003-04 Enrollment: 912 . . . . (609) 522-4157

Housing: Homeownership rate: 39.8% (2005); Median home value: $151,630 (2005); Median rent: $490 per month (2000); Median age of housing: 52 years (2000).

Safety: Violent crime rate: 151.0 per 10,000 population; Property crime rate: 1,193.1 per 10,000 population (2004).
Newspapers: Wildwood Leader (General - Circulation 4,250)
Transportation: Commute to work: 70.2% car, 8.9% public transportation, 15.6% walk, 2.0% work from home (2000); Travel time to work: 48.7% less than 15 minutes, 28.5% 15 to 30 minutes, 8.6% 30 to 45 minutes, 5.6% 45 to 60 minutes, 8.6% 60 minutes or more (2000)
Additional Information Contacts
Greater Wildwood Chamber of Commerce . . . . (609) 729-4000
  http://www.gwcoc.com

WILDWOOD CREST (borough). Covers a land area of 1.152 square miles and a water area of 0.154 square miles. Located at 38.97° N. Lat.; 74.83° W. Long. Elevation is 9 feet.
Population: 3,631 (1990); 3,980 (2000); 3,850 (2005); 3,714 (2010 projected); Race: 94.3% White, 1.5% Black, 0.5% Asian, 5.0% Hispanic of any race (2005); Density: 3,341.1 persons per square mile (2005); Average household size: 2.14 (2005); Median age: 47.5 (2005); Males per 100 females: 87.9 (2005); Marriage status: 21.6% never married, 54.5% now married, 12.8% widowed, 11.1% divorced (2000); Foreign born: 3.2% (2000); Ancestry (includes multiple ancestries): 29.6% Irish, 23.9% Italian, 22.8% German, 11.6% English, 7.8% Polish (2000).
Economy: Resort borough. Single-family building permits issued: 96 (2005); Multi-family building permits issued: 261 (2005); Employment by occupation: 12.7% management, 26.6% professional, 18.3% services, 29.4% sales, 0.3% farming, 7.1% construction, 5.6% production (2000).
Income: Per capita income: $25,115 (2005); Median household income: $35,483 (2005); Average household income: $52,786 (2005); Percent of households with income of $100,000 or more: 13.8% (2005); Poverty rate: 6.0% (2000).
Education: Percent of population age 25 and over with: High school diploma (including GED) or higher: 79.2% (2005); Bachelor's degree or higher: 26.2% (2005); Master's degree or higher: 8.8% (2005).
School District(s)
Wildwood Crest Borough (PK-08)
  2003-04 Enrollment: 340 . . . . (609) 729-3760
Housing: Homeownership rate: 66.8% (2005); Median home value: $258,902 (2005); Median rent: $525 per month (2000); Median age of housing: 42 years (2000).
Safety: Violent crime rate: 33.2 per 10,000 population; Property crime rate: 391.2 per 10,000 population (2004).
Transportation: Commute to work: 88.5% car, 0.6% public transportation, 4.9% walk, 3.7% work from home (2000); Travel time to work: 49.0% less than 15 minutes, 33.8% 15 to 30 minutes, 5.5% 30 to 45 minutes, 4.4% 45 to 60 minutes, 7.3% 60 minutes or more (2000)

WOODBINE (borough). Covers a land area of 7.997 square miles and a water area of 0 square miles. Located at 39.23° N. Lat.; 74.81° W. Long. Elevation is 40 feet.
History: In 1880s it was developed as a Jewish agricultural community supported by Baron de Hirsch. Incorporated 1903.
Population: 2,678 (1990); 2,716 (2000); 2,682 (2005); 2,661 (2010 projected); Race: 54.5% White, 32.1% Black, 0.0% Asian, 22.9% Hispanic of any race (2005); Density: 335.4 persons per square mile (2005); Average household size: 3.46 (2005); Median age: 36.1 (2005); Males per 100 females: 142.9 (2005); Marriage status: 49.6% never married, 35.5% now married, 6.1% widowed, 8.8% divorced (2000); Foreign born: 1.3% (2000); Ancestry (includes multiple ancestries): 40.3% Other groups, 6.3% German, 6.0% Irish, 5.6% Italian, 4.4% Polish (2000).
Economy: Agricultural area. Single-family building permits issued: 7 (2005); Multi-family building permits issued: 0 (2005); Employment by occupation: 6.6% management, 14.4% professional, 33.4% services, 20.3% sales, 1.2% farming, 9.4% construction, 14.7% production (2000).
Income: Per capita income: $15,764 (2005); Median household income: $35,484 (2005); Average household income: $44,153 (2005); Percent of households with income of $100,000 or more: 7.9% (2005); Poverty rate: 17.9% (2000).
Education: Percent of population age 25 and over with: High school diploma (including GED) or higher: 57.7% (2005); Bachelor's degree or higher: 4.4% (2005); Master's degree or higher: 1.0% (2005).
School District(s)
Woodbine Borough (PK-08)
  2003-04 Enrollment: 283 . . . . (609) 861-5174

Housing: Homeownership rate: 59.0% (2005); Median home value: $133,333 (2005); Median rent: $413 per month (2000); Median age of housing: 34 years (2000).
Safety: Violent crime rate: 14.8 per 10,000 population; Property crime rate: 37.1 per 10,000 population (2004).
Transportation: Commute to work: 90.5% car, 0.2% public transportation, 5.3% walk, 1.5% work from home (2000); Travel time to work: 50.1% less than 15 minutes, 27.9% 15 to 30 minutes, 14.3% 30 to 45 minutes, 3.5% 45 to 60 minutes, 4.3% 60 minutes or more (2000)

Cumberland County

Located in southern New Jersey; bounded on the southwest by Delaware Bay. Covers a land area of 489.30 square miles, a water area of 187.29 square miles, and is located in the Eastern Time Zone. The county government was organized in 1748. County seat is Bridgeton.

Cumberland County is part of the Vineland-Millville-Bridgeton, NJ Metropolitan Statistical Area. The entire metro area includes: Cumberland County, NJ

Weather Station: Millville Municipal Airport   Elevation: 68 feet

	Jan	Feb	Mar	Apr	May	Jun	Jul	Aug	Sep	Oct	Nov	Dec
High	41	44	52	63	73	81	86	84	78	67	56	46
Low	24	25	33	41	51	61	67	65	58	45	37	29
Precip	3.6	3.2	4.3	3.7	3.9	3.3	3.6	4.2	3.4	3.2	3.3	3.6
Snow	5.0	4.7	1.4	0.3	tr	0.0	tr	0.0	0.0	tr	0.2	1.6

High and Low temperatures in degrees Fahrenheit; Precipitation and Snow in inches

Weather Station: Seabrook Farms   Elevation: 88 feet

	Jan	Feb	Mar	Apr	May	Jun	Jul	Aug	Sep	Oct	Nov	Dec
High	41	43	52	62	72	81	86	84	78	67	56	46
Low	24	26	33	42	51	61	66	65	57	45	37	29
Precip	4.1	2.9	4.2	3.4	4.0	3.3	4.4	4.3	3.7	3.5	3.3	3.8
Snow	na	na	na	0.4	0.0	0.0	0.0	0.0	0.0	0.0	0.2	na

High and Low temperatures in degrees Fahrenheit; Precipitation and Snow in inches

Population: 138,053 (1990); 146,438 (2000); 151,111 (2005); 155,968 (2010 projected); Race: 64.2% White, 20.5% Black, 1.0% Asian, 21.8% Hispanic of any race (2005); Density: 308.8 persons per square mile (2005); Average household size: 2.95 (2005); Median age: 35.9 (2005); Males per 100 females: 104.8 (2005).
Religion: Five largest groups: 22.9% Catholic Church, 4.4% The United Methodist Church, 2.1% Assemblies of God, 2.0% American Baptist Churches in the USA, 1.4% Jewish Estimate (2000).
Economy: Unemployment rate: 6.2% (2005); Total civilian labor force: 70,871 (2005); Leading industries: 21.6% manufacturing; 16.2% health care and social assistance; 15.7% retail trade (2004); Farms: 616 totaling 71,097 acres (2002); Companies that employ 500 or more persons: 18 (2004); Companies that employ 100 to 499 persons: 152 (2004); Companies that employ less than 100 persons: 6,173 (2004); Black-owned businesses: n/a (2002); Hispanic-owned businesses: 524 (2002); Asian-owned businesses: 208 (2002); Women-owned businesses: 1,881 (2002); Retail sales per capita: $11,963 (2006). Single-family building permits issued: 597 (2005); Multi-family building permits issued: 33 (2005).
Income: Per capita income: $19,764 (2005); Median household income: $43,817 (2005); Average household income: $55,459 (2005); Percent of households with income of $100,000 or more: 12.2% (2005); Poverty rate: 14.9% (2003); Bankruptcy rate: 11.45% (2005).
Taxes: Total county taxes per capita: $321 (2004); County property taxes per capita: $321 (2004).
Education: Percent of population age 25 and over with: High school diploma (including GED) or higher: 68.4% (2005); Bachelor's degree or higher: 11.7% (2005); Master's degree or higher: 3.7% (2005).
Housing: Homeownership rate: 68.3% (2005); Median home value: $131,334 (2005); Median rent: $518 per month (2000); Median age of housing: 38 years (2000).
Health: Birth rate: 140.8 per 10,000 population (2004); Death rate: 97.6 per 10,000 population (2004); Age-adjusted cancer mortality rate: 221.6 deaths per 100,000 population (2002); Air Quality Index: 90.4% good, 8.5% moderate, 0.8% unhealthy for sensitive individuals, 0.3% unhealthy (percent of days in 2005); Number of physicians: 15.1 per 10,000 population (2004); Hospital beds: 30.6 per 10,000 population (2003); Hospital admissions: 1,335.3 per 10,000 population (2003).
Elections: 2004 Presidential election results: 45.8% Bush, 52.4% Kerry, 0.3% Nader, 0.2% Badnarik

Additional Information Contacts

Cumberland County Government . . . . (856) 453-2125
    http://www.co.cumberland.nj.us
Bridgeton Area Chamber of Commerce. . . . . (856) 455-1312
    http://www.bridgeton-nj-chamber.com
City of Millville . . . . (856) 825-7000
    http://millvillev2.qscend.com
City of Vineland . . . . (856) 794-4060
    http://www.vinelandcity.org
Greater Mercer County Chamber of Commerce . . . . (609) 393-4143
    http://www.mercerchamber.org
Hopewell Township . . . . (609) 737-0605
    http://www.hopewelltwp-nj.com
Millville Chamber of Commerce. . . . . (856) 825-2600
    http://www.millville-nj.com
Vineland Chamber of Commerce. . . . . (856) 691-7400
    http://chamber.vineland.org/index

Cumberland County Communities

BRIDGETON (city). Covers a land area of 6.222 square miles and a water area of 0.226 square miles. Located at 39.43° N. Lat.; 75.23° W. Long. Elevation is 40 feet.

History: Once a rural farm center. Downtown is highly Victorian, but with several 18th-century buildings, including the restored Potter's Tavern, a Revolutionary center in colonial days; and a Presbyterian church (1792). The city's liberty bell, in the county courthouse lobby, rang on July 7, 1776, for the reading of the Declaration of Independence. Settled 1686, Incorporated 1865.

Population: 18,942 (1990); 22,771 (2000); 22,841 (2005); 23,059 (2010 projected); Race: 37.0% White, 39.6% Black, 0.7% Asian, 31.1% Hispanic of any race (2005); Density: 3,671.1 persons per square mile (2005); Average household size: 3.71 (2005); Median age: 31.5 (2005); Males per 100 females: 131.6 (2005); Marriage status: 40.1% never married, 44.7% now married, 7.1% widowed, 8.1% divorced (2000); Foreign born: 12.4% (2000); Ancestry (includes multiple ancestries): 49.3% Other groups, 5.9% German, 5.8% Irish, 5.7% Italian, 4.4% English (2000).

Economy: Highly industrialized, with glassworks, printing, food-processing, textile, and clothing industries. Single-family building permits issued: 167 (2005); Multi-family building permits issued: 0 (2005); Employment by occupation: 5.3% management, 13.9% professional, 23.7% services, 21.6% sales, 5.0% farming, 6.4% construction, 24.2% production (2000).

Income: Per capita income: $11,714 (2005); Median household income: $29,366 (2005); Average household income: $39,645 (2005); Percent of households with income of $100,000 or more: 5.8% (2005); Poverty rate: 26.6% (2000).

Education: Percent of population age 25 and over with: High school diploma (including GED) or higher: 57.2% (2005); Bachelor's degree or higher: 7.2% (2005); Master's degree or higher: 2.6% (2005).

School District(s)

Bridgeton City (PK-12)
    2003-04 Enrollment: 4,761 . . . . (856) 455-8030
Cumberland County Vocational (09-12)
    2003-04 Enrollment: 72 . . . . (856) 451-9000

Housing: Homeownership rate: 47.9% (2005); Median home value: $101,215 (2005); Median rent: $512 per month (2000); Median age of housing: 51 years (2000).

Hospitals: South Jersey Hospital-Bridgeton (252 beds)

Safety: Violent crime rate: 176.1 per 10,000 population; Property crime rate: 472.9 per 10,000 population (2004).

Newspapers: Bridgeton News (Circulation 7,400); Cumberland/Salem Guide (General - Circulation 75,000); Millville News (Circulation 1,200)

Transportation: Commute to work: 88.1% car, 3.7% public transportation, 3.7% walk, 1.8% work from home (2000); Travel time to work: 39.5% less than 15 minutes, 27.7% 15 to 30 minutes, 17.5% 30 to 45 minutes, 5.6% 45 to 60 minutes, 9.7% 60 minutes or more (2000)

Additional Information Contacts

Bridgeton Area Chamber of Commerce. . . . . (856) 455-1312
    http://www.bridgeton-nj-chamber.com

CEDARVILLE (CDP). Covers a land area of 2.267 square miles and a water area of 0.035 square miles. Located at 39.33° N. Lat.; 75.20° W. Long. Elevation is 33 feet.

Population: 796 (1990); 793 (2000); 747 (2005); 728 (2010 projected); Race: 85.7% White, 8.6% Black, 0.4% Asian, 4.8% Hispanic of any race

(2005); Density: 329.5 persons per square mile (2005); Average household size: 2.80 (2005); Median age: 36.8 (2005); Males per 100 females: 100.3 (2005); Marriage status: 26.3% never married, 58.7% now married, 9.5% widowed, 5.5% divorced (2000); Foreign born: 7.9% (2000); Ancestry (includes multiple ancestries): 24.2% German, 19.8% Irish, 19.4% Italian, 17.0% Other groups, 10.9% English (2000).

Economy: Market center for vegetable-growing region; canned vegetables. Employment by occupation: 4.5% management, 16.8% professional, 9.1% services, 18.2% sales, 0.0% farming, 15.1% construction, 36.4% production (2000).

Income: Per capita income: $18,004 (2005); Median household income: $51,285 (2005); Average household income: $49,232 (2005); Percent of households with income of $100,000 or more: 3.0% (2005); Poverty rate: 3.8% (2000).

Education: Percent of population age 25 and over with: High school diploma (including GED) or higher: 73.2% (2005); Bachelor's degree or higher: 10.8% (2005); Master's degree or higher: 2.7% (2005).

School District(s)

Lawrence Township (PK-08)
    2003-04 Enrollment: 478 . . . . (856) 447-4237

Housing: Homeownership rate: 87.6% (2005); Median home value: $118,142 (2005); Median rent: $530 per month (2000); Median age of housing: 60+ years (2000).

Transportation: Commute to work: 85.8% car, 0.0% public transportation, 3.4% walk, 2.6% work from home (2000); Travel time to work: 36.2% less than 15 minutes, 45.8% 15 to 30 minutes, 8.5% 30 to 45 minutes, 3.2% 45 to 60 minutes, 6.4% 60 minutes or more (2000)

COMMERCIAL (township). Covers a land area of 32.459 square miles and a water area of 2.043 square miles. Located at 39.29° N. Lat.; 75.03° W. Long.

History: Incorporated 1874.

Population: 5,026 (1990); 5,259 (2000); 5,471 (2005); 5,692 (2010 projected); Race: 85.7% White, 10.9% Black, 0.2% Asian, 4.5% Hispanic of any race (2005); Density: 168.5 persons per square mile (2005); Average household size: 2.78 (2005); Median age: 34.2 (2005); Males per 100 females: 97.1 (2005); Marriage status: 29.1% never married, 51.4% now married, 7.6% widowed, 11.9% divorced (2000); Foreign born: 1.1% (2000); Ancestry (includes multiple ancestries): 20.8% Other groups, 18.5% Irish, 17.5% German, 13.9% Italian, 13.7% English (2000).

Economy: Rural area with oyster packing and light industry. Single-family building permits issued: 9 (2005); Multi-family building permits issued: 0 (2005); Employment by occupation: 5.8% management, 11.3% professional, 19.6% services, 19.6% sales, 2.7% farming, 13.5% construction, 27.6% production (2000).

Income: Per capita income: $15,744 (2005); Median household income: $37,035 (2005); Average household income: $43,597 (2005); Percent of households with income of $100,000 or more: 4.8% (2005); Poverty rate: 15.8% (2000).

Education: Percent of population age 25 and over with: High school diploma (including GED) or higher: 63.5% (2005); Bachelor's degree or higher: 6.3% (2005); Master's degree or higher: 1.3% (2005).

Housing: Homeownership rate: 79.4% (2005); Median home value: $86,581 (2005); Median rent: $544 per month (2000); Median age of housing: 33 years (2000).

Transportation: Commute to work: 95.7% car, 0.2% public transportation, 0.5% walk, 2.3% work from home (2000); Travel time to work: 24.0% less than 15 minutes, 48.4% 15 to 30 minutes, 14.7% 30 to 45 minutes, 3.3% 45 to 60 minutes, 9.6% 60 minutes or more (2000)

DEERFIELD (township). Aka Deerfield Street. Covers a land area of 16.839 square miles and a water area of 0 square miles. Located at 39.46° N. Lat.; 75.13° W. Long. Elevation is 87 feet.

Population: 2,933 (1990); 2,927 (2000); 3,142 (2005); 3,350 (2010 projected); Race: 78.5% White, 11.9% Black, 1.3% Asian, 7.0% Hispanic of any race (2005); Density: 186.6 persons per square mile (2005); Average household size: 2.85 (2005); Median age: 39.1 (2005); Males per 100 females: 94.8 (2005); Marriage status: 31.2% never married, 51.7% now married, 6.6% widowed, 10.4% divorced (2000); Foreign born: 2.9% (2000); Ancestry (includes multiple ancestries): 24.4% Other groups, 20.7% Italian, 15.6% German, 14.5% Irish, 8.6% Polish (2000).

Economy: Single-family building permits issued: 15 (2005); Multi-family building permits issued: 0 (2005); Employment by occupation: 6.3% management, 14.6% professional, 17.0% services, 27.1% sales, 0.8% farming, 11.1% construction, 23.0% production (2000).

Income: Per capita income: $21,532 (2005); Median household income: $53,034 (2005); Average household income: $60,786 (2005); Percent of households with income of $100,000 or more: 13.9% (2005); Poverty rate: 9.2% (2000).

Education: Percent of population age 25 and over with: High school diploma (including GED) or higher: 73.1% (2005); Bachelor's degree or higher: 10.6% (2005); Master's degree or higher: 2.7% (2005).

Housing: Homeownership rate: 84.0% (2005); Median home value: $145,222 (2005); Median rent: $531 per month (2000); Median age of housing: 36 years (2000).

Transportation: Commute to work: 93.2% car, 0.2% public transportation, 1.6% walk, 2.6% work from home (2000); Travel time to work: 25.8% less than 15 minutes, 50.0% 15 to 30 minutes, 8.5% 30 to 45 minutes, 7.8% 45 to 60 minutes, 7.9% 60 minutes or more (2000)

DELMONT (unincorporated postal area, zip code 08314). Covers a land area of 11.827 square miles and a water area of 0 square miles. Located at 39.21° N. Lat.; 74.94° W. Long. Elevation is 11 feet.

Population: 1,986 (2000); Race: 32.2% White, 53.7% Black, 0.7% Asian, 18.2% Hispanic of any race (2000); Density: 167.9 persons per square mile (2000); Age: 4.1% under 18, 2.2% over 64 (2000); Marriage status: 32.5% never married, 55.3% now married, 2.6% widowed, 9.6% divorced (2000); Foreign born: 6.3% (2000); Ancestry (includes multiple ancestries): 37.8% Other groups, 6.4% German, 5.4% Irish, 4.6% African, 4.0% Italian (2000).

Economy: In marshland near Delaware Bay. Employment by occupation: 7.5% management, 6.1% professional, 27.2% services, 17.7% sales, 0.0% farming, 17.0% construction, 24.5% production (2000).

Income: Per capita income: $6,844 (2000); Median household income: $39,000 (2000); Poverty rate: 6.1% (2000).

Education: Percent of population age 25 and over with: High school diploma (including GED) or higher: 61.8% (2000); Bachelor's degree or higher: 2.3% (2000).

Housing: Homeownership rate: 84.6% (2000); Median home value: $68,400 (2000); Median rent: $475 per month (2000); Median age of housing: 44 years (2000).

Transportation: Commute to work: 95.8% car, 0.0% public transportation, 4.2% walk, 0.0% work from home (2000); Travel time to work: 29.9% less than 15 minutes, 36.1% 15 to 30 minutes, 18.1% 30 to 45 minutes, 6.3% 45 to 60 minutes, 9.7% 60 minutes or more (2000)

DOWNE (township). Covers a land area of 50.758 square miles and a water area of 3.474 square miles. Located at 39.27° N. Lat.; 75.12° W. Long.

Population: 1,702 (1990); 1,631 (2000); 1,564 (2005); 1,532 (2010 projected); Race: 90.9% White, 4.9% Black, 0.3% Asian, 3.9% Hispanic of any race (2005); Density: 30.8 persons per square mile (2005); Average household size: 2.42 (2005); Median age: 41.9 (2005); Males per 100 females: 108.5 (2005); Marriage status: 23.4% never married, 54.8% now married, 10.6% widowed, 11.2% divorced (2000); Foreign born: 1.5% (2000); Ancestry (includes multiple ancestries): 17.4% German, 17.0% Irish, 15.9% Other groups, 14.7% English, 9.7% United States or American (2000).

Economy: Single-family building permits issued: 7 (2005); Multi-family building permits issued: 0 (2005); Employment by occupation: 3.8% management, 13.0% professional, 17.8% services, 25.6% sales, 2.0% farming, 12.8% construction, 25.0% production (2000).

Income: Per capita income: $20,534 (2005); Median household income: $39,795 (2005); Average household income: $49,714 (2005); Percent of households with income of $100,000 or more: 9.1% (2005); Poverty rate: 13.1% (2000).

Education: Percent of population age 25 and over with: High school diploma (including GED) or higher: 71.1% (2005); Bachelor's degree or higher: 7.7% (2005); Master's degree or higher: 2.1% (2005).

Housing: Homeownership rate: 90.7% (2005); Median home value: $109,363 (2005); Median rent: $483 per month (2000); Median age of housing: 40 years (2000).

Transportation: Commute to work: 92.9% car, 1.1% public transportation, 1.1% walk, 3.9% work from home (2000); Travel time to work: 21.5% less than 15 minutes, 39.1% 15 to 30 minutes, 23.2% 30 to 45 minutes, 2.7% 45 to 60 minutes, 13.5% 60 minutes or more (2000)

FAIRFIELD (township). Covers a land area of 42.290 square miles and a water area of 1.515 square miles. Located at 39.38° N. Lat.; 75.21° W. Long.

Population: 5,699 (1990); 6,283 (2000); 6,736 (2005); 7,072 (2010 projected); Race: 43.3% White, 47.2% Black, 0.6% Asian, 10.8% Hispanic of any race (2005); Density: 159.3 persons per square mile (2005); Average household size: 3.54 (2005); Median age: 37.1 (2005); Males per 100 females: 147.4 (2005); Marriage status: 24.1% never married, 59.3% now married, 8.7% widowed, 7.8% divorced (2000); Foreign born: 1.9% (2000); Ancestry (includes multiple ancestries): 37.1% Other groups, 9.2% German, 5.5% Irish, 5.5% Italian, 4.2% English (2000).

Economy: Single-family building permits issued: 11 (2005); Multi-family building permits issued: 0 (2005); Employment by occupation: 6.0% management, 13.9% professional, 22.9% services, 21.6% sales, 0.3% farming, 8.8% construction, 26.5% production (2000).

Income: Per capita income: $20,235 (2005); Median household income: $43,346 (2005); Average household income: $53,136 (2005); Percent of households with income of $100,000 or more: 9.9% (2005); Poverty rate: 11.2% (2000).

Education: Percent of population age 25 and over with: High school diploma (including GED) or higher: 63.1% (2005); Bachelor's degree or higher: 5.1% (2005); Master's degree or higher: 1.5% (2005).

Housing: Homeownership rate: 84.1% (2005); Median home value: $118,305 (2005); Median rent: $510 per month (2000); Median age of housing: 32 years (2000).

Transportation: Commute to work: 93.0% car, 1.5% public transportation, 1.6% walk, 2.9% work from home (2000); Travel time to work: 33.8% less than 15 minutes, 40.6% 15 to 30 minutes, 12.4% 30 to 45 minutes, 4.9% 45 to 60 minutes, 8.3% 60 minutes or more (2000)

FAIRTON (CDP). Covers a land area of 2.821 square miles and a water area of 0.124 square miles. Located at 39.38° N. Lat.; 75.21° W. Long. Elevation is 30 feet.

Population: 1,359 (1990); 2,253 (2000); 2,427 (2005); 2,517 (2010 projected); Race: 55.6% White, 40.3% Black, 1.3% Asian, 15.2% Hispanic of any race (2005); Density: 860.4 persons per square mile (2005); Average household size: 4.65 (2005); Median age: 36.7 (2005); Males per 100 females: 267.2 (2005); Marriage status: 14.5% never married, 71.3% now married, 8.8% widowed, 5.4% divorced (2000); Foreign born: 0.5% (2000); Ancestry (includes multiple ancestries): 10.1% Italian, 9.9% German, 9.8% Other groups, 5.8% Irish, 5.4% English (2000).

Economy: Canned vegetables. Employment by occupation: 6.9% management, 13.3% professional, 22.5% services, 22.9% sales, 0.0% farming, 5.2% construction, 29.1% production (2000).

Income: Per capita income: $22,584 (2005); Median household income: $41,830 (2005); Average household income: $51,580 (2005); Percent of households with income of $100,000 or more: 10.5% (2005); Poverty rate: 5.9% (2000).

Education: Percent of population age 25 and over with: High school diploma (including GED) or higher: 56.0% (2005); Bachelor's degree or higher: 3.4% (2005); Master's degree or higher: 1.5% (2005).

Housing: Homeownership rate: 82.4% (2005); Median home value: $120,732 (2005); Median rent: $524 per month (2000); Median age of housing: 37 years (2000).

Transportation: Commute to work: 91.7% car, 0.0% public transportation, 2.3% walk, 6.1% work from home (2000); Travel time to work: 34.1% less than 15 minutes, 38.9% 15 to 30 minutes, 10.1% 30 to 45 minutes, 5.4% 45 to 60 minutes, 11.4% 60 minutes or more (2000)

GREENWICH (township). Covers a land area of 18.159 square miles and a water area of 0.718 square miles. Located at 39.40° N. Lat.; 75.35° W. Long. Elevation is 14 feet.

History: Seaport in 18th century. Monument (1908) commemorates scene of tea-burning "party," 1774.

Population: 911 (1990); 847 (2000); 932 (2005); 1,019 (2010 projected); Race: 92.9% White, 3.3% Black, 0.2% Asian, 1.8% Hispanic of any race (2005); Density: 51.3 persons per square mile (2005); Average household size: 2.55 (2005); Median age: 43.0 (2005); Males per 100 females: 98.7 (2005); Marriage status: 16.3% never married, 67.6% now married, 6.2% widowed, 9.8% divorced (2000); Foreign born: 0.5% (2000); Ancestry (includes multiple ancestries): 25.3% English, 22.3% German, 16.6% Irish, 11.3% Italian, 10.9% Other groups (2000).

Economy: Canneries. Single-family building permits issued: 9 (2005); Multi-family building permits issued: 0 (2005); Employment by occupation: 18.4% management, 23.6% professional, 11.8% services, 22.3% sales, 1.1% farming, 8.9% construction, 13.9% production (2000).

Income: Per capita income: $26,583 (2005); Median household income: $61,097 (2005); Average household income: $67,877 (2005); Percent of

households with income of $100,000 or more: 20.5% (2005); Poverty rate: 8.0% (2000).

Education: Percent of population age 25 and over with: High school diploma (including GED) or higher: 86.4% (2005); Bachelor's degree or higher: 22.0% (2005); Master's degree or higher: 7.1% (2005).

School District(s)

Greenwich Township (PK-08)

    2003-04 Enrollment: 102 . . . . (856) 451-5513

Housing: Homeownership rate: 86.3% (2005); Median home value: $170,522 (2005); Median rent: $523 per month (2000); Median age of housing: 60+ years (2000).

Transportation: Commute to work: 87.0% car, 1.6% public transportation, 0.9% walk, 10.0% work from home (2000); Travel time to work: 18.5% less than 15 minutes, 40.9% 15 to 30 minutes, 23.4% 30 to 45 minutes, 9.6% 45 to 60 minutes, 7.6% 60 minutes or more (2000)

HEISLERVILLE (unincorporated postal area, zip code 08324).

Covers a land area of 8.166 square miles and a water area of 0.018 square miles. Located at 39.21° N. Lat.; 74.99° W. Long. Elevation is 10 feet.

Population: 451 (2000); Race: 88.1% White, 0.7% Black, 0.0% Asian, 0.0% Hispanic of any race (2000); Density: 55.2 persons per square mile (2000); Age: 37.7% under 18, 8.7% over 64 (2000); Marriage status: 17.0% never married, 66.8% now married, 9.4% widowed, 6.8% divorced (2000); Foreign born: 0.0% (2000); Ancestry (includes multiple ancestries): 26.2% German, 21.2% Irish, 14.1% United States or American, 11.1% Other groups, 10.8% English (2000).

Economy: Employment by occupation: 11.7% management, 16.0% professional, 33.8% services, 10.3% sales, 0.0% farming, 7.5% construction, 20.7% production (2000).

Income: Per capita income: $16,572 (2000); Median household income: $43,833 (2000); Poverty rate: 6.7% (2000).

Education: Percent of population age 25 and over with: High school diploma (including GED) or higher: 73.8% (2000); Bachelor's degree or higher: 5.6% (2000).

Housing: Homeownership rate: 84.7% (2000); Median home value: $85,000 (2000); Median rent: $605 per month (2000); Median age of housing: 45 years (2000).

Transportation: Commute to work: 92.4% car, 1.5% public transportation, 0.0% walk, 4.1% work from home (2000); Travel time to work: 38.1% less than 15 minutes, 30.2% 15 to 30 minutes, 5.8% 30 to 45 minutes, 9.5% 45 to 60 minutes, 16.4% 60 minutes or more (2000)

HOPEWELL (township). Covers a land area of 29.901 square miles and a water area of 0.884 square miles. Located at 39.44° N. Lat.; 75.27° W. Long.

Population: 4,215 (1990); 4,434 (2000); 4,736 (2005); 5,021 (2010 projected); Race: 88.2% White, 6.3% Black, 0.6% Asian, 3.8% Hispanic of any race (2005); Density: 158.4 persons per square mile (2005); Average household size: 2.67 (2005); Median age: 43.3 (2005); Males per 100 females: 91.0 (2005); Marriage status: 22.2% never married, 59.2% now married, 14.7% widowed, 3.9% divorced (2000); Foreign born: 2.5% (2000); Ancestry (includes multiple ancestries): 24.5% German, 16.2% Italian, 14.8% Irish, 14.6% English, 12.5% Other groups (2000).

Economy: Single-family building permits issued: 26 (2005); Multi-family building permits issued: 0 (2005); Employment by occupation: 11.5% management, 21.0% professional, 18.6% services, 22.1% sales, 1.3% farming, 7.7% construction, 17.8% production (2000).

Income: Per capita income: $25,325 (2005); Median household income: $57,047 (2005); Average household income: $66,832 (2005); Percent of households with income of $100,000 or more: 20.1% (2005); Poverty rate: 6.6% (2000).

Education: Percent of population age 25 and over with: High school diploma (including GED) or higher: 82.8% (2005); Bachelor's degree or higher: 18.5% (2005); Master's degree or higher: 7.5% (2005).

Housing: Homeownership rate: 83.4% (2005); Median home value: $146,572 (2005); Median rent: $486 per month (2000); Median age of housing: 35 years (2000).

Transportation: Commute to work: 92.6% car, 1.7% public transportation, 2.1% walk, 3.3% work from home (2000); Travel time to work: 41.7% less than 15 minutes, 29.2% 15 to 30 minutes, 16.5% 30 to 45 minutes, 3.0% 45 to 60 minutes, 9.6% 60 minutes or more (2000)

Additional Information Contacts

Hopewell Township . . . . (609) 737-0605

    http://www.hopewelltwp-nj.com

LAUREL LAKE (CDP). Covers a land area of 1.761 square miles and a water area of 0.106 square miles. Located at 39.32° N. Lat.; 75.03° W. Long. Elevation is 30 feet.

Population: 2,619 (1990); 2,929 (2000); 2,989 (2005); 3,021 (2010 projected); Race: 95.3% White, 1.5% Black, 0.1% Asian, 5.2% Hispanic of any race (2005); Density: 1,697.3 persons per square mile (2005); Average household size: 2.68 (2005); Median age: 32.5 (2005); Males per 100 females: 98.3 (2005); Marriage status: 29.7% never married, 48.2% now married, 8.6% widowed, 13.5% divorced (2000); Foreign born: 1.3% (2000); Ancestry (includes multiple ancestries): 23.1% Irish, 21.1% German, 17.1% Italian, 14.4% English, 14.3% Other groups (2000).

Economy: Employment by occupation: 5.1% management, 6.5% professional, 18.7% services, 23.9% sales, 0.6% farming, 15.4% construction, 29.9% production (2000).

Income: Per capita income: $13,973 (2005); Median household income: $33,111 (2005); Average household income: $37,491 (2005); Percent of households with income of $100,000 or more: 2.9% (2005); Poverty rate: 17.8% (2000).

Education: Percent of population age 25 and over with: High school diploma (including GED) or higher: 59.9% (2005); Bachelor's degree or higher: 4.1% (2005); Master's degree or higher: 0.5% (2005).

Housing: Homeownership rate: 75.5% (2005); Median home value: $70,106 (2005); Median rent: $564 per month (2000); Median age of housing: 27 years (2000).

Transportation: Commute to work: 97.3% car, 0.4% public transportation, 0.0% walk, 1.6% work from home (2000); Travel time to work: 18.0% less than 15 minutes, 58.3% 15 to 30 minutes, 12.4% 30 to 45 minutes, 2.9% 45 to 60 minutes, 8.3% 60 minutes or more (2000)

LAWRENCE (township). Covers a land area of 37.470 square miles and a water area of 0.984 square miles. Located at 39.35° N. Lat.; 75.17° W. Long.

Population: 2,433 (1990); 2,721 (2000); 2,966 (2005); 3,187 (2010 projected); Race: 82.9% White, 8.6% Black, 0.3% Asian, 8.3% Hispanic of any race (2005); Density: 79.2 persons per square mile (2005); Average household size: 2.88 (2005); Median age: 36.8 (2005); Males per 100 females: 98.3 (2005); Marriage status: 23.7% never married, 58.8% now married, 7.1% widowed, 10.3% divorced (2000); Foreign born: 4.0% (2000); Ancestry (includes multiple ancestries): 22.8% Other groups, 19.0% Italian, 17.2% Irish, 16.0% German, 11.4% English (2000).

Economy: Single-family building permits issued: 7 (2005); Multi-family building permits issued: 0 (2005); Employment by occupation: 7.6% management, 13.7% professional, 13.9% services, 21.0% sales, 1.0% farming, 15.7% construction, 27.0% production (2000).

Income: Per capita income: $21,491 (2005); Median household income: $53,937 (2005); Average household income: $60,326 (2005); Percent of households with income of $100,000 or more: 10.7% (2005); Poverty rate: 8.9% (2000).

Education: Percent of population age 25 and over with: High school diploma (including GED) or higher: 75.6% (2005); Bachelor's degree or higher: 11.0% (2005); Master's degree or higher: 2.7% (2005).

Housing: Homeownership rate: 91.7% (2005); Median home value: $139,840 (2005); Median rent: $520 per month (2000); Median age of housing: 33 years (2000).

Transportation: Commute to work: 89.9% car, 0.6% public transportation, 3.1% walk, 2.1% work from home (2000); Travel time to work: 29.7% less than 15 minutes, 42.3% 15 to 30 minutes, 17.1% 30 to 45 minutes, 4.4% 45 to 60 minutes, 6.5% 60 minutes or more (2000)

LEESBURG (unincorporated postal area, zip code 08327). Covers a land area of 8.655 square miles and a water area of 0 square miles. Located at 39.25° N. Lat.; 74.97° W. Long. Elevation is 20 feet.

Population: 2,666 (2000); Race: 45.8% White, 44.3% Black, 0.0% Asian, 10.2% Hispanic of any race (2000); Density: 308.0 persons per square mile (2000); Age: 8.1% under 18, 6.3% over 64 (2000); Marriage status: 42.6% never married, 44.8% now married, 3.8% widowed, 8.8% divorced (2000); Foreign born: 1.6% (2000); Ancestry (includes multiple ancestries): 28.8% Other groups, 7.5% Italian, 7.1% English, 7.0% African, 6.9% Irish (2000).

Economy: Employment by occupation: 4.1% management, 16.2% professional, 24.6% services, 17.9% sales, 1.0% farming, 17.9% construction, 18.2% production (2000).

Income: Per capita income: $23,049 (2000); Median household income: $37,212 (2000); Poverty rate: 8.7% (2000).

Education: Percent of population age 25 and over with: High school diploma (including GED) or higher: 55.7% (2000); Bachelor's degree or higher: 4.3% (2000).
Housing: Homeownership rate: 86.8% (2000); Median home value: $76,400 (2000); Median rent: $525 per month (2000); Median age of housing: 48 years (2000).
Transportation: Commute to work: 99.2% car, 0.0% public transportation, 0.0% walk, 0.8% work from home (2000); Travel time to work: 34.0% less than 15 minutes, 32.9% 15 to 30 minutes, 20.2% 30 to 45 minutes, 8.0% 45 to 60 minutes, 5.0% 60 minutes or more (2000)

MAURICE RIVER (township).
Covers a land area of 93.410 square miles and a water area of 2.313 square miles. Located at 39.32° N. Lat.; 74.93° W. Long. Elevation is 5 feet.
History: Incorporated 1798.
Population: 6,648 (1990); 6,928 (2000); 7,174 (2005); 7,364 (2010 projected); Race: 56.7% White, 34.3% Black, 0.3% Asian, 9.1% Hispanic of any race (2005); Density: 76.8 persons per square mile (2005); Average household size: 5.05 (2005); Median age: 36.6 (2005); Males per 100 females: 272.7 (2005); Marriage status: 33.1% never married, 54.1% now married, 4.3% widowed, 8.4% divorced (2000); Foreign born: 3.1% (2000); Ancestry (includes multiple ancestries): 23.7% Other groups, 13.9% German, 10.4% Irish, 9.2% Italian, 8.7% English (2000).
Economy: Sparsely populated. Single-family building permits issued: 11 (2005); Multi-family building permits issued: 0 (2005); Employment by occupation: 7.9% management, 15.1% professional, 20.6% services, 19.6% sales, 0.7% farming, 13.6% construction, 22.6% production (2000).
Income: Per capita income: $18,762 (2005); Median household income: $48,475 (2005); Average household income: $58,610 (2005); Percent of households with income of $100,000 or more: 13.9% (2005); Poverty rate: 8.1% (2000).
Education: Percent of population age 25 and over with: High school diploma (including GED) or higher: 62.8% (2005); Bachelor's degree or higher: 4.7% (2005); Master's degree or higher: 1.1% (2005).
Housing: Homeownership rate: 88.1% (2005); Median home value: $121,711 (2005); Median rent: $507 per month (2000); Median age of housing: 41 years (2000).
Transportation: Commute to work: 96.1% car, 0.9% public transportation, 0.6% walk, 2.0% work from home (2000); Travel time to work: 28.2% less than 15 minutes, 42.0% 15 to 30 minutes, 15.8% 30 to 45 minutes, 7.1% 45 to 60 minutes, 6.8% 60 minutes or more (2000)

MILLVILLE (city).
Covers a land area of 42.350 square miles and a water area of 2.186 square miles. Located at 39.39° N. Lat.; 75.03° W. Long. Elevation is 37 feet.
History: Settled 1756, incorporated 1866.
Population: 25,992 (1990); 26,847 (2000); 27,364 (2005); 27,953 (2010 projected); Race: 72.3% White, 17.6% Black, 0.9% Asian, 13.0% Hispanic of any race (2005); Density: 646.1 persons per square mile (2005); Average household size: 2.67 (2005); Median age: 34.9 (2005); Males per 100 females: 90.4 (2005); Marriage status: 30.6% never married, 51.6% now married, 8.0% widowed, 9.9% divorced (2000); Foreign born: 2.2% (2000); Ancestry (includes multiple ancestries): 26.5% Other groups, 17.4% German, 15.7% Irish, 13.6% Italian, 13.0% English (2000).
Economy: In a poultry, fruit and vegetable farm area. The principal industries produce glass, tools, canned seafood, and machinery; aircraft engines are repaired in Millville. Unemployment rate: 7.7% (2005); Total civilian labor force: 14,303 (2005); Single-family building permits issued: 160 (2005); Multi-family building permits issued: 0 (2005); Employment by occupation: 8.5% management, 16.3% professional, 19.9% services, 24.5% sales, 0.2% farming, 10.8% construction, 19.8% production (2000).
Income: Per capita income: $20,727 (2005); Median household income: $43,964 (2005); Average household income: $54,851 (2005); Percent of households with income of $100,000 or more: 12.1% (2005); Poverty rate: 15.2% (2000).
Taxes: Total city taxes per capita: $441 (2004); City property taxes per capita: $408 (2004).
Education: Percent of population age 25 and over with: High school diploma (including GED) or higher: 74.1% (2005); Bachelor's degree or higher: 12.2% (2005); Master's degree or higher: 3.2% (2005).
School District(s)
Millville City (PK-12)
    2003-04 Enrollment: 6,226 . . . . (856) 327-7575

Housing: Homeownership rate: 64.2% (2005); Median home value: $127,012 (2005); Median rent: $502 per month (2000); Median age of housing: 38 years (2000).
Safety: Violent crime rate: 78.0 per 10,000 population; Property crime rate: 575.6 per 10,000 population (2004).
Transportation: Commute to work: 91.5% car, 2.8% public transportation, 2.2% walk, 2.1% work from home (2000); Travel time to work: 39.0% less than 15 minutes, 36.6% 15 to 30 minutes, 12.6% 30 to 45 minutes, 5.2% 45 to 60 minutes, 6.6% 60 minutes or more (2000)
Additional Information Contacts
City of Millville . . . . (856) 825-7000
    http://millvillev2.qscend.com
Millville Chamber of Commerce . . . . (856) 825-2600
    http://www.millville-nj.com

NEWPORT (unincorporated postal area, zip code 08345).
Covers a land area of 22.915 square miles and a water area of 0.919 square miles. Located at 39.28° N. Lat.; 75.15° W. Long. Elevation is 9 feet.
Population: 834 (2000); Race: 93.1% White, 4.5% Black, 0.1% Asian, 3.8% Hispanic of any race (2000); Density: 36.4 persons per square mile (2000); Age: 26.2% under 18, 16.9% over 64 (2000); Marriage status: 22.9% never married, 54.3% now married, 10.9% widowed, 11.8% divorced (2000); Foreign born: 0.6% (2000); Ancestry (includes multiple ancestries): 19.8% German, 15.8% English, 15.3% Irish, 11.7% Italian, 11.5% Other groups (2000).
Economy: Sand pits. Employment by occupation: 3.6% management, 13.7% professional, 16.4% services, 25.8% sales, 0.9% farming, 14.9% construction, 24.6% production (2000).
Income: Per capita income: $16,340 (2000); Median household income: $34,063 (2000); Poverty rate: 15.8% (2000).
Education: Percent of population age 25 and over with: High school diploma (including GED) or higher: 71.6% (2000); Bachelor's degree or higher: 6.8% (2000).
School District(s)
Downe Township (PK-08)
    2003-04 Enrollment: 274 . . . . (856) 447-3878
Housing: Homeownership rate: 91.4% (2000); Median home value: $74,900 (2000); Median rent: $517 per month (2000); Median age of housing: 37 years (2000).
Transportation: Commute to work: 90.8% car, 0.9% public transportation, 0.0% walk, 6.8% work from home (2000); Travel time to work: 22.1% less than 15 minutes, 38.9% 15 to 30 minutes, 22.8% 30 to 45 minutes, 0.7% 45 to 60 minutes, 15.5% 60 minutes or more (2000)

PORT ELIZABETH (unincorporated postal area, zip code 08348).
Covers a land area of 3.906 square miles and a water area of 0.129 square miles. Located at 39.31° N. Lat.; 74.98° W. Long. Elevation is 15 feet.
Population: 455 (2000); Race: 90.9% White, 0.0% Black, 1.3% Asian, 0.0% Hispanic of any race (2000); Density: 116.5 persons per square mile (2000); Age: 18.0% under 18, 12.4% over 64 (2000); Marriage status: 11.9% never married, 73.4% now married, 7.7% widowed, 7.1% divorced (2000); Foreign born: 5.4% (2000); Ancestry (includes multiple ancestries): 38.4% German, 19.9% English, 18.5% Italian, 11.0% Irish, 8.9% Scottish (2000).
Economy: Employment by occupation: 7.5% management, 21.6% professional, 24.9% services, 26.3% sales, 0.0% farming, 6.6% construction, 13.1% production (2000).
Income: Per capita income: $21,145 (2000); Median household income: $58,333 (2000); Poverty rate: 11.6% (2000).
Education: Percent of population age 25 and over with: High school diploma (including GED) or higher: 83.4% (2000); Bachelor's degree or higher: 14.6% (2000).
School District(s)
Maurice River Township (PK-08)
    2003-04 Enrollment: 438 . . . . (856) 825-7411
Housing: Homeownership rate: 90.0% (2000); Median home value: $85,300 (2000); Median rent: $281 per month (2000); Median age of housing: 60+ years (2000).
Transportation: Commute to work: 94.4% car, 0.0% public transportation, 1.5% walk, 4.1% work from home (2000); Travel time to work: 52.4% less than 15 minutes, 34.2% 15 to 30 minutes, 3.2% 30 to 45 minutes, 0.0% 45 to 60 minutes, 10.2% 60 minutes or more (2000)

PORT NORRIS (CDP). Covers a land area of 6.372 square miles and a water area of 0.501 square miles. Located at 39.24° N. Lat.; 75.03° W. Long. Elevation is 11 feet.
Population: 1,701 (1990); 1,507 (2000); 1,498 (2005); 1,535 (2010 projected); Race: 64.2% White, 31.1% Black, 0.3% Asian, 5.5% Hispanic of any race (2005); Density: 235.1 persons per square mile (2005); Average household size: 2.91 (2005); Median age: 37.0 (2005); Males per 100 females: 92.3 (2005); Marriage status: 29.5% never married, 54.1% now married, 8.2% widowed, 8.1% divorced (2000); Foreign born: 0.3% (2000); Ancestry (includes multiple ancestries): 35.3% Other groups, 11.6% Irish, 11.0% English, 10.1% German, 7.9% Italian (2000).
Economy: Oysters. Employment by occupation: 4.8% management, 18.7% professional, 19.5% services, 14.7% sales, 6.6% farming, 11.5% construction, 24.2% production (2000).
Income: Per capita income: $17,297 (2005); Median household income: $38,879 (2005); Average household income: $49,748 (2005); Percent of households with income of $100,000 or more: 8.7% (2005); Poverty rate: 16.1% (2000).
Education: Percent of population age 25 and over with: High school diploma (including GED) or higher: 65.6% (2005); Bachelor's degree or higher: 8.7% (2005); Master's degree or higher: 2.3% (2005).
School District(s)
Commercial Township (PK-08)
   2003-04 Enrollment: 763 . . . . (856) 785-0840
Housing: Homeownership rate: 84.1% (2005); Median home value: $106,250 (2005); Median rent: $411 per month (2000); Median age of housing: 60+ years (2000).
Transportation: Commute to work: 94.6% car, 0.0% public transportation, 0.0% walk, 2.0% work from home (2000); Travel time to work: 31.2% less than 15 minutes, 27.6% 15 to 30 minutes, 21.9% 30 to 45 minutes, 5.4% 45 to 60 minutes, 13.9% 60 minutes or more (2000)

ROSENHAYN (CDP). Covers a land area of 2.652 square miles and a water area of 0 square miles. Located at 39.47° N. Lat.; 75.13° W. Long. Elevation is 109 feet.
Population: 1,053 (1990); 1,099 (2000); 1,182 (2005); 1,263 (2010 projected); Race: 70.9% White, 16.7% Black, 0.2% Asian, 11.8% Hispanic of any race (2005); Density: 445.7 persons per square mile (2005); Average household size: 2.90 (2005); Median age: 36.4 (2005); Males per 100 females: 93.5 (2005); Marriage status: 40.3% never married, 45.8% now married, 5.6% widowed, 8.3% divorced (2000); Foreign born: 1.3% (2000); Ancestry (includes multiple ancestries): 32.0% Other groups, 19.3% Italian, 15.5% Irish, 10.9% German, 6.1% English (2000).
Economy: Employment by occupation: 5.6% management, 12.0% professional, 15.9% services, 24.7% sales, 1.0% farming, 16.3% construction, 24.5% production (2000).
Income: Per capita income: $17,387 (2005); Median household income: $42,019 (2005); Average household income: $49,588 (2005); Percent of households with income of $100,000 or more: 7.6% (2005); Poverty rate: 15.7% (2000).
Education: Percent of population age 25 and over with: High school diploma (including GED) or higher: 66.9% (2005); Bachelor's degree or higher: 6.5% (2005); Master's degree or higher: 1.2% (2005).
School District(s)
Deerfield Township (PK-08)
   2003-04 Enrollment: 352 . . . . (856) 451-6610
Housing: Homeownership rate: 80.1% (2005); Median home value: $137,903 (2005); Median rent: $585 per month (2000); Median age of housing: 37 years (2000).
Transportation: Commute to work: 93.8% car, 0.0% public transportation, 0.0% walk, 1.5% work from home (2000); Travel time to work: 30.4% less than 15 minutes, 49.0% 15 to 30 minutes, 10.1% 30 to 45 minutes, 6.1% 45 to 60 minutes, 4.2% 60 minutes or more (2000)

SEABROOK FARMS (CDP). Aka Seabrook. Covers a land area of 2.179 square miles and a water area of 0 square miles. Located at 39.50° N. Lat.; 75.22° W. Long.
Population: 1,466 (1990); 1,719 (2000); 1,726 (2005); 1,733 (2010 projected); Race: 26.9% White, 59.4% Black, 1.5% Asian, 16.3% Hispanic of any race (2005); Density: 792.0 persons per square mile (2005); Average household size: 2.90 (2005); Median age: 21.8 (2005); Males per 100 females: 86.4 (2005); Marriage status: 39.6% never married, 45.5% now married, 6.6% widowed, 8.3% divorced (2000); Foreign born: 6.3%

(2000); Ancestry (includes multiple ancestries): 62.7% Other groups, 6.6% Italian, 6.0% German, 4.1% English, 3.3% Polish (2000).
Economy: Employment by occupation: 1.8% management, 16.8% professional, 19.5% services, 25.3% sales, 2.8% farming, 5.8% construction, 28.1% production (2000).
Income: Per capita income: $12,768 (2005); Median household income: $19,496 (2005); Average household income: $37,038 (2005); Percent of households with income of $100,000 or more: 10.1% (2005); Poverty rate: 34.3% (2000).
Education: Percent of population age 25 and over with: High school diploma (including GED) or higher: 75.7% (2005); Bachelor's degree or higher: 12.1% (2005); Master's degree or higher: 1.8% (2005).
Housing: Homeownership rate: 29.6% (2005); Median home value: $139,394 (2005); Median rent: $409 per month (2000); Median age of housing: 48 years (2000).
Transportation: Commute to work: 90.2% car, 2.9% public transportation, 5.3% walk, 0.0% work from home (2000); Travel time to work: 52.9% less than 15 minutes, 21.8% 15 to 30 minutes, 16.8% 30 to 45 minutes, 0.0% 45 to 60 minutes, 8.5% 60 minutes or more (2000)

SHILOH (borough). Covers a land area of 1.195 square miles and a water area of 0 square miles. Located at 39.45° N. Lat.; 75.29° W. Long. Elevation is 118 feet.
Population: 408 (1990); 534 (2000); 567 (2005); 599 (2010 projected); Race: 94.7% White, 3.2% Black, 0.0% Asian, 3.7% Hispanic of any race (2005); Density: 474.3 persons per square mile (2005); Average household size: 2.71 (2005); Median age: 39.4 (2005); Males per 100 females: 87.7 (2005); Marriage status: 23.7% never married, 65.0% now married, 7.6% widowed, 3.8% divorced (2000); Foreign born: 1.5% (2000); Ancestry (includes multiple ancestries): 17.7% English, 17.5% German, 16.0% Irish, 15.3% United States or American, 13.4% Italian (2000).
Economy: In agricultural region. Single-family building permits issued: 5 (2005); Multi-family building permits issued: 0 (2005); Employment by occupation: 6.5% management, 19.1% professional, 9.7% services, 21.9% sales, 2.9% farming, 16.2% construction, 23.7% production (2000).
Income: Per capita income: $24,757 (2005); Median household income: $59,318 (2005); Average household income: $67,165 (2005); Percent of households with income of $100,000 or more: 18.2% (2005); Poverty rate: 5.8% (2000).
Education: Percent of population age 25 and over with: High school diploma (including GED) or higher: 77.2% (2005); Bachelor's degree or higher: 14.4% (2005); Master's degree or higher: 3.7% (2005).
School District(s)
Shiloh Borough (PK-08)
   2003-04 Enrollment: 72 . . . . (856) 451-5424
Housing: Homeownership rate: 80.9% (2005); Median home value: $146,186 (2005); Median rent: $408 per month (2000); Median age of housing: 60+ years (2000).
Transportation: Commute to work: 94.1% car, 0.0% public transportation, 5.9% walk, 0.0% work from home (2000); Travel time to work: 39.5% less than 15 minutes, 23.2% 15 to 30 minutes, 20.3% 30 to 45 minutes, 8.1% 45 to 60 minutes, 8.9% 60 minutes or more (2000)

STOW CREEK (township). Covers a land area of 18.450 square miles and a water area of 0.419 square miles. Located at 39.45° N. Lat.; 75.34° W. Long.
Population: 1,437 (1990); 1,429 (2000); 1,466 (2005); 1,502 (2010 projected); Race: 93.9% White, 2.9% Black, 0.1% Asian, 1.9% Hispanic of any race (2005); Density: 79.5 persons per square mile (2005); Average household size: 2.62 (2005); Median age: 41.3 (2005); Males per 100 females: 96.3 (2005); Marriage status: 23.9% never married, 64.8% now married, 5.5% widowed, 5.7% divorced (2000); Foreign born: 2.0% (2000); Ancestry (includes multiple ancestries): 21.6% German, 18.3% Irish, 18.0% English, 12.3% Italian, 9.3% Other groups (2000).
Economy: Single-family building permits issued: 4 (2005); Multi-family building permits issued: 0 (2005); Employment by occupation: 9.8% management, 22.6% professional, 13.2% services, 21.0% sales, 1.8% farming, 13.7% construction, 17.8% production (2000).
Income: Per capita income: $26,262 (2005); Median household income: $58,807 (2005); Average household income: $68,873 (2005); Percent of households with income of $100,000 or more: 18.8% (2005); Poverty rate: 6.7% (2000).
Education: Percent of population age 25 and over with: High school diploma (including GED) or higher: 83.2% (2005); Bachelor's degree or higher: 18.9% (2005); Master's degree or higher: 5.8% (2005).

Housing: Homeownership rate: 87.8% (2005); Median home value: $172,742 (2005); Median rent: $463 per month (2000); Median age of housing: 32 years (2000).
Transportation: Commute to work: 93.9% car, 0.0% public transportation, 2.9% walk, 2.0% work from home (2000); Travel time to work: 30.8% less than 15 minutes, 39.4% 15 to 30 minutes, 16.8% 30 to 45 minutes, 5.3% 45 to 60 minutes, 7.7% 60 minutes or more (2000)

UPPER DEERFIELD (township). Covers a land area of 31.104 square miles and a water area of 0.141 square miles. Located at 39.48° N. Lat.; 75.21° W. Long.
History: Incorporated 1922.
Population: 6,927 (1990); 7,556 (2000); 7,780 (2005); 8,025 (2010 projected); Race: 73.5% White, 18.5% Black, 2.8% Asian, 5.5% Hispanic of any race (2005); Density: 250.1 persons per square mile (2005); Average household size: 2.69 (2005); Median age: 36.8 (2005); Males per 100 females: 94.4 (2005); Marriage status: 25.7% never married, 61.2% now married, 7.4% widowed, 5.7% divorced (2000); Foreign born: 3.2% (2000); Ancestry (includes multiple ancestries): 26.1% Other groups, 13.7% German, 13.6% Italian, 13.0% Irish, 12.0% English (2000).
Economy: Single-family building permits issued: 41 (2005); Multi-family building permits issued: 19 (2005); Employment by occupation: 10.6% management, 19.0% professional, 15.3% services, 28.3% sales, 1.1% farming, 6.9% construction, 18.8% production (2000).
Income: Per capita income: $21,231 (2005); Median household income: $50,238 (2005); Average household income: $56,633 (2005); Percent of households with income of $100,000 or more: 13.2% (2005); Poverty rate: 13.7% (2000).
Education: Percent of population age 25 and over with: High school diploma (including GED) or higher: 81.0% (2005); Bachelor's degree or higher: 15.4% (2005); Master's degree or higher: 4.3% (2005).
Housing: Homeownership rate: 76.1% (2005); Median home value: $173,535 (2005); Median rent: $463 per month (2000); Median age of housing: 35 years (2000).
Transportation: Commute to work: 95.1% car, 0.5% public transportation, 0.8% walk, 2.6% work from home (2000); Travel time to work: 45.6% less than 15 minutes, 33.7% 15 to 30 minutes, 9.4% 30 to 45 minutes, 5.3% 45 to 60 minutes, 6.1% 60 minutes or more (2000)

VINELAND (city). Covers a land area of 68.690 square miles and a water area of 0.285 square miles. Located at 39.48° N. Lat.; 75.01° W. Long. Elevation is 106 feet.
History: Charles K. Landis, who arrived in Vineland in 1861, spent 20 years building the colony. He drew farm settlers largely from the Middle Atlantic states and induced many Italian farmers to immigrate to his farms, which he named Vineland. Grapes were grown in large quantities during the early years.
Population: 54,780 (1990); 56,271 (2000); 58,372 (2005); 60,593 (2010 projected); Race: 65.2% White, 14.4% Black, 1.3% Asian, 33.4% Hispanic of any race (2005); Density: 849.8 persons per square mile (2005); Average household size: 2.79 (2005); Median age: 37.1 (2005); Males per 100 females: 92.8 (2005); Marriage status: 28.4% never married, 53.7% now married, 8.3% widowed, 9.7% divorced (2000); Foreign born: 8.1% (2000); Ancestry (includes multiple ancestries): 37.5% Other groups, 22.8% Italian, 9.6% German, 8.4% Irish, 5.9% English (2000).
Economy: Unemployment rate: 5.8% (2005); Total civilian labor force: 29,359 (2005); Single-family building permits issued: 125 (2005); Multi-family building permits issued: 14 (2005); Employment by occupation: 8.5% management, 17.7% professional, 18.0% services, 24.5% sales, 2.0% farming, 9.7% construction, 19.6% production (2000).
Income: Per capita income: $21,736 (2005); Median household income: $45,425 (2005); Average household income: $59,370 (2005); Percent of households with income of $100,000 or more: 13.9% (2005); Poverty rate: 13.8% (2000).
Taxes: Total city taxes per capita: $369 (2004); City property taxes per capita: $345 (2004).
Education: Percent of population age 25 and over with: High school diploma (including GED) or higher: 67.5% (2005); Bachelor's degree or higher: 14.2% (2005); Master's degree or higher: 4.7% (2005).

School District(s)
Vineland City (PK-12)
    2003-04 Enrollment: 10,316 . . . . (856) 794-6700

Two-year College(s)
Cumberland County College (Public)
    Fall 2004 Enrollment: 3,174 . . . . (856) 691-8600
    2005-06 Tuition: In-state $5,370; Out-of-state $9,900
Harrison Career Institute-Vineland (Private, For-profit)
    Fall 2004 Enrollment: 183 . . . . (856) 696-0500
Housing: Homeownership rate: 66.5% (2005); Median home value: $137,002 (2005); Median rent: $535 per month (2000); Median age of housing: 35 years (2000).
Hospitals: South Jersey Hospital - Newcomb (235 beds)
Safety: Violent crime rate: 78.1 per 10,000 population; Property crime rate: 508.4 per 10,000 population (2004).
Newspapers: Daily Journal (Circulation 17,968); Daily Journal This Week (General - Circulation 18,000); The Bridgeton Journal (General - Circulation 15,270)
Transportation: Commute to work: 92.2% car, 2.5% public transportation, 1.9% walk, 1.9% work from home (2000); Travel time to work: 43.8% less than 15 minutes, 29.8% 15 to 30 minutes, 10.5% 30 to 45 minutes, 7.7% 45 to 60 minutes, 8.1% 60 minutes or more (2000)
Additional Information Contacts
City of Vineland . . . . (856) 794-4060
    http://www.vinelandcity.org
Vineland Chamber of Commerce . . . . (856) 691-7400
    http://chamber.vineland.org/index

Essex County

Located in northeastern New Jersey; bounded on the west, north, and east by the Passaic River, and on the southeast by Newark Bay. Covers a land area of 126.27 square miles, a water area of 3.29 square miles, and is located in the Eastern Time Zone. The county government was organized in 1683. County seat is Newark.

Essex County is part of the New York-Northern New Jersey-Long Island, NY-NJ-PA Metropolitan Statistical Area. The entire metro area includes: Edison, NJ Metropolitan Division (Middlesex County, NJ; Monmouth County, NJ; Ocean County, NJ; Somerset County, NJ); Nassau-Suffolk, NY Metropolitan Division (Nassau County, NY; Suffolk County, NY; New York-White Plains-Wayne, NY-NJ Metropolitan Division (Bergen County, NJ; Hudson County, NJ; Passaic County, NJ; Bronx County, NY; Kings County, NY; New York County, NY; Putnam County, NY; Queens County, NY; Richmond County, NY; Rockland County, NY; Westchester County, NY); Newark-Union, NJ-PA Metropolitan Division (Essex County, NJ; Hunterdon County, NJ; Morris County, NJ; Sussex County, NJ; Union County, NJ; Pike County, PA)

Weather Station: Canoe Brook   Elevation: 177 feet

	Jan	Feb	Mar	Apr	May	Jun	Jul	Aug	Sep	Oct	Nov	Dec
High	38	41	50	61	72	80	86	84	77	65	54	43
Low	18	20	29	38	48	57	62	61	53	40	33	24
Precip	4.1	3.1	4.2	4.2	4.7	4.4	4.6	4.8	5.0	4.3	4.5	3.8
Snow	8.7	7.8	4.5	0.8	0.0	0.0	0.0	0.0	0.0	tr	0.6	3.2

High and Low temperatures in degrees Fahrenheit; Precipitation and Snow in inches

Weather Station: Essex Fells Serv Bldg   Elevation: 347 feet

	Jan	Feb	Mar	Apr	May	Jun	Jul	Aug	Sep	Oct	Nov	Dec
High	37	40	49	61	72	79	85	83	76	64	53	42
Low	19	21	28	38	48	57	62	60	52	41	33	24
Precip	4.1	3.2	4.1	4.6	4.9	4.5	4.9	4.4	4.7	4.1	4.4	4.0
Snow	5.6	4.1	3.6	0.7	0.0	0.0	0.0	0.0	0.0	tr	0.3	2.4

High and Low temperatures in degrees Fahrenheit; Precipitation and Snow in inches

Weather Station: Newark Int'l Airport   Elevation: 9 feet

	Jan	Feb	Mar	Apr	May	Jun	Jul	Aug	Sep	Oct	Nov	Dec
High	39	42	51	62	73	81	87	85	77	66	55	44
Low	24	26	34	44	54	64	69	68	60	49	39	30
Precip	3.9	3.0	4.2	3.9	4.4	3.4	4.6	4.0	3.9	3.2	3.9	3.5
Snow	8.4	8.2	4.4	0.8	tr	0.0	0.0	0.0	tr	tr	0.6	2.5

High and Low temperatures in degrees Fahrenheit; Precipitation and Snow in inches

Population: 778,062 (1990); 793,633 (2000); 798,103 (2005); 802,490 (2010 projected); Race: 43.1% White, 41.4% Black, 3.8% Asian, 17.3% Hispanic of any race (2005); Density: 6,320.8 persons per square mile (2005); Average household size: 2.79 (2005); Median age: 35.7 (2005); Males per 100 females: 91.7 (2005).

Religion: Five largest groups: 35.3% Catholic Church, 9.6% Jewish Estimate, 2.7% Muslim Estimate, 2.1% American Baptist Churches in the USA, 1.3% Presbyterian Church (U.S.A.) (2000).

Economy: Unemployment rate: 5.6% (2005); Total civilian labor force: 366,324 (2005); Leading industries: 17.2% health care and social assistance; 9.7% retail trade; 8.9% manufacturing (2004); Farms: 15 totaling 153 acres (2002); Companies that employ 500 or more persons: 137 (2004); Companies that employ 100 to 499 persons: 844 (2004); Companies that employ less than 100 persons: 39,529 (2004); Black-owned businesses: 9,100 (2002); Hispanic-owned businesses: 4,708 (2002); Asian-owned businesses: 4,017 (2002); Women-owned businesses: 17,162 (2002); Retail sales per capita: $9,928 (2006). Single-family building permits issued: 718 (2005); Multi-family building permits issued: 2,410 (2005).

Income: Per capita income: $28,115 (2005); Median household income: $50,898 (2005); Average household income: $77,643 (2005); Percent of households with income of $100,000 or more: 23.3% (2005); Poverty rate: 14.4% (2003); Bankruptcy rate: 6.96% (2005).

Taxes: Total county taxes per capita: $384 (2004); County property taxes per capita: $384 (2004).

Education: Percent of population age 25 and over with: High school diploma (including GED) or higher: 75.1% (2005); Bachelor's degree or higher: 26.8% (2005); Master's degree or higher: 10.6% (2005).

Housing: Homeownership rate: 45.5% (2005); Median home value: $297,664 (2005); Median rent: $611 per month (2000); Median age of housing: 49 years (2000).

Health: Birth rate: 160.6 per 10,000 population (2004); Death rate: 86.6 per 10,000 population (2004); Age-adjusted cancer mortality rate: 208.7 deaths per 100,000 population (2002); Air Quality Index: 66.7% good, 31.4% moderate, 1.9% unhealthy for sensitive individuals, 0.0% unhealthy (percent of days in 2005); Number of physicians: 43.4 per 10,000 population (2004); Hospital beds: 57.0 per 10,000 population (2003); Hospital admissions: 1,901.1 per 10,000 population (2003).

Elections: 2004 Presidential election results: 28.8% Bush, 70.4% Kerry, 0.4% Nader, 0.1% Badnarik

National and State Parks: Edison National Historic Site

Additional Information Contacts

Essex County Government . . . . (973) 621-4492
    http://www.co.essex.nj.us
Bloomfield Township . . . . (973) 680-4006
    http://www.bloomfieldtwpnj.com
Borough of Caldwell. . . . . (973) 226-6100
    http://www.caldwell-nj.com
Borough of Roseland . . . . (973) 226-8080
    http://www.roselandnj.org
City of East Orange . . . . (973) 266-5310
    http://www.eastorange-nj.org
City of Newark . . . . (973) 733-6029
    http://www.ci.newark.nj.us
East Orange Chamber of Commerce . . . . (973) 674-0900
    http://www.orangechamber.biz
Irvington Chamber of Commerce. . . . . (973) 372-4100
    http://www.irvington-nj.com
Livingston Chamber of Commerce . . . . (973) 992-4343
    http://www.livingstonchambernj.com
Maplewood Chamber of Commerce . . . . (973) 761-4333
    http://www.maplewoodchamber.org
Millburn Township . . . . (973) 564-7072
    http://www.twp.millburn.nj.us/muni.htm
Millburn-Short Hills Chamber of Commerce . . . . (973) 379-1198
    http://www.millburn.com/chamber/index.html
Montclair Township . . . . (973) 744-1400
    http://www.montclairnjusa.org
Newark Chamber of Commerce . . . . (973) 522-0099
    http://www.rbp.org
North Essex Chamber of Commerce. . . . . (973) 226-5500
    http://www.northessexchamber.com
North Essex Chamber of Commerce. . . . . (973) 226-5500
    http://www.northessexchamber.com
Nutley Chamber of Commerce . . . . (973) 667-5300
    http://www.nutleychamber.com
Orange Chamber of Commerce. . . . . (973) 676-8725
    http://www.orangechamber.biz
South Orange Chamber of Commerce . . . . (973) 762-4333
    http://www.southorangechamber.com

South Orange Village Township . . . . (973) 378-7805
    http://www.southorange.org
Suburban Essex Chamber of Commerce . . . . (973) 748-2000
    http://www.suburbanessexchamber.com
Tri-County Chamber of Commerce . . . . (973) 831-7788
    http://www.tricounty.org
Verona Chamber of Commerce. . . . . (973) 226-5500
    http://www.veronachamber.org
Verona Township. . . . . (973) 239-3220
    http://www.veronanj.org
West Caldwell Township . . . . (973) 226-2300
    http://www.westcaldwell.com
West Essex Chamber of Commerce . . . . (973) 226-5500
    http://www.wecc.org
West Orange Chamber of Commerce . . . . (973) 731-0360
    http://www.westorangechamber.com
West Orange Township. . . . . (973) 325-4029
    http://www.westorange.org

Essex County Communities

BELLEVILLE (township). Aka Belleville CDP. Covers a land area of 3.344 square miles and a water area of 0.069 square miles. Located at 40.79° N. Lat.; 74.16° W. Long. Elevation is 140 feet.

History: Named for the French translation of "beautiful city". John Stevens's boat, built here in 1798 for the run to N.Y., contained one of the country's 1st steam engines. Settled c.1680, set off from Newark 1839. Incorporated 1910.

Population: 34,095 (1990); 35,928 (2000); 35,367 (2005); 34,854 (2010 projected); Race: 64.9% White, 5.9% Black, 12.5% Asian, 30.3% Hispanic of any race (2005); Density: 10,576.5 persons per square mile (2005); Average household size: 2.64 (2005); Median age: 37.9 (2005); Males per 100 females: 93.9 (2005); Marriage status: 32.0% never married, 51.9% now married, 7.8% widowed, 8.2% divorced (2000); Foreign born: 26.8% (2000); Ancestry (includes multiple ancestries): 37.1% Other groups, 30.9% Italian, 9.4% Irish, 6.9% German, 4.5% Polish (2000).

Economy: Manufacturing includes electrical equipment, optical equipment, gloves and precision instruments. Unemployment rate: 5.3% (2005); Total civilian labor force: 18,337 (2005); Single-family building permits issued: 20 (2005); Multi-family building permits issued: 34 (2005); Employment by occupation: 11.9% management, 18.8% professional, 15.0% services, 31.7% sales, 0.0% farming, 8.1% construction, 14.4% production (2000).

Income: Per capita income: $24,884 (2005); Median household income: $54,998 (2005); Average household income: $65,308 (2005); Percent of households with income of $100,000 or more: 17.3% (2005); Poverty rate: 8.2% (2000).

Taxes: Total city taxes per capita: $796 (2004); City property taxes per capita: $779 (2004).

Education: Percent of population age 25 and over with: High school diploma (including GED) or higher: 78.2% (2005); Bachelor's degree or higher: 21.7% (2005); Master's degree or higher: 5.9% (2005).

School District(s)

Belleville Town (PK-12)
    2003-04 Enrollment: 4,729 . . . . (973) 450-3447

Housing: Homeownership rate: 50.8% (2005); Median home value: $236,281 (2005); Median rent: $697 per month (2000); Median age of housing: 51 years (2000).

Hospitals: Clara Maass Medical Center (575 beds)

Safety: Violent crime rate: 28.2 per 10,000 population; Property crime rate: 235.4 per 10,000 population (2004).

Transportation: Commute to work: 88.7% car, 7.3% public transportation, 2.6% walk, 0.8% work from home (2000); Travel time to work: 21.8% less than 15 minutes, 35.9% 15 to 30 minutes, 25.5% 30 to 45 minutes, 8.3% 45 to 60 minutes, 8.6% 60 minutes or more (2000)

Additional Information Contacts

Tri-County Chamber of Commerce . . . . (973) 831-7788
    http://www.tricounty.org

BLOOMFIELD (township). Aka Bloomfield CDP. Covers a land area of 5.321 square miles and a water area of 0.007 square miles. Located at 40.80° N. Lat.; 74.18° W. Long. Elevation is 131 feet.

History: Named for the Revolutionary War general Joseph Bloomfield, who later became governor of New Jersey, the town was a supply point for both sides during the war. In the 19th century it was a trade and transportation hub. The Presbyterian church here dates from 1796. Settled c.1660. Incorporated as a town 1812, as a city 1900.

Population: 45,142 (1990); 47,683 (2000); 46,821 (2005); 46,031 (2010 projected); Race: 65.1% White, 13.9% Black, 9.0% Asian, 18.8% Hispanic of any race (2005); Density: 8,799.5 persons per square mile (2005); Average household size: 2.52 (2005); Median age: 38.6 (2005); Males per 100 females: 91.7 (2005); Marriage status: 32.1% never married, 53.0% now married, 7.3% widowed, 7.6% divorced (2000); Foreign born: 22.8% (2000); Ancestry (includes multiple ancestries): 30.2% Other groups, 26.4% Italian, 13.9% Irish, 10.2% German, 7.0% Polish (2000).

Economy: Manufacturing includes electrical equipment, adhesives, paints, plastics, rubber products and semiconductor gaskets. Unemployment rate: 4.3% (2005); Total civilian labor force: 26,086 (2005); Single-family building permits issued: 1 (2005); Multi-family building permits issued: 0 (2005); Employment by occupation: 14.0% management, 24.8% professional, 12.0% services, 30.4% sales, 0.1% farming, 6.6% construction, 12.1% production (2000).

Income: Per capita income: $30,682 (2005); Median household income: $63,131 (2005); Average household income: $76,646 (2005); Percent of households with income of $100,000 or more: 24.3% (2005); Poverty rate: 5.9% (2000).

Taxes: Total city taxes per capita: $710 (2004); City property taxes per capita: $700 (2004).

Education: Percent of population age 25 and over with: High school diploma (including GED) or higher: 83.4% (2005); Bachelor's degree or higher: 31.6% (2005); Master's degree or higher: 9.8% (2005).

School District(s)

Bloomfield Township (PK-12)
    2003-04 Enrollment: 6,354 . . . . (973) 680-8555
Essex County Voc-Tech (09-12)
    2003-04 Enrollment: 2,368 . . . . (973) 243-2926
Passaic County Ed Serv Comm (UG-UG)
    2003-04 Enrollment: 451 . . . . (973) 614-8585

Four-year College(s)

Bloomfield College (Private, Not-for-profit, Presbyterian Church (USA))
    Fall 2004 Enrollment: 2,166. . . . . (973) 748-9000
    2005-06 Tuition: In-state $14,850; Out-of-state $14,850

Two-year College(s)

Concorde School of Hair Design-Bloomfield (Private, For-profit)
    Fall 2004 Enrollment: 194 . . . . (973) 680-0099

Housing: Homeownership rate: 53.1% (2005); Median home value: $259,855 (2005); Median rent: $718 per month (2000); Median age of housing: 54 years (2000).

Safety: Violent crime rate: 38.7 per 10,000 population; Property crime rate: 403.0 per 10,000 population (2004).

Newspapers: Belleville Post (General - Circulation 3,212); Nutley Journal (General - Circulation 5,223); The Glen Ridge Paper (General - Circulation 2,000); The Independent Press of Bloomfield (General - Circulation 7,600)

Transportation: Commute to work: 83.1% car, 11.8% public transportation, 2.6% walk, 1.9% work from home (2000); Travel time to work: 21.2% less than 15 minutes, 34.4% 15 to 30 minutes, 24.7% 30 to 45 minutes, 8.2% 45 to 60 minutes, 11.5% 60 minutes or more (2000)

Additional Information Contacts
Bloomfield Township . . . . (973) 680-4006
    http://www.bloomfieldtwpnj.com
Suburban Essex Chamber of Commerce . . . . (973) 748-2000
    http://www.suburbanessexchamber.com

CALDWELL (borough). Covers a land area of 1.186 square miles and a water area of <.001 square miles. Located at 40.83° N. Lat.; 74.27° W. Long. Elevation is 411 feet.

Population: 7,549 (1990); 7,584 (2000); 7,616 (2005); 7,640 (2010 projected); Race: 90.6% White, 2.4% Black, 4.2% Asian, 5.5% Hispanic of any race (2005); Density: 6,423.3 persons per square mile (2005); Average household size: 2.26 (2005); Median age: 40.6 (2005); Males per 100 females: 83.0 (2005); Marriage status: 31.6% never married, 49.7% now married, 9.4% widowed, 9.4% divorced (2000); Foreign born: 12.2% (2000); Ancestry (includes multiple ancestries): 26.3% Italian, 23.1% Irish, 13.8% German, 12.3% Other groups, 11.7% English (2000).

Economy: Single-family building permits issued: 0 (2005); Multi-family building permits issued: 0 (2005); Employment by occupation: 21.6% management, 30.8% professional, 8.5% services, 29.8% sales, 0.0% farming, 4.7% construction, 4.6% production (2000).

Income: Per capita income: $42,588 (2005); Median household income: $72,942 (2005); Average household income: $94,983 (2005); Percent of

households with income of $100,000 or more: 34.1% (2005); Poverty rate: 4.8% (2000).

Education: Percent of population age 25 and over with: High school diploma (including GED) or higher: 90.9% (2005); Bachelor's degree or higher: 44.0% (2005); Master's degree or higher: 18.0% (2005).

School District(s)

Caldwell-West Caldwell (PK-12)
    2003-04 Enrollment: 2,627 . . . . (973) 228-6979

Four-year College(s)

Caldwell College (Private, Not-for-profit, Roman Catholic)
    Fall 2004 Enrollment: 2,172. . . . . (973) 618-3000
    2005-06 Tuition: In-state $18,700; Out-of-state $18,700

Housing: Homeownership rate: 49.1% (2005); Median home value: $350,463 (2005); Median rent: $864 per month (2000); Median age of housing: 46 years (2000).

Safety: Violent crime rate: 13.0 per 10,000 population; Property crime rate: 92.5 per 10,000 population (2004).

Newspapers: The Progress (General - Circulation 8,600)

Transportation: Commute to work: 87.2% car, 4.6% public transportation, 4.7% walk, 3.1% work from home (2000); Travel time to work: 26.1% less than 15 minutes, 34.7% 15 to 30 minutes, 23.7% 30 to 45 minutes, 5.3% 45 to 60 minutes, 10.3% 60 minutes or more (2000)

Additional Information Contacts
Borough of Caldwell. . . . . (973) 226-6100
    http://www.caldwell-nj.com
North Essex Chamber of Commerce . . . . (973) 226-5500
    http://www.northessexchamber.com

CEDAR GROVE (township). Aka Cedar Grove CDP. Covers a land area of 4.222 square miles and a water area of 0.131 square miles. Located at 40.85° N. Lat.; 74.22° W. Long. Elevation is 300 feet.

Population: 12,053 (1990); 12,300 (2000); 12,240 (2005); 12,140 (2010 projected); Race: 90.2% White, 3.1% Black, 5.1% Asian, 3.6% Hispanic of any race (2005); Density: 2,898.9 persons per square mile (2005); Average household size: 2.76 (2005); Median age: 44.9 (2005); Males per 100 females: 87.6 (2005); Marriage status: 23.6% never married, 59.4% now married, 10.2% widowed, 6.8% divorced (2000); Foreign born: 11.0% (2000); Ancestry (includes multiple ancestries): 34.8% Italian, 21.7% Irish, 12.3% Other groups, 12.1% German, 6.7% Polish (2000).

Economy: Manufacturing: gauges, brushes. Largely residential. Overbrook state mental hospital here. Single-family building permits issued: 45 (2005); Multi-family building permits issued: 98 (2005); Employment by occupation: 21.9% management, 29.8% professional, 9.0% services, 29.8% sales, 0.0% farming, 3.7% construction, 5.8% production (2000).

Income: Per capita income: $43,481 (2005); Median household income: $93,049 (2005); Average household income: $118,290 (2005); Percent of households with income of $100,000 or more: 46.0% (2005); Poverty rate: 2.0% (2000).

Education: Percent of population age 25 and over with: High school diploma (including GED) or higher: 88.3% (2005); Bachelor's degree or higher: 41.6% (2005); Master's degree or higher: 14.1% (2005).

School District(s)

Cedar Grove Township (PK-12)
    2003-04 Enrollment: 1,511 . . . . (973) 239-1550
Essex County Ed Serv Comm (UG-UG)
    2003-04 Enrollment: 270 . . . . (973) 239-1511

Housing: Homeownership rate: 79.3% (2005); Median home value: $375,922 (2005); Median rent: $956 per month (2000); Median age of housing: 43 years (2000).

Hospitals: Essex County Hospital Center (340 beds)

Safety: Violent crime rate: 8.9 per 10,000 population; Property crime rate: 145.7 per 10,000 population (2004).

Newspapers: Verona-Cedar Grove Times (General - Circulation 5,118)

Transportation: Commute to work: 88.0% car, 7.4% public transportation, 0.9% walk, 3.7% work from home (2000); Travel time to work: 26.0% less than 15 minutes, 34.7% 15 to 30 minutes, 22.3% 30 to 45 minutes, 7.6% 45 to 60 minutes, 9.5% 60 minutes or more (2000)

Additional Information Contacts
Tri-County Chamber of Commerce . . . . (973) 831-7788
    http://www.tricounty.org

EAST ORANGE (city). Covers a land area of 3.928 square miles and a water area of 0 square miles. Located at 40.76° N. Lat.; 74.21° W. Long. Elevation is 166 feet.

Population: 73,379 (1990); 69,824 (2000); 68,781 (2005); 67,883 (2010 projected); Race: 3.7% White, 89.0% Black, 0.4% Asian, 5.5% Hispanic of any race (2005); Density: 17,511.1 persons per square mile (2005); Average household size: 2.68 (2005); Median age: 34.1 (2005); Males per 100 females: 83.2 (2005); Marriage status: 43.9% never married, 37.6% now married, 8.9% widowed, 9.7% divorced (2000); Foreign born: 18.3% (2000); Ancestry (includes multiple ancestries): 61.8% Other groups, 4.8% Jamaican, 4.1% Haitian, 2.3% African, 2.1% Guyanese (2000).
Economy: Unemployment rate: 7.4% (2005); Total civilian labor force: 29,971 (2005); Single-family building permits issued: 15 (2005); Multi-family building permits issued: 53 (2005); Employment by occupation: 7.6% management, 17.0% professional, 22.2% services, 32.2% sales, 0.0% farming, 5.9% construction, 15.1% production (2000).
Income: Per capita income: $18,697 (2005); Median household income: $37,004 (2005); Average household income: $49,346 (2005); Percent of households with income of $100,000 or more: 10.8% (2005); Poverty rate: 19.2% (2000).
Taxes: Total city taxes per capita: $892 (2004); City property taxes per capita: $874 (2004).
Education: Percent of population age 25 and over with: High school diploma (including GED) or higher: 72.7% (2005); Bachelor's degree or higher: 15.3% (2005); Master's degree or higher: 4.6% (2005).
School District(s)
Agency - East Orange Community CS (KG-04)
    2003-04 Enrollment: 485 . . . . (973) 676-1199
East Orange (PK-12)
    2003-04 Enrollment: 12,403 . . . . (973) 266-5760
Housing: Homeownership rate: 27.0% (2005); Median home value: $195,345 (2005); Median rent: $600 per month (2000); Median age of housing: 49 years (2000).
Hospitals: East Orange General Hospital (211 beds); Veterans Affairs New Jersey Health Care System
Safety: Violent crime rate: 159.8 per 10,000 population; Property crime rate: 605.8 per 10,000 population (2004).
Transportation: Commute to work: 65.3% car, 27.8% public transportation, 3.6% walk, 1.9% work from home (2000); Travel time to work: 15.4% less than 15 minutes, 33.8% 15 to 30 minutes, 23.3% 30 to 45 minutes, 12.1% 45 to 60 minutes, 15.6% 60 minutes or more (2000)
Additional Information Contacts
City of East Orange . . . . (973) 266-5310
    http://www.eastorange-nj.org
East Orange Chamber of Commerce . . . . (973) 674-0900
    http://www.orangechamber.biz

ESSEX FELLS (borough). Covers a land area of 1.409 square miles and a water area of 0.005 square miles. Located at 40.82° N. Lat.; 74.28° W. Long. Elevation is 393 feet.
History: Incorporated 1902.
Population: 2,139 (1990); 2,162 (2000); 2,151 (2005); 2,148 (2010 projected); Race: 97.2% White, 0.3% Black, 1.0% Asian, 1.4% Hispanic of any race (2005); Density: 1,526.2 persons per square mile (2005); Average household size: 2.98 (2005); Median age: 40.1 (2005); Males per 100 females: 96.8 (2005); Marriage status: 17.2% never married, 72.6% now married, 5.4% widowed, 4.7% divorced (2000); Foreign born: 7.3% (2000); Ancestry (includes multiple ancestries): 31.9% Irish, 19.4% Italian, 16.1% German, 13.3% English, 6.8% Polish (2000).
Economy: Residential. Single-family building permits issued: 1 (2005); Multi-family building permits issued: 0 (2005); Employment by occupation: 30.1% management, 35.3% professional, 4.6% services, 26.2% sales, 0.0% farming, 2.4% construction, 1.4% production (2000).
Income: Per capita income: $79,305 (2005); Median household income: $179,518 (2005); Average household income: $236,267 (2005); Percent of households with income of $100,000 or more: 73.5% (2005); Poverty rate: 1.1% (2000).
Education: Percent of population age 25 and over with: High school diploma (including GED) or higher: 97.1% (2005); Bachelor's degree or higher: 72.4% (2005); Master's degree or higher: 31.9% (2005).
School District(s)
Essex Fells Borough (PK-06)
    2003-04 Enrollment: 257 . . . . (973) 226-0505
Housing: Homeownership rate: 96.1% (2005); Median home value: $943,609 (2005); Median rent: $1,313 per month (2000); Median age of housing: 54 years (2000).
Safety: Violent crime rate: 4.6 per 10,000 population; Property crime rate: 64.5 per 10,000 population (2004).

Transportation: Commute to work: 82.7% car, 9.0% public transportation, 1.2% walk, 6.7% work from home (2000); Travel time to work: 25.3% less than 15 minutes, 32.6% 15 to 30 minutes, 19.5% 30 to 45 minutes, 7.4% 45 to 60 minutes, 15.2% 60 minutes or more (2000)
Additional Information Contacts
North Essex Chamber of Commerce . . . . (973) 226-5500
    http://www.northessexchamber.com

FAIRFIELD (township). Aka Fairfield CDP. Covers a land area of 10.452 square miles and a water area of 0.001 square miles. Located at 40.87° N. Lat.; 74.29° W. Long. Elevation is 180 feet.
History: Incorporated 1798.
Population: 7,615 (1990); 7,063 (2000); 7,553 (2005); 8,009 (2010 projected); Race: 95.8% White, 0.6% Black, 2.5% Asian, 3.8% Hispanic of any race (2005); Density: 722.7 persons per square mile (2005); Average household size: 3.01 (2005); Median age: 41.9 (2005); Males per 100 females: 95.7 (2005); Marriage status: 21.9% never married, 67.4% now married, 7.3% widowed, 3.4% divorced (2000); Foreign born: 12.6% (2000); Ancestry (includes multiple ancestries): 45.8% Italian, 14.4% Irish, 13.8% German, 8.1% Other groups, 7.3% Polish (2000).
Economy: Manufacturing: fishing tackle, textiles, sheet metal products, packaging, apparel. Single-family building permits issued: 26 (2005); Multi-family building permits issued: 0 (2005); Employment by occupation: 17.8% management, 24.5% professional, 9.6% services, 32.0% sales, 0.0% farming, 8.6% construction, 7.6% production (2000).
Income: Per capita income: $39,207 (2005); Median household income: $98,371 (2005); Average household income: $117,717 (2005); Percent of households with income of $100,000 or more: 49.0% (2005); Poverty rate: 2.8% (2000).
Education: Percent of population age 25 and over with: High school diploma (including GED) or higher: 86.9% (2005); Bachelor's degree or higher: 34.9% (2005); Master's degree or higher: 11.6% (2005).
School District(s)
Fairfield Township (PK-06)
    2003-04 Enrollment: 759 . . . . (973) 227-5586
Two-year College(s)
Stenotech Career Institute (Private, For-profit)
    Fall 2004 Enrollment: 81 . . . . (973) 882-4875
The Institute for Health Education (Private, For-profit)
    Fall 2004 Enrollment: 16 . . . . (973) 808-1666
Housing: Homeownership rate: 93.4% (2005); Median home value: $440,665 (2005); Median rent: $744 per month (2000); Median age of housing: 36 years (2000).
Safety: Violent crime rate: 25.4 per 10,000 population; Property crime rate: 436.3 per 10,000 population (2004).
Newspapers: Suburban Essex Magazine (General - Circulation 55,000); Vicinity Magazine (General - Circulation 33,000)
Transportation: Commute to work: 92.8% car, 3.1% public transportation, 1.0% walk, 2.5% work from home (2000); Travel time to work: 31.9% less than 15 minutes, 31.7% 15 to 30 minutes, 20.6% 30 to 45 minutes, 7.6% 45 to 60 minutes, 8.2% 60 minutes or more (2000)

GLEN RIDGE (borough). Covers a land area of 1.277 square miles and a water area of 0 square miles. Located at 40.80° N. Lat.; 74.20° W. Long. Elevation is 187 feet.
Population: 7,076 (1990); 7,271 (2000); 7,098 (2005); 6,928 (2010 projected); Race: 88.8% White, 5.4% Black, 3.1% Asian, 4.0% Hispanic of any race (2005); Density: 5,559.5 persons per square mile (2005); Average household size: 2.98 (2005); Median age: 38.2 (2005); Males per 100 females: 95.4 (2005); Marriage status: 19.2% never married, 68.0% now married, 5.3% widowed, 7.5% divorced (2000); Foreign born: 9.0% (2000); Ancestry (includes multiple ancestries): 27.3% Irish, 19.0% German, 18.8% Italian, 12.4% English, 12.3% Other groups (2000).
Economy: Single-family building permits issued: 0 (2005); Multi-family building permits issued: 0 (2005); Employment by occupation: 24.5% management, 37.0% professional, 5.9% services, 26.8% sales, 0.0% farming, 3.4% construction, 2.4% production (2000).
Income: Per capita income: $54,922 (2005); Median household income: $123,422 (2005); Average household income: $162,925 (2005); Percent of households with income of $100,000 or more: 59.7% (2005); Poverty rate: 3.0% (2000).
Education: Percent of population age 25 and over with: High school diploma (including GED) or higher: 96.2% (2005); Bachelor's degree or higher: 66.0% (2005); Master's degree or higher: 31.2% (2005).

School District(s)
Glen Ridge Borough (PK-12)
   2003-04 Enrollment: 1,797 . . . . (973) 429-8302
Housing: Homeownership rate: 91.0% (2005); Median home value: $402,584 (2005); Median rent: $939 per month (2000); Median age of housing: 60+ years (2000).
Safety: Violent crime rate: 20.8 per 10,000 population; Property crime rate: 361.7 per 10,000 population (2004).
Transportation: Commute to work: 69.9% car, 23.7% public transportation, 2.1% walk, 4.1% work from home (2000); Travel time to work: 18.7% less than 15 minutes, 20.6% 15 to 30 minutes, 20.9% 30 to 45 minutes, 13.9% 45 to 60 minutes, 25.9% 60 minutes or more (2000)

IRVINGTON (township). Aka Irvington CDP. Covers a land area of 2.957 square miles and a water area of 0 square miles. Located at 40.72° N. Lat.; 74.23° W. Long. Elevation is 160 feet.
History: Named for Washington Irving, American writer. Settled 1692 as Camptown, renamed 1852. Incorporated 1898.
Population: 61,067 (1990); 60,695 (2000); 59,611 (2005); 58,659 (2010 projected); Race: 8.0% White, 82.9% Black, 0.8% Asian, 8.3% Hispanic of any race (2005); Density: 20,161.7 persons per square mile (2005); Average household size: 2.74 (2005); Median age: 33.0 (2005); Males per 100 females: 88.6 (2005); Marriage status: 44.7% never married, 40.1% now married, 6.8% widowed, 8.4% divorced (2000); Foreign born: 24.2% (2000); Ancestry (includes multiple ancestries): 57.3% Other groups, 9.6% Haitian, 4.3% Jamaican, 2.3% African, 1.9% United States or American (2000).
Economy: Manufacturing: tools, castings, photographic equipment, paints, building materials, and plastic and paper products. Unemployment rate: 6.8% (2005); Total civilian labor force: 28,162 (2005); Single-family building permits issued: 5 (2005); Multi-family building permits issued: 46 (2005); Employment by occupation: 7.2% management, 13.9% professional, 21.7% services, 32.5% sales, 0.0% farming, 5.9% construction, 18.8% production (2000).
Income: Per capita income: $18,732 (2005); Median household income: $41,700 (2005); Average household income: $51,172 (2005); Percent of households with income of $100,000 or more: 10.3% (2005); Poverty rate: 17.4% (2000).
Taxes: Total city taxes per capita: $728 (2004); City property taxes per capita: $706 (2004).
Education: Percent of population age 25 and over with: High school diploma (including GED) or higher: 72.3% (2005); Bachelor's degree or higher: 12.2% (2005); Master's degree or higher: 2.7% (2005).
School District(s)
Irvington Township (PK-12)
   2003-04 Enrollment: 8,830 . . . . (973) 399-6801
Housing: Homeownership rate: 29.2% (2005); Median home value: $192,855 (2005); Median rent: $624 per month (2000); Median age of housing: 46 years (2000).
Hospitals: Irvington General Hospital (157 beds)
Safety: Violent crime rate: 237.3 per 10,000 population; Property crime rate: 556.4 per 10,000 population (2004).
Transportation: Commute to work: 73.1% car, 22.4% public transportation, 2.6% walk, 1.1% work from home (2000); Travel time to work: 11.5% less than 15 minutes, 35.7% 15 to 30 minutes, 27.1% 30 to 45 minutes, 11.6% 45 to 60 minutes, 14.0% 60 minutes or more (2000)
Additional Information Contacts
Irvington Chamber of Commerce. (973) 372-4100
   http://www.irvington-nj.com

LIVINGSTON (township). Aka Livingston CDP. Covers a land area of 13.883 square miles and a water area of 0.186 square miles. Located at 40.78° N. Lat.; 74.32° W. Long. Elevation is 307 feet.
Population: 26,609 (1990); 27,391 (2000); 28,257 (2005); 29,119 (2010 projected); Race: 81.7% White, 1.2% Black, 15.4% Asian, 3.0% Hispanic of any race (2005); Density: 2,035.4 persons per square mile (2005); Average household size: 2.91 (2005); Median age: 41.3 (2005); Males per 100 females: 94.7 (2005); Marriage status: 19.0% never married, 70.4% now married, 6.4% widowed, 4.2% divorced (2000); Foreign born: 18.8% (2000); Ancestry (includes multiple ancestries): 24.8% Other groups, 17.7% Italian, 10.3% Irish, 9.8% Russian, 7.4% German (2000).
Economy: Beverages. Unemployment rate: 2.6% (2005); Total civilian labor force: 14,399 (2005); Single-family building permits issued: 85 (2005); Multi-family building permits issued: 326 (2005); Employment by

occupation: 23.8% management, 32.1% professional, 7.4% services, 29.7% sales, 0.0% farming, 3.9% construction, 3.1% production (2000).
Income: Per capita income: $51,718 (2005); Median household income: $110,471 (2005); Average household income: $150,212 (2005); Percent of households with income of $100,000 or more: 54.6% (2005); Poverty rate: 1.8% (2000).
Taxes: Total city taxes per capita: $666 (2004); City property taxes per capita: $639 (2004).
Education: Percent of population age 25 and over with: High school diploma (including GED) or higher: 93.9% (2005); Bachelor's degree or higher: 57.6% (2005); Master's degree or higher: 26.7% (2005).
School District(s)
Livingston Township (PK-12)
   2003-04 Enrollment: 5,216 . . . . (973) 535-8010
Two-year College(s)
Gibbs College (Private, For-profit)
   Fall 2004 Enrollment: 1,462. . . . . (973) 369-1360
   2005-06 Tuition: In-state $20,147; Out-of-state $20,147
Housing: Homeownership rate: 93.4% (2005); Median home value: $465,917 (2005); Median rent: $1,182 per month (2000); Median age of housing: 42 years (2000).
Hospitals: Saint Barnabas Medical Center (705 beds)
Safety: Violent crime rate: 11.7 per 10,000 population; Property crime rate: 180.3 per 10,000 population (2004).
Newspapers: West Essex Tribune (General - Circulation 7,925)
Transportation: Commute to work: 85.1% car, 8.1% public transportation, 0.5% walk, 5.9% work from home (2000); Travel time to work: 27.3% less than 15 minutes, 31.8% 15 to 30 minutes, 15.9% 30 to 45 minutes, 7.7% 45 to 60 minutes, 17.3% 60 minutes or more (2000)
Additional Information Contacts
Livingston Chamber of Commerce . . . . (973) 992-4343
   http://www.livingstonchambernj.com

MAPLEWOOD (township). Aka Maplewood CDP. Covers a land area of 3.845 square miles and a water area of 0.002 square miles. Located at 40.72° N. Lat.; 74.26° W. Long. Elevation is 136 feet.
Population: 21,593 (1990); 23,868 (2000); 23,489 (2005); 23,136 (2010 projected); Race: 52.9% White, 38.1% Black, 2.7% Asian, 6.2% Hispanic of any race (2005); Density: 6,108.5 persons per square mile (2005); Average household size: 2.84 (2005); Median age: 38.4 (2005); Males per 100 females: 91.1 (2005); Marriage status: 25.8% never married, 60.3% now married, 6.5% widowed, 7.3% divorced (2000); Foreign born: 17.8% (2000); Ancestry (includes multiple ancestries): 29.1% Other groups, 11.8% Irish, 10.0% Italian, 9.5% German, 6.0% English (2000).
Economy: Maps. Single-family building permits issued: 2 (2005); Multi-family building permits issued: 10 (2005); Employment by occupation: 18.8% management, 33.6% professional, 9.1% services, 26.4% sales, 0.0% farming, 4.9% construction, 7.1% production (2000).
Income: Per capita income: $43,367 (2005); Median household income: $92,260 (2005); Average household income: $122,810 (2005); Percent of households with income of $100,000 or more: 45.4% (2005); Poverty rate: 4.4% (2000).
Education: Percent of population age 25 and over with: High school diploma (including GED) or higher: 91.6% (2005); Bachelor's degree or higher: 49.4% (2005); Master's degree or higher: 21.0% (2005).
School District(s)
South Orange-Maplewood (PK-12)
   2003-04 Enrollment: 6,559 . . . . (973) 378-9630
Housing: Homeownership rate: 77.2% (2005); Median home value: $342,792 (2005); Median rent: $851 per month (2000); Median age of housing: 60+ years (2000).
Safety: Violent crime rate: 34.0 per 10,000 population; Property crime rate: 273.0 per 10,000 population (2004).
Newspapers: Irvington Herald (General - Circulation 3,650); News-Record of Maplewood & South Orange (General - Circulation 8,000); Orange Transcript (General - Circulation 2,500); West Orange Chronicle (General - Circulation 5,300)
Transportation: Commute to work: 70.6% car, 21.4% public transportation, 1.7% walk, 5.7% work from home (2000); Travel time to work: 16.3% less than 15 minutes, 30.1% 15 to 30 minutes, 23.3% 30 to 45 minutes, 10.4% 45 to 60 minutes, 19.9% 60 minutes or more (2000)
Additional Information Contacts
Maplewood Chamber of Commerce . . . . (973) 761-4333
   http://www.maplewoodchamber.org

MILLBURN (township). Aka Millburn CDP. Covers a land area of 9.384 square miles and a water area of 0.516 square miles. Located at 40.73° N. Lat.; 74.32° W. Long. Elevation is 140 feet.

History: Named for Samuel Campbell's first "mill on the burn". The Paper Mill Playhouse, the oldest continually running nonprofit playhouse, is here. Settled c.1725. Incorporated 1857.

Population: 18,630 (1990); 19,765 (2000); 19,567 (2005); 19,393 (2010 projected); Race: 88.3% White, 1.0% Black, 9.1% Asian, 2.3% Hispanic of any race (2005); Density: 2,085.1 persons per square mile (2005); Average household size: 2.86 (2005); Median age: 39.1 (2005); Males per 100 females: 94.5 (2005); Marriage status: 17.9% never married, 71.8% now married, 5.4% widowed, 4.9% divorced (2000); Foreign born: 14.7% (2000); Ancestry (includes multiple ancestries): 19.3% Other groups, 13.5% Italian, 12.1% Irish, 11.7% Russian, 11.5% German (2000).

Economy: Includes Short Hills, site of shopping mall. Single-family building permits issued: 43 (2005); Multi-family building permits issued: 0 (2005); Employment by occupation: 30.5% management, 34.9% professional, 4.8% services, 24.6% sales, 0.0% farming, 1.9% construction, 3.2% production (2000).

Income: Per capita income: $77,044 (2005); Median household income: $153,316 (2005); Average household income: $220,308 (2005); Percent of households with income of $100,000 or more: 66.7% (2005); Poverty rate: 1.5% (2000).

Education: Percent of population age 25 and over with: High school diploma (including GED) or higher: 96.6% (2005); Bachelor's degree or higher: 73.9% (2005); Master's degree or higher: 38.2% (2005).

School District(s)

Bergen County Special Services (UG-UG)

    2003-04 Enrollment: 1,982 . . . . (201) 343-6000

Millburn Township (PK-12)

    2003-04 Enrollment: 4,365 . . . . (973) 376-3600

Housing: Homeownership rate: 82.0% (2005); Median home value: $858,578 (2005); Median rent: $995 per month (2000); Median age of housing: 52 years (2000).

Safety: Violent crime rate: 9.1 per 10,000 population; Property crime rate: 332.2 per 10,000 population (2004).

Newspapers: The Item of Millburn & Short Hills (General - Circulation 4,630)

Transportation: Commute to work: 68.1% car, 22.3% public transportation, 3.1% walk, 6.3% work from home (2000); Travel time to work: 21.4% less than 15 minutes, 25.5% 15 to 30 minutes, 15.8% 30 to 45 minutes, 12.2% 45 to 60 minutes, 25.1% 60 minutes or more (2000)

Additional Information Contacts

Millburn Township . . . . (973) 564-7072

    http://www.twp.millburn.nj.us/muni.htm

Millburn-Short Hills Chamber of Commerce . . . . (973) 379-1198

    http://www.millburn.com/chamber/index.html

MONTCLAIR (township). Aka Montclair CDP. Covers a land area of 6.303 square miles and a water area of 0.004 square miles. Located at 40.82° N. Lat.; 74.21° W. Long. Elevation is 300 feet.

History: Named for the French translation of "clear view of mountain". Art museum contains several paintings by George Inness, who lived here. Montclair State University is in Upper Montclair (notable for its many large mansions). Settled c.1666 as part of Newark, set off from Newark 1812, set off from Bloomfield and incorporated 1868.

Population: 37,729 (1990); 38,977 (2000); 38,802 (2005); 38,656 (2010 projected); Race: 59.1% White, 32.0% Black, 3.4% Asian, 6.3% Hispanic of any race (2005); Density: 6,155.9 persons per square mile (2005); Average household size: 2.59 (2005); Median age: 38.4 (2005); Males per 100 females: 87.1 (2005); Marriage status: 31.1% never married, 53.7% now married, 6.8% widowed, 8.4% divorced (2000); Foreign born: 14.5% (2000); Ancestry (includes multiple ancestries): 32.9% Other groups, 13.7% Irish, 10.1% Italian, 9.2% German, 7.6% English (2000).

Economy: Has plants that make chemicals, paint, and metalware. Unemployment rate: 3.5% (2005); Total civilian labor force: 21,345 (2005); Single-family building permits issued: 25 (2005); Multi-family building permits issued: 40 (2005); Employment by occupation: 21.9% management, 36.4% professional, 10.4% services, 23.7% sales, 0.0% farming, 2.7% construction, 4.9% production (2000).

Income: Per capita income: $50,338 (2005); Median household income: $87,550 (2005); Average household income: $129,065 (2005); Percent of households with income of $100,000 or more: 44.2% (2005); Poverty rate: 5.6% (2000).

Taxes: Total city taxes per capita: $2,882 (2004); City property taxes per capita: $2,831 (2004).

Education: Percent of population age 25 and over with: High school diploma (including GED) or higher: 91.7% (2005); Bachelor's degree or higher: 56.5% (2005); Master's degree or higher: 26.6% (2005).

School District(s)

Montclair Town (PK-12)

    2003-04 Enrollment: 6,617 . . . . (973) 509-4010

Four-year College(s)

Montclair State University (Public)

    Fall 2004 Enrollment: 15,637. . . . . (973) 655-4000

    2005-06 Tuition: In-state $7,710; Out-of-state $12,157

Two-year College(s)

Eastern School of Acupuncture and Traditional Medicine (Private, For-profit)

    Fall 2004 Enrollment: n/a. . . . . (973) 746-8717

Mountainside Hospital School of Nursing (Private, Not-for-profit)

    Fall 2004 Enrollment: 142 . . . . (973) 429-6060

    2005-06 Tuition: In-state $9,703; Out-of-state $9,703

Housing: Homeownership rate: 55.7% (2005); Median home value: $453,586 (2005); Median rent: $810 per month (2000); Median age of housing: 60+ years (2000).

Hospitals: Atlantic Health System (365 beds)

Safety: Violent crime rate: 36.3 per 10,000 population; Property crime rate: 264.6 per 10,000 population (2004).

Newspapers: The Montclair Times (General - Circulation 11,715)

Transportation: Commute to work: 66.4% car, 22.0% public transportation, 4.1% walk, 6.3% work from home (2000); Travel time to work: 19.5% less than 15 minutes, 28.4% 15 to 30 minutes, 20.5% 30 to 45 minutes, 10.5% 45 to 60 minutes, 21.1% 60 minutes or more (2000)

Additional Information Contacts

Montclair Township . . . . (973) 744-1400

    http://www.montclairnjusa.org

North Essex Chamber of Commerce. . . . . (973) 226-5500

    http://ww.northessexchamber.com

NEWARK (city). Covers a land area of 23.797 square miles and a water area of 2.165 square miles. Located at 40.73° N. Lat.; 74.18° W. Long. Elevation is 95 feet.

History: Named for Newark in Nottinghamshire, England. Newark was settled in 1666 by Captain Robert Treat and 30 families from New Haven and the vicinity. These former Connecticut citizens wanted self-government and religious freedom. The source of the name Newark remains buried with the original settlers. It was founded as a theocracy with the Puritan Congregational Church in control of village affairs. The severity of ecclesiastical rule at first discouraged new settlers. In 1748 the College of New Jersey, later Princeton University, moved from Elizabethtown to Newark. The college remained until 1756, when it was transferred to Princeton. In 1836, Newark was incorporated as a city.

Population: 275,419 (1990); 273,546 (2000); 281,352 (2005); 288,667 (2010 projected); Race: 26.6% White, 52.1% Black, 1.2% Asian, 31.4% Hispanic of any race (2005); Density: 11,823.0 persons per square mile (2005); Average household size: 2.98 (2005); Median age: 32.0 (2005); Males per 100 females: 95.2 (2005); Marriage status: 43.9% never married, 41.2% now married, 7.5% widowed, 7.4% divorced (2000); Foreign born: 24.1% (2000); Ancestry (includes multiple ancestries): 61.5% Other groups, 5.8% Portuguese, 2.6% Italian, 2.1% Brazilian, 1.8% United States or American (2000).

Economy: Unemployment rate: 8.3% (2005); Total civilian labor force: 104,266 (2005); Single-family building permits issued: 376 (2005); Multi-family building permits issued: 1,695 (2005); Employment by occupation: 6.5% management, 12.5% professional, 21.8% services, 27.5% sales, 0.1% farming, 10.4% construction, 21.2% production (2000).

Income: Per capita income: $14,790 (2005); Median household income: $30,610 (2005); Average household income: $43,033 (2005); Percent of households with income of $100,000 or more: 8.1% (2005); Poverty rate: 28.4% (2000).

Taxes: Total city taxes per capita: $633 (2004); City property taxes per capita: $433 (2004).

Education: Percent of population age 25 and over with: High school diploma (including GED) or higher: 57.9% (2005); Bachelor's degree or higher: 8.9% (2005); Master's degree or higher: 3.0% (2005).

School District(s)

Agency - Discovery CS (04-08)

    2003-04 Enrollment: 87 . . . . (973) 429-8360

Agency - Gray CS (KG-08)
  2003-04 Enrollment: 244 . . . . (973) 678-4637
Agency - Lady Liberty Academy CS (KG-08)
  2003-04 Enrollment: 461 . . . . (973) 639-7805
Agency - Maria L. Varisco-Rogers CS (06-08)
  2003-04 Enrollment: 65 . . . . (973) 621-8209
Agency - Marion P. Thomas Academy CS (KG-06)
  2003-04 Enrollment: 272 . . . . (973) 484-6863
Agency - New Horizons Comm. CS (KG-05)
  2003-04 Enrollment: 492 . . . . (973) 596-9599
Agency - Newark CS (05-08)
  2003-04 Enrollment: 112 . . . . (201) 324-0396
Agency - North Star Academy CS of Newark (05-12)
  2003-04 Enrollment: 268 . . . . (973) 642-0101
Agency - Robert Treat Academy CS (KG-07)
  2003-04 Enrollment: 400 . . . . (973) 482-8811
Agency - Team Academy Charter School (05-06)
  2003-04 Enrollment: 154 . . . . (973) 705-8326
Essex County Voc-Tech (09-12)
  2003-04 Enrollment: 2,368 . . . . (973) 243-2926
Newark City (PK-12)
  2003-04 Enrollment: 46,825 . . . . (973) 733-7333

Four-year College(s)

New Jersey Institute of Technology (Public)
  Fall 2004 Enrollment: 8,249 . . . . (973) 596-3000
  2005-06 Tuition: In-state $9,822; Out-of-state $16,026
Rutgers University-Newark (Public)
  Fall 2004 Enrollment: 10,293 . . . . (973) 353-1766
  2005-06 Tuition: In-state $8,812; Out-of-state $16,410
University of Medicine and Dentistry of New Jersey (Public)
  Fall 2004 Enrollment: 5,329 . . . . (973) 972-4300

Two-year College(s)

Essex County College (Public)
  Fall 2004 Enrollment: 11,268 . . . . (973) 877-3000
  2005-06 Tuition: In-state $4,440; Out-of-state $4,440
New Community Workforce Development Center (Private, Not-for-profit)
  Fall 2004 Enrollment: 77 . . . . (973) 824-6484
PC Age (Private, For-profit)
  Fall 2004 Enrollment: 69 . . . . (973) 565-9800
Star Technical Institute (Private, For-profit)
  Fall 2004 Enrollment: 87 . . . . (973) 639-0789
Housing: Homeownership rate: 23.9% (2005); Median home value: $216,790 (2005); Median rent: $525 per month (2000); Median age of housing: 47 years (2000).
Hospitals: Columbus Hospital (206 beds); Newark Beth Israel Medical Center (665 beds); Saint James Hospital of Newark (182 beds); St. Michael's Medical Center (337 beds); UMDNJ - University Hospital (518 beds)
Safety: Violent crime rate: 102.4 per 10,000 population; Property crime rate: 471.6 per 10,000 population (2004).
Newspapers: City News (Black, General - Circulation 49,500); El Nuevo Coqui (Hispanic - Circulation 10,000); Italian Tribune (Ethnic - Circulation 40,000); Luso Americano (Ethnic - Circulation 24,000); New Community Clarion (Black, General, Hispanic - Circulation 42,000); The Catholic Advocate (Catholic - Circulation 135,698); The New Jersey Citizen (General - Circulation 50,000); The Star-Ledger (Circulation 388,807)
Transportation: Commute to work: 63.0% car, 26.5% public transportation, 7.9% walk, 1.2% work from home (2000); Travel time to work: 18.5% less than 15 minutes, 32.9% 15 to 30 minutes, 24.5% 30 to 45 minutes, 9.9% 45 to 60 minutes, 14.3% 60 minutes or more (2000); Amtrak: Service available.
Additional Information Contacts
City of Newark . . . . (973) 733-6029
  http://www.ci.newark.nj.us
Newark Chamber of Commerce . . . . (973) 522-0099
  http://www.rbp.org

NORTH CALDWELL (borough). Covers a land area of 2.992 square miles and a water area of 0.003 square miles. Located at 40.86° N. Lat.; 74.25° W. Long. Elevation is 460 feet.

History: Incorporated 1898.
Population: 6,706 (1990); 7,375 (2000); 7,384 (2005); 7,368 (2010 projected); Race: 79.1% White, 15.3% Black, 4.6% Asian, 2.3% Hispanic of any race (2005); Density: 2,467.6 persons per square mile (2005); Average household size: 3.54 (2005); Median age: 36.7 (2005); Males per 100

females: 118.3 (2005); Marriage status: 26.0% never married, 65.8% now married, 4.4% widowed, 3.9% divorced (2000); Foreign born: 8.6% (2000); Ancestry (includes multiple ancestries): 24.1% Italian, 10.2% Other groups, 9.0% Russian, 8.1% Irish, 8.0% Polish (2000).
Economy: Single-family building permits issued: 7 (2005); Multi-family building permits issued: 0 (2005); Employment by occupation: 29.5% management, 33.5% professional, 4.5% services, 27.4% sales, 0.0% farming, 2.5% construction, 2.5% production (2000).
Income: Per capita income: $56,729 (2005); Median household income: $134,190 (2005); Average household income: $198,527 (2005); Percent of households with income of $100,000 or more: 65.0% (2005); Poverty rate: 1.2% (2000).
Education: Percent of population age 25 and over with: High school diploma (including GED) or higher: 92.5% (2005); Bachelor's degree or higher: 57.3% (2005); Master's degree or higher: 28.8% (2005).

School District(s)

North Caldwell Borough (PK-06)
  2003-04 Enrollment: 630 . . . . (973) 228-6439
West Essex Regional (07-12)
  2003-04 Enrollment: 1,491 . . . . (973) 228-1200
Housing: Homeownership rate: 96.3% (2005); Median home value: $639,898 (2005); Median rent: $1,509 per month (2000); Median age of housing: 36 years (2000).
Safety: Violent crime rate: 1.3 per 10,000 population; Property crime rate: 35.0 per 10,000 population (2004).
Transportation: Commute to work: 89.1% car, 5.7% public transportation, 0.0% walk, 5.2% work from home (2000); Travel time to work: 26.0% less than 15 minutes, 29.6% 15 to 30 minutes, 24.4% 30 to 45 minutes, 6.3% 45 to 60 minutes, 13.6% 60 minutes or more (2000)
Additional Information Contacts
West Essex Chamber of Commerce . . . . (973) 226-5500
  http://www.wecc.org

NUTLEY (township). Aka Nutley CDP. Covers a land area of 3.368 square miles and a water area of 0.060 square miles. Located at 40.82° N. Lat.; 74.15° W. Long. Elevation is 91 feet.

History: Named for the Old Nutley Manor House owned by the Satterwaite family. Settled 1680. Incorporated 1902. After the Civil War the town was a center for writers and artists. Annie Oakley lived here.
Population: 27,099 (1990); 27,362 (2000); 28,197 (2005); 28,961 (2010 projected); Race: 87.0% White, 1.9% Black, 7.5% Asian, 8.5% Hispanic of any race (2005); Density: 8,370.9 persons per square mile (2005); Average household size: 2.48 (2005); Median age: 40.7 (2005); Males per 100 females: 89.9 (2005); Marriage status: 26.1% never married, 58.1% now married, 8.7% widowed, 7.1% divorced (2000); Foreign born: 14.7% (2000); Ancestry (includes multiple ancestries): 44.5% Italian, 18.2% Irish, 16.0% Other groups, 11.6% German, 7.0% Polish (2000).
Economy: Pharmaceuticals, dyestuffs and machinery are made here. Unemployment rate: 3.6% (2005); Total civilian labor force: 15,358 (2005); Single-family building permits issued: 6 (2005); Multi-family building permits issued: 3 (2005); Employment by occupation: 15.5% management, 25.6% professional, 11.1% services, 31.5% sales, 0.0% farming, 7.4% construction, 8.9% production (2000).
Income: Per capita income: $33,714 (2005); Median household income: $69,472 (2005); Average household income: $83,297 (2005); Percent of households with income of $100,000 or more: 29.7% (2005); Poverty rate: 4.8% (2000).
Taxes: Total city taxes per capita: $943 (2004); City property taxes per capita: $929 (2004).
Education: Percent of population age 25 and over with: High school diploma (including GED) or higher: 86.5% (2005); Bachelor's degree or higher: 33.0% (2005); Master's degree or higher: 10.5% (2005).

School District(s)

Nutley Town (PK-12)
  2003-04 Enrollment: 4,395 . . . . (973) 661-8798

Two-year College(s)

Hohokus School-RETS Nutley (Private, For-profit)
  Fall 2004 Enrollment: 261 . . . . (973) 661-0600
  2005-06 Tuition: In-state $8,840; Out-of-state $8,840
Housing: Homeownership rate: 66.8% (2005); Median home value: $297,529 (2005); Median rent: $764 per month (2000); Median age of housing: 53 years (2000).
Safety: Violent crime rate: 14.8 per 10,000 population; Property crime rate: 127.3 per 10,000 population (2004).

Newspapers: Belleville Times (General - Circulation 2,856); Bloomfield Life (General - Circulation 2,343); Glen Ridge Voice (General - Circulation 729); The Nutley Sun (General - Circulation 4,375)

Transportation: Commute to work: 86.2% car, 8.2% public transportation, 2.4% walk, 2.8% work from home (2000); Travel time to work: 28.1% less than 15 minutes, 33.4% 15 to 30 minutes, 20.5% 30 to 45 minutes, 8.7% 45 to 60 minutes, 9.3% 60 minutes or more (2000)

Additional Information Contacts

Nutley Chamber of Commerce . . . . (973) 667-5300
http://www.nutleychamber.com

ORANGE (CDP). Aka City of Orange Township. Covers a land area of 2.205 square miles and a water area of 0.002 square miles. Located at 40.76° N. Lat.; 74.23° W. Long. Elevation is 204 feet.

Population: 29,925 (1990); 32,868 (2000); 32,432 (2005); 31,982 (2010 projected); Race: 12.1% White, 75.1% Black, 1.3% Asian, 13.8% Hispanic of any race (2005); Density: 14,706.0 persons per square mile (2005); Average household size: 2.81 (2005); Median age: 33.5 (2005); Males per 100 females: 87.3 (2005); Marriage status: 40.5% never married, 41.6% now married, 8.1% widowed, 9.8% divorced (2000); Foreign born: 31.3% (2000); Ancestry (includes multiple ancestries): 51.7% Other groups, 9.9% Haitian, 3.8% Jamaican, 3.2% Italian, 3.2% United States or American (2000).

Economy: Residential city adjacent to Newark. Manufacturing includes metals, paint, electrical equipment, and building materials. Unemployment rate: 6.4% (2005); Total civilian labor force: 14,824 (2005); Single-family building permits issued: 7 (2005); Multi-family building permits issued: 102 (2005); Employment by occupation: 8.5% management, 17.2% professional, 23.1% services, 29.0% sales, 0.2% farming, 7.7% construction, 14.4% production (2000).

Income: Per capita income: $18,091 (2005); Median household income: $39,449 (2005); Average household income: $50,227 (2005); Percent of households with income of $100,000 or more: 10.8% (2005); Poverty rate: 18.8% (2000).

Taxes: Total city taxes per capita: $1,048 (2004); City property taxes per capita: $1,028 (2004).

Education: Percent of population age 25 and over with: High school diploma (including GED) or higher: 72.3% (2005); Bachelor's degree or higher: 16.6% (2005); Master's degree or higher: 6.2% (2005).

School District(s)

City of Orange Township (PK-12)
    2003-04 Enrollment: 4,798 . . . . (973) 677-4040
Essex County Ed Serv Comm (UG-UG)
    2003-04 Enrollment: 270 . . . . (973) 239-1511

Housing: Homeownership rate: 25.2% (2005); Median home value: $206,502 (2005); Median rent: $636 per month (2000); Median age of housing: 45 years (2000).

Safety: Violent crime rate: 116.5 per 10,000 population; Property crime rate: 517.9 per 10,000 population (2004).

Newspapers: East Orange Record (General - Circulation 3,200)

Transportation: Commute to work: 69.2% car, 23.5% public transportation, 5.0% walk, 1.4% work from home (2000); Travel time to work: 15.9% less than 15 minutes, 33.1% 15 to 30 minutes, 27.8% 30 to 45 minutes, 10.5% 45 to 60 minutes, 12.7% 60 minutes or more (2000)

Additional Information Contacts

Orange Chamber of Commerce. . . . . (973) 676-8725
http://www.orangechamber.biz

ROSELAND (borough). Covers a land area of 3.620 square miles and a water area of 0.002 square miles. Located at 40.82° N. Lat.; 74.30° W. Long. Elevation is 356 feet.

History: Incorporated 1908.

Population: 4,847 (1990); 5,298 (2000); 5,286 (2005); 5,294 (2010 projected); Race: 93.4% White, 0.8% Black, 4.7% Asian, 2.8% Hispanic of any race (2005); Density: 1,460.3 persons per square mile (2005); Average household size: 2.42 (2005); Median age: 45.7 (2005); Males per 100 females: 86.6 (2005); Marriage status: 20.3% never married, 62.1% now married, 10.9% widowed, 6.7% divorced (2000); Foreign born: 11.4% (2000); Ancestry (includes multiple ancestries): 38.7% Italian, 23.1% Irish, 12.5% Other groups, 11.4% German, 5.5% English (2000).

Economy: Electronic and photographic equipment. Single-family building permits issued: 36 (2005); Multi-family building permits issued: 0 (2005); Employment by occupation: 23.0% management, 29.7% professional, 7.2% services, 31.3% sales, 0.0% farming, 6.0% construction, 2.8% production (2000).

Income: Per capita income: $49,567 (2005); Median household income: $95,266 (2005); Average household income: $119,858 (2005); Percent of households with income of $100,000 or more: 47.1% (2005); Poverty rate: 1.7% (2000).

Education: Percent of population age 25 and over with: High school diploma (including GED) or higher: 92.1% (2005); Bachelor's degree or higher: 46.6% (2005); Master's degree or higher: 18.8% (2005).

School District(s)

Roseland Borough (PK-06)
    2003-04 Enrollment: 428 . . . . (973) 226-1296

Housing: Homeownership rate: 81.7% (2005); Median home value: $462,704 (2005); Median rent: $1,216 per month (2000); Median age of housing: 32 years (2000).

Safety: Violent crime rate: 13.1 per 10,000 population; Property crime rate: 144.4 per 10,000 population (2004).

Transportation: Commute to work: 92.3% car, 3.9% public transportation, 0.2% walk, 2.9% work from home (2000); Travel time to work: 29.0% less than 15 minutes, 35.1% 15 to 30 minutes, 19.6% 30 to 45 minutes, 3.9% 45 to 60 minutes, 12.4% 60 minutes or more (2000)

Additional Information Contacts

Borough of Roseland . . . . (973) 226-8080
http://www.roselandnj.org
North Essex Chamber of Commerce. . . . . (973) 226-5500
http://www.northessexchamber.com

SHORT HILLS (unincorporated postal area, zip code 07078). Covers a land area of 6.812 square miles and a water area of 0.503 square miles. Located at 40.73° N. Lat.; 74.32° W. Long. Elevation is 220 feet.

Population: 12,849 (2000); Race: 89.8% White, 0.8% Black, 8.0% Asian, 2.5% Hispanic of any race (2000); Density: 1,886.2 persons per square mile (2000); Age: 32.0% under 18, 12.5% over 64 (2000); Marriage status: 15.8% never married, 76.2% now married, 4.6% widowed, 3.4% divorced (2000); Foreign born: 12.8% (2000); Ancestry (includes multiple ancestries): 19.2% Other groups, 11.5% Italian, 11.0% German, 10.6% Irish, 10.1% Russian (2000).

Economy: Employment by occupation: 32.2% management, 33.8% professional, 4.1% services, 26.4% sales, 0.0% farming, 0.6% construction, 2.8% production (2000).

Income: Per capita income: $92,940 (2000); Median household income: $185,466 (2000); Poverty rate: 1.8% (2000).

Education: Percent of population age 25 and over with: High school diploma (including GED) or higher: 97.4% (2000); Bachelor's degree or higher: 79.2% (2000).

School District(s)

Millburn Township (PK-12)
    2003-04 Enrollment: 4,365 . . . . (973) 376-3600

Housing: Homeownership rate: 92.1% (2000); Median home value: $690,800 (2000); Median rent: $1,407 per month (2000); Median age of housing: 48 years (2000).

Transportation: Commute to work: 69.4% car, 22.9% public transportation, 0.7% walk, 6.7% work from home (2000); Travel time to work: 20.9% less than 15 minutes, 24.1% 15 to 30 minutes, 15.8% 30 to 45 minutes, 12.2% 45 to 60 minutes, 26.9% 60 minutes or more (2000)

Additional Information Contacts

Millburn-Short Hills Chamber of Commerce . . . . (973) 379-1198
http://www.millburn.com/chamber/index.html

SOUTH ORANGE VILLAGE (township). Aka South Orange CDP. Covers a land area of 2.853 square miles and a water area of 0.004 square miles. Located at 40.74° N. Lat.; 74.25° W. Long.

Population: 16,268 (1990); 16,964 (2000); 16,864 (2005); 16,767 (2010 projected); Race: 56.1% White, 35.1% Black, 4.0% Asian, 6.1% Hispanic of any race (2005); Density: 5,910.3 persons per square mile (2005); Average household size: 3.04 (2005); Median age: 35.1 (2005); Males per 100 females: 93.0 (2005); Marriage status: 38.1% never married, 50.1% now married, 6.1% widowed, 5.7% divorced (2000); Foreign born: 16.9% (2000); Ancestry (includes multiple ancestries): 31.2% Other groups, 11.8% Irish, 11.1% Italian, 9.3% German, 5.4% Polish (2000).

Economy: Single-family building permits issued: 0 (2005); Multi-family building permits issued: 3 (2005); Employment by occupation: 19.3% management, 33.7% professional, 12.6% services, 26.7% sales, 0.0% farming, 2.6% construction, 5.1% production (2000).

Income: Per capita income: $45,378 (2005); Median household income: $95,127 (2005); Average household income: $133,192 (2005); Percent of

households with income of $100,000 or more: 47.6% (2005); Poverty rate: 5.3% (2000).

Taxes: Total city taxes per capita: $941 (2004); City property taxes per capita: $936 (2004).

Education: Percent of population age 25 and over with: High school diploma (including GED) or higher: 93.4% (2005); Bachelor's degree or higher: 57.1% (2005); Master's degree or higher: 29.0% (2005).

School District(s)
South Orange-Maplewood (PK-12)
    2003-04 Enrollment: 6,559 . . . . (973) 378-9630

Four-year College(s)
Seton Hall University (Private, Not-for-profit, Roman Catholic)
    Fall 2004 Enrollment: 9,824. . . . . (973) 761-9000
    2005-06 Tuition: In-state $23,460; Out-of-state $23,460

Two-year College(s)
Harrison Career Institute-South Orange (Private, For-profit)
    Fall 2004 Enrollment: 161 . . . . (973) 763-9484

Housing: Homeownership rate: 71.8% (2005); Median home value: $421,185 (2005); Median rent: $837 per month (2000); Median age of housing: 60+ years (2000).

Safety: Violent crime rate: 40.5 per 10,000 population; Property crime rate: 299.7 per 10,000 population (2004).

Transportation: Commute to work: 60.7% car, 21.2% public transportation, 10.6% walk, 6.8% work from home (2000); Travel time to work: 23.9% less than 15 minutes, 31.9% 15 to 30 minutes, 18.8% 30 to 45 minutes, 8.2% 45 to 60 minutes, 17.3% 60 minutes or more (2000)

Additional Information Contacts
South Orange Chamber of Commerce . . . . (973) 762-4333
    http://www.southorangechamber.com
South Orange Village Township . . . . (973) 378-7805
    http://www.southorange.org

VERONA (township). Aka Verona CDP. Covers a land area of 2.752 square miles and a water area of 0.022 square miles. Located at 40.83° N. Lat.; 74.24° W. Long. Elevation is 348 feet.

History: Named for Verona, Italy. Incorporated 1907.

Population: 13,597 (1990); 13,533 (2000); 13,300 (2005); 13,086 (2010 projected); Race: 92.9% White, 1.4% Black, 3.4% Asian, 4.1% Hispanic of any race (2005); Density: 4,832.7 persons per square mile (2005); Average household size: 2.40 (2005); Median age: 42.5 (2005); Males per 100 females: 90.2 (2005); Marriage status: 20.8% never married, 62.1% now married, 10.6% widowed, 6.5% divorced (2000); Foreign born: 9.7% (2000); Ancestry (includes multiple ancestries): 34.3% Italian, 22.6% Irish, 13.6% German, 11.5% Other groups, 7.8% Polish (2000).

Economy: Single-family building permits issued: 7 (2005); Multi-family building permits issued: 0 (2005); Employment by occupation: 22.0% management, 29.4% professional, 9.9% services, 29.6% sales, 0.0% farming, 4.0% construction, 5.2% production (2000).

Income: Per capita income: $48,806 (2005); Median household income: $88,984 (2005); Average household income: $116,846 (2005); Percent of households with income of $100,000 or more: 44.2% (2005); Poverty rate: 3.3% (2000).

Education: Percent of population age 25 and over with: High school diploma (including GED) or higher: 92.5% (2005); Bachelor's degree or higher: 49.5% (2005); Master's degree or higher: 18.3% (2005).

School District(s)
Verona Borough (PK-12)
    2003-04 Enrollment: 2,055 . . . . (973) 239-2100

Housing: Homeownership rate: 77.2% (2005); Median home value: $368,808 (2005); Median rent: $838 per month (2000); Median age of housing: 49 years (2000).

Safety: Violent crime rate: 8.9 per 10,000 population; Property crime rate: 133.4 per 10,000 population (2004).

Transportation: Commute to work: 86.0% car, 7.3% public transportation, 2.0% walk, 4.3% work from home (2000); Travel time to work: 23.3% less than 15 minutes, 36.3% 15 to 30 minutes, 20.9% 30 to 45 minutes, 7.8% 45 to 60 minutes, 11.7% 60 minutes or more (2000)

Additional Information Contacts
Verona Chamber of Commerce . . . . (973) 226-5500
    http://www.veronachamber.org
Verona Township . . . . (973) 239-3220
    http://www.veronanj.org

WEST CALDWELL (township). Aka West Caldwell CDP. Covers a land area of 5.050 square miles and a water area of 0 square miles. Located at 40.84° N. Lat.; 74.28° W. Long. Elevation is 240 feet.

History: Incorporated 1904.

Population: 10,422 (1990); 11,233 (2000); 11,081 (2005); 10,955 (2010 projected); Race: 93.7% White, 1.0% Black, 3.7% Asian, 3.4% Hispanic of any race (2005); Density: 2,194.3 persons per square mile (2005); Average household size: 2.78 (2005); Median age: 41.8 (2005); Males per 100 females: 91.0 (2005); Marriage status: 20.0% never married, 65.6% now married, 9.3% widowed, 5.2% divorced (2000); Foreign born: 8.6% (2000); Ancestry (includes multiple ancestries): 35.2% Italian, 21.7% Irish, 14.4% German, 9.1% Other groups, 6.7% English (2000).

Economy: Light manufacturing. Single-family building permits issued: 4 (2005); Multi-family building permits issued: 0 (2005); Employment by occupation: 23.9% management, 25.9% professional, 10.5% services, 30.0% sales, 0.0% farming, 5.7% construction, 3.9% production (2000).

Income: Per capita income: $45,334 (2005); Median household income: $97,542 (2005); Average household income: $124,507 (2005); Percent of households with income of $100,000 or more: 48.4% (2005); Poverty rate: 2.1% (2000).

Taxes: Total city taxes per capita: $895 (2004); City property taxes per capita: $877 (2004).

Education: Percent of population age 25 and over with: High school diploma (including GED) or higher: 93.1% (2005); Bachelor's degree or higher: 47.8% (2005); Master's degree or higher: 18.0% (2005).

School District(s)
Caldwell-West Caldwell (PK-12)
    2003-04 Enrollment: 2,627 . . . . (973) 228-6979
Essex County Voc-Tech (09-12)
    2003-04 Enrollment: 2,368 . . . . (973) 243-2926

Housing: Homeownership rate: 85.8% (2005); Median home value: $414,081 (2005); Median rent: $1,130 per month (2000); Median age of housing: 42 years (2000).

Safety: Violent crime rate: 5.3 per 10,000 population; Property crime rate: 92.6 per 10,000 population (2004).

Transportation: Commute to work: 89.0% car, 4.0% public transportation, 1.3% walk, 5.5% work from home (2000); Travel time to work: 28.6% less than 15 minutes, 34.6% 15 to 30 minutes, 20.6% 30 to 45 minutes, 5.6% 45 to 60 minutes, 10.7% 60 minutes or more (2000)

Additional Information Contacts
North Essex Chamber of Commerce . . . . (973) 226-5500
    http://www.northessexchamber.com
West Caldwell Township . . . . (973) 226-2300
    http://www.westcaldwell.com

WEST ORANGE (township). Aka West Orange CDP. Covers a land area of 12.118 square miles and a water area of 0.112 square miles. Located at 40.78° N. Lat.; 74.25° W. Long. Elevation is 500 feet.

History: Named for the European ruling family of Orange-Nassau. "Glenmont," Thomas Edison's home in Llewellyn Park, and his laboratory, now a museum, are included in the Edison National Historic Site. Set off from Orange 1862. Incorporated 1900.

Population: 39,103 (1990); 44,943 (2000); 44,854 (2005); 44,814 (2010 projected); Race: 62.6% White, 20.8% Black, 8.5% Asian, 12.6% Hispanic of any race (2005); Density: 3,701.3 persons per square mile (2005); Average household size: 2.72 (2005); Median age: 40.5 (2005); Males per 100 females: 89.3 (2005); Marriage status: 25.0% never married, 59.9% now married, 8.7% widowed, 6.4% divorced (2000); Foreign born: 25.6% (2000); Ancestry (includes multiple ancestries): 30.0% Other groups, 16.7% Italian, 10.9% Irish, 6.8% German, 5.8% Russian (2000).

Economy: Unemployment rate: 3.7% (2005); Total civilian labor force: 23,278 (2005); Single-family building permits issued: 7 (2005); Multi-family building permits issued: 0 (2005); Employment by occupation: 18.8% management, 28.5% professional, 11.0% services, 27.9% sales, 0.1% farming, 5.8% construction, 7.9% production (2000).

Income: Per capita income: $39,453 (2005); Median household income: $80,571 (2005); Average household income: $105,903 (2005); Percent of households with income of $100,000 or more: 39.8% (2005); Poverty rate: 5.6% (2000).

Taxes: Total city taxes per capita: $824 (2004); City property taxes per capita: $805 (2004).

Education: Percent of population age 25 and over with: High school diploma (including GED) or higher: 86.2% (2005); Bachelor's degree or higher: 42.9% (2005); Master's degree or higher: 18.8% (2005).

School District(s)

School District(s)
West Orange Town (PK-12)
    2003-04 Enrollment: 6,588 . . . . (973) 669-5430
Housing: Homeownership rate: 70.4% (2005); Median home value:
$324,992 (2005); Median rent: $788 per month (2000); Median age of
housing: 45 years (2000).
Hospitals: Kessler Institute for Rehabilitation (322 beds)
Safety: Violent crime rate: 17.0 per 10,000 population; Property crime rate:
252.1 per 10,000 population (2004).
Transportation: Commute to work: 84.5% car, 9.6% public transportation,
1.8% walk, 3.4% work from home (2000); Travel time to work: 22.0% less
than 15 minutes, 35.7% 15 to 30 minutes, 21.2% 30 to 45 minutes, 7.6%
45 to 60 minutes, 13.6% 60 minutes or more (2000)
Additional Information Contacts
West Orange Chamber of Commerce . . . . (973) 731-0360
    http://www.westorangechamber.com
West Orange Township . . . . (973) 325-4029
    http://www.westorange.org

Gloucester County

Located in southwestern New Jersey; bounded on the west by the
Delaware River and the Pennsylvania border; drained by the Maurice
River. Covers a land area of 324.72 square miles, a water area of 12.20
square miles, and is located in the Eastern Time Zone. The county
government was organized in 1686. County seat is Woodbury.

Gloucester County is part of the Philadelphia-Camden-Wilmington,
PA-NJ-DE-MD Metropolitan Statistical Area. The entire metro area
includes: Camden, NJ Metropolitan Division (Burlington County, NJ;
Camden County, NJ; Gloucester County, NJ); Philadelphia, PA
Metropolitan Division (Bucks County, PA; Chester County, PA; Delaware
County, PA; Montgomery County, PA; Philadelphia County, PA);
Wilmington, DE-MD-NJ Metropolitan Division (New Castle County, DE;
Cecil County, MD; Salem County, NJ)

Weather Station: Glassboro 2 W										Elevation: 98 feet	
	Jan	Feb	Mar	Apr	May	Jun	Jul	Aug	Sep	Oct	Nov	Dec
High	39	42	51	62	72	81	86	84	77	66	55	45
Low	23	25	33	42	52	61	67	65	58	45	37	29
Precip	3.6	2.8	4.2	3.9	4.2	3.8	4.4	4.3	3.4	3.6	3.7	3.8
Snow	na	na	tr	tr	0.0	0.0	0.0	0.0	0.0	tr	tr	1.2

High and Low temperatures in degrees Fahrenheit; Precipitation and Snow in inches

Population: 230,082 (1990); 254,673 (2000); 273,319 (2005); 292,830
(2010 projected); Race: 86.2% White, 9.6% Black, 1.7% Asian, 3.0%
Hispanic of any race (2005); Density: 841.7 persons per square mile
(2005); Average household size: 2.77 (2005); Median age: 37.2 (2005);
Males per 100 females: 94.3 (2005).
Religion: Five largest groups: 37.3% Catholic Church, 3.9% The United
Methodist Church, 2.8% Southern Baptist Convention, 1.4% Episcopal
Church, 1.3% Evangelical Lutheran Church in America (2000).
Economy: Unemployment rate: 4.3% (2005); Total civilian labor force:
147,352 (2005); Leading industries: 20.1% retail trade; 12.9%
manufacturing; 12.6% health care and social assistance (2004); Farms:
692 totaling 50,753 acres (2002); Companies that employ 500 or more
persons: 33 (2004); Companies that employ 100 to 499 persons: 320
(2004); Companies that employ less than 100 persons: 11,538 (2004);
Black-owned businesses: 549 (2002); Hispanic-owned businesses: 295
(2002); Asian-owned businesses: 539 (2002); Women-owned businesses:
4,453 (2002); Retail sales per capita: $13,206 (2006). Single-family
building permits issued: 1,882 (2005); Multi-family building permits issued:
193 (2005).
Income: Per capita income: $26,871 (2005); Median household income:
$62,465 (2005); Average household income: $73,554 (2005); Percent of
households with income of $100,000 or more: 23.1% (2005); Poverty rate:
6.7% (2003); Bankruptcy rate: 7.13% (2005).
Taxes: Total county taxes per capita: $353 (2004); County property taxes
per capita: $353 (2004).
Education: Percent of population age 25 and over with: High school
diploma (including GED) or higher: 84.5% (2005); Bachelor's degree or
higher: 22.2% (2005); Master's degree or higher: 6.5% (2005).
Housing: Homeownership rate: 80.0% (2005); Median home value:
$184,201 (2005); Median rent: $557 per month (2000); Median age of
housing: 29 years (2000).

Health: Birth rate: 114.8 per 10,000 population (2004); Death rate: 87.5 per
10,000 population (2004); Age-adjusted cancer mortality rate: 238.9 deaths
per 100,000 population (2002); Air Quality Index: 82.5% good, 15.6%
moderate, 1.9% unhealthy for sensitive individuals, 0.0% unhealthy
(percent of days in 2005); Number of physicians: 16.1 per 10,000
population (2004); Hospital beds: 9.0 per 10,000 population (2003);
Hospital admissions: 504.9 per 10,000 population (2003).
Elections: 2004 Presidential election results: 46.9% Bush, 52.2% Kerry,
0.6% Nader, 0.1% Badnarik
Additional Information Contacts
Gloucester County Government . . . . (856) 853-3275
    http://www.co.gloucester.nj.us
Borough of Pitman . . . . (856) 589-3522
    http://www.pitman.org
City of Woodbury . . . . (856) 845-1300
    http://www.woodbury.nj.us/cg_city_off.shtml
Deptford Township . . . . (856) 845-5300
    http://www.deptford-nj.org
East Greenwich Township . . . . (856) 423-0654
    http://www.gloucester.lib.nj.us/eastgreenwich
Glassboro Chamber of Commerce . . . . (856) 881-7900
    http://www.glassborochamber.org
Gloucester County Chamber of Commerce . . . . (856) 384-2655
    http://www.gloucestercountychamber.org
Greenwich Township . . . . (856) 423-1038
    http://www.greenwichtwp.com
Harrison Township . . . . (856) 478-4111
    http://www.harrisontwp.us
Logan Township . . . . (856) 467-2670
    http://www.logan-twp.org
Mantua Township . . . . (856) 468-1500
    http://www.mantuatownship.com
Monroe Township . . . . (856) 728-9800
    http://www.monroetownshipnj.org
South Harrison Township . . . . (856) 769-3737
    http://www.southharrison-nj.org
Washington Township . . . . (856) 589-0575
    http://www.twp.washington.nj.us
Washington Township Chamber of Commerce . . . . (856) 227-1776
    http://www.washingtontownshipchamber.org
West Deptford Township . . . . (856) 845-4004
    http://www.westdeptford.com
Woodbury Chamber of Commerce . . . . (856) 845-4056
    http://woodbury.nj.us

Gloucester County Communities

BECKETT (CDP). Covers a land area of 1.767 square miles and a
water area of 0.076 square miles. Located at 39.75° N. Lat.; 75.35° W.
Long.
Population: 3,815 (1990); 4,726 (2000); 4,587 (2005); 4,539 (2010
projected); Race: 77.3% White, 17.4% Black, 2.2% Asian, 3.3% Hispanic of
any race (2005); Density: 2,596.2 persons per square mile (2005); Average
household size: 3.08 (2005); Median age: 33.7 (2005); Males per 100
females: 96.4 (2005); Marriage status: 23.5% never married, 67.5% now
married, 1.7% widowed, 7.3% divorced (2000); Foreign born: 3.9% (2000);
Ancestry (includes multiple ancestries): 34.5% Irish, 22.9% Italian, 22.0%
Other groups, 19.4% German, 11.0% English (2000).
Economy: Employment by occupation: 14.3% management, 26.9%
professional, 10.3% services, 30.0% sales, 0.0% farming, 6.1%
construction, 12.4% production (2000).
Income: Per capita income: $33,288 (2005); Median household income:
$94,667 (2005); Average household income: $102,547 (2005); Percent of
households with income of $100,000 or more: 45.8% (2005); Poverty rate:
3.1% (2000).
Education: Percent of population age 25 and over with: High school
diploma (including GED) or higher: 94.2% (2005); Bachelor's degree or
higher: 29.8% (2005); Master's degree or higher: 8.7% (2005).
Housing: Homeownership rate: 94.2% (2005); Median home value:
$180,301 (2005); Median rent: $927 per month (2000); Median age of
housing: 17 years (2000).
Transportation: Commute to work: 93.6% car, 2.6% public transportation,
1.3% walk, 2.3% work from home (2000); Travel time to work: 19.8% less
than 15 minutes, 30.9% 15 to 30 minutes, 27.2% 30 to 45 minutes, 11.9%
45 to 60 minutes, 10.2% 60 minutes or more (2000)

BRIDGEPORT (unincorporated postal area, zip code 08014). Covers a land area of 4.378 square miles and a water area of 0.009 square miles. Located at 39.80° N. Lat.; 75.34° W. Long. Elevation is 17 feet.
Population: 635 (2000); Race: 100.0% White, 0.0% Black, 0.0% Asian, 0.0% Hispanic of any race (2000); Density: 145.0 persons per square mile (2000); Age: 25.0% under 18, 14.6% over 64 (2000); Marriage status: 25.3% never married, 49.4% now married, 11.7% widowed, 13.6% divorced (2000); Foreign born: 1.8% (2000); Ancestry (includes multiple ancestries): 28.0% German, 24.8% Irish, 22.8% English, 13.2% Polish, 8.4% Italian (2000).
Economy: Employment by occupation: 28.0% management, 5.3% professional, 11.3% services, 36.2% sales, 0.0% farming, 7.9% construction, 11.3% production (2000).
Income: Per capita income: $41,558 (2000); Median household income: $34,853 (2000); Poverty rate: 12.8% (2000).
Education: Percent of population age 25 and over with: High school diploma (including GED) or higher: 76.1% (2000); Bachelor's degree or higher: 6.4% (2000).
Housing: Homeownership rate: 73.9% (2000); Median home value: $99,800 (2000); Median rent: $563 per month (2000); Median age of housing: 60+ years (2000).
Transportation: Commute to work: 95.6% car, 0.0% public transportation, 2.5% walk, 1.9% work from home (2000); Travel time to work: 51.0% less than 15 minutes, 18.9% 15 to 30 minutes, 16.7% 30 to 45 minutes, 2.6% 45 to 60 minutes, 10.9% 60 minutes or more (2000)

CLARKSBORO (unincorporated postal area, zip code 08020). Covers a land area of 5.126 square miles and a water area of 0.077 square miles. Located at 39.80° N. Lat.; 75.22° W. Long. Elevation is 56 feet.
Population: 2,234 (2000); Race: 98.5% White, 0.9% Black, 0.0% Asian, 2.9% Hispanic of any race (2000); Density: 435.9 persons per square mile (2000); Age: 27.3% under 18, 11.8% over 64 (2000); Marriage status: 21.5% never married, 61.6% now married, 8.4% widowed, 8.5% divorced (2000); Foreign born: 3.6% (2000); Ancestry (includes multiple ancestries): 32.3% German, 30.8% Irish, 22.7% Italian, 15.9% English, 7.5% Polish (2000).
Economy: Employment by occupation: 17.0% management, 26.0% professional, 8.6% services, 25.0% sales, 0.7% farming, 9.1% construction, 13.6% production (2000).
Income: Per capita income: $25,359 (2000); Median household income: $71,023 (2000); Poverty rate: 5.3% (2000).
Education: Percent of population age 25 and over with: High school diploma (including GED) or higher: 88.7% (2000); Bachelor's degree or higher: 29.8% (2000).
Housing: Homeownership rate: 82.9% (2000); Median home value: $147,600 (2000); Median rent: $563 per month (2000); Median age of housing: 35 years (2000).
Transportation: Commute to work: 93.6% car, 0.0% public transportation, 0.0% walk, 4.6% work from home (2000); Travel time to work: 20.5% less than 15 minutes, 45.2% 15 to 30 minutes, 17.9% 30 to 45 minutes, 5.7% 45 to 60 minutes, 10.7% 60 minutes or more (2000)

CLAYTON (borough). Covers a land area of 7.180 square miles and a water area of 0.171 square miles. Located at 39.65° N. Lat.; 75.08° W. Long. Elevation is 135 feet.
History: Settled c.1775, incorporated 1924.
Population: 6,188 (1990); 7,139 (2000); 7,162 (2005); 7,274 (2010 projected); Race: 78.3% White, 16.8% Black, 0.8% Asian, 3.4% Hispanic of any race (2005); Density: 997.4 persons per square mile (2005); Average household size: 2.85 (2005); Median age: 34.7 (2005); Males per 100 females: 92.7 (2005); Marriage status: 25.5% never married, 62.9% now married, 5.7% widowed, 5.9% divorced (2000); Foreign born: 4.2% (2000); Ancestry (includes multiple ancestries): 26.6% Irish, 25.4% German, 17.9% Other groups, 14.2% Italian, 9.9% English (2000).
Economy: Manufacturing: bottles, water conditioning equipment, food containers; truck farming. Single-family building permits issued: 23 (2005); Multi-family building permits issued: 0 (2005); Employment by occupation: 9.0% management, 17.3% professional, 12.7% services, 29.4% sales, 0.2% farming, 12.9% construction, 18.5% production (2000).
Income: Per capita income: $24,598 (2005); Median household income: $61,579 (2005); Average household income: $69,929 (2005); Percent of households with income of $100,000 or more: 21.2% (2005); Poverty rate: 2.9% (2000).

Education: Percent of population age 25 and over with: High school diploma (including GED) or higher: 83.8% (2005); Bachelor's degree or higher: 19.1% (2005); Master's degree or higher: 3.9% (2005).
School District(s)
Clayton Borough (PK-12)
   2003-04 Enrollment: 1,386 . . . . (856) 881-8700
Housing: Homeownership rate: 79.6% (2005); Median home value: $149,480 (2005); Median rent: $486 per month (2000); Median age of housing: 36 years (2000).
Safety: Violent crime rate: 19.4 per 10,000 population; Property crime rate: 341.3 per 10,000 population (2004).
Transportation: Commute to work: 94.3% car, 2.3% public transportation, 1.1% walk, 1.8% work from home (2000); Travel time to work: 23.9% less than 15 minutes, 27.9% 15 to 30 minutes, 25.0% 30 to 45 minutes, 12.4% 45 to 60 minutes, 10.8% 60 minutes or more (2000)

DEPTFORD (township). Covers a land area of 17.495 square miles and a water area of 0.081 square miles. Located at 39.82° N. Lat.; 75.12° W. Long.
Population: 24,137 (1990); 26,763 (2000); 28,807 (2005); 30,911 (2010 projected); Race: 81.3% White, 13.9% Black, 1.9% Asian, 3.5% Hispanic of any race (2005); Density: 1,646.5 persons per square mile (2005); Average household size: 2.63 (2005); Median age: 38.6 (2005); Males per 100 females: 94.1 (2005); Marriage status: 27.1% never married, 57.0% now married, 8.3% widowed, 7.5% divorced (2000); Foreign born: 4.2% (2000); Ancestry (includes multiple ancestries): 28.1% Irish, 22.9% Italian, 21.1% German, 15.9% Other groups, 9.8% English (2000).
Economy: Suburban area with retail businesses and light industry. Unemployment rate: 3.0% (2005); Total civilian labor force: 15,424 (2005); Single-family building permits issued: 259 (2005); Multi-family building permits issued: 0 (2005); Employment by occupation: 11.4% management, 15.4% professional, 13.4% services, 29.7% sales, 0.0% farming, 12.3% construction, 17.6% production (2000).
Income: Per capita income: $24,453 (2005); Median household income: $56,358 (2005); Average household income: $63,234 (2005); Percent of households with income of $100,000 or more: 15.3% (2005); Poverty rate: 5.9% (2000).
Taxes: Total city taxes per capita: $491 (2004); City property taxes per capita: $417 (2004).
Education: Percent of population age 25 and over with: High school diploma (including GED) or higher: 80.3% (2005); Bachelor's degree or higher: 15.6% (2005); Master's degree or higher: 4.2% (2005).
School District(s)
Deptford Township (PK-12)
   2003-04 Enrollment: 4,476 . . . . (856) 232-2700
Two-year College(s)
Harrison Career Institute-Deptford (Private, For-profit)
   Fall 2004 Enrollment: 213 . . . . (856) 384-2888
Housing: Homeownership rate: 76.8% (2005); Median home value: $166,079 (2005); Median rent: $563 per month (2000); Median age of housing: 32 years (2000).
Safety: Violent crime rate: 47.1 per 10,000 population; Property crime rate: 539.1 per 10,000 population (2004).
Transportation: Commute to work: 93.0% car, 3.0% public transportation, 1.4% walk, 1.6% work from home (2000); Travel time to work: 30.6% less than 15 minutes, 32.5% 15 to 30 minutes, 23.0% 30 to 45 minutes, 6.9% 45 to 60 minutes, 7.1% 60 minutes or more (2000)
Additional Information Contacts
Deptford Township. . . . . (856) 845-5300
   http://www.deptford-nj.org

EAST GREENWICH (township). Covers a land area of 14.750 square miles and a water area of 0.224 square miles. Located at 39.79° N. Lat.; 75.23° W. Long.
Population: 5,258 (1990); 5,430 (2000); 6,129 (2005); 6,830 (2010 projected); Race: 94.6% White, 3.1% Black, 0.8% Asian, 1.7% Hispanic of any race (2005); Density: 415.5 persons per square mile (2005); Average household size: 2.78 (2005); Median age: 41.5 (2005); Males per 100 females: 92.5 (2005); Marriage status: 20.9% never married, 63.7% now married, 7.7% widowed, 7.7% divorced (2000); Foreign born: 3.5% (2000); Ancestry (includes multiple ancestries): 29.6% Irish, 27.4% German, 20.6% Italian, 15.0% English, 6.9% Other groups (2000).
Economy: Single-family building permits issued: 169 (2005); Multi-family building permits issued: 0 (2005); Employment by occupation: 15.7%

management, 24.9% professional, 9.1% services, 26.4% sales, 0.3% farming, 10.0% construction, 13.5% production (2000).
Income: Per capita income: $31,988 (2005); Median household income: $75,589 (2005); Average household income: $87,523 (2005); Percent of households with income of $100,000 or more: 34.0% (2005); Poverty rate: 3.9% (2000).
Education: Percent of population age 25 and over with: High school diploma (including GED) or higher: 88.0% (2005); Bachelor's degree or higher: 23.9% (2005); Master's degree or higher: 7.2% (2005).
Housing: Homeownership rate: 90.8% (2005); Median home value: $241,873 (2005); Median rent: $555 per month (2000); Median age of housing: 28 years (2000).
Safety: Violent crime rate: 10.1 per 10,000 population; Property crime rate: 130.1 per 10,000 population (2004).
Transportation: Commute to work: 94.2% car, 0.4% public transportation, 0.5% walk, 4.1% work from home (2000); Travel time to work: 25.2% less than 15 minutes, 39.9% 15 to 30 minutes, 19.0% 30 to 45 minutes, 4.6% 45 to 60 minutes, 11.2% 60 minutes or more (2000)
Additional Information Contacts
East Greenwich Township . . . . (856) 423-0654
   http://www.gloucester.lib.nj.us/eastgreenwich

ELK (township). Covers a land area of 19.630 square miles and a water area of 0.082 square miles. Located at 39.67° N. Lat.; 75.14° W. Long.
Population: 3,806 (1990); 3,514 (2000); 3,692 (2005); 3,895 (2010 projected); Race: 83.2% White, 12.8% Black, 0.6% Asian, 3.4% Hispanic of any race (2005); Density: 188.1 persons per square mile (2005); Average household size: 2.72 (2005); Median age: 39.1 (2005); Males per 100 females: 96.2 (2005); Marriage status: 21.1% never married, 62.9% now married, 8.3% widowed, 7.7% divorced (2000); Foreign born: 2.0% (2000); Ancestry (includes multiple ancestries): 24.8% German, 19.0% Other groups, 18.6% Irish, 15.9% English, 14.6% Italian (2000).
Economy: Single-family building permits issued: 38 (2005); Multi-family building permits issued: 0 (2005); Employment by occupation: 9.0% management, 21.6% professional, 17.5% services, 23.5% sales, 0.7% farming, 14.3% construction, 13.5% production (2000).
Income: Per capita income: $23,000 (2005); Median household income: $60,329 (2005); Average household income: $61,789 (2005); Percent of households with income of $100,000 or more: 15.3% (2005); Poverty rate: 8.5% (2000).
Education: Percent of population age 25 and over with: High school diploma (including GED) or higher: 78.2% (2005); Bachelor's degree or higher: 13.6% (2005); Master's degree or higher: 5.2% (2005).
Housing: Homeownership rate: 89.8% (2005); Median home value: $189,235 (2005); Median rent: $540 per month (2000); Median age of housing: 30 years (2000).
Safety: Violent crime rate: 8.2 per 10,000 population; Property crime rate: 235.6 per 10,000 population (2004).
Transportation: Commute to work: 89.2% car, 1.3% public transportation, 3.8% walk, 4.7% work from home (2000); Travel time to work: 24.1% less than 15 minutes, 39.9% 15 to 30 minutes, 19.2% 30 to 45 minutes, 10.4% 45 to 60 minutes, 6.3% 60 minutes or more (2000)

FRANKLIN (township). Covers a land area of 56.011 square miles and a water area of 0.422 square miles. Located at 39.59° N. Lat.; 75.04° W. Long.
Population: 14,482 (1990); 15,466 (2000); 16,267 (2005); 17,181 (2010 projected); Race: 90.2% White, 6.6% Black, 0.4% Asian, 3.9% Hispanic of any race (2005); Density: 290.4 persons per square mile (2005); Average household size: 2.90 (2005); Median age: 37.4 (2005); Males per 100 females: 99.8 (2005); Marriage status: 28.0% never married, 59.1% now married, 5.7% widowed, 7.3% divorced (2000); Foreign born: 2.3% (2000); Ancestry (includes multiple ancestries): 24.1% Irish, 23.8% German, 23.6% Italian, 11.8% English, 10.5% Other groups (2000).
Economy: Single-family building permits issued: 101 (2005); Multi-family building permits issued: 0 (2005); Employment by occupation: 9.2% management, 17.2% professional, 15.0% services, 25.5% sales, 0.6% farming, 17.5% construction, 15.0% production (2000).
Income: Per capita income: $24,395 (2005); Median household income: $64,104 (2005); Average household income: $70,633 (2005); Percent of households with income of $100,000 or more: 22.1% (2005); Poverty rate: 5.1% (2000).
Education: Percent of population age 25 and over with: High school diploma (including GED) or higher: 81.9% (2005); Bachelor's degree or higher: 14.9% (2005); Master's degree or higher: 3.4% (2005).

Housing: Homeownership rate: 88.7% (2005); Median home value: $175,343 (2005); Median rent: $575 per month (2000); Median age of housing: 27 years (2000).
Safety: Violent crime rate: 18.6 per 10,000 population; Property crime rate: 210.2 per 10,000 population (2004).
Transportation: Commute to work: 93.0% car, 1.7% public transportation, 1.9% walk, 2.4% work from home (2000); Travel time to work: 20.1% less than 15 minutes, 33.1% 15 to 30 minutes, 21.4% 30 to 45 minutes, 12.8% 45 to 60 minutes, 12.6% 60 minutes or more (2000)

FRANKLINVILLE (unincorporated postal area, zip code 08322). Covers a land area of 28.418 square miles and a water area of 0.169 square miles. Located at 39.61° N. Lat.; 75.06° W. Long. Elevation is 98 feet.
History: Founded 1800.
Population: 9,357 (2000); Race: 90.3% White, 6.3% Black, 0.5% Asian, 1.8% Hispanic of any race (2000); Density: 329.3 persons per square mile (2000); Age: 28.9% under 18, 8.7% over 64 (2000); Marriage status: 26.7% never married, 61.2% now married, 5.0% widowed, 7.1% divorced (2000); Foreign born: 1.9% (2000); Ancestry (includes multiple ancestries): 25.8% Irish, 25.4% German, 23.2% Italian, 12.4% English, 9.6% Other groups (2000).
Economy: Vegetable farming. Employment by occupation: 8.9% management, 17.9% professional, 15.2% services, 24.8% sales, 0.1% farming, 18.1% construction, 15.1% production (2000).
Income: Per capita income: $19,766 (2000); Median household income: $54,028 (2000); Poverty rate: 5.3% (2000).
Education: Percent of population age 25 and over with: High school diploma (including GED) or higher: 82.7% (2000); Bachelor's degree or higher: 14.9% (2000).
School District(s)
Delsea Regional H.S Dist. (07-12)
   2003-04 Enrollment: 1,989 . . . . (856) 694-0100
Franklin Township (PK-06)
   2003-04 Enrollment: 1,506 . . . . (856) 629-9500
Two-year College(s)
Prism Career Institute (Private, For-profit)
   Fall 2004 Enrollment: 27 . . . . (609) 407-7476
Housing: Homeownership rate: 88.2% (2000); Median home value: $112,700 (2000); Median rent: $561 per month (2000); Median age of housing: 26 years (2000).
Newspapers: Sentinel (General - Circulation 4,500)
Transportation: Commute to work: 93.5% car, 1.9% public transportation, 0.9% walk, 2.9% work from home (2000); Travel time to work: 17.6% less than 15 minutes, 31.0% 15 to 30 minutes, 23.7% 30 to 45 minutes, 12.7% 45 to 60 minutes, 15.1% 60 minutes or more (2000)

GIBBSTOWN (CDP). Aka Greenwich Township. Covers a land area of 1.632 square miles and a water area of 0 square miles. Located at 39.82° N. Lat.; 75.28° W. Long. Elevation is 15 feet.
Population: 3,902 (1990); 3,758 (2000); 3,867 (2005); 4,022 (2010 projected); Race: 96.1% White, 1.3% Black, 0.8% Asian, 2.0% Hispanic of any race (2005); Density: 2,369.2 persons per square mile (2005); Average household size: 2.52 (2005); Median age: 40.7 (2005); Males per 100 females: 96.9 (2005); Marriage status: 23.4% never married, 61.1% now married, 9.0% widowed, 6.5% divorced (2000); Foreign born: 3.9% (2000); Ancestry (includes multiple ancestries): 35.7% Italian, 23.7% Irish, 17.5% German, 12.1% English, 4.4% Polish (2000).
Economy: Employment by occupation: 8.9% management, 19.8% professional, 11.5% services, 26.7% sales, 0.6% farming, 13.3% construction, 19.3% production (2000).
Income: Per capita income: $28,197 (2005); Median household income: $57,740 (2005); Average household income: $70,007 (2005); Percent of households with income of $100,000 or more: 21.5% (2005); Poverty rate: 3.2% (2000).
Education: Percent of population age 25 and over with: High school diploma (including GED) or higher: 86.7% (2005); Bachelor's degree or higher: 16.7% (2005); Master's degree or higher: 2.8% (2005).
School District(s)
Greenwich Township (PK-08)
   2003-04 Enrollment: 537 . . . . (856) 224-4920
Housing: Homeownership rate: 83.7% (2005); Median home value: $174,854 (2005); Median rent: $581 per month (2000); Median age of housing: 42 years (2000).

Transportation: Commute to work: 94.0% car, 1.9% public transportation, 1.1% walk, 1.7% work from home (2000); Travel time to work: 36.7% less than 15 minutes, 32.6% 15 to 30 minutes, 19.9% 30 to 45 minutes, 4.6% 45 to 60 minutes, 6.2% 60 minutes or more (2000)
Additional Information Contacts
Cherry Hill Regional Chamber of Commerce . . . . (856) 667-1600
   http://www.cherryhillregional.com

GLASSBORO (borough). Covers a land area of 9.206 square miles and a water area of 0.014 square miles. Located at 39.70° N. Lat.; 75.11° W. Long. Elevation is 144 feet.
History: Named for the local glass factories. Glassboro State College, renamed Rowan State College in 1992, was the site of a summit meeting (1967) between President Lyndon Johnson and Soviet Premier Aleksei Kosygin. Settled 1775. Incorporated 1920.
Population: 15,581 (1990); 19,068 (2000); 19,201 (2005); 19,516 (2010 projected); Race: 72.7% White, 20.8% Black, 2.8% Asian, 4.3% Hispanic of any race (2005); Density: 2,085.7 persons per square mile (2005); Average household size: 3.05 (2005); Median age: 28.8 (2005); Males per 100 females: 92.1 (2005); Marriage status: 37.6% never married, 50.6% now married, 5.3% widowed, 6.5% divorced (2000); Foreign born: 4.0% (2000); Ancestry (includes multiple ancestries): 21.9% Other groups, 21.5% Italian, 20.2% Irish, 17.0% German, 8.1% English (2000).
Economy: Trade and processing center for a fruit-growing (especially apples) region. Has light manufacturing. The founding industry, glass, is still important. Single-family building permits issued: 61 (2005); Multi-family building permits issued: 0 (2005); Employment by occupation: 12.0% management, 22.1% professional, 17.3% services, 27.5% sales, 0.1% farming, 7.9% construction, 13.1% production (2000).
Income: Per capita income: $20,795 (2005); Median household income: $50,443 (2005); Average household income: $60,952 (2005); Percent of households with income of $100,000 or more: 16.1% (2005); Poverty rate: 15.2% (2000).
Education: Percent of population age 25 and over with: High school diploma (including GED) or higher: 82.2% (2005); Bachelor's degree or higher: 24.2% (2005); Master's degree or higher: 7.6% (2005).

School District(s)
Elk Township (PK-06)
   2003-04 Enrollment: 442 . . . . (856) 881-4551
Glassboro (PK-12)
   2003-04 Enrollment: 2,555 . . . . (856) 881-0123
Gloucester County Spec Services (UG-UG)
   2003-04 Enrollment: 1,095 . . . . (856) 256-0540
Four-year College(s)
Rowan University (Public)
   Fall 2004 Enrollment: 9,688. (856) 256-4000
   2005-06 Tuition: In-state $8,607; Out-of-state $14,901
Housing: Homeownership rate: 62.6% (2005); Median home value: $173,585 (2005); Median rent: $516 per month (2000); Median age of housing: 31 years (2000).
Safety: Violent crime rate: 40.6 per 10,000 population; Property crime rate: 422.3 per 10,000 population (2004).
Transportation: Commute to work: 86.9% car, 2.2% public transportation, 7.3% walk, 2.0% work from home (2000); Travel time to work: 30.6% less than 15 minutes, 26.4% 15 to 30 minutes, 21.7% 30 to 45 minutes, 11.9% 45 to 60 minutes, 9.4% 60 minutes or more (2000)
Additional Information Contacts
Glassboro Chamber of Commerce . . . . (856) 881-7900
   http://www.glassborochamber.org

GREENWICH (township). Covers a land area of 9.316 square miles and a water area of 2.743 square miles. Located at 39.82° N. Lat.; 75.28° W. Long.
History: Incorporated 1881.
Population: 5,102 (1990); 4,879 (2000); 5,050 (2005); 5,266 (2010 projected); Race: 94.2% White, 3.5% Black, 0.7% Asian, 1.9% Hispanic of any race (2005); Density: 542.1 persons per square mile (2005); Average household size: 2.56 (2005); Median age: 41.2 (2005); Males per 100 females: 96.0 (2005); Marriage status: 24.1% never married, 61.3% now married, 8.6% widowed, 6.0% divorced (2000); Foreign born: 3.6% (2000); Ancestry (includes multiple ancestries): 34.8% Italian, 24.7% Irish, 17.6% German, 10.8% English, 6.5% Other groups (2000).
Economy: Single-family building permits issued: 6 (2005); Multi-family building permits issued: 0 (2005); Employment by occupation: 8.6%

management, 19.8% professional, 11.2% services, 27.7% sales, 0.4% farming, 13.3% construction, 19.0% production (2000).
Income: Per capita income: $28,240 (2005); Median household income: $60,611 (2005); Average household income: $71,268 (2005); Percent of households with income of $100,000 or more: 21.6% (2005); Poverty rate: 3.6% (2000).
Education: Percent of population age 25 and over with: High school diploma (including GED) or higher: 87.0% (2005); Bachelor's degree or higher: 17.4% (2005); Master's degree or higher: 3.0% (2005).
Housing: Homeownership rate: 85.4% (2005); Median home value: $176,910 (2005); Median rent: $583 per month (2000); Median age of housing: 40 years (2000).
Safety: Violent crime rate: 15.9 per 10,000 population; Property crime rate: 226.4 per 10,000 population (2004).
Transportation: Commute to work: 94.3% car, 1.7% public transportation, 1.0% walk, 1.7% work from home (2000); Travel time to work: 36.0% less than 15 minutes, 33.6% 15 to 30 minutes, 20.1% 30 to 45 minutes, 4.9% 45 to 60 minutes, 5.5% 60 minutes or more (2000)
Additional Information Contacts
Greenwich Township . . . . (856) 423-1038
   http://www.greenwichtwp.com

GRENLOCH (unincorporated postal area, zip code 08032). Covers a land area of 0.214 square miles and a water area of 0 square miles. Located at 39.77° N. Lat.; 75.06° W. Long.
Population: 399 (2000); Race: 100.0% White, 0.0% Black, 0.0% Asian, 0.0% Hispanic of any race (2000); Density: 1,864.5 persons per square mile (2000); Age: 31.2% under 18, 16.2% over 64 (2000); Marriage status: 16.2% never married, 71.3% now married, 3.6% widowed, 9.0% divorced (2000); Foreign born: 11.9% (2000); Ancestry (includes multiple ancestries): 42.5% Irish, 33.0% German, 12.8% Italian, 9.5% English, 8.2% Greek (2000).
Economy: Employment by occupation: 5.4% management, 11.7% professional, 21.1% services, 16.6% sales, 0.0% farming, 26.5% construction, 18.8% production (2000).
Income: Per capita income: $17,328 (2000); Median household income: $52,857 (2000); Poverty rate: 13.3% (2000).
Education: Percent of population age 25 and over with: High school diploma (including GED) or higher: 82.3% (2000); Bachelor's degree or higher: 7.7% (2000).
Housing: Homeownership rate: 82.4% (2000); Median home value: $96,700 (2000); Median rent: $811 per month (2000); Median age of housing: 60+ years (2000).
Transportation: Commute to work: 100.0% car, 0.0% public transportation, 0.0% walk, 0.0% work from home (2000); Travel time to work: 10.8% less than 15 minutes, 41.0% 15 to 30 minutes, 22.1% 30 to 45 minutes, 0.0% 45 to 60 minutes, 26.2% 60 minutes or more (2000)

HARRISON (township). Covers a land area of 19.133 square miles and a water area of 0.046 square miles. Located at 39.73° N. Lat.; 75.20° W. Long.
Population: 4,669 (1990); 8,788 (2000); 11,017 (2005); 13,136 (2010 projected); Race: 94.9% White, 3.0% Black, 0.9% Asian, 1.9% Hispanic of any race (2005); Density: 575.8 persons per square mile (2005); Average household size: 3.13 (2005); Median age: 36.0 (2005); Males per 100 females: 98.2 (2005); Marriage status: 20.6% never married, 70.3% now married, 3.8% widowed, 5.4% divorced (2000); Foreign born: 2.0% (2000); Ancestry (includes multiple ancestries): 29.7% Irish, 27.4% German, 25.1% Italian, 14.2% English, 7.1% Polish (2000).
Economy: Single-family building permits issued: 208 (2005); Multi-family building permits issued: 0 (2005); Employment by occupation: 19.7% management, 26.6% professional, 6.8% services, 28.6% sales, 1.1% farming, 10.8% construction, 6.4% production (2000).
Income: Per capita income: $34,620 (2005); Median household income: $94,552 (2005); Average household income: $107,653 (2005); Percent of households with income of $100,000 or more: 46.6% (2005); Poverty rate: 3.2% (2000).
Education: Percent of population age 25 and over with: High school diploma (including GED) or higher: 90.8% (2005); Bachelor's degree or higher: 38.2% (2005); Master's degree or higher: 10.6% (2005).
Housing: Homeownership rate: 85.7% (2005); Median home value: $275,207 (2005); Median rent: $452 per month (2000); Median age of housing: 12 years (2000).
Safety: Violent crime rate: 7.7 per 10,000 population; Property crime rate: 181.3 per 10,000 population (2004).

Transportation: Commute to work: 89.2% car, 1.9% public transportation, 2.6% walk, 5.7% work from home (2000); Travel time to work: 22.4% less than 15 minutes, 28.8% 15 to 30 minutes, 26.7% 30 to 45 minutes, 13.0% 45 to 60 minutes, 9.1% 60 minutes or more (2000)
Additional Information Contacts
Harrison Township . . . . (856) 478-4111
    http://www.harrisontwp.us

LOGAN (township). Covers a land area of 22.619 square miles and a water area of 4.206 square miles. Located at 39.78° N. Lat.; 75.34° W. Long.
History: Incorporated 1877.
Population: 5,147 (1990); 6,032 (2000); 6,010 (2005); 6,061 (2010 projected); Race: 80.5% White, 14.6% Black, 1.9% Asian, 2.9% Hispanic of any race (2005); Density: 265.7 persons per square mile (2005); Average household size: 2.97 (2005); Median age: 35.3 (2005); Males per 100 females: 97.8 (2005); Marriage status: 23.3% never married, 64.9% now married, 3.8% widowed, 8.0% divorced (2000); Foreign born: 3.6% (2000); Ancestry (includes multiple ancestries): 30.8% Irish, 20.3% German, 20.1% Italian, 18.4% Other groups, 12.1% English (2000).
Economy: Single-family building permits issued: 0 (2005); Multi-family building permits issued: 0 (2005); Employment by occupation: 14.7% management, 22.9% professional, 10.9% services, 30.0% sales, 0.6% farming, 6.5% construction, 14.4% production (2000).
Income: Per capita income: $34,287 (2005); Median household income: $85,033 (2005); Average household income: $97,012 (2005); Percent of households with income of $100,000 or more: 38.8% (2005); Poverty rate: 4.3% (2000).
Education: Percent of population age 25 and over with: High school diploma (including GED) or higher: 88.9% (2005); Bachelor's degree or higher: 24.5% (2005); Master's degree or higher: 7.5% (2005).
School District(s)
Logan Township (PK-08)
    2003-04 Enrollment: 1,000 . . . . (856) 467-5133
Housing: Homeownership rate: 90.4% (2005); Median home value: $177,086 (2005); Median rent: $645 per month (2000); Median age of housing: 20 years (2000).
Safety: Violent crime rate: 23.1 per 10,000 population; Property crime rate: 204.7 per 10,000 population (2004).
Transportation: Commute to work: 93.9% car, 2.1% public transportation, 1.5% walk, 2.4% work from home (2000); Travel time to work: 25.6% less than 15 minutes, 29.1% 15 to 30 minutes, 25.3% 30 to 45 minutes, 10.3% 45 to 60 minutes, 9.7% 60 minutes or more (2000)
Additional Information Contacts
Logan Township . . . . (856) 467-2670
    http://www.logan-twp.org

MALAGA (unincorporated postal area, zip code 08328). Covers a land area of 1.872 square miles and a water area of 0.155 square miles. Located at 39.57° N. Lat.; 75.05° W. Long. Elevation is 100 feet.
Population: 1,476 (2000); Race: 91.9% White, 3.2% Black, 0.4% Asian, 2.8% Hispanic of any race (2000); Density: 788.4 persons per square mile (2000); Age: 31.3% under 18, 7.8% over 64 (2000); Marriage status: 30.9% never married, 58.0% now married, 5.7% widowed, 5.4% divorced (2000); Foreign born: 0.7% (2000); Ancestry (includes multiple ancestries): 25.5% German, 24.6% Irish, 23.6% Italian, 12.3% English, 9.0% Other groups (2000).
Economy: In fruit and vegetable area. Employment by occupation: 3.4% management, 19.7% professional, 20.6% services, 24.2% sales, 1.0% farming, 18.1% construction, 13.1% production (2000).
Income: Per capita income: $18,250 (2000); Median household income: $58,833 (2000); Poverty rate: 1.5% (2000).
Education: Percent of population age 25 and over with: High school diploma (including GED) or higher: 81.0% (2000); Bachelor's degree or higher: 10.4% (2000).
Housing: Homeownership rate: 81.7% (2000); Median home value: $103,900 (2000); Median rent: $605 per month (2000); Median age of housing: 26 years (2000).
Transportation: Commute to work: 94.4% car, 2.0% public transportation, 2.6% walk, 1.0% work from home (2000); Travel time to work: 24.1% less than 15 minutes, 34.4% 15 to 30 minutes, 17.8% 30 to 45 minutes, 12.4% 45 to 60 minutes, 11.3% 60 minutes or more (2000)

MANTUA (township). Covers a land area of 15.897 square miles and a water area of 0.005 square miles. Located at 39.76° N. Lat.; 75.16° W. Long. Elevation is 38 feet.
Population: 10,074 (1990); 14,217 (2000); 14,319 (2005); 14,528 (2010 projected); Race: 95.2% White, 2.5% Black, 1.0% Asian, 1.4% Hispanic of any race (2005); Density: 900.7 persons per square mile (2005); Average household size: 2.64 (2005); Median age: 37.4 (2005); Males per 100 females: 96.1 (2005); Marriage status: 21.3% never married, 65.6% now married, 5.7% widowed, 7.4% divorced (2000); Foreign born: 3.0% (2000); Ancestry (includes multiple ancestries): 28.1% German, 27.5% Irish, 23.1% Italian, 14.8% English, 7.1% Other groups (2000).
Economy: In suburbanizing area. Single-family building permits issued: 29 (2005); Multi-family building permits issued: 0 (2005); Employment by occupation: 13.1% management, 22.3% professional, 12.6% services, 29.4% sales, 0.2% farming, 10.2% construction, 12.2% production (2000).
Income: Per capita income: $28,132 (2005); Median household income: $65,011 (2005); Average household income: $73,968 (2005); Percent of households with income of $100,000 or more: 21.8% (2005); Poverty rate: 3.6% (2000).
Education: Percent of population age 25 and over with: High school diploma (including GED) or higher: 85.5% (2005); Bachelor's degree or higher: 23.4% (2005); Master's degree or higher: 6.6% (2005).
School District(s)
Mantua Township (PK-06)
    2003-04 Enrollment: 1,518 . . . . (856) 468-2225
Housing: Homeownership rate: 91.9% (2005); Median home value: $182,503 (2005); Median rent: $504 per month (2000); Median age of housing: 20 years (2000).
Safety: Violent crime rate: 18.8 per 10,000 population; Property crime rate: 212.9 per 10,000 population (2004).
Transportation: Commute to work: 94.9% car, 1.3% public transportation, 1.5% walk, 2.0% work from home (2000); Travel time to work: 25.5% less than 15 minutes, 28.2% 15 to 30 minutes, 27.4% 30 to 45 minutes, 10.0% 45 to 60 minutes, 8.9% 60 minutes or more (2000)
Additional Information Contacts
Mantua Township . . . . (856) 468-1500
    http://www.mantuatownship.com

MICKLETON (unincorporated postal area, zip code 08056). Covers a land area of 8.615 square miles and a water area of 0.030 square miles. Located at 39.78° N. Lat.; 75.25° W. Long. Elevation is 68 feet.
Population: 2,469 (2000); Race: 95.7% White, 0.6% Black, 1.9% Asian, 0.0% Hispanic of any race (2000); Density: 286.6 persons per square mile (2000); Age: 23.6% under 18, 18.2% over 64 (2000); Marriage status: 17.8% never married, 71.8% now married, 6.2% widowed, 4.2% divorced (2000); Foreign born: 3.7% (2000); Ancestry (includes multiple ancestries): 30.0% Irish, 23.4% German, 20.2% Italian, 14.1% English, 4.7% United States or American (2000).
Economy: Employment by occupation: 16.2% management, 23.8% professional, 8.6% services, 27.1% sales, 0.0% farming, 10.9% construction, 13.4% production (2000).
Income: Per capita income: $27,029 (2000); Median household income: $66,058 (2000); Poverty rate: 2.0% (2000).
Education: Percent of population age 25 and over with: High school diploma (including GED) or higher: 90.1% (2000); Bachelor's degree or higher: 21.1% (2000).
School District(s)
East Greenwich Township (PK-06)
    2003-04 Enrollment: 620 . . . . (856) 423-0412
Housing: Homeownership rate: 98.5% (2000); Median home value: $160,400 (2000); Median rent: $675 per month (2000); Median age of housing: 19 years (2000).
Transportation: Commute to work: 94.6% car, 1.0% public transportation, 0.6% walk, 3.8% work from home (2000); Travel time to work: 27.9% less than 15 minutes, 36.2% 15 to 30 minutes, 21.0% 30 to 45 minutes, 3.1% 45 to 60 minutes, 11.8% 60 minutes or more (2000)

MONROE (township). Covers a land area of 46.552 square miles and a water area of 0.377 square miles. Located at 39.66° N. Lat.; 74.98° W. Long.
Population: 26,703 (1990); 28,967 (2000); 31,357 (2005); 33,865 (2010 projected); Race: 84.4% White, 11.3% Black, 1.4% Asian, 3.1% Hispanic of any race (2005); Density: 673.6 persons per square mile (2005); Average household size: 2.71 (2005); Median age: 38.5 (2005); Males per 100

females: 94.2 (2005); Marriage status: 24.9% never married, 60.0% now married, 6.7% widowed, 8.4% divorced (2000); Foreign born: 2.9% (2000); Ancestry (includes multiple ancestries): 25.7% Irish, 24.1% Italian, 23.0% German, 15.2% Other groups, 9.6% English (2000).

Economy: Unemployment rate: 5.0% (2005); Total civilian labor force: 16,488 (2005); Single-family building permits issued: 248 (2005); Multi-family building permits issued: 0 (2005); Employment by occupation: 10.3% management, 16.4% professional, 16.2% services, 31.8% sales, 0.2% farming, 11.5% construction, 13.8% production (2000).

Income: Per capita income: $23,819 (2005); Median household income: $56,468 (2005); Average household income: $64,345 (2005); Percent of households with income of $100,000 or more: 18.2% (2005); Poverty rate: 6.2% (2000).

Taxes: Total city taxes per capita: $533 (2004); City property taxes per capita: $480 (2004).

Education: Percent of population age 25 and over with: High school diploma (including GED) or higher: 80.4% (2005); Bachelor's degree or higher: 16.0% (2005); Master's degree or higher: 4.1% (2005).

Housing: Homeownership rate: 84.2% (2005); Median home value: $173,191 (2005); Median rent: $531 per month (2000); Median age of housing: 24 years (2000).

Safety: Violent crime rate: 20.9 per 10,000 population; Property crime rate: 187.7 per 10,000 population (2004).

Transportation: Commute to work: 91.2% car, 3.2% public transportation, 1.7% walk, 2.7% work from home (2000); Travel time to work: 23.2% less than 15 minutes, 27.0% 15 to 30 minutes, 22.8% 30 to 45 minutes, 13.9% 45 to 60 minutes, 13.0% 60 minutes or more (2000)

Additional Information Contacts

Monroe Township . . . . (856) 728-9800
   http://www.monroetownshipnj.org
Monroe Township . . . . (856) 728-9800
   http://www.monroetownshipnj.org

MOUNT ROYAL (unincorporated postal area, zip code 08061). Covers a land area of 1.197 square miles and a water area of <.001 square miles. Located at 39.80° N. Lat.; 75.20° W. Long. Elevation is 39 feet.

Population: 713 (2000); Race: 80.8% White, 17.8% Black, 1.4% Asian, 1.4% Hispanic of any race (2000); Density: 595.5 persons per square mile (2000); Age: 26.9% under 18, 17.3% over 64 (2000); Marriage status: 33.3% never married, 37.4% now married, 12.4% widowed, 16.9% divorced (2000); Foreign born: 2.7% (2000); Ancestry (includes multiple ancestries): 24.0% German, 22.0% Irish, 20.9% Other groups, 15.1% English, 11.0% Italian (2000).

Economy: Employment by occupation: 8.5% management, 23.8% professional, 12.3% services, 26.2% sales, 0.0% farming, 11.2% construction, 18.1% production (2000).

Income: Per capita income: $18,804 (2000); Median household income: $45,313 (2000); Poverty rate: 5.1% (2000).

Education: Percent of population age 25 and over with: High school diploma (including GED) or higher: 80.2% (2000); Bachelor's degree or higher: 11.6% (2000).

Housing: Homeownership rate: 84.5% (2000); Median home value: $134,500 (2000); Median rent: $522 per month (2000); Median age of housing: 36 years (2000).

Transportation: Commute to work: 94.5% car, 0.0% public transportation, 2.4% walk, 3.1% work from home (2000); Travel time to work: 38.1% less than 15 minutes, 21.5% 15 to 30 minutes, 21.9% 30 to 45 minutes, 6.9% 45 to 60 minutes, 11.7% 60 minutes or more (2000)

MULLICA HILL (CDP). Covers a land area of 1.200 square miles and a water area of 0 square miles. Located at 39.73° N. Lat.; 75.22° W. Long. Elevation is 95 feet.

Population: 1,165 (1990); 1,658 (2000); 2,184 (2005); 2,683 (2010 projected); Race: 91.4% White, 6.2% Black, 0.9% Asian, 2.4% Hispanic of any race (2005); Density: 1,820.4 persons per square mile (2005); Average household size: 2.43 (2005); Median age: 37.2 (2005); Males per 100 females: 84.3 (2005); Marriage status: 23.8% never married, 59.2% now married, 6.5% widowed, 10.5% divorced (2000); Foreign born: 1.4% (2000); Ancestry (includes multiple ancestries): 27.8% Italian, 24.5% German, 19.9% Irish, 16.7% English, 7.0% United States or American (2000).

Economy: In rich fruit and produce region. Employment by occupation: 20.8% management, 24.1% professional, 8.0% services, 37.5% sales, 0.0% farming, 7.6% construction, 2.0% production (2000).

Income: Per capita income: $26,915 (2005); Median household income: $47,515 (2005); Average household income: $65,234 (2005); Percent of households with income of $100,000 or more: 22.8% (2005); Poverty rate: 8.1% (2000).

Education: Percent of population age 25 and over with: High school diploma (including GED) or higher: 88.5% (2005); Bachelor's degree or higher: 37.7% (2005); Master's degree or higher: 8.6% (2005).

School District(s)

Clearview Regional (07-12)
   2003-04 Enrollment: 2,192 . . . . (856) 223-2765
Harrison Township (PK-06)
   2003-04 Enrollment: 1,410 . . . . (856) 478-2016

Housing: Homeownership rate: 62.0% (2005); Median home value: $238,913 (2005); Median rent: $407 per month (2000); Median age of housing: 22 years (2000).

Transportation: Commute to work: 86.5% car, 2.0% public transportation, 4.4% walk, 6.0% work from home (2000); Travel time to work: 21.1% less than 15 minutes, 29.8% 15 to 30 minutes, 23.7% 30 to 45 minutes, 13.2% 45 to 60 minutes, 12.3% 60 minutes or more (2000)

NATIONAL PARK (borough). Covers a land area of 0.996 square miles and a water area of 0.443 square miles. Located at 39.86° N. Lat.; 75.18° W. Long. Elevation is 20 feet.

Population: 3,413 (1990); 3,205 (2000); 3,203 (2005); 3,238 (2010 projected); Race: 98.3% White, 0.1% Black, 0.3% Asian, 1.7% Hispanic of any race (2005); Density: 3,217.0 persons per square mile (2005); Average household size: 2.82 (2005); Median age: 37.5 (2005); Males per 100 females: 99.2 (2005); Marriage status: 25.9% never married, 58.9% now married, 6.6% widowed, 8.7% divorced (2000); Foreign born: 0.9% (2000); Ancestry (includes multiple ancestries): 36.1% Irish, 24.5% German, 20.0% Italian, 13.0% English, 7.0% Polish (2000).

Economy: Single-family building permits issued: 4 (2005); Multi-family building permits issued: 0 (2005); Employment by occupation: 8.8% management, 9.9% professional, 18.7% services, 25.3% sales, 0.3% farming, 16.3% construction, 20.7% production (2000).

Income: Per capita income: $21,025 (2005); Median household income: $53,757 (2005); Average household income: $58,630 (2005); Percent of households with income of $100,000 or more: 10.8% (2005); Poverty rate: 7.6% (2000).

Education: Percent of population age 25 and over with: High school diploma (including GED) or higher: 76.5% (2005); Bachelor's degree or higher: 7.1% (2005); Master's degree or higher: 1.2% (2005).

School District(s)

National Park Borough (PK-06)
   2003-04 Enrollment: 338 . . . . (856) 845-6876

Housing: Homeownership rate: 84.8% (2005); Median home value: $136,330 (2005); Median rent: $538 per month (2000); Median age of housing: 48 years (2000).

Safety: Violent crime rate: 21.7 per 10,000 population; Property crime rate: 145.9 per 10,000 population (2004).

Transportation: Commute to work: 94.1% car, 1.7% public transportation, 1.0% walk, 0.4% work from home (2000); Travel time to work: 28.8% less than 15 minutes, 42.3% 15 to 30 minutes, 19.6% 30 to 45 minutes, 4.2% 45 to 60 minutes, 5.1% 60 minutes or more (2000)

NEWFIELD (borough). Covers a land area of 1.699 square miles and a water area of 0 square miles. Located at 39.54° N. Lat.; 75.02° W. Long. Elevation is 120 feet.

Population: 1,592 (1990); 1,616 (2000); 1,632 (2005); 1,667 (2010 projected); Race: 94.7% White, 1.4% Black, 0.7% Asian, 4.7% Hispanic of any race (2005); Density: 960.5 persons per square mile (2005); Average household size: 2.65 (2005); Median age: 39.8 (2005); Males per 100 females: 86.7 (2005); Marriage status: 20.6% never married, 65.8% now married, 5.5% widowed, 8.2% divorced (2000); Foreign born: 3.4% (2000); Ancestry (includes multiple ancestries): 37.7% Italian, 21.5% Irish, 19.7% German, 12.4% English, 11.0% Other groups (2000).

Economy: Manufacturing: powdered metals, glass products. Single-family building permits issued: 4 (2005); Multi-family building permits issued: 0 (2005); Employment by occupation: 10.3% management, 17.1% professional, 14.0% services, 29.7% sales, 0.2% farming, 14.6% construction, 14.0% production (2000).

Income: Per capita income: $23,959 (2005); Median household income: $57,517 (2005); Average household income: $62,634 (2005); Percent of households with income of $100,000 or more: 16.6% (2005); Poverty rate: 6.5% (2000).

Education: Percent of population age 25 and over with: High school diploma (including GED) or higher: 83.5% (2005); Bachelor's degree or higher: 15.8% (2005); Master's degree or higher: 3.7% (2005).

School District(s)

Buena Regional (PK-12)
    2003-04 Enrollment: 2,627 . . . . (856) 697-0800
Franklin Township (PK-06)
    2003-04 Enrollment: 1,506 . . . . (856) 629-9500
Housing: Homeownership rate: 82.1% (2005); Median home value: $162,050 (2005); Median rent: $548 per month (2000); Median age of housing: 43 years (2000).
Safety: Violent crime rate: 0.0 per 10,000 population; Property crime rate: 109.8 per 10,000 population (2004).
Transportation: Commute to work: 94.4% car, 0.6% public transportation, 1.8% walk, 3.2% work from home (2000); Travel time to work: 39.5% less than 15 minutes, 32.7% 15 to 30 minutes, 12.0% 30 to 45 minutes, 5.7% 45 to 60 minutes, 10.1% 60 minutes or more (2000)

OAK VALLEY (CDP).

Covers a land area of 0.704 square miles and a water area of 0 square miles. Located at 39.80° N. Lat.; 75.15° W. Long. Elevation is 60 feet.
Population: 4,055 (1990); 3,747 (2000); 3,611 (2005); 3,510 (2010 projected); Race: 92.7% White, 4.8% Black, 0.8% Asian, 2.8% Hispanic of any race (2005); Density: 5,128.5 persons per square mile (2005); Average household size: 2.81 (2005); Median age: 38.3 (2005); Males per 100 females: 95.4 (2005); Marriage status: 24.2% never married, 60.3% now married, 9.1% widowed, 6.4% divorced (2000); Foreign born: 2.0% (2000); Ancestry (includes multiple ancestries): 33.3% Irish, 27.1% German, 22.0% Italian, 10.5% English, 8.1% Other groups (2000).
Economy: Employment by occupation: 7.9% management, 13.0% professional, 11.5% services, 35.3% sales, 0.0% farming, 12.8% construction, 19.5% production (2000).
Income: Per capita income: $20,883 (2005); Median household income: $54,844 (2005); Average household income: $58,685 (2005); Percent of households with income of $100,000 or more: 11.3% (2005); Poverty rate: 3.7% (2000).
Education: Percent of population age 25 and over with: High school diploma (including GED) or higher: 83.3% (2005); Bachelor's degree or higher: 6.3% (2005); Master's degree or higher: 2.2% (2005).
Housing: Homeownership rate: 91.1% (2005); Median home value: $152,471 (2005); Median rent: $506 per month (2000); Median age of housing: 41 years (2000).
Transportation: Commute to work: 95.1% car, 1.1% public transportation, 1.3% walk, 1.4% work from home (2000); Travel time to work: 35.9% less than 15 minutes, 26.8% 15 to 30 minutes, 21.0% 30 to 45 minutes, 9.6% 45 to 60 minutes, 6.8% 60 minutes or more (2000)

PAULSBORO (borough).

Covers a land area of 1.961 square miles and a water area of 0.659 square miles. Located at 39.83° N. Lat.; 75.24° W. Long. Elevation is 12 feet.
History: Fortified in the Revolution. Settled 1681, incorporated 1904.
Population: 6,577 (1990); 6,160 (2000); 6,097 (2005); 6,094 (2010 projected); Race: 60.9% White, 33.9% Black, 0.5% Asian, 5.7% Hispanic of any race (2005); Density: 3,108.7 persons per square mile (2005); Average household size: 2.56 (2005); Median age: 34.9 (2005); Males per 100 females: 89.3 (2005); Marriage status: 33.3% never married, 47.4% now married, 9.8% widowed, 9.5% divorced (2000); Foreign born: 3.9% (2000); Ancestry (includes multiple ancestries): 36.5% Other groups, 18.2% Italian, 17.7% German, 14.2% Irish, 8.6% English (2000).
Economy: Oil refineries. Manufacturing: fertilizer, chemicals. Agriculture: vegetables, fruit; poultry. Single-family building permits issued: 1 (2005); Multi-family building permits issued: 0 (2005); Employment by occupation: 6.5% management, 9.0% professional, 19.1% services, 31.3% sales, 0.5% farming, 11.0% construction, 22.7% production (2000).
Income: Per capita income: $18,615 (2005); Median household income: $39,429 (2005); Average household income: $47,455 (2005); Percent of households with income of $100,000 or more: 7.4% (2005); Poverty rate: 17.7% (2000).
Education: Percent of population age 25 and over with: High school diploma (including GED) or higher: 75.5% (2005); Bachelor's degree or higher: 6.0% (2005); Master's degree or higher: 2.0% (2005).

School District(s)

Paulsboro Borough (PK-12)
    2003-04 Enrollment: 1,670 . . . . (856) 423-5515

Housing: Homeownership rate: 60.5% (2005); Median home value: $118,042 (2005); Median rent: $462 per month (2000); Median age of housing: 54 years (2000).
Safety: Violent crime rate: 69.8 per 10,000 population; Property crime rate: 420.5 per 10,000 population (2004).
Transportation: Commute to work: 87.4% car, 3.9% public transportation, 5.5% walk, 0.8% work from home (2000); Travel time to work: 45.1% less than 15 minutes, 31.0% 15 to 30 minutes, 15.7% 30 to 45 minutes, 3.5% 45 to 60 minutes, 4.7% 60 minutes or more (2000)

PITMAN (borough).

Covers a land area of 2.294 square miles and a water area of 0.026 square miles. Located at 39.73° N. Lat.; 75.13° W. Long. Elevation is 132 feet.
History: Settled 1871 as place for Methodist camp meetings; incorporated 1905.
Population: 9,365 (1990); 9,331 (2000); 9,267 (2005); 9,275 (2010 projected); Race: 96.8% White, 1.1% Black, 0.6% Asian, 1.9% Hispanic of any race (2005); Density: 4,040.4 persons per square mile (2005); Average household size: 2.65 (2005); Median age: 39.3 (2005); Males per 100 females: 87.4 (2005); Marriage status: 23.9% never married, 60.7% now married, 7.0% widowed, 8.5% divorced (2000); Foreign born: 2.2% (2000); Ancestry (includes multiple ancestries): 31.4% Irish, 28.7% German, 19.3% Italian, 17.4% English, 6.9% Polish (2000).
Economy: Summer resort. Agriculture: fruit, vegetables, dairy and nursery products. Manufacturing: telecommunications. Site of Lipari Landfill, one of nation's worst Federal Superfund sites. Cleanup completed in 1995. Single-family building permits issued: 1 (2005); Multi-family building permits issued: 0 (2005); Employment by occupation: 12.0% management, 30.7% professional, 11.2% services, 24.3% sales, 0.1% farming, 10.2% construction, 11.5% production (2000).
Income: Per capita income: $26,038 (2005); Median household income: $56,524 (2005); Average household income: $67,811 (2005); Percent of households with income of $100,000 or more: 20.4% (2005); Poverty rate: 5.6% (2000).
Education: Percent of population age 25 and over with: High school diploma (including GED) or higher: 87.9% (2005); Bachelor's degree or higher: 31.3% (2005); Master's degree or higher: 10.2% (2005).

School District(s)

Pitman Borough (PK-12)
    2003-04 Enrollment: 1,695 . . . . (856) 589-2145
Housing: Homeownership rate: 74.2% (2005); Median home value: $181,523 (2005); Median rent: $586 per month (2000); Median age of housing: 56 years (2000).
Safety: Violent crime rate: 1.1 per 10,000 population; Property crime rate: 117.8 per 10,000 population (2004).
Transportation: Commute to work: 91.5% car, 3.3% public transportation, 1.9% walk, 2.8% work from home (2000); Travel time to work: 31.2% less than 15 minutes, 35.7% 15 to 30 minutes, 18.0% 30 to 45 minutes, 6.9% 45 to 60 minutes, 8.1% 60 minutes or more (2000)
Additional Information Contacts
Borough of Pitman . . . . (856) 589-3522
    http://www.pitman.org

SEWELL (unincorporated postal area, zip code 08080).

Covers a land area of 30.242 square miles and a water area of 0.059 square miles. Located at 39.75° N. Lat.; 75.10° W. Long. Elevation is 60 feet.
Population: 36,410 (2000); Race: 90.7% White, 4.4% Black, 3.4% Asian, 2.0% Hispanic of any race (2000); Density: 1,204.0 persons per square mile (2000); Age: 30.6% under 18, 7.1% over 64 (2000); Marriage status: 24.5% never married, 66.4% now married, 3.6% widowed, 5.6% divorced (2000); Foreign born: 5.0% (2000); Ancestry (includes multiple ancestries): 33.8% Italian, 27.3% Irish, 20.2% German, 12.1% Other groups, 10.3% English (2000).
Economy: Employment by occupation: 17.2% management, 24.6% professional, 13.5% services, 28.6% sales, 0.2% farming, 7.5% construction, 8.4% production (2000).
Income: Per capita income: $26,109 (2000); Median household income: $70,418 (2000); Poverty rate: 3.3% (2000).
Education: Percent of population age 25 and over with: High school diploma (including GED) or higher: 90.4% (2000); Bachelor's degree or higher: 31.7% (2000).

School District(s)

Deptford Township (PK-12)
    2003-04 Enrollment: 4,476 . . . . (856) 232-2700

Gloucester County Spec Services (UG-UG)
    2003-04 Enrollment: 1,095 . . . . (856) 256-0540
Gloucester County Vocational (09-12)
    2003-04 Enrollment: 362 . . . . (856) 468-1445
Mantua Township (PK-06)
    2003-04 Enrollment: 1,518 . . . . (856) 468-2225
Washington Township (PK-12)
    2003-04 Enrollment: 9,859 . . . . (856) 589-6644
Two-year College(s)
Gloucester County College (Public)
    Fall 2004 Enrollment: 5,636. . . . . (856) 468-5000
    2005-06 Tuition: In-state $2,976; Out-of-state $5,312
Housing: Homeownership rate: 89.7% (2000); Median home value: $149,200 (2000); Median rent: $714 per month (2000); Median age of housing: 15 years (2000).
Transportation: Commute to work: 92.6% car, 2.5% public transportation, 0.8% walk, 3.7% work from home (2000); Travel time to work: 25.6% less than 15 minutes, 24.1% 15 to 30 minutes, 26.4% 30 to 45 minutes, 13.3% 45 to 60 minutes, 10.7% 60 minutes or more (2000)

SOUTH HARRISON (township). Covers a land area of 15.801 square miles and a water area of 0.021 square miles. Located at 39.69° N. Lat.; 75.26° W. Long.
Population: 1,919 (1990); 2,417 (2000); 2,842 (2005); 3,256 (2010 projected); Race: 92.8% White, 3.1% Black, 0.3% Asian, 4.1% Hispanic of any race (2005); Density: 179.9 persons per square mile (2005); Average household size: 2.96 (2005); Median age: 39.1 (2005); Males per 100 females: 101.1 (2005); Marriage status: 21.8% never married, 67.1% now married, 4.5% widowed, 6.6% divorced (2000); Foreign born: 4.6% (2000); Ancestry (includes multiple ancestries): 24.9% Irish, 24.5% German, 23.2% Italian, 15.3% English, 8.9% Other groups (2000).
Economy: Single-family building permits issued: 30 (2005); Multi-family building permits issued: 0 (2005); Employment by occupation: 17.4% management, 22.6% professional, 8.1% services, 25.0% sales, 0.9% farming, 14.3% construction, 11.7% production (2000).
Income: Per capita income: $32,716 (2005); Median household income: $82,277 (2005); Average household income: $95,874 (2005); Percent of households with income of $100,000 or more: 39.2% (2005); Poverty rate: 8.0% (2000).
Education: Percent of population age 25 and over with: High school diploma (including GED) or higher: 86.3% (2005); Bachelor's degree or higher: 27.1% (2005); Master's degree or higher: 9.5% (2005).
Housing: Homeownership rate: 93.4% (2005); Median home value: $285,496 (2005); Median rent: $521 per month (2000); Median age of housing: 20 years (2000).
Safety: Violent crime rate: 3.7 per 10,000 population; Property crime rate: 65.8 per 10,000 population (2004).
Transportation: Commute to work: 89.1% car, 0.5% public transportation, 1.3% walk, 8.0% work from home (2000); Travel time to work: 19.7% less than 15 minutes, 32.8% 15 to 30 minutes, 26.1% 30 to 45 minutes, 10.6% 45 to 60 minutes, 10.8% 60 minutes or more (2000)
Additional Information Contacts
South Harrison Township . . . . (856) 769-3737
    http://www.southharrison-nj.org

SWEDESBORO (borough). Covers a land area of 0.726 square miles and a water area of 0.031 square miles. Located at 39.74° N. Lat.; 75.31° W. Long. Elevation is 68 feet.
History: Settled by Swedes 1641, incorporated 1902. Partly burned by British, 1778. Trinity Church built 1784.
Population: 2,024 (1990); 2,055 (2000); 2,045 (2005); 2,059 (2010 projected); Race: 77.4% White, 16.3% Black, 0.3% Asian, 9.2% Hispanic of any race (2005); Density: 2,817.0 persons per square mile (2005); Average household size: 2.61 (2005); Median age: 36.2 (2005); Males per 100 females: 98.2 (2005); Marriage status: 27.6% never married, 55.8% now married, 6.6% widowed, 10.0% divorced (2000); Foreign born: 3.1% (2000); Ancestry (includes multiple ancestries): 24.4% Other groups, 23.8% German, 16.3% Italian, 13.2% Irish, 10.9% English (2000).
Economy: Tin cans, plastics, closures. Agriculture: poultry. Single-family building permits issued: 2 (2005); Multi-family building permits issued: 0 (2005); Employment by occupation: 12.4% management, 17.1% professional, 11.3% services, 30.9% sales, 0.9% farming, 10.3% construction, 17.2% production (2000).
Income: Per capita income: $24,002 (2005); Median household income: $54,808 (2005); Average household income: $62,337 (2005); Percent of

households with income of $100,000 or more: 18.0% (2005); Poverty rate: 9.7% (2000).
Education: Percent of population age 25 and over with: High school diploma (including GED) or higher: 80.9% (2005); Bachelor's degree or higher: 14.0% (2005); Master's degree or higher: 4.6% (2005).
School District(s)
Swedesboro-Woolwich (PK-06)
    2003-04 Enrollment: 1,076 . . . . (856) 467-0221
Housing: Homeownership rate: 64.6% (2005); Median home value: $153,571 (2005); Median rent: $513 per month (2000); Median age of housing: 60 years (2000).
Safety: Violent crime rate: 29.1 per 10,000 population; Property crime rate: 319.9 per 10,000 population (2004).
Transportation: Commute to work: 93.3% car, 0.0% public transportation, 4.2% walk, 0.6% work from home (2000); Travel time to work: 38.2% less than 15 minutes, 27.1% 15 to 30 minutes, 18.6% 30 to 45 minutes, 11.2% 45 to 60 minutes, 5.0% 60 minutes or more (2000)

THOROFARE (unincorporated postal area, zip code 08086). Aka Thoroughfare. Covers a land area of 5.689 square miles and a water area of 0.092 square miles. Located at 39.84° N. Lat.; 75.18° W. Long. Elevation is 19 feet.
Population: 5,424 (2000); Race: 91.5% White, 7.1% Black, 0.2% Asian, 1.8% Hispanic of any race (2000); Density: 953.3 persons per square mile (2000); Age: 22.6% under 18, 11.5% over 64 (2000); Marriage status: 26.1% never married, 56.1% now married, 6.4% widowed, 11.4% divorced (2000); Foreign born: 0.6% (2000); Ancestry (includes multiple ancestries): 33.8% Irish, 32.7% German, 21.6% Italian, 15.2% English, 9.6% Other groups (2000).
Economy: Manufacturing includes business forms, bearings, electrical connectors, and baked goods. Employment by occupation: 12.4% management, 18.1% professional, 11.2% services, 30.4% sales, 0.3% farming, 10.7% construction, 17.0% production (2000).
Income: Per capita income: $23,886 (2000); Median household income: $51,146 (2000); Poverty rate: 7.0% (2000).
Education: Percent of population age 25 and over with: High school diploma (including GED) or higher: 84.7% (2000); Bachelor's degree or higher: 18.0% (2000).
School District(s)
West Deptford Township (PK-12)
    2003-04 Enrollment: 3,326 . . . . (856) 848-4300
Housing: Homeownership rate: 67.4% (2000); Median home value: $113,300 (2000); Median rent: $623 per month (2000); Median age of housing: 28 years (2000).
Transportation: Commute to work: 95.7% car, 1.5% public transportation, 0.9% walk, 1.5% work from home (2000); Travel time to work: 30.3% less than 15 minutes, 36.1% 15 to 30 minutes, 21.0% 30 to 45 minutes, 8.4% 45 to 60 minutes, 4.2% 60 minutes or more (2000)

TURNERSVILLE (CDP). Covers a land area of 1.485 square miles and a water area of 0.004 square miles. Located at 39.76° N. Lat.; 75.06° W. Long. Elevation is 80 feet.
Population: 3,843 (1990); 3,867 (2000); 3,616 (2005); 3,521 (2010 projected); Race: 92.8% White, 3.9% Black, 2.1% Asian, 1.4% Hispanic of any race (2005); Density: 2,434.4 persons per square mile (2005); Average household size: 3.30 (2005); Median age: 38.0 (2005); Males per 100 females: 93.7 (2005); Marriage status: 23.3% never married, 67.0% now married, 5.0% widowed, 4.6% divorced (2000); Foreign born: 4.1% (2000); Ancestry (includes multiple ancestries): 37.6% Italian, 30.8% Irish, 17.3% German, 12.5% English, 10.5% Other groups (2000).
Economy: Employment by occupation: 17.3% management, 23.2% professional, 8.9% services, 35.1% sales, 0.0% farming, 4.0% construction, 11.5% production (2000).
Income: Per capita income: $32,196 (2005); Median household income: $95,531 (2005); Average household income: $104,393 (2005); Percent of households with income of $100,000 or more: 46.6% (2005); Poverty rate: 3.1% (2005).
Education: Percent of population age 25 and over with: High school diploma (including GED) or higher: 89.0% (2005); Bachelor's degree or higher: 33.9% (2005); Master's degree or higher: 8.9% (2005).
School District(s)
Washington Township (PK-12)
    2003-04 Enrollment: 9,859 . . . . (856) 589-6644

Housing: Homeownership rate: 98.1% (2005); Median home value: $241,563 (2005); Median rent: $816 per month (2000); Median age of housing: 20 years (2000).

Hospitals: Kennedy Memorial Hospitals: UMC Washington Township (146 beds)

Transportation: Commute to work: 89.8% car, 3.4% public transportation, 0.8% walk, 6.0% work from home (2000); Travel time to work: 23.0% less than 15 minutes, 27.4% 15 to 30 minutes, 22.7% 30 to 45 minutes, 13.5% 45 to 60 minutes, 13.4% 60 minutes or more (2000)

Additional Information Contacts

Washington Township Chamber of Commerce . . . . (856) 227-1776
http://www.washingtontownshipchamber.org

VICTORY LAKES (CDP). Covers a land area of 2.398 square miles and a water area of 0.121 square miles. Located at 39.63° N. Lat.; 74.96° W. Long.

Population: 2,160 (1990); 2,118 (2000); 2,330 (2005); 2,552 (2010 projected); Race: 91.3% White, 4.9% Black, 1.0% Asian, 3.8% Hispanic of any race (2005); Density: 971.8 persons per square mile (2005); Average household size: 2.89 (2005); Median age: 37.5 (2005); Males per 100 females: 100.9 (2005); Marriage status: 26.1% never married, 58.6% now married, 6.9% widowed, 8.5% divorced (2000); Foreign born: 1.0% (2000); Ancestry (includes multiple ancestries): 35.0% Irish, 28.4% German, 20.8% Italian, 10.3% Other groups, 10.2% English (2000).

Economy: Employment by occupation: 6.7% management, 19.5% professional, 22.7% services, 26.6% sales, 0.0% farming, 13.5% construction, 11.1% production (2000).

Income: Per capita income: $23,161 (2005); Median household income: $62,333 (2005); Average household income: $66,954 (2005); Percent of households with income of $100,000 or more: 19.5% (2005); Poverty rate: 7.1% (2000).

Education: Percent of population age 25 and over with: High school diploma (including GED) or higher: 80.7% (2005); Bachelor's degree or higher: 12.8% (2005); Master's degree or higher: 2.9% (2005).

Housing: Homeownership rate: 92.3% (2005); Median home value: $156,846 (2005); Median rent: $645 per month (2000); Median age of housing: 30 years (2000).

Transportation: Commute to work: 93.3% car, 2.7% public transportation, 0.7% walk, 2.9% work from home (2000); Travel time to work: 19.6% less than 15 minutes, 26.7% 15 to 30 minutes, 30.7% 30 to 45 minutes, 11.2% 45 to 60 minutes, 11.9% 60 minutes or more (2000)

WASHINGTON (township). Covers a land area of 21.371 square miles and a water area of 0.124 square miles. Located at 39.74° N. Lat.; 75.06° W. Long.

Population: 41,960 (1990); 47,114 (2000); 51,774 (2005); 56,463 (2010 projected); Race: 89.1% White, 5.7% Black, 3.4% Asian, 2.4% Hispanic of any race (2005); Density: 2,422.7 persons per square mile (2005); Average household size: 2.95 (2005); Median age: 37.1 (2005); Males per 100 females: 94.1 (2005); Marriage status: 25.3% never married, 64.0% now married, 5.0% widowed, 5.6% divorced (2000); Foreign born: 4.8% (2000); Ancestry (includes multiple ancestries): 33.9% Italian, 28.9% Irish, 20.0% German, 11.4% Other groups, 9.8% English (2000).

Economy: Unemployment rate: 1.8% (2005); Total civilian labor force: 28,219 (2005); Single-family building permits issued: 65 (2005); Multi-family building permits issued: 0 (2005); Employment by occupation: 16.7% management, 24.1% professional, 12.5% services, 31.0% sales, 0.0% farming, 7.1% construction, 8.6% production (2000).

Income: Per capita income: $30,187 (2005); Median household income: $74,784 (2005); Average household income: $88,460 (2005); Percent of households with income of $100,000 or more: 31.8% (2005); Poverty rate: 3.2% (2000).

Taxes: Total city taxes per capita: $491 (2004); City property taxes per capita: $468 (2004).

Education: Percent of population age 25 and over with: High school diploma (including GED) or higher: 89.9% (2005); Bachelor's degree or higher: 30.4% (2005); Master's degree or higher: 9.0% (2005).

Housing: Homeownership rate: 86.2% (2005); Median home value: $218,805 (2005); Median rent: $710 per month (2000); Median age of housing: 19 years (2000).

Safety: Violent crime rate: 19.1 per 10,000 population; Property crime rate: 245.8 per 10,000 population (2004).

Transportation: Commute to work: 92.6% car, 3.1% public transportation, 0.8% walk, 3.1% work from home (2000); Travel time to work: 24.6% less than 15 minutes, 24.1% 15 to 30 minutes, 25.5% 30 to 45 minutes, 13.2% 45 to 60 minutes, 12.7% 60 minutes or more (2000)

Additional Information Contacts

Washington Township . . . . (856) 589-0575
http://www.twp.washington.nj.us

WENONAH (borough). Covers a land area of 0.973 square miles and a water area of 0 square miles. Located at 39.79° N. Lat.; 75.14° W. Long. Elevation is 60 feet.

History: Incorporated 1883.

Population: 2,331 (1990); 2,317 (2000); 2,318 (2005); 2,348 (2010 projected); Race: 97.6% White, 1.0% Black, 0.7% Asian, 0.9% Hispanic of any race (2005); Density: 2,381.3 persons per square mile (2005); Average household size: 2.69 (2005); Median age: 42.5 (2005); Males per 100 females: 95.3 (2005); Marriage status: 22.5% never married, 67.0% now married, 3.8% widowed, 6.7% divorced (2000); Foreign born: 1.6% (2000); Ancestry (includes multiple ancestries): 33.0% Irish, 27.3% German, 21.6% Italian, 16.1% English, 6.9% Polish (2000).

Economy: Single-family building permits issued: 5 (2005); Multi-family building permits issued: 0 (2005); Employment by occupation: 18.0% management, 36.2% professional, 8.0% services, 23.3% sales, 0.4% farming, 7.5% construction, 6.7% production (2000).

Income: Per capita income: $38,217 (2005); Median household income: $83,287 (2005); Average household income: $101,305 (2005); Percent of households with income of $100,000 or more: 36.2% (2005); Poverty rate: 2.5% (2000).

Education: Percent of population age 25 and over with: High school diploma (including GED) or higher: 97.4% (2005); Bachelor's degree or higher: 42.2% (2005); Master's degree or higher: 15.8% (2005).

School District(s)

Deptford Township (PK-12)
    2003-04 Enrollment: 4,476 . . . . (856) 232-2700
Wenonah Borough (PK-06)
    2003-04 Enrollment: 213 . . . . (856) 468-6000

Housing: Homeownership rate: 89.0% (2005); Median home value: $248,688 (2005); Median rent: $589 per month (2000); Median age of housing: 54 years (2000).

Safety: Violent crime rate: 0.0 per 10,000 population; Property crime rate: 68.7 per 10,000 population (2004).

Transportation: Commute to work: 90.7% car, 2.0% public transportation, 2.0% walk, 5.1% work from home (2000); Travel time to work: 28.9% less than 15 minutes, 28.2% 15 to 30 minutes, 21.7% 30 to 45 minutes, 9.2% 45 to 60 minutes, 12.1% 60 minutes or more (2000)

WEST DEPTFORD (township). Covers a land area of 15.896 square miles and a water area of 1.860 square miles. Located at 39.84° N. Lat.; 75.17° W. Long.

History: Incorporated 1871.

Population: 19,380 (1990); 19,368 (2000); 20,334 (2005); 21,406 (2010 projected); Race: 91.2% White, 6.0% Black, 1.2% Asian, 2.0% Hispanic of any race (2005); Density: 1,279.2 persons per square mile (2005); Average household size: 2.46 (2005); Median age: 38.9 (2005); Males per 100 females: 94.0 (2005); Marriage status: 26.8% never married, 56.3% now married, 6.8% widowed, 10.1% divorced (2000); Foreign born: 1.9% (2000); Ancestry (includes multiple ancestries): 33.2% Irish, 28.1% German, 23.3% Italian, 14.5% English, 8.7% Other groups (2000).

Economy: Single-family building permits issued: 217 (2005); Multi-family building permits issued: 193 (2005); Employment by occupation: 11.0% management, 20.9% professional, 11.3% services, 30.3% sales, 0.2% farming, 9.0% construction, 17.2% production (2000).

Income: Per capita income: $27,208 (2005); Median household income: $56,140 (2005); Average household income: $66,719 (2005); Percent of households with income of $100,000 or more: 18.1% (2005); Poverty rate: 5.3% (2000).

Education: Percent of population age 25 and over with: High school diploma (including GED) or higher: 85.7% (2005); Bachelor's degree or higher: 21.7% (2005); Master's degree or higher: 6.8% (2005).

School District(s)

West Deptford Township (PK-12)
    2003-04 Enrollment: 3,326 . . . . (856) 848-4300

Housing: Homeownership rate: 70.1% (2005); Median home value: $177,367 (2005); Median rent: $614 per month (2000); Median age of housing: 30 years (2000).

Safety: Violent crime rate: 15.4 per 10,000 population; Property crime rate: 217.9 per 10,000 population (2004).

Transportation: Commute to work: 93.4% car, 2.5% public transportation, 1.6% walk, 1.5% work from home (2000); Travel time to work: 31.0% less than 15 minutes, 35.7% 15 to 30 minutes, 21.0% 30 to 45 minutes, 6.8% 45 to 60 minutes, 5.5% 60 minutes or more (2000)
Additional Information Contacts
West Deptford Township . . . . (856) 845-4004
    http://www.westdeptford.com

WESTVILLE (borough). Covers a land area of 0.964 square miles and a water area of 0.392 square miles. Located at 39.86° N. Lat.; 75.12° W. Long. Elevation is 16 feet.
History: Incorporated 1924.
Population: 4,573 (1990); 4,500 (2000); 4,464 (2005); 4,477 (2010 projected); Race: 92.1% White, 3.5% Black, 1.1% Asian, 3.9% Hispanic of any race (2005); Density: 4,628.8 persons per square mile (2005); Average household size: 2.47 (2005); Median age: 38.2 (2005); Males per 100 females: 95.3 (2005); Marriage status: 26.1% never married, 52.6% now married, 8.7% widowed, 12.6% divorced (2000); Foreign born: 2.3% (2000); Ancestry (includes multiple ancestries): 28.6% Irish, 27.2% German, 20.6% Italian, 13.2% English, 6.5% Other groups (2000).
Economy: Oil refining, manufacturing of clothing, chemicals, glass, fabricated metal products. Single-family building permits issued: 6 (2005); Multi-family building permits issued: 0 (2005); Employment by occupation: 8.7% management, 11.8% professional, 15.4% services, 31.2% sales, 0.0% farming, 14.9% construction, 17.9% production (2000).
Income: Per capita income: $21,283 (2005); Median household income: $44,519 (2005); Average household income: $52,366 (2005); Percent of households with income of $100,000 or more: 10.7% (2005); Poverty rate: 8.7% (2000).
Education: Percent of population age 25 and over with: High school diploma (including GED) or higher: 75.7% (2005); Bachelor's degree or higher: 9.0% (2005); Master's degree or higher: 1.2% (2005).
School District(s)
Deptford Township (PK-12)
    2003-04 Enrollment: 4,476 . . . . (856) 232-2700
West Deptford Township (PK-12)
    2003-04 Enrollment: 3,326 . . . . (856) 848-4300
Westville Borough (PK-06)
    2003-04 Enrollment: 406 . . . . (856) 456-0235
Housing: Homeownership rate: 63.9% (2005); Median home value: $133,344 (2005); Median rent: $511 per month (2000); Median age of housing: 52 years (2000).
Safety: Violent crime rate: 15.5 per 10,000 population; Property crime rate: 286.4 per 10,000 population (2004).
Transportation: Commute to work: 91.4% car, 2.2% public transportation, 3.1% walk, 2.1% work from home (2000); Travel time to work: 39.9% less than 15 minutes, 35.4% 15 to 30 minutes, 15.8% 30 to 45 minutes, 4.1% 45 to 60 minutes, 4.7% 60 minutes or more (2000)

WILLIAMSTOWN (CDP). Covers a land area of 6.163 square miles and a water area of 0 square miles. Located at 39.68° N. Lat.; 74.99° W. Long. Elevation is 154 feet.
History: Settled before 1800.
Population: 10,891 (1990); 11,812 (2000); 12,910 (2005); 14,047 (2010 projected); Race: 85.5% White, 10.4% Black, 1.1% Asian, 3.2% Hispanic of any race (2005); Density: 2,094.9 persons per square mile (2005); Average household size: 2.57 (2005); Median age: 38.2 (2005); Males per 100 females: 91.7 (2005); Marriage status: 25.8% never married, 58.6% now married, 6.7% widowed, 8.9% divorced (2000); Foreign born: 3.2% (2000); Ancestry (includes multiple ancestries): 25.1% Italian, 24.7% German, 24.0% Irish, 13.8% Other groups, 10.2% English (2000).
Economy: Manufacturing of clothing, canned goods. Agriculture: poultry; vegetables, fruit. Employment by occupation: 9.5% management, 14.9% professional, 16.0% services, 34.6% sales, 0.0% farming, 10.5% construction, 14.5% production (2000).
Income: Per capita income: $21,948 (2005); Median household income: $48,483 (2005); Average household income: $56,242 (2005); Percent of households with income of $100,000 or more: 13.4% (2005); Poverty rate: 7.5% (2000).
Education: Percent of population age 25 and over with: High school diploma (including GED) or higher: 80.0% (2005); Bachelor's degree or higher: 13.4% (2005); Master's degree or higher: 2.5% (2005).
School District(s)
Buena Regional (PK-12)
    2003-04 Enrollment: 2,627 . . . . (856) 697-0800

Monroe Township (PK-12)
    2003-04 Enrollment: 5,593 . . . . (856) 629-6400
Housing: Homeownership rate: 73.5% (2005); Median home value: $175,718 (2005); Median rent: $520 per month (2000); Median age of housing: 26 years (2000).
Transportation: Commute to work: 90.3% car, 4.8% public transportation, 1.8% walk, 2.4% work from home (2000); Travel time to work: 26.8% less than 15 minutes, 25.5% 15 to 30 minutes, 24.5% 30 to 45 minutes, 12.0% 45 to 60 minutes, 11.3% 60 minutes or more (2000)

WOODBURY (city). Covers a land area of 2.077 square miles and a water area of 0.039 square miles. Located at 39.83° N. Lat.; 75.15° W. Long. Elevation is 57 feet.
History: Named for Henry Wood and his son John, Quaker farmers from Bury, England. Originally a Quaker settlement, Woodbury tried to remain neutral during the American Revolution; however, the armies of both sides occupied the town, and many battles were fought in the vicinity. The city's 18th-century buildings include the Cooper House, where Cornwallis stopped in 1777, and a Friends' meetinghouse. The county historical society has collections in the John Lawrence House (1765). Settled 1683. Incorporated as a city 1871.
Population: 10,904 (1990); 10,307 (2000); 10,509 (2005); 10,778 (2010 projected); Race: 69.0% White, 25.9% Black, 1.1% Asian, 5.1% Hispanic of any race (2005); Density: 5,058.6 persons per square mile (2005); Average household size: 2.48 (2005); Median age: 37.8 (2005); Males per 100 females: 89.1 (2005); Marriage status: 32.7% never married, 47.3% now married, 10.2% widowed, 9.8% divorced (2000); Foreign born: 2.7% (2000); Ancestry (includes multiple ancestries): 25.2% Other groups, 20.8% Irish, 20.1% German, 13.8% Italian, 11.6% English (2000).
Economy: Trade and service center, with petrochemical companies nearby. Single-family building permits issued: 10 (2005); Multi-family building permits issued: 0 (2005); Employment by occupation: 15.2% management, 20.8% professional, 16.1% services, 25.7% sales, 0.3% farming, 7.6% construction, 14.3% production (2000).
Income: Per capita income: $25,237 (2005); Median household income: $46,933 (2005); Average household income: $60,743 (2005); Percent of households with income of $100,000 or more: 15.8% (2005); Poverty rate: 13.5% (2000).
Education: Percent of population age 25 and over with: High school diploma (including GED) or higher: 80.1% (2005); Bachelor's degree or higher: 21.6% (2005); Master's degree or higher: 6.8% (2005).
School District(s)
West Deptford Township (PK-12)
    2003-04 Enrollment: 3,326 . . . . (856) 848-4300
Woodbury City (PK-12)
    2003-04 Enrollment: 1,609 . . . . (856) 853-0123
Housing: Homeownership rate: 58.4% (2005); Median home value: $146,362 (2005); Median rent: $440 per month (2000); Median age of housing: 51 years (2000).
Hospitals: Underwood-Memorial Hospital (305 beds)
Safety: Violent crime rate: 49.5 per 10,000 population; Property crime rate: 462.3 per 10,000 population (2004).
Newspapers: Gloucester County Times (Circulation 24,040)
Transportation: Commute to work: 86.0% car, 5.6% public transportation, 4.3% walk, 2.0% work from home (2000); Travel time to work: 31.1% less than 15 minutes, 35.6% 15 to 30 minutes, 19.6% 30 to 45 minutes, 6.5% 45 to 60 minutes, 7.2% 60 minutes or more (2000)
Additional Information Contacts
City of Woodbury . . . . (856) 845-1300
    http://www.woodbury.nj.us/cg_city_off.shtml
Gloucester County Chamber of Commerce . . . . (856) 384-2655
    http://www.gloucestercountychamber.org
Woodbury Chamber of Commerce . . . . (856) 845-4056
    http://woodbury.nj.us

WOODBURY HEIGHTS (borough). Covers a land area of 1.226 square miles and a water area of 0 square miles. Located at 39.81° N. Lat.; 75.15° W. Long. Elevation is 74 feet.
History: Settled c.1770, incorporated 1915.
Population: 3,392 (1990); 2,988 (2000); 3,009 (2005); 3,063 (2010 projected); Race: 96.1% White, 1.5% Black, 1.2% Asian, 1.6% Hispanic of any race (2005); Density: 2,454.3 persons per square mile (2005); Average household size: 2.85 (2005); Median age: 39.4 (2005); Males per 100 females: 93.3 (2005); Marriage status: 21.7% never married, 67.9% now married, 6.9% widowed, 3.6% divorced (2000); Foreign born: 3.1% (2000);

Ancestry (includes multiple ancestries): 35.1% Irish, 30.3% Italian, 25.8% German, 15.7% English, 5.5% Polish (2000).
Economy: Manufacturing: clothing, concrete blocks. Single-family building permits issued: 8 (2005); Multi-family building permits issued: 0 (2005); Employment by occupation: 6.5% management, 23.2% professional, 11.0% services, 32.0% sales, 0.4% farming, 11.9% construction, 15.0% production (2000).
Income: Per capita income: $27,421 (2005); Median household income: $65,846 (2005); Average household income: $77,252 (2005); Percent of households with income of $100,000 or more: 25.4% (2005); Poverty rate: 4.1% (2000).
Education: Percent of population age 25 and over with: High school diploma (including GED) or higher: 86.6% (2005); Bachelor's degree or higher: 23.0% (2005); Master's degree or higher: 7.9% (2005).

School District(s)

Gateway Regional (07-12)
   2003-04 Enrollment: 1,143 . . . . (856) 848-8172
Woodbury Heights Borough (PK-06)
   2003-04 Enrollment: 253 . . . . (856) 848-7001
Housing: Homeownership rate: 92.4% (2005); Median home value: $187,598 (2005); Median rent: $642 per month (2000); Median age of housing: 39 years (2000).
Safety: Violent crime rate: 26.5 per 10,000 population; Property crime rate: 380.5 per 10,000 population (2004).
Transportation: Commute to work: 93.8% car, 3.2% public transportation, 0.9% walk, 1.5% work from home (2000); Travel time to work: 29.3% less than 15 minutes, 36.3% 15 to 30 minutes, 17.8% 30 to 45 minutes, 7.7% 45 to 60 minutes, 8.9% 60 minutes or more (2000)

WOOLWICH (township). Covers a land area of 20.945 square miles and a water area of 0.236 square miles. Located at 39.73° N. Lat.; 75.30° W. Long.
Population: 1,505 (1990); 3,032 (2000); 6,814 (2005); 10,243 (2010 projected); Race: 91.5% White, 3.9% Black, 1.2% Asian, 3.7% Hispanic of any race (2005); Density: 325.3 persons per square mile (2005); Average household size: 3.18 (2005); Median age: 35.1 (2005); Males per 100 females: 98.3 (2005); Marriage status: 20.4% never married, 72.6% now married, 3.4% widowed, 3.7% divorced (2000); Foreign born: 2.4% (2000); Ancestry (includes multiple ancestries): 28.8% Italian, 28.0% Irish, 27.3% German, 11.0% English, 10.9% Other groups (2000).
Economy: Single-family building permits issued: 387 (2005); Multi-family building permits issued: 0 (2005); Employment by occupation: 21.2% management, 23.5% professional, 8.3% services, 26.5% sales, 2.4% farming, 8.5% construction, 9.6% production (2000).
Income: Per capita income: $37,575 (2005); Median household income: $104,336 (2005); Average household income: $118,853 (2005); Percent of households with income of $100,000 or more: 52.7% (2005); Poverty rate: 2.9% (2000).
Education: Percent of population age 25 and over with: High school diploma (including GED) or higher: 87.8% (2005); Bachelor's degree or higher: 30.0% (2005); Master's degree or higher: 11.7% (2005).

School District(s)

Kingsway Regional (07-12)
   2003-04 Enrollment: 1,751 . . . . (856) 467-4600
Swedesboro-Woolwich (PK-06)
   2003-04 Enrollment: 1,076 . . . . (856) 467-0221
Housing: Homeownership rate: 92.7% (2005); Median home value: $299,178 (2005); Median rent: $542 per month (2000); Median age of housing: 7 years (2000).
Safety: Violent crime rate: 9.0 per 10,000 population; Property crime rate: 239.0 per 10,000 population (2004).
Transportation: Commute to work: 93.2% car, 0.0% public transportation, 0.0% walk, 5.8% work from home (2000); Travel time to work: 19.0% less than 15 minutes, 28.6% 15 to 30 minutes, 27.0% 30 to 45 minutes, 14.6% 45 to 60 minutes, 10.9% 60 minutes or more (2000)

Hudson County

Located in northeastern New Jersey; bounded on the west by the Passaic River and Newark Bay, and on the east by the Hudson River and Upper New York Bay; drained by the Hackensack River. Covers a land area of 46.69 square miles, a water area of 15.74 square miles, and is located in the Eastern Time Zone. The county government was organized in 1840. County seat is Jersey City.

Hudson County is part of the New York-Northern New Jersey-Long Island, NY-NJ-PA Metropolitan Statistical Area. The entire metro area includes: Edison, NJ Metropolitan Division (Middlesex County, NJ; Monmouth County, NJ; Ocean County, NJ; Somerset County, NJ); Nassau-Suffolk, NY Metropolitan Division (Nassau County, NY; Suffolk County, NY); New York-White Plains-Wayne, NY-NJ Metropolitan Division (Bergen County, NJ; Hudson County, NJ; Passaic County, NJ; Bronx County, NY; Kings County, NY; New York County, NY; Putnam County, NY; Queens County, NY; Richmond County, NY; Rockland County, NY; Westchester County, NY); Newark-Union, NJ-PA Metropolitan Division (Essex County, NJ; Hunterdon County, NJ; Morris County, NJ; Sussex County, NJ; Union County, NJ; Pike County, PA)

Population: 553,105 (1990); 608,975 (2000); 605,015 (2005); 600,740 (2010 projected); Race: 54.0% White, 13.2% Black, 9.7% Asian, 41.4% Hispanic of any race (2005); Density: 12,958.8 persons per square mile (2005); Average household size: 2.64 (2005); Median age: 35.4 (2005); Males per 100 females: 97.4 (2005).
Religion: Five largest groups: 52.2% Catholic Church, 2.6% Muslim Estimate, 2.1% Jewish Estimate, 0.9% American Baptist Churches in the USA, 0.6% Assemblies of God (2000).
Economy: Unemployment rate: 5.4% (2005); Total civilian labor force: 290,621 (2005); Leading industries: 15.6% finance & insurance; 11.4% transportation & warehousing; 10.6% health care and social assistance (2004); Farms: n/a totaling n/a acres (2002); Companies that employ 500 or more persons: 106 (2004); Companies that employ 100 to 499 persons: 612 (2004); Companies that employ less than 100 persons: 26,285 (2004); Black-owned businesses: 3,116 (2002); Hispanic-owned businesses: 12,588 (2002); Asian-owned businesses: 5,066 (2002); Women-owned businesses: 11,792 (2002); Retail sales per capita: $9,744 (2006). Single-family building permits issued: 361 (2005); Multi-family building permits issued: 4,137 (2005).
Income: Per capita income: $24,557 (2005); Median household income: $46,499 (2005); Average household income: $64,144 (2005); Percent of households with income of $100,000 or more: 18.0% (2005); Poverty rate: 15.0% (2003); Bankruptcy rate: 7.56% (2005).
Taxes: Total county taxes per capita: $338 (2004); County property taxes per capita: $338 (2004).
Education: Percent of population age 25 and over with: High school diploma (including GED) or higher: 70.6% (2005); Bachelor's degree or higher: 25.7% (2005); Master's degree or higher: 9.1% (2005).
Housing: Homeownership rate: 30.5% (2005); Median home value: $255,898 (2005); Median rent: $638 per month (2000); Median age of housing: 52 years (2000).
Health: Birth rate: 150.3 per 10,000 population (2004); Death rate: 77.7 per 10,000 population (2004); Age-adjusted cancer mortality rate: 188.0 deaths per 100,000 population (2002); Air Quality Index: 81.6% good, 15.6% moderate, 2.7% unhealthy for sensitive individuals, 0.0% unhealthy (percent of days in 2005); Number of physicians: 20.2 per 10,000 population (2004); Hospital beds: 27.1 per 10,000 population (2003); Hospital admissions: 1,107.1 per 10,000 population (2003).
Elections: 2004 Presidential election results: 32.0% Bush, 67.3% Kerry, 0.5% Nader, 0.1% Badnarik

Additional Information Contacts

Hudson County Government . . . . (201) 795-6200
   http://www.hudsoncountynj.org
Bayonne Chamber of Commerce . . . . (201) 436-4333
   http://www.bayonnenj.org/commerce.htm
City of Bayonne . . . . (201) 858-6000
   http://www.bayonnenj.org
City of Hoboken . . . . (201) 420-2000
   http://www.hobokennj.org
City of Jersey City . . . . (201) 547-4900
   http://www.cityofjerseycity.com
Hoboken Chamber of Commerce . . . . (201) 222-1100
   http://www.hobokenchamber.com
Hudson County Chamber of Commerce . . . . (201) 435-7400
   http://www.hudsonchamber.org
Town of Kearny . . . . (201) 955-7400
   http://www.kearnyusa.com
Town of Secaucus . . . . (201) 330-2008
   http://www.townofsecaucus.com
West Hudson-South Bergen Chmbr of Commerce . . . . (201) 991-5600
   http://www.co.bergen.nj.us

Hudson County Communities

BAYONNE (city). Covers a land area of 5.626 square miles and a water area of 5.628 square miles. Located at 40.66° N. Lat.; 74.11° W. Long. Elevation is 49 feet.

History: In 1646, Jacob Jacobsen Roy, a gunner at New Amsterdam, received a patent to a tract of land, called Konstapel's Hoeck ("gunner's point"). Dutch settlement continued until 1664, when the British gained control and renamed the peninsula Constable Hook. In 1869, the township was incorporated as the City of Bayonne. The establishment of the Prentice refinery in 1875 marked the beginning of the city's change. The Standard Oil Company, the Tide Water Oil Company, and others also came. The oil companies brought some financial success but also pollution, fires and strikes.

Population: 61,444 (1990); 61,842 (2000); 60,238 (2005); 58,625 (2010 projected); Race: 76.6% White, 5.5% Black, 4.5% Asian, 20.3% Hispanic of any race (2005); Density: 10,707.1 persons per square mile (2005); Average household size: 2.42 (2005); Median age: 39.5 (2005); Males per 100 females: 91.0 (2005); Marriage status: 32.1% never married, 49.8% now married, 10.5% widowed, 7.6% divorced (2000); Foreign born: 20.2% (2000); Ancestry (includes multiple ancestries): 26.2% Other groups, 20.1% Italian, 18.8% Irish, 17.9% Polish, 6.1% German (2000).

Economy: Unemployment rate: 5.3% (2005); Total civilian labor force: 29,003 (2005); Single-family building permits issued: 23 (2005); Multi-family building permits issued: 46 (2005); Employment by occupation: 11.7% management, 20.2% professional, 14.1% services, 32.1% sales, 0.1% farming, 7.8% construction, 14.0% production (2000).

Income: Per capita income: $24,730 (2005); Median household income: $47,442 (2005); Average household income: $59,579 (2005); Percent of households with income of $100,000 or more: 16.5% (2005); Poverty rate: 10.1% (2000).

Taxes: Total city taxes per capita: $1,949 (2004); City property taxes per capita: $1,931 (2004).

Education: Percent of population age 25 and over with: High school diploma (including GED) or higher: 78.5% (2005); Bachelor's degree or higher: 21.1% (2005); Master's degree or higher: 6.9% (2005).

School District(s)

Bayonne City (PK-12)
 2003-04 Enrollment: 9,430 . . . . (201) 858-5817
Hudson County Vocational (09-12)
 2003-04 Enrollment: 1,351 . . . . (201) 854-6800

Housing: Homeownership rate: 39.9% (2005); Median home value: $261,233 (2005); Median rent: $611 per month (2000); Median age of housing: 57 years (2000).

Hospitals: Bayonne Medical Center (278 beds)

Safety: Violent crime rate: 29.8 per 10,000 population; Property crime rate: 137.8 per 10,000 population (2004).

Newspapers: Bayonne Community News (General - Circulation 28,525)

Transportation: Commute to work: 72.2% car, 17.9% public transportation, 8.1% walk, 1.5% work from home (2000); Travel time to work: 26.5% less than 15 minutes, 25.3% 15 to 30 minutes, 20.9% 30 to 45 minutes, 10.4% 45 to 60 minutes, 16.9% 60 minutes or more (2000)

Additional Information Contacts

Bayonne Chamber of Commerce . . . . (201) 436-4333
 http://www.bayonnenj.org/commerce.htm
City of Bayonne . . . . (201) 858-6000
 http://www.bayonnenj.org

EAST NEWARK (borough). Covers a land area of 0.102 square miles and a water area of 0.019 square miles. Located at 40.75° N. Lat.; 74.16° W. Long. Elevation is 30 feet.

History: Incorporated 1895.

Population: 2,157 (1990); 2,377 (2000); 2,305 (2005); 2,231 (2010 projected); Race: 63.9% White, 1.8% Black, 1.8% Asian, 51.6% Hispanic of any race (2005); Density: 22,623.3 persons per square mile (2005); Average household size: 3.14 (2005); Median age: 34.1 (2005); Males per 100 females: 103.4 (2005); Marriage status: 31.5% never married, 55.9% now married, 5.4% widowed, 7.2% divorced (2000); Foreign born: 53.6% (2000); Ancestry (includes multiple ancestries): 51.7% Other groups, 14.5% Portuguese, 7.7% Italian, 6.5% Brazilian, 6.1% Irish (2000).

Economy: Manufacturing: clothing, textiles, yarn, metal products. Single-family building permits issued: 0 (2005); Multi-family building permits issued: 0 (2005); Employment by occupation: 7.9% management, 7.6% professional, 17.5% services, 26.5% sales, 0.4% farming, 14.3% construction, 25.8% production (2000).

Income: Per capita income: $18,470 (2005); Median household income: $49,836 (2005); Average household income: $58,029 (2005); Percent of households with income of $100,000 or more: 11.3% (2005); Poverty rate: 12.6% (2000).

Education: Percent of population age 25 and over with: High school diploma (including GED) or higher: 60.6% (2005); Bachelor's degree or higher: 13.1% (2005); Master's degree or higher: 5.0% (2005).

School District(s)

East Newark Borough (PK-08)
 2003-04 Enrollment: 297 . . . . (201) 481-6803

Housing: Homeownership rate: 32.9% (2005); Median home value: $241,453 (2005); Median rent: $651 per month (2000); Median age of housing: 52 years (2000).

Safety: Violent crime rate: 42.6 per 10,000 population; Property crime rate: 140.5 per 10,000 population (2004).

Transportation: Commute to work: 70.1% car, 11.6% public transportation, 12.5% walk, 3.1% work from home (2000); Travel time to work: 21.9% less than 15 minutes, 34.3% 15 to 30 minutes, 22.2% 30 to 45 minutes, 8.0% 45 to 60 minutes, 13.5% 60 minutes or more (2000)

GUTTENBERG (town). Covers a land area of 0.193 square miles and a water area of 0.044 square miles. Located at 40.79° N. Lat.; 74.00° W. Long. Elevation is 240 feet.

History: Incorporated 1859.

Population: 8,268 (1990); 10,807 (2000); 11,064 (2005); 11,311 (2010 projected); Race: 63.8% White, 4.1% Black, 7.4% Asian, 57.5% Hispanic of any race (2005); Density: 57,344.0 persons per square mile (2005); Average household size: 2.42 (2005); Median age: 37.3 (2005); Males per 100 females: 93.9 (2005); Marriage status: 32.6% never married, 51.4% now married, 5.1% widowed, 10.8% divorced (2000); Foreign born: 49.2% (2000); Ancestry (includes multiple ancestries): 58.8% Other groups, 9.2% Italian, 6.5% Irish, 4.1% German, 2.7% United States or American (2000).

Economy: Manufacturing: textiles, clothing, knit goods, metal products, vegetable oils. Single-family building permits issued: 8 (2005); Multi-family building permits issued: 17 (2005); Employment by occupation: 16.1% management, 18.3% professional, 13.7% services, 29.7% sales, 0.0% farming, 6.3% construction, 15.9% production (2000).

Income: Per capita income: $32,069 (2005); Median household income: $52,879 (2005); Average household income: $77,189 (2005); Percent of households with income of $100,000 or more: 22.3% (2005); Poverty rate: 13.0% (2000).

Taxes: Total city taxes per capita: $973 (2004); City property taxes per capita: $957 (2004).

Education: Percent of population age 25 and over with: High school diploma (including GED) or higher: 74.6% (2005); Bachelor's degree or higher: 29.5% (2005); Master's degree or higher: 13.2% (2005).

School District(s)

Guttenberg Town (PK-08)
 2003-04 Enrollment: 968 . . . . (201) 861-3100

Housing: Homeownership rate: 35.4% (2005); Median home value: $258,925 (2005); Median rent: $722 per month (2000); Median age of housing: 28 years (2000).

Safety: Violent crime rate: 37.8 per 10,000 population; Property crime rate: 165.5 per 10,000 population (2004).

Transportation: Commute to work: 50.2% car, 39.7% public transportation, 6.0% walk, 3.4% work from home (2000); Travel time to work: 11.4% less than 15 minutes, 24.5% 15 to 30 minutes, 28.2% 30 to 45 minutes, 18.2% 45 to 60 minutes, 17.6% 60 minutes or more (2000)

HARRISON (town). Covers a land area of 1.221 square miles and a water area of 0.095 square miles. Located at 40.74° N. Lat.; 74.15° W. Long. Elevation is 30 feet.

History: Named for William Henry Harrison, ninth President of the U.S. Incorporated 1869.

Population: 13,425 (1990); 14,424 (2000); 14,158 (2005); 13,908 (2010 projected); Race: 61.7% White, 1.2% Black, 12.8% Asian, 39.2% Hispanic of any race (2005); Density: 11,593.3 persons per square mile (2005); Average household size: 2.83 (2005); Median age: 36.1 (2005); Males per 100 females: 104.3 (2005); Marriage status: 32.8% never married, 54.0% now married, 6.9% widowed, 6.3% divorced (2000); Foreign born: 56.0% (2000); Ancestry (includes multiple ancestries): 49.3% Other groups, 13.6% Portuguese, 8.0% Polish, 7.7% Irish, 7.6% Italian (2000).

Economy: The town has several foundries. Manufacturing includes plastics, paperboard, and metal products. Single-family building permits issued: 2 (2005); Multi-family building permits issued: 69 (2005);

Employment by occupation: 7.1% management, 16.3% professional, 21.3% services, 24.3% sales, 0.0% farming, 10.1% construction, 20.7% production (2000).

Income: Per capita income: $20,470 (2005); Median household income: $47,111 (2005); Average household income: $57,432 (2005); Percent of households with income of $100,000 or more: 14.5% (2005); Poverty rate: 12.4% (2000).

Education: Percent of population age 25 and over with: High school diploma (including GED) or higher: 69.3% (2005); Bachelor's degree or higher: 20.8% (2005); Master's degree or higher: 10.0% (2005).

School District(s)

Harrison Town (PK-12)
   2003-04 Enrollment: 2,005 . . . . (973) 483-4627

Housing: Homeownership rate: 32.1% (2005); Median home value: $256,767 (2005); Median rent: $639 per month (2000); Median age of housing: 48 years (2000).

Safety: Violent crime rate: 30.6 per 10,000 population; Property crime rate: 247.2 per 10,000 population (2004).

Transportation: Commute to work: 64.7% car, 18.4% public transportation, 14.3% walk, 1.1% work from home (2000); Travel time to work: 22.7% less than 15 minutes, 28.9% 15 to 30 minutes, 25.7% 30 to 45 minutes, 9.4% 45 to 60 minutes, 13.3% 60 minutes or more (2000)

HOBOKEN (city). Covers a land area of 1.276 square miles and a water area of 0.701 square miles. Located at 40.74° N. Lat.; 74.03° W. Long. Elevation is 5 feet.

History: Named for the Delaware Indian translation of "land of the tobacco pipe". As early as 1640, the Lenni Lenape territory of Hobocan Hackingh ("land of the tobacco pipe") was settled by the Dutch of New Amsterdam. Shortly after, the settlers were driven out. Peter Stuyvesant bought the land back, and later his relatives sold it to Samuel Bayard. Colonel John Stevens, inventor and financier, purchased the entire area. In 1804, he mapped the territory into what he called the "New City of Hoboken" and auctioned the lots in New York. Hoboken soon acquired world fame as a resort. Organized baseball had its beginnings in Hoboken in 1846 when Hoboken's Knickerbocker Giants played against New York. Industrial development began when Hoboken became a city in 1855.

Population: 33,387 (1990); 38,577 (2000); 39,692 (2005); 40,660 (2010 projected); Race: 83.5% White, 3.8% Black, 3.7% Asian, 16.3% Hispanic of any race (2005); Density: 31,113.2 persons per square mile (2005); Average household size: 1.95 (2005); Median age: 32.9 (2005); Males per 100 females: 104.5 (2005); Marriage status: 56.1% never married, 33.1% now married, 5.0% widowed, 5.7% divorced (2000); Foreign born: 14.5% (2000); Ancestry (includes multiple ancestries): 26.6% Other groups, 20.8% Italian, 19.2% Irish, 10.7% German, 5.5% English (2000).

Economy: Unemployment rate: 2.6% (2005); Total civilian labor force: 27,838 (2005); Single-family building permits issued: 19 (2005); Multi-family building permits issued: 426 (2005); Employment by occupation: 30.1% management, 30.9% professional, 6.6% services, 25.9% sales, 0.0% farming, 1.9% construction, 4.6% production (2000).

Income: Per capita income: $53,627 (2005); Median household income: $79,504 (2005); Average household income: $103,481 (2005); Percent of households with income of $100,000 or more: 39.2% (2005); Poverty rate: 11.0% (2000).

Taxes: Total city taxes per capita: $563 (2004); City property taxes per capita: $473 (2004).

Education: Percent of population age 25 and over with: High school diploma (including GED) or higher: 83.2% (2005); Bachelor's degree or higher: 59.5% (2005); Master's degree or higher: 18.6% (2005).

School District(s)

Agency - Elysian CS of Hoboken (KG-08)
   2003-04 Enrollment: 270 . . . . (201) 876-0102
Agency - Hoboken CS (KG-12)
   2003-04 Enrollment: 261 . . . . (201) 963-0222
Hoboken City (PK-12)
   2003-04 Enrollment: 2,218 . . . . (201) 420-2151

Four-year College(s)

Stevens Institute of Technology (Private, Not-for-profit)
   Fall 2004 Enrollment: 4,638 . . . . (201) 216-5100
   2005-06 Tuition: In-state $30,240; Out-of-state $30,240

Housing: Homeownership rate: 22.7% (2005); Median home value: $402,808 (2005); Median rent: $953 per month (2000); Median age of housing: 53 years (2000).

Hospitals: St. Mary Hospital (266 beds)

Safety: Violent crime rate: 36.0 per 10,000 population; Property crime rate: 364.2 per 10,000 population (2004).

Newspapers: Hoboken Reporter (General - Circulation 16,661); Jersey City Reporter (General - Circulation 21,460); North Bergen Reporter (General - Circulation 20,085); Secaucus Reporter (General - Circulation 6,443); Weehawken Reporter (General - Circulation 5,617); West New York/Union City Reporter (General - Circulation 10,840)

Transportation: Commute to work: 29.0% car, 57.2% public transportation, 10.3% walk, 2.8% work from home (2000); Travel time to work: 11.9% less than 15 minutes, 17.0% 15 to 30 minutes, 37.1% 30 to 45 minutes, 24.6% 45 to 60 minutes, 9.4% 60 minutes or more (2000)

Additional Information Contacts

City of Hoboken . . . . (201) 420-2000
   http://www.hobokennj.org
Hoboken Chamber of Commerce . . . . (201) 222-1100
   http://www.hobokenchamber.com

JERSEY CITY (city). Covers a land area of 14.916 square miles and a water area of 6.195 square miles. Located at 40.72° N. Lat.; 74.06° W. Long. Elevation is 83 feet.

History: Named for the state of New Jersey, which was named for the island of Jersey in the English Channel. The site of Jersey City was first important as a North Jersey gateway for the Dutch traders who settled Manhattan. Probably the first permanent settlement was made shortly after 1629, when Michael Pauw bought a tract. The year 1834 was a turning point in the city's growth. A treaty setting the line between New York and New Jersey in the middle of the Hudson River gave the city access to its own water line.

Population: 228,543 (1990); 240,055 (2000); 238,552 (2005); 236,962 (2010 projected); Race: 32.3% White, 27.6% Black, 16.9% Asian, 29.3% Hispanic of any race (2005); Density: 15,993.0 persons per square mile (2005); Average household size: 2.70 (2005); Median age: 34.1 (2005); Males per 100 females: 96.5 (2005); Marriage status: 40.0% never married, 45.9% now married, 6.9% widowed, 7.2% divorced (2000); Foreign born: 34.0% (2000); Ancestry (includes multiple ancestries): 60.0% Other groups, 6.6% Italian, 5.6% Irish, 3.0% Polish, 2.7% German (2000).

Economy: Unemployment rate: 5.9% (2005); Total civilian labor force: 111,108 (2005); Single-family building permits issued: 170 (2005); Multi-family building permits issued: 2,908 (2005); Employment by occupation: 12.8% management, 20.1% professional, 15.9% services, 30.5% sales, 0.1% farming, 5.1% construction, 15.5% production (2000).

Income: Per capita income: $22,933 (2005); Median household income: $44,395 (2005); Average household income: $61,408 (2005); Percent of households with income of $100,000 or more: 16.4% (2005); Poverty rate: 18.6% (2000).

Taxes: Total city taxes per capita: $571 (2004); City property taxes per capita: $521 (2004).

Education: Percent of population age 25 and over with: High school diploma (including GED) or higher: 72.8% (2005); Bachelor's degree or higher: 28.0% (2005); Master's degree or higher: 9.6% (2005).

School District(s)

Agency - C.R.E.A.T.E. CS (09-11)
   2003-04 Enrollment: 289 . . . . (201) 659-3808
Agency - Gateway CS (06-08)
   2003-04 Enrollment: 177 . . . . (201) 653-0016
Agency - Jersey City Comm. CS (KG-06)
   2003-04 Enrollment: 404 . . . . (201) 433-2288
Agency - Jersey City Golden Door CS (KG-08)
   2003-04 Enrollment: 488 . . . . (201) 795-4400
Agency - Learning Community CS (KG-08)
   2003-04 Enrollment: 308 . . . . (201) 332-0900
Agency - Liberty Academy CS (KG-08)
   2003-04 Enrollment: 385 . . . . (201) 395-9400
Agency - Schomburg CS (PK-05)
   2003-04 Enrollment: 543 . . . . (201) 451-8888
Agency - Soaring Heights CS (KG-08)
   2003-04 Enrollment: 171 . . . . (201) 798-4408
Agency - University Academy CS (09-10)
   2003-04 Enrollment: 282 . . . . (201) 200-3200
Hudson County Vocational (09-12)
   2003-04 Enrollment: 1,351 . . . . (201) 854-6800
Jersey City (PK-12)
   2003-04 Enrollment: 35,161 . . . . (201) 915-6202

Four-year College(s)
New Jersey City University (Public)
    Fall 2004 Enrollment: 8,799 . . . . (201) 200-2000
    2005-06 Tuition: In-state $7,040; Out-of-state $12,076
Saint Peters College (Private, Not-for-profit, Roman Catholic)
    Fall 2004 Enrollment: 3,152 . . . . (201) 915-9000
    2005-06 Tuition: In-state $21,190; Out-of-state **$21,190**
University of Phoenix-Jersey City Campus (Private, For-profit)
    Fall 2004 Enrollment: 188 . . . . (201) 610-1408
    2005-06 Tuition: In-state $12,750; Out-of-state $12,750
Two-year College(s)
Harrison Career Institute-Jersey City (Private, For-profit)
    Fall 2004 Enrollment: 192 . . . . (201) 222-1700
Hudson County Community College (Public)
    Fall 2004 Enrollment: 6,492 . . . . (201) 714-7100
    2005-06 Tuition: In-state $5,553; Out-of-state $7,893
Micro Tech Training Center (Private, For-profit)
    Fall 2004 Enrollment: 364 . . . . (201) 216-9901
Natural Motion Institute of Hair Design (Private, For-profit)
    Fall 2004 Enrollment: 106 . . . . (201) 659-0303
PC Tech Learning Center (Private, For-profit)
    Fall 2004 Enrollment: 94 . . . . (201) 761-0038
The Chubb Institute-Jersey City (Private, For-profit)
    Fall 2004 Enrollment: 617 . . . . (201) 876-3800
Housing: Homeownership rate: 28.1% (2005); Median home value: $221,527 (2005); Median rent: $614 per month (2000); Median age of housing: 52 years (2000).
Hospitals: Christ Hospital (381 beds); Greenville Hospital (100 beds); Jersey City Medical Center (609 beds)
Safety: Violent crime rate: 120.2 per 10,000 population; Property crime rate: 341.3 per 10,000 population (2004).
Newspapers: El Nuevo Hudson (Hispanic - Circulation 67,000); The Filipino Express (Asian, General - Circulation 19,000); The Jersey Journal (Circulation 60,000)
Transportation: Commute to work: 49.7% car, 39.5% public transportation, 8.0% walk, 1.8% work from home (2000); Travel time to work: 14.2% less than 15 minutes, 30.3% 15 to 30 minutes, 26.9% 30 to 45 minutes, 13.8% 45 to 60 minutes, 14.9% 60 minutes or more (2000)
Additional Information Contacts
City of Jersey City . . . . (201) 547-4900
    http://www.cityofjerseycity.com
Hudson County Chamber of Commerce . . . . (201) 435-7400
    http://www.hudsonchamber.org

KEARNY (town). Covers a land area of 9.139 square miles and a water area of 1.048 square miles. Located at 40.76° N. Lat.; 74.13° W. Long. Elevation is 125 feet.
History: Named for Philip Kearny (1814-1862), hero of the Mexican and Civil Wars. Incorporated 1899
Population: 34,874 (1990); 40,513 (2000); 39,548 (2005); 38,549 (2010 projected); Race: 73.0% White, 4.9% Black, 5.2% Asian, 30.8% Hispanic of any race (2005); Density: 4,327.6 persons per square mile (2005); Average household size: 3.02 (2005); Median age: 36.4 (2005); Males per 100 females: 107.8 (2005); Marriage status: 33.0% never married, 53.4% now married, 6.7% widowed, 7.0% divorced (2000); Foreign born: 38.2% (2000); Ancestry (includes multiple ancestries): 34.6% Other groups, 13.4% Irish, 12.1% Italian, 11.8% Portuguese, 7.8% Polish (2000).
Economy: The town is the site of shipyards and dry docks. Manufacturing includes chemicals, textiles, plastics, food and electronic equipment. Kearny contains many tidal wetlands between the Passaic and the Hackensack rivers that were filled for industrial and recreational purposes. One development project was the construction of the Meadowlands racetrack and arena, located near the town of Kearny. Unemployment rate: 5.2% (2005); Total civilian labor force: 18,514 (2005); Single-family building permits issued: 0 (2005); Multi-family building permits issued: 8 (2005); Employment by occupation: 11.3% management, 15.5% professional, 15.0% services, 29.7% sales, 0.1% farming, 11.5% construction, 17.0% production (2000).
Income: Per capita income: $23,365 (2005); Median household income: $54,983 (2005); Average household income: $68,205 (2005); Percent of households with income of $100,000 or more: 19.1% (2005); Poverty rate: 8.6% (2000).
Taxes: Total city taxes per capita: $568 (2004); City property taxes per capita: $549 (2004).

Education: Percent of population age 25 and over with: High school diploma (including GED) or higher: 70.9% (2005); Bachelor's degree or higher: 17.4% (2005); Master's degree or higher: 6.6% (2005).
School District(s)
Hudson County Vocational (09-12)
    2003-04 Enrollment: 1,351 . . . . (201) 854-6800
Kearny Town (PK-12)
    2003-04 Enrollment: 5,888 . . . . (201) 955-5021
Housing: Homeownership rate: 47.9% (2005); Median home value: $256,679 (2005); Median rent: $676 per month (2000); Median age of housing: 57 years (2000).
Hospitals: West Hudson Hospital (217 beds)
Safety: Violent crime rate: 26.9 per 10,000 population; Property crime rate: 275.1 per 10,000 population (2004).
Newspapers: Observer (General - Circulation 26,000)
Transportation: Commute to work: 78.2% car, 14.0% public transportation, 6.1% walk, 1.0% work from home (2000); Travel time to work: 21.8% less than 15 minutes, 31.5% 15 to 30 minutes, 24.8% 30 to 45 minutes, 8.5% 45 to 60 minutes, 13.4% 60 minutes or more (2000)
Additional Information Contacts
Town of Kearny . . . . (201) 955-7400
    http://www.kearnyusa.com
West Hudson-South Bergen Chmbr of Commerce . . . . (201) 991-5600
    http://www.co.bergen.nj.us

NORTH BERGEN (township). Covers a land area of 5.196 square miles and a water area of 0.420 square miles. Located at 40.79° N. Lat.; 74.02° W. Long. Elevation is 200 feet.
History: Named for the town of Bergen-op-zoom in the Netherlands. Incorporated 1861.
Population: 48,414 (1990); 58,092 (2000); 58,153 (2005); 58,206 (2010 projected); Race: 65.7% White, 3.0% Black, 6.3% Asian, 62.7% Hispanic of any race (2005); Density: 11,191.3 persons per square mile (2005); Average household size: 2.77 (2005); Median age: 37.5 (2005); Males per 100 females: 92.4 (2005); Marriage status: 30.3% never married, 53.8% now married, 7.8% widowed, 8.1% divorced (2000); Foreign born: 46.8% (2000); Ancestry (includes multiple ancestries): 63.8% Other groups, 10.5% Italian, 5.7% Irish, 4.5% German, 2.6% United States or American (2000).
Economy: Manufacturing: ink, electrical equipment, radio parts, apparel, machinery, textiles, fiber optics, metal cans, foods, paper boxes. Unemployment rate: 5.4% (2005); Total civilian labor force: 27,068 (2005); Single-family building permits issued: 28 (2005); Multi-family building permits issued: 292 (2005); Employment by occupation: 10.9% management, 15.9% professional, 14.4% services, 31.5% sales, 0.1% farming, 6.7% construction, 20.4% production (2000).
Income: Per capita income: $21,490 (2005); Median household income: $45,374 (2005); Average household income: $58,758 (2005); Percent of households with income of $100,000 or more: 15.1% (2005); Poverty rate: 11.1% (2000).
Taxes: Total city taxes per capita: $682 (2004); City property taxes per capita: $665 (2004).
Education: Percent of population age 25 and over with: High school diploma (including GED) or higher: 68.7% (2005); Bachelor's degree or higher: 19.4% (2005); Master's degree or higher: 7.1% (2005).
School District(s)
Hudson County Vocational (09-12)
    2003-04 Enrollment: 1,351 . . . . (201) 854-6800
North Bergen Township (PK-12)
    2003-04 Enrollment: 7,989 . . . . (201) 295-3985
Housing: Homeownership rate: 36.8% (2005); Median home value: $263,892 (2005); Median rent: $679 per month (2000); Median age of housing: 46 years (2000).
Hospitals: Palisades Medical Center (202 beds)
Safety: Violent crime rate: 18.5 per 10,000 population; Property crime rate: 218.7 per 10,000 population (2004).
Transportation: Commute to work: 67.3% car, 25.4% public transportation, 4.7% walk, 1.4% work from home (2000); Travel time to work: 17.9% less than 15 minutes, 30.3% 15 to 30 minutes, 24.1% 30 to 45 minutes, 12.0% 45 to 60 minutes, 15.6% 60 minutes or more (2000)
Additional Information Contacts
Hudson County Chamber of Commerce . . . . (201) 435-7400
    http://www.hudsonchamber.org

SECAUCUS (town).

SECAUCUS (town). Covers a land area of 5.886 square miles and a water area of 0.631 square miles. Located at 40.78° N. Lat.; 74.06° W. Long. Elevation is 12 feet.

History: Named for the Indian translation of "snake land". Once known as a pig farm center. Has benefited economically from the construction in the 1970s of the professional Meadowlands Sports Complex. Incorporated 1917.

Population: 14,061 (1990); 15,931 (2000); 15,645 (2005); 15,326 (2010 projected); Race: 75.7% White, 5.2% Black, 13.0% Asian, 14.0% Hispanic of any race (2005); Density: 2,658.1 persons per square mile (2005); Average household size: 2.54 (2005); Median age: 41.3 (2005); Males per 100 females: 98.1 (2005); Marriage status: 24.2% never married, 58.5% now married, 8.9% widowed, 8.4% divorced (2000); Foreign born: 20.5% (2000); Ancestry (includes multiple ancestries): 27.5% Italian, 25.7% Other groups, 17.7% Irish, 14.8% German, 7.0% Polish (2000).

Economy: Retail center and area of industrial development, especially in the high-technology fields. Some manufacturing. Has become the site of many corporate headquarters. Single-family building permits issued: 109 (2005); Multi-family building permits issued: 2 (2005); Employment by occupation: 19.6% management, 21.2% professional, 9.0% services, 32.7% sales, 0.1% farming, 7.4% construction, 10.0% production (2000).

Income: Per capita income: $34,243 (2005); Median household income: $67,389 (2005); Average household income: $86,103 (2005); Percent of households with income of $100,000 or more: 29.7% (2005); Poverty rate: 7.6% (2000).

Education: Percent of population age 25 and over with: High school diploma (including GED) or higher: 82.0% (2005); Bachelor's degree or higher: 28.9% (2005); Master's degree or higher: 10.4% (2005).

School District(s)

Hudson County Vocational (09-12)
    2003-04 Enrollment: 1,351 . . . . (201) 854-6800
Secaucus Town (PK-12)
    2003-04 Enrollment: 1,892 . . . . (201) 974-2004

Housing: Homeownership rate: 60.4% (2005); Median home value: $322,773 (2005); Median rent: $788 per month (2000); Median age of housing: 33 years (2000).

Hospitals: Meadowlands Hospital Medical Center (230 beds); Meadowview Nursing Center (550 beds)

Safety: Violent crime rate: 10.7 per 10,000 population; Property crime rate: 442.4 per 10,000 population (2004).

Newspapers: Secaucus Home News (General - Circulation 3,400)

Transportation: Commute to work: 77.5% car, 16.4% public transportation, 4.2% walk, 1.1% work from home (2000); Travel time to work: 29.7% less than 15 minutes, 29.8% 15 to 30 minutes, 17.6% 30 to 45 minutes, 12.3% 45 to 60 minutes, 10.5% 60 minutes or more (2000)

Additional Information Contacts
Town of Secaucus . . . . (201) 330-2008
    http://www.townofsecaucus.com

UNION CITY (city).

UNION CITY (city). Covers a land area of 1.266 square miles and a water area of 0 square miles. Located at 40.76° N. Lat.; 74.03° W. Long. Elevation is 175 feet.

History: Incorporated 1925.

Population: 58,012 (1990); 67,088 (2000); 66,325 (2005); 65,626 (2010 projected); Race: 56.6% White, 3.5% Black, 2.1% Asian, 84.2% Hispanic of any race (2005); Density: 52,375.3 persons per square mile (2005); Average household size: 2.97 (2005); Median age: 34.2 (2005); Males per 100 females: 100.8 (2005); Marriage status: 34.1% never married, 50.5% now married, 6.0% widowed, 9.3% divorced (2000); Foreign born: 58.7% (2000); Ancestry (includes multiple ancestries): 79.9% Other groups, 4.5% Italian, 2.5% United States or American, 2.0% Irish, 1.6% German (2000).

Economy: This densely populated city has many small firms, most of them in the embroidery field. Other manufacturing includes fabricated metal products, consumer goods, machinery, apparel, transportation equipment, electrical goods, and dairy products. Unemployment rate: 6.9% (2005); Total civilian labor force: 27,816 (2005); Single-family building permits issued: 0 (2005); Multi-family building permits issued: 71 (2005); Employment by occupation: 7.9% management, 9.2% professional, 19.2% services, 24.4% sales, 0.1% farming, 7.9% construction, 31.2% production (2000).

Income: Per capita income: $14,914 (2005); Median household income: $33,787 (2005); Average household income: $43,911 (2005); Percent of households with income of $100,000 or more: 7.5% (2005); Poverty rate: 21.4% (2000).

Taxes: Total city taxes per capita: $583 (2004); City property taxes per capita: $558 (2004).

Education: Percent of population age 25 and over with: High school diploma (including GED) or higher: 54.4% (2005); Bachelor's degree or higher: 12.4% (2005); Master's degree or higher: 5.4% (2005).

School District(s)

Union City (PK-12)
    2003-04 Enrollment: 10,436 . . . . (201) 348-5851

Housing: Homeownership rate: 18.1% (2005); Median home value: $250,053 (2005); Median rent: $598 per month (2000); Median age of housing: 55 years (2000).

Safety: Violent crime rate: 48.2 per 10,000 population; Property crime rate: 240.6 per 10,000 population (2004).

Newspapers: Continental (Hispanic - Circulation 38,000); La Tribuna de North Jersey (Hispanic - Circulation 53,000)

Transportation: Commute to work: 51.6% car, 33.2% public transportation, 12.2% walk, 1.4% work from home (2000); Travel time to work: 19.7% less than 15 minutes, 34.0% 15 to 30 minutes, 25.1% 30 to 45 minutes, 10.5% 45 to 60 minutes, 10.7% 60 minutes or more (2000)

WEEHAWKEN (township).

WEEHAWKEN (township). Covers a land area of 0.850 square miles and a water area of 0.657 square miles. Located at 40.76° N. Lat.; 74.02° W. Long. Elevation is 189 feet.

History: Named for an Algonquian Indian translation, whose meaning is uncertain. "Highwood," the James Gore King estate, was the scene in 1804 of the duel between Aaron Burr and Alexander Hamilton. A bronze bust commemorates Hamilton, who was fatally wounded. Incorporated 1859.

Population: 12,395 (1990); 13,501 (2000); 13,263 (2005); 13,011 (2010 projected); Race: 72.1% White, 3.4% Black, 4.9% Asian, 39.6% Hispanic of any race (2005); Density: 15,611.2 persons per square mile (2005); Average household size: 2.22 (2005); Median age: 37.2 (2005); Males per 100 females: 96.0 (2005); Marriage status: 41.0% never married, 43.9% now married, 6.3% widowed, 8.8% divorced (2000); Foreign born: 38.7% (2000); Ancestry (includes multiple ancestries): 46.0% Other groups, 16.0% Italian, 12.0% Irish, 8.0% German, 3.4% English (2000).

Economy: Single-family building permits issued: 0 (2005); Multi-family building permits issued: 4 (2005); Employment by occupation: 18.5% management, 23.7% professional, 13.3% services, 29.1% sales, 0.1% farming, 4.3% construction, 11.1% production (2000).

Income: Per capita income: $36,873 (2005); Median household income: $64,018 (2005); Average household income: $81,110 (2005); Percent of households with income of $100,000 or more: 27.2% (2005); Poverty rate: 11.4% (2000).

Education: Percent of population age 25 and over with: High school diploma (including GED) or higher: 75.6% (2005); Bachelor's degree or higher: 37.1% (2005); Master's degree or higher: 12.7% (2005).

School District(s)

Union City (PK-12)
    2003-04 Enrollment: 10,436 . . . . (201) 348-5851
Weehawken Township (PK-12)
    2003-04 Enrollment: 1,267 . . . . (201) 867-2243

Housing: Homeownership rate: 30.8% (2005); Median home value: $372,130 (2005); Median rent: $719 per month (2000); Median age of housing: 60+ years (2000).

Safety: Violent crime rate: 17.9 per 10,000 population; Property crime rate: 289.4 per 10,000 population (2004).

Transportation: Commute to work: 50.2% car, 41.0% public transportation, 5.4% walk, 2.3% work from home (2000); Travel time to work: 13.5% less than 15 minutes, 28.9% 15 to 30 minutes, 27.1% 30 to 45 minutes, 20.5% 45 to 60 minutes, 10.0% 60 minutes or more (2000)

WEST NEW YORK (town).

WEST NEW YORK (town). Covers a land area of 1.017 square miles and a water area of 0.306 square miles. Located at 40.78° N. Lat.; 74.01° W. Long. Elevation is 185 feet.

History: Named for its location west of New York City. Settled 1790. Incorporated 1898.

Population: 38,125 (1990); 45,768 (2000); 46,072 (2005); 46,325 (2010 projected); Race: 58.5% White, 3.7% Black, 3.2% Asian, 79.5% Hispanic of any race (2005); Density: 45,294.0 persons per square mile (2005); Average household size: 2.74 (2005); Median age: 35.9 (2005); Males per 100 females: 96.7 (2005); Marriage status: 33.0% never married, 51.8% now married, 6.3% widowed, 8.9% divorced (2000); Foreign born: 65.2% (2000); Ancestry (includes multiple ancestries): 71.9% Other groups, 3.9% Italian, 2.6% United States or American, 1.7% German, 1.7% Irish (2000).

Economy: Residential town with some light industry: textiles, clothing; also a leading US embroidery center. The waterfront, 1 mile long, can accommodate oceangoing vessels. Unemployment rate: 5.9% (2005); Total civilian labor force: 19,995 (2005); Single-family building permits issued: 2 (2005); Multi-family building permits issued: 294 (2005); Employment by occupation: 8.7% management, 11.0% professional, 20.1% services, 26.3% sales, 0.2% farming, 7.2% construction, 26.5% production (2000).

Income: Per capita income: $19,395 (2005); Median household income: $37,855 (2005); Average household income: $52,772 (2005); Percent of households with income of $100,000 or more: 12.3% (2005); Poverty rate: 18.9% (2000).

Taxes: Total city taxes per capita: $745 (2004); City property taxes per capita: $718 (2004).

Education: Percent of population age 25 and over with: High school diploma (including GED) or higher: 54.8% (2005); Bachelor's degree or higher: 16.8% (2005); Master's degree or higher: 7.5% (2005).

School District(s)

West New York Town (PK-12)
    2003-04 Enrollment: 7,153 . . . . (201) 902-1123

Two-year College(s)

New Horizon Institute of Cosmetology Inc (Private, For-profit)
    Fall 2004 Enrollment: 207 . . . . (201) 864-6389

Housing: Homeownership rate: 20.4% (2005); Median home value: $255,611 (2005); Median rent: $627 per month (2000); Median age of housing: 49 years (2000).

Safety: Violent crime rate: 28.5 per 10,000 population; Property crime rate: 197.8 per 10,000 population (2004).

Transportation: Commute to work: 51.6% car, 30.6% public transportation, 14.0% walk, 1.9% work from home (2000); Travel time to work: 16.4% less than 15 minutes, 31.6% 15 to 30 minutes, 26.0% 30 to 45 minutes, 13.2% 45 to 60 minutes, 12.8% 60 minutes or more (2000)

Hunterdon County

Located in western New Jersey; bounded on the west by the Delaware River and the Pennsylvania border; drained by the Musconetcong River and the South Branch of the Raritan River; includes the Musconetcong Mountains. Covers a land area of 429.94 square miles, a water area of 7.82 square miles, and is located in the Eastern Time Zone. The county government was organized in 1714. County seat is Flemington.

Hunterdon County is part of the New York-Northern New Jersey-Long Island, NY-NJ-PA Metropolitan Statistical Area. The entire metro area includes: Edison, NJ Metropolitan Division (Middlesex County, NJ; Monmouth County, NJ; Ocean County, NJ; Somerset County, NJ); Nassau-Suffolk, NY Metropolitan Division (Nassau County, NY; Suffolk County, NY); New York-White Plains-Wayne, NY-NJ Metropolitan Division (Bergen County, NJ; Hudson County, NJ; Passaic County, NJ; Bronx County, NY; Kings County, NY; New York County, NY; Putnam County, NY; Queens County, NY; Richmond County, NY; Rockland County, NY; Westchester County, NY); Newark-Union, NJ-PA Metropolitan Division (Essex County, NJ; Hunterdon County, NJ; Morris County, NJ; Sussex County, NJ; Union County, NJ; Pike County, PA)

Weather Station: Flemington 5 NNW									Elevation: 259 feet			
	Jan	Feb	Mar	Apr	May	Jun	Jul	Aug	Sep	Oct	Nov	Dec
High	37	41	50	62	72	81	86	84	76	65	54	43
Low	18	20	28	37	47	56	62	60	53	40	32	24
Precip	4.2	3.1	4.2	4.1	4.8	4.3	4.7	4.0	4.4	4.0	3.9	3.9
Snow	9.9	8.4	5.4	1.0	0.0	0.0	0.0	0.0	0.0	tr	0.6	3.5

High and Low temperatures in degrees Fahrenheit; Precipitation and Snow in inches

Weather Station: Lambertville									Elevation: 65 feet			
	Jan	Feb	Mar	Apr	May	Jun	Jul	Aug	Sep	Oct	Nov	Dec
High	40	43	52	64	75	83	88	86	79	67	55	44
Low	21	23	30	39	49	58	64	62	55	42	34	26
Precip	4.0	2.9	4.2	4.1	4.6	4.2	5.0	4.3	4.5	3.6	3.9	3.8
Snow	7.4	6.1	3.3	0.7	0.0	0.0	0.0	0.0	0.0	tr	0.5	2.4

High and Low temperatures in degrees Fahrenheit; Precipitation and Snow in inches

Population: 107,445 (1990); 121,989 (2000); 130,812 (2005); 140,044 (2010 projected); Race: 93.0% White, 2.5% Black, 2.4% Asian, 3.6% Hispanic of any race (2005); Density: 304.3 persons per square mile (2005); Average household size: 2.77 (2005); Median age: 40.2 (2005); Males per 100 females: 97.6 (2005).

Religion: Five largest groups: 35.7% Catholic Church, 4.0% Presbyterian Church (U.S.A.), 2.8% The United Methodist Church, 1.8% Reformed Church in America, 1.2% Jewish Estimate (2000).

Economy: Unemployment rate: 3.0% (2005); Total civilian labor force: 71,248 (2005); Leading industries: 15.1% retail trade; 13.2% health care and social assistance; 9.5% management of companies & enterprises (2004); Farms: 1,514 totaling 109,241 acres (2002); Companies that employ 500 or more persons: 20 (2004); Companies that employ 100 to 499 persons: 112 (2004); Companies that employ less than 100 persons: 8,204 (2004); Black-owned businesses: n/a (2002); Hispanic-owned businesses: n/a (2002); Asian-owned businesses: 301 (2002); Women-owned businesses: 3,888 (2002); Retail sales per capita: $36,714 (2006). Single-family building permits issued: 436 (2005); Multi-family building permits issued: 70 (2005).

Income: Per capita income: $42,876 (2005); Median household income: $92,003 (2005); Average household income: $117,783 (2005); Percent of households with income of $100,000 or more: 45.1% (2005); Poverty rate: 3.5% (2003); Bankruptcy rate: 2.61% (2005).

Taxes: Total county taxes per capita: $540 (2004); County property taxes per capita: $529 (2004).

Education: Percent of population age 25 and over with: High school diploma (including GED) or higher: 91.5% (2005); Bachelor's degree or higher: 41.8% (2005); Master's degree or higher: 16.3% (2005).

Housing: Homeownership rate: 83.9% (2005); Median home value: $401,458 (2005); Median rent: $771 per month (2000); Median age of housing: 27 years (2000).

Health: Birth rate: 118.3 per 10,000 population (2004); Death rate: 72.1 per 10,000 population (2004); Age-adjusted cancer mortality rate: 188.7 deaths per 100,000 population (2002); Air Quality Index: 86.8% good, 9.9% moderate, 3.3% unhealthy for sensitive individuals, 0.0% unhealthy (percent of days in 2005); Number of physicians: 32.6 per 10,000 population (2004); Hospital beds: 28.2 per 10,000 population (2003); Hospital admissions: 648.3 per 10,000 population (2003).

Elections: 2004 Presidential election results: 59.8% Bush, 39.1% Kerry, 0.7% Nader, 0.3% Badnarik

National and State Parks: Bulls Island State Park; Round Valley State Park; Spruce Run State Park; Voorhees State Park

Additional Information Contacts

Hunterdon County Government . . . . (908) 788-1102
    http://www.co.hunterdon.nj.us
Borough of High Bridge . . . . (908) 638-6455
    http://www.highbridge.org/cncl.html
Clinton Township . . . . (908) 735-8800
    http://www.township.clinton.nj.us
Flemington Chamber of Commerce . . . . (908) 284-8118
    http://www.flemington-nj.com
Hunterdon County Chamber of Commerce . . . . (908) 735-5955
    http://www.hunterdon-chamber.org
Lambertville Chamber of Commerce . . . . (609) 397-0055
    http://www.lambertville.org
Raritan Township . . . . (908) 806-6100
    http://www.raritan-township.com
Readington Township . . . . (908) 534-4051
    http://www.readingtontwp.org
West Amwell Township . . . . (609) 397-2054
    http://www.co.hunterdon.nj.us/mun/wamwell.htm

Hunterdon County Communities

ALEXANDRIA (township). Covers a land area of 27.536 square miles and a water area of 0.104 square miles. Located at 40.58° N. Lat.; 75.03° W. Long.

Population: 3,573 (1990); 4,698 (2000); 5,107 (2005); 5,483 (2010 projected); Race: 96.6% White, 0.9% Black, 0.9% Asian, 2.3% Hispanic of any race (2005); Density: 185.5 persons per square mile (2005); Average household size: 3.08 (2005); Median age: 41.5 (2005); Males per 100 females: 100.3 (2005); Marriage status: 18.2% never married, 69.2% now married, 6.9% widowed, 5.6% divorced (2000); Foreign born: 5.3% (2000); Ancestry (includes multiple ancestries): 28.6% German, 23.4% Italian, 21.2% Irish, 14.1% English, 8.9% Polish (2000).

Economy: Single-family building permits issued: 40 (2005); Multi-family building permits issued: 0 (2005); Employment by occupation: 25.2% management, 24.2% professional, 8.3% services, 28.0% sales, 1.2% farming, 6.8% construction, 6.3% production (2000).

Income: Per capita income: $42,652 (2005); Median household income: $108,010 (2005); Average household income: $129,326 (2005); Percent of households with income of $100,000 or more: 55.0% (2005); Poverty rate: 5.0% (2000).

Education: Percent of population age 25 and over with: High school diploma (including GED) or higher: 93.2% (2005); Bachelor's degree or higher: 39.7% (2005); Master's degree or higher: 15.9% (2005).

Housing: Homeownership rate: 92.3% (2005); Median home value: $466,129 (2005); Median rent: $704 per month (2000); Median age of housing: 27 years (2000).

Transportation: Commute to work: 87.1% car, 2.2% public transportation, 1.9% walk, 7.2% work from home (2000); Travel time to work: 19.4% less than 15 minutes, 23.8% 15 to 30 minutes, 23.7% 30 to 45 minutes, 14.6% 45 to 60 minutes, 18.5% 60 minutes or more (2000)

ANNANDALE (CDP).

Covers a land area of 1.450 square miles and a water area of 0 square miles. Located at 40.64° N. Lat.; 74.88° W. Long. Elevation is 346 feet.

Population: 1,074 (1990); 1,276 (2000); 1,495 (2005); 1,723 (2010 projected); Race: 95.3% White, 0.7% Black, 3.1% Asian, 2.1% Hispanic of any race (2005); Density: 1,031.0 persons per square mile (2005); Average household size: 2.80 (2005); Median age: 40.2 (2005); Males per 100 females: 94.9 (2005); Marriage status: 16.5% never married, 67.2% now married, 12.5% widowed, 3.8% divorced (2000); Foreign born: 13.2% (2000); Ancestry (includes multiple ancestries): 21.1% German, 15.9% United States or American, 14.6% Italian, 14.0% Irish, 8.1% Polish (2000).

Economy: In farm area. Employment by occupation: 18.9% management, 34.0% professional, 12.9% services, 18.0% sales, 0.0% farming, 6.1% construction, 10.0% production (2000).

Income: Per capita income: $36,709 (2005); Median household income: $97,535 (2005); Average household income: $102,772 (2005); Percent of households with income of $100,000 or more: 48.7% (2005); Poverty rate: 1.0% (2000).

Education: Percent of population age 25 and over with: High school diploma (including GED) or higher: 90.0% (2005); Bachelor's degree or higher: 51.1% (2005); Master's degree or higher: 19.4% (2005).

School District(s)

Hunterdon County Vocational (09-12)
    2003-04 Enrollment: n/a . . . . (908) 788-1119
North Hunt/Voorhees Regional (09-12)
    2003-04 Enrollment: 2,779 . . . . (908) 735-2846

Housing: Homeownership rate: 85.4% (2005); Median home value: $365,161 (2005); Median rent: $1,158 per month (2000); Median age of housing: 37 years (2000).

Transportation: Commute to work: 93.6% car, 0.0% public transportation, 0.0% walk, 5.3% work from home (2000); Travel time to work: 27.2% less than 15 minutes, 26.9% 15 to 30 minutes, 27.4% 30 to 45 minutes, 14.7% 45 to 60 minutes, 3.7% 60 minutes or more (2000)

BETHLEHEM (township).

Covers a land area of 20.837 square miles and a water area of 0 square miles. Located at 40.67° N. Lat.; 75.01° W. Long.

Population: 3,104 (1990); 3,820 (2000); 4,127 (2005); 4,411 (2010 projected); Race: 96.9% White, 1.0% Black, 1.5% Asian, 2.1% Hispanic of any race (2005); Density: 198.1 persons per square mile (2005); Average household size: 3.03 (2005); Median age: 39.6 (2005); Males per 100 females: 101.1 (2005); Marriage status: 17.7% never married, 72.6% now married, 3.7% widowed, 6.0% divorced (2000); Foreign born: 4.9% (2000); Ancestry (includes multiple ancestries): 30.5% German, 19.9% Irish, 19.2% Italian, 12.5% Polish, 9.6% English (2000).

Economy: Single-family building permits issued: 15 (2005); Multi-family building permits issued: 0 (2005); Employment by occupation: 21.5% management, 26.4% professional, 8.6% services, 26.9% sales, 0.8% farming, 11.8% construction, 4.0% production (2000).

Income: Per capita income: $41,728 (2005); Median household income: $105,381 (2005); Average household income: $126,439 (2005); Percent of households with income of $100,000 or more: 53.0% (2005); Poverty rate: 1.0% (2000).

Education: Percent of population age 25 and over with: High school diploma (including GED) or higher: 92.0% (2005); Bachelor's degree or higher: 45.0% (2005); Master's degree or higher: 18.5% (2005).

Housing: Homeownership rate: 95.7% (2005); Median home value: $448,321 (2005); Median rent: $677 per month (2000); Median age of housing: 22 years (2000).

Transportation: Commute to work: 89.6% car, 2.1% public transportation, 0.9% walk, 6.8% work from home (2000); Travel time to work: 16.7% less than 15 minutes, 18.9% 15 to 30 minutes, 19.4% 30 to 45 minutes, 19.5% 45 to 60 minutes, 25.5% 60 minutes or more (2000)

BLOOMSBURY (borough).

Covers a land area of 0.908 square miles and a water area of 0 square miles. Located at 40.65° N. Lat.; 75.08° W. Long. Elevation is 333 feet.

Population: 890 (1990); 886 (2000); 833 (2005); 830 (2010 projected); Race: 97.8% White, 0.5% Black, 0.4% Asian, 2.3% Hispanic of any race (2005); Density: 917.2 persons per square mile (2005); Average household size: 2.77 (2005); Median age: 37.2 (2005); Males per 100 females: 92.8 (2005); Marriage status: 20.5% never married, 66.0% now married, 5.1% widowed, 8.4% divorced (2000); Foreign born: 2.8% (2000); Ancestry (includes multiple ancestries): 31.2% German, 28.3% Irish, 20.3% Italian, 15.2% English, 12.4% Polish (2000).

Economy: Gravel pit and fish hatchery nearby. Single-family building permits issued: 1 (2005); Multi-family building permits issued: 0 (2005); Employment by occupation: 16.2% management, 24.3% professional, 14.4% services, 25.4% sales, 0.0% farming, 12.3% construction, 7.4% production (2000).

Income: Per capita income: $29,287 (2005); Median household income: $71,065 (2005); Average household income: $78,978 (2005); Percent of households with income of $100,000 or more: 28.2% (2005); Poverty rate: 3.8% (2000).

Education: Percent of population age 25 and over with: High school diploma (including GED) or higher: 93.7% (2005); Bachelor's degree or higher: 33.0% (2005); Master's degree or higher: 11.8% (2005).

School District(s)

Bloomsbury Borough (PK-08)
    2003-04 Enrollment: 150 . . . . (908) 479-4414

Housing: Homeownership rate: 82.1% (2005); Median home value: $274,324 (2005); Median rent: $750 per month (2000); Median age of housing: 60+ years (2000).

Transportation: Commute to work: 93.9% car, 0.9% public transportation, 1.8% walk, 3.4% work from home (2000); Travel time to work: 20.2% less than 15 minutes, 18.3% 15 to 30 minutes, 26.9% 30 to 45 minutes, 17.9% 45 to 60 minutes, 16.7% 60 minutes or more (2000)

CALIFON (borough).

Covers a land area of 0.965 square miles and a water area of 0.012 square miles. Located at 40.72° N. Lat.; 74.83° W. Long. Elevation is 471 feet.

Population: 1,073 (1990); 1,055 (2000); 1,186 (2005); 1,322 (2010 projected); Race: 98.5% White, 0.0% Black, 1.0% Asian, 0.4% Hispanic of any race (2005); Density: 1,229.0 persons per square mile (2005); Average household size: 2.61 (2005); Median age: 40.2 (2005); Males per 100 females: 92.5 (2005); Marriage status: 18.0% never married, 71.4% now married, 4.9% widowed, 5.8% divorced (2000); Foreign born: 3.8% (2000); Ancestry (includes multiple ancestries): 23.1% Irish, 23.0% German, 22.9% Italian, 17.2% English, 7.7% Polish (2000).

Economy: Fruit, truck, wheat. Single-family building permits issued: 2 (2005); Multi-family building permits issued: 0 (2005); Employment by occupation: 23.0% management, 25.6% professional, 8.1% services, 24.4% sales, 0.0% farming, 11.0% construction, 7.9% production (2000).

Income: Per capita income: $37,574 (2005); Median household income: $91,000 (2005); Average household income: $98,155 (2005); Percent of households with income of $100,000 or more: 44.1% (2005); Poverty rate: 4.3% (2000).

Education: Percent of population age 25 and over with: High school diploma (including GED) or higher: 93.2% (2005); Bachelor's degree or higher: 42.5% (2005); Master's degree or higher: 14.9% (2005).

School District(s)

Califon Borough (PK-08)
    2003-04 Enrollment: 143 . . . . (908) 832-2828
Lebanon Township (PK-08)
    2003-04 Enrollment: 856 . . . . (908) 638-4521
Tewksbury Township (PK-08)
    2003-04 Enrollment: 706 . . . . (908) 439-3101

Housing: Homeownership rate: 87.2% (2005); Median home value: $357,988 (2005); Median rent: $875 per month (2000); Median age of housing: 43 years (2000).

Safety: Violent crime rate: 0.0 per 10,000 population; Property crime rate: 56.2 per 10,000 population (2004).

Transportation: Commute to work: 92.3% car, 1.5% public transportation, 3.0% walk, 3.3% work from home (2000); Travel time to work: 14.5% less

than 15 minutes, 24.0% 15 to 30 minutes, 24.0% 30 to 45 minutes, 17.9% 45 to 60 minutes, 19.5% 60 minutes or more (2000)

CLINTON (town). Covers a land area of 1.374 square miles and a water area of 0.043 square miles. Located at 40.63° N. Lat.; 74.91° W. Long. Elevation is 195 feet.

Population: 2,054 (1990); 2,632 (2000); 2,647 (2005); 2,691 (2010 projected); Race: 90.2% White, 1.6% Black, 4.8% Asian, 5.6% Hispanic of any race (2005); Density: 1,926.9 persons per square mile (2005); Average household size: 2.42 (2005); Median age: 38.6 (2005); Males per 100 females: 95.9 (2005); Marriage status: 21.3% never married, 63.8% now married, 5.6% widowed, 9.4% divorced (2000); Foreign born: 10.8% (2000); Ancestry (includes multiple ancestries): 23.5% German, 21.8% Irish, 21.4% Italian, 15.3% English, 14.2% Other groups (2000).

Economy: Single-family building permits issued: 0 (2005); Multi-family building permits issued: 0 (2005); Employment by occupation: 25.3% management, 33.0% professional, 11.4% services, 21.9% sales, 0.3% farming, 3.8% construction, 4.3% production (2000).

Income: Per capita income: $45,805 (2005); Median household income: $91,443 (2005); Average household income: $110,705 (2005); Percent of households with income of $100,000 or more: 44.7% (2005); Poverty rate: 2.8% (2000).

Education: Percent of population age 25 and over with: High school diploma (including GED) or higher: 93.6% (2005); Bachelor's degree or higher: 49.2% (2005); Master's degree or higher: 20.5% (2005).

School District(s)

Clinton Town (PK-08)
   2003-04 Enrollment: 577 . . . . (908) 735-8512
Clinton Township (PK-08)
   2003-04 Enrollment: 1,949 . . . . (908) 735-8320

Housing: Homeownership rate: 74.6% (2005); Median home value: $359,663 (2005); Median rent: $732 per month (2000); Median age of housing: 30 years (2000).

Safety: Violent crime rate: 7.5 per 10,000 population; Property crime rate: 48.7 per 10,000 population (2004).

Transportation: Commute to work: 87.7% car, 2.3% public transportation, 3.4% walk, 6.6% work from home (2000); Travel time to work: 22.0% less than 15 minutes, 29.8% 15 to 30 minutes, 20.4% 30 to 45 minutes, 17.1% 45 to 60 minutes, 10.6% 60 minutes or more (2000)

Additional Information Contacts
Hunterdon County Chamber of Commerce . . . . (908) 735-5955
   http://www.hunterdon-chamber.org

CLINTON (township). Covers a land area of 30.001 square miles and a water area of 3.933 square miles. Located at 40.63° N. Lat.; 74.86° W. Long. Elevation is 195 feet.

History: Settled in mid-18th century, incorporated 1865.

Population: 10,831 (1990); 12,957 (2000); 14,112 (2005); 15,253 (2010 projected); Race: 86.2% White, 7.4% Black, 2.9% Asian, 5.1% Hispanic of any race (2005); Density: 470.4 persons per square mile (2005); Average household size: 3.11 (2005); Median age: 37.2 (2005); Males per 100 females: 116.6 (2005); Marriage status: 27.5% never married, 62.8% now married, 3.5% widowed, 6.2% divorced (2000); Foreign born: 7.1% (2000); Ancestry (includes multiple ancestries): 24.6% German, 22.8% Italian, 18.7% Irish, 10.9% Other groups, 10.5% English (2000).

Economy: State reformatory nearby. Single-family building permits issued: 67 (2005); Multi-family building permits issued: 0 (2005); Employment by occupation: 27.4% management, 32.0% professional, 6.9% services, 22.5% sales, 0.0% farming, 5.0% construction, 6.2% production (2000).

Income: Per capita income: $43,200 (2005); Median household income: $107,908 (2005); Average household income: $132,781 (2005); Percent of households with income of $100,000 or more: 54.1% (2005); Poverty rate: 0.9% (2000).

Taxes: Total city taxes per capita: $357 (2004); City property taxes per capita: $279 (2004).

Education: Percent of population age 25 and over with: High school diploma (including GED) or higher: 93.1% (2005); Bachelor's degree or higher: 50.4% (2005); Master's degree or higher: 21.8% (2005).

School District(s)

Clinton Town (PK-08)
   2003-04 Enrollment: 577 . . . . (908) 735-8512
Clinton Township (PK-08)
   2003-04 Enrollment: 1,949 . . . . (908) 735-8320

Housing: Homeownership rate: 90.6% (2005); Median home value: $454,595 (2005); Median rent: $911 per month (2000); Median age of housing: 19 years (2000).

Safety: Violent crime rate: 2.9 per 10,000 population; Property crime rate: 54.8 per 10,000 population (2004).

Transportation: Commute to work: 92.1% car, 2.0% public transportation, 0.8% walk, 4.5% work from home (2000); Travel time to work: 20.3% less than 15 minutes, 25.5% 15 to 30 minutes, 25.1% 30 to 45 minutes, 16.3% 45 to 60 minutes, 12.8% 60 minutes or more (2000)

Additional Information Contacts
Clinton Township . . . . (908) 735-8800
   http://www.township.clinton.nj.us
Hunterdon County Chamber of Commerce . . . . (908) 735-5955
   http://www.hunterdon-chamber.org

DELAWARE (township). Covers a land area of 36.744 square miles and a water area of 0.282 square miles. Located at 40.44° N. Lat.; 74.95° W. Long.

Population: 4,537 (1990); 4,478 (2000); 4,754 (2005); 5,045 (2010 projected); Race: 97.4% White, 0.3% Black, 1.3% Asian, 1.2% Hispanic of any race (2005); Density: 129.4 persons per square mile (2005); Average household size: 2.67 (2005); Median age: 44.7 (2005); Males per 100 females: 97.8 (2005); Marriage status: 21.3% never married, 66.6% now married, 4.4% widowed, 7.8% divorced (2000); Foreign born: 4.5% (2000); Ancestry (includes multiple ancestries): 26.4% Irish, 25.5% German, 14.8% Italian, 14.1% English, 8.3% Polish (2000).

Economy: Single-family building permits issued: 18 (2005); Multi-family building permits issued: 0 (2005); Employment by occupation: 21.6% management, 24.5% professional, 12.4% services, 24.1% sales, 0.2% farming, 9.6% construction, 7.6% production (2000).

Income: Per capita income: $47,112 (2005); Median household income: $95,254 (2005); Average household income: $125,362 (2005); Percent of households with income of $100,000 or more: 47.2% (2005); Poverty rate: 3.4% (2000).

Education: Percent of population age 25 and over with: High school diploma (including GED) or higher: 91.2% (2005); Bachelor's degree or higher: 39.3% (2005); Master's degree or higher: 17.9% (2005).

School District(s)

Knowlton Township (PK-06)
   2003-04 Enrollment: 372 . . . . (908) 475-5118

Housing: Homeownership rate: 86.4% (2005); Median home value: $485,423 (2005); Median rent: $1,031 per month (2000); Median age of housing: 38 years (2000).

Safety: Violent crime rate: 4.3 per 10,000 population; Property crime rate: 74.4 per 10,000 population (2004).

Transportation: Commute to work: 89.8% car, 1.2% public transportation, 1.3% walk, 7.7% work from home (2000); Travel time to work: 18.7% less than 15 minutes, 26.7% 15 to 30 minutes, 24.4% 30 to 45 minutes, 12.6% 45 to 60 minutes, 17.6% 60 minutes or more (2000)

EAST AMWELL (township). Covers a land area of 28.679 square miles and a water area of 0.044 square miles. Located at 40.43° N. Lat.; 74.83° W. Long.

Population: 4,379 (1990); 4,455 (2000); 4,598 (2005); 4,773 (2010 projected); Race: 96.7% White, 0.7% Black, 1.1% Asian, 2.1% Hispanic of any race (2005); Density: 160.3 persons per square mile (2005); Average household size: 2.77 (2005); Median age: 42.6 (2005); Males per 100 females: 102.9 (2005); Marriage status: 21.0% never married, 70.9% now married, 2.8% widowed, 5.4% divorced (2000); Foreign born: 6.0% (2000); Ancestry (includes multiple ancestries): 23.1% German, 21.0% Italian, 17.7% Irish, 13.3% English, 10.5% Polish (2000).

Economy: Single-family building permits issued: 13 (2005); Multi-family building permits issued: 0 (2005); Employment by occupation: 22.1% management, 26.3% professional, 5.8% services, 22.6% sales, 0.8% farming, 11.1% construction, 11.4% production (2000).

Income: Per capita income: $44,256 (2005); Median household income: $93,709 (2005); Average household income: $121,327 (2005); Percent of households with income of $100,000 or more: 45.4% (2005); Poverty rate: 1.7% (2000).

Education: Percent of population age 25 and over with: High school diploma (including GED) or higher: 92.2% (2005); Bachelor's degree or higher: 39.5% (2005); Master's degree or higher: 15.9% (2005).

Housing: Homeownership rate: 87.2% (2005); Median home value: $439,086 (2005); Median rent: $772 per month (2000); Median age of housing: 29 years (2000).

Transportation: Commute to work: 87.5% car, 1.4% public transportation, 0.9% walk, 10.0% work from home (2000); Travel time to work: 18.6% less than 15 minutes, 33.1% 15 to 30 minutes, 26.3% 30 to 45 minutes, 9.9% 45 to 60 minutes, 12.1% 60 minutes or more (2000)

FLEMINGTON (borough). Covers a land area of 1.069 square miles and a water area of 0 square miles. Located at 40.50° N. Lat.; 74.85° W. Long. Elevation is 179 feet.
History: Agricultural fairs held here since 1930. Scene (1935) of Hauptmann's trial for kidnapping and murder of Charles A. Lindbergh, Jr. Settled c.1730, incorporated 1910.
Population: 4,047 (1990); 4,200 (2000); 4,240 (2005); 4,323 (2010 projected); Race: 85.1% White, 3.8% Black, 3.7% Asian, 16.4% Hispanic of any race (2005); Density: 3,964.8 persons per square mile (2005); Average household size: 2.36 (2005); Median age: 36.1 (2005); Males per 100 females: 95.8 (2005); Marriage status: 34.4% never married, 44.2% now married, 9.1% widowed, 12.4% divorced (2000); Foreign born: 13.9% (2000); Ancestry (includes multiple ancestries): 22.4% German, 19.3% Other groups, 17.1% Irish, 15.2% Italian, 9.9% English (2000).
Economy: Farm-market center: poultry, vegetables. Manufacturing: metal products, fur coats, consumer goods, concrete products, plastics, dairy products, rubber goods, chemicals. Large-scale discount shopping center. Single-family building permits issued: 1 (2005); Multi-family building permits issued: 60 (2005); Employment by occupation: 10.7% management, 20.9% professional, 20.0% services, 29.2% sales, 1.7% farming, 7.5% construction, 10.0% production (2000).
Income: Per capita income: $26,459 (2005); Median household income: $44,565 (2005); Average household income: $60,090 (2005); Percent of households with income of $100,000 or more: 14.9% (2005); Poverty rate: 6.9% (2000).
Education: Percent of population age 25 and over with: High school diploma (including GED) or higher: 82.3% (2005); Bachelor's degree or higher: 27.1% (2005); Master's degree or higher: 10.9% (2005).
School District(s)
Flemington-Raritan Regional (PK-08)
    2003-04 Enrollment: 3,683 . . . . (908) 284-7561
Hunterdon Central Regional (09-12)
    2003-04 Enrollment: 2,839 . . . . (908) 782-5727
Hunterdon County Ed Ser Comm (UG-UG)
    2003-04 Enrollment: 491 . . . . (908) 806-2729
Hunterdon County Vocational (09-12)
    2003-04 Enrollment: n/a . . . . (908) 788-1119
Housing: Homeownership rate: 38.2% (2005); Median home value: $276,418 (2005); Median rent: $773 per month (2000); Median age of housing: 47 years (2000).
Hospitals: Hunterdon Medical Center (176 beds)
Safety: Violent crime rate: 0.0 per 10,000 population; Property crime rate: 234.5 per 10,000 population (2004).
Newspapers: Hunterdon County Democrat (General - Circulation 23,279); The Hunterdon Observer (General - Circulation 45,900)
Transportation: Commute to work: 83.5% car, 2.0% public transportation, 7.7% walk, 3.4% work from home (2000); Travel time to work: 43.3% less than 15 minutes, 26.2% 15 to 30 minutes, 15.4% 30 to 45 minutes, 8.4% 45 to 60 minutes, 6.7% 60 minutes or more (2000)
Additional Information Contacts
Flemington Chamber of Commerce. . . . . (908) 284-8118
    http://www.flemington-nj.com

FRANKLIN (township). Covers a land area of 22.876 square miles and a water area of 0.042 square miles. Located at 40.57° N. Lat.; 74.93° W. Long. Elevation is 329 feet.
Population: 2,855 (1990); 2,990 (2000); 3,179 (2005); 3,381 (2010 projected); Race: 97.4% White, 0.4% Black, 0.8% Asian, 3.0% Hispanic of any race (2005); Density: 139.0 persons per square mile (2005); Average household size: 2.69 (2005); Median age: 43.5 (2005); Males per 100 females: 97.5 (2005); Marriage status: 17.3% never married, 73.8% now married, 4.3% widowed, 4.7% divorced (2000); Foreign born: 6.9% (2000); Ancestry (includes multiple ancestries): 24.3% German, 16.8% Irish, 16.6% Italian, 14.7% English, 11.6% Polish (2000).
Economy: Single-family building permits issued: 8 (2005); Multi-family building permits issued: 0 (2005); Employment by occupation: 26.0% management, 25.4% professional, 7.3% services, 23.1% sales, 0.2% farming, 9.1% construction, 8.8% production (2000).
Income: Per capita income: $46,776 (2005); Median household income: $103,647 (2005); Average household income: $125,804 (2005); Percent of

households with income of $100,000 or more: 52.0% (2005); Poverty rate: 1.6% (2000).
Education: Percent of population age 25 and over with: High school diploma (including GED) or higher: 93.4% (2005); Bachelor's degree or higher: 44.1% (2005); Master's degree or higher: 16.0% (2005).
Housing: Homeownership rate: 89.3% (2005); Median home value: $468,864 (2005); Median rent: $730 per month (2000); Median age of housing: 34 years (2000).
Safety: Violent crime rate: 3.2 per 10,000 population; Property crime rate: 107.6 per 10,000 population (2004).
Transportation: Commute to work: 87.2% car, 0.7% public transportation, 1.9% walk, 9.0% work from home (2000); Travel time to work: 15.4% less than 15 minutes, 21.7% 15 to 30 minutes, 27.8% 30 to 45 minutes, 16.7% 45 to 60 minutes, 18.4% 60 minutes or more (2000)

FRENCHTOWN (borough). Covers a land area of 1.282 square miles and a water area of 0.062 square miles. Located at 40.52° N. Lat.; 75.06° W. Long. Elevation is 161 feet.
History: Incorporated 1867.
Population: 1,528 (1990); 1,488 (2000); 1,471 (2005); 1,479 (2010 projected); Race: 94.7% White, 0.5% Black, 1.6% Asian, 3.7% Hispanic of any race (2005); Density: 1,147.4 persons per square mile (2005); Average household size: 2.37 (2005); Median age: 40.0 (2005); Males per 100 females: 94.1 (2005); Marriage status: 26.0% never married, 56.8% now married, 5.7% widowed, 11.4% divorced (2000); Foreign born: 6.9% (2000); Ancestry (includes multiple ancestries): 27.8% German, 19.2% Irish, 15.1% English, 10.5% Italian, 7.5% Other groups (2000).
Economy: Manufacturing: electronics, office; hatcheries; poultry, fruit, grain; dairy and nursery products. Single-family building permits issued: 0 (2005); Multi-family building permits issued: 0 (2005); Employment by occupation: 15.1% management, 27.6% professional, 9.4% services, 23.9% sales, 0.0% farming, 12.5% construction, 11.6% production (2000).
Income: Per capita income: $32,788 (2005); Median household income: $61,314 (2005); Average household income: $77,270 (2005); Percent of households with income of $100,000 or more: 21.8% (2005); Poverty rate: 3.3% (2000).
Education: Percent of population age 25 and over with: High school diploma (including GED) or higher: 85.6% (2005); Bachelor's degree or higher: 32.4% (2005); Master's degree or higher: 13.1% (2005).
School District(s)
Delaware Valley Regional (09-12)
    2003-04 Enrollment: 940 . . . . (908) 996-2131
Frenchtown Borough (PK-08)
    2003-04 Enrollment: 128 . . . . (908) 996-2751
Kingwood Township (PK-08)
    2003-04 Enrollment: 479 . . . . (908) 996-2941
Housing: Homeownership rate: 57.9% (2005); Median home value: $278,989 (2005); Median rent: $644 per month (2000); Median age of housing: 60+ years (2000).
Safety: Violent crime rate: 6.5 per 10,000 population; Property crime rate: 196.0 per 10,000 population (2004).
Newspapers: Delaware Valley News (General - Circulation 3,607)
Transportation: Commute to work: 83.6% car, 1.4% public transportation, 6.2% walk, 7.7% work from home (2000); Travel time to work: 18.1% less than 15 minutes, 28.8% 15 to 30 minutes, 22.7% 30 to 45 minutes, 14.8% 45 to 60 minutes, 15.6% 60 minutes or more (2000)

GLEN GARDNER (borough). Covers a land area of 1.562 square miles and a water area of 0 square miles. Located at 40.69° N. Lat.; 74.94° W. Long. Elevation is 405 feet.
Population: 1,665 (1990); 1,902 (2000); 2,032 (2005); 2,181 (2010 projected); Race: 95.5% White, 0.8% Black, 1.5% Asian, 5.2% Hispanic of any race (2005); Density: 1,300.8 persons per square mile (2005); Average household size: 2.32 (2005); Median age: 37.2 (2005); Males per 100 females: 94.8 (2005); Marriage status: 24.4% never married, 57.2% now married, 6.0% widowed, 12.4% divorced (2000); Foreign born: 4.8% (2000); Ancestry (includes multiple ancestries): 33.4% German, 26.7% Irish, 20.2% Italian, 9.7% Polish, 8.6% English (2000).
Economy: Hagedorn Center for Geriatrics nearby. Single-family building permits issued: 3 (2005); Multi-family building permits issued: 0 (2005); Employment by occupation: 22.8% management, 23.2% professional, 12.7% services, 25.4% sales, 0.5% farming, 10.6% construction, 4.8% production (2000).
Income: Per capita income: $33,843 (2005); Median household income: $67,632 (2005); Average household income: $77,863 (2005); Percent of

households with income of $100,000 or more: 27.1% (2005); Poverty rate: 4.5% (2000).

Education: Percent of population age 25 and over with: High school diploma (including GED) or higher: 90.9% (2005); Bachelor's degree or higher: 35.2% (2005); Master's degree or higher: 11.4% (2005).

School District(s)

Hunterdon County Vocational (09-12)

   2003-04 Enrollment: n/a . . . . (908) 788-1119

North Hunt/Voorhees Regional (09-12)

   2003-04 Enrollment: 2,779 . . . . (908) 735-2846

Housing: Homeownership rate: 67.8% (2005); Median home value: $222,727 (2005); Median rent: $789 per month (2000); Median age of housing: 17 years (2000).

Transportation: Commute to work: 95.6% car, 1.2% public transportation, 1.1% walk, 1.9% work from home (2000); Travel time to work: 16.2% less than 15 minutes, 24.4% 15 to 30 minutes, 21.5% 30 to 45 minutes, 18.3% 45 to 60 minutes, 19.6% 60 minutes or more (2000)

HAMPTON (borough).
Covers a land area of 1.536 square miles and a water area of 0 square miles. Located at 40.70° N. Lat.; 74.95° W. Long. Elevation is 500 feet.

Population: 1,515 (1990); 1,546 (2000); 1,605 (2005); 1,660 (2010 projected); Race: 88.1% White, 7.4% Black, 1.2% Asian, 4.0% Hispanic of any race (2005); Density: 1,045.2 persons per square mile (2005); Average household size: 2.77 (2005); Median age: 35.1 (2005); Males per 100 females: 108.7 (2005); Marriage status: 30.0% never married, 55.7% now married, 8.3% widowed, 6.0% divorced (2000); Foreign born: 4.5% (2000); Ancestry (includes multiple ancestries): 29.2% German, 24.1% Irish, 17.7% Italian, 12.4% English, 12.2% Polish (2000).

Economy: Single-family building permits issued: 25 (2005); Multi-family building permits issued: 0 (2005); Employment by occupation: 14.8% management, 18.4% professional, 17.4% services, 24.8% sales, 0.3% farming, 12.8% construction, 11.5% production (2000).

Income: Per capita income: $26,266 (2005); Median household income: $60,165 (2005); Average household income: $70,685 (2005); Percent of households with income of $100,000 or more: 25.0% (2005); Poverty rate: 8.3% (2000).

Taxes: Total city taxes per capita: $664 (2004); City property taxes per capita: $646 (2004).

Education: Percent of population age 25 and over with: High school diploma (including GED) or higher: 86.9% (2005); Bachelor's degree or higher: 22.0% (2005); Master's degree or higher: 6.6% (2005).

School District(s)

Hampton Borough (PK-08)

   2003-04 Enrollment: 208 . . . . (908) 537-4101

Union Township (PK-08)

   2003-04 Enrollment: 658 . . . . (908) 735-5511

Housing: Homeownership rate: 66.4% (2005); Median home value: $270,170 (2005); Median rent: $438 per month (2000); Median age of housing: 39 years (2000).

Transportation: Commute to work: 91.6% car, 1.9% public transportation, 1.9% walk, 3.3% work from home (2000); Travel time to work: 18.5% less than 15 minutes, 28.8% 15 to 30 minutes, 23.1% 30 to 45 minutes, 12.3% 45 to 60 minutes, 17.3% 60 minutes or more (2000)

HIGH BRIDGE (borough).
Covers a land area of 2.411 square miles and a water area of 0.023 square miles. Located at 40.66° N. Lat.; 74.89° W. Long. Elevation is 332 feet.

History: Settled before 1750, incorporated 1898.

Population: 3,886 (1990); 3,776 (2000); 3,821 (2005); 3,904 (2010 projected); Race: 95.9% White, 0.8% Black, 1.7% Asian, 3.0% Hispanic of any race (2005); Density: 1,584.7 persons per square mile (2005); Average household size: 2.59 (2005); Median age: 37.6 (2005); Males per 100 females: 94.8 (2005); Marriage status: 23.0% never married, 64.6% now married, 4.0% widowed, 8.4% divorced (2000); Foreign born: 6.5% (2000); Ancestry (includes multiple ancestries): 27.9% Irish, 27.2% German, 20.8% Italian, 11.3% English, 11.0% Polish (2000).

Economy: Metal products; grain, vegetables. Single-family building permits issued: 7 (2005); Multi-family building permits issued: 0 (2005); Employment by occupation: 18.2% management, 22.2% professional, 14.0% services, 29.0% sales, 0.0% farming, 9.6% construction, 7.1% production (2000).

Income: Per capita income: $33,551 (2005); Median household income: $75,965 (2005); Average household income: $86,130 (2005); Percent of

households with income of $100,000 or more: 29.7% (2005); Poverty rate: 3.2% (2000).

Education: Percent of population age 25 and over with: High school diploma (including GED) or higher: 92.4% (2005); Bachelor's degree or higher: 39.3% (2005); Master's degree or higher: 12.2% (2005).

School District(s)

High Bridge Borough (PK-08)

   2003-04 Enrollment: 469 . . . . (908) 638-4103

Housing: Homeownership rate: 82.8% (2005); Median home value: $261,968 (2005); Median rent: $723 per month (2000); Median age of housing: 36 years (2000).

Safety: Violent crime rate: 2.6 per 10,000 population; Property crime rate: 78.1 per 10,000 population (2004).

Transportation: Commute to work: 90.3% car, 3.2% public transportation, 1.5% walk, 4.8% work from home (2000); Travel time to work: 21.5% less than 15 minutes, 24.6% 15 to 30 minutes, 21.7% 30 to 45 minutes, 18.1% 45 to 60 minutes, 14.2% 60 minutes or more (2000)

Additional Information Contacts

Borough of High Bridge . . . . (908) 638-6455

   http://www.highbridge.org/cncl.html

HOLLAND (township).
Covers a land area of 23.698 square miles and a water area of 0.393 square miles. Located at 40.59° N. Lat.; 75.12° W. Long. Elevation is 400 feet.

Population: 4,884 (1990); 5,124 (2000); 5,347 (2005); 5,603 (2010 projected); Race: 97.8% White, 0.6% Black, 0.5% Asian, 2.2% Hispanic of any race (2005); Density: 225.6 persons per square mile (2005); Average household size: 2.67 (2005); Median age: 42.9 (2005); Males per 100 females: 97.3 (2005); Marriage status: 17.8% never married, 71.6% now married, 6.2% widowed, 4.4% divorced (2000); Foreign born: 2.6% (2000); Ancestry (includes multiple ancestries): 29.2% German, 21.0% Irish, 20.8% Italian, 13.0% Polish, 12.0% English (2000).

Economy: Single-family building permits issued: 14 (2005); Multi-family building permits issued: 0 (2005); Employment by occupation: 18.1% management, 18.7% professional, 11.6% services, 28.0% sales, 0.3% farming, 12.6% construction, 10.5% production (2000).

Income: Per capita income: $36,259 (2005); Median household income: $78,665 (2005); Average household income: $96,939 (2005); Percent of households with income of $100,000 or more: 33.7% (2005); Poverty rate: 2.2% (2000).

Education: Percent of population age 25 and over with: High school diploma (including GED) or higher: 91.0% (2005); Bachelor's degree or higher: 24.6% (2005); Master's degree or higher: 8.4% (2005).

Housing: Homeownership rate: 92.6% (2005); Median home value: $332,998 (2005); Median rent: $786 per month (2000); Median age of housing: 34 years (2000).

Safety: Violent crime rate: 0.0 per 10,000 population; Property crime rate: 63.9 per 10,000 population (2004).

Transportation: Commute to work: 92.4% car, 0.9% public transportation, 0.3% walk, 6.5% work from home (2000); Travel time to work: 14.4% less than 15 minutes, 28.5% 15 to 30 minutes, 25.7% 30 to 45 minutes, 12.3% 45 to 60 minutes, 19.1% 60 minutes or more (2000)

KINGWOOD (township).
Covers a land area of 35.226 square miles and a water area of 0.585 square miles. Located at 40.48° N. Lat.; 75.01° W. Long. Elevation is 480 feet.

Population: 3,329 (1990); 3,782 (2000); 4,126 (2005); 4,471 (2010 projected); Race: 97.4% White, 0.7% Black, 1.0% Asian, 2.3% Hispanic of any race (2005); Density: 117.1 persons per square mile (2005); Average household size: 2.76 (2005); Median age: 40.2 (2005); Males per 100 females: 101.1 (2005); Marriage status: 18.8% never married, 71.4% now married, 4.5% widowed, 5.2% divorced (2000); Foreign born: 4.3% (2000); Ancestry (includes multiple ancestries): 26.3% German, 19.5% Irish, 16.6% Italian, 15.7% English, 13.7% Polish (2000).

Economy: Single-family building permits issued: 20 (2005); Multi-family building permits issued: 0 (2005); Employment by occupation: 12.7% management, 23.8% professional, 18.6% services, 22.4% sales, 0.4% farming, 15.9% construction, 6.2% production (2000).

Income: Per capita income: $35,209 (2005); Median household income: $79,464 (2005); Average household income: $97,107 (2005); Percent of households with income of $100,000 or more: 34.6% (2005); Poverty rate: 2.9% (2000).

Education: Percent of population age 25 and over with: High school diploma (including GED) or higher: 89.0% (2005); Bachelor's degree or higher: 26.6% (2005); Master's degree or higher: 9.6% (2005).

Housing: Homeownership rate: 83.8% (2005); Median home value: $403,779 (2005); Median rent: $687 per month (2000); Median age of housing: 33 years (2000).
Transportation: Commute to work: 88.4% car, 0.0% public transportation, 1.3% walk, 9.4% work from home (2000); Travel time to work: 13.3% less than 15 minutes, 29.7% 15 to 30 minutes, 21.8% 30 to 45 minutes, 17.9% 45 to 60 minutes, 17.3% 60 minutes or more (2000)

LAMBERTVILLE (city). Covers a land area of 1.135 square miles and a water area of 0.117 square miles. Located at 40.36° N. Lat.; 74.94° W. Long. Elevation is 71 feet.

History: Founded 1732; incorporated 1849.
Population: 3,927 (1990); 3,868 (2000); 3,878 (2005); 3,931 (2010 projected); Race: 94.3% White, 1.7% Black, 1.4% Asian, 4.0% Hispanic of any race (2005); Density: 3,417.5 persons per square mile (2005); Average household size: 2.04 (2005); Median age: 45.7 (2005); Males per 100 females: 94.7 (2005); Marriage status: 29.7% never married, 51.4% now married, 8.0% widowed, 11.0% divorced (2000); Foreign born: 5.1% (2000); Ancestry (includes multiple ancestries): 24.0% Italian, 19.3% Irish, 17.7% German, 14.2% English, 5.5% United States or American (2000).
Economy: Manufacturing: industrial ceremics, clothing, luggage; stone quarries. Agriculture: livestock, poultry; vegetables. Single-family building permits issued: 0 (2005); Multi-family building permits issued: 0 (2005); Employment by occupation: 16.2% management, 28.7% professional, 13.0% services, 25.1% sales, 0.5% farming, 8.7% construction, 7.8% production (2000).
Income: Per capita income: $43,687 (2005); Median household income: $63,040 (2005); Average household income: $88,887 (2005); Percent of households with income of $100,000 or more: 29.6% (2005); Poverty rate: 5.9% (2000).
Education: Percent of population age 25 and over with: High school diploma (including GED) or higher: 88.0% (2005); Bachelor's degree or higher: 36.9% (2005); Master's degree or higher: 18.2% (2005).
School District(s)
Hunterdon County Ed Ser Comm (UG-UG)
   2003-04 Enrollment: 491 . . . . (908) 806-2729
Lambertville City (PK-06)
   2003-04 Enrollment: 172 . . . . (609) 397-0183
South Hunterdon Regional (07-12)
   2003-04 Enrollment: 341 . . . . (609) 397-2060
West Amwell Township (PK-06)
   2003-04 Enrollment: 224 . . . . (609) 397-0819
Housing: Homeownership rate: 64.9% (2005); Median home value: $282,282 (2005); Median rent: $738 per month (2000); Median age of housing: 60+ years (2000).
Safety: Violent crime rate: 20.5 per 10,000 population; Property crime rate: 209.9 per 10,000 population (2004).
Transportation: Commute to work: 86.6% car, 1.8% public transportation, 6.6% walk, 3.9% work from home (2000); Travel time to work: 28.1% less than 15 minutes, 25.6% 15 to 30 minutes, 23.4% 30 to 45 minutes, 11.0% 45 to 60 minutes, 11.9% 60 minutes or more (2000)
Additional Information Contacts
Lambertville Chamber of Commerce . . . . (609) 397-0055
   http://www.lambertville.org

LEBANON (borough). Covers a land area of 0.868 square miles and a water area of 0 square miles. Located at 40.64° N. Lat.; 74.83° W. Long. Elevation is 296 feet.

Population: 1,028 (1990); 1,065 (2000); 1,206 (2005); 1,345 (2010 projected); Race: 94.7% White, 0.7% Black, 4.1% Asian, 2.7% Hispanic of any race (2005); Density: 1,389.7 persons per square mile (2005); Average household size: 2.28 (2005); Median age: 40.8 (2005); Males per 100 females: 93.9 (2005); Marriage status: 22.4% never married, 58.8% now married, 6.3% widowed, 12.5% divorced (2000); Foreign born: 6.4% (2000); Ancestry (includes multiple ancestries): 27.2% German, 23.8% Irish, 18.8% Italian, 16.1% English, 7.7% Other groups (2000).
Economy: Single-family building permits issued: 43 (2005); Multi-family building permits issued: 0 (2005); Employment by occupation: 19.9% management, 22.8% professional, 8.5% services, 32.6% sales, 0.0% farming, 8.5% construction, 7.6% production (2000).
Income: Per capita income: $37,380 (2005); Median household income: $72,718 (2005); Average household income: $85,217 (2005); Percent of households with income of $100,000 or more: 31.0% (2005); Poverty rate: 3.6% (2000).

Education: Percent of population age 25 and over with: High school diploma (including GED) or higher: 93.3% (2005); Bachelor's degree or higher: 39.6% (2005); Master's degree or higher: 13.2% (2005).
School District(s)
Clinton Township (PK-08)
   2003-04 Enrollment: 1,949 . . . . (908) 735-8320
Lebanon Borough (PK-06)
   2003-04 Enrollment: 95 . . . . (908) 236-2448
Tewksbury Township (PK-08)
   2003-04 Enrollment: 706 . . . . (908) 439-3101
Housing: Homeownership rate: 78.4% (2005); Median home value: $285,371 (2005); Median rent: $873 per month (2000); Median age of housing: 35 years (2000).
Newspapers: Hunterdon Review (General - Circulation 4,083)
Transportation: Commute to work: 93.2% car, 0.5% public transportation, 2.6% walk, 3.7% work from home (2000); Travel time to work: 23.2% less than 15 minutes, 35.0% 15 to 30 minutes, 23.4% 30 to 45 minutes, 10.3% 45 to 60 minutes, 8.2% 60 minutes or more (2000)
Additional Information Contacts
Hunterdon County Chamber of Commerce . . . . (908) 735-5955
   http://www.hunterdon-chamber.org

LEBANON (township). Covers a land area of 31.687 square miles and a water area of 0.036 square miles. Located at 40.72° N. Lat.; 74.89° W. Long. Elevation is 296 feet.

Population: 5,626 (1990); 5,816 (2000); 6,300 (2005); 6,786 (2010 projected); Race: 96.5% White, 1.0% Black, 1.1% Asian, 2.4% Hispanic of any race (2005); Density: 198.8 persons per square mile (2005); Average household size: 2.93 (2005); Median age: 42.2 (2005); Males per 100 females: 97.4 (2005); Marriage status: 21.3% never married, 66.6% now married, 6.0% widowed, 6.1% divorced (2000); Foreign born: 3.0% (2000); Ancestry (includes multiple ancestries): 29.6% German, 22.2% Irish, 19.6% Italian, 14.2% English, 9.8% Polish (2000).
Economy: Agricultural area; machinery manufacturing. Single-family building permits issued: 9 (2005); Multi-family building permits issued: 0 (2005); Employment by occupation: 18.9% management, 24.9% professional, 9.9% services, 25.7% sales, 0.4% farming, 10.5% construction, 9.6% production (2000).
Income: Per capita income: $38,066 (2005); Median household income: $91,520 (2005); Average household income: $110,610 (2005); Percent of households with income of $100,000 or more: 44.2% (2005); Poverty rate: 2.0% (2000).
Education: Percent of population age 25 and over with: High school diploma (including GED) or higher: 94.2% (2005); Bachelor's degree or higher: 37.0% (2005); Master's degree or higher: 12.8% (2005).
School District(s)
Clinton Township (PK-08)
   2003-04 Enrollment: 1,949 . . . . (908) 735-8320
Lebanon Borough (PK-06)
   2003-04 Enrollment: 95 . . . . (908) 236-2448
Tewksbury Township (PK-08)
   2003-04 Enrollment: 706 . . . . (908) 439-3101
Housing: Homeownership rate: 87.2% (2005); Median home value: $385,746 (2005); Median rent: $655 per month (2000); Median age of housing: 33 years (2000).
Safety: Violent crime rate: 6.4 per 10,000 population; Property crime rate: 101.9 per 10,000 population (2004).
Newspapers: Hunterdon Review (General - Circulation 4,083)
Transportation: Commute to work: 92.3% car, 1.0% public transportation, 1.5% walk, 5.2% work from home (2000); Travel time to work: 16.9% less than 15 minutes, 21.4% 15 to 30 minutes, 20.2% 30 to 45 minutes, 18.4% 45 to 60 minutes, 23.2% 60 minutes or more (2000)
Additional Information Contacts
Hunterdon County Chamber of Commerce . . . . (908) 735-5955
   http://www.hunterdon-chamber.org

MILFORD (borough). Covers a land area of 1.152 square miles and a water area of 0.072 square miles. Located at 40.56° N. Lat.; 75.09° W. Long. Elevation is 300 feet.

Population: 1,273 (1990); 1,195 (2000); 1,133 (2005); 1,131 (2010 projected); Race: 97.0% White, 0.1% Black, 0.5% Asian, 2.7% Hispanic of any race (2005); Density: 983.8 persons per square mile (2005); Average household size: 2.55 (2005); Median age: 40.0 (2005); Males per 100 females: 102.7 (2005); Marriage status: 22.2% never married, 60.8% now married, 7.5% widowed, 9.5% divorced (2000); Foreign born: 2.7% (2000);

Ancestry (includes multiple ancestries): 35.0% German, 18.7% Irish, 13.4% English, 11.8% Italian, 11.1% Polish (2000).
Economy: Paper mill. Agriculture includes poultry; produce, grain; dairy products. Single-family building permits issued: 5 (2005); Multi-family building permits issued: 0 (2005); Employment by occupation: 11.8% management, 20.6% professional, 10.4% services, 29.3% sales, 0.0% farming, 13.0% construction, 15.0% production (2000).
Income: Per capita income: $30,007 (2005); Median household income: $64,433 (2005); Average household income: $76,571 (2005); Percent of households with income of $100,000 or more: 23.6% (2005); Poverty rate: 3.7% (2000).
Education: Percent of population age 25 and over with: High school diploma (including GED) or higher: 88.8% (2005); Bachelor's degree or higher: 26.4% (2005); Master's degree or higher: 6.6% (2005).

School District(s)
Holland Township (PK-08)
   2003-04 Enrollment: 689 . . . . (908) 995-2401
Milford Borough (PK-08)
   2003-04 Enrollment: 113 . . . . (908) 995-4349
Housing: Homeownership rate: 68.2% (2005); Median home value: $246,579 (2005); Median rent: $706 per month (2000); Median age of housing: 45 years (2000).
Transportation: Commute to work: 91.1% car, 3.0% public transportation, 3.7% walk, 1.8% work from home (2000); Travel time to work: 17.8% less than 15 minutes, 27.4% 15 to 30 minutes, 26.5% 30 to 45 minutes, 13.0% 45 to 60 minutes, 15.2% 60 minutes or more (2000)

PITTSTOWN (unincorporated postal area, zip code 08867). Covers a land area of 28.480 square miles and a water area of 0.020 square miles. Located at 40.58° N. Lat.; 74.96° W. Long. Elevation is 400 feet.
Population: 4,384 (2000); Race: 97.1% White, 0.2% Black, 2.2% Asian, 3.4% Hispanic of any race (2000); Density: 153.9 persons per square mile (2000); Age: 29.0% under 18, 9.0% over 64 (2000); Marriage status: 17.9% never married, 74.0% now married, 3.7% widowed, 4.4% divorced (2000); Foreign born: 5.1% (2000); Ancestry (includes multiple ancestries): 27.6% German, 24.1% Italian, 18.5% Irish, 15.5% English, 8.6% Polish (2000).
Economy: Employment by occupation: 27.1% management, 22.1% professional, 8.6% services, 25.3% sales, 1.0% farming, 9.2% construction, 6.7% production (2000).
Income: Per capita income: $36,332 (2000); Median household income: $94,953 (2000); Poverty rate: 4.2% (2000).
Education: Percent of population age 25 and over with: High school diploma (including GED) or higher: 94.7% (2000); Bachelor's degree or higher: 44.5% (2000).

School District(s)
Alexandria Township (PK-08)
   2003-04 Enrollment: 643 . . . . (908) 996-6811
Housing: Homeownership rate: 89.8% (2000); Median home value: $311,500 (2000); Median rent: $725 per month (2000); Median age of housing: 28 years (2000).
Transportation: Commute to work: 85.0% car, 1.2% public transportation, 2.1% walk, 10.0% work from home (2000); Travel time to work: 19.0% less than 15 minutes, 24.7% 15 to 30 minutes, 25.6% 30 to 45 minutes, 12.2% 45 to 60 minutes, 18.5% 60 minutes or more (2000)

RARITAN (township). Covers a land area of 37.839 square miles and a water area of 0.067 square miles. Located at 40.50° N. Lat.; 74.85° W. Long.
Population: 15,581 (1990); 19,809 (2000); 22,547 (2005); 25,206 (2010 projected); Race: 92.0% White, 1.6% Black, 4.3% Asian, 3.6% Hispanic of any race (2005); Density: 595.9 persons per square mile (2005); Average household size: 2.87 (2005); Median age: 38.7 (2005); Males per 100 females: 93.9 (2005); Marriage status: 21.2% never married, 67.3% now married, 4.8% widowed, 6.7% divorced (2000); Foreign born: 8.2% (2000); Ancestry (includes multiple ancestries): 23.5% Italian, 23.1% German, 19.0% Irish, 12.5% English, 10.0% Polish (2000).
Economy: Single-family building permits issued: 75 (2005); Multi-family building permits issued: 0 (2005); Employment by occupation: 25.6% management, 26.8% professional, 9.0% services, 25.0% sales, 0.2% farming, 6.5% construction, 6.8% production (2000).
Income: Per capita income: $44,732 (2005); Median household income: $99,201 (2005); Average household income: $127,363 (2005); Percent of households with income of $100,000 or more: 49.5% (2005); Poverty rate: 2.0% (2000).

Taxes: Total city taxes per capita: $436 (2004); City property taxes per capita: $390 (2004).
Education: Percent of population age 25 and over with: High school diploma (including GED) or higher: 94.2% (2005); Bachelor's degree or higher: 47.9% (2005); Master's degree or higher: 17.6% (2005).
Housing: Homeownership rate: 87.6% (2005); Median home value: $399,209 (2005); Median rent: $847 per month (2000); Median age of housing: 16 years (2000).
Safety: Violent crime rate: 3.7 per 10,000 population; Property crime rate: 107.5 per 10,000 population (2004).
Transportation: Commute to work: 91.1% car, 1.8% public transportation, 1.3% walk, 5.3% work from home (2000); Travel time to work: 25.2% less than 15 minutes, 23.3% 15 to 30 minutes, 21.5% 30 to 45 minutes, 15.4% 45 to 60 minutes, 14.6% 60 minutes or more (2000)
Additional Information Contacts
Raritan Township . . . . (908) 806-6100
   http://www.raritan-township.com

READINGTON (township). Covers a land area of 47.693 square miles and a water area of 0.124 square miles. Located at 40.57° N. Lat.; 74.78° W. Long. Elevation is 200 feet.
History: Incorporated 1798.
Population: 13,297 (1990); 15,803 (2000); 16,609 (2005); 17,508 (2010 projected); Race: 94.3% White, 0.9% Black, 3.2% Asian, 2.5% Hispanic of any race (2005); Density: 348.3 persons per square mile (2005); Average household size: 2.73 (2005); Median age: 40.7 (2005); Males per 100 females: 96.6 (2005); Marriage status: 18.8% never married, 68.8% now married, 5.8% widowed, 6.6% divorced (2000); Foreign born: 7.1% (2000); Ancestry (includes multiple ancestries): 22.6% Irish, 22.2% German, 20.8% Italian, 13.0% Polish, 11.7% English (2000).
Economy: Single-family building permits issued: 19 (2005); Multi-family building permits issued: 0 (2005); Employment by occupation: 24.6% management, 27.5% professional, 6.6% services, 27.0% sales, 0.2% farming, 6.2% construction, 7.9% production (2000).
Income: Per capita income: $49,195 (2005); Median household income: $109,973 (2005); Average household income: $134,205 (2005); Percent of households with income of $100,000 or more: 54.9% (2005); Poverty rate: 1.6% (2000).
Taxes: Total city taxes per capita: $552 (2004); City property taxes per capita: $524 (2004).
Education: Percent of population age 25 and over with: High school diploma (including GED) or higher: 94.5% (2005); Bachelor's degree or higher: 48.1% (2005); Master's degree or higher: 18.6% (2005).

School District(s)
Readington Township (PK-08)
   2003-04 Enrollment: 2,298 . . . . (908) 534-2195
Housing: Homeownership rate: 89.1% (2005); Median home value: $459,631 (2005); Median rent: $802 per month (2000); Median age of housing: 20 years (2000).
Safety: Violent crime rate: 6.1 per 10,000 population; Property crime rate: 101.0 per 10,000 population (2004).
Transportation: Commute to work: 90.9% car, 2.4% public transportation, 0.9% walk, 4.6% work from home (2000); Travel time to work: 17.2% less than 15 minutes, 29.2% 15 to 30 minutes, 23.8% 30 to 45 minutes, 16.0% 45 to 60 minutes, 13.8% 60 minutes or more (2000)
Additional Information Contacts
Hunterdon County Chamber of Commerce . . . . (908) 735-5955
   http://www.hunterdon-chamber.org
Readington Township . . . . (908) 534-4051
   http://www.readingtontwp.org

RINGOES (unincorporated postal area, zip code 08551). Covers a land area of 26.120 square miles and a water area of 0.059 square miles. Located at 40.44° N. Lat.; 74.85° W. Long. Elevation is 226 feet.
Population: 5,082 (2000); Race: 94.0% White, 0.3% Black, 3.6% Asian, 3.3% Hispanic of any race (2000); Density: 194.6 persons per square mile (2000); Age: 26.3% under 18, 10.5% over 64 (2000); Marriage status: 17.6% never married, 74.2% now married, 3.7% widowed, 4.5% divorced (2000); Foreign born: 8.0% (2000); Ancestry (includes multiple ancestries): 20.8% German, 20.4% Italian, 15.0% English, 14.8% Irish, 10.6% Polish (2000).
Economy: Employment by occupation: 22.7% management, 24.7% professional, 7.2% services, 25.0% sales, 0.0% farming, 10.8% construction, 9.7% production (2000).

Income: Per capita income: $39,391 (2000); Median household income: $90,149 (2000); Poverty rate: 2.0% (2000).
Education: Percent of population age 25 and over with: High school diploma (including GED) or higher: 93.0% (2000); Bachelor's degree or higher: 40.8% (2000).
School District(s)
East Amwell Township (PK-08)
   2003-04 Enrollment: 469 . . . . (908) 782-6464
Flemington-Raritan Regional (PK-08)
   2003-04 Enrollment: 3,683 . . . . (908) 284-7561
Housing: Homeownership rate: 86.7% (2000); Median home value: $266,600 (2000); Median rent: $860 per month (2000); Median age of housing: 25 years (2000).
Transportation: Commute to work: 90.1% car, 0.6% public transportation, 0.9% walk, 8.2% work from home (2000); Travel time to work: 19.0% less than 15 minutes, 29.0% 15 to 30 minutes, 25.4% 30 to 45 minutes, 11.2% 45 to 60 minutes, 15.4% 60 minutes or more (2000)

STOCKTON (borough). Covers a land area of 0.546 square miles and a water area of 0.058 square miles. Located at 40.40° N. Lat.; 74.97° W. Long. Elevation is 80 feet.
Population: 629 (1990); 560 (2000); 551 (2005); 555 (2010 projected); Race: 98.4% White, 0.0% Black, 1.1% Asian, 0.9% Hispanic of any race (2005); Density: 1,010.0 persons per square mile (2005); Average household size: 2.22 (2005); Median age: 41.7 (2005); Males per 100 females: 88.7 (2005); Marriage status: 25.7% never married, 57.5% now married, 6.8% widowed, 10.1% divorced (2000); Foreign born: 1.4% (2000); Ancestry (includes multiple ancestries): 25.3% Italian, 23.2% German, 20.3% Irish, 16.9% English, 8.4% United States or American (2000).
Economy: Single-family building permits issued: 0 (2005); Multi-family building permits issued: 0 (2005); Employment by occupation: 12.4% management, 27.4% professional, 9.6% services, 25.8% sales, 0.0% farming, 9.2% construction, 15.6% production (2000).
Income: Per capita income: $29,868 (2005); Median household income: $55,392 (2005); Average household income: $66,361 (2005); Percent of households with income of $100,000 or more: 18.5% (2005); Poverty rate: 2.0% (2000).
Education: Percent of population age 25 and over with: High school diploma (including GED) or higher: 86.5% (2005); Bachelor's degree or higher: 31.0% (2005); Master's degree or higher: 12.0% (2005).
School District(s)
Stockton Borough (PK-06)
   2003-04 Enrollment: 58 . . . . (609) 397-2012
Housing: Homeownership rate: 68.1% (2005); Median home value: $326,364 (2005); Median rent: $742 per month (2000); Median age of housing: 60+ years (2000).
Transportation: Commute to work: 86.0% car, 1.3% public transportation, 5.0% walk, 5.0% work from home (2000); Travel time to work: 29.6% less than 15 minutes, 27.1% 15 to 30 minutes, 24.6% 30 to 45 minutes, 7.4% 45 to 60 minutes, 11.3% 60 minutes or more (2000)

TEWKSBURY (township). Covers a land area of 31.628 square miles and a water area of 0.019 square miles. Located at 40.69° N. Lat.; 74.78° W. Long.
Population: 4,601 (1990); 5,541 (2000); 5,972 (2005); 6,421 (2010 projected); Race: 96.3% White, 0.5% Black, 2.5% Asian, 1.9% Hispanic of any race (2005); Density: 188.8 persons per square mile (2005); Average household size: 2.74 (2005); Median age: 45.0 (2005); Males per 100 females: 96.5 (2005); Marriage status: 14.9% never married, 76.2% now married, 2.9% widowed, 6.0% divorced (2000); Foreign born: 4.9% (2000); Ancestry (includes multiple ancestries): 22.9% German, 22.4% Irish, 19.6% Italian, 13.3% English, 6.7% Polish (2000).
Economy: Single-family building permits issued: 21 (2005); Multi-family building permits issued: 10 (2005); Employment by occupation: 35.1% management, 30.5% professional, 7.0% services, 20.2% sales, 1.0% farming, 3.5% construction, 2.6% production (2000).
Income: Per capita income: $73,015 (2005); Median household income: $157,877 (2005); Average household income: $199,838 (2005); Percent of households with income of $100,000 or more: 68.4% (2005); Poverty rate: 2.7% (2000).
Education: Percent of population age 25 and over with: High school diploma (including GED) or higher: 95.8% (2005); Bachelor's degree or higher: 59.3% (2005); Master's degree or higher: 25.9% (2005).

Housing: Homeownership rate: 91.5% (2005); Median home value: $802,563 (2005); Median rent: $1,162 per month (2000); Median age of housing: 28 years (2000).
Safety: Violent crime rate: 0.0 per 10,000 population; Property crime rate: 56.0 per 10,000 population (2004).
Transportation: Commute to work: 85.0% car, 1.2% public transportation, 0.9% walk, 12.5% work from home (2000); Travel time to work: 15.2% less than 15 minutes, 26.6% 15 to 30 minutes, 26.2% 30 to 45 minutes, 15.9% 45 to 60 minutes, 16.0% 60 minutes or more (2000)

THREE BRIDGES (unincorporated postal area, zip code 08887). Covers a land area of 0.348 square miles and a water area of 0 square miles. Located at 40.52° N. Lat.; 74.79° W. Long. Elevation is 140 feet.
Population: 994 (2000); Race: 91.3% White, 8.7% Asian, 0.7% Hispanic of any race (2000); Density: 2,856.3 persons per square mile (2000); Age: 13.8% under 18, 17.4% over 64 (2000); Marriage status: 20.1% never married, 57.5% now married, 9.8% widowed, 12.5% divorced (2000); Foreign born: 9.5% (2000); Ancestry (includes multiple ancestries): 27.7% Irish, 22.0% German, 17.2% Italian, 14.1% English, 11.5% Other groups (2000).
Economy: Employment by occupation: 15.1% management, 43.3% professional, 8.7% services, 20.7% sales, 0.0% farming, 5.7% construction, 6.5% production (2000).
Income: Per capita income: $40,967 (2000); Median household income: $53,828 (2000); Poverty rate: 0.9% (2000).
Education: Percent of population age 25 and over with: High school diploma (including GED) or higher: 89.8% (2000); Bachelor's degree or higher: 35.3% (2000).
School District(s)
Readington Township (PK-08)
   2003-04 Enrollment: 2,298 . . . . (908) 534-2195
Housing: Homeownership rate: 71.0% (2000); Median home value: $134,600 (2000); Median rent: $1,047 per month (2000); Median age of housing: 16 years (2000).
Transportation: Commute to work: 95.7% car, 2.7% public transportation, 0.0% walk, 1.5% work from home (2000); Travel time to work: 16.4% less than 15 minutes, 39.6% 15 to 30 minutes, 21.1% 30 to 45 minutes, 11.2% 45 to 60 minutes, 11.7% 60 minutes or more (2000)

UNION (township). Covers a land area of 18.968 square miles and a water area of 1.625 square miles. Located at 40.63° N. Lat.; 74.97° W. Long. Elevation is 300 feet.
Population: 5,074 (1990); 6,160 (2000); 6,453 (2005); 6,814 (2010 projected); Race: 80.1% White, 14.6% Black, 2.0% Asian, 5.7% Hispanic of any race (2005); Density: 340.2 persons per square mile (2005); Average household size: 3.62 (2005); Median age: 39.0 (2005); Males per 100 females: 74.4 (2005); Marriage status: 28.1% never married, 59.3% now married, 3.7% widowed, 8.9% divorced (2000); Foreign born: 5.6% (2000); Ancestry (includes multiple ancestries): 24.5% German, 20.0% Italian, 17.2% Irish, 14.8% Other groups, 11.0% English (2000).
Economy: Single-family building permits issued: 15 (2005); Multi-family building permits issued: 0 (2005); Employment by occupation: 27.9% management, 27.0% professional, 6.8% services, 24.4% sales, 0.4% farming, 7.5% construction, 6.0% production (2000).
Income: Per capita income: $34,189 (2005); Median household income: $95,348 (2005); Average household income: $118,238 (2005); Percent of households with income of $100,000 or more: 47.7% (2005); Poverty rate: 1.6% (2000).
Taxes: Total city taxes per capita: $6,608 (2004); City property taxes per capita: $6,461 (2004).
Education: Percent of population age 25 and over with: High school diploma (including GED) or higher: 76.7% (2005); Bachelor's degree or higher: 31.6% (2005); Master's degree or higher: 11.5% (2005).
Housing: Homeownership rate: 85.3% (2005); Median home value: $425,833 (2005); Median rent: $876 per month (2000); Median age of housing: 21 years (2000).
Transportation: Commute to work: 89.8% car, 1.5% public transportation, 2.2% walk, 5.7% work from home (2000); Travel time to work: 22.7% less than 15 minutes, 21.0% 15 to 30 minutes, 25.7% 30 to 45 minutes, 12.6% 45 to 60 minutes, 18.0% 60 minutes or more (2000)

WEST AMWELL (township). Covers a land area of 21.723 square miles and a water area of 0.176 square miles. Located at 40.37° N. Lat.; 74.91° W. Long.

Population: 2,259 (1990); 2,383 (2000); 2,978 (2005); 3,537 (2010 projected); Race: 98.1% White, 0.5% Black, 0.9% Asian, 0.8% Hispanic of any race (2005); Density: 137.1 persons per square mile (2005); Average household size: 2.46 (2005); Median age: 45.4 (2005); Males per 100 females: 100.0 (2005); Marriage status: 18.8% never married, 67.7% now married, 6.8% widowed, 6.7% divorced (2000); Foreign born: 4.6% (2000); Ancestry (includes multiple ancestries): 22.3% German, 20.2% Italian, 20.1% Irish, 12.3% English, 8.6% Polish (2000).
Economy: Single-family building permits issued: 15 (2005); Multi-family building permits issued: 0 (2005); Employment by occupation: 15.9% management, 26.2% professional, 10.5% services, 25.6% sales, 1.4% farming, 10.7% construction, 9.8% production (2000).
Income: Per capita income: $39,258 (2005); Median household income: $79,526 (2005); Average household income: $96,603 (2005); Percent of households with income of $100,000 or more: 34.3% (2005); Poverty rate: 1.6% (2000).
Education: Percent of population age 25 and over with: High school diploma (including GED) or higher: 89.7% (2005); Bachelor's degree or higher: 37.1% (2005); Master's degree or higher: 12.7% (2005).
Housing: Homeownership rate: 84.0% (2005); Median home value: $371,124 (2005); Median rent: $748 per month (2000); Median age of housing: 41 years (2000).
Safety: Violent crime rate: 0.0 per 10,000 population; Property crime rate: 125.5 per 10,000 population (2004).
Transportation: Commute to work: 91.1% car, 1.2% public transportation, 1.3% walk, 5.8% work from home (2000); Travel time to work: 23.5% less than 15 minutes, 31.2% 15 to 30 minutes, 24.8% 30 to 45 minutes, 10.4% 45 to 60 minutes, 10.1% 60 minutes or more (2000)
Additional Information Contacts
West Amwell Township . . . . (609) 397-2054
    http://www.co.hunterdon.nj.us/mun/wamwell.htm

WHITE HOUSE STATION (CDP). Aka White Station. Covers a land area of 1.288 square miles and a water area of 0.038 square miles. Located at 40.61° N. Lat.; 74.77° W. Long.
Population: 1,287 (1990); 1,951 (2000); 2,087 (2005); 2,239 (2010 projected); Race: 95.4% White, 1.1% Black, 1.3% Asian, 2.9% Hispanic of any race (2005); Density: 1,620.8 persons per square mile (2005); Average household size: 2.17 (2005); Median age: 42.2 (2005); Males per 100 females: 88.2 (2005); Marriage status: 20.1% never married, 56.1% now married, 11.7% widowed, 12.1% divorced (2000); Foreign born: 8.7% (2000); Ancestry (includes multiple ancestries): 21.4% German, 18.2% Polish, 16.1% Irish, 12.9% English, 9.5% Italian (2000).
Economy: Poultry; grain; fruit; dairy. Pharmaceuticals. Employment by occupation: 20.2% management, 28.1% professional, 7.3% services, 30.0% sales, 0.0% farming, 7.7% construction, 6.6% production (2000).
Income: Per capita income: $46,504 (2005); Median household income: $83,667 (2005); Average household income: $101,063 (2005); Percent of households with income of $100,000 or more: 39.8% (2005); Poverty rate: 1.4% (2000).
Education: Percent of population age 25 and over with: High school diploma (including GED) or higher: 96.0% (2005); Bachelor's degree or higher: 42.3% (2005); Master's degree or higher: 12.3% (2005).
Housing: Homeownership rate: 83.4% (2005); Median home value: $310,066 (2005); Median rent: $730 per month (2000); Median age of housing: 13 years (2000).
Transportation: Commute to work: 91.9% car, 3.0% public transportation, 1.8% walk, 3.2% work from home (2000); Travel time to work: 20.1% less than 15 minutes, 26.6% 15 to 30 minutes, 28.6% 30 to 45 minutes, 14.4% 45 to 60 minutes, 10.3% 60 minutes or more (2000)

WHITEHOUSE STATION (unincorporated postal area, zip code 08889). Covers a land area of 23.110 square miles and a water area of 0.046 square miles. Located at 40.61° N. Lat.; 74.77° W. Long. Elevation is 182 feet.
Population: 9,369 (2000); Race: 95.1% White, 0.7% Black, 2.9% Asian, 2.1% Hispanic of any race (2000); Density: 405.4 persons per square mile (2000); Age: 26.4% under 18, 9.1% over 64 (2000); Marriage status: 18.2% never married, 69.6% now married, 5.6% widowed, 6.6% divorced (2000); Foreign born: 7.4% (2000); Ancestry (includes multiple ancestries): 22.8% Irish, 21.3% German, 19.4% Italian, 13.5% Polish, 13.1% English (2000).
Economy: Employment by occupation: 25.9% management, 26.3% professional, 6.4% services, 27.1% sales, 0.5% farming, 5.1% construction, 8.6% production (2000).

Income: Per capita income: $42,958 (2000); Median household income: $95,476 (2000); Poverty rate: 1.5% (2000).
Education: Percent of population age 25 and over with: High school diploma (including GED) or higher: 94.8% (2000); Bachelor's degree or higher: 50.4% (2000).

School District(s)
Readington Township (PK-08)
    2003-04 Enrollment: 2,298 . . . . (908) 534-2195
Housing: Homeownership rate: 90.5% (2000); Median home value: $278,100 (2000); Median rent: $658 per month (2000); Median age of housing: 23 years (2000).
Transportation: Commute to work: 90.0% car, 2.6% public transportation, 1.2% walk, 4.8% work from home (2000); Travel time to work: 17.7% less than 15 minutes, 29.6% 15 to 30 minutes, 23.1% 30 to 45 minutes, 16.6% 45 to 60 minutes, 13.0% 60 minutes or more (2000)

Mercer County

Located in western New Jersey; bounded on the west by the Delaware River and the Pennsylvania border; drained by the Millstone River and Crosswicks Creek. Covers a land area of 225.93 square miles, a water area of 2.91 square miles, and is located in the Eastern Time Zone. The county government was organized in 1838. County seat is Trenton.

Mercer County is part of the Trenton-Ewing, NJ Metropolitan Statistical Area. The entire metro area includes: Mercer County, NJ

Weather Station: Hightstown 2 W   Elevation: 98 feet

	Jan	Feb	Mar	Apr	May	Jun	Jul	Aug	Sep	Oct	Nov	Dec
High	39	41	50	61	72	81	85	84	77	66	55	44
Low	21	23	31	40	49	58	64	62	55	43	35	27
Precip	3.7	2.8	4.0	4.0	4.3	4.0	4.8	4.7	4.1	3.5	3.8	3.7
Snow	7.1	7.4	3.6	0.9	tr	0.0	0.0	0.0	0.0	tr	0.4	2.6

High and Low temperatures in degrees Fahrenheit; Precipitation and Snow in inches

Population: 325,804 (1990); 350,761 (2000); 367,375 (2005); 384,713 (2010 projected); Race: 65.5% White, 20.0% Black, 6.6% Asian, 11.4% Hispanic of any race (2005); Density: 1,626.1 persons per square mile (2005); Average household size: 2.77 (2005); Median age: 36.9 (2005); Males per 100 females: 95.5 (2005).
Religion: Five largest groups: 31.2% Catholic Church, 3.3% Muslim Estimate, 2.8% Presbyterian Church (U.S.A.), 2.6% Jewish Estimate, 1.9% Episcopal Church (2000).
Economy: Unemployment rate: 3.8% (2005); Total civilian labor force: 194,658 (2005); Leading industries: 13.3% health care and social assistance; 11.6% professional (2004); Farms: 304 totaling 25,070 acres (2002); Companies that employ 500 or more persons: 70 (2004); Companies that employ 100 to 499 persons: 512 (2004); Companies that employ less than 100 persons: 19,365 (2004); Black-owned businesses: 1,493 (2002); Hispanic-owned businesses: 844 (2002); Asian-owned businesses: 1,941 (2002); Women-owned businesses: 7,353 (2002); Retail sales per capita: $15,050 (2006). Single-family building permits issued: 1,221 (2005); Multi-family building permits issued: 75 (2005).
Income: Per capita income: $32,519 (2005); Median household income: $65,719 (2005); Average household income: $88,605 (2005); Percent of households with income of $100,000 or more: 29.5% (2005); Poverty rate: 8.1% (2003); Bankruptcy rate: 5.12% (2004).
Taxes: Total county taxes per capita: $479 (2004); County property taxes per capita: $475 (2004).
Education: Percent of population age 25 and over with: High school diploma (including GED) or higher: 81.9% (2005); Bachelor's degree or higher: 34.2% (2005); Master's degree or higher: 15.6% (2005).
Housing: Homeownership rate: 67.1% (2005); Median home value: $235,142 (2005); Median rent: $645 per month (2000); Median age of housing: 40 years (2000).
Health: Birth rate: 132.2 per 10,000 population (2004); Death rate: 73.2 per 10,000 population (2004); Age-adjusted cancer mortality rate: 192.3 deaths per 100,000 population (2002); Air Quality Index: 82.5% good, 15.3% moderate, 2.2% unhealthy for sensitive individuals, 0.0% unhealthy (percent of days in 2005); Number of physicians: 39.5 per 10,000 population (2004); Hospital beds: 50.0 per 10,000 population (2003); Hospital admissions: 1,733.7 per 10,000 population (2003).
Elections: 2004 Presidential election results: 37.9% Bush, 61.3% Kerry, 0.6% Nader, 0.2% Badnarik
National and State Parks: Princeton Battlefield State Park; Washington Crossing State Park

Additional Information Contacts
Mercer County Government. . . . . (609) 989-6584
    http://www.mercercounty.org
Borough of Hightstown. . . . . (609) 490-5100
    http://www.hightstownborough.com
Borough of Pennington . . . . (609) 737-0276
    http://www.penningtonboro.org
City of Trenton . . . . (609) 989-3185
    http://www.ci.trenton.nj.us/cigovdepts.html
East Windsor Township. . . . . (609) 443-4000
    http://www.east-windsor.nj.us
East Windsor-Hightstown Chamber of Commerce . . . . . . (609) 448-4412
    http://www.east-windsor.nj.us
Ewing Township. . . . . (609) 883-2900
    http://www.ewingtwp.net
Hamilton Township . . . . (609) 890-3654
    http://www.hamiltonnj.com
Hightstown-East Windsor Chamber of Commerce . . . . . . (609) 448-4412
    http://www.east-windsor.nj.us
Lawrence Township. . . . . (609) 844-7000
    http://www.lawrencetwp.com
Mercer County Chamber of Commerce. . . . . (609) 393-4143
    http://www.mercerchamber.org
Princeton Chamber of Commerce . . . . (609) 520-1776
    http://www.princetonchamber.org
Princeton Chamber of Commerce. . . . . (609) 924-1776
    http://www.princetonchamber.org
Princeton Online . . . . (609) 737-7901
    http://www.princetonol.com
Princeton Township . . . . (609) 924-5704
    http://www.princetontwp.org
Washington Township . . . . (609) 918-0002
    http://www.washington-twp.org

Mercer County Communities

EAST WINDSOR (township). Covers a land area of 15.645 square miles and a water area of 0.054 square miles. Located at 40.26° N. Lat.; 74.53° W. Long.
History: Incorporated 1798.
Population: 22,583 (1990); 24,919 (2000); 27,376 (2005); 29,734 (2010 projected); Race: 68.8% White, 9.4% Black, 12.8% Asian, 18.3% Hispanic of any race (2005); Density: 1,749.8 persons per square mile (2005); Average household size: 2.63 (2005); Median age: 36.8 (2005); Males per 100 females: 95.9 (2005); Marriage status: 24.8% never married, 60.7% now married, 5.7% widowed, 8.8% divorced (2000); Foreign born: 23.1% (2000); Ancestry (includes multiple ancestries): 34.1% Other groups, 12.6% Irish, 11.8% Italian, 11.5% German, 9.5% Polish (2000).
Economy: Unemployment rate: 2.8% (2005); Total civilian labor force: 16,591 (2005); Single-family building permits issued: 93 (2005); Multi-family building permits issued: 0 (2005); Employment by occupation: 19.2% management, 26.2% professional, 9.6% services, 28.9% sales, 0.1% farming, 3.6% construction, 12.4% production (2000).
Income: Per capita income: $33,927 (2005); Median household income: $74,074 (2005); Average household income: $88,418 (2005); Percent of households with income of $100,000 or more: 32.8% (2005); Poverty rate: 5.3% (2000).
Taxes: Total city taxes per capita: $371 (2004); City property taxes per capita: $346 (2004).
Education: Percent of population age 25 and over with: High school diploma (including GED) or higher: 88.3% (2005); Bachelor's degree or higher: 41.9% (2005); Master's degree or higher: 15.4% (2005).
School District(s)
East Windsor Regional (PK-12)
    2003-04 Enrollment: 5,152 . . . . (609) 443-7704
Housing: Homeownership rate: 60.5% (2005); Median home value: $228,821 (2005); Median rent: $733 per month (2000); Median age of housing: 25 years (2000).
Safety: Violent crime rate: 8.6 per 10,000 population; Property crime rate: 150.7 per 10,000 population (2004).
Transportation: Commute to work: 86.9% car, 7.7% public transportation, 1.4% walk, 2.8% work from home (2000); Travel time to work: 18.5% less than 15 minutes, 35.5% 15 to 30 minutes, 19.7% 30 to 45 minutes, 9.0% 45 to 60 minutes, 17.4% 60 minutes or more (2000)
Additional Information Contacts

East Windsor Township. . . . . (609) 443-4000
    http://www.east-windsor.nj.us
East Windsor-Hightstown Chamber of Commerce . . . . . . (609) 448-4412
    http://www.east-windsor.nj.us

EWING (township). Aka Ewing CDP. Covers a land area of 15.334 square miles and a water area of 0.265 square miles. Located at 40.26° N. Lat.; 74.78° W. Long. Elevation is 140 feet.
History: Incorporated 1834. College of N.J., formerly Trenton State College.
Population: 34,185 (1990); 35,707 (2000); 37,051 (2005); 38,478 (2010 projected); Race: 65.7% White, 26.8% Black, 2.9% Asian, 5.3% Hispanic of any race (2005); Density: 2,416.2 persons per square mile (2005); Average household size: 2.80 (2005); Median age: 38.0 (2005); Males per 100 females: 93.5 (2005); Marriage status: 35.6% never married, 49.8% now married, 7.2% widowed, 7.4% divorced (2000); Foreign born: 8.2% (2000); Ancestry (includes multiple ancestries): 27.4% Other groups, 16.7% Italian, 15.4% Irish, 14.0% German, 10.1% English (2000).
Economy: Five miles North of Trenton. Printing establishments. Unemployment rate: 2.9% (2005); Total civilian labor force: 20,143 (2005); Single-family building permits issued: 24 (2005); Multi-family building permits issued: 0 (2005); Employment by occupation: 13.7% management, 25.0% professional, 15.9% services, 30.1% sales, 0.1% farming, 5.8% construction, 9.5% production (2000).
Income: Per capita income: $27,949 (2005); Median household income: $64,127 (2005); Average household income: $75,014 (2005); Percent of households with income of $100,000 or more: 23.6% (2005); Poverty rate: 6.4% (2000).
Taxes: Total city taxes per capita: $303 (2004); City property taxes per capita: $293 (2004).
Education: Percent of population age 25 and over with: High school diploma (including GED) or higher: 84.4% (2005); Bachelor's degree or higher: 29.4% (2005); Master's degree or higher: 12.2% (2005).
School District(s)
Ewing Township (PK-12)
    2003-04 Enrollment: 4,178 . . . . (609) 538-9800
Four-year College(s)
The College of New Jersey (Public)
    Fall 2004 Enrollment: 6,812. . . . . (609) 771-1855
    2005-06 Tuition: In-state $9,857; Out-of-state $15,120
Two-year College(s)
Harrison Career Institute-Ewing (Private, For-profit)
    Fall 2004 Enrollment: 243 . . . . (609) 656-4303
Housing: Homeownership rate: 73.8% (2005); Median home value: $209,039 (2005); Median rent: $677 per month (2000); Median age of housing: 41 years (2000).
Safety: Violent crime rate: 24.7 per 10,000 population; Property crime rate: 257.1 per 10,000 population (2004).
Newspapers: Ewing People (General - Circulation 15,200)
Transportation: Commute to work: 87.5% car, 2.8% public transportation, 6.9% walk, 2.4% work from home (2000); Travel time to work: 40.4% less than 15 minutes, 35.3% 15 to 30 minutes, 12.0% 30 to 45 minutes, 4.7% 45 to 60 minutes, 7.6% 60 minutes or more (2000)
Additional Information Contacts
Ewing Township. . . . . (609) 883-2900
    http://www.ewingtwp.net

HAMILTON (township). Covers a land area of 39.451 square miles and a water area of 0.921 square miles. Located at 40.21° N. Lat.; 74.69° W. Long.
History: Incorporated 1842.
Population: 86,453 (1990); 87,109 (2000); 91,002 (2005); 95,176 (2010 projected); Race: 82.3% White, 9.3% Black, 3.2% Asian, 6.5% Hispanic of any race (2005); Density: 2,306.7 persons per square mile (2005); Average household size: 2.57 (2005); Median age: 40.2 (2005); Males per 100 females: 91.8 (2005); Marriage status: 25.8% never married, 58.2% now married, 8.3% widowed, 7.7% divorced (2000); Foreign born: 9.5% (2000); Ancestry (includes multiple ancestries): 26.0% Italian, 18.3% Irish, 16.5% German, 14.3% Other groups, 12.3% Polish (2000).
Economy: Unemployment rate: 2.6% (2005); Total civilian labor force: 51,047 (2005); Single-family building permits issued: 492 (2005); Multi-family building permits issued: 5 (2005); Employment by occupation: 14.5% management, 22.3% professional, 13.4% services, 30.5% sales, 0.1% farming, 8.4% construction, 10.8% production (2000).

Income: Per capita income: $29,571 (2005); Median household income: $65,040 (2005); Average household income: $75,634 (2005); Percent of households with income of $100,000 or more: 24.8% (2005); Poverty rate: 4.2% (2000).

Taxes: Total city taxes per capita: $484 (2004); City property taxes per capita: $459 (2004).

Education: Percent of population age 25 and over with: High school diploma (including GED) or higher: 83.0% (2005); Bachelor's degree or higher: 22.5% (2005); Master's degree or higher: 7.2% (2005).

School District(s)

Agency - Pace CS of Hamilton (KG-03)
   2003-04 Enrollment: 124 . . . . (609) 587-2288
Hamilton Township (PK-12)
   2003-04 Enrollment: 14,074 . . . . (609) 890-3723

Housing: Homeownership rate: 74.7% (2005); Median home value: $214,397 (2005); Median rent: $662 per month (2000); Median age of housing: 40 years (2000).

Hospitals: Robert Wood Johnson University Hospital

Safety: Violent crime rate: 17.6 per 10,000 population; Property crime rate: 190.2 per 10,000 population (2004).

Transportation: Commute to work: 93.7% car, 3.0% public transportation, 0.9% walk, 1.8% work from home (2000); Travel time to work: 25.8% less than 15 minutes, 43.2% 15 to 30 minutes, 17.2% 30 to 45 minutes, 5.7% 45 to 60 minutes, 8.0% 60 minutes or more (2000)

Additional Information Contacts

Greater Mercer County Chamber of Commerce . . . . (609) 393-4143
   http://mercerchamber.org
Hamilton Township . . . . (609) 890-3654
   http://www.hamiltonnj.com

HIGHTSTOWN (borough). Covers a land area of 1.227 square miles and a water area of 0.020 square miles. Located at 40.27° N. Lat.; 74.52° W. Long. Elevation is 84 feet.

History: Seat of Peddie Preparatory School. Nearby is former Jersey Homesteads, now Roosevelt borough. Settled 1721, incorporated 1853.

Population: 4,896 (1990); 5,216 (2000); 5,352 (2005); 5,521 (2010 projected); Race: 73.8% White, 7.6% Black, 2.9% Asian, 25.1% Hispanic of any race (2005); Density: 4,362.8 persons per square mile (2005); Average household size: 2.66 (2005); Median age: 36.9 (2005); Males per 100 females: 103.5 (2005); Marriage status: 26.4% never married, 57.4% now married, 7.1% widowed, 9.1% divorced (2000); Foreign born: 21.1% (2000); Ancestry (includes multiple ancestries): 27.7% Other groups, 15.8% Irish, 14.7% German, 9.6% English, 8.4% Italian (2000).

Economy: Trade center in agricultural area: vegetables, nursery products. In the process of suburbanizing. Manufacturing: textiles. Single-family building permits issued: 10 (2005); Multi-family building permits issued: 0 (2005); Employment by occupation: 19.1% management, 23.0% professional, 13.6% services, 23.1% sales, 0.5% farming, 6.9% construction, 13.8% production (2000).

Income: Per capita income: $34,634 (2005); Median household income: $76,906 (2005); Average household income: $91,916 (2005); Percent of households with income of $100,000 or more: 34.3% (2005); Poverty rate: 7.3% (2000).

Education: Percent of population age 25 and over with: High school diploma (including GED) or higher: 81.7% (2005); Bachelor's degree or higher: 39.4% (2005); Master's degree or higher: 17.4% (2005).

School District(s)

East Windsor Regional (PK-12)
   2003-04 Enrollment: 5,152 . . . . (609) 443-7704

Housing: Homeownership rate: 60.1% (2005); Median home value: $217,865 (2005); Median rent: $701 per month (2000); Median age of housing: 42 years (2000).

Safety: Violent crime rate: 29.9 per 10,000 population; Property crime rate: 177.6 per 10,000 population (2004).

Newspapers: Register-News (General - Circulation 7,977)

Transportation: Commute to work: 85.9% car, 2.5% public transportation, 4.4% walk, 3.2% work from home (2000); Travel time to work: 18.6% less than 15 minutes, 33.8% 15 to 30 minutes, 24.1% 30 to 45 minutes, 13.2% 45 to 60 minutes, 10.3% 60 minutes or more (2000)

Additional Information Contacts

Borough of Hightstown. . . . . (609) 490-5100
   http://www.hightstownborough.com
Hightstown-East Windsor Chamber of Commerce . . . . (609) 448-4412
   http://www.east-windsor.nj.us

HOPEWELL (borough). Covers a land area of 0.687 square miles and a water area of 0 square miles. Located at 40.38° N. Lat.; 74.76° W. Long. Elevation is 200 feet.

Population: 1,969 (1990); 2,035 (2000); 2,047 (2005); 2,075 (2010 projected); Race: 94.9% White, 0.8% Black, 1.1% Asian, 2.8% Hispanic of any race (2005); Density: 2,981.1 persons per square mile (2005); Average household size: 2.49 (2005); Median age: 40.6 (2005); Males per 100 females: 94.6 (2005); Marriage status: 21.9% never married, 64.0% now married, 5.6% widowed, 8.5% divorced (2000); Foreign born: 7.7% (2000); Ancestry (includes multiple ancestries): 23.4% German, 20.6% Irish, 18.4% English, 13.6% Italian, 9.5% Other groups (2000).

Economy: Single-family building permits issued: 1 (2005); Multi-family building permits issued: 0 (2005); Employment by occupation: 13.6% management, 41.7% professional, 10.0% services, 20.0% sales, 0.0% farming, 9.2% construction, 5.5% production (2000).

Income: Per capita income: $45,085 (2005); Median household income: $95,093 (2005); Average household income: $111,906 (2005); Percent of households with income of $100,000 or more: 46.8% (2005); Poverty rate: 2.1% (2000).

Education: Percent of population age 25 and over with: High school diploma (including GED) or higher: 89.7% (2005); Bachelor's degree or higher: 53.9% (2005); Master's degree or higher: 28.9% (2005).

School District(s)

Hopewell Valley Regional (PK-12)
   2003-04 Enrollment: 3,879 . . . . (609) 737-0105

Housing: Homeownership rate: 72.8% (2005); Median home value: $352,247 (2005); Median rent: $744 per month (2000); Median age of housing: 60+ years (2000).

Safety: Violent crime rate: 9.7 per 10,000 population; Property crime rate: 97.2 per 10,000 population (2004).

Newspapers: Hopewell Valley News (General - Circulation 3,300); The Beacon (General - Circulation 3,840); The Lawrence Ledger (General - Circulation 3,000)

Transportation: Commute to work: 89.3% car, 0.7% public transportation, 2.6% walk, 6.4% work from home (2000); Travel time to work: 25.1% less than 15 minutes, 37.7% 15 to 30 minutes, 22.3% 30 to 45 minutes, 4.8% 45 to 60 minutes, 10.0% 60 minutes or more (2000)

HOPEWELL (township). Covers a land area of 58.112 square miles and a water area of 0.544 square miles. Located at 40.33° N. Lat.; 74.79° W. Long. Elevation is 200 feet.

History: Has Baptist Church (1748); monument (1865) to John Hart, who lived here; historical museum. State children's home— the former Lindbergh estate deeded (1941) to state. Settled before 1700, incorporated 1891.

Population: 11,569 (1990); 16,105 (2000); 17,080 (2005); 18,100 (2010 projected); Race: 85.6% White, 6.6% Black, 5.7% Asian, 2.9% Hispanic of any race (2005); Density: 293.9 persons per square mile (2005); Average household size: 2.88 (2005); Median age: 39.8 (2005); Males per 100 females: 103.1 (2005); Marriage status: 19.4% never married, 69.7% now married, 5.0% widowed, 5.9% divorced (2000); Foreign born: 7.7% (2000); Ancestry (includes multiple ancestries): 18.9% Irish, 17.8% German, 16.0% Italian, 15.2% English, 12.8% Other groups (2000).

Economy: In agricultural region: produce, dairy products. Manufacturing: metal products, telecommunications, engineering research, and canned goods. Single-family building permits issued: 129 (2005); Multi-family building permits issued: 0 (2005); Employment by occupation: 23.1% management, 38.0% professional, 8.4% services, 20.2% sales, 0.3% farming, 5.6% construction, 4.4% production (2000).

Income: Per capita income: $52,038 (2005); Median household income: $114,036 (2005); Average household income: $148,130 (2005); Percent of households with income of $100,000 or more: 57.4% (2005); Poverty rate: 1.1% (2000).

Taxes: Total city taxes per capita: $573 (2004); City property taxes per capita: $561 (2004).

Education: Percent of population age 25 and over with: High school diploma (including GED) or higher: 92.8% (2005); Bachelor's degree or higher: 55.6% (2005); Master's degree or higher: 27.6% (2005).

Housing: Homeownership rate: 93.1% (2005); Median home value: $397,422 (2005); Median rent: $833 per month (2000); Median age of housing: 31 years (2000).

Safety: Violent crime rate: 10.7 per 10,000 population; Property crime rate: 58.0 per 10,000 population (2004).

Newspapers: Hopewell Valley News (General - Circulation 3,300); The Beacon (General - Circulation 3,840); The Lawrence Ledger (General - Circulation 3,000)

Transportation: Commute to work: 88.8% car, 4.4% public transportation, 0.3% walk, 5.9% work from home (2000); Travel time to work: 19.1% less than 15 minutes, 43.6% 15 to 30 minutes, 15.3% 30 to 45 minutes, 8.3% 45 to 60 minutes, 13.8% 60 minutes or more (2000)

Additional Information Contacts

Greater Mercer County Chamber of Commerce . . . . (609) 393-4143
http://www.mercerchamber.org

LAWRENCE (township).

Covers a land area of 22.141 square miles and a water area of 0.038 square miles. Located at 40.27° N. Lat.; 74.72° W. Long. Elevation is 60 feet.

History: Incorporated 1798.

Population: 25,787 (1990); 29,159 (2000); 31,742 (2005); 34,242 (2010 projected); Race: 75.4% White, 9.5% Black, 10.8% Asian, 5.5% Hispanic of any race (2005); Density: 1,433.6 persons per square mile (2005); Average household size: 2.65 (2005); Median age: 37.6 (2005); Males per 100 females: 89.0 (2005); Marriage status: 28.5% never married, 57.4% now married, 6.6% widowed, 7.4% divorced (2000); Foreign born: 17.5% (2000); Ancestry (includes multiple ancestries): 20.6% Other groups, 17.1% Italian, 14.6% Irish, 12.5% German, 11.7% Polish (2000).

Economy: Unemployment rate: 2.2% (2005); Total civilian labor force: 17,641 (2005); Single-family building permits issued: 131 (2005); Multi-family building permits issued: 0 (2005); Employment by occupation: 19.5% management, 34.3% professional, 10.5% services, 25.2% sales, 0.0% farming, 4.5% construction, 5.9% production (2000).

Income: Per capita income: $38,434 (2005); Median household income: $78,283 (2005); Average household income: $100,618 (2005); Percent of households with income of $100,000 or more: 36.0% (2005); Poverty rate: 4.9% (2000).

Taxes: Total city taxes per capita: $615 (2004); City property taxes per capita: $551 (2004).

Education: Percent of population age 25 and over with: High school diploma (including GED) or higher: 89.2% (2005); Bachelor's degree or higher: 50.5% (2005); Master's degree or higher: 24.2% (2005).

Housing: Homeownership rate: 69.6% (2005); Median home value: $268,927 (2005); Median rent: $842 per month (2000); Median age of housing: 24 years (2000).

Safety: Violent crime rate: 16.4 per 10,000 population; Property crime rate: 358.8 per 10,000 population (2004).

Transportation: Commute to work: 87.2% car, 5.3% public transportation, 3.4% walk, 3.5% work from home (2000); Travel time to work: 27.8% less than 15 minutes, 40.3% 15 to 30 minutes, 13.5% 30 to 45 minutes, 6.5% 45 to 60 minutes, 11.9% 60 minutes or more (2000)

Additional Information Contacts

Lawrence Township. . . . . (609) 844-7000
http://www.lawrencetwp.com

LAWRENCEVILLE (CDP).

Covers a land area of 1.039 square miles and a water area of 0 square miles. Located at 40.30° N. Lat.; 74.73° W. Long. Elevation is 123 feet.

History: Lawrenceville School for Boys (1810) and Rider University are located here. Settled 1692.

Population: 3,437 (1990); 4,081 (2000); 4,196 (2005); 4,310 (2010 projected); Race: 87.0% White, 3.3% Black, 7.5% Asian, 4.1% Hispanic of any race (2005); Density: 4,037.1 persons per square mile (2005); Average household size: 2.30 (2005); Median age: 40.5 (2005); Males per 100 females: 84.2 (2005); Marriage status: 28.2% never married, 57.9% now married, 4.0% widowed, 9.9% divorced (2000); Foreign born: 16.5% (2000); Ancestry (includes multiple ancestries): 18.6% Irish, 18.1% Italian, 16.9% Other groups, 13.6% German, 13.2% English (2000).

Economy: Turbine manufacturing. Employment by occupation: 19.7% management, 40.7% professional, 8.7% services, 24.8% sales, 0.0% farming, 2.8% construction, 3.4% production (2000).

Income: Per capita income: $43,431 (2005); Median household income: $85,430 (2005); Average household income: $99,745 (2005); Percent of households with income of $100,000 or more: 40.0% (2005); Poverty rate: 1.7% (2000).

Education: Percent of population age 25 and over with: High school diploma (including GED) or higher: 96.6% (2005); Bachelor's degree or higher: 71.4% (2005); Master's degree or higher: 32.8% (2005).

School District(s)
Lawrence Township (PK-12)
2003-04 Enrollment: 4,852 . . . . (609) 530-8609
Four-year College(s)
Rider University (Private, Not-for-profit)
Fall 2004 Enrollment: 5,502 . . . . (609) 896-5000
2005-06 Tuition: In-state $22,910; Out-of-state $22,910

Housing: Homeownership rate: 81.4% (2005); Median home value: $248,993 (2005); Median rent: $936 per month (2000); Median age of housing: 16 years (2000).

Hospitals: St. Lawrence Rehabilitation Center (152 beds)

Transportation: Commute to work: 92.0% car, 4.5% public transportation, 0.8% walk, 2.2% work from home (2000); Travel time to work: 26.2% less than 15 minutes, 44.2% 15 to 30 minutes, 10.2% 30 to 45 minutes, 6.3% 45 to 60 minutes, 13.1% 60 minutes or more (2000)

MERCERVILLE-HAMILTON SQUARE (CDP).

Covers a land area of 7.705 square miles and a water area of 0 square miles. Located at 40.23° N. Lat.; 74.67° W. Long.

Population: 26,873 (1990); 26,419 (2000); 26,648 (2005); 26,989 (2010 projected); Race: 93.1% White, 1.7% Black, 2.9% Asian, 3.2% Hispanic of any race (2005); Density: 3,458.4 persons per square mile (2005); Average household size: 2.78 (2005); Median age: 42.0 (2005); Males per 100 females: 92.0 (2005); Marriage status: 21.2% never married, 64.8% now married, 8.9% widowed, 5.1% divorced (2000); Foreign born: 6.9% (2000); Ancestry (includes multiple ancestries): 29.1% Italian, 21.8% Irish, 18.4% German, 13.9% Polish, 12.8% English (2000).

Economy: Employment by occupation: 17.7% management, 24.3% professional, 12.0% services, 29.1% sales, 0.0% farming, 7.6% construction, 9.3% production (2000).

Income: Per capita income: $32,047 (2005); Median household income: $77,065 (2005); Average household income: $88,014 (2005); Percent of households with income of $100,000 or more: 32.5% (2005); Poverty rate: 2.2% (2000).

Education: Percent of population age 25 and over with: High school diploma (including GED) or higher: 85.9% (2005); Bachelor's degree or higher: 28.0% (2005); Master's degree or higher: 8.9% (2005).

Housing: Homeownership rate: 88.9% (2005); Median home value: $249,037 (2005); Median rent: $768 per month (2000); Median age of housing: 39 years (2000).

Transportation: Commute to work: 94.0% car, 2.7% public transportation, 0.7% walk, 2.1% work from home (2000); Travel time to work: 25.9% less than 15 minutes, 41.5% 15 to 30 minutes, 17.6% 30 to 45 minutes, 5.6% 45 to 60 minutes, 9.4% 60 minutes or more (2000)

PENNINGTON (borough).

Covers a land area of 0.963 square miles and a water area of 0.001 square miles. Located at 40.32° N. Lat.; 74.79° W. Long. Elevation is 211 feet.

History: Pennington School for boys (1838) here. Settled 1708, incorporated 1890.

Population: 2,537 (1990); 2,696 (2000); 2,708 (2005); 2,743 (2010 projected); Race: 95.0% White, 2.6% Black, 0.8% Asian, 1.3% Hispanic of any race (2005); Density: 2,813.4 persons per square mile (2005); Average household size: 2.62 (2005); Median age: 41.2 (2005); Males per 100 females: 92.3 (2005); Marriage status: 20.0% never married, 66.0% now married, 7.1% widowed, 6.9% divorced (2000); Foreign born: 5.8% (2000); Ancestry (includes multiple ancestries): 24.0% German, 20.1% English, 18.2% Irish, 13.4% Italian, 6.9% Other groups (2000).

Economy: Single-family building permits issued: 2 (2005); Multi-family building permits issued: 0 (2005); Employment by occupation: 26.4% management, 37.8% professional, 4.6% services, 24.2% sales, 0.0% farming, 3.3% construction, 3.7% production (2000).

Income: Per capita income: $51,870 (2005); Median household income: $105,901 (2005); Average household income: $135,085 (2005); Percent of households with income of $100,000 or more: 52.7% (2005); Poverty rate: 2.4% (2000).

Education: Percent of population age 25 and over with: High school diploma (including GED) or higher: 97.0% (2005); Bachelor's degree or higher: 69.3% (2005); Master's degree or higher: 32.8% (2005).

School District(s)
Hopewell Valley Regional (PK-12)
2003-04 Enrollment: 3,879 . . . . (609) 737-0105
Mercer County Vocational (09-12)
2003-04 Enrollment: 140 . . . . (609) 586-2129

Housing: Homeownership rate: 84.6% (2005); Median home value: $430,769 (2005); Median rent: $796 per month (2000); Median age of housing: 47 years (2000).

Safety: Violent crime rate: 0.0 per 10,000 population; Property crime rate: 110.1 per 10,000 population (2004).

Newspapers: Pennington Post (General - Circulation 4,000)

Transportation: Commute to work: 84.5% car, 3.2% public transportation, 6.3% walk, 5.8% work from home (2000); Travel time to work: 31.8% less than 15 minutes, 45.5% 15 to 30 minutes, 7.5% 30 to 45 minutes, 4.6% 45 to 60 minutes, 10.6% 60 minutes or more (2000)

Additional Information Contacts

Borough of Pennington . . . . (609) 737-0276
   http://www.penningtonboro.org

PRINCETON (borough).

Covers a land area of 1.848 square miles and a water area of 0 square miles. Located at 40.35° N. Lat.; 74.65° W. Long. Elevation is 215 feet.

History: A half-dozen Quaker families settled in the Princeton area in 1696. At first the settlement was called Stony Brook after the small stream that bordered two sides of the area, but in 1724 the residents chose the name Prince's Town (later shortened to Princeton), supposedly because of the proximity to King's Town (Kingston). Princeton University was moved to Princeton from Newark in the middle of the 18th century. In 1777, the first state legislature met at Princeton. The original state seal, the first in the new nation, was adopted.

Population: 12,064 (1990); 14,203 (2000); 14,194 (2005); 14,135 (2010 projected); Race: 78.8% White, 5.5% Black, 8.7% Asian, 8.3% Hispanic of any race (2005); Density: 7,681.4 persons per square mile (2005); Average household size: 4.38 (2005); Median age: 24.6 (2005); Males per 100 females: 109.1 (2005); Marriage status: 24.6% never married, 66.6% now married, 5.3% widowed, 3.5% divorced (2000); Foreign born: 14.2% (2000); Ancestry (includes multiple ancestries): 14.4% Other groups, 7.3% Irish, 6.7% English, 6.5% German, 3.9% Italian (2000).

Economy: Single-family building permits issued: 14 (2005); Multi-family building permits issued: 2 (2005); Employment by occupation: 14.1% management, 48.6% professional, 18.7% services, 13.9% sales, 0.2% farming, 2.3% construction, 2.2% production (2000).

Income: Per capita income: $30,255 (2005); Median household income: $76,455 (2005); Average household income: $120,483 (2005); Percent of households with income of $100,000 or more: 39.0% (2005); Poverty rate: 9.0% (2000).

Taxes: Total city taxes per capita: $600 (2004); City property taxes per capita: $535 (2004).

Education: Percent of population age 25 and over with: High school diploma (including GED) or higher: 89.0% (2005); Bachelor's degree or higher: 61.3% (2005); Master's degree or higher: 40.5% (2005).

School District(s)

Agency - Princeton CS (KG-08)
   2003-04 Enrollment: 278 . . . . (609) 924-0575
Princeton Regional (PK-12)
   2003-04 Enrollment: 3,304 . . . . (609) 924-9322

Four-year College(s)

Princeton Theological Seminary (Private, Not-for-profit, Presbyterian Church (USA))
   Fall 2004 Enrollment: 766 . . . . (609) 921-8300
Princeton University (Private, Not-for-profit)
   Fall 2004 Enrollment: 6,708 . . . . (609) 258-3000
   2005-06 Tuition: In-state $31,450; Out-of-state $31,450

Housing: Homeownership rate: 46.6% (2005); Median home value: $542,199 (2005); Median rent: $872 per month (2000); Median age of housing: 60+ years (2000).

Hospitals: University Medical Center at Princeton (308 beds)

Safety: Violent crime rate: 16.8 per 10,000 population; Property crime rate: 350.4 per 10,000 population (2004).

Newspapers: Tempo (General - Circulation 5,175); The Princeton Packet (General - Circulation 14,130); Town Topics (General - Circulation 14,500); U.S. 1 (General - Circulation 19,000)

Transportation: Commute to work: 50.6% car, 4.9% public transportation, 35.6% walk, 5.8% work from home (2000); Travel time to work: 53.4% less than 15 minutes, 25.2% 15 to 30 minutes, 10.6% 30 to 45 minutes, 2.8% 45 to 60 minutes, 8.1% 60 minutes or more (2000)

Additional Information Contacts

Princeton Chamber of Commerce . . . . (609) 924-1776
   http://www.princetonchamber.org

Princeton Online . . . . (609) 737-7901
   http://www.princetonol.com

PRINCETON (township).

Covers a land area of 16.384 square miles and a water area of 0.231 square miles. Located at 40.35° N. Lat.; 74.65° W. Long. Elevation is 215 feet.

History: Settled late 1600s, called Stony Brook until 1724. British, and later, Colonial troops occupied Nassau Hall (of Princeton University) as barracks. Site of a battle (Jan. 3, 1777) in which George Washington surprised and defeated a superior British force. A monument with sculptures commemorates the battle. The Continental Congress met in Nassau Hall June—Nov. 1783. Paul Robeson born here and Albert Einstein spent the last 20 years of his life here. Incorporated 1713.

Population: 13,150 (1990); 16,027 (2000); 16,710 (2005); 17,469 (2010 projected); Race: 77.3% White, 4.8% Black, 12.5% Asian, 5.8% Hispanic of any race (2005); Density: 1,019.9 persons per square mile (2005); Average household size: 2.67 (2005); Median age: 41.3 (2005); Males per 100 females: 93.4 (2005); Marriage status: 23.8% never married, 65.6% now married, 4.3% widowed, 6.3% divorced (2000); Foreign born: 25.4% (2000); Ancestry (includes multiple ancestries): 22.9% Other groups, 13.4% English, 11.6% German, 10.8% Irish, 8.0% Italian (2000).

Economy: A leading education center, it is the seat of Princeton University, the Institute for Advanced Study, Princeton Theological Seminary, Westminster Choir College, St. Joseph's College and other institutions. Home to numerous national and international corporate research centers and headquarters. The Educational Testing Service (ETS) is centered here. Single-family building permits issued: 12 (2005); Multi-family building permits issued: 68 (2005); Employment by occupation: 22.7% management, 48.3% professional, 8.5% services, 15.8% sales, 0.2% farming, 1.4% construction, 3.1% production (2000).

Income: Per capita income: $63,056 (2005); Median household income: $108,984 (2005); Average household income: $165,845 (2005); Percent of households with income of $100,000 or more: 53.1% (2005); Poverty rate: 5.7% (2000).

Education: Percent of population age 25 and over with: High school diploma (including GED) or higher: 94.2% (2005); Bachelor's degree or higher: 75.5% (2005); Master's degree or higher: 47.8% (2005).

School District(s)

Agency - Princeton CS (KG-08)
   2003-04 Enrollment: 278 . . . . (609) 924-0575
Princeton Regional (PK-12)
   2003-04 Enrollment: 3,304 . . . . (609) 924-9322

Four-year College(s)

Princeton Theological Seminary (Private, Not-for-profit, Presbyterian Church (USA)
   Fall 2004 Enrollment: 766 . . . . (609) 921-8300
Princeton University (Private, Not-for-profit)
   Fall 2004 Enrollment: 6,708 . . . . (609) 258-3000
   2005-06 Tuition: In-state $31,450; Out-of-state $31,450

Housing: Homeownership rate: 70.5% (2005); Median home value: $680,678 (2005); Median rent: $702 per month (2000); Median age of housing: 37 years (2000).

Hospitals: University Medical Center at Princeton (308 beds)

Safety: Violent crime rate: 3.5 per 10,000 population; Property crime rate: 102.1 per 10,000 population (2004).

Newspapers: Tempo (General - Circulation 5,175); The Princeton Packet (General - Circulation 14,130); Town Topics (General - Circulation 14,500); U.S. 1 (General - Circulation 19,000)

Transportation: Commute to work: 69.2% car, 8.1% public transportation, 10.1% walk, 9.4% work from home (2000); Travel time to work: 43.3% less than 15 minutes, 27.1% 15 to 30 minutes, 11.8% 30 to 45 minutes, 5.1% 45 to 60 minutes, 12.7% 60 minutes or more (2000)

Additional Information Contacts

Princeton Chamber of Commerce . . . . (609) 924-1776
   http://www.princetonchamber.org
Princeton Township . . . . (609) 924-5704
   http://www.princetontwp.org

PRINCETON JUNCTION (CDP).

Covers a land area of 1.865 square miles and a water area of 0 square miles. Located at 40.31° N. Lat.; 74.62° W. Long. Elevation is 80 feet.

Population: 2,362 (1990); 2,382 (2000); 2,505 (2005); 2,630 (2010 projected); Race: 83.9% White, 2.3% Black, 11.3% Asian, 3.9% Hispanic of any race (2005); Density: 1,342.9 persons per square mile (2005); Average household size: 2.80 (2005); Median age: 40.2 (2005); Males per 100

females: 98.7 (2005); Marriage status: 20.7% never married, 69.7% now married, 4.2% widowed, 5.5% divorced (2000); Foreign born: 11.9% (2000); Ancestry (includes multiple ancestries): 22.4% German, 21.4% English, 20.9% Irish, 18.5% Other groups, 10.9% Italian (2000).
Economy: Employment by occupation: 24.9% management, 44.7% professional, 3.1% services, 21.7% sales, 0.0% farming, 3.0% construction, 2.6% production (2000).
Income: Per capita income: $53,189 (2005); Median household income: $131,347 (2005); Average household income: $147,985 (2005); Percent of households with income of $100,000 or more: 63.5% (2005); Poverty rate: 1.5% (2000).
Education: Percent of population age 25 and over with: High school diploma (including GED) or higher: 96.8% (2005); Bachelor's degree or higher: 75.3% (2005); Master's degree or higher: 41.1% (2005).

School District(s)
West Windsor-Plainsboro Regional (PK-12)
    2003-04 Enrollment: 9,238 . . . . (609) 716-5040
Housing: Homeownership rate: 87.1% (2005); Median home value: $424,138 (2005); Median rent: $733 per month (2000); Median age of housing: 37 years (2000).
Newspapers: West Windsor-Plainsboro News (General - Circulation 3,500)
Transportation: Commute to work: 72.0% car, 21.4% public transportation, 1.7% walk, 4.6% work from home (2000); Travel time to work: 29.4% less than 15 minutes, 28.6% 15 to 30 minutes, 11.3% 30 to 45 minutes, 5.6% 45 to 60 minutes, 25.2% 60 minutes or more (2000); Amtrak: Service available.
Additional Information Contacts
Princeton Chamber of Commerce . . . . (609) 520-1776
    http://www.princetonchamber.org

PRINCETON NORTH (CDP). Covers a land area of 1.619 square miles and a water area of 0 square miles. Located at 40.36° N. Lat.; 74.65° W. Long.
Population: 4,386 (1990); 4,528 (2000); 4,436 (2005); 4,425 (2010 projected); Race: 80.4% White, 4.0% Black, 7.5% Asian, 10.0% Hispanic of any race (2005); Density: 2,740.0 persons per square mile (2005); Average household size: 2.55 (2005); Median age: 45.4 (2005); Males per 100 females: 92.5 (2005); Marriage status: 24.0% never married, 61.7% now married, 6.3% widowed, 8.0% divorced (2000); Foreign born: 26.1% (2000); Ancestry (includes multiple ancestries): 21.3% Other groups, 13.9% English, 12.2% Irish, 8.5% German, 8.2% Italian (2000).
Economy: Employment by occupation: 14.2% management, 46.3% professional, 14.7% services, 17.8% sales, 0.2% farming, 2.6% construction, 4.2% production (2000).
Income: Per capita income: $52,742 (2005); Median household income: $108,217 (2005); Average household income: $134,693 (2005); Percent of households with income of $100,000 or more: 54.1% (2005); Poverty rate: 6.0% (2000).
Education: Percent of population age 25 and over with: High school diploma (including GED) or higher: 91.7% (2005); Bachelor's degree or higher: 71.7% (2005); Master's degree or higher: 45.2% (2005).
Housing: Homeownership rate: 81.5% (2005); Median home value: $520,089 (2005); Median rent: $997 per month (2000); Median age of housing: 45 years (2000).
Transportation: Commute to work: 72.1% car, 5.0% public transportation, 8.8% walk, 11.8% work from home (2000); Travel time to work: 38.6% less than 15 minutes, 32.6% 15 to 30 minutes, 15.4% 30 to 45 minutes, 4.4% 45 to 60 minutes, 9.0% 60 minutes or more (2000)

TITUSVILLE (unincorporated postal area, zip code 08560). Covers a land area of 13.107 square miles and a water area of 0 square miles. Located at 40.31° N. Lat.; 74.85° W. Long. Elevation is 61 feet.
Population: 3,468 (2000); Race: 93.9% White, 0.5% Black, 2.2% Asian, 1.9% Hispanic of any race (2000); Density: 264.6 persons per square mile (2000); Age: 22.4% under 18, 15.4% over 64 (2000); Marriage status: 21.6% never married, 67.3% now married, 4.7% widowed, 6.5% divorced (2000); Foreign born: 4.9% (2000); Ancestry (includes multiple ancestries): 24.0% Irish, 20.5% German, 17.7% Italian, 15.4% English, 11.4% Polish (2000).
Economy: Employment by occupation: 22.2% management, 29.6% professional, 11.2% services, 23.1% sales, 1.2% farming, 6.7% construction, 5.9% production (2000).
Income: Per capita income: $44,648 (2000); Median household income: $89,821 (2000); Poverty rate: 0.8% (2000).

Education: Percent of population age 25 and over with: High school diploma (including GED) or higher: 95.7% (2000); Bachelor's degree or higher: 56.2% (2000).

School District(s)
Hopewell Valley Regional (PK-12)
    2003-04 Enrollment: 3,879 . . . . (609) 737-0105
Housing: Homeownership rate: 92.7% (2000); Median home value: $227,900 (2000); Median rent: $605 per month (2000); Median age of housing: 39 years (2000).
Transportation: Commute to work: 90.8% car, 3.9% public transportation, 1.0% walk, 4.2% work from home (2000); Travel time to work: 25.7% less than 15 minutes, 43.3% 15 to 30 minutes, 14.3% 30 to 45 minutes, 6.1% 45 to 60 minutes, 10.6% 60 minutes or more (2000)

TRENTON (city). Covers a land area of 7.657 square miles and a water area of 0.489 square miles. Located at 40.22° N. Lat.; 74.75° W. Long. Elevation is 54 feet.
History: The first settler in Trenton was Mahlon Stacy, an English Quaker, who took up a grant of land in 1679 and built a log mill and clapboard house. The little hamlet that developed was called The Falls. Recognizing the commercial possibilities of the site, William Trent, a Philadelphia merchant, in 1714 bought the holdings from Stacy's son. Trent called his settlement "Trent's Town," later shortened to Trenton. On December 26, 1776, Trenton was the scene of one of the most decisive battles of the Revolution. Washington executed the now-famous crossing of the ice-choked Delaware and mounted a successful surprise attack on the Hessians in Trenton. Trenton was chosen as the state capital in 1790 and, two years later, was incorporated as a city.
Population: 88,675 (1990); 85,403 (2000); 85,338 (2005); 85,887 (2010 projected); Race: 29.0% White, 52.9% Black, 1.1% Asian, 25.3% Hispanic of any race (2005); Density: 11,145.1 persons per square mile (2005); Average household size: 2.89 (2005); Median age: 33.0 (2005); Males per 100 females: 99.1 (2005); Marriage status: 42.9% never married, 38.7% now married, 8.3% widowed, 10.1% divorced (2000); Foreign born: 14.1% (2000); Ancestry (includes multiple ancestries): 55.4% Other groups, 7.3% Italian, 4.5% Irish, 3.8% Polish, 3.7% German (2000).
Economy: Unemployment rate: 9.3% (2005); Total civilian labor force: 38,470 (2005); Single-family building permits issued: 7 (2005); Multi-family building permits issued: 0 (2005); Employment by occupation: 7.6% management, 13.9% professional, 25.8% services, 27.6% sales, 0.3% farming, 8.4% construction, 16.3% production (2000).
Income: Per capita income: $16,118 (2005); Median household income: $34,193 (2005); Average household income: $45,196 (2005); Percent of households with income of $100,000 or more: 8.1% (2005); Poverty rate: 21.1% (2000).
Taxes: Total city taxes per capita: $854 (2004); City property taxes per capita: $827 (2004).
Education: Percent of population age 25 and over with: High school diploma (including GED) or higher: 62.2% (2005); Bachelor's degree or higher: 9.3% (2005); Master's degree or higher: 3.5% (2005).

School District(s)
Agency - Emily Fisher CS of Advanced Studies (06-12)
    2003-04 Enrollment: 300 . . . . (609) 656-1444
Agency - Granville CS (KG-10)
    2003-04 Enrollment: 564 . . . . (609) 656-1300
Agency - International CS of Trenton (KG-05)
    2003-04 Enrollment: 85 . . . . (609) 394-3111
Agency - The Village CS (KG-06)
    2003-04 Enrollment: 289 . . . . (609) 695-0110
Agency - Trenton Community CS (KG-09)
    2003-04 Enrollment: 585 . . . . (609) 394-0068
Chesterfield Township (PK-06)
    2003-04 Enrollment: 268 . . . . (609) 298-6900
Hamilton Township (PK-12)
    2003-04 Enrollment: 14,074 . . . . (609) 890-3723
Mercer County Special Service (UG-UG)
    2003-04 Enrollment: 1,752 . . . . (609) 588-8400
Mercer County Vocational (09-12)
    2003-04 Enrollment: 140 . . . . (609) 586-2129
Trenton City (PK-12)
    2003-04 Enrollment: 13,227 . . . . (609) 989-2744

Four-year College(s)
Thomas Edison State College (Public)
    Fall 2004 Enrollment: 11,000 . . . . (609) 984-1100

Two-year College(s)

Saint Francis Medical Center School of Nursing (Private, Not-for-profit, Roman Catholic)

    Fall 2004 Enrollment: 74 . . . . (609) 599-5190

    2005-06 Tuition: In-state $8,000; Out-of-state $8,000

St Francis Medical Center-School of Radiologic Technology (Private, Not-for-profit, Roman Catholic)

    Fall 2004 Enrollment: 16 . . . . (609) 599-5234

    2005-06 Tuition: In-state $6,358; Out-of-state $6,358

Housing: Homeownership rate: 45.1% (2005); Median home value: $101,484 (2005); Median rent: $532 per month (2000); Median age of housing: 60+ years (2000).

Hospitals: Capital Health System at Fuld (589 beds); Capital Health System, Mercer Campus (589 beds); St. Francis Medical Center (274 beds); Trenton Psychiatric Hospital (379 beds)

Safety: Violent crime rate: 158.0 per 10,000 population; Property crime rate: 442.9 per 10,000 population (2004).

Newspapers: The Monitor (Catholic, Religious - Circulation 45,000); The Nubian News (Black, Ethnic, Hispanic - Circulation 15,000); The Times (Circulation 73,354); The Trentonian (Circulation 45,775)

Transportation: Commute to work: 79.3% car, 11.6% public transportation, 5.9% walk, 1.6% work from home (2000); Travel time to work: 29.5% less than 15 minutes, 40.1% 15 to 30 minutes, 17.2% 30 to 45 minutes, 6.2% 45 to 60 minutes, 7.0% 60 minutes or more (2000); Amtrak: Service available.

Additional Information Contacts

City of Trenton . . . . (609) 989-3185

    http://www.ci.trenton.nj.us/cigovdepts.html

Mercer County Chamber of Commerce . . . . (609) 393-4143

    http://www.mercerchamber.org

TWIN RIVERS (CDP).

Covers a land area of 1.256 square miles and a water area of 0.046 square miles. Located at 40.26° N. Lat.; 74.48° W. Long. Elevation is 120 feet.

Population: 7,715 (1990); 7,422 (2000); 7,166 (2005); 6,942 (2010 projected); Race: 71.5% White, 11.6% Black, 7.9% Asian, 18.3% Hispanic of any race (2005); Density: 5,703.2 persons per square mile (2005); Average household size: 2.65 (2005); Median age: 39.0 (2005); Males per 100 females: 97.7 (2005); Marriage status: 26.1% never married, 59.3% now married, 4.3% widowed, 10.3% divorced (2000); Foreign born: 18.5% (2000); Ancestry (includes multiple ancestries): 37.3% Other groups, 11.5% Polish, 10.2% Irish, 10.2% Italian, 9.4% German (2000).

Economy: Employment by occupation: 15.8% management, 24.1% professional, 12.0% services, 32.0% sales, 0.4% farming, 4.1% construction, 11.6% production (2000).

Income: Per capita income: $31,346 (2005); Median household income: $70,579 (2005); Average household income: $83,070 (2005); Percent of households with income of $100,000 or more: 28.0% (2005); Poverty rate: 4.6% (2000).

Education: Percent of population age 25 and over with: High school diploma (including GED) or higher: 90.2% (2005); Bachelor's degree or higher: 37.3% (2005); Master's degree or higher: 11.9% (2005).

Housing: Homeownership rate: 73.9% (2005); Median home value: $170,282 (2005); Median rent: $719 per month (2000); Median age of housing: 26 years (2000).

Transportation: Commute to work: 86.5% car, 7.5% public transportation, 1.9% walk, 2.6% work from home (2000); Travel time to work: 23.1% less than 15 minutes, 31.2% 15 to 30 minutes, 19.0% 30 to 45 minutes, 8.5% 45 to 60 minutes, 18.2% 60 minutes or more (2000)

WASHINGTON (township).

Covers a land area of 20.475 square miles and a water area of 0.023 square miles. Located at 40.22° N. Lat.; 74.60° W. Long.

Population: 5,915 (1990); 10,275 (2000); 11,584 (2005); 12,846 (2010 projected); Race: 88.9% White, 3.0% Black, 6.2% Asian, 3.1% Hispanic of any race (2005); Density: 565.8 persons per square mile (2005); Average household size: 2.57 (2005); Median age: 38.5 (2005); Males per 100 females: 91.9 (2005); Marriage status: 17.9% never married, 67.2% now married, 6.9% widowed, 8.1% divorced (2000); Foreign born: 8.7% (2000); Ancestry (includes multiple ancestries): 25.7% Italian, 23.9% Irish, 19.7% German, 12.1% Other groups, 11.3% Polish (2000).

Economy: Single-family building permits issued: 147 (2005); Multi-family building permits issued: 0 (2005); Employment by occupation: 29.5% management, 27.9% professional, 6.3% services, 26.2% sales, 0.0% farming, 4.6% construction, 5.4% production (2000).

Income: Per capita income: $40,807 (2005); Median household income: $86,180 (2005); Average household income: $103,794 (2005); Percent of households with income of $100,000 or more: 40.8% (2005); Poverty rate: 3.7% (2000).

Taxes: Total city taxes per capita: $368 (2004); City property taxes per capita: $343 (2004).

Education: Percent of population age 25 and over with: High school diploma (including GED) or higher: 92.3% (2005); Bachelor's degree or higher: 46.8% (2005); Master's degree or higher: 14.9% (2005).

Housing: Homeownership rate: 89.0% (2005); Median home value: $298,801 (2005); Median rent: $711 per month (2000); Median age of housing: 11 years (2000).

Safety: Violent crime rate: 8.9 per 10,000 population; Property crime rate: 98.3 per 10,000 population (2004).

Transportation: Commute to work: 89.0% car, 5.8% public transportation, 0.1% walk, 4.6% work from home (2000); Travel time to work: 16.8% less than 15 minutes, 40.4% 15 to 30 minutes, 19.5% 30 to 45 minutes, 8.4% 45 to 60 minutes, 14.9% 60 minutes or more (2000)

Additional Information Contacts

Washington Township . . . . (609) 918-0002

    http://www.washington-twp.org

WEST WINDSOR (township).

Covers a land area of 26.006 square miles and a water area of 0.320 square miles. Located at 40.29° N. Lat.; 74.61° W. Long.

History: Population growth in recent decades. Incorporated 1798.

Population: 16,021 (1990); 21,907 (2000); 25,191 (2005); 28,307 (2010 projected); Race: 65.1% White, 2.7% Black, 29.0% Asian, 4.5% Hispanic of any race (2005); Density: 968.7 persons per square mile (2005); Average household size: 3.05 (2005); Median age: 37.0 (2005); Males per 100 females: 97.9 (2005); Marriage status: 19.5% never married, 72.2% now married, 3.3% widowed, 5.0% divorced (2000); Foreign born: 22.4% (2000); Ancestry (includes multiple ancestries): 30.9% Other groups, 15.3% Irish, 14.5% Italian, 12.8% German, 10.0% English (2000).

Economy: Single-family building permits issued: 159 (2005); Multi-family building permits issued: 0 (2005); Employment by occupation: 32.0% management, 39.0% professional, 4.5% services, 20.5% sales, 0.0% farming, 1.6% construction, 2.4% production (2000).

Income: Per capita income: $56,893 (2005); Median household income: $138,926 (2005); Average household income: $172,944 (2005); Percent of households with income of $100,000 or more: 67.8% (2005); Poverty rate: 2.5% (2000).

Taxes: Total city taxes per capita: $620 (2004); City property taxes per capita: $593 (2004).

Education: Percent of population age 25 and over with: High school diploma (including GED) or higher: 96.9% (2005); Bachelor's degree or higher: 73.9% (2005); Master's degree or higher: 38.9% (2005).

Two-year College(s)

Mercer County Community College (Public)

    Fall 2004 Enrollment: 9,033 . . . . (609) 586-4800

    2005-06 Tuition: In-state $2,916; Out-of-state $4,524

Housing: Homeownership rate: 81.8% (2005); Median home value: $511,876 (2005); Median rent: $1,132 per month (2000); Median age of housing: 16 years (2000).

Safety: Violent crime rate: 6.6 per 10,000 population; Property crime rate: 217.6 per 10,000 population (2004).

Transportation: Commute to work: 70.9% car, 21.6% public transportation, 1.2% walk, 5.5% work from home (2000); Travel time to work: 21.8% less than 15 minutes, 27.7% 15 to 30 minutes, 10.5% 30 to 45 minutes, 6.9% 45 to 60 minutes, 33.1% 60 minutes or more (2000)

Additional Information Contacts

Mercer County Chamber of Commerce . . . . (609) 393-4143

    http://www.mercerchamber.org

WHITE HORSE (CDP).

Covers a land area of 3.186 square miles and a water area of 0.132 square miles. Located at 40.19° N. Lat.; 74.70° W. Long. Elevation is 70 feet.

Population: 9,456 (1990); 9,373 (2000); 9,689 (2005); 10,047 (2010 projected); Race: 90.8% White, 3.8% Black, 2.2% Asian, 4.8% Hispanic of any race (2005); Density: 3,041.0 persons per square mile (2005); Average household size: 2.48 (2005); Median age: 43.1 (2005); Males per 100 females: 91.2 (2005); Marriage status: 23.6% never married, 59.9% now married, 9.6% widowed, 6.9% divorced (2000); Foreign born: 7.1% (2000); Ancestry (includes multiple ancestries): 25.6% Italian, 19.6% Irish, 17.4% German, 12.5% Polish, 9.0% Other groups (2000).

Economy: Employment by occupation: 15.3% management, 19.4% professional, 13.5% services, 33.8% sales, 0.0% farming, 9.3% construction, 8.8% production (2000).
Income: Per capita income: $29,159 (2005); Median household income: $65,420 (2005); Average household income: $72,301 (2005); Percent of households with income of $100,000 or more: 23.2% (2005); Poverty rate: 3.9% (2000).
Education: Percent of population age 25 and over with: High school diploma (including GED) or higher: 83.8% (2005); Bachelor's degree or higher: 17.4% (2005); Master's degree or higher: 5.2% (2005).
Housing: Homeownership rate: 86.2% (2005); Median home value: $212,492 (2005); Median rent: $779 per month (2000); Median age of housing: 42 years (2000).
Transportation: Commute to work: 95.8% car, 2.6% public transportation, 0.4% walk, 1.1% work from home (2000); Travel time to work: 29.1% less than 15 minutes, 46.9% 15 to 30 minutes, 14.1% 30 to 45 minutes, 4.2% 45 to 60 minutes, 5.8% 60 minutes or more (2000)

YARDVILLE-GROVEVILLE (CDP). Covers a land area of 3.444 square miles and a water area of 0.018 square miles. Located at 40.18° N. Lat.; 74.67° W. Long.
Population: 9,248 (1990); 9,208 (2000); 10,085 (2005); 10,948 (2010 projected); Race: 92.0% White, 3.4% Black, 2.4% Asian, 3.5% Hispanic of any race (2005); Density: 2,928.3 persons per square mile (2005); Average household size: 2.64 (2005); Median age: 40.0 (2005); Males per 100 females: 95.5 (2005); Marriage status: 21.5% never married, 66.4% now married, 5.7% widowed, 6.5% divorced (2000); Foreign born: 6.6% (2000); Ancestry (includes multiple ancestries): 29.2% Italian, 21.7% German, 19.7% Irish, 13.7% Polish, 11.4% English (2000).
Economy: Employment by occupation: 15.3% management, 23.6% professional, 13.8% services, 29.7% sales, 0.1% farming, 7.6% construction, 9.8% production (2000).
Income: Per capita income: $30,069 (2005); Median household income: $69,335 (2005); Average household income: $79,114 (2005); Percent of households with income of $100,000 or more: 27.7% (2005); Poverty rate: 1.4% (2000).
Education: Percent of population age 25 and over with: High school diploma (including GED) or higher: 88.1% (2005); Bachelor's degree or higher: 23.0% (2005); Master's degree or higher: 6.1% (2005).

School District(s)
Hamilton Township (PK-12)
   2003-04 Enrollment: 14,074 . . . . (609) 890-3723
Housing: Homeownership rate: 81.0% (2005); Median home value: $235,377 (2005); Median rent: $601 per month (2000); Median age of housing: 39 years (2000).
Transportation: Commute to work: 95.3% car, 1.9% public transportation, 0.3% walk, 1.9% work from home (2000); Travel time to work: 24.8% less than 15 minutes, 45.6% 15 to 30 minutes, 17.9% 30 to 45 minutes, 4.5% 45 to 60 minutes, 7.2% 60 minutes or more (2000)

Middlesex County

Located in eastern New Jersey; bounded on the east by Raritan Bay and Arthur Kill; drained by the Raritan, Millstone, and South Rivers. Covers a land area of 309.72 square miles, a water area of 12.79 square miles, and is located in the Eastern Time Zone. The county government was organized in 1683. County seat is New Brunswick.

Middlesex County is part of the New York-Northern New Jersey-Long Island, NY-NJ-PA Metropolitan Statistical Area. The entire metro area includes: Edison, NJ Metropolitan Division (Middlesex County, NJ; Monmouth County, NJ; Ocean County, NJ; Somerset County, NJ); Nassau-Suffolk, NY Metropolitan Division (Nassau County, NY; Suffolk County, NY); New York-White Plains-Wayne, NY-NJ Metropolitan Division (Bergen County, NJ; Hudson County, NJ; Passaic County, NJ; Bronx County, NY; Kings County, NY; New York County, NY; Putnam County, NY; Queens County, NY; Richmond County, NY; Rockland County, NY; Westchester County, NY); Newark-Union, NJ-PA Metropolitan Division (Essex County, NJ; Hunterdon County, NJ; Morris County, NJ; Sussex County, NJ; Union County, NJ; Pike County, PA)

Weather Station: New Brunswick 3 SE   Elevation: 85 feet

	Jan	Feb	Mar	Apr	May	Jun	Jul	Aug	Sep	Oct	Nov	Dec
High	38	41	50	61	71	80	85	83	77	65	54	43
Low	21	23	31	40	50	59	64	63	55	43	35	27
Precip	4.0	3.0	4.1	4.2	4.5	3.9	5.0	4.4	4.3	3.5	4.0	3.9
Snow	8.9	8.3	4.5	1.0	tr	0.0	0.0	0.0	0.0	tr	0.6	3.1

High and Low temperatures in degrees Fahrenheit; Precipitation and Snow in inches

Population: 671,940 (1990); 750,162 (2000); 794,310 (2005); 840,448 (2010 projected); Race: 63.3% White, 9.6% Black, 17.1% Asian, 15.9% Hispanic of any race (2005); Density: 2,564.6 persons per square mile (2005); Average household size: 2.83 (2005); Median age: 36.8 (2005); Males per 100 females: 97.0 (2005).
Religion: Five largest groups: 45.7% Catholic Church, 6.0% Jewish Estimate, 1.0% Presbyterian Church (U.S.A.), 0.9% Muslim Estimate, 0.8% American Baptist Churches in the USA (2000).
Economy: Unemployment rate: 4.1% (2005); Total civilian labor force: 418,637 (2005); Leading industries: 12.1% administration (2004); Farms: 275 totaling 21,824 acres (2002); Companies that employ 500 or more persons: 175 (2004); Companies that employ 100 to 499 persons: 1,142 (2004); Companies that employ less than 100 persons: 41,157 (2004); Black-owned businesses: 2,993 (2002); Hispanic-owned businesses: 3,961 (2002); Asian-owned businesses: 9,457 (2002); Women-owned businesses: 13,258 (2002); Retail sales per capita: $14,516 (2006). Single-family building permits issued: 1,774 (2005); Multi-family building permits issued: 1,432 (2005).
Income: Per capita income: $30,428 (2005); Median household income: $69,549 (2005); Average household income: $85,334 (2005); Percent of households with income of $100,000 or more: 29.9% (2005); Poverty rate: 7.4% (2003); Bankruptcy rate: 4.29% (2005).
Taxes: Total county taxes per capita: $293 (2004); County property taxes per capita: $282 (2004).
Education: Percent of population age 25 and over with: High school diploma (including GED) or higher: 84.4% (2005); Bachelor's degree or higher: 33.2% (2005); Master's degree or higher: 12.6% (2005).
Housing: Homeownership rate: 66.7% (2005); Median home value: $267,710 (2005); Median rent: $770 per month (2000); Median age of housing: 33 years (2000).
Health: Birth rate: 141.8 per 10,000 population (2004); Death rate: 72.2 per 10,000 population (2004); Age-adjusted cancer mortality rate: 186.8 deaths per 100,000 population (2002); Air Quality Index: 73.2% good, 24.1% moderate, 2.7% unhealthy for sensitive individuals, 0.0% unhealthy (percent of days in 2005); Number of physicians: 36.2 per 10,000 population (2004); Hospital beds: 24.8 per 10,000 population (2003); Hospital admissions: 1,193.9 per 10,000 population (2003).
Elections: 2004 Presidential election results: 42.8% Bush, 56.3% Kerry, 0.6% Nader, 0.1% Badnarik.
National and State Parks: Cheesequake State Park; Edison State Park
Additional Information Contacts
Middlesex County Government . . . . (732) 745-3080
   http://www.co.middlesex.nj.us
Borough of Carteret . . . . (732) 541-3801
   http://www.ci.carteret.nj.us
Borough of Sayreville . . . . (732) 390-7007
   http://www.sayreville.com
Borough of South Plainfield . . . . (908) 226-7606
   http://www.southplainfieldnj.com
Borough of South River . . . . (732) 257-1999
   http://www.southrivernj.org
Borough of Spotswood . . . . (732) 251-0700
   http://www.spotswoodboro.com
City of New Brunswick . . . . (732) 745-5004
   http://www.cityofnewbrunswick.org
City of Perth Amboy . . . . (732) 826-0290
   http://www.ci.perthamboy.nj.us
Cranbury Township . . . . (609) 395-0900
   http://www.cranburytownship.org
East Brunswick Chamber of Commerce . . . . (732) 257-3009
   http://www.ebnjchamber.org
East Brunswick Township . . . . (732) 390-6810
   http://www.eastbrunswick.org
Edison Chamber of Commerce . . . . (732) 494-0300
   http://www.edisonchamber.com
Edison Township . . . . (732) 248-7200
   http://www.edisonnj.org

Metuchen Chamber of Commerce . . . . (732) 548-2964
   http://www.metuchenchamber.com
Middlesex Chamber of Commerce . . . . (732) 394-0220
   http://wwwpmcoc.org
Middlesex County Chamber of Commerce . . . . (732) 821-1700
   http://www.mcrcc.org
North Brunswick Township . . . . (732) 247-0922
   http://www.northbrunswickonline.com
Old Bridge Chamber of Commerce . . . . (732) 607-6340
   http://www.oldbridge.com/OB_Home.htm
Old Bridge Township . . . . (732) 721-5600
   http://www.oldbridge.com
Perth Amboy Chamber of Commerce . . . . (732) 442-7400
   http://perthamboychamber.com
Piscataway Chamber of Commerce . . . . (732) 394-0220
   http://www.pmcoc.org
Piscataway Township . . . . (732) 562-2301
   http://www.piscatawaynj.org
Plainsboro Township . . . . (609) 799-0909
   http://www.plainsboronj.com
Sayreville Chamber of Commerce . . . . (732) 607-6340
   http://www.oldbridge.com/OB_Home.htm
South Brunswick Chamber of Commerce . . . . (732) 297-2051
   http://www.sbchamber.com
South Brunswick Township . . . . (732) 329-4000
   http://www.twp.south-brunswick.nj.us
South Plainfield Chamber of Commerce . . . . (732) 394-0220
   http://www.pmcoc.org
Woodbridge Chamber of Commerce . . . . (732) 636-4040
   http://www.woodbridgechamber.org
Woodbridge Township . . . . (732) 634-4500
   http://www.twp.woodbridge.nj.us

Middlesex County Communities

AVENEL (CDP). Covers a land area of 3.442 square miles and a water area of 0.020 square miles. Located at 40.58° N. Lat.; 74.28° W. Long. Elevation is 84 feet.
Population: 15,504 (1990); 17,552 (2000); 19,139 (2005); 20,648 (2010 projected); Race: 45.3% White, 20.7% Black, 24.4% Asian, 11.1% Hispanic of any race (2005); Density: 5,560.3 persons per square mile (2005); Average household size: 3.36 (2005); Median age: 36.5 (2005); Males per 100 females: 132.2 (2005); Marriage status: 29.0% never married, 57.0% now married, 5.7% widowed, 8.2% divorced (2000); Foreign born: 25.9% (2000); Ancestry (includes multiple ancestries): 36.7% Other groups, 12.8% Italian, 12.3% Irish, 7.7% German, 6.7% Polish (2000).
Economy: Employment by occupation: 12.9% management, 24.7% professional, 10.4% services, 27.4% sales, 0.7% farming, 6.7% construction, 17.2% production (2000).
Income: Per capita income: $22,871 (2005); Median household income: $63,959 (2005); Average household income: $73,276 (2005); Percent of households with income of $100,000 or more: 24.9% (2005); Poverty rate: 9.6% (2000).
Education: Percent of population age 25 and over with: High school diploma (including GED) or higher: 79.9% (2005); Bachelor's degree or higher: 26.0% (2005); Master's degree or higher: 8.6% (2005).
School District(s)
Woodbridge Township (PK-12)
   2003-04 Enrollment: 14,056 . . . . (732) 602-8549
Housing: Homeownership rate: 53.4% (2005); Median home value: $230,234 (2005); Median rent: $794 per month (2000); Median age of housing: 36 years (2000).
Transportation: Commute to work: 84.6% car, 8.6% public transportation, 4.8% walk, 1.0% work from home (2000); Travel time to work: 26.2% less than 15 minutes, 29.2% 15 to 30 minutes, 20.9% 30 to 45 minutes, 8.8% 45 to 60 minutes, 15.0% 60 minutes or more (2000)

BROWNVILLE (CDP). Covers a land area of 0.942 square miles and a water area of 0 square miles. Located at 40.40° N. Lat.; 74.29° W. Long.
Population: 2,521 (1990); 2,660 (2000); 2,694 (2005); 2,726 (2010 projected); Race: 81.1% White, 5.5% Black, 9.5% Asian, 7.2% Hispanic of any race (2005); Density: 2,859.7 persons per square mile (2005); Average household size: 2.29 (2005); Median age: 41.2 (2005); Males per 100 females: 83.3 (2005); Marriage status: 21.1% never married, 54.9% now married, 12.3% widowed, 11.7% divorced (2000); Foreign born: 17.5%

(2000); Ancestry (includes multiple ancestries): 24.9% Italian, 21.1% Other groups, 18.2% Irish, 11.1% German, 8.4% Russian (2000).
Economy: Employment by occupation: 22.3% management, 28.0% professional, 5.2% services, 32.3% sales, 0.0% farming, 6.2% construction, 6.0% production (2000).
Income: Per capita income: $32,838 (2005); Median household income: $66,894 (2005); Average household income: $75,161 (2005); Percent of households with income of $100,000 or more: 29.1% (2005); Poverty rate: 6.3% (2000).
Education: Percent of population age 25 and over with: High school diploma (including GED) or higher: 87.7% (2005); Bachelor's degree or higher: 31.3% (2005); Master's degree or higher: 13.4% (2005).
Housing: Homeownership rate: 72.6% (2005); Median home value: $216,424 (2005); Median rent: $240 per month (2000); Median age of housing: 16 years (2000).
Transportation: Commute to work: 80.9% car, 15.1% public transportation, 1.5% walk, 1.7% work from home (2000); Travel time to work: 12.1% less than 15 minutes, 21.7% 15 to 30 minutes, 19.9% 30 to 45 minutes, 18.8% 45 to 60 minutes, 27.5% 60 minutes or more (2000)

CARTERET (borough). Aka Roosevelt. Covers a land area of 4.362 square miles and a water area of 0.631 square miles. Located at 40.58° N. Lat.; 74.23° W. Long. Elevation is 16 feet.
History: Named for Sir George Carteret, who received a grant for what is now the state of New Jersey. Incorporated 1906.
Population: 19,025 (1990); 20,709 (2000); 21,901 (2005); 23,158 (2010 projected); Race: 62.2% White, 11.0% Black, 10.3% Asian, 28.5% Hispanic of any race (2005); Density: 5,020.7 persons per square mile (2005); Average household size: 2.96 (2005); Median age: 37.7 (2005); Males per 100 females: 95.1 (2005); Marriage status: 28.3% never married, 55.0% now married, 8.8% widowed, 7.9% divorced (2000); Foreign born: 23.4% (2000); Ancestry (includes multiple ancestries): 37.4% Other groups, 14.3% Italian, 12.9% Irish, 12.3% Polish, 7.2% German (2000).
Economy: It has oil and copper refineries and industries that produce steel and chemicals. Single-family building permits issued: 29 (2005); Multi-family building permits issued: 381 (2005); Employment by occupation: 9.2% management, 12.4% professional, 14.9% services, 33.4% sales, 0.1% farming, 8.9% construction, 21.1% production (2000).
Income: Per capita income: $20,667 (2005); Median household income: $50,702 (2005); Average household income: $60,486 (2005); Percent of households with income of $100,000 or more: 15.1% (2005); Poverty rate: 11.0% (2000).
Taxes: Total city taxes per capita: $697 (2004); City property taxes per capita: $658 (2004).
Education: Percent of population age 25 and over with: High school diploma (including GED) or higher: 74.9% (2005); Bachelor's degree or higher: 13.0% (2005); Master's degree or higher: 3.7% (2005).
School District(s)
Carteret Borough (PK-12)
   2003-04 Enrollment: 3,957 . . . . (732) 541-8961
Housing: Homeownership rate: 68.4% (2005); Median home value: $222,955 (2005); Median rent: $658 per month (2000); Median age of housing: 44 years (2000).
Safety: Violent crime rate: 25.2 per 10,000 population; Property crime rate: 191.7 per 10,000 population (2004).
Transportation: Commute to work: 88.4% car, 6.3% public transportation, 3.0% walk, 1.3% work from home (2000); Travel time to work: 24.9% less than 15 minutes, 32.4% 15 to 30 minutes, 24.0% 30 to 45 minutes, 9.8% 45 to 60 minutes, 8.9% 60 minutes or more (2000)
Additional Information Contacts
Borough of Carteret . . . . (732) 541-3801
   http://www.ci.carteret.nj.us

CLEARBROOK PARK (CDP). Covers a land area of 0.852 square miles and a water area of 0.015 square miles. Located at 40.31° N. Lat.; 74.46° W. Long.
Population: 2,853 (1990); 3,053 (2000); 3,367 (2005); 3,682 (2010 projected); Race: 98.2% White, 1.0% Black, 0.3% Asian, 0.7% Hispanic of any race (2005); Density: 3,953.6 persons per square mile (2005); Average household size: 1.54 (2005); Median age: 77.2 (2005); Males per 100 females: 66.4 (2005); Marriage status: 3.7% never married, 64.4% now married, 28.0% widowed, 4.0% divorced (2000); Foreign born: 6.9% (2000); Ancestry (includes multiple ancestries): 18.7% Russian, 15.1% Other groups, 14.2% Polish, 11.7% Italian, 8.8% United States or American (2000).

Economy: Employment by occupation: 18.3% management, 23.3% professional, 2.2% services, 40.5% sales, 0.0% farming, 8.2% construction, 7.5% production (2000).

Income: Per capita income: $32,405 (2005); Median household income: $39,924 (2005); Average household income: $49,935 (2005); Percent of households with income of $100,000 or more: 9.1% (2005); Poverty rate: 2.2% (2000).

Education: Percent of population age 25 and over with: High school diploma (including GED) or higher: 90.6% (2005); Bachelor's degree or higher: 27.0% (2005); Master's degree or higher: 8.9% (2005).

Housing: Homeownership rate: 95.6% (2005); Median home value: $191,598 (2005); Median rent: $654 per month (2000); Median age of housing: 19 years (2000).

Transportation: Commute to work: 86.0% car, 10.0% public transportation, 0.0% walk, 3.9% work from home (2000); Travel time to work: 4.5% less than 15 minutes, 32.5% 15 to 30 minutes, 26.1% 30 to 45 minutes, 10.8% 45 to 60 minutes, 26.1% 60 minutes or more (2000)

COLONIA (CDP).

Covers a land area of 3.877 square miles and a water area of 0.007 square miles. Located at 40.59° N. Lat.; 74.31° W. Long. Elevation is 60 feet.

Population: 18,161 (1990); 17,811 (2000); 17,900 (2005); 18,133 (2010 projected); Race: 83.9% White, 5.1% Black, 7.3% Asian, 6.2% Hispanic of any race (2005); Density: 4,617.0 persons per square mile (2005); Average household size: 2.85 (2005); Median age: 40.8 (2005); Males per 100 females: 93.8 (2005); Marriage status: 22.1% never married, 63.7% now married, 8.2% widowed, 6.0% divorced (2000); Foreign born: 15.2% (2000); Ancestry (includes multiple ancestries): 24.6% Italian, 20.0% Irish, 17.9% Other groups, 14.7% Polish, 14.4% German (2000).

Economy: Employment by occupation: 16.0% management, 21.0% professional, 9.8% services, 31.3% sales, 0.1% farming, 10.3% construction, 11.4% production (2000).

Income: Per capita income: $31,521 (2005); Median household income: $75,001 (2005); Average household income: $89,711 (2005); Percent of households with income of $100,000 or more: 32.7% (2005); Poverty rate: 2.2% (2000).

Education: Percent of population age 25 and over with: High school diploma (including GED) or higher: 86.4% (2005); Bachelor's degree or higher: 24.6% (2005); Master's degree or higher: 8.0% (2005).

School District(s)

Woodbridge Township (PK-12)

   2003-04 Enrollment: 14,056 . . . . (732) 602-8549

Housing: Homeownership rate: 89.7% (2005); Median home value: $288,552 (2005); Median rent: $666 per month (2000); Median age of housing: 42 years (2000).

Transportation: Commute to work: 89.6% car, 5.9% public transportation, 0.8% walk, 3.1% work from home (2000); Travel time to work: 22.6% less than 15 minutes, 32.2% 15 to 30 minutes, 23.6% 30 to 45 minutes, 9.1% 45 to 60 minutes, 12.5% 60 minutes or more (2000)

CONCORDIA (CDP).

Covers a land area of 1.052 square miles and a water area of 0.029 square miles. Located at 40.31° N. Lat.; 74.44° W. Long.

Population: 2,683 (1990); 3,658 (2000); 4,143 (2005); 4,613 (2010 projected); Race: 98.8% White, 0.4% Black, 0.5% Asian, 0.4% Hispanic of any race (2005); Density: 3,938.2 persons per square mile (2005); Average household size: 1.65 (2005); Median age: 74.5 (2005); Males per 100 females: 71.8 (2005); Marriage status: 3.4% never married, 74.1% now married, 19.2% widowed, 3.2% divorced (2000); Foreign born: 9.0% (2000); Ancestry (includes multiple ancestries): 22.0% Russian, 18.2% Other groups, 16.0% Polish, 9.2% United States or American, 7.9% Italian (2000).

Economy: Employment by occupation: 22.4% management, 18.2% professional, 5.7% services, 48.8% sales, 0.0% farming, 0.0% construction, 4.9% production (2000).

Income: Per capita income: $37,597 (2005); Median household income: $47,120 (2005); Average household income: $62,106 (2005); Percent of households with income of $100,000 or more: 14.8% (2005); Poverty rate: 1.9% (2000).

Education: Percent of population age 25 and over with: High school diploma (including GED) or higher: 94.3% (2005); Bachelor's degree or higher: 31.0% (2005); Master's degree or higher: 11.8% (2005).

Housing: Homeownership rate: 98.2% (2005); Median home value: $254,542 (2005); Median rent: $550 per month (2000); Median age of housing: 13 years (2000).

Transportation: Commute to work: 77.9% car, 5.7% public transportation, 0.0% walk, 13.2% work from home (2000); Travel time to work: 8.4% less than 15 minutes, 31.4% 15 to 30 minutes, 21.0% 30 to 45 minutes, 11.2% 45 to 60 minutes, 28.0% 60 minutes or more (2000)

CRANBURY (township).

Aka Cranbury Center. Covers a land area of 13.413 square miles and a water area of 0.039 square miles. Located at 40.30° N. Lat.; 74.51° W. Long. Elevation is 103 feet.

History: Cranbury Inn (built 18th century) and 1st Presbyterian Church (1734) here. David Brainerd, Indian missionary, lived nearby.

Population: 2,500 (1990); 3,227 (2000); 3,553 (2005); 3,876 (2010 projected); Race: 87.1% White, 1.7% Black, 9.3% Asian, 1.9% Hispanic of any race (2005); Density: 264.9 persons per square mile (2005); Average household size: 3.02 (2005); Median age: 39.8 (2005); Males per 100 females: 93.7 (2005); Marriage status: 17.2% never married, 72.1% now married, 6.0% widowed, 4.7% divorced (2000); Foreign born: 11.5% (2000); Ancestry (includes multiple ancestries): 20.2% Irish, 17.5% German, 15.8% Italian, 13.4% Other groups, 12.6% English (2000).

Economy: Manufacturing of pharmaceutical supplies, cosmetics, fertilizer. Single-family building permits issued: 2 (2005); Multi-family building permits issued: 0 (2005); Employment by occupation: 29.8% management, 30.6% professional, 8.0% services, 23.6% sales, 0.0% farming, 2.1% construction, 5.8% production (2000).

Income: Per capita income: $58,944 (2005); Median household income: $134,787 (2005); Average household income: $177,736 (2005); Percent of households with income of $100,000 or more: 63.9% (2005); Poverty rate: 1.6% (2000).

Education: Percent of population age 25 and over with: High school diploma (including GED) or higher: 93.4% (2005); Bachelor's degree or higher: 61.5% (2005); Master's degree or higher: 27.1% (2005).

School District(s)

Cranbury Township (PK-08)

   2003-04 Enrollment: 602 . . . . (609) 395 1700

Housing: Homeownership rate: 86.0% (2005); Median home value: $552,752 (2005); Median rent: $673 per month (2000); Median age of housing: 25 years (2000).

Safety: Violent crime rate: 0.0 per 10,000 population; Property crime rate: 196.4 per 10,000 population (2004).

Transportation: Commute to work: 81.4% car, 9.5% public transportation, 2.3% walk, 5.4% work from home (2000); Travel time to work: 25.8% less than 15 minutes, 29.9% 15 to 30 minutes, 16.4% 30 to 45 minutes, 8.5% 45 to 60 minutes, 19.3% 60 minutes or more (2000)

Additional Information Contacts

Cranbury Township . . . . (609) 395-0900
   http://www.cranburytownship.org

CRANBURY (CDP).

Covers a land area of 1.238 square miles and a water area of 0.016 square miles. Located at 40.30° N. Lat.; 74.51° W. Long.

Population: 1,348 (1990); 2,008 (2000); 2,264 (2005); 2,512 (2010 projected); Race: 85.8% White, 1.4% Black, 10.8% Asian, 1.5% Hispanic of any race (2005); Density: 1,828.3 persons per square mile (2005); Average household size: 2.92 (2005); Median age: 39.2 (2005); Males per 100 females: 91.9 (2005); Marriage status: 16.0% never married, 71.7% now married, 7.3% widowed, 5.0% divorced (2000); Foreign born: 11.7% (2000); Ancestry (includes multiple ancestries): 22.5% Irish, 17.9% German, 13.8% English, 13.5% Italian, 12.3% Other groups (2000).

Economy: Employment by occupation: 27.6% management, 33.2% professional, 9.1% services, 23.6% sales, 0.0% farming, 2.0% construction, 4.5% production (2000).

Income: Per capita income: $61,779 (2005); Median household income: $133,704 (2005); Average household income: $179,942 (2005); Percent of households with income of $100,000 or more: 61.7% (2005); Poverty rate: 2.2% (2000).

Education: Percent of population age 25 and over with: High school diploma (including GED) or higher: 93.3% (2005); Bachelor's degree or higher: 64.9% (2005); Master's degree or higher: 31.8% (2005).

School District(s)

Cranbury Township (PK-08)

   2003-04 Enrollment: 602 . . . . (609) 395-1700

Housing: Homeownership rate: 84.1% (2005); Median home value: $506,250 (2005); Median rent: $713 per month (2000); Median age of housing: 37 years (2000).

Transportation: Commute to work: 79.0% car, 9.2% public transportation, 2.9% walk, 4.0% work from home (2000); Travel time to work: 26.7% less

than 15 minutes, 29.6% 15 to 30 minutes, 17.7% 30 to 45 minutes, 8.9% 45 to 60 minutes, 17.1% 60 minutes or more (2000)

DAYTON (CDP). Covers a land area of 2.129 square miles and a water area of 0 square miles. Located at 40.38° N. Lat.; 74.51° W. Long. Elevation is 120 feet.

Population: 4,321 (1990); 6,235 (2000); 6,881 (2005); 7,523 (2010 projected); Race: 53.3% White, 11.2% Black, 31.1% Asian, 6.0% Hispanic of any race (2005); Density: 3,232.6 persons per square mile (2005); Average household size: 3.10 (2005); Median age: 35.1 (2005); Males per 100 females: 93.8 (2005); Marriage status: 18.8% never married, 70.6% now married, 3.6% widowed, 7.0% divorced (2000); Foreign born: 25.9% (2000); Ancestry (includes multiple ancestries): 39.8% Other groups, 17.0% Italian, 10.0% German, 9.0% Irish, 6.1% English (2000).
Economy: In rapidly suburbanizing area. Employment by occupation: 22.7% management, 33.8% professional, 6.2% services, 23.2% sales, 0.0% farming, 5.6% construction, 8.6% production (2000).
Income: Per capita income: $33,939 (2005); Median household income: $94,225 (2005); Average household income: $105,147 (2005); Percent of households with income of $100,000 or more: 44.9% (2005); Poverty rate: 2.4% (2000).
Education: Percent of population age 25 and over with: High school diploma (including GED) or higher: 95.0% (2005); Bachelor's degree or higher: 50.2% (2005); Master's degree or higher: 19.8% (2005).
School District(s)
South Brunswick Township (PK-12)
   2003-04 Enrollment: 8,506 . . . . (732) 297-7800
Housing: Homeownership rate: 79.7% (2005); Median home value: $262,797 (2005); Median rent: $928 per month (2000); Median age of housing: 14 years (2000).
Newspapers: Cranbury Press (General - Circulation 4,500); South Brunswick's Central Post (General - Circulation 5,000)
Transportation: Commute to work: 89.3% car, 6.5% public transportation, 1.6% walk, 2.6% work from home (2000); Travel time to work: 19.4% less than 15 minutes, 25.6% 15 to 30 minutes, 21.3% 30 to 45 minutes, 11.3% 45 to 60 minutes, 22.5% 60 minutes or more (2000)

DUNELLEN (borough). Covers a land area of 1.038 square miles and a water area of 0 square miles. Located at 40.59° N. Lat.; 74.46° W. Long. Elevation is 60 feet.

History: Incorporated 1887.
Population: 6,528 (1990); 6,823 (2000); 7,114 (2005); 7,443 (2010 projected); Race: 79.0% White, 4.6% Black, 4.5% Asian, 20.1% Hispanic of any race (2005); Density: 6,854.2 persons per square mile (2005); Average household size: 2.84 (2005); Median age: 37.0 (2005); Males per 100 females: 101.4 (2005); Marriage status: 26.2% never married, 58.9% now married, 6.0% widowed, 8.8% divorced (2000); Foreign born: 16.2% (2000); Ancestry (includes multiple ancestries): 26.2% Irish, 24.9% Other groups, 19.2% Italian, 18.6% German, 9.8% Polish (2000).
Economy: Industrial machinery, adhesives, pumps; commercial printing. Residential. Single-family building permits issued: 5 (2005); Multi-family building permits issued: 15 (2005); Employment by occupation: 14.5% management, 20.9% professional, 12.7% services, 26.1% sales, 0.3% farming, 10.4% construction, 15.0% production (2000).
Income: Per capita income: $28,812 (2005); Median household income: $69,233 (2005); Average household income: $81,107 (2005); Percent of households with income of $100,000 or more: 27.8% (2005); Poverty rate: 3.3% (2000).
Education: Percent of population age 25 and over with: High school diploma (including GED) or higher: 86.4% (2005); Bachelor's degree or higher: 22.5% (2005); Master's degree or higher: 6.3% (2005).
School District(s)
Dunellen Borough (PK-12)
   2003-04 Enrollment: 1,130 . . . . (732) 968-3226
Housing: Homeownership rate: 69.0% (2005); Median home value: $252,725 (2005); Median rent: $718 per month (2000); Median age of housing: 55 years (2000).
Safety: Violent crime rate: 38.3 per 10,000 population; Property crime rate: 205.5 per 10,000 population (2004).
Transportation: Commute to work: 86.0% car, 6.4% public transportation, 3.1% walk, 3.5% work from home (2000); Travel time to work: 23.8% less than 15 minutes, 37.2% 15 to 30 minutes, 20.3% 30 to 45 minutes, 6.7% 45 to 60 minutes, 11.9% 60 minutes or more (2000)

EAST BRUNSWICK (township). Aka East Brunswick CDP. Covers a land area of 21.954 square miles and a water area of 0.425 square miles. Located at 40.43° N. Lat.; 74.40° W. Long.

History: Named for the city and duchy in central Germany. Incorporated 1860.
Population: 43,548 (1990); 46,756 (2000); 49,033 (2005); 51,532 (2010 projected); Race: 73.1% White, 3.1% Black, 19.5% Asian, 5.1% Hispanic of any race (2005); Density: 2,233.5 persons per square mile (2005); Average household size: 2.84 (2005); Median age: 39.8 (2005); Males per 100 females: 94.7 (2005); Marriage status: 22.2% never married, 66.6% now married, 5.7% widowed, 5.5% divorced (2000); Foreign born: 23.5% (2000); Ancestry (includes multiple ancestries): 26.7% Other groups, 15.0% Italian, 13.7% Irish, 11.5% Polish, 10.6% German (2000).
Economy: Residential and commercial. Unemployment rate: 3.2% (2005); Total civilian labor force: 26,686 (2005); Single-family building permits issued: 15 (2005); Multi-family building permits issued: 0 (2005); Employment by occupation: 19.2% management, 30.3% professional, 7.6% services, 29.9% sales, 0.0% farming, 5.7% construction, 7.3% production (2000).
Income: Per capita income: $37,404 (2005); Median household income: $85,134 (2005); Average household income: $106,012 (2005); Percent of households with income of $100,000 or more: 40.5% (2005); Poverty rate: 2.8% (2000).
Taxes: Total city taxes per capita: $593 (2004); City property taxes per capita: $568 (2004).
Education: Percent of population age 25 and over with: High school diploma (including GED) or higher: 92.1% (2005); Bachelor's degree or higher: 47.1% (2005); Master's degree or higher: 19.6% (2005).
School District(s)
East Brunswick Township (PK-12)
   2003-04 Enrollment: 9,141 . . . . (732) 613-6705
Middlesex County Vocational (09-12)
   2003-04 Enrollment: 2,315 . . . . (732) 257-3300
Housing: Homeownership rate: 84.3% (2005); Median home value: $327,744 (2005); Median rent: $813 per month (2000); Median age of housing: 28 years (2000).
Safety: Violent crime rate: 7.6 per 10,000 population; Property crime rate: 170.9 per 10,000 population (2004).
Newspapers: Home News Tribune (Circulation 62,499)
Transportation: Commute to work: 85.0% car, 10.3% public transportation, 1.1% walk, 3.1% work from home (2000); Travel time to work: 19.8% less than 15 minutes, 24.9% 15 to 30 minutes, 21.4% 30 to 45 minutes, 11.3% 45 to 60 minutes, 22.6% 60 minutes or more (2000)
Additional Information Contacts
East Brunswick Chamber of Commerce . . . . (732) 257-3009
   http://www.ebnjchamber.org
East Brunswick Township . . . . (732) 390-6810
   http://www.eastbrunswick.org

EDISON (township). Aka Edison CDP; Piscatawaytown. Covers a land area of 30.122 square miles and a water area of 0.568 square miles. Located at 40.53° N. Lat.; 74.37° W. Long. Elevation is 100 feet.

Population: 88,680 (1990); 97,687 (2000); 101,153 (2005); 104,974 (2010 projected); Race: 51.7% White, 7.4% Black, 35.6% Asian, 7.7% Hispanic of any race (2005); Density: 3,358.1 persons per square mile (2005); Average household size: 2.78 (2005); Median age: 37.4 (2005); Males per 100 females: 96.8 (2005); Marriage status: 25.5% never married, 62.7% now married, 5.8% widowed, 6.0% divorced (2000); Foreign born: 33.1% (2000); Ancestry (includes multiple ancestries): 41.0% Other groups, 14.8% Italian, 11.0% Irish, 8.7% German, 7.4% Polish (2000).
Economy: Residential; manufacturing of chemicals, metal products, electrical and electronic equipment, machinery, and instruments. Newspaper printing. Unemployment rate: 3.5% (2005); Total civilian labor force: 55,274 (2005); Single-family building permits issued: 95 (2005); Multi-family building permits issued: 42 (2005); Employment by occupation: 17.4% management, 30.2% professional, 8.9% services, 28.0% sales, 0.0% farming, 5.2% construction, 10.2% production (2000).
Income: Per capita income: $34,836 (2005); Median household income: $77,543 (2005); Average household income: $95,775 (2005); Percent of households with income of $100,000 or more: 34.8% (2005); Poverty rate: 4.8% (2000).
Taxes: Total city taxes per capita: $2,079 (2004); City property taxes per capita: $2,039 (2004).

Education: Percent of population age 25 and over with: High school diploma (including GED) or higher: 87.7% (2005); Bachelor's degree or higher: 42.6% (2005); Master's degree or higher: 17.3% (2005).

School District(s)

Edison Township (PK-12)
    2003-04 Enrollment: 13,293 . . . . (732) 452-4900
Middlesex County Ed Ser Comm (UG-UG)
    2003-04 Enrollment: 1,165 . . . . (732) 777-9848
Middlesex County Vocational (09-12)
    2003-04 Enrollment: 2,315 . . . . (732) 257-3300

Four-year College(s)

Rabbi Jacob Joseph School (Private, Not-for-profit)
    Fall 2004 Enrollment: 44 . . . . (732) 985-6533
    2005-06 Tuition: In-state $8,150; Out-of-state $8,150

Two-year College(s)

Cittone Institute (Private, For-profit)
    Fall 2004 Enrollment: 618 . . . . (732) 548-8798
    2005-06 Tuition: In-state $11,944; Out-of-state $11,944
Middlesex County College (Public)
    Fall 2004 Enrollment: 12,984. (732) 548-6000
    2005-06 Tuition: In-state $5,438; Out-of-state $5,438
PC Age II (Private, For-profit)
    Fall 2004 Enrollment: 35 . . . . (973) 565-9800

Housing: Homeownership rate: 63.6% (2005); Median home value: $289,760 (2005); Median rent: $847 per month (2000); Median age of housing: 29 years (2000).
Hospitals: John F Kennedy Medical Center (509 beds)
Safety: Violent crime rate: 21.3 per 10,000 population; Property crime rate: 243.5 per 10,000 population (2004).
Newspapers: The Epoch Times (New Jersey) (Asian, Ethnic - Circulation 50,000)
Transportation: Commute to work: 84.8% car, 10.9% public transportation, 2.0% walk, 1.8% work from home (2000); Travel time to work: 21.6% less than 15 minutes, 31.8% 15 to 30 minutes, 19.4% 30 to 45 minutes, 9.6% 45 to 60 minutes, 17.6% 60 minutes or more (2000)

Additional Information Contacts

Edison Chamber of Commerce . . . . (732) 494-0300
    http://www.edisonchamber.com
Edison Township . . . . (732) 248-7200
    http://www.edisonnj.org

FORDS (CDP). Covers a land area of 2.592 square miles and a water area of 0.004 square miles. Located at 40.53° N. Lat.; 74.31° W. Long. Elevation is 116 feet.
Population: 14,392 (1990); 15,032 (2000); 15,565 (2005); 16,183 (2010 projected); Race: 65.4% White, 7.3% Black, 20.9% Asian, 11.5% Hispanic of any race (2005); Density: 6,006.1 persons per square mile (2005); Average household size: 2.72 (2005); Median age: 38.7 (2005); Males per 100 females: 94.4 (2005); Marriage status: 24.1% never married, 60.0% now married, 8.1% widowed, 7.8% divorced (2000); Foreign born: 21.9% (2000); Ancestry (includes multiple ancestries): 29.3% Other groups, 18.1% Irish, 17.9% Italian, 12.3% Polish, 11.7% German (2000).
Economy: Chemicals, plastics, metal products, clothing. Employment by occupation: 14.0% management, 22.0% professional, 10.9% services, 29.2% sales, 0.1% farming, 9.7% construction, 14.3% production (2000).
Income: Per capita income: $29,138 (2005); Median household income: $68,274 (2005); Average household income: $79,330 (2005); Percent of households with income of $100,000 or more: 27.9% (2005); Poverty rate: 3.4% (2000).
Education: Percent of population age 25 and over with: High school diploma (including GED) or higher: 86.3% (2005); Bachelor's degree or higher: 28.3% (2005); Master's degree or higher: 9.2% (2005).

School District(s)

Woodbridge Township (PK-12)
    2003-04 Enrollment: 14,056 . . . . (732) 602-8549

Housing: Homeownership rate: 72.5% (2005); Median home value: $251,692 (2005); Median rent: $744 per month (2000); Median age of housing: 44 years (2000).
Transportation: Commute to work: 88.1% car, 8.5% public transportation, 1.6% walk, 1.6% work from home (2000); Travel time to work: 27.0% less than 15 minutes, 29.2% 15 to 30 minutes, 22.7% 30 to 45 minutes, 7.7% 45 to 60 minutes, 13.4% 60 minutes or more (2000)

HEATHCOTE (CDP). Covers a land area of 2.627 square miles and a water area of 0.005 square miles. Located at 40.38° N. Lat.; 74.57° W. Long.
Population: 3,112 (1990); 4,755 (2000); 5,255 (2005); 5,710 (2010 projected); Race: 62.9% White, 11.7% Black, 21.3% Asian, 5.3% Hispanic of any race (2005); Density: 2,000.6 persons per square mile (2005); Average household size: 2.38 (2005); Median age: 38.2 (2005); Males per 100 females: 88.0 (2005); Marriage status: 24.3% never married, 58.6% now married, 4.2% widowed, 12.8% divorced (2000); Foreign born: 23.4% (2000); Ancestry (includes multiple ancestries): 30.8% Other groups, 19.7% Italian, 14.6% German, 13.8% Irish, 8.7% Polish (2000).
Economy: Employment by occupation: 27.5% management, 32.8% professional, 5.9% services, 25.8% sales, 0.0% farming, 3.8% construction, 4.3% production (2000).
Income: Per capita income: $47,657 (2005); Median household income: $95,155 (2005); Average household income: $113,209 (2005); Percent of households with income of $100,000 or more: 46.6% (2005); Poverty rate: 2.4% (2000).
Education: Percent of population age 25 and over with: High school diploma (including GED) or higher: 94.9% (2005); Bachelor's degree or higher: 58.8% (2005); Master's degree or higher: 26.3% (2005).
Housing: Homeownership rate: 80.5% (2005); Median home value: $303,299 (2005); Median rent: $1,046 per month (2000); Median age of housing: 13 years (2000).
Transportation: Commute to work: 87.2% car, 7.1% public transportation, 1.6% walk, 3.9% work from home (2000); Travel time to work: 18.6% less than 15 minutes, 29.9% 15 to 30 minutes, 24.5% 30 to 45 minutes, 9.1% 45 to 60 minutes, 17.8% 60 minutes or more (2000)

HELMETTA (borough). Covers a land area of 0.847 square miles and a water area of 0.050 square miles. Located at 40.38° N. Lat.; 74.42° W. Long. Elevation is 44 feet.
History: Former snuff manufacturing center in 19th century.
Population: 1,211 (1990); 1,825 (2000); 2,035 (2005); 2,241 (2010 projected); Race: 90.8% White, 3.2% Black, 3.3% Asian, 7.4% Hispanic of any race (2005); Density: 2,401.4 persons per square mile (2005); Average household size: 2.41 (2005); Median age: 37.2 (2005); Males per 100 females: 99.7 (2005); Marriage status: 24.0% never married, 59.2% now married, 3.9% widowed, 12.9% divorced (2000); Foreign born: 9.1% (2000); Ancestry (includes multiple ancestries): 22.4% Irish, 19.9% Italian, 18.0% German, 17.2% Polish, 11.0% Other groups (2000).
Economy: In suburbanizing area. Single-family building permits issued: 1 (2005); Multi-family building permits issued: 0 (2005); Employment by occupation: 13.2% management, 15.9% professional, 15.3% services, 31.4% sales, 0.0% farming, 10.0% construction, 14.2% production (2000).
Income: Per capita income: $30,434 (2005); Median household income: $67,569 (2005); Average household income: $73,293 (2005); Percent of households with income of $100,000 or more: 21.3% (2005); Poverty rate: 3.3% (2000).
Education: Percent of population age 25 and over with: High school diploma (including GED) or higher: 88.7% (2005); Bachelor's degree or higher: 18.5% (2005); Master's degree or higher: 3.2% (2005).
Housing: Homeownership rate: 88.9% (2005); Median home value: $193,723 (2005); Median rent: $948 per month (2000); Median age of housing: 14 years (2000).
Safety: Violent crime rate: 30.4 per 10,000 population; Property crime rate: 55.7 per 10,000 population (2004).
Transportation: Commute to work: 93.7% car, 3.4% public transportation, 0.8% walk, 2.0% work from home (2000); Travel time to work: 19.8% less than 15 minutes, 34.1% 15 to 30 minutes, 18.6% 30 to 45 minutes, 11.5% 45 to 60 minutes, 16.0% 60 minutes or more (2000)

HIGHLAND PARK (borough). Covers a land area of 1.839 square miles and a water area of 0 square miles. Located at 40.50° N. Lat.; 74.42° W. Long. Elevation is 74 feet.
History: Named, originally, Raritan Falls. Incorporated 1905.
Population: 13,279 (1990); 13,999 (2000); 14,311 (2005); 14,717 (2010 projected); Race: 67.1% White, 7.7% Black, 17.3% Asian, 9.9% Hispanic of any race (2005); Density: 7,783.8 persons per square mile (2005); Average household size: 2.41 (2005); Median age: 36.3 (2005); Males per 100 females: 94.5 (2005); Marriage status: 32.8% never married, 52.8% now married, 5.9% widowed, 8.4% divorced (2000); Foreign born: 29.2% (2000); Ancestry (includes multiple ancestries): 33.1% Other groups, 9.8% Italian, 9.1% Irish, 8.1% German, 7.8% Russian (2000).

Economy: Single-family building permits issued: 8 (2005); Multi-family building permits issued: 46 (2005); Employment by occupation: 13.6% management, 48.0% professional, 8.2% services, 19.9% sales, 0.0% farming, 3.4% construction, 7.0% production (2000).

Income: Per capita income: $32,879 (2005); Median household income: $60,672 (2005); Average household income: $79,015 (2005); Percent of households with income of $100,000 or more: 25.7% (2005); Poverty rate: 8.4% (2000).

Taxes: Total city taxes per capita: $518 (2004); City property taxes per capita: $497 (2004).

Education: Percent of population age 25 and over with: High school diploma (including GED) or higher: 90.9% (2005); Bachelor's degree or higher: 59.2% (2005); Master's degree or higher: 35.1% (2005).

School District(s)

Highland Park Borough (PK-12)

  2003-04 Enrollment: 1,606 . . . . (732) 572-6990

Housing: Homeownership rate: 41.5% (2005); Median home value: $290,918 (2005); Median rent: $802 per month (2000); Median age of housing: 47 years (2000).

Safety: Violent crime rate: 7.7 per 10,000 population; Property crime rate: 143.1 per 10,000 population (2004).

Transportation: Commute to work: 81.4% car, 10.9% public transportation, 3.9% walk, 2.5% work from home (2000); Travel time to work: 32.0% less than 15 minutes, 29.9% 15 to 30 minutes, 15.8% 30 to 45 minutes, 8.4% 45 to 60 minutes, 13.9% 60 minutes or more (2000)

ISELIN (CDP). Covers a land area of 3.134 square miles and a water area of 0 square miles. Located at 40.57° N. Lat.; 74.31° W. Long. Elevation is 64 feet.

Population: 16,218 (1990); 16,698 (2000); 17,537 (2005); 18,449 (2010 projected); Race: 54.8% White, 6.9% Black, 33.0% Asian, 6.9% Hispanic of any race (2005); Density: 5,595.3 persons per square mile (2005); Average household size: 2.80 (2005); Median age: 38.3 (2005); Males per 100 females: 98.0 (2005); Marriage status: 24.1% never married, 60.9% now married, 8.5% widowed, 6.5% divorced (2000); Foreign born: 27.5% (2000); Ancestry (includes multiple ancestries): 35.1% Other groups, 18.3% Irish, 18.1% Italian, 11.7% German, 9.6% Polish (2000).

Economy: Employment by occupation: 15.6% management, 24.3% professional, 9.9% services, 30.7% sales, 0.1% farming, 8.3% construction, 11.0% production (2000).

Income: Per capita income: $31,366 (2005); Median household income: $73,225 (2005); Average household income: $87,527 (2005); Percent of households with income of $100,000 or more: 30.4% (2005); Poverty rate: 3.2% (2000).

Education: Percent of population age 25 and over with: High school diploma (including GED) or higher: 85.4% (2005); Bachelor's degree or higher: 33.2% (2005); Master's degree or higher: 11.3% (2005).

School District(s)

Woodbridge Township (PK-12)

  2003-04 Enrollment: 14,056 . . . . (732) 602-8549

Two-year College(s)

Sanford-Brown Institute (Private, For-profit)

  Fall 2004 Enrollment: 630 . . . . (732) 623-5740

Housing: Homeownership rate: 74.6% (2005); Median home value: $246,145 (2005); Median rent: $891 per month (2000); Median age of housing: 40 years (2000).

Transportation: Commute to work: 83.4% car, 12.7% public transportation, 1.4% walk, 1.5% work from home (2000); Travel time to work: 26.6% less than 15 minutes, 27.0% 15 to 30 minutes, 17.5% 30 to 45 minutes, 11.5% 45 to 60 minutes, 17.5% 60 minutes or more (2000); Amtrak: Service available.

Additional Information Contacts

Middlesex County Chamber of Commerce . . . . (732) 821-1700

  http://www.mcrcc.org

JAMESBURG (borough). Covers a land area of 0.843 square miles and a water area of 0.003 square miles. Located at 40.35° N. Lat.; 74.43° W. Long. Elevation is 65 feet.

History: Incorporated 1887.

Population: 5,294 (1990); 6,025 (2000); 6,661 (2005); 7,274 (2010 projected); Race: 80.3% White, 9.0% Black, 2.6% Asian, 13.9% Hispanic of any race (2005); Density: 7,902.8 persons per square mile (2005); Average household size: 2.80 (2005); Median age: 36.7 (2005); Males per 100 females: 95.7 (2005); Marriage status: 27.4% never married, 55.2% now married, 7.5% widowed, 9.9% divorced (2000); Foreign born: 11.3%

(2000); Ancestry (includes multiple ancestries): 25.3% Italian, 19.6% Other groups, 18.9% German, 15.4% Polish, 14.9% Irish (2000).

Economy: Some light industry. Single-family building permits issued: 0 (2005); Multi-family building permits issued: 0 (2005); Employment by occupation: 11.4% management, 15.5% professional, 13.5% services, 30.8% sales, 0.0% farming, 10.2% construction, 18.7% production (2000).

Income: Per capita income: $26,184 (2005); Median household income: $65,810 (2005); Average household income: $73,243 (2005); Percent of households with income of $100,000 or more: 25.4% (2005); Poverty rate: 3.5% (2000).

Education: Percent of population age 25 and over with: High school diploma (including GED) or higher: 82.7% (2005); Bachelor's degree or higher: 20.1% (2005); Master's degree or higher: 5.0% (2005).

School District(s)

Jamesburg Borough (PK-08)

  2003-04 Enrollment: 693 . . . . (732) 521-0303

Monroe Township (PK-12)

  2003-04 Enrollment: 4,124 . . . . (732) 521-2111

Housing: Homeownership rate: 68.8% (2005); Median home value: $233,010 (2005); Median rent: $682 per month (2000); Median age of housing: 30 years (2000).

Safety: Violent crime rate: 13.8 per 10,000 population; Property crime rate: 101.2 per 10,000 population (2004).

Transportation: Commute to work: 91.7% car, 2.0% public transportation, 2.7% walk, 3.1% work from home (2000); Travel time to work: 29.3% less than 15 minutes, 26.4% 15 to 30 minutes, 23.8% 30 to 45 minutes, 8.7% 45 to 60 minutes, 11.8% 60 minutes or more (2000)

KEASBEY (unincorporated postal area, zip code 08832). Aka Keasbeys. Part of the Census Designated Place of Fords. Covers a land area of 2.349 square miles and a water area of 0.029 square miles. Located at 40.51° N. Lat.; 74.30° W. Long. Elevation is 20 feet.

Population: 3,018 (2000); Race: 33.7% White, 21.1% Black, 14.5% Asian, 41.7% Hispanic of any race (2000); Density: 1,285.0 persons per square mile (2000); Age: 29.8% under 18, 4.8% over 64 (2000); Marriage status: 33.3% never married, 57.2% now married, 3.2% widowed, 6.3% divorced (2000); Foreign born: 35.9% (2000); Ancestry (includes multiple ancestries): 65.8% Other groups, 5.6% Jamaican, 5.2% Irish, 4.1% Italian, 3.1% Hungarian (2000).

Economy: Employment by occupation: 9.2% management, 31.8% professional, 14.3% services, 28.4% sales, 0.0% farming, 1.9% construction, 14.3% production (2000).

Income: Per capita income: $20,342 (2000); Median household income: $51,411 (2000); Poverty rate: 12.3% (2000).

Education: Percent of population age 25 and over with: High school diploma (including GED) or higher: 76.0% (2000); Bachelor's degree or higher: 29.3% (2000).

Housing: Homeownership rate: 18.7% (2000); Median home value: $116,000 (2000); Median rent: $784 per month (2000); Median age of housing: 24 years (2000).

Transportation: Commute to work: 84.8% car, 8.7% public transportation, 5.1% walk, 0.9% work from home (2000); Travel time to work: 28.2% less than 15 minutes, 33.6% 15 to 30 minutes, 17.2% 30 to 45 minutes, 7.7% 45 to 60 minutes, 13.3% 60 minutes or more (2000)

KENDALL PARK (CDP). Covers a land area of 3.724 square miles and a water area of 0 square miles. Located at 40.41° N. Lat.; 74.56° W. Long. Elevation is 200 feet.

Population: 7,127 (1990); 9,006 (2000); 8,942 (2005); 8,953 (2010 projected); Race: 75.5% White, 4.6% Black, 16.3% Asian, 4.9% Hispanic of any race (2005); Density: 2,401.2 persons per square mile (2005); Average household size: 3.04 (2005); Median age: 37.0 (2005); Males per 100 females: 95.3 (2005); Marriage status: 20.4% never married, 68.1% now married, 5.2% widowed, 6.4% divorced (2000); Foreign born: 16.6% (2000); Ancestry (includes multiple ancestries): 25.1% Other groups, 23.0% Italian, 19.3% Irish, 15.6% German, 9.5% Polish (2000).

Economy: Employment by occupation: 17.4% management, 26.3% professional, 12.7% services, 27.4% sales, 0.0% farming, 7.5% construction, 8.7% production (2000).

Income: Per capita income: $33,641 (2005); Median household income: $87,772 (2005); Average household income: $102,204 (2005); Percent of households with income of $100,000 or more: 42.4% (2005); Poverty rate: 2.9% (2000).

Education: Percent of population age 25 and over with: High school diploma (including GED) or higher: 92.6% (2005); Bachelor's degree or higher: 37.7% (2005); Master's degree or higher: 13.4% (2005).

School District(s)

South Brunswick Township (PK-12)

    2003-04 Enrollment: 8,506 . . . . (732) 297-7800

Housing: Homeownership rate: 88.4% (2005); Median home value: $288,243 (2005); Median rent: $696 per month (2000); Median age of housing: 33 years (2000).

Transportation: Commute to work: 88.7% car, 7.2% public transportation, 1.0% walk, 2.7% work from home (2000); Travel time to work: 18.7% less than 15 minutes, 34.1% 15 to 30 minutes, 19.4% 30 to 45 minutes, 10.4% 45 to 60 minutes, 17.3% 60 minutes or more (2000)

KINGSTON (CDP).

Covers a land area of 0.897 square miles and a water area of 0.015 square miles. Located at 40.37° N. Lat.; 74.61° W. Long.

Population: 1,057 (1990); 1,292 (2000); 1,339 (2005); 1,378 (2010 projected); Race: 70.1% White, 8.5% Black, 11.7% Asian, 14.3% Hispanic of any race (2005); Density: 1,493.3 persons per square mile (2005); Average household size: 2.35 (2005); Median age: 38.7 (2005); Males per 100 females: 94.1 (2005); Marriage status: 31.4% never married, 52.8% now married, 8.2% widowed, 7.5% divorced (2000); Foreign born: 21.8% (2000); Ancestry (includes multiple ancestries): 20.6% Other groups, 18.7% Italian, 16.5% Irish, 14.5% English, 10.2% German (2000).

Economy: Employment by occupation: 23.3% management, 36.8% professional, 11.6% services, 22.9% sales, 0.0% farming, 3.8% construction, 1.7% production (2000).

Income: Per capita income: $43,277 (2005); Median household income: $78,726 (2005); Average household income: $101,841 (2005); Percent of households with income of $100,000 or more: 34.4% (2005); Poverty rate: 1.0% (2000).

Education: Percent of population age 25 and over with: High school diploma (including GED) or higher: 92.3% (2005); Bachelor's degree or higher: 65.9% (2005); Master's degree or higher: 31.3% (2005).

School District(s)

Hunterdon County Ed Ser Comm (UG-UG)

    2003-04 Enrollment: 491 . . . . (908) 806-2729

Housing: Homeownership rate: 48.0% (2005); Median home value: $386,923 (2005); Median rent: $819 per month (2000); Median age of housing: 25 years (2000).

Transportation: Commute to work: 93.9% car, 3.2% public transportation, 1.8% walk, 1.1% work from home (2000); Travel time to work: 26.7% less than 15 minutes, 34.6% 15 to 30 minutes, 22.1% 30 to 45 minutes, 5.5% 45 to 60 minutes, 11.1% 60 minutes or more (2000)

LAURENCE HARBOR (CDP).

Covers a land area of 2.817 square miles and a water area of 0.061 square miles. Located at 40.45° N. Lat.; 74.24° W. Long. Elevation is 27 feet.

Population: 6,445 (1990); 6,227 (2000); 6,833 (2005); 7,437 (2010 projected); Race: 88.9% White, 4.4% Black, 2.4% Asian, 7.8% Hispanic of any race (2005); Density: 2,425.4 persons per square mile (2005); Average household size: 2.69 (2005); Median age: 37.9 (2005); Males per 100 females: 104.0 (2005); Marriage status: 27.3% never married, 55.1% now married, 6.3% widowed, 11.3% divorced (2000); Foreign born: 8.6% (2000); Ancestry (includes multiple ancestries): 25.9% Irish, 22.9% Italian, 17.3% German, 16.1% Other groups, 14.0% Polish (2000).

Economy: Employment by occupation: 11.7% management, 12.3% professional, 14.9% services, 32.2% sales, 0.0% farming, 12.4% construction, 16.5% production (2000).

Income: Per capita income: $28,020 (2005); Median household income: $66,623 (2005); Average household income: $75,318 (2005); Percent of households with income of $100,000 or more: 23.7% (2005); Poverty rate: 5.6% (2000).

Education: Percent of population age 25 and over with: High school diploma (including GED) or higher: 84.7% (2005); Bachelor's degree or higher: 16.0% (2005); Master's degree or higher: 3.1% (2005).

School District(s)

Old Bridge Township (PK-12)

    2003-04 Enrollment: 10,119 . . . . (732) 290-3976

Housing: Homeownership rate: 76.6% (2005); Median home value: $203,950 (2005); Median rent: $745 per month (2000); Median age of housing: 43 years (2000).

Transportation: Commute to work: 90.3% car, 4.2% public transportation, 1.7% walk, 2.3% work from home (2000); Travel time to work: 16.4% less

than 15 minutes, 30.8% 15 to 30 minutes, 23.9% 30 to 45 minutes, 13.2% 45 to 60 minutes, 15.7% 60 minutes or more (2000)

MADISON PARK (CDP).

Covers a land area of 1.643 square miles and a water area of 0.020 square miles. Located at 40.45° N. Lat.; 74.29° W. Long. Elevation is 140 feet.

Population: 7,490 (1990); 6,929 (2000); 7,329 (2005); 7,731 (2010 projected); Race: 47.8% White, 16.3% Black, 23.4% Asian, 14.9% Hispanic of any race (2005); Density: 4,459.5 persons per square mile (2005); Average household size: 2.83 (2005); Median age: 34.3 (2005); Males per 100 females: 96.9 (2005); Marriage status: 28.5% never married, 57.6% now married, 5.7% widowed, 8.3% divorced (2000); Foreign born: 35.7% (2000); Ancestry (includes multiple ancestries): 39.4% Other groups, 15.7% Irish, 11.6% Italian, 7.3% German, 7.3% Polish (2000).

Economy: Employment by occupation: 13.0% management, 21.4% professional, 13.3% services, 31.3% sales, 0.0% farming, 6.6% construction, 14.4% production (2000).

Income: Per capita income: $23,622 (2005); Median household income: $58,777 (2005); Average household income: $66,767 (2005); Percent of households with income of $100,000 or more: 17.5% (2005); Poverty rate: 8.0% (2000).

Education: Percent of population age 25 and over with: High school diploma (including GED) or higher: 84.6% (2005); Bachelor's degree or higher: 26.9% (2005); Master's degree or higher: 9.3% (2005).

Housing: Homeownership rate: 27.8% (2005); Median home value: $243,456 (2005); Median rent: $698 per month (2000); Median age of housing: 35 years (2000).

Transportation: Commute to work: 83.2% car, 11.5% public transportation, 3.0% walk, 1.6% work from home (2000); Travel time to work: 16.4% less than 15 minutes, 23.8% 15 to 30 minutes, 24.7% 30 to 45 minutes, 12.7% 45 to 60 minutes, 22.3% 60 minutes or more (2000)

METUCHEN (borough).

Covers a land area of 2.741 square miles and a water area of 0 square miles. Located at 40.54° N. Lat.; 74.36° W. Long. Elevation is 117 feet.

History: Named for the Indian name for the area. In June 1777, a brief but bloody skirmish occurred here between British troops under Gen. William Howe and a small American force led by William Alexander. Settled before 1700. Incorporated 1900.

Population: 12,804 (1990); 12,840 (2000); 13,459 (2005); 14,140 (2010 projected); Race: 82.3% White, 5.3% Black, 8.7% Asian, 4.8% Hispanic of any race (2005); Density: 4,910.6 persons per square mile (2005); Average household size: 2.58 (2005); Median age: 40.5 (2005); Males per 100 females: 92.4 (2005); Marriage status: 25.0% never married, 60.5% now married, 7.2% widowed, 7.3% divorced (2000); Foreign born: 14.2% (2000); Ancestry (includes multiple ancestries): 22.3% Irish, 20.9% Other groups, 17.2% Italian, 14.5% German, 8.7% Polish (2000).

Economy: Chiefly residential; light manufacturing includes fabricated metal products, packaging equipment, consumer goods, machinery, and electric appliances. Single-family building permits issued: 12 (2005); Multi-family building permits issued: 2 (2005); Employment by occupation: 20.3% management, 32.9% professional, 7.1% services, 27.6% sales, 0.0% farming, 4.2% construction, 7.8% production (2000).

Income: Per capita income: $43,691 (2005); Median household income: $89,390 (2005); Average household income: $111,753 (2005); Percent of households with income of $100,000 or more: 43.4% (2005); Poverty rate: 3.9% (2000).

Education: Percent of population age 25 and over with: High school diploma (including GED) or higher: 92.0% (2005); Bachelor's degree or higher: 48.8% (2005); Master's degree or higher: 19.7% (2005).

School District(s)

Metuchen Borough (PK-12)

    2003-04 Enrollment: 1,872 . . . . (732) 321-8714

Woodbridge Township (PK-12)

    2003-04 Enrollment: 14,056 . . . . (732) 602-8549

Housing: Homeownership rate: 80.2% (2005); Median home value: $329,193 (2005); Median rent: $783 per month (2000); Median age of housing: 47 years (2000).

Safety: Violent crime rate: 10.5 per 10,000 population; Property crime rate: 153.1 per 10,000 population (2004).

Transportation: Commute to work: 76.1% car, 16.7% public transportation, 2.7% walk, 4.3% work from home (2000); Travel time to work: 26.0% less than 15 minutes, 25.3% 15 to 30 minutes, 18.9% 30 to 45 minutes, 12.0% 45 to 60 minutes, 17.7% 60 minutes or more (2000)

Additional Information Contacts

Metuchen Chamber of Commerce. . . . . (732) 548-2964
  http://www.metuchenchamber.com

MIDDLESEX (borough).

MIDDLESEX (borough). Covers a land area of 3.498 square miles and a water area of 0.025 square miles. Located at 40.57° N. Lat.; 74.50° W. Long. Elevation is 61 feet.

History: Named for the former Middlesex county in England, now part of London. Incorporated 1913.

Population: 13,055 (1990); 13,717 (2000); 14,110 (2005); 14,597 (2010 projected); Race: 83.7% White, 4.1% Black, 5.1% Asian, 12.4% Hispanic of any race (2005); Density: 4,033.5 persons per square mile (2005); Average household size: 2.71 (2005); Median age: 39.0 (2005); Males per 100 females: 95.8 (2005); Marriage status: 23.8% never married, 58.5% now married, 8.9% widowed, 8.8% divorced (2000); Foreign born: 12.7% (2000); Ancestry (includes multiple ancestries): 26.0% Italian, 20.3% Irish, 19.4% German, 16.8% Other groups, 14.5% Polish (2000).

Economy: Diversified manufacturing includes adhesives, plastics, and chemicals. Single-family building permits issued: 5 (2005); Multi-family building permits issued: 0 (2005); Employment by occupation: 14.1% management, 20.8% professional, 11.3% services, 30.5% sales, 0.0% farming, 9.9% construction, 13.4% production (2000).

Income: Per capita income: $31,230 (2005); Median household income: $69,967 (2005); Average household income: $84,125 (2005); Percent of households with income of $100,000 or more: 29.6% (2005); Poverty rate: 3.6% (2000).

Taxes: Total city taxes per capita: $798 (2004); City property taxes per capita: $786 (2004).

Education: Percent of population age 25 and over with: High school diploma (including GED) or higher: 85.5% (2005); Bachelor's degree or higher: 23.5% (2005); Master's degree or higher: 6.3% (2005).

School District(s)
Middlesex Borough (PK-12)
  2003-04 Enrollment: 2,179 . . . . (732) 317-6000
Housing: Homeownership rate: 74.8% (2005); Median home value: $268,426 (2005); Median rent: $782 per month (2000); Median age of housing: 41 years (2000).

Safety: Violent crime rate: 11.4 per 10,000 population; Property crime rate: 91.6 per 10,000 population (2004).

Transportation: Commute to work: 89.8% car, 3.1% public transportation, 3.0% walk, 2.8% work from home (2000); Travel time to work: 30.4% less than 15 minutes, 37.4% 15 to 30 minutes, 16.6% 30 to 45 minutes, 8.4% 45 to 60 minutes, 7.3% 60 minutes or more (2000)

Additional Information Contacts
Middlesex Chamber of Commerce . . . . (732) 394-0220
  http://wwwpmcoc.org

MILLTOWN (borough).

MILLTOWN (borough). Covers a land area of 1.572 square miles and a water area of 0.032 square miles. Located at 40.45° N. Lat.; 74.43° W. Long. Elevation is 60 feet.

History: Settled before 1800, incorporated 1889.

Population: 6,968 (1990); 7,000 (2000); 7,241 (2005); 7,526 (2010 projected); Race: 92.7% White, 1.1% Black, 3.3% Asian, 4.9% Hispanic of any race (2005); Density: 4,605.2 persons per square mile (2005); Average household size: 2.62 (2005); Median age: 40.5 (2005); Males per 100 females: 94.3 (2005); Marriage status: 26.4% never married, 59.2% now married, 7.4% widowed, 7.0% divorced (2000); Foreign born: 7.6% (2000); Ancestry (includes multiple ancestries): 27.5% Italian, 22.5% Irish, 22.2% German, 14.0% Polish, 8.4% Other groups (2000).

Economy: Manufacturing: health-care products, typewriter and computer ribbons, paper products; sand, gravel, clay pits. Agriculture: poultry; fruit; dairy products. Single-family building permits issued: 3 (2005); Multi-family building permits issued: 0 (2005); Employment by occupation: 13.3% management, 25.2% professional, 13.1% services, 29.8% sales, 0.0% farming, 9.3% construction, 9.2% production (2000).

Income: Per capita income: $35,570 (2005); Median household income: $80,482 (2005); Average household income: $93,179 (2005); Percent of households with income of $100,000 or more: 36.7% (2005); Poverty rate: 2.3% (2000).

Taxes: Total city taxes per capita: $523 (2004); City property taxes per capita: $472 (2004).

Education: Percent of population age 25 and over with: High school diploma (including GED) or higher: 86.9% (2005); Bachelor's degree or higher: 27.3% (2005); Master's degree or higher: 7.4% (2005).

School District(s)
Milltown Borough (PK-08)
  2003-04 Enrollment: 699 . . . . (732) 828-0300
Housing: Homeownership rate: 83.6% (2005); Median home value: $285,422 (2005); Median rent: $691 per month (2000); Median age of housing: 44 years (2000).

Safety: Violent crime rate: 15.2 per 10,000 population; Property crime rate: 202.1 per 10,000 population (2004).

Transportation: Commute to work: 92.4% car, 2.9% public transportation, 1.3% walk, 2.1% work from home (2000); Travel time to work: 27.8% less than 15 minutes, 34.9% 15 to 30 minutes, 17.9% 30 to 45 minutes, 10.5% 45 to 60 minutes, 8.8% 60 minutes or more (2000)

MONMOUTH JUNCTION (CDP).

MONMOUTH JUNCTION (CDP). Covers a land area of 1.496 square miles and a water area of 0.010 square miles. Located at 40.38° N. Lat.; 74.54° W. Long. Elevation is 91 feet.

Population: 1,570 (1990); 2,721 (2000); 2,677 (2005); 2,688 (2010 projected); Race: 70.9% White, 7.0% Black, 17.5% Asian, 5.3% Hispanic of any race (2005); Density: 1,789.8 persons per square mile (2005); Average household size: 3.21 (2005); Median age: 35.9 (2005); Males per 100 females: 97.6 (2005); Marriage status: 22.5% never married, 65.5% now married, 2.9% widowed, 9.2% divorced (2000); Foreign born: 12.6% (2000); Ancestry (includes multiple ancestries): 20.8% Italian, 20.2% Other groups, 16.2% German, 15.3% Irish, 10.7% English (2000).

Economy: Employment by occupation: 27.3% management, 25.9% professional, 8.2% services, 26.6% sales, 0.0% farming, 3.5% construction, 8.5% production (2000).

Income: Per capita income: $39,965 (2005); Median household income: $110,884 (2005); Average household income: $127,485 (2005); Percent of households with income of $100,000 or more: 56.0% (2005); Poverty rate: 5.1% (2000).

Education: Percent of population age 25 and over with: High school diploma (including GED) or higher: 93.8% (2005); Bachelor's degree or higher: 50.4% (2005); Master's degree or higher: 19.6% (2005).

School District(s)
South Brunswick Township (PK-12)
  2003-04 Enrollment: 8,506 . . . . (732) 297-7800
Housing: Homeownership rate: 95.3% (2005); Median home value: $303,070 (2005); Median rent: $753 per month (2000); Median age of housing: 15 years (2000).

Transportation: Commute to work: 92.3% car, 3.2% public transportation, 0.4% walk, 3.0% work from home (2000); Travel time to work: 25.5% less than 15 minutes, 25.0% 15 to 30 minutes, 21.7% 30 to 45 minutes, 8.8% 45 to 60 minutes, 18.9% 60 minutes or more (2000)

Additional Information Contacts
Middlesex County Chamber of Commerce . . . . (732) 821-1700
  http://www.mcrcc.org

MONROE (township).

MONROE (township). Covers a land area of 41.943 square miles and a water area of 0.102 square miles. Located at 40.33° N. Lat.; 74.43° W. Long.

History: Incorporated 1838.

Population: 22,235 (1990); 27,999 (2000); 33,224 (2005); 38,095 (2010 projected); Race: 92.2% White, 3.1% Black, 2.8% Asian, 2.9% Hispanic of any race (2005); Density: 792.1 persons per square mile (2005); Average household size: 2.22 (2005); Median age: 50.8 (2005); Males per 100 females: 85.3 (2005); Marriage status: 12.7% never married, 67.4% now married, 15.3% widowed, 4.6% divorced (2000); Foreign born: 8.1% (2000); Ancestry (includes multiple ancestries): 20.7% Italian, 14.4% Irish, 13.7% Other groups, 12.7% Polish, 12.2% German (2000).

Economy: Unemployment rate: 4.6% (2005); Total civilian labor force: 12,089 (2005); Single-family building permits issued: 659 (2005); Multi-family building permits issued: 0 (2005); Employment by occupation: 20.0% management, 19.7% professional, 10.5% services, 30.8% sales, 0.4% farming, 8.5% construction, 10.1% production (2000).

Income: Per capita income: $36,727 (2005); Median household income: $61,428 (2005); Average household income: $81,129 (2005); Percent of households with income of $100,000 or more: 27.5% (2005); Poverty rate: 3.3% (2000).

Taxes: Total city taxes per capita: $632 (2004); City property taxes per capita: $566 (2004).

Education: Percent of population age 25 and over with: High school diploma (including GED) or higher: 90.2% (2005); Bachelor's degree or higher: 29.8% (2005); Master's degree or higher: 10.4% (2005).

Housing: Homeownership rate: 94.9% (2005); Median home value: $272,124 (2005); Median rent: $777 per month (2000); Median age of housing: 17 years (2000).

Safety: Violent crime rate: 4.7 per 10,000 population; Property crime rate: 62.7 per 10,000 population (2004).

Transportation: Commute to work: 87.7% car, 6.1% public transportation, 1.3% walk, 4.3% work from home (2000); Travel time to work: 19.7% less than 15 minutes, 26.3% 15 to 30 minutes, 22.1% 30 to 45 minutes, 10.9% 45 to 60 minutes, 21.0% 60 minutes or more (2000)

NEW BRUNSWICK (city).

Covers a land area of 5.227 square miles and a water area of 0.521 square miles. Located at 40.48° N. Lat.; 74.44° W. Long. Elevation is 80 feet.

History: Named for the city and duchy in central Germany. The area around New Brunswick was occupied by the Lenni Lenape people when John Inian and ten associates from Long Island bought about 10,000 acres in 1681. Inian's group established an English hegemony which was not threatened until 1730 when Dutch settlers from Albany began to change the national character of the community. The name Brunswick, in honor of King George I, also Duke of Brunswick, first appears in court records of 1724. New Brunswick soon became one of the leading agricultural depots of the Colony.

Population: 41,711 (1990); 48,573 (2000); 50,624 (2005); 52,995 (2010 projected); Race: 46.7% White, 20.3% Black, 5.9% Asian, 47.4% Hispanic of any race (2005); Density: 9,685.9 persons per square mile (2005); Average household size: 3.78 (2005); Median age: 24.8 (2005); Males per 100 females: 98.3 (2005); Marriage status: 56.5% never married, 34.1% now married, 3.2% widowed, 6.1% divorced (2000); Foreign born: 33.4% (2000); Ancestry (includes multiple ancestries): 55.6% Other groups, 7.3% Italian, 7.0% Irish, 5.3% German, 3.5% Polish (2000).

Economy: Unemployment rate: 4.4% (2005); Total civilian labor force: 26,563 (2005); Single-family building permits issued: 29 (2005); Multi-family building permits issued: 197 (2005); Employment by occupation: 6.7% management, 18.2% professional, 22.4% services, 26.5% sales, 0.5% farming, 4.6% construction, 21.2% production (2000).

Income: Per capita income: $15,545 (2005); Median household income: $41,394 (2005); Average household income: $55,212 (2005); Percent of households with income of $100,000 or more: 12.5% (2005); Poverty rate: 27.0% (2000).

Taxes: Total city taxes per capita: $956 (2004); City property taxes per capita: $921 (2004).

Education: Percent of population age 25 and over with: High school diploma (including GED) or higher: 63.3% (2005); Bachelor's degree or higher: 19.7% (2005); Master's degree or higher: 7.7% (2005).

School District(s)
Agency - Greater Brunswick CS (KG-08)
   2003-04 Enrollment: 141 . . . . (732) 246-5661
Middlesex County Vocational (09-12)
   2003-04 Enrollment: 2,315 . . . . (732) 257-3300
New Brunswick City (PK-12)
   2003-04 Enrollment: 6,989 . . . . (732) 745-5414

Four-year College(s)
New Brunswick Theological Seminary (Private, Not-for-profit, Reformed Church in America)
   Fall 2004 Enrollment: 237 . . . . (732) 247-5241
Rutgers University-New Brunswick/Piscataway (Public)
   Fall 2004 Enrollment: 34,696 . . . . (732) 932-1766
   2005-06 Tuition: In-state $9,221; Out-of-state $16,819

Housing: Homeownership rate: 26.5% (2005); Median home value: $206,845 (2005); Median rent: $747 per month (2000); Median age of housing: 46 years (2000).

Hospitals: Robert Wood Johnson University Hospital; Saint Peter's University Hospital (422 beds)

Safety: Violent crime rate: 70.2 per 10,000 population; Property crime rate: 389.8 per 10,000 population (2004).

Transportation: Commute to work: 72.0% car, 11.3% public transportation, 12.9% walk, 1.3% work from home (2000); Travel time to work: 33.0% less than 15 minutes, 36.0% 15 to 30 minutes, 18.1% 30 to 45 minutes, 5.7% 45 to 60 minutes, 7.1% 60 minutes or more (2000); Amtrak: Service available.

Additional Information Contacts
City of New Brunswick . . . . (732) 745-5004
   http://www.cityofnewbrunswick.org
Middlesex County Chamber of Commerce . . . . (732) 821-1700
   http://www.mcrcc.org

NORTH BRUNSWICK TOWNSHIP (township).

Aka North Brunswick Township CDP. Covers a land area of 12.022 square miles and a water area of 0.234 square miles. Located at 40.45° N. Lat.; 74.47° W. Long.

Population: 31,287 (1990); 36,287 (2000); 39,208 (2005); 42,142 (2010 projected); Race: 55.7% White, 16.8% Black, 17.6% Asian, 13.1% Hispanic of any race (2005); Density: 3,261.2 persons per square mile (2005); Average household size: 2.67 (2005); Median age: 36.6 (2005); Males per 100 females: 99.2 (2005); Marriage status: 26.5% never married, 60.1% now married, 5.4% widowed, 8.0% divorced (2000); Foreign born: 24.4% (2000); Ancestry (includes multiple ancestries): 34.7% Other groups, 16.9% Italian, 12.4% Irish, 8.7% German, 6.8% Polish (2000).

Economy: Unemployment rate: 3.7% (2005); Total civilian labor force: 21,752 (2005); Single-family building permits issued: 79 (2005); Multi-family building permits issued: 198 (2005); Employment by occupation: 18.7% management, 27.6% professional, 9.3% services, 28.4% sales, 0.0% farming, 5.2% construction, 10.7% production (2000).

Income: Per capita income: $31,132 (2005); Median household income: $67,476 (2005); Average household income: $82,811 (2005); Percent of households with income of $100,000 or more: 27.8% (2005); Poverty rate: 4.7% (2000).

Taxes: Total city taxes per capita: $550 (2004); City property taxes per capita: $516 (2004).

Education: Percent of population age 25 and over with: High school diploma (including GED) or higher: 86.1% (2005); Bachelor's degree or higher: 37.3% (2005); Master's degree or higher: 14.4% (2005).

School District(s)
North Brunswick Township (PK-12)
   2003-04 Enrollment: 5,519 . . . . (732) 289-3030

Four-year College(s)
DeVry University-New Jersey (Private, For-profit)
   Fall 2004 Enrollment: 2,007 . . . . (732) 435-4880
   2005-06 Tuition: In-state $12,200; Out-of-state $12,200

Two-year College(s)
The Chubb Institute-North Brunswick (Private, For-profit)
   Fall 2004 Enrollment: 594 . . . . (732) 448-2600

Housing: Homeownership rate: 62.6% (2005); Median home value: $262,416 (2005); Median rent: $842 per month (2000); Median age of housing: 24 years (2000).

Safety: Violent crime rate: 20.4 per 10,000 population; Property crime rate: 236.6 per 10,000 population (2004).

Transportation: Commute to work: 88.4% car, 7.8% public transportation, 1.4% walk, 1.7% work from home (2000); Travel time to work: 23.8% less than 15 minutes, 34.9% 15 to 30 minutes, 17.3% 30 to 45 minutes, 9.0% 45 to 60 minutes, 14.9% 60 minutes or more (2000)

Additional Information Contacts
Middlesex County Chamber of Commerce . . . . (732) 821-1700
   http://www.mcrcc.org
North Brunswick Township . . . . (732) 247-0922
   http://www.northbrunswickonline.com

OLD BRIDGE (township).

Covers a land area of 38.086 square miles and a water area of 2.573 square miles. Located at 40.41° N. Lat.; 74.30° W. Long. Elevation is 30 feet.

Population: 56,655 (1990); 60,456 (2000); 65,076 (2005); 69,739 (2010 projected); Race: 74.9% White, 6.3% Black, 13.2% Asian, 9.4% Hispanic of any race (2005); Density: 1,708.7 persons per square mile (2005); Average household size: 2.81 (2005); Median age: 37.5 (2005); Males per 100 females: 96.2 (2005); Marriage status: 24.4% never married, 61.2% now married, 6.7% widowed, 7.8% divorced (2000); Foreign born: 18.4% (2000); Ancestry (includes multiple ancestries): 24.6% Other groups, 24.4% Italian, 20.5% Irish, 11.4% German, 9.6% Polish (2000).

Economy: Concrete blocks. Unemployment rate: 3.1% (2005); Total civilian labor force: 34,179 (2005); Single-family building permits issued: 302 (2005); Multi-family building permits issued: 318 (2005); Employment by occupation: 16.4% management, 20.8% professional, 11.2% services, 31.4% sales, 0.1% farming, 9.3% construction, 10.8% production (2000).

Income: Per capita income: $30,209 (2005); Median household income: $72,338 (2005); Average household income: $84,642 (2005); Percent of households with income of $100,000 or more: 30.4% (2005); Poverty rate: 4.2% (2000).

Taxes: Total city taxes per capita: $479 (2004); City property taxes per capita: $456 (2004).

Education: Percent of population age 25 and over with: High school diploma (including GED) or higher: 88.3% (2005); Bachelor's degree or higher: 29.6% (2005); Master's degree or higher: 8.9% (2005).

School District(s)
Old Bridge Township (PK-12)
    2003-04 Enrollment: 10,119 . . . . (732) 290-3976
Two-year College(s)
Charles E Gregory School of Nursing (Private, Not-for-profit)
    Fall 2004 Enrollment: 154 . . . . (732) 607-6500
    2005-06 Tuition: In-state $8,795; Out-of-state $9,295

Housing: Homeownership rate: 68.5% (2005); Median home value: $268,257 (2005); Median rent: $723 per month (2000); Median age of housing: 32 years (2000).

Hospitals: Old Bridge Regional Hospital (113 beds)

Safety: Violent crime rate: 9.0 per 10,000 population; Property crime rate: 164.1 per 10,000 population (2004).

Transportation: Commute to work: 84.5% car, 11.4% public transportation, 1.2% walk, 2.2% work from home (2000); Travel time to work: 16.4% less than 15 minutes, 22.6% 15 to 30 minutes, 22.1% 30 to 45 minutes, 13.4% 45 to 60 minutes, 25.4% 60 minutes or more (2000)

Additional Information Contacts
Old Bridge Chamber of Commerce . . . . (732) 607-6340
    http://www.oldbridge.com/OB_Home.htm
Old Bridge Township . . . . (732) 721-5600
    http://www.oldbridge.com

OLD BRIDGE (CDP). Covers a land area of 7.050 square miles and a water area of 0.124 square miles. Located at 40.39° N. Lat.; 74.33° W. Long.

Population: 21,913 (1990); 22,833 (2000); 23,123 (2005); 23,637 (2010 projected); Race: 82.0% White, 4.7% Black, 9.3% Asian, 8.3% Hispanic of any race (2005); Density: 3,279.7 persons per square mile (2005); Average household size: 3.12 (2005); Median age: 37.7 (2005); Males per 100 females: 96.5 (2005); Marriage status: 22.2% never married, 65.6% now married, 6.5% widowed, 5.6% divorced (2000); Foreign born: 14.6% (2000); Ancestry (includes multiple ancestries): 29.5% Italian, 22.6% Irish, 20.2% Other groups, 11.2% Polish, 11.1% German (2000).

Economy: Employment by occupation: 17.3% management, 20.1% professional, 10.5% services, 32.1% sales, 0.1% farming, 10.6% construction, 9.4% production (2000).

Income: Per capita income: $30,186 (2005); Median household income: $81,887 (2005); Average household income: $93,611 (2005); Percent of households with income of $100,000 or more: 35.8% (2005); Poverty rate: 2.9% (2000).

Education: Percent of population age 25 and over with: High school diploma (including GED) or higher: 90.0% (2005); Bachelor's degree or higher: 28.6% (2005); Master's degree or higher: 7.8% (2005).

School District(s)
Old Bridge Township (PK-12)
    2003-04 Enrollment: 10,119 . . . . (732) 290-3976
Two-year College(s)
Charles E Gregory School of Nursing (Private, Not-for-profit)
    Fall 2004 Enrollment: 154 . . . . (732) 607-6500
    2005-06 Tuition: In-state $8,795; Out-of-state $9,295

Housing: Homeownership rate: 88.6% (2005); Median home value: $278,745 (2005); Median rent: $701 per month (2000); Median age of housing: 34 years (2000).

Hospitals: Old Bridge Regional Hospital (113 beds)

Transportation: Commute to work: 74.7% car, 12.1% public transportation, 0.8% walk, 2.6% work from home (2000); Travel time to work: 17.6% less than 15 minutes, 20.1% 15 to 30 minutes, 21.6% 30 to 45 minutes, 12.8% 45 to 60 minutes, 27.9% 60 minutes or more (2000)

Additional Information Contacts
Old Bridge Chamber of Commerce . . . . (732) 607-6340
    http://www.oldbridge.com/OB_Home.htm

PARLIN (unincorporated postal area, zip code 08859). Part of the Borough of Sayreville. Covers a land area of 6.165 square miles and a water area of 0.222 square miles. Located at 40.46° N. Lat.; 74.30° W. Long. Elevation is 89 feet.

Population: 20,129 (2000); Race: 73.6% White, 8.0% Black, 11.7% Asian, 8.6% Hispanic of any race (2000); Density: 3,265.3 persons per square mile (2000); Age: 24.4% under 18, 11.6% over 64 (2000); Marriage status: 24.0% never married, 61.1% now married, 7.1% widowed, 7.8% divorced (2000); Foreign born: 22.6% (2000); Ancestry (includes multiple

ancestries): 26.6% Other groups, 21.1% Italian, 19.5% Irish, 13.4% Polish, 9.8% German (2000).

Economy: Employment by occupation: 13.8% management, 22.4% professional, 12.0% services, 30.8% sales, 0.1% farming, 8.8% construction, 12.1% production (2000).

Income: Per capita income: $24,508 (2000); Median household income: $60,486 (2000); Poverty rate: 5.1% (2000).

Education: Percent of population age 25 and over with: High school diploma (including GED) or higher: 86.2% (2000); Bachelor's degree or higher: 25.9% (2000).

School District(s)
Middlesex County Ed Ser Comm (UG-UG)
    2003-04 Enrollment: 1,165 . . . . (732) 777-9848
Old Bridge Township (PK-12)
    2003-04 Enrollment: 10,119 . . . . (732) 290-3976
Sayreville Borough (PK-12)
    2003-04 Enrollment: 5,924 . . . . (732) 525-5224

Housing: Homeownership rate: 64.3% (2000); Median home value: $151,400 (2000); Median rent: $685 per month (2000); Median age of housing: 34 years (2000).

Transportation: Commute to work: 85.2% car, 11.2% public transportation, 1.4% walk, 1.7% work from home (2000); Travel time to work: 18.1% less than 15 minutes, 24.8% 15 to 30 minutes, 24.1% 30 to 45 minutes, 12.9% 45 to 60 minutes, 20.1% 60 minutes or more (2000)

PERTH AMBOY (city). Covers a land area of 4.782 square miles and a water area of 1.198 square miles. Located at 40.51° N. Lat.; 74.27° W. Long. Elevation is 65 feet.

History: Named for an Earl of Perth, a Scottish earl who permitted immigration to Middlesex County. Perth Amboy's history goes back to 1651, when a tract of land was purchased by Dutchman Augustine Herman. Known as "Ambo Point," the settlement developed slowly, having only three buildings in 1683. The population took a sudden spurt when the Earl of Perth permitted the immigration of nearly 200 oppressed Scots in 1685. Other Scots, English merchants, and French Huguenots came soon after. In 1718, Perth Amboy was granted the charter that makes it the oldest incorporated city in New Jersey.

Population: 41,967 (1990); 47,303 (2000); 49,071 (2005); 51,076 (2010 projected); Race: 43.1% White, 9.7% Black, 1.8% Asian, 75.4% Hispanic of any race (2005); Density: 10,261.7 persons per square mile (2005); Average household size: 3.31 (2005); Median age: 32.3 (2005); Males per 100 females: 99.2 (2005); Marriage status: 34.8% never married, 50.6% now married, 6.2% widowed, 8.5% divorced (2000); Foreign born: 35.7% (2000); Ancestry (includes multiple ancestries): 70.1% Other groups, 5.1% Polish, 2.9% Italian, 2.0% Irish, 1.9% Hungarian (2000).

Economy: Unemployment rate: 8.5% (2005); Total civilian labor force: 21,848 (2005); Single-family building permits issued: 21 (2005); Multi-family building permits issued: 157 (2005); Employment by occupation: 7.5% management, 10.0% professional, 17.4% services, 25.0% sales, 0.1% farming, 8.7% construction, 31.3% production (2000).

Income: Per capita income: $16,674 (2005); Median household income: $42,802 (2005); Average household income: $54,304 (2005); Percent of households with income of $100,000 or more: 12.9% (2005); Poverty rate: 17.6% (2000).

Taxes: Total city taxes per capita: $417 (2004); City property taxes per capita: $402 (2004).

Education: Percent of population age 25 and over with: High school diploma (including GED) or higher: 55.9% (2005); Bachelor's degree or higher: 10.2% (2005); Master's degree or higher: 3.6% (2005).

School District(s)
Middlesex County Vocational (09-12)
    2003-04 Enrollment: 2,315 . . . . (732) 257-3300
Perth Amboy City (PK-12)
    2003-04 Enrollment: 9,762 . . . . (732) 376-6279
Two-year College(s)
Reignbow Beauty Academy (Private, For-profit)
    Fall 2004 Enrollment: 238 . . . . (732) 442-6007

Housing: Homeownership rate: 39.9% (2005); Median home value: $219,986 (2005); Median rent: $642 per month (2000); Median age of housing: 48 years (2000).

Hospitals: Raritan Bay Medical Center (522 beds)

Safety: Violent crime rate: 31.6 per 10,000 population; Property crime rate: 210.5 per 10,000 population (2004).

Transportation: Commute to work: 82.8% car, 7.0% public transportation, 6.6% walk, 1.0% work from home (2000); Travel time to work: 30.5% less

than 15 minutes, 38.4% 15 to 30 minutes, 18.2% 30 to 45 minutes, 6.4% 45 to 60 minutes, 6.6% 60 minutes or more (2000)

Additional Information Contacts

City of Perth Amboy . . . . (732) 826-0290
  http://www.ci.perthamboy.nj.us
Perth Amboy Chamber of Commerce . . . . (732) 442-7400
  http://perthamboychamber.com

PISCATAWAY (township).

Covers a land area of 18.776 square miles and a water area of 0.197 square miles. Located at 40.55° N. Lat.; 74.46° W. Long. Elevation is 100 feet.

History: St. James Episcopal Church (1837), here, is reproduction of earlier church destroyed by tornado in 1835. Site of branch campuses of Rutgers University. Township incorporated 1693.

Population: 47,089 (1990); 50,482 (2000); 52,711 (2005); 55,192 (2010 projected); Race: 42.1% White, 21.1% Black, 29.8% Asian, 9.4% Hispanic of any race (2005); Density: 2,807.3 persons per square mile (2005); Average household size: 3.04 (2005); Median age: 34.8 (2005); Males per 100 females: 98.3 (2005); Marriage status: 30.8% never married, 58.4% now married, 4.6% widowed, 6.2% divorced (2000); Foreign born: 29.8% (2000); Ancestry (includes multiple ancestries): 48.3% Other groups, 12.3% Italian, 9.4% Irish, 8.7% German, 6.7% Polish (2000).

Economy: Manufacturing: chemicals, fabricated metal products, pharmaceuticals, electronic equipment. Unemployment rate: 3.9% (2005); Total civilian labor force: 29,525 (2005); Single-family building permits issued: 154 (2005); Multi-family building permits issued: 76 (2005); Employment by occupation: 14.0% management, 31.7% professional, 8.8% services, 27.4% sales, 0.0% farming, 5.9% construction, 12.2% production (2000).

Income: Per capita income: $30,387 (2005); Median household income: $77,923 (2005); Average household income: $91,242 (2005); Percent of households with income of $100,000 or more: 33.9% (2005); Poverty rate: 3.8% (2000).

Taxes: Total city taxes per capita: $513 (2004); City property taxes per capita: $489 (2004).

Education: Percent of population age 25 and over with: High school diploma (including GED) or higher: 88.7% (2005); Bachelor's degree or higher: 41.3% (2005); Master's degree or higher: 17.0% (2005).

School District(s)

Middlesex County Ed Ser Comm (UG-UG)
  2003-04 Enrollment: 1,165 . . . . (732) 777-9848
Middlesex County Vocational (09-12)
  2003-04 Enrollment: 2,315 . . . . (732) 257-3300
Piscataway Township (PK-12)
  2003-04 Enrollment: 6,991 . . . . (732) 572-2289

Two-year College(s)

Katharine Gibbs School (Private, For-profit)
  Fall 2004 Enrollment: 711 . . . . (732) 885-1580
  2005-06 Tuition: In-state $16,273; Out-of-state $16,273
Somerset School of Massage Therapy
  Fall 2004 Enrollment: 50 . . . . (732) 885-3400

Housing: Homeownership rate: 68.9% (2005); Median home value: $269,494 (2005); Median rent: $774 per month (2000); Median age of housing: 31 years (2000).

Hospitals: UMDNJ-University Behavioral Healthcare/Piscataway (64 beds)

Safety: Violent crime rate: 11.3 per 10,000 population; Property crime rate: 116.0 per 10,000 population (2004).

Transportation: Commute to work: 88.5% car, 6.0% public transportation, 2.7% walk, 2.1% work from home (2000); Travel time to work: 27.4% less than 15 minutes, 33.3% 15 to 30 minutes, 18.4% 30 to 45 minutes, 9.2% 45 to 60 minutes, 11.7% 60 minutes or more (2000)

Additional Information Contacts

Piscataway Chamber of Commerce . . . . (732) 394-0220
  http://www.pmcoc.org
Piscataway Township . . . . (732) 562-2301
  http://www.piscatawaynj.org

PLAINSBORO (township).

Covers a land area of 11.838 square miles and a water area of 0.412 square miles. Located at 40.33° N. Lat.; 74.59° W. Long. Elevation is 80 feet.

Population: 14,213 (1990); 20,215 (2000); 21,335 (2005); 22,464 (2010 projected); Race: 49.6% White, 6.5% Black, 39.6% Asian, 5.2% Hispanic of any race (2005); Density: 1,802.3 persons per square mile (2005); Average household size: 2.36 (2005); Median age: 34.3 (2005); Males per 100 females: 102.7 (2005); Marriage status: 29.1% never married, 62.3% now

married, 2.2% widowed, 6.3% divorced (2000); Foreign born: 34.5% (2000); Ancestry (includes multiple ancestries): 42.2% Other groups, 11.4% Irish, 11.4% German, 10.0% Italian, 6.4% Polish (2000).

Economy: Many corporate office parks have moved to the region. Single-family building permits issued: 56 (2005); Multi-family building permits issued: 0 (2005); Employment by occupation: 25.7% management, 43.4% professional, 5.1% services, 20.4% sales, 0.0% farming, 2.1% construction, 3.2% production (2000).

Income: Per capita income: $47,133 (2005); Median household income: $87,374 (2005); Average household income: $111,347 (2005); Percent of households with income of $100,000 or more: 41.7% (2005); Poverty rate: 3.0% (2000).

Education: Percent of population age 25 and over with: High school diploma (including GED) or higher: 97.3% (2005); Bachelor's degree or higher: 70.3% (2005); Master's degree or higher: 31.3% (2005).

School District(s)

West Windsor-Plainsboro Regional (PK-12)
  2003-04 Enrollment: 9,238 . . . . (609) 716-5040
West Windsor-Plainsboro Regional (PK-12)
  2003-04 Enrollment: 9,238 . . . . (609) 716-5040

Housing: Homeownership rate: 42.1% (2005); Median home value: $365,831 (2005); Median rent: $850 per month (2000); Median age of housing: 16 years (2000).

Safety: Violent crime rate: 5.2 per 10,000 population; Property crime rate: 84.0 per 10,000 population (2004).

Transportation: Commute to work: 83.8% car, 11.7% public transportation, 0.5% walk, 3.4% work from home (2000); Travel time to work: 23.1% less than 15 minutes, 29.8% 15 to 30 minutes, 15.2% 30 to 45 minutes, 9.2% 45 to 60 minutes, 22.6% 60 minutes or more (2000)

Additional Information Contacts

Middlesex County Chamber of Commerce . . . . (732) 821-1700
  http://www.mcrcc.org
Plainsboro Township . . . . (609) 799-0909
  http://www.plainsboronj.com

PLAINSBORO CENTER (CDP).

Covers a land area of 0.673 square miles and a water area of 0 square miles. Located at 40.33° N. Lat.; 74.59° W. Long.

Population: 1,464 (1990); 2,209 (2000); 2,227 (2005); 2,276 (2010 projected); Race: 46.2% White, 3.3% Black, 47.2% Asian, 4.6% Hispanic of any race (2005); Density: 3,311.5 persons per square mile (2005); Average household size: 2.21 (2005); Median age: 33.0 (2005); Males per 100 females: 107.9 (2005); Marriage status: 29.6% never married, 62.8% now married, 2.1% widowed, 5.5% divorced (2000); Foreign born: 43.9% (2000); Ancestry (includes multiple ancestries): 49.5% Other groups, 14.3% German, 11.2% Irish, 9.6% Italian, 4.5% English (2000).

Economy: Employment by occupation: 17.1% management, 53.8% professional, 2.9% services, 18.5% sales, 0.0% farming, 3.8% construction, 3.9% production (2000).

Income: Per capita income: $45,791 (2005); Median household income: $84,590 (2005); Average household income: $101,068 (2005); Percent of households with income of $100,000 or more: 38.5% (2005); Poverty rate: 3.8% (2000).

Education: Percent of population age 25 and over with: High school diploma (including GED) or higher: 98.2% (2005); Bachelor's degree or higher: 75.0% (2005); Master's degree or higher: 31.6% (2005).

Housing: Homeownership rate: 27.6% (2005); Median home value: $343,137 (2005); Median rent: $863 per month (2000); Median age of housing: 24 years (2000).

Transportation: Commute to work: 84.0% car, 11.9% public transportation, 2.4% walk, 1.6% work from home (2000); Travel time to work: 26.1% less than 15 minutes, 32.9% 15 to 30 minutes, 14.8% 30 to 45 minutes, 10.1% 45 to 60 minutes, 16.1% 60 minutes or more (2000)

PORT READING (CDP).

Covers a land area of 2.229 square miles and a water area of 0.621 square miles. Located at 40.57° N. Lat.; 74.24° W. Long. Elevation is 20 feet.

Population: 3,977 (1990); 3,829 (2000); 3,906 (2005); 3,992 (2010 projected); Race: 88.4% White, 3.6% Black, 2.7% Asian, 9.8% Hispanic of any race (2005); Density: 1,752.2 persons per square mile (2005); Average household size: 2.82 (2005); Median age: 39.8 (2005); Males per 100 females: 96.6 (2005); Marriage status: 25.9% never married, 56.6% now married, 9.1% widowed, 8.4% divorced (2000); Foreign born: 9.7% (2000); Ancestry (includes multiple ancestries): 34.6% Italian, 23.7% Irish, 11.5% Polish, 11.2% German, 10.1% Other groups (2000).

Economy: Employment by occupation: 11.6% management, 19.2% professional, 10.2% services, 34.7% sales, 0.0% farming, 9.1% construction, 15.3% production (2000).
Income: Per capita income: $28,542 (2005); Median household income: $67,411 (2005); Average household income: $80,471 (2005); Percent of households with income of $100,000 or more: 27.1% (2005); Poverty rate: 3.2% (2000).
Education: Percent of population age 25 and over with: High school diploma (including GED) or higher: 81.4% (2005); Bachelor's degree or higher: 14.8% (2005); Master's degree or higher: 4.5% (2005).

School District(s)
Woodbridge Township (PK-12)
   2003-04 Enrollment: 14,056 . . . . (732) 602-8549
Housing: Homeownership rate: 86.4% (2005); Median home value: $249,698 (2005); Median rent: $688 per month (2000); Median age of housing: 39 years (2000).
Transportation: Commute to work: 93.2% car, 3.3% public transportation, 1.4% walk, 0.7% work from home (2000); Travel time to work: 30.8% less than 15 minutes, 34.8% 15 to 30 minutes, 19.9% 30 to 45 minutes, 7.0% 45 to 60 minutes, 7.4% 60 minutes or more (2000)

PRINCETON MEADOWS (CDP). Covers a land area of 2.172 square miles and a water area of 0.019 square miles. Located at 40.33° N. Lat.; 74.56° W. Long.
Population: 9,459 (1990); 13,436 (2000); 14,550 (2005); 15,632 (2010 projected); Race: 47.1% White, 8.2% Black, 40.0% Asian, 5.8% Hispanic of any race (2005); Density: 6,700.1 persons per square mile (2005); Average household size: 2.31 (2005); Median age: 33.3 (2005); Males per 100 females: 103.4 (2005); Marriage status: 33.3% never married, 58.2% now married, 1.6% widowed, 6.9% divorced (2000); Foreign born: 34.4% (2000); Ancestry (includes multiple ancestries): 43.2% Other groups, 10.7% Italian, 10.5% German, 10.3% Irish, 7.4% Polish (2000).
Economy: Employment by occupation: 26.3% management, 40.5% professional, 5.7% services, 22.5% sales, 0.0% farming, 1.8% construction, 3.2% production (2000).
Income: Per capita income: $45,097 (2005); Median household income: $81,995 (2005); Average household income: $103,844 (2005); Percent of households with income of $100,000 or more: 37.4% (2005); Poverty rate: 3.4% (2000).
Education: Percent of population age 25 and over with: High school diploma (including GED) or higher: 96.9% (2005); Bachelor's degree or higher: 68.4% (2005); Master's degree or higher: 28.0% (2005).
Housing: Homeownership rate: 33.5% (2005); Median home value: $273,370 (2005); Median rent: $846 per month (2000); Median age of housing: 15 years (2000).
Transportation: Commute to work: 85.0% car, 12.2% public transportation, 0.2% walk, 2.0% work from home (2000); Travel time to work: 20.2% less than 15 minutes, 30.8% 15 to 30 minutes, 16.0% 30 to 45 minutes, 9.2% 45 to 60 minutes, 23.9% 60 minutes or more (2000)

ROSSMOOR (CDP). Covers a land area of 0.903 square miles and a water area of 0 square miles. Located at 40.33° N. Lat.; 74.47° W. Long.
Population: 3,231 (1990); 3,129 (2000); 3,421 (2005); 3,704 (2010 projected); Race: 97.5% White, 1.2% Black, 0.6% Asian, 0.4% Hispanic of any race (2005); Density: 3,790.4 persons per square mile (2005); Average household size: 1.45 (2005); Median age: 77.7 (2005); Males per 100 females: 50.2 (2005); Marriage status: 8.4% never married, 50.0% now married, 34.3% widowed, 7.3% divorced (2000); Foreign born: 7.6% (2000); Ancestry (includes multiple ancestries): 17.4% Irish, 14.4% Italian, 14.0% German, 13.0% English, 7.4% Polish (2000).
Economy: Employment by occupation: 6.8% management, 24.7% professional, 13.1% services, 40.1% sales, 0.0% farming, 0.0% construction, 15.4% production (2000).
Income: Per capita income: $35,486 (2005); Median household income: $37,120 (2005); Average household income: $51,196 (2005); Percent of households with income of $100,000 or more: 10.0% (2005); Poverty rate: 4.3% (2000).
Education: Percent of population age 25 and over with: High school diploma (including GED) or higher: 83.1% (2005); Bachelor's degree or higher: 24.9% (2005); Master's degree or higher: 8.0% (2005).
Housing: Homeownership rate: 94.6% (2005); Median home value: $137,793 (2005); Median rent: $445 per month (2000); Median age of housing: 25 years (2000).
Transportation: Commute to work: 80.8% car, 2.4% public transportation, 7.2% walk, 9.6% work from home (2000); Travel time to work: 32.6% less

than 15 minutes, 29.2% 15 to 30 minutes, 29.7% 30 to 45 minutes, 2.1% 45 to 60 minutes, 6.4% 60 minutes or more (2000)

SAYREVILLE (borough). Covers a land area of 15.900 square miles and a water area of 2.849 square miles. Located at 40.46° N. Lat.; 74.32° W. Long. Elevation is 41 feet.
History: Named for James F. Sayer, Jr., founder of Sayer and Fisher Brick Company. Incorporated 1919.
Population: 34,986 (1990); 40,377 (2000); 42,789 (2005); 45,332 (2010 projected); Race: 70.0% White, 10.5% Black, 13.9% Asian, 9.2% Hispanic of any race (2005); Density: 2,691.1 persons per square mile (2005); Average household size: 2.70 (2005); Median age: 37.6 (2005); Males per 100 females: 97.2 (2005); Marriage status: 25.9% never married, 60.4% now married, 6.9% widowed, 6.8% divorced (2000); Foreign born: 20.1% (2000); Ancestry (includes multiple ancestries): 23.1% Other groups, 20.1% Polish, 18.6% Italian, 18.5% Irish, 10.7% German (2000).
Economy: Manufacturing includes chemicals, plastics, steel, steel reinforcing, adhesives. Unemployment rate: 3.9% (2005); Total civilian labor force: 22,678 (2005); Single-family building permits issued: 59 (2005); Multi-family building permits issued: 0 (2005); Employment by occupation: 14.0% management, 21.5% professional, 11.8% services, 31.3% sales, 0.1% farming, 9.3% construction, 12.0% production (2000).
Income: Per capita income: $28,692 (2005); Median household income: $66,868 (2005); Average household income: $77,330 (2005); Percent of households with income of $100,000 or more: 26.0% (2005); Poverty rate: 4.7% (2000).
Taxes: Total city taxes per capita: $436 (2004); City property taxes per capita: $418 (2004).
Education: Percent of population age 25 and over with: High school diploma (including GED) or higher: 85.8% (2005); Bachelor's degree or higher: 25.7% (2005); Master's degree or higher: 7.7% (2005).

School District(s)
Sayreville Borough (PK-12)
   2003-04 Enrollment: 5,924 . . . . (732) 525-5224
Housing: Homeownership rate: 66.3% (2005); Median home value: $257,160 (2005); Median rent: $713 per month (2000); Median age of housing: 32 years (2000).
Safety: Violent crime rate: 19.8 per 10,000 population; Property crime rate: 171.6 per 10,000 population (2004).
Transportation: Commute to work: 88.4% car, 8.6% public transportation, 1.0% walk, 1.4% work from home (2000); Travel time to work: 19.1% less than 15 minutes, 27.5% 15 to 30 minutes, 23.1% 30 to 45 minutes, 12.5% 45 to 60 minutes, 17.8% 60 minutes or more (2000)
Additional Information Contacts
Borough of Sayreville . . . . (732) 390-7007
   http://www.sayreville.com
Sayreville Chamber of Commerce . . . . (732) 607-6340
   http://www.oldbridge.com/OB_Home.htm

SEWAREN (CDP). Covers a land area of 0.952 square miles and a water area of 0.050 square miles. Located at 40.55° N. Lat.; 74.26° W. Long. Elevation is 40 feet.
Population: 2,569 (1990); 2,780 (2000); 2,929 (2005); 3,092 (2010 projected); Race: 81.7% White, 7.4% Black, 5.6% Asian, 11.8% Hispanic of any race (2005); Density: 3,077.5 persons per square mile (2005); Average household size: 2.71 (2005); Median age: 38.7 (2005); Males per 100 females: 93.3 (2005); Marriage status: 23.3% never married, 56.0% now married, 9.3% widowed, 11.4% divorced (2000); Foreign born: 15.0% (2000); Ancestry (includes multiple ancestries): 21.3% Italian, 20.7% Other groups, 17.2% Irish, 16.8% Polish, 9.9% Hungarian (2000).
Economy: Chemicals and petroleum products; large power plant. Employment by occupation: 12.7% management, 13.8% professional, 11.2% services, 35.5% sales, 0.4% farming, 10.7% construction, 15.6% production (2000).
Income: Per capita income: $28,582 (2005); Median household income: $68,500 (2005); Average household income: $77,588 (2005); Percent of households with income of $100,000 or more: 28.8% (2005); Poverty rate: 3.5% (2000).
Education: Percent of population age 25 and over with: High school diploma (including GED) or higher: 84.4% (2005); Bachelor's degree or higher: 16.8% (2005); Master's degree or higher: 5.0% (2005).

School District(s)
Woodbridge Township (PK-12)
   2003-04 Enrollment: 14,056 . . . . (732) 602-8549

Housing: Homeownership rate: 80.4% (2005); Median home value: $252,481 (2005); Median rent: $630 per month (2000); Median age of housing: 42 years (2000).
Transportation: Commute to work: 81.6% car, 11.3% public transportation, 1.0% walk, 5.3% work from home (2000); Travel time to work: 25.7% less than 15 minutes, 34.8% 15 to 30 minutes, 18.1% 30 to 45 minutes, 10.0% 45 to 60 minutes, 11.5% 60 minutes or more (2000)

SOCIETY HILL (CDP).
Covers a land area of 1.371 square miles and a water area of 0 square miles. Located at 40.53° N. Lat.; 74.45° W. Long.
Population: 3,577 (1990); 3,804 (2000); 3,948 (2005); 4,132 (2010 projected); Race: 39.2% White, 17.8% Black, 37.4% Asian, 6.2% Hispanic of any race (2005); Density: 2,879.0 persons per square mile (2005); Average household size: 3.01 (2005); Median age: 35.6 (2005); Males per 100 females: 97.8 (2005); Marriage status: 30.3% never married, 57.8% now married, 4.4% widowed, 7.5% divorced (2000); Foreign born: 31.1% (2000); Ancestry (includes multiple ancestries): 52.2% Other groups, 16.5% Italian, 10.6% Irish, 8.9% German, 3.1% English (2000).
Economy: Employment by occupation: 18.4% management, 40.7% professional, 4.6% services, 27.3% sales, 0.0% farming, 2.2% construction, 6.7% production (2000).
Income: Per capita income: $36,520 (2005); Median household income: $96,377 (2005); Average household income: $109,655 (2005); Percent of households with income of $100,000 or more: 47.7% (2005); Poverty rate: 4.3% (2000).
Education: Percent of population age 25 and over with: High school diploma (including GED) or higher: 95.0% (2005); Bachelor's degree or higher: 53.9% (2005); Master's degree or higher: 26.8% (2005).
Housing: Homeownership rate: 81.8% (2005); Median home value: $302,597 (2005); Median rent: $1,070 per month (2000); Median age of housing: 15 years (2000).
Transportation: Commute to work: 84.5% car, 11.4% public transportation, 0.9% walk, 1.5% work from home (2000); Travel time to work: 32.8% less than 15 minutes, 29.5% 15 to 30 minutes, 14.4% 30 to 45 minutes, 5.6% 45 to 60 minutes, 17.7% 60 minutes or more (2000)

SOUTH AMBOY (city).
Covers a land area of 1.551 square miles and a water area of 1.152 square miles. Located at 40.48° N. Lat.; 74.28° W. Long. Elevation is 99 feet.
History: Clay dug here since early 19th century. Terminal (1832) of the Camden and Amboy, state's first railroad, became an important coal port. Settled 1651; incorporated as borough 1888, as city 1908. Damaged (1950) by explosion of munitions.
Population: 7,863 (1990); 7,913 (2000); 8,082 (2005); 8,293 (2010 projected); Race: 92.6% White, 1.1% Black, 1.5% Asian, 8.9% Hispanic of any race (2005); Density: 5,211.1 persons per square mile (2005); Average household size: 2.67 (2005); Median age: 38.0 (2005); Males per 100 females: 96.9 (2005); Marriage status: 28.8% never married, 52.7% now married, 10.5% widowed, 8.0% divorced (2000); Foreign born: 9.0% (2000); Ancestry (includes multiple ancestries): 26.9% Irish, 25.8% Polish, 16.7% Italian, 12.8% German, 10.6% Other groups (2000).
Economy: Manufacturing: steel products, rubber and plastic goods. Clay. Transships coal. Single-family building permits issued: 2 (2005); Multi-family building permits issued: 0 (2005); Employment by occupation: 8.5% management, 14.2% professional, 15.9% services, 33.7% sales, 0.0% farming, 11.3% construction, 16.4% production (2000).
Income: Per capita income: $25,222 (2005); Median household income: $54,600 (2005); Average household income: $67,139 (2005); Percent of households with income of $100,000 or more: 17.7% (2005); Poverty rate: 7.4% (2000).
Education: Percent of population age 25 and over with: High school diploma (including GED) or higher: 80.8% (2005); Bachelor's degree or higher: 12.3% (2005); Master's degree or higher: 3.2% (2005).
School District(s)
Sayreville Borough (PK-12)
    2003-04 Enrollment: 5,924 . . . . (732) 525-5224
South Amboy City (PK-12)
    2003-04 Enrollment: 1,224 . . . . (732) 525-2102
Housing: Homeownership rate: 63.2% (2005); Median home value: $231,660 (2005); Median rent: $677 per month (2000); Median age of housing: 57 years (2000).
Safety: Violent crime rate: 24.7 per 10,000 population; Property crime rate: 171.9 per 10,000 population (2004).
Newspapers: Amboy Beacon (General - Circulation 21,000)

Transportation: Commute to work: 87.9% car, 5.9% public transportation, 4.2% walk, 1.4% work from home (2000); Travel time to work: 25.6% less than 15 minutes, 33.2% 15 to 30 minutes, 21.1% 30 to 45 minutes, 9.1% 45 to 60 minutes, 11.0% 60 minutes or more (2000)
Additional Information Contacts
Old Bridge Chamber of Commerce . . . . (732) 607-6340
    http://www.oldbridge.com/OB_Home.htm

SOUTH BRUNSWICK (township).
Covers a land area of 40.860 square miles and a water area of 0.239 square miles. Located at 40.39° N. Lat.; 74.54° W. Long.
History: Incorporated 1798.
Population: 25,792 (1990); 37,734 (2000); 41,061 (2005); 44,355 (2010 projected); Race: 64.0% White, 8.7% Black, 22.8% Asian, 6.2% Hispanic of any race (2005); Density: 1,004.9 persons per square mile (2005); Average household size: 2.85 (2005); Median age: 35.8 (2005); Males per 100 females: 94.5 (2005); Marriage status: 22.2% never married, 65.9% now married, 4.4% widowed, 7.5% divorced (2000); Foreign born: 21.6% (2000); Ancestry (includes multiple ancestries): 30.9% Other groups, 19.2% Italian, 14.0% Irish, 13.4% German, 8.1% Polish (2000).
Economy: Printing and plastics industries. Unemployment rate: 3.0% (2005); Total civilian labor force: 22,923 (2005); Single-family building permits issued: 188 (2005); Multi-family building permits issued: 0 (2005); Employment by occupation: 22.7% management, 31.1% professional, 8.0% services, 26.2% sales, 0.0% farming, 5.4% construction, 6.5% production (2000).
Income: Per capita income: $38,628 (2005); Median household income: $93,875 (2005); Average household income: $109,831 (2005); Percent of households with income of $100,000 or more: 45.8% (2005); Poverty rate: 3.1% (2000).
Taxes: Total city taxes per capita: $561 (2004); City property taxes per capita: $532 (2004).
Education: Percent of population age 25 and over with: High school diploma (including GED) or higher: 93.3% (2005); Bachelor's degree or higher: 49.3% (2005); Master's degree or higher: 20.1% (2005).
Housing: Homeownership rate: 75.1% (2005); Median home value: $311,807 (2005); Median rent: $864 per month (2000); Median age of housing: 16 years (2000).
Safety: Violent crime rate: 8.2 per 10,000 population; Property crime rate: 124.1 per 10,000 population (2004).
Transportation: Commute to work: 88.8% car, 6.8% public transportation, 1.1% walk, 2.9% work from home (2000); Travel time to work: 19.0% less than 15 minutes, 32.0% 15 to 30 minutes, 21.2% 30 to 45 minutes, 9.3% 45 to 60 minutes, 18.5% 60 minutes or more (2000)
Additional Information Contacts
South Brunswick Chamber of Commerce . . . . (732) 297-2051
    http://www.sbchamber.com
South Brunswick Township . . . . (732) 329-4000
    http://www.twp.south-brunswick.nj.us

SOUTH PLAINFIELD (borough).
Covers a land area of 8.357 square miles and a water area of 0.037 square miles. Located at 40.58° N. Lat.; 74.41° W. Long. Elevation is 67 feet.
History: Named for its flat, open surroundings. Incorporated 1926.
Population: 20,489 (1990); 21,810 (2000); 23,441 (2005); 25,089 (2010 projected); Race: 73.0% White, 9.7% Black, 9.6% Asian, 11.3% Hispanic of any race (2005); Density: 2,804.9 persons per square mile (2005); Average household size: 3.06 (2005); Median age: 38.8 (2005); Males per 100 females: 96.5 (2005); Marriage status: 24.2% never married, 62.5% now married, 7.5% widowed, 5.8% divorced (2000); Foreign born: 14.8% (2000); Ancestry (includes multiple ancestries): 25.0% Italian, 22.7% Other groups, 16.5% Irish, 15.7% German, 11.4% Polish (2000).
Economy: Seat of several research and consulting firms. Manufacturing includes chemicals, plastics, spices and flavorings, cosmetics, rubber products, pigments, electrical machinery and structural steel. Single-family building permits issued: 23 (2005); Multi-family building permits issued: 0 (2005); Employment by occupation: 16.3% management, 21.2% professional, 10.7% services, 27.9% sales, 0.0% farming, 8.6% construction, 15.2% production (2000).
Income: Per capita income: $28,133 (2005); Median household income: $75,045 (2005); Average household income: $85,521 (2005); Percent of households with income of $100,000 or more: 32.0% (2005); Poverty rate: 3.4% (2000).
Taxes: Total city taxes per capita: $620 (2004); City property taxes per capita: $593 (2004).

Education: Percent of population age 25 and over with: High school diploma (including GED) or higher: 84.1% (2005); Bachelor's degree or higher: 24.0% (2005); Master's degree or higher: 6.8% (2005).

School District(s)

South Plainfield Borough (PK-12)
2003-04 Enrollment: 3,906 . . . . (908) 754-4620

Two-year College(s)

Central Career School (Private, For-profit)
Fall 2004 Enrollment: 66 . . . . (908) 412-8600
Engine City Technical Institute (Private, For-profit)
Fall 2004 Enrollment: 130 . . . . (800) 305-3487

Housing: Homeownership rate: 88.7% (2005); Median home value: $270,031 (2005); Median rent: $878 per month (2000); Median age of housing: 42 years (2000).

Safety: Violent crime rate: 20.8 per 10,000 population; Property crime rate: 183.3 per 10,000 population (2004).

Transportation: Commute to work: 92.2% car, 3.0% public transportation, 1.6% walk, 1.8% work from home (2000); Travel time to work: 30.7% less than 15 minutes, 33.7% 15 to 30 minutes, 19.3% 30 to 45 minutes, 8.0% 45 to 60 minutes, 8.3% 60 minutes or more (2000)

Additional Information Contacts
Borough of South Plainfield . . . . (908) 226-7606
http://www.southplainfieldnj.com
South Plainfield Chamber of Commerce . . . . (732) 394-0220
http://www.pmcoc.org

SOUTH RIVER (borough). Covers a land area of 2.814 square miles and a water area of 0.126 square miles. Located at 40.44° N. Lat.; 74.38° W. Long. Elevation is 80 feet.

History: Named for a local tributary of the Raritan River. Settled 1720. Incorporated 1898.

Population: 13,692 (1990); 15,322 (2000); 16,379 (2005); 17,476 (2010 projected); Race: 79.3% White, 7.0% Black, 4.6% Asian, 11.3% Hispanic of any race (2005); Density: 5,820.3 persons per square mile (2005); Average household size: 2.75 (2005); Median age: 37.5 (2005); Males per 100 females: 98.9 (2005); Marriage status: 27.3% never married, 58.7% now married, 6.8% widowed, 7.2% divorced (2000); Foreign born: 26.3% (2000); Ancestry (includes multiple ancestries): 18.9% Polish, 18.5% Other groups, 14.6% Italian, 13.0% Irish, 12.5% German (2000).

Economy: Manufacturing includes clothing, furniture, and handkerchiefs. Single-family building permits issued: 1 (2005); Multi-family building permits issued: 0 (2005); Employment by occupation: 10.1% management, 17.3% professional, 12.0% services, 28.8% sales, 0.0% farming, 16.4% construction, 15.4% production (2000).

Income: Per capita income: $27,349 (2005); Median household income: $61,115 (2005); Average household income: $75,120 (2005); Percent of households with income of $100,000 or more: 23.8% (2005); Poverty rate: 4.9% (2000).

Education: Percent of population age 25 and over with: High school diploma (including GED) or higher: 76.1% (2005); Bachelor's degree or higher: 21.2% (2005); Master's degree or higher: 6.5% (2005).

School District(s)

South River Borough (PK-12)
2003-04 Enrollment: 2,247 . . . . (732) 613-4000

Housing: Homeownership rate: 68.8% (2005); Median home value: $245,300 (2005); Median rent: $683 per month (2000); Median age of housing: 46 years (2000).

Safety: Violent crime rate: 16.1 per 10,000 population; Property crime rate: 152.3 per 10,000 population (2004).

Transportation: Commute to work: 89.5% car, 4.4% public transportation, 3.0% walk, 2.0% work from home (2000); Travel time to work: 24.0% less than 15 minutes, 28.0% 15 to 30 minutes, 22.6% 30 to 45 minutes, 10.4% 45 to 60 minutes, 15.0% 60 minutes or more (2000)

Additional Information Contacts
Borough of South River . . . . (732) 257-1999
http://www.southrivernj.org

SPOTSWOOD (borough). Covers a land area of 2.325 square miles and a water area of 0.170 square miles. Located at 40.39° N. Lat.; 74.39° W. Long. Elevation is 31 feet.

History: Site of Revolutionary ironworks. Incorporated 1908.

Population: 7,983 (1990); 7,880 (2000); 8,403 (2005); 8,948 (2010 projected); Race: 92.9% White, 1.9% Black, 3.2% Asian, 5.4% Hispanic of any race (2005); Density: 3,614.8 persons per square mile (2005); Average household size: 2.51 (2005); Median age: 40.7 (2005); Males per 100

females: 94.7 (2005); Marriage status: 22.1% never married, 61.0% now married, 9.7% widowed, 7.2% divorced (2000); Foreign born: 7.9% (2000); Ancestry (includes multiple ancestries): 26.0% Irish, 24.4% Italian, 19.8% German, 16.6% Polish, 9.7% Other groups (2000).

Economy: Single-family building permits issued: 25 (2005); Multi-family building permits issued: 0 (2005); Employment by occupation: 11.6% management, 16.3% professional, 11.3% services, 31.2% sales, 0.0% farming, 13.3% construction, 16.4% production (2000).

Income: Per capita income: $28,571 (2005); Median household income: $62,331 (2005); Average household income: $71,716 (2005); Percent of households with income of $100,000 or more: 24.2% (2005); Poverty rate: 4.3% (2000).

Education: Percent of population age 25 and over with: High school diploma (including GED) or higher: 83.4% (2005); Bachelor's degree or higher: 18.6% (2005); Master's degree or higher: 4.2% (2005).

School District(s)

Monroe Township (PK-12)
2003-04 Enrollment: 4,124 . . . . (732) 521-2111

Housing: Homeownership rate: 79.8% (2005); Median home value: $239,635 (2005); Median rent: $665 per month (2000); Median age of housing: 37 years (2000).

Safety: Violent crime rate: 15.7 per 10,000 population; Property crime rate: 107.3 per 10,000 population (2004).

Transportation: Commute to work: 93.1% car, 4.0% public transportation, 0.5% walk, 1.8% work from home (2000); Travel time to work: 23.6% less than 15 minutes, 28.3% 15 to 30 minutes, 21.1% 30 to 45 minutes, 10.6% 45 to 60 minutes, 16.6% 60 minutes or more (2000)

Additional Information Contacts
Borough of Spotswood . . . . (732) 251-0700
http://www.spotswoodboro.com

WHITTINGHAM (CDP). Covers a land area of 1.008 square miles and a water area of 0.006 square miles. Located at 40.32° N. Lat.; 74.44° W. Long.

Population: 518 (1990); 2,483 (2000); 3,375 (2005); 4,197 (2010 projected); Race: 98.4% White, 0.7% Black, 0.5% Asian, 0.8% Hispanic of any race (2005); Density: 3,347.1 persons per square mile (2005); Average household size: 1.83 (2005); Median age: 69.3 (2005); Males per 100 females: 82.9 (2005); Marriage status: 2.3% never married, 81.8% now married, 12.2% widowed, 3.7% divorced (2000); Foreign born: 7.3% (2000); Ancestry (includes multiple ancestries): 19.0% Russian, 16.0% Other groups, 13.9% Polish, 11.9% Italian, 8.6% United States or American (2000).

Economy: Employment by occupation: 23.8% management, 20.7% professional, 4.0% services, 44.1% sales, 0.0% farming, 2.3% construction, 5.1% production (2000).

Income: Per capita income: $40,907 (2005); Median household income: $57,511 (2005); Average household income: $74,667 (2005); Percent of households with income of $100,000 or more: 19.8% (2005); Poverty rate: 2.3% (2000).

Education: Percent of population age 25 and over with: High school diploma (including GED) or higher: 94.3% (2005); Bachelor's degree or higher: 36.9% (2005); Master's degree or higher: 17.3% (2005).

Housing: Homeownership rate: 98.4% (2005); Median home value: $380,762 (2005); Median rent: $545 per month (2000); Median age of housing: 3 years (2000).

Transportation: Commute to work: 74.1% car, 13.0% public transportation, 0.0% walk, 13.0% work from home (2000); Travel time to work: 7.8% less than 15 minutes, 27.3% 15 to 30 minutes, 18.1% 30 to 45 minutes, 10.5% 45 to 60 minutes, 36.3% 60 minutes or more (2000)

WOODBRIDGE (township). Covers a land area of 23.009 square miles and a water area of 1.210 square miles. Located at 40.56° N. Lat.; 74.29° W. Long. Elevation is 34 feet.

History: Named for Woodbridge in Suffolk, England. Woodbridge was settled by 1665 by Puritans from Massachusetts Bay and New Hampshire. In 1751 in Woodbridge, James Parker established the first press in New Jersey.

Population: 93,086 (1990); 97,203 (2000); 102,335 (2005); 107,774 (2010 projected); Race: 63.7% White, 9.8% Black, 18.8% Asian, 11.5% Hispanic of any race (2005); Density: 4,447.6 persons per square mile (2005); Average household size: 2.82 (2005); Median age: 38.0 (2005); Males per 100 females: 101.1 (2005); Marriage status: 25.7% never married, 58.9% now married, 7.9% widowed, 7.5% divorced (2000); Foreign born: 21.5%

(2000); Ancestry (includes multiple ancestries): 29.2% Other groups, 18.2% Italian, 16.8% Irish, 11.0% Polish, 10.9% German (2000).
Economy: Unemployment rate: 3.9% (2005); Total civilian labor force: 52,899 (2005); Single-family building permits issued: 1 (2005); Multi-family building permits issued: 0 (2005); Employment by occupation: 13.9% management, 23.4% professional, 10.5% services, 30.0% sales, 0.2% farming, 8.4% construction, 13.6% production (2000).
Income: Per capita income: $28,992 (2005); Median household income: $68,745 (2005); Average household income: $81,101 (2005); Percent of households with income of $100,000 or more: 28.2% (2005); Poverty rate: 4.8% (2000).
Taxes: Total city taxes per capita: $400 (2004); City property taxes per capita: $391 (2004).
Education: Percent of population age 25 and over with: High school diploma (including GED) or higher: 84.1% (2005); Bachelor's degree or higher: 27.4% (2005); Master's degree or higher: 9.2% (2005).

School District(s)
Middlesex County Vocational (09-12)
    2003-04 Enrollment: 2,315 . . . . (732) 257-3300
Woodbridge Township (PK-12)
    2003-04 Enrollment: 14,056 . . . . (732) 602-8549

Housing: Homeownership rate: 69.7% (2005); Median home value: $251,983 (2005); Median rent: $794 per month (2000); Median age of housing: 41 years (2000).
Hospitals: Woodbridge Developmental Center
Safety: Violent crime rate: 31.3 per 10,000 population; Property crime rate: 281.3 per 10,000 population (2004).
Transportation: Commute to work: 86.5% car, 8.9% public transportation, 2.1% walk, 1.7% work from home (2000); Travel time to work: 26.6% less than 15 minutes, 29.8% 15 to 30 minutes, 19.9% 30 to 45 minutes, 9.3% 45 to 60 minutes, 14.5% 60 minutes or more (2000)
Additional Information Contacts
Woodbridge Chamber of Commerce . . . . (732) 636-4040
    http://www.woodbridgechamber.org
Woodbridge Township . . . . (732) 634-4500
    http://www.twp.woodbridge.nj.us

WOODBRIDGE (CDP).
Covers a land area of 3.873 square miles and a water area of 0.006 square miles. Located at 40.55° N. Lat.; 74.28° W. Long.
Population: 17,434 (1990); 18,309 (2000); 19,677 (2005); 21,107 (2010 projected); Race: 67.5% White, 8.8% Black, 17.3% Asian, 12.5% Hispanic of any race (2005); Density: 5,080.3 persons per square mile (2005); Average household size: 2.52 (2005); Median age: 37.5 (2005); Males per 100 females: 93.7 (2005); Marriage status: 27.6% never married, 55.6% now married, 8.6% widowed, 8.2% divorced (2000); Foreign born: 19.1% (2000); Ancestry (includes multiple ancestries): 27.8% Other groups, 16.7% Italian, 16.6% Irish, 12.0% Polish, 10.1% German (2000).
Economy: Employment by occupation: 13.3% management, 27.1% professional, 10.4% services, 28.7% sales, 0.0% farming, 7.9% construction, 12.7% production (2000).
Income: Per capita income: $32,596 (2005); Median household income: $69,418 (2005); Average household income: $81,741 (2005); Percent of households with income of $100,000 or more: 29.3% (2005); Poverty rate: 5.8% (2000).
Education: Percent of population age 25 and over with: High school diploma (including GED) or higher: 85.9% (2005); Bachelor's degree or higher: 31.0% (2005); Master's degree or higher: 10.9% (2005).

School District(s)
Middlesex County Vocational (09-12)
    2003-04 Enrollment: 2,315 . . . . (732) 257-3300
Woodbridge Township (PK-12)
    2003-04 Enrollment: 14,056 . . . . (732) 602-8549

Housing: Homeownership rate: 60.9% (2005); Median home value: $239,050 (2005); Median rent: $840 per month (2000); Median age of housing: 40 years (2000).
Hospitals: Woodbridge Developmental Center
Transportation: Commute to work: 77.3% car, 10.0% public transportation, 2.3% walk, 1.4% work from home (2000); Travel time to work: 27.7% less than 15 minutes, 28.6% 15 to 30 minutes, 17.5% 30 to 45 minutes, 9.8% 45 to 60 minutes, 16.5% 60 minutes or more (2000)
Additional Information Contacts
Woodbridge Chamber of Commerce . . . . (732) 636-4040
    http://www.woodbridgechamber.org

Monmouth County

Located in eastern New Jersey; bounded on the east by the Atlantic Ocean, and on the north by Raritan and Sandy Hook Bays; drained by the Metedeconk, Manasquan, and Shark Rivers. Covers a land area of 471.94 square miles, a water area of 193.18 square miles, and is located in the Eastern Time Zone. The county government was organized in 1683. County seat is Freehold.

Monmouth County is part of the New York-Northern New Jersey-Long Island, NY-NJ-PA Metropolitan Statistical Area. The entire metro area includes: Edison, NJ Metropolitan Division (Middlesex County, NJ; Monmouth County, NJ; Ocean County, NJ; Somerset County, NJ); Nassau-Suffolk, NY Metropolitan Division (Nassau County, NY; Suffolk County, NY); New York-White Plains-Wayne, NY-NJ Metropolitan Division (Bergen County, NJ; Hudson County, NJ; Passaic County, NJ; Bronx County, NY; Kings County, NY; New York County, NY; Putnam County, NY; Queens County, NY; Richmond County, NY; Rockland County, NY; Westchester County, NY); Newark-Union, NJ-PA Metropolitan Division (Essex County, NJ; Hunterdon County, NJ; Morris County, NJ; Sussex County, NJ; Union County, NJ; Pike County, PA)

Population: 552,964 (1990); 615,301 (2000); 639,747 (2005); 665,216 (2010 projected); Race: 83.5% White, 7.9% Black, 4.5% Asian, 7.3% Hispanic of any race (2005); Density: 1,355.6 persons per square mile (2005); Average household size: 2.73 (2005); Median age: 38.8 (2005); Males per 100 females: 94.9 (2005).
Religion: Five largest groups: 47.0% Catholic Church, 10.6% Jewish Estimate, 2.1% The United Methodist Church, 1.5% Muslim Estimate, 1.3% Presbyterian Church (U.S.A.) (2000).
Economy: Unemployment rate: 4.0% (2005); Total civilian labor force: 328,107 (2005); Leading industries: 18.1% retail trade; 14.8% health care and social assistance; 8.9% professional (2004); Farms: 892 totaling 47,198 acres (2002); Companies that employ 500 or more persons: 61 (2004); Companies that employ 100 to 499 persons: 686 (2004); Companies that employ less than 100 persons: 38,328 (2004); Black-owned businesses: 1,383 (2002); Hispanic-owned businesses: 1,623 (2002); Asian-owned businesses: 2,994 (2002); Women-owned businesses: 14,817 (2002); Retail sales per capita: $17,389 (2006). Single-family building permits issued: 1,932 (2005); Multi-family building permits issued: 652 (2005).
Income: Per capita income: $36,363 (2005); Median household income: $74,080 (2005); Average household income: $98,565 (2005); Percent of households with income of $100,000 or more: 35.1% (2005); Poverty rate: 6.5% (2003); Bankruptcy rate: 4.37% (2005).
Taxes: Total county taxes per capita: $410 (2004); County property taxes per capita: $404 (2004).
Education: Percent of population age 25 and over with: High school diploma (including GED) or higher: 87.8% (2005); Bachelor's degree or higher: 34.6% (2005); Master's degree or higher: 12.8% (2005).
Housing: Homeownership rate: 74.9% (2005); Median home value: $341,510 (2005); Median rent: $687 per month (2000); Median age of housing: 33 years (2000).
Health: Birth rate: 127.1 per 10,000 population (2004); Death rate: 80.6 per 10,000 population (2004); Age-adjusted cancer mortality rate: 212.8 deaths per 100,000 population (2002); Air Quality Index: 90.7% good, 7.1% moderate, 2.2% unhealthy for sensitive individuals, 0.0% unhealthy (percent of days in 2005); Number of physicians: 37.9 per 10,000 population (2004); Hospital beds: 23.6 per 10,000 population (2003); Hospital admissions: 1,291.0 per 10,000 population (2003).
Elections: 2004 Presidential election results: 54.6% Bush, 44.6% Kerry, 0.6% Nader, 0.1% Badnarik
National and State Parks: Allaire State Park
Additional Information Contacts
Monmouth County Government . . . . (732) 431-7387
    http://www.shore.co.monmouth.nj.us
Aberdeen Township . . . . (732) 583-4200
    http://atnj0109.web.aplus.net
Asbury Park Chamber of Commerce . . . . (732) 775-7676
    http://www.asburyparkchamber.com
Belmar Chamber of Commerce . . . . (732) 681-2900
    http://www.belmar.com/index.asp
Borough of Atlantic Highlands . . . . (732) 291-1444
    http://www.ahnj.com/ahnj
Borough of Brielle . . . . (732) 528-6600
    http://www.briellenj.com

Borough of Eatontown . . . . (609) 267-5723
    http://www.eastampton.com
Borough of Englishtown . . . . (732) 446-9235
    http://www.englishtownnj.com
Borough of Fair Haven . . . . (732) 747-0214
    http://www.fairhavennj.net/pages/departments/clerk.html
Borough of Manasquan . . . . (732) 223-0544
    http://www.manasquan-nj.com/public/default.asp
Borough of Neptune City . . . . (732) 776-7224
    http://www.neptunecitynj.com
Borough of Spring Lake Heights . . . . (732) 449-3503
    http://www.springlakehts.com
Borough of Tinton Falls . . . . (732) 542-3400
    http://www.tintonfalls.com
City of Asbury Park . . . . (732) 775-2100
    http://www.cityofasburypark.com
City of Long Branch . . . . (732) 222-7000
    http://www.longbranch.org/ieindex.html
Colts Neck Township . . . . (732) 462-5470
    http://www.colts-neck.nj.us
Eastern Monmouth Chamber of Commerce . . . . (732) 741-0055
    http://www.emacc.org
Farmingdale Chamber of Commerce . . . . (732) 751-0641
    http://www.wmchamber.com
Freehold Township . . . . (732) 294-2000
    http://www.twp.freehold.nj.us
Holmdel Township Chamber of Commerce . . . . (732) 946-3239
    http://www.holmdeltownship.com
Howell Chamber of Commerce . . . . (732) 363-4114
    http://howellchamber.com
Howell Township . . . . (732) 938-4500
    http://www.twp.howell.nj.us
Keyport Chamber of Commerce . . . . (732) 264-3626
    http://www.northernmonmouth.com
Long Branch Chamber of Commerce . . . . (732) 222-0400
    http://www.longbranch.org
Manalapan Township . . . . (732) 446-3200
    http://www.twp.manalapan.nj.us
Manasquan Chamber of Commerce . . . . (732) 223-8303
    http://www.manasquanchamber.com
Marlboro Township . . . . (732) 536-0200
    http://www.marlboro-nj.gov
Matawan-Aberdeen Chamber of Commerce . . . . (732) 290-1125
    http://www.visitmonmouth.com/tourism/Chambers.asp
Middletown Township . . . . (732) 615-2000
    http://www.middletownnj.org
Millstone Township . . . . (609) 208-9325
    http://www.millstone.nj.us
Northern Monmouth Cty Chamber of Commerce . . . . (732) 291-7870
    http://www.northernmonmouth.com
Northern Monmouth Cty Chamber of Commerce . . . . (732) 291-7870
    http://www.northernmonmouth.org
Ocean Grove Chamber of Commerce . . . . (732) 774-1391
    http://www.oceangrovenj.com
Ocean Township . . . . (732) 531-5000
    http://www.oceantwp.org
Ocean Township Chamber of Commerce . . . . (732) 728-1888
    http://www.oceantwpchamber.org
Southern Monmouth Chamber of Commerce . . . . (732) 974-1151
    http://www.smcconline.org
Wall Township . . . . (732) 449-8444
    http://www.wallnj.com
Western Monmouth Chamber of Commerce . . . . (732) 462-3030
    http://www.wmchamber.com

Monmouth County Communities

ABERDEEN (township). Covers a land area of 5.537 square miles and a water area of 2.218 square miles. Located at 40.41° N. Lat.; 74.22° W. Long.
Population: 16,818 (1990); 17,454 (2000); 19,245 (2005); 20,972 (2010 projected); Race: 77.8% White, 11.7% Black, 6.4% Asian, 8.2% Hispanic of any race (2005); Density: 3,475.7 persons per square mile (2005); Average household size: 2.67 (2005); Median age: 38.5 (2005); Males per 100 females: 95.3 (2005); Marriage status: 25.7% never married, 61.7% now

married, 5.8% widowed, 6.8% divorced (2000); Foreign born: 11.5% (2000); Ancestry (includes multiple ancestries): 23.0% Italian, 22.9% Irish, 22.5% Other groups, 13.1% German, 7.6% Polish (2000).
Economy: Single-family building permits issued: 22 (2005); Multi-family building permits issued: 0 (2005); Employment by occupation: 17.8% management, 24.4% professional, 11.9% services, 28.9% sales, 0.1% farming, 6.9% construction, 10.1% production (2000).
Income: Per capita income: $33,861 (2005); Median household income: $77,516 (2005); Average household income: $90,318 (2005); Percent of households with income of $100,000 or more: 33.9% (2005); Poverty rate: 4.7% (2000).
Taxes: Total city taxes per capita: $518 (2004); City property taxes per capita: $499 (2004).
Education: Percent of population age 25 and over with: High school diploma (including GED) or higher: 87.5% (2005); Bachelor's degree or higher: 33.8% (2005); Master's degree or higher: 11.3% (2005).

School District(s)
Bayshore Jointure Comm (UG-UG)
    2003-04 Enrollment: 68 . . . . (732) 708-9215
Matawan-Aberdeen Regional (PK-12)
    2003-04 Enrollment: 3,953 . . . . (732) 290-2705
Housing: Homeownership rate: 77.5% (2005); Median home value: $263,753 (2005); Median rent: $716 per month (2000); Median age of housing: 34 years (2000).
Safety: Violent crime rate: 19.6 per 10,000 population; Property crime rate: 132.6 per 10,000 population (2004).
Transportation: Commute to work: 83.9% car, 11.3% public transportation, 1.7% walk, 2.4% work from home (2000); Travel time to work: 18.7% less than 15 minutes, 27.3% 15 to 30 minutes, 22.2% 30 to 45 minutes, 11.3% 45 to 60 minutes, 20.5% 60 minutes or more (2000)
Additional Information Contacts
Aberdeen Township . . . . (732) 583-4200
    http://atnj0109.web.aplus.net
Matawan-Aberdeen Chamber of Commerce . . . . (732) 290-1125
    http://www.visitmonmouth.com/tourism/Chambers.asp

ALLENHURST (borough). Covers a land area of 0.261 square miles and a water area of 0.018 square miles. Located at 40.23° N. Lat.; 74.00° W. Long. Elevation is 24 feet.
Population: 759 (1990); 718 (2000); 710 (2005); 697 (2010 projected); Race: 97.2% White, 1.0% Black, 0.4% Asian, 2.5% Hispanic of any race (2005); Density: 2,720.0 persons per square mile (2005); Average household size: 2.46 (2005); Median age: 43.1 (2005); Males per 100 females: 104.6 (2005); Marriage status: 23.2% never married, 62.6% now married, 8.7% widowed, 5.6% divorced (2000); Foreign born: 3.2% (2000); Ancestry (includes multiple ancestries): 36.1% Irish, 31.7% Italian, 13.1% German, 9.4% English, 7.3% Polish (2000).
Economy: Resort borough. Single-family building permits issued: 0 (2005); Multi-family building permits issued: 0 (2005); Employment by occupation: 19.9% management, 30.8% professional, 9.0% services, 34.5% sales, 0.0% farming, 2.0% construction, 3.9% production (2000).
Income: Per capita income: $50,993 (2005); Median household income: $94,792 (2005); Average household income: $125,277 (2005); Percent of households with income of $100,000 or more: 47.4% (2005); Poverty rate: 3.8% (2000).
Education: Percent of population age 25 and over with: High school diploma (including GED) or higher: 96.0% (2005); Bachelor's degree or higher: 57.8% (2005); Master's degree or higher: 21.3% (2005).
Housing: Homeownership rate: 72.3% (2005); Median home value: $646,959 (2005); Median rent: $703 per month (2000); Median age of housing: 60+ years (2000).
Safety: Violent crime rate: 0.0 per 10,000 population; Property crime rate: 478.2 per 10,000 population (2004).
Transportation: Commute to work: 82.3% car, 8.8% public transportation, 2.3% walk, 6.6% work from home (2000); Travel time to work: 24.1% less than 15 minutes, 32.6% 15 to 30 minutes, 14.3% 30 to 45 minutes, 7.3% 45 to 60 minutes, 21.6% 60 minutes or more (2000)

ALLENTOWN (borough). Covers a land area of 0.608 square miles and a water area of 0.017 square miles. Located at 40.17° N. Lat.; 74.58° W. Long. Elevation is 82 feet.
History: Imlay mansion (c.1790) here.
Population: 1,828 (1990); 1,882 (2000); 1,853 (2005); 1,835 (2010 projected); Race: 91.9% White, 5.0% Black, 0.5% Asian, 1.7% Hispanic of any race (2005); Density: 3,049.4 persons per square mile (2005); Average

household size: 2.60 (2005); Median age: 39.4 (2005); Males per 100 females: 89.9 (2005); Marriage status: 23.1% never married, 63.7% now married, 5.8% widowed, 7.4% divorced (2000); Foreign born: 2.9% (2000); Ancestry (includes multiple ancestries): 25.5% Irish, 21.9% German, 17.8% Italian, 13.1% English, 9.4% Polish (2000).

Economy: Produce. Single-family building permits issued: 1 (2005); Multi-family building permits issued: 0 (2005); Employment by occupation: 19.5% management, 27.6% professional, 11.8% services, 26.6% sales, 0.1% farming, 6.3% construction, 8.3% production (2000).

Income: Per capita income: $39,336 (2005); Median household income: $90,289 (2005); Average household income: $102,374 (2005); Percent of households with income of $100,000 or more: 43.4% (2005); Poverty rate: 2.3% (2000).

Education: Percent of population age 25 and over with: High school diploma (including GED) or higher: 92.3% (2005); Bachelor's degree or higher: 41.1% (2005); Master's degree or higher: 15.8% (2005).

School District(s)
Upper Freehold Regional (PK-12)
    2003-04 Enrollment: 2,040 . . . . (609) 259-7292

Housing: Homeownership rate: 77.0% (2005); Median home value: $277,358 (2005); Median rent: $696 per month (2000); Median age of housing: 44 years (2000).

Safety: Violent crime rate: 0.0 per 10,000 population; Property crime rate: 96.2 per 10,000 population (2004).

Transportation: Commute to work: 90.9% car, 1.6% public transportation, 2.7% walk, 4.4% work from home (2000); Travel time to work: 21.0% less than 15 minutes, 31.2% 15 to 30 minutes, 27.9% 30 to 45 minutes, 9.2% 45 to 60 minutes, 10.7% 60 minutes or more (2000)

ALLENWOOD (CDP). Covers a land area of 1.810 square miles and a water area of 0.020 square miles. Located at 40.14° N. Lat.; 74.10° W. Long. Elevation is 68 feet.

Population: 772 (1990); 935 (2000); 908 (2005); 948 (2010 projected); Race: 97.2% White, 0.0% Black, 2.0% Asian, 2.2% Hispanic of any race (2005); Density: 501.6 persons per square mile (2005); Average household size: 2.93 (2005); Median age: 40.8 (2005); Males per 100 females: 108.3 (2005); Marriage status: 31.5% never married, 60.8% now married, 2.3% widowed, 5.5% divorced (2000); Foreign born: 2.3% (2000); Ancestry (includes multiple ancestries): 31.6% Irish, 29.5% German, 18.8% Italian, 15.9% English, 8.6% Greek (2000).

Economy: Employment by occupation: 21.9% management, 26.1% professional, 6.4% services, 24.0% sales, 0.0% farming, 18.1% construction, 3.6% production (2000).

Income: Per capita income: $56,528 (2005); Median household income: $137,647 (2005); Average household income: $165,573 (2005); Percent of households with income of $100,000 or more: 70.6% (2005); Poverty rate: 0.0% (2000).

Education: Percent of population age 25 and over with: High school diploma (including GED) or higher: 98.8% (2005); Bachelor's degree or higher: 39.8% (2005); Master's degree or higher: 15.8% (2005).

School District(s)
Wall Township (PK-12)
    2003-04 Enrollment: 4,360 . . . . (732) 556-2000

Housing: Homeownership rate: 92.9% (2005); Median home value: $537,500 (2005); Median rent: $275 per month (2000); Median age of housing: 19 years (2000).

Transportation: Commute to work: 90.5% car, 0.0% public transportation, 2.2% walk, 7.3% work from home (2000); Travel time to work: 35.9% less than 15 minutes, 24.3% 15 to 30 minutes, 19.3% 30 to 45 minutes, 6.1% 45 to 60 minutes, 14.5% 60 minutes or more (2000)

ASBURY PARK (city). Covers a land area of 1.430 square miles and a water area of 0.169 square miles. Located at 40.22° N. Lat.; 74.01° W. Long. Elevation is 21 feet.

History: Named for Francis Asbury (1745-1816), Methodist Episcopal Church bishop. Incorporated 1897. Asbury Park was developed by James A. Bradley in the 1870s to be a Methodist campground. Childhood home of Stephen Crane.

Population: 16,799 (1990); 16,930 (2000); 16,636 (2005); 16,515 (2010 projected); Race: 22.3% White, 62.4% Black, 0.8% Asian, 18.7% Hispanic of any race (2005); Density: 11,636.4 persons per square mile (2005); Average household size: 2.51 (2005); Median age: 32.3 (2005); Males per 100 females: 89.5 (2005); Marriage status: 47.1% never married, 33.6% now married, 9.0% widowed, 10.4% divorced (2000); Foreign born: 18.7%

(2000); Ancestry (includes multiple ancestries): 56.7% Other groups, 5.8% Haitian, 4.9% Irish, 4.4% Italian, 2.7% German (2000).

Economy: Manufacturing of electronics, apparel, plastics and candy. Single-family building permits issued: 30 (2005); Multi-family building permits issued: 3 (2005); Employment by occupation: 6.1% management, 15.0% professional, 24.8% services, 28.8% sales, 0.3% farming, 9.4% construction, 15.6% production (2000).

Income: Per capita income: $14,129 (2005); Median household income: $24,485 (2005); Average household income: $34,604 (2005); Percent of households with income of $100,000 or more: 4.6% (2005); Poverty rate: 30.1% (2000).

Taxes: Total city taxes per capita: $723 (2004); City property taxes per capita: $694 (2004).

Education: Percent of population age 25 and over with: High school diploma (including GED) or higher: 67.8% (2005); Bachelor's degree or higher: 11.2% (2005); Master's degree or higher: 3.5% (2005).

School District(s)
Agency - Hope Academy CS (KG-07)
    2003-04 Enrollment: 149 . . . . (732) 918-6669
Asbury Park City (PK-12)
    2003-04 Enrollment: 3,181 . . . . (732) 776-2606

Housing: Homeownership rate: 19.6% (2005); Median home value: $159,190 (2005); Median rent: $570 per month (2000); Median age of housing: 49 years (2000).

Safety: Violent crime rate: 213.6 per 10,000 population; Property crime rate: 635.3 per 10,000 population (2004).

Newspapers: The Coaster (General - Circulation 5,300); Tri-City News (Alternative, General - Circulation 8,000)

Transportation: Commute to work: 75.2% car, 15.5% public transportation, 6.0% walk, 0.9% work from home (2000); Travel time to work: 29.1% less than 15 minutes, 36.6% 15 to 30 minutes, 17.7% 30 to 45 minutes, 6.8% 45 to 60 minutes, 9.8% 60 minutes or more (2000)

Additional Information Contacts
Asbury Park Chamber of Commerce . . . . (732) 775-7676
    http://www.asburyparkchamber.com
City of Asbury Park . . . . (732) 775-2100
    http://www.cityofasburypark.com

ATLANTIC HIGHLANDS (borough). Covers a land area of 1.236 square miles and a water area of 3.272 square miles. Located at 40.41° N. Lat.; 74.03° W. Long. Elevation is 26 feet.

Population: 4,629 (1990); 4,705 (2000); 4,631 (2005); 4,584 (2010 projected); Race: 93.4% White, 2.5% Black, 1.5% Asian, 4.4% Hispanic of any race (2005); Density: 3,745.6 persons per square mile (2005); Average household size: 2.34 (2005); Median age: 41.8 (2005); Males per 100 females: 94.3 (2005); Marriage status: 22.3% never married, 56.0% now married, 10.0% widowed, 11.6% divorced (2000); Foreign born: 6.3% (2000); Ancestry (includes multiple ancestries): 30.8% Irish, 21.4% German, 17.0% Italian, 10.5% English, 8.4% Other groups (2000).

Economy: Single-family building permits issued: 9 (2005); Multi-family building permits issued: 0 (2005); Employment by occupation: 17.1% management, 29.5% professional, 15.1% services, 27.3% sales, 0.0% farming, 6.5% construction, 4.6% production (2000).

Income: Per capita income: $44,792 (2005); Median household income: $77,168 (2005); Average household income: $104,711 (2005); Percent of households with income of $100,000 or more: 37.5% (2005); Poverty rate: 4.9% (2000).

Education: Percent of population age 25 and over with: High school diploma (including GED) or higher: 91.1% (2005); Bachelor's degree or higher: 35.5% (2005); Master's degree or higher: 11.4% (2005).

School District(s)
Atlantic Highlands Borough (PK-06)
    2003-04 Enrollment: 339 . . . . (732) 291-2020
Bayshore Jointure Comm (UG-UG)
    2003-04 Enrollment: 68 . . . . (732) 708-9215

Housing: Homeownership rate: 67.8% (2005); Median home value: $318,511 (2005); Median rent: $739 per month (2000); Median age of housing: 46 years (2000).

Safety: Violent crime rate: 4.3 per 10,000 population; Property crime rate: 132.6 per 10,000 population (2004).

Transportation: Commute to work: 83.4% car, 10.2% public transportation, 2.1% walk, 4.0% work from home (2000); Travel time to work: 26.9% less than 15 minutes, 27.3% 15 to 30 minutes, 13.9% 30 to 45 minutes, 10.1% 45 to 60 minutes, 21.8% 60 minutes or more (2000)

Additional Information Contacts

Borough of Atlantic Highlands . . . . (732) 291-1444
http://www.ahnj.com/ahnj

AVON-BY-THE-SEA (borough). Covers a land area of 0.426 square miles and a water area of 0.121 square miles. Located at 40.19° N. Lat.; 74.01° W. Long. Elevation is 22 feet.
Population: 2,165 (1990); 2,244 (2000); 2,237 (2005); 2,250 (2010 projected); Race: 96.5% White, 0.7% Black, 1.1% Asian, 2.8% Hispanic of any race (2005); Density: 5,246.5 persons per square mile (2005); Average household size: 2.14 (2005); Median age: 45.6 (2005); Males per 100 females: 94.2 (2005); Marriage status: 27.2% never married, 51.4% now married, 12.4% widowed, 9.0% divorced (2000); Foreign born: 3.4% (2000); Ancestry (includes multiple ancestries): 45.6% Irish, 20.5% Italian, 17.2% German, 7.9% English, 6.6% Polish (2000).
Economy: Single-family building permits issued: 15 (2005); Multi-family building permits issued: 0 (2005); Employment by occupation: 17.9% management, 32.8% professional, 11.4% services, 26.5% sales, 0.3% farming, 6.2% construction, 4.9% production (2000).
Income: Per capita income: $48,357 (2005); Median household income: $72,327 (2005); Average household income: $103,043 (2005); Percent of households with income of $100,000 or more: 34.9% (2005); Poverty rate: 2.7% (2000).
Education: Percent of population age 25 and over with: High school diploma (including GED) or higher: 92.7% (2005); Bachelor's degree or higher: 48.1% (2005); Master's degree or higher: 21.3% (2005).

School District(s)
Avon Borough (PK-08)
   2003-04 Enrollment: 121 . . . . (732) 775-4328
Housing: Homeownership rate: 60.4% (2005); Median home value: $610,406 (2005); Median rent: $712 per month (2000); Median age of housing: 60+ years (2000).
Safety: Violent crime rate: 4.4 per 10,000 population; Property crime rate: 422.4 per 10,000 population (2004).
Transportation: Commute to work: 83.0% car, 5.5% public transportation, 3.7% walk, 6.0% work from home (2000); Travel time to work: 26.6% less than 15 minutes, 25.9% 15 to 30 minutes, 12.8% 30 to 45 minutes, 7.1% 45 to 60 minutes, 27.6% 60 minutes or more (2000)

BELFORD (CDP). Covers a land area of 1.265 square miles and a water area of 0.051 square miles. Located at 40.42° N. Lat.; 74.08° W. Long. Elevation is 10 feet.
Population: 1,501 (1990); 1,340 (2000); 1,435 (2005); 1,530 (2010 projected); Race: 96.7% White, 0.1% Black, 1.0% Asian, 4.5% Hispanic of any race (2005); Density: 1,134.0 persons per square mile (2005); Average household size: 3.06 (2005); Median age: 37.1 (2005); Males per 100 females: 97.1 (2005); Marriage status: 26.9% never married, 60.9% now married, 4.1% widowed, 8.1% divorced (2000); Foreign born: 2.7% (2000); Ancestry (includes multiple ancestries): 44.0% Irish, 38.2% Italian, 23.6% German, 9.7% Other groups, 8.6% Polish (2000).
Economy: Largely residential. Employment by occupation: 9.3% management, 17.9% professional, 10.2% services, 34.1% sales, 2.3% farming, 16.4% construction, 9.8% production (2000).
Income: Per capita income: $32,131 (2005); Median household income: $81,944 (2005); Average household income: $98,177 (2005); Percent of households with income of $100,000 or more: 32.0% (2005); Poverty rate: 3.2% (2000).
Education: Percent of population age 25 and over with: High school diploma (including GED) or higher: 89.2% (2005); Bachelor's degree or higher: 16.8% (2005); Master's degree or higher: 3.4% (2005).

School District(s)
Middletown Township (PK-12)
   2003-04 Enrollment: 10,777 . . . . (732) 706-6002
Housing: Homeownership rate: 86.6% (2005); Median home value: $262,136 (2005); Median rent: $768 per month (2000); Median age of housing: 48 years (2000).
Transportation: Commute to work: 86.9% car, 9.7% public transportation, 1.5% walk, 0.8% work from home (2000); Travel time to work: 24.0% less than 15 minutes, 28.4% 15 to 30 minutes, 16.7% 30 to 45 minutes, 10.5% 45 to 60 minutes, 20.5% 60 minutes or more (2000)

BELMAR (borough). Covers a land area of 1.021 square miles and a water area of 0.673 square miles. Located at 40.17° N. Lat.; 74.02° W. Long. Elevation is 19 feet.
History: Incorporated 1890.

Population: 5,877 (1990); 6,045 (2000); 5,970 (2005); 5,930 (2010 projected); Race: 91.1% White, 2.8% Black, 1.2% Asian, 8.9% Hispanic of any race (2005); Density: 5,848.3 persons per square mile (2005); Average household size: 2.01 (2005); Median age: 40.2 (2005); Males per 100 females: 101.8 (2005); Marriage status: 39.8% never married, 39.6% now married, 7.3% widowed, 13.3% divorced (2000); Foreign born: 8.6% (2000); Ancestry (includes multiple ancestries): 35.2% Irish, 19.3% Italian, 16.9% German, 14.4% Other groups, 8.7% Polish (2000).
Economy: Fishing; boating. Single-family building permits issued: 20 (2005); Multi-family building permits issued: 7 (2005); Employment by occupation: 15.0% management, 25.1% professional, 13.9% services, 27.8% sales, 0.0% farming, 9.4% construction, 8.8% production (2000).
Income: Per capita income: $33,233 (2005); Median household income: $50,635 (2005); Average household income: $66,687 (2005); Percent of households with income of $100,000 or more: 18.5% (2005); Poverty rate: 8.6% (2000).
Education: Percent of population age 25 and over with: High school diploma (including GED) or higher: 89.1% (2005); Bachelor's degree or higher: 33.8% (2005); Master's degree or higher: 11.9% (2005).

School District(s)
Belmar Borough (PK-08)
   2003-04 Enrollment: 571 . . . . (732) 280-9218
Housing: Homeownership rate: 47.5% (2005); Median home value: $305,336 (2005); Median rent: $694 per month (2000); Median age of housing: 54 years (2000).
Safety: Violent crime rate: 29.9 per 10,000 population; Property crime rate: 609.9 per 10,000 population (2004).
Transportation: Commute to work: 87.4% car, 5.4% public transportation, 2.8% walk, 3.1% work from home (2000); Travel time to work: 28.3% less than 15 minutes, 29.6% 15 to 30 minutes, 14.4% 30 to 45 minutes, 7.9% 45 to 60 minutes, 19.8% 60 minutes or more (2000)
Additional Information Contacts
Belmar Chamber of Commerce . . . . (732) 681-2900
http://www.belmar.com/index.asp

BRADLEY BEACH (borough). Covers a land area of 0.592 square miles and a water area of 0.024 square miles. Located at 40.20° N. Lat.; 74.01° W. Long. Elevation is 20 feet.
History: Developed in the 1870s by James A. Bradley, a brush manufacturer from New York City. Settled c.1858, incorporated 1893.
Population: 4,475 (1990); 4,793 (2000); 4,775 (2005); 4,799 (2010 projected); Race: 87.0% White, 3.7% Black, 1.6% Asian, 15.5% Hispanic of any race (2005); Density: 8,067.2 persons per square mile (2005); Average household size: 2.04 (2005); Median age: 38.9 (2005); Males per 100 females: 99.7 (2005); Marriage status: 41.8% never married, 41.0% now married, 5.7% widowed, 11.4% divorced (2000); Foreign born: 11.2% (2000); Ancestry (includes multiple ancestries): 24.2% Irish, 22.0% Italian, 18.8% Other groups, 15.0% German, 7.3% English (2000).
Economy: Fisheries. Single-family building permits issued: 20 (2005); Multi-family building permits issued: 25 (2005); Employment by occupation: 9.8% management, 22.7% professional, 17.0% services, 29.9% sales, 0.0% farming, 9.7% construction, 10.8% production (2000).
Income: Per capita income: $29,217 (2005); Median household income: $47,207 (2005); Average household income: $59,570 (2005); Percent of households with income of $100,000 or more: 14.5% (2005); Poverty rate: 9.2% (2000).
Education: Percent of population age 25 and over with: High school diploma (including GED) or higher: 81.5% (2005); Bachelor's degree or higher: 25.0% (2005); Master's degree or higher: 10.0% (2005).

School District(s)
Bradley Beach Borough (PK-08)
   2003-04 Enrollment: 345 . . . . (732) 775-4413
Housing: Homeownership rate: 41.9% (2005); Median home value: $281,336 (2005); Median rent: $673 per month (2000); Median age of housing: 55 years (2000).
Safety: Violent crime rate: 33.3 per 10,000 population; Property crime rate: 468.5 per 10,000 population (2004).
Transportation: Commute to work: 86.0% car, 6.8% public transportation, 3.1% walk, 1.5% work from home (2000); Travel time to work: 28.5% less than 15 minutes, 33.8% 15 to 30 minutes, 10.1% 30 to 45 minutes, 10.6% 45 to 60 minutes, 17.0% 60 minutes or more (2000)

BRIELLE (borough). Covers a land area of 1.776 square miles and a water area of 0.594 square miles. Located at 40.10° N. Lat.; 74.06° W. Long. Elevation is 30 feet.

History: Named after Brielle, Netherlands, because of the many windmills once used here. Most of the town (the Salt Works and 50 homes and buildings) was burned (April 1778) by the British. Only the home of Dirck (or Derrick) Longstreet, a loyal British subject, escaped the flames; now known as The Boxwood Cottage(built 1760) and still used as a residence.
Population: 4,406 (1990); 4,893 (2000); 5,063 (2005); 5,254 (2010 projected); Race: 93.0% White, 2.8% Black, 0.7% Asian, 4.2% Hispanic of any race (2005); Density: 2,850.1 persons per square mile (2005); Average household size: 2.51 (2005); Median age: 43.9 (2005); Males per 100 females: 92.1 (2005); Marriage status: 18.3% never married, 63.4% now married, 8.2% widowed, 10.1% divorced (2000); Foreign born: 3.2% (2000); Ancestry (includes multiple ancestries): 32.6% Irish, 22.0% Italian, 21.2% German, 11.7% English, 7.1% Other groups (2000).
Economy: Sports-fishing and recreational-boating center. Single-family building permits issued: 22 (2005); Multi-family building permits issued: 0 (2005); Employment by occupation: 21.4% management, 34.6% professional, 10.1% services, 21.8% sales, 0.7% farming, 4.8% construction, 6.5% production (2000).
Income: Per capita income: $42,770 (2005); Median household income: $80,157 (2005); Average household income: $107,520 (2005); Percent of households with income of $100,000 or more: 38.7% (2005); Poverty rate: 3.9% (2000).
Education: Percent of population age 25 and over with: High school diploma (including GED) or higher: 94.9% (2005); Bachelor's degree or higher: 44.8% (2005); Master's degree or higher: 14.7% (2005).
School District(s)
Brielle Borough (PK-08)
   2003-04 Enrollment: 678 . . . . (732) 528-6400
Housing: Homeownership rate: 83.7% (2005); Median home value: $477,974 (2005); Median rent: $1,034 per month (2000); Median age of housing: 33 years (2000).
Safety: Violent crime rate: 8.0 per 10,000 population; Property crime rate: 71.6 per 10,000 population (2004).
Transportation: Commute to work: 90.1% car, 3.1% public transportation, 1.7% walk, 4.8% work from home (2000); Travel time to work: 30.6% less than 15 minutes, 26.0% 15 to 30 minutes, 16.6% 30 to 45 minutes, 9.3% 45 to 60 minutes, 17.5% 60 minutes or more (2000)
Additional Information Contacts
Borough of Brielle . . . . (732) 528-6600
   http://www.briellenj.com

CLARKSBURG (unincorporated postal area, zip code 08510). Covers a land area of 8.154 square miles and a water area of 0.068 square miles. Located at 40.18° N. Lat.; 74.42° W. Long. Elevation is 200 feet.
Population: 2,128 (2000); Race: 93.5% White, 5.5% Black, 0.0% Asian, 2.0% Hispanic of any race (2000); Density: 261.0 persons per square mile (2000); Age: 30.0% under 18, 9.1% over 64 (2000); Marriage status: 21.0% never married, 70.7% now married, 5.3% widowed, 3.0% divorced (2000); Foreign born: 6.1% (2000); Ancestry (includes multiple ancestries): 29.0% Irish, 25.4% Italian, 19.6% German, 13.7% Polish, 10.7% Other groups (2000).
Economy: Employment by occupation: 21.8% management, 31.8% professional, 9.9% services, 22.6% sales, 0.0% farming, 8.5% construction, 5.4% production (2000).
Income: Per capita income: $34,431 (2000); Median household income: $88,575 (2000); Poverty rate: 9.0% (2000).
Education: Percent of population age 25 and over with: High school diploma (including GED) or higher: 89.0% (2000); Bachelor's degree or higher: 44.7% (2000).
School District(s)
Millstone Township (PK-08)
   2003-04 Enrollment: 1,735 . . . . (732) 446-0890
Housing: Homeownership rate: 96.5% (2000); Median home value: $312,600 (2000); Median rent: $689 per month (2000); Median age of housing: 16 years (2000).
Transportation: Commute to work: 90.6% car, 3.0% public transportation, 0.8% walk, 5.6% work from home (2000); Travel time to work: 18.1% less than 15 minutes, 28.9% 15 to 30 minutes, 18.5% 30 to 45 minutes, 18.2% 45 to 60 minutes, 16.2% 60 minutes or more (2000)

CLIFFWOOD (unincorporated postal area, zip code 07721). Covers a land area of 0.878 square miles and a water area of 0 square miles. Located at 40.43° N. Lat.; 74.23° W. Long. Elevation is 80 feet.
Population: 2,573 (2000); Race: 47.6% White, 44.1% Black, 3.5% Asian, 9.7% Hispanic of any race (2000); Density: 2,931.2 persons per square

mile (2000); Age: 27.4% under 18, 6.4% over 64 (2000); Marriage status: 29.6% never married, 58.3% now married, 5.2% widowed, 6.9% divorced (2000); Foreign born: 13.7% (2000); Ancestry (includes multiple ancestries): 46.6% Other groups, 13.4% Italian, 10.4% Irish, 3.9% German, 3.4% Polish (2000).
Economy: Employment by occupation: 10.3% management, 21.6% professional, 16.1% services, 33.4% sales, 0.0% farming, 3.9% construction, 14.7% production (2000).
Income: Per capita income: $23,740 (2000); Median household income: $47,906 (2000); Poverty rate: 7.4% (2000).
Education: Percent of population age 25 and over with: High school diploma (including GED) or higher: 86.4% (2000); Bachelor's degree or higher: 23.1% (2000).
School District(s)
Matawan-Aberdeen Regional (PK-12)
   2003-04 Enrollment: 3,953 . . . . (732) 290-2705
Housing: Homeownership rate: 56.8% (2000); Median home value: $145,600 (2000); Median rent: $710 per month (2000); Median age of housing: 25 years (2000).
Transportation: Commute to work: 91.0% car, 7.3% public transportation, 1.2% walk, 0.5% work from home (2000); Travel time to work: 16.6% less than 15 minutes, 35.5% 15 to 30 minutes, 25.0% 30 to 45 minutes, 7.3% 45 to 60 minutes, 15.6% 60 minutes or more (2000)

CLIFFWOOD BEACH (CDP). Covers a land area of 0.929 square miles and a water area of 0.023 square miles. Located at 40.44° N. Lat.; 74.21° W. Long. Elevation is 43 feet.
Population: 3,480 (1990); 3,538 (2000); 3,811 (2005); 4,077 (2010 projected); Race: 77.2% White, 15.8% Black, 1.4% Asian, 11.0% Hispanic of any race (2005); Density: 4,103.1 persons per square mile (2005); Average household size: 3.08 (2005); Median age: 37.4 (2005); Males per 100 females: 98.5 (2005); Marriage status: 30.6% never married, 53.3% now married, 9.4% widowed, 6.8% divorced (2000); Foreign born: 8.2% (2000); Ancestry (includes multiple ancestries): 27.3% Irish, 24.6% Other groups, 21.5% Italian, 12.6% German, 6.7% English (2000).
Economy: Employment by occupation: 7.2% management, 15.4% professional, 14.5% services, 32.7% sales, 0.0% farming, 14.7% construction, 15.6% production (2000).
Income: Per capita income: $27,773 (2005); Median household income: $69,520 (2005); Average household income: $84,679 (2005); Percent of households with income of $100,000 or more: 27.1% (2005); Poverty rate: 5.5% (2000).
Education: Percent of population age 25 and over with: High school diploma (including GED) or higher: 75.9% (2005); Bachelor's degree or higher: 15.0% (2005); Master's degree or higher: 7.3% (2005).
School District(s)
Old Bridge Township (PK-12)
   2003-04 Enrollment: 10,119 . . . . (732) 290-3976
Housing: Homeownership rate: 88.9% (2005); Median home value: $204,107 (2005); Median rent: $712 per month (2000); Median age of housing: 42 years (2000).
Transportation: Commute to work: 91.4% car, 2.5% public transportation, 2.9% walk, 1.5% work from home (2000); Travel time to work: 22.7% less than 15 minutes, 28.8% 15 to 30 minutes, 26.7% 30 to 45 minutes, 11.6% 45 to 60 minutes, 10.2% 60 minutes or more (2000)

COLTS NECK (township). Covers a land area of 31.427 square miles and a water area of 0.676 square miles. Located at 40.30° N. Lat.; 74.18° W. Long. Elevation is 74 feet.
History: Incorporated 1847.
Population: 8,559 (1990); 12,331 (2000); 11,836 (2005); 11,548 (2010 projected); Race: 84.4% White, 8.0% Black, 4.2% Asian, 4.7% Hispanic of any race (2005); Density: 376.6 persons per square mile (2005); Average household size: 3.48 (2005); Median age: 33.2 (2005); Males per 100 females: 107.7 (2005); Marriage status: 24.2% never married, 68.8% now married, 3.7% widowed, 3.3% divorced (2000); Foreign born: 8.6% (2000); Ancestry (includes multiple ancestries): 24.6% Italian, 22.8% Irish, 17.0% Other groups, 16.8% German, 7.5% Polish (2000).
Economy: Single-family building permits issued: 19 (2005); Multi-family building permits issued: 0 (2005); Employment by occupation: 25.8% management, 26.7% professional, 9.8% services, 26.1% sales, 0.2% farming, 5.7% construction, 5.7% production (2000).
Income: Per capita income: $54,078 (2005); Median household income: $130,090 (2005); Average household income: $182,966 (2005); Percent of

households with income of $100,000 or more: 59.8% (2005); Poverty rate: 2.8% (2000).

Taxes: Total city taxes per capita: $237 (2004); City property taxes per capita: $193 (2004).

Education: Percent of population age 25 and over with: High school diploma (including GED) or higher: 95.0% (2005); Bachelor's degree or higher: 48.1% (2005); Master's degree or higher: 19.5% (2005).

School District(s)

Colts Neck Township (PK-08)
   2003-04 Enrollment: 1,544 . . . . (732) 946-0055
Freehold Regional (09-12)
   2003-04 Enrollment: 10,935 . . . . (732) 792-7300
Monmouth County Vocational (09-12)
   2003-04 Enrollment: 1,856 . . . . (732) 431-7942
Monmouth-Ocean Ed Serv Comm (UG-UG)
   2003-04 Enrollment: 218 . . . . (732) 389-5555

Housing: Homeownership rate: 83.6% (2005); Median home value: $723,181 (2005); Median rent: $922 per month (2000); Median age of housing: 24 years (2000).

Safety: Violent crime rate: 7.5 per 10,000 population; Property crime rate: 108.8 per 10,000 population (2004).

Transportation: Commute to work: 73.2% car, 9.4% public transportation, 4.1% walk, 9.2% work from home (2000); Travel time to work: 23.6% less than 15 minutes, 30.4% 15 to 30 minutes, 13.6% 30 to 45 minutes, 9.2% 45 to 60 minutes, 23.1% 60 minutes or more (2000)

Additional Information Contacts

Colts Neck Township . . . . (732) 462-5470
   http://www.colts-neck.nj.us
Western Monmouth Chamber of Commerce . . . . (732) 462-3030
   http://www.wmchamber.com

CREAMRIDGE (unincorporated postal area, zip code 08514). Covers a land area of 28.504 square miles and a water area of 0.305 square miles. Located at 40.13° N. Lat.; 74.48° W. Long.

Population: 3,096 (2000); Race: 91.9% White, 1.3% Black, 1.4% Asian, 4.7% Hispanic of any race (2000); Density: 108.6 persons per square mile (2000); Age: 26.7% under 18, 10.7% over 64 (2000); Marriage status: 18.0% never married, 71.5% now married, 3.6% widowed, 6.8% divorced (2000); Foreign born: 6.3% (2000); Ancestry (includes multiple ancestries): 23.7% German, 23.7% Irish, 22.2% Italian, 16.6% English, 10.3% Polish (2000).

Economy: Employment by occupation: 19.4% management, 19.0% professional, 15.5% services, 28.4% sales, 2.4% farming, 6.8% construction, 8.5% production (2000).

Income: Per capita income: $28,260 (2000); Median household income: $71,711 (2000); Poverty rate: 7.5% (2000).

Education: Percent of population age 25 and over with: High school diploma (including GED) or higher: 89.8% (2000); Bachelor's degree or higher: 31.5% (2000).

Housing: Homeownership rate: 88.6% (2000); Median home value: $217,600 (2000); Median rent: $674 per month (2000); Median age of housing: 25 years (2000).

Transportation: Commute to work: 89.3% car, 2.1% public transportation, 0.9% walk, 6.0% work from home (2000); Travel time to work: 21.2% less than 15 minutes, 24.4% 15 to 30 minutes, 26.5% 30 to 45 minutes, 20.0% 45 to 60 minutes, 7.9% 60 minutes or more (2000)

DEAL (borough). Covers a land area of 1.215 square miles and a water area of 0.079 square miles. Located at 40.24° N. Lat.; 73.99° W. Long. Elevation is 33 feet.

Population: 1,179 (1990); 1,070 (2000); 1,074 (2005); 1,087 (2010 projected); Race: 93.7% White, 1.4% Black, 0.3% Asian, 5.8% Hispanic of any race (2005); Density: 883.8 persons per square mile (2005); Average household size: 2.41 (2005); Median age: 44.8 (2005); Males per 100 females: 100.0 (2005); Marriage status: 23.4% never married, 60.1% now married, 11.1% widowed, 5.3% divorced (2000); Foreign born: 12.6% (2000); Ancestry (includes multiple ancestries): 23.7% Other groups, 16.8% Syrian, 12.0% Italian, 10.1% Irish, 6.9% United States or American (2000).

Economy: Resort borough. Single-family building permits issued: 8 (2005); Multi-family building permits issued: 0 (2005); Employment by occupation: 18.7% management, 19.0% professional, 14.7% services, 39.9% sales, 0.0% farming, 4.3% construction, 3.4% production (2000).

Income: Per capita income: $35,973 (2005); Median household income: $55,123 (2005); Average household income: $86,792 (2005); Percent of

households with income of $100,000 or more: 27.0% (2005); Poverty rate: 11.2% (2000).

Education: Percent of population age 25 and over with: High school diploma (including GED) or higher: 88.5% (2005); Bachelor's degree or higher: 26.8% (2005); Master's degree or higher: 8.3% (2005).

School District(s)

Deal Borough (PK-08)
   2003-04 Enrollment: 129 . . . . (732) 531-0410

Housing: Homeownership rate: 67.4% (2005); Median home value: $858,333 (2005); Median rent: $853 per month (2000); Median age of housing: 52 years (2000).

Safety: Violent crime rate: 18.6 per 10,000 population; Property crime rate: 788.5 per 10,000 population (2004).

Newspapers: The Jewish Voice (Jewish - Circulation 15,000)

Transportation: Commute to work: 83.9% car, 9.9% public transportation, 0.3% walk, 3.8% work from home (2000); Travel time to work: 24.3% less than 15 minutes, 21.6% 15 to 30 minutes, 10.3% 30 to 45 minutes, 10.0% 45 to 60 minutes, 33.7% 60 minutes or more (2000)

EAST FREEHOLD (CDP). Covers a land area of 2.954 square miles and a water area of 0 square miles. Located at 40.27° N. Lat.; 74.23° W. Long. Elevation is 180 feet.

Population: 3,842 (1990); 4,936 (2000); 5,471 (2005); 5,994 (2010 projected); Race: 85.5% White, 4.1% Black, 7.9% Asian, 4.2% Hispanic of any race (2005); Density: 1,851.8 persons per square mile (2005); Average household size: 2.98 (2005); Median age: 37.6 (2005); Males per 100 females: 95.7 (2005); Marriage status: 19.0% never married, 71.9% now married, 4.3% widowed, 4.8% divorced (2000); Foreign born: 13.3% (2000); Ancestry (includes multiple ancestries): 27.7% Italian, 21.0% Irish, 17.9% Other groups, 12.4% German, 8.2% English (2000).

Economy: Employment by occupation: 22.8% management, 25.7% professional, 7.7% services, 28.3% sales, 0.5% farming, 8.4% construction, 6.5% production (2000).

Income: Per capita income: $46,101 (2005); Median household income: $114,678 (2005); Average household income: $137,600 (2005); Percent of households with income of $100,000 or more: 57.7% (2005); Poverty rate: 2.6% (2000).

Education: Percent of population age 25 and over with: High school diploma (including GED) or higher: 94.1% (2005); Bachelor's degree or higher: 48.9% (2005); Master's degree or higher: 19.6% (2005).

Housing: Homeownership rate: 85.9% (2005); Median home value: $431,502 (2005); Median rent: $746 per month (2000); Median age of housing: 22 years (2000).

Transportation: Commute to work: 90.1% car, 6.5% public transportation, 0.7% walk, 2.6% work from home (2000); Travel time to work: 22.1% less than 15 minutes, 25.7% 15 to 30 minutes, 13.0% 30 to 45 minutes, 16.1% 45 to 60 minutes, 23.2% 60 minutes or more (2000)

EATONTOWN (borough). Covers a land area of 5.918 square miles and a water area of 0.008 square miles. Located at 40.29° N. Lat.; 74.05° W. Long. Elevation is 46 feet.

History: Named for Thomas Eaton, who built a gristmill here c.1670. The mill's site is a landmark.

Population: 13,800 (1990); 14,008 (2000); 14,346 (2005); 14,645 (2010 projected); Race: 72.1% White, 11.5% Black, 10.0% Asian, 7.8% Hispanic of any race (2005); Density: 2,423.9 persons per square mile (2005); Average household size: 2.43 (2005); Median age: 38.3 (2005); Males per 100 females: 95.3 (2005); Marriage status: 26.6% never married, 56.1% now married, 8.2% widowed, 9.1% divorced (2000); Foreign born: 16.5% (2000); Ancestry (includes multiple ancestries): 26.3% Other groups, 21.4% Italian, 19.2% Irish, 14.1% German, 8.1% English (2000).

Economy: A residential borough. Single-family building permits issued: 27 (2005); Multi-family building permits issued: 0 (2005); Employment by occupation: 16.0% management, 28.7% professional, 13.3% services, 28.5% sales, 0.0% farming, 5.3% construction, 8.1% production (2000).

Income: Per capita income: $30,877 (2005); Median household income: $60,949 (2005); Average household income: $73,463 (2005); Percent of households with income of $100,000 or more: 23.7% (2005); Poverty rate: 5.7% (2000).

Taxes: Total city taxes per capita: $564 (2004); City property taxes per capita: $514 (2004).

Education: Percent of population age 25 and over with: High school diploma (including GED) or higher: 88.9% (2005); Bachelor's degree or higher: 33.1% (2005); Master's degree or higher: 13.1% (2005).

Eatontown Borough (PK-08)
  2003-04 Enrollment: 1,378 . . . . (732) 542-1310
Housing: Homeownership rate: 51.0% (2005); Median home value: $281,641 (2005); Median rent: $702 per month (2000); Median age of housing: 32 years (2000).
Safety: Violent crime rate: 24.6 per 10,000 population; Property crime rate: 404.3 per 10,000 population (2004).
Transportation: Commute to work: 92.4% car, 3.1% public transportation, 1.4% walk, 2.7% work from home (2000); Travel time to work: 42.2% less than 15 minutes, 30.2% 15 to 30 minutes, 10.9% 30 to 45 minutes, 6.1% 45 to 60 minutes, 10.5% 60 minutes or more (2000)
Additional Information Contacts
Borough of Eatontown . . . . (609) 267-5723
  http://www.eastampton.com
Eastern Monmouth Chamber of Commerce . . . . (732) 741-0055
  http://www.emacc.org

ENGLISHTOWN (borough). Covers a land area of 0.569 square miles and a water area of 0.011 square miles. Located at 40.29° N. Lat.; 74.36° W. Long. Elevation is 70 feet.
History: American troops camped here just before the battle of Monmouth (1778).
Population: 1,268 (1990); 1,764 (2000); 1,802 (2005); 1,851 (2010 projected); Race: 86.2% White, 4.7% Black, 5.3% Asian, 8.2% Hispanic of any race (2005); Density: 3,169.0 persons per square mile (2005); Average household size: 2.74 (2005); Median age: 36.1 (2005); Males per 100 females: 93.3 (2005); Marriage status: 21.6% never married, 59.5% now married, 9.3% widowed, 9.6% divorced (2000); Foreign born: 11.8% (2000); Ancestry (includes multiple ancestries): 26.0% Italian, 19.0% Other groups, 18.5% Irish, 13.8% German, 11.6% Polish (2000).
Economy: Site of thoroughbred race track. Single-family building permits issued: 46 (2005); Multi-family building permits issued: 0 (2005); Employment by occupation: 15.3% management, 16.0% professional, 15.6% services, 27.1% sales, 0.1% farming, 13.3% construction, 12.6% production (2000).
Income: Per capita income: $26,981 (2005); Median household income: $64,050 (2005); Average household income: $74,003 (2005); Percent of households with income of $100,000 or more: 26.0% (2005); Poverty rate: 7.2% (2000)
Education: Percent of population age 25 and over with: High school diploma (including GED) or higher: 81.7% (2005); Bachelor's degree or higher: 19.0% (2005); Master's degree or higher: 6.0% (2005).
School District(s)
Freehold Regional (09-12)
  2003-04 Enrollment: 10,935 . . . . (732) 792-7300
Housing: Homeownership rate: 66.8% (2005); Median home value: $262,500 (2005); Median rent: $665 per month (2000); Median age of housing: 17 years (2000).
Safety: Violent crime rate: 27.8 per 10,000 population; Property crime rate: 66.6 per 10,000 population (2004).
Transportation: Commute to work: 87.7% car, 7.6% public transportation, 2.6% walk, 1.2% work from home (2000); Travel time to work: 25.7% less than 15 minutes, 24.8% 15 to 30 minutes, 16.4% 30 to 45 minutes, 12.9% 45 to 60 minutes, 20.1% 60 minutes or more (2000)
Additional Information Contacts
Borough of Englishtown . . . . (732) 446-9235
  http://www.englishtownnj.com
Western Monmouth Chamber of Commerce . . . . (732) 462-3030
  http://www.wmchamber.com

FAIR HAVEN (borough). Covers a land area of 1.668 square miles and a water area of 0.008 square miles. Located at 40.36° N. Lat.; 74.03° W. Long. Elevation is 40 feet.
History: Incorporated 1912.
Population: 5,270 (1990); 5,937 (2000); 5,963 (2005); 6,034 (2010 projected); Race: 94.6% White, 3.4% Black, 1.0% Asian, 1.4% Hispanic of any race (2005); Density: 3,574.9 persons per square mile (2005); Average household size: 3.03 (2005); Median age: 37.7 (2005); Males per 100 females: 94.2 (2005); Marriage status: 18.0% never married, 70.8% now married, 5.6% widowed, 5.6% divorced (2000); Foreign born: 4.7% (2000); Ancestry (includes multiple ancestries): 31.2% Irish, 22.1% German, 16.6% Italian, 12.0% English, 9.1% Other groups (2000).
Economy: Largely residential. Single-family building permits issued: 13 (2005); Multi-family building permits issued: 0 (2005); Employment by

occupation: 21.1% management, 34.6% professional, 6.9% services, 27.1% sales, 0.2% farming, 6.2% construction, 4.0% production (2000).
Income: Per capita income: $52,954 (2005); Median household income: $117,537 (2005); Average household income: $160,118 (2005); Percent of households with income of $100,000 or more: 57.2% (2005); Poverty rate: 2.3% (2000).
Education: Percent of population age 25 and over with: High school diploma (including GED) or higher: 97.1% (2005); Bachelor's degree or higher: 61.7% (2005); Master's degree or higher: 26.3% (2005).
School District(s)
Fair Haven Borough (PK-08)
  2003-04 Enrollment: 1,020 . . . . (732) 747-2294
Housing: Homeownership rate: 93.5% (2005); Median home value: $552,826 (2005); Median rent: $1,060 per month (2000); Median age of housing: 49 years (2000).
Safety: Violent crime rate: 6.7 per 10,000 population; Property crime rate: 78.5 per 10,000 population (2004).
Transportation: Commute to work: 78.3% car, 13.4% public transportation, 0.7% walk, 7.3% work from home (2000); Travel time to work: 31.8% less than 15 minutes, 22.7% 15 to 30 minutes, 12.3% 30 to 45 minutes, 7.5% 45 to 60 minutes, 25.7% 60 minutes or more (2000)
Additional Information Contacts
Borough of Fair Haven . . . . (732) 747-0214
  http://www.fairhavennj.net/pages/departments/clerk.html

FAIRVIEW (CDP). Covers a land area of 1.285 square miles and a water area of 0.005 square miles. Located at 40.36° N. Lat.; 74.08° W. Long. Elevation is 112 feet.
Population: 3,853 (1990); 3,942 (2000); 3,714 (2005); 3,506 (2010 projected); Race: 95.7% White, 0.5% Black, 2.1% Asian, 4.8% Hispanic of any race (2005); Density: 2,890.3 persons per square mile (2005); Average household size: 2.94 (2005); Median age: 38.2 (2005); Males per 100 females: 101.0 (2005); Marriage status: 23.0% never married, 65.4% now married, 6.0% widowed, 5.5% divorced (2000); Foreign born: 5.1% (2000); Ancestry (includes multiple ancestries): 33.0% Italian, 31.5% Irish, 16.9% German, 12.9% Polish, 8.7% English (2000).
Economy: Employment by occupation: 15.3% management, 23.6% professional, 11.8% services, 30.5% sales, 0.3% farming, 10.7% construction, 7.9% production (2000).
Income: Per capita income: $36,981 (2005); Median household income: $96,706 (2005); Average household income: $108,747 (2005); Percent of households with income of $100,000 or more: 47.1% (2005); Poverty rate: 1.8% (2000).
Education: Percent of population age 25 and over with: High school diploma (including GED) or higher: 93.2% (2005); Bachelor's degree or higher: 38.3% (2005); Master's degree or higher: 10.9% (2005).
Housing: Homeownership rate: 93.7% (2005); Median home value: $346,569 (2005); Median rent: $887 per month (2000); Median age of housing: 44 years (2000).
Transportation: Commute to work: 84.3% car, 10.9% public transportation, 2.1% walk, 2.7% work from home (2000); Travel time to work: 23.3% less than 15 minutes, 29.0% 15 to 30 minutes, 16.4% 30 to 45 minutes, 6.1% 45 to 60 minutes, 25.2% 60 minutes or more (2000)

FARMINGDALE (borough). Covers a land area of 0.534 square miles and a water area of 0 square miles. Located at 40.19° N. Lat.; 74.17° W. Long. Elevation is 79 feet.
Population: 1,462 (1990); 1,587 (2000); 1,573 (2005); 1,571 (2010 projected); Race: 92.7% White, 0.8% Black, 2.9% Asian, 4.4% Hispanic of any race (2005); Density: 2,946.0 persons per square mile (2005); Average household size: 2.50 (2005); Median age: 36.4 (2005); Males per 100 females: 101.9 (2005); Marriage status: 26.7% never married, 58.8% now married, 5.0% widowed, 9.5% divorced (2000); Foreign born: 5.7% (2000); Ancestry (includes multiple ancestries): 19.5% Italian, 19.2% Irish, 19.2% German, 13.5% English, 8.8% Other groups (2000).
Economy: Manufacturing: concrete products. Naval Ammunition Depot just North. Single-family building permits issued: 2 (2005); Multi-family building permits issued: 0 (2005); Employment by occupation: 11.6% management, 21.2% professional, 14.5% services, 27.6% sales, 0.0% farming, 13.7% construction, 11.3% production (2000).
Income: Per capita income: $23,350 (2005); Median household income: $50,452 (2005); Average household income: $58,282 (2005); Percent of households with income of $100,000 or more: 9.7% (2005); Poverty rate: 5.7% (2000).

Education: Percent of population age 25 and over with: High school diploma (including GED) or higher: 88.4% (2005); Bachelor's degree or higher: 19.0% (2005); Master's degree or higher: 6.3% (2005).

School District(s)

Farmingdale Borough (PK-08)
   2003-04 Enrollment: 154 . . . . (732) 938-9611
Freehold Regional (09-12)
   2003-04 Enrollment: 10,935 . . . . (732) 792-7300
Howell Township (PK-08)
   2003-04 Enrollment: 7,648 . . . . (732) 751-2480

Housing: Homeownership rate: 53.8% (2005); Median home value: $263,043 (2005); Median rent: $655 per month (2000); Median age of housing: 39 years (2000).

Transportation: Commute to work: 92.1% car, 0.5% public transportation, 4.8% walk, 2.1% work from home (2000); Travel time to work: 25.5% less than 15 minutes, 39.7% 15 to 30 minutes, 14.4% 30 to 45 minutes, 9.0% 45 to 60 minutes, 11.3% 60 minutes or more (2000).

Additional Information Contacts

Farmingdale Chamber of Commerce . . . . (732) 751-0641
   http://www.wmchamber.com

FORT MONMOUTH (unincorporated postal area, zip code 07703).
Covers a land area of 0.941 square miles and a water area of 0 square miles. Located at 40.31° N. Lat.; 74.04° W. Long.

Population: 439 (2000); Race: 60.4% White, 17.6% Black, 0.0% Asian, 20.4% Hispanic of any race (2000); Density: 466.5 persons per square mile (2000); Age: 12.9% under 18, 0.0% over 64 (2000); Marriage status: 56.3% never married, 34.8% now married, 0.0% widowed, 8.8% divorced (2000); Foreign born: 8.4% (2000); Ancestry (includes multiple ancestries): 38.7% Other groups, 22.4% Irish, 18.4% German, 14.0% English, 11.6% French (except Basque) (2000).

Economy: Employment by occupation: 14.9% management, 14.9% professional, 32.8% services, 11.9% sales, 0.0% farming, 7.5% construction, 17.9% production (2000).

Income: Per capita income: $19,104 (2000); Median household income: $87,669 (2000); Poverty rate: 0.0% (2000).

Education: Percent of population age 25 and over with: High school diploma (including GED) or higher: 85.0% (2000); Bachelor's degree or higher: 35.6% (2000).

Housing: Homeownership rate: 12.5% (2000); Median home value: $225,000 (2000); Median rent: $1,075 per month (2000); Median age of housing: 60+ years (2000).

Hospitals: Patterson Army Health Clinic

Transportation: Commute to work: 57.2% car, 2.5% public transportation, 34.8% walk, 5.5% work from home (2000); Travel time to work: 85.0% less than 15 minutes, 9.4% 15 to 30 minutes, 2.3% 30 to 45 minutes, 3.3% 45 to 60 minutes, 0.0% 60 minutes or more (2000)

FREEHOLD (borough). Covers a land area of 1.995 square miles and a water area of 0 square miles. Located at 40.26° N. Lat.; 74.27° W. Long. Elevation is 178 feet.

History: Named for the freeholders, or landowners, who established the county. Settled c.1650, called Monmouth Courthouse (1715-1801). Incorporated as a town 1869, as a borough 1919. The Revolutionary War battle of Monmouth took place here in 1778, notable in part because of Mary Ludwig, alias Molly Pitcher. Women who would carry water to the soldiers during battle were given the name Molly Pitcher. While Mary Ludwig was performing this task, her husband, a soldier, was overcome by the heat. Mary took his place in the battle and was later rewarded with a soldier's pension.

Population: 10,742 (1990); 10,976 (2000); 11,547 (2005); 12,133 (2010 projected); Race: 70.1% White, 14.7% Black, 2.6% Asian, 36.1% Hispanic of any race (2005); Density: 5,787.3 persons per square mile (2005); Average household size: 3.00 (2005); Median age: 34.5 (2005); Males per 100 females: 106.8 (2005); Marriage status: 34.1% never married, 49.8% now married, 6.9% widowed, 9.2% divorced (2000); Foreign born: 20.6% (2000); Ancestry (includes multiple ancestries): 41.2% Other groups, 17.2% Irish, 10.7% Italian, 8.8% German, 6.5% English (2000).

Economy: A farm trade center, with some diversified industry, including telecommunications equipment. Site of Freehold Raceway, thoroughbred horse racetrack. Single-family building permits issued: 21 (2005); Multi-family building permits issued: 0 (2005); Employment by occupation: 11.9% management, 14.1% professional, 25.3% services, 25.4% sales, 0.7% farming, 10.0% construction, 12.6% production (2000).

Income: Per capita income: $22,233 (2005); Median household income: $54,940 (2005); Average household income: $66,099 (2005); Percent of households with income of $100,000 or more: 17.6% (2005); Poverty rate: 12.0% (2000).

Education: Percent of population age 25 and over with: High school diploma (including GED) or higher: 75.6% (2005); Bachelor's degree or higher: 19.4% (2005); Master's degree or higher: 4.6% (2005).

School District(s)

Freehold Borough (PK-08)
   2003-04 Enrollment: 1,465 . . . . (732) 761-2102
Freehold Regional (09-12)
   2003-04 Enrollment: 10,935 . . . . (732) 792-7300
Freehold Township (PK-08)
   2003-04 Enrollment: 4,787 . . . . (732) 462-8400
Howell Township (PK-08)
   2003-04 Enrollment: 7,648 . . . . (732) 751-2480
Monmouth County Vocational (09-12)
   2003-04 Enrollment: 1,856 . . . . (732) 431-7942

Housing: Homeownership rate: 59.8% (2005); Median home value: $226,559 (2005); Median rent: $707 per month (2000); Median age of housing: 45 years (2000).

Hospitals: CentraState Medical Health Care System (241 beds)

Safety: Violent crime rate: 47.6 per 10,000 population; Property crime rate: 272.0 per 10,000 population (2004).

Newspapers: Atlanticville (General - Circulation 20,000); News Transcript (General - Circulation 40,000); North/South Brunswick Sentinel (General - Circulation 23,000); Sentinel (General - Circulation 18,000); Suburban (General - Circulation 25,572); The Examiner (General - Circulation 5,000); The Hub (General - Circulation 20,000); The Independent (General - Circulation 35,026); Tri-Town News (General - Circulation 36,000)

Transportation: Commute to work: 80.3% car, 10.0% public transportation, 5.0% walk, 2.1% work from home (2000); Travel time to work: 34.5% less than 15 minutes, 27.7% 15 to 30 minutes, 14.5% 30 to 45 minutes, 10.2% 45 to 60 minutes, 13.1% 60 minutes or more (2000)

Additional Information Contacts

Western Monmouth Chamber of Commerce . . . . (732) 462-3030
   http://www.wmchamber.com

FREEHOLD (township). Covers a land area of 38.451 square miles and a water area of 0.079 square miles. Located at 40.24° N. Lat.; 74.27° W. Long. Elevation is 178 feet.

History: An early settlement in the Freehold district was made about 1650. A permanent village was established in 1715 by Scots from New Aberdeen, who had earlier left England because of persecution by Charles II. They chose the name of Monmouth Court House from Monmouthshire in England. The name was changed to Freehold in 1801 by the postal authorities to avoid confusion with other Monmouths in the county.

Population: 24,710 (1990); 31,537 (2000); 34,314 (2005); 36,963 (2010 projected); Race: 86.1% White, 5.2% Black, 5.6% Asian, 6.1% Hispanic of any race (2005); Density: 892.4 persons per square mile (2005); Average household size: 2.89 (2005); Median age: 39.4 (2005); Males per 100 females: 98.0 (2005); Marriage status: 20.2% never married, 65.6% now married, 7.5% widowed, 6.8% divorced (2000); Foreign born: 11.2% (2000); Ancestry (includes multiple ancestries): 26.1% Italian, 18.2% Irish, 17.0% Other groups, 12.9% German, 10.2% Polish (2000).

Economy: Unemployment rate: 3.2% (2005); Total civilian labor force: 17,800 (2005); Single-family building permits issued: 26 (2005); Multi-family building permits issued: 305 (2005); Employment by occupation: 20.4% management, 25.4% professional, 9.2% services, 32.2% sales, 0.2% farming, 6.6% construction, 6.0% production (2000).

Income: Per capita income: $38,034 (2005); Median household income: $89,547 (2005); Average household income: $108,833 (2005); Percent of households with income of $100,000 or more: 43.6% (2005); Poverty rate: 3.9% (2000).

Taxes: Total city taxes per capita: $373 (2004); City property taxes per capita: $343 (2004).

Education: Percent of population age 25 and over with: High school diploma (including GED) or higher: 88.7% (2005); Bachelor's degree or higher: 37.5% (2005); Master's degree or higher: 13.0% (2005).

School District(s)

Freehold Borough (PK-08)
   2003-04 Enrollment: 1,465 . . . . (732) 761-2102
Freehold Regional (09-12)
   2003-04 Enrollment: 10,935 . . . . (732) 792-7300

Freehold Township (PK-08)
2003-04 Enrollment: 4,787 . . . . (732) 462-8400
Howell Township (PK-08)
2003-04 Enrollment: 7,648 . . . . (732) 751-2480
Monmouth County Vocational (09-12)
2003-04 Enrollment: 1,856 . . . . (732) 431-7942
Housing: Homeownership rate: 87.1% (2005); Median home value: $356,165 (2005); Median rent: $809 per month (2000); Median age of housing: 19 years (2000).
Hospitals: CentraState Medical Health Care System (241 beds)
Safety: Violent crime rate: 13.0 per 10,000 population; Property crime rate: 287.9 per 10,000 population (2004).
Newspapers: Atlanticville (General - Circulation 20,000); News Transcript (General - Circulation 40,000); North/South Brunswick Sentinel (General - Circulation 23,000); Sentinel (General - Circulation 18,000); Suburban (General - Circulation 25,572); The Examiner (General - Circulation 5,000); The Hub (General - Circulation 20,000); The Independent (General - Circulation 35,026); Tri-Town News (General - Circulation 36,000)
Transportation: Commute to work: 86.2% car, 8.1% public transportation, 0.7% walk, 4.5% work from home (2000); Travel time to work: 23.5% less than 15 minutes, 22.8% 15 to 30 minutes, 16.3% 30 to 45 minutes, 11.9% 45 to 60 minutes, 25.4% 60 minutes or more (2000)
Additional Information Contacts
Freehold Township . . . . (732) 294-2000
http://www.twp.freehold.nj.us
Western Monmouth Chamber of Commerce . . . . (732) 462-3030
http://www.wmchamber.com

HAZLET (township). Covers a land area of 5.622 square miles and a water area of 0.040 square miles. Located at 40.42° N. Lat.; 74.17° W. Long. Elevation is 60 feet.
History: Incorporated 1848.
Population: 21,976 (1990); 21,378 (2000); 21,341 (2005); 21,419 (2010 projected); Race: 92.7% White, 1.2% Black, 3.4% Asian, 7.0% Hispanic of any race (2005); Density: 3,795.7 persons per square mile (2005); Average household size: 2.90 (2005); Median age: 39.6 (2005); Males per 100 females: 92.3 (2005); Marriage status: 22.8% never married, 64.2% now married, 6.9% widowed, 6.1% divorced (2000); Foreign born: 7.8% (2000); Ancestry (includes multiple ancestries): 32.9% Irish, 32.9% Italian, 14.7% German, 11.1% Other groups, 7.7% Polish (2000).
Economy: Major industry is flavors and fragrance company. Single-family building permits issued: 25 (2005); Multi-family building permits issued: 0 (2005); Employment by occupation: 15.3% management, 18.1% professional, 12.9% services, 31.8% sales, 0.2% farming, 10.6% construction, 11.1% production (2000).
Income: Per capita income: $29,243 (2005); Median household income: $73,766 (2005); Average household income: $84,281 (2005); Percent of households with income of $100,000 or more: 29.5% (2005); Poverty rate: 3.4% (2000).
Education: Percent of population age 25 and over with: High school diploma (including GED) or higher: 83.8% (2005); Bachelor's degree or higher: 19.1% (2005); Master's degree or higher: 6.0% (2005).
School District(s)
Hazlet Township (PK-12)
2003-04 Enrollment: 3,561 . . . . (732) 264-8402
Housing: Homeownership rate: 90.0% (2005); Median home value: $280,785 (2005); Median rent: $394 per month (2000); Median age of housing: 36 years (2000).
Safety: Violent crime rate: 3.7 per 10,000 population; Property crime rate: 122.0 per 10,000 population (2004).
Transportation: Commute to work: 84.2% car, 13.1% public transportation, 0.9% walk, 1.3% work from home (2000); Travel time to work: 26.1% less than 15 minutes, 20.0% 15 to 30 minutes, 19.2% 30 to 45 minutes, 9.6% 45 to 60 minutes, 25.1% 60 minutes or more (2000)

HIGHLANDS (borough). Covers a land area of 0.762 square miles and a water area of 0.561 square miles. Located at 40.40° N. Lat.; 73.98° W. Long. Elevation is 10 feet.
History: Settled before 1675, incorporated 1887.
Population: 4,802 (1990); 5,097 (2000); 5,172 (2005); 5,286 (2010 projected); Race: 94.4% White, 1.9% Black, 1.1% Asian, 5.0% Hispanic of any race (2005); Density: 6,787.6 persons per square mile (2005); Average household size: 2.05 (2005); Median age: 40.7 (2005); Males per 100 females: 99.8 (2005); Marriage status: 31.5% never married, 42.2% now married, 6.8% widowed, 19.5% divorced (2000); Foreign born: 6.0%

(2000); Ancestry (includes multiple ancestries): 33.7% Irish, 19.5% Italian, 16.8% German, 8.9% Other groups, 8.2% Polish (2000).
Economy: Residential. Part of Gateway National Recreation Area just Northeast. Single-family building permits issued: 11 (2005); Multi-family building permits issued: 0 (2005); Employment by occupation: 13.0% management, 21.9% professional, 16.6% services, 28.2% sales, 0.8% farming, 10.7% construction, 8.8% production (2000).
Income: Per capita income: $34,819 (2005); Median household income: $55,255 (2005); Average household income: $70,640 (2005); Percent of households with income of $100,000 or more: 19.9% (2005); Poverty rate: 12.3% (2000).
Education: Percent of population age 25 and over with: High school diploma (including GED) or higher: 87.8% (2005); Bachelor's degree or higher: 25.2% (2005); Master's degree or higher: 8.9% (2005).
School District(s)
Henry Hudson Regional (07-12)
2003-04 Enrollment: 483 . . . . (732) 872-0900
Highlands Borough (PK-06)
2003-04 Enrollment: 312 . . . . (732) 872-1476
Housing: Homeownership rate: 54.5% (2005); Median home value: $221,759 (2005); Median rent: $654 per month (2000); Median age of housing: 38 years (2000).
Safety: Violent crime rate: 22.2 per 10,000 population; Property crime rate: 162.8 per 10,000 population (2004).
Transportation: Commute to work: 82.4% car, 8.5% public transportation, 5.3% walk, 3.3% work from home (2000); Travel time to work: 19.8% less than 15 minutes, 25.5% 15 to 30 minutes, 20.9% 30 to 45 minutes, 11.8% 45 to 60 minutes, 22.0% 60 minutes or more (2000)

HOLMDEL (township). Covers a land area of 17.965 square miles and a water area of 0.121 square miles. Located at 40.38° N. Lat.; 74.17° W. Long. Elevation is 100 feet.
Population: 11,532 (1990); 15,781 (2000); 17,252 (2005); 18,672 (2010 projected); Race: 77.3% White, 0.7% Black, 20.0% Asian, 2.7% Hispanic of any race (2005); Density: 960.3 persons per square mile (2005); Average household size: 3.14 (2005); Median age: 41.8 (2005); Males per 100 females: 91.8 (2005); Marriage status: 19.6% never married, 69.6% now married, 6.4% widowed, 4.3% divorced (2000); Foreign born: 18.8% (2000); Ancestry (includes multiple ancestries): 28.0% Italian, 23.8% Other groups, 16.7% Irish, 12.0% German, 5.6% Polish (2000).
Economy: AT&T Bell Laboratories here. Single-family building permits issued: 24 (2005); Multi-family building permits issued: 0 (2005); Employment by occupation: 28.7% management, 35.5% professional, 5.6% services, 22.5% sales, 0.0% farming, 4.0% construction, 3.7% production (2000).
Income: Per capita income: $54,650 (2005); Median household income: $124,910 (2005); Average household income: $170,451 (2005); Percent of households with income of $100,000 or more: 60.0% (2005); Poverty rate: 3.4% (2000).
Education: Percent of population age 25 and over with: High school diploma (including GED) or higher: 91.0% (2005); Bachelor's degree or higher: 54.4% (2005); Master's degree or higher: 28.0% (2005).
School District(s)
Holmdel Township (PK-12)
2003-04 Enrollment: 3,617 . . . . (732) 946-1800
Housing: Homeownership rate: 94.5% (2005); Median home value: $636,117 (2005); Median rent: $1,317 per month (2000); Median age of housing: 17 years (2000).
Hospitals: Bayshore Community Hospital (225 beds)
Safety: Violent crime rate: 7.7 per 10,000 population; Property crime rate: 132.3 per 10,000 population (2004).
Transportation: Commute to work: 81.2% car, 13.1% public transportation, 1.4% walk, 3.8% work from home (2000); Travel time to work: 27.4% less than 15 minutes, 26.8% 15 to 30 minutes, 13.4% 30 to 45 minutes, 6.5% 45 to 60 minutes, 25.9% 60 minutes or more (2000)
Additional Information Contacts
Holmdel Township Chamber of Commerce . . . . (732) 946-3239
http://www.holmdeltownship.com

HOWELL (township). Covers a land area of 60.913 square miles and a water area of 0.095 square miles. Located at 40.16° N. Lat.; 74.20° W. Long.
History: Incorporated 1801.
Population: 38,987 (1990); 48,903 (2000); 50,595 (2005); 52,332 (2010 projected); Race: 89.3% White, 3.7% Black, 3.7% Asian, 6.0% Hispanic of

any race (2005); Density: 830.6 persons per square mile (2005); Average household size: 3.04 (2005); Median age: 36.7 (2005); Males per 100 females: 95.5 (2005); Marriage status: 21.6% never married, 66.3% now married, 6.3% widowed, 5.8% divorced (2000); Foreign born: 8.9% (2000); Ancestry (includes multiple ancestries): 30.7% Italian, 24.2% Irish, 16.5% German, 14.6% Other groups, 9.9% Polish (2000).

Economy: Light industry. Unemployment rate: 3.6% (2005); Total civilian labor force: 26,350 (2005); Single-family building permits issued: 250 (2005); Multi-family building permits issued: 0 (2005); Employment by occupation: 17.1% management, 21.3% professional, 12.6% services, 30.8% sales, 0.3% farming, 8.4% construction, 9.5% production (2000).

Income: Per capita income: $30,950 (2005); Median household income: $78,934 (2005); Average household income: $93,944 (2005); Percent of households with income of $100,000 or more: 35.5% (2005); Poverty rate: 4.2% (2000).

Taxes: Total city taxes per capita: $347 (2004); City property taxes per capita: $300 (2004).

Education: Percent of population age 25 and over with: High school diploma (including GED) or higher: 88.1% (2005); Bachelor's degree or higher: 28.9% (2005); Master's degree or higher: 8.8% (2005).

School District(s)

Howell Township (PK-08)
  2003-04 Enrollment: 7,648 . . . . (732) 751-2480

Housing: Homeownership rate: 89.1% (2005); Median home value: $284,518 (2005); Median rent: $643 per month (2000); Median age of housing: 18 years (2000).

Safety: Violent crime rate: 10.1 per 10,000 population; Property crime rate: 122.8 per 10,000 population (2004).

Transportation: Commute to work: 90.2% car, 5.6% public transportation, 0.8% walk, 2.6% work from home (2000); Travel time to work: 17.4% less than 15 minutes, 30.3% 15 to 30 minutes, 18.5% 30 to 45 minutes, 9.7% 45 to 60 minutes, 24.1% 60 minutes or more (2000)

Additional Information Contacts

Howell Chamber of Commerce . . . . (732) 363-4114
  http://howellchamber.com

Howell Township . . . . (732) 938-4500
  http://www.twp.howell.nj.us

INTERLAKEN (borough). Covers a land area of 0.352 square miles and a water area of 0.043 square miles. Located at 40.23° N. Lat.; 74.01° W. Long. Elevation is 21 feet.

Population: 910 (1990); 900 (2000); 899 (2005); 906 (2010 projected); Race: 98.4% White, 0.0% Black, 0.2% Asian, 1.2% Hispanic of any race (2005); Density: 2,553.4 persons per square mile (2005); Average household size: 2.29 (2005); Median age: 49.5 (2005); Males per 100 females: 92.1 (2005); Marriage status: 19.0% never married, 63.8% now married, 9.4% widowed, 7.7% divorced (2000); Foreign born: 4.3% (2000); Ancestry (includes multiple ancestries): 30.0% Irish, 29.2% Italian, 15.4% German, 13.1% English, 7.8% Polish (2000).

Economy: Single-family building permits issued: 0 (2005); Multi-family building permits issued: 0 (2005); Employment by occupation: 23.1% management, 31.5% professional, 8.0% services, 27.9% sales, 0.0% farming, 5.1% construction, 4.4% production (2000).

Income: Per capita income: $57,492 (2005); Median household income: $98,611 (2005); Average household income: $131,514 (2005); Percent of households with income of $100,000 or more: 49.4% (2005); Poverty rate: 3.0% (2000).

Education: Percent of population age 25 and over with: High school diploma (including GED) or higher: 97.8% (2005); Bachelor's degree or higher: 53.4% (2005); Master's degree or higher: 21.7% (2005).

Housing: Homeownership rate: 95.7% (2005); Median home value: $474,167 (2005); Median rent: $1,071 per month (2000); Median age of housing: 60+ years (2000).

Safety: Violent crime rate: 0.0 per 10,000 population; Property crime rate: 143.8 per 10,000 population (2004).

Transportation: Commute to work: 85.0% car, 9.6% public transportation, 0.0% walk, 5.0% work from home (2000); Travel time to work: 29.3% less than 15 minutes, 30.0% 15 to 30 minutes, 14.6% 30 to 45 minutes, 5.5% 45 to 60 minutes, 20.6% 60 minutes or more (2000)

KEANSBURG (borough). Covers a land area of 1.078 square miles and a water area of 15.749 square miles. Located at 40.44° N. Lat.; 74.13° W. Long. Elevation is 13 feet.

History: Named for John Kean, a United States senator. Incorporated 1917.

Population: 11,079 (1990); 10,732 (2000); 10,574 (2005); 10,471 (2010 projected); Race: 92.2% White, 2.6% Black, 1.5% Asian, 9.4% Hispanic of any race (2005); Density: 9,807.8 persons per square mile (2005); Average household size: 2.71 (2005); Median age: 35.6 (2005); Males per 100 females: 96.1 (2005); Marriage status: 31.0% never married, 48.3% now married, 10.1% widowed, 10.6% divorced (2000); Foreign born: 7.3% (2000); Ancestry (includes multiple ancestries): 34.6% Irish, 23.5% Italian, 17.2% German, 13.7% Other groups, 6.4% Polish (2000).

Economy: Resort borough. Fishing. Single-family building permits issued: 7 (2005); Multi-family building permits issued: 14 (2005); Employment by occupation: 9.2% management, 11.7% professional, 16.9% services, 30.6% sales, 0.3% farming, 14.2% construction, 17.0% production (2000).

Income: Per capita income: $19,502 (2005); Median household income: $39,476 (2005); Average household income: $51,648 (2005); Percent of households with income of $100,000 or more: 12.2% (2005); Poverty rate: 17.7% (2000).

Education: Percent of population age 25 and over with: High school diploma (including GED) or higher: 69.8% (2005); Bachelor's degree or higher: 9.4% (2005); Master's degree or higher: 2.8% (2005).

School District(s)

Keansburg Borough (PK-12)
  2003-04 Enrollment: 2,194 . . . . (732) 787-7578

Housing: Homeownership rate: 53.1% (2005); Median home value: $172,715 (2005); Median rent: $639 per month (2000); Median age of housing: 45 years (2000).

Safety: Violent crime rate: 50.8 per 10,000 population; Property crime rate: 273.5 per 10,000 population (2004).

Transportation: Commute to work: 90.1% car, 5.5% public transportation, 2.7% walk, 1.3% work from home (2000); Travel time to work: 30.3% less than 15 minutes, 22.9% 15 to 30 minutes, 22.6% 30 to 45 minutes, 11.2% 45 to 60 minutes, 13.0% 60 minutes or more (2000)

KEYPORT (borough). Covers a land area of 1.412 square miles and a water area of 0.010 square miles. Located at 40.43° N. Lat.; 74.20° W. Long. Elevation is 36 feet.

History: Settled before 1700, incorporated 1908.

Population: 7,586 (1990); 7,568 (2000); 7,512 (2005); 7,506 (2010 projected); Race: 84.5% White, 6.5% Black, 2.8% Asian, 12.6% Hispanic of any race (2005); Density: 5,318.7 persons per square mile (2005); Average household size: 2.28 (2005); Median age: 39.8 (2005); Males per 100 females: 93.9 (2005); Marriage status: 27.2% never married, 49.6% now married, 12.0% widowed, 11.2% divorced (2000); Foreign born: 10.8% (2000); Ancestry (includes multiple ancestries): 26.8% Irish, 20.8% Italian, 18.8% Other groups, 16.0% German, 9.6% Polish (2000).

Economy: Resort and fishing center with harbor on Raritan Bay. Manufacturing: rubber goods, clothing. Single-family building permits issued: 15 (2005); Multi-family building permits issued: 0 (2005); Employment by occupation: 15.0% management, 17.5% professional, 16.5% services, 31.0% sales, 0.3% farming, 8.3% construction, 11.4% production (2000).

Income: Per capita income: $28,591 (2005); Median household income: $51,713 (2005); Average household income: $64,857 (2005); Percent of households with income of $100,000 or more: 18.7% (2005); Poverty rate: 7.8% (2000).

Taxes: Total city taxes per capita: $518 (2004); City property taxes per capita: $492 (2004).

Education: Percent of population age 25 and over with: High school diploma (including GED) or higher: 82.9% (2005); Bachelor's degree or higher: 15.9% (2005); Master's degree or higher: 6.6% (2005).

School District(s)

Keyport Borough (PK-12)
  2003-04 Enrollment: 1,448 . . . . (732) 264-2840

Housing: Homeownership rate: 50.0% (2005); Median home value: $243,625 (2005); Median rent: $629 per month (2000); Median age of housing: 46 years (2000).

Safety: Violent crime rate: 17.2 per 10,000 population; Property crime rate: 161.4 per 10,000 population (2004).

Transportation: Commute to work: 83.1% car, 8.4% public transportation, 4.3% walk, 2.5% work from home (2000); Travel time to work: 30.2% less than 15 minutes, 28.2% 15 to 30 minutes, 17.7% 30 to 45 minutes, 6.3% 45 to 60 minutes, 17.7% 60 minutes or more (2000)

Additional Information Contacts

Keyport Chamber of Commerce . . . . (732) 264-3626
  http://www.northernmonmouth.com

LEONARDO (CDP). Covers a land area of 0.624 square miles and a water area of 0.010 square miles. Located at 40.41° N. Lat.; 74.06° W. Long. Elevation is 20 feet.

Population: 3,788 (1990); 2,823 (2000); 2,730 (2005); 2,660 (2010 projected); Race: 97.5% White, 0.4% Black, 0.5% Asian, 5.3% Hispanic of any race (2005); Density: 4,374.1 persons per square mile (2005); Average household size: 2.80 (2005); Median age: 38.2 (2005); Males per 100 females: 100.6 (2005); Marriage status: 30.9% never married, 53.9% now married, 4.7% widowed, 10.4% divorced (2000); Foreign born: 1.9% (2000); Ancestry (includes multiple ancestries): 35.2% Irish, 28.1% Italian, 22.0% German, 12.2% English, 7.7% Other groups (2000).

Economy: Employment by occupation: 9.2% management, 20.0% professional, 18.2% services, 31.7% sales, 0.0% farming, 12.4% construction, 8.4% production (2000).

Income: Per capita income: $28,346 (2005); Median household income: $71,330 (2005); Average household income: $79,369 (2005); Percent of households with income of $100,000 or more: 28.6% (2005); Poverty rate: 4.1% (2000).

Education: Percent of population age 25 and over with: High school diploma (including GED) or higher: 88.9% (2005); Bachelor's degree or higher: 16.8% (2005); Master's degree or higher: 2.8% (2005).

School District(s)
Bayshore Jointure Comm (UG-UG)
    2003-04 Enrollment: 68 . . . . (732) 708-9215
Middletown Township (PK-12)
    2003-04 Enrollment: 10,777 . . . . (732) 706-6002

Housing: Homeownership rate: 85.8% (2005); Median home value: $260,631 (2005); Median rent: $727 per month (2000); Median age of housing: 52 years (2000).

Transportation: Commute to work: 88.8% car, 5.7% public transportation, 3.0% walk, 2.6% work from home (2000); Travel time to work: 15.2% less than 15 minutes, 34.5% 15 to 30 minutes, 16.7% 30 to 45 minutes, 16.0% 45 to 60 minutes, 17.6% 60 minutes or more (2000)

LINCROFT (CDP). Covers a land area of 5.620 square miles and a water area of 0.183 square miles. Located at 40.33° N. Lat.; 74.12° W. Long. Elevation is 66 feet.

Population: 6,214 (1990); 6,255 (2000); 6,337 (2005); 6,458 (2010 projected); Race: 93.2% White, 0.7% Black, 4.3% Asian, 2.8% Hispanic of any race (2005); Density: 1,127.6 persons per square mile (2005); Average household size: 2.90 (2005); Median age: 41.2 (2005); Males per 100 females: 98.0 (2005); Marriage status: 19.9% never married, 70.1% now married, 7.4% widowed, 2.5% divorced (2000); Foreign born: 8.1% (2000); Ancestry (includes multiple ancestries): 31.1% Irish, 30.7% Italian, 14.3% German, 10.6% Other groups, 10.1% Polish (2000).

Economy: Employment by occupation: 25.1% management, 28.8% professional, 8.2% services, 28.8% sales, 0.0% farming, 4.0% construction, 5.2% production (2000).

Income: Per capita income: $44,733 (2005); Median household income: $105,009 (2005); Average household income: $129,320 (2005); Percent of households with income of $100,000 or more: 52.6% (2005); Poverty rate: 5.6% (2000).

Education: Percent of population age 25 and over with: High school diploma (including GED) or higher: 92.2% (2005); Bachelor's degree or higher: 49.2% (2005); Master's degree or higher: 21.3% (2005).

School District(s)
Middletown Township (PK-12)
    2003-04 Enrollment: 10,777 . . . . (732) 706-6002
Monmouth County Vocational (09-12)
    2003-04 Enrollment: 1,856 . . . . (732) 431-7942

Two-year College(s)
Brookdale Community College (Public)
    Fall 2004 Enrollment: 13,083. (732) 224-2345
    2005-06 Tuition: In-state $4,866; Out-of-state $5,862

Housing: Homeownership rate: 86.2% (2005); Median home value: $501,596 (2005); Median rent: $386 per month (2000); Median age of housing: 32 years (2000).

Transportation: Commute to work: 85.4% car, 8.9% public transportation, 1.3% walk, 3.9% work from home (2000); Travel time to work: 24.1% less than 15 minutes, 32.2% 15 to 30 minutes, 13.2% 30 to 45 minutes, 9.6% 45 to 60 minutes, 21.0% 60 minutes or more (2000)

LITTLE SILVER (borough). Covers a land area of 2.772 square miles and a water area of 0.603 square miles. Located at 40.33° N. Lat.; 74.04° W. Long. Elevation is 38 feet.

History: Fort Monmouth nearby. Incorporated 1923.

Population: 5,721 (1990); 6,170 (2000); 6,112 (2005); 6,093 (2010 projected); Race: 96.9% White, 0.3% Black, 1.7% Asian, 1.4% Hispanic of any race (2005); Density: 2,205.3 persons per square mile (2005); Average household size: 2.73 (2005); Median age: 42.2 (2005); Males per 100 females: 93.7 (2005); Marriage status: 17.2% never married, 71.3% now married, 6.3% widowed, 5.1% divorced (2000); Foreign born: 5.8% (2000); Ancestry (includes multiple ancestries): 31.2% Irish, 26.3% Italian, 19.8% German, 13.1% English, 4.5% Other groups (2000).

Economy: Single-family building permits issued: 23 (2005); Multi-family building permits issued: 0 (2005); Employment by occupation: 26.7% management, 32.6% professional, 5.8% services, 28.4% sales, 0.2% farming, 4.4% construction, 1.9% production (2000).

Income: Per capita income: $55,159 (2005); Median household income: $111,158 (2005); Average household income: $150,573 (2005); Percent of households with income of $100,000 or more: 55.3% (2005); Poverty rate: 0.8% (2000).

Taxes: Total city taxes per capita: $970 (2004); City property taxes per capita: $966 (2004).

Education: Percent of population age 25 and over with: High school diploma (including GED) or higher: 96.9% (2005); Bachelor's degree or higher: 60.5% (2005); Master's degree or higher: 22.1% (2005).

School District(s)
Little Silver Borough (PK-08)
    2003-04 Enrollment: 839 . . . . (732) 741-2188
Red Bank Regional (09-12)
    2003-04 Enrollment: 1,346 . . . . (908) 842-7884

Housing: Homeownership rate: 96.5% (2005); Median home value: $542,391 (2005); Median rent: $1,125 per month (2000); Median age of housing: 45 years (2000).

Safety: Violent crime rate: 3.2 per 10,000 population; Property crime rate: 154.1 per 10,000 population (2004).

Transportation: Commute to work: 77.2% car, 15.4% public transportation, 0.8% walk, 6.3% work from home (2000); Travel time to work: 39.2% less than 15 minutes, 21.5% 15 to 30 minutes, 8.6% 30 to 45 minutes, 3.8% 45 to 60 minutes, 26.9% 60 minutes or more (2000)

LOCH ARBOUR (village). Covers a land area of 0.097 square miles and a water area of 0.038 square miles. Located at 40.23° N. Lat.; 74.00° W. Long. Elevation is 24 feet.

Population: 380 (1990); 280 (2000); 265 (2005); 261 (2010 projected); Race: 93.2% White, 2.6% Black, 1.1% Asian, 0.8% Hispanic of any race (2005); Density: 2,739.0 persons per square mile (2005); Average household size: 2.28 (2005); Median age: 44.0 (2005); Males per 100 females: 107.0 (2005); Marriage status: 29.6% never married, 48.9% now married, 5.2% widowed, 16.3% divorced (2000); Foreign born: 0.7% (2000); Ancestry (includes multiple ancestries): 39.3% Irish, 22.5% Italian, 17.8% German, 11.3% English, 9.5% Other groups (2000).

Economy: Single-family building permits issued: 1 (2005); Multi-family building permits issued: 0 (2005); Employment by occupation: 20.7% management, 38.7% professional, 6.7% services, 22.7% sales, 0.0% farming, 8.0% construction, 3.3% production (2000).

Income: Per capita income: $43,821 (2005); Median household income: $80,000 (2005); Average household income: $100,108 (2005); Percent of households with income of $100,000 or more: 32.8% (2005); Poverty rate: 4.8% (2000).

Education: Percent of population age 25 and over with: High school diploma (including GED) or higher: 100.0% (2005); Bachelor's degree or higher: 49.7% (2005); Master's degree or higher: 20.1% (2005).

Housing: Homeownership rate: 74.1% (2005); Median home value: $550,000 (2005); Median rent: $705 per month (2000); Median age of housing: 60+ years (2000).

Safety: Violent crime rate: 0.0 per 10,000 population; Property crime rate: 324.9 per 10,000 population (2004).

Transportation: Commute to work: 79.1% car, 7.4% public transportation, 8.8% walk, 4.7% work from home (2000); Travel time to work: 43.3% less than 15 minutes, 20.6% 15 to 30 minutes, 12.1% 30 to 45 minutes, 5.0% 45 to 60 minutes, 19.1% 60 minutes or more (2000)

LONG BRANCH (city). Covers a land area of 5.216 square miles and a water area of 0.973 square miles. Located at 40.29° N. Lat.; 73.99° W. Long. Elevation is 19 feet.

History: Named for the longest branch of the Shrewsbury River, which runs through the town. Presidents Grant, Hayes, Garfield, and Arthur summered here, and President Wilson's summer house, now part of Monmouth College, was at West Long Branch. President Garfield died in Long Branch in 1881. Historical museum. Settled 1740. Incorporated 1904.

Population: 28,658 (1990); 31,340 (2000); 31,681 (2005); 32,189 (2010 projected); Race: 66.7% White, 18.2% Black, 1.7% Asian, 24.4% Hispanic of any race (2005); Density: 6,073.9 persons per square mile (2005); Average household size: 2.50 (2005); Median age: 36.2 (2005); Males per 100 females: 95.0 (2005); Marriage status: 35.9% never married, 46.4% now married, 6.4% widowed, 11.2% divorced (2000); Foreign born: 19.7% (2000); Ancestry (includes multiple ancestries): 36.9% Other groups, 17.5% Italian, 11.2% Irish, 6.6% German, 4.1% English (2000).

Economy: Manufacturing: apparel, cabinetmaking, electronic products. Art center. Monmouth Park Racetrack nearby. Unemployment rate: 5.2% (2005); Total civilian labor force: 15,648 (2005); Single-family building permits issued: 7 (2005); Multi-family building permits issued: 0 (2005); Employment by occupation: 10.1% management, 18.5% professional, 20.5% services, 28.2% sales, 0.2% farming, 10.5% construction, 12.1% production (2000).

Income: Per capita income: $22,854 (2005); Median household income: $42,816 (2005); Average household income: $56,663 (2005); Percent of households with income of $100,000 or more: 13.5% (2005); Poverty rate: 16.7% (2000).

Taxes: Total city taxes per capita: $758 (2004); City property taxes per capita: $725 (2004).

Education: Percent of population age 25 and over with: High school diploma (including GED) or higher: 76.4% (2005); Bachelor's degree or higher: 20.2% (2005); Master's degree or higher: 7.2% (2005).

School District(s)
Long Branch City (PK-12)
   2003-04 Enrollment: 5,264 . . . . (908) 571-2868
Two-year College(s)
Monmouth County Vocational School District (Public)
   Fall 2004 Enrollment: 194 . . . . (732) 431-7944

Housing: Homeownership rate: 42.5% (2005); Median home value: $240,849 (2005); Median rent: $670 per month (2000); Median age of housing: 42 years (2000).

Hospitals: Monmouth Medical Center (526 beds)

Safety: Violent crime rate: 46.3 per 10,000 population; Property crime rate: 232.5 per 10,000 population (2004).

Transportation: Commute to work: 85.1% car, 6.6% public transportation, 4.5% walk, 1.9% work from home (2000); Travel time to work: 31.1% less than 15 minutes, 31.0% 15 to 30 minutes, 17.7% 30 to 45 minutes, 6.0% 45 to 60 minutes, 14.2% 60 minutes or more (2000)

Additional Information Contacts
City of Long Branch . . . . (732) 222-7000
   http://www.longbranch.org/ieindex.html
Long Branch Chamber of Commerce . . . . (732) 222-0400
   http://www.longbranch.org

MANALAPAN (township). Covers a land area of 30.817 square miles and a water area of 0.050 square miles. Located at 40.29° N. Lat.; 74.33° W. Long. Elevation is 160 feet.

History: Incorporated 1848. Former farm community.

Population: 26,731 (1990); 33,423 (2000); 36,308 (2005); 39,023 (2010 projected); Race: 91.4% White, 1.7% Black, 5.0% Asian, 4.1% Hispanic of any race (2005); Density: 1,178.2 persons per square mile (2005); Average household size: 3.10 (2005); Median age: 38.5 (2005); Males per 100 females: 92.9 (2005); Marriage status: 20.3% never married, 69.1% now married, 6.9% widowed, 3.7% divorced (2000); Foreign born: 10.4% (2000); Ancestry (includes multiple ancestries): 27.9% Italian, 17.2% Other groups, 13.1% Irish, 11.7% Polish, 10.0% Russian (2000).

Economy: Growing suburb. Unemployment rate: 3.0% (2005); Total civilian labor force: 18,118 (2005); Single-family building permits issued: 289 (2005); Multi-family building permits issued: 0 (2005); Employment by occupation: 21.6% management, 25.4% professional, 8.2% services, 31.9% sales, 0.1% farming, 6.8% construction, 6.0% production (2000).

Income: Per capita income: $40,055 (2005); Median household income: $98,592 (2005); Average household income: $123,764 (2005); Percent of

households with income of $100,000 or more: 49.2% (2005); Poverty rate: 3.8% (2000).

Taxes: Total city taxes per capita: $453 (2004); City property taxes per capita: $429 (2004).

Education: Percent of population age 25 and over with: High school diploma (including GED) or higher: 92.4% (2005); Bachelor's degree or higher: 39.5% (2005); Master's degree or higher: 14.7% (2005).

School District(s)
Manalapan-Englishtown Regional (PK-08)
   2003-04 Enrollment: 5,640 . . . . (732) 446-5506

Housing: Homeownership rate: 94.3% (2005); Median home value: $406,172 (2005); Median rent: $920 per month (2000); Median age of housing: 19 years (2000).

Safety: Violent crime rate: 5.6 per 10,000 population; Property crime rate: 79.1 per 10,000 population (2004).

Transportation: Commute to work: 81.9% car, 13.0% public transportation, 0.7% walk, 3.8% work from home (2000); Travel time to work: 18.7% less than 15 minutes, 21.0% 15 to 30 minutes, 18.0% 30 to 45 minutes, 10.0% 45 to 60 minutes, 32.2% 60 minutes or more (2000)

Additional Information Contacts
Manalapan Township . . . . (732) 446-3200
   http://www.twp.manalapan.nj.us
Western Monmouth Chamber of Commerce . . . . (732) 462-3030
   http://www.wmchamber.com

MANASQUAN (borough). Covers a land area of 1.378 square miles and a water area of 1.153 square miles. Located at 40.11° N. Lat.; 74.04° W. Long. Elevation is 28 feet.

History: Incorporated 1887.

Population: 5,357 (1990); 6,310 (2000); 6,498 (2005); 6,720 (2010 projected); Race: 97.7% White, 0.5% Black, 0.4% Asian, 5.6% Hispanic of any race (2005); Density: 4,716.1 persons per square mile (2005); Average household size: 2.43 (2005); Median age: 40.2 (2005); Males per 100 females: 97.9 (2005); Marriage status: 28.0% never married, 55.6% now married, 8.3% widowed, 8.1% divorced (2000); Foreign born: 4.6% (2000); Ancestry (includes multiple ancestries): 33.2% Irish, 21.9% Italian, 17.2% German, 10.1% English, 6.2% Other groups (2000).

Economy: Fishing; wood millwork. Single-family building permits issued: 56 (2005); Multi-family building permits issued: 0 (2005); Employment by occupation: 13.6% management, 26.1% professional, 14.0% services, 31.0% sales, 0.3% farming, 6.6% construction, 8.4% production (2000).

Income: Per capita income: $39,799 (2005); Median household income: $79,384 (2005); Average household income: $96,679 (2005); Percent of households with income of $100,000 or more: 34.6% (2005); Poverty rate: 3.1% (2000).

Taxes: Total city taxes per capita: $763 (2004); City property taxes per capita: $750 (2004).

Education: Percent of population age 25 and over with: High school diploma (including GED) or higher: 93.1% (2005); Bachelor's degree or higher: 40.1% (2005); Master's degree or higher: 13.0% (2005).

School District(s)
Manasquan Borough (PK-12)
   2003-04 Enrollment: 1,804 . . . . (732) 528-8800

Housing: Homeownership rate: 70.5% (2005); Median home value: $473,543 (2005); Median rent: $729 per month (2000); Median age of housing: 47 years (2000).

Safety: Violent crime rate: 23.2 per 10,000 population; Property crime rate: 221.4 per 10,000 population (2004).

Newspapers: The Coast Star (General - Circulation 13,000)

Transportation: Commute to work: 84.9% car, 4.9% public transportation, 5.1% walk, 3.4% work from home (2000); Travel time to work: 34.0% less than 15 minutes, 20.7% 15 to 30 minutes, 17.9% 30 to 45 minutes, 7.8% 45 to 60 minutes, 19.6% 60 minutes or more (2000)

Additional Information Contacts
Borough of Manasquan . . . . (732) 223-0544
   http://www.manasquan-nj.com/public/default.asp
Manasquan Chamber of Commerce . . . . (732) 223-8303
   http://www.manasquanchamber.com

MARLBORO (township). Covers a land area of 30.594 square miles and a water area of 0 square miles. Located at 40.33° N. Lat.; 74.26° W. Long. Elevation is 173 feet.

Population: 27,974 (1990); 36,398 (2000); 40,010 (2005); 43,433 (2010 projected); Race: 81.0% White, 1.8% Black, 15.6% Asian, 3.4% Hispanic of any race (2005); Density: 1,307.8 persons per square mile (2005); Average

household size: 3.16 (2005); Median age: 38.3 (2005); Males per 100 females: 98.1 (2005); Marriage status: 19.3% never married, 72.9% now married, 5.0% widowed, 2.8% divorced (2000); Foreign born: 15.4% (2000); Ancestry (includes multiple ancestries): 25.0% Other groups, 20.1% Italian, 10.8% Russian, 10.6% Irish, 10.6% Polish (2000).

Economy: In suburbanizing agricultural area. Marlboro State Hospital nearby. Unemployment rate: 2.7% (2005); Total civilian labor force: 20,147 (2005); Single-family building permits issued: 180 (2005); Multi-family building permits issued: 15 (2005); Employment by occupation: 26.5% management, 28.7% professional, 6.3% services, 28.7% sales, 0.0% farming, 4.2% construction, 5.7% production (2000).

Income: Per capita income: $44,428 (2005); Median household income: $116,775 (2005); Average household income: $140,304 (2005); Percent of households with income of $100,000 or more: 58.1% (2005); Poverty rate: 3.5% (2000).

Taxes: Total city taxes per capita: $453 (2004); City property taxes per capita: $433 (2004).

Education: Percent of population age 25 and over with: High school diploma (including GED) or higher: 94.0% (2005); Bachelor's degree or higher: 52.6% (2005); Master's degree or higher: 22.7% (2005).

School District(s)

Freehold Regional (09-12)
  2003-04 Enrollment: 10,935 . . . . (732) 792-7300
Marlboro Township (PK-08)
  2003-04 Enrollment: 6,084 . . . . (732) 972-2015

Housing: Homeownership rate: 96.5% (2005); Median home value: $473,247 (2005); Median rent: $1,127 per month (2000); Median age of housing: 15 years (2000).

Safety: Violent crime rate: 3.8 per 10,000 population; Property crime rate: 98.4 per 10,000 population (2004).

Transportation: Commute to work: 77.8% car, 17.3% public transportation, 0.4% walk, 4.1% work from home (2000); Travel time to work: 17.4% less than 15 minutes, 18.6% 15 to 30 minutes, 16.0% 30 to 45 minutes, 10.5% 45 to 60 minutes, 37.4% 60 minutes or more (2000)

Additional Information Contacts
Marlboro Township . . . . (732) 536-0200
  http://www.marlboro-nj.gov
Western Monmouth Chamber of Commerce . . . . (732) 462-3030
  http://www.wmchamber.com

MATAWAN (borough).
Covers a land area of 2.279 square miles and a water area of 0.116 square miles. Located at 40.41° N. Lat.; 74.23° W. Long. Elevation is 55 feet.

History: Has 18th-century buildings. Called New Aberdeen before 1715, incorporated 1895.

Population: 9,315 (1990); 8,910 (2000); 8,869 (2005); 8,007 (2010 projected); Race: 80.2% White, 6.7% Black, 9.6% Asian, 7.7% Hispanic of any race (2005); Density: 3,891.1 persons per square mile (2005); Average household size: 2.47 (2005); Median age: 38.2 (2005); Males per 100 females: 97.9 (2005); Marriage status: 28.7% never married, 56.6% now married, 5.6% widowed, 9.1% divorced (2000); Foreign born: 14.9% (2000); Ancestry (includes multiple ancestries): 23.9% Irish, 21.2% Italian, 18.0% Other groups, 14.4% German, 8.9% Polish (2000).

Economy: Manufacturing: metal goods, rubber and plastic goods, concrete products.. Single-family building permits issued: 0 (2005); Multi-family building permits issued: 0 (2005); Employment by occupation: 19.5% management, 22.5% professional, 12.7% services, 28.2% sales, 0.0% farming, 8.2% construction, 8.9% production (2000).

Income: Per capita income: $35,012 (2005); Median household income: $72,433 (2005); Average household income: $86,533 (2005); Percent of households with income of $100,000 or more: 31.4% (2005); Poverty rate: 5.4% (2000).

Education: Percent of population age 25 and over with: High school diploma (including GED) or higher: 88.4% (2005); Bachelor's degree or higher: 30.7% (2005); Master's degree or higher: 11.7% (2005).

School District(s)

Matawan-Aberdeen Regional (PK-12)
  2003-04 Enrollment: 3,953 . . . . (732) 290-2705
Old Bridge Township (PK-12)
  2003-04 Enrollment: 10,119 . . . . (732) 290-3976

Housing: Homeownership rate: 58.9% (2005); Median home value: $295,669 (2005); Median rent: $740 per month (2000); Median age of housing: 35 years (2000).

Safety: Violent crime rate: 6.7 per 10,000 population; Property crime rate: 118.6 per 10,000 population (2004).

Transportation: Commute to work: 81.9% car, 13.1% public transportation, 2.9% walk, 1.9% work from home (2000); Travel time to work: 24.2% less than 15 minutes, 26.5% 15 to 30 minutes, 17.7% 30 to 45 minutes, 9.2% 45 to 60 minutes, 22.4% 60 minutes or more (2000)

Additional Information Contacts
Matawan-Aberdeen Chamber of Commerce . . . . (732) 290-1125
  http://www.visitmonmouth.com/tourism/Chambers.asp

MIDDLETOWN (township).
Covers a land area of 41.121 square miles and a water area of 18.226 square miles. Located at 40.39° N. Lat.; 74.09° W. Long. Elevation is 100 feet.

History: Middletown was originally a Baptist settlement, the first Baptist church in the state having been organized here in 1668.

Population: 68,220 (1990); 66,327 (2000); 66,972 (2005); 67,901 (2010 projected); Race: 94.7% White, 1.1% Black, 2.6% Asian, 3.8% Hispanic of any race (2005); Density: 1,628.6 persons per square mile (2005); Average household size: 2.81 (2005); Median age: 39.8 (2005); Males per 100 females: 95.2 (2005); Marriage status: 22.2% never married, 64.7% now married, 7.6% widowed, 5.5% divorced (2000); Foreign born: 6.4% (2000); Ancestry (includes multiple ancestries): 32.8% Irish, 28.9% Italian, 17.4% German, 8.8% English, 8.7% Polish (2000).

Economy: Unemployment rate: 3.2% (2005); Total civilian labor force: 35,764 (2005); Single-family building permits issued: 105 (2005); Multi-family building permits issued: 0 (2005); Employment by occupation: 18.7% management, 23.1% professional, 11.0% services, 30.5% sales, 0.2% farming, 8.2% construction, 8.3% production (2000).

Income: Per capita income: $39,905 (2005); Median household income: $87,584 (2005); Average household income: $112,085 (2005); Percent of households with income of $100,000 or more: 41.9% (2005); Poverty rate: 3.1% (2000).

Taxes: Total city taxes per capita: $594 (2004); City property taxes per capita: $565 (2004).

Education: Percent of population age 25 and over with: High school diploma (including GED) or higher: 90.7% (2005); Bachelor's degree or higher: 34.9% (2005); Master's degree or higher: 12.5% (2005).

School District(s)

Middletown Township (PK-12)
  2003-04 Enrollment: 10,777 . . . . (732) 706-6002

Housing: Homeownership rate: 85.8% (2005); Median home value: $355,781 (2005); Median rent: $738 per month (2000); Median age of housing: 35 years (2000).

Safety: Violent crime rate: 9.6 per 10,000 population; Property crime rate: 104.2 per 10,000 population (2004).

Newspapers: The Courier (General - Circulation 8,000)

Transportation: Commute to work: 84.6% car, 11.5% public transportation, 1.0% walk, 2.6% work from home (2000); Travel time to work: 22.2% less than 15 minutes, 27.0% 15 to 30 minutes, 16.1% 30 to 45 minutes, 10.1% 45 to 60 minutes, 24.6% 60 minutes or more (2000)

Additional Information Contacts
Middletown Township . . . . (732) 615-2000
  http://www.middletownnj.org
Northern Monmouth Cty Chamber of Commerce . . . . (732) 291-7870
  http://www.northernmonmouth.com

MILLSTONE (township).
Covers a land area of 36.760 square miles and a water area of 0.424 square miles. Located at 40.21° N. Lat.; 74.43° W. Long.

Population: 5,069 (1990); 8,970 (2000); 10,041 (2005); 11,070 (2010 projected); Race: 91.8% White, 2.2% Black, 4.3% Asian, 3.7% Hispanic of any race (2005); Density: 273.2 persons per square mile (2005); Average household size: 3.37 (2005); Median age: 37.3 (2005); Males per 100 females: 99.4 (2005); Marriage status: 18.0% never married, 75.2% now married, 3.9% widowed, 3.0% divorced (2000); Foreign born: 6.6% (2000); Ancestry (includes multiple ancestries): 27.6% Italian, 22.2% Irish, 17.2% German, 14.8% Polish, 10.2% Other groups (2000).

Economy: Single-family building permits issued: 44 (2005); Multi-family building permits issued: 0 (2005); Employment by occupation: 25.6% management, 26.0% professional, 9.2% services, 26.9% sales, 0.9% farming, 6.4% construction, 4.9% production (2000).

Income: Per capita income: $45,349 (2005); Median household income: $121,720 (2005); Average household income: $150,834 (2005); Percent of households with income of $100,000 or more: 61.8% (2005); Poverty rate: 4.9% (2000).

Education: Percent of population age 25 and over with: High school diploma (including GED) or higher: 92.1% (2005); Bachelor's degree or higher: 42.7% (2005); Master's degree or higher: 16.0% (2005).
Housing: Homeownership rate: 95.5% (2005); Median home value: $547,729 (2005); Median rent: $770 per month (2000); Median age of housing: 12 years (2000).
Transportation: Commute to work: 88.2% car, 4.8% public transportation, 1.1% walk, 5.6% work from home (2000); Travel time to work: 16.3% less than 15 minutes, 23.5% 15 to 30 minutes, 23.8% 30 to 45 minutes, 17.3% 45 to 60 minutes, 19.1% 60 minutes or more (2000)
Additional Information Contacts
Millstone Township . . . . (609) 208-9325
    http://www.millstone.nj.us
Western Monmouth Chamber of Commerce . . . . (732) 462-3030
    http://www.wmchamber.com

MONMOUTH BEACH (borough). Covers a land area of 1.072 square miles and a water area of 0.853 square miles. Located at 40.33° N. Lat.; 73.98° W. Long. Elevation is 9 feet.
Population: 3,303 (1990); 3,595 (2000); 3,642 (2005); 3,716 (2010 projected); Race: 97.3% White, 0.5% Black, 0.9% Asian, 2.4% Hispanic of any race (2005); Density: 3,398.3 persons per square mile (2005); Average household size: 2.19 (2005); Median age: 46.3 (2005); Males per 100 females: 89.0 (2005); Marriage status: 20.2% never married, 56.2% now married, 10.8% widowed, 12.9% divorced (2000); Foreign born: 5.9% (2000); Ancestry (includes multiple ancestries): 36.6% Irish, 22.8% Italian, 14.9% German, 9.5% English, 6.2% Other groups (2000).
Economy: Resort borough. Single-family building permits issued: 12 (2005); Multi-family building permits issued: 0 (2005); Employment by occupation: 25.7% management, 29.2% professional, 6.7% services, 27.0% sales, 0.0% farming, 6.7% construction, 4.7% production (2000).
Income: Per capita income: $59,883 (2005); Median household income: $93,857 (2005); Average household income: $130,988 (2005); Percent of households with income of $100,000 or more: 46.5% (2005); Poverty rate: 1.9% (2000).
Education: Percent of population age 25 and over with: High school diploma (including GED) or higher: 94.4% (2005); Bachelor's degree or higher: 49.0% (2005); Master's degree or higher: 19.0% (2005).
School District(s)
Monmouth Beach Borough (PK-08)
    2003-04 Enrollment: 315 . . . . (732) 222-6139
Housing: Homeownership rate: 82.1% (2005); Median home value: $491,987 (2005); Median rent: $918 per month (2000); Median age of housing: 27 years (2000).
Safety: Violent crime rate: 0.0 per 10,000 population; Property crime rate: 85.1 per 10,000 population (2004).
Transportation: Commute to work: 84.9% car, 8.3% public transportation, 0.5% walk, 4.7% work from home (2000); Travel time to work: 21.7% less than 15 minutes, 29.6% 15 to 30 minutes, 12.0% 30 to 45 minutes, 7.4% 45 to 60 minutes, 29.2% 60 minutes or more (2000)

MORGANVILLE (CDP). Covers a land area of 5.949 square miles and a water area of 0 square miles. Located at 40.33° N. Lat.; 74.29° W. Long. Elevation is 115 feet.
Population: 9,841 (1990); 11,255 (2000); 11,705 (2005); 12,157 (2010 projected); Race: 84.3% White, 1.8% Black, 12.4% Asian, 3.8% Hispanic of any race (2005); Density: 1,967.6 persons per square mile (2005); Average household size: 3.05 (2005); Median age: 40.6 (2005); Males per 100 females: 95.3 (2005); Marriage status: 18.4% never married, 73.9% now married, 4.7% widowed, 3.0% divorced (2000); Foreign born: 13.9% (2000); Ancestry (includes multiple ancestries): 24.0% Other groups, 15.7% Italian, 12.9% Russian, 12.0% Polish, 11.2% Irish (2000).
Economy: Employment by occupation: 25.6% management, 30.7% professional, 6.4% services, 28.8% sales, 0.0% farming, 4.0% construction, 4.5% production (2000).
Income: Per capita income: $45,427 (2005); Median household income: $114,858 (2005); Average household income: $138,507 (2005); Percent of households with income of $100,000 or more: 57.1% (2005); Poverty rate: 1.7% (2000).
Education: Percent of population age 25 and over with: High school diploma (including GED) or higher: 96.4% (2005); Bachelor's degree or higher: 54.1% (2005); Master's degree or higher: 23.7% (2005).
School District(s)
Marlboro Township (PK-08)
    2003-04 Enrollment: 6,084 . . . . (732) 972-2015

Housing: Homeownership rate: 97.2% (2005); Median home value: $454,286 (2005); Median rent: $959 per month (2000); Median age of housing: 21 years (2000).
Transportation: Commute to work: 78.8% car, 17.1% public transportation, 0.3% walk, 3.2% work from home (2000); Travel time to work: 18.8% less than 15 minutes, 16.8% 15 to 30 minutes, 17.7% 30 to 45 minutes, 9.2% 45 to 60 minutes, 37.5% 60 minutes or more (2000)

NAVESINK (CDP). Covers a land area of 0.900 square miles and a water area of 0.008 square miles. Located at 40.40° N. Lat.; 74.03° W. Long. Elevation is 50 feet.
Population: 1,913 (1990); 1,962 (2000); 1,962 (2005); 1,985 (2010 projected); Race: 87.2% White, 9.0% Black, 1.3% Asian, 3.0% Hispanic of any race (2005); Density: 2,178.8 persons per square mile (2005); Average household size: 3.08 (2005); Median age: 41.8 (2005); Males per 100 females: 96.0 (2005); Marriage status: 20.9% never married, 59.6% now married, 12.0% widowed, 7.6% divorced (2000); Foreign born: 8.3% (2000); Ancestry (includes multiple ancestries): 33.9% Irish, 22.5% Other groups, 19.7% German, 16.1% English, 11.5% Italian (2000).
Economy: Employment by occupation: 19.3% management, 16.8% professional, 16.2% services, 36.0% sales, 0.8% farming, 4.6% construction, 6.3% production (2000).
Income: Per capita income: $34,796 (2005); Median household income: $97,614 (2005); Average household income: $105,812 (2005); Percent of households with income of $100,000 or more: 48.4% (2005); Poverty rate: 1.6% (2000).
Education: Percent of population age 25 and over with: High school diploma (including GED) or higher: 88.0% (2005); Bachelor's degree or higher: 28.1% (2005); Master's degree or higher: 6.4% (2005).
School District(s)
Middletown Township (PK-12)
    2003-04 Enrollment: 10,777 . . . . (732) 706-6002
Housing: Homeownership rate: 88.1% (2005); Median home value: $380,242 (2005); Median rent: $913 per month (2000); Median age of housing: 44 years (2000).
Transportation: Commute to work: 85.6% car, 11.7% public transportation, 0.8% walk, 1.9% work from home (2000); Travel time to work: 26.1% less than 15 minutes, 10.7% 15 to 30 minutes, 17.7% 30 to 45 minutes, 8.2% 45 to 60 minutes, 37.3% 60 minutes or more (2000)
Additional Information Contacts
Northern Monmouth Cty Chamber of Commerce . . . . (732) 291-7870
    http://www.northernmonmouth.org

NEPTUNE (township). Aka Neptune City. Covers a land area of 8.225 square miles and a water area of 0.536 square miles. Located at 40.20° N. Lat.; 74.03° W. Long.
History: Incorporated 1879.
Population: 28,148 (1990); 27,690 (2000); 28,766 (2005); 29,905 (2010 projected); Race: 53.4% White, 40.0% Black, 1.2% Asian, 6.5% Hispanic of any race (2005); Density: 3,497.6 persons per square mile (2005); Average household size: 2.49 (2005); Median age: 40.7 (2005); Males per 100 females: 88.1 (2005); Marriage status: 31.0% never married, 48.8% now married, 10.1% widowed, 10.1% divorced (2000); Foreign born: 7.3% (2000); Ancestry (includes multiple ancestries): 35.3% Other groups, 14.5% Irish, 12.3% Italian, 11.7% German, 7.5% English (2000).
Economy: Manufacturing: apparel, electrical equipment, fabricated metal products; ironworks. Includes Ocean Grove resort. Unemployment rate: 6.0% (2005); Total civilian labor force: 14,501 (2005); Single-family building permits issued: 6 (2005); Multi-family building permits issued: 155 (2005); Employment by occupation: 14.0% management, 22.9% professional, 16.1% services, 28.4% sales, 0.1% farming, 7.5% construction, 11.0% production (2000).
Income: Per capita income: $26,130 (2005); Median household income: $50,871 (2005); Average household income: $64,037 (2005); Percent of households with income of $100,000 or more: 18.3% (2005); Poverty rate: 11.7% (2000).
Taxes: Total city taxes per capita: $614 (2004); City property taxes per capita: $579 (2004).
Education: Percent of population age 25 and over with: High school diploma (including GED) or higher: 83.9% (2005); Bachelor's degree or higher: 23.4% (2005); Master's degree or higher: 8.2% (2005).
School District(s)
Monmouth County Vocational (09-12)
    2003-04 Enrollment: 1,856 . . . . (732) 431-7942

Neptune Township (PK-12)
2003-04 Enrollment: 4,559 . . . . (732) 776-2001
Housing: Homeownership rate: 64.8% (2005); Median home value:
$234,037 (2005); Median rent: $603 per month (2000); Median age of
housing: 43 years (2000).
Hospitals: Jersey Shore Medical Center (529 beds)
Safety: Violent crime rate: 41.2 per 10,000 population; Property crime rate:
425.1 per 10,000 population (2004).
Newspapers: Asbury Park Press (Circulation 167,161)
Transportation: Commute to work: 88.9% car, 4.5% public transportation,
2.4% walk, 3.1% work from home (2000); Travel time to work: 31.4% less
than 15 minutes, 35.1% 15 to 30 minutes, 13.7% 30 to 45 minutes, 6.9%
45 to 60 minutes, 12.8% 60 minutes or more (2000)

NEPTUNE CITY (borough). Aka Neptune. Covers a land area of
0.909 square miles and a water area of 0 square miles. Located at 40.20°
N. Lat.; 74.03° W. Long. Elevation is 15 feet.
History: Incorporated 1881.
Population: 4,997 (1990); 5,218 (2000); 5,203 (2005); 5,229 (2010
projected); Race: 79.8% White, 11.8% Black, 3.2% Asian, 6.6% Hispanic of
any race (2005); Density: 5,726.2 persons per square mile (2005); Average
household size: 2.34 (2005); Median age: 41.2 (2005); Males per 100
females: 88.5 (2005); Marriage status: 27.3% never married, 49.7% now
married, 11.7% widowed, 11.3% divorced (2000); Foreign born: 8.0%
(2000); Ancestry (includes multiple ancestries): 29.3% Irish, 18.7% Other
groups, 17.9% Italian, 14.1% German, 11.8% English (2000).
Economy: Resort borough near Atlantic coast. Single-family building
permits issued: 11 (2005); Multi-family building permits issued: 0 (2005);
Employment by occupation: 8.3% management, 18.9% professional,
17.2% services, 26.6% sales, 0.3% farming, 14.4% construction, 14.2%
production (2000).
Income: Per capita income: $24,811 (2005); Median household income:
$48,003 (2005); Average household income: $57,121 (2005); Percent of
households with income of $100,000 or more: 13.9% (2005); Poverty rate:
5.5% (2000).
Taxes: Total city taxes per capita: $672 (2004); City property taxes per
capita: $646 (2004).
Education: Percent of population age 25 and over with: High school
diploma (including GED) or higher: 82.3% (2005); Bachelor's degree or
higher: 17.1% (2005); Master's degree or higher: 4.7% (2005).
School District(s)
Neptune City (PK-08)
2003-04 Enrollment: 445 . . . . (732) 775-5319
Housing: Homeownership rate: 59.6% (2005); Median home value:
$204,569 (2005); Median rent: $680 per month (2000); Median age of
housing: 41 years (2000).
Safety: Violent crime rate: 30.6 per 10,000 population; Property crime rate:
410.9 per 10,000 population (2004).
Transportation: Commute to work: 90.8% car, 2.5% public transportation,
4.3% walk, 1.2% work from home (2000); Travel time to work: 39.6% less
than 15 minutes, 33.6% 15 to 30 minutes, 10.8% 30 to 45 minutes, 6.2%
45 to 60 minutes, 9.8% 60 minutes or more (2000)
Additional Information Contacts
Borough of Neptune City . . . . (732) 776-7224
http://www.neptunecitynj.com

NORTH MIDDLETOWN (CDP). Covers a land area of 0.460
square miles and a water area of 0 square miles. Located at 40.44° N. Lat.;
74.11° W. Long.
Population: 3,018 (1990); 3,165 (2000); 3,131 (2005); 3,134 (2010
projected); Race: 94.0% White, 1.9% Black, 1.5% Asian, 5.8% Hispanic of
any race (2005); Density: 6,805.7 persons per square mile (2005); Average
household size: 3.09 (2005); Median age: 33.5 (2005); Males per 100
females: 95.8 (2005); Marriage status: 27.7% never married, 55.9% now
married, 8.2% widowed, 8.1% divorced (2000); Foreign born: 2.9% (2000);
Ancestry (includes multiple ancestries): 33.3% Irish, 28.2% Italian, 20.6%
German, 12.4% Polish, 8.4% Other groups (2000).
Economy: Employment by occupation: 12.2% management, 11.2%
professional, 11.8% services, 39.1% sales, 0.0% farming, 10.8%
construction, 14.9% production (2000).
Income: Per capita income: $21,153 (2005); Median household income:
$60,554 (2005); Average household income: $65,445 (2005); Percent of
households with income of $100,000 or more: 16.4% (2005); Poverty rate:
6.3% (2000).

Education: Percent of population age 25 and over with: High school
diploma (including GED) or higher: 81.6% (2005); Bachelor's degree or
higher: 10.4% (2005); Master's degree or higher: 1.2% (2005).
School District(s)
Middletown Township (PK-12)
2003-04 Enrollment: 10,777 . . . . (732) 706-6002
Housing: Homeownership rate: 76.3% (2005); Median home value:
$227,041 (2005); Median rent: $843 per month (2000); Median age of
housing: 47 years (2000).
Transportation: Commute to work: 88.4% car, 9.6% public transportation,
1.2% walk, 0.4% work from home (2000); Travel time to work: 24.3% less
than 15 minutes, 29.3% 15 to 30 minutes, 17.0% 30 to 45 minutes, 12.4%
45 to 60 minutes, 17.0% 60 minutes or more (2000)

OAKHURST (CDP). Covers a land area of 1.616 square miles and a
water area of 0 square miles. Located at 40.26° N. Lat.; 74.02° W. Long.
Elevation is 40 feet.
Population: 4,130 (1990); 4,152 (2000); 4,001 (2005); 3,895 (2010
projected); Race: 95.9% White, 0.9% Black, 2.1% Asian, 2.2% Hispanic of
any race (2005); Density: 2,476.5 persons per square mile (2005); Average
household size: 2.93 (2005); Median age: 39.2 (2005); Males per 100
females: 98.3 (2005); Marriage status: 20.7% never married, 67.4% now
married, 5.6% widowed, 6.3% divorced (2000); Foreign born: 10.5%
(2000); Ancestry (includes multiple ancestries): 25.2% Italian, 22.5% Irish,
14.3% German, 8.4% English, 7.9% Other groups (2000).
Economy: Employment by occupation: 17.7% management, 22.7%
professional, 11.9% services, 33.7% sales, 0.0% farming, 6.9%
construction, 7.2% production (2000).
Income: Per capita income: $33,896 (2005); Median household income:
$86,582 (2005); Average household income: $99,353 (2005); Percent of
households with income of $100,000 or more: 38.8% (2005); Poverty rate:
2.4% (2000).
Education: Percent of population age 25 and over with: High school
diploma (including GED) or higher: 90.6% (2005); Bachelor's degree or
higher: 36.8% (2005); Master's degree or higher: 13.9% (2005).
School District(s)
Ocean Township (PK-12)
2003-04 Enrollment: 4,982 . . . . (732) 531-5600
Two-year College(s)
Harrison Career Institute-Oakhurst (Private, For-profit)
Fall 2004 Enrollment: 136 . . . . (732) 493-1660
Housing: Homeownership rate: 94.5% (2005); Median home value:
$327,551 (2005); Median rent: $761 per month (2000); Median age of
housing: 36 years (2000).
Transportation: Commute to work: 91.8% car, 4.5% public transportation,
1.0% walk, 2.3% work from home (2000); Travel time to work: 41.4% less
than 15 minutes, 29.4% 15 to 30 minutes, 12.8% 30 to 45 minutes, 3.6%
45 to 60 minutes, 12.8% 60 minutes or more (2000)

OCEAN (township). Covers a land area of 11.034 square miles and a
water area of 0.086 square miles. Located at 40.24° N. Lat.; 74.03° W.
Long.
History: Incorporated 1849.
Population: 25,058 (1990); 26,959 (2000); 28,241 (2005); 29,565 (2010
projected); Race: 81.7% White, 5.9% Black, 7.7% Asian, 5.7% Hispanic of
any race (2005); Density: 2,559.5 persons per square mile (2005); Average
household size: 2.60 (2005); Median age: 39.4 (2005); Males per 100
females: 93.3 (2005); Marriage status: 24.2% never married, 60.4% now
married, 6.7% widowed, 8.7% divorced (2000); Foreign born: 15.7%
(2000); Ancestry (includes multiple ancestries): 21.0% Italian, 19.2% Other
groups, 18.2% Irish, 12.9% German, 7.2% English (2000).
Economy: Unemployment rate: 3.5% (2005); Total civilian labor force:
14,535 (2005); Single-family building permits issued: 126 (2005);
Multi-family building permits issued: 0 (2005); Employment by occupation:
14.9% management, 26.7% professional, 12.7% services, 31.9% sales,
0.1% farming, 6.2% construction, 7.6% production (2000).
Income: Per capita income: $34,356 (2005); Median household income:
$69,071 (2005); Average household income: $88,881 (2005); Percent of
households with income of $100,000 or more: 30.9% (2005); Poverty rate:
5.0% (2000).
Education: Percent of population age 25 and over with: High school
diploma (including GED) or higher: 89.9% (2005); Bachelor's degree or
higher: 38.8% (2005); Master's degree or higher: 16.0% (2005).

School District(s)
Ocean Township (PK-12)
  2003-04 Enrollment: 4,982 . . . . (732) 531-5600

Two-year College(s)
Concorde School of Hair Design-Wanamassa (Private, For-profit)
  Fall 2004 Enrollment: 89 . . . . (732) 493-1355
Housing: Homeownership rate: 65.7% (2005); Median home value: $347,816 (2005); Median rent: $642 per month (2000); Median age of housing: 33 years (2000).
Safety: Violent crime rate: 15.1 per 10,000 population; Property crime rate: 238.1 per 10,000 population (2004).
Transportation: Commute to work: 90.7% car, 4.7% public transportation, 1.3% walk, 2.4% work from home (2000); Travel time to work: 34.8% less than 15 minutes, 34.2% 15 to 30 minutes, 12.2% 30 to 45 minutes, 4.4% 45 to 60 minutes, 14.4% 60 minutes or more (2000)
Additional Information Contacts
Ocean Township . . . . (732) 531-5000
  http://www.oceantwp.org
Ocean Township Chamber of Commerce . . . . (732) 728-1888
  http://www.oceantwpchamber.org

OCEAN GROVE (CDP). Covers a land area of 0.356 square miles and a water area of 0.039 square miles. Located at 40.21° N. Lat.; 74.00° W. Long. Elevation is 20 feet.
Population: 4,818 (1990); 4,256 (2000); 4,337 (2005); 4,445 (2010 projected); Race: 92.9% White, 4.2% Black, 1.1% Asian, 3.7% Hispanic of any race (2005); Density: 12,184.1 persons per square mile (2005); Average household size: 1.78 (2005); Median age: 47.3 (2005); Males per 100 females: 84.1 (2005); Marriage status: 37.9% never married, 36.2% now married, 11.0% widowed, 14.8% divorced (2000); Foreign born: 7.1% (2000); Ancestry (includes multiple ancestries): 22.0% Irish, 20.5% German, 16.3% English, 15.2% Italian, 8.8% Other groups (2000).
Economy: Employment by occupation: 19.5% management, 26.4% professional, 12.4% services, 27.9% sales, 0.4% farming, 6.8% construction, 6.7% production (2000).
Income: Per capita income: $32,122 (2005); Median household income: $38,123 (2005); Average household income: $55,306 (2005); Percent of households with income of $100,000 or more: 12.2% (2005); Poverty rate: 13.3% (2000).
Education: Percent of population age 25 and over with: High school diploma (including GED) or higher: 88.2% (2005); Bachelor's degree or higher: 36.1% (2005); Master's degree or higher: 14.4% (2005).
Housing: Homeownership rate: 42.8% (2005); Median home value: $259,818 (2005); Median rent: $604 per month (2000); Median age of housing: 60+ years (2000).
Transportation: Commute to work: 76.4% car, 8.6% public transportation, 5.4% walk, 6.8% work from home (2000); Travel time to work: 26.7% less than 15 minutes, 33.2% 15 to 30 minutes, 13.7% 30 to 45 minutes, 7.5% 45 to 60 minutes, 18.9% 60 minutes or more (2000)
Additional Information Contacts
Ocean Grove Chamber of Commerce . . . . (732) 774-1391
  http://www.oceangrovenj.com

OCEANPORT (borough). Covers a land area of 3.222 square miles and a water area of 0.635 square miles. Located at 40.31° N. Lat.; 74.01° W. Long. Elevation is 24 feet.
History: Fort Monmouth nearby. Incorporated 1920.
Population: 6,146 (1990); 5,807 (2000); 5,981 (2005); 6,162 (2010 projected); Race: 95.5% White, 1.9% Black, 0.8% Asian, 2.4% Hispanic of any race (2005); Density: 1,856.1 persons per square mile (2005); Average household size: 2.81 (2005); Median age: 41.2 (2005); Males per 100 females: 98.2 (2005); Marriage status: 24.1% never married, 61.3% now married, 8.4% widowed, 6.2% divorced (2000); Foreign born: 3.8% (2000); Ancestry (includes multiple ancestries): 34.8% Italian, 25.6% Irish, 16.7% German, 9.7% English, 7.8% Polish (2000).
Economy: Largely residential, computer manufacturing. Single-family building permits issued: 12 (2005); Multi-family building permits issued: 0 (2005); Employment by occupation: 19.0% management, 25.6% professional, 8.2% services, 32.0% sales, 0.0% farming, 8.1% construction, 7.1% production (2000).
Income: Per capita income: $41,227 (2005); Median household income: $88,323 (2005); Average household income: $113,876 (2005); Percent of households with income of $100,000 or more: 41.3% (2005); Poverty rate: 2.7% (2000).

Education: Percent of population age 25 and over with: High school diploma (including GED) or higher: 90.8% (2005); Bachelor's degree or higher: 35.9% (2005); Master's degree or higher: 11.1% (2005).
School District(s)
Oceanport Borough (PK-08)
  2003-04 Enrollment: 784 . . . . (732) 544-8588
Housing: Homeownership rate: 88.2% (2005); Median home value: $397,473 (2005); Median rent: $543 per month (2000); Median age of housing: 34 years (2000).
Safety: Violent crime rate: 5.0 per 10,000 population; Property crime rate: 118.5 per 10,000 population (2004).
Transportation: Commute to work: 85.1% car, 5.6% public transportation, 4.4% walk, 3.7% work from home (2000); Travel time to work: 41.8% less than 15 minutes, 28.4% 15 to 30 minutes, 8.1% 30 to 45 minutes, 6.0% 45 to 60 minutes, 15.6% 60 minutes or more (2000)

PERRINEVILLE (unincorporated postal area, zip code 08535). Covers a land area of 5.350 square miles and a water area of 0.039 square miles. Located at 40.22° N. Lat.; 74.45° W. Long. Elevation is 150 feet.
Population: 2,073 (2000); Race: 88.2% White, 6.4% Black, 3.3% Asian, 2.1% Hispanic of any race (2000); Density: 387.4 persons per square mile (2000); Age: 36.4% under 18, 3.7% over 64 (2000); Marriage status: 13.9% never married, 81.2% now married, 0.1% widowed, 4.8% divorced (2000); Foreign born: 9.1% (2000); Ancestry (includes multiple ancestries): 24.2% Italian, 23.7% Irish, 11.7% German, 10.2% Other groups, 8.8% Polish (2000).
Economy: Employment by occupation: 30.0% management, 26.2% professional, 6.3% services, 29.2% sales, 0.0% farming, 4.0% construction, 4.3% production (2000).
Income: Per capita income: $39,372 (2000); Median household income: $118,412 (2000); Poverty rate: 1.8% (2000).
Education: Percent of population age 25 and over with: High school diploma (including GED) or higher: 95.2% (2000); Bachelor's degree or higher: 48.1% (2000).
Housing: Homeownership rate: 94.8% (2000); Median home value: $367,400 (2000); Median rent: $950 per month (2000); Median age of housing: 9 years (2000).
Transportation: Commute to work: 85.8% car, 8.2% public transportation, 0.0% walk, 6.0% work from home (2000); Travel time to work: 15.0% less than 15 minutes, 15.0% 15 to 30 minutes, 26.3% 30 to 45 minutes, 20.3% 45 to 60 minutes, 23.4% 60 minutes or more (2000)

PORT MONMOUTH (CDP). Covers a land area of 1.321 square miles and a water area of 0.020 square miles. Located at 40.43° N. Lat.; 74.10° W. Long. Elevation is 9 feet.
Population: 3,558 (1990); 3,742 (2000); 4,032 (2005); 4,309 (2010 projected); Race: 95.0% White, 1.6% Black, 0.4% Asian, 7.8% Hispanic of any race (2005); Density: 3,052.7 persons per square mile (2005); Average household size: 2.90 (2005); Median age: 36.4 (2005); Males per 100 females: 95.3 (2005); Marriage status: 26.6% never married, 56.3% now married, 8.3% widowed, 8.7% divorced (2000); Foreign born: 4.5% (2000); Ancestry (includes multiple ancestries): 39.4% Irish, 23.2% Italian, 20.9% German, 9.4% Polish, 9.2% Other groups (2000).
Economy: Employment by occupation: 11.0% management, 13.8% professional, 19.4% services, 30.6% sales, 0.5% farming, 10.7% construction, 13.8% production (2000).
Income: Per capita income: $23,943 (2005); Median household income: $59,934 (2005); Average household income: $69,170 (2005); Percent of households with income of $100,000 or more: 20.2% (2005); Poverty rate: 10.5% (2000).
Education: Percent of population age 25 and over with: High school diploma (including GED) or higher: 81.9% (2005); Bachelor's degree or higher: 15.1% (2005); Master's degree or higher: 3.0% (2005).
School District(s)
Middletown Township (PK-12)
  2003-04 Enrollment: 10,777 . . . . (732) 706-6002
Housing: Homeownership rate: 77.7% (2005); Median home value: $245,408 (2005); Median rent: $621 per month (2000); Median age of housing: 42 years (2000).
Transportation: Commute to work: 91.8% car, 5.7% public transportation, 1.6% walk, 0.0% work from home (2000); Travel time to work: 22.7% less than 15 minutes, 30.8% 15 to 30 minutes, 21.7% 30 to 45 minutes, 8.7% 45 to 60 minutes, 16.1% 60 minutes or more (2000)

RAMTOWN (CDP). Covers a land area of 2.065 square miles and a water area of 0 square miles. Located at 40.11° N. Lat.; 74.14° W. Long. Elevation is 80 feet.
Population: 3,846 (1990); 5,932 (2000); 6,418 (2005); 6,882 (2010 projected); Race: 92.4% White, 1.9% Black, 2.3% Asian, 7.5% Hispanic of any race (2005); Density: 3,108.3 persons per square mile (2005); Average household size: 3.44 (2005); Median age: 33.4 (2005); Males per 100 females: 97.0 (2005); Marriage status: 20.3% never married, 73.0% now married, 1.9% widowed, 4.9% divorced (2000); Foreign born: 7.6% (2000); Ancestry (includes multiple ancestries): 46.8% Italian, 24.1% Irish, 14.8% German, 10.0% Other groups, 8.4% Polish (2000).
Economy: Employment by occupation: 14.7% management, 22.2% professional, 12.2% services, 30.6% sales, 0.0% farming, 10.9% construction, 9.4% production (2000).
Income: Per capita income: $27,345 (2005); Median household income: $84,969 (2005); Average household income: $94,203 (2005); Percent of households with income of $100,000 or more: 37.1% (2005); Poverty rate: 3.1% (2000).
Education: Percent of population age 25 and over with: High school diploma (including GED) or higher: 91.9% (2005); Bachelor's degree or higher: 25.9% (2005); Master's degree or higher: 7.8% (2005).
Housing: Homeownership rate: 95.7% (2005); Median home value: $274,366 (2005); Median rent: $994 per month (2000); Median age of housing: 14 years (2000).
Transportation: Commute to work: 94.1% car, 3.3% public transportation, 0.6% walk, 1.8% work from home (2000); Travel time to work: 19.6% less than 15 minutes, 27.3% 15 to 30 minutes, 19.0% 30 to 45 minutes, 9.8% 45 to 60 minutes, 24.3% 60 minutes or more (2000)

RED BANK (borough). Covers a land area of 1.784 square miles and a water area of 0.374 square miles. Located at 40.34° N. Lat.; 74.06° W. Long. Elevation is 39 feet.
History: Named for the color of the soil. An early shipping center. Landmarks include Old Christ Church (1769) and the Allen House (1667). Fort Monmouth to South. Count Basie born here. Incorporated 1908.
Population: 10,636 (1990); 11,844 (2000); 11,796 (2005); 11,806 (2010 projected); Race: 67.9% White, 17.4% Black, 2.4% Asian, 23.2% Hispanic of any race (2005); Density: 6,612.2 persons per square mile (2005); Average household size: 2.27 (2005); Median age: 39.0 (2005); Males per 100 females: 93.6 (2005); Marriage status: 35.5% never married, 42.6% now married, 12.2% widowed, 9.6% divorced (2000); Foreign born: 15.0% (2000); Ancestry (includes multiple ancestries): 32.3% Other groups, 19.6% Irish, 14.0% Italian, 11.3% German, 6.5% English (2000).
Economy: Summer and winter resort and residential suburb with some light industry. Single-family building permits issued: 3 (2005); Multi-family building permits issued: 0 (2005); Employment by occupation: 15.6% management, 21.0% professional, 19.5% services, 29.8% sales, 0.2% farming, 6.5% construction, 7.4% production (2000).
Income: Per capita income: $30,571 (2005); Median household income: $53,306 (2005); Average household income: $68,630 (2005); Percent of households with income of $100,000 or more: 20.9% (2005); Poverty rate: 12.0% (2000).
Education: Percent of population age 25 and over with: High school diploma (including GED) or higher: 81.0% (2005); Bachelor's degree or higher: 31.1% (2005); Master's degree or higher: 10.4% (2005).
School District(s)
Agency - The Red Bank CS (KG-08)
    2003-04 Enrollment: 189 . . . . (732) 450-2092
Middletown Township (PK-12)
    2003-04 Enrollment: 10,777 . . . . (732) 706-6002
Red Bank Borough (PK-08)
    2003-04 Enrollment: 767 . . . . (732) 758-1506
Housing: Homeownership rate: 47.2% (2005); Median home value: $282,496 (2005); Median rent: $738 per month (2000); Median age of housing: 51 years (2000).
Hospitals: Riverview Medical Center (475 beds)
Safety: Violent crime rate: 36.2 per 10,000 population; Property crime rate: 239.2 per 10,000 population (2004).
Newspapers: The Two River Times (General - Circulation 10,000)
Transportation: Commute to work: 76.0% car, 12.7% public transportation, 7.1% walk, 2.1% work from home (2000); Travel time to work: 32.7% less than 15 minutes, 28.2% 15 to 30 minutes, 12.4% 30 to 45 minutes, 7.9% 45 to 60 minutes, 18.7% 60 minutes or more (2000)
Additional Information Contacts

Eastern Monmouth Chamber of Commerce . . . . (732) 741-0055
    http://www.emacc.org

ROOSEVELT (borough). Aka Jersey Homesteads. Covers a land area of 1.956 square miles and a water area of 0.002 square miles. Located at 40.21° N. Lat.; 74.47° W. Long. Elevation is 152 feet.
History: Founded 1933 as Jersey Homesteads by Federal Resettlement Administration as government-aided experiment in cooperative agriculture and manufacturing for garment workers; sold 1940, later renamed in honor of Franklin D. Roosevelt.
Population: 884 (1990); 933 (2000); 938 (2005); 950 (2010 projected); Race: 87.5% White, 2.2% Black, 2.7% Asian, 5.8% Hispanic of any race (2005); Density: 479.5 persons per square mile (2005); Average household size: 2.78 (2005); Median age: 40.6 (2005); Males per 100 females: 93.8 (2005); Marriage status: 23.4% never married, 63.4% now married, 5.3% widowed, 7.9% divorced (2000); Foreign born: 8.6% (2000); Ancestry (includes multiple ancestries): 22.5% Irish, 17.0% Other groups, 14.9% German, 10.1% Italian, 9.7% Polish (2000).
Economy: Single-family building permits issued: 1 (2005); Multi-family building permits issued: 0 (2005); Employment by occupation: 17.1% management, 29.5% professional, 9.5% services, 20.5% sales, 0.0% farming, 13.9% construction, 9.5% production (2000).
Income: Per capita income: $28,273 (2005); Median household income: $69,306 (2005); Average household income: $78,694 (2005); Percent of households with income of $100,000 or more: 24.0% (2005); Poverty rate: 4.3% (2000).
Education: Percent of population age 25 and over with: High school diploma (including GED) or higher: 93.0% (2005); Bachelor's degree or higher: 44.3% (2005); Master's degree or higher: 17.9% (2005).
School District(s)
Roosevelt Borough (PK-06)
    2003-04 Enrollment: 105 . . . . (609) 448-2798
Housing: Homeownership rate: 87.2% (2005); Median home value: $236,975 (2005); Median rent: $657 per month (2000); Median age of housing: 60+ years (2000).
Transportation: Commute to work: 90.5% car, 0.9% public transportation, 2.2% walk, 6.5% work from home (2000); Travel time to work: 17.1% less than 15 minutes, 28.4% 15 to 30 minutes, 24.9% 30 to 45 minutes, 15.7% 45 to 60 minutes, 13.9% 60 minutes or more (2000)

RUMSON (borough). Covers a land area of 5.225 square miles and a water area of 2.010 square miles. Located at 40.37° N. Lat.; 74.00° W. Long. Elevation is 40 feet.
History: Settled c.1700, incorporated 1907.
Population: 6,701 (1990); 7,137 (2000); 7,408 (2005); 7,708 (2010 projected); Race: 97.6% White, 0.2% Black, 1.1% Asian, 1.5% Hispanic of any race (2005); Density: 1,417.8 persons per square mile (2005); Average household size: 2.96 (2005); Median age: 39.3 (2005); Males per 100 females: 93.9 (2005); Marriage status: 16.8% never married, 70.9% now married, 6.3% widowed, 6.0% divorced (2000); Foreign born: 4.1% (2000); Ancestry (includes multiple ancestries): 33.4% Irish, 17.9% German, 16.4% Italian, 13.8% English, 6.2% Polish (2000).
Economy: Resort borough. Estate center; boating. Single-family building permits issued: 34 (2005); Multi-family building permits issued: 0 (2005); Employment by occupation: 26.3% management, 33.1% professional, 5.2% services, 28.4% sales, 0.0% farming, 4.5% construction, 2.5% production (2000).
Income: Per capita income: $69,800 (2005); Median household income: $146,909 (2005); Average household income: $205,251 (2005); Percent of households with income of $100,000 or more: 63.9% (2005); Poverty rate: 3.2% (2000).
Education: Percent of population age 25 and over with: High school diploma (including GED) or higher: 97.0% (2005); Bachelor's degree or higher: 64.2% (2005); Master's degree or higher: 25.0% (2005).
School District(s)
Rumson Borough (PK-08)
    2003-04 Enrollment: 1,006 . . . . (732) 842-4747
Rumson-Fair Haven Regional (09-12)
    2003-04 Enrollment: 845 . . . . (732) 842-5456
Housing: Homeownership rate: 90.3% (2005); Median home value: $805,118 (2005); Median rent: $1,045 per month (2000); Median age of housing: 48 years (2000).
Safety: Violent crime rate: 1.4 per 10,000 population; Property crime rate: 118.2 per 10,000 population (2004).

Transportation: Commute to work: 76.4% car, 18.2% public transportation, 0.5% walk, 4.3% work from home (2000); Travel time to work: 26.2% less than 15 minutes, 22.7% 15 to 30 minutes, 10.8% 30 to 45 minutes, 8.6% 45 to 60 minutes, 31.7% 60 minutes or more (2000)

SEA BRIGHT (borough).
Covers a land area of 0.639 square miles and a water area of 0.488 square miles. Located at 40.37° N. Lat.; 73.97° W. Long. Elevation is 10 feet.
Population: 1,693 (1990); 1,818 (2000); 1,790 (2005); 1,774 (2010 projected); Race: 94.1% White, 1.7% Black, 2.8% Asian, 5.6% Hispanic of any race (2005); Density: 2,803.1 persons per square mile (2005); Average household size: 1.77 (2005); Median age: 42.7 (2005); Males per 100 females: 110.6 (2005); Marriage status: 37.3% never married, 42.7% now married, 4.9% widowed, 15.1% divorced (2000); Foreign born: 11.9% (2000); Ancestry (includes multiple ancestries): 28.1% Irish, 19.8% German, 15.3% Italian, 12.7% Other groups, 11.0% English (2000).
Economy: Resort borough in estate area. Single-family building permits issued: 15 (2005); Multi-family building permits issued: 0 (2005); Employment by occupation: 20.3% management, 26.6% professional, 9.9% services, 29.8% sales, 1.0% farming, 5.5% construction, 6.8% production (2000).
Income: Per capita income: $50,318 (2005); Median household income: $66,733 (2005); Average household income: $89,267 (2005); Percent of households with income of $100,000 or more: 30.6% (2005); Poverty rate: 7.6% (2000).
Education: Percent of population age 25 and over with: High school diploma (including GED) or higher: 91.3% (2005); Bachelor's degree or higher: 47.0% (2005); Master's degree or higher: 18.5% (2005).
Housing: Homeownership rate: 54.3% (2005); Median home value: $346,465 (2005); Median rent: $816 per month (2000); Median age of housing: 31 years (2000).
Safety: Violent crime rate: 0.0 per 10,000 population; Property crime rate: 171.7 per 10,000 population (2004).
Transportation: Commute to work: 76.6% car, 13.1% public transportation, 3.8% walk, 5.0% work from home (2000); Travel time to work: 14.6% less than 15 minutes, 29.9% 15 to 30 minutes, 14.9% 30 to 45 minutes, 7.2% 45 to 60 minutes, 33.4% 60 minutes or more (2000)

SEA GIRT (borough).
Covers a land area of 1.060 square miles and a water area of 0.391 square miles. Located at 40.13° N. Lat.; 74.03° W. Long. Elevation is 19 feet.
Population: 2,099 (1990); 2,148 (2000); 2,231 (2005); 2,323 (2010 projected); Race: 99.0% White, 0.1% Black, 0.3% Asian, 1.8% Hispanic of any race (2005); Density: 2,105.2 persons per square mile (2005); Average household size: 2.23 (2005); Median age: 51.9 (2005); Males per 100 females: 87.8 (2005); Marriage status: 19.3% never married, 67.2% now married, 9.2% widowed, 4.4% divorced (2000); Foreign born: 3.0% (2000); Ancestry (includes multiple ancestries): 45.3% Irish, 22.5% Italian, 20.8% German, 12.8% English, 6.4% Polish (2000).
Economy: Resort borough. Single-family building permits issued: 32 (2005); Multi-family building permits issued: 0 (2005); Employment by occupation: 30.4% management, 26.5% professional, 8.3% services, 31.2% sales, 0.0% farming, 1.5% construction, 2.0% production (2000).
Income: Per capita income: $71,593 (2005); Median household income: $108,500 (2005); Average household income: $158,428 (2005); Percent of households with income of $100,000 or more: 53.4% (2005); Poverty rate: 3.5% (2000).
Education: Percent of population age 25 and over with: High school diploma (including GED) or higher: 96.4% (2005); Bachelor's degree or higher: 58.6% (2005); Master's degree or higher: 23.4% (2005).
School District(s)
Sea Girt Borough (PK-08)
    2003-04 Enrollment: 183 . . . . (732) 449-3422
Wall Township (PK-12)
    2003-04 Enrollment: 4,360 . . . . (732) 556-2000
Housing: Homeownership rate: 89.6% (2005); Median home value: $970,165 (2005); Median rent: $990 per month (2000); Median age of housing: 49 years (2000).
Safety: Violent crime rate: 13.6 per 10,000 population; Property crime rate: 63.3 per 10,000 population (2004).
Transportation: Commute to work: 82.0% car, 7.8% public transportation, 0.8% walk, 8.0% work from home (2000); Travel time to work: 24.5% less than 15 minutes, 18.1% 15 to 30 minutes, 18.0% 30 to 45 minutes, 7.2% 45 to 60 minutes, 32.3% 60 minutes or more (2000)
Additional Information Contacts

Southern Monmouth Chamber of Commerce . . . . (732) 974-1151
http://www.smcconline.org

SHARK RIVER HILLS (CDP).
Covers a land area of 0.841 square miles and a water area of 0.073 square miles. Located at 40.19° N. Lat.; 74.04° W. Long. Elevation is 240 feet.
Population: 4,228 (1990); 3,878 (2000); 3,803 (2005); 3,738 (2010 projected); Race: 97.1% White, 0.7% Black, 0.8% Asian, 1.4% Hispanic of any race (2005); Density: 4,521.1 persons per square mile (2005); Average household size: 2.51 (2005); Median age: 42.3 (2005); Males per 100 females: 94.4 (2005); Marriage status: 25.5% never married, 58.5% now married, 7.1% widowed, 8.9% divorced (2000); Foreign born: 4.0% (2000); Ancestry (includes multiple ancestries): 26.0% Italian, 24.5% Irish, 23.3% German, 15.5% English, 10.2% Polish (2000).
Economy: Employment by occupation: 18.5% management, 27.5% professional, 12.9% services, 24.5% sales, 0.0% farming, 7.8% construction, 8.8% production (2000).
Income: Per capita income: $37,401 (2005); Median household income: $81,807 (2005); Average household income: $94,010 (2005); Percent of households with income of $100,000 or more: 35.4% (2005); Poverty rate: 1.9% (2000).
Education: Percent of population age 25 and over with: High school diploma (including GED) or higher: 89.8% (2005); Bachelor's degree or higher: 33.4% (2005); Master's degree or higher: 10.2% (2005).
Housing: Homeownership rate: 95.6% (2005); Median home value: $259,813 (2005); Median rent: $722 per month (2000); Median age of housing: 36 years (2000).
Transportation: Commute to work: 93.9% car, 2.3% public transportation, 0.4% walk, 3.2% work from home (2000); Travel time to work: 33.0% less than 15 minutes, 35.8% 15 to 30 minutes, 14.6% 30 to 45 minutes, 4.0% 45 to 60 minutes, 12.6% 60 minutes or more (2000)

SHREWSBURY (borough).
Covers a land area of 2.206 square miles and a water area of 0.017 square miles. Located at 40.32° N. Lat.; 74.05° W. Long. Elevation is 133 feet.
Population: 3,096 (1990); 3,590 (2000); 3,789 (2005); 3,994 (2010 projected); Race: 96.6% White, 0.5% Black, 1.7% Asian, 2.3% Hispanic of any race (2005); Density: 1,717.3 persons per square mile (2005); Average household size: 3.03 (2005); Median age: 38.9 (2005); Males per 100 females: 98.8 (2005); Marriage status: 17.1% never married, 68.4% now married, 7.2% widowed, 7.3% divorced (2000); Foreign born: 7.4% (2000); Ancestry (includes multiple ancestries): 29.5% Irish, 24.8% Italian, 20.7% German, 12.7% English, 5.7% Polish (2000).
Economy: Single-family building permits issued: 28 (2005); Multi-family building permits issued: 0 (2005); Employment by occupation: 21.5% management, 29.2% professional, 8.4% services, 31.5% sales, 0.0% farming, 5.1% construction, 4.4% production (2000).
Income: Per capita income: $46,505 (2005); Median household income: $103,975 (2005); Average household income: $139,872 (2005); Percent of households with income of $100,000 or more: 51.5% (2005); Poverty rate: 1.0% (2000).
Education: Percent of population age 25 and over with: High school diploma (including GED) or higher: 91.3% (2005); Bachelor's degree or higher: 48.8% (2005); Master's degree or higher: 19.8% (2005).
School District(s)
Shrewsbury Borough (PK-08)
    2003-04 Enrollment: 574 . . . . (732) 747-0882
Housing: Homeownership rate: 95.4% (2005); Median home value: $427,547 (2005); Median rent: $788 per month (2000); Median age of housing: 45 years (2000).
Safety: Violent crime rate: 13.3 per 10,000 population; Property crime rate: 245.2 per 10,000 population (2004).
Newspapers: Holmdel Happenings (General - Circulation 4,800); Lincroft Village News (General - Circulation 4,800); The Country Press (General - Circulation 5,500)
Transportation: Commute to work: 86.7% car, 7.6% public transportation, 1.4% walk, 4.4% work from home (2000); Travel time to work: 38.5% less than 15 minutes, 19.7% 15 to 30 minutes, 12.4% 30 to 45 minutes, 8.9% 45 to 60 minutes, 20.5% 60 minutes or more (2000)

SHREWSBURY (township).
Covers a land area of 0.094 square miles and a water area of 0 square miles. Located at 40.31° N. Lat.; 74.07° W. Long. Elevation is 133 feet.
History: Has 18th-century church. Settled 1665, incorporated 1926.

Population: 986 (1990); 1,098 (2000); 1,082 (2005); 1,073 (2010 projected); Race: 60.3% White, 20.1% Black, 11.7% Asian, 8.2% Hispanic of any race (2005); Density: 11,455.3 persons per square mile (2005); Average household size: 2.06 (2005); Median age: 36.5 (2005); Males per 100 females: 95.3 (2005); Marriage status: 37.0% never married, 39.4% now married, 5.2% widowed, 18.4% divorced (2000); Foreign born: 17.6% (2000); Ancestry (includes multiple ancestries): 29.6% Other groups, 20.2% Irish, 17.9% Italian, 15.3% German, 6.3% English (2000).
Economy: Single-family building permits issued: 0 (2005); Multi-family building permits issued: 0 (2005); Employment by occupation: 9.7% management, 20.3% professional, 12.3% services, 36.2% sales, 0.0% farming, 7.5% construction, 14.0% production (2000).
Income: Per capita income: $26,761 (2005); Median household income: $38,861 (2005); Average household income: $53,436 (2005); Percent of households with income of $100,000 or more: 8.0% (2005); Poverty rate: 8.8% (2000).
Education: Percent of population age 25 and over with: High school diploma (including GED) or higher: 82.4% (2005); Bachelor's degree or higher: 20.3% (2005); Master's degree or higher: 5.6% (2005).

School District(s)
Shrewsbury Borough (PK-08)
    2003-04 Enrollment: 574 . . . . (732) 747-0882
Housing: Homeownership rate: 49.8% (2005); Median home value: $94,340 (2005); Median rent: $768 per month (2000); Median age of housing: 46 years (2000).
Newspapers: Holmdel Happenings (General - Circulation 4,800); Lincroft Village News (General - Circulation 4,800); The Country Press (General - Circulation 5,500)
Transportation: Commute to work: 83.7% car, 5.5% public transportation, 6.0% walk, 3.0% work from home (2000); Travel time to work: 37.4% less than 15 minutes, 37.3% 15 to 30 minutes, 10.0% 30 to 45 minutes, 4.2% 45 to 60 minutes, 11.1% 60 minutes or more (2000)

SOUTH BELMAR (borough). Covers a land area of 0.247 square miles and a water area of 0.014 square miles. Located at 40.17° N. Lat.; 74.02° W. Long. Elevation is 14 feet.
Population: 1,482 (1990); 1,806 (2000); 1,795 (2005); 1,798 (2010 projected); Race: 81.8% White, 5.7% Black, 1.3% Asian, 13.0% Hispanic of any race (2005); Density: 7,278.3 persons per square mile (2005); Average household size: 2.16 (2005); Median age: 37.5 (2005); Males per 100 females: 103.1 (2005); Marriage status: 38.0% never married, 41.6% now married, 9.7% widowed, 10.7% divorced (2000); Foreign born: 7.8% (2000); Ancestry (includes multiple ancestries): 32.7% Irish, 20.1% Other groups, 16.2% Italian, 15.7% German, 8.5% English (2000).
Economy: Resort borough. Employment by occupation: 13.0% management, 21.4% professional, 16.5% services, 23.9% sales, 0.6% farming, 10.9% construction, 13.7% production (2000).
Income: Per capita income: $32,251 (2005); Median household income: $58,730 (2005); Average household income: $69,747 (2005); Percent of households with income of $100,000 or more: 17.2% (2005); Poverty rate: 7.5% (2000).
Education: Percent of population age 25 and over with: High school diploma (including GED) or higher: 87.3% (2005); Bachelor's degree or higher: 25.3% (2005); Master's degree or higher: 6.6% (2005).

School District(s)
Agency - Academy Charter High School (09-12)
    2003-04 Enrollment: 231 . . . . (732) 681-8377
Housing: Homeownership rate: 59.9% (2005); Median home value: $222,750 (2005); Median rent: $708 per month (2000); Median age of housing: 47 years (2000).
Safety: Violent crime rate: 38.7 per 10,000 population; Property crime rate: 127.2 per 10,000 population (2004).
Transportation: Commute to work: 88.8% car, 2.7% public transportation, 3.8% walk, 2.1% work from home (2000); Travel time to work: 31.0% less than 15 minutes, 28.1% 15 to 30 minutes, 22.4% 30 to 45 minutes, 5.2% 45 to 60 minutes, 13.3% 60 minutes or more (2000)

SPRING LAKE (borough). Aka Spring Lake Beach. Covers a land area of 1.310 square miles and a water area of 0.403 square miles. Located at 40.15° N. Lat.; 74.02° W. Long. Elevation is 25 feet.
History: St. Catharines Roman Catholic Church here was built by Margaret and Martin Maloney as a tribute to their 16-year-old daughter Catharine Maloney, who died of T.B. in 1900 (all three are buried in the church). The church is an example of Roman Renaissance and baroque architecture modeled after the Santa Marie del Popolo in Rome. Incorporated 1892.

Population: 3,499 (1990); 3,567 (2000); 3,733 (2005); 3,911 (2010 projected); Race: 98.6% White, 0.4% Black, 0.3% Asian, 0.7% Hispanic of any race (2005); Density: 2,850.5 persons per square mile (2005); Average household size: 2.39 (2005); Median age: 48.9 (2005); Males per 100 females: 87.8 (2005); Marriage status: 20.1% never married, 64.1% now married, 10.0% widowed, 5.7% divorced (2000); Foreign born: 1.9% (2000); Ancestry (includes multiple ancestries): 50.7% Irish, 20.8% Italian, 19.5% German, 7.2% English, 5.8% Polish (2000).
Economy: Single-family building permits issued: 24 (2005); Multi-family building permits issued: 0 (2005); Employment by occupation: 27.0% management, 26.2% professional, 10.0% services, 29.6% sales, 0.0% farming, 4.7% construction, 2.4% production (2000).
Income: Per capita income: $64,725 (2005); Median household income: $109,350 (2005); Average household income: $152,971 (2005); Percent of households with income of $100,000 or more: 54.5% (2005); Poverty rate: 2.6% (2000).
Education: Percent of population age 25 and over with: High school diploma (including GED) or higher: 96.5% (2005); Bachelor's degree or higher: 59.3% (2005); Master's degree or higher: 26.4% (2005).

School District(s)
Spring Lake Borough (PK-08)
    2003-04 Enrollment: 296 . . . . (732) 449-6380
Housing: Homeownership rate: 79.2% (2005); Median home value: $1 million+ (2005); Median rent: $1,169 per month (2000); Median age of housing: 57 years (2000).
Safety: Violent crime rate: 2.7 per 10,000 population; Property crime rate: 288.8 per 10,000 population (2004).
Transportation: Commute to work: 81.6% car, 5.3% public transportation, 5.0% walk, 7.1% work from home (2000); Travel time to work: 28.5% less than 15 minutes, 23.0% 15 to 30 minutes, 15.6% 30 to 45 minutes, 7.6% 45 to 60 minutes, 25.3% 60 minutes or more (2000)

SPRING LAKE HEIGHTS (borough). Covers a land area of 1.324 square miles and a water area of 0.020 square miles. Located at 40.15° N. Lat.; 74.04° W. Long. Elevation is 54 feet.
History: Incorporated 1927.
Population: 5,341 (1990); 5,227 (2000); 5,273 (2005); 5,356 (2010 projected); Race: 96.9% White, 1.1% Black, 0.4% Asian, 2.5% Hispanic of any race (2005); Density: 3,982.4 persons per square mile (2005); Average household size: 2.05 (2005); Median age: 49.9 (2005); Males per 100 females: 82.5 (2005); Marriage status: 25.8% never married, 48.3% now married, 14.0% widowed, 11.8% divorced (2000); Foreign born: 3.9% (2000); Ancestry (includes multiple ancestries): 42.2% Irish, 22.3% German, 14.0% Italian, 12.2% English, 6.1% Polish (2000).
Economy: Single-family building permits issued: 25 (2005); Multi-family building permits issued: 0 (2005); Employment by occupation: 17.2% management, 27.8% professional, 15.7% services, 29.1% sales, 0.0% farming, 4.7% construction, 5.5% production (2000).
Income: Per capita income: $39,934 (2005); Median household income: $61,323 (2005); Average household income: $81,642 (2005); Percent of households with income of $100,000 or more: 25.2% (2005); Poverty rate: 7.5% (2000).
Education: Percent of population age 25 and over with: High school diploma (including GED) or higher: 89.1% (2005); Bachelor's degree or higher: 38.2% (2005); Master's degree or higher: 12.0% (2005).

School District(s)
Spring Lake Heights Borough (PK-08)
    2003-04 Enrollment: 391 . . . . (732) 449-6149
Housing: Homeownership rate: 61.9% (2005); Median home value: $384,904 (2005); Median rent: $808 per month (2000); Median age of housing: 34 years (2000).
Safety: Violent crime rate: 1.9 per 10,000 population; Property crime rate: 85.1 per 10,000 population (2004).
Transportation: Commute to work: 83.2% car, 7.9% public transportation, 1.3% walk, 7.1% work from home (2000); Travel time to work: 27.5% less than 15 minutes, 24.2% 15 to 30 minutes, 13.9% 30 to 45 minutes, 10.5% 45 to 60 minutes, 23.9% 60 minutes or more (2000)
Additional Information Contacts
Borough of Spring Lake Heights . . . . (732) 449-3503
    http://www.springlakehts.com

STRATHMORE (CDP). Covers a land area of 1.844 square miles and a water area of 0.013 square miles. Located at 40.40° N. Lat.; 74.21° W. Long. Elevation is 140 feet.

Population: 7,060 (1990); 6,740 (2000); 7,244 (2005); 7,737 (2010 projected); Race: 86.9% White, 3.2% Black, 7.2% Asian, 5.5% Hispanic of any race (2005); Density: 3,927.6 persons per square mile (2005); Average household size: 2.83 (2005); Median age: 40.3 (2005); Males per 100 females: 94.4 (2005); Marriage status: 20.0% never married, 70.9% now married, 5.6% widowed, 3.5% divorced (2000); Foreign born: 9.5% (2000); Ancestry (includes multiple ancestries): 25.9% Italian, 22.8% Irish, 17.8% Other groups, 14.4% German, 6.7% Polish (2000).

Economy: Employment by occupation: 24.3% management, 27.7% professional, 8.9% services, 29.8% sales, 0.2% farming, 4.5% construction, 4.6% production (2000).

Income: Per capita income: $37,694 (2005); Median household income: $94,398 (2005); Average household income: $106,536 (2005); Percent of households with income of $100,000 or more: 45.5% (2005); Poverty rate: 2.3% (2000).

Education: Percent of population age 25 and over with: High school diploma (including GED) or higher: 94.8% (2005); Bachelor's degree or higher: 48.9% (2005); Master's degree or higher: 15.0% (2005).

Housing: Homeownership rate: 93.4% (2005); Median home value: $327,427 (2005); Median rent: $734 per month (2000); Median age of housing: 34 years (2000).

Transportation: Commute to work: 77.9% car, 16.4% public transportation, 1.6% walk, 3.3% work from home (2000); Travel time to work: 17.6% less than 15 minutes, 23.4% 15 to 30 minutes, 18.2% 30 to 45 minutes, 11.4% 45 to 60 minutes, 29.3% 60 minutes or more (2000)

TINTON FALLS (borough). Aka New Shrewsbury. Covers a land area of 15.588 square miles and a water area of 0.032 square miles. Located at 40.27° N. Lat.; 74.09° W. Long. Elevation is 42 feet.

History: Named for Tintern in Monmouthshire, England. Incorporated 1950.

Population: 12,473 (1990); 15,053 (2000); 16,313 (2005); 17,588 (2010 projected); Race: 80.1% White, 11.6% Black, 5.0% Asian, 5.5% Hispanic of any race (2005); Density: 1,046.5 persons per square mile (2005); Average household size: 2.50 (2005); Median age: 38.3 (2005); Males per 100 females: 91.4 (2005); Marriage status: 23.6% never married, 60.5% now married, 6.5% widowed, 9.4% divorced (2000); Foreign born: 10.0% (2000); Ancestry (includes multiple ancestries): 23.2% Other groups, 22.6% Italian, 21.2% Irish, 14.3% German, 7.4% English (2000).

Economy: Manufacturing: telecommunications and tungsten products, inks. Single-family building permits issued: 53 (2005); Multi-family building permits issued: 28 (2005); Employment by occupation: 21.3% management, 24.8% professional, 11.2% services, 30.9% sales, 0.3% farming, 4.8% construction, 6.8% production (2000).

Income: Per capita income: $37,439 (2005); Median household income: $78,436 (2005); Average household income: $93,432 (2005); Percent of households with income of $100,000 or more: 35.4% (2005); Poverty rate: 3.9% (2000).

Education: Percent of population age 25 and over with: High school diploma (including GED) or higher: 92.5% (2005); Bachelor's degree or higher: 42.4% (2005); Master's degree or higher: 14.5% (2005).

School District(s)
Monmouth County Vocational (09-12)
    2003-04 Enrollment: 1,856 . . . . (732) 431-7942
Monmouth Regional (09-12)
    2003-04 Enrollment: 1,355 . . . . (732) 542-1170
Monmouth-Ocean Ed Serv Comm (UG-UG)
    2003-04 Enrollment: 218 . . . . (732) 389-5555
Tinton Falls (PK-08)
    2003-04 Enrollment: 1,797 . . . . (732) 460-2404

Housing: Homeownership rate: 83.7% (2005); Median home value: $292,662 (2005); Median rent: $1,046 per month (2000); Median age of housing: 16 years (2000).

Safety: Violent crime rate: 8.1 per 10,000 population; Property crime rate: 169.7 per 10,000 population (2004).

Transportation: Commute to work: 89.2% car, 6.1% public transportation, 1.1% walk, 2.9% work from home (2000); Travel time to work: 27.1% less than 15 minutes, 34.6% 15 to 30 minutes, 9.7% 30 to 45 minutes, 9.8% 45 to 60 minutes, 18.7% 60 minutes or more (2000)

Additional Information Contacts
Borough of Tinton Falls . . . . (732) 542-3400
    http://www.tintonfalls.com

UNION BEACH (borough). Covers a land area of 1.876 square miles and a water area of 0.055 square miles. Located at 40.44° N. Lat.; 74.17° W. Long. Elevation is 9 feet.

History: Incorporated 1925.

Population: 6,156 (1990); 6,649 (2000); 6,764 (2005); 6,921 (2010 projected); Race: 93.8% White, 0.9% Black, 1.4% Asian, 9.9% Hispanic of any race (2005); Density: 3,606.4 persons per square mile (2005); Average household size: 3.09 (2005); Median age: 35.9 (2005); Males per 100 females: 101.7 (2005); Marriage status: 26.9% never married, 57.2% now married, 6.7% widowed, 9.2% divorced (2000); Foreign born: 5.1% (2000); Ancestry (includes multiple ancestries): 27.0% Irish, 26.5% Italian, 19.8% German, 12.7% Other groups, 9.0% Polish (2000).

Economy: Single-family building permits issued: 7 (2005); Multi-family building permits issued: 0 (2005); Employment by occupation: 10.1% management, 12.7% professional, 14.2% services, 29.3% sales, 0.0% farming, 16.4% construction, 17.2% production (2000).

Income: Per capita income: $25,325 (2005); Median household income: $70,720 (2005); Average household income: $78,182 (2005); Percent of households with income of $100,000 or more: 27.9% (2005); Poverty rate: 4.8% (2000).

Taxes: Total city taxes per capita: $516 (2004); City property taxes per capita: $510 (2004).

Education: Percent of population age 25 and over with: High school diploma (including GED) or higher: 79.0% (2005); Bachelor's degree or higher: 8.6% (2005); Master's degree or higher: 2.1% (2005).

School District(s)
Union Beach (PK-08)
    2003-04 Enrollment: 1,038 . . . . (732) 264-5405

Housing: Homeownership rate: 83.9% (2005); Median home value: $231,692 (2005); Median rent: $780 per month (2000); Median age of housing: 46 years (2000).

Safety: Violent crime rate: 20.6 per 10,000 population; Property crime rate: 128.1 per 10,000 population (2004).

Transportation: Commute to work: 89.0% car, 7.0% public transportation, 2.0% walk, 1.3% work from home (2000); Travel time to work: 25.3% less than 15 minutes, 28.1% 15 to 30 minutes, 22.3% 30 to 45 minutes, 10.4% 45 to 60 minutes, 13.9% 60 minutes or more (2000)

UPPER FREEHOLD (township). Covers a land area of 46.861 square miles and a water area of 0.273 square miles. Located at 40.15° N. Lat.; 74.52° W. Long.

Population: 3,277 (1990); 4,282 (2000); 6,826 (2005); 9,123 (2010 projected); Race: 94.4% White, 0.8% Black, 1.7% Asian, 3.6% Hispanic of any race (2005); Density: 145.7 persons per square mile (2005); Average household size: 2.97 (2005); Median age: 39.0 (2005); Males per 100 females: 101.8 (2005); Marriage status: 20.7% never married, 70.0% now married, 3.4% widowed, 5.8% divorced (2000); Foreign born: 5.4% (2000); Ancestry (includes multiple ancestries): 22.1% German, 21.7% Italian, 20.1% Irish, 15.1% English, 11.3% Polish (2000).

Economy: Single-family building permits issued: 62 (2005); Multi-family building permits issued: 0 (2005); Employment by occupation: 23.6% management, 17.5% professional, 14.7% services, 24.2% sales, 3.1% farming, 8.8% construction, 8.1% production (2000).

Income: Per capita income: $36,905 (2005); Median household income: $88,914 (2005); Average household income: $108,932 (2005); Percent of households with income of $100,000 or more: 42.7% (2005); Poverty rate: 4.0% (2000).

Education: Percent of population age 25 and over with: High school diploma (including GED) or higher: 88.6% (2005); Bachelor's degree or higher: 36.4% (2005); Master's degree or higher: 9.6% (2005).

Housing: Homeownership rate: 87.1% (2005); Median home value: $452,998 (2005); Median rent: $658 per month (2000); Median age of housing: 25 years (2000).

Transportation: Commute to work: 85.5% car, 2.8% public transportation, 2.2% walk, 6.8% work from home (2000); Travel time to work: 20.6% less than 15 minutes, 26.2% 15 to 30 minutes, 26.0% 30 to 45 minutes, 14.6% 45 to 60 minutes, 12.6% 60 minutes or more (2000)

WALL (township). Covers a land area of 30.617 square miles and a water area of 0.798 square miles. Located at 40.15° N. Lat.; 74.07° W. Long.

History: Incorporated 1851.

Population: 20,256 (1990); 25,261 (2000); 26,318 (2005); 27,393 (2010 projected); Race: 96.9% White, 0.6% Black, 1.4% Asian, 1.8% Hispanic of

any race (2005); Density: 859.6 persons per square mile (2005); Average household size: 2.64 (2005); Median age: 41.6 (2005); Males per 100 females: 93.6 (2005); Marriage status: 20.9% never married, 64.7% now married, 7.1% widowed, 7.3% divorced (2000); Foreign born: 4.0% (2000); Ancestry (includes multiple ancestries): 34.9% Irish, 25.7% Italian, 20.9% German, 11.5% English, 8.2% Polish (2000).
Economy: Unemployment rate: 2.7% (2005); Total civilian labor force: 13,592 (2005); Single-family building permits issued: 122 (2005); Multi-family building permits issued: 93 (2005); Employment by occupation: 18.0% management, 26.5% professional, 9.7% services, 27.6% sales, 0.5% farming, 10.1% construction, 7.8% production (2000).
Income: Per capita income: $40,332 (2005); Median household income: $86,847 (2005); Average household income: $106,277 (2005); Percent of households with income of $100,000 or more: 41.9% (2005); Poverty rate: 2.3% (2000).
Taxes: Total city taxes per capita: $701 (2004); City property taxes per capita: $605 (2004).
Education: Percent of population age 25 and over with: High school diploma (including GED) or higher: 91.7% (2005); Bachelor's degree or higher: 39.1% (2005); Master's degree or higher: 14.0% (2005).

School District(s)
Monmouth County Vocational (09-12)
    2003-04 Enrollment: 1,856 . . . . (732) 431-7942
Wall Township (PK-12)
    2003-04 Enrollment: 4,360 . . . . (732) 556-2000

Two-year College(s)
Stuart School of Business Administration (Private, For-profit)
    Fall 2004 Enrollment: 92 . . . . (732) 681-7200

Housing: Homeownership rate: 86.1% (2005); Median home value: $401,500 (2005); Median rent: $752 per month (2000); Median age of housing: 30 years (2000).
Safety: Violent crime rate: 9.1 per 10,000 population; Property crime rate: 144.0 per 10,000 population (2004).
Transportation: Commute to work: 92.4% car, 3.1% public transportation, 0.8% walk, 3.3% work from home (2000); Travel time to work: 29.9% less than 15 minutes, 31.6% 15 to 30 minutes, 13.7% 30 to 45 minutes, 7.6% 45 to 60 minutes, 17.2% 60 minutes or more (2000)
Additional Information Contacts
Southern Monmouth Chamber of Commerce . . . . (732) 974-1151
    http://www.smcconline.org
Wall Township . . . . (732) 449-8444
    http://www.wallnj.com

WANAMASSA (CDP).
Covers a land area of 1.123 square miles and a water area of 0.009 square miles. Located at 40.23° N. Lat.; 74.02° W. Long. Elevation is 34 feet.
Population: 4,530 (1990); 4,551 (2000); 4,572 (2005); 4,627 (2010 projected); Race: 93.9% White, 1.1% Black, 3.1% Asian, 3.6% Hispanic of any race (2005); Density: 4,070.1 persons per square mile (2005); Average household size: 2.73 (2005); Median age: 39.7 (2005); Males per 100 females: 95.1 (2005); Marriage status: 21.7% never married, 61.9% now married, 7.0% widowed, 9.4% divorced (2000); Foreign born: 7.0% (2000); Ancestry (includes multiple ancestries): 28.4% Irish, 26.5% Italian, 18.5% German, 12.1% Other groups, 11.3% English (2000).
Economy: Employment by occupation: 13.1% management, 27.8% professional, 9.2% services, 32.9% sales, 0.6% farming, 8.7% construction, 7.8% production (2000).
Income: Per capita income: $31,909 (2005); Median household income: $71,429 (2005); Average household income: $87,151 (2005); Percent of households with income of $100,000 or more: 27.9% (2005); Poverty rate: 1.6% (2000).
Education: Percent of population age 25 and over with: High school diploma (including GED) or higher: 91.8% (2005); Bachelor's degree or higher: 33.0% (2005); Master's degree or higher: 11.8% (2005).

School District(s)
Ocean Township (PK-12)
    2003-04 Enrollment: 4,982 . . . . (732) 531-5600
Housing: Homeownership rate: 89.1% (2005); Median home value: $270,125 (2005); Median rent: $688 per month (2000); Median age of housing: 46 years (2000).
Transportation: Commute to work: 89.8% car, 4.2% public transportation, 1.0% walk, 3.2% work from home (2000); Travel time to work: 35.7% less than 15 minutes, 35.7% 15 to 30 minutes, 10.4% 30 to 45 minutes, 4.0% 45 to 60 minutes, 14.2% 60 minutes or more (2000)

WEST BELMAR (CDP).
Covers a land area of 0.478 square miles and a water area of 0 square miles. Located at 40.17° N. Lat.; 74.03° W. Long. Elevation is 24 feet.
Population: 2,498 (1990); 2,606 (2000); 2,469 (2005); 2,375 (2010 projected); Race: 94.7% White, 0.9% Black, 1.7% Asian, 3.2% Hispanic of any race (2005); Density: 5,163.7 persons per square mile (2005); Average household size: 2.62 (2005); Median age: 37.8 (2005); Males per 100 females: 96.6 (2005); Marriage status: 24.3% never married, 60.9% now married, 4.5% widowed, 10.3% divorced (2000); Foreign born: 7.9% (2000); Ancestry (includes multiple ancestries): 31.9% Irish, 23.9% Italian, 20.5% German, 12.0% English, 10.0% Other groups (2000).
Economy: Employment by occupation: 10.5% management, 19.5% professional, 9.9% services, 31.6% sales, 0.4% farming, 17.0% construction, 11.0% production (2000).
Income: Per capita income: $25,712 (2005); Median household income: $61,565 (2005); Average household income: $67,391 (2005); Percent of households with income of $100,000 or more: 17.6% (2005); Poverty rate: 3.1% (2000).
Education: Percent of population age 25 and over with: High school diploma (including GED) or higher: 88.9% (2005); Bachelor's degree or higher: 20.8% (2005); Master's degree or higher: 5.0% (2005).
Housing: Homeownership rate: 77.2% (2005); Median home value: $252,442 (2005); Median rent: $699 per month (2000); Median age of housing: 52 years (2000).
Transportation: Commute to work: 95.9% car, 2.4% public transportation, 0.4% walk, 0.0% work from home (2000); Travel time to work: 36.8% less than 15 minutes, 36.2% 15 to 30 minutes, 10.5% 30 to 45 minutes, 5.7% 45 to 60 minutes, 10.8% 60 minutes or more (2000)

WEST FREEHOLD (CDP).
Covers a land area of 5.867 square miles and a water area of 0 square miles. Located at 40.23° N. Lat.; 74.29° W. Long. Elevation is 190 feet.
Population: 11,166 (1990); 12,498 (2000); 12,971 (2005); 13,460 (2010 projected); Race: 90.3% White, 2.0% Black, 4.6% Asian, 6.2% Hispanic of any race (2005); Density: 2,210.9 persons per square mile (2005); Average household size: 2.66 (2005); Median age: 41.8 (2005); Males per 100 females: 92.8 (2005); Marriage status: 20.1% never married, 64.7% now married, 7.4% widowed, 7.8% divorced (2000); Foreign born: 11.4% (2000); Ancestry (includes multiple ancestries): 24.9% Italian, 18.6% Irish, 15.6% Other groups, 13.9% German, 12.2% Polish (2000).
Economy: Employment by occupation: 19.2% management, 25.5% professional, 9.2% services, 35.5% sales, 0.0% farming, 5.5% construction, 5.1% production (2000).
Income: Per capita income: $37,078 (2005); Median household income: $83,317 (2005); Average household income: $98,025 (2005); Percent of households with income of $100,000 or more: 39.4% (2005); Poverty rate: 4.7% (2000).
Education: Percent of population age 25 and over with: High school diploma (including GED) or higher: 90.6% (2005); Bachelor's degree or higher: 39.9% (2005); Master's degree or higher: 12.6% (2005).
Housing: Homeownership rate: 86.6% (2005); Median home value: $350,191 (2005); Median rent: $770 per month (2000); Median age of housing: 22 years (2000).
Transportation: Commute to work: 85.7% car, 9.6% public transportation, 0.1% walk, 3.8% work from home (2000); Travel time to work: 24.8% less than 15 minutes, 21.6% 15 to 30 minutes, 17.9% 30 to 45 minutes, 10.7% 45 to 60 minutes, 25.0% 60 minutes or more (2000)

WEST LONG BRANCH (borough).
Covers a land area of 2.888 square miles and a water area of 0.019 square miles. Located at 40.29° N. Lat.; 74.01° W. Long. Elevation is 20 feet.
History: "Shadow Lawn," here, was President Wilson's summer White House, which now is the main building of Monmouth College. Settled 1711, incorporated 1908.
Population: 7,690 (1990); 8,258 (2000); 8,182 (2005); 8,104 (2010 projected); Race: 94.3% White, 2.2% Black, 1.0% Asian, 3.3% Hispanic of any race (2005); Density: 2,833.6 persons per square mile (2005); Average household size: 3.37 (2005); Median age: 32.6 (2005); Males per 100 females: 87.4 (2005); Marriage status: 30.5% never married, 57.2% now married, 7.2% widowed, 5.1% divorced (2000); Foreign born: 7.0% (2000); Ancestry (includes multiple ancestries): 36.1% Italian, 20.5% Irish, 13.4% German, 9.7% Other groups, 7.3% English (2000).
Economy: Single-family building permits issued: 6 (2005); Multi-family building permits issued: 0 (2005); Employment by occupation: 15.0%

management, 24.1% professional, 15.0% services, 31.5% sales, 0.0% farming, 10.0% construction, 4.4% production (2000).
Income: Per capita income: $29,978 (2005); Median household income: $79,110 (2005); Average household income: $98,738 (2005); Percent of households with income of $100,000 or more: 37.4% (2005); Poverty rate: 4.5% (2000).
Taxes: Total city taxes per capita: $518 (2004); City property taxes per capita: $492 (2004).
Education: Percent of population age 25 and over with: High school diploma (including GED) or higher: 87.2% (2005); Bachelor's degree or higher: 35.1% (2005); Master's degree or higher: 14.4% (2005).

School District(s)
Shore Regional (09-12)
    2003-04 Enrollment: 835 . . . . (732) 222-9300
West Long Branch Borough (PK-08)
    2003-04 Enrollment: 759 . . . . (732) 222-5900

Four-year College(s)
Monmouth University (Private, Not-for-profit)
    Fall 2004 Enrollment: 6,329. . . . . (732) 571-3400
    2005-06 Tuition: In-state $20,662; Out-of-state $20,662
Housing: Homeownership rate: 84.9% (2005); Median home value: $359,291 (2005); Median rent: $605 per month (2000); Median age of housing: 41 years (2000).
Safety: Violent crime rate: 25.4 per 10,000 population; Property crime rate: 375.9 per 10,000 population (2004).
Transportation: Commute to work: 83.8% car, 3.3% public transportation, 6.2% walk, 5.2% work from home (2000); Travel time to work: 46.7% less than 15 minutes, 28.1% 15 to 30 minutes, 8.7% 30 to 45 minutes, 5.2% 45 to 60 minutes, 11.2% 60 minutes or more (2000)

YORKETOWN (CDP). Covers a land area of 2.404 square miles and a water area of 0 square miles. Located at 40.30° N. Lat.; 74.33° W. Long.
Population: 6,313 (1990); 6,712 (2000); 6,275 (2005); 5,933 (2010 projected); Race: 94.0% White, 1.9% Black, 2.5% Asian, 3.8% Hispanic of any race (2005); Density: 2,609.7 persons per square mile (2005); Average household size: 3.37 (2005); Median age: 37.7 (2005); Males per 100 females: 95.2 (2005); Marriage status: 22.4% never married, 69.3% now married, 4.6% widowed, 3.7% divorced (2000); Foreign born: 6.6% (2000); Ancestry (includes multiple ancestries): 31.7% Italian, 18.6% Irish, 14.7% Other groups, 10.7% Polish, 9.8% German (2000).
Economy: Employment by occupation: 23.7% management, 24.4% professional, 5.6% services, 32.9% sales, 0.0% farming, 7.0% construction, 6.3% production (2000).
Income: Per capita income: $37,000 (2005); Median household income: $105,863 (2005); Average household income: $124,322 (2005); Percent of households with income of $100,000 or more: 53.4% (2005); Poverty rate: 2.7% (2000).
Education: Percent of population age 25 and over with: High school diploma (including GED) or higher: 94.7% (2005); Bachelor's degree or higher: 37.6% (2005); Master's degree or higher: 10.6% (2005).
Housing: Homeownership rate: 95.5% (2005); Median home value: $380,868 (2005); Median rent: $1,367 per month (2000); Median age of housing: 28 years (2000).
Transportation: Commute to work: 83.1% car, 13.2% public transportation, 0.0% walk, 2.6% work from home (2000); Travel time to work: 15.8% less than 15 minutes, 25.9% 15 to 30 minutes, 14.6% 30 to 45 minutes, 9.1% 45 to 60 minutes, 34.6% 60 minutes or more (2000)

Morris County

Located in northern New Jersey; bounded on the southeast and east by the Passaic River; includes many lakes and mountain ridges; drained by the Pequannock, Rockaway, Whippany, and Musconetcong Rivers. Covers a land area of 468.99 square miles, a water area of 12.29 square miles, and is located in the Eastern Time Zone. The county government was organized in 1739. County seat is Morristown.

Morris County is part of the New York-Northern New Jersey-Long Island, NY-NJ-PA Metropolitan Statistical Area. The entire metro area includes: Edison, NJ Metropolitan Division (Middlesex County, NJ; Monmouth County, NJ; Ocean County, NJ; Somerset County, NJ); Nassau-Suffolk, NY Metropolitan Division (Nassau County, NY; Suffolk County, NY); New York-White Plains-Wayne, NY-NJ Metropolitan Division (Bergen County, NJ; Hudson County, NJ; Passaic County, NJ; Bronx County, NY; Kings County, NY; New York County, NY; Putnam County, NY; Queens County,

NY; Richmond County, NY; Rockland County, NY; Westchester County, NY); Newark-Union, NJ-PA Metropolitan Division (Essex County, NJ; Hunterdon County, NJ; Morris County, NJ; Sussex County, NJ; Union County, NJ; Pike County, PA)

Weather Station: Boonton 1 SE   Elevation: 278 feet

	Jan	Feb	Mar	Apr	May	Jun	Jul	Aug	Sep	Oct	Nov	Dec
High	36	39	48	60	71	79	84	82	75	64	52	41
Low	18	20	29	39	48	57	62	61	52	41	33	24
Precip	3.9	3.1	4.2	4.4	4.8	4.6	4.7	4.1	4.6	4.2	4.5	3.9
Snow	8.9	9.0	5.1	0.8	0.0	0.0	0.0	0.0	0.0	tr	0.8	3.6

High and Low temperatures in degrees Fahrenheit; Precipitation and Snow in inches

Weather Station: Long Valley   Elevation: 547 feet

	Jan	Feb	Mar	Apr	May	Jun	Jul	Aug	Sep	Oct	Nov	Dec
High	36	39	48	60	70	77	82	80	72	63	52	41
Low	17	18	26	35	45	54	59	58	50	38	31	22
Precip	4.2	3.3	4.2	4.6	4.9	4.7	5.0	4.8	4.9	4.3	4.4	4.0
Snow	10.5	8.9	6.3	1.9	0.0	0.0	0.0	0.0	0.0	0.2	1.0	4.9

High and Low temperatures in degrees Fahrenheit; Precipitation and Snow in inches

Population: 421,574 (1990); 470,212 (2000); 489,732 (2005); 510,077 (2010 projected); Race: 85.6% White, 2.8% Black, 7.3% Asian, 9.3% Hispanic of any race (2005); Density: 1,044.2 persons per square mile (2005); Average household size: 2.75 (2005); Median age: 39.3 (2005); Males per 100 females: 96.3 (2005).
Religion: Five largest groups: 38.1% Catholic Church, 7.1% Jewish Estimate, 2.5% Presbyterian Church (U.S.A.), 2.0% The United Methodist Church, 1.7% Episcopal Church (2000).
Economy: Unemployment rate: 3.2% (2005); Total civilian labor force: 267,847 (2005); Leading industries: 11.7% retail trade; 11.2% professional (2004); Farms: 407 totaling 17,233 acres (2002); Companies that employ 500 or more persons: 128 (2004); Companies that employ 100 to 499 persons: 805 (2004); Companies that employ less than 100 persons: 34,360 (2004); Black-owned businesses: 648 (2002); Hispanic-owned businesses: 1,939 (2002); Asian-owned businesses: 2,948 (2002); Women-owned businesses: 11,322 (2002); Retail sales per capita: $23,238 (2006). Single-family building permits issued: 927 (2005); Multi-family building permits issued: 1,576 (2005).
Income: Per capita income: $42,536 (2005); Median household income: $88,278 (2005); Average household income: $116,046 (2005); Percent of households with income of $100,000 or more: 42.8% (2005); Poverty rate: 4.2% (2003); Bankruptcy rate: 2.79% (2005).
Taxes: Total county taxes per capita: $399 (2004); County property taxes per capita: $398 (2004).
Education: Percent of population age 25 and over with: High school diploma (including GED) or higher: 90.5% (2005); Bachelor's degree or higher: 43.9% (2005); Master's degree or higher: 16.9% (2005).
Housing: Homeownership rate: 75.9% (2005); Median home value: $399,933 (2005); Median rent: $813 per month (2000); Median age of housing: 35 years (2000).
Health: Birth rate: 127.6 per 10,000 population (2004); Death rate: 71.2 per 10,000 population (2004); Age-adjusted cancer mortality rate: 197.9 deaths per 100,000 population (2002); Air Quality Index: 85.2% good, 13.7% moderate, 1.1% unhealthy for sensitive individuals, 0.0% unhealthy (percent of days in 2005); Number of physicians: 41.1 per 10,000 population (2004); Hospital beds: 65.9 per 10,000 population (2003); Hospital admissions: 2,202.0 per 10,000 population (2003).
Elections: 2004 Presidential election results: 57.5% Bush, 41.7% Kerry, 0.5% Nader, 0.1% Badnarik
National and State Parks: Farny State Park; Fort Nonsense Historical National Park; Great Swamp National Wildlife Refuge; Hacklebarney State Park; Hopatcong State Park; Morristown National Historical Park; Washington Headquarters National Park
Additional Information Contacts
Morris County Government . . . . (973) 285-6010
    http://www.co.morris.nj.us
Boonton Township . . . . (973) 402-4002
    http://www.boontontownship.com
Borough of Butler . . . . (973) 838-7200
    http://www.butlerborough.com
Borough of Chester . . . . (908) 879-5361
    http://www.chesterborough.org
Borough of Florham Park . . . . (973) 410-5300
    http://www.florhamparkboro.net
Borough of Lincoln Park . . . . (973) 694-6100
    http://www.lincolnpark.org

Borough of Madison............................(973) 593-3042
    http://www.rosenet.org/gov
Borough of Mendham ....(973) 543-7152
    http://www.mendhamnj.org
Borough of Mount Arlington.......................(973) 398-6832
    http://www.ci.mount-arlington.nj.us
Borough of Mountain Lakes........................(973) 334-1413
    http://www.mtnlakes.org
Borough of Netcong...........................(973) 347-0252
    http://www.netcong.org
Chatham Area Chamber of Commerce................(973) 635-2444
    http://www.chathamarea.com
Chatham Township ....(973) 635-4600
    http://www.chathamtownship.org
Chester Township ....(908) 879-5100
    http://www.chestertownship.org
Denville Chamber of Commerce ....(973) 627-1340
    http://www.denville-nj.com
Denville Township ....(973) 625-8300
    http://www.denvillenj.org
Hanover Township ....(973) 428-2500
    http://www.hanovertownship.com
Jefferson Township ....(973) 208-6129
    http://www.jeffersontownship.net
Jefferson Township Chamber of Commerce ....(973) 663-2240
    http://www.jeffersontownshipchamber.org
Livingston-East Hanover Chamber of Commerce ....(973) 992-4343
    http://www.livingstonchambernj.com
Long Hill Township ....(908) 647-8000
    http://www.longhillnj.org
Madison Chamber of Commerce.....................(973) 377-7830
    http://www.rosenet.org/chamber
Mendham Township.............................(973) 543-4555
    http://www.mendhamtownship.org
Mine Hill Township................................(973) 366-9031
    http://www.minehill.com
Montville Township ....(973) 331-3302
    http://www.montville-township.org
Montville Township Chamber of Commerce ....(973) 263-3300
    http://www.montville-township.org
Morris County Chamber of Commerce ....(973) 539-3882
    http://www.morrischamber.org
Morris Township ....(973) 326-7360
    http://www.morristwp.com
Morristown Chamber of Commerce..................(973) 539-3882
    http://www.morrischamber.org
Mount Olive Area Chamber of Commerce.............(973) 691-0109
    http://mountolivechambernj.com
Mount Olive Area Chamber of Commerce.............(973) 671-0109
    http://www.mtolivechambernj.com
Mount Olive Township ....(973) 691-0900
    http://www.mountolivetownship.com
Parsippany Chamber of Commerce..................(973) 402-6400
    http://www.njpacc.org
Parsippany-Troy Hills Township ....(973) 263-4357
    http://www.parsippany.net
Pequannock Township...........................(973) 835-5700
    http://www.pequannocktownship.org
Randolph Chamber of Commerce...................(973) 361-3462
    http://www.randolphchamber.org
Randolph Township............................(973) 989-7100
    http://www.randolphnj.org
Roxbury Area Chamber of Commerce................(973) 770-0740
    http://www.roxburychamber.org
Roxbury Chamber of Commerce ....(973) 770-07.4
    http://www.roxburychamber.org
Roxbury Township.............................(973) 448-2000
    http://www.roxburynj.us
Town of Boonton ....(973) 402-9410
    http://www.boonton.org
Tri-County Chamber of Commerce ....(973) 831-7788
    http://www.tricounty.org/directory/city/Butler
Tri-Town Chamber of Commerce ....(973) 334-4117
    http://www.tritownchamber.org
Washington Township ....(908) 876-3315
    http://www.washtwpmorris.org

Morris County Communities

BOONTON (town). Covers a land area of 2.347 square miles and a water area of 0.120 square miles. Located at 40.90° N. Lat.; 74.40° W. Long. Elevation is 431 feet.

Population: 8,296 (1990); 8,496 (2000); 8,431 (2005); 8,427 (2010 projected); Race: 79.8% White, 4.5% Black, 9.5% Asian, 8.6% Hispanic of any race (2005); Density: 3,591.9 persons per square mile (2005); Average household size: 2.56 (2005); Median age: 38.6 (2005); Males per 100 females: 99.7 (2005); Marriage status: 27.2% never married, 56.1% now married, 8.2% widowed, 8.5% divorced (2000); Foreign born: 16.3% (2000); Ancestry (includes multiple ancestries): 24.3% Italian, 20.8% Irish, 18.7% Other groups, 16.3% German, 7.0% English (2000).

Economy: Single-family building permits issued: 31 (2005); Multi-family building permits issued: 0 (2005); Employment by occupation: 16.1% management, 24.8% professional, 11.4% services, 28.1% sales, 0.0% farming, 7.3% construction, 12.3% production (2000).

Income: Per capita income: $36,791 (2005); Median household income: $76,184 (2005); Average household income: $93,005 (2005); Percent of households with income of $100,000 or more: 34.7% (2005); Poverty rate: 6.7% (2000).

Education: Percent of population age 25 and over with: High school diploma (including GED) or higher: 85.8% (2005); Bachelor's degree or higher: 32.6% (2005); Master's degree or higher: 9.4% (2005).

School District(s)

Boonton Town (PK-12)
    2003-04 Enrollment: 1,395 ....(973) 335-3994
Boonton Township (PK-08)
    2003-04 Enrollment: 547........................(973) 334-4162
Morris County Vocational (09-12)
    2003-04 Enrollment: 182.......................(973) 627-4600

Housing: Homeownership rate: 59.3% (2005); Median home value: $336,713 (2005); Median rent: $817 per month (2000); Median age of housing: 58 years (2000).

Hospitals: Saint Clare's Hospital-Boonton Township (106 beds)

Safety: Violent crime rate: 18.9 per 10,000 population; Property crime rate: 88.4 per 10,000 population (2004).

Transportation: Commute to work: 90.8% car, 2.7% public transportation, 3.3% walk, 2.6% work from home (2000); Travel time to work: 31.5% less than 15 minutes, 39.5% 15 to 30 minutes, 16.2% 30 to 45 minutes, 5.2% 45 to 60 minutes, 7.6% 60 minutes or more (2000)

Additional Information Contacts

Town of Boonton ....(973) 402-9410
    http://www.boonton.org
Tri-Town Chamber of Commerce ....(973) 334-4117
    http://www.tritownchamber.org

BOONTON (township). Covers a land area of 8.425 square miles and a water area of 0.164 square miles. Located at 40.93° N. Lat.; 74.43° W. Long. Elevation is 431 feet.

History: Was iron center in mid-19th century. First Bakelite factory here. Settled 1760, incorporated 1867.

Population: 3,202 (1990); 4,287 (2000); 4,372 (2005); 4,486 (2010 projected); Race: 92.1% White, 1.0% Black, 4.9% Asian, 2.7% Hispanic of any race (2005); Density: 519.0 persons per square mile (2005); Average household size: 2.91 (2005); Median age: 43.2 (2005); Males per 100 females: 99.2 (2005); Marriage status: 20.6% never married, 67.1% now married, 6.4% widowed, 5.9% divorced (2000); Foreign born: 8.3% (2000); Ancestry (includes multiple ancestries): 24.5% Italian, 22.9% German, 18.8% Irish, 12.1% English, 8.7% Polish (2000).

Economy: Manufacturing: plastics, electrical and radio equipment, apparel. Agriculture: dairy products; livestock; vegetables. Single-family building permits issued: 16 (2005); Multi-family building permits issued: 0 (2005); Employment by occupation: 25.4% management, 29.1% professional, 6.2% services, 28.8% sales, 0.0% farming, 6.2% construction, 4.1% production (2000).

Income: Per capita income: $54,199 (2005); Median household income: $108,991 (2005); Average household income: $155,737 (2005); Percent of households with income of $100,000 or more: 53.8% (2005); Poverty rate: 1.3% (2000).

Education: Percent of population age 25 and over with: High school diploma (including GED) or higher: 93.1% (2005); Bachelor's degree or higher: 46.0% (2005); Master's degree or higher: 17.0% (2005).

Housing: Homeownership rate: 92.8% (2005); Median home value: $538,653 (2005); Median rent: $980 per month (2000); Median age of housing: 37 years (2000).
Hospitals: Saint Clare's Hospital-Boonton Township (106 beds)
Safety: Violent crime rate: 2.3 per 10,000 population; Property crime rate: 64.1 per 10,000 population (2004).
Transportation: Commute to work: 84.1% car, 3.2% public transportation, 1.9% walk, 10.3% work from home (2000); Travel time to work: 26.0% less than 15 minutes, 35.9% 15 to 30 minutes, 19.6% 30 to 45 minutes, 9.1% 45 to 60 minutes, 9.4% 60 minutes or more (2000)
Additional Information Contacts
Boonton Township . . . . (973) 402-4002
 http://www.boontontownship.com
Tri-Town Chamber of Commerce . . . . (973) 334-4117
 http://www.tritownchamber.org

BUDD LAKE (CDP). Covers a land area of 5.853 square miles and a water area of 0.592 square miles. Located at 40.86° N. Lat.; 74.74° W. Long. Elevation is 1,060 feet.
Population: 7,272 (1990); 8,100 (2000); 8,002 (2005); 7,840 (2010 projected); Race: 84.1% White, 4.3% Black, 7.4% Asian, 8.4% Hispanic of any race (2005); Density: 1,367.1 persons per square mile (2005); Average household size: 2.83 (2005); Median age: 35.2 (2005); Males per 100 females: 99.3 (2005); Marriage status: 25.0% never married, 60.7% now married, 4.2% widowed, 10.0% divorced (2000); Foreign born: 13.3% (2000); Ancestry (includes multiple ancestries): 26.4% Italian, 19.5% German, 19.4% Irish, 16.8% Other groups, 8.7% Polish (2000).
Economy: Resort village. Employment by occupation: 15.3% management, 24.7% professional, 12.0% services, 23.9% sales, 0.0% farming, 9.4% construction, 14.6% production (2000).
Income: Per capita income: $29,140 (2005); Median household income: $71,059 (2005); Average household income: $82,434 (2005); Percent of households with income of $100,000 or more: 26.9% (2005); Poverty rate: 3.3% (2000).
Education: Percent of population age 25 and over with: High school diploma (including GED) or higher: 90.3% (2005); Bachelor's degree or higher: 29.5% (2005); Master's degree or higher: 7.2% (2005).
Housing: Homeownership rate: 68.1% (2005); Median home value: $291,041 (2005); Median rent: $694 per month (2000); Median age of housing: 32 years (2000).
Transportation: Commute to work: 95.8% car, 1.3% public transportation, 0.2% walk, 2.0% work from home (2000); Travel time to work: 16.7% less than 15 minutes, 23.6% 15 to 30 minutes, 26.0% 30 to 45 minutes, 16.8% 45 to 60 minutes, 16.8% 60 minutes or more (2000)
Additional Information Contacts
Mount Olive Area Chamber of Commerce . . . . (973) 671-0109
 http://www.mtolivechambernj.com

BUTLER (borough). Covers a land area of 2.079 square miles and a water area of 0.015 square miles. Located at 40.99° N. Lat.; 74.34° W. Long. Elevation is 480 feet.
History: St. Anthony's Monastery (Franciscan) here. Settled 1695, incorporated 1901.
Population: 7,392 (1990); 7,420 (2000); 8,253 (2005); 9,052 (2010 projected); Race: 93.4% White, 0.8% Black, 2.3% Asian, 6.4% Hispanic of any race (2005); Density: 3,969.5 persons per square mile (2005); Average household size: 2.54 (2005); Median age: 39.4 (2005); Males per 100 females: 97.6 (2005); Marriage status: 24.3% never married, 61.6% now married, 7.4% widowed, 6.6% divorced (2000); Foreign born: 9.8% (2000); Ancestry (includes multiple ancestries): 26.7% Irish, 24.9% Italian, 20.5% German, 11.2% Polish, 10.2% Other groups (2000).
Economy: Manufacturing: plastics, paper, and concrete products. Residential area. Single-family building permits issued: 0 (2005); Multi-family building permits issued: 0 (2005); Employment by occupation:

17.0% management, 18.2% professional, 12.8% services, 30.6% sales, 0.1% farming, 9.4% construction, 11.9% production (2000).
Income: Per capita income: $29,540 (2005); Median household income: $61,509 (2005); Average household income: $73,793 (2005); Percent of households with income of $100,000 or more: 21.9% (2005); Poverty rate: 5.0% (2000).
Taxes: Total city taxes per capita: $539 (2004); City property taxes per capita: $527 (2004).
Education: Percent of population age 25 and over with: High school diploma (including GED) or higher: 85.2% (2005); Bachelor's degree or higher: 23.7% (2005); Master's degree or higher: 7.3% (2005).
Housing: Homeownership rate: 65.6% (2005); Median home value: $297,290 (2005); Median rent: $739 per month (2000); Median age of housing: 47 years (2000).
Safety: Violent crime rate: 14.7 per 10,000 population; Property crime rate: 152.0 per 10,000 population (2004).
Transportation: Commute to work: 91.4% car, 2.4% public transportation, 3.1% walk, 2.4% work from home (2000); Travel time to work: 23.4% less than 15 minutes, 37.0% 15 to 30 minutes, 26.2% 30 to 45 minutes, 7.3% 45 to 60 minutes, 6.1% 60 minutes or more (2000)
Additional Information Contacts
Borough of Butler . . . . (973) 838-7200
 http://www.butlerborough.com
Tri-County Chamber of Commerce . . . . (973) 831-7788
 http://www.tricounty.org/directory/city/Butler

CEDAR KNOLLS (unincorporated postal area, zip code 07927). Aka Monroe-Cedar Knoll. Covers a land area of 1.931 square miles and a water area of 0 square miles. Located at 40.82° N. Lat.; 74.45° W. Long. Elevation is 340 feet.
Population: 3,163 (2000); Race: 89.8% White, 0.0% Black, 9.5% Asian, 2.5% Hispanic of any race (2000); Density: 1,637.7 persons per square mile (2000); Age: 23.4% under 18, 13.4% over 64 (2000); Marriage status: 27.7% never married, 59.6% now married, 6.5% widowed, 6.2% divorced (2000); Foreign born: 15.5% (2000); Ancestry (includes multiple ancestries): 34.8% Italian, 22.4% Irish, 14.2% German, 13.0% Other groups, 10.1% English (2000).
Economy: Employment by occupation: 19.9% management, 20.2% professional, 10.2% services, 33.4% sales, 0.0% farming, 6.5% construction, 9.7% production (2000).
Income: Per capita income: $32,717 (2000); Median household income: $82,453 (2000); Poverty rate: 1.0% (2000).
Education: Percent of population age 25 and over with: High school diploma (including GED) or higher: 88.4% (2000); Bachelor's degree or higher: 37.2% (2000).
Housing: Homeownership rate: 88.2% (2000); Median home value: $255,000 (2000); Median rent: $910 per month (2000); Median age of housing: 35 years (2000).
Transportation: Commute to work: 94.2% car, 2.5% public transportation, 0.5% walk, 2.6% work from home (2000); Travel time to work: 33.0% less than 15 minutes, 36.9% 15 to 30 minutes, 17.0% 30 to 45 minutes, 7.4% 45 to 60 minutes, 5.8% 60 minutes or more (2000)

CHATHAM (borough). Covers a land area of 2.413 square miles and a water area of 0.001 square miles. Located at 40.74° N. Lat.; 74.38° W. Long. Elevation is 244 feet.
Population: 8,007 (1990); 8,460 (2000); 8,453 (2005); 8,472 (2010 projected); Race: 95.2% White, 0.1% Black, 3.2% Asian, 3.1% Hispanic of any race (2005); Density: 3,503.0 persons per square mile (2005); Average household size: 2.71 (2005); Median age: 38.4 (2005); Males per 100 females: 92.3 (2005); Marriage status: 19.1% never married, 70.3% now married, 4.7% widowed, 5.9% divorced (2000); Foreign born: 9.8% (2000); Ancestry (includes multiple ancestries): 30.3% Irish, 19.6% Italian, 17.4% English, 16.4% German, 7.3% Other groups (2000).
Economy: Single-family building permits issued: 9 (2005); Multi-family building permits issued: 0 (2005); Employment by occupation: 32.0% management, 30.5% professional, 7.3% services, 24.0% sales, 0.0% farming, 2.5% construction, 3.8% production (2000).
Income: Per capita income: $59,709 (2005); Median household income: $119,373 (2005); Average household income: $159,974 (2005); Percent of

households with income of $100,000 or more: 57.7% (2005); Poverty rate: 2.2% (2000).

Education: Percent of population age 25 and over with: High school diploma (including GED) or higher: 96.6% (2005); Bachelor's degree or higher: 66.7% (2005); Master's degree or higher: 28.1% (2005).

School District(s)

School District of the Chathams (PK-12)

    2003-04 Enrollment: 3,199 . . . . (973) 635-5656

Housing: Homeownership rate: 78.7% (2005); Median home value: $630,734 (2005); Median rent: $1,018 per month (2000); Median age of housing: 53 years (2000).

Safety: Violent crime rate: 8.2 per 10,000 population; Property crime rate: 102.4 per 10,000 population (2004).

Newspapers: Chatham Courier (General - Circulation 6,000); Chatham Courier (General - Circulation 4,000).

Transportation: Commute to work: 74.6% car, 18.2% public transportation, 2.3% walk, 4.3% work from home (2000); Travel time to work: 27.5% less than 15 minutes, 29.3% 15 to 30 minutes, 13.9% 30 to 45 minutes, 6.7% 45 to 60 minutes, 22.5% 60 minutes or more (2000)

Additional Information Contacts

Chatham Area Chamber of Commerce . . . . (973) 635-2444

    http://www.chathamarea.com

CHATHAM (township). Covers a land area of 9.330 square miles and a water area of 0.018 square miles. Located at 40.72° N. Lat.; 74.41° W. Long. Elevation is 244 feet.

History: Has pre-Revolutionary inn. Settled 1749, incorporated 1897.

Population: 9,266 (1990); 10,086 (2000); 10,094 (2005); 10,178 (2010 projected); Race: 92.9% White, 0.5% Black, 5.5% Asian, 2.1% Hispanic of any race (2005); Density: 1,081.9 persons per square mile (2005); Average household size: 2.55 (2005); Median age: 41.5 (2005); Males per 100 females: 91.7 (2005); Marriage status: 21.5% never married, 66.0% now married, 6.1% widowed, 6.4% divorced (2000); Foreign born: 12.0% (2000); Ancestry (includes multiple ancestries): 24.2% Irish, 19.7% German, 19.3% Italian, 14.7% English, 10.0% Other groups (2000).

Economy: Hothouse flowers. Manufacturing: metal products, plastic resins, thermostats, sponge and rubber products. Single-family building permits issued: 44 (2005); Multi-family building permits issued: 0 (2005); Employment by occupation: 30.5% management, 33.1% professional, 5.2% services, 26.3% sales, 0.0% farming, 2.7% construction, 2.3% production (2000).

Income: Per capita income: $70,216 (2005); Median household income: $125,102 (2005); Average household income: $178,577 (2005); Percent of households with income of $100,000 or more: 59.3% (2005); Poverty rate: 2.7% (2000).

Education: Percent of population age 25 and over with: High school diploma (including GED) or higher: 96.6% (2005); Bachelor's degree or higher: 65.6% (2005); Master's degree or higher: 31.6% (2005).

Housing: Homeownership rate: 83.5% (2005); Median home value: $650,246 (2005); Median rent: $1,238 per month (2000); Median age of housing: 34 years (2000).

Safety: Violent crime rate: 0.0 per 10,000 population; Property crime rate: 48.3 per 10,000 population (2004).

Newspapers: Chatham Courier (General - Circulation 6,000)

Transportation: Commute to work: 78.3% car, 14.8% public transportation, 0.9% walk, 5.6% work from home (2000); Travel time to work: 26.6% less than 15 minutes, 26.2% 15 to 30 minutes, 18.6% 30 to 45 minutes, 5.9% 45 to 60 minutes, 22.8% 60 minutes or more (2000)

Additional Information Contacts

Chatham Area Chamber of Commerce . . . . (973) 635-2444

    http://www.chathamarea.com

Chatham Township . . . . (973) 635-4600

    http://www.chathamtownship.org

CHESTER (borough). Covers a land area of 1.538 square miles and a water area of 0 square miles. Located at 40.78° N. Lat.; 74.69° W. Long. Elevation is 846 feet.

Population: 1,214 (1990); 1,635 (2000); 1,663 (2005); 1,703 (2010 projected); Race: 93.5% White, 1.0% Black, 1.7% Asian, 9.2% Hispanic of any race (2005); Density: 1,081.2 persons per square mile (2005); Average household size: 2.67 (2005); Median age: 40.3 (2005); Males per 100 females: 100.8 (2005); Marriage status: 22.1% never married, 62.5% now married, 6.9% widowed, 8.5% divorced (2000); Foreign born: 12.3% (2000); Ancestry (includes multiple ancestries): 21.7% Italian, 18.5% Irish, 17.8% German, 11.9% Other groups, 11.3% English (2000).

Economy: Single-family building permits issued: 1 (2005); Multi-family building permits issued: 0 (2005); Employment by occupation: 25.3% management, 24.3% professional, 13.6% services, 23.6% sales, 0.0% farming, 6.4% construction, 6.8% production (2000).

Income: Per capita income: $51,678 (2005); Median household income: $95,833 (2005); Average household income: $137,335 (2005); Percent of households with income of $100,000 or more: 48.3% (2005); Poverty rate: 5.2% (2000).

Education: Percent of population age 25 and over with: High school diploma (including GED) or higher: 90.3% (2005); Bachelor's degree or higher: 48.5% (2005); Master's degree or higher: 20.0% (2005).

School District(s)

Chester Township (PK-08)

    2003-04 Enrollment: 1,286 . . . . (908) 879-7383

West Morris Regional (09-12)

    2003-04 Enrollment: 2,402 . . . . (908) 879-6404

Housing: Homeownership rate: 77.8% (2005); Median home value: $482,065 (2005); Median rent: $741 per month (2000); Median age of housing: 29 years (2000).

Hospitals: Kessler Institute for Rehabilitation (72 beds)

Safety: Violent crime rate: 24.0 per 10,000 population; Property crime rate: 168.0 per 10,000 population (2004).

Newspapers: Mount Olive Chronicle (General - Circulation 3,034); Observer-Tribune (General - Circulation 6,723); Randolph Reporter (General - Circulation 4,000); Roxbury Register (General - Circulation 3,011)

Transportation: Commute to work: 87.3% car, 1.4% public transportation, 6.2% walk, 3.7% work from home (2000); Travel time to work: 24.2% less than 15 minutes, 29.0% 15 to 30 minutes, 26.4% 30 to 45 minutes, 10.7% 45 to 60 minutes, 9.7% 60 minutes or more (2000)

Additional Information Contacts

Borough of Chester . . . . (908) 879-5361

    http://www.chesterborough.org

CHESTER (township). Covers a land area of 29.327 square miles and a water area of 0.014 square miles. Located at 40.78° N. Lat.; 74.68° W. Long. Elevation is 846 feet.

Population: 5,981 (1990); 7,282 (2000); 7,831 (2005); 8,381 (2010 projected); Race: 94.7% White, 1.3% Black, 2.6% Asian, 3.3% Hispanic of any race (2005); Density: 267.0 persons per square mile (2005); Average household size: 3.11 (2005); Median age: 40.4 (2005); Males per 100 females: 96.5 (2005); Marriage status: 19.2% never married, 73.0% now married, 5.0% widowed, 2.8% divorced (2000); Foreign born: 9.1% (2000); Ancestry (includes multiple ancestries): 22.4% Italian, 20.6% German, 19.6% Irish, 14.2% English, 8.4% Polish (2000).

Economy: In agricultural area. Single-family building permits issued: 18 (2005); Multi-family building permits issued: 0 (2005); Employment by occupation: 32.8% management, 28.8% professional, 5.7% services, 23.8% sales, 0.2% farming, 6.0% construction, 2.5% production (2000).

Income: Per capita income: $64,028 (2005); Median household income: $139,189 (2005); Average household income: $198,086 (2005); Percent of households with income of $100,000 or more: 65.0% (2005); Poverty rate: 2.3% (2000).

Education: Percent of population age 25 and over with: High school diploma (including GED) or higher: 96.3% (2005); Bachelor's degree or higher: 63.7% (2005); Master's degree or higher: 30.7% (2005).

School District(s)

Chester Township (PK-08)

    2003-04 Enrollment: 1,286 . . . . (908) 879-7383

West Morris Regional (09-12)

    2003-04 Enrollment: 2,402 . . . . (908) 879-6404

Housing: Homeownership rate: 92.9% (2005); Median home value: $684,409 (2005); Median rent: $1,176 per month (2000); Median age of housing: 28 years (2000).

Hospitals: Kessler Institute for Rehabilitation (72 beds)

Safety: Violent crime rate: 3.9 per 10,000 population; Property crime rate: 66.0 per 10,000 population (2004).

Newspapers: Mount Olive Chronicle (General - Circulation 3,034); Observer-Tribune (General - Circulation 6,723); Randolph Reporter (General - Circulation 4,000); Roxbury Register (General - Circulation 3,011)

Transportation: Commute to work: 85.2% car, 4.2% public transportation, 0.8% walk, 9.2% work from home (2000); Travel time to work: 15.7% less than 15 minutes, 20.9% 15 to 30 minutes, 30.2% 30 to 45 minutes, 14.3% 45 to 60 minutes, 18.9% 60 minutes or more (2000)

Additional Information Contacts
Chester Township . . . . (908) 879-5100
  http://www.chestertownship.org

DENVILLE (township). Covers a land area of 12.106 square miles and a water area of 0.521 square miles. Located at 40.88° N. Lat.; 74.48° W. Long. Elevation is 513 feet.
Population: 13,812 (1990); 15,824 (2000); 16,018 (2005); 16,274 (2010 projected); Race: 91.5% White, 1.4% Black, 5.4% Asian, 3.2% Hispanic of any race (2005); Density: 1,323.1 persons per square mile (2005); Average household size: 2.60 (2005); Median age: 41.3 (2005); Males per 100 females: 93.8 (2005); Marriage status: 19.0% never married, 66.0% now married, 8.6% widowed, 6.4% divorced (2000); Foreign born: 10.6% (2000); Ancestry (includes multiple ancestries): 26.1% Italian, 25.1% Irish, 19.6% German, 11.0% Other groups, 8.5% English (2000).
Economy: Largely residential. Single-family building permits issued: 43 (2005); Multi-family building permits issued: 14 (2005); Employment by occupation: 22.1% management, 26.7% professional, 7.1% services, 29.3% sales, 0.1% farming, 7.7% construction, 7.0% production (2000).
Income: Per capita income: $44,828 (2005); Median household income: $88,797 (2005); Average household income: $116,298 (2005); Percent of households with income of $100,000 or more: 42.8% (2005); Poverty rate: 2.8% (2000).
Taxes: Total city taxes per capita: $613 (2004); City property taxes per capita: $557 (2004).
Education: Percent of population age 25 and over with: High school diploma (including GED) or higher: 92.3% (2005); Bachelor's degree or higher: 44.1% (2005); Master's degree or higher: 17.1% (2005).
School District(s)
Denville Township (PK-08)
  2003-04 Enrollment: 1,959 . . . . (973) 366-1001
Morris County Vocational (09-12)
  2003-04 Enrollment: 182 . . . . (973) 627-4600
Two-year College(s)
Morris County Vocational School District (Public)
  Fall 2004 Enrollment: n/a . . . . (201) 627-4600
Housing: Homeownership rate: 86.0% (2005); Median home value: $367,869 (2005); Median rent: $1,049 per month (2000); Median age of housing: 37 years (2000).
Hospitals: Saint Clare's Hospital-Denville (331 beds)
Safety: Violent crime rate: 8.7 per 10,000 population; Property crime rate: 116.6 per 10,000 population (2004).
Newspapers: The Citizen Of Morris County (General - Circulation 10,100)
Transportation: Commute to work: 91.5% car, 4.0% public transportation, 0.6% walk, 3.5% work from home (2000); Travel time to work: 24.9% less than 15 minutes, 32.7% 15 to 30 minutes, 22.1% 30 to 45 minutes, 10.3% 45 to 60 minutes, 10.0% 60 minutes or more (2000)
Additional Information Contacts
Denville Chamber of Commerce . . . . (973) 627-1340
  http://www.denville-nj.com
Denville Township . . . . (973) 625-8300
  http://www.denvillenj.org

DOVER (town). Covers a land area of 2.679 square miles and a water area of 0.025 square miles. Located at 40.88° N. Lat.; 74.55° W. Long. Elevation is 800 feet.
History: Named for Robert Dover (1575-1641), an English lawyer. In an iron ore area, the town grew as an iron manufacturing center on the old Morris Canal. Settled 1722. Incorporated as town 1869.
Population: 15,150 (1990); 18,188 (2000); 18,631 (2005); 19,126 (2010 projected); Race: 67.1% White, 7.3% Black, 2.6% Asian, 66.1% Hispanic of any race (2005); Density: 6,953.5 persons per square mile (2005); Average household size: 3.42 (2005); Median age: 35.4 (2005); Males per 100 females: 107.2 (2005); Marriage status: 32.2% never married, 52.9% now married, 6.1% widowed, 8.8% divorced (2000); Foreign born: 42.8% (2000); Ancestry (includes multiple ancestries): 56.6% Other groups, 7.3% Italian, 6.5% Irish, 5.4% German, 4.4% English (2000).
Economy: Has iron and steelworks as well as a wide variety of manufacturing. The U.S. Army Picatinny Arsenal is nearby. Single-family building permits issued: 10 (2005); Multi-family building permits issued: 0 (2005); Employment by occupation: 7.5% management, 11.9% professional, 20.9% services, 25.7% sales, 0.0% farming, 8.9% construction, 25.0% production (2000).
Income: Per capita income: $19,284 (2005); Median household income: $57,127 (2005); Average household income: $65,173 (2005); Percent of

households with income of $100,000 or more: 20.3% (2005); Poverty rate: 13.4% (2000).
Education: Percent of population age 25 and over with: High school diploma (including GED) or higher: 66.9% (2005); Bachelor's degree or higher: 12.4% (2005); Master's degree or higher: 4.4% (2005).
School District(s)
Dover Town (PK-12)
  2003-04 Enrollment: 3,391 . . . . (973) 989-2000
Rockaway Township (PK-08)
  2003-04 Enrollment: 2,985 . . . . (973) 627-8200
Two-year College(s)
Joe Kubert School of Cartoon and Graphic Art (Private, For-profit)
  Fall 2004 Enrollment: 101 . . . . (973) 361-1327
  2005-06 Tuition: In-state $14,550; Out-of-state $14,550
Housing: Homeownership rate: 53.3% (2005); Median home value: $254,485 (2005); Median rent: $782 per month (2000); Median age of housing: 47 years (2000).
Hospitals: Saint Clare's Hospital-Dover (60 beds)
Safety: Violent crime rate: 29.2 per 10,000 population; Property crime rate: 229.7 per 10,000 population (2004).
Transportation: Commute to work: 84.6% car, 4.6% public transportation, 3.1% walk, 1.3% work from home (2000); Travel time to work: 33.1% less than 15 minutes, 38.1% 15 to 30 minutes, 18.7% 30 to 45 minutes, 5.1% 45 to 60 minutes, 4.9% 60 minutes or more (2000)

EAST HANOVER (township). Covers a land area of 8.157 square miles and a water area of 0.002 square miles. Located at 40.82° N. Lat.; 74.36° W. Long.
Population: 9,920 (1990); 11,393 (2000); 11,485 (2005); 11,604 (2010 projected); Race: 84.9% White, 0.6% Black, 13.1% Asian, 3.1% Hispanic of any race (2005); Density: 1,407.9 persons per square mile (2005); Average household size: 2.90 (2005); Median age: 42.4 (2005); Males per 100 females: 94.7 (2005); Marriage status: 22.1% never married, 66.9% now married, 6.8% widowed, 4.1% divorced (2000); Foreign born: 18.6% (2000); Ancestry (includes multiple ancestries): 41.8% Italian, 16.1% Other groups, 12.9% Irish, 12.3% German, 7.0% Polish (2000).
Economy: Single-family building permits issued: 25 (2005); Multi-family building permits issued: 0 (2005); Employment by occupation: 20.5% management, 23.8% professional, 13.0% services, 26.5% sales, 0.0% farming, 8.2% construction, 8.0% production (2000).
Income: Per capita income: $36,043 (2005); Median household income: $88,674 (2005); Average household income: $103,984 (2005); Percent of households with income of $100,000 or more: 41.5% (2005); Poverty rate: 1.7% (2000).
Education: Percent of population age 25 and over with: High school diploma (including GED) or higher: 88.3% (2005); Bachelor's degree or higher: 34.1% (2005); Master's degree or higher: 13.9% (2005).
School District(s)
East Hanover Township (PK-08)
  2003-04 Enrollment: 1,136 . . . . (973) 887-2112
Hanover Park Regional (09-12)
  2003-04 Enrollment: 1,448 . . . . (973) 887-0320
Housing: Homeownership rate: 93.9% (2005); Median home value: $499,441 (2005); Median rent: $1,255 per month (2000); Median age of housing: 27 years (2000).
Safety: Violent crime rate: 6.9 per 10,000 population; Property crime rate: 176.9 per 10,000 population (2004).
Transportation: Commute to work: 94.1% car, 3.0% public transportation, 0.6% walk, 2.4% work from home (2000); Travel time to work: 32.1% less than 15 minutes, 33.4% 15 to 30 minutes, 19.2% 30 to 45 minutes, 7.3% 45 to 60 minutes, 8.0% 60 minutes or more (2000)
Additional Information Contacts
Livingston-East Hanover Chamber of Commerce . . . . (973) 992-4343
  http://www.livingstonchambernj.com

FLANDERS (unincorporated postal area, zip code 07836). Covers a land area of 16.229 square miles and a water area of 0.011 square miles. Located at 40.84° N. Lat.; 74.70° W. Long. Elevation is 679 feet.
Population: 12,217 (2000); Race: 88.3% White, 3.9% Black, 6.1% Asian, 4.1% Hispanic of any race (2000); Density: 752.8 persons per square mile (2000); Age: 27.6% under 18, 5.9% over 64 (2000); Marriage status: 24.6% never married, 66.5% now married, 3.9% widowed, 5.1% divorced (2000); Foreign born: 11.3% (2000); Ancestry (includes multiple ancestries): 23.7% Irish, 23.6% Italian, 20.7% German, 14.0% Other groups, 9.3% English (2000).

Economy: Employment by occupation: 24.1% management, 26.3% professional, 9.0% services, 25.4% sales, 0.1% farming, 6.6% construction, 8.6% production (2000).
Income: Per capita income: $34,086 (2000); Median household income: $76,040 (2000); Poverty rate: 2.0% (2000).
Education: Percent of population age 25 and over with: High school diploma (including GED) or higher: 94.8% (2000); Bachelor's degree or higher: 43.4% (2000).

School District(s)

Mount Olive Township (PK-12)
   2003-04 Enrollment: 4,961 . . . . (973) 691-4008
Housing: Homeownership rate: 64.3% (2000); Median home value: $236,900 (2000); Median rent: $771 per month (2000); Median age of housing: 25 years (2000).
Transportation: Commute to work: 92.8% car, 1.7% public transportation, 0.8% walk, 4.5% work from home (2000); Travel time to work: 16.8% less than 15 minutes, 21.6% 15 to 30 minutes, 24.3% 30 to 45 minutes, 20.2% 45 to 60 minutes, 17.1% 60 minutes or more (2000)

FLORHAM PARK (borough). Covers a land area of 7.435 square miles and a water area of 0.016 square miles. Located at 40.77° N. Lat.; 74.39° W. Long. Elevation is 240 feet.

History: Campus of Farleigh Dickinson University and College of St. Elizabeth. Site of Little Red Schoolhouse (1897) now on National Registry. Incorporated 1899.
Population: 8,521 (1990); 8,857 (2000); 11,244 (2005); 13,374 (2010 projected); Race: 93.3% White, 1.3% Black, 4.2% Asian, 2.5% Hispanic of any race (2005); Density: 1,512.4 persons per square mile (2005); Average household size: 2.67 (2005); Median age: 45.3 (2005); Males per 100 females: 87.0 (2005); Marriage status: 22.5% never married, 64.7% now married, 7.4% widowed, 5.4% divorced (2000); Foreign born: 10.5% (2000); Ancestry (includes multiple ancestries): 27.4% Itallan, 23.1% Irish, 15.1% German, 10.3% English, 9.0% Other groups (2000).
Economy: Light industry, petroleum research. Single-family building permits issued: 16 (2005); Multi-family building permits issued: 0 (2005); Employment by occupation: 24.6% management, 30.5% professional, 10.6% services, 25.2% sales, 0.0% farming, 5.0% construction, 4.0% production (2000).
Income: Per capita income: $51,315 (2005); Median household income: $101,925 (2005); Average household income: $134,944 (2005); Percent of households with income of $100,000 or more: 50.8% (2005); Poverty rate: 5.8% (2000).
Education: Percent of population age 25 and over with: High school diploma (including GED) or higher: 92.2% (2005); Bachelor's degree or higher: 57.7% (2005); Master's degree or higher: 24.4% (2005).

School District(s)

Florham Park Borough (PK-08)
   2003-04 Enrollment: 974 . . . . (973) 822-3880
Housing: Homeownership rate: 86.1% (2005); Median home value: $515,280 (2005); Median rent: $731 per month (2000); Median age of housing: 34 years (2000).
Safety: Violent crime rate: 3.2 per 10,000 population; Property crime rate: 92.1 per 10,000 population (2004).
Transportation: Commute to work: 86.9% car, 6.1% public transportation, 1.3% walk, 4.6% work from home (2000); Travel time to work: 32.5% less than 15 minutes, 33.2% 15 to 30 minutes, 15.5% 30 to 45 minutes, 6.6% 45 to 60 minutes, 12.2% 60 minutes or more (2000)

Additional Information Contacts

Borough of Florham Park. . . . . (973) 410-5300
   http://www.florhamparkboro.net
Morris County Chamber of Commerce . . . . (973) 539-3882
   http://www.morrischamber.org

GILLETTE (unincorporated postal area, zip code 07933). Covers a land area of 6.783 square miles and a water area of 0 square miles. Located at 40.68° N. Lat.; 74.47° W. Long. Elevation is 248 feet.

Population: 3,278 (2000); Race: 90.1% White, 0.6% Black, 5.7% Asian, 1.6% Hispanic of any race (2000); Density: 483.3 persons per square mile (2000); Age: 27.1% under 18, 13.7% over 64 (2000); Marriage status: 19.0% never married, 68.9% now married, 5.6% widowed, 6.5% divorced (2000); Foreign born: 11.2% (2000); Ancestry (includes multiple ancestries): 26.7% Irish, 23.5% German, 22.1% Italian, 12.3% Other groups, 6.8% English (2000).

Economy: Employment by occupation: 21.4% management, 26.4% professional, 8.6% services, 31.6% sales, 0.0% farming, 5.1% construction, 6.9% production (2000).
Income: Per capita income: $43,323 (2000); Median household income: $81,862 (2000); Poverty rate: 3.8% (2000).
Education: Percent of population age 25 and over with: High school diploma (including GED) or higher: 94.3% (2000); Bachelor's degree or higher: 49.3% (2000).

School District(s)

Long Hill Township (PK-08)
   2003-04 Enrollment: 1,159 . . . . (908) 647-1200
Housing: Homeownership rate: 90.8% (2000); Median home value: $280,100 (2000); Median rent: $840 per month (2000); Median age of housing: 36 years (2000).
Transportation: Commute to work: 87.1% car, 8.3% public transportation, 0.0% walk, 4.6% work from home (2000); Travel time to work: 19.8% less than 15 minutes, 31.7% 15 to 30 minutes, 27.7% 30 to 45 minutes, 5.8% 45 to 60 minutes, 15.0% 60 minutes or more (2000)

GREEN VILLAGE (unincorporated postal area, zip code 07935). Covers a land area of 4.552 square miles and a water area of 0.012 square miles. Located at 40.73° N. Lat.; 74.45° W. Long. Elevation is 254 feet.

Population: 515 (2000); Race: 100.0% White, 0.0% Black, 0.0% Asian, 1.3% Hispanic of any race (2000); Density: 113.1 persons per square mile (2000); Age: 29.9% under 18, 28.7% over 64 (2000); Marriage status: 8.4% never married, 66.1% now married, 21.3% widowed, 4.3% divorced (2000); Foreign born: 14.0% (2000); Ancestry (includes multiple ancestries): 30.1% United States or American, 15.7% Italian, 15.5% German, 8.5% Irish, 7.2% Dutch (2000).
Economy: Employment by occupation: 16.0% management, 32.0% professional, 4.6% services, 43.4% sales, 0.0% farming, 4.0% construction, 0.0% production (2000).
Income: Per capita income: $23,659 (2000); Median household income: $42,639 (2000); Poverty rate: 2.1% (2000).
Education: Percent of population age 25 and over with: High school diploma (including GED) or higher: 93.1% (2000); Bachelor's degree or higher: 29.6% (2000).
Housing: Homeownership rate: 68.6% (2000); Median home value: $363,500 (2000); Median rent: $1,113 per month (2000); Median age of housing: 60+ years (2000).
Transportation: Commute to work: 68.6% car, 11.4% public transportation, 0.0% walk, 20.0% work from home (2000); Travel time to work: 20.7% less than 15 minutes, 14.3% 15 to 30 minutes, 31.4% 30 to 45 minutes, 3.6% 45 to 60 minutes, 30.0% 60 minutes or more (2000)

HANOVER (township). Covers a land area of 10.663 square miles and a water area of 0.029 square miles. Located at 40.82° N. Lat.; 74.43° W. Long. Elevation is 200 feet.

History: Incorporated 1928.
Population: 11,538 (1990); 12,898 (2000); 13,789 (2005); 14,688 (2010 projected); Race: 87.2% White, 1.2% Black, 9.9% Asian, 4.2% Hispanic of any race (2005); Density: 1,293.1 persons per square mile (2005); Average household size: 2.67 (2005); Median age: 41.7 (2005); Males per 100 females: 95.3 (2005); Marriage status: 24.4% never married, 63.2% now married, 6.8% widowed, 5.6% divorced (2000); Foreign born: 15.7% (2000); Ancestry (includes multiple ancestries): 30.4% Italian, 21.1% Irish, 15.5% German, 13.4% Other groups, 9.7% Polish (2000).
Economy: Manufacturing: food products, electronic parts, lubricants, pharmaceuticals, office machines, and plastics. Single-family building permits issued: 32 (2005); Multi-family building permits issued: 0 (2005); Employment by occupation: 21.0% management, 25.1% professional, 9.3% services, 30.0% sales, 0.0% farming, 7.5% construction, 7.1% production (2000).
Income: Per capita income: $45,322 (2005); Median household income: $96,538 (2005); Average household income: $120,007 (2005); Percent of households with income of $100,000 or more: 48.0% (2005); Poverty rate: 1.2% (2000).
Taxes: Total city taxes per capita: $727 (2004); City property taxes per capita: $713 (2004).
Education: Percent of population age 25 and over with: High school diploma (including GED) or higher: 89.6% (2005); Bachelor's degree or higher: 41.6% (2005); Master's degree or higher: 15.2% (2005).
Housing: Homeownership rate: 92.0% (2005); Median home value: $441,270 (2005); Median rent: $1,004 per month (2000); Median age of housing: 36 years (2000).

Safety: Violent crime rate: 11.9 per 10,000 population; Property crime rate: 129.4 per 10,000 population (2004).
Transportation: Commute to work: 93.4% car, 2.4% public transportation, 1.2% walk, 2.9% work from home (2000); Travel time to work: 35.4% less than 15 minutes, 35.6% 15 to 30 minutes, 16.4% 30 to 45 minutes, 5.9% 45 to 60 minutes, 6.8% 60 minutes or more (2000)
Additional Information Contacts
Hanover Township . . . . (973) 428-2500
  http://www.hanovertownship.com

HARDING (township). Covers a land area of 20.437 square miles and a water area of 0.036 square miles. Located at 40.74° N. Lat.; 74.49° W. Long.
Population: 3,649 (1990); 3,180 (2000); 3,302 (2005); 3,438 (2010 projected); Race: 96.9% White, 0.3% Black, 1.3% Asian, 1.8% Hispanic of any race (2005); Density: 161.6 persons per square mile (2005); Average household size: 2.71 (2005); Median age: 46.5 (2005); Males per 100 females: 94.5 (2005); Marriage status: 14.5% never married, 72.3% now married, 8.7% widowed, 4.4% divorced (2000); Foreign born: 6.2% (2000); Ancestry (includes multiple ancestries): 19.9% Irish, 19.6% Italian, 19.1% German, 12.7% United States or American, 9.6% English (2000).
Economy: Single-family building permits issued: 10 (2005); Multi-family building permits issued: 0 (2005); Employment by occupation: 32.1% management, 29.2% professional, 8.1% services, 23.4% sales, 0.0% farming, 5.4% construction, 1.7% production (2000).
Income: Per capita income: $75,515 (2005); Median household income: $125,000 (2005); Average household income: $203,056 (2005); Percent of households with income of $100,000 or more: 58.2% (2005); Poverty rate: 1.1% (2000).
Education: Percent of population age 25 and over with: High school diploma (including GED) or higher: 97.6% (2005); Bachelor's degree or higher: 66.5% (2005); Master's degree or higher: 32.3% (2005).
Housing: Homeownership rate: 92.5% (2005); Median home value: $1 million+ (2005); Median rent: $1,080 per month (2000); Median age of housing: 35 years (2000).
Safety: Violent crime rate: 3.0 per 10,000 population; Property crime rate: 24.4 per 10,000 population (2004).
Transportation: Commute to work: 84.6% car, 7.6% public transportation, 1.0% walk, 6.7% work from home (2000); Travel time to work: 24.4% less than 15 minutes, 26.6% 15 to 30 minutes, 24.4% 30 to 45 minutes, 6.9% 45 to 60 minutes, 17.6% 60 minutes or more (2000)

JEFFERSON (township). Covers a land area of 40.632 square miles and a water area of 2.412 square miles. Located at 40.98° N. Lat.; 74.57° W. Long.
Population: 17,776 (1990); 19,717 (2000); 21,298 (2005); 22,867 (2010 projected); Race: 95.6% White, 0.9% Black, 1.2% Asian, 4.1% Hispanic of any race (2005); Density: 524.2 persons per square mile (2005); Average household size: 2.75 (2005); Median age: 38.8 (2005); Males per 100 females: 98.5 (2005); Marriage status: 20.5% never married, 66.1% now married, 4.9% widowed, 8.5% divorced (2000); Foreign born: 6.3% (2000); Ancestry (includes multiple ancestries): 25.7% Italian, 22.9% Irish, 21.7% German, 11.6% English, 10.0% Polish (2000).
Economy: Incorporated 1809. Single-family building permits issued: 116 (2005); Multi-family building permits issued: 0 (2005); Employment by occupation: 17.1% management, 20.7% professional, 10.6% services, 30.1% sales, 0.1% farming, 12.4% construction, 9.1% production (2000).
Income: Per capita income: $34,127 (2005); Median household income: $79,107 (2005); Average household income: $93,554 (2005); Percent of households with income of $100,000 or more: 34.3% (2005); Poverty rate: 2.4% (2000).
Taxes: Total city taxes per capita: $730 (2004); City property taxes per capita: $700 (2004).
Education: Percent of population age 25 and over with: High school diploma (including GED) or higher: 89.7% (2005); Bachelor's degree or higher: 27.8% (2005); Master's degree or higher: 7.1% (2005).
Housing: Homeownership rate: 88.6% (2005); Median home value: $283,295 (2005); Median rent: $754 per month (2000); Median age of housing: 36 years (2000).
Safety: Violent crime rate: 4.8 per 10,000 population; Property crime rate: 139.9 per 10,000 population (2004).
Transportation: Commute to work: 94.5% car, 1.9% public transportation, 0.5% walk, 2.4% work from home (2000); Travel time to work: 15.9% less than 15 minutes, 24.3% 15 to 30 minutes, 25.4% 30 to 45 minutes, 18.1% 45 to 60 minutes, 16.3% 60 minutes or more (2000)

Additional Information Contacts
Jefferson Township . . . . (973) 208-6129
  http://www.jeffersontownship.net
Jefferson Township Chamber of Commerce . . . . (973) 663-2240
  http://www.jeffersontownshipchamber.org

KENVIL (unincorporated postal area, zip code 07847). Covers a land area of 2.928 square miles and a water area of 0.039 square miles. Located at 40.87° N. Lat.; 74.69° W. Long. Elevation is 719 feet.
Population: 1,498 (2000); Race: 95.1% White, 0.5% Black, 0.0% Asian, 12.7% Hispanic of any race (2000); Density: 511.6 persons per square mile (2000); Age: 27.7% under 18, 11.6% over 64 (2000); Marriage status: 21.9% never married, 59.2% now married, 9.0% widowed, 10.0% divorced (2000); Foreign born: 8.2% (2000); Ancestry (includes multiple ancestries): 30.7% Italian, 22.5% German, 20.3% Irish, 12.7% Other groups, 12.1% Polish (2000).
Economy: Employment by occupation: 6.9% management, 16.5% professional, 10.6% services, 35.6% sales, 0.0% farming, 19.2% construction, 11.2% production (2000).
Income: Per capita income: $21,857 (2000); Median household income: $51,750 (2000); Poverty rate: 6.8% (2000).
Education: Percent of population age 25 and over with: High school diploma (including GED) or higher: 84.2% (2000); Bachelor's degree or higher: 16.0% (2000).
Housing: Homeownership rate: 69.6% (2000); Median home value: $167,100 (2000); Median rent: $658 per month (2000); Median age of housing: 51 years (2000).
Transportation: Commute to work: 92.6% car, 0.0% public transportation, 2.4% walk, 2.8% work from home (2000); Travel time to work: 42.3% less than 15 minutes, 21.0% 15 to 30 minutes, 19.9% 30 to 45 minutes, 8.4% 45 to 60 minutes, 8.4% 60 minutes or more (2000)

KINNELON (borough). Covers a land area of 17.888 square miles and a water area of 0.927 square miles. Located at 40.99° N. Lat.; 74.37° W. Long. Elevation is 700 feet.
Population: 8,708 (1990); 9,365 (2000); 9,539 (2005); 9,771 (2010 projected); Race: 95.1% White, 0.7% Black, 3.1% Asian, 2.7% Hispanic of any race (2005); Density: 533.3 persons per square mile (2005); Average household size: 3.07 (2005); Median age: 40.3 (2005); Males per 100 females: 99.2 (2005); Marriage status: 16.3% never married, 75.1% now married, 4.2% widowed, 4.4% divorced (2000); Foreign born: 9.6% (2000); Ancestry (includes multiple ancestries): 25.4% Italian, 23.9% Irish, 19.1% German, 11.3% English, 8.4% Polish (2000).
Economy: Single-family building permits issued: 32 (2005); Multi-family building permits issued: 0 (2005); Employment by occupation: 28.0% management, 31.0% professional, 6.6% services, 25.5% sales, 0.0% farming, 4.7% construction, 4.2% production (2000).
Income: Per capita income: $49,838 (2005); Median household income: $120,728 (2005); Average household income: $152,997 (2005); Percent of households with income of $100,000 or more: 60.0% (2005); Poverty rate: 2.6% (2000).
Education: Percent of population age 25 and over with: High school diploma (including GED) or higher: 96.4% (2005); Bachelor's degree or higher: 57.5% (2005); Master's degree or higher: 25.2% (2005).
School District(s)
Kinnelon Borough (PK-12)
  2003-04 Enrollment: 2,157 . . . . (973) 838-1418
Housing: Homeownership rate: 97.0% (2005); Median home value: $571,525 (2005); Median rent: $1,288 per month (2000); Median age of housing: 35 years (2000).
Safety: Violent crime rate: 6.3 per 10,000 population; Property crime rate: 89.1 per 10,000 population (2004).
Newspapers: Suburban Trends (General - Circulation 14,000)
Transportation: Commute to work: 87.4% car, 4.6% public transportation, 0.9% walk, 7.0% work from home (2000); Travel time to work: 17.0% less than 15 minutes, 25.0% 15 to 30 minutes, 33.3% 30 to 45 minutes, 11.2% 45 to 60 minutes, 13.4% 60 minutes or more (2000)

LAKE HIAWATHA (unincorporated postal area, zip code 07034). Covers a land area of 1.190 square miles and a water area of 0 square miles. Located at 40.88° N. Lat.; 74.38° W. Long. Elevation is 280 feet.
Population: 9,320 (2000); Race: 78.8% White, 2.5% Black, 13.5% Asian, 7.1% Hispanic of any race (2000); Density: 7,831.8 persons per square mile (2000); Age: 20.3% under 18, 8.9% over 64 (2000); Marriage status: 31.0% never married, 57.0% now married, 5.3% widowed, 6.6% divorced

(2000); Foreign born: 22.6% (2000); Ancestry (includes multiple ancestries): 26.4% Other groups, 21.6% Italian, 17.3% Irish, 15.3% German, 7.0% Polish (2000).

Economy: Employment by occupation: 17.5% management, 22.5% professional, 11.3% services, 29.1% sales, 0.0% farming, 8.3% construction, 11.4% production (2000).

Income: Per capita income: $27,729 (2000); Median household income: $60,187 (2000); Poverty rate: 3.7% (2000).

Education: Percent of population age 25 and over with: High school diploma (including GED) or higher: 89.8% (2000); Bachelor's degree or higher: 32.5% (2000).

School District(s)

Parsippany-Troy Hills Township (PK-12)
    2003-04 Enrollment: 7,201 . . . . (973) 263-7250

Housing: Homeownership rate: 61.4% (2000); Median home value: $174,300 (2000); Median rent: $767 per month (2000); Median age of housing: 41 years (2000).

Transportation: Commute to work: 92.8% car, 3.4% public transportation, 1.9% walk, 1.7% work from home (2000); Travel time to work: 24.4% less than 15 minutes, 37.8% 15 to 30 minutes, 22.6% 30 to 45 minutes, 7.6% 45 to 60 minutes, 7.6% 60 minutes or more (2000)

LAKE HOPATCONG (unincorporated postal area, zip code 07849).

Aka Espanong. Covers a land area of 7.151 square miles and a water area of 0.023 square miles. Located at 40.96° N. Lat.; 74.61° W. Long. Elevation is 940 feet.

Population: 7,086 (2000); Race: 97.7% White, 0.2% Black, 0.2% Asian, 3.9% Hispanic of any race (2000); Density: 990.9 persons per square mile (2000); Age: 26.2% under 18, 8.9% over 64 (2000); Marriage status: 22.9% never married, 61.0% now married, 6.5% widowed, 9.6% divorced (2000); Foreign born: 3.7% (2000); Ancestry (includes multiple ancestries): 27.9% Irish, 24.6% Italian, 17.4% German, 12.0% English, 10.2% Polish (2000).

Economy: Employment by occupation: 14.7% management, 20.4% professional, 10.0% services, 30.7% sales, 0.0% farming, 14.1% construction, 10.1% production (2000).

Income: Per capita income: $27,061 (2000); Median household income: $63,785 (2000); Poverty rate: 3.1% (2000).

Education: Percent of population age 25 and over with: High school diploma (including GED) or higher: 87.3% (2000); Bachelor's degree or higher: 23.1% (2000)

School District(s)

Jefferson Township (PK-12)
    2003-04 Enrollment: 3,694 . . . . (973) 663-5780

Housing: Homeownership rate: 84.8% (2000); Median home value: $155,500 (2000); Median rent: $766 per month (2000); Median age of housing: 40 years (2000).

Transportation: Commute to work: 94.6% car, 1.5% public transportation, 0.3% walk, 3.2% work from home (2000); Travel time to work: 15.0% less than 15 minutes, 33.8% 15 to 30 minutes, 22.3% 30 to 45 minutes, 15.5% 45 to 60 minutes, 13.5% 60 minutes or more (2000)

Additional Information Contacts

Jefferson Township Chamber of Commerce . . . . (973) 663-2240
    http://www.jeffersontownshipchamber.org

LAKE TELEMARK (CDP). Covers a land area of 2.217 square miles

and a water area of 0.039 square miles. Located at 40.95° N. Lat.; 74.49° W. Long. Elevation is 740 feet.

Population: 1,108 (1990); 1,202 (2000); 1,335 (2005); 1,443 (2010 projected); Race: 97.1% White, 0.4% Black, 1.0% Asian, 3.7% Hispanic of any race (2005); Density: 602.1 persons per square mile (2005); Average household size: 2.96 (2005); Median age: 38.1 (2005); Males per 100 females: 105.4 (2005); Marriage status: 14.6% never married, 70.6% now married, 5.0% widowed, 9.8% divorced (2000); Foreign born: 12.4% (2000); Ancestry (includes multiple ancestries): 28.9% Irish, 28.2% Italian, 17.5% German, 12.7% Other groups, 11.0% Polish (2000).

Economy: Employment by occupation: 15.9% management, 9.9% professional, 10.4% services, 41.7% sales, 0.0% farming, 9.4% construction, 12.8% production (2000).

Income: Per capita income: $29,852 (2005); Median household income: $81,731 (2005); Average household income: $88,365 (2005); Percent of households with income of $100,000 or more: 35.3% (2005); Poverty rate: 1.1% (2000).

Education: Percent of population age 25 and over with: High school diploma (including GED) or higher: 93.2% (2005); Bachelor's degree or higher: 26.4% (2005); Master's degree or higher: 3.7% (2005).

Housing: Homeownership rate: 93.8% (2005); Median home value: $270,455 (2005); Median rent: $875 per month (2000); Median age of housing: 40 years (2000).

Transportation: Commute to work: 94.2% car, 2.8% public transportation, 1.1% walk, 1.9% work from home (2000); Travel time to work: 15.9% less than 15 minutes, 31.7% 15 to 30 minutes, 23.8% 30 to 45 minutes, 17.7% 45 to 60 minutes, 10.9% 60 minutes or more (2000)

LANDING (unincorporated postal area, zip code 07850). Covers a land

area of 3.463 square miles and a water area of 0.012 square miles. Located at 40.90° N. Lat.; 74.65° W. Long. Elevation is 940 feet.

Population: 6,827 (2000); Race: 92.0% White, 3.7% Black, 2.7% Asian, 6.4% Hispanic of any race (2000); Density: 1,971.6 persons per square mile (2000); Age: 28.5% under 18, 7.4% over 64 (2000); Marriage status: 21.4% never married, 64.1% now married, 5.8% widowed, 8.7% divorced (2000); Foreign born: 10.6% (2000); Ancestry (includes multiple ancestries): 27.6% Irish, 26.3% Italian, 20.7% German, 13.4% Other groups, 9.6% Polish (2000).

Economy: Resort village. In suburbanizing area. Boating; state park nearby. Employment by occupation: 17.9% management, 17.9% professional, 13.2% services, 29.4% sales, 0.0% farming, 10.0% construction, 11.6% production (2000).

Income: Per capita income: $25,433 (2000); Median household income: $66,295 (2000); Poverty rate: 3.1% (2000).

Education: Percent of population age 25 and over with: High school diploma (including GED) or higher: 89.0% (2000); Bachelor's degree or higher: 23.2% (2000).

School District(s)

Roxbury Township (PK-12)
    2003-04 Enrollment: 4,817 . . . . (973) 584-6867

Housing: Homeownership rate: 77.9% (2000); Median home value: $158,500 (2000); Median rent: $757 per month (2000); Median age of housing: 34 years (2000).

Transportation: Commute to work: 94.9% car, 2.1% public transportation, 0.0% walk, 1.9% work from home (2000); Travel time to work: 18.2% less than 15 minutes, 23.5% 15 to 30 minutes, 24.6% 30 to 45 minutes, 17.6% 45 to 60 minutes, 16.1% 60 minutes or more (2000)

LEDGEWOOD (unincorporated postal area, zip code 07852). Covers

a land area of 2.723 square miles and a water area of 0.017 square miles. Located at 40.87° N. Lat.; 74.65° W. Long. Elevation is 737 feet.

Population: 2,558 (2000); Race: 94.9% White, 0.6% Black, 4.3% Asian, 3.8% Hispanic of any race (2000); Density: 939.5 persons per square mile (2000); Age: 17.9% under 18, 18.9% over 64 (2000); Marriage status: 23.6% never married, 56.2% now married, 10.0% widowed, 10.2% divorced (2000); Foreign born: 11.7% (2000); Ancestry (includes multiple ancestries): 25.7% Italian, 19.6% Irish, 16.2% German, 14.7% English, 10.8% Other groups (2000).

Economy: Employment by occupation: 22.9% management, 26.0% professional, 12.5% services, 27.4% sales, 0.0% farming, 8.2% construction, 3.0% production (2000).

Income: Per capita income: $30,835 (2000); Median household income: $63,750 (2000); Poverty rate: 3.4% (2000).

Education: Percent of population age 25 and over with: High school diploma (including GED) or higher: 83.6% (2000); Bachelor's degree or higher: 36.4% (2000).

Housing: Homeownership rate: 82.9% (2000); Median home value: $195,000 (2000); Median rent: $632 per month (2000); Median age of housing: 5 years (2000).

Transportation: Commute to work: 89.9% car, 2.6% public transportation, 4.0% walk, 2.8% work from home (2000); Travel time to work: 19.3% less than 15 minutes, 21.2% 15 to 30 minutes, 24.3% 30 to 45 minutes, 15.6% 45 to 60 minutes, 19.6% 60 minutes or more (2000)

Additional Information Contacts

Roxbury Area Chamber of Commerce . . . . (973) 770-0740
    http://www.roxburychamber.org

LINCOLN PARK (borough). Covers a land area of 6.729 square

miles and a water area of 0.237 square miles. Located at 40.92° N. Lat.; 74.29° W. Long. Elevation is 180 feet.

History: Named for Abraham Lincoln, 16th President of the U.S. Incorporated 1922.

Population: 10,978 (1990); 10,930 (2000); 10,889 (2005); 10,913 (2010 projected); Race: 88.3% White, 2.2% Black, 6.1% Asian, 7.1% Hispanic of any race (2005); Density: 1,618.1 persons per square mile (2005); Average

household size: 2.67 (2005); Median age: 41.8 (2005); Males per 100 females: 92.9 (2005); Marriage status: 23.7% never married, 61.7% now married, 6.7% widowed, 7.9% divorced (2000); Foreign born: 13.5% (2000); Ancestry (includes multiple ancestries): 26.7% Italian, 19.2% Irish, 16.6% German, 13.0% Other groups, 9.9% Polish (2000).

Economy: Vegetable farming; manufacturing of fixtures, chemicals, machinery. Single-family building permits issued: 0 (2005); Multi-family building permits issued: 0 (2005); Employment by occupation: 16.7% management, 25.9% professional, 8.3% services, 29.7% sales, 0.2% farming, 8.4% construction, 10.8% production (2000).

Income: Per capita income: $36,852 (2005); Median household income: $79,814 (2005); Average household income: $96,461 (2005); Percent of households with income of $100,000 or more: 34.8% (2005); Poverty rate: 2.8% (2000).

Taxes: Total city taxes per capita: $715 (2004); City property taxes per capita: $715 (2004).

Education: Percent of population age 25 and over with: High school diploma (including GED) or higher: 86.2% (2005); Bachelor's degree or higher: 32.8% (2005); Master's degree or higher: 10.9% (2005).

School District(s)
Lincoln Park Borough (PK-08)
   2003-04 Enrollment: 1,055 . . . . (973) 696-5500

Housing: Homeownership rate: 76.0% (2005); Median home value: $291,348 (2005); Median rent: $879 per month (2000); Median age of housing: 33 years (2000).

Safety: Violent crime rate: 3.7 per 10,000 population; Property crime rate: 86.8 per 10,000 population (2004).

Transportation: Commute to work: 92.7% car, 2.8% public transportation, 0.7% walk, 2.4% work from home (2000); Travel time to work: 24.0% less than 15 minutes, 39.0% 15 to 30 minutes, 21.1% 30 to 45 minutes, 6.9% 45 to 60 minutes, 9.0% 60 minutes or more (2000)

Additional Information Contacts
Borough of Lincoln Park. . . . . (973) 694-6100
   http://www.lincolnpark.org
Tri-County Chamber of Commerce . . . . (973) 831-7788
   http://www.tricounty.org

LONG HILL (township). Covers a land area of 12.075 square miles and a water area of 0.002 square miles. Located at 40.67° N. Lat.; 74.49° W. Long. Elevation is 300 feet.

Population: 7,826 (1990); 8,777 (2000); 8,795 (2005); 8,861 (2010 projected); Race: 91.9% White, 0.4% Black, 5.3% Asian, 4.0% Hispanic of any race (2005); Density: 728.3 persons per square mile (2005); Average household size: 2.77 (2005); Median age: 40.3 (2005); Males per 100 females: 94.5 (2005); Marriage status: 20.5% never married, 68.7% now married, 5.5% widowed, 5.2% divorced (2000); Foreign born: 11.3% (2000); Ancestry (includes multiple ancestries): 28.2% Italian, 22.8% Irish, 20.5% German, 11.2% Other groups, 7.9% Polish (2000).

Economy: Single-family building permits issued: 4 (2005); Multi-family building permits issued: 0 (2005); Employment by occupation: 22.4% management, 26.0% professional, 11.9% services, 27.6% sales, 0.3% farming, 4.5% construction, 7.3% production (2000).

Income: Per capita income: $49,468 (2005); Median household income: $102,181 (2005); Average household income: $136,226 (2005); Percent of households with income of $100,000 or more: 50.9% (2005); Poverty rate: 3.3% (2000).

Taxes: Total city taxes per capita: $1,332 (2004); City property taxes per capita: $1,332 (2004).

Education: Percent of population age 25 and over with: High school diploma (including GED) or higher: 93.8% (2005); Bachelor's degree or higher: 49.4% (2005); Master's degree or higher: 19.0% (2005).

Housing: Homeownership rate: 85.6% (2005); Median home value: $475,849 (2005); Median rent: $886 per month (2000); Median age of housing: 37 years (2000).

Safety: Violent crime rate: 5.7 per 10,000 population; Property crime rate: 118.9 per 10,000 population (2004).

Transportation: Commute to work: 87.4% car, 6.5% public transportation, 1.6% walk, 4.4% work from home (2000); Travel time to work: 22.8% less than 15 minutes, 32.8% 15 to 30 minutes, 24.7% 30 to 45 minutes, 7.4% 45 to 60 minutes, 12.2% 60 minutes or more (2000)

Additional Information Contacts
Long Hill Township. . . . . (908) 647-8000
   http://www.longhillnj.org

LONG VALLEY (CDP). Covers a land area of 4.717 square miles and a water area of 0 square miles. Located at 40.78° N. Lat.; 74.77° W. Long. Elevation is 532 feet.

Population: 1,733 (1990); 1,818 (2000); 1,761 (2005); 1,705 (2010 projected); Race: 97.2% White, 0.6% Black, 0.9% Asian, 1.5% Hispanic of any race (2005); Density: 373.3 persons per square mile (2005); Average household size: 2.72 (2005); Median age: 39.6 (2005); Males per 100 females: 103.1 (2005); Marriage status: 21.6% never married, 67.9% now married, 3.1% widowed, 7.4% divorced (2000); Foreign born: 4.2% (2000); Ancestry (includes multiple ancestries): 22.9% Irish, 20.6% German, 20.5% Italian, 9.8% English, 8.5% Other groups (2000).

Economy: Employment by occupation: 21.6% management, 22.4% professional, 19.4% services, 20.8% sales, 0.0% farming, 9.2% construction, 6.7% production (2000).

Income: Per capita income: $42,569 (2005); Median household income: $95,833 (2005); Average household income: $114,950 (2005); Percent of households with income of $100,000 or more: 47.3% (2005); Poverty rate: 4.3% (2000).

Education: Percent of population age 25 and over with: High school diploma (including GED) or higher: 91.6% (2005); Bachelor's degree or higher: 45.8% (2005); Master's degree or higher: 16.4% (2005).

School District(s)
Washington Township (PK-08)
   2003-04 Enrollment: 3,073 . . . . (908) 876-4172

Housing: Homeownership rate: 86.1% (2005); Median home value: $364,496 (2005); Median rent: $841 per month (2000); Median age of housing: 36 years (2000).

Transportation: Commute to work: 88.4% car, 0.0% public transportation, 0.8% walk, 10.0% work from home (2000); Travel time to work: 20.2% less than 15 minutes, 21.3% 15 to 30 minutes, 19.0% 30 to 45 minutes, 18.5% 45 to 60 minutes, 21.0% 60 minutes or more (2000)

MADISON (borough). Covers a land area of 4.200 square miles and a water area of 0 square miles. Located at 40.75° N. Lat.; 74.41° W. Long. Elevation is 261 feet.

History: Named for James Madison, fourth President of the U.S. Seat of Drew University and part of Fairleigh Dickinson University. Originally called Bottle Hill, it was renamed in 1834. Sayre House (1745) in Madison was Gen. Anthony Wayne's headquarters. Noted for its roses. Settled 1685. Incorporated 1889.

Population: 15,945 (1990); 16,530 (2000); 16,470 (2005); 16,503 (2010 projected); Race: 88.9% White, 2.6% Black, 4.4% Asian, 7.6% Hispanic of any race (2005); Density: 3,921.3 persons per square mile (2005); Average household size: 3.01 (2005); Median age: 35.1 (2005); Males per 100 females: 90.2 (2005); Marriage status: 31.7% never married, 56.6% now married, 5.7% widowed, 6.0% divorced (2000); Foreign born: 13.4% (2000); Ancestry (includes multiple ancestries): 23.6% Italian, 19.7% Irish, 13.5% Other groups, 12.9% German, 11.0% English (2000).

Economy: Corporate headquarters. Single-family building permits issued: 32 (2005); Multi-family building permits issued: 0 (2005); Employment by occupation: 22.1% management, 30.8% professional, 9.8% services, 27.6% sales, 0.1% farming, 2.8% construction, 6.8% production (2000).

Income: Per capita income: $42,930 (2005); Median household income: $94,771 (2005); Average household income: $126,213 (2005); Percent of households with income of $100,000 or more: 47.3% (2005); Poverty rate: 3.4% (2000).

Taxes: Total city taxes per capita: $713 (2004); City property taxes per capita: $674 (2004).

Education: Percent of population age 25 and over with: High school diploma (including GED) or higher: 90.7% (2005); Bachelor's degree or higher: 56.6% (2005); Master's degree or higher: 25.9% (2005).

School District(s)
Madison Borough (PK-12)
   2003-04 Enrollment: 2,290 . . . . (973) 593-3100

Four-year College(s)
Drew University (Private, Not-for-profit, United Methodist)
   Fall 2004 Enrollment: 2,675 . . . . (973) 408-3000
   2005-06 Tuition: In-state $31,286; Out-of-state $31,286
Fairleigh Dickinson University-College at Florham (Private, Not-for-profit)
   Fall 2004 Enrollment: 3,684. . . . . (973) 443-8500
   2005-06 Tuition: In-state $24,364; Out-of-state $24,364

Housing: Homeownership rate: 67.1% (2005); Median home value: $606,755 (2005); Median rent: $960 per month (2000); Median age of housing: 47 years (2000).

Safety: Violent crime rate: 5.8 per 10,000 population; Property crime rate: 87.3 per 10,000 population (2004).

Newspapers: Florham Park Eagle (General - Circulation 1,862); Hanover Eagle (General - Circulation 4,000); Madison Eagle (General - Circulation 4,000); Morris News Bee (General - Circulation 3,500)

Transportation: Commute to work: 75.6% car, 9.2% public transportation, 9.4% walk, 5.0% work from home (2000); Travel time to work: 36.7% less than 15 minutes, 28.9% 15 to 30 minutes, 13.8% 30 to 45 minutes, 5.9% 45 to 60 minutes, 14.7% 60 minutes or more (2000)

Additional Information Contacts

Borough of Madison. . . . . (973) 593-3042
   http://www.rosenet.org/gov
Madison Chamber of Commerce. (973) 377-7830
   http://www.rosenet.org/chamber

MENDHAM (borough). Covers a land area of 6.023 square miles and a water area of 0.021 square miles. Located at 40.77° N. Lat.; 74.60° W. Long. Elevation is 618 feet.

Population: 4,890 (1990); 5,097 (2000); 5,165 (2005); 5,264 (2010 projected); Race: 96.9% White, 0.5% Black, 1.5% Asian, 3.2% Hispanic of any race (2005); Density: 857.5 persons per square mile (2005); Average household size: 2.84 (2005); Median age: 43.2 (2005); Males per 100 females: 90.7 (2005); Marriage status: 19.2% never married, 67.5% now married, 7.8% widowed, 5.4% divorced (2000); Foreign born: 8.2% (2000); Ancestry (includes multiple ancestries): 26.9% Irish, 21.1% Italian, 21.0% German, 13.1% English, 7.7% Polish (2000).

Economy: Single-family building permits issued: 2 (2005); Multi-family building permits issued: 0 (2005); Employment by occupation: 29.3% management, 25.9% professional, 6.0% services, 32.4% sales, 0.6% farming, 3.2% construction, 2.5% production (2000).

Income: Per capita income: $53,200 (2005); Median household income: $122,115 (2005); Average household income: $150,427 (2005); Percent of households with income of $100,000 or more: 58.2% (2005); Poverty rate: 4.1% (2000).

Education: Percent of population age 25 and over with: High school diploma (including GED) or higher: 95.3% (2005); Bachelor's degree or higher: 62.1% (2005); Master's degree or higher: 27.7% (2005).

School District(s)

Mendham Borough (PK-08)
   2003-04 Enrollment: 672. . . . . (973) 543-2295
West Morris Regional (09-12)
   2003-04 Enrollment: 2,402 . . . . (908) 879-6404

Two-year College(s)

Assumption College for Sisters (Private, Not-for-profit, Roman Catholic)
   Fall 2004 Enrollment: 35 . . . . (973) 543-6528
   2005-06 Tuition: In-state $3,300; Out-of-state $3,300

Housing: Homeownership rate: 85.8% (2005); Median home value: $643,468 (2005); Median rent: $1,092 per month (2000); Median age of housing: 29 years (2000).

Safety: Violent crime rate: 1.9 per 10,000 population; Property crime rate: 77.4 per 10,000 population (2004).

Transportation: Commute to work: 85.6% car, 3.8% public transportation, 2.0% walk, 8.5% work from home (2000); Travel time to work: 21.6% less than 15 minutes, 31.0% 15 to 30 minutes, 22.9% 30 to 45 minutes, 10.5% 45 to 60 minutes, 14.1% 60 minutes or more (2000)

Additional Information Contacts

Borough of Mendham . . . . (973) 543-7152
   http://www.mendhamnj.org

MENDHAM (township). Covers a land area of 17.859 square miles and a water area of 0.123 square miles. Located at 40.78° N. Lat.; 74.58° W. Long. Elevation is 618 feet.

History: Has pre-Revolutionary tavern. Settled before 1750, incorporated 1906.

Population: 4,537 (1990); 5,400 (2000); 5,701 (2005); 6,012 (2010 projected); Race: 95.3% White, 1.1% Black, 2.3% Asian, 1.5% Hispanic of any race (2005); Density: 319.2 persons per square mile (2005); Average household size: 3.09 (2005); Median age: 40.6 (2005); Males per 100 females: 96.7 (2005); Marriage status: 16.3% never married, 75.8% now married, 4.8% widowed, 3.1% divorced (2000); Foreign born: 7.5% (2000); Ancestry (includes multiple ancestries): 21.2% German, 19.1% Irish, 18.2% Italian, 10.9% English, 7.7% United States or American (2000).

Economy: Single-family building permits issued: 5 (2005); Multi-family building permits issued: 0 (2005); Employment by occupation: 34.3%

management, 26.0% professional, 5.8% services, 26.0% sales, 0.0% farming, 4.7% construction, 3.2% production (2000).

Income: Per capita income: $68,992 (2005); Median household income: $155,542 (2005); Average household income: $212,860 (2005); Percent of households with income of $100,000 or more: 69.5% (2005); Poverty rate: 1.8% (2000).

Taxes: Total city taxes per capita: $1,058 (2004); City property taxes per capita: $1,005 (2004).

Education: Percent of population age 25 and over with: High school diploma (including GED) or higher: 97.9% (2005); Bachelor's degree or higher: 71.4% (2005); Master's degree or higher: 34.7% (2005).

School District(s)

Mendham Borough (PK-08)
   2003-04 Enrollment: 672. . . . . (973) 543-2295
West Morris Regional (09-12)
   2003-04 Enrollment: 2,402 . . . . (908) 879-6404

Two-year College(s)

Assumption College for Sisters (Private, Not-for-profit, Roman Catholic)
   Fall 2004 Enrollment: 35 . . . . (973) 543-6528
   2005-06 Tuition: In-state $3,300; Out-of-state $3,300

Housing: Homeownership rate: 95.6% (2005); Median home value: $895,278 (2005); Median rent: $956 per month (2000); Median age of housing: 27 years (2000).

Safety: Violent crime rate: 8.8 per 10,000 population; Property crime rate: 74.3 per 10,000 population (2004).

Transportation: Commute to work: 89.5% car, 3.8% public transportation, 0.2% walk, 5.7% work from home (2000); Travel time to work: 13.8% less than 15 minutes, 38.1% 15 to 30 minutes, 19.3% 30 to 45 minutes, 10.1% 45 to 60 minutes, 18.6% 60 minutes or more (2000)

Additional Information Contacts

Mendham Township. . . . . (973) 543-4555
   http://www.mendhamtownship.org

MILLINGTON (unincorporated postal area, zip code 07946). Covers a land area of 3.615 square miles and a water area of 0 square miles. Located at 40.67° N. Lat.; 74.52° W. Long. Elevation is 340 feet.

Population: 3,000 (2000); Race: 93.7% White, 0.5% Black, 3.7% Asian, 4.0% Hispanic of any race (2000); Density: 829.9 persons per square mile (2000); Age: 28.3% under 18, 12.5% over 64 (2000); Marriage status: 18.5% never married, 71.9% now married, 5.1% widowed, 4.5% divorced (2000); Foreign born: 9.4% (2000); Ancestry (includes multiple ancestries): 32.1% Italian, 19.5% Irish, 19.0% German, 8.8% Other groups, 8.6% Polish (2000).

Economy: Employment by occupation: 28.0% management, 31.8% professional, 6.6% services, 26.0% sales, 0.0% farming, 3.1% construction, 4.7% production (2000).

Income: Per capita income: $47,602 (2000); Median household income: $105,511 (2000); Poverty rate: 3.7% (2000).

Education: Percent of population age 25 and over with: High school diploma (including GED) or higher: 95.8% (2000); Bachelor's degree or higher: 58.9% (2000).

School District(s)

Long Hill Township (PK-08)
   2003-04 Enrollment: 1,159 . . . . (908) 647-1200

Housing: Homeownership rate: 90.3% (2000); Median home value: $333,500 (2000); Median rent: $635 per month (2000); Median age of housing: 37 years (2000).

Transportation: Commute to work: 86.8% car, 6.8% public transportation, 0.0% walk, 5.8% work from home (2000); Travel time to work: 19.1% less than 15 minutes, 32.8% 15 to 30 minutes, 24.5% 30 to 45 minutes, 11.8% 45 to 60 minutes, 11.8% 60 minutes or more (2000)

MINE HILL (township). Covers a land area of 2.995 square miles and a water area of 0.013 square miles. Located at 40.87° N. Lat.; 74.60° W. Long. Elevation is 840 feet.

History: Iron mine here opened 1858, reopened 1939, since closed.

Population: 3,333 (1990); 3,679 (2000); 3,686 (2005); 3,724 (2010 projected); Race: 90.1% White, 4.0% Black, 2.5% Asian, 10.2% Hispanic of any race (2005); Density: 1,230.9 persons per square mile (2005); Average household size: 2.67 (2005); Median age: 39.2 (2005); Males per 100 females: 95.0 (2005); Marriage status: 22.1% never married, 61.7% now married, 8.4% widowed, 7.8% divorced (2000); Foreign born: 11.5% (2000); Ancestry (includes multiple ancestries): 23.5% Irish, 20.5% Italian, 20.1% German, 19.5% Other groups, 10.4% English (2000).

Economy: Ships crushed stone, sand. Single-family building permits issued: 3 (2005); Multi-family building permits issued: 0 (2005); Employment by occupation: 20.8% management, 19.7% professional, 9.9% services, 28.8% sales, 0.4% farming, 10.9% construction, 9.5% production (2000).

Income: Per capita income: $30,706 (2005); Median household income: $70,342 (2005); Average household income: $81,957 (2005); Percent of households with income of $100,000 or more: 27.7% (2005); Poverty rate: 5.6% (2000).

Education: Percent of population age 25 and over with: High school diploma (including GED) or higher: 90.9% (2005); Bachelor's degree or higher: 27.8% (2005); Master's degree or higher: 9.1% (2005).

School District(s)

Mine Hill Township (PK-06)
    2003-04 Enrollment: 384 . . . . (973) 366-0590

Housing: Homeownership rate: 89.9% (2005); Median home value: $256,172 (2005); Median rent: $1,045 per month (2000); Median age of housing: 42 years (2000).

Safety: Violent crime rate: 10.8 per 10,000 population; Property crime rate: 91.7 per 10,000 population (2004).

Transportation: Commute to work: 97.4% car, 0.8% public transportation, 0.4% walk, 0.9% work from home (2000); Travel time to work: 18.8% less than 15 minutes, 31.5% 15 to 30 minutes, 24.7% 30 to 45 minutes, 15.0% 45 to 60 minutes, 10.1% 60 minutes or more (2000)

Additional Information Contacts

Mine Hill Township. . . . . (973) 366-9031
    http://www.minehill.com

MONTVILLE (township). Covers a land area of 18.871 square miles and a water area of 0.263 square miles. Located at 40.90° N. Lat.; 74.35° W. Long. Elevation is 300 feet.

Population: 15,647 (1990); 20,839 (2000); 21,431 (2005); 22,033 (2010 projected); Race: 82.2% White, 1.0% Black, 15.1% Asian, 3.0% Hispanic of any race (2005); Density: 1,135.6 persons per square mile (2005); Average household size: 2.77 (2005); Median age: 40.2 (2005); Males per 100 females: 95.1 (2005); Marriage status: 20.8% never married, 68.3% now married, 6.2% widowed, 4.7% divorced (2000); Foreign born: 17.2% (2000); Ancestry (includes multiple ancestries): 26.8% Italian, 18.3% Other groups, 14.3% Irish, 13.7% German, 9.3% Polish (2000).

Economy: Manufacturing: drugs, crushed stone. Single-family building permits issued: 49 (2005); Multi-family building permits issued: 0 (2005); Employment by occupation: 23.8% management, 30.1% professional, 6.1% services, 28.6% sales, 0.0% farming, 5.7% construction, 5.7% production (2000).

Income: Per capita income: $47,677 (2005); Median household income: $99,244 (2005); Average household income: $131,015 (2005); Percent of households with income of $100,000 or more: 49.5% (2005); Poverty rate: 3.8% (2000).

Taxes: Total city taxes per capita: $517 (2004); City property taxes per capita: $517 (2004).

Education: Percent of population age 25 and over with: High school diploma (including GED) or higher: 93.6% (2005); Bachelor's degree or higher: 51.5% (2005); Master's degree or higher: 20.2% (2005).

School District(s)

Montville Township (PK-12)
    2003-04 Enrollment: 4,030 . . . . (973) 331-7117

Housing: Homeownership rate: 81.9% (2005); Median home value: $548,314 (2005); Median rent: $1,049 per month (2000); Median age of housing: 21 years (2000).

Safety: Violent crime rate: 3.3 per 10,000 population; Property crime rate: 101.6 per 10,000 population (2004).

Newspapers: The Montville Magazine (General - Circulation 8,900)

Transportation: Commute to work: 90.1% car, 5.0% public transportation, 1.0% walk, 3.6% work from home (2000); Travel time to work: 22.3% less than 15 minutes, 37.9% 15 to 30 minutes, 21.1% 30 to 45 minutes, 7.2% 45 to 60 minutes, 11.6% 60 minutes or more (2000)

Additional Information Contacts

Montville Township . . . . (973) 331-3302
    http://www.montville-township.org
Montville Township Chamber of Commerce . . . . (973) 263-3300
    http://www.montville-township.org

MORRIS (township). Covers a land area of 15.760 square miles and a water area of 0.049 square miles. Located at 40.79° N. Lat.; 74.49° W. Long.

Population: 19,849 (1990); 21,796 (2000); 21,751 (2005); 21,845 (2010 projected); Race: 88.1% White, 5.4% Black, 4.3% Asian, 4.7% Hispanic of any race (2005); Density: 1,380.1 persons per square mile (2005); Average household size: 2.65 (2005); Median age: 42.4 (2005); Males per 100 females: 90.0 (2005); Marriage status: 21.3% never married, 67.4% now married, 5.4% widowed, 5.9% divorced (2000); Foreign born: 10.7% (2000); Ancestry (includes multiple ancestries): 21.5% Irish, 18.2% Italian, 15.1% Other groups, 14.5% German, 10.5% English (2000).

Economy: Single-family building permits issued: 14 (2005); Multi-family building permits issued: 0 (2005); Employment by occupation: 29.6% management, 33.1% professional, 6.6% services, 24.0% sales, 0.0% farming, 3.7% construction, 3.0% production (2000).

Income: Per capita income: $61,244 (2005); Median household income: $120,394 (2005); Average household income: $159,682 (2005); Percent of households with income of $100,000 or more: 59.0% (2005); Poverty rate: 3.8% (2000).

Education: Percent of population age 25 and over with: High school diploma (including GED) or higher: 95.3% (2005); Bachelor's degree or higher: 63.8% (2005); Master's degree or higher: 29.8% (2005).

Housing: Homeownership rate: 85.5% (2005); Median home value: $543,659 (2005); Median rent: $929 per month (2000); Median age of housing: 33 years (2000).

Safety: Violent crime rate: 11.2 per 10,000 population; Property crime rate: 77.7 per 10,000 population (2004).

Transportation: Commute to work: 84.5% car, 7.1% public transportation, 1.7% walk, 6.1% work from home (2000); Travel time to work: 27.5% less than 15 minutes, 36.4% 15 to 30 minutes, 16.7% 30 to 45 minutes, 5.6% 45 to 60 minutes, 13.8% 60 minutes or more (2000)

Additional Information Contacts

Morris Township. . . . . (973) 326-7360
    http://www.morristwp.com

MORRIS PLAINS (borough). Covers a land area of 2.594 square miles and a water area of 0.023 square miles. Located at 40.83° N. Lat.; 74.48° W. Long. Elevation is 399 feet.

History: State mental hospital (1871) nearby. Incorporated 1926.

Population: 4,815 (1990); 5,236 (2000); 5,782 (2005); 6,301 (2010 projected); Race: 92.3% White, 1.2% Black, 5.1% Asian, 3.1% Hispanic of any race (2005); Density: 2,229.3 persons per square mile (2005); Average household size: 2.65 (2005); Median age: 42.0 (2005); Males per 100 females: 93.2 (2005); Marriage status: 18.8% never married, 66.7% now married, 9.0% widowed, 5.5% divorced (2000); Foreign born: 9.7% (2000); Ancestry (includes multiple ancestries): 29.7% Irish, 24.8% Italian, 21.2% German, 9.5% English, 9.0% Other groups (2000).

Economy: Pharmaceuticals, tea, electrical equipment and office equipment are produced here. Single-family building permits issued: 8 (2005); Multi-family building permits issued: 49 (2005); Employment by occupation: 24.8% management, 31.8% professional, 8.9% services, 25.3% sales, 0.0% farming, 5.6% construction, 3.6% production (2000).

Income: Per capita income: $44,539 (2005); Median household income: $97,545 (2005); Average household income: $117,685 (2005); Percent of households with income of $100,000 or more: 48.5% (2005); Poverty rate: 2.4% (2000).

Education: Percent of population age 25 and over with: High school diploma (including GED) or higher: 94.1% (2005); Bachelor's degree or higher: 50.7% (2005); Master's degree or higher: 21.2% (2005).

School District(s)

Educ Serv Comm Morris Co (PK-PK)
    2003-04 Enrollment: 272 . . . . (973) 540-8844
Hanover Township (PK-08)
    2003-04 Enrollment: 1,504 . . . . (973) 515-2404
Morris Plains Borough (PK-08)
    2003-04 Enrollment: 583 . . . . (973) 538-1650
Morris School District (PK-12)
    2003-04 Enrollment: 4,876 . . . . (973) 292-2300
Parsippany-Troy Hills Township (PK-12)
    2003-04 Enrollment: 7,201 . . . . (973) 263-7250

Two-year College(s)

Artistic Academy of Hair Design (Private, For-profit)
    Fall 2004 Enrollment: 109 . . . . (973) 656-1401

Housing: Homeownership rate: 91.7% (2005); Median home value: $440,882 (2005); Median rent: $935 per month (2000); Median age of housing: 43 years (2000).

Hospitals: Greystone Park Psychiatric Hospital (605 beds)

Safety: Violent crime rate: 10.8 per 10,000 population; Property crime rate: 217.9 per 10,000 population (2004).
Transportation: Commute to work: 85.9% car, 6.6% public transportation, 1.5% walk, 5.1% work from home (2000); Travel time to work: 27.1% less than 15 minutes, 40.3% 15 to 30 minutes, 15.6% 30 to 45 minutes, 6.9% 45 to 60 minutes, 10.2% 60 minutes or more (2000)

MORRISTOWN (town). Covers a land area of 2.942 square miles and a water area of 0.063 square miles. Located at 40.79° N. Lat.; 74.47° W. Long. Elevation is 327 feet.
History: Named for Lewis Morris (1671-1746), colonial statesman. When, about 1710, word came to the settlement at Newark that iron ore was plentiful beyond the Watchung Mountains, a small number of pioneers struck out on a wilderness road to engage in a new industry. One group selected a site that is now part of Morristown, and named their new village West Hanover. In 1739 a new county was laid out and named in honor of Lewis Morris, the first governor of New Jersey. The court martial of General Benedict Arnold took place in Morristown in 1780.
Population: 16,189 (1990); 18,544 (2000); 18,896 (2005); 19,325 (2010 projected); Race: 65.6% White, 14.9% Black, 4.2% Asian, 34.5% Hispanic of any race (2005); Density: 6,423.5 persons per square mile (2005); Average household size: 2.60 (2005); Median age: 36.8 (2005); Males per 100 females: 101.7 (2005); Marriage status: 39.0% never married, 44.3% now married, 6.9% widowed, 9.8% divorced (2000); Foreign born: 32.4% (2000); Ancestry (includes multiple ancestries): 41.6% Other groups, 14.4% Irish, 10.8% Italian, 7.5% German, 6.1% English (2000).
Economy: Single-family building permits issued: 7 (2005); Multi-family building permits issued: 11 (2005); Employment by occupation: 19.6% management, 21.8% professional, 21.4% services, 20.6% sales, 0.4% farming, 7.0% construction, 9.1% production (2000).
Income: Per capita income: $33,112 (2005); Median household income: $64,719 (2005); Average household income: $84,864 (2005); Percent of households with income of $100,000 or more: 29.5% (2005); Poverty rate: 11.5% (2000).
Taxes: Total city taxes per capita: $1,117 (2004); City property taxes per capita: $1,058 (2004).
Education: Percent of population age 25 and over with: High school diploma (including GED) or higher: 82.1% (2005); Bachelor's degree or higher: 38.1% (2005); Master's degree or higher: 15.4% (2005).

School District(s)
Agency - Unity CS (KG-08)
   2003-04 Enrollment: 105 . . . . (973) 292-1808
Educ Serv Comm Morris Co (PK-PK)
   2003-04 Enrollment: 272 . . . . (973) 540-8844
Mendham Borough (PK-08)
   2003-04 Enrollment: 672 . . . . (973) 543-2295
Morris School District (PK-12)
   2003-04 Enrollment: 4,876 . . . . (973) 292-2300

Four-year College(s)
College of Saint Elizabeth (Private, Not-for-profit, Roman Catholic)
   Fall 2004 Enrollment: 1,976. (973) 290-4000
   2005-06 Tuition: In-state $18,640; Out-of-state $18,640
Rabbinical College of America (Private, Not-for-profit)
   Fall 2004 Enrollment: 257 . . . . (973) 267-9404
   2005-06 Tuition: In-state $8,700; Out-of-state $8,700
Housing: Homeownership rate: 38.9% (2005); Median home value: $343,207 (2005); Median rent: $862 per month (2000); Median age of housing: 46 years (2000).
Hospitals: Morristown Memorial Hospital (561 beds)
Safety: Violent crime rate: 69.7 per 10,000 population; Property crime rate: 386.8 per 10,000 population (2004).
Transportation: Commute to work: 79.8% car, 6.3% public transportation, 7.7% walk, 2.1% work from home (2000); Travel time to work: 33.1% less than 15 minutes, 36.8% 15 to 30 minutes, 15.9% 30 to 45 minutes, 5.5% 45 to 60 minutes, 8.7% 60 minutes or more (2000)
Additional Information Contacts
Morristown Chamber of Commerce. . . . . (973) 539-3882
   http://www.morrischamber.org

MOUNT ARLINGTON (borough). Covers a land area of 2.113 square miles and a water area of 0.720 square miles. Located at 40.91° N. Lat.; 74.64° W. Long. Elevation is 1,000 feet.
Population: 3,630 (1990); 4,663 (2000); 5,138 (2005); 5,600 (2010 projected); Race: 89.7% White, 2.3% Black, 4.6% Asian, 5.5% Hispanic of any race (2005); Density: 2,431.9 persons per square mile (2005); Average

household size: 2.38 (2005); Median age: 40.2 (2005); Males per 100 females: 91.5 (2005); Marriage status: 23.2% never married, 60.0% now married, 7.5% widowed, 9.4% divorced (2000); Foreign born: 9.8% (2000); Ancestry (includes multiple ancestries): 24.7% Irish, 24.2% Italian, 23.8% German, 10.1% Other groups, 9.0% English (2000).
Economy: Single-family building permits issued: 30 (2005); Multi-family building permits issued: 163 (2005); Employment by occupation: 14.8% management, 22.8% professional, 10.4% services, 32.7% sales, 0.0% farming, 10.0% construction, 9.3% production (2000).
Income: Per capita income: $38,142 (2005); Median household income: $77,311 (2005); Average household income: $90,263 (2005); Percent of households with income of $100,000 or more: 32.7% (2005); Poverty rate: 3.3% (2000).
Education: Percent of population age 25 and over with: High school diploma (including GED) or higher: 90.6% (2005); Bachelor's degree or higher: 36.5% (2005); Master's degree or higher: 11.5% (2005).

School District(s)
Mount Arlington Borough (PK-08)
   2003-04 Enrollment: 448 . . . . (973) 398-6400
Housing: Homeownership rate: 81.2% (2005); Median home value: $273,877 (2005); Median rent: $770 per month (2000); Median age of housing: 29 years (2000).
Safety: Violent crime rate: 4.0 per 10,000 population; Property crime rate: 138.6 per 10,000 population (2004).
Transportation: Commute to work: 94.6% car, 2.1% public transportation, 0.3% walk, 2.5% work from home (2000); Travel time to work: 18.3% less than 15 minutes, 28.1% 15 to 30 minutes, 23.8% 30 to 45 minutes, 16.9% 45 to 60 minutes, 12.9% 60 minutes or more (2000)
Additional Information Contacts
Borough of Mount Arlington . . . . (973) 398-6832
   http://www.ci.mount-arlington.nj.us

MOUNT OLIVE (township). Covers a land area of 30.354 square miles and a water area of 0.703 square miles. Located at 40.86° N. Lat.; 74.73° W. Long. Elevation is 960 feet.
History: Incorporated 1871.
Population: 21,306 (1990); 24,193 (2000); 26,135 (2005); 28,004 (2010 projected); Race: 83.7% White, 4.5% Black, 7.7% Asian, 7.3% Hispanic of any race (2005); Density: 861.0 persons per square mile (2005); Average household size: 2.66 (2005); Median age: 35.7 (2005); Males per 100 females: 100.8 (2005); Marriage status: 26.2% never married, 61.7% now married, 4.3% widowed, 7.9% divorced (2000); Foreign born: 13.0% (2000); Ancestry (includes multiple ancestries): 22.7% Irish, 22.7% Italian, 19.6% German, 18.2% Other groups, 8.8% Polish (2000).
Economy: Unemployment rate: 3.6% (2005); Total civilian labor force: 14,768 (2005); Single-family building permits issued: 106 (2005); Multi-family building permits issued: 0 (2005); Employment by occupation: 19.1% management, 24.7% professional, 10.7% services, 26.2% sales, 0.2% farming, 7.9% construction, 11.2% production (2000).
Income: Per capita income: $34,020 (2005); Median household income: $74,094 (2005); Average household income: $89,922 (2005); Percent of households with income of $100,000 or more: 30.8% (2005); Poverty rate: 3.1% (2000).
Taxes: Total city taxes per capita: $611 (2004); City property taxes per capita: $582 (2004).
Education: Percent of population age 25 and over with: High school diploma (including GED) or higher: 92.1% (2005); Bachelor's degree or higher: 36.9% (2005); Master's degree or higher: 11.5% (2005).
Housing: Homeownership rate: 55.7% (2005); Median home value: $329,211 (2005); Median rent: $763 per month (2000); Median age of housing: 27 years (2000).
Safety: Violent crime rate: 6.2 per 10,000 population; Property crime rate: 118.2 per 10,000 population (2004).
Transportation: Commute to work: 94.1% car, 1.5% public transportation, 0.6% walk, 3.1% work from home (2000); Travel time to work: 17.4% less than 15 minutes, 22.1% 15 to 30 minutes, 24.3% 30 to 45 minutes, 19.0% 45 to 60 minutes, 17.1% 60 minutes or more (2000)
Additional Information Contacts
Mount Olive Area Chamber of Commerce. . . . . (973) 691-0109
   http://mountolivechambernj.com
Mount Olive Township . . . . (973) 691-0900
   http://www.mountolivetownship.com

MOUNTAIN LAKES (borough). Covers a land area of 2.672 square miles and a water area of 0.221 square miles. Located at 40.88° N. Lat.; 74.44° W. Long. Elevation is 513 feet.

History: Settled 1915 as real estate development, incorporated 1924.

Population: 3,842 (1990); 4,256 (2000); 4,344 (2005); 4,457 (2010 projected); Race: 91.8% White, 0.4% Black, 6.1% Asian, 1.8% Hispanic of any race (2005); Density: 1,626.0 persons per square mile (2005); Average household size: 3.25 (2005); Median age: 38.7 (2005); Males per 100 females: 98.2 (2005); Marriage status: 15.0% never married, 77.6% now married, 3.9% widowed, 3.5% divorced (2000); Foreign born: 9.8% (2000); Ancestry (includes multiple ancestries): 21.9% Irish, 18.0% German, 17.7% Italian, 11.9% English, 10.1% Other groups (2000).

Economy: Single-family building permits issued: 8 (2005); Multi-family building permits issued: 0 (2005); Employment by occupation: 33.8% management, 35.0% professional, 6.0% services, 19.8% sales, 0.0% farming, 2.9% construction, 2.6% production (2000).

Income: Per capita income: $66,103 (2005); Median household income: $155,479 (2005); Average household income: $214,935 (2005); Percent of households with income of $100,000 or more: 69.8% (2005); Poverty rate: 2.0% (2000).

Education: Percent of population age 25 and over with: High school diploma (including GED) or higher: 98.4% (2005); Bachelor's degree or higher: 76.0% (2005); Master's degree or higher: 34.9% (2005).

School District(s)
Mountain Lakes Borough (PK-12)
    2003-04 Enrollment: 1,842 . . . . (973) 334-8280

Housing: Homeownership rate: 96.3% (2005); Median home value: $831,330 (2005); Median rent: $1,554 per month (2000); Median age of housing: 53 years (2000).

Safety: Violent crime rate: 2.3 per 10,000 population; Property crime rate: 212.1 per 10,000 population (2004).

Transportation: Commute to work: 81.4% car, 7.8% public transportation, 1.3% walk, 8.7% work from home (2000); Travel time to work: 26.9% less than 15 minutes, 29.3% 15 to 30 minutes, 19.9% 30 to 45 minutes, 7.7% 45 to 60 minutes, 16.1% 60 minutes or more (2000)

Additional Information Contacts
Borough of Mountain Lakes. . . . . (973) 334-1413
    http://www.mtnlakes.org
Tri-Town Chamber of Commerce . . . . (973) 334-4117
    http://www.tritownchamber.org

NETCONG (borough). Covers a land area of 0.841 square miles and a water area of 0.057 square miles. Located at 40.89° N. Lat.; 74.70° W. Long. Elevation is 882 feet.

History: Incorporated 1894; grew as residence for iron miners and ironworkers.

Population: 2,858 (1990); 2,580 (2000); 2,638 (2005); 2,712 (2010 projected); Race: 93.4% White, 1.3% Black, 1.9% Asian, 9.1% Hispanic of any race (2005); Density: 3,135.8 persons per square mile (2005); Average household size: 2.53 (2005); Median age: 39.6 (2005); Males per 100 females: 97.6 (2005); Marriage status: 26.5% never married, 57.4% now married, 7.3% widowed, 8.8% divorced (2000); Foreign born: 10.4% (2000); Ancestry (includes multiple ancestries): 38.9% Italian, 21.5% Irish, 17.6% German, 12.6% Other groups, 9.1% English (2000).

Economy: In resort area. Manufacturing: machinery, consumer goods. Agriculture: poultry; fruit, vegetables. Single-family building permits issued: 5 (2005); Multi-family building permits issued: 0 (2005); Employment by occupation: 11.2% management, 20.2% professional, 18.3% services, 26.7% sales, 0.0% farming, 9.5% construction, 14.2% production (2000).

Income: Per capita income: $27,816 (2005); Median household income: $63,245 (2005); Average household income: $70,430 (2005); Percent of households with income of $100,000 or more: 21.5% (2005); Poverty rate: 3.1% (2000).

Education: Percent of population age 25 and over with: High school diploma (including GED) or higher: 84.6% (2005); Bachelor's degree or higher: 21.8% (2005); Master's degree or higher: 6.3% (2005).

School District(s)
Netcong Borough (PK-08)
    2003-04 Enrollment: 291 . . . . (973) 347-0020

Housing: Homeownership rate: 64.5% (2005); Median home value: $234,987 (2005); Median rent: $688 per month (2000); Median age of housing: 53 years (2000).

Safety: Violent crime rate: 24.2 per 10,000 population; Property crime rate: 338.8 per 10,000 population (2004).

Transportation: Commute to work: 90.2% car, 3.0% public transportation, 2.1% walk, 3.8% work from home (2000); Travel time to work: 30.5% less than 15 minutes, 29.1% 15 to 30 minutes, 18.4% 30 to 45 minutes, 10.2% 45 to 60 minutes, 11.8% 60 minutes or more (2000)

Additional Information Contacts
Borough of Netcong. . . . . (973) 347-0252
    http://www.netcong.org

NEW VERNON (unincorporated postal area, zip code 07976). Covers a land area of 4.876 square miles and a water area of 0.001 square miles. Located at 40.73° N. Lat.; 74.48° W. Long. Elevation is 320 feet.

Population: 729 (2000); Race: 100.0% White, 0.0% Black, 0.0% Asian, 0.0% Hispanic of any race (2000); Density: 149.5 persons per square mile (2000); Age: 29.2% under 18, 9.0% over 64 (2000); Marriage status: 15.7% never married, 75.5% now married, 6.2% widowed, 2.6% divorced (2000); Foreign born: 3.2% (2000); Ancestry (includes multiple ancestries): 24.3% Italian, 17.4% United States or American, 14.7% German, 10.1% European, 9.3% Irish (2000).

Economy: Employment by occupation: 20.4% management, 31.2% professional, 12.0% services, 21.3% sales, 0.0% farming, 13.3% construction, 1.9% production (2000).

Income: Per capita income: $59,844 (2000); Median household income: $74,750 (2000); Poverty rate: 1.1% (2000).

Education: Percent of population age 25 and over with: High school diploma (including GED) or higher: 96.6% (2000); Bachelor's degree or higher: 64.7% (2000).

School District(s)
Harding Township (PK-08)
    2003-04 Enrollment: 336 . . . . (973) 267-6398

Housing: Homeownership rate: 94.5% (2000); Median home value: $729,700 (2000); Median rent: $575 per month (2000); Median age of housing: 40 years (2000).

Transportation: Commute to work: 87.3% car, 5.6% public transportation, 1.9% walk, 5.2% work from home (2000); Travel time to work: 34.2% less than 15 minutes, 28.0% 15 to 30 minutes, 22.5% 30 to 45 minutes, 4.9% 45 to 60 minutes, 10.4% 60 minutes or more (2000)

PARSIPPANY-TROY HILLS (township). Covers a land area of 23.942 square miles and a water area of 1.476 square miles. Located at 40.86° N. Lat.; 74.42° W. Long.

Population: 48,982 (1990); 50,649 (2000); 51,723 (2005); 53,033 (2010 projected); Race: 70.0% White, 3.1% Black, 21.7% Asian, 8.6% Hispanic of any race (2005); Density: 2,160.3 persons per square mile (2005); Average household size: 2.55 (2005); Median age: 39.6 (2005); Males per 100 females: 98.0 (2005); Marriage status: 26.7% never married, 60.5% now married, 5.6% widowed, 7.1% divorced (2000); Foreign born: 26.8% (2000); Ancestry (includes multiple ancestries): 29.3% Other groups, 20.9% Italian, 15.2% Irish, 12.9% German, 7.0% Polish (2000).

Economy: Unemployment rate: 3.0% (2005); Total civilian labor force: 30,559 (2005); Single-family building permits issued: 48 (2005); Multi-family building permits issued: 0 (2005); Employment by occupation: 20.7% management, 26.4% professional, 9.0% services, 28.6% sales, 0.1% farming, 6.1% construction, 9.2% production (2000).

Income: Per capita income: $37,455 (2005); Median household income: $77,012 (2005); Average household income: $95,031 (2005); Percent of households with income of $100,000 or more: 34.8% (2005); Poverty rate: 3.9% (2000).

Taxes: Total city taxes per capita: $710 (2004); City property taxes per capita: $669 (2004).

Education: Percent of population age 25 and over with: High school diploma (including GED) or higher: 89.7% (2005); Bachelor's degree or higher: 43.0% (2005); Master's degree or higher: 15.4% (2005).

School District(s)
Parsippany-Troy Hills Township (PK-12)
    2003-04 Enrollment: 7,201 . . . . (973) 263-7250

Two-year College(s)
The Chubb Institute-Parsippany (Private, For-profit)
    Fall 2004 Enrollment: 667 . . . . (973) 630-4900

Housing: Homeownership rate: 59.9% (2005); Median home value: $368,351 (2005); Median rent: $771 per month (2000); Median age of housing: 35 years (2000).

Safety: Violent crime rate: 6.8 per 10,000 population; Property crime rate: 161.2 per 10,000 population (2004).

Newspapers: Daily Record (Circulation 44,352); Svoboda (Ethnic - Circulation 7,800); The Ukrainian Weekly (Ethnic, General - Circulation 7,500)

Transportation: Commute to work: 91.8% car, 3.6% public transportation, 1.7% walk, 2.5% work from home (2000); Travel time to work: 25.3% less than 15 minutes, 38.8% 15 to 30 minutes, 20.3% 30 to 45 minutes, 7.1% 45 to 60 minutes, 8.5% 60 minutes or more (2000)

Additional Information Contacts

Parsippany Chamber of Commerce. . . . . (973) 402-6400
　　http://www.njpacc.org
Parsippany-Troy Hills Township . . . . (973) 263-4357
　　http://www.parsippany.net

PEQUANNOCK (township). Covers a land area of 7.067 square miles and a water area of 0.144 square miles. Located at 40.96° N. Lat.; 74.29° W. Long. Elevation is 180 feet.

History: Incorporated 1798.

Population: 12,844 (1990); 13,888 (2000); 14,975 (2005); 16,055 (2010 projected); Race: 96.2% White, 0.3% Black, 2.0% Asian, 3.5% Hispanic of any race (2005); Density: 2,118.9 persons per square mile (2005); Average household size: 2.72 (2005); Median age: 40.2 (2005); Males per 100 females: 93.7 (2005); Marriage status: 20.9% never married, 66.3% now married, 6.8% widowed, 6.0% divorced (2000); Foreign born: 7.1% (2000); Ancestry (includes multiple ancestries): 29.2% Italian, 26.5% Irish, 17.7% German, 9.0% English, 8.2% Dutch (2000).

Economy: Single-family building permits issued: 12 (2005); Multi-family building permits issued: 234 (2005); Employment by occupation: 19.9% management, 23.9% professional, 10.0% services, 32.4% sales, 0.1% farming, 6.7% construction, 6.9% production (2000).

Income: Per capita income: $37,806 (2005); Median household income: $86,938 (2005); Average household income: $101,774 (2005); Percent of households with income of $100,000 or more: 40.5% (2005); Poverty rate: 3.0% (2000).

Education: Percent of population age 25 and over with: High school diploma (including GED) or higher: 92.9% (2005); Bachelor's degree or higher: 37.7% (2005); Master's degree or higher: 11.5% (2005).

School District(s)

Pequannock Township (PK-12)
　　2003-04 Enrollment: 2,541 . . . . (973) 616-6040

Housing: Homeownership rate: 89.6% (2005); Median home value: $387,261 (2005); Median rent: $680 per month (2000); Median age of housing: 40 years (2000).

Safety: Violent crime rate: 3.4 per 10,000 population; Property crime rate: 129.4 per 10,000 population (2004).

Transportation: Commute to work: 90.5% car, 4.3% public transportation, 0.8% walk, 3.8% work from home (2000); Travel time to work: 27.4% less than 15 minutes, 32.9% 15 to 30 minutes, 22.6% 30 to 45 minutes, 7.2% 45 to 60 minutes, 10.0% 60 minutes or more (2000)

Additional Information Contacts

Pequannock Township. . . . . (973) 835-5700
　　http://www.pequannocktownship.org
Tri-County Chamber of Commerce . . . . (973) 831-7788
　　http://www.tricounty.org

PINE BROOK (unincorporated postal area, zip code 07058). Covers a land area of 2.998 square miles and a water area of 0 square miles. Located at 40.87° N. Lat.; 74.34° W. Long. Elevation is 183 feet.

Population: 5,207 (2000); Race: 76.1% White, 0.2% Black, 20.2% Asian, 2.9% Hispanic of any race (2000); Density: 1,736.7 persons per square mile (2000); Age: 24.3% under 18, 8.4% over 64 (2000); Marriage status: 24.7% never married, 66.9% now married, 4.7% widowed, 3.7% divorced (2000); Foreign born: 24.8% (2000); Ancestry (includes multiple ancestries): 26.0% Other groups, 23.0% Italian, 12.1% Irish, 10.9% German, 9.2% Polish (2000).

Economy: Employment by occupation: 24.0% management, 30.6% professional, 6.5% services, 26.9% sales, 0.0% farming, 4.3% construction, 7.8% production (2000).

Income: Per capita income: $41,205 (2000); Median household income: $90,286 (2000); Poverty rate: 4.6% (2000).

Education: Percent of population age 25 and over with: High school diploma (including GED) or higher: 94.9% (2000); Bachelor's degree or higher: 55.6% (2000).

School District(s)

Montville Township (PK-12)
　　2003-04 Enrollment: 4,030 . . . . (973) 331-7117

Housing: Homeownership rate: 60.1% (2000); Median home value: $356,800 (2000); Median rent: $1,076 per month (2000); Median age of housing: 24 years (2000).

Transportation: Commute to work: 90.2% car, 5.2% public transportation, 1.6% walk, 3.1% work from home (2000); Travel time to work: 23.0% less than 15 minutes, 38.4% 15 to 30 minutes, 20.9% 30 to 45 minutes, 5.6% 45 to 60 minutes, 12.1% 60 minutes or more (2000)

POMPTON PLAINS (unincorporated postal area, zip code 07444). Covers a land area of 5.399 square miles and a water area of 0.051 square miles. Located at 40.96° N. Lat.; 74.29° W. Long. Elevation is 181 feet.

History: On site of a prehistoric lake.

Population: 9,227 (2000); Race: 97.1% White, 0.0% Black, 2.6% Asian, 2.8% Hispanic of any race (2000); Density: 1,708.9 persons per square mile (2000); Age: 26.6% under 18, 12.4% over 64 (2000); Marriage status: 22.3% never married, 65.7% now married, 5.8% widowed, 6.2% divorced (2000); Foreign born: 6.2% (2000); Ancestry (includes multiple ancestries): 30.1% Italian, 25.1% Irish, 17.0% German, 9.5% Dutch, 8.6% English (2000).

Economy: Employment by occupation: 20.2% management, 24.8% professional, 9.9% services, 31.8% sales, 0.1% farming, 6.3% construction, 6.9% production (2000).

Income: Per capita income: $32,724 (2000); Median household income: $76,854 (2000); Poverty rate: 3.0% (2000).

Education: Percent of population age 25 and over with: High school diploma (including GED) or higher: 93.5% (2000); Bachelor's degree or higher: 42.7% (2000).

School District(s)

Pequannock Township (PK-12)
　　2003-04 Enrollment: 2,541 . . . . (973) 616-6040

Housing: Homeownership rate: 91.5% (2000); Median home value: $252,600 (2000); Median rent: $697 per month (2000); Median age of housing: 41 years (2000).

Hospitals: Chilton Memorial Hospital (256 beds)

Transportation: Commute to work: 91.1% car, 4.2% public transportation, 0.6% walk, 3.7% work from home (2000); Travel time to work: 26.6% less than 15 minutes, 32.9% 15 to 30 minutes, 22.4% 30 to 45 minutes, 7.3% 45 to 60 minutes, 10.8% 60 minutes or more (2000)

RANDOLPH (township). Covers a land area of 20.964 square miles and a water area of 0.116 square miles. Located at 40.84° N. Lat.; 74.57° W. Long.

History: Incorporated 1806.

Population: 19,974 (1990); 24,847 (2000); 25,864 (2005); 26,948 (2010 projected); Race: 83.7% White, 2.2% Black, 10.9% Asian, 5.9% Hispanic of any race (2005); Density: 1,233.7 persons per square mile (2005); Average household size: 2.85 (2005); Median age: 37.4 (2005); Males per 100 females: 98.5 (2005); Marriage status: 22.0% never married, 69.5% now married, 4.0% widowed, 4.5% divorced (2000); Foreign born: 16.1% (2000); Ancestry (includes multiple ancestries): 20.8% Other groups, 19.3% Italian, 17.0% Irish, 16.2% German, 7.2% Polish (2000).

Economy: Manufacturing: knives, metal parts, plastic package closures. Unemployment rate: 2.8% (2005); Total civilian labor force: 14,039 (2005); Single-family building permits issued: 35 (2005); Multi-family building permits issued: 0 (2005); Employment by occupation: 28.2% management, 30.7% professional, 7.4% services, 23.5% sales, 0.0% farming, 4.5% construction, 5.7% production (2000).

Income: Per capita income: $51,139 (2005); Median household income: $115,209 (2005); Average household income: $145,158 (2005); Percent of households with income of $100,000 or more: 56.3% (2005); Poverty rate: 1.4% (2000).

Education: Percent of population age 25 and over with: High school diploma (including GED) or higher: 95.4% (2005); Bachelor's degree or higher: 58.9% (2005); Master's degree or higher: 25.5% (2005).

School District(s)

Randolph Township (PK-12)
　　2003-04 Enrollment: 5,624 . . . . (973) 328-2775

Two-year College(s)

County College of Morris (Public)
　　Fall 2004 Enrollment: 8,422. . . . . (973) 328-5000
　　2005-06 Tuition: In-state $5,795; Out-of-state $7,925

Housing: Homeownership rate: 74.1% (2005); Median home value: $525,993 (2005); Median rent: $848 per month (2000); Median age of housing: 24 years (2000).

Safety: Violent crime rate: 4.7 per 10,000 population; Property crime rate: 98.2 per 10,000 population (2004).
Transportation: Commute to work: 90.2% car, 3.0% public transportation, 0.7% walk, 5.7% work from home (2000); Travel time to work: 17.5% less than 15 minutes, 33.2% 15 to 30 minutes, 26.5% 30 to 45 minutes, 11.5% 45 to 60 minutes, 11.3% 60 minutes or more (2000)
Additional Information Contacts
Randolph Chamber of Commerce . . . . (973) 361-3462
   http://www.randolphchamber.org
Randolph Township . . . . (973) 989-7100
   http://www.randolphnj.org

RIVERDALE (borough). Aka Riverdale-Pompton. Covers a land area of 2.056 square miles and a water area of 0.015 square miles. Located at 40.99° N. Lat.; 74.31° W. Long. Elevation is 232 feet.
History: Incorporated 1923.
Population: 2,370 (1990); 2,498 (2000); 2,685 (2005); 2,874 (2010 projected); Race: 91.8% White, 1.3% Black, 3.6% Asian, 5.3% Hispanic of any race (2005); Density: 1,306.2 persons per square mile (2005); Average household size: 2.67 (2005); Median age: 39.1 (2005); Males per 100 females: 95.8 (2005); Marriage status: 25.7% never married, 59.1% now married, 6.8% widowed, 8.4% divorced (2000); Foreign born: 9.1% (2000); Ancestry (includes multiple ancestries): 33.5% Italian, 24.2% Irish, 17.3% German, 7.9% Other groups, 7.9% Polish (2000).
Economy: Sand, gravel. Single-family building permits issued: 20 (2005); Multi-family building permits issued: 924 (2005); Employment by occupation: 20.9% management, 15.3% professional, 8.6% services, 33.9% sales, 0.0% farming, 11.2% construction, 10.1% production (2000).
Income: Per capita income: $37,752 (2005); Median household income: $85,613 (2005); Average household income: $100,410 (2005); Percent of households with income of $100,000 or more: 40.9% (2005); Poverty rate: 5.3% (2000).
Education: Percent of population age 25 and over with: High school diploma (including GED) or higher: 89.1% (2005); Bachelor's degree or higher: 31.1% (2005); Master's degree or higher: 8.5% (2005).

School District(s)
Riverdale Borough (PK-08)
   2003-04 Enrollment: 284 . . . . (973) 839-1304
Housing: Homeownership rate: 82.6% (2005); Median home value: $327,215 (2005); Median rent: $872 per month (2000); Median age of housing: 44 years (2000).
Safety: Violent crime rate: 3.8 per 10,000 population; Property crime rate: 255.3 per 10,000 population (2004).
Transportation: Commute to work: 92.7% car, 3.4% public transportation, 1.3% walk, 2.4% work from home (2000); Travel time to work: 26.8% less than 15 minutes, 46.1% 15 to 30 minutes, 13.2% 30 to 45 minutes, 4.5% 45 to 60 minutes, 9.3% 60 minutes or more (2000)
Additional Information Contacts
Tri-County Chamber of Commerce . . . . (973) 831-7788
   http://www.tricounty.org

ROCKAWAY (borough). Covers a land area of 2.089 square miles and a water area of 0.017 square miles. Located at 40.90° N. Lat.; 74.51° W. Long. Elevation is 534 feet.
Population: 6,243 (1990); 6,473 (2000); 6,425 (2005); 6,419 (2010 projected); Race: 84.7% White, 1.6% Black, 8.0% Asian, 11.8% Hispanic of any race (2005); Density: 3,075.9 persons per square mile (2005); Average household size: 2.61 (2005); Median age: 39.7 (2005); Males per 100 females: 95.3 (2005); Marriage status: 25.7% never married, 58.0% now married, 7.2% widowed, 9.1% divorced (2000); Foreign born: 15.4% (2000); Ancestry (includes multiple ancestries): 21.0% German, 21.0% Italian, 19.2% Irish, 19.1% Other groups, 10.2% Polish (2000).
Economy: Single-family building permits issued: 0 (2005); Multi-family building permits issued: 0 (2005); Employment by occupation: 14.8% management, 21.3% professional, 10.9% services, 32.4% sales, 0.4% farming, 7.2% construction, 13.1% production (2000).
Income: Per capita income: $30,544 (2005); Median household income: $66,224 (2005); Average household income: $78,867 (2005); Percent of households with income of $100,000 or more: 25.4% (2005); Poverty rate: 5.0% (2000).
Taxes: Total city taxes per capita: $569 (2004); City property taxes per capita: $546 (2004).
Education: Percent of population age 25 and over with: High school diploma (including GED) or higher: 89.7% (2005); Bachelor's degree or higher: 28.6% (2005); Master's degree or higher: 7.6% (2005).

School District(s)
Educ Serv Comm Morris Co (PK-PK)
   2003-04 Enrollment: 272 . . . . (973) 540-8844
Morris County Vocational (09-12)
   2003-04 Enrollment: 182 . . . . (973) 627-4600
Morris Hills Regional (09-12)
   2003-04 Enrollment: 2,696 . . . . (973) 664-2291
Rockaway Borough (PK-08)
   2003-04 Enrollment: 608 . . . . (973) 625-8601
Rockaway Township (PK-08)
   2003-04 Enrollment: 2,985 . . . . (973) 627-8200
Housing: Homeownership rate: 68.8% (2005); Median home value: $296,135 (2005); Median rent: $804 per month (2000); Median age of housing: 45 years (2000).
Safety: Violent crime rate: 7.7 per 10,000 population; Property crime rate: 114.3 per 10,000 population (2004).
Newspapers: Parsippany Life (General - Circulation 20,000)
Transportation: Commute to work: 95.7% car, 1.1% public transportation, 1.9% walk, 1.3% work from home (2000); Travel time to work: 27.9% less than 15 minutes, 34.8% 15 to 30 minutes, 17.6% 30 to 45 minutes, 10.2% 45 to 60 minutes, 9.4% 60 minutes or more (2000)

ROCKAWAY (township). Covers a land area of 42.819 square miles and a water area of 3.172 square miles. Located at 40.93° N. Lat.; 74.52° W. Long. Elevation is 534 feet.
History: Settled 1739, incorporated 1894.
Population: 19,668 (1990); 22,930 (2000); 25,952 (2005); 28,796 (2010 projected); Race: 87.0% White, 3.0% Black, 6.5% Asian, 7.6% Hispanic of any race (2005); Density: 606.1 persons per square mile (2005); Average household size: 2.82 (2005); Median age: 38.7 (2005); Males per 100 females: 97.9 (2005); Marriage status: 20.7% never married, 68.2% now married, 4.4% widowed, 6.7% divorced (2000); Foreign born: 13.2% (2000); Ancestry (includes multiple ancestries): 23.4% Italian, 19.3% Irish, 15.7% Other groups, 15.2% German, 10.0% Polish (2000).
Economy: Manufacturing: machinery, fabricated metal products; nursery products. Unemployment rate: 2.3% (2005); Total civilian labor force: 14,188 (2005); Single-family building permits issued: 38 (2005); Multi-family building permits issued: 133 (2005); Employment by occupation: 21.2% management, 26.3% professional, 9.8% services, 28.2% sales, 0.0% farming, 6.2% construction, 8.2% production (2000).
Income: Per capita income: $40,788 (2005); Median household income: $94,606 (2005); Average household income: $114,865 (2005); Percent of households with income of $100,000 or more: 46.1% (2005); Poverty rate: 2.4% (2000).
Education: Percent of population age 25 and over with: High school diploma (including GED) or higher: 92.9% (2005); Bachelor's degree or higher: 41.9% (2005); Master's degree or higher: 12.7% (2005).

School District(s)
Educ Serv Comm Morris Co (PK-PK)
   2003-04 Enrollment: 272 . . . . (973) 540-8844
Morris County Vocational (09-12)
   2003-04 Enrollment: 182 . . . . (973) 627-4600
Morris Hills Regional (09-12)
   2003-04 Enrollment: 2,696 . . . . (973) 664-2291
Rockaway Borough (PK-08)
   2003-04 Enrollment: 608 . . . . (973) 625-8601
Rockaway Township (PK-08)
   2003-04 Enrollment: 2,985 . . . . (973) 627-8200
Housing: Homeownership rate: 83.4% (2005); Median home value: $332,854 (2005); Median rent: $876 per month (2000); Median age of housing: 35 years (2000).
Safety: Violent crime rate: 8.3 per 10,000 population; Property crime rate: 157.8 per 10,000 population (2004).
Newspapers: Parsippany Life (General - Circulation 20,000)
Transportation: Commute to work: 94.4% car, 2.0% public transportation, 0.8% walk, 2.5% work from home (2000); Travel time to work: 21.1% less than 15 minutes, 30.8% 15 to 30 minutes, 24.2% 30 to 45 minutes, 13.0% 45 to 60 minutes, 10.9% 60 minutes or more (2000)

ROXBURY (township). Covers a land area of 21.374 square miles and a water area of 0.531 square miles. Located at 40.87° N. Lat.; 74.65° W. Long.
History: Incorporated 1798.
Population: 20,858 (1990); 23,883 (2000); 24,645 (2005); 25,465 (2010 projected); Race: 91.8% White, 2.2% Black, 3.7% Asian, 6.0% Hispanic of

any race (2005); Density: 1,153.0 persons per square mile (2005); Average household size: 2.80 (2005); Median age: 39.0 (2005); Males per 100 females: 96.4 (2005); Marriage status: 22.8% never married, 64.7% now married, 6.2% widowed, 6.3% divorced (2000); Foreign born: 10.1% (2000); Ancestry (includes multiple ancestries): 27.8% Italian, 21.0% Irish, 19.2% German, 11.8% Other groups, 10.3% Polish (2000).
Economy: Single-family building permits issued: 52 (2005); Multi-family building permits issued: 48 (2005); Employment by occupation: 18.9% management, 24.1% professional, 10.4% services, 29.9% sales, 0.1% farming, 8.9% construction, 7.7% production (2000).
Income: Per capita income: $35,817 (2005); Median household income: $83,239 (2005); Average household income: $99,682 (2005); Percent of households with income of $100,000 or more: 38.2% (2005); Poverty rate: 2.7% (2000).
Taxes: Total city taxes per capita: $631 (2004); City property taxes per capita: $609 (2004).
Education: Percent of population age 25 and over with: High school diploma (including GED) or higher: 90.1% (2005); Bachelor's degree or higher: 34.2% (2005); Master's degree or higher: 10.1% (2005).
Housing: Homeownership rate: 84.1% (2005); Median home value: $322,276 (2005); Median rent: $704 per month (2000); Median age of housing: 29 years (2000).
Safety: Violent crime rate: 10.9 per 10,000 population; Property crime rate: 141.6 per 10,000 population (2004).
Transportation: Commute to work: 94.2% car, 1.3% public transportation, 1.2% walk, 2.8% work from home (2000); Travel time to work: 22.4% less than 15 minutes, 23.0% 15 to 30 minutes, 24.2% 30 to 45 minutes, 15.8% 45 to 60 minutes, 14.7% 60 minutes or more (2000)
Additional Information Contacts
Roxbury Chamber of Commerce . . . . (973) 770-07.4
   http://www.roxburychamber.org
Roxbury Township . . . . (973) 440-2000
   http://www.roxburynj.us

STIRLING (unincorporated postal area, zip code 07980).
Covers a land area of 2.193 square miles and a water area of 0.002 square miles. Located at 40.67° N. Lat.; 74.49° W. Long. Elevation is 240 feet.
Population: 2,499 (2000); Race: 93.9% White, 1.4% Black, 4.1% Asian, 6.3% Hispanic of any race (2000); Density: 1,139.5 persons per square mile (2000); Age: 23.1% under 18, 12.0% over 64 (2000); Marriage status: 24.4% never married, 65.2% now married, 5.9% widowed, 4.4% divorced (2000); Foreign born: 13.4% (2000); Ancestry (includes multiple ancestries): 31.3% Italian, 21.7% Irish, 18.6% German, 12.6% Other groups, 8.9% Polish (2000).
Economy: Manufacturing of metal products, clothing, clay products. Employment by occupation: 18.4% management, 20.5% professional, 19.9% services, 25.2% sales, 0.9% farming, 5.1% construction, 10.1% production (2000).
Income: Per capita income: $36,311 (2000); Median household income: $71,250 (2000); Poverty rate: 2.2% (2000).
Education: Percent of population age 25 and over with: High school diploma (including GED) or higher: 91.0% (2000); Bachelor's degree or higher: 38.7% (2000).
School District(s)
Long Hill Township (PK-08)
   2003-04 Enrollment: 1,159 . . . . (908) 647-1200
Housing: Homeownership rate: 72.4% (2000); Median home value: $272,700 (2000); Median rent: $950 per month (2000); Median age of housing: 37 years (2000).
Newspapers: Echoes-Sentinel (General - Circulation 7,000)
Transportation: Commute to work: 88.2% car, 4.4% public transportation, 4.5% walk, 2.9% work from home (2000); Travel time to work: 28.8% less than 15 minutes, 33.9% 15 to 30 minutes, 22.2% 30 to 45 minutes, 5.1% 45 to 60 minutes, 10.0% 60 minutes or more (2000)

SUCCASUNNA-KENVIL (CDP).
Covers a land area of 6.670 square miles and a water area of 0.115 square miles. Located at 40.86° N. Lat.; 74.64° W. Long.
Population: 11,785 (1990); 12,569 (2000); 12,758 (2005); 12,969 (2010 projected); Race: 92.6% White, 1.4% Black, 4.2% Asian, 4.9% Hispanic of any race (2005); Density: 1,912.7 persons per square mile (2005); Average household size: 2.98 (2005); Median age: 39.0 (2005); Males per 100 females: 98.4 (2005); Marriage status: 21.0% never married, 68.7% now married, 5.8% widowed, 4.5% divorced (2000); Foreign born: 9.9% (2000);

Ancestry (includes multiple ancestries): 28.4% Italian, 19.6% German, 19.5% Irish, 11.0% Other groups, 10.3% Polish (2000).
Economy: Employment by occupation: 18.8% management, 25.8% professional, 8.7% services, 30.7% sales, 0.1% farming, 8.6% construction, 7.2% production (2000).
Income: Per capita income: $38,681 (2005); Median household income: $95,479 (2005); Average household income: $114,172 (2005); Percent of households with income of $100,000 or more: 46.6% (2005); Poverty rate: 2.4% (2000).
Education: Percent of population age 25 and over with: High school diploma (including GED) or higher: 91.6% (2005); Bachelor's degree or higher: 39.1% (2005); Master's degree or higher: 10.8% (2005).
School District(s)
Roxbury Township (PK-12)
   2003-04 Enrollment: 4,817 . . . . (973) 584-6867
Two-year College(s)
Capri Institute (Private, For-profit)
   Fall 2004 Enrollment: 75 . . . . (800) 232-2774
Housing: Homeownership rate: 92.4% (2005); Median home value: $353,946 (2005); Median rent: $773 per month (2000); Median age of housing: 32 years (2000).
Transportation: Commute to work: 94.8% car, 0.9% public transportation, 1.2% walk, 2.9% work from home (2000); Travel time to work: 23.9% less than 15 minutes, 22.1% 15 to 30 minutes, 24.4% 30 to 45 minutes, 15.8% 45 to 60 minutes, 13.8% 60 minutes or more (2000)

TOWACO (unincorporated postal area, zip code 07082).
Covers a land area of 5.975 square miles and a water area of 0 square miles. Located at 40.92° N. Lat.; 74.34° W. Long. Elevation is 240 feet.
Population: 4,723 (2000); Race: 89.6% White, 0.1% Black, 8.8% Asian, 1.5% Hispanic of any race (2000); Density: 790.5 persons per square mile (2000); Age: 25.0% under 18, 11.4% over 64 (2000); Marriage status: 19.3% never married, 69.6% now married, 4.9% widowed, 6.2% divorced (2000); Foreign born: 11.3% (2000); Ancestry (includes multiple ancestries): 30.9% Italian, 16.4% Irish, 15.7% German, 12.0% Other groups, 10.4% Polish (2000).
Economy: Employment by occupation: 19.9% management, 28.4% professional, 7.0% services, 30.9% sales, 0.0% farming, 6.5% construction, 7.3% production (2000).
Income: Per capita income: $36,871 (2000); Median household income: $93,485 (2000); Poverty rate: 3.4% (2000).
Education: Percent of population age 25 and over with: High school diploma (including GED) or higher: 93.6% (2000); Bachelor's degree or higher: 45.3% (2000).
School District(s)
Montville Township (PK-12)
   2003-04 Enrollment: 4,030 . . . . (973) 331-7117
Housing: Homeownership rate: 94.5% (2000); Median home value: $296,200 (2000); Median rent: $960 per month (2000); Median age of housing: 31 years (2000).
Transportation: Commute to work: 89.8% car, 5.8% public transportation, 0.8% walk, 3.4% work from home (2000); Travel time to work: 19.5% less than 15 minutes, 37.4% 15 to 30 minutes, 22.2% 30 to 45 minutes, 9.0% 45 to 60 minutes, 11.9% 60 minutes or more (2000)

VICTORY GARDENS (borough).
Covers a land area of 0.146 square miles and a water area of 0 square miles. Located at 40.87° N. Lat.; 74.54° W. Long. Elevation is 660 feet.
Population: 1,314 (1990); 1,546 (2000); 1,528 (2005); 1,519 (2010 projected); Race: 47.5% White, 20.0% Black, 7.0% Asian, 56.3% Hispanic of any race (2005); Density: 10,459.4 persons per square mile (2005); Average household size: 2.74 (2005); Median age: 33.7 (2005); Males per 100 females: 92.7 (2005); Marriage status: 34.6% never married, 52.4% now married, 4.7% widowed, 8.3% divorced (2000); Foreign born: 36.7% (2000); Ancestry (includes multiple ancestries): 64.2% Other groups, 7.6% United States or American, 3.6% Irish, 2.8% Italian, 2.8% German (2000).
Economy: Single-family building permits issued: 0 (2005); Multi-family building permits issued: 0 (2005); Employment by occupation: 8.5% management, 5.0% professional, 24.1% services, 30.1% sales, 0.0% farming, 8.8% construction, 23.5% production (2000).
Income: Per capita income: $22,698 (2005); Median household income: $51,701 (2005); Average household income: $62,267 (2005); Percent of households with income of $100,000 or more: 9.3% (2005); Poverty rate: 8.4% (2000).

Education: Percent of population age 25 and over with: High school diploma (including GED) or higher: 69.9% (2005); Bachelor's degree or higher: 10.1% (2005); Master's degree or higher: 1.2% (2005).
Housing: Homeownership rate: 40.9% (2005); Median home value: $183,708 (2005); Median rent: $722 per month (2000); Median age of housing: 36 years (2000).
Transportation: Commute to work: 91.6% car, 3.2% public transportation, 3.5% walk, 0.9% work from home (2000); Travel time to work: 26.7% less than 15 minutes, 46.9% 15 to 30 minutes, 17.7% 30 to 45 minutes, 5.7% 45 to 60 minutes, 3.0% 60 minutes or more (2000)

WASHINGTON (township).
Covers a land area of 44.863 square miles and a water area of <.001 square miles. Located at 40.79° N. Lat.; 74.79° W. Long.
Population: 15,839 (1990); 17,592 (2000); 18,505 (2005); 19,423 (2010 projected); Race: 96.0% White, 0.8% Black, 2.0% Asian, 2.7% Hispanic of any race (2005); Density: 412.5 persons per square mile (2005); Average household size: 3.01 (2005); Median age: 39.1 (2005); Males per 100 females: 96.0 (2005); Marriage status: 20.7% never married, 69.8% now married, 4.8% widowed, 4.8% divorced (2000); Foreign born: 6.0% (2000); Ancestry (includes multiple ancestries): 25.5% Irish, 23.6% Italian, 22.0% German, 11.8% English, 8.2% Polish (2000).
Economy: Single-family building permits issued: 45 (2005); Multi-family building permits issued: 0 (2005); Employment by occupation: 26.8% management, 28.1% professional, 9.6% services, 24.7% sales, 0.2% farming, 5.9% construction, 4.6% production (2000).
Income: Per capita income: $44,286 (2005); Median household income: $112,612 (2005); Average household income: $131,557 (2005); Percent of households with income of $100,000 or more: 56.9% (2005); Poverty rate: 2.3% (2000).
Taxes: Total city taxes per capita: $563 (2004); City property taxes per capita: $548 (2004).
Education: Percent of population age 25 and over with: High school diploma (including GED) or higher: 96.2% (2005); Bachelor's degree or higher: 53.2% (2005); Master's degree or higher: 20.0% (2005).
Housing: Homeownership rate: 87.8% (2005); Median home value: $443,270 (2005); Median rent: $899 per month (2000); Median age of housing: 22 years (2000).
Safety: Violent crime rate: 7.6 per 10,000 population; Property crime rate: 70.8 per 10,000 population (2004).
Transportation: Commute to work: 89.8% car, 2.1% public transportation, 1.4% walk, 5.5% work from home (2000); Travel time to work: 18.8% less than 15 minutes, 19.5% 15 to 30 minutes, 23.8% 30 to 45 minutes, 17.4% 45 to 60 minutes, 20.5% 60 minutes or more (2000)
Additional Information Contacts
Washington Township . . . . (908) 876-3315
　http://www.washtwpmorris.org

WHARTON (borough).
Covers a land area of 2.185 square miles and a water area of 0.026 square miles. Located at 40.89° N. Lat.; 74.58° W. Long. Elevation is 660 feet.
History: Incorporated 1895.
Population: 5,405 (1990); 6,298 (2000); 6,206 (2005); 6,150 (2010 projected); Race: 78.4% White, 5.3% Black, 3.2% Asian, 29.0% Hispanic of any race (2005); Density: 2,840.3 persons per square mile (2005); Average household size: 2.74 (2005); Median age: 37.4 (2005); Males per 100 females: 94.8 (2005); Marriage status: 27.5% never married, 54.0% now married, 8.0% widowed, 10.5% divorced (2000); Foreign born: 13.8% (2000); Ancestry (includes multiple ancestries): 29.2% Other groups, 20.8% Irish, 19.9% German, 12.5% Italian, 10.2% English (2000).
Economy: Chemicals. Single-family building permits issued: 1 (2005); Multi-family building permits issued: 0 (2005); Employment by occupation: 18.9% management, 15.4% professional, 12.1% services, 31.5% sales, 0.3% farming, 8.5% construction, 13.4% production (2000).
Income: Per capita income: $27,095 (2005); Median household income: $62,592 (2005); Average household income: $73,903 (2005); Percent of households with income of $100,000 or more: 25.7% (2005); Poverty rate: 8.3% (2000).
Education: Percent of population age 25 and over with: High school diploma (including GED) or higher: 80.9% (2005); Bachelor's degree or higher: 22.9% (2005); Master's degree or higher: 8.0% (2005).
School District(s)
Jefferson Township (PK-12)
　2003-04 Enrollment: 3,694 . . . . (973) 663-5780

Rockaway Township (PK-08)
　2003-04 Enrollment: 2,985 . . . . (973) 627-8200
Wharton Borough (PK-08)
　2003-04 Enrollment: 857 . . . . (973) 361-2592
Housing: Homeownership rate: 62.4% (2005); Median home value: $268,076 (2005); Median rent: $761 per month (2000); Median age of housing: 44 years (2000).
Safety: Violent crime rate: 14.4 per 10,000 population; Property crime rate: 233.0 per 10,000 population (2004).
Transportation: Commute to work: 94.4% car, 3.0% public transportation, 0.9% walk, 1.1% work from home (2000); Travel time to work: 26.3% less than 15 minutes, 30.9% 15 to 30 minutes, 23.2% 30 to 45 minutes, 9.4% 45 to 60 minutes, 10.2% 60 minutes or more (2000)
Additional Information Contacts
Jefferson Township Chamber of Commerce . . . . (973) 663-2240
　http://www.jeffersontownshipchamber.org

WHITE MEADOW LAKE (CDP).
Covers a land area of 4.095 square miles and a water area of 0.520 square miles. Located at 40.91° N. Lat.; 74.51° W. Long.
Population: 8,475 (1990); 9,052 (2000); 9,163 (2005); 9,336 (2010 projected); Race: 90.2% White, 1.9% Black, 5.3% Asian, 5.7% Hispanic of any race (2005); Density: 2,237.7 persons per square mile (2005); Average household size: 2.96 (2005); Median age: 37.9 (2005); Males per 100 females: 97.4 (2005); Marriage status: 20.2% never married, 72.3% now married, 3.5% widowed, 4.0% divorced (2000); Foreign born: 9.6% (2000); Ancestry (includes multiple ancestries): 23.6% Italian, 21.7% Irish, 14.9% Other groups, 14.3% German, 12.6% Polish (2000).
Economy: Employment by occupation: 20.2% management, 30.5% professional, 9.3% services, 25.5% sales, 0.0% farming, 6.4% construction, 8.2% production (2000).
Income: Per capita income: $40,101 (2005); Median household income: $97,555 (2005); Average household income: $118,656 (2005); Percent of households with income of $100,000 or more: 48.1% (2005); Poverty rate: 2.3% (2000).
Education: Percent of population age 25 and over with: High school diploma (including GED) or higher: 95.6% (2005); Bachelor's degree or higher: 41.9% (2005); Master's degree or higher: 13.8% (2005).
Housing: Homeownership rate: 94.8% (2005); Median home value: $315,371 (2005); Median rent: $961 per month (2000); Median age of housing: 36 years (2000).
Transportation: Commute to work: 95.1% car, 1.3% public transportation, 0.7% walk, 2.4% work from home (2000); Travel time to work: 23.3% less than 15 minutes, 29.8% 15 to 30 minutes, 23.8% 30 to 45 minutes, 13.7% 45 to 60 minutes, 9.4% 60 minutes or more (2000)

Ocean County

Located in eastern New Jersey; bounded on the east by the Atlantic Ocean, with Island Beach Peninsula and Long Beach Island enclosing Barnegat Bay; drained by the Toms and Metedeconk Rivers. Covers a land area of 636.28 square miles, a water area of 279.60 square miles, and is located in the Eastern Time Zone. The county government was organized in 1850. County seat is Toms River.

Ocean County is part of the New York-Northern New Jersey-Long Island, NY-NJ-PA Metropolitan Statistical Area. The entire metro area includes: Edison, NJ Metropolitan Division (Middlesex County, NJ; Monmouth County, NJ; Ocean County, NJ; Somerset County, NJ); Nassau-Suffolk, NY Metropolitan Division (Nassau County, NY; Suffolk County, NY); New York-White Plains-Wayne, NY-NJ Metropolitan Division (Bergen County, NJ; Hudson County, NJ; Passaic County, NJ; Bronx County, NY; Kings County, NY; New York County, NY; Putnam County, NY; Queens County, NY; Richmond County, NY; Rockland County, NY; Westchester County, NY); Newark-Union, NJ-PA Metropolitan Division (Essex County, NJ; Hunterdon County, NJ; Morris County, NJ; Sussex County, NJ; Union County, NJ; Pike County, PA)

Weather Station: Toms River　　　　　　　　　Elevation: 98 feet

	Jan	Feb	Mar	Apr	May	Jun	Jul	Aug	Sep	Oct	Nov	Dec
High	42	44	52	62	72	81	86	85	78	67	57	47
Low	21	22	30	38	49	58	63	62	54	42	34	26
Precip	4.1	3.3	4.4	4.2	4.2	3.5	4.4	5.0	3.8	3.7	4.1	4.1
Snow	na	2.2	0.4	tr	0.0	0.0	0.0	0.0	0.0	0.0	tr	na

High and Low temperatures in degrees Fahrenheit; Precipitation and Snow in inches

Weather Station: Tuckerton   Elevation: 19 feet

	Jan	Feb	Mar	Apr	May	Jun	Jul	Aug	Sep	Oct	Nov	Dec
High	41	44	52	62	71	80	86	84	78	67	57	47
Low	23	24	32	40	50	60	66	65	58	45	37	28
Precip	3.9	3.2	4.5	4.1	3.6	3.1	4.1	4.8	3.2	3.3	3.8	3.7
Snow	6.1	6.7	2.0	0.4	tr	0.0	0.0	0.0	0.0	tr	0.4	2.3

High and Low temperatures in degrees Fahrenheit; Precipitation and Snow in inches

Population: 433,203 (1990); 510,916 (2000); 561,292 (2005); 614,076 (2010 projected); Race: 92.3% White, 3.2% Black, 1.4% Asian, 6.1% Hispanic of any race (2005); Density: 882.2 persons per square mile (2005); Average household size: 2.54 (2005); Median age: 41.0 (2005); Males per 100 females: 91.1 (2005).

Religion: Five largest groups: 41.6% Catholic Church, 2.3% Jewish Estimate, 1.9% The United Methodist Church, 1.3% Evangelical Lutheran Church in America, 1.3% Presbyterian Church (U.S.A.) (2000).

Economy: Unemployment rate: 4.5% (2005); Total civilian labor force: 250,176 (2005); Leading industries: 22.2% retail trade; 21.6% health care and social assistance; 9.3% accommodation & food services (2004); Farms: 217 totaling 12,239 acres (2002); Companies that employ 500 or more persons: 34 (2004); Companies that employ 100 to 499 persons: 372 (2004); Companies that employ less than 100 persons: 23,919 (2004); Black-owned businesses: n/a (2002); Hispanic-owned businesses: 963 (2002); Asian-owned businesses: 1,059 (2002); Women-owned businesses: 10,924 (2002); Retail sales per capita: $14,146 (2006). Single-family building permits issued: 2,743 (2005); Multi-family building permits issued: 161 (2005).

Income: Per capita income: $26,615 (2005); Median household income: $53,136 (2005); Average household income: $67,114 (2005); Percent of households with income of $100,000 or more: 19.1% (2005); Poverty rate: 8.1% (2003); Bankruptcy rate: 5.30% (2005).

Taxes: Total county taxes per capita: $405 (2004); County property taxes per capita: $404 (2004).

Education: Percent of population age 25 and over with: High school diploma (including GED) or higher: 83.0% (2005); Bachelor's degree or higher: 19.5% (2005); Master's degree or higher: 6.1% (2005).

Housing: Homeownership rate: 83.0% (2005); Median home value: $219,343 (2005); Median rent: $702 per month (2000); Median age of housing: 25 years (2000).

Health: Birth rate: 131.1 per 10,000 population (2004); Death rate: 125.9 per 10,000 population (2004); Age-adjusted cancer mortality rate: 207.1 deaths per 100,000 population (2002); Air Quality Index: 78.8% good, 16.2% moderate, 4.7% unhealthy for sensitive individuals, 0.4% unhealthy (percent of days in 2005); Number of physicians: 16.1 per 10,000 population (2004); Hospital beds: 23.6 per 10,000 population (2003); Hospital admissions: 1,199.3 per 10,000 population (2003).

Elections: 2004 Presidential election results: 60.2% Bush, 39.0% Kerry, 0.7% Nader, 0.1% Badnarik.

National and State Parks: Barnegat Lighthouse State Park; Barnegat Lighthouse State Park; Barnegat National Wildlife Refuge; Double Trouble State Park; Edwin B Forsythe National Wildlife Refuge; Island Beach State Park; Jackson State Forest; Lebanon State Forest; Sedge Islands State Wildlife Management Areas

Additional Information Contacts

Ocean County Government . . . . (732) 244-2121
  http://www.oceancountygov.com
Barnegat Township . . . . (609) 698-0080
  http://www.ci.barnegat.nj.us
Bay Head Chamber of Commerce . . . . (800) 422-9433
  http://www.BayHead.org
Berkeley Township Chamber of Commerce . . . . (908) 464-2700
  http://www.berkeleyheightstwp.com/links.cfm
Borough of Barnegat Light . . . . (609) 494-9196
  http://www.barnlight.com
Borough of Beach Haven . . . . (609) 492-4548
  http://www.longbeachisland.com/beach_haven.html
Borough of Beachwood . . . . (732) 286-6000
  http://www.beachwoodusa.com
Borough of Harvey Cedars . . . . (609) 361-6000
  http://www.harveycedars.org
Borough of Island Heights . . . . (732) 349-0220
  http://www.oceancountygov.com/history/default.htm
Borough of Lavallette . . . . (732) 793-7477
  http://lavalletteboro.com
Borough of Mantoloking . . . . (732) 899-6600
  http://www.mantoloking.org

Borough of Point Pleasant . . . . (732) 892-3434
  http://www.ptboro.com
Borough of Point Pleasant Beach . . . . (732) 892-1118
  http://www.pointpleasantbeach.org
Borough of Ship Bottom . . . . (609) 494-2171
  http://www.shipbottom.org
Brick Township . . . . (732) 262-1000
  http://www.branchburg.nj.us
Brick Township Chamber of Commerc . . . . (732) 477-4949
  http://www.brickchamber.com
Dover Township . . . . (732) 341-1000
  http://www.townshipofdover.com
Greater Lacey Township Chamber of Commerce . . . . (609) 693-8312
  http://www.greaterlacey.com
Greater Lacey Township Chamber of Commerce . . . . (609) 693-8312
  http://www.laceybusiness.com
Jackson Chamber of Commerce . . . . (732) 833-0005
  http://www.jacksonchamber.com
Lacey Township . . . . (609) 693-1100
  http://www.laceytownship.org
Lacey Township Chamber of Commerce . . . . (609) 693-8312
  http://www.laceybusiness.com
Lakewood Chamber of Commerce . . . . (732) 363-0012
  http://mylakewoodchamber.com
Lakewood Township . . . . (732) 364-2500
  http://www.twp.lakewood.nj.us
Little Egg Harbor Township . . . . (609) 296-7241
  http://www.leht.com
Long Beach Township . . . . (609) 361-1000
  http://longbeachtownship.com
Manchester Township . . . . (732) 657-8121
  http://manchestertownshipnj.org
Ocean County Chamber of Commerce . . . . (732) 349-0220
  http://www.oc-chamber.com
Ocean Township . . . . (609) 693-3302
  http://www.oceantwp.com
Plumsted Township . . . . (609) 758-2241
  http://www.plumsted.org
Point Pleasant Beach Chamber of Commerce . . . . (732) 899-2424
  http://www.pointpleasantbeachnj.com
Southern Ocean County Chamber of Commerce . . . . (609) 492-7211
  http://www.discoversouthernocean.org
Southern Ocean County Chamber of Commerce . . . . (609) 494-7211
  http://www.discoversouthernocean.org
Stafford Township . . . . (609) 597-1000
  http://twp.stafford.nj.us
Toms River-Ocean County Chamber of Commerce . . . . . . (732) 349-0220
  http://www.oc-chamber.com

Ocean County Communities

BARNEGAT (township). Covers a land area of 34.673 square miles and a water area of 6.157 square miles. Located at 39.76° N. Lat.; 74.26° W. Long. Elevation is 43 feet.

Population: 12,235 (1990); 15,270 (2000); 19,056 (2005); 22,680 (2010 projected); Race: 94.1% White, 2.5% Black, 1.0% Asian, 4.7% Hispanic of any race (2005); Density: 549.6 persons per square mile (2005); Average household size: 2.76 (2005); Median age: 38.7 (2005); Males per 100 females: 93.1 (2005); Marriage status: 21.6% never married, 63.8% now married, 7.9% widowed, 6.7% divorced (2000); Foreign born: 4.1% (2000); Ancestry (includes multiple ancestries): 27.8% Italian, 26.6% Irish, 22.3% German, 9.4% English, 8.5% Polish (2000).

Economy: Single-family building permits issued: 386 (2005); Multi-family building permits issued: 0 (2005); Employment by occupation: 9.3% management, 17.6% professional, 18.2% services, 29.6% sales, 0.0% farming, 12.0% construction, 13.3% production (2000).

Income: Per capita income: $22,848 (2005); Median household income: $55,758 (2005); Average household income: $62,780 (2005); Percent of households with income of $100,000 or more: 16.0% (2005); Poverty rate: 6.2% (2000).

Education: Percent of population age 25 and over with: High school diploma (including GED) or higher: 84.8% (2005); Bachelor's degree or higher: 16.0% (2005); Master's degree or higher: 4.4% (2005).

School District(s)

Barnegat Township (PK-08)

    2003-04 Enrollment: 2,376 . . . . (609) 698-5800

Housing: Homeownership rate: 90.2% (2005); Median home value: $102,903 (2005); Median rent: $741 per month (2000); Median age of housing: 19 years (2000).

Safety: Violent crime rate: 16.3 per 10,000 population; Property crime rate: 103.6 per 10,000 population (2004).

Transportation: Commute to work: 93.9% car, 1.8% public transportation, 1.4% walk, 2.5% work from home (2000); Travel time to work: 25.3% less than 15 minutes, 26.8% 15 to 30 minutes, 17.4% 30 to 45 minutes, 13.1% 45 to 60 minutes, 17.4% 60 minutes or more (2000)

Additional Information Contacts

Barnegat Township . . . . (609) 698-0080

    http://www.ci.barnegat.nj.us

BARNEGAT (CDP). Covers a land area of 2.678 square miles and a water area of 0.002 square miles. Located at 39.75° N. Lat.; 74.22° W. Long.

Population: 1,248 (1990); 1,690 (2000); 2,100 (2005); 2,495 (2010 projected); Race: 95.2% White, 0.3% Black, 1.6% Asian, 3.6% Hispanic of any race (2005); Density: 784.2 persons per square mile (2005); Average household size: 2.83 (2005); Median age: 36.1 (2005); Males per 100 females: 105.7 (2005); Marriage status: 28.2% never married, 57.0% now married, 6.2% widowed, 8.6% divorced (2000); Foreign born: 3.2% (2000); Ancestry (includes multiple ancestries): 26.6% German, 21.9% Irish, 18.6% English, 13.8% Italian, 8.9% United States or American (2000).

Economy: Employment by occupation: 2.8% management, 23.9% professional, 13.3% services, 24.4% sales, 0.0% farming, 18.5% construction, 17.3% production (2000).

Income: Per capita income: $25,851 (2005); Median household income: $63,081 (2005); Average household income: $73,259 (2005); Percent of households with income of $100,000 or more: 26.0% (2005); Poverty rate: 6.0% (2000).

Education: Percent of population age 25 and over with: High school diploma (including GED) or higher: 86.0% (2005); Bachelor's degree or higher: 18.8% (2005); Master's degree or higher: 6.6% (2005).

Housing: Homeownership rate: 84.9% (2005); Median home value: $252,035 (2005); Median rent: $647 per month (2000); Median age of housing: 40 years (2000).

Transportation: Commute to work: 85.9% car, 0.8% public transportation, 0.0% walk, 3.8% work from home (2000); Travel time to work: 33.5% less than 15 minutes, 20.3% 15 to 30 minutes, 17.1% 30 to 45 minutes, 9.5% 45 to 60 minutes, 19.6% 60 minutes or more (2000)

BARNEGAT LIGHT (borough). Covers a land area of 0.723 square miles and a water area of 0.135 square miles. Located at 39.75° N. Lat.; 74.11° W. Long. Elevation is 10 feet.

History: Site of abandoned Barnegat Lighthouse (1855), replaced (1930) by lightship, then replaced by a Texas Tower, which was destroyed by a storm; two tower attendants died in the storm. A floating light off the coast now serves as beacon. Formerly Barnegat City.

Population: 675 (1990); 764 (2000); 836 (2005); 904 (2010 projected); Race: 98.0% White, 0.7% Black, 0.4% Asian, 0.8% Hispanic of any race (2005); Density: 1,156.4 persons per square mile (2005); Average household size: 2.04 (2005); Median age: 54.7 (2005); Males per 100 females: 105.4 (2005); Marriage status: 14.8% never married, 61.7% now married, 14.5% widowed, 8.9% divorced (2000); Foreign born: 3.2% (2000); Ancestry (includes multiple ancestries): 28.0% Irish, 23.2% German, 17.4% English, 14.6% Italian, 8.7% Polish (2000).

Economy: Fishing. Single-family building permits issued: 22 (2005); Multi-family building permits issued: 0 (2005); Employment by occupation: 12.7% management, 28.1% professional, 13.0% services, 23.3% sales, 6.5% farming, 11.3% construction, 5.1% production (2000).

Income: Per capita income: $41,520 (2005); Median household income: $60,691 (2005); Average household income: $84,474 (2005); Percent of households with income of $100,000 or more: 26.2% (2005); Poverty rate: 4.7% (2000).

Education: Percent of population age 25 and over with: High school diploma (including GED) or higher: 92.1% (2005); Bachelor's degree or higher: 39.3% (2005); Master's degree or higher: 17.8% (2005).

Housing: Homeownership rate: 87.8% (2005); Median home value: $536,250 (2005); Median rent: $658 per month (2000); Median age of housing: 28 years (2000).

Safety: Violent crime rate: 24.8 per 10,000 population; Property crime rate: 297.8 per 10,000 population (2004).

Transportation: Commute to work: 80.4% car, 0.0% public transportation, 7.0% walk, 11.9% work from home (2000); Travel time to work: 48.8% less than 15 minutes, 11.1% 15 to 30 minutes, 7.1% 30 to 45 minutes, 7.5% 45 to 60 minutes, 25.4% 60 minutes or more (2000)

Additional Information Contacts

Borough of Barnegat Light . . . . (609) 494-9196

    http://www.barnlight.com

BAY HEAD (borough). Covers a land area of 0.591 square miles and a water area of 0.114 square miles. Located at 40.06° N. Lat.; 74.04° W. Long. Elevation is 9 feet.

History: Noted for beautiful turn-of-the-century architecture.

Population: 1,226 (1990); 1,238 (2000); 1,293 (2005); 1,361 (2010 projected); Race: 97.4% White, 0.2% Black, 0.8% Asian, 1.9% Hispanic of any race (2005); Density: 2,187.3 persons per square mile (2005); Average household size: 2.08 (2005); Median age: 51.1 (2005); Males per 100 females: 91.8 (2005); Marriage status: 20.5% never married, 60.8% now married, 8.3% widowed, 10.4% divorced (2000); Foreign born: 1.8% (2000); Ancestry (includes multiple ancestries): 34.6% Irish, 22.5% German, 21.8% English, 19.1% Italian, 7.8% Polish (2000).

Economy: Single-family building permits issued: 5 (2005); Multi-family building permits issued: 0 (2005); Employment by occupation: 23.3% management, 24.2% professional, 8.7% services, 28.0% sales, 0.0% farming, 12.2% construction, 3.7% production (2000).

Income: Per capita income: $60,901 (2005); Median household income: $92,135 (2005); Average household income: $126,600 (2005); Percent of households with income of $100,000 or more: 45.5% (2005); Poverty rate: 3.0% (2000).

Education: Percent of population age 25 and over with: High school diploma (including GED) or higher: 97.3% (2005); Bachelor's degree or higher: 52.7% (2005); Master's degree or higher: 19.9% (2005).

School District(s)

Bay Head Borough (PK-08)

    2003-04 Enrollment: 89 . . . . (732) 892-0668

Housing: Homeownership rate: 82.2% (2005); Median home value: $781,798 (2005); Median rent: $693 per month (2000); Median age of housing: 49 years (2000).

Safety: Violent crime rate: 0.0 per 10,000 population; Property crime rate: 457.8 per 10,000 population (2004).

Transportation: Commute to work: 80.6% car, 5.4% public transportation, 4.9% walk, 8.5% work from home (2000); Travel time to work: 32.3% less than 15 minutes, 24.7% 15 to 30 minutes, 14.5% 30 to 45 minutes, 8.4% 45 to 60 minutes, 20.1% 60 minutes or more (2000)

Additional Information Contacts

Bay Head Chamber of Commerce. . . . . (800) 422-9433

    http://www.BayHead.org

BAYVILLE (unincorporated postal area, zip code 08721). Covers a land area of 18.848 square miles and a water area of 0.125 square miles. Located at 39.90° N. Lat.; 74.16° W. Long. Elevation is 37 feet.

Population: 17,148 (2000); Race: 95.7% White, 1.5% Black, 0.8% Asian, 4.2% Hispanic of any race (2000); Density: 909.8 persons per square mile (2000); Age: 24.9% under 18, 14.4% over 64 (2000); Marriage status: 23.3% never married, 62.2% now married, 6.9% widowed, 7.6% divorced (2000); Foreign born: 4.8% (2000); Ancestry (includes multiple ancestries): 26.5% Irish, 25.9% Italian, 20.0% German, 9.4% Polish, 8.2% Other groups (2000).

Economy: Employment by occupation: 11.2% management, 17.0% professional, 13.7% services, 31.0% sales, 0.0% farming, 14.6% construction, 12.5% production (2000).

Income: Per capita income: $22,448 (2000); Median household income: $52,778 (2000); Poverty rate: 5.0% (2000).

Education: Percent of population age 25 and over with: High school diploma (including GED) or higher: 83.8% (2000); Bachelor's degree or higher: 14.6% (2000).

School District(s)

Berkeley Township (PK-06)

    2003-04 Enrollment: 1,983 . . . . (732) 269-2233

Central Regional (07-12)

    2003-04 Enrollment: 2,357 . . . . (732) 269-1100

Housing: Homeownership rate: 85.9% (2000); Median home value: $130,600 (2000); Median rent: $633 per month (2000); Median age of housing: 22 years (2000).

Newspapers: Urner Barry's Yellow Sheet (Circulation 1,500); Urner Barry's Price Current (Circulation 3,000)

Transportation: Commute to work: 93.4% car, 2.8% public transportation, 0.6% walk, 2.4% work from home (2000); Travel time to work: 20.6% less than 15 minutes, 32.3% 15 to 30 minutes, 20.3% 30 to 45 minutes, 9.6% 45 to 60 minutes, 17.2% 60 minutes or more (2000)
Additional Information Contacts
Toms River-Ocean County Chamber of Commerce . . . . . . (732) 349-0220
  http://www.oc-chamber.com

BEACH HAVEN (borough). Covers a land area of 0.982 square miles and a water area of 1.343 square miles. Located at 39.56° N. Lat.; 74.24° W. Long. Elevation is 10 feet.

Population: 1,475 (1990); 1,278 (2000); 1,296 (2005); 1,331 (2010 projected); Race: 98.7% White, 0.1% Black, 0.7% Asian, 6.6% Hispanic of any race (2005); Density: 1,320.2 persons per square mile (2005); Average household size: 2.15 (2005); Median age: 48.1 (2005); Males per 100 females: 87.6 (2005); Marriage status: 22.7% never married, 56.0% now married, 11.3% widowed, 10.0% divorced (2000); Foreign born: 4.2% (2000); Ancestry (includes multiple ancestries): 28.7% Irish, 24.9% German, 15.6% English, 14.7% Italian, 6.5% Other groups (2000).
Economy: Fishing. Single-family building permits issued: 39 (2005); Multi-family building permits issued: 0 (2005); Employment by occupation: 15.4% management, 24.7% professional, 15.3% services, 25.1% sales, 0.0% farming, 12.4% construction, 7.1% production (2000).
Income: Per capita income: $36,880 (2005); Median household income: $60,156 (2005); Average household income: $78,910 (2005); Percent of households with income of $100,000 or more: 26.2% (2005); Poverty rate: 3.7% (2000).
Education: Percent of population age 25 and over with: High school diploma (including GED) or higher: 90.5% (2005); Bachelor's degree or higher: 35.8% (2005); Master's degree or higher: 14.2% (2005).
School District(s)
Beach Haven Borough (PK-06)
  2003-04 Enrollment: 90 . . . . (609) 492-7411
Housing: Homeownership rate: 77.8% (2005); Median home value: $473,295 (2005); Median rent: $603 per month (2000); Median age of housing: 34 years (2000).
Safety: Violent crime rate: 15.2 per 10,000 population; Property crime rate: 849.1 per 10,000 population (2004).
Transportation: Commute to work: 82.7% car, 1.6% public transportation, 7.4% walk, 2.5% work from home (2000); Travel time to work: 48.0% less than 15 minutes, 17.8% 15 to 30 minutes, 8.6% 30 to 45 minutes, 6.0% 45 to 60 minutes, 19.6% 60 minutes or more (2000)
Additional Information Contacts
Borough of Beach Haven . . . . (609) 492-4548
  http://www.longbeachisland.com/beach_haven.html

BEACH HAVEN WEST (CDP). Covers a land area of 2.019 square miles and a water area of 0.146 square miles. Located at 39.66° N. Lat.; 74.23° W. Long. Elevation is 5 feet.

Population: 4,237 (1990); 4,444 (2000); 4,533 (2005); 4,722 (2010 projected); Race: 97.6% White, 0.4% Black, 0.7% Asian, 2.7% Hispanic of any race (2005); Density: 2,244.9 persons per square mile (2005); Average household size: 2.09 (2005); Median age: 53.1 (2005); Males per 100 females: 94.3 (2005); Marriage status: 18.0% never married, 65.4% now married, 9.9% widowed, 6.7% divorced (2000); Foreign born: 3.1% (2000); Ancestry (includes multiple ancestries): 27.5% Irish, 25.1% Italian, 24.4% German, 10.3% Polish, 9.4% English (2000).
Economy: Employment by occupation: 16.0% management, 16.1% professional, 14.3% services, 28.0% sales, 0.0% farming, 15.0% construction, 10.7% production (2000).
Income: Per capita income: $40,685 (2005); Median household income: $61,391 (2005); Average household income: $84,910 (2005); Percent of households with income of $100,000 or more: 25.0% (2005); Poverty rate: 3.8% (2000).
Education: Percent of population age 25 and over with: High school diploma (including GED) or higher: 81.9% (2005); Bachelor's degree or higher: 19.8% (2005); Master's degree or higher: 6.5% (2005).
Housing: Homeownership rate: 89.0% (2005); Median home value: $260,209 (2005); Median rent: $685 per month (2000); Median age of housing: 26 years (2000).
Transportation: Commute to work: 96.1% car, 1.0% public transportation, 0.4% walk, 2.5% work from home (2000); Travel time to work: 27.5% less than 15 minutes, 19.2% 15 to 30 minutes, 15.0% 30 to 45 minutes, 11.8% 45 to 60 minutes, 26.5% 60 minutes or more (2000)

BEACHWOOD (borough). Covers a land area of 2.761 square miles and a water area of 0 square miles. Located at 39.93° N. Lat.; 74.19° W. Long. Elevation is 40 feet.

Population: 9,324 (1990); 10,375 (2000); 10,873 (2005); 11,472 (2010 projected); Race: 94.8% White, 1.2% Black, 1.2% Asian, 5.5% Hispanic of any race (2005); Density: 3,937.6 persons per square mile (2005); Average household size: 2.95 (2005); Median age: 35.7 (2005); Males per 100 females: 97.4 (2005); Marriage status: 25.1% never married, 61.1% now married, 5.1% widowed, 8.7% divorced (2000); Foreign born: 3.8% (2000); Ancestry (includes multiple ancestries): 28.3% Italian, 25.5% Irish, 21.7% German, 9.7% Polish, 8.6% Other groups (2000).
Economy: Resort borough on Toms River. Single-family building permits issued: 15 (2005); Multi-family building permits issued: 0 (2005); Employment by occupation: 9.0% management, 16.7% professional, 18.5% services, 28.8% sales, 0.0% farming, 14.6% construction, 12.4% production (2000).
Income: Per capita income: $25,737 (2005); Median household income: $66,327 (2005); Average household income: $75,776 (2005); Percent of households with income of $100,000 or more: 22.0% (2005); Poverty rate: 4.5% (2000).
Education: Percent of population age 25 and over with: High school diploma (including GED) or higher: 87.4% (2005); Bachelor's degree or higher: 13.2% (2005); Master's degree or higher: 3.4% (2005).
School District(s)
Toms River Regional (PK-12)
  2003-04 Enrollment: 19,190 . . . . (732) 505-5510
Housing: Homeownership rate: 88.7% (2005); Median home value: $189,240 (2005); Median rent: $761 per month (2000); Median age of housing: 27 years (2000).
Safety: Violent crime rate: 10.2 per 10,000 population; Property crime rate: 153.9 per 10,000 population (2004).
Transportation: Commute to work: 95.1% car, 1.0% public transportation, 0.7% walk, 2.4% work from home (2000); Travel time to work: 26.8% less than 15 minutes, 33.8% 15 to 30 minutes, 17.1% 30 to 45 minutes, 6.6% 45 to 60 minutes, 15.7% 60 minutes or more (2000)
Additional Information Contacts
Borough of Beachwood . . . . (732) 286-6000
  http://www.beachwoodusa.com

BERKELEY (township). Covers a land area of 42.895 square miles and a water area of 12.901 square miles. Located at 39.94° N. Lat.; 74.19° W. Long.

Population: 37,321 (1990); 39,991 (2000); 42,830 (2005); 45,898 (2010 projected); Race: 96.6% White, 1.5% Black, 0.5% Asian, 3.0% Hispanic of any race (2005); Density: 998.5 persons per square mile (2005); Average household size: 2.01 (2005); Median age: 65.6 (2005); Males per 100 females: 81.1 (2005); Marriage status: 13.1% never married, 62.8% now married, 18.6% widowed, 5.6% divorced (2000); Foreign born: 6.7% (2000); Ancestry (includes multiple ancestries): 29.4% Italian, 21.4% Irish, 17.3% German, 9.2% Polish, 6.8% English (2000).
Economy: Unemployment rate: 5.5% (2005); Total civilian labor force: 12,529 (2005); Single-family building permits issued: 108 (2005); Multi-family building permits issued: 3 (2005); Employment by occupation: 10.7% management, 16.7% professional, 14.5% services, 33.2% sales, 0.0% farming, 12.8% construction, 12.1% production (2000).
Income: Per capita income: $25,328 (2005); Median household income: $38,021 (2005); Average household income: $50,500 (2005); Percent of households with income of $100,000 or more: 9.5% (2005); Poverty rate: 5.4% (2000).
Taxes: Total city taxes per capita: $376 (2004); City property taxes per capita: $353 (2004).
Education: Percent of population age 25 and over with: High school diploma (including GED) or higher: 73.0% (2005); Bachelor's degree or higher: 10.7% (2005); Master's degree or higher: 2.9% (2005).
Housing: Homeownership rate: 92.6% (2005); Median home value: $178,292 (2005); Median rent: $642 per month (2000); Median age of housing: 19 years (2000).
Safety: Violent crime rate: 7.8 per 10,000 population; Property crime rate: 159.8 per 10,000 population (2004).
Transportation: Commute to work: 93.7% car, 2.5% public transportation, 0.5% walk, 2.7% work from home (2000); Travel time to work: 20.2% less than 15 minutes, 33.3% 15 to 30 minutes, 19.8% 30 to 45 minutes, 8.6% 45 to 60 minutes, 18.1% 60 minutes or more (2000)
Additional Information Contacts

Berkeley Township Chamber of Commerce . . . . (908) 464-2700
http://www.berkeleyheightstwp.com/links.cfm

BRICK (township).
Covers a land area of 26.234 square miles and a water area of 6.026 square miles. Located at 40.06° N. Lat.; 74.11° W. Long.

History: Incorporated 1850.

Population: 66,423 (1990); 76,119 (2000); 79,396 (2005); 83,464 (2010 projected); Race: 95.2% White, 1.2% Black, 1.3% Asian, 4.7% Hispanic of any race (2005); Density: 3,026.4 persons per square mile (2005); Average household size: 2.55 (2005); Median age: 39.6 (2005); Males per 100 females: 91.4 (2005); Marriage status: 22.2% never married, 59.9% now married, 9.2% widowed, 8.7% divorced (2000); Foreign born: 5.7% (2000); Ancestry (includes multiple ancestries): 30.4% Italian, 28.9% Irish, 20.8% German, 9.2% Polish, 8.5% English (2000).

Economy: Residential and resort area with some light industry, commercial development. Unemployment rate: 4.2% (2005); Total civilian labor force: 40,405 (2005); Single-family building permits issued: 129 (2005); Multi-family building permits issued: 13 (2005); Employment by occupation: 12.4% management, 18.7% professional, 15.0% services, 31.0% sales, 0.2% farming, 11.6% construction, 11.2% production (2000).

Income: Per capita income: $28,415 (2005); Median household income: $59,752 (2005); Average household income: $72,133 (2005); Percent of households with income of $100,000 or more: 20.8% (2005); Poverty rate: 4.5% (2000).

Taxes: Total city taxes per capita: $546 (2004); City property taxes per capita: $524 (2004).

Education: Percent of population age 25 and over with: High school diploma (including GED) or higher: 86.6% (2005); Bachelor's degree or higher: 19.3% (2005); Master's degree or higher: 5.5% (2005).

School District(s)
Brick Township (PK-12)
    2003-04 Enrollment: 12,065 . . . . (732) 785-3002
Ocean County Vocational (09-12)
    2003-04 Enrollment: 196 . . . . (732) 240-6414
Two-year College(s)
Capri Institute of Hair Design (Private, For-profit)
    Fall 2004 Enrollment: 160 . . . . (800) 232-2774

Housing: Homeownership rate: 82.9% (2005); Median home value: $233,056 (2005); Median rent: $704 per month (2000); Median age of housing: 26 years (2000).

Hospitals: Medical Center of Ocean County (237 beds)

Safety: Violent crime rate: 12.5 per 10,000 population; Property crime rate: 168.0 per 10,000 population (2004).

Newspapers: Brick Township Town News & Sampler (General - Circulation 5,000)

Transportation: Commute to work: 94.9% car, 2.0% public transportation, 0.8% walk, 1.8% work from home (2000); Travel time to work: 22.3% less than 15 minutes, 32.6% 15 to 30 minutes, 17.1% 30 to 45 minutes, 9.3% 45 to 60 minutes, 18.6% 60 minutes or more (2000)

Additional Information Contacts
Brick Township. . . . . (732) 262-1000
    http://www.branchburg.nj.us
Brick Township Chamber of Commerc . . . . (732) 477-4949
    http://www.brickchamber.com

CEDAR GLEN LAKES (CDP).
Covers a land area of 0.670 square miles and a water area of 0 square miles. Located at 39.95° N. Lat.; 74.39° W. Long.

Population: 1,620 (1990); 1,617 (2000); 1,718 (2005); 1,853 (2010 projected); Race: 98.0% White, 0.9% Black, 0.6% Asian, 1.8% Hispanic of any race (2005); Density: 2,564.2 persons per square mile (2005); Average household size: 1.40 (2005); Median age: 76.4 (2005); Males per 100 females: 58.2 (2005); Marriage status: 8.3% never married, 52.0% now married, 31.2% widowed, 8.5% divorced (2000); Foreign born: 16.4% (2000); Ancestry (includes multiple ancestries): 23.7% Irish, 19.0% German, 17.7% Italian, 11.1% English, 5.7% Polish (2000).

Economy: Employment by occupation: 34.7% management, 8.9% professional, 11.9% services, 17.8% sales, 0.0% farming, 0.0% construction, 26.7% production (2000).

Income: Per capita income: $24,530 (2005); Median household income: $24,017 (2005); Average household income: $34,346 (2005); Percent of households with income of $100,000 or more: 3.6% (2005); Poverty rate: 3.7% (2000).

Education: Percent of population age 25 and over with: High school diploma (including GED) or higher: 60.4% (2005); Bachelor's degree or higher: 8.4% (2005); Master's degree or higher: 3.3% (2005).

Housing: Homeownership rate: 98.1% (2005); Median home value: $75,410 (2005); Median rent: $289 per month (2000); Median age of housing: 25 years (2000).

Transportation: Commute to work: 92.1% car, 7.9% public transportation, 0.0% walk, 0.0% work from home (2000); Travel time to work: 8.9% less than 15 minutes, 44.6% 15 to 30 minutes, 17.8% 30 to 45 minutes, 20.8% 45 to 60 minutes, 7.9% 60 minutes or more (2000)

CEDAR GLEN WEST (CDP).
Covers a land area of 1.087 square miles and a water area of 0 square miles. Located at 40.04° N. Lat.; 74.29° W. Long. Elevation is 90 feet.

Population: 1,396 (1990); 1,376 (2000); 1,355 (2005); 1,399 (2010 projected); Race: 97.0% White, 1.9% Black, 0.1% Asian, 1.2% Hispanic of any race (2005); Density: 1,246.5 persons per square mile (2005); Average household size: 1.43 (2005); Median age: 74.0 (2005); Males per 100 females: 56.3 (2005); Marriage status: 8.9% never married, 36.3% now married, 41.2% widowed, 13.6% divorced (2000); Foreign born: 10.9% (2000); Ancestry (includes multiple ancestries): 21.2% German, 20.4% Irish, 18.9% Italian, 12.4% English, 8.1% Other groups (2000).

Economy: Employment by occupation: 14.4% management, 25.2% professional, 11.7% services, 26.8% sales, 0.0% farming, 2.7% construction, 19.1% production (2000).

Income: Per capita income: $24,696 (2005); Median household income: $25,257 (2005); Average household income: $35,410 (2005); Percent of households with income of $100,000 or more: 3.9% (2005); Poverty rate: 8.1% (2000).

Education: Percent of population age 25 and over with: High school diploma (including GED) or higher: 67.4% (2005); Bachelor's degree or higher: 7.3% (2005); Master's degree or higher: 2.3% (2005).

Housing: Homeownership rate: 95.4% (2005); Median home value: $52,520 (2005); Median rent: $406 per month (2000); Median age of housing: 34 years (2000).

Transportation: Commute to work: 100.0% car, 0.0% public transportation, 0.0% walk, 0.0% work from home (2000); Travel time to work: 24.5% less than 15 minutes, 36.9% 15 to 30 minutes, 19.0% 30 to 45 minutes, 5.5% 45 to 60 minutes, 14.1% 60 minutes or more (2000)

CRESTWOOD VILLAGE (CDP).
Covers a land area of 4.393 square miles and a water area of 0.026 square miles. Located at 39.95° N. Lat.; 74.35° W. Long. Elevation is 133 feet.

Population: 8,179 (1990); 8,392 (2000); 9,307 (2005); 10,306 (2010 projected); Race: 98.0% White, 1.0% Black, 0.3% Asian, 1.5% Hispanic of any race (2005); Density: 2,118.4 persons per square mile (2005); Average household size: 1.45 (2005); Median age: 76.9 (2005); Males per 100 females: 57.3 (2005); Marriage status: 7.2% never married, 53.8% now married, 31.1% widowed, 8.0% divorced (2000); Foreign born: 12.0% (2000); Ancestry (includes multiple ancestries): 22.2% German, 19.0% Irish, 16.3% Italian, 13.6% English, 6.3% Polish (2000).

Economy: Employment by occupation: 5.1% management, 14.9% professional, 17.6% services, 37.7% sales, 0.0% farming, 7.1% construction, 17.6% production (2000).

Income: Per capita income: $25,211 (2005); Median household income: $26,538 (2005); Average household income: $36,337 (2005); Percent of households with income of $100,000 or more: 3.5% (2005); Poverty rate: 7.1% (2000).

Education: Percent of population age 25 and over with: High school diploma (including GED) or higher: 66.1% (2005); Bachelor's degree or higher: 9.7% (2005); Master's degree or higher: 3.2% (2005).

Housing: Homeownership rate: 96.0% (2005); Median home value: $77,205 (2005); Median rent: $663 per month (2000); Median age of housing: 24 years (2000).

Transportation: Commute to work: 93.7% car, 0.0% public transportation, 2.7% walk, 2.7% work from home (2000); Travel time to work: 27.8% less than 15 minutes, 25.7% 15 to 30 minutes, 12.9% 30 to 45 minutes, 14.8% 45 to 60 minutes, 18.8% 60 minutes or more (2000)

DOVER (township).
Covers a land area of 40.971 square miles and a water area of 11.964 square miles. Located at 39.97° N. Lat.; 74.14° W. Long.

Population: 76,417 (1990); 89,706 (2000); 95,235 (2005); 101,452 (2010 projected); Race: 92.3% White, 2.2% Black, 2.8% Asian, 5.8% Hispanic of any race (2005); Density: 2,324.5 persons per square mile (2005); Average

household size: 2.64 (2005); Median age: 40.2 (2005); Males per 100 females: 93.2 (2005); Marriage status: 24.0% never married, 59.4% now married, 8.6% widowed, 8.0% divorced (2000); Foreign born: 7.0% (2000); Ancestry (includes multiple ancestries): 31.5% Italian, 24.2% Irish, 18.8% German, 10.4% Other groups, 9.0% Polish (2000).
Economy: Unemployment rate: 4.8% (2005); Total civilian labor force: 47,515 (2005); Single-family building permits issued: 252 (2005); Multi-family building permits issued: 0 (2005); Employment by occupation: 13.0% management, 21.3% professional, 15.6% services, 30.6% sales, 0.1% farming, 10.1% construction, 9.2% production (2000).
Income: Per capita income: $28,443 (2005); Median household income: $60,259 (2005); Average household income: $74,584 (2005); Percent of households with income of $100,000 or more: 22.9% (2005); Poverty rate: 5.7% (2000).
Taxes: Total city taxes per capita: $432 (2004); City property taxes per capita: $416 (2004).
Education: Percent of population age 25 and over with: High school diploma (including GED) or higher: 86.3% (2005); Bachelor's degree or higher: 23.7% (2005); Master's degree or higher: 8.0% (2005).
Housing: Homeownership rate: 83.6% (2005); Median home value: $251,697 (2005); Median rent: $685 per month (2000); Median age of housing: 28 years (2000).
Safety: Violent crime rate: 12.9 per 10,000 population; Property crime rate: 199.9 per 10,000 population (2004).
Transportation: Commute to work: 93.9% car, 1.8% public transportation, 0.9% walk, 2.7% work from home (2000); Travel time to work: 30.0% less than 15 minutes, 30.6% 15 to 30 minutes, 14.2% 30 to 45 minutes, 7.5% 45 to 60 minutes, 17.8% 60 minutes or more (2000)
Additional Information Contacts
Dover Township . . . . (732) 341-1000
http://www.townshipofdover.com

DOVER BEACHES NORTH (CDP). Covers a land area of 0.980 square miles and a water area of 0.621 square miles. Located at 39.99° N. Lat.; 74.06° W. Long.
Population: 1,685 (1990); 1,785 (2000); 1,847 (2005); 1,930 (2010 projected); Race: 98.6% White, 0.2% Black, 0.6% Asian, 1.7% Hispanic of any race (2005); Density: 1,885.1 persons per square mile (2005); Average household size: 1.80 (2005); Median age: 58.4 (2005); Males per 100 females: 90.0 (2005); Marriage status: 15.4% never married, 63.0% now married, 16.3% widowed, 5.2% divorced (2000); Foreign born: 3.1% (2000); Ancestry (includes multiple ancestries): 28.5% Irish, 22.7% German, 19.8% Italian, 11.9% Polish, 8.9% English (2000).
Economy: Employment by occupation: 13.9% management, 26.1% professional, 17.5% services, 32.2% sales, 0.0% farming, 5.0% construction, 5.4% production (2000).
Income: Per capita income: $42,028 (2005); Median household income: $55,000 (2005); Average household income: $75,511 (2005); Percent of households with income of $100,000 or more: 21.5% (2005); Poverty rate: 5.4% (2000).
Education: Percent of population age 25 and over with: High school diploma (including GED) or higher: 87.8% (2005); Bachelor's degree or higher: 29.6% (2005); Master's degree or higher: 10.8% (2005).
Housing: Homeownership rate: 91.7% (2005); Median home value: $342,576 (2005); Median rent: $709 per month (2000); Median age of housing: 41 years (2000).
Transportation: Commute to work: 87.8% car, 6.9% public transportation, 0.0% walk, 5.4% work from home (2000); Travel time to work: 17.0% less than 15 minutes, 20.9% 15 to 30 minutes, 11.5% 30 to 45 minutes, 15.3% 45 to 60 minutes, 35.2% 60 minutes or more (2000)

DOVER BEACHES SOUTH (CDP). Covers a land area of 0.621 square miles and a water area of 0.446 square miles. Located at 39.95° N. Lat.; 74.07° W. Long.
Population: 1,546 (1990); 1,594 (2000); 1,677 (2005); 1,777 (2010 projected); Race: 98.7% White, 0.1% Black, 0.3% Asian, 2.3% Hispanic of any race (2005); Density: 2,702.3 persons per square mile (2005); Average household size: 1.81 (2005); Median age: 50.0 (2005); Males per 100 females: 95.2 (2005); Marriage status: 23.5% never married, 50.8% now married, 16.8% widowed, 8.9% divorced (2000); Foreign born: 4.7% (2000); Ancestry (includes multiple ancestries): 41.3% Italian, 28.9% Irish, 14.5% German, 12.1% Polish, 10.4% English (2000).
Economy: Employment by occupation: 12.7% management, 16.1% professional, 17.0% services, 33.9% sales, 0.0% farming, 17.2% construction, 3.0% production (2000).

Income: Per capita income: $31,582 (2005); Median household income: $44,844 (2005); Average household income: $57,195 (2005); Percent of households with income of $100,000 or more: 15.4% (2005); Poverty rate: 10.0% (2000).
Education: Percent of population age 25 and over with: High school diploma (including GED) or higher: 82.3% (2005); Bachelor's degree or higher: 21.1% (2005); Master's degree or higher: 5.8% (2005).
Housing: Homeownership rate: 73.3% (2005); Median home value: $271,277 (2005); Median rent: $636 per month (2000); Median age of housing: 40 years (2000).
Transportation: Commute to work: 91.8% car, 1.1% public transportation, 1.8% walk, 2.4% work from home (2000); Travel time to work: 28.5% less than 15 minutes, 20.3% 15 to 30 minutes, 18.2% 30 to 45 minutes, 17.4% 45 to 60 minutes, 15.6% 60 minutes or more (2000)

EAGLESWOOD (township). Covers a land area of 16.369 square miles and a water area of 2.486 square miles. Located at 39.65° N. Lat.; 74.30° W. Long.
Population: 1,476 (1990); 1,441 (2000); 1,583 (2005); 1,731 (2010 projected); Race: 99.1% White, 0.0% Black, 0.2% Asian, 1.4% Hispanic of any race (2005); Density: 96.7 persons per square mile (2005); Average household size: 2.59 (2005); Median age: 39.4 (2005); Males per 100 females: 101.9 (2005); Marriage status: 20.2% never married, 64.0% now married, 7.9% widowed, 7.9% divorced (2000); Foreign born: 1.9% (2000); Ancestry (includes multiple ancestries): 27.3% Irish, 21.6% German, 17.0% English, 13.9% Italian, 9.2% United States or American (2000).
Economy: Single-family building permits issued: 27 (2005); Multi-family building permits issued: 0 (2005); Employment by occupation: 8.1% management, 10.9% professional, 15.2% services, 27.0% sales, 0.6% farming, 26.5% construction, 11.7% production (2000).
Income: Per capita income: $22,798 (2005); Median household income: $46,636 (2005); Average household income: $58,971 (2005); Percent of households with income of $100,000 or more: 15.8% (2005); Poverty rate: 3.5% (2000).
Education: Percent of population age 25 and over with: High school diploma (including GED) or higher: 75.9% (2005); Bachelor's degree or higher: 10.2% (2005); Master's degree or higher: 2.5% (2005).
Housing: Homeownership rate: 87.4% (2005); Median home value: $197,481 (2005); Median rent: $553 per month (2000); Median age of housing: 34 years (2000).
Transportation: Commute to work: 92.8% car, 0.7% public transportation, 1.5% walk, 4.0% work from home (2000); Travel time to work: 29.0% less than 15 minutes, 26.7% 15 to 30 minutes, 22.7% 30 to 45 minutes, 8.0% 45 to 60 minutes, 13.5% 60 minutes or more (2000)

FORKED RIVER (CDP). Covers a land area of 2.890 square miles and a water area of 7.425 square miles. Located at 39.82° N. Lat.; 74.18° W. Long. Elevation is 13 feet.
Population: 4,265 (1990); 4,914 (2000); 5,167 (2005); 5,464 (2010 projected); Race: 97.0% White, 0.7% Black, 0.4% Asian, 4.3% Hispanic of any race (2005); Density: 1,787.8 persons per square mile (2005); Average household size: 2.56 (2005); Median age: 38.5 (2005); Males per 100 females: 97.8 (2005); Marriage status: 20.5% never married, 65.9% now married, 5.8% widowed, 7.7% divorced (2000); Foreign born: 1.4% (2000); Ancestry (includes multiple ancestries): 32.2% Italian, 22.6% Irish, 19.9% German, 10.6% Polish, 9.1% English (2000).
Economy: Fishing. State marina. Employment by occupation: 12.8% management, 12.6% professional, 20.0% services, 30.4% sales, 0.0% farming, 12.9% construction, 11.3% production (2000).
Income: Per capita income: $29,213 (2005); Median household income: $66,604 (2005); Average household income: $74,159 (2005); Percent of households with income of $100,000 or more: 26.4% (2005); Poverty rate: 7.6% (2000).
Education: Percent of population age 25 and over with: High school diploma (including GED) or higher: 83.7% (2005); Bachelor's degree or higher: 17.7% (2005); Master's degree or higher: 3.0% (2005).
School District(s)
Lacey Township (PK-12)
    2003-04 Enrollment: 5,323 . . . . (609) 971-2002
Housing: Homeownership rate: 86.2% (2005); Median home value: $222,628 (2005); Median rent: $731 per month (2000); Median age of housing: 25 years (2000).
Transportation: Commute to work: 96.0% car, 1.6% public transportation, 0.8% walk, 1.0% work from home (2000); Travel time to work: 19.5% less

than 15 minutes, 28.9% 15 to 30 minutes, 21.3% 30 to 45 minutes, 6.9% 45 to 60 minutes, 23.4% 60 minutes or more (2000)

Additional Information Contacts
Greater Lacey Township Chamber of Commerce . . . . (609) 693-8312
http://www.greaterlacey.com

HARVEY CEDARS (borough). Covers a land area of 0.546 square miles and a water area of 0.647 square miles. Located at 39.70° N. Lat.; 74.13° W. Long. Elevation is 9 feet.

Population: 357 (1990); 359 (2000); 368 (2005); 382 (2010 projected); Race: 95.7% White, 0.8% Black, 0.3% Asian, 5.7% Hispanic of any race (2005); Density: 673.6 persons per square mile (2005); Average household size: 2.14 (2005); Median age: 53.6 (2005); Males per 100 females: 103.3 (2005); Marriage status: 15.4% never married, 72.0% now married, 7.2% widowed, 5.3% divorced (2000); Foreign born: 4.0% (2000); Ancestry (includes multiple ancestries): 24.4% English, 24.1% German, 21.2% Irish, 13.3% Polish, 9.9% Italian (2000).
Economy: Artists' summer colony here. Single-family building permits issued: 17 (2005); Multi-family building permits issued: 0 (2005); Employment by occupation: 23.9% management, 17.9% professional, 14.9% services, 26.9% sales, 0.0% farming, 13.4% construction, 3.0% production (2000).
Income: Per capita income: $41,997 (2005); Median household income: $78,448 (2005); Average household income: $89,855 (2005); Percent of households with income of $100,000 or more: 35.5% (2005); Poverty rate: 5.1% (2000).
Education: Percent of population age 25 and over with: High school diploma (including GED) or higher: 95.2% (2005); Bachelor's degree or higher: 47.4% (2005); Master's degree or higher: 14.4% (2005).
Housing: Homeownership rate: 80.2% (2005); Median home value: $763,514 (2005); Median rent: $739 per month (2000); Median age of housing: 25 years (2000).
Safety: Violent crime rate: 0.0 per 10,000 population; Property crime rate: 425.5 per 10,000 population (2004).
Transportation: Commute to work: 75.4% car, 0.0% public transportation, 16.2% walk, 8.5% work from home (2000); Travel time to work: 59.7% less than 15 minutes, 17.6% 15 to 30 minutes, 11.8% 30 to 45 minutes, 1.7% 45 to 60 minutes, 9.2% 60 minutes or more (2000)

Additional Information Contacts
Borough of Harvey Cedars . . . . (609) 361-6000
http://www.harveycedars.org

HOLIDAY CITY SOUTH (CDP). Covers a land area of 1.876 square miles and a water area of 0.008 square miles. Located at 39.95° N. Lat.; 74.23° W. Long.

Population: 5,452 (1990); 4,047 (2000); 3,937 (2005); 3,852 (2010 projected); Race: 94.2% White, 5.1% Black, 0.2% Asian, 1.1% Hispanic of any race (2005); Density: 2,099.0 persons per square mile (2005); Average household size: 1.66 (2005); Median age: 75.1 (2005); Males per 100 females: 74.0 (2005); Marriage status: 6.6% never married, 65.3% now married, 24.3% widowed, 3.9% divorced (2000); Foreign born: 7.8% (2000); Ancestry (includes multiple ancestries): 40.3% Italian, 13.8% Irish, 12.0% German, 9.5% Polish, 6.5% Other groups (2000).
Economy: Employment by occupation: 7.5% management, 9.8% professional, 19.9% services, 50.4% sales, 0.0% farming, 0.0% construction, 12.4% production (2000).
Income: Per capita income: $20,912 (2005); Median household income: $28,297 (2005); Average household income: $34,738 (2005); Percent of households with income of $100,000 or more: 1.9% (2005); Poverty rate: 6.5% (2000).
Education: Percent of population age 25 and over with: High school diploma (including GED) or higher: 63.8% (2005); Bachelor's degree or higher: 7.2% (2005); Master's degree or higher: 2.0% (2005).
Housing: Homeownership rate: 97.4% (2005); Median home value: $175,065 (2005); Median rent: $397 per month (2000); Median age of housing: 15 years (2000).
Transportation: Commute to work: 95.8% car, 1.7% public transportation, 0.0% walk, 2.5% work from home (2000); Travel time to work: 22.0% less than 15 minutes, 39.9% 15 to 30 minutes, 5.3% 30 to 45 minutes, 9.2% 45 to 60 minutes, 23.7% 60 minutes or more (2000)

HOLIDAY CITY-BERKELEY (CDP). Covers a land area of 5.759 square miles and a water area of 0 square miles. Located at 39.96° N. Lat.; 74.26° W. Long.

Population: 14,293 (1990); 13,884 (2000); 13,842 (2005); 13,982 (2010 projected); Race: 98.8% White, 0.5% Black, 0.3% Asian, 1.3% Hispanic of any race (2005); Density: 2,403.6 persons per square mile (2005); Average household size: 1.59 (2005); Median age: 77.0 (2005); Males per 100 females: 66.0 (2005); Marriage status: 6.3% never married, 61.2% now married, 28.5% widowed, 4.1% divorced (2000); Foreign born: 8.6% (2000); Ancestry (includes multiple ancestries): 30.2% Italian, 17.9% Irish, 15.6% German, 9.0% Polish, 7.2% English (2000).
Economy: Employment by occupation: 10.3% management, 12.2% professional, 16.0% services, 44.7% sales, 0.0% farming, 3.7% construction, 13.0% production (2000).
Income: Per capita income: $25,187 (2005); Median household income: $31,740 (2005); Average household income: $39,735 (2005); Percent of households with income of $100,000 or more: 3.4% (2005); Poverty rate: 6.0% (2000).
Education: Percent of population age 25 and over with: High school diploma (including GED) or higher: 63.4% (2005); Bachelor's degree or higher: 7.0% (2005); Master's degree or higher: 2.3% (2005).
Housing: Homeownership rate: 96.6% (2005); Median home value: $145,275 (2005); Median rent: $715 per month (2000); Median age of housing: 20 years (2000).
Transportation: Commute to work: 93.3% car, 1.4% public transportation, 0.6% walk, 4.0% work from home (2000); Travel time to work: 21.6% less than 15 minutes, 31.6% 15 to 30 minutes, 22.0% 30 to 45 minutes, 4.4% 45 to 60 minutes, 20.4% 60 minutes or more (2000)

HOLIDAY HEIGHTS (CDP). Covers a land area of 4.999 square miles and a water area of 0 square miles. Located at 39.94° N. Lat.; 74.24° W. Long.

Population: 737 (1990); 2,389 (2000); 2,704 (2005); 3,033 (2010 projected); Race: 99.3% White, 0.3% Black, 0.2% Asian, 1.6% Hispanic of any race (2005); Density: 540.9 persons per square mile (2005); Average household size: 1.71 (2005); Median age: 72.9 (2005); Males per 100 females: 78.0 (2005); Marriage status: 4.2% never married, 79.3% now married, 14.2% widowed, 2.4% divorced (2000); Foreign born: 8.3% (2000); Ancestry (includes multiple ancestries): 43.1% Italian, 14.2% Irish, 11.6% German, 7.4% Polish, 4.4% Other groups (2000).
Economy: Employment by occupation: 0.0% management, 16.7% professional, 21.4% services, 38.1% sales, 0.0% farming, 7.1% construction, 16.7% production (2000).
Income: Per capita income: $22,469 (2005); Median household income: $32,880 (2005); Average household income: $38,404 (2005); Percent of households with income of $100,000 or more: 2.2% (2005); Poverty rate: 2.0% (2000).
Education: Percent of population age 25 and over with: High school diploma (including GED) or higher: 74.2% (2005); Bachelor's degree or higher: 8.8% (2005); Master's degree or higher: 2.6% (2005).
Housing: Homeownership rate: 99.2% (2005); Median home value: $234,019 (2005); Median rent: $725 per month (2000); Median age of housing: 8 years (2000).
Transportation: Commute to work: 100.0% car, 0.0% public transportation, 0.0% walk, 0.0% work from home (2000); Travel time to work: 14.9% less than 15 minutes, 47.0% 15 to 30 minutes, 11.9% 30 to 45 minutes, 0.0% 45 to 60 minutes, 26.2% 60 minutes or more (2000)

ISLAND HEIGHTS (borough). Covers a land area of 0.602 square miles and a water area of 0.272 square miles. Located at 39.94° N. Lat.; 74.14° W. Long. Elevation is 30 feet.

Population: 1,422 (1990); 1,751 (2000); 1,877 (2005); 2,016 (2010 projected); Race: 97.3% White, 0.1% Black, 0.8% Asian, 1.7% Hispanic of any race (2005); Density: 3,118.6 persons per square mile (2005); Average household size: 2.44 (2005); Median age: 42.5 (2005); Males per 100 females: 93.1 (2005); Marriage status: 26.1% never married, 58.7% now married, 7.8% widowed, 7.3% divorced (2000); Foreign born: 4.9% (2000); Ancestry (includes multiple ancestries): 31.6% Irish, 22.9% German, 19.4% Italian, 16.0% English, 6.7% Polish (2000).
Economy: Resort borough. Single-family building permits issued: 11 (2005); Multi-family building permits issued: 0 (2005); Employment by occupation: 17.6% management, 25.4% professional, 10.9% services, 24.8% sales, 0.0% farming, 14.6% construction, 6.7% production (2000).
Income: Per capita income: $33,765 (2005); Median household income: $68,543 (2005); Average household income: $82,308 (2005); Percent of households with income of $100,000 or more: 30.0% (2005); Poverty rate: 4.1% (2000).

Education: Percent of population age 25 and over with: High school diploma (including GED) or higher: 90.9% (2005); Bachelor's degree or higher: 33.3% (2005); Master's degree or higher: 12.7% (2005).

School District(s)

Island Heights Borough (PK-06)

2003-04 Enrollment: 105 . . . . (732) 929-1222

Housing: Homeownership rate: 87.3% (2005); Median home value: $272,277 (2005); Median rent: $764 per month (2000); Median age of housing: 47 years (2000).

Safety: Violent crime rate: 21.6 per 10,000 population; Property crime rate: 97.4 per 10,000 population (2004).

Transportation: Commute to work: 89.3% car, 0.9% public transportation, 0.9% walk, 7.3% work from home (2000); Travel time to work: 34.5% less than 15 minutes, 27.3% 15 to 30 minutes, 17.3% 30 to 45 minutes, 8.7% 45 to 60 minutes, 12.2% 60 minutes or more (2000)

Additional Information Contacts

Borough of Island Heights . . . . (732) 349-0220
http://www.oceancountygov.com/history/default.htm

JACKSON (township). Covers a land area of 100.058 square miles and a water area of 0.752 square miles. Located at 40.10° N. Lat.; 74.33° W. Long.

Population: 33,262 (1990); 42,816 (2000); 52,671 (2005); 62,149 (2010 projected); Race: 90.4% White, 4.3% Black, 2.2% Asian, 6.7% Hispanic of any race (2005); Density: 526.4 persons per square mile (2005); Average household size: 3.03 (2005); Median age: 35.7 (2005); Males per 100 females: 95.8 (2005); Marriage status: 22.1% never married, 64.3% now married, 6.2% widowed, 7.4% divorced (2000); Foreign born: 6.3% (2000); Ancestry (includes multiple ancestries): 26.4% Italian, 23.5% Irish, 17.7% German, 13.3% Other groups, 11.2% Polish (2000).

Economy: Site of Six Flags Great Adventure Theme Park with looping roller coasters and drive-through animal safari park. Unemployment rate: 3.9% (2005); Total civilian labor force: 26,517 (2005); Single-family building permits issued: 209 (2005); Multi-family building permits issued: 0 (2005); Employment by occupation: 14.2% management, 20.9% professional, 13.8% services, 27.3% sales, 0.1% farming, 12.3% construction, 11.4% production (2000).

Income: Per capita income: $28,136 (2005); Median household income: $75,590 (2005); Average household income: $84,943 (2005); Percent of households with income of $100,000 or more: 32.1% (2005); Poverty rate: 3.7% (2000).

Taxes: Total city taxes per capita: $434 (2004); City property taxes per capita: $397 (2004).

Education: Percent of population age 25 and over with: High school diploma (including GED) or higher: 86.9% (2005); Bachelor's degree or higher: 23.1% (2005); Master's degree or higher: 6.1% (2005).

School District(s)

Jackson Township (PK-12)

2003-04 Enrollment: 9,762 . . . . (732) 833-4600

Manchester Township (PK-12)

2003-04 Enrollment: 3,580 . . . . (732) 350-5900

Ocean County Vocational (09-12)

2003-04 Enrollment: 196 . . . . (732) 240-6414

Housing: Homeownership rate: 87.2% (2005); Median home value: $262,264 (2005); Median rent: $739 per month (2000); Median age of housing: 20 years (2000).

Safety: Violent crime rate: 12.6 per 10,000 population; Property crime rate: 114.4 per 10,000 population (2004).

Transportation: Commute to work: 93.7% car, 2.4% public transportation, 0.9% walk, 2.7% work from home (2000); Travel time to work: 16.6% less than 15 minutes, 30.7% 15 to 30 minutes, 20.6% 30 to 45 minutes, 12.0% 45 to 60 minutes, 20.1% 60 minutes or more (2000)

Additional Information Contacts

Jackson Chamber of Commerce . . . . (732) 833-0005
http://www.jacksonchamber.com

LACEY (township). Covers a land area of 83.999 square miles and a water area of 14.523 square miles. Located at 39.85° N. Lat.; 74.23° W. Long. Elevation is 109 feet.

Population: 22,141 (1990); 25,346 (2000); 26,537 (2005); 27,980 (2010 projected); Race: 97.6% White, 0.4% Black, 0.6% Asian, 2.5% Hispanic of any race (2005); Density: 315.9 persons per square mile (2005); Average household size: 2.70 (2005); Median age: 38.7 (2005); Males per 100 females: 95.5 (2005); Marriage status: 20.0% never married, 64.2% now married, 8.5% widowed, 7.2% divorced (2000); Foreign born: 2.7% (2000);

Ancestry (includes multiple ancestries): 31.1% Italian, 26.2% Irish, 20.8% German, 9.7% Polish, 9.4% English (2000).

Economy: Incorporated 1871. Unemployment rate: 4.6% (2005); Total civilian labor force: 13,480 (2005); Single-family building permits issued: 63 (2005); Multi-family building permits issued: 0 (2005); Employment by occupation: 10.4% management, 19.5% professional, 16.5% services, 29.3% sales, 0.0% farming, 14.3% construction, 10.1% production (2000).

Income: Per capita income: $27,201 (2005); Median household income: $64,427 (2005); Average household income: $73,146 (2005); Percent of households with income of $100,000 or more: 23.3% (2005); Poverty rate: 4.5% (2000).

Taxes: Total city taxes per capita: $200 (2004); City property taxes per capita: $185 (2004).

Education: Percent of population age 25 and over with: High school diploma (including GED) or higher: 86.1% (2005); Bachelor's degree or higher: 19.5% (2005); Master's degree or higher: 5.9% (2005).

Housing: Homeownership rate: 90.7% (2005); Median home value: $229,981 (2005); Median rent: $763 per month (2000); Median age of housing: 23 years (2000).

Safety: Violent crime rate: 11.0 per 10,000 population; Property crime rate: 211.2 per 10,000 population (2004).

Transportation: Commute to work: 96.5% car, 0.9% public transportation, 0.5% walk, 1.8% work from home (2000); Travel time to work: 23.7% less than 15 minutes, 29.2% 15 to 30 minutes, 19.9% 30 to 45 minutes, 7.8% 45 to 60 minutes, 19.4% 60 minutes or more (2000)

Additional Information Contacts

Lacey Township . . . . (609) 693-1100
http://www.laceytownship.org

Lacey Township Chamber of Commerce . . . . (609) 693-8312
http://www.laceybusiness.com

LAKEHURST (borough). Covers a land area of 0.922 square miles and a water area of 0.089 square miles. Located at 40.01° N. Lat.; 74.32° W. Long. Elevation is 72 feet.

History: Early-20th-century resort area. Site of the Lakehurst Naval Air Station (est. 1919) and Air Warfare Center. The *Shenandoah* (1923) was the first airship to use the station, and transatlantic airships made it their U.S. terminal from 1924. The crash and burning of the *Hindenburg*, occurred here (May 6, 1937) as the hydrogen-filled German zeppelin was being moored. Center for U.S. Navy blimps until 1940s. Incorporated 1921.

Population: 3,078 (1990); 2,522 (2000); 2,614 (2005); 2,733 (2010 projected); Race: 84.6% White, 7.0% Black, 2.3% Asian, 9.0% Hispanic of any race (2005); Density: 2,833.6 persons per square mile (2005); Average household size: 2.84 (2005); Median age: 32.4 (2005); Males per 100 females: 106.0 (2005); Marriage status: 24.4% never married, 61.2% now married, 6.1% widowed, 8.3% divorced (2000); Foreign born: 9.2% (2000); Ancestry (includes multiple ancestries): 22.0% German, 21.3% Irish, 20.1% Other groups, 16.7% Italian, 8.6% Polish (2000).

Economy: Resort area. It is important as the site of the Lakehurst Naval Air Station and Air Warfare Center. Single-family building permits issued: 1 (2005); Multi-family building permits issued: 0 (2005); Employment by occupation: 8.7% management, 11.7% professional, 27.1% services, 21.4% sales, 0.5% farming, 17.7% construction, 12.9% production (2000).

Income: Per capita income: $21,562 (2005); Median household income: $49,914 (2005); Average household income: $61,264 (2005); Percent of households with income of $100,000 or more: 12.8% (2005); Poverty rate: 7.1% (2000).

Education: Percent of population age 25 and over with: High school diploma (including GED) or higher: 73.2% (2005); Bachelor's degree or higher: 7.4% (2005); Master's degree or higher: 3.1% (2005).

School District(s)

Lakehurst Borough (PK-08)

2003-04 Enrollment: 510 . . . . (732) 657-5741

Ocean County Vocational (09-12)

2003-04 Enrollment: 196 . . . . (732) 240-6414

Housing: Homeownership rate: 67.3% (2005); Median home value: $149,107 (2005); Median rent: $699 per month (2000); Median age of housing: 43 years (2000).

Safety: Violent crime rate: 15.4 per 10,000 population; Property crime rate: 134.6 per 10,000 population (2004).

Transportation: Commute to work: 91.5% car, 0.3% public transportation, 5.0% walk, 1.9% work from home (2000); Travel time to work: 40.6% less than 15 minutes, 31.5% 15 to 30 minutes, 8.7% 30 to 45 minutes, 8.1% 45 to 60 minutes, 11.2% 60 minutes or more (2000)

LAKEWOOD (township). Covers a land area of 24.818 square miles and a water area of 0.297 square miles. Located at 40.08° N. Lat.; 74.20° W. Long. Elevation is 91 feet.

History: Named for its location in a wooded area near two lakes. Lakewood was first called Washington Furnace, because of a smelter established in 1812. Later the community became known as Bergen Works and next as Bricksburg.

Population: 45,019 (1990); 60,352 (2000); 67,602 (2005); 75,083 (2010 projected); Race: 78.3% White, 11.7% Black, 1.5% Asian, 17.4% Hispanic of any race (2005); Density: 2,723.9 persons per square mile (2005); Average household size: 3.08 (2005); Median age: 31.5 (2005); Males per 100 females: 92.2 (2005); Marriage status: 23.7% never married, 58.3% now married, 11.2% widowed, 6.8% divorced (2000); Foreign born: 13.8% (2000); Ancestry (includes multiple ancestries): 31.2% Other groups, 9.9% Italian, 9.2% Irish, 7.6% German, 6.1% Polish (2000).

Economy: Unemployment rate: 4.4% (2005); Total civilian labor force: 23,505 (2005); Single-family building permits issued: 364 (2005); Multi-family building permits issued: 0 (2005); Employment by occupation: 9.9% management, 23.4% professional, 16.6% services, 26.2% sales, 0.2% farming, 8.4% construction, 15.2% production (2000).

Income: Per capita income: $18,405 (2005); Median household income: $40,433 (2005); Average household income: $55,819 (2005); Percent of households with income of $100,000 or more: 13.8% (2005); Poverty rate: 19.8% (2000).

Taxes: Total city taxes per capita: $393 (2004); City property taxes per capita: $369 (2004).

Education: Percent of population age 25 and over with: High school diploma (including GED) or higher: 78.4% (2005); Bachelor's degree or higher: 20.9% (2005); Master's degree or higher: 8.2% (2005).

School District(s)

Lakewood Township (PK-12)
    2003-04 Enrollment: 5,807 . . . . (732) 905-3633
Monmouth-Ocean Ed Serv Comm (UG-UG)
    2003-04 Enrollment: 218 . . . . (732) 389-5555

Four-year College(s)

Beth Medrash Govoha (Private, Not-for-profit)
    Fall 2004 Enrollment: 4,333. (732) 367-1060
Georgian Court University (Private, Not-for-profit, Roman Catholic)
    Fall 2004 Enrollment: 3,065. (732) 364-2200
    2005-06 Tuition: In-state $19,100; Out-of-state $19,100

Two-year College(s)

Star Technical Institute (Private, For-profit)
    Fall 2004 Enrollment: 268 . . . . (732) 901-9710

Housing: Homeownership rate: 61.9% (2005); Median home value: $208,957 (2005); Median rent: $740 per month (2000); Median age of housing: 26 years (2000).

Hospitals: Kimball Medical Center (350 beds)

Safety: Violent crime rate: 33.2 per 10,000 population; Property crime rate: 260.7 per 10,000 population (2004).

Transportation: Commute to work: 84.3% car, 4.3% public transportation, 5.4% walk, 4.4% work from home (2000); Travel time to work: 36.4% less than 15 minutes, 28.4% 15 to 30 minutes, 14.3% 30 to 45 minutes, 5.6% 45 to 60 minutes, 15.3% 60 minutes or more (2000)

Additional Information Contacts

Lakewood Chamber of Commerce . . . . (732) 363-0012
    http://mylakewoodchamber.com
Lakewood Township . . . . (732) 364-2500
    http://www.twp.lakewood.nj.us

LAKEWOOD (CDP). Covers a land area of 7.157 square miles and a water area of 0.204 square miles. Located at 40.09° N. Lat.; 74.21° W. Long.

Population: 26,093 (1990); 36,065 (2000); 40,530 (2005); 45,110 (2010 projected); Race: 79.4% White, 10.2% Black, 1.0% Asian, 20.0% Hispanic of any race (2005); Density: 5,663.1 persons per square mile (2005); Average household size: 4.07 (2005); Median age: 23.9 (2005); Males per 100 females: 102.0 (2005); Marriage status: 27.9% never married, 60.2% now married, 6.1% widowed, 5.8% divorced (2000); Foreign born: 15.6% (2000); Ancestry (includes multiple ancestries): 37.0% Other groups, 6.0% United States or American, 5.6% Polish, 3.6% Italian, 3.4% German (2000).

Economy: Employment by occupation: 9.0% management, 26.6% professional, 17.7% services, 23.3% sales, 0.3% farming, 8.1% construction, 15.1% production (2000).

Income: Per capita income: $12,631 (2005); Median household income: $33,283 (2005); Average household income: $50,273 (2005); Percent of households with income of $100,000 or more: 11.5% (2005); Poverty rate: 29.1% (2000).

Education: Percent of population age 25 and over with: High school diploma (including GED) or higher: 73.9% (2005); Bachelor's degree or higher: 21.1% (2005); Master's degree or higher: 9.2% (2005).

School District(s)

Lakewood Township (PK-12)
    2003-04 Enrollment: 5,807 . . . . (732) 905-3633
Monmouth-Ocean Ed Serv Comm (UG-UG)
    2003-04 Enrollment: 218 . . . . (732) 389-5555

Four-year College(s)

Beth Medrash Govoha (Private, Not-for-profit)
    Fall 2004 Enrollment: 4,333. (732) 367-1060
Georgian Court University (Private, Not-for-profit, Roman Catholic)
    Fall 2004 Enrollment: 3,065. (732) 364-2200
    2005-06 Tuition: In-state $19,100; Out-of-state $19,100

Two-year College(s)

Star Technical Institute (Private, For-profit)
    Fall 2004 Enrollment: 268 . . . . (732) 901-9710

Housing: Homeownership rate: 42.9% (2005); Median home value: $234,268 (2005); Median rent: $732 per month (2000); Median age of housing: 29 years (2000).

Hospitals: Kimball Medical Center (350 beds)

Transportation: Commute to work: 56.1% car, 5.3% public transportation, 8.8% walk, 6.3% work from home (2000); Travel time to work: 43.3% less than 15 minutes, 26.0% 15 to 30 minutes, 12.4% 30 to 45 minutes, 4.2% 45 to 60 minutes, 14.0% 60 minutes or more (2000)

Additional Information Contacts

Lakewood Chamber of Commerce . . . . (732) 363-0012
    http://mylakewoodchamber.com

LANOKA HARBOR (unincorporated postal area, zip code 08734). Covers a land area of 6.232 square miles and a water area of 0.021 square miles. Located at 39.86° N. Lat.; 74.16° W. Long. Elevation is 10 feet.

Population: 7,361 (2000); Race: 99.0% White, 0.1% Black, 0.3% Asian, 1.6% Hispanic of any race (2000); Density: 1,181.2 persons per square mile (2000); Age: 29.2% under 18, 10.2% over 64 (2000); Marriage status: 23.4% never married, 62.1% now married, 7.8% widowed, 6.6% divorced (2000); Foreign born: 3.0% (2000); Ancestry (includes multiple ancestries): 30.5% Italian, 27.1% Irish, 19.0% German, 10.4% Polish, 8.6% English (2000).

Economy: Employment by occupation: 9.6% management, 22.1% professional, 13.4% services, 29.2% sales, 0.0% farming, 13.7% construction, 12.1% production (2000).

Income: Per capita income: $22,354 (2000); Median household income: $66,928 (2000); Poverty rate: 2.5% (2000).

Education: Percent of population age 25 and over with: High school diploma (including GED) or higher: 87.1% (2000); Bachelor's degree or higher: 21.6% (2000).

School District(s)

Lacey Township (PK-12)
    2003-04 Enrollment: 5,323 . . . . (609) 971-2002

Housing: Homeownership rate: 93.0% (2000); Median home value: $145,900 (2000); Median rent: $702 per month (2000); Median age of housing: 21 years (2000).

Transportation: Commute to work: 96.6% car, 0.3% public transportation, 0.1% walk, 2.7% work from home (2000); Travel time to work: 24.3% less than 15 minutes, 29.2% 15 to 30 minutes, 19.3% 30 to 45 minutes, 8.5% 45 to 60 minutes, 18.7% 60 minutes or more (2000)

Additional Information Contacts

Greater Lacey Township Chamber of Commerce . . . . (609) 693-8312
    http://www.laceybusiness.com

LAVALLETTE (borough). Covers a land area of 0.804 square miles and a water area of 0.124 square miles. Located at 39.96° N. Lat.; 74.07° W. Long. Elevation is 5 feet.

Population: 2,299 (1990); 2,665 (2000); 2,751 (2005); 2,869 (2010 projected); Race: 97.8% White, 0.3% Black, 0.1% Asian, 2.0% Hispanic of any race (2005); Density: 3,422.1 persons per square mile (2005); Average household size: 2.17 (2005); Median age: 55.8 (2005); Males per 100 females: 85.1 (2005); Marriage status: 17.4% never married, 58.9% now married, 14.2% widowed, 9.6% divorced (2000); Foreign born: 3.3%

(2000); Ancestry (includes multiple ancestries): 35.3% Italian, 25.3% Irish, 14.7% German, 10.7% Polish, 8.9% English (2000).

Economy: Resort borough. Single-family building permits issued: 20 (2005); Multi-family building permits issued: 0 (2005); Employment by occupation: 21.6% management, 18.8% professional, 9.8% services, 30.0% sales, 0.0% farming, 12.4% construction, 7.5% production (2000).

Income: Per capita income: $33,960 (2005); Median household income: $50,450 (2005); Average household income: $72,228 (2005); Percent of households with income of $100,000 or more: 19.6% (2005); Poverty rate: 8.0% (2000).

Education: Percent of population age 25 and over with: High school diploma (including GED) or higher: 85.1% (2005); Bachelor's degree or higher: 26.5% (2005); Master's degree or higher: 10.7% (2005).

School District(s)

Lavallette Borough (PK-08)

   2003-04 Enrollment: 154 . . . . (732) 793-7722

Housing: Homeownership rate: 75.2% (2005); Median home value: $552,570 (2005); Median rent: $698 per month (2000); Median age of housing: 38 years (2000).

Safety: Violent crime rate: 7.3 per 10,000 population; Property crime rate: 175.5 per 10,000 population (2004).

Transportation: Commute to work: 89.1% car, 2.1% public transportation, 3.2% walk, 4.0% work from home (2000); Travel time to work: 27.3% less than 15 minutes, 30.8% 15 to 30 minutes, 16.9% 30 to 45 minutes, 5.5% 45 to 60 minutes, 19.5% 60 minutes or more (2000)

Additional Information Contacts

Borough of Lavallette . . . . (732) 793-7477
   http://lavalletteboro.com

LEISURE KNOLL (CDP). Covers a land area of 0.885 square miles and a water area of 0 square miles. Located at 40.01° N. Lat.; 74.28° W. Long.

Population: 2,707 (1990); 2,467 (2000); 2,514 (2005); 2,604 (2010 projected); Race: 98.6% White, 0.6% Black, 0.4% Asian, 0.8% Hispanic of any race (2005); Density: 2,841.3 persons per square mile (2005); Average household size: 1.53 (2005); Median age: 76.7 (2005); Males per 100 females: 68.0 (2005); Marriage status: 3.7% never married, 68.3% now married, 25.9% widowed, 2.1% divorced (2000); Foreign born: 7.3% (2000); Ancestry (includes multiple ancestries): 22.4% German, 21.4% Irish, 20.9% Italian, 10.6% English, 5.7% Polish (2000).

Economy: Employment by occupation: 7.9% management, 18.8% professional, 6.7% services, 46.4% sales, 0.0% farming, 0.0% construction, 20.1% production (2000).

Income: Per capita income: $30,576 (2005); Median household income: $38,987 (2005); Average household income: $46,728 (2005); Percent of households with income of $100,000 or more: 5.9% (2005); Poverty rate: 2.4% (2000).

Education: Percent of population age 25 and over with: High school diploma (including GED) or higher: 84.0% (2005); Bachelor's degree or higher: 18.1% (2005); Master's degree or higher: 7.6% (2005).

Housing: Homeownership rate: 97.9% (2005); Median home value: $176,768 (2005); Median rent: $762 per month (2000); Median age of housing: 16 years (2000).

Transportation: Commute to work: 100.0% car, 0.0% public transportation, 0.0% walk, 0.0% work from home (2000); Travel time to work: 32.9% less than 15 minutes, 43.1% 15 to 30 minutes, 0.0% 30 to 45 minutes, 8.0% 45 to 60 minutes, 16.0% 60 minutes or more (2000)

LEISURE VILLAGE (CDP). Covers a land area of 1.234 square miles and a water area of 0.094 square miles. Located at 40.04° N. Lat.; 74.18° W. Long. Elevation is 60 feet.

Population: 4,295 (1990); 4,443 (2000); 4,622 (2005); 4,865 (2010 projected); Race: 93.3% White, 3.2% Black, 0.6% Asian, 7.2% Hispanic of any race (2005); Density: 3,746.1 persons per square mile (2005); Average household size: 1.58 (2005); Median age: 72.4 (2005); Males per 100 females: 55.6 (2005); Marriage status: 13.1% never married, 41.7% now married, 34.9% widowed, 10.3% divorced (2000); Foreign born: 8.9% (2000); Ancestry (includes multiple ancestries): 20.9% Irish, 18.4% Italian, 17.1% German, 10.4% Other groups, 9.3% English (2000).

Economy: Employment by occupation: 4.6% management, 13.3% professional, 20.1% services, 34.0% sales, 0.0% farming, 5.7% construction, 22.3% production (2000).

Income: Per capita income: $24,597 (2005); Median household income: $27,500 (2005); Average household income: $38,599 (2005); Percent of

households with income of $100,000 or more: 4.2% (2005); Poverty rate: 6.9% (2000).

Education: Percent of population age 25 and over with: High school diploma (including GED) or higher: 74.6% (2005); Bachelor's degree or higher: 12.8% (2005); Master's degree or higher: 3.6% (2005).

Housing: Homeownership rate: 80.3% (2005); Median home value: $109,960 (2005); Median rent: $864 per month (2000); Median age of housing: 33 years (2000).

Transportation: Commute to work: 94.9% car, 2.8% public transportation, 0.9% walk, 0.9% work from home (2000); Travel time to work: 26.9% less than 15 minutes, 40.9% 15 to 30 minutes, 17.2% 30 to 45 minutes, 7.9% 45 to 60 minutes, 7.1% 60 minutes or more (2000)

LEISURE VILLAGE EAST (CDP). Covers a land area of 1.596 square miles and a water area of 0 square miles. Located at 40.03° N. Lat.; 74.17° W. Long. Elevation is 40 feet.

Population: 1,989 (1990); 4,597 (2000); 5,007 (2005); 5,448 (2010 projected); Race: 99.0% White, 0.4% Black, 0.2% Asian, 1.3% Hispanic of any race (2005); Density: 3,137.6 persons per square mile (2005); Average household size: 1.66 (2005); Median age: 71.9 (2005); Males per 100 females: 65.8 (2005); Marriage status: 5.6% never married, 66.2% now married, 21.1% widowed, 7.1% divorced (2000); Foreign born: 7.6% (2000); Ancestry (includes multiple ancestries): 29.1% Italian, 18.7% Irish, 14.7% German, 10.2% English, 6.7% Polish (2000).

Economy: Employment by occupation: 12.1% management, 19.3% professional, 13.7% services, 44.9% sales, 0.0% farming, 2.5% construction, 7.5% production (2000).

Income: Per capita income: $33,042 (2005); Median household income: $40,280 (2005); Average household income: $54,819 (2005); Percent of households with income of $100,000 or more: 11.7% (2005); Poverty rate: 2.2% (2000).

Education: Percent of population age 25 and over with: High school diploma (including GED) or higher: 85.0% (2005); Bachelor's degree or higher: 21.4% (2005); Master's degree or higher: 6.9% (2005).

Housing: Homeownership rate: 94.7% (2005); Median home value: $220,808 (2005); Median rent: $554 per month (2000); Median age of housing: 12 years (2000).

Transportation: Commute to work: 93.6% car, 1.3% public transportation, 0.0% walk, 5.2% work from home (2000); Travel time to work: 22.3% less than 15 minutes, 33.6% 15 to 30 minutes, 12.1% 30 to 45 minutes, 11.6% 45 to 60 minutes, 20.5% 60 minutes or more (2000)

LEISURE VILLAGE WEST-PINE LAKE PARK (CDP). Covers a land area of 3.801 square miles and a water area of 0 square miles. Located at 40.00° N. Lat.; 74.26° W. Long.

Population: 10,139 (1990); 11,085 (2000); 12,510 (2005); 13,975 (2010 projected); Race: 92.0% White, 3.4% Black, 1.3% Asian, 4.8% Hispanic of any race (2005); Density: 3,290.9 persons per square mile (2005); Average household size: 2.25 (2005); Median age: 48.0 (2005); Males per 100 females: 86.1 (2005); Marriage status: 16.5% never married, 62.2% now married, 15.3% widowed, 6.0% divorced (2000); Foreign born: 5.6% (2000); Ancestry (includes multiple ancestries): 22.3% Italian, 20.8% Irish, 19.5% German, 10.8% Other groups, 9.0% Polish (2000).

Economy: Employment by occupation: 10.9% management, 15.2% professional, 16.5% services, 25.9% sales, 0.0% farming, 14.4% construction, 17.1% production (2000).

Income: Per capita income: $26,979 (2005); Median household income: $50,076 (2005); Average household income: $60,833 (2005); Percent of households with income of $100,000 or more: 13.3% (2005); Poverty rate: 4.1% (2000).

Education: Percent of population age 25 and over with: High school diploma (including GED) or higher: 83.2% (2005); Bachelor's degree or higher: 16.1% (2005); Master's degree or higher: 5.1% (2005).

Housing: Homeownership rate: 90.0% (2005); Median home value: $169,247 (2005); Median rent: $740 per month (2000); Median age of housing: 21 years (2000).

Transportation: Commute to work: 96.0% car, 0.7% public transportation, 0.2% walk, 2.3% work from home (2000); Travel time to work: 21.5% less than 15 minutes, 31.8% 15 to 30 minutes, 16.3% 30 to 45 minutes, 15.0% 45 to 60 minutes, 15.4% 60 minutes or more (2000)

LITTLE EGG HARBOR (township). Covers a land area of 49.107 square miles and a water area of 24.068 square miles. Located at 39.61° N. Lat.; 74.35° W. Long.

History: Incorporated 1798.

Population: 13,294 (1990); 15,945 (2000); 19,977 (2005); 23,838 (2010 projected); Race: 95.6% White, 0.9% Black, 0.6% Asian, 3.9% Hispanic of any race (2005); Density: 406.8 persons per square mile (2005); Average household size: 2.54 (2005); Median age: 39.6 (2005); Males per 100 females: 92.9 (2005); Marriage status: 19.8% never married, 62.1% now married, 9.7% widowed, 8.4% divorced (2000); Foreign born: 3.1% (2000); Ancestry (includes multiple ancestries): 24.9% Italian, 24.0% German, 23.6% Irish, 11.1% English, 9.3% Polish (2000).
Economy: Single-family building permits issued: 259 (2005); Multi-family building permits issued: 0 (2005); Employment by occupation: 10.5% management, 15.9% professional, 22.1% services, 27.9% sales, 0.4% farming, 13.3% construction, 10.0% production (2000).
Income: Per capita income: $23,871 (2005); Median household income: $49,957 (2005); Average household income: $60,644 (2005); Percent of households with income of $100,000 or more: 13.3% (2005); Poverty rate: 6.5% (2000).
Taxes: Total city taxes per capita: $684 (2004); City property taxes per capita: $625 (2004).
Education: Percent of population age 25 and over with: High school diploma (including GED) or higher: 80.8% (2005); Bachelor's degree or higher: 15.1% (2005); Master's degree or higher: 4.6% (2005).

School District(s)
Little Egg Harbor Township (PK-06)
   2003-04 Enrollment: 1,844 . . . . (609) 296-3295
Housing: Homeownership rate: 79.9% (2005); Median home value: $172,051 (2005); Median rent: $658 per month (2000); Median age of housing: 22 years (2000).
Safety: Violent crime rate: 16.5 per 10,000 population; Property crime rate: 192.6 per 10,000 population (2004).
Transportation: Commute to work: 94.7% car, 1.9% public transportation, 0.8% walk, 2.2% work from home (2000); Travel time to work: 18.5% less than 15 minutes, 21.8% 15 to 30 minutes, 34.1% 30 to 45 minutes, 11.2% 45 to 60 minutes, 14.3% 60 minutes or more (2000)
Additional Information Contacts
Little Egg Harbor Township . . . . (609) 296-7241
   http://www.leht.com

LONG BEACH (township). Aka Beach Haven Park. Covers a land area of 5.307 square miles and a water area of 16.686 square miles. Located at 39.60° N. Lat.; 74.20° W. Long. Elevation is 10 feet.
History: Incorporated 1899.
Population: 3,412 (1990); 3,329 (2000); 3,499 (2005); 3,712 (2010 projected); Race: 98.3% White, 0.4% Black, 0.4% Asian, 2.7% Hispanic of any race (2005); Density: 659.3 persons per square mile (2005); Average household size: 1.99 (2005); Median age: 57.2 (2005); Males per 100 females: 91.1 (2005); Marriage status: 14.9% never married, 65.5% now married, 11.4% widowed, 8.1% divorced (2000); Foreign born: 3.7% (2000); Ancestry (includes multiple ancestries): 25.0% Irish, 24.5% German, 16.5% English, 14.7% Italian, 10.3% Polish (2000).
Economy: Resort and summer art colony communities on coastal Long Beach Island. Single-family building permits issued: 113 (2005); Multi-family building permits issued: 20 (2005); Employment by occupation: 14.0% management, 19.5% professional, 16.0% services, 32.2% sales, 0.0% farming, 8.7% construction, 9.7% production (2000).
Income: Per capita income: $38,598 (2005); Median household income: $55,400 (2005); Average household income: $76,672 (2005); Percent of households with income of $100,000 or more: 24.1% (2005); Poverty rate: 5.1% (2000).
Education: Percent of population age 25 and over with: High school diploma (including GED) or higher: 91.8% (2005); Bachelor's degree or higher: 36.5% (2005); Master's degree or higher: 12.8% (2005).
Housing: Homeownership rate: 86.1% (2005); Median home value: $551,611 (2005); Median rent: $644 per month (2000); Median age of housing: 30 years (2000).
Safety: Violent crime rate: 20.3 per 10,000 population; Property crime rate: 544.6 per 10,000 population (2004).
Transportation: Commute to work: 88.2% car, 0.3% public transportation, 4.1% walk, 6.4% work from home (2000); Travel time to work: 33.7% less than 15 minutes, 20.4% 15 to 30 minutes, 10.8% 30 to 45 minutes, 5.0% 45 to 60 minutes, 30.1% 60 minutes or more (2000)
Additional Information Contacts
Long Beach Township . . . . (609) 361-1000
   http://longbeachtownship.com

MANAHAWKIN (CDP). Covers a land area of 1.824 square miles and a water area of 0.089 square miles. Located at 39.69° N. Lat.; 74.25° W. Long. Elevation is 32 feet.
Population: 1,683 (1990); 2,004 (2000); 2,077 (2005); 2,143 (2010 projected); Race: 96.1% White, 0.1% Black, 1.6% Asian, 2.0% Hispanic of any race (2005); Density: 1,139.0 persons per square mile (2005); Average household size: 2.58 (2005); Median age: 41.3 (2005); Males per 100 females: 88.0 (2005); Marriage status: 21.0% never married, 69.5% now married, 3.6% widowed, 5.9% divorced (2000); Foreign born: 1.8% (2000); Ancestry (includes multiple ancestries): 26.9% Irish, 24.2% German, 21.1% English, 13.4% Italian, 7.9% United States or American (2000).
Economy: Employment by occupation: 5.8% management, 21.5% professional, 17.5% services, 27.1% sales, 0.8% farming, 18.6% construction, 8.8% production (2000).
Income: Per capita income: $31,457 (2005); Median household income: $73,668 (2005); Average household income: $80,710 (2005); Percent of households with income of $100,000 or more: 25.7% (2005); Poverty rate: 3.4% (2000).
Education: Percent of population age 25 and over with: High school diploma (including GED) or higher: 87.8% (2005); Bachelor's degree or higher: 19.0% (2005); Master's degree or higher: 5.9% (2005).

School District(s)
Monmouth-Ocean Ed Serv Comm (UG-UG)
   2003-04 Enrollment: 218 . . . . (732) 389-5555
Southern Regional (07-12)
   2003-04 Enrollment: 4,163 . . . . (609) 597-9481
Stafford Township (PK-06)
   2003-04 Enrollment: 2,727 . . . . (609) 978-5708
Housing: Homeownership rate: 83.9% (2005); Median home value: $242,529 (2005); Median rent: $565 per month (2000); Median age of housing: 31 years (2000).
Hospitals: Southern Ocean County Hospital (134 beds)
Newspapers: Beach Haven Times (General - Circulation 7,500); Beacon Mail-Bag (General - Circulation 50,000); Forked River Gazette (General - Circulation 20,000); Lacey Beacon (General - Circulation 2,955); The Beacon (General - Circulation 13,093); The Summertime Islander (General - Circulation 36,000); Tuckerton Beacon (General - Circulation 4,300)
Transportation: Commute to work: 97.0% car, 1.2% public transportation, 0.9% walk, 0.9% work from home (2000); Travel time to work: 50.0% less than 15 minutes, 23.6% 15 to 30 minutes, 10.6% 30 to 45 minutes, 4.2% 45 to 60 minutes, 11.6% 60 minutes or more (2000)
Additional Information Contacts
Southern Ocean County Chamber of Commerce . . . . (609) 492-7211
   http://www.discoversouthernocean.org

MANCHESTER (township). Covers a land area of 82.599 square miles and a water area of 0.290 square miles. Located at 39.97° N. Lat.; 74.34° W. Long.
History: Incorporated 1865.
Population: 35,976 (1990); 38,928 (2000); 43,586 (2005); 48,357 (2010 projected); Race: 93.9% White, 3.0% Black, 1.0% Asian, 3.1% Hispanic of any race (2005); Density: 527.7 persons per square mile (2005); Average household size: 1.86 (2005); Median age: 67.5 (2005); Males per 100 females: 74.1 (2005); Marriage status: 12.4% never married, 58.4% now married, 22.4% widowed, 6.9% divorced (2000); Foreign born: 7.7% (2000); Ancestry (includes multiple ancestries): 21.4% Irish, 20.6% Italian, 20.0% German, 9.8% English, 8.7% Other groups (2000).
Economy: Unemployment rate: 5.5% (2005); Total civilian labor force: 11,226 (2005); Single-family building permits issued: 11 (2005); Multi-family building permits issued: 13 (2005); Employment by occupation: 11.1% management, 16.3% professional, 17.8% services, 27.1% sales, 0.1% farming, 12.2% construction, 15.5% production (2000).
Income: Per capita income: $26,444 (2005); Median household income: $34,458 (2005); Average household income: $48,696 (2005); Percent of households with income of $100,000 or more: 9.3% (2005); Poverty rate: 5.5% (2000).
Taxes: Total city taxes per capita: $339 (2004); City property taxes per capita: $295 (2004).
Education: Percent of population age 25 and over with: High school diploma (including GED) or higher: 75.7% (2005); Bachelor's degree or higher: 12.9% (2005); Master's degree or higher: 4.1% (2005).

School District(s)
Manchester Township (PK-12)
   2003-04 Enrollment: 3,580 . . . . (732) 350-5900

Housing: Homeownership rate: 91.6% (2005); Median home value: $120,521 (2005); Median rent: $832 per month (2000); Median age of housing: 22 years (2000).
Safety: Violent crime rate: 5.9 per 10,000 population; Property crime rate: 86.8 per 10,000 population (2004).
Newspapers: The Advance News (General - Circulation 25,000)
Transportation: Commute to work: 95.8% car, 0.6% public transportation, 0.9% walk, 1.8% work from home (2000); Travel time to work: 23.9% less than 15 minutes, 29.7% 15 to 30 minutes, 17.7% 30 to 45 minutes, 13.8% 45 to 60 minutes, 14.9% 60 minutes or more (2000)
Additional Information Contacts
Manchester Township . . . . (732) 657-8121
   http://manchestertownshipnj.org

MANTOLOKING (borough). Covers a land area of 0.441 square miles and a water area of 0.220 square miles. Located at 40.04° N. Lat.; 74.05° W. Long. Elevation is 7 feet.
Population: 384 (1990); 423 (2000); 435 (2005); 452 (2010 projected); Race: 97.2% White, 2.1% Black, 0.5% Asian, 0.9% Hispanic of any race (2005); Density: 985.8 persons per square mile (2005); Average household size: 2.00 (2005); Median age: 59.0 (2005); Males per 100 females: 95.9 (2005); Marriage status: 11.9% never married, 67.4% now married, 13.6% widowed, 7.1% divorced (2000); Foreign born: 6.5% (2000); Ancestry (includes multiple ancestries): 22.2% German, 20.6% English, 19.8% Irish, 9.2% United States or American, 9.2% Italian (2000).
Economy: Resort borough. Single-family building permits issued: 4 (2005); Multi-family building permits issued: 0 (2005); Employment by occupation: 48.2% management, 16.8% professional, 0.0% services, 28.5% sales, 0.0% farming, 5.1% construction, 1.5% production (2000).
Income: Per capita income: $91,309 (2005); Median household income: $121,111 (2005); Average household income: $181,938 (2005); Percent of households with income of $100,000 or more: 58.7% (2005); Poverty rate: 0.8% (2000).
Education: Percent of population age 25 and over with: High school diploma (including GED) or higher: 98.9% (2005); Bachelor's degree or higher: 59.6% (2005); Master's degree or higher: 20.3% (2005).
Housing: Homeownership rate: 93.6% (2005); Median home value: $1 million+ (2005); Median rent: $2,000+ per month (2000); Median age of housing: 41 years (2000).
Safety: Violent crime rate: 0.0 per 10,000 population; Property crime rate: 222.7 per 10,000 population (2004).
Transportation: Commute to work: 81.8% car, 6.6% public transportation, 0.0% walk, 11.7% work from home (2000); Travel time to work: 14.9% less than 15 minutes, 23.1% 15 to 30 minutes, 10.7% 30 to 45 minutes, 8.3% 45 to 60 minutes, 43.0% 60 minutes or more (2000)
Additional Information Contacts
Borough of Mantoloking . . . . (732) 899-6600
   http://www.mantoloking.org

MYSTIC ISLAND (CDP). Covers a land area of 7.619 square miles and a water area of 0.152 square miles. Located at 39.56° N. Lat.; 74.37° W. Long.
Population: 7,357 (1990); 8,694 (2000); 10,724 (2005); 12,673 (2010 projected); Race: 96.2% White, 0.7% Black, 0.5% Asian, 3.6% Hispanic of any race (2005); Density: 1,407.6 persons per square mile (2005); Average household size: 2.47 (2005); Median age: 42.7 (2005); Males per 100 females: 94.2 (2005); Marriage status: 19.0% never married, 60.6% now married, 12.0% widowed, 8.4% divorced (2000); Foreign born: 3.4% (2000); Ancestry (includes multiple ancestries): 25.5% Italian, 24.4% Irish, 22.1% German, 11.0% English, 10.1% Polish (2000).
Economy: Employment by occupation: 8.4% management, 14.4% professional, 23.4% services, 28.0% sales, 0.3% farming, 12.6% construction, 12.9% production (2000).
Income: Per capita income: $21,676 (2005); Median household income: $46,131 (2005); Average household income: $53,569 (2005); Percent of households with income of $100,000 or more: 10.0% (2005); Poverty rate: 7.8% (2000).
Education: Percent of population age 25 and over with: High school diploma (including GED) or higher: 78.5% (2005); Bachelor's degree or higher: 13.1% (2005); Master's degree or higher: 4.0% (2005).
Housing: Homeownership rate: 84.6% (2005); Median home value: $157,635 (2005); Median rent: $697 per month (2000); Median age of housing: 25 years (2000).
Transportation: Commute to work: 95.6% car, 2.0% public transportation, 1.1% walk, 1.0% work from home (2000); Travel time to work: 14.1% less

than 15 minutes, 19.1% 15 to 30 minutes, 38.1% 30 to 45 minutes, 12.4% 45 to 60 minutes, 16.4% 60 minutes or more (2000)

NEW EGYPT (CDP). Covers a land area of 4.024 square miles and a water area of 0.044 square miles. Located at 40.06° N. Lat.; 74.53° W. Long. Elevation is 78 feet.
Population: 2,402 (1990); 2,519 (2000); 2,736 (2005); 2,960 (2010 projected); Race: 90.6% White, 2.2% Black, 1.6% Asian, 7.5% Hispanic of any race (2005); Density: 679.9 persons per square mile (2005); Average household size: 2.76 (2005); Median age: 35.9 (2005); Males per 100 females: 100.7 (2005); Marriage status: 25.2% never married, 60.7% now married, 3.6% widowed, 10.5% divorced (2000); Foreign born: 6.9% (2000); Ancestry (includes multiple ancestries): 27.6% German, 19.1% Irish, 18.6% English, 16.1% Italian, 8.3% Polish (2000).
Economy: Agriculture. Manufacturing: apparel, canned cranberries. Employment by occupation: 8.5% management, 13.3% professional, 20.9% services, 26.3% sales, 1.4% farming, 13.8% construction, 15.7% production (2000).
Income: Per capita income: $21,804 (2005); Median household income: $54,031 (2005); Average household income: $59,798 (2005); Percent of households with income of $100,000 or more: 11.7% (2005); Poverty rate: 7.6% (2000).
Education: Percent of population age 25 and over with: High school diploma (including GED) or higher: 81.3% (2005); Bachelor's degree or higher: 15.5% (2005); Master's degree or higher: 6.7% (2005).
School District(s)
Plumsted Township (PK-12)
   2003-04 Enrollment: 1,772 . . . . (609) 758-6800
Housing: Homeownership rate: 71.5% (2005); Median home value: $207,765 (2005); Median rent: $623 per month (2000); Median age of housing: 47 years (2000).
Newspapers: New Egypt Press (General - Circulation 4,000)
Transportation: Commute to work: 90.2% car, 0.0% public transportation, 3.1% walk, 2.8% work from home (2000); Travel time to work: 17.7% less than 15 minutes, 31.8% 15 to 30 minutes, 31.3% 30 to 45 minutes, 9.8% 45 to 60 minutes, 9.4% 60 minutes or more (2000)

NORTH BEACH HAVEN (CDP). Covers a land area of 1.748 square miles and a water area of 0 square miles. Located at 39.60° N. Lat.; 74.21° W. Long. Elevation is 4 feet.
Population: 2,413 (1990); 2,427 (2000); 2,548 (2005); 2,694 (2010 projected); Race: 98.4% White, 0.5% Black, 0.2% Asian, 3.6% Hispanic of any race (2005); Density: 1,457.5 persons per square mile (2005); Average household size: 2.01 (2005); Median age: 55.4 (2005); Males per 100 females: 89.7 (2005); Marriage status: 15.5% never married, 63.1% now married, 12.1% widowed, 9.4% divorced (2000); Foreign born: 3.5% (2000); Ancestry (includes multiple ancestries): 25.8% Irish, 23.3% German, 19.4% English, 15.9% Italian, 10.4% Polish (2000).
Economy: Employment by occupation: 13.2% management, 19.6% professional, 14.4% services, 35.8% sales, 0.0% farming, 10.1% construction, 6.9% production (2000).
Income: Per capita income: $35,981 (2005); Median household income: $50,189 (2005); Average household income: $71,853 (2005); Percent of households with income of $100,000 or more: 20.7% (2005); Poverty rate: 5.8% (2000).
Education: Percent of population age 25 and over with: High school diploma (including GED) or higher: 91.6% (2005); Bachelor's degree or higher: 34.5% (2005); Master's degree or higher: 12.0% (2005).
Housing: Homeownership rate: 84.1% (2005); Median home value: $472,857 (2005); Median rent: $634 per month (2000); Median age of housing: 36 years (2000).
Transportation: Commute to work: 88.7% car, 0.0% public transportation, 4.9% walk, 4.9% work from home (2000); Travel time to work: 35.3% less than 15 minutes, 18.9% 15 to 30 minutes, 12.5% 30 to 45 minutes, 3.8% 45 to 60 minutes, 29.5% 60 minutes or more (2000)

OCEAN (township). Covers a land area of 20.798 square miles and a water area of 11.227 square miles. Located at 39.79° N. Lat.; 74.21° W. Long.
Population: 5,416 (1990); 6,450 (2000); 7,736 (2005); 8,990 (2010 projected); Race: 96.9% White, 0.9% Black, 0.5% Asian, 3.9% Hispanic of any race (2005); Density: 372.0 persons per square mile (2005); Average household size: 2.66 (2005); Median age: 38.1 (2005); Males per 100 females: 98.8 (2005); Marriage status: 22.7% never married, 59.1% now married, 8.1% widowed, 10.1% divorced (2000); Foreign born: 1.4%

(2000); Ancestry (includes multiple ancestries): 29.4% Irish, 23.1% German, 21.3% Italian, 11.1% English, 10.2% Polish (2000).
Economy: In fishing and resort area. Single-family building permits issued: 212 (2005); Multi-family building permits issued: 0 (2005); Employment by occupation: 8.1% management, 17.0% professional, 19.2% services, 23.2% sales, 0.0% farming, 21.8% construction, 10.6% production (2000).
Income: Per capita income: $27,837 (2005); Median household income: $57,171 (2005); Average household income: $73,475 (2005); Percent of households with income of $100,000 or more: 20.9% (2005); Poverty rate: 7.8% (2000).
Education: Percent of population age 25 and over with: High school diploma (including GED) or higher: 86.0% (2005); Bachelor's degree or higher: 15.9% (2005); Master's degree or higher: 5.1% (2005).
Housing: Homeownership rate: 84.3% (2005); Median home value: $184,195 (2005); Median rent: $674 per month (2000); Median age of housing: 30 years (2000).
Safety: Violent crime rate: 13.8 per 10,000 population; Property crime rate: 140.4 per 10,000 population (2004).
Transportation: Commute to work: 94.0% car, 1.8% public transportation, 0.8% walk, 2.2% work from home (2000); Travel time to work: 27.9% less than 15 minutes, 26.5% 15 to 30 minutes, 17.1% 30 to 45 minutes, 11.9% 45 to 60 minutes, 16.6% 60 minutes or more (2000)
Additional Information Contacts
Ocean Township . . . . (609) 693-3302
  http://www.oceantwp.com

OCEAN ACRES (CDP). Covers a land area of 5.852 square miles and a water area of 0.089 square miles. Located at 39.74° N. Lat.; 74.28° W. Long.
Population: 5,587 (1990); 13,155 (2000); 15,305 (2005); 17,451 (2010 projected); Race: 95.7% White, 1.3% Black, 1.0% Asian, 3.6% Hispanic of any race (2005); Density: 2,615.4 persons per square mile (2005); Average household size: 2.82 (2005); Median age: 36.7 (2005); Males per 100 females: 96.5 (2005); Marriage status: 17.9% never married, 71.1% now married, 5.9% widowed, 5.1% divorced (2000); Foreign born: 5.1% (2000); Ancestry (includes multiple ancestries): 28.3% Irish, 27.8% Italian, 22.9% German, 10.4% English, 9.5% Polish (2000).
Economy: Employment by occupation: 9.9% management, 19.8% professional, 16.7% services, 29.1% sales, 0.0% farming, 13.6% construction, 10.9% production (2000).
Income: Per capita income: $25,518 (2005); Median household income: $64,697 (2005); Average household income: $71,504 (2005); Percent of households with income of $100,000 or more: 21.4% (2005); Poverty rate: 3.5% (2000).
Education: Percent of population age 25 and over with: High school diploma (including GED) or higher: 86.6% (2005); Bachelor's degree or higher: 17.4% (2005); Master's degree or higher: 3.4% (2005).
Housing: Homeownership rate: 94.4% (2005); Median home value: $228,040 (2005); Median rent: $780 per month (2000); Median age of housing: 8 years (2000).
Transportation: Commute to work: 97.0% car, 0.6% public transportation, 0.5% walk, 0.9% work from home (2000); Travel time to work: 27.9% less than 15 minutes, 22.7% 15 to 30 minutes, 17.9% 30 to 45 minutes, 12.3% 45 to 60 minutes, 19.2% 60 minutes or more (2000)

OCEAN GATE (borough). Covers a land area of 0.437 square miles and a water area of 0.002 square miles. Located at 39.92° N. Lat.; 74.13° W. Long. Elevation is 7 feet.
Population: 2,078 (1990); 2,076 (2000); 2,131 (2005); 2,213 (2010 projected); Race: 95.9% White, 1.3% Black, 1.3% Asian, 2.6% Hispanic of any race (2005); Density: 4,874.8 persons per square mile (2005); Average household size: 2.50 (2005); Median age: 36.8 (2005); Males per 100 females: 90.1 (2005); Marriage status: 25.7% never married, 52.4% now married, 8.1% widowed, 13.7% divorced (2000); Foreign born: 0.5% (2000); Ancestry (includes multiple ancestries): 32.5% Italian, 31.4% Irish, 19.7% German, 9.7% Polish, 8.3% English (2000).
Economy: Single-family building permits issued: 17 (2005); Multi-family building permits issued: 0 (2005); Employment by occupation: 7.3% management, 13.7% professional, 16.7% services, 31.0% sales, 0.0% farming, 18.3% construction, 13.0% production (2000).
Income: Per capita income: $23,144 (2005); Median household income: $47,926 (2005); Average household income: $57,819 (2005); Percent of households with income of $100,000 or more: 13.5% (2005); Poverty rate: 10.3% (2000).

Education: Percent of population age 25 and over with: High school diploma (including GED) or higher: 81.3% (2005); Bachelor's degree or higher: 7.3% (2005); Master's degree or higher: 0.6% (2005).
School District(s)
Ocean Gate Borough (PK-06)
  2003-04 Enrollment: 190 . . . . (732) 269-3023
Housing: Homeownership rate: 69.6% (2005); Median home value: $181,646 (2005); Median rent: $670 per month (2000); Median age of housing: 45 years (2000).
Safety: Violent crime rate: 33.0 per 10,000 population; Property crime rate: 146.0 per 10,000 population (2004).
Transportation: Commute to work: 93.6% car, 2.7% public transportation, 1.6% walk, 1.0% work from home (2000); Travel time to work: 16.5% less than 15 minutes, 33.9% 15 to 30 minutes, 23.7% 30 to 45 minutes, 8.0% 45 to 60 minutes, 17.8% 60 minutes or more (2000)
Additional Information Contacts
Ocean County Chamber of Commerce . . . . (732) 349-0220
  http://www.oc-chamber.com

PINE BEACH (borough). Covers a land area of 0.623 square miles and a water area of 0.006 square miles. Located at 39.93° N. Lat.; 74.17° W. Long. Elevation is 20 feet.
Population: 1,954 (1990); 1,950 (2000); 2,034 (2005); 2,138 (2010 projected); Race: 98.2% White, 0.2% Black, 0.6% Asian, 3.2% Hispanic of any race (2005); Density: 3,265.1 persons per square mile (2005); Average household size: 2.50 (2005); Median age: 41.9 (2005); Males per 100 females: 94.6 (2005); Marriage status: 21.7% never married, 62.0% now married, 8.1% widowed, 8.1% divorced (2000); Foreign born: 2.6% (2000); Ancestry (includes multiple ancestries): 29.2% German, 27.7% Irish, 25.2% Italian, 12.6% English, 9.1% Polish (2000).
Economy: In resort, fishing area. Single-family building permits issued: 7 (2005); Multi-family building permits issued: 0 (2005); Employment by occupation: 11.9% management, 27.2% professional, 13.9% services, 27.5% sales, 0.0% farming, 12.8% construction, 6.8% production (2000).
Income: Per capita income: $32,187 (2005); Median household income: $70,143 (2005); Average household income: $80,328 (2005); Percent of households with income of $100,000 or more: 30.7% (2005); Poverty rate: 3.5% (2000).
Education: Percent of population age 25 and over with: High school diploma (including GED) or higher: 90.8% (2005); Bachelor's degree or higher: 32.7% (2005); Master's degree or higher: 11.6% (2005).
School District(s)
Toms River Regional (PK-12)
  2003-04 Enrollment: 19,190 . . . . (732) 505-5510
Housing: Homeownership rate: 88.6% (2005); Median home value: $254,391 (2005); Median rent: $691 per month (2000); Median age of housing: 40 years (2000).
Safety: Violent crime rate: 9.9 per 10,000 population; Property crime rate: 143.6 per 10,000 population (2004).
Transportation: Commute to work: 95.5% car, 0.4% public transportation, 0.2% walk, 3.3% work from home (2000); Travel time to work: 26.0% less than 15 minutes, 29.4% 15 to 30 minutes, 20.4% 30 to 45 minutes, 8.8% 45 to 60 minutes, 15.4% 60 minutes or more (2000)
Additional Information Contacts
Ocean County Chamber of Commerce . . . . (732) 349-0220
  http://www.oc-chamber.com

PINE RIDGE AT CRESTWOOD (CDP). Covers a land area of 1.715 square miles and a water area of 0 square miles. Located at 39.95° N. Lat.; 74.32° W. Long.
Population: 2,334 (1990); 2,025 (2000); 2,198 (2005); 2,372 (2010 projected); Race: 98.5% White, 0.6% Black, 0.3% Asian, 1.0% Hispanic of any race (2005); Density: 1,282.0 persons per square mile (2005); Average household size: 1.47 (2005); Median age: 76.3 (2005); Males per 100 females: 62.6 (2005); Marriage status: 10.1% never married, 47.6% now married, 34.5% widowed, 7.8% divorced (2000); Foreign born: 6.0% (2000); Ancestry (includes multiple ancestries): 23.6% Italian, 20.9% German, 19.5% Irish, 11.5% English, 8.2% Polish (2000).
Economy: Employment by occupation: 9.3% management, 11.9% professional, 34.7% services, 29.7% sales, 3.4% farming, 7.2% construction, 3.8% production (2000).
Income: Per capita income: $22,841 (2005); Median household income: $24,010 (2005); Average household income: $33,559 (2005); Percent of households with income of $100,000 or more: 4.3% (2005); Poverty rate: 5.7% (2000).

Education: Percent of population age 25 and over with: High school diploma (including GED) or higher: 63.5% (2005); Bachelor's degree or higher: 4.6% (2005); Master's degree or higher: 1.6% (2005).
Housing: Homeownership rate: 95.9% (2005); Median home value: $37,488 (2005); Median rent: $313 per month (2000); Median age of housing: 21 years (2000).
Transportation: Commute to work: 96.1% car, 0.0% public transportation, 3.9% walk, 0.0% work from home (2000); Travel time to work: 27.9% less than 15 minutes, 36.7% 15 to 30 minutes, 17.5% 30 to 45 minutes, 15.3% 45 to 60 minutes, 2.6% 60 minutes or more (2000)

PLUMSTED (township). Covers a land area of 40.016 square miles and a water area of 0.198 square miles. Located at 40.07° N. Lat.; 74.50° W. Long.

Population: 6,005 (1990); 7,275 (2000); 8,300 (2005); 9,331 (2010 projected); Race: 93.6% White, 2.1% Black, 0.8% Asian, 4.6% Hispanic of any race (2005); Density: 207.4 persons per square mile (2005); Average household size: 2.91 (2005); Median age: 36.7 (2005); Males per 100 females: 99.4 (2005); Marriage status: 24.1% never married, 65.0% now married, 4.5% widowed, 6.4% divorced (2000); Foreign born: 4.6% (2000); Ancestry (includes multiple ancestries): 24.4% German, 22.6% Irish, 18.1% Italian, 15.2% English, 8.5% Other groups (2000).
Economy: Single-family building permits issued: 36 (2005); Multi-family building permits issued: 2 (2005); Employment by occupation: 12.7% management, 17.6% professional, 12.7% services, 27.4% sales, 1.1% farming, 13.5% construction, 15.0% production (2000).
Income: Per capita income: $26,504 (2005); Median household income: $70,226 (2005); Average household income: $76,378 (2005); Percent of households with income of $100,000 or more: 27.1% (2005); Poverty rate: 5.0% (2000).
Education: Percent of population age 25 and over with: High school diploma (including GED) or higher: 84.3% (2005); Bachelor's degree or higher: 17.5% (2005); Master's degree or higher: 4.3% (2005).
Housing: Homeownership rate: 85.3% (2005); Median home value: $261,251 (2005); Median rent: $632 per month (2000); Median age of housing: 27 years (2000).
Safety: Violent crime rate: 8.7 per 10,000 population; Property crime rate: 75.4 per 10,000 population (2004).
Transportation: Commute to work: 93.9% car, 0.0% public transportation, 1.0% walk, 3.4% work from home (2000); Travel time to work: 17.8% less than 15 minutes, 23.7% 15 to 30 minutes, 34.3% 30 to 45 minutes, 13.6% 45 to 60 minutes, 10.6% 60 minutes or more (2000)
Additional Information Contacts
Plumsted Township . . . . (609) 758-2241
  http://www.plumsted.org

POINT PLEASANT (borough). Covers a land area of 3.535 square miles and a water area of 0.628 square miles. Located at 40.08° N. Lat.; 74.07° W. Long. Elevation is 16 feet.

History: Named to promote the city as a pleasant place to live. Settled 1850. Incorporated 1920.
Population: 18,177 (1990); 19,306 (2000); 20,106 (2005); 21,112 (2010 projected); Race: 97.6% White, 0.3% Black, 0.6% Asian, 3.0% Hispanic of any race (2005); Density: 5,687.9 persons per square mile (2005); Average household size: 2.53 (2005); Median age: 39.8 (2005); Males per 100 females: 93.4 (2005); Marriage status: 23.2% never married, 58.8% now married, 8.1% widowed, 9.9% divorced (2000); Foreign born: 3.1% (2000); Ancestry (includes multiple ancestries): 32.7% Irish, 25.2% Italian, 21.5% German, 10.0% Polish, 10.0% English (2000).
Economy: Nearby Point Pleasant Beach is a summer seaside resort. Single-family building permits issued: 42 (2005); Multi-family building permits issued: 0 (2005); Employment by occupation: 13.7% management, 22.4% professional, 15.7% services, 28.8% sales, 0.2% farming, 10.5% construction, 8.7% production (2000).
Income: Per capita income: $29,825 (2005); Median household income: $63,242 (2005); Average household income: $75,117 (2005); Percent of households with income of $100,000 or more: 24.8% (2005); Poverty rate: 3.2% (2000).
Education: Percent of population age 25 and over with: High school diploma (including GED) or higher: 88.4% (2005); Bachelor's degree or higher: 27.8% (2005); Master's degree or higher: 7.7% (2005).
School District(s)
Point Pleasant Borough (PK-12)
  2003-04 Enrollment: 3,238 . . . . (732) 701-1900

Two-year College(s)
Shore Academy (Private, For-profit)
  Fall 2004 Enrollment: n/a. . . . . (732) 899-3337
Housing: Homeownership rate: 79.5% (2005); Median home value: $275,460 (2005); Median rent: $746 per month (2000); Median age of housing: 36 years (2000).
Safety: Violent crime rate: 7.0 per 10,000 population; Property crime rate: 166.7 per 10,000 population (2004).
Transportation: Commute to work: 95.5% car, 1.6% public transportation, 0.9% walk, 1.4% work from home (2000); Travel time to work: 31.6% less than 15 minutes, 26.0% 15 to 30 minutes, 16.8% 30 to 45 minutes, 8.5% 45 to 60 minutes, 17.1% 60 minutes or more (2000)
Additional Information Contacts
Borough of Point Pleasant . . . . (732) 892-3434
  http://www.ptboro.com

POINT PLEASANT BEACH (borough). Covers a land area of 1.438 square miles and a water area of 0.280 square miles. Located at 40.09° N. Lat.; 74.04° W. Long. Elevation is 10 feet.

History: Incorporated 1886.
Population: 5,112 (1990); 5,314 (2000); 5,456 (2005); 5,664 (2010 projected); Race: 95.3% White, 0.4% Black, 1.1% Asian, 6.1% Hispanic of any race (2005); Density: 3,794.8 persons per square mile (2005); Average household size: 2.25 (2005); Median age: 43.0 (2005); Males per 100 females: 102.7 (2005); Marriage status: 29.0% never married, 53.5% now married, 9.6% widowed, 8.0% divorced (2000); Foreign born: 5.8% (2000); Ancestry (includes multiple ancestries): 28.5% Irish, 22.2% Italian, 19.5% German, 13.8% English, 8.4% Polish (2000).
Economy: Resort borough. Single-family building permits issued: 17 (2005); Multi-family building permits issued: 0 (2005); Employment by occupation: 11.3% management, 25.7% professional, 16.0% services, 29.9% sales, 2.6% farming, 8.3% construction, 6.2% production (2000).
Income: Per capita income: $35,060 (2005); Median household income: $60,232 (2005); Average household income: $78,283 (2005); Percent of households with income of $100,000 or more: 24.5% (2005); Poverty rate: 6.1% (2000).
Taxes: Total city taxes per capita: $889 (2004); City property taxes per capita: $815 (2004).
Education: Percent of population age 25 and over with: High school diploma (including GED) or higher: 87.3% (2005); Bachelor's degree or higher: 34.4% (2005); Master's degree or higher: 11.6% (2005).
School District(s)
Point Pleasant Beach Borough (PK-12)
  2003-04 Enrollment: 956 . . . . (732) 899-8840
Housing: Homeownership rate: 62.3% (2005); Median home value: $398,778 (2005); Median rent: $703 per month (2000); Median age of housing: 47 years (2000).
Hospitals: Medical Center of Ocean County, Brook Division (426 beds)
Safety: Violent crime rate: 33.1 per 10,000 population; Property crime rate: 470.5 per 10,000 population (2004).
Newspapers: Ocean Star (General - Circulation 5,300)
Transportation: Commute to work: 83.8% car, 5.3% public transportation, 5.6% walk, 2.3% work from home (2000); Travel time to work: 29.7% less than 15 minutes, 19.7% 15 to 30 minutes, 18.5% 30 to 45 minutes, 7.6% 45 to 60 minutes, 24.4% 60 minutes or more (2000)
Additional Information Contacts
Borough of Point Pleasant Beach . . . . (732) 892-1118
  http://www.pointpleasantbeach.org
Point Pleasant Beach Chamber of Commerce . . . . (732) 899-2424
  http://www.pointpleasantbeachnj.com

SEASIDE HEIGHTS (borough). Covers a land area of 0.611 square miles and a water area of 0.146 square miles. Located at 39.94° N. Lat.; 74.07° W. Long. Elevation is 7 feet.

Population: 2,366 (1990); 3,155 (2000); 3,462 (2005); 3,790 (2010 projected); Race: 89.7% White, 3.8% Black, 0.9% Asian, 11.4% Hispanic of any race (2005); Density: 5,664.5 persons per square mile (2005); Average household size: 2.18 (2005); Median age: 33.8 (2005); Males per 100 females: 106.1 (2005); Marriage status: 36.0% never married, 40.2% now married, 7.3% widowed, 16.5% divorced (2000); Foreign born: 7.5% (2000); Ancestry (includes multiple ancestries): 25.7% Italian, 19.0% Irish, 18.4% Other groups, 18.1% German, 7.8% English (2000).
Economy: Resort borough. Boatyards, recreational facilities. Single-family building permits issued: 27 (2005); Multi-family building permits issued: 5 (2005); Employment by occupation: 9.6% management, 12.5%

professional, 28.0% services, 25.4% sales, 0.7% farming, 11.2% construction, 12.5% production (2000).
Income: Per capita income: $20,889 (2005); Median household income: $28,583 (2005); Average household income: $43,414 (2005); Percent of households with income of $100,000 or more: 8.6% (2005); Poverty rate: 24.1% (2000).
Education: Percent of population age 25 and over with: High school diploma (including GED) or higher: 76.2% (2005); Bachelor's degree or higher: 15.7% (2005); Master's degree or higher: 3.6% (2005).

School District(s)
Seaside Heights Borough (PK-06)
    2003-04 Enrollment: 322 . . . . (732) 793-8485
Housing: Homeownership rate: 28.2% (2005); Median home value: $206,838 (2005); Median rent: $604 per month (2000); Median age of housing: 39 years (2000).
Safety: Violent crime rate: 246.7 per 10,000 population; Property crime rate: 808.9 per 10,000 population (2004).
Transportation: Commute to work: 83.8% car, 2.9% public transportation, 11.6% walk, 0.3% work from home (2000); Travel time to work: 29.2% less than 15 minutes, 28.3% 15 to 30 minutes, 19.8% 30 to 45 minutes, 6.5% 45 to 60 minutes, 16.3% 60 minutes or more (2000)

SEASIDE PARK (borough). Covers a land area of 0.650 square miles and a water area of 0.114 square miles. Located at 39.92° N. Lat.; 74.07° W. Long. Elevation is 6 feet.
Population: 1,871 (1990); 2,263 (2000); 2,234 (2005); 2,254 (2010 projected); Race: 97.5% White, 0.2% Black, 0.9% Asian, 2.7% Hispanic of any race (2005); Density: 3,436.9 persons per square mile (2005); Average household size: 1.96 (2005); Median age: 46.3 (2005); Males per 100 females: 96.5 (2005); Marriage status: 27.7% never married, 53.4% now married, 10.3% widowed, 8.6% divorced (2000); Foreign born: 4.0% (2000); Ancestry (includes multiple ancestries): 24.0% Irish, 23.4% Italian, 19.5% German, 10.7% English, 7.6% Polish (2000).
Economy: Resort borough. Single-family building permits issued: 14 (2005); Multi-family building permits issued: 0 (2005); Employment by occupation: 13.8% management, 21.8% professional, 13.9% services, 31.3% sales, 0.0% farming, 11.3% construction, 8.1% production (2000).
Income: Per capita income: $35,325 (2005); Median household income: $48,953 (2005); Average household income: $69,406 (2005); Percent of households with income of $100,000 or more: 23.5% (2005); Poverty rate: 8.6% (2000).
Education: Percent of population age 25 and over with: High school diploma (including GED) or higher: 87.7% (2005); Bachelor's degree or higher: 34.0% (2005); Master's degree or higher: 11.7% (2005).

School District(s)
Seaside Park Borough (PK-06)
    2003-04 Enrollment: 121 . . . . (732) 793-0177
Housing: Homeownership rate: 60.2% (2005); Median home value: $377,273 (2005); Median rent: $636 per month (2000); Median age of housing: 48 years (2000).
Safety: Violent crime rate: 21.7 per 10,000 population; Property crime rate: 190.6 per 10,000 population (2004).
Transportation: Commute to work: 92.6% car, 0.5% public transportation, 4.3% walk, 2.1% work from home (2000); Travel time to work: 31.0% less than 15 minutes, 31.3% 15 to 30 minutes, 13.3% 30 to 45 minutes, 9.7% 45 to 60 minutes, 14.7% 60 minutes or more (2000)

SHIP BOTTOM (borough). Covers a land area of 0.695 square miles and a water area of 0.299 square miles. Located at 39.64° N. Lat.; 74.18° W. Long. Elevation is 10 feet.
Population: 1,352 (1990); 1,384 (2000); 1,439 (2005); 1,511 (2010 projected); Race: 96.5% White, 0.4% Black, 0.7% Asian, 6.9% Hispanic of any race (2005); Density: 2,070.2 persons per square mile (2005); Average household size: 2.08 (2005); Median age: 49.6 (2005); Males per 100 females: 93.7 (2005); Marriage status: 22.7% never married, 49.9% now married, 12.7% widowed, 14.8% divorced (2000); Foreign born: 5.5% (2000); Ancestry (includes multiple ancestries): 30.5% Irish, 22.9% German, 21.4% Italian, 12.5% English, 9.6% Polish (2000).
Economy: Resort borough. Single-family building permits issued: 24 (2005); Multi-family building permits issued: 0 (2005); Employment by occupation: 14.9% management, 18.8% professional, 19.7% services, 26.6% sales, 0.5% farming, 11.8% construction, 7.7% production (2000).
Income: Per capita income: $35,321 (2005); Median household income: $52,337 (2005); Average household income: $73,344 (2005); Percent of

households with income of $100,000 or more: 21.9% (2005); Poverty rate: 8.2% (2000).
Education: Percent of population age 25 and over with: High school diploma (including GED) or higher: 88.8% (2005); Bachelor's degree or higher: 25.2% (2005); Master's degree or higher: 9.3% (2005).

School District(s)
Long Beach Island (PK-06)
    2003-04 Enrollment: 314 . . . . (609) 494-2341
Housing: Homeownership rate: 76.8% (2005); Median home value: $433,333 (2005); Median rent: $700 per month (2000); Median age of housing: 37 years (2000).
Safety: Violent crime rate: 21.0 per 10,000 population; Property crime rate: 671.8 per 10,000 population (2004).
Transportation: Commute to work: 86.7% car, 0.6% public transportation, 5.6% walk, 5.3% work from home (2000); Travel time to work: 41.3% less than 15 minutes, 23.9% 15 to 30 minutes, 9.8% 30 to 45 minutes, 4.7% 45 to 60 minutes, 20.3% 60 minutes or more (2000)
Additional Information Contacts
Borough of Ship Bottom . . . . (609) 494-2171
    http://www.shipbottom.org
Southern Ocean County Chamber of Commerce . . . . (609) 494-7211
    http://www.discoversouthernocean.org

SILVER RIDGE (CDP). Covers a land area of 0.440 square miles and a water area of 0 square miles. Located at 39.96° N. Lat.; 74.23° W. Long. Elevation is 40 feet.
Population: 1,138 (1990); 1,211 (2000); 1,158 (2005); 1,129 (2010 projected); Race: 99.1% White, 0.3% Black, 0.3% Asian, 1.7% Hispanic of any race (2005); Density: 2,634.4 persons per square mile (2005); Average household size: 1.55 (2005); Median age: 73.1 (2005); Males per 100 females: 67.8 (2005); Marriage status: 9.3% never married, 51.1% now married, 31.0% widowed, 8.7% divorced (2000); Foreign born: 8.6% (2000); Ancestry (includes multiple ancestries): 20.8% German, 20.4% Irish, 17.7% Italian, 11.2% English, 9.1% Polish (2000).
Economy: Employment by occupation: 14.6% management, 22.9% professional, 11.7% services, 44.2% sales, 0.0% farming, 2.9% construction, 3.8% production (2000).
Income: Per capita income: $26,304 (2005); Median household income: $34,837 (2005); Average household income: $40,668 (2005); Percent of households with income of $100,000 or more: 3.5% (2005); Poverty rate: 3.9% (2000).
Education: Percent of population age 25 and over with: High school diploma (including GED) or higher: 78.0% (2005); Bachelor's degree or higher: 12.1% (2005); Master's degree or higher: 4.5% (2005).
Housing: Homeownership rate: 92.7% (2005); Median home value: $130,407 (2005); Median rent: $625 per month (2000); Median age of housing: 26 years (2000).
Transportation: Commute to work: 96.3% car, 0.0% public transportation, 0.0% walk, 3.7% work from home (2000); Travel time to work: 5.3% less than 15 minutes, 41.3% 15 to 30 minutes, 26.9% 30 to 45 minutes, 13.0% 45 to 60 minutes, 13.5% 60 minutes or more (2000)

SOUTH TOMS RIVER (borough). Covers a land area of 1.160 square miles and a water area of 0.058 square miles. Located at 39.94° N. Lat.; 74.21° W. Long. Elevation is 31 feet.
Population: 3,869 (1990); 3,634 (2000); 3,743 (2005); 3,895 (2010 projected); Race: 71.7% White, 22.1% Black, 0.5% Asian, 11.0% Hispanic of any race (2005); Density: 3,225.9 persons per square mile (2005); Average household size: 3.32 (2005); Median age: 32.0 (2005); Males per 100 females: 93.8 (2005); Marriage status: 33.6% never married, 50.9% now married, 6.0% widowed, 9.5% divorced (2000); Foreign born: 2.6% (2000); Ancestry (includes multiple ancestries): 26.9% Other groups, 20.9% Irish, 15.2% Italian, 11.9% German, 9.1% United States or American (2000).
Economy: Single-family building permits issued: 9 (2005); Multi-family building permits issued: 0 (2005); Employment by occupation: 4.3% management, 12.5% professional, 22.4% services, 31.3% sales, 0.6% farming, 14.5% construction, 14.5% production (2000).
Income: Per capita income: $17,666 (2005); Median household income: $48,373 (2005); Average household income: $58,726 (2005); Percent of households with income of $100,000 or more: 11.7% (2005); Poverty rate: 12.6% (2000).
Education: Percent of population age 25 and over with: High school diploma (including GED) or higher: 74.1% (2005); Bachelor's degree or higher: 5.6% (2005); Master's degree or higher: 1.4% (2005).

School District(s)
Toms River Regional (PK-12)
2003-04 Enrollment: 19,190 . . . . (732) 505-5510
Housing: Homeownership rate: 81.5% (2005); Median home value: $138,608 (2005); Median rent: $586 per month (2000); Median age of housing: 36 years (2000).
Safety: Violent crime rate: 37.5 per 10,000 population; Property crime rate: 244.0 per 10,000 population (2004).
Transportation: Commute to work: 95.6% car, 1.3% public transportation, 0.9% walk, 1.1% work from home (2000); Travel time to work: 26.7% less than 15 minutes, 38.9% 15 to 30 minutes, 17.8% 30 to 45 minutes, 7.4% 45 to 60 minutes, 9.1% 60 minutes or more (2000)

STAFFORD (township). Covers a land area of 46.529 square miles and a water area of 8.293 square miles. Located at 39.70° N. Lat.; 74.26° W. Long.
History: Incorporated 1798.
Population: 13,325 (1990); 22,532 (2000); 25,147 (2005); 27,843 (2010 projected); Race: 96.2% White, 1.0% Black, 1.1% Asian, 3.1% Hispanic of any race (2005); Density: 540.5 persons per square mile (2005); Average household size: 2.63 (2005); Median age: 40.0 (2005); Males per 100 females: 94.8 (2005); Marriage status: 18.9% never married, 67.1% now married, 7.7% widowed, 6.3% divorced (2000); Foreign born: 4.4% (2000); Ancestry (includes multiple ancestries): 29.4% Irish, 24.7% Italian, 23.0% German, 11.2% English, 9.1% Polish (2000).
Economy: Single-family building permits issued: 231 (2005); Multi-family building permits issued: 84 (2005); Employment by occupation: 11.0% management, 20.3% professional, 16.0% services, 28.9% sales, 0.3% farming, 14.0% construction, 9.4% production (2000).
Income: Per capita income: $29,809 (2005); Median household income: $65,375 (2005); Average household income: $78,074 (2005); Percent of households with income of $100,000 or more: 24.6% (2005); Poverty rate: 4.0% (2000).
Taxes: Total city taxes per capita: $792 (2004); City property taxes per capita: $747 (2004).
Education: Percent of population age 25 and over with: High school diploma (including GED) or higher: 84.9% (2005); Bachelor's degree or higher: 18.7% (2005); Master's degree or higher: 4.5% (2005).
Housing: Homeownership rate: 90.8% (2005); Median home value: $239,111 (2005); Median rent: $674 per month (2000); Median age of housing: 20 years (2000).
Safety: Violent crime rate: 17.6 per 10,000 population; Property crime rate: 252.4 per 10,000 population (2004).
Transportation: Commute to work: 96.6% car, 0.7% public transportation, 0.5% walk, 1.6% work from home (2000); Travel time to work: 32.0% less than 15 minutes, 22.3% 15 to 30 minutes, 15.7% 30 to 45 minutes, 11.6% 45 to 60 minutes, 18.4% 60 minutes or more (2000)
Additional Information Contacts
Stafford Township . . . . (609) 597-1000
http://twp.stafford.nj.us

SURF CITY (borough). Covers a land area of 0.724 square miles and a water area of 0.198 square miles. Located at 39.66° N. Lat.; 74.16° W. Long. Elevation is 10 feet.
History: Settled 1690 by whalers.
Population: 1,375 (1990); 1,442 (2000); 1,523 (2005); 1,617 (2010 projected); Race: 97.8% White, 0.1% Black, 0.5% Asian, 2.4% Hispanic of any race (2005); Density: 2,102.2 persons per square mile (2005); Average household size: 2.03 (2005); Median age: 52.8 (2005); Males per 100 females: 91.6 (2005); Marriage status: 20.7% never married, 56.7% now married, 13.2% widowed, 9.4% divorced (2000); Foreign born: 3.2% (2000); Ancestry (includes multiple ancestries): 27.9% Irish, 23.9% German, 19.1% Italian, 17.9% English, 7.8% Polish (2000).
Economy: Resort borough. Single-family building permits issued: 38 (2005); Multi-family building permits issued: 0 (2005); Employment by occupation: 15.8% management, 16.6% professional, 15.4% services, 35.5% sales, 0.8% farming, 7.6% construction, 8.1% production (2000).
Income: Per capita income: $34,731 (2005); Median household income: $46,980 (2005); Average household income: $70,527 (2005); Percent of households with income of $100,000 or more: 16.7% (2005); Poverty rate: 7.5% (2000).
Education: Percent of population age 25 and over with: High school diploma (including GED) or higher: 87.4% (2005); Bachelor's degree or higher: 25.6% (2005); Master's degree or higher: 6.2% (2005).

School District(s)
Long Beach Island (PK-06)
2003-04 Enrollment: 314 . . . . (609) 494-2341
Housing: Homeownership rate: 76.9% (2005); Median home value: $413,415 (2005); Median rent: $621 per month (2000); Median age of housing: 35 years (2000).
Safety: Violent crime rate: 6.6 per 10,000 population; Property crime rate: 192.7 per 10,000 population (2004).
Newspapers: Beachcomber (General - Circulation 10,500); The SandPaper (General - Circulation 18,000)
Transportation: Commute to work: 85.6% car, 0.3% public transportation, 7.3% walk, 5.0% work from home (2000); Travel time to work: 49.9% less than 15 minutes, 15.3% 15 to 30 minutes, 8.6% 30 to 45 minutes, 6.0% 45 to 60 minutes, 20.2% 60 minutes or more (2000)

TOMS RIVER (CDP). Covers a land area of 39.371 square miles and a water area of 1.237 square miles. Located at 39.97° N. Lat.; 74.16° W. Long. Elevation is 40 feet.
Population: 73,186 (1990); 86,327 (2000); 91,711 (2005); 97,745 (2010 projected); Race: 92.0% White, 2.3% Black, 2.9% Asian, 6.0% Hispanic of any race (2005); Density: 2,329.4 persons per square mile (2005); Average household size: 2.69 (2005); Median age: 39.7 (2005); Males per 100 females: 93.2 (2005); Marriage status: 24.2% never married, 59.5% now married, 8.2% widowed, 8.0% divorced (2000); Foreign born: 7.1% (2000); Ancestry (includes multiple ancestries): 31.5% Italian, 24.1% Irish, 18.8% German, 10.7% Other groups, 8.9% Polish (2000).
Economy: Employment by occupation: 13.0% management, 21.3% professional, 15.5% services, 30.5% sales, 0.1% farming, 10.1% construction, 9.4% production (2000).
Income: Per capita income: $28,112 (2005); Median household income: $60,880 (2005); Average household income: $75,029 (2005); Percent of households with income of $100,000 or more: 23.2% (2005); Poverty rate: 5.6% (2000).
Education: Percent of population age 25 and over with: High school diploma (including GED) or higher: 86.4% (2005); Bachelor's degree or higher: 23.7% (2005); Master's degree or higher: 8.0% (2005).
School District(s)
Ocean County Vocational (09-12)
2003-04 Enrollment: 196 . . . . (732) 240-6414
Toms River Regional (PK-12)
2003-04 Enrollment: 19,190 . . . . (732) 505-5510
Two-year College(s)
Ocean County College (Public)
Fall 2004 Enrollment: 8,335. . . . . (732) 255-0326
2005-06 Tuition: In-state $3,672; Out-of-state $5,616
Ocean County Vocational-Technical School (Public)
Fall 2004 Enrollment: 421 . . . . (732) 473-3100
Performance Training (Private, For-profit)
Fall 2004 Enrollment: n/a. . . . . (732) 505-9119
Housing: Homeownership rate: 83.6% (2005); Median home value: $249,612 (2005); Median rent: $687 per month (2000); Median age of housing: 26 years (2000).
Hospitals: Community Medical Center (595 beds); HealthSouth Rehabilitation Hospital of Toms River (80 beds)
Newspapers: Ocean County Observer (Circulation 18,794); Ocean County Reporter (General - Circulation 100,000)
Transportation: Commute to work: 94.0% car, 1.7% public transportation, 0.9% walk, 2.7% work from home (2000); Travel time to work: 30.2% less than 15 minutes, 31.0% 15 to 30 minutes, 14.1% 30 to 45 minutes, 7.1% 45 to 60 minutes, 17.5% 60 minutes or more (2000)
Additional Information Contacts
Ocean County Chamber of Commerce . . . . (732) 349-0220
http://www.oc-chamber.com

TUCKERTON (borough). Covers a land area of 3.657 square miles and a water area of 0.119 square miles. Located at 39.60° N. Lat.; 74.33° W. Long. Elevation is 23 feet.
History: Settled c.1700; incorporated 1901. Important 18th-century port; raided by British, 1778.
Population: 3,087 (1990); 3,517 (2000); 3,666 (2005); 3,854 (2010 projected); Race: 96.9% White, 0.3% Black, 0.5% Asian, 3.7% Hispanic of any race (2005); Density: 1,002.5 persons per square mile (2005); Average household size: 2.35 (2005); Median age: 39.1 (2005); Males per 100 females: 98.9 (2005); Marriage status: 22.7% never married, 55.5% now married, 9.7% widowed, 12.1% divorced (2000); Foreign born: 2.7%

(2000); Ancestry (includes multiple ancestries): 27.1% Irish, 25.3% German, 17.9% Italian, 10.5% English, 9.0% Polish (2000).
Economy: Boatyards; fishing. Single-family building permits issued: 14 (2005); Multi-family building permits issued: 21 (2005); Employment by occupation: 11.5% management, 16.9% professional, 16.7% services, 27.4% sales, 1.0% farming, 15.4% construction, 11.0% production (2000).
Income: Per capita income: $22,868 (2005); Median household income: $45,545 (2005); Average household income: $53,070 (2005); Percent of households with income of $100,000 or more: 11.3% (2005); Poverty rate: 7.9% (2000).
Education: Percent of population age 25 and over with: High school diploma (including GED) or higher: 84.6% (2005); Bachelor's degree or higher: 13.3% (2005); Master's degree or higher: 4.5% (2005).

School District(s)
Pinelands Regional (07-12)
   2003-04 Enrollment: 2,061 . . . . (609) 296-3106
Tuckerton Borough (PK-06)
   2003-04 Enrollment: 344 . . . . (609) 296-2858
Housing: Homeownership rate: 72.0% (2005); Median home value: $177,273 (2005); Median rent: $626 per month (2000); Median age of housing: 31 years (2000).
Safety: Violent crime rate: 8.2 per 10,000 population; Property crime rate: 178.7 per 10,000 population (2004).
Transportation: Commute to work: 93.8% car, 1.6% public transportation, 2.0% walk, 2.0% work from home (2000); Travel time to work: 24.9% less than 15 minutes, 24.1% 15 to 30 minutes, 31.1% 30 to 45 minutes, 11.0% 45 to 60 minutes, 8.9% 60 minutes or more (2000)

VISTA CENTER (CDP). Covers a land area of 3.452 square miles and a water area of 0.029 square miles. Located at 40.15° N. Lat.; 74.32° W. Long.
Population: 384 (1990); 541 (2000); 691 (2005); 838 (2010 projected); Race: 90.3% White, 5.2% Black, 1.6% Asian, 7.4% Hispanic of any race (2005); Density: 200.2 persons per square mile (2005); Average household size: 3.21 (2005); Median age: 36.0 (2005); Males per 100 females: 103.8 (2005); Marriage status: 18.9% never married, 76.2% now married, 0.0% widowed, 4.9% divorced (2000); Foreign born: 7.7% (2000); Ancestry (includes multiple ancestries): 21.7% Other groups, 16.7% United States or American, 15.8% Irish, 15.2% Italian, 11.0% German (2000).
Economy: Employment by occupation: 28.6% management, 8.7% professional, 18.1% services, 26.6% sales, 0.0% farming, 12.1% construction, 6.0% production (2000).
Income: Per capita income: $40,702 (2005); Median household income: $109,409 (2005); Average household income: $130,814 (2005); Percent of households with income of $100,000 or more: 58.1% (2005); Poverty rate: 1.1% (2000).
Education: Percent of population age 25 and over with: High school diploma (including GED) or higher: 90.0% (2005); Bachelor's degree or higher: 37.7% (2005); Master's degree or higher: 5.7% (2005).
Housing: Homeownership rate: 89.8% (2005); Median home value: $282,632 (2005); Median rent: $n/a per month (2000); Median age of housing: 22 years (2000).
Transportation: Commute to work: 87.8% car, 3.1% public transportation, 1.6% walk, 7.5% work from home (2000); Travel time to work: 23.1% less than 15 minutes, 18.8% 15 to 30 minutes, 18.5% 30 to 45 minutes, 23.9% 45 to 60 minutes, 15.7% 60 minutes or more (2000)

WARETOWN (CDP). Covers a land area of 0.934 square miles and a water area of 0 square miles. Located at 39.79° N. Lat.; 74.18° W. Long. Elevation is 15 feet.
Population: 1,264 (1990); 1,582 (2000); 1,916 (2005); 2,245 (2010 projected); Race: 97.2% White, 0.6% Black, 0.4% Asian, 3.0% Hispanic of any race (2005); Density: 2,052.1 persons per square mile (2005); Average household size: 2.49 (2005); Median age: 40.7 (2005); Males per 100 females: 98.8 (2005); Marriage status: 21.2% never married, 58.0% now married, 9.3% widowed, 11.4% divorced (2000); Foreign born: 2.0% (2000); Ancestry (includes multiple ancestries): 33.8% Irish, 18.8% German, 13.8% Italian, 12.7% Polish, 8.9% English (2000).
Economy: Employment by occupation: 11.0% management, 15.6% professional, 21.7% services, 21.3% sales, 0.0% farming, 20.7% construction, 9.7% production (2000).
Income: Per capita income: $26,662 (2005); Median household income: $53,611 (2005); Average household income: $66,344 (2005); Percent of households with income of $100,000 or more: 18.1% (2005); Poverty rate: 5.6% (2000).

Education: Percent of population age 25 and over with: High school diploma (including GED) or higher: 84.5% (2005); Bachelor's degree or higher: 14.3% (2005); Master's degree or higher: 3.7% (2005).

School District(s)
Ocean County Vocational (09-12)
   2003-04 Enrollment: 196 . . . . (732) 240-6414
Ocean Township (PK-06)
   2003-04 Enrollment: 625 . . . . (609) 693-3329
Housing: Homeownership rate: 82.5% (2005); Median home value: $192,407 (2005); Median rent: $648 per month (2000); Median age of housing: 35 years (2000).
Transportation: Commute to work: 95.4% car, 0.0% public transportation, 3.2% walk, 1.5% work from home (2000); Travel time to work: 38.3% less than 15 minutes, 16.2% 15 to 30 minutes, 24.4% 30 to 45 minutes, 5.8% 45 to 60 minutes, 15.4% 60 minutes or more (2000)

WEST CREEK (unincorporated postal area, zip code 08092). Covers a land area of 16.629 square miles and a water area of 0.058 square miles. Located at 39.65° N. Lat.; 74.28° W. Long. Elevation is 10 feet.
Population: 3,003 (2000); Race: 98.3% White, 0.0% Black, 0.1% Asian, 0.7% Hispanic of any race (2000); Density: 180.6 persons per square mile (2000); Age: 26.8% under 18, 14.8% over 64 (2000); Marriage status: 19.7% never married, 61.8% now married, 9.3% widowed, 9.2% divorced (2000); Foreign born: 2.0% (2000); Ancestry (includes multiple ancestries): 33.8% Irish, 19.1% German, 17.5% Italian, 13.7% English, 5.8% Polish (2000).
Economy: Employment by occupation: 9.8% management, 21.0% professional, 14.4% services, 25.8% sales, 2.3% farming, 18.4% construction, 8.3% production (2000).
Income: Per capita income: $25,267 (2000); Median household income: $44,792 (2000); Poverty rate: 5.3% (2000).
Education: Percent of population age 25 and over with: High school diploma (including GED) or higher: 82.3% (2000); Bachelor's degree or higher: 17.8% (2000).

School District(s)
Eagleswood Township (PK-06)
   2003-04 Enrollment: 178 . . . . (609) 597-3663
Housing: Homeownership rate: 83.1% (2000); Median home value: $128,600 (2000); Median rent: $317 per month (2000); Median age of housing: 26 years (2000).
Transportation: Commute to work: 94.2% car, 0.4% public transportation, 0.8% walk, 4.2% work from home (2000); Travel time to work: 30.4% less than 15 minutes, 30.6% 15 to 30 minutes, 15.9% 30 to 45 minutes, 12.2% 45 to 60 minutes, 10.9% 60 minutes or more (2000)

WHITING (unincorporated postal area, zip code 08759). Aka Whitings. Covers a land area of 23.382 square miles and a water area of 0.056 square miles. Located at 39.94° N. Lat.; 74.36° W. Long. Elevation is 173 feet.
Population: 17,417 (2000); Race: 98.0% White, 0.7% Black, 0.2% Asian, 2.0% Hispanic of any race (2000); Density: 744.9 persons per square mile (2000); Age: 4.2% under 18, 72.2% over 64 (2000); Marriage status: 9.5% never married, 55.5% now married, 28.5% widowed, 6.5% divorced (2000); Foreign born: 9.8% (2000); Ancestry (includes multiple ancestries): 21.0% Irish, 20.4% German, 18.3% Italian, 11.8% English, 7.7% Polish (2000).
Economy: Employment by occupation: 9.8% management, 18.8% professional, 19.3% services, 27.6% sales, 0.3% farming, 9.9% construction, 14.2% production (2000).
Income: Per capita income: $22,538 (2000); Median household income: $23,914 (2000); Poverty rate: 6.0% (2000).
Education: Percent of population age 25 and over with: High school diploma (including GED) or higher: 68.5% (2000); Bachelor's degree or higher: 10.1% (2000).

School District(s)
Manchester Township (PK-12)
   2003-04 Enrollment: 3,580 . . . . (732) 350-5900
Housing: Homeownership rate: 93.7% (2000); Median home value: $58,300 (2000); Median rent: $1,255 per month (2000); Median age of housing: 23 years (2000).
Transportation: Commute to work: 94.6% car, 1.1% public transportation, 1.7% walk, 1.3% work from home (2000); Travel time to work: 19.7% less than 15 minutes, 28.9% 15 to 30 minutes, 19.9% 30 to 45 minutes, 14.4% 45 to 60 minutes, 17.1% 60 minutes or more (2000)
Additional Information Contacts

Greater Lacey Township Chamber of Commerce . . . . (609) 693-8312
http://www.laceybusiness.com

Passaic County

Located in northern New Jersey; bounded on the north by New York; includes part of the Ramapo Mountains, and Greenwood Lake. Covers a land area of 185.29 square miles, a water area of 11.76 square miles, and is located in the Eastern Time Zone. The county government was organized in 1837. County seat is Paterson.

Passaic County is part of the New York-Northern New Jersey-Long Island, NY-NJ-PA Metropolitan Statistical Area. The entire metro area includes: Edison, NJ Metropolitan Division (Middlesex County, NJ; Monmouth County, NJ; Ocean County, NJ; Somerset County, NJ); Nassau-Suffolk, NY Metropolitan Division (Nassau County, NY; Suffolk County, NY); New York-White Plains-Wayne, NY-NJ Metropolitan Division (Bergen County, NJ; Hudson County, NJ; Passaic County, NJ; Bronx County, NY; Kings County, NY; New York County, NY; Putnam County, NY; Queens County, NY; Richmond County, NY; Rockland County, NY; Westchester County, NY); Newark-Union, NJ-PA Metropolitan Division (Essex County, NJ; Hunterdon County, NJ; Morris County, NJ; Sussex County, NJ; Union County, NJ; Pike County, PA)

Weather Station: Charlotteburg Reservoir									Elevation: 757 feet		
	Jan	Feb	Mar	Apr	May	Jun	Jul	Aug	Sep	Oct	Nov	Dec
High	35	38	47	58	69	77	83	81	73	63	51	40
Low	16	17	26	35	45	54	59	57	49	38	31	22
Precip	4.2	3.4	4.6	4.6	4.8	4.4	4.6	4.6	5.1	4.4	4.7	4.0
Snow	10.2	9.7	7.1	1.9	tr	0.0	0.0	0.0	0.0	0.1	0.9	4.6

High and Low temperatures in degrees Fahrenheit; Precipitation and Snow in inches

Weather Station: Little Falls									Elevation: 147 feet		
	Jan	Feb	Mar	Apr	May	Jun	Jul	Aug	Sep	Oct	Nov	Dec
High	38	41	49	61	72	80	86	84	76	65	54	43
Low	20	22	30	40	50	59	65	63	55	42	35	26
Precip	4.1	3.1	4.3	4.4	4.9	4.4	4.4	4.5	5.2	4.0	4.4	3.8
Snow	na	na	2.3	tr	0.0	0.0	0.0	0.0	0.0	0.0	tr	na

High and Low temperatures in degrees Fahrenheit; Precipitation and Snow in inches

Population: 453,380 (1990); 489,049 (2000); 501,734 (2005); 514,883 (2010 projected); Race: 60.1% White, 12.9% Black, 3.8% Asian, 33.6% Hispanic of any race (2005); Density: 2,707.8 persons per square mile (2005); Average household size: 3.02 (2005); Median age: 35.6 (2005); Males per 100 females: 94.7 (2005).
Religion: Five largest groups: 32.8% Catholic Church, 4.6% Muslim Estimate, 3.5% Jewish Estimate, 1.1% Assemblies of God, 0.9% American Baptist Churches in the USA (2000).
Economy: Unemployment rate: 5.4% (2005); Total civilian labor force: 236,900 (2005); Leading industries: 14.9% retail trade; 14.6% manufacturing; 13.5% health care and social assistance (2004); Farms: 70 totaling 1,526 acres (2002); Companies that employ 500 or more persons: 73 (2004); Companies that employ 100 to 499 persons: 499 (2004); Companies that employ less than 100 persons: 24,359 (2004); Black-owned businesses: 1,833 (2002); Hispanic-owned businesses: 6,921 (2002); Asian-owned businesses: 2,261 (2002); Women-owned businesses: 10,375 (2002); Retail sales per capita: $15,492 (2006). Single-family building permits issued: 230 (2005); Multi-family building permits issued: 417 (2005).
Income: Per capita income: $23,985 (2005); Median household income: $54,993 (2005); Average household income: $71,519 (2005); Percent of households with income of $100,000 or more: 22.4% (2005); Poverty rate: 12.6% (2003); Bankruptcy rate: 5.12% (2005).
Taxes: Total county taxes per capita: $362 (2004); County property taxes per capita: $362 (2004).
Education: Percent of population age 25 and over with: High school diploma (including GED) or higher: 73.1% (2005); Bachelor's degree or higher: 21.0% (2005); Master's degree or higher: 7.0% (2005).
Housing: Homeownership rate: 56.1% (2005); Median home value: $292,669 (2005); Median rent: $653 per month (2000); Median age of housing: 46 years (2000).
Health: Birth rate: 172.8 per 10,000 population (2004); Death rate: 84.7 per 10,000 population (2004); Age-adjusted cancer mortality rate: 193.2 deaths per 100,000 population (2002); Air Quality Index: 81.3% good, 15.2% moderate, 3.5% unhealthy for sensitive individuals, 0.0% unhealthy (percent of days in 2005); Number of physicians: 22.2 per 10,000

population (2004); Hospital beds: 29.9 per 10,000 population (2003); Hospital admissions: 1,009.1 per 10,000 population (2003).
Elections: 2004 Presidential election results: 43.9% Bush, 55.4% Kerry, 0.5% Nader, 0.1% Badnarik
National and State Parks: Abram S Hewitt State Forest; Norvin Green State Forest; Ringwood Manor State Park; Rough Mountain State Forest; Wawayanda State Park
Additional Information Contacts
Passaic County Government . . . . (973) 881-4402
http://www.passaiccountynj.org
Borough of Hawthorne . . . . (973) 427-5555
http://www.hawthornenj.org
Borough of Ringwood . . . . (973) 962-7037
http://www.ringwoodnj.net
Borough of West Paterson . . . . (973) 345-8100
http://www.westpaterson.com
City of Passaic . . . . (973) 365-5500
http://www.cityofpassaic.com
City of Paterson . . . . (973) 321-1310
http://www.patcity.com
Hawthorne Chamber of Commerce . . . . (973) 427-5078
http://www.hawthornechamber.com
North Jersey Regional Chamber of Commerce . . . . (973) 226-5500
http://www.njrcc.org
North Jersey Regional Chamber of Commerce . . . . (973) 470-9300
http://www.njrcc.org
Paterson Chamber of Commerce . . . . (973) 881-7300
http://www.greaterpatersoncc.org
Pompton Lakes Chamber of Commerce . . . . (973) 839-0187
http://www.pomptonlakes.org
Ringwood Chamber of Commerce . . . . (973) 835-7998
http://ringwoodchamber.com
Wayne Township . . . . (973) 694-1800
http://www.waynetownship.com
West Milford Chamber of Commerce. . . . . (973) 728-3150
http://www.westmilford.com
West Milford Township. . . . . (973) 728-7000
http://www.westmilford.org

Passaic County Communities

BLOOMINGDALE (borough). Covers a land area of 8.801 square miles and a water area of 0.409 square miles. Located at 41.01° N. Lat.; 74.33° W. Long. Elevation is 280 feet.
History: Incorporated 1918.
Population: 7,530 (1990); 7,610 (2000); 7,737 (2005); 7,894 (2010 projected); Race: 94.8% White, 0.4% Black, 2.5% Asian, 5.2% Hispanic of any race (2005); Density: 879.1 persons per square mile (2005); Average household size: 2.65 (2005); Median age: 39.5 (2005); Males per 100 females: 97.1 (2005); Marriage status: 22.7% never married, 63.2% now married, 7.4% widowed, 6.7% divorced (2000); Foreign born: 10.1% (2000); Ancestry (includes multiple ancestries): 27.3% Italian, 26.7% Irish, 19.8% German, 11.5% Polish, 8.0% English (2000).
Economy: Residential. Single-family building permits issued: 2 (2005); Multi-family building permits issued: 0 (2005); Employment by occupation: 14.3% management, 23.1% professional, 13.4% services, 28.2% sales, 0.0% farming, 7.4% construction, 13.6% production (2000).
Income: Per capita income: $31,231 (2005); Median household income: $72,533 (2005); Average household income: $82,294 (2005); Percent of households with income of $100,000 or more: 28.0% (2005); Poverty rate: 3.4% (2000).
Education: Percent of population age 25 and over with: High school diploma (including GED) or higher: 87.8% (2005); Bachelor's degree or higher: 25.7% (2005); Master's degree or higher: 7.7% (2005).
School District(s)
Bloomingdale Borough (PK-08)
    2003-04 Enrollment: 725 . . . . (973) 838-3282
Housing: Homeownership rate: 74.2% (2005); Median home value: $277,174 (2005); Median rent: $868 per month (2000); Median age of housing: 40 years (2000).
Safety: Violent crime rate: 3.9 per 10,000 population; Property crime rate: 117.5 per 10,000 population (2004).
Transportation: Commute to work: 92.6% car, 3.4% public transportation, 1.6% walk, 2.2% work from home (2000); Travel time to work: 19.2% less

than 15 minutes, 34.4% 15 to 30 minutes, 27.4% 30 to 45 minutes, 9.7% 45 to 60 minutes, 9.2% 60 minutes or more (2000)

Additional Information Contacts
Tri-County Chamber of Commerce . . . . (973) 831-7788
http://www.tricounty.org

CLIFTON (city).
Covers a land area of 11.295 square miles and a water area of 0.104 square miles. Located at 40.86° N. Lat.; 74.15° W. Long. Elevation is 233 feet.

History: Named for the cliffs in the area. Settled 1685 and incorporated 1917

Population: 70,869 (1990); 78,672 (2000); 79,679 (2005); 80,742 (2010 projected); Race: 70.8% White, 3.6% Black, 7.2% Asian, 26.0% Hispanic of any race (2005); Density: 7,054.4 persons per square mile (2005); Average household size: 2.64 (2005); Median age: 39.8 (2005); Males per 100 females: 92.2 (2005); Marriage status: 26.9% never married, 56.0% now married, 9.7% widowed, 7.5% divorced (2000); Foreign born: 29.2% (2000); Ancestry (includes multiple ancestries): 29.7% Other groups, 19.2% Italian, 14.6% Polish, 9.8% Irish, 8.7% German (2000).

Economy: Steel, textile equipment, chemical, plastics, clothing, and electronic industries. Unemployment rate: 4.6% (2005); Total civilian labor force: 40,302 (2005); Single-family building permits issued: 28 (2005); Multi-family building permits issued: 94 (2005); Employment by occupation: 12.7% management, 19.6% professional, 11.7% services, 30.9% sales, 0.0% farming, 8.4% construction, 16.6% production (2000).

Income: Per capita income: $26,365 (2005); Median household income: $56,303 (2005); Average household income: $69,239 (2005); Percent of households with income of $100,000 or more: 21.1% (2005); Poverty rate: 6.3% (2000).

Taxes: Total city taxes per capita: $609 (2004); City property taxes per capita: $586 (2004).

Education: Percent of population age 25 and over with: High school diploma (including GED) or higher: 78.6% (2005); Bachelor's degree or higher: 23.8% (2005); Master's degree or higher: 7.5% (2005).

School District(s)
Agency - Classical Academy CS of Clifton (06-08)
    2003-04 Enrollment: 101 . . . . (973) 278-7707
Clifton City (PK-12)
    2003-04 Enrollment: 10,984 . . . . (973) 470-2260
Essex County Ed Serv Comm (UG-UG)
    2003-04 Enrollment: 270 . . . . (973) 239-1511
Passaic County Ed Serv Comm (UG-UG)
    2003-04 Enrollment: 451 . . . . (973) 614-8585

Two-year College(s)
Capri Institute of Hair Design (Private, For-profit)
    Fall 2004 Enrollment: 151 . . . . (800) 232-2774
Harrison Career Institute-Clifton (Private, For-profit)
    Fall 2004 Enrollment: 156 . . . . (973) 253-0444
Keyskills Learning
    Fall 2004 Enrollment: 78 . . . . (973) 778-8136

Housing: Homeownership rate: 60.7% (2005); Median home value: $285,091 (2005); Median rent: $705 per month (2000); Median age of housing: 50 years (2000).

Safety: Violent crime rate: 28.9 per 10,000 population; Property crime rate: 261.1 per 10,000 population (2004).

Newspapers: Clifton Journal (General - Circulation 35,000); North Jersey Prospector (General - Circulation 63,000); Post Eagle (General - Circulation 16,000); Su Guia (Hispanic - Circulation 15,000); The Beacon (Catholic, Religious - Circulation 33,519)

Transportation: Commute to work: 88.6% car, 6.6% public transportation, 2.1% walk, 2.0% work from home (2000); Travel time to work: 27.9% less than 15 minutes, 39.8% 15 to 30 minutes, 19.1% 30 to 45 minutes, 6.1% 45 to 60 minutes, 7.1% 60 minutes or more (2000)

Additional Information Contacts
North Jersey Regional Chamber of Commerce . . . . (973) 470-9300
http://www.njrcc.org

HALEDON (borough).
Covers a land area of 1.160 square miles and a water area of <.001 square miles. Located at 40.93° N. Lat.; 74.18° W. Long. Elevation is 300 feet.

History: Incorporated 1908.

Population: 6,951 (1990); 8,252 (2000); 8,524 (2005); 8,817 (2010 projected); Race: 67.2% White, 8.5% Black, 5.6% Asian, 29.5% Hispanic of any race (2005); Density: 7,345.8 persons per square mile (2005); Average household size: 3.03 (2005); Median age: 35.8 (2005); Males per 100

females: 89.8 (2005); Marriage status: 31.0% never married, 54.2% now married, 7.8% widowed, 7.0% divorced (2000); Foreign born: 26.1% (2000); Ancestry (includes multiple ancestries): 35.4% Other groups, 18.6% Italian, 9.6% Irish, 8.8% German, 6.4% Dutch (2000).

Economy: Manufacturing: textiles, pharmaceuticals. Single-family building permits issued: 5 (2005); Multi-family building permits issued: 4 (2005); Employment by occupation: 11.7% management, 16.3% professional, 14.7% services, 31.0% sales, 0.0% farming, 9.6% construction, 16.7% production (2000).

Income: Per capita income: $20,661 (2005); Median household income: $49,675 (2005); Average household income: $61,342 (2005); Percent of households with income of $100,000 or more: 15.7% (2005); Poverty rate: 10.6% (2000).

Education: Percent of population age 25 and over with: High school diploma (including GED) or higher: 77.4% (2005); Bachelor's degree or higher: 18.4% (2005); Master's degree or higher: 6.1% (2005).

School District(s)
Haledon Borough (PK-08)
    2003-04 Enrollment: 1,033 . . . . (973) 790-9087
Passaic County Manchester Regional (09-12)
    2003-04 Enrollment: 788 . . . . (973) 956-2560

Housing: Homeownership rate: 49.8% (2005); Median home value: $271,373 (2005); Median rent: $735 per month (2000); Median age of housing: 54 years (2000).

Safety: Violent crime rate: 10.6 per 10,000 population; Property crime rate: 133.5 per 10,000 population (2004).

Transportation: Commute to work: 88.9% car, 3.5% public transportation, 4.3% walk, 2.3% work from home (2000); Travel time to work: 30.8% less than 15 minutes, 41.0% 15 to 30 minutes, 18.0% 30 to 45 minutes, 4.7% 45 to 60 minutes, 5.6% 60 minutes or more (2000)

Additional Information Contacts
North Essex Chamber of Commerce . . . . (973) 226-5500
http://www.northessexchamber.com

HASKELL (unincorporated postal area, zip code 07420).
Part of the Borough of Wanaque. Covers a land area of 2.550 square miles and a water area of 0.042 square miles. Located at 41.02° N. Lat.; 74.29° W. Long. Elevation is 220 feet.

Population: 4,767 (2000); Race: 89.7% White, 0.0% Black, 2.8% Asian, 7.3% Hispanic of any race (2000); Density: 1,869.5 persons per square mile (2000); Age: 25.3% under 18, 15.1% over 64 (2000); Marriage status: 22.9% never married, 59.6% now married, 7.3% widowed, 10.2% divorced (2000); Foreign born: 12.3% (2000); Ancestry (includes multiple ancestries): 23.4% German, 21.5% Italian, 16.0% Irish, 13.3% Other groups, 8.1% Dutch (2000).

Economy: Employment by occupation: 12.4% management, 13.1% professional, 19.6% services, 30.0% sales, 0.0% farming, 10.5% construction, 14.4% production (2000).

Income: Per capita income: $20,891 (2000); Median household income: $60,428 (2000); Poverty rate: 3.6% (2000).

Education: Percent of population age 25 and over with: High school diploma (including GED) or higher: 78.9% (2000); Bachelor's degree or higher: 14.8% (2000).

School District(s)
Wanaque Borough (PK-08)
    2003-04 Enrollment: 1,069 . . . . (973) 835-8202

Housing: Homeownership rate: 79.3% (2000); Median home value: $144,600 (2000); Median rent: $855 per month (2000); Median age of housing: 46 years (2000).

Transportation: Commute to work: 92.1% car, 2.2% public transportation, 2.8% walk, 2.9% work from home (2000); Travel time to work: 21.2% less than 15 minutes, 40.9% 15 to 30 minutes, 25.2% 30 to 45 minutes, 4.4% 45 to 60 minutes, 8.4% 60 minutes or more (2000)

HAWTHORNE (borough).
Covers a land area of 3.396 square miles and a water area of 0.022 square miles. Located at 40.95° N. Lat.; 74.15° W. Long. Elevation is 100 feet.

History: Named for Nathaniel Hawthorne, 19th century American novelist. Settled 1850. Incorporated 1898.

Population: 17,084 (1990); 18,218 (2000); 18,378 (2005); 18,581 (2010 projected); Race: 92.4% White, 0.9% Black, 2.1% Asian, 9.8% Hispanic of any race (2005); Density: 5,412.0 persons per square mile (2005); Average household size: 2.53 (2005); Median age: 39.3 (2005); Males per 100 females: 92.1 (2005); Marriage status: 24.9% never married, 57.9% now married, 8.9% widowed, 8.3% divorced (2000); Foreign born: 13.9%

(2000); Ancestry (includes multiple ancestries): 33.5% Italian, 17.9% Irish, 14.7% German, 13.1% Other groups, 11.1% Dutch (2000).

Economy: Residential suburb, with some light manufacturing. Single-family building permits issued: 1 (2005); Multi-family building permits issued: 16 (2005); Employment by occupation: 15.7% management, 20.2% professional, 14.4% services, 32.1% sales, 0.1% farming, 8.6% construction, 8.9% production (2000).

Income: Per capita income: $31,057 (2005); Median household income: $62,678 (2005); Average household income: $78,307 (2005); Percent of households with income of $100,000 or more: 23.8% (2005); Poverty rate: 3.4% (2000).

Taxes: Total city taxes per capita: $602 (2004); City property taxes per capita: $568 (2004).

Education: Percent of population age 25 and over with: High school diploma (including GED) or higher: 84.1% (2005); Bachelor's degree or higher: 25.5% (2005); Master's degree or higher: 7.9% (2005).

School District(s)

Hawthorne Borough (PK-12)
 2003-04 Enrollment: 2,345 . . . . (973) 423-6401

Two-year College(s)

Roman Academy of Beauty Culture (Private, For-profit)
 Fall 2004 Enrollment: 178 . . . . (973) 423-2223

Housing: Homeownership rate: 65.2% (2005); Median home value: $326,189 (2005); Median rent: $860 per month (2000); Median age of housing: 51 years (2000).

Safety: Violent crime rate: 5.9 per 10,000 population; Property crime rate: 138.4 per 10,000 population (2004).

Newspapers: Hawthorne Press (General - Circulation 10,500)

Transportation: Commute to work: 92.0% car, 3.4% public transportation, 1.4% walk, 2.6% work from home (2000); Travel time to work: 33.8% less than 15 minutes, 35.3% 15 to 30 minutes, 17.8% 30 to 45 minutes, 5.8% 45 to 60 minutes, 7.3% 60 minutes or more (2000)

Additional Information Contacts

Borough of Hawthorne . . . . (973) 427-5555
 http://www.hawthornenj.org
Hawthorne Chamber of Commerce . . . . (973) 427-5078
 http://www.hawthornechamber.com

HEWITT (unincorporated postal area, zip code 07421). Covers a land area of 25.348 square miles and a water area of 0.806 square miles. Located at 41.17° N. Lat.; 74.37° W. Long. Elevation is 420 feet.

Population: 7,639 (2000); Race: 95.2% White, 0.7% Black, 1.0% Asian, 3.9% Hispanic of any race (2000); Density: 301.4 persons per square mile (2000); Age: 28.7% under 18, 6.4% over 64 (2000); Marriage status: 22.7% never married, 64.4% now married, 3.8% widowed, 9.2% divorced (2000); Foreign born: 3.7% (2000); Ancestry (includes multiple ancestries): 26.6% Irish, 26.1% Italian, 25.8% German, 10.1% Polish, 8.8% English (2000).

Economy: Employment by occupation: 15.3% management, 17.0% professional, 11.7% services, 29.9% sales, 0.0% farming, 14.3% construction, 11.9% production (2000).

Income: Per capita income: $26,367 (2000); Median household income: $67,229 (2000); Poverty rate: 4.5% (2000).

Education: Percent of population age 25 and over with: High school diploma (including GED) or higher: 90.0% (2000); Bachelor's degree or higher: 22.5% (2000).

School District(s)

West Milford Township (PK-12)
 2003-04 Enrollment: 4,878 . . . . (973) 697-1700

Housing: Homeownership rate: 86.0% (2000); Median home value: $149,900 (2000); Median rent: $722 per month (2000); Median age of housing: 42 years (2000).

Newspapers: Journal America (General - Circulation 75,000)

Transportation: Commute to work: 92.8% car, 2.9% public transportation, 0.7% walk, 3.3% work from home (2000); Travel time to work: 12.1% less than 15 minutes, 12.4% 15 to 30 minutes, 28.0% 30 to 45 minutes, 23.5% 45 to 60 minutes, 24.0% 60 minutes or more (2000)

LITTLE FALLS (township). Aka Little Falls CDP. Covers a land area of 2.754 square miles and a water area of 0.075 square miles. Located at 40.88° N. Lat.; 74.22° W. Long. Elevation is 360 feet.

History: Named for the falls on the Passaic River. Settled 1711.

Population: 11,294 (1990); 10,855 (2000); 11,021 (2005); 11,231 (2010 projected); Race: 91.3% White, 0.5% Black, 4.7% Asian, 6.3% Hispanic of any race (2005); Density: 4,002.1 persons per square mile (2005); Average household size: 2.29 (2005); Median age: 42.1 (2005); Males per 100

females: 90.4 (2005); Marriage status: 26.9% never married, 55.3% now married, 8.8% widowed, 9.0% divorced (2000); Foreign born: 13.7% (2000); Ancestry (includes multiple ancestries): 34.6% Italian, 20.0% Irish, 12.3% German, 11.9% Other groups, 7.3% Polish (2000).

Economy: Large laundry plant. Manufacturing includes metal products, athletic goods, concrete products. Single-family building permits issued: 8 (2005); Multi-family building permits issued: 0 (2005); Employment by occupation: 20.1% management, 23.5% professional, 9.5% services, 32.4% sales, 0.0% farming, 6.3% construction, 8.1% production (2000).

Income: Per capita income: $37,229 (2005); Median household income: $68,200 (2005); Average household income: $85,120 (2005); Percent of households with income of $100,000 or more: 28.7% (2005); Poverty rate: 4.6% (2000).

Education: Percent of population age 25 and over with: High school diploma (including GED) or higher: 85.4% (2005); Bachelor's degree or higher: 34.9% (2005); Master's degree or higher: 12.4% (2005).

School District(s)

Little Falls Township (PK-08)
 2003-04 Enrollment: 896 . . . . (973) 256-1034
Passaic Valley Regional (09-12)
 2003-04 Enrollment: 1,260 . . . . (973) 890-2560

Housing: Homeownership rate: 69.8% (2005); Median home value: $322,432 (2005); Median rent: $837 per month (2000); Median age of housing: 44 years (2000).

Safety: Violent crime rate: 15.0 per 10,000 population; Property crime rate: 303.4 per 10,000 population (2004).

Transportation: Commute to work: 89.0% car, 6.5% public transportation, 1.6% walk, 1.9% work from home (2000); Travel time to work: 30.7% less than 15 minutes, 33.9% 15 to 30 minutes, 19.6% 30 to 45 minutes, 6.0% 45 to 60 minutes, 9.8% 60 minutes or more (2000)

Additional Information Contacts

North Jersey Regional Chamber of Commerce . . . . (973) 226-5500
 http://www.njrcc.org

NEWFOUNDLAND (unincorporated postal area, zip code 07435). Covers a land area of 9.561 square miles and a water area of 0.243 square miles. Located at 41.04° N. Lat.; 74.43° W. Long. Elevation is 760 feet.

Population: 2,155 (2000); Race: 95.0% White, 0.7% Black, 0.0% Asian, 2.3% Hispanic of any race (2000); Density: 225.4 persons per square mile (2000); Age: 22.6% under 18, 15.4% over 64 (2000); Marriage status: 24.3% never married, 64.6% now married, 6.1% widowed, 5.0% divorced (2000); Foreign born: 6.3% (2000); Ancestry (includes multiple ancestries): 30.8% German, 23.2% Irish, 21.4% Italian, 7.7% Dutch, 7.5% English (2000).

Economy: Employment by occupation: 18.2% management, 30.0% professional, 6.9% services, 24.3% sales, 0.0% farming, 10.8% construction, 9.7% production (2000).

Income: Per capita income: $34,274 (2000); Median household income: $79,762 (2000); Poverty rate: 3.0% (2000).

Education: Percent of population age 25 and over with: High school diploma (including GED) or higher: 94.4% (2000); Bachelor's degree or higher: 36.2% (2000).

Housing: Homeownership rate: 84.1% (2000); Median home value: $222,200 (2000); Median rent: $768 per month (2000); Median age of housing: 42 years (2000).

Newspapers: Aim Action News (General, Native American - Circulation 22,000)

Transportation: Commute to work: 90.9% car, 0.9% public transportation, 1.7% walk, 6.5% work from home (2000); Travel time to work: 18.3% less than 15 minutes, 23.0% 15 to 30 minutes, 32.0% 30 to 45 minutes, 16.0% 45 to 60 minutes, 10.7% 60 minutes or more (2000)

Additional Information Contacts

Jefferson Township Chamber of Commerce . . . . (973) 663-2240
 http://www.jeffersontownshipchamber.org

NORTH HALEDON (borough). Covers a land area of 3.443 square miles and a water area of 0.034 square miles. Located at 40.96° N. Lat.; 74.18° W. Long. Elevation is 250 feet.

History: Incorporated 1901.

Population: 8,106 (1990); 7,920 (2000); 8,806 (2005); 9,612 (2010 projected); Race: 94.7% White, 1.6% Black, 1.1% Asian, 4.0% Hispanic of any race (2005); Density: 2,557.9 persons per square mile (2005); Average household size: 3.05 (2005); Median age: 40.7 (2005); Males per 100 females: 89.2 (2005); Marriage status: 21.5% never married, 64.7% now married, 8.6% widowed, 5.1% divorced (2000); Foreign born: 13.4%

(2000); Ancestry (includes multiple ancestries): 33.5% Italian, 17.6% Dutch, 15.1% German, 10.8% Other groups, 10.3% Irish (2000).
Economy: Single-family building permits issued: 11 (2005); Multi-family building permits issued: 0 (2005); Employment by occupation: 16.6% management, 26.4% professional, 17.1% services, 23.6% sales, 0.2% farming, 9.4% construction, 6.7% production (2000).
Income: Per capita income: $36,173 (2005); Median household income: $87,103 (2005); Average household income: $106,107 (2005); Percent of households with income of $100,000 or more: 41.0% (2005); Poverty rate: 4.0% (2000).
Education: Percent of population age 25 and over with: High school diploma (including GED) or higher: 88.0% (2005); Bachelor's degree or higher: 33.5% (2005); Master's degree or higher: 9.7% (2005).

School District(s)
North Haledon Borough (PK-08)
   2003-04 Enrollment: 643 . . . . (973) 427-8993
Housing: Homeownership rate: 89.0% (2005); Median home value: $374,272 (2005); Median rent: $849 per month (2000); Median age of housing: 43 years (2000).
Safety: Violent crime rate: 7.1 per 10,000 population; Property crime rate: 97.6 per 10,000 population (2004).
Transportation: Commute to work: 89.5% car, 0.8% public transportation, 6.9% walk, 2.3% work from home (2000); Travel time to work: 33.4% less than 15 minutes, 38.1% 15 to 30 minutes, 16.4% 30 to 45 minutes, 7.1% 45 to 60 minutes, 5.0% 60 minutes or more (2000)

OAK RIDGE (unincorporated postal area, zip code 07438). Covers a land area of 32.031 square miles and a water area of 1.053 square miles. Located at 41.03° N. Lat.; 74.50° W. Long. Elevation is 900 feet.
Population: 11,901 (2000); Race: 96.8% White, 0.7% Black, 0.6% Asian, 2.8% Hispanic of any race (2000); Density: 371.5 persons per square mile (2000); Age: 28.1% under 18, 8.2% over 64 (2000); Marriage status: 18.4% never married, 69.1% now married, 4.3% widowed, 8.2% divorced (2000); Foreign born: 7.4% (2000); Ancestry (includes multiple ancestries): 26.8% Italian, 24.0% German, 19.7% Irish, 10.3% English, 10.1% Polish (2000).
Economy: Employment by occupation: 19.1% management, 19.2% professional, 10.6% services, 30.2% sales, 0.0% farming, 11.7% construction, 9.2% production (2000).
Income: Per capita income: $29,541 (2000); Median household income: $75,813 (2000); Poverty rate: 2.4% (2000).
Education: Percent of population age 25 and over with: High school diploma (including GED) or higher: 90.8% (2000); Bachelor's degree or higher: 30.1% (2000).

School District(s)
Jefferson Township (PK-12)
   2003-04 Enrollment: 3,694 . . . . (973) 663-5780
West Milford Township (PK-12)
   2003-04 Enrollment: 4,878 . . . . (973) 697-1700
Housing: Homeownership rate: 90.6% (2000); Median home value: $197,000 (2000); Median rent: $717 per month (2000); Median age of housing: 31 years (2000).
Transportation: Commute to work: 94.7% car, 1.9% public transportation, 0.7% walk, 1.9% work from home (2000); Travel time to work: 15.5% less than 15 minutes, 17.9% 15 to 30 minutes, 28.0% 30 to 45 minutes, 20.7% 45 to 60 minutes, 17.9% 60 minutes or more (2000)
Additional Information Contacts
Jefferson Township Chamber of Commerce . . . . (973) 663-2240
   http://www.jeffersontownshipchamber.org

PASSAIC (city). Covers a land area of 3.112 square miles and a water area of 0.100 square miles. Located at 40.85° N. Lat.; 74.12° W. Long. Elevation is 115 feet.
History: Named for the Delaware Indian translation of "peace" or "valley". Dutch traders were the first settlers of Passaic ("peaceful valley"). In 1678, Hartman Micheilsen established a fur trading post. Dutch, Irish and German families settled to farm the land. Slavic immigrants followed, attracted by rising industry. In 1854 the town's name was changed to Passaic, after the river around which its life centered. It was chartered as a city in 1873.
Population: 58,914 (1990); 67,861 (2000); 68,690 (2005); 69,648 (2010 projected); Race: 32.7% White, 12.3% Black, 4.6% Asian, 69.0% Hispanic of any race (2005); Density: 22,071.1 persons per square mile (2005); Average household size: 3.59 (2005); Median age: 29.3 (2005); Males per 100 females: 100.0 (2005); Marriage status: 38.3% never married, 48.9% now married, 5.8% widowed, 7.0% divorced (2000); Foreign born: 45.8%

(2000); Ancestry (includes multiple ancestries): 73.0% Other groups, 3.5% Polish, 2.6% Italian, 2.3% United States or American, 1.1% Irish (2000).
Economy: Unemployment rate: 6.8% (2005); Total civilian labor force: 28,204 (2005); Single-family building permits issued: 8 (2005); Multi-family building permits issued: 45 (2005); Employment by occupation: 6.4% management, 11.6% professional, 17.4% services, 23.6% sales, 0.3% farming, 7.2% construction, 33.5% production (2000).
Income: Per capita income: $13,390 (2005); Median household income: $35,964 (2005); Average household income: $47,242 (2005); Percent of households with income of $100,000 or more: 8.4% (2005); Poverty rate: 21.2% (2000).
Taxes: Total city taxes per capita: $550 (2004); City property taxes per capita: $535 (2004).
Education: Percent of population age 25 and over with: High school diploma (including GED) or higher: 54.8% (2005); Bachelor's degree or higher: 13.1% (2005); Master's degree or higher: 4.9% (2005).

School District(s)
Passaic City (PK-12)
   2003-04 Enrollment: 12,162 . . . . (973) 470-5201
Passaic County Ed Serv Comm (UG-UG)
   2003-04 Enrollment: 451 . . . . (973) 614-8585
Housing: Homeownership rate: 26.8% (2005); Median home value: $247,458 (2005); Median rent: $587 per month (2000); Median age of housing: 55 years (2000).
Hospitals: General Hospital Center at Passaic (303 beds); Passaic Beth Israel Hospital (223 beds); St. Mary's Hospital (226 beds)
Safety: Violent crime rate: 99.0 per 10,000 population; Property crime rate: 291.9 per 10,000 population (2004).
Newspapers: Slovak Catholic Falcon (Catholic, Religious - Circulation 12,000)
Transportation: Commute to work: 66.3% car, 18.7% public transportation, 9.8% walk, 1.4% work from home (2000); Travel time to work: 22.8% less than 15 minutes, 38.6% 15 to 30 minutes, 22.8% 30 to 45 minutes, 6.7% 45 to 60 minutes, 9.1% 60 minutes or more (2000)
Additional Information Contacts
City of Passaic . . . . (973) 365-5500
   http://www.cityofpassaic.com

PATERSON (city). Covers a land area of 8.442 square miles and a water area of 0.291 square miles. Located at 40.91° N. Lat.; 74.16° W. Long. Elevation is 70 feet.
History: Named for William Paterson (1745-1806), attorney and legislator. Dutch settlers were early attracted to the great cataract on the Passaic and in 1679 they obtained the first tract of land within the present bounds of Paterson. In 1791, Alexander Hamilton, Secretary of the Treasury, helped form the Society for Establishing Useful Manufactures. Paterson grew out of the Society's 700 acres above and below the Passaic Falls and was named for William Paterson, the governor of New Jersey.
Population: 140,891 (1990); 149,222 (2000); 151,822 (2005); 154,698 (2010 projected); Race: 28.6% White, 32.1% Black, 1.9% Asian, 54.3% Hispanic of any race (2005); Density: 17,983.3 persons per square mile (2005); Average household size: 3.41 (2005); Median age: 31.1 (2005); Males per 100 females: 95.9 (2005); Marriage status: 39.3% never married, 46.3% now married, 6.1% widowed, 8.3% divorced (2000); Foreign born: 32.8% (2000); Ancestry (includes multiple ancestries): 69.4% Other groups, 4.7% Italian, 3.2% Jamaican, 3.2% United States or American, 1.6% Irish (2000).
Economy: Unemployment rate: 8.6% (2005); Total civilian labor force: 58,944 (2005); Single-family building permits issued: 0 (2005); Multi-family building permits issued: 0 (2005); Employment by occupation: 5.8% management, 10.9% professional, 20.2% services, 27.7% sales, 0.2% farming, 7.8% construction, 27.4% production (2000).
Income: Per capita income: $14,284 (2005); Median household income: $36,122 (2005); Average household income: $47,432 (2005); Percent of households with income of $100,000 or more: 9.3% (2005); Poverty rate: 22.2% (2000).
Taxes: Total city taxes per capita: $566 (2004); City property taxes per capita: $559 (2004).
Education: Percent of population age 25 and over with: High school diploma (including GED) or higher: 58.4% (2005); Bachelor's degree or higher: 8.1% (2005); Master's degree or higher: 2.8% (2005).

School District(s)
Agency - Great Falls CS
   2003-04 Enrollment: n/a . . . . (973) 587-6102

Agency - Paterson CS for Sci/Tech (06-09)
2003-04 Enrollment: 143 . . . . (973) 247-0600
Agency - Paterson CS for Urban Leadership (KG-04)
2003-04 Enrollment: n/a . . . . (973) 684-6591
Paterson City (PK-12)
2003-04 Enrollment: 27,734 . . . . (973) 321-0980

Two-year College(s)
Passaic County Community College (Public)
Fall 2004 Enrollment: 6,989 . . . . (973) 684-6800
2005-06 Tuition: In-state $2,748; Out-of-state $4,938
Housing: Homeownership rate: 31.4% (2005); Median home value: $237,361 (2005); Median rent: $611 per month (2000); Median age of housing: 50 years (2000).
Hospitals: Barnert Hospital (256 beds); St. Joseph's Regional Medical Center (700 beds)
Safety: Violent crime rate: 80.1 per 10,000 population; Property crime rate: 306.3 per 10,000 population (2004).
Transportation: Commute to work: 78.9% car, 12.2% public transportation, 5.9% walk, 1.0% work from home (2000); Travel time to work: 25.0% less than 15 minutes, 42.3% 15 to 30 minutes, 20.7% 30 to 45 minutes, 5.7% 45 to 60 minutes, 6.4% 60 minutes or more (2000)
Additional Information Contacts
City of Paterson . . . . (973) 321-1310
http://www.patcity.com
Paterson Chamber of Commerce . . . . (973) 881-7300
http://ww.greaterpatersoncc.org

POMPTON LAKES (borough). Covers a land area of 2.967 square miles and a water area of 0.189 square miles. Located at 41.00° N. Lat.; 74.28° W. Long. Elevation is 220 feet.
History: Named for several man-made lakes in the area. Settled 1682 by the Dutch. Several pre-Revolutionary houses remain. Incorporated 1895.
Population: 10,539 (1990); 10,640 (2000); 11,322 (2005); 11,980 (2010 projected); Race: 91.8% White, 1.4% Black, 3.4% Asian, 7.3% Hispanic of any race (2005); Density: 3,815.6 persons per square mile (2005); Average household size: 2.72 (2005); Median age: 38.2 (2005); Males per 100 females: 93.7 (2005); Marriage status: 24.7% never married, 58.0% now married, 8.3% widowed, 9.0% divorced (2000); Foreign born: 10.3% (2000); Ancestry (includes multiple ancestries): 26.5% Italian, 23.2% Irish, 20.6% German, 12.9% Other groups, 8.5% English (2000).
Economy: Manufacturing: ordnance and machinery. Single-family building permits issued: 1 (2005); Multi-family building permits issued: 0 (2005); Employment by occupation: 16.0% management, 23.1% professional, 11.4% services, 27.4% sales, 0.0% farming, 10.6% construction, 11.6% production (2000).
Income: Per capita income: $31,409 (2005); Median household income: $75,733 (2005); Average household income: $85,197 (2005); Percent of households with income of $100,000 or more: 31.3% (2005); Poverty rate: 3.2% (2000).
Education: Percent of population age 25 and over with: High school diploma (including GED) or higher: 88.6% (2005); Bachelor's degree or higher: 28.1% (2005); Master's degree or higher: 7.8% (2005).

School District(s)
Pompton Lakes Borough (PK-12)
2003-04 Enrollment: 1,910 . . . . (973) 835-4334

Two-year College(s)
Institute for Therapeutic Massage
Fall 2004 Enrollment: 171 . . . . (973) 839-6131
Housing: Homeownership rate: 76.7% (2005); Median home value: $283,645 (2005); Median rent: $836 per month (2000); Median age of housing: 43 years (2000).
Safety: Violent crime rate: 10.7 per 10,000 population; Property crime rate: 123.6 per 10,000 population (2004).
Transportation: Commute to work: 90.7% car, 5.0% public transportation, 1.6% walk, 1.9% work from home (2000); Travel time to work: 26.8% less than 15 minutes, 35.0% 15 to 30 minutes, 25.5% 30 to 45 minutes, 5.9% 45 to 60 minutes, 6.8% 60 minutes or more (2000)
Additional Information Contacts
Pompton Lakes Chamber of Commerce . . . . (973) 839-0187
http://www.pomptonlakes.org

PROSPECT PARK (borough). Covers a land area of 0.480 square miles and a water area of 0.002 square miles. Located at 40.93° N. Lat.; 74.17° W. Long. Elevation is 250 feet.
History: Incorporated 1901.

Population: 5,053 (1990); 5,779 (2000); 5,773 (2005); 5,792 (2010 projected); Race: 54.0% White, 16.2% Black, 3.1% Asian, 48.4% Hispanic of any race (2005); Density: 12,031.2 persons per square mile (2005); Average household size: 3.26 (2005); Median age: 31.7 (2005); Males per 100 females: 92.1 (2005); Marriage status: 31.4% never married, 56.1% now married, 5.0% widowed, 7.6% divorced (2000); Foreign born: 31.6% (2000); Ancestry (includes multiple ancestries): 51.3% Other groups, 9.1% Italian, 7.5% Dutch, 6.8% German, 5.4% Irish (2000).
Economy: Manufacturing: metal products, textiles. Single-family building permits issued: 2 (2005); Multi-family building permits issued: 0 (2005); Employment by occupation: 6.7% management, 15.5% professional, 17.5% services, 32.1% sales, 0.0% farming, 8.9% construction, 19.3% production (2000).
Income: Per capita income: $18,968 (2005); Median household income: $51,416 (2005); Average household income: $61,756 (2005); Percent of households with income of $100,000 or more: 13.8% (2005); Poverty rate: 10.0% (2000).
Education: Percent of population age 25 and over with: High school diploma (including GED) or higher: 68.2% (2005); Bachelor's degree or higher: 12.4% (2005); Master's degree or higher: 3.2% (2005).

School District(s)
Passaic County Ed Serv Comm (UG-UG)
2003-04 Enrollment: 451 . . . . (973) 614-8585
Prospect Park Borough (PK-08)
2003-04 Enrollment: 798 . . . . (973) 720-1992
Housing: Homeownership rate: 47.9% (2005); Median home value: $245,580 (2005); Median rent: $754 per month (2000); Median age of housing: 54 years (2000).
Safety: Violent crime rate: 18.9 per 10,000 population; Property crime rate: 233.2 per 10,000 population (2004).
Transportation: Commute to work: 89.1% car, 5.8% public transportation, 2.9% walk, 1.0% work from home (2000); Travel time to work: 28.2% less than 15 minutes, 43.2% 15 to 30 minutes, 19.5% 30 to 45 minutes, 4.1% 45 to 60 minutes, 5.0% 60 minutes or more (2000)

RINGWOOD (borough). Covers a land area of 25.249 square miles and a water area of 2.781 square miles. Located at 41.09° N. Lat.; 74.26° W. Long. Elevation is 470 feet.
History: Named for the Ringwood Company, producer of iron. Iron was found nearby in 1730; mines and works were developed from 1764 by Peter Hasenclever, who made Ringwood Manor his headquarters. His successor, Robert Erskine, produced munitions during the American Revolution. Presented to the state in 1936, the estate (95 acres 38 ha) became (1939) a park and the manor house was converted into a Museum. Ringwood Manor has been designated a national historic landmark.
Population: 12,623 (1990); 12,396 (2000); 12,829 (2005); 13,269 (2010 projected); Race: 93.5% White, 1.6% Black, 1.1% Asian, 5.2% Hispanic of any race (2005); Density: 508.1 persons per square mile (2005); Average household size: 2.98 (2005); Median age: 38.3 (2005); Males per 100 females: 100.3 (2005); Marriage status: 22.2% never married, 66.9% now married, 4.5% widowed, 6.3% divorced (2000); Foreign born: 8.7% (2000); Ancestry (includes multiple ancestries): 26.7% Italian, 25.1% Irish, 23.5% German, 8.8% Other groups, 8.3% English (2000).
Economy: Single-family building permits issued: 33 (2005); Multi-family building permits issued: 0 (2005); Employment by occupation: 17.8% management, 26.7% professional, 8.2% services, 28.4% sales, 0.0% farming, 10.8% construction, 8.0% production (2000).
Income: Per capita income: $37,128 (2005); Median household income: $92,905 (2005); Average household income: $110,076 (2005); Percent of households with income of $100,000 or more: 44.6% (2005); Poverty rate: 2.8% (2000).
Education: Percent of population age 25 and over with: High school diploma (including GED) or higher: 91.5% (2005); Bachelor's degree or higher: 39.2% (2005); Master's degree or higher: 11.8% (2005).

School District(s)
Passaic County Ed Serv Comm (UG-UG)
2003-04 Enrollment: 451 . . . . (973) 614-8585
Ringwood Borough (PK-08)
2003-04 Enrollment: 1,464 . . . . (973) 962-7028
Housing: Homeownership rate: 94.4% (2005); Median home value: $313,043 (2005); Median rent: $1,056 per month (2000); Median age of housing: 35 years (2000).
Safety: Violent crime rate: 7.0 per 10,000 population; Property crime rate: 61.0 per 10,000 population (2004).

Transportation: Commute to work: 92.9% car, 2.7% public transportation, 0.2% walk, 3.8% work from home (2000); Travel time to work: 13.4% less than 15 minutes, 23.3% 15 to 30 minutes, 35.1% 30 to 45 minutes, 14.1% 45 to 60 minutes, 14.2% 60 minutes or more (2000)

Additional Information Contacts
Borough of Ringwood . . . . (973) 962-7037
   http://www.ringwoodnj.net
Ringwood Chamber of Commerce. (973) 835-7998
   http://ringwoodchamber.com

TOTOWA (borough). Covers a land area of 3.997 square miles and a water area of 0.051 square miles. Located at 40.90° N. Lat.; 74.21° W. Long. Elevation is 200 feet.

History: Named for an Indian translation, whose meaning is uncertain. Incorporated 1898.

Population: 10,177 (1990); 9,892 (2000); 10,231 (2005); 10,591 (2010 projected); Race: 92.1% White, 1.3% Black, 2.4% Asian, 8.4% Hispanic of any race (2005); Density: 2,559.6 persons per square mile (2005); Average household size: 2.81 (2005); Median age: 43.6 (2005); Males per 100 females: 89.7 (2005); Marriage status: 27.2% never married, 57.2% now married, 9.7% widowed, 5.9% divorced (2000); Foreign born: 13.3% (2000); Ancestry (includes multiple ancestries): 44.5% Italian, 13.0% Irish, 11.3% German, 9.4% Other groups, 5.8% Polish (2000).

Economy: Diverse manufacturing. Single-family building permits issued: 47 (2005); Multi-family building permits issued: 0 (2005); Employment by occupation: 11.9% management, 15.0% professional, 14.2% services, 31.2% sales, 0.0% farming, 10.9% construction, 16.8% production (2000).

Income: Per capita income: $29,800 (2005); Median household income: $66,865 (2005); Average household income: $82,184 (2005); Percent of households with income of $100,000 or more: 28.4% (2005); Poverty rate: 4.1% (2000).

Education: Percent of population age 25 and over with: High school diploma (including GED) or higher: 73.7% (2005); Bachelor's degree or higher: 17.9% (2005); Master's degree or higher: 4.2% (2005).

School District(s)
Totowa Borough (PK-08)
   2003-04 Enrollment: 969 . . . . (973) 956-2125
Housing: Homeownership rate: 81.4% (2005); Median home value: $317,288 (2005); Median rent: $829 per month (2000); Median age of housing: 46 years (2000).

Safety: Violent crime rate: 10.9 per 10,000 population; Property crime rate: 312.9 per 10,000 population (2004).

Newspapers: The Italian Voice (La Voce Italiana) (Ethnic, General - Circulation 6,000)

Transportation: Commute to work: 90.7% car, 2.6% public transportation, 3.5% walk, 3.3% work from home (2000); Travel time to work: 39.1% less than 15 minutes, 40.4% 15 to 30 minutes, 10.9% 30 to 45 minutes, 4.5% 45 to 60 minutes, 5.1% 60 minutes or more (2000)

Additional Information Contacts
Tri-County Chamber of Commerce . . . . (973) 831-7788
   http://www.tricounty.org

WANAQUE (borough). Aka Wanaque-Midvale. Covers a land area of 7.978 square miles and a water area of 1.230 square miles. Located at 41.04° N. Lat.; 74.28° W. Long. Elevation is 240 feet.

History: Named for the Algonquian Indian translation of "place of sassafras". Incorporated 1918.

Population: 9,711 (1990); 10,266 (2000); 10,588 (2005); 10,926 (2010 projected); Race: 89.4% White, 1.6% Black, 3.8% Asian, 6.7% Hispanic of any race (2005); Density: 1,327.1 persons per square mile (2005); Average household size: 2.98 (2005); Median age: 39.2 (2005); Males per 100 females: 93.2 (2005); Marriage status: 24.3% never married, 61.3% now married, 6.4% widowed, 8.1% divorced (2000); Foreign born: 12.6% (2000); Ancestry (includes multiple ancestries): 25.7% Italian, 20.0% Irish, 18.9% German, 13.3% Other groups, 9.1% Polish (2000).

Economy: Includes manufacturing of candles, metal products and precision ceramics in villages of Haskell and Midvale. Single-family building permits issued: 0 (2005); Multi-family building permits issued: 227 (2005); Employment by occupation: 13.2% management, 18.1% professional, 15.9% services, 32.2% sales, 0.0% farming, 8.6% construction, 11.9% production (2000).

Income: Per capita income: $31,434 (2005); Median household income: $79,419 (2005); Average household income: $92,366 (2005); Percent of households with income of $100,000 or more: 33.9% (2005); Poverty rate: 3.3% (2000).

Education: Percent of population age 25 and over with: High school diploma (including GED) or higher: 84.4% (2005); Bachelor's degree or higher: 22.4% (2005); Master's degree or higher: 7.8% (2005).

School District(s)
Lakeland Regional (09-12)
   2003-04 Enrollment: 1,050 . . . . (973) 835-1900
Wanaque Borough (PK-08)
   2003-04 Enrollment: 1,069 . . . . (973) 835-8202
Housing: Homeownership rate: 80.1% (2005); Median home value: $278,366 (2005); Median rent: $843 per month (2000); Median age of housing: 41 years (2000).

Safety: Violent crime rate: 12.4 per 10,000 population; Property crime rate: 128.7 per 10,000 population (2004).

Transportation: Commute to work: 92.9% car, 2.8% public transportation, 2.1% walk, 2.1% work from home (2000); Travel time to work: 19.7% less than 15 minutes, 35.6% 15 to 30 minutes, 26.1% 30 to 45 minutes, 9.4% 45 to 60 minutes, 9.3% 60 minutes or more (2000)

WAYNE (township). Aka Wayne CDP. Covers a land area of 23.824 square miles and a water area of 1.365 square miles. Located at 40.94° N. Lat.; 74.25° W. Long. Elevation is 180 feet.

History: Named for General Anthony Wayne, Pennsylvania soldier and statesman. Incorporated 1847.

Population: 47,025 (1990); 54,069 (2000); 56,420 (2005); 58,773 (2010 projected); Race: 88.7% White, 1.9% Black, 6.3% Asian, 6.3% Hispanic of any race (2005); Density: 2,368.2 persons per square mile (2005); Average household size: 2.90 (2005); Median age: 40.5 (2005); Males per 100 females: 90.3 (2005); Marriage status: 23.3% never married, 61.9% now married, 8.8% widowed, 6.0% divorced (2000); Foreign born: 16.3% (2000); Ancestry (includes multiple ancestries): 29.9% Italian, 15.9% Irish, 14.7% Other groups, 12.9% German, 9.1% Polish (2000).

Economy: Industrial township. Leading products are: paper bags, sheet metal, munitions, lubricants, scales, household products, electrical parts, plastic laminates, navigation equipment, pharmaceuticals and security systems. Willowbrook, one of the largest shopping centers in the US, is here. Unemployment rate: 3.2% (2005); Total civilian labor force: 29,001 (2005); Single-family building permits issued: 24 (2005); Multi-family building permits issued: 0 (2005); Employment by occupation: 22.0% management, 25.3% professional, 9.7% services, 29.2% sales, 0.1% farming, 6.0% construction, 7.7% production (2000).

Income: Per capita income: $39,664 (2005); Median household income: $91,604 (2005); Average household income: $113,138 (2005); Percent of households with income of $100,000 or more: 45.1% (2005); Poverty rate: 2.8% (2000).

Taxes: Total city taxes per capita: $780 (2004); City property taxes per capita: $755 (2004).

Education: Percent of population age 25 and over with: High school diploma (including GED) or higher: 89.1% (2005); Bachelor's degree or higher: 41.6% (2005); Master's degree or higher: 15.4% (2005).

School District(s)
Passaic County Vocational (09-12)
   2003-04 Enrollment: 2,399 . . . . (973) 389-4202
Wayne Township (PK-12)
   2003-04 Enrollment: 9,097 . . . . (973) 633-3032
Four-year College(s)
William Paterson University of New Jersey (Public)
   Fall 2004 Enrollment: 11,409. . . . . (973) 720-2000
   2005-06 Tuition: In-state $8,740; Out-of-state $13,856
Two-year College(s)
Allied Medical and Technical Institute (Private, For-profit)
   Fall 2004 Enrollment: 141 . . . . (973) 837-1818
Berdan Institute (Private, For-profit)
   Fall 2004 Enrollment: 270 . . . . (973) 837-1818
   2005-06 Tuition: In-state $8,625; Out-of-state $8,625
Housing: Homeownership rate: 81.7% (2005); Median home value: $445,771 (2005); Median rent: $887 per month (2000); Median age of housing: 35 years (2000).

Hospitals: Wayne General Hospital (225 beds)

Safety: Violent crime rate: 5.8 per 10,000 population; Property crime rate: 232.3 per 10,000 population (2004).

Transportation: Commute to work: 89.4% car, 5.3% public transportation, 1.9% walk, 3.2% work from home (2000); Travel time to work: 25.6% less than 15 minutes, 32.8% 15 to 30 minutes, 21.4% 30 to 45 minutes, 8.6% 45 to 60 minutes, 11.5% 60 minutes or more (2000)

Additional Information Contacts

Tri-County Chamber of Commerce . . . . (973) 831-7788
　http://www.tricounty.org
Wayne Township . . . . (973) 694-1800
　http://www.waynetownship.com

WEST MILFORD (township). Aka West Milford CDP. Covers a land
area of 75.437 square miles and a water area of 4.971 square miles.
Located at 41.11° N. Lat.; 74.38° W. Long. Elevation is 710 feet.
Population: 25,631 (1990); 26,410 (2000); 28,568 (2005); 30,605 (2010
projected); Race: 94.5% White, 1.3% Black, 1.0% Asian, 4.1% Hispanic of
any race (2005); Density: 378.7 persons per square mile (2005); Average
household size: 2.85 (2005); Median age: 38.0 (2005); Males per 100
females: 99.8 (2005); Marriage status: 22.5% never married, 65.7% now
married, 5.0% widowed, 6.7% divorced (2000); Foreign born: 5.8% (2000);
Ancestry (includes multiple ancestries): 26.3% Italian, 25.4% Irish, 24.7%
German, 10.5% English, 9.7% Polish (2000).
Economy: Building supplies. Unemployment rate: 4.0% (2005); Total
civilian labor force: 16,008 (2005); Single-family building permits issued: 47
(2005); Multi-family building permits issued: 15 (2005); Employment by
occupation: 15.0% management, 20.2% professional, 10.8% services,
29.5% sales, 0.1% farming, 13.2% construction, 11.1% production (2000).
Income: Per capita income: $32,792 (2005); Median household income:
$82,500 (2005); Average household income: $92,701 (2005); Percent of
households with income of $100,000 or more: 36.7% (2005); Poverty rate:
4.1% (2000).
Taxes: Total city taxes per capita: $657 (2004); City property taxes per
capita: $635 (2004).
Education: Percent of population age 25 and over with: High school
diploma (including GED) or higher: 89.2% (2005); Bachelor's degree or
higher: 27.2% (2005); Master's degree or higher: 8.0% (2005).

School District(s)
West Milford Township (PK-12)
　2003-04 Enrollment: 4,878 . . . . (973) 697-1700
Housing: Homeownership rate: 89.6% (2005); Median home value:
$273,859 (2005); Median rent: $754 per month (2000); Median age of
housing: 37 years (2000).
Safety: Violent crime rate: 8.2 per 10,000 population; Property crime rate:
153.3 per 10,000 population (2004).
Transportation: Commute to work: 92.2% car, 2.2% public transportation,
1.4% walk, 4.0% work from home (2000); Travel time to work: 13.5% less
than 15 minutes, 17.8% 15 to 30 minutes, 30.5% 30 to 45 minutes, 20.4%
45 to 60 minutes, 17.7% 60 minutes or more (2000)
Additional Information Contacts
West Milford Chamber of Commerce. . . . . (973) 728-3150
　http://www.westmilford.com
West Milford Township. . . . . (973) 728-7000
　http://www.westmilford.org

WEST PATERSON (borough). Covers a land area of 2.957 square
miles and a water area of 0.135 square miles. Located at 40.89° N. Lat.;
74.19° W. Long. Elevation is 330 feet.
History: Named for William Paterson (1745-1806), attorney and legislator.
Incorporated 1914.
Population: 10,982 (1990); 10,987 (2000); 11,346 (2005); 11,724 (2010
projected); Race: 84.2% White, 3.8% Black, 4.2% Asian, 13.2% Hispanic of
any race (2005); Density: 3,836.9 persons per square mile (2005); Average
household size: 2.49 (2005); Median age: 39.3 (2005); Males per 100
females: 93.1 (2005); Marriage status: 27.4% never married, 58.3% now
married, 5.9% widowed, 8.4% divorced (2000); Foreign born: 21.0%
(2000); Ancestry (includes multiple ancestries): 40.5% Italian, 17.9% Other
groups, 15.4% Irish, 10.8% German, 7.0% Polish (2000).
Economy: Electric, electronic, and photographic products. Single-family
building permits issued: 13 (2005); Multi-family building permits issued: 16
(2005); Employment by occupation: 15.2% management, 24.3%
professional, 12.1% services, 28.6% sales, 0.0% farming, 7.3%
construction, 12.5% production (2000).
Income: Per capita income: $32,967 (2005); Median household income:
$68,138 (2005); Average household income: $81,734 (2005); Percent of
households with income of $100,000 or more: 28.2% (2005); Poverty rate:
3.4% (2000).
Education: Percent of population age 25 and over with: High school
diploma (including GED) or higher: 81.9% (2005); Bachelor's degree or
higher: 25.5% (2005); Master's degree or higher: 8.3% (2005).

School District(s)
West Paterson Borough (PK-08)
　2003-04 Enrollment: 959 . . . . (973) 278-5535
Four-year College(s)
Berkeley College (Private, For-profit)
　Fall 2004 Enrollment: 2,313 . . . . (973) 278-5400
　2005-06 Tuition: In-state $16,950; Out-of-state $16,950
Housing: Homeownership rate: 57.3% (2005); Median home value:
$324,188 (2005); Median rent: $785 per month (2000); Median age of
housing: 39 years (2000).
Safety: Violent crime rate: 22.9 per 10,000 population; Property crime rate:
208.2 per 10,000 population (2004).
Newspapers: The Herald News (Circulation 40,000); Today Newspaper
(General - Circulation 16,931)
Transportation: Commute to work: 92.4% car, 2.7% public transportation,
0.8% walk, 3.1% work from home (2000); Travel time to work: 30.5% less
than 15 minutes, 39.1% 15 to 30 minutes, 18.4% 30 to 45 minutes, 6.1%
45 to 60 minutes, 5.9% 60 minutes or more (2000)
Additional Information Contacts
Borough of West Paterson. . . . . (973) 345-8100
　http://www.westpaterson.com

Salem County

Located in southwestern New Jersey; bounded on the west and south by
the Delaware River and the Delaware border; drained by the Maurice and
Salem Rivers. Covers a land area of 337.88 square miles, a water area of
34.69 square miles, and is located in the Eastern Time Zone. The county
government was organized in 1694. County seat is Salem.

Salem County is part of the Philadelphia-Camden-Wilmington,
PA-NJ-DE-MD Metropolitan Statistical Area. The entire metro area
includes: Camden, NJ Metropolitan Division (Burlington County, NJ;
Camden County, NJ; Gloucester County, NJ); Philadelphia, PA
Metropolitan Division (Bucks County, PA; Chester County, PA; Delaware
County, PA; Montgomery County, PA; Philadelphia County, PA);
Wilmington, DE-MD-NJ Metropolitan Division (New Castle County, DE;
Cecil County, MD; Salem County, NJ)

Weather Station: Woodstown　　　　　　　　　Elevation: 49 feet

	Jan	Feb	Mar	Apr	May	Jun	Jul	Aug	Sep	Oct	Nov	Dec
High	41	44	54	65	76	84	88	86	79	68	57	46
Low	24	25	32	41	51	60	65	63	57	45	37	29
Precip	3.7	2.8	4.1	3.8	3.9	3.9	4.4	4.2	3.9	3.5	3.6	3.7
Snow	5.7	5.0	2.6	0.5	tr	0.0	0.0	0.0	0.0	0.1	0.3	2.3

High and Low temperatures in degrees Fahrenheit; Precipitation and Snow in inches

Population: 65,294 (1990); 64,285 (2000); 65,200 (2005); 66,137 (2010
projected); Race: 80.7% White, 15.0% Black, 0.7% Asian, 4.7% Hispanic of
any race (2005); Density: 193.0 persons per square mile (2005); Average
household size: 2.62 (2005); Median age: 38.8 (2005); Males per 100
females: 93.7 (2005).
Religion: Five largest groups: 11.7% Catholic Church, 6.8% The United
Methodist Church, 2.7% American Baptist Churches in the USA, 2.4%
Presbyterian Church (U.S.A.), 1.4% Episcopal Church (2000).
Economy: Unemployment rate: 4.8% (2005); Total civilian labor force:
31,383 (2005); Leading industries: 16.7% manufacturing; 13.8% retail
trade; 8.8% accommodation & food services (2004); Farms: 753 totaling
96,238 acres (2002); Companies that employ 500 or more persons: 9
(2004); Companies that employ 100 to 499 persons: 50 (2004); Companies
that employ less than 100 persons: 2,580 (2004); Black-owned businesses:
107 (2002); Hispanic-owned businesses: n/a (2002); Asian-owned
businesses: n/a (2002); Women-owned businesses: 1,270 (2002); Retail
sales per capita: $10,207 (2006). Single-family building permits issued: 285
(2005); Multi-family building permits issued: 12 (2005).
Income: Per capita income: $24,055 (2005); Median household income:
$51,026 (2005); Average household income: $62,025 (2005); Percent of
households with income of $100,000 or more: 16.2% (2005); Poverty rate:
9.3% (2003); Bankruptcy rate: 7.37% (2005).
Taxes: Total county taxes per capita: $542 (2004); County property taxes
per capita: $542 (2004).
Education: Percent of population age 25 and over with: High school
diploma (including GED) or higher: 79.5% (2005); Bachelor's degree or
higher: 15.3% (2005); Master's degree or higher: 4.0% (2005).

Housing: Homeownership rate: 73.3% (2005); Median home value: $165,450 (2005); Median rent: $516 per month (2000); Median age of housing: 42 years (2000).
Health: Birth rate: 107.5 per 10,000 population (2004); Death rate: 104.9 per 10,000 population (2004); Age-adjusted cancer mortality rate: 239.0 deaths per 100,000 population (2002); Number of physicians: 12.7 per 10,000 population (2004); Hospital beds: 17.0 per 10,000 population (2003); Hospital admissions: 791.4 per 10,000 population (2003).
Elections: 2004 Presidential election results: 52.8% Bush, 46.2% Kerry, 0.6% Nader, 0.3% Badnarik
National and State Parks: Fort Mott State Park; Killcohook National Wildlife Refuge; Parvin State Park; Supawna Meadows National Wildlife Refuge
Additional Information Contacts
Salem County Government . . . . (856) 935-7510
   http://www.salemco.org
Pennsville Township . . . . (856) 678-3089
   http://www.pennsville.org
Pittsgrove Township. . . . . (856) 358-2300
   http://www.pittsgrovetownship.com
Salem County Chamber of Commerce . . . . (856) 299-6699
   http://www.salemnjchamber.homestead.com
Salem County Chamber of Commerce . . . . (856) 935-7510
   http://www.salemnjchamber.homestead.com

Salem County Communities

ALLOWAY (township). Covers a land area of 32.845 square miles and a water area of 0.329 square miles. Located at 39.56° N. Lat.; 75.32° W. Long. Elevation is 41 feet.
Population: 2,795 (1990); 2,774 (2000); 2,881 (2005); 2,991 (2010 projected); Race: 91.1% White, 6.8% Black, 0.3% Asian, 2.9% Hispanic of any race (2005); Density: 87.7 persons per square mile (2005); Average household size: 2.88 (2005); Median age: 37.8 (2005); Males per 100 females: 103.2 (2005); Marriage status: 20.8% never married, 66.3% now married, 7.6% widowed, 5.2% divorced (2000); Foreign born: 1.7% (2000); Ancestry (includes multiple ancestries): 21.8% German, 16.5% Irish, 15.8% English, 13.6% Other groups, 9.4% Italian (2000).
Economy: Single-family building permits issued: 34 (2005); Multi-family building permits issued: 0 (2005); Employment by occupation: 12.8% management, 18.6% professional, 12.0% services, 23.4% sales, 1.8% farming, 16.4% construction, 15.0% production (2000).
Income: Per capita income: $26,344 (2005); Median household income: $63,985 (2005); Average household income: $75,347 (2005); Percent of households with income of $100,000 or more: 22.6% (2005); Poverty rate: 8.2% (2000).
Education: Percent of population age 25 and over with: High school diploma (including GED) or higher: 87.4% (2005); Bachelor's degree or higher: 20.5% (2005); Master's degree or higher: 6.6% (2005).
School District(s)
Alloway Township (PK-08)
   2003-04 Enrollment: 493 . . . . (856) 935-1622
Housing: Homeownership rate: 88.3% (2005); Median home value: $230,000 (2005); Median rent: $575 per month (2000); Median age of housing: 37 years (2000).
Transportation: Commute to work: 92.2% car, 0.5% public transportation, 2.1% walk, 4.5% work from home (2000); Travel time to work: 24.8% less than 15 minutes, 37.6% 15 to 30 minutes, 22.7% 30 to 45 minutes, 5.6% 45 to 60 minutes, 9.2% 60 minutes or more (2000)

ALLOWAY (CDP). Covers a land area of 6.968 square miles and a water area of 0.185 square miles. Located at 39.56° N. Lat.; 75.35° W. Long.
Population: 1,380 (1990); 1,128 (2000); 1,169 (2005); 1,212 (2010 projected); Race: 92.0% White, 5.8% Black, 0.0% Asian, 0.9% Hispanic of any race (2005); Density: 167.8 persons per square mile (2005); Average household size: 2.83 (2005); Median age: 38.2 (2005); Males per 100 females: 105.4 (2005); Marriage status: 22.3% never married, 61.7% now married, 10.5% widowed, 5.4% divorced (2000); Foreign born: 1.2% (2000); Ancestry (includes multiple ancestries): 28.9% German, 19.8% Irish, 17.1% English, 10.7% Italian, 7.5% Other groups (2000).
Economy: Employment by occupation: 11.9% management, 18.4% professional, 10.1% services, 23.1% sales, 1.3% farming, 18.2% construction, 16.9% production (2000).

Income: Per capita income: $26,729 (2005); Median household income: $62,781 (2005); Average household income: $75,042 (2005); Percent of households with income of $100,000 or more: 21.3% (2005); Poverty rate: 11.2% (2000).
Education: Percent of population age 25 and over with: High school diploma (including GED) or higher: 86.7% (2005); Bachelor's degree or higher: 22.9% (2005); Master's degree or higher: 7.7% (2005).
Housing: Homeownership rate: 86.4% (2005); Median home value: $204,245 (2005); Median rent: $525 per month (2000); Median age of housing: 48 years (2000).
Transportation: Commute to work: 85.4% car, 0.0% public transportation, 2.5% walk, 2.9% work from home (2000); Travel time to work: 30.8% less than 15 minutes, 28.5% 15 to 30 minutes, 27.5% 30 to 45 minutes, 5.3% 45 to 60 minutes, 7.9% 60 minutes or more (2000)

CARNEYS POINT (township). Covers a land area of 17.499 square miles and a water area of 0.252 square miles. Located at 39.70° N. Lat.; 75.46° W. Long. Elevation is 19 feet.
Population: 8,443 (1990); 7,684 (2000); 7,584 (2005); 7,488 (2010 projected); Race: 77.0% White, 17.0% Black, 1.0% Asian, 5.0% Hispanic of any race (2005); Density: 433.4 persons per square mile (2005); Average household size: 2.42 (2005); Median age: 39.6 (2005); Males per 100 females: 92.2 (2005); Marriage status: 26.2% never married, 54.1% now married, 9.5% widowed, 10.2% divorced (2000); Foreign born: 3.9% (2000); Ancestry (includes multiple ancestries): 20.1% Other groups, 18.3% German, 16.9% Irish, 15.8% Italian, 10.7% English (2000).
Economy: Increasingly suburbanized area. Single-family building permits issued: 33 (2005); Multi-family building permits issued: 10 (2005); Employment by occupation: 8.4% management, 16.9% professional, 14.0% services, 26.8% sales, 0.4% farming, 10.5% construction, 23.0% production (2000).
Income: Per capita income: $22,402 (2005); Median household income: $44,631 (2005); Average household income: $54,009 (2005); Percent of households with income of $100,000 or more: 11.9% (2005); Poverty rate: 10.8% (2000).
Education: Percent of population age 25 and over with: High school diploma (including GED) or higher: 77.5% (2005); Bachelor's degree or higher: 14.0% (2005); Master's degree or higher: 3.7% (2005).
School District(s)
Penns Grv-Carney's Point Regional (PK-12)
   2003-04 Enrollment: 2,371 . . . . (856) 299-4250
Two-year College(s)
Salem Community College (Public)
   Fall 2004 Enrollment: 1,163. . . . . (856) 299-2100
   2005-06 Tuition: In-state $3,605; Out-of-state $3,605
Housing: Homeownership rate: 70.4% (2005); Median home value: $138,407 (2005); Median rent: $543 per month (2000); Median age of housing: 44 years (2000).
Safety: Violent crime rate: 19.6 per 10,000 population; Property crime rate: 210.2 per 10,000 population (2004).
Transportation: Commute to work: 97.4% car, 0.4% public transportation, 0.5% walk, 0.6% work from home (2000); Travel time to work: 33.6% less than 15 minutes, 41.1% 15 to 30 minutes, 12.6% 30 to 45 minutes, 5.8% 45 to 60 minutes, 7.0% 60 minutes or more (2000)
Additional Information Contacts
Salem County Chamber of Commerce . . . . (856) 935-7510
   http://www.salemnjchamber.homestead.com

CARNEYS POINT (CDP). Covers a land area of 8.747 square miles and a water area of 0.106 square miles. Located at 39.70° N. Lat.; 75.47° W. Long.
Population: 7,686 (1990); 6,914 (2000); 6,815 (2005); 6,732 (2010 projected); Race: 75.1% White, 18.6% Black, 1.0% Asian, 5.3% Hispanic of any race (2005); Density: 779.1 persons per square mile (2005); Average household size: 2.40 (2005); Median age: 39.2 (2005); Males per 100 females: 91.9 (2005); Marriage status: 26.7% never married, 52.8% now married, 10.4% widowed, 10.1% divorced (2000); Foreign born: 4.1% (2000); Ancestry (includes multiple ancestries): 22.0% Other groups, 17.7% German, 16.9% Irish, 16.7% Italian, 11.7% English (2000).
Economy: Employment by occupation: 8.4% management, 16.9% professional, 14.7% services, 26.8% sales, 0.2% farming, 9.9% construction, 23.2% production (2000).
Income: Per capita income: $21,487 (2005); Median household income: $43,308 (2005); Average household income: $51,396 (2005); Percent of

households with income of $100,000 or more: 10.8% (2005); Poverty rate: 11.8% (2000).

Education: Percent of population age 25 and over with: High school diploma (including GED) or higher: 77.8% (2005); Bachelor's degree or higher: 13.8% (2005); Master's degree or higher: 3.6% (2005).

School District(s)
Penns Grv-Carney's Point Regional (PK-12)
   2003-04 Enrollment: 2,371 . . . . (856) 299-4250

Two-year College(s)
Salem Community College (Public)
   Fall 2004 Enrollment: 1,163. . . . . (856) 299-2100
   2005-06 Tuition: In-state $3,605; Out-of-state $3,605

Housing: Homeownership rate: 68.6% (2005); Median home value: $135,566 (2005); Median rent: $547 per month (2000); Median age of housing: 44 years (2000).

Transportation: Commute to work: 85.7% car, 0.4% public transportation, 0.6% walk, 0.4% work from home (2000); Travel time to work: 33.7% less than 15 minutes, 40.5% 15 to 30 minutes, 13.7% 30 to 45 minutes, 5.1% 45 to 60 minutes, 7.0% 60 minutes or more (2000)

Additional Information Contacts
Salem County Chamber of Commerce . . . . (856) 935-7510
   http://www.salemnjchamber.homestead.com

ELMER (borough).
Covers a land area of 0.865 square miles and a water area of 0.014 square miles. Located at 39.59° N. Lat.; 75.17° W. Long. Elevation is 118 feet.

History: Incorporated 1893.

Population: 1,571 (1990); 1,384 (2000); 1,366 (2005); 1,352 (2010 projected); Race: 96.7% White, 0.7% Black, 0.7% Asian, 2.0% Hispanic of any race (2005); Density: 1,578.7 persons per square mile (2005); Average household size: 2.60 (2005); Median age: 39.0 (2005); Males per 100 females: 93.2 (2005); Marriage status: 23.7% never married, 60.8% now married, 8.4% widowed, 7.1% divorced (2000); Foreign born: 1.2% (2000); Ancestry (includes multiple ancestries): 26.2% Irish, 25.6% German, 22.7% English, 7.8% Other groups, 7.2% Italian (2000).

Economy: Agricultural shipping center (vegetables). Single-family building permits issued: 1 (2005); Multi-family building permits issued: 0 (2005); Employment by occupation: 6.7% management, 18.7% professional, 12.8% services, 29.3% sales, 0.3% farming, 11.2% construction, 21.0% production (2000).

Income: Per capita income: $24,400 (2005); Median household income: $54,128 (2005); Average household income: $62,913 (2005); Percent of households with income of $100,000 or more: 16.0% (2005); Poverty rate: 5.3% (2000).

Education: Percent of population age 25 and over with: High school diploma (including GED) or higher: 85.3% (2005); Bachelor's degree or higher: 14.9% (2005); Master's degree or higher: 3.9% (2005).

School District(s)
Elmer Borough (PK-06)
   2003-04 Enrollment: 76 . . . . (609) 358-6761
Salem County Special Services (UG-UG)
   2003-04 Enrollment: 152 . . . . (856) 769-5181

Housing: Homeownership rate: 71.5% (2005); Median home value: $168,045 (2005); Median rent: $561 per month (2000); Median age of housing: 60+ years (2000).

Hospitals: South Jersey Hospital System - Elmer Division (91 beds)

Safety: Violent crime rate: 0.0 per 10,000 population; Property crime rate: 108.7 per 10,000 population (2004).

Newspapers: Elmer Times (General - Circulation 2,100)

Transportation: Commute to work: 93.0% car, 0.3% public transportation, 4.1% walk, 1.9% work from home (2000); Travel time to work: 31.6% less than 15 minutes, 33.2% 15 to 30 minutes, 22.3% 30 to 45 minutes, 8.2% 45 to 60 minutes, 4.7% 60 minutes or more (2000)

ELSINBORO (township).
Covers a land area of 12.266 square miles and a water area of 1.060 square miles. Located at 39.53° N. Lat.; 75.49° W. Long.

Population: 1,170 (1990); 1,092 (2000); 1,075 (2005); 1,060 (2010 projected); Race: 95.2% White, 3.5% Black, 0.0% Asian, 0.8% Hispanic of any race (2005); Density: 87.6 persons per square mile (2005); Average household size: 2.32 (2005); Median age: 45.4 (2005); Males per 100 females: 88.9 (2005); Marriage status: 15.5% never married, 66.0% now married, 7.2% widowed, 11.4% divorced (2000); Foreign born: 0.6% (2000); Ancestry (includes multiple ancestries): 24.9% German, 21.0%

Irish, 17.3% English, 11.3% United States or American, 8.2% Other groups (2000).

Economy: Single-family building permits issued: 1 (2005); Multi-family building permits issued: 0 (2005); Employment by occupation: 7.7% management, 22.1% professional, 14.2% services, 26.2% sales, 0.9% farming, 12.3% construction, 16.6% production (2000).

Income: Per capita income: $29,374 (2005); Median household income: $58,486 (2005); Average household income: $68,055 (2005); Percent of households with income of $100,000 or more: 19.0% (2005); Poverty rate: 1.7% (2000).

Education: Percent of population age 25 and over with: High school diploma (including GED) or higher: 83.8% (2005); Bachelor's degree or higher: 16.3% (2005); Master's degree or higher: 6.7% (2005).

Housing: Homeownership rate: 86.0% (2005); Median home value: $170,960 (2005); Median rent: $544 per month (2000); Median age of housing: 46 years (2000).

Safety: Violent crime rate: 9.2 per 10,000 population; Property crime rate: 119.5 per 10,000 population (2004).

Transportation: Commute to work: 90.8% car, 2.3% public transportation, 0.9% walk, 4.3% work from home (2000); Travel time to work: 33.6% less than 15 minutes, 37.1% 15 to 30 minutes, 15.1% 30 to 45 minutes, 9.2% 45 to 60 minutes, 4.9% 60 minutes or more (2000)

LOWER ALLOWAYS CREEK (township).
Covers a land area of 46.778 square miles and a water area of 25.804 square miles. Located at 39.47° N. Lat.; 75.45° W. Long.

Population: 1,858 (1990); 1,851 (2000); 1,925 (2005); 1,999 (2010 projected); Race: 96.7% White, 1.6% Black, 0.8% Asian, 0.7% Hispanic of any race (2005); Density: 41.2 persons per square mile (2005); Average household size: 2.63 (2005); Median age: 40.4 (2005); Males per 100 females: 93.3 (2005); Marriage status: 22.0% never married, 65.1% now married, 6.3% widowed, 6.6% divorced (2000); Foreign born: 0.8% (2000); Ancestry (includes multiple ancestries): 27.4% German, 17.6% English, 15.2% United States or American, 14.9% Irish, 7.3% Other groups (2000).

Economy: Single-family building permits issued: 1 (2005); Multi-family building permits issued: 0 (2005); Employment by occupation: 7.3% management, 19.3% professional, 18.6% services, 21.9% sales, 0.9% farming, 12.9% construction, 19.2% production (2000).

Income: Per capita income: $25,918 (2005); Median household income: $60,977 (2005); Average household income: $68,066 (2005); Percent of households with income of $100,000 or more: 17.1% (2005); Poverty rate: 7.3% (2000).

Education: Percent of population age 25 and over with: High school diploma (including GED) or higher: 82.4% (2005); Bachelor's degree or higher: 11.5% (2005); Master's degree or higher: 2.1% (2005).

Housing: Homeownership rate: 81.2% (2005); Median home value: $188,190 (2005); Median rent: $515 per month (2000); Median age of housing: 35 years (2000).

Safety: Violent crime rate: 0.0 per 10,000 population; Property crime rate: 68.1 per 10,000 population (2004).

Transportation: Commute to work: 94.9% car, 0.8% public transportation, 0.7% walk, 2.4% work from home (2000); Travel time to work: 32.2% less than 15 minutes, 40.9% 15 to 30 minutes, 13.6% 30 to 45 minutes, 9.5% 45 to 60 minutes, 3.8% 60 minutes or more (2000)

MANNINGTON (township).
Covers a land area of 34.780 square miles and a water area of 3.643 square miles. Located at 39.61° N. Lat.; 75.40° W. Long.

Population: 1,693 (1990); 1,559 (2000); 1,579 (2005); 1,609 (2010 projected); Race: 77.3% White, 19.6% Black, 0.4% Asian, 3.4% Hispanic of any race (2005); Density: 45.4 persons per square mile (2005); Average household size: 2.86 (2005); Median age: 44.1 (2005); Males per 100 females: 96.1 (2005); Marriage status: 18.9% never married, 68.7% now married, 6.7% widowed, 5.7% divorced (2000); Foreign born: 1.6% (2000); Ancestry (includes multiple ancestries): 18.6% English, 17.1% German, 16.5% Other groups, 15.2% Irish, 8.1% Italian (2000).

Economy: Single-family building permits issued: 5 (2005); Multi-family building permits issued: 2 (2005); Employment by occupation: 14.3% management, 24.5% professional, 10.1% services, 26.7% sales, 2.0% farming, 7.5% construction, 15.0% production (2000).

Income: Per capita income: $27,107 (2005); Median household income: $57,713 (2005); Average household income: $71,667 (2005); Percent of households with income of $100,000 or more: 21.2% (2005); Poverty rate: 6.9% (2000).

Education: Percent of population age 25 and over with: High school diploma (including GED) or higher: 75.7% (2005); Bachelor's degree or higher: 20.6% (2005); Master's degree or higher: 5.9% (2005).

School District(s)
Salem County Vocational (09-12)

    2003-04 Enrollment: 490 . . . . (856) 769-0101

Housing: Homeownership rate: 83.9% (2005); Median home value: $187,162 (2005); Median rent: $531 per month (2000); Median age of housing: 47 years (2000).

Transportation: Commute to work: 90.0% car, 2.1% public transportation, 1.5% walk, 6.5% work from home (2000); Travel time to work: 32.5% less than 15 minutes, 37.1% 15 to 30 minutes, 18.2% 30 to 45 minutes, 6.3% 45 to 60 minutes, 5.8% 60 minutes or more (2000)

MONROEVILLE (unincorporated postal area, zip code 08343).
Covers a land area of 34.923 square miles and a water area of 0.067 square miles. Located at 39.63° N. Lat.; 75.15° W. Long. Elevation is 140 feet.

Population: 4,596 (2000); Race: 93.5% White, 2.4% Black, 0.0% Asian, 4.7% Hispanic of any race (2000); Density: 131.6 persons per square mile (2000); Age: 28.1% under 18, 11.1% over 64 (2000); Marriage status: 24.5% never married, 61.6% now married, 6.2% widowed, 7.7% divorced (2000); Foreign born: 1.5% (2000); Ancestry (includes multiple ancestries): 26.2% German, 25.9% Irish, 20.0% English, 14.9% Italian, 8.0% Other groups (2000).

Economy: Employment by occupation: 12.8% management, 19.5% professional, 13.3% services, 24.1% sales, 1.3% farming, 12.4% construction, 16.6% production (2000).

Income: Per capita income: $20,020 (2000); Median household income: $55,546 (2000); Poverty rate: 7.1% (2000).

Education: Percent of population age 25 and over with: High school diploma (including GED) or higher: 82.6% (2000); Bachelor's degree or higher: 17.4% (2000).

School District(s)
Upper Pittsgrove Township (PK-08)

    2003-04 Enrollment: 426 . . . . (856) 358-8163

Housing: Homeownership rate: 92.3% (2000); Median home value: $125,700 (2000); Median rent: $601 per month (2000); Median age of housing: 32 years (2000).

Transportation: Commute to work: 92.2% car, 1.3% public transportation, 1.9% walk, 4.6% work from home (2000); Travel time to work: 26.8% less than 15 minutes, 36.1% 15 to 30 minutes, 18.4% 30 to 45 minutes, 12.3% 45 to 60 minutes, 6.5% 60 minutes or more (2000)

OLDMANS (township). Covers a land area of 19.967 square miles and a water area of 0.334 square miles. Located at 39.74° N. Lat.; 75.41° W. Long. Elevation is 15 feet.

Population: 1,683 (1990); 1,798 (2000); 1,801 (2005); 1,811 (2010 projected); Race: 87.6% White, 8.2% Black, 0.2% Asian, 5.3% Hispanic of any race (2005); Density: 90.2 persons per square mile (2005); Average household size: 2.70 (2005); Median age: 40.1 (2005); Males per 100 females: 101.0 (2005); Marriage status: 26.7% never married, 61.1% now married, 6.4% widowed, 5.7% divorced (2000); Foreign born: 2.4% (2000); Ancestry (includes multiple ancestries): 22.4% Irish, 21.6% German, 21.4% Italian, 14.6% Other groups, 13.7% English (2000).

Economy: Single-family building permits issued: 3 (2005); Multi-family building permits issued: 0 (2005); Employment by occupation: 9.1% management, 16.7% professional, 10.7% services, 28.0% sales, 0.6% farming, 12.4% construction, 22.6% production (2000).

Income: Per capita income: $27,740 (2005); Median household income: $68,503 (2005); Average household income: $74,689 (2005); Percent of households with income of $100,000 or more: 24.3% (2005); Poverty rate: 8.1% (2000).

Education: Percent of population age 25 and over with: High school diploma (including GED) or higher: 82.0% (2005); Bachelor's degree or higher: 11.0% (2005); Master's degree or higher: 3.2% (2005).

Housing: Homeownership rate: 86.7% (2005); Median home value: $181,597 (2005); Median rent: $583 per month (2000); Median age of housing: 46 years (2000).

Transportation: Commute to work: 95.3% car, 0.7% public transportation, 1.6% walk, 2.3% work from home (2000); Travel time to work: 39.6% less than 15 minutes, 31.8% 15 to 30 minutes, 17.8% 30 to 45 minutes, 6.0% 45 to 60 minutes, 4.8% 60 minutes or more (2000)

OLIVET (CDP). Covers a land area of 2.494 square miles and a water area of 0.198 square miles. Located at 39.54° N. Lat.; 75.16° W. Long. Elevation is 115 feet.

Population: 1,315 (1990); 1,420 (2000); 1,433 (2005); 1,440 (2010 projected); Race: 94.1% White, 1.7% Black, 2.4% Asian, 1.9% Hispanic of any race (2005); Density: 574.6 persons per square mile (2005); Average household size: 3.04 (2005); Median age: 39.8 (2005); Males per 100 females: 104.7 (2005); Marriage status: 13.0% never married, 77.1% now married, 2.4% widowed, 7.4% divorced (2000); Foreign born: 2.9% (2000); Ancestry (includes multiple ancestries): 25.1% Italian, 22.7% Irish, 19.0% German, 18.7% English, 10.1% Other groups (2000).

Economy: Employment by occupation: 12.1% management, 37.6% professional, 10.7% services, 18.9% sales, 1.2% farming, 11.1% construction, 8.4% production (2000).

Income: Per capita income: $35,427 (2005); Median household income: $82,345 (2005); Average household income: $107,787 (2005); Percent of households with income of $100,000 or more: 35.5% (2005); Poverty rate: 3.7% (2000).

Education: Percent of population age 25 and over with: High school diploma (including GED) or higher: 96.9% (2005); Bachelor's degree or higher: 41.6% (2005); Master's degree or higher: 12.3% (2005).

Housing: Homeownership rate: 97.2% (2005); Median home value: $235,747 (2005); Median rent: $n/a per month (2000); Median age of housing: 18 years (2000).

Transportation: Commute to work: 95.2% car, 0.0% public transportation, 0.0% walk, 2.2% work from home (2000); Travel time to work: 10.7% less than 15 minutes, 42.3% 15 to 30 minutes, 27.2% 30 to 45 minutes, 11.3% 45 to 60 minutes, 8.5% 60 minutes or more (2000)

PEDRICKTOWN (unincorporated postal area, zip code 08067).
Covers a land area of 18.531 square miles and a water area of 0.124 square miles. Located at 39.74° N. Lat.; 75.41° W. Long. Elevation is 10 feet.

Population: 1,641 (2000); Race: 85.5% White, 10.6% Black, 0.2% Asian, 2.6% Hispanic of any race (2000); Density: 88.6 persons per square mile (2000); Age: 24.8% under 18, 11.1% over 64 (2000); Marriage status: 26.9% never married, 62.5% now married, 5.9% widowed, 4.7% divorced (2000); Foreign born: 2.2% (2000); Ancestry (includes multiple ancestries): 22.1% Italian, 22.0% German, 20.6% Irish, 15.6% Other groups, 12.1% English (2000).

Economy: Employment by occupation: 9.2% management, 16.7% professional, 11.2% services, 27.2% sales, 0.6% farming, 12.4% construction, 22.7% production (2000).

Income: Per capita income: $22,549 (2000); Median household income: $57,708 (2000); Poverty rate: 7.6% (2000).

Education: Percent of population age 25 and over with: High school diploma (including GED) or higher: 82.0% (2000); Bachelor's degree or higher: 10.7% (2000).

School District(s)
Oldmans Township (PK-08)

    2003-04 Enrollment: 234 . . . . (856) 299-4240

Housing: Homeownership rate: 85.4% (2000); Median home value: $104,600 (2000); Median rent: $583 per month (2000); Median age of housing: 45 years (2000).

Transportation: Commute to work: 95.2% car, 0.7% public transportation, 1.7% walk, 2.2% work from home (2000); Travel time to work: 40.8% less than 15 minutes, 31.1% 15 to 30 minutes, 17.2% 30 to 45 minutes, 6.4% 45 to 60 minutes, 4.5% 60 minutes or more (2000)

PENNS GROVE (borough). Covers a land area of 0.926 square miles and a water area of 0 square miles. Located at 39.72° N. Lat.; 75.46° W. Long. Elevation is 12 feet.

History: Settled 1675, incorporated 1894.

Population: 5,228 (1990); 4,886 (2000); 4,824 (2005); 4,771 (2010 projected); Race: 45.4% White, 41.5% Black, 0.4% Asian, 21.5% Hispanic of any race (2005); Density: 5,208.8 persons per square mile (2005); Average household size: 2.66 (2005); Median age: 31.3 (2005); Males per 100 females: 86.3 (2005); Marriage status: 36.5% never married, 45.9% now married, 7.9% widowed, 9.8% divorced (2000); Foreign born: 3.6% (2000); Ancestry (includes multiple ancestries): 45.0% Other groups, 11.4% Italian, 11.0% German, 9.0% Irish, 5.3% United States or American (2000).

Economy: Manufacturing: chemicals, apparel, lumber products. Agriculture: poultry; fruit, produce; dairy products. Single-family building permits issued: 4 (2005); Multi-family building permits issued: 0 (2005); Employment by occupation: 4.0% management, 15.2% professional, 20.3% services, 23.8% sales, 1.3% farming, 8.3% construction, 27.0% production (2000).

Income: Per capita income: $15,496 (2005); Median household income: $30,311 (2005); Average household income: $40,689 (2005); Percent of households with income of $100,000 or more: 6.6% (2005); Poverty rate: 21.0% (2000).

Education: Percent of population age 25 and over with: High school diploma (including GED) or higher: 66.1% (2005); Bachelor's degree or higher: 7.4% (2005); Master's degree or higher: 1.5% (2005).

School District(s)

Penns Grv-Carney's Point Regional (PK-12)
    2003-04 Enrollment: 2,371 . . . . (856) 299-4250
Housing: Homeownership rate: 46.0% (2005); Median home value: $112,117 (2005); Median rent: $425 per month (2000); Median age of housing: 50 years (2000).

Safety: Violent crime rate: 67.7 per 10,000 population; Property crime rate: 424.7 per 10,000 population (2004).

Transportation: Commute to work: 87.6% car, 3.7% public transportation, 3.5% walk, 1.9% work from home (2000); Travel time to work: 29.9% less than 15 minutes, 44.4% 15 to 30 minutes, 14.6% 30 to 45 minutes, 3.9% 45 to 60 minutes, 7.1% 60 minutes or more (2000)

PENNSVILLE (township). Aka Pennsville Center. Covers a land area of 23.101 square miles and a water area of 1.709 square miles. Located at 39.65° N. Lat.; 75.51° W. Long. Elevation is 19 feet.

History: Named for William Penn (1644-1718), founder of Pennsylvania. Pennsville was once known as a center for sturgeon and shad fishermen. The region around Pennsville was settled by Swedes after 1640.

Population: 13,794 (1990); 13,194 (2000); 13,161 (2005); 13,141 (2010 projected); Race: 96.3% White, 1.1% Black, 1.0% Asian, 1.9% Hispanic of any race (2005); Density: 569.7 persons per square mile (2005); Average household size: 2.44 (2005); Median age: 40.3 (2005); Males per 100 females: 93.1 (2005); Marriage status: 22.5% never married, 58.9% now married, 9.4% widowed, 9.2% divorced (2000); Foreign born: 3.2% (2000); Ancestry (includes multiple ancestries): 22.1% German, 22.0% Irish, 17.1% English, 13.6% Italian, 7.6% Other groups (2000).

Economy: Single-family building permits issued: 53 (2005); Multi-family building permits issued: 0 (2005); Employment by occupation: 10.2% management, 18.1% professional, 14.4% services, 27.5% sales, 0.4% farming, 11.6% construction, 17.9% production (2000).

Income: Per capita income: $25,079 (2005); Median household income: $53,097 (2005); Average household income: $61,034 (2005); Percent of households with income of $100,000 or more: 14.0% (2005); Poverty rate: 4.9% (2000).

Taxes: Total city taxes per capita: $225 (2004); City property taxes per capita: $203 (2004).

Education: Percent of population age 25 and over with: High school diploma (including GED) or higher: 82.0% (2005); Bachelor's degree or higher: 13.7% (2005); Master's degree or higher: 2.6% (2005).

School District(s)

Pennsville (PK-12)
    2003-04 Enrollment: 2,105 . . . . (856) 540-6210
Housing: Homeownership rate: 75.1% (2005); Median home value: $158,483 (2005); Median rent: $575 per month (2000); Median age of housing: 40 years (2000).

Safety: Violent crime rate: 10.6 per 10,000 population; Property crime rate: 235.4 per 10,000 population (2004).

Transportation: Commute to work: 96.2% car, 0.5% public transportation, 1.2% walk, 1.0% work from home (2000); Travel time to work: 33.6% less than 15 minutes, 37.5% 15 to 30 minutes, 16.9% 30 to 45 minutes, 7.5% 45 to 60 minutes, 4.6% 60 minutes or more (2000)

Additional Information Contacts

Pennsville Township . . . . (856) 678-3089
    http://www.pennsville.org

PENNSVILLE (CDP). Covers a land area of 10.477 square miles and a water area of 0.110 square miles. Located at 39.65° N. Lat.; 75.51° W. Long.

Population: 12,306 (1990); 11,657 (2000); 11,516 (2005); 11,374 (2010 projected); Race: 96.8% White, 0.9% Black, 0.9% Asian, 1.9% Hispanic of any race (2005); Density: 1,099.2 persons per square mile (2005); Average household size: 2.45 (2005); Median age: 40.1 (2005); Males per 100 females: 92.7 (2005); Marriage status: 22.6% never married, 58.9% now

married, 9.3% widowed, 9.3% divorced (2000); Foreign born: 2.9% (2000); Ancestry (includes multiple ancestries): 22.7% German, 22.6% Irish, 18.0% English, 13.8% Italian, 7.7% Other groups (2000).

Economy: Employment by occupation: 10.5% management, 17.9% professional, 14.2% services, 26.6% sales, 0.4% farming, 11.8% construction, 18.6% production (2000).

Income: Per capita income: $25,008 (2005); Median household income: $53,905 (2005); Average household income: $61,151 (2005); Percent of households with income of $100,000 or more: 14.2% (2005); Poverty rate: 5.1% (2000).

Education: Percent of population age 25 and over with: High school diploma (including GED) or higher: 82.1% (2005); Bachelor's degree or higher: 13.0% (2005); Master's degree or higher: 2.2% (2005).

School District(s)

Pennsville (PK-12)
    2003-04 Enrollment: 2,105 . . . . (856) 540-6210
Housing: Homeownership rate: 76.8% (2005); Median home value: $155,429 (2005); Median rent: $566 per month (2000); Median age of housing: 41 years (2000).

Transportation: Commute to work: 86.9% car, 0.6% public transportation, 1.4% walk, 1.0% work from home (2000); Travel time to work: 32.1% less than 15 minutes, 37.5% 15 to 30 minutes, 17.5% 30 to 45 minutes, 8.3% 45 to 60 minutes, 4.6% 60 minutes or more (2000)

PILESGROVE (township). Covers a land area of 34.908 square miles and a water area of 0.144 square miles. Located at 39.65° N. Lat.; 75.31° W. Long.

Population: 3,250 (1990); 3,923 (2000); 4,116 (2005); 4,285 (2010 projected); Race: 83.6% White, 12.9% Black, 1.1% Asian, 2.9% Hispanic of any race (2005); Density: 117.9 persons per square mile (2005); Average household size: 3.20 (2005); Median age: 40.8 (2005); Males per 100 females: 106.2 (2005); Marriage status: 26.5% never married, 58.9% now married, 7.7% widowed, 6.9% divorced (2000); Foreign born: 1.7% (2000); Ancestry (includes multiple ancestries): 17.8% German, 17.7% English, 15.1% Other groups, 13.9% Irish, 13.1% Italian (2000).

Economy: Single-family building permits issued: 56 (2005); Multi-family building permits issued: 0 (2005); Employment by occupation: 13.5% management, 24.6% professional, 13.1% services, 21.8% sales, 1.3% farming, 11.1% construction, 14.7% production (2000).

Income: Per capita income: $30,396 (2005); Median household income: $75,341 (2005); Average household income: $90,474 (2005); Percent of households with income of $100,000 or more: 33.2% (2005); Poverty rate: 3.4% (2000).

Education: Percent of population age 25 and over with: High school diploma (including GED) or higher: 87.9% (2005); Bachelor's degree or higher: 23.0% (2005); Master's degree or higher: 6.6% (2005).

Housing: Homeownership rate: 88.8% (2005); Median home value: $256,840 (2005); Median rent: $522 per month (2000); Median age of housing: 30 years (2000).

Transportation: Commute to work: 93.1% car, 0.4% public transportation, 2.3% walk, 3.7% work from home (2000); Travel time to work: 28.2% less than 15 minutes, 32.8% 15 to 30 minutes, 20.1% 30 to 45 minutes, 10.1% 45 to 60 minutes, 8.8% 60 minutes or more (2000)

PITTSGROVE (township). Covers a land area of 45.187 square miles and a water area of 0.739 square miles. Located at 39.53° N. Lat.; 75.13° W. Long.

History: Incorporated 1798.

Population: 8,090 (1990); 8,893 (2000); 9,338 (2005); 9,771 (2010 projected); Race: 88.0% White, 8.1% Black, 0.5% Asian, 4.2% Hispanic of any race (2005); Density: 206.7 persons per square mile (2005); Average household size: 2.91 (2005); Median age: 39.1 (2005); Males per 100 females: 97.4 (2005); Marriage status: 24.4% never married, 61.9% now married, 6.4% widowed, 7.3% divorced (2000); Foreign born: 2.0% (2000); Ancestry (includes multiple ancestries): 26.1% German, 20.3% Irish, 18.6% Italian, 14.0% English, 13.1% Other groups (2000).

Economy: Agriculture: vegetable farming. Single-family building permits issued: 51 (2005); Multi-family building permits issued: 0 (2005); Employment by occupation: 9.5% management, 18.9% professional, 14.6% services, 22.5% sales, 0.5% farming, 14.2% construction, 19.8% production (2000).

Income: Per capita income: $25,894 (2005); Median household income: $65,148 (2005); Average household income: $74,480 (2005); Percent of households with income of $100,000 or more: 23.5% (2005); Poverty rate: 5.0% (2000).

Education: Percent of population age 25 and over with: High school diploma (including GED) or higher: 78.8% (2005); Bachelor's degree or higher: 15.9% (2005); Master's degree or higher: 4.2% (2005).

School District(s)
Pittsgrove Township (PK-12)
   2003-04 Enrollment: 1,878 . . . . (609) 358-3094

Housing: Homeownership rate: 90.5% (2005); Median home value: $183,918 (2005); Median rent: $528 per month (2000); Median age of housing: 25 years (2000).

Transportation: Commute to work: 94.2% car, 0.3% public transportation, 1.5% walk, 2.8% work from home (2000); Travel time to work: 26.2% less than 15 minutes, 36.6% 15 to 30 minutes, 18.9% 30 to 45 minutes, 9.0% 45 to 60 minutes, 9.3% 60 minutes or more (2000)

Additional Information Contacts
Pittsgrove Township. . . . . (856) 358-2300
   http://www.pittsgrovetownship.com

QUINTON (township). Covers a land area of 24.173 square miles and a water area of 0.368 square miles. Located at 39.52° N. Lat.; 75.39° W. Long. Elevation is 17 feet.

History: Monument marks Revolutionary battle site.

Population: 2,511 (1990); 2,786 (2000); 2,827 (2005); 2,878 (2010 projected); Race: 84.0% White, 12.6% Black, 0.3% Asian, 1.7% Hispanic of any race (2005); Density: 116.9 persons per square mile (2005); Average household size: 2.56 (2005); Median age: 40.0 (2005); Males per 100 females: 98.9 (2005); Marriage status: 23.6% never married, 61.0% now married, 8.4% widowed, 7.0% divorced (2000); Foreign born: 1.8% (2000); Ancestry (includes multiple ancestries): 22.7% German, 18.6% Other groups, 16.9% Irish, 14.1% English, 8.5% United States or American (2000).

Economy: Single-family building permits issued: 10 (2005); Multi-family building permits issued: 0 (2005); Employment by occupation: 8.0% management, 16.7% professional, 15.9% services, 22.6% sales, 1.4% farming, 13.4% construction, 21.9% production (2000).

Income: Per capita income: $21,852 (2005); Median household income: $46,756 (2005); Average household income: $55,622 (2005); Percent of households with income of $100,000 or more: 10.8% (2005); Poverty rate: 9.3% (2000).

Education: Percent of population age 25 and over with: High school diploma (including GED) or higher: 72.1% (2005); Bachelor's degree or higher: 10.3% (2005); Master's degree or higher: 2.2% (2005).

School District(s)
Quinton Township (PK-08)
   2003-04 Enrollment: 359 . . . . (856) 935-2379

Housing: Homeownership rate: 84.3% (2005); Median home value: $146,393 (2005); Median rent: $557 per month (2000); Median age of housing: 38 years (2000).

Transportation: Commute to work: 94.0% car, 1.0% public transportation, 0.4% walk, 2.8% work from home (2000); Travel time to work: 27.6% less than 15 minutes, 34.6% 15 to 30 minutes, 23.2% 30 to 45 minutes, 7.6% 45 to 60 minutes, 7.1% 60 minutes or more (2000)

SALEM (city). Covers a land area of 2.610 square miles and a water area of 0.186 square miles. Located at 39.57° N. Lat.; 75.46° W. Long. Elevation is 19 feet.

History: In 1675, John Fenwick and a group of English Quakers settled the region and founded the city of New Salem, the first permanent English-speaking settlement on the Delaware River. The city of New Salem became a port of entry for vessels, and trade and industry prospered. Salem saw fighting and plundering during the Revolutionary War. It also began to decline as a river port as industry became more firmly established, especially with the arrival of a railroad in 1863.

Population: 6,883 (1990); 5,857 (2000); 5,778 (2005); 5,709 (2010 projected); Race: 34.7% White, 59.6% Black, 0.2% Asian, 5.6% Hispanic of any race (2005); Density: 2,214.0 persons per square mile (2005); Average household size: 2.45 (2005); Median age: 32.7 (2005); Males per 100 females: 81.9 (2005); Marriage status: 40.1% never married, 41.0% now married, 10.0% widowed, 8.9% divorced (2000); Foreign born: 0.8% (2000); Ancestry (includes multiple ancestries): 58.6% Other groups, 6.9% German, 4.9% English, 4.8% Irish, 3.8% Italian (2000).

Economy: Single-family building permits issued: 5 (2005); Multi-family building permits issued: 0 (2005); Employment by occupation: 5.4% management, 15.0% professional, 21.5% services, 22.7% sales, 0.0% farming, 10.1% construction, 25.4% production (2000).

Income: Per capita income: $16,107 (2005); Median household income: $28,629 (2005); Average household income: $38,297 (2005); Percent of households with income of $100,000 or more: 5.5% (2005); Poverty rate: 26.6% (2000).

Education: Percent of population age 25 and over with: High school diploma (including GED) or higher: 68.1% (2005); Bachelor's degree or higher: 8.1% (2005); Master's degree or higher: 1.8% (2005).

School District(s)
Elsinboro Township (PK-08)
   2003-04 Enrollment: 118 . . . . (856) 935-3817
Lower Alloways Creek (PK-08)
   2003-04 Enrollment: 221 . . . . (856) 935-2707
Mannington Township (PK-08)
   2003-04 Enrollment: 188 . . . . (856) 935-1078
Salem City (PK-12)
   2003-04 Enrollment: 1,518 . . . . (856) 935-3800

Housing: Homeownership rate: 41.2% (2005); Median home value: $112,298 (2005); Median rent: $374 per month (2000); Median age of housing: 54 years (2000).

Hospitals: Memorial Hospital of Salem County (152 beds)

Safety: Violent crime rate: 123.4 per 10,000 population; Property crime rate: 596.5 per 10,000 population (2004).

Newspapers: Today's Sunbeam (Circulation 9,850)

Transportation: Commute to work: 81.8% car, 7.0% public transportation, 8.5% walk, 0.0% work from home (2000); Travel time to work: 35.6% less than 15 minutes, 29.7% 15 to 30 minutes, 23.9% 30 to 45 minutes, 3.7% 45 to 60 minutes, 7.1% 60 minutes or more (2000)

Additional Information Contacts
Salem County Chamber of Commerce . . . . (856) 299-6699
   http://www.salemnjchamber.homestead.com

UPPER PITTSGROVE (township). Covers a land area of 40.386 square miles and a water area of 0.072 square miles. Located at 39.61° N. Lat.; 75.20° W. Long.

Population: 3,171 (1990); 3,468 (2000); 3,641 (2005); 3,807 (2010 projected); Race: 95.3% White, 1.7% Black, 0.2% Asian, 3.8% Hispanic of any race (2005); Density: 90.2 persons per square mile (2005); Average household size: 2.86 (2005); Median age: 40.0 (2005); Males per 100 females: 98.9 (2005); Marriage status: 23.1% never married, 61.7% now married, 8.0% widowed, 7.2% divorced (2000); Foreign born: 3.6% (2000); Ancestry (includes multiple ancestries): 26.3% German, 19.8% English, 18.5% Irish, 11.1% Italian, 8.2% Other groups (2000).

Economy: Single-family building permits issued: 7 (2005); Multi-family building permits issued: 0 (2005); Employment by occupation: 12.0% management, 19.6% professional, 14.6% services, 24.5% sales, 2.2% farming, 10.6% construction, 16.6% production (2000).

Income: Per capita income: $25,930 (2005); Median household income: $61,025 (2005); Average household income: $72,582 (2005); Percent of households with income of $100,000 or more: 21.6% (2005); Poverty rate: 8.5% (2000).

Education: Percent of population age 25 and over with: High school diploma (including GED) or higher: 81.6% (2005); Bachelor's degree or higher: 18.9% (2005); Master's degree or higher: 5.8% (2005).

Housing: Homeownership rate: 85.1% (2005); Median home value: $196,467 (2005); Median rent: $525 per month (2000); Median age of housing: 36 years (2000).

Transportation: Commute to work: 91.7% car, 0.9% public transportation, 3.3% walk, 4.1% work from home (2000); Travel time to work: 29.9% less than 15 minutes, 35.4% 15 to 30 minutes, 19.7% 30 to 45 minutes, 7.4% 45 to 60 minutes, 7.6% 60 minutes or more (2000)

WOODSTOWN (borough). Covers a land area of 1.587 square miles and a water area of 0.037 square miles. Located at 39.65° N. Lat.; 75.32° W. Long. Elevation is 47 feet.

History: Has 18th-century Friends' meetinghouse. Quaker center since settlement before 1725; incorporated 1882.

Population: 3,154 (1990); 3,136 (2000); 3,304 (2005); 3,465 (2010 projected); Race: 84.6% White, 13.3% Black, 0.7% Asian, 1.9% Hispanic of any race (2005); Density: 2,081.4 persons per square mile (2005); Average household size: 2.42 (2005); Median age: 39.0 (2005); Males per 100 females: 87.7 (2005); Marriage status: 21.3% never married, 57.9% now married, 11.0% widowed, 9.8% divorced (2000); Foreign born: 3.3% (2000); Ancestry (includes multiple ancestries): 20.2% Irish, 19.9% German, 17.6% English, 11.8% Other groups, 9.1% Italian (2000).

Economy: In agricultural region; manufacturing of bricks, clothing. Single-family building permits issued: 21 (2005); Multi-family building permits issued: 0 (2005); Employment by occupation: 9.8% management, 30.7% professional, 14.5% services, 22.0% sales, 0.3% farming, 5.6% construction, 17.2% production (2000).

Income: Per capita income: $28,469 (2005); Median household income: $49,898 (2005); Average household income: $67,438 (2005); Percent of households with income of $100,000 or more: 19.5% (2005); Poverty rate: 5.5% (2000).

Education: Percent of population age 25 and over with: High school diploma (including GED) or higher: 92.7% (2005); Bachelor's degree or higher: 31.7% (2005); Master's degree or higher: 9.7% (2005).

School District(s)

Salem County Vocational (09-12)

2003-04 Enrollment: 490 . . . . (856) 769-0101

Woodstown-Pilesgrove Regional (PK-12)

2003-04 Enrollment: 1,700 . . . . (856) 769-1664

Housing: Homeownership rate: 59.4% (2005); Median home value: $186,060 (2005); Median rent: $560 per month (2000); Median age of housing: 52 years (2000).

Safety: Violent crime rate: 27.4 per 10,000 population; Property crime rate: 97.5 per 10,000 population (2004).

Transportation: Commute to work: 92.2% car, 0.4% public transportation, 3.8% walk, 3.6% work from home (2000); Travel time to work: 26.5% less than 15 minutes, 38.1% 15 to 30 minutes, 21.4% 30 to 45 minutes, 6.4% 45 to 60 minutes, 7.7% 60 minutes or more (2000)

Somerset County

Located in north central New Jersey; bounded on the northeast by the Passaic River; includes Appalachian ridges in the northwest, and part of the Watchung Mountains in the northeast; drained by the Millstone River and branches of the Raritan River. Covers a land area of 304.69 square miles, a water area of 0.36 square miles, and is located in the Eastern Time Zone. The county government was organized in 1688. County seat is Somerville.

Somerset County is part of the New York-Northern New Jersey-Long Island, NY-NJ-PA Metropolitan Statistical Area. The entire metro area includes: Edison, NJ Metropolitan Division (Middlesex County, NJ; Monmouth County, NJ; Ocean County, NJ; Somerset County, NJ); Nassau-Suffolk, NY Metropolitan Division (Nassau County, NY; Suffolk County, NY); New York-White Plains-Wayne, NY-NJ Metropolitan Division (Bergen County, NJ; Hudson County, NJ; Passaic County, NJ; Bronx County, NY; Kings County, NY; New York County, NY; Putnam County, NY; Queens County, NY; Richmond County, NY; Rockland County, NY; Westchester County, NY); Newark-Union, NJ-PA Metropolitan Division (Essex County, NJ; Hunterdon County, NJ; Morris County, NJ; Sussex County, NJ; Union County, NJ; Pike County, PA)

Weather Station: Somerville 3 NW									Elevation: 157 feet		
	Jan	Feb	Mar	Apr	May	Jun	Jul	Aug	Sep	Oct	Nov	Dec
High	37	40	49	61	72	80	85	83	75	64	53	42
Low	18	20	28	37	47	56	62	60	52	41	33	24
Precip	3.8	2.8	3.9	4.1	4.4	4.2	4.8	4.4	4.3	3.9	3.9	3.7
Snow	8.8	8.4	5.1	1.4	0.0	0.0	0.0	0.0	0.0	tr	0.7	3.1

High and Low temperatures in degrees Fahrenheit; Precipitation and Snow in inches

Population: 240,360 (1990); 297,490 (2000); 317,736 (2005); 338,913 (2010 projected); Race: 74.9% White, 8.5% Black, 11.0% Asian, 10.7% Hispanic of any race (2005); Density: 1,042.8 persons per square mile (2005); Average household size: 2.73 (2005); Median age: 38.4 (2005); Males per 100 females: 96.2 (2005).

Religion: Five largest groups: 39.9% Catholic Church, 3.7% Jewish Estimate, 2.1% American Baptist Churches in the USA, 2.1% Presbyterian Church (U.S.A.), 1.8% Reformed Church in America (2000).

Economy: Unemployment rate: 3.3% (2005); Total civilian labor force: 175,411 (2005); Leading industries: 11.9% professional (2004); Farms: 442 totaling 36,237 acres (2002); Companies that employ 500 or more persons: 75 (2004); Companies that employ 100 to 499 persons: 509 (2004); Companies that employ less than 100 persons: 19,190 (2004); Black-owned businesses: 1,284 (2002); Hispanic-owned businesses: 1,032 (2002); Asian-owned businesses: 2,610 (2002); Women-owned businesses: 8,530 (2002); Retail sales per capita: $19,549 (2006). Single-family building permits issued: 818 (2005); Multi-family building permits issued: 402 (2005).

Income: Per capita income: $42,521 (2005); Median household income: $86,925 (2005); Average household income: $115,416 (2005); Percent of households with income of $100,000 or more: 42.2% (2005); Poverty rate: 4.7% (2003); Bankruptcy rate: 2.93% (2005).

Taxes: Total county taxes per capita: $465 (2004); County property taxes per capita: $465 (2004).

Education: Percent of population age 25 and over with: High school diploma (including GED) or higher: 89.6% (2005); Bachelor's degree or higher: 46.8% (2005); Master's degree or higher: 19.4% (2005).

Housing: Homeownership rate: 77.5% (2005); Median home value: $365,824 (2005); Median rent: $813 per month (2000); Median age of housing: 27 years (2000).

Health: Birth rate: 145.6 per 10,000 population (2004); Death rate: 66.3 per 10,000 population (2004); Age-adjusted cancer mortality rate: 196.8 deaths per 100,000 population (2002); Number of physicians: 44.7 per 10,000 population (2004); Hospital beds: 18.4 per 10,000 population (2003); Hospital admissions: 583.6 per 10,000 population (2003).

Elections: 2004 Presidential election results: 51.7% Bush, 47.4% Kerry, 0.6% Nader, 0.2% Badnarik.

National and State Parks: Delaware and Raritan Canal State Park; Washington Rock State Park

Additional Information Contacts

Somerset County Government . . . . (908) 231-7030
http://www.co.somerset.nj.us

Bedminster Township . . . . (908) 212-7000
http://bedminster.us

Bernards Township . . . . (908) 766-2510
http://www.bernards.org

Borough of North Plainfield . . . . (908) 769-2900
http://www.northplainfield.org

Borough of Somerville . . . . (908) 725-2300
http://www.somervillenj.org

Borough of Watchung . . . . (908) 756-0080
http://watchungnj.com

Bound Brook Chamber of Commerce . . . . (732) 356-7273
http://www.boundbrook.com/Content/179/14.aspx

Branchburg Township . . . . (908) 526-1300
http://www.branchburg.nj.us

Franklin Township . . . . (908) 735-5212
http://www.franklintwpnj.org

Franklin Township Chamber of Commerce . . . . (732) 545-7044
http://franklinchamber.com

Hillsborough Township . . . . (908) 369-4313
http://www.harrisontwp.us

Montgomery County Chamber of Commerce . . . . (908) 725-1552
http://www.somersetbusinesspartnership.com

Montgomery Township . . . . (908) 359-8211
http://www.montgomery.nj.us

Raritan Chamber of Commerce . . . . (908) 429-0555
http://www.somersetbusinesspartnership.com

Somerset County Business Partnership . . . . (908) 218-4300
http://www.somersetbusinesspartnership.com

Somerset County Chamber of Commerce . . . . (908) 725-1552
http://www.somersetbusinesspartnership.com

Warren Township . . . . (908) 753-8000
http://www.warrennj.org

Somerset County Communities

BASKING RIDGE (unincorporated postal area, zip code 07920). Covers a land area of 21.635 square miles and a water area of 0.023 square miles. Located at 40.67° N. Lat.; 74.57° W. Long. Elevation is 320 feet.

History: Basking Ridge received its name from early 18th-century settlers who had seen wild animals come up from the lowlands to bask in the sun.

Population: 24,600 (2000); Race: 88.7% White, 1.6% Black, 7.9% Asian, 2.6% Hispanic of any race (2000); Density: 1,137.1 persons per square mile (2000); Age: 27.3% under 18, 12.6% over 64 (2000); Marriage status: 19.6% never married, 67.8% now married, 5.8% widowed, 6.8% divorced (2000); Foreign born: 12.7% (2000); Ancestry (includes multiple ancestries): 23.0% Irish, 19.3% Italian, 18.4% German, 13.6% Other groups, 10.8% English (2000).

Economy: Employment by occupation: 33.7% management, 30.4% professional, 5.3% services, 23.3% sales, 0.0% farming, 3.4% construction, 3.8% production (2000).

Income: Per capita income: $54,753 (2000); Median household income: $105,471 (2000); Poverty rate: 1.4% (2000).

Education: Percent of population age 25 and over with: High school diploma (including GED) or higher: 95.9% (2000); Bachelor's degree or higher: 66.9% (2000).

School District(s)

Bernards Township (PK-12)

   2003-04 Enrollment: 5,100 . . . . (908) 204-2600

Housing: Homeownership rate: 86.7% (2000); Median home value: $370,100 (2000); Median rent: $1,368 per month (2000); Median age of housing: 16 years (2000).

Transportation: Commute to work: 88.1% car, 5.6% public transportation, 0.6% walk, 5.2% work from home (2000); Travel time to work: 21.8% less than 15 minutes, 31.8% 15 to 30 minutes, 21.8% 30 to 45 minutes, 9.5% 45 to 60 minutes, 15.1% 60 minutes or more (2000)

BEDMINSTER (township).
Covers a land area of 26.471 square miles and a water area of 0.003 square miles. Located at 40.66° N. Lat.; 74.65° W. Long. Elevation is 198 feet.

Population: 7,063 (1990); 8,302 (2000); 8,404 (2005); 8,602 (2010 projected); Race: 87.5% White, 1.8% Black, 8.5% Asian, 4.9% Hispanic of any race (2005); Density: 317.5 persons per square mile (2005); Average household size: 1.92 (2005); Median age: 41.2 (2005); Males per 100 females: 86.7 (2005); Marriage status: 26.4% never married, 54.3% now married, 5.3% widowed, 14.0% divorced (2000); Foreign born: 14.7% (2000); Ancestry (includes multiple ancestries): 19.8% Irish, 18.9% Italian, 18.8% German, 13.7% Other groups, 10.3% English (2000).

Economy: A telecommunications center. Peapack Ski Area to Northwest. Single-family building permits issued: 2 (2005); Multi-family building permits issued: 0 (2005); Employment by occupation: 32.1% management, 26.4% professional, 6.9% services, 27.4% sales, 0.4% farming, 2.3% construction, 4.5% production (2000).

Income: Per capita income: $57,367 (2005); Median household income: $76,092 (2005); Average household income: $109,936 (2005); Percent of households with income of $100,000 or more: 35.0% (2005); Poverty rate: 3.1% (2000).

Education: Percent of population age 25 and over with: High school diploma (including GED) or higher: 96.2% (2005); Bachelor's degree or higher: 60.4% (2005); Master's degree or higher: 22.6% (2005).

School District(s)

Bedminster Township (PK-08)

   2003-04 Enrollment: 597 . . . . (908) 234-0768

Housing: Homeownership rate: 80.3% (2005); Median home value: $329,582 (2005); Median rent: $1,299 per month (2000); Median age of housing: 15 years (2000).

Safety: Violent crime rate: 1.2 per 10,000 population; Property crime rate: 60.8 per 10,000 population (2004).

Transportation: Commute to work: 86.6% car, 3.2% public transportation, 2.5% walk, 7.3% work from home (2000); Travel time to work: 21.3% less than 15 minutes, 35.8% 15 to 30 minutes, 21.7% 30 to 45 minutes, 9.7% 45 to 60 minutes, 11.5% 60 minutes or more (2000)

Additional Information Contacts

Bedminster Township . . . . (908) 212-7000
  http://bedminster.us

BELLE MEAD (unincorporated postal area, zip code 08502).
Covers a land area of 27.687 square miles and a water area of 0 square miles. Located at 40.46° N. Lat.; 74.63° W. Long. Elevation is 114 feet.

Population: 19,217 (2000); Race: 86.9% White, 2.8% Black, 8.8% Asian, 2.7% Hispanic of any race (2000); Density: 694.1 persons per square mile (2000); Age: 34.7% under 18, 5.2% over 64 (2000); Marriage status: 18.0% never married, 76.1% now married, 2.9% widowed, 3.0% divorced (2000); Foreign born: 11.8% (2000); Ancestry (includes multiple ancestries): 20.8% Italian, 19.5% Irish, 16.1% German, 14.9% Other groups, 12.1% Polish (2000).

Economy: Employment by occupation: 30.5% management, 34.2% professional, 5.5% services, 22.1% sales, 0.4% farming, 3.6% construction, 3.6% production (2000).

Income: Per capita income: $41,723 (2000); Median household income: $114,854 (2000); Poverty rate: 1.6% (2000).

Education: Percent of population age 25 and over with: High school diploma (including GED) or higher: 95.7% (2000); Bachelor's degree or higher: 61.2% (2000).

School District(s)

Hillsborough Township (PK-12)

   2003-04 Enrollment: 7,782 . . . . (908) 369-0030

Housing: Homeownership rate: 90.6% (2000); Median home value: $320,800 (2000); Median rent: $1,151 per month (2000); Median age of housing: 14 years (2000).

Hospitals: Carrier Clinic (2 beds)

Transportation: Commute to work: 90.8% car, 3.5% public transportation, 0.6% walk, 4.7% work from home (2000); Travel time to work: 13.4% less than 15 minutes, 33.2% 15 to 30 minutes, 26.4% 30 to 45 minutes, 11.0% 45 to 60 minutes, 15.9% 60 minutes or more (2000)

BERNARDS (township).
Covers a land area of 24.004 square miles and a water area of 0.010 square miles. Located at 40.68° N. Lat.; 74.57° W. Long.

History: Incorporated 1798.

Population: 17,199 (1990); 24,575 (2000); 26,802 (2005); 28,948 (2010 projected); Race: 85.0% White, 1.6% Black, 11.7% Asian, 3.1% Hispanic of any race (2005); Density: 1,116.6 persons per square mile (2005); Average household size: 2.69 (2005); Median age: 40.1 (2005); Males per 100 females: 95.4 (2005); Marriage status: 19.4% never married, 68.0% now married, 5.8% widowed, 6.8% divorced (2000); Foreign born: 12.5% (2000); Ancestry (includes multiple ancestries): 23.5% Irish, 19.1% Italian, 18.7% German, 13.3% Other groups, 11.0% English (2000).

Economy: Unemployment rate: 2.5% (2005); Total civilian labor force: 13,887 (2005); Single-family building permits issued: 23 (2005); Multi-family building permits issued: 0 (2005); Employment by occupation: 33.9% management, 30.2% professional, 5.3% services, 23.7% sales, 0.0% farming, 3.2% construction, 3.8% production (2000).

Income: Per capita income: $63,558 (2005); Median household income: $131,167 (2005); Average household income: $170,442 (2005); Percent of households with income of $100,000 or more: 62.7% (2005); Poverty rate: 1.3% (2000).

Taxes: Total city taxes per capita: $777 (2004); City property taxes per capita: $745 (2004).

Education: Percent of population age 25 and over with: High school diploma (including GED) or higher: 95.9% (2005); Bachelor's degree or higher: 67.9% (2005); Master's degree or higher: 31.5% (2005).

Housing: Homeownership rate: 86.9% (2005); Median home value: $587,682 (2005); Median rent: $1,365 per month (2000); Median age of housing: 15 years (2000).

Safety: Violent crime rate: 0.8 per 10,000 population; Property crime rate: 63.5 per 10,000 population (2004).

Transportation: Commute to work: 88.1% car, 5.6% public transportation, 0.7% walk, 5.3% work from home (2000); Travel time to work: 21.5% less than 15 minutes, 32.2% 15 to 30 minutes, 21.5% 30 to 45 minutes, 9.6% 45 to 60 minutes, 15.2% 60 minutes or more (2000)

Additional Information Contacts

Bernards Township . . . . (908) 766-2510
  http://www.bernards.org

BERNARDSVILLE (borough).
Covers a land area of 12.930 square miles and a water area of 0.014 square miles. Located at 40.71° N. Lat.; 74.57° W. Long. Elevation is 400 feet.

History: Settled early 18th century, incorporated 1924.

Population: 6,597 (1990); 7,345 (2000); 7,668 (2005); 8,042 (2010 projected); Race: 92.3% White, 0.2% Black, 3.3% Asian, 7.7% Hispanic of any race (2005); Density: 593.1 persons per square mile (2005); Average household size: 2.71 (2005); Median age: 41.1 (2005); Males per 100 females: 96.9 (2005); Marriage status: 17.6% never married, 69.6% now married, 5.4% widowed, 7.4% divorced (2000); Foreign born: 12.5% (2000); Ancestry (includes multiple ancestries): 24.7% Irish, 21.8% Italian, 19.2% German, 15.8% English, 8.5% Other groups (2000).

Economy: In agricultural, resort area; engineering, laminated materials. Single-family building permits issued: 10 (2005); Multi-family building permits issued: 0 (2005); Employment by occupation: 29.5% management, 23.4% professional, 12.6% services, 23.9% sales, 0.0% farming, 5.0% construction, 5.5% production (2000).

Income: Per capita income: $71,451 (2005); Median household income: $126,394 (2005); Average household income: $190,515 (2005); Percent of households with income of $100,000 or more: 59.4% (2005); Poverty rate: 2.8% (2000).

Taxes: Total city taxes per capita: $1,053 (2004); City property taxes per capita: $1,017 (2004).

Education: Percent of population age 25 and over with: High school diploma (including GED) or higher: 92.8% (2005); Bachelor's degree or higher: 60.5% (2005); Master's degree or higher: 24.7% (2005).

School District(s)

Somerset Hills Regional (PK-12)

   2003-04 Enrollment: 1,915 . . . . (908) 630-3010

Housing: Homeownership rate: 83.8% (2005); Median home value: $674,817 (2005); Median rent: $982 per month (2000); Median age of housing: 42 years (2000).

Safety: Violent crime rate: 2.6 per 10,000 population; Property crime rate: 109.0 per 10,000 population (2004).

Newspapers: The Bernardsville News (General - Circulation 8,689)

Transportation: Commute to work: 81.4% car, 6.5% public transportation, 2.9% walk, 7.3% work from home (2000); Travel time to work: 28.5% less than 15 minutes, 25.6% 15 to 30 minutes, 22.2% 30 to 45 minutes, 7.6% 45 to 60 minutes, 16.2% 60 minutes or more (2000)

BOUND BROOK (borough).

Covers a land area of 1.706 square miles and a water area of 0 square miles. Located at 40.56° N. Lat.; 74.54° W. Long. Elevation is 48 feet.

History: During the American Revolution, George Washington maintained an outpost here, and American forces were defeated (April 1777) by those of British General Cornwallis. Local attractions include Washington's campgrounds and several 18th-century houses. Settled 1681, incorporated 1891

Population: 9,487 (1990); 10,155 (2000); 10,208 (2005); 10,353 (2010 projected); Race: 79.1% White, 2.6% Black, 3.2% Asian, 46.3% Hispanic of any race (2005); Density: 5,984.7 persons per square mile (2005); Average household size: 2.86 (2005); Median age: 35.6 (2005); Males per 100 females: 108.9 (2005); Marriage status: 30.6% never married, 53.7% now married, 7.6% widowed, 8.1% divorced (2000); Foreign born: 35.9% (2000); Ancestry (includes multiple ancestries): 39.1% Other groups, 18.7% Italian, 11.9% Irish, 9.9% German, 8.3% Polish (2000).

Economy: Largely residential, it produces chemicals, pharmaceuticals, and dyes. Single-family building permits issued: 3 (2005); Multi-family building permits issued: 0 (2005); Employment by occupation: 10.1% management, 15.7% professional, 18.8% services, 25.1% sales, 0.5% farming, 8.8% construction, 21.1% production (2000).

Income: Per capita income: $23,238 (2005); Median household income: $49,955 (2005); Average household income: $65,542 (2005); Percent of households with income of $100,000 or more: 17.6% (2005); Poverty rate: 10.9% (2000).

Education: Percent of population age 25 and over with: High school diploma (including GED) or higher: 75.2% (2005); Bachelor's degree or higher: 22.9% (2005); Master's degree or higher: 7.2% (2005).

School District(s)

Bound Brook Borough (PK-12)

   2003-04 Enrollment: 1,679 . . . . (732) 271-2830

Housing: Homeownership rate: 52.5% (2005); Median home value: $255,943 (2005); Median rent: $768 per month (2000); Median age of housing: 51 years (2000).

Safety: Violent crime rate: 12.7 per 10,000 population; Property crime rate: 211.3 per 10,000 population (2004).

Transportation: Commute to work: 83.4% car, 4.9% public transportation, 4.2% walk, 1.3% work from home (2000); Travel time to work: 30.6% less than 15 minutes, 39.2% 15 to 30 minutes, 16.1% 30 to 45 minutes, 6.1% 45 to 60 minutes, 8.1% 60 minutes or more (2000)

Additional Information Contacts

Bound Brook Chamber of Commerce . . . . (732) 356-7273

   http://www.boundbrook.com/Content/179/14.aspx

BRANCHBURG (township).

Covers a land area of 20.255 square miles and a water area of 0 square miles. Located at 40.56° N. Lat.; 74.71° W. Long.

Population: 10,958 (1990); 14,566 (2000); 15,028 (2005); 15,610 (2010 projected); Race: 88.5% White, 2.3% Black, 7.6% Asian, 3.4% Hispanic of any race (2005); Density: 741.9 persons per square mile (2005); Average household size: 2.72 (2005); Median age: 38.7 (2005); Males per 100 females: 96.8 (2005); Marriage status: 20.3% never married, 68.6% now married, 4.4% widowed, 6.6% divorced (2000); Foreign born: 10.7% (2000); Ancestry (includes multiple ancestries): 21.3% Italian, 18.7% German, 18.2% Irish, 13.1% Other groups, 10.2% English (2000).

Economy: Single-family building permits issued: 15 (2005); Multi-family building permits issued: 0 (2005); Employment by occupation: 29.0% management, 26.8% professional, 5.8% services, 25.3% sales, 0.0% farming, 6.6% construction, 6.6% production (2000).

Income: Per capita income: $47,395 (2005); Median household income: $107,702 (2005); Average household income: $129,149 (2005); Percent of households with income of $100,000 or more: 53.8% (2005); Poverty rate: 1.9% (2000).

Education: Percent of population age 25 and over with: High school diploma (including GED) or higher: 94.8% (2005); Bachelor's degree or higher: 53.6% (2005); Master's degree or higher: 23.1% (2005).

School District(s)

Branchburg Township (PK-08)

   2003-04 Enrollment: 1,933 . . . . (908) 722-3265

Housing: Homeownership rate: 88.5% (2005); Median home value: $428,386 (2005); Median rent: $943 per month (2000); Median age of housing: 17 years (2000).

Safety: Violent crime rate: 1.3 per 10,000 population; Property crime rate: 81.6 per 10,000 population (2004).

Transportation: Commute to work: 93.1% car, 2.2% public transportation, 0.7% walk, 3.1% work from home (2000); Travel time to work: 17.3% less than 15 minutes, 33.8% 15 to 30 minutes, 24.7% 30 to 45 minutes, 13.3% 45 to 60 minutes, 11.0% 60 minutes or more (2000)

Additional Information Contacts

Branchburg Township . . . . (908) 526-1300

   http://www.branchburg.nj.us

BRIDGEWATER (township).

Covers a land area of 32.447 square miles and a water area of 0.092 square miles. Located at 40.59° N. Lat.; 74.61° W. Long.

History: Incorporated 1798.

Population: 32,509 (1990); 42,940 (2000); 44,492 (2005); 46,314 (2010 projected); Race: 81.0% White, 2.5% Black, 13.9% Asian, 6.2% Hispanic of any race (2005); Density: 1,371.2 persons per square mile (2005); Average household size: 2.72 (2005); Median age: 39.3 (2005); Males per 100 females: 93.7 (2005); Marriage status: 20.1% never married, 67.7% now married, 6.3% widowed, 5.9% divorced (2000); Foreign born: 15.8% (2000); Ancestry (includes multiple ancestries): 21.3% Italian, 19.7% Other groups, 17.1% Irish, 16.7% German, 11.8% Polish (2000).

Economy: Industrial with manufacturing: telecommunications and office equipment, clothing. Rapidly expanding suburb. Unemployment rate: 3.0% (2005); Total civilian labor force: 24,687 (2005); Single-family building permits issued: 44 (2005); Multi-family building permits issued: 6 (2005); Employment by occupation: 24.0% management, 29.7% professional, 7.6% services, 25.9% sales, 0.1% farming, 6.8% construction, 5.9% production (2000).

Income: Per capita income: $44,716 (2005); Median household income: $97,929 (2005); Average household income: $120,417 (2005); Percent of households with income of $100,000 or more: 48.7% (2005); Poverty rate: 2.1% (2000).

Taxes: Total city taxes per capita: $308 (2004); City property taxes per capita: $288 (2004).

Education: Percent of population age 25 and over with: High school diploma (including GED) or higher: 91.8% (2005); Bachelor's degree or higher: 49.7% (2005); Master's degree or higher: 21.8% (2005).

School District(s)

Bridgewater-Raritan Regional (PK-12)

   2003-04 Enrollment: 8,894 . . . . (908) 685-2777

Somerset County Ed Serv Comm (09-12)

   2003-04 Enrollment: 294 . . . . (908) 707-8558

Somerset County Vocational (09-12)

   2003-04 Enrollment: 339 . . . . (908) 526-8900

Two-year College(s)

Somerset County Technology Institute (Public)

   Fall 2004 Enrollment: 545 . . . . (908) 526-8900

   2005-06 Tuition: In-state $5,000; Out-of-state $5,000

Housing: Homeownership rate: 85.5% (2005); Median home value: $408,829 (2005); Median rent: $952 per month (2000); Median age of housing: 24 years (2000).

Safety: Violent crime rate: 3.4 per 10,000 population; Property crime rate: 143.1 per 10,000 population (2004).

Newspapers: Courier News (Circulation 43,000)

Transportation: Commute to work: 91.4% car, 3.5% public transportation, 0.7% walk, 3.8% work from home (2000); Travel time to work: 24.7% less than 15 minutes, 31.0% 15 to 30 minutes, 22.4% 30 to 45 minutes, 11.4% 45 to 60 minutes, 10.5% 60 minutes or more (2000)

FAR HILLS (borough). Covers a land area of 4.860 square miles and a water area of 0.055 square miles. Located at 40.68° N. Lat.; 74.63° W. Long. Elevation is 140 feet.
Population: 657 (1990); 859 (2000); 925 (2005); 993 (2010 projected); Race: 95.1% White, 1.2% Black, 2.5% Asian, 3.7% Hispanic of any race (2005); Density: 190.3 persons per square mile (2005); Average household size: 2.29 (2005); Median age: 45.7 (2005); Males per 100 females: 91.5 (2005); Marriage status: 24.5% never married, 62.1% now married, 5.8% widowed, 7.7% divorced (2000); Foreign born: 11.7% (2000); Ancestry (includes multiple ancestries): 23.0% Irish, 16.5% German, 14.5% English, 13.8% Italian, 11.6% Other groups (2000).
Economy: In country-estate area that is suburbanizing. Single-family building permits issued: 1 (2005); Multi-family building permits issued: 0 (2005); Employment by occupation: 35.6% management, 19.9% professional, 13.2% services, 21.0% sales, 0.9% farming, 6.9% construction, 2.5% production (2000).
Income: Per capita income: $79,486 (2005); Median household income: $127,049 (2005); Average household income: $181,993 (2005); Percent of households with income of $100,000 or more: 58.2% (2005); Poverty rate: 2.5% (2000).
Education: Percent of population age 25 and over with: High school diploma (including GED) or higher: 94.9% (2005); Bachelor's degree or higher: 58.2% (2005); Master's degree or higher: 23.3% (2005).
Housing: Homeownership rate: 77.0% (2005); Median home value: $777,083 (2005); Median rent: $1,139 per month (2000); Median age of housing: 33 years (2000).
Safety: Violent crime rate: 0.0 per 10,000 population; Property crime rate: 33.0 per 10,000 population (2004).
Transportation: Commute to work: 81.3% car, 6.1% public transportation, 1.4% walk, 10.3% work from home (2000); Travel time to work: 26.8% less than 15 minutes, 31.8% 15 to 30 minutes, 15.6% 30 to 45 minutes, 13.5% 45 to 60 minutes, 12.2% 60 minutes or more (2000)

FRANKLIN (township). Covers a land area of 46.774 square miles and a water area of 0.073 square miles. Located at 40.49° N. Lat.; 74.51° W. Long.
History: Formerly farm area: corn, barley, wheat. Incorporated 1798.
Population: 42,780 (1990); 50,903 (2000); 56,558 (2005); 62,189 (2010 projected); Race: 47.7% White, 28.5% Black, 16.3% Asian, 10.1% Hispanic of any race (2005); Density: 1,209.2 persons per square mile (2005); Average household size: 2.64 (2005); Median age: 37.6 (2005); Males per 100 females: 92.7 (2005); Marriage status: 28.6% never married, 57.0% now married, 6.4% widowed, 8.0% divorced (2000); Foreign born: 23.2% (2000); Ancestry (includes multiple ancestries): 37.3% Other groups, 12.0% Italian, 10.0% Irish, 8.5% German, 6.9% Polish (2000).
Economy: Suburban development and service industries. Unemployment rate: 4.0% (2005); Total civilian labor force: 32,388 (2005); Single-family building permits issued: 518 (2005); Multi-family building permits issued: 69 (2005); Employment by occupation: 21.0% management, 30.7% professional, 9.1% services, 25.4% sales, 0.1% farming, 5.1% construction, 8.6% production (2000).
Income: Per capita income: $34,682 (2005); Median household income: $74,230 (2005); Average household income: $90,420 (2005); Percent of households with income of $100,000 or more: 31.7% (2005); Poverty rate: 5.1% (2000).
Taxes: Total city taxes per capita: $588 (2004); City property taxes per capita: $532 (2004).
Education: Percent of population age 25 and over with: High school diploma (including GED) or higher: 88.3% (2005); Bachelor's degree or higher: 43.4% (2005); Master's degree or higher: 16.1% (2005).
Housing: Homeownership rate: 71.9% (2005); Median home value: $267,829 (2005); Median rent: $838 per month (2000); Median age of housing: 21 years (2000).
Safety: Violent crime rate: 20.2 per 10,000 population; Property crime rate: 137.6 per 10,000 population (2004).
Transportation: Commute to work: 89.7% car, 6.2% public transportation, 1.1% walk, 2.1% work from home (2000); Travel time to work: 18.2% less than 15 minutes, 38.2% 15 to 30 minutes, 19.3% 30 to 45 minutes, 10.5% 45 to 60 minutes, 13.8% 60 minutes or more (2000)
Additional Information Contacts
Franklin Township . . . . (908) 735-5212
   http://www.franklintwpnj.org
Franklin Township . . . . (908) 735-5212
   http://www.franklintwpnj.org

Franklin Township Chamber of Commerce . . . . (732) 873-1717
   http://www.franklinchamber.com

FRANKLIN PARK (unincorporated postal area, zip code 08823). Covers a land area of 3.700 square miles and a water area of 0 square miles. Located at 40.43° N. Lat.; 74.55° W. Long.
Population: 7,389 (2000); Race: 49.9% White, 22.3% Black, 22.8% Asian, 5.7% Hispanic of any race (2000); Density: 1,996.8 persons per square mile (2000); Age: 23.1% under 18, 7.5% over 64 (2000); Marriage status: 30.9% never married, 53.1% now married, 5.5% widowed, 10.5% divorced (2000); Foreign born: 26.2% (2000); Ancestry (includes multiple ancestries): 43.9% Other groups, 10.5% Italian, 9.7% Irish, 7.4% German, 6.3% Polish (2000).
Economy: Employment by occupation: 25.5% management, 29.1% professional, 5.5% services, 29.9% sales, 0.0% farming, 2.8% construction, 7.2% production (2000).
Income: Per capita income: $32,755 (2000); Median household income: $64,051 (2000); Poverty rate: 3.2% (2000).
Education: Percent of population age 25 and over with: High school diploma (including GED) or higher: 92.0% (2000); Bachelor's degree or higher: 47.5% (2000).
School District(s)
Franklin Township (PK-12)
   2003-04 Enrollment: 6,840 . . . . (732) 873-2400
Housing: Homeownership rate: 83.4% (2000); Median home value: $144,300 (2000); Median rent: $1,035 per month (2000); Median age of housing: 10 years (2000).
Transportation: Commute to work: 88.0% car, 8.4% public transportation, 1.3% walk, 1.8% work from home (2000); Travel time to work: 7.6% less than 15 minutes, 41.9% 15 to 30 minutes, 20.9% 30 to 45 minutes, 10.4% 45 to 60 minutes, 19.2% 60 minutes or more (2000)

GLADSTONE (unincorporated postal area, zip code 07934). Aka Peapack and Gladstone. Covers a land area of 5.126 square miles and a water area of 0 square miles. Located at 40.71° N. Lat.; 74.68° W. Long. Elevation is 260 feet.
Population: 1,482 (2000); Race: 99.3% White, 0.2% Black, 0.2% Asian, 1.2% Hispanic of any race (2000); Density: 289.1 persons per square mile (2000); Age: 26.3% under 18, 14.5% over 64 (2000); Marriage status: 20.2% never married, 68.5% now married, 3.6% widowed, 7.8% divorced (2000); Foreign born: 7.8% (2000); Ancestry (includes multiple ancestries): 22.6% German, 19.4% English, 19.0% Irish, 18.6% Italian, 9.7% Polish (2000).
Economy: Employment by occupation: 40.6% management, 20.0% professional, 3.7% services, 27.9% sales, 0.3% farming, 4.1% construction, 3.4% production (2000).
Income: Per capita income: $60,789 (2000); Median household income: $104,078 (2000); Poverty rate: 2.7% (2000).
Education: Percent of population age 25 and over with: High school diploma (including GED) or higher: 94.3% (2000); Bachelor's degree or higher: 59.7% (2000).
Housing: Homeownership rate: 80.4% (2000); Median home value: $430,900 (2000); Median rent: $1,057 per month (2000); Median age of housing: 45 years (2000).
Transportation: Commute to work: 83.8% car, 5.9% public transportation, 4.8% walk, 5.5% work from home (2000); Travel time to work: 20.6% less than 15 minutes, 26.6% 15 to 30 minutes, 19.5% 30 to 45 minutes, 12.1% 45 to 60 minutes, 21.1% 60 minutes or more (2000)

GREEN BROOK (township). Covers a land area of 4.579 square miles and a water area of 0 square miles. Located at 40.60° N. Lat.; 74.48° W. Long.
Population: 4,456 (1990); 5,654 (2000); 6,823 (2005); 7,897 (2010 projected); Race: 85.0% White, 2.1% Black, 10.7% Asian, 5.0% Hispanic of any race (2005); Density: 1,489.9 persons per square mile (2005); Average household size: 2.94 (2005); Median age: 41.4 (2005); Males per 100 females: 92.6 (2005); Marriage status: 21.4% never married, 65.9% now married, 8.0% widowed, 4.7% divorced (2000); Foreign born: 13.1% (2000); Ancestry (includes multiple ancestries): 24.0% Italian, 20.2% Irish, 17.5% German, 16.9% Other groups, 10.9% Polish (2000).
Economy: Single-family building permits issued: 39 (2005); Multi-family building permits issued: 0 (2005); Employment by occupation: 22.0% management, 24.6% professional, 7.7% services, 28.1% sales, 0.0% farming, 8.5% construction, 9.2% production (2000).

Income: Per capita income: $43,025 (2005); Median household income: $95,526 (2005); Average household income: $125,193 (2005); Percent of households with income of $100,000 or more: 47.3% (2005); Poverty rate: 2.4% (2000).

Education: Percent of population age 25 and over with: High school diploma (including GED) or higher: 87.9% (2005); Bachelor's degree or higher: 40.0% (2005); Master's degree or higher: 15.1% (2005).

School District(s)
Green Brook Township (PK-08)
    2003-04 Enrollment: 905 . . . . (732) 968-1051

Housing: Homeownership rate: 90.3% (2005); Median home value: $391,543 (2005); Median rent: $1,023 per month (2000); Median age of housing: 35 years (2000).

Safety: Violent crime rate: 10.6 per 10,000 population; Property crime rate: 189.9 per 10,000 population (2004).

Transportation: Commute to work: 90.8% car, 3.7% public transportation, 1.2% walk, 3.6% work from home (2000); Travel time to work: 19.8% less than 15 minutes, 32.3% 15 to 30 minutes, 24.7% 30 to 45 minutes, 9.2% 45 to 60 minutes, 14.1% 60 minutes or more (2000)

HILLSBOROUGH (township).
Covers a land area of 54.689 square miles and a water area of 0.099 square miles. Located at 40.50° N. Lat.; 74.65° W. Long. Elevation is 100 feet.

History: Incorporated 1798.

Population: 28,842 (1990); 36,634 (2000); 38,125 (2005); 39,790 (2010 projected); Race: 83.4% White, 4.1% Black, 9.0% Asian, 5.9% Hispanic of any race (2005); Density: 697.1 persons per square mile (2005); Average household size: 2.90 (2005); Median age: 36.8 (2005); Males per 100 females: 98.2 (2005); Marriage status: 21.9% never married, 67.6% now married, 3.9% widowed, 6.6% divorced (2000); Foreign born: 12.1% (2000); Ancestry (includes multiple ancestries): 22.7% Italian, 18.1% Irish, 17.3% Other groups, 16.6% German, 13.1% Polish (2000).

Economy: Brick manufacturing. Unemployment rate: 3.0% (2005); Total civilian labor force: 21,823 (2005); Single-family building permits issued: 15 (2005); Multi-family building permits issued: 0 (2005); Employment by occupation: 24.3% management, 29.0% professional, 8.3% services, 25.6% sales, 0.5% farming, 5.7% construction, 6.7% production (2000).

Income: Per capita income: $39,060 (2005); Median household income: $94,135 (2005); Average household income: $112,509 (2005); Percent of households with income of $100,000 or more: 46.2% (2005); Poverty rate: 3.1% (2000).

Taxes: Total city taxes per capita: $394 (2004); City property taxes per capita: $360 (2004).

Education: Percent of population age 25 and over with: High school diploma (including GED) or higher: 92.7% (2005); Bachelor's degree or higher: 46.9% (2005); Master's degree or higher: 16.5% (2005).

Housing: Homeownership rate: 83.6% (2005); Median home value: $379,678 (2005); Median rent: $841 per month (2000); Median age of housing: 19 years (2000).

Safety: Violent crime rate: 5.0 per 10,000 population; Property crime rate: 94.0 per 10,000 population (2004).

Newspapers: Hillsborough Beacon (General - Circulation 4,500); The Manville News (General - Circulation 1,500)

Transportation: Commute to work: 92.0% car, 2.2% public transportation, 1.2% walk, 3.8% work from home (2000); Travel time to work: 18.5% less than 15 minutes, 32.9% 15 to 30 minutes, 24.6% 30 to 45 minutes, 12.1% 45 to 60 minutes, 12.0% 60 minutes or more (2000)

Additional Information Contacts
Hillsborough Township. . . . . (908) 369-4313
    http://www.harrisontwp.us
Somerset County Chamber of Commerce. . . . . (908) 725-1552
    http://www.somersetbusinesspartnership.com

MANVILLE (borough).
Covers a land area of 2.482 square miles and a water area of 0 square miles. Located at 40.53° N. Lat.; 74.59° W. Long. Elevation is 60 feet.

History: Named for the Johns-Manville Corporation, an asbestos products company. Laid out 1906. Incorporated 1929.

Population: 10,567 (1990); 10,343 (2000); 10,478 (2005); 10,723 (2010 projected); Race: 94.9% White, 0.6% Black, 1.7% Asian, 7.5% Hispanic of any race (2005); Density: 4,221.9 persons per square mile (2005); Average household size: 2.49 (2005); Median age: 41.1 (2005); Males per 100 females: 97.4 (2005); Marriage status: 26.5% never married, 54.5% now married, 10.7% widowed, 8.3% divorced (2000); Foreign born: 13.5%

(2000); Ancestry (includes multiple ancestries): 29.1% Polish, 20.5% Italian, 15.3% German, 12.4% Irish, 7.9% Other groups (2000).

Economy: Single-family building permits issued: 5 (2005); Multi-family building permits issued: 0 (2005); Employment by occupation: 10.9% management, 14.8% professional, 14.8% services, 30.7% sales, 0.2% farming, 12.1% construction, 16.5% production (2000).

Income: Per capita income: $25,803 (2005); Median household income: $56,126 (2005); Average household income: $64,216 (2005); Percent of households with income of $100,000 or more: 17.9% (2005); Poverty rate: 3.8% (2000).

Education: Percent of population age 25 and over with: High school diploma (including GED) or higher: 78.3% (2005); Bachelor's degree or higher: 13.8% (2005); Master's degree or higher: 3.7% (2005).

School District(s)
Manville Borough (PK-12)
    2003-04 Enrollment: 1,355 . . . . (908) 231-8545

Housing: Homeownership rate: 70.1% (2005); Median home value: $243,298 (2005); Median rent: $697 per month (2000); Median age of housing: 45 years (2000).

Safety: Violent crime rate: 6.7 per 10,000 population; Property crime rate: 227.2 per 10,000 population (2004).

Transportation: Commute to work: 95.3% car, 0.7% public transportation, 2.5% walk, 0.9% work from home (2000); Travel time to work: 33.2% less than 15 minutes, 40.8% 15 to 30 minutes, 12.8% 30 to 45 minutes, 6.0% 45 to 60 minutes, 7.2% 60 minutes or more (2000)

Additional Information Contacts
Franklin Township Chamber of Commerce . . . . (732) 873-1717
    http://www.franklinchamber.com

MARTINSVILLE (unincorporated postal area, zip code 08836).
Covers a land area of 5.542 square miles and a water area of 0.064 square miles. Located at 40.59° N. Lat.; 74.55° W. Long. Elevation is 306 feet.

Population: 3,962 (2000); Race: 92.9% White, 0.6% Black, 4.5% Asian, 0.5% Hispanic of any race (2000); Density: 714.9 persons per square mile (2000); Age: 27.4% under 18, 12.5% over 64 (2000); Marriage status: 17.3% never married, 74.7% now married, 5.6% widowed, 2.5% divorced (2000); Foreign born: 9.1% (2000); Ancestry (includes multiple ancestries): 20.6% Italian, 19.1% German, 18.0% Irish, 12.0% Polish, 9.5% Other groups (2000).

Economy: Employment by occupation: 28.6% management, 29.9% professional, 5.1% services, 25.0% sales, 0.0% farming, 8.1% construction, 3.3% production (2000).

Income: Per capita income: $53,167 (2000); Median household income: $113,639 (2000); Poverty rate: 1.5% (2000).

Education: Percent of population age 25 and over with: High school diploma (including GED) or higher: 94.7% (2000); Bachelor's degree or higher: 55.6% (2000).

Housing: Homeownership rate: 97.3% (2000); Median home value: $358,200 (2000); Median rent: $870 per month (2000); Median age of housing: 34 years (2000).

Transportation: Commute to work: 89.8% car, 3.3% public transportation, 1.4% walk, 5.5% work from home (2000); Travel time to work: 20.8% less than 15 minutes, 37.0% 15 to 30 minutes, 20.9% 30 to 45 minutes, 10.3% 45 to 60 minutes, 10.9% 60 minutes or more (2000)

MILLSTONE (borough).
Covers a land area of 0.749 square miles and a water area of 0 square miles. Located at 40.49° N. Lat.; 74.59° W. Long. Elevation is 60 feet.

Population: 450 (1990); 410 (2000); 414 (2005); 422 (2010 projected); Race: 97.8% White, 0.7% Black, 1.2% Asian, 4.8% Hispanic of any race (2005); Density: 552.4 persons per square mile (2005); Average household size: 2.38 (2005); Median age: 46.7 (2005); Males per 100 females: 95.3 (2005); Marriage status: 23.7% never married, 63.5% now married, 5.6% widowed, 7.3% divorced (2000); Foreign born: 4.6% (2000); Ancestry (includes multiple ancestries): 21.1% Irish, 19.9% Italian, 19.9% Polish, 19.2% German, 7.2% English (2000).

Economy: Single-family building permits issued: 0 (2005); Multi-family building permits issued: 0 (2005); Employment by occupation: 12.9% management, 40.0% professional, 8.3% services, 21.3% sales, 0.0% farming, 9.6% construction, 7.9% production (2000).

Income: Per capita income: $45,574 (2005); Median household income: $95,192 (2005); Average household income: $108,434 (2005); Percent of households with income of $100,000 or more: 47.1% (2005); Poverty rate: 4.6% (2000).

Education: Percent of population age 25 and over with: High school diploma (including GED) or higher: 91.6% (2005); Bachelor's degree or higher: 39.0% (2005); Master's degree or higher: 16.5% (2005).
Housing: Homeownership rate: 87.9% (2005); Median home value: $340,833 (2005); Median rent: $688 per month (2000); Median age of housing: 46 years (2000).
Transportation: Commute to work: 93.2% car, 0.0% public transportation, 3.0% walk, 3.4% work from home (2000); Travel time to work: 23.9% less than 15 minutes, 34.1% 15 to 30 minutes, 25.2% 30 to 45 minutes, 7.1% 45 to 60 minutes, 9.7% 60 minutes or more (2000)

MONTGOMERY (township). Covers a land area of 32.618 square miles and a water area of 0 square miles. Located at 40.43° N. Lat.; 74.66° W. Long. Elevation is 120 feet.

History: Incorporated 1798.
Population: 9,612 (1990); 17,481 (2000); 22,480 (2005); 27,160 (2010 projected); Race: 80.6% White, 2.1% Black, 15.2% Asian, 2.6% Hispanic of any race (2005); Density: 689.2 persons per square mile (2005); Average household size: 3.03 (2005); Median age: 37.3 (2005); Males per 100 females: 97.3 (2005); Marriage status: 17.5% never married, 74.4% now married, 3.1% widowed, 4.9% divorced (2000); Foreign born: 14.5% (2000); Ancestry (includes multiple ancestries): 18.3% Irish, 17.5% Italian, 17.2% Other groups, 15.3% German, 10.1% Polish (2000).
Economy: Single-family building permits issued: 17 (2005); Multi-family building permits issued: 0 (2005); Employment by occupation: 31.7% management, 38.0% professional, 4.5% services, 20.1% sales, 0.2% farming, 2.9% construction, 2.5% production (2000).
Income: Per capita income: $52,261 (2005); Median household income: $133,333 (2005); Average household income: $157,827 (2005); Percent of households with income of $100,000 or more: 67.4% (2005); Poverty rate: 1.5% (2000).
Education: Percent of population age 25 and over with: High school diploma (including GED) or higher: 97.3% (2005); Bachelor's degree or higher: 70.1% (2005); Master's degree or higher: 34.7% (2005).
Housing: Homeownership rate: 86.7% (2005); Median home value: $558,200 (2005); Median rent: $1,094 per month (2000); Median age of housing: 11 years (2000).
Safety: Violent crime rate: 1.9 per 10,000 population; Property crime rate: 97.8 per 10,000 population (2004).
Transportation: Commute to work: 87.9% car, 5.4% public transportation, 1.0% walk, 5.2% work from home (2000); Travel time to work: 14.1% less than 15 minutes, 34.1% 15 to 30 minutes, 26.1% 30 to 45 minutes, 8.7% 45 to 60 minutes, 17.0% 60 minutes or more (2000)
Additional Information Contacts
Montgomery County Chamber of Commerce . . . . (908) 725-1552
    http://www.somersetbusinesspartnership.com
Montgomery Township. . . . . (908) 359-8211
    http://www.montgomery.nj.us

NESHANIC STATION (unincorporated postal area, zip code 08853). Covers a land area of 31.821 square miles and a water area of 0.021 square miles. Located at 40.51° N. Lat.; 74.72° W. Long. Elevation is 100 feet.

Population: 12,241 (2000); Race: 92.4% White, 1.1% Black, 5.3% Asian, 2.3% Hispanic of any race (2000); Density: 384.7 persons per square mile (2000); Age: 29.7% under 18, 7.2% over 64 (2000); Marriage status: 19.7% never married, 71.4% now married, 4.4% widowed, 4.4% divorced (2000); Foreign born: 8.2% (2000); Ancestry (includes multiple ancestries): 22.9% Italian, 18.8% Irish, 16.9% German, 14.2% Polish, 10.7% Other groups (2000).
Economy: Employment by occupation: 28.6% management, 26.9% professional, 5.9% services, 25.7% sales, 0.2% farming, 7.3% construction, 5.5% production (2000).
Income: Per capita income: $37,964 (2000); Median household income: $100,432 (2000); Poverty rate: 2.4% (2000).
Education: Percent of population age 25 and over with: High school diploma (including GED) or higher: 93.1% (2000); Bachelor's degree or higher: 50.0% (2000).
School District(s)
Branchburg Township (PK-08)
    2003-04 Enrollment: 1,933 . . . . (908) 722-3265
Housing: Homeownership rate: 88.6% (2000); Median home value: $279,700 (2000); Median rent: $934 per month (2000); Median age of housing: 16 years (2000).

Transportation: Commute to work: 90.5% car, 2.7% public transportation, 1.5% walk, 4.7% work from home (2000); Travel time to work: 16.7% less than 15 minutes, 28.6% 15 to 30 minutes, 26.1% 30 to 45 minutes, 14.0% 45 to 60 minutes, 14.6% 60 minutes or more (2000)

NORTH PLAINFIELD (borough). Covers a land area of 2.790 square miles and a water area of 0 square miles. Located at 40.62° N. Lat.; 74.43° W. Long. Elevation is 100 feet.

History: Named for its location north of Plainfield. Settled 1736. Incorporated 1885. A Revolutionary War cemetery is here.
Population: 18,824 (1990); 21,103 (2000); 21,195 (2005); 21,512 (2010 projected); Race: 55.2% White, 16.4% Black, 5.9% Asian, 40.8% Hispanic of any race (2005); Density: 7,597.9 persons per square mile (2005); Average household size: 2.99 (2005); Median age: 35.1 (2005); Males per 100 females: 98.3 (2005); Marriage status: 29.9% never married, 55.9% now married, 5.9% widowed, 8.4% divorced (2000); Foreign born: 33.1% (2000); Ancestry (includes multiple ancestries): 46.9% Other groups, 13.9% Italian, 10.2% Irish, 10.1% German, 4.9% English (2000).
Economy: Single-family building permits issued: 2 (2005); Multi-family building permits issued: 0 (2005); Employment by occupation: 11.7% management, 19.2% professional, 12.7% services, 26.5% sales, 0.3% farming, 8.7% construction, 21.0% production (2000).
Income: Per capita income: $23,944 (2005); Median household income: $60,561 (2005); Average household income: $70,862 (2005); Percent of households with income of $100,000 or more: 20.9% (2005); Poverty rate: 6.4% (2000).
Education: Percent of population age 25 and over with: High school diploma (including GED) or higher: 80.1% (2005); Bachelor's degree or higher: 26.2% (2005); Master's degree or higher: 9.3% (2005).
School District(s)
North Plainfield Borough (PK-12)
    2003-04 Enrollment: 3,352 . . . . (908) 769-6060
Two-year College(s)
Reignbow Beauty Academy (Private, For-profit)
    Fall 2004 Enrollment: 106 . . . . (908) 754-4247
Housing: Homeownership rate: 58.8% (2005); Median home value: $243,964 (2005); Median rent: $759 per month (2000); Median age of housing: 48 years (2000).
Safety: Violent crime rate: 29.2 per 10,000 population; Property crime rate: 227.9 per 10,000 population (2004).
Transportation: Commute to work: 89.6% car, 4.4% public transportation, 1.8% walk, 2.0% work from home (2000); Travel time to work: 18.8% less than 15 minutes, 35.8% 15 to 30 minutes, 25.8% 30 to 45 minutes, 9.4% 45 to 60 minutes, 10.1% 60 minutes or more (2000)
Additional Information Contacts
Borough of North Plainfield . . . . (908) 769-2900
    http://www.northplainfield.org

PEAPACK AND GLADSTONE (borough). Covers a land area of 5.800 square miles and a water area of 0 square miles. Located at 40.71° N. Lat.; 74.66° W. Long.

Population: 2,111 (1990); 2,433 (2000); 2,470 (2005); 2,533 (2010 projected); Race: 93.9% White, 3.6% Black, 1.2% Asian, 5.2% Hispanic of any race (2005); Density: 425.9 persons per square mile (2005); Average household size: 2.95 (2005); Median age: 39.8 (2005); Males per 100 females: 98.1 (2005); Marriage status: 20.5% never married, 68.3% now married, 5.2% widowed, 6.0% divorced (2000); Foreign born: 12.1% (2000); Ancestry (includes multiple ancestries): 20.2% German, 19.0% Italian, 17.8% Irish, 14.7% English, 6.4% Polish (2000).
Economy: Single-family building permits issued: 1 (2005); Multi-family building permits issued: 0 (2005); Employment by occupation: 28.0% management, 23.7% professional, 12.8% services, 26.4% sales, 0.7% farming, 4.5% construction, 3.8% production (2000).
Income: Per capita income: $55,494 (2005); Median household income: $117,344 (2005); Average household income: $163,145 (2005); Percent of households with income of $100,000 or more: 56.6% (2005); Poverty rate: 4.2% (2000).
Education: Percent of population age 25 and over with: High school diploma (including GED) or higher: 93.0% (2005); Bachelor's degree or higher: 56.9% (2005); Master's degree or higher: 19.2% (2005).
Housing: Homeownership rate: 78.5% (2005); Median home value: $776,163 (2005); Median rent: $1,043 per month (2000); Median age of housing: 45 years (2000).
Hospitals: Matheny School and Hospital (87 beds)

Safety: Violent crime rate: 0.0 per 10,000 population; Property crime rate: 84.9 per 10,000 population (2004).
Transportation: Commute to work: 79.8% car, 4.7% public transportation, 8.2% walk, 7.1% work from home (2000); Travel time to work: 22.9% less than 15 minutes, 27.7% 15 to 30 minutes, 19.6% 30 to 45 minutes, 14.5% 45 to 60 minutes, 15.3% 60 minutes or more (2000)

RARITAN (borough). Covers a land area of 2.035 square miles and a water area of 0 square miles. Located at 40.57° N. Lat.; 74.63° W. Long. Elevation is 76 feet.
History: Incorporated 1868.
Population: 5,798 (1990); 6,338 (2000); 6,401 (2005); 6,535 (2010 projected); Race: 83.3% White, 1.3% Black, 11.4% Asian, 11.4% Hispanic of any race (2005); Density: 3,144.8 persons per square mile (2005); Average household size: 2.47 (2005); Median age: 39.0 (2005); Males per 100 females: 93.5 (2005); Marriage status: 24.0% never married, 59.0% now married, 8.1% widowed, 8.8% divorced (2000); Foreign born: 23.4% (2000); Ancestry (includes multiple ancestries): 34.1% Italian, 18.7% Other groups, 13.5% German, 11.0% Irish, 10.1% Polish (2000).
Economy: Manufacturing of metal products. Single-family building permits issued: 4 (2005); Multi-family building permits issued: 242 (2005); Employment by occupation: 15.2% management, 21.6% professional, 14.8% services, 27.2% sales, 0.0% farming, 8.8% construction, 12.4% production (2000).
Income: Per capita income: $30,625 (2005); Median household income: $59,179 (2005); Average household income: $75,434 (2005); Percent of households with income of $100,000 or more: 24.4% (2005); Poverty rate: 6.4% (2000).
Education: Percent of population age 25 and over with: High school diploma (including GED) or higher: 77.1% (2005); Bachelor's degree or higher: 26.6% (2005); Master's degree or higher: 8.9% (2005).
School District(s)
Bridgewater-Raritan Regional (PK-12)
    2003-04 Enrollment: 8,894 . . . . (908) 685-2777
Somerset County Ed Serv Comm (09-12)
    2003-04 Enrollment: 294 . . . . (908) 707-8558
Housing: Homeownership rate: 62.9% (2005); Median home value: $290,027 (2005); Median rent: $717 per month (2000); Median age of housing: 48 years (2000).
Safety: Violent crime rate: 12.5 per 10,000 population; Property crime rate: 207.7 per 10,000 population (2004).
Transportation: Commute to work: 89.7% car, 2.3% public transportation, 3.8% walk, 3.0% work from home (2000); Travel time to work: 38.7% less than 15 minutes, 31.4% 15 to 30 minutes, 14.8% 30 to 45 minutes, 8.5% 45 to 60 minutes, 6.6% 60 minutes or more (2000)
Additional Information Contacts
Raritan Chamber of Commerce . . . . (908) 429-0555
    http://www.somersetbusinesspartnership.com

ROCKY HILL (borough). Covers a land area of 0.674 square miles and a water area of 0 square miles. Located at 40.40° N. Lat.; 74.63° W. Long. Elevation is 100 feet.
History: Washington wrote his farewell address to the army here, 1783. A state historical site is here.
Population: 693 (1990); 662 (2000); 668 (2005); 683 (2010 projected); Race: 94.9% White, 1.3% Black, 0.4% Asian, 4.8% Hispanic of any race (2005); Density: 990.9 persons per square mile (2005); Average household size: 2.28 (2005); Median age: 45.3 (2005); Males per 100 females: 101.8 (2005); Marriage status: 18.4% never married, 70.9% now married, 4.3% widowed, 6.4% divorced (2000); Foreign born: 11.1% (2000); Ancestry (includes multiple ancestries): 19.8% German, 17.3% English, 14.4% Italian, 13.1% Irish, 7.3% Other groups (2000).
Economy: Major source of terra cotta for facings on Manhattan building facades. Single-family building permits issued: 0 (2005); Multi-family building permits issued: 0 (2005); Employment by occupation: 19.4% management, 41.8% professional, 8.0% services, 18.6% sales, 0.0% farming, 6.6% construction, 5.6% production (2000).
Income: Per capita income: $54,001 (2005); Median household income: $94,643 (2005); Average household income: $123,114 (2005); Percent of households with income of $100,000 or more: 47.4% (2005); Poverty rate: 2.7% (2000).
Education: Percent of population age 25 and over with: High school diploma (including GED) or higher: 96.0% (2005); Bachelor's degree or higher: 59.8% (2005); Master's degree or higher: 29.2% (2005).

Housing: Homeownership rate: 80.5% (2005); Median home value: $432,308 (2005); Median rent: $775 per month (2000); Median age of housing: 39 years (2000).
Transportation: Commute to work: 89.7% car, 3.2% public transportation, 1.4% walk, 5.7% work from home (2000); Travel time to work: 37.8% less than 15 minutes, 38.1% 15 to 30 minutes, 15.8% 30 to 45 minutes, 2.0% 45 to 60 minutes, 6.3% 60 minutes or more (2000)

SKILLMAN (unincorporated postal area, zip code 08558). Covers a land area of 15.329 square miles and a water area of 0 square miles. Located at 40.41° N. Lat.; 74.70° W. Long. Elevation is 120 feet.
Population: 5,202 (2000); Race: 91.4% White, 0.8% Black, 6.7% Asian, 2.3% Hispanic of any race (2000); Density: 339.4 persons per square mile (2000); Age: 30.0% under 18, 8.2% over 64 (2000); Marriage status: 17.2% never married, 73.7% now married, 3.0% widowed, 6.1% divorced (2000); Foreign born: 9.7% (2000); Ancestry (includes multiple ancestries): 19.7% German, 19.5% Italian, 18.1% Irish, 12.9% English, 12.4% Other groups (2000).
Economy: Employment by occupation: 30.8% management, 36.0% professional, 5.4% services, 20.4% sales, 0.3% farming, 4.3% construction, 2.8% production (2000).
Income: Per capita income: $55,876 (2000); Median household income: $126,027 (2000); Poverty rate: 1.2% (2000).
Education: Percent of population age 25 and over with: High school diploma (including GED) or higher: 97.2% (2000); Bachelor's degree or higher: 70.0% (2000).
School District(s)
Montgomery Township (PK-12)
    2003-04 Enrollment: 4,721 . . . . (908) 874-5201
Housing: Homeownership rate: 92.6% (2000); Median home value: $382,800 (2000); Median rent: $981 per month (2000); Median age of housing: 20 years (2000).
Transportation: Commute to work: 85.0% car, 5.1% public transportation, 0.8% walk, 8.1% work from home (2000); Travel time to work: 18.6% less than 15 minutes, 31.9% 15 to 30 minutes, 27.6% 30 to 45 minutes, 6.2% 45 to 60 minutes, 15.7% 60 minutes or more (2000)

SOMERSET (CDP). Covers a land area of 5.330 square miles and a water area of 0.028 square miles. Located at 40.49° N. Lat.; 74.48° W. Long. Elevation is 125 feet.
Population: 22,070 (1990); 23,040 (2000); 23,979 (2005); 25,090 (2010 projected); Race: 38.4% White, 40.3% Black, 9.7% Asian, 15.5% Hispanic of any race (2005); Density: 4,498.8 persons per square mile (2005); Average household size: 2.82 (2005); Median age: 36.8 (2005); Males per 100 females: 95.1 (2005); Marriage status: 30.5% never married, 56.0% now married, 5.9% widowed, 7.6% divorced (2000); Foreign born: 22.8% (2000); Ancestry (includes multiple ancestries): 43.1% Other groups, 8.6% Italian, 7.7% Irish, 6.2% German, 5.6% Polish (2000).
Economy: Manufacturing includes electrical and electronic products, computers, cosmetics, plastics, paint primers. Employment by occupation: 16.2% management, 28.4% professional, 11.3% services, 26.3% sales, 0.2% farming, 5.7% construction, 11.9% production (2000).
Income: Per capita income: $28,919 (2005); Median household income: $69,399 (2005); Average household income: $80,607 (2005); Percent of households with income of $100,000 or more: 27.7% (2005); Poverty rate: 7.0% (2000).
Education: Percent of population age 25 and over with: High school diploma (including GED) or higher: 84.8% (2005); Bachelor's degree or higher: 36.3% (2005); Master's degree or higher: 12.7% (2005).
School District(s)
Agency - Franklin CS (KG-06)
    2003-04 Enrollment: n/a . . . . (732) 764-4102
Franklin Township (PK-12)
    2003-04 Enrollment: 6,840 . . . . (732) 873-2400
Housing: Homeownership rate: 67.8% (2005); Median home value: $268,206 (2005); Median rent: $832 per month (2000); Median age of housing: 34 years (2000).
Newspapers: Somerset Spectator (General - Circulation 3,000)
Transportation: Commute to work: 89.8% car, 5.7% public transportation, 1.4% walk, 2.1% work from home (2000); Travel time to work: 23.0% less than 15 minutes, 37.4% 15 to 30 minutes, 18.6% 30 to 45 minutes, 9.1% 45 to 60 minutes, 11.9% 60 minutes or more (2000)
Additional Information Contacts
Franklin Township Chamber of Commerce . . . . (732) 545-7044
    http://franklinchamber.com

SOMERVILLE (borough). Covers a land area of 2.361 square miles and a water area of 0 square miles. Located at 40.57° N. Lat.; 74.60° W. Long. Elevation is 54 feet.

History: Named for Somerset County, which was named for Lord John Berkeley, Duke of Somerset. Of interest are the Wallace House, residence of George Washington 1778-1779, and the old Dutch parsonage (1751; now a museum). Settled 1683. Incorporated as a borough 1909.

Population: 11,632 (1990); 12,423 (2000); 12,421 (2005); 12,521 (2010 projected); Race: 66.7% White, 13.6% Black, 9.5% Asian, 22.2% Hispanic of any race (2005); Density: 5,261.5 persons per square mile (2005); Average household size: 2.63 (2005); Median age: 37.0 (2005); Males per 100 females: 103.1 (2005); Marriage status: 33.3% never married, 49.5% now married, 8.3% widowed, 8.9% divorced (2000); Foreign born: 22.5% (2000); Ancestry (includes multiple ancestries): 33.4% Other groups, 15.1% Italian, 13.4% Irish, 12.9% German, 6.8% Polish (2000).

Economy: Electronic parts and pharmaceuticals. Single-family building permits issued: 10 (2005); Multi-family building permits issued: 0 (2005); Employment by occupation: 13.9% management, 23.6% professional, 16.5% services, 26.0% sales, 0.0% farming, 8.7% construction, 11.4% production (2000).

Income: Per capita income: $25,159 (2005); Median household income: $55,377 (2005); Average household income: $64,216 (2005); Percent of households with income of $100,000 or more: 16.5% (2005); Poverty rate: 7.7% (2000).

Education: Percent of population age 25 and over with: High school diploma (including GED) or higher: 81.8% (2005); Bachelor's degree or higher: 31.9% (2005); Master's degree or higher: 10.7% (2005).

School District(s)

Branchburg Township (PK-08)
    2003-04 Enrollment: 1,933 . . . . (908) 722-3265
Hillsborough Township (PK-12)
    2003-04 Enrollment: 7,782 . . . . (908) 369-0030
Somerville Borough (PK-12)
    2003-04 Enrollment: 2,236 . . . . (908) 218-4101

Two-year College(s)

Raritan Valley Community College (Public)
    Fall 2004 Enrollment: 6,451 . . . . (908) 526-1200
    2005-06 Tuition: In-state $3,160; Out-of-state $3,160

Housing: Homeownership rate: 48.3% (2005); Median home value: $252,735 (2005); Median rent: $743 per month (2000); Median age of housing: 48 years (2000).

Hospitals: Somerset Medical Center (355 beds)

Safety: Violent crime rate: 32.1 per 10,000 population; Property crime rate: 201.2 per 10,000 population (2004).

Newspapers: Cranford Chronicle (General - Circulation 4,754); Record-Press (General - Circulation 10,000); Somerset Messenger Gazette (General - Circulation 4,743); The Chronicle (General - Circulation 4,743); The Reporter (General - Circulation 3,140); The Review (General - Circulation 4,743)

Transportation: Commute to work: 87.9% car, 3.2% public transportation, 5.1% walk, 2.3% work from home (2000); Travel time to work: 36.7% less than 15 minutes, 33.5% 15 to 30 minutes, 17.1% 30 to 45 minutes, 6.0% 45 to 60 minutes, 6.7% 60 minutes or more (2000)

Additional Information Contacts

Borough of Somerville . . . . (908) 725-2300
    http://www.somervillenj.org
Somerset County Business Partnership . . . . (908) 218-4300
    http://www.somersetbusinesspartnership.com
Somerset County Chamber of Commerce. . . . . (908) 725-1552
    http://www.somersetbusinesspartnership.com

SOUTH BOUND BROOK (borough). Covers a land area of 0.779 square miles and a water area of 0 square miles. Located at 40.55° N. Lat.; 74.53° W. Long. Elevation is 45 feet.

History: Baron von Steuben had headquarters here, 1778-1779. Incorporated 1907.

Population: 4,185 (1990); 4,492 (2000); 4,523 (2005); 4,603 (2010 projected); Race: 74.3% White, 7.7% Black, 5.3% Asian, 31.1% Hispanic of any race (2005); Density: 5,805.1 persons per square mile (2005); Average household size: 2.81 (2005); Median age: 36.8 (2005); Males per 100 females: 106.1 (2005); Marriage status: 34.6% never married, 49.9% now married, 6.4% widowed, 9.0% divorced (2000); Foreign born: 22.2% (2000); Ancestry (includes multiple ancestries): 33.3% Other groups, 15.3% German, 14.4% Italian, 12.7% Polish, 12.3% Irish (2000).

Economy: Industrial borough. Single-family building permits issued: 44 (2005); Multi-family building permits issued: 77 (2005); Employment by occupation: 8.8% management, 14.9% professional, 16.6% services, 30.0% sales, 0.7% farming, 9.2% construction, 19.8% production (2000).

Income: Per capita income: $20,894 (2005); Median household income: $50,587 (2005); Average household income: $58,735 (2005); Percent of households with income of $100,000 or more: 12.6% (2005); Poverty rate: 6.7% (2000).

Education: Percent of population age 25 and over with: High school diploma (including GED) or higher: 78.6% (2005); Bachelor's degree or higher: 17.7% (2005); Master's degree or higher: 6.7% (2005).

School District(s)

South Bound Brook (PK-08)
    2003-04 Enrollment: 508 . . . . (908) 356-0018

Housing: Homeownership rate: 58.0% (2005); Median home value: $228,843 (2005); Median rent: $701 per month (2000); Median age of housing: 46 years (2000).

Safety: Violent crime rate: 11.0 per 10,000 population; Property crime rate: 22.1 per 10,000 population (2004).

Transportation: Commute to work: 92.1% car, 1.6% public transportation, 3.8% walk, 1.3% work from home (2000); Travel time to work: 29.5% less than 15 minutes, 44.9% 15 to 30 minutes, 12.4% 30 to 45 minutes, 5.3% 45 to 60 minutes, 7.9% 60 minutes or more (2000)

WARREN (township). Aka Warrenville. Covers a land area of 19.668 square miles and a water area of 0 square miles. Located at 40.63° N. Lat.; 74.50° W. Long.

History: Incorporated 1806.

Population: 10,733 (1990); 14,259 (2000); 15,838 (2005); 17,414 (2010 projected); Race: 83.9% White, 1.4% Black, 12.8% Asian, 3.9% Hispanic of any race (2005); Density: 805.3 persons per square mile (2005); Average household size: 3.10 (2005); Median age: 39.7 (2005); Males per 100 females: 99.1 (2005); Marriage status: 18.7% never married, 72.9% now married, 4.6% widowed, 3.8% divorced (2000); Foreign born: 15.7% (2000); Ancestry (includes multiple ancestries): 23.5% Italian, 18.2% Other groups, 13.8% German, 13.4% Irish, 8.0% Polish (2000).

Economy: Residential with some light industry. Single-family building permits issued: 30 (2005); Multi-family building permits issued: 0 (2005); Employment by occupation: 27.5% management, 30.4% professional, 8.1% services, 23.4% sales, 0.1% farming, 5.1% construction, 5.5% production (2000).

Income: Per capita income: $57,208 (2005); Median household income: $125,234 (2005); Average household income: $176,440 (2005); Percent of households with income of $100,000 or more: 59.5% (2005); Poverty rate: 2.1% (2000).

Education: Percent of population age 25 and over with: High school diploma (including GED) or higher: 93.6% (2005); Bachelor's degree or higher: 58.5% (2005); Master's degree or higher: 28.5% (2005).

School District(s)

Warren Township (PK-08)
    2003-04 Enrollment: 2,229 . . . . (732) 560-8700
Watchung Hills Regional (09-12)
    2003-04 Enrollment: 1,735 . . . . (908) 647-4890

Housing: Homeownership rate: 92.4% (2005); Median home value: $696,594 (2005); Median rent: $975 per month (2000); Median age of housing: 26 years (2000).

Safety: Violent crime rate: 4.5 per 10,000 population; Property crime rate: 100.9 per 10,000 population (2004).

Transportation: Commute to work: 89.4% car, 4.3% public transportation, 0.8% walk, 5.0% work from home (2000); Travel time to work: 19.5% less than 15 minutes, 30.8% 15 to 30 minutes, 25.2% 30 to 45 minutes, 10.5% 45 to 60 minutes, 14.0% 60 minutes or more (2000)

Additional Information Contacts

Warren Township. . . . . (908) 753-8000
    http://www.warrennj.org

WATCHUNG (borough). Covers a land area of 6.016 square miles and a water area of 0.018 square miles. Located at 40.63° N. Lat.; 74.44° W. Long. Elevation is 181 feet.

History: Incorporated 1926.

Population: 5,207 (1990); 5,613 (2000); 5,815 (2005); 6,069 (2010 projected); Race: 79.9% White, 4.5% Black, 12.6% Asian, 3.9% Hispanic of any race (2005); Density: 966.5 persons per square mile (2005); Average household size: 2.62 (2005); Median age: 44.6 (2005); Males per 100 females: 96.1 (2005); Marriage status: 18.8% never married, 70.7% now married, 5.4% widowed, 5.1% divorced (2000); Foreign born: 15.3% (2000); Ancestry (includes multiple ancestries): 17.5% Other groups, 16.4% Italian, 16.0% German, 15.7% Irish, 8.0% Polish (2000).

Economy: Single-family building permits issued: 35 (2005); Multi-family building permits issued: 8 (2005); Employment by occupation: 23.8% management, 35.0% professional, 7.4% services, 21.9% sales, 0.0% farming, 5.8% construction, 6.0% production (2000).

Income: Per capita income: $63,007 (2005); Median household income: $120,413 (2005); Average household income: $164,535 (2005); Percent of households with income of $100,000 or more: 58.0% (2005); Poverty rate: 2.2% (2000).

Education: Percent of population age 25 and over with: High school diploma (including GED) or higher: 93.8% (2005); Bachelor's degree or higher: 57.1% (2005); Master's degree or higher: 31.5% (2005).

School District(s)

Watchung Borough (PK-08)

   2003-04 Enrollment: 647 . . . . (908) 755-8121

Housing: Homeownership rate: 81.3% (2005); Median home value: $697,954 (2005); Median rent: $784 per month (2000); Median age of housing: 35 years (2000).

Safety: Violent crime rate: 5.2 per 10,000 population; Property crime rate: 621.3 per 10,000 population (2004).

Transportation: Commute to work: 87.0% car, 4.2% public transportation, 0.0% walk, 8.5% work from home (2000); Travel time to work: 21.0% less than 15 minutes, 34.5% 15 to 30 minutes, 28.0% 30 to 45 minutes, 5.5% 45 to 60 minutes, 11.1% 60 minutes or more (2000)

Additional Information Contacts

Borough of Watchung . . . . (908) 756-0080
   http://watchungnj.com

Sussex County

Located in northwestern New Jersey; bounded on the west by the Delaware River and the Pennsylvania border, and on the north by New York; mountainous area, includes the Kittatinny Mountains and High Point, the highest point in the state (1,801 ft); drained by the Musconetcong, Wallkill, and Pequest Rivers. Covers a land area of 521.26 square miles, a water area of 14.73 square miles, and is located in the Eastern Time Zone. The county government was organized in 1753. County seat is Newton.

Sussex County is part of the New York-Northern New Jersey-Long Island, NY-NJ-PA Metropolitan Statistical Area. The entire metro area includes: Edison, NJ Metropolitan Division (Middlesex County, NJ; Monmouth County, NJ; Ocean County, NJ; Somerset County, NJ); Nassau-Suffolk, NY Metropolitan Division (Nassau County, NY; Suffolk County, NY); New York-White Plains-Wayne, NY-NJ Metropolitan Division (Bergen County, NJ; Hudson County, NJ; Passaic County, NJ; Bronx County, NY; Kings County, NY; New York County, NY; Putnam County, NY; Queens County, NY; Richmond County, NY; Rockland County, NY; Westchester County, NY); Newark-Union, NJ-PA Metropolitan Division (Essex County, NJ; Hunterdon County, NJ; Morris County, NJ; Sussex County, NJ; Union County, NJ; Pike County, PA)

Weather Station: Newton Saint Pauls Abbey									Elevation: 597 feet		
	Jan	Feb	Mar	Apr	May	Jun	Jul	Aug	Sep	Oct	Nov	Dec
High	34	37	46	59	70	78	83	81	73	62	50	39
Low	14	16	25	35	45	54	59	57	49	37	30	21
Precip	3.5	2.8	3.7	4.1	4.3	4.5	4.3	4.4	4.6	3.8	3.9	3.4
Snow	11.1	9.9	7.4	2.0	tr	0.0	0.0	0.0	0.0	0.1	1.9	5.4

High and Low temperatures in degrees Fahrenheit; Precipitation and Snow in inches

Population: 130,676 (1990); 144,166 (2000); 154,441 (2005); 165,191 (2010 projected); Race: 94.7% White, 1.3% Black, 1.5% Asian, 4.7% Hispanic of any race (2005); Density: 296.3 persons per square mile (2005); Average household size: 2.80 (2005); Median age: 38.2 (2005); Males per 100 females: 98.0 (2005).

Religion: Five largest groups: 31.0% Catholic Church, 2.8% Jewish Estimate, 2.8% The United Methodist Church, 2.7% Presbyterian Church (U.S.A.), 1.1% Episcopal Church (2000).

Economy: Unemployment rate: 3.8% (2005); Total civilian labor force: 83,100 (2005); Leading industries: 17.9% retail trade; 16.5% health care and social assistance; 10.9% accommodation & food services (2004); Farms: 1,029 totaling 75,496 acres (2002); Companies that employ 500 or more persons: 6 (2004); Companies that employ 100 to 499 persons: 78 (2004); Companies that employ less than 100 persons: 7,345 (2004); Black-owned businesses: n/a (2002); Hispanic-owned businesses: n/a

(2002); Asian-owned businesses: 172 (2002); Women-owned businesses: 3,829 (2002); Retail sales per capita: $12,031 (2006). Single-family building permits issued: 666 (2005); Multi-family building permits issued: 2 (2005).

Income: Per capita income: $31,475 (2005); Median household income: $73,496 (2005); Average household income: $87,693 (2005); Percent of households with income of $100,000 or more: 31.2% (2005); Poverty rate: 4.8% (2003); Bankruptcy rate: 4.54% (2005).

Taxes: Total county taxes per capita: $400 (2004); County property taxes per capita: $399 (2004).

Education: Percent of population age 25 and over with: High school diploma (including GED) or higher: 89.8% (2005); Bachelor's degree or higher: 27.3% (2005); Master's degree or higher: 8.7% (2005).

Housing: Homeownership rate: 82.8% (2005); Median home value: $254,880 (2005); Median rent: $680 per month (2000); Median age of housing: 31 years (2000).

Health: Birth rate: 113.3 per 10,000 population (2004); Death rate: 65.0 per 10,000 population (2004); Age-adjusted cancer mortality rate: 209.7 deaths per 100,000 population (2002); Number of physicians: 14.6 per 10,000 population (2004); Hospital beds: 9.7 per 10,000 population (2003); Hospital admissions: 711.9 per 10,000 population (2003).

Elections: 2004 Presidential election results: 64.1% Bush, 34.6% Kerry, 0.7% Nader, 0.2% Badnarik

National and State Parks: Appalachian National Scenic Trail; Cranberry State Park; High Point State Park; Musconetcong State Park; Stokes State Forest; Swartswood State Park

Additional Information Contacts

Sussex County Government . . . . (973) 579-0210
   http://www.sussex.nj.us
Borough of Hopatcong. . . . . (973) 770-1200
   http://www.hopatcong.org
Byram Township . . . . (973) 347-2500
   http://byramtwp.org
Franklin Township Chamber of Commerce . . . . (732) 873-1717
   http://www.franklinchamber.com
Fredon Township . . . . (973) 383-7025
   http://twp.fredon.nj.us
Green Township. . . . . (908) 852-9333
   http://www.greentwp.com
Montague Township. . . . . (973) 293-7300
   http://www.montaguenj.org
Sussex County Chamber of Commerce . . . . (973) 579-1811
   http://www.sussexcountychamber.org
Vernon Chamber of Commerce. . . . . (973) 764-0764
   http://www.vernonchamber.com
Vernon Township . . . . (973) 764-4055
   http://www.vernontwp.com/township
Wantage Township . . . . (973) 875-7192
   http://www.wantagetwp.com

Sussex County Communities

ANDOVER (borough). Covers a land area of 1.456 square miles and a water area of 0.012 square miles. Located at 40.98° N. Lat.; 74.74° W. Long. Elevation is 646 feet.

Population: 666 (1990); 658 (2000); 744 (2005); 842 (2010 projected); Race: 90.3% White, 2.8% Black, 3.5% Asian, 3.2% Hispanic of any race (2005); Density: 511.0 persons per square mile (2005); Average household size: 2.50 (2005); Median age: 38.4 (2005); Males per 100 females: 104.4 (2005); Marriage status: 32.7% never married, 50.9% now married, 3.3% widowed, 13.1% divorced (2000); Foreign born: 5.5% (2000); Ancestry (includes multiple ancestries): 23.9% Irish, 19.9% German, 17.8% Italian, 11.6% English, 9.1% Other groups (2000).

Economy: Single-family building permits issued: 0 (2005); Multi-family building permits issued: 0 (2005); Employment by occupation: 13.9% management, 13.7% professional, 10.4% services, 30.0% sales, 2.4% farming, 14.4% construction, 15.1% production (2000).

Income: Per capita income: $32,114 (2005); Median household income: $72,388 (2005); Average household income: $80,176 (2005); Percent of households with income of $100,000 or more: 30.2% (2005); Poverty rate: 2.8% (2000).

Education: Percent of population age 25 and over with: High school diploma (including GED) or higher: 84.0% (2005); Bachelor's degree or higher: 20.0% (2005); Master's degree or higher: 6.5% (2005).

Housing: Homeownership rate: 59.7% (2005); Median home value: $250,000 (2005); Median rent: $671 per month (2000); Median age of housing: 60+ years (2000).

Transportation: Commute to work: 92.3% car, 0.7% public transportation, 3.8% walk, 3.1% work from home (2000); Travel time to work: 27.5% less than 15 minutes, 30.0% 15 to 30 minutes, 15.1% 30 to 45 minutes, 13.4% 45 to 60 minutes, 13.9% 60 minutes or more (2000)

ANDOVER (township). Covers a land area of 20.184 square miles and a water area of 0.571 square miles. Located at 41.01° N. Lat.; 74.73° W. Long. Elevation is 646 feet.

History: Furnished iron in Revolution.

Population: 5,313 (1990); 6,033 (2000); 6,548 (2005); 7,073 (2010 projected); Race: 92.8% White, 2.5% Black, 3.0% Asian, 3.2% Hispanic of any race (2005); Density: 324.4 persons per square mile (2005); Average household size: 3.15 (2005); Median age: 42.0 (2005); Males per 100 females: 93.4 (2005); Marriage status: 23.8% never married, 60.8% now married, 8.8% widowed, 6.6% divorced (2000); Foreign born: 7.4% (2000); Ancestry (includes multiple ancestries): 24.7% German, 23.3% Irish, 18.6% Italian, 8.0% English, 7.8% Other groups (2000).

Economy: Iron ore. Single-family building permits issued: 31 (2005); Multi-family building permits issued: 0 (2005); Employment by occupation: 20.5% management, 25.2% professional, 9.6% services, 28.5% sales, 0.0% farming, 7.1% construction, 9.0% production (2000).

Income: Per capita income: $36,203 (2005); Median household income: $89,770 (2005); Average household income: $109,538 (2005); Percent of households with income of $100,000 or more: 42.5% (2005); Poverty rate: 3.5% (2000).

Education: Percent of population age 25 and over with: High school diploma (including GED) or higher: 84.4% (2005); Bachelor's degree or higher: 29.0% (2005); Master's degree or higher: 8.9% (2005).

Housing: Homeownership rate: 84.6% (2005); Median home value: $264,748 (2005); Median rent: $920 per month (2000); Median age of housing: 30 years (2000).

Safety: Violent crime rate: 10.8 per 10,000 population; Property crime rate: 47.8 per 10,000 population (2004).

Transportation: Commute to work: 94.4% car, 1.1% public transportation, 0.2% walk, 3.8% work from home (2000); Travel time to work: 26.9% less than 15 minutes, 25.1% 15 to 30 minutes, 13.9% 30 to 45 minutes, 10.9% 45 to 60 minutes, 23.1% 60 minutes or more (2000)

AUGUSTA (unincorporated postal area, zip code 07822). Covers a land area of 6.888 square miles and a water area of 0.002 square miles. Located at 41.14° N. Lat.; 74.69° W. Long. Elevation is 498 feet.

Population: 843 (2000); Race: 99.1% White, 0.0% Black, 0.0% Asian, 0.9% Hispanic of any race (2000); Density: 122.4 persons per square mile (2000); Age: 26.7% under 18, 8.5% over 64 (2000); Marriage status: 20.7% never married, 71.3% now married, 2.8% widowed, 5.1% divorced (2000); Foreign born: 2.0% (2000); Ancestry (includes multiple ancestries): 39.1% German, 24.0% Irish, 18.6% Italian, 15.1% Dutch, 11.4% English (2000).

Economy: Employment by occupation: 18.3% management, 22.8% professional, 16.7% services, 17.3% sales, 0.0% farming, 19.8% construction, 5.1% production (2000).

Income: Per capita income: $27,740 (2000); Median household income: $75,525 (2000); Poverty rate: 2.7% (2000).

Education: Percent of population age 25 and over with: High school diploma (including GED) or higher: 92.2% (2000); Bachelor's degree or higher: 24.6% (2000).

Housing: Homeownership rate: 88.4% (2000); Median home value: $202,000 (2000); Median rent: $434 per month (2000); Median age of housing: 21 years (2000).

Transportation: Commute to work: 84.5% car, 2.9% public transportation, 4.0% walk, 7.3% work from home (2000); Travel time to work: 21.2% less than 15 minutes, 20.5% 15 to 30 minutes, 9.3% 30 to 45 minutes, 9.9% 45 to 60 minutes, 39.1% 60 minutes or more (2000)

BRANCHVILLE (borough). Covers a land area of 0.594 square miles and a water area of 0 square miles. Located at 41.14° N. Lat.; 74.74° W. Long. Elevation is 800 feet.

History: Appalachian Trail to Northwest.

Population: 865 (1990); 845 (2000); 781 (2005); 781 (2010 projected); Race: 98.2% White, 0.3% Black, 0.3% Asian, 1.7% Hispanic of any race (2005); Density: 1,313.9 persons per square mile (2005); Average household size: 2.32 (2005); Median age: 42.8 (2005); Males per 100 females: 86.8 (2005); Marriage status: 20.5% never married, 57.0% now

married, 11.3% widowed, 11.1% divorced (2000); Foreign born: 2.1% (2000); Ancestry (includes multiple ancestries): 24.9% English, 24.3% German, 21.1% Irish, 10.5% Italian, 8.9% Other groups (2000).

Economy: Single-family building permits issued: 2 (2005); Multi-family building permits issued: 0 (2005); Employment by occupation: 8.2% management, 21.2% professional, 13.0% services, 29.3% sales, 0.5% farming, 13.7% construction, 14.2% production (2000).

Income: Per capita income: $24,873 (2005); Median household income: $48,578 (2005); Average household income: $56,454 (2005); Percent of households with income of $100,000 or more: 13.9% (2005); Poverty rate: 4.4% (2000).

Education: Percent of population age 25 and over with: High school diploma (including GED) or higher: 85.5% (2005); Bachelor's degree or higher: 18.4% (2005); Master's degree or higher: 6.9% (2005).

School District(s)

Frankford Township (PK-08)

   2003-04 Enrollment: 763 . . . . (973) 948-3727

Housing: Homeownership rate: 64.7% (2005); Median home value: $238,843 (2005); Median rent: $588 per month (2000); Median age of housing: 60+ years (2000).

Transportation: Commute to work: 91.2% car, 1.2% public transportation, 2.7% walk, 4.4% work from home (2000); Travel time to work: 32.6% less than 15 minutes, 36.8% 15 to 30 minutes, 11.6% 30 to 45 minutes, 11.1% 45 to 60 minutes, 8.0% 60 minutes or more (2000)

BYRAM (township). Covers a land area of 21.068 square miles and a water area of 1.107 square miles. Located at 40.96° N. Lat.; 74.72° W. Long.

Population: 8,404 (1990); 8,254 (2000); 8,711 (2005); 9,210 (2010 projected); Race: 94.9% White, 1.3% Black, 1.7% Asian, 3.9% Hispanic of any race (2005); Density: 413.5 persons per square mile (2005); Average household size: 2.87 (2005); Median age: 37.9 (2005); Males per 100 females: 98.9 (2005); Marriage status: 20.8% never married, 70.0% now married, 3.6% widowed, 5.6% divorced (2000); Foreign born: 6.1% (2000); Ancestry (includes multiple ancestries): 27.2% Irish, 25.9% Italian, 22.0% German, 10.2% Polish, 7.8% Other groups (2000).

Economy: Manufacturing: glass, pharmaceuticals. Single-family building permits issued: 18 (2005); Multi-family building permits issued: 0 (2005); Employment by occupation: 21.6% management, 22.9% professional, 10.2% services, 28.4% sales, 0.1% farming, 9.1% construction, 7.7% production (2000).

Income: Per capita income: $35,651 (2005); Median household income: $90,004 (2005); Average household income: $102,256 (2005); Percent of households with income of $100,000 or more: 42.2% (2005); Poverty rate: 1.7% (2000).

Education: Percent of population age 25 and over with: High school diploma (including GED) or higher: 94.0% (2005); Bachelor's degree or higher: 31.8% (2005); Master's degree or higher: 9.2% (2005).

Housing: Homeownership rate: 92.9% (2005); Median home value: $276,561 (2005); Median rent: $823 per month (2000); Median age of housing: 32 years (2000).

Safety: Violent crime rate: 9.3 per 10,000 population; Property crime rate: 83.6 per 10,000 population (2004).

Transportation: Commute to work: 94.8% car, 1.4% public transportation, 0.5% walk, 2.9% work from home (2000); Travel time to work: 15.8% less than 15 minutes, 24.3% 15 to 30 minutes, 18.4% 30 to 45 minutes, 19.3% 45 to 60 minutes, 22.2% 60 minutes or more (2000)

Additional Information Contacts

Byram Township . . . . (973) 347-2500
  http://byramtwp.org

CRANDON LAKES (CDP). Covers a land area of 2.531 square miles and a water area of 0.135 square miles. Located at 41.12° N. Lat.; 74.84° W. Long.

Population: 1,177 (1990); 1,180 (2000); 1,183 (2005); 1,200 (2010 projected); Race: 97.7% White, 0.3% Black, 0.5% Asian, 1.9% Hispanic of any race (2005); Density: 467.3 persons per square mile (2005); Average household size: 2.89 (2005); Median age: 36.4 (2005); Males per 100 females: 96.5 (2005); Marriage status: 21.5% never married, 63.1% now married, 6.9% widowed, 8.6% divorced (2000); Foreign born: 4.7% (2000); Ancestry (includes multiple ancestries): 23.5% Irish, 22.5% German, 19.9% Italian, 12.3% Polish, 10.3% English (2000).

Economy: Employment by occupation: 9.2% management, 15.5% professional, 18.3% services, 22.4% sales, 0.0% farming, 16.5% construction, 18.1% production (2000).

Income: Per capita income: $27,098 (2005); Median household income: $66,071 (2005); Average household income: $78,380 (2005); Percent of households with income of $100,000 or more: 28.4% (2005); Poverty rate: 1.5% (2000).

Education: Percent of population age 25 and over with: High school diploma (including GED) or higher: 89.8% (2005); Bachelor's degree or higher: 23.7% (2005); Master's degree or higher: 0.0% (2005).

Housing: Homeownership rate: 93.4% (2005); Median home value: $187,871 (2005); Median rent: $867 per month (2000); Median age of housing: 34 years (2000).

Transportation: Commute to work: 97.4% car, 0.0% public transportation, 0.0% walk, 2.6% work from home (2000); Travel time to work: 12.9% less than 15 minutes, 35.4% 15 to 30 minutes, 19.0% 30 to 45 minutes, 10.3% 45 to 60 minutes, 22.4% 60 minutes or more (2000)

FRANKFORD (township). Covers a land area of 34.114 square miles and a water area of 1.312 square miles. Located at 41.15° N. Lat.; 74.74° W. Long.

Population: 5,100 (1990); 5,420 (2000); 5,806 (2005); 6,161 (2010 projected); Race: 97.7% White, 0.4% Black, 0.4% Asian, 2.4% Hispanic of any race (2005); Density: 170.2 persons per square mile (2005); Average household size: 2.89 (2005); Median age: 42.5 (2005); Males per 100 females: 95.8 (2005); Marriage status: 21.9% never married, 64.6% now married, 7.4% widowed, 6.1% divorced (2000); Foreign born: 3.0% (2000); Ancestry (includes multiple ancestries): 25.7% German, 23.9% Irish, 16.9% Italian, 13.8% English, 8.7% Dutch (2000).

Economy: Incorporated 1798. Single-family building permits issued: 19 (2005); Multi-family building permits issued: 0 (2005); Employment by occupation: 16.0% management, 21.1% professional, 16.7% services, 23.7% sales, 0.4% farming, 11.2% construction, 10.8% production (2000).

Income: Per capita income: $28,008 (2005); Median household income: $70,313 (2005); Average household income: $78,767 (2005); Percent of households with income of $100,000 or more: 27.8% (2005); Poverty rate: 5.1% (2000).

Education: Percent of population age 25 and over with: High school diploma (including GED) or higher: 88.6% (2005); Bachelor's degree or higher: 25.3% (2005); Master's degree or higher: 7.9% (2005).

Housing: Homeownership rate: 89.4% (2005); Median home value: $287,687 (2005); Median rent: $595 per month (2000); Median age of housing: 30 years (2000).

Transportation: Commute to work: 93.5% car, 1.4% public transportation, 1.5% walk, 2.6% work from home (2000); Travel time to work: 23.0% less than 15 minutes, 31.2% 15 to 30 minutes, 13.2% 30 to 45 minutes, 9.5% 45 to 60 minutes, 23.2% 60 minutes or more (2000)

FRANKLIN (borough). Covers a land area of 4.486 square miles and a water area of 0.061 square miles. Located at 41.11° N. Lat.; 74.58° W. Long. Elevation is 621 feet.

History: Former zinc mines. A museum here commemorates the area's mining past. Incorporated 1913.

Population: 4,977 (1990); 5,160 (2000); 5,293 (2005); 5,468 (2010 projected); Race: 93.6% White, 0.8% Black, 2.1% Asian, 6.2% Hispanic of any race (2005); Density: 1,179.8 persons per square mile (2005); Average household size: 2.72 (2005); Median age: 37.6 (2005); Males per 100 females: 91.3 (2005); Marriage status: 24.8% never married, 56.8% now married, 8.6% widowed, 9.8% divorced (2000); Foreign born: 7.4% (2000); Ancestry (includes multiple ancestries): 22.0% German, 21.9% Irish, 20.1% Italian, 10.5% Other groups, 10.2% English (2000).

Economy: Textiles, clothing. Single-family building permits issued: 9 (2005); Multi-family building permits issued: 0 (2005); Employment by occupation: 13.9% management, 11.6% professional, 15.0% services, 28.6% sales, 0.0% farming, 12.3% construction, 18.6% production (2000).

Income: Per capita income: $22,355 (2005); Median household income: $49,815 (2005); Average household income: $60,446 (2005); Percent of households with income of $100,000 or more: 13.8% (2005); Poverty rate: 7.0% (2000).

Education: Percent of population age 25 and over with: High school diploma (including GED) or higher: 86.8% (2005); Bachelor's degree or higher: 15.6% (2005); Master's degree or higher: 4.8% (2005).

School District(s)

Franklin Borough (PK-08)
  2003-04 Enrollment: 609 . . . . (973) 827-9775
Hardyston Township (PK-08)
  2003-04 Enrollment: 789 . . . . (973) 827-3600

Housing: Homeownership rate: 72.7% (2005); Median home value: $186,073 (2005); Median rent: $642 per month (2000); Median age of housing: 46 years (2000).

Safety: Violent crime rate: 9.5 per 10,000 population; Property crime rate: 245.9 per 10,000 population (2004).

Transportation: Commute to work: 95.3% car, 0.5% public transportation, 1.4% walk, 2.2% work from home (2000); Travel time to work: 25.2% less than 15 minutes, 19.0% 15 to 30 minutes, 17.0% 30 to 45 minutes, 17.8% 45 to 60 minutes, 21.0% 60 minutes or more (2000)

FREDON (township). Covers a land area of 17.757 square miles and a water area of 0.185 square miles. Located at 41.03° N. Lat.; 74.82° W. Long. Elevation is 706 feet.

Population: 2,904 (1990); 2,860 (2000); 3,266 (2005); 3,657 (2010 projected); Race: 96.3% White, 0.9% Black, 0.9% Asian, 3.1% Hispanic of any race (2005); Density: 183.9 persons per square mile (2005); Average household size: 2.86 (2005); Median age: 40.2 (2005); Males per 100 females: 95.0 (2005); Marriage status: 20.8% never married, 69.7% now married, 4.4% widowed, 5.0% divorced (2000); Foreign born: 4.9% (2000); Ancestry (includes multiple ancestries): 23.1% German, 23.0% Irish, 21.3% Italian, 11.7% English, 10.2% Polish (2000).

Economy: Single-family building permits issued: 25 (2005); Multi-family building permits issued: 0 (2005); Employment by occupation: 17.6% management, 24.1% professional, 14.4% services, 26.7% sales, 0.3% farming, 8.9% construction, 8.1% production (2000).

Income: Per capita income: $33,543 (2005); Median household income: $80,263 (2005); Average household income: $95,893 (2005); Percent of households with income of $100,000 or more: 35.5% (2005); Poverty rate: 2.2% (2000).

Education: Percent of population age 25 and over with: High school diploma (including GED) or higher: 92.9% (2005); Bachelor's degree or higher: 33.9% (2005); Master's degree or higher: 10.9% (2005).

Housing: Homeownership rate: 92.1% (2005); Median home value: $335,573 (2005); Median rent: $656 per month (2000); Median age of housing: 25 years (2000).

Transportation: Commute to work: 93.2% car, 1.0% public transportation, 1.0% walk, 4.8% work from home (2000); Travel time to work: 25.8% less than 15 minutes, 25.1% 15 to 30 minutes, 14.7% 30 to 45 minutes, 12.5% 45 to 60 minutes, 21.9% 60 minutes or more (2000)

Additional Information Contacts

Fredon Township . . . . (973) 383-7025
  http://twp.fredon.nj.us

GLENWOOD (unincorporated postal area, zip code 07418). Covers a land area of 6.161 square miles and a water area of 0.061 square miles. Located at 41.23° N. Lat.; 74.48° W. Long. Elevation is 580 feet.

Population: 2,751 (2000); Race: 96.3% White, 0.7% Black, 0.4% Asian, 0.3% Hispanic of any race (2000); Density: 446.5 persons per square mile (2000); Age: 31.7% under 18, 7.4% over 64 (2000); Marriage status: 23.7% never married, 69.6% now married, 2.9% widowed, 3.9% divorced (2000); Foreign born: 4.1% (2000); Ancestry (includes multiple ancestries): 31.1% Irish, 28.7% German, 24.2% Italian, 8.2% English, 8.0% Polish (2000).

Economy: Employment by occupation: 15.2% management, 20.4% professional, 15.2% services, 26.9% sales, 0.0% farming, 11.8% construction, 10.5% production (2000).

Income: Per capita income: $26,820 (2000); Median household income: $82,055 (2000); Poverty rate: 1.2% (2000).

Education: Percent of population age 25 and over with: High school diploma (including GED) or higher: 95.0% (2000); Bachelor's degree or higher: 25.4% (2000).

Housing: Homeownership rate: 93.8% (2000); Median home value: $162,600 (2000); Median rent: $733 per month (2000); Median age of housing: 24 years (2000).

Transportation: Commute to work: 94.1% car, 1.5% public transportation, 0.0% walk, 3.4% work from home (2000); Travel time to work: 23.8% less than 15 minutes, 20.0% 15 to 30 minutes, 10.7% 30 to 45 minutes, 8.4% 45 to 60 minutes, 37.1% 60 minutes or more (2000)

GREEN (township). Covers a land area of 16.179 square miles and a water area of 0.128 square miles. Located at 40.97° N. Lat.; 74.78° W. Long.

Population: 2,812 (1990); 3,220 (2000); 3,545 (2005); 3,872 (2010 projected); Race: 95.7% White, 1.1% Black, 1.2% Asian, 4.7% Hispanic of any race (2005); Density: 219.1 persons per square mile (2005); Average household size: 3.03 (2005); Median age: 37.5 (2005); Males per 100

females: 104.3 (2005); Marriage status: 19.5% never married, 73.2% now married, 3.1% widowed, 4.2% divorced (2000); Foreign born: 8.2% (2000); Ancestry (includes multiple ancestries): 26.2% Irish, 22.9% Italian, 17.7% German, 13.1% Polish, 10.2% English (2000).

Economy: Single-family building permits issued: 16 (2005); Multi-family building permits issued: 0 (2005); Employment by occupation: 25.5% management, 21.4% professional, 7.0% services, 28.6% sales, 0.2% farming, 9.4% construction, 8.0% production (2000).

Income: Per capita income: $39,988 (2005); Median household income: $98,936 (2005); Average household income: $120,167 (2005); Percent of households with income of $100,000 or more: 49.1% (2005); Poverty rate: 1.6% (2000).

Education: Percent of population age 25 and over with: High school diploma (including GED) or higher: 93.8% (2005); Bachelor's degree or higher: 34.4% (2005); Master's degree or higher: 10.7% (2005).

Housing: Homeownership rate: 92.5% (2005); Median home value: $298,661 (2005); Median rent: $830 per month (2000); Median age of housing: 25 years (2000).

Transportation: Commute to work: 92.7% car, 2.0% public transportation, 1.2% walk, 3.7% work from home (2000); Travel time to work: 11.3% less than 15 minutes, 28.6% 15 to 30 minutes, 16.5% 30 to 45 minutes, 16.9% 45 to 60 minutes, 26.8% 60 minutes or more (2000)

Additional Information Contacts

Green Township. . . . . (908) 852-9333
  http://www.greentwp.com

HAMBURG (borough). Covers a land area of 1.156 square miles and a water area of 0.006 square miles. Located at 41.15° N. Lat.; 74.57° W. Long. Elevation is 453 feet.

History: "Gingerbread Castle" here has scenes from various fairy tales. Incorporated 1920.

Population: 2,566 (1990); 3,105 (2000); 3,648 (2005); 4,170 (2010 projected); Race: 91.6% White, 1.0% Black, 2.8% Asian, 5.7% Hispanic of any race (2005); Density: 3,156.4 persons per square mile (2005); Average household size: 2.62 (2005); Median age: 36.3 (2005); Males per 100 females: 93.5 (2005); Marriage status: 21.3% never married, 62.9% now married, 4.0% widowed, 11.7% divorced (2000); Foreign born: 5.8% (2000); Ancestry (includes multiple ancestries): 24.6% Italian, 23.0% German, 21.6% Irish, 12.0% English, 10.2% Other groups (2000).

Economy: In suburbanizing area. Single-family building permits issued: 8 (2005); Multi-family building permits issued: 0 (2005); Employment by occupation: 14.3% management, 21.5% professional, 13.0% services, 26.7% sales, 0.2% farming, 10.2% construction, 14.0% production (2000).

Income: Per capita income: $28,112 (2005); Median household income: $65,107 (2005); Average household income: $73,370 (2005); Percent of households with income of $100,000 or more: 18.6% (2005); Poverty rate: 4.6% (2000).

Education: Percent of population age 25 and over with: High school diploma (including GED) or higher: 89.2% (2005); Bachelor's degree or higher: 19.9% (2005); Master's degree or higher: 6.2% (2005).

School District(s)

Hamburg Borough (PK-08)
  2003-04 Enrollment: 401 . . . . (973) 827-7440
Hardyston Township (PK-08)
  2003-04 Enrollment: 789 . . . . (973) 827-3600
Wallkill Valley Regional (09-12)
  2003-04 Enrollment: 869 . . . . (973) 827-4100

Housing: Homeownership rate: 74.7% (2005); Median home value: $185,213 (2005); Median rent: $729 per month (2000); Median age of housing: 20 years (2000).

Safety: Violent crime rate: 8.5 per 10,000 population; Property crime rate: 88.1 per 10,000 population (2004).

Transportation: Commute to work: 92.5% car, 0.7% public transportation, 3.4% walk, 2.6% work from home (2000); Travel time to work: 25.4% less than 15 minutes, 15.3% 15 to 30 minutes, 16.3% 30 to 45 minutes, 18.0% 45 to 60 minutes, 24.9% 60 minutes or more (2000)

HAMPTON (township). Covers a land area of 24.624 square miles and a water area of 0.687 square miles. Located at 41.10° N. Lat.; 74.80° W. Long.

Population: 4,352 (1990); 4,943 (2000); 5,248 (2005); 5,576 (2010 projected); Race: 96.7% White, 1.3% Black, 0.7% Asian, 2.7% Hispanic of any race (2005); Density: 213.1 persons per square mile (2005); Average household size: 2.62 (2005); Median age: 41.0 (2005); Males per 100 females: 95.2 (2005); Marriage status: 20.7% never married, 65.6% now

married, 6.8% widowed, 6.9% divorced (2000); Foreign born: 3.6% (2000); Ancestry (includes multiple ancestries): 25.3% Irish, 24.2% German, 20.0% Italian, 12.7% English, 10.2% Polish (2000).

Economy: Single-family building permits issued: 20 (2005); Multi-family building permits issued: 0 (2005); Employment by occupation: 13.6% management, 23.6% professional, 12.8% services, 25.4% sales, 0.5% farming, 12.9% construction, 11.2% production (2000).

Income: Per capita income: $30,593 (2005); Median household income: $69,983 (2005); Average household income: $79,985 (2005); Percent of households with income of $100,000 or more: 29.8% (2005); Poverty rate: 2.0% (2000).

Education: Percent of population age 25 and over with: High school diploma (including GED) or higher: 91.6% (2005); Bachelor's degree or higher: 27.5% (2005); Master's degree or higher: 7.3% (2005).

Housing: Homeownership rate: 89.0% (2005); Median home value: $241,140 (2005); Median rent: $793 per month (2000); Median age of housing: 26 years (2000).

Transportation: Commute to work: 91.2% car, 2.6% public transportation, 1.0% walk, 5.1% work from home (2000); Travel time to work: 23.1% less than 15 minutes, 23.8% 15 to 30 minutes, 15.2% 30 to 45 minutes, 9.6% 45 to 60 minutes, 28.4% 60 minutes or more (2000)

HARDYSTON (township). Covers a land area of 32.094 square miles and a water area of 0.545 square miles. Located at 41.10° N. Lat.; 74.55° W. Long.

History: Incorporated 1798.

Population: 4,844 (1990); 6,171 (2000); 7,936 (2005); 9,586 (2010 projected); Race: 94.3% White, 1.2% Black, 2.0% Asian, 4.8% Hispanic of any race (2005); Density: 247.3 persons per square mile (2005); Average household size: 2.63 (2005); Median age: 39.8 (2005); Males per 100 females: 97.1 (2005); Marriage status: 22.6% never married, 62.5% now married, 5.7% widowed, 9.2% divorced (2000); Foreign born: 4.8% (2000); Ancestry (includes multiple ancestries): 23.0% Italian, 22.0% German, 21.4% Irish, 12.3% English, 9.1% Other groups (2000).

Economy: Single-family building permits issued: 195 (2005); Multi-family building permits issued: 0 (2005); Employment by occupation: 17.0% management, 19.1% professional, 12.7% services, 26.5% sales, 0.3% farming, 12.6% construction, 11.8% production (2000).

Income: Per capita income: $35,685 (2005); Median household income: $79,041 (2005); Average household income: $93,710 (2005); Percent of households with income of $100,000 or more: 35.3% (2005); Poverty rate: 4.7% (2000).

Education: Percent of population age 25 and over with: High school diploma (including GED) or higher: 90.8% (2005); Bachelor's degree or higher: 27.3% (2005); Master's degree or higher: 10.5% (2005).

Housing: Homeownership rate: 83.0% (2005); Median home value: $257,468 (2005); Median rent: $638 per month (2000); Median age of housing: 28 years (2000).

Safety: Violent crime rate: 1.3 per 10,000 population; Property crime rate: 140.6 per 10,000 population (2004).

Transportation: Commute to work: 95.4% car, 1.4% public transportation, 1.0% walk, 2.0% work from home (2000); Travel time to work: 17.0% less than 15 minutes, 17.8% 15 to 30 minutes, 17.8% 30 to 45 minutes, 19.0% 45 to 60 minutes, 28.4% 60 minutes or more (2000)

HIGHLAND LAKE (CDP). Covers a land area of 5.042 square miles and a water area of 1.027 square miles. Located at 41.17° N. Lat.; 74.46° W. Long.

Population: 4,449 (1990); 5,051 (2000); 5,176 (2005); 5,316 (2010 projected); Race: 94.6% White, 1.6% Black, 0.6% Asian, 6.1% Hispanic of any race (2005); Density: 1,026.5 persons per square mile (2005); Average household size: 2.77 (2005); Median age: 37.0 (2005); Males per 100 females: 98.8 (2005); Marriage status: 18.8% never married, 67.7% now married, 5.8% widowed, 7.7% divorced (2000); Foreign born: 6.8% (2000); Ancestry (includes multiple ancestries): 26.0% Irish, 23.4% Italian, 23.3% German, 8.4% Polish, 7.4% English (2000).

Economy: Employment by occupation: 9.7% management, 19.4% professional, 14.5% services, 32.4% sales, 0.0% farming, 11.0% construction, 13.0% production (2000).

Income: Per capita income: $27,715 (2005); Median household income: $66,184 (2005); Average household income: $76,837 (2005); Percent of households with income of $100,000 or more: 21.6% (2005); Poverty rate: 3.5% (2000).

Education: Percent of population age 25 and over with: High school diploma (including GED) or higher: 92.9% (2005); Bachelor's degree or higher: 22.8% (2005); Master's degree or higher: 7.8% (2005).
Housing: Homeownership rate: 89.3% (2005); Median home value: $214,560 (2005); Median rent: $778 per month (2000); Median age of housing: 37 years (2000).
Transportation: Commute to work: 94.8% car, 1.1% public transportation, 0.0% walk, 3.4% work from home (2000); Travel time to work: 15.4% less than 15 minutes, 13.0% 15 to 30 minutes, 18.0% 30 to 45 minutes, 26.6% 45 to 60 minutes, 26.9% 60 minutes or more (2000)

HIGHLAND LAKES (unincorporated postal area, zip code 07422).
Covers a land area of 15.364 square miles and a water area of 1.144 square miles. Located at 41.18° N. Lat.; 74.45° W. Long. Elevation is 1,260 feet.
Population: 7,177 (2000); Race: 96.5% White, 0.4% Black, 0.8% Asian, 4.0% Hispanic of any race (2000); Density: 467.1 persons per square mile (2000); Age: 30.9% under 18, 6.9% over 64 (2000); Marriage status: 20.7% never married, 68.6% now married, 3.8% widowed, 6.9% divorced (2000); Foreign born: 5.6% (2000); Ancestry (includes multiple ancestries): 27.9% Italian, 26.5% Irish, 23.2% German, 10.8% Polish, 6.6% English (2000).
Economy: Employment by occupation: 12.0% management, 21.8% professional, 11.7% services, 30.1% sales, 0.0% farming, 11.7% construction, 12.7% production (2000).
Income: Per capita income: $24,004 (2000); Median household income: $67,222 (2000); Poverty rate: 2.9% (2000).
Education: Percent of population age 25 and over with: High school diploma (including GED) or higher: 94.8% (2000); Bachelor's degree or higher: 24.7% (2000).
Housing: Homeownership rate: 92.6% (2000); Median home value: $137,900 (2000); Median rent: $769 per month (2000); Median age of housing: 34 years (2000).
Transportation: Commute to work: 95.4% car, 0.8% public transportation, 0.4% walk, 2.6% work from home (2000); Travel time to work: 14.7% less than 15 minutes, 13.3% 15 to 30 minutes, 18.0% 30 to 45 minutes, 24.2% 45 to 60 minutes, 29.8% 60 minutes or more (2000)

HOPATCONG (borough).
Covers a land area of 10.960 square miles and a water area of 1.379 square miles. Located at 40.93° N. Lat.; 74.66° W. Long. Elevation is 1,000 feet.
Population: 15,693 (1990); 15,888 (2000); 16,205 (2005); 16,658 (2010 projected); Race: 91.6% White, 2.5% Black, 2.0% Asian, 8.4% Hispanic of any race (2005); Density: 1,478.6 persons per square mile (2005); Average household size: 2.77 (2005); Median age: 37.3 (2005); Males per 100 females: 101.5 (2005); Marriage status: 24.6% never married, 62.2% now married, 4.6% widowed, 8.6% divorced (2000); Foreign born: 6.5% (2000); Ancestry (includes multiple ancestries): 25.8% Italian, 24.3% Irish, 20.7% German, 12.1% Other groups, 7.8% English (2000).
Economy: Resorts include Landing, Mt. Arlington, Lake Hopatcong. Single-family building permits issued: 14 (2005); Multi-family building permits issued: 0 (2005); Employment by occupation: 14.5% management, 18.0% professional, 10.2% services, 33.6% sales, 0.0% farming, 11.0% construction, 12.6% production (2000).
Income: Per capita income: $31,132 (2005); Median household income: $75,505 (2005); Average household income: $86,294 (2005); Percent of households with income of $100,000 or more: 30.1% (2005); Poverty rate: 3.0% (2000).
Taxes: Total city taxes per capita: $576 (2004); City property taxes per capita: $558 (2004).
Education: Percent of population age 25 and over with: High school diploma (including GED) or higher: 89.4% (2005); Bachelor's degree or higher: 19.3% (2005); Master's degree or higher: 4.5% (2005).
School District(s)
Hopatcong (PK-12)
    2003-04 Enrollment: 3,187 . . . . (973) 398-8801
Housing: Homeownership rate: 87.4% (2005); Median home value: $229,685 (2005); Median rent: $778 per month (2000); Median age of housing: 39 years (2000).
Safety: Violent crime rate: 8.6 per 10,000 population; Property crime rate: 84.5 per 10,000 population (2004).
Transportation: Commute to work: 94.4% car, 2.4% public transportation, 0.7% walk, 2.4% work from home (2000); Travel time to work: 16.4% less than 15 minutes, 25.6% 15 to 30 minutes, 20.3% 30 to 45 minutes, 16.0% 45 to 60 minutes, 21.7% 60 minutes or more (2000)
Additional Information Contacts

Borough of Hopatcong. . . . . (973) 770-1200
    http://www.hopatcong.org

LAFAYETTE (township).
Covers a land area of 18.024 square miles and a water area of 0.034 square miles. Located at 41.11° N. Lat.; 74.67° W. Long. Elevation is 533 feet.
Population: 1,902 (1990); 2,300 (2000); 2,486 (2005); 2,675 (2010 projected); Race: 96.7% White, 1.4% Black, 0.7% Asian, 3.8% Hispanic of any race (2005); Density: 137.9 persons per square mile (2005); Average household size: 2.98 (2005); Median age: 39.8 (2005); Males per 100 females: 101.1 (2005); Marriage status: 20.2% never married, 70.1% now married, 3.9% widowed, 5.8% divorced (2000); Foreign born: 5.3% (2000); Ancestry (includes multiple ancestries): 22.7% German, 22.5% Irish, 18.3% Italian, 11.5% English, 8.3% Polish (2000).
Economy: Single-family building permits issued: 15 (2005); Multi-family building permits issued: 0 (2005); Employment by occupation: 19.1% management, 21.3% professional, 11.0% services, 24.9% sales, 1.3% farming, 13.8% construction, 8.6% production (2000).
Income: Per capita income: $36,704 (2005); Median household income: $95,395 (2005); Average household income: $108,787 (2005); Percent of households with income of $100,000 or more: 47.1% (2005); Poverty rate: 3.7% (2000).
Education: Percent of population age 25 and over with: High school diploma (including GED) or higher: 91.9% (2005); Bachelor's degree or higher: 33.4% (2005); Master's degree or higher: 11.3% (2005).
School District(s)
Lafayette Township (PK-08)
    2003-04 Enrollment: 368 . . . . (973) 875-3344
Housing: Homeownership rate: 88.6% (2005); Median home value: $380,000 (2005); Median rent: $650 per month (2000); Median age of housing: 23 years (2000).
Transportation: Commute to work: 90.4% car, 2.1% public transportation, 0.8% walk, 5.5% work from home (2000); Travel time to work: 24.1% less than 15 minutes, 21.2% 15 to 30 minutes, 16.7% 30 to 45 minutes, 14.6% 45 to 60 minutes, 23.3% 60 minutes or more (2000)

LAKE MOHAWK (CDP). Aka Sparta.
Covers a land area of 5.000 square miles and a water area of 1.151 square miles. Located at 41.01° N. Lat.; 74.66° W. Long.
Population: 8,955 (1990); 9,755 (2000); 10,493 (2005); 11,267 (2010 projected); Race: 96.2% White, 0.5% Black, 1.4% Asian, 3.3% Hispanic of any race (2005); Density: 2,098.8 persons per square mile (2005); Average household size: 2.61 (2005); Median age: 40.1 (2005); Males per 100 females: 94.0 (2005); Marriage status: 17.9% never married, 69.5% now married, 6.0% widowed, 6.6% divorced (2000); Foreign born: 7.7% (2000); Ancestry (includes multiple ancestries): 27.1% Irish, 23.0% German, 22.2% Italian, 11.0% English, 8.5% Polish (2000).
Economy: Employment by occupation: 24.6% management, 25.0% professional, 9.8% services, 27.5% sales, 0.0% farming, 6.5% construction, 6.6% production (2000).
Income: Per capita income: $40,102 (2005); Median household income: $92,150 (2005); Average household income: $104,734 (2005); Percent of households with income of $100,000 or more: 45.1% (2005); Poverty rate: 1.7% (2000).
Education: Percent of population age 25 and over with: High school diploma (including GED) or higher: 93.7% (2005); Bachelor's degree or higher: 46.9% (2005); Master's degree or higher: 17.1% (2005).
Housing: Homeownership rate: 88.6% (2005); Median home value: $331,471 (2005); Median rent: $399 per month (2000); Median age of housing: 36 years (2000).
Transportation: Commute to work: 91.5% car, 2.6% public transportation, 0.3% walk, 4.6% work from home (2000); Travel time to work: 15.2% less than 15 minutes, 24.7% 15 to 30 minutes, 16.9% 30 to 45 minutes, 14.5% 45 to 60 minutes, 28.7% 60 minutes or more (2000)

LAYTON (unincorporated postal area, zip code 07851).
Covers a land area of 30.682 square miles and a water area of 0.661 square miles. Located at 41.17° N. Lat.; 74.88° W. Long. Elevation is 547 feet.
Population: 250 (2000); Race: 98.1% White, 0.0% Black, 0.0% Asian, 0.0% Hispanic of any race (2000); Density: 8.1 persons per square mile (2000); Age: 20.5% under 18, 20.5% over 64 (2000); Marriage status: 20.5% never married, 66.4% now married, 8.7% widowed, 4.4% divorced (2000); Foreign born: 3.0% (2000); Ancestry (includes multiple ancestries): 28.7% German, 22.8% Irish, 18.3% Italian, 17.2% English, 11.2% Polish (2000).

Economy: Employment by occupation: 13.5% management, 12.0% professional, 16.5% services, 31.6% sales, 0.0% farming, 13.5% construction, 12.8% production (2000).
Income: Per capita income: $21,019 (2000); Median household income: $49,583 (2000); Poverty rate: 3.0% (2000).
Education: Percent of population age 25 and over with: High school diploma (including GED) or higher: 81.0% (2000); Bachelor's degree or higher: 19.0% (2000).

School District(s)

Sandyston-Walpack Township (PK-06)
    2003-04 Enrollment: 181 . . . . (973) 948-4450
Housing: Homeownership rate: 70.9% (2000); Median home value: $158,800 (2000); Median rent: $325 per month (2000); Median age of housing: 56 years (2000).
Transportation: Commute to work: 85.7% car, 1.5% public transportation, 4.5% walk, 6.8% work from home (2000); Travel time to work: 20.2% less than 15 minutes, 39.5% 15 to 30 minutes, 10.5% 30 to 45 minutes, 10.5% 45 to 60 minutes, 19.4% 60 minutes or more (2000)

MONTAGUE (township). Covers a land area of 44.009 square miles and a water area of 1.329 square miles. Located at 41.30° N. Lat.; 74.74° W. Long. Elevation is 519 feet.
Population: 2,832 (1990); 3,412 (2000); 3,716 (2005); 4,026 (2010 projected); Race: 94.7% White, 1.8% Black, 0.8% Asian, 4.7% Hispanic of any race (2005); Density: 84.4 persons per square mile (2005); Average household size: 2.61 (2005); Median age: 38.3 (2005); Males per 100 females: 105.1 (2005); Marriage status: 21.1% never married, 61.9% now married, 4.9% widowed, 12.1% divorced (2000); Foreign born: 3.9% (2000); Ancestry (includes multiple ancestries): 22.6% Italian, 20.7% German, 20.3% Irish, 12.5% English, 7.2% Other groups (2000).
Economy: Single-family building permits issued: 44 (2005); Multi-family building permits issued: 2 (2005); Employment by occupation: 10.3% management, 15.4% professional, 16.3% services, 28.5% sales, 0.0% farming, 17.0% construction, 12.5% production (2000).
Income: Per capita income: $23,304 (2005); Median household income: $49,871 (2005); Average household income: $60,785 (2005); Percent of households with income of $100,000 or more: 15.0% (2005); Poverty rate: 12.0% (2000).
Taxes: Total city taxes per capita: $226 (2004); City property taxes per capita: $205 (2004).
Education: Percent of population age 25 and over with: High school diploma (including GED) or higher: 80.3% (2005); Bachelor's degree or higher: 14.5% (2005); Master's degree or higher: 5.9% (2005).

School District(s)

Montague Township (PK-08)
    2003-04 Enrollment: 375 . . . . (973) 293-7131
Housing: Homeownership rate: 73.4% (2005); Median home value: $191,698 (2005); Median rent: $667 per month (2000); Median age of housing: 26 years (2000).
Transportation: Commute to work: 95.9% car, 1.3% public transportation, 0.4% walk, 2.0% work from home (2000); Travel time to work: 13.1% less than 15 minutes, 18.4% 15 to 30 minutes, 27.1% 30 to 45 minutes, 11.0% 45 to 60 minutes, 30.4% 60 minutes or more (2000)
Additional Information Contacts
Montague Township . . . . (973) 293-7300
    http://www.montaguenj.org

NEWTON (town). Covers a land area of 3.097 square miles and a water area of 0.006 square miles. Located at 41.05° N. Lat.; 74.75° W. Long. Elevation is 608 feet.
History: Don Bosco College and Little Flower Monastery (Benedictine) nearby. Settled c.1760, incorporated 1864.
Population: 7,521 (1990); 8,244 (2000); 8,466 (2005); 8,741 (2010 projected); Race: 89.5% White, 4.5% Black, 2.8% Asian, 5.2% Hispanic of any race (2005); Density: 2,733.3 persons per square mile (2005); Average household size: 2.51 (2005); Median age: 38.6 (2005); Males per 100 females: 93.1 (2005); Marriage status: 27.3% never married, 49.8% now married, 10.3% widowed, 12.6% divorced (2000); Foreign born: 8.2% (2000); Ancestry (includes multiple ancestries): 21.0% Irish, 18.8% German, 14.1% English, 14.0% Italian, 10.7% Other groups (2000).
Economy: Dairying center. Manufacturing: clothing, plastics, pharmaceuticals, metal fabrication. Fur processing. Poultry, fruit. Single-family building permits issued: 0 (2005); Multi-family building permits issued: 0 (2005); Employment by occupation: 12.1% management, 20.7%

professional, 16.5% services, 29.9% sales, 0.0% farming, 7.5% construction, 13.2% production (2000).
Income: Per capita income: $22,953 (2005); Median household income: $46,680 (2005); Average household income: $55,775 (2005); Percent of households with income of $100,000 or more: 13.8% (2005); Poverty rate: 11.2% (2000).
Education: Percent of population age 25 and over with: High school diploma (including GED) or higher: 83.4% (2005); Bachelor's degree or higher: 18.9% (2005); Master's degree or higher: 6.6% (2005).

School District(s)

Andover Regional (PK-08)
    2003-04 Enrollment: 770 . . . . (973) 383-3746
Fredon Township (PK-06)
    2003-04 Enrollment: 317 . . . . (973) 383-4151
Hampton Township (PK-06)
    2003-04 Enrollment: 477 . . . . (973) 383-5300
Kittatinny Regional (07-12)
    2003-04 Enrollment: 1,316 . . . . (973) 383-1800
Newton Town (PK-12)
    2003-04 Enrollment: 1,779 . . . . (973) 383-7392

Two-year College(s)

Sussex County Community College (Public)
    Fall 2004 Enrollment: 3,153 . . . . (973) 300-2100
    2005-06 Tuition: In-state $4,860; Out-of-state $4,860
Housing: Homeownership rate: 48.2% (2005); Median home value: $225,763 (2005); Median rent: $635 per month (2000); Median age of housing: 48 years (2000).
Hospitals: Newton Memorial Hospital (162 beds)
Safety: Violent crime rate: 10.7 per 10,000 population; Property crime rate: 221.4 per 10,000 population (2004).
Newspapers: The New Jersey Herald (Circulation 16,719)
Transportation: Commute to work: 87.8% car, 1.4% public transportation, 6.0% walk, 3.1% work from home (2000); Travel time to work: 36.1% less than 15 minutes, 24.4% 15 to 30 minutes, 15.7% 30 to 45 minutes, 11.9% 45 to 60 minutes, 12.0% 60 minutes or more (2000)
Additional Information Contacts
Sussex County Chamber of Commerce . . . . (973) 579-1811
    http://www.sussexcountychamber.org

OGDENSBURG (borough). Covers a land area of 2.285 square miles and a water area of 0.018 square miles. Located at 41.08° N. Lat.; 74.59° W. Long. Elevation is 693 feet.
History: Incorporated 1914.
Population: 2,722 (1990); 2,638 (2000); 2,663 (2005); 2,713 (2010 projected); Race: 97.1% White, 0.2% Black, 1.1% Asian, 5.3% Hispanic of any race (2005); Density: 1,165.7 persons per square mile (2005); Average household size: 2.94 (2005); Median age: 36.9 (2005); Males per 100 females: 102.7 (2005); Marriage status: 24.6% never married, 63.8% now married, 4.6% widowed, 7.0% divorced (2000); Foreign born: 6.0% (2000); Ancestry (includes multiple ancestries): 25.9% Italian, 25.5% Irish, 20.4% German, 10.3% English, 9.7% Polish (2000).
Economy: Single-family building permits issued: 6 (2005); Multi-family building permits issued: 0 (2005); Employment by occupation: 14.2% management, 19.5% professional, 11.0% services, 29.4% sales, 0.0% farming, 10.2% construction, 15.7% production (2000).
Income: Per capita income: $28,258 (2005); Median household income: $70,188 (2005); Average household income: $83,149 (2005); Percent of households with income of $100,000 or more: 28.1% (2005); Poverty rate: 5.7% (2000).
Education: Percent of population age 25 and over with: High school diploma (including GED) or higher: 89.2% (2005); Bachelor's degree or higher: 19.9% (2005); Master's degree or higher: 5.8% (2005).

School District(s)

Ogdensburg Borough (PK-08)
    2003-04 Enrollment: 451 . . . . (973) 827-7127
Housing: Homeownership rate: 84.1% (2005); Median home value: $235,185 (2005); Median rent: $639 per month (2000); Median age of housing: 38 years (2000).
Safety: Violent crime rate: 3.7 per 10,000 population; Property crime rate: 29.9 per 10,000 population (2004).
Transportation: Commute to work: 95.2% car, 2.0% public transportation, 1.2% walk, 1.5% work from home (2000); Travel time to work: 16.1% less than 15 minutes, 28.4% 15 to 30 minutes, 20.4% 30 to 45 minutes, 17.2% 45 to 60 minutes, 17.8% 60 minutes or more (2000)

SANDYSTON (township). Covers a land area of 42.607 square miles and a water area of 0.698 square miles. Located at 41.21° N. Lat.; 74.80° W. Long.

Population: 1,732 (1990); 1,825 (2000); 1,944 (2005); 2,069 (2010 projected); Race: 97.5% White, 0.5% Black, 0.5% Asian, 1.8% Hispanic of any race (2005); Density: 45.6 persons per square mile (2005); Average household size: 2.65 (2005); Median age: 41.4 (2005); Males per 100 females: 100.0 (2005); Marriage status: 21.1% never married, 63.8% now married, 7.8% widowed, 7.3% divorced (2000); Foreign born: 3.7% (2000); Ancestry (includes multiple ancestries): 26.9% German, 20.7% Irish, 17.2% Italian, 15.3% English, 6.3% Polish (2000).

Economy: Single-family building permits issued: 12 (2005); Multi-family building permits issued: 0 (2005); Employment by occupation: 15.1% management, 19.0% professional, 13.9% services, 26.0% sales, 0.2% farming, 12.8% construction, 13.1% production (2000).

Income: Per capita income: $26,500 (2005); Median household income: $61,480 (2005); Average household income: $70,160 (2005); Percent of households with income of $100,000 or more: 19.5% (2005); Poverty rate: 5.4% (2000).

Education: Percent of population age 25 and over with: High school diploma (including GED) or higher: 87.3% (2005); Bachelor's degree or higher: 24.6% (2005); Master's degree or higher: 7.6% (2005).

Housing: Homeownership rate: 88.1% (2005); Median home value: $243,750 (2005); Median rent: $742 per month (2000); Median age of housing: 42 years (2000).

Transportation: Commute to work: 91.4% car, 0.4% public transportation, 3.5% walk, 4.5% work from home (2000); Travel time to work: 18.2% less than 15 minutes, 28.8% 15 to 30 minutes, 14.3% 30 to 45 minutes, 10.6% 45 to 60 minutes, 28.1% 60 minutes or more (2000)

SPARTA (township). Covers a land area of 37.394 square miles and a water area of 1.828 square miles. Located at 41.03° N. Lat.; 74.63° W. Long. Elevation is 712 feet.

History: Has reproductions of historic colonial houses.

Population: 15,053 (1990); 18,080 (2000); 19,794 (2005); 21,516 (2010 projected); Race: 96.1% White, 0.3% Black, 1.8% Asian, 3.6% Hispanic of any race (2005); Density: 529.3 persons per square mile (2005); Average household size: 2.90 (2005); Median age: 38.6 (2005); Males per 100 females: 97.5 (2005); Marriage status: 18.5% never married, 70.7% now married, 4.9% widowed, 5.8% divorced (2000); Foreign born: 7.0% (2000); Ancestry (includes multiple ancestries): 27.6% Irish, 23.3% German, 22.6% Italian, 11.2% English, 8.1% Polish (2000).

Economy: In recreational area. Single-family building permits issued: 75 (2005); Multi-family building permits issued: 0 (2005); Employment by occupation: 27.0% management, 23.0% professional, 8.4% services, 28.1% sales, 0.0% farming, 6.0% construction, 7.5% production (2000).

Income: Per capita income: $42,566 (2005); Median household income: $102,925 (2005); Average household income: $123,341 (2005); Percent of households with income of $100,000 or more: 51.5% (2005); Poverty rate: 1.5% (2000).

Education: Percent of population age 25 and over with: High school diploma (including GED) or higher: 94.6% (2005); Bachelor's degree or higher: 50.1% (2005); Master's degree or higher: 17.6% (2005).

School District(s)

Agency - Sussex County CS for Technology (07-08)
2003-04 Enrollment: 94 . . . . (973) 383-6700
Sparta Township (PK-12)
2003-04 Enrollment: 4,025 . . . . (973) 729-7886
Sussex County Ed Serv Comm (UG-UG)
2003-04 Enrollment: 46 . . . . (973) 383-6700
Sussex County Vocational (09-12)
2003-04 Enrollment: 686 . . . . (973) 383-6700

Housing: Homeownership rate: 89.9% (2005); Median home value: $359,139 (2005); Median rent: $710 per month (2000); Median age of housing: 31 years (2000).

Safety: Violent crime rate: 2.1 per 10,000 population; Property crime rate: 47.0 per 10,000 population (2004).

Transportation: Commute to work: 91.3% car, 2.2% public transportation, 1.2% walk, 4.8% work from home (2000); Travel time to work: 18.0% less than 15 minutes, 20.2% 15 to 30 minutes, 18.8% 30 to 45 minutes, 17.7% 45 to 60 minutes, 25.3% 60 minutes or more (2000)

STANHOPE (borough). Covers a land area of 1.873 square miles and a water area of 0.335 square miles. Located at 40.91° N. Lat.; 74.70° W. Long. Elevation is 882 feet.

History: Produced iron in American Revolution. Waterloo Village, restored colonial village and site of a summer musical festival, 5 miles to West. Settled 1714, incorporated 1904.

Population: 3,393 (1990); 3,584 (2000); 3,750 (2005); 3,938 (2010 projected); Race: 92.4% White, 1.7% Black, 2.0% Asian, 5.4% Hispanic of any race (2005); Density: 2,002.3 persons per square mile (2005); Average household size: 2.56 (2005); Median age: 38.6 (2005); Males per 100 females: 91.1 (2005); Marriage status: 24.1% never married, 59.9% now married, 3.3% widowed, 12.7% divorced (2000); Foreign born: 5.2% (2000); Ancestry (includes multiple ancestries): 22.9% Italian, 21.4% German, 20.4% Irish, 9.6% English, 7.9% Polish (2000).

Economy: Manufacturing: metal and stone products. Agriculture: poultry; dairy products. Single-family building permits issued: 0 (2005); Multi-family building permits issued: 0 (2005); Employment by occupation: 13.4% management, 27.3% professional, 8.6% services, 34.7% sales, 0.0% farming, 6.3% construction, 9.8% production (2000).

Income: Per capita income: $32,590 (2005); Median household income: $71,568 (2005); Average household income: $83,185 (2005); Percent of households with income of $100,000 or more: 27.9% (2005); Poverty rate: 2.2% (2000).

Education: Percent of population age 25 and over with: High school diploma (including GED) or higher: 91.7% (2005); Bachelor's degree or higher: 32.4% (2005); Master's degree or higher: 7.5% (2005).

School District(s)

Byram Township (PK-08)
2003-04 Enrollment: 1,223 . . . . (973) 347-1019
Lenape Valley Regional (09-12)
2003-04 Enrollment: 966 . . . . (973) 347-7600
Stanhope Borough (PK-08)
2003-04 Enrollment: 468 . . . . (973) 347-0008

Housing: Homeownership rate: 80.9% (2005); Median home value: $210,382 (2005); Median rent: $782 per month (2000); Median age of housing: 33 years (2000).

Safety: Violent crime rate: 10.8 per 10,000 population; Property crime rate: 67.3 per 10,000 population (2004).

Transportation: Commute to work: 93.6% car, 2.0% public transportation, 1.8% walk, 2.6% work from home (2000); Travel time to work: 21.7% less than 15 minutes, 24.7% 15 to 30 minutes, 25.1% 30 to 45 minutes, 13.9% 45 to 60 minutes, 14.6% 60 minutes or more (2000)

STILLWATER (township). Covers a land area of 27.118 square miles and a water area of 1.256 square miles. Located at 41.06° N. Lat.; 74.85° W. Long. Elevation is 460 feet.

Population: 4,099 (1990); 4,267 (2000); 4,466 (2005); 4,690 (2010 projected); Race: 97.6% White, 0.2% Black, 0.6% Asian, 3.1% Hispanic of any race (2005); Density: 164.7 persons per square mile (2005); Average household size: 2.82 (2005); Median age: 38.4 (2005); Males per 100 females: 97.9 (2005); Marriage status: 23.6% never married, 65.3% now married, 3.1% widowed, 8.1% divorced (2000); Foreign born: 3.3% (2000); Ancestry (includes multiple ancestries): 25.3% German, 23.2% Irish, 22.4% Italian, 12.0% English, 7.4% Polish (2000).

Economy: Single-family building permits issued: 14 (2005); Multi-family building permits issued: 0 (2005); Employment by occupation: 12.7% management, 21.1% professional, 10.1% services, 27.0% sales, 0.0% farming, 16.5% construction, 12.6% production (2000).

Income: Per capita income: $28,790 (2005); Median household income: $73,552 (2005); Average household income: $81,120 (2005); Percent of households with income of $100,000 or more: 28.6% (2005); Poverty rate: 2.8% (2000).

Education: Percent of population age 25 and over with: High school diploma (including GED) or higher: 92.1% (2005); Bachelor's degree or higher: 26.9% (2005); Master's degree or higher: 8.4% (2005).

School District(s)

Stillwater Township (PK-06)
2003-04 Enrollment: 426 . . . . (973) 383-6171

Housing: Homeownership rate: 87.4% (2005); Median home value: $250,316 (2005); Median rent: $622 per month (2000); Median age of housing: 37 years (2000).

Safety: Violent crime rate: 2.3 per 10,000 population; Property crime rate: 36.1 per 10,000 population (2004).

Transportation: Commute to work: 92.8% car, 0.5% public transportation, 0.8% walk, 5.9% work from home (2000); Travel time to work: 10.5% less than 15 minutes, 33.4% 15 to 30 minutes, 17.5% 30 to 45 minutes, 12.2% 45 to 60 minutes, 26.4% 60 minutes or more (2000)

STOCKHOLM (unincorporated postal area, zip code 07460). Covers a land area of 31.636 square miles and a water area of 0.624 square miles. Located at 41.09° N. Lat.; 74.52° W. Long. Elevation is 1,058 feet.
Population: 3,602 (2000); Race: 99.4% White, 0.2% Black, 0.0% Asian, 4.7% Hispanic of any race (2000); Density: 113.9 persons per square mile (2000); Age: 30.3% under 18, 5.6% over 64 (2000); Marriage status: 19.8% never married, 70.2% now married, 4.2% widowed, 5.8% divorced (2000); Foreign born: 2.6% (2000); Ancestry (includes multiple ancestries): 25.7% Italian, 21.7% Irish, 20.8% German, 9.2% English, 8.5% Polish (2000).
Economy: Employment by occupation: 14.1% management, 20.6% professional, 12.5% services, 26.7% sales, 0.0% farming, 14.4% construction, 11.8% production (2000).
Income: Per capita income: $26,992 (2000); Median household income: $69,459 (2000); Poverty rate: 5.5% (2000).
Education: Percent of population age 25 and over with: High school diploma (including GED) or higher: 92.8% (2000); Bachelor's degree or higher: 24.4% (2000).
Housing: Homeownership rate: 92.6% (2000); Median home value: $151,600 (2000); Median rent: $908 per month (2000); Median age of housing: 38 years (2000).
Transportation: Commute to work: 94.9% car, 1.2% public transportation, 1.0% walk, 1.9% work from home (2000); Travel time to work: 11.4% less than 15 minutes, 20.6% 15 to 30 minutes, 18.5% 30 to 45 minutes, 27.3% 45 to 60 minutes, 22.2% 60 minutes or more (2000)
Additional Information Contacts
Jefferson Township Chamber of Commerce . . . . (973) 663-2240
    http://www.jeffersontownshipchamber.org

SUSSEX (borough). Covers a land area of 0.596 square miles and a water area of 0.025 square miles. Located at 41.20° N. Lat.; 74.60° W. Long. Elevation is 464 feet.
Population: 2,201 (1990); 2,145 (2000); 2,201 (2005); 2,277 (2010 projected); Race: 95.5% White, 1.4% Black, 1.5% Asian, 4.0% Hispanic of any race (2005); Density: 3,691.8 persons per square mile (2005); Average household size: 2.33 (2005); Median age: 37.0 (2005); Males per 100 females: 91.9 (2005); Marriage status: 30.0% never married, 48.2% now married, 7.6% widowed, 14.1% divorced (2000); Foreign born: 1.6% (2000); Ancestry (includes multiple ancestries): 20.2% Irish, 17.5% Italian, 16.0% German, 13.6% English, 6.8% United States or American (2000).
Economy: Single-family building permits issued: 10 (2005); Multi-family building permits issued: 0 (2005); Employment by occupation: 6.9% management, 10.5% professional, 22.5% services, 26.4% sales, 0.8% farming, 10.5% construction, 22.4% production (2000).
Income: Per capita income: $20,377 (2005); Median household income: $37,284 (2005); Average household income: $47,057 (2005); Percent of households with income of $100,000 or more: 8.3% (2005); Poverty rate: 11.0% (2000).
Education: Percent of population age 25 and over with: High school diploma (including GED) or higher: 75.1% (2005); Bachelor's degree or higher: 10.9% (2005); Master's degree or higher: 2.5% (2005).
School District(s)
High Point Regional (09-12)
    2003-04 Enrollment: 1,540 . . . . (973) 875-7204
Sussex-Wantage Regional (PK-08)
    2003-04 Enrollment: 1,829 . . . . (973) 875-3175
Housing: Homeownership rate: 38.4% (2005); Median home value: $192,647 (2005); Median rent: $582 per month (2000); Median age of housing: 49 years (2000).
Hospitals: Saint Clare's Hospital-Sussex (106 beds)
Transportation: Commute to work: 90.0% car, 2.4% public transportation, 4.9% walk, 0.6% work from home (2000); Travel time to work: 28.4% less than 15 minutes, 30.9% 15 to 30 minutes, 12.5% 30 to 45 minutes, 11.0% 45 to 60 minutes, 17.2% 60 minutes or more (2000)

VERNON (township). Covers a land area of 68.394 square miles and a water area of 2.142 square miles. Located at 41.19° N. Lat.; 74.49° W. Long. Elevation is 564 feet.
History: Incorporated 1798.
Population: 21,196 (1990); 24,686 (2000); 25,767 (2005); 26,995 (2010 projected); Race: 95.6% White, 1.1% Black, 0.9% Asian, 5.2% Hispanic of

any race (2005); Density: 376.7 persons per square mile (2005); Average household size: 2.90 (2005); Median age: 36.4 (2005); Males per 100 females: 102.3 (2005); Marriage status: 23.4% never married, 65.9% now married, 3.9% widowed, 6.8% divorced (2000); Foreign born: 5.1% (2000); Ancestry (includes multiple ancestries): 28.4% Irish, 26.7% Italian, 25.5% German, 9.5% Polish, 8.1% English (2000).
Economy: Manufacturing of metal and machine parts. Vernon Valley-Great Gorge and Theme Park here. Unemployment rate: 3.3% (2005); Total civilian labor force: 13,755 (2005); Single-family building permits issued: 54 (2005); Multi-family building permits issued: 0 (2005); Employment by occupation: 13.4% management, 21.0% professional, 12.4% services, 28.3% sales, 0.2% farming, 12.6% construction, 12.0% production (2000).
Income: Per capita income: $29,249 (2005); Median household income: $74,167 (2005); Average household income: $84,507 (2005); Percent of households with income of $100,000 or more: 28.6% (2005); Poverty rate: 2.9% (2000).
Education: Percent of population age 25 and over with: High school diploma (including GED) or higher: 92.9% (2005); Bachelor's degree or higher: 25.3% (2005); Master's degree or higher: 7.7% (2005).
School District(s)
Vernon Township (PK-12)
    2003-04 Enrollment: 5,500 . . . . (973) 764-2900
Housing: Homeownership rate: 85.2% (2005); Median home value: $240,144 (2005); Median rent: $783 per month (2000); Median age of housing: 25 years (2000).
Safety: Violent crime rate: 6.2 per 10,000 population; Property crime rate: 149.1 per 10,000 population (2004).
Transportation: Commute to work: 95.3% car, 0.7% public transportation, 0.5% walk, 2.7% work from home (2000); Travel time to work: 18.5% less than 15 minutes, 16.2% 15 to 30 minutes, 14.5% 30 to 45 minutes, 19.1% 45 to 60 minutes, 31.7% 60 minutes or more (2000)
Additional Information Contacts
Vernon Chamber of Commerce . . . . (973) 764-0764
    http://www.vernonchamber.com
Vernon Township . . . . (973) 764-4055
    http://www.vernontwp.com/township

VERNON VALLEY (CDP). Aka Vernon Valley Lake. Covers a land area of 2.643 square miles and a water area of 0.041 square miles. Located at 41.23° N. Lat.; 74.48° W. Long.
Population: 1,788 (1990); 1,737 (2000); 1,660 (2005); 1,637 (2010 projected); Race: 95.7% White, 1.0% Black, 1.4% Asian, 3.7% Hispanic of any race (2005); Density: 628.0 persons per square mile (2005); Average household size: 3.14 (2005); Median age: 37.3 (2005); Males per 100 females: 101.2 (2005); Marriage status: 26.2% never married, 65.7% now married, 3.4% widowed, 4.6% divorced (2000); Foreign born: 4.0% (2000); Ancestry (includes multiple ancestries): 32.2% German, 30.3% Irish, 23.3% Italian, 11.4% Polish, 5.9% French (except Basque) (2000).
Economy: Employment by occupation: 12.5% management, 15.6% professional, 17.2% services, 29.5% sales, 0.0% farming, 11.9% construction, 13.3% production (2000).
Income: Per capita income: $27,465 (2005); Median household income: $82,733 (2005); Average household income: $86,186 (2005); Percent of households with income of $100,000 or more: 34.6% (2005); Poverty rate: 1.9% (2000).
Education: Percent of population age 25 and over with: High school diploma (including GED) or higher: 94.1% (2005); Bachelor's degree or higher: 20.7% (2005); Master's degree or higher: 6.6% (2005).
Housing: Homeownership rate: 94.3% (2005); Median home value: $249,467 (2005); Median rent: $625 per month (2000); Median age of housing: 26 years (2000).
Transportation: Commute to work: 95.1% car, 2.0% public transportation, 0.0% walk, 1.3% work from home (2000); Travel time to work: 25.9% less than 15 minutes, 20.3% 15 to 30 minutes, 12.2% 30 to 45 minutes, 7.9% 45 to 60 minutes, 33.6% 60 minutes or more (2000)

WALPACK (township). Covers a land area of 24.066 square miles and a water area of 0.650 square miles. Located at 41.12° N. Lat.; 74.91° W. Long.
Population: 67 (1990); 41 (2000); 36 (2005); 36 (2010 projected); Race: 100.0% White, 0.0% Black, 0.0% Asian, 0.0% Hispanic of any race (2005); Density: 1.5 persons per square mile (2005); Average household size: 2.00 (2005); Median age: 51.7 (2005); Males per 100 females: 100.0 (2005); Marriage status: 0.0% never married, 86.5% now married, 13.5% widowed,

0.0% divorced (2000); Foreign born: 0.0% (2000); Ancestry (includes multiple ancestries): 75.7% Irish, 37.8% German, 13.5% Polish, 13.5% Hungarian, 13.5% Other groups (2000).

Economy: Single-family building permits issued: 0 (2005); Multi-family building permits issued: 0 (2005); Employment by occupation: 0.0% management, 0.0% professional, 55.6% services, 0.0% sales, 0.0% farming, 44.4% construction, 0.0% production (2000).

Income: Per capita income: $18,194 (2005); Median household income: $31,667 (2005); Average household income: $36,389 (2005); Percent of households with income of $100,000 or more: 0.0% (2005); Poverty rate: 0.0% (2000).

Education: Percent of population age 25 and over with: High school diploma (including GED) or higher: 63.3% (2005); Bachelor's degree or higher: 0.0% (2005); Master's degree or higher: 0.0% (2005).

Housing: Homeownership rate: 44.4% (2005); Median home value: $420,000 (2005); Median rent: $300 per month (2000); Median age of housing: 60+ years (2000).

Transportation: Commute to work: 100.0% car, 0.0% public transportation, 0.0% walk, 0.0% work from home (2000); Travel time to work: 27.8% less than 15 minutes, 27.8% 15 to 30 minutes, 0.0% 30 to 45 minutes, 0.0% 45 to 60 minutes, 44.4% 60 minutes or more (2000)

WANTAGE (township). Covers a land area of 67.120 square miles and a water area of 0.418 square miles. Located at 41.24° N. Lat.; 74.63° W. Long. Elevation is 410 feet.

History: Incorporated 1798.

Population: 9,462 (1990); 10,387 (2000); 11,421 (2005); 12,461 (2010 projected); Race: 96.5% White, 0.8% Black, 0.9% Asian, 3.9% Hispanic of any race (2005); Density: 170.2 persons per square mile (2005); Average household size: 2.98 (2005); Median age: 37.3 (2005); Males per 100 females: 96.7 (2005); Marriage status: 23.0% never married, 64.3% now married, 6.2% widowed, 6.5% divorced (2000); Foreign born: 4.7% (2000); Ancestry (includes multiple ancestries): 24.7% German, 20.5% Irish, 16.9% Italian, 15.1% English, 9.1% Dutch (2000).

Economy: Single-family building permits issued: 79 (2005); Multi-family building permits issued: 0 (2005); Employment by occupation: 11.0% management, 20.7% professional, 15.1% services, 26.9% sales, 1.0% farming, 13.1% construction, 12.1% production (2000).

Income: Per capita income: $25,887 (2005); Median household income: $65,872 (2005); Average household income: $76,917 (2005); Percent of households with income of $100,000 or more: 24.6% (2005); Poverty rate: 4.9% (2000).

Taxes: Total city taxes per capita: $291 (2004); City property taxes per capita: $240 (2004).

Education: Percent of population age 25 and over with: High school diploma (including GED) or higher: 84.4% (2005); Bachelor's degree or higher: 19.7% (2005); Master's degree or higher: 7.7% (2005).

School District(s)

Sussex-Wantage Regional (PK-08)

    2003-04 Enrollment: 1,829 . . . . (973) 875-3175

Housing: Homeownership rate: 88.0% (2005); Median home value: $254,606 (2005); Median rent: $654 per month (2000); Median age of housing: 25 years (2000).

Transportation: Commute to work: 92.6% car, 0.6% public transportation, 1.2% walk, 4.9% work from home (2000); Travel time to work: 17.8% less than 15 minutes, 31.9% 15 to 30 minutes, 13.2% 30 to 45 minutes, 9.9% 45 to 60 minutes, 27.2% 60 minutes or more (2000)

Additional Information Contacts

Wantage Township . . . . (973) 875-7192
    http://www.wantagetwp.com

Union County

Located in northeastern New Jersey; bounded on the northwest by the Passaic River, and on the east by Newark Bay and Arthur Kill; drained by the Rahway River. Covers a land area of 103.29 square miles, a water area of 2.17 square miles, and is located in the Eastern Time Zone. The county government was organized in 1857. County seat is Elizabeth.

Union County is part of the New York-Northern New Jersey-Long Island, NY-NJ-PA Metropolitan Statistical Area. The entire metro area includes: Edison, NJ Metropolitan Division (Middlesex County, NJ; Monmouth County, NJ; Ocean County, NJ; Somerset County, NJ); Nassau-Suffolk, NY Metropolitan Division (Nassau County, NY; Suffolk County, NY); New York-White Plains-Wayne, NY-NJ Metropolitan Division (Bergen County, NJ; Hudson County, NJ; Passaic County, NJ; Bronx County, NY; Kings County, NY; New York County, NY; Putnam County, NY; Queens County, NY; Richmond County, NY; Rockland County, NY; Westchester County, NY); Newark-Union, NJ-PA Metropolitan Division (Essex County, NJ; Hunterdon County, NJ; Morris County, NJ; Sussex County, NJ; Union County, NJ; Pike County, PA)

Weather Station: Cranford										Elevation: 72 feet		
	Jan	Feb	Mar	Apr	May	Jun	Jul	Aug	Sep	Oct	Nov	Dec
High	40	44	52	64	74	82	87	85	78	67	56	45
Low	21	23	30	39	48	58	63	62	55	43	35	27
Precip	4.0	3.1	4.2	4.2	4.8	4.1	5.2	4.3	4.5	4.0	4.5	4.0
Snow	7.2	6.6	3.7	0.4	0.0	0.0	0.0	0.0	0.0	tr	0.5	2.2

High and Low temperatures in degrees Fahrenheit; Precipitation and Snow in inches

Weather Station: Plainfield										Elevation: 88 feet		
	Jan	Feb	Mar	Apr	May	Jun	Jul	Aug	Sep	Oct	Nov	Dec
High	38	42	52	63	74	82	87	85	77	66	54	43
Low	22	24	31	40	50	59	64	63	55	44	36	28
Precip	4.0	3.1	4.1	4.0	4.7	4.0	5.3	4.2	4.5	4.0	4.1	3.7
Snow	9.2	8.7	4.4	0.6	tr	0.0	0.0	0.0	0.0	tr	0.6	3.1

High and Low temperatures in degrees Fahrenheit; Precipitation and Snow in inches

Population: 493,963 (1990); 522,541 (2000); 531,611 (2005); 540,944 (2010 projected); Race: 62.8% White, 21.7% Black, 4.0% Asian, 23.5% Hispanic of any race (2005); Density: 5,146.8 persons per square mile (2005); Average household size: 2.83 (2005); Median age: 37.6 (2005); Males per 100 females: 93.4 (2005).

Religion: Five largest groups: 48.2% Catholic Church, 5.8% Jewish Estimate, 2.3% Presbyterian Church (U.S.A.), 1.9% American Baptist Churches in the USA, 1.3% Episcopal Church (2000).

Economy: Unemployment rate: 4.7% (2005); Total civilian labor force: 267,292 (2005); Leading industries: 12.9% manufacturing; 12.4% retail trade; 11.6% health care and social assistance (2004); Farms: 18 totaling 182 acres (2002); Companies that employ 500 or more persons: 87 (2004); Companies that employ 100 to 499 persons: 685 (2004); Companies that employ less than 100 persons: 28,660 (2004); Black-owned businesses: 3,648 (2002); Hispanic-owned businesses: 4,972 (2002); Asian-owned businesses: 2,300 (2002); Women-owned businesses: 11,023 (2002); Retail sales per capita: $16,211 (2006). Single-family building permits issued: 599 (2005); Multi-family building permits issued: 679 (2005).

Income: Per capita income: $30,309 (2005); Median household income: $62,755 (2005); Average household income: $85,059 (2005); Percent of households with income of $100,000 or more: 27.6% (2005); Poverty rate: 9.9% (2003); Bankruptcy rate: 5.34% (2005).

Taxes: Total county taxes per capita: $369 (2004); County property taxes per capita: $360 (2004).

Education: Percent of population age 25 and over with: High school diploma (including GED) or higher: 78.8% (2005); Bachelor's degree or higher: 27.9% (2005); Master's degree or higher: 10.6% (2005).

Housing: Homeownership rate: 61.2% (2005); Median home value: $293,027 (2005); Median rent: $676 per month (2000); Median age of housing: 47 years (2000).

Health: Birth rate: 149.6 per 10,000 population (2004); Death rate: 82.9 per 10,000 population (2004); Age-adjusted cancer mortality rate: 190.2 deaths per 100,000 population (2002); Air Quality Index: 58.1% good, 39.5% moderate, 2.5% unhealthy for sensitive individuals, 0.0% unhealthy (percent of days in 2005); Number of physicians: 28.4 per 10,000 population (2004); Hospital beds: 29.2 per 10,000 population (2003); Hospital admissions: 817.1 per 10,000 population (2003).

Elections: 2004 Presidential election results: 40.6% Bush, 58.7% Kerry, 0.5% Nader, 0.1% Badnarik

Additional Information Contacts

Union County Government . . . . (908) 527-4100
    http://www.unioncountynj.org
Borough of Fanwood . . . . (908) 322-8236
    http://www.visitfanwood.com/borough
Borough of New Providence . . . . (908) 665-1400
    http://www.newprov.org
Borough of Roselle Park . . . . (908) 245-6180
    http://www.rosellepark.org
Central Jersey Chamber of Commerc . . . . (908) 756-7250
    http://www.plainfield.com
City of Elizabeth . . . . (908) 820-4133
    http://www.elizabethnj.org
City of Plainfield . . . . (908) 753-3222
    http://www.plainfield.com/city

City of Rahway...................................... (732) 827-2100
　http://www.cityofrahway.com
City of Summit .... (908) 273-6400
　http://www.ci.summit.nj.us
Clark Township .... (735) 381-5395
　http://www.ourclark.com
Cranford Chamber of Commerce..................... (908) 272-6114
　http://www.cranford.com/chamber
Cranford Township................................... (908) 709-7200
　http://www.cranford.com/township
Fanwood Chamber of Commerce .... (908) 352-0900
　http://www.unioncountynj.org
Gateway Regional Chamber of Commerce .... (908) 352-0900
　http://www.gatewaychamber.com/members/union_county.asp
Greater Elizabeth Area Chamber of Commerce .... (908) 355-7600
　http://www.elizabethchamber.com
Rahway Chamber of Commerce .... (732) 499-0210
　http://www.cityofrahway.com
Scotch Plains Chamber of Commerce................. (908) 233-3021
　http://www.scotchplainsnj.com
Scotch Plains Township.............................. (908) 322-6700
　http://www.scotchplainsnj.com
Suburban Chamber of Commerce.................... (908) 522-1700
　http://www.suburbanchambers.org
Suburban Chambers of Commerce .... (908) 522-1700
　http://www.suburbanchambers.org
Town of Westfield .... (908) 789-4040
　http://www.westfieldnj.govoffice2.com
Union County Chamber of Commerce................. (908) 352-0900
　http://www.suburbanchambers.org
Union Township .... (908) 527-4000
　http://www.unioncountynj.org
Union Township Chamber of Commerce............... (908) 688-2777
　http://www.unionchamber.com
Westfield Chamber of Commerce .... (908) 233-3021
　http://www.westfieldchamber.com

Union County Communities

BERKELEY HEIGHTS (township). Aka Berkeley Heights CDP.
Covers a land area of 6.263 square miles and a water area of 0.011 square
miles. Located at 40.67° N. Lat.; 74.43° W. Long. Elevation is 220 feet.
Population: 11,980 (1990); 13,407 (2000); 13,637 (2005); 13,880 (2010
projected); Race: 89.3% White, 1.1% Black, 8.0% Asian, 5.0% Hispanic of
any race (2005); Density: 2,177.4 persons per square mile (2005); Average
household size: 2.96 (2005); Median age: 40.4 (2005); Males per 100
females: 91.1 (2005); Marriage status: 17.7% never married, 70.7% now
married, 6.8% widowed, 4.8% divorced (2000); Foreign born: 13.8%
(2000); Ancestry (includes multiple ancestries): 25.4% Italian, 22.5% Irish,
17.3% German, 13.9% Other groups, 9.0% English (2000).
Economy: Manufacturing: chemicals, metal products, electronics. Suburb.
Single-family building permits issued: 26 (2005); Multi-family building
permits issued: 6 (2005); Employment by occupation: 25.0% management,
31.6% professional, 8.8% services, 26.7% sales, 0.0% farming, 4.8%
construction, 3.1% production (2000).
Income: Per capita income: $52,597 (2005); Median household income:
$124,076 (2005); Average household income: $154,963 (2005); Percent of
households with income of $100,000 or more: 60.8% (2005); Poverty rate:
2.1% (2000).
Education: Percent of population age 25 and over with: High school
diploma (including GED) or higher: 92.4% (2005); Bachelor's degree or
higher: 52.0% (2005); Master's degree or higher: 23.1% (2005).
School District(s)
Berkeley Heights Township (PK-12)
　2003-04 Enrollment: 2,797 .... (908) 464-1718
Housing: Homeownership rate: 91.6% (2005); Median home value:
$517,824 (2005); Median rent: $1,141 per month (2000); Median age of
housing: 38 years (2000).
Hospitals: Runnells Specialized Hospital of Union County (369 beds)
Safety: Violent crime rate: 5.1 per 10,000 population; Property crime rate:
63.7 per 10,000 population (2004).
Transportation: Commute to work: 81.0% car, 10.4% public
transportation, 2.1% walk, 5.7% work from home (2000); Travel time to
work: 26.3% less than 15 minutes, 30.6% 15 to 30 minutes, 19.8% 30 to 45
minutes, 7.8% 45 to 60 minutes, 15.6% 60 minutes or more (2000)

Additional Information Contacts
Suburban Chambers of Commerce .... (908) 522-1700
　http://www.suburbanchambers.org

CLARK (township). Aka Clark CDP. Covers a land area of 4.345 square
miles and a water area of 0.141 square miles. Located at 40.62° N. Lat.;
74.30° W. Long. Elevation is 80 feet.
History: Named for Abraham Clark (1726-1794), a signer of the
Declaration of Independence. Incorporated 1864.
Population: 14,629 (1990); 14,597 (2000); 14,726 (2005); 14,868 (2010
projected); Race: 94.9% White, 0.4% Black, 3.1% Asian, 4.5% Hispanic of
any race (2005); Density: 3,389.3 persons per square mile (2005); Average
household size: 2.55 (2005); Median age: 44.0 (2005); Males per 100
females: 90.9 (2005); Marriage status: 21.1% never married, 64.6% now
married, 9.1% widowed, 5.2% divorced (2000); Foreign born: 11.1%
(2000); Ancestry (includes multiple ancestries): 31.5% Italian, 18.8% Irish,
17.7% Polish, 16.2% German, 6.6% Other groups (2000).
Economy: Manufacturing: machinery, metal products, consumer products,
building materials, chemical products, gypsum board. Single-family building
permits issued: 46 (2005); Multi-family building permits issued: 0 (2005);
Employment by occupation: 14.7% management, 22.3% professional,
10.8% services, 34.5% sales, 0.0% farming, 8.6% construction, 9.1%
production (2000).
Income: Per capita income: $35,934 (2005); Median household income:
$78,348 (2005); Average household income: $91,042 (2005); Percent of
households with income of $100,000 or more: 34.1% (2005); Poverty rate:
1.7% (2000).
Education: Percent of population age 25 and over with: High school
diploma (including GED) or higher: 88.0% (2005); Bachelor's degree or
higher: 28.2% (2005); Master's degree or higher: 8.8% (2005).
School District(s)
Clark Township (PK-12)
　2003-04 Enrollment: 2,760 .... (732) 574-9600
Housing: Homeownership rate: 80.9% (2005); Median home value:
$339,370 (2005); Median rent: $856 per month (2000); Median age of
housing: 41 years (2000).
Safety: Violent crime rate: 2.7 per 10,000 population; Property crime rate:
123.6 per 10,000 population (2004).
Newspapers: Suburban News (General - Circulation 94,000)
Transportation: Commute to work: 92.5% car, 3.9% public transportation,
0.4% walk, 3.1% work from home (2000); Travel time to work: 29.5% less
than 15 minutes, 33.9% 15 to 30 minutes, 21.5% 30 to 45 minutes, 8.1%
45 to 60 minutes, 6.9% 60 minutes or more (2000)
Additional Information Contacts
Clark Township .... (735) 381-5395
　http://www.ourclark.com

CRANFORD (township). Aka Cranford CDP. Covers a land area of
4.820 square miles and a water area of 0.020 square miles. Located at
40.65° N. Lat.; 74.30° W. Long. Elevation is 81 feet.
History: Named for the Crane family, descendants of Stephen Crane.
Union County college here. Incorporated 1871.
Population: 22,633 (1990); 22,578 (2000); 22,690 (2005); 22,831 (2010
projected); Race: 93.3% White, 2.5% Black, 2.3% Asian, 5.0% Hispanic of
any race (2005); Density: 4,707.4 persons per square mile (2005); Average
household size: 2.65 (2005); Median age: 41.5 (2005); Males per 100
females: 91.0 (2005); Marriage status: 22.1% never married, 64.5% now
married, 8.0% widowed, 5.5% divorced (2000); Foreign born: 8.7% (2000);
Ancestry (includes multiple ancestries): 25.4% Italian, 24.6% Irish, 18.1%
German, 12.0% Polish, 10.2% Other groups (2000).
Economy: Printing. Manufacturing: metal products, fire extinguishers.
Single-family building permits issued: 19 (2005); Multi-family building
permits issued: 2 (2005); Employment by occupation: 21.5% management,
29.1% professional, 9.1% services, 27.1% sales, 0.0% farming, 6.9%
construction, 6.2% production (2000).
Income: Per capita income: $40,301 (2005); Median household income:
$88,799 (2005); Average household income: $106,050 (2005); Percent of
households with income of $100,000 or more: 42.2% (2005); Poverty rate:
2.5% (2000).
Education: Percent of population age 25 and over with: High school
diploma (including GED) or higher: 91.3% (2005); Bachelor's degree or
higher: 42.7% (2005); Master's degree or higher: 15.8% (2005).
School District(s)
Cranford Township (PK-12)
　2003-04 Enrollment: 3,642 .... (908) 709-6202

Two-year College(s)
Union County College (Public)
    Fall 2004 Enrollment: 11,058. . . . . (908) 709-7000
    2005-06 Tuition: In-state $4,279; Out-of-state $4,279
Housing: Homeownership rate: 82.5% (2005); Median home value: $364,237 (2005); Median rent: $792 per month (2000); Median age of housing: 51 years (2000).
Safety: Violent crime rate: 4.4 per 10,000 population; Property crime rate: 113.9 per 10,000 population (2004).
Newspapers: Round About Peterstown (General - Circulation 5,000)
Transportation: Commute to work: 83.6% car, 11.2% public transportation, 1.4% walk, 3.5% work from home (2000); Travel time to work: 24.8% less than 15 minutes, 31.7% 15 to 30 minutes, 19.9% 30 to 45 minutes, 8.8% 45 to 60 minutes, 14.8% 60 minutes or more (2000)
Additional Information Contacts
Cranford Chamber of Commerce. . . . . (908) 272-6114
    http://www.cranford.com/chamber
Cranford Township. . . . . (908) 709-7200
    http://www.cranford.com/township

ELIZABETH (city). Covers a land area of 12.221 square miles and a water area of 1.434 square miles. Located at 40.66° N. Lat.; 74.20° W. Long. Elevation is 38 feet.
History: Named for Lady Elizabeth, wife of Sir George Carteret, grantee of the land. The history of Elizabeth, oldest English settlement in New Jersey, began in 1664, when the English ended Dutch control of New Netherland. Three Long Islanders bought a large tract extending from Raritan River to Newark Bay. Philip Carteret arrived as the first English governor of New Jersey. He picked a spot for his capital and named it Elizabethtown in honor of the wife of his cousin, Sir George Carteret. Elizabethtown was chartered in 1740 as the "Free Borough and town of Elizabeth." A city charter was issued in 1855. In 1873, the Singer Sewing Machine Company came to Elizabeth.
Population: 109,978 (1990); 120,568 (2000); 124,189 (2005); 127,800 (2010 projected); Race: 53.5% White, 20.1% Black, 2.0% Asian, 56.1% Hispanic of any race (2005); Density: 10,161.7 persons per square mile (2005); Average household size: 3.02 (2005); Median age: 33.7 (2005); Males per 100 females: 98.7 (2005); Marriage status: 35.5% never married, 49.6% now married, 6.3% widowed, 8.6% divorced (2000); Foreign born: 43.9% (2000); Ancestry (includes multiple ancestries): 59.4% Other groups, 5.5% Portuguese, 5.0% Italian, 3.5% Polish, 3.3% Irish (2000).
Economy: Unemployment rate: 6.7% (2005); Total civilian labor force: 54,199 (2005); Single-family building permits issued: 2 (2005); Multi-family building permits issued: 460 (2005); Employment by occupation: 6.9% management, 11.4% professional, 17.8% services, 25.9% sales, 0.1% farming, 9.5% construction, 28.4% production (2000).
Income: Per capita income: $16,691 (2005); Median household income: $39,428 (2005); Average household income: $49,840 (2005); Percent of households with income of $100,000 or more: 10.1% (2005); Poverty rate: 17.8% (2000).
Taxes: Total city taxes per capita: $752 (2004); City property taxes per capita: $649 (2004).
Education: Percent of population age 25 and over with: High school diploma (including GED) or higher: 61.5% (2005); Bachelor's degree or higher: 12.0% (2005); Master's degree or higher: 4.2% (2005).
School District(s)
Elizabeth City (PK-12)
    2003-04 Enrollment: 21,998 . . . . (908) 436-5010
Two-year College(s)
Drake College of Business (Private, For-profit)
    Fall 2004 Enrollment: 415 . . . . (908) 352-5509
    2005-06 Tuition: In-state $3,800; Out-of-state $3,800
Housing: Homeownership rate: 29.4% (2005); Median home value: $246,851 (2005); Median rent: $616 per month (2000); Median age of housing: 48 years (2000).
Hospitals: St. Elizabeth Hospital (329 beds); Trinitas Hospital (315 beds)
Safety: Violent crime rate: 55.3 per 10,000 population; Property crime rate: 445.2 per 10,000 population (2004).
Newspapers: La Voz (Hispanic - Circulation 38,000); Mensaje (General, Hispanic - Circulation 52,000)
Transportation: Commute to work: 76.9% car, 14.7% public transportation, 4.9% walk, 1.1% work from home (2000); Travel time to work: 22.9% less than 15 minutes, 36.2% 15 to 30 minutes, 21.9% 30 to 45 minutes, 9.0% 45 to 60 minutes, 9.9% 60 minutes or more (2000)
Additional Information Contacts

City of Elizabeth. . . . . (908) 820-4133
    http://www.elizabethnj.org
Greater Elizabeth Area Chamber of Commerce . . . . (908) 355-7600
    http://www.elizabethchamber.com

FANWOOD (borough). Covers a land area of 1.338 square miles and a water area of 0 square miles. Located at 40.64° N. Lat.; 74.38° W. Long. Elevation is 157 feet.
History: Settled before 1780, incorporated 1895.
Population: 7,075 (1990); 7,174 (2000); 7,285 (2005); 7,409 (2010 projected); Race: 87.9% White, 5.3% Black, 4.3% Asian, 4.9% Hispanic of any race (2005); Density: 5,446.4 persons per square mile (2005); Average household size: 2.74 (2005); Median age: 39.7 (2005); Males per 100 females: 92.3 (2005); Marriage status: 17.6% never married, 70.4% now married, 7.4% widowed, 4.5% divorced (2000); Foreign born: 12.0% (2000); Ancestry (includes multiple ancestries): 23.2% Italian, 23.0% Irish, 20.6% German, 13.8% Other groups, 6.4% Polish (2000).
Economy: Manufacturing: packaging, air hoses. Single-family building permits issued: 13 (2005); Multi-family building permits issued: 0 (2005); Employment by occupation: 23.9% management, 31.5% professional, 6.0% services, 28.1% sales, 0.0% farming, 5.1% construction, 5.4% production (2000).
Income: Per capita income: $42,162 (2005); Median household income: $99,465 (2005); Average household income: $114,573 (2005); Percent of households with income of $100,000 or more: 49.7% (2005); Poverty rate: 3.4% (2000).
Education: Percent of population age 25 and over with: High school diploma (including GED) or higher: 94.9% (2005); Bachelor's degree or higher: 50.8% (2005); Master's degree or higher: 18.3% (2005).
Housing: Homeownership rate: 91.8% (2005); Median home value: $358,224 (2005); Median rent: $1,077 per month (2000); Median age of housing: 47 years (2000).
Safety: Violent crime rate: 8.2 per 10,000 population; Property crime rate: 127.3 per 10,000 population (2004).
Transportation: Commute to work: 83.1% car, 11.0% public transportation, 1.9% walk, 3.7% work from home (2000); Travel time to work: 19.1% less than 15 minutes, 26.5% 15 to 30 minutes, 23.3% 30 to 45 minutes, 11.1% 45 to 60 minutes, 20.0% 60 minutes or more (2000)
Additional Information Contacts
Borough of Fanwood . . . . (908) 322-8236
    http://www.visitfanwood.com/borough
Fanwood Chamber of Commerce . . . . (908) 352-0900
    http://www.unioncountynj.org

GARWOOD (borough). Covers a land area of 0.660 square miles and a water area of 0 square miles. Located at 40.65° N. Lat.; 74.32° W. Long. Elevation is 100 feet.
History: Incorporated 1903.
Population: 4,227 (1990); 4,153 (2000); 4,166 (2005); 4,196 (2010 projected); Race: 95.0% White, 0.4% Black, 1.5% Asian, 6.5% Hispanic of any race (2005); Density: 6,312.6 persons per square mile (2005); Average household size: 2.36 (2005); Median age: 40.1 (2005); Males per 100 females: 93.9 (2005); Marriage status: 29.5% never married, 53.0% now married, 10.9% widowed, 6.6% divorced (2000); Foreign born: 10.5% (2000); Ancestry (includes multiple ancestries): 29.2% Italian, 25.4% Irish, 16.1% German, 11.7% Polish, 10.1% Other groups (2000).
Economy: Manufacturing: metal products, vitamins, paper, and plastics. Single-family building permits issued: 8 (2005); Multi-family building permits issued: 44 (2005); Employment by occupation: 15.6% management, 22.8% professional, 10.5% services, 32.0% sales, 0.0% farming, 10.6% construction, 8.4% production (2000).
Income: Per capita income: $31,526 (2005); Median household income: $61,816 (2005); Average household income: $73,796 (2005); Percent of households with income of $100,000 or more: 25.1% (2005); Poverty rate: 5.1% (2000).
Education: Percent of population age 25 and over with: High school diploma (including GED) or higher: 86.5% (2005); Bachelor's degree or higher: 27.6% (2005); Master's degree or higher: 11.2% (2005).
School District(s)
Garwood Borough (PK-08)
    2003-04 Enrollment: 394 . . . . (908) 789-0165
Housing: Homeownership rate: 63.1% (2005); Median home value: $287,546 (2005); Median rent: $808 per month (2000); Median age of housing: 55 years (2000).

Safety: Violent crime rate: 7.2 per 10,000 population; Property crime rate: 147.8 per 10,000 population (2004).
Transportation: Commute to work: 87.2% car, 7.2% public transportation, 4.0% walk, 0.6% work from home (2000); Travel time to work: 34.1% less than 15 minutes, 28.5% 15 to 30 minutes, 17.1% 30 to 45 minutes, 9.8% 45 to 60 minutes, 10.5% 60 minutes or more (2000)

HILLSIDE (township). Aka Hillside CDP. Covers a land area of 2.790 square miles and a water area of 0 square miles. Located at 40.69° N. Lat.; 74.22° W. Long. Elevation is 100 feet.

History: Named for its location in a hilly area. Incorporated 1913.
Population: 21,047 (1990); 21,747 (2000); 21,945 (2005); 22,113 (2010 projected); Race: 35.0% White, 50.1% Black, 3.1% Asian, 16.0% Hispanic of any race (2005); Density: 7,864.6 persons per square mile (2005); Average household size: 3.06 (2005); Median age: 36.8 (2005); Males per 100 females: 89.0 (2005); Marriage status: 31.9% never married, 54.1% now married, 7.9% widowed, 6.1% divorced (2000); Foreign born: 27.4% (2000); Ancestry (includes multiple ancestries): 52.3% Other groups, 11.0% Portuguese, 5.0% Polish, 4.1% Italian, 3.3% Irish (2000).
Economy: Mixed industry, including metal products and frozen juices. Single-family building permits issued: 15 (2005); Multi-family building permits issued: 20 (2005); Employment by occupation: 11.4% management, 16.2% professional, 14.7% services, 30.2% sales, 0.1% farming, 9.1% construction, 18.3% production (2000).
Income: Per capita income: $25,145 (2005); Median household income: $64,499 (2005); Average household income: $76,834 (2005); Percent of households with income of $100,000 or more: 22.4% (2005); Poverty rate: 5.3% (2000).
Education: Percent of population age 25 and over with: High school diploma (including GED) or higher: 75.7% (2005); Bachelor's degree or higher: 18.3% (2005); Master's degree or higher: 5.4% (2005).
School District(s)
Hillside Township (PK-12)
   2003-04 Enrollment: 3,626 . . . . (908) 352-7664
Housing: Homeownership rate: 70.8% (2005); Median home value: $230,420 (2005); Median rent: $697 per month (2000); Median age of housing: 51 years (2000).
Safety: Violent crime rate: 54.9 per 10,000 population; Property crime rate: 360.9 per 10,000 population (2004).
Transportation: Commute to work: 84.1% car, 10.7% public transportation, 3.7% walk, 1.4% work from home (2000); Travel time to work: 21.5% less than 15 minutes, 36.8% 15 to 30 minutes, 23.8% 30 to 45 minutes, 8.8% 45 to 60 minutes, 9.1% 60 minutes or more (2000)
Additional Information Contacts
Gateway Regional Chamber of Commerce . . . . (908) 352-0900
   http://www.gatewaychamber.com/members/union_county.asp

KENILWORTH (borough). Covers a land area of 2.141 square miles and a water area of 0.002 square miles. Located at 40.67° N. Lat.; 74.29° W. Long. Elevation is 91 feet.

History: Incorporated 1907.
Population: 7,574 (1990); 7,675 (2000); 7,750 (2005); 7,849 (2010 projected); Race: 89.9% White, 2.5% Black, 3.4% Asian, 11.0% Hispanic of any race (2005); Density: 3,619.9 persons per square mile (2005); Average household size: 2.67 (2005); Median age: 41.0 (2005); Males per 100 females: 94.7 (2005); Marriage status: 26.2% never married, 56.0% now married, 10.3% widowed, 7.4% divorced (2000); Foreign born: 17.6% (2000); Ancestry (includes multiple ancestries): 32.9% Italian, 17.8% German, 14.3% Irish, 13.7% Polish, 13.5% Other groups (2000).
Economy: Manufacturing: machinery, fabricated metal products, paper products, plastics. Single-family building permits issued: 17 (2005); Multi-family building permits issued: 4 (2005); Employment by occupation: 15.5% management, 14.9% professional, 16.2% services, 31.3% sales, 0.2% farming, 10.6% construction, 11.2% production (2000).
Income: Per capita income: $28,033 (2005); Median household income: $64,416 (2005); Average household income: $74,684 (2005); Percent of households with income of $100,000 or more: 22.8% (2005); Poverty rate: 2.0% (2000).
Education: Percent of population age 25 and over with: High school diploma (including GED) or higher: 80.1% (2005); Bachelor's degree or higher: 15.2% (2005); Master's degree or higher: 4.0% (2005).
School District(s)
Kenilworth Borough (PK-12)
   2003-04 Enrollment: 1,340 . . . . (908) 276-1644

Morris-Union Joint (UG-UG)
   2003-04 Enrollment: 586 . . . . (908) 464-7625
Two-year College(s)
Capri Institute of Hair Design (Private, For-profit)
   Fall 2004 Enrollment: 148 . . . . (800) 232-2774
Housing: Homeownership rate: 77.6% (2005); Median home value: $287,017 (2005); Median rent: $850 per month (2000); Median age of housing: 47 years (2000).
Safety: Violent crime rate: 5.1 per 10,000 population; Property crime rate: 188.7 per 10,000 population (2004).
Newspapers: Freie Zeitung (General - Circulation 6,000)
Transportation: Commute to work: 93.9% car, 2.7% public transportation, 1.0% walk, 1.5% work from home (2000); Travel time to work: 32.0% less than 15 minutes, 33.7% 15 to 30 minutes, 18.2% 30 to 45 minutes, 8.6% 45 to 60 minutes, 7.5% 60 minutes or more (2000)

LINDEN (city). Covers a land area of 10.806 square miles and a water area of 0.414 square miles. Located at 40.63° N. Lat.; 74.25° W. Long. Elevation is 10 feet.

History: During the first half of the 20th century, Linden changed from an agricultural district to a city of diverse manufacturing. The city, named for Linden, Germany and the linden trees in the vicinity, was part of Elizabeth until 1861. Incorporated 1925.
Population: 36,701 (1990); 39,394 (2000); 40,010 (2005); 40,630 (2010 projected); Race: 61.9% White, 24.5% Black, 2.6% Asian, 18.8% Hispanic of any race (2005); Density: 3,702.5 persons per square mile (2005); Average household size: 2.65 (2005); Median age: 39.1 (2005); Males per 100 females: 91.3 (2005); Marriage status: 29.6% never married, 53.0% now married, 9.7% widowed, 7.7% divorced (2000); Foreign born: 26.3% (2000); Ancestry (includes multiple ancestries): 31.1% Other groups, 18.0% Polish, 10.3% Italian, 9.0% Irish, 6.8% German (2000).
Economy: Manufacturing: chemicals, petroleum products, plastics, advertising signs, transportation equipment. Unemployment rate: 5.2% (2005); Total civilian labor force: 20,624 (2005); Single-family building permits issued: 36 (2005); Multi-family building permits issued: 21 (2005); Employment by occupation: 9.1% management, 13.8% professional, 14.9% services, 32.3% sales, 0.1% farming, 9.2% construction, 20.5% production (2000).
Income: Per capita income: $23,092 (2005); Median household income: $50,888 (2005); Average household income: $61,069 (2005); Percent of households with income of $100,000 or more: 15.6% (2005); Poverty rate: 6.4% (2000).
Taxes: Total city taxes per capita: $808 (2004); City property taxes per capita: $788 (2004).
Education: Percent of population age 25 and over with: High school diploma (including GED) or higher: 78.2% (2005); Bachelor's degree or higher: 14.2% (2005); Master's degree or higher: 4.5% (2005).
School District(s)
Linden City (PK-12)
   2003-04 Enrollment: 6,508 . . . . (908) 486-5818
Two-year College(s)
Hohokus School of Trade and Technical Sciences (Private, For-profit)
   Fall 2004 Enrollment: 35 . . . . (908) 486-9353
Housing: Homeownership rate: 57.7% (2005); Median home value: $245,060 (2005); Median rent: $705 per month (2000); Median age of housing: 46 years (2000).
Safety: Violent crime rate: 37.1 per 10,000 population; Property crime rate: 377.0 per 10,000 population (2004).
Transportation: Commute to work: 87.6% car, 7.1% public transportation, 3.5% walk, 0.9% work from home (2000); Travel time to work: 30.1% less than 15 minutes, 34.2% 15 to 30 minutes, 18.4% 30 to 45 minutes, 8.0% 45 to 60 minutes, 9.2% 60 minutes or more (2000)

MOUNTAINSIDE (borough). Covers a land area of 4.024 square miles and a water area of 0.033 square miles. Located at 40.68° N. Lat.; 74.35° W. Long. Elevation is 142 feet.

History: Incorporated 1895.
Population: 6,616 (1990); 6,602 (2000); 6,679 (2005); 6,761 (2010 projected); Race: 94.7% White, 1.1% Black, 2.9% Asian, 3.9% Hispanic of any race (2005); Density: 1,659.9 persons per square mile (2005); Average household size: 2.67 (2005); Median age: 47.2 (2005); Males per 100 females: 89.6 (2005); Marriage status: 16.2% never married, 70.8% now married, 9.6% widowed, 3.4% divorced (2000); Foreign born: 13.3% (2000); Ancestry (includes multiple ancestries): 23.4% Italian, 20.1% German, 15.5% Irish, 12.2% Polish, 9.3% Other groups (2000).

Economy: Single-family building permits issued: 21 (2005); Multi-family building permits issued: 0 (2005); Employment by occupation: 24.8% management, 28.0% professional, 10.0% services, 27.6% sales, 0.0% farming, 5.6% construction, 4.0% production (2000).
Income: Per capita income: $51,388 (2005); Median household income: $107,985 (2005); Average household income: $134,998 (2005); Percent of households with income of $100,000 or more: 53.8% (2005); Poverty rate: 3.0% (2000).
Education: Percent of population age 25 and over with: High school diploma (including GED) or higher: 92.9% (2005); Bachelor's degree or higher: 48.5% (2005); Master's degree or higher: 22.2% (2005).

School District(s)
Morris-Union Joint (UG-UG)
   2003-04 Enrollment: 586 . . . . (908) 464-7625
Mountainside Borough (PK-08)
   2003-04 Enrollment: 672 . . . . (908) 232-3232
Housing: Homeownership rate: 94.6% (2005); Median home value: $566,202 (2005); Median rent: $916 per month (2000); Median age of housing: 44 years (2000).
Hospitals: Children's Specialized Hospital (117 beds)
Safety: Violent crime rate: 6.0 per 10,000 population; Property crime rate: 95.4 per 10,000 population (2004).
Transportation: Commute to work: 86.4% car, 6.2% public transportation, 1.1% walk, 5.0% work from home (2000); Travel time to work: 26.0% less than 15 minutes, 33.2% 15 to 30 minutes, 20.2% 30 to 45 minutes, 7.8% 45 to 60 minutes, 12.8% 60 minutes or more (2000)

Additional Information Contacts
Union County Chamber of Commerce . . . . (908) 352-0900
   http://www.suburbanchambers.org

NEW PROVIDENCE (borough). Covers a land area of 3.679 square miles and a water area of 0 square miles. Located at 40.70° N. Lat.; 74.40° W. Long. Elevation is 220 feet.
History: Named for the fact that all escaped injury when a church balcony collapsed. Originally called Turkey Town, its name was changed to New Providence in 1778. Settled c.1720, set off and incorporated 1899.
Population: 11,439 (1990); 11,907 (2000); 11,996 (2005); 12,123 (2010 projected); Race: 88.6% White, 1.1% Black, 8.3% Asian, 4.3% Hispanic of any race (2005); Density: 3,261.1 persons per square mile (2005); Average household size: 2.70 (2005); Median age: 39.9 (2005); Males per 100 females: 94.4 (2005); Marriage status: 20.2% never married, 67.7% now married, 7.0% widowed, 5.2% divorced (2000); Foreign born: 17.9% (2000); Ancestry (includes multiple ancestries): 25.9% Italian, 21.9% Irish, 15.9% German, 14.0% Other groups, 8.7% English (2000).
Economy: Largely residential but has some light industry. Roses and fruit are grown here commercially. Single-family building permits issued: 25 (2005); Multi-family building permits issued: 10 (2005); Employment by occupation: 25.4% management, 34.7% professional, 7.3% services, 24.1% sales, 0.0% farming, 5.2% construction, 3.3% production (2000).
Income: Per capita income: $50,471 (2005); Median household income: $105,325 (2005); Average household income: $134,631 (2005); Percent of households with income of $100,000 or more: 52.4% (2005); Poverty rate: 1.8% (2000).
Taxes: Total city taxes per capita: $830 (2004); City property taxes per capita: $802 (2004).
Education: Percent of population age 25 and over with: High school diploma (including GED) or higher: 95.1% (2005); Bachelor's degree or higher: 58.0% (2005); Master's degree or higher: 27.4% (2005).

School District(s)
Morris-Union Joint (UG-UG)
   2003-04 Enrollment: 586 . . . . (908) 464-7625
New Providence Borough (PK-12)
   2003-04 Enrollment: 2,185 . . . . (908) 464-9050
Housing: Homeownership rate: 76.1% (2005); Median home value: $500,786 (2005); Median rent: $887 per month (2000); Median age of housing: 43 years (2000).
Safety: Violent crime rate: 5.8 per 10,000 population; Property crime rate: 82.9 per 10,000 population (2004).
Newspapers: Berkeley Heights/New Providence Independent Press (General - Circulation 55,000); Independent Press (General - Circulation 40,750); The Berkeley Heights/New Providence Dispatch (General - Circulation 1,000); The Madison Independent Press (General - Circulation 35,200); The Millburn/Short Hills Independent Press (General - Circulation 7,450); The Summit Herald (General - Circulation 2,154); The Summit/Chatham Independent Press (General - Circulation 8,450)

Transportation: Commute to work: 81.4% car, 12.5% public transportation, 2.0% walk, 3.5% work from home (2000); Travel time to work: 28.7% less than 15 minutes, 30.4% 15 to 30 minutes, 18.9% 30 to 45 minutes, 6.6% 45 to 60 minutes, 15.4% 60 minutes or more (2000)

Additional Information Contacts
Borough of New Providence . . . . (908) 665-1400
   http://www.newprov.org
Suburban Chamber of Commerce . . . . (908) 522-1700
   http://www.suburbanchambers.org

PLAINFIELD (city). Covers a land area of 6.038 square miles and a water area of 0.001 square miles. Located at 40.61° N. Lat.; 74.41° W. Long. Elevation is 110 feet.
History: Named for its location on a beautiful plain. Among the several 18th-century buildings remaining are a Friends' meetinghouse (1788), the Martine house (1717), and the Nathaniel Drake House (1746), known as Washington's Headquarters. Nearby Washington Rock, overlooking the piedmont, is reputed to be the vantage point from which George Washington watched British troop movements. Settled 1684 by Friends. Incorporated as a city 1869.
Population: 46,567 (1990); 47,829 (2000); 48,048 (2005); 48,283 (2010 projected); Race: 21.1% White, 59.4% Black, 0.9% Asian, 30.8% Hispanic of any race (2005); Density: 7,958.0 persons per square mile (2005); Average household size: 3.19 (2005); Median age: 33.8 (2005); Males per 100 females: 96.5 (2005); Marriage status: 40.1% never married, 44.5% now married, 6.6% widowed, 8.8% divorced (2000); Foreign born: 23.7% (2000); Ancestry (includes multiple ancestries): 70.0% Other groups, 3.0% Jamaican, 2.5% Italian, 2.2% Irish, 2.2% German (2000).
Economy: Diversified industries, including printing and the manufacturing of of chemicals, machinery, electronic equipment and transportation equipment. Unemployment rate: 6.6% (2005); Total civilian labor force: 25,329 (2005); Single-family building permits issued: 16 (2005); Multi-family building permits issued: 2 (2005); Employment by occupation: 10.5% management, 13.5% professional, 17.7% services, 27.3% sales, 0.1% farming, 8.4% construction, 22.5% production (2000).
Income: Per capita income: $20,974 (2005); Median household income: $51,416 (2005); Average household income: $65,753 (2005); Percent of households with income of $100,000 or more: 19.7% (2005); Poverty rate: 15.9% (2000).
Taxes: Total city taxes per capita: $759 (2004); City property taxes per capita: $746 (2004).
Education: Percent of population age 25 and over with: High school diploma (including GED) or higher: 70.0% (2005); Bachelor's degree or higher: 18.1% (2005); Master's degree or higher: 6.0% (2005).

School District(s)
Agency - Queen City Academy CS (KG-08)
   2003-04 Enrollment: 177 . . . . (908) 756-0291
Plainfield City (PK-12)
   2003-04 Enrollment: 8,119 . . . . (908) 731-4335

Two-year College(s)
Muhlenberg Regional Medical Center-Harold B. & Dorothy A. Snyder Schools-Sc (Private, Not-for-profit)
   Fall 2004 Enrollment: 365 . . . . (908) 668-2400
   2005-06 Tuition: In-state $13,847; Out-of-state $13,847
Muhlenberg Regional Medical Center-Harold B. & Dorothy A. Snyder Schools-Sc (Private, Not-for-profit)
   Fall 2004 Enrollment: 113 . . . . (908) 668-2194
   2005-06 Tuition: In-state $13,666; Out-of-state $13,666
duCret School of Arts (Private, Not-for-profit)
   Fall 2004 Enrollment: 56 . . . . (908) 757-7171
   2005-06 Tuition: In-state $7,100; Out-of-state $7,100
Housing: Homeownership rate: 49.0% (2005); Median home value: $220,769 (2005); Median rent: $657 per month (2000); Median age of housing: 51 years (2000).
Hospitals: Muhlenberg Regional Medical Center (406 beds)
Safety: Violent crime rate: 114.1 per 10,000 population; Property crime rate: 329.0 per 10,000 population (2004).
Transportation: Commute to work: 82.9% car, 8.8% public transportation, 3.9% walk, 1.3% work from home (2000); Travel time to work: 19.4% less than 15 minutes, 35.9% 15 to 30 minutes, 25.6% 30 to 45 minutes, 7.6% 45 to 60 minutes, 11.6% 60 minutes or more (2000)

Additional Information Contacts
Central Jersey Chamber of Commerc . . . . (908) 756-7250
   http://www.plainfield.com

City of Plainfield . . . . (908) 753-3222
    http://www.plainfield.com/city

RAHWAY (city). Covers a land area of 3.989 square miles and a water area of 0.050 square miles. Located at 40.60° N. Lat.; 74.28° W. Long. Elevation is 20 feet.

History: Named, possibly, for the Indian translation of "in the middle of the woods". The British were routed in skirmishes here in 1777. One of the signers of the Declaration of Independence and 42 Revolutionary soldiers are buried in the Rahway cemetery. Settled c.1720 as part of Elizabethtown. Incorporated 1858.

Population: 25,325 (1990); 26,500 (2000); 26,838 (2005); 27,194 (2010 projected); Race: 54.1% White, 30.7% Black, 3.9% Asian, 17.7% Hispanic of any race (2005); Density: 6,727.5 persons per square mile (2005); Average household size: 2.65 (2005); Median age: 38.2 (2005); Males per 100 females: 92.0 (2005); Marriage status: 29.0% never married, 54.0% now married, 8.6% widowed, 8.4% divorced (2000); Foreign born: 17.2% (2000); Ancestry (includes multiple ancestries): 39.3% Other groups, 12.0% Italian, 11.4% Irish, 10.0% German, 9.5% Polish (2000).

Economy: Manufacturing includes plastics, clothing, pharmaceuticals, and electrical equipment. Unemployment rate: 5.0% (2005); Total civilian labor force: 14,157 (2005); Single-family building permits issued: 130 (2005); Multi-family building permits issued: 61 (2005); Employment by occupation: 13.2% management, 17.4% professional, 13.4% services, 31.1% sales, 0.0% farming, 9.6% construction, 15.3% production (2000).

Income: Per capita income: $25,261 (2005); Median household income: $56,524 (2005); Average household income: $66,875 (2005); Percent of households with income of $100,000 or more: 18.5% (2005); Poverty rate: 7.1% (2000).

Taxes: Total city taxes per capita: $861 (2004); City property taxes per capita: $821 (2004).

Education: Percent of population age 25 and over with: High school diploma (including GED) or higher: 81.3% (2005); Bachelor's degree or higher: 18.3% (2005); Master's degree or higher: 5.4% (2005).

School District(s)
Rahway City (PK-12)
    2003-04 Enrollment: 4,155 . . . . (732) 396-1020

Housing: Homeownership rate: 62.2% (2005); Median home value: $232,489 (2005); Median rent: $669 per month (2000); Median age of housing: 47 years (2000).

Hospitals: Robert Wood Johnson Memorial Hospital at Rahway (311 beds)

Safety: Violent crime rate: 34.1 per 10,000 population; Property crime rate: 249.9 per 10,000 population (2004).

Newspapers: The Atom Tabloid (General - Circulation 23,000); The News Record (General - Circulation 1,875); The Patriot (General - Circulation 1,285).

Transportation: Commute to work: 84.2% car, 9.4% public transportation, 3.5% walk, 1.9% work from home (2000); Travel time to work: 26.8% less than 15 minutes, 32.2% 15 to 30 minutes, 21.8% 30 to 45 minutes, 8.5% 45 to 60 minutes, 10.7% 60 minutes or more (2000)

Additional Information Contacts
City of Rahway . . . . (732) 827-2100
    http://www.cityofrahway.com
Rahway Chamber of Commerce . . . . (732) 499-0210
    http://www.cityofrahway.com

ROSELLE (borough). Covers a land area of 2.643 square miles and a water area of 0.010 square miles. Located at 40.65° N. Lat.; 74.26° W. Long. Elevation is 78 feet.

History: Named for John C. Rose, the town's developer. Thomas Edison had a laboratory here, and Roselle was the world's first community to have incandescent bulbs light its streets. Abraham Clark, a signer of the Declaration of Independence, born here. Set off from Linden 1890. Incorporated 1894.

Population: 20,314 (1990); 21,274 (2000); 21,430 (2005); 21,592 (2010 projected); Race: 29.4% White, 56.0% Black, 2.5% Asian, 20.2% Hispanic of any race (2005); Density: 8,107.9 persons per square mile (2005); Average household size: 2.87 (2005); Median age: 36.4 (2005); Males per 100 females: 89.0 (2005); Marriage status: 33.5% never married, 50.3% now married, 7.6% widowed, 8.6% divorced (2000); Foreign born: 22.9% (2000); Ancestry (includes multiple ancestries): 49.1% Other groups, 8.0% Haitian, 7.7% Irish, 6.5% Italian, 5.7% German (2000).

Economy: Chiefly residential, the borough has some industry. Single-family building permits issued: 2 (2005); Multi-family building permits

issued: 6 (2005); Employment by occupation: 9.5% management, 15.6% professional, 15.7% services, 33.7% sales, 0.0% farming, 6.7% construction, 18.8% production (2000).

Income: Per capita income: $23,677 (2005); Median household income: $58,125 (2005); Average household income: $67,718 (2005); Percent of households with income of $100,000 or more: 21.0% (2005); Poverty rate: 7.5% (2000).

Education: Percent of population age 25 and over with: High school diploma (including GED) or higher: 77.7% (2005); Bachelor's degree or higher: 17.4% (2005); Master's degree or higher: 4.9% (2005).

School District(s)
Roselle Borough (PK-12)
    2003-04 Enrollment: 2,899 . . . . (908) 298-2040

Housing: Homeownership rate: 60.3% (2005); Median home value: $204,041 (2005); Median rent: $649 per month (2000); Median age of housing: 47 years (2000).

Safety: Violent crime rate: 31.1 per 10,000 population; Property crime rate: 237.8 per 10,000 population (2004).

Transportation: Commute to work: 81.6% car, 12.3% public transportation, 2.6% walk, 1.7% work from home (2000); Travel time to work: 19.4% less than 15 minutes, 36.8% 15 to 30 minutes, 21.9% 30 to 45 minutes, 10.2% 45 to 60 minutes, 11.7% 60 minutes or more (2000)

ROSELLE PARK (borough). Covers a land area of 1.223 square miles and a water area of 0 square miles. Located at 40.66° N. Lat.; 74.26° W. Long. Elevation is 85 feet.

History: Named for John C. Rose, the town's developer. Founded c.1700. Incorporated 1901.

Population: 12,805 (1990); 13,281 (2000); 13,301 (2005); 13,365 (2010 projected); Race: 77.0% White, 3.1% Black, 10.1% Asian, 21.9% Hispanic of any race (2005); Density: 10,872.0 persons per square mile (2005); Average household size: 2.62 (2005); Median age: 38.2 (2005); Males per 100 females: 95.9 (2005); Marriage status: 29.1% never married, 56.5% now married, 7.0% widowed, 7.5% divorced (2000); Foreign born: 24.8% (2000); Ancestry (includes multiple ancestries): 28.9% Other groups, 25.2% Italian, 20.0% Irish, 12.4% German, 7.8% Polish (2000).

Economy: Mainly residential, the borough produces some light industrial goods, such as rugs and leather products. Single-family building permits issued: 7 (2005); Multi-family building permits issued: 0 (2005); Employment by occupation: 14.2% management, 20.5% professional, 14.5% services, 30.7% sales, 0.0% farming, 7.4% construction, 12.7% production (2000).

Income: Per capita income: $26,075 (2005); Median household income: $57,780 (2005); Average household income: $68,200 (2005); Percent of households with income of $100,000 or more: 18.9% (2005); Poverty rate: 4.3% (2000).

Education: Percent of population age 25 and over with: High school diploma (including GED) or higher: 82.9% (2005); Bachelor's degree or higher: 25.9% (2005); Master's degree or higher: 7.7% (2005).

School District(s)
Roselle Park Borough (PK-12)
    2003-04 Enrollment: 2,101 . . . . (908) 245-1197

Housing: Homeownership rate: 58.4% (2005); Median home value: $252,810 (2005); Median rent: $745 per month (2000); Median age of housing: 52 years (2000).

Safety: Violent crime rate: 17.9 per 10,000 population; Property crime rate: 161.2 per 10,000 population (2004).

Transportation: Commute to work: 84.5% car, 8.5% public transportation, 4.7% walk, 1.3% work from home (2000); Travel time to work: 31.5% less than 15 minutes, 31.8% 15 to 30 minutes, 19.9% 30 to 45 minutes, 6.3% 45 to 60 minutes, 10.5% 60 minutes or more (2000)

Additional Information Contacts
Borough of Roselle Park . . . . (908) 245-6180
    http://www.rosellepark.org

SCOTCH PLAINS (township). Aka Scotch Plains CDP. Covers a land area of 9.081 square miles and a water area of 0.014 square miles. Located at 40.63° N. Lat.; 74.37° W. Long. Elevation is 151 feet.

History: Named for the Scottish families from Perth Amboy, New Jersey, settlers from the 1680s. Settled 1684 by Scotch Presbyterians and Quakers.

Population: 21,200 (1990); 22,732 (2000); 22,995 (2005); 23,280 (2010 projected); Race: 77.3% White, 11.8% Black, 7.9% Asian, 4.8% Hispanic of any race (2005); Density: 2,532.3 persons per square mile (2005); Average household size: 2.69 (2005); Median age: 39.4 (2005); Males per 100

females: 92.4 (2005); Marriage status: 23.2% never married, 64.2% now married, 7.2% widowed, 5.4% divorced (2000); Foreign born: 15.7% (2000); Ancestry (includes multiple ancestries): 22.5% Italian, 22.3% Other groups, 18.3% Irish, 13.4% German, 10.1% Polish (2000).
Economy: Light manufacturing. Single-family building permits issued: 72 (2005); Multi-family building permits issued: 0 (2005); Employment by occupation: 22.6% management, 32.8% professional, 7.0% services, 27.2% sales, 0.0% farming, 4.6% construction, 5.7% production (2000).
Income: Per capita income: $45,599 (2005); Median household income: $92,798 (2005); Average household income: $122,230 (2005); Percent of households with income of $100,000 or more: 45.6% (2005); Poverty rate: 3.0% (2000).
Education: Percent of population age 25 and over with: High school diploma (including GED) or higher: 92.2% (2005); Bachelor's degree or higher: 49.7% (2005); Master's degree or higher: 19.9% (2005).

School District(s)
Scotch Plains-Fanwood Regional (PK-12)
    2003-04 Enrollment: 5,004 . . . . (908) 232-6161
Union County Ed Serv Comm (09-12)
    2003-04 Enrollment: 629 . . . . (908) 233-9317
Union County Vocational (09-12)
    2003-04 Enrollment: 498 . . . . (908) 889-2900

Two-year College(s)
Union County Vocational Technical School (Public)
    Fall 2004 Enrollment: 109 . . . . (908) 889-8288
    2005-06 Tuition: In-state $7,500; Out-of-state $7,500
Housing: Homeownership rate: 78.6% (2005); Median home value: $402,016 (2005); Median rent: $877 per month (2000); Median age of housing: 41 years (2000).
Safety: Violent crime rate: 8.7 per 10,000 population; Property crime rate: 109.9 per 10,000 population (2004).
Transportation: Commute to work: 82.6% car, 12.0% public transportation, 0.6% walk, 4.2% work from home (2000); Travel time to work: 20.8% less than 15 minutes, 30.7% 15 to 30 minutes, 21.0% 30 to 45 minutes, 10.0% 45 to 60 minutes, 17.5% 60 minutes or more (2000)
Additional Information Contacts
Scotch Plains Chamber of Commerce . . . . (908) 233-3021
    http://www.scotchplainsnj.com
Scotch Plains Township . . . . (908) 322-6700
    http://www.scotchplainsnj.com

SPRINGFIELD (township). Aka Springfield CDP.
Covers a land area of 5.150 square miles and a water area of 0.004 square miles. Located at 40.70° N. Lat.; 74.32° W. Long. Elevation is 97 feet.
History: Named for the local springs that fed the headwaters of the Rahway River. Settled c.1717. Church and several other buildings burned by British, 1780; Bret Harte's poem *Caldwell of Springfield* commemorates Chaplain James Caldwell's aid to defenders. Present church was built 1791.
Population: 13,420 (1990); 14,429 (2000); 14,908 (2005); 15,364 (2010 projected); Race: 88.4% White, 3.9% Black, 5.4% Asian, 5.6% Hispanic of any race (2005); Density: 2,894.8 persons per square mile (2005); Average household size: 2.44 (2005); Median age: 43.2 (2005); Males per 100 females: 90.2 (2005); Marriage status: 20.7% never married, 64.0% now married, 8.9% widowed, 6.4% divorced (2000); Foreign born: 20.4% (2000); Ancestry (includes multiple ancestries): 21.0% Italian, 18.7% Other groups, 10.7% German, 10.3% Russian, 10.2% Irish (2000).
Economy: Manufacturing: chemicals, laboratory equipment, electronic products, rubber goods. Single-family building permits issued: 10 (2005); Multi-family building permits issued: 25 (2005); Employment by occupation: 21.4% management, 28.3% professional, 9.9% services, 27.6% sales, 0.1% farming, 5.8% construction, 6.9% production (2000).
Income: Per capita income: $42,629 (2005); Median household income: $84,875 (2005); Average household income: $104,050 (2005); Percent of households with income of $100,000 or more: 39.8% (2005); Poverty rate: 3.1% (2000).
Taxes: Total city taxes per capita: $1,037 (2004); City property taxes per capita: $1,005 (2004).
Education: Percent of population age 25 and over with: High school diploma (including GED) or higher: 90.1% (2005); Bachelor's degree or higher: 46.5% (2005); Master's degree or higher: 16.5% (2005).

School District(s)
Springfield Township (PK-12)
    2003-04 Enrollment: 2,083 . . . . (973) 376-1025

Housing: Homeownership rate: 73.7% (2005); Median home value: $385,109 (2005); Median rent: $979 per month (2000); Median age of housing: 43 years (2000).
Safety: Violent crime rate: 7.4 per 10,000 population; Property crime rate: 199.1 per 10,000 population (2004).
Transportation: Commute to work: 86.7% car, 7.9% public transportation, 1.6% walk, 3.6% work from home (2000); Travel time to work: 25.6% less than 15 minutes, 34.2% 15 to 30 minutes, 22.5% 30 to 45 minutes, 7.0% 45 to 60 minutes, 10.8% 60 minutes or more (2000)

SUMMIT (city).
Covers a land area of 6.054 square miles and a water area of 0.021 square miles. Located at 40.71° N. Lat.; 74.36° W. Long. Elevation is 388 feet.
History: Named for its location on the crest of First Watchung Mountain. Situated on a ridge of Watchung Mt., it was the site of an important American lookout post during the Revolutionary War. Settled c.1720, set off from Springfield and New Providence and established 1869. Incorporated 1899.
Population: 19,757 (1990); 21,131 (2000); 21,307 (2005); 21,518 (2010 projected); Race: 87.3% White, 3.9% Black, 4.8% Asian, 13.5% Hispanic of any race (2005); Density: 3,519.8 persons per square mile (2005); Average household size: 2.73 (2005); Median age: 37.9 (2005); Males per 100 females: 94.3 (2005); Marriage status: 23.5% never married, 64.7% now married, 6.2% widowed, 5.6% divorced (2000); Foreign born: 18.3% (2000); Ancestry (includes multiple ancestries): 20.6% Irish, 20.4% Other groups, 15.3% Italian, 14.9% German, 13.0% English (2000).
Economy: Commuter railroad. Pharmaceuticals manufacturing; several major companies have research facilities here. Single-family building permits issued: 21 (2005); Multi-family building permits issued: 2 (2005); Employment by occupation: 27.6% management, 31.0% professional, 10.6% services, 22.4% sales, 0.1% farming, 3.5% construction, 4.9% production (2000).
Income: Per capita income: $61,726 (2005); Median household income: $110,222 (2005); Average household income: $168,045 (2005); Percent of households with income of $100,000 or more: 53.9% (2005); Poverty rate: 4.2% (2000).
Taxes: Total city taxes per capita: $3,040 (2004); City property taxes per capita: $3,027 (2004).
Education: Percent of population age 25 and over with: High school diploma (including GED) or higher: 92.3% (2005); Bachelor's degree or higher: 61.1% (2005); Master's degree or higher: 29.8% (2005).

School District(s)
Summit City (PK-12)
    2003-04 Enrollment: 3,515 . . . . (908) 273-3023
Housing: Homeownership rate: 67.6% (2005); Median home value: $702,402 (2005); Median rent: $997 per month (2000); Median age of housing: 51 years (2000).
Hospitals: Overlook Hospital (504 beds)
Safety: Violent crime rate: 6.1 per 10,000 population; Property crime rate: 182.1 per 10,000 population (2004).
Transportation: Commute to work: 73.3% car, 16.2% public transportation, 4.2% walk, 5.9% work from home (2000); Travel time to work: 27.1% less than 15 minutes, 28.4% 15 to 30 minutes, 15.0% 30 to 45 minutes, 7.7% 45 to 60 minutes, 21.7% 60 minutes or more (2000)
Additional Information Contacts
City of Summit . . . . (908) 273-6400
    http://www.ci.summit.nj.us
Suburban Chamber of Commerce . . . . (908) 522-1700
    http://www.suburbanchambers.org

UNION (township). Aka Union CDP.
Covers a land area of 9.116 square miles and a water area of <.001 square miles. Located at 40.69° N. Lat.; 74.27° W. Long. Elevation is 93 feet.
History: Named for patriotism during the Civil War. Site of a Revolutionary battle in 1780. Seat of Kean University of New Jersey. Settled 1749 by colonists from Connecticut, set off from Elizabethtown 1808.
Population: 50,189 (1990); 54,405 (2000); 56,128 (2005); 57,811 (2010 projected); Race: 60.8% White, 24.2% Black, 9.0% Asian, 11.8% Hispanic of any race (2005); Density: 6,157.1 persons per square mile (2005); Average household size: 2.82 (2005); Median age: 39.7 (2005); Males per 100 females: 88.8 (2005); Marriage status: 28.0% never married, 55.4% now married, 9.9% widowed, 6.6% divorced (2000); Foreign born: 24.6% (2000); Ancestry (includes multiple ancestries): 28.8% Other groups, 17.2% Italian, 10.2% German, 9.9% Irish, 9.0% Polish (2000).

Economy: Steel and metal products, paint manufacturing. Unemployment rate: 4.2% (2005); Total civilian labor force: 28,601 (2005); Single-family building permits issued: 21 (2005); Multi-family building permits issued: 16 (2005); Employment by occupation: 14.3% management, 23.6% professional, 12.1% services, 31.1% sales, 0.0% farming, 7.9% construction, 11.0% production (2000).

Income: Per capita income: $28,198 (2005); Median household income: $66,566 (2005); Average household income: $78,745 (2005); Percent of households with income of $100,000 or more: 27.1% (2005); Poverty rate: 4.2% (2000).

Taxes: Total city taxes per capita: $762 (2004); City property taxes per capita: $745 (2004).

Education: Percent of population age 25 and over with: High school diploma (including GED) or higher: 80.9% (2005); Bachelor's degree or higher: 26.6% (2005); Master's degree or higher: 8.4% (2005).

School District(s)

Morris-Union Joint (UG-UG)
    2003-04 Enrollment: 586 . . . . (908) 464-7625
Union Township (PK-12)
    2003-04 Enrollment: 8,105 . . . . (908) 851-6420

Four-year College(s)

Kean University (Public)
    Fall 2004 Enrollment: 12,897 . . . . (908) 737-5326
    2005-06 Tuition: In-state $7,506; Out-of-state $10,139

Two-year College(s)

European Academy of Cosmetology (Private, For-profit)
    Fall 2004 Enrollment: 135 . . . . (908) 686-4422
Healthcare Training Institute (Private, For-profit)
    Fall 2004 Enrollment: n/a . . . . (908) 851-7711
Lincoln Technical Institute (Private, For-profit)
    Fall 2004 Enrollment: 1,351 . . . . (908) 964-7800
    2005-06 Tuition: In-state $19,868; Out-of-state $19,868

Housing: Homeownership rate: 76.0% (2005); Median home value: $267,641 (2005); Median rent: $774 per month (2000); Median age of housing: 47 years (2000).

Hospitals: Union Hospital (201 beds)

Safety: Violent crime rate: 35.7 per 10,000 population; Property crime rate: 296.3 per 10,000 population (2004).

Newspapers: Echo Leader (General - Circulation 2,800); Elizabeth/Hillside Gazette Leader (General - Circulation 1,500); Rahway Progress (General - Circulation 1,500); Roselle Spectator (General - Circulation 1,700); Spectator Leader (General - Circulation 2,450); Summit Observer (General - Circulation 1,400); The Eagle (General - Circulation 1,500); The Leader (General - Circulation 2,824); The Leader (General - Circulation 1,700); Union Leader (General - Circulation 7,039)

Transportation: Commute to work: 86.8% car, 6.9% public transportation, 3.7% walk, 2.0% work from home (2000); Travel time to work: 27.6% less than 15 minutes, 34.6% 15 to 30 minutes, 19.9% 30 to 45 minutes, 8.0% 45 to 60 minutes, 9.8% 60 minutes or more (2000)

Additional Information Contacts

Union Township . . . . (908) 527-4000
    http://www.unioncountynj.org
Union Township Chamber of Commerce . . . . (908) 688-2777
    http://www.unionchamber.com

VAUXHALL (unincorporated postal area, zip code 07088). Covers a land area of 0.341 square miles and a water area of 0 square miles. Located at 40.71° N. Lat.; 74.28° W. Long. Elevation is 133 feet.

Population: 3,411 (2000); Race: 4.4% White, 87.9% Black, 1.4% Asian, 2.1% Hispanic of any race (2000); Density: 10,014.8 persons per square mile (2000); Age: 23.4% under 18, 14.6% over 64 (2000); Marriage status: 37.7% never married, 38.2% now married, 11.6% widowed, 12.5% divorced (2000); Foreign born: 9.7% (2000); Ancestry (includes multiple ancestries): 74.6% Other groups, 4.1% African, 3.5% Jamaican, 2.5% Italian, 2.2% Haitian (2000).

Economy: Employment by occupation: 8.8% management, 15.5% professional, 20.0% services, 38.5% sales, 0.0% farming, 5.0% construction, 12.2% production (2000).

Income: Per capita income: $20,710 (2000); Median household income: $43,030 (2000); Poverty rate: 8.2% (2000).

Education: Percent of population age 25 and over with: High school diploma (including GED) or higher: 76.8% (2000); Bachelor's degree or higher: 17.5% (2000).

Housing: Homeownership rate: 61.8% (2000); Median home value: $121,600 (2000); Median rent: $706 per month (2000); Median age of housing: 46 years (2000).

Transportation: Commute to work: 79.1% car, 13.6% public transportation, 3.1% walk, 2.9% work from home (2000); Travel time to work: 25.4% less than 15 minutes, 31.7% 15 to 30 minutes, 20.7% 30 to 45 minutes, 10.6% 45 to 60 minutes, 11.6% 60 minutes or more (2000)

WESTFIELD (town). Covers a land area of 6.732 square miles and a water area of 0.015 square miles. Located at 40.65° N. Lat.; 74.34° W. Long. Elevation is 126 feet.

History: Named for its location in the area west of Elizabeth. A Revolutionary War cemetery is here. Settled late 17th century as part of Elizabethtown. Incorporated 1903.

Population: 28,911 (1990); 29,644 (2000); 30,066 (2005); 30,550 (2010 projected); Race: 89.7% White, 3.8% Black, 4.2% Asian, 3.6% Hispanic of any race (2005); Density: 4,465.8 persons per square mile (2005); Average household size: 2.79 (2005); Median age: 39.1 (2005); Males per 100 females: 92.4 (2005); Marriage status: 20.5% never married, 68.2% now married, 6.5% widowed, 4.8% divorced (2000); Foreign born: 9.1% (2000); Ancestry (includes multiple ancestries): 22.9% Irish, 20.1% Italian, 17.1% German, 13.7% Other groups, 11.2% English (2000).

Economy: Unemployment rate: 2.5% (2005); Total civilian labor force: 15,546 (2005); Single-family building permits issued: 92 (2005); Multi-family building permits issued: 0 (2005); Employment by occupation: 25.7% management, 34.8% professional, 7.6% services, 24.1% sales, 0.1% farming, 3.3% construction, 4.5% production (2000).

Income: Per capita income: $54,617 (2005); Median household income: $113,812 (2005); Average household income: $151,543 (2005); Percent of households with income of $100,000 or more: 56.0% (2005); Poverty rate: 2.7% (2000).

Education: Percent of population age 25 and over with: High school diploma (including GED) or higher: 95.3% (2005); Bachelor's degree or higher: 62.4% (2005); Master's degree or higher: 29.7% (2005).

School District(s)

Union County Ed Serv Comm (09-12)
    2003-04 Enrollment: 629 . . . . (908) 233-9317
Westfield Town (PK-12)
    2003-04 Enrollment: 5,909 . . . . (908) 789-4420

Housing: Homeownership rate: 81.5% (2005); Median home value: $544,583 (2005); Median rent: $981 per month (2000); Median age of housing: 52 years (2000).

Safety: Violent crime rate: 1.3 per 10,000 population; Property crime rate: 114.7 per 10,000 population (2004).

Newspapers: Westfield Leader (General - Circulation 7,500)

Transportation: Commute to work: 78.2% car, 14.3% public transportation, 2.1% walk, 4.9% work from home (2000); Travel time to work: 25.9% less than 15 minutes, 25.2% 15 to 30 minutes, 19.0% 30 to 45 minutes, 9.3% 45 to 60 minutes, 20.6% 60 minutes or more (2000)

Additional Information Contacts

Town of Westfield . . . . (908) 789-4040
    http://www.westfieldnj.govoffice2.com
Westfield Chamber of Commerce . . . . (908) 233-3021
    http://www.westfieldchamber.com

WINFIELD (township). Covers a land area of 0.176 square miles and a water area of 0 square miles. Located at 40.63° N. Lat.; 74.29° W. Long. Elevation is 40 feet.

Population: 1,576 (1990); 1,514 (2000); 1,517 (2005); 1,527 (2010 projected); Race: 96.3% White, 0.4% Black, 0.1% Asian, 2.8% Hispanic of any race (2005); Density: 8,595.3 persons per square mile (2005); Average household size: 2.15 (2005); Median age: 40.5 (2005); Males per 100 females: 85.2 (2005); Marriage status: 27.6% never married, 46.8% now married, 13.9% widowed, 11.7% divorced (2000); Foreign born: 2.8% (2000); Ancestry (includes multiple ancestries): 32.0% Irish, 25.9% German, 23.8% Italian, 18.8% Polish, 8.5% English (2000).

Economy: Single-family building permits issued: 0 (2005); Multi-family building permits issued: 0 (2005); Employment by occupation: 6.6% management, 12.2% professional, 19.0% services, 32.3% sales, 0.5% farming, 12.0% construction, 17.4% production (2000).

Income: Per capita income: $22,988 (2005); Median household income: $41,524 (2005); Average household income: $49,325 (2005); Percent of households with income of $100,000 or more: 9.8% (2005); Poverty rate: 7.5% (2000).

Education: Percent of population age 25 and over with: High school diploma (including GED) or higher: 79.2% (2005); Bachelor's degree or higher: 8.1% (2005); Master's degree or higher: 1.9% (2005).

School District(s)

Winfield Township (PK-08)
    2003-04 Enrollment: 128 . . . . (908) 486-7410

Housing: Homeownership rate: 20.5% (2005); Median home value: $91,176 (2005); Median rent: $344 per month (2000); Median age of housing: 55 years (2000).

Safety: Violent crime rate: 0.0 per 10,000 population; Property crime rate: 157.0 per 10,000 population (2004).

Transportation: Commute to work: 93.2% car, 1.4% public transportation, 3.6% walk, 1.2% work from home (2000); Travel time to work: 30.7% less than 15 minutes, 37.7% 15 to 30 minutes, 18.6% 30 to 45 minutes, 6.5% 45 to 60 minutes, 6.5% 60 minutes or more (2000)

Warren County

Located in northwestern New Jersey; hilly area, bounded on the west by the Delaware River and the Pennsylvania border, and on the east and southeast by the Musconetcong River; drained by the Pohatcong and Pequest Rivers. Covers a land area of 357.87 square miles, a water area of 4.89 square miles, and is located in the Eastern Time Zone. The county government was organized in 1824. County seat is Belvidere.

Warren County is part of the Allentown-Bethlehem-Easton, PA-NJ Metropolitan Statistical Area. The entire metro area includes: Warren County, NJ; Carbon County, PA; Lehigh County, PA; Northampton County, PA

Population: 91,716 (1990); 102,437 (2000); 111,957 (2005); 121,930 (2010 projected); Race: 92.6% White, 2.7% Black, 1.8% Asian, 5.3% Hispanic of any race (2005); Density: 312.8 persons per square mile (2005); Average household size: 2.63 (2005); Median age: 38.6 (2005); Males per 100 females: 95.3 (2005).

Religion: Five largest groups: 30.2% Catholic Church, 4.8% The United Methodist Church, 3.8% Presbyterian Church (U.S.A.), 2.6% Evangelical Lutheran Church in America, 1.7% Episcopal Church (2000).

Economy: Unemployment rate: 3.8% (2005); Total civilian labor force: 59,557 (2005); Leading industries: 21.5% retail trade; 16.3% health care and social assistance; 15.4% manufacturing (2004); Farms: 814 totaling 78,042 acres (2002); Companies that employ 500 or more persons: 9 (2004); Companies that employ 100 to 499 persons: 89 (2004); Companies that employ less than 100 persons: 5,622 (2004); Black-owned businesses: n/a (2002); Hispanic-owned businesses: 198 (2002); Asian-owned businesses: 160 (2002); Women-owned businesses: 1,926 (2002); Retail sales per capita: $18,496 (2006). Single-family building permits issued: 441 (2005); Multi-family building permits issued: 119 (2005).

Income: Per capita income: $29,409 (2005); Median household income: $63,861 (2005); Average household income: $76,637 (2005); Percent of households with income of $100,000 or more: 24.9% (2005); Poverty rate: 6.1% (2003); Bankruptcy rate: 5.57% (2005).

Taxes: Total county taxes per capita: $435 (2004); County property taxes per capita: $434 (2004).

Education: Percent of population age 25 and over with: High school diploma (including GED) or higher: 84.9% (2005); Bachelor's degree or higher: 24.5% (2005); Master's degree or higher: 7.6% (2005).

Housing: Homeownership rate: 73.4% (2005); Median home value: $241,701 (2005); Median rent: $621 per month (2000); Median age of housing: 37 years (2000).

Health: Birth rate: 126.7 per 10,000 population (2004); Death rate: 78.7 per 10,000 population (2004); Age-adjusted cancer mortality rate: 192.5 deaths per 100,000 population (2002); Air Quality Index: 66.4% good, 32.8% moderate, 0.9% unhealthy for sensitive individuals, 0.0% unhealthy (percent of days in 2005); Number of physicians: 16.6 per 10,000 population (2004); Hospital beds: 20.5 per 10,000 population (2003); Hospital admissions: 992.8 per 10,000 population (2003).

Elections: 2004 Presidential election results: 61.3% Bush, 37.4% Kerry, 0.9% Nader, 0.2% Badnarik.

National and State Parks: Jenny Jump State Forest; Stephens State Park; Worthington State Forest

Additional Information Contacts

Warren County Government . . . . (908) 475-6500
    http://www.warrennet.org/warrencounty
Allamuchy Township . . . . (908) 852-5132
    http://www.allamuchynj.org

Franklin Township . . . . (908) 689-3994
    http://www.franklintwpwarren.org
Phillipsburg Chamber of Commerce . . . . (908) 859-5161
    http://www.phillipsburgnj.com
Town of Hackettstown . . . . (908) 852-3130
    http://www.hackettstown.net
Warren County Regional Chamber of Commerce . . . . (908) 852-1253
    http://www.warrencountychamber.org
Washington Township . . . . (908) 689-7200
    http://www.washington-twp-warren.org

Warren County Communities

ALLAMUCHY (township). Covers a land area of 20.539 square miles and a water area of 0.229 square miles. Located at 40.92° N. Lat.; 74.83° W. Long. Elevation is 620 feet.

Population: 3,484 (1990); 3,877 (2000); 3,962 (2005); 4,095 (2010 projected); Race: 93.4% White, 1.5% Black, 3.0% Asian, 3.6% Hispanic of any race (2005); Density: 192.9 persons per square mile (2005); Average household size: 2.26 (2005); Median age: 45.1 (2005); Males per 100 females: 86.9 (2005); Marriage status: 16.2% never married, 65.6% now married, 7.0% widowed, 11.2% divorced (2000); Foreign born: 9.9% (2000); Ancestry (includes multiple ancestries): 20.2% German, 19.8% Irish, 18.1% Italian, 14.6% Polish, 9.8% English (2000).

Economy: Single-family building permits issued: 51 (2005); Multi-family building permits issued: 0 (2005); Employment by occupation: 26.4% management, 22.6% professional, 6.9% services, 29.2% sales, 0.9% farming, 5.5% construction, 8.5% production (2000).

Income: Per capita income: $46,042 (2005); Median household income: $78,281 (2005); Average household income: $103,766 (2005); Percent of households with income of $100,000 or more: 39.1% (2005); Poverty rate: 1.8% (2000).

Education: Percent of population age 25 and over with: High school diploma (including GED) or higher: 94.6% (2005); Bachelor's degree or higher: 43.6% (2005); Master's degree or higher: 15.0% (2005).

School District(s)

Allamuchy Township (PK-08)
    2003-04 Enrollment: 345 . . . . (908) 852-1894

Housing: Homeownership rate: 85.2% (2005); Median home value: $273,188 (2005); Median rent: $896 per month (2000); Median age of housing: 19 years (2000).

Transportation: Commute to work: 94.2% car, 1.3% public transportation, 0.7% walk, 3.1% work from home (2000); Travel time to work: 15.5% less than 15 minutes, 25.8% 15 to 30 minutes, 19.4% 30 to 45 minutes, 21.2% 45 to 60 minutes, 18.1% 60 minutes or more (2000)

Additional Information Contacts

Allamuchy Township . . . . (908) 852-5132
    http://www.allamuchynj.org

ALLAMUCHY-PANTHER VALLEY (CDP). Covers a land area of 5.716 square miles and a water area of 0.086 square miles. Located at 40.91° N. Lat.; 74.82° W. Long.

Population: 2,764 (1990); 3,125 (2000); 3,205 (2005); 3,323 (2010 projected); Race: 94.1% White, 1.5% Black, 3.2% Asian, 3.0% Hispanic of any race (2005); Density: 560.7 persons per square mile (2005); Average household size: 2.15 (2005); Median age: 46.7 (2005); Males per 100 females: 85.9 (2005); Marriage status: 16.1% never married, 65.8% now married, 6.8% widowed, 11.4% divorced (2000); Foreign born: 9.7% (2000); Ancestry (includes multiple ancestries): 20.4% Italian, 20.3% German, 19.8% Irish, 16.2% Polish, 7.8% English (2000).

Economy: Employment by occupation: 27.7% management, 22.9% professional, 5.0% services, 32.6% sales, 1.2% farming, 4.2% construction, 6.5% production (2000).

Income: Per capita income: $47,527 (2005); Median household income: $76,203 (2005); Average household income: $102,094 (2005); Percent of households with income of $100,000 or more: 38.1% (2005); Poverty rate: 1.6% (2000).

Education: Percent of population age 25 and over with: High school diploma (including GED) or higher: 95.5% (2005); Bachelor's degree or higher: 45.5% (2005); Master's degree or higher: 16.2% (2005).

Housing: Homeownership rate: 86.9% (2005); Median home value: $263,165 (2005); Median rent: $942 per month (2000); Median age of housing: 19 years (2000).

Transportation: Commute to work: 95.2% car, 0.8% public transportation, 0.6% walk, 2.9% work from home (2000); Travel time to work: 13.2% less

than 15 minutes, 22.6% 15 to 30 minutes, 22.8% 30 to 45 minutes, 21.2% 45 to 60 minutes, 20.2% 60 minutes or more (2000)

ALPHA (borough).
Covers a land area of 1.698 square miles and a water area of 0.038 square miles. Located at 40.66° N. Lat.; 75.16° W. Long. Elevation is 299 feet.

History: Incorporated 1911.

Population: 2,502 (1990); 2,482 (2000); 2,481 (2005); 2,515 (2010 projected); Race: 95.9% White, 0.6% Black, 1.8% Asian, 2.8% Hispanic of any race (2005); Density: 1,461.4 persons per square mile (2005); Average household size: 2.46 (2005); Median age: 39.1 (2005); Males per 100 females: 96.6 (2005); Marriage status: 23.2% never married, 59.6% now married, 9.9% widowed, 7.4% divorced (2000); Foreign born: 2.0% (2000); Ancestry (includes multiple ancestries): 26.3% German, 21.0% Italian, 15.8% Irish, 9.3% Hungarian, 8.0% Polish (2000).

Economy: Manufactures electronic equipment, paper products. Single-family building permits issued: 1 (2005); Multi-family building permits issued: 0 (2005); Employment by occupation: 5.8% management, 15.6% professional, 17.7% services, 33.2% sales, 0.0% farming, 12.0% construction, 15.7% production (2000).

Income: Per capita income: $22,104 (2005); Median household income: $44,579 (2005); Average household income: $54,128 (2005); Percent of households with income of $100,000 or more: 9.0% (2005); Poverty rate: 7.6% (2000).

Education: Percent of population age 25 and over with: High school diploma (including GED) or higher: 80.5% (2005); Bachelor's degree or higher: 11.9% (2005); Master's degree or higher: 4.4% (2005).

School District(s)
Alpha Borough (PK-08)
    2003-04 Enrollment: 286 . . . . (908) 454-5000

Housing: Homeownership rate: 71.1% (2005); Median home value: $176,859 (2005); Median rent: $631 per month (2000); Median age of housing: 50 years (2000).

Safety: Violent crime rate: 16.0 per 10,000 population; Property crime rate: 63.9 per 10,000 population (2004).

Transportation: Commute to work: 92.0% car, 0.9% public transportation, 3.6% walk, 2.6% work from home (2000); Travel time to work: 30.2% less than 15 minutes, 29.6% 15 to 30 minutes, 17.5% 30 to 45 minutes, 9.9% 45 to 60 minutes, 12.8% 60 minutes or more (2000)

ASBURY (unincorporated postal area, zip code 08802).
Aka Ludlow-Asbury. Covers a land area of 27.078 square miles and a water area of 0 square miles. Located at 40.66° N. Lat.; 75.03° W. Long. Elevation is 360 feet.

Population: 3,933 (2000); Race: 96.6% White, 0.8% Black, 1.6% Asian, 2.7% Hispanic of any race (2000); Density: 145.2 persons per square mile (2000); Age: 28.7% under 18, 9.4% over 64 (2000); Marriage status: 19.5% never married, 69.6% now married, 4.8% widowed, 6.0% divorced (2000); Foreign born: 4.5% (2000); Ancestry (includes multiple ancestries): 30.7% German, 22.0% Italian, 18.1% Irish, 13.9% Polish, 11.1% English (2000).

Economy: Employment by occupation: 17.9% management, 24.6% professional, 9.1% services, 24.8% sales, 0.7% farming, 14.7% construction, 8.1% production (2000).

Income: Per capita income: $31,849 (2000); Median household income: $77,079 (2000); Poverty rate: 1.6% (2000).

Education: Percent of population age 25 and over with: High school diploma (including GED) or higher: 89.9% (2000); Bachelor's degree or higher: 36.5% (2000).

School District(s)
Bethlehem Township (PK-08)
    2003-04 Enrollment: 639 . . . . (908) 537-4044

Housing: Homeownership rate: 90.3% (2000); Median home value: $239,900 (2000); Median rent: $660 per month (2000); Median age of housing: 25 years (2000).

Transportation: Commute to work: 87.4% car, 2.2% public transportation, 3.0% walk, 6.7% work from home (2000); Travel time to work: 18.7% less than 15 minutes, 21.2% 15 to 30 minutes, 19.7% 30 to 45 minutes, 16.3% 45 to 60 minutes, 24.1% 60 minutes or more (2000)

BEATYESTOWN (CDP).
Covers a land area of 3.008 square miles and a water area of 0 square miles. Located at 40.82° N. Lat.; 74.84° W. Long.

Population: 3,966 (1990); 3,223 (2000); 3,224 (2005); 3,269 (2010 projected); Race: 89.0% White, 2.2% Black, 2.7% Asian, 9.5% Hispanic of any race (2005); Density: 1,071.8 persons per square mile (2005); Average

household size: 2.69 (2005); Median age: 35.8 (2005); Males per 100 females: 96.0 (2005); Marriage status: 24.8% never married, 60.6% now married, 4.8% widowed, 9.8% divorced (2000); Foreign born: 7.9% (2000); Ancestry (includes multiple ancestries): 22.6% Italian, 22.1% German, 16.9% Irish, 13.3% Other groups, 9.2% Polish (2000).

Economy: Employment by occupation: 12.7% management, 22.3% professional, 15.1% services, 25.4% sales, 0.5% farming, 10.5% construction, 13.6% production (2000).

Income: Per capita income: $33,877 (2005); Median household income: $70,931 (2005); Average household income: $91,093 (2005); Percent of households with income of $100,000 or more: 32.9% (2005); Poverty rate: 2.3% (2000).

Education: Percent of population age 25 and over with: High school diploma (including GED) or higher: 92.5% (2005); Bachelor's degree or higher: 28.9% (2005); Master's degree or higher: 9.6% (2005).

Housing: Homeownership rate: 59.5% (2005); Median home value: $259,339 (2005); Median rent: $669 per month (2000); Median age of housing: 25 years (2000).

Transportation: Commute to work: 92.8% car, 0.5% public transportation, 2.0% walk, 3.7% work from home (2000); Travel time to work: 25.7% less than 15 minutes, 23.1% 15 to 30 minutes, 23.9% 30 to 45 minutes, 9.1% 45 to 60 minutes, 18.2% 60 minutes or more (2000)

BELVIDERE (town).
Covers a land area of 1.325 square miles and a water area of 0.021 square miles. Located at 40.82° N. Lat.; 75.07° W. Long. Elevation is 257 feet.

History: Settled 1759, laid out 1799, incorporated 1845.

Population: 2,669 (1990); 2,771 (2000); 2,770 (2005); 2,808 (2010 projected); Race: 97.8% White, 0.7% Black, 0.5% Asian, 3.5% Hispanic of any race (2005); Density: 2,091.0 persons per square mile (2005); Average household size: 2.52 (2005); Median age: 37.3 (2005); Males per 100 females: 92.8 (2005); Marriage status: 25.7% never married, 56.9% now married, 8.2% widowed, 9.1% divorced (2000); Foreign born: 2.5% (2000); Ancestry (includes multiple ancestries): 29.8% German, 25.3% Irish, 13.2% Italian, 11.0% English, 8.3% Polish (2000).

Economy: Manufacturing includes vitamins, transportation equipment; dairy products. Single-family building permits issued: 2 (2005); Multi-family building permits issued: 0 (2005); Employment by occupation: 12.4% management, 22.9% professional, 13.8% services, 26.6% sales, 0.1% farming, 8.4% construction, 15.8% production (2000).

Income: Per capita income: $26,765 (2005); Median household income: $57,439 (2005); Average household income: $67,200 (2005); Percent of households with income of $100,000 or more: 18.2% (2005); Poverty rate: 3.4% (2000).

Education: Percent of population age 25 and over with: High school diploma (including GED) or higher: 83.9% (2005); Bachelor's degree or higher: 26.2% (2005); Master's degree or higher: 7.6% (2005).

School District(s)
Belvidere Town (PK-12)
    2003-04 Enrollment: 983 . . . . (908) 475-6600
White Township (PK-08)
    2003-04 Enrollment: 454 . . . . (908) 475-4773

Housing: Homeownership rate: 66.2% (2005); Median home value: $179,434 (2005); Median rent: $533 per month (2000); Median age of housing: 60+ years (2000).

Safety: Violent crime rate: 10.7 per 10,000 population; Property crime rate: 17.9 per 10,000 population (2004).

Transportation: Commute to work: 90.4% car, 0.9% public transportation, 3.8% walk, 3.1% work from home (2000); Travel time to work: 39.0% less than 15 minutes, 22.9% 15 to 30 minutes, 15.4% 30 to 45 minutes, 7.4% 45 to 60 minutes, 15.4% 60 minutes or more (2000)

BLAIRSTOWN (township).
Covers a land area of 31.021 square miles and a water area of 0.753 square miles. Located at 40.97° N. Lat.; 74.99° W. Long. Elevation is 348 feet.

History: Blair Academy for boys (1848) here.

Population: 5,331 (1990); 5,747 (2000); 6,073 (2005); 6,449 (2010 projected); Race: 97.9% White, 0.3% Black, 0.8% Asian, 2.7% Hispanic of any race (2005); Density: 195.8 persons per square mile (2005); Average household size: 2.76 (2005); Median age: 41.2 (2005); Males per 100 females: 99.4 (2005); Marriage status: 20.6% never married, 66.5% now married, 5.7% widowed, 7.1% divorced (2000); Foreign born: 5.2% (2000); Ancestry (includes multiple ancestries): 26.1% German, 21.4% Italian, 21.3% Irish, 14.5% English, 8.3% Polish (2000).

Economy: In hilly region. Fruit, vegetables; poultry. Single-family building permits issued: 18 (2005); Multi-family building permits issued: 0 (2005); Employment by occupation: 16.1% management, 28.2% professional, 7.2% services, 22.3% sales, 0.6% farming, 13.5% construction, 12.2% production (2000).
Income: Per capita income: $32,619 (2005); Median household income: $76,162 (2005); Average household income: $89,999 (2005); Percent of households with income of $100,000 or more: 32.7% (2005); Poverty rate: 4.5% (2000).
Education: Percent of population age 25 and over with: High school diploma (including GED) or higher: 86.7% (2005); Bachelor's degree or higher: 29.5% (2005); Master's degree or higher: 12.5% (2005).

School District(s)

Blairstown Township (PK-06)
   2003-04 Enrollment: 792 . . . . (908) 362-6111
North Warren Regional (07-12)
   2003-04 Enrollment: 1,053 . . . . (908) 362-9342
Housing: Homeownership rate: 85.0% (2005); Median home value: $311,626 (2005); Median rent: $759 per month (2000); Median age of housing: 25 years (2000).
Safety: Violent crime rate: 1.7 per 10,000 population; Property crime rate: 51.4 per 10,000 population (2004).
Transportation: Commute to work: 89.3% car, 2.2% public transportation, 2.8% walk, 4.9% work from home (2000); Travel time to work: 21.5% less than 15 minutes, 15.8% 15 to 30 minutes, 21.7% 30 to 45 minutes, 11.6% 45 to 60 minutes, 29.4% 60 minutes or more (2000)

BRASS CASTLE (CDP). Covers a land area of 2.918 square miles and a water area of 0.010 square miles. Located at 40.76° N. Lat.; 75.00° W. Long. Elevation is 460 feet.
Population: 1,419 (1990); 1,507 (2000); 1,611 (2005); 1,724 (2010 projected); Race: 97.8% White, 1.2% Black, 0.3% Asian, 1.9% Hispanic of any race (2005); Density: 552.1 persons per square mile (2005); Average household size: 2.92 (2005); Median age: 39.3 (2005); Males per 100 females: 94.1 (2005); Marriage status: 23.4% never married, 66.9% now married, 4.4% widowed, 5.3% divorced (2000); Foreign born: 2.7% (2000); Ancestry (includes multiple ancestries): 24.0% German, 22.1% Italian, 17.7% Irish, 8.7% Polish, 8.1% French (except Basque) (2000).
Economy: Employment by occupation: 18.9% management, 24.3% professional, 7.4% services, 27.4% sales, 0.7% farming, 12.1% construction, 9.3% production (2000).
Income: Per capita income: $36,284 (2005); Median household income: $95,037 (2005); Average household income: $105,842 (2005); Percent of households with income of $100,000 or more: 45.1% (2005); Poverty rate: 4.3% (2000).
Education: Percent of population age 25 and over with: High school diploma (including GED) or higher: 91.5% (2005); Bachelor's degree or higher: 26.4% (2005); Master's degree or higher: 2.8% (2005).
Housing: Homeownership rate: 94.0% (2005); Median home value: $259,564 (2005); Median rent: $490 per month (2000); Median age of housing: 35 years (2000).
Transportation: Commute to work: 95.8% car, 0.0% public transportation, 0.0% walk, 4.2% work from home (2000); Travel time to work: 32.2% less than 15 minutes, 22.3% 15 to 30 minutes, 13.4% 30 to 45 minutes, 11.0% 45 to 60 minutes, 21.1% 60 minutes or more (2000)

COLUMBIA (unincorporated postal area, zip code 07832). Covers a land area of 52.135 square miles and a water area of 0.262 square miles. Located at 40.93° N. Lat.; 75.06° W. Long. Elevation is 300 feet.
Population: 3,539 (2000); Race: 98.2% White, 0.5% Black, 0.7% Asian, 1.4% Hispanic of any race (2000); Density: 67.9 persons per square mile (2000); Age: 27.4% under 18, 10.7% over 64 (2000); Marriage status: 20.5% never married, 68.1% now married, 4.8% widowed, 6.5% divorced (2000); Foreign born: 2.8% (2000); Ancestry (includes multiple ancestries): 28.8% German, 21.1% Irish, 17.0% Italian, 12.7% English, 8.5% Polish (2000).
Economy: Employment by occupation: 14.7% management, 19.7% professional, 13.6% services, 24.2% sales, 1.0% farming, 12.2% construction, 14.5% production (2000).
Income: Per capita income: $24,484 (2000); Median household income: $64,850 (2000); Poverty rate: 3.9% (2000).
Education: Percent of population age 25 and over with: High school diploma (including GED) or higher: 87.8% (2000); Bachelor's degree or higher: 24.7% (2000).

Housing: Homeownership rate: 87.0% (2000); Median home value: $192,200 (2000); Median rent: $648 per month (2000); Median age of housing: 27 years (2000).
Transportation: Commute to work: 93.1% car, 1.9% public transportation, 1.3% walk, 3.3% work from home (2000); Travel time to work: 22.6% less than 15 minutes, 17.7% 15 to 30 minutes, 21.8% 30 to 45 minutes, 12.8% 45 to 60 minutes, 25.1% 60 minutes or more (2000)

FRANKLIN (township). Covers a land area of 23.989 square miles and a water area of 0.044 square miles. Located at 40.72° N. Lat.; 75.05° W. Long.
Population: 2,404 (1990); 2,768 (2000); 3,336 (2005); 3,889 (2010 projected); Race: 95.9% White, 1.2% Black, 1.4% Asian, 3.0% Hispanic of any race (2005); Density: 139.1 persons per square mile (2005); Average household size: 2.82 (2005); Median age: 38.4 (2005); Males per 100 females: 102.2 (2005); Marriage status: 20.5% never married, 67.3% now married, 6.6% widowed, 5.5% divorced (2000); Foreign born: 3.7% (2000); Ancestry (includes multiple ancestries): 27.0% German, 21.3% Italian, 18.5% Irish, 13.9% Polish, 13.8% English (2000).
Economy: Single-family building permits issued: 8 (2005); Multi-family building permits issued: 0 (2005); Employment by occupation: 14.2% management, 14.5% professional, 13.4% services, 27.1% sales, 1.2% farming, 15.7% construction, 13.9% production (2000).
Income: Per capita income: $31,706 (2005); Median household income: $78,913 (2005); Average household income: $88,533 (2005); Percent of households with income of $100,000 or more: 32.4% (2005); Poverty rate: 3.1% (2000).
Education: Percent of population age 25 and over with: High school diploma (including GED) or higher: 86.8% (2005); Bachelor's degree or higher: 21.2% (2005); Master's degree or higher: 6.5% (2005).
Housing: Homeownership rate: 86.8% (2005); Median home value: $281,019 (2005); Median rent: $560 per month (2000); Median age of housing: 31 years (2000).
Transportation: Commute to work: 92.1% car, 0.4% public transportation, 2.1% walk, 5.2% work from home (2000); Travel time to work: 18.1% less than 15 minutes, 29.6% 15 to 30 minutes, 15.7% 30 to 45 minutes, 17.3% 45 to 60 minutes, 19.3% 60 minutes or more (2000)
Additional Information Contacts
Franklin Township . . . . (908) 689-3994
   http://www.franklintwpwarren.org

FRELINGHUYSEN (township). Covers a land area of 23.435 square miles and a water area of 0.119 square miles. Located at 40.95° N. Lat.; 74.89° W. Long.
Population: 1,923 (1990); 2,083 (2000); 2,270 (2005); 2,487 (2010 projected); Race: 97.4% White, 0.4% Black, 0.5% Asian, 4.0% Hispanic of any race (2005); Density: 96.9 persons per square mile (2005); Average household size: 2.83 (2005); Median age: 41.2 (2005); Males per 100 females: 97.4 (2005); Marriage status: 19.9% never married, 67.2% now married, 5.7% widowed, 7.2% divorced (2000); Foreign born: 4.7% (2000); Ancestry (includes multiple ancestries): 24.3% German, 23.3% Italian, 23.0% Irish, 12.0% English, 9.5% Polish (2000).
Economy: Single-family building permits issued: 16 (2005); Multi-family building permits issued: 0 (2005); Employment by occupation: 16.8% management, 26.2% professional, 12.9% services, 24.1% sales, 0.4% farming, 12.0% construction, 7.6% production (2000).
Income: Per capita income: $34,441 (2005); Median household income: $82,549 (2005); Average household income: $96,563 (2005); Percent of households with income of $100,000 or more: 36.6% (2005); Poverty rate: 2.3% (2000).
Education: Percent of population age 25 and over with: High school diploma (including GED) or higher: 89.8% (2005); Bachelor's degree or higher: 33.5% (2005); Master's degree or higher: 12.7% (2005).
Housing: Homeownership rate: 88.4% (2005); Median home value: $331,500 (2005); Median rent: $619 per month (2000); Median age of housing: 24 years (2000).
Transportation: Commute to work: 88.9% car, 1.4% public transportation, 2.0% walk, 7.5% work from home (2000); Travel time to work: 15.7% less than 15 minutes, 29.5% 15 to 30 minutes, 17.8% 30 to 45 minutes, 11.9% 45 to 60 minutes, 25.1% 60 minutes or more (2000)

GREAT MEADOWS-VIENNA (CDP). Covers a land area of 4.219 square miles and a water area of 0 square miles. Located at 40.86° N. Lat.; 74.89° W. Long.

Population: 1,108 (1990); 1,264 (2000); 1,437 (2005); 1,583 (2010 projected); Race: 95.5% White, 1.3% Black, 1.4% Asian, 1.7% Hispanic of any race (2005); Density: 340.6 persons per square mile (2005); Average household size: 3.07 (2005); Median age: 36.5 (2005); Males per 100 females: 97.4 (2005); Marriage status: 17.2% never married, 74.8% now married, 4.1% widowed, 4.0% divorced (2000); Foreign born: 9.1% (2000); Ancestry (includes multiple ancestries): 25.9% German, 18.9% Italian, 16.2% Irish, 12.5% Polish, 10.5% Other groups (2000).
Economy: Employment by occupation: 18.9% management, 14.0% professional, 20.6% services, 23.1% sales, 0.0% farming, 9.3% construction, 14.1% production (2000).
Income: Per capita income: $33,185 (2005); Median household income: $79,775 (2005); Average household income: $101,896 (2005); Percent of households with income of $100,000 or more: 34.6% (2005); Poverty rate: 1.4% (2000).
Education: Percent of population age 25 and over with: High school diploma (including GED) or higher: 90.4% (2005); Bachelor's degree or higher: 30.1% (2005); Master's degree or higher: 9.1% (2005).
School District(s)
Great Meadows Regional (PK-08)
    2003-04 Enrollment: 1,066 . . . . (908) 637-6576
Housing: Homeownership rate: 86.3% (2005); Median home value: $276,761 (2005); Median rent: $679 per month (2000); Median age of housing: 34 years (2000).
Transportation: Commute to work: 90.9% car, 2.0% public transportation, 5.7% walk, 0.7% work from home (2000); Travel time to work: 36.1% less than 15 minutes, 21.7% 15 to 30 minutes, 17.0% 30 to 45 minutes, 9.3% 45 to 60 minutes, 15.9% 60 minutes or more (2000)

GREENWICH (township). Covers a land area of 10.554 square miles and a water area of 0 square miles. Located at 40.68° N. Lat.; 75.11° W. Long.
Population: 1,899 (1990); 4,365 (2000); 5,457 (2005); 6,502 (2010 projected); Race: 89.3% White, 4.4% Black, 3.6% Asian, 6.3% Hispanic of any race (2005); Density: 517.1 persons per square mile (2005); Average household size: 3.14 (2005); Median age: 35.2 (2005); Males per 100 females: 97.4 (2005); Marriage status: 15.4% never married, 75.9% now married, 4.5% widowed, 4.2% divorced (2000); Foreign born: 5.8% (2000); Ancestry (includes multiple ancestries): 24.3% German, 23.4% Irish, 20.2% Italian, 10.0% English, 9.8% Other groups (2000).
Economy: Single-family building permits issued: 10 (2005); Multi-family building permits issued: 2 (2005); Employment by occupation: 24.7% management, 23.9% professional, 9.2% services, 27.4% sales, 0.0% farming, 7.1% construction, 7.7% production (2000).
Income: Per capita income: $39,015 (2005); Median household income: $105,794 (2005); Average household income: $122,430 (2005); Percent of households with income of $100,000 or more: 53.7% (2005); Poverty rate: 2.4% (2000).
Education: Percent of population age 25 and over with: High school diploma (including GED) or higher: 92.0% (2005); Bachelor's degree or higher: 40.7% (2005); Master's degree or higher: 11.8% (2005).
Housing: Homeownership rate: 92.9% (2005); Median home value: $365,179 (2005); Median rent: $767 per month (2000); Median age of housing: 8 years (2000).
Safety: Violent crime rate: 3.8 per 10,000 population; Property crime rate: 206.5 per 10,000 population (2004).
Transportation: Commute to work: 94.7% car, 1.6% public transportation, 0.0% walk, 3.2% work from home (2000); Travel time to work: 16.5% less than 15 minutes, 15.6% 15 to 30 minutes, 23.9% 30 to 45 minutes, 21.4% 45 to 60 minutes, 22.7% 60 minutes or more (2000)

HACKETTSTOWN (town). Covers a land area of 3.703 square miles and a water area of 0 square miles. Located at 40.85° N. Lat.; 74.82° W. Long. Elevation is 571 feet.
History: Seat of Centenary College. Incorporated 1853.
Population: 8,120 (1990); 10,403 (2000); 10,898 (2005); 11,525 (2010 projected); Race: 86.8% White, 3.2% Black, 4.1% Asian, 12.2% Hispanic of any race (2005); Density: 2,943.1 persons per square mile (2005); Average household size: 2.47 (2005); Median age: 36.7 (2005); Males per 100 females: 93.8 (2005); Marriage status: 26.6% never married, 57.0% now married, 7.4% widowed, 9.0% divorced (2000); Foreign born: 12.5% (2000); Ancestry (includes multiple ancestries): 20.1% German, 19.1% Irish, 18.4% Italian, 14.0% Other groups, 8.4% English (2000).
Economy: In fertile Musconetcong Valley. Metal products, machinery, plastics; vegetables, dairy products. State fish hatcheries located here.

Single-family building permits issued: 8 (2005); Multi-family building permits issued: 66 (2005); Employment by occupation: 13.7% management, 19.8% professional, 14.7% services, 28.6% sales, 0.2% farming, 11.2% construction, 12.0% production (2000).
Income: Per capita income: $27,646 (2005); Median household income: $56,785 (2005); Average household income: $65,976 (2005); Percent of households with income of $100,000 or more: 17.1% (2005); Poverty rate: 4.8% (2000).
Education: Percent of population age 25 and over with: High school diploma (including GED) or higher: 87.3% (2005); Bachelor's degree or higher: 24.5% (2005); Master's degree or higher: 7.0% (2005).
School District(s)
Hackettstown (PK-12)
    2003-04 Enrollment: 1,980 . . . . (908) 850-6500
Warren County Special Service (UG-UG)
    2003-04 Enrollment: 176 . . . . (908) 852-5222
Four-year College(s)
Centenary College (Private, Not-for-profit, United Methodist)
    Fall 2004 Enrollment: 2,339 . . . . (908) 852-1400
    2005-06 Tuition: In-state $19,840; Out-of-state $19,840
Housing: Homeownership rate: 48.3% (2005); Median home value: $243,266 (2005); Median rent: $648 per month (2000); Median age of housing: 34 years (2000).
Hospitals: Hackettstown Community Hospital (106 beds)
Safety: Violent crime rate: 14.8 per 10,000 population; Property crime rate: 150.6 per 10,000 population (2004).
Newspapers: The Star-Gazette (General - Circulation 4,569); Warren Reporter (General - Circulation 4,400)
Transportation: Commute to work: 91.2% car, 1.6% public transportation, 4.6% walk, 2.1% work from home (2000); Travel time to work: 30.3% less than 15 minutes, 18.1% 15 to 30 minutes, 18.5% 30 to 45 minutes, 16.4% 45 to 60 minutes, 16.6% 60 minutes or more (2000)
Additional Information Contacts
Town of Hackettstown . . . . (908) 852-3130
    http://www.hackettstown.net
Warren County Regional Chamber of Commerce . . . . (908) 852-1253
    http://www.warrencountychamber.org

HARDWICK (township). Covers a land area of 36.485 square miles and a water area of 1.438 square miles. Located at 41.02° N. Lat.; 74.96° W. Long. Elevation is 860 feet.
Population: 1,220 (1990); 1,464 (2000); 1,536 (2005); 1,605 (2010 projected); Race: 95.8% White, 0.8% Black, 0.6% Asian, 3.6% Hispanic of any race (2005); Density: 42.1 persons per square mile (2005); Average household size: 2.85 (2005); Median age: 40.6 (2005); Males per 100 females: 97.9 (2005); Marriage status: 17.6% never married, 71.1% now married, 4.0% widowed, 7.3% divorced (2000); Foreign born: 4.4% (2000); Ancestry (includes multiple ancestries): 29.3% German, 21.7% Irish, 20.7% Italian, 13.6% English, 9.6% Polish (2000).
Economy: Single-family building permits issued: 10 (2005); Multi-family building permits issued: 0 (2005); Employment by occupation: 20.5% management, 22.6% professional, 11.7% services, 26.3% sales, 1.1% farming, 10.5% construction, 7.2% production (2000).
Income: Per capita income: $35,239 (2005); Median household income: $85,698 (2005); Average household income: $99,100 (2005); Percent of households with income of $100,000 or more: 38.2% (2005); Poverty rate: 2.6% (2000).
Education: Percent of population age 25 and over with: High school diploma (including GED) or higher: 91.9% (2005); Bachelor's degree or higher: 29.8% (2005); Master's degree or higher: 9.6% (2005).
Housing: Homeownership rate: 90.0% (2005); Median home value: $309,130 (2005); Median rent: $625 per month (2000); Median age of housing: 23 years (2000).
Transportation: Commute to work: 89.7% car, 1.2% public transportation, 2.0% walk, 6.8% work from home (2000); Travel time to work: 22.2% less than 15 minutes, 18.5% 15 to 30 minutes, 19.3% 30 to 45 minutes, 11.3% 45 to 60 minutes, 28.7% 60 minutes or more (2000)

HARMONY (township). Covers a land area of 23.812 square miles and a water area of 0.328 square miles. Located at 40.76° N. Lat.; 75.12° W. Long. Elevation is 482 feet.
Population: 2,653 (1990); 2,729 (2000); 2,841 (2005); 2,981 (2010 projected); Race: 97.6% White, 1.0% Black, 0.4% Asian, 2.0% Hispanic of any race (2005); Density: 119.3 persons per square mile (2005); Average household size: 2.65 (2005); Median age: 41.1 (2005); Males per 100

females: 97.4 (2005); Marriage status: 20.4% never married, 65.4% now married, 7.0% widowed, 7.3% divorced (2000); Foreign born: 1.4% (2000); Ancestry (includes multiple ancestries): 29.7% German, 17.9% Irish, 16.0% Italian, 8.8% English, 7.3% Dutch (2000).

Economy: Single-family building permits issued: 18 (2005); Multi-family building permits issued: 10 (2005); Employment by occupation: 10.5% management, 18.6% professional, 12.9% services, 29.4% sales, 0.3% farming, 14.2% construction, 14.1% production (2000).

Income: Per capita income: $28,915 (2005); Median household income: $67,537 (2005); Average household income: $75,920 (2005); Percent of households with income of $100,000 or more: 21.7% (2005); Poverty rate: 4.5% (2000).

Education: Percent of population age 25 and over with: High school diploma (including GED) or higher: 84.4% (2005); Bachelor's degree or higher: 16.0% (2005); Master's degree or higher: 5.3% (2005).

Housing: Homeownership rate: 88.3% (2005); Median home value: $247,852 (2005); Median rent: $598 per month (2000); Median age of housing: 43 years (2000).

Transportation: Commute to work: 92.7% car, 0.6% public transportation, 1.2% walk, 4.9% work from home (2000); Travel time to work: 25.1% less than 15 minutes, 30.3% 15 to 30 minutes, 17.1% 30 to 45 minutes, 15.1% 45 to 60 minutes, 12.4% 60 minutes or more (2000)

HOPE (township). Covers a land area of 18.499 square miles and a water area of 0.181 square miles. Located at 40.91° N. Lat.; 74.97° W. Long. Elevation is 433 feet.

History: Has 18th-century buildings, including stone mill built 1768 by Moravian settlers.

Population: 1,719 (1990); 1,891 (2000); 2,108 (2005); 2,344 (2010 projected); Race: 97.7% White, 0.7% Black, 0.6% Asian, 2.2% Hispanic of any race (2005); Density: 114.0 persons per square mile (2005); Average household size: 2.68 (2005); Median age: 40.1 (2005); Males per 100 females: 99.6 (2005); Marriage status: 19.8% never married, 68.4% now married, 5.8% widowed, 6.0% divorced (2000); Foreign born: 4.1% (2000); Ancestry (includes multiple ancestries): 28.2% German, 21.9% Italian, 20.9% Irish, 10.5% English, 8.5% Polish (2000).

Economy: Amusement park. Single-family building permits issued: 7 (2005); Multi-family building permits issued: 0 (2005); Employment by occupation: 18.4% management, 17.7% professional, 11.9% services, 29.0% sales, 0.5% farming, 11.4% construction, 11.0% production (2000).

Income: Per capita income: $30,567 (2005); Median household income: $68,364 (2005); Average household income: $81,978 (2005); Percent of households with income of $100,000 or more: 26.7% (2005); Poverty rate: 1.9% (2000).

Education: Percent of population age 25 and over with: High school diploma (including GED) or higher: 90.8% (2005); Bachelor's degree or higher: 26.8% (2005); Master's degree or higher: 8.0% (2005).

School District(s)

Hope Township (PK-08)
    2003-04 Enrollment: 248 . . . . (908) 459-4242

Housing: Homeownership rate: 89.2% (2005); Median home value: $281,920 (2005); Median rent: $603 per month (2000); Median age of housing: 31 years (2000).

Transportation: Commute to work: 91.1% car, 0.6% public transportation, 3.4% walk, 4.7% work from home (2000); Travel time to work: 20.0% less than 15 minutes, 22.7% 15 to 30 minutes, 22.5% 30 to 45 minutes, 10.4% 45 to 60 minutes, 24.5% 60 minutes or more (2000)

INDEPENDENCE (township). Covers a land area of 19.840 square miles and a water area of 0.048 square miles. Located at 40.86° N. Lat.; 74.85° W. Long.

Population: 3,940 (1990); 5,603 (2000); 5,835 (2005); 6,124 (2010 projected); Race: 93.3% White, 1.7% Black, 2.3% Asian, 5.7% Hispanic of any race (2005); Density: 294.1 persons per square mile (2005); Average household size: 2.56 (2005); Median age: 38.3 (2005); Males per 100 females: 94.1 (2005); Marriage status: 21.6% never married, 65.4% now married, 5.1% widowed, 7.9% divorced (2000); Foreign born: 7.3% (2000); Ancestry (includes multiple ancestries): 23.6% Irish, 23.1% German, 20.3% Italian, 11.3% Polish, 10.0% Other groups (2000).

Economy: Single-family building permits issued: 14 (2005); Multi-family building permits issued: 0 (2005); Employment by occupation: 19.3% management, 20.7% professional, 14.8% services, 26.5% sales, 0.0% farming, 9.9% construction, 8.9% production (2000).

Income: Per capita income: $36,433 (2005); Median household income: $79,875 (2005); Average household income: $93,240 (2005); Percent of

households with income of $100,000 or more: 34.4% (2005); Poverty rate: 2.8% (2000).

Education: Percent of population age 25 and over with: High school diploma (including GED) or higher: 91.3% (2005); Bachelor's degree or higher: 35.6% (2005); Master's degree or higher: 9.9% (2005).

Housing: Homeownership rate: 78.9% (2005); Median home value: $260,495 (2005); Median rent: $683 per month (2000); Median age of housing: 16 years (2000).

Safety: Violent crime rate: 3.4 per 10,000 population; Property crime rate: 84.1 per 10,000 population (2004).

Transportation: Commute to work: 92.2% car, 1.9% public transportation, 2.1% walk, 3.7% work from home (2000); Travel time to work: 22.3% less than 15 minutes, 24.5% 15 to 30 minutes, 19.0% 30 to 45 minutes, 11.8% 45 to 60 minutes, 22.4% 60 minutes or more (2000)

KNOWLTON (township). Covers a land area of 24.779 square miles and a water area of 0.531 square miles. Located at 40.92° N. Lat.; 75.06° W. Long. Elevation is 720 feet.

Population: 2,543 (1990); 2,977 (2000); 3,060 (2005); 3,165 (2010 projected); Race: 96.8% White, 0.4% Black, 1.0% Asian, 2.5% Hispanic of any race (2005); Density: 123.5 persons per square mile (2005); Average household size: 2.86 (2005); Median age: 38.5 (2005); Males per 100 females: 102.1 (2005); Marriage status: 21.8% never married, 66.7% now married, 5.0% widowed, 6.4% divorced (2000); Foreign born: 4.3% (2000); Ancestry (includes multiple ancestries): 26.6% German, 21.8% Irish, 15.6% Italian, 11.9% English, 8.3% Polish (2000).

Economy: Single-family building permits issued: 13 (2005); Multi-family building permits issued: 0 (2005); Employment by occupation: 14.7% management, 20.3% professional, 15.5% services, 21.9% sales, 0.8% farming, 12.2% construction, 14.6% production (2000).

Income: Per capita income: $28,726 (2005); Median household income: $72,150 (2005); Average household income: $81,775 (2005); Percent of households with income of $100,000 or more: 29.1% (2005); Poverty rate: 3.5% (2000).

Education: Percent of population age 25 and over with: High school diploma (including GED) or higher: 87.1% (2005); Bachelor's degree or higher: 26.8% (2005); Master's degree or higher: 6.6% (2005).

Housing: Homeownership rate: 87.4% (2005); Median home value: $277,119 (2005); Median rent: $578 per month (2000); Median age of housing: 28 years (2000).

Transportation: Commute to work: 94.9% car, 1.4% public transportation, 1.1% walk, 2.0% work from home (2000); Travel time to work: 21.7% less than 15 minutes, 21.3% 15 to 30 minutes, 19.7% 30 to 45 minutes, 14.4% 45 to 60 minutes, 22.9% 60 minutes or more (2000)

LIBERTY (township). Covers a land area of 11.801 square miles and a water area of 0.206 square miles. Located at 40.87° N. Lat.; 74.95° W. Long.

Population: 2,493 (1990); 2,765 (2000); 2,966 (2005); 3,190 (2010 projected); Race: 97.0% White, 0.4% Black, 0.6% Asian, 4.1% Hispanic of any race (2005); Density: 251.3 persons per square mile (2005); Average household size: 2.78 (2005); Median age: 38.5 (2005); Males per 100 females: 98.4 (2005); Marriage status: 22.1% never married, 65.6% now married, 5.9% widowed, 6.5% divorced (2000); Foreign born: 6.2% (2000); Ancestry (includes multiple ancestries): 23.8% German, 22.5% Irish, 20.9% Italian, 13.4% Polish, 11.9% English (2000).

Economy: Single-family building permits issued: 7 (2005); Multi-family building permits issued: 0 (2005); Employment by occupation: 14.0% management, 20.6% professional, 11.3% services, 22.0% sales, 1.5% farming, 14.8% construction, 15.8% production (2000).

Income: Per capita income: $26,874 (2005); Median household income: $67,389 (2005); Average household income: $74,442 (2005); Percent of households with income of $100,000 or more: 23.6% (2005); Poverty rate: 3.5% (2000).

Education: Percent of population age 25 and over with: High school diploma (including GED) or higher: 88.2% (2005); Bachelor's degree or higher: 25.4% (2005); Master's degree or higher: 8.7% (2005).

Housing: Homeownership rate: 88.8% (2005); Median home value: $245,845 (2005); Median rent: $535 per month (2000); Median age of housing: 30 years (2000).

Transportation: Commute to work: 93.9% car, 1.5% public transportation, 0.5% walk, 2.7% work from home (2000); Travel time to work: 17.8% less than 15 minutes, 26.8% 15 to 30 minutes, 18.4% 30 to 45 minutes, 12.8% 45 to 60 minutes, 24.3% 60 minutes or more (2000)

LOPATCONG (township). Covers a land area of 7.077 square miles and a water area of 0.062 square miles. Located at 40.70° N. Lat.; 75.16° W. Long.
Population: 5,052 (1990); 5,765 (2000); 8,890 (2005); 11,708 (2010 projected); Race: 94.7% White, 1.6% Black, 2.5% Asian, 3.0% Hispanic of any race (2005); Density: 1,256.1 persons per square mile (2005); Average household size: 2.69 (2005); Median age: 41.7 (2005); Males per 100 females: 87.0 (2005); Marriage status: 17.8% never married, 63.2% now married, 12.5% widowed, 6.5% divorced (2000); Foreign born: 4.6% (2000); Ancestry (includes multiple ancestries): 24.3% Italian, 20.0% German, 18.5% Irish, 8.4% Polish, 8.3% English (2000).
Economy: Incorporated 1851. Single-family building permits issued: 101 (2005); Multi-family building permits issued: 12 (2005); Employment by occupation: 16.1% management, 26.9% professional, 13.1% services, 24.6% sales, 0.6% farming, 9.6% construction, 9.3% production (2000).
Income: Per capita income: $26,323 (2005); Median household income: $58,735 (2005); Average household income: $68,810 (2005); Percent of households with income of $100,000 or more: 22.2% (2005); Poverty rate: 6.4% (2000).
Education: Percent of population age 25 and over with: High school diploma (including GED) or higher: 82.8% (2005); Bachelor's degree or higher: 22.6% (2005); Master's degree or higher: 7.2% (2005).
Housing: Homeownership rate: 78.2% (2005); Median home value: $251,216 (2005); Median rent: $585 per month (2000); Median age of housing: 29 years (2000).
Safety: Violent crime rate: 8.9 per 10,000 population; Property crime rate: 96.3 per 10,000 population (2004).
Transportation: Commute to work: 94.7% car, 1.1% public transportation, 1.4% walk, 2.3% work from home (2000); Travel time to work: 34.7% less than 15 minutes, 14.4% 15 to 30 minutes, 16.1% 30 to 45 minutes, 13.9% 45 to 60 minutes, 21.0% 60 minutes or more (2000)

MANSFIELD (township). Covers a land area of 29.922 square miles and a water area of 0.018 square miles. Located at 40.80° N. Lat.; 74.90° W. Long.
History: Incorporated 1798.
Population: 7,154 (1990); 6,653 (2000); 6,988 (2005); 7,401 (2010 projected); Race: 88.8% White, 5.5% Black, 1.8% Asian, 6.2% Hispanic of any race (2005); Density: 233.5 persons per square mile (2005); Average household size: 2.89 (2005); Median age: 38.0 (2005); Males per 100 females: 95.4 (2005); Marriage status: 22.1% never married, 65.2% now married, 5.9% widowed, 6.8% divorced (2000); Foreign born: 5.5% (2000); Ancestry (includes multiple ancestries): 20.3% German, 19.0% Italian, 17.9% Irish, 9.8% Other groups, 9.1% Polish (2000).
Economy: Single-family building permits issued: 16 (2005); Multi-family building permits issued: 6 (2005); Employment by occupation: 13.6% management, 23.4% professional, 14.0% services, 26.0% sales, 0.3% farming, 10.8% construction, 11.9% production (2000).
Income: Per capita income: $31,051 (2005); Median household income: $76,336 (2005); Average household income: $88,631 (2005); Percent of households with income of $100,000 or more: 34.6% (2005); Poverty rate: 3.9% (2000).
Education: Percent of population age 25 and over with: High school diploma (including GED) or higher: 88.4% (2005); Bachelor's degree or higher: 27.4% (2005); Master's degree or higher: 9.3% (2005).
Housing: Homeownership rate: 72.9% (2005); Median home value: $270,733 (2005); Median rent: $669 per month (2000); Median age of housing: 27 years (2000).
Safety: Violent crime rate: 3.6 per 10,000 population; Property crime rate: 135.3 per 10,000 population (2004).
Transportation: Commute to work: 90.3% car, 0.7% public transportation, 2.5% walk, 5.3% work from home (2000); Travel time to work: 27.2% less than 15 minutes, 22.5% 15 to 30 minutes, 20.9% 30 to 45 minutes, 10.1% 45 to 60 minutes, 19.4% 60 minutes or more (2000)

OXFORD (township). Aka Oxford Center. Covers a land area of 5.936 square miles and a water area of 0.079 square miles. Located at 40.80° N. Lat.; 74.99° W. Long. Elevation is 460 feet.
History: Once an important iron-mining region.
Population: 1,790 (1990); 2,307 (2000); 2,727 (2005); 3,138 (2010 projected); Race: 94.7% White, 2.0% Black, 0.8% Asian, 5.1% Hispanic of any race (2005); Density: 459.4 persons per square mile (2005); Average household size: 2.59 (2005); Median age: 37.8 (2005); Males per 100 females: 98.5 (2005); Marriage status: 20.8% never married, 63.2% now

married, 7.4% widowed, 8.6% divorced (2000); Foreign born: 3.6% (2000); Ancestry (includes multiple ancestries): 27.0% German, 26.0% Irish, 18.2% Italian, 9.2% English, 8.1% Polish (2000).
Economy: Single-family building permits issued: 5 (2005); Multi-family building permits issued: 0 (2005); Employment by occupation: 13.2% management, 17.3% professional, 17.1% services, 24.7% sales, 0.4% farming, 12.2% construction, 15.1% production (2000).
Income: Per capita income: $27,134 (2005); Median household income: $62,405 (2005); Average household income: $70,204 (2005); Percent of households with income of $100,000 or more: 19.3% (2005); Poverty rate: 4.0% (2000).
Education: Percent of population age 25 and over with: High school diploma (including GED) or higher: 82.2% (2005); Bachelor's degree or higher: 19.8% (2005); Master's degree or higher: 5.0% (2005).
School District(s)
Oxford Township (PK-08)
    2003-04 Enrollment: 317 . . . . (908) 453-4101
Housing: Homeownership rate: 84.2% (2005); Median home value: $181,561 (2005); Median rent: $538 per month (2000); Median age of housing: 39 years (2000).
Safety: Violent crime rate: 3.8 per 10,000 population; Property crime rate: 34.1 per 10,000 population (2004).
Transportation: Commute to work: 96.1% car, 0.5% public transportation, 0.4% walk, 2.9% work from home (2000); Travel time to work: 20.6% less than 15 minutes, 22.3% 15 to 30 minutes, 12.9% 30 to 45 minutes, 13.1% 45 to 60 minutes, 31.1% 60 minutes or more (2000)

OXFORD (CDP). Covers a land area of 5.254 square miles and a water area of 0 square miles. Located at 40.80° N. Lat.; 74.99° W. Long.
Population: 1,784 (1990); 2,283 (2000); 2,699 (2005); 3,106 (2010 projected); Race: 94.7% White, 2.0% Black, 0.9% Asian, 5.2% Hispanic of any race (2005); Density: 513.7 persons per square mile (2005); Average household size: 2.58 (2005); Median age: 37.7 (2005); Males per 100 females: 98.3 (2005); Marriage status: 20.9% never married, 63.1% now married, 7.4% widowed, 8.5% divorced (2000); Foreign born: 3.7% (2000); Ancestry (includes multiple ancestries): 27.1% German, 25.8% Irish, 17.9% Italian, 9.1% English, 8.2% Polish (2000).
Economy: Employment by occupation: 13.3% management, 17.1% professional, 17.1% services, 24.8% sales, 0.4% farming, 12.1% construction, 15.2% production (2000).
Income: Per capita income: $27,278 (2005); Median household income: $62,597 (2005); Average household income: $70,452 (2005); Percent of households with income of $100,000 or more: 19.4% (2005); Poverty rate: 4.0% (2000).
Education: Percent of population age 25 and over with: High school diploma (including GED) or higher: 82.0% (2005); Bachelor's degree or higher: 19.8% (2005); Master's degree or higher: 5.1% (2005).
School District(s)
Oxford Township (PK-08)
    2003-04 Enrollment: 317 . . . . (908) 453-4101
Housing: Homeownership rate: 84.3% (2005); Median home value: $181,452 (2005); Median rent: $538 per month (2000); Median age of housing: 38 years (2000).
Transportation: Commute to work: 88.2% car, 0.5% public transportation, 0.4% walk, 2.9% work from home (2000); Travel time to work: 20.3% less than 15 minutes, 22.4% 15 to 30 minutes, 13.0% 30 to 45 minutes, 13.1% 45 to 60 minutes, 31.2% 60 minutes or more (2000)

PHILLIPSBURG (town). Covers a land area of 3.224 square miles and a water area of 0.114 square miles. Located at 40.68° N. Lat.; 75.18° W. Long. Elevation is 314 feet.
History: Phillipsburg was long ago the site of a Native American village called Chintewink.
Population: 15,757 (1990); 15,166 (2000); 15,132 (2005); 15,285 (2010 projected); Race: 88.4% White, 5.4% Black, 1.2% Asian, 8.1% Hispanic of any race (2005); Density: 4,693.1 persons per square mile (2005); Average household size: 2.49 (2005); Median age: 36.6 (2005); Males per 100 females: 92.4 (2005); Marriage status: 28.4% never married, 51.1% now married, 10.1% widowed, 10.4% divorced (2000); Foreign born: 4.1% (2000); Ancestry (includes multiple ancestries): 23.8% German, 18.3% Irish, 17.3% Italian, 11.6% Other groups, 8.4% English (2000).
Economy: Single-family building permits issued: 10 (2005); Multi-family building permits issued: 0 (2005); Employment by occupation: 8.2% management, 11.9% professional, 18.9% services, 29.5% sales, 0.1% farming, 8.7% construction, 22.7% production (2000).

Income: Per capita income: $20,743 (2005); Median household income: $41,153 (2005); Average household income: $51,002 (2005); Percent of households with income of $100,000 or more: 9.5% (2005); Poverty rate: 13.4% (2000).
Taxes: Total city taxes per capita: $535 (2004); City property taxes per capita: $519 (2004).
Education: Percent of population age 25 and over with: High school diploma (including GED) or higher: 71.3% (2005); Bachelor's degree or higher: 9.0% (2005); Master's degree or higher: 2.3% (2005).

School District(s)
Harmony Township (PK-08)
   2003-04 Enrollment: 313 . . . . (908) 859-1001
Lopatcong Township (PK-08)
   2003-04 Enrollment: 874 . . . . (908) 859-0800
Phillipsburg Town (PK-12)
   2003-04 Enrollment: 3,715 . . . . (908) 454-3400
Pohatcong Township (PK-08)
   2003-04 Enrollment: 385 . . . . (908) 859-8155
Housing: Homeownership rate: 56.9% (2005); Median home value: $133,631 (2005); Median rent: $518 per month (2000); Median age of housing: 60+ years (2000).
Hospitals: Warren Hospital (214 beds)
Safety: Violent crime rate: 17.0 per 10,000 population; Property crime rate: 171.4 per 10,000 population (2004).
Transportation: Commute to work: 90.8% car, 1.4% public transportation, 4.4% walk, 1.6% work from home (2000); Travel time to work: 41.7% less than 15 minutes, 27.1% 15 to 30 minutes, 13.0% 30 to 45 minutes, 8.6% 45 to 60 minutes, 9.6% 60 minutes or more (2000)
Additional Information Contacts
Phillipsburg Chamber of Commerce . . . . (908) 859-5161
   http://www.phillipsburgnj.com

POHATCONG (township).
Covers a land area of 13.326 square miles and a water area of 0.279 square miles. Located at 40.66° N. Lat.; 75.16° W. Long.
Population: 3,619 (1990); 3,416 (2000); 3,438 (2005); 3,506 (2010 projected); Race: 97.3% White, 0.7% Black, 0.4% Asian, 3.1% Hispanic of any race (2005); Density: 258.0 persons per square mile (2005); Average household size: 2.50 (2005); Median age: 40.9 (2005); Males per 100 females: 99.1 (2005); Marriage status: 21.2% never married, 65.9% now married, 5.5% widowed, 7.4% divorced (2000); Foreign born: 2.0% (2000); Ancestry (includes multiple ancestries): 28.7% German, 20.4% Irish, 18.5% Italian, 12.9% English, 7.8% Polish (2000).
Economy: Single-family building permits issued: 10 (2005); Multi-family building permits issued: 0 (2005); Employment by occupation: 14.9% management, 20.1% professional, 13.1% services, 28.2% sales, 0.3% farming, 13.5% construction, 9.8% production (2000).
Income: Per capita income: $27,262 (2005); Median household income: $58,457 (2005); Average household income: $67,870 (2005); Percent of households with income of $100,000 or more: 16.2% (2005); Poverty rate: 4.3% (2000).
Education: Percent of population age 25 and over with: High school diploma (including GED) or higher: 86.1% (2005); Bachelor's degree or higher: 17.6% (2005); Master's degree or higher: 5.9% (2005).
Housing: Homeownership rate: 86.5% (2005); Median home value: $204,392 (2005); Median rent: $619 per month (2000); Median age of housing: 52 years (2000).
Safety: Violent crime rate: 46.2 per 10,000 population; Property crime rate: 548.8 per 10,000 population (2004).
Transportation: Commute to work: 93.2% car, 1.0% public transportation, 1.5% walk, 3.6% work from home (2000); Travel time to work: 26.7% less than 15 minutes, 24.6% 15 to 30 minutes, 22.4% 30 to 45 minutes, 11.7% 45 to 60 minutes, 14.7% 60 minutes or more (2000)

PORT MURRAY (unincorporated postal area, zip code 07865).
Covers a land area of 11.299 square miles and a water area of 0.002 square miles. Located at 40.78° N. Lat.; 74.90° W. Long. Elevation is 594 feet.
Population: 2,010 (2000); Race: 87.7% White, 10.5% Black, 0.0% Asian, 0.9% Hispanic of any race (2000); Density: 177.9 persons per square mile (2000); Age: 25.7% under 18, 8.2% over 64 (2000); Marriage status: 22.6% never married, 69.3% now married, 4.2% widowed, 3.9% divorced (2000); Foreign born: 3.6% (2000); Ancestry (includes multiple ancestries): 20.4% Irish, 18.7% Italian, 17.4% German, 17.1% English, 9.5% Other groups (2000).

Economy: Employment by occupation: 13.4% management, 25.6% professional, 15.8% services, 25.5% sales, 0.0% farming, 12.1% construction, 7.7% production (2000).
Income: Per capita income: $25,076 (2000); Median household income: $70,607 (2000); Poverty rate: 4.8% (2000).
Education: Percent of population age 25 and over with: High school diploma (including GED) or higher: 90.3% (2000); Bachelor's degree or higher: 28.2% (2000).

School District(s)
Mansfield Township (PK-06)
   2003-04 Enrollment: 811 . . . . (908) 689-3212
Housing: Homeownership rate: 84.5% (2000); Median home value: $169,400 (2000); Median rent: $645 per month (2000); Median age of housing: 36 years (2000).
Transportation: Commute to work: 85.1% car, 0.8% public transportation, 4.3% walk, 8.9% work from home (2000); Travel time to work: 26.8% less than 15 minutes, 27.3% 15 to 30 minutes, 20.9% 30 to 45 minutes, 6.1% 45 to 60 minutes, 18.9% 60 minutes or more (2000)

STEWARTSVILLE (unincorporated postal area, zip code 08886).
Covers a land area of 13.127 square miles and a water area of 0.044 square miles. Located at 40.69° N. Lat.; 75.11° W. Long. Elevation is 320 feet.
Population: 4,854 (2000); Race: 93.7% White, 2.8% Black, 1.7% Asian, 3.8% Hispanic of any race (2000); Density: 369.8 persons per square mile (2000); Age: 33.1% under 18, 5.7% over 64 (2000); Marriage status: 14.7% never married, 77.5% now married, 3.9% widowed, 4.0% divorced (2000); Foreign born: 5.8% (2000); Ancestry (includes multiple ancestries): 24.8% German, 21.7% Italian, 21.2% Irish, 10.1% Polish, 9.5% Other groups (2000).
Economy: Employment by occupation: 24.2% management, 24.1% professional, 8.1% services, 26.8% sales, 0.0% farming, 9.4% construction, 7.5% production (2000).
Income: Per capita income: $32,376 (2000); Median household income: $86,131 (2000); Poverty rate: 2.2% (2000).
Education: Percent of population age 25 and over with: High school diploma (including GED) or higher: 92.4% (2000); Bachelor's degree or higher: 37.5% (2000).

School District(s)
Greenwich Township (PK-08)
   2003-04 Enrollment: 947 . . . . (908) 859-2022
Housing: Homeownership rate: 90.8% (2000); Median home value: $231,400 (2000); Median rent: $677 per month (2000); Median age of housing: 10 years (2000).
Transportation: Commute to work: 93.4% car, 1.4% public transportation, 1.0% walk, 3.8% work from home (2000); Travel time to work: 19.0% less than 15 minutes, 16.7% 15 to 30 minutes, 22.9% 30 to 45 minutes, 20.2% 45 to 60 minutes, 21.3% 60 minutes or more (2000)

WASHINGTON (borough).
Covers a land area of 1.957 square miles and a water area of <.001 square miles. Located at 40.76° N. Lat.; 74.97° W. Long. Elevation is 463 feet.
Population: 6,474 (1990); 6,712 (2000); 6,797 (2005); 6,972 (2010 projected); Race: 87.5% White, 6.1% Black, 2.4% Asian, 6.0% Hispanic of any race (2005); Density: 3,473.3 persons per square mile (2005); Average household size: 2.45 (2005); Median age: 36.5 (2005); Males per 100 females: 99.9 (2005); Marriage status: 28.7% never married, 53.6% now married, 7.5% widowed, 10.2% divorced (2000); Foreign born: 8.8% (2000); Ancestry (includes multiple ancestries): 20.3% German, 16.6% Italian, 16.3% Irish, 10.4% Other groups, 9.2% Polish (2000).
Economy: Single-family building permits issued: 10 (2005); Multi-family building permits issued: 0 (2005); Employment by occupation: 12.0% management, 21.5% professional, 14.1% services, 25.8% sales, 0.0% farming, 11.4% construction, 15.2% production (2000).
Income: Per capita income: $25,317 (2005); Median household income: $50,780 (2005); Average household income: $62,011 (2005); Percent of households with income of $100,000 or more: 16.8% (2005); Poverty rate: 5.6% (2000).
Taxes: Total city taxes per capita: $485 (2004); City property taxes per capita: $479 (2004).
Education: Percent of population age 25 and over with: High school diploma (including GED) or higher: 83.5% (2005); Bachelor's degree or higher: 22.8% (2005); Master's degree or higher: 8.0% (2005).

School District(s)

Franklin Township (PK-06)
   2003-04 Enrollment: 386 . . . . (908) 689-2958

Warren County Vocational (09-12)
   2003-04 Enrollment: 387 . . . . (908) 835-2814

Warren Hills Regional (07-12)
   2003-04 Enrollment: 2,216 . . . . (908) 689-3143

Washington Borough (PK-06)
   2003-04 Enrollment: 562 . . . . (908) 689-0241

Washington Township (PK-06)
   2003-04 Enrollment: 687 . . . . (908) 689-1119

Two-year College(s)

Warren County Community College (Public)
   Fall 2004 Enrollment: 1,332 . . . . (908) 835-9222
   2005-06 Tuition: In-state $2,580; Out-of-state $3,060

Housing: Homeownership rate: 52.0% (2005); Median home value: $176,356 (2005); Median rent: $625 per month (2000); Median age of housing: 56 years (2000).

Safety: Violent crime rate: 14.5 per 10,000 population; Property crime rate: 194.9 per 10,000 population (2004).

Transportation: Commute to work: 93.9% car, 0.9% public transportation, 1.9% walk, 2.3% work from home (2000); Travel time to work: 20.8% less than 15 minutes, 31.8% 15 to 30 minutes, 21.3% 30 to 45 minutes, 11.8% 45 to 60 minutes, 14.3% 60 minutes or more (2000)

WASHINGTON (township). Covers a land area of 17.577 square miles and a water area of 0.017 square miles. Located at 40.74° N. Lat.; 74.98° W. Long. Elevation is 463 feet.

History: Settled 1741; incorporated 1868.

Population: 5,367 (1990); 6,248 (2000); 6,829 (2005); 7,441 (2010 projected); Race: 94.4% White, 2.6% Black, 1.3% Asian, 3.0% Hispanic of any race (2005); Density: 388.5 persons per square mile (2005); Average household size: 2.97 (2005); Median age: 37.9 (2005); Males per 100 females: 95.1 (2005); Marriage status: 21.8% never married, 68.6% now married, 4.5% widowed, 5.1% divorced (2000); Foreign born: 4.1% (2000); Ancestry (includes multiple ancestries): 27.2% German, 19.0% Irish, 16.6% Italian, 10.3% Polish, 9.8% English (2000).

Economy: Manufacturing: wire and cable, apparel, porcelain and brass products. Agriculture: corn, oats, hay; nursery and dairy products. Single-family building permits issued: 30 (2005); Multi-family building permits issued: 0 (2005); Employment by occupation: 18.2% management, 19.2% professional, 12.7% services, 30.4% sales, 0.5% farming, 12.0% construction, 7.0% production (2000).

Income: Per capita income: $35,128 (2005); Median household income: $90,605 (2005); Average household income: $104,083 (2005); Percent of households with income of $100,000 or more: 42.4% (2005); Poverty rate: 3.1% (2000).

Education: Percent of population age 25 and over with: High school diploma (including GED) or higher: 90.8% (2005); Bachelor's degree or higher: 32.1% (2005); Master's degree or higher: 8.9% (2005).

School District(s)

Franklin Township (PK-06)
   2003-04 Enrollment: 386 . . . . (908) 689-2958

Warren County Vocational (09-12)
   2003-04 Enrollment: 387 . . . . (908) 835-2814

Warren Hills Regional (07-12)
   2003-04 Enrollment: 2,216 . . . . (908) 689-3143

Washington Borough (PK-06)
   2003-04 Enrollment: 562 . . . . (908) 689-0241

Washington Township (PK-06)
   2003-04 Enrollment: 687 . . . . (908) 689-1119

Two-year College(s)

Warren County Community College (Public)
   Fall 2004 Enrollment: 1,332 . . . . (908) 835-9222
   2005-06 Tuition: In-state $2,580; Out-of-state $3,060

Housing: Homeownership rate: 89.4% (2005); Median home value: $279,080 (2005); Median rent: $645 per month (2000); Median age of housing: 30 years (2000).

Safety: Violent crime rate: 6.0 per 10,000 population; Property crime rate: 156.2 per 10,000 population (2004).

Transportation: Commute to work: 92.5% car, 1.1% public transportation, 1.7% walk, 4.7% work from home (2000); Travel time to work: 24.0% less than 15 minutes, 18.6% 15 to 30 minutes, 16.1% 30 to 45 minutes, 17.1% 45 to 60 minutes, 24.2% 60 minutes or more (2000)

Additional Information Contacts

Washington Township . . . . (908) 689-7200
   http://www.washington-twp-warren.org

WHITE (township). Covers a land area of 27.370 square miles and a water area of 0.380 square miles. Located at 40.83° N. Lat.; 75.05° W. Long.

Population: 3,603 (1990); 4,245 (2000); 5,563 (2005); 6,800 (2010 projected); Race: 95.7% White, 1.4% Black, 1.0% Asian, 2.7% Hispanic of any race (2005); Density: 203.3 persons per square mile (2005); Average household size: 2.48 (2005); Median age: 42.5 (2005); Males per 100 females: 99.4 (2005); Marriage status: 19.2% never married, 64.8% now married, 9.8% widowed, 6.1% divorced (2000); Foreign born: 5.1% (2000); Ancestry (includes multiple ancestries): 30.0% German, 15.8% Irish, 14.7% Italian, 12.8% English, 7.0% Polish (2000).

Economy: Single-family building permits issued: 76 (2005); Multi-family building permits issued: 23 (2005); Employment by occupation: 15.1% management, 17.8% professional, 14.5% services, 26.4% sales, 0.4% farming, 11.9% construction, 13.9% production (2000).

Income: Per capita income: $28,669 (2005); Median household income: $62,355 (2005); Average household income: $70,233 (2005); Percent of households with income of $100,000 or more: 22.7% (2005); Poverty rate: 4.9% (2000).

Education: Percent of population age 25 and over with: High school diploma (including GED) or higher: 81.2% (2005); Bachelor's degree or higher: 22.0% (2005); Master's degree or higher: 5.4% (2005).

Housing: Homeownership rate: 79.0% (2005); Median home value: $249,466 (2005); Median rent: $416 per month (2000); Median age of housing: 24 years (2000).

Transportation: Commute to work: 95.4% car, 0.0% public transportation, 1.0% walk, 3.6% work from home (2000); Travel time to work: 24.1% less than 15 minutes, 25.1% 15 to 30 minutes, 19.0% 30 to 45 minutes, 12.6% 45 to 60 minutes, 19.2% 60 minutes or more (2000);

CDP = Census Designated Place

CDP = Census Designated Place

CDP = Census Designated Place

CDP = Census Designated Place

COMPARATIVE STATISTICS

Population

Place	1990	2000	2005 Estimate	2010 Projection
Atlantic City (city)	37,986	40,517	40,543	41,058
Bayonne (city)	61,444	61,842	60,238	58,625
Belleville (twp)	34,095	35,928	35,367	34,854
Bergenfield (borough)	24,458	26,247	26,165	26,081
Berkeley (twp)	37,321	39,991	42,830	45,898
Bernards (twp)	17,199	24,575	26,802	28,948
Bloomfield (twp)	45,142	47,683	46,821	46,031
Brick (twp)	66,423	76,119	79,396	83,464
Bridgewater (twp)	32,509	42,940	44,492	46,314
Camden (city)	87,492	79,904	80,605	81,402
Cherry Hill (twp)	69,348	69,965	71,986	74,000
Clifton (city)	70,869	78,672	79,679	80,742
Deptford (twp)	24,137	26,763	28,807	30,911
Dover (twp)	76,417	89,706	95,235	101,452
East Brunswick (twp)	43,548	46,756	49,033	51,532
East Orange (city)	73,379	69,824	68,781	67,883
East Windsor (twp)	22,583	24,919	27,376	29,734
Edison (twp)	88,680	97,687	101,153	104,974
Egg Harbor (twp)	24,970	30,726	37,251	43,441
Elizabeth (city)	109,978	120,568	124,189	127,800
Englewood (city)	24,850	26,203	26,073	25,995
Evesham (twp)	35,309	42,275	48,039	53,719
Ewing (twp)	34,185	35,707	37,051	38,478
Fair Lawn (borough)	30,548	31,637	31,564	31,559
Fort Lee (borough)	31,997	35,461	37,654	39,738
Franklin (twp)	42,780	50,903	56,558	62,189
Freehold (twp)	24,710	31,537	34,314	36,963
Galloway (twp)	23,360	31,209	35,254	39,238
Garfield (city)	26,727	29,786	29,662	29,605
Gloucester (twp)	53,797	64,350	66,628	68,741
Hackensack (city)	37,049	42,677	43,636	44,742
Hamilton (twp)	86,453	87,109	91,002	95,176
Hillsborough (twp)	28,842	36,634	38,125	39,790
Hoboken (city)	33,387	38,577	39,692	40,660
Howell (twp)	38,987	48,903	50,595	52,332
Irvington (twp)	61,067	60,695	59,611	58,659
Jackson (twp)	33,262	42,816	52,671	62,149
Jersey City (city)	228,543	240,055	238,552	236,962
Kearny (town)	34,874	40,513	39,548	38,549
Lacey (twp)	22,141	25,346	26,537	27,980
Lakewood (twp)	45,019	60,352	67,602	75,083
Lakewood (cdp)	26,093	36,065	40,530	45,110
Lawrence (twp)	25,787	29,159	31,742	34,242
Linden (city)	36,701	39,394	40,010	40,630
Livingston (twp)	26,609	27,391	28,257	29,119
Long Branch (city)	28,658	31,340	31,681	32,189
Manalapan (twp)	26,731	33,423	36,308	39,023
Manchester (twp)	35,976	38,928	43,586	48,357
Marlboro (twp)	27,974	36,398	40,010	43,433
Mercerville-Ham. Sq. (cdp)	26,873	26,419	26,648	26,989

Place	1990	2000	2005 Estimate	2010 Projection
Middletown (twp)	68,220	66,327	66,972	67,901
Millville (city)	25,992	26,847	27,364	27,953
Monroe (twp)	22,235	27,999	33,224	38,095
Monroe (twp)	26,703	28,967	31,357	33,865
Montclair (twp)	37,729	38,977	38,802	38,656
Mount Laurel (twp)	30,270	40,221	40,630	41,385
Mount Olive (twp)	21,306	24,193	26,135	28,004
Neptune (twp)	28,148	27,690	28,766	29,905
New Brunswick (city)	41,711	48,573	50,624	52,995
Newark (city)	275,419	273,546	281,352	288,667
North Bergen (twp)	48,414	58,092	58,153	58,206
North Brunswick (twp)	31,287	36,287	39,208	42,142
Nutley (twp)	27,099	27,362	28,197	28,961
Ocean (twp)	25,058	26,959	28,241	29,565
Old Bridge (twp)	56,655	60,456	65,076	69,739
Orange (cdp)	29,925	32,868	32,432	31,982
Paramus (borough)	25,004	25,737	26,904	27,950
Parsippany-Troy Hills (twp)	48,982	50,649	51,723	53,033
Passaic (city)	58,914	67,861	68,690	69,648
Paterson (city)	140,891	149,222	151,822	154,698
Pemberton (twp)	31,335	28,691	29,269	30,089
Pennsauken (twp)	34,764	35,737	35,923	36,169
Perth Amboy (city)	41,967	47,303	49,071	51,076
Piscataway (twp)	47,089	50,482	52,711	55,192
Plainfield (city)	46,567	47,829	48,048	48,283
Rahway (city)	25,325	26,500	26,838	27,194
Randolph (twp)	19,974	24,847	25,864	26,948
Rockaway (twp)	19,668	22,930	25,952	28,796
Sayreville (borough)	34,986	40,377	42,789	45,332
South Brunswick (twp)	25,792	37,734	41,061	44,355
Stafford (twp)	13,325	22,532	25,147	27,843
Teaneck (twp)	37,825	39,260	40,406	41,593
Toms River (cdp)	73,186	86,327	91,711	97,745
Trenton (city)	88,675	85,403	85,338	85,887
Union (twp)	50,189	54,405	56,128	57,811
Union City (city)	58,012	67,088	66,325	65,626
Vernon (twp)	21,196	24,686	25,767	26,995
Vineland (city)	54,780	56,271	58,372	60,593
Voorhees (twp)	24,559	28,126	28,741	29,316
Wall (twp)	20,256	25,261	26,318	27,393
Washington (twp)	41,960	47,114	51,774	56,463
Wayne (twp)	47,025	54,069	56,420	58,773
West Milford (twp)	25,631	26,410	28,568	30,605
West New York (town)	38,125	45,768	46,072	46,325
West Orange (twp)	39,103	44,943	44,854	44,814
West Windsor (twp)	16,021	21,907	25,191	28,307
Westfield (town)	28,911	29,644	30,066	30,550
Willingboro (twp)	36,291	33,008	33,118	33,563
Winslow (twp)	30,087	34,611	35,465	36,338
Woodbridge (twp)	93,086	97,203	102,335	107,774

Physical Characteristics

Place	Density (persons per square mile)	Land Area (square miles)	Water Area (square miles)	Elevation (feet)
Atlantic City (city)	3,572.1	11.35	6.00	8
Bayonne (city)	10,707.1	5.63	5.63	49
Belleville (twp)	10,576.5	3.34	0.07	140
Bergenfield (borough)	9,037.1	2.90	0.00	93
Berkeley (twp)	998.5	42.90	12.90	n/a
Bernards (twp)	1,116.6	24.00	0.01	n/a
Bloomfield (twp)	8,799.5	5.32	0.01	131
Brick (twp)	3,026.4	26.23	6.03	n/a
Bridgewater (twp)	1,371.2	32.45	0.09	n/a
Camden (city)	9,136.5	8.82	1.56	33
Cherry Hill (twp)	2,968.2	24.25	0.11	40
Clifton (city)	7,054.4	11.30	0.10	233
Deptford (twp)	1,646.5	17.50	0.08	n/a
Dover (twp)	2,324.5	40.97	11.96	n/a
East Brunswick (twp)	2,233.5	21.95	0.43	n/a
East Orange (city)	17,511.1	3.93	0.00	166
East Windsor (twp)	1,749.8	15.65	0.05	n/a
Edison (twp)	3,358.1	30.12	0.57	100
Egg Harbor (twp)	553.1	67.35	7.61	n/a
Elizabeth (city)	10,161.7	12.22	1.43	38
Englewood (city)	5,295.6	4.92	0.01	44
Evesham (twp)	1,626.2	29.54	0.17	n/a
Ewing (twp)	2,416.2	15.33	0.27	140
Fair Lawn (borough)	6,106.9	5.17	0.05	100
Fort Lee (borough)	14,867.6	2.53	0.35	313
Franklin (twp)	1,209.2	46.77	0.07	n/a
Freehold (twp)	892.4	38.45	0.08	178
Galloway (twp)	389.6	90.49	24.31	n/a
Garfield (city)	13,917.8	2.13	0.06	36
Gloucester (twp)	2,869.3	23.22	0.10	n/a
Hackensack (city)	10,591.0	4.12	0.19	22
Hamilton (twp)	2,306.7	39.45	0.92	n/a
Hillsborough (twp)	697.1	54.69	0.10	100
Hoboken (city)	31,113.2	1.28	0.70	5
Howell (twp)	830.6	60.91	0.09	n/a
Irvington (twp)	20,161.7	2.96	0.00	160
Jackson (twp)	526.4	100.06	0.75	n/a
Jersey City (city)	15,993.0	14.92	6.20	83
Kearny (town)	4,327.6	9.14	1.05	125
Lacey (twp)	315.9	84.00	14.52	109
Lakewood (twp)	2,723.9	24.82	0.30	91
Lakewood (cdp)	5,663.1	7.16	0.20	n/a
Lawrence (twp)	1,433.6	22.14	0.04	60
Linden (city)	3,702.5	10.81	0.41	10
Livingston (twp)	2,035.4	13.88	0.19	307
Long Branch (city)	6,073.9	5.22	0.97	19
Manalapan (twp)	1,178.2	30.82	0.05	160
Manchester (twp)	527.7	82.60	0.29	n/a
Marlboro (twp)	1,307.8	30.59	0.00	173
Mercerville-Ham. Sq. (cdp)	3,458.4	7.71	0.00	n/a

Place	Density (persons per square mile)	Land Area (square miles)	Water Area (square miles)	Elevation (feet)
Middletown (twp)	1,628.6	41.12	18.23	100
Millville (city)	646.1	42.35	2.19	37
Monroe (twp)	792.1	41.94	0.10	n/a
Monroe (twp)	673.6	46.55	0.38	n/a
Montclair (twp)	6,155.9	6.30	0.00	300
Mount Laurel (twp)	1,863.1	21.81	0.12	80
Mount Olive (twp)	861.0	30.35	0.70	960
Neptune (twp)	3,497.6	8.22	0.54	n/a
New Brunswick (city)	9,685.9	5.23	0.52	80
Newark (city)	11,823.0	23.80	2.17	95
North Bergen (twp)	11,191.3	5.20	0.42	200
North Brunswick (twp)	3,261.2	12.02	0.23	n/a
Nutley (twp)	8,370.9	3.37	0.06	91
Ocean (twp)	2,559.5	11.03	0.09	n/a
Old Bridge (twp)	1,708.7	38.09	2.57	30
Orange (cdp)	14,706.0	2.21	0.00	204
Paramus (borough)	2,569.1	10.47	0.00	56
Parsippany-Troy Hills (twp)	2,160.3	23.94	1.48	n/a
Passaic (city)	22,071.1	3.11	0.10	115
Paterson (city)	17,983.3	8.44	0.29	70
Pemberton (twp)	474.6	61.68	0.82	60
Pennsauken (twp)	3,410.0	10.53	1.65	65
Perth Amboy (city)	10,261.7	4.78	1.20	65
Piscataway (twp)	2,807.3	18.78	0.20	100
Plainfield (city)	7,950.0	6.04	0.00	110
Rahway (city)	6,727.5	3.99	0.05	20
Randolph (twp)	1,233.7	20.96	0.12	n/a
Rockaway (twp)	606.1	42.82	3.17	534
Sayreville (borough)	2,691.1	15.90	2.85	41
South Brunswick (twp)	1,004.9	40.86	0.24	n/a
Stafford (twp)	540.5	46.53	8.29	n/a
Teaneck (twp)	6,675.5	6.05	0.20	92
Toms River (cdp)	2,329.4	39.37	1.24	40
Trenton (city)	11,145.1	7.66	0.49	54
Union (twp)	6,157.1	9.12	0.00	93
Union City (city)	52,375.3	1.27	0.00	175
Vernon (twp)	376.7	68.39	2.14	564
Vineland (city)	849.8	68.69	0.29	106
Voorhees (twp)	2,477.0	11.60	0.03	n/a
Wall (twp)	859.6	30.62	0.80	n/a
Washington (twp)	2,422.7	21.37	0.12	n/a
Wayne (twp)	2,368.2	23.82	1.37	180
West Milford (twp)	378.7	75.44	4.97	710
West New York (town)	45,294.0	1.02	0.31	185
West Orange (twp)	3,701.3	12.12	0.11	500
West Windsor (twp)	968.7	26.01	0.32	n/a
Westfield (town)	4,465.8	6.73	0.02	126
Willingboro (twp)	4,307.1	7.69	0.33	60
Winslow (twp)	614.7	57.70	0.40	114
Woodbridge (twp)	4,447.6	23.01	1.21	34

NOTE: Population Density figures as of 2005; Land Area and Water Area figures as of 2000.

Population by Race/Hispanic Origin

Place	White Alone[1] (%)	Black Alone[1] (%)	Asian Alone[1] (%)	Hispanic[2] (%)
Atlantic City (city)	25.6	41.3	12.0	28.8
Bayonne (city)	76.6	5.5	4.5	20.3
Belleville (twp)	64.9	5.9	12.5	30.3
Bergenfield (borough)	54.5	8.2	25.3	21.7
Berkeley (twp)	96.6	1.5	0.5	3.0
Bernards (twp)	85.0	1.6	11.7	3.1
Bloomfield (twp)	65.1	13.9	9.0	18.8
Brick (twp)	95.2	1.2	1.3	4.7
Bridgewater (twp)	81.0	2.5	13.9	6.2
Camden (city)	16.5	51.8	2.7	42.3
Cherry Hill (twp)	83.1	5.3	9.2	2.9
Clifton (city)	70.8	3.6	7.2	26.0
Deptford (twp)	81.3	13.9	1.9	3.5
Dover (twp)	92.3	2.2	2.8	5.8
East Brunswick (twp)	73.1	3.1	19.5	5.1
East Orange (city)	3.7	89.0	0.4	5.5
East Windsor (twp)	68.8	9.4	12.8	18.3
Edison (twp)	51.7	7.4	35.6	7.7
Egg Harbor (twp)	78.4	10.1	5.5	8.1
Elizabeth (city)	53.5	20.1	2.0	56.1
Englewood (city)	40.7	38.8	5.5	25.7
Evesham (twp)	89.7	3.5	4.9	2.5
Ewing (twp)	65.7	26.8	2.9	5.3
Fair Lawn (borough)	89.8	0.8	5.9	6.9
Fort Lee (borough)	57.0	2.0	36.4	9.5
Franklin (twp)	47.7	28.5	16.3	10.1
Freehold (twp)	86.1	5.2	5.6	6.1
Galloway (twp)	74.5	10.5	9.4	7.1
Garfield (city)	77.7	3.4	3.2	26.0
Gloucester (twp)	79.3	14.5	2.7	3.9
Hackensack (city)	48.4	24.5	9.0	31.5
Hamilton (twp)	82.3	9.3	3.2	6.5
Hillsborough (twp)	83.4	4.1	9.0	5.9
Hoboken (city)	83.5	3.8	3.7	16.3
Howell (twp)	89.3	3.7	3.7	6.0
Irvington (twp)	8.0	82.9	0.8	8.3
Jackson (twp)	90.4	4.3	2.2	6.7
Jersey City (city)	32.3	27.6	16.9	29.3
Kearny (town)	73.0	4.9	5.2	30.8
Lacey (twp)	97.6	0.4	0.6	2.5
Lakewood (twp)	78.3	11.7	1.5	17.4
Lakewood (cdp)	79.4	10.2	1.0	20.0
Lawrence (twp)	75.4	9.5	10.8	5.5
Linden (city)	61.9	24.5	2.6	18.8
Livingston (twp)	81.7	1.2	15.4	3.0
Long Branch (city)	66.7	18.2	1.7	24.4
Manalapan (twp)	91.4	1.7	5.0	4.1
Manchester (twp)	93.9	3.0	1.0	3.1
Marlboro (twp)	81.0	1.8	15.6	3.4
Mercerville-Ham. Sq. (cdp)	93.1	1.7	2.9	3.2

Place	White Alone[1] (%)	Black Alone[1] (%)	Asian Alone[1] (%)	Hispanic[2] (%)
Middletown (twp)	94.7	1.1	2.6	3.8
Millville (city)	72.3	17.6	0.9	13.0
Monroe (twp)	92.2	3.1	2.8	2.9
Monroe (twp)	84.4	11.3	1.4	3.1
Montclair (twp)	59.1	32.0	3.4	6.3
Mount Laurel (twp)	84.6	8.1	4.7	2.7
Mount Olive (twp)	83.7	4.5	7.7	7.3
Neptune (twp)	53.4	40.0	1.2	6.5
New Brunswick (city)	46.7	20.3	5.9	47.4
Newark (city)	26.6	52.1	1.2	31.4
North Bergen (twp)	65.7	3.0	6.3	62.7
North Brunswick (twp)	55.7	16.8	17.6	13.1
Nutley (twp)	87.0	1.9	7.5	8.5
Ocean (twp)	81.7	5.9	7.7	5.7
Old Bridge (twp)	74.9	6.3	13.2	9.4
Orange (cdp)	12.1	75.1	1.3	13.8
Paramus (borough)	75.3	1.3	20.5	5.9
Parsippany-Troy Hills (twp)	70.0	3.1	21.7	8.6
Passaic (city)	32.7	12.3	4.6	69.0
Paterson (city)	28.6	32.1	1.9	54.3
Pemberton (twp)	63.1	25.3	3.1	9.8
Pennsauken (twp)	52.1	28.2	5.1	18.7
Perth Amboy (city)	43.1	9.7	1.8	75.4
Piscataway (twp)	42.1	21.1	29.8	9.4
Plainfield (city)	21.1	59.4	0.9	30.8
Rahway (city)	54.1	30.7	3.9	17.7
Randolph (twp)	83.7	2.2	10.9	5.9
Rockaway (twp)	87.0	3.0	6.5	7.6
Sayreville (borough)	70.0	10.5	13.9	9.2
South Brunswick (twp)	64.0	8.7	22.8	6.2
Stafford (twp)	96.2	1.0	1.1	3.1
Teaneck (twp)	52.4	30.1	7.9	12.9
Toms River (cdp)	92.0	2.3	2.9	6.0
Trenton (city)	29.0	52.9	1.1	25.3
Union (twp)	60.8	24.2	9.0	11.8
Union City (city)	56.6	3.5	2.1	84.2
Vernon (twp)	95.6	1.1	0.9	5.2
Vineland (city)	65.2	14.4	1.3	33.4
Voorhees (twp)	75.6	9.4	12.1	2.8
Wall (twp)	96.9	0.6	1.4	1.8
Washington (twp)	89.1	5.7	3.4	2.4
Wayne (twp)	88.7	1.9	6.3	6.3
West Milford (twp)	94.5	1.3	1.0	4.1
West New York (town)	58.5	3.7	3.2	79.5
West Orange (twp)	62.6	20.8	8.5	12.6
West Windsor (twp)	65.1	2.7	29.0	4.5
Westfield (town)	89.7	3.8	4.2	3.6
Willingboro (twp)	17.9	72.8	1.8	6.6
Winslow (twp)	61.9	32.2	1.3	5.0
Woodbridge (twp)	63.7	9.8	18.8	11.5

NOTE: Data as of 2005; (1) Figures are not in combination with any other race; (2) Persons of Hispanic Origin may be of any race

Avg. Household Size, Median Age, Male/Female Ratio & Foreign Born

Place	Average Household Size (persons)	Median Age (years)	Male/Female Ratio (males per 100 females)	Foreign Born (%)
Atlantic City (city)	2.58	35.3	97.4	24.7
Bayonne (city)	2.42	39.5	91.0	20.2
Belleville (twp)	2.64	37.9	93.9	26.8
Bergenfield (borough)	2.97	38.8	92.3	32.1
Berkeley (twp)	2.01	65.6	81.1	6.7
Bernards (twp)	2.69	40.1	95.4	12.5
Bloomfield (twp)	2.52	38.6	91.7	22.8
Brick (twp)	2.55	39.6	91.4	5.7
Bridgewater (twp)	2.72	39.3	93.7	15.8
Camden (city)	3.29	27.9	95.1	8.9
Cherry Hill (twp)	2.63	43.1	91.7	12.5
Clifton (city)	2.64	39.8	92.2	29.2
Deptford (twp)	2.63	38.6	94.1	4.2
Dover (twp)	2.64	40.2	93.2	7.0
East Brunswick (twp)	2.84	39.8	94.7	23.5
East Orange (city)	2.68	34.1	83.2	18.3
East Windsor (twp)	2.63	36.8	95.9	23.1
Edison (twp)	2.78	37.4	96.8	33.1
Egg Harbor (twp)	2.74	36.9	95.1	8.4
Elizabeth (city)	3.02	33.7	98.7	43.9
Englewood (city)	2.85	38.8	89.8	30.8
Evesham (twp)	2.65	37.0	94.0	6.5
Ewing (twp)	2.80	38.0	93.5	8.2
Fair Lawn (borough)	2.69	43.1	91.4	26.8
Fort Lee (borough)	2.16	43.3	88.8	44.7
Franklin (twp)	2.64	37.6	92.7	23.2
Freehold (twp)	2.89	39.4	98.0	11.2
Galloway (twp)	2.89	34.9	92.3	11.2
Garfield (city)	2.70	37.3	95.9	39.1
Gloucester (twp)	2.74	35.9	95.1	4.9
Hackensack (city)	2.38	38.2	99.3	33.8
Hamilton (twp)	2.57	40.2	91.8	9.5
Hillsborough (twp)	2.90	36.8	98.2	12.1
Hoboken (city)	1.95	32.9	104.5	14.5
Howell (twp)	3.04	36.7	95.5	8.9
Irvington (twp)	2.74	33.0	88.6	24.2
Jackson (twp)	3.03	35.7	95.8	6.3
Jersey City (city)	2.70	34.1	96.5	34.0
Kearny (town)	3.02	36.4	107.8	38.2
Lacey (twp)	2.70	38.7	95.5	2.7
Lakewood (twp)	3.08	31.5	92.2	13.8
Lakewood (cdp)	4.07	23.9	102.0	15.6
Lawrence (twp)	2.65	37.6	89.0	17.5
Linden (city)	2.65	39.1	91.3	26.3
Livingston (twp)	2.91	41.3	94.7	18.8
Long Branch (city)	2.50	36.2	95.0	19.7
Manalapan (twp)	3.10	38.5	92.9	10.4
Manchester (twp)	1.86	67.5	74.1	7.7
Marlboro (twp)	3.16	38.3	98.1	15.4
Mercerville-Ham. Sq. (cdp)	2.78	42.0	92.0	6.9

Place	Average Household Size (persons)	Median Age (years)	Male/Female Ratio (males per 100 females)	Foreign Born (%)
Middletown (twp)	2.81	39.8	95.2	6.4
Millville (city)	2.67	34.9	90.4	2.2
Monroe (twp)	2.22	59.8	85.3	8.1
Monroe (twp)	2.71	38.5	94.2	2.9
Montclair (twp)	2.59	38.4	87.1	14.5
Mount Laurel (twp)	2.39	40.0	89.8	6.9
Mount Olive (twp)	2.66	35.7	100.8	13.0
Neptune (twp)	2.49	40.7	88.1	7.3
New Brunswick (city)	3.78	24.8	98.3	33.4
Newark (city)	2.98	32.0	95.2	24.1
North Bergen (twp)	2.77	37.5	92.4	46.8
North Brunswick (twp)	2.67	36.6	99.2	24.4
Nutley (twp)	2.48	40.7	89.9	14.7
Ocean (twp)	2.60	39.4	93.3	15.7
Old Bridge (twp)	2.81	37.5	96.2	18.4
Orange (cdp)	2.81	33.5	87.3	31.3
Paramus (borough)	3.15	44.5	94.8	25.1
Parsippany-Troy Hills (twp)	2.55	39.6	98.0	26.8
Passaic (city)	3.59	29.3	100.0	45.8
Paterson (city)	3.41	31.1	95.9	32.8
Pemberton (twp)	2.78	35.5	96.6	7.1
Pennsauken (twp)	2.90	37.1	92.5	7.9
Perth Amboy (city)	3.31	32.3	99.2	35.7
Piscataway (twp)	3.04	34.8	98.3	29.8
Plainfield (city)	3.19	33.8	96.5	23.7
Rahway (city)	2.65	38.2	92.0	17.2
Randolph (twp)	2.85	37.4	98.5	16.1
Rockaway (twp)	2.82	38.7	97.9	13.2
Sayreville (borough)	2.70	37.6	97.2	20.1
South Brunswick (twp)	2.85	35.8	94.5	21.6
Stafford (twp)	2.63	40.0	94.8	4.4
Teaneck (twp)	2.94	38.9	90.6	24.0
Toms River (cdp)	2.69	39.7	93.2	7.1
Trenton (city)	2.89	33.0	99.1	14.1
Union (twp)	2.82	39.7	88.8	24.6
Union City (city)	2.97	34.2	100.8	58.7
Vernon (twp)	2.90	36.4	102.3	5.1
Vineland (city)	2.79	37.1	92.8	8.1
Voorhees (twp)	2.65	38.0	92.6	13.4
Wall (twp)	2.64	41.6	93.6	4.0
Washington (twp)	2.95	37.1	94.1	4.8
Wayne (twp)	2.90	40.5	90.3	16.3
West Milford (twp)	2.85	38.0	99.8	5.8
West New York (town)	2.74	35.9	96.7	65.2
West Orange (twp)	2.72	40.5	89.3	25.6
West Windsor (twp)	3.05	37.0	97.9	22.4
Westfield (town)	2.79	39.1	92.4	9.1
Willingboro (twp)	3.01	38.3	89.7	8.2
Winslow (twp)	2.95	35.4	97.1	3.8
Woodbridge (twp)	2.82	38.0	101.1	21.5

NOTE: Average Household Size, Median Age, and Male/Female Ratio figures as of 2005. Foreign Born figures as of 2000.

Five Largest Ancestry Groups

Place	Group 1	Group 2	Group 3	Group 4	Group 5
Atlantic City (city)	Other (65.1%)	Italian (4.9%)	Irish (4.1%)	American (2.4%)	German (2.0%)
Bayonne (city)	Other (26.2%)	Italian (20.1%)	Irish (18.8%)	Polish (17.9%)	German (6.1%)
Belleville (twp)	Other (37.1%)	Italian (30.9%)	Irish (9.4%)	German (6.9%)	Polish (4.5%)
Bergenfield (borough)	Other (42.1%)	Italian (16.8%)	Irish (16.2%)	German (10.7%)	English (3.6%)
Berkeley (twp)	Italian (29.4%)	Irish (21.4%)	German (17.3%)	Polish (9.2%)	English (6.8%)
Bernards (twp)	Irish (23.5%)	Italian (19.1%)	German (18.7%)	Other (13.3%)	English (11.0%)
Bloomfield (twp)	Other (30.2%)	Italian (26.4%)	Irish (13.9%)	German (10.2%)	Polish (7.0%)
Brick (twp)	Italian (30.4%)	Irish (28.9%)	German (20.8%)	Polish (9.2%)	English (8.5%)
Bridgewater (twp)	Italian (21.3%)	Other (19.7%)	Irish (17.1%)	German (16.7%)	Polish (11.8%)
Camden (city)	Other (70.8%)	Irish (2.0%)	German (1.6%)	Italian (1.5%)	African (1.3%)
Cherry Hill (twp)	Other (21.0%)	Irish (17.0%)	Italian (16.8%)	German (13.7%)	Russian (8.0%)
Clifton (city)	Other (29.7%)	Italian (19.2%)	Polish (14.6%)	Irish (9.8%)	German (8.7%)
Deptford (twp)	Irish (28.1%)	Italian (22.9%)	German (21.1%)	Other (15.9%)	English (9.8%)
Dover (twp)	Italian (31.5%)	Irish (24.2%)	German (18.8%)	Other (10.4%)	Polish (9.0%)
East Brunswick (twp)	Other (26.7%)	Italian (15.0%)	Irish (13.7%)	Polish (11.5%)	German (10.6%)
East Orange (city)	Other (61.8%)	Jamaican (4.8%)	Haitian (4.1%)	African (2.3%)	Guyanese (2.1%)
East Windsor (twp)	Other (34.1%)	Irish (12.6%)	Italian (11.8%)	German (11.5%)	Polish (9.5%)
Edison (twp)	Other (41.0%)	Italian (14.8%)	Irish (11.0%)	German (8.7%)	Polish (7.4%)
Egg Harbor (twp)	Irish (23.1%)	Other (23.0%)	German (18.2%)	Italian (17.4%)	English (10.4%)
Elizabeth (city)	Other (59.4%)	Portuguese (5.5%)	Italian (5.0%)	Polish (3.5%)	Irish (3.3%)
Englewood (city)	Other (55.5%)	Jamaican (5.0%)	Italian (4.5%)	American (3.6%)	Irish (3.6%)
Evesham (twp)	Irish (27.8%)	Italian (26.6%)	German (20.4%)	Other (11.3%)	English (9.9%)
Ewing (twp)	Other (27.4%)	Italian (16.7%)	Irish (15.4%)	German (14.0%)	English (10.1%)
Fair Lawn (borough)	Other (19.7%)	Italian (19.7%)	Russian (11.7%)	German (10.0%)	Irish (9.9%)
Fort Lee (borough)	Other (44.7%)	Italian (11.7%)	Russian (8.1%)	Irish (4.9%)	German (4.1%)
Franklin (twp)	Other (37.3%)	Italian (12.0%)	Irish (10.0%)	German (8.5%)	Polish (6.9%)
Freehold (twp)	Italian (26.1%)	Irish (18.2%)	Other (17.0%)	German (12.9%)	Polish (10.2%)
Galloway (twp)	Other (23.8%)	Irish (20.7%)	Italian (19.5%)	German (19.1%)	English (8.2%)
Garfield (city)	Polish (24.9%)	Other (24.4%)	Italian (19.5%)	Irish (6.7%)	German (5.5%)
Gloucester (twp)	Italian (29.3%)	Irish (25.8%)	German (19.1%)	Other (17.1%)	English (8.2%)
Hackensack (city)	Other (48.7%)	Italian (13.7%)	Irish (7.4%)	German (5.7%)	Polish (3.3%)
Hamilton (twp)	Italian (26.0%)	Irish (18.3%)	German (16.5%)	Other (14.3%)	Polish (12.3%)
Hillsborough (twp)	Italian (22.7%)	Irish (18.1%)	Other (17.3%)	German (16.6%)	Polish (13.1%)
Hoboken (city)	Other (26.6%)	Italian (20.8%)	Irish (19.2%)	German (10.7%)	English (5.5%)
Howell (twp)	Italian (30.7%)	Irish (24.2%)	German (16.5%)	Other (14.6%)	Polish (9.9%)
Irvington (twp)	Other (57.3%)	Haitian (9.6%)	Jamaican (4.3%)	African (2.3%)	American (1.9%)
Jackson (twp)	Italian (26.4%)	Irish (23.5%)	German (17.7%)	Other (13.3%)	Polish (11.2%)
Jersey City (city)	Other (60.0%)	Italian (6.6%)	Irish (5.6%)	Polish (3.0%)	German (2.7%)
Kearny (town)	Other (34.6%)	Irish (13.4%)	Italian (12.1%)	Portuguese (11.8%)	Polish (7.8%)
Lacey (twp)	Italian (31.1%)	Irish (26.2%)	German (20.8%)	Polish (9.7%)	English (9.4%)
Lakewood (twp)	Other (31.2%)	Italian (9.9%)	Irish (9.2%)	German (7.6%)	Polish (6.1%)
Lakewood (cdp)	Other (37.0%)	American (6.0%)	Polish (5.6%)	Italian (3.6%)	German (3.4%)
Lawrence (twp)	Other (20.6%)	Italian (17.1%)	Irish (14.6%)	German (12.5%)	Polish (11.7%)
Linden (city)	Other (31.1%)	Polish (18.0%)	Italian (10.3%)	Irish (9.0%)	German (6.8%)
Livingston (twp)	Other (24.8%)	Italian (17.7%)	Irish (10.3%)	Russian (9.8%)	German (7.4%)
Long Branch (city)	Other (36.9%)	Italian (17.5%)	Irish (11.2%)	German (6.6%)	English (4.1%)
Manalapan (twp)	Italian (27.9%)	Other (17.2%)	Irish (13.1%)	Polish (11.7%)	Russian (10.0%)
Manchester (twp)	Irish (21.4%)	Italian (20.6%)	German (20.0%)	English (9.8%)	Other (8.7%)
Marlboro (twp)	Other (25.0%)	Italian (20.1%)	Russian (10.8%)	Irish (10.6%)	Polish (10.6%)
Mercerville-Ham. Sq. (cdp)	Italian (29.1%)	Irish (21.8%)	German (18.4%)	Polish (13.9%)	English (12.8%)

Place	Group 1	Group 2	Group 3	Group 4	Group 5
Middletown (twp)	Irish (32.8%)	Italian (28.9%)	German (17.4%)	English (8.8%)	Polish (8.7%)
Millville (city)	Other (26.5%)	German (17.4%)	Irish (15.7%)	Italian (13.6%)	English (13.0%)
Monroe (twp)	Italian (20.7%)	Irish (14.4%)	Other (13.7%)	Polish (12.7%)	German (12.2%)
Monroe (twp)	Irish (25.7%)	Italian (24.1%)	German (23.0%)	Other (15.2%)	English (9.6%)
Montclair (twp)	Other (32.9%)	Irish (13.7%)	Italian (10.1%)	German (9.2%)	English (7.6%)
Mount Laurel (twp)	Irish (21.1%)	Italian (19.7%)	German (19.0%)	Other (15.9%)	English (12.0%)
Mount Olive (twp)	Irish (22.7%)	Italian (22.7%)	German (19.6%)	Other (18.2%)	Polish (8.8%)
Neptune (twp)	Other (35.3%)	Irish (14.5%)	Italian (12.3%)	German (11.7%)	English (7.5%)
New Brunswick (city)	Other (55.6%)	Italian (7.3%)	Irish (7.0%)	German (5.3%)	Polish (3.5%)
Newark (city)	Other (61.5%)	Portuguese (5.8%)	Italian (2.6%)	Brazilian (2.1%)	American (1.8%)
North Bergen (twp)	Other (63.8%)	Italian (10.5%)	Irish (5.7%)	German (4.5%)	American (2.6%)
North Brunswick (twp)	Other (34.7%)	Italian (16.9%)	Irish (12.4%)	German (8.7%)	Polish (6.8%)
Nutley (twp)	Italian (44.5%)	Irish (18.2%)	Other (16.0%)	German (11.6%)	Polish (7.0%)
Ocean (twp)	Italian (21.0%)	Other (19.2%)	Irish (18.2%)	German (12.9%)	English (7.2%)
Old Bridge (twp)	Other (24.6%)	Italian (24.4%)	Irish (20.5%)	German (11.4%)	Polish (9.6%)
Orange (cdp)	Other (51.7%)	Haitian (9.9%)	Jamaican (3.8%)	Italian (3.2%)	American (3.2%)
Paramus (borough)	Other (24.1%)	Italian (23.8%)	Irish (14.4%)	German (12.6%)	Polish (6.8%)
Parsippany-Troy Hills (twp)	Other (29.3%)	Italian (20.9%)	Irish (15.2%)	German (12.9%)	Polish (7.0%)
Passaic (city)	Other (73.0%)	Polish (3.5%)	Italian (2.6%)	American (2.3%)	Irish (1.1%)
Paterson (city)	Other (69.4%)	Italian (4.7%)	Jamaican (3.2%)	American (3.2%)	Irish (1.6%)
Pemberton (twp)	Other (34.2%)	German (16.1%)	Irish (15.5%)	Italian (8.8%)	English (7.4%)
Pennsauken (twp)	Other (36.8%)	Irish (18.4%)	Italian (14.3%)	German (14.3%)	English (6.8%)
Perth Amboy (city)	Other (70.1%)	Polish (5.1%)	Italian (2.9%)	Irish (2.0%)	Hungarian (1.9%)
Piscataway (twp)	Other (48.3%)	Italian (12.3%)	Irish (9.4%)	German (8.7%)	Polish (6.7%)
Plainfield (city)	Other (70.0%)	Jamaican (3.0%)	Italian (2.5%)	Irish (2.2%)	German (2.2%)
Rahway (city)	Other (39.3%)	Italian (12.0%)	Irish (11.4%)	German (10.0%)	Polish (9.5%)
Randolph (twp)	Other (20.8%)	Italian (19.3%)	Irish (17.0%)	German (16.2%)	Polish (7.2%)
Rockaway (twp)	Italian (23.4%)	Irish (19.3%)	Other (15.7%)	German (15.2%)	Polish (10.0%)
Sayreville (borough)	Other (23.1%)	Polish (20.1%)	Italian (18.6%)	Irish (18.5%)	German (10.7%)
South Brunswick (twp)	Other (30.9%)	Italian (19.2%)	Irish (14.0%)	German (13.4%)	Polish (8.1%)
Stafford (twp)	Irish (29.4%)	Italian (24.7%)	German (23.0%)	English (11.2%)	Polish (9.1%)
Teaneck (twp)	Other (43.0%)	Italian (6.2%)	German (6.0%)	Russian (5.3%)	Irish (5.1%)
Toms River (cdp)	Italian (31.5%)	Irish (24.1%)	German (18.8%)	Other (10.7%)	Polish (8.9%)
Trenton (city)	Other (55.4%)	Italian (7.3%)	Irish (4.5%)	Polish (3.8%)	German (3.7%)
Union (twp)	Other (28.8%)	Italian (17.2%)	German (10.2%)	Irish (9.9%)	Polish (9.0%)
Union City (city)	Other (79.9%)	Italian (4.5%)	American (2.5%)	Irish (2.0%)	German (1.6%)
Vernon (twp)	Irish (28.4%)	Italian (26.7%)	German (25.5%)	Polish (9.5%)	English (8.1%)
Vineland (city)	Other (37.5%)	Italian (22.8%)	German (9.6%)	Irish (8.4%)	English (5.9%)
Voorhees (twp)	Other (25.1%)	Italian (19.5%)	Irish (18.1%)	German (14.3%)	English (8.3%)
Wall (twp)	Irish (34.9%)	Italian (25.7%)	German (20.9%)	English (11.5%)	Polish (8.2%)
Washington (twp)	Italian (33.9%)	Irish (28.9%)	German (20.0%)	Other (11.4%)	English (9.8%)
Wayne (twp)	Italian (29.9%)	Irish (15.9%)	Other (14.7%)	German (12.9%)	Polish (9.1%)
West Milford (twp)	Italian (26.3%)	Irish (25.4%)	German (24.7%)	English (10.5%)	Polish (9.7%)
West New York (town)	Other (71.9%)	Italian (3.9%)	American (2.6%)	German (1.7%)	Irish (1.7%)
West Orange (twp)	Other (30.0%)	Italian (16.7%)	Irish (10.9%)	German (6.8%)	Russian (5.8%)
West Windsor (twp)	Other (30.9%)	Irish (15.3%)	Italian (14.5%)	German (12.8%)	English (10.0%)
Westfield (town)	Irish (22.9%)	Italian (20.1%)	German (17.1%)	Other (13.7%)	English (11.2%)
Willingboro (twp)	Other (64.2%)	German (6.9%)	Irish (6.0%)	English (3.9%)	Italian (3.5%)
Winslow (twp)	Other (31.0%)	Italian (20.1%)	Irish (19.6%)	German (17.3%)	English (6.7%)
Woodbridge (twp)	Other (29.2%)	Italian (18.2%)	Irish (16.8%)	Polish (11.0%)	German (10.9%)

NOTE: Data as of 2000; "Other" includes Hispanic and race groups. Please refer to the Explanation of Data for more information.

Marriage Status

Place	Never Married (%)	Now Married (%)	Widowed (%)	Divorced (%)
Atlantic City (city)	38.8	40.5	9.6	11.2
Bayonne (city)	32.1	49.8	10.5	7.6
Belleville (twp)	32.0	51.9	7.8	8.2
Bergenfield (borough)	26.4	59.5	7.9	6.2
Berkeley (twp)	13.1	62.8	18.6	5.6
Bernards (twp)	19.4	68.0	5.8	6.8
Bloomfield (twp)	32.1	53.0	7.3	7.6
Brick (twp)	22.2	59.9	9.2	8.7
Bridgewater (twp)	20.1	67.7	6.3	5.9
Camden (city)	47.8	36.6	6.4	9.2
Cherry Hill (twp)	22.4	62.3	8.7	6.5
Clifton (city)	26.9	56.0	9.7	7.5
Deptford (twp)	27.1	57.0	8.3	7.5
Dover (twp)	24.0	59.4	8.6	8.0
East Brunswick (twp)	22.2	66.6	5.7	5.5
East Orange (city)	43.9	37.6	8.9	9.7
East Windsor (twp)	24.8	60.7	5.7	8.8
Edison (twp)	25.5	62.7	5.8	6.0
Egg Harbor (twp)	24.2	59.4	6.4	10.0
Elizabeth (city)	35.5	49.6	6.3	8.6
Englewood (city)	29.6	53.4	7.7	9.4
Evesham (twp)	23.3	63.6	5.3	7.8
Ewing (twp)	35.6	49.8	7.2	7.4
Fair Lawn (borough)	21.9	63.1	9.0	5.9
Fort Lee (borough)	23.2	59.1	9.1	8.6
Franklin (twp)	28.6	57.0	6.4	8.0
Freehold (twp)	20.2	65.6	7.5	6.8
Galloway (twp)	27.8	57.3	5.3	9.6
Garfield (city)	30.8	52.7	8.6	7.9
Gloucester (twp)	28.4	58.4	5.3	7.9
Hackensack (city)	35.3	46.5	6.9	11.3
Hamilton (twp)	25.8	58.2	8.3	7.7
Hillsborough (twp)	21.9	67.6	3.9	6.6
Hoboken (city)	56.1	33.1	5.0	5.7
Howell (twp)	21.6	66.3	6.3	5.8
Irvington (twp)	44.7	40.1	6.8	8.4
Jackson (twp)	22.1	64.3	6.2	7.4
Jersey City (city)	40.0	45.9	6.9	7.2
Kearny (town)	33.0	53.4	6.7	7.0
Lacey (twp)	20.0	64.2	8.5	7.2
Lakewood (twp)	23.7	58.3	11.2	6.8
Lakewood (cdp)	27.9	60.2	6.1	5.8
Lawrence (twp)	28.5	57.4	6.6	7.4
Linden (city)	29.6	53.0	9.7	7.7
Livingston (twp)	19.0	70.4	6.4	4.2
Long Branch (city)	35.9	46.4	6.4	11.2
Manalapan (twp)	20.3	69.1	6.9	3.7
Manchester (twp)	12.4	58.4	22.4	6.9
Marlboro (twp)	19.3	72.9	5.0	2.8
Mercerville-Ham. Sq. (cdp)	21.2	64.8	8.9	5.1

Place	Never Married (%)	Now Married (%)	Widowed (%)	Divorced (%)
Middletown (twp)	22.2	64.7	7.6	5.5
Millville (city)	30.6	51.6	8.0	9.9
Monroe (twp)	12.7	67.4	15.3	4.6
Monroe (twp)	24.9	60.0	6.7	8.4
Montclair (twp)	31.1	53.7	6.8	8.4
Mount Laurel (twp)	23.0	61.9	7.2	7.9
Mount Olive (twp)	26.2	61.7	4.3	7.9
Neptune (twp)	31.0	48.8	10.1	10.1
New Brunswick (city)	56.5	34.1	3.2	6.1
Newark (city)	43.9	41.2	7.5	7.4
North Bergen (twp)	30.3	53.8	7.8	8.1
North Brunswick (twp)	26.5	60.1	5.4	8.0
Nutley (twp)	26.1	58.1	8.7	7.1
Ocean (twp)	24.2	60.4	6.7	8.7
Old Bridge (twp)	24.4	61.2	6.7	7.8
Orange (cdp)	40.5	41.6	8.1	9.8
Paramus (borough)	22.2	63.5	9.4	4.8
Parsippany-Troy Hills (twp)	26.7	60.5	5.6	7.1
Passaic (city)	38.3	48.9	5.8	7.0
Paterson (city)	39.3	46.3	6.1	8.3
Pemberton (twp)	28.3	56.6	6.4	8.7
Pennsauken (twp)	30.2	54.6	7.5	7.6
Perth Amboy (city)	34.8	50.6	6.2	8.5
Piscataway (twp)	30.8	58.4	4.6	6.2
Plainfield (city)	40.1	44.5	6.6	8.8
Rahway (city)	29.0	54.0	8.6	8.4
Randolph (twp)	22.0	69.5	4.0	4.5
Rockaway (twp)	20.7	68.2	4.4	6.7
Sayreville (borough)	25.9	60.4	6.9	6.8
South Brunswick (twp)	22.2	65.9	4.4	7.5
Stafford (twp)	18.9	67.1	7.7	6.3
Teaneck (twp)	26.1	59.5	7.6	6.8
Toms River (cdp)	24.2	59.5	8.2	8.0
Trenton (city)	42.9	38.7	8.3	10.1
Union (twp)	28.0	55.4	9.9	6.6
Union City (city)	34.1	50.5	6.0	9.3
Vernon (twp)	23.4	65.9	3.9	6.8
Vineland (city)	28.4	53.7	8.3	9.7
Voorhees (twp)	25.6	61.4	5.8	7.3
Wall (twp)	20.9	64.7	7.1	7.3
Washington (twp)	25.3	64.0	5.0	5.6
Wayne (twp)	23.3	61.9	8.8	6.0
West Milford (twp)	22.5	65.7	5.0	6.7
West New York (town)	33.0	51.8	6.3	8.9
West Orange (twp)	25.0	59.9	8.7	6.4
West Windsor (twp)	19.5	72.2	3.3	5.0
Westfield (town)	20.5	68.2	6.5	4.8
Willingboro (twp)	28.8	56.0	6.8	8.4
Winslow (twp)	25.1	61.9	5.2	7.7
Woodbridge (twp)	25.7	58.9	7.9	7.5

NOTE: Data as of 2000

Employment and Building Permits Issued

Place	Unemployment Rate (%)	Total Civilian Labor Force	Single-Family Building Permits	Multi-Family Building Permits
Atlantic City (city)	8.0	17,676	70	31
Bayonne (city)	5.3	29,003	23	46
Belleville (twp)	5.3	18,337	20	34
Bergenfield (borough)	3.5	13,921	16	103
Berkeley (twp)	5.5	12,529	108	3
Bernards (twp)	2.5	13,887	23	0
Bloomfield (twp)	4.3	26,086	1	0
Brick (twp)	4.2	40,405	129	13
Bridgewater (twp)	3.0	24,687	44	6
Camden (city)	10.1	27,051	1	16
Cherry Hill (twp)	2.9	38,277	31	124
Clifton (city)	4.6	40,302	28	94
Deptford (twp)	3.0	15,424	259	0
Dover (twp)	4.8	47,515	252	0
East Brunswick (twp)	3.2	26,686	15	0
East Orange (city)	7.4	29,971	15	53
East Windsor (twp)	2.8	16,591	93	0
Edison (twp)	3.5	55,274	95	42
Egg Harbor (twp)	4.2	20,689	519	0
Elizabeth (city)	6.7	54,199	2	460
Englewood (city)	4.6	13,380	22	663
Evesham (twp)	2.7	27,407	46	0
Ewing (twp)	2.9	20,143	24	0
Fair Lawn (borough)	3.6	16,566	13	14
Fort Lee (borough)	2.8	18,926	29	8
Franklin (twp)	4.0	32,388	518	69
Freehold (twp)	3.2	17,800	26	305
Galloway (twp)	4.5	18,850	348	0
Garfield (city)	6.4	15,665	0	38
Gloucester (twp)	2.4	36,895	181	93
Hackensack (city)	5.0	24,027	3	101
Hamilton (twp)	2.6	51,047	492	5
Hillsborough (twp)	3.0	21,823	15	0
Hoboken (city)	2.6	27,838	19	426
Howell (twp)	3.6	26,350	250	0
Irvington (twp)	6.8	28,162	5	46
Jackson (twp)	3.9	26,517	209	0
Jersey City (city)	5.9	111,108	170	2,908
Kearny (town)	5.2	18,514	0	8
Lacey (twp)	4.6	13,480	63	0
Lakewood (twp)	4.4	23,505	364	0
Lakewood (cdp)	n/a	n/a	n/a	n/a
Lawrence (twp)	2.2	17,641	131	0
Linden (city)	5.2	20,624	36	21
Livingston (twp)	2.6	14,399	85	326
Long Branch (city)	5.2	15,648	7	0
Manalapan (twp)	3.0	18,118	289	0
Manchester (twp)	5.5	11,226	11	13
Marlboro (twp)	2.7	20,147	180	15
Mercerville-Ham. Sq. (cdp)	n/a	n/a	n/a	n/a

Place	Unemployment Rate (%)	Total Civilian Labor Force	Single-Family Building Permits	Multi-Family Building Permits
Middletown (twp)	3.2	35,764	105	0
Millville (city)	7.7	14,303	160	0
Monroe (twp)	4.6	12,089	659	0
Monroe (twp)	5.0	16,488	248	0
Montclair (twp)	3.5	21,345	25	40
Mount Laurel (twp)	3.1	23,193	1	0
Mount Olive (twp)	3.6	14,768	106	0
Neptune (twp)	6.0	14,501	6	155
New Brunswick (city)	4.4	26,563	29	197
Newark (city)	8.3	104,266	376	1,695
North Bergen (twp)	5.4	27,068	28	292
North Brunswick (twp)	3.7	21,752	79	198
Nutley (twp)	3.6	15,358	6	3
Ocean (twp)	3.5	14,535	126	0
Old Bridge (twp)	3.1	34,179	302	318
Orange (cdp)	6.4	14,824	7	102
Paramus (borough)	3.4	12,824	46	15
Parsippany-Troy Hills (twp)	3.0	30,559	48	0
Passaic (city)	6.8	28,204	8	45
Paterson (city)	8.6	58,944	0	0
Pemberton (twp)	5.5	14,780	68	0
Pennsauken (twp)	5.3	17,769	15	79
Perth Amboy (city)	8.5	21,848	21	157
Piscataway (twp)	3.9	29,525	154	76
Plainfield (city)	6.6	25,329	16	2
Rahway (city)	5.0	14,157	130	61
Randolph (twp)	2.8	14,039	35	0
Rockaway (twp)	2.3	14,188	38	133
Sayreville (borough)	3.9	22,678	59	0
South Brunswick (twp)	3.0	22,923	188	0
Stafford (twp)	n/a	n/a	231	84
Teaneck (twp)	3.5	20,460	9	85
Toms River (cdp)	n/a	n/a	n/a	n/a
Trenton (city)	9.3	38,470	7	0
Union (twp)	4.2	28,601	21	16
Union City (city)	6.9	27,816	0	71
Vernon (twp)	3.3	13,755	54	0
Vineland (city)	5.8	29,359	125	14
Voorhees (twp)	2.8	16,079	125	152
Wall (twp)	2.7	13,592	122	93
Washington (twp)	1.8	28,219	65	0
Wayne (twp)	3.2	29,001	24	0
West Milford (twp)	4.0	16,008	47	15
West New York (town)	5.9	19,995	2	294
West Orange (twp)	3.7	23,278	7	0
West Windsor (twp)	n/a	n/a	159	0
Westfield (town)	2.5	15,546	92	0
Willingboro (twp)	5.6	16,798	42	29
Winslow (twp)	5.9	19,418	538	0
Woodbridge (twp)	3.9	52,899	1	0

NOTE: Unemployment Rate and Civilian Labor Force are 2005 annual averages; Building permit data covers 2005; n/a not available.

Employment by Occupation

Place	Sales	Professional	Management	Services	Production	Construction
Atlantic City (city)	22.3	8.3	5.4	48.5	10.4	4.9
Bayonne (city)	32.1	20.2	11.7	14.1	14.0	7.8
Belleville (twp)	31.7	18.8	11.9	15.0	14.4	8.1
Bergenfield (borough)	29.3	23.8	14.2	14.3	11.3	7.0
Berkeley (twp)	33.2	16.7	10.7	14.5	12.1	12.8
Bernards (twp)	23.7	30.2	33.9	5.3	3.8	3.2
Bloomfield (twp)	30.4	24.8	14.0	12.0	12.1	6.6
Brick (twp)	31.0	18.7	12.4	15.0	11.2	11.6
Bridgewater (twp)	25.9	29.7	24.0	7.6	5.9	6.8
Camden (city)	25.1	11.8	4.9	25.5	25.7	6.7
Cherry Hill (twp)	28.4	33.1	19.8	9.5	5.5	3.7
Clifton (city)	30.9	19.6	12.7	11.7	16.6	8.4
Deptford (twp)	29.7	15.4	11.4	13.4	17.6	12.3
Dover (twp)	30.6	21.3	13.0	15.6	9.2	10.1
East Brunswick (twp)	29.9	30.3	19.2	7.6	7.3	5.7
East Orange (city)	32.2	17.0	7.6	22.2	15.1	5.9
East Windsor (twp)	28.9	26.2	19.2	9.6	12.4	3.6
Edison (twp)	28.0	30.2	17.4	8.9	10.2	5.2
Egg Harbor (twp)	25.9	17.1	9.6	27.3	9.2	10.9
Elizabeth (city)	25.9	11.4	6.9	17.8	28.4	9.5
Englewood (city)	27.2	22.7	16.0	16.0	12.4	5.6
Evesham (twp)	31.1	26.8	21.2	9.7	6.1	5.1
Ewing (twp)	30.1	25.0	13.7	15.9	9.5	5.8
Fair Lawn (borough)	29.3	30.7	17.4	9.1	7.8	5.8
Fort Lee (borough)	30.9	26.2	25.4	8.3	5.9	3.3
Franklin (twp)	25.4	30.7	21.0	9.1	8.6	5.1
Freehold (twp)	32.2	25.4	20.4	9.2	6.0	6.6
Galloway (twp)	27.6	17.6	11.2	28.5	7.0	8.2
Garfield (city)	28.2	12.3	8.2	15.5	20.7	14.6
Gloucester (twp)	31.3	20.3	13.6	13.3	11.4	10.1
Hackensack (city)	29.8	21.1	14.5	14.9	13.6	6.1
Hamilton (twp)	30.5	22.3	14.5	13.4	10.8	8.4
Hillsborough (twp)	25.6	29.0	24.3	8.3	6.7	5.7
Hoboken (city)	25.9	30.9	30.1	6.6	4.6	1.9
Howell (twp)	30.8	21.3	17.1	12.6	9.5	8.4
Irvington (twp)	32.5	13.9	7.2	21.7	18.8	5.9
Jackson (twp)	27.3	20.9	14.2	13.8	11.4	12.3
Jersey City (city)	30.5	20.1	12.8	15.9	15.5	5.1
Kearny (town)	29.7	15.5	11.3	15.0	17.0	11.5
Lacey (twp)	29.3	19.5	10.4	16.5	10.1	14.3
Lakewood (twp)	26.2	23.4	9.9	16.6	15.2	8.4
Lakewood (cdp)	23.3	26.6	9.0	17.7	15.1	8.1
Lawrence (twp)	25.2	34.3	19.5	10.5	5.9	4.5
Linden (city)	32.3	13.8	9.1	14.9	20.5	9.2
Livingston (twp)	29.7	32.1	23.8	7.4	3.1	3.9
Long Branch (city)	28.2	18.5	10.1	20.5	12.1	10.5
Manalapan (twp)	31.9	25.4	21.6	8.2	6.0	6.8
Manchester (twp)	27.1	16.3	11.1	17.8	15.5	12.2
Marlboro (twp)	28.7	28.7	26.5	6.3	5.7	4.2
Mercerville-Ham. Sq. (cdp)	29.1	24.3	17.7	12.0	9.3	7.6

Place	Sales	Professional	Management	Services	Production	Construction
Middletown (twp)	30.5	23.1	18.7	11.0	8.3	8.2
Millville (city)	24.5	16.3	8.5	19.9	19.8	10.8
Monroe (twp)	30.8	19.7	20.0	10.5	10.1	8.5
Monroe (twp)	31.8	16.4	10.3	16.2	13.8	11.5
Montclair (twp)	23.7	36.4	21.9	10.4	4.9	2.7
Mount Laurel (twp)	30.2	28.4	21.1	9.2	6.2	4.8
Mount Olive (twp)	26.2	24.7	19.1	10.7	11.2	7.9
Neptune (twp)	28.4	22.9	14.0	16.1	11.0	7.5
New Brunswick (city)	26.5	18.2	6.7	22.4	21.2	4.6
Newark (city)	27.5	12.5	6.5	21.8	21.2	10.4
North Bergen (twp)	31.5	15.9	10.9	14.4	20.4	6.7
North Brunswick (twp)	28.4	27.6	18.7	9.3	10.7	5.2
Nutley (twp)	31.5	25.6	15.5	11.1	8.9	7.4
Ocean (twp)	31.9	26.7	14.9	12.7	7.6	6.2
Old Bridge (twp)	31.4	20.8	16.4	11.2	10.8	9.3
Orange (cdp)	29.0	17.2	8.5	23.1	14.4	7.7
Paramus (borough)	33.3	26.3	17.8	9.1	7.2	6.2
Parsippany-Troy Hills (twp)	28.6	26.4	20.7	9.0	9.2	6.1
Passaic (city)	23.6	11.6	6.4	17.4	33.5	7.2
Paterson (city)	27.7	10.9	5.8	20.2	27.4	7.8
Pemberton (twp)	28.8	12.9	8.5	23.0	16.3	10.1
Pennsauken (twp)	31.1	16.8	11.0	16.0	16.9	8.1
Perth Amboy (city)	25.0	10.0	7.5	17.4	31.3	8.7
Piscataway (twp)	27.4	31.7	14.0	8.8	12.2	5.9
Plainfield (city)	27.3	13.5	10.5	17.7	22.5	8.4
Rahway (city)	31.1	17.4	13.2	13.4	15.3	9.6
Randolph (twp)	23.5	30.7	28.2	7.4	5.7	4.5
Rockaway (twp)	28.2	26.3	21.2	9.8	8.2	6.2
Sayreville (borough)	31.3	21.5	14.0	11.8	12.0	9.3
South Brunswick (twp)	26.2	31.1	22.7	8.0	6.5	5.4
Stafford (twp)	28.9	20.3	11.0	16.0	9.4	14.0
Teaneck (twp)	26.8	33.2	20.0	9.4	6.4	4.2
Toms River (cdp)	30.5	21.3	13.0	15.5	9.4	10.1
Trenton (city)	27.6	13.9	7.6	25.8	16.3	8.4
Union (twp)	31.1	23.6	14.3	12.1	11.0	7.9
Union City (city)	24.4	9.2	7.9	19.2	31.2	7.9
Vernon (twp)	28.3	21.0	13.4	12.4	12.0	12.6
Vineland (city)	24.5	17.7	8.5	18.0	19.6	9.7
Voorhees (twp)	27.0	33.3	20.8	10.2	5.2	3.4
Wall (twp)	27.6	26.5	18.0	9.7	7.8	10.1
Washington (twp)	31.0	24.1	16.7	12.5	8.6	7.1
Wayne (twp)	29.2	25.3	22.0	9.7	7.7	6.0
West Milford (twp)	29.5	20.2	15.0	10.8	11.1	13.2
West New York (town)	26.3	11.0	8.7	20.1	26.5	7.2
West Orange (twp)	27.9	28.5	18.8	11.0	7.9	5.8
West Windsor (twp)	20.5	39.0	32.0	4.5	2.4	1.6
Westfield (town)	24.1	34.8	25.7	7.6	4.5	3.3
Willingboro (twp)	30.6	20.5	12.1	15.7	14.8	6.2
Winslow (twp)	28.3	19.9	11.4	15.0	12.9	12.1
Woodbridge (twp)	30.0	23.4	13.9	10.5	13.6	8.4

NOTE: Data as of 2000

Educational Attainment

Place	Percent of Population 25 Years and Over with:		
	High School Diploma including Equivalency	Bachelor's Degree or Higher	Masters's Degree or Higher
Atlantic City (city)	61.7	10.4	3.2
Bayonne (city)	78.5	21.1	6.9
Belleville (twp)	78.2	21.7	5.9
Bergenfield (borough)	86.4	32.1	9.7
Berkeley (twp)	73.0	10.7	2.9
Bernards (twp)	95.9	67.9	31.5
Bloomfield (twp)	83.4	31.6	9.8
Brick (twp)	86.6	19.3	5.5
Bridgewater (twp)	91.8	49.7	21.8
Camden (city)	51.2	5.3	1.8
Cherry Hill (twp)	90.9	46.1	19.0
Clifton (city)	78.6	23.8	7.5
Deptford (twp)	80.3	15.6	4.2
Dover (twp)	86.3	23.7	8.0
East Brunswick (twp)	92.1	47.1	19.6
East Orange (city)	72.7	15.3	4.6
East Windsor (twp)	88.3	41.9	15.4
Edison (twp)	87.7	42.6	17.3
Egg Harbor (twp)	82.8	19.1	5.6
Elizabeth (city)	61.5	12.0	4.2
Englewood (city)	81.9	35.2	15.6
Evesham (twp)	93.2	39.7	12.3
Ewing (twp)	84.4	29.4	12.2
Fair Lawn (borough)	89.9	44.7	17.5
Fort Lee (borough)	89.4	48.6	18.6
Franklin (twp)	88.3	43.4	16.1
Freehold (twp)	88.7	37.5	13.0
Galloway (twp)	87.5	22.9	7.4
Garfield (city)	70.2	14.0	3.8
Gloucester (twp)	85.6	21.8	6.1
Hackensack (city)	79.9	29.4	10.7
Hamilton (twp)	83.0	22.5	7.2
Hillsborough (twp)	92.7	46.9	16.5
Hoboken (city)	83.2	59.5	18.6
Howell (twp)	88.1	28.9	8.8
Irvington (twp)	72.3	12.2	2.7
Jackson (twp)	86.9	23.1	6.1
Jersey City (city)	72.8	28.0	9.6
Kearny (town)	70.9	17.4	6.6
Lacey (twp)	86.1	19.5	5.9
Lakewood (twp)	78.4	20.9	8.2
Lakewood (cdp)	73.9	21.1	9.2
Lawrence (twp)	89.2	50.5	24.2
Linden (city)	78.2	14.2	4.5
Livingston (twp)	93.9	57.6	26.7
Long Branch (city)	76.4	20.2	7.2
Manalapan (twp)	92.4	39.5	14.7
Manchester (twp)	75.7	12.9	4.1
Marlboro (twp)	94.0	52.6	22.7
Mercerville-Ham. Sq. (cdp)	85.9	28.0	8.9

Place	Percent of Population 25 Years and Over with:		
	High School Diploma including Equivalency	Bachelor's Degree or Higher	Masters's Degree or Higher
Middletown (twp)	90.7	34.9	12.5
Millville (city)	74.1	12.2	3.2
Monroe (twp)	90.2	29.8	10.4
Monroe (twp)	80.4	16.0	4.1
Montclair (twp)	91.7	56.5	26.6
Mount Laurel (twp)	92.2	42.1	14.1
Mount Olive (twp)	92.1	36.9	11.5
Neptune (twp)	83.9	23.4	8.2
New Brunswick (city)	63.3	19.7	7.7
Newark (city)	57.9	8.9	3.0
North Bergen (twp)	68.7	19.4	7.1
North Brunswick (twp)	86.1	37.3	14.4
Nutley (twp)	86.5	33.0	10.5
Ocean (twp)	89.9	38.8	16.0
Old Bridge (twp)	88.3	29.6	8.9
Orange (cdp)	72.3	16.6	6.2
Paramus (borough)	86.1	38.6	14.2
Parsippany-Troy Hills (twp)	89.7	43.0	15.4
Passaic (city)	54.8	13.1	4.9
Paterson (city)	58.4	8.1	2.8
Pemberton (twp)	79.8	9.3	2.6
Pennsauken (twp)	77.0	15.3	4.8
Perth Amboy (city)	55.9	10.2	3.6
Piscataway (twp)	88.7	41.3	17.0
Plainfield (city)	70.0	18.1	6.0
Rahway (city)	81.3	18.3	5.4
Randolph (twp)	95.4	58.9	25.5
Rockaway (twp)	92.9	41.9	12.7
Sayreville (borough)	85.8	25.7	7.7
South Brunswick (twp)	93.3	49.3	20.1
Stafford (twp)	84.9	18.7	4.5
Teaneck (twp)	89.5	47.2	22.6
Toms River (cdp)	86.4	23.7	8.0
Trenton (city)	62.2	9.3	3.5
Union (twp)	80.9	26.6	8.4
Union City (city)	54.4	12.4	5.4
Vernon (twp)	92.9	25.3	7.7
Vineland (city)	67.5	14.2	4.7
Voorhees (twp)	91.0	45.9	19.7
Wall (twp)	91.7	39.1	14.0
Washington (twp)	89.9	30.4	9.0
Wayne (twp)	89.1	41.6	15.4
West Milford (twp)	89.2	27.2	8.0
West New York (town)	54.8	16.8	7.5
West Orange (twp)	86.2	42.9	18.8
West Windsor (twp)	96.9	73.9	38.9
Westfield (town)	95.3	62.4	29.7
Willingboro (twp)	87.2	18.9	6.0
Winslow (twp)	81.9	18.5	4.3
Woodbridge (twp)	84.1	27.4	9.2

NOTE: Data as of 2005

Income and Poverty

Place	Average Household Income ($)	Median Household Income ($)	Per Capita Income ($)	Households with income of $100,000+ (%)	Poverty Rate[1] (%)
Atlantic City (city)	42,429	29,580	16,826	7.3	23.6
Bayonne (city)	59,579	47,442	24,730	16.5	10.1
Belleville (twp)	65,308	54,998	24,884	17.3	8.2
Bergenfield (borough)	85,200	71,057	28,880	31.0	3.5
Berkeley (twp)	50,500	38,021	25,328	9.5	5.4
Bernards (twp)	170,442	131,167	63,558	62.7	1.3
Bloomfield (twp)	76,646	63,131	30,682	24.3	5.9
Brick (twp)	72,133	59,752	28,415	20.8	4.5
Bridgewater (twp)	120,417	97,929	44,716	48.7	2.1
Camden (city)	33,681	26,170	10,697	3.1	35.5
Cherry Hill (twp)	97,965	75,708	37,728	34.7	4.0
Clifton (city)	69,239	56,303	26,365	21.1	6.3
Deptford (twp)	63,234	56,358	24,453	15.3	5.9
Dover (twp)	74,584	60,259	28,443	22.9	5.7
East Brunswick (twp)	106,012	85,134	37,404	40.5	2.8
East Orange (city)	49,346	37,004	18,697	10.8	19.2
East Windsor (twp)	88,418	74,074	33,927	32.8	5.3
Edison (twp)	95,775	77,543	34,836	34.8	4.8
Egg Harbor (twp)	68,662	57,882	25,128	19.0	5.4
Elizabeth (city)	49,840	39,428	16,691	10.1	17.8
Englewood (city)	101,592	66,853	35,897	32.5	8.9
Evesham (twp)	91,329	77,094	34,686	33.6	2.8
Ewing (twp)	75,014	64,127	27,949	23.6	6.4
Fair Lawn (borough)	100,775	83,679	37,576	39.7	3.7
Fort Lee (borough)	85,780	62,972	39,673	28.5	7.9
Franklin (twp)	90,420	74,230	34,682	31.7	5.1
Freehold (twp)	108,833	89,547	38,034	43.6	3.9
Galloway (twp)	70,899	60,527	24,897	20.3	6.6
Garfield (city)	58,706	48,326	21,832	14.5	7.8
Gloucester (twp)	73,091	62,190	26,845	22.0	6.2
Hackensack (city)	71,254	56,136	30,382	19.9	9.3
Hamilton (twp)	75,634	65,040	29,571	24.8	4.2
Hillsborough (twp)	112,509	94,135	39,060	46.2	3.1
Hoboken (city)	103,481	79,504	53,627	39.2	11.0
Howell (twp)	93,944	78,934	30,950	35.5	4.2
Irvington (twp)	51,172	41,700	18,732	10.3	17.4
Jackson (twp)	84,943	75,590	28,136	32.1	3.7
Jersey City (city)	61,408	44,395	22,933	16.4	18.6
Kearny (town)	68,205	54,983	23,365	19.1	8.6
Lacey (twp)	73,146	64,427	27,201	23.3	4.5
Lakewood (twp)	55,819	40,433	18,405	13.8	19.8
Lakewood (cdp)	50,273	33,283	12,631	11.5	29.1
Lawrence (twp)	100,618	78,283	38,434	36.0	4.9
Linden (city)	61,069	50,888	23,092	15.6	6.4
Livingston (twp)	150,212	110,471	51,718	54.6	1.8
Long Branch (city)	56,663	42,816	22,854	13.5	16.7
Manalapan (twp)	123,764	98,592	40,055	49.2	3.8
Manchester (twp)	48,696	34,458	26,444	9.3	5.5
Marlboro (twp)	140,304	116,775	44,428	58.1	3.5
Mercerville-Ham. Sq. (cdp)	88,014	77,065	32,047	32.5	2.2

Place	Average Household Income ($)	Median Household Income ($)	Per Capita Income ($)	Households with income of $100,000+ (%)	Poverty Rate[1] (%)
Middletown (twp)	112,085	87,584	39,905	41.9	3.1
Millville (city)	54,851	43,964	20,727	12.1	15.2
Monroe (twp)	81,129	61,428	36,727	27.5	3.3
Monroe (twp)	64,345	56,468	23,819	18.2	6.2
Montclair (twp)	129,065	87,550	50,338	44.2	5.6
Mount Laurel (twp)	89,049	72,050	37,449	32.1	3.1
Mount Olive (twp)	89,922	74,094	34,020	30.8	3.1
Neptune (twp)	64,037	50,871	26,130	18.3	11.7
New Brunswick (city)	55,212	41,394	15,545	12.5	27.0
Newark (city)	43,033	30,610	14,790	8.1	28.4
North Bergen (twp)	58,758	45,374	21,490	15.1	11.1
North Brunswick (twp)	82,811	67,476	31,132	27.8	4.7
Nutley (twp)	83,297	69,472	33,714	29.7	4.8
Ocean (twp)	88,881	69,071	34,356	30.9	5.0
Old Bridge (twp)	84,642	72,338	30,209	30.4	4.2
Orange (cdp)	50,227	39,449	18,091	10.8	18.8
Paramus (borough)	106,144	85,847	34,705	40.8	3.3
Parsippany-Troy Hills (twp)	95,031	77,012	37,455	34.8	3.9
Passaic (city)	47,242	35,964	13,390	8.4	21.2
Paterson (city)	47,432	36,122	14,284	9.3	22.2
Pemberton (twp)	61,414	52,803	22,305	13.6	9.3
Pennsauken (twp)	62,753	53,381	21,805	15.7	8.0
Perth Amboy (city)	54,304	42,802	16,674	12.9	17.6
Piscataway (twp)	91,242	77,923	30,387	33.9	3.8
Plainfield (city)	65,753	51,416	20,974	19.7	15.9
Rahway (city)	66,875	56,524	25,261	18.5	7.1
Randolph (twp)	145,158	115,209	51,139	56.3	1.4
Rockaway (twp)	114,865	94,606	40,788	46.1	2.4
Sayreville (borough)	77,330	66,868	28,692	26.0	4.7
South Brunswick (twp)	109,831	93,875	38,628	45.8	3.1
Stafford (twp)	78,074	65,375	29,809	24.6	4.0
Teaneck (twp)	108,402	82,927	37,230	38.9	4.2
Toms River (cdp)	75,029	60,880	28,112	23.2	5.6
Trenton (city)	45,196	34,193	16,118	8.1	21.1
Union (twp)	78,745	66,566	28,198	27.1	4.2
Union City (city)	43,911	33,787	14,914	7.5	21.4
Vernon (twp)	84,507	74,167	29,249	28.6	2.9
Vineland (city)	59,370	45,425	21,736	13.9	13.8
Voorhees (twp)	103,095	76,287	39,330	36.2	5.7
Wall (twp)	106,277	86,847	40,332	41.9	2.3
Washington (twp)	88,460	74,784	30,187	31.8	3.2
Wayne (twp)	113,138	91,604	39,664	45.1	2.8
West Milford (twp)	92,701	82,500	32,792	36.7	4.1
West New York (town)	52,772	37,855	19,395	12.3	18.9
West Orange (twp)	105,903	80,571	39,453	39.8	5.6
West Windsor (twp)	172,944	138,926	56,893	67.8	2.5
Westfield (town)	151,543	113,812	54,617	56.0	2.7
Willingboro (twp)	77,304	68,351	25,833	23.2	5.9
Winslow (twp)	73,837	64,408	25,288	22.7	6.0
Woodbridge (twp)	81,101	68,745	28,992	28.2	4.8

NOTE: Data as of 2005 except for Poverty Rate which is from 2000; (1) Percentage of population with income below the poverty level

Taxes

Place	Total City Taxes Per Capita ($)	City Property Taxes Per Capita ($)
Atlantic City (city)	3,341	3,261
Bayonne (city)	1,949	1,931
Belleville (twp)	796	779
Bergenfield (borough)	n/a	n/a
Berkeley (twp)	376	353
Bernards (twp)	777	745
Bloomfield (twp)	710	700
Brick (twp)	546	524
Bridgewater (twp)	308	288
Camden (city)	408	383
Cherry Hill (twp)	291	249
Clifton (city)	609	586
Deptford (twp)	491	417
Dover (twp)	432	416
East Brunswick (twp)	593	568
East Orange (city)	892	874
East Windsor (twp)	371	346
Edison (twp)	2,079	2,039
Egg Harbor (twp)	n/a	n/a
Elizabeth (city)	752	649
Englewood (city)	2,718	2,697
Evesham (twp)	351	315
Ewing (twp)	303	293
Fair Lawn (borough)	691	657
Fort Lee (borough)	n/a	n/a
Franklin (twp)	588	532
Freehold (twp)	373	343
Galloway (twp)	329	300
Garfield (city)	494	456
Gloucester (twp)	320	301
Hackensack (city)	1,105	1,080
Hamilton (twp)	484	459
Hillsborough (twp)	394	360
Hoboken (city)	563	473
Howell (twp)	347	300
Irvington (twp)	728	706
Jackson (twp)	434	397
Jersey City (city)	571	521
Kearny (town)	568	549
Lacey (twp)	200	185
Lakewood (twp)	393	369
Lakewood (cdp)	n/a	n/a
Lawrence (twp)	615	551
Linden (city)	808	788
Livingston (twp)	666	639
Long Branch (city)	758	725
Manalapan (twp)	453	429
Manchester (twp)	339	295
Marlboro (twp)	453	433
Mercerville-Ham. Sq. (cdp)	n/a	n/a

Place	Total City Taxes Per Capita ($)	City Property Taxes Per Capita ($)
Middletown (twp)	594	565
Millville (city)	441	408
Monroe (twp)	632	566
Monroe (twp)	533	480
Montclair (twp)	2,882	2,831
Mount Laurel (twp)	532	504
Mount Olive (twp)	611	582
Neptune (twp)	614	579
New Brunswick (city)	956	921
Newark (city)	633	433
North Bergen (twp)	682	665
North Brunswick (twp)	550	516
Nutley (twp)	943	929
Ocean (twp)	n/a	n/a
Old Bridge (twp)	479	456
Orange (cdp)	1,048	1,028
Paramus (borough)	1,036	979
Parsippany-Troy Hills (twp)	710	669
Passaic (city)	550	535
Paterson (city)	566	559
Pemberton (twp)	385	378
Pennsauken (twp)	397	380
Perth Amboy (city)	417	402
Piscataway (twp)	513	489
Plainfield (city)	759	746
Rahway (city)	861	821
Randolph (twp)	n/a	n/a
Rockaway (twp)	n/a	n/a
Sayreville (borough)	436	418
South Brunswick (twp)	561	532
Stafford (twp)	792	747
Teaneck (twp)	932	896
Toms River (cdp)	n/a	n/a
Trenton (city)	854	827
Union (twp)	762	745
Union City (city)	583	558
Vernon (twp)	n/a	n/a
Vineland (city)	369	345
Voorhees (twp)	498	460
Wall (twp)	701	605
Washington (twp)	491	468
Wayne (twp)	780	755
West Milford (twp)	657	635
West New York (town)	745	718
West Orange (twp)	824	805
West Windsor (twp)	620	593
Westfield (town)	n/a	n/a
Willingboro (twp)	538	534
Winslow (twp)	287	262
Woodbridge (twp)	400	391

NOTE: Data as of 2004.

Housing

Place	Homeownership Rate (%)	Median Home Value ($)	Median Age of Housing (years)	Median Rent ($/month)
Atlantic City (city)	29.2	146,634	39	502
Bayonne (city)	39.9	261,233	57	611
Belleville (twp)	50.8	236,281	51	697
Bergenfield (borough)	68.9	290,829	49	794
Berkeley (twp)	92.6	178,292	19	642
Bernards (twp)	86.9	587,682	15	1,365
Bloomfield (twp)	53.1	259,855	54	718
Brick (twp)	82.9	233,056	26	704
Bridgewater (twp)	85.5	408,829	24	952
Camden (city)	45.9	62,798	52	440
Cherry Hill (twp)	82.7	241,286	32	747
Clifton (city)	60.7	285,091	50	705
Deptford (twp)	76.8	166,079	32	563
Dover (twp)	83.6	251,697	28	685
East Brunswick (twp)	84.3	327,744	28	813
East Orange (city)	27.0	195,345	49	600
East Windsor (twp)	60.5	228,821	25	733
Edison (twp)	63.6	289,760	29	847
Egg Harbor (twp)	85.2	195,580	21	608
Elizabeth (city)	29.4	246,851	48	616
Englewood (city)	58.5	310,793	51	768
Evesham (twp)	77.5	237,683	17	765
Ewing (twp)	73.8	209,039	41	677
Fair Lawn (borough)	78.8	345,538	49	863
Fort Lee (borough)	55.8	301,891	33	1,042
Franklin (twp)	71.9	267,829	21	838
Freehold (twp)	87.1	356,165	19	809
Galloway (twp)	73.8	203,238	16	673
Garfield (city)	40.2	281,302	51	694
Gloucester (twp)	72.0	177,891	24	631
Hackensack (city)	32.0	257,745	37	790
Hamilton (twp)	74.7	214,397	40	662
Hillsborough (twp)	83.6	379,678	19	841
Hoboken (city)	22.7	402,808	53	953
Howell (twp)	89.1	284,518	18	643
Irvington (twp)	29.2	192,855	46	624
Jackson (twp)	87.2	262,264	20	739
Jersey City (city)	28.1	221,527	52	614
Kearny (town)	47.9	256,679	57	676
Lacey (twp)	90.7	229,981	23	763
Lakewood (twp)	61.9	208,957	26	740
Lakewood (cdp)	42.9	234,268	29	732
Lawrence (twp)	69.6	268,927	24	842
Linden (city)	57.7	245,060	46	705
Livingston (twp)	93.4	465,917	42	1,182
Long Branch (city)	42.5	240,849	42	670
Manalapan (twp)	94.3	406,172	19	920
Manchester (twp)	91.6	120,521	22	832
Marlboro (twp)	96.5	473,247	15	1,127
Mercerville-Ham. Sq. (cdp)	88.9	249,037	39	768

Place	Homeownership Rate (%)	Median Home Value ($)	Median Age of Housing (years)	Median Rent ($/month)
Middletown (twp)	85.8	355,781	35	738
Millville (city)	64.2	127,012	38	502
Monroe (twp)	94.9	272,124	17	777
Monroe (twp)	84.2	173,191	24	531
Montclair (twp)	55.7	453,586	60+	810
Mount Laurel (twp)	83.1	225,130	15	816
Mount Olive (twp)	55.7	329,211	27	763
Neptune (twp)	64.8	234,037	43	603
New Brunswick (city)	26.5	206,845	46	747
Newark (city)	23.9	216,790	47	525
North Bergen (twp)	36.8	263,892	46	679
North Brunswick (twp)	62.6	262,416	24	842
Nutley (twp)	66.8	297,529	53	764
Ocean (twp)	65.7	347,816	33	642
Old Bridge (twp)	68.5	268,257	32	723
Orange (cdp)	25.2	206,502	45	636
Paramus (borough)	89.9	464,742	42	1,308
Parsippany-Troy Hills (twp)	59.9	368,351	35	771
Passaic (city)	26.8	247,458	55	587
Paterson (city)	31.4	237,361	50	611
Pemberton (twp)	74.1	143,545	29	558
Pennsauken (twp)	80.5	141,329	44	531
Perth Amboy (city)	39.9	219,986	48	642
Piscataway (twp)	68.9	269,494	31	774
Plainfield (city)	49.0	220,769	51	657
Rahway (city)	62.2	232,489	47	669
Randolph (twp)	74.1	525,993	24	848
Rockaway (twp)	83.4	332,854	35	876
Sayreville (borough)	66.3	257,160	32	713
South Brunswick (twp)	75.1	311,807	16	864
Stafford (twp)	90.8	239,111	20	674
Teaneck (twp)	76.8	336,536	54	818
Toms River (cdp)	83.6	249,612	26	687
Trenton (city)	45.1	101,484	60+	532
Union (twp)	76.0	267,641	47	774
Union City (city)	18.1	250,053	55	598
Vernon (twp)	85.2	240,144	25	783
Vineland (city)	66.5	137,002	35	535
Voorhees (twp)	64.6	265,019	17	773
Wall (twp)	86.1	401,500	30	752
Washington (twp)	86.2	218,805	19	710
Wayne (twp)	81.7	445,771	35	887
West Milford (twp)	89.6	273,859	37	754
West New York (town)	20.4	255,611	49	627
West Orange (twp)	70.4	324,992	45	788
West Windsor (twp)	81.8	511,876	16	1,132
Westfield (town)	81.5	544,583	52	981
Willingboro (twp)	92.5	144,055	35	896
Winslow (twp)	82.6	173,022	19	614
Woodbridge (twp)	69.7	251,983	41	794

NOTE: Homeownership Rate and Median Home Value as of 2005; Median Rent and Median Age of Housing as of 2000.

Commute to Work

Place	Automobile (%)	Public Transportation (%)	Walk (%)	Work from Home (%)
Atlantic City (city)	46.7	27.9	21.0	1.2
Bayonne (city)	72.2	17.9	8.1	1.5
Belleville (twp)	88.7	7.3	2.6	0.8
Bergenfield (borough)	83.1	11.6	2.7	1.8
Berkeley (twp)	93.7	2.5	0.5	2.7
Bernards (twp)	88.1	5.6	0.7	5.3
Bloomfield (twp)	83.1	11.8	2.6	1.9
Brick (twp)	94.9	2.0	0.8	1.8
Bridgewater (twp)	91.4	3.5	0.7	3.8
Camden (city)	67.7	20.8	8.5	0.9
Cherry Hill (twp)	87.6	6.9	1.3	3.9
Clifton (city)	88.6	6.6	2.1	2.0
Deptford (twp)	93.0	3.0	1.4	1.6
Dover (twp)	93.9	1.8	0.9	2.7
East Brunswick (twp)	85.0	10.3	1.1	3.1
East Orange (city)	65.3	27.8	3.6	1.9
East Windsor (twp)	86.9	7.7	1.4	2.8
Edison (twp)	84.8	10.9	2.0	1.8
Egg Harbor (twp)	93.8	1.4	1.1	2.2
Elizabeth (city)	76.9	14.7	4.9	1.1
Englewood (city)	73.4	16.6	4.6	3.6
Evesham (twp)	90.6	4.6	1.2	3.1
Ewing (twp)	87.5	2.8	6.9	2.4
Fair Lawn (borough)	82.7	11.4	2.0	3.7
Fort Lee (borough)	73.5	17.6	4.0	4.2
Franklin (twp)	89.7	6.2	1.1	2.1
Freehold (twp)	86.2	8.1	0.7	4.5
Galloway (twp)	93.2	2.6	2.1	1.5
Garfield (city)	89.5	4.6	3.6	1.4
Gloucester (twp)	90.3	6.4	0.7	1.8
Hackensack (city)	74.2	15.6	6.9	1.6
Hamilton (twp)	93.7	3.0	0.9	1.8
Hillsborough (twp)	92.0	2.2	1.2	3.8
Hoboken (city)	29.0	57.2	10.3	2.8
Howell (twp)	90.2	5.6	0.8	2.6
Irvington (twp)	73.1	22.4	2.6	1.1
Jackson (twp)	93.7	2.4	0.9	2.7
Jersey City (city)	49.7	39.5	8.0	1.8
Kearny (town)	78.2	14.0	6.1	1.0
Lacey (twp)	96.5	0.9	0.5	1.8
Lakewood (twp)	84.3	4.3	5.4	4.4
Lakewood (cdp)	56.1	5.3	8.8	6.3
Lawrence (twp)	87.2	5.3	3.4	3.5
Linden (city)	87.6	7.1	3.5	0.9
Livingston (twp)	85.1	8.1	0.5	5.9
Long Branch (city)	85.1	6.6	4.5	1.9
Manalapan (twp)	81.9	13.0	0.7	3.8
Manchester (twp)	95.8	0.6	0.9	1.8
Marlboro (twp)	77.8	17.3	0.4	4.1
Mercerville-Ham. Sq. (cdp)	94.0	2.7	0.7	2.1

Place	Automobile (%)	Public Transportation (%)	Walk (%)	Work from Home (%)
Middletown (twp)	84.6	11.5	1.0	2.6
Millville (city)	91.5	2.8	2.2	2.1
Monroe (twp)	87.7	6.1	1.3	4.3
Monroe (twp)	91.2	3.2	1.7	2.7
Montclair (twp)	66.4	22.0	4.1	6.3
Mount Laurel (twp)	92.1	3.1	0.3	4.0
Mount Olive (twp)	94.1	1.5	0.6	3.1
Neptune (twp)	88.9	4.5	2.4	3.1
New Brunswick (city)	72.0	11.3	12.9	1.3
Newark (city)	63.0	26.5	7.9	1.2
North Bergen (twp)	67.3	25.4	4.7	1.4
North Brunswick (twp)	88.4	7.8	1.4	1.7
Nutley (twp)	86.2	8.2	2.4	2.8
Ocean (twp)	90.7	4.7	1.3	2.4
Old Bridge (twp)	84.5	11.4	1.2	2.2
Orange (cdp)	69.2	23.5	5.0	1.4
Paramus (borough)	87.8	6.6	1.8	3.5
Parsippany-Troy Hills (twp)	91.8	3.6	1.7	2.5
Passaic (city)	66.3	18.7	9.8	1.4
Paterson (city)	78.9	12.2	5.9	1.0
Pemberton (twp)	95.2	1.0	1.4	1.5
Pennsauken (twp)	88.1	6.3	2.0	2.2
Perth Amboy (city)	82.8	7.0	6.6	1.0
Piscataway (twp)	88.5	6.0	2.7	2.1
Plainfield (city)	82.9	8.8	3.9	1.3
Rahway (city)	84.2	9.4	3.5	1.9
Randolph (twp)	90.2	3.0	0.7	5.7
Rockaway (twp)	94.4	2.0	0.8	2.5
Sayreville (borough)	88.4	8.6	1.0	1.4
South Brunswick (twp)	88.8	6.8	1.1	2.9
Stafford (twp)	96.6	0.7	0.5	1.6
Teaneck (twp)	77.7	15.6	2.4	3.7
Toms River (cdp)	94.0	1.7	0.9	2.7
Trenton (city)	79.3	11.6	5.9	1.6
Union (twp)	86.8	6.9	3.7	2.0
Union City (city)	51.6	33.2	12.2	1.4
Vernon (twp)	95.3	0.7	0.5	2.7
Vineland (city)	92.2	2.5	1.9	1.9
Voorhees (twp)	82.8	10.8	1.4	3.9
Wall (twp)	92.4	3.1	0.8	3.3
Washington (twp)	92.6	3.1	0.8	3.1
Wayne (twp)	89.4	5.3	1.9	3.2
West Milford (twp)	92.2	2.2	1.4	4.0
West New York (town)	51.6	30.6	14.0	1.9
West Orange (twp)	84.5	9.6	1.8	3.4
West Windsor (twp)	70.9	21.6	1.2	5.5
Westfield (town)	78.2	14.3	2.1	4.9
Willingboro (twp)	91.6	5.7	1.1	1.1
Winslow (twp)	89.6	6.5	1.0	1.9
Woodbridge (twp)	86.5	8.9	2.1	1.7

NOTE: Data as of 2000

Travel Time to Work

Place	Less than 15 Minutes (%)	15 to 30 Minutes (%)	30 to 45 Minutes (%)	45 to 60 Minutes (%)	60 Minutes or More (%)
Atlantic City (city)	38.1	42.4	12.0	3.2	4.3
Bayonne (city)	26.5	25.3	20.9	10.4	16.9
Belleville (twp)	21.8	35.9	25.5	8.3	8.6
Bergenfield (borough)	22.6	33.1	21.4	9.4	13.6
Berkeley (twp)	20.2	33.3	19.8	8.6	18.1
Bernards (twp)	21.5	32.2	21.5	9.6	15.2
Bloomfield (twp)	21.2	34.4	24.7	8.2	11.5
Brick (twp)	22.3	32.6	17.1	9.3	18.6
Bridgewater (twp)	24.7	31.0	22.4	11.4	10.5
Camden (city)	24.7	40.1	19.1	7.2	8.9
Cherry Hill (twp)	26.8	35.3	19.1	8.8	10.1
Clifton (city)	27.9	39.8	19.1	6.1	7.1
Deptford (twp)	30.6	32.5	23.0	6.9	7.1
Dover (twp)	30.0	30.6	14.2	7.5	17.8
East Brunswick (twp)	19.8	24.9	21.4	11.3	22.6
East Orange (city)	15.4	33.8	23.3	12.1	15.6
East Windsor (twp)	18.5	35.5	19.7	9.0	17.4
Edison (twp)	21.6	31.8	19.4	9.6	17.6
Egg Harbor (twp)	27.7	48.4	14.5	2.8	6.6
Elizabeth (city)	22.9	36.2	21.9	9.0	9.9
Englewood (city)	22.9	29.9	20.6	8.8	17.9
Evesham (twp)	21.9	35.2	20.4	10.6	11.9
Ewing (twp)	40.4	35.3	12.0	4.7	7.6
Fair Lawn (borough)	24.3	33.5	16.7	8.8	16.6
Fort Lee (borough)	20.2	25.2	21.7	14.0	18.9
Franklin (twp)	18.2	38.2	19.3	10.5	13.8
Freehold (twp)	23.5	22.8	16.3	11.9	25.4
Galloway (twp)	24.4	52.3	15.1	2.3	5.9
Garfield (city)	26.4	40.8	20.5	4.9	7.4
Gloucester (twp)	18.9	33.7	24.9	10.3	12.2
Hackensack (city)	28.7	34.9	16.8	7.1	12.5
Hamilton (twp)	25.8	43.2	17.2	5.7	8.0
Hillsborough (twp)	18.5	32.9	24.6	12.1	12.0
Hoboken (city)	11.9	17.0	37.1	24.6	9.4
Howell (twp)	17.4	30.3	18.5	9.7	24.1
Irvington (twp)	11.5	35.7	27.1	11.6	14.0
Jackson (twp)	16.6	30.7	20.6	12.0	20.1
Jersey City (city)	14.2	30.3	26.9	13.8	14.9
Kearny (town)	21.8	31.5	24.8	8.5	13.4
Lacey (twp)	23.7	29.2	19.9	7.8	19.4
Lakewood (twp)	36.4	28.4	14.3	5.6	15.3
Lakewood (cdp)	43.3	26.0	12.4	4.2	14.0
Lawrence (twp)	27.8	40.3	13.5	6.5	11.9
Linden (city)	30.1	34.2	18.4	8.0	9.2
Livingston (twp)	27.3	31.8	15.9	7.7	17.3
Long Branch (city)	31.1	31.0	17.7	6.0	14.2
Manalapan (twp)	18.7	21.0	18.0	10.0	32.2
Manchester (twp)	23.9	29.7	17.7	13.8	14.9
Marlboro (twp)	17.4	18.6	16.0	10.5	37.4
Mercerville-Ham. Sq. (cdp)	25.9	41.5	17.6	5.6	9.4

Place	Less than 15 Minutes (%)	15 to 30 Minutes (%)	30 to 45 Minutes (%)	45 to 60 Minutes (%)	60 Minutes or More (%)
Middletown (twp)	22.2	27.0	16.1	10.1	24.6
Millville (city)	39.0	36.6	12.6	5.2	6.6
Monroe (twp)	19.7	26.3	22.1	10.9	21.0
Monroe (twp)	23.2	27.0	22.8	13.9	13.0
Montclair (twp)	19.5	28.4	20.5	10.5	21.1
Mount Laurel (twp)	24.2	36.4	19.8	8.4	11.2
Mount Olive (twp)	17.4	22.1	24.3	19.0	17.1
Neptune (twp)	31.4	35.1	13.7	6.9	12.8
New Brunswick (city)	33.0	36.0	18.1	5.7	7.1
Newark (city)	18.5	32.9	24.5	9.9	14.3
North Bergen (twp)	17.9	30.3	24.1	12.0	15.6
North Brunswick (twp)	23.8	34.9	17.3	9.0	14.9
Nutley (twp)	28.1	33.4	20.5	8.7	9.3
Ocean (twp)	34.8	34.2	12.2	4.4	14.4
Old Bridge (twp)	16.4	22.6	22.1	13.4	25.4
Orange (cdp)	15.9	33.1	27.8	10.5	12.7
Paramus (borough)	27.0	35.8	18.7	6.1	12.4
Parsippany-Troy Hills (twp)	25.3	38.8	20.3	7.1	8.5
Passaic (city)	22.8	38.6	22.8	6.7	9.1
Paterson (city)	25.0	42.3	20.7	5.7	6.4
Pemberton (twp)	20.6	29.2	24.5	13.5	12.2
Pennsauken (twp)	30.1	40.0	16.2	6.8	6.8
Perth Amboy (city)	30.5	38.4	18.2	6.4	6.6
Piscataway (twp)	27.4	33.3	18.4	9.2	11.7
Plainfield (city)	19.4	35.9	25.6	7.6	11.6
Rahway (city)	26.8	32.2	21.8	8.5	10.7
Randolph (twp)	17.5	33.2	26.5	11.5	11.3
Rockaway (twp)	21.1	30.8	24.2	13.0	10.9
Sayreville (borough)	19.1	27.5	23.1	12.5	17.8
South Brunswick (twp)	19.0	32.0	21.2	9.3	18.5
Stafford (twp)	32.0	22.3	15.7	11.6	18.4
Teaneck (twp)	22.6	27.0	20.7	12.2	17.4
Toms River (cdp)	30.2	31.0	14.1	7.1	17.5
Trenton (city)	29.5	40.1	17.2	6.2	7.0
Union (twp)	27.6	34.6	19.9	8.0	9.8
Union City (city)	19.7	34.0	25.1	10.5	10.7
Vernon (twp)	18.5	16.2	14.5	19.1	31.7
Vineland (city)	43.8	29.8	10.5	7.7	8.1
Voorhees (twp)	21.4	29.2	24.9	12.8	11.7
Wall (twp)	29.9	31.6	13.7	7.6	17.2
Washington (twp)	24.6	24.1	25.5	13.2	12.7
Wayne (twp)	25.6	32.8	21.4	8.6	11.5
West Milford (twp)	13.5	17.8	30.5	20.4	17.7
West New York (town)	16.4	31.6	26.0	13.2	12.8
West Orange (twp)	22.0	35.7	21.2	7.6	13.6
West Windsor (twp)	21.8	27.7	10.5	6.9	33.1
Westfield (town)	25.9	25.2	19.0	9.3	20.6
Willingboro (twp)	19.6	31.4	24.2	10.2	14.6
Winslow (twp)	17.2	28.1	25.5	15.0	14.2
Woodbridge (twp)	26.6	29.8	19.9	9.3	14.5

NOTE: Data as of 2000

Crime

Place	Violent Crime Rate (crimes per 10,000 population)	Property Crime Rate (crimes per 10,000 population)
Atlantic City (city)	170.2	1,143.2
Bayonne (city)	29.8	137.8
Belleville (twp)	28.2	235.4
Bergenfield (borough)	9.5	99.0
Berkeley (twp)	7.8	159.8
Bernards (twp)	0.8	63.5
Bloomfield (twp)	38.7	403.0
Brick (twp)	12.5	168.0
Bridgewater (twp)	3.4	143.1
Camden (city)	226.2	656.1
Cherry Hill (twp)	14.1	309.9
Clifton (city)	28.9	261.1
Deptford (twp)	47.1	539.1
Dover (twp)	12.9	199.9
East Brunswick (twp)	7.6	170.9
East Orange (city)	159.8	605.8
East Windsor (twp)	8.6	150.7
Edison (twp)	21.3	243.5
Egg Harbor (twp)	27.2	272.5
Elizabeth (city)	55.3	445.2
Englewood (city)	21.3	199.3
Evesham (twp)	10.6	152.3
Ewing (twp)	24.7	257.1
Fair Lawn (borough)	17.6	155.0
Fort Lee (borough)	7.2	124.3
Franklin (twp)	20.2	137.6
Freehold (twp)	13.0	287.9
Galloway (twp)	22.9	190.9
Garfield (city)	24.4	179.2
Gloucester (twp)	31.3	244.3
Hackensack (city)	31.7	266.4
Hamilton (twp)	17.6	190.2
Hillsborough (twp)	5.0	94.0
Hoboken (city)	36.0	364.2
Howell (twp)	10.1	122.8
Irvington (twp)	237.3	556.4
Jackson (twp)	12.6	114.4
Jersey City (city)	120.2	341.3
Kearny (town)	26.9	275.1
Lacey (twp)	11.0	211.2
Lakewood (twp)	33.2	260.7
Lakewood (cdp)	n/a	n/a
Lawrence (twp)	16.4	358.8
Linden (city)	37.1	377.0
Livingston (twp)	11.7	180.3
Long Branch (city)	46.3	232.5
Manalapan (twp)	5.6	79.1
Manchester (twp)	5.9	86.8
Marlboro (twp)	3.8	98.4
Mercerville-Ham. Sq. (cdp)	n/a	n/a

Place	Violent Crime Rate (crimes per 10,000 population)	Property Crime Rate (crimes per 10,000 population)
Middletown (twp)	9.6	104.2
Millville (city)	78.0	575.6
Monroe (twp)	4.7	62.7
Monroe (twp)	20.9	187.7
Montclair (twp)	36.3	264.6
Mount Laurel (twp)	10.8	191.9
Mount Olive (twp)	6.2	118.2
Neptune (twp)	41.2	425.1
New Brunswick (city)	70.2	389.8
Newark (city)	102.4	471.6
North Bergen (twp)	18.5	218.7
North Brunswick (twp)	20.4	236.6
Nutley (twp)	14.8	127.3
Ocean (twp)	15.1	238.1
Old Bridge (twp)	9.0	164.1
Orange (cdp)	116.5	517.9
Paramus (borough)	31.5	790.2
Parsippany-Troy Hills (twp)	6.8	161.2
Passaic (city)	99.0	291.9
Paterson (city)	80.1	306.3
Pemberton (twp)	21.3	187.0
Pennsauken (twp)	44.0	366.2
Perth Amboy (city)	31.6	210.5
Piscataway (twp)	11.3	116.0
Plainfield (city)	114.1	329.0
Rahway (city)	34.1	249.9
Randolph (twp)	4.7	98.2
Rockaway (twp)	8.3	157.8
Sayreville (borough)	19.8	171.6
South Brunswick (twp)	8.2	124.1
Stafford (twp)	17.6	252.4
Teaneck (twp)	18.7	186.1
Toms River (cdp)	n/a	n/a
Trenton (city)	158.0	442.9
Union (twp)	35.7	296.3
Union City (city)	48.2	240.6
Vernon (twp)	6.2	149.1
Vineland (city)	78.1	508.4
Voorhees (twp)	24.3	284.2
Wall (twp)	9.1	144.0
Washington (twp)	19.1	245.8
Wayne (twp)	5.8	232.3
West Milford (twp)	8.2	153.3
West New York (town)	28.5	197.8
West Orange (twp)	17.0	252.1
West Windsor (twp)	6.6	217.6
Westfield (town)	1.3	114.7
Willingboro (twp)	35.1	216.4
Winslow (twp)	43.2	193.2
Woodbridge (twp)	31.3	281.3

NOTE: Data as of 2004.

EDUCATION

New Jersey Public School Educational Profile

Category	Value	Category	Value
Schools *(2003-2004)*	2,467	**Diploma Recipients** *(2002-2003)*	77,831
Instructional Level		White, Non-Hispanic	50,429
Primary	1,540	Black, Non-Hispanic	11,944
Middle	437	Asian/Pacific Islander	5,632
High	384	American Indian/Alaskan Native	133
Other Level	106	Hispanic	9,693
Curriculum		**High School Drop-out Rate** (%) *(2001-2002)*	2.5
Regular	2,311	White, Non-Hispanic	1.5
Special Education	83	Black, Non-Hispanic	4.9
Vocational	55	Asian/Pacific Islander	0.9
Alternative	18	American Indian/Alaskan Native	2.2
Type		Hispanic	4.7
Magnet	3	**Staff** *(2003-2004)*	
Charter	51	Teachers	109,076.5
Title I Eligible	1,366	Average Salary ($)	53,663
School-wide Title I	256	Librarians/Media Specialists	1,871.2
Students *(2003-2004)*	1,451,180	Guidance Counselors	3,672.7
Gender (%)		**Ratios** *(2003-2004)*	
Male	51.4	Student/Teacher Ratio	13.3 to 1
Female	48.6	Student/Librarian Ratio	775.5 to 1
Race/Ethnicity (%)		Student/Counselor Ratio	395.1 to 1
White, Non-Hispanic	57.9	**College Entrance Exam Scores** *(2005)*	
Black, Non-Hispanic	17.7	Scholastic Aptitude Test (SAT)	
Asian/Pacific Islander	7.0	Participation Rate (%)	86
American Indian/Alaskan Native	0.2	Mean SAT Reasoning Test Verbal Score	503
Hispanic	17.2	Mean SAT Reasoning Test Math Score	517
Classification (%)		American College Testing Program (ACT)	
Individual Education Program (IEP)	15.4	Participation Rate (%)	6
Migrant *(2002-2003)*	0.1	Average Composite Score	21.3
English Language Learner (ELL)	4.0	Average English Score	20.9
Eligible for Free Lunch Program	20.6	Average Math Score	21.5
Eligible for Reduced-Price Lunch Program	6.3	Average Reading Score	21.7
Current Spending *($ per student in FY 2003)*	12,366	Average Science Score	20.8
Instruction	7,421		
Support Services	4,586		

Note: *For an explanation of data, please refer to the User's Guide in the front of the book*

Number of Schools

Rank	Number	District Name	City
1	77	Newark City	Newark
2	40	Jersey City	Jersey City
3	36	Paterson City	Paterson
4	31	Camden City	Camden
5	26	Elizabeth City	Elizabeth
6	24	Trenton City	Trenton
6	24	Woodbridge Twp	Woodbridge
8	23	Hamilton Twp	Hamilton Square
9	21	East Orange	East Orange
10	19	Cherry Hill Twp	Cherry Hill
10	19	Vineland City	Vineland
12	17	Edison Twp	Edison
12	17	Middletown Twp	Middletown
12	17	Passaic City	Passaic
12	17	Toms River Regional	Toms River
16	16	Clifton City	Clifton
17	15	Old Bridge Twp	Matawan
18	14	Parsippany-Troy Hills Twp	Parsippany
19	13	Pennsauken Twp	Pennsauken
19	13	Plainfield City	Plainfield
19	13	Wayne Twp	Wayne
22	12	Bayonne City	Bayonne
22	12	Brick Twp	Brick
22	12	Gloucester Twp	Blackwood
22	12	Howell Twp	Howell
22	12	Irvington Township	Irvington
22	12	South Brunswick Twp	Monmouth Jct
22	12	Union City	Union City
29	11	Atlantic City	Atlantic City
29	11	Bloomfield Twp	Bloomfield
29	11	East Brunswick Twp	E Brunswick
29	11	Linden City	Linden
29	11	Montclair Town	Montclair
29	11	Pemberton Twp	Pemberton
29	11	Perth Amboy City	Perth Amboy
29	11	Washington Twp	Sewell
29	11	Willingboro Twp	Willingboro
38	10	Bridgewater-Raritan Reg	Bridgewater
38	10	Deptford Twp	Deptford
38	10	Garfield City	Garfield
38	10	Millville City	Millville
38	10	Morris SD	Morristown
38	10	New Brunswick City	New Brunswick
38	10	Piscataway Twp	Piscataway
38	10	Ridgewood Village	Ridgewood
38	10	Union Twp	Union
38	10	W Windsor-Plainsboro Reg	Princeton Jct
38	10	West Orange Town	West Orange
49	9	Belleville Twp	Belleville
49	9	City of Orange Twp	Orange
49	9	Evesham Twp	Marlton
49	9	Fair Lawn Boro	Fair Lawn
49	9	Galloway Twp	Galloway
49	9	Hillsborough Twp	Neshanic
49	9	Jackson Twp	Jackson
49	9	Livingston Twp	Livingston
49	9	Long Branch City	Long Branch
49	9	South Orange-Maplewood	Maplewood
49	9	Westfield Town	Westfield
49	9	Winslow Twp	Atco
61	8	Franklin Twp	Somerset
61	8	Hazlet Twp	Hazlet
61	8	Jefferson Twp	Lake Hopatcong
61	8	Marlboro Twp	Marlboro
61	8	Monmouth County Vocational	Colts Neck
61	8	Mount Laurel Twp	Mount Laurel
61	8	Neptune Twp	Neptune
61	8	Paramus Boro	Paramus
61	8	Scotch Plains-Fanwood Reg	Scotch Plains
61	8	South Plainfield Boro	S Plainfield
61	8	West Milford Twp	West Milford
61	8	West New York Town	West New York
73	7	Bergen County Special Service	Paramus
73	7	Bergenfield Boro	Bergenfield
73	7	Bridgeton City	Bridgeton
73	7	Collingswood Boro	Collingswood
73	7	Cranford Twp	Cranford
73	7	Egg Harbor Twp	W Atlantic City
73	7	Freehold Regional	Freehold
73	7	Hackensack City	Hackensack
73	7	Haddon Twp	Westmont
73	7	Kearny Town	Kearny
73	7	Lawrence Twp	Lawrenceville
73	7	Lodi Borough	Lodi
73	7	Lyndhurst Twp	Lyndhurst
73	7	Mahwah Twp	Mahwah
73	7	Manalapan-Englishtown Reg	Englishtown
73	7	Matawan-Aberdeen Regional	Aberdeen
73	7	Millburn Twp	Millburn
73	7	Montville Twp	Montville
73	7	North Bergen Twp	North Bergen
73	7	Nutley Town	Nutley
73	7	Phillipsburg Town	Phillipsburg
73	7	Roxbury Twp	Succasunna
73	7	Sayreville Boro	Sayreville
73	7	Summit City	Summit
73	7	Teaneck Twp	Teaneck
73	7	Wall Twp	Wall
99	6	Asbury Park City	Asbury Park
99	6	Berkeley Heights Twp	Berkeley Hgts
99	6	Bernards Twp	Basking Ridge
99	6	Buena Regional	Buena
99	6	Caldwell-West Caldwell	West Caldwell
99	6	East Windsor Regional	Hightstown
99	6	Fort Lee Boro	Fort Lee
99	6	Freehold Regional	Englishtown
99	6	Glen Rock Boro	Glen Rock
99	6	Hillside Twp	Hillside
99	6	Hoboken City	Hoboken
99	6	Hopewell Valley Regional	Pennington
99	6	Lacey Twp	Lanoka Harbor
99	6	Lakewood Twp	Lakewood
99	6	Manchester Twp	Whiting
99	6	Middlesex County Vocational	E Brunswick
99	6	Monroe Twp	Williamstown
99	6	Monroe Twp	Monroe Township
99	6	Moorestown Twp	Moorestown
99	6	Mount Olive Twp	Budd Lake
99	6	North Brunswick Twp	North Brunswick
99	6	Pleasantville City	Pleasantville
99	6	Princeton Regional	Princeton
99	6	Rahway City	Rahway
99	6	Randolph Twp	Randolph
99	6	Rockaway Twp	Hibernia
99	6	Roselle Boro	Roselle
99	6	Rutherford Boro	Rutherford
99	6	SD of the Chathams	Chatham
99	6	Tenafly Boro	Tenafly
99	6	Vernon Twp	Vernon
99	6	Verona Boro	Verona
99	6	Westwood Regional	Westwood
132	5	Burlington City	Burlington
132	5	Burlington Twp	Burlington
132	5	Carteret Boro	Carteret
132	5	Cliffside Park Boro	Cliffside Park
132	5	Dover Town	Dover
132	5	Dumont Boro	Dumont
132	5	Elmwood Park	Elmwood Park
132	5	Englewood City	Englewood
132	5	Ewing Twp	Ewing
132	5	Flemington-Raritan Reg	Flemington
132	5	Glassboro	Glassboro
132	5	Haddonfield Boro	Haddonfield
132	5	Hawthorne Boro	Hawthorne
132	5	Hopatcong	Hopatcong
132	5	Madison Boro	Madison
132	5	Medford Twp	Medford
132	5	Mercer County Special Service	Trenton
132	5	Middlesex Boro	Middlesex
132	5	North Arlington Boro	North Arlington
132	5	North Plainfield Boro	N Plainfield
132	5	Ocean Twp	Oakhurst
132	5	Penns Grv-Carney's Pt Reg	Penns Grove
132	5	Pennsville	Pennsville
132	5	Pequannock Twp	Pompton Plains
132	5	Pitman Boro	Pitman
132	5	Ramsey Boro	Ramsey
132	5	Roselle Park Boro	Roselle Park
132	5	Saddle Brook Twp	Saddle Brook
132	5	Sparta Twp	Sparta
132	5	Springfield Twp	Springfield
132	5	Voorhees Twp	Voorhees
132	5	Warren Twp	Warren
132	5	Washington Twp	Long Valley
132	5	West Deptford Twp	West Deptford
132	5	Wyckoff Twp	Wyckoff
167	4	Barnegat Twp	Barnegat
167	4	Bergen County Vocational	Paramus
167	4	Bordentown Regional	Bordentown
167	4	Branchburg Twp	Branchburg
167	4	Cedar Grove Twp	Cedar Grove
167	4	Cinnaminson Twp	Cinnaminson
167	4	Clark Twp	Clark
167	4	Delran Twp	Delran
167	4	Essex County Voc-Tech	West Orange
167	4	Florence Twp	Florence
167	4	Glen Ridge Boro	Glen Ridge
167	4	Hackettstown	Hackettstown
167	4	Hammonton Town	Hammonton
167	4	Hanover Twp	Whippany
167	4	Hasbrouck Heights Boro	Hasbrouck Hgts
167	4	Holmdel Twp	Holmdel
167	4	Keansburg Boro	Keansburg
167	4	Kinnelon Boro	Kinnelon
167	4	Lenape Regional	Shamong
167	4	Lindenwold Boro	Lindenwold
167	4	Lower Twp	Cape May
167	4	Lumberton Twp	Lumberton
167	4	Maple Shade Twp	Maple Shade
167	4	Metuchen Boro	Metuchen
167	4	Middle Twp	Cape May Ct Hse
167	4	Montgomery Twp	Skillman
167	4	Mountain Lakes Boro	Mountain Lakes
167	4	New Milford Boro	New Milford
167	4	New Providence Boro	New Providence
167	4	Oakland Boro	Oakland
167	4	Pine Hill Boro	Pine Hill
167	4	Pittsgrove Twp	Pittsgrove
167	4	Point Pleasant Boro	Pt Pleasant
167	4	Pompton Lakes Boro	Pompton Lakes
167	4	Readington Twp	Whitehouse Stn
167	4	Ridgefield Boro	Ridgefield
167	4	Ridgefield Park Twp	Ridgefield Park
167	4	Secaucus Town	Secaucus
167	4	Spotswood Boro	Spotswood
167	4	Stafford Twp	Manahawkin
167	4	Woodbury City	Woodbury
208	3	Audubon Boro	Audubon
208	3	Berkeley Twp	Bayville
208	3	Black Horse Pike Regional	Blackwood
208	3	Bound Brook Boro	Bound Brook
208	3	Burlington County Spec Serv	Mount Holly
208	3	Clinton Twp	Annandale
208	3	Colts Neck Twp	Colts Neck
208	3	Cresskill Boro	Cresskill
208	3	Denville Twp	Denville
208	3	Franklin Lakes Boro	Franklin Lakes
208	3	Franklin Twp	Franklinville
208	3	Gloucester City	Gloucester City
208	3	Hamilton Twp	Mays Landing
208	3	Harrison Town	Harrison
208	3	Highland Park Boro	Highland Park
208	3	Leonia Boro	Leonia
208	3	Mantua Twp	Sewell
208	3	Newton Town	Newton
208	3	Ocean City	Ocean City
208	3	Paulsboro Boro	Paulsboro
208	3	Plumsted Twp	New Egypt
208	3	Riverside Twp	Riverside
208	3	Salem City	Salem
208	3	Somerset Hills Regional	Bernardsville
208	3	Somerville Boro	Somerville
208	3	South River Boro	South River
208	3	Sussex-Wantage Regional	Wantage
208	3	Tinton Falls	Tinton Falls
208	3	Upper Twp	Petersburg
208	3	Waldwick Boro	Waldwick
208	3	Woodstown-Pilesgrove Reg	Woodstown
239	2	Burlington County Vocational	Westampton Twp
239	2	Camden County Vocational	Sicklerville
239	2	Central Regional	Bayville
239	2	Clearview Regional	Mullica Hill
239	2	Delsea Regional H.S District	Franklinville
239	2	Eastern Camden County Reg	Voorhees
239	2	Greater Egg Harbor Reg	Mays Landing
239	2	Kingsway Regional	Woolwich Twp
239	2	Little Egg Harbor Twp	Little Egg Hbr
239	2	Lower Cape May Regional	Cape May
239	2	Manasquan Boro	Manasquan
239	2	Millstone Twp	Clarksburg
239	2	Morris Hills Regional	Rockaway
239	2	N Hunt/Voorhees Regional	Annandale
239	2	Northern Burlington Reg	Columbus
239	2	Northern Valley Regional	Demarest
239	2	Palisades Park	Palisades Park
239	2	Pascack Valley Regional	Montvale
239	2	Pinelands Regional	Tuckerton
239	2	Ramapo-Indian Hill Reg	Franklin Lakes
239	2	Rancocas Valley Regional	Mount Holly
239	2	Southern Regional	Manahawkin
239	2	Upper Freehold Regional	Allentown
239	2	Warren Hills Regional	Washington
239	2	Washington Twp	Robbinsville
239	2	West Morris Regional	Chester
265	1	High Point Regional	Sussex
265	1	Hunterdon Central Reg	Flemington
265	1	Mainland Regional	Linwood
265	1	Passaic County Vocational	Wayne
265	1	Watchung Hills Regional	Warren

Number of Teachers

Rank	Number	District Name	City
1	3,687	Newark City	Newark
2	2,701	Jersey City	Jersey City

3	2,419	Paterson City	Paterson
4	2,007	Elizabeth City	Elizabeth
5	1,547	Camden City	Camden
6	1,176	Toms River Regional	Toms River
7	1,040	Edison Twp	Edison
8	1,017	Trenton City	Trenton
9	996	Woodbridge Twp	Woodbridge
10	949	Hamilton Twp	Hamilton Square
11	894	Passaic City	Passaic
12	881	East Orange	East Orange
13	850	Vineland City	Vineland
14	823	Union City	Union City
15	818	Cherry Hill Twp	Cherry Hill
16	786	Clifton City	Clifton
17	777	Brick Twp	Brick
18	755	Middletown Twp	Middletown
19	739	Freehold Regional	Englishtown
20	736	Washington Twp	Sewell
21	727	Perth Amboy City	Perth Amboy
22	695	W Windsor-Plainsboro Reg	Princeton Jct
23	670	Old Bridge Twp	Matawan
24	662	Bridgewater-Raritan Reg	Bridgewater
25	660	Jackson Twp	Jackson
26	649	Plainfield City	Plainfield
27	636	Bayonne City	Bayonne
28	625	Wayne Twp	Wayne
29	622	East Brunswick Twp	E Brunswick
30	622	South Brunswick Twp	Monmouth Jct
31	616	Atlantic City	Atlantic City
32	614	Hillsborough Twp	Neshanic
33	592	New Brunswick City	New Brunswick
34	583	Parsippany-Troy Hills Twp	Parsippany
35	567	Irvington Township	Irvington
36	544	Union Twp	Union
37	544	Montclair Town	Montclair
38	544	Gloucester Twp	Blackwood
39	538	Lenape Regional	Shamong
40	530	Howell Twp	Howell
41	520	West New York Town	West New York
42	515	West Orange Town	West Orange
43	514	Winslow Twp	Atco
44	514	Pemberton Twp	Pemberton
45	511	Millville City	Millville
46	506	Franklin Twp	Somerset
47	504	Piscataway Twp	Piscataway
48	489	Long Branch City	Long Branch
49	486	Egg Harbor Twp	W Atlantic City
50	482	North Bergen Twp	North Bergen
51	476	Lakewood Twp	Lakewood
52	469	Willingboro Twp	Willingboro
53	462	South Orange-Maplewood	Maplewood
54	460	Linden City	Linden
55	448	Westfield Town	Westfield
56	445	Bloomfield Twp	Bloomfield
57	427	Pennsauken Twp	Pennsauken
58	418	Livingston Twp	Livingston
59	416	Randolph Twp	Randolph
60	406	Evesham Twp	Marlton
61	406	Morris SD	Morristown
62	400	Bridgeton City	Bridgeton
63	399	Marlboro Twp	Marlboro
64	395	North Brunswick Twp	North Brunswick
65	395	Bernards Twp	Basking Ridge
66	395	Kearny Town	Kearny
67	390	Manalapan-Englishtown Reg	Englishtown
68	387	Sayreville Boro	Sayreville
69	387	Ridgewood Village	Ridgewood
70	382	Pleasantville City	Pleasantville
71	379	Hackensack City	Hackensack
72	375	City of Orange Twp	Orange
73	366	Monroe Twp	Williamstown
74	360	East Windsor Regional	Hightstown
75	352	Mount Olive Twp	Budd Lake
76	352	Garfield City	Garfield
77	350	Fair Lawn Boro	Fair Lawn
78	350	Scotch Plains-Fanwood Reg	Scotch Plains
79	348	Teaneck Twp	Teaneck
80	348	Vernon Twp	Vernon
81	345	Roxbury Twp	Succasunna
82	344	Millburn Twp	Millburn
83	344	Lacey Twp	Lanoka Harbor
84	339	Paramus Boro	Paramus
85	337	Mount Laurel Twp	Mount Laurel
86	334	Phillipsburg Town	Phillipsburg
87	332	West Milford Twp	West Milford
88	330	Montgomery Twp	Skillman
89	328	Neptune Twp	Neptune
90	326	Ocean Twp	Oakhurst
91	326	Wall Twp	Wall
92	325	Galloway Twp	Galloway
93	325	Belleville Town	Belleville
94	323	Ewing Twp	Ewing
95	321	Monroe Twp	Monroe Township
96	321	Hopewell Valley Regional	Pennington
97	310	Lawrence Twp	Lawrenceville
98	307	Asbury Park City	Asbury Park
99	300	Matawan-Aberdeen Regional	Aberdeen
100	298	South Plainfield Boro	S Plainfield
101	296	Moorestown Twp	Moorestown
102	294	Montville Twp	Montville
103	289	Freehold Twp	Freehold
104	289	Burlington Twp	Burlington
105	286	North Plainfield Boro	N Plainfield
106	286	Deptford Twp	Deptford
107	282	Southern Regional	Manahawkin
108	281	Rahway City	Rahway
109	280	Summit City	Summit
110	280	Carteret Boro	Carteret
111	279	Nutley Town	Nutley
112	278	Princeton Regional	Princeton
113	268	Cranford Twp	Cranford
114	266	Bergenfield Boro	Bergenfield
115	266	Manchester Twp	Whiting
116	263	Hazlet Twp	Hazlet
117	262	Flemington-Raritan Reg	Flemington
118	262	Jefferson Twp	Lake Hopatcong
119	262	Mahwah Twp	Mahwah
120	261	Sparta Twp	Sparta
121	260	Greater Egg Harbor Reg	Mays Landing
122	259	Tenafly Boro	Tenafly
123	258	Voorhees Twp	Voorhees
124	257	Black Horse Pike Regional	Blackwood
125	250	Rockaway Twp	Hibernia
126	249	Fort Lee Boro	Fort Lee
127	241	Holmdel Twp	Holmdel
128	237	Englewood City	Englewood
129	233	SD of the Chathams	Chatham
130	231	Middle Twp	Cape May Ct Hse
131	230	Hamilton Twp	Mays Landing
132	230	Lodi Borough	Lodi
133	226	Point Pleasant Boro	Pt Pleasant
134	224	Ramsey Boro	Ramsey
135	222	Dover Town	Dover
136	221	Gloucester City	Gloucester City
137	220	Hillside Twp	Hillside
138	219	Hunterdon Central Reg	Flemington
139	216	Lindenwold Boro	Lindenwold
140	216	Morris Hills Regional	Rockaway
141	216	Keansburg Boro	Keansburg
142	214	Bergen County Vocational	Paramus
143	212	Monmouth County Vocational	Colts Neck
144	211	Ocean City	Ocean City
145	209	Hammonton Town	Hammonton
146	209	Warren Twp	Warren
147	208	N Hunt/Voorhees Regional	Annandale
148	208	Berkeley Heights Twp	Berkeley Hgts
148	208	Hoboken City	Hoboken
150	207	West Deptford Twp	West Deptford
151	206	Westwood Regional	Westwood
152	205	Northern Valley Regional	Demarest
153	205	Middlesex County Vocational	E Brunswick
154	202	Cinnaminson Twp	Cinnaminson
155	201	Roselle Boro	Roselle
156	196	Passaic County Vocational	Wayne
157	193	Hopatcong	Hopatcong
157	193	West Morris Regional	Chester
159	192	Washington Twp	Long Valley
160	192	Penns Grv-Carney's Pt Reg	Penns Grove
160	192	Pine Hill Boro	Pine Hill
162	191	Cliffside Park Boro	Cliffside Park
163	191	Glassboro	Glassboro
164	188	Ramapo-Indian Hill Reg	Franklin Lakes
165	188	Buena Regional	Buena
166	186	Bergen County Special Service	Paramus
167	185	Hawthorne Boro	Hawthorne
168	185	Caldwell-West Caldwell	West Caldwell
169	185	Glen Rock Boro	Glen Rock
170	185	Dumont Boro	Dumont
171	184	Rutherford Boro	Rutherford
172	184	Medford Twp	Medford
173	182	Pequannock Twp	Pompton Plains
174	182	Delran Twp	Delran
175	180	Burlington City	Burlington
176	177	Pinelands Regional	Tuckerton
177	176	Madison Boro	Madison
178	175	Clark Twp	Clark
178	175	Essex County Voc-Tech	West Orange
180	173	Readington Twp	Whitehouse Stn
181	173	Stafford Twp	Manahawkin
182	172	Somerville Boro	Somerville
183	172	Barnegat Twp	Barnegat
184	171	Leonia Boro	Leonia
185	170	New Providence Boro	New Providence
186	169	Camden County Vocational	Sicklerville
187	168	Mountain Lakes Boro	Mountain Lakes
188	167	Haddonfield Boro	Haddonfield
189	166	Ridgefield Park Twp	Ridgefield Park
190	165	Wyckoff Twp	Wyckoff
191	165	Middlesex Boro	Middlesex
192	163	Collingswood Boro	Collingswood
193	161	Roselle Park Boro	Roselle Park
194	160	Springfield Twp	Springfield
195	159	Pennsville	Pennsville
196	159	Branchburg Twp	Branchburg
197	158	Burlington County Vocational	Westampton Twp
198	157	Warren Hills Regional	Washington
199	157	Ridgefield Boro	Ridgefield
200	156	Maple Shade Twp	Maple Shade
201	155	Bordentown Regional	Bordentown
202	154	Metuchen Boro	Metuchen
203	153	Clearview Regional	Mullica Hill
204	152	Burlington County Spec Serv	Mount Holly
205	151	Haddon Twp	Westmont
206	151	Eastern Camden County Reg	Voorhees
207	151	Kinnelon Boro	Kinnelon
208	150	Lower Cape May Regional	Cape May
209	149	Lyndhurst Twp	Lyndhurst
210	149	Hackettstown	Hackettstown
211	149	South River Boro	South River
212	148	Central Regional	Bayville
213	145	Woodbury City	Woodbury
214	145	Northern Burlington Reg	Columbus
215	143	Secaucus Town	Secaucus
216	143	Verona Boro	Verona
217	143	Somerset Hills Regional	Bernardsville
218	141	Lower Twp	Cape May
219	140	New Milford Boro	New Milford
220	139	Upper Freehold Regional	Allentown
221	139	Pitman Boro	Pitman
222	138	Delsea Regional H.S District	Franklinville
223	137	Little Egg Harbor Twp	Little Egg Hbr
224	137	Sussex-Wantage Regional	Wantage
225	137	Mercer County Special Service	Trenton
226	137	Newton Town	Newton
227	136	Clinton Twp	Annandale
228	134	Elmwood Park	Elmwood Park
229	133	Harrison Town	Harrison
230	133	Pompton Lakes Boro	Pompton Lakes
231	133	Spotswood Boro	Spotswood
232	133	Berkeley Twp	Bayville
232	133	Pascack Valley Regional	Montvale
234	132	Pittsgrove Twp	Pittsgrove
234	132	Watchung Hills Regional	Warren
236	131	Upper Twp	Petersburg
237	130	Rancocas Valley Regional	Mount Holly
238	130	Denville Twp	Denville
239	129	Florence Twp	Florence
240	129	Lumberton Twp	Lumberton
241	128	Mainland Regional	Linwood
242	127	Colts Neck Twp	Colts Neck
243	126	Salem City	Salem
244	126	Glen Ridge Boro	Glen Ridge
245	125	Audubon Boro	Audubon
246	124	Woodstown-Pilesgrove Reg	Woodstown
247	123	Washington Twp	Robbinsville
248	123	Millstone Twp	Clarksburg
248	123	Oakland Boro	Oakland
248	123	Plumsted Twp	New Egypt
251	123	Kingsway Regional	Woolwich Twp
252	122	Manasquan Boro	Manasquan
253	122	Tinton Falls	Tinton Falls
254	122	Highland Park Boro	Highland Park
255	121	Franklin Lakes Boro	Franklin Lakes
256	118	Saddle Brook Twp	Saddle Brook
257	117	Hanover Twp	Whippany
258	117	Hasbrouck Heights Boro	Hasbrouck Hgts
259	116	Bound Brook Boro	Bound Brook
260	116	Paulsboro Boro	Paulsboro
261	114	Waldwick Boro	Waldwick
262	113	Cedar Grove Twp	Cedar Grove
262	113	North Arlington Boro	North Arlington
264	111	Palisades Park	Palisades Park
265	107	High Point Regional	Sussex
266	107	Cresskill Boro	Cresskill
267	100	Mantua Twp	Sewell
268	100	Riverside Twp	Riverside
269	94	Franklin Twp	Franklinville

Number of Students

Rank	Number	District Name	City
1	46,825	Newark City	Newark
2	35,161	Jersey City	Jersey City
3	27,734	Paterson City	Paterson
4	21,998	Elizabeth City	Elizabeth
5	19,190	Toms River Regional	Toms River
6	18,997	Camden City	Camden
7	14,074	Hamilton Twp	Hamilton Square

8	14,056	Woodbridge Twp	Woodbridge
9	13,293	Edison Twp	Edison
10	13,227	Trenton City	Trenton
11	12,403	East Orange	East Orange
12	12,162	Passaic City	Passaic
13	12,065	Brick Twp	Brick
14	11,911	Cherry Hill Twp	Cherry Hill
15	10,984	Clifton City	Clifton
16	10,935	Freehold Regional	Englishtown
17	10,777	Middletown Twp	Middletown
18	10,436	Union City	Union City
19	10,316	Vineland City	Vineland
20	10,119	Old Bridge Twp	Matawan
21	9,859	Washington Twp	Sewell
22	9,762	Jackson Twp	Jackson
22	9,762	Perth Amboy City	Perth Amboy
24	9,430	Bayonne City	Bayonne
25	9,238	W Windsor-Plainsboro Reg	Princeton Jct
26	9,141	East Brunswick Twp	E Brunswick
27	9,097	Wayne Twp	Wayne
28	8,894	Bridgewater-Raritan Reg	Bridgewater
29	8,830	Irvington Township	Irvington
30	8,506	South Brunswick Twp	Monmouth Jct
31	8,119	Plainfield City	Plainfield
32	8,105	Union Twp	Union
33	8,090	Gloucester Twp	Blackwood
34	7,989	North Bergen Twp	North Bergen
35	7,782	Hillsborough Twp	Neshanic
36	7,648	Howell Twp	Howell
37	7,290	Atlantic City	Atlantic City
38	7,201	Parsippany-Troy Hills Twp	Parsippany
39	7,153	West New York Town	West New York
40	7,067	Lenape Regional	Shamong
41	6,991	Piscataway Twp	Piscataway
42	6,989	New Brunswick City	New Brunswick
43	6,840	Franklin Twp	Somerset
44	6,805	Egg Harbor Twp	W Atlantic City
45	6,742	Winslow Twp	Atco
46	6,646	Pennsauken Twp	Pennsauken
47	6,617	Montclair Town	Montclair
48	6,588	West Orange Town	West Orange
49	6,559	South Orange-Maplewood	Maplewood
50	6,508	Linden City	Linden
51	6,354	Bloomfield Twp	Bloomfield
52	6,226	Millville City	Millville
53	6,210	Pemberton Twp	Pemberton
54	6,084	Marlboro Twp	Marlboro
55	5,924	Sayreville Boro	Sayreville
56	5,909	Westfield Town	Westfield
57	5,888	Kearny Town	Kearny
58	5,875	Willingboro Twp	Willingboro
59	5,807	Lakewood Twp	Lakewood
60	5,708	Evesham Twp	Marlton
61	5,640	Manalapan-Englishtown Reg	Englishtown
62	5,624	Randolph Twp	Randolph
63	5,593	Monroe Twp	Williamstown
64	5,560	Ridgewood Village	Ridgewood
65	5,519	North Brunswick Twp	North Brunswick
66	5,500	Vernon Twp	Vernon
67	5,323	Lacey Twp	Lanoka Harbor
68	5,264	Long Branch City	Long Branch
69	5,216	Livingston Twp	Livingston
70	5,152	East Windsor Regional	Hightstown
71	5,149	Hackensack City	Hackensack
72	5,100	Bernards Twp	Basking Ridge
73	5,004	Scotch Plains-Fanwood Reg	Scotch Plains
74	4,982	Ocean Twp	Oakhurst
75	4,961	Mount Olive Twp	Budd Lake
76	4,878	West Milford Twp	West Milford
77	4,876	Morris SD	Morristown
78	4,865	Fair Lawn Boro	Fair Lawn
79	4,852	Lawrence Twp	Lawrenceville
80	4,817	Roxbury Twp	Succasunna
81	4,798	City of Orange Twp	Orange
82	4,787	Freehold Twp	Freehold
83	4,761	Bridgeton City	Bridgeton
84	4,729	Belleville Town	Belleville
85	4,726	Mount Laurel Twp	Mount Laurel
86	4,721	Montgomery Twp	Skillman
87	4,587	Garfield City	Garfield
88	4,576	Paramus Boro	Paramus
89	4,559	Neptune Twp	Neptune
90	4,512	Teaneck Twp	Teaneck
91	4,476	Deptford Twp	Deptford
92	4,438	Black Horse Pike Regional	Blackwood
93	4,395	Nutley Town	Nutley
94	4,365	Millburn Twp	Millburn
95	4,360	Wall Twp	Wall
96	4,316	Moorestown Twp	Moorestown
97	4,178	Ewing Twp	Ewing
98	4,163	Southern Regional	Manahawkin
99	4,155	Rahway City	Rahway
100	4,138	Galloway Twp	Galloway
101	4,124	Monroe Twp	Monroe Township
102	4,098	Burlington Twp	Burlington
103	4,067	Pleasantville City	Pleasantville
104	4,030	Montville Twp	Montville
105	4,025	Sparta Twp	Sparta
106	3,957	Carteret Boro	Carteret
107	3,953	Matawan-Aberdeen Regional	Aberdeen
108	3,906	South Plainfield Boro	S Plainfield
109	3,900	Bergenfield Boro	Bergenfield
110	3,879	Hopewell Valley Regional	Pennington
111	3,844	Greater Egg Harbor Reg	Mays Landing
112	3,715	Phillipsburg Town	Phillipsburg
113	3,694	Jefferson Twp	Lake Hopatcong
114	3,683	Flemington-Raritan Reg	Flemington
115	3,642	Cranford Twp	Cranford
116	3,626	Hillside Twp	Hillside
117	3,617	Holmdel Twp	Holmdel
118	3,580	Manchester Twp	Whiting
119	3,561	Hazlet Twp	Hazlet
120	3,519	Voorhees Twp	Voorhees
121	3,515	Summit City	Summit
122	3,461	Fort Lee Boro	Fort Lee
123	3,391	Dover Town	Dover
124	3,372	Hammonton Town	Hammonton
125	3,355	Mahwah Twp	Mahwah
126	3,352	North Plainfield Boro	N Plainfield
127	3,326	West Deptford Twp	West Deptford
128	3,304	Princeton Regional	Princeton
129	3,238	Point Pleasant Boro	Pt Pleasant
130	3,199	SD of the Chathams	Chatham
131	3,187	Hopatcong	Hopatcong
132	3,181	Asbury Park City	Asbury Park
133	3,176	Lodi Borough	Lodi
134	3,128	Tenafly Boro	Tenafly
135	3,073	Washington Twp	Long Valley
136	3,065	Hamilton Twp	Mays Landing
137	3,038	Ramsey Boro	Ramsey
138	3,028	Medford Twp	Medford
139	2,985	Rockaway Twp	Hibernia
140	2,949	Middle Twp	Cape May Ct Hse
141	2,899	Roselle Boro	Roselle
142	2,839	Hunterdon Central Reg	Flemington
143	2,808	Lindenwold Boro	Lindenwold
144	2,803	Englewood City	Englewood
145	2,797	Berkeley Heights Twp	Berkeley Hgts
146	2,780	Delran Twp	Delran
147	2,779	N Hunt/Voorhees Regional	Annandale
148	2,760	Clark Twp	Clark
149	2,727	Cliffside Park Boro	Cliffside Park
149	2,727	Stafford Twp	Manahawkin
151	2,717	Dumont Boro	Dumont
152	2,696	Morris Hills Regional	Rockaway
153	2,663	Westwood Regional	Westwood
154	2,642	Cinnaminson Twp	Cinnaminson
155	2,627	Buena Regional	Buena
155	2,627	Caldwell-West Caldwell	West Caldwell
157	2,620	Camden County Vocational	Sicklerville
158	2,555	Glassboro	Glassboro
159	2,541	Pequannock Twp	Pompton Plains
160	2,472	Burlington County Spec Serv	Mount Holly
161	2,446	Wyckoff Twp	Wyckoff
162	2,431	Pine Hill Boro	Pine Hill
163	2,404	Maple Shade Twp	Maple Shade
164	2,402	West Morris Regional	Chester
165	2,399	Glen Rock Boro	Glen Rock
165	2,399	Passaic County Vocational	Wayne
165	2,399	Rutherford Boro	Rutherford
168	2,376	Barnegat Twp	Barnegat
169	2,371	Penns Grv-Carney's Pt Reg	Penns Grove
170	2,368	Essex County Voc-Tech	West Orange
171	2,357	Central Regional	Bayville
171	2,357	Haddon Twp	Westmont
173	2,345	Hawthorne Boro	Hawthorne
174	2,336	Ridgefield Boro	Ridgefield
175	2,331	Bergen County Vocational	Paramus
176	2,327	Northern Valley Regional	Demarest
177	2,317	Haddonfield Boro	Haddonfield
178	2,315	Middlesex County Vocational	E Brunswick
179	2,298	Readington Twp	Whitehouse Stn
180	2,290	Madison Boro	Madison
181	2,273	Gloucester City	Gloucester City
182	2,269	Rancocas Valley Regional	Mount Holly
183	2,247	South River Boro	South River
184	2,236	Somerville Boro	Somerville
185	2,229	Warren Twp	Warren
186	2,224	Ocean City	Ocean City
187	2,218	Hoboken City	Hoboken
188	2,216	Warren Hills Regional	Washington
189	2,205	Eastern Camden County Reg	Voorhees
190	2,194	Keansburg Boro	Keansburg
191	2,192	Clearview Regional	Mullica Hill
191	2,192	Lyndhurst Twp	Lyndhurst
193	2,185	New Providence Boro	New Providence
194	2,179	Middlesex Boro	Middlesex
195	2,157	Kinnelon Boro	Kinnelon
196	2,134	Ramapo-Indian Hill Reg	Franklin Lakes
197	2,114	Elmwood Park	Elmwood Park
198	2,105	Pennsville	Pennsville
199	2,101	Roselle Park Boro	Roselle Park
200	2,083	Springfield Twp	Springfield
201	2,075	Collingswood Boro	Collingswood
202	2,062	Bordentown Regional	Bordentown
203	2,061	Pinelands Regional	Tuckerton
204	2,055	Verona Boro	Verona
205	2,040	Upper Freehold Regional	Allentown
206	2,005	Harrison Town	Harrison
207	2,000	Lower Twp	Cape May
208	1,989	Delsea Regional H.S District	Franklinville
209	1,983	Berkeley Twp	Bayville
210	1,982	Bergen County Special Service	Paramus
211	1,980	Hackettstown	Hackettstown
212	1,959	Denville Twp	Denville
212	1,959	Ridgefield Park Twp	Ridgefield Park
214	1,949	Clinton Twp	Annandale
215	1,943	New Milford Boro	New Milford
216	1,933	Branchburg Twp	Branchburg
217	1,927	Northern Burlington Reg	Columbus
218	1,919	Burlington City	Burlington
219	1,915	Somerset Hills Regional	Bernardsville
220	1,910	Pompton Lakes Boro	Pompton Lakes
221	1,892	Secaucus Town	Secaucus
222	1,878	Pittsgrove Twp	Pittsgrove
223	1,872	Metuchen Boro	Metuchen
224	1,856	Monmouth County Vocational	Colts Neck
225	1,845	Lower Cape May Regional	Cape May
226	1,844	Little Egg Harbor Twp	Little Egg Hbr
226	1,844	Lumberton Twp	Lumberton
228	1,842	Mountain Lakes Boro	Mountain Lakes
229	1,829	Sussex-Wantage Regional	Wantage
230	1,826	Spotswood Boro	Spotswood
231	1,809	Leonia Boro	Leonia
232	1,804	Manasquan Boro	Manasquan
233	1,803	Burlington County Vocational	Westampton Twp
234	1,797	Glen Ridge Boro	Glen Ridge
234	1,797	Tinton Falls	Tinton Falls
236	1,779	Newton Town	Newton
237	1,772	Plumsted Twp	New Egypt
238	1,767	Upper Twp	Petersburg
239	1,763	Saddle Brook Twp	Saddle Brook
240	1,755	Audubon Boro	Audubon
241	1,752	Mercer County Special Service	Trenton
242	1,751	Kingsway Regional	Woolwich Twp
243	1,735	Millstone Twp	Clarksburg
243	1,735	Watchung Hills Regional	Warren
245	1,700	Woodstown-Pilesgrove Reg	Woodstown
246	1,695	Pitman Boro	Pitman
247	1,692	Oakland Boro	Oakland
248	1,679	Bound Brook Boro	Bound Brook
249	1,671	Franklin Lakes Boro	Franklin Lakes
250	1,670	Paulsboro Boro	Paulsboro
251	1,669	Mainland Regional	Linwood
252	1,641	Florence Twp	Florence
253	1,629	Riverside Twp	Riverside
254	1,624	North Arlington Boro	North Arlington
255	1,614	Pascack Valley Regional	Montvale
256	1,609	Woodbury City	Woodbury
257	1,606	Highland Park Boro	Highland Park
258	1,558	Hasbrouck Heights Boro	Hasbrouck Hgts
259	1,544	Colts Neck Twp	Colts Neck
259	1,544	Washington Twp	Robbinsville
261	1,540	High Point Regional	Sussex
262	1,518	Mantua Twp	Sewell
262	1,518	Salem City	Salem
264	1,514	Palisades Park	Palisades Park
265	1,512	Waldwick Boro	Waldwick
266	1,511	Cedar Grove Twp	Cedar Grove
267	1,509	Cresskill Boro	Cresskill
268	1,506	Franklin Twp	Franklinville
269	1,504	Hanover Twp	Whippany

Male Students

Rank	Percent	District Name	City
1	71.6	Burlington County Spec Serv	Mount Holly
2	71.0	Mercer County Special Service	Trenton
3	64.4	Bergen County Special Service	Paramus
4	58.4	Middlesex County Vocational	E Brunswick
5	55.5	Monmouth County Vocational	Colts Neck
6	55.2	Mantua Twp	Sewell
7	55.2	Lower Twp	Cape May
8	54.9	Ridgefield Boro	Ridgefield
9	54.9	Bergen County Vocational	Paramus
10	54.2	Franklin Twp	Franklinville
11	53.9	North Arlington Boro	North Arlington
12	53.7	Camden County Vocational	Sicklerville

13	53.6	New Milford Boro	New Milford
14	53.5	Cranford Twp	Cranford
15	53.5	Burlington City	Burlington
16	53.4	Hanover Twp	Whippany
17	53.4	Newton Town	Newton
18	53.3	Cinnaminson Twp	Cinnaminson
19	53.3	Keansburg Boro	Keansburg
20	53.2	Rockaway Twp	Hibernia
21	53.2	West Deptford Twp	West Deptford
22	53.1	Pleasantville City	Pleasantville
23	53.0	Phillipsburg Town	Phillipsburg
24	52.9	Cliffside Park Boro	Cliffside Park
25	52.9	Clark Twp	Clark
26	52.8	Sayreville Boro	Sayreville
27	52.8	Palisades Park	Palisades Park
28	52.8	Hoboken City	Hoboken
29	52.8	Mountain Lakes Boro	Mountain Lakes
30	52.8	Lindenwold Boro	Lindenwold
31	52.8	Plumsted Twp	New Egypt
32	52.7	Morris SD	Morristown
33	52.7	Tenafly Boro	Tenafly
34	52.7	Dover Town	Dover
35	52.7	West Milford Twp	West Milford
36	52.6	Ramsey Boro	Ramsey
37	52.6	South River Boro	South River
38	52.6	Glen Rock Boro	Glen Rock
39	52.6	Rahway City	Rahway
40	52.5	Spotswood Boro	Spotswood
41	52.5	Upper Freehold Regional	Allentown
42	52.5	Pennsauken Twp	Pennsauken
43	52.5	Central Regional	Bayville
44	52.5	Berkeley Twp	Bayville
45	52.5	Stafford Twp	Manahawkin
46	52.5	Paulsboro Boro	Paulsboro
47	52.5	Harrison Town	Harrison
48	52.5	Cherry Hill Twp	Cherry Hill
49	52.4	Perth Amboy City	Perth Amboy
50	52.4	Monroe Twp	Monroe Township
51	52.4	Paramus Boro	Paramus
52	52.3	Warren Hills Regional	Washington
53	52.3	Eastern Camden County Reg	Voorhees
54	52.3	Oakland Boro	Oakland
55	52.3	Hillsborough Twp	Neshanic
56	52.2	Clifton City	Clifton
57	52.2	Neptune Twp	Neptune
58	52.2	Middle Twp	Cape May Ct Hse
59	52.1	Lower Cape May Regional	Cape May
60	52.1	Franklin Lakes Boro	Franklin Lakes
61	52.1	Bayonne City	Bayonne
62	52.1	Gloucester Twp	Blackwood
63	52.1	Brick Twp	Brick
64	52.1	Westwood Regional	Westwood
65	52.1	Parsippany-Troy Hills Twp	Parsippany
66	52.1	Middletown Twp	Middletown
67	52.0	Summit City	Summit
68	52.0	Ridgefield Park Twp	Ridgefield Park
69	52.0	Kearny Town	Kearny
70	52.0	Flemington-Raritan Reg	Flemington
71	52.0	Union Twp	Union
72	52.0	Point Pleasant Boro	Pt Pleasant
73	52.0	Burlington County Vocational	Westampton Twp
74	52.0	Springfield Twp	Springfield
75	52.0	Upper Twp	Petersburg
76	52.0	Wall Twp	Wall
77	51.9	Pequannock Twp	Pompton Plains
78	51.9	Bloomfield Twp	Bloomfield
79	51.9	Hopatcong	Hopatcong
80	51.9	Glen Ridge Boro	Glen Ridge
81	51.9	Bound Brook Boro	Bound Brook
82	51.9	Carteret Boro	Carteret
83	51.9	Madison Boro	Madison
84	51.9	Willingboro Twp	Willingboro
85	51.8	North Bergen Twp	North Bergen
86	51.8	New Providence Boro	New Providence
86	51.8	Verona Boro	Verona
88	51.8	Vernon Twp	Vernon
89	51.8	Vineland City	Vineland
90	51.8	Manchester Twp	Whiting
91	51.8	City of Orange Twp	Orange
92	51.8	Lakewood Twp	Lakewood
93	51.8	Livingston Twp	Livingston
94	51.8	Irvington Township	Irvington
95	51.7	Winslow Twp	Atco
96	51.7	Roxbury Twp	Succasunna
97	51.7	Audubon Boro	Audubon
98	51.7	Evesham Twp	Marlton
99	51.7	Belleville Town	Belleville
100	51.7	Berkeley Heights Twp	Berkeley Hgts
101	51.7	Lawrence Twp	Lawrenceville
102	51.7	Little Egg Harbor Twp	Little Egg Hbr
103	51.6	Egg Harbor Twp	W Atlantic City
104	51.6	Kinnelon Boro	Kinnelon
105	51.6	South Plainfield Boro	S Plainfield
106	51.6	Jackson Twp	Jackson
107	51.6	Lumberton Twp	Lumberton
108	51.6	Branchburg Twp	Branchburg
109	51.6	Cedar Grove Twp	Cedar Grove
110	51.6	Hamilton Twp	Mays Landing
111	51.6	Fort Lee Boro	Fort Lee
112	51.5	Mount Laurel Twp	Mount Laurel
113	51.5	East Brunswick Twp	E Brunswick
114	51.5	Westfield Town	Westfield
115	51.5	Voorhees Twp	Voorhees
116	51.5	Hackettstown	Hackettstown
117	51.5	Pittsgrove Twp	Pittsgrove
118	51.5	Metuchen Boro	Metuchen
119	51.5	Montgomery Twp	Skillman
120	51.5	Marlboro Twp	Marlboro
121	51.4	Hamilton Twp	Hamilton Square
122	51.4	Sparta Twp	Sparta
123	51.4	Lacey Twp	Lanoka Harbor
124	51.4	Hawthorne Boro	Hawthorne
125	51.4	Toms River Regional	Toms River
126	51.4	Fair Lawn Boro	Fair Lawn
127	51.4	Princeton Regional	Princeton
128	51.3	Holmdel Twp	Holmdel
129	51.3	Old Bridge Twp	Matawan
130	51.3	Deptford Twp	Deptford
131	51.3	Union City	Union City
132	51.3	Jefferson Twp	Lake Hopatcong
133	51.3	Wayne Twp	Wayne
134	51.3	Bridgeton City	Bridgeton
135	51.3	SD of the Chathams	Chatham
136	51.3	Riverside Twp	Riverside
137	51.3	Jersey City	Jersey City
138	51.3	Newark City	Newark
139	51.3	Mount Olive Twp	Budd Lake
140	51.3	Delsea Regional H.S District	Franklinville
141	51.3	Ewing Twp	Ewing
142	51.3	Somerville Boro	Somerville
143	51.3	Monroe Twp	Williamstown
144	51.3	Watchung Hills Regional	Warren
145	51.3	Mahwah Twp	Mahwah
146	51.3	Black Horse Pike Regional	Blackwood
147	51.2	Tinton Falls	Tinton Falls
148	51.2	East Windsor Regional	Hightstown
149	51.2	Piscataway Twp	Piscataway
150	51.2	Franklin Twp	Somerset
151	51.2	Middlesex Boro	Middlesex
152	51.2	Readington Twp	Whitehouse Stn
153	51.2	Woodbridge Twp	Woodbridge
154	51.2	Washington Twp	Sewell
155	51.2	Maple Shade Twp	Maple Shade
156	51.2	Scotch Plains-Fanwood Reg	Scotch Plains
157	51.2	New Brunswick City	New Brunswick
158	51.2	Lyndhurst Twp	Lyndhurst
159	51.2	Collingswood Boro	Collingswood
160	51.2	Long Branch City	Long Branch
161	51.2	Ocean City	Ocean City
162	51.1	Elmwood Park	Elmwood Park
163	51.1	Plainfield City	Plainfield
164	51.1	Montville Twp	Montville
165	51.1	Morris Hills Regional	Rockaway
166	51.1	Pine Hill Boro	Pine Hill
167	51.1	Secaucus Town	Secaucus
168	51.0	Colts Neck Twp	Colts Neck
169	51.0	Buena Regional	Buena
170	51.0	Northern Burlington Reg	Columbus
171	51.0	South Orange-Maplewood	Maplewood
172	51.0	Haddon Twp	Westmont
173	51.0	Florence Twp	Florence
174	51.0	Kingsway Regional	Woolwich Twp
175	51.0	Rutherford Boro	Rutherford
176	51.0	Bernards Twp	Basking Ridge
177	51.0	Ridgewood Village	Ridgewood
178	50.9	W Windsor-Plainsboro Reg	Princeton Jct
179	50.9	Pemberton Twp	Pemberton
180	50.9	Glassboro	Glassboro
181	50.9	Woodbury City	Woodbury
182	50.9	Randolph Twp	Randolph
183	50.9	Woodstown-Pilesgrove Reg	Woodstown
184	50.8	North Brunswick Twp	North Brunswick
185	50.8	Hillside Twp	Hillside
186	50.8	Teaneck Twp	Teaneck
187	50.8	Bridgewater-Raritan Reg	Bridgewater
188	50.8	Paterson City	Paterson
189	50.8	Matawan-Aberdeen Regional	Aberdeen
190	50.8	Hopewell Valley Regional	Pennington
191	50.8	Howell Twp	Howell
192	50.7	Millburn Twp	Millburn
193	50.7	Ocean Twp	Oakhurst
194	50.7	West New York Town	West New York
195	50.7	Roselle Boro	Roselle
196	50.7	Highland Park Boro	Highland Park
197	50.7	Medford Twp	Medford
198	50.7	Clearview Regional	Mullica Hill
199	50.7	Garfield City	Garfield
200	50.7	Somerset Hills Regional	Bernardsville
201	50.7	Nutley Town	Nutley
202	50.7	Linden City	Linden
203	50.6	West Orange Town	West Orange
204	50.6	Pascack Valley Regional	Montvale
205	50.6	Hackensack City	Hackensack
206	50.6	Galloway Twp	Galloway
207	50.6	Lodi Borough	Lodi
208	50.6	Southern Regional	Manahawkin
209	50.5	Roselle Park Boro	Roselle Park
210	50.5	Atlantic City	Atlantic City
211	50.5	Bordentown Regional	Bordentown
212	50.5	Montclair Town	Montclair
213	50.5	Denville Twp	Denville
214	50.4	Delran Twp	Delran
215	50.4	West Morris Regional	Chester
216	50.4	Elizabeth City	Elizabeth
217	50.4	Bergenfield Boro	Bergenfield
218	50.3	Moorestown Twp	Moorestown
219	50.3	Penns Grv-Carney's Pt Reg	Penns Grove
220	50.3	Millstone Twp	Clarksburg
221	50.3	North Plainfield Boro	N Plainfield
222	50.3	South Brunswick Twp	Monmouth Jct
223	50.3	Trenton City	Trenton
224	50.3	Edison Twp	Edison
225	50.3	Freehold Twp	Freehold
226	50.2	Waldwick Boro	Waldwick
227	50.2	Hunterdon Central Reg	Flemington
228	50.2	Burlington Twp	Burlington
229	50.2	Caldwell-West Caldwell	West Caldwell
230	50.2	Rancocas Valley Regional	Mount Holly
231	50.2	Manasquan Boro	Manasquan
232	50.2	Pinelands Regional	Tuckerton
233	50.2	Hammonton Town	Hammonton
234	50.1	Northern Valley Regional	Demarest
235	50.1	Clinton Twp	Annandale
236	50.1	Englewood City	Englewood
237	50.1	Pennsville	Pennsville
238	50.1	Camden City	Camden
239	50.0	Greater Egg Harbor Reg	Mays Landing
240	50.0	Haddonfield Boro	Haddonfield
241	50.0	Barnegat Twp	Barnegat
241	50.0	Cresskill Boro	Cresskill
241	50.0	Hasbrouck Heights Boro	Hasbrouck Hgts
241	50.0	Millville City	Millville
245	49.9	Manalapan-Englishtown Reg	Englishtown
246	49.9	N Hunt/Voorhees Regional	Annandale
247	49.9	Warren Twp	Warren
248	49.9	Lenape Regional	Shamong
249	49.8	Asbury Park City	Asbury Park
250	49.8	Washington Twp	Long Valley
251	49.8	Washington Twp	Robbinsville
252	49.8	Dumont Boro	Dumont
253	49.8	Passaic City	Passaic
254	49.7	Wyckoff Twp	Wyckoff
255	49.7	East Orange	East Orange
256	49.5	High Point Regional	Sussex
257	49.4	Freehold Regional	Englishtown
258	49.4	Pompton Lakes Boro	Pompton Lakes
259	49.4	Leonia Boro	Leonia
260	49.3	Passaic County Vocational	Wayne
261	49.3	Gloucester City	Gloucester City
262	49.1	Hazlet Twp	Hazlet
263	48.8	Sussex-Wantage Regional	Wantage
264	48.5	Saddle Brook Twp	Saddle Brook
265	48.1	Pitman Boro	Pitman
266	48.0	Mainland Regional	Linwood
267	47.7	Salem City	Salem
268	47.5	Ramapo-Indian Hill Reg	Franklin Lakes
269	43.1	Essex County Voc-Tech	West Orange

Female Students

Rank	Percent	District Name	City
1	56.8	Essex County Voc-Tech	West Orange
2	52.4	Ramapo-Indian Hill Reg	Franklin Lakes
3	52.2	Salem City	Salem
4	51.9	Mainland Regional	Linwood
5	51.8	Pitman Boro	Pitman
6	51.4	Saddle Brook Twp	Saddle Brook
7	51.1	Sussex-Wantage Regional	Wantage
8	50.8	Hazlet Twp	Hazlet
9	50.6	Gloucester City	Gloucester City
10	50.6	Passaic County Vocational	Wayne
11	50.5	Leonia Boro	Leonia
12	50.5	Pompton Lakes Boro	Pompton Lakes
13	50.5	Freehold Regional	Englishtown
14	50.4	High Point Regional	Sussex
15	50.2	East Orange	East Orange
16	50.2	Wyckoff Twp	Wyckoff
17	50.1	Passaic City	Passaic

18	50.1	Dumont Boro	Dumont
19	50.1	Washington Twp	Robbinsville
20	50.1	Washington Twp	Long Valley
21	50.1	Asbury Park City	Asbury Park
22	50.0	Lenape Regional	Shamong
23	50.0	Warren Twp	Warren
24	50.0	N Hunt/Voorhees Regional	Annandale
25	50.0	Manalapan-Englishtown Reg	Englishtown
26	50.0	Barnegat Twp	Barnegat
26	50.0	Cresskill Boro	Cresskill
26	50.0	Hasbrouck Heights Boro	Hasbrouck Hgts
26	50.0	Millville City	Millville
30	49.9	Haddonfield Boro	Haddonfield
31	49.9	Greater Egg Harbor Reg	Mays Landing
32	49.8	Camden City	Camden
33	49.8	Pennsville	Pennsville
34	49.8	Englewood City	Englewood
35	49.8	Clinton Twp	Annandale
36	49.8	Northern Valley Regional	Demarest
37	49.7	Hammonton Town	Hammonton
38	49.7	Pinelands Regional	Tuckerton
39	49.7	Manasquan Boro	Manasquan
40	49.7	Rancocas Valley Regional	Mount Holly
41	49.7	Caldwell-West Caldwell	West Caldwell
42	49.7	Burlington Twp	Burlington
43	49.7	Hunterdon Central Reg	Flemington
44	49.7	Waldwick Boro	Waldwick
45	49.6	Freehold Twp	Freehold
46	49.6	Edison Twp	Edison
47	49.6	Trenton City	Trenton
48	49.6	South Brunswick Twp	Monmouth Jct
49	49.6	North Plainfield Boro	N Plainfield
50	49.6	Millstone Twp	Clarksburg
51	49.6	Penns Grv-Carney's Pt Reg	Penns Grove
52	49.6	Moorestown Twp	Moorestown
53	49.5	Bergenfield Boro	Bergenfield
54	49.5	Elizabeth City	Elizabeth
55	49.5	West Morris Regional	Chester
56	49.5	Delran Twp	Delran
57	49.4	Denville Twp	Denville
58	49.4	Montclair Town	Montclair
59	49.4	Bordentown Regional	Bordentown
60	49.4	Atlantic City	Atlantic City
61	49.4	Roselle Park Boro	Roselle Park
62	49.3	Southern Regional	Manahawkin
63	49.3	Lodi Borough	Lodi
64	49.3	Galloway Twp	Galloway
65	49.3	Hackensack City	Hackensack
66	49.3	Pascack Valley Regional	Montvale
67	49.3	West Orange Town	West Orange
68	49.2	Linden City	Linden
69	49.2	Nutley Town	Nutley
70	49.2	Somerset Hills Regional	Bernardsville
71	49.2	Garfield City	Garfield
72	49.2	Clearview Regional	Mullica Hill
73	49.2	Medford Twp	Medford
74	49.2	Highland Park Boro	Highland Park
75	49.2	Roselle Boro	Roselle
76	49.2	West New York Town	West New York
77	49.2	Ocean Twp	Oakhurst
78	49.2	Millburn Twp	Millburn
79	49.1	Howell Twp	Howell
80	49.1	Hopewell Valley Regional	Pennington
81	49.1	Matawan-Aberdeen Regional	Aberdeen
82	49.1	Paterson City	Paterson
83	49.1	Bridgewater-Raritan Reg	Bridgewater
84	49.1	Teaneck Twp	Teaneck
85	49.1	Hillside Twp	Hillside
86	49.1	North Brunswick Twp	North Brunswick
87	49.0	Woodstown-Pilesgrove Reg	Woodstown
88	49.0	Randolph Twp	Randolph
89	49.0	Woodbury City	Woodbury
90	49.0	Glassboro	Glassboro
91	49.0	Pemberton Twp	Pemberton
92	49.0	W Windsor-Plainsboro Reg	Princeton Jct
93	48.9	Ridgewood Village	Ridgewood
94	48.9	Bernards Twp	Basking Ridge
95	48.9	Rutherford Boro	Rutherford
96	48.9	Kingsway Regional	Woolwich Twp
97	48.9	Florence Twp	Florence
98	48.9	Haddon Twp	Westmont
99	48.9	South Orange-Maplewood	Maplewood
100	48.9	Northern Burlington Reg	Columbus
101	48.9	Buena Regional	Buena
102	48.9	Colts Neck Twp	Colts Neck
103	48.8	Secaucus Town	Secaucus
104	48.8	Pine Hill Boro	Pine Hill
105	48.8	Morris Hills Regional	Rockaway
106	48.8	Montville Twp	Montville
107	48.8	Plainfield City	Plainfield
108	48.8	Elmwood Park	Elmwood Park
109	48.7	Ocean City	Ocean City
110	48.7	Long Branch City	Long Branch
111	48.7	Collingswood Boro	Collingswood
112	48.7	Lyndhurst Twp	Lyndhurst
113	48.7	New Brunswick City	New Brunswick
114	48.7	Scotch Plains-Fanwood Reg	Scotch Plains
115	48.7	Maple Shade Twp	Maple Shade
116	48.7	Washington Twp	Sewell
117	48.7	Woodbridge Twp	Woodbridge
118	48.7	Readington Twp	Whitehouse Stn
119	48.7	Middlesex Boro	Middlesex
120	48.7	Franklin Twp	Somerset
121	48.7	Piscataway Twp	Piscataway
122	48.7	East Windsor Regional	Hightstown
123	48.7	Tinton Falls	Tinton Falls
124	48.6	Black Horse Pike Regional	Blackwood
125	48.6	Mahwah Twp	Mahwah
126	48.6	Watchung Hills Regional	Warren
127	48.6	Monroe Twp	Williamstown
128	48.6	Somerville Boro	Somerville
129	48.6	Ewing Twp	Ewing
130	48.6	Delsea Regional H.S District	Franklinville
131	48.6	Mount Olive Twp	Budd Lake
132	48.6	Newark City	Newark
133	48.6	Jersey City	Jersey City
134	48.6	Riverside Twp	Riverside
135	48.6	SD of the Chathams	Chatham
136	48.6	Bridgeton City	Bridgeton
137	48.6	Wayne Twp	Wayne
138	48.6	Jefferson Twp	Lake Hopatcong
139	48.6	Union City	Union City
140	48.6	Deptford Twp	Deptford
141	48.6	Old Bridge Twp	Matawan
142	48.6	Holmdel Twp	Holmdel
143	48.5	Princeton Regional	Princeton
144	48.5	Fair Lawn Boro	Fair Lawn
145	48.5	Toms River Regional	Toms River
146	48.5	Hawthorne Boro	Hawthorne
147	48.5	Lacey Twp	Lanoka Harbor
148	48.5	Sparta Twp	Sparta
149	48.5	Hamilton Twp	Hamilton Square
150	48.4	Marlboro Twp	Marlboro
151	48.4	Montgomery Twp	Skillman
152	48.4	Metuchen Boro	Metuchen
153	48.4	Pittsgrove Twp	Pittsgrove
154	48.4	Hackettstown	Hackettstown
155	48.4	Voorhees Twp	Voorhees
156	48.4	Westfield Town	Westfield
157	48.4	East Brunswick Twp	E Brunswick
158	48.4	Mount Laurel Twp	Mount Laurel
159	48.3	Fort Lee Boro	Fort Lee
160	48.3	Hamilton Twp	Mays Landing
161	48.3	Cedar Grove Twp	Cedar Grove
162	48.3	Branchburg Twp	Branchburg
163	48.3	Lumberton Twp	Lumberton
164	48.3	Jackson Twp	Jackson
165	48.3	South Plainfield Boro	S Plainfield
166	48.3	Kinnelon Boro	Kinnelon
167	48.3	Egg Harbor Twp	W Atlantic City
168	48.2	Little Egg Harbor Twp	Little Egg Hbr
169	48.2	Lawrence Twp	Lawrenceville
170	48.2	Berkeley Heights Twp	Berkeley Hgts
171	48.2	Belleville Town	Belleville
172	48.2	Evesham Twp	Marlton
173	48.2	Audubon Boro	Audubon
174	48.2	Roxbury Twp	Succasunna
175	48.2	Winslow Twp	Atco
176	48.1	Irvington Township	Irvington
177	48.1	Livingston Twp	Livingston
178	48.1	Lakewood Twp	Lakewood
179	48.1	City of Orange Twp	Orange
180	48.1	Manchester Twp	Whiting
181	48.1	Vineland City	Vineland
182	48.1	Vernon Twp	Vernon
183	48.1	New Providence Boro	New Providence
183	48.1	Verona Boro	Verona
185	48.1	North Bergen Twp	North Bergen
186	48.0	Willingboro Twp	Willingboro
187	48.0	Madison Boro	Madison
188	48.0	Carteret Boro	Carteret
189	48.0	Bound Brook Boro	Bound Brook
190	48.0	Glen Ridge Boro	Glen Ridge
191	48.0	Hopatcong	Hopatcong
192	48.0	Bloomfield Twp	Bloomfield
193	48.0	Pequannock Twp	Pompton Plains
194	47.9	Wall Twp	Wall
195	47.9	Upper Twp	Petersburg
196	47.9	Springfield Twp	Springfield
197	47.9	Burlington County Vocational	Westampton Twp
198	47.9	Point Pleasant Boro	Pt Pleasant
199	47.9	Union Twp	Union
200	47.9	Flemington-Raritan Reg	Flemington
201	47.9	Kearny Town	Kearny
202	47.9	Ridgefield Park Twp	Ridgefield Park
203	47.9	Summit City	Summit
204	47.8	Middletown Twp	Middletown
205	47.8	Parsippany-Troy Hills Twp	Parsippany
206	47.8	Westwood Regional	Westwood
207	47.8	Brick Twp	Brick
208	47.8	Gloucester Twp	Blackwood
209	47.8	Bayonne City	Bayonne
210	47.8	Franklin Lakes Boro	Franklin Lakes
211	47.8	Lower Cape May Regional	Cape May
212	47.7	Middle Twp	Cape May Ct Hse
213	47.7	Neptune Twp	Neptune
214	47.7	Clifton City	Clifton
215	47.6	Hillsborough Twp	Neshanic
216	47.6	Oakland Boro	Oakland
217	47.6	Eastern Camden County Reg	Voorhees
218	47.6	Warren Hills Regional	Washington
219	47.5	Paramus Boro	Paramus
220	47.5	Monroe Twp	Monroe Township
221	47.5	Perth Amboy City	Perth Amboy
222	47.4	Cherry Hill Twp	Cherry Hill
223	47.4	Harrison Town	Harrison
224	47.4	Paulsboro Boro	Paulsboro
225	47.4	Stafford Twp	Manahawkin
226	47.4	Berkeley Twp	Bayville
227	47.4	Central Regional	Bayville
228	47.4	Pennsauken Twp	Pennsauken
229	47.4	Upper Freehold Regional	Allentown
230	47.4	Spotswood Boro	Spotswood
231	47.3	Rahway City	Rahway
232	47.3	Glen Rock Boro	Glen Rock
233	47.3	South River Boro	South River
234	47.3	Ramsey Boro	Ramsey
235	47.2	West Milford Twp	West Milford
236	47.2	Dover Town	Dover
237	47.2	Tenafly Boro	Tenafly
238	47.2	Morris SD	Morristown
239	47.1	Plumsted Twp	New Egypt
240	47.1	Lindenwold Boro	Lindenwold
241	47.1	Mountain Lakes Boro	Mountain Lakes
242	47.1	Hoboken City	Hoboken
243	47.1	Palisades Park	Palisades Park
244	47.1	Sayreville Boro	Sayreville
245	47.0	Clark Twp	Clark
246	47.0	Cliffside Park Boro	Cliffside Park
247	46.9	Phillipsburg Town	Phillipsburg
248	46.8	Pleasantville City	Pleasantville
249	46.7	West Deptford Twp	West Deptford
250	46.7	Rockaway Twp	Hibernia
251	46.6	Keansburg Boro	Keansburg
252	46.6	Cinnaminson Twp	Cinnaminson
253	46.5	Newton Town	Newton
254	46.5	Hanover Twp	Whippany
255	46.4	Burlington City	Burlington
256	46.4	Cranford Twp	Cranford
257	46.3	New Milford Boro	New Milford
258	46.2	Camden County Vocational	Sicklerville
259	46.0	North Arlington Boro	North Arlington
260	45.7	Franklin Twp	Franklinville
261	45.0	Bergen County Vocational	Paramus
262	45.0	Ridgefield Boro	Ridgefield
263	44.7	Lower Twp	Cape May
264	44.7	Mantua Twp	Sewell
265	44.4	Monmouth County Vocational	Colts Neck
266	41.5	Middlesex County Vocational	E Brunswick
267	35.5	Bergen County Special Service	Paramus
268	28.9	Mercer County Special Service	Trenton
269	28.3	Burlington County Spec Serv	Mount Holly

Individual Education Program Students

Rank	Percent	District Name	City
1	31.9	Burlington County Vocational	Westampton Twp
2	26.1	Barnegat Twp	Barnegat
3	25.8	Lower Cape May Regional	Cape May
4	24.7	Keansburg Boro	Keansburg
5	24.2	Pinelands Regional	Tuckerton
6	23.8	Camden County Vocational	Sicklerville
7	23.4	Upper Twp	Petersburg
8	22.4	Sussex-Wantage Regional	Wantage
9	22.2	Middlesex County Vocational	E Brunswick
10	22.1	Bordentown Regional	Bordentown
10	22.1	Mantua Twp	Sewell
12	21.9	Westwood Regional	Westwood
13	21.7	Hamilton Twp	Hamilton Square
14	21.5	Asbury Park City	Asbury Park
15	21.1	Woodbury City	Woodbury
16	21.0	Lower Twp	Cape May
17	20.8	Glassboro	Glassboro
18	20.7	Neptune Twp	Neptune
19	20.4	Morris SD	Morristown
19	20.4	Pemberton Twp	Pemberton
19	20.4	West Deptford Twp	West Deptford
22	20.3	Maple Shade Twp	Maple Shade

22	20.3	Rancocas Valley Regional	Mount Holly
24	20.2	Branchburg Twp	Branchburg
24	20.2	Lumberton Twp	Lumberton
26	20.1	Lyndhurst Twp	Lyndhurst
26	20.1	Passaic City	Passaic
28	20.0	Roselle Boro	Roselle
28	20.0	Washington Twp	Robbinsville
30	19.9	Trenton City	Trenton
31	19.7	Ewing Twp	Ewing
32	19.3	Gloucester City	Gloucester City
32	19.3	Pennsauken Twp	Pennsauken
32	19.3	Vineland City	Vineland
35	19.2	Evesham Twp	Marlton
35	19.2	Middle Twp	Cape May Ct Hse
37	19.1	Millstone Twp	Clarksburg
38	18.8	New Brunswick City	New Brunswick
39	18.7	Florence Twp	Florence
39	18.7	Franklin Twp	Franklinville
39	18.7	North Arlington Boro	North Arlington
42	18.6	Brick Twp	Brick
42	18.6	Pennsville	Pennsville
42	18.6	Pitman Boro	Pitman
42	18.6	Winslow Twp	Atco
46	18.5	Hoboken City	Hoboken
46	18.5	Hopatcong	Hopatcong
46	18.5	Lindenwold Boro	Lindenwold
46	18.5	Millville City	Millville
50	18.3	Bridgeton City	Bridgeton
50	18.3	Cedar Grove Twp	Cedar Grove
50	18.3	Cinnaminson Twp	Cinnaminson
53	18.2	Pleasantville City	Pleasantville
53	18.2	Rahway City	Rahway
55	18.1	Paulsboro Boro	Paulsboro
56	18.0	Burlington City	Burlington
56	18.0	Jackson Twp	Jackson
58	17.8	Pine Hill Boro	Pine Hill
58	17.8	Washington Twp	Sewell
60	17.7	Central Regional	Bayville
60	17.7	Riverside Twp	Riverside
62	17.6	Little Egg Harbor Twp	Little Egg Hbr
63	17.5	Hillsborough Twp	Neshanic
63	17.5	Lakewood Twp	Lakewood
63	17.5	Linden City	Linden
63	17.5	Waldwick Boro	Waldwick
67	17.3	Bergenfield Boro	Bergenfield
67	17.3	Montclair Town	Montclair
67	17.3	Penns Grv-Carney's Pt Reg	Penns Grove
67	17.3	West Milford Twp	West Milford
71	17.2	Deptford Twp	Deptford
71	17.2	Fair Lawn Boro	Fair Lawn
71	17.2	Greater Egg Harbor Reg	Mays Landing
74	17.1	Verona Boro	Verona
75	17.0	Camden City	Camden
75	17.0	Moorestown Twp	Moorestown
77	16.9	Delsea Regional H.S District	Franklinville
77	16.9	Lacey Twp	Lanoka Harbor
77	16.9	Saddle Brook Twp	Saddle Brook
77	16.9	Scotch Plains-Fanwood Reg	Scotch Plains
81	16.8	Englewood City	Englewood
81	16.8	Howell Twp	Howell
81	16.8	Salem City	Salem
81	16.8	Wall Twp	Wall
81	16.8	Westfield Town	Westfield
86	16.7	East Windsor Regional	Hightstown
86	16.7	Egg Harbor Twp	W Atlantic City
86	16.7	Galloway Twp	Galloway
86	16.7	Rockaway Twp	Hibernia
90	16.6	Buena Regional	Buena
90	16.6	Hazlet Twp	Hazlet
90	16.6	Middletown Twp	Middletown
90	16.6	SD of the Chathams	Chatham
94	16.5	Roselle Park Boro	Roselle Park
94	16.5	Tinton Falls	Tinton Falls
96	16.4	Lawrence Twp	Lawrenceville
97	16.3	Belleville Town	Belleville
97	16.3	Monroe Twp	Williamstown
97	16.3	Monroe Twp	Monroe Township
97	16.3	Warren Twp	Warren
97	16.3	Willingboro Twp	Willingboro
102	16.2	Hamilton Twp	Mays Landing
102	16.2	Northern Burlington Reg	Columbus
102	16.2	Sayreville Boro	Sayreville
105	16.1	Pompton Lakes Boro	Pompton Lakes
106	16.0	Manchester Twp	Whiting
106	16.0	Oakland Boro	Oakland
106	16.0	Parsippany-Troy Hills Twp	Parsippany
106	16.0	Pittsgrove Twp	Pittsgrove
110	15.9	Madison Boro	Madison
110	15.9	N Hunt/Voorhees Regional	Annandale
112	15.8	Denville Twp	Denville
112	15.8	Hawthorne Boro	Hawthorne
112	15.8	Mount Laurel Twp	Mount Laurel
112	15.8	Washington Twp	Long Valley
116	15.7	Bayonne City	Bayonne
116	15.7	East Orange	East Orange
116	15.7	Franklin Twp	Somerset
116	15.7	Irvington Township	Irvington
116	15.7	Ridgefield Park Twp	Ridgefield Park
116	15.7	Stafford Twp	Manahawkin
116	15.7	Voorhees Twp	Voorhees
116	15.7	Warren Hills Regional	Washington
124	15.6	East Brunswick Twp	E Brunswick
124	15.6	Mainland Regional	Linwood
124	15.6	North Plainfield Boro	N Plainfield
124	15.6	Princeton Regional	Princeton
128	15.5	Cranford Twp	Cranford
128	15.5	Garfield City	Garfield
128	15.5	Mount Olive Twp	Budd Lake
128	15.5	Phillipsburg Town	Phillipsburg
128	15.5	Ramsey Boro	Ramsey
133	15.4	Gloucester Twp	Blackwood
133	15.4	Livingston Twp	Livingston
135	15.3	Bergen County Vocational	Paramus
135	15.3	Bridgewater-Raritan Reg	Bridgewater
135	15.3	City of Orange Twp	Orange
135	15.3	Hackensack City	Hackensack
135	15.3	Teaneck Twp	Teaneck
140	15.2	Lenape Regional	Shamong
140	15.2	Long Branch City	Long Branch
140	15.2	Medford Twp	Medford
140	15.2	Passaic County Vocational	Wayne
140	15.2	Paterson City	Paterson
140	15.2	South Plainfield Boro	S Plainfield
140	15.2	Springfield Twp	Springfield
140	15.2	Union Twp	Union
148	15.1	Cresskill Boro	Cresskill
148	15.1	Middlesex Boro	Middlesex
148	15.1	Plumsted Twp	New Egypt
148	15.1	Ramapo-Indian Hill Reg	Franklin Lakes
148	15.1	Readington Twp	Whitehouse Stn
153	15.0	Collingswood Boro	Collingswood
153	15.0	Rutherford Boro	Rutherford
155	14.9	Bloomfield Twp	Bloomfield
156	14.8	Haddonfield Boro	Haddonfield
156	14.8	Hopewell Valley Regional	Pennington
156	14.8	New Milford Boro	New Milford
156	14.8	Newark City	Newark
160	14.7	Black Horse Pike Regional	Blackwood
160	14.7	Burlington Twp	Burlington
160	14.7	Elmwood Park	Elmwood Park
163	14.6	Hunterdon Central Reg	Flemington
164	14.5	Audubon Boro	Audubon
164	14.5	Dumont Boro	Dumont
164	14.5	Hillside Twp	Hillside
167	14.4	Glen Rock Boro	Glen Rock
167	14.4	Jefferson Twp	Lake Hopatcong
169	14.3	Piscataway Twp	Piscataway
169	14.3	West New York Town	West New York
171	14.2	Hasbrouck Heights Boro	Hasbrouck Hgts
171	14.2	Morris Hills Regional	Rockaway
171	14.2	Ocean Twp	Oakhurst
174	14.1	Caldwell-West Caldwell	West Caldwell
174	14.1	West Morris Regional	Chester
176	14.0	Freehold Twp	Freehold
176	14.0	Haddon Twp	Westmont
176	14.0	Mahwah Twp	Mahwah
176	14.0	Sparta Twp	Sparta
180	13.9	Bound Brook Boro	Bound Brook
180	13.9	Clearview Regional	Mullica Hill
180	13.9	Manalapan-Englishtown Reg	Englishtown
180	13.9	Tenafly Boro	Tenafly
184	13.8	Pequannock Twp	Pompton Plains
184	13.8	Woodbridge Twp	Woodbridge
186	13.7	Berkeley Twp	Bayville
186	13.7	Hanover Twp	Whippany
186	13.7	Highland Park Boro	Highland Park
189	13.6	New Providence Boro	New Providence
189	13.6	Nutley Town	Nutley
189	13.6	Secaucus Town	Secaucus
189	13.6	Summit City	Summit
193	13.5	Randolph Twp	Randolph
194	13.4	Atlantic City	Atlantic City
194	13.4	Millburn Twp	Millburn
194	13.4	Pascack Valley Regional	Montvale
194	13.4	Toms River Regional	Toms River
194	13.4	West Orange Town	West Orange
199	13.3	South Brunswick Twp	Monmouth Jct
200	13.2	Flemington-Raritan Reg	Flemington
200	13.2	Freehold Regional	Englishtown
200	13.2	South River Boro	South River
203	13.1	Cherry Hill Twp	Cherry Hill
203	13.1	High Point Regional	Sussex
205	13.0	Lodi Borough	Lodi
205	13.0	Metuchen Boro	Metuchen
207	12.9	Delran Twp	Delran
207	12.9	Edison Twp	Edison
207	12.9	Hammonton Town	Hammonton
207	12.9	Harrison Town	Harrison
207	12.9	South Orange Maplewood	Maplewood
212	12.8	Clinton Twp	Annandale
212	12.8	Colts Neck Twp	Colts Neck
214	12.7	Point Pleasant Boro	Pt Pleasant
214	12.7	Watchung Hills Regional	Warren
216	12.6	Montville Twp	Montville
216	12.6	Plainfield City	Plainfield
218	12.5	Fort Lee Boro	Fort Lee
218	12.5	North Brunswick Twp	North Brunswick
218	12.5	Somerset Hills Regional	Bernardsville
221	12.4	Dover Town	Dover
221	12.4	Eastern Camden County Reg	Voorhees
223	12.3	Jersey City	Jersey City
223	12.3	Marlboro Twp	Marlboro
225	12.2	Leonia Boro	Leonia
225	12.2	Matawan-Aberdeen Regional	Aberdeen
225	12.2	Old Bridge Twp	Matawan
225	12.2	Ridgewood Village	Ridgewood
225	12.2	Vernon Twp	Vernon
230	12.1	Essex County Voc-Tech	West Orange
230	12.1	Wayne Twp	Wayne
230	12.1	Woodstown-Pilesgrove Reg	Woodstown
233	12.0	Bernards Twp	Basking Ridge
233	12.0	Kearny Town	Kearny
233	12.0	W Windsor-Plainsboro Reg	Princeton Jct
236	11.9	Montgomery Twp	Skillman
236	11.9	North Bergen Twp	North Bergen
236	11.9	Roxbury Twp	Succasunna
239	11.8	Franklin Lakes Boro	Franklin Lakes
239	11.8	Hackettstown	Hackettstown
239	11.8	Mountain Lakes Boro	Mountain Lakes
242	11.7	Kinnelon Boro	Kinnelon
243	11.6	Clifton City	Clifton
244	11.5	Newton Town	Newton
245	11.4	Elizabeth City	Elizabeth
245	11.4	Kingsway Regional	Woolwich Twp
245	11.4	Northern Valley Regional	Demarest
245	11.4	Palisades Park	Palisades Park
245	11.4	Somerville Boro	Somerville
250	11.0	Southern Regional	Manahawkin
251	10.9	Glen Ridge Boro	Glen Ridge
251	10.9	Holmdel Twp	Holmdel
251	10.9	Perth Amboy City	Perth Amboy
254	10.7	Carteret Boro	Carteret
254	10.7	Ocean City	Ocean City
256	10.5	Spotswood Boro	Spotswood
257	10.3	Wyckoff Twp	Wyckoff
258	10.2	Berkeley Heights Twp	Berkeley Hgts
258	10.2	Clark Twp	Clark
258	10.2	Cliffside Park Boro	Cliffside Park
261	9.4	Paramus Boro	Paramus
262	8.9	Union City	Union City
262	8.9	Upper Freehold Regional	Allentown
264	7.2	Ridgefield Boro	Ridgefield
265	6.8	Manasquan Boro	Manasquan
266	0.0	Bergen County Special Service	Paramus
266	0.0	Burlington County Spec Serv	Mount Holly
266	0.0	Mercer County Special Service	Trenton
266	0.0	Monmouth County Vocational	Colts Neck

English Language Learner Students

Rank	Percent	District Name	City
1	43.8	Union City	Union City
2	26.7	Passaic City	Passaic
3	23.3	New Brunswick City	New Brunswick
4	18.9	Elizabeth City	Elizabeth
5	17.9	Paterson City	Paterson
6	16.2	Palisades Park	Palisades Park
7	15.2	Perth Amboy City	Perth Amboy
8	14.4	Dover Town	Dover
9	14.2	West New York Town	West New York
10	13.0	Plainfield City	Plainfield
11	12.2	Atlantic City	Atlantic City
12	11.5	Bound Brook Boro	Bound Brook
13	11.1	Harrison Town	Harrison
14	10.9	Garfield City	Garfield
15	9.4	North Bergen Twp	North Bergen
16	9.2	Cliffside Park Boro	Cliffside Park
16	9.2	Fort Lee Boro	Fort Lee
18	8.8	Englewood City	Englewood
19	8.7	Leonia Boro	Leonia
19	8.7	Roselle Boro	Roselle
21	8.4	Bridgeton City	Bridgeton
22	8.3	Lakewood Twp	Lakewood
23	7.8	Jersey City	Jersey City
23	7.8	Trenton City	Trenton
25	7.5	North Plainfield Boro	N Plainfield
26	7.4	Newark City	Newark

27	7.1	Kearny Town	Kearny
28	7.0	City of Orange Twp	Orange
28	7.0	Pleasantville City	Pleasantville
30	6.9	Roselle Park Boro	Roselle Park
31	6.8	Tenafly Boro	Tenafly
32	6.6	Hackensack City	Hackensack
33	6.4	Camden City	Camden
33	6.4	Morris SD	Morristown
35	6.3	Lodi Borough	Lodi
36	6.1	Clifton City	Clifton
37	6.0	Carteret Boro	Carteret
37	6.0	Essex County Voc-Tech	West Orange
39	5.9	Parsippany-Troy Hills Twp	Parsippany
40	5.8	East Windsor Regional	Hightstown
41	5.6	Ridgefield Park Twp	Ridgefield Park
42	5.4	Belleville Town	Belleville
42	5.4	Cresskill Boro	Cresskill
44	5.1	Asbury Park City	Asbury Park
44	5.1	Linden City	Linden
46	5.0	West Orange Town	West Orange
47	4.9	Somerville Boro	Somerville
48	4.8	Irvington Township	Irvington
48	4.8	Long Branch City	Long Branch
50	4.7	Bergenfield Boro	Bergenfield
50	4.7	North Arlington Boro	North Arlington
52	4.3	Dumont Boro	Dumont
52	4.3	Hammonton Town	Hammonton
52	4.3	Hillside Twp	Hillside
55	4.2	Highland Park Boro	Highland Park
55	4.2	North Brunswick Twp	North Brunswick
55	4.2	South River Boro	South River
58	4.1	Bloomfield Twp	Bloomfield
59	4.0	Franklin Twp	Somerset
60	3.9	Burlington City	Burlington
60	3.9	Elmwood Park	Elmwood Park
60	3.9	Lindenwold Boro	Lindenwold
60	3.9	Piscataway Twp	Piscataway
60	3.9	Vineland City	Vineland
65	3.7	Middlesex Boro	Middlesex
66	3.6	Galloway Twp	Galloway
66	3.6	Paramus Boro	Paramus
66	3.6	Summit City	Summit
69	3.5	Ridgefield Boro	Ridgefield
70	3.3	Princeton Regional	Princeton
71	3.2	Lawrence Twp	Lawrenceville
71	3.2	Ocean Twp	Oakhurst
73	3.1	Glen Rock Boro	Glen Rock
73	3.1	W Windsor-Plainsboro Reg	Princeton Jct
75	2.9	Upper Freehold Regional	Allentown
76	2.8	Westwood Regional	Westwood
77	2.7	New Milford Boro	New Milford
77	2.7	Old Bridge Twp	Matawan
79	2.6	Penns Grv-Carney's Pt Reg	Penns Grove
80	2.5	East Orange	East Orange
80	2.5	Phillipsburg Town	Phillipsburg
80	2.5	Rahway City	Rahway
80	2.5	Somerset Hills Regional	Bernardsville
84	2.4	Bayonne City	Bayonne
84	2.4	Burlington Twp	Burlington
84	2.4	Edison Twp	Edison
84	2.4	Fair Lawn Boro	Fair Lawn
84	2.4	Hackettstown	Hackettstown
84	2.4	Union Twp	Union
84	2.4	Woodbridge Twp	Woodbridge
91	2.3	Delran Twp	Delran
91	2.3	Egg Harbor Twp	W Atlantic City
91	2.3	Hanover Twp	Whippany
94	2.2	Madison Boro	Madison
94	2.2	Pennsauken Twp	Pennsauken
94	2.2	Teaneck Twp	Teaneck
94	2.2	Waldwick Boro	Waldwick
98	2.1	Collingswood Boro	Collingswood
98	2.1	Ewing Twp	Ewing
100	2.0	Hamilton Twp	Mays Landing
100	2.0	Springfield Twp	Springfield
102	1.9	East Brunswick Twp	E Brunswick
102	1.9	Lyndhurst Twp	Lyndhurst
102	1.9	Mount Olive Twp	Budd Lake
102	1.9	Ridgewood Village	Ridgewood
106	1.8	Buena Regional	Buena
106	1.8	Pompton Lakes Boro	Pompton Lakes
108	1.7	Bordentown Regional	Bordentown
108	1.7	Bridgewater-Raritan Reg	Bridgewater
108	1.7	Millville City	Millville
108	1.7	Nutley Town	Nutley
112	1.6	Flemington-Raritan Reg	Flemington
112	1.6	Livingston Twp	Livingston
112	1.6	Passaic County Vocational	Wayne
112	1.6	Sayreville Boro	Sayreville
112	1.6	Secaucus Town	Secaucus
112	1.6	South Plainfield Boro	S Plainfield
118	1.5	Berkeley Heights Twp	Berkeley Hgts
118	1.5	Hoboken City	Hoboken
118	1.5	Maple Shade Twp	Maple Shade
118	1.5	Marlboro Twp	Marlboro
118	1.5	Matawan-Aberdeen Regional	Aberdeen
118	1.5	Riverside Twp	Riverside
118	1.5	South Orange-Maplewood	Maplewood
125	1.4	Berkeley Twp	Bayville
125	1.4	Manalapan-Englishtown Reg	Englishtown
125	1.4	Saddle Brook Twp	Saddle Brook
125	1.4	Warren Twp	Warren
129	1.3	Greater Egg Harbor Reg	Mays Landing
129	1.3	Hamilton Twp	Hamilton Square
129	1.3	Hasbrouck Heights Boro	Hasbrouck Hgts
129	1.3	Hillsborough Twp	Neshanic
129	1.3	Millburn Twp	Millburn
129	1.3	Montville Twp	Montville
129	1.3	Voorhees Twp	Voorhees
136	1.2	Cherry Hill Twp	Cherry Hill
136	1.2	Gloucester City	Gloucester City
136	1.2	Randolph Twp	Randolph
136	1.2	South Brunswick Twp	Monmouth Jct
136	1.2	Tinton Falls	Tinton Falls
141	1.1	Central Regional	Bayville
141	1.1	Denville Twp	Denville
141	1.1	Florence Twp	Florence
141	1.1	Glassboro	Glassboro
141	1.1	Keansburg Boro	Keansburg
141	1.1	Middlesex County Vocational	E Brunswick
141	1.1	Montclair Town	Montclair
141	1.1	Newton Town	Newton
141	1.1	Northern Valley Regional	Demarest
141	1.1	Rockaway Twp	Hibernia
141	1.1	Roxbury Twp	Succasunna
141	1.1	Warren Hills Regional	Washington
153	1.0	Branchburg Twp	Branchburg
153	1.0	Manasquan Boro	Manasquan
153	1.0	Wall Twp	Wall
153	1.0	Wayne Twp	Wayne
153	1.0	Winslow Twp	Atco
158	0.9	Hawthorne Boro	Hawthorne
158	0.9	Howell Twp	Howell
158	0.9	Little Egg Harbor Twp	Little Egg Hbr
158	0.9	Middle Twp	Cape May Ct Hse
158	0.9	Morris Hills Regional	Rockaway
158	0.9	Plumsted Twp	New Egypt
158	0.9	Rutherford Boro	Rutherford
158	0.9	Woodbury City	Woodbury
158	0.9	Wyckoff Twp	Wyckoff
167	0.8	Brick Twp	Brick
167	0.8	Caldwell-West Caldwell	West Caldwell
167	0.8	Clark Twp	Clark
167	0.8	Deptford Twp	Deptford
167	0.8	Evesham Twp	Marlton
167	0.8	Franklin Lakes Boro	Franklin Lakes
167	0.8	Freehold Regional	Englishtown
167	0.8	Jackson Twp	Jackson
167	0.8	Mahwah Twp	Mahwah
167	0.8	Manchester Twp	Whiting
167	0.8	Millstone Twp	Clarksburg
167	0.8	New Providence Boro	New Providence
179	0.7	Eastern Camden County Reg	Voorhees
179	0.7	Gloucester Twp	Blackwood
179	0.7	Hopatcong	Hopatcong
179	0.7	Lumberton Twp	Lumberton
179	0.7	Metuchen Boro	Metuchen
179	0.7	Monroe Twp	Monroe Township
179	0.7	Mount Laurel Twp	Mount Laurel
179	0.7	Point Pleasant Boro	Pt Pleasant
179	0.7	Ramsey Boro	Ramsey
179	0.7	Southern Regional	Manahawkin
179	0.7	Toms River Regional	Toms River
179	0.7	Watchung Hills Regional	Warren
191	0.6	Colts Neck Twp	Colts Neck
191	0.6	Holmdel Twp	Holmdel
191	0.6	Hunterdon Central Reg	Flemington
191	0.6	Lower Twp	Cape May
191	0.6	Neptune Twp	Neptune
191	0.6	Ocean City	Ocean City
191	0.6	Pascack Valley Regional	Montvale
191	0.6	Pemberton Twp	Pemberton
191	0.6	Pennsville	Pennsville
191	0.6	SD of the Chathams	Chatham
201	0.5	Audubon Boro	Audubon
201	0.5	Barnegat Twp	Barnegat
201	0.5	Bernards Twp	Basking Ridge
201	0.5	Black Horse Pike Regional	Blackwood
201	0.5	Freehold Twp	Freehold
201	0.5	Mainland Regional	Linwood
201	0.5	Monroe Twp	Williamstown
201	0.5	Oakland Boro	Oakland
201	0.5	Pine Hill Boro	Pine Hill
201	0.5	Readington Twp	Whitehouse Stn
201	0.5	Scotch Plains-Fanwood Reg	Scotch Plains
201	0.5	Washington Twp	Robbinsville
213	0.4	Cedar Grove Twp	Cedar Grove
213	0.4	Cinnaminson Twp	Cinnaminson
213	0.4	Jefferson Twp	Lake Hopatcong
213	0.4	Lacey Twp	Lanoka Harbor
213	0.4	Lower Cape May Regional	Cape May
213	0.4	Middletown Twp	Middletown
213	0.4	Montgomery Twp	Skillman
213	0.4	Moorestown Twp	Moorestown
213	0.4	Pequannock Twp	Pompton Plains
213	0.4	Ramapo-Indian Hill Reg	Franklin Lakes
213	0.4	Rancocas Valley Regional	Mount Holly
213	0.4	Spotswood Boro	Spotswood
213	0.4	Verona Boro	Verona
213	0.4	Washington Twp	Sewell
213	0.4	Westfield Town	Westfield
213	0.4	Willingboro Twp	Willingboro
213	0.4	Woodstown-Pilesgrove Reg	Woodstown
230	0.3	Bergen County Vocational	Paramus
230	0.3	Clinton Twp	Annandale
230	0.3	Delsea Regional H.S District	Franklinville
230	0.3	Haddonfield Boro	Haddonfield
230	0.3	Hazlet Twp	Hazlet
230	0.3	Kingsway Regional	Woolwich Twp
230	0.3	Kinnelon Boro	Kinnelon
230	0.3	Lenape Regional	Shamong
230	0.3	Pinelands Regional	Tuckerton
230	0.3	Salem City	Salem
230	0.3	Sparta Twp	Sparta
230	0.3	Sussex-Wantage Regional	Wantage
230	0.3	Washington Twp	Long Valley
230	0.3	West Milford Twp	West Milford
244	0.2	Haddon Twp	Westmont
244	0.2	Hopewell Valley Regional	Pennington
244	0.2	Northern Burlington Reg	Columbus
244	0.2	Stafford Twp	Manahawkin
244	0.2	Vernon Twp	Vernon
244	0.2	West Morris Regional	Chester
250	0.1	Burlington County Vocational	Westampton Twp
250	0.1	Cranford Twp	Cranford
250	0.1	Franklin Twp	Franklinville
250	0.1	Glen Ridge Boro	Glen Ridge
250	0.1	N Hunt/Voorhees Regional	Annandale
250	0.1	Pittsgrove Twp	Pittsgrove
250	0.1	West Deptford Twp	West Deptford
257	0.0	Clearview Regional	Mullica Hill
258	0.0	Bergen County Special Service	Paramus
258	0.0	Burlington County Spec Serv	Mount Holly
258	0.0	Camden County Vocational	Sicklerville
258	0.0	High Point Regional	Sussex
258	0.0	Mantua Twp	Sewell
258	0.0	Medford Twp	Medford
258	0.0	Mercer County Special Service	Trenton
258	0.0	Monmouth County Vocational	Colts Neck
258	0.0	Mountain Lakes Boro	Mountain Lakes
258	0.0	Paulsboro Boro	Paulsboro
258	0.0	Pitman Boro	Pitman
258	0.0	Upper Twp	Petersburg

Migrant Students

Rank	Percent	District Name	City
1	8.4	Bridgeton City	Bridgeton
2	2.2	Hammonton Town	Hammonton
3	1.0	Vineland City	Vineland
4	0.8	Buena Regional	Buena
5	0.6	Penns Grv-Carney's Pt Reg	Penns Grove
6	0.5	Woodstown-Pilesgrove Reg	Woodstown
7	0.4	Kingsway Regional	Woolwich Twp
7	0.4	Winslow Twp	Atco
9	0.3	Hamilton Twp	Mays Landing
10	0.2	Delsea Regional H.S District	Franklinville
10	0.2	Lindenwold Boro	Lindenwold
10	0.2	Pittsgrove Twp	Pittsgrove
13	0.1	Franklin Twp	Franklinville
13	0.1	Greater Egg Harbor Reg	Mays Landing
13	0.1	Lakewood Twp	Lakewood
13	0.1	Millville City	Millville
13	0.1	Northern Burlington Reg	Columbus
13	0.1	Plumsted Twp	New Egypt
19	0.0	Atlantic City	Atlantic City
19	0.0	Camden City	Camden
19	0.0	Galloway Twp	Galloway
19	0.0	Lenape Regional	Shamong
19	0.0	Monroe Twp	Williamstown
19	0.0	Pemberton Twp	Pemberton
25	0.0	Asbury Park City	Asbury Park
25	0.0	Audubon Boro	Audubon
25	0.0	Barnegat Twp	Barnegat
25	0.0	Bayonne City	Bayonne
25	0.0	Belleville Town	Belleville
25	0.0	Bergen County Special Service	Paramus
25	0.0	Bergen County Vocational	Paramus

25	0.0	Bergenfield Boro	Bergenfield
25	0.0	Berkeley Heights Twp	Berkeley Hgts
25	0.0	Berkeley Twp	Bayville
25	0.0	Bernards Twp	Basking Ridge
25	0.0	Black Horse Pike Regional	Blackwood
25	0.0	Bloomfield Twp	Bloomfield
25	0.0	Bordentown Regional	Bordentown
25	0.0	Bound Brook Boro	Bound Brook
25	0.0	Branchburg Twp	Branchburg
25	0.0	Brick Twp	Brick
25	0.0	Bridgewater-Raritan Reg	Bridgewater
25	0.0	Burlington City	Burlington
25	0.0	Burlington County Spec Serv	Mount Holly
25	0.0	Burlington County Vocational	Westampton Twp
25	0.0	Burlington Twp	Burlington
25	0.0	Caldwell-West Caldwell	West Caldwell
25	0.0	Camden County Vocational	Sicklerville
25	0.0	Carteret Boro	Carteret
25	0.0	Cedar Grove Twp	Cedar Grove
25	0.0	Central Regional	Bayville
25	0.0	Cherry Hill Twp	Cherry Hill
25	0.0	Cinnaminson Twp	Cinnaminson
25	0.0	City of Orange Twp	Orange
25	0.0	Clark Twp	Clark
25	0.0	Clearview Regional	Mullica Hill
25	0.0	Cliffside Park Boro	Cliffside Park
25	0.0	Clifton City	Clifton
25	0.0	Clinton Twp	Annandale
25	0.0	Collingswood Boro	Collingswood
25	0.0	Colts Neck Twp	Colts Neck
25	0.0	Cranford Twp	Cranford
25	0.0	Cresskill Boro	Cresskill
25	0.0	Delran Twp	Delran
25	0.0	Denville Twp	Denville
25	0.0	Deptford Twp	Deptford
25	0.0	Dover Town	Dover
25	0.0	Dumont Boro	Dumont
25	0.0	East Brunswick Twp	E Brunswick
25	0.0	East Orange	East Orange
25	0.0	East Windsor Regional	Hightstown
25	0.0	Eastern Camden County Reg	Voorhees
25	0.0	Edison Twp	Edison
25	0.0	Egg Harbor Twp	W Atlantic City
25	0.0	Elizabeth City	Elizabeth
25	0.0	Elmwood Park	Elmwood Park
25	0.0	Englewood City	Englewood
25	0.0	Essex County Voc-Tech	West Orange
25	0.0	Evesham Twp	Marlton
25	0.0	Ewing Twp	Ewing
25	0.0	Fair Lawn Boro	Fair Lawn
25	0.0	Flemington-Raritan Reg	Flemington
25	0.0	Florence Twp	Florence
25	0.0	Fort Lee Boro	Fort Lee
25	0.0	Franklin Lakes Boro	Franklin Lakes
25	0.0	Franklin Twp	Somerset
25	0.0	Freehold Regional	Englishtown
25	0.0	Freehold Twp	Freehold
25	0.0	Garfield City	Garfield
25	0.0	Glassboro	Glassboro
25	0.0	Glen Ridge Boro	Glen Ridge
25	0.0	Glen Rock Boro	Glen Rock
25	0.0	Gloucester City	Gloucester City
25	0.0	Gloucester Twp	Blackwood
25	0.0	Hackensack City	Hackensack
25	0.0	Hackettstown	Hackettstown
25	0.0	Haddon Twp	Westmont
25	0.0	Haddonfield Boro	Haddonfield
25	0.0	Hamilton Twp	Hamilton Square
25	0.0	Hanover Twp	Whippany
25	0.0	Harrison Town	Harrison
25	0.0	Hasbrouck Heights Boro	Hasbrouck Hgts
25	0.0	Hawthorne Boro	Hawthorne
25	0.0	Hazlet Twp	Hazlet
25	0.0	High Point Regional	Sussex
25	0.0	Highland Park Boro	Highland Park
25	0.0	Hillsborough Twp	Neshanic
25	0.0	Hillside Twp	Hillside
25	0.0	Hoboken City	Hoboken
25	0.0	Holmdel Twp	Holmdel
25	0.0	Hopatcong	Hopatcong
25	0.0	Hopewell Valley Regional	Pennington
25	0.0	Howell Twp	Howell
25	0.0	Hunterdon Central Reg	Flemington
25	0.0	Irvington Township	Irvington
25	0.0	Jackson Twp	Jackson
25	0.0	Jefferson Twp	Lake Hopatcong
25	0.0	Jersey City	Jersey City
25	0.0	Keansburg Boro	Keansburg
25	0.0	Kearny Town	Kearny
25	0.0	Kinnelon Boro	Kinnelon
25	0.0	Lacey Twp	Lanoka Harbor
25	0.0	Lawrence Twp	Lawrenceville
25	0.0	Leonia Boro	Leonia
25	0.0	Linden City	Linden
25	0.0	Little Egg Harbor Twp	Little Egg Hbr
25	0.0	Livingston Twp	Livingston
25	0.0	Lodi Borough	Lodi
25	0.0	Long Branch City	Long Branch
25	0.0	Lower Cape May Regional	Cape May
25	0.0	Lower Twp	Cape May
25	0.0	Lumberton Twp	Lumberton
25	0.0	Lyndhurst Twp	Lyndhurst
25	0.0	Madison Boro	Madison
25	0.0	Mahwah Twp	Mahwah
25	0.0	Mainland Regional	Linwood
25	0.0	Manalapan-Englishtown Reg	Englishtown
25	0.0	Manasquan Boro	Manasquan
25	0.0	Manchester Twp	Whiting
25	0.0	Mantua Twp	Sewell
25	0.0	Maple Shade Twp	Maple Shade
25	0.0	Marlboro Twp	Marlboro
25	0.0	Matawan-Aberdeen Regional	Aberdeen
25	0.0	Medford Twp	Medford
25	0.0	Mercer County Special Service	Trenton
25	0.0	Metuchen Boro	Metuchen
25	0.0	Middle Twp	Cape May Ct Hse
25	0.0	Middlesex Boro	Middlesex
25	0.0	Middlesex County Vocational	E Brunswick
25	0.0	Middletown Twp	Middletown
25	0.0	Millburn Twp	Millburn
25	0.0	Millstone Twp	Clarksburg
25	0.0	Monmouth County Vocational	Colts Neck
25	0.0	Monroe Twp	Monroe Township
25	0.0	Montclair Town	Montclair
25	0.0	Montgomery Twp	Skillman
25	0.0	Montville Twp	Montville
25	0.0	Moorestown Twp	Moorestown
25	0.0	Morris Hills Regional	Rockaway
25	0.0	Morris SD	Morristown
25	0.0	Mount Laurel Twp	Mount Laurel
25	0.0	Mount Olive Twp	Budd Lake
25	0.0	Mountain Lakes Boro	Mountain Lakes
25	0.0	N Hunt/Voorhees Regional	Annandale
25	0.0	Neptune Twp	Neptune
25	0.0	New Brunswick City	New Brunswick
25	0.0	New Milford Boro	New Milford
25	0.0	New Providence Boro	New Providence
25	0.0	Newark City	Newark
25	0.0	Newton Town	Newton
25	0.0	North Arlington Boro	North Arlington
25	0.0	North Bergen Twp	North Bergen
25	0.0	North Brunswick Twp	North Brunswick
25	0.0	North Plainfield Boro	N Plainfield
25	0.0	Northern Valley Regional	Demarest
25	0.0	Nutley Town	Nutley
25	0.0	Oakland Boro	Oakland
25	0.0	Ocean City	Ocean City
25	0.0	Ocean Twp	Oakhurst
25	0.0	Old Bridge Twp	Matawan
25	0.0	Palisades Park	Palisades Park
25	0.0	Paramus Boro	Paramus
25	0.0	Parsippany-Troy Hills Twp	Parsippany
25	0.0	Pascack Valley Regional	Montvale
25	0.0	Passaic City	Passaic
25	0.0	Passaic County Vocational	Wayne
25	0.0	Paterson City	Paterson
25	0.0	Paulsboro Boro	Paulsboro
25	0.0	Pennsauken Twp	Pennsauken
25	0.0	Pennsville	Pennsville
25	0.0	Pequannock Twp	Pompton Plains
25	0.0	Perth Amboy City	Perth Amboy
25	0.0	Phillipsburg Town	Phillipsburg
25	0.0	Pine Hill Boro	Pine Hill
25	0.0	Pinelands Regional	Tuckerton
25	0.0	Piscataway Twp	Piscataway
25	0.0	Pitman Boro	Pitman
25	0.0	Plainfield City	Plainfield
25	0.0	Pleasantville City	Pleasantville
25	0.0	Point Pleasant Boro	Pt Pleasant
25	0.0	Pompton Lakes Boro	Pompton Lakes
25	0.0	Princeton Regional	Princeton
25	0.0	Rahway City	Rahway
25	0.0	Ramapo-Indian Hill Reg	Franklin Lakes
25	0.0	Ramsey Boro	Ramsey
25	0.0	Rancocas Valley Regional	Mount Holly
25	0.0	Randolph Twp	Randolph
25	0.0	Readington Twp	Whitehouse Stn
25	0.0	Ridgefield Boro	Ridgefield
25	0.0	Ridgefield Park Twp	Ridgefield Park
25	0.0	Ridgewood Village	Ridgewood
25	0.0	Riverside Twp	Riverside
25	0.0	Rockaway Twp	Hibernia
25	0.0	Roselle Boro	Roselle
25	0.0	Roselle Park Boro	Roselle Park
25	0.0	Roxbury Twp	Succasunna
25	0.0	Rutherford Boro	Rutherford
25	0.0	SD of the Chathams	Chatham
25	0.0	Saddle Brook Twp	Saddle Brook
25	0.0	Salem City	Salem
25	0.0	Sayreville Boro	Sayreville
25	0.0	Scotch Plains-Fanwood Reg	Scotch Plains
25	0.0	Secaucus Town	Secaucus
25	0.0	Somerset Hills Regional	Bernardsville
25	0.0	Somerville Boro	Somerville
25	0.0	South Brunswick Twp	Monmouth Jct
25	0.0	South Orange-Maplewood	Maplewood
25	0.0	South Plainfield Boro	S Plainfield
25	0.0	South River Boro	South River
25	0.0	Southern Regional	Manahawkin
25	0.0	Sparta Twp	Sparta
25	0.0	Spotswood Boro	Spotswood
25	0.0	Springfield Twp	Springfield
25	0.0	Stafford Twp	Manahawkin
25	0.0	Summit City	Summit
25	0.0	Sussex-Wantage Regional	Wantage
25	0.0	Teaneck Twp	Teaneck
25	0.0	Tenafly Boro	Tenafly
25	0.0	Tinton Falls	Tinton Falls
25	0.0	Toms River Regional	Toms River
25	0.0	Trenton City	Trenton
25	0.0	Union City	Union City
25	0.0	Union Twp	Union
25	0.0	Upper Freehold Regional	Allentown
25	0.0	Upper Twp	Petersburg
25	0.0	Vernon Twp	Vernon
25	0.0	Verona Boro	Verona
25	0.0	Voorhees Twp	Voorhees
25	0.0	W Windsor-Plainsboro Reg	Princeton Jct
25	0.0	Waldwick Boro	Waldwick
25	0.0	Wall Twp	Wall
25	0.0	Warren Hills Regional	Washington
25	0.0	Warren Twp	Warren
25	0.0	Washington Twp	Robbinsville
25	0.0	Washington Twp	Long Valley
25	0.0	Washington Twp	Sewell
25	0.0	Watchung Hills Regional	Warren
25	0.0	Wayne Twp	Wayne
25	0.0	West Deptford Twp	West Deptford
25	0.0	West Milford Twp	West Milford
25	0.0	West Morris Regional	Chester
25	0.0	West New York Town	West New York
25	0.0	West Orange Town	West Orange
25	0.0	Westfield Town	Westfield
25	0.0	Westwood Regional	Westwood
25	0.0	Willingboro Twp	Willingboro
25	0.0	Woodbridge Twp	Woodbridge
25	0.0	Woodbury City	Woodbury
25	0.0	Wyckoff Twp	Wyckoff

Students Eligible for Free Lunch

Rank	Percent	District Name	City
1	87.6	Union City	Union City
2	75.6	Asbury Park City	Asbury Park
3	74.8	Camden City	Camden
4	69.0	City of Orange Twp	Orange
5	66.2	Perth Amboy City	Perth Amboy
6	66.1	Bridgeton City	Bridgeton
6	66.1	New Brunswick City	New Brunswick
8	65.2	Hoboken City	Hoboken
9	63.8	Passaic City	Passaic
10	62.8	Essex County Voc-Tech	West Orange
10	62.8	Salem City	Salem
12	60.5	Newark City	Newark
13	59.8	Elizabeth City	Elizabeth
14	59.4	West New York Town	West New York
15	59.0	East Orange	East Orange
16	58.5	Jersey City	Jersey City
17	58.1	Irvington Township	Irvington
18	57.6	Atlantic City	Atlantic City
19	57.3	Plainfield City	Plainfield
20	51.6	Camden County Vocational	Sicklerville
21	51.5	Paterson City	Paterson
22	50.6	Trenton City	Trenton
23	50.3	Long Branch City	Long Branch
24	49.0	Lakewood Twp	Lakewood
25	46.6	Pleasantville City	Pleasantville
26	44.3	Penns Grv-Carney's Pt Reg	Penns Grove
27	43.7	Vineland City	Vineland
28	43.2	Keansburg Boro	Keansburg
29	42.6	Burlington County Spec Serv	Mount Holly
30	42.5	Passaic County Vocational	Wayne
31	42.3	Englewood City	Englewood
32	40.8	North Bergen Twp	North Bergen
33	39.8	Paulsboro Boro	Paulsboro
34	38.3	Harrison Town	Harrison
35	37.8	Mercer County Special Service	Trenton
36	37.1	Lindenwold Boro	Lindenwold

37	36.7	Millville City	Millville
38	35.5	Dover Town	Dover
39	35.2	Carteret Boro	Carteret
40	35.1	Hillside Twp	Hillside
41	34.7	Roselle Boro	Roselle
42	33.7	Gloucester City	Gloucester City
43	33.6	Garfield City	Garfield
44	32.8	Middlesex County Vocational	E Brunswick
45	31.7	Neptune Twp	Neptune
46	31.2	Linden City	Linden
47	31.1	Pennsauken Twp	Pennsauken
48	31.0	Woodbury City	Woodbury
49	30.9	Bound Brook Boro	Bound Brook
50	30.6	Burlington City	Burlington
51	30.2	Hackensack City	Hackensack
52	29.4	Rahway City	Rahway
53	29.0	Phillipsburg Town	Phillipsburg
54	28.3	Willingboro Twp	Willingboro
55	27.4	Bayonne City	Bayonne
56	26.2	Buena Regional	Buena
57	25.4	Winslow Twp	Atco
58	24.9	Pemberton Twp	Pemberton
59	24.8	Cliffside Park Boro	Cliffside Park
60	24.7	Bergen County Special Service	Paramus
61	24.1	Pine Hill Boro	Pine Hill
62	23.6	Pittsgrove Twp	Pittsgrove
63	23.4	Riverside Twp	Riverside
64	23.2	Lodi Borough	Lodi
64	23.2	North Plainfield Boro	N Plainfield
66	23.1	Lower Cape May Regional	Cape May
67	22.9	Lower Twp	Cape May
68	21.9	Hamilton Twp	Mays Landing
69	21.6	Glassboro	Glassboro
70	21.5	Kearny Town	Kearny
71	20.3	Deptford Twp	Deptford
72	20.2	Hammonton Town	Hammonton
73	19.8	Franklin Twp	Somerset
74	19.2	Highland Park Boro	Highland Park
74	19.2	Somerville Boro	Somerville
76	19.0	Belleville Town	Belleville
77	18.8	Little Egg Harbor Twp	Little Egg Hbr
78	18.6	Middle Twp	Cape May Ct Hse
79	17.6	Burlington County Vocational	Westampton Twp
80	17.5	Bloomfield Twp	Bloomfield
81	17.3	Ridgefield Park Twp	Ridgefield Park
82	15.8	Egg Harbor Twp	W Atlantic City
83	15.5	Collingswood Boro	Collingswood
84	15.2	Pinelands Regional	Tuckerton
84	15.2	South River Boro	South River
86	14.9	Monroe Twp	Williamstown
87	14.8	Greater Egg Harbor Reg	Mays Landing
88	14.7	Morris SD	Morristown
89	14.6	West Orange Town	West Orange
90	14.5	Florence Twp	Florence
91	14.1	Newton Town	Newton
92	13.7	Gloucester Twp	Blackwood
93	13.6	Ewing Twp	Ewing
93	13.6	Franklin Twp	Franklinville
95	13.4	Union Twp	Union
96	13.2	Galloway Twp	Galloway
97	13.1	North Brunswick Twp	North Brunswick
98	12.4	Barnegat Twp	Barnegat
98	12.4	Woodbridge Twp	Woodbridge
100	12.2	Delsea Regional H.S District	Franklinville
101	12.1	Elmwood Park	Elmwood Park
101	12.1	Hamilton Twp	Hamilton Square
103	12.0	Maple Shade Twp	Maple Shade
104	11.8	Montclair Town	Montclair
105	11.6	Secaucus Town	Secaucus
106	11.4	South Orange-Maplewood	Maplewood
107	11.3	Manchester Twp	Whiting
107	11.3	Ocean City	Ocean City
109	11.2	Matawan-Aberdeen Regional	Aberdeen
110	11.1	East Windsor Regional	Hightstown
111	10.9	Piscataway Twp	Piscataway
112	10.8	Central Regional	Bayville
113	10.7	Berkeley Twp	Bayville
114	10.6	Palisades Park	Palisades Park
115	10.4	Roselle Park Boro	Roselle Park
116	10.0	Clifton City	Clifton
117	9.9	Sayreville Boro	Sayreville
117	9.9	Teaneck Twp	Teaneck
119	9.5	West Deptford Twp	West Deptford
120	9.2	Sussex-Wantage Regional	Wantage
121	8.9	Bergenfield Boro	Bergenfield
121	8.9	Toms River Regional	Toms River
123	8.6	Pennsville	Pennsville
124	8.3	Lyndhurst Twp	Lyndhurst
124	8.3	Ridgefield Boro	Ridgefield
126	8.2	Burlington Twp	Burlington
127	8.1	Tinton Falls	Tinton Falls
128	7.9	Bordentown Regional	Bordentown
128	7.9	Lacey Twp	Lanoka Harbor
130	7.8	Middlesex Boro	Middlesex
131	7.6	Hackettstown	Hackettstown
131	7.6	Woodstown-Pilesgrove Reg	Woodstown
133	7.5	Old Bridge Twp	Matawan
133	7.5	Pitman Boro	Pitman
135	7.4	Brick Twp	Brick
136	7.2	Black Horse Pike Regional	Blackwood
136	7.2	Stafford Twp	Manahawkin
138	7.1	Hopatcong	Hopatcong
139	6.8	Lawrence Twp	Lawrenceville
140	6.7	Audubon Boro	Audubon
141	6.5	Bergen County Vocational	Paramus
142	6.4	Edison Twp	Edison
142	6.4	Summit City	Summit
144	6.2	Ocean Twp	Oakhurst
144	6.2	Princeton Regional	Princeton
146	6.1	Southern Regional	Manahawkin
147	6.0	Delran Twp	Delran
147	6.0	Mainland Regional	Linwood
147	6.0	South Plainfield Boro	S Plainfield
150	5.8	Manasquan Boro	Manasquan
151	5.7	Warren Hills Regional	Washington
152	5.6	Kingsway Regional	Woolwich Twp
152	5.6	Lumberton Twp	Lumberton
152	5.6	Northern Burlington Reg	Columbus
152	5.6	Plumsted Twp	New Egypt
156	5.4	Fort Lee Boro	Fort Lee
156	5.4	Hawthorne Boro	Hawthorne
156	5.4	Leonia Boro	Leonia
156	5.4	Rancocas Valley Regional	Mount Holly
160	5.3	Hazlet Twp	Hazlet
160	5.3	Pompton Lakes Boro	Pompton Lakes
160	5.3	Washington Twp	Sewell
163	5.2	Howell Twp	Howell
163	5.2	Jackson Twp	Jackson
163	5.2	Spotswood Boro	Spotswood
166	5.1	Saddle Brook Twp	Saddle Brook
167	4.9	North Arlington Boro	North Arlington
168	4.8	Mantua Twp	Sewell
168	4.8	Morris Hills Regional	Rockaway
170	4.7	Haddon Twp	Westmont
170	4.7	Parsippany-Troy Hills Twp	Parsippany
172	4.6	Cinnaminson Twp	Cinnaminson
172	4.6	Wall Twp	Wall
174	4.5	Upper Twp	Petersburg
175	4.4	Jefferson Twp	Lake Hopatcong
176	4.2	Cherry Hill Twp	Cherry Hill
176	4.2	Madison Boro	Madison
176	4.2	Vernon Twp	Vernon
179	4.1	Mount Laurel Twp	Mount Laurel
180	3.9	Eastern Camden County Reg	Voorhees
180	3.9	Middletown Twp	Middletown
180	3.9	West Milford Twp	West Milford
183	3.8	Point Pleasant Boro	Pt Pleasant
183	3.8	Roxbury Twp	Succasunna
185	3.5	Clearview Regional	Mullica Hill
185	3.5	Mount Olive Twp	Budd Lake
185	3.5	New Milford Boro	New Milford
185	3.5	Voorhees Twp	Voorhees
189	3.4	Fair Lawn Boro	Fair Lawn
189	3.4	Freehold Regional	Englishtown
189	3.4	High Point Regional	Sussex
189	3.4	Metuchen Boro	Metuchen
193	3.3	Flemington-Raritan Reg	Flemington
193	3.3	Rockaway Twp	Hibernia
193	3.3	Springfield Twp	Springfield
196	3.2	East Brunswick Twp	E Brunswick
196	3.2	Mahwah Twp	Mahwah
196	3.2	Nutley Town	Nutley
199	3.1	Hillsborough Twp	Neshanic
199	3.1	Monroe Twp	Monroe Township
199	3.1	Moorestown Twp	Moorestown
202	3.0	Dumont Boro	Dumont
203	2.9	South Brunswick Twp	Monmouth Jct
203	2.9	Wayne Twp	Wayne
205	2.8	Bridgewater-Raritan Reg	Bridgewater
206	2.7	Denville Twp	Denville
207	2.6	Manalapan-Englishtown Reg	Englishtown
208	2.5	Mountain Lakes Boro	Mountain Lakes
209	2.3	Freehold Twp	Freehold
210	2.2	Monmouth County Vocational	Colts Neck
210	2.2	Randolph Twp	Randolph
212	2.0	Evesham Twp	Marlton
212	2.0	Hasbrouck Heights Boro	Hasbrouck Hgts
212	2.0	Scotch Plains-Fanwood Reg	Scotch Plains
212	2.0	Upper Freehold Regional	Allentown
212	2.0	Westwood Regional	Westwood
217	1.8	Hunterdon Central Reg	Flemington
217	1.8	Millstone Twp	Clarksburg
217	1.8	Somerset Hills Regional	Bernardsville
220	1.7	W Windsor-Plainsboro Reg	Princeton Jct
221	1.6	Cranford Twp	Cranford
221	1.6	Medford Twp	Medford
223	1.5	Rutherford Boro	Rutherford
224	1.3	Paramus Boro	Paramus
224	1.3	Ramsey Boro	Ramsey
226	1.2	Lenape Regional	Shamong
226	1.2	Pequannock Twp	Pompton Plains
228	1.1	Cresskill Boro	Cresskill
228	1.1	Sparta Twp	Sparta
228	1.1	Westfield Town	Westfield
231	1.0	Pascack Valley Regional	Montvale
231	1.0	Washington Twp	Robbinsville
233	0.9	Branchburg Twp	Branchburg
233	0.9	Cedar Grove Twp	Cedar Grove
233	0.9	Clark Twp	Clark
233	0.9	Clinton Twp	Annandale
233	0.9	Haddonfield Boro	Haddonfield
233	0.9	Marlboro Twp	Marlboro
233	0.9	Readington Twp	Whitehouse Stn
240	0.8	Hopewell Valley Regional	Pennington
240	0.8	Ridgewood Village	Ridgewood
242	0.7	Berkeley Heights Twp	Berkeley Hgts
242	0.7	Bernards Twp	Basking Ridge
242	0.7	Colts Neck Twp	Colts Neck
242	0.7	New Providence Boro	New Providence
242	0.7	Oakland Boro	Oakland
242	0.7	Waldwick Boro	Waldwick
248	0.5	Caldwell-West Caldwell	West Caldwell
248	0.5	Glen Rock Boro	Glen Rock
248	0.5	Hanover Twp	Whippany
248	0.5	Livingston Twp	Livingston
248	0.5	Millburn Twp	Millburn
248	0.5	Montgomery Twp	Skillman
248	0.5	Montville Twp	Montville
248	0.5	Warren Twp	Warren
248	0.5	Washington Twp	Long Valley
248	0.5	West Morris Regional	Chester
258	0.4	Kinnelon Boro	Kinnelon
258	0.4	N Hunt/Voorhees Regional	Annandale
258	0.4	Watchung Hills Regional	Warren
261	0.3	Holmdel Twp	Holmdel
261	0.3	SD of the Chathams	Chatham
261	0.3	Tenafly Boro	Tenafly
261	0.3	Wyckoff Twp	Wyckoff
265	0.2	Franklin Lakes Boro	Franklin Lakes
265	0.2	Verona Boro	Verona
267	0.1	Northern Valley Regional	Demarest
268	0.0	Glen Ridge Boro	Glen Ridge
268	0.0	Ramapo-Indian Hill Reg	Franklin Lakes

Students Eligible for Reduced-Price Lunch

Rank	Percent	District Name	City
1	19.5	Hillside Twp	Hillside
2	19.4	Garfield City	Garfield
3	17.6	Passaic County Vocational	Wayne
4	17.3	Dover Town	Dover
5	17.1	Essex County Voc-Tech	West Orange
6	16.6	Keansburg Boro	Keansburg
7	15.7	Lower Twp	Cape May
8	15.6	Pleasantville City	Pleasantville
9	15.4	Lindenwold Boro	Lindenwold
9	15.4	Long Branch City	Long Branch
11	15.2	West New York Town	West New York
12	14.5	Linden City	Linden
12	14.5	Perth Amboy City	Perth Amboy
14	14.3	Pemberton Twp	Pemberton
15	14.0	Pennsauken Twp	Pennsauken
16	13.9	Bound Brook Boro	Bound Brook
17	13.6	Hoboken City	Hoboken
18	13.5	Camden County Vocational	Sicklerville
19	13.4	Gloucester City	Gloucester City
20	13.3	Lodi Borough	Lodi
21	13.2	Englewood City	Englewood
22	13.1	Carteret Boro	Carteret
22	13.1	City of Orange Twp	Orange
22	13.1	North Bergen Twp	North Bergen
25	13.0	Rahway City	Rahway
25	13.0	Vineland City	Vineland
27	12.9	Cliffside Park Boro	Cliffside Park
27	12.9	Elizabeth City	Elizabeth
29	12.5	Willingboro Twp	Willingboro
30	12.3	Jersey City	Jersey City
30	12.3	Roselle Boro	Roselle
32	11.9	Plainfield City	Plainfield
33	11.7	Hackensack City	Hackensack
33	11.7	Paulsboro Boro	Paulsboro
35	11.4	Bridgeton City	Bridgeton
35	11.4	Irvington Township	Irvington
37	11.3	New Brunswick City	New Brunswick
38	11.2	North Plainfield Boro	N Plainfield
38	11.2	Paterson City	Paterson

38	11.2	Ridgefield Park Twp	Ridgefield Park
41	11.0	Burlington City	Burlington
41	11.0	Penns Grv-Carney's Pt Reg	Penns Grove
43	10.9	Buena Regional	Buena
44	10.8	Harrison Town	Harrison
45	10.7	Atlantic City	Atlantic City
45	10.7	Hamilton Twp	Mays Landing
47	10.6	Little Egg Harbor Twp	Little Egg Hbr
47	10.6	Millville City	Millville
47	10.6	Pine Hill Boro	Pine Hill
50	10.3	East Orange	East Orange
51	10.1	Burlington County Spec Serv	Mount Holly
51	10.1	Middlesex County Vocational	E Brunswick
51	10.1	Woodbury City	Woodbury
54	9.9	Lakewood Twp	Lakewood
54	9.9	Trenton City	Trenton
56	9.8	Burlington County Vocational	Westampton Twp
56	9.8	Maple Shade Twp	Maple Shade
56	9.8	Passaic City	Passaic
59	9.7	Bloomfield Twp	Bloomfield
59	9.7	Neptune Twp	Neptune
59	9.7	South River Boro	South River
62	9.4	Egg Harbor Twp	W Atlantic City
62	9.4	Mercer County Special Service	Trenton
64	9.3	Deptford Twp	Deptford
64	9.3	Elmwood Park	Elmwood Park
64	9.3	Galloway Twp	Galloway
67	9.2	Newark City	Newark
67	9.2	Pinelands Regional	Tuckerton
69	9.1	Belleville Town	Belleville
69	9.1	Kearny Town	Kearny
69	9.1	Roselle Park Boro	Roselle Park
72	8.9	Bergen County Special Service	Paramus
72	8.9	Glassboro	Glassboro
72	8.9	Lower Cape May Regional	Cape May
75	8.8	Salem City	Salem
76	8.7	Bayonne City	Bayonne
77	8.6	Riverside Twp	Riverside
77	8.6	Union Twp	Union
79	8.5	Collingswood Boro	Collingswood
79	8.5	Phillipsburg Town	Phillipsburg
81	8.4	Palisades Park	Palisades Park
82	8.3	Ewing Twp	Ewing
83	8.1	Middle Twp	Cape May Ct Hse
84	8.0	Gloucester Twp	Blackwood
85	7.9	Delsea Regional H.S District	Franklinville
85	7.9	Monroe Twp	Williamstown
87	7.8	Barnegat Twp	Barnegat
88	7.7	Greater Egg Harbor Reg	Mays Landing
88	7.7	Highland Park Boro	Highland Park
88	7.7	Pittsgrove Twp	Pittsgrove
88	7.7	West Orange Town	West Orange
92	7.5	Franklin Twp	Franklinville
93	7.4	Franklin Twp	Somerset
93	7.4	Somerville Boro	Somerville
95	7.3	Central Regional	Bayville
96	7.2	Teaneck Twp	Teaneck
97	7.0	Asbury Park City	Asbury Park
98	6.9	North Brunswick Twp	North Brunswick
99	6.8	Morris SD	Morristown
99	6.8	West Deptford Twp	West Deptford
99	6.8	Winslow Twp	Atco
102	6.6	East Windsor Regional	Hightstown
102	6.6	Middlesex Boro	Middlesex
102	6.6	South Orange-Maplewood	Maplewood
105	6.5	Hamilton Twp	Hamilton Square
106	6.4	Florence Twp	Florence
106	6.4	Sayreville Boro	Sayreville
106	6.4	Secaucus Town	Secaucus
106	6.4	Sussex-Wantage Regional	Wantage
110	6.3	Matawan-Aberdeen Regional	Aberdeen
110	6.3	Stafford Twp	Manahawkin
112	6.2	Woodbridge Twp	Woodbridge
113	6.1	Berkeley Twp	Bayville
113	6.1	Hammonton Town	Hammonton
113	6.1	Newton Town	Newton
113	6.1	Piscataway Twp	Piscataway
117	6.0	Lyndhurst Twp	Lyndhurst
118	5.9	Tinton Falls	Tinton Falls
119	5.8	Bordentown Regional	Bordentown
120	5.7	Bergenfield Boro	Bergenfield
120	5.7	Manchester Twp	Whiting
120	5.7	Pitman Boro	Pitman
123	5.6	Mainland Regional	Linwood
123	5.6	Southern Regional	Manahawkin
125	5.5	Lacey Twp	Lanoka Harbor
126	5.4	Brick Twp	Brick
127	5.2	Hopatcong	Hopatcong
127	5.2	Old Bridge Twp	Matawan
129	5.1	Black Horse Pike Regional	Blackwood
129	5.1	Hackettstown	Hackettstown
129	5.1	Montclair Town	Montclair
132	4.9	Audubon Boro	Audubon
132	4.9	Lawrence Twp	Lawrenceville
132	4.9	Northern Burlington Reg	Columbus
135	4.7	Plumsted Twp	New Egypt
136	4.6	Fort Lee Boro	Fort Lee
137	4.5	South Plainfield Boro	S Plainfield
137	4.5	Union City	Union City
139	4.3	Burlington Twp	Burlington
139	4.3	Hawthorne Boro	Hawthorne
141	4.2	Camden City	Camden
141	4.2	Ridgefield Boro	Ridgefield
141	4.2	Woodstown-Pilesgrove Reg	Woodstown
144	4.1	Pennsville	Pennsville
145	4.0	Mount Olive Twp	Budd Lake
146	3.9	Spotswood Boro	Spotswood
147	3.8	Toms River Regional	Toms River
148	3.7	Leonia Boro	Leonia
148	3.7	Summit City	Summit
150	3.6	Clifton City	Clifton
150	3.6	Delran Twp	Delran
150	3.6	Mantua Twp	Sewell
150	3.6	Ocean City	Ocean City
150	3.6	Parsippany-Troy Hills Twp	Parsippany
155	3.5	Edison Twp	Edison
156	3.4	Jackson Twp	Jackson
156	3.4	North Arlington Boro	North Arlington
158	3.3	Bergen County Vocational	Paramus
158	3.3	Lumberton Twp	Lumberton
158	3.3	Ocean Twp	Oakhurst
158	3.3	Saddle Brook Twp	Saddle Brook
162	3.2	Haddon Twp	Westmont
162	3.2	New Milford Boro	New Milford
162	3.2	Vernon Twp	Vernon
162	3.2	Warren Hills Regional	Washington
166	3.1	Hazlet Twp	Hazlet
166	3.1	Jefferson Twp	Lake Hopatcong
166	3.1	Upper Twp	Petersburg
166	3.1	Washington Twp	Sewell
170	3.0	Kingsway Regional	Woolwich Twp
170	3.0	South Brunswick Twp	Monmouth Jct
172	2.9	Point Pleasant Boro	Pt Pleasant
172	2.9	Roxbury Twp	Succasunna
174	2.8	Rockaway Twp	Hibernia
175	2.7	Cherry Hill Twp	Cherry Hill
175	2.7	Howell Twp	Howell
175	2.7	Princeton Regional	Princeton
178	2.5	Middletown Twp	Middletown
178	2.5	Morris Hills Regional	Rockaway
178	2.5	Voorhees Twp	Voorhees
181	2.4	Mahwah Twp	Mahwah
181	2.4	Mount Laurel Twp	Mount Laurel
183	2.3	East Brunswick Twp	E Brunswick
183	2.3	Eastern Camden County Reg	Voorhees
183	2.3	Fair Lawn Boro	Fair Lawn
183	2.3	High Point Regional	Sussex
183	2.3	Madison Boro	Madison
183	2.3	Metuchen Boro	Metuchen
183	2.3	Nutley Town	Nutley
183	2.3	Springfield Twp	Springfield
183	2.3	West Milford Twp	West Milford
192	2.2	Evesham Twp	Marlton
192	2.2	Manasquan Boro	Manasquan
192	2.2	Wall Twp	Wall
195	1.9	Bridgewater-Raritan Reg	Bridgewater
195	1.9	Cinnaminson Twp	Cinnaminson
195	1.9	Clearview Regional	Mullica Hill
195	1.9	Monroe Twp	Monroe Township
199	1.8	Flemington-Raritan Reg	Flemington
199	1.8	Freehold Twp	Freehold
199	1.8	Monmouth County Vocational	Colts Neck
199	1.8	Mountain Lakes Boro	Mountain Lakes
199	1.8	Rancocas Valley Regional	Mount Holly
204	1.7	Dumont Boro	Dumont
204	1.7	Freehold Regional	Englishtown
204	1.7	Hillsborough Twp	Neshanic
204	1.7	Manalapan-Englishtown Reg	Englishtown
204	1.7	Moorestown Twp	Moorestown
204	1.7	Wayne Twp	Wayne
210	1.6	Oakland Boro	Oakland
210	1.6	Pompton Lakes Boro	Pompton Lakes
212	1.4	Millstone Twp	Clarksburg
212	1.4	W Windsor-Plainsboro Reg	Princeton Jct
212	1.4	Washington Twp	Robbinsville
215	1.3	Medford Twp	Medford
215	1.3	Upper Freehold Regional	Allentown
217	1.1	Clark Twp	Clark
217	1.1	Cranford Twp	Cranford
217	1.1	New Providence Boro	New Providence
220	1.0	Paramus Boro	Paramus
220	1.0	Randolph Twp	Randolph
220	1.0	Rutherford Boro	Rutherford
223	0.9	Colts Neck Twp	Colts Neck
223	0.9	Marlboro Twp	Marlboro
223	0.9	Pequannock Twp	Pompton Plains
223	0.9	Scotch Plains-Fanwood Reg	Scotch Plains
223	0.9	Westwood Regional	Westwood
228	0.8	Ramapo-Indian Hill Reg	Franklin Lakes
228	0.8	Ramsey Boro	Ramsey
228	0.8	Washington Twp	Long Valley
231	0.7	Hopewell Valley Regional	Pennington
231	0.7	Hunterdon Central Reg	Flemington
231	0.7	Somerset Hills Regional	Bernardsville
231	0.7	Sparta Twp	Sparta
231	0.7	Westfield Town	Westfield
236	0.6	Branchburg Twp	Branchburg
236	0.6	Lenape Regional	Shamong
238	0.5	Berkeley Heights Twp	Berkeley Hgts
238	0.5	Bernards Twp	Basking Ridge
238	0.5	Caldwell-West Caldwell	West Caldwell
238	0.5	Glen Rock Boro	Glen Rock
238	0.5	Montgomery Twp	Skillman
238	0.5	N Hunt/Voorhees Regional	Annandale
244	0.4	Livingston Twp	Livingston
244	0.4	Readington Twp	Whitehouse Stn
244	0.4	Ridgewood Village	Ridgewood
244	0.4	Watchung Hills Regional	Warren
248	0.3	Cresskill Boro	Cresskill
248	0.3	Haddonfield Boro	Haddonfield
248	0.3	Hasbrouck Heights Boro	Hasbrouck Hgts
248	0.3	Northern Valley Regional	Demarest
248	0.3	Verona Boro	Verona
253	0.2	Montville Twp	Montville
254	0.1	Cedar Grove Twp	Cedar Grove
254	0.1	Holmdel Twp	Holmdel
254	0.1	Millburn Twp	Millburn
254	0.1	SD of the Chathams	Chatham
254	0.1	Tenafly Boro	Tenafly
254	0.1	Waldwick Boro	Waldwick
260	0.0	West Morris Regional	Chester
260	0.0	Wyckoff Twp	Wyckoff
262	0.0	Clinton Twp	Annandale
262	0.0	Denville Twp	Denville
262	0.0	Franklin Lakes Boro	Franklin Lakes
262	0.0	Glen Ridge Boro	Glen Ridge
262	0.0	Hanover Twp	Whippany
262	0.0	Kinnelon Boro	Kinnelon
262	0.0	Pascack Valley Regional	Montvale
262	0.0	Warren Twp	Warren

Student/Teacher Ratio

Rank	Ratio	District Name	City
1	17.0	Rancocas Valley Regional	Mount Holly
2	16.1	Medford Twp	Medford
3	15.7	Central Regional	Bayville
3	15.7	Freehold Twp	Freehold
5	15.6	North Bergen Twp	North Bergen
5	15.6	Toms River Regional	Toms River
7	15.5	Hammonton Town	Hammonton
7	15.5	Hillside Twp	Hillside
9	15.4	Elmwood Park	Elmwood Park
10	15.3	Black Horse Pike Regional	Blackwood
10	15.3	Sparta Twp	Sparta
10	15.3	Vernon Twp	Vernon
10	15.3	Washington Twp	Long Valley
10	15.3	West Deptford Twp	West Deptford
15	15.1	Franklin Twp	Franklinville
15	15.1	Nutley Town	Nutley
17	15.0	Brick Twp	Brick
18	14.9	Deptford Twp	Deptford
18	14.9	Hopatcong	Hopatcong
18	14.9	Marlboro Twp	Marlboro
18	14.9	Old Bridge Twp	Matawan
22	14.8	Holmdel Twp	Holmdel
22	14.8	Lacey Twp	Lanoka Harbor
22	14.8	South River Boro	South River
25	14.7	Freehold Regional	Englishtown
25	14.7	Gloucester Twp	Blackwood
25	14.7	Sayreville Boro	Sayreville
28	14.6	Delran Twp	Delran
28	14.6	Denville Twp	Denville
28	14.6	Haddon Twp	Westmont
28	14.6	Harrison Town	Harrison
28	14.6	Monroe Twp	Williamstown
28	14.6	Union Twp	Union
34	14.5	Clark Twp	Clark
34	14.5	Irvington Township	Irvington
34	14.5	Wyckoff Twp	Wyckoff
37	14.4	Dumont Boro	Dumont
37	14.4	East Brunswick Twp	E Brunswick
37	14.4	Eastern Camden County Reg	Voorhees
37	14.4	Lyndhurst Twp	Lyndhurst
37	14.4	Manasquan Boro	Manasquan
37	14.4	Mantua Twp	Sewell
37	14.4	Saddle Brook Twp	Saddle Brook
37	14.4	Upper Freehold Regional	Allentown

45	14.3	Bergenfield Boro	Bergenfield
45	14.3	Greater Egg Harbor Reg	Mays Landing
45	14.3	Jackson Twp	Jackson
45	14.3	Rahway City	Rahway
49	14.2	Manalapan-Englishtown Reg	Englishtown
49	14.2	Montgomery Twp	Skillman
49	14.2	Tinton Falls	Tinton Falls
49	14.2	West Milford Twp	West Milford
53	14.1	Belleville Town	Belleville
53	14.1	Berkeley Twp	Bayville
53	14.1	Cherry Hill Twp	Cherry Hill
53	14.1	Clearview Regional	Mullica Hill
53	14.1	Glen Ridge Boro	Glen Ridge
53	14.1	Kingsway Regional	Woolwich Twp
53	14.1	Pennsauken Twp	Pennsauken
53	14.1	Pittsgrove Twp	Pittsgrove
53	14.1	Point Pleasant Boro	Pt Pleasant
53	14.1	Ridgewood Village	Ridgewood
53	14.1	Southern Regional	Manahawkin
64	14.0	Bound Brook Boro	Bound Brook
64	14.0	Caldwell-West Caldwell	West Caldwell
64	14.0	Delsea Regional H.S District	Franklinville
64	14.0	Hamilton Twp	Hamilton Square
64	14.0	Kinnelon Boro	Kinnelon
64	14.0	Moorestown Twp	Moorestown
64	14.0	Plumsted Twp	New Egypt
64	14.0	Pompton Lakes Boro	Pompton Lakes
64	14.0	Riverside Twp	Riverside
64	14.0	Scotch Plains-Fanwood Reg	Scotch Plains
64	14.0	Verona Boro	Verona
64	14.0	Wayne Twp	Wayne
76	13.9	Burlington Twp	Burlington
76	13.9	Cresskill Boro	Cresskill
76	13.9	Howell Twp	Howell
76	13.9	Maple Shade Twp	Maple Shade
76	13.9	North Arlington Boro	North Arlington
76	13.9	Stafford Twp	Manahawkin
82	13.8	Bloomfield Twp	Bloomfield
82	13.8	Carteret Boro	Carteret
82	13.8	Dover Town	Dover
82	13.8	Middletown Twp	Middletown
82	13.8	Millstone Twp	Clarksburg
82	13.8	South Orange-Maplewood	Maplewood
88	13.7	Buena Regional	Buena
88	13.7	Haddonfield Boro	Haddonfield
88	13.7	Jefferson Twp	Lake Hopatcong
88	13.7	Lawrence Twp	Lawrenceville
88	13.7	New Milford Boro	New Milford
88	13.7	North Brunswick Twp	North Brunswick
88	13.7	Ocean Twp	Oakhurst
88	13.7	Roselle Boro	Roselle
96	13.6	Bayonne City	Bayonne
96	13.6	Egg Harbor Twp	W Atlantic City
96	13.6	Fair Lawn Boro	Fair Lawn
96	13.6	Fort Lee Boro	Fort Lee
96	13.6	Kearny Town	Kearny
96	13.6	Lower Twp	Cape May
96	13.6	Pequannock Twp	Pompton Plains
103	13.5	Cliffside Park Boro	Cliffside Park
103	13.5	East Windsor Regional	Hightstown
103	13.5	Flemington-Raritan Reg	Flemington
103	13.5	Linden City	Linden
103	13.5	Lodi Borough	Lodi
103	13.5	Lumberton Twp	Lumberton
103	13.5	Mount Laurel Twp	Mount Laurel
103	13.5	Mount Olive Twp	Budd Lake
103	13.5	Roxbury Twp	Succasunna
103	13.5	Warren Hills Regional	Washington
103	13.5	Woodstown-Pilesgrove Reg	Woodstown
114	13.4	Audubon Boro	Audubon
114	13.4	Hackensack City	Hackensack
114	13.4	Montville Twp	Montville
114	13.4	Oakland Boro	Oakland
114	13.4	Piscataway Twp	Piscataway
114	13.4	SD of the Chathams	Chatham
114	13.4	South Brunswick Twp	Monmouth Jct
114	13.4	Voorhees Twp	Voorhees
114	13.4	Woodbridge Twp	Woodbridge
123	13.3	Bordentown Regional	Bordentown
123	13.3	East Orange	East Orange
123	13.3	Palisades Park	Palisades Park
123	13.3	Wall Twp	Wall
127	13.2	Berkeley Heights Twp	Berkeley Hgts
127	13.2	Clifton City	Clifton
127	13.2	Evesham Twp	Marlton
127	13.2	Northern Burlington Reg	Columbus
127	13.2	Randolph Twp	Randolph
127	13.2	Somerset Hills Regional	Bernardsville
127	13.2	Upper Twp	Petersburg
134	13.1	Bridgewater-Raritan Reg	Bridgewater
134	13.1	Cranford Twp	Cranford
134	13.1	Neptune Twp	Neptune
134	13.1	Ramsey Boro	Ramsey
134	13.1	Waldwick Boro	Waldwick
134	13.1	Washington Twp	Sewell
140	13.0	Barnegat Twp	Barnegat
140	13.0	Cedar Grove Twp	Cedar Grove
140	13.0	Franklin Twp	Somerset
140	13.0	Hasbrouck Heights Boro	Hasbrouck Hgts
140	13.0	Hazlet Twp	Hazlet
140	13.0	Highland Park Boro	Highland Park
140	13.0	Lenape Regional	Shamong
140	13.0	Matawan-Aberdeen Regional	Aberdeen
140	13.0	N Hunt/Voorhees Regional	Annandale
140	13.0	W Windsor-Plainsboro Reg	Princeton Jct
140	13.0	Westfield Town	Westfield
151	12.9	Clinton Twp	Annandale
151	12.9	Hackettstown	Hackettstown
151	12.9	Middlesex Boro	Middlesex
151	12.9	Passaic City	Passaic
151	12.9	Readington Twp	Whitehouse Stn
151	12.9	Ridgefield Boro	Ridgefield
151	12.9	Secaucus Town	Secaucus
151	12.9	South Plainfield Boro	S Plainfield
151	12.9	Spotswood Boro	Spotswood
151	12.9	Watchung Hills Regional	Warren
161	12.8	Glassboro	Glassboro
161	12.8	Glen Rock Boro	Glen Rock
161	12.8	Hunterdon Central Reg	Flemington
161	12.8	Mainland Regional	Linwood
161	12.8	Pennsville	Pennsville
161	12.8	Perth Amboy City	Perth Amboy
161	12.8	Rutherford Boro	Rutherford
161	12.8	Somerville Boro	Somerville
169	12.7	Bernards Twp	Basking Ridge
169	12.7	Edison Twp	Edison
169	12.7	Hamilton Twp	Mays Landing
169	12.7	Newton Town	Newton
169	12.7	Paulsboro Boro	Paulsboro
169	12.7	Roselle Park Boro	Roselle Park
169	12.7	Springfield Twp	Springfield
169	12.7	West New York Town	West New York
177	12.6	Little Egg Harbor Twp	Little Egg Hbr
177	12.6	Madison Boro	Madison
177	12.6	Manchester Twp	Whiting
177	12.6	Middle Twp	Cape May Ct Hse
177	12.6	Millburn Twp	Millburn
177	12.6	Monroe Twp	Monroe Township
177	12.6	New Providence Boro	New Providence
177	12.6	Teaneck Twp	Teaneck
177	12.6	Westwood Regional	Westwood
186	12.5	Cinnaminson Twp	Cinnaminson
186	12.5	Collingswood Boro	Collingswood
186	12.5	Garfield City	Garfield
186	12.5	High Point Regional	Sussex
186	12.5	Paramus Boro	Paramus
186	12.5	Summit City	Summit
186	12.5	Sussex-Wantage Regional	Wantage
193	12.4	Hanover Twp	Whippany
193	12.4	Hillsborough Twp	Neshanic
193	12.4	Mahwah Twp	Mahwah
193	12.4	West Morris Regional	Chester
197	12.3	Livingston Twp	Livingston
197	12.3	Lower Cape May Regional	Cape May
197	12.3	West Orange Town	West Orange
200	12.2	Branchburg Twp	Branchburg
200	12.2	City of Orange Twp	Orange
200	12.2	Franklin Lakes Boro	Franklin Lakes
200	12.2	Galloway Twp	Galloway
200	12.2	Hawthorne Boro	Hawthorne
200	12.2	Morris Hills Regional	Rockaway
200	12.2	Trenton City	Trenton
200	12.2	Winslow Twp	Atco
208	12.1	Florence Twp	Florence
208	12.1	Metuchen Boro	Metuchen
208	12.1	Pascack Valley Regional	Montvale
208	12.1	Union City	Union City
208	12.1	Washington Twp	Robbinsville
213	12.0	Ewing Twp	Ewing
213	12.0	Tenafly Boro	Tenafly
213	12.0	Willingboro Twp	Willingboro
216	11.9	Colts Neck Twp	Colts Neck
216	11.9	Essex County Voc-Tech	West Orange
216	11.9	Hopewell Valley Regional	Pennington
216	11.9	Millville City	Millville
216	11.9	Parsippany-Troy Hills Twp	Parsippany
216	11.9	Penns Grv-Carney's Pt Reg	Penns Grove
216	11.9	Plainfield City	Plainfield
223	11.8	Montclair Town	Montclair
223	11.8	Pine Hill Boro	Pine Hill
223	11.8	Princeton Regional	Princeton
226	11.7	Camden County Vocational	Sicklerville
227	11.6	Newark City	Newark
227	11.6	Pitman Boro	Pitman
229	11.5	Atlantic City	Atlantic City
229	11.5	Lakewood Twp	Lakewood
229	11.5	Morris SD	Morristown
229	11.5	North Plainfield Boro	N Plainfield
229	11.5	Vineland City	Vineland
234	11.4	Burlington County Vocational	Westampton Twp
234	11.4	Englewood City	Englewood
234	11.4	Jersey City	Jersey City
234	11.4	Rockaway Twp	Hibernia
234	11.4	Salem City	Salem
239	11.3	Northern Valley Regional	Demarest
239	11.3	Ramapo-Indian Hill Reg	Franklin Lakes
239	11.3	Ridgefield Park Twp	Ridgefield Park
242	11.2	Lindenwold Boro	Lindenwold
242	11.2	Pemberton Twp	Pemberton
244	11.1	Pinelands Regional	Tuckerton
245	11.0	Camden City	Camden
246	10.9	Bridgeton City	Bridgeton
246	10.9	New Brunswick City	New Brunswick
246	10.9	Paterson City	Paterson
249	10.7	Phillipsburg Town	Phillipsburg
250	10.6	Woodbury City	Woodbury
251	10.5	Elizabeth City	Elizabeth
251	10.5	Warren Twp	Warren
253	10.4	Passaic County Vocational	Wayne
254	10.3	Burlington City	Burlington
255	10.2	Ocean City	Ocean City
256	10.0	Hoboken City	Hoboken
256	10.0	Leonia Boro	Leonia
256	10.0	Long Branch City	Long Branch
259	9.8	Mountain Lakes Boro	Mountain Lakes
260	9.7	Asbury Park City	Asbury Park
260	9.7	Gloucester City	Gloucester City
260	9.7	Keansburg Boro	Keansburg
263	9.4	Bergen County Vocational	Paramus
264	9.3	Pleasantville City	Pleasantville
265	8.7	Middlesex County Vocational	E Brunswick
266	8.1	Burlington County Spec Serv	Mount Holly
267	7.2	Monmouth County Vocational	Colts Neck
268	6.4	Mercer County Special Service	Trenton
269	5.3	Bergen County Special Service	Paramus

Student/Librarian Ratio

Rank	Ratio	District Name	City
1	4,880.0	Harrison Town	Harrison
2	3,984.0	Southern Regional	Manahawkin
3	2,887.7	Bayonne City	Bayonne
4	2,771.0	Roselle Boro	Roselle
5	2,707.0	Englewood City	Englewood
6	2,495.5	Union City	Union City
7	2,225.0	Haddon Twp	Westmont
8	2,204.5	Garfield City	Garfield
9	2,199.5	Edison Twp	Edison
10	2,181.0	Maple Shade Twp	Maple Shade
11	2,161.0	Lyndhurst Twp	Lyndhurst
12	2,160.5	Wall Twp	Wall
13	2,031.0	Passaic County Vocational	Wayne
14	1,849.0	Secaucus Town	Secaucus
15	1,732.0	Plumsted Twp	New Egypt
16	1,731.0	Tinton Falls	Tinton Falls
17	1,705.0	Saddle Brook Twp	Saddle Brook
18	1,686.0	Audubon Boro	Audubon
19	1,576.0	North Arlington Boro	North Arlington
20	1,531.2	Toms River Regional	Toms River
21	1,506.8	Pennsauken Twp	Pennsauken
22	1,500.2	North Bergen Twp	North Bergen
23	1,462.1	East Orange	East Orange
24	1,453.0	Middle Twp	Cape May Ct Hse
25	1,404.0	Riverside Twp	Riverside
26	1,360.5	N Hunt/Voorhees Regional	Annandale
27	1,342.0	Burlington Twp	Burlington
28	1,335.0	High Point Regional	Sussex
29	1,327.7	Union Twp	Union
30	1,267.7	Bergenfield Boro	Bergenfield
31	1,235.0	Rancocas Valley Regional	Mount Holly
32	1,203.4	Freehold Regional	Englishtown
33	1,195.3	Holmdel Twp	Holmdel
34	1,186.5	Glen Rock Boro	Glen Rock
35	1,173.0	Cranford Twp	Cranford
36	1,168.4	Greater Egg Harbor Reg	Mays Landing
37	1,158.1	Passaic City	Passaic
38	1,156.0	Northern Valley Regional	Demarest
39	1,135.5	Pine Hill Boro	Pine Hill
40	1,110.1	Elizabeth City	Elizabeth
41	1,089.5	Eastern Camden County Reg	Voorhees
42	1,081.0	Hammonton Town	Hammonton
43	1,077.5	Clearview Regional	Mullica Hill
44	1,076.7	New Brunswick City	New Brunswick
45	1,070.4	Monroe Twp	Williamstown
46	1,066.5	Middlesex Boro	Middlesex
46	1,066.5	Warren Hills Regional	Washington
48	1,061.8	Lawrence Twp	Lawrenceville
49	1,061.5	Ramapo-Indian Hill Reg	Franklin Lakes

50	1,057.9	Bloomfield Twp	Bloomfield
51	1,046.9	Jackson Twp	Jackson
52	1,041.9	Middletown Twp	Middletown
53	1,037.2	Perth Amboy City	Perth Amboy
54	1,036.5	Elmwood Park	Elmwood Park
55	1,014.0	Ridgefield Boro	Ridgefield
56	1,010.3	Monroe Twp	Monroe Township
57	1,007.0	Upper Freehold Regional	Allentown
58	998.5	Sparta Twp	Sparta
59	992.5	Camden County Vocational	Sicklerville
60	974.0	Long Branch City	Long Branch
61	973.5	Matawan-Aberdeen Regional	Aberdeen
62	965.0	Carteret Boro	Carteret
63	957.5	Northern Burlington Reg	Columbus
64	956.4	West Morris Regional	Chester
65	948.7	Sayreville Boro	Sayreville
66	946.9	Egg Harbor Twp	W Atlantic City
67	935.4	Montgomery Twp	Skillman
68	935.3	Hunterdon Central Reg	Flemington
69	934.4	Lenape Regional	Shamong
70	933.0	Pittsgrove Twp	Pittsgrove
71	922.5	Lower Cape May Regional	Cape May
72	915.6	Belleville Town	Belleville
73	909.8	Lakewood Twp	Lakewood
74	901.5	Burlington County Vocational	Westampton Twp
75	901.2	Brick Twp	Brick
76	900.2	North Brunswick Twp	North Brunswick
77	900.0	Jefferson Twp	Lake Hopatcong
78	896.4	Ocean Twp	Oakhurst
79	888.3	Hamilton Twp	Hamilton Square
80	887.3	Vernon Twp	Vernon
81	886.7	Linden City	Linden
82	886.3	Dumont Boro	Dumont
83	883.7	Morris Hills Regional	Rockaway
84	883.0	Manasquan Boro	Manasquan
85	877.0	Teaneck Twp	Teaneck
86	876.0	Mercer County Special Service	Trenton
87	868.0	Kingsway Regional	Woolwich Twp
88	867.5	Little Egg Harbor Twp	Little Egg Hbr
89	864.3	Cliffside Park Boro	Cliffside Park
90	861.5	Spotswood Boro	Spotswood
91	857.3	Buena Regional	Buena
92	856.0	Leonia Boro	Leonia
93	855.8	Hazlet Twp	Hazlet
94	853.5	Watchung Hills Regional	Warren
95	851.5	Millstone Twp	Clarksburg
96	849.7	Lacey Twp	Lanoka Harbor
97	848.7	Marlboro Twp	Marlboro
98	844.6	Hillsborough Twp	Neshanic
99	844.2	Hackensack City	Hackensack
100	841.7	Cinnaminson Twp	Cinnaminson
101	833.5	Bernards Twp	Basking Ridge
102	823.0	Mainland Regional	Linwood
103	822.0	W Windsor-Plainsboro Reg	Princeton Jct
104	806.3	Bridgewater-Raritan Reg	Bridgewater
105	805.5	Pitman Boro	Pitman
106	803.4	Rahway City	Rahway
107	802.8	Washington Twp	Sewell
108	802.0	Pascack Valley Regional	Montvale
109	798.5	Point Pleasant Boro	Pt Pleasant
110	797.5	Gloucester Twp	Blackwood
111	791.3	West Deptford Twp	West Deptford
112	791.2	Mount Olive Twp	Budd Lake
113	790.4	Manalapan-Englishtown Reg	Englishtown
114	790.3	Rutherford Boro	Rutherford
115	783.9	Winslow Twp	Atco
116	782.3	Randolph Twp	Randolph
117	775.7	Central Regional	Bayville
118	769.3	Dover Town	Dover
119	769.0	Woodbury City	Woodbury
120	764.7	Haddonfield Boro	Haddonfield
121	758.7	Hillside Twp	Hillside
122	755.5	Colts Neck Twp	Colts Neck
123	752.5	Waldwick Boro	Waldwick
124	748.3	Readington Twp	Whitehouse Stn
125	744.0	Cresskill Boro	Cresskill
126	742.0	Palisades Park	Palisades Park
127	741.5	Asbury Park City	Asbury Park
128	740.0	Burlington City	Burlington
129	737.9	Old Bridge Twp	Matawan
130	735.7	Somerville Boro	Somerville
130	735.7	South River Boro	South River
132	731.9	Jersey City	Jersey City
133	729.0	Hamilton Twp	Mays Landing
134	725.0	Salem City	Salem
135	717.5	Hopatcong	Hopatcong
136	716.0	Gloucester City	Gloucester City
137	709.5	Atlantic City	Atlantic City
138	705.2	Woodbridge Twp	Woodbridge
139	703.2	West Orange Town	West Orange
140	702.4	Plainfield City	Plainfield
141	701.8	Willingboro Twp	Willingboro
142	696.8	Freehold Twp	Freehold
143	696.0	Hoboken City	Hoboken
143	696.0	Paterson City	Paterson
145	693.7	East Windsor Regional	Hightstown
146	690.7	Trenton City	Trenton
147	688.5	East Brunswick Twp	E Brunswick
148	688.0	Montclair Town	Montclair
149	687.3	Bordentown Regional	Bordentown
150	680.7	Roselle Park Boro	Roselle Park
151	680.0	Collingswood Boro	Collingswood
152	677.3	Piscataway Twp	Piscataway
153	674.7	Millville City	Millville
154	673.0	Kearny Town	Kearny
155	671.4	Manchester Twp	Whiting
156	668.8	Newark City	Newark
157	668.2	Howell Twp	Howell
158	665.7	Roxbury Twp	Succasunna
159	662.5	Galloway Twp	Galloway
160	660.4	North Plainfield Boro	N Plainfield
161	659.8	West New York Town	West New York
162	656.7	Pinelands Regional	Tuckerton
163	650.9	Vineland City	Vineland
164	650.3	Westwood Regional	Westwood
165	648.3	Ewing Twp	Ewing
166	648.0	Delsea Regional H.S District	Franklinville
167	640.1	South Brunswick Twp	Monmouth Jct
168	634.9	Irvington Township	Irvington
169	634.3	Clark Twp	Clark
170	633.3	Denville Twp	Denville
171	631.0	Somerset Hills Regional	Bernardsville
172	627.3	Cherry Hill Twp	Cherry Hill
173	626.7	Berkeley Twp	Bayville
174	626.0	Ramsey Boro	Ramsey
174	626.0	Wayne Twp	Wayne
176	619.7	Metuchen Boro	Metuchen
177	616.6	Neptune Twp	Neptune
178	612.5	Glassboro	Glassboro
179	607.0	Lindenwold Boro	Lindenwold
180	602.8	Stafford Twp	Manahawkin
181	598.6	Evesham Twp	Marlton
182	598.5	Phillipsburg Town	Phillipsburg
183	595.8	Medford Twp	Medford
184	594.7	Moorestown Twp	Moorestown
185	594.3	Fair Lawn Boro	Fair Lawn
186	591.7	South Orange-Maplewood	Maplewood
187	591.0	West Milford Twp	West Milford
188	590.6	Hopewell Valley Regional	Pennington
189	590.3	Glen Ridge Boro	Glen Ridge
190	589.7	Ridgefield Park Twp	Ridgefield Park
191	588.0	Clinton Twp	Annandale
192	587.8	Washington Twp	Long Valley
193	583.6	Hackettstown	Hackettstown
194	581.0	Newton Town	Newton
195	580.0	Upper Twp	Petersburg
196	577.5	Voorhees Twp	Voorhees
197	575.1	Clifton City	Clifton
198	573.0	Franklin Twp	Somerset
199	572.7	Sussex-Wantage Regional	Wantage
200	571.5	Mount Laurel Twp	Mount Laurel
201	570.4	City of Orange Twp	Orange
202	566.3	Montville Twp	Montville
203	565.5	Hawthorne Boro	Hawthorne
204	560.0	Woodstown-Pilesgrove Reg	Woodstown
205	551.8	Berkeley Heights Twp	Berkeley Hgts
206	548.1	Nutley Town	Nutley
207	546.4	Ridgewood Village	Ridgewood
208	546.0	Scotch Plains-Fanwood Reg	Scotch Plains
209	545.3	Lumberton Twp	Lumberton
210	543.5	Bridgeton City	Bridgeton
210	543.5	Flemington-Raritan Reg	Flemington
212	542.8	Mahwah Twp	Mahwah
213	542.3	Bound Brook Boro	Bound Brook
214	541.5	Ocean City	Ocean City
215	541.2	Black Horse Pike Regional	Blackwood
216	540.0	New Providence Boro	New Providence
217	532.8	Delran Twp	Delran
218	530.9	Paramus Boro	Paramus
219	530.6	Rockaway Twp	Hibernia
220	529.7	Highland Park Boro	Highland Park
221	528.8	Westfield Town	Westfield
222	526.3	Keansburg Boro	Keansburg
223	525.7	Florence Twp	Florence
224	523.2	SD of the Chathams	Chatham
225	518.8	Essex County Voc-Tech	West Orange
226	517.7	Lodi Borough	Lodi
227	516.5	Tenafly Boro	Tenafly
228	513.0	Livingston Twp	Livingston
229	509.3	Hasbrouck Heights Boro	Hasbrouck Hgts
230	505.3	Pleasantville City	Pleasantville
231	500.5	Verona Boro	Verona
232	499.0	Washington Twp	Robbinsville
233	498.6	Pequannock Twp	Pompton Plains
234	495.0	Franklin Lakes Boro	Franklin Lakes
235	491.7	Paulsboro Boro	Paulsboro
236	486.0	Hanover Twp	Whippany
237	485.9	Fort Lee Boro	Fort Lee
238	483.7	Millburn Twp	Millburn
239	483.3	Branchburg Twp	Branchburg
240	481.6	Pemberton Twp	Pemberton
240	481.6	South Plainfield Boro	S Plainfield
242	481.3	Lower Twp	Cape May
242	481.3	Mantua Twp	Sewell
244	480.6	Caldwell-West Caldwell	West Caldwell
245	480.4	Wyckoff Twp	Wyckoff
246	477.0	Franklin Twp	Franklinville
247	472.7	Deptford Twp	Deptford
248	470.0	Kinnelon Boro	Kinnelon
249	469.7	Princeton Regional	Princeton
250	468.3	Pompton Lakes Boro	Pompton Lakes
251	466.3	Morris SD	Morristown
252	465.7	Penns Grv-Carney's Pt Reg	Penns Grove
253	457.4	New Milford Boro	New Milford
254	448.8	Barnegat Twp	Barnegat
255	446.2	Camden City	Camden
256	445.0	Middlesex County Vocational	E Brunswick
257	439.8	Warren Twp	Warren
258	433.7	Parsippany-Troy Hills Twp	Parsippany
259	414.0	Oakland Boro	Oakland
260	413.8	Mountain Lakes Boro	Mountain Lakes
261	407.8	Pennsville	Pennsville
262	407.6	Summit City	Summit
263	405.6	Springfield Twp	Springfield
264	368.5	Cedar Grove Twp	Cedar Grove
265	352.9	Madison Boro	Madison
266	n/a	Bergen County Special Service	Paramus
266	n/a	Bergen County Vocational	Paramus
266	n/a	Burlington County Spec Serv	Mount Holly
266	n/a	Monmouth County Vocational	Colts Neck

Student/Counselor Ratio

Rank	Ratio	District Name	City
1	1,146.0	Rockaway Twp	Hibernia
2	991.0	Bergen County Special Service	Paramus
3	979.7	Washington Twp	Long Valley
4	876.0	Mercer County Special Service	Trenton
5	870.0	Upper Twp	Petersburg
6	853.5	Hillside Twp	Hillside
7	851.5	Millstone Twp	Clarksburg
8	803.7	Stafford Twp	Manahawkin
9	752.5	Waldwick Boro	Waldwick
10	729.0	Hanover Twp	Whippany
11	722.0	Mantua Twp	Sewell
12	703.8	Cranford Twp	Cranford
13	689.7	Linden City	Linden
14	668.2	Howell Twp	Howell
15	645.9	Brick Twp	Brick
16	633.3	Denville Twp	Denville
17	626.7	Berkeley Twp	Bayville
18	623.9	Union City	Union City
19	618.0	Burlington County Spec Serv	Mount Holly
20	607.7	Deptford Twp	Deptford
21	594.1	Marlboro Twp	Marlboro
22	592.8	Rutherford Boro	Rutherford
23	592.4	Sussex-Wantage Regional	Wantage
24	577.0	Tinton Falls	Tinton Falls
25	576.2	Cliffside Park Boro	Cliffside Park
26	569.0	Union Twp	Union
27	568.3	Saddle Brook Twp	Saddle Brook
28	566.1	Freehold Twp	Freehold
29	562.8	Hackensack City	Hackensack
30	561.0	Barnegat Twp	Barnegat
31	556.3	Matawan-Aberdeen Regional	Aberdeen
32	553.4	Old Bridge Twp	Matawan
33	547.6	Randolph Twp	Randolph
34	542.3	Bound Brook Boro	Bound Brook
35	542.2	Harrison Town	Harrison
36	540.0	New Providence Boro	New Providence
37	528.8	Kinnelon Boro	Kinnelon
38	527.5	Nutley Town	Nutley
39	527.4	Mount Olive Twp	Budd Lake
40	527.0	Manalapan-Englishtown Reg	Englishtown
41	525.3	North Arlington Boro	North Arlington
42	520.2	Westwood Regional	Westwood
43	519.0	Caldwell-West Caldwell	West Caldwell
44	518.7	Garfield City	Garfield
45	515.1	Plainfield City	Plainfield
46	510.4	Toms River Regional	Toms River
47	507.0	Ridgefield Boro	Ridgefield
48	503.7	Colts Neck Twp	Colts Neck
49	502.1	Rahway City	Rahway
50	500.1	North Bergen Twp	North Bergen
51	499.0	Washington Twp	Robbinsville
52	498.6	Pequannock Twp	Pompton Plains
53	496.0	Cresskill Boro	Cresskill
54	495.0	Voorhees Twp	Voorhees

55	494.7	Palisades Park	Palisades Park
56	491.7	Paulsboro Boro	Paulsboro
57	489.0	Hazlet Twp	Hazlet
58	486.0	Hamilton Twp	Mays Landing
59	483.7	Millburn Twp	Millburn
60	481.3	Lower Twp	Cape May
61	479.6	Manchester Twp	Whiting
62	473.3	Somerset Hills Regional	Bernardsville
63	472.8	West Milford Twp	West Milford
64	471.1	Jackson Twp	Jackson
65	470.1	South Brunswick Twp	Monmouth Jct
66	468.0	Scotch Plains-Fanwood Reg	Scotch Plains
67	466.1	Fair Lawn Boro	Fair Lawn
68	465.4	Monroe Twp	Williamstown
69	463.5	Lacey Twp	Lanoka Harbor
70	459.3	Delran Twp	Delran
71	459.1	Cinnaminson Twp	Cinnaminson
72	458.2	Bergenfield Boro	Bergenfield
73	457.2	Mount Laurel Twp	Mount Laurel
74	456.4	South Orange-Maplewood	Maplewood
75	456.3	Point Pleasant Boro	Pt Pleasant
76	455.7	Gloucester Twp	Blackwood
77	453.0	Middletown Twp	Middletown
78	450.1	North Brunswick Twp	North Brunswick
79	449.0	Readington Twp	Whitehouse Stn
80	448.3	Holmdel Twp	Holmdel
81	447.5	East Brunswick Twp	E Brunswick
82	447.1	Hillsborough Twp	Neshanic
83	443.8	Ocean Twp	Oakhurst
84	443.5	Hawthorne Boro	Hawthorne
85	443.4	Atlantic City	Atlantic City
86	442.7	Tenafly Boro	Tenafly
87	441.6	Evesham Twp	Marlton
87	441.6	Flemington-Raritan Reg	Flemington
89	438.7	Passaic City	Passaic
90	435.9	Dumont Boro	Dumont
91	432.2	Woodbridge Twp	Woodbridge
92	431.3	Clifton City	Clifton
93	426.6	Middlesex Boro	Middlesex
94	425.6	Medford Twp	Medford
95	424.4	Hasbrouck Heights Boro	Hasbrouck Hgts
96	420.3	Ramsey Boro	Ramsey
97	417.6	Hoboken City	Hoboken
98	417.3	Wayne Twp	Wayne
99	416.3	Moorestown Twp	Moorestown
100	415.1	Middle Twp	Cape May Ct Hse
101	413.5	Elizabeth City	Elizabeth
102	412.7	Irvington Township	Irvington
103	409.1	Bloomfield Twp	Bloomfield
104	407.1	Mahwah Twp	Mahwah
105	406.6	Sayreville Boro	Sayreville
106	402.8	Upper Freehold Regional	Allentown
107	401.8	Pennsauken Twp	Pennsauken
108	401.0	Willingboro Twp	Willingboro
109	400.4	Verona Boro	Verona
110	400.3	Wyckoff Twp	Wyckoff
111	400.0	Jefferson Twp	Lake Hopatcong
112	399.9	Montclair Town	Montclair
113	398.6	Hopatcong	Hopatcong
114	395.9	Roselle Boro	Roselle
115	395.5	Glen Rock Boro	Glen Rock
116	393.0	Pleasantville City	Pleasantville
117	392.4	SD of the Chathams	Chatham
118	391.9	Winslow Twp	Atco
119	391.5	Piscataway Twp	Piscataway
120	390.2	Bayonne City	Bayonne
121	389.9	Lakewood Twp	Lakewood
122	388.6	Morris SD	Morristown
123	387.8	Westfield Town	Westfield
124	387.6	Franklin Twp	Somerset
125	387.1	Burlington Twp	Burlington
126	386.6	Branchburg Twp	Branchburg
127	385.6	Newark City	Newark
128	385.3	South Plainfield Boro	S Plainfield
129	384.9	Plumsted Twp	New Egypt
130	383.5	Clinton Twp	Annandale
131	381.5	Belleville Town	Belleville
132	380.0	New Brunswick City	New Brunswick
133	378.9	Newton Town	Newton
134	377.3	East Orange	East Orange
135	377.1	Edison Twp	Edison
136	375.3	Neptune Twp	Neptune
137	373.4	Perth Amboy City	Perth Amboy
138	371.8	Metuchen Boro	Metuchen
139	371.3	Franklin Lakes Boro	Franklin Lakes
140	370.5	Madison Boro	Madison
141	370.2	Elmwood Park	Elmwood Park
142	367.8	Somerville Boro	Somerville
143	367.4	Buena Regional	Buena
144	366.5	Warren Twp	Warren
145	363.1	Sparta Twp	Sparta
146	362.3	Bridgeton City	Bridgeton
147	360.4	Montville Twp	Montville
148	360.3	Hammonton Town	Hammonton
149	360.2	Lyndhurst Twp	Lyndhurst
149	360.2	W Windsor-Plainsboro Reg	Princeton Jct
151	360.1	Wall Twp	Wall
152	359.8	Mountain Lakes Boro	Mountain Lakes
153	358.9	Kearny Town	Kearny
154	355.1	Glassboro	Glassboro
155	354.8	Ridgewood Village	Ridgewood
156	354.2	Glen Ridge Boro	Glen Ridge
157	353.9	Paramus Boro	Paramus
158	351.0	Riverside Twp	Riverside
159	350.9	Carteret Boro	Carteret
160	349.0	Lumberton Twp	Lumberton
161	346.9	East Windsor Regional	Hightstown
161	346.9	Lindenwold Boro	Lindenwold
163	345.2	Egg Harbor Twp	W Atlantic City
164	345.1	Lodi Borough	Lodi
165	344.9	Berkeley Heights Twp	Berkeley Hgts
166	342.7	Galloway Twp	Galloway
167	342.0	Livingston Twp	Livingston
168	341.9	Dover Town	Dover
169	340.1	Fort Lee Boro	Fort Lee
170	339.8	Pennsville	Pennsville
171	338.4	Englewood City	Englewood
172	334.1	Montgomery Twp	Skillman
173	333.6	Cherry Hill Twp	Cherry Hill
174	333.4	Bernards Twp	Basking Ridge
175	332.9	Roxbury Twp	Succasunna
176	331.2	Oakland Boro	Oakland
177	329.6	Asbury Park City	Asbury Park
178	329.2	Mainland Regional	Linwood
179	328.6	Vernon Twp	Vernon
180	327.6	Cedar Grove Twp	Cedar Grove
181	326.7	Lawrence Twp	Lawrenceville
182	326.0	Penns Grv-Carney's Pt Reg	Penns Grove
183	325.9	City of Orange Twp	Orange
184	324.4	Pine Hill Boro	Pine Hill
185	322.5	Paterson City	Paterson
186	322.2	Pitman Boro	Pitman
187	320.2	New Milford Boro	New Milford
188	318.0	West Orange Town	West Orange
189	317.8	Highland Park Boro	Highland Park
190	317.1	Clark Twp	Clark
191	316.5	West Deptford Twp	West Deptford
192	315.4	Florence Twp	Florence
193	315.3	South River Boro	South River
194	314.5	Ridgefield Park Twp	Ridgefield Park
195	313.2	Teaneck Twp	Teaneck
196	312.2	Pompton Lakes Boro	Pompton Lakes
197	310.8	Monroe Twp	Monroe Township
197	310.8	Washington Twp	Sewell
199	307.9	Clearview Regional	Mullica Hill
200	305.7	North Plainfield Boro	N Plainfield
201	304.4	Long Branch City	Long Branch
202	304.2	Pemberton Twp	Pemberton
203	303.6	Millville City	Millville
204	302.2	Summit City	Summit
205	300.9	Freehold Regional	Englishtown
206	300.3	Bridgewater-Raritan Reg	Bridgewater
207	299.2	Ewing Twp	Ewing
208	296.7	Haddon Twp	Westmont
209	294.6	Bordentown Regional	Bordentown
210	291.7	Roselle Park Boro	Roselle Park
211	291.4	Collingswood Boro	Collingswood
212	290.9	Central Regional	Bayville
213	288.4	Princeton Regional	Princeton
214	287.1	Pittsgrove Twp	Pittsgrove
215	286.9	West New York Town	West New York
216	285.3	Leonia Boro	Leonia
217	284.6	Southern Regional	Manahawkin
218	282.6	Camden City	Camden
218	282.6	Trenton City	Trenton
220	280.0	Woodstown-Pilesgrove Reg	Woodstown
221	279.1	Hackettstown	Hackettstown
222	277.7	Delsea Regional H.S District	Franklinville
223	276.2	Phillipsburg Town	Phillipsburg
224	272.6	Maple Shade Twp	Maple Shade
225	268.5	Gloucester City	Gloucester City
226	267.0	High Point Regional	Sussex
227	266.6	Warren Hills Regional	Washington
228	264.3	Burlington City	Burlington
229	261.1	Spotswood Boro	Spotswood
230	260.7	Haddonfield Boro	Haddonfield
231	259.7	Manasquan Boro	Manasquan
232	259.4	Audubon Boro	Audubon
233	256.3	Woodbury City	Woodbury
234	255.5	Rancocas Valley Regional	Mount Holly
235	254.3	Middlesex County Vocational	E Brunswick
236	253.8	Hamilton Twp	Hamilton Square
237	250.9	Greater Egg Harbor Reg	Mays Landing
238	247.7	Hopewell Valley Regional	Pennington
239	246.0	Lower Cape May Regional	Cape May
240	244.0	Jersey City	Jersey City
241	243.3	Secaucus Town	Secaucus
242	241.7	Salem City	Salem
243	240.7	Ocean City	Ocean City
244	239.3	Parsippany-Troy Hills Twp	Parsippany
245	233.9	Keansburg Boro	Keansburg
246	225.3	Springfield Twp	Springfield
247	221.9	Vineland City	Vineland
248	218.9	Pinelands Regional	Tuckerton
249	217.0	Kingsway Regional	Woolwich Twp
250	214.7	Black Horse Pike Regional	Blackwood
251	213.9	Essex County Voc-Tech	West Orange
252	213.4	Watchung Hills Regional	Warren
253	212.8	Northern Burlington Reg	Columbus
254	200.5	Pascack Valley Regional	Montvale
255	200.3	Burlington County Vocational	Westampton Twp
256	200.2	Lenape Regional	Shamong
257	198.1	Eastern Camden County Reg	Voorhees
258	192.7	Northern Valley Regional	Demarest
259	187.1	Hunterdon Central Reg	Flemington
260	183.9	West Morris Regional	Chester
261	176.9	Ramapo-Indian Hill Reg	Franklin Lakes
262	167.8	Morris Hills Regional	Rockaway
263	156.4	N Hunt/Voorhees Regional	Annandale
264	155.6	Bergen County Vocational	Paramus
265	152.7	Camden County Vocational	Sicklerville
266	145.1	Passaic County Vocational	Wayne
267	89.2	Monmouth County Vocational	Colts Neck
268	n/a	Franklin Twp	Franklinville
268	n/a	Little Egg Harbor Twp	Little Egg Hbr

Current Spending per Student in FY2003

Rank	Dollars	District Name	City
1	39,428	Bergen County Special Service	Paramus
2	32,907	Mercer County Special Service	Trenton
3	31,812	Burlington County Spec Serv	Mount Holly
4	24,805	Bergen County Vocational	Paramus
5	22,784	Asbury Park City	Asbury Park
6	21,614	Monmouth County Vocational	Colts Neck
7	20,642	Hoboken City	Hoboken
8	20,350	Middlesex County Vocational	E Brunswick
9	19,113	Passaic County Vocational	Wayne
10	19,083	Pascack Valley Regional	Montvale
11	18,756	Northern Valley Regional	Demarest
12	18,517	Newark City	Newark
13	18,180	New Brunswick City	New Brunswick
14	17,805	Englewood City	Englewood
15	17,270	Trenton City	Trenton
16	17,024	Camden County Vocational	Sicklerville
17	16,491	Keansburg Boro	Keansburg
18	16,452	Pleasantville City	Pleasantville
19	16,275	Burlington County Vocational	Westampton Twp
20	16,213	Essex County Voc-Tech	West Orange
21	16,089	Morris SD	Morristown
22	16,074	Ramapo-Indian Hill Reg	Franklin Lakes
23	15,888	Jersey City	Jersey City
24	15,621	Morris Hills Regional	Rockaway
25	15,586	Long Branch City	Long Branch
26	15,564	Passaic City	Passaic
27	15,257	Irvington Township	Irvington
28	15,225	East Orange	East Orange
29	15,208	Mountain Lakes Boro	Mountain Lakes
29	15,208	Teaneck Twp	Teaneck
31	15,185	City of Orange Twp	Orange
32	15,137	High Point Regional	Sussex
33	15,122	Camden City	Camden
34	15,100	Lakewood Twp	Lakewood
35	14,966	Paterson City	Paterson
36	14,947	Ocean City	Ocean City
37	14,940	Vineland City	Vineland
38	14,863	Hunterdon Central Reg	Flemington
39	14,669	Pemberton Twp	Pemberton
40	14,582	Princeton Regional	Princeton
41	14,490	Phillipsburg Town	Phillipsburg
42	14,379	Atlantic City	Atlantic City
43	14,326	N Hunt/Voorhees Regional	Annandale
44	14,273	Gloucester City	Gloucester City
45	14,214	Plainfield City	Plainfield
46	14,156	Neptune Twp	Neptune
47	14,125	West Morris Regional	Chester
48	13,904	Union City	Union City
49	13,834	Bridgeton City	Bridgeton
50	13,657	Watchung Hills Regional	Warren
51	13,427	Westwood Regional	Westwood
52	13,407	Elizabeth City	Elizabeth
53	13,371	Livingston Twp	Livingston
54	13,367	Franklin Twp	Somerset
55	13,320	Burlington City	Burlington
56	13,266	Harrison Town	Harrison
57	13,263	Parsippany-Troy Hills Twp	Parsippany
58	13,170	Somerset Hills Regional	Bernardsville
59	13,101	Tenafly Boro	Tenafly

60	13,067	Highland Park Boro	Highland Park
61	13,020	Madison Boro	Madison
62	12,842	Paramus Boro	Paramus
63	12,772	W Windsor-Plainsboro Reg	Princeton Jct
64	12,717	Secaucus Town	Secaucus
65	12,708	West Orange Town	West Orange
66	12,701	Hopewell Valley Regional	Pennington
67	12,700	Fair Lawn Boro	Fair Lawn
68	12,634	Woodbury City	Woodbury
69	12,614	Rockaway Twp	Hibernia
70	12,611	West New York Town	West New York
71	12,599	Branchburg Twp	Branchburg
72	12,558	Ridgefield Park Twp	Ridgefield Park
73	12,539	Garfield City	Garfield
74	12,506	Hackensack City	Hackensack
75	12,493	Millburn Twp	Millburn
76	12,487	Perth Amboy City	Perth Amboy
76	12,487	Ridgefield Boro	Ridgefield
78	12,463	Metuchen Boro	Metuchen
79	12,446	Ramsey Boro	Ramsey
80	12,433	Montclair Town	Montclair
81	12,416	Cedar Grove Twp	Cedar Grove
82	12,393	Hanover Twp	Whippany
83	12,389	Ewing Twp	Ewing
84	12,353	Mahwah Twp	Mahwah
85	12,317	Pinelands Regional	Tuckerton
86	12,217	Glen Rock Boro	Glen Rock
87	12,211	Berkeley Heights Twp	Berkeley Hgts
88	12,204	Ridgewood Village	Ridgewood
89	12,183	Millville City	Millville
90	12,181	Summit City	Summit
91	12,140	Northern Burlington Reg	Columbus
92	12,139	Lindenwold Boro	Lindenwold
93	12,113	Saddle Brook Twp	Saddle Brook
94	12,112	Springfield Twp	Springfield
95	12,097	SD of the Chathams	Chatham
96	12,073	Somerville Boro	Somerville
97	12,065	Lawrence Twp	Lawrenceville
98	12,052	Oakland Boro	Oakland
99	12,044	Roselle Boro	Roselle
100	12,034	Rahway City	Rahway
101	11,978	Matawan-Aberdeen Regional	Aberdeen
102	11,924	Lenape Regional	Shamong
103	11,919	Franklin Lakes Boro	Franklin Lakes
104	11,895	East Windsor Regional	Hightstown
105	11,871	Cranford Twp	Cranford
106	11,859	Monroe Twp	Monroe Township
107	11,830	South Orange-Maplewood	Maplewood
108	11,820	Piscataway Twp	Piscataway
108	11,820	Warren Twp	Warren
110	11,817	Cresskill Boro	Cresskill
111	11,780	East Brunswick Twp	E Brunswick
112	11,767	Lower Cape May Regional	Cape May
113	11,760	Newton Town	Newton
114	11,704	Salem City	Salem
115	11,703	Willingboro Twp	Willingboro
116	11,668	Fort Lee Boro	Fort Lee
117	11,660	Caldwell-West Caldwell	West Caldwell
118	11,656	Pine Hill Boro	Pine Hill
119	11,653	Rutherford Boro	Rutherford
120	11,645	Hackettstown	Hackettstown
121	11,624	Black Horse Pike Regional	Blackwood
122	11,606	Hawthorne Boro	Hawthorne
123	11,593	Mount Olive Twp	Budd Lake
124	11,578	Collingswood Boro	Collingswood
125	11,573	Greater Egg Harbor Reg	Mays Landing
126	11,563	West Milford Twp	West Milford
127	11,555	Pennsville	Pennsville
128	11,548	Penns Grv-Carney's Pt Reg	Penns Grove
129	11,541	Edison Twp	Edison
130	11,529	Scotch Plains-Fanwood Reg	Scotch Plains
131	11,498	Westfield Town	Westfield
132	11,496	Roxbury Twp	Succasunna
133	11,480	South Brunswick Twp	Monmouth Jct
134	11,473	Lower Twp	Cape May
135	11,440	Montville Twp	Montville
136	11,432	Lyndhurst Twp	Lyndhurst
137	11,429	Pompton Lakes Boro	Pompton Lakes
138	11,423	Waldwick Boro	Waldwick
139	11,421	Warren Hills Regional	Washington
140	11,410	Bordentown Regional	Bordentown
141	11,364	Wayne Twp	Wayne
142	11,337	Winslow Twp	Atco
143	11,303	Cherry Hill Twp	Cherry Hill
144	11,297	Eastern Camden County Reg	Voorhees
145	11,277	Hillside Twp	Hillside
146	11,251	New Milford Boro	New Milford
147	11,241	Buena Regional	Buena
148	11,231	Pitman Boro	Pitman
149	11,226	Tinton Falls	Tinton Falls
150	11,222	Leonia Boro	Leonia
151	11,221	Florence Twp	Florence
152	11,216	Freehold Regional	Englishtown
153	11,214	Cinnaminson Twp	Cinnaminson
154	11,192	Bernards Twp	Basking Ridge
155	11,175	Bridgewater-Raritan Reg	Bridgewater
156	11,155	Kinnelon Boro	Kinnelon
157	11,142	North Plainfield Boro	N Plainfield
158	11,140	Glassboro	Glassboro
159	11,118	Mainland Regional	Linwood
160	11,112	New Providence Boro	New Providence
161	11,097	Bergenfield Boro	Bergenfield
162	11,069	Delsea Regional H.S District	Franklinville
163	11,059	Upper Freehold Regional	Allentown
164	11,048	Roselle Park Boro	Roselle Park
165	11,041	Middlesex Boro	Middlesex
166	11,028	Sussex-Wantage Regional	Wantage
167	10,990	Lodi Borough	Lodi
168	10,975	Kearny Town	Kearny
169	10,970	Ocean Twp	Oakhurst
170	10,959	Hopatcong	Hopatcong
171	10,951	Dumont Boro	Dumont
172	10,906	Palisades Park	Palisades Park
173	10,882	Hazlet Twp	Hazlet
174	10,878	Maple Shade Twp	Maple Shade
175	10,863	Middletown Twp	Middletown
176	10,861	Old Bridge Twp	Matawan
177	10,855	Jefferson Twp	Lake Hopatcong
178	10,854	Spotswood Boro	Spotswood
179	10,846	Elmwood Park	Elmwood Park
180	10,841	South Plainfield Boro	S Plainfield
181	10,814	Moorestown Twp	Moorestown
182	10,809	Washington Twp	Long Valley
183	10,805	Haddonfield Boro	Haddonfield
184	10,788	Kingsway Regional	Woolwich Twp
185	10,776	Bound Brook Boro	Bound Brook
186	10,733	Wall Twp	Wall
187	10,729	North Brunswick Twp	North Brunswick
188	10,725	Linden City	Linden
189	10,723	Voorhees Twp	Voorhees
190	10,707	Barnegat Twp	Barnegat
191	10,701	Holmdel Twp	Holmdel
192	10,695	Dover Town	Dover
193	10,688	Hasbrouck Heights Boro	Hasbrouck Hgts
194	10,686	Clark Twp	Clark
195	10,674	Readington Twp	Whitehouse Stn
196	10,638	Woodbridge Twp	Woodbridge
197	10,600	Colts Neck Twp	Colts Neck
198	10,586	Bayonne City	Bayonne
199	10,571	Randolph Twp	Randolph
200	10,553	Paulsboro Boro	Paulsboro
201	10,523	Pennsauken Twp	Pennsauken
202	10,489	Washington Twp	Sewell
203	10,481	Little Egg Harbor Twp	Little Egg Hbr
204	10,427	Vernon Twp	Vernon
205	10,417	Cliffside Park Boro	Cliffside Park
206	10,397	Pequannock Twp	Pompton Plains
207	10,378	Union Twp	Union
208	10,359	Manchester Twp	Whiting
209	10,345	Carteret Boro	Carteret
210	10,330	Howell Twp	Howell
211	10,326	Hillsborough Twp	Neshanic
212	10,325	Central Regional	Bayville
213	10,322	Washington Twp	Robbinsville
214	10,319	Verona Boro	Verona
215	10,305	Medford Twp	Medford
216	10,272	Belleville Town	Belleville
217	10,268	Sparta Twp	Sparta
218	10,264	Glen Ridge Boro	Glen Ridge
219	10,250	Nutley Town	Nutley
220	10,249	Middle Twp	Cape May Ct Hse
221	10,229	Clinton Twp	Annandale
222	10,222	Hamilton Twp	Mays Landing
223	10,200	Flemington-Raritan Reg	Flemington
224	10,175	Clearview Regional	Mullica Hill
225	10,157	North Arlington Boro	North Arlington
226	10,153	West Deptford Twp	West Deptford
227	10,143	Rancocas Valley Regional	Mount Holly
228	10,092	Stafford Twp	Manahawkin
229	10,074	Manasquan Boro	Manasquan
230	10,048	Clifton City	Clifton
231	10,020	Hamilton Twp	Hamilton Square
232	10,019	Galloway Twp	Galloway
233	9,978	Riverside Twp	Riverside
234	9,936	Audubon Boro	Audubon
235	9,930	Jackson Twp	Jackson
236	9,913	Haddon Twp	Westmont
237	9,910	Mount Laurel Twp	Mount Laurel
238	9,873	Sayreville Boro	Sayreville
239	9,847	North Bergen Twp	North Bergen
240	9,831	Monroe Twp	Williamstown
241	9,824	Delran Twp	Delran
242	9,768	Wyckoff Twp	Wyckoff
243	9,761	Bloomfield Twp	Bloomfield
244	9,732	Woodstown-Pilesgrove Reg	Woodstown
245	9,680	Montgomery Twp	Skillman
246	9,678	Upper Twp	Petersburg
247	9,640	Evesham Twp	Marlton
248	9,637	Pittsgrove Twp	Pittsgrove
249	9,623	Freehold Twp	Freehold
250	9,598	Hammonton Town	Hammonton
251	9,581	Manalapan-Englishtown Reg	Englishtown
252	9,580	Southern Regional	Manahawkin
253	9,559	Plumsted Twp	New Egypt
254	9,542	Egg Harbor Twp	W Atlantic City
255	9,491	Toms River Regional	Toms River
256	9,471	Denville Twp	Denville
257	9,424	Deptford Twp	Deptford
258	9,418	Berkeley Twp	Bayville
259	9,327	Millstone Twp	Clarksburg
260	9,249	Lacey Twp	Lanoka Harbor
261	9,247	Brick Twp	Brick
262	9,195	Lumberton Twp	Lumberton
263	9,182	Gloucester Twp	Blackwood
264	9,158	Marlboro Twp	Marlboro
265	9,127	Point Pleasant Boro	Pt Pleasant
266	9,099	Franklin Twp	Franklinville
267	8,921	Burlington Twp	Burlington
268	8,728	Mantua Twp	Sewell
269	8,546	South River Boro	South River

Number of Diploma Recipients

Rank	Number	District Name	City
1	2,214	Freehold Regional	Englishtown
2	1,699	Newark City	Newark
3	1,496	Lenape Regional	Shamong
4	1,293	Jersey City	Jersey City
5	1,188	Toms River Regional	Toms River
6	929	Burlington County Vocational	Westampton Twp
7	926	Edison Twp	Edison
8	901	Woodbridge Twp	Woodbridge
9	899	Hamilton Twp	Hamilton Square
10	877	Elizabeth City	Elizabeth
11	872	Trenton City	Trenton
12	846	Cherry Hill Twp	Cherry Hill
13	754	Paterson City	Paterson
14	730	Black Horse Pike Regional	Blackwood
15	703	Clifton City	Clifton
16	696	Middletown Twp	Middletown
17	675	Washington Twp	Sewell
18	668	Brick Twp	Brick
19	648	Greater Egg Harbor Reg	Mays Landing
20	646	East Brunswick Twp	E Brunswick
21	615	Southern Regional	Manahawkin
22	579	Old Bridge Twp	Matawan
23	578	Wayne Twp	Wayne
24	562	Vineland City	Vineland
25	560	Union City	Union City
26	554	W Windsor-Plainsboro Reg	Princeton Jct
27	526	Parsippany-Troy Hills Twp	Parsippany
28	523	Morris Hills Regional	Rockaway
29	521	N Hunt/Voorhees Regional	Annandale
30	512	West Morris Regional	Chester
31	505	Camden City	Camden
32	500	Hunterdon Central Reg	Flemington
33	486	Northern Valley Regional	Demarest
34	482	Union Twp	Union
35	476	Eastern Camden County Reg	Voorhees
36	462	East Orange	East Orange
37	455	Bridgewater-Raritan Reg	Bridgewater
38	451	Millville City	Millville
38	451	Passaic County Vocational	Wayne
40	440	Bayonne City	Bayonne
41	439	Ramapo-Indian Hill Reg	Franklin Lakes
42	435	Jackson Twp	Jackson
43	429	Hillsborough Twp	Neshanic
44	428	Piscataway Twp	Piscataway
45	427	South Brunswick Twp	Monmouth Jct
46	426	North Bergen Twp	North Bergen
47	417	South Orange-Maplewood	Maplewood
48	416	Atlantic City	Atlantic City
49	410	Rancocas Valley Regional	Mount Holly
50	395	Essex County Voc-Tech	West Orange
51	385	Pennsauken Twp	Pennsauken
52	375	Kearny Town	Kearny
53	373	Linden City	Linden
54	370	Pine Hill Boro	Pine Hill
55	367	Pascack Valley Regional	Montvale
56	358	Watchung Hills Regional	Warren
57	357	West New York Town	West New York
58	355	West Orange Town	West Orange
59	353	Livingston Twp	Livingston
60	348	Fair Lawn Boro	Fair Lawn
60	348	Montclair Town	Montclair
60	348	Sayreville Boro	Sayreville
63	347	Egg Harbor Twp	W Atlantic City
64	344	Bloomfield Twp	Bloomfield

65	343	Vernon Twp	Vernon
66	342	Hackensack City	Hackensack
67	333	Randolph Twp	Randolph
68	332	Ridgewood Village	Ridgewood
69	328	Winslow Twp	Atco
70	327	Westfield Town	Westfield
71	325	Belleville Town	Belleville
71	325	Lacey Twp	Lanoka Harbor
71	325	Roxbury Twp	Succasunna
74	322	Perth Amboy City	Perth Amboy
75	316	Morris SD	Morristown
76	314	Camden County Vocational	Sicklerville
76	314	Teaneck Twp	Teaneck
78	311	Lawrence Twp	Lawrenceville
79	310	Pemberton Twp	Pemberton
80	309	North Brunswick Twp	North Brunswick
81	307	Paramus Boro	Paramus
82	302	Irvington Township	Irvington
82	302	Mainland Regional	Linwood
84	299	Ocean City	Ocean City
85	295	Willingboro Twp	Willingboro
86	294	West Milford Twp	West Milford
87	288	Warren Hills Regional	Washington
88	287	Franklin Twp	Somerset
89	286	Ocean Twp	Oakhurst
90	285	Bergen County Vocational	Paramus
91	280	Phillipsburg Town	Phillipsburg
92	276	Plainfield City	Plainfield
93	271	Monmouth County Vocational	Colts Neck
94	268	Lakewood Twp	Lakewood
95	266	Nutley Town	Nutley
96	264	Monroe Twp	Williamstown
97	258	Middlesex County Vocational	E Brunswick
98	257	Clearview Regional	Mullica Hill
99	256	Lower Cape May Regional	Cape May
100	254	Scotch Plains-Fanwood Reg	Scotch Plains
101	253	Delsea Regional H.S District	Franklinville
102	251	Wall Twp	Wall
103	249	Central Regional	Bayville
104	247	High Point Regional	Sussex
105	240	Hopewell Valley Regional	Pennington
106	237	Princeton Regional	Princeton
107	236	South Plainfield Boro	S Plainfield
108	235	Upper Freehold Regional	Allentown
109	233	Neptune Twp	Neptune
110	232	Cranford Twp	Cranford
110	232	Hackettstown	Hackettstown
110	232	Middle Twp	Cape May Ct Hse
110	232	Tenafly Boro	Tenafly
114	231	Bernards Twp	Basking Ridge
114	231	Mount Olive Twp	Budd Lake
116	230	Ewing Twp	Ewing
116	230	Jefferson Twp	Lake Hopatcong
118	227	Cliffside Park Boro	Cliffside Park
118	227	Rahway City	Rahway
118	227	Sparta Twp	Sparta
118	227	West Deptford Twp	West Deptford
122	225	East Windsor Regional	Hightstown
123	224	Point Pleasant Boro	Pt Pleasant
124	223	Kingsway Regional	Woolwich Twp
124	223	Northern Burlington Reg	Columbus
126	222	Bergenfield Boro	Bergenfield
126	222	Moorestown Twp	Moorestown
128	218	Holmdel Twp	Holmdel
128	218	Millburn Twp	Millburn
130	213	Garfield City	Garfield
131	212	Fort Lee Boro	Fort Lee
132	209	City of Orange Twp	Orange
133	208	Montville Twp	Montville
134	207	Hazlet Twp	Hazlet
134	207	Long Branch City	Long Branch
136	204	Pleasantville City	Pleasantville
137	203	Montgomery Twp	Skillman
138	200	Carteret Boro	Carteret
138	200	Cinnaminson Twp	Cinnaminson
140	197	Deptford Twp	Deptford
140	197	Manasquan Boro	Manasquan
142	194	Pinelands Regional	Tuckerton
143	191	Lodi Borough	Lodi
143	191	Matawan-Aberdeen Regional	Aberdeen
145	190	Spotswood Boro	Spotswood
146	189	Clark Twp	Clark
147	188	Buena Regional	Buena
148	184	Ramsey Boro	Ramsey
149	182	Manchester Twp	Whiting
150	181	Delran Twp	Delran
151	180	Dumont Boro	Dumont
152	179	Monroe Twp	Monroe Township
153	175	Haddonfield Boro	Haddonfield
154	174	Mahwah Twp	Mahwah
154	174	Somerville Boro	Somerville
156	171	Berkeley Heights Twp	Berkeley Hgts
156	171	Dover Town	Dover
156	171	Summit City	Summit
159	169	Hillside Twp	Hillside
160	168	Bridgeton City	Bridgeton
161	166	SD of the Chathams	Chatham
161	166	Woodstown-Pilesgrove Reg	Woodstown
163	165	North Plainfield Boro	N Plainfield
164	163	Newton Town	Newton
165	162	Collingswood Boro	Collingswood
165	162	Penns Grv-Carney's Pt Reg	Penns Grove
165	162	Roselle Boro	Roselle
168	161	Caldwell-West Caldwell	West Caldwell
169	160	Haddon Twp	Westmont
169	160	Hopatcong	Hopatcong
171	158	New Brunswick City	New Brunswick
171	158	Ridgefield Park Twp	Ridgefield Park
173	157	Audubon Boro	Audubon
174	151	Pequannock Twp	Pompton Plains
175	150	Gloucester City	Gloucester City
176	149	Englewood City	Englewood
176	149	Rutherford Boro	Rutherford
178	148	Harrison Town	Harrison
178	148	South River Boro	South River
180	145	Burlington Twp	Burlington
181	140	Pompton Lakes Boro	Pompton Lakes
182	139	Glassboro	Glassboro
182	139	Madison Boro	Madison
184	137	Hammonton Town	Hammonton
184	137	Hoboken City	Hoboken
184	137	Westwood Regional	Westwood
187	136	Hawthorne Boro	Hawthorne
187	136	Metuchen Boro	Metuchen
189	134	Lyndhurst Twp	Lyndhurst
189	134	New Providence Boro	New Providence
191	130	Glen Rock Boro	Glen Rock
192	127	Ridgefield Boro	Ridgefield
193	126	Maple Shade Twp	Maple Shade
194	125	Elmwood Park	Elmwood Park
194	125	Pittsgrove Twp	Pittsgrove
196	124	Pennsville	Pennsville
197	123	Somerset Hills Regional	Bernardsville
198	121	Mountain Lakes Boro	Mountain Lakes
199	120	Leonia Boro	Leonia
199	120	Secaucus Town	Secaucus
201	119	Bordentown Regional	Bordentown
202	118	Asbury Park City	Asbury Park
203	114	Verona Boro	Verona
204	113	Kinnelon Boro	Kinnelon
204	113	New Milford Boro	New Milford
206	112	Burlington City	Burlington
206	112	Pitman Boro	Pitman
208	111	Palisades Park	Palisades Park
208	111	Paulsboro Boro	Paulsboro
208	111	Saddle Brook Twp	Saddle Brook
211	110	Springfield Twp	Springfield
212	108	Highland Park Boro	Highland Park
212	108	Middlesex Boro	Middlesex
214	106	North Arlington Boro	North Arlington
215	105	Florence Twp	Florence
216	104	Roselle Park Boro	Roselle Park
217	103	Woodbury City	Woodbury
218	100	Bound Brook Boro	Bound Brook
219	99	Hasbrouck Heights Boro	Hasbrouck Hgts
220	98	Salem City	Salem
221	96	Riverside Twp	Riverside
222	91	Cresskill Boro	Cresskill
223	87	Glen Ridge Boro	Glen Ridge
224	85	Keansburg Boro	Keansburg
225	84	Waldwick Boro	Waldwick
226	82	Cedar Grove Twp	Cedar Grove
227	0	Bergen County Special Service	Paramus
227	0	Burlington County Spec Serv	Mount Holly
227	0	Lindenwold Boro	Lindenwold
227	0	Mercer County Special Service	Trenton
227	0	Passaic City	Passaic
227	0	Plumsted Twp	New Egypt
233	n/a	Barnegat Twp	Barnegat
233	n/a	Berkeley Twp	Bayville
233	n/a	Branchburg Twp	Branchburg
233	n/a	Clinton Twp	Annandale
233	n/a	Colts Neck Twp	Colts Neck
233	n/a	Denville Twp	Denville
233	n/a	Evesham Twp	Marlton
233	n/a	Flemington-Raritan Reg	Flemington
233	n/a	Franklin Lakes Boro	Franklin Lakes
233	n/a	Franklin Twp	Franklinville
233	n/a	Freehold Twp	Freehold
233	n/a	Galloway Twp	Galloway
233	n/a	Gloucester Twp	Blackwood
233	n/a	Hamilton Twp	Mays Landing
233	n/a	Hanover Twp	Whippany
233	n/a	Howell Twp	Howell
233	n/a	Little Egg Harbor Twp	Little Egg Hbr
233	n/a	Lower Twp	Cape May
233	n/a	Lumberton Twp	Lumberton
233	n/a	Manalapan-Englishtown Reg	Englishtown
233	n/a	Mantua Twp	Sewell
233	n/a	Marlboro Twp	Marlboro
233	n/a	Medford Twp	Medford
233	n/a	Millstone Twp	Clarksburg
233	n/a	Mount Laurel Twp	Mount Laurel
233	n/a	Oakland Boro	Oakland
233	n/a	Readington Twp	Whitehouse Stn
233	n/a	Rockaway Twp	Hibernia
233	n/a	Stafford Twp	Manahawkin
233	n/a	Sussex-Wantage Regional	Wantage
233	n/a	Tinton Falls	Tinton Falls
233	n/a	Upper Twp	Petersburg
233	n/a	Voorhees Twp	Voorhees
233	n/a	Warren Twp	Warren
233	n/a	Washington Twp	Robbinsville
233	n/a	Washington Twp	Long Valley
233	n/a	Wyckoff Twp	Wyckoff

High School Drop-out Rate

Rank	Percent	District Name	City
1	14.1	Camden City	Camden
2	14.0	Trenton City	Trenton
3	11.5	Pleasantville City	Pleasantville
4	9.3	Paterson City	Paterson
5	9.0	Asbury Park City	Asbury Park
6	8.6	Jersey City	Jersey City
7	8.3	Passaic City	Passaic
8	8.0	New Brunswick City	New Brunswick
8	8.0	Pinelands Regional	Tuckerton
10	7.9	Millville City	Millville
11	7.8	Atlantic City	Atlantic City
12	7.3	Pine Hill Boro	Pine Hill
13	7.0	City of Orange Twp	Orange
14	6.4	Salem City	Salem
15	5.9	Elizabeth City	Elizabeth
15	5.9	Phillipsburg Town	Phillipsburg
17	5.8	Pennsauken Twp	Pennsauken
18	5.5	Englewood City	Englewood
18	5.5	Hillside Twp	Hillside
18	5.5	Lindenwold Boro	Lindenwold
21	5.4	Collingswood Boro	Collingswood
22	5.2	Plainfield City	Plainfield
23	4.9	East Orange	East Orange
24	4.6	Woodbury City	Woodbury
25	4.5	Bloomfield Twp	Bloomfield
25	4.5	Burlington City	Burlington
25	4.5	Greater Egg Harbor Reg	Mays Landing
28	4.4	Bergenfield Boro	Bergenfield
29	4.3	Central Regional	Bayville
29	4.3	Garfield City	Garfield
31	4.2	Lodi Borough	Lodi
31	4.2	Newark City	Newark
33	4.0	Clifton City	Clifton
33	4.0	South River Boro	South River
35	3.9	Lakewood Twp	Lakewood
35	3.9	Riverside Twp	Riverside
37	3.8	Hackensack City	Hackensack
37	3.8	Rahway City	Rahway
39	3.7	Long Branch City	Long Branch
39	3.7	Perth Amboy City	Perth Amboy
41	3.6	North Bergen Twp	North Bergen
42	3.5	East Windsor Regional	Hightstown
42	3.5	Glassboro	Glassboro
42	3.5	Penns Grv-Carney's Pt Reg	Penns Grove
45	3.4	Irvington Township	Irvington
45	3.4	Kearny Town	Kearny
45	3.4	Pemberton Twp	Pemberton
48	3.3	Bridgeton City	Bridgeton
48	3.3	Hoboken City	Hoboken
48	3.3	Old Bridge Twp	Matawan
51	3.2	Black Horse Pike Regional	Blackwood
51	3.2	Lawrence Twp	Lawrenceville
51	3.2	Vineland City	Vineland
54	3.1	Linden City	Linden
54	3.1	Pitman Boro	Pitman
56	2.8	Dover Town	Dover
56	2.8	Ewing Twp	Ewing
56	2.8	Middle Twp	Cape May Ct Hse
59	2.7	Elmwood Park	Elmwood Park
59	2.7	Newton Town	Newton
59	2.7	Warren Hills Regional	Washington
59	2.7	West Orange Town	West Orange
63	2.6	Winslow Twp	Atco
64	2.5	Egg Harbor Twp	W Atlantic City
64	2.5	Hamilton Twp	Hamilton Square
64	2.5	Mahwah Twp	Mahwah
67	2.4	Teaneck Twp	Teaneck
67	2.4	Toms River Regional	Toms River

Rank	Value	District	Town
69	2.2	Delsea Regional H.S District	Franklinville
69	2.2	Wall Twp	Wall
71	2.1	Clearview Regional	Mullica Hill
71	2.1	Monroe Twp	Williamstown
71	2.1	Plumsted Twp	New Egypt
71	2.1	Roselle Boro	Roselle
71	2.1	Union City	Union City
76	2.0	Audubon Boro	Audubon
76	2.0	Belleville Town	Belleville
76	2.0	Rancocas Valley Regional	Mount Holly
79	1.9	Brick Twp	Brick
79	1.9	Cliffside Park Boro	Cliffside Park
79	1.9	Franklin Twp	Somerset
79	1.9	Paulsboro Boro	Paulsboro
79	1.9	Pennsville	Pennsville
79	1.9	Southern Regional	Manahawkin
79	1.9	Washington Twp	Sewell
79	1.9	West Milford Twp	West Milford
87	1.8	Delran Twp	Delran
87	1.8	Eastern Camden County Reg	Voorhees
87	1.8	Jefferson Twp	Lake Hopatcong
87	1.8	Mainland Regional	Linwood
87	1.8	Moorestown Twp	Moorestown
87	1.8	Palisades Park	Palisades Park
87	1.8	South Orange-Maplewood	Maplewood
94	1.7	Bayonne City	Bayonne
94	1.7	Montclair Town	Montclair
94	1.7	Wayne Twp	Wayne
97	1.6	Buena Regional	Buena
97	1.6	Gloucester City	Gloucester City
97	1.6	Lower Cape May Regional	Cape May
97	1.6	Secaucus Town	Secaucus
97	1.6	Vernon Twp	Vernon
97	1.6	Woodstown-Pilesgrove Reg	Woodstown
103	1.5	Manasquan Boro	Manasquan
103	1.5	Manchester Twp	Whiting
103	1.5	Maple Shade Twp	Maple Shade
103	1.5	Northern Burlington Reg	Columbus
103	1.5	Willingboro Twp	Willingboro
108	1.4	Florence Twp	Florence
108	1.4	Keansburg Boro	Keansburg
108	1.4	Lyndhurst Twp	Lyndhurst
108	1.4	Monroe Twp	Monroe Township
112	1.3	Bordentown Regional	Bordentown
112	1.3	Carteret Boro	Carteret
112	1.3	Deptford Twp	Deptford
112	1.3	Matawan-Aberdeen Regional	Aberdeen
112	1.3	South Brunswick Twp	Monmouth Jct
112	1.3	Woodbridge Twp	Woodbridge
118	1.2	Hammonton Town	Hammonton
118	1.2	Morris Hills Regional	Rockaway
118	1.2	Roxbury Twp	Succasunna
118	1.2	Saddle Brook Twp	Saddle Brook
118	1.2	Union Twp	Union
123	1.1	Burlington County Vocational	Westampton Twp
123	1.1	Fort Lee Boro	Fort Lee
123	1.1	Freehold Regional	Englishtown
123	1.1	New Milford Boro	New Milford
123	1.1	West Deptford Twp	West Deptford
128	1.0	Cinnaminson Twp	Cinnaminson
128	1.0	Kingsway Regional	Woolwich Twp
128	1.0	Lacey Twp	Lanoka Harbor
128	1.0	N Hunt/Voorhees Regional	Annandale
128	1.0	Ridgefield Park Twp	Ridgefield Park
128	1.0	Somerset Hills Regional	Bernardsville
128	1.0	Westwood Regional	Westwood
135	0.9	Camden County Vocational	Sicklerville
135	0.9	Clark Twp	Clark
135	0.9	Middlesex Boro	Middlesex
135	0.9	Middlesex County Vocational	E Brunswick
135	0.9	Middletown Twp	Middletown
135	0.9	Princeton Regional	Princeton
135	0.9	Roselle Park Boro	Roselle Park
135	0.9	Somerville Boro	Somerville
143	0.8	Caldwell-West Caldwell	West Caldwell
143	0.8	Cranford Twp	Cranford
143	0.8	Dumont Boro	Dumont
143	0.8	Morris SD	Morristown
143	0.8	North Brunswick Twp	North Brunswick
143	0.8	Ocean City	Ocean City
143	0.8	Pompton Lakes Boro	Pompton Lakes
150	0.7	Burlington Twp	Burlington
150	0.7	Cherry Hill Twp	Cherry Hill
150	0.7	Fair Lawn Boro	Fair Lawn
150	0.7	Montgomery Twp	Skillman
150	0.7	Mount Olive Twp	Budd Lake
155	0.6	Bridgewater-Raritan Reg	Bridgewater
155	0.6	Hunterdon Central Reg	Flemington
155	0.6	Neptune Twp	Neptune
155	0.6	North Plainfield Boro	N Plainfield
155	0.6	Parsippany-Troy Hills Twp	Parsippany
155	0.6	Passaic County Vocational	Wayne
155	0.6	Sayreville Boro	Sayreville
155	0.6	Spotswood Boro	Spotswood
155	0.6	Summit City	Summit
155	0.6	West Morris Regional	Chester
165	0.5	Berkeley Heights Twp	Berkeley Hgts
165	0.5	Cresskill Boro	Cresskill
165	0.5	Hasbrouck Heights Boro	Hasbrouck Hgts
165	0.5	Jackson Twp	Jackson
165	0.5	Leonia Boro	Leonia
165	0.5	Montville Twp	Montville
165	0.5	Nutley Town	Nutley
165	0.5	Piscataway Twp	Piscataway
165	0.5	Pittsgrove Twp	Pittsgrove
165	0.5	Ridgewood Village	Ridgewood
165	0.5	SD of the Chathams	Chatham
176	0.4	East Brunswick Twp	E Brunswick
176	0.4	Edison Twp	Edison
176	0.4	Hazlet Twp	Hazlet
176	0.4	Hillsborough Twp	Neshanic
176	0.4	Hopatcong	Hopatcong
176	0.4	Lenape Regional	Shamong
176	0.4	Ocean Twp	Oakhurst
176	0.4	Point Pleasant Boro	Pt Pleasant
184	0.3	Cedar Grove Twp	Cedar Grove
184	0.3	Glen Ridge Boro	Glen Ridge
184	0.3	Haddon Twp	Westmont
184	0.3	Harrison Town	Harrison
184	0.3	Mountain Lakes Boro	Mountain Lakes
184	0.3	Ramapo-Indian Hill Reg	Franklin Lakes
184	0.3	Randolph Twp	Randolph
184	0.3	W Windsor-Plainsboro Reg	Princeton Jct
184	0.3	Waldwick Boro	Waldwick
184	0.3	Watchung Hills Regional	Warren
184	0.3	Westfield Town	Westfield
195	0.2	Hackettstown	Hackettstown
195	0.2	Metuchen Boro	Metuchen
195	0.2	Upper Freehold Regional	Allentown
195	0.2	Verona Boro	Verona
199	0.1	Bernards Twp	Basking Ridge
199	0.1	Essex County Voc-Tech	West Orange
199	0.1	Hawthorne Boro	Hawthorne
199	0.1	Holmdel Twp	Holmdel
199	0.1	Paramus Boro	Paramus
199	0.1	Pascack Valley Regional	Montvale
199	0.1	Rutherford Boro	Rutherford
199	0.1	Scotch Plains-Fanwood Reg	Scotch Plains
199	0.1	South Plainfield Boro	S Plainfield
199	0.1	Sparta Twp	Sparta
199	0.1	Tenafly Boro	Tenafly
199	0.1	West New York Town	West New York
211	0.0	Bergen County Vocational	Paramus
211	0.0	Bound Brook Boro	Bound Brook
211	0.0	Glen Rock Boro	Glen Rock
211	0.0	Haddonfield Boro	Haddonfield
211	0.0	High Point Regional	Sussex
211	0.0	Highland Park Boro	Highland Park
211	0.0	Hopewell Valley Regional	Pennington
211	0.0	Kinnelon Boro	Kinnelon
211	0.0	Livingston Twp	Livingston
211	0.0	Madison Boro	Madison
211	0.0	Millburn Twp	Millburn
211	0.0	Monmouth County Vocational	Colts Neck
211	0.0	New Providence Boro	New Providence
211	0.0	North Arlington Boro	North Arlington
211	0.0	Northern Valley Regional	Demarest
211	0.0	Pequannock Twp	Pompton Plains
211	0.0	Ramsey Boro	Ramsey
211	0.0	Ridgefield Boro	Ridgefield
211	0.0	Springfield Twp	Springfield
230	n/a	Barnegat Twp	Barnegat
230	n/a	Bergen County Special Service	Paramus
230	n/a	Berkeley Twp	Bayville
230	n/a	Branchburg Twp	Branchburg
230	n/a	Burlington County Spec Serv	Mount Holly
230	n/a	Clinton Twp	Annandale
230	n/a	Colts Neck Twp	Colts Neck
230	n/a	Denville Twp	Denville
230	n/a	Evesham Twp	Marlton
230	n/a	Flemington-Raritan Reg	Flemington
230	n/a	Franklin Lakes Boro	Franklin Lakes
230	n/a	Franklin Twp	Franklinville
230	n/a	Freehold Twp	Freehold
230	n/a	Galloway Twp	Galloway
230	n/a	Gloucester Twp	Blackwood
230	n/a	Hamilton Twp	Mays Landing
230	n/a	Hanover Twp	Whippany
230	n/a	Howell Twp	Howell
230	n/a	Little Egg Harbor Twp	Little Egg Hbr
230	n/a	Lower Twp	Cape May
230	n/a	Lumberton Twp	Lumberton
230	n/a	Manalapan-Englishtown Reg	Englishtown
230	n/a	Mantua Twp	Sewell
230	n/a	Marlboro Twp	Marlboro
230	n/a	Medford Twp	Medford
230	n/a	Mercer County Special Service	Trenton
230	n/a	Millstone Twp	Clarksburg
230	n/a	Mount Laurel Twp	Mount Laurel
230	n/a	Oakland Boro	Oakland
230	n/a	Readington Twp	Whitehouse Stn
230	n/a	Rockaway Twp	Hibernia
230	n/a	Stafford Twp	Manahawkin
230	n/a	Sussex-Wantage Regional	Wantage
230	n/a	Tinton Falls	Tinton Falls
230	n/a	Upper Twp	Petersburg
230	n/a	Voorhees Twp	Voorhees
230	n/a	Warren Twp	Warren
230	n/a	Washington Twp	Long Valley
230	n/a	Washington Twp	Robbinsville
230	n/a	Wyckoff Twp	Wyckoff

2005 New Jersey NAEP Public School Snapshot
Grade 4 Mathematics

The National Assessment of Educational Progress (NAEP) assesses mathematics in five content areas: number properties and operations; measurement; geometry; data analysis and probability; and algebra. The NAEP mathematics scale ranges from 0 to 500.

Overall Mathematics Results for New Jersey

- In 2005, the average scale score for fourth-grade students in New Jersey was 244. This was higher[1] than their average score in 2003 (239), and was higher than their average score in 1992 (227).

- New Jersey's average score (244) in 2005 was higher than that of the Nation's public schools (237).

- Of the 52 states and other jurisdictions[2] that participated in the 2005 fourth-grade assessment, students' average scale scores in New Jersey were higher than those in 36 jurisdictions, not significantly different from those in 14 jurisdictions, and lower than those in 1 jurisdiction.

- The percentage of students in New Jersey who performed at or above the NAEP Proficient level was 45 percent in 2005. This percentage was greater than that in 2003 (39 percent), and was greater than that in 1992 (25 percent).

- The percentage of students in New Jersey who performed at or above the NAEP Basic level was 86 percent in 2005. This percentage was greater than that in 2003 (80 percent), and was greater than that in 1992 (68 percent).

Student Percentage at NAEP Achievement Levels

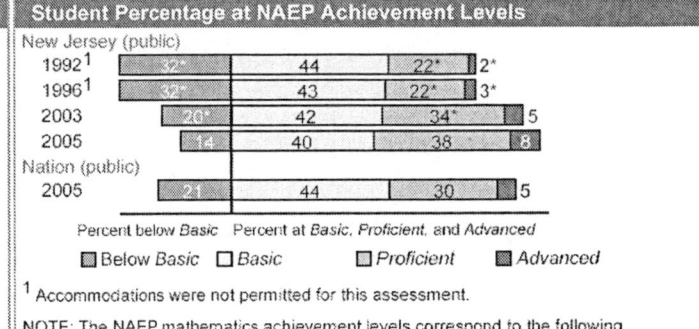

Percent below *Basic*   Percent at *Basic*, *Proficient*, and *Advanced*

■ Below *Basic*   □ *Basic*   ▨ *Proficient*   ▦ *Advanced*

[1] Accommodations were not permitted for this assessment.

NOTE: The NAEP mathematics achievement levels correspond to the following scale points: Below *Basic*, 213 or lower; *Basic*, 214–248; *Proficient*, 249–281; *Advanced*, 282 or above.

Performance of NAEP Reporting Groups in New Jersey

Reporting groups	Percent of students	Average score	Percent below *Basic*	Percent of students at or above *Basic*	Percent of students at or above *Proficient*	Percent *Advanced*
Male	52	246↑	13↓	87↑	47↑	9
Female	48	242↑	16↓	84↑	43↑	6
White	57	251↑	7	93	55	8
Black	18	224↑	33↓	67↑	17↑	1
Hispanic	15	230↑	26	74	25	1
Asian/Pacific Islander	9	264↑	3	97	74↑	26
American Indian/Alaska Native	#	‡	‡	‡	‡	‡
Eligible for free/reduced-price school lunch	29	227↑	31↓	69↑	23↑	2
Not eligible for free/reduced-price school lunch	65	252↑	7↓	93↑	56↑	11

Average Score Gaps Between Selected Groups

- In 2005, male students in New Jersey had an average score that was higher than that of female students by 4 points. In 1992, there was no significant difference between the average score of male and female students.

- In 2005, Black students had an average score that was lower than that of White students by 27 points. This performance gap was narrower than that of 1992 (38 points).

- In 2005, Hispanic students had an average score that was lower than that of White students by 21 points. This performance gap was narrower than that of 1992 (32 points).

- In 2005, students who were eligible for free/reduced-price school lunch, an indicator of poverty, had an average score that was lower than that of students who were not eligible for free/reduced-price school lunch by 24 points. This performance gap was narrower than that of 1996 (32 points).

- In 2005, the score gap between students at the 75th percentile and students at the 25th percentile was 36 points. This performance gap was narrower than that of 1992 (41 points).

Mathematics Scale Scores at Selected Percentiles

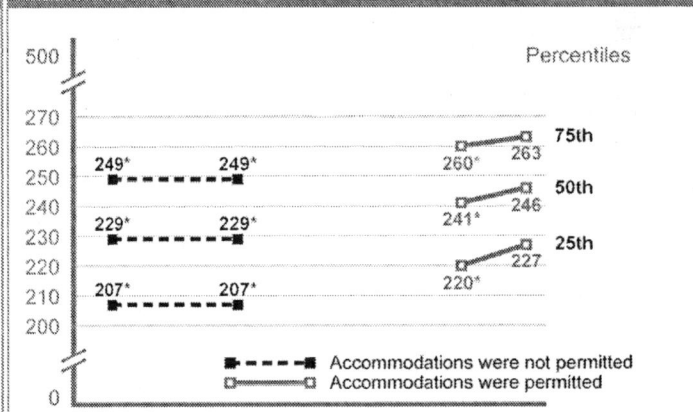

Scores at selected percentiles on the NAEP mathematics scale indicate how well students at lower, middle, and higher levels of the distribution performed.

The estimate rounds to zero.   ‡ Reporting standards not met.

* Significantly different from 2005.   ↑ Significantly higher than 2003. ↓ Significantly lower than 2003.

[1] Comparisons (higher/lower/not different) are based on statistical tests. The .05 level was used for testing statistical significance. Performance comparisons may be affected by differences in exclusion rates across years for students with disabilities (2% nationally in 2005) and English language learners (1% nationally in 2005) in the NAEP samples. Statistical comparisons are calculated on the basis of unrounded scale scores or percentages.
[2] "Other Jurisdictions" refers to the District of Columbia and the Department of Defense Education Activity schools.
NOTE: Detail may not sum to totals because of rounding and because the "Information not available" category for free/reduced-price lunch and the "Unclassifed" category for race/ethnicity are not displayed. Visit http://nces.ed.gov/nationsreportcard/states/ for additional results and detailed information.
SOURCE: U.S. Department of Education, Institute of Education Sciences, National Center for Education Statistics, National Assessment of Educational Progress (NAEP), selected years, 1992–2005 Mathematics Assessments.

2005 New Jersey NAEP Public School Snapshot
Grade 4 Reading

The National Assessment of Educational Progress (NAEP) assesses reading in two content areas: reading for literary experience and to gain information. The NAEP reading scale ranges from 0 to 500.

Overall Reading Results for New Jersey

- In 2005, the average scale score for fourth-grade students in New Jersey was 223. This was not significantly different from[1] their average score in 2003 (225), and was not significantly different from their average score in 1992 (223).
- New Jersey's average score (223) in 2005 was higher than that of the Nation's public schools (217).
- Of the 52 states and other jurisdictions[2] that participated in the 2005 fourth-grade assessment, students' average scale scores in New Jersey were higher than those in 24 jurisdictions, not significantly different from those in 24 jurisdictions, and lower than those in 3 jurisdictions.
- The percentage of students in New Jersey who performed at or above the NAEP *Proficient* level was 37 percent in 2005. This percentage was not significantly different from that in 2003 (39 percent), and was not significantly different from that in 1992 (35 percent).
- The percentage of students in New Jersey who performed at or above the NAEP *Basic* level was 68 percent in 2005. This percentage was not significantly different from that in 2003 (70 percent), and was not significantly different from that in 1992 (69 percent).

Student Percentage at NAEP Achievement Levels

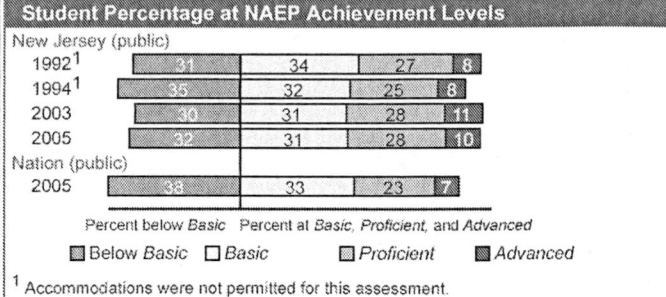

Percent below *Basic*   Percent at *Basic, Proficient,* and *Advanced*

☐ Below *Basic*   ☐ *Basic*   ☐ *Proficient*   ☐ *Advanced*

[1] Accommodations were not permitted for this assessment.

NOTE: The NAEP reading achievement levels correspond to the following scale points: Below *Basic,* 207 or lower; *Basic,* 208–237; *Proficient,* 238–267; *Advanced,* 268 or above.

Performance of NAEP Reporting Groups in New Jersey

Reporting groups	Percent of students	Average score	Percent below *Basic*	Percent of students at or above *Basic*	Percent of students at or above *Proficient*	Percent *Advanced*
Male	53	221	34	66	34	8
Female	47	226	29	71	40	11
White	58	232	21	79	46	12
Black	17	199	58	42	15	3
Hispanic	16	206	51	49	19	3
Asian/Pacific Islander	8	241	16	84	57	21
American Indian/Alaska Native	#	‡	‡	‡	‡	‡
Eligible for free/reduced-price school lunch	28	203	55	45	17	2
Not eligible for free/reduced-price school lunch	66	232	22	78	46	12

Average Score Gaps Between Selected Groups

- In 2005, male students in New Jersey had an average score that was lower than that of female students by 6 points. In 1992, the average score for male students was lower than that of female students by 5 points.
- In 2005, Black students had an average score that was lower than that of White students by 33 points. In 1992, the average score for Black students was lower than that of White students by 35 points.
- In 2005, Hispanic students had an average score that was lower than that of White students by 26 points. This performance gap was narrower than that of 1992 (38 points).
- In 2005, students who were eligible for free/reduced-price school lunch, an indicator of poverty, had an average score that was lower than that of students who were not eligible for free/reduced-price school lunch by 29 points. In 2003, the average score for students who were eligible for free/reduced-price school lunch was lower than the score of those not eligible by 30 points.
- In 2005, the score gap between students at the 75th percentile and students at the 25th percentile was 49 points. In 1992, the score gap between students at the 75th percentile and students at the 25th percentile was 45 points.

Reading Scale Scores at Selected Percentiles

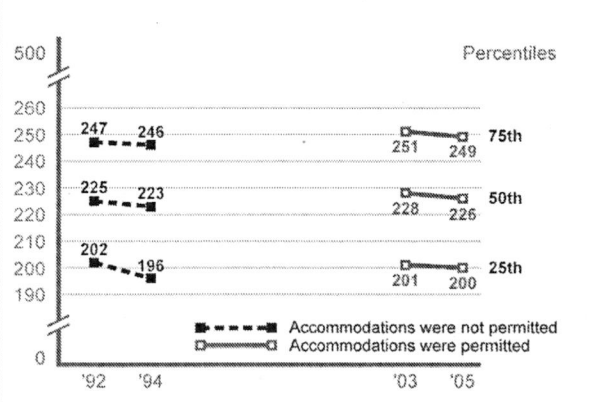

Scores at selected percentiles on the NAEP reading scale indicate how well students at lower, middle, and higher levels of the distribution performed.

\# The estimate rounds to zero.   ‡ Reporting standards not met.

* Significantly different from 2005.   † Significantly higher than 2003. ↓ Significantly lower than 2003.

[1] Comparisons (higher/lower/not different) are based on statistical tests. The .05 level was used for testing statistical significance. Performance comparisons may be affected by differences in exclusion rates across years for students with disabilities (5% nationally in 2005) and English language learners (2% nationally in 2005) in the NAEP samples. Statistical comparisons are calculated on the basis of unrounded scale scores or percentages.

[2] "Other Jurisdictions" refers to the District of Columbia and the Department of Defense Education Activity schools.

NOTE: Detail may not sum to totals because of rounding and because the "Information not available" category for free/reduced-price lunch and the "Unclassifed" category for race/ethnicity are not displayed. Visit http://nces.ed.gov/nationsreportcard/states/ for additional results and detailed information.

SOURCE: U.S. Department of Education, Institute of Education Sciences, National Center for Education Statistics, National Assessment of Educational Progress (NAEP), selected years, 1992–2005 Reading Assessments.

2005 New Jersey NAEP Public School Snapshot
Grade 4 Science

The National Assessment of Educational Progress (NAEP) assesses science in two major dimensions: Fields of Science (Earth, Physical, and Life) and Knowing and Doing Science (Conceptual Understanding, Scientific Investigation, and Practical Reasoning). The NAEP science scale ranges from 0 to 300. Scales are created separately for each grade.

Overall Science Results for New Jersey

- New Jersey's average score (154) in 2005 was higher than that of the nation's public schools (149).[1]
- Of the 44 states and one jurisdiction that participated in the 2005 fourth-grade assessment, students' average scale score in New Jersey was higher than those in 19 jurisdictions, not significantly different from those in 13 jurisdictions, and lower than those in 12 jurisdictions.[2]
- The percentage of students in New Jersey who performed at or above the NAEP *Proficient* level was 32 percent in 2005. This percentage was greater than that in the nation (27 percent).
- The percentage of students in New Jersey who performed at or above the NAEP *Basic* level was 72 percent in 2005. This percentage was greater than that in the nation (66 percent).

Student Percentages at NAEP Achievement Levels

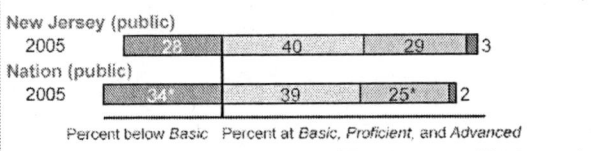

New Jersey (public)
2005: 28 | 40 | 29 | 3

Nation (public)
2005: 34* | 39 | 25* | 2

Percent below *Basic*   Percent at *Basic*, *Proficient*, and *Advanced*

■ Below *Basic*   □ *Basic*   ▪ *Proficient*   ■ *Advanced*

NOTE: The NAEP grade 4 science achievement levels correspond to the following scale points: Below *Basic*, 137 or lower; *Basic*, 138–169; *Proficient*, 170–204; *Advanced*, 205 or above.

Performance of NAEP Reporting Groups in New Jersey: 2005

Reporting groups	Percent of students	Average score	Percent below *Basic*	Percent of students at or above *Basic*	Percent of students at or above *Proficient*	Percent *Advanced*
Male	50	155↑	28↓	72↑	33	3
Female	50	153↑	29↓	71↑	30↑	2
White	58	164↑	15↓	85↑	42↑	4
Black	18	130	60	40	8	#
Hispanic	15↓	137	49	51	10	#
Asian/Pacific Islander	9↑	165↑	14↓	86↑	44↑	6
American Indian/Alaska Native	#	‡	‡	‡	‡	‡
Eligible for free/reduced-price school lunch	28↓	135	54	46	11	#
Not eligible for free/reduced-price school lunch	67↑	162	18	82	40	4

Average Score Gaps Between Selected Groups

- In 2005, male students in New Jersey had an average score that was not significantly different from that of female students. In the nation, the average score for male students was higher than that of female students by 4 points.
- In 2005, Black students had an average score that was lower than that of White students by 33 points. In the nation, the average score for Black students was lower than that of White students by 33 points.
- In 2005, Hispanic students had an average score that was lower than that of White students by 27 points. In the nation, the average score for Hispanic students was lower than that of White students by 29 points.
- In 2005, students who were eligible for free/reduced-price school lunch, an indicator of poverty, had an average score that was lower than that of students who were not eligible for free/reduced-price school lunch by 27 points. In the nation, the average score for students who were eligible for free/reduced-price school lunch was lower than the score of those not eligible by 27 points.
- In 2005, the score gap between students at the 75th percentile and students at the 25th percentile was 40 points. In the nation, the score gap between students at the 75th percentile and students at the 25th percentile was 43 points.

Science Scale Scores at Selected Percentiles

Scale Score Distribution

	25th Percentile	50th Percentile	75th Percentile
New Jersey	135	156	175
Nation (public)	129*	152*	172*

Scores at selected percentiles on the NAEP science scale indicate how well students at lower, middle, and higher levels performed. For example, the data above shows that 75 percent of students in public schools nationally scored below 172, while 75 percent of students in New Jersey scored below 175.

The estimate rounds to zero.   ‡ Reporting standards not met.

* Significantly different from New Jersey.   ↑ Significantly higher than nation (public). ↓ Significantly lower than nation (public).

[1] Comparisons (higher/lower/not different) are based on statistical tests. The .05 level was used for testing statistical significance. Comparisons across jurisdictions and comparisons with the nation or within a jurisdiction across years may be affected by differences in exclusion rates for students with disabilities (SD) and English language learners (ELL). The exclusion rates for SD and ELL in New Jersey were 3 percent and 1 percent in 2005, respectively. Statistical comparisons are calculated on the basis of unrounded scale scores or percentages.

[2] "Jurisdiction" refers to states and the Department of Defense Education Activity schools.

NOTE: Detail may not sum to totals because of rounding and because the "Information not available" category for free/reduced-price school lunch and the "Unclassifed" category for race/ethnicity are not displayed. Visit http://nces.ed.gov/nationsreportcard/states/ for additional results and detailed information.

SOURCE: U.S. Department of Education, Institute of Education Sciences, National Center for Education Statistics, National Assessment of Educational Progress (NAEP), 2005 Science Assessment.

2005 New Jersey NAEP Public School Snapshot
Grade 8 Mathematics

The National Assessment of Educational Progress (NAEP) assesses mathematics in five content areas: number properties and operations; measurement; geometry; data analysis and probability; and algebra. The NAEP mathematics scale ranges from 0 to 500.

Overall Mathematics Results for New Jersey

- In 2005, the average scale score for eighth-grade students in New Jersey was 284. This was not significantly different from[1] their average score in 2003 (281), and was higher than their average score in 1990 (270).

- New Jersey's average score (284) in 2005 was higher than that of the Nation's public schools (278).

- Of the 52 states and other jurisdictions[2] that participated in the 2005 eighth-grade assessment, students' average scale scores in New Jersey were higher than those in 24 jurisdictions, not significantly different from those in 23 jurisdictions, and lower than those in 4 jurisdictions.

- The percentage of students in New Jersey who performed at or above the NAEP *Proficient* level was 36 percent in 2005. This percentage was not significantly different from that in 2003 (33 percent), and was greater than that in 1990 (21 percent).

- The percentage of students in New Jersey who performed at or above the NAEP *Basic* level was 74 percent in 2005. This percentage was not significantly different from that in 2003 (72 percent), and was greater than that in 1990 (58 percent).

Student Percentage at NAEP Achievement Levels

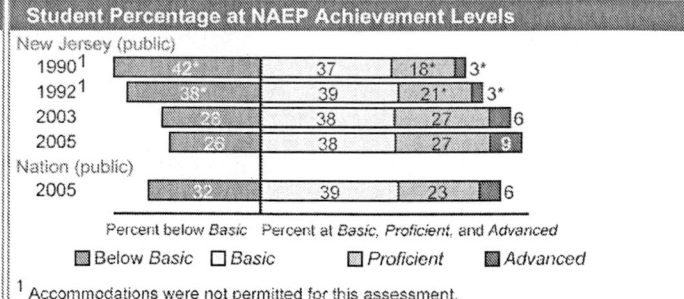

Percent below *Basic*   Percent at *Basic, Proficient,* and *Advanced*

■ Below *Basic*   □ *Basic*   ▨ *Proficient*   ▨ *Advanced*

[1] Accommodations were not permitted for this assessment.

NOTE: The NAEP mathematics achievement levels correspond to the following scale points: Below *Basic*, 261 or lower; *Basic*, 262–298; *Proficient*, 299–332; *Advanced*, 333 or above.

Performance of NAEP Reporting Groups in New Jersey

Reporting groups	Percent of students	Average score	Percent below *Basic*	Percent of students at or above *Basic*	Percent of students at or above *Proficient*	Percent *Advanced*
Male	51	286	25	75	39	10
Female	49	282	27	73	33	7
White	57	295	15	85	47	12
Black	20	260	50	50	11	1
Hispanic	15	264	42	58	15	1
Asian/Pacific Islander	7	309	8	92	63	24
American Indian/Alaska Native	#	‡	‡	‡	‡	‡
Eligible for free/reduced-price school lunch	27	262	46	54	14	1
Not eligible for free/reduced-price school lunch	68	292	19	81	44	11

Average Score Gaps Between Selected Groups

- In 2005, male students in New Jersey had an average score that was not found to be significantly different from that of female students. In 1990, there was no significant difference between the average score of male and female students.

- In 2005, Black students had an average score that was lower than that of White students by 35 points. In 1990, the average score for Black students was lower than that of White students by 38 points.

- In 2005, Hispanic students had an average score that was lower than that of White students by 30 points. In 1990, the average score for Hispanic students was lower than that of White students by 37 points.

- In 2005, students who were eligible for free/reduced-price school lunch, an indicator of poverty, had an average score that was lower than that of students who were not eligible for free/reduced-price school lunch by 30 points. In 2003, the average score for students who were eligible for free/reduced-price school lunch was lower than the score of those not eligible by 34 points.

- In 2005, the score gap between students at the 75th percentile and students at the 25th percentile was 49 points. In 1990, the score gap between students at the 75th percentile and students at the 25th percentile was 49 points.

Mathematics Scale Scores at Selected Percentiles

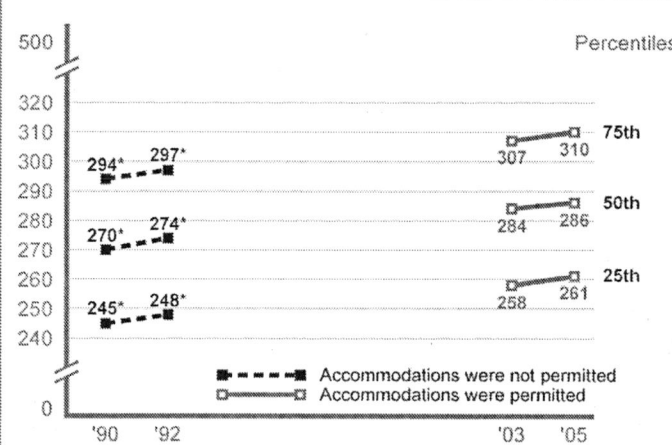

Scores at selected percentiles on the NAEP mathematics scale indicate how well students at lower, middle, and higher levels of the distribution performed.

\# The estimate rounds to zero.

* Significantly different from 2005.

‡ Reporting standards not met.

↑ Significantly higher than 2003. ↓ Significantly lower than 2003.

[1] Comparisons (higher/lower/not different) are based on statistical tests. The .05 level was used for testing statistical significance. Performance comparisons may be affected by differences in exclusion rates across years for students with disabilities (3% nationally in 2005) and English language learners (1% nationally in 2005) in the NAEP samples. Statistical comparisons are calculated on the basis of unrounded scale scores or percentages.

[2] "Other Jurisdictions" refers to the District of Columbia and the Department of Defense Education Activity schools.

NOTE: Detail may not sum to totals because of rounding and because the "Information not available" category for free/reduced-price lunch and the "Unclassifed" category for race/ethnicity are not displayed. Visit http://nces.ed.gov/nationsreportcard/states/ for additional results and detailed information.

SOURCE: U.S. Department of Education, Institute of Education Sciences, National Center for Education Statistics, National Assessment of Educational Progress (NAEP), selected years, 1990–2005 Mathematics Assessments.

2005 New Jersey NAEP Public School Snapshot
Grade 8 Reading

The National Assessment of Educational Progress (NAEP) assesses reading in three content areas: reading for literary experience, to gain information, and to perform a task. The NAEP reading scale ranges from 0 to 500.

Overall Reading Results for New Jersey

- In 2005, the average scale score for eighth-grade students in New Jersey was 269. This was not significantly different from[1] their average score in 2003 (268).
- New Jersey's average score (269) in 2005 was higher than that of the Nation's public schools (260).
- Of the 52 states and other jurisdictions[2] that participated in the 2005 eighth-grade assessment, students' average scale scores in New Jersey were higher than those in 34 jurisdictions, not significantly different from those in 16 jurisdictions, and lower than those in 1 jurisdiction.
- The percentage of students in New Jersey who performed at or above the NAEP *Proficient* level was 38 percent in 2005. This percentage was not significantly different from that in 2003 (37 percent)
- The percentage of students in New Jersey who performed at or above the NAEP *Basic* level was 80 percent in 2005. This percentage was not significantly different from that in 2003 (79 percent).

Student Percentage at NAEP Achievement Levels

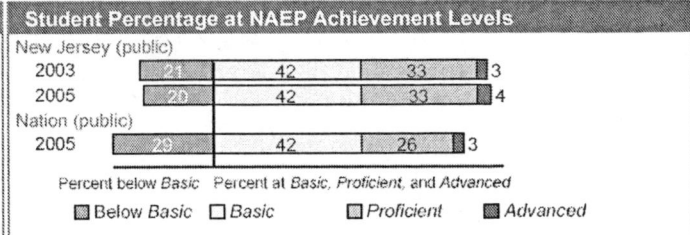

New Jersey (public)
2003: 21 | 42 | 33 | 3
2005: 20 | 42 | 33 | 4
Nation (public)
2005: 29 | 42 | 26 | 3

Percent below *Basic* Percent at *Basic, Proficient,* and *Advanced*

☐ Below *Basic*   ☐ *Basic*   ☐ *Proficient*   ☐ *Advanced*

NOTE: The NAEP reading achievement levels correspond to the following scale points: Below *Basic*, 242 or lower; *Basic*, 243–280; *Proficient*, 281–322; *Advanced*, 323 or above.

Performance of NAEP Reporting Groups in New Jersey

Reporting groups	Percent of students	Average score	Percent below *Basic*	Percent of students at or above *Basic*	*Proficient*	Percent *Advanced*
Male	50	266	23	77	33	3
Female	50	273	17	83	42	6
White	59	278	12	88	48	5
Black	20	251	38	62	14	1
Hispanic	14	251	35	65	14	1
Asian/Pacific Islander	6	291	5	95	66	12
American Indian/Alaska Native	#	‡	‡	‡	‡	‡
Eligible for free/reduced-price school lunch	25	252	37	63	17	1
Not eligible for free/reduced-price school lunch	69	276	14	86	45	5

Average Score Gaps Between Selected Groups

- In 2005, male students in New Jersey had an average score that was lower than that of female students by 8 points. In 2003, the average score for male students was lower than that of female students by 9 points.
- In 2005, Black students had an average score that was lower than that of White students by 27 points. In 2003, the average score for Black students was lower than that of White students by 29 points.
- In 2005, Hispanic students had an average score that was lower than that of White students by 26 points. In 2003, the average score for Hispanic students was lower than that of White students by 28 points.
- In 2005, students who were eligible for free/reduced-price school lunch, an indicator of poverty, had an average score that was lower than that of students who were not eligible for free/reduced-price school lunch by 24 points. In 2003, the average score for students who were eligible for free/reduced-price school lunch was lower than the score of those not eligible by 30 points.
- In 2005, the score gap between students at the 75th percentile and students at the 25th percentile was 43 points. In 2003, the score gap between students at the 75th percentile and students at the 25th percentile was 43 points.

Reading Scale Scores at Selected Percentiles

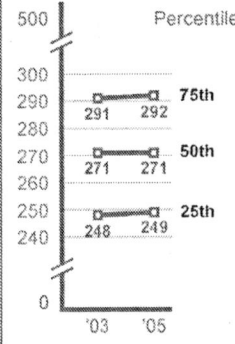

Percentiles

75th: 291 → 292
50th: 271 → 271
25th: 248 → 249

'03 '05

Scores at selected percentiles on the NAEP reading scale indicate how well students at lower, middle, and higher levels of the distribution performed.

The estimate rounds to zero.   ‡ Reporting standards not met.

* Significantly different from 2005.   † Significantly higher than 2003. ↓ Significantly lower than 2003.

[1] Comparisons (higher/lower/not different) are based on statistical tests. The .05 level was used for testing statistical significance. Performance comparisons may be affected by differences in exclusion rates across years for students with disabilities (4% nationally in 2005) and English language learners (1% nationally in 2005) in the NAEP samples. Statistical comparisons are calculated on the basis of unrounded scale scores or percentages.

[2] "Other Jurisdictions" refers to the District of Columbia and the Department of Defense Education Activity schools.

NOTE: Detail may not sum to totals because of rounding and because the "Information not available" category for free/reduced-price lunch and the "Unclassifed" category for race/ethnicity are not displayed. Visit http://nces.ed.gov/nationsreportcard/states/ for additional results and detailed information.

SOURCE: U.S. Department of Education, Institute of Education Sciences, National Center for Education Statistics, National Assessment of Educational Progress (NAEP), selected years, 2003–2005 Reading Assessments.

2005 New Jersey NAEP Public School Snapshot
Grade 8 Science

The National Assessment of Educational Progress (NAEP) assesses science in two major dimensions: Fields of Science (Earth, Physical, and Life) and Knowing and Doing Science (Conceptual Understanding, Scientific Investigation, and Practical Reasoning). The NAEP science scale ranges from 0 to 300. Scales are created separately for each grade.

Overall Science Results for New Jersey

- New Jersey's average score (153) in 2005 was higher than that of the nation's public schools (147).[1]
- Of the 44 states and one jurisdiction that participated in the 2005 eighth-grade assessment, students' average scale score in New Jersey was higher than those in 20 jurisdictions, not significantly different from those in 12 jurisdictions, and lower than those in 12 jurisdictions.[2]
- The percentage of students in New Jersey who performed at or above the NAEP *Proficient* level was 33 percent in 2005. This percentage was greater than that in the nation (27 percent).
- The percentage of students in New Jersey who performed at or above the NAEP *Basic* level was 65 percent in 2005. This percentage was greater than that in the nation (57 percent).

Student Percentages at NAEP Achievement Levels

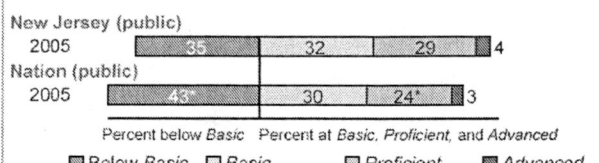

Percent below *Basic*   Percent at *Basic, Proficient,* and *Advanced*

■ Below *Basic*   □ *Basic*   □ *Proficient*   ▨ *Advanced*

NOTE: The NAEP grade 8 science achievement levels correspond to the following scale points: Below *Basic*, 142 or lower; *Basic*, 143–169; *Proficient*, 170–207; *Advanced*, 208 or above.

Performance of NAEP Reporting Groups in New Jersey: 2005

Reporting groups	Percent of students	Average score	Percent below *Basic*	Percent of students at or above *Basic*	*Proficient*	Percent *Advanced*
Male	51	157↑	32↓	68↑	38↑	5↑
Female	49	150↑	38↓	62↑	28	2
White	57	165↑	20↓	80↑	45↑	5
Black	21	131↑	63↓	37↑	11↑	#
Hispanic	15	133↑	61	39	12	1
Asian/Pacific Islander	7	172↑	17↓	83↑	53↑	12↑
American Indian/Alaska Native	#↓	‡	‡	‡	‡	‡
Eligible for free/reduced-price school lunch	27↓	131	62	38	11	#
Not eligible for free/reduced-price school lunch	67↑	162↑	25↓	75↑	42↑	5

Average Score Gaps Between Selected Groups

- In 2005, male students in New Jersey had an average score that was higher than that of female students by 7 points. In the nation, the average score for male students was higher than that of female students by 4 points.
- In 2005, Black students had an average score that was lower than that of White students by 33 points. In the nation, the average score for Black students was lower than that of White students by 37 points.
- In 2005, Hispanic students had an average score that was lower than that of White students by 32 points. In the nation, the average score for Hispanic students was lower than that of White students by 32 points.
- In 2005, students who were eligible for free/reduced-price school lunch, an indicator of poverty, had an average score that was lower than that of students who were not eligible for free/reduced-price school lunch by 31 points. In the nation, the average score for students who were eligible for free/reduced-price school lunch was lower than that of those not eligible by 28 points.
- In 2005, the score gap between students at the 75th percentile and students at the 25th percentile was 46 points. In the nation, the score gap between students at the 75th percentile and students at the 25th percentile was 48 points.

Science Scale Scores at Selected Percentiles

Scale Score Distribution

	25th Percentile	50th Percentile	75th Percentile
New Jersey	131	156	177
Nation (public)	124*	150*	172*

Scores at selected percentiles on the NAEP science scale indicate how well students at lower, middle, and higher levels performed. For example, the data above shows that 75 percent of students in public schools nationally scored below 172, while 75 percent of students in New Jersey scored below 177.

The estimate rounds to zero.   ‡ Reporting standards not met.

* Significantly different from New Jersey.   ↑ Significantly higher than nation (public).   ↓ Significantly lower than nation (public).

[1] Comparisons (higher/lower/not different) are based on statistical tests. The .05 level was used for testing statistical significance. Comparisons across jurisdictions and comparisons with the nation or within a jurisdiction across years may be affected by differences in exclusion rates for students with disabilities (SD) and English language learners (ELL). The exclusion rates for SD and ELL in New Jersey were 3 percent and 1 percent in 2005, respectively. Statistical comparisons are calculated on the basis of unrounded scale scores or percentages.
[2] "Jurisdiction" refers to states and the Department of Defense Education Activity schools.
NOTE: Detail may not sum to totals because of rounding and because the "Information not available" category for free/reduced-price school lunch and the "Unclassifed" category for race/ethnicity are not displayed. Visit http://nces.ed.gov/nationsreportcard/states/ for additional results and detailed information.
SOURCE: U.S. Department of Education, Institute of Education Sciences, National Center for Education Statistics, National Assessment of Educational Progress (NAEP), 2005 Science Assessment.

New Jersey Assessment of Skills and Knowledge (NJASK)
Language Arts Literacy

Language Arts Literacy	Year	Total Enrollment	Number Tested	Percent Not Tested	Proficiency Percentages		
					Partial	Proficient	Advanced
All Students	2004-05	178,878	177,504	0.2	9.5	90.5	0.0
	2003-04	86,113	85,859	0.3	16.4	78.7	5.0

Language Arts Literacy 2004–2005	Total Enrollment	Number Tested	Percent Not Tested	Proficiency Percentages		
				Partial	Proficient	Advanced
Students with Disabilities	27,419	27,319	0.4	43.7	53.7	2.6
Limited English Proficient Students	5,997	5,908	1.5	49.0	50.6	0.4
Male	91,814	91,593	0.2	19.9	77.2	2.9
Female	86,804	86,633	0.2	12.1	80.8	7.1
White	105,605	105,480	0.1	9.8	84.2	6.0
African-American	28,285	28,198	0.3	31.7	66.6	1.7
Asian & Pacific Islander	13,320	13,285	0.3	7.2	82.7	10.7
American Indian/Native American	175	175	0.0	16.8	80.9	2.3
Hispanic	29,956	29,835	0.4	27.7	70.5	1.8
Other Race	1,537	1,485	3.4	17.9	76.0	6.1
Migrant Students	89	89	0.0	46.1	51.7	2.2
Economically Disadvantaged	49,871	49,691	0.4	31.4	67.2	1.4

The state standard for Adequate Yearly Progress (AYP) for language arts literacy is 75% proficient for the school and each subgroup.

New Jersey Assessment of Skills and Knowledge (NJASK)
Mathematics

Mathematics	Year	Total Enrollment	Number Tested	Percent Not Tested	Proficiency Percentages		
					Partial	Proficient	Advanced
All Students	2004-05	178,878	177,704	0.3	16.8	51.3	31.8
	2003-04	86,113	85,831	0.3	26.1	47.1	26.9

Mathematics 2004–2005	Total Enrollment	Number Tested	Percent Not Tested	Proficiency Percentages		
				Partial	Proficient	Advanced
Students with Disabilities	27,419	27,276	0.5	37.3	47.3	15.3
Limited English Proficient Students	178,878	178,849	0.0	39.0	46.9	14.0
Male	91,814	91,538	0.3	17.0	50.6	32.4
Female	86,804	86,637	0.2	16.7	52.1	31.2
White	105,605	105,434	0.2	10.6	52.7	36.7
African-American	28,285	28,165	0.4	35.1	49.7	15.2
Asian & Pacific Islander	13,320	13,294	0.2	6.7	39.6	53.7
American Indian/Native American	175	175	0.0	19.5	44.8	35.6
Hispanic	29,956	29,849	0.4	26.2	53.7	20.2
Other Race	1,537	1,500	2.4	17.6	44.9	37.5
Migrant Students	89	89	0.0	30.3	43.8	25.8
Economically Disadvantaged	49,871	49,681	0.4	31.1	51.2	17.7

The state standard for Adequate Yearly Progress (AYP) for mathematics is 62% proficient for the school and each subgroup.

Grade Eight Proficiency Assessment (GEPA)
Language Arts Literacy

Language Arts Literacy	Year	Total Enrollment	Number Tested	Percent Not Tested	Proficiency Percentages		
					Partial	Proficient	Advanced
All Students	2004-05	100,609	100,208	0.4	25.9	65.5	8.6
	2003-04	101,610	101,218	0.4	26.4	67.6	5.9

Language Arts Literacy 2004–2005	Total Enrollment	Number Tested	Percent Not Tested	Proficiency Percentages		
				Partial	Proficient	Advanced
Students with Disabilities	16,541	16,378	1.0	67.9	30.3	1.7
Limited English Proficient Students	2,363	2,322	1.7	79.2	19.6	1.3
Male	51,587	51,355	0.4	31.8	63.2	4.9
Female	48,965	48,805	0.3	19.6	67.9	12.5
White	60,718	60,569	0.2	16.0	73.3	10.7
African-American	16,554	16,435	0.7	50.0	47.8	2.2
Asian & Pacific Islander	6,533	6,515	0.3	13.8	68.1	18.1
American Indian/Native American	136	136	0.0	35.6	60.0	4.4
Hispanic	15,842	15,746	0.6	43.7	53.3	3.0
Other Race	826	807	2.3	29.1	57.7	13.2
Migrant Students	39	39	*	71.8	25.6	2.6
Economically Disadvantaged	25,639	25,452	0.7	49.3	48.6	2.1

The state standard for Adequate Yearly Progress (AYP) for language arts literacy is 66% proficient for the school and each subgroup.

Grade Eight Proficiency Assessment (GEPA)
Mathematics

Mathematics	Year	Total Enrollment	Number Tested	Percent Not Tested	Proficiency Percentages		
					Partial	Proficient	Advanced
All Students	2004-05	100,609	100,131	0.5	35.4	44.8	19.9
	2003-04	101,610	101,110	0.5	36.0	42.8	21.3

Mathematics 2004-2005	Total Enrollment	Number Tested	Percent Not Tested	Proficiency Percentages		
				Partial	Proficient	Advanced
Students with Disabilities	16,541	16,347	1.2	74.1	22.2	3.7
Limited English Proficient Students	2,363	2,346	0.7	73.0	20.8	6.1
Male	51,587	51,320	0.5	34.6	43.6	21.8
Female	48,965	48,763	0.4	36.2	46.0	17.8
White	60,718	60,532	0.3	23.7	51.3	25.1
African-American	16,554	16,391	1.0	67.6	28.6	3.9
Asian & Pacific Islander	6,533	6,521	0.2	15.3	43.1	41.6
American Indian/Native American	136	134	1.5	45.5	41.8	12.7
Hispanic	15,842	15,743	0.6	55.0	38.0	7.0
Other Race	826	810	1.9	35.7	36.2	28.1
Migrant Students	39	39	*	76.9	23.1	0.0
Economically Disadvantaged	25,639	25,418	0.9	61.0	33.0	6.0

The state standard for Adequate Yearly Progress (AYP) for mathematics is 49% proficient for the school and each subgroup.

High School Proficiency Assessment (HSPA)
Language Arts Literacy

Language Arts Literacy	Year	Total Enrollment	Number Tested	Percent Not Tested	Proficiency Percentages		
					Partial	Proficient	Advanced
All Students	2004-05	91,958	91,152	0.9	15.6	64.1	20.3
	2003-04	86,989	86,138	1.0	16.3	65.7	18.0

Language Arts Literacy 2004–2005	Total Enrollment	Number Tested	Percent Not Tested	Proficiency Percentages		
				Partial	Proficient	Advanced
Students with Disabilities	13,841	13,490	2.5	53.6	43.0	3.5
Limited English Proficient Students	2,387	2,362	1.0	75.8	22.6	1.6
Male	46,276	45,814	1.0	18.6	66.2	15.1
Female	45,419	45,105	0.7	12.5	61.9	25.6
White	57,410	57,090	0.6	8.6	66.1	25.3
African-American	13,578	13,297	2.1	32.9	61.4	5.7
Asian & Pacific Islander	6,647	6,635	0.2	10.7	57.4	31.8
American Indian/Native American	121	119	1.7	19.3	68.9	11.8
Hispanic	12,738	12,581	1.2	31.8	61.5	6.7
Other Race	1,464	1,430	2.3	18.3	59.1	22.6
Migrant Students	14	14	*	*	*	*
Economically Disadvantaged	14,091	13,890	1.4	34.8	60.0	5.2

The state standard for Adequate Yearly Progress (AYP) for language arts literacy is 79% proficient for the school and each subgroup.

High School Proficiency Assessment (HSPA)
Mathematics

Mathematics	Year	Total Enrollment	Number Tested	Percent Not Tested	Proficiency Percentages		
					Partial	Proficient	Advanced
All Students	2004-05	91,958	90,303	1.8	23.2	47.5	29.2
	2003-04	86,989	85,951	1.2	28.3	46.2	25.5

Mathematics 2004–2005	Total Enrollment	Number Tested	Percent Not Tested	Proficiency Percentages		
				Partial	Proficient	Advanced
Students with Disabilities	13,841	13,239	4.3	66.6	27.9	5.5
Limited English Proficient Students	2,387	2,347	1.7	65.4	28.3	6.4
Male	46,276	45,387	1.9	22.5	44.8	32.7
Female	45,419	44,689	1.6	23.8	50.4	25.8
White	57,410	56,710	1.2	14.2	50.1	35.7
African-American	13,578	13,027	4.1	51.3	41.9	6.8
Asian & Pacific Islander	6,647	6,618	0.4	10.1	36.0	53.9
American Indian/Native American	121	118	2.5	34.7	47.5	17.8
Hispanic	12,738	12,425	2.5	41.5	48.5	10.0
Other Race	1,464	1,405	4.0	26.2	43.3	30.5
Migrant Students	14	13	*	*	*	*
Economically Disadvantaged	14,091	13,679	2.9	45.9	45.2	8.9

The state standard for Adequate Yearly Progress (AYP) for mathematics is 64% proficient for the school and each subgroup.

Acadian/Cajun

Top 10 Places Sorted by Number
Based on all places, regardless of population

Place	Number	%
Howell (township) Monmouth County	23	0.05
Burlington (township) Burlington County	18	0.09
Chatham (township) Morris County	17	0.17
Mahwah (township) Bergen County	14	0.06
Carneys Point (township) Salem County	13	0.17
Lumberton (township) Burlington County	11	0.11
Hillsborough (township) Somerset County	9	0.02
Florence (township) Burlington County	8	0.07
Paterson (city) Passaic County	8	0.01
Glen Ridge (borough) Essex County	6	0.08

Top 10 Places Sorted by Percent
Based on all places, regardless of population

Place	Number	%
Chatham (township) Morris County	17	0.17
Carneys Point (township) Salem County	13	0.17
Lumberton (township) Burlington County	11	0.11
Glen Gardner (borough) Hunterdon County	2	0.11
Burlington (township) Burlington County	18	0.09
Glen Ridge (borough) Essex County	6	0.08
Florence (township) Burlington County	8	0.07
Mahwah (township) Bergen County	14	0.06
Bound Brook (borough) Somerset County	6	0.06
Echelon (cdp) Camden County	6	0.06

Top 10 Places Sorted by Percent
Based on places with populations of 10,000 or more

Place	Number	%
Chatham (township) Morris County	17	0.17
Lumberton (township) Burlington County	11	0.11
Burlington (township) Burlington County	18	0.09
Florence (township) Burlington County	8	0.07
Mahwah (township) Bergen County	14	0.06
Bound Brook (borough) Somerset County	6	0.06
Echelon (cdp) Camden County	6	0.06
Howell (township) Monmouth County	23	0.05
Hillsborough (township) Somerset County	9	0.02
Voorhees (township) Camden County	6	0.02

Afghan

Top 10 Places Sorted by Number
Based on all places, regardless of population

Place	Number	%
Parsippany-Troy Hills (township) Morris County	361	0.71
Newark (city) Essex County	162	0.06
Ocean (township) Monmouth County	90	0.33
Jersey City (city) Hudson County	82	0.03
Montville (township) Morris County	65	0.31
Woodbridge (township) Middlesex County	64	0.07
Bayonne (city) Hudson County	59	0.10
Nutley (cdp) Essex County	55	0.20
Marlboro (township) Monmouth County	55	0.15
South Plainfield (borough) Middlesex County	53	0.24

Top 10 Places Sorted by Percent
Based on all places, regardless of population

Place	Number	%
Lawrenceville (cdp) Mercer County	31	0.76
Parsippany-Troy Hills (township) Morris County	361	0.71
Chester (borough) Morris County	11	0.67
Demarest (borough) Bergen County	26	0.54
Somerville (borough) Somerset County	46	0.37
Plumsted (township) Ocean County	25	0.34
Ocean (township) Monmouth County	90	0.33
Beatyestown (cdp) Warren County	10	0.32
Montville (township) Morris County	65	0.31

| Carlstadt (borough) Bergen County | 16 | 0.27 |

Top 10 Places Sorted by Percent
Based on places with populations of 10,000 or more

Place	Number	%
Parsippany-Troy Hills (township) Morris County	361	0.71
Somerville (borough) Somerset County	46	0.37
Ocean (township) Monmouth County	90	0.33
Montville (township) Morris County	65	0.31
South Plainfield (borough) Middlesex County	53	0.24
New Milford (borough) Bergen County	36	0.22
Avenel (cdp) Middlesex County	37	0.21
Secaucus (town) Hudson County	34	0.21
Nutley (cdp) Essex County	55	0.20
Fords (cdp) Middlesex County	27	0.18

African American/Black

Top 10 Places Sorted by Number
Based on all places, regardless of population

Place	Number	%
Newark (city) Essex County	150,384	54.98
Jersey City (city) Hudson County	72,080	30.03
East Orange (city) Essex County	64,797	92.80
Irvington (cdp) Essex County	51,726	85.22
Paterson (city) Passaic County	51,663	34.62
Trenton (city) Mercer County	45,762	53.58
Camden (city) Camden County	44,224	55.35
Plainfield (city) Union County	30,557	63.89
Elizabeth (city) Union County	26,038	21.60
Orange (cdp) Essex County	25,879	78.74

Top 10 Places Sorted by Percent
Based on all places, regardless of population

Place	Number	%
Lawnside (borough) Camden County	2,580	95.84
East Orange (city) Essex County	64,797	92.80
Irvington (cdp) Essex County	51,726	85.22
Orange (cdp) Essex County	25,879	78.74
Willingboro (township) Burlington County	23,069	69.89
Asbury Park (city) Monmouth County	11,240	66.39
Plainfield (city) Union County	30,557	63.89
Pleasantville (city) Atlantic County	11,429	60.11
Salem (city) Salem County	3,484	59.48
Chesilhurst (borough) Camden County	879	57.83

Top 10 Places Sorted by Percent
Based on places with populations of 10,000 or more

Place	Number	%
East Orange (city) Essex County	64,797	92.80
Irvington (cdp) Essex County	51,726	85.22
Orange (cdp) Essex County	25,879	78.74
Willingboro (township) Burlington County	23,069	69.89
Asbury Park (city) Monmouth County	11,240	66.39
Plainfield (city) Union County	30,557	63.89
Pleasantville (city) Atlantic County	11,429	60.11
Camden (city) Camden County	44,224	55.35
Newark (city) Essex County	150,384	54.98
Trenton (city) Mercer County	45,762	53.58

African American/Black: Not Hispanic

Top 10 Places Sorted by Number
Based on all places, regardless of population

Place	Number	%
Newark (city) Essex County	144,900	52.97
Jersey City (city) Hudson County	67,172	27.98
East Orange (city) Essex County	63,742	91.29
Irvington (cdp) Essex County	50,878	83.83
Paterson (city) Passaic County	48,404	32.44
Trenton (city) Mercer County	44,481	52.08
Camden (city) Camden County	40,651	50.87

Plainfield (city) Union County	29,406	61.48
Orange (cdp) Essex County	25,425	77.35
Elizabeth (city) Union County	23,586	19.56

Top 10 Places Sorted by Percent
Based on all places, regardless of population

Place	Number	%
Lawnside (borough) Camden County	2,548	94.65
East Orange (city) Essex County	63,742	91.29
Irvington (cdp) Essex County	50,878	83.83
Orange (cdp) Essex County	25,425	77.35
Willingboro (township) Burlington County	22,507	68.19
Asbury Park (city) Monmouth County	10,864	64.17
Plainfield (city) Union County	29,406	61.48
Salem (city) Salem County	3,388	57.85
Pleasantville (city) Atlantic County	10,927	57.47
Chesilhurst (borough) Camden County	873	57.43

Top 10 Places Sorted by Percent
Based on places with populations of 10,000 or more

Place	Number	%
East Orange (city) Essex County	63,742	91.29
Irvington (cdp) Essex County	50,878	83.83
Orange (cdp) Essex County	25,425	77.35
Willingboro (township) Burlington County	22,507	68.19
Asbury Park (city) Monmouth County	10,864	64.17
Plainfield (city) Union County	29,406	61.48
Pleasantville (city) Atlantic County	10,927	57.47
Newark (city) Essex County	144,900	52.97
Trenton (city) Mercer County	44,481	52.08
Roselle (borough) Union County	11,069	52.03

African American/Black: Hispanic

Top 10 Places Sorted by Number
Based on all places, regardless of population

Place	Number	%
Newark (city) Essex County	5,484	2.00
Jersey City (city) Hudson County	4,908	2.04
Camden (city) Camden County	3,573	4.47
Paterson (city) Passaic County	3,259	2.18
Union City (city) Hudson County	2,559	3.81
Elizabeth (city) Union County	2,452	2.03
Passaic (city) Passaic County	1,958	2.89
New Brunswick (city) Middlesex County	1,487	3.06
West New York (town) Hudson County	1,434	3.13
Perth Amboy (city) Middlesex County	1,420	3.00

Top 10 Places Sorted by Percent
Based on all places, regardless of population

Place	Number	%
Camden (city) Camden County	3,573	4.47
Union City (city) Hudson County	2,559	3.81
West New York (town) Hudson County	1,434	3.13
New Brunswick (city) Middlesex County	1,487	3.06
Perth Amboy (city) Middlesex County	1,420	3.00
Passaic (city) Passaic County	1,958	2.89
Pleasantville (city) Atlantic County	502	2.64
Penns Grove (borough) Salem County	123	2.52
Plainfield (city) Union County	1,151	2.41
Atlantic City (city) Atlantic County	966	2.38

Top 10 Places Sorted by Percent
Based on places with populations of 10,000 or more

Place	Number	%
Camden (city) Camden County	3,573	4.47
Union City (city) Hudson County	2,559	3.81
West New York (town) Hudson County	1,434	3.13
New Brunswick (city) Middlesex County	1,487	3.06
Perth Amboy (city) Middlesex County	1,420	3.00
Passaic (city) Passaic County	1,958	2.89
Pleasantville (city) Atlantic County	502	2.64

Notes: (cdp) census designated place; Refer to the User's Guide in the front of the book for more detailed information.

Place	Number	%
Plainfield (city) Union County	1,151	2.41
Atlantic City (city) Atlantic County	966	2.38
Asbury Park (city) Monmouth County	376	2.22

African, sub-Saharan

Top 10 Places Sorted by Number
Based on all places, regardless of population

Place	Number	%
Newark (city) Essex County	7,114	2.60
Jersey City (city) Hudson County	5,342	2.23
East Orange (city) Essex County	2,774	3.97
Trenton (city) Mercer County	2,555	3.00
Irvington (cdp) Essex County	2,422	4.00
Franklin (township) Somerset County	1,987	3.90
Paterson (city) Passaic County	1,930	1.29
Elizabeth (city) Union County	1,550	1.29
Orange (cdp) Essex County	1,492	4.54
Somerset (cdp) Somerset County	1,426	6.19

Top 10 Places Sorted by Percent
Based on all places, regardless of population

Place	Number	%
Somerset (cdp) Somerset County	1,426	6.19
Orange (cdp) Essex County	1,492	4.54
Irvington (cdp) Essex County	2,422	4.00
East Orange (city) Essex County	2,774	3.97
Maurice River (township) Cumberland County	274	3.95
Woodstown (borough) Salem County	123	3.92
Franklin (township) Somerset County	1,987	3.90
Avenel (cdp) Middlesex County	602	3.43
Madison Park (cdp) Middlesex County	230	3.34
South Orange (cdp) Essex County	560	3.30

Top 10 Places Sorted by Percent
Based on places with populations of 10,000 or more

Place	Number	%
Somerset (cdp) Somerset County	1,426	6.19
Orange (cdp) Essex County	1,492	4.54
Irvington (cdp) Essex County	2,422	4.00
East Orange (city) Essex County	2,774	3.97
Franklin (township) Somerset County	1,987	3.90
Avenel (cdp) Middlesex County	602	3.43
South Orange (cdp) Essex County	560	3.30
Trenton (city) Mercer County	2,555	3.00
Hillside (cdp) Union County	615	2.83
Newark (city) Essex County	7,114	2.60

African, Subsaharan: African

Top 10 Places Sorted by Number
Based on all places, regardless of population

Place	Number	%
Newark (city) Essex County	3,920	1.43
Jersey City (city) Hudson County	3,546	1.48
Paterson (city) Passaic County	1,733	1.16
Trenton (city) Mercer County	1,603	1.88
East Orange (city) Essex County	1,598	2.29
Irvington (cdp) Essex County	1,377	2.27
Franklin (township) Somerset County	1,273	2.50
Elizabeth (city) Union County	1,118	0.93
Camden (city) Camden County	1,006	1.26
Somerset (cdp) Somerset County	964	4.18

Top 10 Places Sorted by Percent
Based on all places, regardless of population

Place	Number	%
Somerset (cdp) Somerset County	964	4.18
Maurice River (township) Cumberland County	274	3.95
Woodstown (borough) Salem County	101	3.22
Pemberton Heights (cdp) Burlington County	64	2.55
Franklin (township) Somerset County	1,273	2.50

Place	Number	%
Orange (cdp) Essex County	801	2.44
Rosenhayn (cdp) Cumberland County	27	2.36
Buena Vista (township) Atlantic County	171	2.30
Penns Grove (borough) Salem County	112	2.30
East Orange (city) Essex County	1,598	2.29

Top 10 Places Sorted by Percent
Based on places with populations of 10,000 or more

Place	Number	%
Somerset (cdp) Somerset County	964	4.18
Franklin (township) Somerset County	1,273	2.50
Orange (cdp) Essex County	801	2.44
East Orange (city) Essex County	1,598	2.29
Irvington (cdp) Essex County	1,377	2.27
Avenel (cdp) Middlesex County	386	2.20
Pleasantville (city) Atlantic County	383	2.01
Trenton (city) Mercer County	1,603	1.88
New Brunswick (city) Middlesex County	793	1.63
Asbury Park (city) Monmouth County	276	1.63

African, Subsaharan: Cape Verdean

Top 10 Places Sorted by Number
Based on all places, regardless of population

Place	Number	%
Jersey City (city) Hudson County	124	0.05
Newark (city) Essex County	96	0.04
Montclair (cdp) Essex County	71	0.18
North Bergen (township) Hudson County	42	0.07
Ocean Acres (cdp) Ocean County	28	0.21
Harrison (town) Hudson County	28	0.19
Stafford (township) Ocean County	28	0.12
Byram (township) Sussex County	25	0.30
Lake Mohawk (cdp) Sussex County	25	0.26
Mount Laurel (township) Burlington County	23	0.06

Top 10 Places Sorted by Percent
Based on all places, regardless of population

Place	Number	%
Princeton Junction (cdp) Mercer County	8	0.33
Byram (township) Sussex County	25	0.30
Holiday Heights (cdp) Ocean County	7	0.30
Lake Mohawk (cdp) Sussex County	25	0.26
East Newark (borough) Hudson County	6	0.25
Ocean Acres (cdp) Ocean County	28	0.21
Harrison (town) Hudson County	28	0.19
Montclair (cdp) Essex County	71	0.18
Stafford (township) Ocean County	28	0.12
Washington Township (cdp) Bergen County	10	0.11

Top 10 Places Sorted by Percent
Based on places with populations of 10,000 or more

Place	Number	%
Ocean Acres (cdp) Ocean County	28	0.21
Harrison (town) Hudson County	28	0.19
Montclair (cdp) Essex County	71	0.18
Stafford (township) Ocean County	28	0.12
North Bergen (township) Hudson County	42	0.07
Tinton Falls (borough) Monmouth County	10	0.07
Mount Laurel (township) Burlington County	23	0.06
Jersey City (city) Hudson County	124	0.05
Warren (township) Somerset County	7	0.05
Newark (city) Essex County	96	0.04

African, Subsaharan: Ethiopian

Top 10 Places Sorted by Number
Based on all places, regardless of population

Place	Number	%
Jersey City (city) Hudson County	221	0.09
East Orange (city) Essex County	149	0.21
West Orange (cdp) Essex County	104	0.23

Place	Number	%
Secaucus (town) Hudson County	48	0.30
Old Bridge (township) Middlesex County	48	0.08
Gloucester (township) Camden County	42	0.07
Winslow (township) Camden County	40	0.12
East Brunswick (cdp) Middlesex County	37	0.08
Camden (city) Camden County	32	0.04
South Brunswick (township) Middlesex County	30	0.08

Top 10 Places Sorted by Percent
Based on all places, regardless of population

Place	Number	%
Roosevelt (borough) Monmouth County	4	0.43
Peapack and Gladstone (borough) Somerset Co.	9	0.37
Secaucus (town) Hudson County	48	0.30
Florham Park (borough) Morris County	24	0.27
West Orange (cdp) Essex County	104	0.23
East Orange (city) Essex County	149	0.21
Phillipsburg (town) Warren County	27	0.18
Highland Park (borough) Middlesex County	22	0.16
Liberty (township) Warren County	4	0.15
Iselin (cdp) Middlesex County	23	0.14

Top 10 Places Sorted by Percent
Based on places with populations of 10,000 or more

Place	Number	%
Secaucus (town) Hudson County	48	0.30
West Orange (cdp) Essex County	104	0.23
East Orange (city) Essex County	149	0.21
Phillipsburg (town) Warren County	27	0.18
Highland Park (borough) Middlesex County	22	0.16
Iselin (cdp) Middlesex County	23	0.14
Winslow (township) Camden County	40	0.12
Ocean City (city) Cape May County	19	0.12
Jersey City (city) Hudson County	221	0.09
Dover (town) Morris County	16	0.09

African, Subsaharan: Ghanian

Top 10 Places Sorted by Number
Based on all places, regardless of population

Place	Number	%
Newark (city) Essex County	868	0.32
Irvington (cdp) Essex County	308	0.51
Sayreville (borough) Middlesex County	289	0.72
Franklin (township) Somerset County	259	0.51
North Brunswick Twp (cdp) Middlesex County	217	0.60
East Orange (city) Essex County	217	0.31
Orange (cdp) Essex County	196	0.60
Somerset (cdp) Somerset County	164	0.71
Union (cdp) Union County	143	0.26
Woodbridge (township) Middlesex County	134	0.14

Top 10 Places Sorted by Percent
Based on all places, regardless of population

Place	Number	%
Little Ferry (borough) Bergen County	91	0.84
Fords (cdp) Middlesex County	116	0.77
Sayreville (borough) Middlesex County	289	0.72
Somerset (cdp) Somerset County	164	0.71
Twin Rivers (cdp) Mercer County	53	0.71
North Brunswick Twp (cdp) Middlesex County	217	0.60
Orange (cdp) Essex County	196	0.60
Wallington (borough) Bergen County	63	0.54
Jamesburg (borough) Middlesex County	32	0.53
Irvington (cdp) Essex County	308	0.51

Top 10 Places Sorted by Percent
Based on places with populations of 10,000 or more

Place	Number	%
Little Ferry (borough) Bergen County	91	0.84
Fords (cdp) Middlesex County	116	0.77
Sayreville (borough) Middlesex County	289	0.72

Notes: (cdp) census designated place; Refer to the User's Guide in the front of the book for more detailed information.

Place	Number	%
Somerset (cdp) Somerset County	164	0.71
North Brunswick Twp (cdp) Middlesex County	217	0.60
Orange (cdp) Essex County	196	0.60
Wallington (borough) Bergen County	63	0.54
Irvington (cdp) Essex County	308	0.51
Franklin (township) Somerset County	259	0.51
Delran (township) Burlington County	80	0.51

African, Subsaharan: Kenyan

Top 10 Places Sorted by Number
Based on all places, regardless of population

Place	Number	%
Jersey City (city) Hudson County	209	0.09
Edison (cdp) Middlesex County	132	0.14
Newark (city) Essex County	85	0.03
Hillside (cdp) Union County	48	0.22
Montclair (cdp) Essex County	48	0.12
Carlstadt (borough) Bergen County	40	0.68
Marlboro (township) Monmouth County	36	0.10
Maplewood (cdp) Essex County	35	0.15
Edgewater (borough) Bergen County	32	0.42
Scotch Plains (cdp) Union County	32	0.14

Top 10 Places Sorted by Percent
Based on all places, regardless of population

Place	Number	%
Peapack and Gladstone (borough) Somerset Co.	23	0.95
Carlstadt (borough) Bergen County	40	0.68
Elmer (borough) Salem County	0	0.58
Edgewater (borough) Bergen County	32	0.42
Jamesburg (borough) Middlesex County	21	0.35
Hillside (cdp) Union County	48	0.22
Maplewood (cdp) Essex County	35	0.15
Edison (cdp) Middlesex County	132	0.14
Scotch Plains (cdp) Union County	32	0.14
Cedar Grove (cdp) Essex County	17	0.14

Top 10 Places Sorted by Percent
Based on places with populations of 10,000 or more

Place	Number	%
Hillside (cdp) Union County	48	0.22
Maplewood (cdp) Essex County	35	0.15
Edison (cdp) Middlesex County	132	0.14
Scotch Plains (cdp) Union County	32	0.14
Cedar Grove (cdp) Essex County	17	0.14
North Plainfield (borough) Somerset County	28	0.13
Montclair (cdp) Essex County	48	0.12
Marlboro (township) Monmouth County	36	0.10
Jersey City (city) Hudson County	209	0.09
Holmdel (township) Monmouth County	13	0.08

African, Subsaharan: Liberian

Top 10 Places Sorted by Number
Based on all places, regardless of population

Place	Number	%
Trenton (city) Mercer County	739	0.87
Newark (city) Essex County	427	0.16
Hamilton (township) Mercer County	187	0.21
East Orange (city) Essex County	162	0.23
Atlantic City (city) Atlantic County	106	0.26
Elizabeth (city) Union County	97	0.08
Irvington (cdp) Essex County	59	0.10
East Windsor (township) Mercer County	58	0.23
Paterson (city) Passaic County	56	0.04
Monroe (township) Gloucester County	50	0.17

Top 10 Places Sorted by Percent
Based on all places, regardless of population

Place	Number	%
Monmouth Junction (cdp) Middlesex County	32	1.32

Place	Number	%
Trenton (city) Mercer County	739	0.87
Harvey Cedars (borough) Ocean County	3	0.85
Lakehurst (borough) Ocean County	12	0.48
Sewaren (cdp) Middlesex County	12	0.43
Twin Rivers (cdp) Mercer County	30	0.40
Brigantine (city) Atlantic County	34	0.27
Atlantic City (city) Atlantic County	106	0.26
Madison Park (cdp) Middlesex County	17	0.25
Plainsboro Center (cdp) Middlesex County	6	0.25

Top 10 Places Sorted by Percent
Based on places with populations of 10,000 or more

Place	Number	%
Trenton (city) Mercer County	739	0.87
Brigantine (city) Atlantic County	34	0.27
Atlantic City (city) Atlantic County	106	0.26
Burlington (township) Burlington County	49	0.24
East Orange (city) Essex County	162	0.23
East Windsor (township) Mercer County	58	0.23
Hamilton (township) Mercer County	187	0.21
Monroe (township) Gloucester County	50	0.17
Newark (city) Essex County	427	0.16
Willingboro (township) Burlington County	48	0.15

African, Subsaharan: Nigerian

Top 10 Places Sorted by Number
Based on all places, regardless of population

Place	Number	%
Newark (city) Essex County	1,325	0.48
Irvington (cdp) Essex County	598	0.99
Union (cdp) Union County	518	0.95
East Orange (city) Essex County	495	0.71
Jersey City (city) Hudson County	449	0.19
Orange (cdp) Essex County	417	1.27
Woodbridge (township) Middlesex County	292	0.30
Franklin (township) Somerset County	277	0.54
South Orange (cdp) Essex County	231	1.36
Piscataway (township) Middlesex County	229	0.45

Top 10 Places Sorted by Percent
Based on all places, regardless of population

Place	Number	%
Brownville (cdp) Middlesex County	37	1.41
South Orange (cdp) Essex County	231	1.36
Mine Hill (township) Morris County	48	1.30
Orange (cdp) Essex County	417	1.27
Irvington (cdp) Essex County	598	0.99
Union (cdp) Union County	518	0.95
Hillside (cdp) Union County	205	0.94
Maplewood (cdp) Essex County	212	0.89
Budd Lake (cdp) Morris County	71	0.86
Madison Park (cdp) Middlesex County	58	0.84

Top 10 Places Sorted by Percent
Based on places with populations of 10,000 or more

Place	Number	%
South Orange (cdp) Essex County	231	1.36
Orange (cdp) Essex County	417	1.27
Irvington (cdp) Essex County	598	0.99
Union (cdp) Union County	518	0.95
Hillside (cdp) Union County	205	0.94
Maplewood (cdp) Essex County	212	0.89
Somerset (cdp) Somerset County	180	0.78
East Orange (city) Essex County	495	0.71
Avenel (cdp) Middlesex County	116	0.66
Montgomery (township) Somerset County	112	0.64

African, Subsaharan: Senegalese

Top 10 Places Sorted by Number
Based on all places, regardless of population

Place	Number	%
Jersey City (city) Hudson County	110	0.05
West New York (town) Hudson County	30	0.07
Montclair (cdp) Essex County	24	0.06
Union City (city) Hudson County	20	0.03
Newark (city) Essex County	15	0.01
Hoboken (city) Hudson County	10	0.03
Edison (cdp) Middlesex County	9	0.01
Washington (borough) Warren County	8	0.12
Pleasantville (city) Atlantic County	8	0.04
North Bergen (township) Hudson County	7	0.01

Top 10 Places Sorted by Percent
Based on all places, regardless of population

Place	Number	%
Washington (borough) Warren County	8	0.12
West New York (town) Hudson County	30	0.07
Montclair (cdp) Essex County	24	0.06
Jersey City (city) Hudson County	110	0.05
Pleasantville (city) Atlantic County	8	0.04
Union City (city) Hudson County	20	0.03
Hoboken (city) Hudson County	10	0.03
Newark (city) Essex County	15	0.01
Edison (cdp) Middlesex County	9	0.01
North Bergen (township) Hudson County	7	0.01

Top 10 Places Sorted by Percent
Based on places with populations of 10,000 or more

Place	Number	%
West New York (town) Hudson County	30	0.07
Montclair (cdp) Essex County	24	0.06
Jersey City (city) Hudson County	110	0.05
Pleasantville (city) Atlantic County	8	0.04
Union City (city) Hudson County	20	0.03
Hoboken (city) Hudson County	10	0.03
Newark (city) Essex County	15	0.01
Edison (cdp) Middlesex County	9	0.01
North Bergen (township) Hudson County	7	0.01
Atlantic City (city) Atlantic County	4	0.01

African, Subsaharan: Sierra Leonean

Top 10 Places Sorted by Number
Based on all places, regardless of population

Place	Number	%
Highland Park (borough) Middlesex County	110	0.79
Lawrence (township) Mercer County	107	0.37
Somerset (cdp) Somerset County	106	0.46
Franklin (township) Somerset County	106	0.21
Pennsauken (cdp) Camden County	90	0.25
North Brunswick Twp (cdp) Middlesex County	89	0.25
Edison (cdp) Middlesex County	81	0.08
Piscataway (township) Middlesex County	74	0.15
Ewing (cdp) Mercer County	67	0.19
Plainfield (city) Union County	54	0.11

Top 10 Places Sorted by Percent
Based on all places, regardless of population

Place	Number	%
Highland Park (borough) Middlesex County	110	0.79
Somerset (cdp) Somerset County	106	0.46
Old Tappan (borough) Bergen County	25	0.46
Lawrence (township) Mercer County	107	0.37
Collingswood (borough) Camden County	38	0.27
Pennsauken (cdp) Camden County	90	0.25
North Brunswick Twp (cdp) Middlesex County	89	0.25
Franklin (township) Somerset County	106	0.21
Ewing (cdp) Mercer County	67	0.19

Notes: (cdp) census designated place; Refer to the User's Guide in the front of the book for more detailed information.

Woodbury (city) Gloucester County | 20 | 0.19

Top 10 Places Sorted by Percent
Based on places with populations of 10,000 or more

Place	Number	%
Highland Park (borough) Middlesex County	110	0.79
Somerset (cdp) Somerset County	106	0.46
Lawrence (township) Mercer County	107	0.37
Collingswood (borough) Camden County	38	0.27
Pennsauken (cdp) Camden County	90	0.25
North Brunswick Twp (cdp) Middlesex County	89	0.25
Franklin (township) Somerset County	106	0.21
Ewing (cdp) Mercer County	67	0.19
Woodbury (city) Gloucester County	20	0.19
Piscataway (township) Middlesex County	74	0.15

African, Subsaharan: Somalian

Top 10 Places Sorted by Number
Based on all places, regardless of population

Place	Number	%
Jersey City (city) Hudson County	49	0.02
Peapack and Gladstone (borough) Somerset Co.	18	0.74
South Orange (cdp) Essex County	17	0.10
Glassboro (borough) Gloucester County	13	0.07
New Brunswick (city) Middlesex County	7	0.01
Plainsboro (township) Middlesex County	6	0.03
Hackensack (city) Bergen County	6	0.01
Plainfield (city) Union County	6	0.01

Top 10 Places Sorted by Percent
Based on all places, regardless of population

Place	Number	%
Peapack and Gladstone (borough) Somerset Co.	18	0.74
South Orange (cdp) Essex County	17	0.10
Glassboro (borough) Gloucester County	13	0.07
Plainsboro (township) Middlesex County	6	0.03
Jersey City (city) Hudson County	49	0.02
New Brunswick (city) Middlesex County	7	0.01
Hackensack (city) Bergen County	6	0.01
Plainfield (city) Union County	6	0.01

Top 10 Places Sorted by Percent
Based on places with populations of 10,000 or more

Place	Number	%
South Orange (cdp) Essex County	17	0.10
Glassboro (borough) Gloucester County	13	0.07
Plainsboro (township) Middlesex County	6	0.03
Jersey City (city) Hudson County	49	0.02
New Brunswick (city) Middlesex County	7	0.01
Hackensack (city) Bergen County	6	0.01
Plainfield (city) Union County	6	0.01

African, Subsaharan: South African

Top 10 Places Sorted by Number
Based on all places, regardless of population

Place	Number	%
Springfield (cdp) Union County	87	0.60
Montclair (cdp) Essex County	63	0.16
Jersey City (city) Hudson County	59	0.02
Deptford (township) Gloucester County	56	0.21
Cherry Hill (township) Camden County	56	0.08
Summit (city) Union County	49	0.23
Fort Lee (borough) Bergen County	48	0.14
Mahwah (township) Bergen County	45	0.19
Parsippany-Troy Hills (township) Morris County	44	0.09
Piscataway (township) Middlesex County	44	0.09

Top 10 Places Sorted by Percent
Based on all places, regardless of population

Place	Number	%
Springfield (cdp) Union County	87	0.60
Haworth (borough) Bergen County	18	0.53
Morris Plains (borough) Morris County	22	0.42
Chester (borough) Morris County	5	0.31
Sandyston (township) Sussex County	5	0.27
Edgewater (borough) Bergen County	19	0.25
Riverdale (borough) Morris County	6	0.24
Summit (city) Union County	49	0.23
Princeton (borough) Mercer County	33	0.23
Greentree (cdp) Camden County	27	0.23

Top 10 Places Sorted by Percent
Based on places with populations of 10,000 or more

Place	Number	%
Springfield (cdp) Union County	87	0.60
Summit (city) Union County	49	0.23
Princeton (borough) Mercer County	33	0.23
Greentree (cdp) Camden County	27	0.23
Deptford (township) Gloucester County	56	0.21
Franklin Lakes (borough) Bergen County	22	0.21
Mahwah (township) Bergen County	45	0.19
Little Falls (cdp) Passaic County	21	0.19
Hillsdale (borough) Bergen County	19	0.19
Jefferson (township) Morris County	36	0.18

African, Subsaharan: Sudanese

Top 10 Places Sorted by Number
Based on all places, regardless of population

Place	Number	%
Jersey City (city) Hudson County	146	0.06
Brigantine (city) Atlantic County	66	0.52
Woodbridge (township) Middlesex County	39	0.04
Avenel (cdp) Middlesex County	25	0.14
Woodstown (borough) Salem County	22	0.70
Princeton Meadows (cdp) Middlesex County	22	0.17
Plainsboro (township) Middlesex County	22	0.11
Irvington (cdp) Essex County	22	0.04
Elmwood Park (borough) Bergen County	18	0.10
Hackensack (city) Bergen County	12	0.03

Top 10 Places Sorted by Percent
Based on all places, regardless of population

Place	Number	%
Woodstown (borough) Salem County	22	0.70
Brigantine (city) Atlantic County	66	0.52
Princeton Meadows (cdp) Middlesex County	22	0.17
Avenel (cdp) Middlesex County	25	0.14
Plainsboro (township) Middlesex County	22	0.11
Elmwood Park (borough) Bergen County	18	0.10
Jersey City (city) Hudson County	146	0.06
South Orange (cdp) Essex County	8	0.05
Woodbridge (township) Middlesex County	39	0.04
Irvington (cdp) Essex County	22	0.04

Top 10 Places Sorted by Percent
Based on places with populations of 10,000 or more

Place	Number	%
Brigantine (city) Atlantic County	66	0.52
Princeton Meadows (cdp) Middlesex County	22	0.17
Avenel (cdp) Middlesex County	25	0.14
Plainsboro (township) Middlesex County	22	0.11
Elmwood Park (borough) Bergen County	18	0.10
Jersey City (city) Hudson County	146	0.06
South Orange (cdp) Essex County	8	0.05
Woodbridge (township) Middlesex County	39	0.04
Irvington (cdp) Essex County	22	0.04
Hackensack (city) Bergen County	12	0.03

African, Subsaharan: Ugandan

Top 10 Places Sorted by Number
Based on all places, regardless of population

Place	Number	%
West New York (town) Hudson County	40	0.09
Avenel (cdp) Middlesex County	20	0.11
Woodbridge (township) Middlesex County	20	0.02
Sayreville (borough) Middlesex County	12	0.03
New Brunswick (city) Middlesex County	11	0.02
East Orange (city) Essex County	10	0.01
Jersey City (city) Hudson County	10	0.00
Bernardsville (borough) Somerset County	9	0.12
Delran (township) Burlington County	7	0.05
West Windsor (township) Mercer County	5	0.02

Top 10 Places Sorted by Percent
Based on all places, regardless of population

Place	Number	%
Bernardsville (borough) Somerset County	9	0.12
Avenel (cdp) Middlesex County	20	0.11
West New York (town) Hudson County	40	0.09
Delran (township) Burlington County	7	0.05
Sayreville (borough) Middlesex County	12	0.03
Woodbridge (township) Middlesex County	20	0.02
New Brunswick (city) Middlesex County	11	0.02
West Windsor (township) Mercer County	5	0.02
East Orange (city) Essex County	10	0.01
Jersey City (city) Hudson County	10	0.00

Top 10 Places Sorted by Percent
Based on places with populations of 10,000 or more

Place	Number	%
Avenel (cdp) Middlesex County	20	0.11
West New York (town) Hudson County	40	0.09
Delran (township) Burlington County	7	0.05
Sayreville (borough) Middlesex County	12	0.03
Woodbridge (township) Middlesex County	20	0.02
New Brunswick (city) Middlesex County	11	0.02
West Windsor (township) Mercer County	5	0.02
East Orange (city) Essex County	10	0.01
Jersey City (city) Hudson County	10	0.00

African, Subsaharan: Zairian

Top 10 Places Sorted by Number
Based on all places, regardless of population

Place	Number	%
Teaneck (cdp) Bergen County	17	0.04
Burlington (township) Burlington County	13	0.06
Newark (city) Essex County	8	0.00
Mount Laurel (township) Burlington County	7	0.02

Top 10 Places Sorted by Percent
Based on all places, regardless of population

Place	Number	%
Burlington (township) Burlington County	13	0.06
Teaneck (cdp) Bergen County	17	0.04
Mount Laurel (township) Burlington County	7	0.02
Newark (city) Essex County	8	0.00

Top 10 Places Sorted by Percent
Based on places with populations of 10,000 or more

Place	Number	%
Burlington (township) Burlington County	13	0.06
Teaneck (cdp) Bergen County	17	0.04
Mount Laurel (township) Burlington County	7	0.02
Newark (city) Essex County	8	0.00

Notes: (cdp) census designated place; Refer to the User's Guide in the front of the book for more detailed information.

African, Subsaharan: Zimbabwean

Top 10 Places Sorted by Number
Based on all places, regardless of population

Place	Number	%
South Orange (cdp) Essex County	17	0.10
Hoboken (city) Hudson County	11	0.03
Tewksbury (township) Hunterdon County	9	0.16
Springfield (cdp) Union County	9	0.06
Fort Lee (borough) Bergen County	7	0.02
Merchantville (borough) Camden County	5	0.13
Bernards (township) Somerset County	5	0.02

Top 10 Places Sorted by Percent
Based on all places, regardless of population

Place	Number	%
Tewksbury (township) Hunterdon County	9	0.16
Merchantville (borough) Camden County	5	0.13
South Orange (cdp) Essex County	17	0.10
Springfield (cdp) Union County	9	0.06
Hoboken (city) Hudson County	11	0.03
Fort Lee (borough) Bergen County	7	0.02
Bernards (township) Somerset County	5	0.02

Top 10 Places Sorted by Percent
Based on places with populations of 10,000 or more

Place	Number	%
South Orange (cdp) Essex County	17	0.10
Springfield (cdp) Union County	9	0.06
Hoboken (city) Hudson County	11	0.03
Fort Lee (borough) Bergen County	7	0.02
Bernards (township) Somerset County	5	0.02

African, Subsaharan: Other

Top 10 Places Sorted by Number
Based on all places, regardless of population

Place	Number	%
Newark (city) Essex County	337	0.12
Jersey City (city) Hudson County	211	0.09
East Orange (city) Essex County	130	0.19
Matawan (borough) Monmouth County	77	0.86
Trenton (city) Mercer County	74	0.09
Edison (cdp) Middlesex County	63	0.06
Edgewater Park (township) Burlington County	61	0.78
Roselle (borough) Union County	57	0.27
South Orange (cdp) Essex County	53	0.31
Piscataway (township) Middlesex County	52	0.10

Top 10 Places Sorted by Percent
Based on all places, regardless of population

Place	Number	%
Matawan (borough) Monmouth County	77	0.86
Edgewater Park (township) Burlington County	61	0.78
Independence (township) Warren County	19	0.34
South Orange (cdp) Essex County	53	0.31
Roselle (borough) Union County	57	0.27
Barrington (borough) Camden County	19	0.27
Burlington (township) Burlington County	51	0.25
Avenel (cdp) Middlesex County	37	0.21
Little Ferry (borough) Bergen County	22	0.20
East Orange (city) Essex County	130	0.19

Top 10 Places Sorted by Percent
Based on places with populations of 10,000 or more

Place	Number	%
South Orange (cdp) Essex County	53	0.31
Roselle (borough) Union County	57	0.27
Burlington (township) Burlington County	51	0.25
Avenel (cdp) Middlesex County	37	0.21
Little Ferry (borough) Bergen County	22	0.20

Place	Number	%
East Orange (city) Essex County	130	0.19
Franklin (township) Gloucester County	28	0.18
Hillsdale (borough) Bergen County	16	0.16
Teaneck (cdp) Bergen County	50	0.13
Dumont (borough) Bergen County	23	0.13

Alaska Native tribes, specified

Top 10 Places Sorted by Number
Based on all places, regardless of population

Place	Number	%
Elizabeth (city) Union County	12	0.01
Ridgefield Park (village) Bergen County	8	0.06
Dover (township) Ocean County	8	0.01
Toms River (cdp) Ocean County	8	0.01
Wyckoff (cdp) Bergen County	6	0.04
Newark (city) Essex County	6	0.00
Mansfield (township) Warren County	5	0.08
Jersey City (city) Hudson County	5	0.00
Audubon (borough) Camden County	4	0.04
Asbury Park (city) Monmouth County	4	0.02

Top 10 Places Sorted by Percent
Based on all places, regardless of population

Place	Number	%
Hopewell (borough) Mercer County	2	0.10
Swedesboro (borough) Gloucester County	2	0.10
Mansfield (township) Warren County	5	0.08
Ridgefield Park (village) Bergen County	8	0.06
Seaside Heights (borough) Ocean County	2	0.06
Island Heights (borough) Ocean County	1	0.06
Erma (cdp) Cape May County	1	0.05
Manahawkin (cdp) Ocean County	1	0.05
Wyckoff (cdp) Bergen County	6	0.04
Audubon (borough) Camden County	4	0.04

Top 10 Places Sorted by Percent
Based on places with populations of 10,000 or more

Place	Number	%
Ridgefield Park (village) Bergen County	8	0.06
Wyckoff (cdp) Bergen County	6	0.04
Asbury Park (city) Monmouth County	4	0.02
Madison (borough) Morris County	4	0.02
Rutherford (borough) Bergen County	3	0.02
Elizabeth (city) Union County	12	0.01
Dover (township) Ocean County	8	0.01
Toms River (cdp) Ocean County	8	0.01
Mount Laurel (township) Burlington County	4	0.01
New Brunswick (city) Middlesex County	4	0.01

Alaska Native: Alaska Athabascan

Top 10 Places Sorted by Number
Based on all places, regardless of population

Place	Number	%
Wyckoff (cdp) Bergen County	5	0.03
Audubon (borough) Camden County	4	0.04
Hopewell (borough) Mercer County	2	0.10
Barrington (borough) Camden County	2	0.03
Hamilton (township) Mercer County	2	0.00
Jersey City (city) Hudson County	2	0.00
Lakehurst (borough) Ocean County	1	0.04
Laurence Harbor (cdp) Middlesex County	1	0.02
Allendale (borough) Bergen County	1	0.01
Dover (town) Morris County	1	0.01

Top 10 Places Sorted by Percent
Based on all places, regardless of population

Place	Number	%
Hopewell (borough) Mercer County	2	0.10
Audubon (borough) Camden County	4	0.04
Lakehurst (borough) Ocean County	1	0.04

Place	Number	%
Wyckoff (cdp) Bergen County	5	0.03
Barrington (borough) Camden County	2	0.03
Laurence Harbor (cdp) Middlesex County	1	0.02
Allendale (borough) Bergen County	1	0.01
Dover (town) Morris County	1	0.01
Echelon (cdp) Camden County	1	0.01
Leisure Village W-Pine Lake Pk (cdp) Ocean Co.	1	0.01

Top 10 Places Sorted by Percent
Based on places with populations of 10,000 or more

Place	Number	%
Wyckoff (cdp) Bergen County	5	0.03
Dover (town) Morris County	1	0.01
Echelon (cdp) Camden County	1	0.01
Leisure Village W-Pine Lake Pk (cdp) Ocean Co.	1	0.01
Little Ferry (borough) Bergen County	1	0.01
Lumberton (township) Burlington County	1	0.01
Ocean City (city) Cape May County	1	0.01
Pine Hill (borough) Camden County	1	0.01
Hamilton (township) Mercer County	2	0.00
Jersey City (city) Hudson County	2	0.00

Alaska Native: Aleut

Top 10 Places Sorted by Number
Based on all places, regardless of population

Place	Number	%
Mansfield (township) Warren County	5	0.08
Dover (township) Ocean County	4	0.00
Toms River (cdp) Ocean County	4	0.00
Bernardsville (borough) Somerset County	2	0.03
Iselin (cdp) Middlesex County	2	0.01
Woodbridge (township) Middlesex County	2	0.00
Seaside Heights (borough) Ocean County	1	0.03
Neptune City (borough) Monmouth County	1	0.02
White (township) Warren County	1	0.02
Franklin (township) Gloucester County	1	0.01

Top 10 Places Sorted by Percent
Based on all places, regardless of population

Place	Number	%
Mansfield (township) Warren County	5	0.08
Bernardsville (borough) Somerset County	2	0.03
Seaside Heights (borough) Ocean County	1	0.03
Neptune City (borough) Monmouth County	1	0.02
White (township) Warren County	1	0.02
Iselin (cdp) Middlesex County	2	0.01
Franklin (township) Gloucester County	1	0.01
Little Falls (cdp) Passaic County	1	0.01
Madison (borough) Morris County	1	0.01
Ventnor City (city) Atlantic County	1	0.01

Top 10 Places Sorted by Percent
Based on places with populations of 10,000 or more

Place	Number	%
Iselin (cdp) Middlesex County	2	0.01
Franklin (township) Gloucester County	1	0.01
Little Falls (cdp) Passaic County	1	0.01
Madison (borough) Morris County	1	0.01
Ventnor City (city) Atlantic County	1	0.01
Dover (township) Ocean County	4	0.00
Toms River (cdp) Ocean County	4	0.00
Woodbridge (township) Middlesex County	2	0.00
Cranford (cdp) Union County	1	0.00
Elizabeth (city) Union County	1	0.00

Alaska Native: Eskimo

Top 10 Places Sorted by Number
Based on all places, regardless of population

Place	Number	%
Ridgefield Park (village) Bergen County	8	0.06

Place	Number	%
Edison (cdp) Middlesex County	4	0.00
Madison (borough) Morris County	3	0.02
Rutherford (borough) Bergen County	3	0.02
Mount Arlington (borough) Morris County	2	0.04
Asbury Park (city) Monmouth County	2	0.01
Berkeley (township) Ocean County	2	0.01
Phillipsburg (town) Warren County	2	0.01
South Brunswick (township) Middlesex County	2	0.01
Jersey City (city) Hudson County	2	0.00

Top 10 Places Sorted by Percent
Based on all places, regardless of population

Place	Number	%
Ridgefield Park (village) Bergen County	8	0.06
Mount Arlington (borough) Morris County	2	0.04
Madison (borough) Morris County	3	0.02
Rutherford (borough) Bergen County	3	0.02
Chesterfield (township) Burlington County	1	0.02
Eastampton (township) Burlington County	1	0.02
Fairfield (township) Cumberland County	1	0.02
Neptune City (borough) Monmouth County	1	0.02
Raritan (borough) Somerset County	1	0.02
Asbury Park (city) Monmouth County	2	0.01

Top 10 Places Sorted by Percent
Based on places with populations of 10,000 or more

Place	Number	%
Ridgefield Park (village) Bergen County	8	0.06
Madison (borough) Morris County	3	0.02
Rutherford (borough) Bergen County	3	0.02
Asbury Park (city) Monmouth County	2	0.01
Berkeley (township) Ocean County	2	0.01
Phillipsburg (town) Warren County	2	0.01
South Brunswick (township) Middlesex County	2	0.01
Colonia (cdp) Middlesex County	1	0.01
Lindenwold (borough) Camden County	1	0.01
Morristown (town) Morris County	1	0.01

Alaska Native: Tlingit-Haida

Top 10 Places Sorted by Number
Based on all places, regardless of population

Place	Number	%
Elizabeth (city) Union County	11	0.01
Mount Laurel (township) Burlington County	4	0.01
Dover (township) Ocean County	4	0.00
Newark (city) Essex County	4	0.00
Toms River (cdp) Ocean County	4	0.00
Swedesboro (borough) Gloucester County	2	0.10
Ocean (township) Ocean County	2	0.03
Upper Deerfield (township) Cumberland County	2	0.03
Asbury Park (city) Monmouth County	2	0.01
Belleville (cdp) Essex County	2	0.01

Top 10 Places Sorted by Percent
Based on all places, regardless of population

Place	Number	%
Swedesboro (borough) Gloucester County	2	0.10
Island Heights (borough) Ocean County	1	0.06
Erma (cdp) Cape May County	1	0.05
Manahawkin (cdp) Ocean County	1	0.05
Ocean (township) Ocean County	2	0.03
Upper Deerfield (township) Cumberland County	2	0.03
Seaside Heights (borough) Ocean County	1	0.03
Belmar (borough) Monmouth County	1	0.02
Ho-Ho-Kus (borough) Bergen County	1	0.02
Elizabeth (city) Union County	11	0.01

Top 10 Places Sorted by Percent
Based on places with populations of 10,000 or more

Place	Number	%
Elizabeth (city) Union County	11	0.01

Place	Number	%
Mount Laurel (township) Burlington County	4	0.01
Asbury Park (city) Monmouth County	2	0.01
Belleville (cdp) Essex County	2	0.01
Bergenfield (borough) Bergen County	2	0.01
Ewing (cdp) Mercer County	2	0.01
Millville (city) Cumberland County	2	0.01
Cinnaminson (township) Burlington County	1	0.01
Colts Neck (township) Monmouth County	1	0.01
Hackettstown (town) Warren County	1	0.01

Alaska Native: All other tribes

Top 10 Places Sorted by Number
Based on all places, regardless of population

Place	Number	%

Top 10 Places Sorted by Percent
Based on all places, regardless of population

Place	Number	%

Top 10 Places Sorted by Percent
Based on places with populations of 10,000 or more

Place	Number	%

Alaska Native tribes, not specified

Top 10 Places Sorted by Number
Based on all places, regardless of population

Place	Number	%
Hamburg (borough) Sussex County	4	0.13
Seaside Heights (borough) Ocean County	4	0.13
Hazlet (township) Monmouth County	4	0.02
Dover (township) Ocean County	4	0.00
Toms River (cdp) Ocean County	4	0.00
Brigantine (city) Atlantic County	2	0.02
Asbury Park (city) Monmouth County	2	0.01
Madison (borough) Morris County	2	0.01
Middle (township) Cape May County	2	0.01
Orange (cdp) Essex County	2	0.01

Top 10 Places Sorted by Percent
Based on all places, regardless of population

Place	Number	%
Hamburg (borough) Sussex County	4	0.13
Seaside Heights (borough) Ocean County	4	0.13
Golden Triangle (cdp) Camden County	1	0.03
Hazlet (township) Monmouth County	4	0.02
Brigantine (city) Atlantic County	2	0.02
Cape May Court House (cdp) Cape May County	1	0.02
Mount Ephraim (borough) Camden County	1	0.02
Asbury Park (city) Monmouth County	2	0.01
Madison (borough) Morris County	2	0.01
Middle (township) Cape May County	2	0.01

Top 10 Places Sorted by Percent
Based on places with populations of 10,000 or more

Place	Number	%
Hazlet (township) Monmouth County	4	0.02
Brigantine (city) Atlantic County	2	0.02
Asbury Park (city) Monmouth County	2	0.01
Madison (borough) Morris County	2	0.01
Middle (township) Cape May County	2	0.01
Orange (cdp) Essex County	2	0.01
Browns Mills (cdp) Burlington County	1	0.01
Hawthorne (borough) Passaic County	1	0.01
Leisure Village W-Pine Lake Pk (cdp) Ocean Co.	1	0.01
Little Egg Harbor (township) Ocean County	1	0.01

American Indian or Alaska Native, not specified

Top 10 Places Sorted by Number
Based on all places, regardless of population

Place	Number	%
Jersey City (city) Hudson County	1,368	0.57
Newark (city) Essex County	1,285	0.47
Paterson (city) Passaic County	918	0.62
Camden (city) Camden County	588	0.74
Elizabeth (city) Union County	548	0.45
Passaic (city) Passaic County	533	0.79
Union City (city) Hudson County	468	0.70
Trenton (city) Mercer County	381	0.45
East Orange (city) Essex County	339	0.49
North Bergen (township) Hudson County	295	0.51

Top 10 Places Sorted by Percent
Based on all places, regardless of population

Place	Number	%
Fairfield (township) Cumberland County	138	2.20
Greenwich (township) Cumberland County	16	1.89
Rockleigh (borough) Bergen County	7	1.79
Lawnside (borough) Camden County	30	1.11
Deerfield (township) Cumberland County	29	0.99
Downe (township) Cumberland County	16	0.98
Egg Harbor City (city) Atlantic County	44	0.97
Lawrence (township) Cumberland County	25	0.92
Bridgeton (city) Cumberland County	207	0.91
Quinton (township) Salem County	24	0.86

Top 10 Places Sorted by Percent
Based on places with populations of 10,000 or more

Place	Number	%
Bridgeton (city) Cumberland County	207	0.91
Passaic (city) Passaic County	533	0.79
Camden (city) Camden County	588	0.74
Union City (city) Hudson County	468	0.70
Asbury Park (city) Monmouth County	113	0.67
Avenel (cdp) Middlesex County	114	0.65
Paterson (city) Passaic County	918	0.62
Hackensack (city) Bergen County	265	0.62
Lindenwold (borough) Camden County	105	0.60
New Brunswick (city) Middlesex County	286	0.59

Albanian

Top 10 Places Sorted by Number
Based on all places, regardless of population

Place	Number	%
Wayne (cdp) Passaic County	466	0.86
Garfield (city) Bergen County	370	1.24
Paterson (city) Passaic County	255	0.17
Lodi (borough) Bergen County	245	1.02
Lincoln Park (borough) Morris County	200	1.83
Pompton Lakes (borough) Passaic County	173	1.63
Cliffside Park (borough) Bergen County	172	0.75
Clifton (city) Passaic County	170	0.22
Totowa (borough) Passaic County	119	1.21
Montville (township) Morris County	117	0.56

Top 10 Places Sorted by Percent
Based on all places, regardless of population

Place	Number	%
Lincoln Park (borough) Morris County	200	1.83
Prospect Park (borough) Passaic County	101	1.75
Pompton Lakes (borough) Passaic County	173	1.63
North Haledon (borough) Passaic County	110	1.39
Garfield (city) Bergen County	370	1.24
Totowa (borough) Passaic County	119	1.21
Erma (cdp) Cape May County	22	1.03
Lodi (borough) Bergen County	245	1.02

Notes: (cdp) census designated place; Refer to the User's Guide in the front of the book for more detailed information.

Place	Number	%
Ventnor City (city) Atlantic County	115	0.89
Netcong (borough) Morris County	23	0.89

Top 10 Places Sorted by Percent
Based on places with populations of 10,000 or more

Place	Number	%
Lincoln Park (borough) Morris County	200	1.83
Pompton Lakes (borough) Passaic County	173	1.63
Garfield (city) Bergen County	370	1.24
Lodi (borough) Bergen County	245	1.02
Ventnor City (city) Atlantic County	115	0.89
Wayne (cdp) Passaic County	466	0.86
Cliffside Park (borough) Bergen County	172	0.75
Montville (township) Morris County	117	0.56
Roselle Park (borough) Union County	72	0.54
Marlton (cdp) Burlington County	41	0.40

Alsatian

Top 10 Places Sorted by Number
Based on all places, regardless of population

Place	Number	%
Montgomery (township) Somerset County	54	0.31
Hamilton (township) Mercer County	40	0.05
Wyckoff (cdp) Bergen County	37	0.22
Holmdel (township) Monmouth County	34	0.22
White Horse (cdp) Mercer County	31	0.32
Princeton (borough) Mercer County	31	0.22
Middletown (township) Monmouth County	27	0.04
Jersey City (city) Hudson County	26	0.01
Mahwah (township) Bergen County	23	0.10
Scotch Plains (cdp) Union County	22	0.10

Top 10 Places Sorted by Percent
Based on all places, regardless of population

Place	Number	%
Cape May Point (borough) Cape May County	4	1.68
Golden Triangle (cdp) Camden County	11	0.33
White Horse (cdp) Mercer County	31	0.32
Montgomery (township) Somerset County	54	0.31
Lebanon (borough) Hunterdon County	3	0.28
Forked River (cdp) Ocean County	13	0.27
Navesink (cdp) Monmouth County	5	0.27
Wyckoff (cdp) Bergen County	37	0.22
Holmdel (township) Monmouth County	34	0.22
Princeton (borough) Mercer County	31	0.22

Top 10 Places Sorted by Percent
Based on places with populations of 10,000 or more

Place	Number	%
Montgomery (township) Somerset County	54	0.31
Wyckoff (cdp) Bergen County	37	0.22
Holmdel (township) Monmouth County	34	0.22
Princeton (borough) Mercer County	31	0.22
Mahwah (township) Bergen County	23	0.10
Scotch Plains (cdp) Union County	22	0.10
Morris (township) Morris County	21	0.10
Westwood (borough) Bergen County	10	0.09
Cherry Hill Mall (cdp) Camden County	11	0.08
Washington (township) Morris County	12	0.07

American Indian tribes, specified

Top 10 Places Sorted by Number
Based on all places, regardless of population

Place	Number	%
Jersey City (city) Hudson County	828	0.34
Newark (city) Essex County	774	0.28
Paterson (city) Passaic County	532	0.36
Camden (city) Camden County	367	0.46
Elizabeth (city) Union County	307	0.25
Bridgeton (city) Cumberland County	280	1.23

Place	Number	%
Trenton (city) Mercer County	276	0.32
Union City (city) Hudson County	275	0.41
Willingboro (township) Burlington County	274	0.83
Vineland (city) Cumberland County	271	0.48

Top 10 Places Sorted by Percent
Based on all places, regardless of population

Place	Number	%
Fairfield (township) Cumberland County	268	4.27
Hopewell (township) Cumberland County	123	2.77
Fairton (cdp) Cumberland County	52	2.31
Greenwich (township) Cumberland County	17	2.01
Lawrence (township) Cumberland County	52	1.91
Deerfield (township) Cumberland County	51	1.74
Downe (township) Cumberland County	25	1.53
Ringwood (borough) Passaic County	182	1.47
Stow Creek (township) Cumberland County	21	1.47
Rosenhayn (cdp) Cumberland County	15	1.36

Top 10 Places Sorted by Percent
Based on places with populations of 10,000 or more

Place	Number	%
Ringwood (borough) Passaic County	182	1.47
Bridgeton (city) Cumberland County	280	1.23
Browns Mills (cdp) Burlington County	120	1.07
Willingboro (township) Burlington County	274	0.83
Pemberton (township) Burlington County	237	0.83
Eatontown (borough) Monmouth County	104	0.74
West Milford (cdp) Passaic County	193	0.73
Millville (city) Cumberland County	183	0.68
Mahwah (township) Bergen County	162	0.67
Wanaque (borough) Passaic County	67	0.65

American Indian: Apache

Top 10 Places Sorted by Number
Based on all places, regardless of population

Place	Number	%
Newark (city) Essex County	13	0.00
South Orange (cdp) Essex County	9	0.05
Howell (township) Monmouth County	9	0.02
Woodbridge (township) Middlesex County	9	0.01
Avenel (cdp) Middlesex County	8	0.05
Gloucester (township) Camden County	8	0.01
Jersey City (city) Hudson County	8	0.00
Country Lake Estates (cdp) Burlington County	7	0.17
Pemberton (township) Burlington County	7	0.02
Middletown (township) Monmouth County	7	0.01

Top 10 Places Sorted by Percent
Based on all places, regardless of population

Place	Number	%
Country Lake Estates (cdp) Burlington County	7	0.17
Pemberton (borough) Burlington County	2	0.17
Estell Manor (city) Atlantic County	2	0.13
Leonardo (cdp) Monmouth County	3	0.11
Hope (township) Warren County	2	0.11
Roosevelt (borough) Monmouth County	1	0.11
Oaklyn (borough) Camden County	4	0.10
Audubon Park (borough) Camden County	1	0.09
Rosenhayn (cdp) Cumberland County	1	0.09
Laurel Lake (cdp) Cumberland County	2	0.07

Top 10 Places Sorted by Percent
Based on places with populations of 10,000 or more

Place	Number	%
South Orange (cdp) Essex County	9	0.05
Avenel (cdp) Middlesex County	8	0.05
Marlton (cdp) Burlington County	4	0.04
Wanaque (borough) Passaic County	4	0.04
Dover (town) Morris County	5	0.03
Branchburg (township) Somerset County	4	0.03

Place	Number	%
Little Egg Harbor (township) Ocean County	4	0.03
Somerville (borough) Somerset County	4	0.03
Lumberton (township) Burlington County	3	0.03
Howell (township) Monmouth County	9	0.02

American Indian: Blackfeet

Top 10 Places Sorted by Number
Based on all places, regardless of population

Place	Number	%
Newark (city) Essex County	96	0.04
Jersey City (city) Hudson County	44	0.02
East Orange (city) Essex County	42	0.06
Willingboro (township) Burlington County	41	0.12
Paterson (city) Passaic County	41	0.03
Winslow (township) Camden County	31	0.09
Atlantic City (city) Atlantic County	26	0.06
Camden (city) Camden County	24	0.03
Hackensack (city) Bergen County	23	0.05
Vineland (city) Cumberland County	20	0.04

Top 10 Places Sorted by Percent
Based on all places, regardless of population

Place	Number	%
Wrightstown (borough) Burlington County	3	0.40
Milford (borough) Hunterdon County	4	0.33
Hi-Nella (borough) Camden County	3	0.29
Whitesboro-Burleigh (cdp) Cape May County	4	0.22
Essex Fells (borough) Essex County	4	0.19
Sussex (borough) Sussex County	4	0.19
Dover Beaches South (cdp) Ocean County	3	0.19
Newfield (borough) Gloucester County	3	0.19
Woodlynne (borough) Camden County	5	0.18
Fairton (cdp) Cumberland County	4	0.18

Top 10 Places Sorted by Percent
Based on places with populations of 10,000 or more

Place	Number	%
Willingboro (township) Burlington County	41	0.12
Tinton Falls (borough) Monmouth County	15	0.10
Red Bank (borough) Monmouth County	12	0.10
Browns Mills (cdp) Burlington County	11	0.10
Winslow (township) Camden County	31	0.09
Pleasantville (city) Atlantic County	15	0.08
Burlington (township) Burlington County	15	0.07
Middle (township) Cape May County	11	0.07
Bellmawr (borough) Camden County	8	0.07
Pine Hill (borough) Camden County	8	0.07

American Indian: Cherokee

Top 10 Places Sorted by Number
Based on all places, regardless of population

Place	Number	%
Newark (city) Essex County	237	0.09
Jersey City (city) Hudson County	224	0.09
Camden (city) Camden County	131	0.16
Willingboro (township) Burlington County	122	0.37
Pemberton (township) Burlington County	111	0.39
Trenton (city) Mercer County	107	0.13
East Orange (city) Essex County	96	0.14
Montclair (cdp) Essex County	95	0.24
Hackensack (city) Bergen County	85	0.20
Atlantic City (city) Atlantic County	81	0.20

Top 10 Places Sorted by Percent
Based on all places, regardless of population

Place	Number	%
West Wildwood (borough) Cape May County	5	1.12
Clementon (borough) Camden County	26	0.52
Lawrence (township) Cumberland County	14	0.51
Presidential Lakes Estates (cdp) Burlington County	12	0.51

Notes: (cdp) census designated place; Refer to the User's Guide in the front of the book for more detailed information.

Place	Number	%
Browns Mills (cdp) Burlington County	56	0.50
Lawnside (borough) Camden County	13	0.48
Hopewell (township) Cumberland County	21	0.47
Shrewsbury (township) Monmouth County	5	0.46
Salem (city) Salem County	26	0.44
Roosevelt (borough) Monmouth County	4	0.43

Top 10 Places Sorted by Percent
Based on places with populations of 10,000 or more

Place	Number	%
Browns Mills (cdp) Burlington County	56	0.50
Pemberton (township) Burlington County	111	0.39
Willingboro (township) Burlington County	122	0.37
Asbury Park (city) Monmouth County	50	0.30
Eatontown (borough) Monmouth County	39	0.28
Neptune (township) Monmouth County	69	0.25
Montclair (cdp) Essex County	95	0.24
South Orange (cdp) Essex County	40	0.24
Pennsville (township) Salem County	32	0.24
Lindenwold (borough) Camden County	37	0.21

American Indian: Cheyenne

Top 10 Places Sorted by Number
Based on all places, regardless of population

Place	Number	%
Franklin (borough) Sussex County	5	0.10
Hardyston (township) Sussex County	4	0.06
Point Pleasant (borough) Ocean County	4	0.02
Linden (city) Union County	4	0.01
Hopewell (township) Mercer County	3	0.02
Scotch Plains (cdp) Union County	3	0.01
Gloucester (township) Camden County	3	0.00
Ocean Grove (cdp) Monmouth County	2	0.05
Cape May Court House (cdp) Cape May County	2	0.04
Somerdale (borough) Camden County	2	0.04

Top 10 Places Sorted by Percent
Based on all places, regardless of population

Place	Number	%
Franklin (borough) Sussex County	5	0.10
Hardwick (township) Warren County	1	0.07
Hardyston (township) Sussex County	4	0.06
Ocean Grove (cdp) Monmouth County	2	0.05
Cape May Court House (cdp) Cape May County	2	0.04
Somerdale (borough) Camden County	2	0.04
Wenonah (borough) Gloucester County	1	0.04
Montvale (borough) Bergen County	2	0.03
Wharton (borough) Morris County	2	0.03
Seaside Heights (borough) Ocean County	1	0.03

Top 10 Places Sorted by Percent
Based on places with populations of 10,000 or more

Place	Number	%
Point Pleasant (borough) Ocean County	4	0.02
Hopewell (township) Mercer County	3	0.02
Linden (city) Union County	4	0.01
Scotch Plains (cdp) Union County	3	0.01
Hazlet (township) Monmouth County	2	0.01
Middle (township) Cape May County	2	0.01
Moorestown-Lenola (cdp) Burlington County	2	0.01
Moorestown (township) Burlington County	2	0.01
Neptune (township) Monmouth County	2	0.01
Pleasantville (city) Atlantic County	2	0.01

American Indian: Chickasaw

Top 10 Places Sorted by Number
Based on all places, regardless of population

Place	Number	%
Rahway (city) Union County	7	0.03
Paterson (city) Passaic County	7	0.00

Place	Number	%
Franklin (township) Gloucester County	5	0.03
Franklin (township) Somerset County	5	0.01
Hillsborough (township) Somerset County	5	0.01
Belmar (borough) Monmouth County	4	0.07
Jersey City (city) Hudson County	4	0.00
Collings Lakes (cdp) Atlantic County	3	0.17
Manasquan (borough) Monmouth County	3	0.05
Buena Vista (township) Atlantic County	3	0.04

Top 10 Places Sorted by Percent
Based on all places, regardless of population

Place	Number	%
Collings Lakes (cdp) Atlantic County	3	0.17
Andover (borough) Sussex County	1	0.15
Sussex (borough) Sussex County	2	0.09
Belmar (borough) Monmouth County	4	0.07
Dover Beaches North (cdp) Ocean County	1	0.06
Manasquan (borough) Monmouth County	3	0.05
Buena Vista (township) Atlantic County	3	0.04
Heathcote (cdp) Middlesex County	2	0.04
Rahway (city) Union County	7	0.03
Franklin (township) Gloucester County	5	0.03

Top 10 Places Sorted by Percent
Based on places with populations of 10,000 or more

Place	Number	%
Rahway (city) Union County	7	0.03
Franklin (township) Gloucester County	5	0.03
Little Falls (cdp) Passaic County	3	0.03
New Providence (borough) Union County	3	0.03
Dover (town) Morris County	3	0.02
Ocean Acres (cdp) Ocean County	2	0.02
Southampton (township) Burlington County	2	0.02
Franklin (township) Somerset County	5	0.01
Hillsborough (township) Somerset County	5	0.01
Somerset (cdp) Somerset County	3	0.01

American Indian: Chippewa

Top 10 Places Sorted by Number
Based on all places, regardless of population

Place	Number	%
Hamilton (township) Atlantic County	16	0.08
Ringwood (borough) Passaic County	8	0.06
Willingboro (township) Burlington County	8	0.02
Jersey City (city) Hudson County	7	0.00
Palmyra (borough) Burlington County	6	0.08
Bellmawr (borough) Camden County	6	0.05
Lower (township) Cape May County	6	0.03
Ewing (cdp) Mercer County	6	0.02
Hampton (township) Sussex County	5	0.10
Raritan (township) Hunterdon County	5	0.03

Top 10 Places Sorted by Percent
Based on all places, regardless of population

Place	Number	%
Seaside Heights (borough) Ocean County	4	0.13
Hampton (borough) Hunterdon County	2	0.13
Hampton (township) Sussex County	5	0.10
Woodstown (borough) Salem County	3	0.10
Elsinboro (township) Salem County	1	0.09
Hamilton (township) Atlantic County	16	0.08
Palmyra (borough) Burlington County	6	0.08
Lakehurst (borough) Ocean County	2	0.08
Berlin (borough) Camden County	4	0.07
Frenchtown (borough) Hunterdon County	1	0.07

Top 10 Places Sorted by Percent
Based on places with populations of 10,000 or more

Place	Number	%
Hamilton (township) Atlantic County	16	0.08
Ringwood (borough) Passaic County	8	0.06

Place	Number	%
Bellmawr (borough) Camden County	6	0.05
Lower (township) Cape May County	6	0.03
Raritan (township) Hunterdon County	5	0.03
South Orange (cdp) Essex County	5	0.03
Hopatcong (borough) Sussex County	4	0.03
Gloucester City (city) Camden County	3	0.03
Willingboro (township) Burlington County	8	0.02
Ewing (cdp) Mercer County	6	0.02

American Indian: Choctaw

Top 10 Places Sorted by Number
Based on all places, regardless of population

Place	Number	%
Jersey City (city) Hudson County	10	0.00
Pennsauken (cdp) Camden County	7	0.02
Berlin (borough) Camden County	6	0.10
Burlington (township) Burlington County	6	0.03
Howell (township) Monmouth County	6	0.01
Wayne (cdp) Passaic County	6	0.01
Morristown (town) Morris County	5	0.03
Lacey (township) Ocean County	5	0.02
North Plainfield (borough) Somerset County	5	0.02
Pemberton (township) Burlington County	5	0.02

Top 10 Places Sorted by Percent
Based on all places, regardless of population

Place	Number	%
Andover (borough) Sussex County	3	0.46
Alpine (borough) Bergen County	3	0.14
Wrightstown (borough) Burlington County	1	0.13
Berlin (borough) Camden County	6	0.10
Kingston (cdp) Middlesex County	1	0.08
Sea Isle City (city) Cape May County	2	0.07
Belford (cdp) Monmouth County	1	0.07
Belmar (borough) Monmouth County	3	0.05
Eastampton (township) Burlington County	3	0.05
Hardyston (township) Sussex County	3	0.05

Top 10 Places Sorted by Percent
Based on places with populations of 10,000 or more

Place	Number	%
Wanaque (borough) Passaic County	4	0.04
Burlington (township) Burlington County	6	0.03
Morristown (town) Morris County	5	0.03
Echelon (cdp) Camden County	3	0.03
Pennsauken (cdp) Camden County	7	0.02
Lacey (township) Ocean County	5	0.02
North Plainfield (borough) Somerset County	5	0.02
Pemberton (township) Burlington County	5	0.02
Asbury Park (city) Monmouth County	4	0.02
Somerville (borough) Somerset County	3	0.02

American Indian: Colville

Top 10 Places Sorted by Number
Based on all places, regardless of population

Place	Number	%
Burlington (city) Burlington County	1	0.01
Ridgefield Park (village) Bergen County	1	0.01
Parsippany-Troy Hills (township) Morris County	1	0.00

Top 10 Places Sorted by Percent
Based on all places, regardless of population

Place	Number	%
Burlington (city) Burlington County	1	0.01
Ridgefield Park (village) Bergen County	1	0.01
Parsippany-Troy Hills (township) Morris County	1	0.00

Notes: (cdp) census designated place; Refer to the User's Guide in the front of the book for more detailed information.

Top 10 Places Sorted by Percent
Based on places with populations of 10,000 or more

Place	Number	%
Ridgefield Park (village) Bergen County	1	0.01
Parsippany-Troy Hills (township) Morris County	1	0.00

American Indian: Comanche

Top 10 Places Sorted by Number
Based on all places, regardless of population

Place	Number	%
Berkeley (township) Ocean County	5	0.01
Brick (township) Ocean County	4	0.01
South Amboy (city) Middlesex County	3	0.04
Somers Point (city) Atlantic County	3	0.03
Delran (township) Burlington County	3	0.02
Jefferson (township) Morris County	3	0.02
Metuchen (borough) Middlesex County	3	0.02
North Brunswick Twp (cdp) Middlesex County	3	0.01
West Milford (cdp) Passaic County	3	0.01
Camden (city) Camden County	3	0.00

Top 10 Places Sorted by Percent
Based on all places, regardless of population

Place	Number	%
Laurel Springs (borough) Camden County	1	0.05
South Amboy (city) Middlesex County	3	0.04
Presidential Lakes Estates (cdp) Burlington County	1	0.04
Quinton (township) Salem County	1	0.04
Somers Point (city) Atlantic County	3	0.03
Laurel Lake (cdp) Cumberland County	1	0.03
Oak Valley (cdp) Gloucester County	1	0.03
Port Monmouth (cdp) Monmouth County	1	0.03
Delran (township) Burlington County	3	0.02
Jefferson (township) Morris County	3	0.02

Top 10 Places Sorted by Percent
Based on places with populations of 10,000 or more

Place	Number	%
Somers Point (city) Atlantic County	3	0.03
Delran (township) Burlington County	3	0.02
Jefferson (township) Morris County	3	0.02
Metuchen (borough) Middlesex County	3	0.02
Keansburg (borough) Monmouth County	2	0.02
Washington (township) Mercer County	2	0.02
Berkeley (township) Ocean County	5	0.01
Brick (township) Ocean County	4	0.01
North Brunswick Twp (cdp) Middlesex County	3	0.01
West Milford (cdp) Passaic County	3	0.01

American Indian: Cree

Top 10 Places Sorted by Number
Based on all places, regardless of population

Place	Number	%
Bayonne (city) Hudson County	6	0.01
East Orange (city) Essex County	6	0.01
Sea Isle City (city) Cape May County	4	0.14
Fanwood (borough) Union County	3	0.04
Hopewell (township) Mercer County	3	0.02
Sayreville (borough) Middlesex County	3	0.01
North Hanover (township) Burlington County	2	0.03
Eatontown (borough) Monmouth County	2	0.01
Galloway (township) Atlantic County	2	0.01
Lawrence (township) Mercer County	2	0.01

Top 10 Places Sorted by Percent
Based on all places, regardless of population

Place	Number	%
Sea Isle City (city) Cape May County	4	0.14
Allentown (borough) Monmouth County	1	0.05

Place	Number	%
Fanwood (borough) Union County	3	0.04
North Hanover (township) Burlington County	2	0.03
High Bridge (borough) Hunterdon County	1	0.03
Hopewell (township) Mercer County	3	0.02
Dennis (township) Cape May County	1	0.02
Eastampton (township) Burlington County	1	0.02
McGuire AFB (cdp) Burlington County	1	0.02
Bayonne (city) Hudson County	6	0.01

Top 10 Places Sorted by Percent
Based on places with populations of 10,000 or more

Place	Number	%
Hopewell (township) Mercer County	3	0.02
Bayonne (city) Hudson County	6	0.01
East Orange (city) Essex County	6	0.01
Sayreville (borough) Middlesex County	3	0.01
Eatontown (borough) Monmouth County	2	0.01
Galloway (township) Atlantic County	2	0.01
Lawrence (township) Mercer County	2	0.01
Teaneck (cdp) Bergen County	2	0.01
West Milford (cdp) Passaic County	2	0.01
Berkeley Heights (cdp) Union County	1	0.01

American Indian: Creek

Top 10 Places Sorted by Number
Based on all places, regardless of population

Place	Number	%
McGuire AFB (cdp) Burlington County	10	0.15
Dover (township) Ocean County	10	0.01
Toms River (cdp) Ocean County	10	0.01
North Hanover (township) Burlington County	9	0.12
Willingboro (township) Burlington County	7	0.02
Perth Amboy (city) Middlesex County	7	0.01
Phillipsburg (town) Warren County	6	0.04
Hamilton (township) Atlantic County	6	0.03
Winslow (township) Camden County	6	0.02
Scotch Plains (cdp) Union County	5	0.02

Top 10 Places Sorted by Percent
Based on all places, regardless of population

Place	Number	%
Lebanon (borough) Hunterdon County	2	0.19
Long Valley (cdp) Morris County	3	0.17
McGuire AFB (cdp) Burlington County	10	0.15
North Hanover (township) Burlington County	9	0.12
Bedminster (township) Somerset County	4	0.05
Independence (township) Warren County	3	0.05
Woodcliff Lake (borough) Bergen County	3	0.05
High Bridge (borough) Hunterdon County	2	0.05
Helmetta (borough) Middlesex County	1	0.05
Pine Ridge at Crestwood (cdp) Ocean County	1	0.05

Top 10 Places Sorted by Percent
Based on places with populations of 10,000 or more

Place	Number	%
Phillipsburg (town) Warren County	6	0.04
Chatham (township) Morris County	4	0.04
Hamilton (township) Atlantic County	6	0.03
Collingswood (borough) Camden County	4	0.03
Guttenberg (town) Hudson County	3	0.03
Willingboro (township) Burlington County	7	0.02
Winslow (township) Camden County	6	0.02
Scotch Plains (cdp) Union County	5	0.02
Aberdeen (township) Monmouth County	4	0.02
Upper (township) Cape May County	3	0.02

American Indian: Crow

Top 10 Places Sorted by Number
Based on all places, regardless of population

Place	Number	%
Jersey City (city) Hudson County	6	0.00
Highland Lake (cdp) Sussex County	5	0.10
Vernon (township) Sussex County	5	0.02
Beverly (city) Burlington County	4	0.15
Wharton (borough) Morris County	4	0.06
Paterson (city) Passaic County	4	0.00
Lumberton (township) Burlington County	3	0.03
Hackensack (city) Bergen County	3	0.01
Barnegat (township) Ocean County	2	0.01
Bridgeton (city) Cumberland County	2	0.01

Top 10 Places Sorted by Percent
Based on all places, regardless of population

Place	Number	%
Beverly (city) Burlington County	4	0.15
Highland Lake (cdp) Sussex County	5	0.10
Wharton (borough) Morris County	4	0.06
Alloway (township) Salem County	1	0.04
Lumberton (township) Burlington County	3	0.03
Montague (township) Sussex County	1	0.03
Vernon (township) Sussex County	5	0.02
Hackensack (city) Bergen County	3	0.01
Barnegat (township) Ocean County	2	0.01
Bridgeton (city) Cumberland County	2	0.01

Top 10 Places Sorted by Percent
Based on places with populations of 10,000 or more

Place	Number	%
Lumberton (township) Burlington County	3	0.03
Vernon (township) Sussex County	5	0.02
Hackensack (city) Bergen County	3	0.01
Barnegat (township) Ocean County	2	0.01
Bridgeton (city) Cumberland County	2	0.01
Englewood (city) Bergen County	2	0.01
Glassboro (borough) Gloucester County	2	0.01
Morris (township) Morris County	2	0.01
Winslow (township) Camden County	2	0.01
Colts Neck (township) Monmouth County	1	0.01

American Indian: Delaware

Top 10 Places Sorted by Number
Based on all places, regardless of population

Place	Number	%
Ringwood (borough) Passaic County	145	1.17
Mahwah (township) Bergen County	131	0.54
West Milford (cdp) Passaic County	88	0.33
Fairfield (township) Cumberland County	76	1.21
Bridgeton (city) Cumberland County	76	0.33
Millville (city) Cumberland County	48	0.18
Vineland (city) Cumberland County	47	0.08
Dover (township) Ocean County	34	0.04
Toms River (cdp) Ocean County	34	0.04
Hopewell (township) Cumberland County	31	0.70

Top 10 Places Sorted by Percent
Based on all places, regardless of population

Place	Number	%
Fairfield (township) Cumberland County	76	1.21
Ringwood (borough) Passaic County	145	1.17
Greenwich (township) Cumberland County	8	0.94
Corbin City (city) Atlantic County	4	0.85
Hopewell (township) Cumberland County	31	0.70
Great Meadows-Vienna (cdp) Warren County	8	0.63
Cedarville (cdp) Cumberland County	5	0.63
Fairton (cdp) Cumberland County	13	0.58
Stow Creek (township) Cumberland County	8	0.56

Notes: (cdp) census designated place; Refer to the User's Guide in the front of the book for more detailed information.

Mahwah (township) Bergen County   131   0.54

Top 10 Places Sorted by Percent
Based on places with populations of 10,000 or more

Place	Number	%
Ringwood (borough) Passaic County	145	1.17
Mahwah (township) Bergen County	131	0.54
West Milford (cdp) Passaic County	88	0.33
Bridgeton (city) Cumberland County	76	0.33
Wanaque (borough) Passaic County	27	0.26
Millville (city) Cumberland County	48	0.18
Westwood (borough) Bergen County	14	0.13
Mount Holly (township) Burlington County	10	0.09
Vineland (city) Cumberland County	47	0.08
Ewing (cdp) Mercer County	25	0.07

American Indian: Houma

Top 10 Places Sorted by Number
Based on all places, regardless of population

Place	Number	%
Hamilton (township) Mercer County	4	0.00
Egg Harbor (township) Atlantic County	2	0.01
Morris (township) Morris County	2	0.01
Lake Mohawk (cdp) Sussex County	1	0.01
Pittsgrove (township) Salem County	1	0.01
Sparta (township) Sussex County	1	0.01
Montclair (cdp) Essex County	1	0.00
Plainfield (city) Union County	1	0.00
Vernon (township) Sussex County	1	0.00

Top 10 Places Sorted by Percent
Based on all places, regardless of population

Place	Number	%
Egg Harbor (township) Atlantic County	2	0.01
Morris (township) Morris County	2	0.01
Lake Mohawk (cdp) Sussex County	1	0.01
Pittsgrove (township) Salem County	1	0.01
Sparta (township) Sussex County	1	0.01
Hamilton (township) Mercer County	4	0.00
Montclair (cdp) Essex County	1	0.00
Plainfield (city) Union County	1	0.00
Vernon (township) Sussex County	1	0.00

Top 10 Places Sorted by Percent
Based on places with populations of 10,000 or more

Place	Number	%
Egg Harbor (township) Atlantic County	2	0.01
Morris (township) Morris County	2	0.01
Sparta (township) Sussex County	1	0.01
Hamilton (township) Mercer County	4	0.00
Montclair (cdp) Essex County	1	0.00
Plainfield (city) Union County	1	0.00
Vernon (township) Sussex County	1	0.00

American Indian: Iroquois

Top 10 Places Sorted by Number
Based on all places, regardless of population

Place	Number	%
Newark (city) Essex County	48	0.02
Brick (township) Ocean County	22	0.03
Willingboro (township) Burlington County	20	0.06
East Orange (city) Essex County	19	0.03
Cliffside Park (borough) Bergen County	17	0.07
Pemberton (township) Burlington County	17	0.06
Dover (township) Ocean County	17	0.02
Toms River (cdp) Ocean County	17	0.02
Browns Mills (cdp) Burlington County	16	0.14
Old Bridge (township) Middlesex County	16	0.03

Top 10 Places Sorted by Percent
Based on all places, regardless of population

Place	Number	%
Port Republic (city) Atlantic County	4	0.39
Branchville (borough) Sussex County	3	0.36
Gibbsboro (borough) Camden County	7	0.29
Alloway (township) Salem County	7	0.25
Englishtown (borough) Monmouth County	4	0.23
Allentown (borough) Monmouth County	4	0.21
White House Station (cdp) Hunterdon County	4	0.21
Seaside Heights (borough) Ocean County	6	0.19
Weymouth (township) Atlantic County	4	0.18
Downe (township) Cumberland County	3	0.18

Top 10 Places Sorted by Percent
Based on places with populations of 10,000 or more

Place	Number	%
Browns Mills (cdp) Burlington County	16	0.14
Little Egg Harbor (township) Ocean County	12	0.08
Wantage (township) Sussex County	8	0.08
Cliffside Park (borough) Bergen County	17	0.07
Aberdeen (township) Monmouth County	12	0.07
Willingboro (township) Burlington County	20	0.06
Pemberton (township) Burlington County	17	0.06
Hopatcong (borough) Sussex County	10	0.06
Denville (township) Morris County	9	0.06
Mantua (township) Gloucester County	9	0.06

American Indian: Kiowa

Top 10 Places Sorted by Number
Based on all places, regardless of population

Place	Number	%
Berkeley (township) Ocean County	5	0.01
Willingboro (township) Burlington County	2	0.01
Clifton (city) Passaic County	2	0.00
Passaic (city) Passaic County	2	0.00
Essex Fells (borough) Essex County	1	0.05
Collingswood (borough) Camden County	1	0.01
Hamilton (township) Mercer County	1	0.00
Vineland (city) Cumberland County	1	0.00

Top 10 Places Sorted by Percent
Based on all places, regardless of population

Place	Number	%
Essex Fells (borough) Essex County	1	0.05
Berkeley (township) Ocean County	5	0.01
Willingboro (township) Burlington County	2	0.01
Collingswood (borough) Camden County	1	0.01
Clifton (city) Passaic County	2	0.00
Passaic (city) Passaic County	2	0.00
Hamilton (township) Mercer County	1	0.00
Vineland (city) Cumberland County	1	0.00

Top 10 Places Sorted by Percent
Based on places with populations of 10,000 or more

Place	Number	%
Berkeley (township) Ocean County	5	0.01
Willingboro (township) Burlington County	2	0.01
Collingswood (borough) Camden County	1	0.01
Clifton (city) Passaic County	2	0.00
Passaic (city) Passaic County	2	0.00
Hamilton (township) Mercer County	1	0.00
Vineland (city) Cumberland County	1	0.00

American Indian: Latin American Indians

Top 10 Places Sorted by Number
Based on all places, regardless of population

Place	Number	%
Jersey City (city) Hudson County	367	0.15

Paterson (city) Passaic County   280   0.19
Union City (city) Hudson County   226   0.34
Newark (city) Essex County   217   0.08
Passaic (city) Passaic County   195   0.29
Elizabeth (city) Union County   193   0.16
Perth Amboy (city) Middlesex County   152   0.32
New Brunswick (city) Middlesex County   145   0.30
West New York (town) Hudson County   133   0.29
Plainfield (city) Union County   104   0.22

Top 10 Places Sorted by Percent
Based on all places, regardless of population

Place	Number	%
Avon-by-the-Sea (borough) Monmouth County	10	0.45
Ship Bottom (borough) Ocean County	6	0.43
Wrightstown (borough) Burlington County	3	0.40
Buena (borough) Atlantic County	15	0.39
Hi-Nella (borough) Camden County	4	0.39
Union City (city) Hudson County	226	0.34
Chesterfield (township) Burlington County	20	0.34
Freehold (borough) Monmouth County	36	0.33
Interlaken (borough) Monmouth County	3	0.33
Perth Amboy (city) Middlesex County	152	0.32

Top 10 Places Sorted by Percent
Based on places with populations of 10,000 or more

Place	Number	%
Union City (city) Hudson County	226	0.34
Freehold (borough) Monmouth County	36	0.33
Perth Amboy (city) Middlesex County	152	0.32
New Brunswick (city) Middlesex County	145	0.30
Passaic (city) Passaic County	195	0.29
West New York (town) Hudson County	133	0.29
Dover (town) Morris County	45	0.25
Princeton (borough) Mercer County	36	0.25
Bridgeton (city) Cumberland County	55	0.24
Harrison (town) Hudson County	34	0.24

American Indian: Lumbee

Top 10 Places Sorted by Number
Based on all places, regardless of population

Place	Number	%
Orange (cdp) Essex County	8	0.02
Merchantville (borough) Camden County	5	0.13
Bound Brook (borough) Somerset County	5	0.05
Williamstown (cdp) Gloucester County	5	0.04
Monroe (township) Gloucester County	5	0.02
Union (cdp) Union County	5	0.01
Upper Pittsgrove (township) Salem County	4	0.12
East Greenwich (township) Gloucester County	4	0.07
Paulsboro (borough) Gloucester County	4	0.06
Mercerville-Hamilton Square (cdp) Mercer County	4	0.02

Top 10 Places Sorted by Percent
Based on all places, regardless of population

Place	Number	%
Andover (borough) Sussex County	2	0.30
Merchantville (borough) Camden County	5	0.13
Upper Pittsgrove (township) Salem County	4	0.12
South Belmar (borough) Monmouth County	2	0.11
East Greenwich (township) Gloucester County	4	0.07
Paulsboro (borough) Gloucester County	4	0.06
Bound Brook (borough) Somerset County	5	0.05
Shamong (township) Burlington County	3	0.05
Gibbstown (cdp) Gloucester County	2	0.05
Hainesport (township) Burlington County	2	0.05

Top 10 Places Sorted by Percent
Based on places with populations of 10,000 or more

Place	Number	%
Bound Brook (borough) Somerset County	5	0.05

Notes: (cdp) census designated place; Refer to the User's Guide in the front of the book for more detailed information.

Place	Number	%
Williamstown (cdp) Gloucester County	5	0.04
Hackettstown (town) Warren County	3	0.03
Orange (cdp) Essex County	8	0.02
Monroe (township) Gloucester County	5	0.02
Mercerville-Hamilton Square (cdp) Mercer County	4	0.02
Rahway (city) Union County	4	0.02
Branchburg (township) Somerset County	3	0.02
Colts Neck (township) Monmouth County	3	0.02
Union (cdp) Union County	5	0.01

American Indian: Menominee

Top 10 Places Sorted by Number
Based on all places, regardless of population

Place	Number	%
Allamuchy-Panther Valley (cdp) Warren County	2	0.06
Allamuchy (township) Warren County	2	0.05
Bernards (township) Somerset County	2	0.01
Jersey City (city) Hudson County	2	0.00
Heathcote (cdp) Middlesex County	1	0.02
Kinnelon (borough) Morris County	1	0.01
Lindenwold (borough) Camden County	1	0.01
Morristown (town) Morris County	1	0.01
Montclair (cdp) Essex County	1	0.00
Parsippany-Troy Hills (township) Morris County	1	0.00

Top 10 Places Sorted by Percent
Based on all places, regardless of population

Place	Number	%
Allamuchy-Panther Valley (cdp) Warren County	2	0.06
Allamuchy (township) Warren County	2	0.05
Heathcote (cdp) Middlesex County	1	0.02
Bernards (township) Somerset County	2	0.01
Kinnelon (borough) Morris County	1	0.01
Lindenwold (borough) Camden County	1	0.01
Morristown (town) Morris County	1	0.01
Jersey City (city) Hudson County	2	0.00
Montclair (cdp) Essex County	1	0.00
Parsippany-Troy Hills (township) Morris County	1	0.00

Top 10 Places Sorted by Percent
Based on places with populations of 10,000 or more

Place	Number	%
Bernards (township) Somerset County	2	0.01
Lindenwold (borough) Camden County	1	0.01
Morristown (town) Morris County	1	0.01
Jersey City (city) Hudson County	2	0.00
Montclair (cdp) Essex County	1	0.00
Parsippany-Troy Hills (township) Morris County	1	0.00
Piscataway (township) Middlesex County	1	0.00
South Brunswick (township) Middlesex County	1	0.00
Vineland (city) Cumberland County	1	0.00

American Indian: Navajo

Top 10 Places Sorted by Number
Based on all places, regardless of population

Place	Number	%
Teaneck (cdp) Bergen County	13	0.03
Jersey City (city) Hudson County	11	0.00
Newark (city) Essex County	11	0.00
Hawthorne (borough) Passaic County	9	0.05
Camden (city) Camden County	8	0.01
North Bergen (township) Hudson County	8	0.01
Trenton (city) Mercer County	7	0.00
Mercerville-Hamilton Square (cdp) Mercer County	6	0.02
West Milford (cdp) Passaic County	6	0.02
Hamilton (township) Mercer County	6	0.01

Top 10 Places Sorted by Percent
Based on all places, regardless of population

Place	Number	%
Port Republic (city) Atlantic County	3	0.29
Lawrence (township) Cumberland County	4	0.15
Harmony (township) Warren County	3	0.11
Elsinboro (township) Salem County	1	0.09
Franklin (borough) Sussex County	4	0.08
Alpha (borough) Warren County	2	0.08
Ogdensburg (borough) Sussex County	2	0.08
Pemberton (borough) Burlington County	1	0.08
Delanco (township) Burlington County	2	0.06
Hawthorne (borough) Passaic County	9	0.05

Top 10 Places Sorted by Percent
Based on places with populations of 10,000 or more

Place	Number	%
Hawthorne (borough) Passaic County	9	0.05
Washington (township) Mercer County	4	0.04
Teaneck (cdp) Bergen County	13	0.03
Colts Neck (township) Monmouth County	4	0.03
Mount Holly (township) Burlington County	3	0.03
Somers Point (city) Atlantic County	3	0.03
Wanaque (borough) Passaic County	3	0.03
Mercerville-Hamilton Square (cdp) Mercer County	6	0.02
West Milford (cdp) Passaic County	6	0.02
Lower (township) Cape May County	4	0.02

American Indian: Osage

Top 10 Places Sorted by Number
Based on all places, regardless of population

Place	Number	%
Raritan (borough) Somerset County	3	0.05
Pleasantville (city) Atlantic County	3	0.02
Bridgewater (township) Somerset County	3	0.01
East Windsor (township) Mercer County	3	0.01
Willingboro (township) Burlington County	3	0.01
Denville (township) Morris County	2	0.01
Ewing (cdp) Mercer County	2	0.01
Wall (township) Monmouth County	2	0.01
Fair Haven (borough) Monmouth County	1	0.02
Highland Lake (cdp) Sussex County	1	0.02

Top 10 Places Sorted by Percent
Based on all places, regardless of population

Place	Number	%
Raritan (borough) Somerset County	3	0.05
Pleasantville (city) Atlantic County	3	0.02
Fair Haven (borough) Monmouth County	1	0.02
Highland Lake (cdp) Sussex County	1	0.02
Pomona (cdp) Atlantic County	1	0.02
Bridgewater (township) Somerset County	3	0.01
East Windsor (township) Mercer County	3	0.01
Willingboro (township) Burlington County	3	0.01
Denville (township) Morris County	2	0.01
Ewing (cdp) Mercer County	2	0.01

Top 10 Places Sorted by Percent
Based on places with populations of 10,000 or more

Place	Number	%
Pleasantville (city) Atlantic County	3	0.02
Bridgewater (township) Somerset County	3	0.01
East Windsor (township) Mercer County	3	0.01
Willingboro (township) Burlington County	3	0.01
Denville (township) Morris County	2	0.01
Ewing (cdp) Mercer County	2	0.01
Wall (township) Monmouth County	2	0.01
Branchburg (township) Somerset County	1	0.01
Browns Mills (cdp) Burlington County	1	0.01
Hackettstown (town) Warren County	1	0.01

American Indian: Ottawa

Top 10 Places Sorted by Number
Based on all places, regardless of population

Place	Number	%
Wharton (borough) Morris County	4	0.06
Haddon (township) Camden County	4	0.03
Jefferson (township) Morris County	3	0.02
Long Branch (city) Monmouth County	3	0.01
Plainsboro Center (cdp) Middlesex County	2	0.09
Deptford (township) Gloucester County	2	0.01
Eatontown (borough) Monmouth County	2	0.01
Plainsboro (township) Middlesex County	2	0.01
Winslow (township) Camden County	2	0.01
Brielle (borough) Monmouth County	1	0.02

Top 10 Places Sorted by Percent
Based on all places, regardless of population

Place	Number	%
Plainsboro Center (cdp) Middlesex County	2	0.09
Wharton (borough) Morris County	4	0.06
Haddon (township) Camden County	4	0.03
Jefferson (township) Morris County	3	0.02
Brielle (borough) Monmouth County	1	0.02
Franklin (borough) Sussex County	1	0.02
Highlands (borough) Monmouth County	1	0.02
Independence (township) Warren County	1	0.02
Upper Freehold (township) Monmouth County	1	0.02
Long Branch (city) Monmouth County	3	0.01

Top 10 Places Sorted by Percent
Based on places with populations of 10,000 or more

Place	Number	%
Haddon (township) Camden County	4	0.03
Jefferson (township) Morris County	3	0.02
Long Branch (city) Monmouth County	3	0.01
Deptford (township) Gloucester County	2	0.01
Eatontown (borough) Monmouth County	2	0.01
Plainsboro (township) Middlesex County	2	0.01
Winslow (township) Camden County	2	0.01
Colts Neck (township) Monmouth County	1	0.01
Berkeley (township) Ocean County	1	0.00
Camden (city) Camden County	1	0.00

American Indian: Paiute

Top 10 Places Sorted by Number
Based on all places, regardless of population

Place	Number	%
Wanamassa (cdp) Monmouth County	9	0.20
Ocean (township) Monmouth County	9	0.03
Carteret (borough) Middlesex County	4	0.02
Neptune City (borough) Monmouth County	3	0.06
Fair Lawn (borough) Bergen County	2	0.01
Buena (borough) Atlantic County	1	0.03
Society Hill (cdp) Middlesex County	1	0.03
Dennis (township) Cape May County	1	0.02
Highlands (borough) Monmouth County	1	0.02
Haledon (borough) Passaic County	1	0.01

Top 10 Places Sorted by Percent
Based on all places, regardless of population

Place	Number	%
Wanamassa (cdp) Monmouth County	9	0.20
Neptune City (borough) Monmouth County	3	0.06
Ocean (township) Monmouth County	9	0.03
Buena (borough) Atlantic County	1	0.03
Society Hill (cdp) Middlesex County	1	0.03
Carteret (borough) Middlesex County	4	0.02
Dennis (township) Cape May County	1	0.02
Highlands (borough) Monmouth County	1	0.02
Fair Lawn (borough) Bergen County	2	0.01

Place	Number	%
Haledon (borough) Passaic County	1	0.01

Top 10 Places Sorted by Percent
Based on places with populations of 10,000 or more

Place	Number	%
Ocean (township) Monmouth County	9	0.03
Carteret (borough) Middlesex County	4	0.02
Fair Lawn (borough) Bergen County	2	0.01
Wyckoff (cdp) Bergen County	1	0.01
Brick (township) Ocean County	1	0.00
Dover (township) Ocean County	1	0.00
Franklin (township) Somerset County	1	0.00
Howell (township) Monmouth County	1	0.00
Jersey City (city) Hudson County	1	0.00
Old Bridge (township) Middlesex County	1	0.00

American Indian: Pima

Top 10 Places Sorted by Number
Based on all places, regardless of population

Place	Number	%
Allenhurst (borough) Monmouth County	2	0.28
Greentree (cdp) Camden County	1	0.01
Harrison (town) Hudson County	1	0.01
Lake Mohawk (cdp) Sussex County	1	0.01
Saddle Brook (cdp) Bergen County	1	0.01
Sparta (township) Sussex County	1	0.01
Upper Saddle River (borough) Bergen County	1	0.01
Washington (township) Morris County	1	0.01
Burlington (township) Burlington County	1	0.00
Cherry Hill (township) Camden County	1	0.00

Top 10 Places Sorted by Percent
Based on all places, regardless of population

Place	Number	%
Allenhurst (borough) Monmouth County	2	0.28
Greentree (cdp) Camden County	1	0.01
Harrison (town) Hudson County	1	0.01
Lake Mohawk (cdp) Sussex County	1	0.01
Saddle Brook (cdp) Bergen County	1	0.01
Sparta (township) Sussex County	1	0.01
Upper Saddle River (borough) Bergen County	1	0.01
Washington (township) Morris County	1	0.01
Burlington (township) Burlington County	1	0.00
Cherry Hill (township) Camden County	1	0.00

Top 10 Places Sorted by Percent
Based on places with populations of 10,000 or more

Place	Number	%
Greentree (cdp) Camden County	1	0.01
Harrison (town) Hudson County	1	0.01
Saddle Brook (cdp) Bergen County	1	0.01
Sparta (township) Sussex County	1	0.01
Washington (township) Morris County	1	0.01
Burlington (township) Burlington County	1	0.00
Cherry Hill (township) Camden County	1	0.00
North Bergen (township) Hudson County	1	0.00

American Indian: Potawatomi

Top 10 Places Sorted by Number
Based on all places, regardless of population

Place	Number	%
Hamilton (township) Atlantic County	5	0.02
Willingboro (township) Burlington County	5	0.02
Berkeley Heights (cdp) Union County	4	0.03
Egg Harbor (township) Atlantic County	4	0.01
Marlboro (township) Monmouth County	4	0.01
Hardyston (township) Sussex County	3	0.05
Lakewood (township) Ocean County	3	0.00
Rio Grande (cdp) Cape May County	2	0.08
Lumberton (township) Burlington County	2	0.02

Place	Number	%
Linden (city) Union County	2	0.01

Top 10 Places Sorted by Percent
Based on all places, regardless of population

Place	Number	%
Rio Grande (cdp) Cape May County	2	0.08
Hardyston (township) Sussex County	3	0.05
Folsom (borough) Atlantic County	1	0.05
Frelinghuysen (township) Warren County	1	0.05
Sea Isle City (city) Cape May County	1	0.04
Berkeley Heights (cdp) Union County	4	0.03
Upper Pittsgrove (township) Salem County	1	0.03
Hamilton (township) Atlantic County	5	0.02
Willingboro (township) Burlington County	5	0.02
Lumberton (township) Burlington County	2	0.02

Top 10 Places Sorted by Percent
Based on places with populations of 10,000 or more

Place	Number	%
Berkeley Heights (cdp) Union County	4	0.03
Hamilton (township) Atlantic County	5	0.02
Willingboro (township) Burlington County	5	0.02
Lumberton (township) Burlington County	2	0.02
Egg Harbor (township) Atlantic County	4	0.01
Marlboro (township) Monmouth County	4	0.01
Linden (city) Union County	2	0.01
Middle (township) Cape May County	2	0.01
Mount Olive (township) Morris County	2	0.01
Barnegat (township) Ocean County	1	0.01

American Indian: Pueblo

Top 10 Places Sorted by Number
Based on all places, regardless of population

Place	Number	%
Paterson (city) Passaic County	45	0.03
Perth Amboy (city) Middlesex County	36	0.08
Jersey City (city) Hudson County	31	0.01
Elizabeth (city) Union County	17	0.01
Newark (city) Essex County	17	0.01
Atlantic City (city) Atlantic County	15	0.04
New Brunswick (city) Middlesex County	15	0.03
Camden (city) Camden County	15	0.02
Union City (city) Hudson County	14	0.02
Ventnor City (city) Atlantic County	12	0.09

Top 10 Places Sorted by Percent
Based on all places, regardless of population

Place	Number	%
Port Norris (cdp) Cumberland County	4	0.27
Lawrence (township) Cumberland County	5	0.18
Brownville (cdp) Middlesex County	3	0.11
Leonardo (cdp) Monmouth County	3	0.11
Ventnor City (city) Atlantic County	12	0.09
Perth Amboy (city) Middlesex County	36	0.08
Commercial (township) Cumberland County	4	0.08
Red Bank (borough) Monmouth County	8	0.07
Franklin (township) Warren County	2	0.07
Eagleswood (township) Ocean County	1	0.07

Top 10 Places Sorted by Percent
Based on places with populations of 10,000 or more

Place	Number	%
Ventnor City (city) Atlantic County	12	0.09
Perth Amboy (city) Middlesex County	36	0.08
Red Bank (borough) Monmouth County	8	0.07
Atlantic City (city) Atlantic County	15	0.04
Dover (town) Morris County	7	0.04
Pleasantville (city) Atlantic County	7	0.04
West Freehold (cdp) Monmouth County	5	0.04
Paterson (city) Passaic County	45	0.03
New Brunswick (city) Middlesex County	15	0.03

Place	Number	%
Bridgeton (city) Cumberland County	7	0.03

American Indian: Puget Sound Salish

Top 10 Places Sorted by Number
Based on all places, regardless of population

Place	Number	%
Medford (township) Burlington County	4	0.02
Edgewater (borough) Bergen County	1	0.01
Keyport (borough) Monmouth County	1	0.01
Ocean City (city) Cape May County	1	0.01
Bloomfield (cdp) Essex County	1	0.00
Burlington (township) Burlington County	1	0.00
Clifton (city) Passaic County	1	0.00
Jersey City (city) Hudson County	1	0.00
Middletown (township) Monmouth County	1	0.00
North Brunswick Twp (cdp) Middlesex County	1	0.00

Top 10 Places Sorted by Percent
Based on all places, regardless of population

Place	Number	%
Medford (township) Burlington County	4	0.02
Edgewater (borough) Bergen County	1	0.01
Keyport (borough) Monmouth County	1	0.01
Ocean City (city) Cape May County	1	0.01
Bloomfield (cdp) Essex County	1	0.00
Burlington (township) Burlington County	1	0.00
Clifton (city) Passaic County	1	0.00
Jersey City (city) Hudson County	1	0.00
Middletown (township) Monmouth County	1	0.00
North Brunswick Twp (cdp) Middlesex County	1	0.00

Top 10 Places Sorted by Percent
Based on places with populations of 10,000 or more

Place	Number	%
Medford (township) Burlington County	4	0.02
Ocean City (city) Cape May County	1	0.01
Bloomfield (cdp) Essex County	1	0.00
Burlington (township) Burlington County	1	0.00
Clifton (city) Passaic County	1	0.00
Jersey City (city) Hudson County	1	0.00
Middletown (township) Monmouth County	1	0.00
North Brunswick Twp (cdp) Middlesex County	1	0.00

American Indian: Seminole

Top 10 Places Sorted by Number
Based on all places, regardless of population

Place	Number	%
Newark (city) Essex County	29	0.01
Jersey City (city) Hudson County	10	0.00
Teaneck (cdp) Bergen County	9	0.02
North Hanover (township) Burlington County	8	0.11
Linden (city) Union County	8	0.02
Trenton (city) Mercer County	8	0.01
Hammonton (town) Atlantic County	7	0.06
Maplewood (cdp) Essex County	7	0.03
Orange (cdp) Essex County	7	0.02
East Orange (city) Essex County	7	0.01

Top 10 Places Sorted by Percent
Based on all places, regardless of population

Place	Number	%
Eagleswood (township) Ocean County	3	0.21
Pemberton (borough) Burlington County	2	0.17
Gibbsboro (borough) Camden County	4	0.16
Navesink (cdp) Monmouth County	3	0.15
Presidential Lakes Estates (cdp) Burlington County	3	0.13
Mansfield (township) Burlington County	6	0.12
North Hanover (township) Burlington County	8	0.11
Fredon (township) Sussex County	3	0.10
Tuckerton (borough) Ocean County	3	0.09

Notes: (cdp) census designated place; Refer to the User's Guide in the front of the book for more detailed information.

Mays Landing (cdp) Atlantic County	2	0.09

Top 10 Places Sorted by Percent
Based on places with populations of 10,000 or more

Place	Number	%
Hammonton (town) Atlantic County	7	0.06
Pine Hill (borough) Camden County	4	0.04
Maplewood (cdp) Essex County	7	0.03
Branchburg (township) Somerset County	5	0.03
Brigantine (city) Atlantic County	4	0.03
Mantua (township) Gloucester County	4	0.03
Williamstown (cdp) Gloucester County	4	0.03
Lumberton (township) Burlington County	3	0.03
Teaneck (cdp) Bergen County	9	0.02
Linden (city) Union County	8	0.02

American Indian: Shoshone

Top 10 Places Sorted by Number
Based on all places, regardless of population

Place	Number	%
Hamilton (township) Atlantic County	6	0.03
Old Bridge (township) Middlesex County	4	0.01
Delran (township) Burlington County	3	0.02
Princeton Meadows (cdp) Middlesex County	3	0.02
Montville (township) Morris County	3	0.01
Plainsboro (township) Middlesex County	3	0.01
Tewksbury (township) Hunterdon County	2	0.04
Ridgefield (borough) Bergen County	2	0.02
Cranford (cdp) Union County	2	0.01
Pennsauken (cdp) Camden County	2	0.01

Top 10 Places Sorted by Percent
Based on all places, regardless of population

Place	Number	%
Waretown (cdp) Ocean County	1	0.06
Tewksbury (township) Hunterdon County	2	0.04
Hamilton (township) Atlantic County	6	0.03
Franklin (township) Hunterdon County	1	0.03
Lambertville (city) Hunterdon County	1	0.03
Delran (township) Burlington County	3	0.02
Princeton Meadows (cdp) Middlesex County	3	0.02
Ridgefield (borough) Bergen County	2	0.02
Ocean (township) Ocean County	1	0.02
Old Bridge (township) Middlesex County	4	0.01

Top 10 Places Sorted by Percent
Based on places with populations of 10,000 or more

Place	Number	%
Hamilton (township) Atlantic County	6	0.03
Delran (township) Burlington County	3	0.02
Princeton Meadows (cdp) Middlesex County	3	0.02
Ridgefield (borough) Bergen County	2	0.02
Old Bridge (township) Middlesex County	4	0.01
Montville (township) Morris County	3	0.01
Plainsboro (township) Middlesex County	3	0.01
Cranford (cdp) Union County	2	0.01
Pennsauken (cdp) Camden County	2	0.01
Willingboro (township) Burlington County	2	0.01

American Indian: Sioux

Top 10 Places Sorted by Number
Based on all places, regardless of population

Place	Number	%
Jersey City (city) Hudson County	20	0.01
Pemberton (township) Burlington County	14	0.05
Camden (city) Camden County	14	0.02
Newark (city) Essex County	14	0.01
Mount Olive (township) Morris County	13	0.05
Browns Mills (cdp) Burlington County	11	0.10
Williamstown (cdp) Gloucester County	11	0.09
Monroe (township) Gloucester County	11	0.04
Evesham (township) Burlington County	11	0.03
Jefferson (township) Morris County	9	0.05

Top 10 Places Sorted by Percent
Based on all places, regardless of population

Place	Number	%
Oldmans (township) Salem County	3	0.17
Fredon (township) Sussex County	4	0.14
Seaside Park (borough) Ocean County	3	0.13
Browns Mills (cdp) Burlington County	11	0.10
Williamstown (cdp) Gloucester County	11	0.09
Maurice River (township) Cumberland County	6	0.09
McGuire AFB (cdp) Burlington County	6	0.09
Montague (township) Sussex County	3	0.09
Shrewsbury (township) Monmouth County	1	0.09
Jamesburg (borough) Middlesex County	5	0.08

Top 10 Places Sorted by Percent
Based on places with populations of 10,000 or more

Place	Number	%
Browns Mills (cdp) Burlington County	11	0.10
Williamstown (cdp) Gloucester County	11	0.09
Wanaque (borough) Passaic County	6	0.06
Waterford (township) Camden County	6	0.06
Pemberton (township) Burlington County	14	0.05
Mount Olive (township) Morris County	13	0.05
Jefferson (township) Morris County	9	0.05
Monroe (township) Gloucester County	11	0.04
Collingswood (borough) Camden County	6	0.04
Pine Hill (borough) Camden County	4	0.04

American Indian: Tohono O'Odham

Top 10 Places Sorted by Number
Based on all places, regardless of population

Place	Number	%
Asbury Park (city) Monmouth County	4	0.02
Swedesboro (borough) Gloucester County	2	0.10
Dover (town) Morris County	2	0.01
North Plainfield (borough) Somerset County	2	0.01
Palisades Park (borough) Bergen County	2	0.01
Newark (city) Essex County	2	0.00
Phillipsburg (town) Warren County	1	0.01
Princeton (township) Mercer County	1	0.01
Sparta (township) Sussex County	1	0.01
West Orange (cdp) Essex County	1	0.00

Top 10 Places Sorted by Percent
Based on all places, regardless of population

Place	Number	%
Swedesboro (borough) Gloucester County	2	0.10
Asbury Park (city) Monmouth County	4	0.02
Dover (town) Morris County	2	0.01
North Plainfield (borough) Somerset County	2	0.01
Palisades Park (borough) Bergen County	2	0.01
Phillipsburg (town) Warren County	1	0.01
Princeton (township) Mercer County	1	0.01
Sparta (township) Sussex County	1	0.01
Newark (city) Essex County	2	0.00
West Orange (cdp) Essex County	1	0.00

Top 10 Places Sorted by Percent
Based on places with populations of 10,000 or more

Place	Number	%
Asbury Park (city) Monmouth County	4	0.02
Dover (town) Morris County	2	0.01
North Plainfield (borough) Somerset County	2	0.01
Palisades Park (borough) Bergen County	2	0.01
Phillipsburg (town) Warren County	1	0.01
Princeton (township) Mercer County	1	0.01
Sparta (township) Sussex County	1	0.01

Newark (city) Essex County	2	0.00
West Orange (cdp) Essex County	1	0.00

American Indian: Ute

Top 10 Places Sorted by Number
Based on all places, regardless of population

Place	Number	%
Wall (township) Monmouth County	4	0.02
Hampton (borough) Hunterdon County	3	0.19
Union City (city) Hudson County	3	0.00
Pittsgrove (township) Salem County	2	0.02
Bradley Beach (borough) Monmouth County	1	0.02
McGuire AFB (cdp) Burlington County	1	0.02
New Hanover (township) Burlington County	1	0.01
Point Pleasant (borough) Ocean County	1	0.01
Atlantic City (city) Atlantic County	1	0.00
Dover (township) Ocean County	1	0.00

Top 10 Places Sorted by Percent
Based on all places, regardless of population

Place	Number	%
Hampton (borough) Hunterdon County	3	0.19
Wall (township) Monmouth County	4	0.02
Pittsgrove (township) Salem County	2	0.02
Bradley Beach (borough) Monmouth County	1	0.02
McGuire AFB (cdp) Burlington County	1	0.02
New Hanover (township) Burlington County	1	0.01
Point Pleasant (borough) Ocean County	1	0.01
Union City (city) Hudson County	3	0.00
Atlantic City (city) Atlantic County	1	0.00
Dover (township) Ocean County	1	0.00

Top 10 Places Sorted by Percent
Based on places with populations of 10,000 or more

Place	Number	%
Wall (township) Monmouth County	4	0.02
Point Pleasant (borough) Ocean County	1	0.01
Union City (city) Hudson County	3	0.00
Atlantic City (city) Atlantic County	1	0.00
Dover (township) Ocean County	1	0.00
Gloucester (township) Camden County	1	0.00
Paramus (borough) Bergen County	1	0.00
Piscataway (township) Middlesex County	1	0.00
Toms River (cdp) Ocean County	1	0.00
Vineland (city) Cumberland County	1	0.00

American Indian: Yakama

Top 10 Places Sorted by Number
Based on all places, regardless of population

Place	Number	%
Rio Grande (cdp) Cape May County	4	0.16
Middle (township) Cape May County	4	0.02
Weehawken (township) Hudson County	2	0.01
Dover (town) Morris County	1	0.01
Mount Holly (township) Burlington County	1	0.01

Top 10 Places Sorted by Percent
Based on all places, regardless of population

Place	Number	%
Rio Grande (cdp) Cape May County	4	0.16
Middle (township) Cape May County	4	0.02
Weehawken (township) Hudson County	2	0.01
Dover (town) Morris County	1	0.01
Mount Holly (township) Burlington County	1	0.01

Top 10 Places Sorted by Percent
Based on places with populations of 10,000 or more

Place	Number	%
Middle (township) Cape May County	4	0.02

Notes: (cdp) census designated place; Refer to the User's Guide in the front of the book for more detailed information.

Weehawken (township) Hudson County | 2 | 0.01
Dover (town) Morris County | 1 | 0.01
Mount Holly (township) Burlington County | 1 | 0.01

American Indian: Yaqui

Top 10 Places Sorted by Number
Based on all places, regardless of population

Place	Number	%
Leonia (borough) Bergen County	3	0.03
Jackson (township) Ocean County	3	0.01
Parsippany-Troy Hills (township) Morris County	3	0.01
Eastampton (township) Burlington County	2	0.03
Wildwood Crest (borough) Cape May County	1	0.03
Glen Rock (borough) Bergen County	1	0.01
Hackettstown (town) Warren County	1	0.01
Highland Park (borough) Middlesex County	1	0.01
Dover (township) Ocean County	1	0.00
East Windsor (township) Mercer County	1	0.00

Top 10 Places Sorted by Percent
Based on all places, regardless of population

Place	Number	%
Leonia (borough) Bergen County	3	0.03
Eastampton (township) Burlington County	2	0.03
Wildwood Crest (borough) Cape May County	1	0.03
Jackson (township) Ocean County	3	0.01
Parsippany-Troy Hills (township) Morris County	3	0.01
Glen Rock (borough) Bergen County	1	0.01
Hackettstown (town) Warren County	1	0.01
Highland Park (borough) Middlesex County	1	0.01
Dover (township) Ocean County	1	0.00
East Windsor (township) Mercer County	1	0.00

Top 10 Places Sorted by Percent
Based on places with populations of 10,000 or more

Place	Number	%
Jackson (township) Ocean County	3	0.01
Parsippany-Troy Hills (township) Morris County	3	0.01
Glen Rock (borough) Bergen County	1	0.01
Hackettstown (town) Warren County	1	0.01
Highland Park (borough) Middlesex County	1	0.01
Dover (township) Ocean County	1	0.00
East Windsor (township) Mercer County	1	0.00
Fort Lee (borough) Bergen County	1	0.00
New Brunswick (city) Middlesex County	1	0.00
Ocean (township) Monmouth County	1	0.00

American Indian: Yuman

Top 10 Places Sorted by Number
Based on all places, regardless of population

Place	Number	%
Jackson (township) Ocean County	3	0.01
Mount Holly (township) Burlington County	1	0.01
Riverside (township) Burlington County	1	0.01
Bridgeton (city) Cumberland County	1	0.00
Jersey City (city) Hudson County	1	0.00

Top 10 Places Sorted by Percent
Based on all places, regardless of population

Place	Number	%
Jackson (township) Ocean County	3	0.01
Mount Holly (township) Burlington County	1	0.01
Riverside (township) Burlington County	1	0.01
Bridgeton (city) Cumberland County	1	0.00
Jersey City (city) Hudson County	1	0.00

Top 10 Places Sorted by Percent
Based on places with populations of 10,000 or more

Place	Number	%
Jackson (township) Ocean County	3	0.01
Mount Holly (township) Burlington County	1	0.01
Bridgeton (city) Cumberland County	1	0.00
Jersey City (city) Hudson County	1	0.00

American Indian: All other tribes

Top 10 Places Sorted by Number
Based on all places, regardless of population

Place	Number	%
Fairfield (township) Cumberland County	168	2.67
Bridgeton (city) Cumberland County	78	0.34
Vineland (city) Cumberland County	66	0.12
Newark (city) Essex County	65	0.02
Millville (city) Cumberland County	63	0.23
Hopewell (township) Cumberland County	62	1.40
Pennsauken (cdp) Camden County	57	0.16
Jersey City (city) Hudson County	44	0.02
Camden (city) Camden County	42	0.05
Upper Deerfield (township) Cumberland County	33	0.44

Top 10 Places Sorted by Percent
Based on all places, regardless of population

Place	Number	%
Fairfield (township) Cumberland County	168	2.67
Hopewell (township) Cumberland County	62	1.40
Fairton (cdp) Cumberland County	29	1.29
Deerfield (township) Cumberland County	32	1.09
Greenwich (township) Cumberland County	8	0.94
Rosenhayn (cdp) Cumberland County	10	0.91
Stow Creek (township) Cumberland County	9	0.63
Downe (township) Cumberland County	10	0.61
Upper Deerfield (township) Cumberland County	33	0.44
Lawrence (township) Cumberland County	11	0.40

Top 10 Places Sorted by Percent
Based on places with populations of 10,000 or more

Place	Number	%
Bridgeton (city) Cumberland County	78	0.34
Millville (city) Cumberland County	63	0.23
Pennsauken (cdp) Camden County	57	0.16
Moorestown-Lenola (cdp) Burlington County	22	0.16
Lindenwold (borough) Camden County	22	0.13
Vineland (city) Cumberland County	66	0.12
Moorestown (township) Burlington County	22	0.12
Lumberton (township) Burlington County	12	0.11
Pemberton (township) Burlington County	30	0.10
Cinnaminson (township) Burlington County	15	0.10

American Indian tribes, not specified

Top 10 Places Sorted by Number
Based on all places, regardless of population

Place	Number	%
Jersey City (city) Hudson County	188	0.08
Newark (city) Essex County	180	0.07
Elizabeth (city) Union County	116	0.10
Paterson (city) Passaic County	91	0.06
Union City (city) Hudson County	67	0.10
East Orange (city) Essex County	57	0.08
Camden (city) Camden County	56	0.07
West New York (town) Hudson County	51	0.11
Passaic (city) Passaic County	44	0.06
Trenton (city) Mercer County	41	0.05

Top 10 Places Sorted by Percent
Based on places with populations of 10,000 or more

Place	Number	%
Jackson (township) Ocean County	3	0.01
Mount Holly (township) Burlington County	1	0.01
Bridgeton (city) Cumberland County	1	0.00
Jersey City (city) Hudson County	1	0.00

Top 10 Places Sorted by Percent
Based on all places, regardless of population

Place	Number	%
Cedarville (cdp) Cumberland County	5	0.63
Salem (city) Salem County	28	0.48
Clinton (town) Hunterdon County	12	0.46
Cape May Point (borough) Cape May County	1	0.41
Fairfield (township) Cumberland County	23	0.37
Oldmans (township) Salem County	5	0.28
Hopewell (borough) Mercer County	5	0.25
Lawrence (township) Cumberland County	6	0.22
Stow Creek (township) Cumberland County	3	0.21
Fieldsboro (borough) Burlington County	1	0.19

Top 10 Places Sorted by Percent
Based on places with populations of 10,000 or more

Place	Number	%
Bridgeton (city) Cumberland County	30	0.13
Bound Brook (borough) Somerset County	13	0.13
Ridgefield Park (village) Bergen County	15	0.12
West New York (town) Hudson County	51	0.11
Elizabeth (city) Union County	116	0.10
Union City (city) Hudson County	67	0.10
Brigantine (city) Atlantic County	13	0.10
Freehold (borough) Monmouth County	11	0.10
Dover (town) Morris County	17	0.09
Lindenwold (borough) Camden County	15	0.09

Arab

Top 10 Places Sorted by Number
Based on all places, regardless of population

Place	Number	%
Jersey City (city) Hudson County	6,764	2.82
Clifton (city) Passaic County	2,641	3.36
Paterson (city) Passaic County	2,634	1.77
Bayonne (city) Hudson County	2,345	3.79
North Bergen (township) Hudson County	1,830	3.14
Wayne (cdp) Passaic County	1,448	2.68
East Brunswick (cdp) Middlesex County	1,307	2.80
Old Bridge (township) Middlesex County	1,140	1.89
Woodbridge (township) Middlesex County	1,027	1.06
Edison (cdp) Middlesex County	1,003	1.03

Top 10 Places Sorted by Percent
Based on all places, regardless of population

Place	Number	%
Deal (borough) Monmouth County	242	22.62
Haledon (borough) Passaic County	699	8.47
Prospect Park (borough) Passaic County	305	5.28
Madison Park (cdp) Middlesex County	327	4.75
Totowa (borough) Passaic County	422	4.26
Fairview (borough) Bergen County	565	4.26
Bayonne (city) Hudson County	2,345	3.79
Washington Township (cdp) Bergen County	316	3.54
Crandon Lakes (cdp) Sussex County	43	3.44
Clifton (city) Passaic County	2,641	3.36

Top 10 Places Sorted by Percent
Based on places with populations of 10,000 or more

Place	Number	%
Fairview (borough) Bergen County	565	4.26
Bayonne (city) Hudson County	2,345	3.79
Clifton (city) Passaic County	2,641	3.36
North Bergen (township) Hudson County	1,830	3.14
Little Falls (cdp) Passaic County	319	2.94
Hawthorne (borough) Passaic County	521	2.86
Jersey City (city) Hudson County	6,764	2.82
East Brunswick (cdp) Middlesex County	1,307	2.80
West Paterson (borough) Passaic County	298	2.71
Wayne (cdp) Passaic County	1,448	2.68

Arab: Arab/Arabic

Top 10 Places Sorted by Number
Based on all places, regardless of population

Place	Number	%
Paterson (city) Passaic County	1,171	0.78
Jersey City (city) Hudson County	770	0.32
Clifton (city) Passaic County	729	0.93
North Bergen (township) Hudson County	416	0.71
Haledon (borough) Passaic County	247	2.99
West New York (town) Hudson County	203	0.44
Prospect Park (borough) Passaic County	194	3.36
Woodbridge (township) Middlesex County	185	0.19
Garfield (city) Bergen County	171	0.57
Fairview (borough) Bergen County	169	1.27

Top 10 Places Sorted by Percent
Based on all places, regardless of population

Place	Number	%
Prospect Park (borough) Passaic County	194	3.36
Haledon (borough) Passaic County	247	2.99
Lavallette (borough) Ocean County	39	1.46
Park Ridge (borough) Bergen County	116	1.33
Fairview (borough) Bergen County	169	1.27
Liberty (township) Warren County	29	1.06
Clifton (city) Passaic County	729	0.93
Secaucus (town) Hudson County	148	0.93
Upper Freehold (township) Monmouth County	38	0.89
Paterson (city) Passaic County	1,171	0.78

Top 10 Places Sorted by Percent
Based on places with populations of 10,000 or more

Place	Number	%
Fairview (borough) Bergen County	169	1.27
Clifton (city) Passaic County	729	0.93
Secaucus (town) Hudson County	148	0.93
Paterson (city) Passaic County	1,171	0.78
West Paterson (borough) Passaic County	82	0.75
North Bergen (township) Hudson County	416	0.71
Guttenberg (town) Hudson County	69	0.65
Garfield (city) Bergen County	171	0.57
Palisades Park (borough) Bergen County	83	0.49
Wallington (borough) Bergen County	56	0.48

Arab: Egyptian

Top 10 Places Sorted by Number
Based on all places, regardless of population

Place	Number	%
Jersey City (city) Hudson County	4,820	2.01
Bayonne (city) Hudson County	1,958	3.17
East Brunswick (cdp) Middlesex County	1,128	2.41
Old Bridge (township) Middlesex County	900	1.49
Edison (cdp) Middlesex County	562	0.58
Woodbridge (township) Middlesex County	562	0.58
North Bergen (township) Hudson County	485	0.83
South Brunswick (township) Middlesex County	363	0.96
Sayreville (borough) Middlesex County	355	0.88
Hamilton (township) Mercer County	301	0.34

Top 10 Places Sorted by Percent
Based on all places, regardless of population

Place	Number	%
Madison Park (cdp) Middlesex County	286	4.15
Crandon Lakes (cdp) Sussex County	43	3.44
Bayonne (city) Hudson County	1,958	3.17
Monmouth Junction (cdp) Middlesex County	66	2.73
East Brunswick (cdp) Middlesex County	1,128	2.41
Brownville (cdp) Middlesex County	62	2.37
Plainsboro Center (cdp) Middlesex County	52	2.19
Jersey City (city) Hudson County	4,820	2.01
Dayton (cdp) Middlesex County	111	1.73

Fanwood (borough) Union County   119   1.66

Top 10 Places Sorted by Percent
Based on places with populations of 10,000 or more

Place	Number	%
Bayonne (city) Hudson County	1,958	3.17
East Brunswick (cdp) Middlesex County	1,128	2.41
Jersey City (city) Hudson County	4,820	2.01
Old Bridge (township) Middlesex County	900	1.49
Avenel (cdp) Middlesex County	259	1.48
Ridgefield Park (village) Bergen County	161	1.25
Fairview (borough) Bergen County	141	1.06
Secaucus (town) Hudson County	159	1.00
South Brunswick (township) Middlesex County	363	0.96
Rutherford (borough) Bergen County	174	0.96

Arab: Iraqi

Top 10 Places Sorted by Number
Based on all places, regardless of population

Place	Number	%
Princeton (township) Mercer County	57	0.36
Passaic (city) Passaic County	55	0.08
Cliffside Park (borough) Bergen County	43	0.19
Paramus (borough) Bergen County	40	0.16
Ridgewood (village) Bergen County	33	0.13
West Paterson (borough) Passaic County	32	0.29
Haworth (borough) Bergen County	29	0.86
Westfield (town) Union County	26	0.09
Washington (township) Mercer County	21	0.20
Livingston (cdp) Essex County	20	0.07

Top 10 Places Sorted by Percent
Based on all places, regardless of population

Place	Number	%
Haworth (borough) Bergen County	29	0.86
Deal (borough) Monmouth County	4	0.37
Princeton (township) Mercer County	57	0.36
West Paterson (borough) Passaic County	32	0.29
Washington (township) Mercer County	21	0.20
Cliffside Park (borough) Bergen County	43	0.19
Paramus (borough) Bergen County	40	0.16
Flemington (borough) Hunterdon County	6	0.14
Ridgewood (village) Bergen County	33	0.13
Glen Rock (borough) Bergen County	15	0.13

Top 10 Places Sorted by Percent
Based on places with populations of 10,000 or more

Place	Number	%
Princeton (township) Mercer County	57	0.36
West Paterson (borough) Passaic County	32	0.29
Washington (township) Mercer County	21	0.20
Cliffside Park (borough) Bergen County	43	0.19
Paramus (borough) Bergen County	40	0.16
Ridgewood (village) Bergen County	33	0.13
Glen Rock (borough) Bergen County	15	0.13
Weehawken (township) Hudson County	15	0.11
Hawthorne (borough) Passaic County	18	0.10
Westfield (town) Union County	26	0.09

Arab: Jordanian

Top 10 Places Sorted by Number
Based on all places, regardless of population

Place	Number	%
Paterson (city) Passaic County	165	0.11
Clifton (city) Passaic County	143	0.18
Jersey City (city) Hudson County	143	0.06
North Bergen (township) Hudson County	120	0.21
Bayonne (city) Hudson County	93	0.15
North Arlington (borough) Bergen County	90	0.59
Garfield (city) Bergen County	82	0.28

Hawthorne (borough) Passaic County   79   0.43
Barclay-Kingston (cdp) Camden County   53   0.49
Cherry Hill (township) Camden County   53   0.08

Top 10 Places Sorted by Percent
Based on all places, regardless of population

Place	Number	%
North Arlington (borough) Bergen County	90	0.59
Barclay-Kingston (cdp) Camden County	53	0.49
Hawthorne (borough) Passaic County	79	0.43
Dayton (cdp) Middlesex County	27	0.42
Keansburg (borough) Monmouth County	43	0.40
Wallington (borough) Bergen County	45	0.39
Echelon (cdp) Camden County	40	0.39
Newton (town) Sussex County	28	0.34
Point Pleasant Beach (borough) Ocean County	18	0.34
Ogdensburg (borough) Sussex County	9	0.34

Top 10 Places Sorted by Percent
Based on places with populations of 10,000 or more

Place	Number	%
North Arlington (borough) Bergen County	90	0.59
Barclay-Kingston (cdp) Camden County	53	0.49
Hawthorne (borough) Passaic County	79	0.43
Keansburg (borough) Monmouth County	43	0.40
Wallington (borough) Bergen County	45	0.39
Echelon (cdp) Camden County	40	0.39
Hasbrouck Heights (borough) Bergen County	37	0.32
Pompton Lakes (borough) Passaic County	31	0.29
Garfield (city) Bergen County	82	0.28
New Milford (borough) Bergen County	42	0.26

Arab: Lebanese

Top 10 Places Sorted by Number
Based on all places, regardless of population

Place	Number	%
Franklin (township) Somerset County	394	0.77
Jersey City (city) Hudson County	387	0.16
North Brunswick Twp (cdp) Middlesex County	381	1.05
North Bergen (township) Hudson County	320	0.55
New Brunswick (city) Middlesex County	223	0.46
Wayne (cdp) Passaic County	196	0.36
Edison (cdp) Middlesex County	185	0.19
Paterson (city) Passaic County	181	0.12
Middletown (township) Monmouth County	169	0.25
Brick (township) Ocean County	169	0.22

Top 10 Places Sorted by Percent
Based on all places, regardless of population

Place	Number	%
Deal (borough) Monmouth County	41	3.83
Leonardo (cdp) Monmouth County	72	2.51
Lavallette (borough) Ocean County	50	1.88
Washington Township (cdp) Bergen County	166	1.86
East Freehold (cdp) Monmouth County	65	1.28
Lawrenceville (cdp) Mercer County	50	1.22
Fair Haven (borough) Monmouth County	72	1.21
Princeton Junction (cdp) Mercer County	29	1.21
North Brunswick Twp (cdp) Middlesex County	381	1.05
Little Falls (cdp) Passaic County	113	1.04

Top 10 Places Sorted by Percent
Based on places with populations of 10,000 or more

Place	Number	%
North Brunswick Twp (cdp) Middlesex County	381	1.05
Little Falls (cdp) Passaic County	113	1.04
Hillsdale (borough) Bergen County	94	0.93
East Hanover (township) Morris County	98	0.86
Wanaque (borough) Passaic County	82	0.80
Franklin (township) Somerset County	394	0.77
Pompton Lakes (borough) Passaic County	79	0.74

Notes: (cdp) census designated place; Refer to the User's Guide in the front of the book for more detailed information.

Place	Number	%
Princeton Meadows (cdp) Middlesex County	84	0.63
Ridgefield (borough) Bergen County	68	0.63
North Bergen (township) Hudson County	320	0.55

Arab: Moroccan

Top 10 Places Sorted by Number
Based on all places, regardless of population

Place	Number	%
Jersey City (city) Hudson County	223	0.09
Paterson (city) Passaic County	115	0.08
West Orange (cdp) Essex County	98	0.22
Lakewood (township) Ocean County	88	0.15
Cherry Hill (township) Camden County	78	0.11
Franklin (township) Somerset County	58	0.11
Cliffside Park (borough) Bergen County	57	0.25
Guttenberg (town) Hudson County	51	0.48
North Bergen (township) Hudson County	50	0.09
Teaneck (cdp) Bergen County	49	0.12

Top 10 Places Sorted by Percent
Based on all places, regardless of population

Place	Number	%
Seaside Heights (borough) Ocean County	34	1.08
Wrightstown (borough) Burlington County	4	0.54
Rochelle Park (cdp) Bergen County	28	0.51
Atlantic Highlands (borough) Monmouth County	23	0.49
Guttenberg (town) Hudson County	51	0.48
Wantage (township) Sussex County	43	0.41
Allenhurst (borough) Monmouth County	3	0.41
Deal (borough) Monmouth County	4	0.37
Leonia (borough) Bergen County	31	0.35
Wenonah (borough) Gloucester County	8	0.35

Top 10 Places Sorted by Percent
Based on places with populations of 10,000 or more

Place	Number	%
Guttenberg (town) Hudson County	51	0.48
Wantage (township) Sussex County	43	0.41
Little Ferry (borough) Bergen County	30	0.28
Cliffside Park (borough) Bergen County	57	0.25
Cherry Hill Mall (cdp) Camden County	31	0.23
West Orange (cdp) Essex County	98	0.22
Ventnor City (city) Atlantic County	28	0.22
Millburn (cdp) Essex County	42	0.21
Greentree (cdp) Camden County	24	0.21
Roselle (borough) Union County	43	0.20

Arab: Palestinian

Top 10 Places Sorted by Number
Based on all places, regardless of population

Place	Number	%
Paterson (city) Passaic County	556	0.37
North Bergen (township) Hudson County	354	0.61
Clifton (city) Passaic County	298	0.38
Passaic (city) Passaic County	207	0.31
Saddle Brook (cdp) Bergen County	143	1.09
Garfield (city) Bergen County	121	0.41
Fairview (borough) Bergen County	120	0.91
Newton (town) Sussex County	94	1.14
Union City (city) Hudson County	88	0.13
Howell (township) Monmouth County	86	0.18

Top 10 Places Sorted by Percent
Based on all places, regardless of population

Place	Number	%
Newton (town) Sussex County	94	1.14
Heathcote (cdp) Middlesex County	51	1.11
Saddle Brook (cdp) Bergen County	143	1.09
Fairview (borough) Bergen County	120	0.91
Haledon (borough) Passaic County	74	0.90

Place	Number	%
North Bergen (township) Hudson County	354	0.61
Prospect Park (borough) Passaic County	35	0.61
Ridgefield (borough) Bergen County	53	0.49
Woodlynne (borough) Camden County	12	0.43
Garfield (city) Bergen County	121	0.41

Top 10 Places Sorted by Percent
Based on places with populations of 10,000 or more

Place	Number	%
Saddle Brook (cdp) Bergen County	143	1.09
Fairview (borough) Bergen County	120	0.91
North Bergen (township) Hudson County	354	0.61
Ridgefield (borough) Bergen County	53	0.49
Garfield (city) Bergen County	121	0.41
Clifton (city) Passaic County	298	0.38
Paterson (city) Passaic County	556	0.37
Elmwood Park (borough) Bergen County	67	0.35
Hillsdale (borough) Bergen County	33	0.33
Passaic (city) Passaic County	207	0.31

Arab: Syrian

Top 10 Places Sorted by Number
Based on all places, regardless of population

Place	Number	%
Clifton (city) Passaic County	1,010	1.28
Wayne (cdp) Passaic County	853	1.58
Haledon (borough) Passaic County	371	4.50
Ocean (township) Monmouth County	337	1.25
Paterson (city) Passaic County	329	0.22
Totowa (borough) Passaic County	287	2.91
Hawthorne (borough) Passaic County	266	1.46
Lodi (borough) Bergen County	215	0.90
Jersey City (city) Hudson County	181	0.08
Deal (borough) Monmouth County	180	16.82

Top 10 Places Sorted by Percent
Based on all places, regardless of population

Place	Number	%
Deal (borough) Monmouth County	180	16.82
Haledon (borough) Passaic County	371	4.50
Totowa (borough) Passaic County	287	2.91
Saddle River (borough) Bergen County	76	2.37
Little Falls (cdp) Passaic County	173	1.59
Wayne (cdp) Passaic County	853	1.58
Hawthorne (borough) Passaic County	266	1.46
Greenwich (township) Warren County	59	1.35
Clifton (city) Passaic County	1,010	1.28
Ocean (township) Monmouth County	337	1.25

Top 10 Places Sorted by Percent
Based on places with populations of 10,000 or more

Place	Number	%
Little Falls (cdp) Passaic County	173	1.59
Wayne (cdp) Passaic County	853	1.58
Hawthorne (borough) Passaic County	266	1.46
Clifton (city) Passaic County	1,010	1.28
Ocean (township) Monmouth County	337	1.25
Colts Neck (township) Monmouth County	130	1.05
New Milford (borough) Bergen County	167	1.02
Lodi (borough) Bergen County	215	0.90
West Freehold (cdp) Monmouth County	97	0.77
Saddle Brook (cdp) Bergen County	97	0.74

Arab: Other

Top 10 Places Sorted by Number
Based on all places, regardless of population

Place	Number	%
Jersey City (city) Hudson County	192	0.08
Ocean (township) Monmouth County	129	0.48
Lodi (borough) Bergen County	113	0.47

Place	Number	%
Edison (cdp) Middlesex County	101	0.10
Fort Lee (borough) Bergen County	91	0.26
Cliffside Park (borough) Bergen County	78	0.34
Paramus (borough) Bergen County	72	0.28
Paterson (city) Passaic County	63	0.04
Hackensack (city) Bergen County	62	0.15
Eatontown (borough) Monmouth County	59	0.42

Top 10 Places Sorted by Percent
Based on all places, regardless of population

Place	Number	%
Port Monmouth (cdp) Monmouth County	27	0.74
Lawrenceville (cdp) Mercer County	24	0.59
Vernon Valley (cdp) Sussex County	10	0.58
Watchung (borough) Somerset County	32	0.57
Twin Rivers (cdp) Mercer County	41	0.55
Lambertville (city) Hunterdon County	20	0.52
North Haledon (borough) Passaic County	40	0.51
Oakhurst (cdp) Monmouth County	21	0.51
Ocean (township) Monmouth County	129	0.48
Lodi (borough) Bergen County	113	0.47

Top 10 Places Sorted by Percent
Based on places with populations of 10,000 or more

Place	Number	%
Ocean (township) Monmouth County	129	0.48
Lodi (borough) Bergen County	113	0.47
Eatontown (borough) Monmouth County	59	0.42
West Paterson (borough) Passaic County	41	0.37
Cliffside Park (borough) Bergen County	78	0.34
Paramus (borough) Bergen County	72	0.28
Weehawken (township) Hudson County	37	0.27
Fort Lee (borough) Bergen County	91	0.26
South River (borough) Middlesex County	39	0.25
Highland Park (borough) Middlesex County	32	0.23

Armenian

Top 10 Places Sorted by Number
Based on all places, regardless of population

Place	Number	%
Cliffside Park (borough) Bergen County	879	3.82
Fort Lee (borough) Bergen County	582	1.64
Paramus (borough) Bergen County	445	1.73
New Milford (borough) Bergen County	367	2.24
Fairview (borough) Bergen County	320	2.41
Palisades Park (borough) Bergen County	320	1.87
Wayne (cdp) Passaic County	309	0.57
Oradell (borough) Bergen County	307	3.82
Ridgefield (borough) Bergen County	294	2.71
North Bergen (township) Hudson County	269	0.46

Top 10 Places Sorted by Percent
Based on all places, regardless of population

Place	Number	%
Cliffside Park (borough) Bergen County	879	3.82
Oradell (borough) Bergen County	307	3.82
Englewood Cliffs (borough) Bergen County	184	3.46
Emerson (borough) Bergen County	200	2.78
Demarest (borough) Bergen County	133	2.75
Ridgefield (borough) Bergen County	294	2.71
Fairview (borough) Bergen County	320	2.41
Old Tappan (borough) Bergen County	128	2.33
New Milford (borough) Bergen County	367	2.24
Allendale (borough) Bergen County	145	2.16

Top 10 Places Sorted by Percent
Based on places with populations of 10,000 or more

Place	Number	%
Cliffside Park (borough) Bergen County	879	3.82
Ridgefield (borough) Bergen County	294	2.71
Fairview (borough) Bergen County	320	2.41

Notes: (cdp) census designated place; Refer to the User's Guide in the front of the book for more detailed information.

Place	Number	%
New Milford (borough) Bergen County	367	2.24
Palisades Park (borough) Bergen County	320	1.87
Paramus (borough) Bergen County	445	1.73
Tenafly (borough) Bergen County	229	1.66
Fort Lee (borough) Bergen County	582	1.64
River Edge (borough) Bergen County	147	1.34
Westwood (borough) Bergen County	142	1.29

Asian

Top 10 Places Sorted by Number
Based on all places, regardless of population

Place	Number	%
Jersey City (city) Hudson County	42,849	17.85
Edison (cdp) Middlesex County	29,669	30.37
Woodbridge (township) Middlesex County	15,042	15.47
Piscataway (township) Middlesex County	13,167	26.08
Fort Lee (borough) Bergen County	11,548	32.57
Parsippany-Troy Hills (township) Morris County	9,870	19.49
East Brunswick (cdp) Middlesex County	8,027	17.17
Palisades Park (borough) Bergen County	7,259	42.52
Old Bridge (township) Middlesex County	7,203	11.91
South Brunswick (township) Middlesex County	7,160	18.97

Top 10 Places Sorted by Percent
Based on all places, regardless of population

Place	Number	%
Palisades Park (borough) Bergen County	7,259	42.52
Plainsboro Center (cdp) Middlesex County	890	40.29
Society Hill (cdp) Middlesex County	1,357	35.67
Fort Lee (borough) Bergen County	11,548	32.57
Plainsboro (township) Middlesex County	6,432	31.82
Princeton Meadows (cdp) Middlesex County	4,211	31.34
Englewood Cliffs (borough) Bergen County	1,634	30.70
Edison (cdp) Middlesex County	29,669	30.37
Leonia (borough) Bergen County	2,446	27.44
Iselin (cdp) Middlesex County	4,409	26.40

Top 10 Places Sorted by Percent
Based on places with populations of 10,000 or more

Place	Number	%
Palisades Park (borough) Bergen County	7,259	42.52
Fort Lee (borough) Bergen County	11,548	32.57
Plainsboro (township) Middlesex County	6,432	31.82
Princeton Meadows (cdp) Middlesex County	4,211	31.34
Edison (cdp) Middlesex County	29,669	30.37
Iselin (cdp) Middlesex County	4,409	26.40
Piscataway (township) Middlesex County	13,167	26.08
West Windsor (township) Mercer County	5,268	24.05
Bergenfield (borough) Bergen County	5,678	21.63
Avenel (cdp) Middlesex County	3,640	20.74

Asian: Bangladeshi

Top 10 Places Sorted by Number
Based on all places, regardless of population

Place	Number	%
Paterson (city) Passaic County	729	0.49
Atlantic City (city) Atlantic County	303	0.75
Jersey City (city) Hudson County	182	0.08
Edison (cdp) Middlesex County	87	0.09
Elizabeth (city) Union County	72	0.06
Newark (city) Essex County	67	0.02
Ventnor City (city) Atlantic County	64	0.50
Woodbridge (township) Middlesex County	50	0.05
Montclair (cdp) Essex County	47	0.12
Hackensack (city) Bergen County	47	0.11

Top 10 Places Sorted by Percent
Based on all places, regardless of population

Place	Number	%
Atlantic City (city) Atlantic County	303	0.75

Place	Number	%
Haledon (borough) Passaic County	42	0.51
Ventnor City (city) Atlantic County	64	0.50
Paterson (city) Passaic County	729	0.49
Monmouth Junction (cdp) Middlesex County	9	0.33
Society Hill (cdp) Middlesex County	12	0.32
Bordentown (city) Burlington County	12	0.30
Berlin (borough) Camden County	18	0.29
Lindenwold (borough) Camden County	44	0.25
Brooklawn (borough) Camden County	6	0.25

Top 10 Places Sorted by Percent
Based on places with populations of 10,000 or more

Place	Number	%
Atlantic City (city) Atlantic County	303	0.75
Ventnor City (city) Atlantic County	64	0.50
Paterson (city) Passaic County	729	0.49
Lindenwold (borough) Camden County	44	0.25
Brigantine (city) Atlantic County	30	0.24
Elmwood Park (borough) Bergen County	39	0.21
Echelon (cdp) Camden County	21	0.20
Avenel (cdp) Middlesex County	22	0.13
Highland Park (borough) Middlesex County	18	0.13
Montclair (cdp) Essex County	47	0.12

Asian: Cambodian

Top 10 Places Sorted by Number
Based on all places, regardless of population

Place	Number	%
Camden (city) Camden County	267	0.33
Pennsauken (cdp) Camden County	122	0.34
Cherry Hill (township) Camden County	65	0.09
Woodlynne (borough) Camden County	28	1.00
Trenton (city) Mercer County	24	0.03
Hamilton (township) Mercer County	23	0.03
Barclay-Kingston (cdp) Camden County	21	0.20
Newark (city) Essex County	15	0.01
Atlantic City (city) Atlantic County	13	0.03
Evesham (township) Burlington County	13	0.03

Top 10 Places Sorted by Percent
Based on all places, regardless of population

Place	Number	%
Woodlynne (borough) Camden County	28	1.00
Pennsauken (cdp) Camden County	122	0.34
Camden (city) Camden County	267	0.33
Barclay-Kingston (cdp) Camden County	21	0.20
Golden Triangle (cdp) Camden County	7	0.20
Rockaway (borough) Morris County	10	0.15
Ashland (cdp) Camden County	11	0.13
Merchantville (borough) Camden County	4	0.11
Cherry Hill (township) Camden County	65	0.09
Wanamassa (cdp) Monmouth County	4	0.09

Top 10 Places Sorted by Percent
Based on places with populations of 10,000 or more

Place	Number	%
Pennsauken (cdp) Camden County	122	0.34
Camden (city) Camden County	267	0.33
Barclay-Kingston (cdp) Camden County	21	0.20
Cherry Hill (township) Camden County	65	0.09
Cherry Hill Mall (cdp) Camden County	10	0.08
Lindenwold (borough) Camden County	11	0.06
Hopatcong (borough) Sussex County	8	0.05
Greentree (cdp) Camden County	6	0.05
Cinnaminson (township) Burlington County	6	0.04
Springdale (cdp) Camden County	6	0.04

Asian: Chinese, except Taiwanese

Top 10 Places Sorted by Number
Based on all places, regardless of population

Place	Number	%
Edison (cdp) Middlesex County	5,824	5.96
Jersey City (city) Hudson County	3,811	1.59
East Brunswick (cdp) Middlesex County	3,245	6.94
Parsippany-Troy Hills (township) Morris County	2,870	5.67
Piscataway (township) Middlesex County	2,478	4.91
Marlboro (township) Monmouth County	2,206	6.06
Fort Lee (borough) Bergen County	1,971	5.56
West Windsor (township) Mercer County	1,820	8.31
Plainsboro (township) Middlesex County	1,729	8.55
Livingston (cdp) Essex County	1,723	6.29

Top 10 Places Sorted by Percent
Based on all places, regardless of population

Place	Number	%
Holmdel (township) Monmouth County	1,574	9.97
Plainsboro (township) Middlesex County	1,729	8.55
Englewood Cliffs (borough) Bergen County	448	8.42
West Windsor (township) Mercer County	1,820	8.31
Society Hill (cdp) Middlesex County	311	8.18
Princeton Meadows (cdp) Middlesex County	1,037	7.72
Harrison (town) Hudson County	1,042	7.22
Plainsboro Center (cdp) Middlesex County	156	7.06
East Brunswick (cdp) Middlesex County	3,245	6.94
Livingston (cdp) Essex County	1,723	6.29

Top 10 Places Sorted by Percent
Based on places with populations of 10,000 or more

Place	Number	%
Holmdel (township) Monmouth County	1,574	9.97
Plainsboro (township) Middlesex County	1,729	8.55
West Windsor (township) Mercer County	1,820	8.31
Princeton Meadows (cdp) Middlesex County	1,037	7.72
Harrison (town) Hudson County	1,042	7.22
East Brunswick (cdp) Middlesex County	3,245	6.94
Livingston (cdp) Essex County	1,723	6.29
Marlboro (township) Monmouth County	2,206	6.06
Edison (cdp) Middlesex County	5,824	5.96
Montgomery (township) Somerset County	1,023	5.85

Asian: Filipino

Top 10 Places Sorted by Number
Based on all places, regardless of population

Place	Number	%
Jersey City (city) Hudson County	16,777	6.99
Bergenfield (borough) Bergen County	3,254	12.40
Edison (cdp) Middlesex County	2,516	2.58
Woodbridge (township) Middlesex County	2,284	2.35
Piscataway (township) Middlesex County	2,235	4.43
Belleville (cdp) Essex County	2,224	6.19
Union (cdp) Union County	2,184	4.01
Bloomfield (cdp) Essex County	1,714	3.59
Clifton (city) Passaic County	1,670	2.12
Old Bridge (township) Middlesex County	1,350	2.23

Top 10 Places Sorted by Percent
Based on all places, regardless of population

Place	Number	%
Bergenfield (borough) Bergen County	3,254	12.40
Jersey City (city) Hudson County	16,777	6.99
New Milford (borough) Bergen County	1,119	6.82
Belleville (cdp) Essex County	2,224	6.19
Dumont (borough) Bergen County	884	5.05
Society Hill (cdp) Middlesex County	187	4.92
Fords (cdp) Middlesex County	677	4.50
Piscataway (township) Middlesex County	2,235	4.43
Union (cdp) Union County	2,184	4.01

Notes: (cdp) census designated place; Refer to the User's Guide in the front of the book for more detailed information.

Raritan (borough) Somerset County   229   3.61

Top 10 Places Sorted by Percent
Based on places with populations of 10,000 or more

Place	Number	%
Bergenfield (borough) Bergen County	3,254	12.40
Jersey City (city) Hudson County	16,777	6.99
New Milford (borough) Bergen County	1,119	6.82
Belleville (cdp) Essex County	2,224	6.19
Dumont (borough) Bergen County	884	5.05
Fords (cdp) Middlesex County	677	4.50
Piscataway (township) Middlesex County	2,235	4.43
Union (cdp) Union County	2,184	4.01
Bloomfield (cdp) Essex County	1,714	3.59
Secaucus (town) Hudson County	549	3.45

Asian: Hmong

Top 10 Places Sorted by Number
Based on all places, regardless of population

Place	Number	%
Franklin (township) Somerset County	8	0.02
Gloucester (township) Camden County	5	0.01
Passaic (city) Passaic County	4	0.01
Somerset (cdp) Somerset County	3	0.01
Colts Neck (township) Monmouth County	2	0.02
Jefferson (township) Morris County	2	0.01
Dover (town) Morris County	1	0.01
East Rutherford (borough) Bergen County	1	0.01
Elizabeth (city) Union County	1	0.00
Galloway (township) Atlantic County	1	0.00

Top 10 Places Sorted by Percent
Based on all places, regardless of population

Place	Number	%
Franklin (township) Somerset County	8	0.02
Colts Neck (township) Monmouth County	2	0.02
Gloucester (township) Camden County	5	0.01
Passaic (city) Passaic County	4	0.01
Somerset (cdp) Somerset County	3	0.01
Jefferson (township) Morris County	2	0.01
Dover (town) Morris County	1	0.01
East Rutherford (borough) Bergen County	1	0.01
Elizabeth (city) Union County	1	0.00
Galloway (township) Atlantic County	1	0.00

Top 10 Places Sorted by Percent
Based on places with populations of 10,000 or more

Place	Number	%
Franklin (township) Somerset County	8	0.02
Colts Neck (township) Monmouth County	2	0.02
Gloucester (township) Camden County	5	0.01
Passaic (city) Passaic County	4	0.01
Somerset (cdp) Somerset County	3	0.01
Jefferson (township) Morris County	2	0.01
Dover (town) Morris County	1	0.01
Elizabeth (city) Union County	1	0.00
Galloway (township) Atlantic County	1	0.00
Newark (city) Essex County	1	0.00

Asian: Indian

Top 10 Places Sorted by Number
Based on all places, regardless of population

Place	Number	%
Edison (cdp) Middlesex County	17,343	17.75
Jersey City (city) Hudson County	14,206	5.92
Woodbridge (township) Middlesex County	8,937	9.19
Piscataway (township) Middlesex County	6,307	12.49
Parsippany-Troy Hills (township) Morris County	4,251	8.39
South Brunswick (township) Middlesex County	3,954	10.48
Franklin (township) Somerset County	3,574	7.02

Plainsboro (township) Middlesex County	3,431	16.97
Old Bridge (township) Middlesex County	3,219	5.32
North Brunswick Twp (cdp) Middlesex County	3,158	8.70

Top 10 Places Sorted by Percent
Based on all places, regardless of population

Place	Number	%
Plainsboro Center (cdp) Middlesex County	603	27.30
Society Hill (cdp) Middlesex County	713	18.74
Edison (cdp) Middlesex County	17,343	17.75
Iselin (cdp) Middlesex County	2,912	17.44
Princeton Meadows (cdp) Middlesex County	2,305	17.16
Plainsboro (township) Middlesex County	3,431	16.97
Dayton (cdp) Middlesex County	980	15.72
Madison Park (cdp) Middlesex County	985	14.22
Avenel (cdp) Middlesex County	2,395	13.65
Piscataway (township) Middlesex County	6,307	12.49

Top 10 Places Sorted by Percent
Based on places with populations of 10,000 or more

Place	Number	%
Edison (cdp) Middlesex County	17,343	17.75
Iselin (cdp) Middlesex County	2,912	17.44
Princeton Meadows (cdp) Middlesex County	2,305	17.16
Plainsboro (township) Middlesex County	3,431	16.97
Avenel (cdp) Middlesex County	2,395	13.65
Piscataway (township) Middlesex County	6,307	12.49
South Brunswick (township) Middlesex County	3,954	10.48
Woodbridge (township) Middlesex County	8,937	9.19
West Windsor (township) Mercer County	1,973	9.01
North Brunswick Twp (cdp) Middlesex County	3,158	8.70

Asian: Indonesian

Top 10 Places Sorted by Number
Based on all places, regardless of population

Place	Number	%
Edison (cdp) Middlesex County	182	0.19
Woodbridge (township) Middlesex County	154	0.16
Avenel (cdp) Middlesex County	108	0.62
Jersey City (city) Hudson County	45	0.02
Secaucus (town) Hudson County	44	0.28
Iselin (cdp) Middlesex County	35	0.21
Metuchen (borough) Middlesex County	30	0.23
Piscataway (township) Middlesex County	30	0.06
South Plainfield (borough) Middlesex County	28	0.13
Trenton (city) Mercer County	22	0.03

Top 10 Places Sorted by Percent
Based on all places, regardless of population

Place	Number	%
Avenel (cdp) Middlesex County	108	0.62
Sea Bright (borough) Monmouth County	6	0.33
Secaucus (town) Hudson County	44	0.28
Metuchen (borough) Middlesex County	30	0.23
Iselin (cdp) Middlesex County	35	0.21
Edison (cdp) Middlesex County	182	0.19
Woodbridge (township) Middlesex County	154	0.16
Middlesex (borough) Middlesex County	19	0.14
Budd Lake (cdp) Morris County	11	0.14
South Plainfield (borough) Middlesex County	28	0.13

Top 10 Places Sorted by Percent
Based on places with populations of 10,000 or more

Place	Number	%
Avenel (cdp) Middlesex County	108	0.62
Secaucus (town) Hudson County	44	0.28
Metuchen (borough) Middlesex County	30	0.23
Iselin (cdp) Middlesex County	35	0.21
Edison (cdp) Middlesex County	182	0.19
Woodbridge (township) Middlesex County	154	0.16
Middlesex (borough) Middlesex County	19	0.14

South Plainfield (borough) Middlesex County	28	0.13
Cedar Grove (cdp) Essex County	12	0.10
Tenafly (borough) Bergen County	11	0.08

Asian: Japanese

Top 10 Places Sorted by Number
Based on all places, regardless of population

Place	Number	%
Fort Lee (borough) Bergen County	2,161	6.09
Jersey City (city) Hudson County	486	0.20
Cliffside Park (borough) Bergen County	424	1.84
Ridgewood (village) Bergen County	423	1.70
Paramus (borough) Bergen County	326	1.27
Tenafly (borough) Bergen County	282	1.27
Leonia (borough) Bergen County	274	3.07
Pemberton (township) Burlington County	270	0.94
Edgewater (borough) Bergen County	247	3.22
West Windsor (township) Mercer County	232	1.06

Top 10 Places Sorted by Percent
Based on all places, regardless of population

Place	Number	%
Fort Lee (borough) Bergen County	2,161	6.09
Demarest (borough) Bergen County	180	3.72
Edgewater (borough) Bergen County	247	3.22
Leonia (borough) Bergen County	274	3.07
Englewood Cliffs (borough) Bergen County	155	2.91
Cresskill (borough) Bergen County	200	2.58
Haworth (borough) Bergen County	84	2.48
Upper Deerfield (township) Cumberland County	160	2.12
Tenafly (borough) Bergen County	282	2.04
Seabrook Farms (cdp) Cumberland County	33	1.92

Top 10 Places Sorted by Percent
Based on places with populations of 10,000 or more

Place	Number	%
Fort Lee (borough) Bergen County	2,161	6.09
Tenafly (borough) Bergen County	282	2.04
Cliffside Park (borough) Bergen County	424	1.84
Ridgewood (village) Bergen County	423	1.70
River Edge (borough) Bergen County	154	1.41
Glen Rock (borough) Bergen County	149	1.29
Paramus (borough) Bergen County	326	1.27
Palisades Park (borough) Bergen County	203	1.19
Ramsey (borough) Bergen County	154	1.07
West Windsor (township) Mercer County	232	1.06

Asian: Korean

Top 10 Places Sorted by Number
Based on all places, regardless of population

Place	Number	%
Palisades Park (borough) Bergen County	6,211	36.38
Fort Lee (borough) Bergen County	6,091	17.18
Edison (cdp) Middlesex County	1,647	1.69
Cliffside Park (borough) Bergen County	1,620	7.04
Ridgefield (borough) Bergen County	1,550	14.31
Leonia (borough) Bergen County	1,537	17.24
Jersey City (city) Hudson County	1,507	0.63
Cherry Hill (township) Camden County	1,409	2.01
Tenafly (borough) Bergen County	1,332	9.65
Paramus (borough) Bergen County	1,253	4.87

Top 10 Places Sorted by Percent
Based on all places, regardless of population

Place	Number	%
Palisades Park (borough) Bergen County	6,211	36.38
Leonia (borough) Bergen County	1,537	17.24
Fort Lee (borough) Bergen County	6,091	17.18
Ridgefield (borough) Bergen County	1,550	14.31
Closter (borough) Bergen County	1,069	12.75

Norwood (borough) Bergen County		730	12.69
Edgewater (borough) Bergen County		908	11.83
Englewood Cliffs (borough) Bergen County		626	11.76
Demarest (borough) Bergen County		508	10.49
Cresskill (borough) Bergen County		784	10.12

Top 10 Places Sorted by Percent
Based on places with populations of 10,000 or more

Place	Number	%
Palisades Park (borough) Bergen County	6,211	36.38
Fort Lee (borough) Bergen County	6,091	17.18
Ridgefield (borough) Bergen County	1,550	14.31
Tenafly (borough) Bergen County	1,332	9.65
Little Ferry (borough) Bergen County	865	8.01
Cliffside Park (borough) Bergen County	1,620	7.04
Rutherford (borough) Bergen County	995	5.49
River Edge (borough) Bergen County	553	5.05
Paramus (borough) Bergen County	1,253	4.87
Greentree (cdp) Camden County	374	3.24

Asian: Laotian

Top 10 Places Sorted by Number
Based on all places, regardless of population

Place	Number	%
Egg Harbor (township) Atlantic County	72	0.23
Pleasantville (city) Atlantic County	58	0.31
Hamilton (township) Atlantic County	36	0.18
Atlantic City (city) Atlantic County	26	0.06
Lodi (borough) Bergen County	23	0.10
Lyndhurst (cdp) Bergen County	19	0.10
Galloway (township) Atlantic County	19	0.06
Jersey City (city) Hudson County	18	0.01
Pomona (cdp) Atlantic County	16	0.40
North Plainfield (borough) Somerset County	14	0.07

Top 10 Places Sorted by Percent
Based on all places, regardless of population

Place	Number	%
Pomona (cdp) Atlantic County	16	0.40
Pleasantville (city) Atlantic County	58	0.31
Egg Harbor (township) Atlantic County	72	0.23
Hamilton (township) Atlantic County	36	0.18
Carlstadt (borough) Bergen County	10	0.17
Mendham (borough) Morris County	8	0.16
East Rutherford (borough) Bergen County	13	0.15
Ogdensburg (borough) Sussex County	4	0.15
Lodi (borough) Bergen County	23	0.10
Lyndhurst (cdp) Bergen County	19	0.10

Top 10 Places Sorted by Percent
Based on places with populations of 10,000 or more

Place	Number	%
Pleasantville (city) Atlantic County	58	0.31
Egg Harbor (township) Atlantic County	72	0.23
Hamilton (township) Atlantic County	36	0.18
Lodi (borough) Bergen County	23	0.10
Lyndhurst (cdp) Bergen County	19	0.10
Leisure Village W-Pine Lake Pk (cdp) Ocean Co.	11	0.10
North Plainfield (borough) Somerset County	14	0.07
Bound Brook (borough) Somerset County	7	0.07
Atlantic City (city) Atlantic County	26	0.06
Galloway (township) Atlantic County	19	0.06

Asian: Malaysian

Top 10 Places Sorted by Number
Based on all places, regardless of population

Place	Number	%
Jersey City (city) Hudson County	56	0.02
East Brunswick (cdp) Middlesex County	17	0.04
Fort Lee (borough) Bergen County	16	0.05

Parsippany-Troy Hills (township) Morris County		15	0.03
Teaneck (cdp) Bergen County		13	0.03
Atlantic City (city) Atlantic County		11	0.03
Piscataway (township) Middlesex County		11	0.02
Paramus (borough) Bergen County		10	0.04
Perth Amboy (city) Middlesex County		10	0.02
Dover (township) Ocean County		10	0.01

Top 10 Places Sorted by Percent
Based on all places, regardless of population

Place	Number	%
South Toms River (borough) Ocean County	8	0.22
Glen Gardner (borough) Hunterdon County	4	0.21
Englewood Cliffs (borough) Bergen County	8	0.15
Hopewell (borough) Mercer County	3	0.15
Far Hills (borough) Somerset County	1	0.12
New Egypt (cdp) Ocean County	2	0.08
Pemberton (borough) Burlington County	1	0.08
River Edge (borough) Bergen County	8	0.07
Edgewater (borough) Bergen County	5	0.07
Lopatcong (township) Warren County	4	0.07

Top 10 Places Sorted by Percent
Based on places with populations of 10,000 or more

Place	Number	%
River Edge (borough) Bergen County	8	0.07
Fort Lee (borough) Bergen County	16	0.05
East Brunswick (cdp) Middlesex County	17	0.04
Paramus (borough) Bergen County	10	0.04
Parsippany-Troy Hills (township) Morris County	15	0.03
Teaneck (cdp) Bergen County	13	0.03
Atlantic City (city) Atlantic County	11	0.03
East Windsor (township) Mercer County	8	0.03
Millburn (cdp) Essex County	6	0.03
Secaucus (town) Hudson County	5	0.03

Asian: Pakistani

Top 10 Places Sorted by Number
Based on all places, regardless of population

Place	Number	%
Jersey City (city) Hudson County	2,617	1.09
Woodbridge (township) Middlesex County	755	0.78
Edison (cdp) Middlesex County	737	0.75
Old Bridge (township) Middlesex County	526	0.87
Madison Park (cdp) Middlesex County	406	5.86
Piscataway (township) Middlesex County	355	0.70
Avenel (cdp) Middlesex County	330	1.88
Atlantic City (city) Atlantic County	309	0.76
Boonton (town) Morris County	300	3.53
Sayreville (borough) Middlesex County	297	0.74

Top 10 Places Sorted by Percent
Based on all places, regardless of population

Place	Number	%
Madison Park (cdp) Middlesex County	406	5.86
Boonton (town) Morris County	300	3.53
Avenel (cdp) Middlesex County	330	1.88
Harrison (town) Hudson County	168	1.16
Monmouth Junction (cdp) Middlesex County	31	1.14
Jersey City (city) Hudson County	2,617	1.09
Iselin (cdp) Middlesex County	164	0.98
Bellmawr (borough) Camden County	100	0.89
Brigantine (city) Atlantic County	111	0.88
Heathcote (cdp) Middlesex County	42	0.88

Top 10 Places Sorted by Percent
Based on places with populations of 10,000 or more

Place	Number	%
Avenel (cdp) Middlesex County	330	1.88
Harrison (town) Hudson County	168	1.16
Jersey City (city) Hudson County	2,617	1.09

Iselin (cdp) Middlesex County		164	0.98
Bellmawr (borough) Camden County		100	0.89
Brigantine (city) Atlantic County		111	0.88
Old Bridge (township) Middlesex County		526	0.87
North Plainfield (borough) Somerset County		170	0.81
Woodbridge (township) Middlesex County		755	0.78
Atlantic City (city) Atlantic County		309	0.76

Asian: Sri Lankan

Top 10 Places Sorted by Number
Based on all places, regardless of population

Place	Number	%
South Brunswick (township) Middlesex County	68	0.18
Woodbridge (township) Middlesex County	55	0.06
Elizabeth (city) Union County	55	0.05
Edison (cdp) Middlesex County	54	0.06
Newark (city) Essex County	40	0.01
North Brunswick Twp (cdp) Middlesex County	38	0.10
Piscataway (township) Middlesex County	36	0.07
Jersey City (city) Hudson County	33	0.01
Lawrence (township) Mercer County	31	0.11
Old Bridge (township) Middlesex County	31	0.05

Top 10 Places Sorted by Percent
Based on all places, regardless of population

Place	Number	%
Lebanon (borough) Hunterdon County	4	0.38
Barnegat Light (borough) Ocean County	2	0.26
Heathcote (cdp) Middlesex County	10	0.21
Kendall Park (cdp) Middlesex County	18	0.20
South Brunswick (township) Middlesex County	68	0.18
Iselin (cdp) Middlesex County	23	0.14
Mountain Lakes (borough) Morris County	6	0.14
Fairfield (cdp) Essex County	9	0.13
Dayton (cdp) Middlesex County	8	0.13
Ramtown (cdp) Monmouth County	8	0.13

Top 10 Places Sorted by Percent
Based on places with populations of 10,000 or more

Place	Number	%
South Brunswick (township) Middlesex County	68	0.18
Iselin (cdp) Middlesex County	23	0.14
Lawrence (township) Mercer County	31	0.11
Montgomery (township) Somerset County	19	0.11
North Brunswick Twp (cdp) Middlesex County	38	0.10
Princeton Meadows (cdp) Middlesex County	14	0.10
Bergenfield (borough) Bergen County	23	0.09
West Windsor (township) Mercer County	19	0.09
Plainsboro (township) Middlesex County	18	0.09
Piscataway (township) Middlesex County	36	0.07

Asian: Taiwanese

Top 10 Places Sorted by Number
Based on all places, regardless of population

Place	Number	%
Edison (cdp) Middlesex County	465	0.48
Parsippany-Troy Hills (township) Morris County	400	0.79
East Brunswick (cdp) Middlesex County	285	0.61
Livingston (cdp) Essex County	269	0.98
West Windsor (township) Mercer County	253	1.15
Holmdel (township) Monmouth County	216	1.37
Montville (township) Morris County	187	0.90
Piscataway (township) Middlesex County	178	0.35
Bridgewater (township) Somerset County	167	0.39
Cherry Hill (township) Camden County	156	0.22

Top 10 Places Sorted by Percent
Based on all places, regardless of population

Place	Number	%
Holmdel (township) Monmouth County	216	1.37

Notes: (cdp) census designated place; Refer to the User's Guide in the front of the book for more detailed information.

East Hanover (township) Morris County	133	1.17
West Windsor (township) Mercer County	253	1.15
Livingston (cdp) Essex County	269	0.98
Montville (township) Morris County	187	0.90
Parsippany-Troy Hills (township) Morris County	400	0.79
Hanover (township) Morris County	102	0.79
Montgomery (township) Somerset County	134	0.77
Lebanon (borough) Hunterdon County	7	0.66
Cranbury (township) Middlesex County	21	0.65

Top 10 Places Sorted by Percent
Based on places with populations of 10,000 or more

Place	Number	%
Holmdel (township) Monmouth County	216	1.37
East Hanover (township) Morris County	133	1.17
West Windsor (township) Mercer County	253	1.15
Livingston (cdp) Essex County	269	0.98
Montville (township) Morris County	187	0.90
Parsippany-Troy Hills (township) Morris County	400	0.79
Hanover (township) Morris County	102	0.79
Montgomery (township) Somerset County	134	0.77
East Brunswick (cdp) Middlesex County	285	0.61
Greentree (cdp) Camden County	69	0.60

Asian: Thai

Top 10 Places Sorted by Number
Based on all places, regardless of population

Place	Number	%
Jersey City (city) Hudson County	171	0.07
Pemberton (township) Burlington County	82	0.29
Bloomfield (cdp) Essex County	62	0.13
Clifton (city) Passaic County	58	0.07
Edison (cdp) Middlesex County	56	0.06
Browns Mills (cdp) Burlington County	49	0.44
Belleville (cdp) Essex County	41	0.11
Rutherford (borough) Bergen County	40	0.22
Nutley (cdp) Essex County	38	0.14
Hoboken (city) Hudson County	36	0.09

Top 10 Places Sorted by Percent
Based on all places, regardless of population

Place	Number	%
Wrightstown (borough) Burlington County	5	0.67
Browns Mills (cdp) Burlington County	49	0.44
Corbin City (city) Atlantic County	2	0.43
Glen Gardner (borough) Hunterdon County	6	0.32
Pemberton (township) Burlington County	82	0.29
Maywood (borough) Bergen County	28	0.29
Pemberton Heights (cdp) Burlington County	7	0.28
North Hanover (township) Burlington County	20	0.27
River Edge (borough) Bergen County	28	0.26
McGuire AFB (cdp) Burlington County	16	0.25

Top 10 Places Sorted by Percent
Based on places with populations of 10,000 or more

Place	Number	%
Browns Mills (cdp) Burlington County	49	0.44
Pemberton (township) Burlington County	82	0.29
River Edge (borough) Bergen County	28	0.26
Rutherford (borough) Bergen County	40	0.22
Lyndhurst (cdp) Bergen County	35	0.18
New Milford (borough) Bergen County	24	0.15
Hasbrouck Heights (borough) Bergen County	17	0.15
Nutley (cdp) Essex County	38	0.14
Glen Rock (borough) Bergen County	16	0.14
Bloomfield (cdp) Essex County	62	0.13

Asian: Vietnamese

Top 10 Places Sorted by Number
Based on all places, regardless of population

Place	Number	%
Jersey City (city) Hudson County	1,701	0.71
Atlantic City (city) Atlantic County	1,352	3.34
Camden (city) Camden County	1,344	1.68
Pennsauken (cdp) Camden County	883	2.47
Piscataway (township) Middlesex County	550	1.09
Cherry Hill (township) Camden County	366	0.52
Belleville (cdp) Essex County	349	0.97
Edison (cdp) Middlesex County	345	0.35
South Plainfield (borough) Middlesex County	339	1.55
Woodbridge (township) Middlesex County	263	0.27

Top 10 Places Sorted by Percent
Based on all places, regardless of population

Place	Number	%
Woodlynne (borough) Camden County	211	7.55
Atlantic City (city) Atlantic County	1,352	3.34
Pennsauken (cdp) Camden County	883	2.47
Victory Gardens (borough) Morris County	30	1.94
Ventnor City (city) Atlantic County	245	1.90
Pomona (cdp) Atlantic County	72	1.79
Camden (city) Camden County	1,344	1.68
South Plainfield (borough) Middlesex County	339	1.55
Shrewsbury (township) Monmouth County	17	1.55
Piscataway (township) Middlesex County	550	1.09

Top 10 Places Sorted by Percent
Based on places with populations of 10,000 or more

Place	Number	%
Atlantic City (city) Atlantic County	1,352	3.34
Pennsauken (cdp) Camden County	883	2.47
Ventnor City (city) Atlantic County	245	1.90
Camden (city) Camden County	1,344	1.68
South Plainfield (borough) Middlesex County	339	1.55
Piscataway (township) Middlesex County	550	1.09
Belleville (cdp) Essex County	349	0.97
Middlesex (borough) Middlesex County	131	0.96
Cherry Hill Mall (cdp) Camden County	122	0.92
Brigantine (city) Atlantic County	113	0.90

Asian: Other Asian, specified

Top 10 Places Sorted by Number
Based on all places, regardless of population

Place	Number	%
Jersey City (city) Hudson County	62	0.03
East Brunswick (cdp) Middlesex County	40	0.09
Newark (city) Essex County	35	0.01
Piscataway (township) Middlesex County	31	0.06
Edison (cdp) Middlesex County	31	0.03
Parsippany-Troy Hills (township) Morris County	29	0.06
Fort Lee (borough) Bergen County	28	0.08
Bergenfield (borough) Bergen County	19	0.07
Willingboro (township) Burlington County	17	0.05
Old Bridge (township) Middlesex County	16	0.03

Top 10 Places Sorted by Percent
Based on all places, regardless of population

Place	Number	%
Rockleigh (borough) Bergen County	6	1.53
Harvey Cedars (borough) Ocean County	1	0.28
Elsinboro (township) Salem County	3	0.27
Monmouth Junction (cdp) Middlesex County	7	0.26
Brownville (cdp) Middlesex County	4	0.15
South Bound Brook (borough) Somerset County	6	0.13
Wrightstown (borough) Burlington County	1	0.13
Ventnor City (city) Atlantic County	14	0.11
East Brunswick (cdp) Middlesex County	40	0.09

Hanover (township) Morris County	11	0.09

Top 10 Places Sorted by Percent
Based on places with populations of 10,000 or more

Place	Number	%
Ventnor City (city) Atlantic County	14	0.11
East Brunswick (cdp) Middlesex County	40	0.09
Hanover (township) Morris County	11	0.09
Fort Lee (borough) Bergen County	28	0.08
Little Ferry (borough) Bergen County	9	0.08
Bergenfield (borough) Bergen County	19	0.07
Red Bank (borough) Monmouth County	8	0.07
Piscataway (township) Middlesex County	31	0.06
Parsippany-Troy Hills (township) Morris County	29	0.06
Harrison (town) Hudson County	8	0.06

Asian: Other Asian, not specified

Top 10 Places Sorted by Number
Based on all places, regardless of population

Place	Number	%
Jersey City (city) Hudson County	1,025	0.43
Newark (city) Essex County	450	0.16
Paterson (city) Passaic County	367	0.25
Parsippany-Troy Hills (township) Morris County	349	0.69
Woodbridge (township) Middlesex County	265	0.27
Clifton (city) Passaic County	253	0.32
North Bergen (township) Hudson County	232	0.40
Camden (city) Camden County	199	0.25
Edison (cdp) Middlesex County	184	0.19
Elizabeth (city) Union County	173	0.14

Top 10 Places Sorted by Percent
Based on all places, regardless of population

Place	Number	%
West Paterson (borough) Passaic County	94	0.86
Little Ferry (borough) Bergen County	91	0.84
Prospect Park (borough) Passaic County	45	0.78
Parsippany-Troy Hills (township) Morris County	349	0.69
Madison Park (cdp) Middlesex County	46	0.66
Edgewater Park (township) Burlington County	51	0.65
Avenel (cdp) Middlesex County	106	0.60
Tuckerton (borough) Ocean County	19	0.54
Victory Gardens (borough) Morris County	8	0.52
Haledon (borough) Passaic County	42	0.51

Top 10 Places Sorted by Percent
Based on places with populations of 10,000 or more

Place	Number	%
West Paterson (borough) Passaic County	94	0.86
Little Ferry (borough) Bergen County	91	0.84
Parsippany-Troy Hills (township) Morris County	349	0.69
Avenel (cdp) Middlesex County	106	0.60
Paramus (borough) Bergen County	114	0.44
Jersey City (city) Hudson County	1,025	0.43
Fort Lee (borough) Bergen County	154	0.43
Cherry Hill Mall (cdp) Camden County	57	0.43
North Bergen (township) Hudson County	232	0.40
Cliffside Park (borough) Bergen County	88	0.38

Assyrian/Chaldean/Syriac

Top 10 Places Sorted by Number
Based on all places, regardless of population

Place	Number	%
New Milford (borough) Bergen County	88	0.54
Wayne (cdp) Passaic County	77	0.14
Springfield (cdp) Union County	70	0.49
Upper Saddle River (borough) Bergen County	60	0.78
Elizabeth (city) Union County	54	0.04
West Paterson (borough) Passaic County	41	0.37
Wyckoff (cdp) Bergen County	37	0.22

Notes: (cdp) census designated place; Refer to the User's Guide in the front of the book for more detailed information.

Place	Number	%
Washington Township (cdp) Bergen County	32	0.36
Ridgefield (borough) Bergen County	25	0.23
Ocean (township) Monmouth County	24	0.09

Top 10 Places Sorted by Percent
Based on all places, regardless of population

Place	Number	%
Upper Saddle River (borough) Bergen County	60	0.78
New Milford (borough) Bergen County	88	0.54
Springfield (cdp) Union County	70	0.49
West Paterson (borough) Passaic County	41	0.37
Washington Township (cdp) Bergen County	32	0.36
Clementon (borough) Camden County	13	0.26
Ridgefield (borough) Bergen County	25	0.23
Wyckoff (cdp) Bergen County	37	0.22
Little Falls (cdp) Passaic County	18	0.17
Pemberton (borough) Burlington County	2	0.17

Top 10 Places Sorted by Percent
Based on places with populations of 10,000 or more

Place	Number	%
New Milford (borough) Bergen County	88	0.54
Springfield (cdp) Union County	70	0.49
West Paterson (borough) Passaic County	41	0.37
Ridgefield (borough) Bergen County	25	0.23
Wyckoff (cdp) Bergen County	37	0.22
Little Falls (cdp) Passaic County	18	0.17
Wayne (cdp) Passaic County	77	0.14
Hanover (township) Morris County	14	0.11
Ocean (township) Monmouth County	24	0.09
Paramus (borough) Bergen County	24	0.09

Australian

Top 10 Places Sorted by Number
Based on all places, regardless of population

Place	Number	%
Jersey City (city) Hudson County	75	0.03
Ridgewood (village) Bergen County	74	0.30
Morris (township) Morris County	54	0.25
Princeton (borough) Mercer County	42	0.30
Moorestown (township) Burlington County	42	0.22
Holmdel (township) Monmouth County	34	0.22
South Orange (cdp) Essex County	32	0.19
East Windsor (township) Mercer County	31	0.12
Manasquan (borough) Monmouth County	28	0.44
Randolph (township) Morris County	28	0.11

Top 10 Places Sorted by Percent
Based on all places, regardless of population

Place	Number	%
Navesink (cdp) Monmouth County	23	1.23
Rocky Hill (borough) Somerset County	6	0.91
Woodbury Heights (borough) Gloucester County	22	0.74
Plainsboro Center (cdp) Middlesex County	15	0.63
Mendham (borough) Morris County	26	0.51
Manasquan (borough) Monmouth County	28	0.44
High Bridge (borough) Hunterdon County	15	0.40
South Belmar (borough) Monmouth County	7	0.39
Brownville (cdp) Middlesex County	10	0.38
Oaklyn (borough) Camden County	14	0.34

Top 10 Places Sorted by Percent
Based on places with populations of 10,000 or more

Place	Number	%
Ridgewood (village) Bergen County	74	0.30
Princeton (borough) Mercer County	42	0.30
Morris (township) Morris County	54	0.25
Moorestown (township) Burlington County	42	0.22
Holmdel (township) Monmouth County	34	0.22
South Orange (cdp) Essex County	32	0.19
Succasunna-Kenvil (cdp) Morris County	22	0.18

Place	Number	%
Clark (cdp) Union County	25	0.17
Mantua (township) Gloucester County	24	0.17
Ridgefield Park (village) Bergen County	20	0.16

Austrian

Top 10 Places Sorted by Number
Based on all places, regardless of population

Place	Number	%
Clifton (city) Passaic County	799	1.02
Manalapan (township) Monmouth County	753	2.25
Marlboro (township) Monmouth County	682	1.87
Monroe (township) Middlesex County	656	2.34
Cherry Hill (township) Camden County	648	0.93
Wayne (cdp) Passaic County	578	1.07
East Brunswick (cdp) Middlesex County	546	1.17
Middletown (township) Monmouth County	520	0.78
Edison (cdp) Middlesex County	503	0.51
Livingston (cdp) Essex County	500	1.83

Top 10 Places Sorted by Percent
Based on all places, regardless of population

Place	Number	%
Whittingham (cdp) Middlesex County	171	7.00
Concordia (cdp) Middlesex County	181	4.90
Clearbrook Park (cdp) Middlesex County	112	3.66
Cape May Point (borough) Cape May County	8	3.36
Vista Center (cdp) Ocean County	22	3.09
Yorketown (cdp) Monmouth County	192	2.87
Morganville (cdp) Monmouth County	299	2.69
Corbin City (city) Atlantic County	12	2.56
White House Station (cdp) Hunterdon County	48	2.54
Millburn (cdp) Essex County	482	2.44

Top 10 Places Sorted by Percent
Based on places with populations of 10,000 or more

Place	Number	%
Morganville (cdp) Monmouth County	299	2.69
Millburn (cdp) Essex County	482	2.44
Monroe (township) Middlesex County	656	2.34
Manalapan (township) Monmouth County	753	2.25
West Freehold (cdp) Monmouth County	267	2.13
Westwood (borough) Bergen County	234	2.13
Glen Rock (borough) Bergen County	241	2.09
Marlboro (township) Monmouth County	682	1.87
Livingston (cdp) Essex County	500	1.83
Warren (township) Somerset County	247	1.73

Basque

Top 10 Places Sorted by Number
Based on all places, regardless of population

Place	Number	%
Kearny (town) Hudson County	55	0.14
Little Falls (cdp) Passaic County	33	0.30
West Paterson (borough) Passaic County	30	0.27
Clifton (city) Passaic County	27	0.03
Newark (city) Essex County	27	0.01
Tenafly (borough) Bergen County	26	0.19
Weehawken (township) Hudson County	26	0.19
Passaic (city) Passaic County	23	0.03
North Brunswick Twp (cdp) Middlesex County	20	0.06
Hillside (cdp) Union County	17	0.08

Top 10 Places Sorted by Percent
Based on all places, regardless of population

Place	Number	%
Frenchtown (borough) Hunterdon County	9	0.60
Little Falls (cdp) Passaic County	33	0.30
West Paterson (borough) Passaic County	30	0.27
Demarest (borough) Bergen County	12	0.25
Keyport (borough) Monmouth County	16	0.21

Place	Number	%
Tenafly (borough) Bergen County	26	0.19
Weehawken (township) Hudson County	26	0.19
Mountainside (borough) Union County	10	0.15
Kearny (town) Hudson County	55	0.14
White Meadow Lake (cdp) Morris County	13	0.14

Top 10 Places Sorted by Percent
Based on places with populations of 10,000 or more

Place	Number	%
Little Falls (cdp) Passaic County	33	0.30
West Paterson (borough) Passaic County	30	0.27
Tenafly (borough) Bergen County	26	0.19
Weehawken (township) Hudson County	26	0.19
Kearny (town) Hudson County	55	0.14
Oakland (borough) Bergen County	12	0.10
Hillside (cdp) Union County	17	0.08
Roxbury (township) Morris County	16	0.07
Guttenberg (town) Hudson County	7	0.07
North Brunswick Twp (cdp) Middlesex County	20	0.06

Belgian

Top 10 Places Sorted by Number
Based on all places, regardless of population

Place	Number	%
Wayne (cdp) Passaic County	141	0.26
Dover (township) Ocean County	106	0.12
Toms River (cdp) Ocean County	106	0.12
Berkeley (township) Ocean County	94	0.24
Mahwah (township) Bergen County	89	0.37
West Milford (cdp) Passaic County	88	0.33
Ridgewood (village) Bergen County	82	0.33
Hamilton (township) Mercer County	80	0.09
Fort Lee (borough) Bergen County	77	0.22
Paterson (city) Passaic County	76	0.05

Top 10 Places Sorted by Percent
Based on all places, regardless of population

Place	Number	%
Annandale (cdp) Hunterdon County	27	2.06
Collings Lakes (cdp) Atlantic County	15	0.91
Stillwater (township) Sussex County	34	0.80
Mendham (borough) Morris County	40	0.78
Oakhurst (cdp) Monmouth County	32	0.78
Fair Haven (borough) Monmouth County	46	0.77
Loch Arbour (village) Monmouth County	2	0.73
Bloomsbury (borough) Hunterdon County	6	0.68
Upper (township) Cape May County	75	0.62
Woodland (township) Burlington County	7	0.60

Top 10 Places Sorted by Percent
Based on places with populations of 10,000 or more

Place	Number	%
Upper (township) Cape May County	75	0.62
Hasbrouck Heights (borough) Bergen County	67	0.57
Clinton (township) Hunterdon County	56	0.43
Mahwah (township) Bergen County	89	0.37
Plainsboro (township) Middlesex County	68	0.34
Branchburg (township) Somerset County	49	0.34
River Edge (borough) Bergen County	37	0.34
West Milford (cdp) Passaic County	88	0.33
Ridgewood (village) Bergen County	82	0.33
Franklin (township) Gloucester County	51	0.33

Brazilian

Top 10 Places Sorted by Number
Based on all places, regardless of population

Place	Number	%
Newark (city) Essex County	5,805	2.12
Kearny (town) Hudson County	1,629	4.02
Elizabeth (city) Union County	1,349	1.12

Notes: (cdp) census designated place; Refer to the User's Guide in the front of the book for more detailed information.

Place	Number	%
Long Branch (city) Monmouth County	890	2.84
Harrison (town) Hudson County	726	5.03
Cliffside Park (borough) Bergen County	503	2.19
Hillside (cdp) Union County	469	2.16
North Bergen (township) Hudson County	384	0.66
South River (borough) Middlesex County	376	2.45
Union (cdp) Union County	331	0.61

Top 10 Places Sorted by Percent
Based on all places, regardless of population

Place	Number	%
East Newark (borough) Hudson County	154	6.48
Harrison (town) Hudson County	726	5.03
Kearny (town) Hudson County	1,629	4.02
Long Branch (city) Monmouth County	890	2.84
South River (borough) Middlesex County	376	2.45
Cliffside Park (borough) Bergen County	503	2.19
Hillside (cdp) Union County	469	2.16
Newark (city) Essex County	5,805	2.12
Fairview (borough) Bergen County	261	1.97
Riverside (township) Burlington County	144	1.82

Top 10 Places Sorted by Percent
Based on places with populations of 10,000 or more

Place	Number	%
Harrison (town) Hudson County	726	5.03
Kearny (town) Hudson County	1,629	4.02
Long Branch (city) Monmouth County	890	2.84
South River (borough) Middlesex County	376	2.45
Cliffside Park (borough) Bergen County	503	2.19
Hillside (cdp) Union County	469	2.16
Newark (city) Essex County	5,805	2.12
Fairview (borough) Bergen County	261	1.97
Delran (township) Burlington County	217	1.40
Elizabeth (city) Union County	1,349	1.12

British

Top 10 Places Sorted by Number
Based on all places, regardless of population

Place	Number	%
Hamilton (township) Mercer County	424	0.49
Hoboken (city) Hudson County	326	0.84
Westfield (town) Union County	284	0.96
Lawrence (township) Mercer County	281	0.96
Jersey City (city) Hudson County	277	0.12
Berkeley Heights (cdp) Union County	262	1.95
Madison (borough) Morris County	247	1.49
Princeton (township) Mercer County	245	1.53
Summit (city) Union County	245	1.16
Montclair (cdp) Essex County	244	0.62

Top 10 Places Sorted by Percent
Based on all places, regardless of population

Place	Number	%
Pennington (borough) Mercer County	74	2.74
Princeton North (cdp) Mercer County	107	2.34
Far Hills (borough) Somerset County	19	2.22
Chatham (township) Morris County	186	2.20
Mendham (borough) Morris County	112	2.20
Peapack and Gladstone (borough) Somerset Co.	53	2.18
Plainsboro Center (cdp) Middlesex County	50	2.11
Ho-Ho-Kus (borough) Bergen County	80	1.97
Hightstown (borough) Mercer County	102	1.96
Berkeley Heights (cdp) Union County	262	1.95

Top 10 Places Sorted by Percent
Based on places with populations of 10,000 or more

Place	Number	%
Berkeley Heights (cdp) Union County	262	1.95
Chatham (township) Morris County	184	1.82
Princeton (township) Mercer County	245	1.53

Place	Number	%
Madison (borough) Morris County	247	1.49
New Providence (borough) Union County	168	1.41
Princeton (borough) Mercer County	190	1.34
Haddonfield (borough) Camden County	140	1.20
Summit (city) Union County	245	1.16
Ocean City (city) Cape May County	173	1.12
Millburn (cdp) Essex County	204	1.03

Bulgarian

Top 10 Places Sorted by Number
Based on all places, regardless of population

Place	Number	%
Brigantine (city) Atlantic County	83	0.66
Randolph (township) Morris County	44	0.18
Jersey City (city) Hudson County	42	0.02
Lodi (borough) Bergen County	39	0.16
New Brunswick (city) Middlesex County	37	0.08
Dover (township) Ocean County	35	0.04
Toms River (cdp) Ocean County	35	0.04
Ventnor City (city) Atlantic County	33	0.26
Washington (township) Mercer County	32	0.31
West Windsor (township) Mercer County	31	0.14

Top 10 Places Sorted by Percent
Based on all places, regardless of population

Place	Number	%
Plainsboro Center (cdp) Middlesex County	17	0.72
Bethlehem (township) Hunterdon County	26	0.68
Frenchtown (borough) Hunterdon County	10	0.67
Brigantine (city) Atlantic County	83	0.66
Harmony (township) Warren County	12	0.44
Green Brook (township) Somerset County	21	0.37
Lincroft (cdp) Monmouth County	22	0.35
National Park (borough) Gloucester County	11	0.34
Hope (township) Warren County	6	0.32
Washington (township) Mercer County	32	0.31

Top 10 Places Sorted by Percent
Based on places with populations of 10,000 or more

Place	Number	%
Brigantine (city) Atlantic County	83	0.66
Washington (township) Mercer County	32	0.31
Ventnor City (city) Atlantic County	33	0.26
Manville (borough) Somerset County	20	0.19
Randolph (township) Morris County	44	0.18
Marlton (cdp) Burlington County	17	0.17
Lodi (borough) Bergen County	39	0.16
New Milford (borough) Bergen County	25	0.15
Princeton (borough) Mercer County	22	0.15
West Windsor (township) Mercer County	31	0.14

Canadian

Top 10 Places Sorted by Number
Based on all places, regardless of population

Place	Number	%
Jersey City (city) Hudson County	212	0.09
Randolph (township) Morris County	182	0.73
Manalapan (township) Monmouth County	167	0.50
Montclair (cdp) Essex County	166	0.42
Bridgewater (township) Somerset County	165	0.38
Teaneck (cdp) Bergen County	163	0.42
Princeton (borough) Mercer County	160	1.13
Lakewood (township) Ocean County	159	0.26
Middletown (township) Monmouth County	156	0.24
Morris (township) Morris County	152	0.70

Top 10 Places Sorted by Percent
Based on all places, regardless of population

Place	Number	%
Mays Landing (cdp) Atlantic County	35	1.53

Place	Number	%
Rockleigh (borough) Bergen County	6	1.50
Millstone (borough) Somerset County	5	1.20
Allendale (borough) Bergen County	80	1.19
Heathcote (cdp) Middlesex County	54	1.17
Princeton (borough) Mercer County	160	1.13
Monmouth Beach (borough) Monmouth County	38	1.06
Cliffwood Beach (cdp) Monmouth County	36	1.02
Princeton Junction (cdp) Mercer County	24	1.00
Norwood (borough) Bergen County	57	0.99

Top 10 Places Sorted by Percent
Based on places with populations of 10,000 or more

Place	Number	%
Princeton (borough) Mercer County	160	1.13
Chatham (township) Morris County	84	0.83
Randolph (township) Morris County	182	0.73
Morris (township) Morris County	152	0.70
Hasbrouck Heights (borough) Bergen County	70	0.60
Washington (township) Morris County	103	0.59
Medford (township) Burlington County	125	0.56
Wantage (township) Sussex County	57	0.55
Jefferson (township) Morris County	106	0.54
Hillsdale (borough) Bergen County	54	0.54

Carpatho Rusyn

Top 10 Places Sorted by Number
Based on all places, regardless of population

Place	Number	%
Colonia (cdp) Middlesex County	33	0.19
Woodbridge (township) Middlesex County	33	0.03
Weehawken (township) Hudson County	30	0.22
Jefferson (township) Morris County	27	0.14
Tenafly (borough) Bergen County	20	0.14
Hanover (township) Morris County	19	0.15
Garfield (city) Bergen County	19	0.06
Linden (city) Union County	19	0.05
Franklin (township) Somerset County	16	0.03
Chatham (borough) Morris County	15	0.18

Top 10 Places Sorted by Percent
Based on all places, regardless of population

Place	Number	%
Alpha (borough) Warren County	8	0.32
Weehawken (township) Hudson County	30	0.22
Interlaken (borough) Monmouth County	2	0.22
Colonia (cdp) Middlesex County	33	0.19
Chatham (borough) Morris County	15	0.18
Dayton (cdp) Middlesex County	11	0.17
Society Hill (cdp) Middlesex County	6	0.16
Hanover (township) Morris County	19	0.15
Jefferson (township) Morris County	27	0.14
Tenafly (borough) Bergen County	20	0.14

Top 10 Places Sorted by Percent
Based on places with populations of 10,000 or more

Place	Number	%
Weehawken (township) Hudson County	30	0.22
Colonia (cdp) Middlesex County	33	0.19
Hanover (township) Morris County	19	0.15
Jefferson (township) Morris County	27	0.14
Tenafly (borough) Bergen County	20	0.14
Cherry Hill Mall (cdp) Camden County	14	0.10
East Hanover (township) Morris County	9	0.08
Florence (township) Burlington County	7	0.07
Garfield (city) Bergen County	19	0.06
Readington (township) Hunterdon County	10	0.06

Notes: (cdp) census designated place; Refer to the User's Guide in the front of the book for more detailed information.

Celtic

Top 10 Places Sorted by Number
Based on all places, regardless of population

Place	Number	%
Budd Lake (cdp) Morris County	51	0.62
Mount Olive (township) Morris County	51	0.21
Jersey City (city) Hudson County	43	0.02
Rockaway (borough) Morris County	40	0.62
Hamilton (township) Mercer County	39	0.04
Middletown (township) Monmouth County	36	0.05
Raritan (township) Hunterdon County	33	0.17
Fair Lawn (borough) Bergen County	32	0.10
Lacey (township) Ocean County	30	0.12
Bernards (township) Somerset County	24	0.10

Top 10 Places Sorted by Percent
Based on all places, regardless of population

Place	Number	%
Budd Lake (cdp) Morris County	51	0.62
Rockaway (borough) Morris County	40	0.62
Riverton (borough) Burlington County	17	0.62
Port Monmouth (cdp) Monmouth County	17	0.47
Shrewsbury (borough) Monmouth County	17	0.47
Wanamassa (cdp) Monmouth County	21	0.46
Ship Bottom (borough) Ocean County	5	0.36
Leonardo (cdp) Monmouth County	8	0.28
Pilesgrove (township) Salem County	10	0.25
Oaklyn (borough) Camden County	10	0.24

Top 10 Places Sorted by Percent
Based on places with populations of 10,000 or more

Place	Number	%
Mount Olive (township) Morris County	51	0.21
Bellmawr (borough) Camden County	23	0.20
Chatham (township) Morris County	20	0.20
Raritan (township) Hunterdon County	33	0.17
Cinnaminson (township) Burlington County	23	0.16
Haddonfield (borough) Camden County	19	0.16
Manville (borough) Somerset County	17	0.16
Hackettstown (town) Warren County	16	0.15
Lacey (township) Ocean County	30	0.12
Fair Lawn (borough) Bergen County	32	0.10

Croatian

Top 10 Places Sorted by Number
Based on all places, regardless of population

Place	Number	%
Cliffside Park (borough) Bergen County	661	2.87
Fairview (borough) Bergen County	607	4.58
Palisades Park (borough) Bergen County	541	3.17
Fort Lee (borough) Bergen County	395	1.11
Ridgefield (borough) Bergen County	366	3.38
North Bergen (township) Hudson County	325	0.56
Brick (township) Ocean County	203	0.27
Clifton (city) Passaic County	197	0.25
Hoboken (city) Hudson County	172	0.44
Boonton (town) Morris County	166	1.95

Top 10 Places Sorted by Percent
Based on all places, regardless of population

Place	Number	%
Fairview (borough) Bergen County	607	4.58
Ridgefield (borough) Bergen County	366	3.38
Palisades Park (borough) Bergen County	541	3.17
Cliffside Park (borough) Bergen County	661	2.87
Lake Telemark (cdp) Morris County	32	2.48
Boonton (town) Morris County	166	1.95
Little Ferry (borough) Bergen County	143	1.32
Plainsboro Center (cdp) Middlesex County	29	1.22
Annandale (cdp) Hunterdon County	15	1.14

Place	Number	%
Fort Lee (borough) Bergen County	395	1.11

Top 10 Places Sorted by Percent
Based on places with populations of 10,000 or more

Place	Number	%
Fairview (borough) Bergen County	607	4.58
Ridgefield (borough) Bergen County	366	3.38
Palisades Park (borough) Bergen County	541	3.17
Cliffside Park (borough) Bergen County	661	2.87
Little Ferry (borough) Bergen County	143	1.32
Fort Lee (borough) Bergen County	395	1.11
Wyckoff (cdp) Bergen County	120	0.73
North Bergen (township) Hudson County	325	0.56
Mahwah (township) Bergen County	128	0.53
Dumont (borough) Bergen County	84	0.48

Cypriot

Top 10 Places Sorted by Number
Based on all places, regardless of population

Place	Number	%
Paramus (borough) Bergen County	96	0.37
South Brunswick (township) Middlesex County	73	0.19
Fairfield (cdp) Essex County	57	0.81
East Brunswick (cdp) Middlesex County	52	0.11
Raritan (township) Hunterdon County	42	0.21
West Orange (cdp) Essex County	38	0.08
North Brunswick Twp (cdp) Middlesex County	34	0.09
Union City (city) Hudson County	28	0.04
Oradell (borough) Bergen County	27	0.34
Leonia (borough) Bergen County	24	0.27

Top 10 Places Sorted by Percent
Based on all places, regardless of population

Place	Number	%
Fairfield (cdp) Essex County	57	0.81
Paramus (borough) Bergen County	96	0.37
Oradell (borough) Bergen County	27	0.34
Leonia (borough) Bergen County	24	0.27
Raritan (township) Hunterdon County	42	0.21
Highlands (borough) Monmouth County	10	0.20
South Brunswick (township) Middlesex County	73	0.19
Emerson (borough) Bergen County	10	0.14
Dumont (borough) Bergen County	22	0.13
Cherry Hill Mall (cdp) Camden County	18	0.13

Top 10 Places Sorted by Percent
Based on places with populations of 10,000 or more

Place	Number	%
Paramus (borough) Bergen County	96	0.37
Raritan (township) Hunterdon County	42	0.21
South Brunswick (township) Middlesex County	73	0.19
Dumont (borough) Bergen County	22	0.13
Cherry Hill Mall (cdp) Camden County	18	0.13
Warren (township) Somerset County	18	0.13
Marlton (cdp) Burlington County	13	0.13
East Brunswick (cdp) Middlesex County	52	0.11
Washington (township) Mercer County	10	0.10
North Brunswick Twp (cdp) Middlesex County	34	0.09

Czech

Top 10 Places Sorted by Number
Based on all places, regardless of population

Place	Number	%
Dover (township) Ocean County	465	0.52
Woodbridge (township) Middlesex County	465	0.48
Toms River (cdp) Ocean County	440	0.51
Hamilton (township) Mercer County	404	0.46
Clifton (city) Passaic County	400	0.51
Bridgewater (township) Somerset County	346	0.81
Wayne (cdp) Passaic County	301	0.56

Place	Number	%
Brick (township) Ocean County	274	0.36
Middletown (township) Monmouth County	264	0.40
Cherry Hill (township) Camden County	248	0.35

Top 10 Places Sorted by Percent
Based on all places, regardless of population

Place	Number	%
Cape May Point (borough) Cape May County	8	3.36
Glen Ridge (borough) Essex County	230	3.16
White House Station (cdp) Hunterdon County	58	3.07
Navesink (cdp) Monmouth County	40	2.14
Califon (borough) Hunterdon County	19	1.80
East Amwell (township) Hunterdon County	75	1.68
Bass River (township) Burlington County	26	1.68
Allenhurst (borough) Monmouth County	12	1.66
Alexandria (township) Hunterdon County	77	1.64
Hampton (borough) Hunterdon County	25	1.62

Top 10 Places Sorted by Percent
Based on places with populations of 10,000 or more

Place	Number	%
Little Ferry (borough) Bergen County	148	1.37
Montgomery (township) Somerset County	184	1.05
Readington (township) Hunterdon County	161	1.02
New Providence (borough) Union County	120	1.01
Pequannock (township) Morris County	139	1.00
Sparta (township) Sussex County	177	0.98
Westwood (borough) Bergen County	108	0.98
Berkeley Heights (cdp) Union County	115	0.86
Oakland (borough) Bergen County	107	0.86
Raritan (township) Hunterdon County	169	0.85

Czechoslovakian

Top 10 Places Sorted by Number
Based on all places, regardless of population

Place	Number	%
Hamilton (township) Mercer County	465	0.53
Woodbridge (township) Middlesex County	399	0.41
Edison (cdp) Middlesex County	364	0.37
Brick (township) Ocean County	304	0.40
Dover (township) Ocean County	280	0.31
Linden (city) Union County	273	0.69
Toms River (cdp) Ocean County	266	0.31
Clifton (city) Passaic County	257	0.33
Bayonne (city) Hudson County	231	0.37
Berkeley (township) Ocean County	228	0.57

Top 10 Places Sorted by Percent
Based on all places, regardless of population

Place	Number	%
Annandale (cdp) Hunterdon County	24	1.83
Rockleigh (borough) Bergen County	7	1.75
White House Station (cdp) Hunterdon County	30	1.59
Allendale (borough) Bergen County	87	1.30
Millstone (township) Monmouth County	113	1.26
Califon (borough) Hunterdon County	13	1.23
Dunellen (borough) Middlesex County	82	1.20
Knowlton (township) Warren County	36	1.19
Seaside Park (borough) Ocean County	27	1.19
Lake Telemark (cdp) Morris County	15	1.16

Top 10 Places Sorted by Percent
Based on places with populations of 10,000 or more

Place	Number	%
Manville (borough) Somerset County	119	1.15
Montville (township) Morris County	152	0.73
Ringwood (borough) Passaic County	88	0.71
Linden (city) Union County	273	0.69
Metuchen (borough) Middlesex County	87	0.68
Raritan (township) Hunterdon County	127	0.64
Bernards (township) Somerset County	156	0.63

Notes: (cdp) census designated place; Refer to the User's Guide in the front of the book for more detailed information.

Place	Number	%
Hasbrouck Heights (borough) Bergen County	73	0.63
Ramsey (borough) Bergen County	89	0.62
Hillsdale (borough) Bergen County	63	0.62

Danish

Top 10 Places Sorted by Number
Based on all places, regardless of population

Place	Number	%
Edison (cdp) Middlesex County	565	0.58
Woodbridge (township) Middlesex County	560	0.58
Middletown (township) Monmouth County	438	0.66
Dover (township) Ocean County	384	0.43
Brick (township) Ocean County	369	0.48
Toms River (cdp) Ocean County	369	0.43
Sayreville (borough) Middlesex County	314	0.78
Bridgewater (township) Somerset County	265	0.62
Jersey City (city) Hudson County	234	0.10
Cranford (cdp) Union County	229	1.01

Top 10 Places Sorted by Percent
Based on all places, regardless of population

Place	Number	%
Mantoloking (borough) Ocean County	14	3.79
Cape May Point (borough) Cape May County	9	3.78
Harvey Cedars (borough) Ocean County	7	1.98
White House Station (cdp) Hunterdon County	36	1.91
Tabernacle (township) Burlington County	135	1.88
Stillwater (township) Sussex County	78	1.83
Loch Arbour (village) Monmouth County	5	1.82
Bloomsbury (borough) Hunterdon County	16	1.81
Lambertville (city) Hunterdon County	69	1.78
Millstone (borough) Somerset County	7	1.68

Top 10 Places Sorted by Percent
Based on places with populations of 10,000 or more

Place	Number	%
Metuchen (borough) Middlesex County	179	1.39
Cranford (cdp) Union County	229	1.01
Fords (cdp) Middlesex County	152	1.00
West Freehold (cdp) Monmouth County	122	0.97
Readington (township) Hunterdon County	151	0.96
Berkeley Heights (cdp) Union County	111	0.83
Branchburg (township) Somerset County	120	0.82
Sayreville (borough) Middlesex County	314	0.78
Sparta (township) Sussex County	141	0.78
Westwood (borough) Bergen County	83	0.75

Dutch

Top 10 Places Sorted by Number
Based on all places, regardless of population

Place	Number	%
Clifton (city) Passaic County	2,091	2.66
Wayne (cdp) Passaic County	2,035	3.76
Hawthorne (borough) Passaic County	2,014	11.06
Brick (township) Ocean County	1,831	2.41
Dover (township) Ocean County	1,730	1.93
Toms River (cdp) Ocean County	1,670	1.93
West Milford (cdp) Passaic County	1,668	6.32
Vernon (township) Sussex County	1,593	6.45
North Haledon (borough) Passaic County	1,394	17.60
Wyckoff (cdp) Bergen County	1,374	8.32

Top 10 Places Sorted by Percent
Based on all places, regardless of population

Place	Number	%
North Haledon (borough) Passaic County	1,394	17.60
Midland Park (borough) Bergen County	1,183	17.03
Hawthorne (borough) Passaic County	2,014	11.06
Crandon Lakes (cdp) Sussex County	115	9.20
Wantage (township) Sussex County	946	9.11

Place	Number	%
Frankford (township) Sussex County	472	8.71
Strathmere (cdp) Cape May County	13	8.33
Wyckoff (cdp) Bergen County	1,374	8.32
Pequannock (township) Morris County	1,141	8.22
Prospect Park (borough) Passaic County	431	7.46

Top 10 Places Sorted by Percent
Based on places with populations of 10,000 or more

Place	Number	%
Hawthorne (borough) Passaic County	2,014	11.06
Wantage (township) Sussex County	946	9.11
Wyckoff (cdp) Bergen County	1,374	8.32
Pequannock (township) Morris County	1,141	8.22
Pompton Lakes (borough) Passaic County	792	7.44
Vernon (township) Sussex County	1,593	6.45
West Milford (cdp) Passaic County	1,668	6.32
Phillipsburg (town) Warren County	938	6.18
Wanaque (borough) Passaic County	621	6.05
Oakland (borough) Bergen County	676	5.42

Eastern European

Top 10 Places Sorted by Number
Based on all places, regardless of population

Place	Number	%
Cherry Hill (township) Camden County	876	1.25
Livingston (cdp) Essex County	743	2.71
Teaneck (cdp) Bergen County	734	1.87
Marlboro (township) Monmouth County	525	1.44
Millburn (cdp) Essex County	495	2.50
Lakewood (township) Ocean County	493	0.82
West Orange (cdp) Essex County	489	1.09
Springdale (cdp) Camden County	434	3.01
Westfield (town) Union County	398	1.34
Edison (cdp) Middlesex County	395	0.40

Top 10 Places Sorted by Percent
Based on all places, regardless of population

Place	Number	%
Springdale (cdp) Camden County	434	3.01
Livingston (cdp) Essex County	743	2.71
Roosevelt (borough) Monmouth County	24	2.59
Woodcliff Lake (borough) Bergen County	145	2.52
Millburn (cdp) Essex County	495	2.50
Princeton Junction (cdp) Mercer County	58	2.43
Highland Park (borough) Middlesex County	315	2.25
Teaneck (cdp) Bergen County	734	1.87
Upper Saddle River (borough) Bergen County	138	1.78
West Windsor (township) Mercer County	386	1.76

Top 10 Places Sorted by Percent
Based on places with populations of 10,000 or more

Place	Number	%
Springdale (cdp) Camden County	434	3.01
Livingston (cdp) Essex County	743	2.71
Millburn (cdp) Essex County	495	2.50
Highland Park (borough) Middlesex County	315	2.25
Teaneck (cdp) Bergen County	734	1.87
West Windsor (township) Mercer County	386	1.76
Tenafly (borough) Bergen County	234	1.69
Morganville (cdp) Monmouth County	172	1.54
Warren (township) Somerset County	207	1.45
Marlboro (township) Monmouth County	525	1.44

English

Top 10 Places Sorted by Number
Based on all places, regardless of population

Place	Number	%
Hamilton (township) Mercer County	8,574	9.83
Dover (township) Ocean County	7,646	8.52
Toms River (cdp) Ocean County	7,326	8.47

Place	Number	%
Brick (township) Ocean County	6,484	8.52
Middletown (township) Monmouth County	5,816	8.77
Cherry Hill (township) Camden County	5,494	7.85
Gloucester (township) Camden County	5,249	8.16
Mount Laurel (township) Burlington County	4,810	11.96
Washington (township) Gloucester County	4,618	9.80
Evesham (township) Burlington County	4,204	9.91

Top 10 Places Sorted by Percent
Based on all places, regardless of population

Place	Number	%
Cape May Point (borough) Cape May County	63	26.47
Greenwich (township) Cumberland County	213	25.30
Branchville (borough) Sussex County	211	24.91
Harvey Cedars (borough) Ocean County	86	24.36
Port Republic (city) Atlantic County	246	23.84
Strathmere (cdp) Cape May County	37	23.72
Elmer (borough) Salem County	314	22.69
Medford Lakes (borough) Burlington County	912	21.85
Bay Head (borough) Ocean County	282	21.83
Princeton Junction (cdp) Mercer County	512	21.42

Top 10 Places Sorted by Percent
Based on places with populations of 10,000 or more

Place	Number	%
Haddonfield (borough) Camden County	2,251	19.31
Pennsville (township) Salem County	2,261	17.07
Upper (township) Cape May County	2,011	16.60
Southampton (township) Burlington County	1,696	16.41
Hopewell (township) Mercer County	2,441	15.16
Wantage (township) Sussex County	1,566	15.08
Haddon (township) Camden County	2,208	15.06
Moorestown-Lenola (cdp) Burlington County	2,062	14.94
Ocean City (city) Cape May County	2,292	14.90
Moorestown (township) Burlington County	2,808	14.77

Estonian

Top 10 Places Sorted by Number
Based on all places, regardless of population

Place	Number	%
Lakewood (township) Ocean County	160	0.27
Jackson (township) Ocean County	126	0.29
West Orange (cdp) Essex County	78	0.17
Old Bridge (township) Middlesex County	74	0.12
Edison (cdp) Middlesex County	53	0.05
Vineland (city) Cumberland County	44	0.08
Summit (city) Union County	43	0.20
Bernards (township) Somerset County	41	0.17
Hackensack (city) Bergen County	41	0.10
Upper Deerfield (township) Cumberland County	36	0.48

Top 10 Places Sorted by Percent
Based on all places, regardless of population

Place	Number	%
Monmouth Junction (cdp) Middlesex County	21	0.87
Salem (city) Salem County	35	0.60
Deerfield (township) Cumberland County	17	0.58
Upper Deerfield (township) Cumberland County	36	0.48
Watchung (borough) Somerset County	25	0.45
Riverton (borough) Burlington County	12	0.43
Spring Lake Heights (borough) Monmouth County	22	0.42
Lawrenceville (cdp) Mercer County	17	0.42
Laurel Lake (cdp) Cumberland County	11	0.39
New Egypt (cdp) Ocean County	10	0.39

Top 10 Places Sorted by Percent
Based on places with populations of 10,000 or more

Place	Number	%
Westwood (borough) Bergen County	35	0.32
Jackson (township) Ocean County	126	0.29
Echelon (cdp) Camden County	29	0.28

Notes: (cdp) census designated place; Refer to the User's Guide in the front of the book for more detailed information.

Place	Number	%
Lakewood (township) Ocean County	160	0.27
Washington (township) Mercer County	26	0.25
Oakland (borough) Bergen County	29	0.23
Denville (township) Morris County	33	0.21
Summit (city) Union County	43	0.20
West Caldwell (cdp) Essex County	21	0.19
West Orange (cdp) Essex County	78	0.17

European

Top 10 Places Sorted by Number
Based on all places, regardless of population

Place	Number	%
Lakewood (township) Ocean County	643	1.07
Teaneck (cdp) Bergen County	571	1.45
Marlboro (township) Monmouth County	474	1.30
Bridgewater (township) Somerset County	402	0.94
Jersey City (city) Hudson County	388	0.16
Vineland (city) Cumberland County	382	0.68
Dover (township) Ocean County	381	0.42
Toms River (cdp) Ocean County	368	0.43
Newark (city) Essex County	365	0.13
Edison (cdp) Middlesex County	351	0.36

Top 10 Places Sorted by Percent
Based on all places, regardless of population

Place	Number	%
Roosevelt (borough) Monmouth County	25	2.69
Harding (township) Morris County	81	2.55
Tenafly (borough) Bergen County	321	2.33
McGuire AFB (cdp) Burlington County	153	2.33
Hampton (township) Sussex County	113	2.29
Rockleigh (borough) Bergen County	9	2.26
Greenwich (township) Cumberland County	18	2.14
Fair Haven (borough) Monmouth County	117	1.97
Frenchtown (borough) Hunterdon County	29	1.95
Great Meadows-Vienna (cdp) Warren County	25	1.90

Top 10 Places Sorted by Percent
Based on places with populations of 10,000 or more

Place	Number	%
Tenafly (borough) Bergen County	321	2.33
Hopewell (township) Mercer County	272	1.69
Millburn (cdp) Essex County	324	1.64
Teaneck (cdp) Bergen County	571	1.45
Warren (township) Somerset County	199	1.40
Moorestown-Lenola (cdp) Burlington County	188	1.36
Princeton (township) Mercer County	210	1.31
Marlboro (township) Monmouth County	474	1.30
Glen Rock (borough) Bergen County	149	1.29
Upper (township) Cape May County	150	1.24

Finnish

Top 10 Places Sorted by Number
Based on all places, regardless of population

Place	Number	%
Jersey City (city) Hudson County	156	0.06
Mount Laurel (township) Burlington County	131	0.33
Little Egg Harbor (township) Ocean County	88	0.55
Manchester (township) Ocean County	87	0.22
Washington (township) Morris County	75	0.43
Middletown (township) Monmouth County	75	0.11
West Milford (cdp) Passaic County	74	0.28
South Brunswick (township) Middlesex County	74	0.20
Dover (township) Ocean County	72	0.08
Toms River (cdp) Ocean County	72	0.08

Top 10 Places Sorted by Percent
Based on all places, regardless of population

Place	Number	%
Millstone (borough) Somerset County	17	4.08

Place	Number	%
Long Valley (cdp) Morris County	29	1.52
Seaside Park (borough) Ocean County	28	1.24
Montvale (borough) Bergen County	64	0.91
Ogdensburg (borough) Sussex County	24	0.91
Peapack and Gladstone (borough) Somerset Co.	22	0.90
Milltown (borough) Middlesex County	61	0.87
Franklin (township) Hunterdon County	26	0.87
Bay Head (borough) Ocean County	11	0.85
Bass River (township) Burlington County	13	0.84

Top 10 Places Sorted by Percent
Based on places with populations of 10,000 or more

Place	Number	%
Little Egg Harbor (township) Ocean County	88	0.55
Washington (township) Morris County	75	0.43
Barclay-Kingston (cdp) Camden County	43	0.40
Hillsdale (borough) Bergen County	39	0.39
Moorestown-Lenola (cdp) Burlington County	51	0.37
Holmdel (township) Monmouth County	55	0.35
Ringwood (borough) Passaic County	44	0.35
Mount Laurel (township) Burlington County	131	0.33
Princeton (township) Mercer County	52	0.32
Hanover (township) Morris County	37	0.29

French, except Basque

Top 10 Places Sorted by Number
Based on all places, regardless of population

Place	Number	%
Brick (township) Ocean County	1,760	2.31
Dover (township) Ocean County	1,758	1.96
Toms River (cdp) Ocean County	1,652	1.91
Middletown (township) Monmouth County	1,511	2.28
Hamilton (township) Mercer County	1,395	1.60
Gloucester (township) Camden County	1,215	1.89
Cherry Hill (township) Camden County	1,096	1.57
Jackson (township) Ocean County	1,086	2.54
Jersey City (city) Hudson County	1,055	0.44
Woodbridge (township) Middlesex County	978	1.01

Top 10 Places Sorted by Percent
Based on all places, regardless of population

Place	Number	%
Walpack (township) Sussex County	4	10.81
Brass Castle (cdp) Warren County	125	8.12
Great Meadows-Vienna (cdp) Warren County	86	6.52
Vernon Valley (cdp) Sussex County	102	5.88
Rocky Hill (borough) Somerset County	38	5.78
Mantoloking (borough) Ocean County	20	5.42
Shark River Hills (cdp) Monmouth County	205	5.33
Roosevelt (borough) Monmouth County	46	4.96
Ship Bottom (borough) Ocean County	68	4.87
Atlantic Highlands (borough) Monmouth County	227	4.82

Top 10 Places Sorted by Percent
Based on places with populations of 10,000 or more

Place	Number	%
Upper (township) Cape May County	445	3.67
Florence (township) Burlington County	367	3.42
Vernon (township) Sussex County	827	3.35
Ocean Acres (cdp) Ocean County	421	3.19
Waterford (township) Camden County	321	3.06
Jefferson (township) Morris County	599	3.04
Princeton (township) Mercer County	488	3.04
Readington (township) Hunterdon County	478	3.02
Wanaque (borough) Passaic County	310	3.02
Somers Point (city) Atlantic County	350	3.01

French Canadian

Top 10 Places Sorted by Number
Based on all places, regardless of population

Place	Number	%
Dover (township) Ocean County	472	0.53
Toms River (cdp) Ocean County	465	0.54
Hamilton (township) Mercer County	460	0.53
Brick (township) Ocean County	393	0.52
Howell (township) Monmouth County	352	0.72
Edison (cdp) Middlesex County	345	0.35
Franklin (township) Somerset County	315	0.62
Middletown (township) Monmouth County	303	0.46
Evesham (township) Burlington County	275	0.65
Jackson (township) Ocean County	263	0.61

Top 10 Places Sorted by Percent
Based on all places, regardless of population

Place	Number	%
Manahawkin (cdp) Ocean County	71	3.38
Rockleigh (borough) Bergen County	13	3.26
Swedesboro (borough) Gloucester County	65	3.16
Princeton Junction (cdp) Mercer County	66	2.76
Knowlton (township) Warren County	76	2.52
Mays Landing (cdp) Atlantic County	55	2.41
Barnegat Light (borough) Ocean County	18	2.33
Long Valley (cdp) Morris County	44	2.30
Califon (borough) Hunterdon County	22	2.09
Spring Lake Heights (borough) Monmouth County	108	2.07

Top 10 Places Sorted by Percent
Based on places with populations of 10,000 or more

Place	Number	%
Metuchen (borough) Middlesex County	184	1.43
Mount Holly (borough) Burlington County	151	1.41
Florence (township) Burlington County	134	1.25
Branchburg (township) Somerset County	178	1.22
Barnegat (township) Ocean County	178	1.16
Hopewell (township) Mercer County	155	0.96
Pennsville (township) Salem County	123	0.93
Keansburg (borough) Monmouth County	98	0.91
Mount Olive (township) Morris County	218	0.90
Jefferson (township) Morris County	173	0.88

German

Top 10 Places Sorted by Number
Based on all places, regardless of population

Place	Number	%
Dover (township) Ocean County	16,833	18.75
Toms River (cdp) Ocean County	16,217	18.76
Brick (township) Ocean County	15,859	20.83
Hamilton (township) Mercer County	14,425	16.53
Gloucester (township) Camden County	12,253	19.05
Middletown (township) Monmouth County	11,573	17.45
Woodbridge (township) Middlesex County	10,547	10.85
Cherry Hill (township) Camden County	9,617	13.75
Washington (township) Gloucester County	9,433	20.02
Evesham (township) Burlington County	8,671	20.44

Top 10 Places Sorted by Percent
Based on all places, regardless of population

Place	Number	%
Walpack (township) Sussex County	14	37.84
Milford (borough) Hunterdon County	418	34.98
Glen Gardner (borough) Hunterdon County	636	33.44
Vernon Valley (cdp) Sussex County	558	32.16
North Cape May (cdp) Cape May County	1,151	31.16
Bloomsbury (borough) Hunterdon County	276	31.15
Corbin City (city) Atlantic County	144	30.77
Strathmere (cdp) Cape May County	48	30.77
Bethlehem (township) Hunterdon County	1,166	30.52

Notes: (cdp) census designated place; Refer to the User's Guide in the front of the book for more detailed information.

White (township) Warren County   1,274   30.01

Top 10 Places Sorted by Percent
Based on places with populations of 10,000 or more

Place	Number	%
Mantua (township) Gloucester County	4,000	28.14
West Deptford (township) Gloucester County	5,435	28.06
Southampton (township) Burlington County	2,715	26.28
Upper (township) Cape May County	3,117	25.73
Vernon (township) Sussex County	6,294	25.50
Cinnaminson (township) Burlington County	3,718	25.47
Waterford (township) Camden County	2,665	25.42
Haddon (township) Camden County	3,695	25.20
Lower (township) Cape May County	5,690	24.80
Williamstown (cdp) Gloucester County	2,923	24.75

German Russian

Top 10 Places Sorted by Number
Based on all places, regardless of population

Place	Number	%
Teaneck (cdp) Bergen County	53	0.13
Willingboro (township) Burlington County	25	0.08
Presidential Lakes Estates (cdp) Burlington Co.	21	0.87
Pemberton (township) Burlington County	21	0.07
Lindenwold (borough) Camden County	18	0.10
Asbury Park (city) Monmouth County	17	0.10
Bridgewater (township) Somerset County	15	0.03
Newark (city) Essex County	13	0.00
Eastampton (township) Burlington County	10	0.16
Egg Harbor (township) Atlantic County	10	0.03

Top 10 Places Sorted by Percent
Based on all places, regardless of population

Place	Number	%
Presidential Lakes Estates (cdp) Burlington Co.	21	0.87
Eastampton (township) Burlington County	10	0.16
Teaneck (cdp) Bergen County	53	0.13
Lindenwold (borough) Camden County	18	0.10
Asbury Park (city) Monmouth County	17	0.10
Westampton (township) Burlington County	7	0.10
Willingboro (township) Burlington County	25	0.08
Berlin (borough) Camden County	5	0.08
Pemberton (township) Burlington County	21	0.07
New Milford (borough) Bergen County	8	0.05

Top 10 Places Sorted by Percent
Based on places with populations of 10,000 or more

Place	Number	%
Teaneck (cdp) Bergen County	53	0.13
Lindenwold (borough) Camden County	18	0.10
Asbury Park (city) Monmouth County	17	0.10
Willingboro (township) Burlington County	25	0.08
Pemberton (township) Burlington County	21	0.07
New Milford (borough) Bergen County	8	0.05
Bridgewater (township) Somerset County	15	0.03
Egg Harbor (township) Atlantic County	10	0.03
Millville (city) Cumberland County	8	0.03
Winslow (township) Camden County	6	0.02

Greek

Top 10 Places Sorted by Number
Based on all places, regardless of population

Place	Number	%
Fort Lee (borough) Bergen County	1,346	3.80
Jersey City (city) Hudson County	1,011	0.42
Edison (cdp) Middlesex County	990	1.01
Cherry Hill (township) Camden County	959	1.37
Dover (township) Ocean County	840	0.94
Toms River (cdp) Ocean County	832	0.96
Clifton (city) Passaic County	746	0.95

Place	Number	%
Brick (township) Ocean County	708	0.93
Wayne (cdp) Passaic County	652	1.20
Palisades Park (borough) Bergen County	610	3.57

Top 10 Places Sorted by Percent
Based on all places, regardless of population

Place	Number	%
Allenwood (cdp) Monmouth County	70	8.58
Englewood Cliffs (borough) Bergen County	386	7.25
Alpine (borough) Bergen County	114	5.22
Vista Center (cdp) Ocean County	31	4.36
Oakhurst (cdp) Monmouth County	177	4.29
Erma (cdp) Cape May County	82	3.84
Stanhope (borough) Sussex County	135	3.83
Fort Lee (borough) Bergen County	1,346	3.80
Golden Triangle (cdp) Camden County	123	3.64
Palisades Park (borough) Bergen County	610	3.57

Top 10 Places Sorted by Percent
Based on places with populations of 10,000 or more

Place	Number	%
Fort Lee (borough) Bergen County	1,346	3.80
Palisades Park (borough) Bergen County	610	3.57
River Edge (borough) Bergen County	375	3.43
Ridgefield (borough) Bergen County	252	2.33
New Milford (borough) Bergen County	373	2.27
Cliffside Park (borough) Bergen County	489	2.13
Ventnor City (city) Atlantic County	255	1.98
Dumont (borough) Bergen County	344	1.97
Wall (township) Monmouth County	484	1.92
North Arlington (borough) Bergen County	287	1.89

Guyanese

Top 10 Places Sorted by Number
Based on all places, regardless of population

Place	Number	%
Jersey City (city) Hudson County	1,986	0.83
East Orange (city) Essex County	1,460	2.09
Newark (city) Essex County	1,313	0.48
Irvington (cdp) Essex County	920	1.52
Orange (cdp) Essex County	821	2.50
Bloomfield (cdp) Essex County	394	0.83
South Plainfield (borough) Middlesex County	342	1.57
Union (cdp) Union County	314	0.58
Englewood (city) Bergen County	306	1.17
Piscataway (township) Middlesex County	269	0.53

Top 10 Places Sorted by Percent
Based on all places, regardless of population

Place	Number	%
Orange (cdp) Essex County	821	2.50
East Orange (city) Essex County	1,460	2.09
Sewaren (cdp) Middlesex County	45	1.60
South Plainfield (borough) Middlesex County	342	1.57
Irvington (cdp) Essex County	920	1.52
Englewood (city) Bergen County	306	1.17
Roselle (borough) Union County	202	0.95
Maplewood (cdp) Essex County	216	0.90
Jersey City (city) Hudson County	1,986	0.83
Bloomfield (cdp) Essex County	394	0.83

Top 10 Places Sorted by Percent
Based on places with populations of 10,000 or more

Place	Number	%
Orange (cdp) Essex County	821	2.50
East Orange (city) Essex County	1,460	2.09
South Plainfield (borough) Middlesex County	342	1.57
Irvington (cdp) Essex County	920	1.52
Englewood (city) Bergen County	306	1.17
Roselle (borough) Union County	202	0.95
Maplewood (cdp) Essex County	216	0.90

Place	Number	%
Jersey City (city) Hudson County	1,986	0.83
Bloomfield (cdp) Essex County	394	0.83
South Orange (cdp) Essex County	116	0.68

Hawaii Native/Pacific Islander

Top 10 Places Sorted by Number
Based on all places, regardless of population

Place	Number	%
Newark (city) Essex County	634	0.23
Jersey City (city) Hudson County	617	0.26
Paterson (city) Passaic County	504	0.34
Trenton (city) Mercer County	369	0.43
Camden (city) Camden County	246	0.31
Elizabeth (city) Union County	229	0.19
East Orange (city) Essex County	212	0.30
Irvington (cdp) Essex County	198	0.33
Union City (city) Hudson County	141	0.21
Plainfield (city) Union County	133	0.28

Top 10 Places Sorted by Percent
Based on all places, regardless of population

Place	Number	%
Rockleigh (borough) Bergen County	6	1.53
Rocky Hill (borough) Somerset County	5	0.76
Chesterfield (township) Burlington County	37	0.62
Woodlynne (borough) Camden County	17	0.61
Elwood-Magnolia (cdp) Atlantic County	8	0.57
Madison (borough) Morris County	91	0.55
McGuire AFB (cdp) Burlington County	30	0.46
Trenton (city) Mercer County	369	0.43
Surf City (borough) Ocean County	6	0.42
Asbury Park (city) Monmouth County	65	0.38

Top 10 Places Sorted by Percent
Based on places with populations of 10,000 or more

Place	Number	%
Madison (borough) Morris County	91	0.55
Trenton (city) Mercer County	369	0.43
Asbury Park (city) Monmouth County	65	0.38
Paterson (city) Passaic County	504	0.34
Orange (cdp) Essex County	111	0.34
Irvington (cdp) Essex County	198	0.33
Camden (city) Camden County	246	0.31
East Orange (city) Essex County	212	0.30
Plainfield (city) Union County	133	0.28
Jersey City (city) Hudson County	617	0.26

Hawaii Native/Pacific Islander: Melanesian

Top 10 Places Sorted by Number
Based on all places, regardless of population

Place	Number	%
Washington (township) Gloucester County	7	0.01
Camden (city) Camden County	5	0.01
Paterson (city) Passaic County	4	0.00
Jersey City (city) Hudson County	3	0.00
Berlin (township) Camden County	2	0.04
Elizabeth (city) Union County	2	0.00
Piscataway (township) Middlesex County	2	0.00
Mays Landing (cdp) Atlantic County	1	0.04
Pennington (borough) Mercer County	1	0.04
Bellmawr (borough) Camden County	1	0.01

Top 10 Places Sorted by Percent
Based on all places, regardless of population

Place	Number	%
Berlin (township) Camden County	2	0.04
Mays Landing (cdp) Atlantic County	1	0.04
Pennington (borough) Mercer County	1	0.04
Washington (township) Gloucester County	7	0.01
Camden (city) Camden County	5	0.01

Notes: (cdp) census designated place; Refer to the User's Guide in the front of the book for more detailed information.

Place	Number	%
Bellmawr (borough) Camden County	1	0.01
Keyport (borough) Monmouth County	1	0.01
Madison (borough) Morris County	1	0.01
New Milford (borough) Bergen County	1	0.01
Paterson (city) Passaic County	4	0.00

Top 10 Places Sorted by Percent
Based on places with populations of 10,000 or more

Place	Number	%
Washington (township) Gloucester County	7	0.01
Camden (city) Camden County	5	0.01
Bellmawr (borough) Camden County	1	0.01
Madison (borough) Morris County	1	0.01
New Milford (borough) Bergen County	1	0.01
Paterson (city) Passaic County	4	0.00
Jersey City (city) Hudson County	3	0.00
Elizabeth (city) Union County	2	0.00
Piscataway (township) Middlesex County	2	0.00
Bloomfield (cdp) Essex County	1	0.00

Hawaii Native/Pacific Islander: Fijian

Top 10 Places Sorted by Number
Based on all places, regardless of population

Place	Number	%
Washington (township) Gloucester County	7	0.01
Camden (city) Camden County	5	0.01
Paterson (city) Passaic County	4	0.00
Jersey City (city) Hudson County	3	0.00
Berlin (township) Camden County	2	0.04
Piscataway (township) Middlesex County	2	0.00
Mays Landing (cdp) Atlantic County	1	0.04
Pennington (borough) Mercer County	1	0.04
Bellmawr (borough) Camden County	1	0.01
Madison (borough) Morris County	1	0.01

Top 10 Places Sorted by Percent
Based on all places, regardless of population

Place	Number	%
Berlin (township) Camden County	2	0.04
Mays Landing (cdp) Atlantic County	1	0.04
Pennington (borough) Mercer County	1	0.04
Washington (township) Gloucester County	7	0.01
Camden (city) Camden County	5	0.01
Bellmawr (borough) Camden County	1	0.01
Madison (borough) Morris County	1	0.01
New Milford (borough) Bergen County	1	0.01
Paterson (city) Passaic County	4	0.00
Jersey City (city) Hudson County	3	0.00

Top 10 Places Sorted by Percent
Based on places with populations of 10,000 or more

Place	Number	%
Washington (township) Gloucester County	7	0.01
Camden (city) Camden County	5	0.01
Bellmawr (borough) Camden County	1	0.01
Madison (borough) Morris County	1	0.01
New Milford (borough) Bergen County	1	0.01
Paterson (city) Passaic County	4	0.00
Jersey City (city) Hudson County	3	0.00
Piscataway (township) Middlesex County	2	0.00
Bloomfield (cdp) Essex County	1	0.00
Clifton (city) Passaic County	1	0.00

Hawaii Native/Pacific Islander: Other Melanesian

Top 10 Places Sorted by Number
Based on all places, regardless of population

Place	Number	%
Keyport (borough) Monmouth County	1	0.01
Cliffside Park (borough) Bergen County	1	0.00

Place	Number	%
East Orange (city) Essex County	1	0.00
Elizabeth (city) Union County	1	0.00
Freehold (township) Monmouth County	1	0.00
Hamilton (township) Mercer County	1	0.00

Top 10 Places Sorted by Percent
Based on all places, regardless of population

Place	Number	%
Keyport (borough) Monmouth County	1	0.01
Cliffside Park (borough) Bergen County	1	0.00
East Orange (city) Essex County	1	0.00
Elizabeth (city) Union County	1	0.00
Freehold (township) Monmouth County	1	0.00
Hamilton (township) Mercer County	1	0.00

Top 10 Places Sorted by Percent
Based on places with populations of 10,000 or more

Place	Number	%
Cliffside Park (borough) Bergen County	1	0.00
East Orange (city) Essex County	1	0.00
Elizabeth (city) Union County	1	0.00
Freehold (township) Monmouth County	1	0.00
Hamilton (township) Mercer County	1	0.00

Hawaii Native/Pacific Islander: Micronesian

Top 10 Places Sorted by Number
Based on all places, regardless of population

Place	Number	%
Trenton (city) Mercer County	158	0.19
Plainfield (city) Union County	54	0.11
Newark (city) Essex County	54	0.02
Jersey City (city) Hudson County	47	0.02
Hamilton (township) Mercer County	24	0.03
Paterson (city) Passaic County	21	0.01
Princeton (borough) Mercer County	20	0.14
Camden (city) Camden County	19	0.02
East Windsor (township) Mercer County	18	0.07
New Brunswick (city) Middlesex County	18	0.04

Top 10 Places Sorted by Percent
Based on all places, regardless of population

Place	Number	%
Lawrence (township) Cumberland County	8	0.29
Trenton (city) Mercer County	158	0.19
Flemington (borough) Hunterdon County	7	0.17
Princeton (borough) Mercer County	20	0.14
Wanamassa (cdp) Monmouth County	6	0.13
Shark River Hills (cdp) Monmouth County	5	0.13
South Hackensack (township) Bergen County	3	0.13
Plainfield (city) Union County	54	0.11
Twin Rivers (cdp) Mercer County	8	0.11
Raritan (borough) Somerset County	7	0.11

Top 10 Places Sorted by Percent
Based on places with populations of 10,000 or more

Place	Number	%
Trenton (city) Mercer County	158	0.19
Princeton (borough) Mercer County	20	0.14
Plainfield (city) Union County	54	0.11
Woodbury (city) Gloucester County	8	0.08
East Windsor (township) Mercer County	18	0.07
Bridgeton (city) Cumberland County	17	0.07
Bound Brook (borough) Somerset County	6	0.06
Hillsborough (township) Somerset County	17	0.05
Roselle (borough) Union County	11	0.05
Asbury Park (city) Monmouth County	8	0.05

Hawaii Native/Pacific Islander: Guamanian or Chamorro

Top 10 Places Sorted by Number
Based on all places, regardless of population

Place	Number	%
Trenton (city) Mercer County	158	0.19
Plainfield (city) Union County	54	0.11
Newark (city) Essex County	54	0.02
Jersey City (city) Hudson County	47	0.02
Hamilton (township) Mercer County	24	0.03
Princeton (borough) Mercer County	20	0.14
Paterson (city) Passaic County	20	0.01
Camden (city) Camden County	19	0.02
East Windsor (township) Mercer County	18	0.07
New Brunswick (city) Middlesex County	18	0.04

Top 10 Places Sorted by Percent
Based on all places, regardless of population

Place	Number	%
Lawrence (township) Cumberland County	8	0.29
Trenton (city) Mercer County	158	0.19
Princeton (borough) Mercer County	20	0.14
Wanamassa (cdp) Monmouth County	6	0.13
Shark River Hills (cdp) Monmouth County	5	0.13
South Hackensack (township) Bergen County	3	0.13
Plainfield (city) Union County	54	0.11
Twin Rivers (cdp) Mercer County	8	0.11
Glen Gardner (borough) Hunterdon County	2	0.11
Roosevelt (borough) Monmouth County	1	0.11

Top 10 Places Sorted by Percent
Based on places with populations of 10,000 or more

Place	Number	%
Trenton (city) Mercer County	158	0.19
Princeton (borough) Mercer County	20	0.14
Plainfield (city) Union County	54	0.11
Woodbury (city) Gloucester County	8	0.08
East Windsor (township) Mercer County	18	0.07
Bridgeton (city) Cumberland County	17	0.07
Bound Brook (borough) Somerset County	6	0.06
Roselle (borough) Union County	10	0.05
Asbury Park (city) Monmouth County	8	0.05
New Brunswick (city) Middlesex County	18	0.04

Hawaii Native/Pacific Islander: Other Micronesian

Top 10 Places Sorted by Number
Based on all places, regardless of population

Place	Number	%
Hillsborough (township) Somerset County	15	0.04
Raritan (borough) Somerset County	7	0.11
Millville (city) Cumberland County	6	0.02
Colonia (cdp) Middlesex County	5	0.03
Woodbridge (township) Middlesex County	5	0.01
Bernards (township) Somerset County	4	0.02
Flemington (borough) Hunterdon County	3	0.07
Middlesex (borough) Middlesex County	3	0.02
East Brunswick (cdp) Middlesex County	3	0.01
Piscataway (township) Middlesex County	3	0.01

Top 10 Places Sorted by Percent
Based on all places, regardless of population

Place	Number	%
Raritan (borough) Somerset County	7	0.11
Flemington (borough) Hunterdon County	3	0.07
Hillsborough (township) Somerset County	15	0.04
Colonia (cdp) Middlesex County	5	0.03
Millville (city) Cumberland County	6	0.02
Bernards (township) Somerset County	4	0.02
Middlesex (borough) Middlesex County	3	0.02

Notes: (cdp) census designated place; Refer to the User's Guide in the front of the book for more detailed information.

Place	Number	%
Fairview (borough) Bergen County	2	0.02
Hackettstown (town) Warren County	2	0.02
Totowa (borough) Passaic County	2	0.02

Top 10 Places Sorted by Percent
Based on places with populations of 10,000 or more

Place	Number	%
Hillsborough (township) Somerset County	15	0.04
Colonia (cdp) Middlesex County	5	0.03
Millville (city) Cumberland County	6	0.02
Bernards (township) Somerset County	4	0.02
Middlesex (borough) Middlesex County	3	0.02
Fairview (borough) Bergen County	2	0.02
Hackettstown (town) Warren County	2	0.02
Woodbridge (township) Middlesex County	5	0.01
East Brunswick (cdp) Middlesex County	3	0.01
Piscataway (township) Middlesex County	3	0.01

Hawaii Native/Pacific Islander: Polynesian

Top 10 Places Sorted by Number
Based on all places, regardless of population

Place	Number	%
Newark (city) Essex County	126	0.05
Jersey City (city) Hudson County	104	0.04
Paterson (city) Passaic County	58	0.04
East Orange (city) Essex County	52	0.07
Camden (city) Camden County	46	0.06
Vineland (city) Cumberland County	45	0.08
Pemberton (township) Burlington County	38	0.13
Woodbridge (township) Middlesex County	29	0.03
New Brunswick (city) Middlesex County	28	0.06
Elizabeth (city) Union County	28	0.02

Top 10 Places Sorted by Percent
Based on all places, regardless of population

Place	Number	%
Rocky Hill (borough) Somerset County	5	0.76
Elwood-Magnolia (cdp) Atlantic County	7	0.50
Surf City (borough) Ocean County	6	0.42
Folsom (borough) Atlantic County	7	0.35
Milford (borough) Hunterdon County	4	0.33
Lawrenceville (cdp) Mercer County	12	0.29
Fort Dix (cdp) Burlington County	21	0.28
West Belmar (cdp) Monmouth County	7	0.27
Gibbsboro (borough) Camden County	6	0.25
McGuire AFB (cdp) Burlington County	14	0.22

Top 10 Places Sorted by Percent
Based on places with populations of 10,000 or more

Place	Number	%
Delran (township) Burlington County	22	0.14
Pemberton (township) Burlington County	38	0.13
Woodbury (city) Gloucester County	11	0.11
Glassboro (borough) Gloucester County	17	0.09
South Orange (cdp) Essex County	15	0.09
Browns Mills (cdp) Burlington County	10	0.09
Vineland (city) Cumberland County	45	0.08
Colonia (cdp) Middlesex County	14	0.08
Cherry Hill Mall (cdp) Camden County	11	0.08
Eatontown (borough) Monmouth County	11	0.08

Hawaii Native/Pacific Islander: Native Hawaiian

Top 10 Places Sorted by Number
Based on all places, regardless of population

Place	Number	%
Newark (city) Essex County	80	0.03
Jersey City (city) Hudson County	57	0.02
Camden (city) Camden County	34	0.04
Pemberton (township) Burlington County	30	0.10
Paterson (city) Passaic County	24	0.02
Vineland (city) Cumberland County	21	0.04
New Brunswick (city) Middlesex County	19	0.04
Galloway (township) Atlantic County	18	0.06
Mount Laurel (township) Burlington County	18	0.04
Passaic (city) Passaic County	17	0.03

Top 10 Places Sorted by Percent
Based on all places, regardless of population

Place	Number	%
Rocky Hill (borough) Somerset County	5	0.76
Elwood-Magnolia (cdp) Atlantic County	7	0.50
Surf City (borough) Ocean County	6	0.42
Gibbsboro (borough) Camden County	6	0.25
Folsom (borough) Atlantic County	5	0.25
West Belmar (cdp) Monmouth County	6	0.23
Mullica (township) Atlantic County	11	0.19
Frelinghuysen (township) Warren County	4	0.19
Fort Dix (cdp) Burlington County	13	0.17
Ho-Ho-Kus (borough) Bergen County	7	0.17

Top 10 Places Sorted by Percent
Based on places with populations of 10,000 or more

Place	Number	%
Pemberton (township) Burlington County	30	0.10
Lindenwold (borough) Camden County	12	0.07
Browns Mills (cdp) Burlington County	8	0.07
Woodbury (city) Gloucester County	7	0.07
Galloway (township) Atlantic County	18	0.06
West Deptford (township) Gloucester County	11	0.06
Brigantine (city) Atlantic County	8	0.06
Red Bank (borough) Monmouth County	7	0.06
Upper (township) Cape May County	7	0.06
Florence (township) Burlington County	6	0.06

Hawaii Native/Pacific Islander: Samoan

Top 10 Places Sorted by Number
Based on all places, regardless of population

Place	Number	%
Newark (city) Essex County	46	0.02
Jersey City (city) Hudson County	45	0.02
Paterson (city) Passaic County	34	0.02
East Orange (city) Essex County	26	0.04
Vineland (city) Cumberland County	16	0.03
Delran (township) Burlington County	14	0.09
Perth Amboy (city) Middlesex County	14	0.03
Kearny (town) Hudson County	13	0.03
Trenton (city) Mercer County	13	0.02
Elizabeth (city) Union County	13	0.01

Top 10 Places Sorted by Percent
Based on all places, regardless of population

Place	Number	%
Milford (borough) Hunterdon County	4	0.33
Wildwood (city) Cape May County	11	0.20
Clementon (borough) Camden County	10	0.20
South Hackensack (township) Bergen County	4	0.18
Lawrenceville (cdp) Mercer County	7	0.17
Hightstown (borough) Mercer County	8	0.15
Leonardo (cdp) Monmouth County	3	0.11
Paulsboro (borough) Gloucester County	6	0.10
Folsom (borough) Atlantic County	2	0.10
Delran (township) Burlington County	14	0.09

Top 10 Places Sorted by Percent
Based on places with populations of 10,000 or more

Place	Number	%
Delran (township) Burlington County	14	0.09
Cherry Hill Mall (cdp) Camden County	9	0.07
Colonia (cdp) Middlesex County	9	0.05
Beachwood (borough) Ocean County	5	0.05

Place	Number	%
Leisure Village W-Pine Lake Pk (cdp) Ocean Co.	5	0.05
East Orange (city) Essex County	26	0.04
Nutley (cdp) Essex County	10	0.04
Jefferson (township) Morris County	8	0.04
Ocean City (city) Cape May County	6	0.04
Ridgefield Park (village) Bergen County	5	0.04

Hawaii Native/Pacific Islander: Tongan

Top 10 Places Sorted by Number
Based on all places, regardless of population

Place	Number	%
Mount Laurel (township) Burlington County	5	0.01
Carneys Point (township) Salem County	2	0.03
Princeton (township) Mercer County	2	0.00
Trenton (city) Mercer County	2	0.00
Mays Landing (cdp) Atlantic County	1	0.04
Colonia (cdp) Middlesex County	1	0.01
Bergenfield (borough) Bergen County	1	0.00
Englewood (city) Bergen County	1	0.00
Galloway (township) Atlantic County	1	0.00
Hamilton (township) Atlantic County	1	0.00

Top 10 Places Sorted by Percent
Based on all places, regardless of population

Place	Number	%
Mays Landing (cdp) Atlantic County	1	0.04
Carneys Point (township) Salem County	2	0.03
Mount Laurel (township) Burlington County	5	0.01
Princeton (township) Mercer County	2	0.01
Colonia (cdp) Middlesex County	1	0.01
Trenton (city) Mercer County	2	0.00
Bergenfield (borough) Bergen County	1	0.00
Englewood (city) Bergen County	1	0.00
Galloway (township) Atlantic County	1	0.00
Hamilton (township) Atlantic County	1	0.00

Top 10 Places Sorted by Percent
Based on places with populations of 10,000 or more

Place	Number	%
Mount Laurel (township) Burlington County	5	0.01
Princeton (township) Mercer County	2	0.01
Colonia (cdp) Middlesex County	1	0.01
Trenton (city) Mercer County	2	0.00
Bergenfield (borough) Bergen County	1	0.00
Englewood (city) Bergen County	1	0.00
Galloway (township) Atlantic County	1	0.00
Hamilton (township) Atlantic County	1	0.00
Lakewood (township) Ocean County	1	0.00
North Bergen (township) Hudson County	1	0.00

Hawaii Native/Pacific Islander: Other Polynesian

Top 10 Places Sorted by Number
Based on all places, regardless of population

Place	Number	%
East Orange (city) Essex County	14	0.02
Glassboro (borough) Gloucester County	9	0.05
Vineland (city) Cumberland County	8	0.01
Middle (township) Cape May County	6	0.04
Cape May Court House (cdp) Cape May County	4	0.09
Little Silver (borough) Monmouth County	3	0.05
Oceanport (borough) Monmouth County	3	0.05
Villas (cdp) Cape May County	3	0.03
Lower (township) Cape May County	3	0.01
Clifton (city) Passaic County	3	0.00

Top 10 Places Sorted by Percent
Based on all places, regardless of population

Place	Number	%
Cape May Court House (cdp) Cape May County	4	0.09

Place	Number	%
Rio Grande (cdp) Cape May County	2	0.08
Glassboro (borough) Gloucester County	9	0.05
Little Silver (borough) Monmouth County	3	0.05
Oceanport (borough) Monmouth County	3	0.05
Middle (township) Cape May County	6	0.04
Villas (cdp) Cape May County	3	0.03
Fort Dix (cdp) Burlington County	2	0.03
East Orange (city) Essex County	14	0.02
Bradley Beach (borough) Monmouth County	1	0.02

Top 10 Places Sorted by Percent
Based on places with populations of 10,000 or more

Place	Number	%
Glassboro (borough) Gloucester County	9	0.05
Middle (township) Cape May County	6	0.04
East Orange (city) Essex County	14	0.02
Vineland (city) Cumberland County	8	0.01
Lower (township) Cape May County	3	0.01
North Arlington (borough) Bergen County	2	0.01
Pemberton (township) Burlington County	2	0.01
South Orange (cdp) Essex County	2	0.01
Summit (city) Union County	2	0.01
Voorhees (township) Camden County	2	0.01

Hawaii Native/Pacific Islander: Other Pacific Islander, specified

Top 10 Places Sorted by Number
Based on all places, regardless of population

Place	Number	%
Jersey City (city) Hudson County	37	0.02
Newark (city) Essex County	34	0.01
Union City (city) Hudson County	15	0.02
Paterson (city) Passaic County	14	0.01
Neptune (township) Monmouth County	10	0.04
East Orange (city) Essex County	10	0.01
Woodbridge (township) Middlesex County	10	0.01
Bayonne (city) Hudson County	9	0.01
Camden (city) Camden County	9	0.01
Teaneck (cdp) Bergen County	8	0.02

Top 10 Places Sorted by Percent
Based on all places, regardless of population

Place	Number	%
Rockleigh (borough) Bergen County	6	1.53
Elsinboro (township) Salem County	3	0.27
Wrightstown (borough) Burlington County	1	0.13
Kingston (cdp) Middlesex County	1	0.08
Chesterfield (township) Burlington County	4	0.07
Eagleswood (township) Ocean County	1	0.07
Neptune (township) Monmouth County	10	0.04
Asbury Park (city) Monmouth County	6	0.04
West Amwell (township) Hunterdon County	1	0.04
Rockaway (township) Morris County	7	0.03

Top 10 Places Sorted by Percent
Based on places with populations of 10,000 or more

Place	Number	%
Neptune (township) Monmouth County	10	0.04
Asbury Park (city) Monmouth County	6	0.04
Rockaway (township) Morris County	7	0.03
Avenel (cdp) Middlesex County	6	0.03
Bridgeton (city) Cumberland County	6	0.03
Lindenwold (borough) Camden County	6	0.03
Raritan (township) Hunterdon County	6	0.03
Jersey City (city) Hudson County	37	0.02
Union City (city) Hudson County	15	0.02
Teaneck (cdp) Bergen County	8	0.02

Hawaii Native/Pacific Islander: Other Pacific Islander, not specified

Top 10 Places Sorted by Number
Based on all places, regardless of population

Place	Number	%
Jersey City (city) Hudson County	426	0.18
Newark (city) Essex County	420	0.15
Paterson (city) Passaic County	407	0.27
Elizabeth (city) Union County	184	0.15
Trenton (city) Mercer County	181	0.21
Camden (city) Camden County	167	0.21
Irvington (cdp) Essex County	159	0.26
East Orange (city) Essex County	139	0.20
Union City (city) Hudson County	100	0.15
Edison (cdp) Middlesex County	94	0.10

Top 10 Places Sorted by Percent
Based on all places, regardless of population

Place	Number	%
Madison (borough) Morris County	87	0.53
Woodlynne (borough) Camden County	12	0.43
Chesterfield (township) Burlington County	20	0.34
Beverly (city) Burlington County	8	0.30
Manahawkin (cdp) Ocean County	6	0.30
Orange (cdp) Essex County	92	0.28
West Long Branch (borough) Monmouth County	23	0.28
Paterson (city) Passaic County	407	0.27
Irvington (cdp) Essex County	159	0.26
Barnegat Light (borough) Ocean County	2	0.26

Top 10 Places Sorted by Percent
Based on places with populations of 10,000 or more

Place	Number	%
Madison (borough) Morris County	87	0.53
Orange (cdp) Essex County	92	0.28
Paterson (city) Passaic County	407	0.27
Irvington (cdp) Essex County	159	0.26
Asbury Park (city) Monmouth County	41	0.24
Trenton (city) Mercer County	181	0.21
Camden (city) Camden County	167	0.21
East Orange (city) Essex County	139	0.20
Jersey City (city) Hudson County	426	0.18
Perth Amboy (city) Middlesex County	81	0.17

Hispanic or Latino

Top 10 Places Sorted by Number
Based on all places, regardless of population

Place	Number	%
Newark (city) Essex County	80,622	29.47
Paterson (city) Passaic County	74,774	50.11
Jersey City (city) Hudson County	67,952	28.31
Elizabeth (city) Union County	59,627	49.46
Union City (city) Hudson County	55,226	82.32
Passaic (city) Passaic County	42,387	62.46
West New York (town) Hudson County	36,038	78.74
North Bergen (township) Hudson County	33,260	57.25
Perth Amboy (city) Middlesex County	33,033	69.83
Camden (city) Camden County	31,019	38.82

Top 10 Places Sorted by Percent
Based on all places, regardless of population

Place	Number	%
Union City (city) Hudson County	55,226	82.32
West New York (town) Hudson County	36,038	78.74
Perth Amboy (city) Middlesex County	33,033	69.83
Passaic (city) Passaic County	42,387	62.46
Dover (town) Morris County	10,539	57.94
North Bergen (township) Hudson County	33,260	57.25
Guttenberg (town) Hudson County	5,871	54.33
Victory Gardens (borough) Morris County	783	50.65

Place	Number	%
Paterson (city) Passaic County	74,774	50.11
Elizabeth (city) Union County	59,627	49.46

Top 10 Places Sorted by Percent
Based on places with populations of 10,000 or more

Place	Number	%
Union City (city) Hudson County	55,226	82.32
West New York (town) Hudson County	36,038	78.74
Perth Amboy (city) Middlesex County	33,033	69.83
Passaic (city) Passaic County	42,387	62.46
Dover (town) Morris County	10,539	57.94
North Bergen (township) Hudson County	33,260	57.25
Guttenberg (town) Hudson County	5,871	54.33
Paterson (city) Passaic County	74,774	50.11
Elizabeth (city) Union County	59,627	49.46
Weehawken (township) Hudson County	5,487	40.64

Hispanic: Central American

Top 10 Places Sorted by Number
Based on all places, regardless of population

Place	Number	%
Elizabeth (city) Union County	6,126	5.08
Union City (city) Hudson County	5,750	8.57
Jersey City (city) Hudson County	4,752	1.98
West New York (town) Hudson County	3,978	8.69
Trenton (city) Mercer County	3,902	4.57
Plainfield (city) Union County	3,846	8.04
Newark (city) Essex County	3,785	1.38
North Bergen (township) Hudson County	2,739	4.71
Paterson (city) Passaic County	2,284	1.53
New Brunswick (city) Middlesex County	2,198	4.53

Top 10 Places Sorted by Percent
Based on all places, regardless of population

Place	Number	%
Bound Brook (borough) Somerset County	1,202	11.84
Fairview (borough) Bergen County	1,283	9.68
West New York (town) Hudson County	3,978	8.69
Union City (city) Hudson County	5,750	8.57
Plainfield (city) Union County	3,846	8.04
North Plainfield (borough) Somerset County	1,311	6.21
Morristown (town) Morris County	1,139	6.14
Guttenberg (town) Hudson County	582	5.39
Elizabeth (city) Union County	6,126	5.08
North Bergen (township) Hudson County	2,739	4.71

Top 10 Places Sorted by Percent
Based on places with populations of 10,000 or more

Place	Number	%
Bound Brook (borough) Somerset County	1,202	11.84
Fairview (borough) Bergen County	1,283	9.68
West New York (town) Hudson County	3,978	8.69
Union City (city) Hudson County	5,750	8.57
Plainfield (city) Union County	3,846	8.04
North Plainfield (borough) Somerset County	1,311	6.21
Morristown (town) Morris County	1,139	6.14
Guttenberg (town) Hudson County	582	5.39
Elizabeth (city) Union County	6,126	5.08
North Bergen (township) Hudson County	2,739	4.71

Hispanic: Costa Rican

Top 10 Places Sorted by Number
Based on all places, regardless of population

Place	Number	%
Bound Brook (borough) Somerset County	941	9.27
Trenton (city) Mercer County	795	0.93
Paterson (city) Passaic County	789	0.53
Summit (city) Union County	640	3.03
Somerville (borough) Somerset County	464	3.74
Elizabeth (city) Union County	323	0.27

Notes: (cdp) census designated place; Refer to the User's Guide in the front of the book for more detailed information.

Place	Number	%
Bridgewater (township) Somerset County	316	0.74
Newark (city) Essex County	282	0.10
Dover (town) Morris County	239	1.31
Hillsborough (township) Somerset County	210	0.57

Top 10 Places Sorted by Percent
Based on all places, regardless of population

Place	Number	%
Bound Brook (borough) Somerset County	941	9.27
Somerville (borough) Somerset County	464	3.74
Raritan (borough) Somerset County	194	3.06
Summit (city) Union County	640	3.03
South Bound Brook (borough) Somerset County	88	1.96
Clinton (town) Hunterdon County	39	1.48
Dover (town) Morris County	239	1.31
Manville (borough) Somerset County	128	1.24
Prospect Park (borough) Passaic County	61	1.06
Frenchtown (borough) Hunterdon County	14	0.94

Top 10 Places Sorted by Percent
Based on places with populations of 10,000 or more

Place	Number	%
Bound Brook (borough) Somerset County	941	9.27
Somerville (borough) Somerset County	464	3.74
Summit (city) Union County	640	3.03
Dover (town) Morris County	239	1.31
Manville (borough) Somerset County	128	1.24
Trenton (city) Mercer County	795	0.93
Springfield (cdp) Union County	108	0.75
Bridgewater (township) Somerset County	316	0.74
Berkeley Heights (cdp) Union County	98	0.73
Hackettstown (town) Warren County	69	0.66

Hispanic: Guatemalan

Top 10 Places Sorted by Number
Based on all places, regardless of population

Place	Number	%
Trenton (city) Mercer County	2,644	3.10
Plainfield (city) Union County	1,443	3.02
Newark (city) Essex County	776	0.28
Fairview (borough) Bergen County	722	5.45
Elizabeth (city) Union County	537	0.45
Union City (city) Hudson County	525	0.78
Jersey City (city) Hudson County	520	0.22
North Bergen (township) Hudson County	467	0.80
Paterson (city) Passaic County	464	0.31
Palisades Park (borough) Bergen County	451	2.64

Top 10 Places Sorted by Percent
Based on all places, regardless of population

Place	Number	%
Fairview (borough) Bergen County	722	5.45
Trenton (city) Mercer County	2,644	3.10
Plainfield (city) Union County	1,443	3.02
Kingston (cdp) Middlesex County	37	2.86
Palisades Park (borough) Bergen County	451	2.64
North Plainfield (borough) Somerset County	431	2.04
Princeton (borough) Mercer County	264	1.86
East Windsor (township) Mercer County	383	1.54
Morristown (town) Morris County	259	1.40
Chester (borough) Morris County	21	1.28

Top 10 Places Sorted by Percent
Based on places with populations of 10,000 or more

Place	Number	%
Fairview (borough) Bergen County	722	5.45
Trenton (city) Mercer County	2,644	3.10
Plainfield (city) Union County	1,443	3.02
Palisades Park (borough) Bergen County	451	2.64
North Plainfield (borough) Somerset County	431	2.04
Princeton (borough) Mercer County	264	1.86

Place	Number	%
East Windsor (township) Mercer County	383	1.54
Morristown (town) Morris County	259	1.40
Cliffside Park (borough) Bergen County	256	1.11
North Bergen (township) Hudson County	467	0.80

Hispanic: Honduran

Top 10 Places Sorted by Number
Based on all places, regardless of population

Place	Number	%
Jersey City (city) Hudson County	2,192	0.91
Union City (city) Hudson County	1,541	2.30
New Brunswick (city) Middlesex County	1,451	2.99
Elizabeth (city) Union County	1,094	0.91
Plainfield (city) Union County	779	1.63
Newark (city) Essex County	657	0.24
Morristown (town) Morris County	638	3.44
West New York (town) Hudson County	542	1.18
North Bergen (township) Hudson County	509	0.88
Atlantic City (city) Atlantic County	450	1.11

Top 10 Places Sorted by Percent
Based on all places, regardless of population

Place	Number	%
Morristown (town) Morris County	638	3.44
New Brunswick (city) Middlesex County	1,451	2.99
Union City (city) Hudson County	1,541	2.30
Plainfield (city) Union County	779	1.63
West New York (town) Hudson County	542	1.18
North Plainfield (borough) Somerset County	237	1.12
Atlantic City (city) Atlantic County	450	1.11
Guttenberg (town) Hudson County	109	1.01
Dover (town) Morris County	176	0.97
Edgewater Park (township) Burlington County	73	0.93

Top 10 Places Sorted by Percent
Based on places with populations of 10,000 or more

Place	Number	%
Morristown (town) Morris County	638	3.44
New Brunswick (city) Middlesex County	1,451	2.99
Union City (city) Hudson County	1,541	2.30
Plainfield (city) Union County	779	1.63
West New York (town) Hudson County	542	1.18
North Plainfield (borough) Somerset County	237	1.12
Atlantic City (city) Atlantic County	450	1.11
Guttenberg (town) Hudson County	109	1.01
Dover (town) Morris County	176	0.97
Jersey City (city) Hudson County	2,192	0.91

Hispanic: Nicaraguan

Top 10 Places Sorted by Number
Based on all places, regardless of population

Place	Number	%
Camden (city) Camden County	607	0.76
Jersey City (city) Hudson County	351	0.15
Elizabeth (city) Union County	277	0.23
New Brunswick (city) Middlesex County	258	0.53
Union City (city) Hudson County	196	0.29
Pennsauken (cdp) Camden County	177	0.50
Paterson (city) Passaic County	177	0.12
Newark (city) Essex County	174	0.06
North Bergen (township) Hudson County	150	0.26
West New York (town) Hudson County	113	0.25

Top 10 Places Sorted by Percent
Based on all places, regardless of population

Place	Number	%
Camden (city) Camden County	607	0.76
New Brunswick (city) Middlesex County	258	0.53
Pennsauken (cdp) Camden County	177	0.50
Woodlynne (borough) Camden County	13	0.46

Place	Number	%
Merchantville (borough) Camden County	15	0.39
Asbury Park (city) Monmouth County	64	0.38
Guttenberg (town) Hudson County	35	0.32
Union City (city) Hudson County	196	0.29
North Bergen (township) Hudson County	150	0.26
West New York (town) Hudson County	113	0.25

Top 10 Places Sorted by Percent
Based on places with populations of 10,000 or more

Place	Number	%
Camden (city) Camden County	607	0.76
New Brunswick (city) Middlesex County	258	0.53
Pennsauken (cdp) Camden County	177	0.50
Asbury Park (city) Monmouth County	64	0.38
Guttenberg (town) Hudson County	35	0.32
Union City (city) Hudson County	196	0.29
North Bergen (township) Hudson County	150	0.26
West New York (town) Hudson County	113	0.25
Harrison (town) Hudson County	35	0.24
Elizabeth (city) Union County	277	0.23

Hispanic: Panamanian

Top 10 Places Sorted by Number
Based on all places, regardless of population

Place	Number	%
Jersey City (city) Hudson County	236	0.10
Newark (city) Essex County	152	0.06
Pemberton (township) Burlington County	107	0.37
Bayonne (city) Hudson County	97	0.16
Willingboro (township) Burlington County	76	0.23
Union City (city) Hudson County	58	0.09
Elizabeth (city) Union County	57	0.05
Plainfield (city) Union County	56	0.12
North Bergen (township) Hudson County	55	0.09
Paterson (city) Passaic County	47	0.03

Top 10 Places Sorted by Percent
Based on all places, regardless of population

Place	Number	%
Pemberton Heights (cdp) Burlington County	31	1.23
Whitesboro-Burleigh (cdp) Cape May County	19	1.03
Browns Mills (cdp) Burlington County	45	0.40
McGuire AFB (cdp) Burlington County	26	0.40
Pemberton (township) Burlington County	107	0.37
Pemberton (borough) Burlington County	4	0.33
Country Lake Estates (cdp) Burlington County	12	0.30
Elwood-Magnolia (cdp) Atlantic County	4	0.29
Presidential Lakes Estates (cdp) Burlington Co.	6	0.26
Victory Gardens (borough) Morris County	4	0.26

Top 10 Places Sorted by Percent
Based on places with populations of 10,000 or more

Place	Number	%
Browns Mills (cdp) Burlington County	45	0.40
Pemberton (township) Burlington County	107	0.37
Willingboro (township) Burlington County	76	0.23
Mount Holly (township) Burlington County	24	0.22
Eatontown (borough) Monmouth County	30	0.21
Burlington (township) Burlington County	40	0.20
Lumberton (township) Burlington County	21	0.20
Bayonne (city) Hudson County	97	0.16
Middle (township) Cape May County	27	0.16
Ridgefield Park (village) Bergen County	18	0.14

Hispanic: Salvadoran

Top 10 Places Sorted by Number
Based on all places, regardless of population

Place	Number	%
Elizabeth (city) Union County	3,518	2.92
Union City (city) Hudson County	3,099	4.62

Notes: (cdp) census designated place; Refer to the User's Guide in the front of the book for more detailed information.

Place	Number	%
West New York (town) Hudson County	2,491	5.44
Newark (city) Essex County	1,565	0.57
North Bergen (township) Hudson County	1,273	2.19
Plainfield (city) Union County	1,260	2.63
Jersey City (city) Hudson County	932	0.39
Paterson (city) Passaic County	514	0.34
North Plainfield (borough) Somerset County	488	2.31
Cliffside Park (borough) Bergen County	467	2.03

Top 10 Places Sorted by Percent
Based on all places, regardless of population

Place	Number	%
West New York (town) Hudson County	2,491	5.44
Union City (city) Hudson County	3,099	4.62
Fairview (borough) Bergen County	456	3.44
Guttenberg (town) Hudson County	318	2.94
Elizabeth (city) Union County	3,518	2.92
Plainfield (city) Union County	1,260	2.63
North Plainfield (borough) Somerset County	488	2.31
North Bergen (township) Hudson County	1,273	2.19
Cliffside Park (borough) Bergen County	467	2.03
Dunellen (borough) Middlesex County	100	1.47

Top 10 Places Sorted by Percent
Based on places with populations of 10,000 or more

Place	Number	%
West New York (town) Hudson County	2,491	5.44
Union City (city) Hudson County	3,099	4.62
Fairview (borough) Bergen County	456	3.44
Guttenberg (town) Hudson County	318	2.94
Elizabeth (city) Union County	3,518	2.92
Plainfield (city) Union County	1,260	2.63
North Plainfield (borough) Somerset County	488	2.31
North Bergen (township) Hudson County	1,273	2.19
Cliffside Park (borough) Bergen County	467	2.03
Weehawken (township) Hudson County	176	1.30

Hispanic: Other Central American

Top 10 Places Sorted by Number
Based on all places, regardless of population

Place	Number	%
West New York (town) Hudson County	351	0.77
Jersey City (city) Hudson County	333	0.14
Elizabeth (city) Union County	320	0.27
Union City (city) Hudson County	242	0.36
Trenton (city) Mercer County	185	0.22
Plainfield (city) Union County	183	0.38
Newark (city) Essex County	179	0.07
North Bergen (township) Hudson County	169	0.29
New Brunswick (city) Middlesex County	147	0.30
Paterson (city) Passaic County	116	0.08

Top 10 Places Sorted by Percent
Based on all places, regardless of population

Place	Number	%
West New York (town) Hudson County	351	0.77
Plainfield (city) Union County	183	0.38
Morristown (town) Morris County	70	0.38
Guttenberg (town) Hudson County	40	0.37
Union City (city) Hudson County	242	0.36
North Plainfield (borough) Somerset County	65	0.31
South Hackensack (township) Bergen County	7	0.31
New Brunswick (city) Middlesex County	147	0.30
North Bergen (township) Hudson County	169	0.29
Fairview (borough) Bergen County	38	0.29

Top 10 Places Sorted by Percent
Based on places with populations of 10,000 or more

Place	Number	%
West New York (town) Hudson County	351	0.77
Plainfield (city) Union County	183	0.38

Place	Number	%
Morristown (town) Morris County	70	0.38
Guttenberg (town) Hudson County	40	0.37
Union City (city) Hudson County	242	0.36
North Plainfield (borough) Somerset County	65	0.31
New Brunswick (city) Middlesex County	147	0.30
North Bergen (township) Hudson County	169	0.29
Fairview (borough) Bergen County	38	0.29
Elizabeth (city) Union County	320	0.27

Hispanic: Cuban

Top 10 Places Sorted by Number
Based on all places, regardless of population

Place	Number	%
Union City (city) Hudson County	10,296	15.35
West New York (town) Hudson County	8,991	19.64
North Bergen (township) Hudson County	7,635	13.14
Elizabeth (city) Union County	7,069	5.86
Newark (city) Essex County	2,962	1.08
Jersey City (city) Hudson County	1,860	0.77
Guttenberg (town) Hudson County	1,203	11.13
Weehawken (township) Hudson County	1,182	8.75
Perth Amboy (city) Middlesex County	918	1.94
Paterson (city) Passaic County	858	0.57

Top 10 Places Sorted by Percent
Based on all places, regardless of population

Place	Number	%
West New York (town) Hudson County	8,991	19.64
Union City (city) Hudson County	10,296	15.35
North Bergen (township) Hudson County	7,635	13.14
Guttenberg (town) Hudson County	1,203	11.13
Weehawken (township) Hudson County	1,182	8.75
Elizabeth (city) Union County	7,069	5.86
Fairview (borough) Bergen County	562	4.24
Ridgefield Park (village) Bergen County	513	3.99
Ridgefield (borough) Bergen County	361	3.33
Harrison (town) Hudson County	438	3.04

Top 10 Places Sorted by Percent
Based on places with populations of 10,000 or more

Place	Number	%
West New York (town) Hudson County	8,991	19.64
Union City (city) Hudson County	10,296	15.35
North Bergen (township) Hudson County	7,635	13.14
Guttenberg (town) Hudson County	1,203	11.13
Weehawken (township) Hudson County	1,182	8.75
Elizabeth (city) Union County	7,069	5.86
Fairview (borough) Bergen County	562	4.24
Ridgefield Park (village) Bergen County	513	3.99
Ridgefield (borough) Bergen County	361	3.33
Harrison (town) Hudson County	438	3.04

Hispanic: Dominican Republic

Top 10 Places Sorted by Number
Based on all places, regardless of population

Place	Number	%
Paterson (city) Passaic County	15,331	10.27
Jersey City (city) Hudson County	9,186	3.83
Perth Amboy (city) Middlesex County	8,897	18.81
Passaic (city) Passaic County	8,865	13.06
Union City (city) Hudson County	7,688	11.46
Newark (city) Essex County	6,266	2.29
West New York (town) Hudson County	3,847	8.41
Elizabeth (city) Union County	3,629	3.01
North Bergen (township) Hudson County	3,228	5.56
New Brunswick (city) Middlesex County	2,855	5.88

Top 10 Places Sorted by Percent
Based on all places, regardless of population

Place	Number	%
Perth Amboy (city) Middlesex County	8,897	18.81
Passaic (city) Passaic County	8,865	13.06
Union City (city) Hudson County	7,688	11.46
Paterson (city) Passaic County	15,331	10.27
West New York (town) Hudson County	3,847	8.41
New Brunswick (city) Middlesex County	2,855	5.88
Weehawken (township) Hudson County	775	5.74
North Bergen (township) Hudson County	3,228	5.56
Prospect Park (borough) Passaic County	305	5.28
Guttenberg (town) Hudson County	550	5.09

Top 10 Places Sorted by Percent
Based on places with populations of 10,000 or more

Place	Number	%
Perth Amboy (city) Middlesex County	8,897	18.81
Passaic (city) Passaic County	8,865	13.06
Union City (city) Hudson County	7,688	11.46
Paterson (city) Passaic County	15,331	10.27
West New York (town) Hudson County	3,847	8.41
New Brunswick (city) Middlesex County	2,855	5.88
Weehawken (township) Hudson County	775	5.74
North Bergen (township) Hudson County	3,228	5.56
Guttenberg (town) Hudson County	550	5.09
Jersey City (city) Hudson County	9,186	3.83

Hispanic: Mexican

Top 10 Places Sorted by Number
Based on all places, regardless of population

Place	Number	%
Passaic (city) Passaic County	13,346	19.67
New Brunswick (city) Middlesex County	7,364	15.16
Paterson (city) Passaic County	5,004	3.35
Bridgeton (city) Cumberland County	3,264	14.33
Perth Amboy (city) Middlesex County	3,056	6.46
West New York (town) Hudson County	2,982	6.52
Lakewood (township) Ocean County	2,825	4.68
Union City (city) Hudson County	2,752	4.10
Jersey City (city) Hudson County	2,495	1.04
Newark (city) Essex County	2,295	0.84

Top 10 Places Sorted by Percent
Based on all places, regardless of population

Place	Number	%
Passaic (city) Passaic County	13,346	19.67
Freehold (borough) Monmouth County	1,903	17.34
New Brunswick (city) Middlesex County	7,364	15.16
Bridgeton (city) Cumberland County	3,264	14.33
Red Bank (borough) Monmouth County	1,171	9.89
Dover (town) Morris County	1,557	8.56
Bound Brook (borough) Somerset County	706	6.95
West New York (town) Hudson County	2,982	6.52
Perth Amboy (city) Middlesex County	3,056	6.46
South Bound Brook (borough) Somerset County	276	6.14

Top 10 Places Sorted by Percent
Based on places with populations of 10,000 or more

Place	Number	%
Passaic (city) Passaic County	13,346	19.67
Freehold (borough) Monmouth County	1,903	17.34
New Brunswick (city) Middlesex County	7,364	15.16
Bridgeton (city) Cumberland County	3,264	14.33
Red Bank (borough) Monmouth County	1,171	9.89
Dover (town) Morris County	1,557	8.56
Bound Brook (borough) Somerset County	706	6.95
West New York (town) Hudson County	2,982	6.52
Perth Amboy (city) Middlesex County	3,056	6.46
Asbury Park (city) Monmouth County	956	5.65

Notes: (cdp) census designated place; Refer to the User's Guide in the front of the book for more detailed information.

Hispanic: Puerto Rican

Top 10 Places Sorted by Number
Based on all places, regardless of population

Place	Number	%
Newark (city) Essex County	39,650	14.49
Jersey City (city) Hudson County	29,777	12.40
Paterson (city) Passaic County	24,013	16.09
Camden (city) Camden County	23,051	28.85
Vineland (city) Cumberland County	13,284	23.61
Perth Amboy (city) Middlesex County	13,145	27.79
Elizabeth (city) Union County	12,989	10.77
Passaic (city) Passaic County	9,122	13.44
Trenton (city) Mercer County	8,952	10.48
Union City (city) Hudson County	7,388	11.01

Top 10 Places Sorted by Percent
Based on all places, regardless of population

Place	Number	%
Elwood-Magnolia (cdp) Atlantic County	428	30.75
Camden (city) Camden County	23,051	28.85
Perth Amboy (city) Middlesex County	13,145	27.79
Vineland (city) Cumberland County	13,284	23.61
Egg Harbor City (city) Atlantic County	880	19.36
Woodbine (borough) Cape May County	478	17.60
Buena (borough) Atlantic County	660	17.04
Woodlynne (borough) Camden County	456	16.31
Paterson (city) Passaic County	24,013	16.09
Washington (township) Burlington County	96	15.46

Top 10 Places Sorted by Percent
Based on places with populations of 10,000 or more

Place	Number	%
Camden (city) Camden County	23,051	28.85
Perth Amboy (city) Middlesex County	13,145	27.79
Vineland (city) Cumberland County	13,284	23.61
Paterson (city) Passaic County	24,013	16.09
Newark (city) Essex County	39,650	14.49
Passaic (city) Passaic County	9,122	13.44
Dover (town) Morris County	2,413	13.27
Jersey City (city) Hudson County	29,777	12.40
Hoboken (city) Hudson County	4,660	12.08
Union City (city) Hudson County	7,388	11.01

Hispanic: South American

Top 10 Places Sorted by Number
Based on all places, regardless of population

Place	Number	%
Elizabeth (city) Union County	14,831	12.30
Paterson (city) Passaic County	13,852	9.28
Newark (city) Essex County	11,134	4.07
Union City (city) Hudson County	10,080	15.03
Jersey City (city) Hudson County	7,807	3.25
North Bergen (township) Hudson County	7,781	13.39
West New York (town) Hudson County	6,237	13.63
Clifton (city) Passaic County	4,305	5.47
Hackensack (city) Bergen County	4,266	10.00
Passaic (city) Passaic County	3,796	5.59

Top 10 Places Sorted by Percent
Based on all places, regardless of population

Place	Number	%
Victory Gardens (borough) Morris County	331	21.41
East Newark (borough) Hudson County	490	20.61
Dover (town) Morris County	3,440	18.91
Union City (city) Hudson County	10,080	15.03
Harrison (town) Hudson County	2,034	14.10
West New York (town) Hudson County	6,237	13.63
North Bergen (township) Hudson County	7,781	13.39
Guttenberg (town) Hudson County	1,410	13.05
Elizabeth (city) Union County	14,831	12.30

| **North Plainfield** (borough) Somerset County | 2,249 | 10.66 |

Top 10 Places Sorted by Percent
Based on places with populations of 10,000 or more

Place	Number	%
Dover (town) Morris County	3,440	18.91
Union City (city) Hudson County	10,080	15.03
Harrison (town) Hudson County	2,034	14.10
West New York (town) Hudson County	6,237	13.63
North Bergen (township) Hudson County	7,781	13.39
Guttenberg (town) Hudson County	1,410	13.05
Elizabeth (city) Union County	14,831	12.30
North Plainfield (borough) Somerset County	2,249	10.66
Hackensack (city) Bergen County	4,266	10.00
Morristown (town) Morris County	1,814	9.78

Hispanic: Argentinean

Top 10 Places Sorted by Number
Based on all places, regardless of population

Place	Number	%
North Bergen (township) Hudson County	414	0.71
Union City (city) Hudson County	404	0.60
Elizabeth (city) Union County	312	0.26
Jersey City (city) Hudson County	300	0.12
Paterson (city) Passaic County	213	0.14
Newark (city) Essex County	213	0.08
West New York (town) Hudson County	179	0.39
Perth Amboy (city) Middlesex County	166	0.35
Clifton (city) Passaic County	160	0.20
Garfield (city) Bergen County	128	0.43

Top 10 Places Sorted by Percent
Based on all places, regardless of population

Place	Number	%
North Bergen (township) Hudson County	414	0.71
Guttenberg (town) Hudson County	76	0.70
Union City (city) Hudson County	404	0.60
Kenilworth (borough) Union County	36	0.47
Weehawken (township) Hudson County	59	0.44
Garfield (city) Bergen County	128	0.43
Prospect Park (borough) Passaic County	24	0.42
Lodi (borough) Bergen County	97	0.40
West New York (town) Hudson County	179	0.39
Fieldsboro (borough) Burlington County	2	0.38

Top 10 Places Sorted by Percent
Based on places with populations of 10,000 or more

Place	Number	%
North Bergen (township) Hudson County	414	0.71
Guttenberg (town) Hudson County	76	0.70
Union City (city) Hudson County	404	0.60
Weehawken (township) Hudson County	59	0.44
Garfield (city) Bergen County	128	0.43
Lodi (borough) Bergen County	97	0.40
West New York (town) Hudson County	179	0.39
Perth Amboy (city) Middlesex County	166	0.35
South River (borough) Middlesex County	54	0.35
Cliffside Park (borough) Bergen County	77	0.33

Hispanic: Bolivian

Top 10 Places Sorted by Number
Based on all places, regardless of population

Place	Number	%
Jersey City (city) Hudson County	244	0.10
Elizabeth (city) Union County	121	0.10
Clifton (city) Passaic County	118	0.15
Passaic (city) Passaic County	103	0.15
Union City (city) Hudson County	71	0.11
Paterson (city) Passaic County	63	0.04
Garfield (city) Bergen County	53	0.18

Orange (cdp) Essex County	52	0.16
Hackensack (city) Bergen County	49	0.11
West New York (town) Hudson County	48	0.10

Top 10 Places Sorted by Percent
Based on all places, regardless of population

Place	Number	%
South Hackensack (township) Bergen County	9	0.40
Deal (borough) Monmouth County	4	0.37
South Amboy (city) Middlesex County	15	0.19
Garfield (city) Bergen County	53	0.18
Bogota (borough) Bergen County	15	0.18
Orange (cdp) Essex County	52	0.16
Clifton (city) Passaic County	118	0.15
Passaic (city) Passaic County	103	0.15
Lodi (borough) Bergen County	33	0.14
Allenhurst (borough) Monmouth County	1	0.14

Top 10 Places Sorted by Percent
Based on places with populations of 10,000 or more

Place	Number	%
Garfield (city) Bergen County	53	0.18
Orange (cdp) Essex County	52	0.16
Clifton (city) Passaic County	118	0.15
Passaic (city) Passaic County	103	0.15
Lodi (borough) Bergen County	33	0.14
Union City (city) Hudson County	71	0.11
Hackensack (city) Bergen County	49	0.11
Jersey City (city) Hudson County	244	0.10
Elizabeth (city) Union County	121	0.10
West New York (town) Hudson County	48	0.10

Hispanic: Chilean

Top 10 Places Sorted by Number
Based on all places, regardless of population

Place	Number	%
Union City (city) Hudson County	352	0.52
North Bergen (township) Hudson County	315	0.54
Dover (town) Morris County	275	1.51
Jersey City (city) Hudson County	269	0.11
Elizabeth (city) Union County	209	0.17
West New York (town) Hudson County	196	0.43
Bayonne (city) Hudson County	128	0.21
Paterson (city) Passaic County	95	0.06
Clifton (city) Passaic County	84	0.11
Newark (city) Essex County	74	0.03

Top 10 Places Sorted by Percent
Based on all places, regardless of population

Place	Number	%
Dover (town) Morris County	275	1.51
Victory Gardens (borough) Morris County	20	1.29
Guttenberg (town) Hudson County	71	0.66
North Bergen (township) Hudson County	315	0.54
Union City (city) Hudson County	352	0.52
Wharton (borough) Morris County	31	0.49
West New York (town) Hudson County	196	0.43
Netcong (borough) Morris County	11	0.43
Weehawken (township) Hudson County	57	0.42
Carlstadt (borough) Bergen County	23	0.39

Top 10 Places Sorted by Percent
Based on places with populations of 10,000 or more

Place	Number	%
Dover (town) Morris County	275	1.51
Guttenberg (town) Hudson County	71	0.66
North Bergen (township) Hudson County	315	0.54
Union City (city) Hudson County	352	0.52
West New York (town) Hudson County	196	0.43
Weehawken (township) Hudson County	57	0.42
Elmwood Park (borough) Bergen County	43	0.23

Notes: (cdp) census designated place; Refer to the User's Guide in the front of the book for more detailed information.

Hackettstown (town) Warren County	24	0.23
Bayonne (city) Hudson County	128	0.21
Harrison (town) Hudson County	30	0.21

Hispanic: Colombian

Top 10 Places Sorted by Number
Based on all places, regardless of population

Place	Number	%
Elizabeth (city) Union County	7,793	6.46
Paterson (city) Passaic County	5,110	3.42
North Bergen (township) Hudson County	3,351	5.77
Union City (city) Hudson County	3,039	4.53
West New York (town) Hudson County	2,664	5.82
Dover (town) Morris County	2,050	11.27
Englewood (city) Bergen County	1,878	7.17
Jersey City (city) Hudson County	1,683	0.70
Hackensack (city) Bergen County	1,634	3.83
Clifton (city) Passaic County	1,581	2.01

Top 10 Places Sorted by Percent
Based on all places, regardless of population

Place	Number	%
Victory Gardens (borough) Morris County	236	15.27
Dover (town) Morris County	2,050	11.27
Morristown (town) Morris County	1,479	7.98
Englewood (city) Bergen County	1,878	7.17
Elizabeth (city) Union County	7,793	6.46
West New York (town) Hudson County	2,664	5.82
North Bergen (township) Hudson County	3,351	5.77
Guttenberg (town) Hudson County	571	5.28
Union City (city) Hudson County	3,039	4.53
Hackensack (city) Bergen County	1,634	3.83

Top 10 Places Sorted by Percent
Based on places with populations of 10,000 or more

Place	Number	%
Dover (town) Morris County	2,050	11.27
Morristown (town) Morris County	1,479	7.98
Englewood (city) Bergen County	1,878	7.17
Elizabeth (city) Union County	7,793	6.46
West New York (town) Hudson County	2,664	5.82
North Bergen (township) Hudson County	3,351	5.77
Guttenberg (town) Hudson County	571	5.28
Union City (city) Hudson County	3,039	4.53
Hackensack (city) Bergen County	1,634	3.83
Fairview (borough) Bergen County	463	3.49

Hispanic: Ecuadorian

Top 10 Places Sorted by Number
Based on all places, regardless of population

Place	Number	%
Newark (city) Essex County	7,611	2.78
Union City (city) Hudson County	3,984	5.94
Jersey City (city) Hudson County	3,920	1.63
North Bergen (township) Hudson County	2,334	4.02
Elizabeth (city) Union County	2,135	1.77
Hackensack (city) Bergen County	2,040	4.78
West New York (town) Hudson County	2,035	4.45
North Plainfield (borough) Somerset County	1,138	5.39
Belleville (cdp) Essex County	1,098	3.06
Plainfield (city) Union County	863	1.80

Top 10 Places Sorted by Percent
Based on all places, regardless of population

Place	Number	%
East Newark (borough) Hudson County	187	7.87
Hightstown (borough) Mercer County	329	6.31
Union City (city) Hudson County	3,984	5.94
North Plainfield (borough) Somerset County	1,138	5.39
Hackensack (city) Bergen County	2,040	4.78

West New York (town) Hudson County	2,035	4.45
North Bergen (township) Hudson County	2,334	4.02
Harrison (town) Hudson County	562	3.90
Guttenberg (town) Hudson County	419	3.88
East Windsor (township) Mercer County	846	3.39

Top 10 Places Sorted by Percent
Based on places with populations of 10,000 or more

Place	Number	%
Union City (city) Hudson County	3,984	5.94
North Plainfield (borough) Somerset County	1,138	5.39
Hackensack (city) Bergen County	2,040	4.78
West New York (town) Hudson County	2,035	4.45
North Bergen (township) Hudson County	2,334	4.02
Harrison (town) Hudson County	562	3.90
Guttenberg (town) Hudson County	419	3.88
East Windsor (township) Mercer County	846	3.39
Dover (town) Morris County	613	3.37
Belleville (cdp) Essex County	1,098	3.06

Hispanic: Paraguayan

Top 10 Places Sorted by Number
Based on all places, regardless of population

Place	Number	%
Bernardsville (borough) Somerset County	145	1.97
Somerville (borough) Somerset County	49	0.39
Peapack and Gladstone (borough) Somerset Co.	35	1.44
Warren (township) Somerset County	31	0.22
Bedminster (township) Somerset County	25	0.30
Bridgewater (township) Somerset County	23	0.05
Jersey City (city) Hudson County	23	0.01
Mendham (borough) Morris County	17	0.33
Far Hills (borough) Somerset County	16	1.86
Bernards (township) Somerset County	16	0.07

Top 10 Places Sorted by Percent
Based on all places, regardless of population

Place	Number	%
Bernardsville (borough) Somerset County	145	1.97
Far Hills (borough) Somerset County	16	1.86
Peapack and Gladstone (borough) Somerset Co.	35	1.44
Chester (borough) Morris County	7	0.43
Somerville (borough) Somerset County	49	0.39
Mendham (borough) Morris County	17	0.33
Bedminster (township) Somerset County	25	0.30
Warren (township) Somerset County	31	0.22
Olivet (cdp) Salem County	3	0.21
Raritan (borough) Somerset County	11	0.17

Top 10 Places Sorted by Percent
Based on places with populations of 10,000 or more

Place	Number	%
Somerville (borough) Somerset County	49	0.39
Warren (township) Somerset County	31	0.22
Manville (borough) Somerset County	12	0.12
Bound Brook (borough) Somerset County	8	0.08
Bernards (township) Somerset County	16	0.07
Madison (borough) Morris County	10	0.06
Bridgewater (township) Somerset County	23	0.05
Scotch Plains (cdp) Union County	8	0.04
Berkeley Heights (cdp) Union County	6	0.04
Lumberton (township) Burlington County	4	0.04

Hispanic: Peruvian

Top 10 Places Sorted by Number
Based on all places, regardless of population

Place	Number	%
Paterson (city) Passaic County	7,038	4.72
Elizabeth (city) Union County	2,830	2.35
Clifton (city) Passaic County	1,788	2.27

Union City (city) Hudson County	1,694	2.53
Passaic (city) Passaic County	1,643	2.42
Kearny (town) Hudson County	1,549	3.82
Newark (city) Essex County	1,405	0.51
Perth Amboy (city) Middlesex County	1,041	2.20
Harrison (town) Hudson County	1,011	7.01
North Bergen (township) Hudson County	848	1.46

Top 10 Places Sorted by Percent
Based on all places, regardless of population

Place	Number	%
East Newark (borough) Hudson County	240	10.10
Harrison (town) Hudson County	1,011	7.01
Paterson (city) Passaic County	7,038	4.72
Kearny (town) Hudson County	1,549	3.82
Prospect Park (borough) Passaic County	186	3.22
Haledon (borough) Passaic County	224	2.71
Garfield (city) Bergen County	761	2.55
Union City (city) Hudson County	1,694	2.53
Passaic (city) Passaic County	1,643	2.42
Elizabeth (city) Union County	2,830	2.35

Top 10 Places Sorted by Percent
Based on places with populations of 10,000 or more

Place	Number	%
Harrison (town) Hudson County	1,011	7.01
Paterson (city) Passaic County	7,038	4.72
Kearny (town) Hudson County	1,549	3.82
Garfield (city) Bergen County	761	2.55
Union City (city) Hudson County	1,694	2.53
Passaic (city) Passaic County	1,643	2.42
Elizabeth (city) Union County	2,830	2.35
Clifton (city) Passaic County	1,788	2.27
Perth Amboy (city) Middlesex County	1,041	2.20
Carteret (borough) Middlesex County	417	2.01

Hispanic: Uruguayan

Top 10 Places Sorted by Number
Based on all places, regardless of population

Place	Number	%
Elizabeth (city) Union County	772	0.64
West Orange (cdp) Essex County	384	0.85
Newark (city) Essex County	239	0.09
Orange (cdp) Essex County	190	0.58
Dover (town) Morris County	157	0.86
North Bergen (township) Hudson County	104	0.18
Union City (city) Hudson County	100	0.15
Kearny (town) Hudson County	98	0.24
Paterson (city) Passaic County	71	0.05
Harrison (town) Hudson County	66	0.46

Top 10 Places Sorted by Percent
Based on all places, regardless of population

Place	Number	%
Dover (town) Morris County	157	0.86
West Orange (cdp) Essex County	384	0.85
Wharton (borough) Morris County	53	0.84
Victory Gardens (borough) Morris County	12	0.78
Elizabeth (city) Union County	772	0.64
East Newark (borough) Hudson County	14	0.59
Orange (cdp) Essex County	190	0.58
Fieldsboro (borough) Burlington County	3	0.57
Harrison (town) Hudson County	66	0.46
Madison Park (cdp) Middlesex County	27	0.39

Top 10 Places Sorted by Percent
Based on places with populations of 10,000 or more

Place	Number	%
Dover (town) Morris County	157	0.86
West Orange (cdp) Essex County	384	0.85
Elizabeth (city) Union County	772	0.64

Notes: (cdp) census designated place; Refer to the User's Guide in the front of the book for more detailed information.

Place	Number	%
Orange (cdp) Essex County	190	0.58
Harrison (town) Hudson County	66	0.46
Roselle Park (borough) Union County	39	0.29
Hillside (cdp) Union County	59	0.27
Kearny (town) Hudson County	98	0.24
Roselle (borough) Union County	44	0.21
Weehawken (township) Hudson County	27	0.20

Hispanic: Venezuelan

Top 10 Places Sorted by Number
Based on all places, regardless of population

Place	Number	%
Elizabeth (city) Union County	296	0.25
Paterson (city) Passaic County	248	0.17
Newark (city) Essex County	246	0.09
Union City (city) Hudson County	218	0.32
Jersey City (city) Hudson County	165	0.07
North Bergen (township) Hudson County	150	0.26
West New York (town) Hudson County	148	0.32
Kearny (town) Hudson County	59	0.15
Perth Amboy (city) Middlesex County	53	0.11
South River (borough) Middlesex County	50	0.33

Top 10 Places Sorted by Percent
Based on all places, regardless of population

Place	Number	%
Guttenberg (town) Hudson County	47	0.43
South River (borough) Middlesex County	50	0.33
Union City (city) Hudson County	218	0.32
West New York (town) Hudson County	148	0.32
Annandale (cdp) Hunterdon County	4	0.31
Harrison (town) Hudson County	41	0.28
North Bergen (township) Hudson County	150	0.26
Elizabeth (city) Union County	296	0.25
Oldmans (township) Salem County	4	0.22
Prospect Park (borough) Passaic County	12	0.21

Top 10 Places Sorted by Percent
Based on places with populations of 10,000 or more

Place	Number	%
Guttenberg (town) Hudson County	47	0.43
South River (borough) Middlesex County	50	0.33
Union City (city) Hudson County	218	0.32
West New York (town) Hudson County	148	0.32
Harrison (town) Hudson County	41	0.28
North Bergen (township) Hudson County	150	0.26
Elizabeth (city) Union County	296	0.25
Fairview (borough) Bergen County	27	0.20
Ocean (township) Monmouth County	50	0.19
Paterson (city) Passaic County	248	0.17

Hispanic: Other South American

Top 10 Places Sorted by Number
Based on all places, regardless of population

Place	Number	%
Jersey City (city) Hudson County	373	0.16
Elizabeth (city) Union County	356	0.30
Newark (city) Essex County	240	0.09
Paterson (city) Passaic County	230	0.15
Union City (city) Hudson County	213	0.32
North Bergen (township) Hudson County	212	0.36
West New York (town) Hudson County	154	0.34
Kearny (town) Hudson County	114	0.28
Passaic (city) Passaic County	108	0.16
Harrison (town) Hudson County	106	0.73

Top 10 Places Sorted by Percent
Based on all places, regardless of population

Place	Number	%
East Newark (borough) Hudson County	26	1.09

Place	Number	%
Harrison (town) Hudson County	106	0.73
Victory Gardens (borough) Morris County	10	0.65
Wharton (borough) Morris County	36	0.57
Guttenberg (town) Hudson County	51	0.47
Dover Beaches South (cdp) Ocean County	6	0.38
North Bergen (township) Hudson County	212	0.36
Stockton (borough) Hunterdon County	2	0.36
West New York (town) Hudson County	154	0.34
Union City (city) Hudson County	213	0.32

Top 10 Places Sorted by Percent
Based on places with populations of 10,000 or more

Place	Number	%
Harrison (town) Hudson County	106	0.73
Guttenberg (town) Hudson County	51	0.47
North Bergen (township) Hudson County	212	0.36
West New York (town) Hudson County	154	0.34
Union City (city) Hudson County	213	0.32
Dover (town) Morris County	58	0.32
Elizabeth (city) Union County	356	0.30
Kearny (town) Hudson County	114	0.28
Weehawken (township) Hudson County	35	0.26
North Plainfield (borough) Somerset County	53	0.25

Hispanic: Other

Top 10 Places Sorted by Number
Based on all places, regardless of population

Place	Number	%
Newark (city) Essex County	14,530	5.31
Paterson (city) Passaic County	13,432	9.00
Elizabeth (city) Union County	13,371	11.09
Jersey City (city) Hudson County	12,075	5.03
Union City (city) Hudson County	11,272	16.80
West New York (town) Hudson County	7,212	15.76
North Bergen (township) Hudson County	6,789	11.69
Passaic (city) Passaic County	5,795	8.54
Perth Amboy (city) Middlesex County	4,294	9.08
Kearny (town) Hudson County	3,402	8.40

Top 10 Places Sorted by Percent
Based on all places, regardless of population

Place	Number	%
Union City (city) Hudson County	11,272	16.80
West New York (town) Hudson County	7,212	15.76
East Newark (borough) Hudson County	317	13.34
Guttenberg (town) Hudson County	1,285	11.89
Dover (town) Morris County	2,134	11.73
North Bergen (township) Hudson County	6,789	11.69
Harrison (town) Hudson County	1,666	11.55
Elizabeth (city) Union County	13,371	11.09
Victory Gardens (borough) Morris County	160	10.35
Fairton (cdp) Cumberland County	220	9.76

Top 10 Places Sorted by Percent
Based on places with populations of 10,000 or more

Place	Number	%
Union City (city) Hudson County	11,272	16.80
West New York (town) Hudson County	7,212	15.76
Guttenberg (town) Hudson County	1,285	11.89
Dover (town) Morris County	2,134	11.73
North Bergen (township) Hudson County	6,789	11.69
Harrison (town) Hudson County	1,666	11.55
Elizabeth (city) Union County	13,371	11.09
North Plainfield (borough) Somerset County	1,966	9.32
Perth Amboy (city) Middlesex County	4,294	9.08
Paterson (city) Passaic County	13,432	9.00

Hungarian

Top 10 Places Sorted by Number
Based on all places, regardless of population

Place	Number	%
Woodbridge (township) Middlesex County	5,000	5.14
Hamilton (township) Mercer County	3,648	4.18
Edison (cdp) Middlesex County	3,121	3.19
Dover (township) Ocean County	1,808	2.01
East Brunswick (cdp) Middlesex County	1,779	3.80
Toms River (cdp) Ocean County	1,755	2.03
Franklin (township) Somerset County	1,717	3.37
Clifton (city) Passaic County	1,688	2.15
North Brunswick Twp (cdp) Middlesex County	1,581	4.36
Brick (township) Ocean County	1,463	1.92

Top 10 Places Sorted by Percent
Based on all places, regardless of population

Place	Number	%
Diamond Beach (cdp) Cape May County	34	25.19
Walpack (township) Sussex County	5	13.51
Fieldsboro (borough) Burlington County	54	10.23
Sewaren (cdp) Middlesex County	278	9.85
Alpha (borough) Warren County	232	9.35
Port Reading (cdp) Middlesex County	326	8.92
Loch Arbour (village) Monmouth County	23	8.36
Florence-Roebling (cdp) Burlington County	646	7.87
Milltown (borough) Middlesex County	526	7.51
Florence (township) Burlington County	802	7.46

Top 10 Places Sorted by Percent
Based on places with populations of 10,000 or more

Place	Number	%
Florence (township) Burlington County	802	7.46
Fords (cdp) Middlesex County	934	6.17
Manville (borough) Somerset County	568	5.51
Metuchen (borough) Middlesex County	694	5.40
Woodbridge (township) Middlesex County	5,000	5.14
Highland Park (borough) Middlesex County	655	4.68
Carteret (borough) Middlesex County	958	4.63
Phillipsburg (town) Warren County	671	4.42
North Brunswick Twp (cdp) Middlesex County	1,581	4.36
Mercerville-Hamilton Square (cdp) Mercer Co.	1,117	4.22

Icelander

Top 10 Places Sorted by Number
Based on all places, regardless of population

Place	Number	%
Brick (township) Ocean County	34	0.04
Elizabeth (city) Union County	26	0.02
Randolph (township) Morris County	22	0.09
Washington (township) Mercer County	21	0.20
Metuchen (borough) Middlesex County	21	0.16
Leonardo (cdp) Monmouth County	18	0.63
Middletown (township) Monmouth County	18	0.03
Andover (township) Sussex County	17	0.28
Morris (township) Morris County	17	0.08
Byram (township) Sussex County	16	0.19

Top 10 Places Sorted by Percent
Based on all places, regardless of population

Place	Number	%
Leonardo (cdp) Monmouth County	18	0.63
Riverdale (borough) Morris County	10	0.40
Far Hills (borough) Somerset County	3	0.35
South Belmar (borough) Monmouth County	6	0.33
Andover (township) Sussex County	17	0.28
Springfield (township) Burlington County	9	0.28
Harrington Park (borough) Bergen County	12	0.25
Washington (township) Mercer County	21	0.20
Hampton (township) Sussex County	10	0.20

Notes: (cdp) census designated place; Refer to the User's Guide in the front of the book for more detailed information.

Place	Number	%
Byram (township) Sussex County	16	0.19

Top 10 Places Sorted by Percent
Based on places with populations of 10,000 or more

Place	Number	%
Washington (township) Mercer County	21	0.20
Metuchen (borough) Middlesex County	21	0.16
Randolph (township) Morris County	22	0.09
Wantage (township) Sussex County	9	0.09
Morris (township) Morris County	17	0.08
Hanover (township) Morris County	10	0.08
South Plainfield (borough) Middlesex County	16	0.07
Hawthorne (borough) Passaic County	12	0.07
Princeton (township) Mercer County	11	0.07
Cedar Grove (cdp) Essex County	9	0.07

Iranian

Top 10 Places Sorted by Number
Based on all places, regardless of population

Place	Number	%
Paramus (borough) Bergen County	425	1.65
Fort Lee (borough) Bergen County	244	0.69
Bernards (township) Somerset County	234	0.95
Franklin (township) Somerset County	202	0.40
Livingston (cdp) Essex County	185	0.68
Morris (township) Morris County	182	0.84
Cliffside Park (borough) Bergen County	182	0.79
Jersey City (city) Hudson County	170	0.07
West Orange (cdp) Essex County	146	0.33
Holmdel (township) Monmouth County	129	0.82

Top 10 Places Sorted by Percent
Based on all places, regardless of population

Place	Number	%
Alpine (borough) Bergen County	43	1.97
Paramus (borough) Bergen County	425	1.65
Lambertville (city) Hunterdon County	51	1.32
Franklin Lakes (borough) Bergen County	109	1.05
Bernards (township) Somerset County	234	0.95
Morris (township) Morris County	182	0.84
Wanaque (borough) Passaic County	86	0.84
Holmdel (township) Monmouth County	129	0.82
Cliffside Park (borough) Bergen County	182	0.79
Brielle (borough) Monmouth County	36	0.74

Top 10 Places Sorted by Percent
Based on places with populations of 10,000 or more

Place	Number	%
Paramus (borough) Bergen County	425	1.65
Franklin Lakes (borough) Bergen County	109	1.05
Bernards (township) Somerset County	234	0.95
Morris (township) Morris County	182	0.84
Wanaque (borough) Passaic County	86	0.84
Holmdel (township) Monmouth County	129	0.82
Cliffside Park (borough) Bergen County	182	0.79
Fort Lee (borough) Bergen County	244	0.69
Livingston (cdp) Essex County	185	0.68
Little Ferry (borough) Bergen County	59	0.55

Irish

Top 10 Places Sorted by Number
Based on all places, regardless of population

Place	Number	%
Brick (township) Ocean County	22,022	28.93
Dover (township) Ocean County	21,766	24.25
Middletown (township) Monmouth County	21,756	32.80
Toms River (cdp) Ocean County	20,815	24.08
Gloucester (township) Camden County	16,582	25.78
Woodbridge (township) Middlesex County	16,323	16.79
Hamilton (township) Mercer County	15,948	18.28
Washington (township) Gloucester County	13,639	28.95
Jersey City (city) Hudson County	13,500	5.62
Old Bridge (township) Middlesex County	12,378	20.47

Top 10 Places Sorted by Percent
Based on all places, regardless of population

Place	Number	%
Walpack (township) Sussex County	28	75.68
Tavistock (borough) Camden County	13	56.52
Spring Lake (borough) Monmouth County	1,807	50.66
West Wildwood (borough) Cape May County	211	46.99
Avon-by-the-Sea (borough) Monmouth County	1,019	45.55
Sea Girt (borough) Monmouth County	972	45.25
Belford (cdp) Monmouth County	627	43.97
Teterboro (borough) Bergen County	7	43.75
Gloucester City (city) Camden County	4,859	42.34
Spring Lake Heights (borough) Monmouth County	2,204	42.17

Top 10 Places Sorted by Percent
Based on places with populations of 10,000 or more

Place	Number	%
Gloucester City (city) Camden County	4,859	42.34
Wall (township) Monmouth County	8,809	34.87
Keansburg (borough) Monmouth County	3,710	34.57
West Deptford (township) Gloucester County	6,423	33.16
Hazlet (township) Monmouth County	7,033	32.90
Middletown (township) Monmouth County	21,756	32.80
Point Pleasant (borough) Ocean County	6,317	32.72
Upper (township) Cape May County	3,933	32.46
Lower (township) Cape May County	7,350	32.03
Bellmawr (borough) Camden County	3,515	31.21

Israeli

Top 10 Places Sorted by Number
Based on all places, regardless of population

Place	Number	%
Fair Lawn (borough) Bergen County	926	2.93
Teaneck (cdp) Bergen County	291	0.74
Cherry Hill (township) Camden County	225	0.32
Tenafly (borough) Bergen County	200	1.45
Millburn (cdp) Essex County	199	1.01
Jersey City (city) Hudson County	197	0.08
Lakewood (township) Ocean County	191	0.32
Englewood (city) Bergen County	181	0.69
East Brunswick (cdp) Middlesex County	178	0.38
Voorhees (township) Camden County	177	0.63

Top 10 Places Sorted by Percent
Based on all places, regardless of population

Place	Number	%
Deal (borough) Monmouth County	36	3.36
Fair Lawn (borough) Bergen County	926	2.93
Closter (borough) Bergen County	136	1.62
Tenafly (borough) Bergen County	200	1.45
Oakhurst (cdp) Monmouth County	57	1.38
Erlton-Ellisburg (cdp) Camden County	109	1.36
Echelon (cdp) Camden County	106	1.02
Millburn (cdp) Essex County	199	1.01
Princeton (township) Mercer County	157	0.98
Englewood Cliffs (borough) Bergen County	47	0.88

Top 10 Places Sorted by Percent
Based on places with populations of 10,000 or more

Place	Number	%
Fair Lawn (borough) Bergen County	926	2.93
Tenafly (borough) Bergen County	200	1.45
Echelon (cdp) Camden County	106	1.02
Millburn (cdp) Essex County	199	1.01
Princeton (township) Mercer County	157	0.98
Highland Park (borough) Middlesex County	114	0.81

Place	Number	%
Teaneck (cdp) Bergen County	291	0.74
Englewood (city) Bergen County	181	0.69
Livingston (cdp) Essex County	176	0.64
Voorhees (township) Camden County	177	0.63

Italian

Top 10 Places Sorted by Number
Based on all places, regardless of population

Place	Number	%
Dover (township) Ocean County	28,261	31.48
Toms River (cdp) Ocean County	27,250	31.52
Brick (township) Ocean County	23,161	30.43
Hamilton (township) Mercer County	22,684	26.00
Middletown (township) Monmouth County	19,142	28.86
Gloucester (township) Camden County	18,860	29.32
Woodbridge (township) Middlesex County	17,734	18.24
Wayne (cdp) Passaic County	16,166	29.87
Washington (township) Gloucester County	15,966	33.89
Jersey City (city) Hudson County	15,731	6.55

Top 10 Places Sorted by Percent
Based on all places, regardless of population

Place	Number	%
Teterboro (borough) Bergen County	11	68.75
Hammonton (town) Atlantic County	6,841	54.28
Ramtown (cdp) Monmouth County	2,914	46.78
Fairfield (cdp) Essex County	3,235	45.80
Nutley (cdp) Essex County	12,183	44.53
Totowa (borough) Passaic County	4,381	44.50
Holiday Heights (cdp) Ocean County	1,017	43.07
East Hanover (township) Morris County	4,759	41.77
Dover Beaches South (cdp) Ocean County	682	41.26
Lyndhurst (cdp) Bergen County	7,914	40.83

Top 10 Places Sorted by Percent
Based on places with populations of 10,000 or more

Place	Number	%
Hammonton (town) Atlantic County	6,841	54.28
Nutley (cdp) Essex County	12,183	44.53
East Hanover (township) Morris County	4,759	41.77
Lyndhurst (cdp) Bergen County	7,914	40.83
West Paterson (borough) Passaic County	4,452	40.52
Hasbrouck Heights (borough) Bergen County	4,486	38.47
Saddle Brook (cdp) Bergen County	4,700	35.73
West Caldwell (cdp) Essex County	3,958	35.24
Cedar Grove (cdp) Essex County	4,278	34.78
Little Falls (cdp) Passaic County	3,755	34.59

Latvian

Top 10 Places Sorted by Number
Based on all places, regardless of population

Place	Number	%
East Brunswick (cdp) Middlesex County	155	0.33
Brick (township) Ocean County	123	0.16
Manchester (township) Ocean County	109	0.28
Fair Lawn (borough) Bergen County	107	0.34
Cherry Hill (township) Camden County	92	0.13
Edison (cdp) Middlesex County	89	0.09
Roxbury (township) Morris County	88	0.37
Montclair (cdp) Essex County	74	0.19
Fort Lee (borough) Bergen County	72	0.20
Vineland (city) Cumberland County	68	0.12

Top 10 Places Sorted by Percent
Based on all places, regardless of population

Place	Number	%
Cedar Glen West (cdp) Ocean County	39	2.81
Lavallette (borough) Ocean County	31	1.16
Bradley Beach (borough) Monmouth County	49	1.02
Rossmoor (cdp) Middlesex County	32	1.02

Notes: (cdp) census designated place; Refer to the User's Guide in the front of the book for more detailed information.

Place	Number	%
Yorketown (cdp) Monmouth County	46	0.69
Leisure Knoll (cdp) Ocean County	17	0.67
Roosevelt (borough) Monmouth County	6	0.65
Saddle River (borough) Bergen County	20	0.62
Mansfield (township) Burlington County	30	0.59
Island Heights (borough) Ocean County	9	0.51

Top 10 Places Sorted by Percent
Based on places with populations of 10,000 or more

Place	Number	%
Highland Park (borough) Middlesex County	62	0.44
Leisure Village W-Pine Lake Pk (cdp) Ocean Co.	44	0.40
Roxbury (township) Morris County	88	0.37
Fair Lawn (borough) Bergen County	107	0.34
East Brunswick (cdp) Middlesex County	155	0.33
Morris (township) Morris County	64	0.29
Haddonfield (borough) Camden County	34	0.29
Freehold (borough) Monmouth County	32	0.29
Manchester (township) Ocean County	109	0.28
Montville (township) Morris County	56	0.27

Lithuanian

Top 10 Places Sorted by Number
Based on all places, regardless of population

Place	Number	%
Woodbridge (township) Middlesex County	738	0.76
Cherry Hill (township) Camden County	656	0.94
Brick (township) Ocean County	575	0.76
Dover (township) Ocean County	517	0.58
Toms River (cdp) Ocean County	510	0.59
Lakewood (township) Ocean County	508	0.84
Bridgewater (township) Somerset County	450	1.05
Kearny (town) Hudson County	442	1.09
Linden (city) Union County	438	1.11
Bayonne (city) Hudson County	408	0.66

Top 10 Places Sorted by Percent
Based on all places, regardless of population

Place	Number	%
Diamond Beach (cdp) Cape May County	32	23.70
Brass Castle (cdp) Warren County	100	6.49
Leisure Knoll (cdp) Ocean County	60	2.36
Washington (township) Warren County	144	2.30
Waretown (cdp) Ocean County	32	1.98
Greentree (cdp) Camden County	213	1.85
Kingwood (township) Hunterdon County	70	1.85
Cranford (cdp) Union County	406	1.80
Crandon Lakes (cdp) Sussex County	21	1.68
Cape May Point (borough) Cape May County	4	1.68

Top 10 Places Sorted by Percent
Based on places with populations of 10,000 or more

Place	Number	%
Greentree (cdp) Camden County	213	1.85
Cranford (cdp) Union County	406	1.80
Waterford (township) Camden County	174	1.66
New Providence (borough) Union County	152	1.28
Marlton (cdp) Burlington County	124	1.21
Linden (city) Union County	438	1.11
Kearny (town) Hudson County	442	1.09
Lacey (township) Ocean County	273	1.08
Bridgewater (township) Somerset County	450	1.05
Washington (township) Morris County	185	1.05

Luxemburger

Top 10 Places Sorted by Number
Based on all places, regardless of population

Place	Number	%
Ocean Acres (cdp) Ocean County	28	0.21
Stafford (township) Ocean County	28	0.12

Place	Number	%
Clinton (township) Hunterdon County	23	0.18
Madison (borough) Morris County	22	0.13
Matawan (borough) Monmouth County	21	0.23
Springdale (cdp) Camden County	18	0.12
Cherry Hill (township) Camden County	18	0.03
Hamilton (township) Mercer County	18	0.02
Morris Plains (borough) Morris County	15	0.29
Oakland (borough) Bergen County	14	0.11

Top 10 Places Sorted by Percent
Based on all places, regardless of population

Place	Number	%
Dover Beaches North (cdp) Ocean County	7	0.42
Morris Plains (borough) Morris County	15	0.29
Plainsboro Center (cdp) Middlesex County	6	0.25
Matawan (borough) Monmouth County	21	0.23
Heathcote (cdp) Middlesex County	10	0.22
Ocean Acres (cdp) Ocean County	28	0.21
Alexandria (township) Hunterdon County	9	0.19
Clinton (township) Hunterdon County	23	0.18
Chester (township) Morris County	11	0.15
Madison (borough) Morris County	22	0.13

Top 10 Places Sorted by Percent
Based on places with populations of 10,000 or more

Place	Number	%
Ocean Acres (cdp) Ocean County	28	0.21
Clinton (township) Hunterdon County	23	0.18
Madison (borough) Morris County	22	0.13
Stafford (township) Ocean County	28	0.12
Springdale (cdp) Camden County	18	0.12
Oakland (borough) Bergen County	14	0.11
Tinton Falls (borough) Monmouth County	13	0.09
Florence (township) Burlington County	10	0.09
Berkeley Heights (cdp) Union County	9	0.07
Maple Shade (township) Burlington County	12	0.06

Macedonian

Top 10 Places Sorted by Number
Based on all places, regardless of population

Place	Number	%
Garfield (city) Bergen County	834	2.80
Elmwood Park (borough) Bergen County	306	1.62
Clifton (city) Passaic County	298	0.38
Paterson (city) Passaic County	281	0.19
Parsippany-Troy Hills (township) Morris County	193	0.38
Lincoln Park (borough) Morris County	140	1.28
Hackensack (city) Bergen County	106	0.25
Pequannock (township) Morris County	82	0.59
Secaucus (town) Hudson County	74	0.47
Wayne (cdp) Passaic County	66	0.12

Top 10 Places Sorted by Percent
Based on all places, regardless of population

Place	Number	%
Garfield (city) Bergen County	834	2.80
Elmwood Park (borough) Bergen County	306	1.62
Lincoln Park (borough) Morris County	140	1.28
Lake Telemark (cdp) Morris County	13	1.01
Bloomingdale (borough) Passaic County	61	0.80
Fairfield (cdp) Essex County	51	0.72
Pequannock (township) Morris County	82	0.59
Peapack and Gladstone (borough) Somerset Co.	14	0.58
Prospect Park (borough) Passaic County	29	0.50
Secaucus (town) Hudson County	74	0.47

Top 10 Places Sorted by Percent
Based on places with populations of 10,000 or more

Place	Number	%
Garfield (city) Bergen County	834	2.80
Elmwood Park (borough) Bergen County	306	1.62

Place	Number	%
Lincoln Park (borough) Morris County	140	1.28
Pequannock (township) Morris County	82	0.59
Secaucus (town) Hudson County	74	0.47
Hasbrouck Heights (borough) Bergen County	47	0.40
Clifton (city) Passaic County	298	0.38
Parsippany-Troy Hills (township) Morris County	193	0.38
Wantage (township) Sussex County	35	0.34
Saddle Brook (cdp) Bergen County	44	0.33

Maltese

Top 10 Places Sorted by Number
Based on all places, regardless of population

Place	Number	%
Bridgewater (township) Somerset County	79	0.18
Old Bridge (township) Middlesex County	64	0.11
East Brunswick (cdp) Middlesex County	61	0.13
Bayonne (city) Hudson County	55	0.09
Hazlet (township) Monmouth County	53	0.25
Howell (township) Monmouth County	49	0.10
Washington (township) Morris County	48	0.27
Secaucus (town) Hudson County	46	0.29
Middletown (township) Monmouth County	46	0.07
Franklin (township) Somerset County	36	0.07

Top 10 Places Sorted by Percent
Based on all places, regardless of population

Place	Number	%
Moonachie (borough) Bergen County	15	0.54
Saddle River (borough) Bergen County	13	0.41
Westampton (township) Burlington County	26	0.36
Secaucus (town) Hudson County	46	0.29
Englishtown (borough) Monmouth County	5	0.28
Washington (township) Morris County	48	0.27
Greenwich (township) Warren County	12	0.27
West Freehold (cdp) Monmouth County	32	0.26
Millstone (township) Monmouth County	23	0.26
Hazlet (township) Monmouth County	53	0.25

Top 10 Places Sorted by Percent
Based on places with populations of 10,000 or more

Place	Number	%
Secaucus (town) Hudson County	46	0.29
Washington (township) Morris County	48	0.27
West Freehold (cdp) Monmouth County	32	0.26
Hazlet (township) Monmouth County	53	0.25
Bridgewater (township) Somerset County	79	0.18
Saddle Brook (cdp) Bergen County	24	0.18
Somerville (borough) Somerset County	21	0.17
Hillside (cdp) Union County	35	0.16
Barclay-Kingston (cdp) Camden County	17	0.16
Morris (township) Morris County	31	0.14

New Zealander

Top 10 Places Sorted by Number
Based on all places, regardless of population

Place	Number	%
Fair Lawn (borough) Bergen County	48	0.15
New Providence (borough) Union County	30	0.25
Upper Freehold (township) Monmouth County	25	0.58
Upper (township) Cape May County	21	0.17
Fort Lee (borough) Bergen County	21	0.06
Newark (city) Essex County	21	0.01
Ramsey (borough) Bergen County	19	0.13
Hoboken (city) Hudson County	19	0.05
Lyndhurst (cdp) Bergen County	18	0.09
Guttenberg (town) Hudson County	17	0.16

Notes: (cdp) census designated place; Refer to the User's Guide in the front of the book for more detailed information.

Top 10 Places Sorted by Percent
Based on all places, regardless of population

Place	Number	%
Upper Freehold (township) Monmouth County	25	0.58
New Providence (borough) Union County	30	0.25
Upper (township) Cape May County	21	0.17
Guttenberg (town) Hudson County	17	0.16
East Amwell (township) Hunterdon County	7	0.16
Woodstown (borough) Salem County	5	0.16
Fair Lawn (borough) Bergen County	48	0.15
Ramsey (borough) Bergen County	19	0.13
Washington (township) Warren County	8	0.13
Rockaway (borough) Morris County	8	0.12

Top 10 Places Sorted by Percent
Based on places with populations of 10,000 or more

Place	Number	%
New Providence (borough) Union County	30	0.25
Upper (township) Cape May County	21	0.17
Guttenberg (town) Hudson County	17	0.16
Fair Lawn (borough) Bergen County	48	0.15
Ramsey (borough) Bergen County	19	0.13
Lyndhurst (cdp) Bergen County	18	0.09
Princeton (township) Mercer County	14	0.09
Greentree (cdp) Camden County	9	0.08
Pompton Lakes (borough) Passaic County	9	0.08
Fort Lee (borough) Bergen County	21	0.06

Northern European

Top 10 Places Sorted by Number
Based on all places, regardless of population

Place	Number	%
Montgomery (township) Somerset County	118	0.68
Hillsdale (borough) Bergen County	81	0.80
Madison (borough) Morris County	70	0.42
North Brunswick Twp (cdp) Middlesex County	70	0.19
Cape May Court House (cdp) Cape May County	59	1.25
Middle (township) Cape May County	59	0.36
Dumont (borough) Bergen County	55	0.31
Jersey City (city) Hudson County	54	0.02
Shiloh (borough) Cumberland County	51	9.51
Mendham (township) Morris County	51	0.94

Top 10 Places Sorted by Percent
Based on all places, regardless of population

Place	Number	%
Shiloh (borough) Cumberland County	51	9.51
Lakehurst (borough) Ocean County	33	1.31
Cape May Court House (cdp) Cape May County	59	1.25
Mendham (township) Morris County	51	0.94
Hillsdale (borough) Bergen County	81	0.80
Hopewell (borough) Mercer County	16	0.79
Montgomery (township) Somerset County	118	0.68
Bloomsbury (borough) Hunterdon County	6	0.68
Princeton Junction (cdp) Mercer County	16	0.67
Fanwood (borough) Union County	41	0.57

Top 10 Places Sorted by Percent
Based on places with populations of 10,000 or more

Place	Number	%
Hillsdale (borough) Bergen County	81	0.80
Montgomery (township) Somerset County	118	0.68
Madison (borough) Morris County	70	0.42
Middle (township) Cape May County	59	0.36
Dumont (borough) Bergen County	55	0.31
Manville (borough) Somerset County	29	0.28
Ringwood (borough) Passaic County	33	0.27
Mount Holly (township) Burlington County	25	0.23
West Windsor (township) Mercer County	49	0.22
Tinton Falls (borough) Monmouth County	31	0.21

Norwegian

Top 10 Places Sorted by Number
Based on all places, regardless of population

Place	Number	%
Middletown (township) Monmouth County	850	1.28
Brick (township) Ocean County	763	1.00
Dover (township) Ocean County	723	0.81
Toms River (cdp) Ocean County	692	0.80
Woodbridge (township) Middlesex County	618	0.64
Old Bridge (township) Middlesex County	585	0.97
Roxbury (township) Morris County	544	2.28
Franklin (township) Somerset County	530	1.04
Hamilton (township) Mercer County	485	0.56
Manchester (township) Ocean County	472	1.21

Top 10 Places Sorted by Percent
Based on all places, regardless of population

Place	Number	%
Lake Telemark (cdp) Morris County	133	10.32
Diamond Beach (cdp) Cape May County	7	5.19
Barnegat Light (borough) Ocean County	38	4.92
Belford (cdp) Monmouth County	68	4.77
Cedar Glen Lakes (cdp) Ocean County	60	3.73
Waretown (cdp) Ocean County	56	3.47
Erma (cdp) Cape May County	69	3.23
Succasunna-Kenvil (cdp) Morris County	376	3.00
Highland Lake (cdp) Sussex County	142	2.85
Princeton Junction (cdp) Mercer County	67	2.80

Top 10 Places Sorted by Percent
Based on places with populations of 10,000 or more

Place	Number	%
Succasunna-Kenvil (cdp) Morris County	376	3.00
Roxbury (township) Morris County	544	2.28
Readington (township) Hunterdon County	334	2.11
Point Pleasant (borough) Ocean County	354	1.83
Medford (township) Burlington County	388	1.74
Rockaway (township) Morris County	394	1.72
Pequannock (township) Morris County	238	1.71
Montgomery (township) Somerset County	294	1.68
Little Egg Harbor (township) Ocean County	256	1.60
Middlesex (borough) Middlesex County	215	1.57

Pennsylvania German

Top 10 Places Sorted by Number
Based on all places, regardless of population

Place	Number	%
Phillipsburg (town) Warren County	251	1.66
Gloucester (township) Camden County	214	0.33
Hamilton (township) Mercer County	140	0.16
Holland (township) Hunterdon County	131	2.56
Deptford (township) Gloucester County	125	0.47
Monroe (township) Gloucester County	122	0.42
Southampton (township) Burlington County	111	1.07
Mantua (township) Gloucester County	104	0.73
Mount Laurel (township) Burlington County	91	0.23
Cherry Hill (township) Camden County	80	0.11

Top 10 Places Sorted by Percent
Based on all places, regardless of population

Place	Number	%
Holland (township) Hunterdon County	131	2.56
Leisuretowne (cdp) Burlington County	47	1.96
Stockton (borough) Hunterdon County	10	1.80
Belvidere (town) Warren County	49	1.77
Lambertville (city) Hunterdon County	66	1.71
Phillipsburg (town) Warren County	251	1.66
Avalon (borough) Cape May County	33	1.54
Manahawkin (cdp) Ocean County	32	1.52
West Cape May (borough) Cape May County	15	1.37

Place	Number	%
Alpha (borough) Warren County	32	1.29

Top 10 Places Sorted by Percent
Based on places with populations of 10,000 or more

Place	Number	%
Phillipsburg (town) Warren County	251	1.66
Southampton (township) Burlington County	111	1.07
Mantua (township) Gloucester County	104	0.73
Deptford (township) Gloucester County	125	0.47
Hopewell (township) Mercer County	75	0.47
Pennsville (township) Salem County	62	0.47
Monroe (township) Gloucester County	122	0.42
Haddon (township) Camden County	62	0.42
Gloucester (township) Camden County	214	0.33
Collingswood (borough) Camden County	47	0.33

Polish

Top 10 Places Sorted by Number
Based on all places, regardless of population

Place	Number	%
Clifton (city) Passaic County	11,451	14.56
Bayonne (city) Hudson County	11,095	17.94
Hamilton (township) Mercer County	10,751	12.32
Woodbridge (township) Middlesex County	10,694	11.00
Sayreville (borough) Middlesex County	8,133	20.14
Dover (township) Ocean County	8,088	9.01
Toms River (cdp) Ocean County	7,691	8.90
Garfield (city) Bergen County	7,431	24.95
Edison (cdp) Middlesex County	7,251	7.42
Jersey City (city) Hudson County	7,215	3.01

Top 10 Places Sorted by Percent
Based on all places, regardless of population

Place	Number	%
Wallington (borough) Bergen County	5,967	51.52
Manville (borough) Somerset County	2,999	29.10
South Amboy (city) Middlesex County	2,042	25.81
Garfield (city) Bergen County	7,431	24.95
East Rutherford (borough) Bergen County	1,791	20.55
Sayreville (borough) Middlesex County	8,133	20.14
Millstone (borough) Somerset County	83	19.90
South River (borough) Middlesex County	2,894	18.89
Winfield (township) Union County	284	18.76
White House Station (cdp) Hunterdon County	343	18.18

Top 10 Places Sorted by Percent
Based on places with populations of 10,000 or more

Place	Number	%
Wallington (borough) Bergen County	5,967	51.52
Manville (borough) Somerset County	2,999	29.10
Garfield (city) Bergen County	7,431	24.95
Sayreville (borough) Middlesex County	8,133	20.14
South River (borough) Middlesex County	2,894	18.89
Linden (city) Union County	7,098	18.02
Bayonne (city) Hudson County	11,095	17.94
Clark (cdp) Union County	2,588	17.73
Colonia (cdp) Middlesex County	2,612	14.71
Clifton (city) Passaic County	11,451	14.56

Portuguese

Top 10 Places Sorted by Number
Based on all places, regardless of population

Place	Number	%
Newark (city) Essex County	15,801	5.78
Elizabeth (city) Union County	6,639	5.51
Kearny (town) Hudson County	4,773	11.78
Union (cdp) Union County	3,725	6.85
Hillside (cdp) Union County	2,391	10.99
Harrison (town) Hudson County	1,961	13.60
South River (borough) Middlesex County	1,432	9.35

Notes: (cdp) census designated place; Refer to the User's Guide in the front of the book for more detailed information.

Place	Number	%
Woodbridge (township) Middlesex County	1,369	1.41
Linden (city) Union County	1,216	3.09
Long Branch (city) Monmouth County	1,067	3.40

Top 10 Places Sorted by Percent
Based on all places, regardless of population

Place	Number	%
East Newark (borough) Hudson County	345	14.51
Harrison (town) Hudson County	1,961	13.60
Kearny (town) Hudson County	4,773	11.78
Hillside (cdp) Union County	2,391	10.99
South River (borough) Middlesex County	1,432	9.35
Union (cdp) Union County	3,725	6.85
Newark (city) Essex County	15,801	5.78
Elizabeth (city) Union County	6,639	5.51
Riverside (township) Burlington County	393	4.97
North Arlington (borough) Bergen County	731	4.82

Top 10 Places Sorted by Percent
Based on places with populations of 10,000 or more

Place	Number	%
Harrison (town) Hudson County	1,961	13.60
Kearny (town) Hudson County	4,773	11.78
Hillside (cdp) Union County	2,391	10.99
South River (borough) Middlesex County	1,432	9.35
Union (cdp) Union County	3,725	6.85
Newark (city) Essex County	15,801	5.78
Elizabeth (city) Union County	6,639	5.51
North Arlington (borough) Bergen County	731	4.82
Colonia (cdp) Middlesex County	689	3.88
Clark (cdp) Union County	500	3.43

Romanian

Top 10 Places Sorted by Number
Based on all places, regardless of population

Place	Number	%
Cherry Hill (township) Camden County	429	0.61
Edison (cdp) Middlesex County	404	0.41
Marlboro (township) Monmouth County	373	1.02
Wayne (cdp) Passaic County	368	0.68
East Brunswick (cdp) Middlesex County	331	0.71
Monroe (township) Middlesex County	285	1.02
Hamilton (township) Mercer County	282	0.32
Union (cdp) Union County	262	0.48
Fort Lee (borough) Bergen County	219	0.62
Livingston (cdp) Essex County	213	0.78

Top 10 Places Sorted by Percent
Based on all places, regardless of population

Place	Number	%
Andover (borough) Sussex County	23	3.50
Kingston (cdp) Middlesex County	42	3.36
Concordia (cdp) Middlesex County	111	3.00
Whittingham (cdp) Middlesex County	65	2.66
Clearbrook Park (cdp) Middlesex County	58	1.90
Florence-Roebling (cdp) Burlington County	149	1.81
Closter (borough) Bergen County	148	1.77
Florence (township) Burlington County	188	1.75
Franklin (borough) Sussex County	70	1.35
Fieldsboro (borough) Burlington County	7	1.33

Top 10 Places Sorted by Percent
Based on places with populations of 10,000 or more

Place	Number	%
Florence (township) Burlington County	188	1.75
South Orange (cdp) Essex County	180	1.06
Marlboro (township) Monmouth County	373	1.02
Monroe (township) Middlesex County	285	1.02
Millburn (cdp) Essex County	201	1.02
Morganville (cdp) Monmouth County	111	1.00
Greentree (cdp) Camden County	111	0.97

Place	Number	%
Highland Park (borough) Middlesex County	132	0.94
Springdale (cdp) Camden County	132	0.92
Tenafly (borough) Bergen County	109	0.79

Russian

Top 10 Places Sorted by Number
Based on all places, regardless of population

Place	Number	%
Cherry Hill (township) Camden County	5,620	8.03
Marlboro (township) Monmouth County	3,914	10.75
Fair Lawn (borough) Bergen County	3,699	11.69
East Brunswick (cdp) Middlesex County	3,627	7.76
Manalapan (township) Monmouth County	3,333	9.97
Edison (cdp) Middlesex County	3,097	3.17
Fort Lee (borough) Bergen County	2,858	8.06
Livingston (cdp) Essex County	2,693	9.83
West Orange (cdp) Essex County	2,620	5.84
Monroe (township) Middlesex County	2,597	9.28

Top 10 Places Sorted by Percent
Based on all places, regardless of population

Place	Number	%
Concordia (cdp) Middlesex County	814	22.02
Whittingham (cdp) Middlesex County	465	19.03
Clearbrook Park (cdp) Middlesex County	573	18.74
Springdale (cdp) Camden County	2,014	13.97
Morganville (cdp) Monmouth County	1,440	12.93
Teterboro (borough) Bergen County	2	12.50
Fair Lawn (borough) Bergen County	3,699	11.69
Millburn (cdp) Essex County	2,309	11.68
Marlboro (township) Monmouth County	3,914	10.75
Springfield (cdp) Union County	1,493	10.35

Top 10 Places Sorted by Percent
Based on places with populations of 10,000 or more

Place	Number	%
Springdale (cdp) Camden County	2,014	13.97
Morganville (cdp) Monmouth County	1,440	12.93
Fair Lawn (borough) Bergen County	3,699	11.69
Millburn (cdp) Essex County	2,309	11.68
Marlboro (township) Monmouth County	3,914	10.75
Springfield (cdp) Union County	1,493	10.35
Greentree (cdp) Camden County	1,149	9.99
Manalapan (township) Monmouth County	3,333	9.97
Livingston (cdp) Essex County	2,693	9.83
Monroe (township) Middlesex County	2,597	9.28

Scandinavian

Top 10 Places Sorted by Number
Based on all places, regardless of population

Place	Number	%
Middletown (township) Monmouth County	113	0.17
Freehold (township) Monmouth County	107	0.34
Evesham (township) Burlington County	96	0.23
Brick (township) Ocean County	95	0.12
Franklin (township) Somerset County	90	0.18
Woodbridge (township) Middlesex County	81	0.08
Randolph (township) Morris County	74	0.30
Jersey City (city) Hudson County	72	0.03
Bloomfield (cdp) Essex County	69	0.14
Keyport (borough) Monmouth County	66	0.87

Top 10 Places Sorted by Percent
Based on all places, regardless of population

Place	Number	%
Elk (township) Gloucester County	47	1.34
Mays Landing (cdp) Atlantic County	28	1.23
Sea Bright (borough) Monmouth County	18	0.99
Branchville (borough) Sussex County	8	0.94
Keyport (borough) Monmouth County	66	0.87

Place	Number	%
Greenwich (township) Cumberland County	7	0.83
Mendham (township) Morris County	41	0.76
Fanwood (borough) Union County	50	0.70
East Amwell (township) Hunterdon County	29	0.65
Mansfield (township) Warren County	42	0.63

Top 10 Places Sorted by Percent
Based on places with populations of 10,000 or more

Place	Number	%
Waterford (township) Camden County	61	0.58
West Freehold (cdp) Monmouth County	60	0.48
River Edge (borough) Bergen County	47	0.43
Barclay-Kingston (cdp) Camden County	40	0.37
Washington (township) Morris County	62	0.35
Ringwood (borough) Passaic County	44	0.35
Freehold (township) Monmouth County	107	0.34
Randolph (township) Morris County	74	0.30
Hanover (township) Morris County	37	0.29
Mount Holly (township) Burlington County	31	0.29

Scotch-Irish

Top 10 Places Sorted by Number
Based on all places, regardless of population

Place	Number	%
Dover (township) Ocean County	1,444	1.61
Toms River (cdp) Ocean County	1,357	1.57
Brick (township) Ocean County	1,266	1.66
Middletown (township) Monmouth County	1,234	1.86
Hamilton (township) Mercer County	964	1.10
Woodbridge (township) Middlesex County	884	0.91
Cherry Hill (township) Camden County	777	1.11
Gloucester (township) Camden County	719	1.12
Kearny (town) Hudson County	646	1.59
Sparta (township) Sussex County	623	3.44

Top 10 Places Sorted by Percent
Based on all places, regardless of population

Place	Number	%
Shiloh (borough) Cumberland County	42	7.84
Loch Arbour (village) Monmouth County	17	6.18
Annandale (cdp) Hunterdon County	63	4.81
New Egypt (cdp) Ocean County	114	4.44
Lake Mohawk (cdp) Sussex County	432	4.43
North Beach Haven (cdp) Ocean County	106	4.35
Corbin City (city) Atlantic County	20	4.27
Long Valley (cdp) Morris County	75	3.93
Kingston (cdp) Middlesex County	48	3.84
Shamong (township) Burlington County	234	3.62

Top 10 Places Sorted by Percent
Based on places with populations of 10,000 or more

Place	Number	%
Sparta (township) Sussex County	623	3.44
Ocean City (city) Cape May County	451	2.93
Moorestown (township) Burlington County	548	2.88
Moorestown-Lenola (cdp) Burlington County	385	2.79
Somers Point (city) Atlantic County	314	2.70
Washington (township) Morris County	435	2.47
Mantua (township) Gloucester County	333	2.34
Medford (township) Burlington County	513	2.31
Haddonfield (borough) Camden County	268	2.30
Madison (borough) Morris County	376	2.27

Scottish

Top 10 Places Sorted by Number
Based on all places, regardless of population

Place	Number	%
Dover (township) Ocean County	1,757	1.96
Toms River (cdp) Ocean County	1,681	1.94
Brick (township) Ocean County	1,517	1.99

Notes: (cdp) census designated place; Refer to the User's Guide in the front of the book for more detailed information.

Hamilton (township) Mercer County	1,401	1.61
Middletown (township) Monmouth County	1,195	1.80
Kearny (town) Hudson County	1,023	2.53
Manchester (township) Ocean County	958	2.46
Montclair (cdp) Essex County	937	2.40
Cherry Hill (township) Camden County	914	1.31
Woodbridge (township) Middlesex County	883	0.91

Top 10 Places Sorted by Percent
Based on all places, regardless of population

Place	Number	%
Strathmere (cdp) Cape May County	12	7.69
Harvey Cedars (borough) Ocean County	25	7.08
Bay Head (borough) Ocean County	81	6.27
Lebanon (borough) Hunterdon County	64	6.01
Tewksbury (township) Hunterdon County	320	5.78
Monmouth Junction (cdp) Middlesex County	134	5.53
Stillwater (township) Sussex County	226	5.30
Fairview (cdp) Monmouth County	192	4.87
Mendham (borough) Morris County	246	4.83
Peapack and Gladstone (borough) Somerset Co.	114	4.69

Top 10 Places Sorted by Percent
Based on places with populations of 10,000 or more

Place	Number	%
Jefferson (township) Morris County	703	3.57
Washington (township) Morris County	613	3.48
Haddonfield (borough) Camden County	388	3.33
Chatham (township) Morris County	333	3.30
Summit (city) Union County	678	3.21
Bernards (township) Somerset County	787	3.20
Hopewell (township) Mercer County	504	3.13
Madison (borough) Morris County	504	3.05
Princeton (township) Mercer County	485	3.03
Barclay-Kingston (cdp) Camden County	324	3.01

Serbian

Top 10 Places Sorted by Number
Based on all places, regardless of population

Place	Number	%
Clifton (city) Passaic County	144	0.18
Toms River (cdp) Ocean County	85	0.10
Dover (township) Ocean County	85	0.09
Paterson (city) Passaic County	82	0.05
Edison (cdp) Middlesex County	78	0.08
Ocean City (city) Cape May County	70	0.46
Plainsboro (township) Middlesex County	70	0.35
Howell (township) Monmouth County	59	0.12
Piscataway (township) Middlesex County	56	0.11
Princeton Meadows (cdp) Middlesex County	51	0.39

Top 10 Places Sorted by Percent
Based on all places, regardless of population

Place	Number	%
Bradley Beach (borough) Monmouth County	26	0.54
Plainsboro Center (cdp) Middlesex County	12	0.51
Manville (borough) Somerset County	48	0.47
Lebanon (borough) Hunterdon County	5	0.47
Ocean City (city) Cape May County	70	0.46
Butler (borough) Morris County	31	0.42
Princeton Meadows (cdp) Middlesex County	51	0.39
Sussex (borough) Sussex County	8	0.37
White Meadow Lake (cdp) Morris County	33	0.36
Plainsboro (township) Middlesex County	70	0.35

Top 10 Places Sorted by Percent
Based on places with populations of 10,000 or more

Place	Number	%
Manville (borough) Somerset County	48	0.47
Ocean City (city) Cape May County	70	0.46
Princeton Meadows (cdp) Middlesex County	51	0.39

Plainsboro (township) Middlesex County	70	0.35
Waterford (township) Camden County	32	0.31
Marlton (cdp) Burlington County	28	0.27
Hawthorne (borough) Passaic County	39	0.21
Ridgewood (village) Bergen County	49	0.20
Springdale (cdp) Camden County	27	0.19
Clifton (city) Passaic County	144	0.18

Slavic

Top 10 Places Sorted by Number
Based on all places, regardless of population

Place	Number	%
Bayonne (city) Hudson County	383	0.62
Hamilton (township) Mercer County	339	0.39
Woodbridge (township) Middlesex County	234	0.24
Edison (cdp) Middlesex County	174	0.18
Trenton (city) Mercer County	159	0.19
Clifton (city) Passaic County	134	0.17
Linden (city) Union County	112	0.28
Bridgewater (township) Somerset County	112	0.26
Franklin (township) Somerset County	111	0.22
Sayreville (borough) Middlesex County	110	0.27

Top 10 Places Sorted by Percent
Based on all places, regardless of population

Place	Number	%
Vernon Valley (cdp) Sussex County	24	1.38
Dover Beaches South (cdp) Ocean County	20	1.21
North Beach Haven (cdp) Ocean County	26	1.07
Pennington (borough) Mercer County	27	1.00
Long Beach (township) Ocean County	33	0.99
Roosevelt (borough) Monmouth County	8	0.86
Florence-Roebling (cdp) Burlington County	68	0.83
North Middletown (cdp) Monmouth County	25	0.78
Beach Haven West (cdp) Ocean County	33	0.77
Wood-Ridge (borough) Bergen County	58	0.76

Top 10 Places Sorted by Percent
Based on places with populations of 10,000 or more

Place	Number	%
Florence (township) Burlington County	79	0.74
Manville (borough) Somerset County	74	0.72
Bayonne (city) Hudson County	383	0.62
Little Falls (cdp) Passaic County	43	0.40
Hamilton (township) Mercer County	339	0.39
Mercerville-Hamilton Square (cdp) Mercer Co.	103	0.39
Branchburg (township) Somerset County	52	0.36
Garfield (city) Bergen County	99	0.33
Avenel (cdp) Middlesex County	57	0.32
Lodi (borough) Bergen County	71	0.30

Slovak

Top 10 Places Sorted by Number
Based on all places, regardless of population

Place	Number	%
Woodbridge (township) Middlesex County	1,833	1.89
Hamilton (township) Mercer County	1,785	2.05
Clifton (city) Passaic County	1,163	1.48
Edison (cdp) Middlesex County	1,097	1.12
Linden (city) Union County	927	2.35
Bayonne (city) Hudson County	857	1.39
Mercerville-Hamilton Square (cdp) Mercer Co.	641	2.42
Carteret (borough) Middlesex County	635	3.07
Perth Amboy (city) Middlesex County	626	1.32
Brick (township) Ocean County	552	0.73

Top 10 Places Sorted by Percent
Based on all places, regardless of population

Place	Number	%
Port Reading (cdp) Middlesex County	142	3.88

Raritan (borough) Somerset County	239	3.77
Manville (borough) Somerset County	388	3.76
Sewaren (cdp) Middlesex County	106	3.76
Millstone (borough) Somerset County	13	3.12
Carteret (borough) Middlesex County	635	3.07
White Horse (cdp) Mercer County	279	2.92
Boonton (township) Morris County	124	2.89
Lopatcong (township) Warren County	163	2.83
Milltown (borough) Middlesex County	189	2.70

Top 10 Places Sorted by Percent
Based on places with populations of 10,000 or more

Place	Number	%
Manville (borough) Somerset County	388	3.76
Carteret (borough) Middlesex County	635	3.07
Readington (township) Hunterdon County	401	2.54
Clark (cdp) Union County	356	2.44
Mercerville-Hamilton Square (cdp) Mercer Co.	641	2.42
Linden (city) Union County	927	2.35
Florence (township) Burlington County	234	2.18
Fords (cdp) Middlesex County	318	2.10
Hamilton (township) Mercer County	1,785	2.05
Woodbridge (township) Middlesex County	1,833	1.89

Slovene

Top 10 Places Sorted by Number
Based on all places, regardless of population

Place	Number	%
Middletown (township) Monmouth County	53	0.08
Edison (cdp) Middlesex County	51	0.05
Woodbridge (township) Middlesex County	38	0.04
Hamilton (township) Mercer County	36	0.04
Florence (township) Burlington County	34	0.32
Ewing (cdp) Mercer County	31	0.09
Florence-Roebling (cdp) Burlington County	28	0.34
Jersey City (city) Hudson County	28	0.01
Burlington (township) Burlington County	27	0.13
Dover (township) Ocean County	27	0.03

Top 10 Places Sorted by Percent
Based on all places, regardless of population

Place	Number	%
Millstone (borough) Somerset County	2	0.48
West Wildwood (borough) Cape May County	2	0.45
Frenchtown (borough) Hunterdon County	6	0.40
Crandon Lakes (cdp) Sussex County	5	0.40
Mullica Hill (cdp) Gloucester County	6	0.36
Far Hills (borough) Somerset County	3	0.35
Florence-Roebling (cdp) Burlington County	28	0.34
Winfield (township) Union County	5	0.33
Florence (township) Burlington County	34	0.32
Caldwell (borough) Essex County	24	0.32

Top 10 Places Sorted by Percent
Based on places with populations of 10,000 or more

Place	Number	%
Florence (township) Burlington County	34	0.32
Highland Park (borough) Middlesex County	23	0.16
Springfield (cdp) Union County	20	0.14
Burlington (township) Burlington County	27	0.13
Point Pleasant (borough) Ocean County	23	0.12
Little Egg Harbor (township) Ocean County	20	0.12
Branchburg (township) Somerset County	18	0.12
Succasunna-Kenvil (cdp) Morris County	14	0.11
Mount Olive (township) Morris County	24	0.10
Carteret (borough) Middlesex County	20	0.10

Notes: (cdp) census designated place; Refer to the User's Guide in the front of the book for more detailed information.

Soviet Union

Top 10 Places Sorted by Number
Based on all places, regardless of population

Place	Number	%
Tenafly (borough) Bergen County	21	0.15
New Milford (borough) Bergen County	21	0.13
Fairview (borough) Bergen County	11	0.08
Ridgewood (village) Bergen County	10	0.04
Newark (city) Essex County	10	0.00
Phillipsburg (town) Warren County	9	0.06
Parsippany-Troy Hills (township) Morris County	9	0.02
Passaic (city) Passaic County	8	0.01
Metuchen (borough) Middlesex County	7	0.05
Fair Lawn (borough) Bergen County	7	0.02

Top 10 Places Sorted by Percent
Based on all places, regardless of population

Place	Number	%
Tenafly (borough) Bergen County	21	0.15
New Milford (borough) Bergen County	21	0.13
Fairview (borough) Bergen County	11	0.08
Washington Township (cdp) Bergen County	6	0.07
Phillipsburg (town) Warren County	9	0.06
Metuchen (borough) Middlesex County	7	0.05
Ridgewood (village) Bergen County	10	0.04
Rutherford (borough) Bergen County	5	0.03
Parsippany-Troy Hills (township) Morris County	9	0.02
Fair Lawn (borough) Bergen County	7	0.02

Top 10 Places Sorted by Percent
Based on places with populations of 10,000 or more

Place	Number	%
Tenafly (borough) Bergen County	21	0.15
New Milford (borough) Bergen County	21	0.13
Fairview (borough) Bergen County	11	0.08
Phillipsburg (town) Warren County	9	0.06
Metuchen (borough) Middlesex County	7	0.05
Ridgewood (village) Bergen County	10	0.04
Rutherford (borough) Bergen County	5	0.03
Parsippany-Troy Hills (township) Morris County	9	0.02
Fair Lawn (borough) Bergen County	7	0.02
Montclair (cdp) Essex County	6	0.02

Swedish

Top 10 Places Sorted by Number
Based on all places, regardless of population

Place	Number	%
Dover (township) Ocean County	994	1.11
Toms River (cdp) Ocean County	981	1.13
Middletown (township) Monmouth County	902	1.36
Brick (township) Ocean County	677	0.89
Manchester (township) Ocean County	524	1.34
Cherry Hill (township) Camden County	516	0.74
Medford (township) Burlington County	490	2.20
Hamilton (township) Mercer County	486	0.56
Woodbridge (township) Middlesex County	479	0.49
Old Bridge (township) Middlesex County	477	0.79

Top 10 Places Sorted by Percent
Based on all places, regardless of population

Place	Number	%
Strathmere (cdp) Cape May County	11	7.05
Brass Castle (cdp) Warren County	103	6.69
Estell Manor (city) Atlantic County	86	5.40
Pennington (borough) Mercer County	111	4.12
Lebanon (borough) Hunterdon County	40	3.76
Roosevelt (borough) Monmouth County	32	3.45
Corbin City (city) Atlantic County	16	3.42
Netcong (borough) Morris County	87	3.37
Great Meadows-Vienna (cdp) Warren County	44	3.34

| Green (township) Sussex County | 103 | 3.21 |

Top 10 Places Sorted by Percent
Based on places with populations of 10,000 or more

Place	Number	%
Montgomery (township) Somerset County	410	2.35
Medford (township) Burlington County	490	2.20
Hopewell (township) Mercer County	315	1.96
Middle (township) Cape May County	306	1.87
Bernards (township) Somerset County	457	1.86
Moorestown (township) Burlington County	337	1.77
Clinton (township) Hunterdon County	228	1.76
Verona (cdp) Essex County	237	1.75
Readington (township) Hunterdon County	275	1.74
Sparta (township) Sussex County	308	1.70

Swiss

Top 10 Places Sorted by Number
Based on all places, regardless of population

Place	Number	%
Brick (township) Ocean County	305	0.40
Montville (township) Morris County	238	1.14
Mahwah (township) Bergen County	226	0.94
Bridgewater (township) Somerset County	211	0.49
Montclair (cdp) Essex County	206	0.53
Wayne (cdp) Passaic County	206	0.38
Toms River (cdp) Ocean County	196	0.23
Dover (township) Ocean County	196	0.22
Cherry Hill (township) Camden County	191	0.27
Edison (cdp) Middlesex County	191	0.20

Top 10 Places Sorted by Percent
Based on all places, regardless of population

Place	Number	%
Hopewell (borough) Mercer County	55	2.70
Silver Ridge (cdp) Ocean County	25	2.07
Waretown (cdp) Ocean County	33	2.04
Glen Ridge (borough) Essex County	124	1.71
Riverdale (borough) Morris County	41	1.64
Harding (township) Morris County	49	1.54
Roseland (borough) Essex County	79	1.49
Hardwick (township) Warren County	21	1.44
Chatham (township) Morris County	140	1.39
Lawrenceville (cdp) Mercer County	56	1.37

Top 10 Places Sorted by Percent
Based on places with populations of 10,000 or more

Place	Number	%
Chatham (township) Morris County	140	1.39
Montville (township) Morris County	238	1.14
Pequannock (township) Morris County	138	0.99
Pompton Lakes (borough) Passaic County	102	0.96
Glen Rock (borough) Bergen County	110	0.95
Mahwah (township) Bergen County	226	0.94
Ringwood (borough) Passaic County	116	0.94
Hawthorne (borough) Passaic County	162	0.89
Oakland (borough) Bergen County	111	0.89
Wyckoff (cdp) Bergen County	145	0.88

Turkish

Top 10 Places Sorted by Number
Based on all places, regardless of population

Place	Number	%
Paterson (city) Passaic County	842	0.56
Clifton (city) Passaic County	839	1.07
Cliffside Park (borough) Bergen County	306	1.33
Wayne (cdp) Passaic County	250	0.46
Fairview (borough) Bergen County	230	1.74
Delran (township) Burlington County	226	1.45
Edison (cdp) Middlesex County	199	0.20

Parsippany-Troy Hills (township) Morris County	196	0.39
Belleville (cdp) Essex County	183	0.51
Fort Lee (borough) Bergen County	172	0.49

Top 10 Places Sorted by Percent
Based on all places, regardless of population

Place	Number	%
Edgewater Park (township) Burlington County	170	2.16
Fairview (borough) Bergen County	230	1.74
Boonton (town) Morris County	142	1.67
New Egypt (cdp) Ocean County	38	1.48
Delran (township) Burlington County	226	1.45
Ridgefield (borough) Bergen County	152	1.40
Pemberton Heights (cdp) Burlington County	34	1.35
Cliffside Park (borough) Bergen County	306	1.33
Haledon (borough) Passaic County	95	1.15
Clifton (city) Passaic County	839	1.07

Top 10 Places Sorted by Percent
Based on places with populations of 10,000 or more

Place	Number	%
Fairview (borough) Bergen County	230	1.74
Delran (township) Burlington County	226	1.45
Ridgefield (borough) Bergen County	152	1.40
Cliffside Park (borough) Bergen County	306	1.33
Clifton (city) Passaic County	839	1.07
Holmdel (township) Monmouth County	146	0.93
Weehawken (township) Hudson County	121	0.90
Lyndhurst (cdp) Bergen County	166	0.86
Palisades Park (borough) Bergen County	139	0.81
Tenafly (borough) Bergen County	102	0.74

Ukrainian

Top 10 Places Sorted by Number
Based on all places, regardless of population

Place	Number	%
Woodbridge (township) Middlesex County	1,848	1.90
Clifton (city) Passaic County	1,795	2.28
Hamilton (township) Mercer County	1,208	1.38
Dover (township) Ocean County	1,139	1.27
Toms River (cdp) Ocean County	1,052	1.22
Edison (cdp) Middlesex County	1,048	1.07
Union (cdp) Union County	1,045	1.92
Cherry Hill (township) Camden County	976	1.39
Fair Lawn (borough) Bergen County	898	2.84
Bayonne (city) Hudson County	772	1.25

Top 10 Places Sorted by Percent
Based on all places, regardless of population

Place	Number	%
Independence (township) Warren County	247	4.41
Millstone (borough) Somerset County	16	3.84
Carteret (borough) Middlesex County	764	3.69
Port Reading (cdp) Middlesex County	130	3.56
Hanover (township) Morris County	454	3.52
Dover Beaches North (cdp) Ocean County	57	3.43
Great Meadows-Vienna (cdp) Warren County	45	3.41
Liberty (township) Warren County	92	3.37
Sewaren (cdp) Middlesex County	93	3.30
Mullica Hill (cdp) Gloucester County	55	3.30

Top 10 Places Sorted by Percent
Based on places with populations of 10,000 or more

Place	Number	%
Carteret (borough) Middlesex County	764	3.69
Hanover (township) Morris County	454	3.52
Manville (borough) Somerset County	318	3.09
Fair Lawn (borough) Bergen County	898	2.84
Clark (cdp) Union County	376	2.58
Springfield (cdp) Union County	348	2.41
Colonia (cdp) Middlesex County	425	2.39

Notes: (cdp) census designated place; Refer to the User's Guide in the front of the book for more detailed information.

Place	Number	%
Branchburg (township) Somerset County	336	2.31
Clifton (city) Passaic County	1,795	2.28
Little Falls (cdp) Passaic County	242	2.23

United States or American

Top 10 Places Sorted by Number
Based on all places, regardless of population

Place	Number	%
Newark (city) Essex County	4,976	1.82
Paterson (city) Passaic County	4,732	3.17
Jersey City (city) Hudson County	4,513	1.88
Elizabeth (city) Union County	3,703	3.07
Lakewood (township) Ocean County	3,043	5.04
Cherry Hill (township) Camden County	2,777	3.97
Dover (township) Ocean County	2,586	2.88
Hamilton (township) Mercer County	2,537	2.91
Toms River (cdp) Ocean County	2,521	2.92
Edison (cdp) Middlesex County	2,356	2.41

Top 10 Places Sorted by Percent
Based on all places, regardless of population

Place	Number	%
Rio Grande (cdp) Cape May County	607	24.52
Vista Center (cdp) Ocean County	119	16.74
Annandale (cdp) Hunterdon County	208	15.87
Whitesboro-Burleigh (cdp) Cape May County	311	15.84
Shiloh (borough) Cumberland County	82	15.30
Lower Alloways Creek (township) Salem County	281	15.18
Harding (township) Morris County	404	12.70
Elsinboro (township) Salem County	123	11.26
Presidential Lakes Estates (cdp) Burlington Co.	246	10.22
Middle (township) Cape May County	1,599	9.75

Top 10 Places Sorted by Percent
Based on places with populations of 10,000 or more

Place	Number	%
Middle (township) Cape May County	1,599	9.75
Tenafly (borough) Bergen County	1,092	7.91
Morganville (township) Monmouth County	850	7.63
Southampton (township) Burlington County	766	7.41
Pennsville (township) Salem County	959	7.24
Livingston (cdp) Essex County	1,927	7.04
Clinton (township) Hunterdon County	901	6.95
Pemberton (township) Burlington County	1,947	6.80
Millburn (cdp) Essex County	1,306	6.61
Browns Mills (cdp) Burlington County	741	6.53

Welsh

Top 10 Places Sorted by Number
Based on all places, regardless of population

Place	Number	%
Cherry Hill (township) Camden County	621	0.89
Gloucester (township) Camden County	563	0.88
Hamilton (township) Mercer County	451	0.52
Dover (township) Ocean County	434	0.48
Brick (township) Ocean County	415	0.55
Lower (township) Cape May County	411	1.79
Middletown (township) Monmouth County	393	0.59
Toms River (cdp) Ocean County	388	0.45
Woodbridge (township) Middlesex County	378	0.39
Washington (township) Gloucester County	358	0.76

Top 10 Places Sorted by Percent
Based on all places, regardless of population

Place	Number	%
Elsinboro (township) Salem County	47	4.30
Quinton (township) Salem County	97	3.48
Stone Harbor (borough) Cape May County	38	3.37
Branchville (borough) Sussex County	27	3.19
Washington (borough) Warren County	196	2.92

Place	Number	%
East Greenwich (township) Gloucester County	157	2.89
Pennington (borough) Mercer County	74	2.74
Alexandria (township) Hunterdon County	127	2.70
Gibbsboro (borough) Camden County	64	2.63
Wenonah (borough) Gloucester County	61	2.63

Top 10 Places Sorted by Percent
Based on places with populations of 10,000 or more

Place	Number	%
Southampton (township) Burlington County	207	2.00
Lower (township) Cape May County	411	1.79
Ocean City (city) Cape May County	261	1.70
Barclay-Kingston (cdp) Camden County	178	1.65
Woodbury (city) Gloucester County	167	1.62
Madison (borough) Morris County	258	1.56
Haddonfield (borough) Camden County	182	1.56
Collingswood (borough) Camden County	219	1.53
Phillipsburg (town) Warren County	220	1.45
Pennsville (township) Salem County	189	1.43

West Indian, excluding Hispanic

Top 10 Places Sorted by Number
Based on all places, regardless of population

Place	Number	%
Irvington (cdp) Essex County	9,590	15.82
East Orange (city) Essex County	7,743	11.08
Newark (city) Essex County	6,424	2.35
Jersey City (city) Hudson County	5,769	2.40
Orange (cdp) Essex County	5,505	16.75
Paterson (city) Passaic County	5,479	3.67
Elizabeth (city) Union County	4,021	3.34
West Orange (cdp) Essex County	2,674	5.96
Teaneck (cdp) Bergen County	2,469	6.29
Plainfield (city) Union County	2,465	5.15

Top 10 Places Sorted by Percent
Based on all places, regardless of population

Place	Number	%
Orange (cdp) Essex County	5,505	16.75
Irvington (cdp) Essex County	9,590	15.82
East Orange (city) Essex County	7,743	11.08
Roselle (borough) Union County	2,331	10.96
Maplewood (cdp) Essex County	2,423	10.15
Asbury Park (city) Monmouth County	1,629	9.62
Englewood (city) Bergen County	2,034	7.76
South Orange (cdp) Essex County	1,177	6.94
Teaneck (cdp) Bergen County	2,469	6.29
West Orange (cdp) Essex County	2,674	5.96

Top 10 Places Sorted by Percent
Based on places with populations of 10,000 or more

Place	Number	%
Orange (cdp) Essex County	5,505	16.75
Irvington (cdp) Essex County	9,590	15.82
East Orange (city) Essex County	7,743	11.08
Roselle (borough) Union County	2,331	10.96
Maplewood (cdp) Essex County	2,423	10.15
Asbury Park (city) Monmouth County	1,629	9.62
Englewood (city) Bergen County	2,034	7.76
South Orange (cdp) Essex County	1,177	6.94
Teaneck (cdp) Bergen County	2,469	6.29
West Orange (cdp) Essex County	2,674	5.96

West Indian: Bahamian, excluding Hispanic

Top 10 Places Sorted by Number
Based on all places, regardless of population

Place	Number	%
Galloway (township) Atlantic County	59	0.19
Jersey City (city) Hudson County	43	0.02

Place	Number	%
Hackensack (city) Bergen County	30	0.07
Princeton Meadows (cdp) Middlesex County	28	0.21
Plainsboro (township) Middlesex County	28	0.14
Irvington (cdp) Essex County	28	0.05
Paterson (city) Passaic County	25	0.02
Hasbrouck Heights (borough) Bergen County	24	0.21
Lawrence (township) Mercer County	22	0.08
Rahway (city) Union County	22	0.08

Top 10 Places Sorted by Percent
Based on all places, regardless of population

Place	Number	%
Sewaren (cdp) Middlesex County	19	0.67
Helmetta (borough) Middlesex County	8	0.44
Whitesboro-Burleigh (cdp) Cape May County	7	0.36
Princeton Meadows (cdp) Middlesex County	28	0.21
Hasbrouck Heights (borough) Bergen County	24	0.21
Galloway (township) Atlantic County	59	0.19
McGuire AFB (cdp) Burlington County	11	0.17
Plainsboro (township) Middlesex County	28	0.14
Chesterfield (township) Burlington County	8	0.13
Victory Gardens (borough) Morris County	2	0.13

Top 10 Places Sorted by Percent
Based on places with populations of 10,000 or more

Place	Number	%
Princeton Meadows (cdp) Middlesex County	28	0.21
Hasbrouck Heights (borough) Bergen County	24	0.21
Galloway (township) Atlantic County	59	0.19
Plainsboro (township) Middlesex County	28	0.14
Wantage (township) Sussex County	11	0.11
Glen Rock (borough) Bergen County	12	0.10
Somerville (borough) Somerset County	12	0.10
Lawrence (township) Mercer County	22	0.08
Rahway (city) Union County	22	0.08
Burlington (township) Burlington County	17	0.08

West Indian: Barbadian, excluding Hispanic

Top 10 Places Sorted by Number
Based on all places, regardless of population

Place	Number	%
Plainfield (city) Union County	270	0.56
East Orange (city) Essex County	193	0.28
Irvington (cdp) Essex County	113	0.19
Franklin (township) Somerset County	92	0.18
Jersey City (city) Hudson County	82	0.03
Montclair (cdp) Essex County	74	0.19
Old Bridge (township) Middlesex County	71	0.12
Maplewood (cdp) Essex County	67	0.28
Willingboro (township) Burlington County	65	0.20
South Plainfield (borough) Middlesex County	64	0.29

Top 10 Places Sorted by Percent
Based on all places, regardless of population

Place	Number	%
Flemington (borough) Hunterdon County	26	0.62
Plainfield (city) Union County	270	0.56
Hackettstown (town) Warren County	42	0.40
Holiday City South (cdp) Ocean County	12	0.30
South Plainfield (borough) Middlesex County	64	0.29
East Orange (city) Essex County	193	0.28
Maplewood (cdp) Essex County	67	0.28
Summit (city) Union County	59	0.28
Asbury Park (city) Monmouth County	45	0.27
Lawnside (borough) Camden County	7	0.26

Top 10 Places Sorted by Percent
Based on places with populations of 10,000 or more

Place	Number	%
Plainfield (city) Union County	270	0.56

Notes: (cdp) census designated place; Refer to the User's Guide in the front of the book for more detailed information.

Place	Number	%
Hackettstown (town) Warren County	42	0.40
South Plainfield (borough) Middlesex County	64	0.29
East Orange (city) Essex County	193	0.28
Maplewood (cdp) Essex County	67	0.20
Summit (city) Union County	59	0.28
Asbury Park (city) Monmouth County	45	0.27
Hillside (cdp) Union County	46	0.21
Willingboro (township) Burlington County	65	0.20
Somerset (cdp) Somerset County	45	0.20

West Indian: Belizean, excluding Hispanic

Top 10 Places Sorted by Number
Based on all places, regardless of population

Place	Number	%
Jersey City (city) Hudson County	153	0.06
Teaneck (cdp) Bergen County	61	0.16
East Orange (city) Essex County	59	0.08
Long Branch (city) Monmouth County	52	0.17
Asbury Park (city) Monmouth County	48	0.28
Passaic (city) Passaic County	40	0.06
Freehold (borough) Monmouth County	34	0.31
Browns Mills (cdp) Burlington County	29	0.26
Pemberton (township) Burlington County	29	0.10
Keyport (borough) Monmouth County	27	0.36

Top 10 Places Sorted by Percent
Based on all places, regardless of population

Place	Number	%
Allentown (borough) Monmouth County	7	0.37
Keyport (borough) Monmouth County	27	0.36
Freehold (borough) Monmouth County	34	0.31
Asbury Park (city) Monmouth County	48	0.28
Browns Mills (cdp) Burlington County	29	0.26
Port Monmouth (cdp) Monmouth County	9	0.25
Eatontown (borough) Monmouth County	26	0.19
Long Branch (city) Monmouth County	52	0.17
Teaneck (cdp) Bergen County	61	0.16
Saddle Brook (cdp) Bergen County	20	0.15

Top 10 Places Sorted by Percent
Based on places with populations of 10,000 or more

Place	Number	%
Freehold (borough) Monmouth County	34	0.31
Asbury Park (city) Monmouth County	48	0.28
Browns Mills (cdp) Burlington County	29	0.26
Eatontown (borough) Monmouth County	26	0.19
Long Branch (city) Monmouth County	52	0.17
Teaneck (cdp) Bergen County	61	0.16
Saddle Brook (cdp) Bergen County	20	0.15
Iselin (cdp) Middlesex County	22	0.13
Pemberton (township) Burlington County	29	0.10
Palisades Park (borough) Bergen County	17	0.10

West Indian: Bermudan, excluding Hispanic

Top 10 Places Sorted by Number
Based on all places, regardless of population

Place	Number	%
Montclair (cdp) Essex County	48	0.12
East Orange (city) Essex County	37	0.05
Plainfield (city) Union County	35	0.07
Irvington (cdp) Essex County	33	0.05
Beckett (cdp) Gloucester County	29	0.60
Logan (township) Gloucester County	29	0.48
Hillsborough (township) Somerset County	25	0.07
Willingboro (township) Burlington County	22	0.07
Hillside (cdp) Union County	20	0.09
Crestwood Village (cdp) Ocean County	19	0.22

Top 10 Places Sorted by Percent
Based on all places, regardless of population

Place	Number	%
Beckett (cdp) Gloucester County	29	0.60
West Amwell (township) Hunterdon County	12	0.50
Logan (township) Gloucester County	29	0.48
Crestwood Village (cdp) Ocean County	19	0.22
Allendale (borough) Bergen County	15	0.22
Montclair (cdp) Essex County	48	0.12
Chesterfield (township) Burlington County	6	0.10
Hillside (cdp) Union County	20	0.09
Plainfield (city) Union County	35	0.07
Hillsborough (township) Somerset County	25	0.07

Top 10 Places Sorted by Percent
Based on places with populations of 10,000 or more

Place	Number	%
Montclair (cdp) Essex County	48	0.12
Hillside (cdp) Union County	20	0.09
Plainfield (city) Union County	35	0.07
Hillsborough (township) Somerset County	25	0.07
Willingboro (township) Burlington County	22	0.07
Westwood (borough) Bergen County	8	0.07
Readington (township) Hunterdon County	10	0.06
East Orange (city) Essex County	37	0.05
Irvington (cdp) Essex County	33	0.05
Manchester (township) Ocean County	19	0.05

West Indian: British West Indian, excluding Hispanic

Top 10 Places Sorted by Number
Based on all places, regardless of population

Place	Number	%
Jersey City (city) Hudson County	377	0.16
East Orange (city) Essex County	260	0.37
Newark (city) Essex County	248	0.09
Teaneck (cdp) Bergen County	196	0.50
Irvington (cdp) Essex County	153	0.25
Hackensack (city) Bergen County	146	0.34
Paterson (city) Passaic County	113	0.08
Englewood (city) Bergen County	106	0.40
Franklin (township) Somerset County	92	0.18
South Orange (cdp) Essex County	79	0.47

Top 10 Places Sorted by Percent
Based on all places, regardless of population

Place	Number	%
Norwood (borough) Bergen County	48	0.83
Ridgefield (borough) Bergen County	60	0.55
Atlantic Highlands (borough) Monmouth County	26	0.55
Teaneck (cdp) Bergen County	196	0.50
East Freehold (cdp) Monmouth County	25	0.49
South Orange (cdp) Essex County	79	0.47
Englewood (city) Bergen County	106	0.40
White (township) Warren County	16	0.38
East Orange (city) Essex County	260	0.37
Hackensack (city) Bergen County	146	0.34

Top 10 Places Sorted by Percent
Based on places with populations of 10,000 or more

Place	Number	%
Ridgefield (borough) Bergen County	60	0.55
Teaneck (cdp) Bergen County	196	0.50
South Orange (cdp) Essex County	79	0.47
Englewood (city) Bergen County	106	0.40
East Orange (city) Essex County	260	0.37
Hackensack (city) Bergen County	146	0.34
Maplewood (cdp) Essex County	62	0.26
Irvington (cdp) Essex County	153	0.25
Bound Brook (borough) Somerset County	25	0.25
Guttenberg (town) Hudson County	23	0.22

West Indian: Dutch West Indian, excluding Hispanic

Top 10 Places Sorted by Number
Based on all places, regardless of population

Place	Number	%
Camden (city) Camden County	45	0.06
Brick (township) Ocean County	33	0.04
Orange (cdp) Essex County	27	0.08
Piscataway (township) Middlesex County	22	0.04
Vineland (city) Cumberland County	21	0.04
Washington (township) Gloucester County	19	0.04
West New York (town) Hudson County	17	0.04
Greenwich (township) Warren County	15	0.34
Monroe (township) Gloucester County	10	0.03
Montclair (cdp) Essex County	8	0.02

Top 10 Places Sorted by Percent
Based on all places, regardless of population

Place	Number	%
Greenwich (township) Warren County	15	0.34
Liberty (township) Warren County	4	0.15
Orange (cdp) Essex County	27	0.08
Newton (town) Sussex County	7	0.08
Fort Dix (cdp) Burlington County	6	0.08
Camden (city) Camden County	45	0.06
Northfield (city) Atlantic County	5	0.06
Brick (township) Ocean County	33	0.04
Piscataway (township) Middlesex County	22	0.04
Vineland (city) Cumberland County	21	0.04

Top 10 Places Sorted by Percent
Based on places with populations of 10,000 or more

Place	Number	%
Orange (cdp) Essex County	27	0.08
Camden (city) Camden County	45	0.06
Brick (township) Ocean County	33	0.04
Piscataway (township) Middlesex County	22	0.04
Vineland (city) Cumberland County	21	0.04
Washington (township) Gloucester County	19	0.04
West New York (town) Hudson County	17	0.04
Monroe (township) Gloucester County	10	0.03
Ramsey (borough) Bergen County	4	0.03
Montclair (cdp) Essex County	8	0.02

West Indian: Haitian, excluding Hispanic

Top 10 Places Sorted by Number
Based on all places, regardless of population

Place	Number	%
Irvington (cdp) Essex County	5,812	9.59
Orange (cdp) Essex County	3,250	9.89
Elizabeth (city) Union County	3,016	2.50
East Orange (city) Essex County	2,852	4.08
Newark (city) Essex County	2,634	0.96
Jersey City (city) Hudson County	1,931	0.80
Roselle (borough) Union County	1,709	8.03
West Orange (cdp) Essex County	1,618	3.61
Linden (city) Union County	1,360	3.45
Maplewood (cdp) Essex County	1,181	4.95

Top 10 Places Sorted by Percent
Based on all places, regardless of population

Place	Number	%
Orange (cdp) Essex County	3,250	9.89
Irvington (cdp) Essex County	5,812	9.59
Roselle (borough) Union County	1,709	8.03
Asbury Park (city) Monmouth County	974	5.75
Maplewood (cdp) Essex County	1,181	4.95
East Orange (city) Essex County	2,852	4.08
West Orange (cdp) Essex County	1,618	3.61
Linden (city) Union County	1,360	3.45

Notes: (cdp) census designated place; Refer to the User's Guide in the front of the book for more detailed information.

Place	Number	%
Pleasantville (city) Atlantic County	575	3.01
South Orange (cdp) Essex County	488	2.88

Top 10 Places Sorted by Percent
Based on places with populations of 10,000 or more

Place	Number	%
Orange (cdp) Essex County	3,250	9.89
Irvington (cdp) Essex County	5,812	9.59
Roselle (borough) Union County	1,709	8.03
Asbury Park (city) Monmouth County	974	5.75
Maplewood (cdp) Essex County	1,181	4.95
East Orange (city) Essex County	2,852	4.08
West Orange (cdp) Essex County	1,618	3.61
Linden (city) Union County	1,360	3.45
Pleasantville (city) Atlantic County	575	3.01
South Orange (cdp) Essex County	488	2.88

West Indian: Jamaican, excluding Hispanic

Top 10 Places Sorted by Number
Based on all places, regardless of population

Place	Number	%
Paterson (city) Passaic County	4,776	3.20
East Orange (city) Essex County	3,368	4.82
Irvington (cdp) Essex County	2,585	4.26
Newark (city) Essex County	2,008	0.73
Plainfield (city) Union County	1,450	3.03
Teaneck (cdp) Bergen County	1,351	3.44
Englewood (city) Bergen County	1,307	4.99
Franklin (township) Somerset County	1,295	2.54
Orange (cdp) Essex County	1,238	3.77
Hackensack (city) Bergen County	1,226	2.87

Top 10 Places Sorted by Percent
Based on all places, regardless of population

Place	Number	%
Englewood (city) Bergen County	1,307	4.99
East Orange (city) Essex County	3,368	4.82
Irvington (cdp) Essex County	2,585	4.26
Somerset (cdp) Somerset County	910	3.95
Orange (cdp) Essex County	1,238	3.77
Teaneck (cdp) Bergen County	1,351	3.44
Paterson (city) Passaic County	4,776	3.20
Prospect Park (borough) Passaic County	180	3.11
Maplewood (cdp) Essex County	735	3.08
Plainfield (city) Union County	1,450	3.03

Top 10 Places Sorted by Percent
Based on places with populations of 10,000 or more

Place	Number	%
Englewood (city) Bergen County	1,307	4.99
East Orange (city) Essex County	3,368	4.82
Irvington (cdp) Essex County	2,585	4.26
Somerset (cdp) Somerset County	910	3.95
Orange (cdp) Essex County	1,238	3.77
Teaneck (cdp) Bergen County	1,351	3.44
Paterson (city) Passaic County	4,776	3.20
Maplewood (cdp) Essex County	735	3.08
Plainfield (city) Union County	1,450	3.03
Hackensack (city) Bergen County	1,226	2.87

West Indian: Trinidadian and Tobagonian, excluding Hispanic

Top 10 Places Sorted by Number
Based on all places, regardless of population

Place	Number	%
Jersey City (city) Hudson County	1,031	0.43
Orange (cdp) Essex County	630	1.92
Newark (city) Essex County	585	0.21
East Orange (city) Essex County	518	0.74
Irvington (cdp) Essex County	491	0.81
Edison (cdp) Middlesex County	294	0.30
Woodbridge (township) Middlesex County	252	0.26
Elizabeth (city) Union County	252	0.21
Union (cdp) Union County	250	0.46
Maplewood (cdp) Essex County	234	0.98

Top 10 Places Sorted by Percent
Based on all places, regardless of population

Place	Number	%
Orange (cdp) Essex County	630	1.92
Neptune City (borough) Monmouth County	76	1.46
Harrington Park (borough) Bergen County	66	1.39
Scotch Plains (cdp) Union County	231	1.02
Maplewood (cdp) Essex County	234	0.98
Irvington (cdp) Essex County	491	0.81
East Orange (city) Essex County	518	0.74
Dayton (cdp) Middlesex County	43	0.67
Roselle (borough) Union County	141	0.66
Mount Arlington (borough) Morris County	31	0.66

Top 10 Places Sorted by Percent
Based on places with populations of 10,000 or more

Place	Number	%
Orange (cdp) Essex County	630	1.92
Scotch Plains (cdp) Union County	231	1.02
Maplewood (cdp) Essex County	234	0.98
Irvington (cdp) Essex County	491	0.81
East Orange (city) Essex County	518	0.74
Roselle (borough) Union County	141	0.66
Bergenfield (borough) Bergen County	169	0.64
Englewood (city) Bergen County	152	0.58
South Orange (cdp) Essex County	90	0.53
Highland Park (borough) Middlesex County	72	0.51

West Indian: U.S. Virgin Islander, excluding Hispanic

Top 10 Places Sorted by Number
Based on all places, regardless of population

Place	Number	%
Elizabeth (city) Union County	40	0.03
Newark (city) Essex County	36	0.01
Plainfield (city) Union County	29	0.06
Jersey City (city) Hudson County	29	0.01
North Brunswick Twp (cdp) Middlesex County	27	0.07
Paterson (city) Passaic County	27	0.02
Irvington (cdp) Essex County	25	0.04
East Orange (city) Essex County	23	0.03
Englewood (city) Bergen County	20	0.08
Orange (cdp) Essex County	19	0.06

Top 10 Places Sorted by Percent
Based on all places, regardless of population

Place	Number	%
McGuire AFB (cdp) Burlington County	14	0.21
Heathcote (cdp) Middlesex County	9	0.20
New Hanover (township) Burlington County	14	0.14
Franklin Lakes (borough) Bergen County	11	0.11
Highland Park (borough) Middlesex County	13	0.09
Englewood (city) Bergen County	20	0.08
Red Bank (borough) Monmouth County	10	0.08
Boonton (town) Morris County	7	0.08
North Brunswick Twp (cdp) Middlesex County	27	0.07
Plainfield (city) Union County	29	0.06

Top 10 Places Sorted by Percent
Based on places with populations of 10,000 or more

Place	Number	%
Franklin Lakes (borough) Bergen County	11	0.11
Highland Park (borough) Middlesex County	13	0.09
Englewood (city) Bergen County	20	0.08

Place	Number	%
Red Bank (borough) Monmouth County	10	0.08
North Brunswick Twp (cdp) Middlesex County	27	0.07
Plainfield (city) Union County	29	0.06
Orange (cdp) Essex County	19	0.06
Point Pleasant (borough) Ocean County	12	0.06
Avenel (cdp) Middlesex County	11	0.06
Princeton Meadows (cdp) Middlesex County	8	0.06

West Indian: West Indian, excluding Hispanic

Top 10 Places Sorted by Number
Based on all places, regardless of population

Place	Number	%
Jersey City (city) Hudson County	923	0.38
Newark (city) Essex County	812	0.30
East Orange (city) Essex County	406	0.58
Teaneck (cdp) Bergen County	363	0.92
Irvington (cdp) Essex County	326	0.54
Montclair (cdp) Essex County	261	0.67
Willingboro (township) Burlington County	228	0.69
Plainfield (city) Union County	227	0.47
Franklin (township) Somerset County	214	0.42
Orange (cdp) Essex County	191	0.58

Top 10 Places Sorted by Percent
Based on all places, regardless of population

Place	Number	%
Annandale (cdp) Hunterdon County	44	3.36
Whitesboro-Burleigh (cdp) Cape May County	31	1.58
Rockleigh (borough) Bergen County	6	1.50
Cliffwood Beach (cdp) Monmouth County	41	1.16
Fairton (cdp) Cumberland County	27	1.16
South Hackensack (township) Bergen County	21	0.93
Teaneck (cdp) Bergen County	363	0.92
Olivet (cdp) Salem County	13	0.88
Greenwich (township) Warren County	31	0.71
Beverly (city) Burlington County	19	0.71

Top 10 Places Sorted by Percent
Based on places with populations of 10,000 or more

Place	Number	%
Teaneck (cdp) Bergen County	363	0.92
Willingboro (township) Burlington County	228	0.69
Montclair (cdp) Essex County	261	0.67
South Orange (cdp) Essex County	107	0.63
East Orange (city) Essex County	406	0.58
Orange (cdp) Essex County	191	0.58
Englewood (city) Bergen County	145	0.55
Aberdeen (township) Monmouth County	95	0.55
Irvington (cdp) Essex County	326	0.54
Maplewood (cdp) Essex County	125	0.52

West Indian: Other, excluding Hispanic

Top 10 Places Sorted by Number
Based on all places, regardless of population

Place	Number	%
Jersey City (city) Hudson County	39	0.02
Orange (cdp) Essex County	23	0.07
Elizabeth (city) Union County	23	0.02
Matawan (borough) Monmouth County	17	0.19
Teaneck (cdp) Bergen County	17	0.04
South Brunswick (township) Middlesex County	16	0.04
Franklin (township) Somerset County	11	0.02
Old Bridge (township) Middlesex County	11	0.02
Chatham (borough) Morris County	10	0.12
Park Ridge (borough) Bergen County	10	0.11

Notes: (cdp) census designated place; Refer to the User's Guide in the front of the book for more detailed information.

Top 10 Places Sorted by Percent
Based on all places, regardless of population

Place	Number	%
Monmouth Junction (cdp) Middlesex County	7	0.29
Matawan (borough) Monmouth County	17	0.19
Pennington (borough) Mercer County	5	0.19
Dayton (cdp) Middlesex County	9	0.14
Chatham (borough) Morris County	10	0.12
Park Ridge (borough) Bergen County	10	0.11
Pine Beach (borough) Ocean County	2	0.10
Orange (cdp) Essex County	23	0.07
Freehold (borough) Monmouth County	8	0.07
Ridgefield (borough) Bergen County	8	0.07

Top 10 Places Sorted by Percent
Based on places with populations of 10,000 or more

Place	Number	%
Orange (cdp) Essex County	23	0.07
Freehold (borough) Monmouth County	8	0.07
Ridgefield (borough) Bergen County	8	0.07
Somerville (borough) Somerset County	7	0.06
Summit (city) Union County	10	0.05
Teaneck (cdp) Bergen County	17	0.04
South Brunswick (township) Middlesex County	16	0.04
Elmwood Park (borough) Bergen County	7	0.04
Jersey City (city) Hudson County	39	0.02
Elizabeth (city) Union County	23	0.02

White

Top 10 Places Sorted by Number
Based on all places, regardless of population

Place	Number	%
Jersey City (city) Hudson County	90,383	37.65
Dover (township) Ocean County	84,835	94.57
Toms River (cdp) Ocean County	81,480	94.39
Newark (city) Essex County	80,495	29.43
Hamilton (township) Mercer County	75,198	86.33
Brick (township) Ocean County	73,643	96.75
Elizabeth (city) Union County	72,547	60.17
Woodbridge (township) Middlesex County	70,514	72.54
Middletown (township) Monmouth County	63,324	95.47
Clifton (city) Passaic County	63,141	80.26

Top 10 Places Sorted by Percent
Based on all places, regardless of population

Place	Number	%
Walpack (township) Sussex County	41	100.00
Pine Valley (borough) Camden County	20	100.00
Bass River (township) Burlington County	1,504	99.60
Sea Girt (borough) Monmouth County	2,138	99.53
Leisure Village East (cdp) Ocean County	4,572	99.46
Eagleswood (township) Ocean County	1,433	99.44
Interlaken (borough) Monmouth County	895	99.44
Dover Beaches South (cdp) Ocean County	1,583	99.31
Holiday City-Berkeley (cdp) Ocean County	13,787	99.30
Beach Haven (borough) Ocean County	1,269	99.30

Top 10 Places Sorted by Percent
Based on places with populations of 10,000 or more

Place	Number	%
Holiday City-Berkeley (cdp) Ocean County	13,787	99.30
Point Pleasant (borough) Ocean County	19,015	98.49
Lacey (township) Ocean County	24,960	98.48
Upper (township) Cape May County	11,908	98.29
Wantage (township) Sussex County	10,196	98.16
Gloucester City (city) Camden County	11,221	97.71
Berkeley (township) Ocean County	39,071	97.70
Sparta (township) Sussex County	17,664	97.70
Wall (township) Monmouth County	24,663	97.63
Stafford (township) Ocean County	21,995	97.62

White: Not Hispanic

Top 10 Places Sorted by Number
Based on all places, regardless of population

Place	Number	%
Dover (township) Ocean County	81,737	91.12
Toms River (cdp) Ocean County	78,438	90.86
Hamilton (township) Mercer County	72,843	83.62
Brick (township) Ocean County	71,379	93.77
Woodbridge (township) Middlesex County	65,106	66.98
Jersey City (city) Hudson County	62,186	25.90
Middletown (township) Monmouth County	61,440	92.63
Cherry Hill (township) Camden County	58,695	83.89
Clifton (city) Passaic County	55,485	70.53
Edison (cdp) Middlesex County	55,459	56.77

Top 10 Places Sorted by Percent
Based on all places, regardless of population

Place	Number	%
Walpack (township) Sussex County	41	100.00
Pine Valley (borough) Camden County	20	100.00
Audubon Park (borough) Camden County	1,089	98.82
Califon (borough) Hunterdon County	1,042	98.77
Avalon (borough) Cape May County	2,115	98.69
Concordia (cdp) Middlesex County	3,607	98.61
Stone Harbor (borough) Cape May County	1,112	98.58
Spring Lake (borough) Monmouth County	3,516	98.57
Stockton (borough) Hunterdon County	552	98.57
Leisure Knoll (cdp) Ocean County	2,430	98.50

Top 10 Places Sorted by Percent
Based on places with populations of 10,000 or more

Place	Number	%
Holiday City-Berkeley (cdp) Ocean County	13,646	98.29
Upper (township) Cape May County	11,784	97.27
Lacey (township) Ocean County	24,530	96.78
Point Pleasant (borough) Ocean County	18,655	96.63
Southampton (township) Burlington County	10,030	96.55
Gloucester City (city) Camden County	11,081	96.49
Medford (township) Burlington County	21,462	96.45
Wall (township) Monmouth County	24,349	96.39
Pennsville (township) Salem County	12,715	96.37
Lower (township) Cape May County	22,025	95.99

White: Hispanic

Top 10 Places Sorted by Number
Based on all places, regardless of population

Place	Number	%
Elizabeth (city) Union County	38,524	31.95
Newark (city) Essex County	38,067	13.92
Union City (city) Hudson County	33,741	50.29
Paterson (city) Passaic County	29,860	20.01
Jersey City (city) Hudson County	28,197	11.75
North Bergen (township) Hudson County	23,319	40.14
West New York (town) Hudson County	22,990	50.23
Perth Amboy (city) Middlesex County	14,661	30.99
Passaic (city) Passaic County	13,328	19.64
Camden (city) Camden County	8,897	11.13

Top 10 Places Sorted by Percent
Based on all places, regardless of population

Place	Number	%
Union City (city) Hudson County	33,741	50.29
West New York (town) Hudson County	22,990	50.23
Dover (town) Morris County	7,310	40.19
North Bergen (township) Hudson County	23,319	40.14
Guttenberg (town) Hudson County	3,930	36.37
Victory Gardens (borough) Morris County	528	34.15
Elizabeth (city) Union County	38,524	31.95
Perth Amboy (city) Middlesex County	14,661	30.99
East Newark (borough) Hudson County	634	26.67

Bound Brook (borough) Somerset County	2,603	25.63

Top 10 Places Sorted by Percent
Based on places with populations of 10,000 or more

Place	Number	%
Union City (city) Hudson County	33,741	50.29
West New York (town) Hudson County	22,990	50.23
Dover (town) Morris County	7,310	40.19
North Bergen (township) Hudson County	23,319	40.14
Guttenberg (town) Hudson County	3,930	36.37
Elizabeth (city) Union County	38,524	31.95
Perth Amboy (city) Middlesex County	14,661	30.99
Bound Brook (borough) Somerset County	2,603	25.63
Weehawken (township) Hudson County	3,404	25.21
Fairview (borough) Bergen County	3,176	23.96

Yugoslavian

Top 10 Places Sorted by Number
Based on all places, regardless of population

Place	Number	%
Clifton (city) Passaic County	278	0.35
Garfield (city) Bergen County	277	0.93
Paterson (city) Passaic County	273	0.18
Wayne (cdp) Passaic County	215	0.40
Howell (township) Monmouth County	200	0.41
Cliffside Park (borough) Bergen County	189	0.82
Belleville (cdp) Essex County	172	0.48
Fort Lee (borough) Bergen County	160	0.45
Mount Olive (township) Morris County	138	0.57
Woodbridge (township) Middlesex County	131	0.13

Top 10 Places Sorted by Percent
Based on all places, regardless of population

Place	Number	%
Great Meadows-Vienna (cdp) Warren County	46	3.49
Annandale (cdp) Hunterdon County	29	2.21
Beckett (cdp) Gloucester County	67	1.39
Vista Center (cdp) Ocean County	9	1.27
Hackettstown (town) Warren County	118	1.13
Logan (township) Gloucester County	67	1.11
Mantoloking (borough) Ocean County	4	1.08
Matawan (borough) Monmouth County	91	1.01
Ramtown (cdp) Monmouth County	60	0.96
Garfield (city) Bergen County	277	0.93

Top 10 Places Sorted by Percent
Based on places with populations of 10,000 or more

Place	Number	%
Hackettstown (town) Warren County	118	1.13
Garfield (city) Bergen County	277	0.93
Ringwood (borough) Passaic County	112	0.90
Cliffside Park (borough) Bergen County	189	0.82
Oakland (borough) Bergen County	91	0.73
Guttenberg (town) Hudson County	69	0.65
Mount Olive (township) Morris County	138	0.57
Fairview (borough) Bergen County	76	0.57
Delran (township) Burlington County	87	0.56
Bergenfield (borough) Bergen County	129	0.49

Notes: (cdp) census designated place; Refer to the User's Guide in the front of the book for more detailed information.

Population

Total Population
Top 10 Places Sorted by Number

Place	Number
Newark, NJ (city) Essex County	273,546
Jersey City, NJ (city) Hudson County	240,055
Paterson, NJ (city) Passaic County	149,222
Elizabeth, NJ (city) Union County	120,568
Edison, NJ (cdp) Middlesex County	97,687
Woodbridge, NJ (township) Middlesex County	97,203
Dover, NJ (township) Ocean County	89,767
Hamilton, NJ (township) Mercer County	87,254
Toms River, NJ (cdp) Ocean County	86,452
Trenton, NJ (city) Mercer County	85,258

Hispanic
Top 10 Places Sorted by Number

Place	Number
Newark, NJ (city) Essex County	80,451
Paterson, NJ (city) Passaic County	74,869
Jersey City, NJ (city) Hudson County	68,032
Elizabeth, NJ (city) Union County	59,746
Union City, NJ (city) Hudson County	55,241
Passaic, NJ (city) Passaic County	42,410
West New York, NJ (town) Hudson County	36,042
North Bergen, NJ (township) Hudson County	33,420
Perth Amboy, NJ (city) Middlesex County	33,042
Camden, NJ (city) Camden County	30,869

Hispanic
Top 10 Places Sorted by Percent of Total Population

Place	Percent
Union City, NJ (city) Hudson County	82.34
West New York, NJ (town) Hudson County	78.75
Perth Amboy, NJ (city) Middlesex County	69.85
Passaic, NJ (city) Passaic County	62.50
Dover, NJ (town) Morris County	58.15
North Bergen, NJ (township) Hudson County	57.42
Guttenberg, NJ (town) Hudson County	53.32
Paterson, NJ (city) Passaic County	50.17
Elizabeth, NJ (city) Union County	49.55
Weehawken, NJ (township) Hudson County	40.60

Argentinian
Top 10 Places Sorted by Number

Place	Number
North Bergen, NJ (township) Hudson County	489

Argentinian
Top 10 Places Sorted by Percent of Hispanic Population

Place	Percent
North Bergen, NJ (township) Hudson County	1.46

Argentinian
Top 10 Places Sorted by Percent of Total Population

Place	Percent
North Bergen, NJ (township) Hudson County	0.84

Bolivian
Top 10 Places Sorted by Number

Place	Number
No places met population threshold.	

Bolivian
Top 10 Places Sorted by Percent of Hispanic Population

Place	Percent
No places met population threshold.	

Bolivian
Top 10 Places Sorted by Percent of Total Population

Place	Percent
No places met population threshold.	

Central American
Top 10 Places Sorted by Number

Place	Number
Union City, NJ (city) Hudson County	6,823
Elizabeth, NJ (city) Union County	6,226
Jersey City, NJ (city) Hudson County	5,036
West New York, NJ (town) Hudson County	4,990
Plainfield, NJ (city) Union County	4,451
Newark, NJ (city) Essex County	4,324
Trenton, NJ (city) Mercer County	3,921
North Bergen, NJ (township) Hudson County	3,023
New Brunswick, NJ (city) Middlesex County	2,421
Paterson, NJ (city) Passaic County	1,997

Central American
Top 10 Places Sorted by Percent of Hispanic Population

Place	Percent
Bound Brook, NJ (borough) Somerset County	41.00
Plainfield, NJ (city) Union County	36.87
Somerville, NJ (borough) Somerset County	33.79
Palisades Park, NJ (borough) Bergen County	25.83
Morris, NJ (town) Morris County	25.48
Fairview, NJ (borough) Bergen County	24.89
Trenton, NJ (city) Mercer County	21.19
City of Orange, NJ (township) Essex County	19.85
Orange, NJ (cdp) Essex County	19.85
East Windsor, NJ (township) Mercer County	18.13

Central American
Top 10 Places Sorted by Percent of Total Population

Place	Percent
Bound Brook, NJ (borough) Somerset County	14.33
West New York, NJ (town) Hudson County	10.90
Union City, NJ (city) Hudson County	10.17
Plainfield, NJ (city) Union County	9.31
Fairview, NJ (borough) Bergen County	9.29
Guttenberg, NJ (town) Hudson County	7.60
Morris, NJ (town) Morris County	6.91
Somerville, NJ (borough) Somerset County	5.72
North Plainfield, NJ (borough) Somerset County	5.28
North Bergen, NJ (township) Hudson County	5.19

Chilean
Top 10 Places Sorted by Number

Place	Number
North Bergen, NJ (township) Hudson County	483

Chilean
Top 10 Places Sorted by Percent of Hispanic Population

Place	Percent
North Bergen, NJ (township) Hudson County	1.45

Chilean
Top 10 Places Sorted by Percent of Total Population

Place	Percent
North Bergen, NJ (township) Hudson County	0.83

Colombian
Top 10 Places Sorted by Number

Place	Number
Elizabeth, NJ (city) Union County	8,112
Paterson, NJ (city) Passaic County	5,025
North Bergen, NJ (township) Hudson County	3,917
Union City, NJ (city) Hudson County	2,821
West New York, NJ (town) Hudson County	2,537
Dover, NJ (town) Morris County	2,328
Englewood, NJ (city) Bergen County	2,137
Hackensack, NJ (city) Bergen County	1,787
Jersey City, NJ (city) Hudson County	1,761
Morris, NJ (town) Morris County	1,444

Colombian
Top 10 Places Sorted by Percent of Hispanic Population

Place	Percent
Englewood, NJ (city) Bergen County	37.69
Morris, NJ (town) Morris County	28.72
Dover, NJ (town) Morris County	22.01
Lodi, NJ (borough) Bergen County	21.19
Bergenfield, NJ (borough) Bergen County	19.61
Piscataway, NJ (township) Middlesex County	18.42
Roselle, NJ (borough) Union County	18.00
Parsippany-Troy Hills, NJ (township) Morris County	16.65
Hackensack, NJ (city) Bergen County	16.05
Elizabeth, NJ (city) Union County	13.58

Colombian
Top 10 Places Sorted by Percent of Total Population

Place	Percent
Dover, NJ (town) Morris County	12.80
Englewood, NJ (city) Bergen County	8.16
Morris, NJ (town) Morris County	7.79
Elizabeth, NJ (city) Union County	6.73
North Bergen, NJ (township) Hudson County	6.73
West New York, NJ (town) Hudson County	5.54
Union City, NJ (city) Hudson County	4.20
Hackensack, NJ (city) Bergen County	4.19
Lodi, NJ (borough) Bergen County	3.81
North Plainfield, NJ (borough) Somerset County	3.76

Costa Rican
Top 10 Places Sorted by Number

Place	Number
Bound Brook, NJ (borough) Somerset County	1,225
Trenton, NJ (city) Mercer County	816
Paterson, NJ (city) Passaic County	804
Somerville, NJ (borough) Somerset County	585
Elizabeth, NJ (city) Union County	432

Costa Rican
Top 10 Places Sorted by Percent of Hispanic Population

Place	Percent
Bound Brook, NJ (borough) Somerset County	34.40
Somerville, NJ (borough) Somerset County	27.69
Trenton, NJ (city) Mercer County	4.41
Paterson, NJ (city) Passaic County	1.07
Elizabeth, NJ (city) Union County	0.72

Costa Rican
Top 10 Places Sorted by Percent of Total Population

Place	Percent
Bound Brook, NJ (borough) Somerset County	12.02
Somerville, NJ (borough) Somerset County	4.69
Trenton, NJ (city) Mercer County	0.96
Paterson, NJ (city) Passaic County	0.54
Elizabeth, NJ (city) Union County	0.36

Cuban
Top 10 Places Sorted by Number

Place	Number
Union City, NJ (city) Hudson County	10,333
West New York, NJ (town) Hudson County	9,754
North Bergen, NJ (township) Hudson County	7,901
Elizabeth, NJ (city) Union County	7,520
Newark, NJ (city) Essex County	3,273
Jersey City, NJ (city) Hudson County	1,955
Guttenberg, NJ (town) Hudson County	1,187
Weehawken, NJ (township) Hudson County	1,157
Paterson, NJ (city) Passaic County	964

Notes: Please refer to the User's Guide for an explanation of data; tables include places with populations > 9,999 and reflect only those areas that meet Summary File 4 population thresholds, therefore there may be less than 10 places listed

Perth Amboy, NJ (city) Middlesex County   849

Cuban
Top 10 Places Sorted by Percent of Hispanic Population

Place	Percent
West New York, NJ (town) Hudson County	27.06
North Bergen, NJ (township) Hudson County	23.64
Weehawken, NJ (township) Hudson County	21.11
Guttenberg, NJ (town) Hudson County	20.82
Union City, NJ (city) Hudson County	18.71
Cliffside Park, NJ (borough) Bergen County	16.23
Union, NJ (cdp) Union County	15.94
Linden, NJ (city) Union County	12.94
Elizabeth, NJ (city) Union County	12.59
Fort Lee, NJ (borough) Bergen County	11.75

Cuban
Top 10 Places Sorted by Percent of Total Population

Place	Percent
West New York, NJ (town) Hudson County	21.31
Union City, NJ (city) Hudson County	15.40
North Bergen, NJ (township) Hudson County	13.57
Guttenberg, NJ (town) Hudson County	11.10
Weehawken, NJ (township) Hudson County	8.57
Elizabeth, NJ (city) Union County	6.24
Fairview, NJ (borough) Bergen County	3.89
Harrison, NJ (town) Hudson County	3.56
Cliffside Park, NJ (borough) Bergen County	2.91
Kearny, NJ (town) Hudson County	1.96

Dominican
Top 10 Places Sorted by Number

Place	Number
Paterson, NJ (city) Passaic County	15,332
Jersey City, NJ (city) Hudson County	9,669
Passaic, NJ (city) Passaic County	9,579
Perth Amboy, NJ (city) Middlesex County	8,773
Union City, NJ (city) Hudson County	7,832
Newark, NJ (city) Essex County	6,414
West New York, NJ (town) Hudson County	3,932
Elizabeth, NJ (city) Union County	3,847
North Bergen, NJ (township) Hudson County	3,053
New Brunswick, NJ (city) Middlesex County	2,435

Dominican
Top 10 Places Sorted by Percent of Hispanic Population

Place	Percent
Perth Amboy, NJ (city) Middlesex County	26.55
Somerset, NJ (cdp) Somerset County	25.92
Passaic, NJ (city) Passaic County	22.59
Teaneck, NJ (cdp) Bergen County	21.83
Paterson, NJ (city) Passaic County	20.48
Franklin, NJ (township) Somerset County	19.67
East Orange, NJ (city) Essex County	18.63
Pleasantville, NJ (city) Atlantic County	18.47
Palisades Park, NJ (borough) Bergen County	16.65
Bergenfield, NJ (borough) Bergen County	16.01

Dominican
Top 10 Places Sorted by Percent of Total Population

Place	Percent
Perth Amboy, NJ (city) Middlesex County	18.55
Passaic, NJ (city) Passaic County	14.12
Union City, NJ (city) Hudson County	11.67
Paterson, NJ (city) Passaic County	10.27
West New York, NJ (town) Hudson County	8.59
Guttenberg, NJ (town) Hudson County	5.79
Weehawken, NJ (township) Hudson County	5.66
North Bergen, NJ (township) Hudson County	5.25
New Brunswick, NJ (city) Middlesex County	5.01
Pleasantville, NJ (city) Atlantic County	4.11

Ecuadorian
Top 10 Places Sorted by Number

Place	Number
Newark, NJ (city) Essex County	8,208
Jersey City, NJ (city) Hudson County	4,375
Union City, NJ (city) Hudson County	4,215
North Bergen, NJ (township) Hudson County	2,216
West New York, NJ (town) Hudson County	2,201
Hackensack, NJ (city) Bergen County	1,889
Elizabeth, NJ (city) Union County	1,774
North Plainfield, NJ (borough) Somerset County	1,322
Belleville, NJ (cdp) Essex County	1,039
Kearny, NJ (town) Hudson County	918

Ecuadorian
Top 10 Places Sorted by Percent of Hispanic Population

Place	Percent
East Windsor, NJ (township) Mercer County	23.07
North Plainfield, NJ (borough) Somerset County	19.02
Hackensack, NJ (city) Bergen County	16.97
Belleville, NJ (cdp) Essex County	12.26
Newark, NJ (city) Essex County	10.20
Harrison, NJ (town) Hudson County	9.30
Weehawken, NJ (township) Hudson County	8.32
Kearny, NJ (town) Hudson County	8.30
Union City, NJ (city) Hudson County	7.63
Plainfield, NJ (city) Union County	7.26

Ecuadorian
Top 10 Places Sorted by Percent of Total Population

Place	Percent
Union City, NJ (city) Hudson County	6.28
North Plainfield, NJ (borough) Somerset County	6.26
West New York, NJ (town) Hudson County	4.81
Hackensack, NJ (city) Bergen County	4.43
North Bergen, NJ (township) Hudson County	3.81
Harrison, NJ (town) Hudson County	3.45
Weehawken, NJ (township) Hudson County	3.38
Dover, NJ (town) Morris County	3.36
East Windsor, NJ (township) Mercer County	3.31
Newark, NJ (city) Essex County	3.00

Guatelmalan
Top 10 Places Sorted by Number

Place	Number
Trenton, NJ (city) Mercer County	2,834
Plainfield, NJ (city) Union County	1,756
Newark, NJ (city) Essex County	854
Jersey City, NJ (city) Hudson County	663
Fairview, NJ (borough) Bergen County	653
Palisades Park, NJ (borough) Bergen County	619
West New York, NJ (town) Hudson County	560
North Bergen, NJ (township) Hudson County	558
Union City, NJ (city) Hudson County	513
East Windsor, NJ (township) Mercer County	510

Guatelmalan
Top 10 Places Sorted by Percent of Hispanic Population

Place	Percent
Palisades Park, NJ (borough) Bergen County	22.21
Trenton, NJ (city) Mercer County	15.32
Plainfield, NJ (city) Union County	14.54
East Windsor, NJ (township) Mercer County	14.25
Fairview, NJ (borough) Bergen County	13.21
North Plainfield, NJ (borough) Somerset County	6.00
Bayonne, NJ (city) Hudson County	3.32
North Bergen, NJ (township) Hudson County	1.67
West New York, NJ (town) Hudson County	1.55
Newark, NJ (city) Essex County	1.06

Guatelmalan
Top 10 Places Sorted by Percent of Total Population

Place	Percent
Fairview, NJ (borough) Bergen County	4.93
Plainfield, NJ (city) Union County	3.67
Palisades Park, NJ (borough) Bergen County	3.63
Trenton, NJ (city) Mercer County	3.32
East Windsor, NJ (township) Mercer County	2.05
North Plainfield, NJ (borough) Somerset County	1.98
West New York, NJ (town) Hudson County	1.22
North Bergen, NJ (township) Hudson County	0.96
Union City, NJ (city) Hudson County	0.76
Bayonne, NJ (city) Hudson County	0.59

Honduran
Top 10 Places Sorted by Number

Place	Number
Jersey City, NJ (city) Hudson County	1,919
Union City, NJ (city) Hudson County	1,855
New Brunswick, NJ (city) Middlesex County	1,825
Elizabeth, NJ (city) Union County	1,036
Plainfield, NJ (city) Union County	926
Morris, NJ (town) Morris County	715
North Bergen, NJ (township) Hudson County	712
West New York, NJ (town) Hudson County	659
Newark, NJ (city) Essex County	645
Passaic, NJ (city) Passaic County	621

Honduran
Top 10 Places Sorted by Percent of Hispanic Population

Place	Percent
Morris, NJ (town) Morris County	14.22
New Brunswick, NJ (city) Middlesex County	9.62
Plainfield, NJ (city) Union County	7.67
Union City, NJ (city) Hudson County	3.36
Jersey City, NJ (city) Hudson County	2.82
North Bergen, NJ (township) Hudson County	2.13
West New York, NJ (town) Hudson County	1.83
Elizabeth, NJ (city) Union County	1.73
Passaic, NJ (city) Passaic County	1.46
Newark, NJ (city) Essex County	0.80

Honduran
Top 10 Places Sorted by Percent of Total Population

Place	Percent
Morris, NJ (town) Morris County	3.86
New Brunswick, NJ (city) Middlesex County	3.76
Union City, NJ (city) Hudson County	2.77
Plainfield, NJ (city) Union County	1.94
West New York, NJ (town) Hudson County	1.44
North Bergen, NJ (township) Hudson County	1.22
Passaic, NJ (city) Passaic County	0.92
Elizabeth, NJ (city) Union County	0.86
Jersey City, NJ (city) Hudson County	0.80
Newark, NJ (city) Essex County	0.24

Mexican
Top 10 Places Sorted by Number

Place	Number
Passaic, NJ (city) Passaic County	13,573
New Brunswick, NJ (city) Middlesex County	7,817
Paterson, NJ (city) Passaic County	5,372
Bridgeton, NJ (city) Cumberland County	3,304
West New York, NJ (town) Hudson County	3,132
Perth Amboy, NJ (city) Middlesex County	2,873
Jersey City, NJ (city) Hudson County	2,712
Union City, NJ (city) Hudson County	2,682
Atlantic City, NJ (city) Atlantic County	2,539
Lakewood, NJ (township) Ocean County	2,512

Notes: Please refer to the User's Guide for an explanation of data; tables include places with populations > 9,999 and reflect only those areas that meet Summary File 4 population thresholds, therefore there may be less than 10 places listed

Mexican
Top 10 Places Sorted by Percent of Hispanic Population

Place	Percent
Bridgeton, NJ (city) Cumberland County	59.61
Freehold, NJ (borough) Monmouth County	51.37
Princeton, NJ (township) Mercer County	47.23
Hammonton, NJ (town) Atlantic County	46.08
Red Bank, NJ (borough) Monmouth County	45.79
Asbury Park, NJ (city) Monmouth County	41.91
New Brunswick, NJ (city) Middlesex County	41.20
Passaic, NJ (city) Passaic County	32.00
Lakewood, NJ (township) Ocean County	28.73
Freehold, NJ (township) Monmouth County	28.36

Mexican
Top 10 Places Sorted by Percent of Total Population

Place	Percent
Passaic, NJ (city) Passaic County	20.00
New Brunswick, NJ (city) Middlesex County	16.09
Bridgeton, NJ (city) Cumberland County	14.51
Freehold, NJ (borough) Monmouth County	14.31
Dover, NJ (town) Morris County	7.96
Red Bank, NJ (borough) Monmouth County	7.76
Hammonton, NJ (town) Atlantic County	6.85
West New York, NJ (town) Hudson County	6.84
Asbury Park, NJ (city) Monmouth County	6.49
Atlantic City, NJ (city) Atlantic County	6.27

Nicaraguan
Top 10 Places Sorted by Number

Place	Number
Camden, NJ (city) Camden County	636
Jersey City, NJ (city) Hudson County	518

Nicaraguan
Top 10 Places Sorted by Percent of Hispanic Population

Place	Percent
Camden, NJ (city) Camden County	2.06
Jersey City, NJ (city) Hudson County	0.76

Nicaraguan
Top 10 Places Sorted by Percent of Total Population

Place	Percent
Camden, NJ (city) Camden County	0.80
Jersey City, NJ (city) Hudson County	0.22

Panamanian
Top 10 Places Sorted by Number

Place	Number
No places met population threshold.	

Panamanian
Top 10 Places Sorted by Percent of Hispanic Population

Place	Percent
No places met population threshold.	

Panamanian
Top 10 Places Sorted by Percent of Total Population

Place	Percent
No places met population threshold.	

Paraguayan
Top 10 Places Sorted by Number

Place	Number
No places met population threshold.	

Paraguayan
Top 10 Places Sorted by Percent of Hispanic Population

Place	Percent
No places met population threshold.	

Paraguayan
Top 10 Places Sorted by Percent of Total Population

Place	Percent
No places met population threshold.	

Peruvian
Top 10 Places Sorted by Number

Place	Number
Paterson, NJ (city) Passaic County	7,375
Elizabeth, NJ (city) Union County	3,136
Passaic, NJ (city) Passaic County	2,000
Union City, NJ (city) Hudson County	1,956
Clifton, NJ (city) Passaic County	1,810
Kearny, NJ (town) Hudson County	1,661
Newark, NJ (city) Essex County	1,512
Perth Amboy, NJ (city) Middlesex County	1,283
Harrison, NJ (town) Hudson County	1,140
North Bergen, NJ (township) Hudson County	955

Peruvian
Top 10 Places Sorted by Percent of Hispanic Population

Place	Percent
Harrison, NJ (town) Hudson County	21.29
Kearny, NJ (town) Hudson County	15.01
Elmwood Park, NJ (borough) Bergen County	12.33
Garfield, NJ (city) Bergen County	12.30
West Orange, NJ (cdp) Essex County	11.99
Clifton, NJ (city) Passaic County	11.60
Carteret, NJ (borough) Middlesex County	10.57
Paterson, NJ (city) Passaic County	9.85
Elizabeth, NJ (city) Union County	5.25
Belleville, NJ (cdp) Essex County	5.11

Peruvian
Top 10 Places Sorted by Percent of Total Population

Place	Percent
Harrison, NJ (town) Hudson County	7.90
Paterson, NJ (city) Passaic County	4.94
Kearny, NJ (town) Hudson County	4.10
Passaic, NJ (city) Passaic County	2.95
Union City, NJ (city) Hudson County	2.92
Perth Amboy, NJ (city) Middlesex County	2.71
Elizabeth, NJ (city) Union County	2.60
Garfield, NJ (city) Bergen County	2.49
Carteret, NJ (borough) Middlesex County	2.46
Clifton, NJ (city) Passaic County	2.30

Puerto Rican
Top 10 Places Sorted by Number

Place	Number
Newark, NJ (city) Essex County	39,568
Jersey City, NJ (city) Hudson County	29,626
Paterson, NJ (city) Passaic County	24,319
Camden, NJ (city) Camden County	23,071
Perth Amboy, NJ (city) Middlesex County	13,623
Elizabeth, NJ (city) Union County	13,321
Vineland, NJ (city) Cumberland County	12,948
Trenton, NJ (city) Mercer County	9,314
Passaic, NJ (city) Passaic County	8,799
Union City, NJ (city) Hudson County	7,751

Puerto Rican
Top 10 Places Sorted by Percent of Hispanic Population

Place	Percent
Monroe, NJ (township) Gloucester County	84.51
Millville, NJ (city) Cumberland County	79.99
Vineland, NJ (city) Cumberland County	76.77
Camden, NJ (city) Camden County	74.74
Winslow, NJ (township) Camden County	72.21
Woodbury, NJ (city) Gloucester County	71.32
Browns Mills, NJ (cdp) Burlington County	70.29
Mount Holly, NJ (township) Burlington County	69.75
Pennsauken, NJ (cdp) Camden County	69.37
Hamilton, NJ (township) Atlantic County	68.75

Puerto Rican
Top 10 Places Sorted by Percent of Total Population

Place	Percent
Camden, NJ (city) Camden County	28.87
Perth Amboy, NJ (city) Middlesex County	28.80
Vineland, NJ (city) Cumberland County	23.01
Paterson, NJ (city) Passaic County	16.30
Newark, NJ (city) Essex County	14.46
Passaic, NJ (city) Passaic County	12.97
Hoboken, NJ (city) Hudson County	12.34
Jersey City, NJ (city) Hudson County	12.34
Union City, NJ (city) Hudson County	11.55
Dover, NJ (town) Morris County	11.24

Salvadoran
Top 10 Places Sorted by Number

Place	Number
Union City, NJ (city) Hudson County	3,876
Elizabeth, NJ (city) Union County	3,679
West New York, NJ (town) Hudson County	3,052
Newark, NJ (city) Essex County	1,791
North Bergen, NJ (township) Hudson County	1,373
Plainfield, NJ (city) Union County	1,341
Jersey City, NJ (city) Hudson County	1,199
Paterson, NJ (city) Passaic County	528
Fairview, NJ (borough) Bergen County	464
Guttenberg, NJ (town) Hudson County	411

Salvadoran
Top 10 Places Sorted by Percent of Hispanic Population

Place	Percent
Plainfield, NJ (city) Union County	11.11
Fairview, NJ (borough) Bergen County	9.38
West New York, NJ (town) Hudson County	8.47
Guttenberg, NJ (town) Hudson County	7.21
Union City, NJ (city) Hudson County	7.02
Elizabeth, NJ (city) Union County	6.16
North Plainfield, NJ (borough) Somerset County	5.05
North Bergen, NJ (township) Hudson County	4.11
Newark, NJ (city) Essex County	2.23
Jersey City, NJ (city) Hudson County	1.76

Salvadoran
Top 10 Places Sorted by Percent of Total Population

Place	Percent
West New York, NJ (town) Hudson County	6.67
Union City, NJ (city) Hudson County	5.78
Guttenberg, NJ (town) Hudson County	3.84
Fairview, NJ (borough) Bergen County	3.50
Elizabeth, NJ (city) Union County	3.05
Plainfield, NJ (city) Union County	2.80
North Bergen, NJ (township) Hudson County	2.36
North Plainfield, NJ (borough) Somerset County	1.66
Newark, NJ (city) Essex County	0.65
Jersey City, NJ (city) Hudson County	0.50

South American
Top 10 Places Sorted by Number

Place	Number
Elizabeth, NJ (city) Union County	15,277
Paterson, NJ (city) Passaic County	14,164
Newark, NJ (city) Essex County	11,954
Union City, NJ (city) Hudson County	10,029
North Bergen, NJ (township) Hudson County	8,469
Jersey City, NJ (city) Hudson County	8,227

Notes: Please refer to the User's Guide for an explanation of data; tables include places with populations > 9,999 and reflect only those areas that meet Summary File 4 population thresholds, therefore there may be less than 10 places listed

Place	
West New York, NJ (town) Hudson County	6,376
Hackensack, NJ (city) Bergen County	4,446
Passaic, NJ (city) Passaic County	4,277
Clifton, NJ (city) Passaic County	4,238

South American
Top 10 Places Sorted by Percent of Hispanic Population

Place	Percent
Englewood, NJ (city) Bergen County	42.26
Harrison, NJ (town) Hudson County	41.33
Lodi, NJ (borough) Bergen County	40.04
Hackensack, NJ (city) Bergen County	39.94
North Plainfield, NJ (borough) Somerset County	38.14
Dover, NJ (town) Morris County	37.22
Morris, NJ (town) Morris County	36.16
Garfield, NJ (city) Bergen County	33.84
Elmwood Park, NJ (borough) Bergen County	33.50
West Orange, NJ (cdp) Essex County	32.41

South American
Top 10 Places Sorted by Percent of Total Population

Place	Percent
Dover, NJ (town) Morris County	21.65
Harrison, NJ (town) Hudson County	15.34
Union City, NJ (city) Hudson County	14.95
North Bergen, NJ (township) Hudson County	14.55
West New York, NJ (town) Hudson County	13.93
Elizabeth, NJ (city) Union County	12.67
North Plainfield, NJ (borough) Somerset County	12.56
Hackensack, NJ (city) Bergen County	10.42
Guttenberg, NJ (town) Hudson County	10.33
Morris, NJ (town) Morris County	9.80

Spaniard
Top 10 Places Sorted by Number

Place	Number
Newark, NJ (city) Essex County	1,335
Kearny, NJ (town) Hudson County	740
Bayonne, NJ (city) Hudson County	578

Spaniard
Top 10 Places Sorted by Percent of Hispanic Population

Place	Percent
Kearny, NJ (town) Hudson County	6.69
Bayonne, NJ (city) Hudson County	5.25
Newark, NJ (city) Essex County	1.66

Spaniard
Top 10 Places Sorted by Percent of Total Population

Place	Percent
Kearny, NJ (town) Hudson County	1.83
Bayonne, NJ (city) Hudson County	0.93
Newark, NJ (city) Essex County	0.49

Uruguayan
Top 10 Places Sorted by Number

Place	Number
Elizabeth, NJ (city) Union County	815
West Orange, NJ (cdp) Essex County	353

Uruguayan
Top 10 Places Sorted by Percent of Hispanic Population

Place	Percent
West Orange, NJ (cdp) Essex County	7.67
Elizabeth, NJ (city) Union County	1.36

Uruguayan
Top 10 Places Sorted by Percent of Total Population

Place	Percent
West Orange, NJ (cdp) Essex County	0.79

Place	
Elizabeth, NJ (city) Union County	0.68

Venezuelan
Top 10 Places Sorted by Number

Place	Number
No places met population threshold.	

Venezuelan
Top 10 Places Sorted by Percent of Hispanic Population

Place	Percent
No places met population threshold.	

Venezuelan
Top 10 Places Sorted by Percent of Total Population

Place	Percent
No places met population threshold.	

Other Hispanic
Top 10 Places Sorted by Number

Place	Number
Paterson, NJ (city) Passaic County	12,581
Elizabeth, NJ (city) Union County	11,735
Newark, NJ (city) Essex County	11,301
Jersey City, NJ (city) Hudson County	10,492
Union City, NJ (city) Hudson County	9,640
North Bergen, NJ (township) Hudson County	5,734
West New York, NJ (town) Hudson County	5,526
Passaic, NJ (city) Passaic County	4,580
Perth Amboy, NJ (city) Middlesex County	3,646
Clifton, NJ (city) Passaic County	3,016

Other Hispanic
Top 10 Places Sorted by Percent of Hispanic Population

Place	Percent
Fairview, NJ (borough) Bergen County	26.86
Ventnor City, NJ (city) Atlantic County	26.17
Teaneck, NJ (cdp) Bergen County	26.07
Ridgefield, NJ (borough) Bergen County	25.72
East Orange, NJ (city) Essex County	25.40
North Plainfield, NJ (borough) Somerset County	25.38
Morris, NJ (town) Morris County	25.34
Ridgefield Park, NJ (village) Bergen County	25.21
Avenel, NJ (cdp) Middlesex County	25.20
Harrison, NJ (town) Hudson County	24.89

Other Hispanic
Top 10 Places Sorted by Percent of Total Population

Place	Percent
Union City, NJ (city) Hudson County	14.37
West New York, NJ (town) Hudson County	12.07
Fairview, NJ (borough) Bergen County	10.02
North Bergen, NJ (township) Hudson County	9.85
Dover, NJ (town) Morris County	9.81
Elizabeth, NJ (city) Union County	9.73
Harrison, NJ (town) Hudson County	9.24
Guttenberg, NJ (town) Hudson County	8.91
Paterson, NJ (city) Passaic County	8.43
North Plainfield, NJ (borough) Somerset County	8.36

Median Age

Total Population
Top 10 Places Sorted by Number

Place	Years
Manchester, NJ (township) Ocean County	67.8
Berkeley, NJ (township) Ocean County	66.4
Monroe, NJ (township) Middlesex County	58.7
Cedar Grove, NJ (cdp) Essex County	43.5
Paramus, NJ (borough) Bergen County	42.9
Springfield, NJ (cdp) Union County	42.2
Fair Lawn, NJ (borough) Bergen County	41.8
Cherry Hill Mall, NJ (cdp) Camden County	41.6
Cherry Hill, NJ (township) Camden County	41.6
West Caldwell, NJ (cdp) Essex County	41.3

Hispanic
Top 10 Places Sorted by Number

Place	Years
Lincoln Park, NJ (borough) Morris County	39.9
Manchester, NJ (township) Ocean County	39.9
Cedar Grove, NJ (cdp) Essex County	39.6
Berkeley, NJ (township) Ocean County	37.8
Montville, NJ (township) Morris County	37.7
Oakland, NJ (borough) Bergen County	37.6
Point Pleasant, NJ (borough) Ocean County	36.8
Wanaque, NJ (borough) Passaic County	36.3
Franklin Lakes, NJ (borough) Bergen County	35.6
Stafford, NJ (township) Ocean County	35.3

Argentinian
Top 10 Places Sorted by Number

Place	Years
North Bergen, NJ (township) Hudson County	34.3

Bolivian
Top 10 Places Sorted by Number

Place	Years
No places met population threshold.	

Central American
Top 10 Places Sorted by Number

Place	Years
Linden, NJ (city) Union County	37.9
West Orange, NJ (cdp) Essex County	35.1
Kearny, NJ (town) Hudson County	32.5
Passaic, NJ (city) Passaic County	32.1
Hamilton, NJ (township) Mercer County	31.6
Perth Amboy, NJ (city) Middlesex County	31.5
Irvington, NJ (cdp) Essex County	31.2
Englewood, NJ (city) Bergen County	31.0
Jersey City, NJ (city) Hudson County	30.7
Lakewood, NJ (township) Ocean County	30.7

Chilean
Top 10 Places Sorted by Number

Place	Years
North Bergen, NJ (township) Hudson County	34.1

Colombian
Top 10 Places Sorted by Number

Place	Years
West New York, NJ (town) Hudson County	37.4
Elmwood Park, NJ (borough) Bergen County	36.7
Passaic, NJ (city) Passaic County	36.6
Atlantic City, NJ (city) Atlantic County	36.5
Weehawken, NJ (township) Hudson County	36.5
Paterson, NJ (city) Passaic County	36.4
North Bergen, NJ (township) Hudson County	36.3
Clifton, NJ (city) Passaic County	36.2
Newark, NJ (city) Essex County	36.2
Union, NJ (cdp) Union County	36.2

Costa Rican
Top 10 Places Sorted by Number

Place	Years
Elizabeth, NJ (city) Union County	31.1
Paterson, NJ (city) Passaic County	28.9
Trenton, NJ (city) Mercer County	27.7
Bound Brook, NJ (borough) Somerset County	27.6
Somerville, NJ (borough) Somerset County	27.4

Notes: Please refer to the User's Guide for an explanation of data; tables include places with populations > 9,999 and reflect only those areas that meet Summary File 4 population thresholds, therefore there may be less than 10 places listed

Cuban
Top 10 Places Sorted by Number

Place	Years
Fort Lee, NJ (borough) Bergen County	54.3
Weehawken, NJ (township) Hudson County	54.3
West New York, NJ (town) Hudson County	53.7
Passaic, NJ (city) Passaic County	52.0
Union City, NJ (city) Hudson County	49.6
Paterson, NJ (city) Passaic County	46.6
Newark, NJ (city) Essex County	46.4
Perth Amboy, NJ (city) Middlesex County	46.1
Guttenberg, NJ (town) Hudson County	46.0
Elizabeth, NJ (city) Union County	45.3

Dominican
Top 10 Places Sorted by Number

Place	Years
Weehawken, NJ (township) Hudson County	34.9
Bloomfield, NJ (cdp) Essex County	33.4
Bergenfield, NJ (borough) Bergen County	33.2
Hoboken, NJ (city) Hudson County	33.2
Kearny, NJ (town) Hudson County	33.0
West New York, NJ (town) Hudson County	32.0
Ridgefield Park, NJ (village) Bergen County	31.9
North Bergen, NJ (township) Hudson County	31.3
Fairview, NJ (borough) Bergen County	30.9
Union City, NJ (city) Hudson County	30.7

Ecuadorian
Top 10 Places Sorted by Number

Place	Years
Elizabeth, NJ (city) Union County	35.5
Weehawken, NJ (township) Hudson County	35.1
Bloomfield, NJ (cdp) Essex County	34.2
Union City, NJ (city) Hudson County	33.6
Harrison, NJ (town) Hudson County	33.3
Jersey City, NJ (city) Hudson County	33.0
West New York, NJ (town) Hudson County	32.4
Clifton, NJ (city) Passaic County	32.2
Bayonne, NJ (city) Hudson County	31.9
Paterson, NJ (city) Passaic County	31.9

Guatelmalan
Top 10 Places Sorted by Number

Place	Years
North Plainfield, NJ (borough) Somerset County	31.9
Bayonne, NJ (city) Hudson County	31.2
Elizabeth, NJ (city) Union County	31.1
West New York, NJ (town) Hudson County	30.6
Newark, NJ (city) Essex County	30.0
Union City, NJ (city) Hudson County	28.3
North Bergen, NJ (township) Hudson County	27.8
Jersey City, NJ (city) Hudson County	27.7
Plainfield, NJ (city) Union County	27.4
East Windsor, NJ (township) Mercer County	26.5

Honduran
Top 10 Places Sorted by Number

Place	Years
Jersey City, NJ (city) Hudson County	32.7
Passaic, NJ (city) Passaic County	32.2
Newark, NJ (city) Essex County	30.1
West New York, NJ (town) Hudson County	29.4
Elizabeth, NJ (city) Union County	29.2
Union City, NJ (city) Hudson County	28.7
North Bergen, NJ (township) Hudson County	28.3
Plainfield, NJ (city) Union County	28.2
Morris, NJ (town) Morris County	25.9
New Brunswick, NJ (city) Middlesex County	25.9

Mexican
Top 10 Places Sorted by Number

Place	Years
Freehold, NJ (township) Monmouth County	27.6
North Bergen, NJ (township) Hudson County	27.1
Bound Brook, NJ (borough) Somerset County	26.7
Vineland, NJ (city) Cumberland County	26.4
Garfield, NJ (city) Bergen County	26.3
Atlantic City, NJ (city) Atlantic County	25.8
Long Branch, NJ (city) Monmouth County	25.7
Dover, NJ (town) Morris County	25.6
Plainfield, NJ (city) Union County	25.6
Elizabeth, NJ (city) Union County	25.5

Nicaraguan
Top 10 Places Sorted by Number

Place	Years
Jersey City, NJ (city) Hudson County	27.8
Camden, NJ (city) Camden County	27.1

Panamanian
Top 10 Places Sorted by Number

Place	Years
No places met population threshold.	

Paraguayan
Top 10 Places Sorted by Number

Place	Years
No places met population threshold.	

Peruvian
Top 10 Places Sorted by Number

Place	Years
West New York, NJ (town) Hudson County	36.2
Harrison, NJ (town) Hudson County	35.7
Woodbridge, NJ (township) Middlesex County	35.0
Elmwood Park, NJ (borough) Bergen County	34.9
West Orange, NJ (cdp) Essex County	34.8
Newark, NJ (city) Essex County	34.3
Jersey City, NJ (city) Hudson County	33.9
Belleville, NJ (cdp) Essex County	33.8
Garfield, NJ (city) Bergen County	33.8
Paterson, NJ (city) Passaic County	33.6

Puerto Rican
Top 10 Places Sorted by Number

Place	Years
Manchester, NJ (township) Ocean County	43.0
Iselin, NJ (cdp) Middlesex County	37.1
Teaneck, NJ (cdp) Bergen County	36.6
Manalapan, NJ (township) Monmouth County	35.9
West New York, NJ (town) Hudson County	35.8
Wayne, NJ (cdp) Passaic County	35.6
New Milford, NJ (borough) Bergen County	35.4
Avenel, NJ (cdp) Middlesex County	35.1
Guttenberg, NJ (town) Hudson County	35.0
North Bergen, NJ (township) Hudson County	34.8

Salvadoran
Top 10 Places Sorted by Number

Place	Years
Jersey City, NJ (city) Hudson County	30.4
Newark, NJ (city) Essex County	30.2
West New York, NJ (town) Hudson County	30.1
North Plainfield, NJ (borough) Somerset County	29.9
Paterson, NJ (city) Passaic County	29.4
North Bergen, NJ (township) Hudson County	28.4
Elizabeth, NJ (city) Union County	28.2
Plainfield, NJ (city) Union County	27.7
Union City, NJ (city) Hudson County	27.4
Fairview, NJ (borough) Bergen County	27.3

South American
Top 10 Places Sorted by Number

Place	Years
Franklin, NJ (township) Somerset County	39.2
Old Bridge, NJ (township) Middlesex County	38.7
North Brunswick Township, NJ (cdp) Middlesex County	38.5
Sayreville, NJ (borough) Middlesex County	38.2
Nutley, NJ (cdp) Essex County	37.6
Rockaway, NJ (township) Morris County	37.4
Bound Brook, NJ (borough) Somerset County	37.1
Hillside, NJ (cdp) Union County	36.9
Atlantic City, NJ (city) Atlantic County	36.3
Elmwood Park, NJ (borough) Bergen County	36.3

Spaniard
Top 10 Places Sorted by Number

Place	Years
Kearny, NJ (town) Hudson County	43.1
Bayonne, NJ (city) Hudson County	40.0
Newark, NJ (city) Essex County	35.8

Uruguayan
Top 10 Places Sorted by Number

Place	Years
Elizabeth, NJ (city) Union County	40.0
West Orange, NJ (cdp) Essex County	25.4

Venezuelan
Top 10 Places Sorted by Number

Place	Years
No places met population threshold.	

Other Hispanic
Top 10 Places Sorted by Number

Place	Years
Avenel, NJ (cdp) Middlesex County	33.2
Parsippany-Troy Hills, NJ (township) Morris County	33.0
East Windsor, NJ (township) Mercer County	32.7
Lodi, NJ (borough) Bergen County	31.7
Fort Lee, NJ (borough) Bergen County	31.2
Nutley, NJ (cdp) Essex County	31.2
Englewood, NJ (city) Bergen County	30.3
Franklin, NJ (township) Somerset County	29.9
Morris, NJ (town) Morris County	29.2
Somerset, NJ (cdp) Somerset County	28.2

Average Household Size

Total Population
Top 10 Places Sorted by Number

Place	Number
Passaic, NJ (city) Passaic County	3.45
Dover, NJ (town) Morris County	3.27
Paterson, NJ (city) Passaic County	3.25
New Brunswick, NJ (city) Middlesex County	3.22
Perth Amboy, NJ (city) Middlesex County	3.20
Colts Neck, NJ (township) Monmouth County	3.16
Franklin Lakes, NJ (borough) Bergen County	3.16
Marlboro, NJ (township) Monmouth County	3.14
Camden, NJ (city) Camden County	3.12
Plainfield, NJ (city) Union County	3.10

Hispanic
Top 10 Places Sorted by Number

Place	Number
Bridgeton, NJ (city) Cumberland County	4.97
New Brunswick, NJ (city) Middlesex County	4.91
Morris, NJ (town) Morris County	4.54
Freehold, NJ (borough) Monmouth County	4.40
Dover, NJ (town) Morris County	4.35
North Plainfield, NJ (borough) Somerset County	4.30

Notes: Please refer to the User's Guide for an explanation of data; tables include places with populations > 9,999 and reflect only those areas that meet Summary File 4 population thresholds, therefore there may be less than 10 places listed

Place	Number
Plainfield, NJ (city) Union County	4.22
Passaic, NJ (city) Passaic County	4.17
South River, NJ (borough) Middlesex County	4.13
Bridgewater, NJ (township) Somerset County	4.11

Argentinian
Top 10 Places Sorted by Number

Place	Number
North Bergen, NJ (township) Hudson County	2.74

Bolivian
Top 10 Places Sorted by Number

Place	Number
No places met population threshold.	

Central American
Top 10 Places Sorted by Number

Place	Number
Morris, NJ (town) Morris County	5.64
New Brunswick, NJ (city) Middlesex County	5.24
Woodbridge, NJ (township) Middlesex County	5.19
Bridgewater, NJ (township) Somerset County	4.95
Dover, NJ (town) Morris County	4.91
Hillside, NJ (cdp) Union County	4.86
Plainfield, NJ (city) Union County	4.82
Trenton, NJ (city) Mercer County	4.54
Kearny, NJ (town) Hudson County	4.47
Englewood, NJ (city) Bergen County	4.40

Chilean
Top 10 Places Sorted by Number

Place	Number
North Bergen, NJ (township) Hudson County	3.82

Colombian
Top 10 Places Sorted by Number

Place	Number
Roselle, NJ (borough) Union County	5.08
Lakewood, NJ (township) Ocean County	4.91
Dover, NJ (town) Morris County	4.53
Morris, NJ (town) Morris County	4.51
North Plainfield, NJ (borough) Somerset County	4.23
Garfield, NJ (city) Bergen County	4.19
Atlantic City, NJ (city) Atlantic County	4.18
Piscataway, NJ (township) Middlesex County	4.18
Englewood, NJ (city) Bergen County	4.15
Union, NJ (cdp) Union County	4.13

Costa Rican
Top 10 Places Sorted by Number

Place	Number
Bound Brook, NJ (borough) Somerset County	4.28
Trenton, NJ (city) Mercer County	4.22
Paterson, NJ (city) Passaic County	3.80
Somerville, NJ (borough) Somerset County	3.75
Elizabeth, NJ (city) Union County	3.54

Cuban
Top 10 Places Sorted by Number

Place	Number
Union, NJ (cdp) Union County	3.65
Harrison, NJ (town) Hudson County	2.98
Elmwood Park, NJ (borough) Bergen County	2.97
Kearny, NJ (town) Hudson County	2.95
Perth Amboy, NJ (city) Middlesex County	2.95
Woodbridge, NJ (township) Middlesex County	2.88
Elizabeth, NJ (city) Union County	2.86
Linden, NJ (city) Union County	2.85
Belleville, NJ (cdp) Essex County	2.83
Fairview, NJ (borough) Bergen County	2.72

Dominican
Top 10 Places Sorted by Number

Place	Number
Somerset, NJ (cdp) Somerset County	5.58
Franklin, NJ (township) Somerset County	5.15
Pleasantville, NJ (city) Atlantic County	4.51
New Brunswick, NJ (city) Middlesex County	4.43
Camden, NJ (city) Camden County	4.36
Atlantic City, NJ (city) Atlantic County	4.35
Paterson, NJ (city) Passaic County	4.27
Perth Amboy, NJ (city) Middlesex County	4.27
Bergenfield, NJ (borough) Bergen County	4.21
Plainfield, NJ (city) Union County	4.21

Ecuadorian
Top 10 Places Sorted by Number

Place	Number
North Plainfield, NJ (borough) Somerset County	5.08
Dover, NJ (town) Morris County	4.82
Plainfield, NJ (city) Union County	4.65
Belleville, NJ (cdp) Essex County	4.50
Passaic, NJ (city) Passaic County	4.38
Bayonne, NJ (city) Hudson County	4.09
East Windsor, NJ (township) Mercer County	4.06
Jersey City, NJ (city) Hudson County	3.88
Paterson, NJ (city) Passaic County	3.88
Bloomfield, NJ (cdp) Essex County	3.82

Guatelmalan
Top 10 Places Sorted by Number

Place	Number
North Bergen, NJ (township) Hudson County	5.47
Trenton, NJ (city) Mercer County	4.80
Plainfield, NJ (city) Union County	4.78
Jersey City, NJ (city) Hudson County	4.48
East Windsor, NJ (township) Mercer County	4.31
North Plainfield, NJ (borough) Somerset County	4.15
Fairview, NJ (borough) Bergen County	3.80
Palisades Park, NJ (borough) Bergen County	3.71
West New York, NJ (town) Hudson County	3.70
Bayonne, NJ (city) Hudson County	3.69

Honduran
Top 10 Places Sorted by Number

Place	Number
Morris, NJ (town) Morris County	5.58
New Brunswick, NJ (city) Middlesex County	5.36
Passaic, NJ (city) Passaic County	4.93
West New York, NJ (town) Hudson County	4.71
Plainfield, NJ (city) Union County	4.65
Elizabeth, NJ (city) Union County	4.45
North Bergen, NJ (township) Hudson County	4.36
Union City, NJ (city) Hudson County	3.64
Jersey City, NJ (city) Hudson County	3.41
Newark, NJ (city) Essex County	3.05

Mexican
Top 10 Places Sorted by Number

Place	Number
New Brunswick, NJ (city) Middlesex County	6.73
Red Bank, NJ (borough) Monmouth County	6.53
Bridgeton, NJ (city) Cumberland County	6.40
Lakewood, NJ (township) Ocean County	6.30
Ventnor City, NJ (city) Atlantic County	5.91
Princeton, NJ (township) Mercer County	5.90
Passaic, NJ (city) Passaic County	5.67
West New York, NJ (town) Hudson County	5.54
Dover, NJ (town) Morris County	5.37
Hammonton, NJ (town) Atlantic County	5.32

Nicaraguan
Top 10 Places Sorted by Number

Place	Number
Camden, NJ (city) Camden County	4.37
Jersey City, NJ (city) Hudson County	4.32

Panamanian
Top 10 Places Sorted by Number

Place	Number
No places met population threshold.	

Paraguayan
Top 10 Places Sorted by Number

Place	Number
No places met population threshold.	

Peruvian
Top 10 Places Sorted by Number

Place	Number
Elmwood Park, NJ (borough) Bergen County	4.68
Carteret, NJ (borough) Middlesex County	4.52
Clifton, NJ (city) Passaic County	4.50
Perth Amboy, NJ (city) Middlesex County	4.42
Belleville, NJ (cdp) Essex County	4.28
Passaic, NJ (city) Passaic County	4.27
Paterson, NJ (city) Passaic County	4.11
West Orange, NJ (cdp) Essex County	4.09
West New York, NJ (town) Hudson County	4.04
Kearny, NJ (town) Hudson County	3.94

Puerto Rican
Top 10 Places Sorted by Number

Place	Number
Hazlet, NJ (township) Monmouth County	4.21
Wayne, NJ (cdp) Passaic County	4.02
Woodbury, NJ (city) Gloucester County	3.97
Brick, NJ (township) Ocean County	3.92
Egg Harbor, NJ (township) Atlantic County	3.75
Manalapan, NJ (township) Monmouth County	3.71
Glassboro, NJ (borough) Gloucester County	3.70
New Brunswick, NJ (city) Middlesex County	3.69
Willingboro, NJ (township) Burlington County	3.64
Union, NJ (cdp) Union County	3.60

Salvadoran
Top 10 Places Sorted by Number

Place	Number
Plainfield, NJ (city) Union County	4.92
North Plainfield, NJ (borough) Somerset County	4.75
Guttenberg, NJ (town) Hudson County	4.61
Elizabeth, NJ (city) Union County	4.41
Paterson, NJ (city) Passaic County	4.27
Union City, NJ (city) Hudson County	4.10
Fairview, NJ (borough) Bergen County	4.08
Newark, NJ (city) Essex County	4.08
West New York, NJ (town) Hudson County	3.84
North Bergen, NJ (township) Hudson County	3.59

South American
Top 10 Places Sorted by Number

Place	Number
Morris, NJ (town) Morris County	4.76
Dover, NJ (town) Morris County	4.63
North Plainfield, NJ (borough) Somerset County	4.60
Trenton, NJ (city) Mercer County	4.51
Lakewood, NJ (township) Ocean County	4.49
Perth Amboy, NJ (city) Middlesex County	4.25
Piscataway, NJ (township) Middlesex County	4.22
West Orange, NJ (cdp) Essex County	4.22
Roselle, NJ (borough) Union County	4.20
Bound Brook, NJ (borough) Somerset County	4.14

Notes: Please refer to the User's Guide for an explanation of data; tables include places with populations > 9,999 and reflect only those areas that meet Summary File 4 population thresholds, therefore there may be less than 10 places listed

Spaniard
Top 10 Places Sorted by Number

Place	Number
Bayonne, NJ (city) Hudson County	3.49
Kearny, NJ (town) Hudson County	3.05
Newark, NJ (city) Essex County	2.67

Uruguayan
Top 10 Places Sorted by Number

Place	Number
West Orange, NJ (cdp) Essex County	5.24
Elizabeth, NJ (city) Union County	3.05

Venezuelan
Top 10 Places Sorted by Number

Place	Number
No places met population threshold.	

Other Hispanic
Top 10 Places Sorted by Number

Place	Number
Summit, NJ (city) Union County	5.45
Dover, NJ (town) Morris County	4.78
North Plainfield, NJ (borough) Somerset County	4.71
North Brunswick Township, NJ (cdp) Middlesex County	4.48
Pennsauken, NJ (cdp) Camden County	4.47
Ventnor City, NJ (city) Atlantic County	4.35
Bridgewater, NJ (township) Somerset County	4.28
Morris, NJ (town) Morris County	4.28
Elmwood Park, NJ (borough) Bergen County	4.23
Paterson, NJ (city) Passaic County	4.11

Language Spoken: English Only

Total Population 5 Years and Over Who Speak English-Only at Home
Top 10 Places Sorted by Number

Place	Number
Newark, NJ (city) Essex County	145,043
Jersey City, NJ (city) Hudson County	112,059
Dover, NJ (township) Ocean County	75,887
Toms River, NJ (cdp) Ocean County	72,926
Hamilton, NJ (township) Mercer County	70,441
Brick, NJ (township) Ocean County	65,747
Woodbridge, NJ (township) Middlesex County	63,332
Paterson, NJ (city) Passaic County	60,023
Trenton, NJ (city) Mercer County	57,142
Middletown, NJ (township) Monmouth County	56,323

Total Population 5 Years and Over Who Speak English-Only at Home
Top 10 Places Sorted by Percent

Place	Percent
Franklin, NJ (township) Gloucester County	94.69
Point Pleasant, NJ (borough) Ocean County	94.54
Monroe, NJ (township) Gloucester County	94.49
Wall, NJ (township) Monmouth County	94.08
Woodbury, NJ (city) Gloucester County	94.05
Beachwood, NJ (borough) Ocean County	93.49
Phillipsburg, NJ (town) Warren County	93.10
Deptford, NJ (township) Gloucester County	92.98
Vernon, NJ (township) Sussex County	92.91
Stafford, NJ (township) Ocean County	92.86

Hispanics 5 Years and Over Who Speak English-Only at Home
Top 10 Places Sorted by Number

Place	Number
Jersey City, NJ (city) Hudson County	7,808
Newark, NJ (city) Essex County	6,504
Paterson, NJ (city) Passaic County	4,383
Elizabeth, NJ (city) Union County	3,357
Camden, NJ (city) Camden County	3,099
Union City, NJ (city) Hudson County	2,669
Perth Amboy, NJ (city) Middlesex County	2,389
Passaic, NJ (city) Passaic County	2,340
Vineland, NJ (city) Cumberland County	2,143
Trenton, NJ (city) Mercer County	1,940

Hispanics 5 Years and Over Who Speak English-Only at Home
Top 10 Places Sorted by Percent

Place	Percent
Wall, NJ (township) Monmouth County	56.32
Pine Hill, NJ (borough) Camden County	56.30
Glassboro, NJ (borough) Gloucester County	54.34
Washington, NJ (township) Gloucester County	52.84
Colts Neck, NJ (township) Monmouth County	49.77
Oakland, NJ (borough) Bergen County	49.44
Marlboro, NJ (township) Monmouth County	49.25
Mount Olive, NJ (township) Morris County	49.06
Vernon, NJ (township) Sussex County	48.99
Monroe, NJ (township) Middlesex County	46.04

Argentinians 5 Years and Over Who Speak English-Only at Home
Top 10 Places Sorted by Number

Place	Number
North Bergen, NJ (township) Hudson County	7

Argentinians 5 Years and Over Who Speak English-Only at Home
Top 10 Places Sorted by Percent

Place	Percent
North Bergen, NJ (township) Hudson County	1.46

Bolivians 5 Years and Over Who Speak English-Only at Home
Top 10 Places Sorted by Number

Place	Number
No places met population threshold.	

Bolivians 5 Years and Over Who Speak English-Only at Home
Top 10 Places Sorted by Percent

Place	Percent
No places met population threshold.	

Central Americans 5 Years and Over Who Speak English-Only at Home
Top 10 Places Sorted by Number

Place	Number
West New York, NJ (town) Hudson County	327
Trenton, NJ (city) Mercer County	289
Elizabeth, NJ (city) Union County	236
Newark, NJ (city) Essex County	234
Jersey City, NJ (city) Hudson County	207
Union City, NJ (city) Hudson County	172
North Bergen, NJ (township) Hudson County	152
Paterson, NJ (city) Passaic County	132
Camden, NJ (city) Camden County	119
Passaic, NJ (city) Passaic County	69

Central Americans 5 Years and Over Who Speak English-Only at Home
Top 10 Places Sorted by Percent

Place	Percent
Irvington, NJ (cdp) Essex County	13.54
Camden, NJ (city) Camden County	12.14
Linden, NJ (city) Union County	9.04
Bloomfield, NJ (cdp) Essex County	9.00
West Orange, NJ (cdp) Essex County	8.74
Clifton, NJ (city) Passaic County	8.59
East Windsor, NJ (township) Mercer County	8.57
Trenton, NJ (city) Mercer County	7.93
Atlantic City, NJ (city) Atlantic County	7.45
Passaic, NJ (city) Passaic County	7.24

Chileans 5 Years and Over Who Speak English-Only at Home
Top 10 Places Sorted by Number

Place	Number
North Bergen, NJ (township) Hudson County	0

Chileans 5 Years and Over Who Speak English-Only at Home
Top 10 Places Sorted by Percent

Place	Percent
North Bergen, NJ (township) Hudson County	0.00

Colombians 5 Years and Over Who Speak English-Only at Home
Top 10 Places Sorted by Number

Place	Number
Elizabeth, NJ (city) Union County	240
Hackensack, NJ (city) Bergen County	200
Paterson, NJ (city) Passaic County	158
West New York, NJ (town) Hudson County	156
Union City, NJ (city) Hudson County	112
North Bergen, NJ (township) Hudson County	104
Clifton, NJ (city) Passaic County	96
Lakewood, NJ (township) Ocean County	89
Jersey City, NJ (city) Hudson County	87
Morris, NJ (town) Morris County	86

Colombians 5 Years and Over Who Speak English-Only at Home
Top 10 Places Sorted by Percent

Place	Percent
Lakewood, NJ (township) Ocean County	24.05
Elmwood Park, NJ (borough) Bergen County	16.38
Hackensack, NJ (city) Bergen County	11.69
Teaneck, NJ (cdp) Bergen County	11.27
Lodi, NJ (borough) Bergen County	8.92
Clifton, NJ (city) Passaic County	7.42
Parsippany-Troy Hills, NJ (township) Morris County	7.21
West New York, NJ (town) Hudson County	6.43
Morris, NJ (town) Morris County	6.22
Piscataway, NJ (township) Middlesex County	6.14

Costa Ricans 5 Years and Over Who Speak English-Only at Home
Top 10 Places Sorted by Number

Place	Number
Trenton, NJ (city) Mercer County	105
Paterson, NJ (city) Passaic County	67
Bound Brook, NJ (borough) Somerset County	51
Somerville, NJ (borough) Somerset County	14
Elizabeth, NJ (city) Union County	2

Costa Ricans 5 Years and Over Who Speak English-Only at Home
Top 10 Places Sorted by Percent

Place	Percent
Trenton, NJ (city) Mercer County	14.32
Paterson, NJ (city) Passaic County	8.82
Bound Brook, NJ (borough) Somerset County	4.52
Somerville, NJ (borough) Somerset County	2.65
Elizabeth, NJ (city) Union County	0.50

Notes: Please refer to the User's Guide for an explanation of data; tables include places with populations > 9,999 and reflect only those areas that meet Summary File 4 population thresholds, therefore there may be less than 10 places listed

Cubans 5 Years and Over Who Speak English-Only at Home
Top 10 Places Sorted by Number

Place	Number
Union City, NJ (city) Hudson County	478
Elizabeth, NJ (city) Union County	441
North Bergen, NJ (township) Hudson County	381
West New York, NJ (town) Hudson County	369
Jersey City, NJ (city) Hudson County	257
Newark, NJ (city) Essex County	213
Belleville, NJ (cdp) Essex County	209
Hoboken, NJ (city) Hudson County	133
Edison, NJ (cdp) Middlesex County	130
Paterson, NJ (city) Passaic County	96

Cubans 5 Years and Over Who Speak English-Only at Home
Top 10 Places Sorted by Percent

Place	Percent
Belleville, NJ (cdp) Essex County	35.91
Edison, NJ (cdp) Middlesex County	23.68
Hoboken, NJ (city) Hudson County	18.24
Bayonne, NJ (city) Hudson County	18.15
Woodbridge, NJ (township) Middlesex County	17.62
Elmwood Park, NJ (borough) Bergen County	17.03
Bloomfield, NJ (cdp) Essex County	15.76
Jersey City, NJ (city) Hudson County	14.29
Harrison, NJ (town) Hudson County	12.50
Union, NJ (cdp) Union County	12.35

Dominicans 5 Years and Over Who Speak English-Only at Home
Top 10 Places Sorted by Number

Place	Number
Paterson, NJ (city) Passaic County	800
Jersey City, NJ (city) Hudson County	679
Perth Amboy, NJ (city) Middlesex County	376
Passaic, NJ (city) Passaic County	349
Newark, NJ (city) Essex County	312
Union City, NJ (city) Hudson County	299
Elizabeth, NJ (city) Union County	201
West New York, NJ (town) Hudson County	173
Camden, NJ (city) Camden County	103
Franklin, NJ (township) Somerset County	88

Dominicans 5 Years and Over Who Speak English-Only at Home
Top 10 Places Sorted by Percent

Place	Percent
Belleville, NJ (cdp) Essex County	15.89
Franklin, NJ (township) Somerset County	11.92
Somerset, NJ (cdp) Somerset County	10.82
Kearny, NJ (town) Hudson County	10.69
Jersey City, NJ (city) Hudson County	7.61
Fairview, NJ (borough) Bergen County	6.90
Hackensack, NJ (city) Bergen County	6.22
Guttenberg, NJ (town) Hudson County	6.09
North Brunswick Township, NJ (cdp) Middlesex County	5.90
Camden, NJ (city) Camden County	5.85

Ecuadorians 5 Years and Over Who Speak English-Only at Home
Top 10 Places Sorted by Number

Place	Number
Newark, NJ (city) Essex County	599
Jersey City, NJ (city) Hudson County	265
Union City, NJ (city) Hudson County	144
North Bergen, NJ (township) Hudson County	88
Elizabeth, NJ (city) Union County	57
North Plainfield, NJ (borough) Somerset County	52
Bloomfield, NJ (cdp) Essex County	48
West New York, NJ (town) Hudson County	44
Passaic, NJ (city) Passaic County	41

Belleville, NJ (cdp) Essex County | 29

Ecuadorians 5 Years and Over Who Speak English-Only at Home
Top 10 Places Sorted by Percent

Place	Percent
Bloomfield, NJ (cdp) Essex County	11.46
Passaic, NJ (city) Passaic County	9.05
Newark, NJ (city) Essex County	7.66
Bayonne, NJ (city) Hudson County	7.14
Jersey City, NJ (city) Hudson County	6.40
North Plainfield, NJ (borough) Somerset County	4.28
North Bergen, NJ (township) Hudson County	4.17
Union City, NJ (city) Hudson County	3.61
Elizabeth, NJ (city) Union County	3.36
East Windsor, NJ (township) Mercer County	3.15

Guatelmalans 5 Years and Over Who Speak English-Only at Home
Top 10 Places Sorted by Number

Place	Number
Trenton, NJ (city) Mercer County	130
Newark, NJ (city) Essex County	117
Jersey City, NJ (city) Hudson County	50
Union City, NJ (city) Hudson County	26
Fairview, NJ (borough) Bergen County	25
North Bergen, NJ (township) Hudson County	25
Bayonne, NJ (city) Hudson County	24
Plainfield, NJ (city) Union County	23
Elizabeth, NJ (city) Union County	17
East Windsor, NJ (township) Mercer County	16

Guatelmalans 5 Years and Over Who Speak English-Only at Home
Top 10 Places Sorted by Percent

Place	Percent
Newark, NJ (city) Essex County	14.44
Jersey City, NJ (city) Hudson County	7.72
Bayonne, NJ (city) Hudson County	7.08
Union City, NJ (city) Hudson County	5.60
Trenton, NJ (city) Mercer County	4.92
North Bergen, NJ (township) Hudson County	4.53
Fairview, NJ (borough) Bergen County	3.92
East Windsor, NJ (township) Mercer County	3.74
Elizabeth, NJ (city) Union County	3.42
West New York, NJ (town) Hudson County	2.65

Hondurans 5 Years and Over Who Speak English-Only at Home
Top 10 Places Sorted by Number

Place	Number
Jersey City, NJ (city) Hudson County	94
Passaic, NJ (city) Passaic County	61
Union City, NJ (city) Hudson County	32
Morris, NJ (town) Morris County	31
New Brunswick, NJ (city) Middlesex County	29
Newark, NJ (city) Essex County	28
Elizabeth, NJ (city) Union County	23
North Bergen, NJ (township) Hudson County	13
Plainfield, NJ (city) Union County	13
West New York, NJ (town) Hudson County	13

Hondurans 5 Years and Over Who Speak English-Only at Home
Top 10 Places Sorted by Percent

Place	Percent
Passaic, NJ (city) Passaic County	10.74
Jersey City, NJ (city) Hudson County	5.35
Newark, NJ (city) Essex County	4.69
Morris, NJ (town) Morris County	4.49
Elizabeth, NJ (city) Union County	2.40
West New York, NJ (town) Hudson County	2.07
North Bergen, NJ (township) Hudson County	1.99

Union City, NJ (city) Hudson County | 1.86
New Brunswick, NJ (city) Middlesex County | 1.78
Plainfield, NJ (city) Union County | 1.47

Mexicans 5 Years and Over Who Speak English-Only at Home
Top 10 Places Sorted by Number

Place	Number
Passaic, NJ (city) Passaic County	674
Newark, NJ (city) Essex County	429
Jersey City, NJ (city) Hudson County	338
New Brunswick, NJ (city) Middlesex County	334
Bridgeton, NJ (city) Cumberland County	240
Paterson, NJ (city) Passaic County	210
Vineland, NJ (city) Cumberland County	194
Camden, NJ (city) Camden County	186
Atlantic City, NJ (city) Atlantic County	183
Lakewood, NJ (township) Ocean County	133

Mexicans 5 Years and Over Who Speak English-Only at Home
Top 10 Places Sorted by Percent

Place	Percent
Garfield, NJ (city) Bergen County	26.24
Old Bridge, NJ (township) Middlesex County	24.18
Franklin, NJ (township) Somerset County	21.66
Newark, NJ (city) Essex County	21.36
Somerset, NJ (cdp) Somerset County	21.18
Edison, NJ (cdp) Middlesex County	19.72
West Orange, NJ (cdp) Essex County	17.30
Dover, NJ (township) Ocean County	15.73
Princeton, NJ (township) Mercer County	15.51
Toms River, NJ (cdp) Ocean County	15.31

Nicaraguans 5 Years and Over Who Speak English-Only at Home
Top 10 Places Sorted by Number

Place	Number
Camden, NJ (city) Camden County	9
Jersey City, NJ (city) Hudson County	0

Nicaraguans 5 Years and Over Who Speak English-Only at Home
Top 10 Places Sorted by Percent

Place	Percent
Camden, NJ (city) Camden County	1.48
Jersey City, NJ (city) Hudson County	0.00

Panamanians 5 Years and Over Who Speak English-Only at Home
Top 10 Places Sorted by Number

Place	Number
No places met population threshold.	

Panamanians 5 Years and Over Who Speak English-Only at Home
Top 10 Places Sorted by Percent

Place	Percent
No places met population threshold.	

Paraguayans 5 Years and Over Who Speak English-Only at Home
Top 10 Places Sorted by Number

Place	Number
No places met population threshold.	

Notes: Please refer to the User's Guide for an explanation of data; tables include places with populations > 9,999 and reflect only those areas that meet Summary File 4 population thresholds, therefore there may be less than 10 places listed

Paraguayans 5 Years and Over Who Speak English-Only at Home
Top 10 Places Sorted by Percent

Place	Percent
No places met population threshold.	

Peruvians 5 Years and Over Who Speak English-Only at Home
Top 10 Places Sorted by Number

Place	Number
Paterson, NJ (city) Passaic County	201
Passaic, NJ (city) Passaic County	146
Elizabeth, NJ (city) Union County	132
Kearny, NJ (town) Hudson County	95
West New York, NJ (town) Hudson County	64
Newark, NJ (city) Essex County	57
Harrison, NJ (town) Hudson County	54
Union City, NJ (city) Hudson County	53
Belleville, NJ (cdp) Essex County	50
Woodbridge, NJ (township) Middlesex County	45

Peruvians 5 Years and Over Who Speak English-Only at Home
Top 10 Places Sorted by Percent

Place	Percent
Belleville, NJ (cdp) Essex County	12.05
Woodbridge, NJ (township) Middlesex County	10.71
West New York, NJ (town) Hudson County	8.08
Passaic, NJ (city) Passaic County	7.78
Kearny, NJ (town) Hudson County	6.28
West Orange, NJ (cdp) Essex County	5.40
Harrison, NJ (town) Hudson County	4.99
Elizabeth, NJ (city) Union County	4.44
Newark, NJ (city) Essex County	3.90
Perth Amboy, NJ (city) Middlesex County	3.02

Puerto Ricans 5 Years and Over Who Speak English-Only at Home
Top 10 Places Sorted by Number

Place	Number
Jersey City, NJ (city) Hudson County	4,413
Newark, NJ (city) Essex County	3,442
Camden, NJ (city) Camden County	2,313
Paterson, NJ (city) Passaic County	2,050
Vineland, NJ (city) Cumberland County	1,706
Perth Amboy, NJ (city) Middlesex County	1,478
Elizabeth, NJ (city) Union County	1,231
Trenton, NJ (city) Mercer County	1,017
Woodbridge, NJ (township) Middlesex County	1,012
Bayonne, NJ (city) Hudson County	904

Puerto Ricans 5 Years and Over Who Speak English-Only at Home
Top 10 Places Sorted by Percent

Place	Percent
Marlboro, NJ (township) Monmouth County	63.08
Freehold, NJ (township) Monmouth County	60.72
Washington, NJ (township) Gloucester County	60.51
West Milford, NJ (cdp) Passaic County	51.34
Bridgewater, NJ (township) Somerset County	50.84
Lyndhurst, NJ (cdp) Bergen County	50.77
Monroe, NJ (township) Gloucester County	48.42
Manalapan, NJ (township) Monmouth County	47.47
Glassboro, NJ (borough) Gloucester County	46.99
Evesham, NJ (township) Burlington County	46.50

Salvadorans 5 Years and Over Who Speak English-Only at Home
Top 10 Places Sorted by Number

Place	Number
West New York, NJ (town) Hudson County	291
Elizabeth, NJ (city) Union County	113
Union City, NJ (city) Hudson County	75
North Bergen, NJ (township) Hudson County	63
Newark, NJ (city) Essex County	44
Paterson, NJ (city) Passaic County	35
Plainfield, NJ (city) Union County	27
Guttenberg, NJ (town) Hudson County	21
Jersey City, NJ (city) Hudson County	20
Fairview, NJ (borough) Bergen County	7

Salvadorans 5 Years and Over Who Speak English-Only at Home
Top 10 Places Sorted by Percent

Place	Percent
West New York, NJ (town) Hudson County	10.27
Paterson, NJ (city) Passaic County	6.72
Guttenberg, NJ (town) Hudson County	5.98
North Bergen, NJ (township) Hudson County	4.93
Elizabeth, NJ (city) Union County	3.28
Newark, NJ (city) Essex County	2.73
Plainfield, NJ (city) Union County	2.24
Union City, NJ (city) Hudson County	2.10
Jersey City, NJ (city) Hudson County	1.77
Fairview, NJ (borough) Bergen County	1.72

South Americans 5 Years and Over Who Speak English-Only at Home
Top 10 Places Sorted by Number

Place	Number
Newark, NJ (city) Essex County	770
Jersey City, NJ (city) Hudson County	488
Elizabeth, NJ (city) Union County	463
Paterson, NJ (city) Passaic County	422
Union City, NJ (city) Hudson County	323
West New York, NJ (town) Hudson County	289
Passaic, NJ (city) Passaic County	252
Clifton, NJ (city) Passaic County	244
North Bergen, NJ (township) Hudson County	233
Hackensack, NJ (city) Bergen County	223

South Americans 5 Years and Over Who Speak English-Only at Home
Top 10 Places Sorted by Percent

Place	Percent
Hoboken, NJ (city) Hudson County	31.12
Dover, NJ (township) Ocean County	26.61
Toms River, NJ (cdp) Ocean County	26.61
Montclair, NJ (cdp) Essex County	21.81
Lakewood, NJ (township) Ocean County	17.83
Irvington, NJ (cdp) Essex County	16.82
Middletown, NJ (township) Monmouth County	16.63
Ocean, NJ (township) Monmouth County	15.63
Secaucus, NJ (town) Hudson County	15.63
East Brunswick, NJ (cdp) Middlesex County	14.94

Spaniards 5 Years and Over Who Speak English-Only at Home
Top 10 Places Sorted by Number

Place	Number
Newark, NJ (city) Essex County	88
Bayonne, NJ (city) Hudson County	43
Kearny, NJ (town) Hudson County	31

Spaniards 5 Years and Over Who Speak English-Only at Home
Top 10 Places Sorted by Percent

Place	Percent
Bayonne, NJ (city) Hudson County	7.52
Newark, NJ (city) Essex County	6.75
Kearny, NJ (town) Hudson County	4.30

Uruguayans 5 Years and Over Who Speak English-Only at Home
Top 10 Places Sorted by Number

Place	Number
West Orange, NJ (cdp) Essex County	19
Elizabeth, NJ (city) Union County	12

Uruguayans 5 Years and Over Who Speak English-Only at Home
Top 10 Places Sorted by Percent

Place	Percent
West Orange, NJ (cdp) Essex County	5.85
Elizabeth, NJ (city) Union County	1.52

Venezuelans 5 Years and Over Who Speak English-Only at Home
Top 10 Places Sorted by Number

Place	Number
No places met population threshold.	

Venezuelans 5 Years and Over Who Speak English-Only at Home
Top 10 Places Sorted by Percent

Place	Percent
No places met population threshold.	

Other Hispanics 5 Years and Over Who Speak English-Only at Home
Top 10 Places Sorted by Number

Place	Number
Jersey City, NJ (city) Hudson County	1,320
Newark, NJ (city) Essex County	1,016
Paterson, NJ (city) Passaic County	666
Elizabeth, NJ (city) Union County	657
Union City, NJ (city) Hudson County	604
Trenton, NJ (city) Mercer County	509
Dover, NJ (township) Ocean County	414
Toms River, NJ (cdp) Ocean County	414
Bayonne, NJ (city) Hudson County	402
Woodbridge, NJ (township) Middlesex County	389

Other Hispanics 5 Years and Over Who Speak English-Only at Home
Top 10 Places Sorted by Percent

Place	Percent
Dover, NJ (township) Ocean County	64.69
Toms River, NJ (cdp) Ocean County	64.69
Howell, NJ (township) Monmouth County	53.12
Brick, NJ (township) Ocean County	51.96
Old Bridge, NJ (township) Middlesex County	31.06
Woodbridge, NJ (township) Middlesex County	29.58
Lodi, NJ (borough) Bergen County	26.08
Bayonne, NJ (city) Hudson County	24.66
Lakewood, NJ (township) Ocean County	23.80
Sayreville, NJ (borough) Middlesex County	23.29

Language Spoken: Spanish

Total Population 5 Years and Over Who Speak Spanish at Home
Top 10 Places Sorted by Number

Place	Number
Newark, NJ (city) Essex County	71,344
Paterson, NJ (city) Passaic County	66,055
Jersey City, NJ (city) Hudson County	57,048
Elizabeth, NJ (city) Union County	54,845
Union City, NJ (city) Hudson County	50,209
Passaic, NJ (city) Passaic County	36,216
West New York, NJ (town) Hudson County	33,201
North Bergen, NJ (township) Hudson County	31,069
Perth Amboy, NJ (city) Middlesex County	28,375

Notes: Please refer to the User's Guide for an explanation of data; tables include places with populations > 9,999 and reflect only those areas that meet Summary File 4 population thresholds, therefore there may be less than 10 places listed

Camden, NJ (city) Camden County	25,498

Total Population 5 Years and Over Who Speak Spanish at Home
Top 10 Places Sorted by Percent

Place	Percent
Union City, NJ (city) Hudson County	80.67
West New York, NJ (town) Hudson County	77.63
Perth Amboy, NJ (city) Middlesex County	65.12
Passaic, NJ (city) Passaic County	59.28
North Bergen, NJ (township) Hudson County	56.93
Dover, NJ (town) Morris County	55.54
Guttenberg, NJ (town) Hudson County	51.39
Elizabeth, NJ (city) Union County	49.19
Paterson, NJ (city) Passaic County	48.33
Weehawken, NJ (township) Hudson County	40.20

Hispanics 5 Years and Over Who Speak Spanish at Home
Top 10 Places Sorted by Number

Place	Number
Newark, NJ (city) Essex County	66,511
Paterson, NJ (city) Passaic County	63,490
Jersey City, NJ (city) Hudson County	53,884
Elizabeth, NJ (city) Union County	51,054
Union City, NJ (city) Hudson County	48,529
Passaic, NJ (city) Passaic County	35,386
West New York, NJ (town) Hudson County	31,725
North Bergen, NJ (township) Hudson County	29,134
Perth Amboy, NJ (city) Middlesex County	27,603
Camden, NJ (city) Camden County	24,395

Hispanics 5 Years and Over Who Speak Spanish at Home
Top 10 Places Sorted by Percent

Place	Percent
Union City, NJ (city) Hudson County	94.61
Bound Brook, NJ (borough) Somerset County	94.55
West New York, NJ (town) Hudson County	94.38
Plainfield, NJ (city) Union County	94.28
Passaic, NJ (city) Passaic County	93.70
North Bergen, NJ (township) Hudson County	93.65
Dover, NJ (town) Morris County	93.39
Paterson, NJ (city) Passaic County	93.31
Elizabeth, NJ (city) Union County	93.02
Weehawken, NJ (township) Hudson County	92.95

Argentinians 5 Years and Over Who Speak Spanish at Home
Top 10 Places Sorted by Number

Place	Number
North Bergen, NJ (township) Hudson County	466

Argentinians 5 Years and Over Who Speak Spanish at Home
Top 10 Places Sorted by Percent

Place	Percent
North Bergen, NJ (township) Hudson County	96.88

Bolivians 5 Years and Over Who Speak Spanish at Home
Top 10 Places Sorted by Number

Place	Number
No places met population threshold.	

Bolivians 5 Years and Over Who Speak Spanish at Home
Top 10 Places Sorted by Percent

Place	Percent
No places met population threshold.	

Central Americans 5 Years and Over Who Speak Spanish at Home
Top 10 Places Sorted by Number

Place	Number
Union City, NJ (city) Hudson County	6,122
Elizabeth, NJ (city) Union County	5,626
Jersey City, NJ (city) Hudson County	4,493
West New York, NJ (town) Hudson County	4,328
Plainfield, NJ (city) Union County	4,044
Newark, NJ (city) Essex County	3,776
Trenton, NJ (city) Mercer County	3,321
North Bergen, NJ (township) Hudson County	2,680
New Brunswick, NJ (city) Middlesex County	2,149
Paterson, NJ (city) Passaic County	1,777

Central Americans 5 Years and Over Who Speak Spanish at Home
Top 10 Places Sorted by Percent

Place	Percent
Weehawken, NJ (township) Hudson County	100.00
Cliffside Park, NJ (borough) Bergen County	98.48
Plainfield, NJ (city) Union County	98.47
Englewood, NJ (city) Bergen County	98.29
Woodbridge, NJ (township) Middlesex County	98.20
North Plainfield, NJ (borough) Somerset County	98.12
Dover, NJ (town) Morris County	97.96
Morris, NJ (town) Morris County	97.47
Palisades Park, NJ (borough) Bergen County	97.44
Long Branch, NJ (city) Monmouth County	97.30

Chileans 5 Years and Over Who Speak Spanish at Home
Top 10 Places Sorted by Number

Place	Number
North Bergen, NJ (township) Hudson County	465

Chileans 5 Years and Over Who Speak Spanish at Home
Top 10 Places Sorted by Percent

Place	Percent
North Bergen, NJ (township) Hudson County	100.00

Colombians 5 Years and Over Who Speak Spanish at Home
Top 10 Places Sorted by Number

Place	Number
Elizabeth, NJ (city) Union County	7,425
Paterson, NJ (city) Passaic County	4,667
North Bergen, NJ (township) Hudson County	3,587
Union City, NJ (city) Hudson County	2,573
West New York, NJ (town) Hudson County	2,260
Dover, NJ (town) Morris County	2,074
Englewood, NJ (city) Bergen County	1,893
Jersey City, NJ (city) Hudson County	1,612
Hackensack, NJ (city) Bergen County	1,511
Morris, NJ (town) Morris County	1,296

Colombians 5 Years and Over Who Speak Spanish at Home
Top 10 Places Sorted by Percent

Place	Percent
Atlantic City, NJ (city) Atlantic County	100.00
Roselle, NJ (borough) Union County	98.98
Linden, NJ (city) Union County	98.79
Perth Amboy, NJ (city) Middlesex County	98.70
North Plainfield, NJ (borough) Somerset County	98.23
Englewood, NJ (city) Bergen County	97.93
Guttenberg, NJ (town) Hudson County	97.38
Dover, NJ (town) Morris County	97.37
Newark, NJ (city) Essex County	97.07
Elizabeth, NJ (city) Union County	96.77

Costa Ricans 5 Years and Over Who Speak Spanish at Home
Top 10 Places Sorted by Number

Place	Number
Bound Brook, NJ (borough) Somerset County	1,077
Paterson, NJ (city) Passaic County	693
Trenton, NJ (city) Mercer County	628
Somerville, NJ (borough) Somerset County	514
Elizabeth, NJ (city) Union County	398

Costa Ricans 5 Years and Over Who Speak Spanish at Home
Top 10 Places Sorted by Percent

Place	Percent
Elizabeth, NJ (city) Union County	99.50
Somerville, NJ (borough) Somerset County	97.35
Bound Brook, NJ (borough) Somerset County	95.48
Paterson, NJ (city) Passaic County	91.18
Trenton, NJ (city) Mercer County	85.68

Cubans 5 Years and Over Who Speak Spanish at Home
Top 10 Places Sorted by Number

Place	Number
Union City, NJ (city) Hudson County	9,549
West New York, NJ (town) Hudson County	9,116
North Bergen, NJ (township) Hudson County	7,253
Elizabeth, NJ (city) Union County	6,718
Newark, NJ (city) Essex County	2,917
Jersey City, NJ (city) Hudson County	1,537
Guttenberg, NJ (town) Hudson County	1,083
Weehawken, NJ (township) Hudson County	1,041
Paterson, NJ (city) Passaic County	851
Perth Amboy, NJ (city) Middlesex County	782

Cubans 5 Years and Over Who Speak Spanish at Home
Top 10 Places Sorted by Percent

Place	Percent
Passaic, NJ (city) Passaic County	98.36
Guttenberg, NJ (town) Hudson County	96.35
West New York, NJ (town) Hudson County	95.83
Union City, NJ (city) Hudson County	95.02
North Bergen, NJ (township) Hudson County	95.01
Perth Amboy, NJ (city) Middlesex County	94.79
Weehawken, NJ (township) Hudson County	94.21
Fairview, NJ (borough) Bergen County	94.19
Elizabeth, NJ (city) Union County	92.96
Kearny, NJ (town) Hudson County	92.08

Dominicans 5 Years and Over Who Speak Spanish at Home
Top 10 Places Sorted by Number

Place	Number
Paterson, NJ (city) Passaic County	13,155
Passaic, NJ (city) Passaic County	8,288
Jersey City, NJ (city) Hudson County	8,240
Perth Amboy, NJ (city) Middlesex County	7,678
Union City, NJ (city) Hudson County	7,012
Newark, NJ (city) Essex County	5,574
West New York, NJ (town) Hudson County	3,508
Elizabeth, NJ (city) Union County	3,261
North Bergen, NJ (township) Hudson County	2,690
New Brunswick, NJ (city) Middlesex County	2,217

Dominicans 5 Years and Over Who Speak Spanish at Home
Top 10 Places Sorted by Percent

Place	Percent
Fort Lee, NJ (borough) Bergen County	100.00
Bayonne, NJ (city) Hudson County	98.03
Clifton, NJ (city) Passaic County	97.50

Notes: Please refer to the User's Guide for an explanation of data; tables include places with populations > 9,999 and reflect only those areas that meet Summary File 4 population thresholds, therefore there may be less than 10 places listed

Place	
North Bergen, NJ (township) Hudson County	96.87
Bergenfield, NJ (borough) Bergen County	96.58
Garfield, NJ (city) Bergen County	96.41
Ridgefield Park, NJ (village) Bergen County	96.41
Weehawken, NJ (township) Hudson County	96.39
New Brunswick, NJ (city) Middlesex County	96.18
Passaic, NJ (city) Passaic County	95.96

Ecuadorians 5 Years and Over Who Speak Spanish at Home
Top 10 Places Sorted by Number

Place	Number
Newark, NJ (city) Essex County	7,138
Jersey City, NJ (city) Hudson County	3,875
Union City, NJ (city) Hudson County	3,832
North Bergen, NJ (township) Hudson County	2,023
West New York, NJ (town) Hudson County	2,018
Hackensack, NJ (city) Bergen County	1,839
Elizabeth, NJ (city) Union County	1,641
North Plainfield, NJ (borough) Somerset County	1,162
Belleville, NJ (cdp) Essex County	980
Kearny, NJ (town) Hudson County	880

Ecuadorians 5 Years and Over Who Speak Spanish at Home
Top 10 Places Sorted by Percent

Place	Percent
Weehawken, NJ (township) Hudson County	100.00
Hackensack, NJ (city) Bergen County	99.84
Harrison, NJ (town) Hudson County	98.54
Plainfield, NJ (city) Union County	97.97
West New York, NJ (town) Hudson County	97.77
Kearny, NJ (town) Hudson County	97.67
Belleville, NJ (cdp) Essex County	97.13
Dover, NJ (town) Morris County	97.02
Paterson, NJ (city) Passaic County	96.93
Clifton, NJ (city) Passaic County	96.91

Guatelmalans 5 Years and Over Who Speak Spanish at Home
Top 10 Places Sorted by Number

Place	Number
Trenton, NJ (city) Mercer County	2,476
Plainfield, NJ (city) Union County	1,582
Newark, NJ (city) Essex County	693
Fairview, NJ (borough) Bergen County	612
Jersey City, NJ (city) Hudson County	598
Palisades Park, NJ (borough) Bergen County	568
North Bergen, NJ (township) Hudson County	527
West New York, NJ (town) Hudson County	514
Elizabeth, NJ (city) Union County	480
Union City, NJ (city) Hudson County	438

Guatelmalans 5 Years and Over Who Speak Spanish at Home
Top 10 Places Sorted by Percent

Place	Percent
North Plainfield, NJ (borough) Somerset County	98.93
Plainfield, NJ (city) Union County	98.57
Palisades Park, NJ (borough) Bergen County	98.10
West New York, NJ (town) Hudson County	97.35
Elizabeth, NJ (city) Union County	96.58
East Windsor, NJ (township) Mercer County	96.26
Fairview, NJ (borough) Bergen County	96.08
North Bergen, NJ (township) Hudson County	95.47
Union City, NJ (city) Hudson County	94.40
Trenton, NJ (city) Mercer County	93.79

Hondurans 5 Years and Over Who Speak Spanish at Home
Top 10 Places Sorted by Number

Place	Number
Union City, NJ (city) Hudson County	1,690
Jersey City, NJ (city) Hudson County	1,657
New Brunswick, NJ (city) Middlesex County	1,603
Elizabeth, NJ (city) Union County	929
Plainfield, NJ (city) Union County	872
Morris, NJ (town) Morris County	660
North Bergen, NJ (township) Hudson County	639
West New York, NJ (town) Hudson County	614
Newark, NJ (city) Essex County	569
Passaic, NJ (city) Passaic County	507

Hondurans 5 Years and Over Who Speak Spanish at Home
Top 10 Places Sorted by Percent

Place	Percent
Plainfield, NJ (city) Union County	98.53
New Brunswick, NJ (city) Middlesex County	98.22
Union City, NJ (city) Hudson County	98.14
North Bergen, NJ (township) Hudson County	98.01
West New York, NJ (town) Hudson County	97.93
Elizabeth, NJ (city) Union County	97.07
Morris, NJ (town) Morris County	95.51
Newark, NJ (city) Essex County	95.31
Jersey City, NJ (city) Hudson County	94.31
Passaic, NJ (city) Passaic County	89.26

Mexicans 5 Years and Over Who Speak Spanish at Home
Top 10 Places Sorted by Number

Place	Number
Passaic, NJ (city) Passaic County	11,004
New Brunswick, NJ (city) Middlesex County	6,407
Paterson, NJ (city) Passaic County	4,492
West New York, NJ (town) Hudson County	2,668
Bridgeton, NJ (city) Cumberland County	2,580
Perth Amboy, NJ (city) Middlesex County	2,425
Union City, NJ (city) Hudson County	2,305
Jersey City, NJ (city) Hudson County	2,035
Atlantic City, NJ (city) Atlantic County	2,016
Lakewood, NJ (township) Ocean County	1,914

Mexicans 5 Years and Over Who Speak Spanish at Home
Top 10 Places Sorted by Percent

Place	Percent
West New York, NJ (town) Hudson County	96.67
Bound Brook, NJ (borough) Somerset County	96.49
Freehold, NJ (borough) Monmouth County	96.41
North Bergen, NJ (township) Hudson County	96.23
Perth Amboy, NJ (city) Middlesex County	96.04
Paterson, NJ (city) Passaic County	95.53
Ventnor City, NJ (city) Atlantic County	95.44
Dover, NJ (town) Morris County	95.40
Hackensack, NJ (city) Bergen County	95.07
New Brunswick, NJ (city) Middlesex County	95.00

Nicaraguans 5 Years and Over Who Speak Spanish at Home
Top 10 Places Sorted by Number

Place	Number
Camden, NJ (city) Camden County	601
Jersey City, NJ (city) Hudson County	474

Nicaraguans 5 Years and Over Who Speak Spanish at Home
Top 10 Places Sorted by Percent

Place	Percent
Jersey City, NJ (city) Hudson County	100.00
Camden, NJ (city) Camden County	98.52

Panamanians 5 Years and Over Who Speak Spanish at Home
Top 10 Places Sorted by Number

Place	Number
No places met population threshold.	

Panamanians 5 Years and Over Who Speak Spanish at Home
Top 10 Places Sorted by Percent

Place	Percent
No places met population threshold.	

Paraguayans 5 Years and Over Who Speak Spanish at Home
Top 10 Places Sorted by Number

Place	Number
No places met population threshold.	

Paraguayans 5 Years and Over Who Speak Spanish at Home
Top 10 Places Sorted by Percent

Place	Percent
No places met population threshold.	

Peruvians 5 Years and Over Who Speak Spanish at Home
Top 10 Places Sorted by Number

Place	Number
Paterson, NJ (city) Passaic County	6,710
Elizabeth, NJ (city) Union County	2,841
Union City, NJ (city) Hudson County	1,828
Passaic, NJ (city) Passaic County	1,730
Clifton, NJ (city) Passaic County	1,663
Newark, NJ (city) Essex County	1,406
Kearny, NJ (town) Hudson County	1,389
Perth Amboy, NJ (city) Middlesex County	1,182
Harrison, NJ (town) Hudson County	1,017
North Bergen, NJ (township) Hudson County	912

Peruvians 5 Years and Over Who Speak Spanish at Home
Top 10 Places Sorted by Percent

Place	Percent
Elmwood Park, NJ (borough) Bergen County	100.00
Garfield, NJ (city) Bergen County	99.29
Carteret, NJ (borough) Middlesex County	98.46
Jersey City, NJ (city) Hudson County	98.08
North Bergen, NJ (township) Hudson County	97.96
Clifton, NJ (city) Passaic County	97.54
Union City, NJ (city) Hudson County	96.87
Paterson, NJ (city) Passaic County	96.42
Perth Amboy, NJ (city) Middlesex County	96.33
Newark, NJ (city) Essex County	96.10

Puerto Ricans 5 Years and Over Who Speak Spanish at Home
Top 10 Places Sorted by Number

Place	Number
Newark, NJ (city) Essex County	32,523
Jersey City, NJ (city) Hudson County	22,441
Paterson, NJ (city) Passaic County	20,300
Camden, NJ (city) Camden County	18,317
Perth Amboy, NJ (city) Middlesex County	11,030
Elizabeth, NJ (city) Union County	10,979
Vineland, NJ (city) Cumberland County	10,320
Passaic, NJ (city) Passaic County	7,373
Trenton, NJ (city) Mercer County	7,348
Union City, NJ (city) Hudson County	6,500

Notes: Please refer to the User's Guide for an explanation of data; tables include places with populations > 9,999 and reflect only those areas that meet Summary File 4 population thresholds, therefore there may be less than 10 places listed

Puerto Ricans 5 Years and Over Who Speak Spanish at Home
Top 10 Places Sorted by Percent

Place	Percent
Passaic, NJ (city) Passaic County	92.07
Paterson, NJ (city) Passaic County	90.71
Union City, NJ (city) Hudson County	90.67
Newark, NJ (city) Essex County	90.28
Elizabeth, NJ (city) Union County	89.74
West New York, NJ (town) Hudson County	89.33
Plainfield, NJ (city) Union County	89.07
Camden, NJ (city) Camden County	88.76
Browns Mills, NJ (cdp) Burlington County	88.44
Ventnor City, NJ (city) Atlantic County	88.31

Salvadorans 5 Years and Over Who Speak Spanish at Home
Top 10 Places Sorted by Number

Place	Number
Union City, NJ (city) Hudson County	3,493
Elizabeth, NJ (city) Union County	3,333
West New York, NJ (town) Hudson County	2,532
Newark, NJ (city) Essex County	1,565
North Bergen, NJ (township) Hudson County	1,216
Plainfield, NJ (city) Union County	1,177
Jersey City, NJ (city) Hudson County	1,111
Paterson, NJ (city) Passaic County	469
Fairview, NJ (borough) Bergen County	401
Guttenberg, NJ (town) Hudson County	330

Salvadorans 5 Years and Over Who Speak Spanish at Home
Top 10 Places Sorted by Percent

Place	Percent
North Plainfield, NJ (borough) Somerset County	100.00
Fairview, NJ (borough) Bergen County	98.28
Jersey City, NJ (city) Hudson County	98.23
Union City, NJ (city) Hudson County	97.90
Plainfield, NJ (city) Union County	97.76
Newark, NJ (city) Essex County	97.27
Elizabeth, NJ (city) Union County	96.72
North Bergen, NJ (township) Hudson County	95.07
Guttenberg, NJ (town) Hudson County	94.02
Paterson, NJ (city) Passaic County	90.02

South Americans 5 Years and Over Who Speak Spanish at Home
Top 10 Places Sorted by Number

Place	Number
Elizabeth, NJ (city) Union County	13,985
Paterson, NJ (city) Passaic County	12,911
Newark, NJ (city) Essex County	10,500
Union City, NJ (city) Hudson County	9,196
North Bergen, NJ (township) Hudson County	7,804
Jersey City, NJ (city) Hudson County	7,352
West New York, NJ (town) Hudson County	5,744
Hackensack, NJ (city) Bergen County	4,046
Passaic, NJ (city) Passaic County	3,749
Clifton, NJ (city) Passaic County	3,742

South Americans 5 Years and Over Who Speak Spanish at Home
Top 10 Places Sorted by Percent

Place	Percent
Fairview, NJ (borough) Bergen County	100.00
Hillside, NJ (cdp) Union County	98.98
Bound Brook, NJ (borough) Somerset County	98.23
Englewood, NJ (city) Bergen County	98.15
Atlantic City, NJ (city) Atlantic County	98.06
Guttenberg, NJ (town) Hudson County	97.90
Plainfield, NJ (city) Union County	97.81
Roselle, NJ (borough) Union County	97.77
East Windsor, NJ (township) Mercer County	97.56

Place	
Dover, NJ (town) Morris County	97.53

Spaniards 5 Years and Over Who Speak Spanish at Home
Top 10 Places Sorted by Number

Place	Number
Newark, NJ (city) Essex County	1,210
Kearny, NJ (town) Hudson County	637
Bayonne, NJ (city) Hudson County	484

Spaniards 5 Years and Over Who Speak Spanish at Home
Top 10 Places Sorted by Percent

Place	Percent
Newark, NJ (city) Essex County	92.86
Kearny, NJ (town) Hudson County	88.35
Bayonne, NJ (city) Hudson County	84.62

Uruguayans 5 Years and Over Who Speak Spanish at Home
Top 10 Places Sorted by Number

Place	Number
Elizabeth, NJ (city) Union County	778
West Orange, NJ (cdp) Essex County	306

Uruguayans 5 Years and Over Who Speak Spanish at Home
Top 10 Places Sorted by Percent

Place	Percent
Elizabeth, NJ (city) Union County	98.48
West Orange, NJ (cdp) Essex County	94.15

Venezuelans 5 Years and Over Who Speak Spanish at Home
Top 10 Places Sorted by Number

Place	Number
No places met population threshold.	

Venezuelans 5 Years and Over Who Speak Spanish at Home
Top 10 Places Sorted by Percent

Place	Percent
No places met population threshold.	

Other Hispanics 5 Years and Over Who Speak Spanish at Home
Top 10 Places Sorted by Number

Place	Number
Paterson, NJ (city) Passaic County	9,874
Elizabeth, NJ (city) Union County	8,940
Newark, NJ (city) Essex County	8,465
Union City, NJ (city) Hudson County	7,694
Jersey City, NJ (city) Hudson County	7,655
North Bergen, NJ (township) Hudson County	4,451
West New York, NJ (town) Hudson County	4,376
Passaic, NJ (city) Passaic County	3,529
Perth Amboy, NJ (city) Middlesex County	2,717
Clifton, NJ (city) Passaic County	2,267

Other Hispanics 5 Years and Over Who Speak Spanish at Home
Top 10 Places Sorted by Percent

Place	Percent
Elmwood Park, NJ (borough) Bergen County	95.78
Somerville, NJ (borough) Somerset County	95.71
Paterson, NJ (city) Passaic County	93.40
Morris, NJ (town) Morris County	93.36
West New York, NJ (town) Hudson County	92.65
Union City, NJ (city) Hudson County	92.48
Bound Brook, NJ (borough) Somerset County	92.06

Place	
Weehawken, NJ (township) Hudson County	91.99
North Plainfield, NJ (borough) Somerset County	91.91
North Bergen, NJ (township) Hudson County	91.87

Foreign Born

Total Population
Top 10 Places Sorted by Number

Place	Number
Jersey City, NJ (city) Hudson County	81,554
Newark, NJ (city) Essex County	66,057
Elizabeth, NJ (city) Union County	52,975
Paterson, NJ (city) Passaic County	48,924
Union City, NJ (city) Hudson County	39,378
Edison, NJ (cdp) Middlesex County	32,351
Passaic, NJ (city) Passaic County	31,101
West New York, NJ (town) Hudson County	29,831
North Bergen, NJ (township) Hudson County	27,216
Clifton, NJ (city) Passaic County	22,992

Total Population
Top 10 Places Sorted by Percent

Place	Percent
West New York, NJ (town) Hudson County	65.18
Union City, NJ (city) Hudson County	58.70
Palisades Park, NJ (borough) Bergen County	56.96
Harrison, NJ (town) Hudson County	56.00
Guttenberg, NJ (town) Hudson County	49.18
Fairview, NJ (borough) Bergen County	48.39
North Bergen, NJ (township) Hudson County	46.76
Passaic, NJ (city) Passaic County	45.83
Fort Lee, NJ (borough) Bergen County	44.74
Elizabeth, NJ (city) Union County	43.94

Hispanic
Top 10 Places Sorted by Number

Place	Number
Union City, NJ (city) Hudson County	36,249
Paterson, NJ (city) Passaic County	35,719
Elizabeth, NJ (city) Union County	34,566
Newark, NJ (city) Essex County	28,947
West New York, NJ (town) Hudson County	26,468
Jersey City, NJ (city) Hudson County	25,388
Passaic, NJ (city) Passaic County	23,924
North Bergen, NJ (township) Hudson County	19,838
Perth Amboy, NJ (city) Middlesex County	13,866
New Brunswick, NJ (city) Middlesex County	11,575

Hispanic
Top 10 Places Sorted by Percent

Place	Percent
Bound Brook, NJ (borough) Somerset County	78.29
Morris, NJ (town) Morris County	77.84
West New York, NJ (town) Hudson County	73.44
New Providence, NJ (borough) Union County	71.05
Hanover, NJ (township) Morris County	69.74
City of Orange, NJ (township) Essex County	68.78
Orange, NJ (cdp) Essex County	68.78
Harrison, NJ (town) Hudson County	67.67
Fairview, NJ (borough) Bergen County	67.18
Springfield, NJ (cdp) Union County	66.84

Argentinian
Top 10 Places Sorted by Number

Place	Number
North Bergen, NJ (township) Hudson County	368

Argentinian
Top 10 Places Sorted by Percent

Place	Percent
North Bergen, NJ (township) Hudson County	75.26

Notes: Please refer to the User's Guide for an explanation of data; tables include places with populations > 9,999 and reflect only those areas that meet Summary File 4 population thresholds, therefore there may be less than 10 places listed

Bolivian
Top 10 Places Sorted by Number

Place	Number
No places met population threshold.	

Bolivian
Top 10 Places Sorted by Percent

Place	Percent
No places met population threshold.	

Central American
Top 10 Places Sorted by Number

Place	Number
Union City, NJ (city) Hudson County	5,542
Elizabeth, NJ (city) Union County	5,252
West New York, NJ (town) Hudson County	4,173
Jersey City, NJ (city) Hudson County	3,944
Plainfield, NJ (city) Union County	3,797
Trenton, NJ (city) Mercer County	3,310
Newark, NJ (city) Essex County	3,288
North Bergen, NJ (township) Hudson County	2,289
New Brunswick, NJ (city) Middlesex County	2,002
Paterson, NJ (city) Passaic County	1,583

Central American
Top 10 Places Sorted by Percent

Place	Percent
Cliffside Park, NJ (borough) Bergen County	93.56
Bloomfield, NJ (cdp) Essex County	91.98
Morris, NJ (town) Morris County	90.94
Bound Brook, NJ (borough) Somerset County	90.07
Atlantic City, NJ (city) Atlantic County	89.21
City of Orange, NJ (township) Essex County	89.08
Orange, NJ (cdp) Essex County	89.08
Bridgewater, NJ (township) Somerset County	88.25
Lakewood, NJ (township) Ocean County	86.21
Plainfield, NJ (city) Union County	85.31

Chilean
Top 10 Places Sorted by Number

Place	Number
North Bergen, NJ (township) Hudson County	411

Chilean
Top 10 Places Sorted by Percent

Place	Percent
North Bergen, NJ (township) Hudson County	85.09

Colombian
Top 10 Places Sorted by Number

Place	Number
Elizabeth, NJ (city) Union County	6,917
Paterson, NJ (city) Passaic County	4,061
North Bergen, NJ (township) Hudson County	3,236
Union City, NJ (city) Hudson County	2,238
West New York, NJ (town) Hudson County	2,171
Dover, NJ (town) Morris County	1,939
Englewood, NJ (city) Bergen County	1,711
Hackensack, NJ (city) Bergen County	1,395
Jersey City, NJ (city) Hudson County	1,328
Morris, NJ (town) Morris County	1,313

Colombian
Top 10 Places Sorted by Percent

Place	Percent
Lakewood, NJ (township) Ocean County	93.19
Morris, NJ (town) Morris County	90.93
Kearny, NJ (town) Hudson County	90.24
Piscataway, NJ (township) Middlesex County	88.28
Atlantic City, NJ (city) Atlantic County	87.55
North Plainfield, NJ (borough) Somerset County	87.14

West New York, NJ (town) Hudson County	85.57
Elizabeth, NJ (city) Union County	85.27
Perth Amboy, NJ (city) Middlesex County	84.68
Linden, NJ (city) Union County	83.82

Costa Rican
Top 10 Places Sorted by Number

Place	Number
Bound Brook, NJ (borough) Somerset County	1,138
Trenton, NJ (city) Mercer County	764
Paterson, NJ (city) Passaic County	659
Somerville, NJ (borough) Somerset County	472
Elizabeth, NJ (city) Union County	366

Costa Rican
Top 10 Places Sorted by Percent

Place	Percent
Trenton, NJ (city) Mercer County	93.63
Bound Brook, NJ (borough) Somerset County	92.90
Elizabeth, NJ (city) Union County	84.72
Paterson, NJ (city) Passaic County	81.97
Somerville, NJ (borough) Somerset County	80.68

Cuban
Top 10 Places Sorted by Number

Place	Number
Union City, NJ (city) Hudson County	8,749
West New York, NJ (town) Hudson County	8,205
North Bergen, NJ (township) Hudson County	5,808
Elizabeth, NJ (city) Union County	5,802
Newark, NJ (city) Essex County	2,360
Jersey City, NJ (city) Hudson County	1,221
Guttenberg, NJ (town) Hudson County	1,016
Weehawken, NJ (township) Hudson County	964
Perth Amboy, NJ (city) Middlesex County	752
Paterson, NJ (city) Passaic County	674

Cuban
Top 10 Places Sorted by Percent

Place	Percent
Passaic, NJ (city) Passaic County	92.59
Perth Amboy, NJ (city) Middlesex County	88.57
Guttenberg, NJ (town) Hudson County	85.59
Union City, NJ (city) Hudson County	84.67
West New York, NJ (town) Hudson County	84.12
Weehawken, NJ (township) Hudson County	83.32
Fairview, NJ (borough) Bergen County	81.40
Elizabeth, NJ (city) Union County	77.15
North Bergen, NJ (township) Hudson County	73.51
Newark, NJ (city) Essex County	72.11

Dominican
Top 10 Places Sorted by Number

Place	Number
Paterson, NJ (city) Passaic County	11,569
Passaic, NJ (city) Passaic County	7,216
Jersey City, NJ (city) Hudson County	6,867
Perth Amboy, NJ (city) Middlesex County	6,467
Union City, NJ (city) Hudson County	5,980
Newark, NJ (city) Essex County	4,737
West New York, NJ (town) Hudson County	3,216
Elizabeth, NJ (city) Union County	2,817
North Bergen, NJ (township) Hudson County	2,132
New Brunswick, NJ (city) Middlesex County	1,840

Dominican
Top 10 Places Sorted by Percent

Place	Percent
West New York, NJ (town) Hudson County	81.79
Weehawken, NJ (township) Hudson County	78.01
Atlantic City, NJ (city) Atlantic County	76.43
Union City, NJ (city) Hudson County	76.35

New Brunswick, NJ (city) Middlesex County	75.56
Paterson, NJ (city) Passaic County	75.46
Passaic, NJ (city) Passaic County	75.33
Kearny, NJ (town) Hudson County	74.05
Newark, NJ (city) Essex County	73.85
Perth Amboy, NJ (city) Middlesex County	73.71

Ecuadorian
Top 10 Places Sorted by Number

Place	Number
Newark, NJ (city) Essex County	7,060
Union City, NJ (city) Hudson County	3,577
Jersey City, NJ (city) Hudson County	3,390
North Bergen, NJ (township) Hudson County	1,747
West New York, NJ (town) Hudson County	1,722
Hackensack, NJ (city) Bergen County	1,685
Elizabeth, NJ (city) Union County	1,618
North Plainfield, NJ (borough) Somerset County	1,145
Belleville, NJ (cdp) Essex County	891
Kearny, NJ (town) Hudson County	797

Ecuadorian
Top 10 Places Sorted by Percent

Place	Percent
Dover, NJ (town) Morris County	91.67
Elizabeth, NJ (city) Union County	91.21
Hackensack, NJ (city) Bergen County	89.20
Plainfield, NJ (city) Union County	88.03
Kearny, NJ (town) Hudson County	86.82
North Plainfield, NJ (borough) Somerset County	86.61
Newark, NJ (city) Essex County	86.01
Belleville, NJ (cdp) Essex County	85.76
Union City, NJ (city) Hudson County	84.86
East Windsor, NJ (township) Mercer County	83.66

Guatelmalan
Top 10 Places Sorted by Number

Place	Number
Trenton, NJ (city) Mercer County	2,315
Plainfield, NJ (city) Union County	1,517
Newark, NJ (city) Essex County	706
Fairview, NJ (borough) Bergen County	568
Jersey City, NJ (city) Hudson County	555
Palisades Park, NJ (borough) Bergen County	548
West New York, NJ (town) Hudson County	486
Elizabeth, NJ (city) Union County	466
Union City, NJ (city) Hudson County	436
North Bergen, NJ (township) Hudson County	420

Guatelmalan
Top 10 Places Sorted by Percent

Place	Percent
Elizabeth, NJ (city) Union County	92.46
Palisades Park, NJ (borough) Bergen County	88.53
Fairview, NJ (borough) Bergen County	86.98
West New York, NJ (town) Hudson County	86.79
Plainfield, NJ (city) Union County	86.39
Union City, NJ (city) Hudson County	84.99
Jersey City, NJ (city) Hudson County	83.71
Newark, NJ (city) Essex County	82.67
North Plainfield, NJ (borough) Somerset County	82.01
Trenton, NJ (city) Mercer County	81.69

Honduran
Top 10 Places Sorted by Number

Place	Number
New Brunswick, NJ (city) Middlesex County	1,496
Jersey City, NJ (city) Hudson County	1,469
Union City, NJ (city) Hudson County	1,452
Elizabeth, NJ (city) Union County	922
Plainfield, NJ (city) Union County	815
Morris, NJ (town) Morris County	667
West New York, NJ (town) Hudson County	562

Notes: Please refer to the User's Guide for an explanation of data; tables include places with populations > 9,999 and reflect only those areas that meet Summary File 4 population thresholds, therefore there may be less than 10 places listed

Place	Number
North Bergen, NJ (township) Hudson County	521
Passaic, NJ (city) Passaic County	465
Newark, NJ (city) Essex County	461

Honduran
Top 10 Places Sorted by Percent

Place	Percent
Morris, NJ (town) Morris County	93.29
Elizabeth, NJ (city) Union County	89.00
Plainfield, NJ (city) Union County	88.01
West New York, NJ (town) Hudson County	85.28
New Brunswick, NJ (city) Middlesex County	81.97
Union City, NJ (city) Hudson County	78.27
Jersey City, NJ (city) Hudson County	76.55
Passaic, NJ (city) Passaic County	74.88
North Bergen, NJ (township) Hudson County	73.17
Newark, NJ (city) Essex County	71.47

Mexican
Top 10 Places Sorted by Number

Place	Number
Passaic, NJ (city) Passaic County	9,568
New Brunswick, NJ (city) Middlesex County	6,205
Paterson, NJ (city) Passaic County	3,892
West New York, NJ (town) Hudson County	2,441
Bridgeton, NJ (city) Cumberland County	2,338
Perth Amboy, NJ (city) Middlesex County	2,215
Union City, NJ (city) Hudson County	2,072
Atlantic City, NJ (city) Atlantic County	1,919
Jersey City, NJ (city) Hudson County	1,713
Lakewood, NJ (township) Ocean County	1,551

Mexican
Top 10 Places Sorted by Percent

Place	Percent
Roselle, NJ (borough) Union County	82.95
New Brunswick, NJ (city) Middlesex County	79.38
Dover, NJ (town) Morris County	79.35
West New York, NJ (town) Hudson County	77.94
Union City, NJ (city) Hudson County	77.26
Perth Amboy, NJ (city) Middlesex County	77.10
Elizabeth, NJ (city) Union County	76.83
Freehold, NJ (borough) Monmouth County	75.88
Atlantic City, NJ (city) Atlantic County	75.58
Asbury Park, NJ (city) Monmouth County	75.34

Nicaraguan
Top 10 Places Sorted by Number

Place	Number
Camden, NJ (city) Camden County	554
Jersey City, NJ (city) Hudson County	404

Nicaraguan
Top 10 Places Sorted by Percent

Place	Percent
Camden, NJ (city) Camden County	87.11
Jersey City, NJ (city) Hudson County	77.99

Panamanian
Top 10 Places Sorted by Number

Place	Number
No places met population threshold.	

Panamanian
Top 10 Places Sorted by Percent

Place	Percent
No places met population threshold.	

Paraguayan
Top 10 Places Sorted by Number

Place	Number
No places met population threshold.	

Paraguayan
Top 10 Places Sorted by Percent

Place	Percent
No places met population threshold.	

Peruvian
Top 10 Places Sorted by Number

Place	Number
Paterson, NJ (city) Passaic County	6,089
Elizabeth, NJ (city) Union County	2,721
Union City, NJ (city) Hudson County	1,760
Passaic, NJ (city) Passaic County	1,670
Clifton, NJ (city) Passaic County	1,514
Kearny, NJ (town) Hudson County	1,286
Newark, NJ (city) Essex County	1,283
Perth Amboy, NJ (city) Middlesex County	1,027
Harrison, NJ (town) Hudson County	993
North Bergen, NJ (township) Hudson County	813

Peruvian
Top 10 Places Sorted by Percent

Place	Percent
West New York, NJ (town) Hudson County	92.71
Union City, NJ (city) Hudson County	89.98
Jersey City, NJ (city) Hudson County	87.85
Carteret, NJ (borough) Middlesex County	87.84
Harrison, NJ (town) Hudson County	87.11
Elizabeth, NJ (city) Union County	86.77
North Bergen, NJ (township) Hudson County	85.13
Newark, NJ (city) Essex County	84.85
West Orange, NJ (cdp) Essex County	84.24
Clifton, NJ (city) Passaic County	83.65

Puerto Rican
Top 10 Places Sorted by Number

Place	Number
Jersey City, NJ (city) Hudson County	605
Newark, NJ (city) Essex County	541
Paterson, NJ (city) Passaic County	350
Elizabeth, NJ (city) Union County	271
Perth Amboy, NJ (city) Middlesex County	231
Camden, NJ (city) Camden County	225
New Brunswick, NJ (city) Middlesex County	158
Passaic, NJ (city) Passaic County	158
Union City, NJ (city) Hudson County	133
Atlantic City, NJ (city) Atlantic County	121

Puerto Rican
Top 10 Places Sorted by Percent

Place	Percent
City of Orange, NJ (township) Essex County	7.34
Orange, NJ (cdp) Essex County	7.34
Wayne, NJ (cdp) Passaic County	5.45
Lindenwold, NJ (borough) Camden County	5.30
Secaucus, NJ (town) Hudson County	4.57
New Brunswick, NJ (city) Middlesex County	4.54
Plainfield, NJ (city) Union County	4.14
New Milford, NJ (borough) Bergen County	3.90
Weehawken, NJ (township) Hudson County	3.60
Parsippany-Troy Hills, NJ (township) Morris County	3.59

Salvadoran
Top 10 Places Sorted by Number

Place	Number
Union City, NJ (city) Hudson County	3,163
Elizabeth, NJ (city) Union County	2,997
West New York, NJ (town) Hudson County	2,548
Newark, NJ (city) Essex County	1,324
Plainfield, NJ (city) Union County	1,127
North Bergen, NJ (township) Hudson County	1,068
Jersey City, NJ (city) Hudson County	904
Paterson, NJ (city) Passaic County	375
Fairview, NJ (borough) Bergen County	359
Guttenberg, NJ (town) Hudson County	287

Salvadoran
Top 10 Places Sorted by Percent

Place	Percent
Plainfield, NJ (city) Union County	84.04
West New York, NJ (town) Hudson County	83.49
Union City, NJ (city) Hudson County	81.60
Elizabeth, NJ (city) Union County	81.46
North Bergen, NJ (township) Hudson County	77.79
North Plainfield, NJ (borough) Somerset County	77.78
Fairview, NJ (borough) Bergen County	77.37
Jersey City, NJ (city) Hudson County	75.40
Newark, NJ (city) Essex County	73.93
Paterson, NJ (city) Passaic County	71.02

South American
Top 10 Places Sorted by Number

Place	Number
Elizabeth, NJ (city) Union County	13,060
Paterson, NJ (city) Passaic County	11,591
Newark, NJ (city) Essex County	10,180
Union City, NJ (city) Hudson County	8,499
North Bergen, NJ (township) Hudson County	6,927
Jersey City, NJ (city) Hudson County	6,436
West New York, NJ (town) Hudson County	5,404
Hackensack, NJ (city) Bergen County	3,679
Passaic, NJ (city) Passaic County	3,540
Clifton, NJ (city) Passaic County	3,361

South American
Top 10 Places Sorted by Percent

Place	Percent
Morris, NJ (town) Morris County	91.42
Irvington, NJ (cdp) Essex County	90.15
Bound Brook, NJ (borough) Somerset County	89.63
Palisades Park, NJ (borough) Bergen County	88.78
City of Orange, NJ (township) Essex County	88.51
Orange, NJ (cdp) Essex County	88.51
Atlantic City, NJ (city) Atlantic County	87.99
Harrison, NJ (town) Hudson County	87.08
Carteret, NJ (borough) Middlesex County	86.84
Lakewood, NJ (township) Ocean County	86.65

Spaniard
Top 10 Places Sorted by Number

Place	Number
Newark, NJ (city) Essex County	1,069
Kearny, NJ (town) Hudson County	528
Bayonne, NJ (city) Hudson County	404

Spaniard
Top 10 Places Sorted by Percent

Place	Percent
Newark, NJ (city) Essex County	80.07
Kearny, NJ (town) Hudson County	71.35
Bayonne, NJ (city) Hudson County	69.90

Uruguayan
Top 10 Places Sorted by Number

Place	Number
Elizabeth, NJ (city) Union County	627
West Orange, NJ (cdp) Essex County	230

Notes: Please refer to the User's Guide for an explanation of data; tables include places with populations > 9,999 and reflect only those areas that meet Summary File 4 population thresholds, therefore there may be less than 10 places listed

Uruguayan
Top 10 Places Sorted by Percent

Place	Percent
Elizabeth, NJ (city) Union County	76.93
West Orange, NJ (cdp) Essex County	65.16

Venezuelan
Top 10 Places Sorted by Number

Place	Number
No places met population threshold.	

Venezuelan
Top 10 Places Sorted by Percent

Place	Percent
No places met population threshold.	

Other Hispanic
Top 10 Places Sorted by Number

Place	Number
Paterson, NJ (city) Passaic County	5,957
Elizabeth, NJ (city) Union County	5,939
Newark, NJ (city) Essex County	5,455
Union City, NJ (city) Hudson County	5,139
Jersey City, NJ (city) Hudson County	4,436
West New York, NJ (town) Hudson County	2,888
North Bergen, NJ (township) Hudson County	2,235
Passaic, NJ (city) Passaic County	2,093
Perth Amboy, NJ (city) Middlesex County	1,596
Kearny, NJ (town) Hudson County	1,523

Other Hispanic
Top 10 Places Sorted by Percent

Place	Percent
Bound Brook, NJ (borough) Somerset County	80.50
Morris, NJ (town) Morris County	76.84
Summit, NJ (city) Union County	72.07
Dover, NJ (town) Morris County	67.83
City of Orange, NJ (township) Essex County	66.52
Orange, NJ (cdp) Essex County	66.52
Ventnor City, NJ (city) Atlantic County	64.49
Parsippany-Troy Hills, NJ (township) Morris County	61.68
Palisades Park, NJ (borough) Bergen County	61.09
Englewood, NJ (city) Bergen County	60.24

Foreign-Born Naturalized Citizens

Total Population
Top 10 Places Sorted by Number

Place	Number
Jersey City, NJ (city) Hudson County	33,609
Newark, NJ (city) Essex County	21,412
Elizabeth, NJ (city) Union County	19,345
Paterson, NJ (city) Passaic County	17,263
North Bergen, NJ (township) Hudson County	14,485
Union City, NJ (city) Hudson County	14,462
Edison, NJ (cdp) Middlesex County	14,460
Clifton, NJ (city) Passaic County	11,677
West New York, NJ (town) Hudson County	11,009
Woodbridge, NJ (township) Middlesex County	9,502

Total Population
Top 10 Places Sorted by Percent

Place	Percent
North Bergen, NJ (township) Hudson County	24.89
West New York, NJ (town) Hudson County	24.05
Union City, NJ (city) Hudson County	21.56
Fairview, NJ (borough) Bergen County	21.17
Fort Lee, NJ (borough) Bergen County	21.06
Palisades Park, NJ (borough) Bergen County	20.97
Cliffside Park, NJ (borough) Bergen County	20.79
Guttenberg, NJ (town) Hudson County	20.50

Weehawken, NJ (township) Hudson County	19.41
Ridgefield, NJ (borough) Bergen County	18.36

Hispanic
Top 10 Places Sorted by Number

Place	Number
Union City, NJ (city) Hudson County	13,044
Elizabeth, NJ (city) Union County	11,105
Paterson, NJ (city) Passaic County	10,750
North Bergen, NJ (township) Hudson County	10,133
West New York, NJ (town) Hudson County	9,831
Jersey City, NJ (city) Hudson County	8,671
Newark, NJ (city) Essex County	8,275
Passaic, NJ (city) Passaic County	4,856
Perth Amboy, NJ (city) Middlesex County	3,385
Clifton, NJ (city) Passaic County	3,135

Hispanic
Top 10 Places Sorted by Percent

Place	Percent
Franklin Lakes, NJ (borough) Bergen County	41.85
Springfield, NJ (cdp) Union County	37.56
Scotch Plains, NJ (cdp) Union County	35.67
Rutherford, NJ (borough) Bergen County	34.95
Ridgefield, NJ (borough) Bergen County	34.92
Hanover, NJ (township) Morris County	32.82
Paramus, NJ (borough) Bergen County	32.58
Livingston, NJ (cdp) Essex County	30.46
Cranford, NJ (cdp) Union County	30.42
Cedar Grove, NJ (cdp) Essex County	30.32

Argentinian
Top 10 Places Sorted by Number

Place	Number
North Bergen, NJ (township) Hudson County	126

Argentinian
Top 10 Places Sorted by Percent

Place	Percent
North Bergen, NJ (township) Hudson County	25.77

Bolivian
Top 10 Places Sorted by Number

Place	Number
No places met population threshold.	

Bolivian
Top 10 Places Sorted by Percent

Place	Percent
No places met population threshold.	

Central American
Top 10 Places Sorted by Number

Place	Number
Jersey City, NJ (city) Hudson County	1,315
Elizabeth, NJ (city) Union County	1,195
Union City, NJ (city) Hudson County	1,165
Newark, NJ (city) Essex County	881
North Bergen, NJ (township) Hudson County	703
West New York, NJ (town) Hudson County	684
Paterson, NJ (city) Passaic County	509
Trenton, NJ (city) Mercer County	505
Plainfield, NJ (city) Union County	436
Perth Amboy, NJ (city) Middlesex County	232

Central American
Top 10 Places Sorted by Percent

Place	Percent
Linden, NJ (city) Union County	37.12
West Orange, NJ (cdp) Essex County	36.50

Fort Lee, NJ (borough) Bergen County	30.13
Perth Amboy, NJ (city) Middlesex County	28.71
Jersey City, NJ (city) Hudson County	26.11
Paterson, NJ (city) Passaic County	25.49
Clifton, NJ (city) Passaic County	24.25
Hillside, NJ (cdp) Union County	23.45
North Bergen, NJ (township) Hudson County	23.26
Passaic, NJ (city) Passaic County	21.57

Chilean
Top 10 Places Sorted by Number

Place	Number
North Bergen, NJ (township) Hudson County	187

Chilean
Top 10 Places Sorted by Percent

Place	Percent
North Bergen, NJ (township) Hudson County	38.72

Colombian
Top 10 Places Sorted by Number

Place	Number
Elizabeth, NJ (city) Union County	1,915
Paterson, NJ (city) Passaic County	1,329
North Bergen, NJ (township) Hudson County	1,262
Union City, NJ (city) Hudson County	763
West New York, NJ (town) Hudson County	735
Englewood, NJ (city) Bergen County	606
Hackensack, NJ (city) Bergen County	597
Clifton, NJ (city) Passaic County	539
Jersey City, NJ (city) Hudson County	516
Passaic, NJ (city) Passaic County	485

Colombian
Top 10 Places Sorted by Percent

Place	Percent
Elmwood Park, NJ (borough) Bergen County	53.46
Union, NJ (cdp) Union County	45.54
Teaneck, NJ (cdp) Bergen County	44.84
Clifton, NJ (city) Passaic County	40.31
Piscataway, NJ (township) Middlesex County	37.33
Linden, NJ (city) Union County	36.73
Woodbridge, NJ (township) Middlesex County	36.18
Passaic, NJ (city) Passaic County	35.30
North Plainfield, NJ (borough) Somerset County	34.93
Weehawken, NJ (township) Hudson County	34.59

Costa Rican
Top 10 Places Sorted by Number

Place	Number
Paterson, NJ (city) Passaic County	98
Trenton, NJ (city) Mercer County	58
Elizabeth, NJ (city) Union County	57
Somerville, NJ (borough) Somerset County	43
Bound Brook, NJ (borough) Somerset County	20

Costa Rican
Top 10 Places Sorted by Percent

Place	Percent
Elizabeth, NJ (city) Union County	13.19
Paterson, NJ (city) Passaic County	12.19
Somerville, NJ (borough) Somerset County	7.35
Trenton, NJ (city) Mercer County	7.11
Bound Brook, NJ (borough) Somerset County	1.63

Cuban
Top 10 Places Sorted by Number

Place	Number
Union City, NJ (city) Hudson County	5,477
West New York, NJ (town) Hudson County	5,360
North Bergen, NJ (township) Hudson County	4,343

Notes: Please refer to the User's Guide for an explanation of data; tables include places with populations > 9,999 and reflect only those areas that meet Summary File 4 population thresholds, therefore there may be less than 10 places listed

Place	Number
Elizabeth, NJ (city) Union County	3,524
Newark, NJ (city) Essex County	1,596
Jersey City, NJ (city) Hudson County	750
Weehawken, NJ (township) Hudson County	726
Guttenberg, NJ (town) Hudson County	641
Paterson, NJ (city) Passaic County	487
Hoboken, NJ (city) Hudson County	398

Cuban
Top 10 Places Sorted by Percent

Place	Percent
Woodbridge, NJ (township) Middlesex County	63.21
Weehawken, NJ (township) Hudson County	62.75
Fort Lee, NJ (borough) Bergen County	62.73
North Bergen, NJ (township) Hudson County	54.97
West New York, NJ (town) Hudson County	54.95
Cliffside Park, NJ (borough) Bergen County	54.41
Guttenberg, NJ (town) Hudson County	54.00
Union City, NJ (city) Hudson County	53.00
Hoboken, NJ (city) Hudson County	52.72
Belleville, NJ (cdp) Essex County	51.89

Dominican
Top 10 Places Sorted by Number

Place	Number
Paterson, NJ (city) Passaic County	3,188
Jersey City, NJ (city) Hudson County	2,125
Union City, NJ (city) Hudson County	1,893
Passaic, NJ (city) Passaic County	1,815
Perth Amboy, NJ (city) Middlesex County	1,564
Newark, NJ (city) Essex County	1,469
North Bergen, NJ (township) Hudson County	1,044
West New York, NJ (town) Hudson County	906
Elizabeth, NJ (city) Union County	794
Clifton, NJ (city) Passaic County	604

Dominican
Top 10 Places Sorted by Percent

Place	Percent
Ridgefield Park, NJ (village) Bergen County	45.38
Bloomfield, NJ (cdp) Essex County	43.17
Bergenfield, NJ (borough) Bergen County	42.51
Teaneck, NJ (cdp) Bergen County	37.42
Fairview, NJ (borough) Bergen County	35.62
Fort Lee, NJ (borough) Bergen County	35.39
Hoboken, NJ (city) Hudson County	34.57
North Bergen, NJ (township) Hudson County	34.20
Clifton, NJ (city) Passaic County	33.11
Weehawken, NJ (township) Hudson County	32.59

Ecuadorian
Top 10 Places Sorted by Number

Place	Number
Jersey City, NJ (city) Hudson County	1,221
Union City, NJ (city) Hudson County	1,217
Newark, NJ (city) Essex County	1,027
North Bergen, NJ (township) Hudson County	829
West New York, NJ (town) Hudson County	494
Elizabeth, NJ (city) Union County	395
Belleville, NJ (cdp) Essex County	339
Hackensack, NJ (city) Bergen County	309
Kearny, NJ (town) Hudson County	264
Paterson, NJ (city) Passaic County	200

Ecuadorian
Top 10 Places Sorted by Percent

Place	Percent
Bayonne, NJ (city) Hudson County	41.08
North Bergen, NJ (township) Hudson County	37.41
Belleville, NJ (cdp) Essex County	32.63
Union City, NJ (city) Hudson County	28.87
Kearny, NJ (town) Hudson County	28.76
Jersey City, NJ (city) Hudson County	27.91

Place	Percent
Clifton, NJ (city) Passaic County	26.93
Passaic, NJ (city) Passaic County	25.58
Paterson, NJ (city) Passaic County	23.23
West New York, NJ (town) Hudson County	22.44

Guatelmalan
Top 10 Places Sorted by Number

Place	Number
Trenton, NJ (city) Mercer County	399
Newark, NJ (city) Essex County	213
Plainfield, NJ (city) Union County	172
Elizabeth, NJ (city) Union County	165
North Bergen, NJ (township) Hudson County	111
West New York, NJ (town) Hudson County	106
Jersey City, NJ (city) Hudson County	101
Union City, NJ (city) Hudson County	96
North Plainfield, NJ (borough) Somerset County	91
Bayonne, NJ (city) Hudson County	76

Guatelmalan
Top 10 Places Sorted by Percent

Place	Percent
Elizabeth, NJ (city) Union County	32.74
Newark, NJ (city) Essex County	24.94
North Plainfield, NJ (borough) Somerset County	21.82
Bayonne, NJ (city) Hudson County	20.82
North Bergen, NJ (township) Hudson County	19.89
West New York, NJ (town) Hudson County	18.93
Union City, NJ (city) Hudson County	18.71
Jersey City, NJ (city) Hudson County	15.23
Trenton, NJ (city) Mercer County	14.08
Plainfield, NJ (city) Union County	9.79

Honduran
Top 10 Places Sorted by Number

Place	Number
Jersey City, NJ (city) Hudson County	446
Union City, NJ (city) Hudson County	353
North Bergen, NJ (township) Hudson County	188
West New York, NJ (town) Hudson County	184
Elizabeth, NJ (city) Union County	175
Passaic, NJ (city) Passaic County	142
New Brunswick, NJ (city) Middlesex County	112
Newark, NJ (city) Essex County	84
Plainfield, NJ (city) Union County	68
Morris, NJ (town) Morris County	32

Honduran
Top 10 Places Sorted by Percent

Place	Percent
West New York, NJ (town) Hudson County	27.92
North Bergen, NJ (township) Hudson County	26.40
Jersey City, NJ (city) Hudson County	23.24
Passaic, NJ (city) Passaic County	22.87
Union City, NJ (city) Hudson County	19.03
Elizabeth, NJ (city) Union County	16.89
Newark, NJ (city) Essex County	13.02
Plainfield, NJ (city) Union County	7.34
New Brunswick, NJ (city) Middlesex County	6.14
Morris, NJ (town) Morris County	4.48

Mexican
Top 10 Places Sorted by Number

Place	Number
Passaic, NJ (city) Passaic County	674
Paterson, NJ (city) Passaic County	308
Atlantic City, NJ (city) Atlantic County	281
Bridgeton, NJ (city) Cumberland County	278
New Brunswick, NJ (city) Middlesex County	226
Newark, NJ (city) Essex County	207
Vineland, NJ (city) Cumberland County	184
Perth Amboy, NJ (city) Middlesex County	171
West New York, NJ (town) Hudson County	154

Place	Number
Camden, NJ (city) Camden County	141

Mexican
Top 10 Places Sorted by Percent

Place	Percent
Hackensack, NJ (city) Bergen County	14.80
West Orange, NJ (cdp) Essex County	12.98
Toms River, NJ (cdp) Ocean County	12.65
Dover, NJ (township) Ocean County	12.54
Bound Brook, NJ (borough) Somerset County	11.94
Atlantic City, NJ (city) Atlantic County	11.07
Vineland, NJ (city) Cumberland County	10.97
Bayonne, NJ (city) Hudson County	9.62
North Bergen, NJ (township) Hudson County	9.39
Newark, NJ (city) Essex County	9.07

Nicaraguan
Top 10 Places Sorted by Number

Place	Number
Camden, NJ (city) Camden County	161
Jersey City, NJ (city) Hudson County	119

Nicaraguan
Top 10 Places Sorted by Percent

Place	Percent
Camden, NJ (city) Camden County	25.31
Jersey City, NJ (city) Hudson County	22.97

Panamanian
Top 10 Places Sorted by Number

Place	Number
No places met population threshold.	

Panamanian
Top 10 Places Sorted by Percent

Place	Percent
No places met population threshold.	

Paraguayan
Top 10 Places Sorted by Number

Place	Number
No places met population threshold.	

Paraguayan
Top 10 Places Sorted by Percent

Place	Percent
No places met population threshold.	

Peruvian
Top 10 Places Sorted by Number

Place	Number
Paterson, NJ (city) Passaic County	2,133
Elizabeth, NJ (city) Union County	609
Kearny, NJ (town) Hudson County	521
Passaic, NJ (city) Passaic County	461
Newark, NJ (city) Essex County	437
Clifton, NJ (city) Passaic County	433
Union City, NJ (city) Hudson County	425
North Bergen, NJ (township) Hudson County	395
Jersey City, NJ (city) Hudson County	315
Harrison, NJ (town) Hudson County	266

Peruvian
Top 10 Places Sorted by Percent

Place	Percent
North Bergen, NJ (township) Hudson County	41.36
Jersey City, NJ (city) Hudson County	36.80
Woodbridge, NJ (township) Middlesex County	31.79
Belleville, NJ (cdp) Essex County	31.64

Notes: Please refer to the User's Guide for an explanation of data; tables include places with populations > 9,999 and reflect only those areas that meet Summary File 4 population thresholds, therefore there may be less than 10 places listed

Place	
Kearny, NJ (town) Hudson County	31.37
Garfield, NJ (city) Bergen County	29.69
Paterson, NJ (city) Passaic County	28.92
Newark, NJ (city) Essex County	28.90
West New York, NJ (town) Hudson County	28.31
West Orange, NJ (cdp) Essex County	24.28

Puerto Rican
Top 10 Places Sorted by Number

Place	Number
Jersey City, NJ (city) Hudson County	280
Newark, NJ (city) Essex County	246
Paterson, NJ (city) Passaic County	161
Elizabeth, NJ (city) Union County	112
Camden, NJ (city) Camden County	96
New Brunswick, NJ (city) Middlesex County	94
Perth Amboy, NJ (city) Middlesex County	84
Passaic, NJ (city) Passaic County	80
Union City, NJ (city) Hudson County	65
Trenton, NJ (city) Mercer County	62

Puerto Rican
Top 10 Places Sorted by Percent

Place	Percent
Wayne, NJ (cdp) Passaic County	4.88
New Milford, NJ (borough) Bergen County	3.90
Secaucus, NJ (town) Hudson County	3.11
New Brunswick, NJ (city) Middlesex County	2.70
Weehawken, NJ (township) Hudson County	2.67
Franklin, NJ (township) Somerset County	2.57
Woodbury, NJ (city) Gloucester County	2.41
West New York, NJ (town) Hudson County	2.24
Rutherford, NJ (borough) Bergen County	2.15
Elmwood Park, NJ (borough) Bergen County	2.10

Salvadoran
Top 10 Places Sorted by Number

Place	Number
Elizabeth, NJ (city) Union County	642
Union City, NJ (city) Hudson County	508
Jersey City, NJ (city) Hudson County	458
Newark, NJ (city) Essex County	363
North Bergen, NJ (township) Hudson County	323
West New York, NJ (town) Hudson County	280
Paterson, NJ (city) Passaic County	223
Plainfield, NJ (city) Union County	124
North Plainfield, NJ (borough) Somerset County	87
Fairview, NJ (borough) Bergen County	75

Salvadoran
Top 10 Places Sorted by Percent

Place	Percent
Paterson, NJ (city) Passaic County	42.23
Jersey City, NJ (city) Hudson County	38.20
North Plainfield, NJ (borough) Somerset County	24.79
North Bergen, NJ (township) Hudson County	23.53
Newark, NJ (city) Essex County	20.27
Elizabeth, NJ (city) Union County	17.45
Guttenberg, NJ (town) Hudson County	16.55
Fairview, NJ (borough) Bergen County	16.16
Union City, NJ (city) Hudson County	13.11
Plainfield, NJ (city) Union County	9.25

South American
Top 10 Places Sorted by Number

Place	Number
Paterson, NJ (city) Passaic County	4,013
Elizabeth, NJ (city) Union County	3,512
North Bergen, NJ (township) Hudson County	2,908
Union City, NJ (city) Hudson County	2,683
Jersey City, NJ (city) Hudson County	2,391
Newark, NJ (city) Essex County	2,117
West New York, NJ (town) Hudson County	1,759
Clifton, NJ (city) Passaic County	1,406
Passaic, NJ (city) Passaic County	1,167
Hackensack, NJ (city) Bergen County	1,128

South American
Top 10 Places Sorted by Percent

Place	Percent
Franklin, NJ (township) Somerset County	54.65
Old Bridge, NJ (township) Middlesex County	53.65
Nutley, NJ (cdp) Essex County	49.28
Teaneck, NJ (cdp) Bergen County	46.20
Union, NJ (cdp) Union County	44.09
Fort Lee, NJ (borough) Bergen County	43.65
Fairview, NJ (borough) Bergen County	42.04
Brick, NJ (township) Ocean County	41.15
Hoboken, NJ (city) Hudson County	40.04
Dover, NJ (township) Ocean County	39.80

Spaniard
Top 10 Places Sorted by Number

Place	Number
Newark, NJ (city) Essex County	341
Kearny, NJ (town) Hudson County	259
Bayonne, NJ (city) Hudson County	174

Spaniard
Top 10 Places Sorted by Percent

Place	Percent
Kearny, NJ (town) Hudson County	35.00
Bayonne, NJ (city) Hudson County	30.10
Newark, NJ (city) Essex County	25.54

Uruguayan
Top 10 Places Sorted by Number

Place	Number
Elizabeth, NJ (city) Union County	224
West Orange, NJ (cdp) Essex County	88

Uruguayan
Top 10 Places Sorted by Percent

Place	Percent
Elizabeth, NJ (city) Union County	27.48
West Orange, NJ (cdp) Essex County	24.93

Venezuelan
Top 10 Places Sorted by Number

Place	Number
No places met population threshold.	

Venezuelan
Top 10 Places Sorted by Percent

Place	Percent
No places met population threshold.	

Other Hispanic
Top 10 Places Sorted by Number

Place	Number
Paterson, NJ (city) Passaic County	2,032
Elizabeth, NJ (city) Union County	1,799
Jersey City, NJ (city) Hudson County	1,663
Union City, NJ (city) Hudson County	1,566
Newark, NJ (city) Essex County	1,418
North Bergen, NJ (township) Hudson County	962
West New York, NJ (town) Hudson County	899
Clifton, NJ (city) Passaic County	763
Passaic, NJ (city) Passaic County	620
Kearny, NJ (town) Hudson County	486

Other Hispanic
Top 10 Places Sorted by Percent

Place	Percent
Elmwood Park, NJ (borough) Bergen County	32.63
Lodi, NJ (borough) Bergen County	29.75
Parsippany-Troy Hills, NJ (township) Morris County	28.81
Belleville, NJ (cdp) Essex County	28.03
Rahway, NJ (city) Union County	26.66
Union, NJ (cdp) Union County	26.28
Clifton, NJ (city) Passaic County	25.30
Pleasantville, NJ (city) Atlantic County	23.77
Teaneck, NJ (cdp) Bergen County	23.39
Franklin, NJ (township) Somerset County	23.27

High School Graduates

Total Populations 25 Years and Over Who are High School Graduates
Top 10 Places Sorted by Number

Place	Number
Jersey City, NJ (city) Hudson County	112,835
Newark, NJ (city) Essex County	95,163
Edison, NJ (cdp) Middlesex County	59,269
Woodbridge, NJ (township) Middlesex County	57,841
Dover, NJ (township) Ocean County	53,856
Paterson, NJ (city) Passaic County	51,535
Toms River, NJ (cdp) Ocean County	51,381
Hamilton, NJ (township) Mercer County	50,700
Elizabeth, NJ (city) Union County	46,875
Brick, NJ (township) Ocean County	45,894

Total Populations 25 Years and Over Who are High School Graduates
Top 10 Places Sorted by Percent

Place	Percent
Plainsboro, NJ (township) Middlesex County	97.29
West Windsor, NJ (township) Mercer County	96.91
Princeton Meadows, NJ (cdp) Middlesex County	96.85
Millburn, NJ (cdp) Essex County	96.57
Ridgewood, NJ (village) Bergen County	95.88
Bernards, NJ (township) Somerset County	95.81
Randolph, NJ (township) Morris County	95.68
Westfield, NJ (town) Union County	95.36
Morris, NJ (township) Morris County	95.12
New Providence, NJ (borough) Union County	95.08

Hispanics 25 Years and Over Who are High School Graduates
Top 10 Places Sorted by Number

Place	Number
Jersey City, NJ (city) Hudson County	22,042
Newark, NJ (city) Essex County	21,248
Paterson, NJ (city) Passaic County	21,224
Elizabeth, NJ (city) Union County	20,424
Union City, NJ (city) Hudson County	17,334
North Bergen, NJ (township) Hudson County	14,121
West New York, NJ (town) Hudson County	10,980
Passaic, NJ (city) Passaic County	9,468
Perth Amboy, NJ (city) Middlesex County	8,347
Clifton, NJ (city) Passaic County	6,558

Hispanics 25 Years and Over Who are High School Graduates
Top 10 Places Sorted by Percent

Place	Percent
New Providence, NJ (borough) Union County	97.52
Saddle Brook, NJ (cdp) Bergen County	96.76
Pequannock, NJ (township) Morris County	95.15
Denville, NJ (township) Morris County	94.44
Westfield, NJ (town) Union County	94.00
Vernon, NJ (township) Sussex County	92.73
Cherry Hill Mall, NJ (cdp) Camden County	92.15
Rockaway, NJ (township) Morris County	91.38

Notes: Please refer to the User's Guide for an explanation of data; tables include places with populations > 9,999 and reflect only those areas that meet Summary File 4 population thresholds, therefore there may be less than 10 places listed

Place	Percent
Browns Mills, NJ (cdp) Burlington County	91.30
River Edge, NJ (borough) Bergen County	91.00

Argentinians 25 Years and Over Who are High School Graduates
Top 10 Places Sorted by Number

Place	Number
North Bergen, NJ (township) Hudson County	205

Argentinians 25 Years and Over Who are High School Graduates
Top 10 Places Sorted by Percent

Place	Percent
North Bergen, NJ (township) Hudson County	53.25

Bolivians 25 Years and Over Who are High School Graduates
Top 10 Places Sorted by Number

Place	Number
No places met population threshold.	

Bolivians 25 Years and Over Who are High School Graduates
Top 10 Places Sorted by Percent

Place	Percent
No places met population threshold.	

Central Americans 25 Years and Over Who are High School Graduates
Top 10 Places Sorted by Number

Place	Number
Elizabeth, NJ (city) Union County	1,658
Jersey City, NJ (city) Hudson County	1,624
Union City, NJ (city) Hudson County	1,344
West New York, NJ (town) Hudson County	1,088
Newark, NJ (city) Essex County	1,069
North Bergen, NJ (township) Hudson County	1,054
Trenton, NJ (city) Mercer County	701
Plainfield, NJ (city) Union County	696
Paterson, NJ (city) Passaic County	627
New Brunswick, NJ (city) Middlesex County	417

Central Americans 25 Years and Over Who are High School Graduates
Top 10 Places Sorted by Percent

Place	Percent
Woodbridge, NJ (township) Middlesex County	79.90
Fort Lee, NJ (borough) Bergen County	77.58
West Orange, NJ (cdp) Essex County	73.79
Englewood, NJ (city) Bergen County	68.80
Bridgewater, NJ (township) Somerset County	62.98
Bloomfield, NJ (cdp) Essex County	62.83
Clifton, NJ (city) Passaic County	62.58
East Windsor, NJ (township) Mercer County	57.55
North Bergen, NJ (township) Hudson County	56.82
Long Branch, NJ (city) Monmouth County	55.75

Chileans 25 Years and Over Who are High School Graduates
Top 10 Places Sorted by Number

Place	Number
North Bergen, NJ (township) Hudson County	260

Chileans 25 Years and Over Who are High School Graduates
Top 10 Places Sorted by Percent

Place	Percent
North Bergen, NJ (township) Hudson County	79.03

Colombians 25 Years and Over Who are High School Graduates
Top 10 Places Sorted by Number

Place	Number
Elizabeth, NJ (city) Union County	3,276
Paterson, NJ (city) Passaic County	2,191
North Bergen, NJ (township) Hudson County	1,826
Union City, NJ (city) Hudson County	1,270
West New York, NJ (town) Hudson County	1,110
Dover, NJ (town) Morris County	958
Hackensack, NJ (city) Bergen County	945
Englewood, NJ (city) Bergen County	897
Jersey City, NJ (city) Hudson County	830
Clifton, NJ (city) Passaic County	742

Colombians 25 Years and Over Who are High School Graduates
Top 10 Places Sorted by Percent

Place	Percent
Woodbridge, NJ (township) Middlesex County	84.82
Kearny, NJ (town) Hudson County	83.70
Teaneck, NJ (cdp) Bergen County	83.69
Lodi, NJ (borough) Bergen County	81.72
Hackensack, NJ (city) Bergen County	79.35
Union, NJ (cdp) Union County	79.18
Linden, NJ (city) Union County	79.02
Clifton, NJ (city) Passaic County	78.85
Parsippany-Troy Hills, NJ (township) Morris County	77.00
Perth Amboy, NJ (city) Middlesex County	76.67

Costa Ricans 25 Years and Over Who are High School Graduates
Top 10 Places Sorted by Number

Place	Number
Bound Brook, NJ (borough) Somerset County	326
Paterson, NJ (city) Passaic County	277
Elizabeth, NJ (city) Union County	217
Somerville, NJ (borough) Somerset County	190
Trenton, NJ (city) Mercer County	177

Costa Ricans 25 Years and Over Who are High School Graduates
Top 10 Places Sorted by Percent

Place	Percent
Elizabeth, NJ (city) Union County	68.45
Paterson, NJ (city) Passaic County	56.07
Somerville, NJ (borough) Somerset County	53.52
Bound Brook, NJ (borough) Somerset County	46.91
Trenton, NJ (city) Mercer County	34.64

Cubans 25 Years and Over Who are High School Graduates
Top 10 Places Sorted by Number

Place	Number
Union City, NJ (city) Hudson County	4,189
North Bergen, NJ (township) Hudson County	3,869
West New York, NJ (town) Hudson County	3,475
Elizabeth, NJ (city) Union County	3,317
Newark, NJ (city) Essex County	1,206
Jersey City, NJ (city) Hudson County	941
Guttenberg, NJ (town) Hudson County	586
Weehawken, NJ (township) Hudson County	585
Cliffside Park, NJ (borough) Bergen County	438
Union, NJ (cdp) Union County	419

Cubans 25 Years and Over Who are High School Graduates
Top 10 Places Sorted by Percent

Place	Percent
Bloomfield, NJ (cdp) Essex County	91.03
Union, NJ (cdp) Union County	87.47
Belleville, NJ (cdp) Essex County	85.71

Place	Percent
Edison, NJ (cdp) Middlesex County	82.38
Cliffside Park, NJ (borough) Bergen County	82.18
Bayonne, NJ (city) Hudson County	76.52
Linden, NJ (city) Union County	75.45
Woodbridge, NJ (township) Middlesex County	75.31
Fort Lee, NJ (borough) Bergen County	69.89
Passaic, NJ (city) Passaic County	67.18

Dominicans 25 Years and Over Who are High School Graduates
Top 10 Places Sorted by Number

Place	Number
Paterson, NJ (city) Passaic County	3,754
Jersey City, NJ (city) Hudson County	2,682
Union City, NJ (city) Hudson County	2,404
Passaic, NJ (city) Passaic County	2,241
Perth Amboy, NJ (city) Middlesex County	1,727
Newark, NJ (city) Essex County	1,599
Elizabeth, NJ (city) Union County	1,274
North Bergen, NJ (township) Hudson County	1,194
West New York, NJ (town) Hudson County	1,065
Clifton, NJ (city) Passaic County	639

Dominicans 25 Years and Over Who are High School Graduates
Top 10 Places Sorted by Percent

Place	Percent
Palisades Park, NJ (borough) Bergen County	90.34
Ridgefield Park, NJ (village) Bergen County	86.67
Woodbridge, NJ (township) Middlesex County	82.58
Teaneck, NJ (cdp) Bergen County	82.17
Fort Lee, NJ (borough) Bergen County	81.63
Bergenfield, NJ (borough) Bergen County	77.67
Fairview, NJ (borough) Bergen County	75.40
North Brunswick Township, NJ (cdp) Middlesex County	71.86
Bloomfield, NJ (cdp) Essex County	69.30
Garfield, NJ (city) Bergen County	66.22

Ecuadorians 25 Years and Over Who are High School Graduates
Top 10 Places Sorted by Number

Place	Number
Newark, NJ (city) Essex County	2,700
Union City, NJ (city) Hudson County	1,719
Jersey City, NJ (city) Hudson County	1,703
North Bergen, NJ (township) Hudson County	1,125
West New York, NJ (town) Hudson County	905
Elizabeth, NJ (city) Union County	855
Hackensack, NJ (city) Bergen County	723
Belleville, NJ (cdp) Essex County	534
Kearny, NJ (town) Hudson County	462
North Plainfield, NJ (borough) Somerset County	427

Ecuadorians 25 Years and Over Who are High School Graduates
Top 10 Places Sorted by Percent

Place	Percent
Bloomfield, NJ (cdp) Essex County	88.03
Belleville, NJ (cdp) Essex County	82.28
Clifton, NJ (city) Passaic County	79.17
Bayonne, NJ (city) Hudson County	77.23
Kearny, NJ (town) Hudson County	77.00
North Bergen, NJ (township) Hudson County	74.11
Passaic, NJ (city) Passaic County	73.25
Dover, NJ (town) Morris County	70.51
East Windsor, NJ (township) Mercer County	66.82
Elizabeth, NJ (city) Union County	63.95

Guatelmalans 25 Years and Over Who are High School Graduates
Top 10 Places Sorted by Number

Place	Number
Trenton, NJ (city) Mercer County	471

Notes: Please refer to the User's Guide for an explanation of data; tables include places with populations > 9,999 and reflect only those areas that meet Summary File 4 population thresholds, therefore there may be less than 10 places listed

Place	
Plainfield, NJ (city) Union County	258
Elizabeth, NJ (city) Union County	182
West New York, NJ (town) Hudson County	169
East Windsor, NJ (township) Mercer County	161
North Bergen, NJ (township) Hudson County	143
North Plainfield, NJ (borough) Somerset County	143
Bayonne, NJ (city) Hudson County	138
Jersey City, NJ (city) Hudson County	128
Newark, NJ (city) Essex County	127

Guatelmalans 25 Years and Over Who are High School Graduates
Top 10 Places Sorted by Percent

Place	Percent
Bayonne, NJ (city) Hudson County	62.16
East Windsor, NJ (township) Mercer County	58.97
Elizabeth, NJ (city) Union County	52.75
North Plainfield, NJ (borough) Somerset County	51.25
North Bergen, NJ (township) Hudson County	44.69
West New York, NJ (town) Hudson County	41.73
Trenton, NJ (city) Mercer County	30.27
Jersey City, NJ (city) Hudson County	29.91
Plainfield, NJ (city) Union County	26.49
Union City, NJ (city) Hudson County	23.84

Hondurans 25 Years and Over Who are High School Graduates
Top 10 Places Sorted by Number

Place	Number
Jersey City, NJ (city) Hudson County	668
Union City, NJ (city) Hudson County	491
Elizabeth, NJ (city) Union County	330
New Brunswick, NJ (city) Middlesex County	259
North Bergen, NJ (township) Hudson County	257
Morris, NJ (town) Morris County	202
West New York, NJ (town) Hudson County	179
Plainfield, NJ (city) Union County	178
Newark, NJ (city) Essex County	147
Passaic, NJ (city) Passaic County	107

Hondurans 25 Years and Over Who are High School Graduates
Top 10 Places Sorted by Percent

Place	Percent
North Bergen, NJ (township) Hudson County	62.38
Elizabeth, NJ (city) Union County	52.13
Jersey City, NJ (city) Hudson County	51.98
Morris, NJ (town) Morris County	47.98
West New York, NJ (town) Hudson County	44.75
Union City, NJ (city) Hudson County	42.04
Newark, NJ (city) Essex County	36.12
Plainfield, NJ (city) Union County	32.90
Passaic, NJ (city) Passaic County	27.94
New Brunswick, NJ (city) Middlesex County	25.69

Mexicans 25 Years and Over Who are High School Graduates
Top 10 Places Sorted by Number

Place	Number
Passaic, NJ (city) Passaic County	1,455
New Brunswick, NJ (city) Middlesex County	1,026
Paterson, NJ (city) Passaic County	865
Jersey City, NJ (city) Hudson County	794
Newark, NJ (city) Essex County	528
Atlantic City, NJ (city) Atlantic County	516
West New York, NJ (town) Hudson County	453
Union City, NJ (city) Hudson County	406
Perth Amboy, NJ (city) Middlesex County	402
Dover, NJ (town) Morris County	303

Mexicans 25 Years and Over Who are High School Graduates
Top 10 Places Sorted by Percent

Place	Percent
North Bergen, NJ (township) Hudson County	69.35
Brick, NJ (township) Ocean County	67.06
Bound Brook, NJ (borough) Somerset County	60.28
Jersey City, NJ (city) Hudson County	59.03
Hackensack, NJ (city) Bergen County	57.07
Bayonne, NJ (city) Hudson County	53.07
Somerset, NJ (cdp) Somerset County	52.56
Freehold, NJ (township) Monmouth County	52.51
Franklin, NJ (township) Somerset County	51.79
Asbury Park, NJ (city) Monmouth County	51.31

Nicaraguans 25 Years and Over Who are High School Graduates
Top 10 Places Sorted by Number

Place	Number
Jersey City, NJ (city) Hudson County	203
Camden, NJ (city) Camden County	95

Nicaraguans 25 Years and Over Who are High School Graduates
Top 10 Places Sorted by Percent

Place	Percent
Jersey City, NJ (city) Hudson County	67.00
Camden, NJ (city) Camden County	28.19

Panamanians 25 Years and Over Who are High School Graduates
Top 10 Places Sorted by Number

Place	Number
No places met population threshold.	

Panamanians 25 Years and Over Who are High School Graduates
Top 10 Places Sorted by Percent

Place	Percent
No places met population threshold.	

Paraguayans 25 Years and Over Who are High School Graduates
Top 10 Places Sorted by Number

Place	Number
No places met population threshold.	

Paraguayans 25 Years and Over Who are High School Graduates
Top 10 Places Sorted by Percent

Place	Percent
No places met population threshold.	

Peruvians 25 Years and Over Who are High School Graduates
Top 10 Places Sorted by Number

Place	Number
Paterson, NJ (city) Passaic County	3,598
Elizabeth, NJ (city) Union County	1,549
Passaic, NJ (city) Passaic County	978
Union City, NJ (city) Hudson County	962
Clifton, NJ (city) Passaic County	924
Kearny, NJ (town) Hudson County	809
Newark, NJ (city) Essex County	695
Perth Amboy, NJ (city) Middlesex County	619
Harrison, NJ (town) Hudson County	551
North Bergen, NJ (township) Hudson County	514

Peruvians 25 Years and Over Who are High School Graduates
Top 10 Places Sorted by Percent

Place	Percent
Belleville, NJ (cdp) Essex County	90.63
Woodbridge, NJ (township) Middlesex County	88.40
Elmwood Park, NJ (borough) Bergen County	88.04
Garfield, NJ (city) Bergen County	81.82
North Bergen, NJ (township) Hudson County	80.94
Clifton, NJ (city) Passaic County	80.14
Jersey City, NJ (city) Hudson County	77.00
Kearny, NJ (town) Hudson County	76.68
Perth Amboy, NJ (city) Middlesex County	75.95
Elizabeth, NJ (city) Union County	75.71

Puerto Ricans 25 Years and Over Who are High School Graduates
Top 10 Places Sorted by Number

Place	Number
Jersey City, NJ (city) Hudson County	9,420
Newark, NJ (city) Essex County	9,320
Paterson, NJ (city) Passaic County	6,357
Camden, NJ (city) Camden County	4,100
Elizabeth, NJ (city) Union County	4,096
Perth Amboy, NJ (city) Middlesex County	3,841
Vineland, NJ (city) Cumberland County	3,421
Trenton, NJ (city) Mercer County	2,361
Union City, NJ (city) Hudson County	2,319
Passaic, NJ (city) Passaic County	2,309

Puerto Ricans 25 Years and Over Who are High School Graduates
Top 10 Places Sorted by Percent

Place	Percent
Hillsborough, NJ (township) Somerset County	95.74
Rutherford, NJ (borough) Bergen County	95.55
Colonia, NJ (cdp) Middlesex County	90.21
Fort Lee, NJ (borough) Bergen County	89.75
Cherry Hill, NJ (township) Camden County	89.49
Browns Mills, NJ (cdp) Burlington County	88.62
Teaneck, NJ (cdp) Bergen County	88.54
Aberdeen, NJ (township) Monmouth County	87.74
Fords, NJ (cdp) Middlesex County	87.13
Fair Lawn, NJ (borough) Bergen County	86.78

Salvadorans 25 Years and Over Who are High School Graduates
Top 10 Places Sorted by Number

Place	Number
Elizabeth, NJ (city) Union County	688
Union City, NJ (city) Hudson County	536
West New York, NJ (town) Hudson County	524
Newark, NJ (city) Essex County	473
North Bergen, NJ (township) Hudson County	463
Jersey City, NJ (city) Hudson County	356
Plainfield, NJ (city) Union County	141
Guttenberg, NJ (town) Hudson County	110
Paterson, NJ (city) Passaic County	104
Fairview, NJ (borough) Bergen County	87

Salvadorans 25 Years and Over Who are High School Graduates
Top 10 Places Sorted by Percent

Place	Percent
North Bergen, NJ (township) Hudson County	55.38
Guttenberg, NJ (town) Hudson County	51.89
Jersey City, NJ (city) Hudson County	47.21
Newark, NJ (city) Essex County	43.63
Paterson, NJ (city) Passaic County	37.14
North Plainfield, NJ (borough) Somerset County	36.92
Fairview, NJ (borough) Bergen County	33.46
Elizabeth, NJ (city) Union County	32.38
West New York, NJ (town) Hudson County	27.00

Notes: Please refer to the User's Guide for an explanation of data; tables include places with populations > 9,999 and reflect only those areas that meet Summary File 4 population thresholds, therefore there may be less than 10 places listed

Place	
Union City, NJ (city) Hudson County	24.87

South Americans 25 Years and Over Who are High School Graduates
Top 10 Places Sorted by Number

Place	Number
Elizabeth, NJ (city) Union County	6,606
Paterson, NJ (city) Passaic County	6,499
Union City, NJ (city) Hudson County	4,429
Newark, NJ (city) Essex County	4,218
North Bergen, NJ (township) Hudson County	4,121
Jersey City, NJ (city) Hudson County	3,503
West New York, NJ (town) Hudson County	2,753
Clifton, NJ (city) Passaic County	2,247
Hackensack, NJ (city) Bergen County	2,099
Passaic, NJ (city) Passaic County	1,990

South Americans 25 Years and Over Who are High School Graduates
Top 10 Places Sorted by Percent

Place	Percent
Fort Lee, NJ (borough) Bergen County	92.07
Franklin, NJ (township) Somerset County	91.04
Dumont, NJ (borough) Bergen County	88.96
Woodbridge, NJ (township) Middlesex County	88.34
Wayne, NJ (cdp) Passaic County	88.08
Rockaway, NJ (township) Morris County	87.87
Teaneck, NJ (cdp) Bergen County	87.58
East Brunswick, NJ (cdp) Middlesex County	87.55
Bridgewater, NJ (township) Somerset County	86.56
Lodi, NJ (borough) Bergen County	86.43

Spaniards 25 Years and Over Who are High School Graduates
Top 10 Places Sorted by Number

Place	Number
Newark, NJ (city) Essex County	433
Kearny, NJ (town) Hudson County	269
Bayonne, NJ (city) Hudson County	149

Spaniards 25 Years and Over Who are High School Graduates
Top 10 Places Sorted by Percent

Place	Percent
Kearny, NJ (town) Hudson County	48.38
Newark, NJ (city) Essex County	43.00
Bayonne, NJ (city) Hudson County	37.63

Uruguayans 25 Years and Over Who are High School Graduates
Top 10 Places Sorted by Number

Place	Number
Elizabeth, NJ (city) Union County	296
West Orange, NJ (cdp) Essex County	110

Uruguayans 25 Years and Over Who are High School Graduates
Top 10 Places Sorted by Percent

Place	Percent
West Orange, NJ (cdp) Essex County	59.78
Elizabeth, NJ (city) Union County	50.95

Venezuelans 25 Years and Over Who are High School Graduates
Top 10 Places Sorted by Number

Place	Number
No places met population threshold.	

Venezuelans 25 Years and Over Who are High School Graduates
Top 10 Places Sorted by Percent

Place	Percent
No places met population threshold.	

Other Hispanics 25 Years and Over Who are High School Graduates
Top 10 Places Sorted by Number

Place	Number
Elizabeth, NJ (city) Union County	3,039
Jersey City, NJ (city) Hudson County	2,891
Newark, NJ (city) Essex County	2,875
Paterson, NJ (city) Passaic County	2,737
Union City, NJ (city) Hudson County	2,178
North Bergen, NJ (township) Hudson County	1,432
West New York, NJ (town) Hudson County	1,262
Clifton, NJ (city) Passaic County	1,047
Passaic, NJ (city) Passaic County	922
Kearny, NJ (town) Hudson County	863

Other Hispanics 25 Years and Over Who are High School Graduates
Top 10 Places Sorted by Percent

Place	Percent
Brick, NJ (township) Ocean County	85.48
Summit, NJ (city) Union County	85.33
Sayreville, NJ (borough) Middlesex County	83.98
Teaneck, NJ (cdp) Bergen County	83.30
Old Bridge, NJ (township) Middlesex County	83.14
Howell, NJ (township) Monmouth County	82.51
Lodi, NJ (borough) Bergen County	81.57
Belleville, NJ (cdp) Essex County	80.76
Wayne, NJ (cdp) Passaic County	79.19
Parsippany-Troy Hills, NJ (township) Morris County	78.47

College Graduates

Total Populations 25 Years and Over Who are Four-Year College Graduates
Top 10 Places Sorted by Number

Place	Number
Jersey City, NJ (city) Hudson County	42,676
Edison, NJ (cdp) Middlesex County	28,642
Cherry Hill, NJ (township) Camden County	22,831
Woodbridge, NJ (township) Middlesex County	18,463
Hoboken, NJ (city) Hudson County	17,007
Parsippany-Troy Hills, NJ (township) Morris County	15,748
Middletown, NJ (township) Monmouth County	15,634
Franklin, NJ (township) Somerset County	15,620
Wayne, NJ (cdp) Passaic County	15,497
Montclair, NJ (cdp) Essex County	15,291

Total Populations 25 Years and Over Who are Four-Year College Graduates
Top 10 Places Sorted by Percent

Place	Percent
Princeton, NJ (township) Mercer County	75.90
Millburn, NJ (cdp) Essex County	74.03
West Windsor, NJ (township) Mercer County	73.92
Plainsboro, NJ (township) Middlesex County	70.27
Princeton Meadows, NJ (cdp) Middlesex County	68.17
Bernards, NJ (township) Somerset County	67.44
Ridgewood, NJ (village) Bergen County	66.75
Morris, NJ (township) Morris County	63.58
Westfield, NJ (town) Union County	62.54
Tenafly, NJ (borough) Bergen County	62.15

Hispanics 25 Years and Over Who are Four-Year College Graduates
Top 10 Places Sorted by Number

Place	Number
Jersey City, NJ (city) Hudson County	4,408
Elizabeth, NJ (city) Union County	3,605
North Bergen, NJ (township) Hudson County	3,209
Union City, NJ (city) Hudson County	3,190
Newark, NJ (city) Essex County	2,607
West New York, NJ (town) Hudson County	2,436
Paterson, NJ (city) Passaic County	2,365
Passaic, NJ (city) Passaic County	1,254
Clifton, NJ (city) Passaic County	1,118
Perth Amboy, NJ (city) Middlesex County	1,078

Hispanics 25 Years and Over Who are Four-Year College Graduates
Top 10 Places Sorted by Percent

Place	Percent
Millburn, NJ (cdp) Essex County	58.88
Westfield, NJ (town) Union County	57.82
Voorhees, NJ (township) Camden County	53.66
Verona, NJ (cdp) Essex County	50.32
Oakland, NJ (borough) Bergen County	48.76
Berkeley Heights, NJ (cdp) Union County	47.95
South Orange, NJ (cdp) Essex County	46.05
Mount Laurel, NJ (township) Burlington County	45.99
Denville, NJ (township) Morris County	45.83
Bernards, NJ (township) Somerset County	45.63

Argentinians 25 Years and Over Who are Four-Year College Graduates
Top 10 Places Sorted by Number

Place	Number
North Bergen, NJ (township) Hudson County	44

Argentinians 25 Years and Over Who are Four-Year College Graduates
Top 10 Places Sorted by Percent

Place	Percent
North Bergen, NJ (township) Hudson County	11.43

Bolivians 25 Years and Over Who are Four-Year College Graduates
Top 10 Places Sorted by Number

Place	Number
No places met population threshold.	

Bolivians 25 Years and Over Who are Four-Year College Graduates
Top 10 Places Sorted by Percent

Place	Percent
No places met population threshold.	

Central Americans 25 Years and Over Who are Four-Year College Graduates
Top 10 Places Sorted by Number

Place	Number
Jersey City, NJ (city) Hudson County	260
North Bergen, NJ (township) Hudson County	211
Union City, NJ (city) Hudson County	209
Elizabeth, NJ (city) Union County	183
West New York, NJ (town) Hudson County	168
Plainfield, NJ (city) Union County	131
Paterson, NJ (city) Passaic County	117
Newark, NJ (city) Essex County	96
Morris, NJ (town) Morris County	87
Bayonne, NJ (city) Hudson County	71

Notes: Please refer to the User's Guide for an explanation of data; tables include places with populations > 9,999 and reflect only those areas that meet Summary File 4 population thresholds, therefore there may be less than 10 places listed

Central Americans 25 Years and Over Who are Four-Year College Graduates
Top 10 Places Sorted by Percent

Place	Percent
Clifton, NJ (city) Passaic County	20.65
Hackensack, NJ (city) Bergen County	20.36
Fort Lee, NJ (borough) Bergen County	17.94
Bloomfield, NJ (cdp) Essex County	16.78
Bridgewater, NJ (township) Somerset County	16.57
Englewood, NJ (city) Bergen County	15.38
Linden, NJ (city) Union County	14.57
Atlantic City, NJ (city) Atlantic County	13.61
East Windsor, NJ (township) Mercer County	13.39
Weehawken, NJ (township) Hudson County	12.56

Chileans 25 Years and Over Who are Four-Year College Graduates
Top 10 Places Sorted by Number

Place	Number
North Bergen, NJ (township) Hudson County	87

Chileans 25 Years and Over Who are Four-Year College Graduates
Top 10 Places Sorted by Percent

Place	Percent
North Bergen, NJ (township) Hudson County	26.44

Colombians 25 Years and Over Who are Four-Year College Graduates
Top 10 Places Sorted by Number

Place	Number
Elizabeth, NJ (city) Union County	571
North Bergen, NJ (township) Hudson County	286
West New York, NJ (town) Hudson County	257
Paterson, NJ (city) Passaic County	230
Jersey City, NJ (city) Hudson County	199
Hackensack, NJ (city) Bergen County	174
Union City, NJ (city) Hudson County	153
Englewood, NJ (city) Bergen County	142
Dover, NJ (town) Morris County	141
Clifton, NJ (city) Passaic County	113

Colombians 25 Years and Over Who are Four-Year College Graduates
Top 10 Places Sorted by Percent

Place	Percent
Kearny, NJ (town) Hudson County	33.23
Teaneck, NJ (cdp) Bergen County	31.72
Union, NJ (cdp) Union County	30.50
Parsippany-Troy Hills, NJ (township) Morris County	23.00
Edison, NJ (cdp) Middlesex County	19.71
Guttenberg, NJ (town) Hudson County	18.88
Woodbridge, NJ (township) Middlesex County	18.30
Weehawken, NJ (township) Hudson County	16.72
Piscataway, NJ (township) Middlesex County	16.44
Lakewood, NJ (township) Ocean County	15.98

Costa Ricans 25 Years and Over Who are Four-Year College Graduates
Top 10 Places Sorted by Number

Place	Number
Bound Brook, NJ (borough) Somerset County	34
Paterson, NJ (city) Passaic County	34
Elizabeth, NJ (city) Union County	31
Somerville, NJ (borough) Somerset County	27
Trenton, NJ (city) Mercer County	4

Costa Ricans 25 Years and Over Who are Four-Year College Graduates
Top 10 Places Sorted by Percent

Place	Percent
Elizabeth, NJ (city) Union County	9.78
Somerville, NJ (borough) Somerset County	7.61
Paterson, NJ (city) Passaic County	6.88
Bound Brook, NJ (borough) Somerset County	4.89
Trenton, NJ (city) Mercer County	0.78

Cubans 25 Years and Over Who are Four-Year College Graduates
Top 10 Places Sorted by Number

Place	Number
North Bergen, NJ (township) Hudson County	1,334
Union City, NJ (city) Hudson County	1,185
West New York, NJ (town) Hudson County	1,009
Elizabeth, NJ (city) Union County	885
Jersey City, NJ (city) Hudson County	361
Weehawken, NJ (township) Hudson County	244
Guttenberg, NJ (town) Hudson County	201
Cliffside Park, NJ (borough) Bergen County	197
Union, NJ (cdp) Union County	189
Newark, NJ (city) Essex County	188

Cubans 25 Years and Over Who are Four-Year College Graduates
Top 10 Places Sorted by Percent

Place	Percent
Bloomfield, NJ (cdp) Essex County	54.14
Union, NJ (cdp) Union County	39.46
Cliffside Park, NJ (borough) Bergen County	36.96
Fort Lee, NJ (borough) Bergen County	35.69
Edison, NJ (cdp) Middlesex County	30.21
Woodbridge, NJ (township) Middlesex County	26.93
Jersey City, NJ (city) Hudson County	25.58
Weehawken, NJ (township) Hudson County	23.80
Harrison, NJ (town) Hudson County	23.38
Bayonne, NJ (city) Hudson County	21.90

Dominicans 25 Years and Over Who are Four-Year College Graduates
Top 10 Places Sorted by Number

Place	Number
Jersey City, NJ (city) Hudson County	595
Paterson, NJ (city) Passaic County	459
Union City, NJ (city) Hudson County	404
Passaic, NJ (city) Passaic County	305
Newark, NJ (city) Essex County	296
Perth Amboy, NJ (city) Middlesex County	291
Elizabeth, NJ (city) Union County	264
North Bergen, NJ (township) Hudson County	233
West New York, NJ (town) Hudson County	201
Weehawken, NJ (township) Hudson County	136

Dominicans 25 Years and Over Who are Four-Year College Graduates
Top 10 Places Sorted by Percent

Place	Percent
Weehawken, NJ (township) Hudson County	26.93
Ridgefield Park, NJ (village) Bergen County	26.67
Palisades Park, NJ (borough) Bergen County	26.47
Fairview, NJ (borough) Bergen County	24.60
Bloomfield, NJ (cdp) Essex County	22.33
Teaneck, NJ (cdp) Bergen County	22.24
Bergenfield, NJ (borough) Bergen County	21.84
Guttenberg, NJ (town) Hudson County	19.79
Fort Lee, NJ (borough) Bergen County	19.43
Garfield, NJ (city) Bergen County	19.30

Ecuadorians 25 Years and Over Who are Four-Year College Graduates
Top 10 Places Sorted by Number

Place	Number
Newark, NJ (city) Essex County	465
Jersey City, NJ (city) Hudson County	344
Union City, NJ (city) Hudson County	297
North Bergen, NJ (township) Hudson County	262
Elizabeth, NJ (city) Union County	232
West New York, NJ (town) Hudson County	156
Kearny, NJ (town) Hudson County	126
Bloomfield, NJ (cdp) Essex County	96
Belleville, NJ (cdp) Essex County	94
Hackensack, NJ (city) Bergen County	82

Ecuadorians 25 Years and Over Who are Four-Year College Graduates
Top 10 Places Sorted by Percent

Place	Percent
Bloomfield, NJ (cdp) Essex County	33.80
Kearny, NJ (town) Hudson County	21.00
Elizabeth, NJ (city) Union County	17.35
North Bergen, NJ (township) Hudson County	17.26
Harrison, NJ (town) Hudson County	15.93
Belleville, NJ (cdp) Essex County	14.48
Bayonne, NJ (city) Hudson County	13.37
Clifton, NJ (city) Passaic County	12.50
Jersey City, NJ (city) Hudson County	11.91
West New York, NJ (town) Hudson County	10.58

Guatelmalans 25 Years and Over Who are Four-Year College Graduates
Top 10 Places Sorted by Number

Place	Number
Trenton, NJ (city) Mercer County	52
West New York, NJ (town) Hudson County	42
Union City, NJ (city) Hudson County	37
East Windsor, NJ (township) Mercer County	36
North Bergen, NJ (township) Hudson County	25
Elizabeth, NJ (city) Union County	24
Bayonne, NJ (city) Hudson County	21
Jersey City, NJ (city) Hudson County	19
Newark, NJ (city) Essex County	14
Palisades Park, NJ (borough) Bergen County	13

Guatelmalans 25 Years and Over Who are Four-Year College Graduates
Top 10 Places Sorted by Percent

Place	Percent
East Windsor, NJ (township) Mercer County	13.19
Union City, NJ (city) Hudson County	12.25
West New York, NJ (town) Hudson County	10.37
Bayonne, NJ (city) Hudson County	9.46
North Bergen, NJ (township) Hudson County	7.81
Elizabeth, NJ (city) Union County	6.96
Jersey City, NJ (city) Hudson County	4.44
Palisades Park, NJ (borough) Bergen County	4.00
Trenton, NJ (city) Mercer County	3.34
North Plainfield, NJ (borough) Somerset County	2.51

Hondurans 25 Years and Over Who are Four-Year College Graduates
Top 10 Places Sorted by Number

Place	Number
Union City, NJ (city) Hudson County	85
Jersey City, NJ (city) Hudson County	83
Plainfield, NJ (city) Union County	71
North Bergen, NJ (township) Hudson County	47
Morris, NJ (town) Morris County	44
West New York, NJ (town) Hudson County	38
Newark, NJ (city) Essex County	34
New Brunswick, NJ (city) Middlesex County	19
Elizabeth, NJ (city) Union County	16

Notes: Please refer to the User's Guide for an explanation of data; tables include places with populations > 9,999 and reflect only those areas that meet Summary File 4 population thresholds, therefore there may be less than 10 places listed

Passaic, NJ (city) Passaic County — 7

Hondurans 25 Years and Over Who are Four-Year College Graduates
Top 10 Places Sorted by Percent

Place	Percent
Plainfield, NJ (city) Union County	13.12
North Bergen, NJ (township) Hudson County	11.41
Morris, NJ (town) Morris County	10.45
West New York, NJ (town) Hudson County	9.50
Newark, NJ (city) Essex County	8.35
Union City, NJ (city) Hudson County	7.28
Jersey City, NJ (city) Hudson County	6.46
Elizabeth, NJ (city) Union County	2.53
New Brunswick, NJ (city) Middlesex County	1.88
Passaic, NJ (city) Passaic County	1.83

Mexicans 25 Years and Over Who are Four-Year College Graduates
Top 10 Places Sorted by Number

Place	Number
Jersey City, NJ (city) Hudson County	253
Passaic, NJ (city) Passaic County	167
New Brunswick, NJ (city) Middlesex County	105
Paterson, NJ (city) Passaic County	72
West New York, NJ (town) Hudson County	63
Union City, NJ (city) Hudson County	59
Newark, NJ (city) Essex County	57
Elizabeth, NJ (city) Union County	55
Atlantic City, NJ (city) Atlantic County	49
Franklin, NJ (township) Somerset County	46

Mexicans 25 Years and Over Who are Four-Year College Graduates
Top 10 Places Sorted by Percent

Place	Percent
Jersey City, NJ (city) Hudson County	18.81
Franklin, NJ (township) Somerset County	18.33
West Orange, NJ (cdp) Essex County	16.37
Somerset, NJ (cdp) Somerset County	16.28
Princeton, NJ (township) Mercer County	15.19
Freehold, NJ (township) Monmouth County	15.06
Brick, NJ (township) Ocean County	13.53
Old Bridge, NJ (township) Middlesex County	11.57
Bound Brook, NJ (borough) Somerset County	9.76
Bayonne, NJ (city) Hudson County	9.22

Nicaraguans 25 Years and Over Who are Four-Year College Graduates
Top 10 Places Sorted by Number

Place	Number
Jersey City, NJ (city) Hudson County	45
Camden, NJ (city) Camden County	0

Nicaraguans 25 Years and Over Who are Four-Year College Graduates
Top 10 Places Sorted by Percent

Place	Percent
Jersey City, NJ (city) Hudson County	14.85
Camden, NJ (city) Camden County	0.00

Panamanians 25 Years and Over Who are Four-Year College Graduates
Top 10 Places Sorted by Number

Place	Number

No places met population threshold.

Panamanians 25 Years and Over Who are Four-Year College Graduates
Top 10 Places Sorted by Percent

Place	Percent

No places met population threshold.

Paraguayans 25 Years and Over Who are Four-Year College Graduates
Top 10 Places Sorted by Number

Place	Number

No places met population threshold.

Paraguayans 25 Years and Over Who are Four-Year College Graduates
Top 10 Places Sorted by Percent

Place	Percent

No places met population threshold.

Peruvians 25 Years and Over Who are Four-Year College Graduates
Top 10 Places Sorted by Number

Place	Number
Paterson, NJ (city) Passaic County	482
Elizabeth, NJ (city) Union County	279
Kearny, NJ (town) Hudson County	220
Jersey City, NJ (city) Hudson County	127
Clifton, NJ (city) Passaic County	109
Union City, NJ (city) Hudson County	106
Passaic, NJ (city) Passaic County	98
Newark, NJ (city) Essex County	95
North Bergen, NJ (township) Hudson County	87
Harrison, NJ (town) Hudson County	73

Peruvians 25 Years and Over Who are Four-Year College Graduates
Top 10 Places Sorted by Percent

Place	Percent
Kearny, NJ (town) Hudson County	20.85
Jersey City, NJ (city) Hudson County	19.87
Woodbridge, NJ (township) Middlesex County	16.30
Belleville, NJ (cdp) Essex County	15.63
North Bergen, NJ (township) Hudson County	13.70
Elizabeth, NJ (city) Union County	13.64
Elmwood Park, NJ (borough) Bergen County	13.59
Carteret, NJ (borough) Middlesex County	13.31
West New York, NJ (town) Hudson County	11.68
West Orange, NJ (cdp) Essex County	10.29

Puerto Ricans 25 Years and Over Who are Four-Year College Graduates
Top 10 Places Sorted by Number

Place	Number
Jersey City, NJ (city) Hudson County	1,428
Newark, NJ (city) Essex County	705
Paterson, NJ (city) Passaic County	464
Perth Amboy, NJ (city) Middlesex County	415
Elizabeth, NJ (city) Union County	402
Vineland, NJ (city) Cumberland County	372
Hoboken, NJ (city) Hudson County	346
North Bergen, NJ (township) Hudson County	345
Clifton, NJ (city) Passaic County	312
Camden, NJ (city) Camden County	287

Puerto Ricans 25 Years and Over Who are Four-Year College Graduates
Top 10 Places Sorted by Percent

Place	Percent
Hillsborough, NJ (township) Somerset County	47.87
Montclair, NJ (cdp) Essex County	47.59
Rutherford, NJ (borough) Bergen County	35.27
Fort Lee, NJ (borough) Bergen County	33.24

(continued from West Orange row):

Place	Percent
West Orange, NJ (cdp) Essex County	32.71
Bridgewater, NJ (township) Somerset County	31.15
Parsippany-Troy Hills, NJ (township) Morris County	31.14
Wayne, NJ (cdp) Passaic County	30.65
Middletown, NJ (township) Monmouth County	30.30
Evesham, NJ (township) Burlington County	28.77

Salvadorans 25 Years and Over Who are Four-Year College Graduates
Top 10 Places Sorted by Number

Place	Number
North Bergen, NJ (township) Hudson County	107
Elizabeth, NJ (city) Union County	73
West New York, NJ (town) Hudson County	66
Jersey City, NJ (city) Hudson County	60
Union City, NJ (city) Hudson County	47
Plainfield, NJ (city) Union County	42
Paterson, NJ (city) Passaic County	34
North Plainfield, NJ (borough) Somerset County	25
Newark, NJ (city) Essex County	24
Fairview, NJ (borough) Bergen County	20

Salvadorans 25 Years and Over Who are Four-Year College Graduates
Top 10 Places Sorted by Percent

Place	Percent
North Bergen, NJ (township) Hudson County	12.80
Paterson, NJ (city) Passaic County	12.14
North Plainfield, NJ (borough) Somerset County	11.68
Jersey City, NJ (city) Hudson County	7.96
Fairview, NJ (borough) Bergen County	7.69
Plainfield, NJ (city) Union County	5.31
Elizabeth, NJ (city) Union County	3.44
West New York, NJ (town) Hudson County	3.40
Newark, NJ (city) Essex County	2.21
Union City, NJ (city) Hudson County	2.18

South Americans 25 Years and Over Who are Four-Year College Graduates
Top 10 Places Sorted by Number

Place	Number
Elizabeth, NJ (city) Union County	1,242
Jersey City, NJ (city) Hudson County	859
Paterson, NJ (city) Passaic County	836
North Bergen, NJ (township) Hudson County	801
Newark, NJ (city) Essex County	670
Union City, NJ (city) Hudson County	650
West New York, NJ (town) Hudson County	604
Kearny, NJ (town) Hudson County	509
Hackensack, NJ (city) Bergen County	351
Clifton, NJ (city) Passaic County	345

South Americans 25 Years and Over Who are Four-Year College Graduates
Top 10 Places Sorted by Percent

Place	Percent
East Brunswick, NJ (cdp) Middlesex County	45.14
Hoboken, NJ (city) Hudson County	37.30
Teaneck, NJ (cdp) Bergen County	35.29
Montclair, NJ (cdp) Essex County	34.68
Franklin, NJ (township) Somerset County	29.97
Fort Lee, NJ (borough) Bergen County	28.64
Secaucus, NJ (town) Hudson County	27.85
Bloomfield, NJ (cdp) Essex County	27.78
Bridgewater, NJ (township) Somerset County	27.19
Roselle Park, NJ (borough) Union County	27.10

Spaniards 25 Years and Over Who are Four-Year College Graduates
Top 10 Places Sorted by Number

Place	Number
Newark, NJ (city) Essex County	116
Kearny, NJ (town) Hudson County	83

Notes: Please refer to the User's Guide for an explanation of data; tables include places with populations > 9,999 and reflect only those areas that meet Summary File 4 population thresholds, therefore there may be less than 10 places listed

Bayonne, NJ (city) Hudson County   15

Spaniards 25 Years and Over Who are Four-Year College Graduates
Top 10 Places Sorted by Percent

Place	Percent
Kearny, NJ (town) Hudson County	14.93
Newark, NJ (city) Essex County	11.52
Bayonne, NJ (city) Hudson County	3.79

Uruguayans 25 Years and Over Who are Four-Year College Graduates
Top 10 Places Sorted by Number

Place	Number
Elizabeth, NJ (city) Union County	43
West Orange, NJ (cdp) Essex County	0

Uruguayans 25 Years and Over Who are Four-Year College Graduates
Top 10 Places Sorted by Percent

Place	Percent
Elizabeth, NJ (city) Union County	7.40
West Orange, NJ (cdp) Essex County	0.00

Venezuelans 25 Years and Over Who are Four-Year College Graduates
Top 10 Places Sorted by Number

Place	Number
No places met population threshold.	

Venezuelans 25 Years and Over Who are Four-Year College Graduates
Top 10 Places Sorted by Percent

Place	Percent
No places met population threshold.	

Other Hispanics 25 Years and Over Who are Four-Year College Graduates
Top 10 Places Sorted by Number

Place	Number
Elizabeth, NJ (city) Union County	559
Jersey City, NJ (city) Hudson County	545
Newark, NJ (city) Essex County	479
Union City, NJ (city) Hudson County	369
Paterson, NJ (city) Passaic County	366
North Bergen, NJ (township) Hudson County	251
West New York, NJ (town) Hudson County	242
Clifton, NJ (city) Passaic County	200
Edison, NJ (cdp) Middlesex County	187
Passaic, NJ (city) Passaic County	181

Other Hispanics 25 Years and Over Who are Four-Year College Graduates
Top 10 Places Sorted by Percent

Place	Percent
Fort Lee, NJ (borough) Bergen County	37.26
Hoboken, NJ (city) Hudson County	32.64
Wayne, NJ (cdp) Passaic County	31.79
Summit, NJ (city) Union County	29.33
Edison, NJ (cdp) Middlesex County	27.38
Ridgefield, NJ (borough) Bergen County	26.90
Bridgewater, NJ (township) Somerset County	25.97
Harrison, NJ (town) Hudson County	24.24
Cliffside Park, NJ (borough) Bergen County	23.45
Nutley, NJ (cdp) Essex County	23.05

Median Household Income

Total Population
Top 10 Places Sorted by Number

Place	Dollars
Franklin Lakes, NJ (borough) Bergen County	132,373
Millburn, NJ (cdp) Essex County	130,848
West Windsor, NJ (township) Mercer County	116,335
Colts Neck, NJ (township) Monmouth County	109,190
Berkeley Heights, NJ (cdp) Union County	107,716
Bernards, NJ (township) Somerset County	107,204
Ridgewood, NJ (village) Bergen County	104,286
Warren, NJ (township) Somerset County	103,677
Wyckoff, NJ (cdp) Bergen County	103,614
Morris, NJ (township) Morris County	101,902

Hispanic
Top 10 Places Sorted by Number

Place	Dollars
Franklin Lakes, NJ (borough) Bergen County	179,036
Wyckoff, NJ (cdp) Bergen County	120,813
West Caldwell, NJ (cdp) Essex County	112,610
Denville, NJ (township) Morris County	104,457
Marlboro, NJ (township) Monmouth County	103,813
West Windsor, NJ (township) Mercer County	99,329
Cedar Grove, NJ (cdp) Essex County	96,798
Berkeley Heights, NJ (cdp) Union County	94,795
Verona, NJ (cdp) Essex County	94,260
Ridgewood, NJ (village) Bergen County	93,241

Argentinian
Top 10 Places Sorted by Number

Place	Dollars
North Bergen, NJ (township) Hudson County	30,962

Bolivian
Top 10 Places Sorted by Number

Place	Dollars
No places met population threshold.	

Central American
Top 10 Places Sorted by Number

Place	Dollars
Woodbridge, NJ (township) Middlesex County	73,542
Hillside, NJ (cdp) Union County	67,292
Englewood, NJ (city) Bergen County	64,375
Fort Lee, NJ (borough) Bergen County	64,125
Morris, NJ (town) Morris County	57,500
West Orange, NJ (cdp) Essex County	56,724
Somerville, NJ (borough) Somerset County	56,042
East Windsor, NJ (township) Mercer County	55,592
Bloomfield, NJ (cdp) Essex County	54,750
Bridgewater, NJ (township) Somerset County	51,635

Chilean
Top 10 Places Sorted by Number

Place	Dollars
North Bergen, NJ (township) Hudson County	61,875

Colombian
Top 10 Places Sorted by Number

Place	Dollars
Union, NJ (cdp) Union County	77,378
Teaneck, NJ (cdp) Bergen County	69,417
Woodbridge, NJ (township) Middlesex County	64,375
Piscataway, NJ (township) Middlesex County	59,676
Clifton, NJ (city) Passaic County	56,364
Edison, NJ (cdp) Middlesex County	56,250
Kearny, NJ (town) Hudson County	55,417
Garfield, NJ (city) Bergen County	54,554
Englewood, NJ (city) Bergen County	53,750

Dover, NJ (town) Morris County   52,279

Costa Rican
Top 10 Places Sorted by Number

Place	Dollars
Somerville, NJ (borough) Somerset County	58,375
Trenton, NJ (city) Mercer County	41,339
Bound Brook, NJ (borough) Somerset County	37,969
Paterson, NJ (city) Passaic County	35,250
Elizabeth, NJ (city) Union County	30,500

Cuban
Top 10 Places Sorted by Number

Place	Dollars
Union, NJ (cdp) Union County	75,801
Edison, NJ (cdp) Middlesex County	70,954
Elmwood Park, NJ (borough) Bergen County	65,625
Fort Lee, NJ (borough) Bergen County	65,357
Woodbridge, NJ (township) Middlesex County	65,125
Bloomfield, NJ (cdp) Essex County	63,125
Bayonne, NJ (city) Hudson County	58,661
Linden, NJ (city) Union County	56,591
Cliffside Park, NJ (borough) Bergen County	54,875
Kearny, NJ (town) Hudson County	54,432

Dominican
Top 10 Places Sorted by Number

Place	Dollars
Teaneck, NJ (cdp) Bergen County	72,702
Woodbridge, NJ (township) Middlesex County	63,875
Bergenfield, NJ (borough) Bergen County	60,250
Ridgefield Park, NJ (village) Bergen County	56,875
Palisades Park, NJ (borough) Bergen County	56,607
Fort Lee, NJ (borough) Bergen County	51,500
Bloomfield, NJ (cdp) Essex County	48,542
Clifton, NJ (city) Passaic County	45,938
Pleasantville, NJ (city) Atlantic County	44,375
Garfield, NJ (city) Bergen County	44,191

Ecuadorian
Top 10 Places Sorted by Number

Place	Dollars
Dover, NJ (town) Morris County	70,234
Bloomfield, NJ (cdp) Essex County	50,543
North Plainfield, NJ (borough) Somerset County	50,125
Kearny, NJ (town) Hudson County	49,598
Belleville, NJ (cdp) Essex County	49,259
East Windsor, NJ (township) Mercer County	48,558
North Bergen, NJ (township) Hudson County	44,618
Plainfield, NJ (city) Union County	44,167
Passaic, NJ (city) Passaic County	44,000
Harrison, NJ (town) Hudson County	42,308

Guatelmalan
Top 10 Places Sorted by Number

Place	Dollars
East Windsor, NJ (township) Mercer County	55,592
Jersey City, NJ (city) Hudson County	53,750
North Bergen, NJ (township) Hudson County	52,625
Trenton, NJ (city) Mercer County	48,083
West New York, NJ (town) Hudson County	48,000
Plainfield, NJ (city) Union County	47,546
Bayonne, NJ (city) Hudson County	46,429
North Plainfield, NJ (borough) Somerset County	46,000
Elizabeth, NJ (city) Union County	41,563
Fairview, NJ (borough) Bergen County	36,932

Honduran
Top 10 Places Sorted by Number

Place	Dollars
Morris, NJ (town) Morris County	61,500
Elizabeth, NJ (city) Union County	50,000

Notes: Please refer to the User's Guide for an explanation of data; tables include places with populations > 9,999 and reflect only those areas that meet Summary File 4 population thresholds, therefore there may be less than 10 places listed

Place		Dollars
New Brunswick, NJ (city) Middlesex County		43,561
North Bergen, NJ (township) Hudson County		39,722
Plainfield, NJ (city) Union County		39,333
West New York, NJ (town) Hudson County		37,292
Jersey City, NJ (city) Hudson County		36,346
Passaic, NJ (city) Passaic County		31,250
Union City, NJ (city) Hudson County		28,793
Newark, NJ (city) Essex County		25,461

Mexican
Top 10 Places Sorted by Number

Place	Dollars
Brick, NJ (township) Ocean County	91,981
Freehold, NJ (township) Monmouth County	81,652
Edison, NJ (cdp) Middlesex County	66,442
Woodbridge, NJ (township) Middlesex County	57,656
Red Bank, NJ (borough) Monmouth County	52,422
New Brunswick, NJ (city) Middlesex County	49,156
Dover, NJ (town) Morris County	47,798
Somerset, NJ (cdp) Somerset County	47,679
Franklin, NJ (township) Somerset County	47,292
Garfield, NJ (city) Bergen County	46,696

Nicaraguan
Top 10 Places Sorted by Number

Place	Dollars
Jersey City, NJ (city) Hudson County	53,571
Camden, NJ (city) Camden County	44,310

Panamanian
Top 10 Places Sorted by Number

Place	Dollars
No places met population threshold.	

Paraguayan
Top 10 Places Sorted by Number

Place	Dollars
No places met population threshold.	

Peruvian
Top 10 Places Sorted by Number

Place	Dollars
Elmwood Park, NJ (borough) Bergen County	63,000
Clifton, NJ (city) Passaic County	53,529
Carteret, NJ (borough) Middlesex County	52,625
North Bergen, NJ (township) Hudson County	50,511
Woodbridge, NJ (township) Middlesex County	50,417
Kearny, NJ (town) Hudson County	46,691
Perth Amboy, NJ (city) Middlesex County	43,523
Paterson, NJ (city) Passaic County	42,610
Belleville, NJ (cdp) Essex County	42,500
Garfield, NJ (city) Bergen County	39,464

Puerto Rican
Top 10 Places Sorted by Number

Place	Dollars
Freehold, NJ (township) Monmouth County	94,819
West Milford, NJ (cdp) Passaic County	92,440
Parsippany-Troy Hills, NJ (township) Morris County	85,992
Bergenfield, NJ (borough) Bergen County	83,770
Colonia, NJ (cdp) Middlesex County	82,338
Wayne, NJ (cdp) Passaic County	79,700
Fair Lawn, NJ (borough) Bergen County	79,342
Hillsborough, NJ (township) Somerset County	78,461
Manalapan, NJ (township) Monmouth County	75,874
Bridgewater, NJ (township) Somerset County	73,750

Salvadoran
Top 10 Places Sorted by Number

Place	Dollars
Plainfield, NJ (city) Union County	50,000

Place	Dollars
Fairview, NJ (borough) Bergen County	48,750
North Plainfield, NJ (borough) Somerset County	45,781
Elizabeth, NJ (city) Union County	42,532
Guttenberg, NJ (town) Hudson County	39,286
Newark, NJ (city) Essex County	38,750
Jersey City, NJ (city) Hudson County	38,675
North Bergen, NJ (township) Hudson County	37,697
Paterson, NJ (city) Passaic County	34,063
West New York, NJ (town) Hudson County	32,894

South American
Top 10 Places Sorted by Number

Place	Dollars
Montclair, NJ (cdp) Essex County	92,690
Secaucus, NJ (town) Hudson County	80,686
Wayne, NJ (cdp) Passaic County	74,479
Palisades Park, NJ (borough) Bergen County	72,500
Union, NJ (cdp) Union County	72,321
Franklin, NJ (township) Somerset County	69,375
Teaneck, NJ (cdp) Bergen County	68,917
Middletown, NJ (township) Monmouth County	68,854
Fort Lee, NJ (borough) Bergen County	68,641
Piscataway, NJ (township) Middlesex County	68,625

Spaniard
Top 10 Places Sorted by Number

Place	Dollars
Kearny, NJ (town) Hudson County	68,542
Bayonne, NJ (city) Hudson County	47,083
Newark, NJ (city) Essex County	45,417

Uruguayan
Top 10 Places Sorted by Number

Place	Dollars
West Orange, NJ (cdp) Essex County	48,750
Elizabeth, NJ (city) Union County	35,125

Venezuelan
Top 10 Places Sorted by Number

Place	Dollars
No places met population threshold.	

Other Hispanic
Top 10 Places Sorted by Number

Place	Dollars
Bridgewater, NJ (township) Somerset County	95,510
Ridgefield, NJ (borough) Bergen County	77,631
Nutley, NJ (cdp) Essex County	71,838
Howell, NJ (township) Monmouth County	71,667
Wayne, NJ (cdp) Passaic County	71,429
Dover, NJ (township) Ocean County	70,882
Toms River, NJ (cdp) Ocean County	70,882
Old Bridge, NJ (township) Middlesex County	67,679
Teaneck, NJ (cdp) Bergen County	67,344
Sayreville, NJ (borough) Middlesex County	67,143

Per Capita Income

Total Population
Top 10 Places Sorted by Number

Place	Dollars
Millburn, NJ (cdp) Essex County	76,796
Summit, NJ (city) Union County	62,598
Franklin Lakes, NJ (borough) Bergen County	59,763
Bernards, NJ (township) Somerset County	56,521
Princeton, NJ (township) Mercer County	56,360
Morris, NJ (township) Morris County	54,782
Tenafly, NJ (borough) Bergen County	53,170
Ridgewood, NJ (village) Bergen County	51,658
Warren, NJ (township) Somerset County	49,475
Wyckoff, NJ (cdp) Bergen County	49,375

Hispanic
Top 10 Places Sorted by Number

Place	Dollars
Franklin Lakes, NJ (borough) Bergen County	44,597
Denville, NJ (township) Morris County	43,301
Metuchen, NJ (borough) Middlesex County	38,622
West Paterson, NJ (borough) Passaic County	38,502
Wyckoff, NJ (cdp) Bergen County	37,867
Cranford, NJ (cdp) Union County	35,413
Montville, NJ (township) Morris County	34,941
West Caldwell, NJ (cdp) Essex County	33,642
Warren, NJ (township) Somerset County	33,499
Bernards, NJ (township) Somerset County	33,406

Argentinian
Top 10 Places Sorted by Number

Place	Dollars
North Bergen, NJ (township) Hudson County	26,338

Bolivian
Top 10 Places Sorted by Number

Place	Dollars
No places met population threshold.	

Central American
Top 10 Places Sorted by Number

Place	Dollars
West Orange, NJ (cdp) Essex County	26,962
North Bergen, NJ (township) Hudson County	21,602
Linden, NJ (city) Union County	19,171
Bridgewater, NJ (township) Somerset County	18,766
Lakewood, NJ (township) Ocean County	18,271
Fort Lee, NJ (borough) Bergen County	17,727
Perth Amboy, NJ (city) Middlesex County	17,651
Hillside, NJ (cdp) Union County	16,815
Hamilton, NJ (township) Mercer County	16,497
Clifton, NJ (city) Passaic County	16,140

Chilean
Top 10 Places Sorted by Number

Place	Dollars
North Bergen, NJ (township) Hudson County	19,125

Colombian
Top 10 Places Sorted by Number

Place	Dollars
Elmwood Park, NJ (borough) Bergen County	41,215
Union, NJ (cdp) Union County	22,228
Teaneck, NJ (cdp) Bergen County	20,782
Woodbridge, NJ (township) Middlesex County	19,922
Clifton, NJ (city) Passaic County	19,623
Linden, NJ (city) Union County	19,550
Lodi, NJ (borough) Bergen County	18,504
Passaic, NJ (city) Passaic County	17,756
Garfield, NJ (city) Bergen County	17,639
Plainfield, NJ (city) Union County	17,608

Costa Rican
Top 10 Places Sorted by Number

Place	Dollars
Elizabeth, NJ (city) Union County	14,981
Somerville, NJ (borough) Somerset County	14,643
Trenton, NJ (city) Mercer County	11,577
Paterson, NJ (city) Passaic County	11,273
Bound Brook, NJ (borough) Somerset County	10,514

Cuban
Top 10 Places Sorted by Number

Place	Dollars
Cliffside Park, NJ (borough) Bergen County	39,249
Bloomfield, NJ (cdp) Essex County	36,568

Notes: Please refer to the User's Guide for an explanation of data; tables include places with populations > 9,999 and reflect only those areas that meet Summary File 4 population thresholds, therefore there may be less than 10 places listed

Fort Lee, NJ (borough) Bergen County	35,870
Edison, NJ (cdp) Middlesex County	33,455
Woodbridge, NJ (township) Middlesex County	28,275
Union, NJ (cdp) Union County	25,569
Weehawken, NJ (township) Hudson County	25,448
Bayonne, NJ (city) Hudson County	25,400
Linden, NJ (city) Union County	23,286
Belleville, NJ (cdp) Essex County	22,388

Dominican
Top 10 Places Sorted by Number

Place	Dollars
Palisades Park, NJ (borough) Bergen County	23,136
Woodbridge, NJ (township) Middlesex County	22,387
Fort Lee, NJ (borough) Bergen County	22,168
Bloomfield, NJ (cdp) Essex County	22,153
Ridgefield Park, NJ (village) Bergen County	20,744
Teaneck, NJ (cdp) Bergen County	19,560
Kearny, NJ (town) Hudson County	17,732
North Bergen, NJ (township) Hudson County	16,762
Hackensack, NJ (city) Bergen County	16,202
Fairview, NJ (borough) Bergen County	15,659

Ecuadorian
Top 10 Places Sorted by Number

Place	Dollars
Harrison, NJ (town) Hudson County	18,483
Kearny, NJ (town) Hudson County	17,782
Bloomfield, NJ (cdp) Essex County	17,740
Elizabeth, NJ (city) Union County	17,373
North Bergen, NJ (township) Hudson County	16,442
Belleville, NJ (cdp) Essex County	14,654
Dover, NJ (town) Morris County	14,393
East Windsor, NJ (township) Mercer County	14,358
Clifton, NJ (city) Passaic County	14,117
Newark, NJ (city) Essex County	13,438

Guatelmalan
Top 10 Places Sorted by Number

Place	Dollars
North Bergen, NJ (township) Hudson County	25,216
North Plainfield, NJ (borough) Somerset County	15,633
Palisades Park, NJ (borough) Bergen County	13,976
Elizabeth, NJ (city) Union County	13,662
Jersey City, NJ (city) Hudson County	13,525
West New York, NJ (town) Hudson County	13,063
Newark, NJ (city) Essex County	13,025
Bayonne, NJ (city) Hudson County	12,981
Trenton, NJ (city) Mercer County	11,897
Union City, NJ (city) Hudson County	11,592

Honduran
Top 10 Places Sorted by Number

Place	Dollars
Morris, NJ (town) Morris County	14,746
Union City, NJ (city) Hudson County	12,876
Jersey City, NJ (city) Hudson County	12,662
Elizabeth, NJ (city) Union County	12,369
North Bergen, NJ (township) Hudson County	12,346
New Brunswick, NJ (city) Middlesex County	10,576
Plainfield, NJ (city) Union County	9,590
Newark, NJ (city) Essex County	9,306
Passaic, NJ (city) Passaic County	8,969
West New York, NJ (town) Hudson County	8,758

Mexican
Top 10 Places Sorted by Number

Place	Dollars
Brick, NJ (township) Ocean County	40,526
West Orange, NJ (cdp) Essex County	19,730
Woodbridge, NJ (township) Middlesex County	16,237
Garfield, NJ (city) Bergen County	14,488
Freehold, NJ (township) Monmouth County	14,255

Jersey City, NJ (city) Hudson County	13,485
Elizabeth, NJ (city) Union County	13,294
Perth Amboy, NJ (city) Middlesex County	12,785
North Bergen, NJ (township) Hudson County	12,775
Edison, NJ (cdp) Middlesex County	12,194

Nicaraguan
Top 10 Places Sorted by Number

Place	Dollars
Jersey City, NJ (city) Hudson County	14,933
Camden, NJ (city) Camden County	10,894

Panamanian
Top 10 Places Sorted by Number

Place	Dollars
No places met population threshold.	

Paraguayan
Top 10 Places Sorted by Number

Place	Dollars
No places met population threshold.	

Peruvian
Top 10 Places Sorted by Number

Place	Dollars
Jersey City, NJ (city) Hudson County	19,721
Woodbridge, NJ (township) Middlesex County	19,337
North Bergen, NJ (township) Hudson County	17,908
Kearny, NJ (town) Hudson County	16,930
Carteret, NJ (borough) Middlesex County	16,041
Clifton, NJ (city) Passaic County	15,469
Garfield, NJ (city) Bergen County	14,726
Belleville, NJ (cdp) Essex County	14,552
Paterson, NJ (city) Passaic County	14,301
Elmwood Park, NJ (borough) Bergen County	14,244

Puerto Rican
Top 10 Places Sorted by Number

Place	Dollars
Rutherford, NJ (borough) Bergen County	36,793
Hillsborough, NJ (township) Somerset County	34,397
Collingswood, NJ (borough) Camden County	34,219
West Milford, NJ (cdp) Passaic County	32,859
Montclair, NJ (cdp) Essex County	32,340
Fort Lee, NJ (borough) Bergen County	32,085
Freehold, NJ (township) Monmouth County	30,345
Colonia, NJ (cdp) Middlesex County	29,123
Manalapan, NJ (township) Monmouth County	28,705
Ewing, NJ (cdp) Mercer County	27,388

Salvadoran
Top 10 Places Sorted by Number

Place	Dollars
North Bergen, NJ (township) Hudson County	26,926
Jersey City, NJ (city) Hudson County	16,961
North Plainfield, NJ (borough) Somerset County	15,867
Newark, NJ (city) Essex County	13,996
West New York, NJ (town) Hudson County	13,914
Fairview, NJ (borough) Bergen County	13,186
Elizabeth, NJ (city) Union County	11,442
Plainfield, NJ (city) Union County	11,324
Paterson, NJ (city) Passaic County	10,290
Union City, NJ (city) Hudson County	9,737

South American
Top 10 Places Sorted by Number

Place	Dollars
Franklin, NJ (township) Somerset County	37,268
Nutley, NJ (cdp) Essex County	31,072
Rockaway, NJ (township) Morris County	27,358
Montclair, NJ (cdp) Essex County	27,097

Elmwood Park, NJ (borough) Bergen County	26,910
Palisades Park, NJ (borough) Bergen County	26,117
Wayne, NJ (cdp) Passaic County	25,070
Hoboken, NJ (city) Hudson County	24,060
Teaneck, NJ (cdp) Bergen County	23,955
Middletown, NJ (township) Monmouth County	23,579

Spaniard
Top 10 Places Sorted by Number

Place	Dollars
Kearny, NJ (town) Hudson County	28,187
Newark, NJ (city) Essex County	21,374
Bayonne, NJ (city) Hudson County	16,190

Uruguayan
Top 10 Places Sorted by Number

Place	Dollars
Elizabeth, NJ (city) Union County	17,044
West Orange, NJ (cdp) Essex County	12,840

Venezuelan
Top 10 Places Sorted by Number

Place	Dollars
No places met population threshold.	

Other Hispanic
Top 10 Places Sorted by Number

Place	Dollars
Fort Lee, NJ (borough) Bergen County	24,207
Parsippany-Troy Hills, NJ (township) Morris County	22,121
Edison, NJ (cdp) Middlesex County	21,563
Ridgefield, NJ (borough) Bergen County	20,045
Sayreville, NJ (borough) Middlesex County	18,834
Wayne, NJ (cdp) Passaic County	18,633
Dover, NJ (township) Ocean County	18,609
Toms River, NJ (cdp) Ocean County	18,609
Franklin, NJ (township) Somerset County	18,348
Bridgewater, NJ (township) Somerset County	18,216

Poverty Status

Total Populations with Income Below Poverty Level
Top 10 Places Sorted by Number

Place	Number
Newark, NJ (city) Essex County	74,263
Jersey City, NJ (city) Hudson County	44,075
Paterson, NJ (city) Passaic County	32,474
Camden, NJ (city) Camden County	26,786
Elizabeth, NJ (city) Union County	20,963
Trenton, NJ (city) Mercer County	17,222
Passaic, NJ (city) Passaic County	14,249
Union City, NJ (city) Hudson County	14,244
East Orange, NJ (city) Essex County	13,159
New Brunswick, NJ (city) Middlesex County	11,454

Total Populations with Income Below Poverty Level
Top 10 Places Sorted by Percent

Place	Percent
Camden, NJ (city) Camden County	35.52
Asbury Park, NJ (city) Monmouth County	30.13
Newark, NJ (city) Essex County	28.40
New Brunswick, NJ (city) Middlesex County	27.05
Bridgeton, NJ (city) Cumberland County	26.64
Atlantic City, NJ (city) Atlantic County	23.65
Paterson, NJ (city) Passaic County	22.19
Union City, NJ (city) Hudson County	21.37
Passaic, NJ (city) Passaic County	21.19
Trenton, NJ (city) Mercer County	21.13

Notes: Please refer to the User's Guide for an explanation of data; tables include places with populations > 9,999 and reflect only those areas that meet Summary File 4 population thresholds, therefore there may be less than 10 places listed

Hispanics with Income Below Poverty Level
Top 10 Places Sorted by Number

Place	Number
Newark, NJ (city) Essex County	23,270
Paterson, NJ (city) Passaic County	15,658
Jersey City, NJ (city) Hudson County	14,612
Union City, NJ (city) Hudson County	12,234
Camden, NJ (city) Camden County	12,042
Elizabeth, NJ (city) Union County	10,902
Passaic, NJ (city) Passaic County	10,552
West New York, NJ (town) Hudson County	7,256
Perth Amboy, NJ (city) Middlesex County	6,153
Trenton, NJ (city) Mercer County	4,431

Hispanics with Income Below Poverty Level
Top 10 Places Sorted by Percent

Place	Percent
Bridgeton, NJ (city) Cumberland County	40.28
Camden, NJ (city) Camden County	40.21
Asbury Park, NJ (city) Monmouth County	38.10
East Orange, NJ (city) Essex County	34.79
Millville, NJ (city) Cumberland County	33.64
Irvington, NJ (cdp) Essex County	32.43
Newark, NJ (city) Essex County	29.44
Glassboro, NJ (borough) Gloucester County	29.24
Hammonton, NJ (town) Atlantic County	28.31
Mount Holly, NJ (township) Burlington County	27.64

Argentinians with Income Below Poverty Level
Top 10 Places Sorted by Number

Place	Number
North Bergen, NJ (township) Hudson County	55

Argentinians with Income Below Poverty Level
Top 10 Places Sorted by Percent

Place	Percent
North Bergen, NJ (township) Hudson County	11.25

Bolivians with Income Below Poverty Level
Top 10 Places Sorted by Number

Place	Number
No places met population threshold.	

Bolivians with Income Below Poverty Level
Top 10 Places Sorted by Percent

Place	Percent
No places met population threshold.	

Central Americans with Income Below Poverty Level
Top 10 Places Sorted by Number

Place	Number
Union City, NJ (city) Hudson County	1,671
Plainfield, NJ (city) Union County	1,187
Elizabeth, NJ (city) Union County	1,132
Newark, NJ (city) Essex County	919
West New York, NJ (town) Hudson County	886
Trenton, NJ (city) Mercer County	755
Jersey City, NJ (city) Hudson County	700
Paterson, NJ (city) Passaic County	451
Bound Brook, NJ (borough) Somerset County	426
North Bergen, NJ (township) Hudson County	371

Central Americans with Income Below Poverty Level
Top 10 Places Sorted by Percent

Place	Percent
Irvington, NJ (cdp) Essex County	50.35
City of Orange, NJ (township) Essex County	37.34
Orange, NJ (cdp) Essex County	37.34
Bound Brook, NJ (borough) Somerset County	29.18
Long Branch, NJ (city) Monmouth County	29.11
Weehawken, NJ (township) Hudson County	29.10

Place	
Plainfield, NJ (city) Union County	27.18
Union City, NJ (city) Hudson County	24.60
Paterson, NJ (city) Passaic County	22.58
Pallsades Park, NJ (borough) Bergen County	22.36

Chileans with Income Below Poverty Level
Top 10 Places Sorted by Number

Place	Number
North Bergen, NJ (township) Hudson County	23

Chileans with Income Below Poverty Level
Top 10 Places Sorted by Percent

Place	Percent
North Bergen, NJ (township) Hudson County	4.76

Colombians with Income Below Poverty Level
Top 10 Places Sorted by Number

Place	Number
Elizabeth, NJ (city) Union County	1,293
Paterson, NJ (city) Passaic County	835
Union City, NJ (city) Hudson County	766
West New York, NJ (town) Hudson County	510
Dover, NJ (town) Morris County	488
North Bergen, NJ (township) Hudson County	383
Newark, NJ (city) Essex County	344
Jersey City, NJ (city) Hudson County	256
Passaic, NJ (city) Passaic County	255
Hackensack, NJ (city) Bergen County	237

Colombians with Income Below Poverty Level
Top 10 Places Sorted by Percent

Place	Percent
Lakewood, NJ (township) Ocean County	35.88
Perth Amboy, NJ (city) Middlesex County	33.87
Newark, NJ (city) Essex County	32.98
Union City, NJ (city) Hudson County	27.24
Plainfield, NJ (city) Union County	22.50
Dover, NJ (town) Morris County	21.36
West New York, NJ (town) Hudson County	20.10
Atlantic City, NJ (city) Atlantic County	19.53
Passaic, NJ (city) Passaic County	18.56
Paterson, NJ (city) Passaic County	16.68

Costa Ricans with Income Below Poverty Level
Top 10 Places Sorted by Number

Place	Number
Bound Brook, NJ (borough) Somerset County	341
Paterson, NJ (city) Passaic County	300
Trenton, NJ (city) Mercer County	299
Elizabeth, NJ (city) Union County	80
Somerville, NJ (borough) Somerset County	64

Costa Ricans with Income Below Poverty Level
Top 10 Places Sorted by Percent

Place	Percent
Paterson, NJ (city) Passaic County	37.31
Trenton, NJ (city) Mercer County	36.64
Bound Brook, NJ (borough) Somerset County	27.84
Elizabeth, NJ (city) Union County	18.52
Somerville, NJ (borough) Somerset County	11.05

Cubans with Income Below Poverty Level
Top 10 Places Sorted by Number

Place	Number
Union City, NJ (city) Hudson County	1,964
West New York, NJ (town) Hudson County	1,692
Elizabeth, NJ (city) Union County	1,060
Newark, NJ (city) Essex County	703
North Bergen, NJ (township) Hudson County	675
Jersey City, NJ (city) Hudson County	275
Paterson, NJ (city) Passaic County	185

Place	
Weehawken, NJ (township) Hudson County	184
Guttenberg, NJ (town) Hudson County	176
Hoboken, NJ (city) Hudson County	113

Cubans with Income Below Poverty Level
Top 10 Places Sorted by Percent

Place	Percent
Newark, NJ (city) Essex County	21.95
Paterson, NJ (city) Passaic County	19.76
Union City, NJ (city) Hudson County	19.12
Passaic, NJ (city) Passaic County	17.72
West New York, NJ (town) Hudson County	17.35
Weehawken, NJ (township) Hudson County	15.90
Hoboken, NJ (city) Hudson County	15.48
Guttenberg, NJ (town) Hudson County	15.08
Elizabeth, NJ (city) Union County	14.23
Jersey City, NJ (city) Hudson County	14.15

Dominicans with Income Below Poverty Level
Top 10 Places Sorted by Number

Place	Number
Paterson, NJ (city) Passaic County	2,872
Passaic, NJ (city) Passaic County	2,388
Jersey City, NJ (city) Hudson County	1,891
Perth Amboy, NJ (city) Middlesex County	1,835
Union City, NJ (city) Hudson County	1,811
Newark, NJ (city) Essex County	1,644
West New York, NJ (town) Hudson County	866
Elizabeth, NJ (city) Union County	756
New Brunswick, NJ (city) Middlesex County	586
Camden, NJ (city) Camden County	567

Dominicans with Income Below Poverty Level
Top 10 Places Sorted by Percent

Place	Percent
East Orange, NJ (city) Essex County	41.01
Somerset, NJ (cdp) Somerset County	38.51
Franklin, NJ (township) Somerset County	35.94
Camden, NJ (city) Camden County	29.67
Belleville, NJ (cdp) Essex County	27.81
Newark, NJ (city) Essex County	26.11
Passaic, NJ (city) Passaic County	25.12
New Brunswick, NJ (city) Middlesex County	24.91
Hoboken, NJ (city) Hudson County	24.64
Union City, NJ (city) Hudson County	23.22

Ecuadorians with Income Below Poverty Level
Top 10 Places Sorted by Number

Place	Number
Newark, NJ (city) Essex County	1,698
Jersey City, NJ (city) Hudson County	647
Union City, NJ (city) Hudson County	625
West New York, NJ (town) Hudson County	354
Hackensack, NJ (city) Bergen County	239
Elizabeth, NJ (city) Union County	237
Plainfield, NJ (city) Union County	228
North Bergen, NJ (township) Hudson County	226
Paterson, NJ (city) Passaic County	170
Passaic, NJ (city) Passaic County	168

Ecuadorians with Income Below Poverty Level
Top 10 Places Sorted by Percent

Place	Percent
Passaic, NJ (city) Passaic County	32.56
Weehawken, NJ (township) Hudson County	31.80
Plainfield, NJ (city) Union County	26.00
Newark, NJ (city) Essex County	20.77
Paterson, NJ (city) Passaic County	19.88
West New York, NJ (town) Hudson County	16.13
Union City, NJ (city) Hudson County	14.87
Jersey City, NJ (city) Hudson County	14.85
Elizabeth, NJ (city) Union County	13.42
Hackensack, NJ (city) Bergen County	12.82

Notes: Please refer to the User's Guide for an explanation of data; tables include places with populations > 9,999 and reflect only those areas that meet Summary File 4 population thresholds, therefore there may be less than 10 places listed

Guatelmalans with Income Below Poverty Level
Top 10 Places Sorted by Number

Place	Number
Trenton, NJ (city) Mercer County	429
Plainfield, NJ (city) Union County	420
Fairview, NJ (borough) Bergen County	209
Newark, NJ (city) Essex County	172
Palisades Park, NJ (borough) Bergen County	161
West New York, NJ (town) Hudson County	136
North Bergen, NJ (township) Hudson County	129
Union City, NJ (city) Hudson County	94
Jersey City, NJ (city) Hudson County	73
Elizabeth, NJ (city) Union County	42

Guatelmalans with Income Below Poverty Level
Top 10 Places Sorted by Percent

Place	Percent
Fairview, NJ (borough) Bergen County	32.01
Palisades Park, NJ (borough) Bergen County	26.01
West New York, NJ (town) Hudson County	24.29
Plainfield, NJ (city) Union County	24.11
North Bergen, NJ (township) Hudson County	23.12
Newark, NJ (city) Essex County	20.14
Union City, NJ (city) Hudson County	18.65
Trenton, NJ (city) Mercer County	15.22
Jersey City, NJ (city) Hudson County	11.20
Elizabeth, NJ (city) Union County	8.33

Hondurans with Income Below Poverty Level
Top 10 Places Sorted by Number

Place	Number
Union City, NJ (city) Hudson County	579
Plainfield, NJ (city) Union County	409
Elizabeth, NJ (city) Union County	332
New Brunswick, NJ (city) Middlesex County	294
Jersey City, NJ (city) Hudson County	272
Newark, NJ (city) Essex County	214
Passaic, NJ (city) Passaic County	153
West New York, NJ (town) Hudson County	149
Morris, NJ (town) Morris County	105
North Bergen, NJ (township) Hudson County	79

Hondurans with Income Below Poverty Level
Top 10 Places Sorted by Percent

Place	Percent
Plainfield, NJ (city) Union County	44.17
Newark, NJ (city) Essex County	33.18
Elizabeth, NJ (city) Union County	32.14
Union City, NJ (city) Hudson County	31.43
Passaic, NJ (city) Passaic County	24.64
West New York, NJ (town) Hudson County	22.61
New Brunswick, NJ (city) Middlesex County	16.26
Morris, NJ (town) Morris County	14.69
Jersey City, NJ (city) Hudson County	14.17
North Bergen, NJ (township) Hudson County	11.22

Mexicans with Income Below Poverty Level
Top 10 Places Sorted by Number

Place	Number
Passaic, NJ (city) Passaic County	4,101
New Brunswick, NJ (city) Middlesex County	2,118
Paterson, NJ (city) Passaic County	1,517
Bridgeton, NJ (city) Cumberland County	1,313
West New York, NJ (town) Hudson County	897
Lakewood, NJ (township) Ocean County	854
Union City, NJ (city) Hudson County	802
Newark, NJ (city) Essex County	768
Atlantic City, NJ (city) Atlantic County	665
Jersey City, NJ (city) Hudson County	662

Mexicans with Income Below Poverty Level
Top 10 Places Sorted by Percent

Place	Percent
Somerset, NJ (cdp) Somerset County	46.86
Plainfield, NJ (city) Union County	46.03
Asbury Park, NJ (city) Monmouth County	45.45
Franklin, NJ (township) Somerset County	44.08
Roselle, NJ (borough) Union County	43.87
Freehold, NJ (township) Monmouth County	43.49
Trenton, NJ (city) Mercer County	42.49
Princeton, NJ (township) Mercer County	40.47
Bridgeton, NJ (city) Cumberland County	40.31
Freehold, NJ (borough) Monmouth County	39.63

Nicaraguans with Income Below Poverty Level
Top 10 Places Sorted by Number

Place	Number
Jersey City, NJ (city) Hudson County	28
Camden, NJ (city) Camden County	24

Nicaraguans with Income Below Poverty Level
Top 10 Places Sorted by Percent

Place	Percent
Jersey City, NJ (city) Hudson County	5.41
Camden, NJ (city) Camden County	3.77

Panamanians with Income Below Poverty Level
Top 10 Places Sorted by Number

Place	Number
No places met population threshold.	

Panamanians with Income Below Poverty Level
Top 10 Places Sorted by Percent

Place	Percent
No places met population threshold.	

Paraguayans with Income Below Poverty Level
Top 10 Places Sorted by Number

Place	Number
No places met population threshold.	

Paraguayans with Income Below Poverty Level
Top 10 Places Sorted by Percent

Place	Percent
No places met population threshold.	

Peruvians with Income Below Poverty Level
Top 10 Places Sorted by Number

Place	Number
Paterson, NJ (city) Passaic County	855
Elizabeth, NJ (city) Union County	460
Union City, NJ (city) Hudson County	393
Passaic, NJ (city) Passaic County	215
Newark, NJ (city) Essex County	200
Harrison, NJ (town) Hudson County	191
Perth Amboy, NJ (city) Middlesex County	187
West New York, NJ (town) Hudson County	162
Kearny, NJ (town) Hudson County	124
Garfield, NJ (city) Bergen County	118

Peruvians with Income Below Poverty Level
Top 10 Places Sorted by Percent

Place	Percent
Union City, NJ (city) Hudson County	20.25
West New York, NJ (town) Hudson County	19.68
Elmwood Park, NJ (borough) Bergen County	17.55
Carteret, NJ (borough) Middlesex County	17.26
Harrison, NJ (town) Hudson County	16.83
Garfield, NJ (city) Bergen County	16.30
Perth Amboy, NJ (city) Middlesex County	14.71

Place	Percent
Elizabeth, NJ (city) Union County	14.70
Jersey City, NJ (city) Hudson County	13.79
Newark, NJ (city) Essex County	13.47

Puerto Ricans with Income Below Poverty Level
Top 10 Places Sorted by Number

Place	Number
Newark, NJ (city) Essex County	14,181
Camden, NJ (city) Camden County	9,457
Jersey City, NJ (city) Hudson County	8,117
Paterson, NJ (city) Passaic County	6,004
Elizabeth, NJ (city) Union County	3,256
Perth Amboy, NJ (city) Middlesex County	2,568
Vineland, NJ (city) Cumberland County	2,502
Trenton, NJ (city) Mercer County	2,373
Passaic, NJ (city) Passaic County	2,118
Union City, NJ (city) Hudson County	1,958

Puerto Ricans with Income Below Poverty Level
Top 10 Places Sorted by Percent

Place	Percent
Asbury Park, NJ (city) Monmouth County	45.48
East Orange, NJ (city) Essex County	44.06
Camden, NJ (city) Camden County	42.30
Bridgeton, NJ (city) Cumberland County	40.05
Newark, NJ (city) Essex County	36.59
Glassboro, NJ (borough) Gloucester County	35.53
Millville, NJ (city) Cumberland County	34.38
Mount Holly, NJ (township) Burlington County	30.89
Hoboken, NJ (city) Hudson County	30.11
Irvington, NJ (cdp) Essex County	29.26

Salvadorans with Income Below Poverty Level
Top 10 Places Sorted by Number

Place	Number
Union City, NJ (city) Hudson County	906
Elizabeth, NJ (city) Union County	593
West New York, NJ (town) Hudson County	558
Plainfield, NJ (city) Union County	310
Newark, NJ (city) Essex County	258
Jersey City, NJ (city) Hudson County	197
North Bergen, NJ (township) Hudson County	113
Guttenberg, NJ (town) Hudson County	67
Paterson, NJ (city) Passaic County	55
North Plainfield, NJ (borough) Somerset County	43

Salvadorans with Income Below Poverty Level
Top 10 Places Sorted by Percent

Place	Percent
Plainfield, NJ (city) Union County	24.39
Union City, NJ (city) Hudson County	23.43
West New York, NJ (town) Hudson County	18.40
Guttenberg, NJ (town) Hudson County	16.83
Jersey City, NJ (city) Hudson County	16.43
Elizabeth, NJ (city) Union County	16.22
Newark, NJ (city) Essex County	14.73
North Plainfield, NJ (borough) Somerset County	12.61
Paterson, NJ (city) Passaic County	10.42
North Bergen, NJ (township) Hudson County	8.23

South Americans with Income Below Poverty Level
Top 10 Places Sorted by Number

Place	Number
Elizabeth, NJ (city) Union County	2,436
Newark, NJ (city) Essex County	2,391
Paterson, NJ (city) Passaic County	2,003
Union City, NJ (city) Hudson County	1,983
Jersey City, NJ (city) Hudson County	1,294
West New York, NJ (town) Hudson County	1,179
North Bergen, NJ (township) Hudson County	817
Dover, NJ (town) Morris County	708
Passaic, NJ (city) Passaic County	678
Hackensack, NJ (city) Bergen County	642

Notes: Please refer to the User's Guide for an explanation of data; tables include places with populations > 9,999 and reflect only those areas that meet Summary File 4 population thresholds, therefore there may be less than 10 places listed

South Americans with Income Below Poverty Level
Top 10 Places Sorted by Percent

Place	Percent
Irvington, NJ (cdp) Essex County	28.82
Long Branch, NJ (city) Monmouth County	27.84
Plainfield, NJ (city) Union County	24.33
Lakewood, NJ (township) Ocean County	23.63
Weehawken, NJ (township) Hudson County	21.14
Newark, NJ (city) Essex County	20.23
Atlantic City, NJ (city) Atlantic County	20.14
New Brunswick, NJ (city) Middlesex County	20.00
Union City, NJ (city) Hudson County	19.89
West New York, NJ (town) Hudson County	18.54

Spaniards with Income Below Poverty Level
Top 10 Places Sorted by Number

Place	Number
Newark, NJ (city) Essex County	190
Bayonne, NJ (city) Hudson County	82
Kearny, NJ (town) Hudson County	15

Spaniards with Income Below Poverty Level
Top 10 Places Sorted by Percent

Place	Percent
Newark, NJ (city) Essex County	14.65
Bayonne, NJ (city) Hudson County	14.19
Kearny, NJ (town) Hudson County	2.03

Uruguayans with Income Below Poverty Level
Top 10 Places Sorted by Number

Place	Number
Elizabeth, NJ (city) Union County	154
West Orange, NJ (cdp) Essex County	28

Uruguayans with Income Below Poverty Level
Top 10 Places Sorted by Percent

Place	Percent
Elizabeth, NJ (city) Union County	18.90
West Orange, NJ (cdp) Essex County	7.93

Venezuelans with Income Below Poverty Level
Top 10 Places Sorted by Number

Place	Number
No places met population threshold.	

Venezuelans with Income Below Poverty Level
Top 10 Places Sorted by Percent

Place	Percent
No places met population threshold.	

Other Hispanics with Income Below Poverty Level
Top 10 Places Sorted by Number

Place	Number
Paterson, NJ (city) Passaic County	2,603
Newark, NJ (city) Essex County	2,474
Union City, NJ (city) Hudson County	2,022
Elizabeth, NJ (city) Union County	1,916
Jersey City, NJ (city) Hudson County	1,661
West New York, NJ (town) Hudson County	1,219
Camden, NJ (city) Camden County	1,097
Passaic, NJ (city) Passaic County	945
Perth Amboy, NJ (city) Middlesex County	709
North Bergen, NJ (township) Hudson County	626

Other Hispanics with Income Below Poverty Level
Top 10 Places Sorted by Percent

Place	Percent
Camden, NJ (city) Camden County	42.83
East Orange, NJ (city) Essex County	38.47
Irvington, NJ (cdp) Essex County	36.09

Hoboken, NJ (city) Hudson County	32.00
Vineland, NJ (city) Cumberland County	30.72
Fort Lee, NJ (borough) Bergen County	25.13
Newark, NJ (city) Essex County	22.23
Trenton, NJ (city) Mercer County	22.23
West New York, NJ (town) Hudson County	22.16
Dover, NJ (town) Morris County	21.68

Homeownership

Total Populations Who Own Their Own Homes
Top 10 Places Sorted by Number

Place	Number
Dover, NJ (township) Ocean County	28,026
Toms River, NJ (cdp) Ocean County	26,527
Hamilton, NJ (township) Mercer County	25,170
Jersey City, NJ (city) Hudson County	24,965
Brick, NJ (township) Ocean County	24,609
Woodbridge, NJ (township) Middlesex County	24,404
Edison, NJ (cdp) Middlesex County	22,462
Cherry Hill, NJ (township) Camden County	21,751
Newark, NJ (city) Essex County	21,750
Middletown, NJ (township) Monmouth County	20,070

Total Populations Who Own Their Own Homes
Top 10 Places Sorted by Percent

Place	Percent
Marlboro, NJ (township) Monmouth County	96.21
Franklin Lakes, NJ (borough) Bergen County	95.12
Monroe, NJ (township) Middlesex County	94.80
Ringwood, NJ (borough) Passaic County	94.45
Manalapan, NJ (township) Monmouth County	93.98
Livingston, NJ (cdp) Essex County	93.75
Oakland, NJ (borough) Bergen County	93.23
Berkeley, NJ (township) Ocean County	92.95
Wyckoff, NJ (cdp) Bergen County	92.82
Succasunna-Kenvil, NJ (cdp) Morris County	92.49

Hispanics Who Own Their Own Homes
Top 10 Places Sorted by Number

Place	Number
Paterson, NJ (city) Passaic County	5,052
Newark, NJ (city) Essex County	4,539
Elizabeth, NJ (city) Union County	4,318
Jersey City, NJ (city) Hudson County	3,943
North Bergen, NJ (township) Hudson County	3,605
Camden, NJ (city) Camden County	3,386
Perth Amboy, NJ (city) Middlesex County	2,798
Union City, NJ (city) Hudson County	2,623
Vineland, NJ (city) Cumberland County	2,060
Clifton, NJ (city) Passaic County	1,846

Hispanics Who Own Their Own Homes
Top 10 Places Sorted by Percent

Place	Percent
Oakland, NJ (borough) Bergen County	100.00
Ringwood, NJ (borough) Passaic County	100.00
Monroe, NJ (township) Middlesex County	95.74
Willingboro, NJ (township) Burlington County	95.53
Marlboro, NJ (township) Monmouth County	93.85
Franklin Lakes, NJ (borough) Bergen County	93.04
Wyckoff, NJ (cdp) Bergen County	92.11
Paramus, NJ (borough) Bergen County	90.55
Stafford, NJ (township) Ocean County	90.00
Manalapan, NJ (township) Monmouth County	89.02

Argentinians Who Own Their Own Homes
Top 10 Places Sorted by Number

Place	Number
North Bergen, NJ (township) Hudson County	46

Argentinians Who Own Their Own Homes
Top 10 Places Sorted by Percent

Place	Percent
North Bergen, NJ (township) Hudson County	23.47

Bolivians Who Own Their Own Homes
Top 10 Places Sorted by Number

Place	Number
No places met population threshold.	

Bolivians Who Own Their Own Homes
Top 10 Places Sorted by Percent

Place	Percent
No places met population threshold.	

Central Americans Who Own Their Own Homes
Top 10 Places Sorted by Number

Place	Number
Elizabeth, NJ (city) Union County	352
Jersey City, NJ (city) Hudson County	307
Newark, NJ (city) Essex County	230
North Bergen, NJ (township) Hudson County	195
Trenton, NJ (city) Mercer County	183
Camden, NJ (city) Camden County	161
Union City, NJ (city) Hudson County	146
Plainfield, NJ (city) Union County	143
West New York, NJ (town) Hudson County	122
Paterson, NJ (city) Passaic County	114

Central Americans Who Own Their Own Homes
Top 10 Places Sorted by Percent

Place	Percent
Woodbridge, NJ (township) Middlesex County	76.47
Camden, NJ (city) Camden County	64.40
Clifton, NJ (city) Passaic County	56.52
Hillside, NJ (cdp) Union County	52.53
West Orange, NJ (cdp) Essex County	48.15
Fort Lee, NJ (borough) Bergen County	46.99
Hamilton, NJ (township) Mercer County	41.21
Linden, NJ (city) Union County	38.79
Bloomfield, NJ (cdp) Essex County	35.48
Perth Amboy, NJ (city) Middlesex County	33.66

Chileans Who Own Their Own Homes
Top 10 Places Sorted by Number

Place	Number
North Bergen, NJ (township) Hudson County	57

Chileans Who Own Their Own Homes
Top 10 Places Sorted by Percent

Place	Percent
North Bergen, NJ (township) Hudson County	33.73

Colombians Who Own Their Own Homes
Top 10 Places Sorted by Number

Place	Number
Elizabeth, NJ (city) Union County	475
Paterson, NJ (city) Passaic County	422
North Bergen, NJ (township) Hudson County	262
Dover, NJ (town) Morris County	233
Clifton, NJ (city) Passaic County	196
Jersey City, NJ (city) Hudson County	148
Hackensack, NJ (city) Bergen County	144
Englewood, NJ (city) Bergen County	141
Passaic, NJ (city) Passaic County	108
Union, NJ (cdp) Union County	106

Notes: Please refer to the User's Guide for an explanation of data; tables include places with populations > 9,999 and reflect only those areas that meet Summary File 4 population thresholds, therefore there may be less than 10 places listed

Colombians Who Own Their Own Homes
Top 10 Places Sorted by Percent

Place	Percent
Union, NJ (cdp) Union County	80.92
Teaneck, NJ (cdp) Bergen County	78.20
Woodbridge, NJ (township) Middlesex County	70.91
Linden, NJ (city) Union County	56.05
Piscataway, NJ (township) Middlesex County	49.02
Clifton, NJ (city) Passaic County	44.55
Garfield, NJ (city) Bergen County	42.93
Dover, NJ (town) Morris County	42.06
Plainfield, NJ (city) Union County	39.88
Roselle, NJ (borough) Union County	39.20

Costa Ricans Who Own Their Own Homes
Top 10 Places Sorted by Number

Place	Number
Trenton, NJ (city) Mercer County	34
Elizabeth, NJ (city) Union County	24
Paterson, NJ (city) Passaic County	21
Bound Brook, NJ (borough) Somerset County	17
Somerville, NJ (borough) Somerset County	0

Costa Ricans Who Own Their Own Homes
Top 10 Places Sorted by Percent

Place	Percent
Elizabeth, NJ (city) Union County	19.83
Trenton, NJ (city) Mercer County	17.80
Paterson, NJ (city) Passaic County	10.34
Bound Brook, NJ (borough) Somerset County	6.07
Somerville, NJ (borough) Somerset County	0.00

Cubans Who Own Their Own Homes
Top 10 Places Sorted by Number

Place	Number
North Bergen, NJ (township) Hudson County	1,467
Elizabeth, NJ (city) Union County	1,222
Union City, NJ (city) Hudson County	1,105
West New York, NJ (town) Hudson County	845
Newark, NJ (city) Essex County	400
Jersey City, NJ (city) Hudson County	246
Union, NJ (cdp) Union County	195
Weehawken, NJ (township) Hudson County	180
Cliffside Park, NJ (borough) Bergen County	178
Linden, NJ (city) Union County	178

Cubans Who Own Their Own Homes
Top 10 Places Sorted by Percent

Place	Percent
Union, NJ (cdp) Union County	85.53
Woodbridge, NJ (township) Middlesex County	69.06
Linden, NJ (city) Union County	63.35
Fort Lee, NJ (borough) Bergen County	62.90
Edison, NJ (cdp) Middlesex County	62.15
Belleville, NJ (cdp) Essex County	60.58
Kearny, NJ (town) Hudson County	60.08
Cliffside Park, NJ (borough) Bergen County	57.79
Bloomfield, NJ (cdp) Essex County	52.70
Harrison, NJ (town) Hudson County	52.00

Dominicans Who Own Their Own Homes
Top 10 Places Sorted by Number

Place	Number
Paterson, NJ (city) Passaic County	952
Perth Amboy, NJ (city) Middlesex County	647
Passaic, NJ (city) Passaic County	525
Jersey City, NJ (city) Hudson County	405
Newark, NJ (city) Essex County	365
North Bergen, NJ (township) Hudson County	282
Camden, NJ (city) Camden County	279
Elizabeth, NJ (city) Union County	255
Union City, NJ (city) Hudson County	250
Clifton, NJ (city) Passaic County	208

Dominicans Who Own Their Own Homes
Top 10 Places Sorted by Percent

Place	Percent
Bergenfield, NJ (borough) Bergen County	88.27
Teaneck, NJ (cdp) Bergen County	73.00
Pleasantville, NJ (city) Atlantic County	65.70
Ridgefield Park, NJ (village) Bergen County	63.11
Woodbridge, NJ (township) Middlesex County	59.40
Camden, NJ (city) Camden County	57.29
Palisades Park, NJ (borough) Bergen County	53.54
Clifton, NJ (city) Passaic County	52.79
Bloomfield, NJ (cdp) Essex County	43.88
North Brunswick Township, NJ (cdp) Middlesex County	43.40

Ecuadorians Who Own Their Own Homes
Top 10 Places Sorted by Number

Place	Number
Newark, NJ (city) Essex County	353
Jersey City, NJ (city) Hudson County	295
North Bergen, NJ (township) Hudson County	223
Union City, NJ (city) Hudson County	210
North Plainfield, NJ (borough) Somerset County	135
Belleville, NJ (cdp) Essex County	116
Kearny, NJ (town) Hudson County	97
Bloomfield, NJ (cdp) Essex County	96
Elizabeth, NJ (city) Union County	94
Paterson, NJ (city) Passaic County	89

Ecuadorians Who Own Their Own Homes
Top 10 Places Sorted by Percent

Place	Percent
Bloomfield, NJ (cdp) Essex County	59.26
North Plainfield, NJ (borough) Somerset County	43.97
Belleville, NJ (cdp) Essex County	41.28
Paterson, NJ (city) Passaic County	37.24
Clifton, NJ (city) Passaic County	31.41
Kearny, NJ (town) Hudson County	29.94
North Bergen, NJ (township) Hudson County	27.70
Plainfield, NJ (city) Union County	25.23
Dover, NJ (town) Morris County	24.37
Jersey City, NJ (city) Hudson County	22.40

Guatelmalans Who Own Their Own Homes
Top 10 Places Sorted by Number

Place	Number
Trenton, NJ (city) Mercer County	127
Newark, NJ (city) Essex County	60
Elizabeth, NJ (city) Union County	47
Plainfield, NJ (city) Union County	34
North Plainfield, NJ (borough) Somerset County	33
Bayonne, NJ (city) Hudson County	26
West New York, NJ (town) Hudson County	26
Jersey City, NJ (city) Hudson County	25
East Windsor, NJ (township) Mercer County	22
North Bergen, NJ (township) Hudson County	20

Guatelmalans Who Own Their Own Homes
Top 10 Places Sorted by Percent

Place	Percent
North Plainfield, NJ (borough) Somerset County	31.13
Elizabeth, NJ (city) Union County	25.27
Newark, NJ (city) Essex County	24.29
Bayonne, NJ (city) Hudson County	23.64
Trenton, NJ (city) Mercer County	21.86
East Windsor, NJ (township) Mercer County	18.33
West New York, NJ (town) Hudson County	18.18
Jersey City, NJ (city) Hudson County	16.45
North Bergen, NJ (township) Hudson County	13.99
Plainfield, NJ (city) Union County	8.04

Hondurans Who Own Their Own Homes
Top 10 Places Sorted by Number

Place	Number
Elizabeth, NJ (city) Union County	71
North Bergen, NJ (township) Hudson County	59
Jersey City, NJ (city) Hudson County	49
Plainfield, NJ (city) Union County	49
Union City, NJ (city) Hudson County	48
New Brunswick, NJ (city) Middlesex County	39
Passaic, NJ (city) Passaic County	24
Morris, NJ (town) Morris County	12
Newark, NJ (city) Essex County	12
West New York, NJ (town) Hudson County	0

Hondurans Who Own Their Own Homes
Top 10 Places Sorted by Percent

Place	Percent
North Bergen, NJ (township) Hudson County	34.91
Elizabeth, NJ (city) Union County	25.91
Plainfield, NJ (city) Union County	18.85
Passaic, NJ (city) Passaic County	15.00
New Brunswick, NJ (city) Middlesex County	9.61
Union City, NJ (city) Hudson County	9.58
Morris, NJ (town) Morris County	9.23
Jersey City, NJ (city) Hudson County	8.11
Newark, NJ (city) Essex County	7.55
West New York, NJ (town) Hudson County	0.00

Mexicans Who Own Their Own Homes
Top 10 Places Sorted by Number

Place	Number
Passaic, NJ (city) Passaic County	237
Camden, NJ (city) Camden County	133
Paterson, NJ (city) Passaic County	125
New Brunswick, NJ (city) Middlesex County	105
Clifton, NJ (city) Passaic County	101
Perth Amboy, NJ (city) Middlesex County	96
Bridgeton, NJ (city) Cumberland County	95
Jersey City, NJ (city) Hudson County	90
Vineland, NJ (city) Cumberland County	84
Atlantic City, NJ (city) Atlantic County	83

Mexicans Who Own Their Own Homes
Top 10 Places Sorted by Percent

Place	Percent
Dover, NJ (township) Ocean County	39.20
Toms River, NJ (cdp) Ocean County	39.20
Hackensack, NJ (city) Bergen County	36.84
Woodbridge, NJ (township) Middlesex County	34.62
Camden, NJ (city) Camden County	33.59
West Orange, NJ (cdp) Essex County	32.65
Clifton, NJ (city) Passaic County	32.58
North Bergen, NJ (township) Hudson County	29.20
Freehold, NJ (township) Monmouth County	28.89
Ventnor City, NJ (city) Atlantic County	24.44

Nicaraguans Who Own Their Own Homes
Top 10 Places Sorted by Number

Place	Number
Camden, NJ (city) Camden County	121
Jersey City, NJ (city) Hudson County	48

Nicaraguans Who Own Their Own Homes
Top 10 Places Sorted by Percent

Place	Percent
Camden, NJ (city) Camden County	64.71
Jersey City, NJ (city) Hudson County	30.97

Panamanians Who Own Their Own Homes
Top 10 Places Sorted by Number

Place	Number
No places met population threshold.	

Notes: Please refer to the User's Guide for an explanation of data; tables include places with populations > 9,999 and reflect only those areas that meet Summary File 4 population thresholds, therefore there may be less than 10 places listed

Panamanians Who Own Their Own Homes
Top 10 Places Sorted by Percent

Place	Percent
No places met population threshold.	

Paraguayans Who Own Their Own Homes
Top 10 Places Sorted by Number

Place	Number
No places met population threshold.	

Paraguayans Who Own Their Own Homes
Top 10 Places Sorted by Percent

Place	Percent
No places met population threshold.	

Peruvians Who Own Their Own Homes
Top 10 Places Sorted by Number

Place	Number
Paterson, NJ (city) Passaic County	722
Clifton, NJ (city) Passaic County	198
Elizabeth, NJ (city) Union County	156
Kearny, NJ (town) Hudson County	146
North Bergen, NJ (township) Hudson County	122
Perth Amboy, NJ (city) Middlesex County	104
Passaic, NJ (city) Passaic County	100
Belleville, NJ (cdp) Essex County	85
Jersey City, NJ (city) Hudson County	78
Newark, NJ (city) Essex County	77

Peruvians Who Own Their Own Homes
Top 10 Places Sorted by Percent

Place	Percent
Belleville, NJ (cdp) Essex County	63.91
North Bergen, NJ (township) Hudson County	46.56
West Orange, NJ (cdp) Essex County	43.90
Elmwood Park, NJ (borough) Bergen County	41.94
Woodbridge, NJ (township) Middlesex County	40.00
Clifton, NJ (city) Passaic County	39.13
Carteret, NJ (borough) Middlesex County	38.31
Perth Amboy, NJ (city) Middlesex County	35.74
Paterson, NJ (city) Passaic County	33.64
Kearny, NJ (town) Hudson County	31.95

Puerto Ricans Who Own Their Own Homes
Top 10 Places Sorted by Number

Place	Number
Camden, NJ (city) Camden County	2,608
Newark, NJ (city) Essex County	2,175
Jersey City, NJ (city) Hudson County	1,812
Paterson, NJ (city) Passaic County	1,745
Vineland, NJ (city) Cumberland County	1,734
Perth Amboy, NJ (city) Middlesex County	1,453
Trenton, NJ (city) Mercer County	1,125
Elizabeth, NJ (city) Union County	851
Pennsauken, NJ (cdp) Camden County	735
Woodbridge, NJ (township) Middlesex County	689

Puerto Ricans Who Own Their Own Homes
Top 10 Places Sorted by Percent

Place	Percent
Marlboro, NJ (township) Monmouth County	100.00
West Milford, NJ (cdp) Passaic County	100.00
Manalapan, NJ (township) Monmouth County	97.74
Willingboro, NJ (township) Burlington County	93.77
Freehold, NJ (township) Monmouth County	93.22
Bridgewater, NJ (township) Somerset County	87.50
South Plainfield, NJ (borough) Middlesex County	87.27
Hillsborough, NJ (township) Somerset County	84.85
Manchester, NJ (township) Ocean County	84.51
Fair Lawn, NJ (borough) Bergen County	81.98

Salvadorans Who Own Their Own Homes
Top 10 Places Sorted by Number

Place	Number
Elizabeth, NJ (city) Union County	167
Newark, NJ (city) Essex County	122
Jersey City, NJ (city) Hudson County	97
North Bergen, NJ (township) Hudson County	82
West New York, NJ (town) Hudson County	71
Union City, NJ (city) Hudson County	58
Plainfield, NJ (city) Union County	52
Paterson, NJ (city) Passaic County	45
North Plainfield, NJ (borough) Somerset County	31
Guttenberg, NJ (town) Hudson County	18

Salvadorans Who Own Their Own Homes
Top 10 Places Sorted by Percent

Place	Percent
North Plainfield, NJ (borough) Somerset County	31.31
Paterson, NJ (city) Passaic County	30.41
Newark, NJ (city) Essex County	26.35
Jersey City, NJ (city) Hudson County	25.87
North Bergen, NJ (township) Hudson County	21.24
Elizabeth, NJ (city) Union County	18.93
Guttenberg, NJ (town) Hudson County	17.82
Plainfield, NJ (city) Union County	14.94
Fairview, NJ (borough) Bergen County	9.09
West New York, NJ (town) Hudson County	8.66

South Americans Who Own Their Own Homes
Top 10 Places Sorted by Number

Place	Number
Paterson, NJ (city) Passaic County	1,301
Elizabeth, NJ (city) Union County	1,006
North Bergen, NJ (township) Hudson County	735
Newark, NJ (city) Essex County	621
Jersey City, NJ (city) Hudson County	600
Clifton, NJ (city) Passaic County	561
Union City, NJ (city) Hudson County	420
Dover, NJ (town) Morris County	352
Kearny, NJ (town) Hudson County	328
Belleville, NJ (cdp) Essex County	279

South Americans Who Own Their Own Homes
Top 10 Places Sorted by Percent

Place	Percent
East Brunswick, NJ (cdp) Middlesex County	81.82
Wayne, NJ (cdp) Passaic County	77.35
Teaneck, NJ (cdp) Bergen County	76.84
Union, NJ (cdp) Union County	74.84
Franklin, NJ (township) Somerset County	74.62
Middletown, NJ (township) Monmouth County	73.55
Dumont, NJ (borough) Bergen County	72.46
Nutley, NJ (township) Essex County	69.34
Dover, NJ (township) Ocean County	67.42
Toms River, NJ (cdp) Ocean County	67.42

Spaniards Who Own Their Own Homes
Top 10 Places Sorted by Number

Place	Number
Kearny, NJ (town) Hudson County	202
Newark, NJ (city) Essex County	135
Bayonne, NJ (city) Hudson County	102

Spaniards Who Own Their Own Homes
Top 10 Places Sorted by Percent

Place	Percent
Kearny, NJ (town) Hudson County	73.72
Bayonne, NJ (city) Hudson County	64.15
Newark, NJ (city) Essex County	26.06

Uruguayans Who Own Their Own Homes
Top 10 Places Sorted by Number

Place	Number
Elizabeth, NJ (city) Union County	138
West Orange, NJ (cdp) Essex County	50

Uruguayans Who Own Their Own Homes
Top 10 Places Sorted by Percent

Place	Percent
West Orange, NJ (cdp) Essex County	51.02
Elizabeth, NJ (city) Union County	40.23

Venezuelans Who Own Their Own Homes
Top 10 Places Sorted by Number

Place	Number
No places met population threshold.	

Venezuelans Who Own Their Own Homes
Top 10 Places Sorted by Percent

Place	Percent
No places met population threshold.	

Other Hispanics Who Own Their Own Homes
Top 10 Places Sorted by Number

Place	Number
Paterson, NJ (city) Passaic County	641
Newark, NJ (city) Essex County	570
Elizabeth, NJ (city) Union County	542
Jersey City, NJ (city) Hudson County	439
North Bergen, NJ (township) Hudson County	378
Union City, NJ (city) Hudson County	258
Clifton, NJ (city) Passaic County	240
Woodbridge, NJ (township) Middlesex County	175
Perth Amboy, NJ (city) Middlesex County	174
Bayonne, NJ (city) Hudson County	152

Other Hispanics Who Own Their Own Homes
Top 10 Places Sorted by Percent

Place	Percent
Howell, NJ (township) Monmouth County	83.78
Dover, NJ (township) Ocean County	82.05
Toms River, NJ (cdp) Ocean County	82.05
Hamilton, NJ (township) Mercer County	71.65
Union, NJ (cdp) Union County	69.59
Old Bridge, NJ (township) Middlesex County	66.43
Wayne, NJ (cdp) Passaic County	64.02
Roselle, NJ (borough) Union County	63.56
Pleasantville, NJ (city) Atlantic County	63.23
Brick, NJ (township) Ocean County	61.98

Median Gross Rent

All Specified Renter-Occupied Housing Units
Top 10 Places Sorted by Number

Place	Dollars/Month
Bernards, NJ (township) Somerset County	1,494
Paramus, NJ (borough) Bergen County	1,483
Marlboro, NJ (township) Monmouth County	1,334
Franklin Lakes, NJ (borough) Bergen County	1,313
Berkeley Heights, NJ (cdp) Union County	1,248
Livingston, NJ (cdp) Essex County	1,244
Ridgewood, NJ (village) Bergen County	1,220
Tinton Falls, NJ (borough) Monmouth County	1,198
West Windsor, NJ (township) Mercer County	1,198
West Caldwell, NJ (cdp) Essex County	1,193

Specified Housing Units Rented by Hispanics
Top 10 Places Sorted by Number

Place	Dollars/Month
Clinton, NJ (township) Hunterdon County	1,875

Notes: Please refer to the User's Guide for an explanation of data; tables include places with populations > 9,999 and reflect only those areas that meet Summary File 4 population thresholds, therefore there may be less than 10 places listed

Warren, NJ (township) Somerset County	1,775
Livingston, NJ (cdp) Essex County	1,734
Bernards, NJ (township) Somerset County	1,567
Lawrence, NJ (township) Mercer County	1,409
Montville, NJ (township) Morris County	1,385
Stafford, NJ (township) Ocean County	1,375
New Providence, NJ (borough) Union County	1,325
Lincoln Park, NJ (borough) Morris County	1,288
Marlboro, NJ (township) Monmouth County	1,266

Specified Housing Units Rented by Argentinians
Top 10 Places Sorted by Number

Place	Dollars/Month
North Bergen, NJ (township) Hudson County	864

Specified Housing Units Rented by Bolivians
Top 10 Places Sorted by Number

Place	Dollars/Month

No places met population threshold.

Specified Housing Units Rented by Central Americans
Top 10 Places Sorted by Number

Place	Dollars/Month
Morris, NJ (town) Morris County	1,181
Bridgewater, NJ (township) Somerset County	1,145
Englewood, NJ (city) Bergen County	965
Linden, NJ (city) Union County	924
Fort Lee, NJ (borough) Bergen County	920
Dover, NJ (town) Morris County	904
North Plainfield, NJ (borough) Somerset County	904
Somerville, NJ (borough) Somerset County	901
Fairview, NJ (borough) Bergen County	883
New Brunswick, NJ (city) Middlesex County	874

Specified Housing Units Rented by Chileans
Top 10 Places Sorted by Number

Place	Dollars/Month
North Bergen, NJ (township) Hudson County	887

Specified Housing Units Rented by Colombians
Top 10 Places Sorted by Number

Place	Dollars/Month
Union, NJ (cdp) Union County	1,277
Woodbridge, NJ (township) Middlesex County	1,250
Teaneck, NJ (cdp) Bergen County	1,188
Dover, NJ (town) Morris County	975
Lakewood, NJ (township) Ocean County	950
Elmwood Park, NJ (borough) Bergen County	885
Garfield, NJ (city) Bergen County	877
Morris, NJ (town) Morris County	872
North Plainfield, NJ (borough) Somerset County	852
Linden, NJ (city) Union County	850

Specified Housing Units Rented by Costa Ricans
Top 10 Places Sorted by Number

Place	Dollars/Month
Trenton, NJ (city) Mercer County	915
Somerville, NJ (borough) Somerset County	893
Bound Brook, NJ (borough) Somerset County	850
Paterson, NJ (city) Passaic County	830
Elizabeth, NJ (city) Union County	715

Specified Housing Units Rented by Cubans
Top 10 Places Sorted by Number

Place	Dollars/Month
Union, NJ (cdp) Union County	1,232
Fort Lee, NJ (borough) Bergen County	1,100
Woodbridge, NJ (township) Middlesex County	1,019
Belleville, NJ (cdp) Essex County	901
Cliffside Park, NJ (borough) Bergen County	825

Kearny, NJ (town) Hudson County	816
Bloomfield, NJ (cdp) Essex County	815
Linden, NJ (city) Union County	794
Edison, NJ (cdp) Middlesex County	791
Elmwood Park, NJ (borough) Bergen County	789

Specified Housing Units Rented by Dominicans
Top 10 Places Sorted by Number

Place	Dollars/Month
Ridgefield Park, NJ (village) Bergen County	1,016
Fort Lee, NJ (borough) Bergen County	973
Pleasantville, NJ (city) Atlantic County	919
Guttenberg, NJ (town) Hudson County	885
Kearny, NJ (town) Hudson County	877
Palisades Park, NJ (borough) Bergen County	869
Clifton, NJ (city) Passaic County	864
Teaneck, NJ (cdp) Bergen County	850
Somerset, NJ (cdp) Somerset County	847
Franklin, NJ (township) Somerset County	841

Specified Housing Units Rented by Ecuadorians
Top 10 Places Sorted by Number

Place	Dollars/Month
Dover, NJ (town) Morris County	1,074
North Plainfield, NJ (borough) Somerset County	971
Bayonne, NJ (city) Hudson County	870
North Bergen, NJ (township) Hudson County	849
Kearny, NJ (town) Hudson County	835
Belleville, NJ (cdp) Essex County	823
Clifton, NJ (city) Passaic County	811
East Windsor, NJ (township) Mercer County	791
Weehawken, NJ (township) Hudson County	775
Bloomfield, NJ (cdp) Essex County	767

Specified Housing Units Rented by Guatelmalans
Top 10 Places Sorted by Number

Place	Dollars/Month
North Bergen, NJ (township) Hudson County	944
Fairview, NJ (borough) Bergen County	903
North Plainfield, NJ (borough) Somerset County	861
East Windsor, NJ (township) Mercer County	833
Plainfield, NJ (city) Union County	794
Palisades Park, NJ (borough) Bergen County	789
Trenton, NJ (city) Mercer County	778
Bayonne, NJ (city) Hudson County	756
Elizabeth, NJ (city) Union County	714
Union City, NJ (city) Hudson County	686

Specified Housing Units Rented by Hondurans
Top 10 Places Sorted by Number

Place	Dollars/Month
Morris, NJ (town) Morris County	1,099
New Brunswick, NJ (city) Middlesex County	886
North Bergen, NJ (township) Hudson County	775
West New York, NJ (town) Hudson County	709
Elizabeth, NJ (city) Union County	703
Union City, NJ (city) Hudson County	694
Plainfield, NJ (city) Union County	691
Passaic, NJ (city) Passaic County	649
Newark, NJ (city) Essex County	616
Jersey City, NJ (city) Hudson County	599

Specified Housing Units Rented by Mexicans
Top 10 Places Sorted by Number

Place	Dollars/Month
Dover, NJ (town) Morris County	1,103
New Brunswick, NJ (city) Middlesex County	983
Franklin, NJ (township) Somerset County	894
Somerset, NJ (cdp) Somerset County	892
North Bergen, NJ (township) Hudson County	885
Clifton, NJ (city) Passaic County	875
Princeton, NJ (township) Mercer County	870
Hackensack, NJ (city) Bergen County	867

Brick, NJ (township) Ocean County	860
Freehold, NJ (borough) Monmouth County	855

Specified Housing Units Rented by Nicaraguans
Top 10 Places Sorted by Number

Place	Dollars/Month
Camden, NJ (city) Camden County	732
Jersey City, NJ (city) Hudson County	663

Specified Housing Units Rented by Panamanians
Top 10 Places Sorted by Number

Place	Dollars/Month

No places met population threshold.

Specified Housing Units Rented by Paraguayans
Top 10 Places Sorted by Number

Place	Dollars/Month

No places met population threshold.

Specified Housing Units Rented by Peruvians
Top 10 Places Sorted by Number

Place	Dollars/Month
Elmwood Park, NJ (borough) Bergen County	896
Woodbridge, NJ (township) Middlesex County	860
North Bergen, NJ (township) Hudson County	845
Garfield, NJ (city) Bergen County	836
Clifton, NJ (city) Passaic County	832
Belleville, NJ (cdp) Essex County	823
West Orange, NJ (cdp) Essex County	810
Kearny, NJ (town) Hudson County	803
Paterson, NJ (city) Passaic County	770
Harrison, NJ (town) Hudson County	760

Specified Housing Units Rented by Puerto Ricans
Top 10 Places Sorted by Number

Place	Dollars/Month
Bridgewater, NJ (township) Somerset County	1,250
Fair Lawn, NJ (borough) Bergen County	1,143
Manalapan, NJ (township) Monmouth County	1,125
Wayne, NJ (cdp) Passaic County	1,114
Bergenfield, NJ (borough) Bergen County	1,070
Hazlet, NJ (township) Monmouth County	1,054
Elmwood Park, NJ (borough) Bergen County	1,047
Willingboro, NJ (township) Burlington County	986
Secaucus, NJ (town) Hudson County	982
Fort Lee, NJ (borough) Bergen County	974

Specified Housing Units Rented by Salvadorans
Top 10 Places Sorted by Number

Place	Dollars/Month
North Plainfield, NJ (borough) Somerset County	942
Fairview, NJ (borough) Bergen County	841
Plainfield, NJ (city) Union County	829
Paterson, NJ (city) Passaic County	816
Guttenberg, NJ (town) Hudson County	760
Elizabeth, NJ (city) Union County	734
West New York, NJ (town) Hudson County	710
North Bergen, NJ (township) Hudson County	708
Newark, NJ (city) Essex County	688
Union City, NJ (city) Hudson County	686

Specified Housing Units Rented by South Americans
Top 10 Places Sorted by Number

Place	Dollars/Month
East Brunswick, NJ (cdp) Middlesex County	1,125
Dover, NJ (township) Ocean County	1,106
Toms River, NJ (cdp) Ocean County	1,106
Nutley, NJ (cdp) Essex County	1,050
New Brunswick, NJ (city) Middlesex County	1,034
Secaucus, NJ (town) Hudson County	1,023
Union, NJ (cdp) Union County	1,007

Notes: Please refer to the User's Guide for an explanation of data; tables include places with populations > 9,999 and reflect only those areas that meet Summary File 4 population thresholds, therefore there may be less than 10 places listed

Place	
Teaneck, NJ (cdp) Bergen County	1,000
Dover, NJ (town) Morris County	984
Fort Lee, NJ (borough) Bergen County	983

Specified Housing Units Rented by Spaniards
Top 10 Places Sorted by Number

Place	Dollars/Month
Bayonne, NJ (city) Hudson County	789
Kearny, NJ (town) Hudson County	771
Newark, NJ (city) Essex County	682

Specified Housing Units Rented by Uruguayans
Top 10 Places Sorted by Number

Place	Dollars/Month
West Orange, NJ (cdp) Essex County	886
Elizabeth, NJ (city) Union County	736

Specified Housing Units Rented by Venezuelans
Top 10 Places Sorted by Number

Place	Dollars/Month
No places met population threshold.	

Specified Housing Units Rented by Other Hispanics
Top 10 Places Sorted by Number

Place	Dollars/Month
Teaneck, NJ (cdp) Bergen County	1,518
Bridgewater, NJ (township) Somerset County	1,323
Summit, NJ (city) Union County	1,215
Edison, NJ (cdp) Middlesex County	986
Nutley, NJ (cdp) Essex County	965
Piscataway, NJ (township) Middlesex County	965
Wayne, NJ (cdp) Passaic County	960
Ridgefield Park, NJ (village) Bergen County	956
Dover, NJ (town) Morris County	948
Bergenfield, NJ (borough) Bergen County	932

Median Home Value

All Specified Owner-Occupied Housing Units
Top 10 Places Sorted by Number

Place	Dollars
Franklin Lakes, NJ (borough) Bergen County	609,400
Millburn, NJ (cdp) Essex County	549,000
Summit, NJ (city) Union County	469,200
Hoboken, NJ (city) Hudson County	428,900
Warren, NJ (township) Somerset County	427,200
Colts Neck, NJ (township) Monmouth County	425,500
Wyckoff, NJ (cdp) Bergen County	417,500
Princeton, NJ (township) Mercer County	417,000
Tenafly, NJ (borough) Bergen County	403,600
Ridgewood, NJ (village) Bergen County	387,200

Specified Housing Units Owned and Occupied by Hispanics
Top 10 Places Sorted by Number

Place	Dollars
Franklin Lakes, NJ (borough) Bergen County	628,700
Hoboken, NJ (city) Hudson County	425,000
Montville, NJ (township) Morris County	417,400
Wyckoff, NJ (cdp) Bergen County	404,500
Millburn, NJ (cdp) Essex County	400,000
Warren, NJ (township) Somerset County	387,500
Madison, NJ (borough) Morris County	383,300
Princeton, NJ (township) Mercer County	380,000
Berkeley Heights, NJ (cdp) Union County	336,100
Montclair, NJ (cdp) Essex County	324,400

Specified Housing Units Owned and Occupied by Argentinians
Top 10 Places Sorted by Number

Place	Dollars
North Bergen, NJ (township) Hudson County	112,500

Specified Housing Units Owned and Occupied by Bolivians
Top 10 Places Sorted by Number

Place	Dollars
No places met population threshold.	

Specified Housing Units Owned and Occupied by Central Americans
Top 10 Places Sorted by Number

Place	Dollars
Fort Lee, NJ (borough) Bergen County	265,600
Passaic, NJ (city) Passaic County	265,000
North Bergen, NJ (township) Hudson County	238,600
West Orange, NJ (cdp) Essex County	236,100
Englewood, NJ (city) Bergen County	203,600
Hackensack, NJ (city) Bergen County	187,500
West New York, NJ (town) Hudson County	179,200
Union City, NJ (city) Hudson County	173,200
Woodbridge, NJ (township) Middlesex County	170,000
Guttenberg, NJ (town) Hudson County	162,500

Specified Housing Units Owned and Occupied by Chileans
Top 10 Places Sorted by Number

Place	Dollars
North Bergen, NJ (township) Hudson County	112,500

Specified Housing Units Owned and Occupied by Colombians
Top 10 Places Sorted by Number

Place	Dollars
West New York, NJ (town) Hudson County	552,100
Union City, NJ (city) Hudson County	321,400
Elmwood Park, NJ (borough) Bergen County	220,000
Morris, NJ (town) Morris County	200,000
Teaneck, NJ (cdp) Bergen County	195,800
Lodi, NJ (borough) Bergen County	192,500
Bergenfield, NJ (borough) Bergen County	192,000
Parsippany-Troy Hills, NJ (township) Morris County	185,900
Hackensack, NJ (city) Bergen County	181,100
Englewood, NJ (city) Bergen County	180,000

Specified Housing Units Owned and Occupied by Costa Ricans
Top 10 Places Sorted by Number

Place	Dollars
Elizabeth, NJ (city) Union County	95,000
Trenton, NJ (city) Mercer County	48,100
Bound Brook, NJ (borough) Somerset County	0
Paterson, NJ (city) Passaic County	0
Somerville, NJ (borough) Somerset County	0

Specified Housing Units Owned and Occupied by Cubans
Top 10 Places Sorted by Number

Place	Dollars
Cliffside Park, NJ (borough) Bergen County	328,800
Fort Lee, NJ (borough) Bergen County	275,000
Weehawken, NJ (township) Hudson County	239,300
Edison, NJ (cdp) Middlesex County	196,900
Bayonne, NJ (city) Hudson County	195,000
Union, NJ (cdp) Union County	185,100
Elmwood Park, NJ (borough) Bergen County	181,900
Newark, NJ (city) Essex County	176,500
Woodbridge, NJ (township) Middlesex County	172,700

Place	
Bloomfield, NJ (cdp) Essex County	168,200

Specified Housing Units Owned and Occupied by Dominicans
Top 10 Places Sorted by Number

Place	Dollars
Weehawken, NJ (township) Hudson County	275,000
Fort Lee, NJ (borough) Bergen County	260,400
Palisades Park, NJ (borough) Bergen County	255,800
Fairview, NJ (borough) Bergen County	252,500
Garfield, NJ (city) Bergen County	225,000
Hackensack, NJ (city) Bergen County	193,100
North Bergen, NJ (township) Hudson County	192,700
Bergenfield, NJ (borough) Bergen County	192,500
Guttenberg, NJ (town) Hudson County	187,500
Somerset, NJ (cdp) Somerset County	187,500

Specified Housing Units Owned and Occupied by Ecuadorians
Top 10 Places Sorted by Number

Place	Dollars
Hackensack, NJ (city) Bergen County	193,400
North Bergen, NJ (township) Hudson County	170,000
Clifton, NJ (city) Passaic County	166,700
Paterson, NJ (city) Passaic County	165,000
Bloomfield, NJ (cdp) Essex County	159,000
Bayonne, NJ (city) Hudson County	152,100
Belleville, NJ (cdp) Essex County	149,400
Dover, NJ (town) Morris County	148,200
East Windsor, NJ (township) Mercer County	146,400
Kearny, NJ (town) Hudson County	145,300

Specified Housing Units Owned and Occupied by Guatelmalans
Top 10 Places Sorted by Number

Place	Dollars
North Plainfield, NJ (borough) Somerset County	156,300
Plainfield, NJ (city) Union County	143,800
Bayonne, NJ (city) Hudson County	137,500
Elizabeth, NJ (city) Union County	137,500
West New York, NJ (town) Hudson County	119,200
East Windsor, NJ (township) Mercer County	90,800
Newark, NJ (city) Essex County	75,000
Trenton, NJ (city) Mercer County	49,400
Fairview, NJ (borough) Bergen County	0
Jersey City, NJ (city) Hudson County	0

Specified Housing Units Owned and Occupied by Hondurans
Top 10 Places Sorted by Number

Place	Dollars
North Bergen, NJ (township) Hudson County	260,500
Passaic, NJ (city) Passaic County	166,700
Jersey City, NJ (city) Hudson County	156,300
Elizabeth, NJ (city) Union County	154,400
New Brunswick, NJ (city) Middlesex County	152,100
Morris, NJ (town) Morris County	137,500
Union City, NJ (city) Hudson County	130,400
Plainfield, NJ (city) Union County	104,800
Newark, NJ (city) Essex County	0
West New York, NJ (town) Hudson County	0

Specified Housing Units Owned and Occupied by Mexicans
Top 10 Places Sorted by Number

Place	Dollars
Princeton, NJ (township) Mercer County	450,000
North Bergen, NJ (township) Hudson County	275,000
West Orange, NJ (cdp) Essex County	263,300
Bound Brook, NJ (borough) Somerset County	190,600
Woodbridge, NJ (township) Middlesex County	189,400
Freehold, NJ (township) Monmouth County	187,500
Hackensack, NJ (city) Bergen County	187,500

Notes: Please refer to the User's Guide for an explanation of data; tables include places with populations > 9,999 and reflect only those areas that meet Summary File 4 population thresholds, therefore there may be less than 10 places listed

Paterson, NJ (city) Passaic County ... 178,800
Clifton, NJ (city) Passaic County ... 162,100
Dover, NJ (town) Morris County ... 161,000

Specified Housing Units Owned and Occupied by Nicaraguans
Top 10 Places Sorted by Number

Place	Dollars
Jersey City, NJ (city) Hudson County	90,600
Camden, NJ (city) Camden County	37,300

Specified Housing Units Owned and Occupied by Panamanians
Top 10 Places Sorted by Number

Place	Dollars
No places met population threshold.	

Specified Housing Units Owned and Occupied by Paraguayans
Top 10 Places Sorted by Number

Place	Dollars
No places met population threshold.	

Specified Housing Units Owned and Occupied by Peruvians
Top 10 Places Sorted by Number

Place	Dollars
Garfield, NJ (city) Bergen County	204,200
Elmwood Park, NJ (borough) Bergen County	188,700
Newark, NJ (city) Essex County	173,200
Harrison, NJ (town) Hudson County	162,500
Union City, NJ (city) Hudson County	160,400
Clifton, NJ (city) Passaic County	156,100
North Bergen, NJ (township) Hudson County	154,800
Kearny, NJ (town) Hudson County	152,000
Belleville, NJ (cdp) Essex County	144,800
Passaic, NJ (city) Passaic County	142,800

Specified Housing Units Owned and Occupied by Puerto Ricans
Top 10 Places Sorted by Number

Place	Dollars
Hoboken, NJ (city) Hudson County	550,000
Montclair, NJ (cdp) Essex County	300,000
Wayne, NJ (cdp) Passaic County	287,000
Bridgewater, NJ (township) Somerset County	245,000
Marlboro, NJ (township) Monmouth County	237,500
Secaucus, NJ (town) Hudson County	233,300
South Brunswick, NJ (township) Middlesex County	231,300
West Orange, NJ (cdp) Essex County	229,400
Cliffside Park, NJ (borough) Bergen County	229,200
Rutherford, NJ (borough) Bergen County	223,900

Specified Housing Units Owned and Occupied by Salvadorans
Top 10 Places Sorted by Number

Place	Dollars
West New York, NJ (town) Hudson County	187,500
Union City, NJ (city) Hudson County	183,900
Jersey City, NJ (city) Hudson County	173,400
North Plainfield, NJ (borough) Somerset County	148,200
Elizabeth, NJ (city) Union County	132,400
Paterson, NJ (city) Passaic County	129,700
North Bergen, NJ (township) Hudson County	124,000
Guttenberg, NJ (town) Hudson County	121,400
Plainfield, NJ (city) Union County	116,400
Newark, NJ (city) Essex County	99,600

Specified Housing Units Owned and Occupied by South Americans
Top 10 Places Sorted by Number

Place	Dollars
Fort Lee, NJ (borough) Bergen County	375,000
Montclair, NJ (cdp) Essex County	332,100
Palisades Park, NJ (borough) Bergen County	275,000
Secaucus, NJ (town) Hudson County	263,600
Wayne, NJ (cdp) Passaic County	249,000
Hoboken, NJ (city) Hudson County	239,600
Rockaway, NJ (township) Morris County	222,700
Ocean, NJ (township) Monmouth County	221,400

Bridgewater, NJ (township) Somerset County ... 219,200
Elmwood Park, NJ (borough) Bergen County ... 205,500

Specified Housing Units Owned and Occupied by Spaniards
Top 10 Places Sorted by Number

Place	Dollars
Bayonne, NJ (city) Hudson County	275,000
Kearny, NJ (town) Hudson County	172,700
Newark, NJ (city) Essex County	162,500

Specified Housing Units Owned and Occupied by Uruguayans
Top 10 Places Sorted by Number

Place	Dollars
West Orange, NJ (cdp) Essex County	162,500
Elizabeth, NJ (city) Union County	129,800

Specified Housing Units Owned and Occupied by Venezuelans
Top 10 Places Sorted by Number

Place	Dollars
No places met population threshold.	

Specified Housing Units Owned and Occupied by Other Hispanics
Top 10 Places Sorted by Number

Place	Dollars
Weehawken, NJ (township) Hudson County	1 Mil.+
Fort Lee, NJ (borough) Bergen County	332,100
Bridgewater, NJ (township) Somerset County	331,600
Morris, NJ (town) Morris County	252,300
Wayne, NJ (cdp) Passaic County	246,300
Summit, NJ (city) Union County	240,000
Palisades Park, NJ (borough) Bergen County	240,000
Bergenfield, NJ (borough) Bergen County	221,200
Parsippany-Troy Hills, NJ (township) Morris County	218,300
Cliffside Park, NJ (borough) Bergen County	214,500

Notes: Please refer to the User's Guide for an explanation of data; tables include places with populations > 9,999 and reflect only those areas that meet Summary File 4 population thresholds, therefore there may be less than 10 places listed

Population

Total Population
Top 10 Places Sorted by Number

Place	Number
Newark, NJ (city) Essex County	273,546
Jersey City, NJ (city) Hudson County	240,055
Paterson, NJ (city) Passaic County	149,222
Elizabeth, NJ (city) Union County	120,568
Edison, NJ (township) Middlesex County	97,687
Woodbridge, NJ (township) Middlesex County	97,203
Dover, NJ (township) Ocean County	89,767
Hamilton, NJ (township) Mercer County	87,254
Toms River, NJ (cdp) Ocean County	86,452
Trenton, NJ (city) Mercer County	85,258

Asian
Top 10 Places Sorted by Number

Place	Number
Jersey City, NJ (city) Hudson County	39,070
Edison, NJ (township) Middlesex County	28,438
Woodbridge, NJ (township) Middlesex County	13,949
Piscataway, NJ (township) Middlesex County	12,562
Fort Lee, NJ (borough) Bergen County	11,004
Parsippany-Troy Hills, NJ (township) Morris County	9,048
East Brunswick, NJ (township) Middlesex County	7,634
Palisades Park, NJ (borough) Bergen County	7,002
South Brunswick, NJ (township) Middlesex County	6,888
Cherry Hill, NJ (township) Camden County	6,595

Asian
Top 10 Places Sorted by Percent of Total Population

Place	Percent
Palisades Park, NJ (borough) Bergen County	41.01
Plainsboro Center, NJ (cdp) Middlesex County	35.34
Society Hill, NJ (cdp) Middlesex County	34.51
Fort Lee, NJ (borough) Bergen County	31.03
Plainsboro, NJ (township) Middlesex County	30.49
Princeton Meadows, NJ (cdp) Middlesex County	29.26
Edison, NJ (township) Middlesex County	29.11
Englewood Cliffs, NJ (borough) Bergen County	29.01
Leonia, NJ (borough) Bergen County	26.25
Piscataway, NJ (township) Middlesex County	24.88

Native Hawaiian and Other Pacific Islander
Top 10 Places Sorted by Number

Place	Number
No places met population threshold.	

Native Hawaiian and Other Pacific Islander
Top 10 Places Sorted by Percent of Asian Population

Place	Percent
No places met population threshold.	

Native Hawaiian and Other Pacific Islander
Top 10 Places Sorted by Percent of Total Population

Place	Percent
No places met population threshold.	

Asian Indian
Top 10 Places Sorted by Number

Place	Number
Edison, NJ (township) Middlesex County	16,349
Jersey City, NJ (city) Hudson County	13,384
Woodbridge, NJ (township) Middlesex County	8,806
Piscataway, NJ (township) Middlesex County	5,941
Parsippany-Troy Hills, NJ (township) Morris County	4,120
South Brunswick, NJ (township) Middlesex County	3,861
Franklin, NJ (township) Somerset County	3,311
Plainsboro, NJ (township) Middlesex County	3,266
North Brunswick, NJ (township) Middlesex County	3,010
Clifton, NJ (city) Passaic County	2,925

Asian Indian
Top 10 Places Sorted by Percent of Asian Population

Place	Percent
Iselin, NJ (cdp) Middlesex County	70.74
Roselle Park, NJ (borough) Union County	70.64
North Bergen, NJ (township) Hudson County	67.24
Carteret, NJ (borough) Middlesex County	66.55
Avenel, NJ (cdp) Middlesex County	66.23
Passaic, NJ (city) Passaic County	65.85
Plainsboro Center, NJ (cdp) Middlesex County	64.68
East Windsor, NJ (township) Mercer County	63.14
Woodbridge, NJ (township) Middlesex County	63.13
Elmwood Park, NJ (borough) Bergen County	62.03

Asian Indian
Top 10 Places Sorted by Percent of Total Population

Place	Percent
Plainsboro Center, NJ (cdp) Middlesex County	22.86
Society Hill, NJ (cdp) Middlesex County	19.43
Iselin, NJ (cdp) Middlesex County	16.97
Edison, NJ (township) Middlesex County	16.74
Princeton Meadows, NJ (cdp) Middlesex County	16.45
Plainsboro, NJ (township) Middlesex County	16.16
Dayton, NJ (cdp) Middlesex County	15.26
Avenel, NJ (cdp) Middlesex County	12.44
Piscataway, NJ (township) Middlesex County	11.77
Madison Park, NJ (cdp) Middlesex County	10.26

Bangladeshi
Top 10 Places Sorted by Number

Place	Number
Paterson, NJ (city) Passaic County	459

Bangladeshi
Top 10 Places Sorted by Percent of Asian Population

Place	Percent
Paterson, NJ (city) Passaic County	16.52

Bangladeshi
Top 10 Places Sorted by Percent of Total Population

Place	Percent
Paterson, NJ (city) Passaic County	0.31

Cambodian
Top 10 Places Sorted by Number

Place	Number
No places met population threshold.	

Cambodian
Top 10 Places Sorted by Percent of Asian Population

Place	Percent
No places met population threshold.	

Cambodian
Top 10 Places Sorted by Percent of Total Population

Place	Percent
No places met population threshold.	

Chinese (except Taiwanese)
Top 10 Places Sorted by Number

Place	Number
Edison, NJ (township) Middlesex County	5,826
East Brunswick, NJ (township) Middlesex County	3,100
Jersey City, NJ (city) Hudson County	2,907
Marlboro, NJ (township) Monmouth County	2,627
Parsippany-Troy Hills, NJ (township) Morris County	2,616
Piscataway, NJ (township) Middlesex County	2,495
Cherry Hill, NJ (township) Camden County	1,833
West Windsor, NJ (township) Mercer County	1,816
Fort Lee, NJ (borough) Bergen County	1,724
Plainsboro, NJ (township) Middlesex County	1,674

Chinese (except Taiwanese)
Top 10 Places Sorted by Percent of Asian Population

Place	Percent
Harrison, NJ (town) Hudson County	74.70
Holmdel, NJ (township) Monmouth County	61.95
Morganville, NJ (cdp) Monmouth County	61.15
Marlboro, NJ (township) Monmouth County	57.74
Hazlet, NJ (township) Monmouth County	51.84
East Hanover, NJ (township) Morris County	49.48
Bernards, NJ (township) Somerset County	48.75
Montgomery, NJ (township) Somerset County	46.68
Hanover, NJ (township) Morris County	45.51
Highland Park, NJ (borough) Middlesex County	44.76

Chinese (except Taiwanese)
Top 10 Places Sorted by Percent of Total Population

Place	Percent
Holmdel, NJ (township) Monmouth County	10.25
Harrison, NJ (town) Hudson County	9.11
West Windsor, NJ (township) Mercer County	8.29
Plainsboro, NJ (township) Middlesex County	8.28
Englewood Cliffs, NJ (borough) Bergen County	7.33
Marlboro, NJ (township) Monmouth County	7.22
Princeton Meadows, NJ (cdp) Middlesex County	6.72
Greentree, NJ (cdp) Camden County	6.71
East Brunswick, NJ (township) Middlesex County	6.63
Highland Park, NJ (borough) Middlesex County	6.16

Fijian
Top 10 Places Sorted by Number

Place	Number
No places met population threshold.	

Fijian
Top 10 Places Sorted by Percent of Asian Population

Place	Percent
No places met population threshold.	

Fijian
Top 10 Places Sorted by Percent of Total Population

Place	Percent
No places met population threshold.	

Filipino
Top 10 Places Sorted by Number

Place	Number
Jersey City, NJ (city) Hudson County	16,459
Bergenfield, NJ (borough) Bergen County	3,228
Edison, NJ (township) Middlesex County	2,572
Piscataway, NJ (township) Middlesex County	2,153
Union, NJ (township) Union County	2,131
Belleville, NJ (township) Essex County	2,129
Woodbridge, NJ (township) Middlesex County	1,939
Bloomfield, NJ (township) Essex County	1,589
Cherry Hill, NJ (township) Camden County	1,479
Bayonne, NJ (city) Hudson County	1,329

Filipino
Top 10 Places Sorted by Percent of Asian Population

Place	Percent
Bergenfield, NJ (borough) Bergen County	60.37
Bayonne, NJ (city) Hudson County	51.14
Belleville, NJ (township) Essex County	50.35
Union, NJ (township) Union County	50.05
Lakewood, NJ (township) Ocean County	47.28
Rahway, NJ (city) Union County	44.91
Washington, NJ (township) Gloucester County	44.07
Jersey City, NJ (city) Hudson County	42.13
New Milford, NJ (borough) Bergen County	41.24
Gloucester, NJ (township) Camden County	39.92

Notes: Please refer to the User's Guide for an explanation of data; tables reflect only those areas that meet Summary File 4 population thresholds, therefore there may be less than 10 places listed

Filipino
Top 10 Places Sorted by Percent of Total Population

Place	Percent
Bergenfield, NJ (borough) Bergen County	12.30
Jersey City, NJ (city) Hudson County	6.86
Belleville, NJ (township) Essex County	5.93
New Milford, NJ (borough) Bergen County	5.81
Fords, NJ (cdp) Middlesex County	4.35
Piscataway, NJ (township) Middlesex County	4.26
Secaucus, NJ (town) Hudson County	4.01
Union, NJ (township) Union County	3.92
Little Ferry, NJ (borough) Bergen County	3.56
Dumont, NJ (borough) Bergen County	3.46

Guamanian or Chamorro
Top 10 Places Sorted by Number

Place	Number
No places met population threshold.	

Guamanian or Chamorro
Top 10 Places Sorted by Percent of Asian Population

Place	Percent
No places met population threshold.	

Guamanian or Chamorro
Top 10 Places Sorted by Percent of Total Population

Place	Percent
No places met population threshold.	

Hawaiian, Native
Top 10 Places Sorted by Number

Place	Number
No places met population threshold.	

Hawaiian, Native
Top 10 Places Sorted by Percent of Asian Population

Place	Percent
No places met population threshold.	

Hawaiian, Native
Top 10 Places Sorted by Percent of Total Population

Place	Percent
No places met population threshold.	

Hmong
Top 10 Places Sorted by Number

Place	Number
No places met population threshold.	

Hmong
Top 10 Places Sorted by Percent of Asian Population

Place	Percent
No places met population threshold.	

Hmong
Top 10 Places Sorted by Percent of Total Population

Place	Percent
No places met population threshold.	

Indonesian
Top 10 Places Sorted by Number

Place	Number
No places met population threshold.	

Indonesian
Top 10 Places Sorted by Percent of Asian Population

Place	Percent
No places met population threshold.	

Indonesian
Top 10 Places Sorted by Percent of Total Population

Place	Percent
No places met population threshold.	

Japanese
Top 10 Places Sorted by Number

Place	Number
Fort Lee, NJ (borough) Bergen County	2,008
Ridgewood, NJ (village) Bergen County	447
Cliffside Park, NJ (borough) Bergen County	446

Japanese
Top 10 Places Sorted by Percent of Asian Population

Place	Percent
Ridgewood, NJ (village) Bergen County	21.17
Fort Lee, NJ (borough) Bergen County	18.25
Cliffside Park, NJ (borough) Bergen County	16.83

Japanese
Top 10 Places Sorted by Percent of Total Population

Place	Percent
Fort Lee, NJ (borough) Bergen County	5.66
Cliffside Park, NJ (borough) Bergen County	1.94
Ridgewood, NJ (village) Bergen County	1.79

Korean
Top 10 Places Sorted by Number

Place	Number
Fort Lee, NJ (borough) Bergen County	5,911
Palisades Park, NJ (borough) Bergen County	5,902
Cliffside Park, NJ (borough) Bergen County	1,482
Jersey City, NJ (city) Hudson County	1,481
Leonia, NJ (borough) Bergen County	1,459
Paramus, NJ (borough) Bergen County	1,390
Ridgefield, NJ (borough) Bergen County	1,341
Edison, NJ (township) Middlesex County	1,261
Tenafly, NJ (borough) Bergen County	1,179
Cherry Hill, NJ (township) Camden County	1,017

Korean
Top 10 Places Sorted by Percent of Asian Population

Place	Percent
Palisades Park, NJ (borough) Bergen County	84.29
Ridgefield, NJ (borough) Bergen County	75.51
Browns Mills, NJ (cdp) Burlington County	73.22
Norwood, NJ (borough) Bergen County	73.07
Old Tappan, NJ (borough) Bergen County	62.73
Leonia, NJ (borough) Bergen County	62.35
Pemberton, NJ (township) Burlington County	58.17
Closter, NJ (borough) Bergen County	57.61
Harrington Park, NJ (borough) Bergen County	57.18
Cliffside Park, NJ (borough) Bergen County	55.92

Korean
Top 10 Places Sorted by Percent of Total Population

Place	Percent
Palisades Park, NJ (borough) Bergen County	34.57
Fort Lee, NJ (borough) Bergen County	16.67
Leonia, NJ (borough) Bergen County	16.37
Norwood, NJ (borough) Bergen County	13.35
Englewood Cliffs, NJ (borough) Bergen County	12.70
Ridgefield, NJ (borough) Bergen County	12.38
Closter, NJ (borough) Bergen County	11.83
Edgewater, NJ (borough) Bergen County	11.74
Demarest, NJ (borough) Bergen County	10.67
Alpine, NJ (borough) Bergen County	10.31

Laotian
Top 10 Places Sorted by Number

Place	Number
No places met population threshold.	

Laotian
Top 10 Places Sorted by Percent of Asian Population

Place	Percent
No places met population threshold.	

Laotian
Top 10 Places Sorted by Percent of Total Population

Place	Percent
No places met population threshold.	

Malaysian
Top 10 Places Sorted by Number

Place	Number
No places met population threshold.	

Malaysian
Top 10 Places Sorted by Percent of Asian Population

Place	Percent
No places met population threshold.	

Malaysian
Top 10 Places Sorted by Percent of Total Population

Place	Percent
No places met population threshold.	

Pakistani
Top 10 Places Sorted by Number

Place	Number
Jersey City, NJ (city) Hudson County	1,878
Edison, NJ (township) Middlesex County	674
Old Bridge, NJ (township) Middlesex County	526
Woodbridge, NJ (township) Middlesex County	467

Pakistani
Top 10 Places Sorted by Percent of Asian Population

Place	Percent
Old Bridge, NJ (township) Middlesex County	8.11
Jersey City, NJ (city) Hudson County	4.81
Woodbridge, NJ (township) Middlesex County	3.35
Edison, NJ (township) Middlesex County	2.37

Pakistani
Top 10 Places Sorted by Percent of Total Population

Place	Percent
Old Bridge, NJ (township) Middlesex County	0.87
Jersey City, NJ (city) Hudson County	0.78
Edison, NJ (township) Middlesex County	0.69
Woodbridge, NJ (township) Middlesex County	0.48

Samoan
Top 10 Places Sorted by Number

Place	Number
No places met population threshold.	

Samoan
Top 10 Places Sorted by Percent of Asian Population

Place	Percent
No places met population threshold.	

Samoan
Top 10 Places Sorted by Percent of Total Population

Place	Percent
No places met population threshold.	

Sri Lankan
Top 10 Places Sorted by Number

Place	Number
No places met population threshold.	

Notes: Please refer to the User's Guide for an explanation of data; tables reflect only those areas that meet Summary File 4 population thresholds, therefore there may be less than 10 places listed

Sri Lankan
Top 10 Places Sorted by Percent of Asian Population

Place	Percent
No places met population threshold.	

Sri Lankan
Top 10 Places Sorted by Percent of Total Population

Place	Percent
No places met population threshold.	

Taiwanese
Top 10 Places Sorted by Number

Place	Number
Edison, NJ (township) Middlesex County	663

Taiwanese
Top 10 Places Sorted by Percent of Asian Population

Place	Percent
Edison, NJ (township) Middlesex County	2.33

Taiwanese
Top 10 Places Sorted by Percent of Total Population

Place	Percent
Edison, NJ (township) Middlesex County	0.68

Thai
Top 10 Places Sorted by Number

Place	Number
No places met population threshold.	

Thai
Top 10 Places Sorted by Percent of Asian Population

Place	Percent
No places met population threshold.	

Thai
Top 10 Places Sorted by Percent of Total Population

Place	Percent
No places met population threshold.	

Tongan
Top 10 Places Sorted by Number

Place	Number
No places met population threshold.	

Tongan
Top 10 Places Sorted by Percent of Asian Population

Place	Percent
No places met population threshold.	

Tongan
Top 10 Places Sorted by Percent of Total Population

Place	Percent
No places met population threshold.	

Vietnamese
Top 10 Places Sorted by Number

Place	Number
Camden, NJ (city) Camden County	1,419
Jersey City, NJ (city) Hudson County	1,394
Atlantic City, NJ (city) Atlantic County	1,187
Pennsauken, NJ (township) Camden County	692
Belleville, NJ (township) Essex County	424
South Plainfield, NJ (borough) Middlesex County	366
Woodlynne, NJ (borough) Camden County	285

Vietnamese
Top 10 Places Sorted by Percent of Asian Population

Place	Percent
Woodlynne, NJ (borough) Camden County	78.30
Camden, NJ (city) Camden County	61.35
Pennsauken, NJ (township) Camden County	44.47
Atlantic City, NJ (city) Atlantic County	28.73
South Plainfield, NJ (borough) Middlesex County	20.78
Belleville, NJ (township) Essex County	10.03
Jersey City, NJ (city) Hudson County	3.57

Vietnamese
Top 10 Places Sorted by Percent of Total Population

Place	Percent
Woodlynne, NJ (borough) Camden County	10.19
Atlantic City, NJ (city) Atlantic County	2.93
Pennsauken, NJ (township) Camden County	1.94
Camden, NJ (city) Camden County	1.78
South Plainfield, NJ (borough) Middlesex County	1.68
Belleville, NJ (township) Essex County	1.18
Jersey City, NJ (city) Hudson County	0.58

Median Age

Total Population
Top 10 Places Sorted by Number

Place	Years
Monroe, NJ (township) Middlesex County	58.7
Saddle River, NJ (borough) Bergen County	47.1
Englewood Cliffs, NJ (borough) Bergen County	45.1
Alpine, NJ (borough) Bergen County	44.4
Springdale, NJ (cdp) Camden County	44.2
Watchung, NJ (borough) Somerset County	44.1
Cedar Grove, NJ (township) Essex County	43.5
Erlton-Ellisburg, NJ (cdp) Camden County	43.2
Clark, NJ (township) Union County	43.1
Paramus, NJ (borough) Bergen County	42.9

Asian
Top 10 Places Sorted by Number

Place	Years
Moorestown, NJ (township) Burlington County	46.4
Pemberton, NJ (township) Burlington County	46.0
Browns Mills, NJ (cdp) Burlington County	45.1
Monroe, NJ (township) Middlesex County	43.8
Saddle River, NJ (borough) Bergen County	42.9
West Caldwell, NJ (township) Essex County	42.1
West Freehold, NJ (cdp) Monmouth County	42.1
Emerson, NJ (borough) Bergen County	41.3
Alpine, NJ (borough) Bergen County	41.1
White Meadow Lake, NJ (cdp) Morris County	41.0

Native Hawaiian and Other Pacific Islander
Top 10 Places Sorted by Number

Place	Years
No places met population threshold.	

Asian Indian
Top 10 Places Sorted by Number

Place	Years
Warren, NJ (township) Somerset County	41.4
Holmdel, NJ (township) Monmouth County	39.3
Princeton, NJ (township) Mercer County	38.6
Livingston, NJ (township) Essex County	38.3
Teaneck, NJ (township) Bergen County	38.2
Rockaway, NJ (township) Morris County	37.1
Montville, NJ (township) Morris County	36.7
Rutherford, NJ (borough) Bergen County	36.5
Washington, NJ (township) Gloucester County	36.5
Freehold, NJ (township) Monmouth County	36.4

Bangladeshi
Top 10 Places Sorted by Number

Place	Years
Paterson, NJ (city) Passaic County	26.3

Cambodian
Top 10 Places Sorted by Number

Place	Years
No places met population threshold.	

Chinese (except Taiwanese)
Top 10 Places Sorted by Number

Place	Years
Atlantic City, NJ (city) Atlantic County	41.5
Montclair, NJ (township) Essex County	40.8
Tenafly, NJ (borough) Bergen County	40.3
Springdale, NJ (cdp) Camden County	39.9
Greentree, NJ (cdp) Camden County	39.6
Hazlet, NJ (township) Monmouth County	39.6
Paramus, NJ (borough) Bergen County	39.4
West Orange, NJ (township) Essex County	39.3
Bernards, NJ (township) Somerset County	39.1
Cherry Hill, NJ (township) Camden County	39.1

Fijian
Top 10 Places Sorted by Number

Place	Years
No places met population threshold.	

Filipino
Top 10 Places Sorted by Number

Place	Years
Freehold, NJ (township) Monmouth County	49.6
Washington, NJ (township) Gloucester County	42.9
Parsippany-Troy Hills, NJ (township) Morris County	41.4
South Brunswick, NJ (township) Middlesex County	41.1
West Orange, NJ (township) Essex County	40.4
Colonia, NJ (cdp) Middlesex County	39.9
South Plainfield, NJ (borough) Middlesex County	39.9
Passaic, NJ (city) Passaic County	39.8
Atlantic City, NJ (city) Atlantic County	39.5
Fair Lawn, NJ (borough) Bergen County	39.2

Guamanian or Chamorro
Top 10 Places Sorted by Number

Place	Years
No places met population threshold.	

Hawaiian, Native
Top 10 Places Sorted by Number

Place	Years
No places met population threshold.	

Hmong
Top 10 Places Sorted by Number

Place	Years
No places met population threshold.	

Indonesian
Top 10 Places Sorted by Number

Place	Years
No places met population threshold.	

Japanese
Top 10 Places Sorted by Number

Place	Years
Ridgewood, NJ (village) Bergen County	39.7
Fort Lee, NJ (borough) Bergen County	33.4
Cliffside Park, NJ (borough) Bergen County	31.8

Notes: Please refer to the User's Guide for an explanation of data; tables reflect only those areas that meet Summary File 4 population thresholds, therefore there may be less than 10 places listed

Korean
Top 10 Places Sorted by Number

Place	Years
Alpine, NJ (borough) Bergen County	41.0
Pemberton, NJ (township) Burlington County	40.9
Browns Mills, NJ (cdp) Burlington County	40.4
Harrington Park, NJ (borough) Bergen County	40.2
Wayne, NJ (township) Passaic County	39.1
Livingston, NJ (township) Essex County	38.9
Demarest, NJ (borough) Bergen County	38.8
Englewood Cliffs, NJ (borough) Bergen County	38.4
Bayonne, NJ (city) Hudson County	38.3
Closter, NJ (borough) Bergen County	37.9

Laotian
Top 10 Places Sorted by Number

Place	Years
No places met population threshold.	

Malaysian
Top 10 Places Sorted by Number

Place	Years
No places met population threshold.	

Pakistani
Top 10 Places Sorted by Number

Place	Years
Old Bridge, NJ (township) Middlesex County	32.4
Jersey City, NJ (city) Hudson County	28.9
Edison, NJ (township) Middlesex County	27.2
Woodbridge, NJ (township) Middlesex County	23.9

Samoan
Top 10 Places Sorted by Number

Place	Years
No places met population threshold.	

Sri Lankan
Top 10 Places Sorted by Number

Place	Years
No places met population threshold.	

Taiwanese
Top 10 Places Sorted by Number

Place	Years
Edison, NJ (township) Middlesex County	37.2

Thai
Top 10 Places Sorted by Number

Place	Years
No places met population threshold.	

Tongan
Top 10 Places Sorted by Number

Place	Years
No places met population threshold.	

Vietnamese
Top 10 Places Sorted by Number

Place	Years
Woodlynne, NJ (borough) Camden County	32.2
Atlantic City, NJ (city) Atlantic County	31.4
Camden, NJ (city) Camden County	30.7
Pennsauken, NJ (township) Camden County	29.8
Jersey City, NJ (city) Hudson County	29.6
Belleville, NJ (township) Essex County	29.0
South Plainfield, NJ (borough) Middlesex County	28.3

Average Household Size

Total Population
Top 10 Places Sorted by Number

Place	Number
Passaic, NJ (city) Passaic County	3.45
Dover, NJ (town) Morris County	3.27
Paterson, NJ (city) Passaic County	3.25
New Brunswick, NJ (city) Middlesex County	3.22
Perth Amboy, NJ (city) Middlesex County	3.20
Colts Neck, NJ (township) Monmouth County	3.16
Franklin Lakes, NJ (borough) Bergen County	3.16
Marlboro, NJ (township) Monmouth County	3.14
Camden, NJ (city) Camden County	3.12
Dayton, NJ (cdp) Middlesex County	3.09

Asian
Top 10 Places Sorted by Number

Place	Number
Woodlynne, NJ (borough) Camden County	4.79
Boonton, NJ (town) Morris County	4.76
South Plainfield, NJ (borough) Middlesex County	4.51
Deptford, NJ (township) Gloucester County	4.44
Harrington Park, NJ (borough) Bergen County	4.39
Raritan, NJ (borough) Somerset County	4.37
Succasunna-Kenvil, NJ (cdp) Morris County	4.35
Pomona, NJ (cdp) Atlantic County	4.32
Northfield, NJ (city) Atlantic County	4.22
Paterson, NJ (city) Passaic County	4.22

Native Hawaiian and Other Pacific Islander
Top 10 Places Sorted by Number

Place	Number
No places met population threshold.	

Asian Indian
Top 10 Places Sorted by Number

Place	Number
Dumont, NJ (borough) Bergen County	5.16
South Plainfield, NJ (borough) Middlesex County	4.89
Paterson, NJ (city) Passaic County	4.84
Paramus, NJ (borough) Bergen County	4.58
Bergenfield, NJ (borough) Bergen County	4.41
Galloway, NJ (township) Atlantic County	4.29
Fair Lawn, NJ (borough) Bergen County	4.25
Clifton, NJ (city) Passaic County	4.15
Dover, NJ (township) Ocean County	4.01
Rockaway, NJ (township) Morris County	4.01

Bangladeshi
Top 10 Places Sorted by Number

Place	Number
Paterson, NJ (city) Passaic County	5.20

Cambodian
Top 10 Places Sorted by Number

Place	Number
No places met population threshold.	

Chinese (except Taiwanese)
Top 10 Places Sorted by Number

Place	Number
Springdale, NJ (cdp) Camden County	4.57
Hazlet, NJ (township) Monmouth County	3.99
Warren, NJ (township) Somerset County	3.66
Marlboro, NJ (township) Monmouth County	3.62
Montgomery, NJ (township) Somerset County	3.58
Cherry Hill, NJ (township) Camden County	3.57
Morganville, NJ (cdp) Monmouth County	3.56
West Windsor, NJ (township) Mercer County	3.54
Holmdel, NJ (township) Monmouth County	3.53
Randolph, NJ (township) Morris County	3.53

Fijian
Top 10 Places Sorted by Number

Place	Number
No places met population threshold.	

Filipino
Top 10 Places Sorted by Number

Place	Number
Bergenfield, NJ (borough) Bergen County	4.44
South Plainfield, NJ (borough) Middlesex County	4.32
Fair Lawn, NJ (borough) Bergen County	4.29
Union, NJ (township) Union County	4.24
East Brunswick, NJ (township) Middlesex County	4.21
Piscataway, NJ (township) Middlesex County	4.16
Voorhees, NJ (township) Camden County	4.08
Belleville, NJ (township) Essex County	4.07
Edison, NJ (township) Middlesex County	4.03
Howell, NJ (township) Monmouth County	3.97

Guamanian or Chamorro
Top 10 Places Sorted by Number

Place	Number
No places met population threshold.	

Hawaiian, Native
Top 10 Places Sorted by Number

Place	Number
No places met population threshold.	

Hmong
Top 10 Places Sorted by Number

Place	Number
No places met population threshold.	

Indonesian
Top 10 Places Sorted by Number

Place	Number
No places met population threshold.	

Japanese
Top 10 Places Sorted by Number

Place	Number
Ridgewood, NJ (village) Bergen County	3.11
Fort Lee, NJ (borough) Bergen County	2.49
Cliffside Park, NJ (borough) Bergen County	2.09

Korean
Top 10 Places Sorted by Number

Place	Number
Paramus, NJ (borough) Bergen County	4.16
Harrington Park, NJ (borough) Bergen County	4.15
Ridgewood, NJ (village) Bergen County	4.02
Browns Mills, NJ (cdp) Burlington County	3.99
Englewood Cliffs, NJ (borough) Bergen County	3.94
Norwood, NJ (borough) Bergen County	3.88
Leonia, NJ (borough) Bergen County	3.79
Cresskill, NJ (borough) Bergen County	3.75
Old Tappan, NJ (borough) Bergen County	3.75
Piscataway, NJ (township) Middlesex County	3.74

Laotian
Top 10 Places Sorted by Number

Place	Number
No places met population threshold.	

Malaysian
Top 10 Places Sorted by Number

Place	Number
No places met population threshold.	

Notes: Please refer to the User's Guide for an explanation of data; tables reflect only those areas that meet Summary File 4 population thresholds, therefore there may be less than 10 places listed

Pakistani
Top 10 Places Sorted by Number

Place	Number
Woodbridge, NJ (township) Middlesex County	4.56
Jersey City, NJ (city) Hudson County	4.45
Old Bridge, NJ (township) Middlesex County	4.24
Edison, NJ (township) Middlesex County	4.03

Samoan
Top 10 Places Sorted by Number

Place	Number
No places met population threshold.	

Sri Lankan
Top 10 Places Sorted by Number

Place	Number
No places met population threshold.	

Taiwanese
Top 10 Places Sorted by Number

Place	Number
Edison, NJ (township) Middlesex County	4.02

Thai
Top 10 Places Sorted by Number

Place	Number
No places met population threshold.	

Tongan
Top 10 Places Sorted by Number

Place	Number
No places met population threshold.	

Vietnamese
Top 10 Places Sorted by Number

Place	Number
Woodlynne, NJ (borough) Camden County	5.41
South Plainfield, NJ (borough) Middlesex County	4.40
Pennsauken, NJ (township) Camden County	4.36
Camden, NJ (city) Camden County	4.19
Belleville, NJ (township) Essex County	3.96
Atlantic City, NJ (city) Atlantic County	3.66
Jersey City, NJ (city) Hudson County	3.47

Language Spoken: English Only

Total Population 5 Years and Over Who Speak English-Only at Home
Top 10 Places Sorted by Number

Place	Number
Newark, NJ (city) Essex County	145,043
Jersey City, NJ (city) Hudson County	112,059
Dover, NJ (township) Ocean County	75,887
Toms River, NJ (cdp) Ocean County	72,926
Hamilton, NJ (township) Mercer County	70,441
Brick, NJ (township) Ocean County	65,747
Woodbridge, NJ (township) Middlesex County	63,332
Paterson, NJ (city) Passaic County	60,023
Trenton, NJ (city) Mercer County	57,142
Middletown, NJ (township) Monmouth County	56,323

Total Population 5 Years and Over Who Speak English-Only at Home
Top 10 Places Sorted by Percent

Place	Percent
Medford, NJ (township) Burlington County	94.68
Deptford, NJ (township) Gloucester County	92.98
Cinnaminson, NJ (township) Burlington County	92.46
Glassboro, NJ (borough) Gloucester County	92.21
Washington, NJ (township) Gloucester County	92.16

Place	
Winslow, NJ (township) Camden County	92.13
Brick, NJ (township) Ocean County	92.08
Moorestown, NJ (township) Burlington County	92.05
Gloucester, NJ (township) Camden County	91.82
Evesham, NJ (township) Burlington County	91.27

Asians 5 Years and Over Who Speak English-Only at Home
Top 10 Places Sorted by Number

Place	Number
Jersey City, NJ (city) Hudson County	4,788
Edison, NJ (township) Middlesex County	2,360
Piscataway, NJ (township) Middlesex County	1,289
Woodbridge, NJ (township) Middlesex County	1,178
Cherry Hill, NJ (township) Camden County	947
Old Bridge, NJ (township) Middlesex County	941
East Brunswick, NJ (township) Middlesex County	930
New Brunswick, NJ (city) Middlesex County	859
Bergenfield, NJ (borough) Bergen County	825
Bloomfield, NJ (township) Essex County	771

Asians 5 Years and Over Who Speak English-Only at Home
Top 10 Places Sorted by Percent

Place	Percent
Irvington, NJ (township) Essex County	43.81
Montclair, NJ (township) Essex County	43.41
Maplewood, NJ (township) Essex County	41.54
Brick, NJ (township) Ocean County	37.61
Medford, NJ (township) Burlington County	36.09
Jackson, NJ (township) Ocean County	33.29
East Freehold, NJ (cdp) Monmouth County	32.77
Middletown, NJ (township) Monmouth County	32.74
Budd Lake, NJ (cdp) Morris County	32.46
New Brunswick, NJ (city) Middlesex County	32.28

Native Hawaiian and Other Pacific Islanders 5 Years and Over Who Speak English-Only at Home
Top 10 Places Sorted by Number

Place	Number
No places met population threshold.	

Native Hawaiian and Other Pacific Islanders 5 Years and Over Who Speak English-Only at Home
Top 10 Places Sorted by Percent

Place	Percent
No places met population threshold.	

Asian Indians 5 Years and Over Who Speak English-Only at Home
Top 10 Places Sorted by Number

Place	Number
Jersey City, NJ (city) Hudson County	1,351
Edison, NJ (township) Middlesex County	1,180
Woodbridge, NJ (township) Middlesex County	543
Newark, NJ (city) Essex County	500
Piscataway, NJ (township) Middlesex County	437
Bloomfield, NJ (township) Essex County	364
Franklin, NJ (township) Somerset County	328
Bergenfield, NJ (borough) Bergen County	315
East Brunswick, NJ (township) Middlesex County	310
New Brunswick, NJ (city) Middlesex County	305

Asian Indians 5 Years and Over Who Speak English-Only at Home
Top 10 Places Sorted by Percent

Place	Percent
Montclair, NJ (township) Essex County	47.33
Newark, NJ (city) Essex County	42.30
Middletown, NJ (township) Monmouth County	32.60
Warren, NJ (township) Somerset County	30.99
Freehold, NJ (township) Monmouth County	30.75
South Plainfield, NJ (borough) Middlesex County	29.46

Place	
Dover, NJ (township) Ocean County	29.00
Toms River, NJ (cdp) Ocean County	29.00
New Brunswick, NJ (city) Middlesex County	28.27
Bernards, NJ (township) Somerset County	28.00

Bangladeshis 5 Years and Over Who Speak English-Only at Home
Top 10 Places Sorted by Number

Place	Number
Paterson, NJ (city) Passaic County	9

Bangladeshis 5 Years and Over Who Speak English-Only at Home
Top 10 Places Sorted by Percent

Place	Percent
Paterson, NJ (city) Passaic County	2.29

Cambodians 5 Years and Over Who Speak English-Only at Home
Top 10 Places Sorted by Number

Place	Number
No places met population threshold.	

Cambodians 5 Years and Over Who Speak English-Only at Home
Top 10 Places Sorted by Percent

Place	Percent
No places met population threshold.	

Chinese (except Taiwanese) 5 Years and Over Who Speak English-Only at Home
Top 10 Places Sorted by Number

Place	Number
Edison, NJ (township) Middlesex County	407
Jersey City, NJ (city) Hudson County	317
East Brunswick, NJ (township) Middlesex County	304
Holmdel, NJ (township) Monmouth County	203
West Windsor, NJ (township) Mercer County	193
Piscataway, NJ (township) Middlesex County	192
South Brunswick, NJ (township) Middlesex County	191
Randolph, NJ (township) Morris County	165
Tenafly, NJ (borough) Bergen County	165
Bridgewater, NJ (township) Somerset County	164

Chinese (except Taiwanese) 5 Years and Over Who Speak English-Only at Home
Top 10 Places Sorted by Percent

Place	Percent
Montclair, NJ (township) Essex County	36.62
New Brunswick, NJ (city) Middlesex County	34.23
Hoboken, NJ (city) Hudson County	30.17
Middletown, NJ (township) Monmouth County	25.97
Randolph, NJ (township) Morris County	24.92
Manalapan, NJ (township) Monmouth County	23.75
Tenafly, NJ (borough) Bergen County	23.01
Voorhees, NJ (township) Camden County	20.38
Aberdeen, NJ (township) Monmouth County	19.61
Bernards, NJ (township) Somerset County	19.20

Fijians 5 Years and Over Who Speak English-Only at Home
Top 10 Places Sorted by Number

Place	Number
No places met population threshold.	

Fijians 5 Years and Over Who Speak English-Only at Home
Top 10 Places Sorted by Percent

Place	Percent
No places met population threshold.	

Notes: Please refer to the User's Guide for an explanation of data; tables reflect only those areas that meet Summary File 4 population thresholds, therefore there may be less than 10 places listed

Filipinos 5 Years and Over Who Speak English-Only at Home
Top 10 Places Sorted by Number

Place	Number
Jersey City, NJ (city) Hudson County	2,497
Piscataway, NJ (township) Middlesex County	515
Edison, NJ (township) Middlesex County	491
Cherry Hill, NJ (township) Camden County	464
Bergenfield, NJ (borough) Bergen County	443
Woodbridge, NJ (township) Middlesex County	380
Belleville, NJ (township) Essex County	371
Old Bridge, NJ (township) Middlesex County	359
Union, NJ (township) Union County	352
Clifton, NJ (city) Passaic County	339

Filipinos 5 Years and Over Who Speak English-Only at Home
Top 10 Places Sorted by Percent

Place	Percent
East Brunswick, NJ (township) Middlesex County	40.57
Colonia, NJ (cdp) Middlesex County	34.27
Cherry Hill, NJ (township) Camden County	33.02
Dover, NJ (township) Ocean County	32.63
Toms River, NJ (cdp) Ocean County	32.63
Old Bridge, NJ (township) Middlesex County	29.97
Secaucus, NJ (town) Hudson County	29.78
Parsippany-Troy Hills, NJ (township) Morris County	29.33
Clifton, NJ (city) Passaic County	28.90
Howell, NJ (township) Monmouth County	28.70

Guamanians or Chamorros 5 Years and Over Who Speak English-Only at Home
Top 10 Places Sorted by Number

Place	Number
No places met population threshold.	

Guamanians or Chamorros 5 Years and Over Who Speak English-Only at Home
Top 10 Places Sorted by Percent

Place	Percent
No places met population threshold.	

Hawaiian Natives 5 Years and Over Who Speak English-Only at Home
Top 10 Places Sorted by Number

Place	Number
No places met population threshold.	

Hawaiian Natives 5 Years and Over Who Speak English-Only at Home
Top 10 Places Sorted by Percent

Place	Percent
No places met population threshold.	

Hmongs 5 Years and Over Who Speak English-Only at Home
Top 10 Places Sorted by Number

Place	Number
No places met population threshold.	

Hmongs 5 Years and Over Who Speak English-Only at Home
Top 10 Places Sorted by Percent

Place	Percent
No places met population threshold.	

Indonesians 5 Years and Over Who Speak English-Only at Home
Top 10 Places Sorted by Number

Place	Number
No places met population threshold.	

Indonesians 5 Years and Over Who Speak English-Only at Home
Top 10 Places Sorted by Percent

Place	Percent
No places met population threshold.	

Japanese 5 Years and Over Who Speak English-Only at Home
Top 10 Places Sorted by Number

Place	Number
Fort Lee, NJ (borough) Bergen County	79
Cliffside Park, NJ (borough) Bergen County	27
Ridgewood, NJ (village) Bergen County	25

Japanese 5 Years and Over Who Speak English-Only at Home
Top 10 Places Sorted by Percent

Place	Percent
Cliffside Park, NJ (borough) Bergen County	6.46
Ridgewood, NJ (village) Bergen County	5.71
Fort Lee, NJ (borough) Bergen County	4.57

Koreans 5 Years and Over Who Speak English-Only at Home
Top 10 Places Sorted by Number

Place	Number
Fort Lee, NJ (borough) Bergen County	278
Jersey City, NJ (city) Hudson County	235
Palisades Park, NJ (borough) Bergen County	177
West Orange, NJ (township) Essex County	97
Edgewater, NJ (borough) Bergen County	95
Hamilton, NJ (township) Mercer County	86
West Windsor, NJ (township) Mercer County	86
Edison, NJ (township) Middlesex County	85
Parsippany-Troy Hills, NJ (township) Morris County	84
Livingston, NJ (township) Essex County	60

Koreans 5 Years and Over Who Speak English-Only at Home
Top 10 Places Sorted by Percent

Place	Percent
Hamilton, NJ (township) Mercer County	20.28
West Windsor, NJ (township) Mercer County	20.05
Parsippany-Troy Hills, NJ (township) Morris County	18.58
West Orange, NJ (township) Essex County	16.14
Jersey City, NJ (city) Hudson County	16.12
North Brunswick, NJ (township) Middlesex County	13.51
East Brunswick, NJ (township) Middlesex County	13.02
Edgewater, NJ (borough) Bergen County	11.09
Pemberton, NJ (township) Burlington County	10.37
Demarest, NJ (borough) Bergen County	9.86

Laotians 5 Years and Over Who Speak English-Only at Home
Top 10 Places Sorted by Number

Place	Number
No places met population threshold.	

Laotians 5 Years and Over Who Speak English-Only at Home
Top 10 Places Sorted by Percent

Place	Percent
No places met population threshold.	

Malaysians 5 Years and Over Who Speak English-Only at Home
Top 10 Places Sorted by Number

Place	Number
No places met population threshold.	

Malaysians 5 Years and Over Who Speak English-Only at Home
Top 10 Places Sorted by Percent

Place	Percent
No places met population threshold.	

Pakistanis 5 Years and Over Who Speak English-Only at Home
Top 10 Places Sorted by Number

Place	Number
Jersey City, NJ (city) Hudson County	58
Edison, NJ (township) Middlesex County	55
Old Bridge, NJ (township) Middlesex County	34
Woodbridge, NJ (township) Middlesex County	20

Pakistanis 5 Years and Over Who Speak English-Only at Home
Top 10 Places Sorted by Percent

Place	Percent
Edison, NJ (township) Middlesex County	9.24
Old Bridge, NJ (township) Middlesex County	6.73
Woodbridge, NJ (township) Middlesex County	4.72
Jersey City, NJ (city) Hudson County	3.39

Samoans 5 Years and Over Who Speak English-Only at Home
Top 10 Places Sorted by Number

Place	Number
No places met population threshold.	

Samoans 5 Years and Over Who Speak English-Only at Home
Top 10 Places Sorted by Percent

Place	Percent
No places met population threshold.	

Sri Lankans 5 Years and Over Who Speak English-Only at Home
Top 10 Places Sorted by Number

Place	Number
No places met population threshold.	

Sri Lankans 5 Years and Over Who Speak English-Only at Home
Top 10 Places Sorted by Percent

Place	Percent
No places met population threshold.	

Taiwanese 5 Years and Over Who Speak English-Only at Home
Top 10 Places Sorted by Number

Place	Number
Edison, NJ (township) Middlesex County	6

Taiwanese 5 Years and Over Who Speak English-Only at Home
Top 10 Places Sorted by Percent

Place	Percent
Edison, NJ (township) Middlesex County	0.97

Notes: Please refer to the User's Guide for an explanation of data; tables reflect only those areas that meet Summary File 4 population thresholds, therefore there may be less than 10 places listed

Thais 5 Years and Over Who Speak English-Only at Home
Top 10 Places Sorted by Number

Place	Number
No places met population threshold.	

Thais 5 Years and Over Who Speak English-Only at Home
Top 10 Places Sorted by Percent

Place	Percent
No places met population threshold.	

Tongans 5 Years and Over Who Speak English-Only at Home
Top 10 Places Sorted by Number

Place	Number
No places met population threshold.	

Tongans 5 Years and Over Who Speak English-Only at Home
Top 10 Places Sorted by Percent

Place	Percent
No places met population threshold.	

Vietnamese 5 Years and Over Who Speak English-Only at Home
Top 10 Places Sorted by Number

Place	Number
Jersey City, NJ (city) Hudson County	110
Pennsauken, NJ (township) Camden County	56
Camden, NJ (city) Camden County	47
Belleville, NJ (township) Essex County	22
Woodlynne, NJ (borough) Camden County	5
South Plainfield, NJ (borough) Middlesex County	4
Atlantic City, NJ (city) Atlantic County	0

Vietnamese 5 Years and Over Who Speak English-Only at Home
Top 10 Places Sorted by Percent

Place	Percent
Pennsauken, NJ (township) Camden County	8.89
Jersey City, NJ (city) Hudson County	8.11
Belleville, NJ (township) Essex County	5.99
Camden, NJ (city) Camden County	3.60
Woodlynne, NJ (borough) Camden County	1.98
South Plainfield, NJ (borough) Middlesex County	1.19
Atlantic City, NJ (city) Atlantic County	0.00

Foreign Born

Total Population
Top 10 Places Sorted by Number

Place	Number
Jersey City, NJ (city) Hudson County	81,554
Newark, NJ (city) Essex County	66,057
Elizabeth, NJ (city) Union County	52,975
Paterson, NJ (city) Passaic County	48,924
Union City, NJ (city) Hudson County	39,378
Edison, NJ (township) Middlesex County	32,351
Passaic, NJ (city) Passaic County	31,101
West New York, NJ (town) Hudson County	29,831
North Bergen, NJ (township) Hudson County	27,216
Clifton, NJ (city) Passaic County	22,992

Total Population
Top 10 Places Sorted by Percent

Place	Percent
West New York, NJ (town) Hudson County	65.18
Union City, NJ (city) Hudson County	58.70
Palisades Park, NJ (borough) Bergen County	56.96
Harrison, NJ (town) Hudson County	56.00

Place	Percent
Guttenberg, NJ (town) Hudson County	49.18
Fairview, NJ (borough) Bergen County	48.39
North Bergen, NJ (township) Hudson County	46.76
Passaic, NJ (city) Passaic County	45.83
Fort Lee, NJ (borough) Bergen County	44.74
Plainsboro Center, NJ (cdp) Middlesex County	43.95

Asian
Top 10 Places Sorted by Number

Place	Number
Jersey City, NJ (city) Hudson County	30,962
Edison, NJ (township) Middlesex County	21,742
Woodbridge, NJ (township) Middlesex County	10,927
Piscataway, NJ (township) Middlesex County	9,377
Fort Lee, NJ (borough) Bergen County	8,878
Parsippany-Troy Hills, NJ (township) Morris County	6,954
Palisades Park, NJ (borough) Bergen County	5,827
East Brunswick, NJ (township) Middlesex County	5,549
South Brunswick, NJ (township) Middlesex County	5,018
Franklin, NJ (township) Somerset County	4,802

Asian
Top 10 Places Sorted by Percent

Place	Percent
Absecon, NJ (city) Atlantic County	90.57
Plainsboro Center, NJ (cdp) Middlesex County	89.74
Fairview, NJ (borough) Bergen County	89.10
East Rutherford, NJ (borough) Bergen County	87.86
Maple Shade, NJ (township) Burlington County	87.44
Keyport, NJ (borough) Monmouth County	87.31
West New York, NJ (town) Hudson County	86.97
Highland Park, NJ (borough) Middlesex County	86.55
Matawan, NJ (borough) Monmouth County	86.23
Edgewater, NJ (borough) Bergen County	85.94

Native Hawaiian and Other Pacific Islander
Top 10 Places Sorted by Number

Place	Number
No places met population threshold.	

Native Hawaiian and Other Pacific Islander
Top 10 Places Sorted by Percent

Place	Percent
No places met population threshold.	

Asian Indian
Top 10 Places Sorted by Number

Place	Number
Edison, NJ (township) Middlesex County	13,119
Jersey City, NJ (city) Hudson County	11,080
Woodbridge, NJ (township) Middlesex County	7,243
Piscataway, NJ (township) Middlesex County	4,604
Parsippany-Troy Hills, NJ (township) Morris County	3,411
South Brunswick, NJ (township) Middlesex County	2,746
Plainsboro, NJ (township) Middlesex County	2,705
Franklin, NJ (township) Somerset County	2,525
North Brunswick, NJ (township) Middlesex County	2,391
Iselin, NJ (cdp) Middlesex County	2,304

Asian Indian
Top 10 Places Sorted by Percent

Place	Percent
Plainsboro Center, NJ (cdp) Middlesex County	92.99
Atlantic City, NJ (city) Atlantic County	90.50
Lodi, NJ (borough) Bergen County	88.89
Highland Park, NJ (borough) Middlesex County	88.04
Maple Shade, NJ (township) Burlington County	88.02
Ocean, NJ (township) Monmouth County	87.15
Hackensack, NJ (city) Bergen County	86.57
Avenel, NJ (cdp) Middlesex County	86.17
West New York, NJ (town) Hudson County	85.37
Kearny, NJ (town) Hudson County	84.91

Bangladeshi
Top 10 Places Sorted by Number

Place	Number
Paterson, NJ (city) Passaic County	373

Bangladeshi
Top 10 Places Sorted by Percent

Place	Percent
Paterson, NJ (city) Passaic County	81.26

Cambodian
Top 10 Places Sorted by Number

Place	Number
No places met population threshold.	

Cambodian
Top 10 Places Sorted by Percent

Place	Percent
No places met population threshold.	

Chinese (except Taiwanese)
Top 10 Places Sorted by Number

Place	Number
Edison, NJ (township) Middlesex County	4,094
Jersey City, NJ (city) Hudson County	2,279
East Brunswick, NJ (township) Middlesex County	2,042
Parsippany-Troy Hills, NJ (township) Morris County	1,911
Piscataway, NJ (township) Middlesex County	1,834
Marlboro, NJ (township) Monmouth County	1,577
Fort Lee, NJ (borough) Bergen County	1,272
Cherry Hill, NJ (township) Camden County	1,217
Plainsboro, NJ (township) Middlesex County	1,162
West Windsor, NJ (township) Mercer County	1,091

Chinese (except Taiwanese)
Top 10 Places Sorted by Percent

Place	Percent
Princeton, NJ (township) Mercer County	85.32
Atlantic City, NJ (city) Atlantic County	84.72
Kearny, NJ (town) Hudson County	84.41
Highland Park, NJ (borough) Middlesex County	84.11
Paramus, NJ (borough) Bergen County	83.01
Harrison, NJ (town) Hudson County	82.80
Dover, NJ (township) Ocean County	82.07
Toms River, NJ (cdp) Ocean County	81.36
Hazlet, NJ (township) Monmouth County	80.58
Sayreville, NJ (borough) Middlesex County	79.37

Fijian
Top 10 Places Sorted by Number

Place	Number
No places met population threshold.	

Fijian
Top 10 Places Sorted by Percent

Place	Percent
No places met population threshold.	

Filipino
Top 10 Places Sorted by Number

Place	Number
Jersey City, NJ (city) Hudson County	12,534
Bergenfield, NJ (borough) Bergen County	2,386
Edison, NJ (township) Middlesex County	1,824
Belleville, NJ (township) Essex County	1,624
Piscataway, NJ (township) Middlesex County	1,584
Union, NJ (township) Union County	1,490
Woodbridge, NJ (township) Middlesex County	1,392
Bloomfield, NJ (township) Essex County	1,254
Cherry Hill, NJ (township) Camden County	1,027
Bayonne, NJ (city) Hudson County	987

Notes: Please refer to the User's Guide for an explanation of data; tables reflect only those areas that meet Summary File 4 population thresholds, therefore there may be less than 10 places listed

Filipino
Top 10 Places Sorted by Percent

Place	Percent
Elizabeth, NJ (city) Union County	86.14
Atlantic City, NJ (city) Atlantic County	84.93
Passaic, NJ (city) Passaic County	81.75
Little Ferry, NJ (borough) Bergen County	80.73
Fair Lawn, NJ (borough) Bergen County	80.41
Bloomfield, NJ (township) Essex County	78.92
South Brunswick, NJ (township) Middlesex County	78.70
Wayne, NJ (township) Passaic County	78.65
Somerset, NJ (cdp) Somerset County	77.12
Dumont, NJ (borough) Bergen County	76.86

Guamanian or Chamorro
Top 10 Places Sorted by Number

Place	Number
No places met population threshold.	

Guamanian or Chamorro
Top 10 Places Sorted by Percent

Place	Percent
No places met population threshold.	

Hawaiian, Native
Top 10 Places Sorted by Number

Place	Number
No places met population threshold.	

Hawaiian, Native
Top 10 Places Sorted by Percent

Place	Percent
No places met population threshold.	

Hmong
Top 10 Places Sorted by Number

Place	Number
No places met population threshold.	

Hmong
Top 10 Places Sorted by Percent

Place	Percent
No places met population threshold.	

Indonesian
Top 10 Places Sorted by Number

Place	Number
No places met population threshold.	

Indonesian
Top 10 Places Sorted by Percent

Place	Percent
No places met population threshold.	

Japanese
Top 10 Places Sorted by Number

Place	Number
Fort Lee, NJ (borough) Bergen County	1,682
Ridgewood, NJ (village) Bergen County	409
Cliffside Park, NJ (borough) Bergen County	393

Japanese
Top 10 Places Sorted by Percent

Place	Percent
Ridgewood, NJ (village) Bergen County	91.50
Cliffside Park, NJ (borough) Bergen County	88.12
Fort Lee, NJ (borough) Bergen County	83.76

Korean
Top 10 Places Sorted by Number

Place	Number
Palisades Park, NJ (borough) Bergen County	4,988
Fort Lee, NJ (borough) Bergen County	4,834
Jersey City, NJ (city) Hudson County	1,256
Cliffside Park, NJ (borough) Bergen County	1,216
Leonia, NJ (borough) Bergen County	1,136
Paramus, NJ (borough) Bergen County	1,114
Ridgefield, NJ (borough) Bergen County	1,037
Edison, NJ (township) Middlesex County	979
Tenafly, NJ (borough) Bergen County	967
Edgewater, NJ (borough) Bergen County	798

Korean
Top 10 Places Sorted by Percent

Place	Percent
Hackensack, NJ (city) Bergen County	88.89
Edgewater, NJ (borough) Bergen County	88.57
Ridgewood, NJ (village) Bergen County	85.44
Jersey City, NJ (city) Hudson County	84.81
Demarest, NJ (borough) Bergen County	84.72
Palisades Park, NJ (borough) Bergen County	84.51
Bayonne, NJ (city) Hudson County	83.39
Little Ferry, NJ (borough) Bergen County	83.20
Wayne, NJ (township) Passaic County	82.57
Cliffside Park, NJ (borough) Bergen County	82.05

Laotian
Top 10 Places Sorted by Number

Place	Number
No places met population threshold.	

Laotian
Top 10 Places Sorted by Percent

Place	Percent
No places met population threshold.	

Malaysian
Top 10 Places Sorted by Number

Place	Number
No places met population threshold.	

Malaysian
Top 10 Places Sorted by Percent

Place	Percent
No places met population threshold.	

Pakistani
Top 10 Places Sorted by Number

Place	Number
Jersey City, NJ (city) Hudson County	1,467
Edison, NJ (township) Middlesex County	452
Old Bridge, NJ (township) Middlesex County	409
Woodbridge, NJ (township) Middlesex County	373

Pakistani
Top 10 Places Sorted by Percent

Place	Percent
Woodbridge, NJ (township) Middlesex County	79.87
Jersey City, NJ (city) Hudson County	78.12
Old Bridge, NJ (township) Middlesex County	77.76
Edison, NJ (township) Middlesex County	67.06

Samoan
Top 10 Places Sorted by Number

Place	Number
No places met population threshold.	

Samoan
Top 10 Places Sorted by Percent

Place	Percent
No places met population threshold.	

Sri Lankan
Top 10 Places Sorted by Number

Place	Number
No places met population threshold.	

Sri Lankan
Top 10 Places Sorted by Percent

Place	Percent
No places met population threshold.	

Taiwanese
Top 10 Places Sorted by Number

Place	Number
Edison, NJ (township) Middlesex County	472

Taiwanese
Top 10 Places Sorted by Percent

Place	Percent
Edison, NJ (township) Middlesex County	71.19

Thai
Top 10 Places Sorted by Number

Place	Number
No places met population threshold.	

Thai
Top 10 Places Sorted by Percent

Place	Percent
No places met population threshold.	

Tongan
Top 10 Places Sorted by Number

Place	Number
No places met population threshold.	

Tongan
Top 10 Places Sorted by Percent

Place	Percent
No places met population threshold.	

Vietnamese
Top 10 Places Sorted by Number

Place	Number
Camden, NJ (city) Camden County	1,181
Jersey City, NJ (city) Hudson County	1,117
Atlantic City, NJ (city) Atlantic County	932
Pennsauken, NJ (township) Camden County	552
Belleville, NJ (township) Essex County	356
South Plainfield, NJ (borough) Middlesex County	277
Woodlynne, NJ (borough) Camden County	217

Vietnamese
Top 10 Places Sorted by Percent

Place	Percent
Belleville, NJ (township) Essex County	83.96
Camden, NJ (city) Camden County	83.23
Jersey City, NJ (city) Hudson County	80.13
Pennsauken, NJ (township) Camden County	79.77
Atlantic City, NJ (city) Atlantic County	78.52
Woodlynne, NJ (borough) Camden County	76.14
South Plainfield, NJ (borough) Middlesex County	75.68

Notes: Please refer to the User's Guide for an explanation of data; tables reflect only those areas that meet Summary File 4 population thresholds, therefore there may be less than 10 places listed

Foreign-Born Naturalized Citizens

Total Population
Top 10 Places Sorted by Number

Place	Number
Jersey City, NJ (city) Hudson County	33,609
Newark, NJ (city) Essex County	21,412
Elizabeth, NJ (city) Union County	19,345
Paterson, NJ (city) Passaic County	17,263
North Bergen, NJ (township) Hudson County	14,485
Union City, NJ (city) Hudson County	14,462
Edison, NJ (township) Middlesex County	14,460
Clifton, NJ (city) Passaic County	11,677
West New York, NJ (town) Hudson County	11,009
Woodbridge, NJ (township) Middlesex County	9,502

Total Population
Top 10 Places Sorted by Percent

Place	Percent
Englewood Cliffs, NJ (borough) Bergen County	25.40
North Bergen, NJ (township) Hudson County	24.89
West New York, NJ (town) Hudson County	24.05
Union City, NJ (city) Hudson County	21.56
Fairview, NJ (borough) Bergen County	21.17
Fort Lee, NJ (borough) Bergen County	21.06
Palisades Park, NJ (borough) Bergen County	20.97
Cliffside Park, NJ (borough) Bergen County	20.79
Guttenberg, NJ (town) Hudson County	20.50
Weehawken, NJ (township) Hudson County	19.41

Asian
Top 10 Places Sorted by Number

Place	Number
Jersey City, NJ (city) Hudson County	13,927
Edison, NJ (township) Middlesex County	8,567
Piscataway, NJ (township) Middlesex County	4,092
Woodbridge, NJ (township) Middlesex County	3,699
Parsippany-Troy Hills, NJ (township) Morris County	3,309
East Brunswick, NJ (township) Middlesex County	3,017
Cherry Hill, NJ (township) Camden County	2,832
Fort Lee, NJ (borough) Bergen County	2,699
Old Bridge, NJ (township) Middlesex County	2,255
South Brunswick, NJ (township) Middlesex County	2,223

Asian
Top 10 Places Sorted by Percent

Place	Percent
Hillsdale, NJ (borough) Bergen County	59.61
Neptune, NJ (township) Monmouth County	59.44
Willingboro, NJ (township) Burlington County	58.70
Medford, NJ (township) Burlington County	58.30
Monroe, NJ (township) Middlesex County	58.08
Cinnaminson, NJ (township) Burlington County	57.54
Barclay-Kingston, NJ (cdp) Camden County	56.63
Cranbury, NJ (township) Middlesex County	53.15
Moorestown, NJ (township) Burlington County	52.90
West Caldwell, NJ (township) Essex County	52.78

Native Hawaiian and Other Pacific Islander
Top 10 Places Sorted by Number

Place	Number
No places met population threshold.	

Native Hawaiian and Other Pacific Islander
Top 10 Places Sorted by Percent

Place	Percent
No places met population threshold.	

Asian Indian
Top 10 Places Sorted by Number

Place	Number
Jersey City, NJ (city) Hudson County	4,300
Edison, NJ (township) Middlesex County	4,185
Woodbridge, NJ (township) Middlesex County	1,930
Piscataway, NJ (township) Middlesex County	1,722
Parsippany-Troy Hills, NJ (township) Morris County	1,306
Clifton, NJ (city) Passaic County	1,134
East Brunswick, NJ (township) Middlesex County	1,009
South Brunswick, NJ (township) Middlesex County	1,001
North Bergen, NJ (township) Hudson County	993
Old Bridge, NJ (township) Middlesex County	917

Asian Indian
Top 10 Places Sorted by Percent

Place	Percent
Gloucester, NJ (township) Camden County	55.77
Rutherford, NJ (borough) Bergen County	52.30
Greentree, NJ (cdp) Camden County	48.81
Freehold, NJ (township) Monmouth County	48.55
Cherry Hill, NJ (township) Camden County	46.27
Manalapan, NJ (township) Monmouth County	45.99
Rockaway, NJ (township) Morris County	45.32
Warren, NJ (township) Somerset County	45.00
Livingston, NJ (township) Essex County	44.97
Dover, NJ (township) Ocean County	42.19

Bangladeshi
Top 10 Places Sorted by Number

Place	Number
Paterson, NJ (city) Passaic County	149

Bangladeshi
Top 10 Places Sorted by Percent

Place	Percent
Paterson, NJ (city) Passaic County	32.46

Cambodian
Top 10 Places Sorted by Number

Place	Number
No places met population threshold.	

Cambodian
Top 10 Places Sorted by Percent

Place	Percent
No places met population threshold.	

Chinese (except Taiwanese)
Top 10 Places Sorted by Number

Place	Number
Edison, NJ (township) Middlesex County	2,151
East Brunswick, NJ (township) Middlesex County	1,285
Marlboro, NJ (township) Monmouth County	1,105
Parsippany-Troy Hills, NJ (township) Morris County	1,022
Piscataway, NJ (township) Middlesex County	830
Jersey City, NJ (city) Hudson County	809
Cherry Hill, NJ (township) Camden County	755
West Windsor, NJ (township) Mercer County	719
Bridgewater, NJ (township) Somerset County	689
Holmdel, NJ (township) Monmouth County	685

Chinese (except Taiwanese)
Top 10 Places Sorted by Percent

Place	Percent
Scotch Plains, NJ (township) Union County	66.09
West Orange, NJ (township) Essex County	51.78
Voorhees, NJ (township) Camden County	50.81
Morganville, NJ (cdp) Monmouth County	50.39
Hazlet, NJ (township) Monmouth County	49.61
East Hanover, NJ (township) Morris County	49.35
New Providence, NJ (borough) Union County	49.33
Hanover, NJ (township) Morris County	49.02
Montville, NJ (township) Morris County	48.58
North Brunswick, NJ (township) Middlesex County	48.14

Fijian
Top 10 Places Sorted by Number

Place	Number
No places met population threshold.	

Fijian
Top 10 Places Sorted by Percent

Place	Percent
No places met population threshold.	

Filipino
Top 10 Places Sorted by Number

Place	Number
Jersey City, NJ (city) Hudson County	6,932
Bergenfield, NJ (borough) Bergen County	1,212
Edison, NJ (township) Middlesex County	997
Piscataway, NJ (township) Middlesex County	878
Cherry Hill, NJ (township) Camden County	802
Belleville, NJ (township) Essex County	801
Union, NJ (township) Union County	792
Bloomfield, NJ (township) Essex County	743
Woodbridge, NJ (township) Middlesex County	719
Clifton, NJ (city) Passaic County	594

Filipino
Top 10 Places Sorted by Percent

Place	Percent
Colonia, NJ (cdp) Middlesex County	62.12
West Orange, NJ (township) Essex County	54.57
Washington, NJ (township) Gloucester County	54.41
Cherry Hill, NJ (township) Camden County	54.23
Gloucester, NJ (township) Camden County	54.17
North Brunswick, NJ (township) Middlesex County	53.41
Passaic, NJ (city) Passaic County	52.12
Parsippany-Troy Hills, NJ (township) Morris County	52.10
Teaneck, NJ (township) Bergen County	50.23
Dumont, NJ (borough) Bergen County	49.59

Guamanian or Chamorro
Top 10 Places Sorted by Number

Place	Number
No places met population threshold.	

Guamanian or Chamorro
Top 10 Places Sorted by Percent

Place	Percent
No places met population threshold.	

Hawaiian, Native
Top 10 Places Sorted by Number

Place	Number
No places met population threshold.	

Hawaiian, Native
Top 10 Places Sorted by Percent

Place	Percent
No places met population threshold.	

Hmong
Top 10 Places Sorted by Number

Place	Number
No places met population threshold.	

Hmong
Top 10 Places Sorted by Percent

Place	Percent
No places met population threshold.	

Notes: Please refer to the User's Guide for an explanation of data; tables reflect only those areas that meet Summary File 4 population thresholds, therefore there may be less than 10 places listed

Indonesian
Top 10 Places Sorted by Number

Place	Number
No places met population threshold.	

Indonesian
Top 10 Places Sorted by Percent

Place	Percent
No places met population threshold.	

Japanese
Top 10 Places Sorted by Number

Place	Number
Fort Lee, NJ (borough) Bergen County	90
Cliffside Park, NJ (borough) Bergen County	68
Ridgewood, NJ (village) Bergen County	25

Japanese
Top 10 Places Sorted by Percent

Place	Percent
Cliffside Park, NJ (borough) Bergen County	15.25
Ridgewood, NJ (village) Bergen County	5.59
Fort Lee, NJ (borough) Bergen County	4.48

Korean
Top 10 Places Sorted by Number

Place	Number
Fort Lee, NJ (borough) Bergen County	1,555
Palisades Park, NJ (borough) Bergen County	1,291
Edison, NJ (township) Middlesex County	476
Cliffside Park, NJ (borough) Bergen County	452
Jersey City, NJ (city) Hudson County	390
Tenafly, NJ (borough) Bergen County	355
Paramus, NJ (borough) Bergen County	349
Closter, NJ (borough) Bergen County	341
Leonia, NJ (borough) Bergen County	312
Ridgefield, NJ (borough) Bergen County	311

Korean
Top 10 Places Sorted by Percent

Place	Percent
Hamilton, NJ (township) Mercer County	55.40
Pemberton, NJ (township) Burlington County	49.63
Browns Mills, NJ (cdp) Burlington County	48.00
Parsippany-Troy Hills, NJ (township) Morris County	44.16
West Orange, NJ (township) Essex County	42.63
Bayonne, NJ (city) Hudson County	41.69
Woodbridge, NJ (township) Middlesex County	39.72
Englewood Cliffs, NJ (borough) Bergen County	39.20
Livingston, NJ (township) Essex County	38.99
Edison, NJ (township) Middlesex County	37.75

Laotian
Top 10 Places Sorted by Number

Place	Number
No places met population threshold.	

Laotian
Top 10 Places Sorted by Percent

Place	Percent
No places met population threshold.	

Malaysian
Top 10 Places Sorted by Number

Place	Number
No places met population threshold.	

Malaysian
Top 10 Places Sorted by Percent

Place	Percent
No places met population threshold.	

Pakistani
Top 10 Places Sorted by Number

Place	Number
Jersey City, NJ (city) Hudson County	620
Old Bridge, NJ (township) Middlesex County	262
Edison, NJ (township) Middlesex County	220
Woodbridge, NJ (township) Middlesex County	166

Pakistani
Top 10 Places Sorted by Percent

Place	Percent
Old Bridge, NJ (township) Middlesex County	49.81
Woodbridge, NJ (township) Middlesex County	35.55
Jersey City, NJ (city) Hudson County	33.01
Edison, NJ (township) Middlesex County	32.64

Samoan
Top 10 Places Sorted by Number

Place	Number
No places met population threshold.	

Samoan
Top 10 Places Sorted by Percent

Place	Percent
No places met population threshold.	

Sri Lankan
Top 10 Places Sorted by Number

Place	Number
No places met population threshold.	

Sri Lankan
Top 10 Places Sorted by Percent

Place	Percent
No places met population threshold.	

Taiwanese
Top 10 Places Sorted by Number

Place	Number
Edison, NJ (township) Middlesex County	227

Taiwanese
Top 10 Places Sorted by Percent

Place	Percent
Edison, NJ (township) Middlesex County	34.24

Thai
Top 10 Places Sorted by Number

Place	Number
No places met population threshold.	

Thai
Top 10 Places Sorted by Percent

Place	Percent
No places met population threshold.	

Tongan
Top 10 Places Sorted by Number

Place	Number
No places met population threshold.	

Tongan
Top 10 Places Sorted by Percent

Place	Percent
No places met population threshold.	

Vietnamese
Top 10 Places Sorted by Number

Place	Number
Jersey City, NJ (city) Hudson County	530
Atlantic City, NJ (city) Atlantic County	486
Camden, NJ (city) Camden County	349
Pennsauken, NJ (township) Camden County	263
South Plainfield, NJ (borough) Middlesex County	188
Belleville, NJ (township) Essex County	160
Woodlynne, NJ (borough) Camden County	114

Vietnamese
Top 10 Places Sorted by Percent

Place	Percent
South Plainfield, NJ (borough) Middlesex County	51.37
Atlantic City, NJ (city) Atlantic County	40.94
Woodlynne, NJ (borough) Camden County	40.00
Jersey City, NJ (city) Hudson County	38.02
Pennsauken, NJ (township) Camden County	38.01
Belleville, NJ (township) Essex County	37.74
Camden, NJ (city) Camden County	24.59

High School Graduates

Total Populations 25 Years and Over Who are High School Graduates
Top 10 Places Sorted by Number

Place	Number
Jersey City, NJ (city) Hudson County	112,835
Newark, NJ (city) Essex County	95,163
Edison, NJ (township) Middlesex County	59,269
Woodbridge, NJ (township) Middlesex County	57,841
Dover, NJ (township) Ocean County	53,856
Paterson, NJ (city) Passaic County	51,535
Toms River, NJ (cdp) Ocean County	51,381
Hamilton, NJ (township) Mercer County	50,700
Elizabeth, NJ (city) Union County	46,875
Brick, NJ (township) Ocean County	45,894

Total Populations 25 Years and Over Who are High School Graduates
Top 10 Places Sorted by Percent

Place	Percent
Plainsboro Center, NJ (cdp) Middlesex County	98.23
Montgomery, NJ (township) Somerset County	97.32
Plainsboro, NJ (township) Middlesex County	97.29
West Windsor, NJ (township) Mercer County	96.91
Princeton Meadows, NJ (cdp) Middlesex County	96.85
Chatham, NJ (township) Morris County	96.63
Millburn, NJ (township) Essex County	96.57
Morganville, NJ (cdp) Monmouth County	96.43
Bedminster, NJ (township) Somerset County	96.22
Glen Rock, NJ (borough) Bergen County	96.05

Asians 25 Years and Over Who are High School Graduates
Top 10 Places Sorted by Number

Place	Number
Jersey City, NJ (city) Hudson County	21,923
Edison, NJ (township) Middlesex County	16,835
Woodbridge, NJ (township) Middlesex County	8,417
Fort Lee, NJ (borough) Bergen County	7,194
Piscataway, NJ (township) Middlesex County	6,905
Parsippany-Troy Hills, NJ (township) Morris County	5,301
East Brunswick, NJ (township) Middlesex County	4,394
Palisades Park, NJ (borough) Bergen County	4,344
South Brunswick, NJ (township) Middlesex County	4,214
Franklin, NJ (township) Somerset County	4,203

Notes: Please refer to the User's Guide for an explanation of data; tables reflect only those areas that meet Summary File 4 population thresholds, therefore there may be less than 10 places listed

Asians 25 Years and Over Who are High School Graduates
Top 10 Places Sorted by Percent

Place	Percent
Budd Lake, NJ (cdp) Morris County	100.00
Franklin Lakes, NJ (borough) Bergen County	100.00
Heathcote, NJ (cdp) Middlesex County	100.00
Long Hill, NJ (township) Morris County	100.00
Plainsboro Center, NJ (cdp) Middlesex County	98.87
Randolph, NJ (township) Morris County	98.61
Barclay-Kingston, NJ (cdp) Camden County	98.43
Morganville, NJ (cdp) Monmouth County	98.41
Oakland, NJ (borough) Bergen County	98.41
Somerset, NJ (cdp) Somerset County	98.14

Native Hawaiian and Other Pacific Islanders 25 Years and Over Who are High School Graduates
Top 10 Places Sorted by Number

Place	Number
No places met population threshold.	

Native Hawaiian and Other Pacific Islanders 25 Years and Over Who are High School Graduates
Top 10 Places Sorted by Percent

Place	Percent
No places met population threshold.	

Asian Indians 25 Years and Over Who are High School Graduates
Top 10 Places Sorted by Number

Place	Number
Edison, NJ (township) Middlesex County	9,784
Jersey City, NJ (city) Hudson County	6,788
Woodbridge, NJ (township) Middlesex County	5,419
Piscataway, NJ (township) Middlesex County	3,413
Parsippany-Troy Hills, NJ (township) Morris County	2,356
South Brunswick, NJ (township) Middlesex County	2,279
Plainsboro, NJ (township) Middlesex County	2,101
Franklin, NJ (township) Somerset County	2,019
North Brunswick, NJ (township) Middlesex County	1,866
Old Bridge, NJ (township) Middlesex County	1,571

Asian Indians 25 Years and Over Who are High School Graduates
Top 10 Places Sorted by Percent

Place	Percent
Montgomery, NJ (township) Somerset County	100.00
Plainsboro Center, NJ (cdp) Middlesex County	100.00
Randolph, NJ (township) Morris County	100.00
Middletown, NJ (township) Monmouth County	98.32
Plainsboro, NJ (township) Middlesex County	98.04
Mahwah, NJ (township) Bergen County	97.81
Fort Lee, NJ (borough) Bergen County	97.77
West Windsor, NJ (township) Mercer County	97.55
Princeton Meadows, NJ (cdp) Middlesex County	97.42
Bernards, NJ (township) Somerset County	97.20

Bangladeshis 25 Years and Over Who are High School Graduates
Top 10 Places Sorted by Number

Place	Number
Paterson, NJ (city) Passaic County	139

Bangladeshis 25 Years and Over Who are High School Graduates
Top 10 Places Sorted by Percent

Place	Percent
Paterson, NJ (city) Passaic County	59.40

Cambodians 25 Years and Over Who are High School Graduates
Top 10 Places Sorted by Number

Place	Number
No places met population threshold.	

Cambodians 25 Years and Over Who are High School Graduates
Top 10 Places Sorted by Percent

Place	Percent
No places met population threshold.	

Chinese (except Taiwanese) 25 Years and Over Who are High School Graduates
Top 10 Places Sorted by Number

Place	Number
Edison, NJ (township) Middlesex County	3,278
East Brunswick, NJ (township) Middlesex County	1,812
Jersey City, NJ (city) Hudson County	1,746
Parsippany-Troy Hills, NJ (township) Morris County	1,618
Piscataway, NJ (township) Middlesex County	1,480
Marlboro, NJ (township) Monmouth County	1,479
Fort Lee, NJ (borough) Bergen County	1,137
West Windsor, NJ (township) Mercer County	1,107
Plainsboro, NJ (township) Middlesex County	1,046
Cherry Hill, NJ (township) Camden County	995

Chinese (except Taiwanese) 25 Years and Over Who are High School Graduates
Top 10 Places Sorted by Percent

Place	Percent
Somerset, NJ (cdp) Somerset County	100.00
Randolph, NJ (township) Morris County	99.09
Hanover, NJ (township) Morris County	98.89
Millburn, NJ (township) Essex County	98.20
Montville, NJ (township) Morris County	97.99
Princeton, NJ (township) Mercer County	97.51
Morganville, NJ (cdp) Monmouth County	97.44
Paramus, NJ (borough) Bergen County	97.37
Princeton Meadows, NJ (cdp) Middlesex County	97.23
Montclair, NJ (township) Essex County	97.17

Fijians 25 Years and Over Who are High School Graduates
Top 10 Places Sorted by Number

Place	Number
No places met population threshold.	

Fijians 25 Years and Over Who are High School Graduates
Top 10 Places Sorted by Percent

Place	Percent
No places met population threshold.	

Filipinos 25 Years and Over Who are High School Graduates
Top 10 Places Sorted by Number

Place	Number
Jersey City, NJ (city) Hudson County	10,197
Bergenfield, NJ (borough) Bergen County	1,867
Edison, NJ (township) Middlesex County	1,701
Belleville, NJ (township) Essex County	1,271
Union, NJ (township) Union County	1,268
Woodbridge, NJ (township) Middlesex County	1,195
Piscataway, NJ (township) Middlesex County	1,181
Bloomfield, NJ (township) Essex County	1,076
Cherry Hill, NJ (township) Camden County	864
Old Bridge, NJ (township) Middlesex County	794

Filipinos 25 Years and Over Who are High School Graduates
Top 10 Places Sorted by Percent

Place	Percent
East Brunswick, NJ (township) Middlesex County	100.00
Franklin, NJ (township) Somerset County	100.00
Little Ferry, NJ (borough) Bergen County	100.00
Nutley, NJ (township) Essex County	100.00
Somerset, NJ (cdp) Somerset County	100.00
Union City, NJ (city) Hudson County	100.00
Edison, NJ (township) Middlesex County	99.42
Howell, NJ (township) Monmouth County	98.40
Old Bridge, NJ (township) Middlesex County	98.39
Teaneck, NJ (township) Bergen County	98.39

Guamanians or Chamorros 25 Years and Over Who are High School Graduates
Top 10 Places Sorted by Number

Place	Number
No places met population threshold.	

Guamanians or Chamorros 25 Years and Over Who are High School Graduates
Top 10 Places Sorted by Percent

Place	Percent
No places met population threshold.	

Hawaiian Natives 25 Years and Over Who are High School Graduates
Top 10 Places Sorted by Number

Place	Number
No places met population threshold.	

Hawaiian Natives 25 Years and Over Who are High School Graduates
Top 10 Places Sorted by Percent

Place	Percent
No places met population threshold.	

Hmongs 25 Years and Over Who are High School Graduates
Top 10 Places Sorted by Number

Place	Number
No places met population threshold.	

Hmongs 25 Years and Over Who are High School Graduates
Top 10 Places Sorted by Percent

Place	Percent
No places met population threshold.	

Indonesians 25 Years and Over Who are High School Graduates
Top 10 Places Sorted by Number

Place	Number
No places met population threshold.	

Indonesians 25 Years and Over Who are High School Graduates
Top 10 Places Sorted by Percent

Place	Percent
No places met population threshold.	

Japanese 25 Years and Over Who are High School Graduates
Top 10 Places Sorted by Number

Place	Number
Fort Lee, NJ (borough) Bergen County	1,316
Cliffside Park, NJ (borough) Bergen County	335

Notes: Please refer to the User's Guide for an explanation of data; tables reflect only those areas that meet Summary File 4 population thresholds, therefore there may be less than 10 places listed

Place	
Ridgewood, NJ (village) Bergen County	288

Japanese 25 Years and Over Who are High School Graduates
Top 10 Places Sorted by Percent

Place	Percent
Ridgewood, NJ (village) Bergen County	100.00
Fort Lee, NJ (borough) Bergen County	98.50
Cliffside Park, NJ (borough) Bergen County	96.26

Koreans 25 Years and Over Who are High School Graduates
Top 10 Places Sorted by Number

Place	Number
Fort Lee, NJ (borough) Bergen County	3,745
Palisades Park, NJ (borough) Bergen County	3,669
Jersey City, NJ (city) Hudson County	1,003
Cliffside Park, NJ (borough) Bergen County	985
Leonia, NJ (borough) Bergen County	847
Edison, NJ (township) Middlesex County	780
Edgewater, NJ (borough) Bergen County	688
Paramus, NJ (borough) Bergen County	653
Ridgefield, NJ (borough) Bergen County	641
Tenafly, NJ (borough) Bergen County	568

Koreans 25 Years and Over Who are High School Graduates
Top 10 Places Sorted by Percent

Place	Percent
Harrington Park, NJ (borough) Bergen County	100.00
Parsippany-Troy Hills, NJ (township) Morris County	100.00
Demarest, NJ (borough) Bergen County	98.51
Old Tappan, NJ (borough) Bergen County	97.54
Englewood Cliffs, NJ (borough) Bergen County	96.70
Hackensack, NJ (city) Bergen County	96.69
Leonia, NJ (borough) Bergen County	95.92
Ridgewood, NJ (village) Bergen County	95.77
River Edge, NJ (borough) Bergen County	95.76
Edgewater, NJ (borough) Bergen County	95.29

Laotians 25 Years and Over Who are High School Graduates
Top 10 Places Sorted by Number

Place	Number
No places met population threshold.	

Laotians 25 Years and Over Who are High School Graduates
Top 10 Places Sorted by Percent

Place	Percent
No places met population threshold.	

Malaysians 25 Years and Over Who are High School Graduates
Top 10 Places Sorted by Number

Place	Number
No places met population threshold.	

Malaysians 25 Years and Over Who are High School Graduates
Top 10 Places Sorted by Percent

Place	Percent
No places met population threshold.	

Pakistanis 25 Years and Over Who are High School Graduates
Top 10 Places Sorted by Number

Place	Number
Jersey City, NJ (city) Hudson County	763
Edison, NJ (township) Middlesex County	332
Old Bridge, NJ (township) Middlesex County	284

Place	
Woodbridge, NJ (township) Middlesex County	199

Pakistanis 25 Years and Over Who are High School Graduates
Top 10 Places Sorted by Percent

Place	Percent
Old Bridge, NJ (township) Middlesex County	91.91
Woodbridge, NJ (township) Middlesex County	89.64
Edison, NJ (township) Middlesex County	88.06
Jersey City, NJ (city) Hudson County	74.29

Samoans 25 Years and Over Who are High School Graduates
Top 10 Places Sorted by Number

Place	Number
No places met population threshold.	

Samoans 25 Years and Over Who are High School Graduates
Top 10 Places Sorted by Percent

Place	Percent
No places met population threshold.	

Sri Lankans 25 Years and Over Who are High School Graduates
Top 10 Places Sorted by Number

Place	Number
No places met population threshold.	

Sri Lankans 25 Years and Over Who are High School Graduates
Top 10 Places Sorted by Percent

Place	Percent
No places met population threshold.	

Taiwanese 25 Years and Over Who are High School Graduates
Top 10 Places Sorted by Number

Place	Number
Edison, NJ (township) Middlesex County	357

Taiwanese 25 Years and Over Who are High School Graduates
Top 10 Places Sorted by Percent

Place	Percent
Edison, NJ (township) Middlesex County	92.73

Thais 25 Years and Over Who are High School Graduates
Top 10 Places Sorted by Number

Place	Number
No places met population threshold.	

Thais 25 Years and Over Who are High School Graduates
Top 10 Places Sorted by Percent

Place	Percent
No places met population threshold.	

Tongans 25 Years and Over Who are High School Graduates
Top 10 Places Sorted by Number

Place	Number
No places met population threshold.	

Tongans 25 Years and Over Who are High School Graduates
Top 10 Places Sorted by Percent

Place	Percent
No places met population threshold.	

Vietnamese 25 Years and Over Who are High School Graduates
Top 10 Places Sorted by Number

Place	Number
Atlantic City, NJ (city) Atlantic County	476
Jersey City, NJ (city) Hudson County	476
Camden, NJ (city) Camden County	337
Pennsauken, NJ (township) Camden County	195
Belleville, NJ (township) Essex County	192
South Plainfield, NJ (borough) Middlesex County	172
Woodlynne, NJ (borough) Camden County	52

Vietnamese 25 Years and Over Who are High School Graduates
Top 10 Places Sorted by Percent

Place	Percent
Belleville, NJ (township) Essex County	68.09
South Plainfield, NJ (borough) Middlesex County	66.93
Atlantic City, NJ (city) Atlantic County	54.03
Jersey City, NJ (city) Hudson County	53.36
Pennsauken, NJ (township) Camden County	47.56
Camden, NJ (city) Camden County	35.62
Woodlynne, NJ (borough) Camden County	32.30

College Graduates

Total Populations 25 Years and Over Who are Four-Year College Graduates
Top 10 Places Sorted by Number

Place	Number
Jersey City, NJ (city) Hudson County	42,676
Edison, NJ (township) Middlesex County	28,642
Cherry Hill, NJ (township) Camden County	22,831
Woodbridge, NJ (township) Middlesex County	18,463
Hoboken, NJ (city) Hudson County	17,007
Parsippany-Troy Hills, NJ (township) Morris County	15,748
Middletown, NJ (township) Monmouth County	15,634
Franklin, NJ (township) Somerset County	15,620
Wayne, NJ (township) Passaic County	15,497
Montclair, NJ (township) Essex County	15,291

Total Populations 25 Years and Over Who are Four-Year College Graduates
Top 10 Places Sorted by Percent

Place	Percent
Princeton, NJ (township) Mercer County	75.90
Plainsboro Center, NJ (cdp) Middlesex County	74.25
Millburn, NJ (township) Essex County	74.03
West Windsor, NJ (township) Mercer County	73.92
Plainsboro, NJ (township) Middlesex County	70.27
Montgomery, NJ (township) Somerset County	70.16
Princeton Meadows, NJ (cdp) Middlesex County	68.17
Bernards, NJ (township) Somerset County	67.44
Ridgewood, NJ (village) Bergen County	66.75
Chatham, NJ (township) Morris County	65.74

Asians 25 Years and Over Who are Four-Year College Graduates
Top 10 Places Sorted by Number

Place	Number
Jersey City, NJ (city) Hudson County	14,554
Edison, NJ (township) Middlesex County	13,256
Woodbridge, NJ (township) Middlesex County	6,685
Piscataway, NJ (township) Middlesex County	5,338
Fort Lee, NJ (borough) Bergen County	4,714
Parsippany-Troy Hills, NJ (township) Morris County	3,998
South Brunswick, NJ (township) Middlesex County	3,515

Notes: Please refer to the User's Guide for an explanation of data; tables reflect only those areas that meet Summary File 4 population thresholds, therefore there may be less than 10 places listed

Place	Number
Plainsboro, NJ (township) Middlesex County	3,435
East Brunswick, NJ (township) Middlesex County	3,338
Franklin, NJ (township) Somerset County	3,310

Asians 25 Years and Over Who are Four-Year College Graduates
Top 10 Places Sorted by Percent

Place	Percent
Bernards, NJ (township) Somerset County	89.47
Hopewell, NJ (township) Mercer County	89.30
Heathcote, NJ (cdp) Middlesex County	89.04
New Providence, NJ (borough) Union County	87.70
Montgomery, NJ (township) Somerset County	87.46
Plainsboro Center, NJ (cdp) Middlesex County	86.31
Plainsboro, NJ (township) Middlesex County	85.05
Princeton Meadows, NJ (cdp) Middlesex County	84.27
Dayton, NJ (cdp) Middlesex County	83.88
Morganville, NJ (cdp) Monmouth County	83.47

Native Hawaiian and Other Pacific Islanders 25 Years and Over Who are Four-Year College Graduates
Top 10 Places Sorted by Number

Place	Number
No places met population threshold.	

Native Hawaiian and Other Pacific Islanders 25 Years and Over Who are Four-Year College Graduates
Top 10 Places Sorted by Percent

Place	Percent
No places met population threshold.	

Asian Indians 25 Years and Over Who are Four-Year College Graduates
Top 10 Places Sorted by Number

Place	Number
Edison, NJ (township) Middlesex County	8,037
Woodbridge, NJ (township) Middlesex County	4,673
Jersey City, NJ (city) Hudson County	4,574
Piscataway, NJ (township) Middlesex County	2,753
South Brunswick, NJ (township) Middlesex County	2,047
Plainsboro, NJ (township) Middlesex County	1,913
Parsippany-Troy Hills, NJ (township) Morris County	1,837
Franklin, NJ (township) Somerset County	1,581
North Brunswick, NJ (township) Middlesex County	1,480
Sayreville, NJ (borough) Middlesex County	1,299

Asian Indians 25 Years and Over Who are Four-Year College Graduates
Top 10 Places Sorted by Percent

Place	Percent
Randolph, NJ (township) Morris County	97.92
Bernards, NJ (township) Somerset County	95.24
Dayton, NJ (cdp) Middlesex County	94.26
Highland Park, NJ (borough) Middlesex County	93.52
Montgomery, NJ (township) Somerset County	91.49
Plainsboro Center, NJ (cdp) Middlesex County	90.56
Scotch Plains, NJ (township) Union County	90.39
Bridgewater, NJ (township) Somerset County	89.75
Plainsboro, NJ (township) Middlesex County	89.27
Fords, NJ (cdp) Middlesex County	89.12

Bangladeshis 25 Years and Over Who are Four-Year College Graduates
Top 10 Places Sorted by Number

Place	Number
Paterson, NJ (city) Passaic County	34

Bangladeshis 25 Years and Over Who are Four-Year College Graduates
Top 10 Places Sorted by Percent

Place	Percent
Paterson, NJ (city) Passaic County	14.53

Cambodians 25 Years and Over Who are Four-Year College Graduates
Top 10 Places Sorted by Number

Place	Number
No places met population threshold.	

Cambodians 25 Years and Over Who are Four-Year College Graduates
Top 10 Places Sorted by Percent

Place	Percent
No places met population threshold.	

Chinese (except Taiwanese) 25 Years and Over Who are Four-Year College Graduates
Top 10 Places Sorted by Number

Place	Number
Edison, NJ (township) Middlesex County	2,463
Jersey City, NJ (city) Hudson County	1,356
East Brunswick, NJ (township) Middlesex County	1,311
Parsippany-Troy Hills, NJ (township) Morris County	1,244
Marlboro, NJ (township) Monmouth County	1,185
Piscataway, NJ (township) Middlesex County	1,179
Plainsboro, NJ (township) Middlesex County	935
West Windsor, NJ (township) Mercer County	892
Bridgewater, NJ (township) Somerset County	815
Holmdel, NJ (township) Monmouth County	782

Chinese (except Taiwanese) 25 Years and Over Who are Four-Year College Graduates
Top 10 Places Sorted by Percent

Place	Percent
Princeton, NJ (township) Mercer County	91.65
Bernards, NJ (township) Somerset County	90.05
Princeton Meadows, NJ (cdp) Middlesex County	87.79
Montgomery, NJ (township) Somerset County	87.17
Plainsboro, NJ (township) Middlesex County	86.49
New Providence, NJ (borough) Union County	84.62
Hanover, NJ (township) Morris County	84.12
Lawrence, NJ (township) Mercer County	84.02
Millburn, NJ (township) Essex County	83.76
Morganville, NJ (cdp) Monmouth County	83.12

Fijians 25 Years and Over Who are Four-Year College Graduates
Top 10 Places Sorted by Number

Place	Number
No places met population threshold.	

Fijians 25 Years and Over Who are Four-Year College Graduates
Top 10 Places Sorted by Percent

Place	Percent
No places met population threshold.	

Filipinos 25 Years and Over Who are Four-Year College Graduates
Top 10 Places Sorted by Number

Place	Number
Jersey City, NJ (city) Hudson County	6,842
Edison, NJ (township) Middlesex County	1,242
Bergenfield, NJ (borough) Bergen County	1,186
Union, NJ (township) Union County	980
Belleville, NJ (township) Essex County	906
Woodbridge, NJ (township) Middlesex County	895
Bloomfield, NJ (township) Essex County	869
Piscataway, NJ (township) Middlesex County	852
Old Bridge, NJ (township) Middlesex County	620
Cherry Hill, NJ (township) Camden County	618

Filipinos 25 Years and Over Who are Four-Year College Graduates
Top 10 Places Sorted by Percent

Place	Percent
North Brunswick, NJ (township) Middlesex County	87.70
East Brunswick, NJ (township) Middlesex County	87.24
Franklin, NJ (township) Somerset County	85.48
Somerset, NJ (cdp) Somerset County	80.66
South Brunswick, NJ (township) Middlesex County	80.10
Bloomfield, NJ (township) Essex County	78.93
Sayreville, NJ (borough) Middlesex County	78.93
Freehold, NJ (township) Monmouth County	78.75
Parsippany-Troy Hills, NJ (township) Morris County	77.87
Old Bridge, NJ (township) Middlesex County	76.83

Guamanians or Chamorros 25 Years and Over Who are Four-Year College Graduates
Top 10 Places Sorted by Number

Place	Number
No places met population threshold.	

Guamanians or Chamorros 25 Years and Over Who are Four-Year College Graduates
Top 10 Places Sorted by Percent

Place	Percent
No places met population threshold.	

Hawaiian Natives 25 Years and Over Who are Four-Year College Graduates
Top 10 Places Sorted by Number

Place	Number
No places met population threshold.	

Hawaiian Natives 25 Years and Over Who are Four-Year College Graduates
Top 10 Places Sorted by Percent

Place	Percent
No places met population threshold.	

Hmongs 25 Years and Over Who are Four-Year College Graduates
Top 10 Places Sorted by Number

Place	Number
No places met population threshold.	

Hmongs 25 Years and Over Who are Four-Year College Graduates
Top 10 Places Sorted by Percent

Place	Percent
No places met population threshold.	

Indonesians 25 Years and Over Who are Four-Year College Graduates
Top 10 Places Sorted by Number

Place	Number
No places met population threshold.	

Indonesians 25 Years and Over Who are Four-Year College Graduates
Top 10 Places Sorted by Percent

Place	Percent
No places met population threshold.	

Japanese 25 Years and Over Who are Four-Year College Graduates
Top 10 Places Sorted by Number

Place	Number
Fort Lee, NJ (borough) Bergen County	907
Ridgewood, NJ (village) Bergen County	249

Notes: Please refer to the User's Guide for an explanation of data; tables reflect only those areas that meet Summary File 4 population thresholds, therefore there may be less than 10 places listed

Cliffside Park, NJ (borough) Bergen County — 208

Japanese 25 Years and Over Who are Four-Year College Graduates
Top 10 Places Sorted by Percent

Place	Percent
Ridgewood, NJ (village) Bergen County	86.46
Fort Lee, NJ (borough) Bergen County	67.89
Cliffside Park, NJ (borough) Bergen County	59.77

Koreans 25 Years and Over Who are Four-Year College Graduates
Top 10 Places Sorted by Number

Place	Number
Fort Lee, NJ (borough) Bergen County	2,357
Palisades Park, NJ (borough) Bergen County	1,682
Cliffside Park, NJ (borough) Bergen County	610
Jersey City, NJ (city) Hudson County	598
Leonia, NJ (borough) Bergen County	518
Edison, NJ (township) Middlesex County	505
Edgewater, NJ (borough) Bergen County	497
Closter, NJ (borough) Bergen County	422
Paramus, NJ (borough) Bergen County	375
Wayne, NJ (township) Passaic County	373

Koreans 25 Years and Over Who are Four-Year College Graduates
Top 10 Places Sorted by Percent

Place	Percent
West Windsor, NJ (township) Mercer County	79.84
Alpine, NJ (borough) Bergen County	73.58
Ridgewood, NJ (village) Bergen County	73.24
Hackensack, NJ (city) Bergen County	72.05
Closter, NJ (borough) Bergen County	71.28
Englewood Cliffs, NJ (borough) Bergen County	69.82
Edgewater, NJ (borough) Bergen County	68.84
Harrington Park, NJ (borough) Bergen County	68.38
Wayne, NJ (township) Passaic County	68.19
West Orange, NJ (township) Essex County	66.67

Laotians 25 Years and Over Who are Four-Year College Graduates
Top 10 Places Sorted by Number

Place	Number
No places met population threshold.	

Laotians 25 Years and Over Who are Four-Year College Graduates
Top 10 Places Sorted by Percent

Place	Percent
No places met population threshold.	

Malaysians 25 Years and Over Who are Four-Year College Graduates
Top 10 Places Sorted by Number

Place	Number
No places met population threshold.	

Malaysians 25 Years and Over Who are Four-Year College Graduates
Top 10 Places Sorted by Percent

Place	Percent
No places met population threshold.	

Pakistanis 25 Years and Over Who are Four-Year College Graduates
Top 10 Places Sorted by Number

Place	Number
Jersey City, NJ (city) Hudson County	433
Edison, NJ (township) Middlesex County	269
Old Bridge, NJ (township) Middlesex County	207

Woodbridge, NJ (township) Middlesex County — 99

Pakistanis 25 Years and Over Who are Four-Year College Graduates
Top 10 Places Sorted by Percent

Place	Percent
Edison, NJ (township) Middlesex County	71.35
Old Bridge, NJ (township) Middlesex County	66.99
Woodbridge, NJ (township) Middlesex County	44.59
Jersey City, NJ (city) Hudson County	42.16

Samoans 25 Years and Over Who are Four-Year College Graduates
Top 10 Places Sorted by Number

Place	Number
No places met population threshold.	

Samoans 25 Years and Over Who are Four-Year College Graduates
Top 10 Places Sorted by Percent

Place	Percent
No places met population threshold.	

Sri Lankans 25 Years and Over Who are Four-Year College Graduates
Top 10 Places Sorted by Number

Place	Number
No places met population threshold.	

Sri Lankans 25 Years and Over Who are Four-Year College Graduates
Top 10 Places Sorted by Percent

Place	Percent
No places met population threshold.	

Taiwanese 25 Years and Over Who are Four-Year College Graduates
Top 10 Places Sorted by Number

Place	Number
Edison, NJ (township) Middlesex County	317

Taiwanese 25 Years and Over Who are Four-Year College Graduates
Top 10 Places Sorted by Percent

Place	Percent
Edison, NJ (township) Middlesex County	82.34

Thais 25 Years and Over Who are Four-Year College Graduates
Top 10 Places Sorted by Number

Place	Number
No places met population threshold.	

Thais 25 Years and Over Who are Four-Year College Graduates
Top 10 Places Sorted by Percent

Place	Percent
No places met population threshold.	

Tongans 25 Years and Over Who are Four-Year College Graduates
Top 10 Places Sorted by Number

Place	Number
No places met population threshold.	

Tongans 25 Years and Over Who are Four-Year College Graduates
Top 10 Places Sorted by Percent

Place	Percent
No places met population threshold.	

Vietnamese 25 Years and Over Who are Four-Year College Graduates
Top 10 Places Sorted by Number

Place	Number
Jersey City, NJ (city) Hudson County	186
Belleville, NJ (township) Essex County	83
Pennsauken, NJ (township) Camden County	70
Camden, NJ (city) Camden County	66
Atlantic City, NJ (city) Atlantic County	59
South Plainfield, NJ (borough) Middlesex County	37
Woodlynne, NJ (borough) Camden County	3

Vietnamese 25 Years and Over Who are Four-Year College Graduates
Top 10 Places Sorted by Percent

Place	Percent
Belleville, NJ (township) Essex County	29.43
Jersey City, NJ (city) Hudson County	20.85
Pennsauken, NJ (township) Camden County	17.07
South Plainfield, NJ (borough) Middlesex County	14.40
Camden, NJ (city) Camden County	6.98
Atlantic City, NJ (city) Atlantic County	6.70
Woodlynne, NJ (borough) Camden County	1.86

Median Household Income

Total Population
Top 10 Places Sorted by Number

Place	Dollars
Saddle River, NJ (borough) Bergen County	134,289
Franklin Lakes, NJ (borough) Bergen County	132,373
Millburn, NJ (township) Essex County	130,848
Alpine, NJ (borough) Bergen County	130,740
Montgomery, NJ (township) Somerset County	118,850
West Windsor, NJ (township) Mercer County	116,335
Holmdel, NJ (township) Monmouth County	112,879
Cranbury, NJ (township) Middlesex County	111,680
Colts Neck, NJ (township) Monmouth County	109,190
Berkeley Heights, NJ (township) Union County	107,716

Asian
Top 10 Places Sorted by Number

Place	Dollars
Saddle River, NJ (borough) Bergen County	194,640
Moorestown, NJ (township) Burlington County	184,586
Cranbury, NJ (township) Middlesex County	161,769
Warren, NJ (township) Somerset County	158,816
Montgomery, NJ (township) Somerset County	136,301
Bernards, NJ (township) Somerset County	132,683
Wyckoff, NJ (township) Bergen County	132,300
Green Brook, NJ (township) Somerset County	130,889
Hopewell, NJ (township) Mercer County	129,801
Holmdel, NJ (township) Monmouth County	129,322

Native Hawaiian and Other Pacific Islander
Top 10 Places Sorted by Number

Place	Dollars
No places met population threshold.	

Asian Indian
Top 10 Places Sorted by Number

Place	Dollars
Warren, NJ (township) Somerset County	176,569
Bernards, NJ (township) Somerset County	156,915
Montgomery, NJ (township) Somerset County	153,791
West Windsor, NJ (township) Mercer County	146,885

Notes: Please refer to the User's Guide for an explanation of data; tables reflect only those areas that meet Summary File 4 population thresholds, therefore there may be less than 10 places listed

Place	Dollars
Bridgewater, NJ (township) Somerset County	145,490
Mahwah, NJ (township) Bergen County	129,690
Scotch Plains, NJ (township) Union County	126,618
Wayne, NJ (township) Passaic County	126,503
Marlboro, NJ (township) Monmouth County	125,271
Montville, NJ (township) Morris County	123,454

Bangladeshi
Top 10 Places Sorted by Number

Place	Dollars
Paterson, NJ (city) Passaic County	32,411

Cambodian
Top 10 Places Sorted by Number

Place	Dollars
No places met population threshold.	

Chinese (except Taiwanese)
Top 10 Places Sorted by Number

Place	Dollars
Englewood Cliffs, NJ (borough) Bergen County	200,001
Warren, NJ (township) Somerset County	142,984
Holmdel, NJ (township) Monmouth County	139,211
Montgomery, NJ (township) Somerset County	134,367
West Windsor, NJ (township) Mercer County	132,330
Hanover, NJ (township) Morris County	130,918
Bernards, NJ (township) Somerset County	130,561
Bridgewater, NJ (township) Somerset County	125,597
Montville, NJ (township) Morris County	120,500
Marlboro, NJ (township) Monmouth County	117,303

Fijian
Top 10 Places Sorted by Number

Place	Dollars
No places met population threshold.	

Filipino
Top 10 Places Sorted by Number

Place	Dollars
Livingston, NJ (township) Essex County	117,601
Howell, NJ (township) Monmouth County	109,992
North Brunswick, NJ (township) Middlesex County	109,672
Paramus, NJ (borough) Bergen County	108,116
Clifton, NJ (city) Passaic County	102,672
Dumont, NJ (borough) Bergen County	102,526
Washington, NJ (township) Gloucester County	102,134
Wayne, NJ (township) Passaic County	101,949
Union, NJ (township) Union County	101,179
West Orange, NJ (township) Essex County	100,991

Guamanian or Chamorro
Top 10 Places Sorted by Number

Place	Dollars
No places met population threshold.	

Hawaiian, Native
Top 10 Places Sorted by Number

Place	Dollars
No places met population threshold.	

Hmong
Top 10 Places Sorted by Number

Place	Dollars
No places met population threshold.	

Indonesian
Top 10 Places Sorted by Number

Place	Dollars
No places met population threshold.	

Japanese
Top 10 Places Sorted by Number

Place	Dollars
Ridgewood, NJ (village) Bergen County	123,293
Fort Lee, NJ (borough) Bergen County	75,865
Cliffside Park, NJ (borough) Bergen County	65,750

Korean
Top 10 Places Sorted by Number

Place	Dollars
Alpine, NJ (borough) Bergen County	171,479
Englewood Cliffs, NJ (borough) Bergen County	108,831
Demarest, NJ (borough) Bergen County	100,000
Norwood, NJ (borough) Bergen County	98,646
West Windsor, NJ (township) Mercer County	96,481
West Orange, NJ (township) Essex County	92,491
Closter, NJ (borough) Bergen County	83,352
Old Tappan, NJ (borough) Bergen County	82,840
Parsippany-Troy Hills, NJ (township) Morris County	82,046
Cresskill, NJ (borough) Bergen County	71,875

Laotian
Top 10 Places Sorted by Number

Place	Dollars
No places met population threshold.	

Malaysian
Top 10 Places Sorted by Number

Place	Dollars
No places met population threshold.	

Pakistani
Top 10 Places Sorted by Number

Place	Dollars
Edison, NJ (township) Middlesex County	68,295
Old Bridge, NJ (township) Middlesex County	66,750
Woodbridge, NJ (township) Middlesex County	51,944
Jersey City, NJ (city) Hudson County	37,171

Samoan
Top 10 Places Sorted by Number

Place	Dollars
No places met population threshold.	

Sri Lankan
Top 10 Places Sorted by Number

Place	Dollars
No places met population threshold.	

Taiwanese
Top 10 Places Sorted by Number

Place	Dollars
Edison, NJ (township) Middlesex County	95,163

Thai
Top 10 Places Sorted by Number

Place	Dollars
No places met population threshold.	

Tongan
Top 10 Places Sorted by Number

Place	Dollars
No places met population threshold.	

Vietnamese
Top 10 Places Sorted by Number

Place	Dollars
South Plainfield, NJ (borough) Middlesex County	65,288
Woodlynne, NJ (borough) Camden County	55,000

Place	Dollars
Atlantic City, NJ (city) Atlantic County	54,250
Belleville, NJ (township) Essex County	52,917
Pennsauken, NJ (township) Camden County	38,750
Jersey City, NJ (city) Hudson County	36,071
Camden, NJ (city) Camden County	35,000

Per Capita Income

Total Population
Top 10 Places Sorted by Number

Place	Dollars
Saddle River, NJ (borough) Bergen County	85,934
Alpine, NJ (borough) Bergen County	76,995
Millburn, NJ (township) Essex County	76,796
Chatham, NJ (township) Morris County	65,497
Summit, NJ (city) Union County	62,598
Franklin Lakes, NJ (borough) Bergen County	59,763
Watchung, NJ (borough) Somerset County	58,653
Englewood Cliffs, NJ (borough) Bergen County	57,399
Bernards, NJ (township) Somerset County	56,521
Princeton, NJ (township) Mercer County	56,360

Asian
Top 10 Places Sorted by Number

Place	Dollars
Saddle River, NJ (borough) Bergen County	101,616
Moorestown, NJ (township) Burlington County	62,102
Watchung, NJ (borough) Somerset County	58,038
Colts Neck, NJ (township) Monmouth County	57,788
Hopewell, NJ (township) Mercer County	57,581
Alpine, NJ (borough) Bergen County	56,747
Chatham, NJ (township) Morris County	52,506
Guttenberg, NJ (town) Hudson County	51,251
Bernards, NJ (township) Somerset County	50,892
Cranbury, NJ (township) Middlesex County	48,925

Native Hawaiian and Other Pacific Islander
Top 10 Places Sorted by Number

Place	Dollars
No places met population threshold.	

Asian Indian
Top 10 Places Sorted by Number

Place	Dollars
Bernards, NJ (township) Somerset County	67,934
Montville, NJ (township) Morris County	58,050
Warren, NJ (township) Somerset County	55,959
Montgomery, NJ (township) Somerset County	54,172
Scotch Plains, NJ (township) Union County	53,428
Livingston, NJ (township) Essex County	50,008
Holmdel, NJ (township) Monmouth County	47,531
Randolph, NJ (township) Morris County	46,150
Princeton, NJ (township) Mercer County	45,741
Bridgewater, NJ (township) Somerset County	45,291

Bangladeshi
Top 10 Places Sorted by Number

Place	Dollars
Paterson, NJ (city) Passaic County	8,171

Cambodian
Top 10 Places Sorted by Number

Place	Dollars
No places met population threshold.	

Chinese (except Taiwanese)
Top 10 Places Sorted by Number

Place	Dollars
Englewood Cliffs, NJ (borough) Bergen County	61,036
Lawrence, NJ (township) Mercer County	51,123
New Providence, NJ (borough) Union County	48,735
Bridgewater, NJ (township) Somerset County	47,897

Notes: Please refer to the User's Guide for an explanation of data; tables reflect only those areas that meet Summary File 4 population thresholds, therefore there may be less than 10 places listed

Place	Dollars
Bernards, NJ (township) Somerset County	47,784
Montclair, NJ (township) Essex County	47,224
Montville, NJ (township) Morris County	44,624
Holmdel, NJ (township) Monmouth County	41,902
Millburn, NJ (township) Essex County	39,629
Warren, NJ (township) Somerset County	39,258

Fijian
Top 10 Places Sorted by Number

Place	Dollars
No places met population threshold.	

Filipino
Top 10 Places Sorted by Number

Place	Dollars
Freehold, NJ (township) Monmouth County	41,349
Secaucus, NJ (town) Hudson County	38,309
North Brunswick, NJ (township) Middlesex County	36,775
Dover, NJ (township) Ocean County	33,426
Toms River, NJ (cdp) Ocean County	33,426
Franklin, NJ (township) Somerset County	32,064
Washington, NJ (township) Gloucester County	31,941
Paramus, NJ (borough) Bergen County	30,621
South Brunswick, NJ (township) Middlesex County	30,093
Teaneck, NJ (township) Bergen County	29,950

Guamanian or Chamorro
Top 10 Places Sorted by Number

Place	Dollars
No places met population threshold.	

Hawaiian, Native
Top 10 Places Sorted by Number

Place	Dollars
No places met population threshold.	

Hmong
Top 10 Places Sorted by Number

Place	Dollars
No places met population threshold.	

Indonesian
Top 10 Places Sorted by Number

Place	Dollars
No places met population threshold.	

Japanese
Top 10 Places Sorted by Number

Place	Dollars
Cliffside Park, NJ (borough) Bergen County	51,674
Ridgewood, NJ (village) Bergen County	48,407
Fort Lee, NJ (borough) Bergen County	42,503

Korean
Top 10 Places Sorted by Number

Place	Dollars
Alpine, NJ (borough) Bergen County	62,822
West Windsor, NJ (township) Mercer County	40,483
Parsippany-Troy Hills, NJ (township) Morris County	36,333
Demarest, NJ (borough) Bergen County	35,036
Norwood, NJ (borough) Bergen County	33,996
Englewood Cliffs, NJ (borough) Bergen County	32,835
Edgewater, NJ (borough) Bergen County	27,641
Closter, NJ (borough) Bergen County	26,661
Old Tappan, NJ (borough) Bergen County	26,594
Jersey City, NJ (city) Hudson County	25,957

Laotian
Top 10 Places Sorted by Number

Place	Dollars
No places met population threshold.	

Malaysian
Top 10 Places Sorted by Number

Place	Dollars
No places met population threshold.	

Pakistani
Top 10 Places Sorted by Number

Place	Dollars
Edison, NJ (township) Middlesex County	24,735
Old Bridge, NJ (township) Middlesex County	18,890
Jersey City, NJ (city) Hudson County	12,578
Woodbridge, NJ (township) Middlesex County	11,505

Samoan
Top 10 Places Sorted by Number

Place	Dollars
No places met population threshold.	

Sri Lankan
Top 10 Places Sorted by Number

Place	Dollars
No places met population threshold.	

Taiwanese
Top 10 Places Sorted by Number

Place	Dollars
Edison, NJ (township) Middlesex County	25,150

Thai
Top 10 Places Sorted by Number

Place	Dollars
No places met population threshold.	

Tongan
Top 10 Places Sorted by Number

Place	Dollars
No places met population threshold.	

Vietnamese
Top 10 Places Sorted by Number

Place	Dollars
Jersey City, NJ (city) Hudson County	17,294
Atlantic City, NJ (city) Atlantic County	17,139
South Plainfield, NJ (borough) Middlesex County	14,796
Belleville, NJ (township) Essex County	14,185
Woodlynne, NJ (borough) Camden County	11,009
Pennsauken, NJ (township) Camden County	9,783
Camden, NJ (city) Camden County	9,119

Poverty Status

Total Populations with Income Below Poverty Level
Top 10 Places Sorted by Number

Place	Number
Newark, NJ (city) Essex County	74,263
Jersey City, NJ (city) Hudson County	44,075
Paterson, NJ (city) Passaic County	32,474
Camden, NJ (city) Camden County	26,786
Elizabeth, NJ (city) Union County	20,963
Trenton, NJ (city) Mercer County	17,222
Passaic, NJ (city) Passaic County	14,249
Union City, NJ (city) Hudson County	14,244
New Brunswick, NJ (city) Middlesex County	11,454
Lakewood, NJ (township) Ocean County	11,440

Total Populations with Income Below Poverty Level
Top 10 Places Sorted by Percent

Place	Percent
Camden, NJ (city) Camden County	35.52
Newark, NJ (city) Essex County	28.40
New Brunswick, NJ (city) Middlesex County	27.05
Atlantic City, NJ (city) Atlantic County	23.65
Paterson, NJ (city) Passaic County	22.19
Union City, NJ (city) Hudson County	21.37
Passaic, NJ (city) Passaic County	21.19
Trenton, NJ (city) Mercer County	21.13
Lakewood, NJ (township) Ocean County	19.78
West New York, NJ (town) Hudson County	18.92

Asians with Income Below Poverty Level
Top 10 Places Sorted by Number

Place	Number
Jersey City, NJ (city) Hudson County	3,902
Edison, NJ (township) Middlesex County	1,530
Fort Lee, NJ (borough) Bergen County	1,096
Palisades Park, NJ (borough) Bergen County	834
Newark, NJ (city) Essex County	780
Paterson, NJ (city) Passaic County	773
New Brunswick, NJ (city) Middlesex County	669
Camden, NJ (city) Camden County	589
Woodbridge, NJ (township) Middlesex County	566
Atlantic City, NJ (city) Atlantic County	535

Asians with Income Below Poverty Level
Top 10 Places Sorted by Percent

Place	Percent
New Brunswick, NJ (city) Middlesex County	35.49
Trenton, NJ (city) Mercer County	30.10
Newark, NJ (city) Essex County	28.67
Paterson, NJ (city) Passaic County	27.82
Camden, NJ (city) Camden County	26.13
Browns Mills, NJ (cdp) Burlington County	25.10
Collingswood, NJ (borough) Camden County	23.64
Glassboro, NJ (borough) Gloucester County	19.85
Leonia, NJ (borough) Bergen County	19.23
East Rutherford, NJ (borough) Bergen County	19.09

Native Hawaiian and Other Pacific Islanders with Income Below Poverty Level
Top 10 Places Sorted by Number

Place	Number
No places met population threshold.	

Native Hawaiian and Other Pacific Islanders with Income Below Poverty Level
Top 10 Places Sorted by Percent

Place	Percent
No places met population threshold.	

Asian Indians with Income Below Poverty Level
Top 10 Places Sorted by Number

Place	Number
Jersey City, NJ (city) Hudson County	1,466
Edison, NJ (township) Middlesex County	748
Paterson, NJ (city) Passaic County	499
Woodbridge, NJ (township) Middlesex County	396
New Brunswick, NJ (city) Middlesex County	280
North Bergen, NJ (township) Hudson County	266
Passaic, NJ (city) Passaic County	244
Newark, NJ (city) Essex County	225
Kearny, NJ (town) Hudson County	212
Avenel, NJ (cdp) Middlesex County	175

Asian Indians with Income Below Poverty Level
Top 10 Places Sorted by Percent

Place	Percent
Paterson, NJ (city) Passaic County	31.84

Notes: Please refer to the User's Guide for an explanation of data; tables reflect only those areas that meet Summary File 4 population thresholds, therefore there may be less than 10 places listed

New Brunswick, NJ (city) Middlesex County	30.50
Kearny, NJ (town) Hudson County	26.01
West New York, NJ (town) Hudson County	25.91
Newark, NJ (city) Essex County	19.96
Montclair, NJ (township) Essex County	18.84
Secaucus, NJ (town) Hudson County	18.57
Princeton, NJ (township) Mercer County	18.34
Atlantic City, NJ (city) Atlantic County	18.01
Union City, NJ (city) Hudson County	16.78

Bangladeshis with Income Below Poverty Level
Top 10 Places Sorted by Number

Place	Number
Paterson, NJ (city) Passaic County	165

Bangladeshis with Income Below Poverty Level
Top 10 Places Sorted by Percent

Place	Percent
Paterson, NJ (city) Passaic County	35.95

Cambodians with Income Below Poverty Level
Top 10 Places Sorted by Number

Place	Number
No places met population threshold.	

Cambodians with Income Below Poverty Level
Top 10 Places Sorted by Percent

Place	Percent
No places met population threshold.	

Chinese (except Taiwanese) with Income Below Poverty Level
Top 10 Places Sorted by Number

Place	Number
Jersey City, NJ (city) Hudson County	410
Edison, NJ (township) Middlesex County	389
Harrison, NJ (town) Hudson County	246
East Brunswick, NJ (township) Middlesex County	221
Piscataway, NJ (township) Middlesex County	208
Fort Lee, NJ (borough) Bergen County	160
Kearny, NJ (town) Hudson County	151
West Windsor, NJ (township) Mercer County	112
New Brunswick, NJ (city) Middlesex County	107
Marlboro, NJ (township) Monmouth County	100

Chinese (except Taiwanese) with Income Below Poverty Level
Top 10 Places Sorted by Percent

Place	Percent
New Brunswick, NJ (city) Middlesex County	37.41
Harrison, NJ (town) Hudson County	18.72
Kearny, NJ (town) Hudson County	16.56
Jersey City, NJ (city) Hudson County	14.12
Highland Park, NJ (borough) Middlesex County	10.32
Piscataway, NJ (township) Middlesex County	9.74
Fort Lee, NJ (borough) Bergen County	9.28
Wayne, NJ (township) Passaic County	7.71
North Brunswick, NJ (township) Middlesex County	7.60
Berkeley Heights, NJ (township) Union County	7.23

Fijians with Income Below Poverty Level
Top 10 Places Sorted by Number

Place	Number
No places met population threshold.	

Fijians with Income Below Poverty Level
Top 10 Places Sorted by Percent

Place	Percent
No places met population threshold.	

Filipinos with Income Below Poverty Level
Top 10 Places Sorted by Number

Place	Number
Jersey City, NJ (city) Hudson County	694
Fair Lawn, NJ (borough) Bergen County	109
Elizabeth, NJ (city) Union County	108
Belleville, NJ (township) Essex County	106
Bergenfield, NJ (borough) Bergen County	88
Old Bridge, NJ (township) Middlesex County	77
Clifton, NJ (city) Passaic County	55
Edison, NJ (township) Middlesex County	51
Newark, NJ (city) Essex County	43
Dover, NJ (township) Ocean County	36

Filipinos with Income Below Poverty Level
Top 10 Places Sorted by Percent

Place	Percent
Fair Lawn, NJ (borough) Bergen County	20.34
Elizabeth, NJ (city) Union County	11.01
Newark, NJ (city) Essex County	7.54
Little Ferry, NJ (borough) Bergen County	7.03
Voorhees, NJ (township) Camden County	6.85
Old Bridge, NJ (township) Middlesex County	6.04
Rahway, NJ (city) Union County	5.26
Belleville, NJ (township) Essex County	4.98
Lodi, NJ (borough) Bergen County	4.78
Dover, NJ (township) Ocean County	4.55

Guamanians or Chamorros with Income Below Poverty Level
Top 10 Places Sorted by Number

Place	Number
No places met population threshold.	

Guamanians or Chamorros with Income Below Poverty Level
Top 10 Places Sorted by Percent

Place	Percent
No places met population threshold.	

Hawaiian Natives with Income Below Poverty Level
Top 10 Places Sorted by Number

Place	Number
No places met population threshold.	

Hawaiian Natives with Income Below Poverty Level
Top 10 Places Sorted by Percent

Place	Percent
No places met population threshold.	

Hmongs with Income Below Poverty Level
Top 10 Places Sorted by Number

Place	Number
No places met population threshold.	

Hmongs with Income Below Poverty Level
Top 10 Places Sorted by Percent

Place	Percent
No places met population threshold.	

Indonesians with Income Below Poverty Level
Top 10 Places Sorted by Number

Place	Number
No places met population threshold.	

Indonesians with Income Below Poverty Level
Top 10 Places Sorted by Percent

Place	Percent
No places met population threshold.	

Japanese with Income Below Poverty Level
Top 10 Places Sorted by Number

Place	Number
Fort Lee, NJ (borough) Bergen County	130
Cliffside Park, NJ (borough) Bergen County	41
Ridgewood, NJ (village) Bergen County	0

Japanese with Income Below Poverty Level
Top 10 Places Sorted by Percent

Place	Percent
Cliffside Park, NJ (borough) Bergen County	9.19
Fort Lee, NJ (borough) Bergen County	6.47
Ridgewood, NJ (village) Bergen County	0.00

Koreans with Income Below Poverty Level
Top 10 Places Sorted by Number

Place	Number
Palisades Park, NJ (borough) Bergen County	779
Fort Lee, NJ (borough) Bergen County	704
Leonia, NJ (borough) Bergen County	354
Jersey City, NJ (city) Hudson County	297
Ridgefield, NJ (borough) Bergen County	206
Edison, NJ (township) Middlesex County	204
Little Ferry, NJ (borough) Bergen County	187
Cliffside Park, NJ (borough) Bergen County	153
Ridgewood, NJ (village) Bergen County	125
Pemberton, NJ (township) Burlington County	118

Koreans with Income Below Poverty Level
Top 10 Places Sorted by Percent

Place	Percent
Browns Mills, NJ (cdp) Burlington County	27.14
Little Ferry, NJ (borough) Bergen County	25.34
Leonia, NJ (borough) Bergen County	24.26
Pemberton, NJ (township) Burlington County	22.10
Ridgewood, NJ (village) Bergen County	21.93
River Edge, NJ (borough) Bergen County	20.30
Jersey City, NJ (city) Hudson County	20.05
Bayonne, NJ (city) Hudson County	19.66
Edison, NJ (township) Middlesex County	16.18
Ridgefield, NJ (borough) Bergen County	15.36

Laotians with Income Below Poverty Level
Top 10 Places Sorted by Number

Place	Number
No places met population threshold.	

Laotians with Income Below Poverty Level
Top 10 Places Sorted by Percent

Place	Percent
No places met population threshold.	

Malaysians with Income Below Poverty Level
Top 10 Places Sorted by Number

Place	Number
No places met population threshold.	

Malaysians with Income Below Poverty Level
Top 10 Places Sorted by Percent

Place	Percent
No places met population threshold.	

Pakistanis with Income Below Poverty Level
Top 10 Places Sorted by Number

Place	Number
Jersey City, NJ (city) Hudson County	427
Old Bridge, NJ (township) Middlesex County	75
Woodbridge, NJ (township) Middlesex County	24
Edison, NJ (township) Middlesex County	0

Notes: Please refer to the User's Guide for an explanation of data; tables reflect only those areas that meet Summary File 4 population thresholds, therefore there may be less than 10 places listed

Pakistanis with Income Below Poverty Level
Top 10 Places Sorted by Percent

Place	Percent
Jersey City, NJ (city) Hudson County	22.74
Old Bridge, NJ (township) Middlesex County	14.26
Woodbridge, NJ (township) Middlesex County	5.14
Edison, NJ (township) Middlesex County	0.00

Samoans with Income Below Poverty Level
Top 10 Places Sorted by Number

Place	Number
No places met population threshold.	

Samoans with Income Below Poverty Level
Top 10 Places Sorted by Percent

Place	Percent
No places met population threshold.	

Sri Lankans with Income Below Poverty Level
Top 10 Places Sorted by Number

Place	Number
No places met population threshold.	

Sri Lankans with Income Below Poverty Level
Top 10 Places Sorted by Percent

Place	Percent
No places met population threshold.	

Taiwanese with Income Below Poverty Level
Top 10 Places Sorted by Number

Place	Number
Edison, NJ (township) Middlesex County	67

Taiwanese with Income Below Poverty Level
Top 10 Places Sorted by Percent

Place	Percent
Edison, NJ (township) Middlesex County	10.11

Thais with Income Below Poverty Level
Top 10 Places Sorted by Number

Place	Number
No places met population threshold.	

Thais with Income Below Poverty Level
Top 10 Places Sorted by Percent

Place	Percent
No places met population threshold.	

Tongans with Income Below Poverty Level
Top 10 Places Sorted by Number

Place	Number
No places met population threshold.	

Tongans with Income Below Poverty Level
Top 10 Places Sorted by Percent

Place	Percent
No places met population threshold.	

Vietnamese with Income Below Poverty Level
Top 10 Places Sorted by Number

Place	Number
Jersey City, NJ (city) Hudson County	377
Camden, NJ (city) Camden County	346
Belleville, NJ (township) Essex County	103
Pennsauken, NJ (township) Camden County	80
Atlantic City, NJ (city) Atlantic County	73
South Plainfield, NJ (borough) Middlesex County	39
Woodlynne, NJ (borough) Camden County	32

Vietnamese with Income Below Poverty Level
Top 10 Places Sorted by Percent

Place	Percent
Jersey City, NJ (city) Hudson County	27.30
Camden, NJ (city) Camden County	24.82
Belleville, NJ (township) Essex County	24.29
Woodlynne, NJ (borough) Camden County	11.68
Pennsauken, NJ (township) Camden County	11.66
South Plainfield, NJ (borough) Middlesex County	10.66
Atlantic City, NJ (city) Atlantic County	6.15

Homeownership

Total Populations Who Own Their Own Homes
Top 10 Places Sorted by Number

Place	Number
Dover, NJ (township) Ocean County	28,026
Toms River, NJ (cdp) Ocean County	26,527
Hamilton, NJ (township) Mercer County	25,170
Jersey City, NJ (city) Hudson County	24,965
Brick, NJ (township) Ocean County	24,609
Woodbridge, NJ (township) Middlesex County	24,404
Edison, NJ (township) Middlesex County	22,462
Cherry Hill, NJ (township) Camden County	21,751
Newark, NJ (city) Essex County	21,750
Middletown, NJ (township) Monmouth County	20,070

Total Populations Who Own Their Own Homes
Top 10 Places Sorted by Percent

Place	Percent
Morganville, NJ (cdp) Monmouth County	97.07
Cinnaminson, NJ (township) Burlington County	96.26
Marlboro, NJ (township) Monmouth County	96.21
Washington, NJ (township) Bergen County	96.05
Holmdel, NJ (township) Monmouth County	95.51
White Meadow Lake, NJ (cdp) Morris County	95.47
Franklin Lakes, NJ (borough) Bergen County	95.12
Haworth, NJ (borough) Bergen County	94.97
Monroe, NJ (township) Middlesex County	94.80
Harrington Park, NJ (borough) Bergen County	94.18

Asians Who Own Their Own Homes
Top 10 Places Sorted by Number

Place	Number
Jersey City, NJ (city) Hudson County	4,309
Edison, NJ (township) Middlesex County	4,213
East Brunswick, NJ (township) Middlesex County	1,757
Piscataway, NJ (township) Middlesex County	1,678
Woodbridge, NJ (township) Middlesex County	1,649
South Brunswick, NJ (township) Middlesex County	1,631
Parsippany-Troy Hills, NJ (township) Morris County	1,549
Cherry Hill, NJ (township) Camden County	1,487
Fort Lee, NJ (borough) Bergen County	1,409
Franklin, NJ (township) Somerset County	1,327

Asians Who Own Their Own Homes
Top 10 Places Sorted by Percent

Place	Percent
Cranbury, NJ (township) Middlesex County	100.00
Franklin Lakes, NJ (borough) Bergen County	100.00
Greentree, NJ (cdp) Camden County	100.00
Hopewell, NJ (township) Mercer County	100.00
Marlboro, NJ (township) Monmouth County	97.61
Morganville, NJ (cdp) Monmouth County	96.73
Monroe, NJ (township) Middlesex County	96.53
Old Tappan, NJ (borough) Bergen County	96.50
Manalapan, NJ (township) Monmouth County	95.89
Green Brook, NJ (township) Somerset County	95.87

Native Hawaiian and Other Pacific Islanders Who Own Their Own Homes
Top 10 Places Sorted by Number

Place	Number
No places met population threshold.	

Native Hawaiian and Other Pacific Islanders Who Own Their Own Homes
Top 10 Places Sorted by Percent

Place	Percent
No places met population threshold.	

Asian Indians Who Own Their Own Homes
Top 10 Places Sorted by Number

Place	Number
Edison, NJ (township) Middlesex County	1,893
Jersey City, NJ (city) Hudson County	969
South Brunswick, NJ (township) Middlesex County	882
Woodbridge, NJ (township) Middlesex County	822
Piscataway, NJ (township) Middlesex County	695
Franklin, NJ (township) Somerset County	664
East Brunswick, NJ (township) Middlesex County	548
Bridgewater, NJ (township) Somerset County	539
Parsippany-Troy Hills, NJ (township) Morris County	534
North Brunswick, NJ (township) Middlesex County	521

Asian Indians Who Own Their Own Homes
Top 10 Places Sorted by Percent

Place	Percent
Greentree, NJ (cdp) Camden County	100.00
Warren, NJ (township) Somerset County	100.00
Paramus, NJ (borough) Bergen County	97.30
Manalapan, NJ (township) Monmouth County	95.97
Marlboro, NJ (township) Monmouth County	95.82
Howell, NJ (township) Monmouth County	95.09
Branchburg, NJ (township) Somerset County	94.51
Hanover, NJ (township) Morris County	93.75
Freehold, NJ (township) Monmouth County	93.55
South Plainfield, NJ (borough) Middlesex County	90.68

Bangladeshis Who Own Their Own Homes
Top 10 Places Sorted by Number

Place	Number
Paterson, NJ (city) Passaic County	48

Bangladeshis Who Own Their Own Homes
Top 10 Places Sorted by Percent

Place	Percent
Paterson, NJ (city) Passaic County	48.48

Cambodians Who Own Their Own Homes
Top 10 Places Sorted by Number

Place	Number
No places met population threshold.	

Cambodians Who Own Their Own Homes
Top 10 Places Sorted by Percent

Place	Percent
No places met population threshold.	

Chinese (except Taiwanese) Who Own Their Own Homes
Top 10 Places Sorted by Number

Place	Number
Edison, NJ (township) Middlesex County	1,264
East Brunswick, NJ (township) Middlesex County	825
Marlboro, NJ (township) Monmouth County	732
Parsippany-Troy Hills, NJ (township) Morris County	610
West Windsor, NJ (township) Mercer County	465
Livingston, NJ (township) Essex County	464
Fort Lee, NJ (borough) Bergen County	425

Notes: Please refer to the User's Guide for an explanation of data; tables reflect only those areas that meet Summary File 4 population thresholds, therefore there may be less than 10 places listed

Holmdel, NJ (township) Monmouth County	420
Bridgewater, NJ (township) Somerset County	411
Cherry Hill, NJ (township) Camden County	408

Chinese (except Taiwanese) Who Own Their Own Homes
Top 10 Places Sorted by Percent

Place	Percent
Englewood Cliffs, NJ (borough) Bergen County	100.00
Greentree, NJ (cdp) Camden County	100.00
Marlboro, NJ (township) Monmouth County	100.00
Morganville, NJ (cdp) Monmouth County	100.00
Springdale, NJ (cdp) Camden County	100.00
Livingston, NJ (township) Essex County	98.10
Holmdel, NJ (township) Monmouth County	96.33
Manalapan, NJ (township) Monmouth County	96.06
West Windsor, NJ (township) Mercer County	95.29
Bernards, NJ (township) Somerset County	94.27

Fijians Who Own Their Own Homes
Top 10 Places Sorted by Number

Place	Number
No places met population threshold.	

Fijians Who Own Their Own Homes
Top 10 Places Sorted by Percent

Place	Percent
No places met population threshold.	

Filipinos Who Own Their Own Homes
Top 10 Places Sorted by Number

Place	Number
Jersey City, NJ (city) Hudson County	2,354
Bergenfield, NJ (borough) Bergen County	531
Edison, NJ (township) Middlesex County	489
Union, NJ (township) Union County	435
Woodbridge, NJ (township) Middlesex County	374
Cherry Hill, NJ (township) Camden County	368
Piscataway, NJ (township) Middlesex County	363
Bloomfield, NJ (township) Essex County	311
Belleville, NJ (township) Essex County	289
Clifton, NJ (city) Passaic County	288

Filipinos Who Own Their Own Homes
Top 10 Places Sorted by Percent

Place	Percent
Colonia, NJ (cdp) Middlesex County	100.00
Freehold, NJ (township) Monmouth County	100.00
South Plainfield, NJ (borough) Middlesex County	100.00
Paramus, NJ (borough) Bergen County	95.00
Washington, NJ (township) Gloucester County	92.61
Howell, NJ (township) Monmouth County	92.50
Union, NJ (township) Union County	90.81
Cherry Hill, NJ (township) Camden County	90.64
Livingston, NJ (township) Essex County	90.28
Fair Lawn, NJ (borough) Bergen County	90.21

Guamanians or Chamorros Who Own Their Own Homes
Top 10 Places Sorted by Number

Place	Number
No places met population threshold.	

Guamanians or Chamorros Who Own Their Own Homes
Top 10 Places Sorted by Percent

Place	Percent
No places met population threshold.	

Hawaiian Natives Who Own Their Own Homes
Top 10 Places Sorted by Number

Place	Number
No places met population threshold.	

Hawaiian Natives Who Own Their Own Homes
Top 10 Places Sorted by Percent

Place	Percent
No places met population threshold.	

Hmongs Who Own Their Own Homes
Top 10 Places Sorted by Number

Place	Number
No places met population threshold.	

Hmongs Who Own Their Own Homes
Top 10 Places Sorted by Percent

Place	Percent
No places met population threshold.	

Indonesians Who Own Their Own Homes
Top 10 Places Sorted by Number

Place	Number
No places met population threshold.	

Indonesians Who Own Their Own Homes
Top 10 Places Sorted by Percent

Place	Percent
No places met population threshold.	

Japanese Who Own Their Own Homes
Top 10 Places Sorted by Number

Place	Number
Fort Lee, NJ (borough) Bergen County	103
Cliffside Park, NJ (borough) Bergen County	41
Ridgewood, NJ (village) Bergen County	41

Japanese Who Own Their Own Homes
Top 10 Places Sorted by Percent

Place	Percent
Ridgewood, NJ (village) Bergen County	35.04
Cliffside Park, NJ (borough) Bergen County	21.24
Fort Lee, NJ (borough) Bergen County	13.75

Koreans Who Own Their Own Homes
Top 10 Places Sorted by Number

Place	Number
Fort Lee, NJ (borough) Bergen County	535
Palisades Park, NJ (borough) Bergen County	337
Cherry Hill, NJ (township) Camden County	196
Paramus, NJ (borough) Bergen County	185
Closter, NJ (borough) Bergen County	180
Livingston, NJ (township) Essex County	179
Edison, NJ (township) Middlesex County	178
Wayne, NJ (township) Passaic County	169
Edgewater, NJ (borough) Bergen County	165
Cliffside Park, NJ (borough) Bergen County	157

Koreans Who Own Their Own Homes
Top 10 Places Sorted by Percent

Place	Percent
Old Tappan, NJ (borough) Bergen County	100.00
Harrington Park, NJ (borough) Bergen County	94.12
Browns Mills, NJ (cdp) Burlington County	90.79
Alpine, NJ (borough) Bergen County	90.32
Livingston, NJ (township) Essex County	86.47
Englewood Cliffs, NJ (borough) Bergen County	81.22
Pemberton, NJ (township) Burlington County	75.00
Cresskill, NJ (borough) Bergen County	73.23
Cherry Hill, NJ (township) Camden County	72.32

Wayne, NJ (township) Passaic County	71.31

Laotians Who Own Their Own Homes
Top 10 Places Sorted by Number

Place	Number
No places met population threshold.	

Laotians Who Own Their Own Homes
Top 10 Places Sorted by Percent

Place	Percent
No places met population threshold.	

Malaysians Who Own Their Own Homes
Top 10 Places Sorted by Number

Place	Number
No places met population threshold.	

Malaysians Who Own Their Own Homes
Top 10 Places Sorted by Percent

Place	Percent
No places met population threshold.	

Pakistanis Who Own Their Own Homes
Top 10 Places Sorted by Number

Place	Number
Jersey City, NJ (city) Hudson County	138
Edison, NJ (township) Middlesex County	105
Old Bridge, NJ (township) Middlesex County	65
Woodbridge, NJ (township) Middlesex County	53

Pakistanis Who Own Their Own Homes
Top 10 Places Sorted by Percent

Place	Percent
Old Bridge, NJ (township) Middlesex County	59.63
Edison, NJ (township) Middlesex County	56.76
Woodbridge, NJ (township) Middlesex County	54.08
Jersey City, NJ (city) Hudson County	32.78

Samoans Who Own Their Own Homes
Top 10 Places Sorted by Number

Place	Number
No places met population threshold.	

Samoans Who Own Their Own Homes
Top 10 Places Sorted by Percent

Place	Percent
No places met population threshold.	

Sri Lankans Who Own Their Own Homes
Top 10 Places Sorted by Number

Place	Number
No places met population threshold.	

Sri Lankans Who Own Their Own Homes
Top 10 Places Sorted by Percent

Place	Percent
No places met population threshold.	

Taiwanese Who Own Their Own Homes
Top 10 Places Sorted by Number

Place	Number
Edison, NJ (township) Middlesex County	140

Taiwanese Who Own Their Own Homes
Top 10 Places Sorted by Percent

Place	Percent
Edison, NJ (township) Middlesex County	83.83

Notes: Please refer to the User's Guide for an explanation of data; tables reflect only those areas that meet Summary File 4 population thresholds, therefore there may be less than 10 places listed

Thais Who Own Their Own Homes
Top 10 Places Sorted by Number

Place	Number
No places met population threshold.	

Thais Who Own Their Own Homes
Top 10 Places Sorted by Percent

Place	Percent
No places met population threshold.	

Tongans Who Own Their Own Homes
Top 10 Places Sorted by Number

Place	Number
No places met population threshold.	

Tongans Who Own Their Own Homes
Top 10 Places Sorted by Percent

Place	Percent
No places met population threshold.	

Vietnamese Who Own Their Own Homes
Top 10 Places Sorted by Number

Place	Number
Atlantic City, NJ (city) Atlantic County	185
Camden, NJ (city) Camden County	146
Pennsauken, NJ (township) Camden County	111
Jersey City, NJ (city) Hudson County	89
South Plainfield, NJ (borough) Middlesex County	58
Woodlynne, NJ (borough) Camden County	47
Belleville, NJ (township) Essex County	35

Vietnamese Who Own Their Own Homes
Top 10 Places Sorted by Percent

Place	Percent
Woodlynne, NJ (borough) Camden County	79.66
Pennsauken, NJ (township) Camden County	74.00
Atlantic City, NJ (city) Atlantic County	65.60
South Plainfield, NJ (borough) Middlesex County	59.79
Camden, NJ (city) Camden County	40.67
Belleville, NJ (township) Essex County	33.33
Jersey City, NJ (city) Hudson County	21.34

Median Gross Rent

All Specified Renter-Occupied Housing Units
Top 10 Places Sorted by Number

Place	Dollars/Month
Demarest, NJ (borough) Bergen County	2,000+
Englewood Cliffs, NJ (borough) Bergen County	2,000+
Washington, NJ (township) Bergen County	1,909
Alpine, NJ (borough) Bergen County	1,844
Allendale, NJ (borough) Bergen County	1,778
Haworth, NJ (borough) Bergen County	1,625
Cresskill, NJ (borough) Bergen County	1,571
Holmdel, NJ (township) Monmouth County	1,512
East Hanover, NJ (township) Morris County	1,504
Bernards, NJ (township) Somerset County	1,494

Specified Housing Units Rented by Asians
Top 10 Places Sorted by Number

Place	Dollars/Month
Allendale, NJ (borough) Bergen County	2,000+
Alpine, NJ (borough) Bergen County	2,000+
Branchburg, NJ (township) Somerset County	2,000+
Demarest, NJ (borough) Bergen County	2,000+
Emerson, NJ (borough) Bergen County	2,000+
Englewood Cliffs, NJ (borough) Bergen County	2,000+
Glen Rock, NJ (borough) Bergen County	2,000+
Harrington Park, NJ (borough) Bergen County	2,000+
Oradell, NJ (borough) Bergen County	2,000+
Saddle River, NJ (borough) Bergen County	2,000+

Specified Housing Units Rented by Native Hawaiian and Other Pacific Islanders
Top 10 Places Sorted by Number

Place	Dollars/Month
No places met population threshold.	

Specified Housing Units Rented by Asian Indians
Top 10 Places Sorted by Number

Place	Dollars/Month
Hanover, NJ (township) Morris County	2,000+
Livingston, NJ (township) Essex County	2,000+
Freehold, NJ (township) Monmouth County	1,875
Manalapan, NJ (township) Monmouth County	1,875
Holmdel, NJ (township) Monmouth County	1,750
Paramus, NJ (borough) Bergen County	1,625
Montgomery, NJ (township) Somerset County	1,579
Lawrence, NJ (township) Mercer County	1,380
Marlboro, NJ (township) Monmouth County	1,375
Fort Lee, NJ (borough) Bergen County	1,319

Specified Housing Units Rented by Bangladeshis
Top 10 Places Sorted by Number

Place	Dollars/Month
Paterson, NJ (city) Passaic County	863

Specified Housing Units Rented by Cambodians
Top 10 Places Sorted by Number

Place	Dollars/Month
No places met population threshold.	

Specified Housing Units Rented by Chinese (except Taiwanese)
Top 10 Places Sorted by Number

Place	Dollars/Month
Bernards, NJ (township) Somerset County	2,000+
Hanover, NJ (township) Morris County	2,000+
Tenafly, NJ (borough) Bergen County	2,000+
Manalapan, NJ (township) Monmouth County	1,875
Berkeley Heights, NJ (township) Union County	1,777
Freehold, NJ (township) Monmouth County	1,531
Holmdel, NJ (township) Monmouth County	1,500
Toms River, NJ (cdp) Ocean County	1,393
Livingston, NJ (township) Essex County	1,375
Montville, NJ (township) Morris County	1,375

Specified Housing Units Rented by Fijians
Top 10 Places Sorted by Number

Place	Dollars/Month
No places met population threshold.	

Specified Housing Units Rented by Filipinos
Top 10 Places Sorted by Number

Place	Dollars/Month
Livingston, NJ (township) Essex County	1,625
Fair Lawn, NJ (borough) Bergen County	1,375
Teaneck, NJ (township) Bergen County	1,344
Union, NJ (township) Union County	1,241
Franklin, NJ (township) Somerset County	1,208
Howell, NJ (township) Monmouth County	1,125
South Brunswick, NJ (township) Middlesex County	1,125
North Brunswick, NJ (township) Middlesex County	1,076
Dover, NJ (township) Ocean County	1,071
Toms River, NJ (cdp) Ocean County	1,071

Specified Housing Units Rented by Guamanians or Chamorros
Top 10 Places Sorted by Number

Place	Dollars/Month
No places met population threshold.	

Specified Housing Units Rented by Hawaiian Natives
Top 10 Places Sorted by Number

Place	Dollars/Month
No places met population threshold.	

Specified Housing Units Rented by Hmongs
Top 10 Places Sorted by Number

Place	Dollars/Month
No places met population threshold.	

Specified Housing Units Rented by Indonesians
Top 10 Places Sorted by Number

Place	Dollars/Month
No places met population threshold.	

Specified Housing Units Rented by Japanese
Top 10 Places Sorted by Number

Place	Dollars/Month
Ridgewood, NJ (village) Bergen County	2,000+
Fort Lee, NJ (borough) Bergen County	1,822
Cliffside Park, NJ (borough) Bergen County	1,556

Specified Housing Units Rented by Koreans
Top 10 Places Sorted by Number

Place	Dollars/Month
Alpine, NJ (borough) Bergen County	2,000+
Demarest, NJ (borough) Bergen County	2,000+
Englewood Cliffs, NJ (borough) Bergen County	2,000+
Harrington Park, NJ (borough) Bergen County	2,000+
Paramus, NJ (borough) Bergen County	2,000+
Cresskill, NJ (borough) Bergen County	1,875
Ridgewood, NJ (village) Bergen County	1,648
Tenafly, NJ (borough) Bergen County	1,527
Norwood, NJ (borough) Bergen County	1,500
Livingston, NJ (township) Essex County	1,469

Specified Housing Units Rented by Laotians
Top 10 Places Sorted by Number

Place	Dollars/Month
No places met population threshold.	

Specified Housing Units Rented by Malaysians
Top 10 Places Sorted by Number

Place	Dollars/Month
No places met population threshold.	

Specified Housing Units Rented by Pakistanis
Top 10 Places Sorted by Number

Place	Dollars/Month
Edison, NJ (township) Middlesex County	1,098
Woodbridge, NJ (township) Middlesex County	881
Jersey City, NJ (city) Hudson County	769
Old Bridge, NJ (township) Middlesex County	761

Specified Housing Units Rented by Samoans
Top 10 Places Sorted by Number

Place	Dollars/Month
No places met population threshold.	

Specified Housing Units Rented by Sri Lankans
Top 10 Places Sorted by Number

Place	Dollars/Month
No places met population threshold.	

Specified Housing Units Rented by Taiwanese
Top 10 Places Sorted by Number

Place	Dollars/Month
Edison, NJ (township) Middlesex County	1,375

Notes: Please refer to the User's Guide for an explanation of data; tables reflect only those areas that meet Summary File 4 population thresholds, therefore there may be less than 10 places listed

Specified Housing Units Rented by Thais
Top 10 Places Sorted by Number.

Place	Dollars/Month
No places met population threshold.	

Specified Housing Units Rented by Tongans
Top 10 Places Sorted by Number.

Place	Dollars/Month
No places met population threshold.	

Specified Housing Units Rented by Vietnamese
Top 10 Places Sorted by Number.

Place	Dollars/Month
South Plainfield, NJ (borough) Middlesex County	975
Woodlynne, NJ (borough) Camden County	914
Belleville, NJ (township) Essex County	743
Jersey City, NJ (city) Hudson County	642
Atlantic City, NJ (city) Atlantic County	628
Pennsauken, NJ (township) Camden County	572
Camden, NJ (city) Camden County	531

Median Home Value

All Specified Owner-Occupied Housing Units
Top 10 Places Sorted by Number.

Place	Dollars
Alpine, NJ (borough) Bergen County	1 Mil.+
Saddle River, NJ (borough) Bergen County	970,100
Franklin Lakes, NJ (borough) Bergen County	609,400
Millburn, NJ (township) Essex County	549,000
Englewood Cliffs, NJ (borough) Bergen County	507,100
Summit, NJ (city) Union County	469,200
Chatham, NJ (township) Morris County	449,000
Old Tappan, NJ (borough) Bergen County	436,900
Watchung, NJ (borough) Somerset County	429,400
Hoboken, NJ (city) Hudson County	428,900

Specified Housing Units Owned and Occupied by Asians
Top 10 Places Sorted by Number.

Place	Dollars
Alpine, NJ (borough) Bergen County	1 Mil.+
Saddle River, NJ (borough) Bergen County	1 Mil.+
Franklin Lakes, NJ (borough) Bergen County	722,700
Watchung, NJ (borough) Somerset County	554,200
Weehawken, NJ (township) Hudson County	535,700
Warren, NJ (township) Somerset County	527,700
Englewood Cliffs, NJ (borough) Bergen County	524,000
Millburn, NJ (township) Essex County	475,000
West New York, NJ (town) Hudson County	467,600
Summit, NJ (city) Union County	462,500

Specified Housing Units Owned and Occupied by Native Hawaiian and Other Pacific Islanders
Top 10 Places Sorted by Number.

Place	Dollars
No places met population threshold.	

Specified Housing Units Owned and Occupied by Asian Indians
Top 10 Places Sorted by Number.

Place	Dollars
West New York, NJ (town) Hudson County	1 Mil.+
Warren, NJ (township) Somerset County	493,200
Scotch Plains, NJ (township) Union County	461,100
Montgomery, NJ (township) Somerset County	445,200
Holmdel, NJ (township) Monmouth County	443,600
Summit, NJ (city) Union County	443,300
Bernards, NJ (township) Somerset County	437,500
West Windsor, NJ (township) Mercer County	404,600
Mahwah, NJ (township) Bergen County	361,400
Montville, NJ (township) Morris County	356,000

Specified Housing Units Owned and Occupied by Bangladeshis
Top 10 Places Sorted by Number.

Place	Dollars
Paterson, NJ (city) Passaic County	56,600

Specified Housing Units Owned and Occupied by Cambodians
Top 10 Places Sorted by Number.

Place	Dollars
No places met population threshold.	

Specified Housing Units Owned and Occupied by Chinese (except Taiwanese)
Top 10 Places Sorted by Number.

Place	Dollars
Warren, NJ (township) Somerset County	608,200
Englewood Cliffs, NJ (borough) Bergen County	562,500
Princeton, NJ (township) Mercer County	444,000
Bernards, NJ (township) Somerset County	432,400
Millburn, NJ (township) Essex County	417,100
Berkeley Heights, NJ (township) Union County	392,900
Hanover, NJ (township) Morris County	381,800
Holmdel, NJ (township) Monmouth County	374,600
Tenafly, NJ (borough) Bergen County	370,700
Montville, NJ (township) Morris County	370,500

Specified Housing Units Owned and Occupied by Fijians
Top 10 Places Sorted by Number.

Place	Dollars
No places met population threshold.	

Specified Housing Units Owned and Occupied by Filipinos
Top 10 Places Sorted by Number.

Place	Dollars
Paramus, NJ (borough) Bergen County	333,900
North Brunswick, NJ (township) Middlesex County	257,800
Freehold, NJ (township) Monmouth County	256,300
South Brunswick, NJ (township) Middlesex County	253,700
Parsippany-Troy Hills, NJ (township) Morris County	253,100
New Milford, NJ (borough) Bergen County	252,900
Livingston, NJ (township) Essex County	231,100
East Brunswick, NJ (township) Middlesex County	230,000
Fair Lawn, NJ (borough) Bergen County	221,500
Secaucus, NJ (town) Hudson County	221,100

Specified Housing Units Owned and Occupied by Guamanians or Chamorros
Top 10 Places Sorted by Number.

Place	Dollars
No places met population threshold.	

Specified Housing Units Owned and Occupied by Hawaiian Natives
Top 10 Places Sorted by Number.

Place	Dollars
No places met population threshold.	

Specified Housing Units Owned and Occupied by Hmongs
Top 10 Places Sorted by Number.

Place	Dollars
No places met population threshold.	

Specified Housing Units Owned and Occupied by Indonesians
Top 10 Places Sorted by Number.

Place	Dollars
No places met population threshold.	

Specified Housing Units Owned and Occupied by Japanese
Top 10 Places Sorted by Number.

Place	Dollars
Ridgewood, NJ (village) Bergen County	295,000
Fort Lee, NJ (borough) Bergen County	32,500
Cliffside Park, NJ (borough) Bergen County	0

Specified Housing Units Owned and Occupied by Koreans
Top 10 Places Sorted by Number.

Place	Dollars
Alpine, NJ (borough) Bergen County	1 Mil.+
Englewood Cliffs, NJ (borough) Bergen County	494,200
Demarest, NJ (borough) Bergen County	450,000
Cliffside Park, NJ (borough) Bergen County	436,700
Old Tappan, NJ (borough) Bergen County	430,000
Norwood, NJ (borough) Bergen County	367,600
West Windsor, NJ (township) Mercer County	364,600
Parsippany-Troy Hills, NJ (township) Morris County	363,900
Wayne, NJ (township) Passaic County	351,900
Paramus, NJ (borough) Bergen County	341,300

Specified Housing Units Owned and Occupied by Laotians
Top 10 Places Sorted by Number.

Place	Dollars
No places met population threshold.	

Specified Housing Units Owned and Occupied by Malaysians
Top 10 Places Sorted by Number.

Place	Dollars
No places met population threshold.	

Specified Housing Units Owned and Occupied by Pakistanis
Top 10 Places Sorted by Number.

Place	Dollars
Edison, NJ (township) Middlesex County	268,800
Old Bridge, NJ (township) Middlesex County	218,100
Jersey City, NJ (city) Hudson County	166,300
Woodbridge, NJ (township) Middlesex County	137,500

Specified Housing Units Owned and Occupied by Samoans
Top 10 Places Sorted by Number.

Place	Dollars
No places met population threshold.	

Specified Housing Units Owned and Occupied by Sri Lankans
Top 10 Places Sorted by Number.

Place	Dollars
No places met population threshold.	

Specified Housing Units Owned and Occupied by Taiwanese
Top 10 Places Sorted by Number.

Place	Dollars
Edison, NJ (township) Middlesex County	195,000

Notes: Please refer to the User's Guide for an explanation of data; tables reflect only those areas that meet Summary File 4 population thresholds, therefore there may be less than 10 places listed

Specified Housing Units Owned and Occupied by Thais
Top 10 Places Sorted by Number

Place	Dollars
No places met population threshold.	

Specified Housing Units Owned and Occupied by Tongans
Top 10 Places Sorted by Number

Place	Dollars
No places met population threshold.	

Specified Housing Units Owned and Occupied by Vietnamese
Top 10 Places Sorted by Number

Place	Dollars
South Plainfield, NJ (borough) Middlesex County	177,400
Jersey City, NJ (city) Hudson County	162,500
Belleville, NJ (township) Essex County	158,600
Atlantic City, NJ (city) Atlantic County	90,800
Pennsauken, NJ (township) Camden County	81,900
Woodlynne, NJ (borough) Camden County	48,500
Camden, NJ (city) Camden County	38,800

Notes: Please refer to the User's Guide for an explanation of data; tables reflect only those areas that meet Summary File 4 population thresholds, therefore there may be less than 10 places listed

NEW JERSEY

PHYSICAL FEATURES. New Jersey, though one of the smaller states, has a varied topography. In the northwestern part a section comprising about one-fifth of the area of the State is known as the Highlands and Kittatinny Valley. This region is traversed by several low mountain ridges extending northeasterly across the State with valleys and rolling hills between. The highest of these ranges is the Kittatinny, which rises from the banks of the Delaware River at the famous Delaware Water Gap. To the eastward the region is studded with numerous lakes, some of the largest of which are Lakes Hopatcong, Mohawk, and Greenwood. Elevations up to 1,800 feet above sea level are found in the Kittatinny Mountains near the New York State line.

South and east of the Highlands is a region of about equal area known as the Red Sandstone Plain, or the Piedmont of New Jersey. It is generally hilly in its northwestern part, becoming rolling and then flat toward the south and southeast. At its northeastern corner are the Palisades, cliffs which rise abruptly from the Hudson River to heights of 200 to 500 feet. The seacoast section extends from Sandy Hook to Cape May, or about 125 miles. This area is characterized by long stretches of sandy beaches. Tidewater marshes become numerous toward the south.

In the southern interior a region known as the Pines is covered with scrubby forests of pine and some oak. The land is low and some of it is swampy. In fact, most of the State that lies south of a line connecting Jersey City and Trenton is low and flat with few elevations higher than 100 feet above mean sea level, these being mainly in Monmouth County.

About 30 percent of the area of New Jersey drains into the Delaware River and Delaware Bay, which form the western boundary. Nearly half of Sussex County, in the northwest, drains northward through the Wallkill River into the Hudson River of New York. The remainder of the State drains directly into the Atlantic Ocean through the Passaic, Hackensack, and Raritan Rivers in the north, and a number of small rivers and streams in the south.

GENERAL CLIMATE. The extreme length of the State is 166 miles and its greatest width only about 65. The difference in climate is quite marked between the southern tip at Cape May and the northern extremity in the Kittatinny Mountains. The former locality is almost surrounded by water and is fairly well removed from the influence of the frequent storms that cross the Great Lakes region and move out the St. Lawrence Valley. The northern extremity is well within the zone of influence of these storms and, in addition, lies at elevations varying from 800 to 1,800 feet. The influence of these high elevations on the temperature is considerable. The differences between these two localities are particularly marked in the winter, Cape May having a normal January temperature about the same as that of southwestern Virginia, while that of Layton, in the extreme northwest, is similar to that of the northern area of Ohio. Since the prevailing winds are mostly offshore, the ocean influence does not have full effect.

TEMPERATURE. Temperature differences between the northern and southern parts of the State are greatest in winter and least in summer. Nearly every weather station has registered readings of 100°F. or higher at some time, and all of them have records of zero or below. In the northern Highland area, the average date of last freeze (32°F.) in spring is about May 2, and that of the first in fall, October 12. On the seacoast corresponding dates are April 6 and November 9, while in the central and southern interior the dates are April 23 and October 19. Freeze-free days in the northern Highlands average 163, with 217 along the seacoast and 179 in the central and southern interior.

PRECIPITATION. Northern New Jersey is near enough to the paths of the storms which cross the Great Lakes region and pass down the St. Lawrence Valley to receive part of its precipitation from that source. However, the heaviest general rains are produced by coastal storms of tropical origin. The centers of these storms usually pass some distance offshore, with heaviest rainfall and strongest wind near the coast. On several occasions tropical storms have moved inland along the south Atlantic coast, and then moved northward either through or to the west of New Jersey. The damage by high tides to coastal installations during the passage of a tropical storm is often severe, whether the storm passes offshore or inland.

The average annual precipitation ranges from about 40 inches along the southeast coast to 51 inches in north-central parts of the State. In other sections the annual averages are mostly between 43 and 47 inches. Rainfall is well distributed during the warm months. Heavy 24-hour falls of seven or eight inches are occasionally recorded. Brief periods of drought during the growing season are not uncommon, but prolonged droughts are relatively rare, occurring on the average once in 15 years. Flooding in New Jersey is usually caused by heavy general rains, at times associated with storms of tropical origin. Local flooding results from ice gorging.

The season during which measurable quantities of snow are likely to fall extends from about October 15 to April 20 in the Highlands, and from about November 15 to March 15 in the vicinity of Cape May. Average seasonal amounts range from about 13 inches at Cape May to nearly 50 inches in the Highlands. Snowfalls of 10 or more inches in a single storm are occasional occurrences.

The number of days a month with measurable precipitation averages eight for each of the fall months (September, October, and November) and nine to 12 for the other months of the year; the average yearly number is 120. Midday relative humidity averages 68 percent along the seacoast and 57 percent or less at inland locations.

Normally, sunshine varies from slightly over one-half of the possible amount in the northern counties to about 60 percent in the south. The prevailing wind is from the northwest from October to April, inclusive, and from the southwest for the other months of the year.

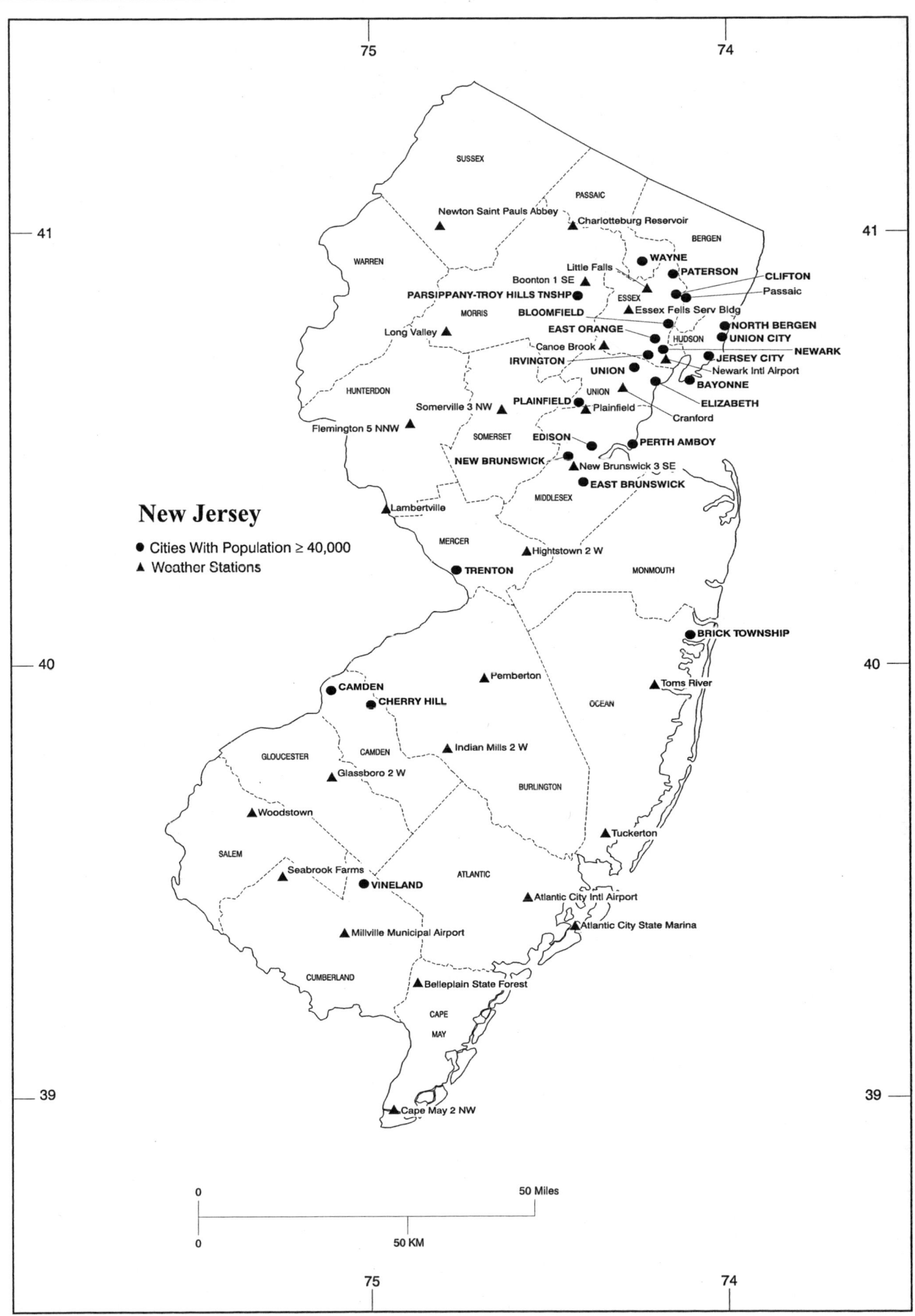

SUSSEX

PASSAIC

Newton Saint Pauls Abbey ▲   ● Charlotteburg Reservoir

BERGEN

WARREN

● WAYNE

Little Falls   ● PATERSON   ● CLIFTON

Boonton 1 SE ▲   ▲   Passaic

PARSIPPANY-TROY HILLS TNSHP ●   ESSEX

MORRIS   BLOOMFIELD   ▲ Essex Fells Serv Bldg

Long Valley ▲   EAST ORANGE   ● NORTH BERGEN
● UNION CITY
Canoe Brook ▲   HUDSON   ● JERSEY CITY   NEWARK
IRVINGTON   Newark Intl Airport
UNION   ▲   ● BAYONNE
HUNTERDON   UNION   ELIZABETH

Somerville 3 NW ▲   PLAINFIELD   ▲ Plainfield
Cranford
Flemington 5 NNW ▲   SOMERSET   EDISON ●   ● PERTH AMBOY

NEW BRUNSWICK ▲   ▲ New Brunswick 3 SE
● EAST BRUNSWICK
Lambertville   MIDDLESEX

MERCER   ▲ Hightstown 2 W   MONMOUTH

New Jersey

● Cities With Population ≥ 40,000
▲ Weather Stations   ● TRENTON

● BRICK TOWNSHIP

● CAMDEN   ▲ Pemberton   ▲ Toms River

● CHERRY HILL   OCEAN

GLOUCESTER   CAMDEN   ▲ Indian Mills 2 W   BURLINGTON

▲ Glassboro 2 W

▲ Woodstown   ▲ Tuckerton

SALEM

▲ Seabrook Farms   ATLANTIC

● VINELAND   ▲ Atlantic City Intl Airport

▲ Millville Municipal Airport   ▲ Atlantic City State Marina

CUMBERLAND   ▲ Belleplain State Forest

CAPE

MAY

▲ Cape May 2 NW

0   50 Miles

0   50 KM

New Jersey Weather Stations by County

County	Station Name
Atlantic	Atlantic City Int'l Airport Atlantic City State Marina
Burlington	Indian Mills 2 W Pemberton
Cape May	Belleplain State Forest Cape May 2 NW
Cumberland	Millville Municipal Airport Seabrook Farms
Essex	Canoe Brook Essex Fells Serv Bldg Newark Int'l Airport
Gloucester	Glassboro 2 W
Hunterdon	Flemington 5 NNW Lambertville
Mercer	Hightstown 2 W
Middlesex	New Brunswick 3 SE
Morris	Boonton 1 SE Long Valley
Ocean	Toms River Tuckerton
Passaic	Charlotteburg Reservoir Little Falls
Salem	Woodstown
Somerset	Somerville 3 NW
Sussex	Newton Saint Pauls Abbey
Union	Cranford Plainfield

New Jersey Weather Stations by City

City	Station Name	Miles
Bayonne	Canoe Brook	13
	Cranford	10
	Essex Fells Serv Bldg	14
	Little Falls	16
	Newark Int'l Airport	5
	Plainfield	15
	New York Avenue V Brooklyn, NY	8
	New York Central Park Observatory, NY	11
	New York JFK Int'l Airport, NY	17
	New York Laguardia Airport, NY	15
Bloomfield	Boonton 1 SE	13
	Canoe Brook	9
	Cranford	12
	Essex Fells Serv Bldg	5
	Little Falls	6
	Newark Int'l Airport	6
	Plainfield	18
	New York Avenue V Brooklyn, NY	18
	New York Central Park Observatory, NY	12
	New York Laguardia Airport, NY	16
Brick Twp	Toms River	10
Camden	Glassboro 2 W	14
	Indian Mills 2 W	19
	Marcus Hook, PA	19
	Philadelphia Int'l Airport, PA	9
Cherry Hill	Glassboro 2 W	13
	Indian Mills 2 W	13
	Pemberton	17
	Philadelphia Int'l Airport, PA	13
Clifton	Boonton 1 SE	13
	Canoe Brook	13
	Charlotteburg Reservoir	18
	Cranford	17
	Essex Fells Serv Bldg	7
	Little Falls	4
	Newark Int'l Airport	11
	Dobbs Ferry Ardsley, NY	19
	New York Central Park Observatory, NY	11
	New York Laguardia Airport, NY	15
E. Brunswick	Cranford	16
	Hightstown 2 W	14
	New Brunswick 3 SE	3
	Plainfield	12
	Somerville 3 NW	17
East Orange	Boonton 1 SE	14
	Canoe Brook	7
	Cranford	9
	Essex Fells Serv Bldg	6
	Little Falls	8
	Newark Int'l Airport	4
	Plainfield	15
	New York Avenue V Brooklyn, NY	16
	New York Central Park Observatory, NY	13
	New York Laguardia Airport, NY	17
Edison	Canoe Brook	16
	Cranford	10

City	Station Name	Miles
Edison (cont.)	Hightstown 2 W	20
	Newark Int'l Airport	18
	New Brunswick 3 SE	4
	Plainfield	6
	Somerville 3 NW	14
Elizabeth	Boonton 1 SE	19
	Canoe Brook	9
	Cranford	5
	Essex Fells Serv Bldg	12
	Little Falls	15
	Newark Int'l Airport	4
	New Brunswick 3 SE	18
	Plainfield	11
	New York Avenue V Brooklyn, NY	13
	New York Central Park Observatory, NY	15
	New York Laguardia Airport, NY	19
Irvington	Boonton 1 SE	15
	Canoe Brook	6
	Cranford	6
	Essex Fells Serv Bldg	8
	Little Falls	11
	Newark Int'l Airport	3
	Plainfield	12
	New York Avenue V Brooklyn, NY	16
	New York Central Park Observatory, NY	14
	New York Laguardia Airport, NY	19
Jersey City	Canoe Brook	15
	Cranford	13
	Essex Fells Serv Bldg	14
	Little Falls	14
	Newark Int'l Airport	6
	Plainfield	19
	New York Avenue V Brooklyn, NY	10
	New York Central Park Observatory, NY	7
	New York JFK Int'l Airport, NY	15
	New York Laguardia Airport, NY	10
New Brunswick	Canoe Brook	19
	Cranford	14
	Hightstown 2 W	17
	New Brunswick 3 SE	2
	Plainfield	8
	Somerville 3 NW	12
Newark	Boonton 1 SE	16
	Canoe Brook	8
	Cranford	8
	Essex Fells Serv Bldg	8
	Little Falls	10
	Newark Int'l Airport	2
	Plainfield	15
	New York Avenue V Brooklyn, NY	14
	New York Central Park Observatory, NY	12
	New York Laguardia Airport, NY	16
North Bergen	Canoe Brook	17
	Cranford	18
	Essex Fells Serv Bldg	14
	Little Falls	13
	Newark Int'l Airport	10
	Dobbs Ferry Ardsley, NY	17

New Jersey Weather Stations by City

City	Station Name	Miles
North Bergen (cont.)	New York Avenue V Brooklyn, NY	14
	New York Central Park Observatory, NY	3
	New York JFK Int'l Airport, NY	15
	New York Laguardia Airport, NY	7
Parsippany	Boonton 1 SE	3
	Canoe Brook	9
	Charlotteburg Reservoir	12
	Cranford	16
	Essex Fells Serv Bldg	8
	Little Falls	10
	Long Valley	20
	Newark Int'l Airport	16
	Plainfield	18
Passaic	Boonton 1 SE	14
	Canoe Brook	14
	Charlotteburg Reservoir	20
	Cranford	17
	Essex Fells Serv Bldg	8
	Little Falls	6
	Newark Int'l Airport	10
	Dobbs Ferry Ardsley, NY	18
	New York Avenue V Brooklyn, NY	19
	New York Central Park Observatory, NY	10
	New York Laguardia Airport, NY	14
Paterson	Boonton 1 SE	12
	Canoe Brook	15
	Charlotteburg Reservoir	16
	Cranford	20
	Essex Fells Serv Bldg	9
	Little Falls	4
	Newark Int'l Airport	14
	Dobbs Ferry Ardsley, NY	18
	New York Central Park Observatory, NY	14
	New York Laguardia Airport, NY	17
Perth Amboy	Canoe Brook	17
	Cranford	9
	Newark Int'l Airport	15
	New Brunswick 3 SE	9
	Plainfield	9
	Somerville 3 NW	20
	New York Avenue V Brooklyn, NY	16
Plainfield	Boonton 1 SE	20
	Canoe Brook	10
	Cranford	7
	Essex Fells Serv Bldg	17
	Newark Int'l Airport	14
	New Brunswick 3 SE	10
	Plainfield	1
	Somerville 3 NW	11
Trenton	Hightstown 2 W	11
	Lambertville	14
	Pemberton	18
Union	Boonton 1 SE	16
	Canoe Brook	6
	Cranford	4
	Essex Fells Serv Bldg	9
	Little Falls	13
	Newark Int'l Airport	5

City	Station Name	Miles
Union (cont.)	New Brunswick 3 SE	18
	Plainfield	10
	New York Avenue V Brooklyn, NY	16
	New York Central Park Observatory, NY	17
Union City	Canoe Brook	17
	Cranford	16
	Essex Fells Serv Bldg	14
	Little Falls	13
	Newark Int'l Airport	9
	Dobbs Ferry Ardsley, NY	19
	New York Avenue V Brooklyn, NY	12
	New York Central Park Observatory, NY	4
	New York JFK Int'l Airport, NY	15
	New York Laguardia Airport, NY	8
Vineland	Belleplain State Forest	18
	Glassboro 2 W	18
	Millville Municipal Airport	8
	Seabrook Farms	12
	Woodstown	20
Wayne	Boonton 1 SE	9
	Canoe Brook	15
	Charlotteburg Reservoir	11
	Essex Fells Serv Bldg	8
	Little Falls	4
	Newark Int'l Airport	16
	New York Central Park Observatory, NY	18

Note: Miles is the distance between the geographic center of the city and the weather station.

New Jersey Weather Stations by Elevation

Feet	Station Name
757	Charlotteburg Reservoir
597	Newton Saint Pauls Abbey
547	Long Valley
347	Essex Fells Serv Bldg
278	Boonton 1 SE
259	Flemington 5 NNW
177	Canoe Brook
157	Somerville 3 NW
147	Little Falls
98	Glassboro 2 W
98	Hightstown 2 W
98	Indian Mills 2 W
98	Toms River
88	Plainfield
88	Seabrook Farms
85	New Brunswick 3 SE
72	Cranford
68	Millville Municipal Airport
65	Lambertville
59	Atlantic City Int'l Airport
59	Pemberton
49	Woodstown
29	Belleplain State Forest
19	Cape May 2 NW
19	Tuckerton
9	Atlantic City State Marina
9	Newark Int'l Airport

Atlantic City Int'l Airport

The Atlantic City National Weather Service Office is located at the National Aviation Facilities Experimental Center, Pomona, which is about 10 miles west-northwest of Atlantic City and the Atlantic Ocean. The surrounding terrain is fairly flat at an elevation of 50 to 60 feet above sea level. Vegetation in the area consists of scrub pine and low underbrush, but clearing for the air facility has been quite extensive. Bays and salt marshes are as near as 6 miles east of the airport. Atlantic City is located on Abescon Island on the southeast coast of New Jersey. Surrounding terrain, composed of tidal marshes and beach sand, is flat and lies slightly above sea level. The climate is principally continental in character. However, the moderating influence of the Atlantic Ocean is apparent throughout the year, being more marked in the city than at the airport. As a result, summers are relatively cooler and winters milder than elsewhere at the same latitude.

Land and sea breezes, local circulations resulting from the differential heating and cooling of the land and sea, often prevail. These winds occur when moderate or intense storms are not present in the area, thus enabling the local circulation to overcome the general wind pattern. During the warm season sea breezes in the late morning and afternoon hours prevent excessive heating. Frequently, the temperature at Atlantic City during the afternoon hours in the summer averages several degrees lower than at the airport and the airport averages several degrees lower than localities farther inland. On occasions, sea breezes have lowered the temperature as much as 15 to 20 degrees within a half hour. However, the major effect of the sea breeze at the airport is preventing the temperature from rising above the 80's. Because the change in ocean temperature lags behind the air temperature from season to season, the weather tends to remain comparatively mild late into the fall, but on the other hand, warming is retarded in the spring. Normal ocean temperatures range from an average near 37 degrees in January to near 72 degrees in August.

Precipitation is moderate and well distributed throughout the year, with June the driest month and August the wettest. Tropical storms or hurricanes occasionally bring excessive rainfall to the area. The bulk of winter precipitation results from storms which move northeastward along or near the east coast of the United States. Snowfall is considerably less than elsewhere at the same latitude and does not remain long on the ground. Precipitation, often beginning as snow, will frequently become mixed with or change to rain while continuing as snow over more interior sections. In addition, ice storms and resultant glaze are relatively infrequent.

Atlantic City Int'l Airport *Atlantic County* Elevation: 59 ft. Latitude: 39° 27' N Longitude: 74° 34' W

	JAN	FEB	MAR	APR	MAY	JUN	JUL	AUG	SEP	OCT	NOV	DEC	YEAR
Mean Maximum Temp. (°F)	41.8	44.1	51.5	61.3	71.1	80.0	85.1	83.4	76.8	66.3	56.1	46.6	63.7
Mean Temp. (°F)	32.5	34.5	41.6	50.6	60.5	69.6	75.3	73.5	66.4	55.2	45.9	37.1	53.6
Mean Minimum Temp. (°F)	23.1	24.9	31.5	39.8	49.8	59.2	65.5	63.5	56.0	44.0	35.7	27.5	43.4
Extreme Maximum Temp. (°F)	72	75	87	92	96	100	101	100	99	87	81	77	101
Extreme Minimum Temp. (°F)	-9	-11	5	20	26	37	42	40	34	20	10	-2	-11
Days Maximum Temp. ≥90°F	0	0	0	0	1	3	8	5	1	0	0	0	18
Days Maximum Temp. ≤ 32°F	6	4	0	0	0	0	0	0	0	0	0	3	13
Days Minimum Temp. ≤ 32°F	25	21	17	6	0	0	0	0	0	3	12	22	106
Days Minimum Temp. ≤ 0°F	1	0	0	0	0	0	0	0	0	0	0	0	1
Heating Degree Days (base 65°F)	1,000	855	721	431	180	29	1	5	66	313	568	859	5,028
Cooling Degree Days (base 65°F)	0	0	1	6	52	184	347	272	118	18	1	0	999
Mean Precipitation (in.)	3.47	2.96	3.99	3.59	3.39	2.75	3.73	4.15	3.02	2.95	3.23	3.09	40.32
Maximum Precipitation (in.)	7.1	5.8	9.3	7.6	6.7	6.4	13.1	12.0	6.3	6.6	9.6	7.3	50.4
Minimum Precipitation (in.)	0.6	0.8	0.7	0.8	0.5	0.7	0.5	0.4	0.4	0.1	0.7	0.6	25.3
Maximum 24-hr. Precipitation (in.)	2.5	2.6	2.7	2.9	4.1	2.8	6.5	6.4	3.9	2.5	2.8	1.9	6.5
Days With ≥0.1" Precipitation	7	6	7	7	7	6	6	6	5	5	6	6	74
Days With ≥1.0" Precipitation	1	1	1	1	1	1	1	1	1	1	1	1	12
Mean Snowfall (in.)	4.8	5.1	1.1	0.4	trace	trace	trace	0.0	0.0	trace	0.3	1.6	13.3
Maximum Snowfall (in.)	20	35	18	4	trace	0	0	0	0	trace	8	9	50
Maximum 24-hr. Snowfall (in.)	14	17	12	4	trace	0	0	0	0	trace	8	7	17
Days With ≥1.0" Snow Depth	4	3	1	0	0	0	0	0	0	0	0	1	9
Thunderstorm Days	< 1	< 1	1	2	4	5	7	5	2	1	1	< 1	28
Foggy Days	12	11	13	13	15	16	19	19	16	14	12	12	172
Predominant Sky Cover	OVR	OVR	OVR	OVR	OVR	OVR	OVR	OVR	OVR	OVR	OVR	OVR	OVR
Mean Relative Humidity 7am (%)	78	78	78	77	79	81	84	87	87	87	83	79	81
Mean Relative Humidity 4pm (%)	60	57	55	54	57	58	60	62	61	59	61	61	59
Mean Dewpoint (°F)	22	23	30	38	50	60	65	65	58	47	37	27	44
Prevailing Wind Direction	WNW	WNW	WNW	S	S	S	S	S	N	NW	WNW	WNW	WNW
Prevailing Wind Speed (mph)	14	14	15	12	12	10	10	9	8	10	13	14	12
Maximum Wind Gust (mph)	78	64	68	67	55	64	81	62	83	58	69	71	83

Atlantic City State Marina

The Atlantic City State Marina is located on Abescon Island on the southeast coast of New Jersey. Surrounding terrain, composed of tidal marshes and beach sand, is flat and lies slightly above sea level. The climate is principally continental in character. However, the moderating influence of the Atlantic Ocean is apparent throughout the year, being more marked in the city than at the airport. As a result, summers are relatively cooler and winters milder than elsewhere at the same latitude.

Land and sea breezes, local circulations resulting from the differential heating and cooling of the land and sea, often prevail. These winds occur when moderate or intense storms are not present in the area, thus enabling the local circulation to overcome the general wind pattern. During the warm season sea breezes in the late morning and afternoon hours prevent excessive heating. Frequently, the temperature at Atlantic City during the afternoon hours in the summer averages several degrees lower than at the airport and the airport averages several degrees lower than localities farther inland. On occasions, sea breezes have lowered the temperature as much as 15 to 20 degrees within a half hour. However, the major effect of the sea breeze at the airport is preventing the temperature from rising above the 80s. Because the change in ocean temperature lags behind the air temperature from season to season, the weather tends to remain comparatively mild late into the fall, but on the other hand, warming is retarded in the spring. Normal ocean temperatures range from an average near 37 degrees in January to near 72 degrees in August.

Precipitation is moderate and well distributed throughout the year, with June the driest month and August the wettest. Tropical storms or hurricanes occasionally bring excessive rainfall to the area. The bulk of winter precipitation results from storms which move northeastward along or near the east coast of the United States. Snowfall is considerably less than elsewhere at the same latitude and does not remain long on the ground. Precipitation, often beginning as snow, will frequently become mixed with or change to rain while continuing as snow over more interior sections. In addition, ice storms and resultant glaze are relatively infrequent.

Atlantic City State Marina *Atlantic County*   Elevation: 9 ft.   Latitude: 39° 23' N   Longitude: 74° 26' W

	JAN	FEB	MAR	APR	MAY	JUN	JUL	AUG	SEP	OCT	NOV	DEC	YEAR
Mean Maximum Temp. (°F)	40.7	42.9	49.1	57.6	66.2	74.7	80.6	79.9	74.1	64.4	55.0	46.8	61.0
Mean Temp. (°F)	34.3	36.4	42.7	51.1	60.1	68.7	74.7	74.2	68.2	57.9	48.5	40.4	54.8
Mean Minimum Temp. (°F)	27.9	29.9	36.3	44.5	54.0	62.8	68.7	68.4	62.2	51.4	41.9	33.8	48.5
Extreme Maximum Temp. (°F)	69	72	82	90	93	97	101	102	92	89	78	74	102
Extreme Minimum Temp. (°F)	-3	4	12	22	38	45	53	50	42	27	19	4	-3
Days Maximum Temp. ≥90°F	0	0	0	0	0	0	3	1	0	0	0	0	4
Days Maximum Temp. ≤ 32°F	6	4	0	0	0	0	0	0	0	0	0	2	12
Days Minimum Temp. ≤ 32°F	21	16	9	1	0	0	0	0	0	0	4	13	64
Days Minimum Temp. ≤ 0°F	0	0	0	0	0	0	0	0	0	0	0	0	0
Heating Degree Days (base 65°F)	944	801	683	413	176	21	1	1	31	231	490	757	4,549
Cooling Degree Days (base 65°F)	0	0	0	1	38	158	334	301	145	23	1	0	1,001
Mean Precipitation (in.)	3.44	2.96	3.77	3.21	3.04	2.43	3.20	3.82	2.78	2.82	2.97	3.38	37.82
Maximum Precipitation (in.)	8.4	6.9	8.5	6.9	8.8	7.3	11.1	14.8	5.8	5.9	8.9	6.8	62.2
Minimum Precipitation (in.)	0.3	0.8	0.7	0.8	0.3	0.3	0.3	0.9	0.5	trace	0.8	0.7	27.5
Maximum 24-hr. Precipitation (in.)	2.5	2.5	3.3	4.0	3.1	3.6	6.6	7.3	3.0	2.9	3.7	3.3	7.3
Days With ≥0.1" Precipitation	7	6	7	7	6	5	5	5	5	5	6	6	70
Days With ≥1.0" Precipitation	1	1	1	1	0	1	1	1	1	1	1	1	11
Mean Snowfall (in.)	na	na	na	na	na	na	na	na	na	na	na	na	na
Maximum Snowfall (in.)	13	13	10	1	0	0	0	0	0	0	3	5	29
Maximum 24-hr. Snowfall (in.)	11	9	8	1	0	0	0	0	0	0	3	4	11
Days With ≥1.0" Snow Depth	na	na	na	na	na	na	na	na	na	na	na	na	na
Thunderstorm Days	0	< 1	2	2	5	5	6	2	1	1	0	0	24
Foggy Days	7	7	12	9	13	15	12	11	7	13	18	10	134
Predominant Sky Cover	na	na	na	na	na	na	na	na	na	na	na	na	na
Mean Relative Humidity 7am (%)	na	na	na	na	na	na	na	na	na	na	na	na	na
Mean Relative Humidity 4pm (%)	na	na	na	na	na	na	na	na	na	na	na	na	na
Mean Dewpoint (°F)	na	na	na	na	na	na	na	na	na	na	na	na	na
Prevailing Wind Direction	na	na	na	na	na	na	na	na	na	na	na	na	na
Prevailing Wind Speed (mph)	na	na	na	na	na	na	na	na	na	na	na	na	na
Maximum Wind Gust (mph)	67	69	87	63	53	51	52	71	67	67	67	67	87

Newark Int'l Airport

Terrain in vicinity of the station is flat and rather marshy. To the northwest are ridges oriented roughly in a south-southwest to north-northeast direction. They rise to an elevation of about 200 feet at 4.5 to five miles and to 500 to 600 feet at seven to eight miles. All winds between west-northwest and north-northwest are downslope and therefore are subject to some adiabatic temperature increase. This effect is evident in the rapid improvement which normally occurs with shift of wind to westerly, following a coastal storm or frontal passage. The drying effect of the downslope winds accounts for the relatively few local thunderstorms occurring at the station, compared to areas to the west. Easterly winds, particularly southeasterly, moderate the temperature because of the influence of the Atlantic Ocean.

Temperature falls of five to 15 degrees, depending on the season, are not uncommon when the wind backs from southwesterly to southeasterly. Periods of very hot weather, lasting as long as a week, are associated with a west-southwest air flow which has a long trajectory over land. Extremes of cold are related to rapidly moving outbreaks of cold air traveling southeastward from the Hudson Bay region. Temperatures of zero or below occur in one winter out of four, but are much more common several miles to the west of the station. Average dates of the last occurrence in spring and the first occurrence in autumn of temperatures as low as 32 degrees are in mid-April and the end of October or early November. Areas to the west of the station experience a growing season at least a month shorter than that at the airport.

A considerable amount of precipitation is realized from the Northeasters of the Atlantic coast. These storms, more typical of the fall and winter, generally last for a period of two days and commonly produce between one and two inches of precipitation. Storms producing four inches or more of snow occur from two to five times a winter. Snowstorms producing eight inches or more have occurred in about one-half the winters. As many as three such storms have been experienced in one winter. The frequency and intensity of snow storms and the duration of snow cover increase dramatically within a few miles to the west of the station.

Newark Int'l Airport *Essex County*   Elevation: 9 ft.   Latitude: 40° 43' N   Longitude: 74° 11' W

	JAN	FEB	MAR	APR	MAY	JUN	JUL	AUG	SEP	OCT	NOV	DEC	YEAR
Mean Maximum Temp. (°F)	38.7	41.9	50.9	62.1	72.7	81.4	86.5	84.6	77.0	65.8	54.8	44.1	63.4
Mean Temp. (°F)	31.6	34.2	42.5	53.0	63.4	72.5	78.0	76.3	68.6	57.2	47.1	37.1	55.1
Mean Minimum Temp. (°F)	24.3	26.5	34.1	43.7	54.2	63.6	69.4	68.0	60.2	48.5	39.4	30.2	46.8
Extreme Maximum Temp. (°F)	70	74	86	94	99	102	105	100	100	88	81	76	105
Extreme Minimum Temp. (°F)	-8	-1	7	16	36	46	54	45	41	29	16	-1	-8
Days Maximum Temp. ≥90°F	0	0	0	0	2	5	10	7	2	0	0	0	26
Days Maximum Temp. ≤ 32°F	9	5	1	0	0	0	0	0	0	0	0	4	19
Days Minimum Temp. ≤ 32°F	24	20	12	1	0	0	0	0	0	0	6	18	81
Days Minimum Temp. ≤ 0°F	1	0	0	0	0	0	0	0	0	0	0	0	1
Heating Degree Days (base 65°F)	1,030	863	693	365	114	11	0	1	38	255	531	857	4,758
Cooling Degree Days (base 65°F)	0	0	0	3	78	259	423	359	156	21	1	0	1,309
Mean Precipitation (in.)	3.89	3.02	4.21	3.92	4.36	3.37	4.60	4.00	3.92	3.22	3.94	3.53	45.98
Maximum Precipitation (in.)	10.1	5.9	11.1	11.1	10.2	6.4	10.0	11.8	10.3	8.2	11.5	9.5	65.5
Minimum Precipitation (in.)	0.4	0.8	1.1	0.9	0.5	0.1	0.9	0.4	0.1	0.2	0.5	0.3	26.1
Maximum 24-hr. Precipitation (in.)	2.9	2.4	2.7	2.8	4.0	3.0	3.5	5.9	4.7	4.0	6.7	2.8	6.7
Days With ≥0.1" Precipitation	7	6	7	7	7	6	7	6	6	5	6	7	77
Days With ≥1.0" Precipitation	1	1	1	1	1	1	1	1	1	1	1	1	12
Mean Snowfall (in.)	8.4	8.2	4.4	0.8	trace	0.0	0.0	0.0	trace	trace	0.6	2.5	24.9
Maximum Snowfall (in.)	27	33	26	14	trace	0	0	0	0	trace	9	29	66
Maximum 24-hr. Snowfall (in.)	14	18	13	13	trace	0	0	0	0	trace	5	26	26
Days With ≥1.0" Snow Depth	10	7	2	0	0	0	0	0	0	0	0	2	21
Thunderstorm Days	< 1	< 1	2	3	6	9	11	8	4	2	1	< 1	46
Foggy Days	9	9	10	9	11	10	9	10	11	11	9	10	118
Predominant Sky Cover	OVR	OVR	OVR	OVR	OVR	OVR	OVR	OVR	OVR	OVR	OVR	OVR	OVR
Mean Relative Humidity 7am (%)	73	71	69	67	70	71	72	76	79	78	76	74	73
Mean Relative Humidity 4pm (%)	58	54	51	48	51	51	52	54	55	53	57	59	54
Mean Dewpoint (°F)	21	21	27	36	48	57	63	63	56	45	35	25	42
Prevailing Wind Direction	WSW	NW	NW	NW	SW	SW	SW	SW	SW	SW	SW	WNW	SW
Prevailing Wind Speed (mph)	12	16	16	16	10	9	9	9	8	9	9	14	12
Maximum Wind Gust (mph)	62	60	67	62	58	83	69	68	67	55	63	61	83

Belleplain State Forest *Cape May County*   Elevation: 29 ft.   Latitude: 39° 15' N   Longitude: 74° 52' W

	JAN	FEB	MAR	APR	MAY	JUN	JUL	AUG	SEP	OCT	NOV	DEC	YEAR
Mean Maximum Temp. (°F)	43.9	46.7	54.9	65.7	74.8	82.3	86.7	85.0	79.3	68.7	58.6	48.9	66.3
Mean Temp. (°F)	33.6	35.7	43.1	52.5	61.9	70.3	75.6	73.8	67.6	56.5	47.2	38.4	54.7
Mean Minimum Temp. (°F)	23.2	24.6	31.3	39.3	49.0	58.4	64.4	62.6	55.9	44.3	35.8	27.8	43.0
Extreme Maximum Temp. (°F)	72	74	88	93	96	99	103	100	97	88	82	78	103
Extreme Minimum Temp. (°F)	-14	-9	5	14	24	38	43	38	33	21	9	-9	-14
Days Maximum Temp. ≥90°F	0	0	0	0	1	4	9	6	2	0	0	0	22
Days Maximum Temp. ≤ 32°F	4	2	0	0	0	0	0	0	0	0	0	2	8
Days Minimum Temp. ≤ 32°F	25	21	18	8	1	0	0	0	0	5	13	21	112
Days Minimum Temp. ≤ 0°F	1	0	0	0	0	0	0	0	0	0	0	0	1
Heating Degree Days (base 65°F)	967	822	673	376	145	24	1	4	52	276	528	818	4,686
Cooling Degree Days (base 65°F)	0	0	2	7	57	196	348	274	131	22	1	0	1,038
Mean Precipitation (in.)	3.80	3.01	4.08	3.72	3.65	2.90	3.63	5.19	3.67	3.82	3.34	3.51	44.32
Days With ≥0.1" Precipitation	7	6	7	7	7	5	6	6	5	5	6	6	73
Days With ≥1.0" Precipitation	1	1	1	1	1	1	1	2	1	1	1	1	13
Mean Snowfall (in.)	3.2	4.3	1.0	trace	0.0	0.0	0.0	0.0	0.0	trace	0.2	0.8	9.5
Days With ≥1.0" Snow Depth	4	2	0	0	0	0	0	0	0	0	0	1	7

Boonton 1 SE *Morris County*   Elevation: 278 ft.   Latitude: 40° 54' N   Longitude: 74° 24' W

	JAN	FEB	MAR	APR	MAY	JUN	JUL	AUG	SEP	OCT	NOV	DEC	YEAR
Mean Maximum Temp. (°F)	35.7	38.8	48.1	59.7	70.8	78.9	83.9	82.4	75.0	63.6	52.4	41.1	60.9
Mean Temp. (°F)	26.9	29.3	38.5	49.2	59.7	68.1	73.1	71.5	63.8	52.2	42.9	32.8	50.7
Mean Minimum Temp. (°F)	17.9	19.7	28.7	38.7	48.5	57.3	62.3	60.7	52.5	40.6	33.4	24.4	40.4
Extreme Maximum Temp. (°F)	65	69	82	92	96	95	100	97	94	83	78	68	100
Extreme Minimum Temp. (°F)	-15	-8	5	17	28	38	47	40	32	20	9	-6	-15
Days Maximum Temp. ≥90°F	0	0	0	0	0	2	5	3	1	0	0	0	11
Days Maximum Temp. ≤ 32°F	11	8	1	0	0	0	0	0	0	0	0	5	25
Days Minimum Temp. ≤ 32°F	29	25	21	6	0	0	0	0	0	6	14	25	126
Days Minimum Temp. ≤ 0°F	2	1	0	0	0	0	0	0	0	0	0	0	3
Heating Degree Days (base 65°F)	1,176	1,002	817	471	194	35	4	8	103	395	656	992	5,853
Cooling Degree Days (base 65°F)	0	0	0	3	38	142	274	219	73	5	0	0	754
Mean Precipitation (in.)	3.92	3.06	4.15	4.40	4.79	4.62	4.70	4.05	4.64	4.17	4.45	3.87	50.82
Days With ≥0.1" Precipitation	6	6	7	8	8	8	7	7	6	6	6	6	81
Days With ≥1.0" Precipitation	1	1	1	1	1	1	2	1	1	1	2	1	14
Mean Snowfall (in.)	8.9	9.0	5.1	0.8	0.0	0.0	0.0	0.0	0.0	trace	0.8	3.6	28.2
Days With ≥1.0" Snow Depth	na	na	3	0	0	0	0	0	0	0	0	na	na

Canoe Brook *Essex County*   Elevation: 177 ft.   Latitude: 40° 45' N   Longitude: 74° 21' W

	JAN	FEB	MAR	APR	MAY	JUN	JUL	AUG	SEP	OCT	NOV	DEC	YEAR
Mean Maximum Temp. (°F)	37.8	40.8	49.7	61.2	71.9	80.4	85.6	83.8	76.5	65.3	53.9	43.0	62.5
Mean Temp. (°F)	27.9	30.2	39.1	49.5	59.8	68.7	74.0	72.3	64.7	52.9	43.4	33.6	51.3
Mean Minimum Temp. (°F)	17.9	19.5	28.5	37.8	47.6	57.0	62.3	60.7	52.9	40.5	33.0	24.2	40.2
Extreme Maximum Temp. (°F)	69	75	89	94	95	100	103	99	99	88	80	76	103
Extreme Minimum Temp. (°F)	-15	-15	-1	18	25	36	44	39	31	19	10	-8	-15
Days Maximum Temp. ≥90°F	0	0	0	0	1	3	8	6	2	0	0	0	20
Days Maximum Temp. ≤ 32°F	9	6	1	0	0	0	0	0	0	0	0	5	21
Days Minimum Temp. ≤ 32°F	29	25	21	8	1	0	0	0	0	6	16	26	132
Days Minimum Temp. ≤ 0°F	2	1	0	0	0	0	0	0	0	0	0	0	3
Heating Degree Days (base 65°F)	1,149	981	802	468	198	37	4	8	94	378	645	971	5,735
Cooling Degree Days (base 65°F)	0	0	2	5	41	163	303	245	93	8	0	0	860
Mean Precipitation (in.)	4.06	3.09	4.21	4.22	4.66	4.35	4.61	4.77	4.97	4.26	4.49	3.78	51.47
Days With ≥0.1" Precipitation	7	6	7	7	8	7	7	6	6	6	6	6	79
Days With ≥1.0" Precipitation	1	1	1	1	1	1	1	1	1	1	1	1	12
Mean Snowfall (in.)	8.7	7.8	4.5	0.8	0.0	0.0	0.0	0.0	0.0	trace	0.6	3.2	25.6
Days With ≥1.0" Snow Depth	14	11	4	0	0	0	0	0	0	0	0	3	32

Cape May 2 NW *Cape May County*   Elevation: 19 ft.   Latitude: 38° 57' N   Longitude: 74° 56' W

	JAN	FEB	MAR	APR	MAY	JUN	JUL	AUG	SEP	OCT	NOV	DEC	YEAR
Mean Maximum Temp. (°F)	41.4	43.1	50.3	59.7	69.1	78.0	83.7	82.7	77.1	66.3	56.2	46.9	62.9
Mean Temp. (°F)	34.2	35.7	42.6	51.5	60.8	69.8	75.6	74.6	68.9	58.0	48.6	39.5	55.0
Mean Minimum Temp. (°F)	27.0	28.3	34.9	43.2	52.6	61.6	67.4	66.5	60.5	49.6	41.0	32.0	47.0
Extreme Maximum Temp. (°F)	68	71	82	88	95	96	100	96	95	88	78	76	100
Extreme Minimum Temp. (°F)	-2	-1	10	22	33	43	53	45	40	30	20	6	-2
Days Maximum Temp. ≥90°F	0	0	0	0	0	1	5	3	1	0	0	0	10
Days Maximum Temp. ≤ 32°F	6	4	1	0	0	0	0	0	0	0	0	2	13
Days Minimum Temp. ≤ 32°F	22	19	11	2	0	0	0	0	0	1	5	16	76
Days Minimum Temp. ≤ 0°F	0	0	0	0	0	0	0	0	0	0	0	0	0
Heating Degree Days (base 65°F)	947	821	688	402	158	17	0	2	31	233	486	785	4,570
Cooling Degree Days (base 65°F)	0	0	0	3	44	184	355	306	157	24	1	0	1,074
Mean Precipitation (in.)	3.64	3.06	4.09	3.48	3.61	3.00	3.16	3.63	3.19	3.56	3.24	3.56	41.22
Days With ≥0.1" Precipitation	7	7	7	7	7	5	5	5	5	5	6	7	73
Days With ≥1.0" Precipitation	1	1	1	1	1	1	1	1	1	1	1	1	12
Mean Snowfall (in.)	4.0	6.2	1.7	trace	0.0	0.0	0.0	0.0	0.0	trace	0.3	1.3	13.5
Days With ≥1.0" Snow Depth	3	5	1	0	0	0	0	0	0	0	0	1	10

Charlotteburg Reservoir *Passaic County*   Elevation: 757 ft.   Latitude: 41° 02' N   Longitude: 74° 26' W

	JAN	FEB	MAR	APR	MAY	JUN	JUL	AUG	SEP	OCT	NOV	DEC	YEAR
Mean Maximum Temp. (°F)	35.1	37.9	46.8	58.3	69.4	77.3	82.6	80.8	73.4	62.8	51.4	40.2	59.7
Mean Temp. (°F)	25.4	27.5	36.2	46.9	57.4	65.7	70.8	68.9	61.3	50.5	41.3	31.1	48.6
Mean Minimum Temp. (°F)	15.6	16.9	25.5	35.5	45.2	54.0	58.9	57.0	49.1	38.1	31.2	22.0	37.4
Extreme Maximum Temp. (°F)	65	74	85	92	94	95	100	97	94	85	79	73	100
Extreme Minimum Temp. (°F)	-24	-12	2	13	24	34	41	36	29	20	9	-11	-24
Days Maximum Temp. ≥90°F	0	0	0	0	0	1	4	2	0	0	0	0	7
Days Maximum Temp. ≤ 32°F	12	9	2	0	0	0	0	0	0	0	0	7	30
Days Minimum Temp. ≤ 32°F	29	26	25	11	1	0	0	0	1	9	18	27	147
Days Minimum Temp. ≤ 0°F	3	2	0	0	0	0	0	0	0	0	0	1	6
Heating Degree Days (base 65°F)	1,222	1,054	888	540	253	66	11	25	151	446	704	1,044	6,404
Cooling Degree Days (base 65°F)	0	0	0	3	24	99	208	152	46	3	0	0	535
Mean Precipitation (in.)	4.23	3.38	4.56	4.55	4.75	4.44	4.62	4.56	5.10	4.38	4.66	3.99	53.22
Days With ≥0.1" Precipitation	7	6	7	7	8	7	7	7	6	6	6	6	80
Days With ≥1.0" Precipitation	1	1	1	2	1	1	2	1	2	1	2	1	16
Mean Snowfall (in.)	10.2	9.7	7.1	1.9	trace	0.0	0.0	0.0	0.0	0.1	0.9	4.6	34.5
Days With ≥1.0" Snow Depth	14	13	6	1	0	0	0	0	0	0	1	5	40

Cranford *Union County*   Elevation: 72 ft.   Latitude: 40° 39' N   Longitude: 74° 18' W

	JAN	FEB	MAR	APR	MAY	JUN	JUL	AUG	SEP	OCT	NOV	DEC	YEAR
Mean Maximum Temp. (°F)	40.1	43.7	52.5	63.7	73.9	82.1	87.0	84.8	77.5	66.6	55.6	44.6	64.3
Mean Temp. (°F)	30.8	33.5	41.4	51.2	61.2	70.0	75.2	73.3	66.1	54.7	45.2	35.8	53.2
Mean Minimum Temp. (°F)	21.4	23.3	30.3	38.7	48.5	57.9	63.4	61.8	54.6	42.8	34.8	27.0	42.0
Extreme Maximum Temp. (°F)	70	75	90	96	96	98	102	99	99	87	80	76	102
Extreme Minimum Temp. (°F)	-10	-6	1	12	24	32	42	39	33	22	14	-5	-10
Days Maximum Temp. ≥90°F	0	0	0	0	1	5	11	6	2	0	0	0	25
Days Maximum Temp. ≤ 32°F	7	4	1	0	0	0	0	0	0	0	0	3	15
Days Minimum Temp. ≤ 32°F	26	23	18	7	1	0	0	0	0	4	13	23	115
Days Minimum Temp. ≤ 0°F	1	0	0	0	0	0	0	0	0	0	0	0	1
Heating Degree Days (base 65°F)	1,055	883	726	413	158	24	1	5	70	322	587	897	5,141
Cooling Degree Days (base 65°F)	0	0	2	5	49	188	337	266	107	11	0	0	965
Mean Precipitation (in.)	3.99	3.13	4.18	4.21	4.84	4.14	5.22	4.30	4.48	4.01	4.47	3.96	50.93
Days With ≥0.1" Precipitation	7	6	7	7	8	7	7	7	6	6	7	7	82
Days With ≥1.0" Precipitation	1	1	1	1	2	1	1	1	1	1	1	1	13
Mean Snowfall (in.)	7.2	6.6	3.7	0.4	0.0	0.0	0.0	0.0	0.0	trace	0.5	2.2	20.6
Days With ≥1.0" Snow Depth	12	9	3	0	0	0	0	0	0	0	0	2	26

Essex Fells Serv Bldg *Essex County*   Elevation: 347 ft.   Latitude: 40° 50' N   Longitude: 74° 17' W

	JAN	FEB	MAR	APR	MAY	JUN	JUL	AUG	SEP	OCT	NOV	DEC	YEAR
Mean Maximum Temp. (°F)	36.8	40.1	49.2	60.7	71.5	79.5	84.7	82.9	75.6	64.5	53.1	41.6	61.7
Mean Temp. (°F)	27.8	30.7	38.7	49.3	59.7	68.1	73.4	71.6	64.0	52.8	43.3	33.0	51.0
Mean Minimum Temp. (°F)	18.6	20.6	28.2	37.8	47.8	56.6	62.1	60.0	52.3	41.0	33.4	24.3	40.2
Extreme Maximum Temp. (°F)	67	75	89	94	92	96	101	98	99	87	83	74	101
Extreme Minimum Temp. (°F)	-14	-4	0	15	26	38	45	36	32	21	12	-6	-14
Days Maximum Temp. ≥90°F	0	0	0	0	1	2	6	4	1	0	0	0	14
Days Maximum Temp. ≤ 32°F	10	7	1	0	0	0	0	0	0	0	0	5	23
Days Minimum Temp. ≤ 32°F	28	25	22	7	0	0	0	0	0	5	15	26	128
Days Minimum Temp. ≤ 0°F	1	0	0	0	0	0	0	0	0	0	0	0	1
Heating Degree Days (base 65°F)	1,148	962	808	470	195	38	3	9	102	380	645	985	5,745
Cooling Degree Days (base 65°F)	0	0	1	4	36	137	274	214	76	7	0	0	749
Mean Precipitation (in.)	4.11	3.17	4.06	4.58	4.86	4.51	4.85	4.41	4.70	4.06	4.39	4.02	51.72
Days With ≥0.1" Precipitation	6	5	6	7	8	7	7	7	6	5	6	6	76
Days With ≥1.0" Precipitation	1	1	1	2	1	1	1	1	2	1	1	1	14
Mean Snowfall (in.)	5.6	4.1	3.6	0.7	0.0	0.0	0.0	0.0	0.0	trace	0.3	2.4	16.7
Days With ≥1.0" Snow Depth	na	na	1	0	0	0	0	0	0	0	0	1	na

Flemington 5 NNW *Hunterdon County*   Elevation: 259 ft.   Latitude: 40° 34' N   Longitude: 74° 53' W

	JAN	FEB	MAR	APR	MAY	JUN	JUL	AUG	SEP	OCT	NOV	DEC	YEAR
Mean Maximum Temp. (°F)	37.2	40.5	49.6	61.6	72.3	80.7	85.9	83.9	76.4	65.2	53.6	42.6	62.5
Mean Temp. (°F)	27.8	30.2	38.7	49.3	59.6	68.4	74.0	71.9	64.5	52.8	43.0	33.5	51.1
Mean Minimum Temp. (°F)	18.2	19.9	27.8	36.9	46.9	56.0	62.0	59.9	52.5	40.4	32.3	24.4	39.8
Extreme Maximum Temp. (°F)	67	73	88	94	95	96	104	101	100	86	81	75	104
Extreme Minimum Temp. (°F)	-18	-10	-6	18	26	34	45	38	29	19	10	-9	-18
Days Maximum Temp. ≥90°F	0	0	0	0	1	3	9	5	2	0	0	0	20
Days Maximum Temp. ≤ 32°F	10	7	1	0	0	0	0	0	0	0	0	5	23
Days Minimum Temp. ≤ 32°F	28	25	22	9	1	0	0	0	0	7	17	26	135
Days Minimum Temp. ≤ 0°F	2	1	0	0	0	0	0	0	0	0	0	0	3
Heating Degree Days (base 65°F)	1,148	976	810	470	195	35	3	10	94	377	653	968	5,739
Cooling Degree Days (base 65°F)	0	0	1	4	38	144	301	234	85	7	0	0	814
Mean Precipitation (in.)	4.24	3.07	4.18	4.11	4.82	4.31	4.67	3.95	4.43	3.97	3.90	3.93	49.58
Days With ≥0.1" Precipitation	7	6	7	7	8	7	7	6	6	6	6	7	80
Days With ≥1.0" Precipitation	1	1	1	1	1	1	2	1	1	1	1	1	13
Mean Snowfall (in.)	9.9	8.4	5.4	1.0	0.0	0.0	0.0	0.0	0.0	trace	0.6	3.5	28.8
Days With ≥1.0" Snow Depth	14	9	4	0	0	0	0	0	0	0	0	4	31

Glassboro 2 W *Gloucester County*   Elevation: 98 ft.   Latitude: 39° 44' N   Longitude: 75° 06' W

	JAN	FEB	MAR	APR	MAY	JUN	JUL	AUG	SEP	OCT	NOV	DEC	YEAR
Mean Maximum Temp. (°F)	39.3	42.4	51.2	62.1	72.3	81.0	85.8	84.2	77.3	65.8	55.3	44.8	63.5
Mean Temp. (°F)	31.3	33.9	42.1	52.0	62.1	71.0	76.2	74.6	67.5	55.6	46.4	36.9	54.1
Mean Minimum Temp. (°F)	23.2	25.3	33.0	42.0	51.7	60.9	66.6	64.9	57.8	45.5	37.4	28.9	44.8
Extreme Maximum Temp. (°F)	71	75	85	93	95	100	101	99	99	86	80	73	101
Extreme Minimum Temp. (°F)	-8	-2	5	18	31	43	51	45	38	23	15	1	-8
Days Maximum Temp. ≥90°F	0	0	0	0	1	4	8	5	2	0	0	0	20
Days Maximum Temp. ≤ 32°F	8	5	1	0	0	0	0	0	0	0	0	3	17
Days Minimum Temp. ≤ 32°F	26	22	15	3	0	0	0	0	0	1	10	21	98
Days Minimum Temp. ≤ 0°F	1	0	0	0	0	0	0	0	0	0	0	0	1
Heating Degree Days (base 65°F)	1,038	872	704	393	143	19	1	3	51	299	554	866	4,943
Cooling Degree Days (base 65°F)	0	0	2	8	61	215	370	300	131	17	1	0	1,105
Mean Precipitation (in.)	3.64	2.83	4.15	3.89	4.22	3.75	4.36	4.28	3.44	3.59	3.69	3.79	45.63
Days With ≥0.1" Precipitation	7	6	7	7	8	6	7	6	5	5	6	7	77
Days With ≥1.0" Precipitation	1	1	1	1	1	1	1	1	1	1	1	1	12
Mean Snowfall (in.)	na	na	trace	trace	0.0	0.0	0.0	0.0	0.0	trace	trace	1.2	na
Days With ≥1.0" Snow Depth	na	na	1	0	0	0	0	0	0	0	0	3	na

Hightstown 2 W *Mercer County*   Elevation: 98 ft.   Latitude: 40° 16' N   Longitude: 74° 34' W

	JAN	FEB	MAR	APR	MAY	JUN	JUL	AUG	SEP	OCT	NOV	DEC	YEAR
Mean Maximum Temp. (°F)	38.6	41.4	50.2	61.4	72.0	80.6	85.5	83.7	76.7	65.5	54.6	43.8	62.8
Mean Temp. (°F)	30.0	32.4	40.7	50.5	60.7	69.4	74.6	72.9	65.7	54.2	45.0	35.5	52.6
Mean Minimum Temp. (°F)	21.4	23.4	31.1	39.6	49.3	58.2	63.7	62.0	54.5	42.9	35.3	27.2	42.4
Extreme Maximum Temp. (°F)	70	75	88	93	95	98	102	97	98	88	80	76	102
Extreme Minimum Temp. (°F)	-12	-8	4	18	28	39	45	40	33	23	11	-5	-12
Days Maximum Temp. ≥90°F	0	0	0	0	1	3	8	5	1	0	0	0	18
Days Maximum Temp. ≤ 32°F	9	6	1	0	0	0	0	0	0	0	0	4	20
Days Minimum Temp. ≤ 32°F	27	23	18	6	0	0	0	0	0	4	13	23	114
Days Minimum Temp. ≤ 0°F	1	0	0	0	0	0	0	0	0	0	0	0	1
Heating Degree Days (base 65°F)	1,076	913	749	435	173	30	3	7	79	338	595	907	5,305
Cooling Degree Days (base 65°F)	0	0	1	6	48	173	317	249	101	12	1	0	908
Mean Precipitation (in.)	3.70	2.77	3.96	4.00	4.33	3.97	4.82	4.71	4.14	3.47	3.75	3.68	47.30
Days With ≥0.1" Precipitation	7	6	7	7	8	7	7	6	6	6	6	7	80
Days With ≥1.0" Precipitation	1	1	1	1	1	1	2	1	1	1	1	1	13
Mean Snowfall (in.)	7.1	7.4	3.6	0.9	trace	0.0	0.0	0.0	0.0	trace	0.4	2.6	22.0
Days With ≥1.0" Snow Depth	9	7	3	0	0	0	0	0	0	0	0	3	22

Indian Mills 2 W *Burlington County*   Elevation: 98 ft.   Latitude: 39° 48' N   Longitude: 74° 47' W

	JAN	FEB	MAR	APR	MAY	JUN	JUL	AUG	SEP	OCT	NOV	DEC	YEAR
Mean Maximum Temp. (°F)	41.2	44.7	53.2	64.6	74.8	82.8	87.5	85.7	78.8	67.8	57.0	46.4	65.4
Mean Temp. (°F)	31.5	34.2	42.1	51.9	61.9	70.3	75.4	73.6	66.6	55.3	45.9	36.7	53.8
Mean Minimum Temp. (°F)	21.8	23.6	30.9	39.0	48.9	57.8	63.2	61.5	54.5	42.7	34.7	26.9	42.1
Extreme Maximum Temp. (°F)	72	77	90	95	97	100	103	100	99	90	82	76	103
Extreme Minimum Temp. (°F)	-18	-12	-3	18	24	36	40	36	31	18	12	-4	-18
Days Maximum Temp. ≥90°F	0	0	0	0	2	5	11	8	2	0	0	0	28
Days Maximum Temp. ≤ 32°F	7	4	0	0	0	0	0	0	0	0	0	2	13
Days Minimum Temp. ≤ 32°F	26	22	18	8	1	0	0	0	0	6	14	22	117
Days Minimum Temp. ≤ 0°F	1	0	0	0	0	0	0	0	0	0	0	0	1
Heating Degree Days (base 65°F)	1,032	865	706	398	150	22	1	5	66	313	570	871	4,999
Cooling Degree Days (base 65°F)	0	0	2	10	64	198	343	275	122	19	2	0	1,035
Mean Precipitation (in.)	4.02	3.06	4.35	4.01	3.98	3.58	4.31	4.92	3.52	3.41	3.67	4.01	46.84
Days With ≥0.1" Precipitation	7	6	7	7	8	6	7	6	5	5	6	7	77
Days With ≥1.0" Precipitation	1	1	1	1	1	1	1	1	1	1	1	1	12
Mean Snowfall (in.)	6.7	5.2	2.3	0.6	0.0	0.0	0.0	0.0	0.0	trace	0.3	2.1	17.2
Days With ≥1.0" Snow Depth	7	5	1	0	0	0	0	0	0	0	0	2	15

Lambertville *Hunterdon County*   Elevation: 65 ft.   Latitude: 40° 22' N   Longitude: 74° 57' W

	JAN	FEB	MAR	APR	MAY	JUN	JUL	AUG	SEP	OCT	NOV	DEC	YEAR
Mean Maximum Temp. (°F)	39.7	43.1	52.4	63.9	74.8	83.0	87.6	85.8	78.6	67.2	55.4	44.4	64.6
Mean Temp. (°F)	30.3	33.0	41.4	51.4	62.0	70.7	75.7	73.9	66.6	54.8	44.9	35.3	53.3
Mean Minimum Temp. (°F)	21.1	22.9	30.4	38.8	49.2	58.4	63.7	62.0	54.6	42.5	34.3	26.2	42.0
Extreme Maximum Temp. (°F)	69	75	88	95	95	98	103	100	100	88	82	75	103
Extreme Minimum Temp. (°F)	-11	-9	1	13	25	38	45	39	32	22	12	-1	-11
Days Maximum Temp. ≥90°F	0	0	0	0	1	5	11	8	2	0	0	0	27
Days Maximum Temp. ≤ 32°F	8	4	0	0	0	0	0	0	0	0	0	3	15
Days Minimum Temp. ≤ 32°F	27	23	19	8	0	0	0	0	0	5	14	23	119
Days Minimum Temp. ≤ 0°F	1	1	0	0	0	0	0	0	0	0	0	0	2
Heating Degree Days (base 65°F)	1,068	896	726	410	141	18	1	4	65	322	597	913	5,161
Cooling Degree Days (base 65°F)	0	0	1	7	57	199	346	280	117	15	0	0	1,022
Mean Precipitation (in.)	3.96	2.90	4.23	4.08	4.56	4.15	5.01	4.28	4.47	3.62	3.87	3.84	48.97
Days With ≥0.1" Precipitation	7	6	8	7	8	7	7	7	6	6	6	7	82
Days With ≥1.0" Precipitation	1	1	1	1	1	1	2	1	1	1	1	1	13
Mean Snowfall (in.)	7.4	6.1	3.3	0.7	0.0	0.0	0.0	0.0	0.0	trace	0.5	2.4	20.4
Days With ≥1.0" Snow Depth	10	6	2	0	0	0	0	0	0	0	0	2	20

Little Falls *Passaic County*   Elevation: 147 ft.   Latitude: 40° 53' N   Longitude: 74° 14' W

	JAN	FEB	MAR	APR	MAY	JUN	JUL	AUG	SEP	OCT	NOV	DEC	YEAR
Mean Maximum Temp. (°F)	37.6	40.7	49.4	61.2	71.7	80.5	85.8	83.5	75.8	64.6	53.7	42.6	62.3
Mean Temp. (°F)	28.9	31.5	39.8	50.6	60.9	69.9	75.2	73.4	65.3	53.6	44.4	34.3	52.3
Mean Minimum Temp. (°F)	20.1	22.2	30.2	39.9	49.9	59.2	64.6	63.1	54.8	42.5	35.0	25.9	42.3
Extreme Maximum Temp. (°F)	67	75	88	95	96	96	103	99	98	87	83	74	103
Extreme Minimum Temp. (°F)	-10	-6	3	17	30	40	40	43	33	23	14	-6	-10
Days Maximum Temp. ≥90°F	0	0	0	0	1	4	8	4	1	0	0	0	18
Days Maximum Temp. ≤ 32°F	10	6	1	0	0	0	0	0	0	0	0	5	22
Days Minimum Temp. ≤ 32°F	28	23	19	5	0	0	0	0	0	4	12	24	115
Days Minimum Temp. ≤ 0°F	1	0	0	0	0	0	0	0	0	0	0	0	1
Heating Degree Days (base 65°F)	1,115	942	776	434	172	27	2	5	80	355	613	948	5,469
Cooling Degree Days (base 65°F)	0	0	2	6	51	187	335	270	96	7	0	0	954
Mean Precipitation (in.)	4.07	3.10	4.32	4.42	4.93	4.42	4.43	4.46	5.23	4.04	4.44	3.83	51.69
Days With ≥0.1" Precipitation	7	6	7	7	8	7	7	6	6	6	6	7	80
Days With ≥1.0" Precipitation	1	1	1	1	1	1	1	1	2	1	1	1	13
Mean Snowfall (in.)	na	na	2.3	trace	0.0	0.0	0.0	0.0	0.0	0.0	trace	na	na
Days With ≥1.0" Snow Depth	na	6	2	0	0	0	0	0	0	0	0	na	na

Long Valley *Morris County*   Elevation: 547 ft.   Latitude: 40° 47' N   Longitude: 74° 47' W

	JAN	FEB	MAR	APR	MAY	JUN	JUL	AUG	SEP	OCT	NOV	DEC	YEAR
Mean Maximum Temp. (°F)	36.3	39.4	48.1	59.8	69.9	77.2	81.9	79.9	72.3	62.6	52.2	41.1	60.0
Mean Temp. (°F)	26.5	28.8	37.0	47.4	57.6	65.5	70.5	68.8	61.0	50.4	41.5	31.7	48.9
Mean Minimum Temp. (°F)	16.6	18.1	25.8	35.0	45.2	53.7	59.1	57.7	49.6	38.2	30.7	22.3	37.7
Extreme Maximum Temp. (°F)	68	76	85	93	93	94	99	95	95	87	80	73	99
Extreme Minimum Temp. (°F)	-18	-12	-2	15	26	34	40	35	26	19	4	-11	-18
Days Maximum Temp. ≥90°F	0	0	0	0	0	1	3	1	0	0	0	0	5
Days Maximum Temp. ≤ 32°F	11	7	2	0	0	0	0	0	0	0	0	6	26
Days Minimum Temp. ≤ 32°F	29	26	25	12	2	0	0	0	0	10	19	27	150
Days Minimum Temp. ≤ 0°F	3	2	0	0	0	0	0	0	0	0	0	1	6
Heating Degree Days (base 65°F)	1,187	1,016	862	525	244	66	11	22	157	448	699	1,024	6,261
Cooling Degree Days (base 65°F)	0	0	0	2	21	89	201	148	43	3	0	0	507
Mean Precipitation (in.)	4.19	3.28	4.18	4.60	4.87	4.71	5.04	4.82	4.91	4.28	4.42	3.98	53.28
Days With ≥0.1" Precipitation	7	6	7	7	9	7	8	7	7	6	6	7	84
Days With ≥1.0" Precipitation	1	1	1	1	1	1	1	2	2	1	1	1	14
Mean Snowfail (in.)	10.5	8.9	6.3	1.9	0.0	0.0	0.0	0.0	0.0	0.2	1.0	4.9	33.7
Days With ≥1.0" Snow Depth	na	na	na	0	0	0	0	0	0	0	0	na	na

Millville Municipal Airport *Cumberland County*   Elevation: 68 ft.   Latitude: 39° 22' N   Longitude: 75° 04' W

	JAN	FEB	MAR	APR	MAY	JUN	JUL	AUG	SEP	OCT	NOV	DEC	YEAR
Mean Maximum Temp. (°F)	41.1	43.8	52.1	62.8	72.7	81.2	86.0	84.4	77.7	66.7	56.4	46.3	64.3
Mean Temp. (°F)	32.5	34.6	42.4	52.0	62.0	70.9	76.4	74.8	67.8	56.1	46.6	37.5	54.5
Mean Minimum Temp. (°F)	24.0	25.4	32.7	41.1	51.2	60.6	66.8	65.1	57.9	45.5	36.9	28.7	44.6
Extreme Maximum Temp. (°F)	71	75	86	91	96	99	101	101	97	90	82	77	101
Extreme Minimum Temp. (°F)	-10	-6	5	20	30	40	44	44	37	23	12	2	-10
Days Maximum Temp. ≥90°F	0	0	0	0	1	3	9	5	2	0	0	0	20
Days Maximum Temp. ≤ 32°F	7	5	1	0	0	0	0	0	0	0	0	3	16
Days Minimum Temp. ≤ 32°F	25	21	16	5	0	0	0	0	0	2	11	21	101
Days Minimum Temp. ≤ 0°F	0	0	0	0	0	0	0	0	0	0	0	0	0
Heating Degree Days (base 65°F)	999	852	694	392	144	18	1	2	47	288	546	845	4,828
Cooling Degree Days (base 65°F)	0	0	2	7	61	208	378	306	137	21	1	0	1,121
Mean Precipitation (in.)	3.55	3.22	4.32	3.66	3.92	3.32	3.59	4.24	3.37	3.20	3.28	3.62	43.29
Days With ≥0.1" Precipitation	6	6	7	7	7	6	6	5	5	5	6	6	72
Days With ≥1.0" Precipitation	1	1	1	1	1	1	1	1	1	1	1	1	12
Mean Snowfall (in.)	5.0	4.7	1.4	0.3	trace	0.0	trace	0.0	0.0	trace	0.2	1.6	13.2
Days With ≥1.0" Snow Depth	5	5	1	0	0	0	0	0	0	0	0	2	13

New Brunswick 3 SE *Middlesex County*   Elevation: 85 ft.   Latitude: 40° 28' N   Longitude: 74° 26' W

	JAN	FEB	MAR	APR	MAY	JUN	JUL	AUG	SEP	OCT	NOV	DEC	YEAR
Mean Maximum Temp. (°F)	38.0	41.0	49.7	60.8	71.3	79.9	85.2	83.4	76.5	65.3	54.3	43.5	62.4
Mean Temp. (°F)	29.5	31.9	40.3	50.3	60.5	69.4	74.8	73.1	65.7	54.2	44.9	35.1	52.5
Mean Minimum Temp. (°F)	21.0	22.8	30.8	39.7	49.6	58.7	64.4	62.8	54.9	43.0	35.3	26.7	42.5
Extreme Maximum Temp. (°F)	70	75	88	94	95	97	103	100	98	88	80	76	103
Extreme Minimum Temp. (°F)	-13	-7	6	16	30	40	45	40	35	25	13	-7	-13
Days Maximum Temp. ≥90°F	0	0	0	0	1	3	7	4	1	0	0	0	16
Days Maximum Temp. ≤ 32°F	9	6	1	0	0	0	0	0	0	0	0	4	20
Days Minimum Temp. ≤ 32°F	27	23	19	5	0	0	0	0	0	3	12	23	112
Days Minimum Temp. ≤ 0°F	1	0	0	0	0	0	0	0	0	0	0	0	1
Heating Degree Days (base 65°F)	1,093	927	761	441	177	29	2	5	73	339	598	919	5,364
Cooling Degree Days (base 65°F)	0	0	1	4	44	172	323	260	103	11	0	0	918
Mean Precipitation (in.)	4.03	3.00	4.11	4.15	4.50	3.89	4.96	4.36	4.29	3.47	4.03	3.87	48.66
Days With ≥0.1" Precipitation	7	6	7	6	8	7	7	6	6	6	6	7	79
Days With ≥1.0" Precipitation	1	1	1	1	1	1	2	1	1	1	1	1	13
Mean Snowfall (in.)	8.9	8.3	4.5	1.0	trace	0.0	0.0	0.0	0.0	trace	0.6	3.1	26.4
Days With ≥1.0" Snow Depth	12	9	3	0	0	0	0	0	0	0	0	3	27

Newton Saint Pauls Abbey *Sussex County*   Elevation: 597 ft.   Latitude: 41° 02' N   Longitude: 74° 48' W

	JAN	FEB	MAR	APR	MAY	JUN	JUL	AUG	SEP	OCT	NOV	DEC	YEAR
Mean Maximum Temp. (°F)	34.2	37.5	46.5	58.6	69.9	78.0	83.0	80.9	73.2	62.1	50.3	39.1	59.4
Mean Temp. (°F)	24.2	26.8	35.9	47.0	57.5	66.1	71.0	69.0	61.1	49.7	40.0	30.1	48.2
Mean Minimum Temp. (°F)	14.2	16.1	25.2	35.3	45.1	54.2	59.0	57.1	49.0	37.2	29.7	21.0	36.9
Extreme Maximum Temp. (°F)	65	71	83	91	95	96	101	95	95	85	80	72	101
Extreme Minimum Temp. (°F)	-26	-17	-5	14	24	33	40	35	27	16	7	-11	-26
Days Maximum Temp. ≥90°F	0	0	0	0	0	2	5	2	1	0	0	0	10
Days Maximum Temp. ≤ 32°F	12	9	2	0	0	0	0	0	0	0	1	7	31
Days Minimum Temp. ≤ 32°F	28	26	24	12	2	0	0	0	1	11	20	27	151
Days Minimum Temp. ≤ 0°F	4	3	0	0	0	0	0	0	0	0	0	1	8
Heating Degree Days (base 65°F)	1,258	1,072	896	537	249	63	12	25	158	471	743	1,077	6,561
Cooling Degree Days (base 65°F)	0	0	1	3	24	105	216	159	48	3	0	0	559
Mean Precipitation (in.)	3.50	2.76	3.65	4.08	4.32	4.47	4.34	4.41	4.55	3.82	3.94	3.41	47.25
Days With ≥0.1" Precipitation	7	6	7	7	8	7	7	6	7	6	7	6	81
Days With ≥1.0" Precipitation	1	0	1	1	1	1	1	1	1	1	1	1	11
Mean Snowfall (in.)	11.1	9.9	7.4	2.0	trace	0.0	0.0	0.0	0.0	0.1	1.9	5.4	37.8
Days With ≥1.0" Snow Depth	17	14	7	1	0	0	0	0	0	0	1	8	48

Pemberton *Burlington County*   Elevation: 59 ft.   Latitude: 39° 58' N   Longitude: 74° 41' W

	JAN	FEB	MAR	APR	MAY	JUN	JUL	AUG	SEP	OCT	NOV	DEC	YEAR
Mean Maximum Temp. (°F)	41.6	45.2	53.5	64.0	74.8	82.4	87.0	85.5	79.1	68.2	57.3	46.5	65.4
Mean Temp. (°F)	31.8	34.6	42.3	51.4	61.7	69.9	74.8	73.7	67.0	55.7	46.3	37.1	53.9
Mean Minimum Temp. (°F)	22.0	24.0	31.0	38.7	48.6	57.3	62.6	61.9	54.8	43.1	35.3	27.6	42.2
Extreme Maximum Temp. (°F)	70	77	91	93	95	98	104	101	98	91	82	75	104
Extreme Minimum Temp. (°F)	-17	-12	-2	16	25	36	41	37	32	20	8	-2	-17
Days Maximum Temp. ≥90°F	0	0	0	0	1	5	10	8	2	0	0	0	26
Days Maximum Temp. ≤ 32°F	6	3	0	0	0	0	0	0	0	0	0	2	11
Days Minimum Temp. ≤ 32°F	26	22	18	8	1	0	0	0	0	6	13	21	115
Days Minimum Temp. ≤ 0°F	1	1	0	0	0	0	0	0	0	0	0	0	2
Heating Degree Days (base 65°F)	1,023	852	701	409	149	25	2	5	61	300	556	858	4,941
Cooling Degree Days (base 65°F)	0	0	3	6	58	185	329	280	131	18	2	0	1,012
Mean Precipitation (in.)	3.88	2.90	4.20	3.83	4.29	4.09	4.51	5.14	3.66	3.50	3.53	3.84	47.37
Days With ≥0.1" Precipitation	7	6	8	7	8	7	6	6	6	5	6	7	79
Days With ≥1.0" Precipitation	1	1	1	1	1	1	1	2	1	1	1	1	13
Mean Snowfall (in.)	5.9	5.7	2.5	0.5	0.0	0.0	0.0	0.0	0.0	trace	0.3	2.0	16.9
Days With ≥1.0" Snow Depth	7	5	2	0	0	0	0	0	0	0	0	2	16

Plainfield *Union County*   Elevation: 88 ft.   Latitude: 40° 36' N   Longitude: 74° 24' W

	JAN	FEB	MAR	APR	MAY	JUN	JUL	AUG	SEP	OCT	NOV	DEC	YEAR
Mean Maximum Temp. (°F)	37.9	42.3	51.8	62.9	73.7	81.7	86.6	84.9	77.4	65.9	53.9	42.7	63.5
Mean Temp. (°F)	30.1	33.3	41.7	51.5	61.9	70.4	75.5	73.9	66.4	54.8	44.8	35.3	53.3
Mean Minimum Temp. (°F)	22.3	24.2	31.5	40.2	50.0	59.0	64.2	62.8	55.4	43.7	35.7	27.8	43.1
Extreme Maximum Temp. (°F)	68	76	91	97	99	100	104	100	100	88	82	74	104
Extreme Minimum Temp. (°F)	-8	-4	5	18	29	40	45	40	33	23	14	-3	-8
Days Maximum Temp. ≥90°F	0	0	0	0	2	5	10	7	2	0	0	0	26
Days Maximum Temp. ≤ 32°F	10	5	1	0	0	0	0	0	0	0	0	4	20
Days Minimum Temp. ≤ 32°F	26	23	17	5	0	0	0	0	0	3	12	22	108
Days Minimum Temp. ≤ 0°F	1	0	0	0	0	0	0	0	0	0	0	0	1
Heating Degree Days (base 65°F)	1,074	889	718	405	145	20	2	4	64	320	599	913	5,153
Cooling Degree Days (base 65°F)	0	0	2	7	57	195	344	282	112	12	0	0	1,011
Mean Precipitation (in.)	3.99	3.05	4.11	3.97	4.66	3.96	5.29	4.23	4.47	3.98	4.10	3.69	49.50
Days With ≥0.1" Precipitation	7	6	8	7	8	7	7	7	6	6	6	7	82
Days With ≥1.0" Precipitation	1	1	1	1	1	1	2	1	1	1	1	1	13
Mean Snowfall (in.)	9.2	8.7	4.4	0.6	trace	0.0	0.0	0.0	0.0	trace	0.6	3.1	26.6
Days With ≥1.0" Snow Depth	13	10	3	0	0	0	0	0	0	0	0	3	29

Seabrook Farms *Cumberland County*   Elevation: 88 ft.   Latitude: 39° 30' N   Longitude: 75° 14' W

	JAN	FEB	MAR	APR	MAY	JUN	JUL	AUG	SEP	OCT	NOV	DEC	YEAR
Mean Maximum Temp. (°F)	40.9	43.1	51.7	62.5	72.3	81.5	85.9	84.5	78.0	66.9	55.7	45.6	64.0
Mean Temp. (°F)	32.5	34.3	42.5	52.1	61.9	71.3	76.1	74.6	67.5	56.1	46.5	37.4	54.4
Mean Minimum Temp. (°F)	24.1	25.5	33.3	41.6	51.5	61.1	66.4	64.6	57.1	45.3	37.3	29.1	44.7
Extreme Maximum Temp. (°F)	70	74	86	92	95	100	100	100	98	88	80	74	100
Extreme Minimum Temp. (°F)	-13	0	9	24	33	41	49	44	36	24	15	5	-13
Days Maximum Temp. ≥90°F	0	0	0	0	1	4	8	5	2	0	0	0	20
Days Maximum Temp. ≤ 32°F	7	5	1	0	0	0	0	0	0	0	0	3	16
Days Minimum Temp. ≤ 32°F	25	21	15	4	0	0	0	0	0	2	10	21	98
Days Minimum Temp. ≤ 0°F	0	0	0	0	0	0	0	0	0	0	0	0	0
Heating Degree Days (base 65°F)	1,000	859	692	392	146	17	1	2	51	286	550	850	4,846
Cooling Degree Days (base 65°F)	0	0	3	8	63	228	376	303	132	19	1	0	1,133
Mean Precipitation (in.)	4.05	2.85	4.17	3.35	3.96	3.28	4.35	4.31	3.71	3.52	3.30	3.84	44.69
Days With ≥0.1" Precipitation	7	6	7	6	7	6	7	6	6	5	6	6	75
Days With ≥1.0" Precipitation	1	1	1	1	1	1	1	1	1	1	1	1	12
Mean Snowfall (in.)	na	na	na	0.4	0.0	0.0	0.0	0.0	0.0	0.0	0.2	na	na
Days With ≥1.0" Snow Depth	na	na	na	0	0	0	0	0	0	0	0	na	na

Somerville 3 NW *Somerset County* Elevation: 157 ft. Latitude: 40° 36' N Longitude: 74° 38' W

	JAN	FEB	MAR	APR	MAY	JUN	JUL	AUG	SEP	OCT	NOV	DEC	YEAR
Mean Maximum Temp. (°F)	36.8	39.8	49.3	60.9	71.6	79.9	85.0	82.8	75.4	64.0	53.2	41.8	61.7
Mean Temp. (°F)	27.6	29.8	38.6	49.1	59.4	68.1	73.4	71.6	63.9	52.3	43.0	33.0	50.8
Mean Minimum Temp. (°F)	18.3	19.8	27.8	37.2	47.2	56.3	61.7	60.2	52.4	40.5	32.7	24.1	39.9
Extreme Maximum Temp. (°F)	68	75	83	94	94	96	103	97	99	85	80	73	103
Extreme Minimum Temp. (°F)	-16	-10	2	18	26	37	45	38	32	21	10	-7	-16
Days Maximum Temp. ≥90°F	0	0	0	0	1	2	7	4	1	0	0	0	15
Days Maximum Temp. ≤ 32°F	10	7	1	0	0	0	0	0	0	0	0	5	23
Days Minimum Temp. ≤ 32°F	28	25	22	9	1	0	0	0	0	6	17	26	134
Days Minimum Temp. ≤ 0°F	2	1	0	0	0	0	0	0	0	0	0	0	3
Heating Degree Days (base 65°F)	1,154	988	813	475	200	35	4	9	103	392	653	986	5,812
Cooling Degree Days (base 65°F)	0	0	0	3	35	140	278	217	76	7	0	0	756
Mean Precipitation (in.)	3.77	2.83	3.88	4.07	4.39	4.16	4.83	4.39	4.33	3.90	3.89	3.70	48.14
Days With ≥0.1" Precipitation	7	6	7	7	8	7	8	7	6	6	6	7	82
Days With ≥1.0" Precipitation	1	0	1	1	1	1	1	1	1	1	1	1	11
Mean Snowfall (in.)	8.8	8.4	5.1	1.4	0.0	0.0	0.0	0.0	0.0	trace	0.7	3.1	27.5
Days With ≥1.0" Snow Depth	13	11	4	0	0	0	0	0	0	0	0	4	32

Toms River *Ocean County* Elevation: 98 ft. Latitude: 39° 57' N Longitude: 74° 13' W

	JAN	FEB	MAR	APR	MAY	JUN	JUL	AUG	SEP	OCT	NOV	DEC	YEAR
Mean Maximum Temp. (°F)	41.6	43.8	51.8	62.1	72.4	80.9	86.3	84.6	78.2	67.2	57.2	46.7	64.4
Mean Temp. (°F)	31.3	33.1	41.0	50.2	60.6	69.3	74.9	73.1	66.3	54.7	45.9	36.3	53.0
Mean Minimum Temp. (°F)	20.8	22.3	30.0	38.3	48.8	57.6	63.4	61.7	54.2	42.3	34.5	25.9	41.7
Extreme Maximum Temp. (°F)	72	75	87	93	99	102	105	101	99	91	85	76	105
Extreme Minimum Temp. (°F)	-19	-8	3	12	28	39	46	39	33	21	9	-3	-19
Days Maximum Temp. ≥90°F	0	0	0	0	1	4	10	7	2	0	0	0	24
Days Maximum Temp. ≤ 32°F	6	4	0	0	0	0	0	0	0	0	0	2	12
Days Minimum Temp. ≤ 32°F	27	23	19	8	0	0	0	0	0	5	14	24	120
Days Minimum Temp. ≤ 0°F	1	1	0	0	0	0	0	0	0	0	0	0	2
Heating Degree Days (base 65°F)	1,039	895	739	442	179	31	2	5	65	322	568	882	5,169
Cooling Degree Days (base 65°F)	0	0	2	4	53	174	328	255	109	11	1	0	937
Mean Precipitation (in.)	4.13	3.30	4.38	4.17	4.15	3.50	4.39	4.98	3.78	3.65	4.08	4.12	48.63
Days With ≥0.1" Precipitation	7	6	7	7	7	7	7	6	6	6	7	7	80
Days With ≥1.0" Precipitation	1	1	1	1	1	1	1	2	1	1	1	1	13
Mean Snowfall (in.)	na	2.2	0.4	trace	0.0	0.0	0.0	0.0	0.0	0.0	trace	na	na
Days With ≥1.0" Snow Depth	na	na	0	0	0	0	0	0	0	0	0	na	na

Tuckerton *Ocean County* Elevation: 19 ft. Latitude: 39° 36' N Longitude: 74° 21' W

	JAN	FEB	MAR	APR	MAY	JUN	JUL	AUG	SEP	OCT	NOV	DEC	YEAR
Mean Maximum Temp. (°F)	41.3	43.7	51.7	61.6	71.5	80.4	85.5	84.1	77.6	66.7	57.0	46.7	64.0
Mean Temp. (°F)	32.1	34.0	41.8	50.9	60.9	70.1	75.7	74.3	67.6	56.1	47.0	37.4	54.0
Mean Minimum Temp. (°F)	22.9	24.3	31.9	40.1	50.4	59.8	65.8	64.5	57.5	45.5	37.0	28.0	44.0
Extreme Maximum Temp. (°F)	74	74	87	92	97	101	104	100	98	87	85	76	104
Extreme Minimum Temp. (°F)	-7	-4	5	19	27	38	45	41	35	25	10	-2	-7
Days Maximum Temp. ≥90°F	0	0	0	0	1	4	9	6	2	0	0	0	22
Days Maximum Temp. ≤ 32°F	6	4	0	0	0	0	0	0	0	0	0	2	12
Days Minimum Temp. ≤ 32°F	25	22	17	6	0	0	0	0	0	2	11	21	104
Days Minimum Temp. ≤ 0°F	1	0	0	0	0	0	0	0	0	0	0	0	1
Heating Degree Days (base 65°F)	1,012	868	712	423	166	22	1	4	53	287	534	849	4,931
Cooling Degree Days (base 65°F)	0	0	0	6	55	199	362	297	135	20	1	0	1,075
Mean Precipitation (in.)	3.86	3.20	4.46	4.12	3.60	3.08	4.11	4.84	3.23	3.27	3.82	3.73	45.32
Days With ≥0.1" Precipitation	7	6	7	6	7	6	6	7	5	5	6	6	74
Days With ≥1.0" Precipitation	1	1	1	1	1	1	1	1	1	1	1	1	12
Mean Snowfall (in.)	6.1	6.7	2.0	0.4	trace	0.0	0.0	0.0	0.0	trace	0.4	2.3	17.9
Days With ≥1.0" Snow Depth	6	5	2	0	0	0	0	0	0	0	0	2	15

Woodstown *Salem County* Elevation: 49 ft. Latitude: 39° 39' N Longitude: 75° 19' W

	JAN	FEB	MAR	APR	MAY	JUN	JUL	AUG	SEP	OCT	NOV	DEC	YEAR
Mean Maximum Temp. (°F)	41.3	44.4	53.8	65.5	75.5	83.7	88.2	86.2	79.4	67.8	56.9	46.2	65.8
Mean Temp. (°F)	32.5	34.8	43.2	53.1	63.1	71.9	76.7	74.7	68.1	56.6	47.0	37.4	54.9
Mean Minimum Temp. (°F)	23.7	25.0	32.5	40.7	50.7	60.0	65.2	63.4	56.7	45.3	37.0	28.6	44.1
Extreme Maximum Temp. (°F)	71	76	88	93	96	101	102	102	99	90	80	75	102
Extreme Minimum Temp. (°F)	-13	-6	-3	18	29	43	43	42	35	20	8	-2	-13
Days Maximum Temp. ≥90°F	0	0	0	0	2	6	13	9	2	0	0	0	32
Days Maximum Temp. ≤ 32°F	6	4	0	0	0	0	0	0	0	0	0	3	13
Days Minimum Temp. ≤ 32°F	25	22	16	5	0	0	0	0	0	3	11	21	103
Days Minimum Temp. ≤ 0°F	1	0	0	0	0	0	0	0	0	0	0	0	1
Heating Degree Days (base 65°F)	1,001	848	673	359	119	13	1	2	47	273	537	847	4,720
Cooling Degree Days (base 65°F)	0	0	2	10	72	237	388	310	145	23	1	0	1,188
Mean Precipitation (in.)	3.72	2.83	4.07	3.80	3.94	3.89	4.40	4.21	3.85	3.50	3.57	3.71	45.49
Days With ≥0.1" Precipitation	7	5	7	7	7	6	7	6	6	5	6	6	75
Days With ≥1.0" Precipitation	1	1	1	1	1	1	1	1	1	1	1	1	12
Mean Snowfall (in.)	5.7	5.0	2.6	0.5	trace	0.0	0.0	0.0	0.0	0.1	0.3	2.3	16.5
Days With ≥1.0" Snow Depth	7	6	2	0	0	0	0	0	0	0	0	3	17

Annual Extreme Maximum Temperature

	Highest				Lowest	
Rank	Station Name	°F		Rank	Station Name	°F
1	Newark Int'l Airport	105		1	Long Valley	99
1	Toms River	105		2	Boonton 1 SE	100
3	Flemington 5 NNW	104		2	Cape May 2 NW	100
3	Pemberton	104		2	Charlotteburg Reservoir	100
3	Plainfield	104		2	Seabrook Farms	100
3	Tuckerton	104		6	Atlantic City Int'l Airport	101
7	Belleplain State Forest	103		6	Essex Fells Serv Bldg	101
7	Canoe Brook	103		6	Glassboro 2 W	101
7	Indian Mills 2 W	103		6	Millville Municipal Airport	101
7	Lambertville	103		6	Newton Saint Pauls Abbey	101
7	Little Falls	103		11	Atlantic City State Marina	102
7	New Brunswick 3 SE	103		11	Cranford	102
7	Somerville 3 NW	103		11	Hightstown 2 W	102
14	Atlantic City State Marina	102		11	Woodstown	102
14	Cranford	102		15	Belleplain State Forest	103
14	Hightstown 2 W	102		15	Canoe Brook	103
14	Woodstown	102		15	Indian Mills 2 W	103
18	Atlantic City Int'l Airport	101		15	Lambertville	103
18	Essex Fells Serv Bldg	101		15	Little Falls	103
18	Glassboro 2 W	101		15	New Brunswick 3 SE	103
18	Millville Municipal Airport	101		15	Somerville 3 NW	103
18	Newton Saint Pauls Abbey	101		22	Flemington 5 NNW	104
23	Boonton 1 SE	100		22	Pemberton	104
23	Cape May 2 NW	100		22	Plainfield	104
23	Charlotteburg Reservoir	100		22	Tuckerton	104

Annual Mean Maximum Temperature

	Highest				Lowest	
Rank	Station Name	°F		Rank	Station Name	°F
1	Belleplain State Forest	66.3		1	Newton Saint Pauls Abbey	59.4
2	Woodstown	65.8		2	Charlotteburg Reservoir	59.7
3	Indian Mills 2 W	65.4		3	Long Valley	60.0
3	Pemberton	65.4		4	Boonton 1 SE	60.9
5	Lambertville	64.6		5	Atlantic City State Marina	61.0
6	Toms River	64.4		6	Essex Fells Serv Bldg	61.7
7	Cranford	64.3		6	Somerville 3 NW	61.7
7	Millville Municipal Airport	64.3		8	Little Falls	62.3
9	Seabrook Farms	64.0		9	New Brunswick 3 SE	62.4
9	Tuckerton	64.0		10	Canoe Brook	62.5
11	Atlantic City Int'l Airport	63.7		10	Flemington 5 NNW	62.5
12	Glassboro 2 W	63.5		12	Hightstown 2 W	62.8
12	Plainfield	63.5		13	Cape May 2 NW	62.9
14	Newark Int'l Airport	63.4		14	Newark Int'l Airport	63.4
15	Cape May 2 NW	62.9		15	Glassboro 2 W	63.5
16	Hightstown 2 W	62.8		15	Plainfield	63.5
17	Canoe Brook	62.5		17	Atlantic City Int'l Airport	63.7
17	Flemington 5 NNW	62.5		18	Seabrook Farms	64.0
19	New Brunswick 3 SE	62.4		18	Tuckerton	64.0
20	Little Falls	62.3		20	Cranford	64.3
21	Essex Fells Serv Bldg	61.7		20	Millville Municipal Airport	64.3
21	Somerville 3 NW	61.7		22	Toms River	64.4
23	Atlantic City State Marina	61.0		23	Lambertville	64.6
24	Boonton 1 SE	60.9		24	Indian Mills 2 W	65.4
25	Long Valley	60.0		24	Pemberton	65.4

Annual Mean Temperature

Highest			Lowest		
Rank	Station Name	°F	Rank	Station Name	°F
1	Newark Int'l Airport	55.1	1	Newton Saint Pauls Abbey	48.2
2	Cape May 2 NW	55.0	2	Charlotteburg Reservoir	48.6
3	Woodstown	54.9	3	Long Valley	48.9
4	Atlantic City State Marina	54.8	4	Boonton 1 SE	50.7
5	Belleplain State Forest	54.7	5	Somerville 3 NW	50.8
6	Millville Municipal Airport	54.5	6	Essex Fells Serv Bldg	51.0
7	Seabrook Farms	54.4	7	Flemington 5 NNW	51.1
8	Glassboro 2 W	54.1	8	Canoe Brook	51.3
9	Tuckerton	54.0	9	Little Falls	52.3
10	Pemberton	53.9	10	New Brunswick 3 SE	52.5
11	Indian Mills 2 W	53.8	11	Hightstown 2 W	52.6
12	Atlantic City Int'l Airport	53.6	12	Toms River	53.0
13	Lambertville	53.3	13	Cranford	53.2
13	Plainfield	53.3	14	Lambertville	53.3
15	Cranford	53.2	14	Plainfield	53.3
16	Toms River	53.0	16	Atlantic City Int'l Airport	53.6
17	Hightstown 2 W	52.6	17	Indian Mills 2 W	53.8
18	New Brunswick 3 SE	52.5	18	Pemberton	53.9
19	Little Falls	52.3	19	Tuckerton	54.0
20	Canoe Brook	51.3	20	Glassboro 2 W	54.1
21	Flemington 5 NNW	51.1	21	Seabrook Farms	54.4
22	Essex Fells Serv Bldg	51.0	22	Millville Municipal Airport	54.5
23	Somerville 3 NW	50.8	23	Belleplain State Forest	54.7
24	Boonton 1 SE	50.7	24	Atlantic City State Marina	54.8
25	Long Valley	48.9	25	Woodstown	54.9

Annual Mean Minimum Temperature

Highest			Lowest		
Rank	Station Name	°F	Rank	Station Name	°F
1	Atlantic City State Marina	48.5	1	Newton Saint Pauls Abbey	36.9
2	Cape May 2 NW	47.0	2	Charlotteburg Reservoir	37.4
3	Newark Int'l Airport	46.8	3	Long Valley	37.7
4	Glassboro 2 W	44.8	4	Flemington 5 NNW	39.8
5	Seabrook Farms	44.7	5	Somerville 3 NW	39.9
6	Millville Municipal Airport	44.6	6	Canoe Brook	40.2
7	Woodstown	44.1	6	Essex Fells Serv Bldg	40.2
8	Tuckerton	44.0	8	Boonton 1 SE	40.4
9	Atlantic City Int'l Airport	43.4	9	Toms River	41.7
10	Plainfield	43.1	10	Cranford	42.0
11	Belleplain State Forest	43.0	10	Lambertville	42.0
12	New Brunswick 3 SE	42.5	12	Indian Mills 2 W	42.1
13	Hightstown 2 W	42.4	13	Pemberton	42.2
14	Little Falls	42.3	14	Little Falls	42.3
15	Pemberton	42.2	15	Hightstown 2 W	42.4
16	Indian Mills 2 W	42.1	16	New Brunswick 3 SE	42.5
17	Cranford	42.0	17	Belleplain State Forest	43.0
17	Lambertville	42.0	18	Plainfield	43.1
19	Toms River	41.7	19	Atlantic City Int'l Airport	43.4
20	Boonton 1 SE	40.4	20	Tuckerton	44.0
21	Canoe Brook	40.2	21	Woodstown	44.1
21	Essex Fells Serv Bldg	40.2	22	Millville Municipal Airport	44.6
23	Somerville 3 NW	39.9	23	Seabrook Farms	44.7
24	Flemington 5 NNW	39.8	24	Glassboro 2 W	44.8
25	Long Valley	37.7	25	Newark Int'l Airport	46.8

Annual Extreme Minimum Temperature

	Highest				Lowest	
Rank	Station Name	°F		Rank	Station Name	°F
1	Cape May 2 NW	-2		1	Newton Saint Pauls Abbey	-26
2	Atlantic City State Marina	-3		2	Charlotteburg Reservoir	-24
3	Tuckerton	-7		3	Toms River	-19
4	Glassboro 2 W	-8		4	Flemington 5 NNW	-18
4	Newark Int'l Airport	-8		4	Indian Mills 2 W	-18
4	Plainfield	-8		4	Long Valley	-18
7	Cranford	-10		7	Pemberton	-17
7	Little Falls	-10		8	Somerville 3 NW	-16
7	Millville Municipal Airport	-10		9	Boonton 1 SE	-15
10	Atlantic City Int'l Airport	-11		9	Canoe Brook	-15
10	Lambertville	-11		11	Belleplain State Forest	-14
12	Hightstown 2 W	-12		11	Essex Fells Serv Bldg	-14
13	New Brunswick 3 SE	-13		13	New Brunswick 3 SE	-13
13	Seabrook Farms	-13		13	Seabrook Farms	-13
13	Woodstown	-13		13	Woodstown	-13
16	Belleplain State Forest	-14		16	Hightstown 2 W	-12
16	Essex Fells Serv Bldg	-14		17	Atlantic City Int'l Airport	-11
18	Boonton 1 SE	-15		17	Lambertville	-11
18	Canoe Brook	-15		19	Cranford	-10
20	Somerville 3 NW	-16		19	Little Falls	-10
21	Pemberton	-17		19	Millville Municipal Airport	-10
22	Flemington 5 NNW	-18		22	Glassboro 2 W	-8
22	Indian Mills 2 W	-18		22	Newark Int'l Airport	-8
22	Long Valley	-18		22	Plainfield	-8
25	Toms River	-19		25	Tuckerton	-7

July Mean Maximum Temperature

	Highest				Lowest	
Rank	Station Name	°F		Rank	Station Name	°F
1	Woodstown	88.2		1	Atlantic City State Marina	80.6
2	Lambertville	87.6		2	Long Valley	81.9
3	Indian Mills 2 W	87.5		3	Charlotteburg Reservoir	82.6
4	Cranford	87.0		4	Newton Saint Pauls Abbey	83.0
4	Pemberton	87.0		5	Cape May 2 NW	83.7
6	Belleplain State Forest	86.7		6	Boonton 1 SE	83.9
7	Plainfield	86.6		7	Essex Fells Serv Bldg	84.7
8	Newark Int'l Airport	86.5		8	Somerville 3 NW	85.0
9	Toms River	86.3		9	Atlantic City Int'l Airport	85.1
10	Millville Municipal Airport	86.0		10	New Brunswick 3 SE	85.2
11	Flemington 5 NNW	85.9		11	Hightstown 2 W	85.5
11	Seabrook Farms	85.9		11	Tuckerton	85.5
13	Glassboro 2 W	85.8		13	Canoe Brook	85.6
13	Little Falls	85.8		14	Glassboro 2 W	85.8
15	Canoe Brook	85.6		14	Little Falls	85.8
16	Hightstown 2 W	85.5		16	Flemington 5 NNW	85.9
16	Tuckerton	85.5		16	Seabrook Farms	85.9
18	New Brunswick 3 SE	85.2		18	Millville Municipal Airport	86.0
19	Atlantic City Int'l Airport	85.1		19	Toms River	86.3
20	Somerville 3 NW	85.0		20	Newark Int'l Airport	86.5
21	Essex Fells Serv Bldg	84.7		21	Plainfield	86.6
22	Boonton 1 SE	83.9		22	Belleplain State Forest	86.7
23	Cape May 2 NW	83.7		23	Cranford	87.0
24	Newton Saint Pauls Abbey	83.0		23	Pemberton	87.0
25	Charlotteburg Reservoir	82.6		25	Indian Mills 2 W	87.5

January Mean Minimum Temperature

	Highest				Lowest	
Rank	Station Name	°F		Rank	Station Name	°F
1	Atlantic City State Marina	27.9		1	Newton Saint Pauls Abbey	14.2
2	Cape May 2 NW	27.0		2	Charlotteburg Reservoir	15.6
3	Newark Int'l Airport	24.3		3	Long Valley	16.6
4	Seabrook Farms	24.1		4	Boonton 1 SE	17.9
5	Millville Municipal Airport	24.0		4	Canoe Brook	17.9
6	Woodstown	23.7		6	Flemington 5 NNW	18.2
7	Belleplain State Forest	23.2		7	Somerville 3 NW	18.3
7	Glassboro 2 W	23.2		8	Essex Fells Serv Bldg	18.6
9	Atlantic City Int'l Airport	23.1		9	Little Falls	20.1
10	Tuckerton	22.9		10	Toms River	20.8
11	Plainfield	22.3		11	New Brunswick 3 SE	21.0
12	Pemberton	22.0		12	Lambertville	21.1
13	Indian Mills 2 W	21.8		13	Cranford	21.4
14	Cranford	21.4		13	Hightstown 2 W	21.4
14	Hightstown 2 W	21.4		15	Indian Mills 2 W	21.8
16	Lambertville	21.1		16	Pemberton	22.0
17	New Brunswick 3 SE	21.0		17	Plainfield	22.3
18	Toms River	20.8		18	Tuckerton	22.9
19	Little Falls	20.1		19	Atlantic City Int'l Airport	23.1
20	Essex Fells Serv Bldg	18.6		20	Belleplain State Forest	23.2
21	Somerville 3 NW	18.3		20	Glassboro 2 W	23.2
22	Flemington 5 NNW	18.2		22	Woodstown	23.7
23	Boonton 1 SE	17.9		23	Millville Municipal Airport	24.0
23	Canoe Brook	17.9		24	Seabrook Farms	24.1
25	Long Valley	16.6		25	Newark Int'l Airport	24.3

Number of Annual Heating Degree Days

	Highest				Lowest	
Rank	Station Name	Num.		Rank	Station Name	Num.
1	Newton Saint Pauls Abbey	6,561		1	Atlantic City State Marina	4,549
2	Charlotteburg Reservoir	6,404		2	Cape May 2 NW	4,570
3	Long Valley	6,261		3	Belleplain State Forest	4,686
4	Boonton 1 SE	5,853		4	Woodstown	4,720
5	Somerville 3 NW	5,812		5	Newark Int'l Airport	4,758
6	Essex Fells Serv Bldg	5,745		6	Millville Municipal Airport	4,828
7	Flemington 5 NNW	5,739		7	Seabrook Farms	4,846
8	Canoe Brook	5,735		8	Tuckerton	4,931
9	Little Falls	5,469		9	Pemberton	4,941
10	New Brunswick 3 SE	5,364		10	Glassboro 2 W	4,943
11	Hightstown 2 W	5,305		11	Indian Mills 2 W	4,999
12	Toms River	5,169		12	Atlantic City Int'l Airport	5,028
13	Lambertville	5,161		13	Cranford	5,141
14	Plainfield	5,153		14	Plainfield	5,153
15	Cranford	5,141		15	Lambertville	5,161
16	Atlantic City Int'l Airport	5,028		16	Toms River	5,169
17	Indian Mills 2 W	4,999		17	Hightstown 2 W	5,305
18	Glassboro 2 W	4,943		18	New Brunswick 3 SE	5,364
19	Pemberton	4,941		19	Little Falls	5,469
20	Tuckerton	4,931		20	Canoe Brook	5,735
21	Seabrook Farms	4,846		21	Flemington 5 NNW	5,739
22	Millville Municipal Airport	4,828		22	Essex Fells Serv Bldg	5,745
23	Newark Int'l Airport	4,758		23	Somerville 3 NW	5,812
24	Woodstown	4,720		24	Boonton 1 SE	5,853
25	Belleplain State Forest	4,686		25	Long Valley	6,261

Number of Annual Cooling Degree Days

Highest			Lowest		
Rank	Station Name	Num.	Rank	Station Name	Num.
1	Newark Int'l Airport	1,309	1	Long Valley	507
2	Woodstown	1,188	2	Charlotteburg Reservoir	535
3	Seabrook Farms	1,133	3	Newton Saint Pauls Abbey	559
4	Millville Municipal Airport	1,121	4	Essex Fells Serv Bldg	749
5	Glassboro 2 W	1,105	5	Boonton 1 SE	754
6	Tuckerton	1,075	6	Somerville 3 NW	756
7	Cape May 2 NW	1,074	7	Flemington 5 NNW	814
8	Belleplain State Forest	1,038	8	Canoe Brook	860
9	Indian Mills 2 W	1,035	9	Hightstown 2 W	908
10	Lambertville	1,022	10	New Brunswick 3 SE	918
11	Pemberton	1,012	11	Toms River	937
12	Plainfield	1,011	12	Little Falls	954
13	Atlantic City State Marina	1,001	13	Cranford	965
14	Atlantic City Int'l Airport	999	14	Atlantic City Int'l Airport	999
15	Cranford	965	15	Atlantic City State Marina	1,001
16	Little Falls	954	16	Plainfield	1,011
17	Toms River	937	17	Pemberton	1,012
18	New Brunswick 3 SE	918	18	Lambertville	1,022
19	Hightstown 2 W	908	19	Indian Mills 2 W	1,035
20	Canoe Brook	860	20	Belleplain State Forest	1,038
21	Flemington 5 NNW	814	21	Cape May 2 NW	1,074
22	Somerville 3 NW	756	22	Tuckerton	1,075
23	Boonton 1 SE	754	23	Glassboro 2 W	1,105
24	Essex Fells Serv Bldg	749	24	Millville Municipal Airport	1,121
25	Newton Saint Pauls Abbey	559	25	Seabrook Farms	1,133

Annual Precipitation

Highest			Lowest		
Rank	Station Name	Inches	Rank	Station Name	Inches
1	Long Valley	53.28	1	Atlantic City State Marina	37.82
2	Charlotteburg Reservoir	53.22	2	Atlantic City Int'l Airport	40.32
3	Essex Fells Serv Bldg	51.72	3	Cape May 2 NW	41.22
4	Little Falls	51.69	4	Millville Municipal Airport	43.29
5	Canoe Brook	51.47	5	Belleplain State Forest	44.32
6	Cranford	50.93	6	Seabrook Farms	44.69
7	Boonton 1 SE	50.82	7	Tuckerton	45.32
8	Flemington 5 NNW	49.58	8	Woodstown	45.49
9	Plainfield	49.50	9	Glassboro 2 W	45.63
10	Lambertville	48.97	10	Newark Int'l Airport	45.98
11	New Brunswick 3 SE	48.66	11	Indian Mills 2 W	46.84
12	Toms River	48.63	12	Newton Saint Pauls Abbey	47.25
13	Somerville 3 NW	48.14	13	Hightstown 2 W	47.30
14	Pemberton	47.37	14	Pemberton	47.37
15	Hightstown 2 W	47.30	15	Somerville 3 NW	48.14
16	Newton Saint Pauls Abbey	47.25	16	Toms River	48.63
17	Indian Mills 2 W	46.84	17	New Brunswick 3 SE	48.66
18	Newark Int'l Airport	45.98	18	Lambertville	48.97
19	Glassboro 2 W	45.63	19	Plainfield	49.50
20	Woodstown	45.49	20	Flemington 5 NNW	49.58
21	Tuckerton	45.32	21	Boonton 1 SE	50.82
22	Seabrook Farms	44.69	22	Cranford	50.93
23	Belleplain State Forest	44.32	23	Canoe Brook	51.47
24	Millville Municipal Airport	43.29	24	Little Falls	51.69
25	Cape May 2 NW	41.22	25	Essex Fells Serv Bldg	51.72

Number of Days Annually With ≥ 0.1" Precipitation

	Highest			Lowest	
Rank	**Station Name**	**Days**	**Rank**	**Station Name**	**Days**
1	Long Valley	84	1	Atlantic City State Marina	70
2	Cranford	82	2	Millville Municipal Airport	72
2	Lambertville	82	3	Belleplain State Forest	73
2	Plainfield	82	3	Cape May 2 NW	73
2	Somerville 3 NW	82	5	Atlantic City Int'l Airport	74
6	Boonton 1 SE	81	5	Tuckerton	74
6	Newton Saint Pauls Abbey	81	7	Seabrook Farms	75
8	Charlotteburg Reservoir	80	7	Woodstown	75
8	Flemington 5 NNW	80	9	Essex Fells Serv Bldg	76
8	Hightstown 2 W	80	10	Glassboro 2 W	77
8	Little Falls	80	10	Indian Mills 2 W	77
8	Toms River	80	10	Newark Int'l Airport	77
13	Canoe Brook	79	13	Canoe Brook	79
13	New Brunswick 3 SE	79	13	New Brunswick 3 SE	79
13	Pemberton	79	13	Pemberton	79
16	Glassboro 2 W	77	16	Charlotteburg Reservoir	80
16	Indian Mills 2 W	77	16	Flemington 5 NNW	80
16	Newark Int'l Airport	77	16	Hightstown 2 W	80
19	Essex Fells Serv Bldg	76	16	Little Falls	80
20	Seabrook Farms	75	16	Toms River	80
20	Woodstown	75	21	Boonton 1 SE	81
22	Atlantic City Int'l Airport	74	21	Newton Saint Pauls Abbey	81
22	Tuckerton	74	23	Cranford	82
24	Belleplain State Forest	73	23	Lambertville	82
24	Cape May 2 NW	73	23	Plainfield	82

Number of Days Annually With ≥ 1.0" Precipitation

	Highest			Lowest	
Rank	**Station Name**	**Days**	**Rank**	**Station Name**	**Days**
1	Charlotteburg Reservoir	16	1	Atlantic City State Marina	11
2	Boonton 1 SE	14	1	Newton Saint Pauls Abbey	11
2	Essex Fells Serv Bldg	14	1	Somerville 3 NW	11
2	Long Valley	14	4	Atlantic City Int'l Airport	12
5	Belleplain State Forest	13	4	Canoe Brook	12
5	Cranford	13	4	Cape May 2 NW	12
5	Flemington 5 NNW	13	4	Glassboro 2 W	12
5	Hightstown 2 W	13	4	Indian Mills 2 W	12
5	Lambertville	13	4	Millville Municipal Airport	12
5	Little Falls	13	4	Newark Int'l Airport	12
5	New Brunswick 3 SE	13	4	Seabrook Farms	12
5	Pemberton	13	4	Tuckerton	12
5	Plainfield	13	4	Woodstown	12
5	Toms River	13	14	Belleplain State Forest	13
15	Atlantic City Int'l Airport	12	14	Cranford	13
15	Canoe Brook	12	14	Flemington 5 NNW	13
15	Cape May 2 NW	12	14	Hightstown 2 W	13
15	Glassboro 2 W	12	14	Lambertville	13
15	Indian Mills 2 W	12	14	Little Falls	13
15	Millville Municipal Airport	12	14	New Brunswick 3 SE	13
15	Newark Int'l Airport	12	14	Pemberton	13
15	Seabrook Farms	12	14	Plainfield	13
15	Tuckerton	12	14	Toms River	13
15	Woodstown	12	24	Boonton 1 SE	14
25	Atlantic City State Marina	11	24	Essex Fells Serv Bldg	14

Annual Snowfall

	Highest			Lowest	
Rank	Station Name	Inches	Rank	Station Name	Inches
1	Newton Saint Pauls Abbey	37.8	1	Belleplain State Forest	9.5
2	Charlotteburg Reservoir	34.5	2	Millville Municipal Airport	13.2
3	Long Valley	33.7	3	Atlantic City Int'l Airport	13.3
4	Flemington 5 NNW	28.8	4	Cape May 2 NW	13.5
5	Boonton 1 SE	28.2	5	Woodstown	16.5
6	Somerville 3 NW	27.5	6	Essex Fells Serv Bldg	16.7
7	Plainfield	26.6	7	Pemberton	16.9
8	New Brunswick 3 SE	26.4	8	Indian Mills 2 W	17.2
9	Canoe Brook	25.6	9	Tuckerton	17.9
10	Newark Int'l Airport	24.9	10	Lambertville	20.4
11	Hightstown 2 W	22.0	11	Cranford	20.6
12	Cranford	20.6	12	Hightstown 2 W	22.0
13	Lambertville	20.4	13	Newark Int'l Airport	24.9
14	Tuckerton	17.9	14	Canoe Brook	25.6
15	Indian Mills 2 W	17.2	15	New Brunswick 3 SE	26.4
16	Pemberton	16.9	16	Plainfield	26.6
17	Essex Fells Serv Bldg	16.7	17	Somerville 3 NW	27.5
18	Woodstown	16.5	18	Boonton 1 SE	28.2
19	Cape May 2 NW	13.5	19	Flemington 5 NNW	28.8
20	Atlantic City Int'l Airport	13.3	20	Long Valley	33.7
21	Millville Municipal Airport	13.2	21	Charlotteburg Reservoir	34.5
22	Belleplain State Forest	9.5	22	Newton Saint Pauls Abbey	37.8

Note: See User's Guide for explanation of data.

Deadliest Storm Events in New Jersey: April 1981 - April 2006

Rank	Location or County	Date	Storm Event	Fatalities	Injuries	Property Damage ($mil.)	Crop Damage ($mil.)
1	Camden, Mercer, Middlesex, Monmouth, Ocean, and Somerset Counties	7/4/1999	Excessive Heat	17	160	0.0	0.0
2	Statewide	7/1/1995	Unseasonably Warm	10	0	0.0	0.0
3	Northeastern New Jersey	7/4/1999	Excessive Heat	10	0	0.0	0.0
4	Southwestern and West Central New Jersey	7/13/1995	Heat Wave	7	0	0.0	0.0
5	Eastern Monmouth County	8/14/1995	Rip Currents/Heavy Surf	4	0	0.0	0.0
6	Northwestern New Jersey	1/28/2005	Extreme Cold/Wind Chill	4	0	0.0	0.0
7	Statewide	1/7/1996	Blizzard	3	0	18.8	0.0
8	Hunterdon County	3/18/1989	Thunderstorm Wind	2	0	0.0	0.0
9	Coastal New Jersey	8/29/1996	Rough Surf	2	1	0.0	0.0
10	Bergen County	9/16/1999	Flood	2	0	17.5	0.0
11	Somerset County	9/16/1999	Flash Flood	2	100	358.0	0.0
12	Statewide	8/6/2001	Excessive Heat	2	0	0.0	0.0
13	Statewide	9/11/2002	Wind	2	2	0.0	0.0
14	Walpack Township	8/10/2003	Heavy Rain	2	0	0.0	0.0
15	Southern New Jersey	7/18/2005	Excessive Heat	2	0	0.0	0.0

Most Destructive Storm Events in New Jersey: April 1981 - April 2006

Rank	Location or County	Date	Storm Event	Fatalities	Injuries	Property Damage ($mil.)	Crop Damage ($mil.)
1	Somerset County	9/16/1999	Flash Flood	2	100	358.0	0.0
2	Southeastern Sussex and Western Morris Counties	8/12/2000	Flood	0	0	166.5	0.0
3	Atlantic County	8/20/1997	Flash Flood	0	0	54.0	0.0
4	Burlington County	7/12/2004	Flash Flood	0	0	50.0	0.0
5	Mercer County	9/16/1999	Flash Flood	0	5	32.0	0.0
6	Somerset County	10/19/1996	Flash Flood	0	0	31.0	0.0
7	Morris County	9/16/1999	Flash Flood	0	6	30.0	0.0
8	Hunterdon County	4/2/2005	Flood	0	0	30.0	0.0
9	Middlesex County	9/16/1999	Flash Flood	0	72	28.0	0.0
10	Warren County	9/18/2004	Flood	0	0	28.0	0.0
11	Central New Jersey	1/7/1996	Blizzard	3	0	18.8	0.0
12	Bergen County	9/16/1999	Flood	2	0	17.5	0.0
13	Coastal New Jersey	2/4/1998	Coastal Flooding/Erosion	0	0	17.0	0.0
14	Statewide	1/22/2005	Winter Storm	0	0	16.2	0.0
15	Coastal New Jersey	1/28/1998	Coastal Flooding/Erosion	0	0	15.0	0.0
16	Coastal New Jersey	1/7/1996	Erosion/Coastal Flood	0	0	14.2	0.0
17	Morris County	8/12/2000	Flood	0	0	12.0	0.0
18	Bergen, Essex, Hudson, Passaic, and Union Counties	4/2/2005	Flood	0	0	12.0	0.0
19	Southern New Jersey	2/16/2003	Winter Storm	0	2	11.5	0.0
20	Sykesville	6/22/1996	Thunderstorm Wind	0	0	11.0	1.0
21	Mercer, Middlesex, Monmouth, Morris, Somerset, Sussex, and Warren Counties	1/22/2005	Heavy Snow	0	0	11.0	0.0
22	Camden, Hunterdon, Mercer, Morris, Somerset, Sussex, and Warren Counties	1/19/1996	Flood	0	1	10.7	0.0
23	Southeastern Middlesex County	7/17/2005	Flash Flood	0	0	10.3	0.0
24	Monmouth County	8/2/2002	Thunderstorm Wind (72 kts.)	0	0	10.2	0.0

NEW JERSEY

nationalatlas.gov™
Where We Are

CONGRESSIONAL DISTRICTS
109th Congress (January 2005 - January 2007)

The Constitution prescribes Congressional apportionment based on decennial census population data. Each state has at least one Representative, no matter how small its population. Since 1941, distribution of Representatives has been based on total U.S. population, so that the average population per Representative has the least possible variation between one state and any other. Congress fixes the number of voting Representatives at each apportionment. States delineate the district boundaries. The first House of Representatives in 1789 had 65 members; currently there are 435. There are non-voting delegates from American Samoa, the District of Columbia, Guam, Puerto Rico, and the Virgin Islands.

CONNECTICUT

NEW YORK

NEW YORK

NEW YORK

ATLANTIC OCEAN

PENNSYLVANIA

MARYLAND

DELAWARE

Sussex
Passaic
Warren
Morris
Bergen
Hunterdon
Somerset
Union
Essex
Hudson
Middlesex
Mercer
Monmouth
Burlington
Ocean
Camden
Gloucester
Salem
Atlantic
Cumberland
Cape May

5
11
8
9
10
13
6
7
12
4
3
1
2

Paterson
Newark
Jersey City
Elizabeth
New Brunswick
Trenton
Asbury Park
Toms River
Ocean
Camden
Glassboro
Salem
Salem
Bridgeton
Vineland
Millville
Atlantic City
Ocean City
Cape May

Delaware Bay

1
2
3
4
5
6
7
8
9
10
11
12
13

MILES
0 10 20 30 40
Albers equal area projection

The **National Atlas** of the United States of America®

U.S. Department of the Interior
U.S. Geological Survey

NEW JERSEY - Core Based Statistical Areas and Counties

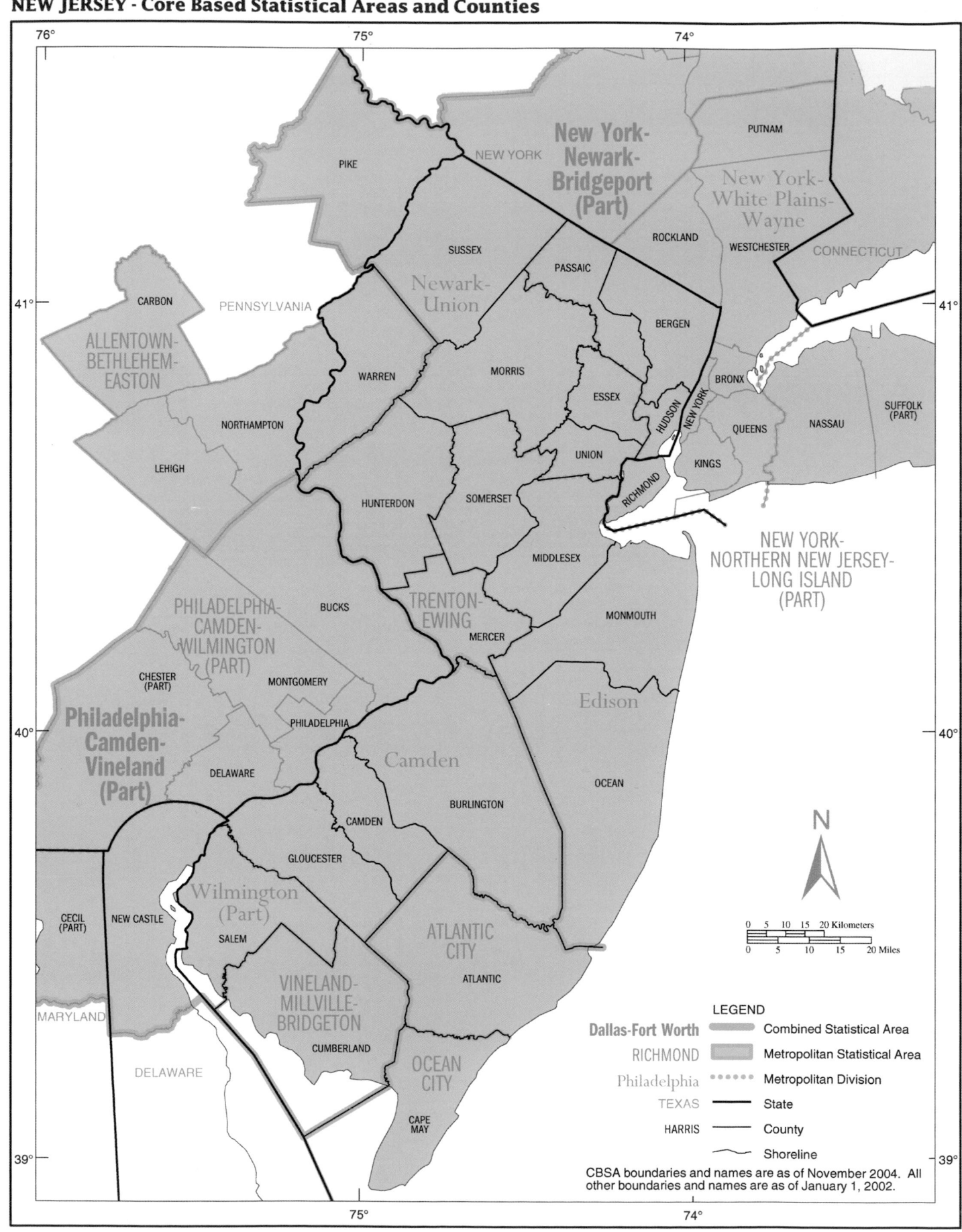

Population (2005)

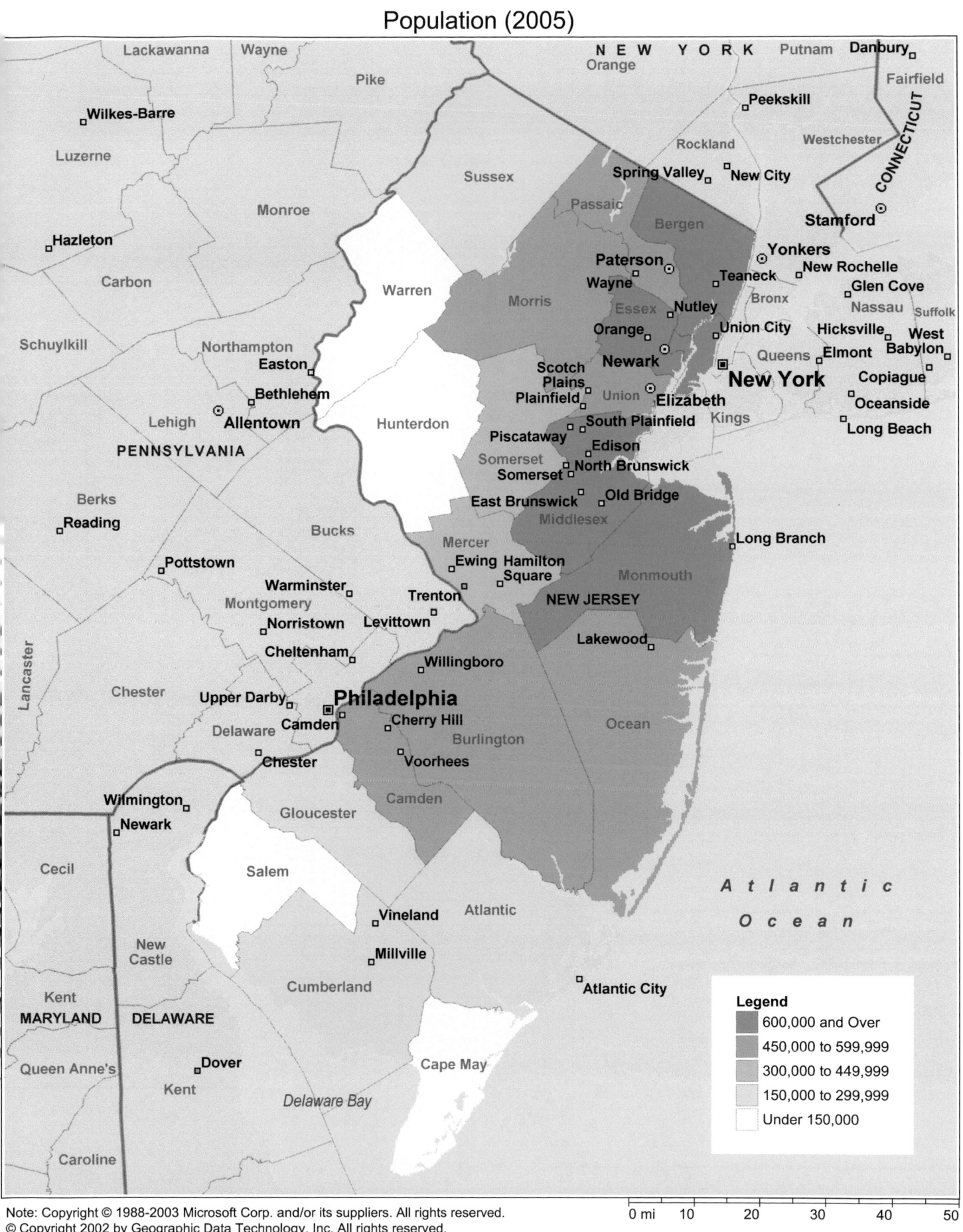

Legend

- 600,000 and Over
- 450,000 to 599,999
- 300,000 to 449,999
- 150,000 to 299,999
- Under 150,000

0 mi 10 20 30 40 50

Percent White (2005)

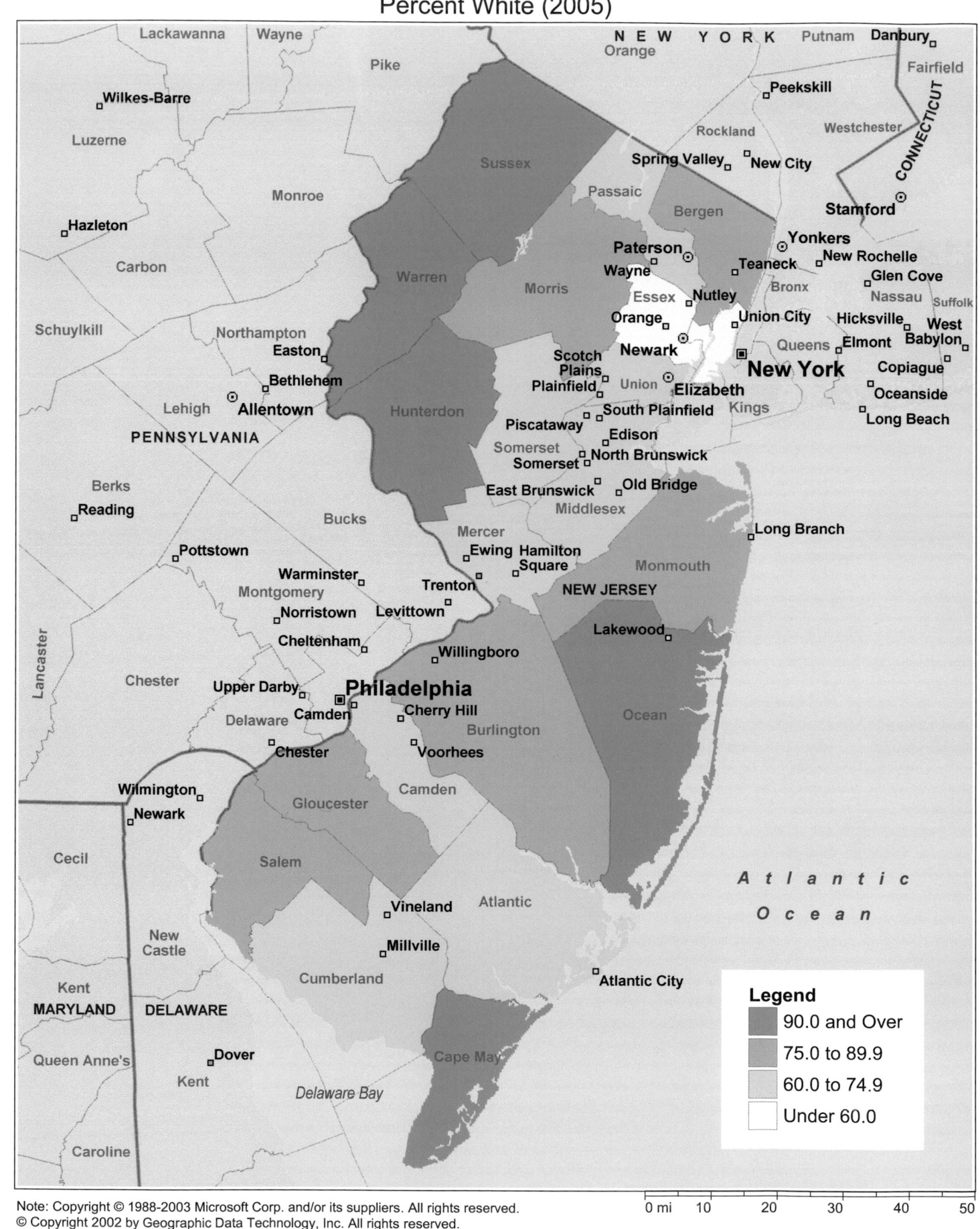

Legend

- 90.0 and Over
- 75.0 to 89.9
- 60.0 to 74.9
- Under 60.0

0 mi   10   20   30   40   50

Percent Black (2005)

Lackawanna | Wayne | Pike | **N E W   Y O R K** | Orange | Putnam | **Danbury** | Fairfield

Wilkes-Barre | Sussex | Rockland | Peekskill | Westchester | CONNECTICUT

Luzerne | Monroe | Warren | Morris | Passaic | Bergen | Spring Valley | New City | Stamford

Hazleton | Carbon | | | | | Paterson | Wayne | Teaneck | Yonkers | New Rochelle | Glen Cove | Nassau | Suffolk

Schuylkill | Northampton | Easton | Essex | Nutley | Bronx | Union City | Hicksville | West Babylon

Lehigh | Bethlehem | Allentown | Hunterdon | Orange | Newark | Queens | Elmont | Copiague

PENNSYLVANIA | Scotch Plains | Plainfield | Union | Elizabeth | New York | Oceanside | Long Beach

Berks | | South Plainfield | Kings

Reading | Bucks | Piscataway | Edison | Somerset | North Brunswick

Pottstown | Somerset | Somerset | Old Bridge

Warminster | Montgomery | East Brunswick | Middlesex | Long Branch

Norristown | Levittown | Mercer | Ewing | Hamilton Square | Monmouth

Lancaster | Cheltenham | Trenton | NEW JERSEY

Chester | Willingboro | Lakewood

Upper Darby | Philadelphia | Cherry Hill | Burlington | Ocean

Delaware | Camden | Voorhees

Wilmington | Chester | Camden

Newark | Gloucester | Atlantic

Cecil | Salem | **A t l a n t i c**

New Castle | Vineland | Atlantic | **O c e a n**

Kent | Millville

MARYLAND | DELAWARE | Cumberland | Atlantic City

Queen Anne's | Dover | Cape May

Caroline | Kent | Delaware Bay

Legend
- 15.0 and Over
- 10.0 to 14.9
- 5.0 to 9.9
- Under 5.0

0 mi   10   20   30   40   50

Percent Asian (2005)

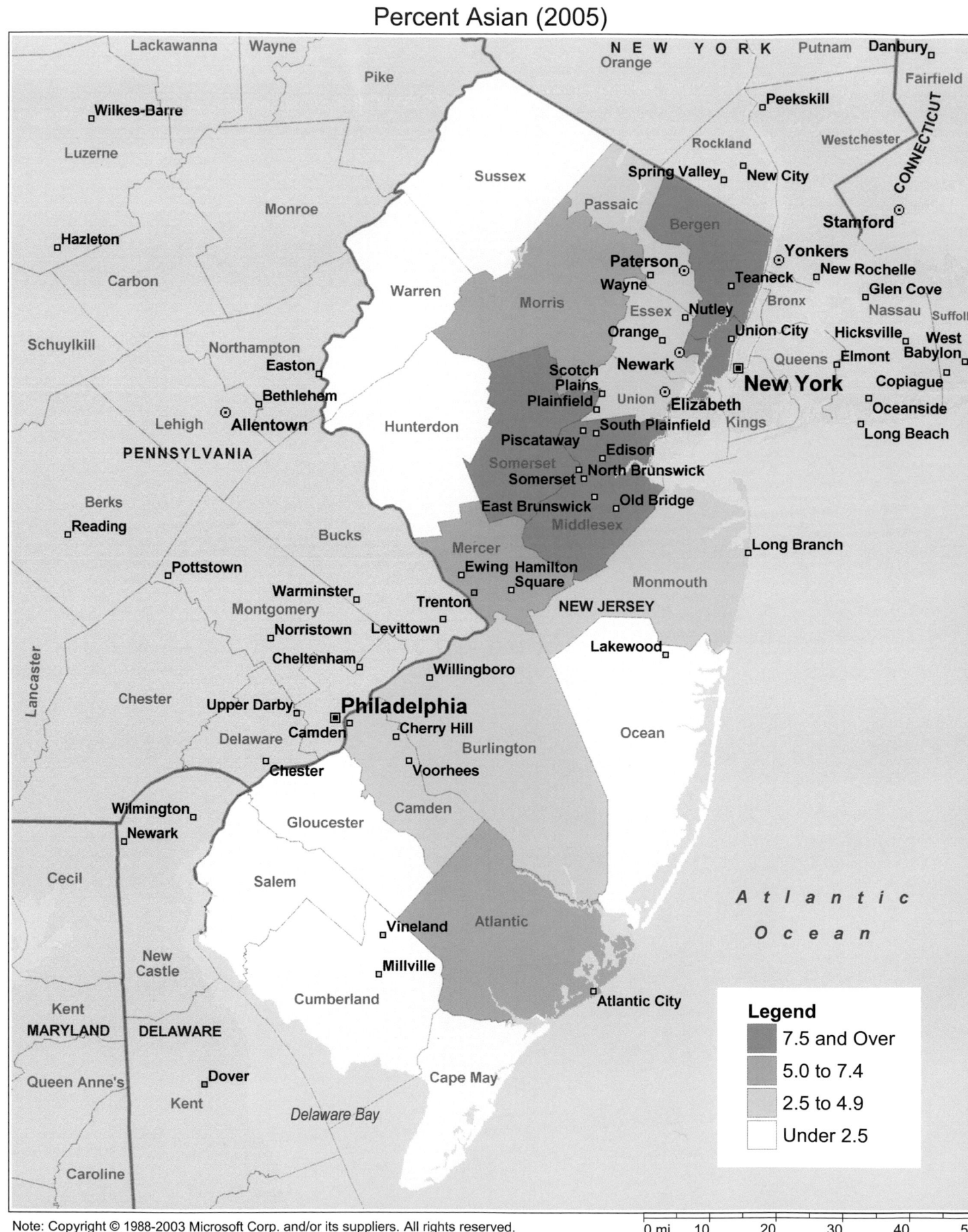

Legend
- 7.5 and Over
- 5.0 to 7.4
- 2.5 to 4.9
- Under 2.5

Percent Hispanic (2005)

N E W   Y O R K

Lackawanna
Wayne
Orange
Putnam
Danbury
Fairfield
Pike
Peekskill
Wilkes-Barre
Rockland
Westchester
CONNECTICUT
Luzerne
Sussex
Spring Valley
New City
Monroe
Passaic
Bergen
Stamford
Hazleton
Yonkers
New Rochelle
Carbon
Warren
Morris
Paterson
Wayne
Teaneck
Glen Cove
Nassau
Suffolk
Schuylkill
Northampton
Essex
Nutley
Bronx
Easton
Orange
Newark
Union City
Hicksville
West Babylon
Bethlehem
Scotch Plains
Queens
Elmont
Lehigh
Allentown
Plainfield
Union
Elizabeth
Copiague
PENNSYLVANIA
Hunterdon
South Plainfield
Kings
Oceanside
Piscataway
Edison
Long Beach
Somerset
North Brunswick
Berks
Somerset
New York
Reading
Bucks
East Brunswick
Old Bridge
Middlesex
Pottstown
Mercer
Ewing Hamilton Square
Long Branch
Warminster
Monmouth
Montgomery
Trenton
NEW JERSEY
Norristown
Levittown
Cheltenham
Lakewood
Willingboro
Lancaster
Chester
Upper Darby
Philadelphia
Delaware
Camden
Cherry Hill
Burlington
Ocean
Chester
Voorhees
Wilmington
Camden
Newark
Gloucester
Cecil
Salem
Atlantic Ocean
New Castle
Vineland
Atlantic
Millville
Kent
MARYLAND
DELAWARE
Cumberland
Atlantic City
Queen Anne's
Dover
Kent
Cape May
Caroline
Delaware Bay

Legend
15.0 and Over
10.0 to 14.9
5.0 to 9.9
Under 5.0

0 mi   10   20   30   40   50

Average Household Size (2005)

NEW YORK

Lackawanna
Wayne
Orange
Putnam
Danbury
Fairfield

Pike

Wilkes-Barre
Peekskill

Luzerne
Rockland
Westchester
CONNECTICUT

Monroe
Bergen
Stamford

Hazleton
Carbon
Spring Valley
New City

Warren
Passaic
Yonkers
New Rochelle

Schuylkill
Morris
Paterson
Teaneck
Glen Cove

Northampton
Wayne
Nassau
Suffolk

Easton
Essex
Nutley
Bronx

Bethlehem
Orange
Union City
Hicksville
West Babylon

Lehigh
Allentown
Newark
Queens
Elmont

PENNSYLVANIA
Scotch Plains
New York
Copiague

Berks
Hunterdon
Plainfield
Union
Elizabeth
Kings
Oceanside

Reading
Piscataway
South Plainfield
Long Beach

Somerset
Edison

Somerset
North Brunswick

Bucks
East Brunswick
Old Bridge

Pottstown
Mercer
Middlesex

Warminster
Ewing
Hamilton Square
Long Branch

Montgomery
Trenton
Monmouth

Norristown
Levittown
NEW JERSEY

Cheltenham
Lakewood

Chester
Willingboro

Upper Darby
Philadelphia
Cherry Hill
Burlington
Ocean

Delaware
Camden

Chester
Voorhees

Wilmington
Gloucester
Camden

Newark
Salem

Cecil
Atlantic
Atlantic Ocean

New Castle
Vineland

Kent
Millville

MARYLAND
DELAWARE
Cumberland
Atlantic City

Queen Anne's
Dover

Kent
Cape May

Caroline
Delaware Bay

Legend

■	2.80 and Over
■	2.70 to 2.79
■	2.60 to 2.69
□	Under 2.60

0 mi   10   20   30   40   50

Median Age (2005)

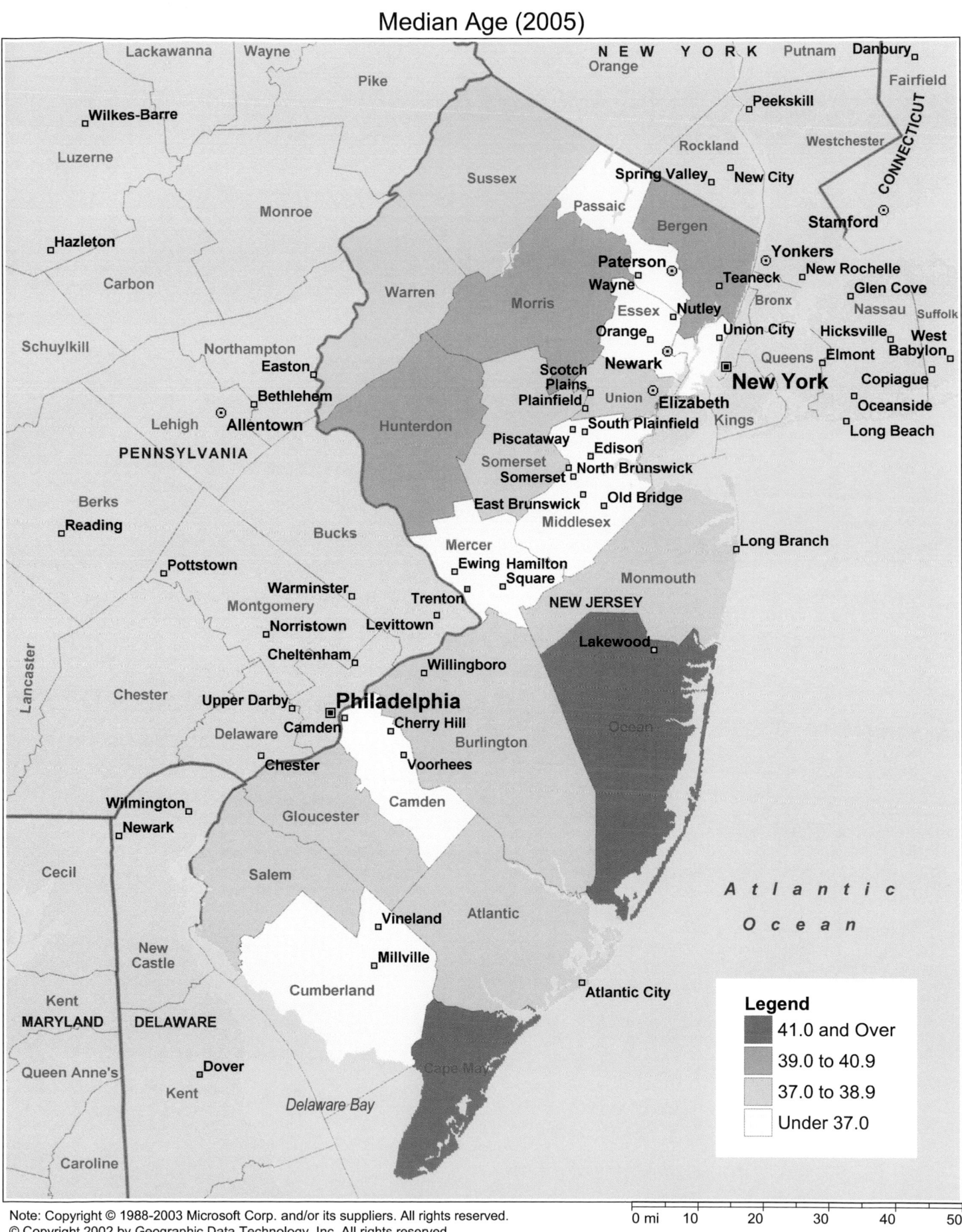

Legend

- 41.0 and Over
- 39.0 to 40.9
- 37.0 to 38.9
- Under 37.0

Median Household Income (2005)

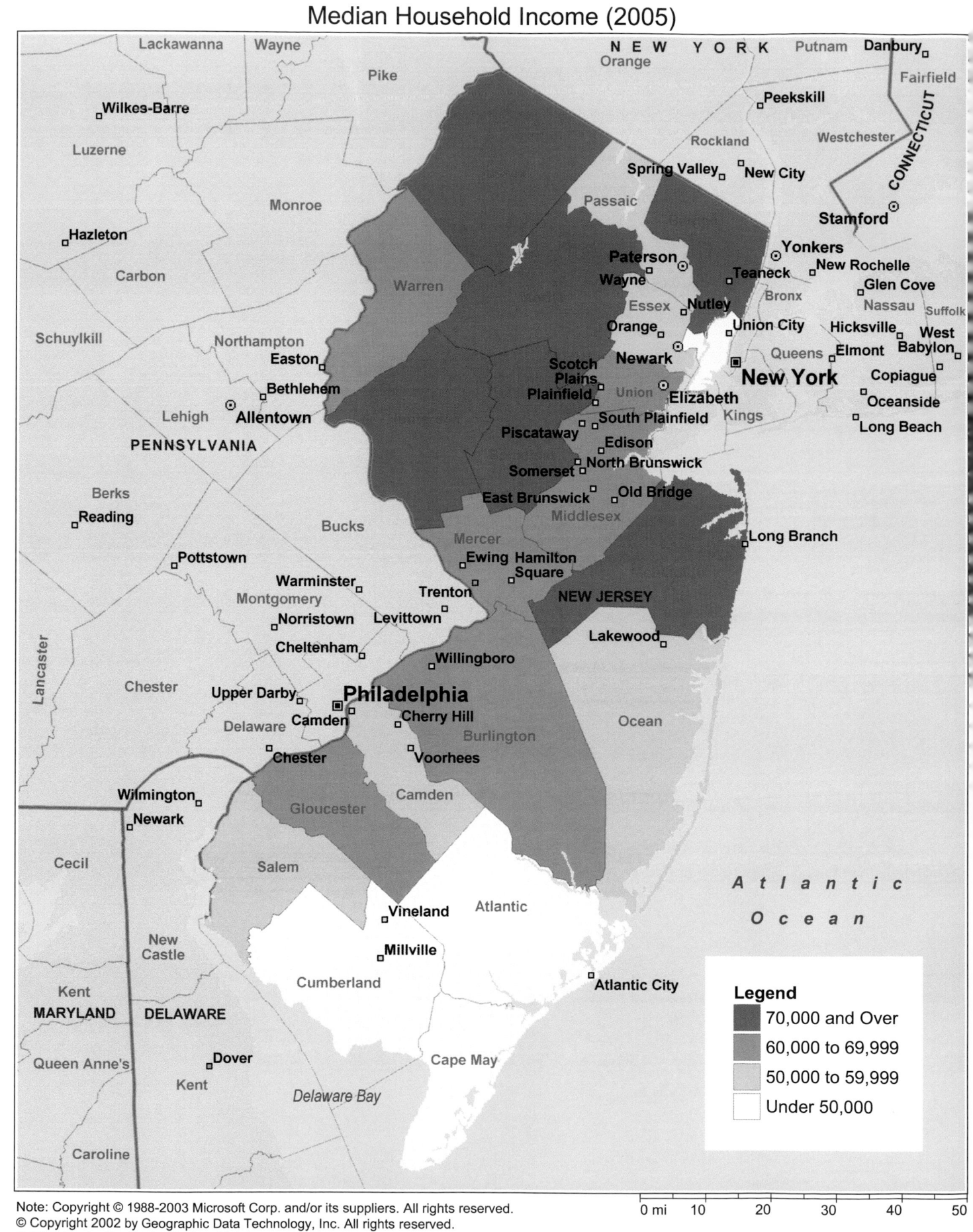

Percent of Population Living Below Poverty Level (2003)

NEW YORK

Lackawanna
Wayne
Orange
Putnam
Danbury
Fairfield

Pike

Wilkes-Barre
Sussex
Peekskill
Rockland
Westchester
CONNECTICUT

Luzerne
Monroe
Spring Valley
New City

Hazleton
Bergen
Stamford

Carbon
Warren
Morris
Paterson
Wayne
Yonkers
New Rochelle
Teaneck
Glen Cove

Schuylkill
Bronx
Nassau
Suffolk

Northampton
Nutley
Hicksville
West
Babylon

Easton
Orange
Union City
Elmont

Bethlehem
Scotch
Plains
Newark
Queens
Copiague

Lehigh
Allentown
Plainfield
Union
Elizabeth
New York
Oceanside

PENNSYLVANIA
Hunterdon
South Plainfield
Kings
Long Beach

Piscataway
Edison

Somerset
North Brunswick

Berks
Somerset
Old Bridge

Reading
East Brunswick
Middlesex

Bucks
Mercer
Long Branch

Pottstown
Ewing
Hamilton
Square
Monmouth

Warminster
Trenton
NEW JERSEY

Montgomery
Norristown
Levittown
Lakewood

Lancaster
Cheltenham

Chester
Willingboro
Ocean

Upper Darby
Philadelphia
Cherry Hill
Burlington

Wilmington
Delaware
Camden

Newark
Chester
Voorhees

Cecil
Gloucester

Salem
Atlantic
Ocean

New
Castle
Vineland

Millville

Kent
MARYLAND
DELAWARE
Atlantic City

Queen Anne's
Dover
Cape May

Kent
Delaware Bay

Caroline

Legend

■	10.0 and Over
■	7.5 to 9.9
■	5.0 to 7.4
□	Under 5.0

0 mi   10   20   30   40   50

Median Home Value (2005)

NEW YORK
Orange · Putnam · Danbury
Fairfield

Lackawanna · Wayne
Pike

Wilkes-Barre
Peekskill
Rockland · Westchester
CONNECTICUT

Luzerne
Sussex
Passaic
Spring Valley · New City

Monroe
Stamford

Hazleton
Warren
Paterson · Yonkers · New Rochelle
Wayne · Teaneck · Glen Cove
Bronx · Nassau · Suffolk
Nutley

Carbon
Essex
Orange · Union City · Hicksville · West Babylon
Newark · Queens · Elmont

Schuylkill
Northampton
Scotch Plains · Elizabeth · Copiague
Easton
Plainfield · Union · Kings · Oceanside
Bethlehem · South Plainfield · Long Beach
New York

Lehigh · Allentown
Piscataway
Edison

PENNSYLVANIA
Somerset · North Brunswick
East Brunswick · Old Bridge
Middlesex

Berks
Bucks
Mercer
Reading
Long Branch
Ewing · Hamilton Square

Pottstown
Trenton · NEW JERSEY
Warminster
Montgomery · Levittown
Norristown · Lakewood
Cheltenham · Willingboro

Lancaster
Chester
Upper Darby · Philadelphia · Cherry Hill
Camden · Burlington
Delaware · Ocean
Chester · Voorhees

Wilmington · Camden
Newark

Cecil
Salem · Atlantic

New Castle
Vineland

Kent
Millville
MARYLAND · DELAWARE
Atlantic City

Queen Anne's
Dover
Cape May
Kent

Caroline
Delaware Bay

Atlantic Ocean

Legend

■	300,000 and Over
■	250,000 to 299,999
■	200,000 to 249,999
□	Under 200,000

0 mi   10   20   30   40   50

Median Home Value (2005)

NEW YORK

Lackawanna
Wayne
Pike
Orange
Putnam
Danbury
Fairfield

Wilkes-Barre
Luzerne
Sussex
Rockland
Westchester
Peekskill

Hazleton
Carbon
Monroe
Warren
Passaic
Spring Valley
New City

CONNECTICUT

Stamford

Schuylkill
Northampton
Easton
Bethlehem
Paterson
Wayne
Essex
Nutley
Bronx

Yonkers
New Rochelle
Glen Cove
Nassau
Suffolk

Lehigh
Allentown
Orange
Newark
Union City
Hicksville
West Babylon
Elmont
Queens

PENNSYLVANIA

Scotch Plains
Plainfield
Union
Elizabeth
Kings

Copiague
Oceanside
Long Beach

Berks
Reading
Bucks
Piscataway
South Plainfield
Edison
North Brunswick
Somerset
East Brunswick
Old Bridge
Middlesex

Long Branch

Pottstown
Warminster
Montgomery
Norristown
Levittown
Trenton
Mercer
Ewing
Hamilton Square

NEW JERSEY

Cheltenham
Willingboro
Lakewood

Lancaster
Chester
Upper Darby
Camden
Philadelphia
Cherry Hill
Burlington
Voorhees

Delaware
Chester
Ocean

Wilmington
Newark
Gloucester
Camden

Cecil
New Castle
Salem
Atlantic

Atlantic Ocean

Vineland
Millville

Kent
MARYLAND
DELAWARE
Cumberland
Atlantic City

Queen Anne's
Dover
Kent
Cape May

Caroline
Delaware Bay

Legend

■	300,000 and Over
■	250,000 to 299,999
■	200,000 to 249,999
□	Under 200,000

0 mi   10   20   30   40   50

High School Graduates* (2005)

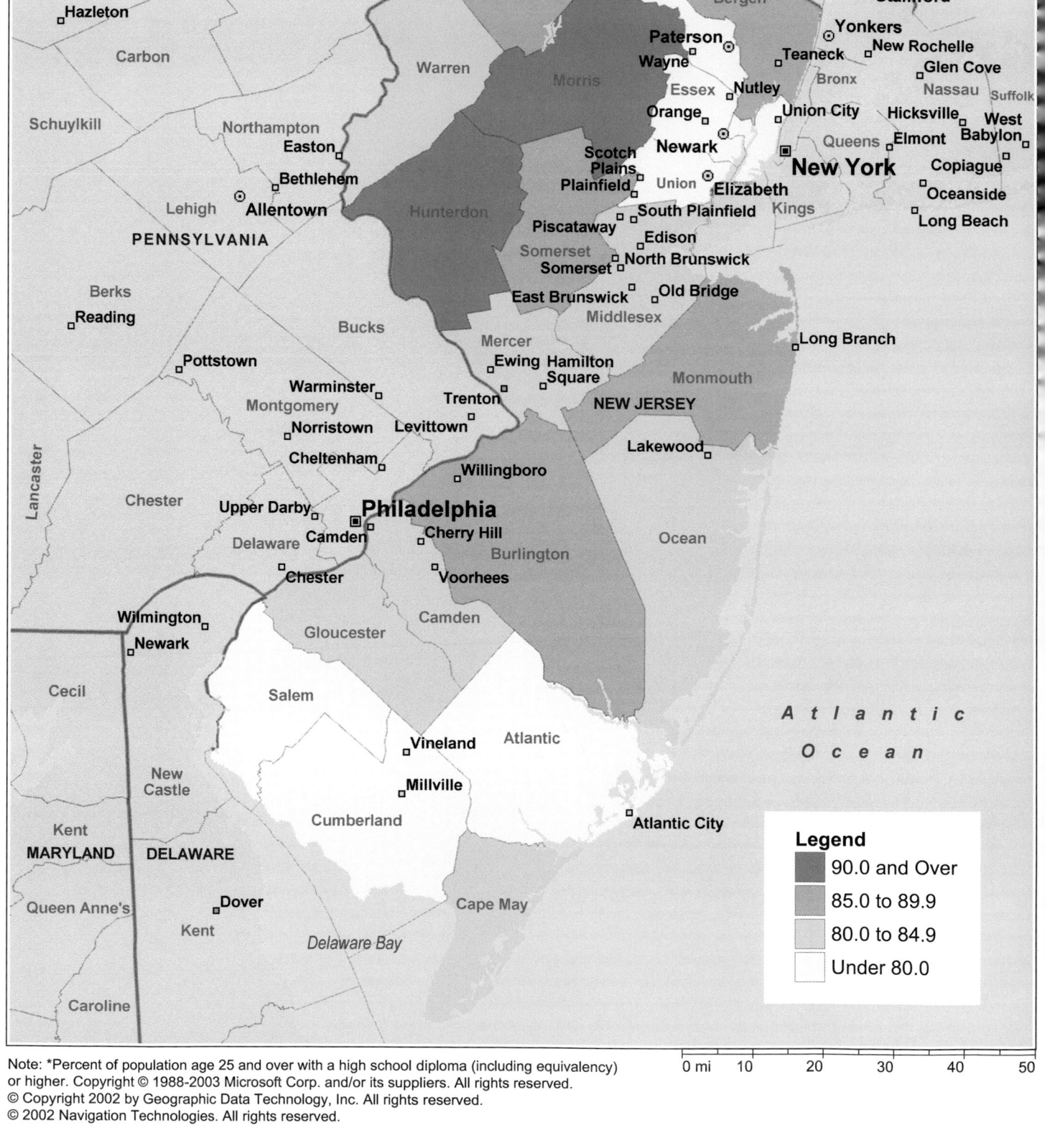

Legend

- 90.0 and Over
- 85.0 to 89.9
- 80.0 to 84.9
- Under 80.0

0 mi 10 20 30 40 50

College Graduates* (2005)

NEW YORK

Lackawanna Wayne
Orange Putnam Danbury
Pike Fairfield
Wilkes-Barre
Peekskill
Luzerne Monroe Rockland Westchester
Hazleton Spring Valley New City
Carbon Sussex Bergen Stamford
Schuylkill Warren Yonkers
Northampton Morris Paterson Teaneck New Rochelle
Easton Wayne Glen Cove
Bethlehem Essex Nutley Bronx Nassau Suffolk
Lehigh Allentown Orange Union City Hicksville West Babylon
PENNSYLVANIA Hunterdon Newark Queens Elmont
Scotch Plains Union New York Copiague
Berks Plainfield Elizabeth Oceanside
Reading South Plainfield Kings Long Beach
Piscataway Somerset Edison
Bucks Somerset North Brunswick
East Brunswick Old Bridge
Pottstown Mercer Middlesex
Warminster Ewing Hamilton Monmouth Long Branch
Montgomery Trenton Square
Norristown Levittown NEW JERSEY
Cheltenham Lakewood
Willingboro
Chester Upper Darby Philadelphia Ocean
Delaware Camden Cherry Hill
Chester Voorhees Burlington
Lancaster Wilmington Camden
Newark Gloucester Atlantic
Cecil Salem Ocean
New Castle Vineland Atlantic
Millville
Kent Cumberland Atlantic City
MARYLAND DELAWARE
Queen Anne's Dover
Kent Cape May
Delaware Bay
Caroline

Legend
30.0 and Over
25.0 to 29.9
20.0 to 24.9
Under 20.0

Note: *Percent of population age 25 and over with a Bachelor's Degree or higher.

0 mi 10 20 30 40 50

Percent of Population Who Voted for George Bush in 2004

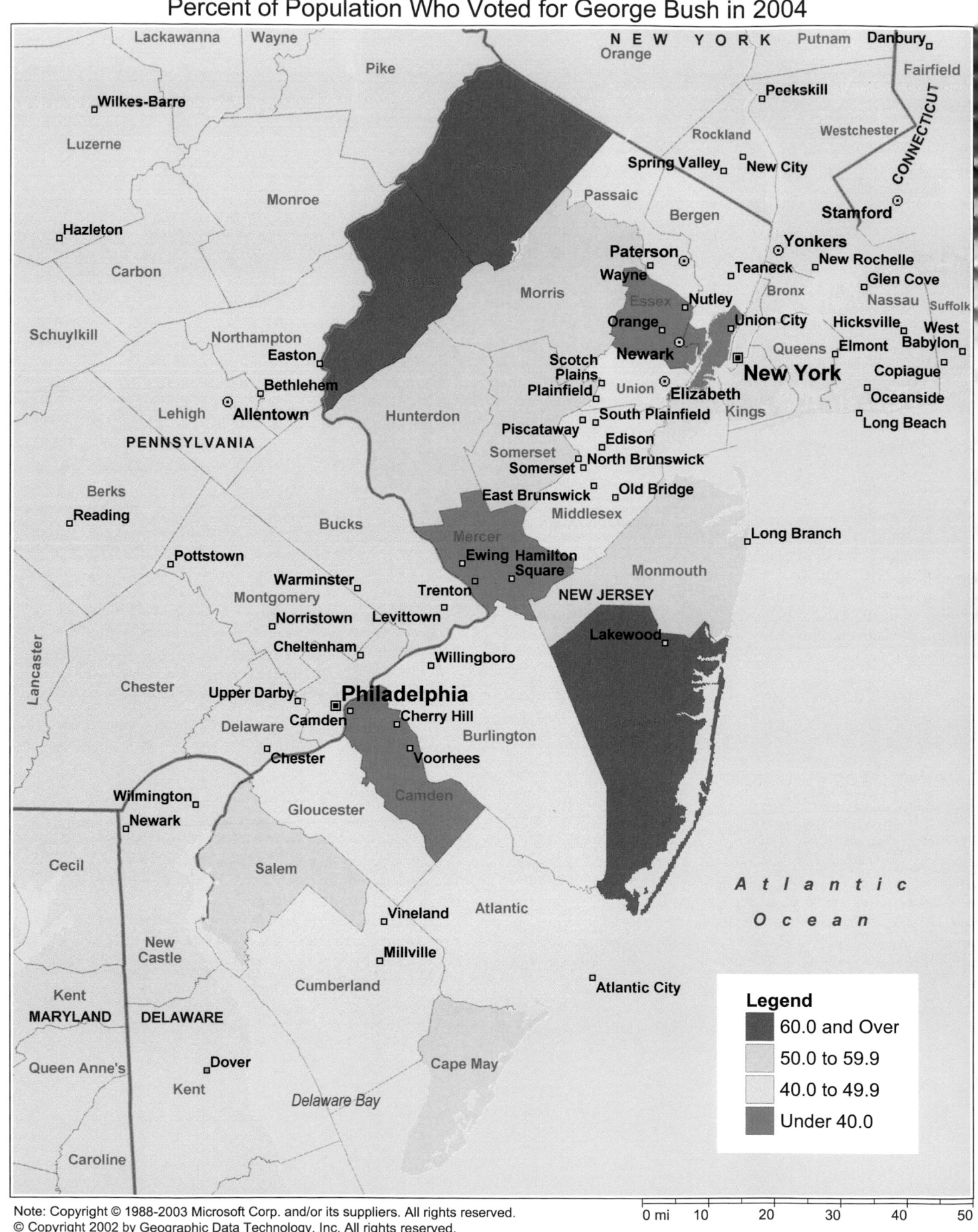

Legend
- 60.0 and Over
- 50.0 to 59.9
- 40.0 to 49.9
- Under 40.0

Also Available from Grey House Publishing
Statistical & Demographic Reference Books

Profiles of New York ♦ Profiles of Florida ♦ Profiles of Texas ♦ Profiles of Illinois ♦ Profiles of Michigan ♦ Profiles of Ohio ♦ Profiles of New Jersey ♦ Profiles of Pennsylvania

Packed with over 50 pieces of data that make up a complete, user-friendly profile of each state, these directories go even further by then pulling selected data and providing it in ranking list form for even easier comparisons between the 100 largest towns and cities! The careful layout gives the user an easy-to-read snapshot of every single place and county in the state, from the biggest metropolis to the smallest unincorporated hamlet. The richness of each place or county profile is astounding in its depth, from history to weather, all packed in an easy-to-navigate, compact format. No need for piles of multiple sources with this volume on your desk. Here is a look at just a few of the data sets you'll find in each profile: History, Geography, Climate, Population, Vital Statistics, Economy, Income, Taxes, Education, Housing, Health & Environment, Public Safety, Newspapers, Transportation, Presidential Election Results, Information Contacts and Chambers of Commerce. As an added bonus, there is a section on Selected Statistics, where data from the 100 largest towns and cities is arranged into easy-to-use charts. Each of 22 different data points has its own two-page spread with the cities listed in alpha order so researchers can easily compare and rank cities. A remarkable compilation that offers overviews and insights into each corner of the state, our *Profiles of... Series* goes beyond Census statistics, beyond metro area coverage, beyond the 100 best places to live. Drawn from official census information, other government statistics and original research, you will have at your fingertips data that's available nowhere else in one single source. Data will be published on additional states in 2007 and 2008.

Profiles of New York: 800 pages; Softcover ISBN 1-59237-161-2; $149.00 ♦ Profiles of Florida: 800 pages; Softcover ISBN 1-59237-110-8; $149.00 ♦ Profiles of Texas: 800 pages; Softcover ISBN 1-59237-111-6; $149.00 ♦ Profiles of Illinois: 800 pages; Softcover ISBN 1-59237-148-5; $149.00 ♦ Profiles of Michigan: 800 pages; Softcover ISBN 1-59237-149-3; $149.00 ♦ Profiles of Ohio: 800 pages; Softcover ISBN 1-59237-175-2; $149.00 ♦ Profiles of New Jersey: 800 pages; Softcover ISBN 1-59237-209-0; $149.00 ♦ Profiles of Pennsylvania: 800 pages; Softcover ISBN 1-59237-210-4; $149.00

America's Top-Rated Cities, 2006

America's Top-Rated Cities provides current, comprehensive statistical information and other essential data in one easy-to-use source on the 100 "top" cities that have been cited as the best for business and living in the U.S. This handbook allows readers to see, at a glance, a concise social, business, economic, demographic and environmental profile of each city, including brief evaluative comments. In addition to detailed data on Cost of Living, Finances, Real Estate, Education, Major Employers, Media, Crime and Climate, city reports now include Housing Vacancies, Tax Audits, Bankruptcy, Presidential Election Results and more. This outstanding source of information will be widely used in any reference collection.

> *"The only source of its kind that brings together all of this information into one easy-to-use source. It will be beneficial to many business and public libraries." –ARBA*

2,500 pages, 4 Volume Set; Softcover ISBN 1-59237-076-4, $195.00

America's Top-Rated Smaller Cities, 2006/07

A perfect companion to *America's Top-Rated Cities, America's Top-Rated Smaller Cities* provides current, comprehensive business and living profiles of smaller cities (population 25,000-99,999) that have been cited as the best for business and living in the United States. Sixty cities make up this 2004 edition of *America's Top-Rated Smaller Cities*, all are top-ranked by Population Growth, Median Income, Unemployment Rate and Crime Rate. City reports reflect the most current data available on a wide-range of statistics, including Employment & Earnings, Household Income, Unemployment Rate, Population Characteristics, Taxes, Cost of Living, Education, Health Care, Public Safety, Recreation, Media, Air & Water Quality and much more. Plus, each city report contains a Background of the City, and an Overview of the State Finances. *America's Top-Rated Smaller Cities* offers a reliable, one-stop source for statistical data that, before now, could only be found scattered in hundreds of sources. This volume is designed for a wide range of readers: individuals considering relocating a residence or business; professionals considering expanding their business or changing careers; general and market researchers; real estate consultants; human resource personnel; urban planners and investors.

> *"Provides current, comprehensive statistical information in one easy-to-use source... Recommended for public and academic libraries and specialized collections." –Library Journal*

1,100 pages; Softcover ISBN 1-59237-135-3, $160.00

To preview any of our Directories Risk-Free for 30 days, call (800) 562-2139 or fax to (518) 789-0556

Profiles of America: Facts, Figures & Statistics for Every Populated Place in the United States

Profiles of America is the only source that pulls together, in one place, statistical, historical and descriptive information about every place in the United States in an easy-to-use format. This award winning reference set, now in its second edition, compiles statistics and data from over 20 different sources – the latest census information has been included along with more than nine brand new statistical topics This Four-Volume Set details over 40,000 places, from the biggest metropolis to the smallest unincorporated hamlet, and provides statistical details and information on over 50 different topics including Geography, Climate, Population, Vital Statistics, Economy, Income, Taxes, Education, Housing, Health & Environment, Public Safety, Newspapers, Transportation, Presidential Election Results and Information Contacts or Chambers of Commerce. Profiles are arranged, for ease-of-use, by state and then by county. Each county begins with a County-Wide Overview and is followed by information for each Community in that particular county. The Community Profiles within the county are arranged alphabetically. *Profiles of America* is a virtual snapshot of America at your fingertips and a unique compilation of information that will be widely used in any reference collection.

A Library Journal Best Reference Book "An outstanding compilation." –Library Journal

10,000 pages; Four Volume Set; Softcover ISBN 1-891482-80-7, $595.00

The Comparative Guide to American Suburbs, 2005

The Comparative Guide to American Suburbs is a one-stop source for Statistics on the 2,000+ suburban communities surrounding the 50 largest metropolitan areas – their population characteristics, income levels, economy, school system and important data on how they compare to one another. Organized into 50 Metropolitan Area chapters, each chapter contains an overview of the Metropolitan Area, a detailed Map followed by a comprehensive Statistical Profile of each Suburban Community, including Contact Information, Physical Characteristics, Population Characteristics, Income, Economy, Unemployment Rate, Cost of Living, Education, Chambers of Commerce and more. Next, statistical data is sorted into Ranking Tables that rank the suburbs by twenty different criteria, including Population, Per Capita Income, Unemployment Rate, Crime Rate, Cost of Living and more. *The Comparative Guide to American Suburbs* is the best source for locating data on suburbs. Those looking to relocate, as well as those doing preliminary market research, will find this an invaluable timesaving resource.

"Public and academic libraries will find this compilation useful…The work draws together figures from many sources and will be especially helpful for job relocation decisions." – Booklist

1,700 pages; Softcover ISBN 1-59237-004-7, $130.00

Weather America, A Thirty-Year Summary of Statistical Weather Data and Rankings

This valuable resource provides extensive climatological data for over 4,000 National and Cooperative Weather Stations throughout the United States. *Weather America* begins with a new Major Storms section that details major storm events of the nation and a National Rankings section that details rankings for several data elements, such as Maximum Temperature and Precipitation. The main body of *Weather America* is organized into 50 state sections. Each section provides a Data Table on each Weather Station, organized alphabetically, that provides statistics on Maximum and Minimum Temperatures, Precipitation, Snowfall, Extreme Temperatures, Foggy Days, Humidity and more. State sections contain two brand new features in this edition – a City Index and a narrative Description of the climatic conditions of the state. Each section also includes a revised Map of the State that includes not only weather stations, but cities and towns.

"Best Reference Book of the Year." –Library Journal

2,013 pages; Softcover ISBN 1-891482-29-7, $175.00

The Asian Databook: Statistics for all US Counties & Cities with Over 10,000 Population

This is the first-ever resource that compiles statistics and rankings on the US Asian population. *The Asian Databook* presents over 20 statistical data points for each city and county, arranged alphabetically by state, then alphabetically by place name. Data reported for each place includes Population, Languages Spoken at Home, Foreign-Born, Educational Attainment, Income Figures, Poverty Status, Homeownership, Home Values & Rent, and more. Next, in the Rankings Section, the top 75 places are listed for each data element. These easy-to-access ranking tables allow the user to quickly determine trends and population characteristics. This kind of comparative data can not be found elsewhere, in print or on the web, in a format that's as easy-to-use or more concise. A useful resource for those searching for demographics data, career search and relocation information and also for market research. With data ranging from Ancestry to Education, *The Asian Databook* presents a useful compilation of information that will be a much-needed resource in the reference collection of any public or academic library along with the marketing collection of any company whose primary focus in on the Asian population.

1,000 pages; Softcover ISBN 1-59237-044-6 $150.00

To preview any of our Directories Risk-Free for 30 days, call (800) 562-2139 or fax to (518) 789-0556

The Hispanic Databook: Statistics for all US Counties & Cities with Over 10,000 Population

Previously published by Toucan Valley Publications, this second edition has been completely updated with figures from the latest census and has been broadly expanded to include dozens of new data elements and a brand new Rankings section. The Hispanic population in the United States has increased over 42% in the last 10 years and accounts for 12.5% of the total US population. For ease-of-use, *The Hispanic Databook* presents over 20 statistical data points for each city and county, arranged alphabetically by state, then alphabetically by place name. Data reported for each place includes Population, Languages Spoken at Home, Foreign-Born, Educational Attainment, Income Figures, Poverty Status, Homeownership, Home Values & Rent, and more. Next, in the Rankings Section, the top 25 places are listed for each data element. These easy-to-access ranking tables allow the user to quickly determine trends and population characteristics. This kind of comparative data can not be found elsewhere, in print or on the web, in a format that's as easy-to-use or more concise. A useful resource for those searching for demographics data, career search and relocation information and also for market research. With data ranging from Ancestry to Education, *The Hispanic Databook* presents a useful compilation of information that will be a much-needed resource in the reference collection of any public or academic library along with the marketing collection of any company whose primary focus in on the Hispanic population.

"This accurate, clearly presented volume of selected Hispanic demographics is recommended for large public libraries and research collections."-Library Journal

1,000 pages; Softcover ISBN 1-59237-008-X, $150.00

Ancestry in America: A Comparative Guide to Over 200 Ethnic Backgrounds

This brand new reference work pulls together thousands of comparative statistics on the Ethnic Backgrounds of all populated places in the United States with populations over 10,000. Never before has this kind of information been reported in a single volume. Section One, Statistics by Place, is made up of a list of over 200 ancestry and race categories arranged alphabetically by each of the 5,000 different places with populations over 10,000. The population number of the ancestry group in that city or town is provided along with the percent that group represents of the total population. This informative city-by-city section allows the user to quickly and easily explore the ethnic makeup of all major population bases in the United States. Section Two, Comparative Rankings, contains three tables for each ethnicity and race. In the first table, the top 150 populated places are ranked by population number for that particular ancestry group, regardless of population. In the second table, the top 150 populated places are ranked by the percent of the total population for that ancestry group. In the third table, those top 150 populated places with 10,000 population are ranked by population number for each ancestry group. These easy-to-navigate tables allow users to see ancestry population patterns and make city-by-city comparisons as well. Plus, as an added bonus with the purchase of *Ancestry in America*, a free companion CD-ROM is available that lists statistics and rankings for all of the 35,000 populated places in the United States. This brand new, information-packed resource will serve a wide-range or research requests for demographics, population characteristics, relocation information and much more. *Ancestry in America: A Comparative Guide to Over 200 Ethnic Backgrounds* will be an important acquisition to all reference collections.

"This compilation will serve a wide range of research requests for population characteristics ... it offers much more detail than other sources." –Booklist

1,500 pages; Softcover ISBN 1-59237-029-2, $225.00

The American Tally: Statistics & Comparative Rankings for U.S. Cities with Populations over 10,000

This important statistical handbook compiles, all in one place, comparative statistics on all U.S. cities and towns with a 10,000+ population. *The American Tally* provides statistical details on over 4,000 cities and towns and profiles how they compare with one another in Population Characteristics, Education, Language & Immigration, Income & Employment and Housing. Each section begins with an alphabetical listing of cities by state, allowing for quick access to both the statistics and relative rankings of any city. Next, the highest and lowest cities are listed in each statistic. These important, informative lists provide quick reference to which cities are at both extremes of the spectrum for each statistic. Unlike any other reference, *The American Tally* provides quick, easy access to comparative statistics – a must-have for any reference collection.

"A solid library reference." -Bookwatch

500 pages; Softcover ISBN 1-930956-29-0, $125.00

To preview any of our Directories Risk-Free for 30 days, call (800) 562-2139 or fax to (518) 789-0556

The Grey House Handbook on Alternative Energy, 2006

This is the first ever resource to pull together information, resources and statistics for all types of Alternative Energy, including Hydro, Wind, Solar, Coal, Natural Gas and Atomic Energy sources. The Handbook begins with an informative Introduction to Alternative Energy Resources, including editorial on the history of energy, the necessity of using alternative energy, conservation and the economics of using alternative energy sources. Plus, handy charts are also included that cover uses of energy sources today; forecasts of energy sources and the availability of energy sources in the future. Next, readers will find chapters on each Type of Energy Source. Chapters begin with an Introduction to the specific energy source, History, Strengths & Drawbacks, Industrial & Residential Use and Trends. Several articles are also included for each energy source, followed by Resources, including Associations, Magazines, Trade Shows and Vendors. The Grey House Handbook on Alternative Energy also contains a informative, useful section on Statistics. These charts allow for easy location of very specific data. A handy Glossary and section on Public Energy Companies is also included for easy reference. Three indexes, Product Index, Subject Index and Entry Name Index allow the user to locate specific resources quickly and easily. As the need for alternative energy sources continues to grow, having access to these resources will become more and more important. This first edition will prove useful to the reference collections public and academic libraries.

800 pages; Softcover ISBN 1-59237-134-5; $165.00

The Environmental Resource Handbook, 2005/06

The Environmental Resource Handbook is the most up-to-date and comprehensive source for Environmental Resources and Statistics. Section I: Resources provides detailed contact information for thousands of information sources, including Associations & Organizations, Awards & Honors, Conferences, Foundations & Grants, Environmental Health, Government Agencies, National Parks & Wildlife Refuges, Publications, Research Centers, Educational Programs, Green Product Catalogs, Consultants and much more. Section II: Statistics, provides statistics and rankings on hundreds of important topics, including Children's Environmental Index, Municipal Finances, Toxic Chemicals, Recycling, Climate, Air & Water Quality and more. This kind of up-to-date environmental data, all in one place, is not available anywhere else on the market place today. This vast compilation of resources and statistics is a must-have for all public and academic libraries as well as any organization with a primary focus on the environment.

> *"...the intrinsic value of the information make it worth consideration by libraries with environmental collections and environmentally concerned users."* —Booklist

1,000 pages; Softcover ISBN 1-59237-090-X, $155.00 ◆ Online Database $300.00

To preview any of our Directories Risk-Free for 30 days, call (800) 562-2139 or fax to (518) 789-0556

Grey House Publishing
Business Directories

The Rauch Guide to the US Adhesives & Sealants, Cosmetics & Toiletries, Ink, Paint, Plastics, Pulp & Paper and Rubber Industries

The Rauch Guides are known worldwide for their comprehensive marketing information. Acquired by Grey House Publishing in 2005, new updated and revised editions will be published throughout 2005 and 2006. Each Guide provides market facts and figures in a highly organized format, ideal for today's busy personnel, serving as ready-references for top executives as well as the industry newcomer. *The Rauch Guides* save time and money by organizing widely scattered information and providing estimates for important business decisions, some of which are available nowhere else. Each Guide is organized into several information-packed chapters. After a brief introduction, the ECONOMICS section provides data on industry shipments; long-term growth and forecasts; prices; company performance; employment, expenditures, and productivity; transportation and geographical patterns; packaging; foreign trade; and government regulations. Next, TECHNOLOGY & RAW MATERIALS provide market, technical, and raw material information for chemicals, equipment and related materials, including market size and leading suppliers, prices, end uses, and trends. PRODUCTS & MARKETS provide information for each major industry product, including market size and historical trends, leading suppliers, five-year forecasts, industry structure, and major end uses. For easy access, each *Guide* contains a chapter on INDUSTRY ACTIVITIES, ORGANIZATIONS & SOURCES OF INFORMATION with detailed information on meetings, exhibits, and trade shows, sources of statistical information, trade associations, technical and professional societies, and trade and technical periodials. Next, the COMPANY DIRECTORY profiles major industry companies, both public and private. Generally several hundred companies are analyzed. Information includes complete contact information, web address, estimated total and domestic sales, product description, and recent mergers and acquisitions. Each Guide also contains several APPENDICES that provide a cross-reference of suppliers, subsidiaries and divisions. The Rauch Guides will prove to be an invaluable source of market information, company data, trends and forecasts that anyone in these fast-paced industries.

The Rauch Guide to the U.S. Paint Industry Softcover ISBN 1-59237-127-2 $595 ♦ The Rauch Guide to the U.S. Plastics Industry Softcover ISBN 1-59237-128-0 $595 ♦ The Rauch Guide to the U.S. Adhesives and Sealants Industry Softcover ISBN 1-59237-129-9 $595 ♦ The Rauch Guide to the U.S. Ink Industry Softcover ISBN 1-59237-126-4 $595 ♦ The Rauch Guide to the U.S. Rubber Industry Softcover ISBN 1-59237-130-2 $595 ♦ The Rauch Guide to the U.S. Pulp and Paper Industry Softcover ISBN 1-59237-131-0 $595 ♦ The Rauch Guide to the U.S. Cosmetic and Toiletries Industry Softcover ISBN 1-59237-132-9 $895

The Directory of Business Information Resources, 2007

With 100% verification, over 1,000 new listings and more than 12,000 updates, this 2007 edition of *The Directory of Business Information Resources* is the most up-to-date source for contacts in over 98 business areas – from advertising and agriculture to utilities and wholesalers. This carefully researched volume details: the Associations representing each industry; the Newsletters that keep members current; the Magazines and Journals - with their "Special Issues" - that are important to the trade, the Conventions that are "must attends," Databases, Directories and Industry Web Sites that provide access to must-have marketing resources. Includes contact names, phone & fax numbers, web sites and e-mail addresses. This one-volume resource is a gold mine of information and would be a welcome addition to any reference collection.

"This is a most useful and easy-to-use addition to any researcher's library." – The Information Professionals Institute

2,500 pages; Softcover ISBN 1-59237-146-9, $195.00 ♦ Online Database $495.00

Nations of the World, 2006 A Political, Economic and Business Handbook

This completely revised edition covers all the nations of the world in an easy-to-use, single volume. Each nation is profiled in a single chapter that includes Key Facts, Political & Economic Issues, a Country Profile and Business Information. In this fast-changing world, it is extremely important to make sure that the most up-to-date information is included in your reference collection. This edition is just the answer. Each of the 200+ country chapters have been carefully reviewed by a political expert to make sure that the text reflects the most current information on Politics, Travel Advisories, Economics and more. You'll find such vital information as a Country Map, Population Characteristics, Inflation, Agricultural Production, Foreign Debt, Political History, Foreign Policy, Regional Insecurity, Economics, Trade & Tourism, Historical Profile, Political Systems, Ethnicity, Languages, Media, Climate, Hotels, Chambers of Commerce, Banking, Travel Information and more. Five Regional Chapters follow the main text and include a Regional Map, an Introductory Article, Key Indicators and Currencies for the Region. As an added bonus, an all-inclusive CD-ROM is available as a companion to the printed text. Noted for its sophisticated, up-to-date and reliable compilation of political, economic and business information, this brand new edition will be an important acquisition to any public, academic or special library reference collection.

"A useful addition to both general reference collections and business collections." – RUSQ

1,700 pages; Print Version Only Softcover ISBN 1-59237-0079-9, $155.00

To preview any of our Directories Risk-Free for 30 days, call (800) 562-2139 or fax to (518) 789-0556

The Directory of Venture Capital & Private Equity Firms, 2006

This edition has been extensively updated and broadly expanded to offer direct access to over 2,800 Domestic and International Venture Capital Firms, including address, phone & fax numbers, e-mail addresses and web sites for both primary and branch locations. Entries include details on the firm's Mission Statement, Industry Group Preferences, Geographic Preferences, Average and Minimum Investments and Investment Criteria. You'll also find details that are available nowhere else, including the Firm's Portfolio Companies and extensive information on each of the firm's Managing Partners, such as Education, Professional Background and Directorships held, along with the Partner's E-mail Address. *The Directory of Venture Capital & Private Equity Firms* offers five important indexes: Geographic Index, Executive Name Index, Portfolio Company Index, Industry Preference Index and College & University Index. With its comprehensive coverage and detailed, extensive information on each company, *The Directory of Venture Capital & Private Equity Firms* is an important addition to any finance collection.

"The sheer number of listings, the descriptive information provided and the outstanding indexing make this directory a better value than its principal competitor, Pratt's Guide to Venture Capital Sources. Recommended for business collections in large public, academic and business libraries." —Choice

1,300 pages; Softcover ISBN 1-59237-102-7, $450.00 ◆ Online Database (includes a free copy of the directory) $889.00

The Directory of Mail Order Catalogs, 2006

Published since 1981, this updated edition features 100% verification of data and is the premier source of information on the mail order catalog industry. Details over 12,000 consumer catalog companies with 44 different product chapters from Animals to Toys & Games. Contains detailed contact information including e-mail addresses and web sites along with important business details such as employee size, years in business, sales volume, catalog size, number of catalogs mailed and more. Four indexes provide quick access to information: Catalog & Company Name Index, Geographic Index, Product Index and Web Sites Index.

"This is a godsend for those looking for information." —Reference Book Review

1,700 pages; Softcover ISBN 1-59237-103-5 $250.00 ◆ Online Database (includes a free copy of the directory) $495.00

The Directory of Business to Business Catalogs, 2006

The completely updated *Directory of Business to Business Catalogs*, provides details on over 6,000 suppliers of everything from computers to laboratory supplies... office products to office design... marketing resources to safety equipment... landscaping to maintenance suppliers... building construction and much more. Detailed entries offer mailing address, phone & fax numbers, e-mail addresses, web sites, key contacts, sales volume, employee size, catalog printing information and more. Jut about every kind of product a business needs in its day-to-day operations is covered in this carefully-researched volume. Three indexes are provided for at-a-glance access to information: Catalog & Company Name Index, Geographic Index and Web Sites Index.

"An excellent choice for libraries... wishing to supplement their business supplier resources." —Booklist

800 pages; Softcover ISBN 1-59237-105-1, $165.00 ◆ Online Database (includes a free copy of the directory) $325.00

Sports Market Place Directory, 2006

For over 20 years, this comprehensive, up-to-date directory has offered direct access to the Who, What, When & Where of the Sports Industry. With over 20,000 updates and enhancements, the *Sports Market Place Directory* is the most detailed, comprehensive and current sports business reference source available. In 1,800 information-packed pages, *Sports Market Place Directory* profiles contact information and key executives for: Single Sport Organizations, Professional Leagues, Multi-Sport Organizations, Disabled Sports, High School & Youth Sports, Military Sports, Olympic Organizations, Media, Sponsors, Sponsorship & Marketing Event Agencies, Event & Meeting Calendars, Professional Services, College Sports, Manufacturers & Retailers, Facilities and much more. *The Sports Market Place Directory* provides organization's contact information with detailed descriptions including: Key Contacts, physical, mailing, email and web addresses plus phone and fax numbers. Plus, nine important indexes make sure that you can find the information you're looking for quickly and easily: Entry Index, Single Sport Index, Media Index, Sponsor Index, Agency Index, Manufacturers Index, Brand Name Index, Facilities Index and Executive/Geographic Index. For over twenty years, *The Sports Market Place Directory* has assisted thousands of individuals in their pursuit of a career in the sports industry. Why not use "THE SOURCE" that top recruiters, headhunters and career placement centers use to find information on or about sports organizations and key hiring contacts.

1,800 pages; Softcover ISBN 1-59237-139-6, $225.00 ◆ Online Database $479.00

To preview any of our Directories Risk-Free for 30 days, call (800) 562-2139 or fax to (518) 789-0556

Thomas Food and Beverage Market Place, 2006

Thomas Food and Beverage Market Place is bigger and better than ever with thousands of new companies, thousands of updates to existing companies and two revised and enhanced product category indexes. This comprehensive directory profiles over 18,000 Food & Beverage Manufacturers, 12,000 Equipment & Supply Companies, 2,200 Transportation & Warehouse Companies, 2,000 Brokers & Wholesalers, 8,000 Importers & Exporters, 900 Industry Resources and hundreds of Mail Order Catalogs. Listings include detailed Contact Information, Sales Volumes, Key Contacts, Brand & Product Information, Packaging Details and much more. *Thomas Food and Beverage Market Place* is available as a three-volume printed set, a subscription-based Online Database via the Internet, on CD-ROM, as well as mailing lists and a licensable database.

"An essential purchase for those in the food industry but will also be useful in public libraries where needed. Much of the information will be difficult and time consuming to locate without this handy three-volume ready-reference source." –ARBA

,500 pages, 3 Volume Set; Softcover ISBN 1-59237-096-9, $495.00 ◆ CD-ROM $695.00 ◆ CD-ROM & 3 Volume Set Combo $895.00 ◆ Online Database $695.00 ◆ Online Database & 3 Volume Set Combo, $895.00

The Grey House Homeland Security Directory, 2006

This updated edition features the latest contact information for government and private organizations involved with Homeland Security along with the latest product information and provides detailed profiles of nearly 1,000 Federal & State Organizations & Agencies and over 3,000 Officials and Key Executives involved with Homeland Security. These listings are incredibly detailed and include Mailing Address, Phone & Fax Numbers, Email Addresses & Web Sites, a complete Description of the Agency and a complete list of the Officials and Key Executives associated with the Agency. Next, *The Grey House Homeland Security Directory* provides the go-to source for Homeland Security Products & Services. This section features over 2,000 Companies that provide Consulting, Products or Services. With this Buyer's Guide at their fingertips, users can locate suppliers of everything from Training Materials to Access Controls, from Perimeter Security to BioTerrorism Countermeasures and everything in between – complete with contact information and product descriptions. A handy Product Locator Index is provided to quickly and easily locate suppliers of a particular product. Lastly, an Information Resources Section provides immediate access to contact information for hundreds of Associations, Newsletters, Magazines, Trade Shows, Databases and Directories that focus on Homeland Security. This comprehensive, information-packed resource will be a welcome tool for any company or agency that is in need of Homeland Security information and will be a necessary acquisition for the reference collection of all public libraries and large school districts.

"Compiles this information in one place and is discerning in content. A useful purchase for public and academic libraries." –Booklist

300 pages; Softcover ISBN 1-59237-084-5, $195.00 ◆ Online Database (includes a free copy of the directory) $385.00

The Grey House Transportation Security Directory & Handbook

This brand new title is the only reference of its kind that brings together current data on Transportation Security. With information on everything from Regulatory Authorities to Security Equipment, this top-flight database brings together the relevant information necessary for creating and maintaining a security plan for a wide range of transportation facilities. With this current, comprehensive directory at the ready you'll have immediate access to: Regulatory Authorities & Legislation; Information Resources; Sample Security Plans & Checklists; Contact Data for Major Airports, Seaports, Railroads, Trucking Companies and Oil Pipelines; Security Service Providers; Recommended Equipment & Product Information and more. Using the *Grey House Transportation Security Directory & Handbook*, managers will be able to quickly and easily assess their current security plans; develop contacts to create and maintain new security procedures; and source the products and services necessary to adequately maintain a secure environment. This valuable resource is a must for all Security Managers at Airports, Seaports, Railroads, Trucking Companies and Oil Pipelines.

300 pages; Softcover ISBN 1-59237-075-6, $195

To preview any of our Directories Risk-Free for 30 days, call (800) 562-2139 or fax to (518) 789-0556

The Grey House Safety & Security Directory, 2006

The Grey House Safety & Security Directory is the most comprehensive reference tool and buyer's guide for the safety and security industry. Arranged by safety topic, each chapter begins with OSHA regulations for the topic, followed by Training Articles written by top professionals in the field and Self-Inspection Checklists. Next, each topic contains Buyer's Guide sections that feature related products and services. Topics include Administration, Insurance, Loss Control & Consulting, Protective Equipment & Apparel, Noise & Vibration, Facilities Monitoring & Maintenance, Employee Health Maintenance & Ergonomics, Retail Food Services, Machine Guards, Process Guidelines & Tool Handling, Ordinary Materials Handling, Hazardous Materials Handling, Workplace Preparation & Maintenance, Electrical Lighting & Safety, Fire & Rescue and Security. The Buyer's Guide sections are carefully indexed within each topic area to ensure that you can find the supplies needed to meet OSHA's regulations. Six important indexes make finding information and product manufacturers quick and easy: Geographical Index of Manufacturers and Distributors, Company Profile Index, Brand Name Index, Product Index, Index of Web Sites and Index of Advertisers. This comprehensive, up-to-date reference will provide every tool necessary to make sure a business is in compliance with OSHA regulations and locate the products and services needed to meet those regulations.

"Presents industrial safety information for engineers, plant managers, risk managers, and construction site supervisors..." —Choic

1,500 pages, 2 Volume Set; Softcover ISBN 1-59237-104-3, $225.00

The Grey House Biometric Information Directory, 2006

The Biometric Information Directory is the only comprehensive source for current biometric industry information. This 2006 edition is the first published by Grey House. With 100% updated information, this latest edition offers a complete, current look, in both print and online form, of biometric companies and products – one of the fastest growing industries in today's economy. Detailed profiles of manufacturers of the latest biometric technology, including Finger, Voice, Face, Hand, Signature, Iris, Vein and Palm Identification systems. Data on the companies include key executives, company size and a detailed, indexed description of their product line. Plus, the Directory also includes valuable business resources, and current editorial make this edition the easiest way for the business community and consumers alike to access the largest, most current compilation of biometric industry information available on the market today. The new edition boasts increased numbers of companies, contact names and company data, with over 700 manufacturers and service providers. Information in the directory includes: Editorial on Advancements in Biometrics; Profiles of 700+ companies listed with contact information; Organizations, Trade & Educational Associations, Publications, Conferences, Trade Shows and Expositions Worldwide; Web Site Index; Biometric & Vendors Services Index by Types of Biometrics; and a Glossary of Biometric Terms. This resource will be an important source for anyone who is considering the use of a biometric product, investing in the development of biometric technology, support existing marketing and sales efforts and will be an important acquisition for the business reference collection for large public and business libraries.

800 pages; Softcover ISBN 1-59237-121-3, $225

The Grey House Performing Arts Directory, 2007

The Grey House Performing Arts Directory is the most comprehensive resource covering the Performing Arts. This important directory provides current information on over 8,500 Dance Companies, Instrumental Music Programs, Opera Companies, Choral Groups, Theater Companies, Performing Arts Series and Performing Arts Facilities. Plus, this edition now contains a brand new section on Artist Management Groups. In addition to mailing address, phone & fax numbers, e-mail addresses and web sites, dozens of other fields of available information include mission statement, key contacts, facilities, seating capacity, season, attendance and more. This directory also provides an important Information Resources section that covers hundreds of Performing Arts Associations, Magazines, Newsletters, Trade Shows, Directories, Databases and Industry Web Sites. Five indexes provide immediate access to this wealth of information: Entry Name, Executive Name, Performance Facilities, Geographic and Information Resources. *The Grey House Performing Arts Directory* pulls together thousands of Performing Arts Organizations, Facilities and Information Resources into an easy-to-use source – this kind of comprehensiveness and extensive detail is not available in any resource on the market place today.

"Immensely useful and user-friendly ... recommended for public, academic and certain special library reference collections." —Booklis

1,500 pages; Softcover ISBN 1-59237-138-8, $185.00 ◆ Online Database $335.00

To preview any of our Directories Risk-Free for 30 days, call (800) 562-2139 or fax to (518) 789-0556

New York State Directory, 2006/07

The New York State Directory, published annually since 1983, is a comprehensive and easy-to-use guide to accessing public officials and private sector organizations and individuals who influence public policy in the state of New York. *The New York State Directory* includes important information on all New York state legislators and congressional representatives, including biographies and key committee assignments. It also includes staff rosters for all branches of New York state government and for federal agencies and departments that impact the state policy process. Following the state government section are 25 chapters covering policy areas from agriculture through veterans' affairs. Each chapter identifies the state, local and federal agencies and officials that formulate or implement policy. In addition, each chapter contains a roster of private sector experts and advocates who influence the policy process. The directory also offers appendices that include statewide party officials; chambers of commerce; lobbying organizations; public and private universities and colleges; television, radio and print media; and local government agencies and officials.

New York State Directory - 800 pages; Softcover ISBN 1-59237-145-0; $145.00
New York State Directory with Profiles of New York – 2 volumes; 1,600 pages; Softcover ISBN 1-59237-162-0; $225

Research Services Directory: Commercial & Corporate Research Centers

This Ninth Edition provides access to well over 8,000 independent Commercial Research Firms, Corporate Research Centers and Laboratories offering contract services for hands-on, basic or applied research. *Research Services Directory* covers the thousands of types of research companies, including Biotechnology & Pharmaceutical Developers, Consumer Product Research, Defense Contractors, Electronics & Software Engineers, Think Tanks, Forensic Investigators, Independent Commercial Laboratories, Information Brokers, Market & Survey Research Companies, Medical Diagnostic Facilities, Product Research & Development Firms and more. Each entry provides the company's name, mailing address, phone & fax numbers, key contacts, web site, e-mail address, as well as a company description and research and technical fields served. Four indexes provide immediate access to this wealth of information: Research Firms Index, Geographic Index, Personnel Name Index and Subject Index.

"An important source for organizations in need of information about laboratories, individuals and other facilities." –ARBA

,400 pages; Softcover ISBN 1-59237-003-9, $395.00 ✦ Online Database (includes a free copy of the directory) $850.00

International Business and Trade Directories

Completely updated, the Third Edition of *International Business and Trade Directories* now contains more than 10,000 entries, over 2,000 more than the last edition, making this directory the most comprehensive resource of the worlds business and trade directories. Entries include content descriptions, price, publisher's name and address, web site and e-mail addresses, phone and fax numbers and editorial staff. Organized by industry group, and then by region, this resource puts over 10,000 industry-specific business and trade directories at the reader's fingertips. Three indexes are included for quick access to information: Geographic Index, Publisher Index and Title Index. Public, college and corporate libraries, as well as individuals and corporations seeking critical market information will want to add this directory to their marketing collection.

"Reasonably priced for a work of this type, this directory should appeal to larger academic, public and corporate libraries with an international focus." –Library Journal

,800 pages; Softcover ISBN 1-930956-63-0, $225.00 ✦ Online Database (includes a free copy of the directory) $450.00

To preview any of our Directories Risk-Free for 30 days, call (800) 562-2139 or fax to (518) 789-0556

Sedgwick Press
Health Directories

The Complete Directory for People with Disabilities, 2007

A wealth of information, now in one comprehensive sourcebook. Completely updated, this edition contains more information than ever before, including thousands of new entries and enhancements to existing entries and thousands of additional web sites and e-mail addresses. This up-to-date directory is the most comprehensive resource available for people with disabilities, detailing Independent Living Centers, Rehabilitation Facilities, State & Federal Agencies, Associations, Support Groups, Periodicals & Books, Assistive Devices, Employment & Education Programs, Camps and Travel Groups. Each year, more libraries, schools, colleges, hospitals, rehabilitation centers and individuals add *The Complete Directory for People with Disabilities* to their collections, making sure that this information is readily available to the families, individuals and professionals who can benefit most from the amazing wealth of resources cataloged here.

"No other reference tool exists to meet the special needs of the disabled in one convenient resource for information." –Library Journal

1,200 pages; Softcover ISBN 1-59237-147-7, $165.00 ◆ Online Database $215.00 ◆ Online Database & Directory Combo $300.00

The Complete Directory for People with Chronic Illness, 2005/06

Thousands of hours of research have gone into this completely updated 2005/06 edition – several new chapters have been added along with thousands of new entries and enhancements to existing entries. Plus, each chronic illness chapter has been reviewed by an medical expert in the field. This widely-hailed directory is structured around the 90 most prevalent chronic illnesses – from Asthma to Cancer to Wilson's Disease – and provides a comprehensive overview of the support services and information resources available for people diagnosed with a chronic illness. Each chronic illness has its own chapter and contains a brief description in layman's language, followed by important resources for National & Local Organizations, State Agencies, Newsletters, Books & Periodicals, Libraries & Research Centers, Support Groups & Hotlines, Web Sites and much more. This directory is an important resource for health care professionals, the collections of hospital and health care libraries, as well as an invaluable tool for people with a chronic illness and their support network.

"A must purchase for all hospital and health care libraries and is strongly recommended for all public library reference departments." –ARBA

1,200 pages; Softcover ISBN 1-59237-081-0, $165.00 ◆ Online Database $215.00 ◆ Online Database & Directory Combo $300.00

The Grey House Rare Disorders Directory, 2006/07

This directory is the most comprehensive resource bringing together hard-to-find information on over 700 rare disorders, including rare cancers, muscular and genetic disorders, and more. This 2006/07 contains the most up-to-date information on each disorder. Written in layman's language, by physicians and faculty at Yale University School of Medicine and Yale New Haven Children's Hospital, the information in this directory is presented in a clear, understandable format, with helpful Cross-References running through the text. The Grey House Rare Disorders Directory is divided into five sections: Disorder Descriptions, Associations & Support Groups, Magazines, Journals & Periodicals, Government Agencies and Treatment Centers. Approximately 20 million, or 1 in every 12, Americans is affected with a rare disorder, so this directory serves a surprisingly wide range of the population. The Grey House Rare Disorders Directory will be an invaluable tool for the thousands of families that have been struck with a rare or "orphan" disease, who feel that they have no place to turn and will be a much-used addition to the reference collection of any public or academic library.

800 pages; Softcover ISBN 1-59237-123-X, $165.00

The Complete Learning Disabilities Directory, 2007

The Complete Learning Disabilities Directory is the most comprehensive database of Programs, Services, Curriculum Materials, Professional Meetings & Resources, Camps, Newsletters and Support Groups for teachers, students and families concerned with learning disabilities. This information-packed directory includes information about Associations & Organizations, Schools, Colleges & Testing Materials, Government Agencies, Legal Resources and much more. For quick, easy access to information, this directory contains four indexes: Entry Name Index, Subject Index and Geographic Index. With every passing year, the field of learning disabilities attracts more attention and the network of caring, committed and knowledgeable professionals grows every day. This directory is an invaluable research tool for these parents, students and professionals.

"Due to its wealth and depth of coverage, parents, teachers and others… should find this an invaluable resource." –Booklist

900 pages; Softcover ISBN 1-59237-122-1, $145.00 ◆ Online Database $195.00 ◆ Online Database & Directory Combo $280.00

To preview any of our Directories Risk-Free for 30 days, call (800) 562-2139 or fax to (518) 789-0556

The Complete Mental Health Directory, 2006/07

This is the most comprehensive resource covering the field of behavioral health, with critical information for both the layman and the mental health professional. For the layman, this directory offers understandable descriptions of 25 Mental Health Disorders as well as detailed information on Associations, Media, Support Groups and Mental Health Facilities. For the professional, *The Complete Mental Health Directory* offers critical and comprehensive information on Managed Care Organizations, Information Systems, Government Agencies and Provider Organizations. This comprehensive volume of needed information will be widely used in any reference collection.

"… the strength of this directory is that it consolidates widely dispersed information into a single volume." —*Booklist*

00 pages; Softcover ISBN 1-59237-124-8, $165.00 ◆ Online Database $215.00 ◆ Online & Directory Combo $300.00

Older Americans Information Directory, 2006/07

Completely updated for 2006/07, this sixth edition has been completely revised and now contains 1,000 new listings, over 8,000 updates to existing listings and over 3,000 brand new e-mail addresses and web sites. You'll find important resources for Older Americans including National, Regional, State & Local Organizations, Government Agencies, Research Centers, Libraries & Information Centers, Legal Resources, Discount Travel Information, Continuing Education Programs, Disability Aids & Assistive Devices, Health, Print Media and Electronic Media. Three indexes: Entry Index, Subject Index and Geographic Index make it easy to find just the right source of information. This comprehensive guide to resources for Older Americans will be a welcome addition to any reference collection.

"Highly recommended for academic, public, health science and consumer libraries…" —*Choice*

,200 pages; Softcover ISBN 1-59237-136-1, $165.00 ◆ Online Database $215.00 ◆ Online Database & Directory Combo $300.00

The Complete Directory for Pediatric Disorders, 2007

This important directory provides parents and caregivers with information about Pediatric Conditions, Disorders, Diseases and Disabilities, including Blood Disorders, Bone & Spinal Disorders, Brain Defects & Abnormalities, Chromosomal Disorders, Congenital Heart Defects, Movement Disorders, Neuromuscular Disorders and Pediatric Tumors & Cancers. This carefully written directory offers: understandable Descriptions of 15 major bodily systems; Descriptions of more than 200 Disorders and a Resources Section, detailing National Agencies & Associations, State Associations, Online Services, Libraries & Resource Centers, Research Centers, Support Groups & Hotlines, Camps, Books and Periodicals. This resource will provide immediate access to information crucial to families and caregivers when coping with children's illnesses.

"Recommended for public and consumer health libraries." —*Library Journal*

,200 pages; Softcover ISBN 1-59237-150-7 $165.00 ◆ Online Database $215.00 ◆ Online Database & Directory Combo $300.00

The Directory of Drug & Alcohol Residential Rehabilitation Facilities

This brand new directory is the first-ever resource to bring together, all in one place, data on the thousands of drug and alcohol residential rehabilitation facilities in the United States. *The Directory of Drug & Alcohol Residential Rehabilitation Facilities* covers over 1,000 facilities, with detailed contact information for each one, including mailing address, phone and fax numbers, email addresses and web sites, mission statement, type of treatment programs, cost, average length of stay, numbers of residents and counselors, accreditation, insurance plans accepted, type of environment, religious affiliation, education components and much more. It also contains a helpful chapter on General Resources that provides contact information for Associations, Print & Electronic Media, Support Groups and Conferences. Multiple indexes allow the user to pinpoint the facilities that meet very specific criteria. This time-saving tool is what so many counselors, parents and medical professionals have been asking for. *The Directory of Drug & Alcohol Residential Rehabilitation Facilities* will be a helpful tool in locating the right source for treatment for a wide range of individuals. This comprehensive directory will be an important acquisition for all reference collections: public and academic libraries, case managers, social workers, state agencies and many more.

"This is an excellent, much needed directory that fills an important gap…" —*Booklist*

300 pages; Softcover ISBN 1-59237-031-4, $135.00

To preview any of our Directories Risk-Free for 30 days, call (800) 562-2139 or fax to (518) 789-0556

Sedgwick Press
Education Directories

The Comparative Guide to American Elementary & Secondary Schools, 2006

The only guide of its kind, this award winning compilation offers a snapshot profile of every public school district in the United States serving 1,500 or more students – more than 5,900 districts are covered. Organized alphabetically by district within state, each chapter begins with a Statistical Overview of the state. Each district listing includes contact information (name, address, phone number and web site) plus Grades Served, the Numbers of Students and Teachers and the Number of Regular, Special Education, Alternative and Vocational Schools in the district along with statistics on Student/Classroom Teacher Ratios, Drop Out Rates, Ethnicity, the Numbers of Librarians and Guidance Counselors and District Expenditures per student. As an added bonus, *The Comparative Guide to American Elementary and Secondary Schools* provides important ranking tables, both by state and nationally, for each data element. For easy navigation through this wealth of information, this handbook contains a useful City Index that lists all districts that operate schools within a city. These important comparative statistics are necessary for anyone considering relocation or doing comparative research or their own district and would be a perfect acquisition for any public library or school district library.

"This straightforward guide is an easy way to find general information. Valuable for academic and large public library collections." –ARB.

2,400 pages; Softcover ISBN 1-59237-137-X, $125.00

Educators Resource Directory, 2005/06

Educators Resource Directory is a comprehensive resource that provides the educational professional with thousands of resources and statistical data for professional development. This directory saves hours of research time by providing immediate access to Association & Organizations, Conferences & Trade Shows, Educational Research Centers, Employment Opportunities & Teaching Abroad, School Library Services, Scholarships, Financial Resources, Professional Consultants, Computer Software & Testing Resources and much more. Plus, this comprehensive directory also includes a section on Statistics and Rankings with over 100 tables, including statistics on Average Teacher Salaries, SAT/ACT scores, Revenues & Expenditures and more. These important statistics will allow the user to see how their school rates among others, make relocation decisions and so much more. For quick access to information, this directory contains four indexes: Entry & Publisher Index, Geographic Index, a Subject & Grade Index and Web Sites Index. *Educators Resource Directory* will be a well-used addition to the reference collection of any school district, education department or public library.

"Recommended for all collections that serve elementary and secondary school professionals." –Choic

1,000 pages; Softcover ISBN 1-59237-080-2, $145.00 ◆ Online Database $195.00 ◆ Online Database & Directory Combo $280.00

To preview any of our Directories Risk-Free for 30 days, call (800) 562-2139 or fax to (518) 789-0556

Sedgwick Press
Hospital & Health Plan Directories

The Comparative Guide to American Hospitals

This brand new title is the first ever resource to compare all of the nation's hospitals by 17 measures of quality in the treatment of heart attack, heart failure and pneumonia. This data is based on the recently announced Hospital Compare, produced by Medicare, and is available in print and in a unique and user-friendly format from Grey House Publishing, along with extra contact information from Grey House's *Directory of Hospital Personnel*. *The Comparative Guide to American Hospitals* provides a snapshot profile of each of the nations 6,000 hospitals. These informative profiles illustrate how the hospital rates in 17 important areas: Heart Attack Care (% who receive Aspirin at Arrival, Aspirin at Discharge, ACE Inhibitor for LVSD, Beta Blocker at Arrival, Beta Blocker at Discharge, Thrombolytic Agent Received, PTCA Received and Adult Smoking Cessation Advice); Heart Failure (% who receive LVF Assessment, ACE Inhibitor for LVSD, Discharge Instructions, Adult Smoking Cessation Advice); and Pneumonia (% who receive Initial Antibiotic Timing, Pneumococcal Vaccination, Oxygenation Assessment, Blood Culture Performed and Adult Smoking Cessation Advice). Each profile includes the raw percentage for that hospital, the state average, the US average and data on the top hospital. For easy access to contact information, each profile includes the hospitals address, phone and fax numbers, email and web addresses, type and accreditation along with 5 top key administrations. These profiles will allow the user to quickly identify the quality of the hospital and have the necessary information at their fingertips to make contact with that hospital. Most importantly, *The Comparative Guide to American Hospitals* provides an easy-to-use Ranking Table for each of the data elements to allow the user to quickly locate the hospitals with the best level of service. This brand new title will be a must for the reference collection at all public, medical and academic libraries.

1,500 pages; Softcover ISBN 1-59237-109-4 $175.00

The Directory of Hospital Personnel, 2006

The Directory of Hospital Personnel is the best resource you can have at your fingertips when researching or marketing a product or service to the hospital market. A "Who's Who" of the hospital universe, this directory puts you in touch with over 150,000 key decision-makers. With 100% verification of data you can rest assured that you will reach the right person with just one call. Every hospital in the U.S. is profiled, listed alphabetically by city within state. Plus, three easy-to-use, cross-referenced indexes put the facts at your fingertips faster and more easily than any other directory. Hospital Name Index, Bed Size Index and Personnel Index. *The Directory of Hospital Personnel* is the only complete source for key hospital decision-makers by name. Whether you want to define or restructure sales territories... locate hospitals with the purchasing power to accept your proposals... keep track of important contacts or colleagues... or find information on which insurance plans are accepted, *The Directory of Hospital Personnel* gives you the information you need – easily, efficiently, effectively and accurately.

"Recommended for college, university and medical libraries." -ARBA

2,500 pages; Softcover ISBN 1-59237-107-8 $275.00 ♦ Online Database $545.00 ♦ Online Database & Directory Combo, $650.00

The Directory of Health Care Group Purchasing Organizations, 2006

This comprehensive directory provides the important data you need to get in touch with over 800 Group Purchasing Organizations. By providing in-depth information on this growing market and its members, *The Directory of Health Care Group Purchasing Organizations* fills a major need for the most accurate and comprehensive information on over 800 GPOs – Mailing Address, Phone & Fax Numbers, E-mail Addresses, Key Contacts, Purchasing Agents, Group Descriptions, Membership Categorization, Standard Vendor Proposal Requirements, Membership Fees & Terms, Expanded Services, Total Member Beds & Outpatient Visits represented and more. Five indexes provide a number of ways to locate the right GPO: Alphabetical Index, Expanded Services Index, Organization Type Index, Geographic Index and Member Institution Index. With its comprehensive and detailed information on each purchasing organization, *The Directory of Health Care Group Purchasing Organizations* is the go-to source for anyone looking to target this market.

"The information is clearly arranged and easy to access...recommended for those needing this very specialized information." –ARBA

1,000 pages; Softcover ISBN 1-59237-0091-8, $325.00 ♦ Online Database, $650.00 ♦ Online Database & Directory Combo, $750.00

The HMO/PPO Directory, 2006

The HMO/PPO Directory is a comprehensive source that provides detailed information about Health Maintenance Organizations and Preferred Provider Organizations nationwide. This comprehensive directory details more information about more managed health care organizations than ever before. Over 1,100 HMOs, PPOs and affiliated companies are listed, arranged alphabetically by state. Detailed listings include Key Contact Information, Prescription Drug Benefits, Enrollment, Geographical Areas served, Affiliated Physicians & Hospitals, Federal Qualifications, Status, Year Founded, Managed Care Partners, Employer References, Fees & Payment Information and more. Plus, five years of historical information is included related to Revenues, Net Income, Medical Loss Ratios, Membership Enrollment and Number of Patient Complaints. Five easy-to-use, cross-referenced indexes will put this vast array of information at your fingertips immediately: HMO Index, PPO Index, Other Providers Index, Personnel Index and Enrollment Index. *The HMO/PPO Directory* provides the most comprehensive information on the most companies available on the market place today.

> *"Helpful to individuals requesting certain HMO/PPO issues such as co-payment costs, subscription costs and patient complaints. Individuals concerned (or those with questions) about their insurance may find this text to be of use to them." -ARB.*

600 pages; Softcover ISBN 1-59237-100-0, $275.00 ◆ Online Database, $495.00 ◆ Online Database & Directory Combo, $600.00

The Directory of Independent Ambulatory Care Centers

This first edition of *The Directory of Independent Ambulatory Care Centers* provides access to detailed information that, before now, could only be found scattered in hundreds of different sources. This comprehensive and up-to-date directory pulls together a vast array of contact information for over 7,200 Ambulatory Surgery Centers, Ambulatory General and Urgent Care Clinics, and Diagnostic Imaging Centers that are not affiliated with a hospital or major medical center. Detailed listings include Mailing Address, Phone & Fax Numbers, E-mail and Web Site addresses, Contact Name and Phone Numbers of the Medical Director and other Key Executives and Purchasing Agents, Specialties & Services Offered, Year Founded, Numbers of Employees and Surgeons, Number of Operating Rooms, Number of Cases seen per year, Overnight Options, Contracted Services and much more. Listings are arranged by State, by Center Category and then alphabetically by Organization Name. Two indexes provide quick and easy access to this wealth of information: Entry Name Index and Specialty/Service Index. *The Directory of Independent Ambulatory Care Centers* is a must-have resource for anyone marketing a product or service to this important industry and will be an invaluable tool for those searching for a local care center that will meet their specific needs.

> *"Among the numerous hospital directories, no other provides information on independent ambulatory centers. A handy, well-organized resource that would be useful in medical center libraries and public libraries." –Choice*

986 pages; Softcover ISBN 1-930956-90-8, $185.00 ◆ Online Database, $365.00 ◆ Online Database & Directory Combo, $450.00

Mackenzie & Harris
General Reference Titles

The Value of a Dollar 1600-1859, The Colonial Era to The Civil War

Following the format of the widely acclaimed, *The Value of a Dollar, 1860-2004*, *The Value of a Dollar 1600-1859*, *The Colonial Era to The Civil War* records the actual prices of thousands of items that consumers purchased from the Colonial Era to the Civil War. Our editorial department had been flooded with requests from users of our Value of a Dollar for the same type of information, just from an earlier time period. This new volume is just the answer – with pricing data from 1600 to 1859. Arranged into five-year chapters, each 5-year chapter includes a Historical Snapshot, Consumer Expenditures, Investments, Selected Income, Income/Standard Jobs, Food Basket, Standard Prices and Miscellany. There is also a section on Trends. This informative section charts the change in price over time and provides added detail on the reasons prices changed within the time period, including industry developments, changes in consumer attitudes and important historical facts. This fascinating survey will serve a wide range of research needs and will be useful in all high school, public and academic library reference collections.

500 pages; Hardcover ISBN 1-59237-094-2, $135.00

The Value of a Dollar 1860-2004, Third Edition

A guide to practical economy, *The Value of a Dollar* records the actual prices of thousands of items that consumers purchased from the Civil War to the present, along with facts about investment options and income opportunities. This brand new Third Edition boasts a brand new addition to each five-year chapter, a section on Trends. This informative section charts the change in price over time and provides added detail on the reasons prices changed within the time period, including industry developments, changes in consumer attitudes and important historical facts. Plus, a brand new chapter for 2000-2004 has been added. Each 5-year chapter includes a Historical Snapshot, Consumer Expenditures, Investments, Selected Income, Income/Standard Jobs, Food Basket, Standard Prices and Miscellany. This interesting and useful publication will be widely used in any reference collection.

"Recommended for high school, college and public libraries." –*ARBA*

500 pages; Hardcover ISBN 1-59237-074-8, $135.00

Working Americans 1880-1999
Volume I: The Working Class, Volume II: The Middle Class, Volume III: The Upper Class

Each of the volumes in the *Working Americans 1880-1999* series focuses on a particular class of Americans, The Working Class, The Middle Class and The Upper Class over the last 120 years. Chapters in each volume focus on one decade and profile three to five families. Family Profiles include real data on Income & Job Descriptions, Selected Prices of the Times, Annual Income, Annual Budgets, Family Finances, Life at Work, Life at Home, Life in the Community, Working Conditions, Cost of Living, Amusements and much more. Each chapter also contains an Economic Profile with Average Wages of other Professions, a selection of Typical Pricing, Key Events & Inventions, News Profiles, Articles from Local Media and Illustrations. The *Working Americans* series captures the lifestyles of each of the classes from the last twelve decades, covers a vast array of occupations and ethnic backgrounds and travels the entire nation. These interesting and useful compilations of portraits of the American Working, Middle and Upper Classes during the last 120 years will be an important addition to any high school, public or academic library reference collection.

"These interesting, unique compilations of economic and social facts, figures and graphs will support multiple research needs. They will engage and enlighten patrons in high school, public and academic library collections." –*Booklist*

Volume I: The Working Class ♦ 558 pages; Hardcover ISBN 1-891482-81-5, $145.00 ♦ Volume II: The Middle Class ♦ 591 pages; Hardcover ISBN 1-891482-72-6; $145.00 ♦ Volume III: The Upper Class ♦ 567 pages; Hardcover ISBN 1-930956-38-X, $145.00

Working Americans 1880-1999 Volume IV: Their Children

This Fourth Volume in the highly successful *Working Americans 1880-1999* series focuses on American children, decade by decade from 1880 to 1999. This interesting and useful volume introduces the reader to three children in each decade, one from each of the Working, Middle and Upper classes. Like the first three volumes in the series, the individual profiles are created from interviews, diaries, statistical studies, biographies and news reports. Profiles cover a broad range of ethnic backgrounds, geographic area and lifestyles – everything from an orphan in Memphis in 1882, following the Yellow Fever epidemic of 1878 to an eleven-year-old nephew of a beer baron and owner of the New York Yankees in New York City in 1921. Chapters also contain important supplementary materials including News Features as well as information on everything from Schools to Parks, Infectious Diseases to Childhood Fears along with Entertainment, Family Life and much more to provide an informative overview of the lifestyles of children from each decade. This interesting account of what life was like for Children in the Working, Middle and Upper Classes will be a welcome addition to the reference collection of any high school, public or academic library.

500 pages; Hardcover ISBN 1-930956-35-5, $145.00

To preview any of our Directories Risk-Free for 30 days, call (800) 562-2139 or fax to (518) 789-0556

Working Americans 1880-2003 Volume V: Americans At War

Working Americans 1880-2003 Volume V: Americans At War is divided into 11 chapters, each covering a decade from 1880-2003 and examines the lives of Americans during the time of war, including declared conflicts, one-time military actions, protests, and preparations for war. Each decade includes several personal profiles, whether on the battlefield or on the homefront, that tell the stories of civilians, soldiers, and officers during the decade. The profiles examine: Life at Home; Life at Work; and Life in the Community. Each decade also includes an Economic Profile with statistical comparisons, a Historical Snapshot, News Profiles, local News Articles, and Illustrations that provide a solid historical background to the decade being examined. Profiles range widely not only geographically, but also emotionally, from that of a girl whose leg was torn off in a blast during WWI, to the boredom of being stationed in the Dakotas as the Indian Wars were drawing to a close. As in previous volumes of the *Working Americans* series, information is presented in narrative form, but hard facts and real-life situations back up each story. The basis of the profiles come from diaries, private print books, personal interviews, family histories, estate documents and magazine articles. For easy reference, *Working Americans 1880-2003 Volume V: Americans At War* includes an in-depth Subject Index. The *Working Americans* series has become an important reference for public libraries, academic libraries and high school libraries. This fifth volume will be a welcome addition to all of these types of reference collections.

600 pages; Hardcover ISBN 1-59237-024-1; $145.00
Five Volume Set (Volumes I-V), Hardcover ISBN 1-59237-034-9, $675.00

Working Americans 1880-2005 Volume VI: Women at Work

Unlike any other volume in the *Working Americans* series, this Sixth Volume, is the first to focus on a particular gender of Americans. *Volume VI: Women at Work*, traces what life was like for working women from the 1860's to the present time. Beginning with the life of a maid in 1890 and a store clerk in 1900 and ending with the life and times of the modern working women, this text captures the struggle, strengths and changing perception of the American woman at work. Each chapter focuses on one decade and profiles three to five women with real data on Income & Job Descriptions, Selected Prices of the Times, Annual Income, Annual Budgets, Family Finances, Life at Work, Life at Home, Life in the Community, Working Conditions, Cost of Living, Amusements and much more. For even broader access to the events, economics and attitude towards women throughout the past 130 years, each chapter is supplemented with News Profiles, Articles from Local Media, Illustrations, Economic Profiles, Typical Pricing, Key Events, Inventions and more. This important volume illustrates what life was like for working women over time and allows the reader to develop an understanding of the changing role of women at work. These interesting and useful compilations of portraits of women at work will be an important addition to any high school, public or academic library reference collection.

600 pages; Hardcover ISBN 1-59237-063-2; $145.00

Working Americans 1880-2005 Volume VII: Social Movements

The newest addition to the widely-successful *Working Americans* series, *Volume VII: Social Movements* explores how Americans sought and fought for change from the 1880s to the present time. Following the format of previous volumes in the Working Americans series, the text examines the lives of 34 individuals who have worked -- often behind the scenes --- to bring about change. Issues include topics as diverse as the Anti-smoking movement of 1901 to efforts by Native Americans to reassert their long lost rights. Along the way, the book will profile individuals brave enough to demand suffrage for Kansas women in 1912 or demand an end to lynching during a March on Washington in 1923. Each profile is enriched with real data on Income & Job Descriptions, Selected Prices of the Times, Annual Incomes & Budgets, Life at Work, Life at Home, Life in the Community, along with News Features, Key Events, and Illustrations. The depth of information contained in each profile allow the user to explore the private, financial and public lives of these subjects, deepening our understanding of how calls for change took place in our society. A must-purchase for the reference collections of high school libraries, public libraries and academic libraries.

600 pages; Hardcover ISBN 1-59237-101-9; $145.00
Seven Volume Set (Volumes I-VII), Hardcover ISBN 1-59237-133-7, $945.00

The Encyclopedia of Warrior Peoples & Fighting Groups

Many military groups throughout the world have excelled in their craft either by fortuitous circumstances, outstanding leadership, or intense training. This new second edition of The Encyclopedia of Warrior Peoples and Fighting Groups explores the origins and leadership of these outstanding combat forces, chronicles their conquests and accomplishments, examines the circumstances surrounding their decline or disbanding, and assesses their influence on the groups and methods of warfare that followed. This edition has been completely updated with information through 2005 and contains over 20 new entries. Readers will encounter ferocious tribes, charismatic leaders, and daring militias, from ancient times to the present, including Amazons, Buffalo Soldiers, Green Berets, Iron Brigade, Kamikazes, Peoples of the Sea, Polish Winged Hussars, Sacred Band of Thebes, Teutonic Knights, and Texas Rangers. With over 100 alphabetical entries, numerous cross-references and illustrations, a comprehensive bibliography, and index, the Encyclopedia of Warrior Peoples and Fighting Groups is a valuable resource for readers seeking insight into the bold history of distinguished fighting forces.

"This work is especially useful for high school students, undergraduates, and general
readers with an interest in military history." –Library Journal

Pub. Date: May 2006; Hardcover ISBN 1-59237-116-7; $135.00

To preview any of our Directories Risk-Free for 30 days, call (800) 562-2139 or fax to (518) 789-0556

The Encyclopedia of Invasions & Conquests, From the Ancient Times to the Present

Throughout history, invasions and conquests have played a remarkable role in shaping our world and defining our boundaries, both physically and culturally. This second edition of the popular Encyclopedia of Invasions & Conquests, a comprehensive guide to over 50 invasions, conquests, battles and occupations from ancient times to the present, takes readers on a journey that includes the Roman conquest of Britain, the Portuguese colonization of Brazil, and the Iraqi invasion of Kuwait, to name a few. New articles will explore the late 20th and 21st centuries, with a specific focus on recent conflicts in Afghanistan, Kuwait, Iraq, Yugoslavia, Grenada and Chechnya. Categories of entries include countries, invasions and conquests, and individuals. In addition to covering the military aspects of invasions and conquests, entries cover some of the political, economic, and cultural aspects, for example, the effects of a conquest on the invade country's political and monetary system and in its language and religion. The entries on leaders – among them Sargon, Alexander the Great, William the Conqueror, and Adolf Hitler – deal with the people who sought to gain control, expand power, or exert religious or political influence over others through military means. Revised and updated for this second edition, entries are arranged alphabetically within historical periods. Each chapter provides a map to help readers locate key areas and geographical features, and bibliographical references appear at the end of each entry. Other useful features include cross-references, a cumulative bibliography and a comprehensive subject index. This authoritative, well-organized, lucidly written volume will prove invaluable for a variety of readers, including high school students, military historians, members of the armed forces, history buffs and hobbyists.

"Engaging writing, sensible organization, nice illustrations, interesting and obscure facts, and useful maps make this book a pleasure to read." –ARBA

Pub. Date: March 2006; Hardcover ISBN 1-59237-114-0; $135.00

Encyclopedia of Prisoners of War & Internment

This authoritative second edition provides a valuable overview of the history of prisoners of war and interned civilians, from earliest times to the present. Written by an international team of experts in the field of POW studies, this fascinating and thought-provoking volume includes entries on a wide range of subjects including the Crusades, Plains Indian Warfare, concentration camps, the two world wars, and famous POWs throughout history, as well as atrocities, escapes, and much more. Written in a clear and easily understandable style, this informative reference details over 350 entries, 30% larger than the first edition, that survey the history of prisoners of war and interned civilians from the earliest times to the present, with emphasis on the 19th and 20th centuries. Medical conditions, international law, exchanges of prisoners, organizations working on behalf of POWs, and trials associated with the treatment of captives are just some of the themes explored. Entries range from the Ardeatine Caves Massacre to Kurt Vonnegut. Entries are arranged alphabetically, plus illustrations and maps are provided for easy reference. The text also includes an introduction, bibliography, appendix of selected documents, and end-of-entry reading suggestions. This one-of-a-kind reference will be a helpful addition to the reference collections of all public libraries, high schools, and university libraries and will prove invaluable to historians and military enthusiasts.

"Thorough and detailed yet accessible to the lay reader. Of special interest to subject specialists and historians; recommended for public and academic libraries." - Library Journal

Pub. Date: March 2006; Hardcover ISBN 1-59237-120-5; $135.00

The Religious Right, A Reference Handbook

Timely and unbiased, this third edition updates and expands its examination of the religious right and its influence on our government, citizens, society, and politics. From the fight to outlaw the teaching of Darwin's theory of evolution to the struggle to outlaw abortion, the religious right is continually exerting an influence on public policy. This text explores the influence of religion on legislation and society, while examining the alignment of the religious right with the political right. A historical survey of the movement highlights the shift to "hands-on" approach to politics and the struggle to present a unified front. The coverage offers a critical historical survey of the religious right movement, focusing on its increased involvement in the political arena, attempts to forge coalitions, and notable successes and failures. The text offers complete coverage of biographies of the men and women who have advanced the cause and an up to date chronology illuminate the movement's goals, including their accomplishments and failures. This edition offers an extensive update to all sections along with several brand new entries. Two new sections complement this third edition, a chapter on legal issues and court decisions and a chapter on demographic statistics and electoral patterns. To aid in further research, The Religious Right, offers an entire section of annotated listings of print and non-print resources, as well as of organizations affiliated with the religious right, and those opposing it. Comprehensive in its scope, this work offers easy-to-read, pertinent information for those seeking to understand the religious right and its evolving role in American society. A must for libraries of all sizes, university religion departments, activists, high schools and for those interested in the evolving role of the religious right.

" Recommended for all public and academic libraries." - Library Journal

Pub. Date: November 2006; Hardcover ISBN 1-59237-113-2; $135.00

To preview any of our Directories Risk-Free for 30 days, call (800) 562-2139 or fax to (518) 789-0556

From Suffrage to the Senate, An Encyclopedia of American Women in Politics

From Suffrage to the Senate is a comprehensive and valuable compendium of biographies of leading women in U.S. politics, past and present, and an examination of the wide range of women's movements. Up to date through 2006, this dynamically illustrated reference work explores American women's path to political power and social equality from the struggle for the right to vote and the abolition of slavery to the first African American woman in the U.S. Senate and beyond. This new edition includes over 150 new entries and a brand new section on trends and demographics of women in politics. The in-depth coverage also traces the political heritage of the abolition, labor, suffrage, temperance, and reproductive rights movements. The alphabetically arranged entries include biographies of every woman from across the political spectrum who has served in the U.S. House and Senate, along with women in the Judiciary and the U.S. Cabinet and, new to this edition, biographies of activists and political consultants. Bibliographical references follow each entry. For easy reference, a handy chronology is provided detailing 150 years of women's history. This up-to-date reference will be a must-purchase for women's studies departments, high schools and public libraries and will be a handy resource for those researching the key players in women's politics, past and present.

"An engaging tool that would be useful in high school, public, and academic libraries looking for an overview of the political history of women in the US." –Bookli

Pub. Date: October 2006; Two Volume Set; Hardcover ISBN 1-59237-117-5; $195.00

An African Biographical Dictionary

This landmark second edition is the only biographical dictionary to bring together, in one volume, cultural, social and political leaders – both historical and contemporary – of the sub-Saharan region. Over 800 biographical sketches of prominent Africans, as well as foreigners who have affected the continent's history, are featured, 150 more than the previous edition. The wide spectrum of leaders includes religious figures, writers, politicians, scientists, entertainers, sports personalities and more. Access to these fascinating individuals is provided in a user-friendly format. The biographies are arranged alphabetically, cross-referenced and indexed. Entries include the country or countries in which the person was significant and the commonly accepted dates of birth and death. Each biographical sketch is chronologically written; entries for cultural personalities add an evaluation of their work. This information is followed by a selection of references often found in university and public libraries, including autobiographies and principal biographical works. Appendixes list each individual by country and by field of accomplishment – rulers, musicians, explorers, missionaries, businessmen, physicists – nearly thirty categories in all. Another convenient appendix lists heads of state since independence by country. Up-to-date and representative of African societies as a whole, An African Biographical Dictionary provides a wealth of vital information for students of African culture and is an indispensable reference guide for anyone interested in African affairs.

"An unquestionable convenience to have these concise, informative biographies gathered into one source, indexed, and analyzed by appendixes listing entrants by nation and occupational field." –Wilson Library Bulletin

Pub. Date: July 2006; Hardcover ISBN 1-59237-112-4; $125.00

American Environmental Leaders, From Colonial Times to the Present

A comprehensive and diverse award winning collection of biographies of the most important figures in American environmentalism. Few subjects arouse the passions the way the environment does. How will we feed an ever-increasing population and how can that food be made safe for consumption? Who decides how land is developed? How can environmental policies be made fair for everyone, including multiethnic groups, women, children, and the poor? American Environmental Leaders presents more than 350 biographies of men and women who have devoted their lives to studying, debating, and organizing these and other controversial issues over the last 200 years. In addition to the scientists who have analyzed how human actions affect nature, we are introduced to poets, landscape architects, presidents, painters, activists, even sanitation engineers, and others who have forever altered how we think about the environment. The easy to use A–Z format provides instant access to these fascinating individuals, and frequent cross references indicate others with whom individuals worked (and sometimes clashed). End of entry references provide users with a starting point for further research.

"Highly recommended for high school, academic, and public libraries needing environmental biographical information." –Library Journal/Starred Review

Two Volume Set; Hardcover ISBN 1-57607-385-8 $175.00

World Cultural Leaders of the Twentieth Century

An expansive two volume set that covers 450 worldwide cultural icons, World Cultural Leaders of the Twentieth Century includes each person's works, achievements, and professional careers in a thorough essay. Who was the originator of the term "documentary"? Which poet married the daughter of the famed novelist Thomas Mann in order to help her escape Nazi Germany? Which British writer served as an agent in Russia against the Bolsheviks before the 1917 revolution? These and many more questions are answered in this illuminating text. A handy two volume set that makes it easy to look up 450 worldwide cultural icons: novelists, poets, playwrights, painters, sculptors, architects, dancers, choreographers, actors, directors, filmmakers, singers, composers, and musicians. World Cultural Leaders of the Twentieth Century provides entries (many of them illustrated) covering the person's works, achievements, and professional career in a thorough essay and offers interesting facts and statistics. Entries are fully cross-referenced so that readers can learn how various individuals influenced others. A thorough general index completes the coverage.

"Fills a need for handy, concise information on a wide array of international cultural figures."-ARBA

Two Volume Set; Hardcover ISBN 1-57607-038-7 $175.00

To preview any of our Directories Risk-Free for 30 days, call (800) 562-2139 or fax to (518) 789-0556